W9-BZO-176

ORLAND PARK PUBLIC LIBRARY
14921 Ravinia Avenue
Orland Park, Illinois 60462
708-428-5100

OCT   2012

AMERICAN WRITERS

AMERICAN WRITERS

JAY PARINI
Editor

SUPPLEMENT XXIII

CHARLES SCRIBNER'S SONS
A part of Gale, Cengage Learning

GALE
CENGAGE Learning®

Detroit • New York • San Francisco • New Haven, Conn • Waterville, Maine • London

ORLAND PARK PUBLIC LIBRARY

Ref
920.03
Ame...

American Writers Supplement XXIII

Editor in Chief: Jay Parini

Project Editor: Lisa Kumar

Permissions: Robyn Young

Composition and Electronic Capture: Gary Leach

Manufacturing: Cynde Lentz

Publisher: Jim Draper

Product Manager: Philip J. Virta

© 2013 Charles Scribner's Sons, a part of Gale, Cengage Learning

ALL RIGHTS RESERVED. No part of this work covered by the copyright herein may be reproduced, transmitted, stored, or used in any form or by any means graphic, electronic, or mechanical, including but not limited to photocopying, recording, scanning, digitizing, taping, Web distribution, information networks, or information storage and retrieval systems, except as permitted under Section 107 or 108 of the 1976 United States Copyright Act, without the prior written permission of the publisher.

This publication is a creative work fully protected by all applicable copyright laws, as well as by misappropriation, trade secret, unfair competition, and other applicable laws. The authors and editors of this work have added value to the underlying factual material herein through one or more of the following: unique and original selection, coordination, expression, arrangement, and classification of the information.

For product information and technology assistance, contact us at **Gale Customer Support, 1-800-877-4253.** For permission to use material from this text or product, submit all requests online at **www.cengage.com/permissions** Further permissions questions can be emailed to **permissionrequest@cengage.com**

While every effort has been made to ensure the reliability of the information presented in this publication, Gale, a part of Cengage Learning, does not guarantee the accuracy of the data contained herein. Gale accepts no payment for listing; and inclusion in the publication of any organization, agency, institution, publication, service, or individual does not imply endorsement of the editors or publisher. Errors brought to the attention of the publisher and verified to the satisfaction of the publisher will be corrected in future editions.

EDITORIAL DATA PRIVACY POLICY. Does this publication contain information about you as an individual? If so, for more information about our editorial data privacy policies, please see our Privacy Statement at www.gale.cengage.com

LIBRARY OF CONGRESS CATALOGING-IN-PUBLICATION DATA

American writers: a collection of literary biographies / Leonard Unger, editor in chief.
   p. cm.
   The 4-vol. main set consists of 97 of the pamphlets originally published as the University of Minnesota pamphlets on American writers; some have been rev. and updated. The supplements cover writers not included in the original series.
   Supplement 2, has editor in chief, A. Walton Litz; Retrospective suppl. 1, c1998, was edited by A. Walton Litz & Molly Weigel; Suppl. 5-7 have as editor-in-chief, Jay Parini.
   Includes bibliographies and index.
   Contents: v. 1. Henry Adams to T.S. Eliot — v. 2. Ralph Waldo Emerson to Carson McCullers — v. 3. Archibald MacLeish to George Santayana — v. 4. Isaac Bashevis Singer to Richard Wright — Supplement\[s\]: 1, pt. 1. Jane Addams to Sidney Lanier. 1, pt. 2. Vachel Lindsay to Elinor Wylie. 2, pt. 1. W.H. Auden to O. Henry. 2, pt. 2. Robinson Jeffers to Yvor Winters. — 4, pt. 1. Maya Angelou to Linda Hogan. 4, pt. 2. Susan Howe to Gore Vidal — Suppl. 5. Russell Banks to Charles Wright — Suppl. 6. Don DeLillo to W. D. Snodgrass — Suppl. 7. Julia Alvarez to Tobias Wolff — Suppl. 8. T.C. Boyle to August Wilson. — Suppl. 11 Toni Cade Bambara to Richard Yates.
   ISBN 978-1-4144-8025-1
   1. American literature—History and criticism. 2. American literature—Bio-bibliography. 3. Authors, American—Biography. I. Unger, Leonard. II. Litz, A. Walton. III. Weigel, Molly. IV. Parini, Jay. V. University of Minnesota pamphlets on American writers.

PS129 .A55
810'.9
\[B\]   73-001759

ISBN-13: 978-1-4144-8025-1
ISBN-10: 1-4144-8025-3

Charles Scribner's Sons an imprint of Gale, Cengage Learning
27500 Drake Rd.
Farmington Hills, MI, 48331-3535

Printed in Mexico
1 2 3 4 5 6 7 16 15 14 13 12

Acknowledgments

The editors wish to thank the copyright holders of the excerpted criticism included in this volume and the permissions managers of many book and magazine publishing companies for assisting us in securing reproduction rights. We are also grateful to the staffs of the Detroit Public Library, the Library of Congress, the University of Detroit Mercy Library, Wayne State University Purdy/Kresge Library Complex, and the University of Michigan Libraries for making their resources available to us. Following is a list of the copyright holders who have granted us permission to reproduce material in this volume of *American Writers*. Every effort has been made to trace copyright, but if omissions have been made, please let us know.

COPYRIGHTED EXCERPTS IN *AMERICAN WRITERS*, VOLUME 23, WERE REPRODUCED FROM THE FOLLOWING BOOKS:

ASCH, SHOLEM. *Christian Herald,* v. 52, January, 1944. Copyright © 1944 by Christian Herald Association. Reproduced by permission.

BALAKIAN, PETER. Balakian, Peter. From *Dyer's Thistle.* Carnegie Mellon University Press, 1996. Copyright © Carnegie Mellon University Press, 1996. Reproduced by permission. / Balakian, Peter. From *Ziggurat.* University of Chicago Press, 2010. Copyright © University of Chicago Press, 2010. Reproduced by permission of the publisher and the author.

BENEDICT, PINCKNEY. Rodger Cunningham, "Letter to the Editor, Heat Over 'Town Smokes'," *The New York Times,* September 27, 1987. Copyright © 1987 by Rodger Cunningham. Reproduced by permission.

CROOKER, BARBARA. "Interview with Barbara Crooker," *The Writer's Almanac Bookshelf.* http://writersalmanac.publicradio.org. Copyright © Prairie Home Productions. Reproduced by permission. / Harry Humes, "Review of Writing Home," *www.barbaracrooker.com.* Reproduced by permission. / Barbara Crooker, "The Lost Children," *Poetry Review,* 1984. Copyright © 1984 by Barbara Crooker. Reproduced by permission of the author. / Barbara Crooker, "A Congregaton of Grackles," *Potomac Review,* 2006. http://cms.montgomerycollege.edu. Copyright © 2006 by Barbara Crooker. Reproduced by permission of the author. / Brown, Fleda. From *Line Dance.* Word Press, 2008. Copyright © Word Press, 2008. Reproduced by permission. / Crooker, Barbara. From *Line Dance.* Word Press, 2008. Copyright © Barbara Crooker, 2008. Reproduced by permission of the author. / Crooker, Barbara. From *More.* C&R Press, 2010. Copyright © Barbara Crooker, 2010. Reproduced by permission of the author. / Crooker, Barbara. From *Ordinary Life.* Byline Press, 2001. Copyright © Barbara Crooker, 2001. Reproduced by permission of the author. / Crooker, Barbara. From *Radiance.* Word Press, 2005. Copyright © Barbara

ACKNOWLEDGEMENTS

Crooker, 2005. Reproduced by permission of the author. / Crooker, Barbara. From *The White Poems.* Barnwood, 2001. Copyright © Barbara Crooker, 2001. Reproduced by permission of the author. / Keillor, Garrison. From *Radiance.* Word Press, 2005. Copyright © Word Press, 2005. Reproduced by permission. / McCourt, Frank. From *More.* C&R Press, 2010. Copyright © C&R Press, 2010. / Plath, Sylvia. From *Crossing the water: transitional poems.* Harper & Row, 1971. Copyright © Harper & Row, 1971. / Schulman, Grace. From *Radiance.* Word Press, 2005. Copyright © Word Press, 2005. Reproduced by permission. / Springstein, Bruce. From *More.* C&R Press, 2010. Copyright © C&R Press, 2010. / Wormser, Baron. From *Radiance.* Word Press, 2005. Copyright © Word Press, 2005. Reproduced by permission.

DYBEK, STUART. Dybek, Stuart. From *Brass Knuckles.* University of Pittsburgh Press, 1979. Copyright © Stuart Dybek, 1979. Reproduced by permission of the author. / Dybek, Stuart. From *The Story of Mist.* State Street Press Chapbooks, 1993. Copyright © State Street Press Chapbooks, 1993. Reproduced by permission of the author. / *The Prose Poem: An International Journal,* v. 3, 1994. Copyright © *The Prose Poem: An International Journal,* 1994. Reproduced by permission of the publisher. / *TriQuarterly,* January 1, 2006 for "A Conversation with Stuart Dybek" by Donna Seaman. Copyright © 2006 by Donna Seaman. Reproduced by permission of the author.

EXLEY, FREDERICK. *New Statesman,* July 5, 1999. Copyright © 1999 New Statesman, Ltd. Reproduced by permission.

HADAS, RACHEL. Hadas, Rachel. From *Laws.* Zoo Press, 2004. Copyright © Rachel Hadas, 2004. Reproduced by permission of the author. / Hadas, Rachel. From *Living in Time.* Rutgers University Press, 1990. Copyright © Rutgers University Press, 1990. Reproduced by permission of Rutgers, The State University. / Hadas, Rachel. From *Mirrors of Astonishment.* Rutgers University Press, 1992. Copyright © Rutgers University Press, 1992. Reproduced by permission of Rutgers, The State University. / Hadas,

Rachel. From *Other Worlds than This.* Rutgers University Press, 1994. Copyright © Rutgers University Press, 1994. Reproduced by permission of Rutgers, The State University. / Hadas, Rachel. From *Pass It On.* Princeton University Press, 1989. Copyright © Princeton University Press, 1989. Reproduced by permission. / Hadas, Rachel. From *Starting from Troy.* David R. Godine, 1975. Copyright © Rachel Hadas, 1975. Reproduced by permission of the author. / Hadas, Rachel. From *The Ache of Appetite.* Copper Beech Press, 2010. Copyright © Rachel Hadas, 2010. Reproduced by permission of the author. / Hadas, Rachel. From *The River of Forgetfulness.* David Robert Books, 2006. Copyright © David Robert Books, 2006. Reproduced by permission. / Hadas, Rachel. From *Three Poets in Conversation.* Between The Lines, 2006. Copyright © Rachel Hadas, 2006. Reproduced by permission of the author. / Hadas, Rachel. From *Unending Dialogue.* Faber and Faber, 1993. Copyright © Faber and Faber, 1993. Reproduced by permission. / Rachel Hadas, "Lower Level, Room EE," "Lunch the Day after Thanksgiving," "Nine Tiles," "Orange," "Six of One," "Thank You and Goodbye," "The Changes," from *The Empty Bed.* © 1995 by Rachel Hadas. Reprinted by permission of Wesleyan University Press. / Rachel Hadas "Chiasmus," "Last Trip to Greece," "On Myth," "Rag Rug," "The Blue Bead," "The Hinge," "The Red Hat," "Two and One," "Upon My Mother's Death," from *Halfway Down the Hall.* © 1998 by Rachel Hadas. Reprinted by permission of Wesleyan University Press. / Rachel Hadas, "Thick and Thin" from *Indelible.* © 2001 by Rachel Hadas. Reprinted with permission of Wesleyan University Press. / Rachel Hadas, "Little by Little," "Philemon and Baucis" from *A Son From Sleep.* © 1987 by Rachel Hadas. Reprinted by permission of Wesleyan University Press. / Rachel Hadas, "Marriage Rhapsody," "The Trial for Arson," from *Slow Transparency.* © 1983 by Rachel Hadas. Reprinted by permission of Wesleyan University Press.

HIRSHFIELD, JANE. *Chicago Review,* Copyright © 1994 by *Chicago Review.* Reproduced by permission of the publisher. / Cynthia Haven. "Kitchen Ants and Everyday Epiphanies," *Po-*

ACKNOWLEDGEMENTS

etry Foundation. www.poetryfoundation.org. Copyright © Poetry Foundation. Reproduced by permission. / *Library Journal,* October 1, 1997; February 15, 2001; v. 102, February 1, 2006; v. 136, August 1, 2011. Copyright © 1997, 2001, 2006, 2011. Library Journals LLC, a wholly owned subsidiary of Media Source, Inc. No redistribution permitted. / *Publishers Weekly,* December 5, 2005. Reproduced from *Publishers Weekly,* published by the PWxyz, LLC, by permission. / *Washington Independent Book Review,* August 30, 2011. Copyright © 2011 by *Washington Independent Book Review.* Reproduced by permission of the publisher. / *The Washington Post,* September 15, 2011 for "In 'Come, Thief,' a stealth meditation of quotidian human experience," by Steven Ratiner. Copyright © Steven Ratiner, 2011. Reprinted with permission of the author. / *The Women's Review of Books,* 1994, July 2001. Copyright © 1994, 2001 by Old City Publishing. Reproduced by permission of the publisher.

KENNY, MAURICE. Kenny, Maurice. From *Between Two Rivers.* White Pine Press, 1987. Copyright © 1987 by Maurice Kenny. Reproduced by permission. / Kenny, Maurice. From *Blackrobe.* North Country Community College Press, 1982. Copyright © Maurice Kenny, 1982. Reproduced by permission of the author. / Kenny, Maurice. From *Carving Hawk: New and Selected Poems 1953-2000.* White Pine Press, 2002. Copyright © 2002 by Maurice Kenny. Reproduced by permission. / Kenny, Maurice. From *Connotations.* White Pine Press, 2008. Copyright © 2008 by Maurice Kenny. Reproduced by permission. / Kenny, Maurice. From *The Mama Poems.* White Pine Press, 2008. Copyright © White Pine Press, 2008. Reproduced by permission. / Kenny, Maurice. From *Only As Far As Brooklyn.* Good Gay Poets Press, 1979. Copyright © Maurice Kenny, 1979. Reproduced by permission of the author. / Kenny, Maurice. From *Tekonwatonti/Molly Brant.* White Pine Press, 1992. Copyright © 1992 by Maurice Kenny. Reproduced by permission.

Le SUEUR, MERIDEL. Le Sueur, Meridel. From *Rites of Ancient Ripening.* Vanilla Press, Inc., 1975. Copyright © Vanilla Press, Inc., 1975. / Le Sueur, Meridel. From *Walt Whitman: The Measure of His Song.* Holy Cow! Press, 1981. Copyright © Meridel LeSueur. Reproduced by permission of The Meridel Le Sueur Family Circle. / Le Sueur, Meridel. From *Women on the Breadlines.* West End Press, 1977. Copyright © Meridel Le Sueur, 1977. Reproduced by permission.

O'HARA, FRANK. O'Hara, Frank. From *Lunch Poems.* City Lights Books, 1964. Copyright © City Lights Books, 1964. Reproduced by permission. / O'Hara, Frank. From *The Collected Poems of Frank O'Hara.* University of California Press, 1995.

SCHOOLCRAFT, JANE JOHNSTON. Johnston Schoolcraft, Jane. From *The Sound the Stars Make Rushing Through the Sky,* pp. 89, 92, 109, 114, 117-18, 130, 136, 138-139, 141-43, 207, 215. University of Pennsylvania Press, 2007. Copyright © University of Pennsylvania Press, 2007. Reprinted with permission of the University of Pennsylvania Press.

SCHOTT, PENELOPE SCAMBLY. Bernadette Geyer, "review of Six Lips," *berniE-zine,* April 7, 2008. rantsravesreviews.homestead.com. Copyright © berniE-zine. Reproduced by permission. / Cooperman, Robert. From *A is for Anne: Mistress Hutchinson Disturbs the Commonwealth.* Turning Point, 2007. Copyright © Robert Cooperman, 2007. Reproduced by permission. / Dickinson, Stephanie. From *Under Taos Mountain: The Terrible Quarrel of Magpie and Tia.* Rain Mountain Press, 2009. Copyright © Rain Mountain Press, 2009. Reproduced by permission. / Gillan, Maria Mazziotti. From *Baiting the Void.* Dream Horse Press, 2005. Copyright © Maria Mazziotti Gillian, 2005. Reproduced by permission of the author. / Inez, Colette. From *The Pest Maiden: A Story of Lobotomy.* Turning Point, 2004. Copyright © Colette Inez, 2004. Reproduced by permission of the author. / Keyes, Claire. "Interview with Penelope Schott," July, 2011; "Interview with Penelope Schott," July 28, 2011; "Biography of Penelope Schott," August 28, 2011. Reproduced by permission of the author. / Komunyakaa, Yusef. From *Crow Mercies.* Calyx Books, 2010.

ACKNOWLEDGEMENTS

Copyright © Calyx Books, 2010. Reproduced by permission. / Nye, Naomi Shihab. From *Crow Mercies*. Calyx Books, 2010. Copyright © Calyx Books, 2010. Reproduced by permission. / *Publishers Weekly*, April 25, 1986. Reproduced from *Publishers Weekly*, published by the PWxyz, LLC, by permission. / Schott, Penelope. From *A is for Anne: Mistress Hutchinson Disturbs the Commonwealth*. Turning Point, 2007. Copyright © Turning Point, 2007. Reproduced by permission. / Schott, Penelope. From *Crow Mercies*. Calyx Books, 2010. Copyright © Calyx Books, 2010. Reproduced by permission. / Schott, Penelope. From *Penelope: The Story of the Half-Scalped Woman*. University Press of Florida, 1999. Copyright © University Press of Florida, 1999. Reprinted with the permission of the University Press of Florida. / Schott, Penelope. From *The Pest Maiden: A Story of Lobotomy*. Turning Point, 2004. Copyright © Turning Point, 2004. Reproduced by permission. / Schott, Penelope. From *These Are My Same Hands*, 1989. Copyright © State Street Press Chapbooks, 1989. / Schott, Penelope. From *Under Taos Mountain: The Terrible Quarrel of Magpie and Tia*. Rain Mountain Press, 2009. Copyright © Rain Mountain Press, 2009. Reproduced by permission. / Schott, Penelope Scambly. From *Baiting the Void*. Dream Horse Press, 2005. Copyright © Penelope Scambly Schott, 2005. Reproduced by permission of the author. / Schott, Penelope Scambly. From *May the Generations Die in the Right Order*. Main Street Rag, 2007. Copyright © Penelope Scambly Schott, 2007. Reproduced by permission of the author. / Schott, Penelope Scambly. From *The Perfect Mother*. Snake Nation Press, 1994. Copyright © Penelope Scambly Schott, 1994. Reproduced by permission of the author./ Schott, Penelope Scambly. From *Six Lips*. Mayapple Press, 2009. Copyright © Penelope Scambly Schott, 2009. Reproduced by permission of the author. / Schott, Penelope Scambly. From *Wave Amplitude in the Mona Passage*. Palanquin Press, 1998. Copyright © Penelope Scambly Schott, 1998. Reproduced by permission of the author. / *Small Press Review*, v. 39, Nov-Dec, 2007. Copyright © Dustbooks, 2007. Reproduced by permission.

SMITH, BETTY. Smith, Betty. From *A Tree Grows In Brooklyn/Maggie Now*. Harper & Row, 1947. Copyright © Harper & Row, 1947.

STROUT, ELIZABETH. *Bangor Daily News*, July 10, 2006. Copyright © *Bangor Daily News, 2006. Reproduced by permission. / Contra Costa Times,* April 2, 2000. Copyright © Media News Group, 2000. Reproduced by permission.

List of Subjects

Introduction | xi

List of Contributors | xiii

SHOLEM ASCH | 1
Jack Fischel

PETER BALAKIAN | 19
Hovig Tchalian

PINCKNEY BENEDICT | 35
Louis H. Palmer III

BARBARA CROOKER | 51
Janet McCann

STUART DYBEK | 67
Judith Kitchen

ZEE EDGELL | 83
J. Roger Kurtz

FREDERICK EXLEY | 97
Tom Cerasulo

RACHEL HADAS | 111
Kim Bridgford

JANE HIRSHFIELD | 129
Susan Carol Hauser

MAURICE KENNY | 143
Nicholas Spengler

MERIDEL Le SUEUR | 161
Robert Buckeye

GEORGE LIPPARD | 177
Jonas Prida

CHERRÍE MORAGA | 193
L. Bailey McDaniel

FRANK O'HARA | 207
Stephen Ross

JANE JOHNSTON SCHOOLCRAFT | 223
Cheri Johnson

PENELOPE SCAMBLY SCHOTT | 239
Claire Keyes

BETTY SMITH | 257
Sari Fordham

ELIZABETH STROUT | 273
Phoebe Jackson

JEAN THOMPSON | 289
Rachel Hall

Cumulative Index | 307

Introduction

In his *Autobiography,* Malcolm X wrote: "The ability to read awoke inside me some long dormant craving to be mentally alive." That is, reading stimulates the senses and wakens the mind; it satisfies a deep craving to understand the world we inhabit. It opens doors that we didn't even know were there. This is true of all kinds of reading, but it seems especially true of that kind of writing we put into the category of literature: poems and plays, novels, stories, memoires, essays. This kind of imaginative writing, especially at the highest levels of accomplishment, enhances our lives by waking us, making available to use large chunks of experience that we might not otherwise access.

This is the twenty-third supplement of *American Writers.* In these pages we offer a range of articles on authors from a wide variety of genres; they are (for the most part) well-known authors who have aspired to the kind of writing that appealed to Malcolm X, as in the opening quotation. Each writer discussed has a substantial body of work in print, and yet none of them has been featured in this series before. Readers who wish to examine into their work will find many things here to attract and sustain them: biographical and critical (as well as historical) context, close readings of individual poems, plays, or works of fiction or nonfiction, and supplementary material that will make this work more available.

This project has its origins in a series of critical and biographical monographs that appeared between 1959 and 1972. The *Minnesota Pamphlets on American Writers* achieved fame in their time; they were incisively written and informative, treating ninety-seven American writers in a format and style that attracted a devoted following of readers. The series proved invaluable to a generation of students and teach-ers, who could depend on these reliable and interesting critiques of major figures. The idea of reprinting these essays occurred to Charles Scribner, Jr. (1921-1995). The series appeared in four volumes entitled *American Writers: A Collection of Literary Biographies* (1974).

Twenty-two supplements have already appeared in as many years, treating hundreds of American writers: poets, novelists, playwrights, screenwriters, essayists, and autobiographers, even a handful of literary critics who have managed to create texts that somebody might want to read in future years. The idea behind each supplement has been consistent with the original series: to provide knowledgeable essays aimed at the general reader. These essays often rise to a high level of craft and critical vision, but they are also meant to introduce a body of work of some importance in the history of American literature, and to provide a sense of the scope and nature of the career under review. Each article puts the author at hand in the context of his or her time.

Supplement twenty-three treats a range of authors from the past and present. Most of the writers included here are modern or contemporary, with the exceptions of three nineteenth century writers: Jane Johnstone Schoolcraft, one of the first Native American authors of note, George Lippard, and Sholem Asch (born in 1880). Peter Balakian, Pinckney Benedict, Barbara Crooker, Stuart Dybek, Zee Edgell, Frederick Exley, Rachel Hadas, Jane Hirshfield, Maurice Kenny, Meridel Le Sueur, Cherríe Moraga, Frank O'Hara, Penelope Scambly Schott, Betty Smith, Elizabeth Strout, and Jean Thompson. While each of these writers has been written about in journals and newspapers, few of them—Frank O'Hara might be an exception—have had the kind of sustained critical at-

INTRODUCTION

tention they deserve, and we hope to provide a beginning here, as the work certainly deserves close reading and rereading.

Going back to Malcolm X: our writers waken us to the world we live in, to the possibilities within the mind itself. The articles in this volume examine an especially strong group of American writers in a variety of genres, all of them responsive to the world they inhabited or inhabit. The articles will assist interested readers in coming closer to the work at hand, providing information and astute critical guides to the lives of each author and their writing itself, moving through an astonishing range of texts that have over two centuries helped to shape this country and its values.

—JAY PARINI

Contributors

Kim Bridgford. Kim Bridgford is the director of the West Chester University Poetry Center and the West Chester University Poetry Conference, the largest all-poetry writing conference in the United States. As editor of *Mezzo Cammin,* she was the founder of The *Mezzo Cammin* Women POets Timeline Project, which was launched at the National Museum of Women in the Arts in Washington on March 27, 2010, and will eventually be the largest database of women poets in the world. She is the author of five books of poetry. RACHEL HADAS

Robert Buckeye. Robert Buckeye is author of four works of fiction, *Pressure Drop, The Munch Case, Left,* and *Still Lives* as well as a history of staff at Middlebury College. A study of English novelist Ann Quin is forthcoming from The Dalkey Archive Press. He has also published fiction, articles and reviews on literature, film and art in magazines. For more than thirty years he was Abernethy Curator of American Literature and College Archivist at Middlebury College. MERIDEL Le SUEUR

Tom Cerasulo. Tom Cerasulo is an associate professor of English at Elms College in Chicopee, Massachusetts, where he also holds The Shaughness Family Chair for the Study of the Humanities. He has published on film adaptations, on ethnicity, and on the cultural history of American authorship. Recent work appears in *Arizona Quarterly, MELUS, Studies in American Culture, Twentieth-Century Literature,* and *Critical Companion to Eugene O'Neill.* He is the author of *Authors Out Here: Fitzgerald, West, Parker, and Schulberg in Hollywood* (University of South Carolina Press, 2010). FREDERICK EXLEY

Jack Fischel. Jack Fischel is Emeritus Professor of History at Millersville University and presently Visiting Professor of the Humanities at Messiah College. He is the auhtor of a number books on the Holocaust and his essay on Leon Uris appeared in Supplement XX of *American Writers.* SHOLEM ASCH

Sari Fordham. Sari Fordham is a creative nonfiction writer and an Assistant Professor of English at La Sierra University. BETTY SMITH

Rachel Hall. Rachel Hall teaches creative writing and literature at the State University of New York at Geneseo, where she holds the Chancellor's Award for Excellence in Teaching. Her fiction has appeared in numerous publications, including *Gettysburg Review, Crab Orchard Review, Water~Stone,* and *New Letters* which awarded her their Alexander Cappon Fiction prize. She has also received honors and awards from *Lilith, Glimmer Train,* the Bread Loaf Writers' Conference and the Constance Saltonstall Foundation for the Arts. JEAN THOMPSON

Susan Carol Hauser. Susan Carol Hauser is a poet, essayist and natural history writer. Her most recent book is *My Kind of River Journey: Seeking Passage on the Mississippi.* Her other books include *Outside after Dark: New & Selected Poems, You Can Write a Memoir,* and *Wild Rice Cooking.* Her awards include a 2011 Minnesota State Arts Board Initiative Grant and a 2010 McKnight Artist Fellowship, Loft Award in Poetry. She is a freelance writer and has been a commentator on Minnesota and National Public Radio. JANE HIRSHFIELD

Phoebe Jackson. Phoebe Jackson is an associate professor of American literature at William

CONTRIBUTORS

Paterson University. She is co-editor of *Public Works: Student Writing as Public Text.* Her research interests include twentieth-century American women writers, working-class fiction, and composition studies. ELIZABETH STROUT

Cheri Johnson. Cheri Johnson's fiction, poetry, and reviews have appeared in magazines such as *Glimmer Train Stories, Pleiades, Puerto Del Sol, New South, The Rio Grande Review,* and *Provincetown Arts.* Her chapbook of poems, *Fun & Games,* was published in 2009 by Finishing Line Press, and she has won fellowships from The McKnight Foundation, The Bush Foundation, and the Fine Arts Work Center in Provincetown. She studied literature and writing at Augsburg College, Hollins University, and The University of Minnesota. Raised in northern Minnesota, she currently lives in Minneapolis. JANE JOHNSTON SCHOOLCRAFT

Claire Keyes. Claire Keyes is Professor Emerita at Salem State University in Massachusetts. In addition to two books of poems, she has published *The Aesthetics of Power: The Poetry of Adrienne Rich* (University of Georgia Press). For the *American Writers* series, she has contributed essays about Annie Finch and Jennifer Egan. PENELOPE SCAMBLY SCHOTT

Judith Kitchen. Judith Kitchen lives in Port Townsend, WA, and teaches in the Rainier Writing Workshop low-residency MFA at Pacific Lutheran University in Tacoma, WA. She is the author of three books of personal essays, a novel, a collection of poems, and a critical study of the work of William Stafford. She regularly reviews poetry for *The Georgia Review,* where she serves as an Advisory and Contributing Editor. STUART DYBEK

J. Roger Kurtz. J. Roger Kurtz is Professor of World Literatures at the College at Brockport, State University of New York. He is the author of *Urban Obsessions, Urban Fears: The Postcolonial Kenyan Novel,* and of *Nyarloka's Gift: The Writing of Marjorie Oludhe Macgoye,* as

well as of essays on Chimamanda Adichie, Daniachew Worku, Derek Walcott, Ngugi wa Thiong'o, Meja Mwangi, David Maillu, and Lloyd Fernando. ZEE EDGELL

Janet McCann. Janet McCann's poetry has been published in a number of journals, including *Kansas Quarterly, Parnassus, Nimrod, Sou'Wester, New York Quarterly, Tendril,* and *Poetry Australia.* A 1989 NEA Creative Writing Fellowship winner, she has taught at Texas A & M University since 1969. She has co-edited two anthologies, *Odd Angles of Heaven* (1994) and *Place of Passage* (2000); co-authored two textbooks; and written a book on Wallace Stevens, *The Celestial Possible: Wallace Stevens Revisited* (1996). Her most recent poetry collection is *Emily's Dress* (Pecan Grove Press, 2004). BARBARA CROOKER

L. Bailey McDaniel. L. Bailey McDaniel is Assistant Professor of English at Oakland University. Her research and publications explore modern U.S. and post-colonial drama, paying particular attention to the ways in which ideologies of race, gender, class, and sexuality inform political hierarchies. CHERRÍE MORAGA

Louis H. Palmer III. Louis H. Palmer III is an Associate Professor in the English Department at Castleton State College in Castleton, Vermont. He teaches courses in American Literature, Public Speaking, and Composition. Research interests include regional literatures, the Gothic, and vampires. He serves as Gothic Chair for the Popular Culture Association. He has just completed *Vampires in the New World* (ABC-CLIO, 2012), an historical survey of the vampire figure in American literature and film. PINCKNEY BENEDICT

Jonas Prida. Jonas Prida holds a Ph.D. in English from Tulane University, with a focus on the popular literature and culture in antebellum America. He is an assistant professor of English at the College of St. Joseph, located in Rutland, Vermont. In addition to his research in 1840s and 1850s popular fiction, he also investigates

CONTRIBUTORS

pulp literature such as *Weird Tales,* exploitation movies, and heroic fantasy. GEORGE LIPPARD

Stephen Ross. Stephen Ross is a doctoral candidate and lecturer in the English department at the University of Oxford. He is currently completing a thesis on John Ashbery. His essays and reviews on contemporary poetry and other subjects have appeared in the *Times Literary Supplement, PN Review, The Wolf, Jacket,* and *Tower Poetry.* He is a founding editor of the literary web-journal, *Wave Composition,* and a senior editor for the *Oxonian Review.* FRANK O'HARA

Nicholas Spengler. Nicholas Spengler is a poet and essayist from Burlington, Vermont. He received an MSc with Distinction in Literature and Transatlanticism from the University of Edinburgh, where he wrote a dissertation titled "Cynosures and Other Stars: Political and Sexual Orientations in the Works of Herman Melville, Jean Genet, and Reinaldo Arenas." He received a BA in English and American Literatures from Middlebury College. An essay, "'Como un condenado': Reinaldo Arenas and Castro's 'Camp'," is forthcoming in *Transgression and Its Limits,* a book-length title from Cambridge Scholars Publishing. MAURICE KENNY

Hovig Tchalian. Hovig Tchalian teaches writing and professional communication at the University of Southern California. He is also co-founder of *Critics' Forum,* an online journal that publishes essays about Armenian diasporan art and culture. His review of Peter Balakian's *Ziggurat* appeared in 2011 in *Harvard Review.* PETER BALAKIAN

AMERICAN WRITERS

SHOLEM ASCH

(1880—1957)

Jack Fischel

IN 1936 THE novelist and critic Ludwig Lewisohn was asked to name the world's "ten greatest living Jews." The list he produced included Albert Einstein, Sigmund Freud, Henri Bergson, Martin Buber, and Louis D. Brandeis. Only one writer was considered great enough to be grouped with these eminent figures: Sholem Asch (Siegel, *The Controversial Sholem Asch*, p. 8). Indeed, until 1939 Sholem Asch was among the most celebrated Yiddish writers in the United States, if not the world. Asch wrote all of his fiction in Yiddish, and many of his eighteen novels were first excerpted in Abraham Cahan's *Forverts* (*Forward*), New York's leading Yiddish-language newspaper. His works, translated into English by translators such as Willa and Edwin Muir and Maurice Samuel, were targeted toward first- and second-generation Jewish audiences.

Asch's fiction concerned itself with aspects of Jewish life both in America (*The Mother, Uncle Moses, East River*) and in Europe, the setting for his idealized shtetl and descriptions of the everyday lives of common Jews (*The Little Town,* "Kola Road"). His subjects included the Jewish underworld (*Mottke, the Thief*), prostitution (*God of Vengeance*), religious piety (*Reb Shloyme nogid, Salvation*), Jewish reaction to anti-Semitism (*Kiddush Ha-Shem, The War Goes On*), intermarriage (*Salvation, East River*), the exploitation of workers in New York's garment industry (*Uncle Moses, East River*), and Jewish involvement in the Russian revolutions of 1905 and 1917 (in *Three Cities,* his condemnation of the Bolsheviks is as devastating as Arthur Koestler's later denunciation of Stalinism in *Darkness at Noon*). His most important and controversial effort as a novelist, however, was to heal the breach between Judaism and Christianity (*The Nazarene, The Apostle,* and *Mary*).

A recurrent theme found in Asch's fiction is that of the Jewish longing for the Messiah, a divinely sent redeemer who will relieve the suffering of the Jews and bring about the end of days, wherein there will be peace on earth as mirrored in the Jewish Sabbath. Where Asch departs from traditional Judaism, however, is that he rejected the belief that the Messiah would redeem only the Jews. Rather, he argued that since God was universal, the Messiah's mission would be to redeem all of mankind. For Jews, the coming of the Messiah necessitated belief in one God by observing the laws of the Torah; for gentiles, salvation required the acceptance of Jesus as the Christ. Christianity and Judaism were, for Asch, two branches of a single monotheistic religion wherein both worshipped the same God. Asch believed that without monotheism, civilization would descend into chaos and anarchy.

Early on in his career, Asch was influenced by the radical Russian writers Maxim Gorky and Mikhail Artsybashev and became a strong advocate of both the Russian revolutionary movement in general and the Social Democrats in particular. But this did not last. As someone who observed the Russian Revolution of 1917, he quickly became disillusioned with bolshevism, but he was aware of its attraction for many intellectuals who saw in Marxism the secularization of the messianic idea, wherein they substituted faith in God for faith in dialectical materialism. Asch was critical of this belief in a secular utopia, and he included among his fictional characters Zachary Mirkin in *Three Cities* (1933) and Nathan Davidowsky in *East River,* (1946) who represented Marxist thought only to become increasingly disillusioned with the belief in secular salvation.

1

SHOLEM ASCH

In his Christological novels, Asch emphasized the Jewish roots of Christianity but also gave credence to the divinity of Jesus. At the height of his fame as a Yiddish writer, Asch's reputation underwent a dramatic reversal within the Jewish community with the publication of the first of his three novels about Jesus Christ, *The Nazarene* (1939); this was followed by *The Apostle* (1943), based on the life of the apostle Paul, and *Mary* (1949). The publication of *The Nazarene,* largely acclaimed by the non-Jewish reading public, quickly became a best seller. Asch's life of Jesus, however, coincided with Nazi Germany's invasion of Poland in 1939, with all of the subsequent consequences for the millions of Europe's Jews. Given the long history of church-based anti-Semitism, and the fact that an ostensibly Christian country, Germany, was embarking on the destruction of European Jewry, Asch's sympathetic portrayal of Jesus and his apparent acceptance of the Immaculate Conception (*Mary*) was at best a case of bad timing. He was subsequently vilified by his peers, including Cahan and members of the *Forward* staff, of promoting Christianity and being an apostate Jew. As a consequence, his long relationship with Cahan, who refused to publish excerpts of *The Nazarene,* came to an acrimonious end. Soon after their break, Cahan attacked Asch's seeming turn to Christianity in a book written in Yiddish that translates as "Sholem Asch's New Way" (1941). Despite the controversy, however, *The Nazarene* received positive reviews in the mainstream American press, which also included favorable reviews by such Jewish American intellectuals as Alfred Kazin and Clifton Fadiman.

The success of *The Nazarene,* however, came with a price. Asch was maligned and boycotted by his fellow writers of Yiddish fiction and found publishing opportunities in the Yiddish press closed to him, with the exception of the Communist newspaper *Morgen Freiheit,* despite his earlier criticism of the Soviet Union. Asch's publication of *The Apostle* in 1943 further rekindled attacks against him, but at the same time, this fictional biography of the apostle Paul became a best seller, and in the following year several of his supporters (unsuccessfully) urged

the Nobel Prize committee to award him its 1943 literature award.

In response to the criticism that he had abandoned Judaism for Christianity, Asch published two nonfiction works in which he attempted to defend himself against the accusation that he had become an apostate. In *What I Believe* (1941) and *One Destiny: An Epistle to the Christians* (1945), Asch explained that, in the Christological novels, he was attempting to show that Christianity and Judaism were linked by a common bond and derived from the same belief system. Foreshadowing the emergence of the term "Judeo-Christian tradition," which came into use following World War II, Asch made the argument he attributed to Paul in *The Apostle:* that while the Torah is the religious authority for the Jews' belief in God, and Jesus is the intermediary for the Christians' belief in God, the two religions are not mutually exclusive but rather believe in the same God through different intercessions. His explanation, however, did not satisfy his critics, whose suspicions about Asch and his Christian sentiments were reinforced by his comments in an interview with the *Christian Herald* in January 1944. The interview must be viewed in the context of the times, when millions of Jews had already been murdered by the Nazis and their Axis helpers in the heart of an ostensibly Christian Europe. Asch informs his interviewer that "Jesus Christ, to me, is the outstanding personality of all time, all his history, both as Son of God and as Son of Man." He further states that he viewed Paul as "the greatest Jewish patriot ... who compromised the minor laws in order to have the major doctrine accepted.... but if he had not done it, Christianity today would be just another Jewish sect." (As background, it is worth remembering that dietary laws and circumcision were among the "small things" from the Torah that Paul absolved gentile converts from observing, and that, early in his career, Asch embroiled himself in controversy when he condemned—in a Polish anti-Semitic newspaper—the Jewish practice of ritual circumcision as barbaric.) Elsewhere in the interview Asch states that Christians must know more about Judaism and Jews more about Christianity and concludes,

"who knows—maybe some day we shall be worshipping under one roof." Irving Howe, in his *World of Our Fathers,* states that to charge Asch with proselytizing for Christianity was outrageous but notes that "the mere fact that Asch had chosen to write about Jesus in a sympathetic vein struck many of his Yiddish readers as a provocation" (p. 450). Referring to the interview in the *Christian Herald,* Howe notes that Asch showed little moral tact when, asked which Christian saint might best become the heavenly patron of the Jews, Asch replied that his candidate was Peter. Howe quotes the response of the Yiddish writer Hayim Greenberg, who rebuked Asch by noting that Peter was commonly recognized as the founder of the Catholic Church. "Yet you [Asch] decided that our patron saint should be the man who stands at the fountainhead of the papal dynasty.... what a lack of elementary decency towards your own people" (Howe, p. 450).

Although Asch was rejected by the Yiddish writing establishment, he did not back down from his admiration for Jesus and his disciples, although in his work he made a distinction between the organized churches and what he perceived as the positive moral ethos of Christianity. This is expressed in his 1946 novel *East River,* where the subject of intermarriage between his Jewish and Catholic characters challenges one of the major taboos in the Jewish community (he had already introduced this motif in *Salvation*). In this widely read and critically praised novel, Asch contends that often it is the dogmatic adherence to religious doctrine in both religions that prevents a reconciliation between Christians and Jews. Asch's response to this critique of institutional rigidity (among both his Jewish and Catholic characters) is exemplified by one the novel's primary characters, Moshe Wolf, a deeply pious Orthodox Jew and the father of two of the author's protagonists, who comes to accept his baptized grandchild despite his deep hurt in regard to his son's marriage to Mary, a Catholic. Asch writes of Mary, who believes that Jesus sent her to Moshe Wolf,

> it sometimes seemed to her that Moshe Wolf was not one individual Jew—he was all Jews; ... and his struggle to keep the faith was the struggle of all Israel. And at the same time he was struggling against the generations to give his grandchild a place in his heart. He was risking everything—his religion, all his moral values, and his portion in the life hereafter. He was risking everything for his deep, human love.
>
> (p. 395)

Although Asch presented himself in his novels as a mediator between Christians and Jews, his critics interpreted his efforts differently. Perhaps the harshest of his detractors was Herman (Chaim) Lieberman, a leading columnist of the *Forward,* who, in his book *The Christianity of Sholem Asch: An Appraisal from the Jewish Viewpoint* (1953), accuses Asch in his Christological novels of undertaking a veritable crusade on behalf of the Christian faith and at the same time both distorting and sometimes slandering Judaism. In *East River,* Lieberman argues, Asch lauds the Christian side, and the Jewish side is belittled. For example, Lieberman charges that a number of Jews in the novel are depicted as being concerned only with money. Thus, states Lieberman, Asch reinforces the slanderous stereotype of the money-loving Jew "so often encountered in Christian novels" (p. 209). Lieberman provides many other examples where he insists Asch denigrates Jews and Judaism and concludes that *East River* is an anti-Jewish book.

In his aptly titled *The Controversial Sholem Asch* (1976), the closest work in English that approximates a biography of his subject, Ben Siegel argues that those who closely monitored Asch's writings through the years would not have been surprised by the publication of *The Nazarene.* According to Siegel, the novel marked the culmination of Asch's preoccupation with the personality of Jesus, an interest that began as early as 1904 and is prefigured in his subsequent fiction. What fascinated Asch was Jesus' self-sacrifice to God, and this obeisance to the God of Israel is often idealized in his fiction in the form of a rabbi or the Jewish people, as exemplified in such novels as *Kiddush Ha-Shem* (1926) and *Salvation* (1934). For Asch, both Jesus and Paul are placed within the teachings of Judaism and their message is representative of those within Judaism who value the spirit of Judaism as op-

SHOLEM ASCH

posed to rigid adherence to the letter of the law. As early as his novella *The Little Town* (1904), Asch wrote of the spiritual affinity of all who worshipped Judaism's deity, but he also expressed his partiality for the advocates of the law's spirit rather than its letter, as well as his disdain for scholarly legalists "who feel superior to their strong-backed, ill-educated brethren" (p. 146). Siegel points to Reb Daavidle of *The Little Town,* a character who foreshadows not only Yechiel in *Salvation* but also Jesus in *The Nazarene* and Paul in *The Apostle,* as an example of a pious rabbi who displays deep compassion for the town's unlettered poor. This compassion not only angers his affluent congregation but leads to his dismissal as its rabbi.

EARLY LIFE AND CAREER

Writing about his great-grandfather, David Mazower summed up the many contradictions that characterized the life of Sholem Asch, describing him as

> a youth who had turned his back on a rabbinical career but never stopped searching for faith; a passionate Jew who harbored a deep mistrust of organized religion; a *bon vivant* who prided himself on being a man of the people; an activist deeply involved in politics but impatient of political parties; and a writer adored by the Jewish masses and later virtually excommunicated …
>
> (p. 3)

Sholem Asch was born on November 1, 1880, in Kutno, Russian Poland, to his devoutly Hasidic parents, Moyshe Gombiner Asch, a cattle dealer and innkeeper, and Malka Frayde, the daughter of the rabbi of Lenshits. Malka was Moyshe Asch's second wife; he was formerly married to Rude Shmit, who bore Moyshe seven children and died in 1879. According to David Mazower, a number of Asch's fictional father-figures are based on Moyshe Asch, with the novellas *The Little Town* (published in Hebrew in 1904) and *Reb Shloyme nogid* (1913) the most closely drawn from life (Mazower, p. 6).

The fourth of ten children, seven boys and three girls, Sholem was the product of a tradi-

tional Jewish education, which included studying the Talmud, Midrash, Psalms, and religious texts. His father assumed that he would become a rabbi since he was the only one of his children who excelled in religious studies, but Asch had become enamored of secular learning soon after teaching himself German with the aid of Moses Mendelssohn's translation of the Bible. (Early literary influences included Leo Tolstoy, Fyodor Dostoevsky, and later on, Miguel de Cervantes, Charles Dickens, and Maxim Gorky; as a mature novelist he admired Thomas Mann and Ernest Hemingway, among others). Like many Orthodox Jewish parents of the time, Moyshe and Malka disapproved of secular education, and for this reason Sholem moved to the nearby town of Wlo-clawek, a more cosmopolitan hub located on the Vistula River. There he supported himself as a letter writer for the illiterate Jewish townspeople, an experience that offered him insights into the needs and longings of his fellow Jews. Asch would later write that "until that time I was a completely orthodox believing Jew. Later I was convinced that the simple Jew … the common man, stands on a much higher ethical level than the learned Hasid" (Siegel, p. 15).

Asch's writing career was stimulated by his wide reading in European literature, and in 1900 he traveled to Warsaw, where he met Isaac Leib Peretz, who is regarded as one of the three great classical Yiddish writers together with Mendele Mokher Sefarim and Sholom Aleichem. Peretz became something of a mentor for Asch and convinced him to switch from writing in Hebrew to Yiddish. (His critics would contend that, although Asch was a good storyteller, his Yiddish had a great deal to be desired.) Soon after, Asch published his first Yiddish story, "Moyshele" (Little Moses), which appeared in the journal *Der Yud* in 1900. His reputation, however, was established with the publication of his first book of stories under the title of *In a shlekhter tsayt* (1902; In a bad time). It was also in Warsaw that he married Mathilde Shapiro, the daughter of the Polish-Jewish writer Menakhem Mendel Shapiro, in 1901. The couple had four children (among them the novelist Nathan Asch and Moses "Moe" Asch, founder of Folkway Records). His mar-

riage to Mathilde afforded Asch a degree of financial security that allowed him to become a full-time writer.

Asch's importance as a fiction writer, however, commenced in 1904 with the publication of *A shtetl* (translated as *The Little Town,* 1907), a novella that described the idyllic home life of Reb Yekhezkel Gombiner (modeled after his own father), a pious Hasidic timber merchant whose connection to nature is the source of his wealth. In this work Asch established himself in the forefront of new Yiddish writers. In the same year, his play *Tsurikgekumen* (The return) launched his career as a dramatist, and the work had a successful run with the Kraków Polish Theater. This was followed by the play *Meshiekhs tsaytn* (1906; Times of the Messiah), which was produced as *The Return to Zion,* starring the Russian actress W. P. Komisarjevsky. In 1907 Komisarjevsky produced Asch's most controversial play, *Got fun nekome* (translated as *The God of Vengeance,* 1918) in Saint Petersburg, in Russian. (Because the play included prostitution and a lesbian relationship, the New York production of the play in 1923 resulted in the arrest of the cast on obscenity charges.)

By 1917 Asch, in addition to his plays, had published three major novels: *Reb Shloyme nogid: A poeme fun yidishn leben* (1913; Shloyme the wealthy: A poem of Jewish life); *Meri* (1913; not to be confused with his 1949 Christological novel, *Mary*), and its sequel *Der veg tsu zikh* (1917; The road to one's self). In both of the latter novels, Asch described the sociopolitical issues surrounding the 1905 Russian Revolution, wherein he focused on the wealthy Jewish elite of Saint Petersburg and the poverty of Jewish workers in Ukraine. Asch's politics would be further elaborated in what is perhaps his best novel, *Three Cities: A Trilogy* (*Farn mabl* [Before the flood]), published in 1933. Asch exhibited great sympathy for the working class but believed that both the 1905 and 1917 revolutions were fundamentally hostile to Jews, and subsequently he became a bitter opponent of the Soviet Union (until 1943–1944, when he supported the Soviets against Nazi Germany).

Asch's rise to prominence was accompanied by his own efforts not only to promote his work but to enhance the prominence of Yiddish literature in the non-Jewish world. Mazower notes that Asch, from his earliest days as a writer, was determined that Yiddish literature should take its place as an integral part of European culture, and toward this end he marketed himself by meeting with publishers, newspaper editors, and theater directors from Odessa and Moscow to Warsaw and beyond. The result was that Asch was the first Yiddish writer to reach a general European audience through the translation of his fiction.

In 1907 Asch traveled to Palestine, where the experience of visiting the holy places, he would later claim, reinforced his intention to write about Jesus. In 1910 he arrived in the United States but decided after a short stay to move his family to France, settling in Châtillon, a suburb outside Paris. With the outbreak of war in 1914 Asch and his family returned to the United States, where he became a naturalized citizen in 1920, moving to a large house on Staten Island. It was also during this period that Asch became a salaried and regular employee of the *Forward,* at the time the most widely read Yiddish newspaper in America, thus commencing a relationship that would last for nearly twenty-five years. Asch also involved himself in Jewish causes, becoming a founder of the American Jewish Joint Distribution Committee (JDC, or the "Joint") in 1914 and coming to know Jewish communal leaders such as Cyrus Adler, Judah Magnes, Jacob Schiff, and Felix Warburg. His first major work published in America was *Motke ganef* (1916), which was serialized both in the *Forward* and in the Warsaw newspaper *Haynt;* the novel was translated by Willa and Edwin Muir and published as *Mottke, the Thief* by Putnam in 1935. (Through all of Asch's later travails, Putnam would remain his publisher.) This tale of an amoral Jewish gangster living in the Warsaw slums was soon followed in 1918 by *Onkl Mozes* (*Uncle Moses,* 1920), a novel inspired by Asch's impressions of impoverished immigrant life in New York's Lower East Side. In 1919 Asch visited Europe on a fact-finding mission for the JDC and was shocked by

the conditions of the Jews he found in Lithuania. His experience was so disturbing that he suffered a nervous breakdown after his return to the United States. The pogroms directed toward Jews both during and after World War 1 was the inspiration for his next major work, *Kidesh ha-Shem* (1919; Sanctification of the name; translated as *Kiddush Ha-Shem: An Epic of 1648,* 1926), one of the earliest historical novels in modern Yiddish literature. The novel was based on the anti-Semitic Khmelnytsky massacre of Jews in mid-seventeenth-century Ukraine and Poland. In this work of fiction, Asch wrote of the moral obligation of Jews to save their own lives unless motivated to martyrdom by their faith. The novel was followed by *Di kishef-makherin fun Kastilye* (1921; The witch of Castile, translated into English in 1980 as *The Witch from Castile*), whose theme of self-sacrifice, like that of *Kiddush Ha-Shem,* is Asch's account of a young woman's resolute martyrdom for her Jewish faith.

His reputation fully established as a major Yiddish novelist, Asch was the recipient of an unusual gift on his fortieth birthday when a number of his New York admirers formed a committee, headed by Rabbi Judah Magnes, to publish his collected works in twelve volumes, with an introduction by the Yiddish critic and his future biographer Samuel Charney, better known under his pen name as "S. Niger." *Sholem Asch: Zayn lebn un zayne verk* (1960; Sholem Asch: His life and his work) is written in Yiddish and has yet to be translated into English. In 1932 Asch was elected honorary president of the Yiddish PEN club.

A few years later Asch received the Polish Republic's Polonia Restituta decoration from Joseph Pilsudski, the dictator of Poland. At a time when Polish anti-Semitism was intensifying, Asch's acceptance of the honor created another controversy in the Jewish world, and although he defended his decision, Asch would later have doubts as to whether he should have acknowledged the receipt of the award.

Charles Madison has written that Asch, more than any other Yiddish writer, was subjected to criticism from the early years of his growing successful career. Some of it, Madison claims, was

owing to his personality, which some viewed as "egotistical, impulsive, inconsiderate, and avid for praise" (p. 243). Madison cites Shlomo Rosenberg, Asch's longtime secretary and editor, who wrote that "Asch had ... a weakness for titles, the rich, and ... Gentiles" (p. 243). Madison notes that, when still a young man, Asch was honored in Odessa by a number of distinguished Yiddish writers such as Hayim Nahman Bialik and Mendele, but, "because they praised him as a Yiddish writer, he interrupted to exclaim, 'I am not a Yiddish artist, I am a universal artist' " (p. 243).

Not really enamored of America, Asch returned to Poland in 1924, and then took up residence in Paris, where he became part of an intellectual circle that included artists such as Marc Chagall and Man Ray. (It is worth noting that Chagall, like Asch, was criticized for his paintings of the crucifixion of Jesus, which he described as symbols of martyred Jews everywhere and the victims of the Holocaust.) Asch's relationships with the colony of Parisian artists resulted in his being frequently asked to sit for portraits and sculptures. Among the many portraits of Asch that have survived are those by Chagall, Leopold Gottlieb, Emil Orlik, and Saul Raskin, together with busts by Jacob Epstein, Chana Orloff, and Moryce Lipschitz.

Although Asch's life in Paris was intellectually stimulating, he could not ignore the ever-worsening condition of the Jews in Germany. Determined to add his voice to those opposed to Hitler, Asch wrote the novel *Bam opgrunt* (1936; At the abyss; published that year as *The War Goes On*), which dissects the ways in which the Jewish minority was scapegoated for the chaotic economic conditions that made possible the Nazi seizure of power. As the threat of war intensified in Europe, Asch returned permanently to the United States in 1938.

The next year saw the publication of *The Nazarene* (1939; published in Yiddish as *Der man fun natseres,* 1943), with all of the concomitant controversy that was to follow. Although deeply hurt by the controversy over his Christological novels, Asch spent the last decade of his life returning to fiction with Jewish themes and settings, with the exception of the last of his Chris-

tological trilogy, *Mary,* published in 1949. In response to *Mary,* perhaps the most "Christian" of the novels about Jesus, Chaim Lieberman angrily wrote *The Christianity of Sholem Asch: An Appraisal from the Jewish Viewpoint,* his savage attack on Asch. The publication of *Mary* also led to an open break with Maurice Samuel, the translator of many of Asch's books.

Despite the controversy surrounding the Christological novels, the books had attained favorable attention in the Christian world, and Asch was certain it would lead to his being awarded a Nobel Prize. Maurice Samuel reported that winning the Nobel Prize was "a kind of mania with him." When he did not receive it, "he could not understand why Thomas Mann should have got it and not he" (Siegel, p. 253). His failure to receive the prize darkened Asch's final years.

Among Asch's more notable works of fiction following the publication of *Mary* is *East River* (*1st River,* both 1946), a novel dealing with the subject of intermarriage and the exploitation of Jewish workers in the garment industry by Jewish factory owners—including a harrowing description of the Triangle Shirtwaist Factory fire in New York City in March 1911—and the attempt of his Jewish characters to reconcile the realities of American life with religious tradition. In the same year he published *The Burning Bush* (*Der brenendiker dorn,* both 1946), a collection of short stories dealing with Nazi atrocities. These short stories were Asch's response to the criticism that he had not used his considerable talents to chronicle the Nazi extermination campaign against the Jews. In his next book, *Tales of My People* (1948), Asch returns to life in the shtetl but also includes a series of short tales about Jewish suffering during the Holocaust. Additional works during this period include *Moses* (*Moyshe,* both 1951); *A Passage in the Night* (1953; *Grosman un zun* [Grosman and Son], 1954); his last completed novel, *The Prophet* (1955; *Der novi,* 1956), about Deutero-Isaiah; and a number of short stories, including "Kola Street," which he wrote for Irving Howe and Eliezer Greenberg's collection of Yiddish short stories, *A Treasury of Yiddish Stories* (1954).

Because he wrote for the communist Yiddish paper *Morgen Freiheit* during the war years and wrote positively about the Soviet Union in the fight against Hitlerism in his 1945 short book *One Destiny: An Epistle to the Christians,* Asch was asked to appear several times in 1952 before Senator Joseph McCarthy and the House Committee on Un-American Activities. In the same year he made his first visit to the State of Israel where the controversy over his Christological novels followed him, especially among Orthodox Jews. But there were others who welcomed him, including the mayor of Bat Yam, who invited Asch to build a home. Asch accepted and spent his last years in the coastal town in the suburb of Tel Aviv with his wife, Mathilde. Asch made provisions for his house in Bat Yam to be converted into a museum after his death. The house is now the Sholem Asch Museum.

In 1957 he and Matilda decided to visit London, even though he was in the process of writing a novel to be called "Abraham and Sarah." On July 10, as he sat at his desk, Asch suffered a stroke and died the same day. Unlike the one hundred thousand people who lined the New York streets in 1916 for the funeral that accompanied Sholom Aleichem's hearse from the Bronx all the way to Brooklyn, or the similar number of Warsaw Jews who had followed Peretz's funeral procession in 1915, Asch's funeral was a low-key affair attended by relatives, friends, and a small number of Yiddish writers—a few dozen mourners at most. The controversy over his Christological novels had taken its toll, resulting in Jewish apathy to his passing. Asch is buried in the Golders Green cemetery in London.

Given Sholem Asch's body of work, the discussion that follows offers a representative sample of his fiction and only those of his works in English translation.

THE LITTLE TOWN

The novella *The Little Town* first appeared in serial form in 1904, and was later published in the 1948 collection *Tales of My People*; it is based

on Asch's memories of Kutno. Although Asch is praised more for his engaging storytelling than for his style as a writer, *The Little Town* is an exception. The novella is a combination of both storytelling and style, wherein Asch celebrates life in the Polish shtetl and the surrounding countryside. Unlike many other writers of Yiddish fiction, Asch displays a love of nature as well as an earthiness among his characters. Absent is any hint of tsarist oppression or anti-Semitism among the Christian peasants. On the contrary, Jewish townsmen and gentile peasants live in peace and contentment, devoid of poverty or fear of one another. Although narrative plotlines are replaced with vignettes of daily life among the Jewish inhabitants, the character of Yekhezkel Gombiner (modeled after Moshe Gombiner Asch) and his family link the various scenes. The story takes place during the nine months that precede the Jewish High Holy Days, and a series of incidents during this period govern the action of the work: the local Hasidim replace the unlettered but "saintly" rabbi with their own "wonder" rabbi; Yekhezkel's daughter is promised in an arranged marriage to a fellow merchant's son fresh from the yeshiva; the town of Kasner is abuzz with wedding preparations; a fire sets the synagogue ablaze.

The Sabbath is beautifully portrayed, as is Asch's description of the preparation of the foods for the day of rest. Summer fades, and the townspeople prepare for the most sacred days of the Jewish calendar. It is evident that Asch is engaged in nostalgia for the traditional Jewish town of his youth, a simple and humble way of life that was quickly disappearing.

GOD OF VENGEANCE

Almost at the same time that Asch wrote the nostalgic *Little Town,* he took notice of the shady characters who also inhabited small Jewish towns. Asch's realism did not shy away from writing about the Jewish "underworld," a subject most Yiddish writers avoided in their fiction. Asch wrote six plays, of which *God of Vengeance* was the most successful as well as the most controversial.

First performed in 1907, the play tells the story of Yankel Chapchovich and his wife, Sore, a former prostitute, who own a brothel in a large Polish town. As staged, Yankel, Sore, and their daughter, Rivkele, live in upstairs quarters, with the brothel located downstairs. The parents are determined to protect Rivkele's innocence, hoping to arrange her marriage to a rabbi. Toward this end they place a Torah scroll in her room as an offering (bribe?) to God to protect Rivkele's purity. The parents, however, are unaware that Rivkele already has a lover—Manke, a young prostitute in Yankel's employ who plies her trade downstairs in the brothel. Rivkele and Manke's relationship is disclosed as they are caught kissing one another, and Yankel's plan to purchase God's protection through the placement of the Torah in Rivkele's room leads to a wrenching result. As the play concludes, Rivkele is banished downstairs to the brothel—God's vengeance for Yankel desecrating the Torah.

Although the play's depiction of Jewish pimps, prostitutes, and lesbian lovers did not cause controversy when it was performed in Europe, the work created a scandal when it was staged at the Apollo Theater in New York City in 1923. The cast, producer, and theater manager were charged with presenting an obscene and immoral play. But this was not all. The theater received letters from patrons who charged that the play was anti-Semitic, an accusation reinforced by Rabbi Joseph Silverman of Fifth Avenue's Temple Emanu-El, who stated that "This play libels the Jewish religion. Even the greatest of anti-Semites could not have written such a thing" (Seidman, p. 54). Subsequently a trial was held, wherein a New York jury fined the producer and the actor Rudolph Schildkraut, who portrayed Yankel, $200.

God of Vengeance is the only full-length, original Asch drama translated into English to date. Along with H. Leivick's *The Golem* and S. Ansky's *The Dybuk, God of Vengeance* remains among the most familiar Yiddish plays known to non-Yiddish-speaking audiences. Yet when Asch provided a copy of the play in its formative stage to Peretz, the response of his mentor to the still-unpublished play was to "burn it, Asch, burn it."

He gave this advice not because he thought the play was poorly written or salacious but because Yankel's act of piety in commissioning a Torah scroll was implausible and foreign to Jewish sensibilities. Give charity to poor people? Yes, but not commission a scribe to copy a Torah scroll. For Peretz, using the scroll for "effect" would constitute sacrilege to Jewish viewers and could only work with a non-Jewish audience ignorant of the central role of the Torah in Jewish life (Seidman).

Despite the controversy surrounding the play, *God of Vengeance* established Asch's international reputation, and thanks to the intercession of Abraham Cahan, who defended it in the pages of the *Forward,* the play ultimately found acceptance by Yiddish audiences in America. In the 1940s, with Nazi Germany bent on the destruction of European Jewry and the controversy surrounding his publication of *The Nazarene* and *The Apostle,* Asch forbade the play's further production, although a 1946 Yiddish performance of it in London was attempted before it was blocked by the censor at the request of the chief rabbi and other community leaders. Since the later twentieth century there has been a renewed interest in the play, and it has been presented in various theaters in the United States.

MOTTKE, THE THIEF

Along with *The God of Vengeance* and the novel *Der toyter mentsh* (1920; The dead man), *Mottke, the Thief,* first published in Yiddish in 1916, was one of three works in which Sholem Asch wrote about the Jewish underworld. During the first two decades of the twentieth century, when the works were written, the Jewish presence in the sex trade and other criminal activities had become an uncomfortable subject in the American Jewish community. Asch's critics charged that representation of Jews as prostitutes, brothel keepers, or gangsters fed into anti-Semitic stereotypes. This was of concern because the perception of large-scale Jewish involvement in crime was used to promote anti-immigration legislation by nativist groups.

This was the context in which Asch wrote his novel of the Warsaw underworld, featuring an immoral Jewish gangster. Asch portrays Mottke as an earthy crook who goes through his adolescent years engaged in thievery and fistfights without any seeming awareness of right from wrong. He decides early on that life is a vicious battleground where only the strong survive. Exhibiting no pangs of conscience, Mottke steals from peddlers and children and engages in physical altercations with others in his neighborhood. He has no use for school and avoids going to classes. This delinquent life is enabled by his mother, Red Slatke, who is the only character until late in the novel for whom Mottke shows any warmth. By the age of fourteen Mottke has become a skilled thief, and the town is terrified by his presence. As the story unfolds, Mottke runs away from home, joins a traveling vaudeville-like act, and eventually leaves with Mary, a rope dancer in the troupe, who subsequently becomes a prostitute with Mottke as her pimp. Having left the vaudeville team, Mottke and Mary are pursued by Kanarik, her other suitor, whom Mottke murders, stealing his papers and assuming his identity. He and Mary then establish themselves among the Warsaw ghetto underworld.

In Warsaw, Mottke becomes rich, powerful, and feared for his acts of violence. But soon he seeks a modicum of respectability as he falls in love with Chanele, a beautiful and proper Jewish young lady. Mottke decides to forgo his life as a criminal, proposes to Chanele, and subsequently tells her about the murder. She reveals this to her parents, who in turn demand that the police arrest him. As the novel reaches its conclusion, Mottke, who did not believe Chanele would betray him, is arrested and goes almost willingly to prison.

More than a few Jewish readers found the character of Mottke as loathsome as that of Yankel Chapchovich in *God of Vengeance.* Consequently Asch, not for the last time, was embroiled in controversy over his portrayal of Jewish characters specifically and Judaism in general.

SHOLEM ASCH

KIDDUSH HA-SHEM: AN EPIC OF 1648

Following his return to the United States after his disheartening 1919 mission to Lithuania, where Asch encountered epidemics, pogroms, hunger, and unemployment among the Jewish population, he joined the JDC's effort to raise funds for the victims. One fund-raising tactic he used was to go on stage after the performance of a Yiddish play and make a stirring appeal for donations from his audience. But this was not all that he did. To encourage his Jewish audiences not to despair about the future of their brethren in Europe, he used his fiction to demonstrate how, in earlier periods of Jewish history, faith and courage had turned tragedy into spiritual victories in the form of martyrdom. Such is the subject of his play *Maranen* (1922; The Marranos) and the novel *The Witch of Castile,* in which a Jewish girl with a Madonna's face is martyred when she is burned at the stake in sixteenth-century Rome.

Kiddush Ha-Shem describes the Khmelnytsky Uprising against absentee Polish landlords in Ukraine in 1648–1649, named for the Cossack chieftain who was responsible for the slaughter of as many as five hundred thousand Jews. In this novel of martyrdom and treachery, the Poles, who had promised to fight alongside the Jews, betray them to the Cossacks, who promptly perpetrate a massacre. In Asch's telling, the Jews are willing to fight back but are persuaded not to do so by a holy Jewish tailor, omnipresent throughout the novel, who persuades them to martyr themselves in the name of God. (Siegel suggests that the tailor is really a *lamedvovnik* of Jewish folklore, one of the supposedly thirty-six secret saints whose collective righteousness makes possible the world's continuation despite its wickedness.) Asch viewed the 1918–1919 pogroms in Lithuania as a recurrence of the Khmelnytsky massacres, and by retelling the earlier events and glorifying their martyrs, he hoped to comfort the Jews in their present situation. As Asch tells the story, the Jews of 1648–1649 faced annihilation, but the remnant survived because of their undying faith in God.

Despite the brutality inflicted by the Cossacks, Asch does not detail the excesses of the pogrom's perpetrators. Rather, his novel emphasizes the restraint, dignity, and spirituality of the Jews, including that of Deborah, a beautiful Jewess captured by the Cossacks who allows herself to be killed rather than submit to her captor. Asch has her utter the *Shema* as her last words: " 'Hear, O Israel, the Lord our God, the Lord is One.' ... And she became silent." As Ben Siegel points out, the author's restraint in re-creating the devastating pogrom is summed up in his inclusion of a Jewish chronicle of the time, "We are ashamed to write down all that the Cossacks and Tatars did unto the Jews, lest we disgrace the species man, which is created in the image of God" (p. 68).

THREE CITIES: A TRILOGY

In Asch's first best seller translated into English, Chomsky, one of his reoccurring characters in *Three Cities,* tells Zachary Mirkin, the novel's protagonist,

> the main thing ... is to believe in everything one does. God does not care in what fashion you believe in Him, so long as you believe there is a power for good directing the world.... That is why it does not matter whether the things you have to do are small or great; they all come from one source, they all have one purpose: to accomplish God's work on earth.
>
> (*Three Cities,* p. 515)

On one level, *Three Cities* (1933) is a sweeping novel about Jewish life in the years between 1910 and 1920, portraying the culture of aristocratic Jews in Saint Petersburg, the poverty of the Jewish masses in Warsaw, and the immediate, tenuous aftermath of the Bolshevik Revolution in Moscow, three threads that are tied together by the character of Mirkin, the son of a wealthy Russian entrepreneur. Yet Chomsky's words to Mirkin, which mark the turning point in Mirkin's search for meaning in his life, also reflect the religious philosophy that will reach a climax in Asch's Christological novels: his view that Christians and Jews worship the same God and seek the same objective of bringing about the Messianic age, which for Asch means establishing peace on earth and redressing the poverty of the masses. This exchange between Chomsky

and Mirkin is not the only instance where Asch promotes his Judeo-Christian synthesis. Early in the novel, Asch introduces Madame Kvasniecova, a Jewish convert to the Orthodox Russian Church who continues to observe both religions: "In the evening when Easter and Passover fell on the same date, she celebrated the Seder and in the morning she went to church joining other worshippers, saying: 'Christ is risen.' " Elsewhere Asch writes that "side by side with her Christmas tree gleamed the eight candles of the old Jewish Menorah" (p. 107).

In his essay "Russia Between Myth and Reality: From *Meri* to *Three Cities*," Mikhail Krutikov argues that the Russian critic Akim Volynsky (Chaim Flekser), who insisted that literature should concern itself with religious problems, influenced Asch's quest for a bridge linking Judaism and Christianity. Krutikov maintains that Volynsky influenced Asch's later Christological writings.

In addition to religion, *Three Cities* contains other themes, most importantly the revolution in Russia. In his earlier work *Meri* (1913), Asch dealt with the 1905 revolution in Russia and then wrote a sequel whose title translates as "The Road to One's Self" (1915). In both of these novels he describes the role played by Jewish intellectuals in the early reform and revolutionary movements and their rejection of their traditional Jewish upbringing. Asch examines their belief that a socialist Russia would liberate Jews and their willingness to sacrifice their lives and careers for the cause, then chronicles their disillusionment by the failure of the 1905 revolution and the subsequent brutal pogroms that followed.

Three Cities was Asch's most ambitious work to date. According to Siegel, he had hoped the novel would gain him the stature of a Thomas Mann. To some degree his expectation was realized when the book received high praise from critics and attained popularity with the public. The influence of Leo Tolstoy is apparent in the grand scope of the novel, which calls to mind *War and Peace,* especially in the similarities between Zachary Mirkin and Count Pierre Bezukhov.

The Jews of Saint Petersburg, as Asch depicts them, are an assimilated and wealthy group of Russian patriots. In addition to Zachary Mirkin, Asch's portrait of the city's Jewish elite includes Solomon Ossipovitch Halperin, a prominent attorney who, despite his distance from his Jewish roots, is always ready to help Jewish victims of tsarist arbitrary rule; and Gabriel Haimovitch Mirkin, Zachary's father, described by Asch as one of the wealthiest men in all of Russia. One of the novel's major plots revolves around the two families' interaction, which includes a number of complicated relationships: Zachary, who is committed to wed Nina, Gabriel Mirken's daughter, secretly lusts for her mother. Zachary leaves Saint Petersburg, having broken his engagement to Nina, but his father subsequently marries Nina.

It has been pointed out that, in describing the wealthy elements of Saint Petersburg Jewry, Asch neglected to include in his novel any mention of the rich Jewish intellectual and cultural presence in the city—which, as Mikhail Krutikov points out, Asch was himself a part of. Rather, what Asch attempts to convey in this riveting novel is that the price these wealthy Jews must pay for their success is alienation from their people.

The "Warsaw" part of the trilogy finds Zachary residing in the poorest sections of the city searching for his Jewish identity. Zachary, having never consorted with poor Jews or spoken Yiddish, is devoid of any knowledge of Jews or Judaism. It is Chomsky who gives direction to Zachary's search for meaning as a Jew (Chomsky is reminiscent of the tailor in *Kiddush Ha-Shem*). In Warsaw, Zachary engages with an assortment of Jewish characters including its radical elements. As the novel shifts to Moscow, he becomes involved with the Bolsheviks during the revolution of 1917, only to become disillusioned with the cynicism and cruelty of the movement.

For Asch, the Bolshevik Revolution not only failed to rid the country of anti-Semitism, it destroyed Russian Jewry as a social and cultural group. As Krutikov notes, Asch " represents both Russian revolutions, of 1905 and 1917, as outbursts of a destructive energy hidden in the Russian soul. Jews inevitably become victims of

these explosions of human anger, no matter whether they try to be on the winning side or on the losing side" (p. 101).

Ironically, the novel's real hero is not Zachary but his father, Gabriel Mirkin, and Solomon Halperin, who are killed for their principles. Halperin is murdered by the Whites, the opponents of the Bolsheviks, when he refuses to hide his Jewish identity in the face of death, an example of Asch's use of the *Kiddush Ha-Shem* motif. As the trilogy concludes, Zachary finds himself alienated from the new Bolshevik Russia, and, having acquired a semblance of Jewish identity, he returns to Warsaw, casting his lot and hopes with the new state of Poland.

SALVATION

Initially titled "The Psalm Jew," *Salvation* was written in 1934, at a time when Nazi Germany was already engaged in persecuting its Jewish population. Indeed, on May 10, 1933, German students burned upward of twenty-five thousand volumes of "un-German" books, which included Asch's *Mottke, the Thief.* Just as his reaction to the pogroms of 1918–1919 in Ukraine was to write *Kiddush Ha-Shem* to provide comfort to its Jewish victims, Asch's immediate response to Nazi anti-Semitism was to write *Salvation.* Siegel contends that in writing *Salvation,* Asch was determined to underscore as much of Jewish sanctity as he could, hoping thereby to emphasize the moral superiority of the Jews to the Nazis.

Salvation is Asch's celebration of Hasidic life, in which he probes its piety and mysticism without overlooking its shortcomings. The novel centers around Yechiel, the son of a rigidly orthodox Hasidic family in which learning the Talmud and strict adherence to religious detail is fundamental to everyday life. Yechiel is viewed by his father as a disappointment because of his seeming lack of aptitude for absorbing religious texts. However, Yechiel does exhibit a strong sense of elation in his perception of God and his surroundings. Everything in his daily life, like doing cartwheels, whistling though his teeth, or counting to two hundred, is done for God's glory.

Over the course of the novel the community's view of him evolves from seeing him as a fool to seeing him as a mystic who is drawn to the meek and the poor. Yechiel joins a "psalm fellowship" of workers, who, because of his piety, make him their leader with the status of rabbi, calling him "the Psalm Jew."

Yechiel's personal journey to holiness, however, is less dependent on the laws of the Torah than it is on the wisdom derived from his heart. But Yechiel's good intentions do not always bring about positive results. Crucial to the story is how Yechiel impulsively invokes God's name to promise a barren couple that they will bear a child within the year. The consequences of this promise are devastating and make up the final third of the novel. Yechiel comes to a tragic end, and as he affirms his faith in the Mosaic law at the moment of his death, it is a Judaism of compassion, not of legalisms. For Asch, the Hasidic Judaism he approved of was one of faith, prayers, and its simplified conceptions of God, Messiah, and afterlife. But Asch reveals his disdain for Hasidic practices that were so remote and austere that many of its adherents were deprived of the human compassion and joy it had long espoused. Because of Yechiel's emphasis on the values of faith above form or ritual, and his embrace of deviation from the norm of Hasidic life, he is reprimanded by a group of rabbis for showing kindness to a follower of Sabbatai Zevi, the seventeenth-century false messiah. (In 1908 Asch had written a play, *Sabbatai Zevi,* sympathetic to the messianic pretender who converted to Islam.) *Salvation* anticipates Asch's subsequent "Christological" novels, and Yechiel is a prototype of Jesus.

CROSSING OVER? THE CHRISTOLOGICAL NOVELS

The Nazarene (1939) is the retelling of the life and death of Jesus by two men: a Polish anti-Semite, Pan Viadomsky, who claims that in a past life, as a Roman aide to Pontius Pilate, he had witnessed the events of Christ's life leading to the crucifixion; and a young rabbi who is enlisted by Viadomsky to interpret ancient

SHOLEM ASCH

Hebrew documents. The novel received favorable reviews in the non-Yiddish press and quickly became a best seller. Described by Asch as "the main product of my life-work" (Siegel, p. 130), he hoped that by placing Jesus within the context of Judaism he would make a major contribution to a better understanding between Christians and Jews, thus forging a reconciliation between the faiths and eliminating the causes for the past injustices and sins committed against Jews in the name of Jesus. Asch believed that Jesus was the finest expression of the Jewish spirit whose martyrdom had been turned into a weapon against his own people by their enemies. "I want to show in this book," Asch stated, "how far Christianity has departed from the original Christian faith, which was almost the same as the Jewish faith" (Siegel, p. 131).Writing the book against the background of the Nazis' barbaric attacks against the Jews, Asch sought to defend the Jews from Christian calumny by exposing the enemies of the Jews as defilers of Christianity as conceived by its founders. As Madison notes, to strengthen his argument, Asch was determined to follow the *New Testament* and accept the miracles and mysticism without question. By depicting Jesus as a pious Jew, he hoped to demonstrate the falseness of the anti-Jewish slander voiced by later followers of Jesus. In an interview with the *Chicago Daily News* in 1945, Asch stated that "I consider the birth of Jesus (Christmas) a Jewish holiday also. In this happy event we Jews have an equal share with all the people in the world, and we have good reason to thank and praise God thereof" (quoted in Lieberman, p. 250).

The Nazarene is a faithful retelling of the life of Jesus as recounted in the New Testament. What Asch does with his story, however, is to fill in those aspects of the Nazarene's life not accounted for in the Gospels. The result is a Jesus who preaches a Judaism closer to Yechiel's Hasidic piety in *Salvation* than the Christianity that justified the Crusades and the Inquisition in his name or, as Orville Prescott put it in a review of another Asch book in 1945, that of "the nations nominally called Christian, not one [of which] has ever acted in a Christian fashion" (p. 17).

In Judaism, the belief in a Messiah reflects the expectation that his arrival will be to deliver *all* of Israel from oppression and traditionally has little to do with individual salvation. For Jews, the Messianic ideal begins with Moses, who is the prototype of the redeemer who delivered Israel from slavery. In Jewish history Jesus is only one of many who have appeared in times of great troubles and attained a following as the Messiah. Indeed, Sabbatai Zevi, the seventeenth-century false messiah, may have had more followers than did Jesus in his own time. More significantly, the Messiah in Jewish tradition is a flesh-and-blood person and under no circumstances God incarnated as a person. The Trinity, as the doctrine evolved over time, is as alien to Judaism as the pagan belief that the Roman emperor was God incarnated. As someone who was educated in the Orthodox Jewish tradition, Asch was fully aware why most Jews throughout history have rejected Jesus as the Messiah. Yet in *The Nazarene,* Asch overlooks the issue of Jesus' divinity when he writes this exchange between a rabbi and a Messianist:

> The only difference between us was that in their belief the Messiah had already been once on earth, and was due to return, and we said that this could not be, that the Messiah could not have been on earth and mankind remain unredeemed from evil, but full of wickedness. Our belief was that the Messiah was yet to come, theirs that he was to come again.
>
> (pp. 692–693)

Asch argues that the early Christians were observant Jews who followed both the laws of the Torah and a belief in Jesus as the Messiah. Son of Man? Son of God? Asch is not prepared to accept this as the real reason for the parting of the ways between Jews and Christians. Rather, he blames the split on the pagan elements that entered into Christianity much later on and turned Jews into Christ-killers. Indeed, Asch is clear that the Romans, in complicity with a small number of corrupt high priests (Sadducees), were responsible for the Crucifixion.

In *The Apostle* (1943) Asch draws a sympathetic picture of Saul/Paul, who, having failed to convince Jews outside of Jerusalem to accept Jesus, takes the "good news" to the gentiles and

13

eliminates circumcision and the dietary laws, core doctrines of Judaism, thereby becoming the effective founder of Christianity. Despite Paul's abrogation of the laws of the Torah, Asch insists that Christianity was the culminating step in Jewish religious development through its spread of monotheism to the pagan world.

In *Mary* (1949), Asch's sympathies for Christian doctrine are apparent in his acknowledgment of the Immaculate Conception. Asch describes how Joseph claims Jesus as his son lest Mary be persecuted by the Jews for blasphemy. In his effort to link Judaism and Christianity as two branches of the same religion, Asch contends that the three wise men who travel to the manger in Bethlehem were not kings but the Jewish patriarchs Abraham, Isaac, and Jacob. Elsewhere Asch portrays Jesus as performing miracles and, in the end, to having arisen from the dead. Indeed, *Mary,* of the three novels, is the most sympathetic to the Christian version of the events of Jesus' life and death as told in the New Testament.

Asch, however, does rehabilitate the Pharisees, a term with pejorative connotations in subsequent Christian history. Asch describes the Pharisees as "the authority to whom Israel looked for guidance ... not the depraved House of Herod, nor the corrupt clique of the High Priest. ... Joseph (the earthly father of Jesus) knew ... that their laws and regulations served but one object—to protect Jewry as by an iron wall from the incursion of paganism and the abominations which abounded throughout the Gentile world" (*Mary,* p. 64). Elsewhere, Asch accuses the Pharisees of shutting out the great mass of Jewry beyond the pale of sanctity because they were not competent to understand the many regulations that constituted the Mosaic law. The criticism of the scribes allows Asch to contrast the mantle of holiness among the learned few with the teaching of Jesus, which embraced the many.

The controversy over the trilogy has been described elsewhere in this essay; suffice to say here that Asch's sensitivity and reverence toward Jesus may have elicited charges of apostasy because his accusers did not understand his objective in writing the novels. It is true that, in

his effort to reconcile Christianity and Judaism, Asch deemphasizes the theological differences that prevent an accord between the faiths, such as Christian belief in the Trinity, original sin, and Christ's divinity. But it is also true that Asch, who was critical of rigid Orthodox adherence to the doctrines of the Torah, saw a commonality in the two religions in the ethical teachings of Jesus. In the Christological novels Asch attributes Jesus' teachings, including the Sermon on the Mount, to the moral teachings of the rabbis and the prophets, thus concluding that Christians have no choice theologically but to accept Israel's God.

Although it would require a theological expert to discern the nuances of Asch's celebration of Jesus, the reaction of Asch's critics to the Christological novels is easily understood considering that, in their minds, he was extolling Jesus at a time when European Jewry was being slaughtered throughout Christian Europe as well as providing grist for Christians to convert Jews. There have been those, however, who have understood what Asch was trying to accomplish. Ben Siegel, for example, points to a particular passage in *The Nazarene* that demonstrates Asch was not an apostate who had crossed over to Christianity. In this passage, writes Siegel, Rabbi Nicodemon, whom Asch considers the embodiment of the tolerance and wisdom of Judaism, attempts to protect Jesus from the Romans and Sadducees, and in speaking to a number of his opponents, he states what in essence is Asch's purpose in writing the novels. According to Siegel, "Nicodemon concludes. ... that Yeshua's doctrine is valid only for non-Jews, 'for those that are born without the spirit, or for such as would deny the spirit.' Yeshua has been sent, states this Pharisee rabbi, to bring solace to the nations by moving them close to One God's 'great light.' For the suffering Jews, however, the Messiah's advent still lies in the future" (Siegel, p. 135).

EAST RIVER

East River (1946), like Asch's earlier work, *Uncle Moses* (English ed., 1920), is a tale of American

Jewish immigrant life. Unlike the earlier novel, which takes place on the Jewish Lower East Side of Manhattan, *East River* is set farther uptown in a more diverse neighborhood of Jews and Irish Catholics around East Forty-Eighth Street, allowing Asch to bring together the dynamics of Christian-Jewish relations as one of the central stories in the novel.

East River centers around Moshe Wolf, a devout, nearly bankrupt grocer whose two sons, Irving and Nathan, like many second-generation Jewish immigrants, do not share their parents' devotion to traditional religion. When Irving marries Mary, a devout Catholic, Moshe Wolf reacts by saying the Kaddish (prayer for the dead). Asch uses the relationship of the two brothers to confront the deplorable conditions in the Garment District, where workers in sweatshops—owned, for the most part, by Jewish businessmen—are underpaid and subject to seasonal labor. Irving, who becomes a wealthy clothing manufacturer, introduces the deplorable system of "take-home bundles," a system designed to undermine the nascent garment workers union by doling out the work to nonunion men, women, and children living in the tenements.

Nathan, who contracted polio and is filled with self-pity, is treated by a secular-minded doctor who partially cures him. Subsequently Nathan becomes a spokesman and organizer for the union, but when he attributes his recovery to his newly found belief in God, he loses his socialist followers and his job with the union.

In Nathan, Asch creates a character who mirrors the ethical and religious qualities of Yechiel in *Salvation* and the Jesus of *The Nazarene*. Nathan repeatedly reiterates his belief that only faith in God makes possible social justice or true brotherhood. Nathan's criticism of organized religion mirrors that of Asch when he states "that I, created by God—can conceive of a universal salvation, whereas God—according to the conception of the religious sects—lacks the tolerance to offer salvation to all men" (p. 125).

It is also in *East River* that Asch reveals his feelings about America. Through Nathan, Asch gives expression to his view that America will resolve the exploitation of the working classes as well as the centuries-old conflict between Christians and Jews. In a speech Nathan delivers to a workers' meeting consisting of Jews and gentiles, he says,

> America is our home, ... not a place where we have found a temporary haven. ... It is the country which should be nearest and dearest to us, because it is most closely related to our ideals of a better world order.... We must fight not only for a better physical life, but for a better moral life, too. The sweat system under which our parents work has robbed them of all human dignity. ... They must learn the pride and dignity of free American citizens.
>
> (pp. 307–308)

CONCLUSION

Sholem Asch was a prolific writer whose fiction encompassed the Jewish experience throughout history, and his range of themes brought Yiddish literature into the mainstream of European and American culture. The authorial voice in his fiction evolved from Hasidic Jew to Social Democrat to critic of Marxism and the Bolshevik Revolution. Once settled in America, Asch became a great admirer of the Rhode Island founder Roger Williams and a strong believer in the separation of church and state. He regarded the Declaration of Independence as an almost religious document that, for the first time in history, guaranteed the equality of all men, not because they belonged to one nation or to one faith but because "they have been created equal by the creator of all" (*What I Believe,* p. 178). Indeed, he wrote that the Declaration of Independence should be taught in the churches and synagogues and "should be entered as one of the prayers in the Jewish *siddur* [prayer book]" (p. 178). Asch's love affair with America, however, was not reciprocated. The critic Oscar Cargill noted in 1950 that although Asch was well known in the literary world of American letters and a naturalized American citizen, there was no anthology of American literature that included his fiction, and when "our prominent writers are enumerated, his name is never mentioned" (p. 67).

Asch's reputation suffered dramatically among his Jewish readership after the publication

of *The Nazarene,* the first novel in his trilogy about the life of Jesus. Asch's Christological novels were published at a time when, according to Siegel, reviewers saw "as literary heresy any fictionalizing of Biblical materials." Serious critics, he says, "generally placed Asch's *Bible* novels on a level equidistant between Mann's *Joseph* novels and Lloyd Douglas's *The Robe,*" or, as Milton Hindus put it, "resting squarely in that no man's land between the popular kitsch of the best-seller lists and qualitative literature of serious intent" (Siegel, p. 226).

Despite their place on the best-seller lists, Asch's Christological novels drew attacks from the left of the Jewish spectrum, led by Abraham Cahan, as well as from the Orthodox Jewish right, with both branding him an apostate. This raises the question, Why did Asch write these novels when he could have anticipated this type of reaction? Siegel argues that Asch's major error was poor judgment. Published at a time when Jews anguished over the increasing news of the slaughter of European Jewry by a "Christian" nation, and the seeming indifference of the rest of the Christian world (including the response of the Roosevelt administration to the news of the Nazi extermination campaign against the Jews), Asch's effort to reconcile Jews to their "spiritual brothers" was sheer effrontery. Siegel concludes that Asch was guilty "hardly of apostasy—he was Jewish to his marrow—but, as with *The Nazarene,* of exhibiting abominable timing and taste" (p. 169).

Asch himself believed that by writing his Christological novels he was countering Nazi propaganda, which was in the process of negating Jesus as a Jew (see, for example, Susanna Heschel's 2008 study, *The Aryan Jesus*). But there may be another explanation. Asch may unconsciously have sought the torment that so many of his fictional characters endured. A great admirer of Jesus and Paul, Asch found himself joined with his fictional cast of characters such as Yechiel and *The Nazarene* when he engaged in a literary act of *Kiddush Ha-Shem* (Sanctification of the name) in the aftermath of the publication of the trilogy. In writing the Christological novels, Asch sought to redeem his people from the centuries of Christian persecution by pointing to their shared common belief in one God, thus eliminating the hold of anti-Jewish feeling that had gripped Christianity over the centuries. But Asch must have realized the possibility that his efforts, like those of Jesus, would have tragic consequences. Given the messianic theme that characterizes many of his novels, it is not implausible that Asch, by writing the trilogy, unwittingly invited the hostility and artistic martyrdom he received from his core following.

Selected Bibliography

WORKS (IN ENGLISH) OF SHOLEM ASCH

NOVELS AND SHORT STORIES

Reb Shloyme nogid. Vilne : Vilner farlag fun B.A. Kletskin, 1913.

America. Translated by James Fuchs. New York: Alpha Omega, 1918.

Uncle Moses. Translated by Isaac Goldberg. New York: E. P. Dutton, 1920.

Kiddush Ha-Shem: An Epic of 1648. Translated by Rufus Learsi (Isaac Goldberg). Philadelphia: Jewish Publication Society of America, 1926.

The Mother. Translated by Nathan Ausübel. New York: Horace Liveright, 1930.

Three Cities: A Trilogy. Translated by Willa and Edward Muir. New York: Putnam, 1933.

Salvation. Translated by Willa and Edwin Muir. New York: Putnam, 1934.

Mottke, the Thief. Translated by Willa and Edwin Muir. New York: Putnam, 1935.

The War Goes On. Translated by Willa and Edwin Muir. New York: Putnam, 1936.

The Nazarene. Translated by Maurice Samuel. New York: Putnam, 1939.

Song of the Valley. Translated by Elsa Krauch. New York: Putnam, 1939.

Children of Abraham: The Short Stories of Sholem Asch. Translated by Maurice Samuel. New York: Putnam, 1942.

The Apostle. Translated by Maurice Samuel. New York: Putnam, 1943.

East River: A Novel. Translated by A. H. Gross. New York: Putnam, 1946.

Tales of My People. Translated by Meyer Levin. New York:

Putnam, 1948. (The collection includes the novella *The Little Town* as well as several short stories about the Jewish victims of the Nazis.)

Mary. Translated by Leo Steinberg. New York: Putnam, 1949.

Moses. Translated by Maurice Samuel. New York: Pocket Books, 1951.

A Passage in the Night. Translated by Maurice Samuel. New York: Putnam, 1953.

The Prophet. Translated by Arthur Saul Super. New York: Putnam, 1955.

"Kola Road." Translated by Norbert Guterman. In *A Treasury of Yiddish Stories.* Edited by Irving Howe and Eliezer Greenberg. New York: Meridian, 1958. Pp. 260–275.

Kiddush Ha-Shem: An Epic of 1648 and Sabbatai Zevi: A Tragedy. Translated by Rufus Learsi (Isaac Goldberg). New York: Meridian Books and Philadelphia: Jewish Publication Society of America, 1959.

PLAYS

Winter. Translated by Isaac Goldberg. In *Six Plays of the Yiddish Theatre.* Edited by Isaac Goldberg. Boston: J. W. Luce, 1916.

The God of Vengeance: Drama in Three Acts. Translated by Isaac Goldberg. Boston: Stratford Company, 1918.

Sabbatai Zevi: A Tragedy in Three Acts and Six Scenes with a Prologue and an Epilogue. Translated by Florence Whyte and George Rapall Noyes. Philadelphia: Jewish Publication Society of America, 1930.

NONFICTION

"The Guilty Ones." *Atlantic Monthly* 166:713–714 (December 1940).

What I Believe. Translated by Maurice Samuel. New York: Putnam, 1941.

One Destiny: An Epistle to the Christians. Translated by Milton Hindus. New York: Putnam, 1945.

"My Father and I." *Commentary* 39:55–64 (January 1965).

PAPERS

Sholem Asch's papers are stored at Yale University and at the Sholem Asch Museum, Bat Yam, Israel.

CRITICAL AND BIOGRAPHICAL STUDIES

Cargill, Oscar. "Sholem Asch: Still Immigrant and Alien." *College English,* 12, no. 2:67–74 (November 1950).

Howe, Irving. *World of Our Fathers.* New York: Harcourt Brace Jovanovich, 1976. Pp. 449–450.

Krutikov, Mikhail. *Yiddish Fiction and the Crisis of Modernity, 1905–1914.* Stanford, Calif.: Stanford University Press, 2001.

———. "Russia Between Myth and Reality: From *Meri* to *Three Cities.*" In *Sholem Asch Reconsidered.* Edited by Nanette Stahl. New Haven, Conn.: Yale University Library Gazette, Occasional Supplement, 2004.

Lieberman, Herman (Chaim). *The Christianity of Sholem Asch: An Appraisal from the Jewish Viewpoint.* New York: Philosophical Library, 1953.

Lifson, David. "Sholem Asch." In his *The Yiddish Theatre in America.* New York: Thomas Yoseloff, 1965. Pp. 89–93.

Liptzin, Solomon. "Sholem Asch." In his *The Flowering of Yiddish Literature.* New York: Thomas Yoseloff, 1963. Pp. 178–189.

Madison, Charles A. *Yiddish Literature: Its Scope and Major Writers.* New York: Schocken Books, 1968.

Mazower, David. "Images of a Life." In *Sholem Asch Reconsidered.* Edited by Nanette Stahl. New Haven, Conn.: *Yale University Library Gazette,* Occasional Supplement, 2004.

Niger, Samuel. *Sholem Asch: Zayn lebn un zayne verk* [Sholem Asch: His Life and Work]. New York: Congress for Jewish Culture, 1960. (In Yiddish.)

Samuel, Maurice. *Little Did I Know: Recollections and Reflections.* New York: Knopf, 1963. Pp. 271–275.

Seidman, Naomi. "Staging Tradition: Piety and Scandal in God of Vengeance." In *Sholem Asch Reconsidered.* Edited by Nanette Stahl. New Haven, Conn.: *Yale University Library Gazette,* Occasional Supplement, 2004.

Shulman, Charles E. "Sholem Asch." In his *What It Means to Be a Jew.* New York: Crown, 1960. Pp. 62–67.

Siegel, Ben. *The Controversial Sholem Asch.* Bowling Green, Ohio: Bowling Green University Popular Press, 1976. (There is no recent biography of Sholem Asch, but until one appears, Siegel's book remains an indispensable work on both Asch's life and his fiction.)

Stahl, Nanette, ed. *Sholem Asch Reconsidered.* New Haven, Conn.: Yale University Library Gazette, Occasional Supplement, 2004. (A collection of papers that were presented at a conference at Yale by a number of Asch scholars. The essays are an invaluable source toward an understanding of Asch's most important fiction.)

REVIEWS AND INTERVIEWS

Fadiman, Clifton. "Paul." *New Yorker,* September 18, 1943, p. 90.

Kazin, Alfred. "Neither Jew nor Greek." *New Republic,* November 1, 1943, pp. 626–627.

Mair, John. "New Novels." *New Statesman and Nation,* November 12, 1938, p. 797.

Mead, Frank S. " 'I Had to Write These Things': An Interview with Sholem Asch." *Christian Herald,* January 1944, pp. 13–14, 52.

Prescott, Orville. "Outstanding Novels." *Yale Review* 33:vi–viii (autumn 1943).

———. Review of *One Destiny: An Epistle to the Christians. New York Times,* September 17, 1945, p. 17.

Rosenberg, Harold. "What Love Is Not." *Commentary,* June 3, 1947, p. 593.

Rugoff, Milton. "A Great Novel About the Life of Jesus." *New York Herald Tribune Books,* October 22, 1939, p. 3.

PETER BALAKIAN

(1951—)

Hovig Tchalian

PETER BALAKIAN IS an Armenian American poet, writer, critic, and scholar. His first publication appeared in 1979, a slim volume of poetry intriguingly titled *Father Fisheye*. Since then Balakian has published several more volumes of poetry. All have been well received, including the 2001 retrospective *June-Tree: New and Selected Poems, 1974–2000* (2001) and the more recent and perhaps best-received, *Ziggurat* (2010). In between, Balakian has ventured into other genres, including memoir (*Black Dog of Fate,* 1997), criticism (*Theodore Roethke's Far Fields: The Evolution of His Poetry,* 1989), historical analysis (*The Burning Tigris: The Armenian Genocide and America's Response,* 2003), and translation (most notably, *Armenian Golgotha,* 2009).

The artistic and career development that encompasses the thirty or so years from 1979 to 2010 has seen Balakian the poet come into his own, especially after the publication, ironically, of his memoir, *Black Dog of Fate*. His foray into historical debates, especially those regarding the Armenian Genocide of 1915 at the hands of the Ottoman Turkish government and his staunch support for its recognition, have thrust him into the center of a century-long debate over testimony, evidence, and personal and national identity.

It is notable that poetry collections bracket those thirty years. Poetry has always served as Balakian's creative bedrock. Balakian himself has identified his initial artistic impulse toward natural and lyric poetry, while tracing his influences to such American stalwarts as Theodore Roethke, Emily Dickinson, and Walt Whitman. That poetry has always been shot through with references to his childhood, his upbringing, and the Armenian heritage that served as a haven as well as a foil in his childhood in suburban New Jersey. Such a sense of "in-betweenness" characterizes Balakian's entire body of work, but especially the poetry. In his very first collection, for instance, the poem "Words for My Grandmother" casts a sideways glance at her harrowing past as a genocide survivor. But the title poem of the same collection also includes naturalistic scenes from Balakian's childhood, alongside references to Italian holidays, Christian saints, and medieval folklore.

What ties these and similar themes in the various poetry collections together, and all of them to the more explicitly historical and biographical writings, is Balakian's complex but singular interest in exploring his own identity as a "witness"—of modern American life, his own Armenian past, and their evolving interaction.

BIOGRAPHY

Peter Balakian was born on June 13, 1951, in Teaneck, New Jersey. He spent his early years in his birthplace and then moved with his family to nearby Tenafly, New Jersey. Both are well-to-do suburbs, and Balakian grew up as a typical middle-class American kid. Balakian eventually attended Bucknell University, where he earned a B.A. degree in 1973; then, after earning an M.A. from New York University, he completed his Ph.D. in American civilization at Brown University in 1980. Later that year he joined the faculty of Colgate University in Hamilton, New York, where he is currently the Donald M. and Constance H. Rebar Professor of the Humanities in the Department of English and director of creative writing.

Coming of age in the 1950s and turbulent 1960s, Balakian absorbed both the popular and

countercultural influences around him. But his most immediate influence was arguably his extended Armenian family—his mother and father, three siblings, aunts, and his maternal grandmother, Nafina Aroosian. He describes her, in his memoir, as someone who both fascinated and confused him. She felt a special affection for her grandson and doted on him. But although he felt close to her, she seemed a strange and somewhat enigmatic figure to the all-American boy, who grew up hearing her stories and picking up from her the few words of Armenian he knew.

Balakian's paternal family, who hailed from Constantinople, was of a more "new world," literary bent. His aunt Nona Balakian, for example, was a literary critic and editor at the *New York Times Book Review,* while his aunt Anna Balakian, a prominent critic and scholar of surrealism and symbolism, served as chairman of the Department of Comparative Literature at New York University. Both were influential in Balakian's introduction into the world of letters, including Armenian American writers such as William Saroyan. Significant aspects of both the old world and the new arguably made an equally strong impression on Balakian's early life and (without reading too much into its psychological aspects) aptly represent the two poles between which his literary career would develop.

Nonetheless, Balakian's maternal grandmother, Nafina, was a more immediate presence early in his life. She and her two daughters, Gladys and Lucille, had fled the genocide (the mass killings and deportations of Armenians by the Ottoman Turkish government between 1915 and 1923) and lived together in nearby East Orange, New Jersey. Balakian describes his monthly visits to Nafina's house, which seemed to him a world away. She taught him to bake *choereg* (a traditional Armenian and Middle Eastern soft bread or roll) while watching Yankees games on the tube and listening to Elvis, Fats Domino, and the Shirelles on the radio. She also recited many biblical passages to him, all of which she knew by heart. Nafina had received a traditional Armenian missionary education in Diyarbakir (now in southeastern Turkey, formerly a part of Armenia and once thought to be the ancient Armenian city of Tigranakert), where she had grown up.

Nafina would also tell her grandson enigmatic fables and fairy tales in Armenian. One of them, about a black dog that a poor woman cooks to successfully court Fate's favor, would become the title of his memoir, *Black Dog of Fate.* In fact, many of the events Balakian recounts in the memoir—from the 1962 Yankees-Giants World Series and the Cuban Missile Crisis of the same year to conflicts in Vietnam and Cambodia—make their way into the poetry collections, suffusing them with the strongly autobiographical flavor that characterizes all of his works. That distinct mixture of history both personal and public, ancient and modern, defines Balakian's larger explorations of identity and witness.

The seminal personal event that triggered those explorations once again involved Nafina. A year after writing the poem "Words for My Grandmother," in which he referred tangentially to his grandmother's dark past, Balakian came across her petition for claims to the U.S. State Department against the Ottoman Turkish government for her exile and the murder of her husband and most of her extended family. That document became the basis of "The Claim," arguably the central poem in the collection *Sad Days of Light* (1983), a blend, at once lyrical and jarring, of poetic musings about his grandmother and direct quotations from her legal petition that acts as an extended meditation on history, memory, and personal narrative. The poem's revelation of what Balakian has repeatedly described as a suppressed family secret was the first of many ruminations on the subject.

MYTH AND MEMOIR

The winter of 2009 saw the publication of the tenth-anniversary edition of Balakian's award-winning *Black Dog of Fate: A Memoir.* Along with two new chapters added to the original 1997 text, the book bears, on its cover, the additional subtitle *An American Son Uncovers His Armenian Past.*

The description aptly encompasses not only this volume but Balakian's broader stance vis-à-

vis his Armenian identity. He has consistently cast himself as the outsider looking in or, perhaps more accurately, inward. The metaphor in the subtitle is not, significantly, that of discovering but rather of uncovering. The former suggests a narrative and an identity of accident and distance (signaled in part by the prefix "dis," suggesting separation). For example, from the European perspective, the explorer Christopher Columbus "discovered" the Americas—a discovery that contained an explicit element of accident, since he was actually headed for (and thought he had reached) the East Indies and Cathay. The central trope of discovery is the outsider's chance encounter.

Uncovering the past, as in Balakian's phrasing, has an entirely different valence. As the speaker of his memoir, Balakian uncovers—in effect, unveils—his Armenian heritage. The sense is of something already there that needs to be identified or revealed. The analogy, in this case, is not that of an expedition but a recognition. Balakian is "born" American. But in the course of living his suburban New Jersey life, as the memoir tells it, he makes the requisite effort to find out about his Armenian heritage. (In addition to his grandmother's stories and her legal claim, Balakian also mentions the profound influence on him of Henry Morgenthau, Sr. As American ambassador to Turkey from 1913 until his resignation in 1916, Morgenthau witnessed many of the events surrounding the genocide firsthand. His personal account of those events, published in 1918 under the title *Ambassador Morgenthau's Story,* deeply moved Balakian.)

Unlike the role of discovering, that of uncovering demands the presence of the quintessential insider—the Armenian born into American life, the child growing up in a world at once familiar and unfamiliar, one whose contours conceal the shape of a yet deeper experience. The metaphor of geographical distance is replaced by that of psychological depth, of plumbing one's "true" self. Gone as well is the element of accident that animates the narrative of discovering. Uncovering one's heritage becomes, as in Balakian's memoir, a narrative not of chance but inevitability.

The acts of discovering and uncovering define what we might think of as the two poles demarcating a wider range of writing and experience in Balakian's writings. At one end, defined by the act of uncovering, lies the narrative of depth and inevitability. Here lies the domain of memoir, which uncovers or reveals the speaker's true, "authentic" self, as Balakian does in part in *Black Dog.* At the other end, defined by the act of discovering, lies the narrative of chance and accident. We might think of this domain (admittedly, somewhat reductively) as that of myth or poetry, employing the element of surprise—of unlikely juxtapositions and unexpected finds.

Balakian has himself long been working in this domain. As outlined earlier, he started out writing poetry in the 1970s and 1980s, then moved in the 1990s to memoir (*Black Dog of Fate*) and, later, to history (*Burning Tigris: The Armenian Genocide and America's Response,* 2003). This third genre is what we might, in line with the previous discussion, refer to as the narrative of recovery, defined in both its psychological and historical meanings. Psychologically, the term encompasses the act or effort of recovering from an often traumatic experience, such as killing or genocide. Historically, it envisions the motivated act of rehabilitation, of rescue. In this case, significantly, the "distance" that must be overcome is that of neither space nor depth but of time. As such, recovery is characterized by a narrative of witness and testimony, of loss and redemption. We might say that recovering falls somewhere between discovering and uncovering, between myth and memoir.

Despite its generic categorization, then, Balakian's *Black Dog* is perhaps not a memoir in the truest sense of the word. A memoir tells a life story from the perspective of the teller. And Balakian's certainly does. But while uncovering his Armenian identity, Balakian also attempts to recover the experience of his grandmother Nafina's past. Nafina—whose name is, interestingly, Armenian for Athena—is a genocide survivor who finds herself in Aleppo, Syria, with her two daughters and finally rejoins Balakian's family in New Jersey. In that sense, *Black Dog*

occupies a peculiar position that helps us better understand Balakian's own extended exploration of memory, identity, and witness: vis-à-vis its author, it is indeed a memoir; but in relation to Nafina, the survivor of genocide whose tale the book also tells, it is closer to a history, more akin to *Burning Tigris*.

The tension between memoir and history, survivor narrative and witness account, permeates Balakian's *Black Dog*. The effect is somewhat akin to reading *The Diary of Anne Frank* had her story been recounted through her grandson's experience. Throughout the book, the reader is aware of a subtle tension between Balakian's experience, that of witness, and his grandmother's, that of survivor. As noted earlier, her presence near the family and Balakian's close relationship with her help him discover his true identity. Along with that experience, however, comes her own, that of a brutal, genocidal past. In *Black Dog*, Balakian's own experience sometimes comes to stand in, ironically, tragically, for her loss.

Numerous moments in Balakian's narrative try to take account of this distance separating witness and survivor. Interestingly, Balakian initiates his quest to uncover his own past by way of a historical account. As mentioned above, as a young boy Balakian picked up a copy of Ambassador Morgenthau's account of the genocide. In *Black Dog*, Balakian describes reading the book while riding a bus to work in New York:

> By the time the bus came rattling over the potholes of Knickerbocker Road, I was lost in my father's birthplace. Ships moored along the Bosphorus. The water, green, tepid, caique-flecked, the glitter of silver. Terraced clumps of fig and olive trees. The dome of Hagia Sophia, golden, with minarets jutting up. Men in fezzes. Smells of *shashlik* and sewage in the streets.
>
> (p. 155)

The only discordant note in this initial description is the closing mention of sewage. Having just begun reading the account, Balakian is not yet immersed in its intricacies. He is, as he suggests, "lost" in a world that seems at once fantastic and imaginary. Describing neither his

experience nor his grandmother's, his prose is staid and confident, with the "accidental" air of the explorer, the nonchalance of a tourist.

This apparent calm is broken in a number of places in the narrative, soon after Balakian delves more deeply into Morgenthau's account. A statement near the end of Balakian's book, in which he tries to come to terms with the stories his grandmother has begun telling him, encapsulates the change, signaled by the writer's reference to himself as his grandmother's unknowing "witness":

> When I think of the stories she slipped to me in the odd moments of her daily routines, or the dreams, folktales, and half-repressed images I was privy to during the last six years of her life, it seems clear now that they were part of a truncated narrative about what she had gone through as a young woman. I was her companion, her captive audience, her beloved witness.
>
> (p. 301)

(*Black Dog* recounts how, when the young Balakian fell ill for a time, his grandmother nursed him to health while relating her experiences in often metaphorical, enigmatic language.) And again a bit further on:

> In odd, isolated moments—moments that seemed to be out of time—I had been privy to some of her intense sensory images, to her telescopic memory, to Genocide flashbacks. This was how she told me about her past. The Armenian invocation, *djamangeen gar oo chagar*—there was and there wasn't—was like the intrusive past, which seemed to appear out of time, like lyric memory that had been activated.
>
> (p. 301)

The easy lyricism of the earlier passage, describing the haunts of Balakian's father's childhood, is replaced here by a somewhat circular prose, marked by sometimes tortured metaphors and repeatedly interrupted by references to time. The passages both describe and enact the difficulty of circumscribing the survivor account within the coming-of-age story turned witness narrative. The resulting prose, affecting but also at times jagged and discordant, represents the difficult achievement of *Black Dog* as well as Balakian's larger oeuvre.

The most explicit instances of this tension between recovering and uncovering, between the positions of witness and survivor, respectively, can be found in the two new chapters added to the tenth anniversary edition of *Black Dog*. In them, Balakian tells of his 2005 trip to Aleppo and Der Zor, in Syria. In Aleppo, Balakian discovers records of his grandmother's arrival in the city housed in an Armenian cathedral, the nearest he can get to a diary of her now remote experiences. Later, he is led to the place where she lived in 1915. The narrative begins, once again, quite accidentally. The search initially leads to several miscues and cases of mistaken identity, as directions provided by locals lead Balakian and his guide through similar-looking streets and alleys. The search ends, somewhat anticlimactically, in another ordinary-looking street: "In a couple of minutes," Balakian recounts, "we were standing on a street not much different than many of the streets we had walked down in the past hour" (p. 327).

When he finally locates the house itself, Balakian describes the scene in much the same terms:

> And then I walked farther down the street, until I found myself in front of 45 Ghuri Street. My grandmother's home in 1915. A place never spoken of, never mentioned in her next life in New Jersey, the life in which I knew her. I looked up at an ordinary, ocher-stone two-story building that still seemed to be a residence. … Who lived there now? Who had lived there in the past 90 years? What did it matter? It was a plain house with an archway and a black door and a couple of windows with closed shutters, and it had no Ottoman overhang.
>
> (p. 328)

Balakian's impossible search for recovery leads him to an ordinary house in an ordinary part of town in Aleppo, no closer to his grandmother's experience than "in her next life in New Jersey," in which Balakian "knew her."

The attempt to recover the past as it really was, to bear witness in full, is at the heart of Balakian's *Black Dog of Fate*. It is a topic that has fascinated, even obsessed, the poet and author, in his memoir as well as his more historical work and his poetry. In a poetically charged moment near the middle of the book, Balakian

tries to convey the difficulty of the task, by way of a historical reference to the building of Armenian churches: "I pictured those wind-bitten stone churches built out of the Armenian highlands of Anatolia, with their wooden belfries preferred by Ottoman law so that no bell could be heard. I could hear those wooden clappers making a thump like a muffled throat" (p. 162). The passage is reminiscent of a line in T. S. Eliot's *Waste Land* that describes the Greek mythical character Philomela, whose tongue was cut off to prevent her revealing the identity of her rapist, singing " 'jug jug' to dirty ears" (p. 68). The passage is equally reminiscent of a line in one of Balakian's own poems, "Oriental Rug" (*Dyer's Thistle*, 1996), in which the purple dyes in the tapestry break apart and "gurgle" their "passion in my ear" (p. 52). Like the garbled, inaudible voices in those poems, the muffled "thump" of the clappers conveys in poetic form the difficulty of the inescapably historical task of telling, and by extension righting, the past that permeates much of Balakian's work.

Midway through *Black Dog*, Balakian explicitly mentions, in fact, that he tried to capture his grandmother's experience in one of his poems, "History of Armenia." "The poem," Balakian explains, "can be a headstone in a world of unmarked graves. … There, I could bring the two of us together again and create what she had in her encoded way told me. I realized that she was my beloved witness, and I the receiver of her story" (p. 195). It is difficult not to see in Balakian's act of imagination both an admirable gesture and a tragic reversal of sorts. (Remember that in the earlier passage discussed above, Balakian described himself as his grandmother's "witness." It seems that she has now become his.) While the historical act of recovery would place both Balakian and his grandmother in close proximity to each other—he as the receiver (and reteller) of a brutal past, and she as its conveyer, what Balakian now calls its "witness"—and unite them in the joint effort at historical recovery, as the "originary" teller of her own story, she is at once witness and survivor. It is in moments such as these that Balakian's poetry, in its successes as well as momentary failures, reminds us that its

PETER BALAKIAN

struggle to mend the past, to recover it across the distance of history, often hinges precisely on the fine distinction, the subtle separation, between myth and memoir.

POETRY AND THE PRESENCE OF THE PAST

Balakian has been a poet longer than a historian or memoirist, and a retrospective of his work, titled *June-Tree: New and Selected Poems, 1974–2000,* was published in 2004. With its well-honed lines and mature, confident style, the volume highlights Balakian's development as a poet with selections from his four previous collections and thirteen new works. The majority of the poems speak of loss, both personal and national. The more recent poems speak especially of the effect of the past on the present, its presence in the lives of people, particularly in the Armenian experience.

Balakian has always been a peculiar observer of that experience. Here again is the notion of witnessing, fraught as it is with connotations of serving as an eyewitness—or near eyewitness—to a tragedy or an instance of wrongdoing. As discussed above, Balakian's memoir, *Black Dog of Fate,* casts him as the American-born Armenian unearthing his past. That gesture taps into two experiences simultaneously—not the "Armenian" or the "American" alone (which are difficult to neatly disentangle, either in the memoir or in Balakian's own experience) but the parallel experiences of a man of Armenian ancestry living in the United States and a man of American upbringing confronting Armenian historical reality.

These two "voices" exist simultaneously in Balakian's poems. Only on rare occasions is either voice heard on its own. An early poem, "Graham House, April '76" (originally published in *Father Fisheye,* 1979), could have been written by a fifth-generation American of nameless ancestry, as it reflects all the elements of American life—baseball, fishing, a domestic television set, and a local bar where boys and men spend their off hours. The only shrill tone is sounded by the mention of Beirut. But it is not entirely clear which experience is directed at the flickering TV at this particular moment, the "knowing" concern of the immigrant or the indiscriminate glance of the local. The most compelling moments in the collection bring these two experiences to bear on each other. The interplay and friction between them produce sometimes extraordinary flights of thought, language, and experience.

A poem from Balakian's most recent collection before *June-Tree* (*Dyer's Thistle,* 1996), "Geese Flying over Hamilton, New York," looks back to the loss of human life in Cambodia and elsewhere. In the poem, a radio delivers news, which comes in "like fuzz." It seems that, like the television set earlier, this vehicle of transmission also garbles the message it transmits, as though the events it is reporting have already become irrelevant, lost in a past more tragic for its inaccessibility. The poem concludes with what amounts to a complete separation between then and now, between a past both "warm" and "ordinary" and a present ambient with its own artificial light. The "fuzzy" radio transmission suggests the tragic enormity of news that doesn't get through, what Balakian elsewhere calls "things that stick in the ear" ("After the Survivors Are Gone," *Dyer's Thistle,* p. 91).

Past and present collide in an earlier poem, "The History of Armenia" (*Sad Days of Light,* 1983), in which the speaker imagines his grandmother's genocidal past intruding into the present, in his hometown. As in most of Balakian's writings, the memory of the past lives on in the present. The result, in this case, is almost unbearably brutal, modern construction machinery taking the place of Turkish soldiers (though they are never specifically mentioned but left to the reader's imagination). The poem ends with a description of the early morning deportation of the speaker's grandfather. The conclusion's note of quiet resignation underscores the inhumanity of the act, but with a complete lack of sentimentality that speaks to the power and substance of Balakian's poems.

Balakian's most remarkable poem is undoubtedly "Oriental Rug" (from perhaps the most ef-

fective collection, *Dyer's Thistle*), in which the speaker's imagination meanders with the curves and images woven into the rug of the title, brought from "Eastern Turkey, once Armenia":

The splintering green wool
bled from juniper berries
seemed to seep, even then,

into the wasp-nest cells
breathing in their tubular ways
inside my ear and further back.

(p. 47)

The berries on the rug remind the speaker of wasp cells and somehow transform themselves into the canal of the inner ear and finally lead the mind's eye "further back," into the historical imagination. The poem concludes when the "dyes" come apart and "break the grid of threads" and reconvene in an image of both loneliness and hope:

Tyrian purple from a mollusk shell
lodged in Phoenician sand—
gurgle all your passion in my ear.

(p. 52)

The "passion" in this case "gurgles" into the disembodied "ear" of a beached shell. The things that would "stick in the ear" (as the other poem had it, and as the "clappers" in the revised version of *Black Dog of Fate* also suggest) are released back into the course of human history.

It is impossible, in this brief discussion, to do the rest of the poem justice. Suffice it to say that it represents the best of Balakian's poems in *Dyer's Thistle*, perhaps one of his very best over the last thirty years. If some of the other poems in the collection (such as "Flat Sky of Summer") are somewhat less successful, it is because they sound an occasional note of sentimentality, as do a number of the thirteen new poems, especially "In Armenia, 1987." The result confirms that the most compelling representations of the poet's and his family's past, of his fragmented Armenian experience, have always been those that allow it to speak for itself.

GENOCIDE AND THE HISTORICAL IMAGINATION

The famous opening lines of T. S. Eliot's epic poem *The Waste Land* seem to haunt much of Balakian's historical writing, particularly when it comes to issues of history and memory:

April is the cruellest month, breeding
Lilacs out of the dead land, mixing
Memory and desire, stirring
Dull roots with spring rain.

(p. 63)

Eliot's poetry was a strong influence on Balakian early in his career but also surfaces in his later writings. (The sense of melancholy captured by *The Waste Land* is considered by many scholars to be a direct response to World War I and its immediate aftermath, the same period Balakian revisits in much of his work.) The sense of a simultaneous loss and renewal reflected in the lines just quoted appear and reappear—directly or indirectly, consciously or unconsciously—in various places in Balakian's writings, both poetry and prose. As noted earlier, *Black Dog of Fate* evokes the mythic story of Philomela and the "gagging" (in both senses of the term) of her message, a past tragedy rendered mute and unavailable in the present.

A similar sense of tragedy, this time historical, animates *Burning Tigris: The Armenian Genocide and America's Response*. The book, originally published in 2003 (a *New York Times* and *Publishers Weekly* notable book that year), was rereleased in 2008. A book with a parallel publication history—Samantha Power's *"A Problem from Hell": America and the Age of Genocide,* first published a year earlier, in 2002, and re-released in 2007—offers an interesting contrast and will help elucidate the important features of Balakian's own study and its relevance to his other writings.

The Armenian Genocide constitutes the first chapter of Power's *"A Problem from Hell,"* a moving, brutal, Pulitzer Prize–winning account of America's failure to halt the perpetration of genocide over the course of the twentieth century, the first chapter of which concerns the Armenian Genocide. In *Burning Tigris,* Balakian looks back

to Power, noting in his preface that she and other historians affirm that the Armenian Genocide functions as a "template" for modern genocide (p. xiv). Here, Balakian follows the well-trodden path of many advocates before him in arguing that recognizing past genocides helps prevent future ones. His statement is qualitatively no different, in fact, than what Power also mentions, herself echoing countless others before her: that Hitler justified the Jewish Holocaust based at least in part on history's feeble response to the Armenian Genocide. ("Who today still speaks of the massacre of the Armenians?" Hitler said to his military chiefs in 1939, as they prepared to launch their own war of annihilation [p. 23].)

Balakian's explicit purpose in *Burning Tigris,* however, is also much larger than what this statement alone would suggest: it is to reinstate what came to be known as the plight of "the starving Armenians" as a central, perhaps *the* central, human rights calamity in American history. In *Burning Tigris,* Balakian proposes a historical perspective that would help teach America something about itself by pointing to a crime that coincides with a seminal moment in its own nationhood and identity—its first, abortive foray into the arena of human rights. In this case, however, the crime is not that of the perpetrator but, once again, of the historical witness and advocate turned bystander and accomplice.

Balakian's argument in effect encompasses a second historical tragedy, one akin to genocide denial. Balakian suggests that the crime here is an even more subtle one: the American nation betrays the Armenian victims of the crime by first betraying itself, by forgetting or ignoring the advocacy of many prominent Americans in its own past who called for recognition and response. Among them were the industrialist John D. Rockefeller, the feminist social critic Charlotte Perkins Gilman, the writer Stephen Crane, U.S. Ambassador to Turkey Henry Morgenthau, Sr., former president Theodore Roosevelt, and the poet Ezra Pound—who was also, ironically, instrumental in the final edits to Eliot's *Waste Land,* published in 1922, when debates about the proper response to "the Armenian Question" still raged.

Balakian's argument casts him in the quintessential role of the immigrant's son, speaking at once for his Armenian past and his American present. His approach accomplishes a complex objective: providing the hope and promise of restoring a lost fragment of America's own past through the transformative, redemptive act of restoring to Armenians a measure of social and historical justice already embedded in American political history. In essence, the well-worn path of Balakian's argument about genocide prevention comes across a sideways path into the American psyche; by retracing the arc of the victim's (and his own national) history, a history characterized by obsessively revisiting its own past, Balakian ends up recasting it in terms of the eyewitness's personal and national narrative. Balakian's Armenian-American identity allows entry into the American psyche. And from that perspective, at least, the personal precedes the historical; self-betrayal precedes the betrayal of the victims.

While the explicit argument of Balakian's text is to hold up a mirror to the American conscience, its implicit one is grappling with the central difficulty inherent in any attempt at historical reconstruction—namely, its belatedness, the difficulty in the distanced present of recovering an event now lost to it. (Indeed, the American tragedy simply reenacts history's more primal betrayal—of itself.) What makes Balakian's rendering especially effective, however, is its ability to personalize the historical, to make its belatedness matter to the eyewitness (almost) as much as it does to the victim. In this recapitulation, what appears as another tragic, hopeless attempt at recovery simply reinforces the personal commitment—to recognition, to a clear and unambiguous response. The historical argument in Balakian's text, as in Power's, solidifies into the simple need to act.

America's tragic failure to be true to itself and its own past unites Balakian's book with Power's. Both texts argue that, when viewed from the personal as well as the historical perspective, resistance becomes denial, complacency shades into complicity. In doing so, they follow individual but parallel paths that render them mirror

images of each other. Balakian speaks as the American-born son of Armenian immigrants, carrying that experience with him into the American historical landscape. Power instead takes her (non-Armenian) readers along for a journey into the Armenian (and Jewish and Cambodian) psyche. Both render the position of neutrality an impossible one to inhabit by compelling their audiences to reexamine the role of the historical eyewitness, balanced uneasily between the two poles of victim and perpetrator.

It is hardly surprising, then, that Balakian emphasizes the importance of "survivor accounts," which, he argues, allow readers access to experiences that might otherwise remain unknowable. Without the benefit of that perspective, Power instead begins her narrative several years later. Her first chapter, "Race Murder," opens interestingly in 1921 Berlin, where the Armenian Genocide survivor Soghomon Tehlirian assassinated Mehmet Talaat, Turkey's former interior minister and one of the masterminds behind the genocide.

Power thus begins not with the historical question but, as the instincts of any good reporter or novelist might suggest, with the historical actor. In fact, she begins with the exact moment of the assassination, repeating in the course of her description the words Tehlirian reportedly spoke as he pulled the trigger: "This is to avenge the death of my family!" (p. 1). By beginning with the pathos of Tehlirian's act of vengeance, Power has readers immediately occupy a position other than their own, one with its own peculiar and compelling complexities. Tehlirian is at once a self-appointed avenger and a victim of genocide—Power soon reminds us that Tehlirian was himself dragged to the Syrian desert of Der Zor and clubbed on the head, awaking to find himself in the midst of carnage, the lone survivor among his village and family.

Power's dramatization of Tehlirian's assassination plot addresses Balakian's implicit argument of belatedness—of Armenians pressing for recognition and Americans struggling with response. Tehlirian both has suffered the crime and looks back to its commission six years later,

embodying at once the dual and contradictory roles of victim and latecomer.

In a sense, the scene Power depicts dramatizes the moment of redemption offered by Balakian. Her version of Tehlirian's act reimagines the near-tragedy of American complicity through complacency as a moment of high conviction. In the person of Tehlirian, Power introduces the vagaries of the latecomer only to dissolve them in a moment of action. As a survivor—in essence, a near-victim—Tehlirian has lived to tell about it and, more importantly, to act on his experience and knowledge. Balakian's retracing of the Armenian psyche into the American finds its parallel in Power's substitution of Tehlirian's action for America's own. Without romanticizing the assassination itself, Power uses it as a clear and unmistakable call for response.

Balakian's *Burning Tigris* and Power's *"A Problem from Hell"* share an acute sense of personal identity and responsibility that also appears in Balakian's other works. It is that sensibility that allows the two authors to reimagine the respective roles of the historical witness and the originary victim from within the context of personal and national commitment, a daunting feat normally accomplished in the best fiction. And yet perhaps this is not entirely surprising—many great works of historical writing share with literature a profound sense of the power of the historical imagination. By pointing the way to personal and national advocacy, action and response, the two authors also highlight the hazards of the historical imagination, which expresses itself in the struggle over evidence and countless polemics about points of view. They also express, in their different yet complementary ways, the important turn from the personal to the historical and back again that also suffuses and haunts Balakian's work.

In this instance, Powers reminds us that this "debate" started with the historical actors themselves. She reports an encounter, for example, between Ambassador Morgenthau and Mehmet Talaat in which the latter is said to have offered these chilling words about his government's responsibility (arguably more chill-

ing than Hitler's later declaration about the Armenian Genocide, now in the past): "'We don't give a rap for the future!' he exclaimed. 'We live only in the present!' " He later added to a German reporter: "'We have been reproached for making no distinction between the innocent Armenians and the guilty.' ... 'But that was utterly impossible, in view of the fact that those who were innocent today might be guilty tomorrow' " (p. 8). In moments such as these, *Burning Tigris* and *"A Problem from Hell"* remind us of what Balakian's writings in every genre try to convey, the recognition that it is perhaps the cruelest of April's ironies that the historical imagination itself is what can most easily betray us.

THE TASK OF THE TRANSLATOR: ARMENIAN GOLGOTHA *AND THE CONSPIRACY OF HISTORY*

Balakian's ventures into translation include two texts, *Bloody News from My Friend* by Siamanto (1996) and *Armenian Golgotha: A Memoir of the Armenian Genocide, 1915–1918,* by Grigoris Balakian (with Aris Sevag; 2009). The first renders in English a poetry cycle written by the Armenian poet Atom Yarjanian, better known by his pen name, Siamanto. Siamanto's poems were based on letters Peter Balakian's paternal grandfather, a physician named Diran Balakian, wrote while helping victims in the aftermath of massacres in Adana, Turkey, in 1909. Diran Balakian's life adds yet another link in the chain that ties his grandson to both his Armenian and his literary ancestry.

Armenian Golgotha bears even more directly on Balakian's career as writer and translator. It also addresses the belatedness mentioned above, the "betrayal" of history and evidence that is so central to Balakian's writings. The text is a translation of an Armenian-language memoir of a genocide survivor, the priest Grigoris Balakian, Peter Balakian's great-uncle. In *Armenian Golgotha,* the notion of such a betrayal—history's silent "conspiracy"—extends into the complex process of translation itself. The meaning of translation can be expanded in this instance to encompass not only literary translation, across

languages and cultures, but also historical translation, across time periods. (The Latin for "translation," *translatio,* means "a carrying across.") Understanding just how Balakian addresses the subject of translation, therefore, takes us not only into the process of the translator's own task but also into his uncle's own process of historical translation, of writing and witness.

The text has quickly achieved the status of a classic in the genre of genocide memoir. It is lengthy—the English edition extends to more than five hundred pages. The process of translating it took the better part of ten years, with several translators collaborating with its chief translator, Balakian, to complete it. Understandably, completing a translation of this magnitude may encounter numerous difficulties along the way, some mundane and others profound. As Balakian suggests, for instance, there is the difficulty of his great uncle's early twentieth-century Armenian to contend with. But even this seemingly mundane issue of translation encompasses two distinct aspects, the historical and the cultural. Grigoris Balakian's Armenian has to be translated across the decades and, only then, across the cultural and linguistic threshold from Armenian into English.

As the German Jewish intellectual and critic Walter Benjamin suggests in his essay "The Translator's Task" about the German and French versions of the word "bread": "In *'Brot'* and *'pain,'* the intended object is the same, but the mode of intention differs. It is because of their modes of intention that the two words signify something different to a German or a Frenchman, that they are not regarded as interchangeable, and in fact ultimately seek to exclude one another" (pp. 156–157). In this early statement in Benjamin's essay, the separation of the German and French languages embedded as a fissure in the notion of "pain" itself, rent as it is between two different "modes of intention" (or somewhat more simply, two separate cultural and historical contexts), suggests a fundamental obstacle to overcome, a determining mechanism of translation.

Since English is the modern lingua franca, translating words into English places the transla-

tor at the crossroads of many more than two languages and cultures. In *Armenian Golgotha,* for instance, place names act as potentially divisive obstacles. While Peter Balakian's co-translator, Aris Sevag, only mentions them briefly, he nevertheless hints that making the memoir accessible to the widest possible readership entailed the apparently unthinkable, replacing ancient Armenian place names with their modern Turkish ones, which have, ironically, gained much wider currency.

The act of translating a memoir such as *Armenian Golgotha,* therefore, is fundamentally wedded to history. As Benjamin is acutely aware, times change, and with them historically derived uses and conventions: "For in its continuing life, which could not be so called if it were not the transformation and renewal of a living thing, the original is changed. Established words also have their after-ripening. ... What once sounded fresh may come to sound stale, and what once sounded idiomatic may later sound archaic" (p. 155). The writer of the memoir himself is caught in this historical flux. As Peter Balakian admits, his great-uncle is susceptible to the conventions and faults of his age: "sometimes he essentializes Turks in a racialist way characteristic of the period" (p. xviii).

These at times more mundane considerations become, in Benjamin's rendering, characteristic of the separation of languages and, through the attempt at uniting them, part of a larger struggle that yokes history and language: "If the kinship of languages manifests itself in translation, it does so otherwise than through the vague similarity of original and copy. For it is clear that kinship does not necessarily involve similarity. ... Wherein can the kinship of two languages be sought, apart from a historical kinship?" (p. 156).

It is perhaps not surprising, therefore, that the roles of historical witness and originary writer—much like the roles of survivor and witness in *Black Dog of Fate*—are difficult to disentangle, even at the memoir's inception. In this regard, the struggle of translating *Armenian Golgotha* ninety years after the fact is first manifested in the very act of writing the memoir, an act that is itself caught in the mesh of history.

In his author's preface, Grigoris Balakian clearly expresses his feelings of inadequacy and uneasiness at depicting the events of 1915. In fact, he presents himself as a historian of sorts, one desperately needed by the rapidly dwindling Armenian nation: "Although you had many writers, poets, novelists, playwrights, and especially journalists and editors, you never had a historian" (p. 456).

The feeling of deep ambivalence that the act of committing his observations to print precipitates for Grigoris Balakian has its source in the historical events he is witnessing. The writer sounds as unsure about the prospects of doing justice to what he sees as he is adamant about his need to make the attempt (as his nephew will also later be): "I myself felt both weak at heart and of pen, to write about the great annihilation that surpasses even the bloodiest pages of human history" (p. 454). But as his confession suggests, this unambiguous profession of personal inadequacy primarily reflects the "surpassing" magnitude of the events he sees unfolding before him. Grigoris Balakian makes this aspect of the telling explicit only two pages later in the same preface:

> Never doubt my story of the great crime, and never think that what has been written herein has been in any way exaggerated. On the contrary, I have written the bare minimum, because it is not humanly possible to describe the horrific and ineffable martyrdom of over one million dead sons and daughters.
>
> (p. 454)

As the author puts it, it is his gargantuan task of making "a critical analysis of your [i.e., Armenia's] real inner life hidden behind the curtain" (p. 456) that causes him considerable anxiety: "As you had no historian, it was a thankless task to truthfully write this chapter of contemporary Armenian history with its veiled secret moments and, in so doing, to become everyone's enemy" (p. 457). His "thankless task" encompasses not only witnessing the genocidal events but having to relive them in the retelling, coupled with the awesome burden of conveying them to posterity, whole and intact.

Grigoris Balakian's attempt to reveal the "secrets" hidden behind the historical curtain

bears an uncanny resemblance to Benjamin's description of the translator's encounter with a similar secret, the truth or message lodged in the language of the poet he seeks to translate: "But what then is there in a poem—and even bad translators concede this to be essential—besides a message? Isn't it generally acknowledged to be the incomprehensible, the secret, the 'poetic'? That which the translator can render only insofar as he—also writes poetry?" (p. 152). (That message is also similar to the enigmatic, poetically charged stories that Peter Balakian's grandmother, Nafina, would tell him in "isolated moments" during his childhood.) The truth of the original memoir that Peter Balakian, or any other translator, is concerned about "capturing" corresponds in this particular memoir of genocidal atrocities to what Grigoris Balakian refers to as the "ineffable martyrdom" of the victims, both in turn reflecting what Benjamin locates in the hard, intractable "kernel" that resists any attempt to translate it, through language and across history. As he says, translation

> nevertheless at least points, with wonderful penetration, toward the predetermined, inaccessible domain where languages are reconciled and fulfilled. The original does not attain this domain in every respect, but in it lies that which, in a translation, is more than a message. This essential kernel can be more precisely defined as what is not retranslatable in a translation.
>
> (pp. 157–158)

However, as Grigoris Balakian's own confession illustrates, while the translator's task is critical, it ultimately leads away from him and toward what the writer calls the "thankless task" of recomposition, of historical translation. The memoirist is a historian, because both translate. They are linked in their attempt at being true to the original by their equally uneasy relationship to history— the translator's to the memoir and the memoir's to its own witness.

As such, the memoirist's attempt at rendering the ineffable, the unspeakable, transcends any subsequently simple attempt at fidelity on the translator's part. As Benjamin succinctly defines it, the "distinguishing mark of bad translation" is the "inexact transmission of an inessential content" (p. 152). The act of truthfully translating "content" takes the translator far beyond a simple attempt at fidelity, the narrow effort of being true to the original. It confronts him instead with the much more daunting task of capturing its essence, of representing the "whole" truth, as Grigoris Balakian struggles to do. Benjamin mentions the ideal translator's role as a poet for a reason—not primarily because it makes him a better wordsmith but because it implies that he has what might be called, for lack of a better term, the "sensibility" of a poet. As Peter Balakian reminds us in his own preface, he is both a poet and a translator. But Benjamin's rendering of the act of translation, as well as the circumstances of Grigoris Balakian's memoir, suggest that we should see the reminder as a fundamentally historical act—not a mention of the translator's appropriate skills or abilities so much as a summoning of his correspondingly appropriate identity for taking on his task. The same paradox of personal and public retelling in *Burning Tigris,* an explicitly historical work, reappears in *Armenian Golgotha,* a translation.

Benjamin's emphasis on this correspondence that transcends fidelity points to the central question surrounding any witness account: its value, beyond those of similar ones, in reinstating an otherwise dim historical reality. There are, after all, countless other observer accounts, including perhaps the best known, Ambassador Morgenthau's. What seems to distinguish Grigoris Balakian's account is its status as memoir. Not unlike his nephew in *Black Dog of Fate,* Grigoris Balakian is at once an insider and an outsider, in this case both eyewitness and survivor of the atrocities.

Armenian Golgotha, therefore, bears a unique relationship to the events it describes, one available to only a small handful of eyewitness accounts. As Peter Balakian is aware, "many readers will find that *Armenian Golgotha,* because of its intimacy with Turkish culture and the Anatolian landscape, will be another important text that tells the story of the eradication of the Armenians from inside Turkey and reveals Turkish denial as a continued assault on truth" (p. xx). He is referring in part to the physical, literal

landscape, the wilderness of Anatolia into which Grigoris Balakian escaped and in which he survived for four long years. But beyond that, the words suggest the larger milieu of Anatolian culture, politics, and history that the memoir evokes. It is entirely fitting, therefore, that such a memoir is situated at the crossroads between two cultures, embedded as it is in the Anatolian landscape, intimate with Turkish as well as Armenian history and culture, its status as the ultimate witness against denial in part a result of straddling the threshold between them. It is hardly surprising, then, that in addition to the family connection, Peter Balakian should feel a special affinity for Grigoris Balakian and his powerful account of personal and historical redemption in *Armenian Golgotha.*

Grigoris Balakian's attempt at translating a story across historical and cultural environments points to a question that is central to much of Peter Balakian's writings and a driving force in his exploration of witness accounts: Does someone who is close to an event, whether tragic or not, necessarily convey it better than someone who is not? Or, to put it in terms of Grigoris Balakian's intimacy with Anatolian culture, can we, as a result, conjecture that his memoir captures the writer's deep understanding of the victims' plight better than, say, Morgenthau's? While there is ample reason to do so, claiming the memoirist's status as an insider also presents a difficult conundrum, as Peter Balakian's own writings suggest—the fact itself shields others (in this case, non-Armenians) from the truth. Keeping in mind Benjamin's rendering of the translator's complex and multilayered task, it is worth considering that in Balakian's text, contemporary Armenians' own historical distance from the atrocities in their past is no more preferable to, say, Morgenthau's linguistic or cultural distance from the victims themselves. In fact, as discussed above, not even Grigoris Balakian's own proximity to the events he witnessed gives him an unconditional advantage in its retelling. It is here that Benjamin's characterization of the translator's task is especially pertinent. By recognizing the inherent complexities of translation, he also hints at their ultimate resolution:

Just as fragments of a vessel, in order to be fitted together, must correspond to each other in the tiniest details but need not resemble each other, so translation, instead of making itself resemble the meaning of the original, must lovingly, and in detail, fashion in its own language a counterpart to the original's mode of intention, in order to make both of them recognizable as fragments of a vessel, as fragments of a greater language.

(p. 161)

But while Benjamin's words point to a prophetic resolution, the task of both Balakians is resolutely historical. Peter Balakian's reference to Raphael Lemkin, the Polish Jewish legal scholar who coined the term "genocide" in 1943, is telling in this regard: "While it is likely that Lemkin never read *Armenian Golgotha* because of the obstacle of translation, he had accrued a depth of understanding of the events of 1915 such that his own knowledge of the Armenian Genocide is vividly borne out by and embodied in [Grigoris] Balakian's memoir" (p. xx). Balakian singles out "translation" as the primary "obstacle" facing Lemkin but one that never prevented him from "understanding" the victims' plight. While separated from the events of the genocide by both historical and linguistic distance, Lemkin is able to "translate" the events depicted in *Armenian Golgotha* across the cultural-historical threshold by fashioning the same deep, visceral, understanding that the memoir "embodies." In other words, as a reader, Lemkin displays the kind of identity, the sensibility, required of the ideal translator. Peter Balakian's description of Lemkin here places him once again in the familiar "in-between" space that he occupies in most of his writings. In this translation, he becomes what he envisions in his more biographical and poetic works, the carrier of a personal message across a threshold both cultural and historical.

Such an act of rewriting is, of course, also fraught with a kind of ambiguity at least as complex as the writer's own. As noted earlier, that ambiguity represents in part the uneasy moment of Grigoris Balakian's originary act of composing his memoir. But it is also the subsequent act of rewriting, of translating, the memoir across the cultural-historical divide that opens up the possibility of denial, which purports to be

simply another, or different, rewriting, like the conflicting account in a historical trial presented, in Grigoris Balakian's evocative phrasing, by a "testifier" (p. xxiii). Balakian mentions, for instance, an early and more localized rewriting of history, a disturbingly subtle form of denial: German soldiers Grigoris Balakian meets speak of Armenians as money-hungry "Christian Jews," conflating Turkish rhetoric with German stereotypes, reinterpreting history at the very moment of its making (p. xviii).

In moments such as these, the anonymous conspiracy of history becomes a deliberate vehicle of betrayal. Grigoris Balakian's original account, as much as his great-nephew Peter's translation of it, suggests that the attempt at fidelity complicates the task of the translator. As a result, the burden—better, the responsibility—of translation in its multiple meanings always takes on a deeply historical character. Peter Balakian's translation of *Armenian Golgotha* into English evokes the themes of historical witness that the poet and writer's own works explore, suggesting like them that, while no act of translation is immune to the conspiracy of history, it is also far from irrevocably subject to the betrayal of its agents.

ZIGGURAT *AND THE POETRY OF CONTEMPORARY WITNESS*

Peter Balakian's *Ziggurat* (2010), is a collection of poems new and old. The title refers to pyramid-like structures built by ancient civilizations, most notably the Sumerians, in the historic city of Ur. Although less than half the length of *June-Tree*, this second retrospective of sorts presents Balakian's most mature and compelling writing. It also takes him, and his readers, back to the poetry that grounds and defines his writing.

Perhaps it is more accurate to say that this latest volume effectively combines the major preoccupations of Peter Balakian's writings to date. If it is a retrospective, it is so not only because it brings together some of his earlier poems with new ones. Beyond simply combining the old with the new, it is also deeply con-

cerned—like his other poetry collections, his memoir *Black Dog,* and his historical study *Burning Tigris*—about how the present is powerfully imbued with the past, both ancient and modern. In that sense, this latest volume powerfully condenses more than thirty years of personal and poetic exploration in the span of a compact seventy pages.

The volume was published on the ninth anniversary of the September 11 attacks. Balakian earlier worked as a mail runner in the World Trade Center, delivering letters, documents, and checks by bicycle among the many firms in the financial district. (While Balakian did actually work as a mail runner, one cannot help but notice how apposite its poetic reinvention is to the notion of history and translation identified above.) The extended poem at the center of the volume, "A-Train / Ziggurat / Elegy," reflects on that experience to explore the aftermath of the attacks, both social and personal. In effect, the poem uses the forty-year span that saw the tower's construction and destruction as a microcosm of ancient and modern history. The poem looks back to the rise and fall of other towers—including the ziggurat at Ur and its mythic, Judeo-Christian archetype, the Tower of Babel—and ahead to a modern consciousness rent by historical and psychic calamity. There is an "in-betweenness" here, too—as though we have yet to fully internalize the meaning of the destruction of the twin towers, stuck as it is between ancient lessons we have yet to learn and modern experiences we have yet to understand.

The poem is rich in personal and anecdotal detail. It describes the way construction workers suspended themselves among the scaffolding, tens of stories above ground. Balakian's mail runner rides the A train, delivers the mail, and incessantly rides up and down the tower's enormous, ultramodern glass elevators. Earlier poems such as "Warhol / Blue Jackie" (about Warhol's lithographs of Jackie Kennedy) connect that experience to our own fractured, modern consciousness, much like the "pixilation" in the poem's description of the First Lady's face (p. 10). The very next poem, "World Trade Center / Mail runner / '73," brings us immediately back

to the twin towers and to what is arguably the central image of the entire collection, the simultaneous rise and fall of ambitions—at once literal and metaphorical—seen in various historical periods and places, and especially in the repeating image of ancient staircases and their modern equivalents, elevators: "It was comic to think Bachelard believed elevators / had destroyed the heroism of stair climbing" (p. 11). (Gaston Bachelard was an early twentieth-century French philosopher and critic.) The modern elevator "comically" mimics its ancient counterpart, combining a technological advance with a moral lapse. The poem's last line then sounds the ominous note: "It will come again. Be still. Wait" (p. 11).

The achievement of the volume is its ability to shuttle back and forth (and sideways and across) various episodes and images, while maintaining contact with its touchstone image, the stairs/elevator. Although the ziggurat at Ur looks like a quintessential pyramid, for instance, with its stairs on the outside, Balakian's poem takes us in various places back to its ancient archetype, the biblical Tower of Babel, whose steps may have been housed on the inside, eerily echoing the twin towers built around their massive elevator shafts. In Balakian's poem, the construction of the modern towers ominously repeats the past, the result of living in a fractured, "post-diluvian" (p. 22) existence, of life after the flood, a fall away from a primordial past tragically lost to us.

The image of the stairs/elevator corresponds to a parallel image in *Ziggurat*, that of digging, or excavation. Alongside that of the mail runner, a number of the poems present the shadowy figure of the British archaeologist Leonard Woolley, who headed the excavation and discovery of the Mesopotamian city of Ur in the 1920s. Much like the earlier Warhol lithographs, repeated with minor alterations, the many images in the volume and in Balakian's larger body of work come together in what amounts to a historical collage: the act of digging up the ruins of Ur suggests the pride of the biblical tyrant Nebuchadnezzar and the bombing of the World Trade Center (a perverse kind of excavation) melding into the deeply personal and historical act of excavating the Syrian dessert of Der Zor for remains of Armenian victims of the genocide. (Here too is an echo of Balakian's own digging into his past, to "unearth" the remnants of his own identity.)

By juxtaposing past, present, and future and sifting them repeatedly, *Ziggurat* offers a contemporary, sometimes disturbing perspective on the fundamentally historical question that animates all of Balakian's writing, the role of the witness. The poems in this volume redefine that role by extending and expanding it from a poetic into a more universal one. *Ziggurat* suggests that, like the poet and mail runner, we all inhabit a modern consciousness torn uneasily between past and present, that we are all witnesses.

Selected Bibliography

WORKS OF PETER BALAKIAN

POETRY

Father Fisheye: Poems. New York: Sheep Meadow Press, 1979.

Sad Days of Light: Poems. New York: Sheep Meadow Press, 1983.

Reply from Wilderness Island: Poems. Riverdale-on-Hudson, New York: Sheep Meadow Press, 1988.

Dyer's Thistle: Poems. Pittsburgh: Carnegie Mellon University Press, 1996.

June-Tree: New and Selected Poems, 1974–2000. New York: HarperCollins, 2001.

Ziggurat. Chicago: University of Chicago Press, 2010.

ESSAYS AND MEMOIRS

"Arshile Gorky and the Armenian Genocide." *Art in America,* February 1996, pp. 58–67, 108–109.

Black Dog of Fate: A Memoir. New York: Basic Books, 1997. Tenth anniversary edition, 2009.

"A Memoir Across Generations: Baby-Boom Suburbs, the Armenian Genocide, and Scholarly Corruption in America." *Chronicle of Higher Education,* June 12, 1998, pp. B6–B7.

"From Ezra Pound to Theodore Roosevelt: American Intellectual and Cultural Responses to the Armenian Genocide." In *America and the Armenian Genocide of*

1915. Edited by Jay Winter. Cambridge, U.K.: Cambridge University Press, 2003. Pp. 240–253.

"How a Poet Writes History Without Going Mad." *Chronicle of Higher Education,* May 7, 2004, pp. B10–B13.

"The Armenian Genocide and the Modern Age." *Sydney Papers* 20, no. 2:144–161 (autumn 2008).

"Falling into a Rug: Some Notes on Imagination and the Artifact." In *Crafting Fiction, Poetry, & Memoir: Talks from the Colgate Writers' Conference.* Edited by Matthew Leone. Hamilton, N.Y.: Colgate University Press, 2008. Pp. 11–23.

"Bones." *New York Times Magazine,* December 5, 2008, p. MM74.

ACADEMIC AND HISTORICAL WORKS

Theodore Roethke's Far Fields: The Evolution of His Poetry. Baton Rouge: Louisiana State University Press, 1989.

The Burning Tigris: The Armenian Genocide and America's Response. New York: HarperCollins, 2003.

TRANSLATIONS

With Nevart Yaghlian. *Bloody News from My Friend,* by Siamento. Detroit: Wayne State University Press, 1996.

With Aris Sevag. *Armenian Golgotha: A Memoir of the Armenian Genocide,* by Grigoris Balakian. New York: Knopf, 2009.

EDITED WORKS

With Bruce Smith. *Graham House Review: A Journal of Contemporary Poetry,* 1976–1996.

Ambassador Morgenthau's Story. Detroit: Wayne State University Press, 2003.

CRITICAL AND BIOGRAPHICAL STUDIES

Bartrop, Paul R., and Steven Leonard Jacobs. "Peter Balakian." In their *Fifty Key Thinkers on the Holocaust and Genocide.* Abingdon, Oxon, U.K.: Routledge, 2011. Pp. 19–25.

Foy, John. Review of *Ziggurat. Consequence Magazine* 3, no.1:248–250 (2011).

Frieze, Donna-Lee. " 'And This Is How We Shall Kill You': A Memoir of Evil Intent." *Jewish Daily Forward,* June 5,

2009. http://www.forward.com/articles/106660/. (Review of *American Golgotha.*)

Kalaidjian, Walter. *The Edge of Modernism: American Poetry and the Traumatic Past.* Baltimore: Johns Hopkins University Press, 2006. (First chapter on genocide includes an extended discussion of Balakian.)

Marino, Gigi. "Messenger for the Millennium: Peter Balakian's *Ziggurat.*" *Ararat Magazine,* April 7, 2011. http://araratmagazine.org/2011/04/peter-balakian-ziggurat/.

Russell, James R. "When the Tigris Burned and the Euphrates Ran Red." *Jewish Daily Forward,* January 23, 2004. http://www.forward.com/articles/6170/. (Review of *Burning Tigris.*)

Smith, Dinitia. "A Poet Knits Together Memories of Armenian Horrors." *New York Times,* August 19, 1997. http://www.nytimes.com/1997/08/19/books/a-poet-knits-together-memories-of-armenian-horrors.html?pagewanted=all&src=pm.

Smith, Wendy. "When History and Poetry Collide." *Publishers Weekly,* October 6, 2003.

INTERVIEWS

Jones, Christopher. "Phone Interview with Peter Balakian." *Cortland Review* 22 (February 2003). http://www.cortlandreview.com/issue/22/balakian_i.html.

Presson Mosby, Rebekah. "The Voice of History: An Interview with Peter Balakian." *New Letters* 67, no. 3:46 (2001).

OTHER SOURCES

Benjamin, Walter. "The Translator's Task (Die Aufgabe des Übersetzers)." Translated by Steven Rendall. *TTR: Traduction, Terminologie, Rédaction* 10, no. 2:151–165 (1997). http://www.scribd.com/doc/14029859/The-Task-of-the-TranslatorWalter-Benjamin.

Lipstadt, Deborah E. *Denying the Holocaust: The Growing Assault on Truth and Memory.* New York: Free Press, 1993.

Power, Samantha. *"A Problem from Hell": America and the Age of Genocide.* New York: Basic Books, 2002. Reprinted 2007.

The Waste Land. In *A Broadview Anthology of British Literature Edition: The Waste Land and Other Poems, T. S. Eliot.* Peterborough, Ontario: Broadview Press, 2011.

PINCKNEY BENEDICT

(1964—)

Louis H. Palmer III

PINCKNEY BENEDICT IS primarily known as a short-story writer and novelist but is also a screenwriter, playwright, essayist, and professor. He has published three short-story collections, *Town Smokes* (1987), *The Wrecking Yard* (1992), and *Miracle Boy and Other Stories* (2010), and a novel, *Dogs of God* (1993).

BIOGRAPHY

Benedict was born on April 12, 1964, in Lewisburg, West Virginia, to Ann Farrar Arthur and Cleveland Keith (Cleve) Benedict, a farmer and Republican politician who later served as a U.S. congressman and state commissioner of agriculture. Pinckney Benedict grew up on the family's dairy farm near Lewisburg in Greenbrier County, West Virginia. He attended the Hill School near Philadelphia and then entered Princeton University, receiving a B.A. degree in 1986. He went on to the Iowa Writers' Workshop, receiving his M.F.A. degree from the University of Iowa in 1988. In 1990 he married Laura Philpot (the writer Laura Benedict); they have two children, Nora and Cleveland.

Benedict has taught creative writing at Oberlin College, Ohio State University, Hope College, Princeton University, the Bread Loaf Writers' Conference, Queens University, and Hollins University in Roanoke, Virginia, where he serves on the faculty of the summer Tinker Mountain Writers' Workshop. At the time of this writing, he is a full professor in the English Department at Southern Illinois University in Carbondale, Illinois. With Laura Benedict, he coedits the series of anthologies *Surreal South,* which has published three volumes (2007, 2009, and 2011). A novel, *Wild Bleeding Heart,* is forthcoming. His stories have appeared in *Esquire, StoryQuar-* *terly,* the O. Henry Award series (twice), *Ontario Review, The Oxford Book of American Short Stories,* the *New Stories from the South* series (three times), the Pushcart Prize series (three times), and *Zoetrope: All-Story.* His awards include the *Chicago Tribune*'s Nelson Algren Award for "The Sutton Pie Safe," Britain's Steinbeck Award, and fellowships from the National Endowment for the Arts, the West Virginia Commission on the Arts, the Illinois Arts Council, and the Writers' Workshop at the University of Iowa. His screenplays include *Four Days* (1999) and a script for his novel, *Dogs of God* (forthcoming). He has also tried his hand at graphic stories based on comic books (e.g., "Kentucky Samurai").

TOWN SMOKES *(1987)*

You ought not to try to buy what hasn't been put up for sale.

("The Sutton Pie Safe," p. 10)

The title of this nine-story collection refers to "ready made" cigarettes, the kind that people who are used to rolling their own see as a special luxury. These stories were mostly written when Benedict was an undergraduate at Princeton, working with Joyce Carol Oates and, according to his own account, under the influence of Breece D'J Pancake. Pancake was a West Virginia writer who had committed suicide at the age of twenty-nine, and whose stories were collected posthumously and published in 1983. Like Pancake's, the stories in *Town Smokes* are realist stories that have mainly rural settings and tend to involve hardscrabble lifestyles and uneducated, first-person protagonists, many of whom are young boys or young men. Sometimes the conflict is between groups of people, but often it is caused

by accident or natural catastrophe. Animals, especially cows and dogs, feature prominently, as do firearms, often described in precise detail by an author whom his wife, Laura Benedict, has described as a "gun nut" (*Notes*).

In "The Sutton Pie Safe," the narrator, an older boy, watches the interplay between his father, who has just shot a blacksnake to make himself a belt, his mother, and a woman from town, a judge's wife, who shows up to buy the item named in the title, a wooden cabinet with tin panels made by a famous local craftsman. The father, caught out in the yard without a shirt, gun in one hand, dead snake in the other, is embarrassed and deals with his hurt pride by displaying redneck bravado. He brings the snake into the house and lectures the judge's wife, "'We aren't merchants,' he said. 'And this isn't a furniture shop.'" When the mother tries to mediate, he chastises her, "Don't apologize for me, Sara. … Go ahead and sell the damn breadbox if you want, but just don't apologize for me" (p. 10). The mother points out that they can use the $300 from the sale to fix their collapsing barn, but the father, still angry, takes it out on his son. When the son seems disgusted with a dead mouse that the father cuts out of the snake's belly, the father hacks up the snake, and tells him, "You think about that, the next time you decide you want something" (p. 12).

This is one of the two most anthologized stories from the collection, and the one that won the Nelson Algren Award. Like many stories with innocent or naive narrators, it skillfully manipulates point of view to present us with a portrait of the conflicts between classes and between men and women. It can also be read as a nascent bildungsroman concerning the ways that men learn to be men by way of processing their emotional conflicts through violence and cruelty. That said, the father is not presented as a villain even if he behaves like a boor. In the opening section he demonstrates that wanton violence is wasteful. Discussing the snake, he reflects,

"Boys want to kill everything, don't they?" he said to me, grinning. Then, more seriously, "Not too good an idea to kill a blacksnake. They keep the

mice down, the rats. Better than a cat, really, a good-sized blacksnake."

(p. 2)

This kind of nuance is what saves Benedict from some early critics' accusation that his works display a patronizing attitude toward his poor and often ignorant characters.

In an interview with Thomas E. Douglass, Benedict said that his story "Booze" was one of the first he wrote and was an exaggerated version of a boyhood experience, when a neighbor's hog went feral (p. 71). It is a version of a rural myth of considerable endurance, more recently justified in the true story of "Hogzilla," a thousand-pound wild hog who had achieved legendary status before being killed in the Okefenokee region of Georgia in 2004. Booze is the name of a particularly nasty hog owned by Tobe Fogus, a neighbor of the twelve-year-old narrator. Tobe claimed to have lost his wife to his hogs, but the boys, the narrator and his friend Kenny, don't believe him. They make pocket money by taking care of Tobe's hogs, all except for Booze, a five-hundred-pound Duroc boar, which Tobe considers to be too dangerous for them. One day the boys find Tobe dead in front of his TV and Booze escaped. Booze continues to be seen occasionally. The narrator's father offers a bounty and shoots Booze three times one night when he gets into the garbage, to no avail. Finally Booze attacks the boys when they are out putting in fence posts. Kenny uses a brush hook, a heavy J-shaped blade on the end of a handle (known as "the tool which tamed the South") to split his head. Even in this condition, Booze manages to bite Kenny's ankle before finally dying.

Like "Booze," "Dog" is a story about everyday heroism, on a lesser scale, with more humor than many of the other stories in this collection. When a mangy, vicious dog crawls under his trailer to die, Eldridge must crawl in after it with a feeble flashlight, enduring the taunts of his no-account roommate, Broom. Needing a weapon, they walk the two miles to Fat Ed's, who must endure the taunts of his mother and Broom before giving Eldridge the appropriate pistol. Again Eldridge must make the epic crawl under the trailer to shoot the dog. The narrative leaves us with

him under there, with the dead dog, imagining digger beetles consuming the corpse. "Didn' have nobody in the world to take up for you, did you" (p. 103), he asks the dog, annoyed by Broom's stomping and yelling above in the trailer. Both he and Fat Ed exhibit a stoical response to the constant criticism of the people they live with, who are narcissistically focused on their own needs and wants.

"All the Dead" and "Town Smokes" both deal with young men who have lost their fathers. In "All the Dead," Adonijah's mother rouses him in the middle of the night to search for "his daddy," to which he replies that his "daddy been gone a long time" (p. 33). She means his stepfather, Makepeace, an ironic name because, as we find out, he is unable to fit into the role of an adequate father figure. Adonijah remembers an incident in which he got beaten up by a friend for making fun of him, then returned home to be whipped by Makepeace for losing the fight. In contrast, he expresses admiration for J. W. Daws, the state trooper who killed Adonijah's father, shooting him in the face by mistake during a robbery attempt: "He come to the funeral which must of took more guts than many a man has. He stood next to my mama and give her his handkerchief when she started to cry" (p. 37). The contrast between the brave and empathetic Daws and the violent and prescriptive Makepeace gives him a context in which he can begin to judge for himself what is good behavior. He doesn't blame Daws for killing his father because he realizes that his father was "a good-looken man before he got shot but mebbe not too good when it come to thinken quick" (p. 36).

Adonijah hikes up the mountain to the trailer of Echols Doolittle. "Yo," he calls, which brings out Doolittle armed with a machine pistol. He realizes that Doolittle is "crazy, nuts as a monkey liven up there in the holler," and that his life is in danger. He discovers that Makepeace had been there, "drunk and argumentative" (p. 40), and had shot a hole in the trailer, but that he is gone now. Adonijah walks into town and finds Makepeace, shot in the chest, sitting at the base of the Confederate monument near his truck. Adonijah loads him in and heads for the hospital. Make-

peace tells him that he knew the man who was the model for the Confederate soldier, and that he committed suicide—"et his gun"—in the square (p. 48). "Makepeace laughs and it is a terrible sound. That ain' the way to do it he says" (p. 49). These are his last words, and imply that perhaps he had wanted to kill himself and had decided to provoke Doolittle. Adonijah keeps "headen on down the road toward Heflin as fast as I can go even though there ain' any use in it" (p. 49). The title refers to Adonijah's losses as well as to a comment Doolittle makes: "They's a number of dead men up in there he says. A powerful number" (p. 41)—killed by himself and other men and some by the mountain itself. In this world of death, Adonijah has to prove himself, like his namesake, Solomon's brother in 1 Kings, to be a worthy man.

"Town Smokes" follows another young man off the mountain. He has just buried his father and he puts together his inheritance—six dollars, an old Colt .38 pistol, an arrowhead he found while digging the grave—and follows a railroad track into town. On the way he is waylaid by two boys with a rifle who have been chasing a wild pig. They mock him for being a ridge runner (hillbilly), shatter the arrowhead, and steal his bag and his shoes. Dirty, barefoot, and in the rain, he enters a town ravaged by flash floods, and a kindly storekeeper gives him a pack of Camels. He sits by a washed-out bridge and smokes, imagining the destruction elsewhere. He tells himself that "it is sure as hell I won' go back up the mountain" (p. 168). He has the world all before him, but his lack of resources and his appetite for disaster place him in a questionable position.

"Hackberry" concerns Timmy Lee Purvis, who is living with the teenage former stripper Torrey across from a skinny old man named Hackberry, who sits on his porch drinking beer and listening to an old radio. All three seem to be looking for direction. Torrey, hoping to be taken care of, had allowed Timmy Lee to take her away from her bar job in the Ohio Valley, where they had met while he was in the army. Timmy Lee had left the army for a job at a tire factory. He doesn't want Torrey to go back to

work—he throws a carton of milk at her when she suggests it. Her half-hearted attempt to be a good housewife results in a burned spoon bread. Hackberry listens to a radio talk show for his answers, which are not satisfying, especially to Timmy Lee, who spends more and more time drinking beer on Hackberry's porch. None of the three are good at what they have been doing—Hackberry, for all his listening, can't really evaluate what he hears, Torrey is a clumsy dancer, and, despite his army training, Timmy Lee doesn't do well in a fight. After Hackberry assures him that he can fight his way out of any conflict, Timmy Lee goes out to a bar and gets beaten up by a martial arts expert, then returns to find himself locked out. When Torrey won't let him in, he sits in his car and leans on the horn. The story ends with each person isolated—Hackberry and Torrey in the houses and Timmy Lee in the car, honking for help. Their institutions have failed them, and it looks like they are failing each other.

"Fat Tuesday" concerns a family crawdad boil in Louisiana. Jason and Sara Goddell are hosting the party, which includes various family members and friends. What starts out as a great party goes bad when Cousin Mobrey Davis, "the middle-aged bachelor man" (p. 120), takes off with Jason's seventeen-year-old niece to attend Mardi Gras across the lake in New Orleans. His aunt gets mad and leaves. Meanwhile, his friend Bud refuses to participate and sits inside drinking and watching TV. He spills crawdads all over the TV room. The story ends with Jason and Sara, in decidedly bad moods, picking up the remains of the party. This is probably the least successful story in the collection, maybe because Benedict doesn't seem to have the ear for Cajun speech that he does for the expressions and cadences of the upper South. Except for the crawdads, it could take place anywhere.

Instead of the point of view of a boy, "Water Witch" takes that of the father, named Castle. He has moved his wife and son to Texas, where he has a small cattle farm. A drought has become so bad that the only thing to do is kill the remaining cattle and declare a loss. Castle is, according to the local feed dealer, "about the last one" (p. 136). On the way home with the ammunition he

needs to shoot the cattle, he picks up a hitchhiker who claims to be a water witch. "You feed me he says and I will find you water. I found water in the desert before" (p. 139). Castle brings him home and feeds him, and he talks like a revival preacher of his abilities. Castle resolves to kill him if he's lying. The next day, the witch chooses a spot and they dig deeper and deeper, until one of them can fit in the hole. As the witch prepares to descend, Castle hits him with a shovel, then buries him in the hole. As the family prepares to leave, Castle reflects, "It is just a spot in the ground, like the farm, like the ditch they will dig with the end-loader for all the cattle. It's nothing I can't leave behind me" (p. 148).

The story depicts a kind of environmental madness. From its opening imagery of a locust emerging and dying, to the son's dream of a green and moist home with a spring in the backyard, to Castle's resolution to kill the witch if he proves false, we see the desperation of a person who has made certain assumptions about the world, that it will provide the basics of life—water and growing things—only to find those assumptions betrayed. In this state, the water witch's promises take on a larger significance. If he too fails in his promise, he deserves to be punished. Castle cannot do anything to help his farm or his cattle, but he can punish an itinerant for his false promises. He has found something that he has the power to do.

The publication of this collection in 1987, when Benedict was twenty-three and still at the Iowa Writers' Workshop, created some controversy. A positive review by Dianne McWhorter in the *New York Times Book Review* was criticized for its stereotyping of Appalachians. The regional scholar Rodger Cunningham wrote in a letter to the editor, "'White trash'? 'Dismal sludge'? 'The preferred form of communication is murder'? Come now. Can any group in this country other than Appalachian mountain people be subjected to this sort of ethnic slur by a national magazine in 1987?" ("Heat"). He goes on to suggest that perhaps Benedict writes from a privileged perspective: "no one despises poor mountain people more than some better-off mountain people." The Kentucky

writer Jim Wayne Miller suggested that the fault was more with McWhorter than with Benedict, whose work deserved better, more nuanced readings. He says, of the "distant Savage South" perceived by Northern city folk: "this Appalachia is found more frequently in the assumptions of reviewers" (pp. 32–33). These two perspectives seem to have set the model for much of what was to come. When they learned that Benedict was the son of the Republican congressman and senatorial candidate Cleve Benedict, and that the previous generation of Benedicts had been heirs to Procter & Gamble money, writers such as the poet and sometime gubernatorial candidate Bob Henry Baber dismissed Benedict as a sort of latter-day carpetbagger: "a slick modern local colorist whose technically brilliant work for the most part preys on an Appalachian underclass he knows only enough about to denigrate. His work is dark, ungenerous, violent" (pp. 376–377). Others, such as the historian John Alexander Williams, were more nuanced in their criticism. Writing in 1993, Williams said that he still had hope that Benedict would grow into "an Appalachian writer whom we can read within the realist tradition." He continued, "most of what he has given us consists of updated versions of familiar mountaineer characters seen through a lens still clouded by the perspectives of his upbringing" (p. 174). More recently, in an article based on an interview, George Brosi has described Benedict as "gleeful." He quotes Benedict as saying, "It fundamentally makes my day when some-thing I've written gets up the nose of some stodgy academic or critic.… That's when I know I'm in the ballpark" (p. 13). Like the younger writers of the Harlem Renaissance, Benedict claims to be less concerned with properly representing a people or a class of people and more interested in creating stories, which he describes as an impulse that is a "strange, largely worthless, self-aggrandizing, atavistic, and mostly ancillary function … that I seem to be wired for" (p. 13).

THE WRECKING YARD (1992)

She knew that the watch would tell her when she was clear of the place and its magnetic rocks, which distorted the flow of the days. When she had come to a place where the mechanism's pace came back to itself, that would be time enough to imagine a way back to people and a way to another kind of life. That would be time enough to imagine what that different life might be like.

("Washman," p. 78)

"Getting Over Arnette" sounds like the title to a country song, and sets the tone for the collection by emphasizing an almost slapstick sense of humor. Like Eldridge and Broom in "Dog," Loftus and Bone are two pathetic characters who do not seem to have the skills or abilities to help themselves. Loftus is described as "skinny sad-sack Loftus" (p. 1). He has just been abandoned by his red-headed girlfriend Arnette, who ran off with "some college puke," and Bone is taking him bowling in a lame attempt to distract him. Mostly because of Bone's incompetent flirtation, they get thrown out of the bowling alley by the Rolling Pins, a local women's team. They go into a bar where a stranger makes fun of their bowling shoes as "a style of dress favored on many of the nation's better university campuses," then comments that "you don't neither of you look like something that might be going to college right away" (p. 12), and finally suggests that he has also had sex with Arnette. This is too much for Loftus, who attacks him. He turns out to be a martial arts expert, as in "Hackberry," and hurts both men badly, fracturing Bone's jaw. The story ends with Arnette returned, Bone thankfully silent, and Loftus convinced that his suffering will keep her from leaving him again.

"The Wrecking Yard" is the setting for a story about the parts left over after a convertible goes off a cliff. One missing part is a woman's body, caught in the trees on the side of the mountain. The wrecker drivers watch as rescuers rappel down to her and haul her up. The wrecker driver scavenges the remaining parts, then throws a hubcap off the cliff so that his boss can't add it to his collection. It is a frustrated attempt to give back something after the ravages of the wreck.

In "Rescuing Moon," young Grady comes off the mountain to rescue his mentor from having to live in a private nursing home run by Mrs. Tencher. The old man, Moon, is wheelchair

bound and very weak, but glad to be out of there. "Bunch of coots," he says. Mrs. Tencher tries to keep him out, then threatens him, then tries to use guilt: "Eight different kinds of pills he's got to have, the doctor says, four different times of day. You going to do that for him?" (p. 53). Ellen, the cook, flings a skinned rabbit at the car, and it lands on the windshield. They run over a rooster on the way out. " 'I don't know about you killing this old man,' Moon says, and he is still laughing, 'but you sure as hell did leave that woman's yard full of little dead animals, didn't you?' " (p. 56). Grady, shaken and uncertain about the future, focuses on his driving.

"Washman" is set in the early twentieth century, just as automobiles were being introduced. Gandy, an adventurer who makes his living by armed robbery, becomes obsessed with a hunchback, Washman, who has withered legs and who passes his house periodically on a mule. Gandy decides to kill the mule, but the men end up wounding each other. Washman takes Gandy's woman with him, leaving Gandy lying in the road. A couple in an automobile almost run over him, crash the car, and injure the woman passenger's arm. They take him to the man's father, who is a doctor. At the town clinic, Gandy won't die and won't stop screaming. The townspeople form a vigilance party to kill him. After they do that, they set out up the mountain after Washman. It is a disastrous journey. Men die in a landslide, in a river crossing, and from a rattlesnake bite, and the survivors arrive just as Washman is raping Gandy's woman. They hang him and burn his house, but the fire spreads, killing all of them but one, who gets back to town with the woman, both badly burned. Gandy's woman and the female car passenger are left together, one burned and pregnant and the other with a crippled arm. Almost everyone gets hurt or killed, and Gandy's woman is convinced she is going to give birth to a monster.

"The Panther: A Bedtime Story," like "Washman," takes place in the Appalachian past. A young man goes up the mountain, hunting for a panther that is killing his father's sheep. He finds an old woman, who shares her food with him

because he treats her politely. They eat lamb stew cooked in her cauldron, and she makes an offer:

> I'll show you a thing, the old woman said. It's a thing nobody else has ever seen, and a thing you'll not see again. I show it to you because you got good manners, and 'cause you brought no rifle into my camp, she said.
>
> Okay, the boy said.
>
> Then you follow the path down the mountain, the old woman said, and she pointed the way out to him. You take it straight down the mountain, straight into the valley. And no more hunting the panther, she said, 'cause it ain't what you think it is, and it's the last one of them left.
>
> (p. 96)

As he watches, she transforms into the panther and goes off into the undergrowth. The boy memorizes the way she looks so he can tell his children and grandchildren.

"The Electric Girl" is in the form of a radio play. It begins with Lilly leaving Murphy for her new boyfriend, Charlie Charlie, who works for the circus. Murphy shoots her, then explains what he did to her father on the telephone. In the next scene Charlie Charlie finds Murphy and cuts out his tongue. The story concludes when the Electric Girl from the circus finds Murphy and seduces him, with the sounds of electrical buzzing and the chair creaking. Unfortunately this kills him.

"At the Alhambra" takes place in Nicaragua in 1970. A pilot, Johnnie, and the woman he has brought with him, Anne, are staying at the Alhambra hotel. A local American, Carl, tries to get Johnnie to invest in his ice plant. Anne gets angry and asks Johnnie if he has signed anything, implying that this kind of thing has happened before. She cuts her hand on a broken glass. Later that day, they fly away. Looking at him, she says she wishes he could always be flying.

"Bounty" is another story about dogs. In this one, an outsider, Candles, comes into the county seat to ask the sheriff if he is offering a bounty on dead coyotes. The sheriff tries to pass him along to animal control, and there is some dispute over jurisdiction, until it becomes obvious that Candles has a truck bed full of dead domestic

dogs. While the dogcatcher and the sheriff are deciding whether to arrest Candles, he takes off on foot. He crashes into a kid with an armful of sodas and the sheriff apprehends him. Accompanied by comments from the dogcatcher, his deputy, and the kids drinking sodas, the sheriff loads the dogs back in the truck, tells Candles to dispose of them, and sends him on his way.

"Horton's Ape" takes place in the western desert, at a roadside zoo. A man eating his lunch, Turley, becomes fascinated with a baboon in a cage, who grabs a tourist's camera and takes a series of random Polaroids. The owner, Horton, comes out and tells him what trouble the ape has caused. It had been trained to take things from people as part of a circus act, and so it will often snatch items from people who come near. He has promised the tourist that he will kill the ape to avoid a lawsuit. When Horton goes back in, Turley helps the ape to escape. It embraces him, bites his thumb, then grabs a pig and climbs a saguaro cactus to eat it. Horton comes out and gives Turley a gun, asking him to shoot the ape. Turley does, but it falls on him and breaks his collarbone. The two men hobble inside, leaving the dead ape, the mangled pig, and the shotgun in the parking lot.

"Odom" describes the title character's frustrated attempts to keep his grown son with him in a camp on a mountainside. He plans to clear a space to build a bigger house. After he wrecks his bulldozer, he turns to dynamite, blowing trees and stumps out of the ground. The son drives to town and disappears. Odom searches the local roads on foot, looking for where he could have wrecked. Finally a policeman comes up and says that the boy will be getting out of jail soon. In celebration, or to impress his son with the work he has accomplished, Odom blasts out a huge area. The son does return, and father and son are working together at the end, drilling a hole for another charge.

The stories in *The Wrecking Yard* take a few steps beyond the limitations that the author set for himself in *Town Smokes*. They are less serious and take more risks, as we might expect, but there is also a move away from the strictly realistic toward the fantastic. Electric girls and shape-shifting old women don't belong in a strictly realistic context, and the broad comedy of "Getting Over Arnette" goes beyond its roots in a story like "Dog." Benedict continues to surprise us, and his novel certainly pushes the envelope.

DOGS OF GOD *(1993)*

In this place that we're going to—I've not been there before, but I have an idea—to be a religious man might be a good thing. I suspect that quite a nasty piece of work awaits us.

(Dogs of God, p. 173)

Focus on the apocalypse, or the end-time, seems to wax and wane in literature, according to forces that are not simply related to a calendar predicated on the base-ten numerical system. Certainly, turns of the centuries seem to bring out apocalyptic patterns of one kind or another. In light of the much-hyped "Y2K," followed by the next supposed end-time, 2012, associated with the end of the Mayan calendar, it may help to look back to gain some kind of perspective.

Two hundred years ago the focus was on a clean break with the past, a true New Age of enlightenment guided by reason and supported by rights, sparked by the French and American revolutions and fueled by Romantic fascination with alternate political and spiritual models. Whatever disappointments resulted from Romantic optimism and Enlightenment idealism were further developed and critiqued a hundred years ago at the turn of the previous century, which saw a trend in novels of utopia and dystopia, novels more properly millennial than apocalyptic in the usual sense. A host of new societies—feminist, socialist, fascist—were imagined and described in fiction. At the turn of the last century, Appalachia, recently discovered as a culturally unique region, was being described in utopian and dystopian terms, often both at the same time.

The rest of the twentieth century saw a steady growth in what is now called Appalachian literature, a literature that seems to have alternately followed and resisted national trends. For some reason that does not seem to be related to

the base-ten calendar but might be more properly related to Hiroshima and Vietnam, apocalypse reemerged nationally in the 1960s as a literary fascination. Most of the prominent critics during the sixties—Northrop Frye, R. W. B. Lewis, M. H. Abrams, Leslie Fiedler, and Harold Bloom, to name a few—used the term, often going back to William Blake and the other Romantics for models. The broader intellectual climate of the 1960s was suffused with eschatological terminology—this was the era of the death of the author, the death of the novel, the end of man. At the same time, an emerging postmodern style in fiction often incorporated apocalyptic themes, images, and plots. Thomas Pynchon, Kurt Vonnegut, Anthony Burgess, John Barth, Russell Hoban, and many others come to mind. In Appalachian literature, Gurney Norman's *Divine Right's Trip,* which was serialized in the margins of the *Whole Earth Catalog* in 1971, concluded with an apocalyptic encounter with a dragon in a Kentucky coal mine. This contrasts with the more typical "coming home" resolution that many Appalachian novels share. But despite the constant presence of the Bible as a model and as a cultural link, it is difficult to think of any other Appalachian fictional apocalypses. Cormac McCarthy moved the setting to Texas for his apocalyptic novel *Blood Meridian* (1985). In fiction written by its native writers, Appalachia typically serves as a safe place, a place to return to, either removed from or to be defended against the onslaughts of outside forces.

Pinckney Benedict's *Dogs of God* takes us in a whole 'nother direction. It certainly presents Appalachia—represented by a corner of West Virginia around a fictional community known as El Dorado—as a place apart, but one which serves as a stage for an apocalyptic confrontation between various forces that are presented in such a way as to suggest allegorical implications. It is a confrontation between the forces of a variety of evils, as represented by competing coteries of international and local criminals and federal and local law enforcement agents. The good characters, including the boxer Goody, are mostly helpless against the coercion, corruption, and violence unleashed against them by these organizations of ruthless and brutal men.

El Dorado, once a summer resort, is now an armed camp for marijuana production and distribution. This community is under the iron heel of a twelve-fingered *Ubermensch* with the appropriately Germanic name of Tannhauser. With a motley collection of soldiers of fortune, he replicates on a smaller scale the atrocities of North American colonial history: he captures and enslaves a group of Central American migrant workers, selected members of which he rapes and tortures for his or the group's amusement. Like a good capitalist, he ruthlessly and efficiently eliminates his competition, hippies and hill folk who grow pot in a subsistence economy. He enlists the help of the local "high sheriff" to protect him from legal interference. He captures a wandering "anchorite" and keeps him on a chain within the compound, shouting biblical verses. He uses the enslaved workers to clear a runway just long enough to land a vintage DC-3 cargo plane loaded with contraband weapons. Anticipating a huge profit from the marijuana crop, Tannhauser seems to be the supreme ruler of his little world.

The novel's prologue is a first-person narrative by Goody, an illegal bare-knuckles boxer, describing a match in a machine shop that ends up in a brawl. The audience is divided into two groups, "hillbillies," supporting his opponent, Rolly, and Goody's group, *"guests here, came up from the county seat to take the woodhicks' money. They're all related up in these mountain places. They're all one big family"* (p. 3). The fight ends ambiguously, with Rolly falling and hitting his head against a sawhorse and then a stool—*"I hear both impacts, which sound the same: like the fat part of a baseball bat connecting with a pumpkin"*(p. 3). As the brawl breaks out and both boxers are trampled by the crowd, Goody realizes that Rolly is dead and imagines two scenes: one where he and Rolly congratulate each other on the fight and another where they fight until everyone leaves, even after their eyes have swollen shut, the blows serving to remind them that they are still alive.

This introduction suggests to the reader that the narrative will follow a familiar course, a conflict between the two groups. We expect it to be structured by the us-versus-them, hills-versus-valley, outlands-versus-city dichotomies familiar to us from earlier novels of Appalachian conflict written by non-natives, such as James Dickey's *Deliverance* (1970) and Madison Smartt Bell's *Soldier's Joy* (1989). Instead, Benedict's narrative combines insiders and outsiders (mainly outsiders) into a variety of groupings, effectively deconstructing the binary patterns we are so used to. The characters are presented as so individualized that each is part of a matrix of interests and alliances, and their interactions, loyalties, and even their origins are constantly in question. Goody and the character that the narrative presents as his evil twin, Peanut, are outsiders who come into a complex political and moral environment.

Goody just seems to want to be left in peace, perhaps out of guilt for having killed Rolly. He moves into a remote farmhouse, where he spends his time exercising and joyriding in his muscle car. Forces are at work, however; he finds a human corpse in a canebrake behind the house, and a group of feral dogs chase a deer out in front of his car, causing him to wreck it. In order to make money to repair the car, he agrees to a boxing contest with Tannhauser's champion and right-hand man, Yukon. We later find out that the body was one of Tannhauser's victims.

Peanut, on the other hand, seems to be out for what he can get. He hitchhikes into the area and has an assignation with an older, asthmatic homosexual, whose car he steals and abandons after ramming a police car that stopped him for having a taillight out. He then heads off across country on foot, where he is beset by a herd of wild boars in an abandoned house. He finally arrives, tattered and starving, at El Dorado, where he manages to sneak in past the razor-wired walls of the compound, only to be caught yelling at an owl for taking a possum he was stalking.

Other interested parties include a DEA agent and his assigned helicopter pilot, who cruise over the area looking for marijuana fields; two mysterious, well-dressed Eurotrash "investors," Bodo

and Toma, who arrive in the DC-3 with weapons to be traded for this year's crop; an aging pot grower, Wallace Claymaker, with a much younger wife, Dreama; and finally Dwight, a tour guide at Hidden World Caverns—the local underground attraction.

Conflicts emerge from a confrontation between the DEA helicopter and Claymaker that makes it necessary for the sheriff to change allegiances. Trying to get a closer view of Dreama nude sunbathing, the Feds in their helicopter discover Claymaker's marijuana patch, and he shoots at them with a machine pistol, which he should not have had. Tensions are augmented when the boxing match takes place and Goody beats Tannhauser's man.

Indeed, nature itself seems to turn on the El Dorado gang: the marijuana crop fails, wild boars attack, the earth opens up and men fall through into the caves below. Tannhauser's explanation for all this is offered to Bodo after the fight, as the sheriff is planning to attack the encampment:

> What you've got to know is, there's a ship buried deep in the mountain up there. A ship, and it's poisoning the soil … I mean a spaceship. A life-carrying vessel from beyond the stars. … It crashed and it poisoned the land and nothing that grows up there now is normal. All of it's distorted, mutated, changed.
>
> (p. 281)

As this is a realist novel, what one could draw from this claim is that the adage about absolute power is correct: Tannhauser has finally gone off the deep end. And, like a true paranoid, he sees a government conspiracy behind the actions of the joyriding Peeping Toms from the DEA and the corrupt local sheriff. The forces out to get him include "the National Guard, The Army, The FBI, NSA, CIA" (p. 281). That he is insane is certainly Bodo's conclusion. But subsequent events call this into doubt.

Tannhauser's gang kidnaps Goody after the fight. Just as Peanut is serving as Tannhauser's executioner, strangling Goody, the sheriff attacks. Snipers kill most of the mercenaries, and the deputies herd the illegals into a building and slaughter them. Tannhauser is gutted by Paloma,

the woman he has raped, who then proceeds to cut off his supernumerary digits. He has enough life in him to fire a rocket from a handheld launcher into the chest of Sheriff Faktor, who dies from the impact even though the rocket fails to explode. The DC-3 and the DEA copter collide in midair, killing all aboard. Goody pursues Peanut into the woods, where they fall down a hole into the underground cavern system. Peanut drowns, while Goody finds land and wanders around until he arrives in a cavern where he finds a city, built and occupied by man-sized moth creatures:

> They came at him from every side, and he threw up his maimed hands, crossed his arms before his face in a useless defense, pushing at their packed bristling frantic bodies, striking out as they greedily probed his flesh with their long pointed sucking proboscises, shouting in fury and despair as the jabbering, flapping mass of them poured over him and bore him down.
>
> (p. 364)

Again, this is an event not explainable in a realist framework. Is he hallucinating? Then why is his body "covered in sores, reddened oozing sores like some sort of terrible pox" (pp. 365–366) when he finally emerges into the Hidden World Caverns? Such events serve to make the reader doubt that this is just a story, to encourage us to look for hidden meanings.

"Apocalypse" literally means "unveiling" and was originally the Greek synonym for "revelation." Today the terms have different connotations, but we still use them interchangeably to refer to the last book in the traditional New Testament. The Book of Revelation, predicated on a series of visions by John of Patmos, is densely allegorical, suggesting that "unveiling" is meant to be taken two ways. The first is the terminal unveiling of the world and the spiritual sorting out into appropriate groups—blessed and damned, sheep and goats, and so on. But the second meaning is textual; readers need to unveil the allegorical meaning of the text. *Dogs of God* is not an allegory in the same sense—it makes, as suggested above, the realist claim. It is about a specific time and place—Appalachia today. Nevertheless, there are textual indications that

things signify more than what they say on a literal level. Some possibilities can be suggested here.

When we use the word "apocalyptic" rather than "millennial," at least as it applies to narrative, we tend to look for a movement toward a final battle or confrontation, which results in both the destruction of the world and a subsequent revelation or passage beyond for the chosen. *Dogs of God* follows this narrative structure, building to a final battle in which only one woman and one man are left on the premises—Paloma and the anchorite—while Goody follows an underground path, a harrowing-of-hell or death-and-rebirth of sorts, emerging from the Hidden World Caverns.

There are other influences here well beyond the Bible—Cormac McCarthy and the action film are two obvious enough to have caught the attention of the reviewers—and the novel's textual structures suggest more than a random resemblance between texts. Like a loosely structured version of allegory, *Dogs of God* can be read at differing levels of focus or scale.

Goody's encounters or hallucinations in the underworld, especially the ultimate attack of the moth men, serve to push readers beyond a securely realist reading toward more inferential and allegorical meanings. It makes us look back at the rest of the story looking for new iterations of meaning, new patterns, new additions.

Meanings on the textual level can be suggested by the use of names. To give a few examples, Goody is one of the characters who is closest to goodness, mainly because he doesn't seem to desire anything much, especially power over others. Even when he is fighting, he has to wait to get angry before he can fight effectively. He is contrasted, in his pragmatism, with Dreama, a creature of her own fantastic imagination who frequents the Hidden World Caverns. She can't seem to focus enough to see when she is in danger and so is destroyed by Sheriff Faktor, whose name suggests what the plot reinforces—that he is a factor in what happens. Tannhauser, notable for his Aryan name, blond hair, muscular physique, and megalomania, as well as for his use of torture and forced labor techniques, can be seen as a figure for the twentieth century's

favorite avatar of evil, fascism, or as an Osama bin Laden–like paramilitary leader, growing drug crops to finance his plans to acquire power through violence. The title of the book, *Dogs of God,* refers to the name of the World War II–era smuggling plane, a DC-3 with the name *Domini Canes,* but also to a medieval French term for werewolf, *chiens deus.* Certainly the abundance of feral animal life, packs of wild dogs especially, suggests something about the feral human life the book describes, although one would hesitate to posit a Social Darwinist interpretation. The title itself abbreviates to DOG.

Together, all of these supplemental meanings suggest that we are to see the events of the story in a larger light. Certainly it can be interpreted as an apocalyptic confrontation between the shifting, dominant, many-masked forms of evil and the simple, humble forms of good. But we've heard that one before. It may be more interesting to look at it in closer, more historically embedded terms. The name of the final failed resort, El Dorado, is also the name of the imaginary city of gold that one of the earliest invaders of this continent, Hernando de Soto, used to justify his long campaign of rape, torture, enslavement, and military adventurism, and is representative of the patterns of European colonial domination of the continent. Or to move closer in time and place, the novel reminds us of the neocolonial capitalist invasion of Appalachia, especially the coal regions, since the mid-nineteenth century. As Tannhauser describes it, the history of El Dorado goes something like this: starting as an antebellum spa, it becomes a Confederate hospital, then a Union POW camp, then a turn-of-the-century resort, then a World War II country-club POW camp, then a resort again, then a women's prison, a hippie commune, and finally a paramilitary drug camp with forced laborers. Significantly, we see that at no time in its history was it locally controlled. It has always been a colonial outpost for some outside group to use, and if we accept Tannhauser's space aliens story, there again.

An apocalypse, yes, but also part of a tradition of literature of place. Benedict places El Dorado and its demise both within the context of Appalachia and within the larger context of America. Many of the issues and recurring motifs dealt with in the Appalachian literature tradition—colonization, class conflict, coercion by violence, economic coercion, religious conflict, environmental issues—all emerge in this apocalyptic narrative, often in strange new configurations. And the recurrent question of individual versus group agency finds an interesting twist here. This novel presents the triumph of justice almost as Greek tragedy does, as part of the mechanism of a force beyond the power of the human will. Is this a force inherent in the universe, or localized in the mountains themselves? If the latter, Benedict joins a long tradition in seeing Appalachia as a place that transforms people. Read as an apocalypse, *Dogs of God* seems to have enlarged the scale of such a transformation.

So at any scale—world cataclysm, Western civilization, American expansionism, or local history, the story has resonance. And as an Appalachian story, it has a lot in common with the understandings that Appalachian scholars have come to in recent years. These understandings suggest that, rather than an "us and them" conflict, the history of the region has always involved interpenetrating forces—classes and groups, collaborators and boosters and isolationists—rather than the stereotype of the isolated, ignorant hillbilly.

MIRACLE BOY AND OTHER STORIES *(2010)*

And Vandal, curled deeply into himself, slumbered away in the upper bedroom, twitching from time to time as dreams of the world, full of infinite life as it had never been, and as it would never be, flitted beautifully across the thin, translucent scrim of his mind.

("The Beginnings of Sorrow," p. 145)

The opening story in this collection, "Miracle Boy," tells the story of a boy who had both feet cut off by his father's silage cutter as he was riding on the fender of a tractor. The tractor spilled over into a nest of copperheads. Miracle Boy's father's quick thinking saved his feet. He managed to tourniquet the legs, then dig though the silage to find the feet. When the story opens,

three other boys, Eskimo Pie, Lizard, and Geronimo, decide that they want to see the scars. They ambush Miracle Boy on his way home and strip off his pants and shoes. When Miracle Boy gives his explanation, "Jesus, he made the lame man to walk. ... And Jesus, he made me walk, too" (p. 2), Geronimo counters with, "Did Jesus take your feet off just so he could put them back on you?"(p. 3). Feeling bad, the boys help Miracle Boy to dress and go on his way, but they have thrown the shoes over a power line, so he has to walk home in his socks. The brothers Lizard and Geronimo get beaten by their father for this act, but their mother invites Miracle Boy and his father to their house, where Lizard spends the afternoon watching a movie, in silence, with Miracle Boy.

Eventually Lizard's guilt provokes him to climb the pole and retrieve the shoes. He gets up in the middle of the night and climbs the pole, driving nails in to stand on. Eventually he gets to the transformer near the top of the pole. Clinging to this, he manages to grab one shoe and dislodge the other. By this time, the shoes are weathered and cracked and useless. He delivers them to Miracle Boy's house. The father opens the door and tells Lizard that Miracle Boy doesn't want the shoes. "Your mommy may not know what you are, Miracle Boy's old man said, and his voice was tired and calm. But I do" (p. 11). Lizard apologizes, but the man tells him he is apologizing to the wrong person. Miracle Boy comes to the door, and the story ends with him smiling at Lizard through the screen. The story is about aftereffects, both of the traumatic injury and of the bullying incident, demonstrating that Lizard, Miracle Boy, and their parents all have different trajectories of response.

"Buckeyes" is told from the point of view of a sixth-grade boy whose father drives a wrecker. He and his friends go to the junkyard to see a car full of dead Ohioans that has just come in, found partway down a cliff years after it went over. They pay the junkyard owner with all the change they have, and he tells them they have ten minutes. They find the car and it seems to be just full of old brush, so some of the boys start pushing on it. The brush falls away and they see the

yellowed corpse of a little girl in the back seat, next to the headless corpse of her brother. The owner kicks them out and the narrator goes home, enumerating in his head the things his father has brought back from wrecked cars:

> He's brought home bracelets; two full sets of dentures and an upper plate; a Fuller Brush salesman's sample kit; some tiny atomizers full of cologne that he gave to me, and some miniature bottles of liquor that he kept; a suitcase with a busted handle, full of women's party clothes; several car jacks, with and without handles; spare tires, full of air and flat; packets of bobby pins; a .45 caliber pistol with a broken slide ...
>
> (p. 21)

All of these items either sit around or get given away. The narrator wonders "what terrible next thing will find its way into our house" (p. 22).

In "The Butcher Cock," Ivanhoe, a fifteen-year-old with a defective "pancake heart," and his father, Snag, are racing to get to a cockfight when they wreck the car, plowing along a row of ornamental concrete chickens that leads to the cockfighting arena. They leave the damaged car and rush to the arena, carrying their caged birds. In the process of the evening, most of their birds are killed, including King Tut, Snag's champion. Ivanhoe meets a girl from Irish Mountain, an isolated community of people who are known for sharing each other's dreams. She offers to take him to see the Eye of God, an abandoned radio telescope at the top of the mountain.

The next day Ivanhoe takes his favorite bird, a Kelso Yellow-Leg, and starts to hike up the mountain. He falls asleep under a giant hemlock and dreams that the girl appears, clad in a cloak of live cedar waxwings, and feeds him from her breast. He awakens and continues to climb, wading through a bog to a stream, which he follows to a waterfall. There the girl appears, and he feels himself change into the Kelso Yellow-Leg; he then stands in the falls until the water tears off all his feathers. Down below, his father sees the feathers go by in the stream. Ivanhoe, meanwhile, stripped and plucked, has followed the girl up the streambed to the Eye of God, and they lie together in the dish of the telescope. The final scene is from the perspective of the Kelso

Yellow-Leg: "It fixes its good eye on Ivanhoe and the girl, who seem to be falling asleep beside each other. Soon they will enter each other's dreams. Soon her family will come, the fearful ones" (p. 44). The mountain appears to be an island in a sea of cloud, and the cock crows as the sun rises. Biblical allusions abound here, with the final image of the two young people, naked on an island separate from the world, suggesting the Garden of Eden.

"Pony Car" is from the perspective of Esau, who remembers Uncle Rowdy and his supercharged 1970 Dodge Challenger, the "pony car" of the title, racing to beat a train. Esau seems to be haunted by memories of his father and his uncle, interspersed with comments from Slow Joe Crow, a talking crow in another room, whom Uncle Rowdy taught to talk. Earlier, Esau had gone to town "to pick up something to keep the spirits out, four-by-sixes and sheets of plywood and bags of nails" (p. 48), only to turn around when he sees Uncle Rowdy, long dead, sitting under the Confederate memorial. He flees to the house, but feels besieged by ghosts. Sick of the nursery rhymes he keeps hearing—*Fifteen men on a dead man's chest! Dead men tell no tales!* (p. 48)—he decides to shoot Old Joe Crow, but when he gets to the room the perch is empty, and he remembers that the crow is dead and buried. "It doesn't occur to Esau to wonder how he is still there, still in this place, if he was in the car, and the car was struck" (p. 61). This suggests that Esau is one of the ghosts himself, trapped in the aftermath of a sudden death. Dead men do tell tales.

"Joe Messenger Is Dreaming" is about a man who is sent up to skydive from a high-altitude balloon as part of the preparations for the manned space-flight program. As he prepares to jump from twenty miles above the earth, he remembers his childhood and various episodes from his life, including imagining his wife and daughter talking to him in the present. No one but his commanding officer and the engineers who designed the experiment know what he is doing because it is a classified mission. Finally, ready to return to "conventional time, conventional space" (p. 77), he tumbles forward. At the end of the story we

assume that he didn't make it, because there is no later record of him.

"Mudman" is a golem story set on a failing farm. Tom Snedegar remembers that the people who first cleared the area where he lives had created "mudmen," golems, to work in the lumber mills. To help on this one-man dairy operation, so he won't have to work on the Sabbath, he decides to create a mudman. He builds a frame and fills it with mud, burying a dirt-dauber wasp nest in its chest to serve as a heart. Because he is plagued by groundhogs, he writes KILL GROUNDHOGS on a piece of paper, then amends it to KILL VERMIN and inserts it where the creature's mouth would be. It goes wrong. When he wakes up, all of his fence posts are festooned with groundhogs, but also with every other living thing from the farm: "a pair of sleek red foxes, squirrels, blacksnakes, copperheads, a wrist-thick diamondback" (p. 94), some of them still alive. He finds the mudman watching his wife through a window as she tries to kill a wasp. He asks it to leave her alone.

"She's fucking him," it said.

It was Snedgar's turn to nod. "I know," he said, and he guessed that he had known that she was screwing Carlson the travel agent. He guessed he had known it for quite some time.

(p. 96)

The mudman has its mission, and Snedgar realizes that he will be killed as well if he tries to stop it. "He was not going to get into Heaven and his wife was not going to get into Heaven. That much was sure" (p. 96).

"Bridge of Sighs" is about a father-and-son team who go about killing cattle herds to stop the spread of a cattle disease. The father wears a rubber suit that the boy sees as a kind of superhero outfit. They call it the Exterminator, and "it made him look like a giant insect" (p. 101). The boy's jobs are to distract the farmers while the father kills the cattle and to clean the Exterminator. The boy is also involved in distracting himself, unable to see his father, a "great, big sloppy cheerful man, always whistling and humming around the house," as a killer: "The

Exterminator did the killing" (pp. 101, 100). The bridge of sighs is the gangway that the cattle follow in the slaughterhouse, where the father used to work, and "you never crossed the Bridge of Sighs both ways," except John Keeper, who had preceded the father in his present job. " 'But you left,' I said to my father.' 'No,' he said, 'I'm there yet' " (p. 108). Supposed to be telling an amusing story to the farmer, the boy tells of watching a cartoon on TV and not being able to stop laughing, until he realizes that the cartoon is over and he is seeing a man use a flamethrower on a bunker. He screams, and his father chastises him for upsetting his mother and younger brother. The story ends with the ironic statement, "Nothing was wrong. Nothing wrong at all" (p. 113).

"The Beginnings of Sorrow" is Benedict's attempt at a werewolf tale. While out hunting with his dog, Hark, Vandal Boucher commands Hark to retrieve a duck carcass, and Hark says, "No." As the story progresses, Hark becomes more and more human while Vandal retreats to his room and sleeps most of the time. Bridie, Vandal's wife, who had been bullied by Vandal's father, Xerxes, fights him off with a poker, but she eventually develops some affection for him. Meanwhile, the dead are rising from their graves, and Hark, who now wants to be called Nefas, promises to stand with her. "Bridie stood at the heart of the catastrophe, and so alone was able to see it for what it was: the end of one thing, and the beginning of another that was infinitely worse" (p. 144).

"The Angel's Trumpet" refers to jimsonweed, a poisonous plant that has hallucinogenic properties. The story is about a family catastrophe in a manure tank, told by the only survivor. The narrator's older brother, father, uncle, and two younger brothers all go in sequence into the tank, which is filled with methane, and each succumbs immediately. The narrator, who describes himself as the odd one in the family, a dreamer and novel reader in a group of stolid pragmatists, is fascinated with the cave paintings of prehistoric Europe and with the aurochs, massive ancestors of present-day cattle, that they portray. His father had been a classicist and had given his sons names like Albertus Magnus and Ptolemy Phila-

delphus, but since the surviving son is a primitivist, he goes into the manure tank as he imagines a Paleolithic shaman would have, chewing jimsonweed and painting his visions in the dark, tributes to his lost family. He feels that he is spurred on by the spirit of the Great Bull. The classical rationalism that secured his family's worldview has yielded to a mystical encounter with the ancient occult.

"The World, the Flesh, and the Devil" is the story of a jet pilot who has to crash his Phantom F4B into a ridge in the Allegheny mountains. He is pursued by a pack of wild dogs, and the point of view alternates between his and that of the lead dog, who was once a domestic animal but has forgotten his ties to humans and worked his way through the hierarchy, so that now he leads the pack. The aviator takes refuge in an overgrown barracks surrounded by a cemetery that he recognizes as a leprosarium, a place where lepers were isolated. Sleeping, he hears a voice say, "Dead to the world, be thou alive to God" (p. 179), the words with which priests had once banished lepers. He sees a shining silver man covered in scales and a featureless face, who walks out into the night. "Go home. Go home" (p. 180), the voice tells him. At dawn, he finds the lead dog still waiting, but the pack is gone. The dog has remembered his past with humans, and follows the man.

In "Pig Helmet and the Wall of Life" the narrator introduces the deformed cop, Pig Helmet:

In olden times, you'd have been one of the Civilized People trying like hell, with fire and boiling oil and molten lead and such, to keep him and his kind out, and he'd have been one of the dreaded barbarians, he'd have been the lead barbarian in fact, climbing over your city walls by means of an improvised ladder.

(p. 183)

But now he is an officer of the peace, with a terribly scarred face from his bounty hunter days, when a criminal threw acid on the left side of his face, scarring it and permanently displaying his teeth through his cheek. Feeling bad after having to shoot an Oxycontin addict who had just killed his whole family, then pointed a gun at him, Pig Helmet stops at a religious carnival ride, the Wall

of Life, where a preacher and his sons ride motorcycles around the inside of a cylinder while his daughter stands in a pit of snakes at the bottom. Pig Helmet watches with other spectators from a catwalk at the top of the cylinder. As the motorcycles speed around and the preacher yells out his sermon, Pig Helmet finds himself speaking in tongues and reaching his hand toward the girl with the snakes. In the midst of the chaos, he feels comfort and relief.

In "The Secret Nature of the Mechanical Rabbit," Buddy and Willard drive a van around the countryside collecting puppies. They work for a dogfighter named Little Pig, who feeds puppies to his fighting dog, a half-dingo named Moloch. The title refers to Buddy's previous job at a greyhound course. If a greyhound ever catches the mechanical rabbit, it will never be able to race again. Buddy loved working with the greyhounds but was shocked to see the way that they are slaughtered after they can no longer race. Now he collects the puppies, pretending to want them as pets. At a rural farmhouse, an attractive young woman gives him two puppies. She says that she has heard of people collecting dogs for a laboratory, but she figures that Buddy isn't doing that or he wouldn't be willing to take one of the puppies, who is sick. At the end of the day, after they drop off the puppies, Buddy heads to Moloch's cage with a half-gallon of antifreeze, planning to poison him.

"Mercy" is told from the point of view of a ten-year-old boy whose father runs an Angus cattle farm. The farm next door has been bought by a surgeon, who has built a mansion and introduced a herd of miniature horses, which he doesn't know how to care for. To the boy's father, they are useless: "Can't work them, can't ride them, can't eat them. Useless" (p. 209). The boy is fascinated by them, and worried that they will break through the poorly maintained fence into his father's cattle pasture. Then his father will shoot them, he claims.

As the new owner continues to neglect them, the horses try to get into the Angus pasture. The boy patches the fence continuously, but there is only so much he can do without replacing posts or whole strands of wire. One winter day, in the snow, the fence gives way and the horses dash through. The boy watches in alarm as his father approaches, armed with a hunting rifle. A horse runs up and playfully grabs his father's coat from behind and pulls him over. "The hood of his coat fell away from his face, and I saw that my old man was laughing" (p. 220).

"Zog-19: A Scientific Romance" is a departure for Benedict, a double-plotted story with a science fiction twist. One story concerns Zog-19, an alien from the future who has been put into the body of a small-town farmer on Earth. Being from a tribe of iron people filled with "sentient gas" on an iron planet named Zog, he has trouble adjusting to his existence as a meat body on Earth. When we first see him, he is trying to work a clutch. Meanwhile, in the second plot, we learn about the planet Zog, where, in the future, spacemen from Earth will discover the sentient gas that fills the people and the planet and will take it to power their spaceships after rendering the Zogs powerless. This process will eventually deplete Zog, and a distant descendant of McGinty the farmer will give up space exploration and choose to settle down on a grass planet and farm. Zog-19 learns to be human, and in the future, humans destroy his planet.

Although the stories in the *Miracle Boy* collection have some of the same settings and themes found in the two earlier collections, one can see a general progression from a tight, although never minimalist, realism toward what Pinckney and Laura Benedict refer to as "surrealism"—"the only meaningful response to the failure of rationalism" (p. xi)—in their introduction to *Surreal South '09*. In that introduction they also use the terms "apocalyptic" and "sublime," terms from the past that help us to understand the kind of fictions that emerge in unstable times. Both *Dogs of God* and *Miracle Boy and Other Stories* take us away from the subject matter that earlier critics like Baber and Freeman objected to. These stories follow Benedict's interests without presenting the types of characters who defenders of Appalachian identity find objectionable. The nasty folks in the novel are all outsiders; depraved, yes, but not the sort of depraved hillbillies found in James

Dickey's *Deliverance*. The characters and settings in the *Miracle Boy* stories might be identifiable as West Virginian in some cases, but they are an idiosyncratic bunch, owing more to Kafka than to Li'l Abner. Benedict is still producing work in a strictly realist mode, such as the "Miracle Boy" story, while at the same time investigating his themes of trauma and adaptation in more surrealist modes. One doesn't know what to expect from a Benedict story. We can expect that he will continue to surprise us.

Selected Bibliography

WORKS OF PINCKNEY BENEDICT

NOVELS AND SHORT STORIES

Town Smokes: Stories. Princeton, N.J.: Ontario Review Books, 1987.

The Wrecking Yard. New York: Nan A. Talese, 1992.

Dogs of God. New York: Nan A. Talese, 1993.

Miracle Boy and Other Stories. Winston-Salem, N.C.: Press 53, 2010.

"Kentucky Samurai." *Appalachian Heritage* 38, no. 1:40–43 (winter 2010). (Graphic fiction.)

EDITED VOLUMES

With Laura Benedict. *Surreal South.* Vol. 1. Winston-Salem, N.C.: Press 53, 2007.

With Laura Benedict. *Surreal South '09.* Winston-Salem, N.C.: Press 53, 2009.

With Laura Benedict. *Surreal South '11.* Winston-Salem, N.C.: Press 53, 2011.

CRITICAL AND BIOGRAPHICAL STUDIES

Baber, Bob Henry. "My Exhilerating [*sic*], Self-Destructive, and Near-Criminal Candidacy for the Governorship of West Virginia." *Appalachian Journal* 24, no. 4:368–419 (1997).

Benedict, Laura. *Notes from the Handbasket* (blog), October 15, 2008. http://laurabenedict.blogspot.com/2008/10/octoberguest-pinckney-benedict.html.

Brosi, George. "Pinckney Benedict: A Gleeful Writer." *Appalachian Heritage* 38, no. 1:18–22 (winter 2010).

Cunningham, Rodger. "Heat over *Town Smokes.*" Letter. *New York Times Book Review,* September 27, 1987. http://www.nytimes.com/1987/09/27/books/l-heat-over-town-smokes-028887.html?scp=1&sq="heat_over_town_smokes.

Douglass, Thomas E. Interview with Pinckney Benedict. *Appalachian Journal* 20, no. 1:68–74 (1992).

McWhorter, Diane. "Cigarettes Rolled from the Bible." *New York Times Book Review,* July 12, 1987, p. 13. (Review of *Town Smokes.*)

Miller, Jim Wayne. "New Generation of Savages Sighted in West Virginia." *Appalachian Heritage* 16, no. 4:28–33 (1988).

Williams, John Alexander. "Unpacking Pinckney in Poland." *Appalachian Journal* 20, no. 2:162–177 (winter 1993).

S83 3186

BARBARA CROOKER

(1945—)

Janet McCann

BARBARA CROOKER'S WORK first received wide notice by the poetry world in 2005 with the publication of her first full-length collection, but her reputation was building before that and her readership has continued to grow ever since. Read by not only other poets but general literature addicts, her poems' mixture of sadness and celebration has strong appeal: her work is uncompromising and yet positive. Loss has always been at the center of poetry, but in Crooker's poems the inevitable losses are balanced by the delight of discovery. Moreover, in Crooker's world transience increases awareness of the presence of beauty and the necessity of love, so that her poetry is witness to a hard-won affirmation.

Crooker's poetry is rooted in nature, and it is her images of the natural world that give the poems the luminousness that distinguishes them. For this reason she has often been compared to Mary Oliver, the consummate recorder and interpreter of transcendent nature. Crooker's main subjects are nature and art, together and separately, and her experience as a mother of an autistic son. Her many ekphrastic poems—that is, poems that describe and imaginatively engage with a work of visual art—come in part from her art history minor in college, which taught her to look at paintings with knowledge as well as appreciation. "I see writing as a way to capture experience," she said in an interview with Allison Rivers of C&R Press, "and [using] painting as a portal gives you a visual to draw the audience in." Specific exhibitions—Edward Hopper, Frida Kahlo, Pierre-Auguste Renoir, J. M. W. Turner—have paved the way for poems or poem sequences. Her themes merge and diverge in surprising combinations.

BIOGRAPHY

Barbara Crooker was born November 21, 1945, in Cold Spring, New York, to Emil Vincent and Isabelle Charlotte Smith Poti. Her father was a chemist for Texaco (in analytical infrared spectroscopy) in Glenham, New York. Her mother had been a nurse, but she stopped working after she got married to raise Barbara and her younger brother, James (Jimmy). Crooker grew up in the nearby village of Fishkill, a historic site settled by the Dutch in 1709, with buildings that predate the American Revolution and with some astounding natural scenery in the shadow of Mount Beacon. Born to sweeping hillsides and eighteenth-century houses, she had a typical mid-twentieth-century small-town childhood with the freedom the era allowed, skating on and swimming in Fishkill Creek, biking everywhere. However, she was "always a reader," she reported to Janet McCann, adding, "Bicycling back into the village to go to the library, on my no-speed Schwinn bike with coaster brakes and metal basket, remains one of my earliest and best memories." As a bookish child in a natural paradise, she could hardly grow up to be anything but a writer. Her earliest writing was a reflection of her pleasure in discovery, surrounded by friends and family, of the margins of her world. Writing was only one of the many interests of her active childhood.

If her parents were not particularly poetic-minded, they certainly did not discourage her intellectual and literary interests. Closeness to parents is one of her themes, and parent-child bonds are explored as one of the main sources of energy and love. Asked by McCann if she had support from parents and had fellow writers to share with in childhood, she responded:

ORLAND PARK PUBLIC LIBRARY

BARBARA CROOKER

No other writers, but my parents were readers. Of course, this was before television, before the Internet. … Since I came to writing relatively late in life (late twenties/early thirties), "support" wasn't really an issue. I think they were somewhat bemused if I'd become, say, a novelist, they'd have been thrilled, but poetry left them (as it does most people) somewhat puzzled. In the last years of her life, my mother lived in an assisted living facility nearby, and she pushed the activities director to bring me in to do a reading, which was very dear.

It seems as if Crooker's poetry converted her mother to poetry, not only because a daughter wrote it but because the poems had something to say to her mother's generation as well.

After her pleasant and peaceful elementary school days in Fishkill, Crooker was bused to a large high school, Wappingers Central School, where she edited the newspaper, selecting poems for it but not writing any herself. She received a bachelor's degree in English from Rutgers University in New Jersey in 1967 and later went on to graduate school at Elmira College in New York. In college she majored in English and minored in art history. She even took a creative writing course, but did not actively participate in it. "I didn't actually attend it, little snot that I was, just handed in the assignments via a friend" (McCann interview). She married Michael Gilmartin in 1967, suffered a traumatic stillbirth at term in 1970, and had a child, Stacey Erin, in 1971; the couple was divorced in 1973. She did not do serious writing until she was in her late twenties and going through the painful divorce. She said in an interview with the *Writer's Almanac:*

Although I'd taken courses like "Contemporary American Literature," I was pretty much unaware of what LIVING contemporary writers were up to. My ex had left some of his books behind, including a copy of the *Eagle,* a little magazine from Mansfield State College in northern Pennsylvania. I read it and was blown away by some of the poetry, especially that of Diane Wakoski, who I thought in my ignorance was an undergraduate there. Perhaps if I'd realized she was a famous writer, I'd have been intimidated, but I read her work and the accompanying interview over and over, and tried to figure out how she got from A to B. And then I wrote a couple of poems. And I liked how they turned out, eventually, and so I kept writing.

Crooker's first marriage had been a traditional 1960s marriage, not conducive to achievement on the part of the wife. When the marriage was over, she began to look again at those parts of her life she had given up for the housewife role. As a young woman with a child, she turned to poetry as a way of taking herself back, and she never put it aside. She married Richard Crooker in 1975 and had two more children, Rebecca in 1979 and David in 1984. David, who was normal at birth, developed autism at age two; her son's condition and its demands have always absorbed a good deal of her time and energy.

Early influences, besides all the poets of the past traditionally read, included not only Diane Wakoski but also the fiction writer Asa Baber, who critiqued her manuscript at a conference and sent her to read contemporary poetry in the 1970s, a whole new territory for her. She dabbled with fiction but soon found that her true voice was in poetry. Her poems began to appear in journals, and then chapbooks, and then finally in books. She is only incidentally an academic poet; she did not take the M.F.A. route but instead chose a master's in education (M.S.Ed.). She has taught in several colleges and universities as well as in other contexts such as at writing conferences and festivals.

Crooker's poetry is in the general area sometimes defined as domestic realism, but it goes far beyond the little epiphanies of the breakfast nook some associate with that subgenre. It might be classified as domestic/metaphysical, because while it often begins and ends in the confines of the family, it is shot through with a kind of metaphysical speculation that shows each of its motivating events in a different light. The natural scenes and cityscapes that appear throughout her work merge with its sense of family and community, so that the poems project purpose—to the individual life, to the universe itself, and also to the small discoveries, the openings and closings that make up the greater part of human existence.

Crooker's work is unusual in that it does not change over time in a particular direction. Of course, with three collections within a five-year time span, one would not expect drastic shifts in

style or subject. But these collections do not convey the sense that she is working toward the completion of an overall project that requires stages and steps toward a conclusion, nor does she follow a specific school, fashion, or articulated poetic theory. There is change and development in her poetry, but it seems to be more a widening of range than a change in technique. Her three books have a lot in common, and yet they seem never to repeat. Part of the reason may be that she came to poetry somewhat late and then began to publish quickly as her work became known. Also, she does not settle on some arbitrary subject area for a work, like a historical figure or theoretical position. "The poem is the cry of its occasion," said Wallace Stevens, and so it is with Crooker. The events that occasion these poems are not surprising or startling but rather are drawn from shared women's experience. It is the poet's interpretation of these events, and her placement of them in the wider context of a life, that makes the poems so distinctive.

Crooker is a ravenous reader. Asked by McCann, "What poets, past and present, do you read? Any of them you think of as especially influential?" she responded:

Past: William Butler Yeats, Rumi, Bashō, Emily Dickinson, Gerard Manley Hopkins, Sylvia Plath, Anne Sexton, Elizabeth Bishop. Present: Mary Oliver, Sharon Olds, Harry Humes, Brigit Pegeen Kelly, Charles Wright, Christopher Buckley, Linda Pastan, Lisel Mueller, William Matthews, Maxine Kumin, Billy Collins, Stephen Dunn, Stephen Dobyns, Marilyn Hacker, Fleda Brown, Jeanne Murray Walker, Betsy Sholl, Pat Fargnoli, Mark Doty, Alicia Ostriker, Philip Levine, Ted Kooser, Alison Townsend, Ron Wallace. Who's influencing me now? Ellen Bass, Dorianne Laux, Kim Addonizio, David Kirby, Barbara Hamby, Albert Goldbarth, Barbara Ras. But I try to be open to everybody.

This list is instructive for what is not included as well as what is: more women than men here, but not drastically so; preference for poets whose images are so memorable that reading the name often brings a particular image, a particular poem, to mind. Who thinks of Mark Doty without bringing to mind the fish, the dogs? Or does not recall Oliver's birds, Kumin's horses, Fargnoli's Dufy pictures, and so forth? Missing from her library

are Oulipo poets, Language poets, and the like—simply because the more postmodernist-leaning poems are not experiential, or at least not recognizably so. To the question of whether she identifies with any current groups, she said, "I'd ... ally myself with contemporary spiritual writers. Contemporary nature writers. Ekphrastic writers (poems about art). Writers on disability. I was on a panel on this topic at AWP [the 2010 Association of Writers & Writing Programs conference] in Denver. That's a field we're not done with yet, either." No, not at all—the poetics of disability is a field that is growing rapidly, as more journals are dedicated to the topic and still more readers and writers become aware of its importance to art and to the real world.

So a keen interest in social justice is there, and feminism—she has not created a separate world or aestheticized away the problems of this one. The particular brand of feminism of her work is noteworthy as well. As she told McCann:

Although I wrote a little bit as an undergraduate (both in and out of class), it was threatening to my boyfriend, who became my first husband (and who also wanted to write). What can I say? I was a "good girl," it was the early sixties, and so I stopped. Then we married, had a baby, who died twenty-four hours before she was born. Fifteen months later, we had another baby, and [my husband] ... left. There I was, still in my twenties, and somehow, I managed to figure out that if I gave in to sorrow, I'd be crushed, and that what I needed to do was reinvent myself. And so I did, turning to things I'd pushed aside in favor of that marriage, such as writing, skiing, outdoor sports....

Some of the underlying issues in her poetry concern a woman's right to write. It is interesting to note that in mid-nineteenth-century women's novels the speaker often justified her writing with the notion that, as a special woman, she was given this right so as to warn other women away from self-assertion, even away from writing itself. Of course there is nothing of this theme in Crooker. Rather there is a sense that writing itself, or creating works of art, is a necessary part of a woman's experience, and not only should it not be repressed but it cannot. No circumstances can diminish a poet's need to create—not full-time work, not difficult family situations, caretaking,

lack of privacy. The writer will find a way. Thus, for Crooker, writing became a "re-creation" in the original sense of that word—the poet was remaking herself and her world. This kind of revision was not of the usual sort of writing as therapy, the notion that writing out one's problems would make them go away. Rather, it was the articulation of a different world, which had promises equal to its pains. Her flirtation with fiction was brief; she quickly "fell into the genre" that she was "best suited for." The conditions of her life, including raising an autistic son, were not conducive to long periods of uninterrupted study and writing, but she wrote.

Her first work startles with the gorgeousness of its nature. Because her nature appears transcendent, it is tempting to see it as theology. She was asked by Janet McCann, "Your nature poetry always seems to me knockout—reminds me a little of Mary Oliver. But more visceral, more this world. Any comments on your involvement with nature?" Crooker's answer:

> Frank Lloyd Wright said, "I believe in God, only I spell it Nature," and it seems to me that the closer we are to the natural world, the closer we are to our true spiritual selves. If I could write one line like Dylan Thomas' "The force that through the green fuse drives the flower," I could die happy. "The green fuse," for the animus of nature. Wow. Wallace Stevens said "One of the functions of poetry is that it gives you a keener sense of being alive," and that's one of the things I'm after, being more connected, being more alive in this one life, the one that we're sleepwalking through.

She identifies her spiritual direction in another context: "I consider myself a 'Zen Lutheran,' in that I'm a practicing Lutheran, but incorporate meditation and other Eastern practices into my own personal spirituality." This combination of East and West helps to explain the combination of meditation and spontaneous combustion that characterizes her work. Sometimes a simple scene seems to have a violently pulsing impressionist scene beneath it.

Not one or two but eleven chapbooks preceded the appearance of her first book. Oddly, her first poem published, "The Lost Children," in the *Poetry Review,* remains one of her most frequently reprinted. The lost child becomes everyone's lost children, those lost in all ways, who leave a hole in their mothers' lives that is never filled in: "they are separated from us / in stadiums, … they disappear on beaches, / they shine at night in the stars."

THE CHAPBOOK YEARS: THE WHITE POEMS

The years from 1983 to 2005, from her first chapbook until her first full-length collection, saw her winning awards and praise for her work. Laura Leimbach wrote, "Early in her career, Crooker wrote about family, birth, love, and loss, drawing on the hardship, joy, and bereavement she experienced as a mother." The decades have brought her more of these experiences, and together with her visual imagination that merges art and life, they remain her major themes.

Some of these manuscripts, like that of her first book, won competitions; unlike most chapbooks, they were noticed and reviewed. *Writing Home* (1983) was her first chapbook, shared with the poet Katharyn Machan Aal. Her distinctive style was noted by the poet Harry Humes, who commented that he liked the poems "because they attempt to get through to a power flowing beneath, through, and over things, power of ice, of the roots of jonquils and tulips. And of light, certainly light, because that mostly is what touches the poems." This early comment could as easily be applied to her most recent collection, even though its subjects and images are not at all the same as in the first. After *Writing Home* she published ten more chapbooks before her first book, and their power was remarked upon by Colette Inez, Judson Jerome, Brigit Pegeen Kelly, Walt Franklin, and a host of others.

Crooker's chapbooks have such internal unity that each one is a distinctive work. One tightly knit chapbook is *The White Poems* (2001), which traces the illness and death of Crooker's friend Judy Krol from breast cancer over a three-year period from 1992 to 1995. It begins with a series of facts about breast cancer and quotations from writers on the subject. Although this is arguably the bleakest of Crooker's work, it is not totally dark. Losing a friend, after all, means having experienced friendship and continuing to experi-

ence it in memory. As in other works she intermingles seasonal cycles and natural processes with what happens to her friend. In one of the two introductory poems, "Meditations on Grass," she demonstrates that not only is all flesh grass, but "all grass is flesh"; nature and the rebellious cells echo each other as the cancer overtakes the body by "spreading its rhizomes," and birth processes and death processes are the same (p. 5). She does much the same in the other introductory poem, "Because the Body Is a Flower," in which she develops further the body/plant metaphor and addresses her husband/lover:

Let us lie down and love, here in the flowers,
kiss my skin, for it is petals, the velvet falls of iris,
the heart of the peony, its voluptuous curves.
Let us become flowers, casual and gorgeous. ...

(p. 6)

The two prologue poems are followed by segments organized by year: 1992, 1993, 1994, and 1995, the year of her friend's death. Always the giant cornucopia of nature coexists with and contrasts with the individual human being in her distress: her friend, in the poem "In the Late Summer Garden," knows her cancer has spread, but still "spreads thick butter and honey on toast. / She would like time to stop now, the sky, blue as radium, / the hills, bolts of calico, red & yellow, gold & green" (p. 20). Does this sense of the oneness of the natural world remove the terror of death? Well, no—but it does provide a sense of wholeness that gives nature's processes meaning. The human consciousness seems to be a kind of anomaly. There is the beauty of the world, and only the human mind is not in sync with it. Is it an anodyne to be aware of the whole? Does it help to make art, to create a semi-permanence that way? Yet the dazzle of things living seems to be the strongest force of all. One of the most powerful poems in the sequence is "Equinox," a poem about her friend's short remission during the course of her treatment:

she's come through it all, annealed by fire,
calm settled in her bones like the morning mist in
  valleys
and low places, and her hair's returned, glossy
as a horse chestnut kept in a shirt pocket.

Today a red fox ran through the corn stubble;
he vanished like smoke. I want to praise things
that cannot last.

(p. 17)

Abundant, infinite nature seems to surround the afflicted woman, producing a blending as well as the expected irony. Awareness of transience becomes a metaphysical experience, even a mysterious promise.

The dying woman is even more part of the cycle in "Total Eclipse of the Moon," in which the speaker remembers a past "eclipse party" (p. 11) and conflates it with the waning of her friend's life. The friend has "written her Christmas letter" and "is moving towards lightness, / the still white center of absolute zero." Meanwhile the speaker and her husband watch the moon appear to go out: "Now it's a sliver, a thumbnail, a shred, ..." The white blank of the vanishing applies to both situations.

The poems chronicle the years of cycles and changes, ending with a letter to her now-deceased friend. In some poetry of loss there is a sense that the loss has been lived through, and that the poet is ready to move on. This is never quite the case in *The White Poems*. The death becomes part of the weave of things, a dark strand among the light ones, and it is permanently a presence. There are permanent colors and flavors, and permanent darknesses, and these all form patterns on the eye, heart, spirit. The poems are quick. The images ambush each other, sometimes push each other into the margins. This breathlessness gives us a sense of time elapsing, one experience collapsing into the next. Because these are the "white" poems, they have less impressionistic color than usual for Crooker, but they have some, together with a rich natural background of flowers, birds, and art. In Crooker's vivid color scheme white is often loss, grief—as in the East, it is the color of mourning.

THE CHAPBOOK YEARS: ORDINARY LIFE

Crooker's series of moving poems on autism takes the reader from her son's early childhood through his growing up. In addition to being a

poet and a parent, Crooker has had to be an autism activist, trying to find the best education and support for her son. The autism poems are fascinating for their empathy, for their attempts to see through the autistic child's eyes and feel as he does. It's a tremendous effort to shrug aside so completely one's own frame of reference, but Crooker has done this again and again, even during times in which she was so occupied with taking care of her son that she had very little time for other things, including writing poetry.

Most of the autism poems are in the chapbook *Ordinary Life,* which won the ByLine chapbook competition in 2001. The theme of this book is one of the poet's recurring observations: that ordinary life, however extraordinary it seems in positive or negative ways, has both beauty and purpose. Ordinary life is beautiful, illuminated by flashes of light and color—the repetition of actions motivated by love and even by duty brings with them a shimmer like the paintings of Vincent van Gogh.

We meet her autistic son David early on as a toddler. In "Doing Jigsaw Puzzles" he is four, and his work on the puzzle is compared with a fairy story. The epigraph reads: "In *The Snow Queen,* by Hans Christian Andersen, Kay, who has a splinter of glass from a hobgoblin's shivered mirror in his eye and heart, must solve a puzzle in order to win his freedom" (p. 6). David's fate is compared with Kay's. "A silver splinter of ice / has lodged in his heart; / his blue fingers keep working the puzzle." Kay will be freed: "Soon, Gerda is coming, lips red as summer's roses. / She will thaw his hands; her tears will wash / the splinter out." But for David there is no savior arriving: "An invisible icy membrane / is cast over him like a caul. / Nothing in the world can touch his heart."

This first autism poem is different from most of them in that the speaker is the observer completely; in later ones we see more and more effort to access the child's mind-set and see his world. In "Blowing Soap Bubbles," the two create together "baubles / from breath and film" that "rise in a swirl / of pink & blue, a moment's iridescence" (p. 8). This kind of sharing is what they have—not the usual kind of parent-child

training based on reason and repetition but a mutual endeavor to create an ephemeral art, to "make a strand of hand-blown beads / to grace the throat of the lawn."

Other poems touch on how the child is a sort of artist too—how he and the mother share elements of vision even though he is not completely in touch with reality. The vision of the poet, slightly askew as a poet's vision always is, helps her understand the deeper slant brought about by a condition such as his. She describes his helping her in the kitchen in "Grating Parmesan":

Together, we hold the rind of the cheese,
scrape our knuckles on the metal teeth.
A fresh pungency enters the room.
You put your fingers in the fallen crumbs:
"Snow," you proudly exclaim, and look at me.
Three years old, nearly mute,
but the master of metaphor.
Most of the time, we speak without words.

(p. 29)

This scene describes the strange partnership between the poet and the nearly wordless metaphor master, the autistic child. Most of these poems have the "-ing" verb form in the title, suggesting repeated action, the inevitable repetitions of "ordinary life."

The reader feels the frustration of mother and son as they try to negotiate the labyrinth that is the autistic child's experience of the world. "Autism Poem #20: The Knot Garden" is in a different collection, *Line Dance,* but fits into the sequence. It compares the child's experience to the clear purpose of the natural world:

chevrons of geese wedge their way
across the sky each autumn; they know
where they are going, have purchased
tickets marked "South." Our route is more
circuitous; two steps forward, one step back,
a knot garden where the possibilities diminish
as the years branch on.

As is often the case, the poem ends at a precise yet ambiguous image:

Too soon, we'll arrive
at the alpine altitudes where the vegetation's

BARBARA CROOKER

scarce, the flowers tiny but exquisite,
the foliage barely visible.

(p. 23)

There are many books and poems and poem sequences on the relationship between a mother and a troubled child, as well as hundreds of memoirs on the subject. Chuck Taylor's *Saving Sebastian* and Deborah Digges's *The Stardust Lounge* are examples of memoirs by poets who put the unique pain of having a problem child into both prose and verse. Sandra McPherson has written movingly on this topic. Crooker's poems are unique in that there is no outcome to the issue—it just, like life's other currents, continues. Crooker's autism poems not only are fine poems in their own right, sharing her usual themes of the power of nature and art to change lives, but they are also encouraging to other parents of children who have autism or other developmental problems by showing how love abides there too. They demonstrate that, despite the intense and constant involvement with an autistic child, a pressure that confined daily activities and travel and never let up, Crooker managed to create her poetry.

BOOKS: RADIANCE

Crooker's first full-length collection, *Radiance* (2005), was the winner of the Word Press First Book Prize. Garrison Keillor commented on it: "*Radiance* is a pleasure to read, straight through, for its humor and intelligence and for the sheer bravery of sentiment. It dares to show deep feeling, unguarded by irony. It's a straight-ahead passionate book by a mature poet, and rather suddenly I've become a fan" (back cover). The phrase "unguarded by irony" is telling. It is certainly not the case that there is no irony in Crooker's work. But the irony is not used, as it so often is in contemporary poetry, to hide the emotion that generated the poem, or to suggest that emotion itself is unpoemworthy. The irony is in the human situation and the vast difference between what we want and what is on offer.

For those who did not yet know her from chapbooks and individual poems, the collection clarified the lifelong focus of her work even by its title. Here as elsewhere, she writes about the shapes and colors of life and of art, and of human experiences that are both ordinary and extraordinary, thrown into relief as part of a larger perspective. The works of the Impressionists of course are radiant in her evocations of them. So are the scenes of foreign cities and of her own backyard. And the world remains radiant, despite loss and sadness, which turn out to make beauty even more valued in its fragility. "Death is the mother of beauty" Wallace Stevens says in "Sunday Morning," and while there is plenty of disagreement as to what he meant, it does convey the sense that it is the fragility of beauty that makes us long for it. Art extends that beauty, and makes us even more aware of the passing of time and the inevitability of change, but it offers consolation by providing a rich vision of the time and place that occasioned it. In "Impressionism," the speaker invokes public and private tragedies and talks about the desire to step out of her life

into a painting, perhaps Van Gogh's *Café de la Nuit*. There I'll sit with my glass of absinthe and a Gaulois bleu, until sweet forgetfulness takes me,
and the troubles of this world dissolve into daubs of paint, a blizzard of color and light.

(p. 18)

Radiance is full of real and painted nature, and its titles are filled with real and painted flowers (lilacs, peonies, sunflowers, iris) and birds (grackles, hawks, crows). Yet there are other persistent motifs such as the autistic child, the process of aging, the irretrievability of the past. Since the darker side of life is present and acknowledged, how can these poems make the reader feel so good? Baron Wormser noted, "The poetry of Barbara Crooker revels in the sensory pleasures of living on this remarkable earth yet acknowledges the hard shadows that fall across our joys" (back cover). Yet the colors outweigh the shadows, and even death is white, all colors rather than no color. The overall impression the poems leave is one of the entire spectrum. The world is, at its darkest, beautiful; art is a celebration of this beauty, and poetry—even the act of

57

perception—is homage to it. "How with this rage shall beauty hold a plea, / Whose action is no stronger than a flower?" Shakespeare asks in his Sonnet 65, and answers conventionally that no one can prevent Time from spoiling beauty: "Or who his spoil of beauty can forbid? / O, none, unless this miracle have might, / That in black ink my love may still shine bright."

Crooker's poems seem to want to demonstrate rather than explain this point. The qualities and tones and dimensions of light, its movements and stillness, inhabit the poems to produce a beauty that can hold its own against the rage of the world and the indifference of the universe. The poems do not aestheticize illness, death, or obstacle, but they do illuminate these things so that they are seen as part of something, not as all of human experience. Even the last words of poems of the difficult world provide hope and joy, and a number of them conclude with the word "light." Quoting last lines tends to diminish poems, but the concluding portion of one poem might serve as illustration. From "The Hour of Peonies":

At the end, confined to a wheelchair,
paintbrushes strapped to his arthritic hands,
Renoir said, "the limpidity of the flesh, one wants to
  caress it."
Even after the petals have fallen, the lawn is full of
  snow,
the last act in Swan Lake where the corps de ballet
in their feathered tutus,
kneel and kiss the ground, cover it in light.

(p. 41)

This poem combines themes of the creation of beauty through suffering, the need for beauty, and the recognition of time's inexorable passage and the erasure of beauty—yet the final words are "cover it in light." This becomes the drive and duty of artist and poet, whose activities are their destiny as well as their delight. *Radiance* clearly establishes Crooker's territory, from which she does not depart. This poem illustrates what Garrison Keillor called "sheer bravery of sentiment." She is willing to write directly about emotion, about the human situation, without worrying about traditions or rules, without asking permission.

Radiance is the most miscellaneous of Crooker's books and yet it seems completely cohesive. Grace Schulman commented on its focus, looking at the first poem. "'All That Is Glorious Around Us' refers only obliquely to the name of the Hudson River School art show and to one of its paintings. The real glory of the title poem, and of her poems in this collection, is driving in rain, hanging wash on the line, ... sitting in a café while thinking of daily events, some of them dark. ... I am led on a journey from light to darkness then back again to 'the radiant world'" (back cover). This is ordinary life indeed, but touched with glory.

BOOKS: LINE DANCE

Line Dance appeared in 2008 and covers her earlier themes. But these poems are more active and connected—the lines dance. *Line Dance* is focused and coordinated, even more than her first book, certainly more than most poetry collections. In fact she is working with four concepts: line, breath, dance, and song, weaving them into each section the way a bird builds a nest but also connecting them each to each like the dance in the title poem. The theme of the book is the supreme importance of relationships, and its primary sustained metaphor is the line. Lines are in all the poems, but their contexts and meanings are so different that their presence is unobtrusive. These are lines both real and metaphorical: lines of poetry, clotheslines, lines on skin, likes that mark blanks in texts, chorus lines, umbilical cords, chains of stitches, lines of music, quoted lines of verse by other poets. And the lines *dance.* Her poem "Line" explains:

I'm saying this: the spine, the matrix, the core
of what's laid down, then played over and over,
improvised, embroidered, embellished.
I love the way it moves away and then comes back,
finds itself again, the hard line, the official line,
the line of scrimmage, one down, goal to go.

(p. 31)

Thus stasis and movement are fused in a metaphysical conjunction. The dance is the celebratory, ritual movement that is prompted by beauty and joy not only among humans but in nature as

it expresses itself—trees and sunflowers dance, in addition to children of the fifties, the speaker, and other people, animals, and things. All kinds of beings also create music for the world to dance to—birds, old records, the body, the wind. Reading the book is much like looking through a mythic kaleidoscope in which images and stories connect and disperse, only to reconnect in new forms and shapes. If this book is different from her others it is because of the intensity of the action in it. In other books the energy, the dazzle, is more in the art and nature and less in the observer. Here the physical motion dominates as everything dances. It would seem that both line and dance are part of the cosmos like subatomic particles.

The lines dance most vividly and visually in the title poem. As the dance chain grows at the speaker's daughter's wedding, it turns out to be a mystical linkage of all the important people in the speaker's life, in celebration of a new conjunction. She describes the line, the friends, the relatives, including the bride's half-sister, who is

Connected to my childhood friend in a black
sheath, who holds onto the khaki sports coat

of my writing friend's husband, the dentist, while
his wife, in lilac, wraps her arm around one of
my neighbors, who's linked to a friend from
college in slinky silk slacks,

and there, at the end, is my ex-husband,
the one who didn't want to be married any
more, holding *his* soon-to-be-estranged second
wife, the one he left us for, at arm's length. *Start*

spreading the news: everyone I've ever loved
is here today, even the dead, raising a glass
and dancing, circling around the bride
in her frothy gown, bubbles rising
in a fluted glass, spilling out, running over.

(p. 15)

Thus the dancing chain is the force that connects, overpowers differences and loss, heals. It is an energy that transcends the individuals that make it up and includes even the dead in its vital chain—and yet is composed of these earthly

connections. Form follows meaning as the lines of the poem dance in and out in the zigzag that makes us visualize—and as active readers participate in—the celebration.

Often, the poems gather seemingly disparate ideas and images that all suddenly fall into place. One such poem is "Poem on a Line by Anne Sexton, 'We Are All Writing God's Poem.' " The short poem contains nature, clothing, NPR, a Hubble scientist, a tractor-trailer, Li Po, jeans—these ideas and images cohere around the notion of transience. The central question of the poem is "How can we get up / in the morning, knowing what we do?" But of course we do get up—and then the poem slips into the details of the day with their beauty and evanescence.

At night, the scent of phlox curls
in the open window, while the sky turned red violet,
lavender, thistle, a box of spilled crayons.
The moon spills its milk on the black tabletop
for the thousandth time.

(p. 32)

Critics were quick to respond to the power of these poems. The poet Fleda Brown wrote:

"Barbara Crooker's *Line Dance* reminds me of Bruegel's paintings, canvases spilling over with energy and movement. In Crooker's collection, chickadees, peonies, heartbreak, birth, marriage, death, autism, rock & roll, and Paris appear not as a jumble, but as a gathering and swirl of the sweetness of the earth. Each subject is held and lifted like an offering, dense with metaphor. … Crooker knows and loves life's ordinary details and watches them so closely and skillfully we can almost see the atoms dance. This book makes me glad to be alive" (back cover).

This comment is especially apt because this is the effect that these poems have on so many people. Few contemporary collections make the reader glad to be alive. The compressed vitality communicates itself as joy, even if the subject matter is dark. The word "sweetness" appears in so many other reviews, although these poems are not sweet in any conventional sense. Rather, they say, the world is sweet as well as bitter—sometimes literally, always through images. Many of the poems blend the various kinds of sweetness—pleasure, delight, love, feasts of the

senses, feasts of the spirit. "When the Acacia Blooms" celebrates seeing, eating, and making love. When the acacia blooms,

> bees go crazy get drunk on the honey-soaked air.
> I think I could sit here forever, inhaling

> this sweetness. …

(p. 60)

and the speaker thinks of a village in France, where "everything was aureate / that spring afternoon, like walking into a painting." The speaker remembers making love with her husband there, "our small room, how we / climbed the ladder of each other's body / until the stars showered us with sparks." Finally she comes back to the present and the scent of flowers which brought the memory back into vital life:

> Off in the distance, doves call,

> their long vowels not mournful, but one of those
> sounds that taps into memory's underground river,

> this waterfall of flowers, pouring its hot breath
> onto the stunned air.

More than in any of her other books, in *Line Dance* each poem is a tiny firework, a roman candle perhaps or multicolored rocket exploding colors across the sky, and the reader wants to say, "Oh, wow."

It is interesting to note Crooker's voluminous acknowledgment pages in all her books—not the usual spare, few credits to cutting-edge journals but the diverse lists of a poet who has published pretty much everywhere. How many collections have, like *Line Dance*, forty-three journals listed as containing the poems—some journals including two or three? In fact, *Radiance* has three solid pages of acknowledgments, which include the names of some of the best-known poetry journals as well as some obscure ones, and *More* has an extensive list of credits as well. There is a kind of generous abundance to her lists—journals ask for her poems, she sends them, and they provide pleasure for all kinds of readers. Her poetry has been published throughout the world in at least a dozen countries and has been translated into Italian, German, Korean, Turkish, and Malayalam.

Honesty and its affirmation are rarely found together in contemporary poetry, and never in such vibrant verse as that of *Line Dance*. Definitely not what would be classified as "inspirational verse," it nevertheless inspires, because its central truths about the core of human experience are sound and solid, and because Crooker's earth is both glorious and delicious. The dozens of reviews the book received agree on that.

BOOKS: MORE

Crooker's third book, *More,* was published in 2010. It returns to her familiar landscape but with a slightly altered perspective. It contains a mixture of poetry from art and poetry from life, and always the one contains elements of the other. Crooker has done some more living, and some more observing between books. Her basic approach has not changed, although her subject matter has broadened to include new experiences, and she is now looking at the world from the point of view of someone a little older, a little wiser. But a little sadder? No, although the experiences chronicled here include the declining health of her mother and other troubles. Her theme in this collection is hunger, desire—for more.

Several critics have commented on her intense focus, her "mindfulness," which is the state of awareness that is the goal and the practice of Zen Buddhism. These poems are mindful in a more Western way, sometimes so intense that she seems to be holding a magnifying glass over nature in such a way as to keep it on the edge of bursting into flame. But time does not stop; nor does the thinker, the observer, enter into nirvana. These are mindful more in the way T. S. Eliot's poems are mindful, but in Eliot's poetry the stimulus is always somewhere else in place and in time, whereas Crooker's mindfulness is a full concentration on the present. As for its Western slant, Crooker's focus does not empty the mind, but fills it. Instead of chasing away random thoughts and wild connections, she invites them into the poem.

More is divided into four parts. Part 1 begins with an epigraph from Bruce Springsteen,

"Everybody's got a hungry heart." The poems express desire for food, experience, love, even just to keep breathing. They ask for more, not out of fear but because the air is good. Mother-daughter concerns blend personal life with myth. The story of Demeter and Persephone embodies the near loss of the speaker's daughter in a riding accident. "Demeter" begins:

It was November when my middle daughter
descended to the underworld. She fell
off her horse straight into Coma's arms.

The poem ends neatly with the daughter's return:

up she swam, a slippery rebirth,
and the light that came into the room
was from a different world.

(p. 20)

The details of the daughter's coma and recovery, merged with the mythic search of Demeter for Persephone, give the reader a sense of a mother's fear and confusion as she is poised on the edge of the worst loss imaginable.

The second part is prefaced by a quotation from Thoreau, "There is no remedy to love but to love more." "The Mother Suite" recounts the decline of the speaker's mother in a series of vignettes and meditations. The poem sequence shows the stages of the inevitable loss of the mother, not with a sense of despair but with the sense of loss balanced against the worth of the life lived. The vulnerability of human life is given perspective by a sense that there is some rightness underneath things. This is not a conventionally religious consolation but rather a truth that defies definition. Even the church becomes the symbol of this rightness, rather than the rightness itself. And the pleasures of the senses are testimony to the goodness of the Earth. From the poem section titled "Lemon":

Oh holy church of the lemon, chapel of wedges,
acidic juice, the slick shine—How the oil
clings to your skin, lingers on your fingers,
blesses the flesh of fish swimming in the plate,
kisses the filling of pie on the shelf,
remembers life is bitter,

remembers life is sweet.

(p. 34)

Thus the church blends with the world, transferring its holiness to it and yet retaining it. It is usually the case that some kind of rite commemorates the luminous beauty of the world—secular sacraments that indicate that the human beings are aware of the sacredness of their surroundings and give thanks for them. The echoing verbs almost suggest a chant: *clings, lingers, blesses, kisses, remembers.*

The third section has an intriguing epigraph from Van Gogh. "It is the artist's duty to create a world that is more beautiful, simpler, and more consoling than the one we live in" (p. 39). This is a section of entirely ekphrastic poems, and they could be seen to be about what it is to make a painting, or by extension, to write. Paintings by Claude Monet, J. M. W. Turner, René Magritte, Pierre-Auguste Renoir, Edward Hopper, and others become commentary on life being lived. "For Judy, Whose Husband Is Undergoing Surgery" blends the bright red flowers of Monet's "Poppy Field, Argenteuil" with thoughts of a friend's husband's hospital room—a combination that makes the reader immediately think of Sylvia Plath, for whom the tulips sucked up the oxygen in the poem "Poppies in July." In Crooker's poem,

The detail here is lost in the brush strokes, dots and
   dashes
of red and yellow, green and blue, small exclama-
   tions
of color, the sky pressing down from above. Now
you are trying to decipher the doctor's calligraphy,
the impenetrable code of sonogram and MRI, the
   odds
of choosing this treatment or that. The poppies flare
like matches struck in the dark. …

(p. 43)

The blend of art and life is so complete the reader is not quite sure which details belong to the room, which to the picture; nor does it matter, because the two form one image.

The last section reprises the book's title with its epigraph, "All I really wanted was more," which is identified as "an anonymous, six-word

memoir." This collection provides a surprising response to its central question. Can you have more than you were given? Can you live more than your life affords? The title of one of her last poems in this collection is "Yes." It begins with a quotation from Frank McCourt's *Teacher Man:* "Yes was the best answer to every question." The poem begins "So I said yes to everything," followed by scenes of art and life, all the elements that the speaker says yes to—to art and poetry and travel and finally

> to the sun pouring down on everything
> like Vermeer's milkmaid and her endless
> jug of milk, yes to the winds that pulled the clouds
> apart like taffy, then turned them into a classroom
> of waving hands punched into fists: *yes yes yes.*
>
> (p. 61)

This collection makes more of the notion of consumption and speech—the poem "Salt" merges the word's connotative and denotative meanings. Beginning with the iconic picture of the girl on the Morton's box, it then indicates what the lack of this condiment would mean:

> Ham would not cure. Soup
> would lose its savor. Language
> its fizz. Swimmers would sink
> under heavy waves. Morning's
> eggs, dull on the plate. It speaks
> in tongues, to wake ours up. Even
> when spilled on the table,
> the tiny crystals spell
> their secret names, dots
> to be connected....
>
> (p. 15)

There is always a mystery to flavor, to "the salt of the earth." *More* expresses a hunger for more of the mystery and verve of life, yet marks the pain of the passage through it.

CHARACTERISTIC STYLE AND TECHNIQUE

Crooker's sensuous world is communicated through patterns of image and thought. Consumption is the underlying drive to live, to be. Everything consumes and is consumed; this is the human condition. In Crooker's work fruits and vegetables speak—their sentience is created playfully, yet we are always aware of their place on the food chain. Her particular brand of synesthesia blends appearance and taste. This contributes to the fun of the poems and gives us an occasional sense of being in Willy Wonka country, where everything, even the grass, is there to eat. One poem is titled "Finches, Little Pats of Butter on the Wing" and presents an abundant, edible world that joins vision with taste:

> And now, everything bursts into bloom,
> the great bouquets of trees, our largest
> perennials: double ruffled cherries, purple-
> leafed plum, flowering pear.
>
> (*More*, p. 13)

Other poems personify food—they are sheer fun, of course, but the consumption theme builds in so many poems that it takes on a life of its own:

> Chocolate strolls up to the microphone
> and plays jazz at midnight, the low slow
> notes of a bass clarinet. ...
>
> ("Ode to Chocolate," *More*, p. 17)

And then there are peaches, with their "plush shoulders," served and consumed as a secular sacrament: "slices of sun in the August sky. / Take and eat, for this is the essence of summer" ("Peaches," *More*, p. 30). Sentient vegetables populate "Vegetable Love," the title of which literalizes the Andrew Marvell metaphor in "To His Coy Mistress": "My vegetable love should grow / Vaster than empires, and more slow."

> All over the garden, the whisper of leaves
> passing secrets and gossip, making assignations.
> All of the vegetables bask in the sun,
> languorous as lizards.
>
> (*Radiance*, p. 54)

The pleasures of the senses all seem to be conflated. As in the works of so many poets, especially women poets, there is an abundance of birds and animals—foxes, grackles, crows, wild geese, cows—but in Crooker's work the flora outweighs the fauna, as every conceivable bush, herb, flower, fruit, and tree seems to surface somewhere, carrying its own metaphorical freight with more added by the poet.

Another Crooker technique is the rhythm and

BARBARA CROOKER

pacing of her poems. The poems dart from image to image like hummingbirds, piling up details similar and dissimilar, with little end punctuation and lots of parallelism. Long sentences continuing from line to line are standard. Her rhythms are strong and carefully crafted—she uses repetition, rising and falling rhythms, sound echoes, and occasionally rhyme to control the free verse and make it musical. (She has a few traditionally formal poems in *Line Dance, More,* and elsewhere.) The melody of her poems is another reason for their popularity—their closeness to traditional verse allows lines to stick in the reader's head without the de-energizing effect rhyme and rhythm so often have.

Crooker attacks her subjects directly, usually without any distancing devices like personae or fragmentation. Because the poems tend to be direct, their originality lies in their rich surface, their daring metaphors, and their juxtaposition of ideas and images that dialogue with each other, rather than in the use of postmodernist techniques. The pacing, piled-up sensory detail, and rush of language make the poems fast, faster than the reader, so that their total effect usually does not hit until the reader has finished the poem—at which time individual images interesting in their own right add up to something more.

It might seem odd to compare Barbara Crooker's work with that of Sylvia Plath, but there are some commonalities. The overall directions are opposite, of course—Plath's poems pull down and Crooker's lift up. But the acuteness of vision, the gathering of disparate images as metaphors for the same thing, the use of vivid colors in unconventional ways, are shared by the two poets. The use of specific images is sometimes similar, as both poets have sharp eyes for natural details that communicate mythic meaning. For instance, in Plath's "Black Rook in Rainy Weather," the image of the bird "arranging and rearranging its feathers in the rain" gives the speaker a brief respite from the bleakness she inhabits, and the search for such images then becomes a reason for going on living. Crooker has crow poems too, and sometimes they carry ominous overtones, but "A Congregation of

Grackles" shows the similarity and difference between her poetry and Plath's:

Startled, they pour out of the woods,
a long black scarf unwinding
in the cold west wind.
Their raucous talk, a thousand fingernails
scratching on glass or a chalkboard
shreds the air. Black cross stitches,
embroidering the blue bunting sky,
they are the X, the unknown quantity
in every equation. They mark the spot
where we cross the equinox,
the resurrection of the woods,
moving from darkness
into the light.

(*Radiance*, p. 60)

The black birds are perceived as a "congregation" and drawn into Crooker's vivid world. Plath's rook is a brief separation from the blank, bleak consciousness of her frame of vision, while Crooker's grackles are a joyous irruption into her sight. Crooker's birds are both real and metaphoric; Plath's rook has been carefully stripped of baggage but of course is metaphoric anyway. The lone rook contrasts with the congregation of birds. The rook briefly distracts, while congregations praise.

Crooker's use of the color red is like and unlike Plath's. Both present red as life squared, the vividness living fully in the present. But Plath rejects the red; the tulips, the poppies. Crooker accepts it. Both poets sometimes associate the color red with burning. Plath's burning reds purify and destroy; Crooker's intensify. In Crooker's "Red," the cherries "turn, burning in the dark green sky." At the poem's end it is dark, and the cherries can no longer be seen.

It is one of those soft
summer nights, after a day of bake oven heat,
the air playing with the hair on your neck,
the bare skin of your arms and legs.
In the grass, fireflies rise in their sultry dance,
little love notes that flicker, that burn.

(*Radiance*, p. 51)

Desire, hunger, need drive Crooker's reds. The color tends to represent life that is too intense, too overflowing in Plath, whose flowers are often

63

connected with blood. Yet like Plath, Crooker is one of the few poets whose individual poems would easily be recognizable by someone who had read a single one of her books. Their electricity, their brilliant colors, their rushing rhythms, and their coherent view are constants.

TEACHING AND POETIC PRACTICE

Barbara Crooker is a teaching poet but not an academic poet, and she has a reputation as a fine teacher who does not use standard techniques but finds new ways to open up poetry's possibilities to those who come to her to learn how to write. She adjusts her presentation to the abilities and needs of each group in her workshops. A teaching poet who gives workshops under different banners never knows what to expect from the vastly different groups of would-be poets, but Crooker is able to bring out the poetry in her visitors by ingenious assignments and by openness to different poetics and points of view.

Teaching is always related to practice, and her fellow poets are always interested in issues of practice: Not only where does the poem come from, but what kind of revision process does the poem go through, and what affects the revision? Workshops, putting the work away for a given time, sharing it with trusted friends? Asked by McCann, "Do you belong to any poetry groups? If so, what do they provide you with?" Crooker responded:

> I belong to several, both "real" and "virtual." One of the "real life" ones is with two other women—we've been in workshops together for over thirty years (the other participants have changed over time, and now it's just the three of us). Mostly, that one provides me with a social night out—we do great refreshments! ... The other real time one is with a man who is pretty much my polar opposite in terms of writing. I tend to write big, then whittle down, and don't like to show poems to others until I think they're "done." He likes to bring poems in multiple drafts.... Something I admire is that he has the ability to take a poem that's pretty small in scope and turn it into something larger. When I write small poems I seem to not be able to revise them outward; i.e., they remain small poems. Just a different approach. While I only seem to use about 10 percent of his suggestions, what he says makes me question my choices, hone my aesthetic, and the

changes that I do make are good ones. I'm always laboring in service to the poem.

She is also very direct about her work and her practices. In an unpublished essay, "The Place Where My Poems Are Coming From," she discusses what keeps her work flowing—so many poet-readers who struggle with writer's block are interested in this topic. She mentions her "colony time" at the Virginia Center for the Creative Arts in Amherst, Virginia, and in other places—the "deep quiet" a socially and family-involved poet needs to write. She comments on writing poems that come from other poems—a source adapted by other poets to use in creative writing classes. Crooker keeps bits of work in manila folders and notes other sources as poetry generative: walking, visiting museums, driving, all kinds of travel, and shifting scenes for writing, together with the "magpie sort of mind" that collects images, ideas, ironies, oddments, linguistic mistakes—anything that would stick in the mind of someone who loves language. Even her own mistakes become meat for the poet—as when her misreading of the last word of Alice Fulton's "Concerning Things That Can Be Doubted" resulted in her own poem, "Concerning Things That Can Be Doubled."

Crooker's engagement with the poetry world also includes poems for children in *Highlights for Children,* the *Christian Science Monitor,* and some children's anthologies, and translation: she has translated eight poems of Henryk Wrozynski from Polish to English. She has a strong Web presence and is a prolific reviewer. Crooker's poetry already has a very wide audience, but it will continue to be adopted into classes and taken up by the academic community because it is layered and complex but remains accessible. Her poems can be analyzed for technique as well as content and used to illustrate various subgenres of poetry that are currently commanding interest, such as environmental poetry, ekphrastic work, poetry of myth, dramatic monologue, and the rich, vibrant, image-based poetry that has been around since Ezra Pound and still is an important current in the flow of contemporary poetry. For Crooker, development is not experimenting with new poetic forms but rather looking with differ-

ent perspectives on the issues that are the major concerns of all poets, bringing her unique sensibility to bear on them. Her work has energy that provides excitement seldom found in new poems.

Crooker's theology—if one can use this word to apply to poetry that contains no explicit doctrine—is part of her appeal. Her Zen Lutheran perspective is more a way of looking at the world than a belief, and yet it implies a belief. Her poetry suggests that nothing is wasted—no love, no trial, no life, no experience. There is a dimension in which everything still exists. Change or removal does not cancel out, and we have a perhaps Derridean sense of the original image, word, relationship still present although under erasure. Crooker does not trade in theological absolutes, except rarely and for the most part playfully. Yet her constructed universe has a sense of intention. If the world did not change, then how could renewal occur? Stevens' "Death is the mother of beauty" comes to mind again. And again as in Stevens, the poetry leaves the impression that the cosmos is intentional, even has a kind of sentience, if we can see her playful personifications as conveying anything beyond their play. Moreover, the coherence or wholeness in her vision is metaphysical in itself. Events and things are always part of a pattern, and we can see only part of the pattern. There is a goodness to it, it is *sweet*—a word Crooker that uses often, and that her critics frequently use about her work—even while life baffles and robs us. It is rare to find a poet who leaves the reader with such a sense of awakening.

Selected Bibliography

WORKS OF BARBARA CROOKER

POETRY BOOKS

Radiance: Poems. Cincinnati, Ohio: Word Press, 2005.
Line Dance: Poems. Cincinnati, Ohio: Word Press, 2008.
More: Poems. Chattanooga, Tenn.: C&N Press, 2010.

POETRY CHAPBOOKS

Writing Home: Poems. With Katharyn Machan Aal. Iowa City: Gehry Press, 1983.

Looking for the Comet Halley. New Wilmington, Pa.: Dawn Valley Press, 1987.

Starting from Zero. Kanona, N.Y.: Great Elm Press & Foothills Publishing, 1987.

The Lost Children. Woodside, Calif.: Heyeck Press, 1989.

Obbligato. Stone Mountain, Ga.: Linwood, 1991.

In the Late Summer Garden. Middlebury Center, Pa.: H&H Press, 1998.

Ordinary Life. Edmond, Okla.: ByLine Press, 2001.

The White Poems. Seattle, Wash.: Barnwood, 2001.

Paris (folio edition). Ithaca, N.Y.: Sometimes Y Publications, 2002.

Impressionism. West Hartford, Conn.: Grayson Books, 2004.

Greatest Hits. Columbus, Ohio: Pudding House Press, 2004.

Single poems have appeared in over five hundred anthologies and journals, including the periodicals *Yankee, Christian Science Monitor, Smartish Pace, Beloit Poetry Journal, Nimrod, Denver Quarterly, Tampa Review, Poetry International, Christian Century,* and *America.*

CRITICAL AND BIOGRAPHICAL STUDIES

"Barbara Crooker." *Contemporary Authors Online,* March 18, 2009. http://www.galenet.galegroup.com.

Barbara Crooker's Home Page. http://www.barbaracrooker .com/index.php. (Contains numerous interviews and reviews, arranged chronologically.)

Leimbach, Laura. "Barbara Crooker." Pennsylvania Center for the Book, spring 2009. http://pabook.libraries.psu.edu/ palitmap/bios/Crooker__Barbara.html.

REVIEWS

Atkins, Priscilla. Review of *Radiance. Midwest Quarterly* 48, no. 2:314–315 (winter 2007).

Dacus, Rachel. Review of *Radiance. Midwest Quarterly* 48, no. 2:315–317 (winter 2007).

———. Review of *More. Pedestal Magazine,* 2010. http:// www.thepedestalmagazine.com/gallery.php?item=17539.

Humes, Harry. Review of *Writing Home.* 1983. http://www .barbaracrooker.com/review_interview.php?start=60.

Johnson, Linnea. Review of *Radiance. Prairie Schooner* 81, no. 2:211–216 (summer 2007).

Keyes, Claire. "*Line Dance* by Barbara Crooker." *Rattle,* March 2008. http://www.rattle.com/ereviews/ crookerlinedance.htm.

McCann, Janet. Review of *More. Valparaiso Poetry Review* 12, no. 1 (fall–winter 2010–2011). http://www.valpo.edu/ vpr/v12n1/v12n1prose/mccannreviewcrooker.php.

Moore, Julie L. "Line Dance: Poems." *Christianity and Literature* 54, no. 4:786–790 (2009).

INTERVIEWS

"An Interview with Barbara Crooker." *Poetry Life & Times*, November 1999. http://www.artvilla.com/plt/poetnewsNov99.html.

"Barbara Crooker." *Writer's Almanac Bookshelf.* http://writersalmanac.publicradio.org/bookshelf/crooker.shtml.

Bittner, Russell. "Poet's Corner—An Interview with Barbara Crooker." *Long Story Short*, spring 2009. http://lssarchives.homestead.com/poetscorner-BarbaraCrooker.html.

Geffner, Michael P. "Spotlight Interview: Poet Barbara Crooker." *Mike's Writing Workshop & Newsletter*, January 23, 2009. http://mikeswritingworkshop.blogspot.com/2009/01/spotlight-interview-poet-barbara.html.

"Interview with Barbara Crooker, Poet." *Iambic Admonit*, September 28, 2010. http://iambicadmonit.blogspot.com/2010/09/interview-with-barbara-crooker-poet_28.html.

McCann, Janet. E-mail interview with Barbara Crooker, March 30, 2011.

Rivers, Allison. "Q&A with Barbara Crooker." C&R Press, April 2010. http://www.wix.com/crpress/crpress/more.

STUART DYBEK

(1942—)

Judith Kitchen

STUART DYBEK HAS a growing reputation as a poet and fiction writer. In 2007 he was awarded a John D. and Catherine T. MacArthur Foundation Fellowship, and the very next day he was informed that he had been selected to receive the prestigious Rea Award for the Short Story. The meticulous craftsmanship of his compact body of work—he published just six volumes of poetry and fiction between 1979 and 2006—has established Dybek as a significant voice in American letters.

LIFE

Stuart Dybek grew up on the Southwest Side of Chicago in blue-collar neighborhoods known as Pilsen and Little Village (together known as "the barrio"), composed mostly of immigrant Poles, Czechs, and Hispanics. In such a mix the Catholic Church was the main unifying force. Dybek's father, Stanley, was a foreman at the International Harvester plant, and his mother, Adeline, worked as a truck dispatcher for extra income.

Dybek's childhood covered the entire decade of the 1950s, a somewhat innocent time when neighborhoods such as his were still places where children could be on their own. Dybek and his two younger brothers were allowed to roam the streets, where they encountered many of the situations and characters that populate his stories. All three of his prose collections mine this material; in one of his many interviews he calls those years "a time when each day was filled with characters and stories that, at the time, I didn't realize were anything other than living" (TheWritingDisorder.com). Moving through the streets of his youth, Dybek delves into the memories and legends of his childhood, often blurring the distinctions between reality and dream. One extremely important figure in Dybek's life was Busha, his Polish grandmother, whose myths and superstitions made their way into his tales along with a sense of unconditional love—an emotion that needed no language.

Dybek's education included attending a Catholic high school, but almost from the beginning he resisted the strictures of the church itself. A bit of a rebel and never much interested in school, he claims his major influence was music. After graduation he attended Loyola University as a premed student, dropped out for a while, then returned to earn both B.A. and M.A. degrees. He worked as a caseworker for the Cook County Department of Public Aid, as an elementary school teacher in a Chicago suburb, in advertising, and then, from 1968 to 1970, he taught at a high school on the island of Saint Thomas. In 1973 he received his M.F.A. in writing from the University of Iowa.

Still, Dybek could be said to have received his real education in the jazz clubs and on the streets of Chicago. For years he played the saxophone, but he realized that he was never likely to have sufficient expertise to meet his aspirations. Turning to writing—where he did not have such a recognized set of models—he was able to experiment more freely. In most of his writing, time becomes fluid, allowing him to orchestrate a kind of jazz in the very structure of his individual pieces and in the arrangement of each collection.

Dybek's first books, published almost simultaneously—one poetry (1979), one fiction (1980)—established him as a new figure in the Chicago literary tradition. But Dybek avoided the "realist" reputations of Carl Sandburg, James T. Farrell, Nelson Algren, and Saul Bellow with fiction that contains an element of what others have

called a brand of "magic realism" but he would call the "fantastical." His work was always grounded in the gritty reality of the city, but it also used as a form of imaginative digression the myths, superstitions, and mystery that accompany ethnicity. Dybek had read and admired most of the important midwestern writers—F. Scott Fitzgerald, Ernest Hemingway, John Dos Passos, Sherwood Anderson—yet both his poetry and prose are actually more akin to the work of such non-American writers as Isaac Babel, Franz Kafka, and Jorge Luis Borges.

Over a span of more than thirty years, Dybek has published two books of poetry, three collections of fiction, and a chapbook of short prose pieces he prefers to call "fragments." This comparatively slight output has, however, been notably well received. The six published volumes have earned him numerous awards, including an Ernest Hemingway Citation from the PEN American Center for *Childhood and Other Neighborhoods* in 1981; the Whiting Writers Award in 1985; a Guggenheim Fellowship; two fellowships from the National Endowment for the Arts; a residency at the Rockefeller Foundation's Bellagio Center; an Academy Institute Award in Fiction from the American Academy of Arts and Letters in 1994; the 1995 PEN/Bernard Malamud Prize "for distinctive achievement in the short story"; a Lannan Award in 1998; and the MacArthur Foundation Fellowship awarded in 2007. His stories, published first in such magazines as the *New Yorker, Atlantic, Playboy, Harper's, Ploughshares,* and *Paris Review,* have received four O. Henry Prize Story awards, the Nelson Algren Prize, and inclusion in *Best American Short Stories* as well as the Rea Award for the Short Story.

Dybek taught at Western Michigan University in Kalamazoo for more than thirty years as assistant professor and then professor of English; he continues to serve as a member of the creative writing faculty for the university's Prague Summer Program. In 2006 he was appointed Distinguished Writer in Residence at Northwestern University, thus bringing him full circle, back to the city, if not the lost neighborhoods, of his youth.

A QUESTION OF GENRE: BRASS KNUCKLES *AND* CHILDHOOD AND OTHER NEIGHBORHOODS

From the beginning of his career, Stuart Dybek seems to have published his books in pairs. In 1979 the University of Pittsburgh Press published *Brass Knuckles,* a collection of poetry and prose poems. Following closely on its heels, a collection of stories, *Childhood and Other Neighborhoods,* came out with Viking Press in 1980. Not surprisingly, the subject matter of these two books overlaps: a world of immigrant neighborhoods, ethnic families, and the vestiges of old languages; the poverty and semi-squalor of rooming houses, abandoned factories, littered streets, derelicts, ragmen; the jazz and salsa of memory all transformed through familiarity and imagination. Dybek was clearly experimenting more with form and genre than with subject matter, trying to see what best fit his natural proclivities. Studded with detail, both books give off the gritty realism of their urban setting, yet they also begin to take some of the imaginative leaps that would characterize Dybek's later work, as though he were trying out genres to see which would best support his underlying issues—the amalgam of fantasy and reality.

The first poem in *Brass Knuckles,* "Vivaldi," demonstrates this propensity:

When I met Vivaldi it was dark,
a ragman lashed his horse's bells,
streets tilted into slow wind tunnels,

no, it was another night, in winter,
snow as soft as opium. …

(p. 3)

The shift between the stanzas indicates Dybek's willingness to probe alternative realities. Or, since the speaker never physically "met" Vivaldi, alternative fantasies.

The poems in *Brass Knuckles* re-create the old neighborhood but populate it with characters out of myth (Persephone, Orpheus), religion (Lazarus, Saint Teresa), and history (Bastille Day, Siberia). Ordinary events turn at times grotesque, at times fanciful—a sleepwalker is poised at the edge of a roof, a groom steps off the icing of the

STUART DYBEK

wedding cake, girls remove their clothes in an endless repetition of latent sexuality while young boys play games of imagined ball, set their own dead cat on fire, and, in "Penance," try to imagine, as they go to confession, the "terrible sins of old women" (p. 9).

The city is the backdrop for discovery. Together, boys wander the streets, searching out the mysteries of adult life. Pictured a bit like a revolutionaries "picking up rocks, swept as one through clouds of bursting gas bombs and buckshot into History" (p. 22), together they learn about violence and sexuality. The images of broken windows and all-night Laundromats coalesce until they take on the dimensions of the bombed cities and napalm glare of recent wars. Set against History, the seeming timelessness of the poems narrows to a span of decades: "one sign points to Hiroshima, the other to Saigon" (p. 44).

Within the collection, the prose poems are more successful than the more traditionally lineated poems. Since Dybek's experimentation was not with metaphor in its more usual sense, the lineated poems rely more on narrative than poetic techniques. The lines are energetic more than musical. The prose poems, on the other hand, often make deft moves that propel the poem into new territory—creating a kind of strobe effect as they flicker in and out of reality, moving almost seamlessly from present to past to present, or front to back to front, so that the reader is transported in space and time. "Doors" is perhaps the best example of this double vision:

Across the street they put up a wall of doors from the rooming house they'd knocked down. Doors all darkened the same, like burnt toast, on the outside. But insides different colors: pinks, blues, yellows, dirty white enamels. You could look through the holes where the doorknobs had been into the rubble-filled foundation. Old black men stacking old bricks. Smoke fuming from a wet pile of charred wood. Grey panes of glass broken everywhere. An old woman taking a bath. A small man from India cooking something on a hot plate. A man in his underwear with a hearing aid sitting beside a radio. Two people fucking on a bed. What did you expect?

(p. 7)

Peering through time, into the life of the vanished rooming house, the reader experiences the flashback effect of revived memory. Everything coexists—the tearing down and the building up. The final poem, titled "My Neighborhood," as though to forecast the upcoming collection of fiction, paints the now familiar pattern of urban ethnic life: the dying elms, the drunks and crazies, the bands of boys, and, over and over, "a girl" who, in her various guises, repeatedly finds her way toward eroticism. The speaker is a stand-in for Dybek as he makes not the girls but their mystery his subject—and not their mystery, but memory itself, his obsession:

I have forgotten their names,
the names of the streets we passed,
weather, daydreams, legends,
the precision of fear;
almost forgotten how the winos
looked in the cold,
the language of the Old Country,
stray dogs, grandparents, my brothers.
But the girls are clear
in a world they made a mystery.

(p. 68)

The stories of *Childhood and Other Neighborhoods* expand the themes of the poetry, employing the same images but giving them a different kind of weight. In many ways, the stories of *Childhood* have a sense of portent, of something about to be lost. The book recovers a transient period in the nation's history, reliving a time when the immigrant neighborhoods of the 1950s and 1960s were already in transition. Conflating the "hoods" in his title, Dybek makes his point: childhood (with its charged imagination) becomes a physical place in which memory resides, a place where an otherwise peripheral character like Sterndorf, the "neighborhood drunk," can take on a larger role, where the narrator's grandmother can wish for duck's blood soup and send him out on what turns out to be a journey of mythic proportions. The superstitious world of the immigrant grandparents and the fantasies of the children find common ground. And thus the broader scope of the imaginary is set against the "factual" world of the hard-working, tough-minded parents. In an interview with Benjamin

69

STUART DYBEK

Seaman in 1988, Dybek stated, "The important aspect of using autobiography is not recording what actually happened so much as believing that the material is a great gift worthy of being reimagined."

A good example can be found in the opening of the book's first story, "The Palatski Man":

> He reappeared in spring, some Sunday morning, perhaps Easter, when the twigs of the catalpa trees budded and lawns smelled of mud and breaking seeds. Or Palm Sunday, returning from mass with handfuls of blessed, bending palms to be cut into crosses and pinned on your Sunday dress and the year-old palms removed by her brother, John, from behind the pictures of Jesus with his burning heart and the Virgin with her sad eyes, to be placed dusty and crumbling in an old coffee can and burned in the backyard. And once, walking back from church, Leon Sisca said these are what they lashed Jesus with. And she said no they aren't, they used whips. They used these, he insisted. What do you know, she said. And he told her she was a dumb girl and lashed her across her bare legs with his blessed palms. They stung her; she started to cry, that anyone could do such a thing, and he caught her running down Twenty-fifth street with her skirt flying and got her against a fence, ...
>
> (pp. 1–2)

The first two sentences (with "perhaps" and "or") announce the story's terrain as the subjective, indefinite realm of memory—vivid memory, laced with digression, and told with immediacy, as though the event had resurfaced, intact. The second paragraph recovers the thread: "No, it wasn't that day, but it was in that season on a Sunday that he reappeared" (p. 2). From this beginning, the neighborhood of childhood unfolds—the Palatski man pushes his white cart through the streets ringing "a little golden bell," selling candy apples and *palatski* (two wafers stuck together with honey)—and, inevitably, the question is raised, who is he? This leads to the moment when Mary urges her brother John to follow the Palatski Man into a hobo town that looms, in memory, in almost surreal proportions as a place where the boys had encountered a veritable regiment of ragmen. This memory, in turn, leads to speculation about Ray—one of the boys caught by the ragmen—who subsequently ran away from home and has been unheard from since. Mystery piles on mystery.

As the siblings trail the Palatski man farther and farther into unfamiliar territory, they watch in fascination as he enters a circle of men around a pot of bubbling bright red fluid. "Blood," they think, as the men, almost in ritual, take small pieces of wafer and eat. The fluid is, in reality, used to make candy apples—and it really is, in their imaginations, blood. They have experienced some kind of transformation, and even upon their return to the safety of their neighborhood, something is altered. What is lost is childhood itself, as Mary feels "her breasts swelling like apples from her flat chest" and, hearing his bell, knows it is "time to go" (p. 20).

"The Palatski Man" contains many of the elements found in the other stories of *Childhood:* the flavor of youth itself, the transformative power of imagination, a tinge of danger or suspense, an element of the unknown, a sense of hovering on the brink of knowledge—knowledge that will simultaneously take the characters into a wider world and rob them of the richness of their innocence.

Often the stories involve a set of brothers, or a group of friends (usually three), for whom change is fraught with temptation. References to Catholicism recur so that each story suggests a promise of redemption, or an underlying sense of guilt. "Visions of Budhardin" recounts the return, as an adult, of a neighborhood boy whose early years were plagued by loneliness. Too fat to wear a cossack, he remained on the fringes of the church while other boys acted as altar boys. Budhardin (his oddly different name is never explained) began to tempt the others with pictures of nude women, encouraging acts of "mortal sin." Soon after his only friend, Eugene, was run over by a car, Budhardin left town. Now he has constructed a mechanized elephant and positioned himself inside it. The ensuing scenes are action-packed surrealism. Entering the church, the elephant finds himself accosting, and accosted by, nuns, bumping into vigil candles until he sets the church on fire. Budhardin is then chased by altar boys until he falls, rolling onto a garbage scow where, with the "angelic" Billy Crystal, he sets off for Europe or the Yucatán, depending on the current. Reminiscent of Huckleberry Finn

and Jim, the two resist both church and society: "'South of the border!' Billy Crystal said, his choirboy mouth breaking into a grin. 'Fucking A!'" (p. 87).

In a more realistic vein, "The Long Thoughts" follows two friends through a desultory evening into the small hours of the morning. First, avoiding the parental nagging and sibling squabbling in his apartment, Tom, or "Vulk" as he is known, introduces the narrator to the music of Claude Debussy. Later, the two adolescents aimlessly wander the streets, talking about the lives of artists, music, and literature. Vulk has just been expelled from the Catholic high school and the narrator is following close behind, refusing to do his homework in a kind of generic rebellion. Snow sifts down as they pass the jail, listening to the inmates inside, then make their way to a Laundromat where, past curfew, they evade a punitive policeman. They decide not to set a garage on fire, "Not tonight" (p. 100). All the while, almost in homage to James Joyce's "The Dead," Dybek sets the scene: "It was early in January and the street and trees were pale with snow. … It was snowing lightly again" (p. 91). "An occasional neon sign blinked across the sidewalk snow" (p. 94). "We cut down an alley, jogging through the ruts the garbage trucks had made in the snow, our breath panting out before us" (pp. 99–100). "Our shadows passed through the shadows of trees etched in the snow by the moonlight" (p. 101). Nothing happens and everything happens as the evening is etched in the narrator's memory, a recollection so clear "that for a moment I started to shake, then it slipped away, leaving me with a chill and the cigarette tasting like burned newspaper in the raw air, so I went in" (p. 102).

Childhood ends with a boy climbing the girders of a drawbridge, with all its attendant dangers. Before the final scene, though, he is able to get a long view:

His life spread out before him like the cityscape, suspended in time, rather than the dark, speeding blur it had been on the highways. This was a landscape he was the center of, completely alone, though surrounded by a city. The dreams were over. Out there under plumes of smoke in some glinting neighborhood the girl sat in a classroom over a

math book. Between them was a distance greater than between foreign countries. He could actually *see* from the bridge that in escaping to the city Uncle had merely substituted one kind of isolation for another.

(p. 198)

Place—Chicago itself—becomes what Dybek refers to as "disguised obsession" (Plath). All the stories of *Childhood* present the same rough urban setting but from a number of different perspectives. Although they are similar in circumstance, each story is discrete, allowing Dybek to present different facets of the urban psyche. Alternating the realistic stories (such as "Neighborhood Drunk" or "The Long Thoughts") with ones that he terms more "fabulist" ("Blood Soup" and "The Apprentice," for example), Dybek is able to suggest the ineffable: the untranslatable mysteries and legends, the erotic underpinnings, the potent adolescent dreams; everything that makes a neighborhood simmer with possibility. By using contrasting modes, Dybek fashions a jazz of his own, using counterpoint to create its own tension. His unique voice seems to emanate from setting. Chicago vibrates with its own history as Dybek draws on the melting pot of his ethnic neighborhood to expand on what it means to be American. His careful microscopic study of place results in work with macroscopic resonance.

Since both the poetry and the prose mine the same material, it seems legitimate to ask which genre best suits Dybek's sensibility. In a 2006 interview in *TriQuarterly*, Donna Seaman asked what form he started writing first, and Dybek answered:

They were always simultaneous, and continue to be written in tandem, so to speak. I kind of "collect" in poetry. Writers often keep little journals, and I call mine "A Great Thoughts Notebook," with tongue firmly planted in cheek. In there a lot of stuff gets recorded in a sloppy verse line, and imagery is emphasized. Then I loot that stuff for both stories and poems.

The lines in the notebook usually contain an image, and fiction, Dybek asserts, is as much image-making as it is storytelling. So the two genres are inextricably intertwined as part of his method of

discovery. However, in the Benjamin Seaman interview Dybek admits, "I'm much more conscious of borrowing from poetry for my fiction than vice versa. Why that is I don't really know." Whether that original verse line becomes a poem or a story is determined in the process of exploration. If a character asserts its presence, then the piece will usually take shape as fiction. But because of its inception as a potential poem, it will retain something of what Dybek thinks of as "compression."

HYBRID FORMS: THE COAST OF CHICAGO AND THE STORY OF MIST

The Coast of Chicago (1990) is a group of loosely linked stories. What links them is Chicago itself—its warehouses and alleys, its music clubs and prisons, all joined by the ever-present El, with its latticework of girders, its gleaming rails, lighted cars streaming through the dark. In comparison with the first collection, the stories veer more toward the dream state than the grotesque, more toward the lyrical than the fantastic.

Dividing *The Coast of Chicago* into two types of stories, Dybek elected to interweave the longer, more fanciful stories with short pieces that act more like the prose poems of his earlier collection. These short pieces, printed on gray paper to further set them off, have the feel of being more autobiographical, as though these snippets of life were the repository for the imagination to build on, and from. One of these, "Lights," demonstrates how, in Dybek's hands, a short piece of prose can operate almost as a poem. The piece is clearly prose—narrative and anecdotal—yet it employs many elements of poetry: simile, repetition, assonance, alliteration, even an echo of iambic pentameter. More, "Lights" behaves like a sonnet. That is, prose pieces can take on the trappings of form and thereby take advantage of how that form functions. Here the initial paragraphs serve as the first quartets, then the turn and the longer sestet complicates the memory, provides an adult overlay on the moment. The simile, in conjunction with the

repetition of those "lights," has the powerful effect of a closing couplet. It carries the finality not of insight but what might be termed "retrosight" (an imposing of another image to revitalize the stasis in which the past is locked). It not only invigorates, it animates. And in doing so, it creates its odd synesthesia. Sound winks on, lights up.

The short pieces hover in a limbo somewhere between fiction and nonfiction; the longer stories invoke the imagination. Simultaneously real and surreal, they seem like life as we live it. "Chopin in Winter," for example, brings together three lonely people whose lives share a brief moment, then diverge. "Blight" anchors the setting in reality, mentioning Mayor Richard J. Daley and his declaration that the neighborhood has been designated an Official Blight Area. "It wasn't until we became Blighters that we began to recognize the obscurity that surrounded us" (p. 55). Suddenly the abandoned cars and run-down factories and bag ladies and potholes hold a new fascination. Venturing out from their world, where they play baseball games and Deejo writes songs for his band, the narrator and his friends range farther and farther into other parts of the city, including the great lake that hovers on the horizon of their consciousness. They return each time to notice the music of viaducts and choirs of insects speaking a "language of terror and beauty" (p. 51). "Back to Blight," they say, and keep on saying, returning the story to its home territory, returning from digression to the business at hand—the fusion of the ordinary and the extraordinary.

Taking its cue from the short prose pieces, "Hot Ice" is a sequence of segments that serve as connective tissue between this new book and the older stories. Told from a longer perspective, all the tics smoothed so that the story reads like sanded wood, its characters move through time and space so that Pancho and Manny and Eddie and Antek seem to drift through the narrative like a dream. Resurrecting the earlier scene outside the prison walls, Eddie and Manny now stand there, night after night, calling out to Manny's brother, Pancho. And Pancho disappears, becomes a ghost of a presence, a legend in his own right.

STUART DYBEK

So it is that they make of belief a fine art, trusting the legend about a drowned girl frozen in ice to the point that they search for her in the old abandoned icehouse and think they find her in a frozen block. It becomes imperative to set her free, to hand her back to the elements in which she met her death. In one wild, outlandish moment, they slide the ice block onto an old railway handcar and furiously pump their way along the rails to the lake. With the ice block melting between them, the fantastic feels inevitable. Nothing can stop them as they "row" through the dark.

Dream is partially the state of the book, night scenes lit up and magnified. Taking its title from Edward Hopper's famous painting of a diner at night, the book's long central piece, "Nighthawks," explores not only a fictional version of that diner but all the other possible surrounding scenes. The piece proceeds by association, the way we do in dream. Its short segments act as facets of something larger, fragments of a whole. Images are repeated like reflections as the inhabitants of the night (the insomniacs and shadowy shapes a boy calls "silhouettes") play out their nighttime fantasies. A drummer finds his way from segment to segment, providing the rhythmic glue; a kiss floats over the city, lighting on a person, riding the trains through the night; the blue bulb of the streetlight is caught in a raindrop, and this blue globe of rain falls in scene after scene. In yet a different segment, a man stands looking out over the river, knowing "there is only so much time to change the direction of a life," and suddenly the paragraph shifts to the question, "And what about the memory of the boy left at the window, staring out past his own spattered reflection?" (p. 114). Time collapses; characters merge; images flicker; the language becomes lyrical:

> He can see the blue of that single bulb diffused in the sheen of breakwaters and distant winks of pumping stations, in the vague outlines of freighters far out on what, come morning, will be a horizon. He could glimpse the future passing, reflected in the current, if he weren't watching the streetlight slowly sinking as it swirls into the vortex of a sewer, if he weren't still waiting for the silhouettes to come

for him. He doesn't realize—he won't ever know—that, like them, he's become a shadow.

(p. 115)

In an interview with Robert Birnbaum for the *Morning News,* Dybek stated, "I get more and more interested in thinking of trying to write—I don't even know how to articulate it—a piece of writing that is more about palpability, touch, feel, smells, sensual experience than it is about story." "Nighthawks" fits that description as the night, with its attendant desires, is made palpable through the use of image and lyricism. The brevity of the segments, the repetition of the imagery, and the elevated language conspire to make "Nighthawks" less a "story" and more a sequence of poetic fragments. "I knew a girl who laughed in her sleep" (p. 87) one segment begins, and an astute reader finds that this is a revised version of section 2 of "Dreams," one of the final poems in *Brass Knuckles.* In just such ways, Dybek blurs the distinctions of genre and makes for himself a hybrid form.

One key element in the book is the use of digression as an active creative force. In his interview with James Plath, Dybek discusses the technique:

> Number one, the digressions themselves have to be interesting, in order to justify being there. ... I think anytime you depart from a narrative line you're taking a risk, but you're also opening up the possibility of point/counterpoint, different kinds of pacing—that is, the digressions themselves become rhythmic shifts ... the reader begins to feel a pattern of digressions.

He goes on to explain how following that instinct can help the writer:

> The story gets smarter than the writer, exceeds his initial conception, or starts making moves that the writer doesn't think of fast enough to make on his own. When stories start misbehaving like that, you suddenly reach the point where there's this overwhelming urge to digress from a nice, tidy narrative line, and allow what might have been an easily written story to become far more chancy and complicated. ... There's an undercurrent to it, some kind of chemistry and interplay between the original narrative line and the digressions, that makes for greater resonance and allows the story to throw a longer shadow.

The Coast of Chicago ends with a riff on an image of coffee, but Dybek allows the image to throw a longer shadow as the narrator moves from his memory of his grandmother's coffee to his flight from the neighborhood. "Pet Milk" ends with something close to what Dybek sees as epiphanic as, in a near-reversal of the boy of "Nighthawks," the narrator sees himself coming and going. Time conflates as the train rocks through the night on its way north and the young man looks up from the girl he is kissing and sees his schoolboy self peering in from the platform "on one of those endlessly accumulated afternoons after school when I stood almost outside of time simply waiting for a train, and I thought how much I'd have loved seeing someone like us streaming by" (p. 173).

This could be called a "lyric moment"—one that functions much the way a poem functions with its fusion of time, its reminder of those accumulated afternoons that, in retrospect, make up the entire subject matter of the book. Dybek stated in the interview with James Plath that his interest in his first book of stories was the grotesque, but that with the second book he turned his attention to the lyrical. "I was experimenting with … the combination of the realistic mode with what might be called the lyric mode." Not only do the stories proceed by association, but, as in poems, they employ gaps or juxtapositions where the reader is forced to bridge the divide between the known world and the hidden one. In the 2006 interview with Donna Seaman, Dybek explained the technique by returning to his knowledge of music:

> I was very aware of how important counterpoint is in music, but it never really occurred to me before that it was a tremendously important mechanism that writers of all kinds use in order to create compression and resonance. That when you take two things that are unlike and you put them side by side, a current jumps between them, as in positive and negative, and that this current is often what the reader supplies where there is silence. So the reader is participating in bringing these two things together, and what's happening is that stuff is getting said that you haven't had to write in language.

Another crossbreed made its presence known with the State Street Press publication of a chapbook of short prose pieces in 1993. Titled *The Story of Mist,* the chapbook is a collection of short segments like those in *The Coast of Chicago.* The use of the word "story" in the title suggests the fictional nature of these pieces, and the "mist" of the title alerts the reader to the elusive quality of these moments—as though they were floating in the air, hazy fragments of memory and experience, or brief illuminations of imagination.

At the time, there was no way to describe these pieces; "flash fiction" or "sudden fiction," with its emphasis on speed, did not really give voice to Dybek's interest in compression, and Dybek was increasingly uncomfortable with the term "prose poem" because he intuitively understood not only the fictive nature of his venture but its inherently narrative focus. When an expanded version of the chapbook was published in France as *L'Histoire de la brume,* the translator, Philippe Beget, told him that such pieces did have a term in French—*fragments*—and this terminology, eschewing any generic references in favor of the elusory nature of their short form, satisfied most of Dybek's concerns. The term itself gave him a sense that these pieces had a kind of purpose—to reflect that particular state of mind that captures pieces of the whole.

The range of the seventeen short pieces—from one paragraph to three pages in length—gives some sense of the fragmentary nature of the venture. Some act more like nonfiction "shorts," with their clear references to Dybek's grandmother, Busha, and to the Chicago of his youth; some more like tiny stories peopled by character and event, such as the lifeguard who "kisses" a woman back to life or the woman who wades in a fountain at night and the man who imagines her there in the morning; some behave like prose poems, coalescing around an image or investigating the fantastic; and some resist all definition, save that of "fragment," in their odd juxtapositions or truncated glimpses. "Seven Sentences," a romance of sorts told in seven seemingly unrelated sentences, also shows up ten years later in a book consisting entirely of poems. The title piece follows one image into several semi-related scenarios: "Mist hangs like incense

in the trees"; "Obscured trains uncouple in a dusk that is also obscured"; "a buoy tolls in the mist like the steeple of a little neighborhood church that has drifted out to sea"; and, finally, "A freighter, sounding a melancholy horn, hoists the moon that it's been towing from a moonlit slick, and tows it through the mist" (p. 28).

"I have long been intrigued by the notion of compression in prose, of what defines it, what is its measure, and how is it achieved. … and that nearly automatically opens up the notion of the relationship between the lyrical and the narrative," Dybek stated in the *Vestal Review*. Thus it was natural that his experiments in the two modes would lead to hybrid forms.

In a review of *The Story of Mist* for the *Prose Poem: An International Journal,* Richard Murphy noted that these pieces are similar to the "interchapter" prose poems of *The Coast of Chicago* in their "evocation of the suppressed details and, thus, the informing emotion." He observed that "the works are poetic in their evanescence, the shadings of lost opportunity or loss itself," even though these fragments are, somehow, neither story nor poem: "The poetic usages of balance and antithesis, repetition, evocation rather than statement, as well as connotative diction and imagery, render Dybek's work different from the short story, no matter how short, though the emphasis on the consciousness of character removes it from the French musical poetics associated with the early development of the prose poem."

THRESHOLDS: I SAILED WITH MAGELLAN *AND* STREETS IN THEIR OWN INK

In 2003, when Dybek was about to publish his third collection of fiction, it was clear that in over twenty years of writing he had been far more interested in his own discoveries than he was in producing the requisite novel or in pursuing a traditional literary career. Telling Robert Birnbaum that "books aren't just pages," it was also clear that he was willing to wait as long as it took for a book to emerge from his experimentations. With *I Sailed with Magellan,* Dybek

crossed into new territory—what has been termed a novel in linked stories.

Once again, the Little Village neighborhood is the setting, a few blocks of back-alley fences, brick walls, pawnshops, litter-strewn gutters, factory smoke—and a teeming inner life of tenements filled with music, argument, and love. At least half the life here is overheard, through open windows, across alleys and fences, wafting up stairwells. Sound becomes a central element. The book was, for Dybek, an homage to music; every story has its song, and some more than one.

As opposed to the earlier books, the stories of *I Sailed with Magellan* have one consistent set of characters, or, more precisely, one specific narrator. This is the story of Perry Katzek, a boy growing up on the streets of Chicago's South Side. In certain ways, the stories "act" like a novel in that they are all told from Perry's perspective. This is not quite so much point of view as it is a presiding sensibility—one angle of vision and set of experiences through which the reader can interpret and infer the larger picture. In many ways, having one central character allows the reader more room to predict and project. At the same time, the stories remain just that—stories. They may chronicle a growing awareness of the wider world, but, deliberately disrupting the logic of linearity, they do not attempt to have the narrative arc expected from a sequence of chapters. Instead, the chronology is often interrupted. Tales are abandoned, then picked up by someone else at some other time. The reader is given eleven glimpses into a life that in turn opens out to other lives. Small events are writ large. The ordinary is magnified. What would, in a novel, be background material becomes, in this collection, the digressive foreground from which the "action" of the book will arise.

That action comes from, but is clearly differentiated from, Perry's life. In fact, the narrative and the narrator are usually somewhat distinct from each other, causing the presiding consciousness to play the role of a subnarrator. What is of interest here is the imaginative interplay between the real and the possible, the undercurrents of neighborhood drama, the way Perry's young life connects with a broader social

structure and how he negotiates within this terrain. The book opens with Perry's war-hero uncle, Lefty, taking him on the round of neighborhood bars to sing for Lefty's drinks. From this we learn a bit about Lefty's history, which remains mysteriously elusive right up to the point when he disappears, leaving Perry in charge of his clarinet. Yet Lefty returns in other stories, resurrected in the memories of others, a part of the neighborhood lore.

This device—the resurfacing of a character, or setting—gives the book much of its connective tissue. The same pier where Perry's father took him and his younger brother, Mick, to swim when they were children will recur when, as an adolescent, Perry branches out of the neighborhood with his friends. What was laden with import to a child will appear ordinary to the young man. For example, when the marching band violates neighborhood boundaries and ventures into an area dominated by rival gangs, Perry's escape through the alleys and back to the protective familiarity of the El is presented almost as grotesquerie—vivid, outlandish, menacing. Later, that same territory will appear diminished, ordinary, something to skim over as he rides the trains north to new adventures.

Adventurousness is the point of *I Sailed with Magellan*—the title comes from a song Perry's brother repeated nightly as they went to sleep, but it represents the urge for exploration, the desire to cross boundaries and discover new lands. It represents, as well, the risk one takes in doing so, whether it is a physical expedition or a journey into memory or imagination. In either case, one hovers on the verge of discovery, and it takes courage to step through the portal into the unknown.

"Blue Boy" illustrates this particular risk as Perry recalls the story of the younger brother of a classmate. Ralphie was small, and sickly, and died young, on a Christmas Eve. When the class is asked by the nun to write a Christmas composition dedicated to Ralphie's memory, Perry wants to use his essay to communicate with Camille, the girl who has caught his interest. He begins by telling the story of shopping for Christmas trees with his father, but that takes complicated,

Scroogelike turns. Giving up, he imagines Ralphie's funeral, and this takes him into regions of empathy and imagination new to him. In the end, he flees the apartment and walks through the winter night, thinking not only of Ralphie but of other kids he had known who had died:

> They couldn't feel the cold because they were the cold. Maybe they could hear the wind, but they couldn't see how even colder than earth the boulder of moon looked through the flocked branches of back yard trees. I stopped, made a snowball, hurled it, and the snow knocked from the tree maintained the shape of branches in midair for a moment before disintegrating.
>
> (p. 148)

Perry has seen the world with fresh eyes, and when he returns he crumples his essay, tosses it in the wastebasket, and faces the consequences in school the next morning. Camille, of course, wins the contest, but with something so contrived that Ralphie's older brother angrily protests that "she shouldn't make stuff up about him" (p. 151). But if this were the story, it would be a conventional story. Dybek himself has crossed a threshold, and the story moves in and out of its narrative arc, taking into account not only Perry's growing awareness of others but Camille's self-conscious embarrassment over her breasts, his father's hard, blue-collar life, his father's death, his own inability to bridge the gaps that even love won't bridge. Serious themes are introduced in the form of digressions that, at this stage in Dybek's career, are so deftly handled that they have become a part of the grain. Yet within these important subjects, the story also manages to describe in fantastic detail a parade in which Tito Guízar, the Mexican movie star, rides down the streets on a prancing white horse, waving his sombrero.

I Sailed with Magellan is perhaps the perfect definition of what Dybek claimed he was striving for: "perception changed through intense, sometimes ecstatic moments" (Ligon et al.). Music accentuates this, providing yet another interconnection. Each character seems to make a musical imprint, or have a signature song. In these ways the neighborhood becomes mythic, but not in the manner of the older stories where

STUART DYBEK

fantastical things happened; instead, the ordinary is now seen (or heard) through a prism in which it becomes, at times, miraculous: the parade of the disabled, the shadow of the El, the snow. The ecstatic moments allow for insight into another world, another way of seeing and being.

Many of the stories reproduce this essential gateway into the adult world, fraught with complicating factors. Perhaps one of the most intricate is "Breasts," where Joe, an inept, thuggish hit man, seems to thwart his own mission through a series of lifelike encounters with various women from his past. They appear and disappear in quick succession so that the reader uneasily senses that they are part memory, part desire, and part denial. The story weaves in and out of fantasy/memory so that each woman rises from Joe's drugged stupor and recedes again, as though they were figments of his imagination, conjured to prevent him from doing what he knows he has to do. This alone would make for a delightful story, but because of the interwoven details of the collection, there is more to tell. Joe finally manages to kill his target, Johnny Sovereign, whose death promptly becomes part of neighborhood lore. Another thread is introduced with the appearance of Teo, a street wrestler gone to seed, who now composes poems in his mind. Teo and Zip recount stories of Uncle Lefty, whose presence still pervades the bar. Teo shows up in a blue tank top with a bird mask. His interior monologue hints at further stories:

With a message to carry, there isn't time to ride a thermal of blazing roses, to fade briefly from existence like a daylight moon. What vandal cracked its pane? The boy whose slingshot shoots cat's-eye marbles? The old man with a cane, who baits a tar roof with hard corn then waits with his pellet gun, camouflaged by a yellowed curtain of Bohemian lace?

Falcons that roost among gargoyles, feral cats, high-voltage wires, plate glass that mirrors sky—so many ways to fall from blue. When men fly they know by instinct they defy.

(p. 101)

"Breasts" also makes its convoluted way back to Perry's family, through his father's odd stammer and fierce instructions. Perry's younger brother,

Mick, plays with Johnny Sovereign's son, and this leads to the moment when Mick unwittingly terrifies Johnny's widow. Everything connects but in unexpected ways—ways beyond the realm of logic, ways that can only be understood long afterward, and maybe below the threshold of language.

Language emerges as a particular obsession in *I Sailed with Magellan*; Dybek creates ecstatic states by using what might be termed the poetry of prose. The effect is twofold: at times a story reaches closure in the form of epiphany, with language at its center; at times language opens up the story to further questions, creates its own doorway, so to speak. Take, for example, the device of repetition. After hearing Yehuda Amichai read a poem called "We Did It," Dybek began his own poetic riff on "We Didn't," which diverged quickly into story. Still, its opening is a list poem of sorts:

We didn't in the light; we didn't in darkness. We didn't in the fresh-cut summer grass or in the mounds of autumn leaves or on the snow where moonlight threw down our shadows. We didn't in your room on the canopy bed you slept in, the bed you'd slept in as a child, or in the backseat of my father's rusted Rambler, which smelled of the smoked chubs and kielbasa he delivered on weekends from my uncle Vincent's meat market. We didn't in your mother's Buick Eight, where a rosary twined the rearview mirror like a beaded, black snake with silver, cruciform fangs.

At the dead end of our lovers' lane—a side street of abandoned factories—where I perfected the pinch that springs open a bra, behind the lilac bushes in Marquette Park, where you first touched me through my jeans and your nipples, swollen against transparent cotton, seemed the shade of lilacs; in the balcony of the now defunct Clark Theater, where I wiped popcorn salt from my palms and slid them up your thighs and you whispered, "I feel like Doris Day is watching us," we didn't.

(p. 233)

There are twelve pages between the opening list of where they didn't and the final paragraph—twelve pages in which a police car's flashing lights over the beach interrupt the lovers because the body of a drowned woman has been discovered, and so instead of "the time they did," they

77

encounter the whirring activities and machinations of tragedy. At the end of the story, the narrator somewhat ruefully returns to second-guessing the relationship that didn't quite happen, a repetition of the might-have-beens that were initially comic. In this case, the tinge of humor is part of the poetry, and it also heightens the irony: life intervened, or rather, death intervened until: "because of fate, karma, luck, what does it matter?—we made not doing it a wonder, and yet we didn't, we didn't, we never did" (p. 246). The reader is forced to see the irony in all the lost moments of our lives that make up our time lines just as potently as what we actually did.

So many things don't happen in *I Sailed with Magellan.* Perry and his buddies Stosh and Angel never do make it to the Mexico of their dreams. But they do manage their own small rebellions. Teo writes his poetry and Perry's father swims far out into Lake Michigan, but only in their heads. The reader, however, has experienced the events—the sensations and the emotions and the ecstasy—even knowing that no one has actually escaped the confines of the city. By the end of the book, Perry's family has moved away from Little Village, and thus the neighborhood can remain in the timeless arena of childhood. Even the title of the final story—"Je Reviens"—is given in another language. "I Return" is the one impossibility. The narrator, dressed in a too-small suit from Robert Hall and the inherited topcoat that he doesn't quite fit, inhabits not so much the old spaces of childhood as the fluid state where, as the reader understands, he will sail off the brink into a larger world, enlarged now by both memory and possibility, poised, like Magellan before him, on the threshold of discovering what he already knows.

Within one year, in 2004, *Streets in Their Own Ink* was published. The book's cover proclaims "Poems," and this time the poems are, for the most part, traditionally lineated, many paying attention to more formal aspects of craft. Sound, for example, is more prominent, as in the wonderful progression of the rhymes in "Chord." In "Vespers" and "Autobiography" the cityscape is once again revived in poetry, accompanied by sound until the images reverberate with renewed significance. Opening with "Autobiography" and closing with "Anti-Memoir," *Streets in Their Own Ink* examines the realms of memory and dream in such a way that the two are nearly interchangeable.

WHAT TRANSCENDS GENRE

As of 2012, Stuart Dybek was on the verge of publishing two more simultaneous collections: a much expanded edition of his 1993 chapbook, to be published under the original title, *The Story of Mist*; and a highly autobiographical collection of linked short stories. Many of its pieces have been published as nonfiction, though one chapter, "Vigil," was published in the *Atlantic*'s 2011 fiction issue. Dybek is calling the work a "nonfiction novel," as Frederick Exley called *A Fan's Notes,* just to indicate that it is not memoir he is after. Dybek also has boxes and boxes of uncollected manuscripts—stories and poems that are still waiting for the right framework. He is willing to wait, honing his craft and carefully orchestrating how his work will be presented.

Dybek's works have been favorably reviewed on the occasion of their publication, but, possibly because of the long intervals between books, and possibly because of his mix of genres, there has been relatively little academic work done on his complete oeuvre. He has, however, been interviewed numerous times, enough that he has become adept at articulating the issues that most concern him. With the advent of his two new ventures, and since he has been the recipient of the nation's most prestigious awards, his work will likely begin to attract the additional scholarly attention it deserves.

In the broadest sense, Dybek's vision is one of America; his characters emerge from their ethnicity—from the chaos and hard work and aspirations of the immigrant experience—and dream the big dreams. Often, they come to knowledge as apprentices to someone older. His boys are the equivalent of Huckleberry Finn, and, like Huck, they learn the wonders and responsibilities of freedom. The country is large enough, bighearted enough, to hold his characters' desires and give

them voice. As he takes them into an uncertain future, the one certainty is that his books will enhance and enlarge the nation's literature.

In 2007 Dybek participated in a lengthy discussion with the editors of *Willow Springs,* where they talked about hybrid forms—from the novel in stories, to the prose poem, to the term "creative nonfiction"—and in that interview he maintained that his interest was not in genre per se but in what a melding or mixture might produce: "What one is ideally trying to do is to generate a dynamic interaction between the various elements." The interview makes clear that Dybek has thought extensively about how his arrangement and sequencing act as his own form of jazz, allowing him to extemporize within generic constraints:

> One reason to work with linked stories or a novel in stories is to escape a certain tyranny of chronology, without losing the power of narrative in the process. ... chronology too can invite you to fall into this numbing pattern of first this happened, then next this happened. ... Obviously there's a valence that is necessary as to what moments in our lives or imaginations are important enough to get written about that has nothing to do with chronology.

> At the same time, fiction is a temporal art. Its main subject is time. Its great power is chronology, because chronology has an inescapable way of translating into cause and effect. It's deceptive and illusory, but that's the power of linear narrative. ... But linear narration is only one way to perceive reality, and one of the things I like about a novel in stories is that it offers other ways to look at reality. Stories can be beads on a string but the form of linked stories can also offer a more crystalline, gemlike, faceted form.

Speaking of poetry in the interview, Dybek resists the notion that the poem is close kin to nonfiction. Describing Eliot's *The Waste Land* as a "novel," and asserting the importance of "place" in the work of Robert Frost, he reclaims some fictional terrain for the poem. Dybek goes on to assert that what he does within his work is only "a rearrangement of time, so that one isn't breaking chronology so much as allowing fictional form precedence over it." His experiments, he claims, are ways to free him from a writer's natural sense of control: "Control is only a temporary state. The state you want to get to is surrender."

Nothing demands surrender as much as letting one's work be adapted to the stage. In 2006 Laura Eason used three stories from *The Coast of Chicago* to evoke the mood and timbre of the old neighborhood. Creating an adult Dybek character/narrator, who spends a sleepless night turning over his memories, the production managed to convey both the everyday and the miraculous. By all reports the play functions as a visual representation of the author's imagination—hinging on the character of the author who articulates his need to examine more than one possibility. The theater becomes the canvas on which his vision is represented as the "actors" cast their colors on the plot. In 2007 Claudia Allen adapted *I Sailed with Magellan* for the stage without quite the same success. Trying for more narrative, the play emerged more as a study in family, something that Dybek had resisted in the original. Still, the play gave visual shape to Dybek's earlier assertion in the *Morning News* that "you can inhabit the world of memory in a way that someone can inhabit the world of dreams."

This assertion is reiterated in the more recent interview in *Willow Springs* (Ligon et al.): "I think one of the things you're trying to write about is memory itself; that is, memory itself has become a subject. And so that has a lot to do with your need to re-invent—not to remember."

In summer 2009, speaking with the editors of the literary journal *Our Stories,* Dybek repeated his particular parameters and attempted to place his work in the longer tradition:

> It is that preservation of memory—in "preserving" it, one is, of course, also interpreting it, recreating it, asserting ownership and control over its relative nature—that figures in discussions of writing a personal history, a family history, a tribal history, a global history. As a younger writer, writing when my immigrant and first generation extended family were all alive I looked back to their past, our past. I felt I was writing out of affection and hoped that if they read what I wrote they would feel that. Most of them are gone now. I think I am facing in a different direction now that the past generation is gone, toward the generation beyond mine.

Whatever genre Dybek chooses as he looks to the future, the result will most likely be unconventional. His essential aim will continue

to be reinvention, animating the field of memory and time. That Stuart Dybek has successfully devoted himself to his craft, and to his stated ambitions within the craft, can be measured in his own wry comment to James Plath: "I mean, sometimes I forget that there's a real Chicago."

Selected Bibliography

WORKS OF STUART DYBEK

POETRY
Brass Knuckles. Pittsburgh: University of Pittsburgh Press, 1979.

Streets in Their Own Ink. New York: Farrar, Straus and Giroux, 2004.

PROSE
Childhood and Other Neighborhoods. New York: Viking, 1980. (Stories.)

The Coast of Chicago. New York: Knopf, 1990. (Stories).

I Sailed with Magellan. New York: Farrar, Straus and Giroux, 2003.(Novel in stories.)

OTHER WORKS
The Story of Mist. Brockport, N.Y.: State Street Press, 1993. (Chapbook.)

"Chicago Aquamarine." *America.gov—Engaging the World*. Bureau of International Information Programs, U.S. Department of State, December 9, 2010. http://www .america.gov/st/peopleplace-english/2010/July/ 20100728165158yeldnahc0.3263651.html&distid=ucs. (Article.)

CRITICAL AND BIOGRAPHICAL STUDIES
Gladsky, Thomas S. "From Ethnicity to Multiculturalism: The Fiction of Stuart Dybek." *MELUS* 20, no. 2:105–118 (summer 1995).

Lee, Don. "About Stuart Dybek: A Profile." *Ploughshares* 24, no 1:192–198 (spring 1998). http://www.pshares.org/ read/article-detail.cfm?intArticleID+4466.

REVIEWS
Clewell, David. "Vital Assurances." *Chowder Review* 14:64–67 (spring–summer 1980). (Review of *Brass Knuckles*.)

Dilworth, Sharon. "*I Sailed with Magellan* by Stuart Dybek; *The Stranger at the Palazzo D'Oro* by Paul Theroux." Post-Gazette.com (Pittsburgh, Pa.), February 8, 2004. http://www.post-gazette.com/books/reviews/20040208 shorts0208fnp6.asp.

Febles, Jorge. "Dying Players: Ramírez's 'El Centerfielder' and Dybek's 'Death of the Rightfielder.' " *Confluencia* 12, no. 1:156–167 (fall 1996).

Kakutani, Michiko. "Lyrical Loss and Desolation of Misfits in Chicago." *New York Times,* April 20, 1990, p. C31. (Review of *The Coast of Chicago*.)

Lee, Don. Review of *The Coast of Chicago*. *Ploughshares* 17, no. 1:228–229 (spring 1991).

Miller, Adrienne. "Return of a Master." Review-a-Day, Esquire.com, December 17, 2003. http://www.powells. com/review/2003_12_17.html. (Review of *I Sailed with Magellan*.)

Murphy, Richard. "Stuart Dybek's *The Story of Mist* and Naomi Shihab Nye's *Mint*." *Prose Poem: An International Journal* 3, 1994. http://digitalcommons.providence.edu/ cgi/viewcontent.cgi?article=1240&context=prosepoem.

Saner, Reg. Review of *Brass Knuckles*. *Ohio Review* 25:113–119 (1980).

Ward, Robert. Review of *Childhood and Other Neighborhoods* and *Brass Knuckles*. *Northwest Review* 18, no. 3:149–157 (1980).

INTERVIEWS
Birnbaum, Robert. "Birnbaum v. Stuart Dybek." *Morning News,* October 5, 2005. http://www.themorningnews.org/ article/stuart-dybek.

"Interview: Stuart Dybek, Author." *Chicagoist,* September 14, 2005. http://www.chicagoist.com/2005/09/14/ interview_stuart_dybek_author.php.

Kadetsky, Elizabeth, Justin Nicholes, and Alexis Enrico Santi. "Interview with a Master: Stuart Dybek." *Our Stories,* summer 2009. http://www.ourstories.us/ Summer_2009/Interview_StuartDybek.html.

Ligon, Samuel, Adam O'Connor Rodriguez, Dan J. Vice, and Zachary Vineyard. "A Conversation with Stuart Dybek, May 18, 2007." *Willow Springs* 61, spring 2008. http://www.willowsprings.ewu.edu/interviews/dybek.php.

McCollister, MaryAnne, ed. "An Interview with Stuart Dybek." *Vestal Review* 36, 2011. http://www.vestalreview. net/dybekWeb.html.

Pearce, Barry. "Interview with Stuart Dybek." *Other Voices* 29, fall–winter 1998. http://webdelsol.com/Other_Voices/ DybekInt.htm.

Pearce, Matt. "A Conversation with Stuart Dybek." *Missouri Review* 31, no. 2:116–132 (summer 2008).

Plath, James. "An Interview with Stuart Dybek." *Cream City Review* 15, no. 1:1–13 (1991). http://www.iwu.edu/ ˜jplath/dybek.html.

Rubin, Stan Sanvel. "Stuart Dybek—Fiction." Writers

Forum Video Tape Library, College at Brockport, SUNY, November 10, 1993. Tape no. V-833. 58 min.

Seaman, Benjamin. "A Conversation with Stuart Dybek and Edward Hirsch." *Artful Dodge*, April 1988. http://www3 .wooster.edu/artfuldodge/interviews/dybekhirsch.htm.

Seaman, Donna. "A Conversation with Stuart Dybek." *Triquarterly* 123:15–26 (winter 2006).

"Stuart Dybek: The TNB Self-Interview." *Nervous Breakdown,* December 19, 2009. http://www.thenervous breakdown.com/sdybek/2009/12/stuart-dybek-the-tnb -self-interview/.

TheWritingDisorder.com. "The Art of the Writer with Stuart Dybek," spring 2011.http://www.thewritingdisorder.com/ nonfictiondybek.html.

PLAYS BASED ON THE WORKS OF STUART DYBEK

The Coast of Chicago. Adapted for the stage by Laura Eason. Walkabout Theater Company, Chicago, January 12–February 19, 2006.

I Sailed with Magellan. Adapted for the stage by Claudia Allen. Victory Gardens Theater, Chicago, June 18–July 15, 2007.

ZEE EDGELL

(1940—)

J. Roger Kurtz

THE NOVELIST ZEE Edgell is generally recognized as the most prominent writer to come from the Caribbean nation of Belize. She is an international figure who has spent much of her adult working life based in the United States, but she has also worked for extended periods in Africa, Asia, and the Caribbean. Edgell has published four major novels and a number of short stories, most of which focus on the experience of Belizean women and girls and on the history of Belize itself, with its complex social and racial dynamics.

LIFE

Zee Edgell was born Zelma Inez Tucker on October 21, 1940, in Belize City, the capital of the colony which at that time was known as British Honduras but which changed its name to Belize on achieving independence from Britain on September 21, 1981. Her parents, Clive and Veronica (Walker) Tucker, were both Creole, a term that in the Belizean context generally denotes a combination of African and European ancestry. Her father worked for an import-export company, eventually becoming its director, while her mother was a homemaker who enjoyed and wrote poetry. Zelma was the eldest of nine siblings. Neither of her parents received a formal education, but Zee Edgell herself attended a Catholic school for both her primary and secondary schooling. She describes herself as an average or even mediocre student during those years, noting that her later success would have surprised her teachers. She subsequently attended the Polytechnic of Central London, where she earned a diploma in journalism in 1965, and she also went on to graduate study at the University of the West Indies.

Edgell's early career interests were principally in journalism and education. One of her first jobs was working for the *Daily Gleaner,* a newspaper based in Kingston, Jamaica. From 1966 to 1968 she taught at her alma mater in Belize City, St. Catherine's Academy, which serves as the model for the Catholic girls' school that appears in her first novel, where it is called "St. Cecilia's Academy." During this time she also edited a newspaper in Belize City. In 1968 she married an American, Alvin G. Edgell, who at the time was the local director for the humanitarian agency CARE, and whose career in international development led them to live and work together in Nigeria, Afghanistan, Bangladesh, and Somalia through affiliations with the Peace Corps and other development organizations. Together they raised a daughter (Holly Emma) and a son (Randall Clive). After Belize achieved political independence in 1981, Zee Edgell was appointed to positions in government, working as director of the Women's Bureau (1981–1982) and as director of the Department of Women's Affairs (1986–1987).

Edgell's creative writing received immediate acclaim when her first novel, *Beka Lamb,* was published in 1982 in the prominent Heinemann Caribbean Writers Series, bringing her recognition as the first Belizean writer to reach an international audience. The novel won the 1983 Fawcett Society Book Prize, an award sponsored by a British nonprofit organization that during the 1980s and 1990s recognized new fiction contributing to global awareness of women's issues. Her subsequent novels also appeared in the Caribbean Writers Series, and Zee Edgell's work has now achieved canonical status in the corpus of anglophone Caribbean literature. In 2007 Edgell was declared a Member of the Order

of the British Empire (MBE), an award originally established to recognize military service in World War I but that today recognizes service of a more general nature and may be granted to individuals who are not British citizens. She received an honorary doctoral degree from the University of the West Indies in 2009.

Edgell taught in the Department of English at Kent State University (Ohio) for sixteen years until her retirement in 2009, having achieved the rank of full professor. She primarily taught courses in international literature and creative writing, in addition to doing her own writing and touring for book readings and lectures on the history and literature of Belize. After retirement, she and her husband settled in St. Louis, Missouri.

LITERARY THEMES AND FEATURES

Edgell's novels explore the social and political dynamics of Belizean history through the perspective of female protagonists. These include the teenager Beka Lamb in her first novel, the young professional Pavana Leslie in *In Times Like These* (1991), the mestiza Luz Marina, who is accused of murdering her husband in *The Festival of San Joaquin* (1997), and Leah Lawson, the young slave and eventual slave owner whose full and varied life is told in the historical novel *Time and the River* (2007).

In Edgell's works, the female experience requires a precarious negotiation of dangerous social terrain. Whereas stories about female characters in the works of many other Caribbean women writers tend to focus on the mother-daughter conflict, this is less obviously the case for the women in Edgell's stories, who instead are preoccupied with the struggle to make their way in a patriarchal and racist social sphere that limits, oppresses, or even crushes them. None of her protagonists are heroic or even unusually virtuous; rather, they illustrate the quotidian challenges of everyday individuals in an unjust social structure. These are characters who are struggling to get by and to find joy in their lives, usually under conditions of severely limited resources, knowledge, and social power.

The female protagonists in these novels also serve to remind readers of the important roles played by women throughout Belizean history. The region's major political leaders before, during, and after the independence movement were male. As a result, many accounts of Belizean history emphasize the accomplishments of men. In contrast to these mainstream historical accounts, Edgell's novels bring women's participation in these historical events to the fore, highlighting their accomplishments and bringing to light the activities of women that have been generally overlooked. As she said in an interview with Irma McClaurin, "I think more women than men were in the streets supporting the early leaders. They contributed money and labor. But apart from very token acknowledgment of their contribution, the women were not part of the dialogue. They weren't part of the discourse" ("A Writer's Life"). Edgell's novels serve to refocus that discourse to include women's experience.

More recently, historians have recognized the important role of women in Belizean history, offering confirmation of Edgell's novelistic treatment of this issue. In a survey of women's political movements, *From Colony to Nation: Women Activists and the Gendering of Politics in Belize, 1912–1982,* Anne Macpherson argues that although women were not leaders of the political elite, they played a central role in two key social arenas: in the reform movements of the middle class, and in the popular labor and nationalist movements. It was the alliances among these groups, in which women were key players, that made possible and shaped the independence movement in Belize. Macpherson notes that both Edgell's novels and her work in the Women's Bureau are integrally connected to the struggle for women's political participation in the country. Similarly, Irma McClaurin's ethnographic overview, *Women of Belize: Gender and Change in Central America,* argues that Edgell's novels authentically reflect many facets of the female experience in that country.

Modern Caribbean history is replete with violence, which is a reality that runs throughout Edgell's works. Without highlighting this violence in a sensational or even a particularly dramatic

way, the characters in her novels are tragically vulnerable, both to the social violence of a brutal slave economy as well as to powerful natural forces such as hurricanes and floods that can be especially devastating in an underdeveloped country like Belize. The reality of death is always near at hand for her characters; sickness, accidents, and mental illness are often the fate of those individuals who live on the margins of a country that is also marginalized in the global economy.

To read Edgell's novels is to receive a primer in the history and social composition of Belize. *Beka Lamb* is set in the period of nationalist ferment before independence, highlighting the conflict between those who wished to retain a relationship with Britain as a way of resisting the perceived threat of being overtaken by neighboring Guatemala, and those chafing under British colonialism. Her second and third novels are set in the time period following independence, and they portray the tensions that arise in this nation-building era. Her fourth novel, *Time and the River,* jumps back to the late eighteenth and early nineteenth centuries, at the height of the slavery period, which in Belize was principally centered on the lumber industry. In all these works, the characters and their relationships are carefully calibrated to reflect the coming together of the various racial and ethnic groups that have constituted Belize in recent centuries. In a setting where racial identity is so determinative of social status and of opportunities, Edgell's novels reveal how characters fit into that structure as well as how they complicate or attempt to undermine it.

In its style, Edgell's fiction is grounded in a resolutely realistic mode of narration, growing out of the tradition of British literary realism. In an interview with Renee Shea, Edgell cited Dickens and Twain as formative influences. Her works emphasize verisimilitude in depicting historical and everyday events and in describing the inner and outer lives of individual characters. She does not include fantastic or miraculous elements in the manner of magical realism. The narrative voice is coherent and consistent, the plot is linear and logical, and there is no attempt to deploy the fragmented, multivocal aesthetics of post-modernism. Using either a first-person narrative voice (as in *The Festival of San Joaquin*) or the third person (in the other three novels), Edgell's style is traditional rather than experimental. The narrative is at pains to identify the precise location and historical moment of its events. The innovation and interest of her works lie in their subject matter, in the sympathetic manner in which Edgell introduces us to her often flawed characters, and in their attempts to present what for most readers will be a fresh literary perspective on the history of an often overlooked and marginalized nation.

In literary studies, the term "postcolonial" is frequently used to describe writings from those parts of the world—primarily in Africa, Asia, and the Caribbean—that achieved independence from European colonial rule during the twentieth century. Despite their geographical and cultural differences, and despite the different forms of colonial rule imposed by the British, French, Portuguese, and others, it is generally recognized that postcolonial writers from all these areas share common concerns and challenges, resulting in a recurring set of themes and strategies that define a recognizable postcolonial genre. In this respect Edgell's work is distinctively postcolonial, not only in its subject matter but also in the way that it illustrates many of the typical thematic preoccupations of this category of literature by writers of her generation.

A dominant postcolonial imperative is to narrate the untold facets of the national story, to give voice to individuals who were previously voiceless. In places like Africa or the Caribbean, an overwhelming amount of writing about those regions—fiction, travelogues, histories, ethnographic studies, and the like—has been composed by the colonizers and other outsiders, with the unfortunate result that these writings reflect the blind spots and stereotypes of their authors. Postcolonial authors feel the urge to "write back," to offer an alternative story of their community from the perspective of the colonized subject. Edgell's writing fits firmly within this tradition. She has noted, for example, that the British author Aldous Huxley wrote a travel account in which he described Belize in a dismissive and patronizing

manner, as an "all but uninhabited" region devoid of interest and promise. As Edgell told Renee Shea, "This is one reason why I feel it is necessary to write back" ("Interview," p. 582).

There are additional themes and narrative preoccupations shared by Edgell and other postcolonial writers. Because they have often had access to a level of education that is denied to many of their compatriots, the works of postcolonial writers frequently demonstrate an awareness of and sometimes an uneasiness about their status as intellectuals. Often, their protagonists may be read as allegorically presenting the tensions and dilemmas of being an intellectual in such a setting. They are also often concerned with the question of national identity. What does it mean to be a citizen of a country like Belize, in which many of the original inhabitants have been eradicated and where ethnicity, language, and history make a unified sense of identity difficult? In Edgell's case, these dynamics are particularly relevant in her first novel, where the teenage Beka Lamb seems obviously allegorical of both the nation of Belize as well as of intellectual women leaders like Zee Edgell.

Like many postcolonial writers, Edgell has spent a great deal of her adult life outside of her country of birth. These are the years during which she has created most of her enduring literary art. Perhaps inevitably, her writing contains a certain amount of yearning and nostalgia. "My novels are an attempt to reconstruct the fragmented images and myriad memories of Belize," she admitted to McClaurin ("A Writer's Life"). This reality is typical of many postcolonial writers, who for varying reasons end up creating their literary works abroad.

Finally, it is fair to say that the majority of postcolonial writers believe that art—including the art embodied in their writing—should contain some sort of social relevance for their societies. This attitude explicitly rejects the notion that fine art exists for its own sake, in some rarified reality that is removed from political and social existence. For most postcolonial writers, literature exists to make a positive impact on their world, and their primary responsibility as writers is not so much to their craft as it is to their audience or their people. These works are often described as comprising a "literature of commitment" or, in a term commonly applied to francophone postcolonial works, *littérature engagée*. Although Edgell's writing is not overtly protest literature, nor is it an obvious example of the "disillusionment literature" that many postcolonial writers created in response to unfulfilled social aspirations following independence, her work is nevertheless firmly engaged with Belize's political history, and as such is distinctly within the broader tradition of postcolonial literature.

BEKA LAMB

Zee Edgell's first novel, *Beka Lamb,* has the distinction of being the first novel by a Belizean writer to achieve international recognition, having been published in Heinemann's Caribbean Writers Series in 1982 and having won the Fawcett Society Book Prize the following year. *Beka Lamb* is a coming-of-age story about a young girl growing up in Belize City in the 1950s. Through Beka's story, the novel also highlights the political and historical experiences of Belize from that period.

A salient feature of *Beka Lamb* is its plot structure, with the majority of the novel constituting an elaborate flashback. Beka's best friend, Toycie, has just died under tragic circumstances, and Beka is determined to hold a proper wake for her. Late in the evening, as her parents retire for bed, and while her grandmother attends a political rally in support of nationalist politicians, Beka goes upstairs and ponders the previous eight months of her life and her friendship with Toycie. The lengthy flashback concludes in the final chapter, when we are returned to the present time.

Beka is the fifteen-year-old daughter of Bill and Lilla Lamb. Her father is a modestly successful businessman, head of one of the "few black families on Cashew Street that had much of anything at all" (pp. 20–21). Her parents are politically conservative, eager to advance socially and economically within the existing system, although their prospects are limited because they are Creole. They favor continued political

dependence on England in contrast to the more politically engaged Granny Ivy (Bill's mother), who is interested in independence and a political alliance with the colony's Spanish-speaking neighbors such as Guatemala. Although it is subordinated to Beka's personal story, the political setting in *Beka Lamb* is crucial to the narrative, to the extent that the novel is frequently described as a national allegory.

At the start of the novel, we learn that Beka has just won an essay-writing contest at her school. Winning this contest is something of a surprise, since just the year before, Beka's academic performance was so miserable that her parents, especially her father, now question whether she should return to school. Much of the narrative tension in the first half of the novel revolves around whether or not she will be allowed to go back to St. Cecilia's Academy. Although she has not particularly applied herself, Beka does at some level understand that her education is a rare opportunity for someone of her social position.

Toycie's death, which occurs in the second half, is the more seriously tragic plot element. Toycie was raised in extreme poverty by a foster mother, Miss Eila, having been abandoned at an early age by her parents. The house in which she lives is "not a 'dawg-siddown' or lean-to, but it nearly could have been" (p. 32). During the school year, Toycie spends increasing time with her boyfriend, Emilio Villanueva, and when she has to miss school because of sickness it becomes evident that she is pregnant. Under pressure from his family, Emilio abandons Toycie, and she is expelled from school. Her attempt at suicide fails, and she is committed to the Belize Mental Asylum. Toycie is sent to a rural area for convalescence, and she dies when a tree falls on her during a hurricane.

The ancestry of each character is crucial to their relationships and to the overall plot. Both Beka and Toycie are Creole, but Emilio is *pania* (in this context, a term interchangeable with "mestizo"), meaning that he has mixed Spanish and Native American ancestry. *Panias* occupy a somewhat privileged position in the social order, and most of the students at St. Cecilia's Academy

are either *panias* or *bakras* (white Belizeans). Beka's father works for Mr. Blanco, whose Spanish name and heritage mark his superior social position. When Toycie becomes involved with Emilio, we are reminded of this Creole-mestizo conflict and the vital connection of race to Belizean politics.

Had she survived the school year without these complications, it is likely that Toycie would have won the school's essay competition. Instead, it is won by Beka for a historical paper on her school and her country. In the end, Beka has changed from a lackadaisical student to one who wishes to explore her past more closely. She concludes her wake for Toycie with a sense of relief and even optimism: "her watch-night for Toycie was over and she felt released—there was need no more for guilt or grief over a mourning postponed" (p. 171).

Because of the overt parallels between Belize's emerging political consciousness and the coming-of-age experiences of the adolescent Beka, it is easy to read *Beka Lamb* as a metaphorical commentary on the early growth and development of the nation of Belize. In fact, we might see both Beka and Toycie as representatives of Belizean identity and of the possible directions or outcomes for the country. In this regard, tragedy is mixed with hope, and we are left with an image of possible future growth, although it seems important that healthy national development be based on an authentic, local, Belizean identity. Edgell uses floral imagery to send home this point. Beka's mother never manages to successfully establish the rose bush that she desires in her garden; instead, it is the tropical bougainvillea that will flourish, but only after it has been pruned and managed and prevented from running wild—rather like Beka herself.

In the process, gender issues are brought to the fore, as the options for many Belizean women are shown to be limited or stifling. Toycie and Beka were "different on the street where economic necessity forced many Creole girls to leave school after elementary education to help at home" (p. 34). When Toycie is expelled from school for her pregnancy but Emilio is not, it reveals a profound double standard in the way

women are treated. Beka's father, Bill, is well meaning but authoritarian, and ultimately it is the female characters who drive the plot by offering support and alternative role models to the girls Toycie and Beka. The nuns who teach in Beka's school offer examples of women who either support and submit to a patriarchal system, or who inspire Beka by their resistance to it.

Beka inhabits a landscape marked by death. She and Toycie enjoy spending much of their time in a graveyard near the lighthouse. Baron Bliss's grave is a reminder of the region's colonial heritage, but also of the fragility of life in this area. Beka has two siblings who died young, and Toycie's death is preceded by another funeral, this one for Beka's Great-Grandmother Straker. In a hospital scene, we are told of a "dead house" that is located at the rear of the hospital emergency room, where corpses are stored. All these images offer more than a simple memento mori, as they remind readers of the broader historical violence and destruction attending the colonial experience of the region. At one point, Granny Ivy tells Beka about a childhood memory of a circus that came to town with a polar bear. When the ice machine broke down, the polar bear died. Granny Ivy's strong emotional response to this memory reveals that she is mourning more than the death of a bear, seeing this as symbolic of the general condition of Belize. "Tings bruk down," she says through her tears (p. 16). This is what prompts Beka to begin the wake for her dead friend Toycie, an experience that begins her own journey toward healing.

Beka Lamb offers a particular perspective on the politics and history of Belize, mainly by offering an alternative view of the nationalist period from the perspective of "ordinary" individuals, rather than as a story of the heroic deeds of "great men." Indeed, there is a marvelous parody of that sort of history in a scene where Toycie and Beka are fooling around, staging a mock political rally complete with a rendition of the national anthem and its ironic lyrics: "Oh land of the Gods, by the Carib Sea, our manhood we pledge to thy liberte-ee" (pp. 44–45). Beka's parents support maintaining ties with England as a response to

the threat of annexation by Guatemala, whereas Granny Ivy attends rallies and meetings supporting the nationalist activities of the People's Independence Party and the General Workers' Union, whose leaders are arrested for sedition. As part of her maturation, Beka becomes gradually politicized. She gets some of her inspiration from a nun, Sister Bernadette, who is forbidden from teaching because she is considered too political. Beka's prize-winning essay on the history of the Catholic order that runs her school could easily have become a reiteration of the standard narrative praising the "civilizing mission" of colonialism. Instead, the essay is significant for the way that it draws on local, oral history. In the center of the essay, at its heart, is an account of "how it all looked to Mr. Rabatu, as an acolyte, standing in his robes waiting for them at the wharf" (p. 155). As a minor figure whose experience would not appear in standard written historical accounts, Rabatu and his story represent a "history from below" characterized by on oral accounts of ordinary individuals. Just as Beka succeeds in recasting Belizean history in her essay, Edgell's novel itself offers a new and alternative vision of the national experience.

Zee Edgell reports that she started to write *Beka Lamb* in Nigeria, she worked on it while living in Afghanistan, and she ultimately finished it while living in Bangladesh. The novel has been translated into German and Dutch, and selections have been included in anthologies of postcolonial writing. For a time, *Beka Lamb* was a required literature text for all secondary school students in Belize. Although it includes at times didactic commentary on the sociological realities of contemporary Belize, it is ultimately an effective meditation on the role of education and specifically of writing in the postcolonial Caribbean context. With insightful and evocative writing, Edgell has created an alternately tragic and optimistic tale that promotes an alternative remembrance of Belizean history—in essence serving as a "wake" for the ordinary people who through their actions during the pre-independence period made possible the creation of the present-day nation of Belize.

ZEE EDGELL

IN TIMES LIKE THESE

In Times Like These (1991) is set in 1981, the year of Belizean independence. Part historical novel, part psychological study, and part political thriller, it follows the experience of Pavana Leslie, a young professional woman who has studied in London and who is returning to Belize along with her twin children to contribute to the rebuilding of her nation at a tumultuous and uncertain moment of its history.

At the time of Independence, one of the political dilemmas for anglophone Belize was how to balance British influence against the influence of its Spanish-speaking neighbors. At issue was Guatemala's long-standing territorial interest in Belize, based on contested treaties dating back to the colonial era. Guatemala only recognized Belize's claim to sovereignty ten years after its independence, and the issue has continued to arise from time to time even since then. The driving political conflict of *In Times Like These* is the debate over a three-way political arrangement arrived at in March 1981 between Belize, Britain, and Guatemala, known as the "Heads of Agreement," which stipulated Guatemalan recognition of Belize's independence in exchange for access to ports on the Belizean coast. Strikes and protests against the agreement, on the grounds that it gave away too much to Guatemala, threw the government into crisis just on the eve of independence.

It is into this setting that Pavana Leslie returns to her homeland. She has accepted a governmental position with the newly created Women's Unit funded by the United Nations, and she is immediately swept up in political infighting that seems likely to overwhelm the bureau's ability to promote women's issues in any significant way. This all unfolds against the background of strikes, riots, and public actions protesting the Heads of Agreement, which is further complicated by the fact that Pavana's former lover, Alex Abrams, who is also father of her twins, has shifted political loyalties to become a leading politician in Belize who is trying to promote the Heads of Agreement.

Prior to her return, Pavana has spent a number of years working as a member of the "aided development community" in Somalia. These years have left her cynical about the ineffectiveness of international aid programs and the hypocrisy of aid workers who conduct lives of privilege and ease in nations where they claim to be helping the poor. She is just as cynical about her peers from her student days in London, a group of idealistic West Indian intellectuals who, as Alex puts it, "believed we were destined to pioneer a new breed of men and women in the Caribbean" (p. 279).

In the end, the novel is about the many forms that betrayal can take, about the challenge of holding on to the ideals of honesty when faced by the temptations of power, and about the difficulties of making sound choices in a complex and shifting world. The betrayals are personified by Alex Abrams, whose romance with Pavana is complicated by the presence of his German girlfriend, Helga. When Pavana reveals that she is pregnant, Alex gives her money to get an abortion, but he fails to pick her up at the clinic after her procedure. In any case, Pavana has decided against the abortion and keeps the twins, but she is forever embittered by Alex's treachery. When they return to Belize and she sees that Alex has sold out his earlier student-era ideals in order to take a position of political power, she feels betrayed again. There is some movement toward reconciliation, as Pavana introduces Alex to her children as their father and they begin spending time together. Political events intervene, however, as activists seek to pressure Alex to change his political stance, and the twins are abducted in an attempt to persuade him. Alex's half-brother, a disillusioned revolutionary aptly named Stoner Bennett, is active in the movement to dislodge the governing party; he becomes Alex's antagonist and foil. In the end the twins are safely rescued, but only after Alex himself is shot in a confusing melee. The end is sobering, as Pavana reflects on the betrayals and losses that have accompanied Belizean independence: "She was weeping now for her children, for Alex, for Stoner, for her parents, for herself, for all that had been tried and for all that had failed, for all the misunderstandings, the lies, the betrayals, for

her greater understanding of the underside of a humanity who loved winners" (p. 302).

As with the other novels, this tragic ending is tempered by hope, and Edgell concludes the story on a stoically optimistic note. Although *In Times Like These* illustrates the ways that ideals and good intentions can easily be warped by power, we can be encouraged by the way that Pavana, like Belize itself, has survived numerous difficulties and threats, and is managing to find some measure of self-determination. She does this in the face of a male-dominated system that is both corrupt and violent and that has the effect of stifling women's opportunities. With this novel, as Kristen Mahlis notes, Edgell "transforms the role of mother from passive victim to active educator and guardian" (p. 131), suggesting a way forward not only for women like Pavana but for Belize itself.

THE FESTIVAL OF SAN JOAQUIN *(1997)*

"I am out of gaol now," says the narrator, Luz Marina, at the start of *The Festival of San Joaquin* (p. 1). This is Edgell's third novel, and it offers a departure from her earlier works in two significant ways: for the first time, Edgell has elected to use a first-person narrative voice, and also for the first time she has a protagonist who is not Creole but rather from the mestizo community.

Luz Marina was jailed for fifteen months for killing her abusive husband, Salvador. Through a series of flashbacks and memories, we learn how she has arrived at this point, beginning from the time that she went to work as a domestic servant for Salvador's mother, Doña Catalina, and we follow her as she seeks to regain her standing in society. Like the earlier novels, *The Festival of San Joaquin* offers an incisive look at the experience of ordinary women in Belize and of how their experience is shaped by a violent patriarchal social system. It highlights the complexities of Belizean society, with a particular interest in the mestizo experience. One of the overriding themes is the search to create a healthy home, something that applies most obviously to the character of Luz but also to various other characters and, in a more abstract sense, to the nation of Belize itself.

Several reviewers have repeated the claim that the events in the novel are based on a specific real-life incident. In her interview with Renee Shea, however, Edgell herself noted that the story was actually inspired by several different incidents that she heard about during return visits to Belize.

Luz is born into a poor family in the town of San Joaquin, a small mestizo community some distance from Belize City. Her father, Papá Apolonio, is disabled and cannot always support the family as he would wish, and her mother, Mamá Sofía, blames herself for having only daughters, with no sons to help the family financially. Consequently, at the age of fourteen Luz goes to work as a domestic servant in the household of a prosperous landowning family, where she works for the next seven years. At first Luz finds a certain inspiration and empowerment in working for her employer, Doña Catalina. The money she makes and sends home is a tangible benefit to her family, and her father's health begins to improve.

Soon, however, Luz begins to see the many problems that beset even this well-off household for which she works. Although Doña Catalina is a strong woman, her husband, Don Pablo, neglects her and makes use of their wealth without consulting her. "I am a full partner," Doña Catalina tries to insist (p. 34), but Don Pablo regularly ignores her, and as time passes Luz observes that Doña Catalina has less and less influence and spends more time daydreaming about escape. Luz herself becomes romantically engaged with Salvador, one of the sons in the family. Although he appears to have a number of attractive qualities, he gradually becomes more like his father. He drinks too much and becomes increasingly abusive. At one point Salvador locks Luz in the house with their three children, and he insists on selling a small plot of land that she has inherited. Finally, she accidentally kills him during a violent, drunken attack on her and the children.

When she is released from prison, Luz makes the crucial decision to return home to San Joaquin rather than staying in the capital city where she would have the opportunity for greater anonymity.

Although one of her goals is emotional healing, she is also eager to regain custody of her children, who are in San Joaquin. As she returns to her parents' home, now in greater disarray than ever, one of her immediate challenges is finding work.

The Festival of San Joaquin makes explicit connections between domestic violence against women and exploitation of the land. The frustrations, limitations, and abuse that afflict both wealthy women like Doña Catalina and poorer women like Luz and Mamá Sofía reflect broader economic injustices. "In the novel, patriarchy and capitalism are inextricably bounded," suggests Julie Moody-Freeman (p. 50), noting how landowners such as Don Pablo exploit both their workers and the natural resources of the country. When Luz and her mother join other women in becoming members of an environmental action group to thwart exploitive land sales, this evokes the historical reality of "activist struggles that actually took place in Belize during the 1990s when Belizeans joined with international environmental groups to fight the sale of lands and the burning of trees" (Moody-Freeman, p. 51).

Like Edgell's earlier work, this novel presents and illuminates the complexity of Belize's social makeup. It depicts the encounter and sometimes the merging of various religious practices, as the Catholicism that dominates the town of San Joaquin (and its festival) is counterposed to evangelical Christianity as well as traditional religious beliefs. Tradition and modernity overlap as Luz relies for healing on the advice of her psychologist but insists on retaining a belief in ghosts and spirits that her doctor would like her to abandon. One of the accomplishments of the novel is that even as it highlights ethnic tensions and competing economic interests, it resists the depiction of a clear right or wrong side, except for the fact that in almost all these settings it is women who are most vulnerable and exploited. As Luz's mother notes, referring to women's experiences, "Here in San Joaquin we are always to blame" (p. 18).

Through the novel, the recurring emphasis on homes and houses shapes Luz's narrative, particularly as they relate to the female experience. Luz realizes that Doña Catalina's house, though opulent, is "a killer of women" in a figurative sense (p. 32). Houses can be a trap for women, as they are for Luz and other characters. The narrative tension revolves around what it means for Luz to return home after her incarceration, and whether she can create a new home after this tragic experience.

In the end, Luz Marina is reunited with her children, and there is a certain determination and even optimism that closes her story. Perhaps she can now set about creating the home that she has always desired. Nevertheless, this optimism is tempered by the tragic experiences of the preceding months, by the sense that not a great deal has changed in Belizean society, and by the knowledge that many of the wounds Luz has suffered will never be fully healed.

TIME AND THE RIVER *(2007)*

Time and the River is a historical novel that focuses on the period of Belizean history immediately preceding emancipation. The dates of the events are highlighted in the chapter headings, and they run from May 1798 to July 1822. As a whole, the novel offers an examination of the various ways that individuals sought to establish their identity and their humanity in the convoluted setting of the early years of the Belize settlement. The main narrative line features a love plot, with a series of unrequited and unrequitable romances among the central characters. A second story line focuses on the slave experience, including a series of Belizean slave revolts and the historical moment in 1807 when the slave trade (though not slavery itself) is abolished in the British colonies. As its larger theme, *Time and the River* illuminates the dehumanizing effects of the slavery system, and the difficult choices that are forced on all those who are caught in that system.

The novel's main characters are Leah Lawson and Will McGilvrey, two young slaves in the Belize settlement whose surnames derive from their British slave masters. In Leah's case, Graham Lawson is her master but also her father.

Lawson has fathered other nonwhite children, including Sukie, whose mother is a Miskito Indian and who is forever indignant at her "illegal" enslavement, since she is aware that British law technically forbids the enslavement of the Miskito. Though Lawson's connection to his various nonwhite children is widely known and openly acknowledged, they remain enslaved and it is only his white children who are legally recognized. Over the years, Lawson becomes increasingly dissipated and indebted, and as Leah grows into increasing self-awareness as a teenager, she understands that she and her family represent "the rag-tag end of Graham Lawson's property in slaves, which had once numbered between fifty and one hundred" (p. 36).

Will, meanwhile, is a slave belonging to Thomas McGilvrey. Like Lawson, McGilvrey is a British character who has moved to the Caribbean in the hopes of making a fortune. Will is at least ten years older than Leah, and as a result he is able to remember his childhood in Africa, his capture, and his abduction into slavery. His memories of his mother, from whom he was separated, and of his earlier life in freedom, sustain him and fuel his desire for emancipation. Will is valued for his ability to seek out and harvest the lumber from mahogany trees in the dense forests of the Belizean interior. He is happiest on the top of a tree, looking out over the landscape, since there he can be "alone, in charge of himself, at least for a little while" (p. 12). His dream is to live as free person on his own plot of land, even if it means severing ties with most other people.

At the start of the novel, Will asks Leah to be his "sweetheart." Although it is clear that this would be a good match, and would probably even be approved by their owners, Leah declines because she is already in love with Josiah Potts, the eldest son of an English family. Though she hopes for "a legal marriage, a family and a home" (p. 25), the Potts family makes it clear that a legal union to Josiah is impossible. As one influential member of the community puts it, such a connection "is neither honourable nor creditable" and there is a certain irony in his insistence that Josiah "emancipate" himself from the slave girl Leah (p. 103). When Josiah is shipped off to England for further schooling, this doomed love interest is effectively ended.

This betrayal occurs halfway through the novel and represents a turning point for Leah. She tries to drown herself in the sea but is rescued by Will's master, Thomas McGilvrey, who has by now also become her master in a payment settlement for Lawson's debts. Leah saves enough money to buy freedom for herself and her brother, but McGilvrey refuses to free her, instead offering to marry her. Leah accepts this arrangement, partly because she has no real choice in the matter and partly in the hope of ultimately gaining freedom for herself, her brother, and her mother.

Not surprisingly, Leah's marriage to a slave owner completely changes her relationship with Will, Sukie, and other slaves who were formerly her friends: "In a way, she felt less free than she'd been when she was a slave" (p. 159). She has a son, Edmond, who takes on all the worst features of the slave-owning class and becomes a harsh taskmaster himself. By the time McGilvrey dies, Leah realizes that she has become like him and her other oppressors: "As she grew older her own features were growing to resemble his more and more" (p. 191).

Running throughout the story is a series of references to slave revolts and slave risings, in which Leah's friend Will is a regular participant. None of these revolts are ultimately successful, but they punctuate the story line with the reminder that the human desire for emancipation is irrepressible. Will is involved in one such revolt at the very beginning of the narrative, and at the end he and his friend Sharper are killed when they take part in a later uprising. Will's death seems to awaken Leah's conscience. Although there is no mention of her own death, the novel ends with an epilogue that consists of Leah's last will and testament, in which she bequeaths her land and money to her friends and in which she frees all the slaves over which she has control.

Time and the River demonstrates how fear, violence, and danger are inherent in this place and time. "Leah had grown to womanhood know-

ing that the settlement was often an unpredictable, dangerous place where betrayals were common, revenge was swift (and even deadly), and misfortune was a part of everyday life" (p. 26). The Belizean interior, where Will and other slaves search for mahogany from their bases at upriver camps, is a rugged territory where food can be scarce, wild animals are a threat, and the uncertain weather patterns can unleash violent storms. At the same time, this wild interior is the place where there is some measure of freedom and self-determination for characters like Will. In town, life for slaves can also be hard. Leah notes the high number of "runaways, suicides, slow-downs, murders, insanity and minor rebellions" that are inherent in a slave system (p. 157). The novel makes clear that there are levels of cruelty in slave life, depending on location, tradition, and individual characters. Leah visits the island of Saint George's Caye, for instance, where life "seemed idyllic to her and the lives of the slaves seemed freer, less brutal" (p. 23). Even there, however, the violence of slave revolts, of cruel slave owners, and of occasional military skirmishes with Spanish military forces make life uncertain and dangerous.

The narrative demonstrates how racial and class identity in this setting are complicated and even mutable. The characters represent a complex mix of European, African, Creole, and Indian, with constant influxes of new immigrants speaking new languages. The slaves, Leah realizes early on, "from different parts of Africa, and the various Indian groups lived their lives between the British and the Spanish, doing their best to survive from day to day" (p. 36). Intermarriage confuses the categories even more, and whether one is free or slave is not necessarily tied to race: "She'd often heard of former slave men and women who now owned slaves and were holders of wood-cutting claims along the many rivers and creeks" (pp. 24–25). Leah's own transformation from slave to slave owner illustrates this mutability.

At some point in their relationship, Josiah gives Leah a copy of the novel *Robinson Crusoe*, which she keeps with her and refers to throughout the story. Two things about Crusoe seem to appeal to her. He is an outsider—born in York, "tho' not of that country"—and he is someone who successfully battles the treacherous weather and geography of the Caribbean. Like him, many of the characters in *Time and the River* are outsiders of various types, looking for survival and freedom in a remote European outpost where the weather, geography, and survival itself are uncertain.

CRITICAL RECEPTION

There is a general critical consensus that Zee Edgell's novels offer a unique and important contribution to contemporary world literature. Her writing is routinely praised on aesthetic grounds as well for the nuanced political and social commentary that it offers. In interviews, Edgell resists having her writing pigeonholed or classified as any representative of any particular "type" or school of thought. She denies that she has a particular focus on class (Shea, p. 576) or that she is deliberately creating an alternative national narrative (Rubin and Kurtz, pp. 8–9). Nevertheless, critics who comment on her work regularly note that it contains a compelling exploration of Belizean national identity, that it forces readers to view that identity through the lens of class and caste, and that it offers an alternative historical perspective emphasizing the role of women and ordinary citizens.

Critics frequently describe Edgell's novels as allegorical or at least strongly symbolic of Belize's development as a country. *Beka Lamb*, for instance, appeared at an important moment of political transition for Belize, just at the time of that country's independence, and it is easy to see how Beka's personal story complements and in some ways stands for the national story. As Irma McClaurin notes, "the young protagonist and her country come of age at the same time" (*A Writer's Life*), meaning that Beka serves as a symbol for the emerging nation of Belize itself. *Beka Lamb* can lay claim to being the first Belizean novel, and it is a novel that is fundamentally about the Belizean national story. It is "readily seen as a political fable," writes Roydan Salick (p. 107). The new Beka Lamb that emerges at the end of

the novel, suggests Ervin Beck, stands for the New Belize.

Edgell's other novels continue and extend this exploration of national identity. *In Times Like These* is set at the time of a significant political dispute. Just as the country is negotiating its identity and sovereignty as an autonomous entity, its protagonist, Pavana Leslie, is doing the same on a personal level. By focusing on the mestizo community, *The Festival of San Joaquin* highlights the strong Hispanic components of the national story. Julie Moody-Freeman points out that since Edgell's last novel delves into Belize's colonial past, it should be read first: "I propose a critical re-reading of Edgell's novels—in the order 4, 1, 2, 3—since it illustrates the development of her history of Belize" (p. 34).

In particular, critics tend to highlight the ways that Edgell's novels offer a focus on the female experience and on female contributions to Belizean society. In each of her books, the primary characters are women who struggle to survive in an often violent patriarchal setting. Women are trapped by various forces and often have no opportunity to express themselves. In this respect her work is often compared to the writings of other postcolonial Caribbean women writers, such as Olive Senior, Merle Hodge, and Maryse Condé. "It is in the literature of postcolonial women writers that a sustained focus on the status and significance of women in national formation emerges," notes Kristen Mahlis (p. 125). McClaurin argues that "Edgell has been remarkably successful at reclaiming women's contributions and voices from the annals of Belize's recent past" ("A Writer's Life"), and Moody-Freeman argues that in Edgell's novels women are able to assert themselves and act against oppression. However, they do so in the context of a community, not as isolated individuals (p. 51). Claire Gard says of Luz Marina, the heroine of *The Festival of San Joaquin,* that "the voice that emerges at first is timid and self-deprecating, unused to speaking her thoughts aloud" before it develops in confidence (p. 213). Speaking about *Beka Lamb,* Suzanne Scafe notes that "the body of the woman, presented throughout the narrative as a site of potential exploita-tion, abuse and destruction, is used to signify wider historical and political themes of imperial and colonial exploitation" (p. 26).

The overall result, and what is important about this aspect of Edgell's writing, according to many critics, is the way that her fiction revises or fills in the gaps in the standard histories of Belize. Her novels "challenge nationalist historiography" (Moody-Freeman, p. 33). They offer a "compelling alternative to masculinist concepts of national and national identity" (Mahlis, p. 126). She is a novelist whose works "reproduce and reverse the economies of colour, class and gender power established in colonialist and early anti-colonial narratives" (Scafe, p. 25).

The national story is inevitably tied up with issues of power, and numerous critics argue that Edgell's writing highlights these particular power issues. According to Beck, this is a multilayered process through which Edgell "implies much about the power wielded in relationships involving gender, race, class and empire." Moody-Freeman notes that "her novels reveal the critical links between systems of domination—patriarchy, imperialism, colonialism, capitalism, and neo-colonialism" (p. 34).

For all of Edgell's characters, power is inveterately entwined with issues of race and class, and her novels reveal that these social tensions are complex and resist simple resolution. Salick observes that Edgell's writing highlights the "various racial stories" of Belize (p. 113). Beck identifies seven distinct racial/ethnic groups in Belize, whose social prestige is not coincidentally linked to skin color: expatriates (generally European), *bakras* (white citizens), Creoles (of mixed white and African ancestry), *panias* or mestizos (of mixed Spanish and Native American ancestry), Maya Indians, "coolies" (of East Indian ancestry), and Caribs (of mixed African and Native American ancestry). Edgell's novels foreground the complex relations between these groups at varying historical moments, he asserts.

In interviews, Edgell herself confirms the validity of reading her novels as alternative historical perspectives: "British and American travel writers have written about not only Belize but other parts of the world, and I feel it's very

important to have on the shelf books by Caribbean writers," she told Shea. "Others came and said the 'continent was dark and empty.' But some of us, the Maya, for example, were right there" ("Interview," p. 582).

Different critics classify these features of Edgell's work in slightly different ways. Beck notes that in *Beka Lamb*, for example, Edgell has written a history of Belize, but it is presented and affirmed through unofficial, folk sources. Thus, Edgell offers a history from below, from a truly Belizean point of view. Scafe suggests that Edgell's writings might be called novels of resistance, whereas Adele Newson-Horst prefers the term "neo-resistance narratives" ("Conversation," p. 424), meaning that they present a modern or contemporary account of resistance to slavery, colonialism, or oppression in a previous historical era. Moody-Freeman calls Edgell's work an instance of "activist writing" that refuses to replicate the oppression of imperialism, that points to ways to actively resist that oppression, and that offers a method for "(re)writing/righting wrongs" (p. 51).

CONCLUSION

Zee Edgell's four novels, and to a lesser extent the few short stories that she has published, illuminate the history and social complexity of Belize, primarily from the perspective of various women in that multicultural society. Written alongside her careers in journalism, education, and international development work, Edgell's writing tells the stories of talented but vulnerable women whose lives in many ways reflect and illuminate the development of the nation of Belize. Like the works of many postcolonial writers, they offer an alternative or even a corrective to the mainstream stories about this formerly colonized region. Without shying away from the realities of betrayal, violence, and other tragedies, they offer an ultimately optimistic vision of human nature and of Caribbean cultural identity and its potential future. Zee Edgell's novels will continue to be read as salient and skillful literary reflections on a dynamic period of Caribbean history.

Selected Bibliography

WORKS OF ZEE EDGELL

NOVELS
Beka Lamb. London: Heinemann, 1982.
In Times Like These. Oxford: Heinemann, 1991.
The Festival of San Joaquin. Oxford: Heinemann, 1997.
Time and the River. Portsmouth, N.H: Heinemann, 2007.

SHORT STORIES
"Longtime Story." In *The Whistling Bird: Women Writers from the Caribbean*. Edited by Elaine Campbell and Pierrette Frickey. Boulder, Colo.: Lynne Rienner, 1998.
"My Uncle Theophilus." *Caribbean Writer* 12 (1998). http://www.thecaribbeanwriter.org/index.php?option=com_content&view=article&id=752&catid=15:volume12&Itemid=2&section=volume.
"The Entertainment." *Great River Review* 35:19–27 (fall–winter 2001–2002).
"My Father and the Confederate Soldier." *Calabash* 4, no. 1 (spring–summer 2006). http://www.nyu.edu/calabash/vol4no1/0401022.pdf.

CRITICAL AND BIOGRAPHICAL STUDIES

Beck, Ervin. "Social Insecurity in *Beka Lamb* by Zee Edgell." http://www.goshen.edu/english/ervinb/BekaLamb.htm.
Birbalsingh, Frank, ed. *Frontiers of Caribbean Literature in English*. New York: St. Martin's Press, 1996.
Bromley, Roger. "Reaching a Clearing: Gender Politics in *Beka Lamb*." *Wasafiri* 1, no. 2:10–14 (spring 1985).
Bruner, Charlotte H. "First Novels of Childhood." *CLA Journal* 31:324–338 (1988).
Down, Lorna. "Singing Her Own Song: Women and Selfhood in Zee Edgell's *Beka Lamb*." *ARIEL* 18, no. 4:39–50 (1987).
Evaristo, Bernardine. "Zee Edgell." *Bomb* 82:54–59 (winter 2003).
Flockemann, Miki. " 'Not-Quite Insiders and Not-Quite Outsiders': The 'Process of Womanhood' in *Beka Lamb, Nervous Conditions,* and *Daughters of Twilight*." *Journal of Commonwealth Literature* 27, no. 1:37–47 (1992).
Ganner, Heidi. "Growing Up in Belize: Zee Edgell's *Beka Lamb*." In *Autobiographical and Biographical Writing in the Commonwealth*. Edited by Doireann MacDermott. Barcelona: Editorial USA, 1984. Pp. 89–93.
Gard, Claire. "Zee Edgell: *The Festival of San Joaquin*." *Journal of Gender Studies* 6, no. 2:212–214 (July 1997).

Gikandi, Simon. "Writing After Colonialism: *Crick Crack Monkey* and *Beka Lamb*." In his *Writing in Limbo: Modernism and Caribbean Literature*. Ithaca, N.Y.: Cornell University Press, 1992. Pp. 197–230.

Hunter, Charles. "*Beka Lamb*: Belize's First Novel." *Belizean Studies* 10:14–21 (December 1982).

Macpherson, Anne S. *From Colony to Nation: Women Activists and the Gendering of Politics in Belize, 1912–1982.* Lincoln: University of Nebraska Press, 2007.

Mahlis, Kristen. "Women and Nationhood: Zee Edgell's *In Times Like These*." *ARIEL* 31, no. 3:125–140 (July 2000).

McClaurin, Irma. *Women of Belize: Gender and Change in Central America*. New Brunswick, N.J.: Rutgers University Press, 1996.

Moody-Freeman, Julie. "Zee Edgell: Novelist as Historian/ Archivist (Re)imagining Nation." *African Identities* 7, no. 1:33–53 (February 2009).

Nemhard, Jessica G. "Coming of Age in Belize: A Review of Zee Edgell's *Beka Lamb*." *Belcast Journal of Belizean Affairs* 2:60–61 (December 1985).

Newson-Horst, Adele. "The Fiction of Zee Edgell." In *Caribbean Women Writers: Fiction in English*. Edited by Mary Conde and Thorunn Lonsdale. London: Macmillan, 1999. Pp. 184–201.

———. "Zee Edgell: *Time and the River*." *World Literature Today* 82, no. 1:61–62 (January–February 2008).

O'Callaghan, Evelyn. "Edgell, Zee." In *Encyclopedia of Post-Colonial Literatures in English*. Vol. 1. Edited by Eugene Benson and L. W. Conolly. New York: Routledge, 1994.

Parham, Mary. "Why Toycie Bruk Down: A Study of Zee Edgell's *Beka Lamb*." *Belizean Studies* 21:15–22 (October 1993).

Salick, Roydon. "The Martyred Virgin: A Political Reading of Zee Edgell's *Beka Lamb*." *ARIEL* 32, no. 4:107–18 (2001).

Scafe, Suzanne. "Refusing 'Slave Man's Revenge': Reading the Politics of the Resisting Body in Zee Edgell's *Beka Lamb* and Brenda Flanagan's *You Alone Are Dancing*." *Changing English* 14, no. 1:23–37 (April 2007).

Shea, Renee H. "Gilligan's 'Crisis of Connections': Contemporary Caribbean Women Writers." *English Journal* 81, no. 4:36–40 (April 1992).

———. "Zee Edgell: Belizean Novelist." *Callaloo* 20, no. 3:551–583 (1997).

INTERVIEWS

McClaurin, Irma. "A Writer's Life, a Country's Transition." *Americas* 46, no. 4:38–45 (July–August 1994).

Newson-Horst, Adele. "A Conversation with Zee Edgell." *CLA Journal* 51, no. 4:424–433 (2008).

Rubin, Stan S., and Roger Kurtz. "A Conversation with Zee Edgell." *Great River Review* 35:1–18 (fall–winter 2001–2002).

Shea, Renee H. "Zee Edgell's Home Within: An Interview." *Callaloo* 20, no. 3:574–583 (summer 1997).

"Twenty Questions—The April Interview with Ms. Zelma 'Zee' Edgell." *BELIZEmagazine.com,* April 2004. http:// www.belizemagazine.com/edition02/english/e02 _04questions.htm.

FREDERICK EXLEY

(1929—1992)

Tom Cerasulo

THE ALL-CONSUMING subject of Frederick Exley's writing, and of Frederick Exley's life, was Frederick Exley. By all published accounts, especially his own, he was self-involved, self-medicating, and selfishly irresponsible. Frederick Exley was possessed by an unshakable sense of entitlement and an unquenchable thirst for alcohol. He was a financially unsuccessful writer unfit for any other vocation but writing. He could not hold a job; he would not purchase a house. He sometimes beat his wives and often ignored his children. He was racist, homophobic, misogynistic, and arrogant. In his own writing, Exley described himself as a "mealy-mouthed little wimp," and a "virtually unknown and unheralded author, drunk, child abandoner, and ex-mental patient" (*Last Notes from Home,* pp. 397, 363).

Yet, according to friends and family, he could also be generous, loyal, kind, and irresistibly charming. Frederick Exley is best known for his 1968 literary debut, *A Fan's Notes: A Fictional Memoir,* a book that has achieved cult status among fellow authors, college students, and the counterculture for its frank depiction of a rebel outsider trying to come to terms with the American success myth. But Exley's subsequent autobiographical novels, *Pages from a Cold Island* (1975) and *Last Notes from Home* (1988), each of which he struggled for years to complete, did not receive the critical acclaim of his first, and his worries about being a one-hit wonder in fact play a central role in both works.

Book critics and lay readers alike praise Frederick Exley for his brutal self-scrutiny. He is often hard on America and its value system, but he is even harder on himself and his own failings. In a review of a 1990s reissue of *A Fan's Notes,* Edward Platt states:

A Fan's Notes is, in many ways, an ugly book: Exley is intent on proving that he was as "tough" as his father and he relishes both his own pain, and other people's. Yet his account of his unfulfilled life is an exhilarating one. He writes in a rich, fervid prose that is alive to both the aberrant nature of his tortured mind and the absurdities of life in modern America. And he is funny. Few people have the courage to write honestly about themselves. Exley makes even the boldest of confessions seem like a pallid evasion.

Most fiction writers draw upon their own life experiences for their work, but none are as unabashedly autobiographical as Exley. The protagonist of all three of his books is a novelist named Frederick Exley who, in between episodes of binge drinking and football watching and chasing after women, examines the place of the literary writer in American culture. Nevertheless, at the suggestion of his publisher's legal department, who were worried about libel, *A Fan's Notes* opens with a winking "Note to the Reader" discounting the book's autobiographical elements and jokingly referring to Exley as a "writer of fantasy."

In *Misfit: The Strange Life of Frederick Exley* (1997), Jonathan Yardley reports that *A Fan's Notes* was originally written as nonfiction, but it was released as a work of fiction by Harper & Row to avoid lawsuits and because memoirs from unknown authors did not have the same commercial and critical cachet in the 1960s as they do today. By any measure, *A Fan's Notes* owes far more to reality than it does to fantasy, and it adheres closely, not "loosely," to the pattern of its author's life. As Yardley freely admits, Exley acted as his own best biographer. His three novels are a painstaking—and often painful—record of the "long malaise" that was his time on this earth.

FREDERICK EXLEY

EARLY LIFE

Frederick Earl Exley was born in Watertown, New York, on March 28, 1929, to Charlotte Merkley Exley, a housewife, and Earl Exley, a telephone lineman and local athletic legend. The family already included Frederick's twin sister, Frances, who had been delivered a half-hour earlier, and an older brother, William, who serves as a central figure in Exley's third and final book *Last Notes from Home*. A younger sister, Constance, would later join them.

In the early twentieth century, Watertown, located in northeastern New York State on the Black River, was a thriving manufacturing center. It had its share of wealthy industrialists, but it also had a substantial working class, and town culture was decidedly blue collar and provincial. During Frederick Exley's youth, no airport or highway connected Watertown to the larger world, and its isolation and brutal winters combined to form a close-knit community where stoic self-reliance, hard honest work, and athletic prowess were prized. In these qualities, Exley would find himself falling forever short: "Watertown is not in my marrow, it is my marrow. … I knew that where other men look home with longing and affection, I would look home with loathing and rage, and that loathing would bind me to home as fiercely as love ever does," he said (quoted in Yardley, p. 6). Despite his enmity for his homeland, throughout his life Exley would return to Watertown and the surrounding region again and again, both as subject matter and as a place where he would always be welcome, despite his eccentricities.

Charlotte Exley doted on her son and would forever cater to his every whim, but Earl Exley was more distant and less prone to expressions of love and affection. Frederick longed for his father's approval. As a good—but not great—football and basketball player as a kid, he felt he could never measure up to Earl's legendary athleticism and virility, a fear expressed in *A Fan's Notes* and *Last Notes from Home*. Although he soon grew tired of spending his childhood known as "Earl's boy" around town, he loved and admired his father. Earl's death in 1945, when

Frederick was still in high school, affected Exley deeply. He writes:

> I suffered myself the singular notion that fame was an heirloom passed on from my father. Dead at forty, which never obviates the stuff of myths, my father acquired over the years a nostalgic eminence in Watertown; and, like him, I wanted to have my name called back and bantered about in consecrated whispers. Perhaps unfairly to him (I have his scrapbooks and know what admirable feats are inventoried there), I'm not sure my father's legend was as attributable to his athletic prowess as to his personality. The tales men selected to pass on about him were never so much about a ninety-yard run as about an authentically colorful man having a ball and in an amiable way thumbing his nose at life.
>
> (*A Fan's Notes*, p. 30)

Frederick's last hope of matching his late father's athletic fame on the gridiron was destroyed in a 1946 auto crash, a formative incident in his life that he curiously never wrote about. As a passenger in a wealthy classmate's car, he suffered a permanent injury to his right arm that delayed his high school graduation and ended his football career.

This minor tragedy had an upside. The money he received in a settlement from the girl's father would help fund a college education the working-class Frederick Exley might not otherwise have received. After prepping for a year at John Jay High School in Katonah, New York—where he played basketball and was named to a conference all-star team—he enrolled at Hobart College in Geneva, New York. When a girlfriend ended their relationship, Exley decided to get as far away as possible. He transferred to the University of Southern California in Los Angeles, where he quickly discovered that the handsome football hero Frank Gifford was the big man on campus. Although Gifford would later play a key role in Exley's football fandom and in his creative arsenal, Exley never saw him play at USC. Exley was not even planning to be a writer when he first enrolled in college. He had started at Hobart as a pre-dental major, in keeping with his father's aspirations for him, but at USC he switched to English "with a view to reading The Books, The Novels and The Poems, those pat reassurances that other men had experienced rejection and pain

and loss" (*A Fan's Notes,* p. 59). But Frederick Exley still was not sure college was for him. After considering a military career, he avoided the draft in 1951 when he failed his Selective Service examination because of his damaged arm. In 1952 Exley left school to look for work in New York City. When he could not find anything, he returned to the University of Southern California, graduating with a bachelor's degree in English in 1953.

Over the next decade, Frederick Exley would hold a series of jobs in a variety of cities, spend time as a patient in mental hospitals receiving shock treatments, and fall into an alcohol habit that reached a quart and a half of vodka a day washed down with cheap beer. But as a recent college graduate, he appeared to be headed down the conventional path of the young urban professional. Right after USC, Exley worked in public relations in the railroad industry, at one point becoming managing editor of the *Rocket,* the Rock Island Railroad employee magazine, where his first writing was published. During this time he considered putting down roots in Chicago, the city of his favorite bars and his favorite literary character, Saul Bellow's Augie March. Yet wanderlust—not to mention habitual drunkenness and a hatred of normal working hours—eventually got the best of him. There was always a home base with his loving mother and patient stepfather, Wally, back in upstate New York, but Exley could never stay anyplace long. Three months was his usual limit. Relying on the kindness and wallets of friends, he lived briefly in Phoenix, Arizona, and then moved back to Los Angeles. He also taught high school English in rural New York towns and washed dishes in Miami. At one point, his brother William had taken him into his Baltimore home and Exley had found work as a bartender. But he was fired, twice, for drinking on the job. He received a position as clerk and crier of the courts in Jefferson County, New York. But when a lawyer friend asked him to forge a signature on a check, Exley was fired and the lawyer disbarred.

If Frederick Exley was a poor breadwinner, he was an even poorer husband and father. His first marriage, in 1959, was to Francena Fritz, a social worker he met while staying at Stony Lodge, a private mental hospital. They had a daughter, Pamela Rae, the following year, but Exley's absenteeism, his drinking, his violent behavior, and his solipsism doomed the marriage. Having him around was as bad as not having him around. At her father's insistence, Francena filed for divorce in 1962. Exley's second marriage, to Nancy Glenn, lasted from 1967 to 1971 and produced another daughter, Alexandra. When they met, Nancy had been married to someone else, and at first she had been repulsed by Exley's boorish behavior. Yardley writes:

> Fred made remarks that Nancy thought were sexist and otherwise offended her, but over time their casual chitchat took on a warmer tone. He let it be known that he had something that needed to be typed; he could type he said, but didn't have a typewriter. She said she'd be willing to do the job for him. As she got deeper and deeper into it, she found herself thinking "My God! I can't believe it! Coming out of *this* guy!" It was a long passage about an aluminum siding salesman whom Fred called Mr. Blue, and its sensitivity brought Nancy up short.
>
> (p. 116)

The passage, about a man obsessed by cunnilingus, was part of a longer piece Exley had been writing for years, the book which would become *A Fan's Notes.* The genesis of the manuscript is unclear. Exley did not save drafts and "few of those who were around when *A Fan's Notes* was working its way through Fred's notepads and typewriter had the slightest idea what was taking place" (Yardley, p. 110). He had probably started composing it while in the mental hospital in 1958 and had continued to work on it while staying at his mother's house and during his travels. Nancy's response was typical. Family and friends alike were often surprised that Frederick Exley was producing any pages at all.

A FAN'S NOTES

Exley's fictional memoir is the story of an unsuccessful author, and he had begun writing it as a doctor-prescribed, therapeutic exercise:

> In many ways that book was this book, which I wasn't then ready to write. Without a thought of

organization I wrote vignettes and thirty-page paragraphs about anything and everything I could remember. There are times now when, in nostalgia, I tell myself I'll never again put down the things I did then, but I know I'm only confusing quantity with quality. If nothing else, I wrote a great deal during those months, writing rapidly, furiously, exultantly, heart-sinkingly, and a manuscript of whatever merit began, page by page, filling up the suitcase at the foot of my iron cot.

(pp. 329–330)

These pages were an attempt to understand the jagged failures of his personal and professional lives. After a long gestation, the manuscript had been rejected by fourteen publishers. But a young literary agent named Lynn Nesbit, who would grow to become one of the most powerful people in the book business, decided to take on Frederick Exley as a client. She placed the manuscript with Harper & Row and negotiated a $3,000 author advance. When *A Fan's Notes* was finally published in 1968, now marketed as a work of fiction, Exley was a thirty-nine-year-old first-time novelist.

Episodic rather than plot driven, alternating in style between flowery prose reminiscent of Henry James and hard-boiled realism in the mode of a cynical sportswriter, *A Fan's Notes* is carried along by the power of Exley's captivating narrative voice. Slangy sentences can often veer off in a different diction direction. For example, in describing the audience at a football stadium, Exley writes: "The Brooklyn guys talked all during the game, as much as Brooklyn guys ever talk, which is to say hardly at all. Brooklyn guys issue statements. There is a unity of tone that forbids disagreement. 'Take duh fucking bum outa deah!' or 'Dat guy is a *pro*'—that designation being the highest accolade they allowed a player for making some superb play" (p. 132). Exley is a good storyteller, if at times a boozily rambling one. He creates vivid, often hilarious, character sketches that make the figures come alive. By turns funny and sad, *A Fan's Notes* is the product of a restless, frenetic intelligence.

Exley satirizes American society, but he does not hold himself morally superior to it. In the mode of Saint Augustine, *A Fan's Notes* reads like a confession, warts and all. At one point in the story Exley harasses a mixed-race gay couple just to feel better about himself. Throughout the novel Frederick Exley characterizes Frederick Exley as an unrepentant alcoholic and a junkie for fame. Unlike many memoirs, the book is not the story of one man's triumph over addiction and adversity. There is no catharsis. There are no lessons learned. There is no moral. Exley pities himself, but he does not ask for ours. *A Fan's Notes* pulls off the trick of making the reader care about a thoroughly unlikable narrator. Like Henry Miller or Jack Kerouac, other rebel authors who tend toward the anecdotal, Exley can find occasional moments of beauty in the midst of squalor, and he can forge communal bonds of human kindness with the lowest of drinking companions. Thomas Deegan writes:

Exley, indeed a loner, writes novels full of outcasts. Against the conformity demanded by society, he is interested in originals, people who fail to do the quintessentially American thing of fitting in, of celebrating America's dream of its own success. His cast of characters is a counterculture: eccentrics, mavericks, misfits, liars, obsessives, madmen, criminals—each of them perhaps Exley's own alter ego. But they both publically and privately exhibit courage, strength, and discipline—a kind of competent professionalism in the face of adversity.

(p. 26)

A Fan's Notes draws a line in the sand between America's beautiful losers and its bland winners. There is no middle ground. In America, Exley implies—indeed he shouts it—a person is either a suffering poet or a cheerful drone. The tone of Exley's narrator in *A Fan's Notes,* somewhat like J. D. Salinger's Holden Caulfield in *The Catcher in the Rye* (1951), is that of a psychologically damaged romantic outcast who has reimagined himself as a willing outsider. As in Ken Kesey's *One Flew Over the Cuckoo's Nest* (1962) or Joseph Heller's *Catch-22* (1961), madness seems to be the only sane response to the insane world of the mid-twentieth century.

With its echoes of other authors and its lionization of the literary vocation (William Shakespeare, George Orwell, Aldous Huxley, and Fyodor Dostoevsky are just some of the notables name-checked or discussed), *A Fan's Notes* documents the desperate struggle of the main charac-

ter, here usually called "Ex," to find a place on the roster of esteemed writers. Yet the book's main theme is the quest for fame and glory on any field, a topic even more foregrounded in the American celebrity-obsessed culture of today. Rather than settling for fifteen minutes, however, Exley wants to be famous forever. He longs to have his name and exploits endure. These quests for him inevitably end in failure. His fears that he will never amount to anything, much less achieve greatness, permeate the book. He writes: "Other men might inherit from their fathers a head for figures, a gold pocket watch all encrusted with the oxidized green of age, or an eternally astonished expression; from mine I acquired this need to have my name whispered in reverential tones" (p. 35).

As a young boy, Exley had to share his father with the crowd. *A Fan's Notes* contains an early scene describing Earl's habit of taking a group of local boys with him to high school football games, getting them admitted inside for free by claiming they are all his sons. Frederick recalls one of the kids shouting back at the gatekeeper: "'Yeah! Earl's my ol' man, yuh fucking rat!' I never heard that disclaimer without the blood rushing to my face. And not because of the obscenity" (p. 35).

As a young man, Frederick Exley has an Oedipal yearning to be richer, tougher, and more famous than his dad, who he feels abandoned him by dying. Yet he rejects his own (fictional) twin sons in pursuit of literary fame and the approval of the reading public. What Exley fears most is anonymity: "I had wanted nothing less than to impose myself deep into the mentality of my countrymen, and now quite suddenly it occurred to me that it was possible to live not only without fame but without self, to live and die without having had one's fellows conscious of the microscopic space one occupies upon this planet" (p. 99).

Exley feels that he is forever stuck on the sidelines. *A Fan's Notes* begins with him suffering an alcohol-induced collapse in a bar while waiting for the start of a televised football game. This episode triggers a flood of memories of his boyhood in his father's shadow, his failed at-

tempts at living a straight-laced life of compromise in the world of New York City advertising, his stints in mental hospitals as a diagnosed paranoid schizophrenic, and his pursuit of young women whose beauty and blond hair seem to signify the promise of America. His first love, Bunny Sue Allorgee, is the type of girl usually only heroic football players get to date. But Exley cannot perform sexually with her. She is too seemingly wholesome (despite his disappointment that she is not a virgin), too middle American, too shallow. Allorgee is an allegory for the United States. Exley writes that his "inability to couple had not been with her but with some aspect of America with which I could not have lived successfully" (p. 221). It is also, not insignificantly, a big turnoff to his literary sensibilities that she uses so many exclamation points and dashes in her letters.

Ultimately, Frederick Exley's *A Fan's Notes,* like F. Scott Fitzgerald's *The Great Gatsby* (1925), finds the American success myth illusory. Although he comes to respect his solidly middle-class stepfather whose "strength had not been acquired in pursuit of the dollar but for the reasons most decent men grow strong: by meeting the needs of those people close to them" (p. 224), Exley does not want to be trapped by the obligations of attainment. He rejects materialism and capitalism; he does not want to follow in the footsteps of his friends and buy houses and join country clubs. Like many countercultural authors, such as Kurt Vonnegut and Thomas Pynchon, Exley exhibits a profound distrust of America and its institutions. But more akin to Fitzgerald, Exley still remains half in love with the dreams and aspirations he attacks. He is a romantic outsider looking to belong. Throughout the book, Exley searches in vain for fame and fulfillment, his reach always seeming to exceed his grasp. He is always moving from place to place and from bottle to bottle and from conversation to conversation and from sexual encounter to sexual encounter, following "Exley's Law of Institutional Survival," which calls for him to avoid "attachments, avoid setting myself up for the possibility of experiencing another's defeat" (p. 92). Later he remarks: "I had been unable to give to wife or

sons the emotional nourishment they coveted. The malaise of writing—and it is of no consequence whether the writer is talented or otherwise—is that after a time a man writing arrives at a point outside human relationships, becomes, as it were, ahuman" (p. 359).

Autobiographical novels like *A Fan's Notes* often depict a yearning for stability and continuity, but they also reveal its denial in life. If straight autobiography attempts a realistic representation of self and tries to make order out of the past, Exley's fictionalized autobiography stresses the fragmented nature of experience and the intrusion of mythmaking fantasy into our recollections. Only in watching New York Giants football does Exley find solace and stability. Unlike his own jumbled life, which he recounts here in broken pieces, the narratives of football are straightforward:

> Why did football bring me so to life? I can't say precisely. Part of it was my feeling that football was an island of directness in a world of circumspection. In football a man was asked to do a difficult and brutal job, and he either did it or got out. There was nothing rhetorical or vague about it; I chose to believe that it was not unlike the jobs which all men, in some sunnier past, had been called upon to do. It smacked of something old, something traditional, something unclouded by legerdemain and subterfuge. It had that kind of power over me, drawing me back with the force of something known, scarcely remembered, elusive as integrity—perhaps it was no more than the force of a forgotten childhood. Whatever it was, I gave myself to the Giants utterly. The recompense I gained was the feeling of being alive.
>
> (p. 8)

Football represents to Exley both small town values and big city glamour. It rewards the hard working, the talented, and the deserving. Phillip Sterling writes: "Football players have become the epitome of health, fair play, heroics, and the All-American boy. Football represents America in a way no other sport can, and so, in a grand metaphor where Exley is a non-participant in both football and what it represents, *A Fan's Notes* is a peculiar and pure view of a success-oriented nation and its hero mystique" (p. 39).

A Fan's Notes contains recaps of individual football games and traces the Hall of Fame career of Frank Gifford. Gifford came from the same type of working-class background as Exley, and by the time he joined the New York Giants as their number-one draft choice in 1952 he had already experienced tremendous athletic success in both high school and college. At the University of Southern California he played both offense and defense and had been named an All-American as a senior. Gifford could run, pass, catch, play defensive back, and return punts and kicks. In 1956 he was the NFL's Most Valuable Player and led the Giants to a league championship as a running back. Six times he was named first- or second-team All-NFL. In 1960 a severe head injury suffered in a game against the Philadelphia Eagles put Gifford on the sidelines, and he decided to retire. Yet he missed football and returned in 1962, switching to wide receiver. He became a star once again.

Frank Gifford represents to Frederick Exley everything he himself will never become. When Exley first comes face-to-face with Gifford at USC, he wants to shout at him in hate and envy: "Listen, you son of a bitch, life is not all a goddam football game! You won't always get the girl! Life is rejection and pain and loss" (p. 63). But soon he begins to weigh Gifford's successes against his own failures and live vicariously through him. Gifford is a hero; he is a team player; he has a purpose; he is famous. Exley is a nobody; he is a loner; he is a coward; he has no self-control. When Gifford suffers a season-ending, career-threatening injury at the hands of Philadelphia Eagles linebacker Chuck Bednarik, Exley feels sharp pangs of his own mortality and fragility. But when Gifford makes his comeback, Exley's hope and strength is renewed. As the New York Giants and Frank Gifford go, so goes Frederick Exley. He tells his fiancée that he "had gone each lonely Sunday to the Polo Grounds where Gifford, when I heard the city cheer him, came after a time to represent to me the possible, had sustained for me the illusion that I could escape the bleak anonymity of life" (p. 231).

Exley's sports watching is a reminder, sometimes quite unsettling and sometimes oddly comforting, that he is primarily a passive spectator. He writes: "In a land where movement

is virtue, where the echo of heels clacking rapidly on pavement is inordinately blest, it is a grand, defiant, and edifying gesture to lie down for six months" (p. 185). Often drunk, often immobile on his mother's couch eating Oreos, more interested in being a writer than in actually doing any writing, Exley is a fan rather than a star. If he can be said to have achieved any sort of triumphant epiphany by the end of the book, it would have to be a victory over his delusions of grandeur. He accepts his lot as one of the herd, one of the faceless members of the mass audience he hates.

Of course, the existence of *A Fan's Notes* itself as a tangible object he could put on his bookshelf was proof to Frederick Exley that he was not a complete waste and could accomplish something. But its publication moment was met with little fanfare. No reviews of the novel appeared for three months. When they started coming, they were positive. Some critics found it rambling, overblown, or repetitious, but most were filled with praise. Christopher Lehmann-Haupt in the *New York Times* of December 23, 1968, named the book one of the best of the year. Jack Kroll in *Newsweek* loved its tone of authenticity. However, these good notices had little influence on sales. Fewer than nine thousand of the hardback edition sold, and by 1969 Exley had made only $2,800 in royalties. But foundations and institutions, supporters of the arts, took notice of the new author. *A Fan's Notes* was nominated for the National Book Award, won the William Faulkner Award for best novel of 1968, and received the National Institute of Arts and Letters Rosenthal award to recognize books that are literary successes without being a commercial successes.

The cult of Frederick Exley and *A Fan's Notes* grew slowly but enthusiastically. The Ballantine paperback edition of 1969 would bring the novel to a wider audience, as awestruck readers passed on well-worn copies to friends. The Vintage Contemporaries reprint in 1988 would increase the book's prestige and popularity, and with the publication of a Modern Library edition in 1997 it entered the literary canon.

A 1972 Canadian film version, directed by Eric Till and starring Jerry Orbach, was made by a division of Warner Bros. It was never commercially released in the United States. Exley was supposed to receive a payment of $30,000 for the movie rights, but there are no traces of the payment having been made. Yardley reports the author did not go see it when it was shown at a special screening at the Kennedy Center in Washington, D.C., in January of 1979. But a crowd of his admirers was there in force. One attendee reported back to Exley: "The audience looked like a meeting of a Frederick Exley fan club. I saw the paperback *Fan's Notes* sticking out of several pockets. One guy entertained himself—the showing was delayed a half hour—by reading passages out loud. A lot of intense looking current and former English majors—the kind that look like they wished they had an envelope or something to write poetry on during the day" (quoted in Yardley, p. 152).

A similar crowd would show up whenever Exley made appearances at universities or bookstores. Live readings are an effective means of forming networks and cultivating an audience. This is especially true of countercultural writers. From Walt Whitman to the Beats to Frederick Exley, many "outsider" authors have found literary success by speaking directly to readers, evoking a sense of mutual participation in the fight against alienation, and drawing upon a shared commitment to authenticity and creative risk-taking. Exley's files at the University of Rochester are filled with fan letters expressing solidarity with him, or sexually propositioning him, or asking to meet with him to discuss *A Fan's Notes*. His self-portrait of a monstrous narcissist had managed to speak to a legion of people. The lifelong fan had become a literary star.

PAGES FROM A COLD ISLAND

In the summer of 1969, and on every visit to New York City afterward, Exley frequented a Greenwich Village bar called the Lion's Head, the subject of his 1990 *GQ* article "The Last Great Saloon," a place where hard-drinking, hard-living, Hemingwayesque male writers were held

in high esteem by peers and hangers-on alike. He had received a $10,000 Rockefeller Grant to work on his next book, but acclaim meant more to him than money. He loved hearing from fans of *A Fan's Notes* that the novel had spoken to them, especially if those fans were fellow authors. "Writing is such a lonely business," he told a friend. "You work so much in the dark, and you are always asking yourself if anybody is going to get your message. It goes without saying, then, how gratifying it is to know you have moved one or two readers" (quoted in Yardley, p. 147).

Exley worried that he had started publishing too late and had dissipated himself too much with drink, and therefore he would never "produce what the boys at The Lion's Head called 'a shelf' " (*Pages from a Cold Island,* pp. 11–12). He also felt pressure to have his next novel measure up to the first.

In the fall of 1969 Exley moved to Singer Island, Florida, where he began work on *Pages from a Cold Island,* the second book in a projected trilogy. The writing did not go well. Exley felt that his moment of hope and promise, like that of the 1960s itself, had quickly faded. Lonely and despondent, he kept the manuscript in a trunk for three years and became suicidal. Even going back to the homes and the support system of his mother and sister, now settled in the Alexandria Bay region of New York State near the Saint Lawrence River, had not helped. But a stint teaching at the famous University of Iowa creative writing program in the fall of 1972 had provided a brief period of camaraderie with fellow guest lecturer John Cheever. Yardley writes:

> Fred was in heaven. He was in the company of a writer whom he worshipped in a place that worshipped writers. As he and Cheever strolled through Iowa City, merchants opened their doors and greeted them effusively. Cheever was astonished, and assumed the hullabaloo had been caused by Fred, who in a just a couple of months had become widely known in town. What they actually wanted was to be introduced to Cheever.
>
> (p. 171)

Exley thought he could draw upon his Iowa visit for his new novel, and interviews with the feminist writer Gloria Steinem and the secretary

of the literary critic Edmund Wilson had also yielded interesting material. The book project was saved. In 1974 Exley received a $50,000 advance from Random House, and in 1975 *Pages from a Cold Island* was published.

More a series of essayistic vignettes than a tightly structured and well-plotted novel, *Pages from a Cold Island* is thematically held together by the story of Exley's struggle to complete *Pages from a Cold Island.* For much of the book we are reading about the writing process of the very book we are reading. Here, Edmund Wilson occupies the role of father-substitute and fame paragon that Frank Gifford played in *A Fan's Notes.* Again, this hero remains at a distance.

In *Pages from a Cold Island,* Exley credits Wilson's prose for keeping him alive during his periods of institutionalization. But his only personal contact with Wilson was a brief telephone conversation that ended with the older writer dismissing him:

> "Who are you?" And there was no doubt that he meant was I someone of such eminence that I should be pushing myself on him.
>
> "Well, nobody," I said. "Look, I'm sorry, *really sorry.* I shan't bother you again."
>
> Before ringing off, the great man, in his cooing pitch, spoke his last words to me:
>
> "Stout fellow!"
>
> (p. 159)

Had they talked longer, the two authors would have found they had much in common. For starters, both called upstate New York home—Wilson split his time between Cape Cod and his mother's house in Talcottville. Louis Menand's description of Wilson also sounds a lot like Exley:

> He had three children, each from a different marriage. He moved a lot, usually from one shabby rented place to another, and, thanks to the divorces and, later, the negligence about taxes, money was a serious problem right up to the end. He was a functioning alcoholic but an angry drunk (one cause of the problems in the early marriages). ... Sex seems to have been one place where he felt natural and in control, a zone of wholeness in a world that, for him, was characterized mostly by tension, rupture,

and decay. The other place he must have felt that way, of course, was his writing.

(pp. 86–87)

Throughout the novel, Exley contrasts Wilson's writerly discipline with his own lack of it. Wilson had the talent, courage, and stamina to "hold up to America a mirrored triptych from which, no matter in which direction America turned, she would—to her dismay, horror, and hopefully even enlightenment—be helpless to free herself from the uncompromising plague of her own image" (pp. 267–268), and had therefore succeeded where Exley believes himself to have failed.

What Frederick Exley appears to admire most about Edmund Wilson is that he was a man of letters. He believes that trying to keep Wilson's reputation alive will bring him luck, as if being an admirer of a great literary critic makes Exley himself a more important writer. To be sure, concepts of the "literary" are subject to cultural and historic fluctuations, and although it has connotations of the elite, the respectable, the refined, the noble, the sophisticated, the inspiring, the best that has ever been thought and said, and so on, the term "literature" has no essential qualities and is not an objective category. Yet writing labeled "literary" has worth beyond the commercial, however that worth is defined, which sets it apart from its opposite, "trash," which is not worth keeping. A writer who aspires to write literature, such as Frederick Exley, hopes to stick around.

In addition to Edmund Wilson, Exley also measures himself against the authors Gloria Steinem, Norman Mailer, and his own class of aspiring writers at Iowa. At its core, *Pages from a Cold Island* is an examination of the literary life. And that life seems to be one of suffering for your art. As Exley lectures his students, "'Your real literary life,' I offered as my one piece of tendentiousness, 'will begin the day you accept the conditions, apartness, confusion, loneliness, work, and *work, and work*—the conditions so many of your peers have already accepted and that Edmund Wilson and his stone house so vividly and hauntingly evoke'" (p. 267).

In its depiction of the Iowa Writers Workshop, Exley's novel contributes to an interesting chapter in the history of the profession of authorship. With the increasing popularity of creative writing classes in grammar schools, high schools, and higher education have come inquiries into the pedagogy of creative writing. But for many years, as *Pages from a Cold Island* demonstrates, creative writing programs spent very little time thinking about how to teach creative writing. Like Exley, authors were hired and promoted based on creative publication, not their skill as teachers: the short story in the *Paris Review* was the equivalent of a literary critic's peer-reviewed article in *Modern Fiction Studies*. Creative writing was founded on the belief that literature is not a repository of knowledge but rather a mode of aesthetic and spiritual cultivation. It set itself against the professional study of literature as historical documents to be contextualized or bits of language to be scientifically categorized. Creative writing sought to look at literature from the inside out, teaching students how to read like writers, concentrating not on what literature means but *how* it means. During classroom discussions of assigned reading, Exley does his "best to see to it that the student talked about the novel the author had written. For example, I didn't give one good shit what [literary critic] Lionel Trilling had to say about *Lolita*" (p. 265).

Exley does not have the heart to criticize the writing produced by his students, and in the classroom he behaves more like a moderator than a judge. Yet the members of his workshop have no qualms about tearing each other apart. For them, writing is essentially rewriting. This masochistic process of revision and peer review guides most fiction workshops. People help you keep fixing your piece by constantly telling you why it still is not good enough. In his workshop, Exley uses Wilson and his lonely stone house as the embodiment of the sacrifice, discipline, and hard work needed to become the kind of great author whose work matters, but he also occasionally envisions a more middle-class writing life for himself.

At one point, during an interview with Steinem, he daydreams a version of domestic contentment as a sportswriter:

FREDERICK EXLEY

I'd have a lovely and loving wife named Corinne; three sons named Mike, Toby and Scott; two boxers, Killer and Duchess, with bulging muscles under their fawn coats, and black ferocious masks, and like all boxers they'd be big whining slobbering babies who couldn't even sleep when they were denied access to the boys' beds. I'd have a split-level home somewhere on the north shore of the island, say, at Northport; and just at that moment I was up to here with Corrine, the boys, Killer and Duchess, my boss at the sports desk would telephone me and cry, "Hey, Ex, do not forget you got to fly out to the coast and cover the Mets' five-game stand with the Dodgers." And off I'd wing, to stand in the press box, a paper cup of Coors beer in my hand, the klieg lights dissolving the faces of the crowd into one another, cheering like mad for Seaver and the guys; after which, renewed, I'd fly back to the loving Corinne, Mike, Toby and Scott, Killer and Duchess.

(pp. 122–123)

But this life is not to be. Exley lacks the ability to stay in one place—and with one woman—for long. After a violent relationship with a student ends, one in which Exley has slapped her on several occasions, he leaves Iowa before the term is over.

As in *A Fan's Notes,* women are depicted in an unflattering light in *Pages from a Cold Island,* one bordering on misogyny. The Steinem section finds Exley questioning a radical feminist agenda that he worries may backfire and deliver the country to Richard Nixon in the next presidential election. Exley believes Steinem is hopelessly naive about politics and he treats her condescendingly, even commenting on the size of her breasts during their conversation. She also strikes him as self-promoting, rigid, and insincere. Summing up his thoughts on his interview subject, Exley writes: "Look, Gloria, you want to do something meaningful with your life? Get Friedan and the rest of those meatballs, rent a bus, pack some picnic lunches, go to Wellfleet on the Cape, bow your heads at Edmund Wilson's grave and pay homage to one of the century's great men! Do anything but what you're doing" (p. 130).

Given that he ultimately dismisses her as foolish, it may seem odd that the author devotes so much space to the Steinem section in the book. The material began its life as the article "Saint Gloria and the Troll," which appeared in the July

1974 issue of *Playboy* and won the magazine's silver medal for the year's best nonfiction piece. In fact, needing the money, Exley had sold much of the book off as magazine pieces as he was writing it. This gives *Pages from a Cold Island* a disjointed feel of unrelated fragments yoked together and slapped with a title. Yet, as the book itself self-reflexively makes plain, Frederick Exley was desperate to publish another book. Any book.

Some critics found *Pages from a Cold Island* self-indulgent, gossipy, and sniping. Exley's interview with Steinem winds up being more about him than it is about her, and he lambastes Norman Mailer for the very type of blowhard macho posturing he himself displays here. On the other hand, Bruce Allen's review in *Library Journal* was favorable: "*Inferno* accomplished, here is Exley's *Purgatorio*—an exuberant meditation on the screwy complicities of success and failure, communicated with a wistfully eccentric force all his own. Do not miss it" (p. 1013). But most critics believed that *Pages from a Cold Island* suffered in comparison to *A Fan's Notes,* lacking the previous novel's rooting interest and vividness.

Ronald DeFeo wrote: "although Exley has written a second book, the more we read of it, the more we begin to feel that he has already said all there is to say about himself" (p. 1004). Alfred Kazin, who many literary historians believe took over for Edmund Wilson as America's premier literary critic, called *A Fan's Notes* "a good, amazingly personal book," but he was not a fan of the sequel. As any Iowa workshop student can attest, "write what you know" is a creative writing chestnut, but Frederick Exley's only real subject was Frederick Exley.

LAST NOTES FROM HOME

In the years that followed, Exley descended even more deeply into alcoholism, and his writing career could not pick up momentum. Throughout the late 1970s and early 1980s he received a few journalism assignments from publications such as *Inside Sports, Rolling Stone, GQ,* the *New York Times,* and *Esquire.* Some of these articles were

about football, others were excerpts from a new manuscript about his brother's clandestine career in military espionage, and one was a profile of the English movie actress Sarah Miles. But many of the pieces Exley promised to editors never got written. Moreover, unwavering in his sense of entitlement and his belief that the world should be his handmaiden, he made frequent demands that the magazines pay the expenses for trips and hotels and airfare that were unrelated to his proposed articles. Yardley writes: "What is made clear by these rare ventures into magazine work—fewer than a dozen full-length published pieces—is that freelance journalism simply was not a career for which Fred was made, demanding as it does self-discipline and energy. He expected the magazines to come to him hat in hand, just as he kept expecting fame to arrive, and when they did not he got huffy and took a hike" (pp. 195–196).

In 1984, on the strength of letters from the literary lions William Styron and William Gaddis, Exley received a Guggenheim Foundation grant for $21,000, money he direly needed in order to climb out of debt and pay his tax bill. He also managed to write another book, *Last Notes from Home,* published by Random House in 1988. There were high financial expectations for the novel. The print run was thirty-five thousand copies, a large number for a writer who had much more of a literary reputation than a commercial one. Random House also paid for a full-page advertisement in the *New York Times Book Review* and managed to get a profile about Exley into the mass circulation *People* magazine.

Frederick Exley novels need a hero the storytelling antihero can weigh himself against. In *Last Notes from Home* the subject of the narrator's admiration is his brother William, a retired army officer who served in World War II, Korea, and Vietnam. The novel describes an actual 1973 trip to Hawaii that Frederick and his mother made to visit William, known here as "The Brigadier," as he was dying of cancer. Exley writes:

Until one has crossed the continent and half the Pacific with an aging and ailing mother, a woman twice widowed, a woman who nightly peruses her Bible and accepts literally the three score and ten years meted man by that book, a woman not uncognizant of having buried two spouses and now en route to lay to rest her eldest progeny, a woman doubtless mightily distressed at the unfairness of the Brigadier's being taken at forty-six and perhaps even chagrined and perplexed that her Bible had seemed to betray her, until one has made such a forlorn pilgrimage one can never truly comprehend the absurdity of what the phrasemakers call the Jet Age.

(p. 28)

Family biographical descriptions aside, *Last Notes from Home* is perhaps the least factually based of Exley's novels. Two characters the Exleys meet on the plane spark much of the wild action and screwball comedy. James Seamus Finbarr O'Twoomey could be a public relations man, or an IRA terrorist, or a criminal, or a con man, or some combination of these vocations. He forces Exley to finish writing this very novel we are reading by placing him under house arrest. Robin Glenn is a sexually liberated stewardess whom Exley eventually marries. Their stories intermingle with stories of Exley's boyhood athletic exploits, as well as portraits of other friends and acquaintances. Drinking, carousing, and womanizing—punctuated by periods of taking solace in literature—once again figure prominently in *Last Notes from Home.* The novel ends with the new bride Robin surfing in her wedding dress, a scene which provides the cover image of the hardcover edition of the book. As he watches her, the narrator promises himself that he will hold out promise for himself: "tubby wimp or not, I shall in the end defeat you, Miss America, shall defeat you, learn to live with you, and make you mine" (p. 397).

Despite its fragmented and episodic structure, and its marked tendency toward free association, *Last Notes from Home* achieves some of the cohesion lacking in *Pages from a Cold Island* owing to its emphasis on Exley's brother, to whom the second novel had been dedicated. Thomas Deegan writes: "William is the Gifford of this novel—a man who exhibited toughness, a combination of machismo, strength, and courage, while participating on the public stage of American life. He is the heroic achiever against whom

Exley gauges his own human failings and the failures of American society" (p. 31). In *Last Notes,* a less mean-spirited book than *Pages from a Cold Island,* the sadness that Exley feels at his brother's long, painful death is echoed by the emotional story of the death of a high school sweetheart, Cass, from anorexia.

When Exley was caught deflowering Cass, he tried to save his own skin and "cowardly and cringingly laid it all at Cass's feet, spitting out unforgivable things like, 'She's screwing everybody in town,' and so forth" (p. 313). She is devastated by his betrayal. Her death from self-starvation strikes Exley "with a grief and guilt so burdensome it is something of a marvel that I survived" (p. 315). Frederick Exley partially blames his mistreatment of Cass on the puritanical 1940s and 1950s, but with each passing year he hates himself more and more for what he has done. Then he begins to hate her for making him feel this way:

> It took me a quarter of a century and a lot of living even to say good-bye to Cass. One autumn day I bought a dozen long-stemmed white roses, went to the lovely shaded Brookside Cemetery on the south side of the city, and asked the caretaker to direct me to Cass's grave, which, as it happened, wasn't far from my father's stone. Believe me when I say I'd fully intended to tell Cass I'd forgiven her as well as myself. But when I got to the grave I found I was sobbing so uncontrollably that snot was leaking from my nose, between terrifying, gasping sobs I spat out, *"Fuck you, Cass,"* then walked to my father's grave and laid the long-stemmed white roses there, which in a way was really the first time I'd been mature enough to say good-bye to Dad.
>
> (p. 316)

He will never forgive himself for his cowardice and betrayal, and he will never recover from the loss of his father. In Exley, the past is never past.

Although most reviewers considered it superior to his second novel, many were nonetheless disappointed in Exley's *Last Notes from Home.* They cited the author's now familiar problems with structure, narrative control, rooting interest, and lack of depth in characterization. While some critics hoped that Exley would continue to write now that the proposed trilogy had come to a conclusion, others thought that

Exley's writing gifts were breaking down along with his body, finding his prose increasingly maudlin, rambling, and self-indulgent.

Furthermore, with the United States now under the charismatic spell of Ronald Reagan, the 1980s were not as favorable a climate for America bashing as the 1960s and 1970s had been. Hilma Wolitzer wrote: "unfortunately the author goes off into too many directions on the way to the denouement ... that make the reader less attentive and therefore less sympathetic. Although Mr. Exley's arguments continue to seem valid, they're simply not as compelling as they used to be." Yardley believes that Exley was essentially a one-book writer who frantically tried to remain in the spotlight: "the pathetic eagerness with which he promoted *Last Notes from Home* for a Pulitzer Prize suggests that at the end he was ready to settle for praise in any form" (p. xxviii). The novel did not meet Random House's sales expectations for it.

In the late 1980s Exley also completed a few magazine pieces, most notably "A Fan's Further Notes," about the Giants' triumph over the Broncos in the 1987 Super Bowl, which Exley had attended as a guest of Frank Gifford, who had read *A Fan's Notes* and had been flattered by it. When Gifford threw a publication party for *Last Notes from Home,* it thrilled the author to no end. In 1989 Exley began work on a novel he was calling *Mean Greenwich Time.* Yardley, who viewed the manuscript and Exley's notes for it, writes:

> It was to be "a spy thriller," about "a 43-year-old English professor whom the intelligence community won't leave alone." In his last years he talked about it constantly. He thought that what he had written "is pretty funny"—it isn't—but claimed that he would not cheapen his literary style in order to cultivate the masses. ... Still, his book was going to be a big best-seller, a piece of commercial fiction that would play to the market and rake in the big money that his more serious books had never come close to earning.
>
> (p. 229)

But as his health worsened, the writing would not come. Frederick Exley died in Alexandria Bay, New York, on June 17, 1992, of complica-

tions from two strokes. He was buried next to his parents at Brookside Cemetery in Watertown.

CONCLUSION

Frederick Exley's writing has received scant attention from academic scholars and researchers. Jonathan Yardley's book on him is more an impressionistic musing than it is a full-fledged biography. But Exley continues to be a writer's writer because of his vivid portrayal of his struggle to put words on the page and his passionate search for recognition and acclaim. Other authors take solace in sharing his vocational doubts. In the final analysis, the writing profession really is not a profession at all. Authors do not share a specialized body of knowledge, a common educational background, a code of ethics, or a system of peer review and self-regulation. But Exley lived for literature. He was a fan of other authors, and they often returned his admiration. His late-night phone calls to other writers he considered friends, where he was expected to talk and they were expected to listen, are infamous in literary circles. He was also an active letter writer. The Frederick Exley Papers, housed at the University of Rochester, include correspondence with John Cheever, Don DeLillo, William Styron, John Updike, Kurt Vonnegut, and other esteemed authors of the late twentieth century.

Frederick Exley continues to inspire other writers. Brock Clarke's 2010 novel *Exley* is about a young reader obsessed with Frederick Exley. *A Fan's Notes* also seems to be the template for many fictionalized memoirs of substance abuse, such as James Frey's *A Million Little Pieces* (2003), as well as fandom autobiographies such as *Fever Pitch* (1992), Nick Hornby's account of his devotion to the Arsenal soccer club.

In addition to being a writer's writer, Frederick Exley is also a reader's writer, an author who connects with his audience by baring his soul to them. He invites his readers to join him in his quixotic fight against the world. There are many reports of people being given his books, or finding them somewhere, at a time when they were feeling displaced or defeated. Exley made them feel less alone. In this way, Frederick Exley may be the most successful failure in American literature. "For my heart," he writes in *A Fan's Notes*, "will always be with the drunk, the poet, the prophet, the criminal, the painter, the lunatic, with all whose aims are insulated from the humdrum business of life" (p. 361).

It is a critical commonplace in literary studies that all discourse is socially constructed. For example, whether chiseled on a stone tablet or typed into a notebook computer, all writing is the result of a variety of factors: the psychological and emotional state of the writer, the writer's ideas of what writing is and what it does, the political and social environments in which the writing occurs, the aesthetic and economic pressures that encourage (or can retard) the process, and other variables. But it is also important to remember that writers and readers are individuals seeking out other like-minded individuals, wherever and whenever they might be living. In the poem "Crossing Brooklyn Ferry," Walt Whitman tells his future readers, "I considered long and seriously of you before you were born." Writing is a solitary occupation, but *A Fan's Notes* reminds us that every artist desperately yearns to connect with an audience that does not yet know it was awaiting him.

Selected Bibliography

WORKS OF FREDERICK EXLEY

FICTIONAL MEMOIRS
A Fan's Notes. New York: Harper & Row, 1968; New York: Vintage Contemporaries, 1988.

Pages from a Cold Island. New York: Random House, 1975; New York: Vintage Contemporaries, 1988.

Last Notes from Home. New York: Random House, 1988.

UNCOLLECTED ARTICLES
"Holding Penalties Build Men." *Inside Sports,* November 1981, pp. 105–109.

"A Fan's Further Notes." *Esquire,* June 1987, pp. 150–152.

"The Last Great Saloon." *GQ,* December 1990, pp. 290–295, 340–342.

PAPERS

Frederick Exley's papers and manuscripts are collected at the University of Rochester.

CRITICAL AND BIOGRAPHICAL STUDIES

Cantwell, Mary. "The Hungriest Writer: One Fan's Notes on Frederick Exley." *New York Times,* September 13, 1992, p. 30.

Chabot, Barry C. "The Alternative Vision of Frederick Exley's *A Fan's Notes.*" *Critique* 19, no. 1:87–100 (1977).

Deegan, Thomas. "Frederick Exley." In *Dictionary of Literary Biography.* Vol. 143, *American Novelists Since World War II, Third Series.* Edited by James R. Giles and Wanda H. Giles. Detroit: Gale, 1994. Pp. 24–32.

Howard, Jane. "Frederick Exley." *People,* November 14, 1988, pp. 163–167.

Menand, Louis. "Missionary: Edmund Wilson and American Culture." *New Yorker,* August 8–15, 2005, pp. 82–88.

Platt, Edward. "A Fan's Notes." *New Statesman,* July 5, 1999, p. 59.

Sterling, Philip. "Frederick Exley's *A Fan's Notes*: Football as Metaphor." *Critique* 22, no. 1:39–46 (1980).

Yardley, Jonathan. *Misfit: The Strange Life of Frederick Exley.* New York: Random House, 1997.

REVIEWS

Allen, Bruce. Review of *Pages from A Cold Island. Library Journal,* May 15, 1975, p. 1013.

DeFeo, Ronald. Review of *Pages from a Cold Island. National Review,* September 12, 1975, pp. 1003–1004.

Edwards, Thomas. "A Case of the American Jitters." *New York Review of Books,* January 19, 1989, pp. 36–37. (Review of *Last Notes from Home, A Fan's Notes,* and *Pages from a Cold Island.*)

Gray, Paul. "Books: Surreal Odyssey." *Time,* October 24, 1988, p. 94. (Review of *Last Notes from Home.*)

Kazin, Alfred. Review of *Pages from a Cold Island. New York Times Book Review,* April 20, 1975, p. 4.

Kirn, Walter. "Sad Sack Superman." *Slate,* August 20, 1997. http://www.slate.com. (Review of *A Fan's Notes* and *Misfit,* by Jonathan Yardley.)

Kroll, Jack. "Man in the Mirror." *Newsweek,* May 12, 1975, p 95.

Lehmann-Haupt, Christopher. "Books of the Times: A Sporting Life." *New York Times,* December 23, 1968, p. 37. (Review of *A Fan's Notes.*)

———. "Books of the Times: Sojourning in Hawaii, Roots and All." *New York Times,* September 22, 1988, p. C24. (Review of *Last Notes from Home.*)

Wolitzer, Hilma. "Love and Hate for the Perfect Hero." *New York Times Book Review,* September 25, 1988, p. 14.

RACHEL HADAS

(1948—)

Kim Bridgford

As the daughter of the classicist Moses Hadas, Rachel Hadas has had a lifelong preoccupation with the classics as well as with the country of Greece itself. At the same time, she has made her mark in poetry as a member of the New Formalist movement, although she herself finds such labels limiting. A prolific author—Robert McPhillips calls her "perhaps the most prolific of the New Formalists" (p. 109)—she has also written scholarship and memoir, moving effortlessly from public to private texts, writing not only about her work with AIDS patients but also about the years spent with her husband as he struggled with dementia. Considering the whole of her career, she is perhaps best thought of as a "poet-critic" (*CPR* interview) in the manner of A. E. Stallings, Robert Pinsky, and Timothy Steele, some of the writers she admires.

Given the classical and public grandeur of some of her themes, it is ironic that she is best known for a poignant, accessible poem titled "The Red Hat," which describes the pang of separation as her young son, his bright red hat visible in the distance, gradually leaves his anxious parents behind and walks to school on his own. If there is a common theme to her body of work it is the passage of time, as well as the universality of loss. Ernest J. Smith puts it another way: "Hadas's major theme is memory, how the past continues to re-present itself, both raising and answering questions about how humans define themselves through their lived and imagined experiences" (p. 153). Hadas herself explains, "Not everybody has a talent for happiness, but as far as I can tell, everybody experiences grief" (*Three Poets,* p. 65) Her life has been shaped by the grief associated with two men in her life: the death of her father after her freshman year in college, and the loss of her husband,

the composer George Edwards, who was diagnosed with early-onset dementia in 2005, at age sixty-one, and died in 2011.

Yet throughout her life, Hadas seems to be able to find the importance of the "red hat" in both a literal and symbolic way. As she writes in *Strange Relation* with regard to George during the days of his dementia:

> If I knew how to knit or embroider or crochet, I could do those things during the quiet time I spend visiting George. If I were Penelope and had a small portable loom, I could weave and then unweave. But these coloring books suit me very well. On and off for a week or two, I've been working on a tricky mandala that features pouting-mouthed goldfish and many small bubbles. I sometimes ask George for advice about colors, and he sometimes gives it—a one-word reply suffices, and he's good at those. "Red!" "Purple!"
>
> (p. 195)

BIOGRAPHY

Rachel Chamberlayne Hadas was born on November 8, 1948, to the classics scholar Moses Hadas and Elizabeth Chamberlayne Hadas, who was a high school Latin teacher. Her elder sister, Elizabeth, was born in 1946.

Her father's legacy was complicated and resonant, both for Hadas herself and for others; part of this has to do with the multiple roles he played. As Hadas herself writes, "He was a rabbi, then a professor; then, like many academics in his generation, an O.S.S. operative who, more unusually, took an active interest in Greek politics after the war; and then a professor again, not to mention a talking head on TV and a telelecturer" ("The Many Lives of Moses Hadas"). He also made the classics accessible in translation to

those outside his discipline. As William M. Calder III points out, "That Sophocles is almost as well known as Shakespeare to so many Americans educated after 1945 is largely due to Hadas" ("Many Lives").

It is no surprise, given her background, that Hadas took a degree in classics from Harvard-Radcliffe in 1969. While there she also took a poetry class with Robert Fitzgerald, as did many of the New Formalists, including such poets as Dana Gioia, Mary Jo Salter, and Robert B. Shaw.

Certainly her father profoundly shaped her intellectual influences; yet it was his death while she was in college that determined her life path. Like Sylvia Plath, whose poem "Daddy" traces the profound impact of her father's emotional and intellectual influence, Hadas had an overpowering father figure—also a college professor—to come to terms with. (Hadas subsequently wrote her own "Daddy" poem.) In fact, as Hadas pointed out, "You could … have said my life as a poet began when my father died" (*Three Poets,* p. 49).

After college she began to travel in earnest, shaping her own interests, both moving away from home and going home at the same time, noting, "When I was growing up, we never travelled abroad; my father thought the best way to get work done was to stay home. So in going to Greece I was treating myself to an adventure … going in search of a father who was not only a classicist but who had been in the O.S.S., had spent time in Athens (as well as in Cairo and Cyprus), and had Greek friends" (*Three Poets,* p. 49).

She was friends early on with the poets John Hollander and James Merrill, and these contacts and friendships helped launch her career. John Hollander was a family friend who had accepted her poem "Daddy" for *Harper's* while she was an undergraduate at Harvard. Hadas recounts his having urged her, "If you're going to be in Athens, you absolutely must look up Jimmy Merrill," and so, she says, "I did and I fell in love with Merrill instantly—fell in love with everything about him" (*Three Poets,* p. 50).Merrill, in fact, proofed her first book manuscript.

Her subsequent degrees, in poetry and com-

parative literature, were from Johns Hopkins (1977) and Princeton (1982), respectively. Her prizes include creative writing grants from the Guggenheim Foundation (1988–1989) and Ingram Merrill Foundation (1977, 1994) as well as an award for scholarship from the American Academy and Institute of Arts and Letters (1990). She has lived for many years in New York City; since 1981 she has taught at the Newark, New Jersey, campus of Rutgers University, where she is the Board of Governors Professor of English.

She met Stavros Kondylis, her first husband, during a four-year stay in Greece. This meeting was facilitated through Alan Ansen, a protégé of W. H. Auden and William Burroughs. The three—Ansen, Kondylis, and Hadas—had a complicated relationship; as McPhillips states, "both Ansen and Hadas were in love with Stavros, a blond 'Greek peasant who had, as they say, finished fourth grade' " (p. 109, quoting Hadas' "Mornings in Ormos"). Ultimately this sorted out, and Kondylis and Hadas were married. In another complicated, but more public, case, the two of them found themselves on trial for arson, accused of setting fire to an olive press they owned and ran. Though they were eventually cleared, Hadas explains, "It was a terrible experience, and it taught me that even the most beautiful Greek island isn't necessarily a paradise" (Baer). Although she spoke the language and adapted to local customs, she still stood out as an American and in other ways. As she writes in "Mornings in Ormos,"

I was a woman. Not only that, but a blond who wore shorts or bathing suits and also talked with the men in the coffee houses. Not only that, but an agnostic American whose Jewish name made people assume she was Israeli, while her hair proclaimed her indubitable Scandinavian. Not only that, but the wealthy [sic] wife of an oddly blond, un-Greek looking man. … Whether less or more was expected of me, I was certainly recognizably odd.

(*Living in Time,* p. 182)

Hadas and Kondylis eventually divorced, and on July 22, 1978, she married George Edwards; their son, Jonathan, was born on February 4, 1984. George taught at Columbia University until he was diagnosed with early-onset dementia, the

RACHEL HADAS

subject of Hadas' memoir *Strange Relation*. This difficult period—the grief of losing the loved one before death—was something that Hadas had to come to terms with, and she realized more than ever the importance of her writing to help her to do this. As she writes in "Demeters,"

To force me to pay attention,
life needed poetry. And poetry needed life
in order to flow like blood
through any woman's veins, ...

(reprinted in *Three Poets in Conversation*, p. 91)

STARTING FROM TROY

The title of her first book of poetry, *Starting from Troy* (1975), is appropriate enough, given Hadas' classical upbringing. The phrase "starting from Troy" addresses both the subject matter itself and her relationship with her father; indeed the book is dedicated to him and includes an epigraph from Tacitus. Ernest J. Smith sums up: "This volume shows a clear attraction to the classical subject and to traditional meters and stanza forms, though Hadas exhibits a great deal of lyrical variety from poem to poem" (p. 154).

Standouts in the book include "The Fall of Troy" (which, impressively, was written when Hadas was in high school), "Sappho, Keats," "The Color-Blind Raspberry Picker," "Daddy," "Madame Swann at Home," "Afterword," "Dream Interpretation," and "Scherzo." Of particular note, given Hadas' strong relationship to her father, are "The Fall of Troy," "Daddy," and "Dream Interpretation."

"The Fall of Troy" (p. 7) intertwines the imagery of the household—furniture, upholstery, and all—with the imagery of the classical text, foreshadowing Hadas' own "fall" through the death of her father. Such an intertwining mirrors the mythology of Hadas' youth and preoccupations: "Sing now the heavy furniture of the fall, / the journey's ending." As with many of Hadas' poems, there is more emphasis on the general than on the particular (which is why "The Red Hat," as an anomaly, is so popular), but at the same time, there is always an emotional resonance that makes the reader return, again and

again, to the poem. "Gods sit / changing their own upholsteries of deceit," writes Hadas; such language cannot help staying with the reader.

No female poet can write a poem called "Daddy" (p. 17) without conjuring Sylvia Plath, and Hadas, of course, consciously does that here. She discovers, as Plath does, that "Dead people, no, they don't come back. / That's why they're dead." Yet there is still a lack of closure in that the physical body is gone, but the influence of the father figure is still felt. "No, no forgetting," Hadas says. The irony of this poem is that many years later Hadas would deal with the opposite difficulty: the physical body of her husband being present, but the same grief process taking hold. Moreover, Hadas, while conjuring Plath's "Daddy," might more specifically be referencing Plath's "The Colossus" when she writes, "It would be funny, if I loved you less / life's lavish spread of food for elegies"—lines reminiscent of Plath's envisioning hiding in her father's ear. The tone of Hadas' close to her poem also reminds the reader of Plath's world-weary and somewhat sadomasochistic comment that "Daddy" is "light verse."

The poem "Dream Interpretation" (p. 44–45) conveys, in its fragmented, surreal way, Hadas' continuing preoccupation with dreams as well as her tapping into various ways of thinking about and experiencing life. The poem underscores the inevitability of her father's death—"That was a death that was to happen, my daughter," and the ending illustrates the way a preoccupation can worry a poet for a lifetime: "in its center / my thumb crooks the sudden eyehole / of your absence."

SLOW TRANSPARENCY

Although Hadas' later work is silent about the arson trial she went through in Greece with her first husband, *Slow Transparency* (1983) references it on the cover and discusses it specifically in a few poems. Later, in "Mornings in Ormos," Hadas would "regret" being so candid about it (*Living in Time*, p. 179).

Being on trial abroad for something one did not do would naturally affect any young adult

(presumably community jealousy was the culprit). At the same time, *Slow Transparency,* on the whole, is dreamy, as Hadas moves from her exile on a Greek island, to the aftermath of her trial, to her relationship with a new partner (George Edwards) in the United States.

The swans on the cover are in some ways ironic, considering that swans mate for life and this book is about the dissolution of one relationship and the moving on to another. At the same time, the cover underscores the dreamy, ethereal nature of the book, the opposite of the frightening reality of her court case.

The poetic style is varied, using both short and long lines as well as fixed and more fluid punctuation, emphasizing that the book is about transition. The writing, while including some lovely imagery, is often unclear, as Robert McPhillips notes: "Amid many dazzling shards of Aegean imagery and pleasingly musical phrases, the reader remains somewhat uncertain about the point of many of these poems" (p. 110). As Hadas herself later observed, "Looked *through:* does the visible but opaque carapace of things grow transparent, then, with time? In poem after poem, my 1983 book *Slow Transparency* affirms exactly that. I now think the answer is both yes and no. We look at things until we can see through them, but in the world the things are still there" (Smith, p. 155).

In Greece, Hadas is seen as an exile, never wholly a part of the place, although she swims in it, eats in it, sleeps in it, and marries in it. This feeling is exacerbated in the poem "The Trial for Arson," which examines the case itself and Hadas' emotions. As the voice of the prosecutor says, "How could this woman have been happy here?" (p. 18). Later in the poem, Hadas notes, "I'm accused by those in power / of being who I am; of being here" (p. 19). When the trial is over, and Hadas and her husband are acquitted, people want to go on with the way things were:

"The trial, my children? It's over?"

That will be what they remember about us.
And of our years here, full of light and air,

at this moment I think I will take with me

only this ending, but I will be wrong.

(p. 20)

This poem stands in stark contrast to "Marriage Rhapsody," which takes place in Vermont and enters a new innocence of place, and dreaminess of interior life, which Hadas savors. The poem, which celebrates birds and bees, cats and love, enjoys this new fairy tale:

No, we ourselves
stood ringed with wishes. If it wasn't written
for us, let me have said
that as at the end of a fairy tale
the marriage was accomplished.
But this was not the end.

(p. 88)

A SON FROM SLEEP

Like many mothers, Hadas felt a need to write a book of poems about her child, and *A Son from Sleep* (1987) has a vague, symbolic cast. In some ways, the book continues the love story from the end of *Slow Transparency;* in others, it underscores an archetypal story of connection and exploration. At the same time, the most successful—and memorable—poems are the ones most clearly rendered. Such poems as "Philemon and Baucis" and "Two and One" bring intensity of emotion to the situation.

"Philemon and Baucis" (p. 8) underscores Hadas' jealousy of children whose parents live on into later life. Because Hadas' father died when she was a teenager, there is a lingering resentment about what she has missed. She writes, "My envy of people my age or older / whose parents both are living / takes the form of contempt." Questioning whether "the young do better," she arrives at the conclusion that "Perhaps the clarifier / is a single pinch of death." It is interesting, in light of the birth of her son, that her role as a child is uppermost in her mind.

"Two and One," which is about the relationship of parents and child, shows Hadas at her technical best. A skillful and supple rhymer, she carries iambic dimeter quatrains with an *abba* rhyme scheme through eighteen stanzas—quite a

feat. The poem is both touching and playful. Lines like "Asleep between us this treasure is" (p. 24) and "You light up space / like a single star" (p. 25) show us the tenderness of the transformation and the new supremacy of the child in the family order.

A Son from Sleep does many things: it devotes a single book to family relationships, especially with the child as center; it illustrates a kind of symbolic approach to a topic that has been often handled by others; and it illustrates Hadas' range of forms and approaches. The first line of her poem "Little by Little" might sum up her philosophy: "Let nothing be too big or small to say or see" (p. 40).

PASS IT ON

Hadas' 1989 poetry volume takes the phrase "pass it on" from Catholic religious worship ceremonies—the shaking of hands, or hugging of a neighbor—and extends it to mean all the things it is necessary to pass on. Overall, the book builds on cycles and patterns that sustain us. The first has to do with seasons; the second with the theme of "pass it on"; and the third, while more eclectic, has endings as its common theme.

While the cyclical nature of the seasons is an expected part of the first section, one subtheme is the importance of mothering. This love is in contrast to that of lovers—"that fresh famished love" (p. 13) and other relationships. One particularly telling phrase appears in "Fix It (Winter)," where Hadas admits, "It's not as if I'm lonely. I'm a mother" (p. 17), a voice that echoes Plath in "Morning Song" and elsewhere. Hadas goes on to say in "Over the Edge,"

To be a mother is to be a house
she first must trace
a path away from, wander, and embrace
her rediscovered shape near story's end.

(p. 27)

The theme of seasons, then, has a human shape.

Of the twelve poems in the middle section of the book, four are titled "Pass It On," with each poem given a number: "Past It On, I," "Pass It On, II," and so on. These provide glue for the remaining poems, which are about teaching and generational change. Two standout poems from the section are "Teaching Emily Dickinson," which underscores the collective effort of a poetry class seeking to understand Emily Dickinson, and "Philoctetes," whose infected foot distresses the contemporary, and more sanitary-minded, students in Hadas' classes.

The last section includes—in addition to the touching poem "The Burial of Jonathan Brown"—a series of takes on various words: *silences, angers,* and *goodbyes.* Of these, "Four Angers" is probably most effective, although it is the emotion with which Hadas is most ill at ease: "I'm nothing but an amateur at anger" (p. 66). The poem ends with a touching rendition of the "She loves me, she loves me not" ritual of pulling the petals off of a flower. In the end, we want the outcome to be positive—that is, "she loves me"—or as Hadas admits, "we cry for happy endings / until our lips grow cold" (p. 67).

MIRRORS OF ASTONISHMENT

The title *Mirrors of Astonishment* (1992) reflects the paradox of Hadas' two main topics in this collection of poems: art and love. While in creating, and in loving, there is a mirroring back, a replication, there is also the difference given back in terms of the gaze, and the reaction of, the other.

The book is unusual for Hadas in that it includes so many long poems. This approach gives an air of meditation to her themes, and the stanzas underscore the theme of mirroring.

Several of Hadas' books fall into organizational patterns of three: the first here references art; the second, life moments; and the third, love. Hadas suggests that the second topic ties the first and third together.

Poems that may best illustrate the themes of the first section are "Art," "On Poetry," and "City and Country." The first, "Art," with its eleven eleven-line stanzas, shows the magpie nature of art as it attempts to collect from life. Metaphors abound in the poem, as if to highlight the idea that art comes from every unexpected place.

RACHEL HADAS

Words are compared to people elbowing each other, pancake batter erupting on the stove, flies stuck to flypaper. Art emerges from dreams and provides rest from the noise of life: "Week-long immersion in gabble! … It calls for Sabbath, for sabbatical, / some ritual distilling of the actual" (pp. vi, 3). Ultimately, the poet makes use of it all: "Particular and universal, / elegy, artifact, intrusion: / nothing to do but join the dots I saw" (p. 6).

"On Poetry" distills in another sense, by categorizing the sections as "Lyric," "Trivia," and "Nature" and musing on these topics. In the first, lyric is held up against narrative and defined by contrast. It is not "heroes / who drink wine piss on the beach, weep at sundown, / go to bed"; rather, "lyric's narrow confines / ought to tighten, tighten like a migraine. / Small explosions follow" (p. 10).

Hadas goes on to define trivia as "unmediated / worship of nature" (p. 11). In order to have art, one must have nostalgia, or regret, informing that trivia:

regret for past
hours spent on hands and knees in search
of strawberries remains, and is enough.
Red-stained knees, mouth, fingers—these are sweeter

in the recalling. …

(p. 11)

Finally, nature is both countryside and cityside, and Hadas needs both to make art: "Itself a pied creation, poetry explores a middle ground, / one foot stuck in a rusty pick-up truck, / one hand shading the eyes against // sun, moon, stars" (p. 12). In short, the magpie artist needs it all, but frames it most simply and effectively through contrast.

"City and Country" explores some of the same themes, and also through contrast. While being in a place is important, distance is crucial to understanding that place—the "grass is always greener" phenomenon. The ending of the poem sums up much of the poem and the volume:

Distance is the only magic key.
Distance is the aphrodisiac.

Except for the golden child asleep between us,
everything—including you and me—
looks better at a distance.

This is being written in the country.

(p. 16)

Section 2 is defined by the image of its opening poem, "The Mirror," which resonates with both reflection and brokenness. For, as the poem tells us, the Garden of Eden is the first mirror, from which brokenness emerges. This image goes on through life, mirroring us through generations:

All of us, confronting—sooner, later—
some version of the mirror
recognize our faces cracked with age
suspended in solution for our children
to find themselves within our steady gaze.

(p. 25)

Mirroring can also happen in other ways: through language, through translation, through grief. Another way we are like others is through death; when we leave, others continue the life journey: "Late comes the sense that all will go on without us," Hadas writes (p. 38). Rather than thinking we affect things, things affect us: "laws we thought we had enacted turn, / chisel in hand, and carve us like a stone" (p. 39).

In the end, as Hadas points out in "Genealogies," we are mirrored not only by people but by nature, and in learning through other people, we may not always learn what we want to know. A long passage illustrates the irony of how nature sometimes gives us what we need much better than the people closest to us can:

Mirrors of astonishment, water, trees
spoke through the window of my meditation,
truer than human voices in their weaving
between the phases, inattention giving
way to thirst, or hunger to abundance.
You never taught me how to make a choice,
or make a friend, or how to think of endings.
How to exclude. That choosing means exclusion.
A task I had to come to on my own,
you never taught me how to tell the truth.
Setting things down came second. First you taught
me—
slow pupil, I'm still learning—how to read.

(p. 42)

The last section of the book involves the way we mirror ourselves to ourselves and especially to the beloved. The section begins with "Desire," which, as we might guess, is "Selfish, the dreamer's mirror" (p. 47). The eleven-stanza poem fans out to other observations about relationships, to the self, to nature, and to the other, ending with connection: "The bridge of glances spans a rainbow's reach / from the original mirror of the eye" (p. 57). This is a variation of the saying "the eyes are the mirror to the soul."

The five poems in the section are "Desire," "Happiness," "On Dreams," "Four Poems at the End of Summer," and "Love." The titles themselves illustrate the theme of human mirroring but also reach a kind of apex in a strong love relationship.

The irony is that the last poem does not use lofty images to heighten the importance of love. By contrast, this ten-section poem is not afraid to discuss such an unpoetic subject as human feet (not the metrical kind!) or to mention the sweat that comes from wrestling with a German shepherd. Although Hadas is, in general, a cerebral poet—and knows this about herself— this poem grounds the relationship in physicality: "Used to each other to the point that we / no longer look to one another's gaze / to see what that could tell us; mirrorlike / it gives us back what we already are" (p. 72). The mirrors and identities become fluid, emphasizing a lifetime shared and to come:

I mother you you father me vice versa:
take the exhausted person off, discard
the mom and dadness of who's child, whose child
means less than the warm back we each of us
lie against, the body where we anchor
ourself, the imprint deep as blood.

(p. 76)

THE EMPTY BED

The "empty bed" of the title of this 1995 poetry collection comes from Hadas' experience of going to see her dying mother, only to find her mother's hospital bed stripped and her mother having passed away. The book is a series of such shocks and reverberations of emptiness, the emptiness that comes with death. Ernest J. Smith writes that it is "a volume that established her as one of the major elegists of her generation." Like Elizabeth Bishop in "One Art," Hadas finds "we must be born // already used to loss" ("The Changes," p. 46). The trick is to preserve, or try to capture, as much of each person's "secret self" as possible, "fragile as a leaf of onionskin // or shut up in a box" (p. 45). Anita Helle cites another model: "Hadas' mentor for writing elegies is Auden. She views late twentieth-century cultures of death and mourning in a gay men's health clinic from the perspective of a commuter who moves in from the professional classes as a part-time bedsitter. ... Her poems from *The Empty Bed* include elegies for gay poets who died of AIDS (among them poet and biographer David Kalstone)" (p. 59).

The book is divided into three sections: the first explores the ineffable nature of human experience; the second is a series of elegies; and the last looks at the insistence of life in the face of death.

The theme of the first section seems to be "Love's ladder of illusion, rung by rung" ("Lower Level, Room EE," p. 9). As much as we try to hold on to experience, we find ourselves foiled by time and death. This theme is illustrated in a range of ways, through "the fissures" in her son's soapy back ("Faultlines," p. 3); the elusiveness of joy—"seen out of the corner of my eye / as happiness always is" ("Lunch the Day After Thanksgiving," p. 4); and nature—"An object like a fallen leaf / foreboding autumn leitmotif" ("The Friend," p. 19). No matter what we do, we end up in the same place: "We all are implicated either way, / your muted gaze both says and doesn't say" ("Chiasmus" p. 16). Helle elaborates: "In 'Faultlines,' it [grieving] goes on in the border spaces, where we are split from ourselves and from others. What Hadas calls the 'cracks' and 'fissures' are spaces in which the generic mythologies are reconsidered if not actually rearranged. Powerfully. ... the spaces in between enable a critical vision—here, of her son's body as the fissured map of an already gendered

background. If the genre is thinly sketched across these spaces, if the poet 'strains across a numb abyss,' it is because intimacy is so fragile" (p. 62).

The second section of the book is perhaps the most memorable, both in terms of illustration of her main theme of loss and in terms of the heartfelt response to the deaths of important people in her life. The series reads with a muted anguish, delivering a tribute as well as expressing the inefficacy of being the one left behind. Most of the poems are written for specific people but move outward to general observations about death.

This approach to death can have a witty, even slightly humorous, edge. For example, the first poem, for Gregory Kolovakos, makes reference to "Sleepy's," the mattress company. But it also stands for the way out of this life, as in the eternal rest. Other ways to approach death include courtesy—"Etiquette dictates *That was delicious / when what we mean is Take my plate away*" ("Thank You and Goodbye," p. 28)—and rewritten narratives emphasizing death in "The Wolf in the Bed," as in Hadas' allusion to Gustave Dorés' painting of "Little Red Riding Hood," with grandmother and Red lying side by side, and intermingled with Hadas' own narrative with her mother. In the Hadas poem they are also *read*. Of the elegies, perhaps the most personally moving is "Upon My Mother's Death," with its resonance of loss: "stretching across the boundaries of love, / defying the short time we're let to live, / the scanty sum it's possible to give" (p. 40).

The last section of the volume deals with what has been left behind: people, objects, memories, life forces. Nothing is enough to even the balance with loss. Even in light of an assertive and yowling tomcat, the feeling is that even such a creature who affects so viscerally is forgotten: "The tomcat stayed out first for one night, next / two, then a week, and finally was clean gone, swallowed up in summer's greeny gullet. / Already we forget the way he looked" ("Orange," p. 65).

What, then, lasts? Hadas says that etiquette does: its "sovereign gesture / apportions envy, mourning, greed, delight / each to its own

compartment and perspective" ("Nine Tiles," p. 66). Yet she points out that it is difficult "To know the difference between full and empty" ("Six of One," p. 69). In the end, it is a series of signs, or tracings, that we must interpret and know: "And when we're done with blame, reproach, resentment, / The creaky hinges of the heart can open. ... / My mother sends me out into the snow / in silence where I listen for her voice" ("The Hinge," p. 71).

HALFWAY DOWN THE HALL: NEW AND SELECTED POEMS

Halfway Down the Hall (1998) comprises thirty-three new poems, including Hadas' most famous poem, "The Red Hat," as well as selections from her previous eight books. While most of the choices from earlier volumes are predictable, especially from *Starting from Troy,* there are especially long selections from *Pass It On* and *The Empty Bed.* In fact, there are roughly double the number of poems included from those volumes as from the others, presumably reflecting her preoccupations. Also included in the count is work from Hadas' book on AIDS, *Unending Dialogue* (1991, with Charles Barber et al.), and *Other Worlds Than This* (1994), her book of translations.

Except for "The Red Hat" and "The Blue Bead," the new poetry is more cerebral than some of her work, and engages in some of the stock-taking that comes with middle age and distance from one's youth. One can seem to go "around and around" with one's life. A poem that illustrates this theme is "Rag Rug," with its *ab-bbcb* rhyme scheme underscoring the buildup and fragility of years. Lines such as "I put my face to the folds and smell despair / as palpable as salt air" (p. 3) and "I can't make out her face, / can only conjure up the faintest trace / of an abstracted grace" (p. 3) are noteworthy. Yet most of the poems are more like "Last Trip to Greece," which reveals how much she has changed since her last trip, noticing, for example, gender roles more acutely: "What was new / was how I saw this world as one of men" (p. 5). Sometimes when we return to a place, or a preoccupation, of

an earlier time in life, it no longer retains the magic of our imagination, and there is a loss in that. A poem that touches on this is "Myth":

> Startling in its intimacy,
> personal as apostrophe,
> bristling with proper names,
> rival traditions, counter-claims,
> conservative yet transitory,
> with room for every human story,
> myth is the rumor we pass on
> after due revision.
>
> (p. 36)

Poems like "The Red Hat" and "The Blue Bead" are more specifically direct, personal, and narrative. Although some might argue that these poems are less poetic, at their best their directness resonates with a larger spectrum of readers. Selections from the two poems illustrate this point:

> "I chose the bead. He told me I could choose."
> All the more, then, a treasure not to lose ...
>
> ... but lost by us. That bead is now long gone—
> misplaced, no doubt, in the translation
>
> from one place to another, child to boy.
> Time's seen to it. ...
>
> ("The Blue Bead," p. 18)

> The mornings we turn back to are no more
> than forty minutes longer than before,
> but they feel vastly different—flimsy, strange,
> wavering in the eddies of this change,
> empty, unanchored, perilously light
> since the red hat vanished from our sight.
>
> ("The Red Hat," p. 20)

INDELIBLE

The title of Hadas' 2001 poetry collection focuses on permanence, and yet the voluptuous raspberries on the cover illustrate the difficulty of such a claim. In the end, the issue is not that everything lasts, but rather *what* lasts. The first poem in the collection, "Thick and Thin," reflects on the earliest memories we have and want to savor. As Hadas writes, "That earliest essence—what was it

again? / You spend a lifetime trying to get it back" (p. 3).

The raspberries on the cover refer to the poem "Ghost Jam," which discusses berry picking in high season. Ultimately, though, because of time and the experience of being in time, it is impossible to lose oneself completely in the experience. Hadas writes, "Without the waiting world— ... / how could the berries keep / the mystery of their promise, sweet and black?" (p. 7). That world, for Hadas, is also about paradox— the "arcs of transcendent longing" ("Déjà vu," p. 8) and the possibility of "an emblem, solid sculpted thing / which can be clasped and framed, can be contained" ("Change Is the Stranger," p. 57).

The book becomes a journey to capture parents and children through their earlier selves and through their earlier experiences. In "Fathers and Daughters, Mothers and Sons," Hadas explains:

> If the past
> is the one place where feeling can be seen,
> it still is not a place we can sit down,
> put down our luggage, up our feet, and stay.
> Its only mode is visions of what's been—
> rare and fleeting.
>
> (pp. 83–84)

Finally, though, as she writes in "The Seamy Side," "we tell / each other versions of an endless tale" (p. 101). As such a prolific poet, preoccupied with the past, she is one of those most admirably suited to do that, although she is suggesting that it is part of the human condition.

LAWS

The focus in Hadas' poetry collection *Laws* (2004) shifts from the personal to the communal, to an awareness of how certain general principles—call them "laws," for lack of a better term—govern the human condition. The book is Hadas' effort to look at such elements as pettiness, jealousy, and sorrow from a more literary, or, in some ways, more distilled perspective. As Hadas writes in "The Chorus": "These watchers

locate in their repertory / mythic fragments of some kindred story / and draw them dripping out of memory's well" (p. 3). She writes of her own work:

> Mine used to play the heroine—me me me
> but lately, having had its fill of 'I,'
> tries to discern, despite its vision's flaws,
> a shape. A piece of myth. A pattern. Laws.
>
> (p. 4)

While many of the poems are in iambic meters, Hadas explores, as well, a longer line in this volume. For example, some lines begin on the left-hand margin, and the subsequent sprawl is often indented like a long quotation in a research paper.

In "Pronoun Variations" she explores a man's relationships to his belongings and to his children and a woman's relationships to others and self. Hadas is concerned, as she is in other volumes, with feminist themes. Yet ultimately she is concerned with ways we can shed our pronouns and move into our communal self:

> And in the end I believe we let go our pronouns,
> loose the strings and they rise
> into the sky *I I I I* balloons
> smoke rings *you you you you*
> the breath of life leaving our
> lips as our eyes, closing,
> become the same as anybody's eyes,
> pronouns passing, the great noun persisting.
>
> (p. 14)

Hadas' themes in the book explore a range of collective human concerns. One is scale, as in "The Gaze": "a loss we locals take as personal, / transformed by time, both shrinks and swells at once / to public; limited; historical" (p. 46). Another is desire, as in "Dead Wood, Green Wood": "appetites tightly braided with frustration" (p. 79). A third is mutability: "pushing through dead wood, though not for him, / my father writing letters against time" (p. 81). Given the frailty of human life, Hadas notes, "No wonder we love the dead" ("The Gates," p. 68). Yet out of this there are shining moments Hadas cannot help noticing, as in "The Other Side":

"ankle-deep / in dapples come undone, the human knot / untied and sparkling in another sun" (p. 86).

THE RIVER OF FORGETFULNESS

Thirty years after *Starting from Troy,* Hadas was still preoccupied by certain themes: Greece, loss, relationships. Yet, while at the beginning of her career Hadas erred on the side of the obscure, in more recent years she has moved to the side of clarity. If at times musicality is sacrificed for sense, Hadas remains both prolific and interesting.

The River of Forgetfulness (2006) underscores loss—of fundamental human interaction and complexity—through the use of media, which has become a preoccupation of Hadas in both poetry and prose. At the same time, Hadas' own frame of reference is more literary, so she gives these moments additional resonance through literary parallels, placing them in *Great Expectations* and *David Copperfield,* respectively.

A loss-of-innocence theme is also clear in a poem written for the son of Alicia Stallings, a poet about whom Hadas had already written in prose and who is Hadas' good friend. With the world full of "Anti-Muses," Hadas explains to Jason that

> All arts surround you. From their street
> You've moved into the Muses' house.
> Raised in that haven, lucky boy,
> You'll face the labyrinth of harm
> and bliss. ...
>
> (p. 116)

Art, for Hadas, is what saves us in the face of loss, or at least makes the way easier.

THE ACHE OF APPETITE

The poetry collection *The Ache of Appetite* (2010) is in many ways a companion book to Hadas' memoir *Strange Relation,* as both address her husband's early onset dementia. Hadas points out in her essay "Eating Barley Sugar and Waiting to Be Ninety," from *Living in Time,* that she finds

herself crossing from one book to another, and one genre to another: "Connections, at any rate, once they begin to work take on a life of their own, weaving strands not only in and out of the books I happen to have read but also in and out of poems in the books I have written. I've enjoyed tracing various strands" (p. 164).

Oddly, given the subject matter, the volume is breezier than some of Hadas' earlier poetry books. The poetry is accessible, clear, and often poignant. Unlike many other books, this collection has only two sections, the first emphasizing endings, the second more specifically focused on the personal circumstances of the couple as well as the profundity of loss. Since Hadas so often has books with three sections, this volume runs the risk of having sections that feel heavy, but the directness of the poems eliminates this difficulty.

Hadas continues to focus on time and circumstance. Here one of her themes is getting a distance on experience. In "The Middle Way," for instance, Hadas is attempting to find just the right distance, not too far or too close—a "Three Bears" motif, but in a serious way. In "Attention," Hadas joins distance with perspective, quoting Gerard Manley Hopkins, who says, "What you look hard at seems to look hard / at you" (p. 14). What is left by this experience? Seeing? Understanding? Hadas uses a range of metaphors to indicate how time passes through as a process. One of her most compelling images is that of the "snake that slides invisibly / off into the long grass of the world" (p. 22). As she asks again in "Masque in Green and Black": "In keeping, what is there to gain? / In loving, what is there to lose? / Nothing but breath and heat and days" (p. 30).

The second half of the book is more intense in its presentation, and more heartbreaking. Given the unfairness of her marital situation, Hadas compares herself to the "push me pull you" pencil, sharpened on both ends, saying, "And as I had been punctured, / I wanted to puncture others" (p. 37). One of the most effective poems in this section is "The Hotel," written in an old-timey blues style: "Living with dementia is like riding on a carousel. / I said dementia is like a big old carousel. / And you can't get off, but it turns into a hotel" (p. 62). Parts are self-pitying and true—"Who's going to visit you? Don't expect your friends"—while others are unspeakably sad: "I'd like to cry, but I have no more tears. / I said I'm done crying, I've run out of tears. / Before and now and after, years and years" (p. 62).

In the end, the book is about the depth and chilliness of loss, as the last poem in the collection, "The Cold Hill Side," suggests: *And I awoke and found me here / on the cold hill side* (p. 64).

FORM, CYCLE, INFINITY

Hadas' scholarly study *Form, Cycle, Infinity: Landscape Imagery in the Poetry of Robert Frost and George Seferis* (1985), which grew out of her thesis at Princeton, compares and contrasts two famous poets known for their emphasis on place, and perfectly suits Hadas' position as an American with classical training and four years spent in Greece. The style of the book, while literary, is meditative and conversational, so that one gets a clear sense of the workings of Hadas' intellectual process. She categorizes herself as more of a poet than a scholar.

Beyond their sense of place, the two poets are markedly different, and Hadas' purpose in treating them together has more to do with Hadas' own preoccupations than with any inherent or expected connections between them. In fact, Hadas begins the book by saying, "Robert Frost and George Seferis, two poets who lived at about the same time, wrote in different languages and knew little or nothing of one another's work" (p. 7). She suggests that she uses "synecdoche"—that is, parts of a whole—as a way to approach her topic (p. 10). In this poetic framework, she returns to the somewhat fragmentary resonance of the approach in "Dream Interpretation" from *Starting from Troy*, although now on a scholarly rather than a poetic level. That is to say, the mere bringing of these poets together, and privileging certain aspects of their work, creates a dreamily intuitive sense of connection, which ultimately is

characteristic of Hadas' oeuvre, both poetry and prose.

LIVING IN TIME

Perhaps no phrase in Hadas' work more accurately describes her work than the title of this 1990 volume. The book is an eclectic mix, covering topics that range from reading and teaching to her early adult experiences living in Greece. The first and third sections of the book, which are selections of essays, serve as bookends for the long poem titled "The Dream Machine," which is about her relationship with her son Jonathan but is also dedicated—as is the book itself—to James Merrill and Alan Ansen, two people whose friendships Hadas has cherished and who have so perfected the notion of "living in time." This long blank-verse poem examines the crease between reality and dream as well as major issues about life.

The first essay in the book, "The Cradle and the Bookcase," published in *Southwest Review* and the winner of a McGinnis Award from the journal, details her experiences with reading, placing them not only within her own personal context but within the context of other famous readers—and writers—such as John Milton, Joseph Brodsky, and Marcel Proust. The motivating principle of the essay is the solitary joy that comes with reading, as rich as the taste of one of Proust's madeleines. Hadas notes,

Reading is one of the handful of human experiences that can be felt as joyful at the moment it's taking place; even as the pleasure is greater in retrospect. And unlike a memorable meal, or a hike up a mountain, or an ecstatic hour with a lover, reading effortlessly and innocently offers itself to us again, permits us to compare, to deepen our understanding in an invidious way that lays the blame on nobody should the repeated experience disappoint us.

(p. 3)

Hadas refers to what she calls "an erotics of reading" (p. 7). Later, in an interview with Gloria Brame, she goes on to say that "reading is not just food for thought; it is thoughts. John Hol-

lander has said that writing is a more difficult form of reading" (p. 140).

Hadas posits that the greatest gift, in one of the most profound ways, is passing on a cherished book to someone else. She understands the solemnity, in Louis Malle's film *Au revoir les enfants,* of a Jewish boy sent off to be killed in World War II who passes his beloved books— one might even say "dearly beloved"—to the childhood version of Louis Malle. As Hadas says, "Books not only ... outlast their authors; they can even outlast their owners, which is why it's important to pass your love of a book on to someone else" (p. 22).

"Notes on Teaching" is an idiosyncratic take on the profession. Hadas addresses the subject elsewhere—for example, she has poems about her relationships with students, with the cycle of the school year, and so on—but it is here that she addresses fully the almost indefinable nature of what happens in the classroom:

My sloppy syllabus, my chaotic blackboard technique. My partiality, my impatience, sometimes my sarcasm—unprofessional, I know. And the hair on my forearms rising when I remember Achilles and Lykaon; my vision of Lear and Cordelia's reunion, projected for them on the opaque screen, carved out by the crude instrument, of my body. I serve, I proffer, I cater, and later on I also judge. But what has been assimilated, even what has once been uttered, hangs in the public air, cannot be taken back or taken away.

(pp. 27–28)

The middle section of the book, "The Dream Machine," a more than three-hundred-line blank verse poem for her son, Jonathan, has a weightiness to it both in its length and in its themes. Broken into fourteen sections, the poem addresses the nature of dreams, reality, and time, all standard subjects for Hadas. The poem is triggered by Jonathan's wondering what is true and what isn't, and it becomes a meditation on the nature of the moment versus the nature of one's lifespan and the larger nature of time's wingspan. What lasts, and what does not?

One particularly poignant section describes Jonathan's sponge animals unfolding in the bathtub. Dropped in as capsules and then reveal-

122

RACHEL HADAS

ing themselves, through the hot water of the bath, in their animal shapes, they become a metaphor for the unfolding of time:

> I wonder: does it ever worry you
> that this unfolding is a one-way road?—
> immediately answering my own
> question *Of course not.*
>
> (p. 122)

Jonathan's belief that any phase of the moon except a full moon is "broken" heightens a theme that epitomizes what Hadas' work is all about: "That silver sliver shining in the sky / tells us the broken world is where we are" (p. 140).

Also of interest in the volume is Hadas' candid assessment of her time in Greece. Since this experience in many ways shaped the course of her life, it is noteworthy to have this take on a subject she has often been reticent about. As she writes in the essay "Mornings in Ormos,"

> One trouble with being young is that you don't know who you are supposed to be, let alone who you are; how you are supposed to be acting, let alone feeling. My youthfulness may have been responsible in part for my finding myself at twenty-two married to a Greek peasant.
>
> (p. 175)

Hadas spends some time outlining her relationship not only with Stavros but also with Alan Ansen. She explains,

> Alan, was, I soon learned, in love with Stavros—or that's the way I jealously put it to myself then. Alan and I were very taken by each other; and during the course of my winter in Athens I found myself attached to both Alan and Stavros. And Stavros—did he love us both? ... How much love flew around the streets of Kolonaki that winter!
>
> (p. 177)

In attempting to come to terms with this atypical time, Hadas admits to readers that

> I have avoided talking about my years on Samos. If people want to know about my experiences in Greece, I refer them to *Slow Transparency.* ... (My decision to put a tantalizing reference to some of what did happen on the back of the book is one I regret in a way; still, I somehow wanted to get it off my chest, in however incomplete a fashion.)

> To explain was more than impossible, it was embarrassing. How wildly, how ludicrously improbable that I should ever have been the wife of ... a person who was a world away from me in background, education, interests!
>
> Our economic base was desire.
>
> (p. 179)

In the end, Hadas sees her time in Greece as both a transition and as start to the rest of her life.

MERRILL, CAVAFY, POEMS, AND DREAMS

Of particular note in this 2000 volume of critical and personal essays is the time Hadas spends elucidating her relationship with James Merrill. While certainly her friendship with him is well known, this book takes time to articulate her relationship with his work and the intellectual, scholarly richness Hadas attempts to bring to her own work. In addition, she underscores not only the legacy of friendship and belongings—in life and death—but also the legacy of AIDS, and how their community of friendships informs their small, privileged circle. The book includes, for example, Merrill's description of the scattering of David Kalstone's ashes, when "the white gravel of our friend fanned out" (p. 45).

While Hadas exhibits both her friendship and critical acumen in her evaluation of James Merrill, it seems that her friendship wins out when she writes of Alan Ansen. Her judgment seems colored by the initial formation of their friendship in Greece. She admits in her essay "Fructifying a Cycle: Homage to Alan Ansen" that she sees him—and his poetry—as "magnetic," "addictive," and "dramatic." Of course, the purpose here is homage, but it is unusual for Hadas to take such a perspective, and it is noteworthy how formative, and lasting, her relationship with Ansen was.

An interview at the end of the volume focuses specifically on her books *The Double Legacy* and *Pass It On,* adding a spotlight to Hadas' continuing oeuvre. While joking a bit about a phoenix reference, she says, "I was tried for arson only once!" (p. 131). Yet she also mentions the heat that comes from friendship. She

explains, "I think it was Bishop who wrote something about poets keeping warm by writing to each other" (p. 137). This volume, as a whole, is about warmth of all kinds—warmth of friendship, warmth of reading—that sustains us. Such warmth has a nourishment theme as well. Hadas points out: "as a teacher, a mother, a whatever, I got to spread this feast out for others" (p. 140).

CLASSICS

Classics (2007), with its punning title—conjoining Hadas' fascination with the classics and her own classic essays—is far-ranging in its interests and prolific in its scope. Not only does the book illustrate how Hadas moves from the personal to the literary and back again; it reminds the reader of what other types of writing she has done—reviews of books of translations and anthologies as well as fictitious (and witty) interviews.

The book begins with the title essay, which excavates the author's childhood and her interest in the classics. The essay delves into her upbringing as the daughter of a famous scholar in a particular corner of New York that included even better-known families such as the Trillings (the critic and scholar Lionel Trilling being the most obvious). She describes her exposure to books in general and to Greek texts in particular. "Classics" is about recovering what we can from the past: "So much from my first twelve years comes back to me as I write—back from wherever lost things disappear to. What matters is to trust in the possibility of a return, and one return heralds another" (p. 38).

While Hadas includes many pieces on both Greek texts and Greek topics, perhaps what is surprising is the memorability of some of her reviews, such as "You Know More Than You Think You Do," which compares and contrasts such poetry textbooks as *The Sounds of Poetry,* by Robert Pinsky; *How to Read a Poem: And Fall in Love with Poetry,* by Edward Hirsch; *A Poet's Guide to Poetry,* by Mary Kinzie; and *Making Your Own Days: The Pleasures of Reading and Writing Poetry,* by Kenneth Koch. Hadas errs on the side of the clear and usable, favoring

Pinsky. Yet she pokes fun at all in a mock interview titled "Pages of Illustrations," where Catullus, Humpty-Dumpty, Shakespeare, and Walt Whitman also join the affectionate fun.

Another standout essay is "More Like an Extension of the Spirit: Clothing in Lyric Poems." While one might expect that clothes might play a role in poems, it is the subtle, tender way that Hadas manages to capture their importance that is noteworthy. One stellar example of a poem cited in the essay is "The Blouse" by Mark Rudman, which lovingly delineates the ruination of a favorite blouse at the laundry. Hadas extends this importance of clothing through human objects, and A. E. Stallings, a favorite poet of Hadas, illustrates this point through "Elegy for the Lost Umbrella."

The William Baer interview with Hadas toward the end of the volume is noteworthy as well. A meticulous poet and interviewer, he asks new questions about her early adult life in Greece and new types of questions about her famous poem "The Red Hat." Since Hadas elsewhere in the book discusses her occasional frustration about being e-mailed certain questions about the poem—including factual locations about place and about her own son—it is with some bemusement that she answers the question "Did Jonathan have a red hat?" with "He did wear a red cap sometimes, but it was more like a ski cap" (p. 339).

OTHER WORLDS THAN THIS

Hadas' book of translations, *Other Worlds Than This* (1994), shows her facility in a range of languages, including Latin, French, and modern Greek. Although she does reference themes that are of interest in her own work—the passing of time, the enjoyment of small moments—what is noteworthy is the way in which she chooses to translate poems that often are about the less-than-admirable in human nature. In a way, this volume looks forward to her book of poetry, *Laws,* in which she examines general human impulses. Here, though, the themes are placed within the personal, and often corrupted, situations of the

RACHEL HADAS

speakers. Hadas' personal style as a poet seems best suited for the classical texts in the book, although she is a faithful, and astute, translator in a range of languages.

As Hadas often does, she connects her project with a personal story, and here she frames her volume with a personal essay. Being in the unusual position of having done translations since her adolescence, she can draw the resonance of her experience through all of her translations, in the way that adults often define their later experiences through their pivotal childhood memories. Thus, Hadas' translations are emotionally charged and impactful. Given that she was teaching poetry to AIDS patients during this time, her experience with certain themes, particularly of mortality, is almost visceral.

She offers a marvelous description of the difficulty and responsibility inherent in approaching someone else's text, especially if the style is unlike one's own:

> Translating Baudelaire … had felt to me like a bold, impulsive act. … I had entered each stanza, no, every line of each stanza of those twenty-one poems as a careful servant would enter a room, polishing facets, highlighting ornaments without displacing any important documents, restoring its primal luster to all the crucial and artful original disorder. …
>
> I thought of red and black lacquer, of an ebony box on a mahogany table, of an inlaid dagger in a lamplit corner. Each unit presented its own riddle. Each was a problem I could solve without shattering it only if I moved gently, brushing the faintest layer of the dust of disuse from the arc of an alexandrine or shifting an unintelligible object (love gift? souvenir?) a shade closer to the reddish glow of firelight, while twilight filled the room and in the hearth the dying embers faintly whistled.
>
> (p. xvi–xvii)

Whatever the box, whether it is the witty world of the betrayed Tibullus—whose lover Delia betrays her husband and then betrays him too—or the world-weary Baudelaire, Hadas manages to make her approach sound. Among the poems of Konstantine Karyotakis, who is perhaps the surprise in the volume, "Precautions" is important not only in terms of the morality play in which Hadas is interested but also in terms of the topic

of bullying, which many people might see as more specifically contemporary. Hadas proves that this topic is universal:

> When people plan to hurt you,
> they'll always manage to. …
>
> People with evil in their hearts
> know how to dress it up
>
> persuasively with golden words
> not one of which is true
>
> since what's at stake is nothing less
> than flesh and blood—yes, you.
>
> (p. 141)

UNENDING DIALOGUE: VOICES FROM AN AIDS POETRY WORKSHOP

Unending Dialogue (1991) is a moving collection of poems by students in Hadas' poetry workshop, which was part of Gay Men's Health Crisis in New York City. Although most of the work in the volume is written by students, Hadas bookends the collection with, on the one side, a well-known essay on her experience called "The Lights Must Never Go Out" (it appears also in *Living in Time*) and, on the other, "Out of Your Nakedness, Out of My Nakedness," a series of sixteen poems with her own analysis of the poems therein.

The interior section consists of poems by Charles Barber, Glenn Besco, Dan Conner, Tony J. Giordano, Kevin Imbusch, Glenn Philip Kramer, Raul Martinez-Avila, Gustavo Motta, Michael Pelonero, and James Turtotte. Most memorable in the section are poems by Barber and Conner, and Barber's work is certainly most akin to Hadas'. There is a fragmentary, meditative cast to the collection as a whole, with writing that is both cathartic and revelatory. As Glenn Besco writes about the teddy bear in his poem, "He knows all the secrets of the night nurses" ("A Teddy Bear," p. 31).

The last section is Hadas' own series of takes on many of the same assignments that her students did, as well as her own explications.

The work is uneven, and can feel distant, especially in comparison with the immediacy of her students' circumstances and work. Yet it has taken courage to plumb these depths, and it is admirable that Hadas has done so. There are memorable moments in both the poetry and prose. For example, in referring to *The Iliad*, she writes, "A person with AIDS could live longer now, perhaps, but forever with the knowledge of his sentence. Surely, I wanted to say, they were grateful for extended lives, new treatments, ever-present hope? Maybe it was at the thought of Achilles and Lykaon that this insipid consolation died on my lips" (p. 120). Ultimately, Hadas hopes that the two parts—the prose and poetry—work together to communicate a truth. As she explains, "Perhaps this tissue of talk can be thought of as a kind of drapery that enhances, rather than muffling, the essential nakedness that the poems depict—that they even, I hope, enact" (p. 90).

THE DOUBLE LEGACY: REFLECTIONS ON A PAIR OF DEATHS

Hadas' *Double Legacy* (1995), which simultaneously ponders the death of Hadas' good friend David Kalstone and that of her mother Elizabeth Chamberlayne Hadas, is a series of brief prose meditations on loss and mourning. The two died within six weeks of each other, making this period particularly difficult for Hadas. While one hesitates to use the term "breezy" in referring to these pieces, there is an ease, both in length and style, that invites that reader in. As Hadas writes in the foreword, "the pieces investigate in one way or another what Proust called the intermittences of the heart: the rhythms of grief and mourning, the odd moments of consolation and oblivion, the forms memory takes, the humdrum yet uncanny changes wrought on time. ... in the words of John Ashbery, it's about the privacy of everyone" (pp. x–xi). Although these essays share qualities with others by Hadas, they are as a group more personal, more similar, and more cumulative.

The pieces are arranged chronologically, starting in 1989 and ending in 1993. Kalstone and Hadas died in 1992. The book's structure,

then, is one of psychological buildup, then release. The book is a near contemporary of *Heaven's Coast* (1996), by Mark Doty, which is both a celebration of life and a contemplation of death; both books were part of the burgeoning of memoir in the mid-1990s. Hadas' book has a more essay-like feel than Doty's, and this is not surprising, given her background; yet both offer series of fragments to make sense of death as a whole. Hadas has as her ordinary milieu loss and loneliness, so this book extends and deepens that topic. She uses occasions such as going to the mailbox, reading a storybook, and receiving a postcard as ways to contemplate the texture of existence around them. For example, in going to the mailbox she has the dizzying, surreal experience of meeting her mother out of context, while in a drifting mental state. In other words, she dreams her mother into the scene. As Hadas writes, "Once liminality sinks its roots deep enough, one's vision changes, one's mental weather darkens" ("The Mailbox," p. 5). One might say that the whole book is an exploration of a liminal state.

Within the book, Hadas often interweaves quotations by others in order to provide additional insight into her experience. This is a strategy she employs in other books as well, but there is an additional urgency here, as if there is a hope that the wisdom of others will provide comfort, or provide an insight into the sadness she is experiencing. Yet, as she writes in "Dark Fire," "What's particularly repellent in this complacency is its numbing matter-of-factness. As if sure, it's all in a day's work for a person one loves to be snatched out of sight, plucked right off the earth's surface, eyes extinguished, voice and moods turned irrevocably off, number unlisted forevermore" (p. 143).

The book is about the journey, the process, and at the end Hadas is still searching:

It's something I can't name—some kind of yielding, somehow, through the daily, normal deafness and obstruction of an air lit up with intermittent livid flashes of grief and resignation and desire, of a clear sign, not tangible, not tooth or bone or photograph, but still some kind of sign of who or what you were. Some signal that may or may not fit

in with, but won't be erased by, whatever it is that you have become.

(p. 163)

STRANGE RELATION *(2011)*

Given that Hadas and her husband, George Edwards, were both academics, and very cerebral people, the diagnosis of his early-onset dementia came as a shock. Hadas realized over time that although her husband was still alive, she was experiencing a grief process about the man who was already gone. She also realized how community does not necessarily stand by people who are going through a difficult time. She had to find her own new community through support groups and other poets, and, in order to survive, she had to learn to compartmentalize her life.

Her book *Strange Relation* (2011) captures this sense of loss and isolation, and is both a reflection of the experience of tracing the onset of dementia and her own process dealing with it. The book intersperses poems written during the period with the memoir, so as to emphasize the way dementia affects every aspect of life. As Hadas writes,

> The failure that haunts me today, that has been haunting me for weeks, involves my marriage of nearly thirty years. Much of the failure is mine. I am failing to imagine a future with him; failing to envision how I can summon the strength to go on like this; failing to remember him as he was before this illness stealthily took hold, to conjure him clearly enough so that some significant remnant is left to me. But there's plenty of failure to go around.

(p. 120)

The memoir picks up on the medical underpinnings of such books as Lisa Genova's best-selling *Still Alice* (2009), which attempts both to imitate and explain the effects of dementia. There is a feeling of "Why me?" as there is with all such diagnoses, because, of course, partners didn't necessarily sign on for this life journey. Hadas tries to avoid self-pity by compartmentalizing her life and keeping herself busy.

However, there is a price to be paid for this, too, in that it's difficult to trace the mysterious unfolding of the disease. When decisions need to be made, a jolt comes with them:

> I didn't know what I wanted. I knew what I didn't want. I didn't want to go on living in this cage of silence, this dumb desert, with a man who no longer spoke to me. I had gone so long living in this deepening drought that I hardly noticed it any more. I didn't visit my own thoughts much, until poems and dreams brought me face to face with them.

(p. 87)

CONCLUSION

From her earliest poems as a teenager, Rachel Hadas has been preoccupied with issues of loss, of place, of time. Although her story moved from New York City to Greece and back again, her work is an endless cycling of the places that have been most important to her, including her summer places in Vermont and Maine.

Place has also been important to Hadas as a state of mind, and she has attempted to move beyond the personal to more abstract parts of the human condition; to move beyond self-pity and narcissism to grief, loss, and happiness. Certainly her own experience with her father's death, and with her trial over the olive press in Greece, proved in her personal life that there could be forces beyond her; her work with AIDS patients only strengthened that belief. Her husband's experience with early onset dementia both brought her full circle and made it possible for her to reach out to others going through the same experience.

In her work in a range of genres, the interrelationship of theme, the admirable range of tone, and the continual restless mind are noteworthy attributes. As Robert McPhillips noted of her work mid-career, "The most interesting aesthetic question that Rachel Hadas poses … is whether she will remain content to write a continuous, absorbing, albeit vexingly repetitious poetry, or whether she will work more vigorously at polishing her lyrics. One would feel more certain about her ultimate permanence as a poet if she selected the latter path, though Hadas' talent is obviously substantial" (p. 113).

In a sense, "The Red Hat " serves as a poetic middle distance for her. If that poem contains what people like best in terms of accessible subject matter and music, the rest of her work moves on a continuum from what is more obscure to what is more direct. Yet, from translations to essays to reviews, from lyric poem to long sequence, from short lines to long lines, Hadas always has something to say and something to say well. Although a translation of a Tacitus quotation makes Hadas think of her father, it is applicable to her as well: "Just as men's faces are frail and perishable, so are likenesses of their faces, but the shape of the mind is an eternal thing, one which you cannot hold on to and expose through artistic medium or skill, but by your own manner of life" ("Many Lives"). Rachel Hadas' prolific power may be daunting to many of us, but there is always a way to move forward. Given her experiences, this is both sobering and courageous as well as profoundly human. As she tells herself and us, "Enter the empty room" ("Six of One," *The Empty Bed*, p. 69).

Selected Bibliography

WORKS OF RACHEL HADAS

POETRY
Starting from Troy. Boston: David R. Godine, 1975.

Slow Transparency. Middletown, Conn.: Wesleyan University Press, 1983.

A Son from Sleep. Middletown, Conn.: Wesleyan University Press, 1987.

Pass It On. Princeton, N.J.: Princeton University Press, 1989.

Mirrors of Astonishment. New Brunswick, N.J.: Rutgers University Press, 1992.

The Empty Bed. Middletown, Conn.: Wesleyan University Press, 1995.

Halfway Down the Hall: New and Selected Poems. Middletown, Conn.: Wesleyan University Press, 1998.

Indelible. Middletown, Conn.: Wesleyan University Press, 2001.

Laws. Lincoln, Neb.: Zoo Press, 2004.

The River of Forgetfulness: Poems. Cincinnati, Ohio: David Robert Books, 2006.

The Ache of Appetite Providence, R.I.: Copper Beech Press, 2010.

MEMOIR
"The Many Lives of Moses Hadas." http://www.rachelhadas.com/themanylivesofmoseshadas.html.

The Double Legacy: Reflections on a Pair of Deaths. Boston: Faber and Faber, 1995.

Strange Relation: A Memoir of Marriage, Dementia, and Poetry. Philadelphia: Paul Dry Books, 2011.

SCHOLARSHIP
Form, Cycle, Infinity: Landscape Imagery in the Poetry of Robert Frost and George Seferis. Lewisburg, Pa.: Bucknell University Press, 1985.

Living in Time. New Brunswick, N.J.: Rutgers University Press, 1990.

Merrill, Cavafy, Poems, and Dreams. Ann Arbor: University of Michigan Press, 2000.

Classics: Essays. Cincinnati, Ohio: Textos Books, 2007.

ANTHOLOGY AND TRANSLATION
Unending Dialogue: Voices from an AIDS Poetry Workshop. With Charles Barber et al. Foreword by Tim Sweeney, Gay Men's Health Crisis. Boston: Faber, 1991.

Other Worlds Than This. New Brunswick, N.J.: Rutgers University Press, 1994.

CRITICAL AND BIOGRAPHICAL STUDIES
Helle, Anita. "Elegy as History: Three Women Poets 'By the Century's Deathbed.' " *South Atlantic Review* 61, no. 2:51–68 (1996).

McPhillips, Robert. "Rachel Hadas." In *American Poets Since World War II, Third Series*. Edited by R. S. Gwynn. *Dictionary of Literary Biography*. Vol. 120. Detroit: Gale Research, 1992. Pp. 108–113.

Smith, Ernest J. "Rachel Hadas." In *New Formalist Poets*. Edited by Jonathan N. Barron and Bruce Meyer. *Dictionary of Literary Biography*. Vol. 282. Detroit: Gale, 2003. Pp. 152–159.

INTERVIEWS
Baer, William. "An Interview with Rachel Hadas." In *Classics*, by Rachel Hadas. Cincinnati, Ohio: Textos Books, 2007.

Brame, Gloria Glickstein. "A Poet's Life: An Interview with Rachel Hadas." In *Merrill, Cavafy, Poems, and Dreams*, by Rachel Hadas. Ann Arbor: University of Michigan Press, 2000. Pp. 131–140.

"The CPR Interview: Rachel Hadas." *Contemporary Poetry Review*, 2009. http://www.cprw.com/Misc/hadas.htm.

Three Poets in Conversation: Dick Davis, Rachel Hadas, Timothy Steele. London: Between the Lines, 2006.

JANE HIRSHFIELD

(1953—)

Susan Carol Hauser

JANE HIRSHFIELD IS a poet, essayist, scholar, translator, editor, teacher, and reader/speaker. Her poetry is widely published in books and periodicals, and she is sought after as a teacher and speaker. Lay-ordained in the Zen Buddhist tradition, her training and mindfulness practice permeate her work. Her goal as a writer and in life is to live with as much awareness as possible. She achieves this in part through her poetry, which focuses on concrete imagery as means to removing perceptual barriers to the realities of experience.

BEGINNINGS

Jane B. Hirshfield was born on February 24, 1953, in New York City. Her father, Robert L. Hirshfield, was a clothing manufacturer and her mother, Harriet, a secretary. The Hirshfield family lived on East Twentieth Street and participated actively in New York City life: they attended the ballet and opera, and Hirshfield frequently visited the Metropolitan Museum of Art. These experiences contributed to the richness of her childhood and to her adult life as a poet.

Hirshfield attended Public School 40 in New York and then the Lenox School, a private girls' school, where she served on the editorial staff of the school literary magazine and wrote a three-hundred-line poem as her senior project. Even earlier, however, she had been influenced in her writing by a teacher at PS 40, Mrs. Barlow, and had written regularly throughout her childhood. Mark A. Eaton, writing in the *Dictionary of Literary Biography,* reports that when she was in elementary school, Hirshfield declared her intention to be a writer. On an oversized sheet of paper she wrote, "I want to be a writer when I grow up" (p. 179), although she had forgotten her pronouncement until 1982, when her mother

presented her with the yellowed sheet on the publication of her first book of poems.

In an interview Hirshfield told Bill Moyers that writing contributed to her maturation as a person, that it was a means to both inventing and discovering herself. She described herself as an introvert, writing not to reach an audience but to reach herself.

While the medium of her quest is poetry, the message comes through nature. One of her earliest memories, she told Mark Eaton and Abigail Keegan, recalls a trip at age two to the country, where she remembers having an evocative sensory experience while "lying on my back with the taste of blackberries in my mouth." She holds this event as a foundational awakening to "how the world is supposed to be" ("Diamond at the Center," p. 1). She even found nature in the midst of New York City, in a small box hedge near her family's apartment. It became a favorite hiding place which she made into a secret child's world.

A third influence on the incipient poet was reading literature. At a reading recorded on video at the University of California (*Jane Hirshfield: An Afternoon with the Poet*), Hirshfield recalled that at the age of nine she bought a Peter Pauper Press book of Japanese haiku poetry. It, along with the "wild, colloquial and vivid" poetry of Horace and Catullus, which she read in a Latin class, spoke to her emerging awareness of the transience of the world. That awareness eventually led to the lifelong study of Zen Buddhism.

Hirshfield lived in New York City until she graduated from high school and entered Princeton University in New Jersey, from which she graduated magna cum laude, Phi Beta Kappa in 1973, in that school's first class to include women. She also published her first poem in 1973, in the first year of the *Nation* magazine's

poetry competition, now called the Discovery Award.

After graduating from Princeton, Hirshfield worked for a season at a farm in New Jersey where she shared an old farmhouse with friends (in a poem written twenty years later, "1973," she recalled the time as idyllic). Except for short excursions into the country, her life experience until then had been in metropolitan settings. At the farm, she ate produce freshly picked for breakfast, before picking more to send to market.

The farm was also the site of her first writing studio, a tiny room that she and a friend painted and decorated just for her. Its windows looked out over the barnyard and fields. The sun shone inside as well when they painted the walls yellow and the floor red. It was in this room that Hirshfield not only wrote but had a mystical experience. As she recalls in an essay titled "Early Rooms," one evening while she was listening and writing to Miles Davis' album *Kind of Blue,* she was overtaken by a sense of being in the world unlimited by her self, even by her body, which she described as having "stepped onto and into a scale without measure" (p. 22).

The experience contributed to her subsequent move to California. A usual next step for a Princeton graduate would have been graduate school, but Hirshfield followed a different path, and the next year, 1974, at the age of twenty-one, she became a full-time practitioner of Soto Zen at the San Francisco Zen Center. She practiced at its three residences until 1982. For three of those years, 1975–1978, while she was in monastic practice at Tassajara Zen Mountain Center, she did not write at all, a practice that, in the end, nurtured her writing. Of that experience she has said that "poetry sent me to Buddhist practice, and Buddhist practice returned me to poetry" (Eaton, p. 180).

In a memory reminiscent of her childhood refuge in the box hedge, she recalls in "Early Rooms" that, in the monastery, she came to know that one's place, a place of belonging, can be as small as a pillow, which in Zen practice one sits on during meditation. Other aspects of her practice, she told Eaton and Keegan, especially at Tassajara, also taught her new values of space

and time. There she rose in the morning to watch the sun rise and watched it descend again in the evening. She lived without electricity or piped-in water, learning economy of resources, and she learned silence. The time there, she said, sustained her because she had chosen it, adding that it changed her in profound ways, that it "probably altered my relationship to language in the same way as living without utilities altered my relationship to the physical world. Each in its own way honed me" (p. 5).

Monastic practice in the Zen tradition is generally limited in time and intensive in nature, and Hirshfield saw her life at the center as a training period. The intent, for laypersons especially, is not to retreat from life but to prepare to return to it more fully aware and intentional. Hirshfield told Moyers that it broke her sense of being separate from the world, and increased her understanding of the connected nature of all things in life. This connection is the outright subject or undercurrent of most of Hirshfield's writing, both poetry and prose.

Hirshfield received lay ordination in 1979, meaning that she has taken vows to live according to Zen precepts such as right-mindedness, right generosity, and right-livelihood and that her Buddhist teacher has recognized her practice.

TEAHOUSE PRACTICE: LIVING ZEN

Because of her extensive training in Zen Buddhism, and its obvious migration into the themes and topics of her poetry, Hirshfield is sometimes thought of as a Zen or Buddhist poet, even though she rarely refers directly to Zen or its practices in her work. The connection, however, Hirshfield told Moyers, is readily made by readers, and she uses the metaphor of "Teahouse Practice" to explain how Zen is an invisible current that runs through her work. Although she envisions her poetry as a teahouse practice-path, she is aware that talking about Zen breaks that metaphor. Still, she feels that the poems themselves honor the practice.

In further explicating Zen to Moyers, Hirshfield emphasized that attention is most predict-

ably achieved through the practice of mindfulness, of setting aside assumptions and predictions and of letting the world flow through you rather than you moving through the world. The point is to be awake to your own experience of life, to not miss a thing. Hirshfield notes, however, that it is not as easy as it might sound to lower the barriers to acute perception.

In the context of Zen, poetry and mindfulness are not easily separated. Not only do they arise in similar ways, but they have similar elevating outcomes. As with mindfulness, "A good poem takes something you probably already know as a human being and somehow raises your capacity to feel it to a higher degree. It allows you to know your experience more intensely" (p. 105). This is accomplished in part, and in Hirshfield's work, through transcendence of the barrier between self and the world, inner and outer, subjective and objective, notes Andrew Elkins. He continues, "Her mission is to erase boundaries while keeping everything absolutely clear and vivid in its living, individual integrity" (p. 247). In her poetry, she does this most often through the recognition and explication of objects, in their finest detail, which "all show Hirshfield paying attention to interstices, boundaries in the world that do not stop, circumscribe, or limit perception and that do not separate phenomena but that instead open up a door to other realities of interconnection, in the unattended gaps over which our vision normally skips" (p. 249).

Hirshfield's poetry abounds with images of transcendence, usually through a portal such as a door, gate, or window. In the essay "Close Reading: Windows," she explains what she calls a window-moment, that brief opportunity when the veil between two worlds is lifted:

Many good poems have a kind of window-moment in them—a point at which they change their direction of gaze or thought in a way that suddenly opens a broadened landscape of meaning and feeling. Encountering such a moment, the reader breathes in some new infusion, as steeply perceptible as any physical window's increase of light, scent, sound, or air. The gesture is one of lifting, unlatching, releasing: mind and attention swing open to newly peeled vistas.

(p. 22)

These window-moments allow us to abandon our stance as observers. Like Alice in Wonderland, we do not stop to face our own reflection in the mirror; instead, we travel through the mirror.

It is metaphor that does the work of opening these windows, doors, and gates because it is not accomplished by mere thought. In her interview with Moyers, Hirshfield relates the example of a traditional metaphor for "awakened being," a Buddhist state of enlightenment, which is "snow in a silver bowl." You cannot tell where one begins and the other ends, indicating both containment and vastness. Metaphor is fundamental to Hirshfield's poetry, but it also permeates her prose, illuminating thought. Like the woman in the teahouse by the side of the road, she embodies Zen consciousness without naming it.

WRITING THE MIND AND HEART

Hirshfield's early poem published in the *Nation* in 1973 signaled the beginning of a career that includes not only the writing and publishing of poems, essays, and poetics but also poetry in translation, teaching, editing, and public reading performances. Her first book, *Alaya,* was published in 1982 by Princeton University's Quarterly Review of Literature Press when it received the *Quarterly*'s prize for that year. Her second book, *Of Gravity and Angels,* was published in 1988 and received the Joseph Henry Jackson Award from the San Francisco Foundation. With the publication of her third volume, *The October Palace,* in 1994, Hirshfield began to receive wide critical attention for her work, as the themes and topics that persist through all of her books became more fully formed, including her understanding and presentation of loss, wholeness, and the here and now. As noted by Lois Marie Harrod, Hirshfield has honed her ability to accommodate both the light and dark sides of the human experience: "Though poems in *The October Palace* ... frequently mention loss, it becomes part of the natural and spiritual cycle. Even when a

lover leaves, he is 'somehow, in another shadow of the same water, / still there' ('Just Below the Surface')." Harrod also observed that the poems propose that readers have a role in selecting how they entertain experience in their own lives, even purporting that selection is integral to experience, not optional: "With serene flamboyance, Hirshfield knows that everything can be lost and knows or imagines she knows what she is gaining." Hirshfield iterates in the poem "The Heart as Origami" that "Not one of the lives of this world the heart does not choose" (*October Palace*, p. 82; quoted in Harrod).

The oxymoronic description "serene flamboyance" appropriately evokes Hirshfield's voice, in which she consistently acknowledges a doubleness in the poems: she provides the reader with concrete descriptions from which they can infer value and meaning, especially those that come from nature. Alison Townsend notes that "one of the great delights of this collection is how firmly grounded it is in the tangible world." She quotes Hirshfield's "Even the Vanishing Housed": "It is the way humans know— / through the earth, through the things of the earthy lips stained by what they have tasted" (*October Palace*, p. 67). Townsend contends that Hirshfield's ability to engage readers through the use of carefully selected sensory details arises from her sense that everything has life, including objects such as earth and stones. It is because of ubiquitous life that objects serve successfully as metaphors and give us new ways to see ourselves and the world. "Objects have their own mysterious lives," writes Townsend, "but also serve as containers for feeling and meaning. In 'The House in Winter,' [Hirshfield] considers how 'perhaps it is / that the house only constructs itself / while we look— / opens from room to room, because we look.' ... Simultaneously active and contemplative, the looking makes the speaker (and reader) of the poem necessary to the process described by the poem."

Poems that allow readers to go their own way, by not providing outright interpretation of images or advice on how to take the poems, also risk losing some readers, who might feel constricted by the intensity. Angela Sorby notes that

Hirshfield's poems are "invariably well-constructed, watertight, and under autocratic control," but wonders if they are "too seldom reckless." Jay Hopler also wonders if sometimes the phrasing and syntax are too cryptic, commenting that, sometimes, "by the time we reach the end of the poem we have forgotten where it was we started from and are uncertain why, exactly, we have arrived at this particular point."

Those challenges of the poems, however, are mostly overridden by the beauty of the style and the experience of reading them. Hopler comments on "the lushness of the language," and Harrod on her "magnificent metaphor." These are the qualities that also lend Hirshfield's voice its poetic authority. Townsend elaborates on the effects of her style:

> Possession or owning, the poet seems to say, consists precisely in the recognition of all that will be lost. What matters is the entering or the experiencing which the heart cannot help but do. ... This attitude gives Hirshfield's work a quiet and intense authority. ... There is a stillness at the center of each poem that encourages the reader to rest meditatively and plunge deeply. ... The cumulative effect of this collection is hypnotic. Reading it one feels as if a translucent curtain between worlds has been pulled back; we have been allowed to glimpse mysteries, only to be reminded that they are with us all the time.
>
> (p. 27)

The Lives of the Heart (1997), Hirshfield's fourth published poetry book, continues the refinement of her understanding and acceptance of life's difficulties, joys, and conundrums. Ellen Kaufman characterizes the immediacy of the work:

> The poems are of the moment—each a single gesture encompassing the dichotomies of presence and absence, life and death, being and not-being.... The best are tragic in their unencumbered vision of human limitation; in one, the speaker listens to a piano played movingly—indeed, even more so, because it is played haltingly—and is ashamed "not at my tears, or even at what has been wasted, / but to have been dry-eyed so long."

As in Hirshfield's earlier poems, those in *Lives* are built on compelling and evocative descriptions of objects and places, which she finds luminescent, substantial, and imbued with hope.

Adrian Oktenberg describes this as "a world of ineffable beauty." She also notes Hirshfield's consistent reliance on key images, carried in "words like 'heart,' 'wisdom,' gift,' 'transparency,' 'forgiveness,' 'silence.'" She concludes, "This is a poetry of substance and sustenance, one that we all need, whether we are aware of it or not, full of melancholy and also of joy."

Hirshfield's fifth poetry collection, *Given Sugar, Given Salt* (2001), continues her quintessential themes, including the contemplation of nature and the relationship of self to world, and continues to use close details of objects as a way to express her observations. But there are new qualities as well, says Miriam Sagan, including an ability to embrace more easily life's stresses. She notes that "the tone has changed. These poems are imbued with a sense of loss and change, not grief but acceptance of the uncertain nature of life. They are written from the perspective of a woman in middle age who has lost friends and family and is on increasingly intimate terms with aging and death." Sagan also identifies a theme newly emphasized in the poetry, that of solitude:

> A certain distance is necessary for the creation of poetry and the focused state of mind that sustains writing. Yet solitude is also an uneasy state, for with just a small shift in mood, it becomes loneliness. Like Emily Dickinson, for whom solitude was an entry into a feeling of connection with the world, Hirshfield views apartness as rich.

Sagan sees the poem "Only When I Am Quiet and Do Not Speak" as the book's "poetic treatise on solitude":

> Only when I am quiet for a
> long time
> and do not speak
> do the objects of my life
> draw near.
> Shy, the scissors and spoons,
> the blue mug.
> Hesitant even the towels,
> for all their intimate knowledge
> and scent of fresh bleach.
>
> (*Given Sugar, Given Salt*, p. 23)

Whereas much contemporary poetry that features domestic imagery addresses social concerns, Hirshfield's use of domestic imagery, proposes Sagan, is a means of ordering the world: "Ordinary objects are simultaneously mundane, precarious and precious." In her review of *Given Sugar, Given Salt*, Ellen Kaufman recognizes the potential difficulties of Hirshfield's domestic imagery, not as a social issue but a philosophical one. She notes that Hirshfield's approach makes her work vulnerable to sentimentality, but that Hirshfield does not succumb to it. Rather, it "attempts to speak clearly and plainly while acknowledging the difficulty—perhaps the impossibility—of doing so. ... These are assured, controlled poems that tread carefully where others have trampled."

Published almost twenty years after her first collection, *Given Sugar, Given Salt* reflects both the sweet and the bitter of accrued experience, and, like the best poetry, offers the reader the means to understand both and to integrate them into a life marked by a sense of well-being. Sagan concludes, "They do some of the basic work of lyric poetry: they express one heart and make the reader examine her or his self afresh."

ASSAYING SELF AND WORLD

Published twenty-four years after her first collection, Hirshfield's sixth poetry book, *After* (2006), maintains the themes laced through her previous work, including the paradoxical nature of self and experience, the difficulty of acceptance of life's raw facts, and the grace of acceptance accomplished. A review of *After* in *Publishers Weekly* recognizes that the volume "continues the meditative direction established in 2001's well-received *Given Sugar, Given Salt*." It also recognizes a new form included in the book, a number of poems labeled "Assay," some of which are prose poems, new to Hirshfield's poetry books. The exploratory nature of an assay allows the poet to conjecture about abstractions as well as the concrete. The *Publishers Weekly* reviewer finds that these prose poems "balance out Hirshfield's tropism toward restrained wonder," and points out that an assay has a dual nature: it is "both a try and an exposition: the sky, the words 'of' and 'to' and the writings of Edgar Allan Poe all become such discursive test cases."

JANE HIRSHFIELD

The assays feature the stylistic control familiar in Hirshfield's earlier poems and, says Donna Seaman in her review of *After,* are a "study of characteristics, an analysis to determine the presence or absence of certain components." She finds the poems to be "constructed as cleverly and economically as riddles as [Hirshfield] ponders the nature of hope, envy, certainty, and possibility" and that the "of" and "to" poems "embody the workings of our minds."

The collection also contains some very small poems, absent from the other collections, that have a subtle effect. Hirshfield calls them "pebbles," and, says Seaman, "they send ripples across the reflecting pool of our collective consciousness."

The title of the book, in another gesture uncharacteristic for Hirshfield, alludes to a time in her own life that was fraught with difficult circumstances. These become a theme that unites the poems in the collection. In a profile for the Poetry Foundation, Cynthia Haven quotes her: "I wrote this book during a tsunami of deaths, disappearances, losses. For me, it's a book of elegies— the black thread of death runs through it." Haven comments that "what that black thread stitches together is moments of experience, of memory, of connection."

Although beset by loss during this period of her life, Hirshfield was also expanding her connections. She traveled frequently to teach workshops and give readings, and also traveled abroad. When a selection of her poems, *Uważność* (2002), was published in Polish, the Nobel laureate Czesław Miłosz recognized the overarching humanity of her poetry. In an introduction to the collection, quoted by Haven, he wrote:

> The subject of her poetry is our ordinary life among other people and our continuing encounter with everything Earth brings us: trees, flowers, animals, and birds. Much depends on whether we can treasure each moment in this way, and whether we are able to respond to cats, dogs, and horses with a friendliness equal to that we bring to people. The sensuality of her poetry equally illuminates the great Buddhist virtue of "mindfulness."

Although Hirshfield does not generally make explicit Buddhist references in her poetry, the title of her seventh volume, *Come, Thief* (2011), elicits the connection for many readers: welcoming the thief is common in Buddhist stories and carries an affectionate tone. The title is also an affectionate public invitation of sorts, welcoming the reader into the community of thieves.

The poems in *Come, Thief,* are easily recognized as Hirshfield's. They continue her tradition of attention to objects, especially those in nature and those within her sight, in which she finds meaning and hope, and which she extends to readers, inviting them to enter the poem and the experience. Diane Scharper comments on these "generally short nature poems with an epiphany in which the poet manages to get to the heart of an experience" by bringing herself, qua observer, and the observed into relationship. The best of these poems, writes Scharper,

> notice telling details as experienced in ordinary moments that nevertheless seem connected to the transcendent. Take "The Supple Deer," for instance: the narrator watches deer gracefully jumping through an opening in the fence, noting in an especially resonant metaphor how the deer seem to pour like an arc of water. The poem ends wistfully as the poet wishes to be as "porous" as the deer, allowing the world to pass through her.

The poems also continue Hirshfield's tradition of crystalline writing. In her earlier volumes, this was recognized as control of her language, but with *Come, Thief,* it manifests as clarity rather than as circumscription. Steven Ratiner elaborates:

> Hirshfield's writing seems to contain two very different impulses: a discursive energy that embraces rich elaboration ... countered by a minimalist's love of clear, implicit images. ... When the two work together in a curious counterpoint, the effects can be marvelous, captivating the eye with closely observed detail and delighting the ear with her exacting diction and rhythmical invention.

This counterpoint can be seen as an embodiment of Zen tenets that embrace the contradictory and the mysterious and help to liberate the mind from reason. Paradoxical and puzzling, such statements, called koans, can contribute to spiritual awakening. James Crews writes that *Come, Thief* "rings with a fearless clarity and an attention to

language that never wavers." The individual poems, he continues, call, as they always have, for patience on the part of the reader, but the reward is higher in this new work when it "marries the abstract with the concrete: 'Let reason flow like water around a stone, the stone remains,' she tells us in one of her koan-like lines, suggesting 'reason' has little place in her work and in our lives."

Come, Thief continues forms introduced in her previous volume, *After,* the "assays" and the haiku-like poems she calls "pebbles." Her voice also contributes to consistency in her work, maintaining its richness in imagery and sound. "The lilt and patterns of her language are beautifully osmotic, altering our brain waves and our perception of how all the world's pieces fit together," notes Donna Seaman in her review.

Consistency of form in the poems is echoed in consistency of voice and message in the poems themselves, enhancing Hirshfield's invitation to readers to levitate away from earth even while remaining connected to it. Grace Cavelieri finds this comforting, especially given the difficult scope and sometimes disturbing nature of the ideas than can be inferred from the poems:

> Each poem is an energetic event and a spiritual discipline. A seasoned poet, Hirshfield gives stability in structure because spirit is untamable and art is the way we hold it to form. This is not to say that one poem is like the other, not at all; poetry is a living thing through variance of expansion and compression, and the way space is utilized on the page. She uses different presentations to provide different meanings. Yet her signature is the dewdrop illuminating the universe. This new book is a further awareness of the experience that characterizes Hirshfield's work. She uses actual events that keep us tethered to earth while pondering abstract realities.

Hirshfield's poems have been widely published in literary journals and the national press. In addition to the selected poems published in Polish, a volume of poems selected from her first five American books, *Each Happiness Ringed by Lions* (2005), was published in England prior to the publication there of *After*.

In its development over the years, Hirshfield's poetic voice remains consistent even as it becomes enriched by experience. From the beginning, it has been informed by concrete descriptions of things that range from household items to living and nonliving things in the out-of-doors, coupled with spiritual and philosophical concepts that frame those objects in meaning and from which readers can infer values and even take advice. The poetry, she says, has not so much been guided by a theory of poetics as her poetics has been formed by the development of her poetry. For her, the poetry—its grace and its mind—come first, although there is pleasure in that second harvest, thinking about poetry.

Portals—gates, doors, windows—are ubiquitous in Hirshfield's poems. They mark the cusp between this and that; inside and outside; abstract and concrete; being awake and being asleep; the senses and ideas. Passing through a portal usually signifies transition to another state of mind or another way of being. Poetry itself, for Hirshfield, is a gate. By passing through it, as writer or reader, we can sometimes step away from the limitations of thought and habit and become fully present in the physical and spiritual worlds we inhabit. Under normal circumstances of everyday living, such conscious participation is diminished by distractions that obscure the fuller reality.

In a discussion of Hirshfield's work, Elkins says that "human consciousness does not block or alienate one from non-human nature but is one of the gates through which one can pass to an understanding of that world, our world, the world" (p. 256). Understanding of the human experience is a priority for Hirshfield, as a means to fully engage in life. In Buddhist practice, this is represented as "mindfulness," undistracted attention to what is at hand in the moment, an openness to it, not only in order to enter it but so that it might enter us. Hirshfield sometimes describes her writing as something that has entered her from the outside. In an interview with Katie Bolick for *Atlantic Unbound,* she explained that her book of poems *The Lives of the Heart* is dominated by the idea of the heart because she "simply followed what kept calling me to look at

it." For her, poems can flow in either direction, into her or out from her—they have their own way of being in the world.

For Hirshfield, poetry can also be a means for passing from distraction to mindfulness, and she expresses "gratitude, respect, and wonder at the mysterious informing it offers to all who pass through its gate" (*Nine Gates*, p. viii). The goal for her is a deepened understanding of experience, which she can sometimes accomplish by bringing her experience into words. "Poetry for me," she said in an interview with *Contemporary Authors,* "is an instrument of investigation and a mode of perception, a way of knowing and feeling both self and world."

Published in 1997, *Nine Gates: Entering the Mind of Poetry,* a collection of essays, addresses both the artistic process and the artifacts of poetry. Hirshfield approaches the essays with the same audacity and imagery with which she approaches her poems and brings to them a similar clarity of language. She offers many descriptions of what constitutes a good poem. It makes you wake up, she says, a reference to the Buddhist state of awareness, and makes the world larger, opening new windows onto experience. It moves the margins of awareness, allowing new perspectives. As she explains elsewhere, in an essay published in the *Writer* titled "The Shock of Good Poetry," these new perspectives are experienced as epiphanies—sudden, unexpected realizations: "A good poem shocks us awake, one way or another—through its beauty, its insight, its music, it shakes or seduces the reader out of the common gaze and into a genuine looking."

Often, the difficulty in approaching the threshold that allows us to experience life fully is the knowledge that stepping across leads to a recognition of the darker side of the human experience and of the offerings of the world. Recognition leads to the experiencing of heartache, loss, injustice, and myriad other painful aspects of life. In the Buddhist view, both recognition and experiencing are necessary to the fully experienced life; true suffering comes from denial of reality. Freedom from suffering comes with acknowledgment of suffering. Hirshfield told Eaton and Keegan, "To ignore suffering is not

the path. The path is to be glad to let the lion come into your life and ruin it. That is the only viable route toward a life we can agree to fully live" (p. 7).

This does not mean that the poet must seek out suffering. It is just there and will come to us; the task is to remove the barriers that keep us from experiencing it honestly. This is the job of metaphor, or imagery: to tilt the angle of our view so we can glimpse, and perhaps even stare at, that which surrounds us but is often invisible.

The challenge of revealing happiness—in poetry and in life—is similar. It is not something we must seek elsewhere. It abounds in the world, is underfoot and within, though it is often hidden by barriers of perception. These barriers too can sometimes be subverted through metaphor and imagery. In Buddhist practice, both suffering and happiness can also be revealed through mindfulness practice, attention to the moment, that which is perceivable through the senses. "To know the fullness of being is actually my intention," Hirshfield told Eaton and Keegan, "as a writer and as a person" (p. 7).

Although poetry is at the heart of Hirshfield's work, she is accomplished in related areas: she is a translator, editor, scholar, reader/speaker, and teacher. Her work in each of these areas is consistent with the messages in her poems, including the oneness of all things and the effort toward what she calls "fullness of being."

WHAT IS LOST? TRANSLATING POETRY

Hirshfield has published two volumes of translated poems by women, *The Ink Dark Moon: Love Poems* by Ono no Komachi and Izumi Shikibu (1988), with Mariko Aratani, and *Mirabai: Ecstatic Poems* (2004), with Robert Bly. She also has edited a volume of international poems, *Women in Praise of the Sacred: 43 Centuries of Spiritual Poetry by Women* (1994). This work has its roots in one of her earliest influences, the book of haiku poetry that she bought when she was nine years old. In college she studied literature in translation as part of her self-designed major, along with creative writing. It was the study of

translated, classical-era Japanese and Chinese literature that introduced her to the vocabulary and tenets of Buddhism, a discovery that was instrumental in her spiritual development and path as well as in her development as a poet.

In her interview with Katie Bolick, Hirshfield noted that after many years of translating (in collaboration with native speakers) and working with translations, she realized that the objective core of a given poem can be retained in spite of a variety of translations of that one work. This liberated her, she said, to not rely on an initial draft of a work—to not feel undue loyalty to it. "That part of the process taught me to value a greater openness and playfulness of mind in meeting a poem. ... I understood more fully that there may be a core, inchoate experience you're reaching for, but that there can be many different ways to reach it."

This understanding of poetry in particular and translation in general allows Hirshfield to feel comfortable about the inevitable translation question: What is lost? For her, poetry is not merely an iteration, a translation, of experience. Rather, it extends experience, is a new iteration along the continuum of experience. This is also true in translation from one language to another, though the core intent of the original work will ideally be carried forward in the variant editions. In a chapter on translation, "The World Is Large and Full of Noise," in *Nine Gates,* she writes, "Translation that serves truly will widen our knowledge of what poetry—what humanness— is" (p. 79).

Although Hirshfield's primary stance is not as a feminist writer, her impetus to publish *Women in Praise of the Sacred,* which includes poetry by sixty-six women from around the world, arose from a realization that such a volume did not yet exist. She recognized that the notion that for centuries women had not written or published was an intransigent myth. In her interview with Bolick she said, "Women simply couldn't be kept from doing this deeply human work of recording, shaping, and discovering their experience through words." The earliest author we know by name, she discovered, is a woman, Enheduanna, who wrote forty-three centuries ago,

circa 2300 BCE. As the volume evolved, Hirshfield found the depth and scope of women's writing traditions to be companionable and comforting.

The historic and critical context exhibited in the editing of *Praise* also informs Hirshfield's other works of scholarship. *Nine Gates: Entering the Mind of Poetry* is thoroughly grounded in research, as are scholarly essays published in literary journals, such as "Thoreau's Hound: On Hiddenness" (*American Poetry Review,* May 2002), first delivered as a talk for the Rochester Arts and Lecture Series in May 2001; and "Poetry and Uncertainty" (*American Poetry Review,* November–December 2005).

In 2007 Hirshfield delivered three lectures on poetry at Newcastle University in Great Britain as part of a prestigious series on contemporary poetry. The lectures extend her perceptions of the human situation as put forth in poetry and present them in prose, placing them in the context of three key aspects: hiddenness, uncertainty, and surprise. The lectures are illustrated with examples of poetry from classics to contemporary, from American to international, and were published in England in 2008 as *Hiddenness, Uncertainty, Surprise: Three Generative Energies of Poetry.*

The first lecture, on hiddenness, posits that ultimate beginnings and endings are not available to us and that, because of that, hiddenness and uncertainty are central to both art and life. The second lecture addresses the inevitable uncertainty of human experience and the role of poetry in expanding and enriching knowledge. Surprise in poetry is addressed in the third lecture. Hirshfield says that, because of their emotional impact, poems with the power to astonish the reader are the ones that last.

Hirshfield's scholarship comes, in some ways, from her desire to open the pleasures and necessities of poetry to a wider audience. Although she does not expect or desire mass popularity for poetry, she does envision it as a helpful tool for individuals who wish to examine their lives and to live with more intention. In 2011 she published a "Kindle Single," *The Heart*

of Haiku, an essay for the inexperienced haiku reader on how to read the brief poems.

Hirshfield does not shy away from popular venues for her poetry or her writings about poetry. Her poems appear in sculpture installations, on bus and subway placards, as lyrics to music, and even on an in-flight airline ad curated by U.S. Poet Laureate Billy Collins. She has been featured numerous times on Garrison Keillor's *Writer's Almanac* and interviewed on American Public Media's *The Splendid Table,* a radio program about cooking. She was interviewed in 2007 for Oprah Winfrey's "Live Your Best Life" series for students in *O, The Oprah Magazine,* and *Come, Thief* was included on the Oprah.com 2011 Summer Reading List.

She has become comfortable with such public venues because it is the poems that are presented, not their writer, for she feels that the poet is irrelevant to the value of poetry. She told Cynthia Haven that the poet "doesn't exist except during the moments that she actually writing." The poetry itself, on the other hand, has a historic role in society. Prior to the printed word and then to the printing press, it was the means of preserving knowledge, its rhythms and rhymes functioning as a sort of technology to enhance accuracy in memory. Because of new and more efficient ways to preserve information, said Hirshfield in her interview with Katie Bolick, that role has changed over the last two hundred years: "Now the role of poetry is not simply to hold understanding in place but to help create and hold a realm of experience. Poetry has become a kind of tool for knowing the world in a particular way. ... it is the place where the thinking of the heart, mind, and body come together."

Knowing, understanding, and feeling the realities of the world we live in are crucial for Hirshfield. Without that, we lose our sense of interconnectedness with all that is around us, whether humans, animals, plants, or stones. When we lose that, we fail to grasp a proportional sense of who we are in the universe.

Poetry can help us maintain our perspective, thus helping us to know our lives the way they really are, as opposed to how we want to see them. Commenting to Haven, Hirshfield said she believes that the world can be changed by poetry: "It is made larger, given new windows that open out onto different landscapes and that also shine an altered light back into the known, as opening a new window in what used to be a wall changes not only the wall but the room." Poetry survives because of its own nature, she continued. Human beings innately desire to know and express themselves, and poetry is a method means to that end. "You couldn't kill it with a sledgehammer. ... Poetry can survive on nothing. Pen and ink are cheap."

Although Hirshfield is primarily known for her writing, she also is known for her keen ability to explicate Buddhism. She was interviewed extensively about Buddhist history and practice for the documentary film *The Buddha: The Story of Siddhartha* (PBS, 2010, directed by David Grubin), and in much of her writing about poetry she explicates Buddhist tenets as a means to explicating poems. For her, the two are inextricably linked by their mutual goals, which include achieving knowledge and understanding about the human experience.

GIFTS RECEIVED

Because of her finely tuned artistic, critical, and spiritual sensibilities, Hirshfield has frequently been called upon to judge poetry competitions, including the National Endowment for the Arts Literature Fellowships for Translation (1991, 1992), the National Book Awards in poetry (2003), and the Walt Whitman Award of the Academy of American Poets (2012). She has served as guest editor for the acclaimed literary journal *Ploughshares* (1998) and as poetry editor for the 2004 *Pushcart Prize Anthology.* In their books, Jack Kornfield (*A Path with Heart,* 1993) and Thomas Moore (*Care of the Soul,* 1992; *Soul Mates,* 1994) acknowledged her insightful emendations that contributed to the clarity of their Buddhist spiritual guides. She has served on the advisory board for *Orion Magazine,* has been a consulting editor for *Tricycle* magazine, among others, and holds membership in numerous literary organizations, including PEN American Center, the Authors Guild, and the Associated of Writers & Writing Programs (AWP).

Hirshfield's fluency in discussing writing has led to opportunities in the national media that are not open to most writers. In addition to being called upon to elucidate the mysteries and joys of poetry for Bill Moyers' *Fooling with Words* special on PBS, recorded in 1998 at the Dodge Poetry Festival and telecast in 1999, she was featured in Moyers' expanded interview series later that year, *Sounds of Poetry*.

Honors and prizes for her work are another indication of Hirshfield's accomplishments in her field. Major award fellowships include a Guggenheim Memorial Foundation Fellowship (1985), a Rockefeller Foundation Fellowship at Bellagio Study Center (1995), an Academy of American Poets Fellowship for distinguished poetic achievement (2004), and a National Endowment for the Arts Fellowship (2005). Specific books have earned the Columbia University Translation Center Award (1988) and the Poetry Center Book Award (1994), and *After* was named a "best book of 2006" by the *Washington Post,* the *San Francisco Chronicle,* and the *Financial Times.* Her work has been included in numerous editions of *The Best American* series, including for poetry, spiritual writing, and science nature writing. She received Pushcart Prizes in 1988, 2002, and 2003.

Support for Hirshfield's writing includes awards from the Poetry Society of America (1988, 1989), among many others, and residency fellowships at the Yaddo and MacDowell writer's artists' colonies, where she was able to dedicate significant periods of time to writing.

Readers have become familiar with Hirshfield's poetry not only through her books but from publication in anthologies, journals, literary magazines, and the popular press, including the *New Yorker, Atlantic,* and *Times Literary Supplement.* In addition to Polish, her work has been translated into Chinese, Japanese, Russian, and Portuguese.

STANDING UP IN FRONT

In her personal life, Hirshfield tends toward the reclusive. She told Cynthia Haven that her cottage in northern California is a refuge for her that is reminiscent of her eight years at the Zen Center: "The days when I can stay here entirely and not step outside the gate are a small echo of the monastic experience of non-distraction, concentration, and hunting the deep ore of experience." However, just as poetry has both called to her and entered her, so does the public realm, and when she was asked to stand up with her work and give it literal voice, she did not feel that she could refuse. Poems that begin in solitude and privacy, she says, end up being read in front of large audiences.

Hearing poets speak their own words does provide one way of entry into the rhythms of a poem, but Hirshfield also recommends that readers provide that entry with their own voices, by murmuring them to themselves or reading them aloud. This not only provides an actual voice for the poems, but also awakens a physical response in the body. This helps to bridge the gap between mind and body, opening a door to richer experience.

Alison Townsend, in her review of *October Palace,* comments that reading Hirshfield's work has a hypnotic effect, as though a veil has been pulled back that keeps us from seeing and experiencing a reality that seems to be outside of ourselves. With the "translucent curtain" removed, we are "allowed to glimpse mysteries, only to be reminded that they are with us all the time," writes Townsend.

Stepping outside of a poem in order to read it publicly and stepping outside of the writing process in order to write about it critically are both acts that, for Hirshfield, are tangential to the art itself. Although both provide a pleasure that is related to the poems, they are not essential to—do not have a place in—the creation of the poems. Hirshfield said to Haven that it is not the poet's job to think about the audience and that, in fact, it is detrimental to the creative process.

Hirshfield has read in a wide variety of venues, including the Geraldine Dodge Poetry Festival (1998, 2004, 2008), the Aspen Ideas Festival (2010), and the Bread Loaf Writers Conference (2010, 2012), all in the United States, and in international venues in Poland, China,

Greece, England, and elsewhere. Audio versions of her readings are widely available on the Internet.

In addition to the poetry itself and the poetry readings, Hirshfield brings her energy and spirit to writers and readers in the classroom. Early in her career, from 1980 to 1985, she was a Poet in the Schools in California. As her body of published work grew, she started teaching at writers' conferences and then as a visiting writer in colleges and universities. She has taught at conferences in the United States, including those at Napa Valley, the University of Minnesota–Split Rock, Squaw Valley, and Aspen, and has held visiting-writer faculty positions at Bennington College, University of California–Berkeley, University of Virginia, University of Cincinnati, and Weber State University in Ogden, Utah.

The influences on Hirshfield's writing are eclectic, from the book of haiku she read when she was nine years old, through the Eastern (Chinese, Japanese) and Western (Greek, Roman, North American, including Eskimo) traditions, to her contemporary peers, including Czesław Miłosz. In the course of her writing, which has maintained its stance of Buddhist mindfulness, she has migrated from intense concentration on imagery through nature toward writing that is more inclusive of the "common life we all share" (Eaton and Keegan, p. 18). For Hirshfield, this shift is a surprise, but she finds it interesting and is happy to greet it, to learn what it brings to her. In the documentary *The Buddha: The Story of Siddhartha,* she says there is sometimes a spontaneous transition from knowing our own life to knowing a larger truth about life and the world. After all, she says, Buddhist life is not about personal bliss; it is about being ordinary.

Selected Bibliography

WORKS OF JANE HIRSHFIELD

POETRY

Alaya. Princeton, N.J.: Quarterly Review of Literature Poetry Series, 1982.

Of Gravity and Angels. Middletown, Conn.: Wesleyan University Press, 1988.

The October Palace. New York: HarperCollins, 1994.

The Lives of the Heart. New York: HarperCollins, 1997.

Given Sugar, Given Salt. New York: HarperCollins, 2001.

Uważność. Kraków, Poland: Znak, 2002.

Each Happiness Ringed by Lions. London: Bloodaxe Books, 2005.

After. New York: HarperCollins, 2006.

Come, Thief. New York: Knopf, 2011.

ESSAYS

Nine Gates: Entering the Mind of Poetry. New York: HarperCollins, 1997.

"The Shock of Good Poetry." *Writer* 112, no. 6:9–10 (June 1999).

Hiddenness, Uncertainty, Surprise: Three Generative Energies of Poetry. London: Bloodaxe Books, 2008.

"Early Rooms." *American Poetry Review* 38, no. 1:22–23 (January–February 2009).

"Close Reading: Windows." *Writer's Chronicle* 43, no. 4:22–29 (February 2011).

The Heart of Haiku. Amazon Kindle, 2011.

TRANSLATIONS AND EDITIONS

The Ink Dark Moon: Love Poems by Ono no Komachi and Izumi Shikibu. New York: Scribner, 1988. (Translated by Hirshfield and Mariko Aratani.)

Women in Praise of the Sacred: 43 Centuries of Spiritual Poetry by Women. New York: HarperCollins, 1994. (Edited by Hirshfield.)

Mirabai: Ecstatic Poems: Boston: Beacon Press, 2004. (English versions by Hirshfield and Robert Bly.)

CRITICAL AND BIOGRAPHICAL STUDIES

"Biography: Jane Hirshfield." Poetry Foundation. http://www.poetryfoundation.org/bio/jane-hirshfield..

Eaton, Mark A. "Jane Hirshfield." In *Dictionary of Literary Biography.* Vol. 342, *Twentieth-Century American Nature Poets.* Edited by J. Scott Bryson and Roger Thompson. Detroit: Gale, 2008. Pp. 178–184.

Elkins, Andrew. "California as the World in the Poetry of Jane Hirshfield." In his *Another Place: An Ecocritical Study of Selected Western American Poets.* Fort Worth: Texas Christian University Press, 2002. Pp. 245–290.

Haven, Cynthia. "Kitchen Ants and Everyday Epiphanies." Poetry Foundation. http://www.poetryfoundation.org/article/178400.

"Jane Hirshfield." In *Contemporary Authors Online*. Detroit: Gale, 2008. *Literature Resource Center*, July 23, 2012.

REVIEWS

"After." *Publishers Weekly*, December 5, 2005. http://www.publishersweekly.com/978-0-06-077916-0..

Cavalieri, Grace. "Review of *Come, Thief*." *Washington Independent Review of Books*, August 30, 2011. http://www.washingtonindependentreviewofbooks.com/?s=jane+hirshfield.

Crews, James. "Review of *Come, Thief* by Jane Hirshfield." *Basalt Magazine*, September 13, 2011. http://www.basaltmagazine.com/2011/09/the-strange-happiness-of-jane-hirshfield-review-of-come-thief/.

Harrod, Lois Marie. "*The October Palace*." *Belles Lettres: A Review of Books by Women* 10, no. 1:47–48 (fall 1994).

Hopler, Jay. "*The October Palace*." *Literary Review* 38, no. 2:304–307 (winter 1995).

Kaufman, Ellen. "*The Lives of the Heart*." *Library Journal*, October 1, 1997, p. 86.

———. "*Given Sugar, Given Salt*." *Library Journal*, February 15, 2001, p. 172.

Oktenberg, Adrian. "*The Lives of the Heart*." *Women's Review of Books* 15:16–17 (July 1998).

Ratiner, Steven. "In *Come, Thief*, a Stealth Meditation of Quotidian Human Experience." *Washington Post*, September 15, 2011. http://www.washingtonpost.com/entertainment/books/poetry-review-come-thief-by-jane-hirshfield/2011/06/15/gIQAGCZSVK_story.html.

Sagan. Miriam. "Solitary Splendor." *Women's Review of Books* 18:41 (July 2001). (Review of *Given Sugar, Given Salt*.)

Scharper, Diane. "Hirshfield, Jane. *Come, Thief*." *Library Journal*, August 1, 2011, p. 103.

Seaman, Donna. "Hirshfield, Jane. *After*." *Booklist*, February 1, 2006, p. 17.

———. "*Come, Thief*." *Booklist*, August 1, 2011, p. 14.

Sorby, Angela. "*The October Palace*." *Chicago Review* 40, no. 4:99–100. (fall 1994).

Townsend, Alison. "*The October Palace*." *Women's Review of Books* 13, no. 3:26–27 (December 1995).

Weiss, Theodore. "Of Gravity and Angels." Wesleyan University Press. http://www.upne.com/0-8195-2136-1.html.

INTERVIEWS

Bolick, Katie. "Some Place Not Yet Known: An Interview with Jane Hirshfield." *Atlantic Unbound*, September 18, 1997. http://www.theatlantic.com/past/docs/unbound/bookauth/jhirsh.htm.

Eaton, Mark, and Abigail Keegan. "Diamond at the Center: An Interview with Jane Hirshfield." Center for Interpersonal Studies Through Film and Literature, Oklahoma City University, March 29, 2000. http://www.okcu.edu/film-lit/interviews/interview_Hirshfield.pdf.

Moyers, Bill. "Jane Hirshfield." In *Fooling with Words*. New York: William Morrow, 1999. Pp. 89–113.

VIDEOS

Jane Hirshfield: An Afternoon with the Poet. April 2, 2001. University of California Television. http://www.uctv.tv/search-details.aspx?showID=5668.

The Buddha: The Story of Siddhartha. Directed by David Grubin. PBS, 2010.

MAURICE KENNY

(1929—)

Nicholas Spengler

MAURICE KENNY EMERGED in the 1970s as one of the earliest and most influential voices in contemporary Native American literature. He has also made a significant, if less publicized, contribution to queer American writing of the post-Stonewall era. Indeed, Kenny is one of the more powerful voices in contemporary American letters, no "minority" classification needed. With twenty-five poetry publications and several collections of short stories and essays spanning more than a half-century, Kenny is among the most prolific poets writing today. Born in 1929 to Mohawk and Seneca parents in upstate New York, Kenny grew up in the homeland of his ancestors, the Iroquois, or Haudenosaunee, "People of the Longhouse"; Native dance and other cultural performances have a large presence in his work. Kenny began his career alongside the Beats, publishing his first book-length collection of poems, *Dead Letters Sent* (1958), through Troubadour Press in New York City. After a period of travel and odd jobs, Kenny returned to the literary world and established himself as an integral force in the renaissance of Native American writing from the 1970s into the present. He has published two volumes of selected poems, *Between Two Rivers* (1987) and *Carving Hawk* (2002). A collection of essays from various writers and scholars, *Maurice Kenny: Celebrations of a Mohawk Writer* (2011), edited by Penelope Myrtle Kelsey, represents the bulk of critical studies of his work.

Among his most acclaimed poetry collections are *Blackrobe: Isaac Jogues* (1982), which was nominated for a Pulitzer Prize, and *Tekonwatonti/ Molly Brant* (1992). In both of these historically steeped works, Kenny channels the voices of the Native past as well as those of the ever-increasing European presence in the Americas. These "personae poems" (*Tekonwatonti,* p. 12) weave a narrative thread through multiple perspectives rather than a historical master narrative; the poems assemble meaning collectively, and often discordantly, in matters ranging from the politics of war and religion to the politics of sex and the home.

Kenny writes just as deftly in the lyric mode. He won the American Book Award for *The Mama Poems* (1984), a collection in which the poet elegizes his mother and her Seneca heritage. *Connotations* (2008) is in many ways a companion work, centering on his Mohawk-Irish father, but it begins with a series of ekphrastic poems in which Kenny culls together homoerotic paintings from modern and contemporary artists. Although Kenny privileges a Native worldview in much of his writing, he does not do so to the exclusion of other perspectives. Rather, he invites all voices—Native American and European, male and female, queer and straight—into dramatic discourse.

Kenny's poems display a richness of vision, in the sense of both observation and insight. They communicate a sense of wonder that reflects Kenny's connection to the natural world and to the lives and histories it contains. A longtime resident of both Brooklyn and the Adirondacks of upstate New York, Kenny seeks out the life force—the "blood and mystery," as he phrased it in an interview with this writer—in any landscape. Yet his poems also deploy a razor-sharp irony that stems not only from a deep knowledge of his subjects but also from his uniquely peripheral vantage point as both an American Indian poet and a gay poet. Kenny exposes those dark corners where sexual and national identities meet and become vulnerable to each other. Desire animates Kenny's many voices: lyrical poems of longing for connection,

be it with animals, spirits, a sexual partner, or a tribal community; and dramatic-historical poems of conquest, loss, and lust for the fruits and flesh of the New World.

While his vibrant images of the natural world suggest spiritual peace and fulfillment, a principal force of Kenny's poetry is antagonism. Kenny reveals national heroes as scoundrels and sings the praises of many whom history has beggared and forgotten. Yet he maintains an unruly kinship with his adversaries. In this way, Kenny's poetry is remarkably inclusive—not in the sense of a harmonious whole, but rather of an embattled world of conflicting and overlapping identities, territories, and histories, all of which Kenny's dexterous voice encompasses.

BEGINNINGS

Maurice Kenny writes in his memoir, *On Second Thought* (1995): "Growing up Indian in the United States is very hard to do. Growing up a half-blood is painful. Growing up a writer/poet is almost impossible" (p. 4). From his childhood in Watertown, New York, Kenny cultivated an ambivalent relationship with his Mohawk and Seneca ancestry. His father, Andrew, and his maternal aunt Jennie were great storytellers, and they endowed Kenny with a sense of the past as narration. Nonetheless, the stigma attached to being an Indian drove those narratives underground, if only just beneath the surface. Kenny recalls that his father "would tell stories or sing songs without identifying the source" (p. 53). In that period of the 1930s and 1940s, Andrew Kenny more vocally celebrated his paternal Irish heritage. Moreover, Andrew's Mohawk mother, Mary West, died when he was five years old. Maurice did not have the privilege of Mary's influence: "never did she hold me tight / in her embrace while dancing / in the Longhouse snowy evenings / while the water drum banged / and rattles rattled" (p. 50).

In a poem from *Dancing Back Strong the Nation* (1979), "Going Home," Kenny expresses his incomplete sense of Native belonging, which he attributes, in part, to his father:

from Brooklyn it was a long ride …
to Watertown …
tired rivers and closed paper mills
home to gossipy aunts …
home to cedars and fields and boulders
cold graves under willow and pine
home from Brooklyn to the reservation
that was not home
to songs I could not sing
to dances I could not dance …
home to a Nation, Mohawk
to faces I did not know
and hands that did not recognize me
to names and doors
my father shut

(p. 99)

While Kenny's lyrical self senses the deep natural and human history of this landscape—the "boulders" and "cold graves"—he feels deprived of that cultural continuity on which contemporary Native American identity is largely predicated. In this case, Kenny speaks of the Saint Regis Mohawk reservation at Akwesasne, New York. "Home" for Kenny is inherently unsettled: it is both the Akwesasne community, which he encountered long after his father's death, and the Watertown of "tired rivers and closed paper mills," where his father owned several gas stations and a restaurant. Two visions or dreams of the American landscape play against each other. The poem communicates a sense of loss and longing for the Native culture his father left unnamed. Kenny writes in "Water Drum," another poem from *Connotations,* "I wish he'd beaten that water drum / and offered his song / in the Longhouse night" (p. 76). Without the Native context for his father's songs and stories, without the "names" that anchor identity in language, the poet feels foreign in his own "home."

Kenny's mother, Doris Parker Herrick, was born near Watertown in Cape Vincent, New York, where she grew up with her Seneca mother and English-descended father. After years of marriage to a husband who was repeatedly unfaithful, however, she had no desire to stay in the North Country. Doris left Andrew in 1941, taking twelve-year-old Maurice with her to Bayonne, New Jersey. This arrangement did not last long; Kenny was truant for the better part of a year,

preferring to take the train into Manhattan and catch glimpses of celebrities such as Rita Hayworth and Ginny Simms. Andrew saved him from reform school and brought him back to Watertown, where he finished his schooling.

In the 1950s Kenny attended Butler University in Indiana, where he took his first tentative steps toward being a writer. He found a mentor in the Keats scholar Werner Beyer. A blow to Kenny's fragile confidence as a poet came when, with the encouragement of a close friend and fellow student of poetry, he sent a batch of poems to John Crowe Ransom, whom Kenny retrospectively classifies as "a fine but minor American poet" with "an ear for European classical forms and a restricted rhythm" (*On Second Thought*, p. 6). This classical ear prompted Ransom to dismiss Kenny's attempts at verse with the incisive declaration, "you have no sense of rhythm" (p. 10). The work and financial stress combined with artistic insecurity drove Kenny to a nervous breakdown and a suicide attempt. He recalls waking in a hospital bed with a young black male patient beside him, combing his hair. Kenny writes, with a curious mixture of dread and Eros, "Without [poetry] I should have remained in the shadowy ward in the Indianapolis hospital with the black youth combing my hair over and over again" (p. 22). This undercurrent of sexuality and mortality courses through much of Kenny's work, alongside the promise of continuity through art, performance, and a strong community.

Andrew again recovered his son from the brink of disaster. "It seems now that my father was always bringing me home" (p. 16), Kenny writes, in spite of his complaints about his father's neglect of their Mohawk homeland. In 1956 Kenny spent a year at St. Lawrence University, and his first published poem, "The Hopeless Kill," appeared in the *Watertown Daily Times*.

Kenny would not begin to write explicitly about home, however, until moving to New York City in 1957, where he studied with the poet Louise Bogan at New York University. Bogan urged Kenny to break away from the metered verse and Romantic conceits of Keats and Wordsworth, after whom Kenny had attempted to model himself. Rather, Kenny relates, she encouraged him "to look back, to look at the fields of home, the woods and hills, the chicory and owls, the berries of the sandlots, the voices which were continually speaking, their echoes surrounding us" (p. 35). The "write what you know" dictum served as a solid foundation from which Kenny would explore fresh and largely unknown realms in his poetry. Kenny found another model in the free-verse poetry of Robinson Jeffers, who, Kenny writes, "opened my eyes and spirit to image and symbol" (p. 20). One Jeffers poem in particular, "Hurt Hawks," spoke to him. "I knew from Iroquois lore, tradition, that the hawk was the messenger of the people to the spirit world," Kenny writes. "I became the hawk, the poet, and the messenger" (p. 19).

Admittedly, Kenny's first book-length works, *Dead Letters Sent* (1958) and *With Love to Lesbia* (1959), which include many poems that he produced under Bogan's tutelage, still smack of classical diction and meter. Kenny's own take on Jeffers' hawk is heavily metered, though it reveals Kenny's budding interest in Haudenosaunee tradition.

The poem "Dead Letters Sent (By the Ontario Shores)" is a long poem in blank verse. The influence of Robert Frost on the young poet is clear in the joining of physical labor with metaphysical meditation. The concluding revelation anticipates Kenny's interest in the spirits and voices of the past, tangled with his conflicted feelings about home:

Home is a house of ghosts and shadows, sounds
Which are restless throughout the long dark night,
Dark even when the moon lies asleep on the pillow.
A man can't take the moonlight in his arms.

(p. 33)

Andrew Kenny died in 1957, before getting a chance to see his son's first book of poems. Maurice continued to live in New York City, managing the Marboro bookstore on Fifty-ninth Street, where he met the novelist Willard Motley in 1960. In 1962 Kenny left New York to work for Motley on the outskirts of Mexico City. This was an itinerant and largely unproductive time for Kenny. Andrew had left him and his older sisters

a modest inheritance, and Kenny spent much time and money traveling throughout the southwestern United States and Mexico and "beachcombing" in the U.S. Virgin Islands. Kenny has written little of his time in the islands, though the influence of the landscape on his imagination is clear in the poem "Pissarro: Tropical Impressions," collected in *Connotations*.

Kenny returned to the mainland United States in 1966, working in Chicago as an obituary writer for the *Chicago Sun-Times* before moving back to New York City in 1967. He settled into an apartment in Brooklyn Heights, which would be his home for the following twenty years. In his collection *In the Time of the Present* (2000), Kenny parrots the question he was frequently asked: *"What's a Mohawk living in a big city for?"* "They forget," Kenny responds, "that Mohawks built most of these skyscrapers" (*Carving Hawk,* p. 300). Kenny added in an interview with this author, in reference to an unpublished manuscript that responds to Hart Crane's *The Bridge,* that many Mohawk steelworkers helped to build the Brooklyn Bridge. Kenny's claim to this cityscape is as valid as that of Crane or Walt Whitman, if not more. Indeed, as Susan Ward writes, Kenny is "one of the few Native American writers to look to the city as well as to his rural home for inspiration" (p. 38). Along with the North Country, New York City provides a historical and cultural backdrop to which Kenny returns throughout his works.

Kenny's years in the city also placed him at the center of the publishing world; in the seventies, he worked as coeditor of the *Contact II* literary review and founded Strawberry Press, through which he printed many titles from Native American authors across the country. New York City provided Kenny with the artistic community he would increasingly engage with as he found his voice and became a major figure in the renaissance of Native American literature.

A VOICE EMERGES: I AM THE SUN, NORTH, *AND* DANCING BACK STRONG THE NATION

Fifteen years passed after the appearance of Kenny's first books of poetry before he would publish a new collection, but once he started publishing again in the 1970s he maintained a prolific pace. Kenny attributes this sudden resurgence of creativity to several influences and catalysts. First, he encountered the work of the Native American historian Mari Sandoz, the author of *Cheyenne Autumn* (1953) and *The Battle of the Little Big Horn* (1966), among many other titles. Sandoz was instrumental in developing Kenny's interest in Native history and culture. "Sandoz watered seeds of history in my thinking that my father had planted," Kenny writes (*On Second Thought,* pp. 56–57). Kenny combined the stories of his youth with these histories of massacres and migrations to forge a powerful voice that was at once dynamic and distinctly his own.

A second stimulus came not from written histories but from heated conflicts erupting in the present. In 1973 the Wounded Knee Occupation by American Indian Movement activists developed into a long, heavily armed siege with FBI agents and U.S. marshals surrounding and ultimately razing the South Dakota town; the protests and violence would continue for years on the Pine Ridge Indian Reservation. Kenny had health problems at the time, which kept him from joining the occupation. He wrote "I Am the Sun," a long chant poem, as a direct response to the events unfolding at Wounded Knee. Kenny based the form of the poem on the Ghost Dance, a religious movement that flourished in 1890 among many tribes. The Lakota Sioux version of the Ghost Dance ended tragically in the Massacre at Wounded Knee that year. Kenny first published "I Am the Sun" in 1973 in *Akwesasne Notes,* a publication of the Saint Regis Mohawk Nation in Akwesasne, New York. In 1974, while recovering from a heart attack, Kenny spent what would be the first of many summers at Akwesasne, working with the writers and editors of *Akwesasne Notes.* Thus, Kenny's recovery in his own Native "home" at Akwesasne parallels his poetic effort to recover the ties between the past and the present of the Lakota people at Wounded Knee, using the Ghost Dance as a means of cultural and spiritual continuance.

"I Am the Sun" begins with an epigraph from Black Elk, an Oglala Lakota who survived the massacre of 1890, which ends on the mournful note "the nation's hoop is broken and scattered" (*Carving Hawk,* p. 39). Kenny honors these words and shares Black Elk's mourning: "The arrows broke with Crazy Horse; / The arrows broke with Sitting Bull; / Father, give us back our arrows" (p. 41). However, the poem's message is ultimately one of strength and promise. The 1973 occupation represents for Kenny the beginning of the restoration of the Lakota nation, and by extension, all Native American nations: "We will put the center back / in your country; / We will circle stones and make the hoop / in your country" (p. 41). The images of the stone circle and hoop correspond with the Ghost Dance, a circle dance, thereby reinforcing the theme of life and continuity through gathering, dance, and song.

Dance is more than just a metaphor for cultural continuity in "I Am the Sun"; it is the means by which that continuity is enacted and achieved. The Cherokee writer and scholar Qwo-Li Driskill points out the "relationships between performance and continuance in Kenny's work" (p. 28). Indeed, Kenny's poem is not so much a representation of the Ghost Dance as an attempt to reenact that dance through its chant-like rhythms. It is significant, then, that "I Am the Sun" is among those poems that Kenny frequently performed during his extensive reading tours in the seventies through the nineties. The refrain *Chankpe Opi Wakpala!*—Lakota for "Wounded Knee Creek"—recurs throughout the poem. The creek ties the physical landscape of Wounded Knee to the theme of continuity and endurance. This refrain is more than a motif; it is an act of remembrance and a call to action—a spoken name that links the past to the present. As Craig Womack argues, "Kenny's presentation of poetry is consistent with oral cultures in which the storyteller becomes the story. ... Stories, then, are a re-experiencing of events" (p. 78). The strength of Kenny's poetry is his ability not simply to refer to past events, places, and personages but to become those things. In this sense, "I Am the Sun"—the poem itself, but especially Kenny's performance of it—constitutes what

Driskill calls a "react[ion] to colonial violence through engaged and embodied action and intentional engagement with our traditions" (p. 31). While Kenny could not physically participate in the Wounded Knee Occupation, "I Am the Sun" represents his form of activism and protest. When Kenny writes, "For I am the Sun! ... I stand above the world" (*Carving Hawk,* p. 42), his voice is not that of an individual artist but rather that of the American Indian nations whose courage has humbled him. The renaissance of Native American literature largely grew out of this shared sense among Native writers of narration as restoration.

The dexterity of Kenny's voice is most evident in the later personae poems of *Blackrobe* and *Tekonwatonti/Molly Brant,* but Kenny experiments with many-angled historical perspectives in *North: Poems of Home* (1977). In "Land," Kenny shifts between the North Country in 1976—"wilderness muzzled; forests—kitchen tables and bedposts / of foreign centuries" (*Carving Hawk,* p. 56)—and images of this landscape in the past. Under the heading "1820" he writes of Madame de Feriet, who built her country retreat outside of Watertown: "her mansion lanterns / glow in the clear darkness of the French dream" (p. 56). As opposed to the Native American vision of cultural and environmental continuity, this European dream is not sustainable: "the disillusionment lorried her trunks to France, / her mansion to ashes" (p. 56). The legacy of such "dreams" is the devastated natural world of the present. Kenny concludes the poem on a bitter note: "the gooseberry is diseased, and the elm, / ... / muskrats sterilized, and fields" (p. 58). The connection between the land and its Native inhabitants is implicit; the dying elms and barren fields suggest the foreign-borne diseases that decimated American Indian nations as well.

Kenny uses this historical lens in a similarly disruptive fashion in "Gowane," which begins with an image of the vitality of the land and its indigenous inhabitants: "The great young elms arched in the autumn winds" while "A young man smoked his sumac in the firelight" (p. 50). Yet this harmonious scene in the first stanza changes when Kenny reveals the young man's

mission: "He held watch for the Canarsee this night," for "The foolish strangers who had taken / The tip of Minna-atn, perhaps, were greedy." Kenny uses this history of the Dutch invasion of the island that would become "Manhattan" to challenge the contemporary skyline view of New York City; here, Gowane sees nothing but "a faint light" shining "on Hill Island ... / The bleached-ones' camp." As Kenny does with the Mohawks who built New York's skyscrapers, he reminds us of the Native roots of the city and its names: "For he had been named Gowane, one of little sleep. / He had stood night sentry at the watchful place, Gowanus" (p. 51). Readers familiar with New York will recognize Gowanus as a neighborhood close to Kenny's own Brooklyn Heights, but Kenny's carefully layered history forces a reconsideration of this place in the present. This shifting perspective works both ways as the jpoem ends on a note of hope—"for another day the village was safe"—that is at once sincere, in Gowane's voice, and bitterly ironic in retrospect.

If these poems decry the loss of land for the sake of foreign "dreams," other poems in *North* speak of the endurance of indigenous elements in the landscape. In "Sweetgrass," Kenny writes of the plant, "You hold the darkness of the moist night / and the music of the river and the drum" (*Between Two Rivers*, p. 29). The thriving of this native species represents the continuity of Native American cultures as well; "the music of the river and the drum," like "I Am the Sun," not only creates a sense of connectedness but also represents what Driskill calls "performance as continuance" (p. 26).

Kenny elaborates this performance in *Dancing Back Strong the Nation* (1979), in which dance and song, like Kenny's spoken words, become the vehicles for recalling the past and, in so doing, guarantee the strength of the Native community in future generations. In the afore-mentioned poem "Going Home," the speaker encounters "songs I could not sing" and "dances I could not dance," but other poems in this collection describe this homecoming as a moment of awakening rather than frustration and loss:

I went north in winter
they were dancing in the Longhouse
women danced
old men danced
children danced
We ate cornbread

...

I knew they would dance back strong the Nation
(*Carving Hawk*, p. 62)

While there remains a separation between the speaker and the multiple generations of dancers, the speaker feels welcome in the Akwesasne community he describes. The images of the dance, Driskill argues, "help return the speaker to a continuing tradition" (p. 29). Moreover, Kenny acknowledges the cultural and political importance of performance. In "Dance," he entreats the reader to "listen ... a hundred feet / a hundred feet / move move / move move / from the ancients / into Grandfather's shoes" (*Carving Hawk*, p. 65). The poem conveys the movement of the dance: both the actual steps and their performance through time, a thread through generations. In *I Am the Sun, North,* and *Dancing Back Strong the Nation,* Kenny combines history and performance to hone the deep and dexterous voice that defines his work.

QUEERING THE NATIVE: ONLY AS FAR AS BROOKLYN *AND OTHERS*

Kenny published *Only as Far as Brooklyn* (1979) through a small press called Good Gay Poets. Like the poems of *Dancing Back Strong the Nation*, these poems make a strong declaration of Native identity, but from a queer perspective. Kenny outlines this identity in the poem "Winkte," a Sioux word that one might translate as "male homosexual," though the Sioux term goes beyond the clinical definition of the Euro-American one: "We were special to the Sioux, Cheyenne, Ponca / And the Crow who valued our worth" (*Only as Far as Brooklyn*, p. 11). Queer Natives within these nations enjoyed an elite status, Kenny explains; they "took to the medicine tent" (p. 10) or "married (a second wife) to the chief" (p. 11). Kenny does not shy away from sensual images: "And we were ac-

cepted into the fur robes / Of a young warrior, and lay by his flesh / And knew his mouth and warm groin." The use of the first-person plural renders the poem especially affirmative, given the distinction between "I" and "they" in "I Went North," for example.

Lisa Tatonetti reports that "Winkte" first appeared in the winter 1975–1976 issue of the journal *Gay Sunshine,* along with an essay by Kenny titled "Tinseled Bucks: A Historical Study of Indian Homosexuality" (p. 121). Kenny was not only among the first gay American poets to publish openly queer texts in the post-Stonewall era; Tatonetti rightly identifies these as "the first pieces of contemporary queer Native literature to be published" (p. 120). In fact, it would take the Native community years to catch up. At a 1990 meeting of American Indian nations in Winnipeg, "Two-Spirit" was coined as a positive term for queer Natives of any nation; prior to this meeting, the only available terminology was either a derogatory non-Native anthropological term or one of the Euro-American classifications, such as "gay" or "homosexual" (note, pp. 130–131).

Part of what makes "Winkte" and other poems in *Only as Far as Brooklyn* seem so forward-looking is that they are steeped in the occluded Native traditions of the past. As in "I Am the Sun," Kenny works to restore cultural continuity despite the rupture of colonization and the subjugation of American Indian nations to Euro-American modes of thought. Ironically, as foreign institutions—from Jesuits and the Catholic Church to Hollywood—forced queer Native identities underground, Native communities began to perceive "homosexuality and/or gender variance [as] a 'white man's disease' " (Tatonetti, p. 121). Kenny's explicit writing about queer Native identity might seem like an affront to contemporary Native culture. Yet Kenny's bold work in this area affirms Native culture by breaking the spell of amnesia cast by non-Native interests. As Qwo-Li Driskill observes, "Two-Spirit movements are themselves models for what 'continuance' means" (note, p. 35). *Only as Far as Brooklyn* is not a stray chapter in Kenny's otherwise Native-focused body of work; rather, it lies at the heart of Kenny's poetry, and it

anticipates the deeply felt sensuality and sexuality of Kenny's later attempts to recover Native history and identity.

The first poem in the collection, "Boys," is not overtly queer, but its subtitle, "(Vision)," refers to a line in "Winkte": "We went to the mountain for our puberty vision" (p. 10). Thus, "Boys" is a poem of queer self-identification, as it represents what the speaker encounters during his "puberty vision": "the hawk flew / to the crazy mountain / plums grew large and red / stains hands and teeth"; "the crazy mountain shivered" and called "hawk, hawk / catch me in your talons" (p. 7). The ripe fruit and shivering mountain are sensual images, which the speaker "must remember … to tell the young boys / fishing in the creek" (p. 7). Given Kenny's identification with the hawk, its presence here suggests that this vision is Kenny's; yet the speaker could also be a voice from the past. As in much of Kenny's work, it is difficult to distinguish between the poet himself and the various personae he becomes. The point, of course, is not to make this distinction but to understand that this vision is a tradition that endures across generations, creating a strong nation. "United," near the end of the collection, mourns the loss of certain traditions—"old Medicine Men, / prodded by priest and politician, / no longer wear robes; / nor [are] boys … celebrated on the warpath / and taken in love by strong warriors" (p. 41)—but the speaker concedes, "they remain in lodges and languages / where the vision is honored, / and grandfathers know Nations will gather" (p. 41). Kenny is realistic about the losses that Native cultures have suffered through colonization and acclimation, but he finds spaces within contemporary society "where the vision is honored," and where the promise of cultural continuity still exists.

The poems that fall between "Winkte" and "United" speak to the continuity of contemporary queer Native identity, but they also expose the fissures in national and sexual identities in North American society. In the poems "Papago I" and "Papago II," Tatonetti observes, Kenny "invokes Indigenous history as a metaphor for desire" (p. 127), fusing Native pasts and landscapes with the

Mohawk speaker's sexual encounters with a member of the Tohono O'odham Nation (formerly known as "Papago"). In "Papago I":

Down into the centuries of your breath
my centuries prodded

...

I meant to leave my name whispered
on your mouth because secrets
are long between your Arizona rocks
and my old cedar wood of home.

...

I meant to leave my arms in your arms
and take only the gift of your voice
whispering the motions of my blood,
the taut muscles of our race.

(p. 20)

The union between lovers parallels the solidarity among American Indian nations struggling to preserve their traditions in the present. Yet their union is brief and leaves the speaker longing for continued connection. As a subsequent poem, "After Reading the Greek Poet," attests, Kenny adopts a voice similar to that of C. P. Cavafy by combining the cultural past with the wistful lyricism of the homosexual lover. Kenny's linking of sex, tradition, and landscape, however, is distinctly Native American, as opposed to the European-historical formality of Cavafy's verse. Kenny writes in "Papago II," "With this flesh / I break the rock / of your painted / and sacred mountain" (p. 21). Sex, like dance and other traditional performances, exposes the core of Native American identity.

Kenny also uses images of Native queerness to challenge notions of nationality and sexuality. In another poem describing a sexual encounter, Kenny describes the "Apache who struck coup on a Mohawk / and left the bed victorious" (p. 17). Images like these, argues Tatonetti, "confront stereotypes of Indian stoicism and of the asexual squaw … or the hypersexualized Indian Savage" (p. 130). While Kenny plays with popular notions of Native American masculinity to comic effect, the ironies he exposes are often tragic at the same time. He describes the Apache "hoteled in Oakland … safe from reservation eyes and rules" (p. 17). In an otherwise lighthearted poem of semantic and sexual play, these lines remind the reader that this manifestation of Native and sexual identity was forbidden in the eyes of those American Indian nations that, thanks to the interference of non-Native institutions, perceived homosexuality as something essentially foreign.

Kenny explores the conflicted relationships between Natives and non-Natives in the poem "Santa Fe, New Mexico." He describes "Underground / toilets / in plush / hotels" as the "only place / in town / where an Indian / can touch / an Irishman / with a western / accent / and keep / his Sacred / Mountains" (p. 14). Kenny employs these "underground" encounters between men to destabilize the strict lines between Native and non-Native identities; the boundaries of sexuality and nationality begin to blur. Nonetheless, that these men, both from cultures marked by machismo in contemporary depictions, couple for a few brief moments in a hotel toilet is not a statement of hope for the dissolution of national and sexual stereotypes. Kenny's ironic mention of the Indian's being able to "keep his Sacred Mountains" hints at the long history of Euro-American seizures of Native lands. The toilet is the only place where these men can reveal their sexual identities; outside that tight space, they continue to play their sharply contrasted cultural roles, the Indian "selling / silver and turquoise / under / arcades / to tourists / from Toledo" (p. 15). *Only as Far as Brooklyn* concludes on a more optimistic note with "United," but the preceding poems expose the intersections of national and sexual politics in ways that make the message of "United" stronger and more pertinent to contemporary Native societies.

Only much later did Kenny return to the territory of queer sexuality with the force that he displayed in *Only as Far as Brooklyn*. "Buddies," a one-act play included in *Tortured Skins* (2000), and the poem "El Paso Del Norte" (2001), collected in *Carving Hawk*, describe a hotel-room encounter between a Mohawk and a blond cowboy type, who call each other "Pat Garrett" and "Billy the Kid." The ekphrastic poems that make up the first part of *Connotations* (2008) include poems about Francis Bacon's studies of his lover and John Singer Sargent's studies of male nudes, as well as a poem mocking Freder-

ick Remington's obsession with painting cowboys and " 'injuns' " (p. 28) on horseback. Nonetheless, *Only as Far as Brooklyn* anticipates all of the collections that follow. Explicitly "queer" sexuality notwithstanding, sexuality and nationality pervade Kenny's works, especially in his two collections of "personae poems."

THE STORY STONE: BLACKROBE *AND* TEKONWATONTI/MOLLY BRANT

The stories of Kenny's youth, though largely abstracted from their Native source, instilled in him a keen interest in history, not as a stale act of record-keeping, or as a master text composed by history's "victors," but rather as an act of storytelling: that is, a performance, a dialogue, or a sounding of echoes and voices that do not always resolve themselves into a coherent narrative. *Blackrobe: Isaac Jogues* (1982) and *Tekonwatonti/Molly Brant* (1992) most vividly display Kenny's talents as a storyteller. The prologue to *Tekonwatonti* is a poem titled "Te-Non-An-At-Che," the Haudenosaunee name for the Mohawk River. Like the refrain from "I Am the Sun," the title suggests rivers as the means of, and a metaphor for, continuance. "Te-Non-An-At-Che" tells the Haudenosaunee creation story—"Water was first / ... And water creatures / legends grew" (p. 19)—but it is also the story of the conflicts between Natives and Europeans. Kenny lists the names of American Indian villages, "followed later by" the European cities built over many of those villages: "(The Indian Lost)" (p. 22). North American history thus becomes part of the layering of elements and life forms in the traditional creation story. Kenny's creation story defines the tragic trajectory of *Blackrobe* and *Molly Brant*.

Yet both works begin on a note of hope, with poems about the Peacemaker, a legendary figure who brought union to the five Haudenosaunee tribes: "we are one in a circle" (p. 3), Kenny writes in "Peacemaker," the first poem of *Blackrobe*. The Peacemaker explains, "I stutter / but the man / I send / will tell you / to lean / a pole / and protect / your / house" (p. 5), referring to the "People of the Longhouse." Ayonwatha

emerges as the speaker for the Peacemaker: "I have listened / and will aid the stutterer / to unite the people of this river country" (p. 6). Kenny repeats the message in "Deganawidah: The Peacemaker," at the beginning of *Tekonwatonti*: "Ayonwatha, / speak my tongue," he says, and "Encourage men to gather" (p. 28). These poems not only portray the Haudenosaunee as a nation united against European encroachment, but they also serve as an invocation through which Kenny establishes himself as the speaker of the present, relaying the message of the Peacemaker to the contemporary Haudenosaunee. For Kenny, Womack writes, "poetry [is] an oracular performance as much as a written form" (p. 78). Despite the tragic histories Kenny re-creates in *Blackrobe* and *Tekonwatonti*, his role as the speaker suggests the continuance of Native culture, even in the face of new threats and challenges to contemporary Natives.

The poems of *Blackrobe* revolve around Isaac Jogues, a seventeenth-century Jesuit missionary who made an ill-fated attempt to Christianize the Iroquois, dying at their hands in 1646. In the poem "Little People," Kenny recasts the Haudenosaunee story of a clan that lives in a quarry and cannot hunt but grows strawberries, which it exchanges for meat with a boy from the bear clan; the boy returns home to find famine, and the berries save his people. (Kenny elaborates on this story in "Little Voices" in *The Mama Poems*.) The poet uses this story to allegorize the meeting of Jesuits and Natives: "Three times he came to the woods / (once with his illness) / and stood above the quarry" (p. 7). This unnamed figure comes with "beaver meat" and the "silver cross," but he will not feed the people. His failure to understand the Native values of reciprocation dooms him; as Kenny puts it: "He will need to go to the story stone," suggesting that if he fails to understand and respect Haudenosaunee stories, he will be history himself. As Kiotsaeton, the Mohawk chief, says to Jogues, "[we] will respect your customs / and invite you into the lodge / if you maintain respect for ours" (p. 20). But Jogues does not heed the advice: "the clubs rained upon his head. / Still holding his cross out to us / he sank to the earth" (p. 45).

MAURICE KENNY

Kenny explores the life and gruesome death of Jogues through many voices, complicating the events so that they cannot be reduced to a single story or judgment. Fellow Mohawk poet James Stevens marvels at "how quickly human Isaac Jogues became" (p. 18). In "Rouen, France," Jogues addresses his mother: "Madame! I go to New France. / ... I will have the opportunity / of saving those lost souls for God. / ... Thank you for the tin of tea. / It will be a comfort in the wilds" (p. 10). Kenny contrasts Jogues' inflated sense of pride in his mission with this domestic exchange, rendering Jogues' missionary zeal more foolish than appropriative. When Jogues reaches "New France," however, his tone hints at conquest, cataloging the bounty—and thus, the commercial potential—of this New World. The short poem "First Seeing the St. Lawrence River" reveals this conqueror's perspective: "Blue as Mary's skirt. / Cold as the heathen heart. / Clear as my purpose. / Abundant with fish" (p. 12). In "Approaching the Mohawk Village: Jogues' Journal," Jogues addresses the Natives in his missionary tone: "I have brought my beads and this cross / to cure your souls" (p. 24), but the "Marginal Note" he records casts doubt on his earnestness: "Richly furred / beaver pelts / hang at the / entrance to / each / lodge" (p. 24). Despite the depth of his faith, Jogues shares something in common with the explorer Cavelier de La Salle, who states his purpose clearly: "it was beaver, exploration, / colonization for the French crown / not the souls of infidels" (p. 9). Another "Marginal Note," in "The French Informal Report" of Jogues' death, confirms the ruthless project of colonization that underlies the Jesuits' mission: "Remember / to send / more brandy / for the savages. / They guzzle / with gusto" (p. 51). Regardless of Jogues' ardor, Kenny makes it clear that he works for an imperial cause.

A more personal aspect of Jogues' character is his fascination with the "Naked, reddish brown bodies" (p. 14) he encounters. Kenny expresses the voice of the Mohawk bear clan through a series of poems titled "Bear," in which the speaker complains both of Jogues' proselytizing and of his pederastic desire for Native boys: "he could not bear the sight / of naked flesh, nor two people / coupling in the shadows of the lodge / ... Yet, he stared / at the young boys swimming nude / in the river" (p. 43). These poems appear to conform to the misconception that same-sex desire is European in origin, yet Bear presents just one perspective of many. A woman called Wolf Aunt adopts Blackrobe "before the people of the Bear / could strike a tomahawk / into his shaven head" (p. 37). Her son, Hoantteniate, "Jogues' Adopted 'Wolf Brother,'" reciprocates Jogues' desire and demonstrates that queer sexuality is not foreign:

I trembled
when his warm hand touched
my bare shoulder, when his solemn eyes
sought my furtive glance.

...

(I will miss the touch of his fingers
and his whispering through the corn fields
while reading his book, and the sweet
raisins he offered the boys and myself.)

(p. 53)

The difference between Jogues and his Wolf Brother is that Jogues' attraction represents not only sexual desire but also French imperial desire; Kenny subtly likens lust for Native flesh to lust for beaver pelts. Moreover, Jogues' advocacy for "chastity" (p. 43) coupled with his pederastic desire demonstrates how non-Native institutions managed Native sexuality in such a way that queer sexuality seemed a foreign sickness, like the influenza that Jogues' predecessors carried to the Haudenosaunee; indeed, Bear observes Jogues' "small box / which contains his evil" (p. 38) and associates it with the withering of the corn in the village. In these poems Kenny depicts the kernel of fear that will grow into the Native American homophobia that he challenges in *Only As Far As Brooklyn*.

Jogues does not die for his lust, however, but for his arrogant dismissal of Haudenosaunee culture: "I openly refute their foolish tales / that the world was built on a turtle's back" (p. 36). For this ignorance and intolerance, he will "go to the story stone."

Tekonwatonti/Molly Brant brings these worlds into more intimate collision, representing this woman's largely occluded life. A Mohawk war-

152

rior in her own right, Molly was sister to the Mohawk leader Joseph Brant and wife to Sir William Johnson, a British baronet and agent to the Iroquois. *Tekonwatonti* is a more extensive and complexly layered work, focusing chiefly on the period from the mid-eighteenth century through Molly's leading her people to fight with the British during the American Revolution and her subsequent exile in Ontario. Womack observes that, as in *Blackrobe*, Kenny "reveals characters cumulatively" (p. 80) through the layering of voices—remarkably, without losing the thread of narrative.

The poem "Abbé François Picquet," in the early pages of *Tekonwatonti*, provides a connection to *Blackrobe*; speaking roughly one hundred years after Jogues' death, the priest declares "France / and the Black Robe Jesuits / will dominate / this new world" (p. 37). Picquet treated the Haudenosaunee as slaves, forcing them to build a mission fort on the Saint Lawrence in 1749. In the briefest poem in the collection, Picquet responds to the newly built fort, *La Présentation*: "Ah! / Behold / my dream" (p. 41). Like Madame de Feriet's dream, however, this one is destined to fail, as he will lose his fort to the British during the Seven Years' War.

These historical ironies are more tragic than amusing, for Kenny demonstrates how Natives repeatedly suffer at the hands of these foreign dreams. In the poem "Dreams," Kenny contrasts the Native view of dreams as naturally inspired prophecies and the European sense of dreams as manifest destiny. The Mohawk Chief Hendrick, or Aroniateka, tells his British "ally," Sir William Johnson, " 'Warraghiyagey, I dream you / gave me a beautiful red coat' " (*Tekonwatonti*, p. 61). Johnson uses this opportunity to advance his own "dream": " 'Hendrick, chief of the great Mohawks, / I dreamed you presented me / with 500 acres of good / tillable land.' " The poem concludes with Hendrick: " 'Warranghiyagey, I will never dream again.' / And he signed, reluctantly, the deed." In "His Daily Journal," Johnson writes, "If war promises my dream then I war" (p. 83). This motivation is starkly different from that of Hendrick. Kenny first writes of Hendrick in the epilogue to *Blackrobe*—"if my

warriors are to fight, they are too few; if they are to die, they are too many" (p. 58)—and Kenny echoes these lines in *Tekonwatonti* (p. 98). Molly shares Hendrick's sentiments; when she readies her people to fight in the American Revolution, she says, "This is my passion ... to survive with all around me. / This is why I mount my raven gelding / and cry out at dawn to the young warriors" (p. 145).

Sir William's motive for war, by contrast, is pure greed. Kenny uses Johnson's sexual lust, as he uses Jogues', to convey his desire for land: "the earth is a fallow woman, / ... yielding the zenith / in stratospheric music which men only hear / when eyes are closed, chest and thighs sticky in lustful sweat / ... tendering her to orgasm" (p. 92). Nonetheless, Kenny tempers this blind lust with a series of poems that represents a romantic dialogue between William and Molly. In "Molly Brant to Willie," Molly complains to him that the German settlers in the Province of New York think her a witch: "They believe I prayed their corn / wither in August fields" (p. 71). In "Sir William's Reply to Molly," William writes, "True, you are a witch, alchemist / of September apples, red and savory / ... and the touch / of your small hands, a balm / that drives off storms rearing / in the brain of this aging man" (p. 72). The love between them, Kenny suggests, is real. After all, they are partners in both sex and war: "when we stand and wash away this joy," he tells her, "my penis once again soft / and coiled in a codpiece, you march before / one army and I another ... Molly, I nearly said, / man like man" (p. 95). Even when William leaves his estate to his son by a German indentured servant whom he marries on his death bed, Molly continues to adore him, preferring to blame the son: "Foppish John! Willie knew he'd / rather hold lace than / the reins to an estate" (p. 125). Once again, Kenny mixes sexual and national politics, imagining the domestic disputes, the various expressions of lust, and the shifting allegiances that provide the complex backdrop to war.

The Seneca scholar Penelope Myrtle Kelsey reads both *Blackrobe* and *Tekonwatonti* through the lens of the Haudenosaunee story of the Twins,

in which twin brothers, Flint (or Ice-Skin) and Sapling (or New Tree), populate the world with natural forms. Flint, who killed his mother in birth, creates all of the destructive elements in the world; Sapling, the second son who emerges peacefully, creates all of the beautiful forms. Kelsey suggests that Isaac Jogues' conflicted and misinformed interactions with Kiosaeton and Bear represent the struggle between Flint and Sapling, respectively (p. 118). Likewise, Kelsey likens Molly Brant to Sapling and Molly's husband, William Johnson, along with the American Revolutionaries, to Flint (p. 121). This interpretation is compelling, as the twins' antagonism mirrors the conflicted relationships of Kenny's characters in *Blackrobe* and *Tekonwatonti,* yet as twins they remain two necessary parts to a whole. The parallels only go so far, but the Twins story sheds some light on the sense of kinship Kenny expresses toward both his heroes, like Molly, and his foes, like Jogues or Sir William. The story also portrays an image of the world that, like Kenny's poetry, is contested and irreducible to one narrative or perspective.

Of course, Kenny is still biased toward his heroes, for the sake of cultural continuity. In the poem "George Washington," Kenny betrays the general's mission to destroy the Haudenosaunee. In many ways, Washington accomplished this mission, not only destroying Native villages but also driving Native peoples and cultures into historical obscurity. Through *Tekonwatonti,* however, Kenny allows Molly to triumph, even in defeat and exile. Kenny writes, in Molly's voice, "A people who do not remember: / *rain which falls upon a rock*" (p. 130). As the Peacemaker's speaker, Kenny warns against cultural amnesia, and *Tekonwatonti* concludes with a series of poems about women who do remember their heritage. In "Generations," Kenny writes from the perspective of E. Pauline Johnson, a Mohawk poet and great-granddaughter of William Johnson and Molly Brant. In Kenny's telling she discounts the importance of Sir William's Legacy: "If you open my vein/ … a smear of blood, a bubble, will rise. / That will be his" (p. 181). It is Molly's legacy that is important to her: "My poems drum as a partridge drums on the

earth; / … / What may appear silk is deerskin; / these feathers are not ostrich but hawk" (p. 181). Despite the loss of her people and her homeland to war, Molly survives in the act of "drumming," or re-creating her through writing and speech.

MAKING PEACE WITH HOME: THE MAMA POEMS *AND* CONNOTATIONS

Kenny expresses a similar allegiance with his Native ancestors and dismissal of his European ones in his slim collection *The Mama Poems* (1984). He addresses his great-great-great-grandfather, an English pastor, in the poem "Joshua Clark": "your blood has thinned into a trickle," he writes. "I claim very little and pass nothing on … / not a drop to any vein" (p. 19). Heritage is not about blood for Kenny as much as it is about spirit. He celebrates his mother in the poem "Inheritance"—Kenny associates being on the road with his mother, while his often conflicted homecomings he associates with his father.

Kenny does not depict his relationship with his mother as an easy one, however. On the dedication page of *The Mama Poems,* Kenny quotes the Twins story "from the Mohawk version of the Iroquois creation story." In this version, Flint is called "Left-handed Twin" and Sapling is called "Right-handed Twin": "Right-handed Twin came naturally from his mother. … But his brother, Left-handed Twin, impatiently sprang early from his mother's arm-pit and killed her." In an interview with this author, Kenny related that he was born left-handed but the nuns at the Catholic school he attended in Watertown forced him to write with his right hand, which he does to this day. Thus, Kenny's choice of names—"Left-handed Twin" as opposed to "Flint"—subtly approximates him to the destructive twin. The poem "On the Staten Island Ferry" begins, "You brought me here when I was ten," and it ends, "My father took me home again." Kenny admits, "I wanted to push / you off the ferry into the wake," to see her "fall like Sky-woman fell from the old world" (p. 19), referring again to the Mohawk creation story. As Womack

suggests, Kenny likens himself to the twin who kills his mother, if only in fantasy (p. 93).

Kenny describes the actual deaths and funerals of both parents with detachment. In "Wake," he writes, "they had her clench a blue rosary / which brought meadows to her cheeks / and swallows to her lips / sealed then and finally with paraffin" (p. 11). In *Connotations* (2008), Kenny recalls his father's funeral with uncertainty in the poem "In the Box": "Were there flowers ... it was March? / Were there mass cards? He'd been / excommunicated by a priest with wine / stains on his vestments" (p. 91). But the cool detail of the former and the lack of detail in the latter have more to do with Kenny's distaste for Catholic ceremony than an absence of feeling for his parents. In "Sketch," Kenny writes a more fitting memorial for his father, remembering his "sea-blue eyes, a substantial nose / that cannot deny its beginnings / miles away on a reservation in Canada / that only his mother knew" (*Connotations*, p. 45); Kenny elegizes his mother in "Reverberation." In both poems, Kenny remembers his parents through the Native heritage of his grandmothers. As in *Molly Brant,* Kenny shows his affinity for these Native women he never knew but with whom he feels the strongest attachment or "reverberation." Kenny's "homecoming" to the Adirondacks in the mid-1980s demonstrates the strength of this connection with his Haudenosaunee ancestors, despite his earlier conflicts with home.

HISTORY'S CASUALTIES: FROM GREYHOUNDING THIS AMERICA *TO* IN THE TIME OF THE PRESENT

Even after Kenny's move to the Adirondacks in the mid-eighties, he continued to exercise the "pleasure [of] running" (*Mama,* p. 10), touring the country by Greyhound bus and giving readings at universities and in Native communities around North America. Kenny presents a travelogue of sorts in *Greyhounding This America* (1988), a collection of poems that have as much to do with the landscape and its Native history as they do with the Natives Kenny meets in the present. In "Sand Creek, Colorado," he describes a nighttime visit with a female friend to this massacre site: "thin hands found our faces / ... hungry mouths of children / sought her breasts and would have sucked / had she opened her blouse" (*Carving Hawk,* p. 191). All that remains of the massacred Cheyenne are these hungry spirits and "bones wolves chose not to chew." Kenny distills Native histories into tight lines that speak of lost heroes—"the white bones / of Crazy Horse were never found" (p. 190)—and false heroes that have met their just ends: Kenny concludes "Reno Hill ... Little Bighorn" from *Humors and/or Not So Humorous* (1988) with the line, "Custer sired no children" (*Carving Hawk,* p. 217). Nonetheless, Kenny acknowledges that marauding and massacring non-Natives like Custer have left an indelible mark upon Native societies. Kenny contrasts the proud Native spirits of the past to contemporary Natives, whom Kenny often depicts as tragically submissive in the face of Euro-American institutions, from the Catholic Church to capitalism. In "Canyon de Chelly, Return, 1978," Kenny reminds the reader that "Anasazi youths once scaled / those unscaleable cliffs before Coca / Cola invented rheumatism" (p. 199). Nevertheless, Kenny continues to trust in the power of the landscape to remind Native Americans of their connection to it. In "The Yellowstone," he writes that the river "changes its course slowly, / it forgets the empire, / it leaves an islet in the stream" (p. 195). This "islet," however small, represents a place that foreign empires cannot claim and that the river has seemingly created out of nothing. It also mirrors the Haudenosaunee creation story, in which the earth is made from the turtle's back and thus is called "Turtle Island." Kenny plays with the strict boundaries that non-Native cultures established; the river, as in Kenny's other river poems, is a metaphor for Native American continuity, but it also suggests that natural boundaries are fluid and impermanent, despite non-Native attempts to fix them.

Kenny returns to the theme of reclaiming a lost past in his own Akwesasne homeland in the poem "Dugout," from *The Short and the Long of It* (1990). In the introduction to this long poem, the Adirondack writer and editor Chris Shaw

explains that it is based on the 1984 discovery of two dugout canoes on a private estate near the Akwesasne Reservation. Kenny was among those Mohawk Indians present during the excavation (*Carving Hawk,* p. 235). In the poem, Kenny searches for the stories held in the pair of canoes: "I am the voice / surely there is a story" (p. 238). But Kenny's voice is many voices over the course of the poem: the voice of the present, witnessing the excavation; the voices of the "bodies forgotten" "in the mud" (p. 238), the "four men" he imagines between the two canoes; and the voices narrating the layered sequences of nature images. The story, Kenny writes, "has long ago begun / it's continuous":

> it streams down the handle of the war club
> it is caught in the grip of the Great Law
> it murmurs in the song of the singer
> the pounding of the drum, the arch of the carver
> the cry of every child, the poet's pen
> the raised foot of each dancer who touches earth
> and moves as the squash vine moves, as wind,
> it is the ever-widening circle of the village
> and the fire in the house

(p. 243)

Of all Kenny's poems, this one contains perhaps the most explicit elaboration of Kenny's vision of storytelling as integral to Native American identity, connecting the past with the present and linking the "poet's pen" to other forms of cultural expression and performance.

The poems of *In the Time of the Present* (2000) contrast Native performances with other, non-Native spectacles. In "Photograph: Carlisle Indian School (1879–1918)," Kenny asks, "who is this boy … nationless / non-descriptive in an army uniform / devoid of hair-feather, fetish and paint / … hair cut, tongue cut" (*Carving Hawk,* p. 286). As a non-Native form of representation, the photograph reveals the loss of Native identity for this boy whose appearance is no longer his own but that of the school and its acclimating mission. This contrived representation renders the boy anonymous, a lost spirit: "his is one of the many spirits / Chief Seattle prophesied / would forever roam this once / free and beautiful land" (p. 288). Similarly, in "O / Rain-in-the-face," Kenny addresses the Lakota warrior who was falsely rumored to have eaten Custer's heart at Little Big Horn. The popularity of this rumor was largely due to a poem by John Greenleaf Whittier: "don't you wish you had / torn out Custer's heart / … and eaten it raw / without salt / as ol' Whittier claimed" (*Carving Hawk,* p. 292). Kenny depicts Rain-in-the-face in his later years, reduced to performing the poem about his imaginary deed before crowds at Coney Island. The layered ironies of this poem reflect how Euro-American literature and other media have glorified the great Indian warriors of the past, while forcing those Natives to perform trite pantomimes in the present. Kenny concludes, "O / Rain-in-the-face / I understand why you sold the poem / to the hordes milling the boardwalk / … at Coney Island" (p. 293). In narrating the history of this misrepresentation, however, Kenny restores Rain-in-the-face to the realm of Native storytelling, a form of representation that honors rather than exploits his memory. As Kenny writes in "New Song," "We are listening to the old stories / … We will remember everything knowing who we are" (p. 285).

FICTIONS: RAIN *AND* TORTURED SKINS

Kenny's stories share many of the concerns of his poetry. Their principal focus is contemporary Native American life and its relationship with Native traditions and histories. In "One More," from *Tortured Skins, and Other Fictions* (2000), an old Mohawk man, Henry, mourns the death of a black bear at the hands of a speeding motorist on vacation in the Adirondacks. Henry performs the traditional Haudenosaunee Bear Dance to honor the spirit of the bear. This story follows the pattern of foreign encroachment (the reckless tourist) into a native landscape (native to both the black bear and Henry), with tragic results. Contemporary tourism in Kenny's native Adirondacks becomes a metaphor for, or even an extension of, European colonialism in the Americas. Henry represents the Haudenosaunee commitment to respecting the natural world— environmental stewardship and conservation, in contemporary parlance—that the Bear Dance encapsulates. His performance of this dance

156

confirms the continuance and the integrity of the Haudenosaunee worldview into the present, even in the face of outsiders—be they tourists, Jesuits, generals, or other invasive species.

This neat distinction between "native" and "foreign" practices and beliefs is not so clear in many of Kenny's other stories. In the title story of *Rain and Other Fictions* (1990) the protagonist, "a stranger in that part of the country" (p. 87), witnesses the rain dance of the Santa Ana on fairgrounds at the edge of a New Mexico Pueblo village. Despite the fact that the Santa Ana dance is successful in calling rain from the clouds over the desert, there is a sense of increasing interference from non-Native cultures. The blind old man sitting near the narrator in the crowd watching the dance doubts the efficacy of this performance, given the distractions from other events on the fair grounds:

His ear catches the din of the carnival outside the plaza with the music of the merry-go-round vying with the beat of the drums, the rattles and the pounding feet of the dancers. What chance has rain with this mechanical noise frightening the cloud and the spirits of the sky. His own grandchild begging for cotton candy and a whirl on the Ferris wheel.

(p. 93)

The old man is committed to teaching his young grandson "the steps, the shake of the rattle" to guarantee the continuity of this cultural performance. "The boy will learn," he thinks, striking a note of both hope and fear for the future, as it reveals the old man's anxiety to pass on his culture so that it will live after his own death. Though the rain falls at the story's conclusion, we are left to wonder how much longer the dance will successfully compete with the "mechanical noise" of the world around it.

Likewise, many of the stories in *Tortured Skins* cast doubt on the ability of Haudenosaunee and other native peoples to remember and perform their traditions, and their respect for the natural world, amid the noises and concerns of contemporary North American society. In "Visitation," a young stranger knocks on the door of an old Mohawk couple living on the Akwesasne reservation. The stranger explains that he just wants a glass of water and that he has been turned away at all of the other houses he approached on the reserve. The wife, Agnes, is hesitant to let him in, but her blind husband, Monroe, bids him enter. The stranger reveals himself as a bear spirit, and for their hospitality, he restores Monroe's vision and Agnes' youth. However, Agnes refuses to believe in the reality of this gift, and she wakes the next morning to find that she is still old and her husband is still blind. In an essay on *Tortured Skins,* Nichole Dragone explains the basis for this story in the legend of the Creator who takes the form of a weary stranger, wandering from longhouse to longhouse; each clan turns him away, until he reaches the house of the Bear Clan, which takes him in. For the Bear Clan's hospitality, he honors them as "Keepers of Medicine" (p. 61). Kenny rewrites this story in a contemporary Native setting, suggesting that such legends continue into the present. The ignorance of many of Kenny's characters to these traditional stories calls that continuance into question, yet these stories are not prophecies of the collapse of Native culture so much as they are warnings about the dangers of ignoring the "story stone." Once again, Kenny plays the role of the speaker, entreating the reader to remember these stories that continue to affect the lives of contemporary Native Americans.

ONGOING WORK

Maurice Kenny, eighty-two years old at the time of this writing, remains an active writer and public presence in his home in the Adirondacks and its environs. He continues to write about the Haudenosaunee homeland, its nature and its history; he is revisiting one of the voices from *Tekonwatonti,* Abbé François Picquet, in what he expects will become a book-length work. He also persists in tackling subjects outside Native culture, working on manuscripts that range in subject from Hart Crane to the painter Frida Kahlo, and an expansion of his Francis Bacon poems into a separate collection.

An equally great part of Kenny's continuing work and legacy is his tireless commitment to teaching others. Not only did Kenny edit the

aforementioned *Contact II* and Strawberry Press publications of Native American writing, but he has also made a lifelong vocation of mentoring younger poets and writers. He has taught poetry, fiction, and playwriting workshops at a host of North American universities: St. Lawrence University, Paul Smith's College, the University of Victoria in British Columbia, Lehigh University, the University of Oklahoma, and most recently, the State University of New York College at Potsdam. Although he officially retired in 2010, Kenny continues to teach weekly workshops at Potsdam.

Selected Bibliography

WORKS OF MAURICE KENNY

POETRY

Dead Letters Sent, and Other Poems. New York: Troubadour Press, 1958.

With Love to Lesbia. New York: Aardvark Press, 1959.

I Am the Sun. New York: Dodeca, 1976; Buffalo, N.Y.: White Pine Press, 1979.

North: Poems of Home. Marvin, S.D.: Blue Cloud Quarterly Press, 1977.

Dancing Back Strong the Nation: Poems. Marvin, S.D.: Blue Cloud Quarterly Press, 1979; Fredonia, N.Y.: White Pine Press, 1981.

Only as Far as Brooklyn. Boston: Good Gay Poets Press, 1979.

Kneading the Blood. New York: Strawberry Press, 1981.

Blackrobe: Isaac Jogues, b. March 11, 1604, d. October 18, 1646: Poems. Saranac Lake, N.Y.: North Country Community College Press, 1982.

Boston Tea Party. San Francisco: Soup Press, 1982.

The Smell of Slaughter. Marvin, S.D.: Blue Cloud Quarterly Press, 1982.

The Mama Poems. Buffalo, N.Y.: White Pine Press, 1984.

Is Summer This Bear. Saranac Lake, N.Y.: Chauncy Press, 1985.

Between Two Rivers: Selected Poems, 1956–1984. Fredonia, N.Y.: White Pine Press, 1987.

Greyhounding This America. Chico, Calif.: Heilelberg Graphics, 1988.

Humors and/or Not So Humorous. Buffalo, N.Y.: Swift Kick Press, 1988.

The Short and the Long of It: New Poems. Little Rock: American Native Press Archives, University of Arkansas at Little Rock, 1990.

Last Mornings in Brooklyn. Norman, Okla.: Point Riders Press, 1991.

Tekonwatonti/Molly Brant: Poems of War. Fredonia, N.Y.: White Pine Press, 1992.

In the Time of the Present: New Poems. East Lansing: Michigan State University Press, 2000.

Carving Hawk: New and Selected Poems, 1953–2000. Buffalo, N.Y.: White Pine Press, 2002.

Connotations. Buffalo, N.Y.: White Pine Press, 2008.

Feeding Bears. Potsdam, N.Y.: Many Moons Press, 2010.

STORIES

Rain and Other Fictions. Marvin, S.D.: Blue Cloud Quarterly Press, 1985; East Lansing: Michigan State University Press, 1990.

Tortured Skins, and Other Fictions. East Lansing: Michigan State University Press, 2000.

NONFICTION

On Second Thought: A Compilation. Norman, Okla.: University of Oklahoma Press, 1995.

Backward to Forward: Prose Pieces. Fredonia, N.Y.: White Pine Press, 1997.

CRITICAL AND BIOGRAPHICAL STUDIES

Barron, Patrick. "Maurice Kenny's *Tekonwatonti, Molly Brant*: Poetic Memory and History." *MELUS* 25, nos. 3–4:31–64 (2000).

Brooks, Lisa. "Painting 'Word-Pictures' in Place: Maurice Kenny's Empathetic Imagination of *Tekonwatonti/Molly Brant*." In *Maurice Kenny: Celebrations of a Mohawk Writer*. Edited by Penelope Myrtle Kelsey. Albany: State University of New York Press, 2011.

Bruchac, Joseph. "New Voices from the Longhouse: Some Contemporary Iroquois Writers and Their Relationship to the Tradition of the Ho-de-no-sau-nee." In *Coyote Was Here: Essays on Contemporary Native American Literary History and Political Mobilization*. Edited by Bo Schöler. Aarhus, Denmark: SEKLOS, 1984. Pp. 147–161.

———. "Maurice Kenny: Not Through Height." In *Maurice Kenny: Celebrations of a Mohawk Writer*. Edited by Penelope Myrtle Kelsey. Albany: State University of New York Press, 2011.

Dragone, Nicholle. "Lest We Forget … Remembering Through the Song of the Resilient Spirit." *Studies in the Humanities* 33, no. 2:190–216 (2007).

———. "*Tortured Skins*, Bears, and Our Responsibilities to the Natural World." In *Maurice Kenny: Celebrations of a*

Mohawk Writer. Edited by Penelope Myrtle Kelsey. Albany: State University of New York Press, 2011.

Driskill, Qwo-Li. "Dancing Back Strong Our Nations: Performance as Continuance in Maurice Kenny's Poetry." In *Maurice Kenny: Celebrations of a Mohawk Writer.* Edited by Penelope Myrtle Kelsey. Albany: State University of New York Press, 2011.

Fast, Robin Riley. "Resistant History: Revisiting the Captivity Narrative in 'Captivity' and *Black Robe: Isaac Jogues.*" *American Indian Culture and Research Journal* 23, no. 1:69–86 (1999).

Kelsey, Penelope Myrtle. "Reading the Wampum: An Introduction to the Works of Maurice Kenny." In *Maurice Kenny: Celebrations of a Mohawk Writer.* Edited by Kelsey. Albany: State University of New York Press, 2011.

———. "Tribal Theory Travels: Kanien'kehaka Poet Maurice Kenny and the Gantowisas." In her *Tribal Theory in Native American Literature: Dakota and Haudenosaunee Writing and Indigenous Worldviews.* Lincoln: University of Nebraska Press, 2008. Pp. 112–129.

Schweninger, Lee. "To Name Is to Claim, or Remembering Place: Native American Writers Reclaim the Northeast." In *Coming into Contact: Explorations in Ecocritical Theory and Practice.* Edited by Annie Merrill Ingram et al. Athens: University of Georgia Press, 2007. Pp. 76–92.

Scott, Carolyn D. "Baskets of Sweetgrass: Maurice Kenny's *Dancing Back Strong the Nation* and *I Am the Sun.*" *Studies in American Indian Literature* 7, no. 1:8–13 (winter 1983).

Steinberg, Alan, and Karen Gibson. "Teaching Maurice Kenny's Fiction: Dislocated Characters, Narrators, and Readers." In *Maurice Kenny: Celebrations of a Mohawk Writer.* Edited by Penelope Myrtle Kelsey. Albany: State University of New York Press, 2011.

Stevens, James Thomas. "The Breath and Skin of History." In *Maurice Kenny: Celebrations of a Mohawk Writer.* Edited by Penelope Myrtle Kelsey. Albany: State University of New York Press, 2011.

Tatonetti, Lisa. "Two-Spirit Images in the Work of Maurice Kenny." In *Maurice Kenny: Celebrations of a Mohawk Writer.* Edited by Penelope Myrtle Kelsey. Albany: State University of New York Press, 2011.

Ward, Susan. "Maurice Kenny: How Can Any Self-Respecting Mohawk Live in a Place Like Brooklyn?" In *Maurice Kenny: Celebrations of a Mohawk Writer.* Edited by Penelope Myrtle Kelsey. Albany: State University of New York Press, 2011.

Womack, Craig. "The Spirit of Independence: Maurice Kenny's *Tekonwatonti/Molly Brant: Poems of War.*" In *Maurice Kenny: Celebrations of a Mohawk Writer.* Edited by Penelope Myrtle Kelsey. Albany: State University of New York Press, 2011.

INTERVIEWS

Grant, Elizabeth. "He Walks in Two Worlds: A Visit with Maurice Kenny." *Studies in American Indian Literature* 7, no. 3:17–24 (1995).

Spengler, Nicholas. Interview with Maurice Kenny, March 23, 2011.

Sweeney, Chad. "An Interview with Maurice Kenny." *World Literature Today* 79, no. 2:66–69 (May–August 2005).

MERIDEL LE SUEUR

(1900—1996)

Robert Buckeye

THE RADICAL POPULIST writer Meridel Le Sueur was born on February 22, 1900. Fourteen years after a bomb exploded at Haymarket. Two years after the Spanish-American War. Ten years after the Battle of Wounded Knee. Fourteen years before the massacre of coal miners at Ludlow. Fourteen years before World War I.

> I was born at the beginning of the swiftest and bloodiest century at Murray, Iowa, in a white square puritan house in the corn belt, of two physically beautiful people who had come through the Indian and the Lincoln country, creating the new race of the Americas by enormous and rugged and gay matings with the Dutch, the Indian, the Irish; being preachers, abolitionists, agrarians, radical lawyers on the Lincoln, Illinois circuit.
>
> *(Rites of Ancient Ripening,* back cover)

Her father, William Winston Wharton, was an itinerant preacher whose first parish was in Boise, Idaho; her mother, Marian, was a college graduate. At a summer school in Chicago, Marian took a course in comparative religion against her husband's wishes. Subsequently she read William Ellery Channing and Ralph Waldo Emerson, whose essay "Self-Reliance" was always at hand. The marriage failed, and, by then living in Texas, Marian took her daughter Meridel and two sons from San Antonio to the new state of Oklahoma, where her mother lived. (Texas law prohibited women from getting custody of their children.) Years later her husband would divorce her on grounds of desertion and reading "dangerous literature."

In 1914 Marian Wharton and the children moved to Fort Scott, Kansas, where she became one of the founders of the People's College, along with Eugene Debs, Helen Keller, Charles P. Steinmetz, and Arthur Le Sueur. Wharton was chair of the English Department, Le Sueur president, Debs chancellor. She married Le Sueur and with

him edited and published the Haldeman-Julius *Little Blue Books,* booklets with quotations from Karl Marx, Thomas Jefferson, and Tom Paine that workers could buy for a nickel and put in their back pockets to read during work breaks. (At age seventy-five she would run for the U.S. Senate in Minnesota in opposition to the Korean War.) Arthur Le Sueur was a lawyer and for a brief period the first Socialist mayor of Minot, North Dakota. As a lawyer, he defended the Industrial Workers of the World (IWW) and the Nonpartisan League, the socialist farmers alliance launched in 1915. (In 1934 he would be appointed a municipal judge by the Minnesota governor.)

It was Meridel Le Sueur's first exposure to radical ideas. She met Debs, Helen Keller, John Reed, Theodore Dreiser, Carl Sandburg, Margaret Sanger. Alexander Berkman spent time with the Le Sueur family, and Le Sueur remembered Berkman walking around town with her and talking to her as he would an adult. She read Nathaniel Hawthorne, Emerson, and Edgar Allan Poe in Kansas City one hot summer and did not understand what their writing had to do with Kansas. They did not glimpse the difficulty of living on its barren plains. "Alien" is the term she used to describe their writing.

Marian's mother, Antoinette Lucy, had divorced her husband because he was an alcoholic and drank up the money he earned. She was a third-generation Puritan, an Iowa pioneer, and one of the first white settlers in Oklahoma, carrying a rifle to protect her land. In Oklahoma she helped take care of Marian's three children and raised funds for libraries, believing people who read will not drink.

Antoinette became an organizer for the Woman's Christian Temperance Union (WCTU)

and traveled through Indiana, Illinois, Iowa, the Dakotas, Minnesota, and Texas fighting King Alcohol. Le Sueur remembered accompanying her grandmother on her trips, crying out that "lips that touch liquor shall never touch mine." On one of her trips for the WCTU, Antoinette died on a train. In Le Sueur's *I Hear Men Talking* (1984), the grandmother, Gee, is modeled after Antoinette, repressed by both her Puritan heritage and her husband's drunkenness. Gee would never let her body be seen naked, would love only the Lord. Her love songs were hymns.

(The lyrical, biblical quality of Le Sueur's prose comes from her grandmother's Puritan rhetoric. If she had to escape the denial of the body her grandmother's puritanism practiced, she nevertheless makes use of its rhetoric in her writing; see, in particular, the Invocation at the beginning of *I Hear Men Talking*.)

Le Sueur's other grandmother had come from Illinois. Her mother had been a full-blooded Iroquois who had married a preacher and come west with him. In Oklahoma, Le Sueur grew up among Indians as much as she did whites. She speaks of Zona, a Mandan Indian who worked in the fields and helped out Le Sueur's family at canning time, as one of the three influential women in her life, along with her mother and grandmother Antoinette. Zona taught Le Sueur that violence was linear, love spherical—a phrase that Le Sueur would make use of years later to criticize linear narrative. (When, during the McCarthy era of the 1940s and 1950s, Le Sueur was shadowed by the FBI, she escaped their surveillance by living in trailers on Indian reservations.)

During Le Sueur's teenage years in Fort Scott, life became increasingly difficult with the U.S. entry into World War I, which the Le Sueurs and other socialists protested as an imperialist power struggle paid for with the blood of the working classes. Rocks were thrown through their windows, yellow paint on their car. Antiwar literature was burned on their front lawn. Le Sueur was excluded at school and quit as a freshman. The People's College was torched and axed by reactionaries, forcing the family to leave in 1917 for Saint Paul, Minnesota, where the Nonpartisan League had an office. There, Arthur

Le Sueur worked for the league and continued to defend radicals. Joe Hill, Lincoln Steffens, Big Bill Haywood, and Debs visited. Debs recited the scaffold speech of John Brown in their kitchen. In their basement the Le Sueurs treated opponents of the war who had been tarred and feathered for their opposition. Steffens told them what revolutionary Russia was like.

During this period Meridel Le Sueur briefly attended a progressive open school in Chicago, then she left for New York to study at the American Academy of Dramatic Arts. She lived in a commune with Emma Goldman, engaged in antiwar activities, and acted on the New York stage. She read James Joyce and John Reed and in school studied Sherwood Anderson and Anton Chekhov.

In 1922 she went to Hollywood, working as an extra and stuntwoman in silent movies, acting in alternative theater in Sacramento and Berkeley, and doing radio voices (including that of "Betty Crocker"). She was offered a studio contract if she would have plastic surgery on her nose, but she declined, ending a career before it had begun. Hollywood was a meat market she could no longer stomach. Starlets prostituted themselves to get roles in films, and some had to work as prostitutes on the streets when they didn't get parts. When Le Sueur went to San Francisco to look for work, she began to take notes about the women she met, a practice she would follow later for her writing.

In 1924 Le Sueur joined the Communist Party and began to write for the *Daily Worker*. Her commitment to the party was lifelong. The party was, she felt, like a father to her and its members family. She served on its committees and at one time was chair of the Minnesota-Dakotas District of the Communist Party.

In 1926 she married Harry Rice, a labor organizer. In 1927 her first short story, "Persephone," was published in the *Dial,* and in the same year she was arrested in San Francisco for protesting the execution of Bartolomeo Sacco and Nicola Vanzetti. In 1928 she left California and gave birth to her first child, Rachel, in Minnesota; in 1930, her second, Deborah, was born. Le Sueur and Rice divorced in the early thirties,

so she, like her mother and grandmother before her, would raise children on her own.

To support herself, she worked as a waitress, garment sweatshop worker, mental hospital aide, chauffeur. At the end of long days of work, exhausting work, she put her head under a cold-water faucet in order to write.

The seeds, as Le Sueur would say—again, again, and again—had been sown.

PRAIRIE RADICAL

The fulcrum of America is the Plains, half sea, half land, a high sun as metal and obdurate as the iron horizon, and a man's job to square the circle.

Some men ride on such space, others have to fasten themselves like a tent stake to survive. As I see it Poe dug in and Melville mounted. They are the alternatives.

(Charles Olson, *Call Me Ishmael,* p. 12)

The Midwest, the Great Plains, what the writer Paul Metcalf calls our great "inland ocean," is all there is for Le Sueur, all that needs to be, its fulcrum the only one essential. Her politics, religion, feminism, and aesthetics have been sown in its soil.

"The body repeats the landscape," says Le Sueur (*Ripening,* p. 39). One bleeds into the other: land, body, politics.

Culture is the cry of its people. Writers are no more and no less than the voices of the people, speaking through those who have been silenced. "The poetry is in the bus station," says Le Sueur (quoted in Schleuning, p. 128).

History is its women holding the hands of those who have given birth or lost children, those who have lost work, those they love; its farmers dispossessed by bank foreclosure or drunkenness; its striking workers marching, marching. The renewal of life and seasons in nature is not only the endless cycle of life but also the inevitability of revolution—revolution that will not only overturn capitalism but also the colonization of women.

Le Sueur's politics was developed and expanded by her parents, by her experience of radicals who stopped by the People's College in Fort Scott or in Saint Paul, her experiences in New York and California. The IWW was the greatest influence on her, and its belief that culture comes from the working class she made her own. The poet can only come from the oppressed and be the voice of the oppressed.

However much her politics had been formed by her reading and experience with radicals, its origins came as much, if not more, from her experience on the farms and in the towns of the Great Plains, its sweatshops, mines, and factories. She may have read Marx, but she did not have to read Marx to know why the banker is rich, the poor poor.

Le Sueur's Marxism, anarchism—prairie anarchism, one scholar says—socialism, call it what you will, is a populist politics based on family, land, community. She sees the family not only as the basis for a revolutionary future but also as a core of resistance. She cites Lenin, who argued that the primal relationship between mother and child is the only communality left in a capitalist society.

In her populist model, decisions and actions are taken by everyone together without the guidance of a leader or leadership group. In this sense, her revolutionary society would follow the practice of the Paris Commune, those fighting fascism in Spain (as dramatically rendered in Ken Loach's 1995 film *Land and Freedom*), and the workers' councils in Budapest after the 1956 uprising against the Soviets. A leader, she feels, drives everything in his direction, not that of the movement of the group.

If we cannot separate her politics from her writing—in fact Le Sueur insists we do not—she nevertheless had to free herself from both her grandmother's puritanism and her parents' middle-class background, despite their politics, in order to be able to write about the oppressed.

I do not care for the bourgeois "individual" that I am. ... It is difficult because you are stepping into a dark chaotic passional world of another class, the proletariat, which is still perhaps unconscious of itself, like a great body sleeping, stirring, strange and outside the calculated, expedient world of the bourgeoisie. It is a hard road to leave your own

class and you cannot leave it by pieces or parts; it is a birth and you have to be born whole out of it. In a complete new body. None of the old ideology is any good in it. The creative artist will create no new forms of art or literature for that new hour out of that darkness unless he is willing to go all the way, with full belief, into that darkness.

(*Harvest Song,* pp. 200, 202)

During the McCarthy era, Le Sueur paid heavily for her politics. The FBI told employers and students in her correspondence writing classes that she was a radical whose classes they should not take. When she was hired as a clerk or waitress, they told her employers to fire her. They advised tenants in the rooming house she and her mother ran in Saint Paul to leave. Her phone was tapped. FBI agents sat in cars outside the rooming house to monitor its activity. (One cold day Le Sueur asked agents if she might sit in their car for a moment to get warm because they could not heat the house adequately.)

In 1935 Le Sueur had six stories and five articles published. During the McCarthy era she was effectively blacklisted. In 1950–1951, she published one article, one poem.

Unlike those writers who left America in the twenties for the greater freedom and possibility of Europe, Le Sueur left the country on only two occasions, the first of them a trip to Mexico City in 1968 to protest the government's massacre of students after they had opposed the cost of the 1968 Olympics. For most of her life she lived in Middle America, traveling by bus across it.

Le Sueur had the prairie in her, as Herman Melville the sea, Edgar Allan Poe the street.

We have never been burdened with the old tradition in literature from the old world. Every writer in the Middle West has had to work alone as far as connection with other writers is concerned, therefore he has been in closer contact with the American experience.

(*Harvest Song,* p. 206)

Europe had had its thumb on America for far too long.

It is not appreciated now, I think, the long and hard struggle to break away from European thought and culture. Plato had a terrible grip on our schools. In 1930, you had to be a "European" writer to speak at the University of Minnesota. I heard them hiss Sandburg—a midwestern guitar-playing yokel out of the cornfields.

("Jelly Roll," p. 354)

Like William Carlos Williams, Le Sueur heard the voices of Polish grandmothers, not Poland.

If she followed the path generations of Midwesterners took to escape difficult lives in the Midwest for New York or California, stopping first in Chicago as Theodore Dreiser and Sherwood Anderson did before her, Le Sueur would reject both tradition and the avant-garde, each of them repressive in different ways.

Her hostility to middle-class intellectuals was lifelong. Historically the voice of the Anglo-Saxon was the only voice America could speak through, but it could not, generations of American writers felt, speak to or for America. Le Sueur returned to Middle America, never to leave until feminism brought her attention she had not had since the thirties.

Her portrait of an intellectual in "A Hungry Intellectual" (a short story that appeared in *American Mercury* in 1935 and was reprinted in *Salute to Spring* in 1940) is a dismissal of an elitist eastern establishment that holds America back. It is a devastating assessment of a man who can think but not act, who can neither be depended on nor trusted. However, her anti-intellectualism is less the result of her ninth-grade education than it is the understanding of the dispossessed, who can never forget how education sorts its students in the country's best interests. How they are marked, tagged.

(In the twenties, Frederick Taylor defended his revolutionary principles of scientific management in Congress, arguing that his ideas would free the German or Englishman to do more complex, challenging, and rewarding work. We can always get a Hungarian to lift a shovel, Taylor added.)

Edna St. Vincent Millay referred to Le Sueur derisively as the "corn virgin of the prairies" (*I Hear Men Talking,* p. 226). The voice of those *with* who have nothing to do with those with *less*. Culture—as those without culture know—is

a weapon to be wielded. The conservative philosopher José Ortega y Gasset wrote of those who had stepped onto the stage of history and did not belong there. "Vertical invaders," he called them.

Le Sueur writes for those who have been kept down, held back, cast aside, because, she believes, it is they, not those in power, who hold the future in their hands. "All of culture comes from the oppressed," she notes. "The oppressed are the only repository of culture in monopoly capitalism" (quoted in Schleuning, p. 129).

Even today, the intellectual industry in America does not make room for Le Sueur, except for the case feminism makes. "Speak White" is the Québécois term for such practice. It defines what is acceptable and what is not, what is art and what is less, what is to be excluded. We understand today why Melville lapsed into silence; why Walt Whitman's *Leaves of Grass,* Theodore Dreiser's *Sister Carrie,* and Stephen Crane's *Maggie: A Girl of the Streets* were considered obscene; why Emily Dickinson's poetry was edited for publication. Our hindsight in such matters is a marvelous corrective. Having understood the past better than it did itself, we assume (and congratulate) our better understanding of the present.

What we have done, however, is construct a past which explains, if not justifies, the present (what we mean by institutional legitimacy). In order to understand Le Sueur's writing and life, we have to see how and why she chose to stand outside; what the consequences of it have been. She may have crossed over into the canon or at least earned a place on its margins as a regional, feminist, or political writer, but she is still not read as she should be.

WRITING: MOVING FORWARD

The writer ... consciously or unconsciously, willingly or unwillingly, works in the service of a class and receives his mandate from that class.

(Walter Benjamin, *Moscow Diary,* p. 133)

In 1924 Le Sueur published "Nests" in *Poetry,* followed in 1926 by "Evening in a Lumber Yard"

in *New Masses.* (Neala Schleuning categorizes the piece as a story in her bibliography, John E. Crawford as reportage). In 1927 her story "Persephone" was published in the *Dial,* her first writing to receive attention.

During her lifetime Le Sueur published nineteen books (a novel about Emiliano Zapata remains unpublished), more than sixty stories, thirty-some articles, and poetry. Scholars have seen her work to be a populist version of T. S. Eliot's *Waste Land.* A Communist *Cantos.* Counter myths. Her writing was praised by Sinclair Lewis, Nelson Algren, Carl Sandburg.

This needs qualification. If Le Sueur published in *Poetry* and the *Dial* and later in the *Kenyon Review, Mademoiselle, New Republic, Harper's Bazaar, Women's Home Companion, Scribner's* and *Yale Review,* increasingly she published in leftist periodicals, populist publications, and little magazines that did not align themselves with market-driven, Madison Avenue mainstream publications but in opposition to them. She was published close to thirty times in *Masses and Mainstream, New Masses,* and *Mainstream,* periodicals of the Communist Party. At times she wrote about middle-class women, but she wrote for those whom the *New York Times* does not serve.

Except for five children's books published by Alfred A. Knopf during the McCarthy era that Le Sueur wrote in order to make a living, none of her books have been published by mainstream presses. (Some libraries ban her children's books.) *Worker Writers* (c. 1939) was published by the Works Progress Administration; *Salute to Spring* (1940) by International Publishers, the Communist Party press. Others were published by John E. Crawford's West End Press, which has done so much to make Le Sueur's writing more widely available, and Howard Fast's Blue Heron Press. After the sixties, when feminists become aware of Le Sueur, the Feminist Press brought out a retrospective selection, *Ripening* (1982).

By the time the Depression deepened in the thirties, it was not uncommon for American writers to become radicalized. Some, like George Oppen, stopped writing. Oppen went into neigh-

borhoods as a community organizer to help the poor, explaining, "There are situations which cannot honorably be met by art" (p. 36).

Le Sueur did not need the Depression to radicalize her. As a girl in Oklahoma she saw farm unrest and Socialist activity. Her teenage years at Fort Scott with the People's College, her experiences in New York and California, her protest against the execution of Sacco and Vanzetti that landed her in jail, all foreshadowed the struggles of the thirties. In the thirties she supported strikes, organized protests, helped out on breadlines.

Unlike Oppen, she did not stop writing. Her writing was her politics, even though she would not let politics dictate how and what she wrote. The Communist Party considered her writing to be too lyrical, too negative, too focused on women. Her powerful piece of reportage "Women on the Breadlines" (1932) was excluded by the party from its publication of her *Salute to Spring*. The leftist writer Anna Louise Strong criticized her for having children, although Le Sueur's fellow party member Myra Page defended her, condemning the Communist Party for its stand on children of female members. Without the Communist Party, however, Le Sueur would not have developed as a writer.

It is crucial to understand that Le Sueur's vision of Middle America is not Eliot's or Ezra Pound's. Their audience is not hers, nor does Le Sueur want it to be. She writes for those on the Left; those who have been cast aside; those who reject Madison Avenue; those who have a dream of America that has not been realized. It is political writing. Writing that is and isn't regional, for Le Sueur argues that the region—Middle America—is the country. The future or the end.

It is a mistake to see Le Sueur as an outsider, primitive, Millay's corn virgin, even if she had no formal education and was a woman, rural, radical. One does not have to go to school to be schooled. Like many radical left American writers in the twenties and thirties, Le Sueur rejected both the naturalists and the modernists that followed. She refused to accept the determinism of the naturalists. As much as modernists such as William Faulkner and Ernest Hemingway opposed the mechanized regimentation of modern

life, she did not think they served the people. Sinclair Lewis was facile. Writers like Saul Bellow were elitist. All about themselves.

D. H. Lawrence was an influence.

> He wrote of the trashing of the body in our civilization, of Puritan attitudes towards the body as commodity, and of male-aggression towards the woman-as-property. He was very important to me because he described the body as alienated by economic necessities and the dominance of property rights over human rights, especially oppressive to women.
> (*I Hear Men Talking*, p. 240)

Walt Whitman was always there.

> When I was fifteen and first read Whitman before World War I, he was considered by the Christian culture to be pornographic because he was for the body on this earth with all the senses and life now without waiting for some far-off heaven. … He gave us a body and taught us to sing in our own voice.
> ("Jelly Roll," pp. 353, 356)

On her deathbed in 1996 she had a copy of Whitman on the table by her side. What she read is a gauge of what she wrote. She read to write.

In the thirties, Louis Adamic surveyed the responses of a group of workers who read novels about workers. Conservative workers felt the poverty of their lives had been patronized, while union workers were appalled by what they considered to be the artistic conceits of the books they read. No matter how much writers may empathize, even work with workers, they know they stand outside. There is no common language between the educated and those without education. We are talking here of trains that run on different tracks.

In Clancy Sigal's *Weekend in Dinlock* (1960), a miner forced to paint because he can longer work in the mines learns, once he is discovered as a painter, that his neighbors no longer consider him to be one of them. However, Richard Wright's account of reading Gertrude Stein's *Three Lives* to longshoremen holds out the possibility that the gap might be bridged.

Whether—how?—any writer can find a way down into that darkness, as Le Sueur argued she must do, is not the question here. The question is

what the writer makes of the effort. In short, how does one's thought come to be realized in a face or landscape?

WRITING: INTO THE DARKNESS

These are not stories, but epitaphs marking the lives of women who in wars, depression or holocaust are at the bottom of the social strata, are trampled on, leave no statistic, no record, obituary or remembrance.

(*Women on the Breadlines,* Introduction)

Le Sueur's writing is like waves crashing on a shore. Words piled on words, details crowding details, images clashing with one another. The wash of waves upon a continent, rushing across Middle America, subsiding, only to advance farther in its next surge. Dreams dashed by the next wave only to return in the one following. Beauty inexplicably harsh. Harshness strangely beautiful. As if it were a force of nature. As if it is. A tide that comes in, comes in, comes in. As inevitable as it is urgent. As poetic as it is prosaic.

"We need the storm, the whirlwind, and the earthquake," Frederick Douglass said to the Rochester Ladies' Anti-slavery Society on July 5, 1852, in his holiday oration "What to the Slave Is Your Fourth of July?" (Marcus, p. 12). Like Douglass, Le Sueur called upon the higher power of nature to purify, cleanse. In *I Hear Men Talking,* a cyclone brings a divided town together. Her Invocation to the novella is a prayer for the storm and whirlwind to come. "The only time the reality is revealed, the terrible surface torn aside," she writes in *Corn Village,* "is after some violence. Violence somehow stirs up the deadly becalmed surface, breaks open the body" (p. 22).

Only if nature wipes the slate clean can there be a new beginning. In her story "The Bird" (collected in *I Hear Men Talking*), Floyd, its protagonist, becomes, for the first time, part of a community after a storm at sea. Floods and droughts are common in her writing and unite as much as they divide. Suffering, Le Sueur feels, is not negative but a basis for solidarity. We can be happy alone, but when we suffer, inevitably we suffer together.

There are other storms, contra nature—greed, property, capitalism, individualism of one kind or another—that uproot. If the inevitable natural disasters in Middle America (its tornadoes and cyclones, its droughts and floods, bone-cold winters) cannot be avoided, the unnatural ones (from banks, Wall Street, corporations, the greed and callousness of the capitalist) imposed from outside can.

In a Middle America undone by so much in the twentieth century—an age in which we became homeless, exiles of one kind or another in our own land, and distance became a measure not so much of miles but of alienation and loneliness—migration is, of necessity, both our common experience and the future we must chase. In story after story, Le Sueur tracks the relentless, unceasing, endless movement of Middle America in buses, trains, cars. "Home," John Berger writes, "is no longer a dwelling but the untold story of a life being lived" (*And Our Faces, My Heart, Brief as Photos,* p. 64).

To tell this story, one that has been heard only in its silence, Le Sueur must speak through the voices of those without a voice. She must write stories that have not been written before. Not stories, epitaphs. She sees herself less as a writer than as a witness, less a writer than a scribe.

Le Sueur may use first-person narration in her fiction and reportage, but, as in "Women on the Breadlines," her narrator may be one of those she writes about, not one who stands aside to report, explain, or interpret. In this story, the narrator is one of the unemployed who seeks assistance, like those whose stories she tells. It is not her story but those of everyone around her, which broadens perspective.

In "I Was Marching" (in *Ripening*), the narrator, who has joined the Teamster strike in Minneapolis in 1934, is fearful that she will lose who she is once she joins the strikers. Fearful not of the physical danger but of being swallowed in the crowd. As her involvement in the strike grows, she begins to see herself not as an individual but as part of something other than herself. When it ceases to be her story, it is their story. In losing her individuality she finds it.

The story Le Sueur has to tell has not only not been told before but must be told for a Middle

America patronized by high culture. In order for her to be a voice of Middle America, she must discard her bourgeois background—not put aside her reading of Marx and Whitman so much as to re-situate it, so that their voices are indistinguishable from the voices she hears.

Le Sueur does so in a number of ways. She uses basic subject-verb sentences so that the reader's movement forward is not stopped. Although she shares Left politics with Oppen (both were blacklisted during the McCarthy era) and emphasizes, as he does, the ordinary and everyday, their aesthetics cannot be more different. Oppen's is austere, minimalist, an aesthetics of poverty; his language as bare as Depression streets. Her writing is exuberant, expansive, often joyous, influenced by her grandmother's biblical rhetoric. The inspiration a preacher brings.

She uses "and" for its accumulative effect, as a preacher might, as well as to link one thing to another: the near and far, personal and political, past and present.

> A woman knows when she has to go to work *and* compete with other men, *and* lower the price of all labor, *and* when her children go to work, tiny, in the vast lettuce and beet fields of the Imperial Valley and Texas [emphasis added].
>
> (*Ripening,* p. 172)

She uses repetition not only for emphasis but also to reinforce or change meaning.

> Of the women and girls who told me these stories, only *one* and myself are visible and alive. *One* had a lobotomy and doesn't know her name. *One* died in the snow. Several died of self-induced abortions, from T.B. and syphilis. *One* went mad from the terror of racism.
>
> *One* went to the Fort [Snelling] naked under a cape to stop the war [emphasis added].
>
> (*Women on the Breadlines,* preface)

She may employ stream of consciousness to reduce the distance between writer and reader, subject and object.

> So I began hearing my voice, strange and small, saying as I felt I had no right with death so near in my mind two hours before, that it was nothing I had done yet, only my brother who belonged to the body of my life and of the earth's. I saw them all there smiling that smile I had never seen before as if they loved me and I had to say further that we were all together and I saw the young girls in white dresses who had been walking restless all the afternoon, their arms entwined around fragrant waists, stop to listen.
>
> (*Harvest & Song for My Time,* p. 80)

The style for some writers is there from the beginning and changes little, but Le Sueur never ceased seeking new ways to write, even if for much of her life her writing varied little. Not what she would say—she had that from the beginning—but how she would say it. In the thirties she defended her lyrical Lawrentian writing to the Communist Party. In the seventies she questioned whether she had been right. In the eighties she came to see that most writing is linear—male, rational, destructive—and began to write what she termed "nounless novels." Linear time is arbitrary, in opposition to the natural cycle of seasons and days.

In an essay, "Poets with History and Poets Without History," Marina Tsvetaeva describes the poet with history:

> Everything is for them a touchstone. Of their power, which increases with each new obstacle. Their self-discovery is their coming to self-knowledge through the world, self-knowledge of the soul through the visible world. Their path is the path of experience. As they walk, we physically sense a wind, the air they cleave with their brows. A wind blows from them.
>
> (*Art in the Light of Conscience,* p. 137)

One cannot compare the early work of a poet with history with his or her later work. The poet of history always moves forward. One cannot compare the early work of Le Sueur with the writing at the end of her life. Her early Lawrentian lyricism in "The Horse" (in *Ripening*) is of a different order than the tripartite construction of *The Dread Road,* published in 1991, and her efforts at "nounless novels."

"Never again," Berger says, "will a single story be told as though it were the only one" (*G.,* p. 129). For any writer to choose the story he or

she tells implies that there are other stories the writer chooses not to tell. We may understand this in several ways. First of all—as is obvious—it underlines the importance of the story the writer tells. More importantly, the story that gets told by definition does not tell the whole story, because its perspective is always single, limited.

We have to ask ourselves not only why stories that do not get told fail to get told—what the politics of such decisions are—but also what other stories, facts, information, commentary are necessary to make the story we read more complete. "It is scarcely any longer possible," Berger adds, "to tell a straight story sequentially unfolding in time. And this is because we are too aware of what is continually traversing a story-line laterally" (*The Look of Things,* p. 40).

Le Sueur chooses to oppose linear narrative in several ways. In *The Dread Road,* she will interrupt the narrative with parenthetical asides of what she thinks or contrast it with selections of Edgar Allan Poe's writing that emphasize or enlarge the events of the story in a historical context. Such writing may be characterized as discontinuous narrative or montage, but Le Sueur disrupts the limiting effects of linear narrative in other ways. Although her stories may be about one person, they are never about one person. The story of the one person is seen, subsumed we might say, in relation to others, to geography, economics, society, politics, history.

THE DREAD ROAD *(1991)*

And the poets of the future will never be done with drawing all the figures of the dead child that every politics abandons.

(Jacques Rancière, p. 24)

In the seventies, Meridel Le Sueur took a bus from Albuquerque to Denver. In Albuquerque she met a woman who had given birth to a child in the rest room of the bus station and ended its life. The woman carried the dead child in a zipper bag with red roses on it onto the bus. In 1991, five years before Le Sueur's death at age ninety-six, years in which she received attention she had

not received since the Depression, lauded and celebrated by feminists, including a trip to Nairobi in 1985 for a woman's conference, only the second time she had been out of the country, she wrote the story she had carried with her for twenty years.

The bus ride from Albuquerque to Denver becomes, in Le Sueur's telling, the story of a long march through our buried history. The bus passes through Trinidad, Colorado, twelve miles from the 1914 massacre of miners at Ludlow. (Le Sueur heard the miners' stories when they came to Fort Scott after the murders to commemorate their dead.) Other ghosts are summoned along the way, from the Trail of Tears, Wounded Knee, Laguna, and Black Hawk's crossing to the atomic bomb tests in Nevada before the end of World War II that the government assured everyone would be safe.

The dead child aboard. Who does not die.

Le Sueur tells the story in three parallel tracks. There is a first-person narrator whose grandparents were killed at Ludlow, whose husband died from nuclear radiation (a geologist who believed the government until he realized they lied), and whose son is in a sanitorium in Denver because of nuclear radiation. She befriends the woman who carries the dead child, takes her side, identifies with her, is transformed.

I felt she was glorious in this chemical light, the light from her seemed to contain all history, generative memory, something lost, now remembered. I had let it die.

(p. 13)

A second narrative, comprising journal notes and authorial explanations and interjections, follows the first to comment on what the narrator says or to direct the reader. At times it is the narrator's reaction or additional explanation to the story she tells. At times it is Le Sueur herself who explains or expands what the narrator says or speaks to readers directly, telling them to listen, pay attention.

The third narrative includes selections from the writings of Poe that reinforce or elaborate upon the events of this trip, which travels farther into the past than it does across country. Poe,

notes Le Sueur, "reflected the dread road of his time and the continuing, hidden buried death in America" (p. 61).

The young woman with the dead child has dark, black straight hair like an Indian, a face like Medusa, with a strange glow and smell about her. "Sulphuric," the narrator says.

There is a third woman, a social worker, who is suspicious of the young woman, whom she thinks has cocaine in the zippered bag. Hers is the voice of propriety, repression, dominance.

The bus driver is spooked approaching Trinidad, as is, for different reasons, the elderly narrator, who at this point in her trip to see her son normally takes Valium to calm herself from terrible memories of Ludlow. "This is a piece of road like nothing I ever seen," the driver says. "See now, there's not just mist but it whirls and looks like people running or stopping the bus. Once an old man stood right in front of the headlights signaling something. I put on the brakes but I went right through the old man" (p. 19). As if the dead of Ludlow did not die but remain to trouble our sleep. The social worker tells the driver it's only the wind. Strange things happen.

It's not that strange things happen, but that they are not considered strange.

The narrator carries history in her bones. Her grandparents dead at Ludlow. Her husband dead from nuclear radiation. Her son with one eye down his cheek. The thirteen women and children at Ludlow who hid in a cellar only to be asphyxiated at the strikers' campsite. Eighty-five bullets fired into Louis Tikas. Machine guns on vehicles used against the strikers, one named the "Death Special." A photograph of Rockefeller at a tee of a plush Eastern golf course defending his actions in Ludlow.

The young woman carries history in her child. She had been told to have an abortion but refused. She gives him life but will not let him live because his life will not be life. "He won't be a cheap worker for Mr. Rockefeller or a beet puller being sprayed," she says. "I gave him our own death" (pp. 29, 28). Not the life that is death.

The social worker wants to see what is in the zipped bag and the police to investigate, but the

narrator prevents her from doing so. The mother shows the narrator her dead child and, later, unzips the bag to look at him again: "He looked different now. Tenderly taken down from the cross, he was not a child now but an icon of the dispossessed, of the brutally murdered, of the nuclear holocaust" (p. 38).

After the bus arrives in Denver, the woman disappears. The narrator stays on, hoping to catch news of her. On the fifth day she reads in the paper about a woman who had thrown a dead body across a bar where men were drinking. On the seventh day, she reads that a young woman had stood in the capitol and held a dead baby up, as if it were a sacrifice.

The narrator keeps the child's blue knit cap the woman had given her.

It is like everything Le Sueur has written and nothing like anything she has written. She reaches back to her grandmother's Christianity and welds it to Marx; finds in the feminism for which she is celebrated her prairie anarchism (at several points the narrator acknowledges that her college education has blinded her to life). At the end of her life, Le Sueur gives us a Christ child for an age of capitalism. Brought to us from hell. Who died that we might live.

"PERSEPHONE" (1927)

In "Persephone," her first published story, the unspoken tension between mother and daughter results in the daughter leaving home with a man, a stranger who has only recently come to town. The daughter, referred to only as "Freda's daughter" by the unnamed narrator, is seen by farm boys and old ladies to have "dark things" in her. When she returns home alone, it is "as if she had touched strange fruits and eaten pale and deathless seeds. ... a woman ravished by strangeness" (*Corn Village*, p. 35).

If Le Sueur adapts the myth of Persephone, the Greek goddess of fertility and decay, to Middle America and its myths of the seasons, of the flowering and dying of nature, she also links it to the life elsewhere that draws so many away from the prairies. (The story follows Le Sueur's

own trajectory from Minnesota to New York and California, where she is living when she writes "Persephone.") Freda's daughter did not want what the plains offered, the narrator says, and left chasing a dream, one we follow from birth. She left home not only for the dream of another world but also, Le Sueur implies, to put distance between herself and her mother.

Living is a kind of dying, Le Sueur says, but from death new life will come, as it does every spring. The dream we die from will not die. Kansas is our Hellas. In "Persephone," Le Sueur lays down the track she will follow the rest of her life: planting the pale and deathless seeds of those she sees on the street every day, the strange fruits of Marx and Whitman.

At the end of the story, the narrator accompanies Freda's daughter on a train to … where and why Le Sueur does not say. Suddenly, inexplicably, the story shifts from that of Freda's daughter to that of the narrator. She is overwhelmed by a terror she cannot explain, as she thinks: Who is Freda's daughter? Her husband? Her mother? Who is anyone?

As if at the beginning of her journey, Le Sueur sees how long it will be.

I HEAR MEN TALKING (c. 1933)

In her early writing, young women and girls stand at the beginning of life, uncertain, if not apprehensive, about men and sex at a time when economic disaster and natural calamity make life difficult, if not impossible; political unrest forces them to choose which side they are on. In *I Hear Men Talking,* Penelope is always in motion, in fields and woods, from one place to another in town, one person to another. She has to listen to everything because she is young, innocent, and knows little.

The voices Penelope hears are those of rural, small-town Iowa. Her grandmother Gee speaks for God, against men. Mr. Littlefield complains that he has not been given the opportunities his education deserves. Nina Shelley, who has been raped by Hawk, the man she loves, goes back to him with a gun, only to be shot herself (no one

in town knows which of them did the shooting), and life for her afterward is a reproach. Jenny meets a man passing through town and leaves with him because, she tells Penelope, there is no life in this town. Bac Kelly is the hard-as-steel boy loved by Penelope, who does not yet know what love is but with an attraction for him she must follow. Mona, her mother, and Lowell, a labor organizer, her mother's friend and possibly lover, are shadowy figures.

At the time Le Sueur was writing the novel, Iowa was rife with milk strikes by destitute dairy farmers trying to force a raise in the price of milk as well as penny auctions of foreclosed farms, wherein local farmers banded together to defeat outside monied interests by forcing a quick cutoff in the bidding and returning the property to its owner at a fraction of its value. Penelope is roughly the same age Le Sueur was in Oklahoma before World War I when she first encountered labor unrest. Like "Persephone," *I Hear Men Talking* is an internal narrative as well as a bildungsroman that reflects Le Sueur's own coming-of-age.

While Penelope plays chess with Mr. Littlefield, has fudge with Miss Shelley, listens to her grandmother Gee go on about God and men, and seeks out Bac Kelly, men in her home plan ways to prevent the foreclosure of farms. If Penelope hears what men do to women and one another—the rampant greed for more, more—she also hears what brings men together. "In a little while the corn will be tall enough," Lowell says to her, meaning that once the corn is high enough men can hide in it if the sheriff arrives at a foreclosure. In an explicit passage, Le Sueur links the community formed by joint action to the natural cycle of seasons:

> In a little while the corn will be high and a thousand men could hide in that corn and you couldn't see them, a thousand men in the corn. And Penelope saw the corn growing up and the thousand men like the corn growing tall and murmuring in the wind, standing together rooted in the soil of Kansas, Iowa, Nebraska, the Dakotas, Minnesota, Illinois. She saw them waving like good soil planted with fat ripe corn, marching corn, all moving together.

(p. 79)

171

Bac almost causes a farm to be sold off by tipping off the sheriff about the organizers' plans for a penny auction. He takes Penelope into the woods so that he might have sex with her, but she breaks free from him. He chases after her and tells friends he sees out hunting that they can have her too if they help him. One of them mistakes him for an animal and accidentally kills him.

A cyclone hits. Mr. Littlefield is found dead in the street from no apparent cause. Miss Shelley helps wounded in the hospital. Mrs. Swillman, the wife of the man who controls the town, dies before she can give birth to the child her husband does not want. In the cemetery where Penelope has run to escape Bac, a monument of an angel falls on her.

Everyone speaks of the smell of brimstone and fire in the air after the cyclone hit, as if God has spoken to them through the violence of the storm and brought them together when love could not. In the hospital, Penelope hears their "voices fused together, talking, of what they had seen and would see, of a tide they knew now carried them and did not separate them doing battle against each other" (p. 130).

"TONIGHT IS PART OF THE STRUGGLE" (1935)

March. Men without work. Dirty snow on the ground. They say Leah hasn't the right to have a baby in the Depression. Welfare won't give her milk. You have to nurse the child, they say. "But with worry the milk goes and you have to be thinking at two o'clock, I've got to have milk, at six o'clock I've got to have milk, at six in the morning, at ten at two at six again I've got to have milk" (*Salute to Spring,* p. 119).

The story "Tonight Is Part of the Struggle" (collected in *Salute to Spring*) introduces us to Leah and her husband, Jock, who has been laid off by Ford. They live in one room, what was once the kitchen of a run-down mansion. The baby sleeps in a cracker box. Their poverty and difficult circumstances erode any sense of well-being and respect and cause them to be always at one another. They have nowhere to go because they have no money. The evening is like every other. If they only had somewhere to go. To forget what their lives have become, if only for a few hours.

There is a mass meeting a block away, Jock says. What's a mass meeting? Leah asks. There'll be people there, Jock says. It'll be warm. We won't be alone. At the meeting, Leah doesn't understand much of what the speaker, a Communist organizer, says, but she hears the words "that her body's experience repeated to her. ... They were like words in the first primer" (*Salute to Spring,* p. 125).

For the first time, someone has spoken to them, eased their irritation with one another, brought them closer together. Leah leans forward on Jock's shoulder while she listens. Jock looks at her as if he is a child again. The "tonight like every other night" has at the mass meeting become the "tonight part of the struggle." The roar of the crowd from something the speaker says causes Leah's child to wake and cry out. When the crowd sees Leah lift the child and hold it on her shoulder, everyone laughs. When they hear its "bawl of rebellion," they hear in its cry the speaker's voice that there can be new life.

Throughout this story and in her writing in general, Le Sueur emphasizes that we are part of the natural world: "like a dandelion top in spring sprouting there," "vast ocean of dark people," "great black sea of bodies," "heads like black wheat growing in the same soil, the same wind" (*Salute to Spring,* pp. 123, 125, 126). If the snowstorm outside the hall is a natural image of the unnatural storm the Depression has brought, it is, after all, March, and after March, Le Sueur knows, always knows, new life will come.

THE GIRL (1978)

The Girl is two novels, one written in 1939 but not published, the second revised by Le Sueur for publication by the West End Press in 1978. In the first, Marxist politics play a greater role. In the second, there is more emphasis on sexual politics. In the first version, the child that the

Girl gives birth to at the end of the novel is a boy. In the second, the child is a girl.

The Marxist politics remain. There is a strike at a foundry in Saint Paul, where the novel is set. Butch, who is seeing the Girl, goes to work as a scab. In a confrontation between strikers and scabs, his brother, who has joined him at the foundry, is killed. Amelia, who works for the Workers' Alliance and keeps photos of Sacco and Vanzetti in her room, is spokesman for Le Sueur's politics and instructs the Girl about economic, class, and sexual issues and stresses the need for being together, not alone. She repeats her husband's belief that we don't live just for ourselves.

In the published version, men die or are imprisoned. The Girl's father dies, used up by how he was used. Butch is shot robbing a bank. Hoinck, Belle's man, dies in the same robbery. Only women remain, not to fend for themselves but to help one another because fending for oneself is not possible in a patriarchal world.

At the end of *The Girl,* Clara, a prostitute and friend of the Girl's who has been given electroshock treatment, dies before anyone can get help. Women demonstrate against the injustice and the same day gather around the Girl to herald the birth of her child. (When, earlier, the Girl goes to a welfare agency for assistance they want her to sign a paper permitting them to sterilize her. In Le Sueur's portrayal, government agency workers, like the social worker in *The Dread Road,* assist less than control.)

During the period between 1939 and 1978 Le Sueur's experience included being blacklisted by McCarthy in the forties and fifties and then, in the seventies, given attention by feminists she had not received since her early writing, even if that writing was considered too lyrically Lawrentian and radically feminist for a puritanical and essentially masculine Communist Party. It was in the late 1970s she considered a change in her writing, arguing against linear narrative, male in its need to control, and for what she termed "nounless novels." How much these events influenced Le Sueur in revising *The Girl* is difficult to say. For the first time, she uses a bank robbery, an established noir form, but does not make it integral to the book, except obliquely, as an example of greed or desperation.

The Girl may be two stories, but Le Sueur comes back again and again to the same story. The hunger in us.

The hunger of *not*: a hunger that stretches far back in Middle America, brought about by drought, bank foreclosure, greed, capitalism, dominance of one individual over one another, and, in particular, of men over women. (At one moment the Girl feels like a bird on a spit when Butch leans over her.)

The hunger of *want*: for something more. For a life that is not only survival, even if survival is, Le Sueur says, a form of resistance against what is. The Girl says her father planted a longing in her, one that took her from their village to Saint Paul. After having sex with Butch for the first time, she thinks:

> Something had entered me, broken me open, in some kind of terrible hunger. Some beings, more like hunger, had given me something from their bodies, had come over me, said something—what did he say?—his whole body said something and I cannot remember the words but it would change me forever. You would never be a wall, a closed door, an empty bowl. I could feel my whole front of my body rise like mama's dough … to his good body, to his terrible hunger. … I would always now know the naked skin of man and woman, their heats and hungers, and the awful wonderful need to enter each other, not to be single, alone, hankering.
>
> (p. 51)

Once again, for Le Sueur, violence is necessary to open us up to possibility, life.

There are those who read the novel as an attack on the rational, individualist, predatory male, but it is as much, if not more, about the need we have for one another. The hunger that leads us away from ourselves to another. The Girl says Butch's body had been good to her. At the end of his life, he is the man he might have been, if it were not for the world that formed him. Belle has had thirteen abortions, but her husband Hoinck makes her life life. Clara, who is paid to have sex with men, pays a man once because it means something to her.

If *The Girl* is a radically subversive attack on repressive puritan values in its advocacy of Marx-

ist and feminist politics, it is also a celebration of those whom middle-class people cross the street to avoid. Its language is their language, more so than in her earlier Lawrentian (and more traditional) writing. Its people—Stasia, Ganz, Hoinck—are the immigrants that the dream of America brought across the ocean only to put in its sweatshops and factories, mines and quarries.

At its center is the Girl, as she is in much of Le Sueur's writing, Persephone or Penelope, who learns about life, often from an older woman, and in learning teaches us.

> I have no place but the place of this understanding which is a kind of home too. … I am here, unknown to any at all, and yet known to all.
>
> (p. 121)

There is no more stirring cry of the dispossessed in our literature—the understanding that is a home to the Girl that we refuse to acknowledge, but which Le Sueur insists on.

When they hung Wesley Everett, the IWW leader, in Centralia, Washington, in 1919, they hung him with a long rope, Amelia tells the Girl, "so *they* could all have souvenirs and you go there, in the best houses, you'll find a piece of that rope, and they are glad to show it to you" (p. 136).

Memory is the rope the oppressed keep. The one Le Sueur hands us.

> Of the women and girls who told me these stories, only one and myself are visible and alive. One had a lobotomy and doesn't know her name. One died in the snow. Several died of self-inflicted abortions, from T.B. and syphilis. One went mad from the terror of racism.
>
> One went to the Fort [Snelling] naked under a cape to stop the war. Many disappeared, took to the road, went east or west, were lost in the underground war against women. You cannot find or claim them, or recognize them or say their name. They are outside the economy, the statistics. You cannot even claim the body.
>
> ("Women on the Breadlines," preface)

LEGACY

> You know what a man's painting is like when he has never been out of, say, Indiana, and has never seen a good gallery.
>
> (Ezra Pound, *Selected Letters*, p. 37)

If American writers had to free themselves from the stranglehold Anglo-Saxon culture held over them, they also had to escape a puritan bourgeois morality that held them hostage. There are those, like Pound, Hemingway, F. Scott Fitzgerald, Hart Crane—the list is long—who left. Those, like Henry David Thoreau and Lorine Niedecker, who withdrew. Those, like Charles Reznikoff, Douglas Woolf, and Paul Metcalf, who stood aside. Those, like Melville, who chose silence.

There are also those, like Le Sueur, who walk down paths that bring them no hearing. Because what they write is too political, and politics is not literature. Because it is offensive, obscene. Not American. Primitive. Scrawled on streets, in toilets, on mirrors. Messages all too clear or never understood. Written as they are because it is the only way the writers' hearing can be heard. Writers who "carry the debris of the forbidden to the public square," as Greil Marcus writes, "and make everybody look" (p. 188).

It is not literature. That is to say, it is literature which is not acknowledged or acceptable; writing which, by implication, is its own criticism of accepted critical standards; which is in itself a social history, an aesthetics of denial, an argument for change, testimony for the need to stay alive, to breathe, however it can be done. America is a verb, Europe a noun, Metcalf says. Whatever the verb, it takes us across. That's what verbs do. "Covering ground," Donald Phelps calls it.

Like Le Sueur, some writers cover the ground that is lost, hidden, forbidden. Donald Goines, ground up in ground zero Detroit but who wrote about it before he was. Emily Harvin, a cry from the asylum. Etheridge Knight, sending poems into the world from a cell. D. A. Levy, unofficial poet laureate of Cleveland, whose homage to his city is his poem *ukanhavyrfuckinciti bak*. J. J. Phillips, who went south in the civil rights movement and left *Mojo Hand* behind to tell us where she had gone. Daniel Thompson, who came out of sixties Kent, Ohio, in the wake of John Brown, who once lived in Kent. Don Van Vliet, before he became Captain Beefheart.

Pound was wrong about Indiana. Culture is what you know, what you keep. A swamp. Le

Sueur went all the way, with full belief, into that darkness.

Selected Bibliography

WORKS OF MERIDEL LE SUEUR

NOVELS, SHORT STORIES, AND POETRY

Annunciation. Los Angeles: Platen Press, 1935.

Salute to Spring. New York: International Publishers, 1940.

Corn Village: A Selection. Sauk City, Wis.: Stanton & Lee, 1970.

Rites of Ancient Ripening. . Minneapolis: Vanilla Press, 1975. (Poetry.)

The Girl. Cambridge, Mass.: West End Press, 1978.

Harvest & Song for My Time: Stories. Minneapolis: West End Press, 1982.

I Hear Men Talking: Stories of the Early Decades. Edited and with an afterword by Linda Ray Pratt. Minneapolis: West End Press, 1984.

Winter Prairie Woman. Minneapolis: Minnesota Center for Book Arts, 1990.

The Dread Road. Minneapolis: West End Press, 1991.

COLLECTIONS

Harvest Song: Collected Essays and Stories. Albuquerque, N.Mex.: West End Press, 1990.

Ripening: Selected Work. Edited and with an introduction by Elaine Hedges. Old Westbury, N.Y.: Feminist Press, 1982. New ed., with an afterword by Le Sueur, 1986.

NONFICTION

Worker Writers. [Minneapolis]: Minnesota Works Progress Administration, n.d. [1939].

North Star Country. New York: Duell, Sloan, & Pearce, 1945.

Crusaders: The Radical Legacy of Marian and Arthur Le Sueur. New York: Blue Heron Press, 1955.

Women on the Breadlines. [Cambridge, Mass.]: West End Press, 1977. Reprint 1984.

"Jelly Roll." In *Walt Whitman: The Measure of His Song.* Edited by Jim Perlman, Ed Folsom, and Dan Campion. Minneapolis: Holy Cow! Press, 1981. Pp. 353–356.

Word Is Movement: Journal Notes from Atlanta to Tulsa to Wounded Knee. Tulsa, Okla.: Cardinal Press, 1984.

CHILDREN'S NOVELS

Little Brother of the Wilderness: The Story of Johnny Appleseed. New York: Knopf, 1947.

Nancy Hanks of Wilderness Road: A Story of Abraham Lincoln's Mother. New York: Knopf, 1949.

Sparrow Hawk. New York: Knopf, 1950.

Chanticleeer of Wilderness Road: A Story of Davy Crockett. New York: Knopf, 1951.

The River Road: A Story of Abraham Lincoln. New York: Knopf, 1954.

Conquistadores. New York: Franklin Watts, 1973.

The Mound Builders. New York: Franklin Watts, 1974.

PAPERS

Collections of Le Sueur's papers are held at the Minnesota Historical Society in Saint Paul, Minnesota, and the University of Delaware Library in Newark, Delaware.

CRITICAL AND BIOGRAPHICAL STUDIES

Boehnlein, James M. "Meridel Le Sueur, 'Corn Village,' and Literary Pragmatism." *MidAmerica* 21:82–97 (1994).

Clausen, Jan. *"The Girl." Motheroot Journal* 3:3 (spring 1980).

Coiner, Constance. *Better Red: The Writing and Resistance of Tillie Olsen and Meridel Le Sueur.* New York: Oxford University Press, 1995.

Crawford, John. Afterword to *Harvest Song: Collected Essays and Stories.* Albuquerque, N.Mex.: West End Press, 1990. Pp. 233–241.

———. Afterword to *The Dread Road.* Minneapolis: West End Press, 1991. Pp. 49–60.

Gelfant, Blanche. "'Everybody Steals': Language as Theft in Meridel Le Sueur's *The Girl.*" In *Tradition and the Talents of Women.* Edited by Florence Howe. Urbana: University of Illinois Press, 1991. Pp. 183–210.

Hampl, Patricia. "Meridel Le Sueur, Voice of the Prairie." *MS* 4, no. 2:62–66, 96 (August 1975).

Hedges, Elaine. Introduction to *Ripening: Selected Work.* New York: Feminist Press, 1990. Pp. 1–30.

Pratt, Linda Ray. Afterword to *I Hear Men Talking and Other Stories.* Minneapolis: West End Press, 1984. Pp. 225–237.

———. "Woman Writer in the CP." *Women's Studies* 14, no. 3:247–264 (February 1988)

Schleuning, Neala. *America, Song We Sang Without Knowing.* Mankato, Minn.: Little Red Hen Press, 1983.

Shulman, Robert. *The Power of Political Art: The 1930s Literary Left Reconsidered.* Chapel Hill and London: University of North Carolina Press, 2000. Pp. 41–86.

Tax, Meredith. "Midwestern Original." *Nation,* July 3, 1982, pp. 23–25.

Wald, Alan M. "The Many Lives of Meridel Le Sueur." *Monthly Review* 49, no. 4:23–31 (September 1997).

———. *Exiles from a Future Time: The Forging of the*

Mid-Twentieth-Century Literary Left. Chapel Hill and London: University of North Carolina Press, 2002. Pp. 95–100.

OTHER SOURCES

Benjamin, Walter. *Moscow Diary.* Edited by Gary Smith, translated by Richard Sieburth. Cambridge, Mass.: Harvard University Press, 1986.

Berger, John. *The Look of Things: Essays.* Edited by Nikos Stangos. New York: Viking Press, 1971.

———. *G.* New York: Viking Press, 1972.

———. *And Our Faces, My Heart, Brief as Photos.* New York: Pantheon Books, 1984.

Marcus, Greil. *The Shape of Things to Come: Prophecy and the American Voice.* London: Faber, 2006.

Olson, Charles. *Call Me Ishmael.* San Francisco: City Lights Books, 1947.

Oppen, George. *Selected Prose, Daybooks, and Papers.* Edited and with an introduction by Stephen Cope. Berkeley: University of California Press, 2007.

Pound, Ezra. *Selected Letters, 1907–1941.* Edited by D. D. Paige. New York: New Directions, 1971.

Rabinowitz, Paula. *Labor and Desire: Women's Revolutionary Fiction in Depression America.* Chapel Hill and London: University of North Carolina Press, 1991.

Rancière, Jacques. *Short Voyages to the Land of the People.* Translated by James B. Swenson. Stanford, Calif.: Stanford University Press, 2003.

Tsvetaeva, Marina. *Art in the Light of Conscience: Eight Essays on Poetry.* Translated by Angela Livingstone. Cambridge, Mass.: Harvard University Press, 1992.

GEORGE LIPPARD

(1822—1854)

Jonas Prida

THE POPULAR WRITER, labor organizer, and occasional mystic George Lippard was best known during his lifetime for his 1844 city mystery novel *The Quaker City; or, The Monks of Monk Hall*. This novel sold more than one hundred thousand copies, split Philadelphia into two camps—those who supported Lippard and those who did not—and set a template for the authors in the late 1840s and 1850s who also explored antebellum urban spaces. But Lippard's influence is far larger than spurring the development of a genre of cheaply produced novels about vice and seduction in a rapidly expanding America. In his Revolutionary War novels and short fiction, Lippard also created a mythology for America, including one embroidered piece of history still circulating today: the mass signing of the Declaration of Independence by the delegates on a single day, July 4, 1776. He also founded, organized, and administrated one of the most successful labor organizations of the nineteenth century, the Brotherhood of the Union, and saw himself as a speaker for the rights of laborers against the depredations of capitalists.

At the height of his career in the late 1840s Lippard was one of the most popular authors in America, producing three or four novels a year, running his own newspaper (*Quaker City Weekly*) and engaging political and social questions through a lecture circuit. Friends with fellow purveyor of weird tales Edgar Allan Poe, and successful in a way that Poe never was, Lippard offers a voice and style different from those of more traditional writers of the American Renaissance such as Herman Melville and Nathaniel Hawthorne. Dead before he turned thirty-two, George Lippard left behind a legacy of sensational novels, Revolutionary legends, and explorations into almost every popular anxiety of the 1840s and 1850s.

LIFE

Although almost all writers mine their own experience, Lippard's birth, upbringing, and formative years provided him a nearly inexhaustible source of raw material to write about. Lippard was born April 10, 1822, the fourth of six children, to Daniel B. Lippard and Jemima Ford, who had recently moved from Philadelphia to a farm in Chester County, Pennsylvania. Lippard's German ancestry would play a major role in both his often heterodox religious viewpoints and his interest in alchemy, mesmerism, and secret societies. His father's ancestors fled Germany to escape religious persecution, and his great-grandfather John Libbert—whose name was later changed to Lippard—was a German from the Rhenish Palatinate, an area with a long history of harboring religious dissenters and mystical thinkers. Lippard's father was crippled in a wagon accident in 1824, and this injury would lead to a slow decline in the Lippard family fortunes. By 1825 Lippard's father and mother were incapable of raising their large family, forcing Lippard and his sisters to live with their German-speaking grandfather, Michael, and two maiden aunts. His aunts Catherine and Mary entertained him with stories of the Revolution, stories that would later be part of his series of "Legends of the Revolution." Lippard also saw the family farm slowly sold off in sections to pay debts, a dissolution of home that would become a theme throughout his fiction.

By 1831 Lippard's mother had died, and little was left of the farm; facing desperate economic circumstances, Lippard, his surviving sisters, and his aunts moved into the growing city of Philadelphia. Lippard's father quickly remarried, but a young George had little to no contact with his father or stepmother, a decision that would

later result in Lippard receiving no legacy from his father upon his death in 1837. What few accounts there are of Lippard in this period describe him as a "queer youth" who wore his hair long and spoke in a backcountry accent reflective of his rural upbringing. When possible, the adolescent Lippard spent his time roaming the Brandywine valley and fishing in the Wissahickon River, and both locations would later play important roles in his fiction. At age fifteen he was persuaded by his aunts to go to Catherine Livingston Garretson's Classical School in Rhinebeck, New York, to prepare for the Methodist ministry. Lippard did not last long at the school, finding its emphasis on hierarchy and religious dogma insulting to his belief in an egalitarian, inclusive ministry. Returning to Philadelphia around the time of his father's death, Lippard learned he would receive no part of his father's estate. After a falling out with his surviving aunt, Lippard moved from her Philadelphia residence and began to live an itinerant existence in the depression-wracked city.

Essentially homeless, living in abandoned buildings and staying with artist friends, Lippard found work in a lawyer's office where, he reported, he was exposed to Philadelphia's "social life, hidden sins, and iniquities covered with the cloak of authority" (Reynolds, *George Lippard,* p. 4). Much like his earlier experiences with poverty and religious intolerance, these hidden sins and iniquities would later be fictionalized in a variety of Lippard's writings. In 1841, through his connections at the law office, he was introduced to John S. DuSolle, editor of the *Spirit of the Times,* whose motto, "Democratic and Fearless; Devoted to No Clique, and Bound to No Master," encapsulates the zeitgeist of many of the cheap daily papers of the period. Working under a variety of noms de plume, Lippard started reporting on the courts and submitting articles that poked fun at Philadelphia's literary establishment. During his time at the *Spirit,* Lippard developed his exuberant, at times sensationalistic, writing style and, as importantly, his ability to produce copious amounts of writing quickly. By the time Lippard quit the *Spirit* in April 1842 he probably had met Edgar Allan Poe,

since the offices *Graham's* magazine, where Poe worked at the time, were across the street from the offices of *Spirit of the Times.* This friendship would last until the end of Poe's life.

At the start of 1843 Lippard began writing for a new periodical, *Citizen Soldier,* and became its chief editor six months later. Although less sporting in style and substance than *Spirit of the Times, Citizen Soldier* provided another venue for Lippard's early experimentation with rapidly shifting narrative voice and tone. In addition to developing his skills as a writer, Lippard used *Citizen Soldier* to sharpen his critical wit, contributing a series of satires in his "Spermaceti Papers" that attacked Philadelphia's literary establishment. Elsewhere Lippard used *Soldier* to praise, to little surprise, the works of Washington Irving and James Fenimore Cooper. But he also supported Poe's work and, even more surprising, the novels of Charles Brockden Brown (1771–1810), whose unusual narratives generally elicited distaste at the time. While working at *Citizen Soldier,* Lippard also wrote his first sustained novel, the gothic *Ladye Annabel* (1844), a surprisingly gory tale of betrayal, entombment, and revenge set in fifteenth-century Italy. Lippard sent a completed version of the manuscript to Poe, who thought the style was nervous but exuberant. Upon leaving the newspaper at the end of 1843, Lippard had cultivated an audience who found his anti-elite exuberance entertaining, and it was this combination of fertile audience, anti-establishment tenor, and wildly inventive narratives that would lead to Lippard's greatest publishing success.

In the fall of 1844 Lippard began composing *The Quaker City.* Loosely basing his novel on the 1843 Philadelphia murder trial and acquittal of Singleton Mercer, who had killed Mahlon Heberton because Heberton had seduced Mercer's sister, Lippard took the basics of the case and imbued them with a wide range of cultural anxieties. Setting the events in the sprawling Monk Hall, Lippard's novel satirized politicians, the penny press, religious fanaticism, and sentimental literature and sensationalized the widening gap between rich and poor. The novel was immediately successful; sources claim that within

the first year, sixty thousand copies were sold. Lippard had gone from editor of a minor paper to the best-known author in Philadelphia. In 1844–1845 the novel went through several different editions, with Lippard gaining control over the printing plates by the end of 1845, ensuring ownership of his masterwork.

Over the course of the next two years Lippard began to produce his "Legends of the Revolution" series for the *Saturday Courier.* Already familiar with Revolutionary lore because of his aunts' storytelling and his adolescent experience around the Germantown and Brandywine battlefields, Lippard explored a wide range of Revolutionary experiences and characters for these stories. Part of the legends' appeal was Lippard's scope: he fictionalized the temptation of George Washington and the betrayal of Benedict Arnold, but he also constructed tales about common mechanics and farmers who fought the British to protect their homes. In the *Saturday Courier,* Lippard also published *Blanche of Brandywine* (1846), a Revolutionary-era romance that continued his mixing of large-scale military history with intimate family dynamics and thwarted marriages. Lippard's "Legend" series proved to be exceedingly popular, and the various stories were later collected and published in 1847 as *Washington and His Generals.*

The year 1847 was probably the height of Lippard's personal life and writing career. In addition to *Washington and His Generals,* Lippard published another short Revolutionary War romance, *The Rose of Wissahikon,* and, in response to the American victory in the Mexican-American War, *Legends of Mexico,* which followed a similar pattern to his *Washington and His Generals,* dramatizing both the successes of Zachary Taylor and the hardships of common soldiers. Personally Lippard had become a celebrity in Philadelphia, cultivating his image as a literary outlaw by continuing to wear his hair long and sporting a variety of velvet capes. On May 15 Lippard married Rose Newman, whom he had courted since 1842. Their wedding ceremony did little to reduce the public's fascination with Lippard: the couple married at night on a rock overlooking the Wissahickon River. Later

in the year Lippard had a temperance play produced and ran, unsuccessfully, for a district commissioner post in Philadelphia. By 1848 Lippard was making three to four thousand dollars a year as a writer, a far cry from his days as a destitute squatter five years before.

In addition to two more novels—*'Bel of Prairie Eden,* a romance about the Mexican-American War, and *Paul Ardenheim, the Monk of Wissahikon,* a complicated, semiautobiographical narrative about secret societies and alchemic transformation in Revolutionary-period Pennsylvania—the year 1848 also saw Lippard achieve one of his publishing dreams with the founding of his *Quaker City Weekly.* Disenchanted with his previous experiences with editors and an earlier 1846 failure of his own publishing company, Lippard invested much of his personal fortune and considerable energies into his new weekly. Publishing its first issue in late 1848, the *Quaker City Weekly* would provide Lippard an outlet for his increasingly radical views on bankers, merchants, and the capitalist system in general.

Over the course of the next two years, until the *Weekly* ceased publication in the middle of 1850, Lippard used his periodical to introduce five of his novels. These included two exposés on religious figures and apocalyptic prophecy, *The Memoirs of a Preacher* and its sequel *The Man with the Mask* (both 1849); a mystical journey through time and space in *The Entranced* (1849); a class-infused city mystery set in New York, *The Empire City* (1850); and *The Killers* (1850), Lippard's account of the 1849 election night riots that pitted native Protestants against Catholics and both groups against the African American community. As importantly for Lippard, his newspaper allowed him a forum to publicize his Brotherhood of the Union, a secret society that supported the rights of labor, land and election reform, Fourierism, and cooperation as antidotes to the increasing power of a capitalist class.

The founding of the Brotherhood of the Union in 1849 and the financing of the group dominated Lippard's life and work, as he poured more of his energies and earnings into the project.

The Brotherhood grew rapidly, and Lippard was a frequent speaker at Brotherhood events and rallies. A constant stream of articles appeared in the *Quaker City Weekly* extolling the virtues of the group and secret societies in general, and Lippard printed parts of the organization's rituals and constitution in his periodical. But the cost of running the group—both physically and financially—took its toll on Lippard, and the *Quaker City Weekly* abruptly ceased publication in June 1850.

The two-year period of 1849–1851 also saw several personal tragedies for Lippard, tragedies that exacerbated Lippard's already growing sense of his own mortality. In July, Lippard was visited by a half-shod and tattered Poe, who, while trying to return to Virginia, had been imprisoned for a night in Philadelphia and could not afford the train home. Lippard, along with several other writers and clerks, gathered eleven dollars for Poe's fare, and Lippard hosted the weakened Poe for three days before seeing him leave for Baltimore and his eventual death. In October 1849 Lippard's first daughter Mima died; in May 1850 Rose gave birth to the couple's second child, Paul, but the infant died before his first birthday. In May 1851 Rose Lippard died from tuberculosis; this event, according a biography printed shortly after his death, pushed a distraught Lippard to attempt suicide by throwing himself off Niagara Falls (a friend caught him before he could succeed). Lippard assumed his own death by tuberculosis would soon follow and spent the next two years of his life vacillating between periods of intense melancholy and equally intense work. The deaths in Lippard's family also contributed to his growing interest in spirituality. Already predisposed to alternate versions of the afterlife because of his heterodox religious beliefs, Lippard visited the founders of Spiritualism, the Fox sisters, in Rochester, New York, and gave lectures on Spiritualism in Philadelphia in 1852.

During the last two years of his life Lippard continued to publish, although at a lesser rate. In 1851 he produced one issue of the *White Banner,* which contained a reprint of *The Entranced,* now titled *Adonai: The Pilgrim of Eternity*; some short

stories; and collected Brotherhood of the Union material. In 1852 he released *The Midnight Queen,* a triptych of city mystery stories, one of which included a character from his earlier work *The Empire City.* Lippard continued his reexamination of *The Empire City* in the final work he saw published while living, *New York: Its Upper Ten and Lower Million* (1853), which fills in *The Empire City*'s missing narrative and opens with a moving introduction about his grief for his family.

By early 1854 Lippard was battling increasingly serious health issues, and his prediction the year before that he would die in March 1854 seemed prophetic. He finished his indictment of the Fugitive Slave Law, *Eleanor,* published serially in 1854 after his death, but was visibly weakening. In the last weeks of his life he was unable to write so instead began sketching pictures of his next narrative. On February 9 Lippard died at the age of thirty-one; a medical examination determined the cause of death to be consumption (tuberculosis). Lippard's Philadelphia funeral was an elaborate affair, with members of the Brotherhood of the Union, Odd Fellows, Freemasons, and other members of Philadelphia's writing community mixing with mechanics and German-speaking farmers.

In his brief lifetime Lippard wrote the best-selling novel in America before *Uncle Tom's Cabin* (1853), founded his own newspaper, started a secret society that would influence more mainstream labor organizations, popularized the genre of city mysteries, and mythologized the American Revolution. His sensationalistic narratives and grotesque characters made him wildly popular with working-class readers while alienating him from the critical establishment. Lippard's blending of traditional gothic elements with a journalistic eye for salacious detail, a style only recently popularized by the French writer Eugène Sue, turned a two-year-old murder into popular culture event.

CITY MYSTERIES

If Lippard had done nothing other than write *The Quaker City,* his place in American popular culture would still be secure. The novel, begun in

1844 and published in a longer form in 1845, went through more than twenty printings in addition to being pirated and published under a changed title in England. In this complex, relentlessly economic novel, Lippard explored the class structure in rapidly industrializing Philadelphia, a class structure that, for Lippard and many of his readers, rewarded vice and punished virtue. At the same time, the novel also uses its critique of antebellum capitalism as an avenue to investigate sexuality, charismatic religion, the penny press, sporting culture, secret societies, and the ultimate fate of the American Republic.

The full title of the novel is *The Quaker City; or, The Monks of Monk Hall, a Romance of Philadelphia Life, Mystery, and Crime,* and Lippard exploits all the different components in the title. Philadelphia and its suburbs provide the setting for the novel, but Lippard's city is a confusing, chaotic space where decaying houses loom over zigzagging roads. Little in the urban setting is stable; houses become traps and traps become escape hatches. Multiple characters have multiple identities and names, and forgery and deception are everyday practices. The Monks of Monk Hall are a secret group of Philadelphia's bon ton who use the mansion to drink, gamble, and seduce. Lawyers, merchants, judges, writers, southern planters, and northern businessmen, any group in possession of economic power, found itself incorporated into Lippard's sensationalistic novel. But *The Quaker City* is not only an investigation into the upper ten, to use one of Lippard's stock phrases to describe the elite. Its panoramic gaze includes the poor, social strivers, and criminals. The central crime in the novel is the seduction of the innocent, and the mystery resides both in the characters solving the various crimes and in the world of the city.

As stated earlier, Lippard used the heavily publicized trial of Singleton Mercer and his acquittal of the murder of Mahlon Heberton as the germ of the novel's seduction plot. Assuming the identity of a Spanish gentleman, Mahlon Heberton seduced and abandoned sixteen-year-old Sarah Mercer; after learning of the deed, Sarah's brother, Singleton, spent the next two days tracking down Heberton, eventually hiding himself on a ship that was carrying Heberton across the river to Camden, New Jersey. Before the boat could dock, Singleton surprised Heberton and killed him. The subsequent trial and eventual release of Singleton were closely covered by Philadelphia's newspapers, and the themes of libertinism and familial justice were part of the popular discourse.

It is to Lippard's credit as an imaginative writer that he took the basics of this case and reworked the material into something much more complex and ironic. Instead of replicating the straightforward revenge plot, Lippard made the avenger, Byrnewood Arlington, complicit in the seduction; the opening scene of the novel has Arlington engaged in a night of heavy drinking with his sister's eventual seducer, Gus Lorrimer. As the party grows drunker, Arlington bets Lorrimer a hundred dollars that the girl Lorrimer is about to seduce is not a girl of quality; unknowingly, Arlington has bet on the social position of his sister. He also agrees to participate in the sham marriage that will precede the seduction. Further complicating Arlington's position as avenging hero is that he previously seduced and left a working-class girl. What could be a simple morality tale is turned into a mediation of the shifting identities and values in the antebellum city.

Once the reader enters into Monk Hall, the distortions hinted at in the opening chapters are magnified, turning the mansion into a labyrinth of secret passageways, trapdoors, and hidden rooms. Reading almost as a parody of the gothic haunted house, Monk Hall expands and contracts as the novel's characters plot and scheme against one another. The central figure in Monk Hall is the misshapen Devil-Bug, who acts as doorman and executioner. With one functioning eye, incredible physical strength, and nearly psychopathic glee in seeing his victims' blood, Devil-Bug is one of Lippard's most memorable characters. As with Byrnewood Arlington, Devil-Bug's psychological nuances lift him out of the purely monstrous. Born in a brothel and an outcast as long as he can remember, Devil-Bug revels in the destruction of those around him, gleefully participating in the robbery and murder of the aged Widow Smolby. But Devil-Bug also

plays the role of protector, saving the virginal Mabel from rape at the hands of the unctuous preacher F. A. T. Pyne. In proper Lippardian fashion, after saving Mabel, Devil-Bug learns that she is his long-lost daughter, and he spends the rest of the novel trying to maneuver Mabel into Philadelphia's upper class.

In addition to the Arlington-Lorrimer narrative thread, two other plots wind their way through the three days of action. One of these plots follows the cuckolded merchant Livingstone as he plans revenge against his unfaithful wife, Dora, and her swindler paramour, Colonel Fitz-Cowles. Both Livingstone and Fitz-Cowles are frequent visitors to Monk Hall, and it is in one of the Hall's many bedrooms that Livingstone finds his wife and the Colonel. A three-sided game of deception and murder develops: Livingstone plans to poison Dora; Dora plans to poison Livingstone and marry Fitz-Cowles, who has led Dora to believe that he is a member of royalty; and Fitz-Cowles wants to marry Dora to gain access to the money that will be left to her after her husband's death. A third plot involves Ravoni, a religious mystic who uses mesmerism and performs public "miracles" in order to gain followers for his new religion. Unfortunately for Ravoni, one of his potential new converts is Mabel, and Ravoni's mesmeric powers are not enough to keep Devil-Bug from killing him.

Enfolded in these three plots are multiple subplots, digressions, authorial intrusions, and set pieces. The reading experience replicates Monk Hall; a story will develop, and, right before its resolution, the reader will be dropped to some other place or time in Philadelphia. When these narrative trapdoors are mixed with the protean identities of the characters, the sense that nothing is as it seems permeates the novel. As Lorrimer states early on, "Every thing fleeting and nothing stable, every thing shifting and changing, and nothing substantial" (p. 23). Lippard's Monk Hall becomes a sensationalized microcosm for Philadelphia and the larger American republic, with the seduction of Mary Arlington as the seduction of all women and the crimes of one bank director acting as a stand-in for the organized robbery of capitalism.

The sensationalistic elements to *The Quaker City* were certainly part of its success. Growing out of the penny press and the French school of journalism popularized by Eugène Sue's *The Mysteries of Paris* (1842–1843), and tapping into the public's seemingly limitless desire for violence and sex, sensationalistic writers such as Lippard, George Thompson, and Ned Buntline often skirted the bounds of taste in their efforts to attract attention to their narratives. In *The Quaker City* readers are frequently presented with women in various states of undress, "snowy globes" ready to be exposed. The Reverend F. A. T. Pyne drugs his adopted daughter with opium-laced coffee as he prepares to seduce her; Devil-Bug interrupts the act and tortures Pyne first by threatening to burn his eyes out and then by tickling him. When Livingstone discovers his wife's unfaithfulness, he hallucinates the word *"kill!"* on the walls surrounding him. The novel's most sensationalistic section, bordering on the surreal, is the chapter "Devil-Bug's Dream." During his dream, Devil-Bug is transported to 1950 Philadelphia, where he watches the coronation of America's first king, armies of skeletons floating on coffins battling each other in the Schuylkill River, and the corpses of the poor rising from their graves on the eve of apocalyptic destruction of the city, while the words "Wo Unto Sodom" are emblazed across the sky.

What sets *The Quaker City* apart from other sensational city mysteries is Lippard's continual merging of the sensational with the economic, the sexual with the political. Lippard ties his most outré passages with class-influenced critiques about the power of the dollar in 1840s America. Dora Livingstone, seeking to limit her exposure for adultery, negotiates with Devil-Bug, offering to pay him handsomely for his protection. Devil-Bug, however, is after gold of another kind: sexual favors. The scene culminates with a leering Devil-Bug moving closer and closer to Dora, repeating the words "The goold, good lady, the *goold!*" (p. 358). Power—sexual, economic, political—is at the heart of *The Quaker City*, and part of the novel's continued relevance is its ability to explore how power works, condensing

these explorations into misshaped freaks, ravishing women, and duplicitous men.

After its publication in 1845, *The Quaker City* quickly became a Philadelphia phenomenon. Monk Hall cigars were sold on the streets, and readers tried to connect Lippard's satiric portrayals of politicians and newspaper editors with their real-life counterparts. Hoping to capitalize on the publicity, Lippard wrote a theatrical version of the novel, but when Singleton Mercer, disgruntled about his treatment in the novel, tried to buy two hundred tickets on opening night in hopes of starting trouble, Philadelphia's mayor stepped in and convinced Lippard and the theater to cancel the production. Lippard also claimed that he was forced to carry a sword cane with him as protection against attack. But Lippard was enthusiastically supported by working-class readers who saw the novel as depicting the day-to-day predations of the rich. Lippard became both an embodiment of and a spokesperson for the laboring classes, a class accent that he would continue to speak with throughout the rest of his city mystery novels.

Lippard returned to the city mystery several times over his career. *The Nazarene; or, The Last of the Washingtons*, started in 1846 as a sequel for *The Quaker City* and never completed, emphasized the native Protestant versus immigrant Catholic tension that occasionally turned violent during the 1840s and 1850s. The novel focuses on the machinations of Calvin Wolfe, another of Lippard's stock plutocratic villains, who is orchestrating the sectarian conflict for his own economic gain. Like *The Quaker City*, *The Nazarene* incorporates a secret society, the G.O.O.L.P.O. (Lippard never revealed what the acronym meant, probably due to the novel's unfinished state), and the seduction of working women by rich, older men. Here too is Lippard's characteristic sensationalism; for example, during the initiation ritual for the secret society, an initiate collides with a festering mummy and imagines himself being strangled by the corpse. Unfortunately, the publishing company that Lippard used to produce *The Nazarene* collapsed before the novel was finished, and the existing novel does not complete any of the narratives.

Lippard's more successful city mysteries are *The Empire City; or, New York by Night and Day* (1850) and its follow-up *New York: Its Upper Ten and Lower Million* (1853). Even though Lippard moves the setting to New York City in these two novels, he keeps his mixture of class militancy and sensational sex and violence. *The Empire City*'s plot revolves around two prosperous brothers, Gulian and Charles Van Huyden. After discovering that his wife has been unfaithful with his brother, Gulian apparently kills himself, but before his death he deposits an infant with one of his workmen. Twenty years later, in accordance with Gulian's will, his estate will be divided among the surviving Van Huyden descendants if no direct heir exists. The ensuing narrative incorporates escaped slaves, assumed and mistaken identities, the attempted seduction of a cross-dressing young woman by an older aristocrat, and various forms of working-class revenge. *New York* fills in the twenty-year gap in the first novel, providing backstory and developing the narrative. In *New York,* Lippard packs in almost every popular anxiety of the antebellum period: the Fugitive Slave Law, the Jesuit conspiracy to turn the West into a Catholic kingdom, mesmerism, the penny press, and the widening gap between rich and poor, to name a few, along with his usual descriptions of working-class misery and upper-class decadence. The novel ends with the mechanic hero, Arthur Dermoyne, leading a group west to found a workers' republic. Both *The Empire City* and *New York* are complex, and at times confusing, novels, but Lippard's frenetic energy and imagination lift them above the usual city mystery novels.

In addition to these traditional city mysteries, Lippard wrote several other short narratives that use the city as a backdrop. His *Memoirs of a Preacher, a Revelation of the Church and the Home* (serialized 1848, novel 1849) and its sequel, *The Man with the Mask* (1849) incorporate the Millerite controversy of 1844 along with the Benjamin Onderdonk scandal of the period. William Miller had forecast the year of the Apocalypse—1843 and then 1844 due to a counting error—and the resulting excitement and disappointment with his prophecy was quickly

spread through the popular press. Onderdonk was an Episcopalian minister who was charged with making sexual advances toward several female parishioners. Although Onderdonk was cleared of all charges, the resulting scandal helped make the figure of the salacious clergyman a popular trope. Lippard's novel ties these two anticlerical threads together in a narrative that also includes the Lippardian touches of personal magnetism, disguised identities, and class-conscious crime.

One other cultural event that spawned three Lippard short urban works was Philadelphia's Kensington riots of 1844. A battle between nativist Protestants and immigrant Catholics that lasted for three days, these riots exposed the rapidly developing fault lines that threatened to break the city. Given Lippard's nonsectarian religious beliefs and his working-class allegiance, these riots encapsulated what he saw as the forces of disunification brought about by unchecked industrial expansion. His three short works that investigate the riots—*The Killers: A Narrative of Real Life in Philadelphia* (1849), *The Life and Adventures of Charles Anderson Chester* (1850), and *The Bank Director's Son: A Real and Intensely Interesting Revelation of City Life* (1851)—are essentially the same narrative told in three different forms. *The Killers* first appeared in Lippard's *Quaker City Weekly* in 1849, focusing on the street gang of the same name and later released that same year as a novel. The latter two publications explore the same events and use many of the same characters, with *Charles Anderson Chester* providing more of the criminal backstory propelling the characters. All three novels of course sensationally unveil aristocratic crimes and contain scenes of violence, sexual threats, and urban decay.

Unsurprisingly, given his interest in popular movements and already circulating cultural anxieties, Lippard also approached American racial politics in a variety of ways in his city works, beginning with caricatures of African American figures in *The Quaker City* to more nuanced approaches in *New York: Its Upper Ten and Lower Million*. In addition to exploring the slavery question that threatened Lippard's beloved Union, he consistently supported Native Americans and their rights to land, as seen in *The Nazarene*. Even at his most stereotypical, Lippard seldom wanders into outright racism, imbuing his people of color with intelligence and depth that, while hardly nullifying the racial cast to the description, makes them more tolerable to modern readers.

In *The Quaker City,* the characters of Glow-worm and Musquito work with Devil-Bug to keep the peace, such as it is, in Monk Hall. Glow-worm and Musquito are both described in the racialized language of the period: large lips, bulging eyes, with imposing physical strength and speaking in a slave patois. But the characters are more than simple stereotypes, acting both as agents of Devil-Bug and on their own behalf. During Devil-Bug's suicide, Glow-worm and Musquito push the rock that kills him, acting out a metaphoric slave revolt. Another character, the Creole slave Endymion, is described as one of the handsomest creations on Earth. In addition to his beauty, Endymion also has a quick wit and biting tongue; during one chapter, he soliloquizes about turning the tables on his master, inverting the master-slave relation and forcing Fitz-Cowles to polish his boots.

A similar mixture of stereotypical description and more progressive elements characterize other Lippard works. In his three versions of the Philadelphia riots, a white woman is menaced by a large black man, and instead of permitting the implied violation, she leaps to her death. But in his *Empire City* and *New York* novels, Lippard uses Esther and Randolph, a mixed-race brother and sister, to interrogate the long shadow of miscegenation and the Fugitive Slave Law. Although both consistently pass as white, they are hunted by Harry, their half-brother, and haunted by the knowledge that neither is truly free. Adding intrigue to their background is Lippard's intimation that their grandfather was Thomas Jefferson, a mystery he keeps in place by using dashes in place of letters. But internal evidence in the novel, as well as the persistent antebellum rumors concerning Jefferson's relationship with Sally Hemings, later fictionalized in William Wells Brown's novel *Clotel* (1853), mark Jefferson as the likely candidate. Later in

Empire City, Lippard has the former slave Royal brutally whip Harry, as Royal recites phrases from the Bible.

In *Washington and His Generals,* one of Lippard's heroes of the Battle of Brandywine is the slave Sampson, who, along with his dog "Debbil," avenges the death of his master by slaying British soldiers with a scythe. Mixing the faithful servant with the vengeful spirit, Sampson embodies the contradictions at the center of Lippard's racial politics. Lippard's preoccupation with the freedom inherent in the Revolution collides with his desire to keep the Union intact. Frequently Lippard assails abolitionists, finding their emphasis on ending slavery in the South misguided; for Lippard, the white slavery of capitalism is an equal, if not worse, evil. Complicating matters further is that abolitionists threatened the Union with their political agenda; Lippard dedicated his *Blanche of Brandywine* (1846) to Henry Clay, whose compromises held the states together through much of the 1830s and 1840s. Like many antebellum Americans, Lippard felt that slavery would eventually collapse under its own contradictions. Also like many Americans, Lippard felt that the Fugitive Slave Law forced Northerners to be complicit in slavery, a theme developed in Lippard's final work, *Eleanor; or, Slave Catching in the Quaker City,* published after his death.

HISTORICAL FICTION

Although Lippard is best remembered, and rightly so, for his urban sensationalism, he was as well known in antebellum American for his historical fiction. These romances, or legends, as Lippard preferred to call them, were part of Lippard's new America mythology. Recalling many of the stories his aunts had told him about Revolutionary-era Pennsylvania and possessing an interest in his home state's role in the foundation of America, Lippard wrote multiple novels elaborating and, in some cases, fabricating a history for a new country.

Lippard's best-known collection of Revolutionary legends was *Washington and His Generals* (1847). A collection of stories that Lippard had published in various other periodicals, *Washington* is composed of five interconnected pieces: "The Battle of Germantown," "The Wissahikon," "Benedict Arnold," "The Battle of Brandywine," and "The Fourth of July, 1776." Mixing historical events and figures with those invented in Lippard's fertile imagination, *Washington and His Generals* is a mixture of hagiography of George Washington, a surprisingly evenhanded investigation into the complex figure of Benedict Arnold, horrific battle scenes complete with working-class heroes, and outright historical falsification. These falsifications achieved a life long after Lippard's career ended. One of the stories, found in the Wissahikon section, describes a meeting between Washington and General Howe, leader of the English forces. Howe presents Washington with a letter offering the American general a dukedom if he ends the rebellion. This story, and Washington's subsequent refusal, remained in historical circulation until well into the twentieth century.

The most important legend that turned into historical "fact" was Lippard's version of the signing of the Declaration of Independence and the ringing of the Liberty Bell. In the Lippard legend, which first appeared in the Philadelphia magazine *Saturday Courier* before being reprinted in *Washington and His Generals,* all fifty-six signers did so on July 4 at the urging of an "unknown patriot." Once the document was signed, an elderly bell ringer and a wealthy youngster joined to ring the Liberty Bell and celebrate the moment. Historically, none of Lippard's facts are correct: the Declaration itself was not publically read until July 8; no parts of it were signed until August 1776, with the last signatures coming in 1777; the Liberty Bell itself was unlikely to have been rung because of structural weaknesses in the steeple. However, Lippard's story became wildly popular, erasing the actual events and replacing them with a legend that better reflected what developing America thought about itself. The popularity of Lippard's version eventually became codified during the end of the nineteenth century and remained a staple of American history textbooks. This legend displays many of Lippard's fictional

preoccupations: rich and poor Americans joining in the face of a common enemy, the heroism of common artisans and mechanics, and the importance of unknown, forgotten, or shadowy figures.

Lippard followed up *Washington and His Generals* with a similarly designed collection, *Legends of Mexico* (1847). Again mixing historical fact with fictional license, Lippard follows the American army from the war's beginning to the final battles at Monterrey and Vera Cruz. General Zachary Taylor, like Washington, is portrayed as both a sophisticated military tactician and common soldier, fighting only when forced to and only to protect the Union. Also like *Generals, Legends of Mexico* is liberally sprinkled with mangled corpses, gory battlefields, and forbidden love between American soldiers and their enemies; the consistent strain of gothic elements in Lippard's city mysteries also operates in the Mexican novel. However, unlike *Washington and His Generals,* the source material for *Legends* was much less popular; discontent about the aims of the war and the potential expansion of slavery helped keep *Legends* from achieving the same status as the stories in *Washington and His Generals*. Lippard would expand one of the parts of *Legends* in another Mexican War–themed novel, *'Bel of Prairie Eden* (1848), which uses a marriage plot to explore questions of an American empire and the long-term cost of war.

Also in 1848 Lippard published *Paul Ardenheim, the Monk of Wissahikon,* a historical novel that Lippard, in his prologue, calls "the most improbable book in the world" (p. 10). Set in pre-Revolutionary Pennsylvania, *Ardenheim* mixes history, conspiracy, and romance as it follows the adventures of the titular character. The novel's improbability lies both in its form, as characters appear and disappear with little regard for narrative plausibility, and in its subject matter. Alchemy, mesmerism, secret societies, and alternate history coexist with such standard Lippardian touches as doomed relationships and Tory political intrigue. As in his previous historical novels, Lippard is less concerned with the historical accuracy of these events than in using events to explore various cultural anxieties. In the case of *Ardenheim,* the anxiety is secret societies.

Writing less than a generation after the alleged kidnapping and murder of the anti-Mason William Morgan by Freemasons, and during a decade in which Americans saw papal conspiracies in the form of Catholic immigration and the expansion of a slave empire in the Mexican-American War, Lippard invests *Ardenheim* with a wide range of secret groups and shadowy cabals.

Two secret groups vie for power in *Ardenheim:* the B.H.A.C., which recruits Gilbert Morgan, a local hunter and woodsman, and the Brotherhood of the Rosy Cross, better known as the Rosicrucians. The B.H.A.C. (much like his secret group in *The Nazarene,* Lippard never explains the acronym) makes its class inflection known early in the novel: the password into its secret meeting hall is "Death to the Rich—Life to the Poor" (p. 107). But as the novel progresses Morgan discovers that despite the B.H.A.C.'s outward allegiance to radical politics, it is largely a front for piracy and violence, using its class antagonism to mask personal enrichment. The B.H.A.C. is the counterpoint to Lippard's incorporation of the secretive Rosicrucians, whose ecumenical beliefs in human brotherhood resonated closely with Lippard's own. Paul Ardenheim finds himself in possession of papers allowing him access to Rosicrucian secrets and, as importantly for Lippard's sense of history, a list of previous Rosicrucian members. Unsurprisingly, given Lippard's interest in linking the American Revolution with mythological past, Lawrence Washington, George Washington's older half-brother, is on the list, as is Robenspierre [*sic*]. But indicative of Lippard's version of Rosicrucian inclusiveness, the list also includes a slave, a Native American, and a "Hindoo." Linking the sine qua non of secret societies with figures like Washington, Lippard places the Rosicrucians at the center of most modern history, influencing groups such as the Freemasons and the Illuminati, who, in turn, played parts in the American and French revolutions. In a move similar to the conspiracy against George Washington found in the "Rose of Wissahikon" section of *Washington and His Generals,* what is perceived as history is largely the interplay of these hidden groups.

GEORGE LIPPARD

BROTHERHOOD OF THE UNION

The Brotherhood of the Rosy Cross's three central ideologies—union, freedom, and brotherhood—explain the Rosicrucian influence on Enlightenment Revolutionary moments and its influence on Lippard's own version of Rosicrucianism, the Brotherhood of the Union. The Brotherhood of the Union would consume much of Lippard's time and energies from its beginning in the *Quaker City Weekly* in 1849 until Lippard's death in 1854. Essentially appropriating the previously mentioned Rosicrucian belief in universal brotherhood and adding to it an economic component, the Brotherhood would quickly grow into one of the most important and most militant early labor organizations. In his biography of Lippard, David Reynolds cites evidence that Lippard's Brotherhood directly influenced Uriah Stephens, founder of the Knights of Labor, a group that dominated the American labor movement in the 1870s and 1880s. Using the *Quaker City Weekly* and, after it folded, his novels, connections in the publishing world, and a wide-ranging lecture circuit, Lippard spread the Brotherhood's message of America as a redeemed Palestine of Labor.

Although Lippard had already been using secret societies in his earlier novels—most directly in *The Quaker City, The Nazarene,* and *Paul Ardenheim*—his Illuminati article in a May 1849 issue of the *Quaker City Weekly* is his first direct mention of the power of historical conspiracies. In a June 2 article Lippard wrote that the greatest movements in history were the work of secret societies. Growing from this proposition about the efficacy of hidden groups, Lippard's Brotherhood was introduced soon after. Over the next month Lippard would continue to incorporate the ideology and rituals of the Brotherhood into his *Weekly,* along with letters and testimonies from new members. By the year's end Lippard had written articles explaining the importance of Rosicrucian philosophy and was filling entire pages of his *Weekly* with material for organizing new circles of the Brotherhood, complete with titles for members and diagrams for rituals.

Based on Lippard's idiosyncratic reading of history and the influence of Rosicrucian philosophy, the Brotherhood's motto of Truth, Hope, and Love mixed with the militancy of class antagonism and mutual economic aid. In another of Lippard's articles laying out the agenda of the Brotherhood, he wrote that one of the Union's aims was to combine labor until it ripens into capital. Combination and association should be the ends of movement; only by combining assets and associating with other members of the laboring classes could Lippard's "Palestine of Labor" be formed. This mixture of moral appeal and economic unity made the Brotherhood similar to the various reform movements of the period such as Fourierism and the Brook Farm experiment famously participated in by Lippard's better-known contemporary Nathaniel Hawthorne. But what separated the Brotherhood from these movements were its elaborate ceremonies and occasional appeals to violent class struggle.

In both the *Quaker City Weekly* and then later in the one issue of the *White Banner,* a magazine designed to be a Brotherhood periodical, Lippard outlined his incredibly intricate rituals for the organization. In addition to the Rosicrucian philosophy that underlay much of the Brotherhood's ideology, Lippard appropriated many of his titles and rituals from groups such as the Freemasons and the Odd Fellows, both of which Lippard saw as offshoots of the Rosy Cross. The central symbol of the Brotherhood was a simple circle, emblematic of labor growing into capital and the shared community of all laborers. The titles of various members in the hierarchy display Lippard's deep investment in American history: Chief Washington, Jefferson, Franklin, Wayne, and Fulton. Much like Lippard's legends in *Washington and His Generals,* these titles reflected Lippard's belief that the health and strength of the republic was displayed in the common laborer and mechanic in addition to the politically important. Lippard also detailed the Brotherhood's rituals and temple layout. He included everything from the paraphernalia used in initiation ceremonies—a copy of the Declaration, a New Testament, a goblet, an axe, a folded parchment, and a skull—to the code words used

to greet fellow members. Although there is no small amount of irony in using an easily purchased periodical to promote a secret society, the labor and energy that Lippard invested in the project affirm his seriousness.

Lippard's allegiance to the secret order he invented can also be seen in his exhausting lecture circuit promoting the Brotherhood. Given his growing distaste for cities, he traveled widely across the mid-Atlantic region and into newly developing areas in Ohio. He also went into Virginia, where his Union sympathies collided with the secessionist movement. According to a contemporary biographer, John Bell Bouton, when rumors began to circulate at a post-lecture dinner that he was an abolitionist, Lippard responded with the toast, "Here's to the revolving pistol. The best antidote to a Northern scoundrel who meddles with the opinions of a Southern gentleman upon slavery while traveling in the North; and an equally good course of treatment for a Southern blackguard who interferes with the sentiments of a Northerner while the guest of the South" (p. 95). Lippard's dedication to the Brotherhood and rights of laboring people resonated long after his death. In 1922, on the one hundredth anniversary of his birth, members of the Brotherhood held a mass ceremony at his grave, culminating with a speech praising Lippard for his work defending the poor.

RELIGIOUS AND MYSTIC WRITINGS

Underpinning much of Lippard's writing and labor activism was his religious belief, which incorporated parts of mainstream Methodism, contemporary transcendentalism, and mysticism. As seen in his early life, Lippard's Methodism took on radical forms even as a teenager. Contemporary accounts mention that Lippard would preach to the animals and trees during his walks in rural Pennsylvania. Lippard dropped out of the training to be a Methodist minister after an incident in which the school's ostensibly Christian headmaster refused to share some fruit with the students. Lippard's heterodox beliefs in religious and social equality continued throughout his career, at times in the background of his works and at other times controlling his narratives.

Invectives against "priestcraft" are scattered throughout the majority of Lippard's novels. Losing sight of Christ's message of benevolence and shared humanity, institutionalized religion emphasizes order at the cost of mercy, rote descriptions of the divine, and gospels that reward venality. Seeing these men as tools of the status quo, Lippard frequently contrasts the rigidity and formality of religious institutions with the simple piety of Quakers and other less hierarchical denominations. In his short story "Jesus and the Poor," Lippard has Jesus appear in a Philadelphia church, only to be ignored because of his shabby clothes; Satan's appearance is better received because of his fine clothing and white cravat.

In works such as *Memoirs of a Preacher* and *The Man with the Mask,* Lippard exposes what he sees as the fundamental hypocrisy operating in organized religion, where religious figures use their positions to enrich themselves or to seduce female parishioners. Given the cultural power that religious figures had in antebellum America, Lippard's depictions of these lascivious pastors explore and exploit the popular anxiety Americans had about these men. Their ability to meet with women in the privacy of the home or in the sanctified space of the church allowed clergymen seduction opportunities that few other males of the period had. As seen in the previously discussed Reverend Onderdonk scandal, the popular press and sensationalist fiction took these improprieties, magnified their scale, and circulated them among a variety of readers. Lippard saw the spiritual betrayal of women as worse than the actual physical assault: Lippard's texts are filled with women being "polluted" by their relationships with these men, their purity and innocence forever corrupted. Once corrupted, these women are usually presented two choices—prostitution or suicide—while the men, by virtue of being respectable males, suffer no immediate consequences.

However, these men will be judged for their corruption of innocence. The concept of an "unpardonable sin" appears in several Lippard texts, and its shifting definition mirrors Lippard's religious preoccupations. In *The Quaker City,* an entire chapter is spent describing the mythology

of this sin. When an innocent is seduced, a specific angel rings a bell, indicating that one of these sins has occurred. Once the bell is rung, the seducer will never find peace either on earth or in the afterlife. The later shorter piece "The Life of a Man of the World" (1853) employs this same sin. In the ritual for the Brotherhood of the Union, the unpardonable sin is no longer the act of seduction but the act of betrayal when a worker deprives another worker of the rights and rewards of his labor. This combination of exploitation in the economic and sexual register that underwrites much of *The Quaker City*'s plot also underwrites Lippard's belief in the worst possible sin.

But Lippard's religious vision is more than the standard portrayal of lecherous priests, seduced parishioners, or sanctimonious businessmen that became de rigueur as the city mystery genre developed. His 1851 mystical novel *Adonai: The Pilgrim of Eternity* (titled *The Entranced* when it first appeared serially in 1849) focuses on the time-traveling adventures of Lucius, a friend of Nero who is reformed by the suffering of the Christian martyrs he is overseeing. Lucius falls into a trance and awakens as the titular Adonai in the year 1525, when he meets Martin Luther and encounters the Executioner, a devilish figure accompanying Adonai during his trip through history. Briefly stopping in 1822 to discuss politics with the utopian philosopher Charles Fourier, Adonai and the Executioner then transport themselves to 1848, the year of European revolution, and see Louis Napoleon, Eugène Sue, and the socialist Louis Blanc, among others. After crossing the Atlantic to see the results of the American Revolution, Adonai meets the spirit of George Washington, who can inhabit the bodies of the poor or those enslaved. With the arisen Washington in tow, Adonai and the Executioner visit Philadelphia to see what has happened to the American republic.

As in *Paul Ardenheim*, Rosicrucian philosophy and religious history are interwoven into *Adonai*, which uses figures such as Martin Luther and Fourier as touchstones to explore how tolerance and goodwill are perverted by institutional religion. For Lippard, the revolutionary aspects of Christianity have given way to a church colluding with the upper class in an effort to economically and spiritually control workers; while on the tour of America, the Executioner makes this relationship explicit, describing labor as a sacrifice at the temple of capital. Later in the novel the arisen Washington and Adonai watch as poor laborers march to the sepulchre of Christ, only to be slain by the priesthood before entering. *Adonai* ends much more ambiguously than *Ardenheim* or even *The Quaker City,* with the Executioner's final pessimistic lines drowning out the final images of a dark globe and a white cross.

Lippard's mystical element was not limited to his writing. The same year he completed *Adonai* (1851), he visited the Fox sisters in Rochester, New York, already becoming famous for their spirit rappings and other communications with the world beyond. According to Lippard's biographer John Bell Bouton, in addition to his general curiosity about other worlds, he was motivated by an interest in contacting his recently dead wife. Lippard claimed that he received "three blows from an unseen hand"; seeing this as evidence of his wife's ghostly presence, Lippard proceeded to give lectures about his own form of spiritualism throughout 1852 (p. 72). He claimed that his wife's spirit frequently visited him and, according to Bouton, during one interview Lippard abruptly pointed over Bouton's shoulder, saying, "There is a figure in a shroud there! It is always behind me" (p. 84). In a moment of fiction and biography intersecting, Devil-Bug, Lippard's antihero in *The Quaker City,* is also consistently haunted by a lurking spectral figure. In another quirky twist, in 1870, Olive G. Pettis, a medium and author, published *The Historical Life of Jesus,* allegedly dictated to her by Lippard's spirit. In a 1894 follow-up, *Autobiography by Jesus of Nazareth,* Lippard's spirit provides both part of the introduction and a conclusion, assuring readers that he is still in their midst.

In addition to the spiritualist element displayed in works like *Adonai* and *Paul Ardenheim,* Lippard also explored another popular pseudo-science of the antebellum period,

mesmerism. As mentioned previously, the religious mystic Ravoni uses mesmerism in *The Quaker City* to control Devil-Bug and Ravoni's other adepts. Mesmerism's more scientific version, magnetism, is discussed in *The Memoirs of a Preacher* and *Adonai*. In *Memoirs*, Lippard writes, "It may be that Magnetism is the great tie which binds the great family of Humanity to its God" (p. 84). Magnetic trances allow for time travel (as in *Adonai*), clairvoyance, and the imposition of one will on another. Growing out of the rapidly developing scientific discourse on the importance of electricity (Luigi Galvani's research on electrical impulses was published in 1791), Lippard's interest in magnetism's powers takes on, in addition to seeing through walls and entrancing maidens, particularly gruesome traits: in *Adonai*, an early version of a battery is applied to a corpse in hopes of reanimating it. As we have seen with much of Lippard's work, his incorporation of already existing popular anxieties into his narratives and exploitation of these anxieties in sensational ways act as the pivot around which his class-inflected narratives turn. His city gothics, with their mesmeric enchanters and loathsome slave catchers, and his historical novels, with their cabals and alchemists, mine the raw material of popular fears and desires and cast them into strangely compelling narratives.

CONCLUSION

Although Lippard is justifiably remembered for the sensationalistic *Quaker City*, the arc of his work illuminates a wide variety of antebellum American concerns and anxieties. Increased urbanization and the dislocation of identity and spatial relations are explored in his many city narratives, as is the class antagonism that industrialization brought to the republic. By yoking these losses and antagonisms to his own form of the American gothic, Lippard, like his sorcerer figure Ravoni, reanimates gothic tropes, setting them loose on the American cityscape. In his histories Lippard melds what might have happened with what should have happened, using these stories and legends to construct a history for a new nation. Fearing that the same forces of

capital that were dominating the antebellum political arena would in turn dominate the historical narrative, Lippard vigorously contested this appropriation by lionizing Washington and valorizing mechanics as heroes. The longevity of his Liberty Bell story attests to the power that Lippard's common-person history has had on the narratives Americans tell themselves. The class inflection operating in the city novels, *The Nazarene,* and *Paul Ardenheim* eventually led to Lippard's secretive Brotherhood of the Union and his conspiratorial outlook on historical development and the growth of the monied class. His individualistic take on organized religion, mysticism, and the Jesus figure as friend to, and avenger of, working people informs portions of *The Entranced,* city pieces such as *Memoirs of a Preacher,* and a variety of articles in *Quaker City Weekly.*

It is not surprising that there has been a resurgence in Lippard scholarship. His vision of antebellum America is both joyful and dark, distinctly different from traditional canonical writers from the period but also hauntingly familiar. Sharing Melville's skepticism of fixed identity without Melville's self-doubt, Hawthorne's sense of history without Hawthorne's historical guilt, and Emerson's individuality without Emerson's cultural snobbery, Lippard's sensational narratives tell us of a more contested America. Lippard's America, where poverty hides behind every misfortune and where all things are for sale, may not be as stylistically perfect as Hawthorne's, but it is all the more compelling because of its grotesque reality.

Selected Bibliography

WORKS OF GEORGE LIPPARD

CITY NOVELS
The Quaker City; or, The Monks of Monk Hall. A Romance of Philadelphia Life, Mystery, and Crime. 1845. Edited by David Reynolds. Amherst: University of Massachusetts Press, 1995.

The Nazarene; or, The Last of the Washingtons. A Revelation of Philadelphia, New York, and Washington in the Year 1844. Philadelphia: G. Lippard, 1846.

The Memoirs of a Preacher, a Revelation of the Church and the Home. Philadelphia: Joseph Severns, 1849. Published serially in *Quaker City Weekly* starting in late 1848 and into 1849.

The Man with the Mask: A Sequel to The Memoirs of a Preacher, a Revelation of the Church and the Home. Philadelphia: Joseph Severns [assumed publication date 1849]. Published serially in *Quaker City Weekly*, 1849.

The Empire City; or, New York by Night and Day. New York: Stringer and Townsend, 1850. Published serially in *Quaker City Weekly*, 1850.

The Killers: A Narrative of Real Life in Philadelphia. Philadelphia: Hankison and Bartholomew, 1850. First printed in *Quaker City Weekly*, 1849. Revised and reissued as *The Bank Director's Son: A Real and Intensely Interesting Revelation of City Life*. Philadelphia: E. E. Barclay, 1851.

The Life and Adventures of Charles Anderson Chester, the Notorious Leader of the Philadelphia "Killers." Philadelphia: [n.p.] 1850.

"The Life of a Man of the World." Published as a shorter piece in *The Midnight Queen; or, Leaves from New-York Life*. New York: Garrett, 1853.

The Midnight Queen; or, Leaves from New-York Life. New York: Garrett, 1853.

New York: Its Upper Ten and Lower Million. Cincinnati, Ohio: E. Rulison, 1853.

Eleanor; or, Slave Catching in the Quaker City. Philadelphia Sunday Mercury. Began serialization February 12, 1854.

HISTORICAL NOVELS

Herbert Tracy; or, The Legend of the Black Rangers. A Romance of the Battle-field of Germantown. Philadelphia: R. G. Bedford, 1844. First published as a serial in *United States Saturday Post*, 1842.

The Battle-Day of Germantown. Philadelphia: A. H. Dillard, 1843. Originally published in *Citizen Soldier*, 1843.

The Ladye Annabel; or, The Doom of the Poisoner. A Romance by an Unknown Author. Philadelphia: R. G. Berford, 1844. Published serially in *Citizen Soldier*, 1843–1844.

Blanche of Brandywine; or, September the Eleventh, 1777. A Romance, Combining the Poetry, Legend, and History of the Battle of Brandywine. Philadelphia: G. B. Zieber, 1846.

Legends of Mexico. Philadelphia: T. B. Peterson, 1847.

The Rose of Wissahikon; or, The Fourth of July, 1776. A Romance, Embracing the Secret History of the Declaration of Independence. Philadelphia, G. B. Zieber, 1847. Published serially in *Semi-Annual Pictorial Saturday Courier* (Philadelphia), 1847.

Washington and His Generals; or, Legends of the Revolution. Philadelphia: G. B. Zieber, 1847.

'Bel of Prairie Eden. A Romance of Mexico. Philadelphia: T. B. Peterson, 1848. Published serially in *Uncle Sam*, 1848.

LABOR AND MYSTICAL NOVELS

Paul Ardenheim, the Monk of Wissahikon. Philadelphia: T. B. Peterson, 1848.

The Entranced; or, The Wanderer of Eighteen Centuries. Philadelphia: Joseph Severns [assumed publication date 1849]. Published serially in Lippard's *Quaker City*, 1849. Revised and reprinted as *Adonai: The Pilgrim of Eternity* in Lippard's *White Banner*, 1851.

NEWSPAPERS, PERIODICALS, AND OTHER PUBLICATIONS

Quaker City Weekly. Philadelphia: Joseph Severns, 1848–1850.

The B.G.C. (No official title; probably issued in parts late in 1850 or early 1851. The only existing, and assumed partial, copy of Lippard's rituals for the Brotherhood is held at the American Antiquarian Society, Worcester, Massachusetts.)

The White Banner. Vol. 1. Philadelphia: George Lippard, 1851.

PAPERS

The majority of Lippard's papers are held at the Library Company of Philadelphia. The American Antiquarian Society in Worcester, Massachusetts, also holds facsimiles of many of Lippard's most important papers.

CRITICAL AND BIOGRAPHICAL STUDIES

Ashwill, Gary. "The Mysteries of Capitalism in George Lippard's City Novels." *ESQ: A Journal of the American Renaissance* 40, no. 4:293–317 (1994).

Bouton, John Bell. *The Life and Choice Writings of George Lippard*. New York: H. H. Randall, 1855.

Faflik, David. "Authorship, Ownership, and the Case for Charles Anderson Chester." *Book History* 11:149–167 (2008).

Helwig, Timothy. "Denying the Wages of Whiteness: The Racial Politics of George Lippard's Working-Class Protest." *American Studies* 47, nos. 3–4:87–111 (fall-winter 2006).

Kelly Gray, Elizabeth. "The World by Gaslight: Urban-Gothic Literature and Moral Reform in New York City, 1845–1860." *American Nineteenth Century History* 10, no. 2:137–161 (2009).

Ostrowski, Carl. "Slavery, Labor Reform, and Intertextuality in Antebellum Print Culture: The Slave Narrative and the

City-Mysteries Novel." *African American Review* 40, no. 3:493–506 (fall 2006).

———. "Inside the Temple of Ravoni: George Lippard's Anti-Exposé." *ESQ: A Journal of the American Renaissance* 55, no. 1:1–26 (2009).

Reynolds, David. *George Lippard.* Boston: Twayne, 1982.

———. *George Lippard, Prophet of Protest: Writings of an American Radical, 1822–1854.* New York: P. Lang, 1986.

———. *Beneath the American Renaissance: The Subversive Imagination in the Era of Emerson and Melville.* Cambridge, Mass.: Harvard University Press, 1989.

Ridgely, J. V. "George Lippard's *The Quaker City:* The World of the American Porno-Gothic." *Studies in the Literary Imagination* 7, no. 1: 77–94 (1974).

Streeby, Shelley. "Haunted Houses: George Lippard, Nathaniel Hawthorne, and Middle-Class America." *Criticism* 38, no. 3:443–473 (1996).

———. "Opening Up the Story Paper: George Lippard and the Construction of Class." *Boundary 2* 24, no. 1:177–203 (1997).

———. "American Sensations: Empire, Amnesia, and the Mexican-American War." *American Literary History* 13, no. 1:1–40 (2000).

———. *American Sensations: Class, Empire, and the Production of Popular Culture.* Berkeley: University of California Press, 2002.

Unger, Mary. "'Dens of Iniquity and Holes of Wickedness': George Lippard and the Queer City." *Journal of American Studies* 43, no. 2:319–339 (2009).

CHERRÍE MORAGA

(1952—)

L. Bailey McDaniel

KNOWN MOST NOTABLY as a playwright and essayist, Cherríe L. Moraga is also an accomplished poet, editor, director, and activist. Her contributions to Chicana/o studies, contemporary drama, and queer studies are prolific, and, along with a handful of other writers and intellectuals since the early 1980s, Moraga has been instrumental in establishing Latina/o Studies as a scholarly discipline and area of study in classrooms and research institutions as well as performance venues. Among some of Moraga's more cited works, her 1981 anthology *This Bridge Called My Back: Writings by Radical Women of Color,* coedited with Gloria Anzaldúa, is a landmark text in queer theory, ethnic studies, and feminist criticism. One of the founding voices in what is often referred to as "third-world feminism," Moraga has produced a significant body of dramatic work, poetry, and essays. The form of her published dramatic work ranges from realist and linear narrative to more experimental and expressionistic offerings. The content of all of Moraga's writing, fiction and nonfiction alike, consistently explores the intersections of lesbian subjectivity, mestiza culture, political and spiritual recuperations within the ideologies of Catholicism, and a politics of the body.

BIOGRAPHY

Cherríe L. Moraga was born Cherríe Lawrence in Whittier, California, on September 25, 1952. Moraga's ethnic background is diverse, as her father, Joseph Lawrence, was white, and her mother, Elvira Moraga, was a California-born Chicana. Moraga often publicly credits a childhood spent in her family kitchen, listening in particular to the stories told by her mother, for her profound appreciation for language. She also explains these early memories of her mother's kitchen as the source of her appreciation for the power of storytelling as a means of articulating one's self as well as remaining connected to a heritage that itself can exist as a source of pride and empowerment.

Moraga attended Immaculate Heart College in Los Angeles, where she earned a bachelor of arts degree in 1974. For the three years following her graduation from Immaculate Heart, she worked as a high school teacher and also took courses in writing. In 1977 Moraga began a graduate program in English and went on to earn a master of arts degree in 1980 from San Francisco State University, where, less than a decade before her arrival, the longest campus strike in history, organized by a coalition of ethnically marginalized groups, led to the establishment of the first programs in ethnic area studies. This trajectory in Moraga's postsecondary education, from private Catholic institution to the more politically left and active atmosphere of San Francisco State, is noteworthy in terms of Moraga's own evolving political consciousness, as each stage in her professional training and publication history marks another step toward a more politically overt, at times separatist, canon and ideology.

Cherríe Moraga grew up identifying ethnically and culturally with her Chicana mother's side of the family. Most of Moraga's childhood was spent in San Gabriel, California. As a self-described *guera* (a light or fair-skinned person), Moraga's early experiences as a woman with the features of her mother, which marked her ethnically as Chicana, but also the light skin of her Anglo father, deeply informed her personal and professional beginnings and the continued focus on border culture issues that frequently find focus

in her drama and essays. Indeed, Moraga's family history has informed her work and politics as much as her sexual identity, and the crucial role occupied by (and the near heroic, looming presence of) her mother can be seen in all of her work.

Moraga's mother endured significant economic and racially informed hardships, and for a large part of her life she was the primary source of income for her family. Without any English education, and with a limited fluency in English at all, Moraga's mother was considered illiterate, and further, she encouraged an "English only" atmosphere for Cherríe and her siblings throughout their childhood. This early encouragement to culturally model herself upon or assimilate toward whiteness would have a profound influence on the playwright's later work, particularly in the ways that this early, unintentionally implied "shame" toward ethnic identity—an unspoken message that typically accompanies assimilation—would fuel her works' more explicit pride and celebration of Chicana/o identity and culture. In other words, any perceived or actual white privilege Moraga may have benefited from, through an unintentional ability to "pass" by virtue of her light skin, might now be the source of a powerful motivation to celebrate and focus attention on a Chicano aesthetic—an aesthetic which, in its politically anti-assimilationist tones, reads to some as angrily separatist.

In 1983 Moraga left the West Coast and moved to New York City to pursue writing as a profession. It was there that she began studying with the Cuban American playwright Maria Irene Fornés, who would become a major artistic and personal influence as well as a contributor to Moraga's work in her role as director. In particular, the nods to expressionism and experimental deviations from dramatic realism that define much of Fornés' work would eventually influence many of Moraga's plays.

As a playwright as well as an activist, Moraga remains passionately committed to teaching and to providing political support to other writers, particularly women of color. She has taught classes in drama and writing at numerous institutions, including Stanford University, where she has served for over ten years as artist-in-residence in the Drama Department. At Stanford, Moraga is also an affiliated faculty member of the Center for Comparative Studies in Race and Ethnicity and a core faculty member of the Institute for Diversity in the Arts.

Further underscoring her personal and professional agenda of increased collectivity among women, women of color, and queer women, Moraga frequently works with other writers in her artistic endeavors as well as her academic projects. For example, the text that initially brought Moraga recognition from a wider audience was the anthology *This Bridge Called My Back,* a collection of essays she edited with fellow Chicana activist, writer, and figurehead of third-wave feminism Gloria Anzaldúa. Along with the writers Barbara Smith and Audre Lorde, in 1980 Moraga founded Kitchen Table: Women of Color Press, a publisher explicitly dedicated to publishing the work of American women of color and run exclusively by women of color. In 1988, along with the writers Ana Castillo and Norma Alarcón, Moraga revised the now significantly influential *Bridge Called My Back* into a Spanish-language adaptation, *Esta puente, mi espalda: Voces de mujeres tercermundistas en los Estados Unidos.* One of the key texts that served as the wellspring for what would eventually be termed third-wave feminism, *Bridge* gathers voices from prominent feminists of color who, in their various contributions of essay, poetry, and memoir, call for a greater presence within feminism for race-related discourse and attention to the ways in which ethnicity, class, and sexual orientation, as well as gender, contribute to the politics of identity and social hierarchies. Moraga's first published book as an author, *Loving in the War Years: Lo que nunca pasó por sus labios* (1983), is also considered an important text in Chicano and queer studies and offers a powerful combination of memoir, poetry, and essay as it details Moraga's experiences as a lesbian, a young Catholic, and a Chicana.

Although she had begun to write earlier in her life, Moraga's serious work as a writer did not begin until she had graduated from Immaculate Heart and came out publicly as a

lesbian; after this period, her writing took on the feminist and political tones for which she would eventually be known, and her work became more than a means of expression; it became a way of life. Along with the larger experience of coming out she developed a newfound and deep connection with her mother. Moraga credits the discovery of Judy Grahn's poem "A Woman Is Talking to Death" as a major force that coalesced in her the need to write not only as a lesbian but as a Chicana. These shifts in the way she understood her personal identity as well as her politics coalesced for Moraga in powerful ways in the mid-to-late 1970s, and her own growing acceptance of her sexuality informed an acceptance and celebration of Chicana identity as well as more expansive notions of family and (political) collectivity. In her 1997 memoir written on queer motherhood, *Waiting in the Wings,* she explains that in 1975,

at the age of twenty-two, I came out as a lesbian and named as female the subject of [my] earlier adolescent sexual dream life. Once out, although I did not keep my sexuality secret from the closest members of my family, I knew it could never be fully expressed there. So the search for a *we* that could embrace all the parts of myself took me far beyond the confines of heterosexual family ties. I soon found myself spinning outside the orbit of that familial embrace, separated by thousands of miles of geography and experience. Still, the need for familia, the knowledge of familia, the capacity to create familia remained and has always informed my relationships and my work as an artist, cultural activist, and teacher.

(pp. 17–18)

In this way, Moraga's ethnic identity, sexuality, and even class identification continue to be the dominant influences that inform her dramatic work, her pedagogy, and her broader worldview. Her work's investment in the politics of gender, sexuality, race, and class retain a tight focus on the ways that the personal and public parts of human life overlap and—in essence—how emancipatory strategies that hope to assist those marginalized by dominant culture need to start by reimagining the most basic concepts, such as family. She writes,

I've always experienced my lesbianism as radically different from most white gays and lesbians. For

that reason, I have never been a strong proponent of lesbian marriages (although I've officiated at a few), nor particularly passionate about the domestic partnership campaigns for which my white middle-class gay counterparts continue to rigorously fight. No, I've always longed for something else in my relationships—something woman-centered, something cross-generational, something extended, something sensual, something humilde ante la creadora. In short, something Mexican and familial but without all the cultural constraints.

(*Wings,* p. 18)

Moraga engages, often explicitly, this critique of (white, middle-class) filial ideologies in her plays, many of which either comment on or redefine notions of family. Occasionally, as in the case of *Heroes and Saints* or *Shadow of a Man* (both 1994), for example, this criticism assumes a focus on a feminized and/or queer notion of family that places women (daughters, mothers, sisters, queer siblings) as the foundation of family support and survival or, alternatively (as in *Circle in the Dirt* and *Watsonville* [published in one volume in 2002]), constructing notions of family (and solidarity) that are not reliant on consanguinity. In both cases, Moraga's understanding of *familia* stands in powerful contrast to the patriarchal and/or homophobic models of filiation embedded in Chicano/Catholic culture. Indeed, much of Moraga's work (in all its forms) dedicates itself to exposing what she classifies as the four forces that combine to oppress women: sexism, racism, classism, and homophobia. Further, a sought after political liberation which is invested in and afforded by a reconceptualization of family, sexuality, and spirituality is something to which Moraga returns regularly in her essays and plays. In *Loving in the War Years,* for example, she argues that the sociopolitical control of women begins through heterosexuality itself, and consequently, her queer identity—particularly as a Chicana—contests the "foundation of *la familia,*" the latter itself one of the more powerful sources of women's oppression. Underscoring the interdependence and conflations of oppression shared among Chicano culture, misogyny, and Catholic ideology, Moraga writes:

Living under Capitalist Patriarchy, what is true for "the man" in terms of misogyny is, to a great extent,

true for the Chicano. He too, like any other man, wants to be able to determine how, when, and with whom his women—mother, wife, daughter—are sexual. For without male imposed social and legal control of our reproductive function, reinforced by the Catholic Church, and the social institutionalization of our roles as sexual and domestic servants to men, Chicanas might very freely "choose" to do otherwise, including being sexually independent *from* and/or *with* men. ... The control of women begins through the institution of heterosexuality.

(*Loving,* pp. 110–111)

While Cherríe Moraga's nonfiction, like her activism and teaching, continues to find an audience interested in her exploration of how the personal and political inform each other, often using her own life experiences as subject matter, Moraga's dramatic work also continues to be staged and receive scholarly attention with consistency. From 1991 to 1997, she was the playwright in residence at Brava Theater Center of San Francisco, a frequent venue for Moraga's works. In 1995 Brava produced *Heart of the Earth,* a play that presents Moraga's adaptation of the Mayan Popol Vuh creation myth and was also performed at New York's Public Theater and INTAR Theatre. While serving as Brava's playwright in residence, she also developed the plays *Watsonville: Some Place Not Here,* which premiered in 1996, and *The Hungry Woman: A Mexican Medea,* which eventually received a Bay Area premiere in a co-production with El Téatro Campesino and Stanford University in April 2005.

Cherríe Moraga continues to write and stage her plays across the United States. She is presently completing a memoir on the subject of cultural memory in an amnesiac California, as well as a new collection of essays. She lives in Oakland, California, with her partner, Celia, and her son, Rafael.

CAREER OVERVIEW

Moraga's plays, poetry, and essays have been deeply influenced and informed by her personal and political evolvement. As a scholar, playwright, and poet, Moraga resists easy categorization within different disciplines of area studies (e. g., Chicano studies, queer literature, class-based

studies) because her works explore personal and political ostracism generated by myriad social forces. In her book-length analysis of Moraga's oeuvre, Yvonne Yarbro-Bejarano succinctly describes the playwright's rhetorical and political agenda this way: "Cherríe Moraga's work spans a range of genres and speaks from multiple sites of struggle" (p. xiv). Employing a hybrid of literary forms and reflecting a rich canvas of voices, the artist productively, poetically, and with an unwavering political consciousness "evoke[s] the contradictory ways in which race, class, gender, and sexuality shape identity" (p. xv). This multivalenced and nuanced sensitivity to the different—if often complementary—struggles experienced by those oppressed by dominant culture, regardless of which component of identity facilitates marginalization, is a hallmark of Moraga's work, whether drama or nonfiction.

Much of Moraga's drama and nonfiction unpacks and celebrates a native subjectivity that prioritizes Amerindian ethnicity over Eurocentric identity (including those constructions of the Eurocentric which nod to Moraga's own Anglo background vis-à-vis her white father). What some understand as a militancy or separatism that potentially informs many of her plays, or that is articulated explicitly in her essays, is as much about a celebration and needed refocus on indigenous identity as it is a direct critique of Western and colonially inspired narratives of nation and origination (and the ways the latter are offered at the expense of the former.)

Moraga's politics and her work's dedication to furthering them have not cost her professionally. Her awards are many. Some of the more noteworthy acknowledgments she has earned include the American Book Award/Before Columbus Foundation for *This Bridge Called My Back* in 1986 and both the Will Glickman Playwriting Award and the Drama-Logue Award for Playwriting in 1992. That same year she was also awarded the Bay Area Theatre Critics Circle Award for Best Original Script for her play *Heroes and Saints.* In 1993 Moraga received a National Endowment for the Arts Theater Playwrights' Fellowship, the same year she received the PEN West Literary Award for

Drama. Moraga earned the Kennedy Center for the Performing Arts Fund for New American Plays Award in 1996 and the David R. Kessler Award in honor of her contributions to the field of queer studies in 2000. She was named a USA Fellow by the advocacy group United States Artists in 2007, the same year she was awarded a USA Rockefeller Fellowship.

In 2011 Duke University Press published a collection of Moraga's writings, including essays, poetry, and cultural critique, titled *A Xicana Codex of Changing Consciousness: Writings, 2000–2010,* and her play *Digging Up the Dirt* is scheduled for publication by West End Press in 2012. In January 2012 San Francisco's Brava Theater and Cihuatl productions staged her play *New Fire: To Put Things Right Again,* which, according to its producers, "follows the sacred geography of Indigenous American ancestors to tell a post-modern story of rupture and homecoming." Moraga served as codirector with the play's leading actor, Adelina Anthony.

MAJOR PLAYS

Among Cherríe Moraga's staged and published plays, *Giving Up the Ghost* (premiered 1989), *Shadow of a Man* (premiered 1990), and *Heroes and Saints* (premiered 1992) are best known to audiences and critics and can be found in collections and anthologies that explore ethnic American theater, feminism, and queer studies. As her first professionally staged play, *Giving Up the Ghost* made a strong impression on spectators and scholars for its blend of emotional realism alongside more expressionistic theatrical devices. The play also marks the first of Moraga's many explorations of women's sexuality, motherhood, psychological trauma, and queer identity. Moreover, as these early plays dramatically investigate how these concepts and ideological forces complicate and feed into one another, they focus strongly on the family as a primary site of identity formation and sociopolitical subjectivity. While her later plays perhaps more explicitly pull at the threads of the real-world cultural and political marginalization of queer and ethnic peoples, Moraga's earlier plays set the stage for a

career-long exploration of how (fictional) characters on the margins mirror and challenge the struggles and victories of the real people they are meant to stand for offstage.

GIVING UP THE GHOST

Giving Up the Ghost premiered at the Theater Rhinoceros in San Francisco on February 10, 1989, under the direction of Anita Mattos and José Guadalupe Saucedo, although it had earlier professional exposure, in a slightly different version, at Seattle's Front Room Theater in March 1987 with Laura Esparza as director. In March 1998 another production, utilizing the official published version of the play, was presented by San Diego's Diversionary Theater. This play, Moraga's first, also enjoys interdisciplinary scholarly attention and, as one of three plays included in her anthology *Heroes and Saints and Other Plays* (West End Press, 1994), can be found on university syllabi in disciplines such as theater studies, gender and area studies, literature, and queer theory.

Giving Up the Ghost focuses on three characters: the older, Mexican-born Amalia and two female Chicana figures, Marisa and Corky. The latter two characters are actually the same person but at different stages of life, with Corky representing the teenage version of the character and Marisa portraying the same person in her late twenties. In one of many deviations from dramatic realism, the characters of Corky and Marissa interact with outside characters as well as with each other throughout the play. Through early exposition, the play introduces an adolescent Corky, a young Chicana lesbian in a working-class Los Angeles barrio who will eventually be victimized by and survive a sexual assault from her school's janitor. Corky's adult self, Marisa, is a struggling painter who tries to secure support and mentorship from Amalia, a woman who is old enough to be her mother and who, audiences quickly learn, possesses a certain degree of respect and gravitas from her (nearly all male) professional peers in her artistic circle around the area of California known as El Cen-

tro, a geographic location especially significant for its proximity to Mexico. Geographic and cultural ties to this native land is a theme that will emerge repeatedly throughout the play as well as throughout Moraga's body of work.

Although the older Amalia has strong feelings for Marisa, many of which incorporate complicated and overlapping notions of sexual attraction, mother-daughter affection, and even political affiliation, she is also deeply in love with a former lover, Alejandro (a character audiences never see, but about whom they learn quite a bit). Later in the play, after learning of Alejandro's suicide, Amalia retreats emotionally (and eventually, physically) from Marisa, who in response angrily breaks it off with the woman who has been the love of her life. Like Amalia herself, the never-seen Alejandro is a native Mexican who in the play represents a kind of Latino/ethnic subjectivity that juxtaposes powerfully against the hybridity of Chicano identity occupied by Marisa/Corky. The play concludes with Marisa alone and articulating sentiments, to both Amalia and the audience, that conflate lesbian sexuality with a unique and powerful kind of personal and spiritual receptiveness. In the final moments of the play, in what the audience is to understand as a memory, Marisa recounts Amalia in voice-over: "You make love to me like worship"; Marisa responds to her lover and mentor, "And I nearly died, it was so powerful what she was saying. And I wanted to answer, 'Sí, la mujer es me religion' " (*Heroes*, p. 34). Ending the play on a slightly sad but still triumphant note, in this scene Marisa's powerful final monologue does what Moraga herself will spend the next twenty years accomplishing with countless plays, essays, and autobiography: exploring the relationship between women's emotional and sexual intimacy, political resistance, and family—in all its different formations—as well as the idea of spiritual redemption.

As Moraga's first published and professionally staged play, *Giving Up the Ghost* begins the playwright's long tradition of expressionistic theatrical conventions alongside a qualified reliance on realism, particularly in terms of the characters' emotional landscape. In terms of set design, lighting, casting decisions, dialogue, and even interventions into the space-time continuum within particular plays, Moraga's deviation from dramatic realism emerges from a perspective that assumes that the more linear and self-contained forms of dramatic realism typically upheld in traditional Western drama often help sustain patriarchal, occasionally elitist liberal humanist ideologies and epistemologies. Invoking examples from the ancient Greeks to Arthur Miller or even "feminist" playwrights such as Marsha Norman, literary and dramatic theorists such as Jill Dolan, Richard Schechner, Antonin Artaud, and Bertolt Brecht have all argued powerfully to realistic drama's ability to sustain and promote the (not always inclusive) ideologies and realities of any particular audience.

Often pointing to Aristotelian notions of catharsis in their analyses, critics, playwrights, and theatrical practitioners, including Moraga, point out the ways that audience identification as well as a perceived objectivity/mastery over what transpires on stage reinforces or even coerces the spectator's eye (and point of view) in the most surreptitious and powerful ways. This contrasts strongly to the alienation effect of Brechtian dramaturgy, which (alluding to Brechtian epic theater's ability to "alienate" the audience from the lull of catharsis and suspension of disbelief so praised in realism) prevents the audience from completely forgetting that it is watching an actual "performance." The refusal to engage in realism's intellectual inertia and suspension of critical thinking means that the spectator and reader remain always alienated from any sense of purging or relief (or unified meaning) that would be otherwise produced with more traditional Aristotelian catharsis. Critical thinking on the part of the alienated spectator, in other words, occurs more powerfully when realism, in its prevention of analyses, is circumvented.

In Moraga's broader discussion of theatrical realism alongside (what she understands as) the oppressive state of the for-profit theater institutions operating within the Western theater tradition, she explains,

> The aesthetics of Euro-American theater—what is considered "good art"—remain institutionally

unaltered and secured by the standard theatergoer who pays "good money" to see it; that is, a theater which reflects the world as Middle America understands it, a world which at its core equates free enterprise with freedom. ... Throughout my 12 years of writing for the American theater, over and over again I am referred to the Aristotelian model of the "well-made play." So, good student that I am, I track down Aristotle's *Poetics*. I read it, re-read it, take copious notes. But not until I read the Marxism of Brecht, then Augosto Boal's *Theater of the Oppressed,* does my discomfort with the Aristotelian system begin to make any sense. Aristotle created his poetics within the context of a slave-based economy, an imperialist democracy, not unlike the corporate-controlled democracy we are living under in the United States today. Women and slaves were not free citizens in Aristotle's Greece. ... Today, the very people (Mexican *and* American at once) who take center stage in my plays daily have their citizenship denied, questioned, and/or unauthenticated. These are me, my mother, my cousins, my ancestors, and my children.

("Sour Grapes," pp. 116–117)

In other words, because traditional, canonical Western theater typically relies on middle-class and liberal humanist values and assumes, by default, a white, straight, Christian point of view as the norm, digression from realism (and experimentation with less realistic dramaturgy) is often an attractive alternative to playwrights and practitioners, such as Moraga, interested in using drama and performance as a means of political intervention into race-, gender-, class-, or even sexually based social systems.

For example, Moraga's expressionistic (and less-than-realistic) choice to have two separate characters (Marisa and Corky) represent the same individual but at different points in her life, and further, have them interact with each other at the same moment in time onstage, is certainly not realistic. Actual people, in their right mind and in the real world, cannot split in two and create a doppelgänger of themselves and then carry on a conversation with that separate/same self. In choosing to have one person played by two characters who converse with and influence the lives of each other on stage, Moraga uses (nonrealistic) dramatic representation to imply a more abstract, politically informed argument. Rather than surreptitiously upholding the Western and liberal humanist notion, indeed celebration,

of the individual as a self-contained and whole entity, one that is knowable and definable (often known and defined in patriarchal, racist, or homophobic terms, Moraga would argue), the Marisa/Corky character distribution suggests, among other things, the fragmented nature of the self, or even the ability of one's past to influence the meaning and existence of one's present.

Although the theatrical device of having one actor play multiple parts is now commonly used by more mainstream and commercially successful dramatists (the Pulitzer Prize–winning playwright Tony Kushner, for example), Moraga uses this deviation from naturalistic representation to hint at broader, politically critical assertions about the self—specifically, the ways humans understand reality and knowledge, and the inability to completely "know" or "define" an individual. The audience is powerfully, visually reminded that it is *not* watching an actual person but rather an actor representing a staged version of a person (e.g., spectators can never completely surrender disbelief and begin to feel as if they can ever "know" or define the individual represented). One actor playing multiple parts, then, suggests a kind of multiplicity of subjectivity (individual identity); the inability for one person (or culture) to "know" or define another person (or culture); and in a more literary way, even the ways that particular characters (e.g., the briefly appearing character of Corky's mother, played by the same actor who performs the character of Amalia) become influential on how other characters experience each other over the course of the play.

SHADOW OF A MAN

The often anthologized *Shadow of a Man* won the Fund for New American Plays Award and is often written about critically for its intervention into previous narratives of "American family tragedy," such as those explored in Arthur Miller's cold war masterpiece *Death of a Salesman* (see, for example, Catherine Wiley's "Cherríe Moraga's Radical Revision of *Death of a Salesman*"). Coproduced by Brava and the Eureka Theatre, *Shadow of a Man* premiered in

San Francisco in November 1990 under the direction of Moraga's mentor and friend María Irene Fornés. In May 1992 it was staged both at the Latino Chicago Theater under the direction of Carmen Aguilar and at the Miracle Theater in Portland, Oregon. Subsequent productions were staged at Denver's Su Teatro in January 1995 and at the Cara Mía Theater in Dallas in May 1996.

Told in two acts, *Shadow of a Man* stages the difficulties experienced by a Chicano family in a politically volatile Los Angeles in 1969. The Rodríguez family is made up of the alcoholic, often abusive, cuckolded patriarch Manuel; his long-suffering wife, Hortensia; her sister Rosario; and the three children, the seventeen-year-old Leticia, her brother Rigo (who is never seen but referred to), and the twelve-year-old protagonist, Lupe. The character of Conrado—Manuel's compadre, Hortensia's onetime lover and, it is strongly suggested, Lupe's biological father—enters the play's final scenes. In a climactic moment, audiences learn that Manuel is and likely always was in love with Conrado; when Manuel "loaned" his wife to his best friend, he perhaps used Hortensia as a third party or liaison to connect emotionally and physically with his compadre in ways that his own culture and his own psyche would never permit. Indeed, the play strongly suggests that the trauma of the closet, along with poverty, racism, and eventual betrayal from an overtly assimilating son collectively bring Manuel to suicide. In a play described by some critics as a retelling of an American domestic tragedy, Moraga takes the traditional issues of American family drama (identity conflicts within parent-child relationships, the impact of dysfunctional marriages on future generations, and poverty) and recasts her net to include equally "American" issues faced by families such as racism and homophobia.

The absence of or incomplete "story," a fractured narrative of a people who suffer from political and cultural amnesia, emerges as a concern in many of Moraga's plays and critical essays, and often this "absent story" or (sometimes willful) amnesia finds focus in staged characters who assimilate all too enthusiastically.

With Rigo, the Rodríguez family's prized first-born son, this assimilation-fed amnesia is a painful reminder to the family's failed patriarch that yet another of his functions as a Chicano male has gone unfulfilled. Rigo's betrayals, from Manuel's perspective, include marrying a white woman, neglecting to invite his entire family to the wedding, and, worse, making no mention of his father's angry absence from the ceremony. Rigo even gives his own son the very white name "Sean." Adding insult to injury, regardless of the political resistance demonstrated by many young men of color in 1969 unwilling to fight for a country that would not extend them equal rights, Rigo voluntarily enlists in the military. Rigo's assimilation to white culture and mores stands in a stark contrast to his more ethnically and politically conscious sister Letitia, who voluntarily "gives away" her virginity so that she will no longer be defined by it—not, she explains, to define herself as "worthless" but rather "to know that my worth had nothing to do with it" (*Shadow*, p. 78). She also proudly wears a United Farm Workers jacket, demonstrating her public support for César Chavez's Delano grape boycott; passionately encourages her young sister Lupe to think about college; and angrily critiques a telenovela's use of blond (Eurocentric) actresses to play Mexican maids on television, thereby privileging white aesthetics of female beauty over indigenous ones.

This engagement with assimilation-versus-consciousness, a politically informed dilemma of remembering/forgetting who one is and where one comes from, is performed powerfully in *Shadow of a Man* by Rigo and Letitia; caught in the middle in terms of the play's action and plot as well as its broader politics, the protagonist, Lupe, teeters back and forth between moments of shame and pride. By the play's conclusion, audiences are unclear as to her eventual trajectory. Instead of choosing a confirmation name connected to her favorite saint (as is typical), she chooses the name "Frances" (the given name of Frankie Pacheco, the young girl in her class she admires and likely has romantic feelings for) because, as she says, "I wannu be in her body. When she sits, she doesn't hold her knees

together like my mom and the nuns are always telling me to. She jus' lets them fly and fall wherever they want ... like they was wings instead of knees" (p. 84). Indeed, Frankie's refusal to sit in a ladylike fashion, her rejection of the restrictive gender paradigm set forth by adults and Catholicism, is as much what Lupe finds attractive (or emulate-able, which the confirmation name exercise is supposed to involve) as anything romantic in the young girl's feelings. But while this celebratory moment, which ends the play, might leave readers and spectators to think Lupe's path is one marked by empowerment and increased consciousness, Moraga undercuts the monologue by having Lupe inform the audience that all of the above will be kept private, a secret, a story she won't dare share, thereby continuing the secrecy, perhaps the shame, and shadows of unspoken narrative that ultimately cost her father everything.

To be sure, this engagement with story, memory, and the capacity of (a people's) narrative to redeem, emancipate, and empower informs Moraga's plays at the character level, as with *Shadow of a Man,* but it consistently finds a voice in her essays as well. More than just an important theme that finds resonance on Moraga's stage, the connection between remembering, story, and selfhood is one that holds great power for Moraga in the potential for increased political consciousness and activism.

This consistent attention to the values, histories, and customs of pre-European Americans is often involved in critics' charges of separatism in Moraga's drama and nonfiction. The purported separatism in much of Moraga's work requires proper contextualization, however, and it would be unfair to ascribe (as some critics do) an inflexibility or militancy to her perspective, an accusation that robs her position of nuance. Her perspective on national identity and consciousness is perhaps best exemplified in "Queer Aztlán," a frequently cited essay within her collection of poetry and prose, *The Last Generation.* Among other things, "Queer Aztlán" contends that a separate sense of place, politically and culturally, must exist for "la Chicanada"; for queer Chicanas in particular, those oppressed by

dominant culture have had to face the racism of second-wave feminism as well as the misogyny and homophobia of the Chicano rights movement. The marginalized can thus find themselves without a political, cultural, or filial homeland even among their own people, a people with whom they purportedly share oppressions. In this Moraga explicates her conception of a collective ethno-sexual identity in which communities could be built "on shared cultural values, blood ties, spiritual beliefs, common histories."

Shadow of a Man, like much of Moraga's drama, includes a heavy use of Spanglish, a blend of Spanish and English spoken by native and nonnative English-speaking peoples alike. The decision to write in a language that is neither exclusively English (the language of the oppressor) nor Spanish (the indigenous tongue with which many audiences might *not* be fluent, as was the case for Moraga growing up) brings with it unavoidable political implications. Also significant with regard to Moraga's use of Spanglish throughout *Shadow of a Man,* footnotes are never provided for the non-Spanish speaking reader or spectator, with the exception of one brief (explanatory more than translating) footnote explaining the definition of the term *compadre* early in the play. Yvonne Yarbro-Bejarano points out that Moraga's insistence, in her earlier plays, on including Spanglish as the language to represent and articulate Chicana and Chicana lesbian experience accomplishes more than just a potential (politically productive) discomfort on the part of the Anglo, English-only-speaking spectator. More than just reminding the audience/reader of her or his privilege, the Spanglish-peppered dialogue "insist[s] on Chicano lives and Chicano language as appropriate matter for the theatre, and by creating Chicanas as desiring subjects ... [Moraga] invites Chicanos, including Chicanas and Chicana lesbians, to take up the ideal spectator position monopolized for so long by white, heterosexual, and economically privileged viewers" (p. 25).

Some playwrights and scholars of Latino studies who potentially take issue with a playwright's decision to write in anything *but* Spanish might consider the presence of English

as an accommodation to the colonial tongue or the privileged spectator, or worse, a rhetorical move that might further marginalize the Spanish-speaking audience for whom the work was supposedly written. Yet, as Lisa B. Thompson's review of *Watsonville* and *Circle In the Dirt* points out, Moraga's decision to "mak[e] her work more accessible" actually ends up helping well-meaning but financially burdened "artistic directors who want to mount more representative offerings" (p. 525). In other words, in the most practical sense, rather than a cop-out or compromise, Moraga's refusal to write exclusively in Spanish can be seen as providing additional opportunities for larger audiences to be exposed to her work and ideas, as non-English productions would be far more difficult to justify to budget-wary artistic directors and boards deciding on a production schedule. Moraga herself points out how the "balancing act" of using Spanglish in a performance text "ensures both cultural authenticity and accessibility to a new (more broadly defined) American audience" (*Watsonville*, p. 4).

Many of the themes in *Shadow of a Man* nod to the importance of stories, history, memory, and, as a consequence, "heritage," as it is experienced (and sometimes lacking) in its young protagonist, Lupe—in particular the ways that story, memory, or heritage can feed, productively or perilously, a sense of self. A person is who she is, in other words, in large part because of the stories that she has been told about who she is and who she was (as part of a people). For Moraga, and throughout this play, this importance of (and the function of) story and memory contributes to sexual as well as gendered and ethnic identity. For example, a large part of what gives Lupe a sense of self and redemption as a young Catholic, one who is already dealing with the requisite shame associated with her growing sexuality, is the "story" of Mary Magdalene, one that Lupe remembers, or recounts, in an almost blissful narrative. Tellingly, Mary Magdalene's absence of shame as she engages with Christ is a hallmark of her importance to Lupe, an adolescent who is already being taught, quite well, to feel shame regarding her gendered and sexual self. Similarly, the memories and stories Lupe is told

repeatedly by her mother and aunt about family lore, Chicano cuisine, and various cultural traditions including family history emerge in the play as touchstones of (sometimes positive, occasionally dangerous) narratives that inform Lupe's political subjectivity. These stories, however, are nearly always Chicano-centric and, very often, queer/non-normative in either tone or content. As Catrióna Rueda Esquibel describes, with regard to Chicana and Latina voices that successfully break out and "articulate their own sexuality" from a textual/cultural landscape too narrow/white/Western in its scope, Moraga offers a politically powerful "Chicana sexual imaginary" (p. 64). She continues, "The history of Chicanas, Chicana lesbians, and Chicanas/os is overshadowed by dominant paradigms of Anglo-American history, models of Manifest Destiny, concepts of land and women 'there for the taking,' the erasure of communities of peoples of color who predate Anglo-American immigration" (p. 64). As Esquibel and other cultural critics point out, Moraga as a playwright and activist successfully departs from less inclusive (more Western and frequently hetero-normative) narratives of queer subjectivity. Furthermore, these less inclusive narratives, typically founded on Western/classical notions of lesbian identity, often "erase or distort *histories* of working-class and people of color" (Esquibel, pp. 64, emphasis added).

As Moraga explains in her essay "Sour Grapes," her own take on the significance of memory and heritage within a politicized Chicano subjectivity illuminates explicitly what Lupe's fictional trajectory merely suggests:

I am a half-breed Chicana. The difference between my gringo immigrant side and my native Mexican is that when gringos came to the United States they were supposed to forget their origins. My whitedaddy isn't quite sure what he is. Orphan son of a British (maybe changed-his-name-Irish) Canadian, he thinks. His mother ... French, yes French for sure, cuz there was some French grandmother somewhere, but Missouri is where they all end up. She meeting my grandfather whom I only met once ... they say ... I was too young to remember ... my Dad's history too vague to remember because they came to this country to forget.

(p. 123)

As she does in more than one autobiographical essay and interview, Moraga here asserts the importance of memory, story, and consequently heritage to the part of her identity associated with being a Chicana, while the white component to her background involves lesser (if any) importance to notions of heritage at all. As a play that attaches great importance to storytelling, if not history-documenting, for a family and a people, Moraga's retelling of "a tragic American family" in *Shadow of a Man* achieves political resonance in the ways that it recasts history and narrative itself into a more Chicano-centric landscape. The centrality of memory and narrative to a sense of heritage exists as something quite different for Moraga's Rodríguez family as compared to their white neighbors. The power of story to exist as a source of history, specifically for future generations, and the individual/cultural pride and self-actualization facilitated by these notions of heritage, are an essential component of their story.

HEROES AND SAINTS

By the time that Moraga's *Heroes and Saints* premiered at the Mission Theater in San Francisco in April 1992, she had established a strong reputation among academics and theater practitioners as an activist and writer devoted to the causes and interests of ethnic minorities, the working class and the poor, women, and in particular, queer women of color. *Heroes and Saints* was commissioned by the Los Angeles Theater Center and won the PEN West Drama Award as well as the Will Glickman Prize. With Albert Takazauckas as its director, the San Francisco production was followed by the October 1992 production at the Guadalupe Cultural Arts Center in San Antonio, Texas, with Susana Tubert acting as director. In August 1993 the play was performed at the Borderlands Theater in Tucson, Arizona, with Diane Rodríguez directing. After its success with *Giving Up the Ghost,* the Latino Chicago Theater also continued to stage Moraga's work, with *Heroes and Saints* opening under Juan Ramírez' direction in May 1994. In December of that same year

the play was produced at the Working Theater in New York City with Albert Takazauckas once again directing.

With *Heroes and Saints,* Moraga finds inspiration for the onstage narrative in the offstage drama of real life. As she would do later with her 1996 play *Watsonville: Some Place Not Here,* the playwright employs real-world political activism and social injustice as a springboard for a dramatic retelling on stage. Although fictional, the play is inspired in part by the 1988 United Farm Workers' grape boycott, which protested and attempted to influence the practice of pesticide poisoning of (predominantly Chicano) California farmworkers. The boycott and the resulting thirty-six-day fast by the president of the UFW, Cesar Chávez, combined with the brutal beating of UFW vice-president Dolores Huerta by a San Francisco policeman less than a month after Chávez' hunger strike ended, brought significant visibility to the struggle of California's farmworkers trying desperately, collectively, to fight for their rights. This all occurred within the same decade (1978–1988) that a cancer cluster was discovered in the town of McFarland in California's San Joaquin Valley. The McFarland tragedy included statistically (high) unexplainable cancer diagnoses, predominantly experienced by children born with birth defects, occurring in the relatively small landscape in which many of the chemical atrocities protested by the UFW were taking place.

With this real-life story serving as inspiration, *Heroes and Saints* also takes place in 1988 in the San Joaquin Valley, in the fictional town of McLaughlin. It features characters who are struggling to survive subsistence wages, threats of violence, and varying levels of commitment from strikers as their courage and numbers fluctuate in a desperate attempt to sustain a strike of the cannery and fields that employ them and are likely killing many of them.

Heroes and Saints involves one of Moraga's most obvious deviations from dramatic realism in the representation of its protagonist, Cerezita, who exists merely as a head on a table throughout the majority of the play's narrative. Luis Valdez' play *The Shrunken Head of Pancho Villa* (1963)

served as "a point of departure" for Moraga's dramaturgical choice (*Heroes,* p. 89); Cerezita, as a talking and feeling character, is unrealistic in the sense that she could not exist outside the fictional world of the play, but the emotional catharsis Moraga intends for her to engage in with the audience is based in emotional and dramatic realism. In the company town forced to deal with increasing numbers of children born with birth defects and dying from the use of pesticides, Cerezita, who was born without limbs, lives with her mother Dolores, sister Yolanda (who fears for her own child's future health), and brother Mario, a gay Chicano who endures the AIDS crisis as well as the cultural machismo that eventually forces him to leave McLaughlin. Characters such as Amparo (who loosely represents the real-life Huerta) and Bonnie occupy important roles in the play's exploration of a community's increasing collective power, not to mention the ability of individuals to enact broader change for the larger community. The play also engages the varying involvement of the Catholic Church within leftist politics, particularly the activism and collective resistance of the Chicano population of the American Southwest, most obviously in the character of Father Juan, who fluctuates in his reserve and what he is willing to do to fight for the rights of the workers. From the play's beginning, upon his first meeting with Cerezita—who will develop more than platonic feelings for the young priest—Father Juan performs a role that will be a hallmark in Moraga's future works: a character who represents a Catholicism that performs both a repressive and a liberatory function for its female adherents. Reading to Cerezita from Rosario Castellanos' *Balun Canan,* a text of prose and poetry that explores the experiences of a young, poor Mexican girl after the Revolution, Father Juan's tenderness toward Cerezita, like his politics, is double-edged: on the one hand, it provides encouragement for the increasingly powerful place she will eventually occupy for the play's characters and McLaughlin's battles, but on the other, it undermines her sexual awakening and feeds a shame that haunts many of Moraga's characters who face draconian or restrictive sexual ideologies at the hands of the Catholic Church. As the curtain falls on the burning fields, audiences are left to decide for themselves whether or not Cerezita, and the town's actions, accomplish anything toward real change.

THIS BRIDGE CALLED MY BACK

One of the most influential texts to mark, if not spark, the presence of third-wave (or third-world) feminism is Moraga's landmark anthology *This Bridge Called My Back: Writings by Radical Women of Color,* coedited with Gloria Anzaldúa. As Chela Sandoval submits, "The publication of *This Bridge Called My Back* ... made the presence of U.S. third world feminism impossible to ignore on the same terms as it had been throughout the 1970s" (p. 341). With its first publication in 1981, this collection passionately articulated a lesbian feminist subjectivity that takes care to include discourses of race and class. The first text to put Moraga on a broader literary and political map by virtue of its contributions to gender studies, queer theory, and Chicano studies, *Bridge* features contributions from women writers of Asian, Latino, African, and Native American background. The anthology was also groundbreaking because so many of the voices explicitly represent (or interrogate issues central to) poor and working-class peoples. The text's contributors confront racism, classism, sexism, and homophobia using myriad literary forms, including essays, poems, short stories, and creative and autobiographical pieces.

While many of the essays and entries in *Bridge* are frequently referenced, one of the most widely cited is Norma Alarcon's "The Theoretical Subject(s) of *This Bridge Called My Back* and Anglo-American Feminism," in which she argues for the importance of including discussions of race and class in wider considerations of women's marginalization. In other words, as Alarcon explains, political resistance and change must go beyond merely examining the ways that gender groups have been oppressed; they must also look at the ways, within a particular gender group, that additional sociopolitical subdivisions come into play and are employed as a means of oppression. This component of third-wave

feminism posited by the text stands in powerful contrast to the less-inclusive but also politically active social moment known as second-wave feminism. Also referred to as the women's movement or women's liberation movement, second-wave feminism was concerned with, among other agendas, the ratification of the Equal Rights Amendment, reproductive control, and equal pay for equal work; this social movement, which emerged in the mid- to late 1960s, was populated overwhelmingly by middle-class white women and, from the perspective of third-wave feminism, typically left issues (and oppressions) central to poor women and/or women of color off of its agenda.

In her exploration of (and challenge to) notions of an existent objective "truth" (a truth which some falsely believe exists outside of language, outside of a reality deeply constructed by human culture), Alarcon maintains in *Bridge* that along with the realization of contextual, culturally specific epistemologies comes the conclusion that feminism itself is contextual, culturally specific, and cannot be fairly categorized under one rubric or political umbrella. Indeed, her essay argues, this monolithic way of thinking often results in a hierarchy within the subgroups of those marginalized. This strong focus on the ways that political and social hierarchies dangerously worked in second-wave feminism would become the hallmark of third-wave feminism's political platform. Responding to that less inclusive agenda, this third wave of feminism emerged in the late 1970s and 1980s and explicitly focused on the needs and issues most relevant to women who were also ethnic minorities, poor, or queer and who felt that they had been largely left out of the second wave. As Moraga and Anzaldúa stated in their 1981 introduction to the volume, "We want to express to all women, especially to white, middle-class women, the experiences which divide us as feminists ... we want to create a definition that expands what 'feminist' means" (p. lii). Due in no small part to the political and cultural work inaugurated by Moraga, Anzaldúa, and the contributors of *This Bridge* since the early 1980s, college campuses, political organizations, and collective movements all over the United States have come to incorporate the concerns of class-, race-, and sexuality based marginalization into their broader agendas which previously might have been defined merely in gender.

Selected Bibliography

WORKS OF CHERRÍE MORAGA

DRAMATIC WORKS

Giving Up the Ghost: Teatro in Two Acts. Los Angeles: West End Press, 1986. Republished as *Giving Up the Ghost: A Stage Play in Three Portraits.* Albuquerque, N.Mex.: West End Press, 1994.

Heroes and Saints and Other Plays. Albuquerque, N.Mex.: West End Press, 1994. (Includes *Heroes and Saints, Giving Up the Ghost,* and *Shadow of a Man.*)

The Hungry Woman. Albuquerque, N.Mex.: West End Press, 2001. (Includes *The Hungry Woman* and *Heart of the Earth: A Popul Vuh Story.*)

Watsonville: Some Place Not Here; Circle in the Dirt: El pueblo de East Palo Alto. Albuquerque, N.Mex.: West End Press, 2002.

Digging Up the Dirt. Albuquerque, N.Mex.: West End Press, 2012 [forthcoming].

NONFICTION AND POETRY

Loving in the War Years: Lo que nunca pasó por sus labios. Boston: South End Press, 1983.

The Last Generation: Prose and Poetry. Boston: South End Press, 1993.

Waiting in the Wings: Portrait of a Queer Motherhood. Ithaca, N.Y.: Firebrand Books, 1997.

"Sour Grapes." In *The Color of Theater.* Edited by Roberta Uno and Lucy Mae San Pablo Burns. New York: Continuum, 2002. Pp. 115–132.

"Art in América con Acento." In *Women Writing Resistance: Essays on Latin America and the Caribbean.* Edited by Jennifer Browdy de Hernandez. Cambridge, Mass.: South End Press, 2003.

A Xicana Codex of Changing Consciousness: Writings, 2000–2010. Durham, N.C.: Duke University Press, 2011.

EDITED VOLUMES

This Bridge Called My Back: Writings by Radical Women of Color. With Gloria Anzaldúa. Watertown, Mass.: Perse-

phone Press, 1981. Expanded and revised 3rd ed., Berkeley, Calif.: Third Woman Press, 2002.

Cuentos: Stories by Latinas. With Alma Gómez and Mariana Romo-Carmona. New York: Kitchen Table, Women of Color Press, 1983.

Esta puente, mi espalda: Voces de mujeres tercermundistas en los Estados Unidos. With Ana Castillo. Translated by Castillo and Norma Alarcón. San Francisco: Ism Press, 1988.

The Sexuality of Latinas. With Norma Alarcón and Ana Castillo. Berkeley, Calif.: Third Woman Press, 1993.

CRITICAL AND BIOGRAPHICAL STUDIES

Alarcón, Norma. "The Theoretical Subject(s) of *This Bridge Called My Back* and Anglo-American Feminism." In *Criticism in the Borderlands: Studies in Chicano Literature, Culture, and Ideology.* Edited by Héctor Calderón and José David Saldívar. Durham, N.C., and London: Duke University Press, 1991. Pp. 28–39.

Allatson, Paul. " 'I May Create a Monster': Cherríe Moraga's Hybrid Denial." *Antípodas: Journal of Hispanic and Galician Studies* 11–12:103–121 (1999–2000).

Case, Sue Ellen. "Seduced and Abandoned: Chicanas and Lesbians in Representation." In *Negotiating Performance: Gender, Sexuality, and Theatricality in Latino America.* Edited by Diane Taylor and Juan Villegas. Durham, N.C.: Duke University Press, 1994. Pp. 88–101.

Esquibel, Catrióna Rueda. *With Her Machete in Her Hand: Reading Chicana Lesbians.* Austin: University of Texas Press, 2006.

Gilmore, Leigh. *Autobiographics: A Feminist Theory of Women's Self-Representation.* Ithaca, N.Y.: Cornell University Press, 1994.

Huerta, Jorge. "Cherrie Moraga's *Heroes and Saints,* Chicano Theatre for the '90s." *TheatreForum* 1 (UC San Diego), 1992.

Negrón-Muntaner, Frances. "Cherríe Moraga." In *Latin American Writers on Gay and Lesbian Themes: A Bio-Critical Sourcebook.* Edited by David William Foster. Westport, Conn.: Greenwood Press, 1994. Pp. 254–262.

Ramírez, Elizabeth C. *Chicanas/Latinas in American Theatre: A History of Performance.* Bloomington: Indiana University Press, 2000.

Sandoval, Chela. "U.S. Third World Feminism: The Theory and Method of Oppositional Consciousness in the Postmodern World." In *Geographic Thought: A Praxis Perspective.* Edited by George Henderson and Marvin Waterstone. New York: Routledge, 2009. Pp. 338–355.

Sternbach, Nancy Saporta. " 'A Deep Racial Memory of Love': The Chicana Feminism of Cherrie Moraga." In *Breaking Boundaries: Latina Writing and Critical Readings.* Edited by Asuncion Horno-Delgado, Eliana Ortega, Nina M. Scott, and Nancy Saporta Sternbach. Amherst: Massachusetts University Press, 1989. Pp. 48–61.

Thompson, Lisa B. *"Watsonville/Circle in the Dirt."* *Theatre Journal* 56, no. 3:523–525 (October 2004).

Wiley, Catherine. "Cherríe Moraga's Radical Revision of *Death of a Salesman.*" *American Drama* 11, no. 2:32–46 (summer 2002).

Yarbro-Bejarano, Yvonne. *The Wounded Heart: Writing on Cherríe Moraga.* Austin: University of Texas Press, 2001.

INTERVIEWS

Anderson, Kelly. "Voices of Feminism Oral History Project: Cherríe Moraga." Sophia Smith Collection, Women's History Archives at Smith College, June 6–7, 2005. http://www.smith.edu/library/libs/ssc/vof/transcripts/Moraga.pdf.

Ikas, Karin Rosa. "Cherríe Moraga." In *Chicana Ways: Conversations with Ten Chicana Writers.* Reno: University of Nevada Press, 2002. Pp. 153–174.

Oliver-Rotger, Maria-Antónia. "Interviews and Readings: Cherríe Moraga." *Voices from the Gaps* (website hosted by the University of Minnesota), January 2000. http://voices.cla.umn.edu/readings/moraga_cherrie.html.

FRANK O'HARA

(1926—1966)

Stephen Ross

IN HIS SHORT but intensely productive life, the poet Frank O'Hara came to be one of the most influential and beloved figures of the New York City arts scene of the 1950s and 1960s. Nearly a half-century after his untimely death at the age of forty, he has become a symbol, for many, of the sophisticated, passionate, and frenetic spirit of his extraordinary time and place. Yet, far from cultivating a literary persona or courting fame and prestige as an establishment poet, he allowed his art and his life to bleed casually—some would say recklessly—into one another. The result was one of the most innovative, idiosyncratic, and sublimely unrehearsed poetic achievements of the twentieth century. As John Ashbery writes in his introduction to O'Hara's *Collected Poems* (1971), "His career stands as an unrevised work-in-progress" (p. vii). Along with the work of close friends and collaborators like Ashbery, Kenneth Koch, and James Schuyler, O'Hara's writing is perhaps best known for having formed the nucleus of the so-called New York School of poetry. As a poet and playwright O'Hara experimented with a variety of highly original styles—some formal, most improvised—drenched in the details of his personal life, popular culture, and the contemporary art world; as an art critic and curator at the Museum of Modern Art (MoMA) he championed several generations of major artists (notably the Abstract Expressionists) and helped organize numerous landmark exhibitions in the United States and abroad; as a frequent collaborator with fellow poets, visual artists, composers, and filmmakers he explored the boundaries of form, genre, and artistic medium; and as a wit and bon vivant he cut a legendary figure across mid-century Manhattan.

From the start of his career, O'Hara's work was nourished by deep and precocious learning and by a healthy irreverence for received notions of art and literature. If his work flouted both academic and commercial standards of poetry—beginning with those of the New Criticism that were ascendant at his maturation in the late 1940s—it did so in the service of an exploratory poetics animated as much by visual art, film, classical music, dance, and popular culture as by the poetic tradition. Or rather, poetic traditions, as O'Hara's personal canon extended well beyond the limited purview of American and British poetic models to include other major national traditions, notably the French, German, and Russian. He was as much at home with Arthur Rimbaud, Rainer Maria Rilke, and Vladimir Mayakovsky as he was with William Carlos Williams, W. H. Auden, and Gertrude Stein.

The smoggy hustle-and-bustle glamour of New York City also provided an important stimulus, if not the primary inspiration, for his creative life. While his work partook of a cosmopolitan richness and diversity, it more often than not emerged from and addressed itself to a uniquely Manhattan-centered community of friends, lovers, and fellow artists. Alongside Walt Whitman and Hart Crane, O'Hara stands as one of the city's great poets. His trademark "I do this I do that" poems—breathless, witty narrations of lunchtime rambles across town—have given us one of the most vivid snapshots of the city in the early cold war years.

Yet O'Hara was far more than a verse chronicler of city life. Over his twenty-odd-year career he embraced a wide variety of poetic forms and styles. He wrote odes, elegies, occasional poems, love poems, hate poems, autobiographical poems, sonnets, homages, pastorals, ekphrases, aubades, birthday poems, epithalamiums, serial works, free verse, collages, dialogues, Surrealist imitations,

207

concrete poems, epistolary poems, nonsense verse, poems with musical titles ("Ann Arbor Variations," "Appoggiaturas," "Nocturne," "Rhapsody," etc.), and more than sixty poems simply titled "Poem." There are also several hundred pages of drama. Some poems appear in traditional stanzaic forms with regular line breaks; many others are erratically lineated. Toward the end of his career he wrote a number of poems with conspicuous caesuras, or blank spaces between words used for dramatic effect. He hardly ever used rhyme and regular meter.

As an experimentalist O'Hara broke the mold with works like "Second Avenue" and "Biotherm." At the same time, his finest lyric poems ("In Memory of My Feelings," "To the Harbormaster," "Ode to Joy," to name a few) rank among the most moving and accomplished of the twentieth century. Still other works, such as "Why I Am Not a Painter," "On Seeing Larry Rivers's *Washington Crossing the Delaware* at the Museum of Modern Art," and "Ode to Willem de Kooning," channeled the electrifying spirit of 1950s vanguard painting like no other poems of their time.

O'Hara's aesthetic sensibility was as sharply defined and demanding as it was omnivorous. Throughout his life he drew energy and inspiration from the many artistic communities to which he belonged, developing what the critic Lytle Shaw has called a "poetics of coterie." O'Hara studied classical music and English literature at Harvard, became a world-class expert in the fine arts as an adult, and cultivated interests in many other art forms in which he had received no formal training, notably dance and film. Friends and colleagues have attested that he possessed the uncanny ability to walk into a new exhibition and immediately spot the most innovative work. At the time of his death he was on the verge of taking over as curator of the Museum of Modern Art—a considerable feat for a man with no official curatorial credentials. His reputation now rests, as it did during his lifetime, on the astonishingly free and full-bodied responses to art and life that he offered at every possible opportunity: in conversation with friends, in print journalism, in museum catalogs and monographs, and, most importantly, in the more than five hundred pages of poetry that he left scattered behind him.

Despite the dizzying scope of his artistic interests and involvements, O'Hara's writing emerges most immediately from two key contexts: the early twentieth-century French literary and painterly avant-gardes (Dada, surrealism, cubism) and the American painterly avant-garde of the late 1940s and 1950s (action painting and abstract expressionism). Rather than imitating the styles and discoveries of these various movements, or trying to adapt painterly techniques to writerly ends, he absorbed from these models a more general resistance to programmatic forms of engagement with art. He took from Guillaume Apollinaire and Pierre Reverdy, Willem de Kooning and Jackson Pollock, the license to reimagine constantly the very aims, contours, and materials of art itself. In his seminal monograph on Pollock, he explains, "The basic theory of Surrealism is a far greater liberation from the restrictions of preconceived form than any amount of idiosyncratic experimentation" (*Art Chronicles*, p. 17). For O'Hara, it was the act of breaking free of "preconceived form" and attaining an immediacy of effect that mattered more than any end product; hence his disregard for his work after he finished writing it. He learned from the painters and poets to whom he apprenticed himself that a great artwork can be—and perhaps ought to be—a record of its own coming into existence. The other lesson he learned and repeated from his models was that great art must flow out of an artist's own life, perceptions, and experiences. Or as O'Hara himself has it, "Style at its lowest ebb is method. Style at its highest ebb is personality" (p. 149).

The turning points of O'Hara's career were marked less by the publication of poetry collections (he published only two full-length and several small-scale volumes) than by individual poems and by the constant waxing and waning of platonic and romantic relationships. In a sense, the books and poems were afterthoughts to the more important matter of living the life that fed the poetry.

FRANK O'HARA

EARLY LIFE

Francis Russell O'Hara was born on March 27, 1926, in Baltimore, Maryland, though all his life he believed his birthday was June 27. O'Hara's parents, Katherine Broderick O'Hara and Russell J. O'Hara, most likely disguised the real birth date of their first-born son to cover up the fact that he had been conceived out of wedlock. Along with his younger brother, Philip, and sister, Maureen, O'Hara grew up in the rural setting of Grafton, Massachusetts, where his parents moved in 1927. Russell worked in the farming business of his uncle, J. Frank Donahue, which he would later take over with his brother, Leonard. Throughout his adolescence Frank helped out with the farm chores, though he took no real interest in country life. References to O'Hara's rural childhood and farm-related activities, however, do appear throughout his poems, notably in "Ode to Michael Goldberg ('s Birth and Other Births)," written in 1958.

O'Hara received his primary and secondary education at Catholic schools in Worcester, Massachusetts. At the age of seven he began the intensive musical instruction that he would pursue through college and that would stimulate a lifelong passion for classical music, especially the modern avant-garde. For most of his high school years he made weekly trips to Boston to study piano as a special student at the New England Conservatory. Encouraged by his instructor, Margaret Mason, he planned for a university education at the conservatory, in preparation for a career as a pianist and music critic. World War II intervened, and in 1944 he enlisted in the U.S. Navy, serving as a sonarman third class on the destroyer USS *Nicholas,* based out of Norfolk, Virginia. During his two-year stint he sailed in the South Pacific and to Japan and visited Florida and California, later recording his experiences in an impressionistic travelogue titled *Lament and Chastisement.*

Following his discharge from the navy, O'Hara applied to college with the support of the GI Bill and gained acceptance to Harvard University, where he matriculated in 1946. Around this time he began seriously to write poetry. Though he set out to major in music, he later switched to English, earning a B.A. degree in 1950. At Harvard he involved himself in the artistic life around Cambridge, cofounding the Poets' Theatre, apprenticing at the Brattle Theatre, and publishing poems and short stories in the *Harvard Advocate* at a time when John Ashbery, Kenneth Koch, and Donald Hall served on the editorial board (Koch and Ashbery published O'Hara before they met him). All the while, he continued to read widely and eclectically, with interests ranging from the French Symbolists and Boris Pasternak to the British novelists Ronald Firbank and Ivy Compton-Burnett. He also kept tabs on the latest developments in music and painting, as he would throughout his life, and by his early twenties had already become something of an authority in the fine arts. He made lasting friendships during his college years with the writer V. R. "Bunny" Lang, the photographer George Montgomery, and the visual artist and writer Edward Gorey, with whom he roomed during his sophomore year. Though at times an intense loner—as he had been from his adolescence—O'Hara earned a reputation in college as a gregarious and brilliant young man destined for great things.

In the spring of 1949 O'Hara met John Ashbery at a party in a Cambridge bookshop and the two immediately hit it off. The meeting was to be one of the most fortuitous of each man's life. When Ashbery graduated several weeks later and moved to New York City (having spent as much time with O'Hara as possible before his graduation), they remained in regular contact, sending each other their latest poems and encouraging their respective forays into experimental poetic composition. Around this time O'Hara made several trips to the city and met the poet Kenneth Koch and the painters Fairfield Porter, Jane Freilicher, and Larry Rivers. In the fall of 1950 he moved to Ann Arbor to attend graduate school in creative writing at the University of Michigan. That year he also began, but did not complete, his first and only novel, "4th of July," a semiautobiographical bildungsroman. His early efforts at Michigan earned him a prestigious Hopwood Award in creative writing for his manuscript "A Byzantine Place," containing fifty poems, and a verse play titled *Try! Try!*

After completing his M.A. degree in 1951, O'Hara moved to New York City, where he would make his home for the rest of his life. It was at this time that he landed his first job at the Museum of Modern Art (selling cards at the front desk so as to have access to a Matisse exhibition). Quickly earning a reputation for wit and brilliance, and with a rapidly expanding circle of friends, he soon found himself at the center of the mid-century art world's attention. He became acquainted with most of the major painters of the era, including Willem and Elaine de Kooning, Jackson Pollock, Philip Guston, and Franz Kline, and befriended many members of the so-called second generation of New York School painters, including Grace Hartigan, Joan Mitchell, Helen Frankenthaler, and Michael Goldberg. He also met the poet James Schuyler and the writer Joseph LeSueur, who would become his roommate, lover, and companion for over a decade.

FIRST WRITINGS AND PUBLICATIONS

In 1951 O'Hara's plays *Try! Try!* and *Change Your Bedding!* were produced at the Poets' Theatre in Cambridge, alongside John Ashbery's masque *Everyman.* O'Hara himself was still in Ann Arbor at the time of the production. In the spring of 1952 he published his first poetry collection, *A City Winter and Other Poems.* The slim thirteen-page pamphlet was brought out by the fledgling Tibor de Nagy Gallery, an uptown venue curated by John Bernard Myers. That O'Hara was first published by an art gallery and not by a more traditional press was entirely fitting, since at the start of his career painters, not poets, were the most sympathetic audience for his work. The Tibor de Nagy not only would become an invaluable resource and support center for many of the young painters in O'Hara's friend circle but would also form an early home base for the nascent New York School poets; indeed, it was Myers who coined the title "New York School of poets" in a lightly ironic reference to the New York School of painters. Tibor de Nagy also published Kenneth Koch's and John Ashbery's first collections in 1953.

A City Winter contains fourteen poems selected by Myers from O'Hara's early body of work, accompanied by two drawings by Larry Rivers. Among the works are "Terrestrial Cuckoo" and the beautiful "Jane Awake," two of many poems that would be dedicated to and take their inspiration from the poet's close friend Jane Freilicher. Also included is the title poem, a rhyming, five-part sonnet sequence written in a kind of faux-Elizabethan Surrealist style characteristic of the kind of poems O'Hara was writing during his apprentice phase.

The following year Tibor de Nagy issued a second collection of O'Hara's work, *Oranges: 12 Pastorals,* a suite of prose poems presented in a mimeographed limited edition of only seventy-five copies, secured in three-ring binders. Published to coincide with the Tibor de Nagy's exhibition of Grace Hartigan's *Oranges* poem-pictures (which took their inspiration from the poems), O'Hara's *Oranges* contained twelve of an original nineteen prose poems composed in June–August 1949 in Grafton. O'Hara's "dozen oranges" marked an early stylistic breakthrough, rooted in the French Symbolist and Surrealist poetic traditions, which would serve as a foundation for much important later work.

O'Hara's earliest poems, reaching back to his undergraduate days and sampled in these early Tibor de Nagy publications, show the poet trying on a variety of traditional forms, often with great parodic verve, and eagerly trying to assimilate both American and European models. In her groundbreaking study *Frank O'Hara: Poet Among Painters,* Marjorie Perloff helpfully divides O'Hara's earlier work (1949–1954) into two principle poetic modes: "the clotted, somewhat mannered Surrealist mode of *Oranges: 12 Pastorals*" and "the natural, colloquial, whimsical, light-hearted mode of 'Les Etiquettes Jaunes' ... a mode clearly derived from William Carlos Williams." By Perloff's lights, it was not until O'Hara found a way to "fuse" these modes in the mid-1950s that he was able to compose the works now considered his "central achievement" (pp. 38–39). Indeed, from the start he had begun to forge his distinctive voice through just such a fusion. Consider "Today," a caprice writ-

ten in 1950, in which Williams' influence comes through in the proliferating exclamation marks (a conspicuous feature of both his and O'Hara's early work) and in the foregrounding of "things" as a central and entirely adequate subject for poetry. If O'Hara was not a strict adherent to Williams' famous dictum "No ideas but in things," his poetry never strayed too far from the material world. In a 1955 letter to the painter Fairfield Porter, O'Hara would describe his work as "materialistic" and "full of objects for their own sake" in contrast to the "spiritual" quality and "moral excellence and kind sentiments" of his friend John Ashbery's work (quoted in Gooch, p. 268).

In the period 1952–1953 O'Hara wrote more than ninety poems. In light of his later achievement, the major breakthroughs of this period now seem like important but perhaps not entirely successful experiments that allowed O'Hara to run to excess and thereby discover his limits. The major long poems from this period, "Easter" and "Second Avenue," achieve a degree of verbal density, owing much to Surrealist techniques of "automatic writing," that more or less defies readerly assimilation; they adamantly refuse to be paraphrased. With their abstract word-clusters muscled into irregular stanzaic form, they are arguably the closest O'Hara would come to approximating in writing the "all-over" painterly techniques of the "action painters," as Pollock, de Kooning, Franz Kline, and their ilk had been recently dubbed in an influential article by the critic Harold Rosenberg (Gooch, p. 225). "Easter," according to O'Hara's close friend and collaborator Kenneth Koch, "burst on us all like a bomb" (quoted in the notes to *Collected Poems*, p. 526) when it appeared in the late summer of 1952. Koch presumably refers to the three-and-a-half-page poem's relentless onslaught of free-association imagery blending the scatological, the sexual, and the grotesque in a lurid verbal melee.

"Second Avenue" takes these methods a step further, toning down the racy imagery of "Easter" but radically expanding O'Hara's previous standards of poem length and subject matter. It was to be a new experiment with language in which global meaning was suppressed in favor of local effects. O'Hara seems to have tried for a wholly abstract—that is, nonreferential—way of using language. In an unpublished letter to the editor of a literary journal, which later appeared in the *Collected Poems*, O'Hara explains that the poem's "surface" and its "meaning" are intended to be the same thing, adding, "I hope the poem to *be* the subject, not just about it" (p. 497). Whether or not he achieved this goal, such aims reflect his deep immersion in contemporaneous vanguard developments in other art forms. Like the aleatoric composition methods of his musician friends John Cage and Morton Feldman, the poem's content seems to have been generated by random or chance operations; and in keeping with the abstract expressionist emphasis on the flatness of the canvas, the poem resists symbolic and allegorical depth. O'Hara composed the poem in March–April 1953, in the throes of his first love affair with Larry Rivers. Parts of the poem were written in between posing sessions at Rivers' studio on Second Avenue, others in the company of other artist friends. The poem is a grab bag of popular and high culture references, accounts of meetings and conversations with friends, exotic tableaux, gossip, random snatches of dialogue, parenthetical asides, (mis)quotation, and much else—all propelled by a seemingly inexhaustible reserve of linguistic brio. One section, transcribed in the original French, gives a newspaper account of Bunny Lang's arrival in Haiti, while another details a lunch break with Kenneth Koch, while still another appears to depict a pilot flying through a lightning storm over an amethyst sea. One scene merges into another, pronouns appear without antecedents, words randomly appear in quotation marks, and on several occasions the text descends into pure exclamation. The poem is quite unparaphrasable, as O'Hara had hoped it would be, and shows just how far ahead of his peers he was, in certain respects, by the early 1950s. By contrast, Robert Lowell had just published his second book of impacted formal verse, *The Mills of the Kavanaughs,* while Allen Ginsberg was still several years away from the *succès de scandale* of *Howl.*

His difficult love affair with Larry Rivers had also begun to darken his style, with themes of lovesickness, heartbreak, and betrayal beginning to temper the scrappy giddiness of his early work. In poems like "Hatred," "Invincibility," "River," "To a Friend," "To Larry Rivers," "To the Harbormaster," and "Larry," O'Hara worked through his complicated relationship with Rivers. These feelings are often punningly figured in riverine or aquatic language, the alternatingly caressing and buffeting action of water mirroring, in self-consciously poetical fashion, the complicated love affair itself.

ART NEWS

From late 1953 to January 1955 O'Hara supplemented his income as an editorial associate for the journal *Art News,* writing reviews and essays on the contemporary art world, including short notices on exhibitions of Georges Braque, Paul Klee, Adolph Gottlieb, Jane Freilicher, Grace Hartigan, Helen Frankenthaler, Cy Twombly, Robert Rauschenberg, Salvador Dalí, Joseph Cornell, Max Beckmann, Fairfield Porter, and others. He also published an important essay, "Nature and New American Painting" (1954), featuring the work of Hartigan, Freilicher, Robert De Niro Sr., Larry Rivers, and Elaine de Kooning. O'Hara praises his subjects' respective turns from pure abstraction to more figurative styles of painting, considered a bold move at a time when abstract expressionism was still the ascendant painterly mode (*Standing Still,* pp. 41–51).

Another notable piece written for *Art News* in January 1955, "Porter Paints a Picture," offers an account of Fairfield Porter's painting methods and sensibility by way of cataloguing his meticulous preparations for a painting of his four-year-old daughter. A member of the older generation that included Pollock and Willem de Kooning, Porter had never wavered in his use of figurative painting methods and was one of the painters most favored by the New York School poets (he allowed James Schuyler to stay as a guest at his home on Great Spruce Head Island, Maine, for many years). O'Hara's sympathetic, if not quite exuberant, piece centers on Porter's commitment to figurative painting and to a measured compositional process that counterbalanced the high-flown romanticism of the abstract expressionists. Whether or not O'Hara was consciously in search of this at the time, his work of the mid-1950s too began to veer away from the pure abstraction of "Easter" and "Second Avenue" toward a still diffuse yet more personal style, a style later summed up jokingly in his mock manifesto, "Personism."

O'Hara spent most of February–June 1954 out of the city living with Larry Rivers and his family in Southampton, New York. Much to O'Hara's taste, it was an unconventional domestic situation, with Rivers living apart from his estranged wife with his children and mother-in-law. O'Hara quickly settled in as an honorary member of the family. While in Southampton, he pursued a mostly happy open relationship with Rivers and managed to write some notable poems, including "Southampton Variations" and "Homosexuality." Written in the unfriendly cultural climate of the pre-Stonewall days, the latter poem was defiantly ahead of its time and did not appear in print until 1970, four years after O'Hara's death.

In June 1954 O'Hara and Rivers had their second falling out, this one definitive, and O'Hara returned to New York City, entering an unhappy phase that would persist through the New Year. In 1955 he began rooming with Joe LeSueur, with whom he would share four apartments over the next ten years. The period of his second breakup with Rivers also saw his gradual distancing from Jane Freilicher (who was by then married to fellow painter Joe Hazan) and his increasing attachment to Grace Hartigan—much as O'Hara's affections had shifted from Bunny Lang to Freilicher several years before. Such was the pattern of intimacy and estrangement that tended to characterize his relationships with his closest female friends.

On returning to the city O'Hara enjoyed a short burst of creativity that produced "Mayakovsky," "On the Way to the San Remo," and "Meditations in an Emergency," a prose poem that appeared in the November 1954 issue of *Poetry.* Throughout the summer and fall, he

scraped together an income with art journalism and other odd jobs, including a short stint as the British photographer Cecil Beaton's secretary. Finally in January 1955 he quit his *Art News* post and rejoined the Museum of Modern Art staff, where he would remain for the rest of his life.

MUSEUM OF MODERN ART

O'Hara's artistic achievement from 1955–1966 cannot be understood outside the context of his involvement with the Museum of Modern Art. More than anything else, his career at MoMA anchored and set the pace of his adult life, providing a ballast to the excesses and tumult of his social life. O'Hara in turn was an invaluable asset to the museum for his unique access to the community of Downtown artists who were beginning to make a name for themselves in the wake of the abstract expressionist revolution.

After his first gig at the museum's front desk in the early 1950s, O'Hara rejoined MoMA in 1955 as a special assistant in the International Program, becoming assistant curator of painting and sculpture exhibitions in 1960 and assistant curator in 1965. During his tenure he helped plan landmark traveling exhibitions such as *The New American Painting* (1958–1959), the first abstract expressionist exhibition to tour Europe, and also selected the U.S. representations at a number of international exhibitions through the late 1950s and early 1960s. Other important exhibitions include *The New Spanish Paintings and Sculpture, Robert Motherwell, Franz Kline, David Smith, Reuben Nakian, and Modern Sculpture: U.S.A.*, which he codirected with Museum Director René d'Harnoncourt and which toured abroad in 1965–1966. At the time of O'Hara's death he was planning major retrospectives of Jackson Pollock and Willem de Kooning and was poised to take over as museum curator.

Far from a nine-to-five grind, O'Hara's workdays seem to have been filled with endless diversions: unexpected visits from friends, long phone calls, boozy lunch hours, and, often enough, the dashing off of a poem or two. No doubt working at MoMA in such heady days was also a thrill in its own right. But he was able to manage all of these distractions with the help of his exceptional organizational skills. Despite the office setting, there were major advantages to working at a prestigious institution: namely, the promise of regular trips to Europe to oversee the setup of traveling exhibitions and the opportunity to remain *au fait* with the most important developments in contemporary international art. O'Hara traveled to Europe for the first time in 1958, visiting Spain, Germany, Italy, and France, and would return several more times over the years as a MoMA representative. Though later in life, as he ascended the museum's chain of command, his commitments would begin to swamp him, it is safe to say the job suited O'Hara very well indeed and enabled him to live the adult life of his choosing.

MEDITATIONS IN AN EMERGENCY

By the mid-1950s O'Hara was publishing with some regularity in top-notch publications like *Poetry, Partisan Review,* and *Paris Review* and was also placing work in influential smaller organs like *Folder, Angel Hair, Audit,* and *Evergreen Review.* By his thirtieth year he had amassed enough work for a full-length volume many times over, and in 1957 Grove Press brought out his first major poetry collection, *Meditations in an Emergency.* It was a fitting venue for one of America's most challenging and provocative young poetic voices—the innovative American publishing imprint, founded in 1951, had also published Samuel Beckett's *Waiting for Godot* in 1954 and throughout the decade would publish work by other avant-garde writers, including Alain Robbe-Grillet, Jean Genet, Allen Ginsberg, Robert Duncan, William S. Burroughs, and Jack Kerouac. Though O'Hara remained disinterested all his life in the tedious business of corralling his work for publication, or even keeping it reasonably well organized, *Meditations* ended up offering a strong and representative sampling of his achievement to date. The fifty-two-page volume includes thirty poems, four of

which were recycled from *A City Winter* and three that reach as far back as 1950.

The poems tend to focus on the set palette of themes that would continuously preoccupy O'Hara: love, friendship, the city, pop culture, art, the self, and the mutability of all these things. While poems like "To the Harbormaster," "Invincibility," and "Mayakovsky" mine the rich and volatile vein of his love life, others, such as "To the Film Industry in Crisis" and "For James Dean" address the tragicomedy of 1950s Hollywood (O'Hara would write several heartfelt elegies to Dean, who died in a car crash in 1955). Other poems are similarly addressed to friends, including "For Grace, After a Party" and "For Janice and Kenneth to Voyage." The volume gives a fair sense of O'Hara's stylistic versatility: early neo-Surrealist works like "Blocks" and "Les Étiquettes Jaunes" appear alongside impressively finished later work like "Sleeping on the Wing" and "On Seeing Larry Rivers' *Washington Crossing the Delaware* at the Museum of Modern Art." Tying the whole volume together, the title poem dramatizes a kind of push-and-pull conflict between attentiveness/love and distraction/ disaffection that is writ large across O'Hara's oeuvre. Casting himself as shifty and unaffiliated is candid autobiography as much as it is a deliberately constructed persona that O'Hara would continue to explore and exploit throughout his career. Beneath it all is the question of paying attention, which for O'Hara was a matter of artistic life and death. "The slightest loss of attention leads to death" (quoted in Berkson and LeSueur, p. 161), he once remarked of David Smith's sculpture. O'Hara's "aesthetic of attention" (Perloff, p. 1) relates less to intense focus on a single object than on the capacity to take in all that is occurring around one at a given moment. "I am bored," he writes, "but it's my duty to be attentive, I am needed by things as the sky must be above the earth." To be attentive in this manner in the face of boredom, romantic disaffection, or any of life's other nuisances is to experience "the ecstasy of always bursting forth!" (*Collected Poems*, p. 197). Such was O'Hara's mature artistic credo.

MONOGRAPHS AND MANIFESTOS

In 1959 O'Hara published several important prose pieces: "About Zhivago and His Poems" in *Evergreen Review*; "An Interview with Larry Rivers" in *Horizon;* and *Jackson Pollock,* his first significant art monograph. Published by George Braziller in its "Great American Artists" series, the 125-page retrospective celebration of Pollock's life and work (he had died two years earlier in a car crash) was accompanied by more than eighty reproductions, with sixteen in full color. In the eight years remaining to him O'Hara would go on to publish several other art monographs and catalogs, usually in accompaniment with MoMA exhibitions he helped to organize. These include *New Spanish Painting and Sculpture* (1960), *Franz Kline, a Retrospective Exhibition* (1964), *Arshile Gorky Drawings* (1964–1965), *Robert Motherwell* (1965), *Nakian* (1966), and *David Smith* (1966). He also made numerous shorter contributions to the catalogs of other exhibitions, and in 1961 became art editor of the quarterly *Kulchur.*

For his study of Pollock's tempestuous career, O'Hara adopts an unabashedly rhapsodic, at times even mystical tone, singling out for praise his subject's "lyricism of immediate impact and spiritual clarity" (*Art Chronicles,* p. 25). The artist's ultimate goal, he affirms, is the achievement of this harrowing state of clarity, in which his or her every action is transformed into art "through a singleness of purpose" (p. 26). As with other favorite artists, O'Hara explains that Pollock's aesthetic was not predicated on choosing a style and then exploring its possibilities but was rather a daring process of continuous self-discovery. Less an academic appraisal than a deeply informed encomium (O'Hara had rubbed shoulders with Pollock many times at the famous Cedar Tavern and elsewhere), O'Hara's study reveals the intimate terms on which he engaged with Pollock's work. As a testament to this intimacy he takes a moment in the middle of his study to quote the entirety of his poem, "Digression on *Number 1*, 1948," which draws its inspiration from one of Pollock's first "drip paintings." Though the book received mixed reviews in the arts community for its obvious

bias and seeming lack of rigor, *Jackson Pollock* was a popular publication and remains one of O'Hara's most serious aesthetic statements.

And yet, despite O'Hara's deep sympathies for Pollock, it must be said that writing about Pollock's work demanded a kind of self-regarding critical gravitas that now seems rather at odds with the lighter, nimbler approach to art that was O'Hara's métier. While he celebrated the Abstract Expressionists throughout his adult life and was passionately devoted to their art, he did not share their tendency to self-aggrandize (at least without irony) or to think of his art in terms of heroic struggle. Like Larry Rivers, his work was in many ways a kind of early pop art, simultaneously invested in the challenges of making contemporary art and puckishly dedicated to undermining, or rendering banal, the institution of art itself. O'Hara was quite content to use the great gift of his learning and intelligence simply to amuse himself and his friends—in fact, it was his willingness not to take art too seriously, even while devoting his life to it, that really earned O'Hara his reputation for doing something original and exciting. Nowhere is this playful spirit more in evidence than in "Personism," his mock manifesto of 1959.

"Personism: A Manifesto" provides the perfect counterstatement to *Jackson Pollock.* O'Hara dashed off the short document one afternoon in September 1959 at the behest of Donald Allen, who was preparing an anthology, *The New American Poetry, 1945–1960,* and wished to include contributors' statements. Though Allen ultimately decided against publishing "Personism," it would become a defining statement of O'Hara's poetics from the time LeRoi Jones (Amiri Baraka) published it in his journal, *Yūgen,* in 1961. The irony of this outcome would not have been lost on O'Hara, who gave his statement little thought during its composition and probably none at all after Jones printed it. While readers must be careful of taking it too seriously, it manages to capture something of the essential nonchalance and carelessness of O'Hara's art that would charm so many.

In spite of its facetious tone, "Personism" is studded with throwaway comments and observations that are as memorable as anything O'Hara would write. He scores some important points against establishment poets who would force-feed their readers with weighty moral sentiments, and makes some suggestive comments about the difference between abstraction in painting and in poetry, all the while undermining his own argument with references to his imaginary Personism movement. O'Hara claims to have "founded" Personism following a 1959 lunch with Jones, when he returned to his office to write a love poem. His ironic tone suggests that the spirit of Personism would indeed attract numerous adherents from a younger generation who were drawn to its inspired breeziness, relish for documentary detail, and self-teasing wit. Serious or not, it came as a breath of fresh air in the stuffy academic climate of the 1950s poetry scene.

Though a mere page and a half long, "Personism" crams in references to a variety of poets and painters, including Walt Whitman, Hart Crane, William Carlos Williams, John Keats, Stéphane Mallarmé, Wallace Stevens, Pierre-Jean de Béranger, Alain Robbe-Grillet, Jean Dubuffet, Allen Ginsberg, and LeRoi Jones. By the late 1950s Ginsberg, Jones, and O'Hara had become good acquaintances and high-profile figures on the New York literary scene. All three would appear in Allen's *New American Poetry* in 1960, in which O'Hara was given pride of place with fifteen poems, more than any other poet. The anthology also featured other friends of O'Hara such as John Wieners and the Beat poet Gregory Corso, as well as John Ashbery, James Schuyler, Kenneth Koch, and Barbara Guest, the charter members of the "New York School."

The New American Poetry mapped for American readers an exciting and varied postwar countercultural poetic landscape clustered around San Francisco, New York, and Black Mountain College near Asheville, North Carolina. Allen's anthology delineated a new national vanguard and placed O'Hara more or less at the center of it. One of O'Hara's signature works from *The New American Poetry,* "In Memory of My Feelings," dramatizes "the scene of my selves" (p.

257), figured by O'Hara as a congeries of transparent, serpentine entities and impulses.

The New American Poetry also featured the classic "I do this, I do that" poem, "The Day Lady Died." O'Hara himself coined the phrase to lightly poke fun at his tendency to write poems that read like a kind of cinematic documentary of his activities around New York City. This particular work, one of O'Hara's most anthologized, follows the poet around the city as he prepares to leave for an evening dinner trip to Easthampton. He eats lunch, stops by the bank, then a bookstore, then goes on to a liquor store and a tobacconist, where he buys a newspaper with the headline that the singer Billie Holliday has died. This prompts a memory of seeing Lady Day perform at the 5 Spot. "The Day Lady Died" might seem casual, but it is, like O'Hara's finest "I do this" poems, in fact a masterfully orchestrated performance. O'Hara's touch is light and precise, creating an illusion of vertiginous motion with a few quick, deft strokes, while remaining utterly in control.

Along with *The New American Poetry,* the year 1960 saw the publication of several other volumes. Totem/Corinth Press brought out an edition of *Second Avenue,* featuring the ambitious long poem of seven years earlier; Grove Press published a revised version of *Try! Try!,* his early Hopwood play which had since been produced in New York with a set designed by Larry Rivers; and Tiber Press published *Odes,* with five serigraphs by the painter Mike Goldberg (similar volumes by Ashbery, Koch, and Schuyler also appeared in the Tiber imprint). This last volume featured eight of O'Hara's "odes," poems that, aside from their title, seem to bear little resemblance to the classical form. *Odes* includes several major works that had also appeared in *The New American Poetry,* including "Ode to Joy," "Ode to Willem de Kooning," "Ode: Salute to the French Negro Poets," and "Ode to Michael Goldberg ('s Birth and Other Births)."

PLAYS

Beginning at Harvard, O'Hara was in the habit of writing short to medium-length plays, almost always in a neo-Surrealist mode featuring minimal plot development, witty absurdist quips, and lyrical monologues. He would often name characters after friends, movie stars, and famous historical figures, then neglect to differentiate them from each other once the play was under way. Lines and passages from the plays frequently ended up in his poems, and so it seems appropriate to think of O'Hara's playwriting as an extension of his poetic practice. The *Selected Plays* includes twenty-three pieces, some of which are revised versions of the same play. And as Joe LeSueur points out in his introduction to the *Selected Plays,* an unknown number of O'Hara's plays (three for sure) have been lost (pp. xviii–xix).

O'Hara's plays were performed at venues in New York and Boston, including the Poets' Theatre, Living Theater, Writer's Stage Theatre, and Artists' Theatre. Some plays, however, such as *What Century?* and *Awake in Spain,* feature outrageous stage directions and huge ensemble casts and were clearly not meant for the stage. O'Hara tended to favor eclogues and the Japanese Noh—or rather, very loose interpretations of these ancient forms. *Try! Try!* is an early example of the latter and stages the breakup of a married couple in the wake of the husband's return from World War II. The play reimagines the traditional "love triangle" by draining it of the usual conflict and tension. Jack finally accepts that his wife, Violet, has found a new lover, John, and so the play ends on a satirically deflated note.

"The General Returns from One Place to Another," a late play and one of O'Hara's best, premiered in the spring of 1964 and was published in *Art and Literature* in 1965. This thirty-page, twenty-act play takes place on the South Pacific island of Scurvy and features the nonsensical activities and dialogue of a cast of comically flat characters: the bumptious General, his retinue of aides, and Mrs. Forbes, a wealthy lady on tour. Chiang Kai-shek, General Franco, a salesman, and an assortment of "natives" and "citizens" also make cameo appearances. In the first act the General appears onstage almost nude, wearing galoshes and a toupee; with each subsequent scene he adds a new article of clothing or

military decoration until he is fully attired at the play's ending.

In addition to letting him indulge his playful side, drama offered O'Hara a reliable means of collaborating with friends. Collaborative dramatic works include *Kennech Koch, a Tragedy,* with Larry Rivers; *The Coronation Murder-Mystery,* with Ashbery and Koch on the occasion of James Schuyler's thirty-third birthday; *Flight 115; or, Pas de Fumer sur la Piste,* written with Bill Berkson as they flew in a jetliner over the Atlantic Ocean; *Shopping for Joe,* with Larry Rivers' son, Steven, when he was seven or eight; and *Love on the Hoof,* with Frank Lima, as part of a never-completed Andy Warhol film titled *Messy Lives.*

COLLABORATIONS

O'Hara's chosen artistic medium might have been words, but his work always strained to transcend the domain of the literary. Throughout his career, he not only took inspiration from visual art, music, dance, and film and posed frequently for artist friends but also engaged in multimedia collaborative projects with numerous practitioners, including Larry Rivers, Grace Hartigan, Nell Blaine, Franz Kline, Jane Freilicher, Ned Rorem, Michael Goldberg, Mario Schifano, Willem de Kooning, Elaine de Kooning, Norman Bluhm, Jasper Johns, Joe Brainard, and Alfred Leslie.

From 1957 to 1960 O'Hara collaborated with Rivers on a twelve-plate lithograph series, *Stones.* The two would begin a lithograph by deciding on a title, then one of them would make an initial move, the other would respond, and so on, until the surface was filled with text and images. One of the more striking plates in this series features sketch portraits of the French poets Arthur Rimbaud and Paul Verlaine, ornamented by phallic bullets and lurid text:

The end of all existences
is a pint of blood on a
windowsill—

(quoted in Perloff, p. 104)

On a whim in 1960, O'Hara undertook a similar paper-based project, *Poem-Paintings,* with the painter Norman Bluhm. These twenty-six collaborations featured abstract black-and-white drawings by Bluhm and text by O'Hara, most of which was playful, poetic, or satiric and often based on inside jokes and gossip about mutual friends. One poem-painting has "BANG" written in the four corners of the sheet while another has the text "May! am I a pole?" above looping splatters of black paint. Many of the others are similarly cryptic and amusing. O'Hara's later collaborations with the writer and visual artist Joe Brainard, mostly parodies of old western comics and of the Nancy comic strip character, were done in an even lighter, often raunchy vein.

For many years, little attention was paid to O'Hara's collaboration with the painter and filmmaker Alfred Leslie on the short experimental film *The Last Clean Shirt,* perhaps owing to its poor reception at its Lincoln Center premiere in the fall of 1964 and to the subsequent destruction by fire of the film's original materials in 1966 (Leslie managed to restore the film in 1989). But more recently critics have begun to argue for the importance of this late work in O'Hara's oeuvre both as a token of his poetry's debt to film and as a testament to his commitment to radical progressive politics. The film's action is simple enough: a white woman and black man drive around New York City while the woman chatters away (in Finnish, with subtitles). This long single shot is then repeated three times, each time with different subtitles that were all provided by O'Hara. Many of these subtitles come from lines in his poems. As with his collaborations with Rivers, Bluhm, and others, *The Last Clean Shirt* showcases the adaptability of O'Hara's writing to visual media.

THE "BILL BERKSON POEMS"

For O'Hara, the question of writerly collaboration had as much to do with sharing the pen or typewriter (which he did on numerous occasions) as it did with engaging in a kind of experimental agon with writer friends. O'Hara, Koch, and Ashbery collaborated in this way early in their careers by sharing their most recent work with each other in a friendly game of literary one-upmanship.

Perhaps the most concentrated collaborative effort of this sort that O'Hara undertook was with the younger poet Bill Berkson. O'Hara met Berkson, a student of Kenneth Koch's at Columbia, in 1959, and by April 1960 Berkson began to appear in O'Hara's poems. Though they were never romantically involved, O'Hara and Berkson shared an intimate relationship centered on writing poems to each other in forms and styles they invented together. So close was their bond and so extensive their collaborations that Joe LeSueur dubs the years 1960–1962 the "Bill Berkson Period" (p. 233) in his memoir of living with O'Hara.

The friendship with Berkson inaugurated a new period style in O'Hara's career. Brad Gooch distinguishes between the "open style" of O'Hara's love poems to his boyfriend Vincent Warren (written roughly from 1959 to 1961 and discussed below), and the " 'closed style' of his experimental poems of parody, reportage, dialogue, and ventriloquism to, or in collaboration with, Bill Berkson" (p. 362). The latter poems are classified as "closed" in part because they are filled with inside jokes and nods to Berkson that make them more or less recondite to outsiders. Unlike O'Hara's love poems, they are not "open" to anyone who might have experienced similar feelings. These poems tend to be witty and bracingly off-color, but they can also be frustratingly exclusive. They include the "Hymns of St. Bridget," the "FYI" poems (a series of poems modeled as fake office memos), an epistolary fiction titled *Letters of Angelicus and Fidelio Fobb* (O'Hara as the former, Berkson the latter), and the play *Flight 115*.

These collaborations marked a significant departure for O'Hara from the dense surrealism, impressionistic autobiography, and "I do this" styles of his early and middle years toward a more ludic, collage-based, and chatty aesthetic. For some of O'Hara's close acquaintances, Berkson's influence was not seen as entirely salutary. For others, especially among the younger generation of admirers like Ted Berrigan and Ron Padgett who carried forward the disjunctive conversational element of O'Hara's work, they marked an important phase of O'Hara's

achievement. In any event, the period yielded several unmistakable masterpieces, such as "For the Chinese New Year and Bill Berkson" and "Biotherm." O'Hara began the latter on August 26, 1961, and intended it as a present for Berkson's August 30 birthday. But, as with "Ode to Michael Goldberg ('s Birth and Other Births)" and "Second Avenue," he decided to leave the manuscript in the typewriter and tinker with it, finally finishing up five months later on January 23, 1962. The resultant 464-line poem is among the most unclassifiable and demanding O'Hara would ever write, possibly outpacing "Second Avenue" for sheer quirkiness and scope. While critics have diligently unpacked the poem's cultural references and explicated its meaning and form, it continues to bristle fifty years after its composition.

Critics tend to agree that "Biotherm" is a noteworthy poem of the 1960s, even as they disagree about the nature of its achievement. This is partly to do with the difficulty of nailing down its tone. It casts an astonishingly wide referential net (one passage moves from Wallace Stevens to American tourists to W. C. Fields in a mere six lines), but it is also a profoundly frustrated, angry, and vulgar work that vigorously refuses all notions of hierarchy and scale. In his essay " 'Housing the Deliberations': New York, War, and Frank O'Hara," Geoff Ward observes, "In 'Biotherm' judgment has evolved in a new direction, one less interested in depth and selection, but more minded to view art (and everything else) as part of an always mobile tapestry, a depthless montage" (Hampson and Montgomery, p. 22). We have seen something like the cinematic montage technique and spontaneous superficiality of "Biotherm" before in other work by O'Hara; what we have not seen is the poem's restlessness and grim resignation, bordering on defeatism.

The poem's organizing theme is O'Hara's great affection for Berkson, which he celebrates and alludes to throughout. Some of the more direct passages seem to refer to O'Hara's frustrated attempts to seduce Berkson, while others revel in their private time together at parties and other social events. At infrequent intervals, scenes of pastoral calm will emerge, only to be swept

away or ridiculed in subsequent lines. As in so many earlier love poems, this one concludes with the figure of the lover as a storm-tossed ship's captain. The slackened language and truncated lines cannot help suggesting that by this point the poet was truly weather-beaten and not merely posing for effect. "Biotherm" was to be the last major poem O'Hara would write.

LOVE POEMS (TENTATIVE TITLE) AND LUNCH POEMS

As the 1960s progressed, O'Hara wrote fewer and fewer poems as his MoMA duties and social obligations absorbed more and more of his time. And yet the mid-sixties were among his most productive periods in terms of publications. Two new poetry collections, his last, appeared almost simultaneously: *Lunch Poems* (in late 1964) and *Love Poems (Tentative Title)* in 1965. Both had been in the works for many years, delayed only by O'Hara's typical lack of motivation to gather and type up his poems for the publishers.

Love Poems (Tentative Title) contains sixteen poems and was published by the Tibor de Nagy Gallery. The poems were all written between early 1959 and late 1960, during the rise and fall of O'Hara's great love affair with Vincent Warren, a professional dancer twelve years his junior. John Bernard Myers selected the poems from a larger batch and prepared the volume for publication, as he had done for *A City Winter* thirteen years earlier. He also unwittingly selected the title, which was meant to be provisional but which O'Hara ended up liking.

O'Hara's affair with Warren was the most satisfying of his life, and moved him often to the writing of love poems set in a tender, colloquial key. "You Are Gorgeous and I'm Coming," not included in *Love Poems,* forms an acrostic of Warren's name, while other poems, such as "Poem (V (F) W)," play with his initials. When read alongside Bill Berkson poems, these and other memorable Vincent Warren poems, such as "Having a Coke with You" and "Saint," showcase O'Hara's ease in shuttling between dense experimentalism and expressive romanticism.

As early as 1959 Lawrence Ferlinghetti had broached the idea of publishing a volume of O'Hara's work in his City Lights Books series (which had published Ginsberg's *Howl, and Other Poems* in 1956). O'Hara promised him a batch of poems but was soon distracted by other pursuits. The manuscript was finally ready in 1964 and appeared in the spring of 1965. The pocket-size book sported an arresting orange-and-blue jacket and a back-cover blurb penned by O'Hara himself in the manner of his "I do this" poems: "Often this poet, strolling through the noisy splintered glare of a Manhattan noon, has paused at a sample Olivetti to type up thirty or forty lines of ruminations. ..." (*Lunch*). The sleek, handy volume would come to be the defining artifact of O'Hara's career: bold, dashed off, fleeting, and companionable.

Like *Meditations in an Emergency, Lunch Poems* offers a healthy sampling of O'Hara's work from the period 1953–1964—effectively his entire mature career. The two volumes are in many ways companion pieces reflecting the extremes of O'Hara's personality. *Meditations in an Emergency* suggests deep mental absorption and frenzy, while *Lunch Poems* suggests a more casual affair—these poems, it seems to say, are made for leisurely midday consumption, or perhaps they are just "takeaway."

In keeping with the title, several of the poems were written, or are at least staged, during O'Hara's lunch break. The "I do this" poems collected in *Lunch Poems,* such as "The Day Lady Died," "Personal Poem," and "Adieu to Norman, Bon Jour to Joan and Jean-Paul," have given us the iconic image of O'Hara as urban poet extraordinaire, moving briskly through the city's "luminous humidity" (p. 335) and soaking in its hectic noontime splendor and poignancy. But *Lunch Poems* is also filled with impressionistic tableaux of O'Hara's non-lunchtime activities and whereabouts in New York and abroad: "On the Way to the San Remo" narrates a macabre night stroll to one of O'Hara's favorite bars; "Cambridge" takes a snapshot of a cold and restless O'Hara gazing out his apartment window at a tree and thinking about Boris Pasternak during his one-semester fellowship at the Poets' Theatre

in Cambridge, Massachusetts, in 1956; and "A Little Travel Diary" gives the highlights of a trip around Spain with John Ashbery in 1960. "Lana Turner Has Collapsed!" was infamously composed on the Staten Island Ferry on the way to a 1962 reading with Robert Lowell at Wagner College (Lowell was not amused).

It is difficult to speak about O'Hara's poems after *Lunch Poems,* since what few there are tend to be rather thin achievements (with a few exceptions like "I Love the Way It Goes" and "Fantasy"). In the final years of his life O'Hara's poetic output tapered off sharply. He wrote approximately thirteen poems in 1964, four in 1965, and only two in 1966. His last recorded poem, "Little Elegy for Antonio Machado," was completed on March 27, 1966.

DEATH AND POSTHUMOUS WORKS

In the early hours of July 24, 1966, Frank O'Hara was struck and mortally wounded by a beach taxi on the beach of Fire Island Pines, New York. He was rushed to a local hospital, where he underwent exploratory surgery and was stabilized. Though he was conscious for part of this time and was able to receive some of the visitors who soon began streaming in to show their support (among them Joe LeSueur, Larry Rivers, Willem de Kooning, and Kenneth Koch), he finally succumbed to his injuries at 8:50 p.m. the following day. He was buried on July 28 in the Springs cemetery, near the spot where Jackson Pollock had been laid to rest ten years earlier.

The circumstances of the Fire Island accident were extremely odd (the accident occurred on an otherwise deserted beach; the buggy that hit O'Hara was traveling around fifteen miles an hour) and eyewitnesses' accounts were hazy, so that a mystique has enveloped the event. Speculation that a suicidal O'Hara might have stepped in front of the beach taxi on purpose remains unconvincing; most likely, he died tragically in a senseless and bizarre accident.

Since his death Frank O'Hara's reputation has been consistently on the rise, owing in part to the steady appearance of his collected works in print. In 1967 the Museum of Modern Art published a thirty-poem selection of O'Hara's work titled *In Memory of My Feelings,* edited by Bill Berkson. Four years later, O'Hara's *Collected Poems* appeared in a diligently prepared, 586-page volume edited by Donald Allen and with an introduction by John Ashbery. The *Collected Poems* went on to win the 1972 National Book Award and was followed up by several companion volumes, also edited by Allen, which effectively brought the remainder of O'Hara's surviving poetry into print: *Selected Poems* (1974), *Early Writing* (1977), and *Poems Retrieved* (1977). Much of his prose appeared in 1975 in two volumes, *Art Chronicles 1954–1966* and *Standing Still and Walking in New York,* with a selection of his plays following suit in 1978. O'Hara's three Tibor de Nagy collections were published in a single volume in 2006, and in 2008 Knopf brought out a new *Selected Poems,* edited and introduced by Mark Ford. His collaborations with Bill Berkson are published in *Hymns of St. Bridget and Other Writings* (2001). *Meditations in an Emergency* was reissued by Grove Press in 1967 and remains in print; *Lunch Poems* has never been out of print.

Though early reviewers and critics often typified O'Hara's work as frivolous, flighty, or otherwise superficial (in thinly veiled dismissive allusions to the poet's homosexuality), O'Hara has since the mid-1970s earned a central place of respect within the academic poetry establishment, thanks in large part to the efforts of his many poet and artist friends and to pioneering work by critics like Marjorie Perloff and Charles Altieri. The years since Brad Gooch published the first and only biography of O'Hara in 1993 have brought a new surge of interest in him, with his life and work increasingly conspicuous in articles, essay collections, and monographs. Additionally, O'Hara's work has begun to secure an international audience, with an essay collection on his work published by a British press in 2010 and the first French translations of *Lunch Poems* and *Meditations in an Emergency* appearing, respectively, in 2010 and 2011.

Among fellow artists and poets, O'Hara's importance was recognized in his lifetime and

has never waned. Toward the end of his life he acquired numerous followers and protégés, some of whom would go on to loosely form a second-generation "New York School." The poets Ted Berrigan, Ron Padgett, Frank Lima, Gerard Malanga, Anne Waldman, Tony Towle, and Alice Notley, to name a very few, all carried forward aspects of O'Hara's unique spirit in their own work. His poetics were also foundational for the experimental Language poetry collective of the 1970s and 1980s, whose members were attentive to his foregrounding of the materiality of his texts and to his dispersal of the traditional lyric speaking voice. In subsequent decades, O'Hara's influence has steadily increased among practitioners across the poetic spectrum, from major gay poets like Mark Doty and D. A. Powell to the loose cadre of so-called post avant-garde poets who have followed in the experimental wake of the Language movement and have staged "the scene of their selves" with an intimate, kaleidoscopic lyricism often redolent of O'Hara at his most memorable.

Selected Bibliography

WORKS OF FRANK O'HARA

POETRY

A City Winter and Other Poems. With two drawings by Larry Rivers. New York: Tibor de Nagy Gallery Editions, 1952. (Limited edition of 280.) Reprinted in *Frank O'Hara: Poems from the Tibor de Nagy Editions 1952–1966.*

Oranges: 12 Pastorals. Cover drawings by Grace Hartigan. New York: Tibor de Nagy Gallery Editions, 1953. (Limited edition of 75.) Reprinted, New York: Angel Hair Books, 1969, and in *Frank O'Hara: Poems from the Tibor de Nagy Editions 1952–1966.*

Meditations in an Emergency. New York: Grove Press, 1957; 2nd ed., 1967.

Second Avenue. Cover drawing by Larry Rivers. New York: Totem Press in Association with Corinth Books, 1960.

Odes. Prints by Michael Goldberg. New York: Tiber Press, 1960.

Lunch Poems. San Francisco, Calif.: City Lights Books, Pocket Poets Series No. 19, 1964.

Love Poems (Tentative Title). New York: Tibor de Nagy Gallery Editions, 1965. (Limited edition of 500.) Reprinted in *Frank O'Hara: Poems from the Tibor de Nagy Editions 1952–1966.*

COLLECTIONS AND ANTHOLOGIES

The New American Poetry, 1945–1960. Edited by Donald Allen. New York: Grove Press, 1960. (Landmark anthology containing fifteen O'Hara poems.)

In Memory of My Feelings: A Selection of Poems. Edited by Bill Berkson. New York: Museum of Modern Art, 1967. (Contains thirty O'Hara poems, each accompanied by an illustration by a different artist.)

The Collected Poems of Frank O'Hara. Edited by Donald Allen with an introduction by John Ashbery. New York: Knopf, 1971. First paperback printing, Berkeley: University of California Press, 1995. (Contains a prose supplement including "Personism: A Manifesto," "About Zhivago and His Poems," "Notes on Second Avenue," and other essays.)

The Selected Poems of Frank O'Hara. Edited by Donald Allen. New York: Knopf, 1974. Paperback edition, 1999.

Poems Retrieved. Edited by Donald Allen. Bolinas, Calif.: Grey Fox Press, 1977.

Frank O'Hara: Poems from the Tibor de Nagy Editions 1952–1966. New York: Tibor de Nagy Editions, 2006.

Selected Poems. Edited by Mark Ford. New York: Knopf, 2008.

CRITICISM, ESSAYS, AND ART WRITINGS

Art Chronicles, 1954–1966. New York: G. Braziller, 1975. Revised paperback edition, 1990. (Contains all major exhibition monographs, including *Jackson Pollock, New Spanish Painting and Sculpture, Robert Motherwell,* and *Nakian.*)

Standing Still and Walking in New York. Edited by Donald Allen. Bolinas, Calif.: Grey Fox Press, 1975. (Contains miscellaneous writings on the literature, fine art, and music, and a 1965 interview with Edward Lucie-Smith).

OTHER WORKS

Early Writing. Edited by Donald Allen. Bolinas, Calif.: Grey Fox Press, 1977. (Contains the travelogue *Lament and Chastisement.*)

Selected Plays. Edited by Ron Padgett, Joan Simon, and Anne Waldman. New York: Full Court Press, 1978.

PAPERS

The Donald Allen Collection at the Mandeville Special Collections Library, University of California, San Diego, contains a vast selection of O'Hara materials. The Dodd Center, University of Connecticut, Storrs, features the Allen Collection of Frank O'Hara letters. Other important

archives include the Museum of Modern Art, the Frank O'Hara Estate, the Harry Ransom Center at the University of Texas at Austin, and the New York Public Library.

CRITICAL AND BIOGRAPHICAL STUDIES

Altieri, Charles. "The Significance of Frank O'Hara." *Iowa Review* 4, no. 1:90–104 (winter 1973).

Berkson, Bill, and Joe LeSueur, eds. *Homage to Frank O'Hara.* Cover by Jane Freilicher. Rev. ed., Berkeley: Creative Arts Book Company, 1980.

Diggory, Terence, and Stephen Paul Miller, eds. *The Scene of My Selves: New Work on New York School Poets.* Orono, Maine: National Poetry Foundation, 2001.

Glavey, Brian. "Frank O'Hara Nude with Boots: Queer Ekphrasis and the Statuesque Poet." *American Literature* 79, no. 4:781–806 (December 2007).

Gooch, Brad. *City Poet: The Life and Times of Frank O'Hara.* New York: Knopf, 1993.

Hampson, Robert, and Will Montgomery, eds. *Frank O'Hara Now: New Essays on the New York Poet.* Liverpool, U.K.: Liverpool University Press, 2010.

Lehman, David. *The Last Avant-Garde: The Making of the New York School of Poets.* New York: Doubleday, 1998.

LeSueur, Joe. *Digressions on Some Poems by Frank O'Hara.* New York: Farrar, Straus and Giroux, 2003.

Moramarco, Fred. "John Ashbery and Frank O'Hara: The Painterly Poets." *Journal of Modern Literature* 5, no. 3: 436–462 (September 1976).

Perloff, Marjorie. *Frank O'Hara: Poet Among Painters.* New York: G. Braziller, 1977.

Shaw, Lytle. *Frank O'Hara: The Poetics of Coterie.* Iowa City: University of Iowa Press, 2006.

Silverberg, Mark. *The New York School Poets and the Neo-Avant-Garde: Between Radical Art and Radical Chic.* Farnham, U.K.: Ashgate, 2010.

Smith, Alexander, Jr. *Frank O'Hara: A Comprehensive Bibliography.* New York: Garland, 1979; 2nd printing corrected, 1980.

Sweet, David L. "Parodic Nostalgia for Aesthetic Machismo: Frank O'Hara and Jackson Pollock." *Journal of Modern Literature* 23, nos. 3–4:375–391 (summer 2000).

Ward, Geoff. *Statues of Liberty: The New York School of Poets.* London: Palgrave, 2001.

JANE JOHNSTON SCHOOLCRAFT

(1800—1842)

Cheri Johnson

NAMED JANE BY her Scottish-Irish father and Bamewawagezhikaquay (Woman of the Sound the Stars Make Rushing Through the Sky) by her Ojibwe mother, Jane Johnston Schoolcraft is often credited as being one of the first known American Indian literary writers. Writing from the Upper Peninsula of Michigan Territory in the first half of the nineteenth century, Schoolcraft, fluent in Ojibwe and English, wrote poems in both languages as well as her own versions of traditional Ojibwe stories and fables. She also transcribed and translated tales by individual Ojibwe oral storytellers as well as songs, letters, and speeches into English. Her stories were a key source for Henry Wadsworth Longfellow's *The Song of Hiawatha* (1855), though Longfellow did not credit her for her work. Growing up in the largely French-speaking métis culture of Sault Sainte Marie, Jane Schoolcraft also knew some French and wrote at least one piece of nonfiction prose in that language.

The literary legacy of Schoolcraft has been difficult to trace, as she did not seek publication of her work, aside from several pieces of poetry and prose she contributed to a handwritten magazine, *The Muzzeniegun or Literary Voyager,* written and circulated to friends by her husband, the early anthropologist and folklorist Henry Rowe Schoolcraft, when Jane was in her mid-twenties. The remaining body of her work lies in unorganized, often unsigned papers, journals, letters, and a bound manuscript of her poems compiled and most likely revised by Henry after her death, as well as in Henry's books on American Indian culture, legends, and customs, in which he sometimes attributes particular verses and stories to individual authors—including his wife—but just as often does not. Complicating matters further, Jane Schoolcraft often copied out the poems of others without attributing them, as others did of hers, and the names with which she sometimes signed pieces for the *Muzzeniegun*—"Rosa" and "Leelinau"—at times seem to be her own pen names, at others poetic personas, and at still others pseudonyms for the Ojibwe individuals whose words she transcribed and translated.

All of these issues have contributed to the confusion and scant attention Jane Schoolcraft's work has attracted since her death. In the late decades of the twentieth century, anthologies of women's and American Indian writing began to include Schoolcraft's tales and poems. But it was not until 2007, when Robert Dale Parker (professor of English at the University of Illinois, Urbana-Champaign) published *The Sound the Stars Make Rushing Through the Sky: The Writings of Jane Johnston Schoolcraft* that a collected volume of Schoolcraft's known works even existed. Many of the pieces Parker includes had never been printed before, and one of the pieces that has been most widely anthologized, "The Otagamiad," Parker argues convincingly was likely not written by Jane at all but by her husband Henry (p. 258). Parker's literary biography draws from primary sources that include letters by Jane, to her, and about her (in her lifetime or shortly after her death), her handwritten manuscripts and journals, and published books by Henry and by friends of the Schoolcrafts, as well as the journals of fur traders and explorers (documentation of the cultural and historical milieu in which Jane lived and wrote). Further, he offers a heavily annotated collection of her works wherein he explains the meticulous process, for each piece he includes, by which he

determined that it ought to be attributed to Jane Schoolcraft. A study of Schoolcraft's works as compiled by Parker reveals, in both her English and Ojibwe poetry—although the two bodies of work do differ in significant ways—a prevailing sense of melancholy and anxiousness; an expression of Christian piety and faith; and a deep appreciation and need for the solace of nature, in particular the wild landscape of Michigan's Upper Peninsula. Her prose tales in English often feature children who are left to fend for themselves owing to the death, abandonment, or poor judgment of their parents, and her translations of Ojibwe songs, the free-verse style of which contrasts greatly with the rhymed-and-metered style of most of her poems, are concerned primarily with the theme of love.

LIFE

Born in 1800, the third child of eight, Jane Johnston Schoolcraft, née Jane Johnston, was part of a family notable for its extensive contributions to the written record of its time, as well as for the influence its individual members wielded over the many quickly shifting national, racial, and political spheres of which they were a part. A central family in the Ojibwe-English-French métis culture of Sault Sainte Marie, Jane's parents, John Johnston and Ozhaguscodaywayquay (John called her "Susan"), Jane, and her brothers and sisters participated directly in many of the defining historical moments of that time and place, as Ojibwes and other native peoples negotiated and fought with various white colonialists over the use of their land and Michigan Territory moved from British to American control. John Johnston, who identified as British rather than American throughout his life, even after power changed hands, joined British forces in the War of 1812 battles that occurred on Mackinac Island, alongside his son Lewis; Ozhaguscodaywayquay, with her son Kahmentayha (George), mediated a bloodless resolution to a conflict between Ojibwes and the American governor Lewis Cass; and George, later hired as an agent by the Americans, worked to broker a peaceful boundary between the Ojibwes and their longtime enemies the Sioux.

Like Jane, other members of her family were also active in the growing cultural exchanges of the day. George translated a book of Episcopal hymns into Ojibwe and Ottowa, and several of Jane's brothers and sisters contributed to Henry's collections of American Indian materials and wrote their own poems and songs in English and in native languages. John Johnston also wrote poetry, and much is made, in the journals and memoirs written by the numerous travelers the family hosted during Jane's childhood, of the extent and quality of Johnston's library of English classics and history.

Using this library, John Johnston provided for Jane's education in English (she was especially fond of Shakespeare, though also of the contemporary British moralist and poet Hannah Moore), while her mother, who chose not to speak English, and other Ojibwe family members, most notably her mother's half-brother Waishkey, taught her Ojibwe stories, tradition, and culture. When she was nine, Jane's father took her to Ireland in hopes that his sister would provide a European education for her, but Jane suffered such homesickness and longing for her mother that her father came to bring her home after less than a year (Parker, pp. 15–16). According to Parker, there is no record that Jane had any formal schooling in Ireland or anywhere; despite this fact, many contemporary accounts of her life, following Henry's most likely inflated reference to her Irish education, alongside descriptions of her refined manners and tastes (Henry Schoolcraft, *Personal Memoirs,* p. 107), note that she was schooled in Ireland.

John and Ozhaguscodaywayquay's mixed-race marriage was one of many in Michigan Territory, and, like many of these marriages, it brought together an influential Ojibwe woman from a respected family with an ambitious young man in the fur trade. Born in the north of Ireland in 1762, John Johnston had sought his fortune in 1790 in the United States and Canada as a fur trader, and in the Chequamegon area (now northern Wisconsin), he asked the esteemed war chief and storyteller Waubojeeg for the hand of Ozhaguscodaywayquay, his youngest daughter. Anna Brownell Jameson, a British art and

Shakespeare critic who wrote about the Johnstons and Schoolcrafts after meeting both of the families, includes a version of this story, told to her by Ozhaguscodaywayquay and Jane, in her memoir *Winter Studies and Summer Rambles in Canada* (1838). Jameson reports that Waubojeeg, unimpressed with the casual way he had seen white men treat marriages to Ojibwe women, often making the matches only for the expanded business opportunities a woman's kinship networks would bring him and many times abandoning the marriage after opportunities dried up, at first denied his permission to Johnston. But when Johnston, after convincing Waubojeeg that he was serious, married Ozhaguscodaywayquay, the unhappy bride (who, it appears, had not had a say in the matter) ran back to her father. Waubojeeg beat her with a stick and dragged her back to Johnston (Jameson, vol. 3, pp. 213–215).

Jane Schoolcraft, at the age of twenty-three, would nevertheless praise her grandfather's legacy in a poem, following in a tradition of fierce family loyalty (George, for example, would later publicly defend his father, John Johnston, concerning his allegiance to Britain). This loyalty, despite the brutal circumstances of the parents' marriage, seems to have been built on a deep and loving familial bond, and surviving accounts, including Jane's, speak to the happiness of the family that grew from the union. Upon moving to Sault Sainte Marie, the couple built a successful business (though weakened by the War of 1812) and a log house that was the biggest in the region. Jane was close with both of her parents and participated in the many activities of a lively household, from learning her mother's techniques for preparing maple sugar to presiding over a table in the European style. At the age of fifteen Jane began to write, or at least to save what she wrote, beginning what would be a lifelong habit of composing poems to mark specific happy or mournful events, as in her 1816 "Language Divine!" which, according to an account by Henry, she wrote in her room while waiting to accompany her mother on a visit to a devastated family who had just received news that one of its children had been lost "in a season of great want and scarcity, North of lake Superior, by the hor-

rible spirit cannabalism [*sic*]" (Henry Schoolcraft, "Dawn," p. 244).

Jane nonetheless loved the wild country that could quickly turn so dangerous, as evidenced by the grateful exuberance of another occasional poem, "To the Pine Tree," written in Ojibwe. Though it was almost certainly written when she was an adult, the poem commemorates Jane's wildly happy return as a child from her first and only unhappy trip to Ireland.

In 1822 Henry Schoolcraft arrived in Sault Sainte Marie. As the first official "Indian agent" working on behalf of the newly arrived American government in Michigan Territory, his main task was to establish American authority there. But in his memoirs he describes the British loyalist John Johnston's warm welcome (*Personal Memoirs*, p. 92), and Henry even stayed with the family for a time, until he established his own quarters. He and Jane soon began a courtship. In his account of the new relationship, Parker includes a note written by Jane to Henry five months before their marriage. In her likening of the two of them to Portia and Bassanio in *The Merchant of Venice*, comparing the three caskets Bassanio must choose between to *moccucks* (birchbark containers) of maple sugar prepared by her mother, Jane expresses both her obvious delight at having found a man with whom she can share clever literary references (Henry was a poet himself), and the way she could move with ease between the two worlds of her parents (Parker, pp. 21–22).

Notes like this one were the first in a rich correspondence between Jane and Henry that would span twenty years, prompted by Henry's long absences as he traveled for his work as an Indian agent and for his own research as an anthropologist and writer. Jane's letters to Henry prompted several of her poems, as she would often break into verse in the middle of a thought or write pithy lines in the margins; in the poem "My Ear-Rings," for instance, she laments the loss of a pair of earrings and hints that she would like another. The letters reveal affection between the couple and their mutual interest in each other's creative work, though also a growing loneliness and even resentment on Jane's part for

Henry so often being away. They also reveal attitudes on Henry's part that must have had a strange and conflicting effect on the bilingual, mixed-race Jane, although, for the most part—not entirely—she does not express such thoughts in her letters and creative work. Largely Jane seems to identify as white, and to aspire to a European model of upper-class social status that was also so precious to the ambitious Henry. Still, it is impossible to imagine that it did not give her pause when Henry, in a letter to Jane when she was thirty, describing Jane's childhood "disadvantages," speaks of her having lacked any society to form her and even of her lack of a mother to direct her (Parker, p. 38), despite Ozhaguscodaywayquay's constant, loving, and richly pedagogical presence in Jane's young—and adult—life. At other times Henry speaks fondly and even with a certain kind of respect for Ozhaguscodaywayquay and other native individuals; but it is his condescension, his expressed pity and desire to "save" the amusing cultural artifacts of a race he saw as dying, his enthusiasm for political figures like Andrew Jackson (champion of Indian removal), and his own checkered dealings with native peoples that stand out most prominently in the record of his life that he himself wrote.

In 1823 Jane married Henry. Her parents built a new wing onto their house for the couple, and within a year they had a son, William Henry. Along with Henry's solo trips, the two traveled together to Detroit and to New York—where, Henry reports, many intellectuals and literary types were abuzz over the charming Mrs. Schoolcraft, exoticizing her Ojibwe ancestry and calling her "the northern Pocahontas" (*Personal Memoirs,* pp. 207–208). In the winter of 1826–1827 Jane contributed poems and Ojibwe tales to Henry's *The Muzzeniegun or Literary Voyager* (*muzzeniegun* is Ojibwe for "book").

That same winter, however, William Henry grew sick in one day and died. The toddler's death came on the heels of a stillborn child the previous November, and Jane did not ever quite recover. She wrote at least five poems about William Henry's death, including "To my ever beloved & lamented son William Henry," a poem that circulated widely among her family and friends and drew an offer (which she declined) of possible publication in the *Detroit Gazette* from family friend C. C. Trowbridge (Parker, p. 35). The raw grief and longing to see her son again that in this, one of her earliest poems on the subject, waver on the edge of her own death wish ("But soon my spirit will be free, / And I, my lovely Son shall see") seem no less sharp or desperate in "Sweet Willy," written eight years later: "I cling no more to life below, / It hath no charm for me" (pp. 136, 139).

As Henry continued to travel, Jane managed the household, now at Mackinac Island, about thirty miles from her birthplace of Sault Sainte Marie. She continued to write, had two more children, Janee and Johnston, and, despite her grief and professed loneliness, impressed her visitors as a charming and cheerful host. In *Winter Studies and Summer Rambles,* one of the most valuably detailed sources about Jane and her mother, Anna Jameson tells of staying with Jane Schoolcraft at Mackinac. When Jameson was offered a spur-of-the-moment passage to Sault Sainte Marie, Jane, eager for the chance to see her mother and other Ojibwe relations, decided in the moment to pack up her children and accompany Jameson on the ninety-four-mile water journey that took two days and two nights, in a boat rowed by five voyageurs. In her description of the second night of their voyage, Jameson offers an evocative image of Jane Schoolcraft and the landscape in which she lived: Jane in the small, rocking boat bending over her sleeping children, waving away mosquitoes and singing in a low voice a sad Ojibwe song, as clouds gather and northern lights stream across the sky. Likewise illuminating is Jameson's picture, when the travelers finally arrive at Sault Sainte Marie, of Ozhaguscodaywayquay, whom she calls warm, intelligent, and benevolent, with an easy manner, and with whom Jameson speaks to through Jane, who looks greatly animated and happy (*Winter Studies,* vol. 3, p. 169).

In 1828 Jane's father died, and in her thirties, the melancholy and loneliness that touched her letters and poems deepened; references abound in letters to, from, and about her to her being

unwell, nervous, and weak. Doctors prescribed laudanum, to which she became addicted. In her later years she wrote considerably less and sometimes secluded herself from company. In 1839 Jane received two more big blows. Henry insisted—and Jane eventually capitulated, despite her deep aversion to the idea, for both her own and her children's sake—that Johnston, age nine, and Janee, eleven, be sent to East Coast boarding schools. Jane wrote one of her last poems, "On leaving my children John and Jane at School, in the Atlantic states, and preparing to return to the interior," to mark the sad occasion. She wrote the poem in Ojibwe, the language she generally used with her children. Soon after, Henry was dismissed from his job as agent for the American government in connection to corruption charges. The couple relocated to New York City, where they struggled with Jane's homesickness, Henry's joblessness, and the blow to their pride that Henry's disgrace had brought them. In the early forties Henry made a trip to Europe in order to promote his newly published *Algic Researches*. Jane decided to visit her sister Charlotte in Canada, rather than accompany him, and on May 22, 1842, Charlotte discovered that Jane had died suddenly while sitting in a chair.

AUTHORSHIP AND ATTRIBUTION

Robert Parker, in *The Sound the Stars Make Rushing Through the Sky,* explores the issue of what it means to talk about the life and works of a writer who may not have thought of herself as one. Jane chose not to pursue publication when it does not appear that the means to do so were inaccessible to her, and when other people she was close to, male and female (Henry and Anna Jameson), white and métis (George—although only after Jane's death), were publishing their own work. What constitutes such a writer's works and legacy? When a writer's published works are established, previous drafts and notes, if printed as part of a literary study, are understood and treated as such; but what happens when handwritten copies, revisions, and notes are all a literary scholar has?

In his appendix "Sources and Editorial Procedures," Parker highlights several of the fac-

tors that affect how readers can understand the authorship of Jane Johnston Schoolcraft, including the condition of the handwritten manuscripts in which her work is found, her uncertain intentions for individual works, and the editorial hand of her husband, Henry. Parker, who in the course of researching his book pored over handwritten manuscripts and collections of letters in libraries across the country, reports that tears and ink smears mark some of the pages, making some word choices difficult, even impossible to determine. Often several versions of a specific work exist in the handwriting of multiple people, and sometimes there is no way to determine which one came first or last: Jane's, Henry's, or that of an unknown copyist; or Henry's or her brother William's, with an attribution to Jane. Which copy is the "right" one, when two or three versions differ, and what does it mean for a copy to be "right"? Parker warns against an automatic instinct to prefer any manuscript in Jane's hand over one in someone else's, as she often expressed the wish for others' suggestions and changes, as in the note with which she accompanied a manuscript she gave to Henry for one of his books, asking him to correct whatever he thought could be changed for the better (Parker, p. 231).

Henry often did more than correct small errors, as changes on her manuscripts can attest, whether with Jane's knowledge or permission or not it is not always clear. Many of his changes are likely now invisible, as in the manuscript of her poems he prepared after her death; Henry concludes his introduction to the poems with the statement that the poems "have been selected, ad libitum, from her portfolio, and received a careful and critical revision" (Henry Schoolcraft, "An Introduction," p. 238).

Judging from her letters and notes, Jane saw her husband as a literary collaborator and trusted editor, not a paternalistic colonialist or thief; and yet modern readers might find, in a comparison of Henry's admittedly "free" translation of one of Jane's poems written in Ojibwe (Henry learned Ojibwe upon moving to Michigan Territory) to a literal translation Parker includes alongside the Ojibwe original, a sense of vindication and relief.

Included here are, firstly, Jane's first stanza in Ojibwe of her poem "On leaving my children John and Jane at School"; followed by the first stanza of Henry's translation, and finally the newly translated stanza by Dennis Jones, Heidi Stark, and James Vukelich:

Nyau nin de nain dum
May kow e yaun in
Ain dah nuk ki yaun
Waus sa wa kom eg
Ain dah nuk ki yaun

Ah! when thought reverts to my country so dear,
My heart fills with pleasure, and throbs with a fear:
My country, my country, my own native land,
So lovely in aspect, in features so grand,
Far, far in the West. What are cities to me,
Oh! land of my mother, compared unto thee?

As I am thinking
When I find you
My land
Far in the west
My land

(Parker, pp. 141–142)

Even with Henry's acknowledgment that his translation is "free," his flowery embellishments in the popular style of the day stand in remarkable contrast to the stark, stunned, almost wraith-like quality Jane chose for this particular poem. And the difference is not simply an issue of the nature of the language dictating a particular tone; in "To the Pine Tree," another of Jane's poems in Ojibwe, her speaker speaks ebulliently: "Shing wauk! Shing wauk!"—"The pine! The pine!" (p. 89). Though Jane often wrote her own English poetry in a similarly rhymed-and-metered, romantic style, and perhaps this fact led to Henry's version of "On leaving my children," which he might have imagined Jane would like, his drastic revision of what she actually wrote here speaks to the lengths to which he might have felt privileged and qualified to go when it came to "improving" Jane's work, before and after her death.

Another complicating factor in discussing the work of Jane Johnston Schoolcraft involves her use of the pen names "Rosa" and "Leelinau." At times her use of the names to sign her work feels straightforward enough, as in her poems "Resignation," "Absence," and "Lines to a Friend Asleep," which point clearly to people and experiences in Jane's life; she is using the names as pseudonyms that represent herself, as she used "Leelinau" sometimes to sign letters. But her use of the name "Leelinau" in particular becomes more enigmatic when she uses it to sign "Character of Aboriginal Historical Tradition," a prose piece published as a letter to the editor in the *Muzzeniegun*. The narrator of the piece, a young Ojibwe woman or girl—her age is not quite clear, though she refers to herself as an orphan—speaks of her hope that she will be able, over the course of submitting this and future pieces to the magazine, to illuminate for the editor what Ojibwes think and feel, and to share songs and stories passed on to her by her mother. Her tone is one of, as Parker notes, "self-colonizing abasement" (p. 219), and she speaks at length of the greater knowledge, spirituality, and methods of recording history of whites, who have come to instruct "us poor Indians" (p. 218).

In his introduction to the letter in the magazine, Henry Schoolcraft conflates the narrator with Jane—a move that, Parker asserts, has caused confusion because the narrator is actually a distant relative of Jane's, whose letter Jane transcribed and translated (p. 219). But Parker is not clear about how he comes to this conclusion, apart from his reference to the first paragraph of the letter, in which the narrator describes herself as a relation of a correspondent of the magazine. Several factors, including the content of the letter, with its almost over-the-top kowtowing to whites, the signature, Henry's introduction, and the fact that some of Jane's pieces were passed on to her by her own mother, might provoke another possibility: that this letter is a playful, even satirical persona piece in which Jane blended an imagined character with herself, and that her use of "Leelinau" to sign works and letters could have been a sly and perhaps—even unconsciously—very serious way of making a poetic claim to her own identification as Ojibwe.

To claim that this is so would require evidence that does not exist, as far as scholars yet

know, because Jane in her regular correspondence often espoused the same sorts of repressive colonial ideas concerning native peoples and their relation to whites and expressed her wish that native peoples would give up their benighted ways. Certainly even if "Character of Aboriginal Historical Tradition" is a persona piece, Jane meant it, at least consciously, to be taken straightforwardly, not satirically, and any such satire would have been completely lost on readers like Henry. And yet it feels equally imprudent to claim absolutely that Jane Schoolcraft—the daughter of a woman whom she respected and admired, who continued until she died to live primarily in traditional Ojibwe ways, who by teaching Jane Ojibwe language and culture taught her also to respect them—could not have produced a piece of literature that critiqued the ideas of colonialism through the cloaks of persona and pseudonym. Nonetheless, it is also possible that Jane only signed her own pen name to a letter she transcribed and translated for someone else because she put so much of her own work into the finished prose, which is quite eloquent and writerly; or, of course, that she signed the work "Leelinau" without thinking much about it, for no great reason at all.

To talk about the work of "Jane Johnston Schoolcraft" is, consequently, often an act of trying to pin down an elusive thing. And yet, all of this being said, thanks to the expansive, intelligent, and sensitive—to issues of culture, gender, and race—work of Robert Dale Parker, a body of work by Jane Johnston Schoolcraft as an author does now exist for literary study. While her work as we read it may be made up of the input and revision of multiple people, and conscious as well as unconscious intention, so too is the work of almost every author.

POETRY IN ENGLISH

Of the thirty-nine poems Jane Schoolcraft is known to have written, thirty-five are in English, excluding "Lines written at Castle Island, Lake Superior," which, according to Henry's notes, she originally wrote in Ojibwe, though only the English translation, written either by Henry or

Jane, survives (Parker, p. 92). As a member of a Christian family—both John Johnston and Ozhaguscodaywayquay were active in the church—Jane's earliest poems, written when she was fifteen and sixteen, speak to her Christian faith, in particular to a theme she would continue to develop in poems she wrote as an adult: a speaker's plea, expressed in an apostrophe to God, Christ, or some other figure, that her heart be opened to God's wisdom and will, followed by the expressed certainty that, this wish being granted, she would be content and happy, insusceptible to melancholy and fear. In "Stanzas, Written in 1815 before going to hear my Father read religious services," the speaker appeals to her "Saviour" (p. 155), while in "On Meditation," composed in the iambic rhyming couplets Jane often preferred, the speaker addresses her plea to a "soft maid" and "faithful friend" not clearly identified, perhaps the moon, mentioned earlier (Parker, p. 147). The speaker asks the figure to teach her to know when reason approves or disapproves of her acts; once she learns this lesson, she looks forward to contentment.

Often, however, a speaker frets over a frail nature that finds it difficult to be as strong as she imagines God wants her to be, as in "Sonnet," which laments the death of Jane's son William Henry, and in which she again refers to reason, here as an ideal state or quality with which she feels her own feelings are at odds. Again, the only balm the speaker can imagine is faith in the Cross. The image of a soul in conflict with itself is echoed even more poignantly and with a more forceful declaration of the validity, or at least the depth, of her own feelings in "Resignation," which offers a sharper picture of a struggling speaker grimly trying to keep herself calm and cheerful. Even as the speaker reminds herself that faith, given enough time, will soothe her soul, she expresses the enormity of what needs soothing: hopes that have been lost forever. The latter reference in particular might be read as self-pity but also as anger or resentment, a cynical indictment on the inadequacy of the very method the speaker claims is the best way to heal.

In other poems, a speaker appeals to nature to help her in a struggle against melancholy, as in "To a Bird, Seen Under My Window in the Garden," which uses one of Schoolcraft's favorite words, "pensive," to describe her speaker's experience of passing time. In "To a Bird," Schoolcraft begs the singing creature, who she knows will soon fly away, to stay and ease her lonely, anxious hours, as she ruminates on fleeting pleasures and happiness. Her poetry is often at its most vivid and energetic when she combines natural images with an urgency to witness them before they are gone, as in "Lines to a Friend Asleep," in which the speaker begs her friend to get up and see the fine morning, or in "By an *Ojibwa Female* Pen: Invitation to sisters to a walk in the Garden, after a shower," in which the alert eye of the speaker delivers a close-up look at that which she has seen, and seen quickly vanish, before: gems of sparkling water just about to dry up. In another poem, "To the Miscodeed," Schoolcraft's description of one of the earliest spring flowers in the northern woods highlights the hope and cheerfulness the flower's appearance inspires after a harrowing winter.

In "Pensive Hours," one of Schoolcraft's longest and most complex poems, many of her concerns and themes come together, and the structure of the poem—forty-four lines unbroken into stanzas—helps to create a great tension and breathlessness, as the speaker experiences a kind of personal and spiritual awakening that reverberates out into the world around her, past and present, natural and supernatural. Sitting in her father's hall while he is away, anxious for his safe return, the speaker waits from sunset until moonrise, until, echoed in the shifting ghostliness of that hour, her own thoughts begin to be consumed with ethereal things. In the sound of "St. Mary's"—the river on which Jane lived in her parents' house, during her childhood and the beginning of her marriage—the speaker begins to hear, in the river's "sweet murmurs," "the murmur of voices we know to be kind, / Or war's silken banners unfurled to the wind" (p. 109), probably a reference to one or all of the conflicts between British, Ojibwe, and American forces that Jane had witnessed at Sault Sainte Marie and

Fort Mackinac. Those lines, followed by the couplet, "Now rising, like shouts of the proud daring foe, / Now falling, like whispers congenial and low" (p. 109) show a marked difference from their corresponding lines in what is most likely an earlier version of the poem:

Like the murmur of far distant voices;
Or like warriors waving their banners,
With shouts of defyance rending the air;
Warning all those who approach to beware.

(p. 114)

In the earlier version, a one-dimensional, almost childlike, image of a battle is delivered in a sing-songy rhyme; but in the revision, Schoolcraft does something more poetically complex, as the first line of her linked set of two couplets, speaking of kind, murmuring voices, is connected thematically to the last, with its reference to congenial whispers, while in the middle of the grouping the battle rages, creating a rising and fading effect in the tone and energy of the contrasting images. The half-rhyme of "kind" and "wind" both highlights a further contrast between these two states—war and peace—and connects them, pointing perhaps to a life lived directly in these two extremes, one of sometimes bloody political strife, the other of a deeply loving domestic happiness.

Schoolcraft wrote this poem when she was only twenty, and while some of the lines merely repeat religious sentiments she probably heard in church—"When he sees that the soul to His will loves to bend" (p. 109)—in other places the speaker digs deeper into a personal spiritual reckoning, as when her meditations on Christian divinity lead her to imagine the love of God through her own tenderness for the smallest natural things: "Since even a leaf cannot wither and die, / Unknown to his care, or unseen by his eye" (p. 109).

Perhaps the most mystical image in the poem occurs when, the speaker having found a peaceful moment after ruminating on God, she is "roused" again, this time by her harp, as the night breeze has blown "enchantingly" across its strings (p. 109). In a note written on the manuscript, the harp referred to is described as an "Eo-

JANE JOHNSTON SCHOOLCRAFT

lian harp," a wooden box with a sounding board, and strings stretched across two bridges; the harp is placed in a window so that the wind can blow across it and make music. Named for Aeolus, the Greek god of winds, the eolian or aeolian harp was a popular image for Romantic poets like Samuel Taylor Coleridge, who wrote "The Eolian Harp" in 1795 and published it in his 1796 collection. It is likely that John Johnston had the collection in his library, and with this image Jane Schoolcraft seems to be both placing herself within that Romantic tradition and referring to a real object from her childhood, as her niece would later write about the eolian harp in the Johnston house (Parker, pp. 111–112). Perhaps the reference also had a special significance for Jane, as the harp relied on nature to make its music, as she did for many of her poems.

The music the speaker hears from the harp is so sweet that at length, she says, she "fanceyed some spirit was touching the strings" (p. 109). Although Schoolcraft returns to Christian imagery a few lines later, this image of a spirit in nature—used also in her poem "As watchful spirits in the night"—seems more closely aligned with the pantheistic array of natural and animal spirits in Ojibwe spiritual tradition.

The speaker's devotion and love for her father, in "Pensive Hours," is echoed playfully in a witty note in verse Jane Schoolcraft wrote to John Johnston, in response to his own poem inviting guests to a whist party in 1827. Jane's response reveals a sweet, easy relationship with her father, as well as a bold and blazing wit, undiluted by the self-consciousness and self-reprobation that fill so many of her "real" poems:

A warm welcome doubt me? Let the coward who
  dares
Miscall his attentions:—by the white of his hairs
He shall fight at ten paces—I'll give him the fires,
And I'll part with my life's blood or he with his ires.

(p. 130)

In addition to her use of caesuras and enjambed lines to enliven the rhythm that in some of Schoolcraft's rhymed and metered poems can feel monotonous or juvenile, these lines sparkle

with alliteration—"warm," "welcome," "coward"—that adds greatly to the spirit and sound of the poem.

But Schoolcraft's work would soon return to melancholy, as three weeks later brought the death of William Henry and her series of poems about the event, beginning with her quiet "Elegy" and her more stridently mournful "To my ever beloved and lamented Son William Henry," in which the alternating refrains of "Sweet Willy" and "My Willy" follow the form of Ann Taylor's 1804 "My Mother" (Parker, p. 136). Written eight years later, "Sweet Willy," like "Pensive Hours," combines Christian imagery with traditional Ojibwe language, which is used to describe the time that has passed since William's death: "A hundred moons and more" (p. 138). In these poems Schoolcraft expresses a romantic view of childhood as a time of innocence, guilelessness, and bliss, a view that also finds its way into the poems that speak to her longing for and resentment toward the absent Henry. In "Absence," a poem cycle or poem broken up into four different parts, each part or poem written in English but titled in Ojibwe, the speaker passes the time while her lover is away by roaming the forest and gazing upon her angelic son, while in "The Contrast, a Splenetic Effusion," written when Jane was twenty-three, the year she was married, the speaker talks wistfully of her own simple and blissful childhood. Following a description of the sweetness and easiness with which the speaker interacted with friends as a young girl, Schoolcraft describes an adult relationship between lovers in which the speaker's lover is warm and loving, even worshipful, of her one minute and cold and indifferent the next.

In another version of "The Contrast," probably a revision, Schoolcraft removes the direct references to the speaker's relationship with her lover but expands the scope of the poem to include political references, setting up the "contrast" of the title as one between "days of homebred ease, / When many a rural care could please" to a time in which "The world hath sent its votaries here" (p. 118). Schoolcraft's references to the trappings of colonialism—razed trees, courts, and gold mining, as well as

"fashion's gaze"—are contrasted not only with forests and "the cot the simple Indian loved" but with the books, concerts, and quiet visits with travelers she enjoyed as a child in the house of her father, whom, despite his involvement with the British fur trade, she associates with a tranquil time before colonial invasion (Parker, pp. 117–118).

In her political version of "The Contrast," Schoolcraft identifies with the landscape and concerns of her Ojibwe homeland and yet keeps her own personal identification with being Ojibwe at an arm's remove. In "Invocation: *To my Maternal Grand-father on hearing his descent from Chippewa ancestors misrepresented*," however, while her style is decidedly epic and European, Schoolcraft's intent is so completely Ojibwe that the fiery, indignant tone with which she delivers its primary concern—to debunk a rumor that Waubojeeg was of Sioux ancestry, not Ojibwe—may have baffled or amused white readers, many of whom most likely lumped all American and Canadian native peoples together, as Schoolcraft herself does in "The Contrast" and in another poem, "On the Doric Rock, Lake Superior." "Invocation" appeared in the *Southern Literary Messenger* (edited famously, though some years earlier, by Jane's near-contemporary Edgar Allan Poe) when Henry published it under Jane's name in 1860. In the poem, written as an apostrophe to Waubojeeg, Schoolcraft also defends her grandfather's reputation as a warrior against slanderers in the Ojibwe world, directly taking up her position as his grandchild in order to record for prosperity her Ojibwe family's version of the chief's bravery and valor in battle.

POEMS IN OJIBWE

Of Jane Schoolcraft's four known poems in Ojibwe, "A Psalm, or Supplication for mercy, and confession of Sin, addressed to the Author of Life, in the Odjibway-Algonquin tongue" is the only one closely aligned with the Christian themes so prevalent in her English poetry. The remaining three—"To the Pine Tree," "Lines written at Castle Island, Lake Superior," and "On leaving my children John and Jane at School, in

the Atlantic states, and preparing to return to the interior"—do not seem to make use of Christian imagery or themes, although Henry Schoolcraft, in his free translation of "On leaving my children," added a Christian reference to the last line of the poem (Parker, p. 142).

"A Psalm," written in a first-person plural voice, in a liturgical style, addresses God and Jesus Christ in an expression of Christian belief and a plea for mercy. The spirit of self-blame in several of Schoolcraft's poems in English is particularly acute here, in her use of the harsh words "evil," "bad," and "perverted" (p. 152) to describe the speakers' thoughts and actions (although it should be noted that it is not clear who made the existing translation, which Henry included, with an introduction to the text, in his book *Oneóta; or, The Red Race of America*; a new translation is not yet available). The poem also makes special mention of God's acts of creation—the sun, moon, and stars but also the rain, thunder, hail, and snow—perhaps a pointed replacement of the Ojibwe tradition's mythical explanations for the origin of animals and other elements in nature with the biblical creation myth.

The joyous "To the Pine Tree on first seeing it on returning from Europe," a very different sort of poem, was written, according to Henry, at his own request, after Jane Schoolcraft told him about her happy return from Ireland and he asked her to write a poem that captured those feelings. According to the story Henry told Anna Jameson, Jane, upon first seeing a pine tree on the ride home, cried out, proclaiming that after all she had seen in Europe, there was nothing so lovely as that (Parker, p. 90). The poem celebrates the speaker's cherished native land and the evergreen tree that greets her like a friend. The English translation of this poem, probably by Henry, is not, according to Parker, a literal translation, nor does it follow the rhyme scheme of the original, which is more irregular than the English version's *ababcc* pattern of lines in iambic tetrameter (p. 90).

There is no Ojibwe version available of "Lines written at Castle Island, Lake Superior," which, according to Henry, is also his free translation of the original. Jane wrote the poem

on a trip with her husband and children to an isolated island on the lake, a trip taken in hopes that it would refresh and restore her health (Henry Schoolcraft, "Dawn," p. 252). In the second line of the poem, the speaker describes her trip as a flight from pain and sickness, and we discover that she is transported to raptures by her "native inland sea" (Parker, p. 92), though its isolation and natural beauty also serve as poignant reminders of the elements of society that trouble her regular life. She begs the natural world to reign here always, far from society, with its fears, crimes, misery, and pride. Here, she finishes, there are "no laws to treat my people ill" (p. 92). In this last line, Jane Schoolcraft makes what is perhaps her most direct identification with being Ojibwe and also her most pointed critique of Ojibwes' unjust treatment under self-interested colonial laws. The ways in which this poem is unique in her body of work, as well as the extremes of conflicted feeling in the poem and the fact that so much is at stake for this speaker, make the loss of the Ojibwe original of "Lines written at Castle Island" one of the deepest lacks in the legacy of Jane Schoolcraft.

Referring to the new translation by Jones, Stark, and Vukelich mentioned earlier (included in Parker), "On leaving my children John and Jane at School" is quite likely Schoolcraft's most singular poem. Like "To the Pine Tree," it is lightly punctuated, and the stark, simple language, sometimes obscure and enigmatic, in which thoughts often hang unfinished, give the poem an airy quality. And yet the tone is not light but ponderous; unlike many of her melancholy poems in English, in which a frantic spirit both censures her own feelings and strives to scrabble, with plenty of fancy flash and rhyme, out from under her ennui, here the speaker simply expresses, with frequent repetition, what feels to be a possibly inconsolable emptiness and grief. Following are the last two stanzas of the poem, first in Ojibwe and then in English:

She gwau go sha ween
Ba sho waud e we
Nin zhe ka we yea
Ishe ez hau jau yaun
Ain dah nuk ke yaun

Ain dah nuk ke yaun
Nin zhe ke we yea
Ishe ke way aun e
Nyau ne gush kain dum

But soon
It is close however
To my home I shall return
That is the way that I am, my being
My land

My land
To my home I shall return
I begin to make my way home
Ahh but I am sad

(pp. 141–143)

The last keening line in particular seems to have more in common with some of the Ojibwe songs Jane Schoolcraft translated than with her original poems in English.

PROSE TALES AND STORIES

Notes written on or about Jane Schoolcraft's nine prose tales, which retell traditional Ojibwe legends and myths, do not always make clear the exact nature of the role she took in their production—that is, whether she transcribed stories verbatim from individual Ojibwe storytellers, then translated them into English as literally as possible and left them as is, or rewrote her own original versions of the tales she learned as a child in her own literary style. The style of the stories does vary, and Jane often signed them with her pen name "Leelinau," which, as has been said earlier, she may not have used consistently. Some claims by Henry and later editors that particular stories were taken down verbatim from Ojibwe elders, with no literary embellishment, sometimes seem likely, but at other times such claims seem suspect, given certain stylistic choices and the way explanations of Ojibwe traditions are worked into the fabric of some of the stories for the benefit of a non-Ojibwe audience (Parker, p. 165).

Both Henry and Jane Schoolcraft have been accused by scholars of prudishly "cleaning up" traditional Ojibwe stories for English readers, by

removing or euphemizing references in the original versions to sex and bodily functions (Parker, p. 62). In the case of "Moowis, The Indian Coquette," Jane Schoolcraft appears to have translated a reference to excrement as "dirt," and in a later version of the story, which Henry published under his own name in the *Columbian Lady's and Gentleman's Magazine* after Jane's death, he cleaned up the story even further (p. 167).

Still, Jane's stories do not shy away completely from coarse subjects, and, apart from a few instances, she does not sentimentalize or demonize—or condescend to—the Ojibwe characters, or their traditions and values, in the stories she chose to work with, as she does often with the figures (based on herself, her children, her husband, friends, and more abstract categories of people) who appear in her poems. "Moowis" is the straightforward telling of a botched courtship, in which a young man, full of rage and shame over the indignity he suffers at the hands of a young woman when he tries to lie with her, seeks revenge by letting her fall in love with a man he has made of clothes filled with "the dirt of the village" (p. 166)—most likely excrement, by the way other characters talk about its smell—and brought to life. The equally strange and earthy story "The Little Spirit, or Boy-Man: An Odjibwa Tale" features a boy who stops growing as he grows older (in one version of the story, reports Parker, he is described as the first dwarf a particular village had ever known). With special powers of speed and strength, he revenges himself on several very tall men who slight him, by stealing their fish and shooting arrows into their heads.

In her stories Schoolcraft also often explores the complex philosophical and spiritual ramifications of the stories' themes and plots. In "The Origin of the Robin," she begins by explaining an Ojibwe coming-of-age tradition in which an adolescent boy or girl fasts in order to secure a guardian spirit, who will help mold and establish the child's character and thereby shape his or her future prospects. She goes on to tell a father-and-son story that shows how the tradition is corrupted through personal ambition and greed. The

father, eager that his son should be the best in the tribe at whatever the tribe deems matters most, follows the ruthless logic that his son must consequently fast much longer than the successful people he envies. When, on the ninth and eleventh days of the fast, the boy begs to stop, claiming his visions—rightly, as it turns out—show omens of evil, his father will not relent, until, on the twelfth day, he brings food, but too late. The boy is painting his breast with red and, to his father's horror and grief, turning into a robin and flying away. In a speech he makes to himself, the boy reckons with what has happened to him, explaining it as the result of many complicated factors coming together, not only his own and his father's actions but the decision of the guardian spirit he has secured through this corrupted fast, who has turned out to be neither good nor evil and who will neither save nor condemn him:

> My father has ruined me, as a man; he would not listen to my request; he will now be the loser. I shall be forever happy in my new state, for I have been obedient to my parent; he alone will be the sufferer; for the Spirit is a just one, though not propitious to me. He has shown me pity, and now I must go.
>
> (p. 164)

In "Mishösha, or the Magician and his daughters: A Chippewa Tale or Legend" and "The Forsaken Brother: A Chippewa Tale," Schoolcraft again takes up the theme of a character who is left to fend for him or herself when a guardian's longing for society or society's glories weakens family ties and obligations. In both stories—as well as in "Corn story (or the origin of corn)," the story Longfellow used for Book 5, "Hiawatha's Fasting," of *The Song of Hiawatha*—a family lives secluded from others, until an event causes the family to scatter. In "Mishösha" this precipitating event is a wife's adultery, and in "The Forsaken Brother" it is the death of both of the parents in the family. In order to save himself and his brother, the elder of the two abandoned boys in "Mishösha" must outwit an evil sorcerer and convince a series of animals—seagulls, a giant fish, and a flock of eagles—to submit to the superiority of humankind, while the abandoned

boy in "The Forsaken Brother" seeks the protection of wolves, until he eventually turns into one. In both stories, Schoolcraft is clearly on the side of the forsaken children, but she also describes with sensitivity the process by which the grown children in "The Forsaken Brother" struggle with the promise they made to their father to always protect their youngest brother, against their private longings for the company of others, adventure, and marriage.

Schoolcraft's prose style varies from story to story, and sometimes within a story as well. At times her sentences are infused with the romantically high-strung flourishes and sentimental descriptions of nature that abound in her English poems, as in "Origin of the Miscodeed, or the Maid of Taquimenon," while in "Mishösha" she reports even the more dramatic turns of its plot in a tone that is refined, elegantly rhythmic, and restrained. In "The Forsaken Brother," at the moment when the elder brother, out fishing on the lake, hears the cry of a child he discovers to be the brother he abandoned, Schoolcraft includes an incantatory verse in both Ojibwe and English, with which the little brother both describes the transformation that is happening and performs it:

Neesya, neesya, shyegwuh gushuh!
Ween ne myeengunish!
ne myeengunish!
My brother, my brother,
I am now turning into a Wolf!—
I am turning into a Wolf.

(p. 179)

As in "The Origin of the Robin," the boy's last speech as a human—here intermingled with a wolf's howls, until the howls are all that remain—is also a reproach on the family member who broke or corrupted his ties as guardian.

Jane Schoolcraft's work in prose also includes a short profile of the life of her uncle, her mother's half-brother Waishkey, and a paragraph, written in simple French, as if for a child's edification, on the features of the reindeer.

TRANSCRIPTIONS AND TRANSLATIONS

According to Anna Jameson, the poetic "Peboan and Seegwun (Winter and Spring): A Chippewa Allegory" was told by Jane's mother Ozhaguscodaywayquay and transcribed and translated by her daughter (*Winter Studies,* vol. 3, p. 218). According to Parker, it is probably Jane's work, although it could also be her sister Charlotte's (p. 199). The story, in which an old man and his young visitor, wearing a wreath of sweet grass, exchange accounts of their respective powers, ends with the melting of the old figure of winter and the sprouting of the small pink-and-white flower emblematic of very early spring that appears several times in Jane Schoolcraft's body of work.

Schoolcraft also transcribed nine Ojibwe songs and translated them into English, some in verse and some in literal prose translations. Love is a prevalent theme in these songs, praise of one's lover in particular, as in "Song for a Lover Killed in Battle," "My lover is tall and handsome," and "High heav'd my breast," though "The O-jib-way Maid" takes a cynical view of the subject as it related to the young women of Upper Michigan. The song describes with scorn the tears of a young American man who leaves his Ojibwe lover reluctantly, but who will, no doubt, forget her as soon as she is out of sight.

Jane's verse translations of the songs she chose to work with do not closely resemble, in structure or style, either her poems in English or the English translations of her poems in Ojibwe, aside from the new translation Parker includes in his book of "On leaving my children John and Jane at School." She does not attempt to rewrite the songs in her usual romantic, rhymed-and-metered English style, aside from such a version of "Song of the Okogis, or Frog in Spring," which might have been written by Henry or by Jane and Henry together (Parker, p. 215). The rhymed version with its jaunty ending— "Sunshine, and verdure, and gladness, to all!"— contrasts greatly with Jane's free-verse translation of the song. This excerpt captures, through repetition of two key phrases, the fatigued longing generated by an oppressively long, harsh winter, on the small creatures who speak in the poem:

See how the white spirit presses us,—
Presses us,—presses us, heavy and long;
Presses us down to the frost-bitten earth.
Alas! you are heavy, ye spirits so white,
Alas! you are cold—you are cold—you are cold.

(p. 215)

It is easy to see similarities in these songs to "On leaving my children John and Jane at School," not only thematically—as in the song "A mother's lament for the absence of a child"—but stylistically. "On leaving my children," with its spare, unrhymed lines and multiple repetitions, shares a great deal with the ponderous lines of an unnamed song in which Jane uses internal rather than end rhyme to build the rising energy of the last line:

I seek—I seek our fallen relations;
I go to revenge—revenge the slain;
Our relations, fallen and slain.
And to our foes—our foes, they shall lie:
I go—I go, to lay them low—to lay them low!

(p. 207)

Jane's translations of songs are also like "On leaving my children" in that they express their sentiments freely, without the self-censure so prevalent in many of her poems in English.

Her other translations include the speech of a dying man who, traveling with friends to see his birthplace before he died, made it only part of the way; Jane translated his last words, as reported by his friends when they arrived at Saint Mary's.

CONCLUSION

"Jane—," "Mrs. Henry R. Schoolcraft," "Mrs. H. R. Schoolcraft," "Rosa," "Mrs. Jane Schoolcraft," "J. S.," "Leelinau"—the sheer number of different names with which the writer we now call Jane Johnston Schoolcraft signed her unpublished literary work can perhaps tell us something about the way she saw herself as a writer, but what? The multiple names show a playfulness, but also, perhaps, a writer who did not ever quite feel that she found a way to negotiate all of the ways she identified herself—Ojibwe, Scottish-Irish, métis; British, American, Christian; poet, translator, prose writer; single, married, mother, daughter; female, rural, urban—into one all-encompassing literary identity in which she felt completely comfortable publicly expressing and announcing herself.

Serious discussion of Jane Johnston Schoolcraft's work has suffered from offhanded misogynist dismissals of her nervousness and sentimentality by writers such as her husband's biographer Richard Bremer (Parker, p. 35), and equally by portraits that focus solely on an idealized view of Jane's Ojibwe heritage and ignore or downplay her identification with European writers and Christianity. Certainly some of Schoolcraft's work is weakened by anxiousness and hesitation, and certainly, too, her work as a native Ojibwe speaker writing poems in that language and translating traditional stories makes that body of her work exceptionally valuable. But it is in the whole of Jane Johnston Schoolcraft, with her multiple identities, writing from a unique place and time in American history in two American languages—one long established on this soil but newly written down, the other quite the opposite—that we can truly understand the complicated life she lived and the complex legacy she left us.

In the body of Schoolcraft's work we can see the gleams of literary merit that were beginning to flash across the American frontier as families and businesses settled in and established themselves; the development of English as both a Native American language and a Native American literary language; the effects of colonialism on the literary work of native peoples; a style of poetry, originating from poetry and songs written in Ojibwe, that more closely resembles what would become an American free-verse style than did most of the English-language poetry of the day; and countless other changes in a quickly changing country, including a growing taste for fables and folktales, concurrent with the European rage for fairy tales inspired by the publication of such tales by the Brothers Grimm. Jane Johnston Schoolcraft's legacy will no doubt continue to change and grow as more of her manuscripts are found and published and as modern Ojibwe

236

speakers continue to write new translations of her work.

Selected Bibliography

WORKS OF JANE JOHNSTON SCHOOLCRAFT

The Sound the Stars Make Rushing Through the Sky, The Writings of Jane Johnston Schoolcraft. Edited by Robert Dale Parker. Philadelphia: University of Pennsylvania Press, 2007. (Contains all of Schoolcraft's known works; all quotations from her works in the essay are taken from this source.)

POEMS

"To the Pine Tree on first seeing it on returning from Europe," pp. 89–90.

"To the Miscodeed," p. 91.

"Lines written at Castle Island, Lake Superior," p. 92.

"On the Doric Rock, Lake Superior: To a Friend," p. 94.

" 'My humble present is a purse,' " p. 98.

"Invocation: *To my Maternal Grand-father on hearing his descent from Chippewa ancestors misrepresented,*" pp. 99–102.

"To a Bird, Seen Under My Window in the Garden," p. 104.

"Lines to a Friend Asleep," p. 105.

"By an *Ojibwa Female* Pen: Invitation to sisters to a walk in the Garden, after a shower," p. 108.

"Pensive Hours," pp. 109–114.

"The Contrast, a Splenetic Effusion. March, 1823—," pp. 116–118.

"On Henry's Birthday," p. 119.

"Absence ('Nindahwaymau,' 'Neezhicka,' 'Neenawbame,' 'Ningwisis')," pp. 120–122.

" 'Amid the still retreat of Elmwood's shade,' " p. 124.

"Resignation," p. 125.

"Lines written under affliction," p. 126.

"Relief," p. 128.

"Response [to 'A Metrical Jeu d'esprit, designed as an invitation to a whist party,' by John Johnston]," p. 130.

"Elegy: On the death of my Son William Henry, at St. Mary's," pp. 132–133.

"Sonnet," p. 134.

"To my ever beloved and lamented son William Henry," pp. 135–136.

"Sweet Willy," pp. 138–139.

"Lines Written under severe Pain and Sickness," p. 140.

"On leaving my children John and Jane at School, in the Atlantic states, and preparing to return to the interior," pp. 141–143.

"An answer, to a remonstrance on my being melancholy, by a Gentleman, who, *sometimes* had a *little pleasing* touch of melancholy himself," p. 144.

"Language Divine!" p. 145.

" 'As watchful spirits in the night,' " p. 146.

"On Meditation," p. 147.

" 'Welcome, welcome to my arms,' " p. 149.

"A Psalm, or Supplication for mercy, and confession of Sin, addressed to the Author of Life, in the Odjibway-Algonquin tongue," pp. 150–151.

"On reading Miss Hannah Moore's Christian morals and Practical Piety. 1816," p. 153.

"Stanzas," p. 155.

" 'My heart is gone with him afar,' " p. 156.

"Acrostic," p. 157.

"My Ear-rings," p. 158.

"When the Stormy Winds Do Blow, After Thomas Campbell," p. 159.

"Elegy on the death of my aunt Mrs Kearny of Kilgobbin Glebe Dublin, Ireland," p. 160.

"Spirit of Peace," p. 161.

" 'Let prayer alone our thoughts engage,' " p. 162.

TALES AND STORIES

"The Origin of the Robin," pp. 163–164.

"Moowis, The Indian Coquette," pp. 166–167.

"Mishösha, or the Magician and his daughters: A Chippewa Tale or Legend," pp. 169–175.

"The Forsaken Brother: A Chippewa Tale," pp. 177–180.

"Origin of the Miscodeed, or the Maid of Taquimenon," pp. 181–183.

"Corn story (or the origin of corn)," pp. 184–187.

"The Three Cranberries," p. 189.

"The Little Spirit, or Boy-Man: An Odjibwa Tale," pp. 190–192.

NONFICTION

"Waish-kee, alias Iawba Wadick," pp. 194–195.

"La Renne," p. 197.

"Peboan and Seegwun (Winter and Spring): A Chippewa Allegory," pp. 198–199.

"The O-jib-way Maid," p. 201.

"Song for a Lover Killed in Battle," p. 205.

"Two Songs," pp. 207–208.

"A mother's lament for the absence of a child," p. 210.

" 'My lover is tall and handsome,' " p. 212.

" 'High heav'd my breast,' " p. 213.

"Song of the Okogis, or Frog in Spring," p. 215.

" 'Kaugig ahnahmeauwin / Ever let piety,' " p. 216.

"Character of Aboriginal Historical Tradition," pp. 217–218.

"Dying Speech," p. 220.

CRITICAL AND BIOGRAPHICAL STUDIES

Brazer, Marjorie Cahn. *Harps upon the Willows: The Johnston Family of the Old Northwest.* Edited by the Historical Society of Michigan. Ann Arbor: Historical Society of Michigan, 1993.

Brehm, Victoria. "Great Lakes Indian Literature." In *The Women's Great Lakes Reader.* Edited by Brehm. Duluth, Minn.: Holy Cow! Press, 1998. Pp. 31–34.

———. "Profile: Jane Johnston Schoolcraft." In *The Women's Great Lakes Reader.* Edited by Brehm. Duluth, Minn.: Holy Cow! Press, 1998. Pp. 37–38.

Bremer, Richard G. *Indian Agent and Wilderness Scholar: The Life of Henry Rowe Schoolcraft.* Mount Pleasant: Clarke Historical Library, Central Michigan University, 1987.

Fuller, Margaret. *Summer on the Lakes, in 1843.* 1844. Urbana: University of Illinois Press, 1991.

Gray, Janet. "Jane Johnston Schoolcraft (Bame-wa-wa-ge-zhik-a-quay) 1800–41." In *She Wields a Pen: American Women Poets of the Nineteenth Century.* Edited by Gray. Iowa City: University of Iowa Press, 1997. Pp. 30–33.

Hambleton, Elizabeth, and Elizabeth Warren Stoutamire, eds. *The John Johnston Family of Sault Ste. Marie.* N.p.: John Johnston Family Association, 1992.

Jameson, Anna Brownell. *Winter Studies and Summer Rambles in Canada.* 3 vols. London: Saunders and Otley, 1838.

Miller, Susan Cummins. "Jane Johnston Schoolcraft (Bame-wa-wa-ge-zhik-a-quay) ('Rosa,' 'Leelinau') (Ojibwa) (1800–1841)." In *A Sweet, Separate Intimacy: Women Writers of the American Frontier, 1800–1922.* Edited by Miller. Salt Lake City: University of Utah Press, 2000.

Mumford, Jeremy. "Mixed-Race Identity in a Nineteenth-Century Family: The Schoolcrafts of Saulte Ste. Marie, 1824–27." *Michigan Historical Review* 25, no. 1:1–23 (spring 1999).

Osborn, Chase S., and Stellanova Osborn. *Schoolcraft—Longfellow—Hiawatha.* Lancaster, Pa.: Jacques Cattell Press, 1942.

Parker, Robert Dale, ed. *The Sound the Stars Make Rushing Through the Sky: The Writings of Jane Johnston Schoolcraft.* Philadelphia: University of Pennsylvania Press, 2007.

Ruoff, A. LaVonne Brown. "Early Native American Women Authors: Jane Johnston Schoolcraft, Sarah Winnemucca, S. Alice Callahan, E. Pauline Johnson, and Zitkala-Sa." In *Nineteenth-Century American Women Writers: A Critical Reader.* Edited by Karen L. Kilcup. Oxford, U.K.: Blackwell, 1998.

Schoolcraft, Henry Rowe. *Algic Researches, Comprising Inquiries Respecting the Mental Characteristics of the North American Indians, First Series: Indian Tales and Legends.* 2 vols. New York: Harper & Brothers, 1839.

———. *Personal Memoirs: Thirty Years with the Indian Tribes.* 1851. New York: AMS Press, 1978.

———. "Dawn of Literary Composition by Educated Natives of the Aboriginal Tribes." In *The Sound the Stars Make Rushing Through the Sky: The Writings of Jane Johnston Schoolcraft.* Edited by Robert Dale Parker. Philadelphia: University of Pennsylvania Press, 2007. Pp. 241–254.

———. "An Introduction to the Poetry of Jane Johnston Schoolcraft." In *The Sound the Stars Make Rushing Through the Sky: The Writings of Jane Johnston Schoolcraft.* Edited by Robert Dale Parker. Philadelphia: University of Pennsylvania Press, 2007. Pp. 237–239.

———, ed. *Onoéta; or, The Red Race of America.* New York: Burgess, Stringer, 1844–1845.

Stone-Gordon, Tammrah. "Woman of the Sound the Stars Make Rushing Through the Sky: A Literary Biography of Jane Johnston Schoolcraft." Master's thesis, Michigan State University, 1993.

PENELOPE SCAMBLY SCHOTT

(1942—)

Claire Keyes

PENELOPE SCAMBLY SCHOTT is a major American writer masquerading as a small-press poet. Without a mainstream publisher, she has published her fourteen books with thirteen different publishers. From her first book in 1977 to her 2010 volume, she has forged her own way driven by her passion for poetry and a seemingly bottomless store of creativity. Her latest books have drawn greater attention from readers and reviewers, primarily female. A feminist who aligns herself with no cause, Schott writes her poems from a deep sense of her femaleness.

THEMES AND SUBJECTS

Were it not for the depth of her poetic skills and the full range of her understanding, one could say that Schott's subjects are typical for a contemporary woman poet. She writes about marriage and motherhood, about time and aging, about sex and sexuality, about nature and her affinity with plants and animals. Out of this matrix of subjects she develops her themes. To be human is to be fallible. To be fully human is to experience spiritual growth, even rebirth. To embrace the fullness of one's humanity, one must develop close, loving relationships. To experience transformation, even metamorphosis, is to connect to the ancient mysteries of the self and the universe. In articulating these themes, Penelope Schott embraces the role of the poet as an essential link between the human and the natural world.

BIOGRAPHY

Penelope Scambly Schott was born in Washington, D.C., on April 20, 1942. Her father, Elihu Schott (pronounced "shot") was a lawyer for Pan American Airways. As she says in one of this writer's interviews with her, "he was a punster and word lover and wrote funny occasional verse" (Keyes, July 7, 2011). Her mother, Marian Goldstein Schott, less an influence on Schott as a poet, studied anthropology and later worked in market research. Schott cites her mother, however, as imparting a "relativistic view of cultures" which "made me an observer and an atheist" (July 12, 2011). The family moved to Manhattan, where she lived until she was eleven, wandering all over the city by herself. When she was nine and her sister, Heather, was six, she took both of them to school on the subway. The family moved to Chappaqua, New York, when Schott was in sixth grade.

Schott's parents influenced her in different ways. "My dad was the word person in our house. I miss him several times a day. My mother had no idea who I was but wanted me to be somebody else" (Keyes, July 28, 2011). Her parental relationships serve as recurring subjects in her poetry. Childhood summers were spent with her maternal grandparents in Winnetka, Illinois, outside Chicago. Schott recalls, "At night on the porch my grandmother read poetry aloud. I used to memorize Wordsworth and Sir Walter Scott" (July 12, 2011). These summers made a significant impact on Schott; the youthful protagonist of her novel, *A Little Ignorance* (1986), also spends summers with her grandparents in Illinois.

Schott's companion on these summer trips was Heather, her only sibling. In an interview with Dave Jarecki, Schott says that "my sister got along better with my mother. I got along better with my father." Schott's deep attachment to her father becomes manifest in her poetry. Her relationship with her mother also fuels her poetry,

taking on a powerful intensity during the extended period of her mother's old age and death. In an extended interview, Schott said: "During her long final illness, I very much wanted a loving relationship with her, and I figured that since she wasn't likely to change, my best bet was to be loving toward her. In the five years I had worked as a home health aide with the old and sick, I found I could do that hard and often messy work by loving each client during the time I was with her or him. I figured that if I could love a stranger that way, I could love my mother" (Keyes, August 28, 2011).

Schott's parents arranged for her to go to Peru the summer she was fifteen, and she earned a Certificado de Estudios from the University of San Marcos in Lima. Back in the States, she attended the University of Michigan because her mother had gone to Northwestern and believed in large midwestern universities. She earned a B.A. in history in 1962. For her M.A. and Ph.D. degrees (1968, 1971), she returned to Queens College and the Graduate Center of the City University of New York, where she specialized in medieval English literature. Schott's love for and background in history becomes important in understanding both the narrative poems *Penelope: The Story of the Half-Scalped Woman* (1999) and *A Is for Anne* (2007), about the Puritan-era religious dissident Anne Hutchinson. These works are deeply imbued with historical relevance. She admits, "I see everything in historical terms. Although my graduate work was in English literature, I have always seen and thought in the context of time" (Keyes, July 28, 2011).

Schott's graduate degrees made academic positions possible, and she views this period in her life with practicality: "My Ph.D. was a union card for supporting my children." She took positions at Rutgers University (1971–1978) and was an administrator at Somerset County College (1978–1981). Switching gears, she worked for the Educational Testing Service writing software for adult students. While she also worked as an artist's model and a home health aide, Schott has since 1974 been a teaching consultant for Thomas A. Edison College in Trenton, New Jersey. None

of these positions has been as important as her writing.

In 1962 she married Ernest Kramer and they had two children, Daniel (1963) and Rebecca (1966). This marriage ended in 1969. Daniel teaches theater at Smith College in Northampton, Massachusetts, and Rebecca does dog rescue in Pasadena, California. There was a brief second marriage to a violent alcoholic. Schott has been married to Eric Sweetman, a physicist, since 1985. Marriage, children, divorce, single motherhood, and remarriage are all subjects that have occupied Schott over the course of her writing career.

What does the poet, having been married three times, call herself? Schott has a first, middle, and a last name. Her middle name is intriguing enough to wonder whether it might have some family history attached to it. Not so. She explains:

> I changed my name twice for marriage and then decided, enough of that. The second married name started with an *S*, so my initials were *PSS*. When I went back to Schott, I needed an *S* middle name, therefore Scambly. I looked in the *Oxford English Dictionary* for a good word and found "scambly," which is a dialect word for "makeshift."
>
> (Keyes, July 28, 2011)

"Scambly," or "makeshift." is, perhaps, a key to understanding the prose and poetic works of Penelope Scambly Schott. She is not easily categorized. A novelist as well as a poet, she is as likely to write a historical verse narrative as she is to write a deeply personal love poem. To read Penelope Schott is to witness the constant evolution of a prodigious talent. She is a poet of infinite variety.

EARLY POETRY AND PROSE

Penelope Schott's first three books show her interest in the subjects of marriage and family, time and aging. The title of her first book is an ironic comment on her own inability to achieve marital constancy: "Having been married and divorced twice, / I am trying to understand about marriage," she writes in her first book, *My Grandparents Were Married for Sixty-five Years*

PENELOPE SCAMBLY SCHOTT

(1977; p. 25). In her second book, the novel *A Little Ignorance* (1986), Schott's protagonist is a young girl who must take the journey from ignorance to knowledge of the realities of the adult world. Elsa Marston, writing in *Best Sellers,* found the novel "a superb achievement," mainly because of Schott's style. "The author's gifts as a poet show to remarkable advantage. Both at age 8 and at age 14, Alison's language is appropriate; yet the fine literary quality never falters." Also focusing on Schott's poetic talent, Sybil Steinberg of *Publishers Weekly* praised her for writing "prose of particular precision and clarity." Steinberg went on to conclude that "in [Schott's] fictional debut, she shows talent as a storyteller, too." Schott, however, has turned away from fiction. She says that she "would rather tell stories in poetry" (Keyes, August 28, 2011), and she has kept to that decision. *These Are My Same Hands* (1989), a chapbook, is the precursor of *The Perfect Mother* (1994) and treats the subject of marriage and motherhood with a focus on a disastrous marriage, divorce, and single parenthood. Spiritual rebirth is Schott's major emphasis. Healing comes through the difficult understanding that "what is broken shall be mended" (p. 28).

THE PERFECT MOTHER *(1994)*

In the five years following *These Are My Same Hands,* Schott composed poems that would eventually fill out and embellish *The Perfect Mother*. While the themes in her 1994 volume are similar to her previous collection (she uses ten of the *Hands* poems), the new book emerges as something with more texture and heft.

Marriage as a subject continues to hold Schott's attention. "The Poor Dead Feet of My First Husband" is a requiem for her first marriage. Whatever love she had for him is long gone; still, she writes:

Somebody kind should gather
these small pieces of your death;
somebody kind should murmur
"how sad"; somebody kind,
somebody else.

(p. 41)

Just as she was not the perfect wife, not "somebody kind," she is far from "the perfect mother." We must read the title of this book as ironic. In "Custody," she writes, "I had traded her brother / for my life" of the period when her divorce settlement required joint custody. "It was 1969," she states, and "I was still an idiot" (p. 42). In general, poems about her children are more upbeat.

In a life where failure seems to pursue her, Schott rises to exuberance in a poem about her daughter's first menstruation. She renders this event, communicated by phone, in striking images that have the effect of a heroic simile:

A brilliant globule of blood
rolled out over the surface of the desert
up and down the Continental Divide
through the singing prairies
parting the Mississippi
leaping the Delaware Water Gap
until it spilled in this tall red kitchen
in Rolling Hills, New Jersey
where it skittered across the linoleum
and cracked into hundred of little faceted jewels.

(p. 54)

The excitement she feels is palpable. Her joy makes her "want to shout / *Bless you, my daughter, bless you, bless you / I have created the world in 13 years / and it is good*" (p. 55). The self-congratulatory note in this poem is natural and refreshing in a volume where the poet seems all too aware of how she has not measured up to some ideal of motherhood.

She treats her failures, her fallibility, in a poem where she thinks back in time and finds herself "the perfect mother." "The Woman Who Went Backwards" has no problem dealing with the vicissitudes of life with her children: "when they pounded her French pots on the kitchen floor, / she withstood the noise and gave the right responses." Living her life forward, as we all must, her responses were most likely not as controlled. With gentle humor, Schott concludes:

By the time they were both babies,
she was the perfect mother;

241

she always did the right things,
as the right thing was whatever she did.

(p. 13)

When she comes to rendering her disastrous second marriage, the mood of Schott's poetry darkens. "Landscape with Bottles" depicts life with a drunken, violent husband in seven sections that accumulate details about a marriage gone terribly wrong. She is frightened of him and escapes the house into a wintry backyard: "Between the garage / and thick old lilacs / I crouch, hoping / the small and chilly stars / will not illuminate / my white nightgown." What is striking about this poem is not the subject matter, but Schott's pacing and her control over images. We do not feel as though we are reading a script for a soap opera—this is horrific experience distilled to its emotional essence. Her handling of metaphor is deft. In section 5 she calls the police and watches as "Their car / drifts up the street / like a remote / lighthouse, steady and clear / beyond the reef" (p. 51).

The wrenching pain of marriages gone wrong and of her inadequacies as a single mother resolve in a ten-part poem (which had also appeared in *These Are My Same Hands*) titled "The New Life." Here she has no police officers as recourse, but a loving man. Section 6 of this poem, which depicts "wild white roses at dawn," finds Schott at her most lyrical:

From the yellow center
of the white blossom

I can walk toward you
in palest nakedness;

I can settle onto your skin
like petals into slow water

a veil woven in water.

(p. 58)

Working with a romantic image that might seem trite in other hands, Schott enters the rose, and she approaches her lover/mate from the heart of the flower. Lyrically sensuous, Schott's lines are delicate and suggestive.

Part 3 of *The Perfect Mother* stands back from the central subject matter of this volume to embrace larger philosophical issues and truth. She considers the expansion of the universe, her aging parents, her own aging, the inevitability of time passing, and the cycles of birth, death, and rebirth. "On the Edge of Visible Light," the penultimate poem of the volume (also in *These Hands*), takes the subject of motherhood to its ultimate rendering. The poem is visionary. The woman who stands "in the middle of a field" is not human. "She reflects all colors, shines / clear white." She is, we must imagine, the perfect mother:

She lets me go and come back;
she lets me invent her
In this land beyond violet
where invisible turns visible,
it is never too late.

Mama, I call across fences.
Mama. All this time, Mama,
in the dark furrows of my body,
in the willing flesh of my children,
I was asking for you.

(p. 81)

Clearly, this figure is not her biological mother but a kind of generative power. What this power generates is transformation, or, as Schott says in the last lines of her last poem: "Visit the old people / every week. ... Once they forget who you are, you are / your own mother" (p. 83). This concept of becoming one's own mother, a spiritual rather than a biological power, is intimately connected to the concept of rebirth.

At the end of *The Perfect Mother,* Schott leaves us with this belief in the power of transformation. She achieved this power through her experiences of marriage and motherhood, divorce, and remarriage. Her struggles have led her to a vision of the kind of being she is capable of becoming.

WAVE AMPLITUDE IN THE MONA PASSAGE *(1998)*

Schott's 1998 chapbook is dedicated to "all the sweet old men, especially my father." Elihu Schott's recent death had brought great grief to

Schott, and here she writes some of her most tender lines about him. Her book, however, is not solely elegiac. Around the time of this book's publication, Schott worked as a home health aide, and that work, primarily with the elderly, informs many of these poems. Along with poems about her father and the elderly, Schott moves the arc of her book toward "all things round and generative" (p. 18). From the beginning, Schott has been interested in the seasons of life, and *Wave Amplitude in the Mona Passage* is no different. What is striking, however, is a new boldness in her style.

Schott is daring in her approach to her poetic materials. She challenges the reader to make connections between disparate images. Sometimes this works astoundingly well; other times her poems remain opaque. Since Schott will continue to evolve into a poet who makes daring gestures with unusual couplings that impart a surreal quality to her verse, it is helpful to consider a poem like "Lamentation in Winter," from *Wave Amplitude,* to see how she structures a poem:

When I stroll outside to walk on your grave,
the feet recite their grammar of grief:

*Come back, come back, this time I will know
how to listen.* But white footprints come back

alone. Breath is a wet otter
in the wild Jurassic flowers of the lungs.

What have you done with that other life
where we grappled like large, affectionate beasts?

When I enter a room where music has been,
I expect I will still hear it. Not

this squawk of ducks on the clown-footed lake,
each clapper frozen to its bell.

(p. 5)

While she doesn't identify the "you" in the poem, the reference to "your grave" plus the title suggest her father. She doesn't own the lamentation but gives it to her feet, which "recite their grammar of grief." The second couplet follows logically from the first and extends it. There is no response, and "white footprints come back /

alone." She may speak to the dead person, but she gets only silence. The metaphor in the third couplet leaps into different territory: "Breath is a wet otter / in the wild Jurassic flowers of the lungs." Capturing the difficulty of breathing in the midst of lamentation, her metaphor conveys heaviness and wetness. An otter in one's lungs would certainly make breathing difficult, but this is forcing logic into a metaphor that defies it.

Couplet 4 returns to the poet and her father and a memory of "that other life" where they were together, grappling "like large, affectionate beasts." That life has been taken away. The last two couplets flow into one another and extend the feeling of something missing—not a father but music. The poet is not getting what she expects—not the "music" she wants but discordance: the "squawk of ducks." Even though these couplets flow, there is still the oddness of "each clapper frozen to its bell"—not the sound of ducks but soundlessness and coldness suggestive of death.

Schott's style is characterized by illogic and sudden leaps of imagination for a collage effect. Rather than move sequentially she reaches out for images and metaphors that have the necessary emotional resonance of grief or lamentation. Schott's style puts demands on the reader to be open to suggestion, to make imaginative leaps, and to be patient with unknowing.

Not all Schott's poems are as demanding on the reader, but she is pretty consistent in providing only what is essential, as in "Mr. Trumm's Eyes," an example of her tribute to the "sweet old men." Written in slender couplets and spare in its language, this poem must have emanated from her work with the elderly. She praises Mr. Trumm's eyes for being her "way in" and also her "way home." When he died, she was the one to close his eyes: "I pressed each lid / toward the rim." She considers looking into his dead eyes, "but I'd already been alone." Instead, she recalls his "dead hands," which "were warm / and I placed them / against my face / and was comforted" (p. 6). The tenderness of this poem is typical of Schott's poems for the elderly.

Her treatment of issues of aging and death brings her to her own passage through time. "The

PENELOPE SCAMBLY SCHOTT

Cage of the Body" is about her own experience told through the means of allegory or extended metaphor. There is no context; she plunges directly into her metaphor: "All day I was a bird." She describes where she came from ("Woolworth's Basement") and what she ate and then states: "On my day of being a bird / I grew old and my eggs grew old too." This sense of her own mortality and her lack of fecundity doesn't put a stop to the liveliness of the bird, for "the cage has no door." Schott's playfulness and sensuality plus her flair for imaginative leaps drive the conclusion of the poem:

so I flew up through lace panties

and lodged in my own womb
where I preen myself with my yellow beak

and sometimes, on sweet weekend mornings,
I shiver my white feathers,

I puff up my round blue cheeks
and speak to my featherless man

I tell him: *Come in.*

(p. 25)

PENELOPE: THE STORY OF THE HALF-SCALPED WOMAN *(1999)*

The poems of *Wave Amplitude* do little to prepare us for *Penelope: The Story of the Half-Scalped Woman,* the first of Schott's three book-length narrative poems, where the poet takes on a historical subject who happens to share her first name. Written partially as a result of her move to New Jersey and research into the state's history, this long narrative poem retells the story of Penelope Stout, who was viciously attacked and "half-scalped" by the Lenape Indians on the beach at Sandy Hook, New Jersey. Her husband was murdered. Left for dead, Stout dragged herself to a hollow tree, where she managed to survive for a week or so until a second group of Indians found her and cared for her. In the meantime, she miscarried her first child. Schott's poem about her is a mixture of fact, legend, and her own poetic imagination. While some elements never

occurred (e.g., an encounter with the artist Judith Leyster in Amsterdam), the poems derive their strength and interest from Schott's reweaving of the narrative she researched. Her themes emerge when we discover her narrative emphasis.

Divided into fifty-three sections with separate titles, "Penelope" is best read as a continuous narrative. Stout's survival in the hollow tree, as miraculous as it may seem, is an undisputed part of her legend. Schott renders this episode graphically in "Alive in the Tree":

here in the shell of my tree,
a plunge as if again of the boat,
and my stomach all gaping and lurching again;
and one hand that I think might be mine
grapples and clutches and enters the viscous
hollow; tips of my fingers pulling away

all sticky and spotted with dark flecks.

(p. 15)

Pregnant at the time of these horrible wounds ("my stomach all gaping and lurching"), Stout loses the baby and in "Miscarriage" looks at her feet to see "the white and bloody doll / ... still in the silken sack, skin translucent." The music of Schott's verse deepens the sense of horror with the alliteration of the *s* sound, a low hiss.

Penelope Stout is young, perhaps only twenty (her dates are uncertain) when she survives this ordeal, and her youth certainly helped but does not explain things entirely. Stout's strength would be further tested when she undergoes Indian medicine, described by Schott in a poem of the same name:

I am an empty cask.
Clean water floods my belly,
the guts set gently back.

With needles of fish hook
and sutures of vine,
they lock up my skin.

A poultice of molten resin
singes the loose seam.

Someone is screaming.

(p. 21)

244

PENELOPE SCAMBLY SCHOTT

The grisly details of this "medicine" do not deter Schott from creating the music of the poem. In lines 3–6, the iambs followed by anapests shape the rhythm. Slant and exact rhymes (vine/skin/resin; seam/scream; cask/back/hook) deliver the lyric intensity necessary. Under the care of her Indian captors, Penelope Stout regains her health. She also achieves a new respect for a people of a distinctly different culture. Likewise, the Indians develop an attachment to her. Penelope is rescued from the Indians by a relative, but the strong bond between her and the Lenape endures.

When trouble arises between the Indians and the white settlers, one of her friends, a man called Machk, comes to her farm to warn her and her family, telling her (imagined by Schott):

Go to the tupelo down by the creek.
Do not sleep in this house Go.
Look in the reeds. Take my canoe
and your babies and row.

(p. 38)

It's significant that he tells her to "Go to the tupelo," for trees become a powerful symbol in the book. Primarily, however, Schott wants to emphasize that Penelope was a woman capable of living in two different cultures, that of the white man and that of the Lenape. While readers may or may not make the leap between Penelope's situation and that of contemporary American women, Schott's depiction of her heroine's life and times certainly convinces us of her inner strength and the flexibility of mind that contributed to her survival.

THE PEST MAIDEN *(2004)*

More a victim than a survivor, Viola-Jean Heuser, the central character in *The Pest Maiden,* was a relative of Schott's. Subtitled *A Story of Lobotomy,* the poet's second book-length narrative traces the story of Jean's experience with mental illness, her stay in a mental hospital, and the lobotomy she received in 1954 as a treatment for her illness. Schott doesn't treat this as an isolated event but weaves together Jean's story with poems about the Black Death, the Ghost Dance

of late nineteenth-century America, and madness brought on by poisoning.

As Barbara Crooker states in her review, "While these connections may seem tenuous, [the poem titled] 'The Dances of Madness' stitches them together for us." In her youth, Jean was a dancer; thus the emphasis on dance stems naturally from her story. How and why this talented, exuberant girl was struck with mental illness deeply absorbs Schott. She, too, according to these poems, had her struggles with mental instability. In "The Dances of Madness" she introduces, first, the concept that manifestations of madness "are terrible and various" (p. 14). Among them, she cites "the plague-ridden populace / galloping / horses of madness / infested, infected / neglected, / rejected" by those who still remained unaffected by the plague. Swerving to the New World, she includes "Indian and settler / prairies and centuries / the purple sickness, / sticky as bad bread," a reference to madness brought on by ergotism, a toxic condition caused by ingesting a fungus found in rye grain. In the poem "Ergotism," "That which hath risen / is poison / the bite / the blight" (p. 71). Into this complex mix of madness and plague ("Pest Maiden" is a metaphor for the Black Death), Schott introduces herself and her project: "I am with / them all who are whirling and writhing, / writing the linked stories, the separate choruses / of lost names, / the pain of Jean who spins and spins / in this thickness of dark music" (p. 14).

The Pest Maiden opens up its scope from the personal travails of Jean Heuser to more universal themes. As Colette Inez explains in her blurb for the book, Schott's book is "enlivened with a mix of letters, reports and multi-cultural references to madness." In one instance, Schott includes a found poem titled "How to Perform My New Transorbital Lobotomy" by Walter Freeman, M.D. The originator of the technique proceeds to describe, in detail, the various steps of the operation. What Schott gains in sheer graphic detail and authenticity she loses in poetic power. Poems that rely overmuch on clinical detail lack the artistry of work executed by Schott in *The*

PENELOPE SCAMBLY SCHOTT

Perfect Mother or *Wave Amplitude in the Mona Passage.*

The Pest Maiden is indicative, however, of Schott's enduring interest in history and the historical implications of her subjects. She continues to pursue this interest in *A Is for Anne,* her study of the life and times of the early American pioneer Anne Hutchinson.

A IS FOR ANNE: MISTRESS HUTCHINSON DISTURBS THE COMMONWEALTH *(2007)*

As Penelope Schott researched her narrative poem about Anne Hutchinson, the religious dissident tried, castigated, and exiled from Boston by the Puritan fathers, she discovered an interesting corollary with her own life. Hutchinson's father had been deeply involved in shaping his daughter's mind and her religious beliefs. Elihu Schott had also contributed greatly to his daughter's development, and she dedicates her book to him.

Schott's 2007 profile by Kristen Boyd reveals that she was moved to write on the subject of Hutchinson following her father's illness and death. The resulting book of poems won the 2008 Oregon Book Award in poetry. It also garnered more book reviews than any of Schott's previous publications. As Eleanor Berry points out, "The book combines narrative interest with lyric intensity. It also creates strong and complex characters" (p. 1). Although Schott gives voice to such figures as Governor Winthrop and the Puritan divines who found Anne's words and actions execrable, the primary character is Hutchinson herself, a strong woman mentioned, if at all, as a footnote in American history. As Schott showed in *Penelope,* she is drawn to strong women.

Barbara Crooker encapsulates the essence of Hutchinson's strength in her brief review. She describes Anne as "a beacon in the struggle for civil rights and religious freedom. Some of the issues she grapples with are disturbingly familiar today: intolerance in the name of Christianity, gender discrimination, the right to dissent, civil disobedience." For all its relevance to contempo-

rary issues, *A Is for Anne* makes its impact not as a political tract but as a poem.

Helen Marie Casey explains in her review that "the danger [in long narrative poems] is that the didactic elements of the narrative will overpower the lyrical" (p. 190). While some of Schott's poems border on the didactic, she never loses control of her lyrical power. A poem from Anne's early married life is a case in point. "Awake at Midnight" gives us a snapshot of Anne's frame of mind as she ruminates about the religious controversies swirling about her and her family in Reformation England:

> The moon on the roof
> of the wellhouse
>
> flares
> like an angel's wing.
>
> Is it Papist
> to think so? No,
>
> for God made the earth
> and all its charms—
>
> this unborn child
> dancing in my womb
>
> and our big bedstead
> so warm.
>
> (p. 43)

It's not simply that Schott employs metaphor, the moon flaring "like an angel's wing," but that musicality and rhythm are primary: the internal assonance of "moon" and "roof," the slant rhyme of "charms," "womb," and "warm." Schott deploys a question in the center of her poem, a syntactical strategy to alter and heighten the rhythm. The question ("Is it Papist / to think so?") is also stunning. Anne, definitely not a papist, allows the question to enter her mind, an indication of her intellectual bravery.

Anne's bravery, however, was more than intellectual. The mother of fifteen children, an early settler of colonial America, exiled to Rhode Island and later New York, she met a horrible death. The last poem in the collection, narrated by Anne's daughter Susannah, tells of the Indian

246

raid during which she was captured, the rest of her family killed, and their house set afire. And there is Anne, whose certainty about her salvation stood her in good stead. In her daughter's eyes, she did not waver, even as she was consumed by flames.

The conclusion of the poems reveals that while Anne may have envisioned an afterlife shaped by Christian tenets, her daughter embraces a pagan or pre-Christian belief in the Great Mother, or Gaia. Susannah's view is, of course, Schott's and not surprising since, as Sherry Chandler points out, *A Is for Anne* "was written with feminist intent." In Hutchinson, Schott finds a powerful, charismatic woman, fearless in her belief: an American foremother who is also a vehicle for Schott's views on contemporary society. Feeling strongly that "people need to hear about [Hutchinson]," Schott delivers what the poet Robert Cooperman deems "a biography written with the flame of poetry" (back-cover blurb). Other authors have written biographies of Hutchinson, but Penelope Schott's contribution is that essential "flame of poetry."

ALMOST LEARNING TO LIVE IN THIS WORLD (2004) AND BAITING THE VOID (2005)

These two books are closely allied, and it makes sense to treat them together. Schott's chapbook *Almost Learning to Live in This World* was folded into *Baiting the Void* and contributed twelve poems to the more fully realized collection. This outpouring of poems and Schott's increasing command over her material led naturally to an increased rate of publication. In one of her poems she exclaims, "But hey, I'm sixty" (p. 46), as if to call attention to her level of maturity. Many people reach sixty; few achieve Schott's mastery as a poet.

Some of her old subjects and themes call out to her and she responds. Still very much interested in the aging process and in death, she replies to her husband's question about why she "tends the elderly" with a number of reasons, the most poignant of which is "so someone will love me when I am old" (p. 70). She looks around and admits "the cool women are getting old," a

reference to the women who form her writing group. Her attitude toward death turns positively playful in "Premeditations": "Conjugation means grammar or sex: / I will die, you will die, she will die" (p. 26). Continuing to grieve over her father's death, she addresses him in "My Father's Employment," his job being to be dead:

> I would spend every leaf in my garden
> to cover your wages
>
> for half an hour so you might knock off to sit with me
> here in the striped shade.
>
> (p. 94)

Schott's conceit here is that death "employs" her father; she would employ him differently by engaging him in the simple pleasures of life.

In contrast to her emphasis on aging and death, Schott asserts cheerfulness and a lust for life. At the same time, she exalts women for rituals in which they nurture life. "The Necessity of Lemons" marries a sensuous appreciation of lemons (and by extension other fruits of the earth) with woman's deep connection with the natural world. Written in prose-poem style or little prose pulses, the poem is allegorical in form:

> In each and every valley of the world just such a woman is
> holding her single lemon. From each lemon, one taut thread
> shoots straight up to the sun.
>
> ...
>
> the women with their lemons will keep
> the sun from abandoning the earth.
>
> (pp. 52, 53)

Schott's sense of an intimate bond between human (female) action and the sun as a generating force gives birth to her book title and forms the thematic substrate of this collection. "The women with their lemons" are "baiting the void." It's a call-and-response figure, which becomes clearer in the poem "Under the Sun." At first the poem appears to be an instance of wishful thinking: "I want to locate a landscape / where there has been no killing." Knowing full well there is no such landscape on this earth, she declares a more achievable goal:

I want to paint light, how it flows
into grass like the winged shimmer

of ripe alfalfa, or the pink tinting
of clouds, a blush of unshed blood,

as if I, who hit a girl in seventh grade
and scraped my hand on her braces,

were trying to paint my own way in
to grace, or dash my whole inheritance

of English words at the moiling furnace
of our harsh and dispassionate star.

(p. 67)

Writing as if she were a visual artist (which she is, in part) Schott provides her credo as a poet: to "dash my whole inheritance / of English words" at the sun, thus "baiting the void." There is, of course, something mythic in this sense of the role of the poet, as if Schott were a modern Orpheus whose music had powers to charm all of nature: birds, fish, wild beasts, even to compel rocks to dance. And why not?

Schott's poems speak of a deep affinity with the plant and animal world. She asserts that "I can't disconnect my own flesh from the grace of beasts" (p. 13). Likewise, she senses a connection with the plant world in a poem like "Convolvulus," writing about plants like morning glories as "a green finger of will / [which] wriggles through interstices, clamping / climbing, winding its tubular way" (p. 16). She extrapolates from this behavior: "who knew / the flesh of plants possessed such rich intention?" Schott's question is playful; she would not blatantly anthropomorphize. The poem moves in the opposite direction; her behavior is like that of the plant. She acknowledges "the bone urge to twist this whole life / into interlaced words" (p. 17). This is her nature as an artist, and it's something deep in her bones. Lest she be pretentious, she undercuts this image with: "or only an owl / winging above the intricate stubble, / cruising for voles" (p. 17). Plant or animal, she engages in a life-sustaining activity—the creation of her poems.

Maria Mazziotti Gillian, in a statement on the back cover of *Baiting the Void,* captures its essence: "Penelope Scambly Schott's book … makes us aware of the precarious nature of our ordinary lives." We need a poet of Schott's perception to help guide us along the way, to remind us in her poem "Usual Objects" of the "immense reaches / of one human mind / finding itself / crowded with worlds and still alone" (p. 62). As in "Under the Sun" and "The Necessity of Lemons," this poem has a cosmic reach. Turning back to some "usual objects," Schott gives us some recourse for our loneliness:

But here is a bowl carved from a burl
and elsewhere, a rock and a stone pestle,
its top polished round
by the palms of a woman

usual objects exquisite by use.

(p. 62)

These "usual objects" provide comfort if we would simply pay them some attention. Schott herself is skilled in observing both the external world and that interior space we call the soul.

MAY THE GENERATIONS DIE IN THE RIGHT ORDER *(2007)*

The reviewer Jennifer MacPherson provides one way to read this book. Noting that the book's title "gives the reader the antidote to loss," she extrapolates that Schott's imperative is that we "be alive to the moment, all the wonderful and quirky details in each of our lives" (p. 134). *May the Generations* becomes, then, a further development of Schott's *Learning to Live in This World.*

The initial images in *May the Generations Die in the Right Order* are somber and dark:

When hemlock branches fold down
like the ribs of an old umbrella

When wet midnight skips in the gutter,
spluttering down the rain chain,

you, there, old lady,
WAKE UP.

(p. 9)

PENELOPE SCAMBLY SCHOTT

At this stage in her life, Schott could be considered, at sixty-five, an old lady. Could she be talking to herself? She insists that the old lady in her poem be attentive because "A dream summons." She issues a directive:

Hold out your arms like twin
perches for songbirds. Now trill.
Keep on trilling. Let the pitch rise.

Instead of sleeping, the old woman will become a songstress, maybe a prolific poet? The poem ends, however, on a threatening note:

Your grown children will tell you
when you may sleep again.

See.
They are floating toward you
with sharp umbrellas.
Arriving with hot eyes.

(p. 9)

Initially, it seems that the children want the "trilling" to continue. Those "sharp umbrellas" and "hot eyes" suggest a more sinister desire: to finish her off so that they might take the stage. For the generations to die in the right order, the old lady must go first. It's the natural order of things, but Schott's handling of this theme is ambivalent. The old lady must both "wake up" and pass on. This conflict between waking up and passing on provides the dynamic tension of this collection.

Passing on, that is, death, takes the first position in Schott's four-part structure. In addition, she dedicates her book to Sadie Schott Sweetdog, her beloved canine companion, and writes several poems about her grief over Sadie's dying. Most likely a poem about that grief, "What the Bed Knows," opens up to all grief: "No silence / ever wider than death, no absence / more complete" (p. 6). She grows more philosophical in "Several Short Questions About Crumbs," which actually contains ten questions, such as "entropy being the natural state, why sweep the floor?" (p. 10). This is where crumbs enter, being the end result (the disorder) from the original form or order (the cookie). The poet questions why she "keep[s] on sweeping." She answers her question with other questions that are on the "Wake up" side of

her conundrum: "For the cockeyed dance of the red-painted handle? / Or simply to delight the straw?" (p. 10). Someone who can imagine sweeping the floor as a way to "delight the straw" will not embrace entropy for long.

Moving away from death, section 2 explores "The Art of Living" and section 3 "The Art of Love." As the array of poems makes apparent, opposites or tensions exist even here. For instance, Schott includes a poem titled "Ex-husband" alongside some magnificent love poems to her third husband. As we know from previous volumes, Schott married a violent alcoholic who terrified her. He must be the one she describes here as the man who "tried / to choke me" (p. 45). Happily married now in her sixties, she looks back upon her previous marriage with chagrin:

I was so ashamed
of my fear, my breasts, my need to breathe,

that years later, I am still collecting my words
like rainwater into this bowl.

(p. 45)

Perhaps she is saying that "the art of love" requires knowing, in a sense, what love is not. Not shame, not fear, not desperation.

"Duenna" speaks of good married love with "the family dog" acting as chaperone:

This is the double bed
these are the arms and legs
these are the lips touching the lips
and this is the yellow dog
unwilling to go out in the rain

(p. 52)

The tensions in *May the Generations* are brought into heightened focus in the fourth section, "The Spirit of the World." Whatever that spirit may be—to some it might be God—there is a sense of largeness about it, an expansion of vision. In "Caring for the World," for example, Schott gives us a catalog of unpleasant, even ugly images and then breaks forth with:

Everything living is beautiful and ugly: the gelatinous
  egg sack
and the flexible, transparent quill of the squid.

PENELOPE SCAMBLY SCHOTT

After we put down our old dog, I lay on her couch
  inhaling
the scent of the scent of her leaked urine.

The couch was a meadow and I was a butterfly,
and over my wings the sky kept on flowing.

(p. 70)

What happens here is also metamorphosis: the poet becoming the butterfly, consumed by grief, yes, but also at one in the universe where "the sky kept on flowing."

There is metamorphosis, as well, for Sadie, who assumes the role of the speaker of the following poem, telling the poet: "It was time: I needed to leave you." Sadie continues in a philosophical mode: "Whatever is beautiful is multiple, is what eats and shits / and breathes, is what still wants. You can imagine me / speaking in well-intoned English, if that's what you want" (p. 71). Schott's humor in this passage manages to avert the potential sentimentality of the dead dog speaking comforting words to her mistress.

There is a wonderful mix in this poem of whimsy and wisdom, of seriousness and lightness. Schott has a deft touch here, as elsewhere in the volume.

UNDER TAOS MOUNTAIN: THE TERRIBLE QUARREL OF MAGPIE AND TÍA (2009)

Discovering energy in argument, Penelope Schott develops a chapbook-length quarrel between Magpie, a loquacious bird, and Tía (Auntie), the name the poet assumes for herself. Written while Schott was in residence at the Wurlitzer Foundation in Taos, New Mexico, *Under Taos Mountain* sparkles with the wit of the poet's conceit: a talking bird who seems to understand the poet better than she does herself. At the same time, Schott returns to themes she has been exploring all her writing life: aging and death, a deep connection with the animal world, and her vocation as a writer.

Stephanie Dickinson, on the back cover, finds the chapbook highly charged and exciting. She deems Schott's language "stark yet voluptuous, each word a scavenged jewel." She finds that

"Schott has written a masterful, scintillating allegory. Set in New Mexico whose mythology she deepens and distills, the reader hears dialogue between what is human ... and what is winged and wild." In a poem like "Magpie Exhorts," this interplay between the human and the "winged and wild" connects directly to the poet's vocation. At the beginning, Tía is trying to clean the mud from her boots and Magpie taunts her: "you too were shaped from clay." Tía sasses her back with, "You think I'm a pot?" Magpie doesn't respond to such banter but penetrates to Tía's core:

I think it was words that coiled your sides.
I think you hold a world in your head.

I think the clay breathes, Auntie,
and someday God will shatter you.

(p. 15)

As a writer Tía has shaped her existence, but she is no less vulnerable for that shaping and is mortal like other humans. Tía's riposte is a tad prideful:

Magpie, have you considered
the shards?

A clump of mud, a yellow pad,

one carefully incised line.

Calling her bluff, Magpie admonishes: "That one careful line— / don't sleep until you write it down" (p. 15). Acting as a goad, Magpie exhorts Tía to be at her work. In her own cranky way, Magpie assumes the role of muse.

The relationship between Magpie and Tía is a natural extension of Schott's deep sense of connection with the animal world. Nonetheless, this connection is something she tends to forget. Magpie reminds her, telling her, "You write too much, Auntie. / Let your dreams lie in peace." Tía responds:

But I need to hold onto something:
the hem of the sheet or the heat

of his skin. Or a pen or this pencil
I trimmed to a point with my knife.

250

Magpie finds Tía's dependence on her pencil pathetic and tells her: "Poor old Auntie. You used to be smarter, / you used to suck your thumb." In other words, Tía has lost that innate physicality she lived as a child: her animal nature. Once Magpie calls her attention to this lack, Tía responds: "Magpie, I almost remember: / such a warm, wet dark." Saying this, she receives Magpie's blessing and admonition:

Drop your pencil.

I will rock you back to sleep in a basket
woven from the tails

of shooting stars.

                                        (p. 29)

This magnificent act of mothering is Tía's boon, the metaphorical language just a single instance of the "scavenged jewels" cited by Stephanie Dickinson.

SIX LIPS (2009)

Six Lips has garnered more reviews than any other book by Penelope Schott and for good reason. Were it for the book's language alone, we would find these poems thrilling. But it's more than that, according to Barbara Crooker, for here we have "a woman who has the key to her own life—the mysteries of the body, the layered sense of self between the generations, the compass of belonging to her current life in the Pacific Northwest while still in firm possession of the maps to her other lives." Schott's imagination knows no bounds and she accomplishes her feats with the time-honored tool of language alone. Six lips? At least.

Even so, she doesn't fly off into the stratosphere. Like Robert Frost's climber of birches, she knows that "Earth's the right place for love." She says as much in "Why I Do Not Wish to Float in Space." She opens with a series of questions reminiscent of God lecturing Job on his powers. For example: "Who spread the western horizon to snip / the orange sun in half." She then proceeds to ask an even more impossible question:

Can you feel how our planet spins in a void,
how the shallow mantle, hauling its fur coat
of forest, its slippery skin of ocean, seems
inconsequential over the molten core?

                                        (p. 25)

Note the rightness of the line break after "fur coat" and the aptness of the ocean's "slippery skin." Note also that as the poem builds, it becomes more intimate:

I've lost my footing in the belly of curled roots,
and I'm scared of falling, of lurching clear out
into space—nothing on earth to touch. Pull me
back by a finger, will you?

                                        (p. 25)

The poem takes a surprising turn with the intimate gesture of "Pull me / back by a finger, will you?" Her meditation on the vastness of the universe turns into a love poem, concluding with "Please? / Here, in the motionless house, my face / brushed by your glance." What makes *Six Lips* so compelling is how unpredictable Schott is.

Penelope Scambly Schott is unabashedly female and, as Bernadette Geyer says, "explores the geography of the female body as well as the psyche. Hers are not poems about the negative stereotypes of feminine passivity and reticence. Schott's poems move boldly into surreal territory as her poems navigate rocky emotional currents." "Counting the Body," the long poem that occupies the center of this collection, makes her attitude toward herself abundantly clear. Each section plays with a number. She requires

Six lips to sip the sublime,
two for the mouth and four for the vulva
plump as succulents and shining with dew—
ah, youth; ah, time.

                                        (p. 48)

The naturalness of the rhyme (lips/sip, sublime/ time) and the abundant alliteration characterize her versifying and also lead to the nostalgic note at the end. These are not the poems of a young woman, but youthful exuberance pervades the volume.

In the last section of the poem, she imagines what it would be like "If I Had Ten Thumbs":

I would wear pink leather shoes with velcro straps
I would strike matches on the sole of my shoe
I would suck firmly on my ten wet thumbs
I would practice exactly how to suck
with rapt attention and rhythm
so as to gratify any man
and I would do it
yes I would
do that
yes

(p. 50)

The voice of these poems is often playful and funny. At the same time, the overall tenor of this book is conditioned by the impending death of her mother. The poems get darker as the poet meditates on time and aging. As she says in "Eclipse": "This is the world that ends over and over and then / goes on without us, our tiny smudge of time" (p. 70).

Schott is blessed, however, with a flexible consciousness. At home with animals or the stars, she gives a sense of her life as a succession of lives. Intimately aware of the natural world, Schott suggests the transmigration of her soul into a screech owl or a horse. Such poems tend to be upbeat and thrilling, but the excruciating demise of her mother haunts the speaker of these poems. She finally gives way to addressing her mother's death and dying.

Typically, she refuses sentimentality. In "Heart Failure," she writes: "This is the year I would like to find pity. I would like / to hurt for my mother the way I ache for my children." As much as she would like to develop this feeling, it eludes her: a failure of *her* heart. "I want to be sad that she's eighty-seven and fading." Through her use of anaphora and an accretion of brilliant details, Schott builds up the image of her mother:

She lives in her elegant house like a black pearl
from a broken oyster drifting under reefs in a bay.
She lives in her house like a startled rabbit unable
to finish crossing the road.

(p. 53)

The poem startles when the speaker imagines killing her mother, as an act of pity:

If I had enough pity,
I would dare squeeze her fragile neck and kiss
her forehead as I press down on her windpipe and
 keep
on pressing with my strong and generous thumbs.

(p. 53)

The poem, however, does not end there. Schott's spirit is too magnanimous, and her mother changes, showing a gentle "appreciation" of nature that Schott finds surprising. Her mother "watches the squirrels scamper up black bark / like acrobats of joy." In fact, Schott doesn't recognize the person her mother has become:

This drowning old lady is not my mother. Not
abrupt. As I stroke her knuckles, grace glints
in our salt hands.

(p. 54)

Drowning because she is dying, the mother undergoes a kind of transformation, as does the daughter. For both of them, there is a communion, a touch of being to being. For Julie L. Moore, Schott has "discovered the secret" of being, "and with great generosity and creativity, she has somehow managed both to preserve it and share it with us."

Phebe Davidson also feels that Schott has reached a "secure understanding" in *Six Lips:* "that this fleeting life in which we are engaged is incredibly beautiful, incredibly rich—something worth singing again and again" (p. 4) Through her language and style, but also through her openness, her dexterity, her seemingly boundless range of being in the world, Penelope Scambly Schott commands our utmost attention and respect. She's a stunning poet.

CROW MERCIES (2010)

Had Penelope Scambly Schott's *Crow Mercies* been available in the 1970s, research into the issue of a female aesthetic in poetry would have been considerably enriched. There are many words to describe Schott's verse: "sharp! shiny!" (Naomi Shihab Nye); "surreal" (Peter Sears);

PENELOPE SCAMBLY SCHOTT

"poems that startle and delight the imagination" (Calyx Press release). The sheer femaleness of these poems is most striking.

Crow Mercies, winner of the Sarah Lantz Memorial Poetry Prize from Calyx, one of the premier women's literary magazines, is female in voice and female in experience, be it as daughter, wife, or mother. Female in role model identification—not Odysseus but Penelope. Female in imagery. Female, dare it be said, in being unpredictable? Anything could happen in a Schott poem, either in form or content. Naomi Shihab Nye finds that Schott "is not afraid to startle or jolt. A reader feels electrified," she says in her back-cover note.

Readers might think they have her pegged ("woman poet"), and then she looks and sounds like Wallace Stevens' "Thirteen Ways of Looking at a Blackbird" in her title poem, "Crow Mercies." Like Stevens, Schott has a powerful imagination and is not wary in the least of the surreal. One of the haiku-like segments of "Crow Mercies" reads:

The Art of the Poetic Line
High on a wire:
Clothespins or crows.

(p. 27)

First, she makes an aesthetic flourish, not a sentence, just a flash of provocative words. We expect, as readers, that the subsequent lines will elucidate that flourish. "High on a wire" suggests acrobatic skill. Look, someone is doing something difficult or daring. No way, the third line asserts. It's either "Clothespins or crows." The former is nothing if not domestic and/or female; the latter is the chief signifier of the volume. Crows may be common, but they're plenty smart and can survive almost anywhere. Schott's poem would have us entertain the possibility of mercies flowing from the crow. When she revisits this image at the end of the poem, we get:

Flock
The clothes on the line
flapped white wings.

(p. 29)

Crow is gone. A transformation has occurred. The domestic remains, but with a positive and angelic air.

Crow Mercies is not bound by time or place, only by the limits of the imagination. In section 2 of the collection, the poems range back in time, seeking connections with ancient forebears and with a planet before the emergence of human beings. On a canoe trip in "On the Mullica," the narrator comes across "the last dinosaur." She greets him:

I lift up my paddle like a flag,
but he is too big or too old
or the silver canoe is too bright for him to see me.

(p. 34)

Schott's inventiveness makes the preposterous seem both real and poignant. Not a chance that a dinosaur would appear in even the remotest wilderness, but the longing for that sighting is made palpable. In a subsequent poem, she turns her attention to a small creature, intimately observed, "The Rough-Skinned Newt." In a series of questions she turns the poem toward the lovemaking between the two humans involved:

Did it skitter away from the hissing sticks of our
  fire?
Did its tail tickle your wet ankles?

Was the flash of its underbelly the color of melon?

Most admirable about Schott's poetry is her subtle music. Note the deployment of alliteration and assonance and the internal rhymes:

skitter/hissing/sticks
tail tickle/wet
belly/color/melon

Further questions raise the ante on the human couple:

Would you wrap me in your yellow slicker?
Would we follow the newt beneath the boat?

Would we lie there on moss as if it were sheepskin?
Would we speak of the newt as true believers

253

might converse about ghosts?
Would I put my lips to the stiff hairs on your neck?

I did. I would.

(p. 36)

The success of Schott's poems lies in her willingness to train her observation on seemingly inconsequential things (the newt) and to follow wherever her subject takes her.

As Yusef Komunyakaa points out in his back-cover blurb: Schott "celebrates the naming of small things in order to know basic truths. An accumulative momentum rises out of the mercy of an attentive eye: not for gazing at the surface of things but looking into the heart of what matters, what keeps us fully engaged as humans." That she has a gift for intimacy—be it human or trans-species—draws the reader in.

Section 3 of *Crow Mercies* begins with a poem titled "In Memory" for her mother, Marian Schott (1919–2009). Schott's complex relationship with her mother takes her deeper and deeper into the nature of her own being and into meditations on mortality. In some poems, the death of her mother is both tortuous and liberating, the mother both vicious and beautiful:

Your crusted tongue will flicker
like the tongue of a snake
and
The embroidered nightgown
will lie white on blue skin.

(p. 53)

In another poem, the poet concludes: "I never had a mother." In its starkness, this statement recalls Sylvia Plath in her manic poems about her father. For Schott, however, the death (and denial) of the mother presages her own coming into full being:

Now watch how I swaddle
my body in sunlight.
My mouth is a warm "O"
sucking on the alphabet.

(p. 54)

She becomes, in essence, her own mother and gives birth and sustenance to herself.

Despite this striking nativity scene, Schott is too wise and too honest not to admit the toll of the aging process and her acute sense of mortality. In "The Lesson" she admits, "Now we are older than our mothers / and our cheeks are softer than talc." This sense of being an older woman pervades the closing pages of the volume. Yes, she is wife and lover, daughter and mother, but little prepares her for what it means to be an old woman in twenty-first-century American culture. Thus she explores "cronehood" imaginatively, as in "Encounter in Vindija Cave, Present-Day Croatia: Late October." The narrator meets her counterpart by "walk[ing] backwards for 38,000 years." Her time travel brings her to an ancestress whose "tangles of red curls embraced / the broad planes of freckled cheeks."

Finding her ancient female forebear, the narrator questions: "How long had my species been lonely?" The species she refers to must be the *female* species. While the narrator says she "knelt to [the other woman's] wildness," the ancient one explores her by touching: "Big knuckles lifted my chin." All this leads to a communion of sorts: "We opened our mouths and sang / in a language neither of us knew we knew." In this portrayal of a woman from a time when woman was honored as the essential link to the natural world, Schott finds both sister and mother:

We keened, we psalmed, we spoke woman
and silence. It was cold October, old October
and we curled together on straw.

(p. 73)

October is the right month, of course, for an autumnal meditation on aging.

The amazing arc of this poem reinvigorates the concept of a female aesthetic in Schott's *Crow Mercies*. These are poems whose deepest impulses come from the poet's sense of herself as a woman. Could a man have written them? Perhaps, but to what end? Yes, Gustave Flaubert declared, "I am Madame Bovary," feeling he had entered her psyche and plumbed his psyche to create the bored, passionate French housewife. The womanliness of Schott's poems is infinitely more complex and variegated than Emma Bovary. She is everywoman.

Selected Bibliography

WORKS OF PENELOPE SCAMBLY SCHOTT

Novel

A Little Ignorance. New York: Clarkson N. Potter, 1986.

Poetry

My Grandparents Were Married for Sixty-Five Years. Madison, N.J.: Department of English, Fairleigh Dickinson University, 1977.

These Are My Same Hands. Brockport, N.Y.: State Street Press Chapbooks, 1989.

The Perfect Mother. Valdosta, Ga.: Snake Nation Press, 1994.

Wave Amplitude in the Mona Passage. Aiken, S.C.: Palanquin Press, 1998.

Penelope: The Story of the Half-Scalped Women: A Narrative Poem. Gainesville: University Press of Florida, 1999.

Almost Learning to Live in This World. Columbus, Ohio: Pudding House Press, 2004.

The Pest Maiden: A Story of Lobotomy. Cincinnati, Ohio: Turning Point, 2004.

Baiting the Void. Felton, Calif.: Dream Horse Press, 2005.

A Is for Anne: Mistress Hutchinson Disturbs the Commonwealth. Cincinnati, Ohio: Turning Point, 2007.

May the Generations Die in the Right Order. Charlotte, N.C.: Main Street Rag, 2007.

Six Lips. Bay City, Mich.: Mayapple Press, 2009.

Under Taos Mountain: The Terrible Quarrel of Magpie and Tía. New York: Rain Mountain Press, 2009.

Crow Mercies. Corvallis, Ore.: Calyx Books, 2010.

CRITICAL AND BIOGRAPHICAL STUDIES

Profiles and Articles

Argüello, Edna. "*Penelope: The Story of the Half-Scalped Woman.*" *Courier-News* (New Jersey), March 20, 1999.

Berry, Eleanor. "Oregon Book Award in Poetry Goes to Penelope Scambly Schott." *Oregon State Poetry Association Newsletter* 51, no. 3:1 (December 2008).

Boyd, Kristin. "Speaking Out: Cool Woman Poet Penelope Scambly Schott Tells the Story of Anne Hutchinson in Verse." *Princeton Packet,* May 31, 2007.

Epstein, Eric. "Q & A: The Poet and the Half-Scalped Woman." *New York Times,* May 2, 1999. http://www.nytimes.com/1999/05/02/nyregion/q-a-the-poet-and-the-half-scalped-woman.html.

Reviews

Ayers, Lana Hechtman. "*A Is for Anne.*" *Adirondack Review* 9, no. 1 (spring 2008). http://adirondackreview.homestead.com/Book69.html.

Buckley, Kerri. "Six Lips." *Poets' Quarterly* 2 (winter 2010). http://poetsquarterly.yolasite.com/winter10_schott.php.

Casey, Helen Marie. "History, Poetry, and Genre-Stretching." *South Carolina Review* 40, no. 2:189–191 (spring 2008). (Review of *A Is for Anne.*)

Chandler, Sherry. "*A Is for Anne.*" August 30, 2009. http://sherrychandler.com/2009/08/30/a-is-for-anne/.

Crooker, Barbara. "*Baiting the Void.*" *Cider Press Review* 7, 2006.http://ciderpressreview.com/archive/volume-9/#.T_tumZHs0g8.

———. "*The Pest Maiden.*" *Triplopia* 5, no. 1 (winter 2006).

———. "*A Is for Anne.*" *Small Press Review* 39:11–12 (November–December 2007).

———. "Six Lips." *Cider Press Review* 11, 2010.

Davidson, Phebe. "Review Article: Books by Sander Zulauf, Barbara Crooker, Penelope Scambly Schott, Diane Lockward, Linda Cronin." *Journal of New Jersey Poets* (spring 2011).

Geller, Jeffrey L. *"The Lobotomist: A Maverick Medical Genius and His Tragic Quest to Rid the World of Mental Illness* and *The Pest Maiden: A Story of Lobotomy."* *Psychiatric Services* 56, no. 10:1318–1319 (October 2005). http://ps.psychiatryonline.org/article.aspx?articleid=90665.

Geyer, Bernadette. "Six Lips." *BerniE-zine,* April–May 2010. http://rantsravesreviews.homestead.com/SixLips.html.

Halscheid, Thérése. "*Six Lips.*" *New Pages Book Reviews.* http://www.newpages.com/bookreviews/2010-05/index.htm.

Hansen, Tyler. "Books in Our Backyard: *Crow Mercies.*" *Gazettetimes.com* (Corvallis, Ore.), November 25, 2010. http://www.gazettetimes.com/entertainment/article_027929a4-f85a-11df-b281-001cc4c002e0.html.

Kartali, Lesley. "*Crow Mercies.*" *Elevate Difference,* October 21, 2010. http://elevatedifference.com/review/crow-mercies.

Keyes, Claire. "*A Is for Anne.*" *Rattle,* August 2007. http://www.rattle.com/ereviews/schottpenelope.htm.

———. "*Six Lips.*" *Rattle,* March 2010. http://rattle.com/blog/2010/03/lips-penelope-scambly-schott/.

———. "*Crow Mercies.*" *Fiera Lingue,* September 2010. http://www.fieralingue.it/modules/poemreviews/corner.php?pa=printpage&pid=267.

MacPherson, Jennifer. "*May the Generations Die in the Right Order.*" *Cider Press Review* 9, 2008.

Marston, Elsa. "*A Little Ignorance.*" *Best Sellers,* September 1986, p. 238.

Miller, Peggy. "*The Pest Maiden.*" *Comstock Review,* May 2005. http://www.comstockreview.org/criticspen.html.

Moore, Julie L. "Six Lips." *Rattle,* July 10, 2010. http://rattle.com/blog/2010/07/six-lips-by-penelope-scambly-schott/.

Richards, Moira."Six Lips." *Verse Wisconsin Online* 104

(fall 2010). http://www.versewisconsin.org/Issue104/reviews104/schott.html.

———. "*Under Taos Mountain.*" *Fiddler Crab Review,* July 10, 2011. http://fiddlercrabreview.blogspot.com/.

Steinberg, Sybil. "*A Little Ignorance.*" *Publishers Weekly,* April 25, 1986, p. 64.

Vardaman, Wendy. "Poems Including History—and More." *Women's Review of Books.* March–April 2008, pp. 11–13. (Review of *A is for Anne.*)

Weaver, Julene. "Baiting the Void." *Goodreads,* April 4, 2010. http://www.goodreads.com/review/show/38488744.

INTERVIEWS

"The Habitual Poet: Penelope Scambly Schott." *Poemeleon,* April 5, 2010. (Contributor interview by Schott.) http://www.poemeleon.org/poemeleon-the-blog/2010/4/5/the-habitual-poet-penelope-scambly-schott.html.

Jarecki, Dave. "Interview with Penelope Schott." 2010. http://davejarecki.com/creative/2010/penelope-schott-interview 10.

Keyes, Claire. Interview with Penelope Schott, July 7, 2011.

———. Interview with Penelope Schott, July 12, 2011.

———. Interview with Penelope Schott, July 28, 2011.

———. Interview with Penelope Schott, August 28, 2011.

Lockward, Diane. "An Interview with Penelope Scambly Schott." *Eclectica Magazine* 14, no. 2 (April–May 2010). http://www.eclectica.org/v14n2/lockward.html.

Shaw, B. T. "For a Poet in Portland, There's More Room to be Odd." *Oregonian,* October 9, 2010. http://www.oregonlive.com/books/index.ssf/2010/10/for_a_poet_in_portland_theres.html.

BETTY SMITH

(1896—1972)

Sari Fordham

BETTY SMITH (NÉE Elisabeth Wehner), author of *A Tree Grows in Brooklyn* (1943), wrote books that explored the American dream in the early twentieth century. She populated her novels with the kind of people she knew best: working-class Americans. Her characters worried about money and were employed at condom factories, cafeterias, sanitation departments, and telegraph offices. Women worked too, and the decisions they made about balancing motherhood and their jobs came from necessity and with little fuss. Smith's novels mainly chronicled the lives of women, in prose that was as meticulous about a trip to the butcher shop as it was about the complexities of love. She was interested in getting the ordinary details right, and by doing so, she created rich worlds that readers either recognized or were transported into.

Smith began her writing career as a playwright, honing an aptitude for realistic dialogue that would typify her four novels. She describes the components of successful dialogue in her final novel, *Joy in the Morning* (1963): "Each line of dialogue must: one, characterize the person speaking; two, advance the plot; three, be interesting in itself. Perfect dialogue has all three elements" (pp. 180–181). Smith's dialogue included all three, particularly the first. Her characters spoke in distinct, authentic voices, and readers came to believe they were real people.

BIOGRAPHY

Betty Smith was born Elisabeth Wehner on December 15, 1896, in Brooklyn, New York. Like many of her protagonists, her parents, John Wehner and Katie Hummel Wehner, lived in the tenements and struggled to make ends meet. Smith's maternal grandparents had emigrated from Germany, but her father's family had lived in the United States since the Civil War, a rarity in her neighborhood. Smith's interest in the immigrant experience, however, was not restricted to families of German descent; indeed, Carol Siri Johnson notes that because several of her characters came from Ireland, the editors of one anthology mistakenly included her in a book on Irish American writers.

Smith was the eldest child of three. When the family needed money, she dropped out of school and entered the work force. She was only fourteen. For the next decade she would be in and out of high school, trying to obtain her diploma. Smith's desire for education informed her later writing, as did her many places of employment. She worked in a restaurant, an artificial-flower factory, a department store, a mail order house, a clipping bureau, and a telegraph office, all jobs her protagonists would later inherit.

When she was twenty-three, she eloped with George Smith, an ambitious law student. Her father had died when she was nineteen and her mother had remarried. The couple moved to Ann Arbor, where George obtained his law degree at the University of Michigan and where she once again became a high school student. She stopped attending school when she became pregnant. The Smiths had two daughters, Nancy and Mary. George got a job first as a lawyer and then as a county prosecutor. While it seemed that Betty Smith's educational pursuits were over, it also seemed as if she would no longer be burdened by financial hardship. She had children whom she loved and a successful husband, and by the cultural norms of the day, she had achieved the American dream. The couple, however, was not happy.

In 1928 they returned to University of Michigan. George enrolled in the graduate program, studying for a master's degree in political science, and an appreciative Betty Smith was allowed to take university classes as a special student. She mainly selected creative writing courses. She thrived in the university setting and gained confidence as a writer. In Kenneth Thorpe Rowe's playwriting course, the first two plays she wrote were so good that the professor included them in an anthology he was editing. In 1931 she won the University of Michigan's prestigious Avery Hopwood Award for her play titled "Francine Nolan." She would later give the protagonist of her first novel the same name.

In 1933 Betty and George separated. She was now a single mother without a reliable income. The United States was in the midst of the Great Depression, and President Franklin D. Roosevelt had implemented the New Deal. One of the programs was the Federal Theatre Project (FTP), which was aimed at employing out-of-work artists. Betty Smith and her friend Robert Finch were hired by the FTP to be playwrights in Chapel Hill, North Carolina. The two had met in a writing class while Smith was still married. They would collaborate throughout Finch's life, occasionally be lovers, and, toward the end of his life, finally marry.

Smith, who had moved frequently with her daughters, wanted to create a more permanent home for her children. When they arrived at Chapel Hill, she told her daughter they would stay there "forever" (see Johnson, online dissertation, "Biography: Chapel Hill"). She was true to her word. After her FTP job finished, she remained in North Carolina, patching together funds from judging plays, writing for magazines, and winning scholarships and awards. During this time, she wrote *A Tree Grows in Brooklyn.*

Smith entered her completed manuscript in the Harper & Brothers 125th Anniversary Nonfiction Contest. After two months of waiting for a response, reports Johnson, Smith wrote to the publisher asking to have her novel returned. The editors responded that the manuscript was not eligible for the nonfiction competition but that they would like to consider it as a standard fiction submission. The publishing house eventually bought the novel, and it went on to sell six million copies. Betty Smith, who had once been so poor that when she lost a bag of groceries she had nearly wept, was now a best-selling author and a celebrity.

After her novel was accepted, but before it came out, Smith remarried. Not to Finch, who had left North Carolina, but to Joe Jones, a soldier who wrote a column for the *Chapel Hill Weekly.* Smith had admired his prose and sent him a letter telling him so. They began to correspond, and soon Smith was writing Jones every day. Three months later, they met at Virginia Beach. They not only got engaged during that first meeting, they went to the courthouse and got married as well. Smith later regretted her haste and advised her daughter: "Don't marry the first man that asks you simply because you're flattered. I wish with all my heart that Joe was a heel, then I could divorce him next week" (Johnson, "Biography: Stress"). Smith and Jones' marriage lasted seven years.

Over the next twenty years Betty Smith wrote three more books: *Tomorrow Will Be Better* (1948), *Maggie-Now* (1958), and *Joy in the Morning* (1963). She hired one of the best literary agents at the time, Helen Strauss, to ensure she would be paid fairly and would no longer have to be concerned about money. She divorced Jones, and in 1957 she finally married Robert Finch. They were married for two years, until his death of a heart attack. Finch had been an alcoholic, and while his death devastated Smith, her friends were relieved. A friend wrote her: "Will you forgive me if I say something brutal? We are old friends, Betty, and I claim the privilege. While Bob's death was a terrible emotional shock to you, I feel that for the first time since I've known you, you are now free from what amounted to enslavement to him" (Johnson, "Biography: Common Folk 1858–1972"). Smith's complex relationships with men and her three marriages influenced her novels. Each depicts marriage as challenging at best and unsalvageable at worst, but they also record the tender moments between spouses and the comforts of familiarity. Only minor characters are

given idyllic marriages, and readers can assume that if we knew more, we would see the hardship beneath the sweetness.

Smith remained alone at her home in Chapel Hill until poor health forced her to move to Connecticut to be with her daughter. She died January 17, 1972, of pneumonia. She was seventy-five. All four of Smith's novels were best sellers, but she never received the formal acknowledgment from her peers that she craved. After the Pulitzer Prize committee overlooked *A Tree Grows in Brooklyn,* Smith wrote her editor Elizabeth Lawrence:

> I feel badly that the book did not receive the Pulitzer Award. I would gladly give up the position of best seller and most of the money if my book had been acknowledged as "distinguished" by the judges. I'm so anxious to write something that may be added to the literature of America and winning of this Prize automatically gives a book a place.
>
> (Johnson, "Biography: Stress")

A Tree Grows in Brooklyn, though, had achieved a place in American literature. It was turned into a film in 1945 and again in 1974. It appeared regularly on summer book lists and was recommended by librarians to young readers. The title became a part of popular culture and has been referenced in venues as varied as a Bugs Bunny cartoon ("A Hare Grows in Manhattan"), an episode of the sitcom *Ugly Betty* ("A Tree Grows in Guadalajara"), and Barry Estabrook's 2011 book *Tomatoland* ("A Tomato Grows in Florida"). With her love of books and her desire to be a writer, the protagonist Francie Nolan appealed to readers who saw in her a version of the American dream. Readers warmed to Francie's humanity and were certain that Betty Smith must be Francie Nolan. When asked if the novel was in fact nonfiction, Smith coyly replied that the book represented her life "not as it was, but as it should have been" (Johnson, "Biography: Common Folk 1896–1910").

A TREE GROWS IN BROOKLYN

When *A Tree Grows in Brooklyn* was published in 1943, it was an immediate sensation; according to *Time* magazine (December 20, 1943), it sold 460,000 copies in only four months. Readers picked up the book and felt as if they were finally reading their own stories. Amid the plethora of details, readers recognized their own neighborhoods, their grocers and butchers and penny stores. They recognized the texture of poverty, the stretching of day-old bread from meal to meal. As Smith reported in her author's note to the 1947 edition, many readers felt compelled to write to her. "My family had the same kind of struggle," wrote one fan. "I've never lived in Brooklyn but someone must have told you the story of my life because that's what you wrote," penned another. "I'm boiling mad. You wrote my book before I had a chance to get around to it," wrote still another (p. 7).

A Tree Grows in Brooklyn chronicles the coming of age of Francie Nolan, a girl who grows up poor but who has a rich sense of self. She is a keen observer, both of her family and her beloved neighborhood of Williamsburg in Brooklyn, and the novel throbs with an urgency to record the world before it is lost. Her neighborhood is changing. Trucks are replacing horses and carts. Women are bobbing their hair. World War I looms and then begins. The shifting backdrop reminds readers that nothing stays the same. Parents get older. Relationships become more complex. Childhood becomes adulthood. Francie experiences familiar rites of passage: she gets vaccinated, goes to school, gets her first doll, experiences death, graduates, receives her first pay, and falls in love. In the midst of these events, Francie discovers her mother is not always right and the tea shop she once considered elegant is shabby. Francie confides her disillusionments to her father, and he diagnoses her with a serious case of growing up. The novel documents Francie's journey away from childhood.

If American readers recognize themselves in Francie Nolan, it is in part because her story is a distinctly American one. When the novel begins, Francie is sitting on a fire escape, reading a book. It is Saturday afternoon, and Brooklyn is serene. Growing below Francie is a tree that is native to China, but since it was introduced here, it has flourished in the United States. Both the tree and

the young girl represent the American dream. Betty Smith writes, "Some people called it the Tree of Heaven. No matter where its seed fell, it made a tree which struggled to reach the sky" (p. 9).

Through the story of the Nolans, Betty Smith gives voice to the American belief that if you work hard and get an education, you will have a brighter future. In the United States, each generation has the opportunity to be more successful than the one before it. Francie's parents are second-generation Americans. Her father, Johnny Nolan, comes from an Irish Catholic family. Her mother, Katie Rommely Nolan, comes from a German Catholic family. Francie's grandparents emigrated to America because they wanted their children and their children's children to have a better future. Francie's maternal grandmother explains that although life has been hard here, in America, a carpenter's son doesn't have to be a carpenter. She goes on to say, "In this land, he may be what he will, if he has the good heart and the way of working honestly at the right things" (p. 67).

The novel, however, does not ignore the struggles of upward mobility or the many challenges of poverty. When Francie is born, Johnny is so overwhelmed with the responsibility of being a parent that he gets drunk, fails to show up for the janitorial job he shares with Katie, and loses their only source of income. Katie realizes that she will not be able to depend on her husband financially, and she wonders how she will be able to claim the American dream for her children. Her mother, who is illiterate, says the secret lies in reading and in saving money to buy land. Francie and her younger brother Neeley are shaped by their grandmother's philosophy. Each Saturday, Francie and Neeley join other Brooklyn children in selling rubbish to the junk man, but unlike other children, they put half their pennies in a condensed milk can that serves as the family bank, and each night, before they go to bed, Francie and Neeley read one page of the Bible and one page of Shakespeare.

The Nolan family's determination to be successful is sharpened by their poverty. Out of the four books Smith wrote, the characters in *A Tree Grows in Brooklyn* are the closest to destitution. Patriarch Johnny Nolan is a dreamer and a drunk. "I drink because I don't stand a chance and I know it," he tells Francie as she is ironing his dress shirt (p. 33). He will not fight against adversity, and so he cannot overcome it. He picks up periodic jobs as a singing waiter, and while he brings home his wages, he keeps his tips for drink. Katie supports the family by working as a janitor. The Nolans are poor, and they know the hunger of it. When they do not have enough money, Katie divides up the remaining food in the house and calls it rations. She pretends with the children that they are explorers waiting for help to come. Eventually Johnny brings home money from a job and the family has sugar buns to celebrate. When Francie is older, she asks her mother, "When explorers get hungry and suffer like that, it's for a *reason*. Something big comes out of it. They discover the North Pole. But what big thing comes out of us being hungry like that?" Katie responds, "You found the catch in it." (p. 167).

Poverty carries a more lasting injury than meaningless hunger: it carries shame. Respectable society despises those without money. At school, wealthy children are given the best seats and are fawned on by teachers. Francie is placed in the back of the room, and she once wets herself because the teacher ignores her raised hand. Society's contempt is contrasted with the Nolans' dignity and pride. When the family is particularly tight for money, Katie's sisters suggest she contact Catholic Charities for assistance. "When the time comes," says Katie quietly, "that we have to take charity baskets, I'll plug up the doors and windows and wait until the children are asleep and then turn on every gas jet in the house" (p. 229).

In *A Tree Grows in Brooklyn,* Smith repeatedly critiques how those with money treat those without. In a particularly poignant passage, Francie and Neeley go to the public health office for vaccinations. They go alone because Katie tells them she must work. Katie's absence is vital to the narration and sets in motion Francie's humiliation. Before going to the office, the children make mud pies, and they forget to wash

afterward. Francie is called first to receive her shot. As the nurse cleans a spot for the injection, she creates a white circle on the mud-streaked arm. The doctor looks down at Francie and says to the nurse, "Filth, filth, filth, from morning to night. I know they're poor but they could wash. Water is free and soap is cheap" (p. 114). The doctor continues his harangue, telling the nurse that the world would be better if poor people were sterilized. Francie is too hurt by the doctor's words to feel the injection. Before leaving, she channels Katie's pride and turns to the doctor and says, "My brother is next. His arm is just as dirty as mine so don't be surprised. And you don't have to tell him. You told me" (p. 115).

The Nolan family, led by Katie, is plucky in the face of discrimination and poverty. They draw strength from their extended families and from their belief that they are honest and good and deserve the American dream. While there might not be any point to being hungry, Katie and the children's lives have purpose: life will be better.

Johnny is the only major character not working for a better future. His brothers have died young, and he believes he will follow them. When the family moves into a new apartment, he says it will be the last time *he* moves, not the last time *they* move. Johnny is neither ambitious nor content. He tells his eleven-year-old daughter, "I am not a happy man. I got a wife and children and I don't happen to be a hard-working man. I never wanted a family" (p. 33). In one of the novel's unexplored ironies, ornamental Johnny, with his fine voice and long dancing legs, seems to have been born to be part of the idle rich. Yet if he were wealthy, he would be a villain.

Instead, Smith writes him with sympathy. Johnny might be a flawed character, the ne'er-do-well drunk, but he is also idealistic and romantic. He is adored by his children, particularly Francie, whom he calls "Prima Donna." He is an interesting conversationalist, a talented musician, and a snazzy dresser within his meager financial limits. Like Katie, Johnny wants his children to share in the American dream. While Katie is the more reliable presence, it is Johnny who takes Francie and Neeley to see the ocean so they might imagine a wider world, and it is Johnny

who helps Francie get into a better school. Writes Smith, "He had the same idea that Katie's mother, Mary Rommely, had about education. He wanted to teach his children all he knew so that at fourteen or fifteen, they would know as much as he knew at thirty" (p. 146).

Although Johnny spends his days at the bar (his daughter makes a note in her diary each time he comes home drunk), what prevents him from becoming a stereotype is his self-awareness. Johnny knows he is a drunk, and he knows society judges him. Toward the end of his life he tells his wife, "I can't sing any more. Katie, they laugh at me now when I sing. The last few jobs I had, they hired me to give the people a laugh. It's come to that, now" (p. 211). Johnny might seem like a cautionary tale, but he actually serves as a counterweight to the novel's dominant theme of upward mobility. If Francie is the beneficiary of the American dream, Johnny is the casualty. Early in the novel, he tells his daughter, "Now, it's work hard all the time or be a bum ... no in-between. When I die, nobody will remember me for long. No one will say, 'He was a man who loved his family and believed in the Union.' All they will say is, 'Too bad. But he was nothing but a drunk no matter which way you look at it" (p. 33). Johnny gives voice to those who are not able to realize America's promise. When he and Francie encounter a prostitute while taking a walk, Francie wants to know if the woman is "bad" (p. 132). Johnny tells her, "There are very few bad people. There are just a lot of people that are unlucky" (p. 132).

That Katie's life would have been easier without Johnny is apparent throughout the novel, but it is underscored when a police sergeant notices her during a Tammany-sponsored boat trip and picnic. Sergeant Michael McShane asks Francie if Katie is her mother, and when Francie says yes, he tells her, "Do you be sayin' your prayers to the Little Flower each night askin' that you grow up half as pretty as your mother. Do that now" (p. 141). Katie sees the exchange and later, when Johnny is at the beer tent, asks Francie about it. Francie confirms that that the police officer was talking about Katie, but she omits the man's compliment. Still, Katie hides her rough

hands and says to her daughter, "I work so hard, sometimes I forget that I'm a woman" (p. 141). The implication is clear: Johnny has failed his wife. Two and a half years after Johnny dies, Katie will, in one of the novel's less plausible plot lines, marry Sergeant Michael McShane, whose own unsuitable spouse has also conveniently died.

Johnny's death acts as the novel's hinge. Before he dies, Francie is still a child—despite the earlier proclamation in her diary that "today, I am a woman" (p. 175). After Johnny dies, Francie will irrevocably leave childhood behind. Johnny's inevitable death is hastened by the news that he will again become a father. He stops drinking, stops talking to his family, and comes home one night devastated that despite his sobriety, he has lost his union membership and any chance at a job. Sometime during the night, he leaves. Two days later he is found unconscious on the streets. Smith allows the reader to conjecture whether Johnny remains sober or whether he again turns to alcohol. The family has more pressing concerns. Katie's priority is maintaining family dignity. When the doctor is about to write acute alcoholism and pneumonia as the cause of death, Katie is adamant that he omit alcoholism. "I got two nice children. They're going to grow up to amount to something. It isn't their fault that their father … that he died from what you said" (p. 215). With pressure from the priest, the doctor complies. Some scholars have speculated that Smith's own father was an alcoholic, and they have used this scene as evidence. Like Johnny, Smith's father also died before Christmas and his death certificate also lists pneumonia as the cause of death (Johnson, "Biography: Common Folk 1896–1910").

By the March after Johnny's death, it seems the family will have to choose between eating or education. The Nolans have endured extreme poverty before, but Johnny always managed to get work when they most needed him. Pregnant Katie has lost her extra janitorial jobs because employers felt guilty watching her scrub floors. Without those jobs, the family does not have funds for food. Francie and Neely, who began school together, are supposed to graduate from eighth grade in May. If they graduate, they will be the first in their family to earn a diploma. The Nolans have already used their tin-can bank money to purchase a burial plot, and now it seems Francie, who is older, will have to get her working papers. Katie's sister Sissy says, "It won't be so terrible. Francie's smart and reads a lot and that girl will get herself educated somehow" (p. 229). But the reader believes it is terrible. The novel has convincingly tied the American dream to education, and to a lesser extent, purchasing land. The Nolans have given up one dream; now it seems Francie must sacrifice the other. Before Katie decides on what seems inevitable, a convenient reprieve comes in the form of Mr. McGarrity, the owner of the saloon Johnny frequented. He hires Neely and Francie to help at the bar after school. The conflict between familial need and education, though, has been established. The American dream is not so easily obtained, and that too is part of growing up.

Before Francie graduates from eighth grade, she receives the culmination of the lesson that began when she was vaccinated. Francie, who thrives in school, writes sweet compositions about trees and birds, or she did until her father died. Afterward, she writes about Johnny. She used to receive As, but these new essays receive Cs. The teacher, Miss Garnder, finally asks Francie to remain after class. Miss Garnder tells Francie that a writer "must strive for beauty always," and she uses John Keats to define beauty as "truth" (p. 243). When Francie protests that her stories are true, her teacher tells her:

> Drunkenness is neither truth nor beauty. It's a vice. Drunkards belong in jail, not in stories. And poverty. There is no excuse for that. There's enough for all who want it. People are poor because they're too lazy to work. There's nothing beautiful about laziness.
>
> (p. 243)

Miss Garnder returns Francie's four essays and tells her to burn them while chanting, "I am burning ugliness. I am burning ugliness" (p. 245). The implication is that if in America you can be anything, then destitution is a choice and does not deserve a story. The only American narrative

worth recording is that of success already achieved. While *A Tree Grows in Brooklyn* celebrates America's opportunities, Smith stridently highlights America's intolerance for those who are, as Johnny noted, merely "unlucky" (p. 132). Francie does burn her compositions, but she burns the sweet ones about birds and trees. She recognizes that *these* are the untruthful narratives. She had written about what she had read, not what she knew. After the compositions are burned, Francie thinks, "There goes my writing career" (p. 248). She would rather give up her ambition than be dishonest.

This passage, in which Francie refuses to be censored, reads like metafiction. Smith too is writing the truth about poverty during a time when the lives of the working poor are not conventional subjects. Smith writes about people who are hungry and who look into pots and see only pale bones, but she also writes about Francie's sense of luxury when she pours a cup of coffee down the drain instead of drinking it. Smith gives her characters multidimensional personalities. They are poor, but they are as complicated as the well-to-do. Francie's aunt Sissy works in a condom factory, is illiterate, loves children, and is the first woman in her family to give birth in a hospital.

Francie's teacher defines truth as "things like the stars always being there and the sun always rising and the true nobility of man and mother-love and love for one's country" (p. 243), but Smith explores a more complex reality of mother-love. Katie is an indomitable parent, the steely spine of the narrative. When a sexual predator tries to molest Francie, Katie shoots him in the groin, and when Francie asks her mother about sex, Katie responds with unflinching candor. Throughout the novel, the reader understands that Katie loves her daughter, but the reader also knows that Katie loves her son more. While watching Francie at Christmas, Katie realizes, "She'll find out that I don't love her as much as I love the boy. I cannot help it that this is so" (p. 159). Francie senses her mother's favoritism. Before Katie gives birth to her third child, Francie rationalizes: "She doesn't love me as much as she loves Neeley. But she needs me more than

she needs him and I guess being needed is almost as good as being loved. Maybe better" (p. 251). The truth Smith presents about familial relationships is that while they are neither simple nor flawless, they are powerful.

After graduating from eighth grade, both Francie and Neeley get summer jobs. Francie works first in a factory making flowers, and when she is laid off she becomes a file clerk at a clipping bureau. She is fourteen, but she pretends to be sixteen. She is the fastest reader at the office and is eventually promoted and given a raise. She will now make twenty dollars a week, the lowest salary in the office, but a fortune for the Nolans. Francie longs to begin high school and worries that her mother will want her to postpone her education. Before Katie learns about the raise, though, she tells her children that only one of them can return to school in the fall, and because Neeley does not want to attend school, he must. Francie, Katie says, will fight to get an education. A deeply disappointed Francie tells her mother, "I can only see that you favor Neeley more than me. You fix everything for him and tell me that I can find a way myself. Someday I'll fool you, Mama. I'll do what I think is right for me and it might not be right in your way" (p. 290).

Francie lives in an adult world of work. She makes good money, is able to purchase nice clothing for the first time in her life, and when one job ends, she easily finds another. She also attracts the attention of men. She dates the dependable, handsome, ambitious Ben. "At nineteen," writes Smith, "his life was planned out in a straight unswerving line" (p. 325). She also has one memorable date with Lee, a soldier who is leaving the next day. Lee is not handsome, and he is engaged to someone else, but at the end of the evening, when he asks Francie to wait for him, she says yes. Francie writes him a gushing letter, and his new wife replies. Francie shows the letter to her mother, tells her the story, and asks her mother if she should have slept with Lee. Katie answers first as a mother ("Your whole life might have been ruined") and then as an equal: "I will tell you the truth as a woman. It would have been a very beautiful thing. Because

there is only once that you love that way" (p. 347).

When *A Tree Grows in Brooklyn* ends, the Nolans are on their way to accomplishing the American dream. Katie is about to remarry; her new husband is wealthy by the Nolans' standard, and he promises to support the three children. Neeley is finishing high school, Francie is studying to take the entrance exam for college, and Laurie is a toddler. Like the Tree of Heaven, the Nolans have struggled to reach the sky and have ultimately succeeded. The novel concludes with Francie, who has now come full circle. As a girl, she had sat on the fire escape and gazed into the windows of her neighbors and watched young women gussy up for Saturday night dates. In the last chapter, Francie is getting ready for her own date. She looks out the window and sees a neighborhood child sitting on a fire escape, book in hand, watching her. Francie leans out the window and calls to the girl, but really, she is calling to her old self. "Hello, Francie," she says. And then, after speaking to her young neighbor, she whispers a farewell to her childhood: "Goodbye, Francie" (p. 368).

TOMORROW WILL BE BETTER

One month after the publication of *A Tree Grows in Brooklyn*, Betty Smith's editor, Elizabeth Lawrence, was already asking, "Do you have time these days to give any thought to the next novel?" ("Tomorrow Will Be Better: The Second Novel"). If the heightened expectation was not enough pressure, Smith was also answering fan letters, collaborating on a *Tree Grows in Brooklyn* screenplay and stage play, and being sued by a distant relative for defamation. She had written her first novel in quiet anonymity; now the editorial team at Harper & Brothers wanted to see early drafts and give revision suggestions. The first meeting with her editors was discouraging. Lawrence would later describe the meeting and her concerns about Smith's draft:

> My principal point was that the story failed for us as good theater—that her characters lacked the warm humanity of the people in A TREE and did not take hold of the reader's imagination—that the conflict was so muted as to be almost non-existent. In A TREE the characters were fighting their environment, they were in vigorous contact with life—either acceptance or rejection—and the reader cared dreadfully what happened to them. In the new novel the characters seemed passive, they took what came, drifted—with the result that they remained for the reader as drab as their background.
>
> (Johnson, "Tomorrow Will Be Better")

Smith did not handle the critique well. Despite reassurances from her publishers that they trusted her work, she rotated through several editors before the publication of *Tomorrow Will Be Better*.

The primary tension, writes Johnson, stemmed from Smith's desire to write a serious literary novel and her publisher's determination that she should also write one that was commercially successful. Smith eventually agreed to give the novel a more hopeful ending. She refused, however, to eliminate one aspect of the story that particularly concerned her publisher: a character's latent homosexuality. Harper & Brothers was afraid that the Book of the Month Club, whose support had boosted sales of *A Tree Grows in Brooklyn*, would not select a novel that might offend their readers. Smith held her ground. The Book of the Month Club chose her book anyway. In August 1948, five years after the publication of *A Tree Grows in Brooklyn*, Betty Smith's second novel, *Tomorrow Will Be Better*, was published. It too was a best seller.

While some critics say *A Tree Grows in Brooklyn* is sentimental, the same cannot be asserted about *Tomorrow Will Be Better*. Despite the optimistic title, the novel is grim. Like Smith's first novel, the characters are hoping for a brighter future, but in this narrative, they discover that the American dream is a mirage. While they experience similar burdens (poverty, disappointment, discrimination, death), they rarely find comfort in their mutual struggles. Marriages are unsatisfying and even the relationships between parent and child are tainted by selfishness and miscommunication. Only friendships and work offer a reprieve from loneliness.

The novel's opening is reminiscent of *A Tree Grows in Brooklyn*. We again meet a lone

protagonist on a Saturday, and she too lives in Williamsburg. It is nighttime, though, and winter. Margy is seventeen years old and walking because she does not want to go home. She is making a point to her mother that with employment she has also earned independence. She does not have a boyfriend to go out with, but she is mildly interested in her former classmate Frankie because his full name, Francis Xavier Malone, sounds important. She purposely walks by his house hoping to see him and she does. They share a mild greeting. She does not think Frankie is "much," but he will do until something better comes along (p. 5).

In the first chapter, Smith establishes the tension between settling for what is available and aspiring toward more. Margy's parents, Flo and Henny, have made bitter compromises and, in their clumsy way, want to prevent their daughter from making similar concessions. Flo is particularly concerned about her daughter's resolve. After Margy yields to her in an argument, Flo bemoans, "She asks for a new winter coat and all she gets is a sandwich and she says thanks—for that. She gives in too easy. She ought to have more fight in her" (p. 96). When Margy comes home, her mother accuses her of being out with a boy and insinuates that Margy will get pregnant. Even good-natured Margy finally gets exasperated, and she says, "Let me alone, Mama. Please!"(p. 6). When Margy later goes to bed, she feels contrite and decides that "it's a wonderful thing to have a home and a family" (p. 6). But the chapter does not end with Margy's warm sentiment. Instead, she slips into a reccurring nightmare where she is lost in Brooklyn. A gate prevents her from returning home, and in her dream, it is Frankie who swings the gate shut and locks her out. She wakes up crying.

The dream is not an exact analogy, but it is a warning. Margy's literal home is caustic and Margy yearns to escape. It is the concept of home that she is being prevented from finding. Margy shrugs off the dream: "What a dope," she tells herself (p. 7). She has, writes Smith, "the optimism of the young to whom all of life shines endlessly ahead; the young who are sure they can make their own proud destiny in spite of the tritely spoken wisdom of the older people who have had their chance at licking life and have come out of the unequal fight with bloody and bowed souls" (p. 34). *Tomorrow Will Be Better* documents Margy's "unequal fight."

Margy's unequal fight, however, is more drift than vigor. If the characters in *A Tree Grows in Brooklyn* are actively pursuing the American Dream, those in *Tomorrow Will Be Better* are either passively hoping for it or too preoccupied fighting with each other to work for it. Mild Henny, who has a feud with the trolley driver, surmises one evening that "we shove each other around more than the cops or bosses do. You'd think we'd stick together against the big shovers instead of being little shovers ourselves" (p. 24). He then goes home and fights with his wife. They quarrel so fiercely that Margy, who is a child then, trembles in the corner, and the neighbors bang on the walls and ceiling. Flo is the fiercer of the two. She also berates Margy, believing that "the quicker she learns that the world ain't all hearts and flowers, the better off she'll be" (p. 9). When Flo loses her daughter while running errands (the genesis of Margy's dream), she is panicked. Yet when she finds her daughter, she screams at her and slaps her repeatedly.

The brightest spot in Margy's life is her job. She is hired by Mr. Prentiss, an older man whom she secretly wishes she could marry. Mr. Prentiss, continuing the theme of unhealthy parent-child relationships, still lives with his mother who calls him her "best beau" (p. 52). He cannot get married while she is alive, though he seems interested in both Margy and her red-haired coworker. Margy becomes friends with another colleague, Reenie, and she enjoys the office camaraderie. When Frankie asks her on a date, it seems as if her life is finally beginning. They attend a dance at the Neighborhood Center House, and while there, they overhear the wealthy volunteers mock Frankie's accent. Once they leave the dance, Frankie cries from humiliation, and Margy tells him she believes in him. With those soothing words, Frankie begins to believe he is falling in love and Margy mistakes her "protective glow for love" (p. 108).

Despite disapproval from both sets of parents, who each believe their child should marry someone better, Margy and Frankie court and wed. Margy leaves her beloved job to become a housewife and finds the shift unfulfilling. The days stretch before her, and she searches for tasks to occupy her hands. She misses the office. Moreover, Frankie is embarrassed by her displays of affection and will only have reluctant sex with her in the dark of night. When Margy's friend Reenie gets married and her groom plants a kiss on Margy after the ceremony, Margy thinks: "It must be very wonderful to have sex in marriage" (p. 178).

The reader assumes that Frankie is gay, though Smith never states it outright. Early in the novel, Frankie's mother calls him "sensitive" (p. 86). He rejects the advances of the short-skirt-wearing Irma and asks Margy out because she seems less aggressive. Margy and Frankie do kiss in the halls, though his affection is the most spontaneous following points of stress. Once they are married, he is uncomfortable with her body. He does not seem to enjoy her company and appears miserable to find himself married. He darts out of the apartment each day in order to get to work. One evening, he brings home two of his colleagues, Sandy and Gene.

Smith relies on negative stereotypes to imply that these coworkers are gay. Sandy "wore a severely plain tweed suit, low-heeled brogues and her stiff, straight hair was cut short" and Gene had "wavy blond hair" that Margy thought should be "cut a little shorter" (p. 187). Frankie is expansive with his friends, and when they say goodnight, Margy is so pleased with her transformed husband that she loops her arm in his. Gene appears irritated.

"What a touching domestic scene," he said.

"Don't be petty, dear," Sandy warned him.

Rather viciously, Frankie pulled his arm away from Margy. She looked at him and noticed that a hot red color was mounting in his face as though he had been caught doing something nasty.

(p. 188)

Despite the awkward conclusion of the evening, Frankie feels buoyed. He initiates sex that evening. Margy first thinks, "don't come fooling around me after you've been to a burlesque show," but when Frankie tells her he was "proud" to show off his wife, she disregards her concerns and chooses to be happy (p. 188).

Margy gets pregnant that night. Neither set of parents particularly welcomes the news. Frankie's mother, who has a hostile relationship with Margy, tells her son, "She played a dirty lowdown trick on you" (p. 194). Frankie, who is a flawed character, is not wholly unsympathetic. He tells his mother, "She's only a girl, Mama, and maybe she's scared." (p. 195). While Frankie defends Margy to her mother, he tells his wife that he will see to it that they have no more children. Margy responds with a raw truth that startles her as much as it offends him: "We've got to have children because you and I have nothing between us" (p. 219). They make up later, each apologizing, but their marriage has a "tear" (p. 220).

Their daughter is born dead, a literal metaphor of their union, and both parents grieve. Margy tells her doctor, "Where I carried the baby, it's empty. But the emptiness hurts like it was a live thing" (p. 222). Her pain gives her the courage to start fighting against the fate she had previously accepted. She tells her mother that if her daughter had gotten lost, "I wouldn't've hit her when I found her" (p. 226). Smith allows Flo to be a complex character who does terrible things but is also life's victim. She writes, "Flo's thoughts ran under her daughter's words," and one of those thoughts was: "She never knew that the slap, the scolding was a way of taking it out on her because she made me feel bad because I couldn't do for her all that should have been done" (p. 226). Margy's words to her mother-in-law are particularly sharp and short. After calling her "Mother Malone," Margie simply says, "I hate you" (p. 228).

Margy has turned a corner in her life. When she returns to the apartment she shares with Frankie, she rejects suicide and decides instead that she is "tired of always considering other people and being afraid to do this or that" (p. 239). After she and Frankie have gone over their bills, she announces that she will return to work.

He feels as if she is undermining his authority. During their discussion, he confesses that he is "born a little a certain way" but that he doesn't "want to go around sleeping with fellers"; he just doesn't "want to sleep with anybody" (p. 243). That evening, while Frankie is falling asleep, Margy imagines their future. They will live together for a while. Frankie will eat at his parents' house and she will eat at her parents' house. Soon, they will decide that keeping the apartment is economically irresponsible. When they eventually divorce, others will wonder what happened since "they seemed to get along so well" (p. 245). The novel concludes with Margy's reoccurring dream. For the first time, Margy is not frightened. She awakes motivated. She sits down and writes a letter to her former boss, Mr. Prentiss. *Tomorrow Will Be Better* takes a pessimistic view of the American dream, yet, as Smith's publishers insisted, it ends on an optimistic note.

MAGGIE-NOW

Maggie-Now, Betty Smith's third novel, was published in February 1958. It had been ten years since the publication of *Tomorrow Will Be Better* and fifteen years since *A Tree Grows in Brooklyn,* and the editors at Harper & Brothers were anxious for Smith to publish again. For much of the previous decade, she had dodged their letters and telegrams. *Tomorrow Will Be Better* had sold well, but it had not received the accolades of *A Tree Grows in Brooklyn,* and Smith must have felt the pressure to write another masterpiece this time. In a 1952 letter to her editor, she wrote: "I should have answered your letter long ago. But in the last few months I've developed a sort of dread of writing anything. I sit at the typewriter to write and I begin to feel ill. I think each day of the letters I should answer and it disturbs my day. Yet I cannot make myself sit down to type" (Johnson, "Maggie-Now: Part 1"). Shortly after writing this letter, Smith was seriously injured in a car accident. She was in the hospital for over a month, and when she returned home, she began typing in order to rehabilitate her hand. The

dialogue that emerged eventually turned into *Maggie-Now.*

Like Smith's previous two novels, *Maggie-Now* examines the lives of the working class, and much of the novel plays out in the homes and stores of Williamsburg, Brooklyn. The novel, however, deviates from the rest of Smith's novels in two dramatic ways: the novel opens in County Kilkenny, Ireland, not the United States, and the first character we meet is male, not female. Though the novel is primarily a meditation on marriage, the one continuous character is the unlikeable Patrick Dennis Moore.

Patrick, called Patsy, is a dandy who likes to dance. He enjoys dating the lovely Maggie Rose, but when Maggie Rose's mother asks when he will marry her daughter, he piously replies that he has promised his own mother he will wait until after she dies. Smith writes, "Patsy kept on courting Maggie Rose and enjoying it more because he knew now that he didn't have to give up his freedom. Sure, he intended to marry her someday maybe" (p. 376). Matrimony must wait until it suits *him.* Maggie Rose's mother sends for her son Big Red, who returns from America, gives Patrick a public licking, and gets the priest to announce Patrick and Maggie Rose's wedding during Mass. Maggie Rose is devastated. " 'Why did you come a-tween us?' she sobbed. 'I was willing to wait till his mother died' " (p. 393). Patrick loves Maggie Rose, but he will not be controlled or humiliated. He gets on a boat to the United States and irrevocably leaves behind love and Ireland.

The novel shifts to more familiar terrain, both for Smith and her readers. In Brooklyn, Patrick works for Mike Moriarity, a Tammany ward heeler called the Boss. The Boss and the Missus have a kind, spinster daughter named Mary, about whom the Boss tells Patrick, "don't get idears" (p. 411). Of course, the reader knows Patrick will get ideas, if for no other reason than to get his way. Patrick is not a sympathetic protagonist. He is selfish, childish, and lazy, but he does recognize that Mary is a good girl and the first time he holds her, he realizes that her body doesn't fit with his, not the way Maggie Rose's did, and he thinks sadly, *"we will never fit together"* (p. 424).

Patrick nevertheless marries his wealthy boss's daughter, and it seems as if his fortune will change. Smith, though, has little interest in exploring the inner lives of the wealthy. During the next election, the reform party wins and the Boss is arrested for corruption and promptly dies of a heart attack. The family fortune is confiscated, and the Missus moves to Boston to live with her sister. All that is left for Patrick and Mary is the street-cleaning job the Boss got Patrick and a run-down house the Boss had placed in his daughter's name.

The nuptials of Mary and Patrick introduce the novel's dominant theme: that marriage is an institution that women crave and men endure, and therefore, women are the ones who must make concessions in order to sustain it. Smith does not seem to be making an overtly feminist argument. In her previous books, the aggrieved parties have at least inwardly protested their treatment. The women in *Maggie-Now* are docile and mainly willing to forgo their personal fulfillment in order to please their husbands. Men will be men, and women must be understanding. Patrick's flight to America is a vital part of this narrative. Maggie Rose's family interferes in his autonomy, and he is obligated to object. The tone of the novel is established early: men do not bend their wills for women. Even Big Red, who traveled to Ireland to try to force Patrick to marry his sister, later regretted his action. While *Maggie-Now* also examines friendship, rituals, and faith, it is predominately a meditation on marriage. Ultimately the novel will focus on four couples representing two generations: Big Red and Lottie, Patrick and Mary, Claude and Maggie-Now, and finally, Denny and Tessie.

Big Red and Dotty are peripheral characters, but they serve as the novel's model of a happy, functioning marriage. Dotty caters to Big Red and acquiesces to him, and in return she enjoys the security and affection of marriage. Each evening before Big Red comes home, Dotty dresses up. She greets him with a pan of hot water so that he can soak his feet. She has spent the day preparing a meal "exactly the way Big Red liked it" (p. 380). Big Red rewards her devotion. On laundry days, he lifts the heavy wash boiler onto the stove for her, and at work, he seeks a promotion so that if he dies, Dotty will get a larger widow's pension. They are both affectionate and they satisfactorily fill their traditional roles. Once Big Red dies, Dotty lives on his memory, telling whoever will listen, "And so we stayed sweethearts right up to the end" (p. 476).

Mary and Patrick's marriage is also an example of a traditional union. Patrick is the head of the house, and Mary yields to his authority. Patrick is more cantankerous than Big Red, however, and the two could not be called sweethearts. What Mary wants most is Patrick's love, and Patrick, who is still pining over Maggie Rose, seems unable to give it to her, despite the opportunities Mary provides. Mary remains patient. She even suggests they name their first daughter, Maggie, "after that girl you liked so … you know, Margaret Rose? It's such a pretty name" (p. 440). The premise of the novel seems to be that women must be generous in a marriage, but they cannot expect the same from their husbands. Those whose husbands are also magnanimous, like Dotty's, are the exception. Mary gets pregnant again, late in life, and during her difficult second delivery, the doctors choose to save the baby's life over hers. As she is dying, she whispers to Patrick, "In all our years you never told me …" Patrick replies, "No, I never told you, Mary. But I do" (p. 489). Her sacrifice, in the end, is rewarded.

Their daughter, Maggie-Now, is a "giver," as the nuns at her parochial school observe (p. 447). When her mother dies, she forfeits her adolescence to raise her younger brother, Denny. Maggie-Now's quiet life changes when she attends a salesmanship workshop taught by Claude. He is humorous and speaks fancy but she likes him despite these flaws, and he likes her despite her faith and her seriousness. Their courtship ends when Maggie-Now refuses to renounce Catholicism for Claude. She will not bend her will to his, and so, like Patrick before him, Claude disappears. Claude, however, reappears in the spring. He again asks Maggie-Now to sacrifice her faith. He seems to be testing the degree to which a man can expect compromise from a

woman, and even as he demands submission, he recognizes his churlishness. He thinks, *"I know how she is about her religion. What difference does it make? No faith means anything to me. So I ask her to give it up. Why? Just to own all of her? To prove I'm a man?"* (p. 596). Claude discovers that for Maggie-Now, at least, faith requires a higher allegiance, and he acquiesces in order to get her to marry him.

Claude and Maggie-Now's marriage is marked by exceptional sacrifice, even in the context of this novel. Each spring, when the chinook blows, Claude disappears. He does not say goodbye to Maggie-Now, nor does he write her while he is gone. The first time he leaves, she thinks he is gone for good. But he returns each winter, thin and bedraggled, with a souvenir for Maggie-Now. If their marriage is to work, she must accept this. Like her mother, she does so with aplomb. Writes Smith. "When she saw him, she held out her arms and smiled. She didn't ask him where he'd been. She didn't ask him never to leave her again. She hugged him tight and smiled and said: 'What took you so long?' as though he had just stepped out an hour ago to go to the store" (p. 638).

Maggie-Now and Claude never have children, a hole Maggie-Now fills as a foster mother. Claude reluctantly consents to this new development. It is the second time Maggie-Now has defied his wishes, and the exceptions serve to underscore the rule. Claude is not providing Maggie-Now with the security usually afforded by marriage, and so he cannot expect her also to remain childless. Claude, however, wins their final disagreement posthumously. He comes home one winter particularly gaunt, promising he will not leave her again. He dies instead from a stroke. Maggie-Now plans to bury him with her mother and her grandfather, but she learns that Claude wanted to be cremated. In her shrillest objection, she screams, "I won't allow it!" and then she explains why "It's against our religion" (p. 728). Her brother convinces her to comply: "You always gave Claude everything he wanted. ... Why don't you give him this one last thing he wanted?" (p. 728). In the end, Claude's will prevails over Maggie-Now's faith.

The novel's final couple represents a more modern marriage. Maggie-Now's brother Denny marries Tessie, who believes a husband must also accommodate his wife. During a family disagreement she tells Maggie-Now, "[Denny's] first obligation is to me and the baby" (p. 713). When Denny is offered a chance to open a new butcher shop, she objects because the position would require moving away from both their families. When Maggie-Now discovers that Tessie is influencing her family's future, she tells Denny, "Tessie's a wonderful girl. And she's a smart girl, too. She has one beautiful fault, though. The fault of being very young. Don't ask her what she wants, tell her what you want" (p. 730). Denny heeds Maggie-Now's advice. In keeping with the novel's portrayal of marriage and women's place in it, the book ends with Denny and Tessie moving away from Brooklyn, and with Patrick taking Claude's ashes to the top of the Statue of Liberty and scattering them.

JOY IN THE MORNING

Betty Smith's fourth and final novel was published in 1963, twenty years after the publication of *A Tree Grows in Brooklyn*. When she had completed her first two novels, Harper & Brothers had contacted Smith repeatedly and asked when she would write her next. But after *Maggie-Now*, they were quiet. According to Johnson, when Smith contacted them for an advance for *Joy in the Morning*, the company offered $1,000 and connected the funds to the royalties of *A Tree Grows in Brooklyn*, not the sales of her forthcoming novel. Smith was incensed. Her agent smoothed over the conflict and got Smith a proper advance. In an ironic twist, Smith's publishers had lost faith in her just as she was writing a novel that was the most reminiscent of her first.

Joy in the Morning seems to pick up where *A Tree Grows in Brooklyn* leaves off. The protagonist, Annie, is leaving Brooklyn with her ambitious fiancé, Carl. He is attending law school at a university in the Midwest. Like Francie Nolan, Annie comes from a poor home, loves to read, dreams of becoming a writer, and has a particular

way about her. She is proud and sincere and pays attention to people. *Joy in the Morning,* however, is not a sequel. Annie's family members are not the winsome Nolans. Annie's mother has a bland personality, and her stepfather tried to molest her. Annie is ready to make a new home for herself with Carl.

While Smith's previous novels grapple with larger social issues, *Joy in the Morning* is content to transcribe the first years of a marriage. Annie and Carl are wed in a courthouse. Before they can consummate their marriage, they sit on a porch swing and wait for their room in the boardinghouse to be vacated and cleaned. Carl gets fresh with Annie and she tells him: "Carl, I'm a person. I'm a person that don't like to be grabbed in a swing" (p. 26). With that line, Smith introduces the predominant conflict in the novel, the tension between autonomy and unity.

Annie and Carl must adjust to their new roles as husband and wife, learning to respect each other as independent people while working toward a common future. The women in *Maggie-Now* might have relinquished their selfhood with marriage, but Annie has not. She gets a job, makes her own friends, takes a playwriting class, and writes a play that is selected for an anthology. When Carl is unkind to her friend the florist, who Smith suggests is gay, Annie tells him, "You ought to be ashamed of yourself" (p. 241). Carl agrees, but Annie still wiggles out of his embrace and marches silently for several blocks.

Carl is also a more complex character than the men of *Maggie-Now*. He works several jobs, strives to make good grades, and appreciates Annie for her keen mind. But he also thinks of her as a child. She is not sophisticated, and he teachers her words like "quiz" (p. 65). Yet, it is Annie who charms the dean of his law school. At the end of their meeting, the Dean shakes Carl's hand and tells him that Annie is his "asset" (p. 102). In the hall, Annie asks what "asset" means.

When Annie gets pregnant, the Dean finds her a doctor and helps Carl get in-state tuition and obtain a loan to defray the cost of school. Carl continues to work multiple jobs, and he and Annie fight more. Despite these challenges, Carl and Annie have grown into their marriage. They

no longer seem like two children pretending to be married. They have learned each other's quirks and have smoothed each other's rough edges. Annie has become more sophisticated and Carl has become more compassionate. The novel ends with Carl's graduation. The event they have both sacrificed for is anticlimactic after the birth of their son and the publication of Annie's play. Carl already had a job for the coming year, thanks to the largesse of the Dean, and the future stretches bright and hopeful before Carl and Annie.

The critics dismissed *Joy in the Morning* as a sentimental book, but it was a commercial success. Like all of Smith's novels, it became a best seller, and like *A Like Tree Grows in Brooklyn,* it was turned into a film. The 1965 movie starred Richard Chamberlain as Carl Brown. Forty-five years later, the novel achieved "classic" status when Harper Perennial Modern Classics published an edition on June 29, 2010.

CONCLUSION

Betty Smith was born at the turn of the twentieth century. The United States was significantly changing. The Civil War had ended thirty years earlier, and the transcontinental railroad had opened up California to migration. In Brooklyn, New York, the issue of the day was immigration and assimilation. A million people lived in the borough across the river from Manhattan and more than a third had been born in other nations. Nativists were anxious about national identity, or more specifically, about who should be an American. The year Smith was born, Congress passed a literacy bill that restricted entrance to the United States to immigrants who could read forty words in any language. President Grover Cleveland vetoed the bill because it contradicted American values.

Betty Smith's novels record the time and place of her childhood and young adulthood. Her novels build a world, with attention paid to place and to the details of day-to-day life. Yet they transcend the specifics. Her characters wrestle with universal problems—marriage, work, parents, money. They want to live decent lives and

they hope tomorrow will be brighter than today. They are often immigrants, usually women, and they are observant about themselves and others. *A Tree Grows in Brooklyn* is Betty Smith's most lasting literary legacy, but in each of her novels, she tells the story of America and what it means to be American.

Selected Bibliography

WORKS OF BETTY SMITH

NOVELS

A Tree Grows in Brooklyn. New York: Harper & Brothers, 1943.

Tomorrow Will Be Better. New York: Harper & Brothers, 1948.

Maggie-Now. New York: Harper & Brothers, 1958.

Joy in the Morning. New York: Harper & Row, 1963.

PAPERS

Smith's papers are held in the Southern Historical Collection at the Louis Round Wilson Special Collections Library of the University of North Carolina at Chapel Hill.

FILMS BASED ON THE WORKS OF BETTY SMITH

A Tree Grows in Brooklyn. Directed by Elia Kazan. Screenplay by Tess Slesinger and Frank Davis. Twentieth Century–Fox, 1945.

A Tree Grows in Brooklyn. (Television movie.) Directed by Joseph Hardy. Adapted from the screenplay by Tess Slesinger and Frank Davis. Twentieth Century–Fox Television, 1974.

CRITICAL AND BIOGRAPHICAL STUDIES

REVIEWS AND OTHER SOURCES

"Books: It Happened in Flatbush." *Time,* September 6, 1943, p. 102.

"Books: The Year in Books." *Time,* December 20, 1943, p. 99.

Johnson, Carol Siri. "A Tree Grows in Brooklyn." Ph.D. dissertation, City University of New York, 1994. http://web.njit.edu/˜cjohnson/tree/.

ELIZABETH STROUT

(1956—)

Phoebe Jackson

ALTHOUGH THE FICTION writer Elizabeth Strout has spent much of her adult life in New York City, her childhood in Maine and New Hampshire holds a special place in her work. Maine is the setting for her three novels, *Amy and Isabelle* (1998), *Abide with Me* (2006), and *Olive Kitteridge* (2008). Strout's vivid depictions of small-town New Englanders have earned her a place on the *New York Times* best-seller lists and, for *Olive Kitteridge,* the Pulitzer Prize.

BIOGRAPHY

Strout was born in Portland, Maine, on January 6, 1956. Her father, Richard Strout, who taught at the University of New Hampshire in Durham, was a parasitologist; her mother, Beverly, was a high school writing teacher. Besides living in New Hampshire, the family spent time in nearby South Harpswell, Maine.

From an early age, Strout knew that she wanted to be a writer. However, she did not take a predictable route to achieve her goal. Strout attributes her passion for writing to her mother's influence. As a young girl, she was encouraged by her mother to write down what she was doing and what she had observed. To Lynn Carey of the *Contra Costa Times,* Strout explained, "My mother was a real storyteller. She made the most mundane things interesting. So, from my earliest memory, I thought that's what you did; you made up stories and sentences. My mother was very encouraging. She'd give me notebooks from when I was very little, telling me to write down what I did that day."

As an adolescent, Strout spent a great deal of time by herself. In her short memoir piece "English Lesson" for the *Washington Post* (2009), she reveals that her parents were quite strict with

both her and her brother. They were not allowed to participate in the usual teenage activities like watching TV, going on dates, or spending time with other teenagers. Strout, however, did a great deal of reading and writing. In an interview with Bill Grattan and Lania Knight in *Center,* Strout underscored the significant role that reading played in teaching her to write; as she said, "I learned from reading. I read and read" (p. 28). During this time, Strout also began to send out stories for publication.

In rather unpredictable move, Strout, with her mother's acceptance, dropped out of high school after her junior year. She left high school because of her displeasure with it. Later Strout went on to pursue a bachelor's degree at Bates College in Lewiston, Maine, majoring in English and theater. She graduated in 1977. Of her time at Bates College, Strout wrote in a very short memoir piece for *Ploughshares* that she lacked confidence as a student and was by and large intimated by students around her. One of the memories she does have of her time at Bates was the pleasure she got in discovering that the library held literary journals—a genre of magazines heretofore completely unknown to her. With this new treasure trove of reading material, Strout found herself completely drawn into the narratives that she was reading. From these fictional stories and poems, she got a glimpse of how other people conducted their lives and how they worked through their relationships. Strout concedes that she learned a lot about life from reading the narratives of other writers.

During her time at college, Strout traveled to Oxford, England, for a summer. In a short memoir piece, "English Lesson," written about her experience in England, Strout comically depicts herself as an innocent abroad. When a

meeting with an English man goes awry, she learns firsthand that sexual assumptions can bring about unwanted complications to one's life. With this brief seven-page foray into the memoir, Strout displays her signature self-deprecating manner in the depiction of herself—the same one that shows up in many of her interviews.

After graduating from Bates, Strout took various and sundry jobs—as a secretary, a salesperson, a house cleaner, and a waitress. While working at these jobs, she also managed to find time to write. Doubtful about her ability to succeed as a writer, Strout made a bid for a more conventional career in 1979 by enrolling in the Syracuse University College of Law. About her decision to go to law school, Strout has written that she wanted to do something in her life that constituted a serious endeavor. While there she met and married her first husband, Martin Feinman. Strout graduated from law school in 1982, having completed her law degree with honors (cum laude) and a certificate in gerontology. After graduation Strout practiced law for six months with Legal Services in Syracuse, giving her enough time to realize that law was not the career for her.

Soon thereafter, Strout and Feinman moved to New York City, where she spent the next twelve years raising her daughter, Zarina (born in 1983), teaching as an adjunct at Manhattan Community College, and writing. Becoming a mother, Strout admits, forced her to take advantage of every spare moment she had to write. As she explained in a profile by Ladette Randolph in *Ploughshares:* "For many years my entire writing schedule was around my daughter. ... she was a good baby, and when she napped I would write. Because she napped best when she was in the car, I often drove somewhere, had her fall asleep, and would turn the car off quietly. So for a couple years, my writing time was done in a car in some warehouse parking lot or on a street in New York. Quite honestly, this worked very well" (p.178).

Though she spent all of her free time writing and teaching, Strout never told anyone that she was a writer. She was unwilling to talk about her chosen career for fear of the questions people might ask her or the comments they might make

when they learned she was a writer. Much as she did in her early years, Strout wrote on her own without talking about it.

During this period of her career, Strout published two short stories—"Staying Afloat" in *Redbook* magazine in 1991 and "RUNNING-AWAY" in *Seventeen* in 1992. Living and writing in New York City helped Strout with her writing in immeasurable ways. She came face-to-face with a different way of living, foreign to someone from Maine. And she had the opportunity to observe people in completely new situations and new circumstances. Then in 1994, as a way to find her narrative voice, she signed up to take a stand-up comedy class. This experience led Strout to one of her most significant discoveries about her writing. Standing up in front of an audience, she found herself telling jokes and stories about Maine. That unusual experience led her to the realization that her source of material in writing should be a subject that she knew intimately, in this case New England.

Unlike many writers of her generation, Elizabeth Strout never took a creative writing class in college and is thus by and large self-taught. She attributes her avoidance of creative writing workshops to her fear of showing her writing to so many other people. In her interview with Grattan and Knight, she does talk about a class that she took with Gordon Lish at the New School. She mentions that Lish taught her the importance of the sentence. As she comments, Lish "would say that you have to earn every sentence" (p. 28). In his class, Lish had the students read their sentences aloud and would stop them when he heard any false note. Though this lesson was valuable for her own writing, she found the experience of Lish's commenting on student writing an intimidating one. She notes in the interview that Lish basically "left [her] alone" (p. 28). Reading individual sentences in Strout's fiction, one can see that she took to heart what Lish had to say about the sentence. It is easy to find oneself going back to reread individual sentences because they are so carefully crafted.

Though it would take Strout seven years to write her first novel, *Amy and Isabelle* (1998), her persistence in the long run paid off in the

ELIZABETH STROUT

wide acclaim it received. This novel won both the *Los Angeles Times* Award for First Fiction and the *Chicago Tribune* Heartland Award, and it was short-listed for the PEN Faulkner Award and the British Orange Prize. In the interview with Grattan and Knight, Strout discussed why writing takes such a long time for her. Specifically, she addressed the difficulty of developing her characters. "Some of the characters come to me so slowly that I could just cry. I want faster access, but I don't seem to have it and I don't seem to know how to speed it up. I have to wait. I have to go through the process, bit by bit, finding out little details here and there that seem right. Then gradually the character will come forward." Besides the slow process of developing characters, Strout has talked about her obsession with rewriting. To Katie Bacon of the *Atlantic,* she explained, "I rewrite so much. And I write so many scenes that end up not being in the book. Making those decisions about what the main storyline ultimately will be seems to take me some time." Indeed, she told John Marshall of the *Seattle Post-Intelligencer* that in writing the first part of *Amy and Isabelle,* she wrote almost "100 different versions" of it.

Strout has also spoken frequently about the continued importance of reading for her and for her writing. Among literary influences, Strout counts such canonical worthies as Edith Wharton, Virginia Woolf, Ernest Hemingway, D. H. Lawrence, and Leo Tolstoy. When discussing contemporary writers, she attributes her attention to detail in her novels to reading the journals of John Cheever. In her interview with Grattan and Knight, Strout talked in more specific terms about his influence on her writing: "John Cheever was an enormous influence on me. His journals influenced me tremendously because of the attention he gave to weather, the daily conditions. I recognized, for the first time, certain things about the physical world that could be captured in a phrase, and I think those journals liberated something in me, actually. I read them again and again, and I still do" (p. 29). For Strout, reading continues to perform a very specific role in her writing. In an interview with Robert Birnbaum, she elaborated on its significance for her: "I think

that it's the other half of my job. I mean, it's directly related to writing, I think that one can write as well as one reads." Her love of reading also demonstrates itself in the thoughtful reviews she has written about the books of authors like William Trevor and Carrie Brown and in the introduction she wrote for a Modern Library edition of Edith Wharton's novels *Ethan Frome* and *Summer* (2001).

Strout followed *Amy and Isabelle* with two other novels, *Abide with Me* (2006) and *Olive Kitteridge* (2009). As in her first novel, Strout uses the small towns of rural and coastal Maine as the setting. Her fiction typically concerns itself with the lives of people who inhabit these small towns. From an outsider's perspective, their lives seem to be about everyday, mundane concerns. But like the novel *The Country of the Pointed Firs* (1896) by Sarah Orne Jewett, her nineteenth-century predecessor, Strout's works are populated with characters who reveal that there is more to their individual lives than life in a small town might suggest. Strout, in her writing, is able to marry the small details of life with larger realities, giving the reader insight into the complications that attend all lives. In *Olive Kitteridge,* Strout distills these moments into what she terms the "big bursts" and "little bursts" that constitute everyday living: "Big bursts are things like marriage or children, intimacies that keep you afloat, but these big bursts hold dangerous, unseen currents. Which is why you need the little bursts as well: a friendly clerk at Bradlee's, let's say, or the waitress at Dunkin' Donuts who knows how you like your coffee" (pp. 68–69). While her characters seem like very ordinary people with ordinary problems, Strout imbues them with a dignity that demonstrates how their struggles to get on in life are worthy of the reader's attention.

Her ability to connect to readers through her style of writing and through her interest in people has led to her success as a writer. Both *Amy and Isabelle* and *Olive Kitteridge* were on the *New York Times* best-seller list, and *Olive Kitteridge* won the Pulitzer Prize for fiction in 2009 as well as the Italian Premio Bancarella award in 2010. Along with the publishing success of *Amy and Isabelle,* Oprah Winfrey's Harpo Productions

turned the novel into a film of the same name in 2001, starring Elizabeth Shue. *Olive Kitteridge* too has been optioned as a movie.

In 2011 Strout married the former Maine Attorney General James Tierney. She lives in Brunswick, Maine, and New York City. Having formerly taught at Bard College, Warren Wilson College, and Colgate University as a National Endowment of the Humanities professor, Strout currently teaches in the MFA program at Queens University of Charlotte in Charlotte, North Carolina. For her next project, besides writing about Maine, Strout will use New York City as part of the setting. The narrative focuses on a group of Somali immigrants who reside in Maine but who have connections to lawyers in New York City. This departure of writing about a wholly different cultural and ethnic group will undoubtedly stretch Strout as a writer. But using her background as a lawyer will also provide an important context to these immigrants' plight.

AMY AND ISABELLE

Published in 1998, *Amy and Isabelle* was widely reviewed and praised. Karen Haram of the *San Antonio Express* enthusiastically called it "the kind of immensely readable first novel publishing houses dream of."

Though her novel won acclaim, Strout interestingly did not consider herself a novelist prior to the book's publication because she had written and published only short stories. Speaking to John Marshall of the *Seattle Post-Intelligencer,* Strout commented that the thought of writing a novel actually "scared" her. In actuality, *Amy and Isabelle* began its life as a kernel for a short story. Strout had imagined a scene of a mother who cuts off her daughter's hair. Because she could not get the scene "to work as a short story," she resorted to the novel form (Carey, *Contra Costa Times*). In an interview with Lonnac O'Neal Parker from the *Washington Post,* Strout noted the influence of the *New Yorker* critic Daniel Menaker, who early on recognized her writing ability. Though he had rejected her short story based on the characters of Amy and Isabelle for

the magazine, Menaker took the unusual step of calling Strout to offer words of encouragement. Strout was quite effusive in her praise of Menaker, telling Parker, "The fact that Daniel Mcnaker at *The New Yorker* had called to tell me to keep going, it would be embarrassing for me to tell you how much that meant to me." Menaker, who had moved on to Random House, eventually read the novel and bought it for his publishing house.

Strout's attention to craft is evidenced in the first sentence of the novel: "It was terribly hot that summer Mr. Robertson left town, and for a long while the river seemed dead" (p. 3). With this opening sentence, Strout forecasts the issues of the novel. The hot weather assaults everyone's sensibilities, seemingly acting in concert with all of the events that have occurred during this 1960s summer. Moreover, because Mr. Robertson has been the catalyst for change in Amy and Isabelle's lives, his leave taking has radically altered their former mother-daughter relationship, creating a dead space between them.

The story itself takes place in the mill town of Shirley Falls, Maine. Within this setting, Strout poignantly describes small-town life in Maine in the 1960s. For Strout the setting of this novel is key. As she said in her interview with Grattan and Knight: "I think that sense of place is hugely important for me. I think it took me a long time to realize the phrase "literature is place" and I finally realized that, yes, it is. … So in the novel, the setting is New England in the sense that it's *my* New England. I'm writing from the area that's very familiar to me. And it was place I was embracing in the novel" (p. 35).

Strout begins the narrative in the present and then goes back in time to narrate the six months from January to June before life changes dramatically for Isabelle and her teenage daughter, Amy. Much of the novel takes place in the mill office, where Isabelle is a secretary for her boss, Avery Clark, and where Amy comes to work for a summer job. Along with Amy and Isabelle, there is a cast of other office women with whom Isabelle chooses to have limited interaction.

Isabelle's relationship with her fellow office workers mirrors in many respects the social and

class boundaries found in Shirley Falls. In her novel, Strout narrates the story about working women and, tangentially, the class divisions to be found in small-town America. Divided by a river, the town of Shirley Falls has working-class people like Isabelle's coworkers living on one side and professional people on the other. Isabelle, who came to town when her daughter was young, lives on the "right side" of the tracks in the area known as Oyster Point. But she feels comfortable neither with the Protestant women from Oyster Point nor with the Catholic women from the other side of the river, known as the Basin.

For Isabelle, time is divided between the horrible summer when she learns of her daughter's sexual liaison with her math teacher, Mr. Robertson, and what she calls "the olden days" (p. 11). Amy's relationship with Mr. Robertson sets up the conflict for the rest of the novel. Even though Amy and Isabelle work together over the summer, their interaction is limited: "For the most part they avoided each other's eyes, and Amy did not seem to find it necessary to take on the responsibility of a conversation. *This stranger, my daughter.* It could be a title for something in the *Reader's Digest*, if it hadn't already been done, and maybe it had, because it sounded familiar to Isabelle" (p. 13).

For Isabelle, the discovery of her daughter's relationship with Mr. Robertson suddenly becomes the whole focal point of her life. Through the character of Isabelle, Strout effectively details how one random event in a person's life can totally derail it. "It was like a car accident," Isabelle thinks to herself. "How afterward you kept saying to yourself, If only the truck had already gone through the intersection by the time I got there. If only Mr. Robertson has passed through town before Amy got to high school" (p. 14). But for Isabelle this one event ends up dramatically changing her life for the worse. Only later on will it become apparent that it is an opportunity of growth for both Isabelle and Amy.

The story begins when Mr. Robertson becomes the substitute teacher for Amy's math class. Initially Amy resents Mr. Robertson and the personal questions he asks her in front of the

class: "Amy. Why do you hide behind your hair?" (p. 29). Her hair is her one hallmark of pride, since so many people comment on it. These questions lead her to react in uncharacteristic ways, including showing up late for class and writing obscenities on the bathroom wall. Soon, though, when Mr. Robertson pays her a personal compliment, Amy finds herself feeling special and looking at herself differently. Their after-school meetings progress from driving Amy home to sexual activity in the car. When they are discovered by Isabelle's boss, Avery Clark, who tells Isabelle what he has seen, the relationship between Mr. Robertson and Amy comes to an abrupt halt.

Isabelle's ensuing anger with her daughter results in the scene that Strout had imagined, prior to writing the novel, in which she cuts off Amy's beautiful hair. For Isabelle, Amy's relationship with Mr. Robertson throws into relief the shortcomings in her own life. Since her arrival in Shirley Falls, Isabelle has kept everyone at arm's length, shrouding her past from her coworkers and from her daughter. Isabelle also carries on an active fantasy life about her boss, Avery Clark, an older man who, she imagines, would be better off married to her than to this wife. Moreover, outside of church and her daughter, Isabelle has no social life. Thus, her discovery of Amy's relationship with Mr. Robertson particularly galls her "because the girl had been enjoying the sexual pleasures of a man, while she herself had not" (p. 206).

In many ways, this novel is about women and their daily lives, specifically about working-class women. Within the larger narrative, Strout interweaves the conversations and interactions of the women who work in the office at the mill. She poignantly captures the tensions and dramas that characterize daily life for these women. Their conversations and worries, like the inability of Fat Bev to have a bowel movement or Dottie Brown's hysterectomy and sighting of an UFO, constitute the defining features of their lives.

Many of the novel's narrative threads come together at the end as a consequence of one evening's events, stretching the novel's credibility to a degree. However, Strout continues to offer pithy observations about human behavior that

reward the reader. At one point, she writes, "There was all sorts of unhappiness in Shirley Falls that night. If Isabelle Goodrow had been able to lift the roof off various houses and peer into their domestic depths she would have found an assortment of human miseries" (p. 188). Though Isabelle is unaware of the problems that others face, the omniscient narrator reminds the reader that troubles are experienced and shared by everyone.

On the evening in question, Avery Clark and his wife completely forget about their dinner engagement with Isabelle, who ends up throwing the uneaten dinner in the garbage. When Amy calls Mr. Robertson in Massachusetts the same evening, he pretends that he does not know her. In both scenarios, the men fail to live up to the expectations that Isabelle and Amy harbor. Moreover, Dottie and Bev, Isabelle's coworkers, call and ask Isabelle if they can spend the night at her house because Dottie has just learned that her husband will be leaving her for a younger woman. In effect, Isabelle, Amy, Dottie, and Bev create a momentary community and union of distraught women. Agreeing to let Dottie and Bev stay at her house effectively opens up the door for Isabelle to reveal the secret of her life: that she had become pregnant with Amy after having an affair with another woman's husband. Allowing herself to divulge her secret enables Isabelle to realize that her life is in many ways no different from anyone else's, specifically the women employed at the mill office. Other people have problems not dissimilar to hers. For the first time in the novel, Isabelle actually sees that she has friends in Dottie and Bev, although that friendship has its limitations. As the omniscient narrator observes, "Yes, there had been and still was kindness in this room of shipwrecked women, but secrets remained nevertheless that would have to be borne alone" (p. 285).

Isabelle essentially comes into her own after confronting the crisis with Mr. Robertson and her daughter. She learns that she can open up to her female coworkers and that she does not have to live isolated from others or keep secret her previous life. She also learns that she has a community of women who will support her emotionally and

not criticize her earlier behavior, for which she feels so much shame. Amy, for her part, comes to learn that she has half-sisters and -brothers. She relishes the idea that she will be able to have a relationship with these new family members. Moreover, both women know that Amy will be moving on to become her own person.

At the end of the novel, Strout offers an apostrophe to the town of Shirley Falls. "Oh, Shirley Falls—the darkness coming sooner, one more season passing, one more summer gone; nothing was forever, nothing" (p. 300). Her words elevate the town and its townspeople, suggesting that they exist as part of a continuum of life that includes all of humanity. In *The Country of the Pointed Firs,* Sarah Orne Jewett enlarges the reader's view of Dunnet Landing and its inhabitants beyond that of a quaint Maine village. The same can be said of Strout and her rendering of Shirley Falls. The townspeople are not that dissimilar to the rest of humanity; as the omniscient narrator opines, "Most of them did the best they could, the people of Shirley Falls" (p. 300).

ABIDE WITH ME

For her next novel, *Abide with Me,* published in 2006, Strout's subject is a Congregational minister, Tyler Caskey. This book did not garner the same critical attention as her first. Some reviewers found the story depressing, calling it "a bleak journey" (*Library Journal*) and "dispiriting" (*Kirkus Reviews*). Other reviewers, however, were more positive. Less driven by plot than *Amy and Isabelle, Abide with Me* explores the inner life of its minister protagonist. In an interview with Judy Harrison of the *Bangor Daily News,* Strout talked about her choice of characters: "For a long time, I've been interested in what it was like to be a minister. It always intrigued me. I think it's a very different kind of job than most people have." Her exploration of Tyler Caskey clearly demonstrates how different a job it is. Having lost his wife to cancer, and with one of his two daughters deeply troubled, Tyler struggles to maintain equilibrium in his life while still tending to his congregants, whose sympathies about

his circumstances are short lived. A year after his wife's passing, the congregation wants their "old" minister back. But as Strout's novel reveals, both the minister and his congregation will have to change.

In the opening pages of the novel, readers learn that the tale we will hear about Tyler Caskey and his daughter Katherine has already taken place. But because of its notoriety in rural Maine, it is a story that bears repetition, one that continually changes in its retelling. Strout sets the story off in the farthest reaches of northern New England in the small town of West Annett, Maine. In her interview with Grattan and Knight after the publication of *Amy and Isabelle,* Strout had commented on her interest in "how place and character come up against each other in time. Time and place and character combine and produce a life." In this novel, as in all of her fiction, place contributes significantly to the plot. Living in rural Maine has informed the character of all its inhabitants, whose main activity in life has been to "endure" in a less-than-hospitable environment (p. 55). But this toughness of character also informs the community's relationship to the main character, Tyler Caskey. In a town like West Annett, the minister is a central figure in the community, and gossip about the minister forms a critical part of the townspeople's interaction with each other, especially among the women.

Abide with Me is divided into three books. In Book One, Tyler has spent the past year trying to cope with the death of his wife, Lauren, from cancer. At the forefront of his problems is his daughter, Katherine, who has almost ceased talking altogether. Moreover, she begins to experience behavioral problems that quickly accelerate from problems at school to an incident in church where she has been overheard to say, "I hate God" (p. 85). Though Tyler understands that his daughter is still grieving a year later, he does not seem to grasp that the problem might need more attention. He would prefer to ignore it altogether. But Strout also effectively demonstrates through her use of third-person omniscient narration that many of his congregants have problems of their own.

Because of her interest in perspective, Strout takes the reader into the minds of the other townspeople to see their thoughts about Tyler and about their own lives. Without passing judgment on individual characters, Strout's narration allows the reader to see that each character's problems, regardless of scope, are equally weighted. Equally important to the townspeople is the minister's response to their problems, though they display little regard for his. *Abide with Me* shows that the relationship between the minister and his congregants in a small rural town during the late 1950s was decidedly a one-way affair.

In her narrative, Strout effectively moves back and forth in time to describe Tyler's current situation along with scenes from past. The novel focuses primarily on Tyler's internal struggles. He is unable to accept either Lauren's prognosis of cancer or her ensuing death. After her death, Tyler struggles to find the equilibrium that he had prior to Lauren's passing. Part of his grieving has to do with his inability to recapture "The Feeling"—moments of transcendence and personal exultation he has experienced throughout his life when tending to his Christian values (p. 159). But equally important is his penchant for hero worship for figures like Dietrich Bonhoeffer, the Lutheran pastor who gave his life in the German resistance against the Nazis in World War II. During Tyler's ministry, Bonhoeffer unrealistically stands as a moral compass for Tyler's own behavior and actions.

After Lauren's death, Mrs. Connie Hatch, Tyler's housekeeper, remains the only person with whom Tyler feels any type of personal connection. Otherwise, Tyler tries to avoid personal interaction with the members of his congregation, much to their chagrin. Book One ends with Connie's mysterious disappearance.

Book Two, the shortest of the three, breaks with the current narrative about Tyler's struggles to take the reader back in time to focus on the beginning of Tyler's relationship with Lauren. This section of the book highlights the theme of class difference, a common one in Strout's fiction. Lauren, "a summer girl from Massachusetts," marries Tyler, who hails from rural Maine, ef-

fectively disregarding the economic disparity of their backgrounds (p. 83). After they move to West Annett and try to live on a minister's small salary, it does not take long for money problems to arise between the two. The arrival of two children, Katherine and her younger sibling, Jeannie, in quick succession further accentuates their money problems. Soon thereafter Lauren gets cancer, and Tyler takes what he calls "the unthinkable, unimaginable" action (p. 187). He leaves her pills within easy reach of her grasp, returning later to find her dead.

Book Three picks up where Book One left off, with the disappearance of Connie Hatch. At this point Strout adds more complications to Tyler's life, which eventually will result in a breakdown for him. First, his daughter tells the school psychologist that her father has given Connie a ring. That bit of information gets circulated through gossip to many of the women in town. Then, a month later, Tyler finds a disheveled Connie hiding in the church. She confesses to euthanizing two nursing home patients who were in her care. By doing so, Connie thought she was helping them out of their misery. Though Connie has committed murder, Tyler sees her as a person in need and a person to whom he will continue to minister. His visits to prison on her behalf, however, incur further gossip by the townspeople of West Annett, who find his actions troubling at best.

Overhearing her father talk about Connie, Katherine confesses that she has started the rumor about his supposed relationship with Connie. The confessions by both Connie and his daughter precipitate a moment of crisis for Tyler. Expecting to get in front of his congregation to chastise them for spreading rumors, Tyler does the unexpected. He stands up in front of the full congregation and utters his own confession: "Oh, I am sorry. I can't do this anymore" (p. 271). This unexpected change in their minister brings about a lot of soul-searching on the part of the community and an attendant recognition of the part they have played in his breakdown. The book ends on a hopeful note. Both the community and Tyler have learned from their experience, allow-

ing all of them to accept each other and move on.

Abide by Me is a character study of both Tyler Caskey and the community members of West Annett. As such, it is less engaging as a narrative than *Amy and Isabelle*. Nonetheless, Strout's fiction continues to deliver for the reader by exploring her never-ending fascination with human behavior and, specifically, as she mentioned in her interview with Grattan and Knight, how a person's life, like that of Tyler Caskey, comes to be defined by a time and a place.

OLIVE KITTERIDGE

Elizabeth Strout's Pulitzer Prize–winning third novel, *Olive Kitteridge,* was published in 2008. The book, a linked collection of thirteen stories, remained on the *New York Times* best-seller list for more than fifty weeks. Reviews of the book were extremely positive. Critics were especially taken with the main character, Olive, who forms the link through all of the stories, where sometimes she is the main focus and at the other times plays a walk-on role. Louisa Thomas of the *New York Times* likened Olive to "a planetary body, exerting a strong gravitational pull." But *Olive Kitteridge* is more than just a novel about its main character. Strout demonstrates the breadth of her talent in creating the individual residents of the small coastal town of Crosby, Maine. About the characters, Ann Cummins of the *San Francisco Chronicle* wrote, "Strout has a magnificent gift for humanizing characters." Molly Gloss of the *Washington Post* further observed, "Strout's benevolence toward her characters forms a slender bridge between heartbreak and hope, a dimly glimpsed path through minefields of despair."

What is clearly distinctive about Strout's novel is the obvious pleasure that people get in reading the book. In her review, Jessica Treadway of the *Boston Globe* summed up her experience when she wrote, "*Olive Kitteridge* is chock-full of those moments that make you need to close the page on your finger and look up, in order to absorb the power and poignancy of what you've just read." Similarly, Cummins remarked:

"just a few pages into Elizabeth Strout's new novel in stories, *Olive Kitteridge*, I found myself … experiencing an increasingly rare sensation: the pure joy of reading."

The same enthusiastic response to *Olive Kitteridge* was replicated in a theater performance of two of Strout's stories from the novel, "Tulips" and "River." Word for Word, a theater group based in San Francisco, brought these two stories to the stage in a production directed by Joel Mullennix in September 2010. In his review, Robert Hurwitt of the *San Francisco Chronicle* noted, "Word's *Kitteridge* sends one out of the theater eager to read the whole thing." Because the production was positively received, Word for Word extended the performance for an additional two weeks beyond its regularly scheduled dates.

In an interview with Caitlin Johnson for Failbetter.com, Strout talks about how she came to conceive of her collection of linked stories. As she remarks,

> I wrote the first "Olive" story a number of years ago—the one where she steals her new daughter-in-law's clothes at the wedding reception—and as I wrote it, I understood that this character, Olive Kitteridge, would someday have a book of her own. But as I wrote and sketched more Olive scenes I began to feel that she was such a force to contend with, on the page, and in the lives of those characters who knew her, that it was best to have the story of Olive be episodic in nature.

In the same interview, she explains how her interest in perspective also influenced the form of the novel: "I am always terribly interested in point of view, so to see Olive in tiny glimpses from others in the community allowed the reader to get a fuller picture of her."

A recurrent theme in Strout's fiction, and one that appears in *Olive Kitteridge,* is the theme of loneliness. In her introduction to Edith Wharton's two novels *Summer* and *Ethan Frome* (2001), Strout writes: "The legacy of loneliness is something that Edith Wharton seems to have intuitively understood about her New England towns" (p. xv). The same could be said of Strout's novel. The residents of Crosby, Maine, including Olive, struggle with their own feelings of loneliness and of psychic isolation. In *Olive*

Kitteridge, Strout investigates emotional territory very similar to that Wharton explores in *Summer* and *Ethan Frome*—what Strout describes in the Wharton introduction as people's "longings and their fears, and their desires to live, ultimately, with integrity" (p. xiv). Similarly, Strout imbues her characters with a sense of dignity. In the stories that make up this novel, all of the characters struggle to do the best that they can.

Unlike the settings of her other two novels, which took place in rural Maine, the coastal town of Crosby has registered the changes that have occurred in Maine in the decades since the 1960s. Though Crosby still has a small-town feel to it, the town itself has tourists, and its residents, like the main character's son, move away to other locations. With characters coming and going, the town seems much less isolated than Shirley Falls and West Annett, the fictional locations of Strout's two other novels.

The first story of the collection, "Pharmacy," sets the stage. The reader is introduced to Henry Kitteridge, Olive's husband, who has worked in a pharmacy his whole life. When his former assistant dies, he hires Denise Thibodeau, a young woman straight out of college, who, symbolically enough, is married to another Henry. The year he spends working with Denise is one of his "happiest" (p. 10). Henry's concern and thoughtfulness toward Denise, whose husband dies while she is still in his employ, are in direct contrast to Olive's opinion of her. Olive's acerbic personality allows her free reign to make condescending comments about Denise whenever her name gets mentioned. Much to Henry's dismay, as an act of provocation Olive goes so far as to call Denise "a simpleton" (p. 12). Olive's comments about Denise are matched by equally hostile remarks to her gentle and beleaguered husband. In this initial story, Strout obviously wants the reader to see Olive in a very specific light—as a mean-spirited and unkind wife, with Henry as her foil. But, like all good fiction, the narrative gradually allows readers to become privy to other sides of Olive and other perspectives, so that they must juggle these competing perspectives about a complex person, Olive.

After her husband dies in a hunting accident, Denise eventually leaves the pharmacy to marry Jerry, a local young man, and they move away from Crosby. Henry's only reminder of that coveted year together is the annual birthday card that Denise sends him. Years later, however, waiting for Denise's card to arrive, Henry realizes that Olive has had a similar experience. She has felt affection for another person, Jim O'Casey, a teacher who drove Olive and her son to school every day. But, like Henry, she never acted upon her romantic inclination. When O'Casey dies in a tragic car accident, Olive's loss and grief send her to bed crying every night. It is at this moment of discovery for Henry that the reader grasps a new insight into Olive's suddenly more complex personality.

The book can be divided into two parts: the stories that place Olive at the center and those where she plays a tangential role. In these latter stories, Olive's walk-on appearances to maintain the links between the stories sometimes feels a bit contrived. However, in each of the succeeding short stories after "Pharmacy," where the focus is on Olive, a different aspect of her personality is revealed, requiring a continuous rethinking of Olive as a character.

In the next story of the collection, "Incoming Tide," Kevin Coulson, a former student of Olive's, has returned to Crosby with the possible intent of committing suicide. Olive encounters Kevin parked in his car at the marina, unaware of the rifle he has in the back of his car covered up by a blanket. Seeing him, Olive approaches the car and invites herself in to sit with him. Though Kevin is not exactly pleased to see his former teacher, Olive mentions that she has thought about him over the years after he left town. Unbeknownst to Kevin until their present conversation, Mrs. Kitteridge, his seventh-grade teacher, shares a similar history. Both of them have had a parent who has committed suicide. Olive confesses to Kevin that she worries about her own son, probably a contemporary of Kevin's, who suffers from depression. Her story of her father's suicide and her worries about her son give Kevin pause. Olive's ability to share this knowledge with Kevin, who is clearly troubled

himself, reveals yet another side of her personality. The revelation of a more compassionate side of Olive means the reader has to rethink Olive's continually evolving personality.

This gradual unfolding of Olive's personality through each story makes her one of the most intriguing fictional characters in recent contemporary literature. It is difficult to pin her down as a character because she is so multifaceted. In "A Little Burst," Christopher, Olive's only child, marries a woman, Suzanne, whom Olive does not like. This story takes place the day of their wedding at the reception in Christopher's house, which his parents built for him. Lying down in the bedroom to get away from the guests, Olive is interrupted by the appearance of a young girl. Their conversation exposes the wry side of Olive's personality. The little girl asks her, "What is that on your chin?" "Crumbs," Olive responds. "From little girls I've eaten up. Now go away before I eat you, too" (p. 65). It is comments like those that make Olive a distinct personality, a person who does not curry favor with people, even unsuspecting little girls. But it is also the transgressive side of Olive's personality that surprises the reader, especially her penchant for acting in ways that seem a bit edgy for a middle-aged woman. Angry with Suzanne's self-satisfied persona, Olive takes a Magic Marker and draws a black line on one of Suzanne's sweaters and steals a shoe out of Suzanne's closet that she later throws away. It is this willingness to act on her anger that makes Olive seem all the more real.

Other stories in which Olive figures prominently continue to reveal aspects of her personality that demonstrate her all-too-human nature. In "A Different Road" the storyline stretches the reader's credulity but nonetheless captures interesting aspects of Olive and Henry's relationship. Stopping at a local hospital to use the bathroom implausibly ends up in a hostage situation for Olive and Henry. Two young men trying to steal drugs force Olive, Henry, a doctor, and a nurse into a bathroom, where they are guarded by one of the young men. Forced into a stressful situation where the outcome is unknowable, Olive and Henry unsurprisingly lose their

composure and end up making horrible and painful accusations about one another. In a telling sentence, the omniscient narrator comments, "No, they would never get over that night because they had said things that altered how they saw each other" (p. 124).

In "Tulips" and "Basket of Trips," Christopher and Suzanne have moved to California, much to the chagrin of Olive and Henry, who have both retired. Then Olive and Henry learn that Christopher and Suzanne are getting a divorce. Soon thereafter, Henry suffers a stroke and must be moved into a nursing home, where Olive visits him on a daily basis. Both of these stories, though they deal in large part with two other couples and their marriages, explore Olive's loneliness now that she must live alone. In the first story, "Tulips," Olive goes to visit Roger and Louise Larkin, who shut themselves off from the community after their son was found guilty of murdering a woman. In part Olive visits them to see how they deal with the loneliness and the isolation in their lives, only to learn that Louise and Roger do not ever speak to each other but live on separate floors. In "Basket of Trips," Olive attends the wake of Marlene Bonney, whose husband has recently died. Marlene reveals to Olive that she has only just learned that day about an affair that her husband had with Marlene's cousin, Kerry. Besides feeling aggrieved by her husband's death, she also feels humiliated. This moment of revelation about Marlene's husband helps to form a connection between the women, who will continue to grieve for what they have lost.

A story titled "Security" takes Olive to New York City to visit with Christopher and his new wife, Ann. Christopher invites Olive for the visit on the pretense that Ann has nausea problems owing to her pregnancy. Strout covers quite a bit of ground in this story, in part because it takes place after 9/11 and because life in Brooklyn, compared to Crosby, takes on an otherworldly perspective. Brooklyn seems almost a caricature of urban living, with Christopher and Ann meeting at a divorced singles group. Moreover, Ann has already had two other children by two different men and feeds her children tofu hot dogs.

Olive, in describing to Henry's nurse how she is doing in New York City, wryly comments, "Different country down here" (p. 223). Because Olive's and Christopher's lives are so radically different, it is not surprising that the story ends with an argument and Olive's quick departure from the city. Olive's story in the novel, however, ends on a hopeful note in "River." After Henry dies, Olive finds Jack Kennison, a retired professor whose own wife has recently died, slumped over on the sidewalk during her morning walk on the river path. While she wants to go get help, he replies, "Don't leave me alone" (p. 254), a feeling that Olive has struggled with since her husband's stroke and death. After this incident, Olive and Jack begin to spend time together. In effect, two lonely older people have found each other and as a result have found a reason to carry on.

In her review for the *New York Times,* Louisa Thomas wrote, "It's no coincidence that the two weakest stories are the ones in which [Olive] is merely mentioned. Without her, the book goes adrift, as if it has lost its anchor." While there is no doubt that Olive's character is the driving force behind the whole novel and the aforementioned stories seem a bit out of place as a result, they are not without merit. These stories bear witness to the struggle of individual characters trying to get on in life. In "Ship in a Bottle," Winnie, the younger of two daughters, comes to the realization that her mother is not mentally well. As a result, she decides to forsake her relationship to her mother in order to save her older sister from her mother's machinations. Likewise, in the story "Criminal," Rebecca Brown, a seemingly unbalanced young woman, takes charge of her life by the end of the story, metaphorically and literally leaving men who have controlled her for most of her life. In three other stories, "The Piano Player," "Starving," and "Winter Concert," Olive appears fleetingly. Within each story, all of the main characters come to a better understanding of how they have lived their lives and the changes they must undertake to continue them. In her portraits of life in Crosby, Maine, as in Shirley Falls, Strout

delineates her characters' lives in such a way that readers are led to empathize with them.

MOVING BEYOND THE PULITZER

In addition to writing fiction, Strout has ventured into the genre of nonfiction, publishing short pieces that include "The Swimming Pool," in the collection *Dream Me Home Safely: Writers on Growing up in America* (2003); her "Introduction," as guest editor, to the spring 2010 issue of *Ploughshares;* and "English Lesson" (2009) for the *Washington Post*. In her fiction, Strout tends to prefer using third-person narration, which allows her to shift from character to character in order to tell the story from each person's perspective. For these three short pieces, Strout ventures into new territory with the use of first-person narration. Doing so gives these works a sense of intimacy that connects the reader to the writer almost immediately. In an approach characteristic of her fictional style, Strout uses her keen observational powers to focus on physical details that function symbolically to illuminate aspects of her character's psyche.

In "The Swimming Pool," Strout displays a poet's sensibility by choosing one object, her father's shoes, to tell the larger story of the four summers she spent at the university swimming pool while her father worked in his lab at the University of New Hampshire. In the telling she goes back and forth between past and present, first to set up the exposition of the piece but also to give the reader a sense of what she felt at the time. From her eye-level perspective in the pool, Strout first observes her father's shoes as he walks toward her. The image of his shoes acts as a catalyst to retrieve memories of him and the dynamic of their father-daughter relationship. The memory of those four summers also brings to mind another physical object that "intrigued" her while she would sit waiting in his office to finish working for the day—"a kind of red pencil that could be sharpened, not by a sharpener, but by peeling down the red skin, allowing the waxy red tip to become longer" (pp. 199–200). Orienting a time of her childhood around these two objects—her father's shoes and his red pencil—

she is reminded of the "joy and hope" she felt that remains an intricate part of her life (p. 200).

Strout narrates the other two short memoir pieces from her perspective as a college student. Her "Introduction" in *Ploughshares* begins with her sense of awe and wonderment when she discovers the college library's collection of literary journals and magazines during her first year in college. This seemingly small event—learning about the existence of literary magazines—gives Strout new insights into life experiences, turning a small event into a very meaningful one. Reading the short stories and poems of others enabled her to understand that, as a college student and a person, she was not alone in her feelings of insecurity. Moreover, the piece suggests the sheer pleasure that Strout gets from reading and learning from other writers, a pleasure that continues to feed her intellectually and emotionally to this day.

In the somewhat longer memoir piece "English Lesson," written for the *Washington Post,* Strout tells a story about a miscommunication between her and an English boy. This miscommunication with him while spending the summer in Oxford, England, turns out to empower Strout, as a young college student, in completely unexpected ways. As a result, she suddenly finds herself able to make her own decisions about living in Oxford for the summer. Written with her typical wry sense of humor, the piece also alludes to her fairly circumscribed childhood growing up with parents who were New England proper to a fault. In Strout's family, one did not venture out of a set of strictly enforced behaviors influenced by a long line of New England descendents. Thus, going to England for the summer put Strout on a new path of self-discovery that included an aggressive sexual overture by an English boy, a brief living arrangement at a commune, and finally, a new awareness of self and a determination to find her own way in the world. Because she is unafraid of voicing her self-doubts, Strout's foray into memoir writing make for engaging reading.

Besides her acute attention to details in her fiction, Strout's writing reveals a penchant for certain themes. Critics have talked about the

central focus of community in all of her novels; however, there has been less attention paid to the specific communities that are represented in Strout's narratives. One of Strout's strengths is her exploration of women's life experiences. In *Amy and Isabelle* and *Abide with Me,* Strout goes back in time to the 1960s and 1950s, respectively. In both cases, the reader learns about the cultural limitations women faced during that time period. Regardless of their specific circumstances, however, the communities of women in both novels make do through the support of their relationships with each other. In *Amy and Isabelle,* doing typically gendered work for the time, that of working in an office, the women find a sense of community in their shared work space with other women. The only male figure in the office is Avery Clark, the boss. Otherwise, the men and women are cordoned off into separate spheres: women in the office and men outside doing the hard labor of the mill. The relationships among these women are not without their daily tensions, a consequence in part of being relegated to menial jobs without the opportunity to advance in the workplace. But then it is also an environment where women can share their crises with other women whom they know will be sympathetic. Ultimately, Isabelle Goodrow comes to learn the importance of being part of such a community, where she can share her troubles and her past with the realization that she is not so wholly different from the other women in the office. Likewise, in *Abide with Me* the women frequently get on telephone party lines to gossip about Tyler Caskey, their town minister. But through these shared moments we learn how these women's lives are quite limited; typically for the 1950s, they are isolated in their respective homes, where they are expected to be perfect housewives devoted to cleaning up and taking care of children and to be happy doing so. While the gossip they partake in can seem malicious, from another perspective one can see that it helps to create a bond between these women and acts as a safety valve for their daily frustrations.

In *Olive Kitteridge,* the sense of community for women has changed dramatically between the mid-twentieth and twenty-first centuries. Women can work outside the home and are no longer confined to specific gendered spaces. As such, there is less a sense of female community because the times have changed for women even in a small coastal town like Crosby, Maine. The problems that women confront are different in part because they have different opportunities. In *Olive Kitteridge,* working women, like Angela O'Meara in "The Piano Player" and Rebecca in "Criminal," face self-esteem issues but ultimately take control of their lives. The waitress Patty Howe, in "Incoming Tide," copes with the sadness she feels after suffering a number of miscarriages. And Nina, in "Starving," loses her battle with anorexia. Through the main character of Olive, Strout explores how women deal with all of the problems that life can bring: staying in a marriage, growing old, dealing with adult children, becoming isolated in old age, and a myriad of other problems that women face. In many respects, *Olive Kitteridge* acts as a counterweight to the other two novels that take place in the mid-twentieth century. In the twenty-first century, a sense of female community does not exist in the same manner as it did in former times, for better or worse. Women in *Olive Kitteridge* sometimes make connections with each other. In "Basket of Trips," Olive does offer a type of physical solace when Marlene learns at her husband's funeral that he has had an affair with her cousin. But in other cases, there are missed opportunities. Olive goes to Mrs. Larkin's house, in "Tulips," to try to understand how she lived with her self-imposed loneliness, only to confront an angry and bitter woman who could care less about Olive's problems. These novels that range from the mid-twentieth to the twenty-first centuries serve as a cultural document of the lives of some New England women of the time.

Through her dogged persistence, Strout has achieved her childhood goal of becoming a writer. In interviews, Strout has talked about her tendency to write about ordinary people in her fiction. In her self-deprecating way, she explained that she wrote about things she knew. Since she was ordinary, it was natural that she would write about so-called ordinary people. But these books

about ordinary people in small towns illustrate how much we all share, regardless of our individual circumstances. They are a reminder that most people are just trying to do the best they can in life. For her next novel, Strout has mentioned briefly in interviews that she is writing about Somali immigrants in Maine. This topic takes Strout, as a writer, into relatively new territory for her fiction. She will not only write about the Somali community, but she will also use New York City as part of her setting for the book. Clearly Strout appears to be engaging in a broader cultural panorama. Taking such a risk beyond her normal scope demonstrates how far she has come as well as her willingness to stretch as a writer.

Selected Bibliography

WORKS OF ELIZABETH STROUT

NOVELS
Amy and Isabelle. New York: Random House, 1998.
Abide with Me. New York: Random House, 2006.
Olive Kitteridge. New York: Random House, 2008.

SHORT STORIES
"Staying Afloat." *Redbook*, August 1991, p. 42.
"RUNNINGAWAY." *Seventeen*, August 1992, p. 194.
"A Little Burst." *New Yorker*, June 1, 1998, pp. 70–74.
"Winter Concert." *Ms.*, October–November 1999, pp. 74–80.

NONFICTION
Introduction to *Ethan Frome & Summer.*, by Edith Wharton. New York: Modern Library, 2001. Pp. xi–xviii.
"The Swimming Pool." In *Dream Me Home Safely: Writers on Growing Up in America.* Edited by Susan Richards Shreve. Boston: Houghton Mifflin, 2003. Pp. 197–201.
"English Lesson." *Washington Post,* July 12, 2009. http://www.washingtonpost.com/wp-dyn/content/article/2009/07/02/AR2009070202180.html.
"Introduction." *Ploughshares* 36, no. 1:7–8 (spring 2010).

CRITICAL AND BIOGRAPHICAL STUDIES
"Abide with Me." *Kirkus Reviews,* January 1, 2006, pp 14–15.

Charles, Ron. "Running on Faith." *Washington Post,* March 19, 2006, p. T5. (Review of *Abide with Me.*)
Cummins, Ann. "*Olive Kitteridge* Stories Come Alive." *San Francisco Chronicle,* April 9, 2008. http://articles.sfgate.com/2008-04-09/entertainment/17145353_1_story-collections-elizabeth-strout-olive-kitteridge.
Gloss, Molly. "Family Matters." *Washington Post,* June 8, 2008. http://www.washingtonpost.com/wp-dyn/content/article/2008/06/05/AR2008060504366.html. (Review of *Olive Kitteridge.*)
Haram, Karen. "You Love, You Hurt, You Forgive." *San Antonio Express-News,* January 31, 1999, p. 4G. (Review of *Amy and Isabelle.*)
Harrison, Judy. "Strout's Second Novel Inspires." *Bangor Daily News,* July 10, 2006, p. 6C. (Review of *Abide with Me.*)
Hurwitt, Robert. "Novel's Essence on Stage." *San Francisco Chronicle,* September 6, 2010, p. E1. (Theater Review.)
McClurg, Jocelyn. "Intertwined Lives, Stories." *USA Today,* April 23, 2008. http://www.usatoday.com/life/books/reviews/2008-04-23-kitteridge_N.htm. (Review of *Olive Kitteridge.*)
Randolph, Ladette. "About Elizabeth Strout: A Profile." *Ploughshares* 36, no. 1:174–179 (spring 2010).
Thomas, Louisa. "The Locals." *New York Times,* April 20, 2008, p. 13. (Review of *Olive Kitteridge.*)
Treadway, Jessica. "Emotions Are Raw and Real in *Olive Kitteridge.*" *Boston Globe,* May 25, 2008. http://www.boston.com/ae/books/articles/2008/05/25/emotions_are_raw_and_real_in_olive_kitteridge/.
Wells, Susanne. "*Abide with Me.*" *Library Journal,* October 1, 2005, pp. 69–70.

INTERVIEWS
Bacon, Katie. "Tight-Knit, Loose-Lipped." *Atlantic.com,* March 2006. http://www.theatlantic.com/magazine/archive/2006/03/tight-knit-loose-lipped/4823/.
Birnbaum, Robert. "Elizabeth Strout." *Morning News,* August 26, 2008. http://www.themorningnews.org/archives/birnbaum_v/elizabeth_strout.php.
Carey, Lynn. "Novelist's Childhood Colors Tale." *Contra Costa Times* (California), April 2, 2000, p. C1.
George, Tara. "Long Years to Success." *New York Daily News,* March 20, 1999, p. 17.
Grattan, Bill, and Lania Knight. "A Conversation with Elizabeth Strout." *Center: A Journal of the Literary Arts* 4:27–43 (2005).
Johnson, Caitlin. "Elizabeth Strout: Interview." Failbetter.com, December 16, 2008. http://www.failbetter.com/29/StroutInterview.php?sxnSrc=rcint.
Marshall, John. "Best-Seller: Bright Lights on an Intimate First Novel." *Seattle Post-Intelligencer,* April 1, 1999, p. D1.

Parker, Lonnae O'Neal. "The Life Lines of a Writer." *Washington Post,* May 18, 1999, p. C1.

FILM AND STAGE PRODUCTIONS BASED ON THE WORK OF ELIZABETH STROUT

Amy and Isabelle. Television movie. Teleplay by Joyce Eliason and Lloyd Kramer; produced by Harpo Films. Aired on ABC, March 4, 2001.

Olive Kitteridge. Stage version of "Tulips" and "River" by Word for Word. Directed by Joel Mullennix. Premiered at Theatre Artaud, San Francisco, September 4, 2010.

JEAN THOMPSON

(1950—)

Rachel Hall

JEAN THOMPSON IS the author of several collections of stories and several novels. Over the course of her career Thompson has garnered critical praise and recognition including fellowships from the Guggenheim Foundation and the National Endowment for the Arts. Her collection *Who Do You Love* (1999) was a finalist for the National Book Award for fiction, and her novel *Wide Blue Yonder* (2002) was a *New York Times* Notable Book as well as a *Chicago Tribune* Best Fiction selection. Equally adept at long and short forms, Thompson's work is noted for its precise and original language and its attention to detail of character and place. Also significant is Thompson's willingness to tackle difficult or dark subject matter. She is often compared to Raymond Carver in this regard, as well as for the kind of characters who populate her fiction. Thompson writes about ordinary folks for whom life has not turned out the way they had hoped. Repeatedly book reviewers note that in spite of her unsparing examination of human folly and suffering, Thompson's fiction isn't depressing. Her humor, elegantly precise language, and compassion for her characters prevent grimness.

Thompson's fiction is set primarily in the Midwest, a region she knows well. In her depiction of small towns, with names like Dead Center, Hi Ho, or Superior, Thompson alludes to the hopefulness with which they were settled and their current state of quiet—and not so quiet—desperation. She also captures the mood and culture of the region's college campuses and their awkward relationship with the surrounding farm communities. Less frequently, but with as much insight, Thompson examines the Midwest's cities and suburbs and the allure of these for her characters.

Thompson has been frequently compared to Alice Munro for her understanding of human nature and for the way her stories are as rich and satisfying as novels. Her work, like Munro's, examines relationships between men and women, parents and children, and records the tensions inherent in intimacy and dependence. Thompson's fiction makes frequent use of the retrospective past tense, a technique that allows her to layer past and present and to look at relationships over a long period of time.

Thompson's best-known story, thanks in part to its inclusion in two beloved anthologies, is "Applause, Applause." In 1983 Tobias Wolff edited *Matters of Life and Death: New American Stories* and included "Applause, Applause" alongside stories by Raymond Carver, Ann Beattie, and Richard Yates. In his introduction Wolff writes about his frustration with metafiction and what he calls its self-absorption and focus on style over content. In response to that "white noise," he selected stories for *Matters of Life and Death* that were concerned with "things that matter" told in voices he "couldn't ignore" (p. xi). In the anthology *Children Playing Before a Statue of Hercules* (2005), David Sedaris included "Applause, Applause" as well as stories by such writers as Charles Baxter, Jhumpa Lahiri, Flannery O'Connor, and Alice Munro. As he notes in the introduction, Sedaris chose stories that were important to him as an apprentice writer, and says that these are stories that "I turn to again and again" (p. 5). In addition, Sedaris has promoted Thompson's work on his reading tours, selling her books alongside his own.

EARLY LIFE

Jean Thompson was born in Chicago on January 3, 1950, to Tom and Isabel Thompson.

JEAN THOMPSON

Thompson's mother was a homemaker and her father worked in the food industry, in sales and management, and the family followed his job from Chicago to Memphis, Tennessee, and Louisville, Kentucky. Thompson is the eldest of four children, two girls and two boys, born into a family that valued education. When all her children were in school, Isabel Thompson went to school herself and obtained a graduate degree in history. Tom Thompson earned an MBA at the same time. Thompson's mother taught her to read before she entered kindergarten. In an interview with Max Ruback in the *Writer,* Thompson says she was "an early and voracious reader of whatever I could get my hands on." As a child, she read Charles Dickens, Anton Chekhov, Ray Bradbury, Willa Cather, and Nathaniel Hawthorne—though she admits she was too young to take all of it in—and everything on the family's bookshelves including her parents' old college textbooks.

Thompson didn't start writing in any organized fashion until attending college at the University of Illinois–Urbana, where she worked with Mark Costello. She graduated in 1971 with a major in English. From there, she went to Bowling Green State University, where she received her M.F.A. in 1973. At Bowling Green, Thompson worked with Philip F. O'Connor, who she says was "a wonderful writer and a supportive mentor … who taught me much of what I later taught to others" (Hall, "Questions"). She published her first story while in graduate school in Ball State University's *Forum.*

Thompson began teaching writing at the University of Illinois in 1973. She has also taught at Wichita State University, in Northwestern's graduate extension program, and at Reed College in addition to the Warren Wilson low-residency program for writers. She retired from full-time teaching in 2004. In her interview in the *Writer,* Thompson says that teaching provided her with large blocks of uninterrupted time to write, such as sabbaticals and summers, that no other job offers. She also says there is "a symbiosis between writing and teaching that at the best of times works for everyone's advantage. Issues in your writing get articulated and worked out in the classroom. And the best student writing can engage and excite you." Teaching, though, is not without its challenges, and student work meant Thompson's own projects had to wait. In her teaching she stresses that "writing is a discipline, something that one ought to do with regularity and concentration." Also: "Young writers need to read, read, read."

A frequent reviewer for the *New York Times Book Review,* Thompson is known for her defense of the contemporary short story, what she calls, in a review of a Deborah Eisenberg collection, "that perennially marginalized and disrespected form." Indeed, Thompson takes on none other than Stephen King for his introduction to *The Best American Short Stories 2007.* In his piece, reprinted in the *New York Times Book Review* (September 30, 2007), King argues that the contemporary short story is "written for editors and teachers rather than for readers" and is "airless, somehow, and self-referring," not to mention "show-offy" and "self-important." Thompson's retort, published on Maud Newton's blog, is witty and incisive about the pressures on the short story, a form that is, she admits readily, challenging and demanding. "The world is complex, ambiguous, difficult; it often makes us feel lost and fearful. Any fiction that attempts to do justice to those complexities can seem disquieting," Thompson says.

EARLY WORK

The University of Illinois Press, one of the more distinguished university presses, published Thompson's first book, a collection of stories titled *The Gasoline Wars,* in 1979. The Illinois Short Fiction series published four volumes a year and included such notable writers such as Stephen Minot, Philip F. O'Connor, Robley Wilson, and Nancy Huddleston Packer. Thompson's collection was published when she was just twenty-nine years old. Stories included in the collection had already appeared in important literary journals such as *Ploughshares, Fiction International,* and *Carolina Quarterly* as well as in *Mademoiselle* and later in *The Best American Short Stories 1979.*

The Gasoline Wars was received well by critics. In *Studies in Short Fiction,* Dale Edmonds wrote that "these are wise and wonderful stories." In particular he praised "Applause, Applause" and "Paper Covers Rock" and asserted that the collection "is surely the sine qua non of marital combat stories; beside it, Updike's fine domestic chronicles seem like border skirmishes, without casualties." In the *New Republic,* Dorothy Wickenden called the collection "honest and sympathetic" and said that Thompson has a "resoundingly distinctive voice." In the *Washington Post Book World,* Terence Winch wrote that of the four collections published by the Short Fiction series, Thompson's was "without question the most exciting and accomplished" (p. 14).

"Applause, Applause," singled out by Edmonds, is a remarkable story about the friendship between two writers. It is one of the two stories in this collection to examine the moral and practical difficulties facing writers and those who love them. In "Applause, Applause," Bernie and Ted met in college as aspiring writers. Thompson brings the men—and their wives—together ten years later at Bernie's Adirondack cabin. While the friends once talked openly and honestly about their dreams, they are cagier now and defensive about the ways they have fallen short of their goals or compromised their artistic vision. Thompson brilliantly captures the competition and admiration that coexists between Ted and Bernie, or as Winch put it, "the paradoxical way love and hate combine in human relationships." In addition, Thompson reveals the way "all this gloomy nonsense about artistic accomplishment" (p. 114) gets in the way of both writing and life.

In "Dry Spring," the narrator is the unwilling muse for her husband, Dennis. She has grown to resent his writing and the way it distances them, though she admits that most wives must face this in any number of variations: "A Man and his Work. A Man and his Dog. A Man and his Drinking Buddies. A Man and Anything but his Woman" (p. 68). She isn't allowed to read his work or even ask him how his writing is going. She dislikes that Dennis is the one shaping the narrative—both in his work and in their marriage—and determines that she too has "secret

words just as he did, and [she] was determined to say them" (p. 79).

With a thoughtful symmetry, *The Gasoline Wars* begins and ends with a journey story. In each, a young couple is on the road. Set during the gas shortages of the mid-1970s, the title story focuses as much on the internal obstacles the couple faces along the way as it does on the lines at gas stations and rationing. In "Driving to Oregon," Bert and Mary Ann Lily, an interracial couple, believe they are leaving racism behind when they quit Illinois for the Northwest. Both stories manage to be hopeful even as the couples fret about money and routing. As Wickenden pointed out, Thompson "catches her characters with their defenses down, at critically revealing moments of peevishness, confusion, or sudden, painful self-knowledge."

Indeed, "Paper Covers Rock" is a story that reveals characters at such a moment. The unnamed narrator must admit that the love affair she has initiated is hopeless. She is disappointed to find herself "yearning after something more predictable" (p. 100). Thompson will examine other women characters like this narrator and similarly unsatisfying and complicated romantic situations in later work, most notably in the characters of Mary Ann in *My Wisdom* (1982) and Flora in *The Woman Driver* (1985).

My Wisdom, Thompson's first novel, was published in 1982. Set in the 1960s, *My Wisdom* is a coming-of-age story for Mary Ann Reynolds, the novel's narrator. In the *Los Angeles Times,* Caroline Thompson wrote that "with admirable forthrightness ... [Thompson] tries hard to describe what it felt like to be alive and of age in the late 1960s." And in *Library Journal,* Jackie Cassada called the novel "skillfully written" and noted how Mary Anne's story "echoes the compromises of many a survivor of a traumatic decade." Through the course of the novel Mary Ann travels from her midwestern college campus to "holy Republican Kansas" (p. 86), to eastern Colorado, and ends up in San Francisco. Like the car trip Mary Ann undertakes, the plot of *My Wisdom* is loose and meandering. Mary Ann discovers a lot about herself on this journey, but also about her sister, Jane, whom she has believed to be the

good girl of the family, the one Mary Ann measures herself against.

Mary Ann tells her story in the retrospective past tense, years after the events she recounts. From this vantage point she is able to analyze the past with perspective and wisdom lacking in her youth. To illustrate how much changed and how quickly for Mary Ann and the entire country, the novel opens with Mary Ann describing a movie that she was shown in high school about the dangers of taking drugs. At the time, she is certain that she would never be involved in that activity, but in just a couple of years, the movie is shown at her college as "a kind of camp event, a comedy, because by this time we'd all grown so wise and cynical" (p. 2).

Two events occur early on that propel Mary Ann's education, though not her formal one. First, her largely disinterested boyfriend, Billy, decides to drop out of college and move to San Francisco. Around the same time, Mary Ann gets very sick and misses too much school to make it up. While she is sick, she is consumed by guilt about her sexual activity. She has bought into the idea that "sex is just another form of communication" but begins to feel that she has "gotten something wrong" (p. 44).

In this state of self-loathing and shame, she too drops out of school and begins her own journey west with two friends, a couple named Red and Bunny. When the truck they are driving breaks down in Dead Center, Kansas, Mary Ann is forced to set out alone. To convey what faces Mary Ann at this juncture, as well as to show the polarization of young and old, town and gown, left and right, Thompson has included excerpts from newspaper articles, letters to the editor, even a summary of a political cartoon. In one such document gathered here, the letter writer declares that "I for one am tired of hearing all the crying about the 'innocent students' at Kent State. It's about time they and their kind realized Americans have run out of patience and Hell yes we'll shoot" (p. 85).

The first ride Mary Ann hitches out of Kansas lands her in Luddig, Colorado, where she promptly marries the driver. When she asks her sister Jane to come to the wedding, the tension between the sisters is evident. Jane admits to feeling disappointed in Mary Ann's decision to marry and be "like everybody else" (p. 175). Mary Ann is, she says, "the brave one, the one who would make underground films or raise bees or live on an Indian reservation" (p. 175).

Still, Mary Ann believes she is in love and enjoys her predictable married life. She does chafe at her mother-in-law's expectations and advice, and she makes only one friend, a neighbor, Ramona Baylo, but she doesn't yet regret the life she has given up in settling in Luddig. After Ramona's husband shoots Ramona and their three children, then kills himself in their bungalow, Mary Ann is shocked and devastated. She is grieving her friend, in part, but she is also disillusioned. "I never expected destruction and chaos to track me down here, in this life I had banished them from. I had bargained in good faith and now I had been cheated," she says (p. 226).

When Mary Ann gets to San Francisco, where she is to visit Jane and get over her grief, she finds that she and her sister have traded roles: Mary Ann is the staid married woman and Jane is involved in a radical leftist organization that isn't averse to using violence in its "strategic disruption" (p. 331). It also appears that Jane is involved with a woman, Anne Marie, though the sisters don't address Jane's sexuality directly. The last time Mary Ann sees Jane before she goes underground, they argue about Jane's political involvement. Of Jane's views, Mary Ann says: "You're like everyone else with a rap. You've bought the whole package. It's simple-minded, Janie. Prefab thinking" (p. 335). Jane has exchanged one way of thinking for its opposite. It isn't clear if Mary Ann understands that her behavior is fairly similar.

By the end of the novel, however, looking back on these events, Mary Ann is aware of her own shifts and reversals and sees them as a necessary part of growing up. Coming across a demonstration in the final pages of her story, Mary Ann says this of her generation: "We had learned nothing; the old rant, the old forms were all still with us, too. We pretend to be changing the world, but it is only ourselves we wish to

escape" (p. 360). Part of what she has learned by this point in her life, the wisdom of the title, is that even if our past selves seem not to "have any more in common than second cousins at a vast, boring family reunion," we cannot escape them (p. 3). Not only that, we must learn to understand them if we are to understand who we are. "I was still here, still the same," Mary Ann acknowledges (p. 341).

Little Face and Other Stories was published in 1984. Stories in the collection first appeared in *Southwest Review, Chicago, Kansas Quarterly,* and *Banyan Anthology,* and "Little Face," under the title of "Lessons from an Older Man," in *Mademoiselle.* In *Library Journal,* Janet Boyarin Blundell noted that Thompson's third book is informed by "the powerful yet subtle voice of a sensitive writer." Of Thompson's ten books to date, *Little Face* received the least critical attention following its publication, though the stories are as ambitious as those in her other collections, examining politics, race, and gender with Thompson's usual blend of humor and insight.

The stories in *Little Face* are primarily about relationships. The protagonist of one story claims to "hate the word relationship" for the way it fails to describe the complexities involved in human interactions, and certainly the characters in *Little Face* find themselves in surprising and difficult relationships. The title story, for instance, is about the unlikely affair between Paula, a shy fifteen-year-old, and Willie, who calls himself "the world's oldest graduate student" (p. 61), who meet at the public library. Willie calls her "Little Face" because of the way her hair hides much of her face. Paula likes the nickname because "no one else in the world would ever use it" (p. 54). The secret relationship with Willie thrills her, but she is also aware that it isolates her from her family and schoolmates. In fact, "she wonders how she could live and talk and move among them without them knowing a single thing about her" (p. 56).

Willie manages to be a sympathetic character, aware that the affair is bad for Paula, despite her protestations. He appreciates Paula in a way no one else has, though it is clear, too, that he needs

her. Her innocence and adoration provide counterbalance to his sense of futility and cynicism.

Another May-December relationship occurs in "Naomi Counting Time," though in this case, Miss Greer handles the younger Naomi's worshipful feelings in a less troubling way. Naomi is also fifteen and in need, according to her mother, "of an accomplishment, something to act as leavening, to give her an outside interest" (p. 70). Miss Greer becomes her violin teacher and the object of Naomi's adoration. As in "Little Face," Thompson beautifully captures the adolescent mind in "Naomi." Paula's and Naomi's inarticulate yearnings and self-consciousness are conveyed through precise language and resonant detail. For instance, of Naomi, Thompson writes: "There was too much inside her that wasn't words, too many itches and confusions and untidy longings" (p. 69). Naomi is a diligent, if not gifted, violinist and plays minuets "carefully, much as she's been taught to cut up her meat at the table" (p. 75). Naomi admires Miss Greer, who provides a model of adult womanhood that is an appealing alternative to her practical housewife mother. Naomi admits that "she wanted to *be* Miss Greer" (p. 76). Miss Greer seems unaware of Naomi's infatuation until Naomi follows her on her evening errands, and then Miss Greer is perplexed by Naomi's motivation. She sends Naomi home, somewhat coolly, but at the next lesson, she brings her violin and they play together for the first time. Under Miss Greer's tutelage, Naomi learns an important way to give expression to her feelings.

Even when Thompson's protagonists are both adults, the relationships they find themselves in don't make any more sense, nor are the characters more articulate about their desire or motivations. In "A Courtship," the protagonist knows she has nothing in common with Terry; they don't care for the same music or share a sense of humor or temperament. He is perpetually late, while she is a planner. Terry knows they are incompatible too, and says, "No sense at all, you and me. You want to try it anyway?" (p. 92). Perhaps, Thompson suggests, we can't plan whom we will love even when we can predict the outcome. "Having Words," a darker examination of unlikely pair-

ings, explores the insurmountable challenges of a marriage between a writer and his nonintellectual wife.

It is not just romantic relationships that are unpredictable or surprising. In "Lenny Dying, Pacific Standard Time," the friendship between the narrator and Lenny is another surprising union. The two men became friends in college when both were "socially maladroit" (p. 96), but the narrator isn't sure why they have stayed friends all these years later. Lenny, the narrator says, has an "adversary relationship with life" and "felt betrayed by all misfortune" (p. 96). After college, Lenny takes to calling Jack in the middle of the night when he has had too much to drink, which is frequently. Meanwhile, Jack is a professor, whose "scholarship attracts regular and respectful attention" (p. 101) and whose married life is as orderly as Lenny's is chaotic. The story opens with a call from Lenny's long-suffering wife to notify Jack that Lenny has died in a car accident. Despite the differences in the two men's lives, Jack imagines the last day of Lenny's life, trying to understand how his friend ended up wrapped around a tree while he lectured about Sherwood Anderson to his undergraduate literature students. This kind of empathy can't save Lenny's life, but it says something powerful about friendship, nonetheless.

The relationships in *Little Face* are often improbable, almost always trying, and not entirely satisfying for the participants, but Thompson's characters don't give up. "Somehow we make connections," says Jack, and he might be speaking for all of us.

The Woman Driver (1985), Thompson's second novel, called "an immensely likeable book" by Roberta Smoodin in the *Los Angeles Times*, examines, as the title suggests, gender and desire. The book begins with the protagonist Flora Reynolds' car accident on the day her husband of six years, Gordon, leaves her. Flora notes that "it had been a very ordinary marriage, but its undoing was making her behave in extraordinary ways" (p. 4). Indeed, she admits that the accident was more of a "large, mechanically-assisted tantrum" (p. 10) than an actual accident. This just the beginning of Flora's

bad behavior, however; soon she is involved in an affair with a married man, Mike Maggio. Her best friend, Suzanne, who has been conducting her own affair with him, introduces Mike to Flora. Suzanne claims her relationship with him is over and offers him to the newly single Flora.

Flora and Suzanne have been friends for a long time. "They know everything about each other" (p. 29), Flora claims, and while this will prove untrue, they do have a long history and share a sense of humor. Like many friendships, theirs is based in part on admiration for complementary qualities as well as on envy. Suzanne compares Flora and herself to Snow White and Rose Red, telling Flora "you get to hog all the sweetness and light and angelic qualities. I'm stuck with the coarser stuff" (p. 36). Flora, for her part, admires Suzanne's drive and aplomb. Suzanne has adopted traditionally male qualities in both her professional and personal life. She is "the only truly ambitious woman" Flora knows (p. 34). In her romantic life Suzanne is also ambitious, juggling several relationships at the same time. She jokingly calls these men her beaus or her gentleman friends. Flora eventually agrees to Suzanne's offer, not because she is particularly attracted to Mike but because she is trying to emulate Suzanne's cavalier approach to men and relationships. She accepts Suzanne's offhand challenge to "change the course of things entirely ... [and] make people complain about us" rather than the men (p. 30).

Besides Flora and Suzanne, there is another woman involved with Mike Maggio: his wife, Elizabeth, who is also the mother of his young child. While most of the novel is told in the third-person limited from Flora's perspective, both Suzanne and Elizabeth are given chapters of their own which they narrate in the first person, thus giving the reader an opportunity to see the situation through their eyes. These chapters address a theme Thompson will return to in *City Boy* (2004) and in a number of her short stories, that is, the fine line between being in love and insanity. Contemplating this, Suzanne observes "there was something in me that stayed intact through everything. I wondered if that was all people meant by love, that willingness to lose

yourself. The craziness, the bleeding and jibbering and mess" (p. 78).

Flora's first-person narrative doesn't take place until the final chapter, in which she drives away from Mike, Suzanne, Elizabeth, and the mess they have created. Flora announces herself by saying, "This is me, Flora, driving again ... I know exactly where I'm going" (p. 249). If before she has been "defeated by machinery," afraid to map her own path, she is, by the novel's end, taking control of things and moving to Boston—the reverse trip made by her pioneer grandmother, but brave nonetheless.

The road trip, the journey story, has long been the province of men. *The Woman Driver* is an insightful look at changing gender roles and the resulting tumult. Post-sexual-revolution and post-no-fault divorce, Thompson's female characters still find themselves overly concerned with men. Flora notes that "men could talk blissfully on and on, without, despite, and heedless of women," while she and the other women characters, raised on girls' magazines that encouraged them to take an interest "in cars and football," remain focused on men (p. 50). The novel examines a smart woman's struggle to make sense of the changing attitudes, which offer both increased freedom and increased responsibility.

WHO DO YOU LOVE

Who Do You Love (1999) is Thompson's thickest collection both in number of stories and in its variety and range. All but three of the stories were previously published in prestigious magazines and journals, including the *New Yorker, Story, TriQuarterly,* and *Ploughshares.* The title story won a Pushcart Prize and was reprinted in the *Pushcart Prize XIX* anthology, and the collection's lead story, "All Shall Love Me and Despair," was selected for *The Best American Short Stories 1996.* Published fifteen years after *The Woman Driver, Who Do You Love* went on to be a finalist for the National Book Award. The nomination was a kind of turning point in Thompson's publishing career, and it brought her a larger audience.

Who Do You Love is divided into three sections, a departure from Thompson's usual method of organizing her collections. The first grouping is titled "Who We Love," and the stories explore romantic relationships, though they are, as Katherine Dieckmann noted in her review in the *New York Times Book Review,* "on the verge of fraying." The title story is about an unhappy, disillusioned social worker with the ironically cheerful name of Judy Applebee. Judy's sadness, including a botched suicide attempt, goes largely undetected by those around her. She feels as if she has no right to feel unhappy compared to her clients, whose lives are much harder than hers. She invites serious trouble by shoplifting, walking in dangerous parts of the city alone, and caring too much about the wrong man. Judy is one of the female loners that Dieckmann mentioned in her review who "curl in on themselves in horrid isolation."

"Mercy" is another story of a character who is disillusioned, though in this case Quinn doesn't know he is, nor does he recognize his deep sadness. When he encounters Bonnie Livengood, whose teenage son has died in a drunk driving accident, he is drawn to her physically but also for the opportunity she offers to dwell in sadness not his own. Bonnie warns him when they first meet that she is unkind, and she makes good on this declaration in the story's final scene. In a move Valerie Miner called "Victorian" in the *Women's Review of Books,* the story flashes forward to a much later time. In her essay "The Art and Architecture of the Double Ending," Pamela Painter dubbed this a double ending. Such an ending allows both the devastation of the final scene and the assurance that Quinn will move beyond this moment and come to understand himself and even Bonnie. Thompson's use of the double ending provides an emotionally satisfying ending without diluting the power of the final scene.

In the book's second grouping, "Other Lives," the focus is on the separations between people. Many of the characters in these stories are able to glimpse possibility in the lives of others. In "The Amish," the narrator, ten-year-old Barbara, divides her world into three categories: the farm

families like her own, the hippies at the state university down the road, and the Amish who reside in farms nearby. While Barbara looks wistfully at the Amish and admires their unchanging and orderly ways, it is on campus that her father finds connection and an outlet for his anger and alienation after he returns from Vietnam partially deaf and wholly disenchanted with his government. As Dieckmann noted, "People in Thompson's world all tend to be caught at a moment when the known borders shift." In "The Amish," this moment happens for Barbara when she attends a demonstration where her father speaks out against the war in which he had volunteered to fight. As Barbara puts it, "There weren't enough rules left to know what to expect of the world. I don't think that's such a bad thing, not anymore, at least. … The day I heard my father speak, I learned how allegiances can change: all at once, without decisions" (p. 209). Barbara's upheaval is mirrored and heightened by the changes and shifts taking place in the larger culture. Like "Mercy," "The Amish" ends with a leap in time out of the present of the story to the future, when healing is possible between father and daughter.

In "Fire Dreams" the narrator is, as Miner indicated, "graced with self-irony and a perceptiveness about the local world," but she is isolated from her suburban neighbors by her shabby house and her singleness in this family neighborhood. Though the narrator attempts connection by attending chili suppers or pancake breakfasts at the firehouse next door, by acquiring a dog to walk, even by embarking on an affair with a fireman, she remains an outsider. Only fire seems to remove divisions, unifying the characters in their awe. Describing a fire at the lumberyard, the narrator says, "People drove to the lumberyard fire as if it were a parade. … We were in love with it. We didn't want it to go out. I had a vision of us feeding the flames, of people scurrying to bring it fuel, tossing microwaves, minibikes, Mr. Coffees, La-Z-Boys into the fire" (p. 114). This story in particular earns praise from Miner, who said that Thompson writes "with a renegade spirit and breathless elegance."

The final section is called "Spirits," and the stories here are united by their unsparing look at absence and death. In the collection's final story, "Forever," Hughes, a journalist for a Chicago newspaper, comes to Superior, Indiana, to interview the family of Kelly Poole, who was abducted and violently murdered a year ago. Hughes, like Quinn in "Mercy," doesn't realize he is depressed until he is confronted with the immense unhappiness of Mrs. Poole. The town of Superior, "another small town burdened with a whimsical name" (p. 293), is, like Hughes, depressed and dreary. Thompson, "an acute observer of people and places," as Miner said, describes it vividly and with "lilting, original language." In this grim place, Hughes learns something about kindness and compassion and his own capacity for them.

The stories in all three sections are populated by resilient outsiders who reside in what Dieckmann called a "flattened but desperate universe." It is this aspect of the book that inspires comparison with Raymond Carver, as well as Thompson's compassion for her characters. Stylistically, however, the collection is much closer to Alice Munro, to whom she is frequently compared. Like Munro, Thompson's characters and settings are richly described, vivid and particular. As dark as many of these stories are, critics commended them for their humor and grace.

WIDE BLUE YONDER

Set in Springfield, Illinois, at the end of the last millennium, *Wide Blue Yonder* (2002) is told from the point of view of four characters whose lives will collide like a storm front by the final chapters. Thunderstorms, heat waves, hurricanes, indeed weather of all sorts, are a trope in Thompson's third novel. The novel begins in the perspective of Harvey Sloan, a.k.a. "Local Weather," who is obsessed with the weather and is a marathon viewer of the Weather Channel. When asked about himself, Harvey volunteers the forecast and not much more. After a mental breakdown, the cause of which we learn about gradually, Harvey spent much of his life in mental institutions but now lives alone in a

decaying little house his family purchased for him. Here, he takes refuge in the Weather Channel. Harvey feels a kinship with the various weather people and finds the maps and language of weather reassuring. He is thrilled to learn that a hurricane will share his name. This is as close to violent as Harvey gets; mostly he is a sweet, pliant oddball.

Across the country in Los Angeles, a different type of storm is brewing. Rolando Gottschalk, like Harvey, is a misfit. He has been picked on and ridiculed his whole life for his unusual ethnic background and appearance. Alienated and angry, he claims he will always be "an outsider anywhere" and "could be made into anyone's enemy" (p. 58). He steals a car and sets off to "breathe a different air" (p. 61), fueled only by his anger. Like a violent storm, Rolando destroys anyone whose path crosses his. By the time he arrives in Springfield, he is in a full-blown state of psychosis and has left a trail of wreckage in his wake.

Because of the different ways their alienation manifests, it isn't initially apparent that Harvey and Rolando are similar. Both men have been damaged by the cruelty of others and both are mentally fragile. Thompson's use of the third-person limited point of view as well as the shifts in perspective from chapter to chapter effectively convey the mental state of each man, as well as his particular obsessions and vulnerabilities. Rolando, for instance, comes to believe he is omnipotent. He claims "things happen when he made them happen. He told the car go, it went. Stop, it stopped" (p. 233).

The novel's other major characters are a mother-daughter pair, Elaine Lindstrom and Josie Sloan. Josie is Harvey's great-niece. Though Elaine is divorced from Harvey's nephew, she remains involved in Harvey's care. Elaine, we are told, "believed in responsibilities. Acts of charity. They were positive things you could balance against all the wreckage and mistakes of your life. So far she had a business that worked, a marriage that hadn't, and a daughter that the jury was still out on" (p. 37). While Elaine is a sympathetic and likeable character, she and Josie have hit a stormy patch in their relationship for all the typical reasons. As a result, Elaine finds herself anxious and lonely. After a frustrating conversation with her ex-husband, she notes that she "let her breath out, looked around for someone to complain to, and as usual found no one" (p. 142).

Josie, who is working at Taco Bell when the reader first meets her, is bored with everything: her job, her high school boyfriend, her friends, her parents, and her hometown, though she maintains a worshipful view of Springfield's most famous citizen, Abe Lincoln. Josie is hoping for something more exciting to come along when Mitch Crook, a twenty-five-year-old policeman, enters the Taco Bell where she is working and orders two Gorditas. Seeing him, Josie thinks, "She had stepped off the cliff edge into brilliant air and she knew now what splendid shape her life was meant to take. She would fall in love" (p. 34). While her obsession with Mitch and the relationship that develops between them provides Josie with focus and excitement, it creates more distance and animosity between mother and daughter.

By the end of the novel, Josie learns a lot about excitement and drama; it's not all it's cracked up to be, nor is it true of Springfield, as she claimed early on, "that nothing ever happened here, and you could die of boredom a dozen different ways" (p. 19). After Hurricane Rolando touches down at Harvey's house, where Josie is hiding out in humiliation, all the characters are brought together. The altercation that ends the novel involves the Springfield police department, including Josie's beloved, and brings about the novel's surprising resolution. Each character finds something by the end, even if it's not what they set out to find. Rolando finds religion. Harvey finds a bride. The changes for Josie and Elaine are less dramatic, but no less important. Elaine anticipates the trip they will take together and notes that "the climate between them had shifted in some subtle way" (p. 361).

In the *New York Times Book Review,* Lisa Zeidner praised *Wide Blue Yonder* for its treatment of "ordinary family happiness," material that has been derided as unserious. In an interview with *One Story* ("Q&A"), Thompson said

that "if you look at 'normal' lives long enough, it's like examining a drop of pond water under a microscope, everything teeming and churning." The relationships Thompson examines are complex and complicated. In *Kirkus Reviews,* Bill Geist compared Thompson to Anne Tyler, known for her examination of contemporary family life.

Wide Blue Yonder ends on an optimistic note with a wedding and a reconciliation. In an interview in the *Chicago Tribune,* Thompson said, "*Wide Blue Yonder* is a kind of happy-ending book. The tone of that book is generally light and bright and cheerful, and I kept warning my editor, 'that's not really me.' For me, pessimism drives conflict ... [and] what interests me as a writer are things that are problematic or difficult."

CITY BOY

Indeed, *City Boy* (2004), Thompson's next novel, is a darker, sadder story about addiction, obsessive love, and, as Donna Seaman noted in the *Chicago Tribune,* "painfully acquired self-knowledge." Dail Willis of the *Baltimore Sun* wrote that "the dark and punishing terrain of broken human heart is flawlessly charted" in *City Boy* and commended what she called the "Rosemary's Baby–like sense of dark narrative."

The novel's opening reveals some of this darkness: "They had a bad neighbor. Bad in all the usual ways, and difficult to ignore. Music, noise on the stairs, carelessness about the disposal of garbage. ... His uncarpeted floors were a soundstage. He dropped and bumped and scraped" (p. 1). Perhaps the upstairs neighbor wouldn't be so troubling if the main characters, newlyweds, Jack and Chloe, weren't just starting out their life together, but they are. In addition, Jack, an aspiring novelist, is trying to write beneath the ruckus. In fact, Jack has quit a full-time teaching job to write, while Chloe, in an admirable bit of gender-role reversal, supports them with her first post-MBA job as a bank manager trainee. They chose this apartment believing it promised "a vision of smart urban

living" (p. 2), but this is just one of the illusions Jack and Chloe will have to examine in *City Boy.*

The tensions between Jack and Chloe are evident from the opening chapter, and the reader learns through flashback of their meeting and courtship that Jack has been the one more invested in the relationship and Chloe's caretaker from the start. He understands that it is his job "to soothe and console her," "to talk her down from ledges" (p. 64). Chloe may be supporting them financially, but Jack does the emotional work in this marriage. For a while he accepts this role uncomplainingly, but it cannot sustain Chloe's drinking and dishonesty. This combination has a lethal effect on the young marriage.

Though he is insightful and a careful observer, qualities useful for a writer, Jack is naïve and idealistic. He is blinded by Chloe's beauty from the moment he sees her in a poetry writing class. Of her, he says, "she was exactly the kind of girl who young men wrote poetry about," and he cannot fathom that beauty might mask inner turmoil, cruelty, selfishness (p. 26). Early on, when Chloe's sadness is revealed, it is shocking to Jack: "It had never occurred to Jack before that beautiful girls had the capacity to be unhappy" (p. 35). Chloe, though, is desperately unhappy and needs frequent propping up from Jack and, it will turn out, other men.

As things grow difficult within the marriage, Jack's writing suffers. Without realizing the same might be said of his relationship with Chloe, Jack notes that writing can "jerk you from high to low and back again" (p. 24). The bothersome neighbor, Rich, and his entourage provoke additional difficulties that both illuminate and complicate Jack's relationship to his work and his marriage. For instance, Jack gets involved with a girl from upstairs, Ivory, who walks with a limp from a childhood accident and calls herself a cripple. Ivory is obsessed with Rich, who seems to care little for her. Ivory and Jack have a lot in common, though it pains Jack to admit this. He does come to see that he has "his own crippled part that he stubbornly pretended was invisible: that he loved Chloe more than she would ever love him" (p. 77).

Chloe, too, has a deeply crippled part, though it isn't apparent in her physical bearing. Because Jack isn't in a position to see this side of her, Thompson allows the reader access to several entries in Chloe's journal, which reveal her insecurity and loneliness. In addition, the journal reveals the way drinking, initially a crutch, comes to own her. Though she claims to have quit drinking, the reader, if not Jack, can't be sure, since she writes in her journal that she has never been "totally honest about anything in [her] entire life. … Or not for very long" (p. 278).

Early on Jack has wondered about an elderly neighbor's devotion to her long-dead husband. He asks of her fifty years of mourning, "When do you cross the line between love and crazy?" (p. 57). By the novel's end, it is a question he must ask of himself. After learning of Chloe's affair with her boss, Jack behaves more and more obsessively and erratically, and the novel grows increasingly suspenseful. In the *Nashville Scene*, Pablo Tanguay remarked: "that Thompson is able to achieve such a compelling transformation—from hopeful young love to utter marital destruction—in so short a time frame is testament to her storytelling skills." Indeed, things end very poorly for Jack. While he has gained experience and maturity—that is, something he might write about and the perspective to do so—he has abandoned his dream of writing. In the *Hudson Review*, Thomas Filbin noted the paucity of contemporary tragedies. He commended Thompson's courage in writing one and said of *City Boy*, "This is a genuine tale that does not end cheerfully, only with the bitter taste of experience. Insightful, vivid, and moving, it offers no glib answers, only a well-drawn portrait for our instruction" (p. 510).

THROW LIKE A GIRL

Thompson's fourth collection of stories, *Throw Like a Girl* (2007), collects stories that were previously published in *Another Chicago Magazine, Crab Orchard Review,* and *Mid-American Review*. To throw like a girl is to be weak, ineffectual, and slightly pathetic. Thompson uses the title ironically, as there is little retiring or weak about the female characters that inhabit the twelve stories in *Throw Like a Girl*. In her review in the *New York Times Book Review,* Jennifer Egan called Thompson's characters "some of the most domineering dames to appear in recent fiction." Each story has at its center a girl or woman, and the collection initially seems to trace the movement from youth to experience. It begins with an adolescent protagonist, and the following stories feature young lovers, college students, mothers, divorcées, the long-married, middle-aged women, and grandmothers. The brilliant title story concludes the collection with a death.

The arrangement of the collection isn't as simple as this progression makes it sound, because the movement is interrupted by stories like "The Family Barcus," "Lost," and "Throw Like a Girl," all of which are told in a retrospective past tense and reveal the narrator's younger self as well as an older, more reflective self. Several reviewers remarked that these are the collection's strongest stories, and they both anchor the collection and remind the reader how the older characters we encounter carry the girls they were with them. There is still something "timid, doubtful, self-hating, sad" (p. 291) about them even as they are tough-talking, witty, and accomplished. The arrangement also cautions the reader from thinking that life is an easy progression through the various stages. Even for the characters in Thompson's small towns who "paired off young and got their lives settled quickly," life is rarely as they plan (p. 46).

Thompson's fellow midwesterner Ernest Hemingway claimed that women couldn't write war stories, but *Throw Like a Girl* boldly takes on this traditionally male subject matter. "It Would Not Make Me Tremble to See Ten Thousand Fall" begins with Jack Pardee's enlistment, but it ends with his wife Kelly Ann's. The army is supposed to "make a man out of" Jack, but Kelly Ann becomes a woman even before she enlists, deciding she "was going to have a life worth remembering" rather than the one everyone else has planned for her (p. 69). Kelly Ann's decision to enlist is less about serving her country or being near her husband than it is an opportunity

to be active rather than passive, to have an identity of her own design, not daughter, wife, or mother. The story ends with her imagining her name—K. Pardee—stenciled on her uniform.

Thompson captures the allure of the military for her characters, while unflinchingly examining the dangers and damages of war to individuals and communities. In "Lost," for instance, the narrator falls in love with a Vietnam vet who had "enlisted for the reasons young men usually do, that is, to measure themselves against something big, and to get their growing-up accomplished," but he is scarred from his time there and remains "a soldier all his life" (p. 107). Far from the fighting, in Hi Ho, Iowa, the setting for the story "Pie of the Month," the Iraq war negatively affects peoples' lives. Mrs. Colley, one of the proprietors of the business for which the story is named, needs pharmaceuticals, her "Rainbow pills," to deal with her anxiety about the war. While she can forget about the war for days, it was "like a pie you'd left in the oven, something nagging at you, a task left unfinished" (p. 255). She is not the only one in Hi Ho to suffer; the doctor tells her "there was a lot of War sickness going around lately" (p. 262). Her friend Mrs. Pulliam takes a stand in the end by stamping the phrase NO MORE WAR onto the September apple pies, the quintessential American pie. The citizens of Hi Ho have been largely silent, trusting, and compliant, though in the end, Mrs. Pulliam and Mrs. Colley seem to understand how taking a stand is the first step to "a bigger life" (p. 260).

Egan wrote that *Throw Like A Girl* "finds Thompson preoccupied with a paradox: why do tough, independent-minded women who know they're smarter than the men around them still end up needing those losers, thus engineering their own disappointment?" Indeed, six of the dozen stories here explore unfulfilling relationships between men and women. According to Bruce Allen in his review for the *Boston Globe*, Thompson analyzes these relationships "with trenchant, dispassionate clarity." Thompson's prose is supple and precise, offering insight and humor. For instance, In "A Woman Taken in Adultery," the narrator hints at her motivation for embarking on an affair when she says "sex was

now meant to be the province of my daughters, who were sixteen and fourteen. Their moon waxed while mine waned. ... My daughters flounced and preened and every moment of the day was a drama and they were the stars. Funny old fussbudget Mom! Comic secondary character, equipped with apron and feather duster!" (p. 219).

In *Throw Like a Girl* the relationships that endure are those between women. The title story follows the long friendship of the narrator, Gail, and Janey, who met in college. The story is largely flashback, a kind of love letter to Janey and to youth. As young women the friends decide that certain experiences with men can be disregarded; they "didn't count" (p. 270). In contrast, this friendship does count. The women share an intimacy and honesty and respect despite all they have been through together and apart. In "Holy Week," Olivia Snow, single mother and alcoholic, doesn't believe in a Higher Power, but when her daughter begs her to quit drinking, she promises to do it. Love for her daughter is what she believes in and what might save her. In "A Normal Life," about a couple who have left spouses for each other but find themselves still unsatisfied, Melanie understands part of what she has lost in her divorce and remarriage is her female friends. Even if they aren't the relationships women initially value, these are the ones that sustain, Thompson suggests. They provide valuable connection and consistency in the lives of her female characters.

DO NOT DENY ME

Do Not Deny Me (2009), a *New York Times* Notable Book, takes as its subject matter the lives of average Americans. In the *Miami Herald*, Connie Ogle wrote that Thompson is "an astute observer of the pitfalls of contemporary life, how it isolates and challenges, how it brings out one's worst and best." And in the *New York Times Book Review*, Francine Prose noted that Thompson's characters "could hardly be more ordinary, more like folks down the block" (p. 15). The critics agreed that despite the ordinary lives depicted here, the collection is never grim or predictable.

Thompson's humor leavens the stories and makes the characters—even the least appealing—sympathetic and recognizable to her readers. In addition, as Catherine Brady noted in the *Rumpus,* the precision and originality of Thompson's language enables readers to care deeply about these ordinary figures as they cope with grief, regret, aging, illness, divorce, and financial and romantic woes.

Ogle observed that "the most insightful stories are a matched set": "Wilderness" and "Her Untold Story." The stories, bracketing the rest of the collection, reveal two sides of the character Lynn. In "Wilderness," we see Lynn through the perspective of her old friend, Anna, who comes to visit for Thanksgiving, as Lynn's marriage is floundering. Anna's perceptions of Lynn are, naturally, colored by her own circumstances and disappointments. Of her past, Anna says: "the wreckages of two marriages and more lovers than had strictly been necessary trailed behind her like a busted parachute" (p. 29). When Anna first sees Lynn, she says, "You are the very model of modern Michigan matron" (p. 30), which not surprisingly offends Lynn. The measuring and comparing that goes on between Lynn and Anna is a preoccupation of Thompson's, a theme she returns to again and again. This competition isn't reserved for female characters. We see it early on in "Applause, Applause" and more recently in the relationship between Chip and Ryan in *The Year We Left Home.* Of this kind of complicated, long-term relationship, Thompson says in an interview (with Rachel Hall) on the blog *Work-in-Progress*: "I'm drawn to complexities, in people and in relationships, and how they play out over time. Few of us are entirely blameless (or blameworthy) when it comes to navigating the expectations and disappointments of long-term relationships. There's always a burr beneath the saddle." In "Wilderness," Anna puts it like this to Lynn's teenaged son, who has picked up on the tension between the two women: "When people know each other for a long time, they sort of wear each other out" (p. 51). Indeed, the friendship is finished by the time the weekend is over. When Lynn's husband drops Anna at the train station, he says of an old hobby, "I don't know why things stop being important, they just do" (p. 54). Without knowing it, he is commenting on the friendship between Anna and Lynn as well as his marriage.

When we meet Lynn again in the collection's final story, she is divorced and depressed, wondering if "her life was already used up" (p. 271). Anna is only mentioned as the "ex-friend" who made the stinging comment about Lynn's suburban appearance. But Lynn has more pressing concerns and resentments. Her ex-husband, for instance, is remarried and has started a new family with his younger second wife. He expects Lynn to understand that he can't pay their sons' college tuition, though the divorce agreement clearly states it is his responsibility. When he asks Lynn for flexibility, she turns all her vitriol on him. Lynn eventually tires of "chewing on her own black heart" (p. 281) and tries online dating with bizarre results. In the story's final scene, Lynn and her friend, another divorcée, take up running. Lynn repeats the phrase "joyful in our beings" as she runs. "This small declaration of faith," Brady noted, "beautifully evokes the aims of the work as a whole." Thompson is a master of these resonant and hopeful moments.

While Anna and Lynn are better at spouting criticism than addressing their murkier feelings, many of the other characters in *Do Not Deny Me* can't articulate their thoughts or feelings at all. They know they aren't happy, but they can't explain why. In "Tree House" for instance, Garrison, the father of two grown children, embarks on building an elaborate tree house in his backyard where he can find refuge from life that he finds "too cluttered with bewilderment and pain" (p. 245). In "Escape," Hurley has had a major stroke that has left him unable to speak at all. His wife, Claudine, has long been unhappy in the marriage and is a bitter and impatient caregiver. Despite his lack of speech, Hurley is able to enact his revenge and escape Claudine.

Both "Mr. Rat" and "Smash" are first-person stories that feature corporate types who have adopted the principles of capitalism so thoroughly they think of other people only in terms of what they need from them. Accidents jolt both men out of themselves. For Matthew, in "Mr. Rat,"

empathy may be fleeting, but Thompson suggests this isn't surprising given the language and philosophy of the world in which he works. At a morning meeting, for instance, all employees are asked to respond to questions like: "Have I established ownership of team objectives?" "Have I looked on each new day as an opportunity to excel?" (p. 58). Brady commended Thompson for pointing out the similarly "debased language of a media-saturated culture" and the way it commodifies human suffering. By the end of "Smash," the protagonist is able to imagine the other people involved in his car accident—their lives, their hopes and fears—and in doing so, opens up possibilities that were not available to him before when he maintained "a clear boundary" (p. 140) between himself and others. Asked how he is after the accident, he responds, "I was finer than fine. Newer than new … I was paying complete attention" (p. 143).

The stories in *Do Not Deny Me* offer readers glimpses into the hearts and minds of a wide range of characters, and, like the narrator of "Smash," we are richer for the chance to see into other characters' lives.

THE YEAR WE LEFT HOME

Called an "epic page turner" in *Kirkus Reviews,* Thompson's novel *The Year We Left Home* (2011) covers thirty years in the life of the Erikson family of Grenada, Iowa, from 1973 to 2003. In her online interview with *Work-in-Progress,* Thompson said that she wrote the chapters to have the momentum and impact of short stories. The chapters shift in point of view among the Erikson family and Chip, their cousin. Through the lives of its characters, the novel addresses American history, starting with the aftermath of Vietnam, touching on the farm crisis of the 1980s, and ending with the Iraq War. In its sweep and approach, wrote Jonathan Dee in the *New York Times Book Review,* the novel is like Evan S. Connell's *Mrs. Bridge* and *Mr. Bridge.* The *Kirkus Reviews* writer compared Thompson to Richard Russo for her "ability to put these characters empathetically on the page, in their special setting,

over an extended period of years, with just the right dose of dark humor."

Of the largely Norwegian immigrants who inhabit Grenada, Thompson writes: "They believed in backbreaking labor, followed by more labor, and in privation, thrift, cleanliness, and joyless charity" (p. 3). Cousin Chip never fit in here, and after returning from Vietnam he is even more of an outsider. He becomes, as John Repp wrote in the *Cleveland Plain Dealer,* "the baffled conscience of the tale." The relationship between Chip and Ryan, the eldest Erikson boy, is central to the novel. Ryan, whose point of view both begins and ends the novel, is a golden boy, a former high school track star and A student, but his alienation, though less obvious than his cousin's, is just as profound. It will take him away from Grenada and the watchful eyes of his family to Iowa City for college and then to Chicago, where he ends up working in computers at the right time. Ryan's professional success doesn't alleviate his sense of being an outsider any more than his marriage or fatherhood does. Indeed, his wife, who comes from a similar background, points out that in their haste to leave their origins and reinvent themselves, they have lost a sense of belonging. "It's like we're not from anywhere," she says, articulating the alienation that Ryan cannot (p. 215). Later, Chip, who understands Ryan's uneasy relationship to home, tells him: "you were like me, you had that same spirit in you, you didn't want to hang around with the home folks watching paint dry. You knew there was more out there" (p. 162).

The other Eriksons stay closer to home. Anita, the eldest sister, is the family beauty. Anita has done exactly what was expected of her. She marries a good provider, has two children, and dresses up for her banker husband's business associates. Anita ends up surprising the reader with her honesty, compassion and generosity, to friend and family alike. She is particularly heroic in a scene in which her relatives' farm is being auctioned off by her husband's bank. By the end of the novel, Anita has assumed the mantel of matriarch, but she puts her own stamp on the role, abandoning the kitchen to become a top-selling realtor. Critics commended Thompson for

the surprising way the novel invigorates familiar situations or characters. Dee wrote that "it's this sense of the familiar revivified—of knowing what's coming yet being emotionally outflanked by it anyway—that best characterizes *The Year We Left Home*."

Torrie Erikson's devastating car accident is another example of Thompson's artistry in this regard. The youngest of the Erikson children, Torrie has aspirations of leaving Grenada for the Ivy League, but her recklessness and bad luck leave her dependent on her mother, Audrey, for her most basic care. Torrie's accident is perhaps the most dramatic aspect of the novel's plot, and its effects linger for the Erikson family. Audrey remarks, "she found herself thinking she'd been born into one world, hopeful and normal, and now she lived in another, full of sadness and failure" (p. 183). Eventually Torrie regains her mobility and independence and reenters the world by taking photographs that give expression to her alienation. Chip understands her better than the others: "You didn't give up wanting things because your life had put them out of reach" (p. 291). This understanding allows Chip to connect Torrie with another photographer, Elton, with whom she will, at long last, leave home.

Of all the Erikson children, the reader sees the least of Blake. The younger son, more interested in cars then school, stays in Grenada, marries and has three children, and becomes a general contractor. In his physical labor he resembles his farming relatives. By the end of the novel he has back problems and a permanently weather-chapped face. His narrative reveals that, even in predictable Grenada, change is inevitable. For instance, Blake and his wife struggle financially on their two salaries, while his parents supported more children on a single salary. "The math of the world had got screwed up somehow," he notes (p. 252). Blake is crucial to the novel's ending as he is renovating the old family farmhouse, which Ryan has bought using Anita as a realtor and where Chip will live. The farm reestablishes the Erikson family's ties to each other and to this place. The optimism of this ending is undercut by Blake's son's plans to enlist to fight in Iraq. When Chip learns of these plans, he says "You know you've been handed a fucked-up life when you've seen two useless obscene wars" (p. 323). Still, this doesn't stop Chip from hanging an American flag over the entrance to the farmhouse, saying "Why not, man. It's my goddamned country too. ... It's like family. No matter how fucked up it is, it's the only one you got" (p. 324).

From her earliest stories to *The Year We Left Home*, Thompson's fiction has grappled with the big political and social issues of our age: race, gender, war and its aftermath. One can easily see her fiction on reading lists for classes in American literature, contemporary literature, peace studies, and women's studies. Thompson has many appreciative readers, but surprisingly her work hasn't received much critical study. Perhaps *The Year We Left Home*, which combines Thompson's many strengths in telling the story of our tumultuous times, will prompt the serious consideration Thompson's oeuvre deserves.

Selected Bibliography

WORKS OF JEAN THOMPSON

NOVELS
My Wisdom. New York: Franklin Watts, 1982.

The Woman Driver. New York: Franklin Watts, 1985.

Wide Blue Yonder. New York: Simon & Schuster, 2002.

City Boy. New York: Simon & Schuster, 2004.

The Year We Left Home. New York: Simon & Schuster, 2011.

STORY COLLECTIONS
The Gasoline Wars: Stories. Urbana: University of Illinois Press, 1979.

Little Face and Other Stories. New York: Franklin Watts, 1984.

Who Do You Love: Stories. New York: Harcourt Brace, 1999.

Throw Like a Girl: Stories. New York: Simon & Schuster, 2007.

Do Not Deny Me: Stories. New York: Simon & Schuster, 2009.

UNCOLLECTED WRITING
"Typical Americans." *New York Times Book Review,* June 27, 1999, p. 13. (Review of *Who's Irish?* by Gish Jen.)

"New Hampshire Primary." *New York Times Book Review,* March 5, 2000, p. 16. (Review of *The Suburbs of Heaven,* by Merle Drown.)

"Lives; Where He Was Calling From." *New York Times,* January 13, 2002. http://www.nytimes.com/2002/01/13/magazine/lives-where-he-was-calling-from.html.

"Western Civ." *New York Times,* July 21, 2002, p. F5. (Review of *Half in Love: Stories,* by Maile Meloy.)

"Notorious in New Haven." *New York Times,* March 16, 2003, p. A7. (Review of *Drinking Coffee Elsewhere,* by ZZ Packer.)

"Legends of the Summer." *New York Times,* August 7, 2005, p. F11. (Review of *The Summer He Didn't Die,* by Jim Harrison.)

"Jean Thompson Responds to King's 'What Ails the Short Story.' " Maud Newton (blog), October 12, 2007. http://maudnewton.com/blog/?p=8047.

"Don't Have a Nice Day." *New York Times Book Review,* April 16, 2010, p. 24. (Review of *The Collected Stories of Deborah Eisenberg.*)

"What Men Want Women to Want." *New York Times Book Review,* January 21, 2011, p. 11. (Review of *Woodcuts of Women,* by Dagoberto Gilb.)

"A Rail Car Named Desire." *New York Times Book Review,* May 27, 2011, p. 13. (Review of *The London Train,* by Tessa Hadley.)

ANTHOLOGIES

Matters of Life and Death: New American Stories. Edited by Tobias Wolff. Green Harbor, Mass.: Wampeter Press, 1983.

Children Playing Before a Statue of Hercules. Edited by David Sedaris. New York: Simon & Schuster Paperbacks, 2005.

CRITICAL AND BIOGRAPHICAL STUDIES

Filbin, Thomas. "Up Close and Personal." *Hudson Review* 57, no. 3:509–514 (fall 2004).

Painter, Pamela. "The Art and Architecture of the Double Ending." In *The Open Book: Essays from the Vermont College Postgraduate Writers Conference.* Edited by Kate Fetherston and Roger Weingarten. New Castle, U.K.: Cambridge Scholars Press, 2006. Pp. 202–207.

REVIEWS

Allen, Bruce. "Simple Stories About Complicated Relationships." *Boston Globe,* August 15, 2007. http://articles.boston.com/2007-08-15/news/29227929_1_jean-thompson-high-school-pair-girls/2.

Blundell, Janet Boyarin. "*Little Face and Other Stories.*" *Library Journal,* October 1, 1984, p. 1864.

Brady, Catherine. "*Do Not Deny Me.*" *Rumpus,* May 29, 2009. http://therumpus.net/2009/05/do-not-deny-me/.

Cassada, Jackie. "*My Wisdom.*" *Library Journal,* September 15, 1982, pp. 1771–1772.

Dee, Jonathan. "A Midwestern Family's Withered Roots." *New York Times Book Review,* May 8, 2011, p. 9. (Review of *The Year We Left Home.*)

Dieckmann, Katherine. "Cobra Snake for a Necktie." *New York Times Book Review,* July 25, 1999, p. 14. (Review of *Who Do You Love.*)

Edmonds, Dale. "*The Gasoline Wars.*" *Studies in Short Fiction* 18, no. 2:198–199 (spring 1981).

Egan, Jennifer. "Woman Warriors." *New York Times,* June 17, 2007, p. F9. (Review of *Throw Like a Girl.*)

Geist, Bill. "*Wild Blue Yonder.*" *Kirkus Reviews,* November 1, 2001, p. 1512.

Giles, Jeff. "Heartsick." *Newsweek,* June 13, 1999. http://www.thedailybeast.com/newsweek/1999/06/13/heartsick.html. (Review of *Who Do You Love.*)

Miner, Valerie. "*Who Do You Love: Stories.*" *Women's Review of Books* 17, no. 2:15 (November 1999).

Nelson, Liza. "O's 2011 Summer Reading List: *The Year We Left Home.*" *Oprah,* June 13, 2011. http://www.oprah.com/book-list/Os-2011-Summer-Reading-List.

Ogle, Connie. "*Do Not Deny Me* by Jean Thompson." *Pop Matters,* July 7, 2009. http://www.popmatters.com/pm/review/107230-do-not-deny-me-by-jean-thompson/.

Prose, Francine. "Everyday Misdemeanors." *New York Times Book Review,* July 16, 2009, p. 15. (Review of *Do Not Deny Me.*)

Repp, John. "Jean Thompson's *The Year We Left Home* Is Intimate and Tender." *Cleveland.com,* May 3, 2011. http://www.cleveland.com/books/index.ssf/2011/05/jean_thompsons_intimate_tender.html.

Seaman, Donna. "Jean Thompson Cooks Up a Recipe for Heartache." *Chicago Tribune,* February 1, 2004. http://articles.chicagotribune.com/2004-02-01/entertainment/0401310275_1_jack-and-chloe-raggedy-ann-city-boy.

Smoodin, Roberta. "*The Woman Driver.*" *Los Angeles Times,* August 25, 1985, p. T8.

Tanguay, Pablo. "A Tale of Tangled Sheets." *Nashville Scene,* March 11, 2004. http://www.nashvillescene.com/nashville/a-tale-of-tangled-sheets/Content?oid=118960. (Review of *City Boy.*)

Thompson, Caroline. "Ring of Truth in a Voice of the '60s." *Los Angeles Times,* November 25, 1982, p. 27. (Review of *My Wisdom.*)

Wickenden, Dorothy. "*The Gasoline Wars.*" *New Republic,* March 15, 1980, p. 35.

Willis, Dail. "Jean Thompson's *City Boy:* The Pain of Love." *Baltimore Sun,* February 8, 2004. http://articles.baltimoresun.com/2004-02-08/entertainment/0402080458_1_jean-thompson-city-boy-jack.

Winch, Terence. "Short Stops on the Reading Railroad." *Washington Post Book World,* March 30, 1979, pp. 14–15. (Review of *The Gasoline Wars.*)

"The Year We Left Home." Kirkus Reviews, February 1, 2011. http://www.kirkusreviews.com/search/ ?q=the+year+we+left+home+jean+thompson.

Zeidner, Lisa. "Josie and the Psychopaths." *New York Times Book Review,* December 30, 2001, p. 7. (Review of *Wide Blue Yonder.*)

INTERVIEWS

Elliott, Erin. "Q&A with Jean Thompson." *Washington Independent Review of Books,* June 20, 2011. http://www. washingtonindependentreviewofbooks.com/author-q-and-a/qa-with-jean-thompson/.

Hall, Rachel. " 'Gossiping About Imaginary People': An Interview with Jean Thompson." *Work-in-Progress,* May 31, 2011. http://workinprogressinprogress.blogspot.com/ 2011/05/guest-in-progress-interview-with-jean.html.

———. "Questions for *American Writers* Series." E-mail correspondence with Jean Thompson, August 8, 2011.

"Q&A." *One Story,* May 10, 2008. http://www.one-story. com/index.php?page=story&story_id=105.

Ruback, Max. "Entanglements of the Heart." *Writer* 115, no. 2:39–42 (February 2002).

Tekulve, Susan. "The Way of Stories: An Interview with Jean Thompson." *Del Sol Review.* http://delsolreview. webdelsol.com/epicks5/tekulve.htm.

Cumulative Index

All references include volume numbers in boldface roman numerals followed by page numbers within that volume. Subjects of articles are indicated by boldface type.

A

"A" (Zukofsky), **Supp. III Part 2:** 611, 612, 614, 617, 619, 620, 621, 622, 623, 624, 626, 627, 628, 629, 630, 631; **Supp. IV Part 1:** 154; **Supp. XVI:** 287, *287*

Aal, Katharyn Machan, **Supp. IV Part 1:** 332; **Supp. XXIII:** 54

Aaron, Daniel, **IV:** 429; **Supp. I Part 2:** 647, 650

Aaron's Rod (Lawrence), **Supp. I Part 1:** 255

Abacus (Karr), **Supp. XI: 240–242,** 248, 254

Abádi-Nagy, Zoltán, **Supp. IV Part 1:** 280, 289, 291

"Abandoned Farmhouse" (Kooser), **Supp. XIX:** 117, 119

"Abandoned House, The" (L. Michaels), **Supp. XVI:** 214

"Abandoned Newborn, The" (Olds), **Supp. X:** 207

"Abandoned Stone Schoolhouse in the Nebraska Sandhills, An" (Kooser), **Supp. XIX:** 124–125

"Abba Jacob" (Nelson), **Supp. XVIII:** 177

"Abbé François Picquet"(Kenny), **Supp. XXIII:** 153

Abbey, Edward, **Supp. VIII:** 42; **Supp. X:** 24, 29, 30, 31, 36; **Supp. XIII: 1–18; Supp. XIV:** 179

Abbey's Road (Abbey), **Supp. XIII:** 12

Abbott, Carl, **Supp. XVIII:** 142

Abbott, Edith, **Supp. I Part 1:** 5

Abbott, George, **Supp. IV Part 2:** 585

Abbott, Grace, **Supp. I Part 1:** 5

Abbott, Jack Henry, **Retro. Supp. II:** 210

Abbott, Jacob, **Supp. I Part 1:** 38, 39

Abbott, Lyman, **III:** 293

Abbott, Sean, **Retro. Supp. II:** 213

ABC of Color, An: Selections from Over a Half Century of Writings (Du Bois), **Supp. II Part 1:** 186

ABC of Reading (Pound), **III:** 468, 474–475

"Abdication, An" (Merrill), **Supp. III Part 1:** 326

'Abdu'l-Bahá, **Supp. XX: 117, 122**

Abel, Lionel, **Supp. XIII:** 98

Abel, Sam, **Supp. XIII:** 199

Abelard, Peter, **I:** 14, 22

Abeles, Sigmund, **Supp. VIII:** 272

Abeng (Cliff), **Supp. XXII:** 66, 69–71

Abercrombie, Lascelles, **III:** 471; **Retro. Supp. I:** 127, 128

Abernathy, Milton, **Supp. III Part 2:** 616

Abernon, Edgar Vincent, Viscount d', **Supp. XVI:** 191

Aberration of Starlight (Sorrentino), **Supp. XXI:** 234–235

Abhau, Anna. *See* Mencken, Mrs. August (Anna Abhau)

"Abide with Me" (Hoffman), **Supp. XVIII:** 86

Abide with Me (Strout), **Supp. XXIII:** 273, 275, **278–280,** 285

"Ability" (Emerson), **II:** 6

Abingdon, Alexander, **Supp. XVI:** 99

Abish, Walter, **Supp. V:** 44

"Abishag" (Glück), **Supp. V:** 82

Abney, Lisa, **Supp. XXII:** 9

Abood, Maureen, **Supp. XXII:** 90

"Abortion, The" (Sexton), **Supp. II Part 2:** 682

"Abortions" (Dixon), **Supp. XII:** 153

"About C. D. Wright" (Colburn), **Supp. XV:** 341

"About Effie" (Findley), **Supp. XX: 50**

"About Hospitality" (Jewett), **Retro. Supp. II:** 131

"About Kathryn" (Dubus), **Supp. VII:** 91

"About Language" (Wrigley), **Supp. XVIII:** 300–301

"About Looking Alone at a Place: Arles" (M. F. K. Fisher), **Supp. XVII:** 89, 91

About the House (Auden), **Supp. II Part 1:** 24

About Town: "The New Yorker" and the World It Made (Yagoda), **Supp. VIII:** 151

"About Zhivago and His Poems"(O'Hara), **Supp. XXIII:** 214

"Above Pate Valley" (Snyder), **Supp. VIII:** 293

Above the River (Wright), **Supp. III Part 2:** 589, 606

"Abraham" (Schwartz), **Supp. II Part 2:** 663

Abraham, Nelson Algren. *See* Algren, Nelson

Abraham, Pearl, **Supp. XVII:** 49; **Supp. XX: 177**

"Abraham Davenport" (Whittier), **Supp. I Part 2:** 699

"Abraham Lincoln" (Emerson), **II:** 13

Abraham Lincoln: The Prairie Years (Sandburg), **III:** 580, 587–589, 590

Abraham Lincoln: The Prairie Years and the War Years (Sandburg), **III:** 588, 590

Abraham Lincoln: The War Years (Sandburg), **III:** 588, 589–590; **Supp. XVII:** 105

"Abraham Lincoln Walks at Midnight" (Lindsay), **Supp. I Part 2:** 390–391

"Abram Morrison" (Whittier), **Supp. I Part 2:** 699

Abramovich, Alex, **Supp. X:** 302, 309

Abrams, David, **Supp. XXII:** 61

Abrams, M. H., **Supp. XVI:** 19; **Supp. XXIII:** 42

Abridgment of Universal Geography, An: Together with Sketches of History (Rowson), **Supp. XV:** 243

"Absalom" (Rukeyser), **Supp. VI:** 278–279

Absalom, Absalom! (Faulkner), **II:** 64, 65–67, 72, 223; **IV:** 207; **Retro. Supp. I:** 75, 81, 82, 84, 85, 86, 87, 88, 89, 90, 92, 382; **Supp. V:** 261; **Supp. X:** 51; **Supp. XIV:** 12–13

"Absence"(J. Schoolcraft), **Supp. XXIII:** 228, 231

"Absence of Mercy" (Stone), **Supp. V:** 295

"Absentee, The" (Levertov), **Supp. III Part 1:** 284

Absentee Ownership (Veblen), **Supp. I Part 2:** 642

"Absent-Minded Bartender" (X. J. Kennedy), **Supp. XV:** 159

"Absent Thee from Felicity Awhile" (Wylie), **Supp. I Part 2:** 727, 729

"Absolution" (Fitzgerald), **Retro. Supp. I:** 108

"Absolution" (Sobin), **Supp. XVI:** 289

"Abuelita's Ache" (Mora), **Supp. XIII:** 218

Abysmal Brute, The (London), **II:** 467

Abyssinia and the Imperialists (C. L. R. James), **Supp. XXI:** 166

Abyss of Human Illusion, The (Sorrentino), **Supp. XXI:** 225, 227, 237–238

"Academic Story, An" (Simpson), **Supp. IX:** 279–280

"Academic Zoo, The: Theory—in Practice" (Epstein), **Supp. XIV:** 107–108, 109

"A Capella" (Wrigley), **Supp. XVIII:** 300

"Accident" (Minot), **Supp. VI: 208–209**

"Accident, The" (Southern), **Supp. XI:** 295

"Accident, The" (Strand), **Supp. IV Part 2:** 624

Accident/A Day's News (Wolf), **Supp. IV Part 1:** 310

Accidental Tourist, The (Tyler), **Supp. IV Part 2:** 657, 668–669; **Supp. V:** 227

Accordion Crimes (Proulx), **Supp. VII:** 259–261

"Accountability" (Dunbar), **Supp. II Part 1:** 197, 204

"Account of the Method of Drawing Birds" (Audubon), **Supp. XVI:** 12

"Accusation, The" (Wright), **Supp. III Part 2:** 595

"Accusation of the Inward Man, The" (Taylor), **IV:** 156

"Accusing Message from Dead Father" (Karr), **Supp. XI:** 244

Ace, Goodman, **Supp. IV Part 2:** 574

Ache of Appetite, The (Hadas), **Supp. XXIII: 120–121**

Achievement in American Poetry (Bogan), **Supp. III Part 1:** 63–64

Acker, Kathy, **Supp. XII:1–20; Supp. XXI:** 236

Ackerley, J. R., **Supp. XX:** 237

Ackerman, Diane, **Supp. XIII:** 154

"Acknowledgment" (Lanier), **Supp. I Part 1:** 364

Ackroyd, Peter, **Supp. V:** 233; **Supp. XVII:** 180

"Acquaintance in the Heavens, An" (Dillard), **Supp. VI:** 34

"Acquainted with the Night" (Frost), **II:** 155; **Retro. Supp. I:** 137; **Supp. XXI:** 26

Across Spoon River (Masters), **Supp. I Part 2:** 455, 457, 459, 460, 466, 474–475, 476

Across the Layers: Poems Old and New (Goldbarth), **Supp. XII:** 181, **187–189**

Across the River and into the Trees (Hemingway), **I:** 491; **II:** 255–256, 261; **Retro. Supp. I:** 172, **184–185; Supp. XIX:** 248

"Actfive" (MacLeish), **III:** 18–19, 22

Actfive and Other Poems (MacLeish), **III:** 3, 17–19, 21

Action (Shepard), **Supp. III Part 2:** 446

Active Anthology (Pound), **Supp. III Part 2:** 617

Active Service (Crane), **I:** 409

"Act of Creation and Its Artifact, The" (Sorrentino), **Supp. XXI:** 229, 235

Act of Love, An (Wolfert), **Supp. XXI:** 270**, 275–277**

Act of Love, An: A Completely Retold Version of the Novel (Wolfert), **Supp. XXI:** 276

Acton, Patricia Nassif, **Supp. X:** 233

Acts and Monuments of These Latter and Perilous Days (Fox), **Supp. XXII:** 36

Acts of Faith (Caputo), **Supp. XIX: 29–30**

"Acts of the Apostles, The" (Bronk), **Supp. XXI:** 28

Actual, The (Bellow), **Retro. Supp. II:** 33

"Actual Experience, Preferred Narratives" (Julier), **Supp. IV Part 1:** 211

Acuff, Roy, **Supp. V:** 335

Ada (Nabokov), **Retro. Supp. I:** 265, 266, 270, 276–277, 278, 279

"Ada" (Stein), **IV:** 43

"Adagia" (Stevens), **IV:** 78, 80, 88, 92

"Adagio" (Hull), **Supp. XXI:** 136–137

"Adam" (Hecht), **Supp. X:** 62

"Adam" (W. C. Williams), **Retro. Supp. I:** 422, 423

"Adam and Eve" (Eugene), **Supp. X:** 204

"Adam and Eve" (Shapiro), **Supp. II Part 2:** 708, 712

"Adamantine Practice of Poetry, The" (Wright), **Supp. XV:** 341–342, 343–344

Adam Bede (G. Eliot), **II:** 181

Adamé, Leonard, **Supp. XIII:** 316

Adam & Eve & the City (W. C. Williams), **Retro. Supp. I:** 423

Adamic, Louis, **Supp. XXIII:** 166

"Adamic Purity as Double Agent" (Whalen-Bridge), **Retro. Supp. II:** 211–212

"Adam Robinson Acquires Grandparents and a Little Sister" (P. E. Jones), **Supp. XXII:** 151

"Adams" (Saunders), **Supp. XIX:** 232

Adams, Althea. *See* Thurber, Mrs. James (Althea Adams)

Adams, Annie. *See* Fields, Annie Adams

Adams, Brooks, **Supp. I Part 2:** 484

Adams, Charles, **Supp. I Part 2:** 644

Adams, Charles Francis, **I:** 1, 4; **Supp. I Part 2:** 484

Adams, Franklin P., **Supp. I Part 2:** 653; **Supp. IX:** 190; **Supp. XV:** 294, 297

Adams, Henry, **I:** 1–24, 111, 243, 258; **II:** 278, 542; **III:** 396, 504; **IV:** 191, 349; **Retro. Supp. I:** 53, 59; **Retro. Supp. II:** 207; **Supp. I Part 1:** 299–300, 301, 314; **Supp. I Part 2:** 417, 492, 543, 644; **Supp. II Part 1:** 93–94, 105; **Supp. III Part 2:** 613; **Supp. IV Part 1:** 31, 208

Adams, Mrs. Henry (Marian Hooper), **I:** 1, 5, 10, 17–18

Adams, Henry B., **Supp. I Part 1:** 369

Adams, James Truslow, **Supp. I Part 2:** 481, 484, 486

Adams, J. Donald, **IV:** 438

Adams, John, **I:** 1; **II:** 103, 301; **III:** 17, 473; **Supp. I Part 2:** 483, 506, 507, 509, 510, 511, 517, 518, 520, 524

Adams, John Luther, **Supp. XII:** 209

Adams, John Quincy, **I:** 1, 3, 16–17; **Supp. I Part 2:** 685, 686

Adams, Léonie, **Supp. I Part 2:** 707; **Supp. V:** 79; **Supp. IX:** 229; **Supp. XVII:** 75

Adams, Luella, **Supp. I Part 2:** 652

Adams, Noah, **Supp. XVII:** 218

Adams, Phoebe, **Supp. IV Part 1:** 203; **Supp. VIII:** 124

Adams, Samuel, **Supp. I Part 2:** 516, 525

Adams, Timothy Dow, **Supp. XVI:** 67, 69

Ada; or Ardor (Nabokov), **III:** 247

"Ad Castitatem" (Bogan), **Supp. III Part 1:** 50

Adcock, Betty, **Supp. XVIII:** 181–182, 182

Addams, Jane, **Supp. I Part 1: 1–26; Supp. XI:** 200, 202

Addams, John Huy, **Supp. I Part 1:** 2

"Addendum" (Wright), **Supp. V:** 339

Addiego, John, **Supp. XII:** 182

Adding Machine, The (Rice), **I:** 479

Adding Machine, The: Selected Essays (Burroughs), **Supp. III Part 1:** 93, 97

Addison, Joseph, **I:** 8, 105, 106–107, 108, 114, 131, 300, 304; **III:** 430

"Addressed to a Political Shrimp, or, Fly upon the Wheel" (Freneau), **Supp. II Part 1:** 267

"Address to My Soul" (Wylie), **Supp. I Part 2:** 729

"Address to the Deist, An" (Wheatley), **Supp. XX: 287**

"Address to the Devil" (Jarman), **Supp. XVII:** 114

Address to the Government of the United States on the Cession of Louisiana to the French, An (Brown), **Supp. I Part 1:** 146

"Address to the Scholars of New England" (Ransom), **III:** 491

"Address with Exclamation Points, A" (Simic), **Supp. VIII:** 283

"Adieu to Norman, Bon Jour to Joan and Jean-Paul"(O'Hara), **Supp. XXIII:** 219

Adisa, Opal Palmer, **Supp. XXII:** 66, 74, 78

"Adjutant Bird, The" (Banks), **Supp. V:** 5

Adkins, Nelson F., **II:** 20

Adler, Alfred, **I:** 248

Adler, Betty, **III:** 103

Adler, George J., **III:** 81

Adler, Renata, **Supp. X:** 171

Admiral of the Ocean Sea: A Life of Christopher Columbus (Morison), **Supp. I Part 2:** 486–488

"Admirals" (Chabon), **Supp. XI:** 72

"Admonition, An" (Brodsky), **Supp. VIII:** 33

"Adolescence" (Bidart), **Supp. XV:** 32

"Adolescence" (Dove), **Supp. IV Part 1:** 245

"Adolescence" (Olds), **Supp. X:** 211

"Adolescence II" (Dove), **Supp. IV Part 1:** 242, 244–245

Adolescent's Christmas, An: 1944 (C. Bly), **Supp. XVI:** 31–32

"Adolf Eichmann" (Carruth), **Supp. XVI:** 47

"Adonais" (Shelley), **II:** 516, 540

Adonai: The Pilgrim of Eternity (Lippard), **Supp. XXIII:** 180, 189, 190

Adorno, Theodor, **Supp. I Part 2:** 645, 650; **Supp. IV Part 1:** 301

"Adrienne Rich: The Poetics of Change" (Gelpi), **Supp. I Part 2:** 554

"Adultery" (Banks), **Supp. V:** 15

"Adultery" (Dubus), **Supp. VII:** 85

Adultery and Other Choices (Dubus), **Supp. VII:** 83–85

Adulthood Rites (O. Butler), **Supp. XIII:** 63, **64–65**

Adult Life of Toulouse Lautrec by Henri Toulouse Lautrec, The (Acker), **Supp. XII:** 5, 6, **8–9**

Adventure (London), **II:** 466

Adventures in Ancient Egypt (Goldbarth), **Supp. XII:** 191

Adventures in Value (Cummings), **I:** 430

"Adventures of a Book Reviewer" (Cowley), **Supp. II Part 1:** 137, 142

Adventures of Augie March, The (Bellow), **I:** 144, 147, 149, 150, 151, 152–153, 154, 155, 157, 158–159, 164; **Retro. Supp. II:** 19, 20, **22–23,** 24, 30; **Supp. VIII:** 234, 236–237

Adventures of a Young Man (Dos Passos), **I:** 488, 489, 492

Adventures of Captain Bonneville (Irving), **II:** 312

Adventures of Harry Franco, The: A Tale of the Great Panic (Briggs), **Supp. XVIII:** 1, 2, **5–8**

Adventures of Harry Richmond, The (Meredith), **Supp. XX: 234**

Adventures of Huckleberry Finn, The (Twain), **I:** 307, 506; **II:** 26, 72, 262, 266–268, 290, 418, 430; **III:** 101, 112–113, 357, 554, 558, 577; **IV:** 198, 201–204, 207; **Retro. Supp. I:** 188; **Retro. Supp. II:** 121; **Supp. I Part 1:** 247; **Supp. IV Part 1:** 247, 257; **Supp. IV Part 2:** 502; **Supp. V:** 131; **Supp. VIII:** 198; **Supp. X:** 230; **Supp. XII:** 16; **Supp. XVI:** 222; **Supp. XX: 171; Supp. XXII:** 81

Adventures of Jimmy (Broughton), **Supp. XV:** 146

Adventures of Roderick Random, The (Smollett), **I:** 134

Adventures of the Letter I (Simpson), **Supp. IX:** 266, **273–274**

Adventures of Tom Sawyer, The (Twain), **II:** 26; **III:** 223, 572, 577; **IV:** 199–200, 203, 204; **Supp. I Part 2:** 456, 470; **Supp. XVI:** 66

Adventures While Preaching the Gospel of Beauty (Lindsay), **Supp. I Part 2:** 374, 376, 381, 382–384, 389, 399

Adventures with Ed (Loeffler), **Supp. XIII:** 1

Advertisements for Myself (Mailer), **III:** 27, 35–38, 41–42, 45, 46; **Retro. Supp. II:** 196, 199, 200, 202, 203, 212; **Supp. IV Part 1:** 90, 284; **Supp. XIV:** 157

"Advertisements for Myself on the Way Out" (Mailer), **III:** 37

"Advice to a Prophet" (Wilbur), **Supp. III Part 2:** 555–557

Advice to a Prophet and Other Poems (Wilbur), **Supp. III Part 2:** 554–558

"Advice to a Raven in Russia" (Barlow), **Supp. II Part 1:** 65, 74, 80, 83

"Advice to Players" (Bidart), **Supp. XV:** 35

Advice to the Lovelorn (film), **Retro. Supp. II:** 328

Advice to the Privileged Orders, Part I (Barlow), **Supp. II Part 1:** 80

Aegerter, Lindsay Pentolfe, **Supp. XXII:** 69

"Aeneas and Dido" (Brodsky), **Supp. VIII:** 24–25

"Aeneas at Washington" (Tate), **IV:** 129

Aeneid (Virgil), **I:** 396; **II:** 542; **III:** 124; **Supp. XV:** 23

Aeneus Tacticus, **I:** 136

Aerial View (Barabtarlo), **Retro. Supp. I:** 278

"Aeria the Evanescent" (Sobin), **Supp. XVI:** 292

Aeschylus, **I:** 274, 433; **III:** 398; **IV:** 358, 368, 370; **Retro. Supp. I:** 65; **Supp. I Part 2:** 458, 494

Aesop, **I:** 387; **II:** 154, 169, 302; **III:** 587

Aesthetic (Croce), **III:** 610

"Aesthetics" (Mumford), **Supp. II Part 2:** 476

"Aesthetics of Silence, The" (Sontag), **Supp. III Part 2:** 459

"Aesthetics of the Shah" (Olds), **Supp. X:** 205

"Affair at Coulter's Notch, The" (Bierce), **I:** 202

Affaire de viol, Une (C. Himes). *See Case of Rape, A* (C. Himes)

"Affair of Outposts, An" (Bierce), **I:** 202

Affliction (Banks), **Supp. V:** 15, 16

Affluent Society, The (Galbraith), **Supp. I Part 2:** 648

Afghanistan Picture Show, An: or, How I Saved the World (Vollmann), **Supp. XVII:** 226, **228–229,** 233

"Aficionados, The" (Carver), **Supp. III Part 1:** 137

"Afloat" (Beattie), **Supp. V:** 29

Afloat and Ashore (Cooper), **I:** 351, 355

"Afoot" (P. N. Warren as Kilina), **Supp. XX: 261–262**

Africa, Its Geography, People, and Products (Du Bois), **Supp. II Part 1:** 179

Africa, Its Place in Modern History (Du Bois), **Supp. II Part 1:** 179

"Africa, to My Mother" (D. Diop), **Supp. IV Part 1:** 16

Africana (H. L. Gates, ed.), **Supp. XX: 99**

African American Century, The : How Black Americans Have Shaped Our Country (H. L. Gates), **Supp. XX: 102**

African American Lives (television production), **Supp. XX: 99**

African American Lives 2 (television production), **Supp. XX: 99**

African American National Biography (H. L. Gates, ed.), **Supp. XX: 99**

African American Writers (Smith, ed.), **Supp. XIII:** 115, 127

"African Book" (Hemingway), **II:** 259

"African Chief, The" (Bryant), **Supp. I Part 1:** 168

"African Fragment" (Brooks), **Supp. III Part 1:** 85

African Queen, The (film), **Supp. XI:** 17

"African Roots of War, The" (Du Bois), **Supp. II Part 1:** 174

African Silences (Matthiessen), **Supp. V:** 203

African Treasury, An (Hughes, ed.), **Supp. I Part 1:** 344

"Afrika Revolution" (Baraka), **Supp. II Part 1:** 53

"AFRO-AMERICAN LYRIC" (Baraka), **Supp. II Part 1:** 59

After (Bukiet), **Supp. XVII:** 43, **44–45**

After (Hirshfield), **Supp. XXIII:** 133–135, 139

After All: Last Poems (Matthews), **Supp. IX:** 155, **167–169**

After and Before the Lightning (Ortiz), **Supp. IV Part 2:** 513

"After a Party" (Salinas), **Supp. XIII:** 327

"After Apple-Picking" (Frost), **Retro. Supp. I:** 126, 128

"After Arguing against the Contention That Art Must Come from Discontent" (Stafford), **Supp. XI:** 327

After Confession: Poetry as Autobiography (Harris), **Supp. XIV:** 269

After Confession: Poetry as Autobiography (K. Sontag and D. Graham), **Supp. XV:** 104

"After Cowboy Chicken Came to Town" (Jin), **Supp. XVIII:** 97–98

"After Disappointment" (Jarman), **Supp. XVII:** 118–119

After Disillusion: Poems (Wolf), **Supp. XXII:** 275

After Experience (Snodgrass), **Supp. VI:** 314–316, 317

"After great pain, a formal feeling comes" (Dickinson), **Retro. Supp. I:** 37

"After Hearing a Waltz by Bartók" (Lowell), **II:** 522

After Henry (Didion), **Supp. IV Part 1:** 195, 196, 199, 207, 208, 211

"After Henry" (Didion), **Supp. IV Part 1:** 211

"After Holbein" (Wharton), **IV:** 325; **Retro. Supp. I:** 382

After Ikkyu and Other Poems (Harrison), **Supp. VIII:** 42

"After-Image" (Bierds), **Supp. XVII:** 31–32

"After-Image" (Caldwell), **I:** 309

After-Images: Autobiographical Sketches (Snodgrass), **Supp. VI:** 314, **319–323,** 324, 326–327

After I's (Zukofsky), **Supp. III Part 2:** 628, 629

Afterlife (Monette), **Supp. X:** 153

Afterlife (Updike), **Retro. Supp. I:** 322

Afterlife, The (Levis), **Supp. XI:** 259, **260–264**

"After Magritte" (McClatchy), **Supp. XII:** 264

"After Making Love" (Dunn), **Supp. XI:** 153

Aftermath (Longfellow), **II:** 490

"Aftermath" (Longfellow), **II:** 498

After New Formalism (A. Finch, ed.), **Supp. XVII:** 74

"Afternoon" (Ellison), **Supp. II Part 1:** 238

"Afternoon at MacDowell" (Kenyon), **Supp. VII:** 159

"Afternoon Miracle, An" (O. Henry), **Supp. II Part 1:** 390

Afternoon of a Faun (Hearon), **Supp. VIII: 63–64**

Afternoon of an Author: A Selection of Uncollected Stories and Essays (Fitzgerald), **II:** 94

"Afternoon of a Playwright" (Thurber), **Supp. I Part 2:** 620

Afternoon of the Unreal (Salinas), **Supp. XIII:** 311, **316–318**

"Afternoon with the Old Man, An" (Dubus), **Supp. VII:** 84

"After Punishment Was Done with Me" (Olds), **Supp. X:** 213

"After Reading *Barely and Widely,*" (Zukofsky), **Supp. III Part 2:** 625, 631

"After Reading 'In the Clearing' for the Author, Robert Frost" (Corso), **Supp. XII:** 130

"After Reading *Mickey in the Night Kitchen* for the Third Time before Bed" (Dove), **Supp. IV Part 1:** 249

"After Reading the Greek Poet"(Kenny), **Supp. XXIII:** 150

"After Reading Tu Fu, I Go Outside to the Dwarf Orchard" (Wright), **Supp. V:** 343

"After Reading Wang Wei, I Go Outside to the Full Moon" (Wright), **Supp. V:** 343

After Shocks, Near Escapes (Dobyns), **Supp. XIII: 80–82**

"After Song, An" (W. C. Williams), **Retro. Supp. I:** 413

After Strange Gods (T. S. Eliot), **I:** 588

After Such Knowledge: Memory, History, and the Legacy of the Holocaust (E. Hoffman), **Supp. XVI:** 152–153, **158–161**

"After the Alphabets" (Merwin), **Supp. III Part 1:** 356

"After the Argument" (Dunn), **Supp. XI:** 149

"After the Baptism" (C. Bly), **Supp. XVI:** 40

"After the Burial" (Lowell), **Supp. I Part 2:** 409

"After the Curfew" (Holmes), **Supp. I Part 1:** 308

"After the Death of John Brown" (Thoreau), **IV:** 185

"After the Denim" (Carver), **Supp. III Part 1:** 144

"After the Dentist" (Swenson), **Supp. IV Part 2:** 645

After the Fall (A. Miller), **III:** 148, 149, 156, 161, 162, 163–165, 166

"After the Fire" (Merrill), **Supp. III Part 1:** 328

"After the Flood" (Sanders), **Supp. XVI:** 274–275

After the Fox (film), **Supp. IV Part 2:** 575

After the Genteel Tradition (Cowley), **Supp. II Part 1:** 143

"After the Heart's Interrogation" (Komunyakaa), **Supp. XIII:** 120

After the Lost Generation: A Critical Study of the Writers of Two Wars (Aldridge), **Supp. IV Part 2:** 680; **Supp. XIX:** 250

"After the Night Office—Gethsemani Abbey" (Merton), **Supp. VIII:** 195–196

After the Others (Weigl), **Supp. XIX:** 282, 283–284

"After the Persian" (Bogan), **Supp. III Part 1:** 64

After the Plague (Boyle), **Supp. XX: 20**

"After the Plague" (Boyle), **Supp. XX: 20**

"After the Pleasure Party" (Melville), **III:** 93

"After the Rain" (Halliday), **Supp. XIX:** 91

"After the Resolution" (Dunn), **Supp. XI:** 151

After the Stroke (Sarton), **Supp. VIII:** 264

"After the Surprising Conversions" (Lowell), **I:** 544, 545; **II:** 550; **Retro. Supp. II:** 187

"After 37 Years My Mother Apologizes for My Childhood" (Olds), **Supp. X:** 208

After This (McDermott), **Supp. XVIII:** 155, **166–167**

Afterthoughts (L. P. Smith), **Supp. XIV:** 339, 345

"Afterthoughts on the Rosenbergs" (Fiedler), **Supp. XIII:** 99

"After Twenty Years" (Rich), **Supp. I Part 2:** 559–560

"Afterwake, The" (Rich), **Supp. I Part 2:** 553

"Afterward" (Wharton), **Retro. Supp. I:** 372

"Afterword"(Hadas), **Supp. XXIII:** 113

"After Working Long" (Kenyon), **Supp. VII:** 170

"After Yitzl" (Goldbarth), **Supp. XII:** 186

"After You, My Dear Alphonse" (Jackson), **Supp. IX:** 119

"After Your Death" (Trethewey), **Supp. XXI:** 255

"After Your Nap" (B. Kelly), **Supp. XVII:** 124

"Again" (Dixon), **Supp. XII:** 157

"Again, Kapowsin" (Hugo), **Supp. VI:** 141

"Again Just Now" (Budbill), **Supp. XIX:** 11

"Against" (Goldbarth), **Supp. XII:** 193

"Against Decoration" (Karr), **Supp. XI:** 248

"Against Epiphanies" (C. Baxter), **Supp. XVII:** 20

Against Interpretation (Sontag), **Supp. III Part 2:** 451, 455; **Supp. XIV:** 15

"Against Interpretation" (Sontag), **Supp. III Part 2:** 456–458, 463

"Against Modernity" (Ozick), **Supp. V:** 272

"Against Nature" (Karr), **Supp. XI:** 243

Against Nature (Updike), **Retro. Supp. I:** 323

Against Our Vanishing: Winter Conversations with Allen Grossman on the Theory and Practice of Poetry (Halliday), **Supp. XIX: 82–84,** 88

"Against Realism" (Halliday), **Supp. XIX:** 93

Against the Cold (Bynner), **Supp. XV:** 51

"Against the Crusades" (Stern), **Supp. IX:** 300

Against the Current: As I Remember F. Scott Fitzgerald (Kroll Ring), **Supp. IX:** 63

Agamben, Giorgio, **Supp. XVI:** 289

Agapida, Fray Antonio (pseudonym). *See* Irving, Washington

"Agassiz" (Lowell), **Supp. I Part 2:** 414, 416

Agassiz, Louis, **II:** 343; **Supp. I Part 1:** 312; **Supp. IX:** 180

Âge cassant, L' (Char; Sobin, trans.), **Supp. XVI:** 282

"Aged Wino's Counsel to a Young Man on the Brink of Marriage, The" (X. J. Kennedy), **Supp. XV:** 156

Agee, Emma, **I:** 26

Agee, James, **I:** 25–47, 293; **IV:** 215; **Supp. IX:** 109; **Supp. XIV:** 92; **Supp. XV:** 143

"Agent, The" (Wilbur), **Supp. III Part 2:** 557–561

Age of Anxiety, The (Auden), **Supp. II Part 1:** 2, 19, 21

"Age of Conformity, The" (Howe), **Supp. VI:** 117

Age of Grief, The: A Novella and Stories (Smiley), **Supp. VI:** 292, **299–301**

Age of Innocence, The (Wharton), **IV:** 320–322, 327–328; **Retro. Supp. I:** 372, 374, **380–381; Supp. IV Part 1:** 23

Age of Longing, The (Koestler), **I:** 258

Age of Reason, The (Paine), **Supp. I Part 2:** 503, 515–517, 520

"Age of Strolling, The" (Stern), **Supp. IX:** 297

"Ages, The" (Bryant), **Supp. I Part 1:** 152, 155, 166, 167

"Ages of the Women, The" (Gibran), **Supp. XX: 115**

"Aggrandizement, The" (Bronk), **Supp. XXI:** 32

"Aging" (Jarrell), **II:** 388

Aging and Gender in Literature (George), **Supp. IV Part 2:** 450

"Agio Neró" (Mora), **Supp. XIII:** 224

"Agitato ma non Troppo" (Ransom), **III:** 493

"Agnes of Iowa" (Moore), **Supp. X:** 165, 178

Agnes of Sorrento (Stowe), **Supp. I Part 2:** 592, 595–596

Agnon, S. Y., **Supp. V:** 266

"Agosta the Winged Man and Rasha the Black Dove" (Dove), **Supp. IV Part 1:** 246–247

Agrarian Justice (Paine), **Supp. I Part 2:** 517–518

"Agricultural Show, The" (McKay), **Supp. X:** 139

Agrippa: A Book of the Dead (W. Gibson), **Supp. XVI:** 125

Agua de dos ríos/Water from Two Rivers (Espaillat), **Supp. XXI:** 104, 112–113

Agua Fresca: An Anthology of Raza Poetry (Rodríguez, ed.), **Supp. IV Part 2:** 540

Agua Santa/Holy Water (Mora), **Supp. XIII:** 222–225

Agüero Sisters, The (García), **Supp. XI:** 185–190

Aguiar, Marian, **Supp. XXII:** 68

Aguiar, Sarah Appleton, **Supp. XIII:** 30

Aguilar, Carmen, **Supp. XXIII:** 200

Ah, Wilderness! (O'Neill), **III:** 400–401; **Supp. IV Part 2:** 587

Ah, Wilderness!: The Frontier in American Literature (Humphrey), **Supp. IX:** 104

Ahearn, Barry, **Retro. Supp. I:** 415

Ahearn, Frederick L., Jr., **Supp. XI:** 184

Ahearn, Kerry, **Supp. IV Part 2:** 604

Ahmed Arabi Pasha, **I:** 453

Ahnebrink, Lars, **III:** 328

Ahrens, Sylvia, **Supp. XX: 162**

Ah Sin (Harte), **Supp. II Part 1:** 354–355

"Ah! Sun-flower" (Blake), **III:** 19

Aida (rock musical), **Supp. XXI:** 148

Aidoo, Ama Ato, **Supp. XXII:** 68

AIDS and Its Metaphors (Sontag), **Supp. III Part 2:** 452, 466–468

Aids to Reflection (Coleridge), **II:** 10

Aiieeeee! An Anthology of Asian-American Writers (The Combined Asian Resources Project), **Supp. X:** 292

Aiken, Conrad, **I:** 48–70, 190, 211, 243; **II:** 55, 530, 542; **III:** 458, 460; **Retro. Supp. I:** 55, 56, 57, 58, 60, 62; **Supp. X:** 50, 115; **Supp. XV:** 144, 297, 298, 302, 306, 309; **Supp. XVII:** 135

"Aimless Love" (Collins), **Supp. XXI:** 61

"Aim Was Song, The" (Frost), **Retro. Supp. I:** 133

Ainger, Arthur Campbell, **Supp. XX: 230**

Ainsworth, Linda, **Supp. IV Part 1:** 274

Ainsworth, William, **III:** 423

Air-Conditioned Nightmare, The (H. Miller), **III:** 186

Airing Dirty Laundry (Reed), **Supp. X:** 241

"Air Is Full of Little Holes, The" (Brockmeier), **Supp. XXII:** 60

"Airmail from Mother" (Kooser), **Supp. XIX:** 120

"Air Plant, The" (Crane), **I:** 401

Air Raid: A Verse Play for Radio (MacLeish), **III:** 21

"Airs above the Ground" (Sarton), **Supp. VIII:** 261

Air Tight: A Novel of Red Russia. See We the Living (Rand)

Air Up There, The (film, Glaser), **Supp. XVII:** 9

"Airwaves" (Mason), **Supp. VIII:** 146

Airways, Inc. (Dos Passos), **I:** 482

A Is for Anne: Mistress Hutchinson Disturbs the Commonwealth (Schott), **Supp. XXIII:** 240, **246–247**

"A is for Dining Alone" (M. F. K. Fisher), **Supp. XVII:** 86

Aitken, Robert, **Supp. I Part 2:** 504

Aizenberg, Susan, **Supp. XXI:** 131

Akhmadulina, Bella, **Supp. III Part 1:** 268

Akhmatova, Anna, **Supp. III Part 1:** 268, 269; **Supp. VIII:** 20, 21, 25, 27, 30; **Supp. XXI:** 132

Akhmatova Translations, The (Kenyon), **Supp. VII:** 160

"Akhnilo" (Salter), **Supp. IX:** 260

Akins, Zoë, **Supp. XVI:** 187

Aksenev, Vasily P., **Retro. Supp. I:** 278

"Al Aaraaf" (Poe), **III:** 426–427

Al Aaraaf, Tamerlane, and Minor Poems (Poe), **III:** 410

"Alabama Jones" (Mosher), **Supp. XXII:** 204, 211

"Alain Locke and Cultural Pluralism" (Kallen), **Supp. XIV:** 197

"Alain Locke: Bahá'í Philosopher" (Buck), **Supp. XIV:** 199

Alain Locke: Faith and Philosophy (Buck), **Supp. XIV:** 200

Alarçon, **Supp. XVII:** 74

Alarcón, Justo, **Supp. IV Part 2:** 538, 539, 540

Alarcón, Norma, **Supp. XXIII:** 194, 204–205

À la Recherche du Temps Perdu (Proust), **IV:** 428

"Alarm" (X. J. Kennedy), **Supp. XV:** 163

"Alastor" (Shelley), **Supp. I Part 2:** 728

"Alatus" (Wilbur), **Supp. III Part 2:** 563

Alaya (Hirshfield), **Supp. XXIII:** 131

"Alba" (Creeley), **Supp. IV Part 1:** 150

Alba, Richard D., **Supp. XX: 43**

Albee, Edward, **I:** 71–96, 113; **II:** 558, 591; **III:** 281, 387; **IV:** 4, 230; **Retro. Supp. II:** 104; **Supp. VIII:** 331; **Supp. XIII:** 196, 197

Albers, Joseph, **Supp. IV Part 2:** 621

Alberti, Rafael, **Supp. XV:** 75

Albright, Margery, **Supp. I Part 2:** 613

"Album, The" (Morris), **III:** 220

Alcestiad, The (Wilder), **IV:** 357, 374

"Alchemist, The" (Bogan), **Supp. III Part 1:** 50

"Alchemist in the City, The" (Hopkins), **Supp. IV Part 2:** 639

Alchymist's Journal, The (Connell), **Supp. XIV:** 80

"Alcmena" (Winters), **Supp. II Part 2:** 801

Alcott, Abba. *See* Alcott, Mrs. Amos Bronson (Abigail May)

Alcott, Amos Bronson, **II:** 7, 225; **IV:** 172, 173, 184; **Retro. Supp. I:** 217; **Supp. I Part 1:** 28, 29–32, 35, 39, 41, 45; **Supp. II Part 1:** 290; **Supp. XVI:** 84, 89

Alcott, Mrs. Amos Bronson (Abigail May), **IV:** 184; **Supp. I Part 1:** 29, 30, 31, 32, 35

Alcott, Anna. *See* Pratt, Anna

Alcott, Louisa May, **IV:** 172; **Supp. I Part 1:** 28–46; **Supp. IX:** 128; **Supp. XV:** 338; **Supp. XVI:** 84

Alcott, May, **Supp. I Part 1:** 41

Alcuin: A Dialogue (Brown), **Supp. I Part 1:** 126–127, 133

Alden, Hortense. *See* Farrell, Mrs. James T. (Hortense Alden)

Alden, John, **I:** 471; **II:** 502–503

"Alder Fork, The" (Leopold), **Supp. XIV:** 186

Aldington, Perdita, **Supp. I Part 1:** 258

Aldington, Richard, **II:** 517; **III:** 458, 459, 465, 472; **Retro. Supp. I:** 63, 127; **Supp. I Part 1:** 257–262, 270

Aldington, Mrs. Richard. *See* Doolittle, Hilda

Aldo Leopold: His Life and Work (Meine), **Supp. XIV:** 179

"Aldo Leopold's Intellectual Heritage" (Nash), **Supp. XIV:** 191–192

Aldon, Raymond, **Supp. XV:** 297

Aldrich, Thomas Bailey, **II:** 400; **Supp. II Part 1:** 192; **Supp. XIV:** 45; **Supp. XVIII:** 4

Aldrich, Tom, **Supp. I Part 2:** 415

Aldridge, John W., **Supp. I Part 1:** 196; **Supp. IV Part 1:** 286; **Supp. IV Part 2:** 680, 681; **Supp. VIII:** 189; **Supp. XI:** 228; **Supp. XIX:** 250

Aleck Maury Sportsman (Gordon), **II:** 197, 200, 203–204

Alegría, Claribel, **Supp. IV Part 1:** 208

Aleichem, Sholem, **Supp. XXIII:** 4, 7

Aleichem, Sholom, **IV:** 3, 10; **Supp. IV Part 2:** 585

"Alert Lovers, Hidden Sides, and Ice Travelers: Notes on Poetic Form and Energy" (Dunn), **Supp. XI:** 153

"Ale&sacaron; Debeljak" (Simic), **Supp. VIII:** 279

"Alex" (Oliver), **Supp. VII:** 232

Alexander, Doris, **Supp. XVII:** 99

Alexander, Elizabeth, **Supp. XVIII:** 171, 185, 186; **Supp. XXI:** 246, 257

Alexander, George, **II:** 331

Alexander, Michael, **Retro. Supp. I:** 293

"Alexander Crummell Dead" (Dunbar), **Supp. II Part 1:** 207, 208–209

Alexander's Bridge (Cather), **I:** 313, 314, 316–317, 326; **Retro. Supp. I:** 1, 6, 7, 8

Alexander the Great, **IV:** 322

"Alexandra" (Cather), **Retro. Supp. I:** 7, 9, 17

Alexandrov, V. E., **Retro. Supp. I:** 270

Alexie, Sherman, **Supp. XVIII:** 58

Algic Researches (H. Schoolcraft), **Supp. XXIII:** 227

Algonquin Round Table, **Supp. IX:** 190, 191, 197

Algren, Nelson, **I:** 211; **Supp. V:** 4; **Supp. IX:** 1–18; **Supp. XII:** 126; **Supp. XIII:** 173; **Supp. XIV:** 3; **Supp. XVII:** 161; **Supp. XXI:** 264; **Supp. XXIII:** 165

Alhambra, The (Irving), **II:** 310–311

Ali, Agha Shahid, **Supp. XVII:** 74

Alias Grace (Atwood), **Supp. XIII:** 20, **31–32**

Alice (film; Allen), **Supp. XV:** 2, 11
"Alice Doane's Appeal" (Hawthorne), **II:** 227
"Alice Drops Her Cigarette on the Floor ... " (Findley), **Supp. XX:** 50–51
Alice in Wonderland (Carroll), **Supp. I Part 2:** 622
Alice Ordered Me to Be Made (Notley), **Supp. XXII:** 224, 227, 228
"Alice Ordered Me to Be Made" (Notley), **Supp. XXII:** 227
Alice's Adventures in Wonderland (Carroll), **Supp. XVI:** 261
"Alicia and I Talking on Edna's Steps" (Cisneros), **Supp. VII:** 64
"Alicia Who Sees Mice" (Cisneros), **Supp. VII:** 60
Alien 3 (screenplay, W. Gibson), **Supp. XVI:** 120, 124
"Ali in Havana" (Talese), **Supp. XVII:** 207, 208
Alison, Archibald, **Supp. I Part 1:** 151, 159
Alison's House (Glaspell), **Supp. III Part 1:** 182, 188, 189
Alive (screenplay, Shanley), **Supp. XIV:** 316
Alive and Writing: Interviews with American Authors of the 1980s (McCaffery and Gregory), **Supp. X:** 260
"Alki Beach" (Hugo), **Supp. VI:** 135
Alla Breve Loving (Wright), **Supp. XV:** 339, 340
"Alla Breve Loving" (Wright), **Supp. XV:** 340
"All Around the Town" (Benét), **Supp. XI:** 48, 58
All at Sea (Lardner), **II:** 427
All Aunt Hagar's Children (E. P. Jones), **Supp. XXII:** 140, 143, **150–153**
"All Aunt Hagar's Children" (P. E. Jones), **Supp. XXII:** 151
"All Boy" (Rawlings), **Supp. X:** 222
Allegiances (Stafford), **Supp. XI: 322–323,** 329
"Allegory of the Cave" (Dunn), **Supp. XI:** 150
"Allegory Unlimited" (Cassill), **Supp. XIX:** 266
Allegro, Johnny (film, Tetzloff), **Supp. XVII:** 62
"Allegro, L' " (Milton), **Supp. XIV:** 8
Allen, Brooke, **Supp. VIII:** 153
Allen, Bruce, **Supp. XXII:** 205, 212; **Supp. XXIII:** 106, 300
Allen, Claudia, **Supp. XXIII:** 79
Allen, Dick, **Supp. IX:** 279
Allen, Donald, **Supp. VIII:** 291; **Supp. XIII:** 112; **Supp. XXIII:** 215, 220
Allen, Frank, **Supp. XI:** 126; **Supp. XII:** 186
Allen, Frederick Lewis, **Supp. I Part 2:** 655
Allen, Gay Wilson, **IV:** 352; **Supp. I Part 2:** 418
Allen, Ivan, **Supp. XXII:** 245
Allen, Paula Gunn. *See* Gunn Allen, Paula
Allen, Robert Moore, **Supp. XX:** 164

Allen, Walter, **I:** 505; **III:** 352; **Supp. IV Part 2:** 685; **Supp. IX:** 231
Allen, Woody, **Supp. I Part 2:** 607, 623; **Supp. IV Part 1:** 205; **Supp. X:** 164; **Supp. XI:** 307; **Supp. XV: 1–18;** **Supp. XVII:** 48
"Aller et Retour" (Barnes), Supp. III Part 1: 36
Aller Retour New York (H. Miller), **III:** 178, 182, 183
Allerton, Isaac, **Supp. XXII:** 44
Allessandrini, Goffredo, **Supp. IV Part 2:** 520
Alleys of Eden, The (R. O. Butler), **Supp. XII:** 62, **62–64,** 68
All God's Children Need Traveling Shoes (Angelou), **Supp. IV Part 1:** 2, 9–10, 12–13, 17
All God's Chillun Got Wings (O'Neill), **III:** 387, 391, 393–394
All Gone (Dixon), **Supp. XII:** 148, 149
"All Hallows" (Glück), **Supp. V:** 82
"All I Can Remember" (Jackson), **Supp. IX:** 115
"Alligators, The" (Updike), **IV:** 219
Allingham, John Till, **Supp. XV:** 243
All in the Family (Boyce), **Supp. XXI:** 8
"ALL IN THE STREET" (Baraka), **Supp. II Part 1:** 53
Allison, Dorothy, **Supp. XVIII:** 195
"All I Want" (Tapahonso), **Supp. IV Part 2:** 508
"All Little Colored Children Should Play the Harmonica" (Patchett), **Supp. XII:** 309
"All Mountains" (Doolittle), **Supp. I Part 1:** 271
All My Friends Are Going to Be Strangers (McMurtry), **Supp. V:** 224, 228, 229
All My Pretty Ones (Sexton), **Supp. II Part 2:** 678, 679–683
"All My Pretty Ones" (Sexton), **Supp. II Part 2:** 681–682
"All My Sad Captains" (Jewett), **Retro. Supp. II:** 134
All My Sons (A. Miller), **III:** 148, 149, 150, 151–153, 154, 155, 156, 158, 159, 160, 164, 166
All New People (Lamott), **Supp. XX: 135–136**
"All Night, All Night" (Schwartz), **Supp. II Part 2:** 665
All Night Long (Caldwell), **I:** 297
"All-Night Melodies" (Nelson), **Supp. XVIII:** 185
All-Night Visitors (Major), **Supp. XXII: 173–174**
"All of Us" (Major), **Supp. XXII:** 185
All of What We Loved (Bronk), **Supp. XXI:** 32
"All Our Lost Children: Trauma and Testimony in the Performance of Childhood" (Pace), **Supp. XI:** 245
All Our Yesterdays (Parker), **Supp. XIX: 187–188**
"All Out" (Hecht), **Supp. X:** 72
All Over (Albee), **I:** 91–94
"Allowance" (Minot), **Supp. VI:** 206, 207–208

"Alloy" (Rukeyser), **Supp. VI:** 279
"All Parrots Speak" (Bowles), **Supp. IV Part 1:** 89
Allport, Gordon, **II:** 363–364
All Quiet on the Western Front (Remarque), **Supp. IV Part 1:** 380, 381
"ALL REACTION IS DOOMED-!-!-!" (Baraka), **Supp. II Part 1:** 59
"All Revelation" (Frost), **II:** 160–162
"All Shall Love Me and Despair"(Thompson), **Supp. XXIII:** 295
All Shot Up (C. Himes), **Supp. XVI:** 143, 144
"All Souls" (Gioia), **Supp. XV:** 117
"All Souls" (Wharton), **IV:** 315–316; **Retro. Supp. I:** 382
"All Souls' Night" (Yeats), **Supp. X:** 69
All Souls' Rising (Bell), **Supp. X:** 12, **13–16,** 17
"All-Star Literary Vaudeville" (Wilson), **IV:** 434–435
Allston, Washington, **II:** 298
All Stories Are True (Wideman), **Supp. X:** 320
"All That Is" (Wilbur), **Supp. III Part 2:** 563
All That Was Possible (Sturgis), **Supp. XX: 227, 232, 235–237**
"All the Bearded Irises of Life: Confessions of a Homospiritual" (Walker), **Supp. III Part 2:** 527
"All the Beautiful Are Blameless" (Wright), **Supp. III Part 2:** 597
ALL: The Collected Poems, 1956–1964 (Zukofsky), **Supp. III Part 2:** 630
ALL: The Collected Short Poems, 1923–1958 (Zukofsky), **Supp. III Part 2:** 629
All the Conspirators (Isherwood), **Supp. XIV:** 156, 159, 160
All the Dark and Beautiful Warriors (Hansberry), **Supp. IV Part 1:** 360, 374
All the Days and Nights: The Collected Stories (Maxwell), **Supp. VIII:** 151, 158, 169
"All the Dead Dears" (Plath), **Retro. Supp. II:** 246; **Supp. I Part 2:** 537
"All the Dead"(P. Benedict), **Supp. XXIII:** 37
All the Good People I've Left Behind (Oates), **Supp. II Part 2:** 510, 522, 523
"All the Hippos Were Boiled in Their Tanks" (Burroughs and Kerouac), **Supp. III Part 1:** 94
All the King's Men (Warren), **I:** 489; **IV:** 243, 248–249, 252; **Supp. V:** 261; **Supp. VIII:** 126; **Supp. X:** 1; **Supp. XVIII:** 77, 79
All the Little Live Things (Stegner), **Supp. IV Part 2:** 599, 604, 605, 606, 609–610, 611, 613
All the Pretty Horses (film), **Supp. VIII:** 175
All the Pretty Horses (McCarthy), **Supp. VIII:** 175, **182–183,** 188

All the Sad Young Men (Fitzgerald), **II:** 94; **Retro. Supp. I:** 108

"All the Time in the World" (Dubus), **Supp. VII:** 91

"All the Way to Flagstaff, Arizona" (Bausch), **Supp. VII:** 47, 49

"All This and More" (Karr), **Supp. XI:** 243

All Tomorrow's Parties (W. Gibson), **Supp. XVI:** 119, 121, 123, 124, **130**

"All Too Real" (Vendler), **Supp. V:** 189

All Trivia: Triva, More Trivia, Afterthoughts, Last Words (L. P. Smith), **Supp. XIV:** 339

All-True Travels and Adventures of Lidie Newton (Smiley), **Supp. VI:** 292, **305–307**

All We Need of Hell (Crews), **Supp. XI:** **114**

Almack, Edward, **Supp. IV Part 2:** 435

al-Maghut, Muhammad, **Supp. XIII:** 278

"Almanac" (Swenson), **Supp. IV Part 2:** 641

Almanac of the Dead (Silko), **Supp. IV Part 2:** 558–559, 560, 561, 570–571

Alma: or, The Dead Women (Notley), **Supp. XXII:** 223, 224, 231, 236

Almon, Bert, **Supp. IX:** 93

"Almost" (Untermeyer), **Supp. XV:** 304

Almost Learning to Live in This World (Schott), **Supp. XXIII:** **247–248**

Almost Revolution, The (Priaulx and Ungar), **Supp. XI:** 228

Alnilam (Dickey), **Supp. IV Part 1:** 176, 186, 188–189

"Alone" (Caputo), **Supp. XIX:** 29

"Alone" (Levine), **Supp. V:** 184, 185, 186

"Alone" (Pickering), **Supp. XXI:** 204

"Alone" (Poe), **Retro. Supp. II:** 266

"Alone" (Singer), **IV:** 15

"Alone" (Winters), **Supp. II Part 2:** 786, 811

"Alone and Lonely" (Budbill), **Supp. XIX:** 10

Aloneness (Brooks), **Supp. III Part 1:** 85, 86

Alone with America (Corso), **Supp. XII:** 131

Alone with America (Howard), **Supp. IX:** 326

"Along America's Edges" (Sobin), **Supp. XVI:** 288

"Along the Color Line" (Du Bois), **Supp. II Part 1:** 173

Along the Illinois (Masters), **Supp. I Part 2:** 472

Alouette, L' (Anouilh), **Supp. I Part 1:** 286–288

"Alphabet" (Nye), **Supp. XIII:** 283

Alphabet, An (Doty), **Supp. XI:** 120

Alphabet for Gourmets, An (M. F. K. Fisher), **Supp. XVII:** 86, 87, 92

Alphabet of Grace, The (Buechner), **Supp. XII:** 52

"Alphabet of My Dead, An" (Pinsky), **Supp. VI:** 235, 250

"Alphabet of Subjects, An" (Zukofsky), **Supp. III Part 2:** 624

"Alpine Christ, The" (Jeffers), **Supp. II Part 2:** 415, 419

Alpine Christ and Other Poems, The (Jeffers), **Supp. II Part 2:** 419

"Alpine Idyll, An" (Hemingway), **II:** 249; **Retro. Supp. I:** 176

Al Que Quiere! (W. C. Williams), **Retro. Supp. I:** 414, 416, **417,** 428

Alraune (Ewers; Endore, trans.), **Supp. XVII:** 54

Alsop, Joseph, **II:** 579

"Altar, The" (Herbert), **Supp. IV Part 2:** 646

"Altar, The" (MacLeish), **III:** 4

"Altar Boy" (Fante), **Supp. XI:** 160, 164

"Altar of the Dead, The" (James), **Retro. Supp. I:** 229

"Altars in the Street, The" (Levertov), **Supp. III Part 1:** 280

Alter, Robert, **Supp. XII:** 167

Altgeld, John Peter, **Supp. I Part 2:** 382, 455

Althea (Masters), **Supp. I Part 2:** 455, 459

Altick, Richard, **Supp. I Part 2:** 423

Altieri, Charles, **Supp. VIII:** 297, 303; **Supp. XXIII:** 220

Altman, Robert, **Supp. IX:** 143

"Alto" (C. Frost), **Supp. XV:** 101

"Altra Ego" (Brodsky), **Supp. VIII:** 31–32

A Lume Spento (Pound), **Retro. Supp. I:** 283, 285

"Aluminum House" (F. Barthelme), **Supp. XI:** 26

Alvares, Mosseh, **Supp. V:** 11

Alvarez, A., **Supp. I Part 2:** 526, 527; **Supp. II Part 1:** 99; **Supp. IX:** 248

Alvarez, Joseph A., **Supp. XXII:** 13–14

Alvarez, Julia, **Supp. VII:** 1–21; **Supp. XI:** 177; **Supp. XVII:** 71, 112

"Always a Rose" (L.-Y. Lee), **Supp. XV:** 215, 216

"Always in Good Humor" (Adams), **Supp. XV:** 294

Always Outnumbered, Always Outgunned (Mosley), **Supp. XIII:** 242

"Always the Stories" (Ortiz), **Supp. IV Part 2:** 499, 500, 502, 504, 512

Always the Young Strangers (Sandburg), **III:** 577–578, 579

Always Young and Fair (Richter), **Supp. XVIII:** 215–216

Amadeus (Shaffer), **Supp. XIV:** 330

"Amahl and the Night Visitors: A Guide to the Tenor of Love" (Moore), **Supp. X:** 167

"Am and Am Not" (Olds), **Supp. X:** 212

Amanita, The (Francis), **Supp. IX:** 81

Amaranth (Robinson), **III:** 509, 510, 512, 513, 522, 523

"Amateurs, The" (Swados), **Supp. XIX:** 256

Amazing Adele, The (Barillet and Grédy; Loos, trans.), **Supp. XVI:** 194

Amazing Adventures of Kavalier and Clay, The (Chabon), **Supp. XI:** 68, 76, **77–80; Supp. XXII:** 49

Amazing Adventures of the Escapist, The (Chabon, ed.), **Supp. XIX:** 174

Amazing Science Fiction Stories, **Supp. XVI:** 121

Amazons: An Intimate Memoir by the First Woman to Play in the National Hockey League (DeLillo), **Supp. VI:** 2

Ambassador Morgenthau's Story (Morgenthau), **Supp. XXIII:** 21, 22

Ambassador of Peace, An (Abernon), **Supp. XVI:** 191

Ambassadors, The (H. James), **II:** 320, 333–334, 600; **III:** 517; **IV:** 322; **Retro. Supp. I:** 215, 218, 219, 220, 221, **232–233**

Ambelain, Robert, **Supp. I Part 1:** 260, 273, 274

"Ambition Bird, The" (Sexton), **Supp. II Part 2:** 693

Ambition: The Secret Passion (Epstein), **Supp. XIV:** 113–114

Ambler, Eric, **III:** 57

Ambrose Holt and Family (Glaspell), **Supp. III Part 1:** 175, 181, 184, 187, 188

"Ambrose Seyffert" (Masters), **Supp. I Part 2:** 464

"Ambush" (Komunyakaa), **Supp. XIII:** 122

Amen Corner, The (Baldwin), **Retro. Supp. II:** 5, 7; **Supp. I Part 1:** 48, 51, 54, 55, 56

America (Benét), **Supp. XI:** 46, 47, 51

"America" (Ginsberg), **Supp. II Part 1:** 58–59, 317

"America" (song), **IV:** 410

"America, America!" (poem) (Schwartz), **Supp. II Part 2:** 665

"America, Commerce, and Freedom" (Rowson and Reinagle), **Supp. XV:** 240

"America, Seen Through Photographs, Darkly" (Sontag), **Supp. III Part 2:** 464

"America! America!" (story) (Schwartz), **Supp. II Part 2:** 640, 658–659, 660

America and Americans (Steinbeck), **IV:** 52

"America and the Vidal Chronicles" (Pease), **Supp. IV Part 2:** 687

America as a Civilization (Lerner), **III:** 60

America Behind the Color Line (H. L. Gates), **Supp. XX: 102, 105**

America Beyond the Color Line (television program), **Supp. XX: 99**

America Hispana: A Portrait and a Prospect (W. Frank), **Supp. XX: 76**

"America Independent" (Freneau), **Supp. II Part 1:** 261

America Is Worth Saving (Dreiser), **Retro. Supp. II:** 96

American, The (James), **I:** 226; **II:** 326–327, 328, 331, 334; **IV:** 318; **Retro. Supp. I:** 220, **221,** 228, 376, 381

Americana (DeLillo), **Supp. VI:** 2, **3,** 5, 6, 8, 13, 14

American Adam, The (R. W. B. Lewis), **II:** 457–458; **Supp. XIII:** 93

American Almanac (Leeds), **II:** 110

American Anthem (Doctorow and Suares), **Supp. IV Part 1:** 234

"American Apocalypse" (Gunn Allen), **Supp. IV Part 1:** 325

American Aristocracy (film), **Supp. XVI:** 185–186

American Blood, (Nichols), **Supp. XIII:** 268

American Blues (T. Williams), **IV:** 381, 383

American Buffalo (Mamet), **Supp. XIV:** 239, 241, 242, 244–245, 246, 254, 255

American Caravan: A Yearbook of American Literature (Mumford, ed.), **Supp. II Part 2:** 482

American Cause, The (MacLeish), **III:** 3

American Childhood, An (Dillard), **Supp. VI:** 19–21, 23, 24, 25, 26, 30, 31

"American Childhood in the Dominican Republic, An" (Alvarez), **Supp. VII:** 2, 5

American Child Supreme, An: The Education of a Liberation Ecologist (Nichols), **Supp. XIII:** 256, 257, 258, 264, 265, 266, 267, 268, 269

American Civilization (C. L. R. James), **Supp. XXI:** 169

American Claimant, The (Twain), **IV:** 194, 198–199

American Crisis I (Paine), **Supp. I Part 2:** 508

American Crisis II (Paine), **Supp. I Part 2:** 508

American Crisis XIII (Paine), **Supp. I Part 2:** 509

"American Critic, The" (J. Spingarn), **I:** 266

American Culture, Canons, and the Case of Elizabeth Stoddard (Smith and Weinauer), **Supp. XV:** 270

American Daughter, An (Wasserstein), **Supp. XV:** 330–332, 333

American Democrat, The (Cooper), **I:** 343, 346, 347, 353

American Desert (Everett), **Supp. XVIII:** 62–63

American Diary (Webb), **Supp. I Part 1:** 5

American Drama since World War II (Weales), **IV:** 385

American Dream, An (Mailer), **III:** 27, 33–34, 35, 39, 41, 43, 44; **Retro. Supp. II:** 203, 204–205

American Dream, The (Albee), **I:** 74–76, 77, 89, 94

"American Dreams" (Simpson), **Supp. IX:** 274

American Earth (Caldwell), **I:** 290, 308

"American Emperors" (Poirier), **Supp. IV Part 2:** 690

American Exodus, An (Lange and Taylor), **I:** 293

American Experience, The (Parkes), **Supp. I Part 2:** 617–618

American Express (Corso), **Supp. XII:** 129

"American Express" (Salter), **Supp. IX:** 260–261

"American Fear of Literature, The" (Lewis), **II:** 451

American Female Patriotism (S. Warner as Wetherell), **Supp. XVIII:** 260–261, 262, 263

American Fictions (Hardwick), **Supp. X:** 171

American Fictions, 1940–1980 (Karl), **Supp. IV Part 1:** 384; **Supp. XXI:** 234

"American Financier, The" (Dreiser), **II:** 428

American Folkways (book series), **I:** 290

American Guerilla in the Philippines (Wolfert), **Supp. XXI:** 267

"American Heart of Darkness: The Moral Vision of Five Novels of the Vietnam War" (Palm), **Supp. XXII:** 103

American Heroine: The Life and Legend of Jane Addams (A. F. Davis), **Supp. I Part 1:** 1

American Historical Novel, The (Leisy), **Supp. II Part 1:** 125

"American Horse" (Erdrich), **Supp. IV Part 1:** 333

American Humor: A Study of the National Character (Rourke), **IV:** 339, 352; **Supp. XIX:** 147

American Hunger (Wright), **Supp. IV Part 1:** 11

American Indian Anthology, An (Tvedten, ed.), **Supp. IV Part 2:** 505

"American Indian Women: At the Center of Indigenous Resistance in Contemporary North America" (Jaimes and Halsey), **Supp. IV Part 1:** 331

"American in England, An" (Wylie), **Supp. I Part 2:** 707

American Jitters, The: A Year of the Slump (Wilson), **IV:** 427, 428

American Journal (Hayden), **Supp. II Part 1:** 367

American Journey: The Times of Robert F. Kennedy (Plimpton, ed.), **Supp. XVI:** 245

"American Land Ethic, An" (Momaday), **Supp. IV Part 2:** 488

American Landscape, The, **Supp. I Part 1:** 157

American Language, The (Mencken), **II:** 289, 430; **III:** 100, 104, 105, 108, 111, 119–120

American Language, The: Supplement One (Mencken), **III:** 111

American Language, The: Supplement Two (Mencken), **III:** 111

"American Letter" (MacLeish), **III:** 13

"American Liberty" (Freneau), **Supp. II Part 1:** 257

"American Life in Poetry" (column, Kooser), **Supp. XIX:** 116, 127

American Literary History (Harrison), **Supp. VIII:** 37

American Mercury, **Supp. XI:** 163, 164

American Mind, The (Commager), **Supp. I Part 2:** 650

American Moderns: Bohemian New York and the Creation of a New Century (Stansell), **Supp. XVII:** 106

American Moderns: From Rebellion to Conformity (Geismar), **Supp. IX:** 15; **Supp. XI:** 223

"American Names" (Benét), **Supp. XI:** 47

American Nature Writers (Elder, ed.), **Supp. IX:** 25

American Nature Writers (Winter), **Supp. X:** 104

American Negro, The (W. H. Thomas), **Supp. II Part 1:** 168

American Notebooks, The (Hawthorne), **II:** 226

American Novel Since World War II, The (Klein, ed.), **Supp. XI:** 233

Americano, The (film), **Supp. XVI:** 185

"American Original, An: Learning from a Literary Master" (Wilkinson), **Supp. VIII:** 164, 165, 168

American Ornithology (Wilson), **Supp. XVI:** 4, 6

American Pastoral (P. Roth), **Retro. Supp. II:** 279, 289, 292–293; **Supp. XI:** 68

American Places (Porter, Stegner and Stegner), **Supp. IV Part 2:** 599

"American Poet" (Shapiro), **Supp. II Part 2:** 701

"American Poetry" (Simpson), **Supp. IX:** 272

American Poetry, 1922: A Miscellany (Untermeyer, ed.), **Supp. XV:** 306

"American Poetry and American Life" (Pinsky), **Supp. VI:** 239–240

American Poetry from the Beginning to Whitman (Untermeyer, ed.), **Supp. XV:** 310

American Poetry since 1900 (Untermeyer, ed.), **Supp. XV:** 306

American Poetry since 1945: A Critical Survey (Stepanchev), **Supp. XI:** 312

American Poetry since 1960 (Mesic), **Supp. IV Part 1:** 175

American Poets since World War II Dictionary of Literary Biography (Gwynn, ed.), **Supp. XV:** 343

American Primer, An (Boorstin), **I:** 253

American Primer, An (Whitman), **IV:** 348

"American Primitive" (W. J. Smith), **Supp. XIII:** 333

American Primitive: Poems (Oliver), **Supp. VII:** 234–237, 238

American Procession, An: The Major American Writers from 1830–1930— the Crucial Century (Kazin), **Supp. VIII:** 105–106, 108

"American Prose Writers" articles (Briggs), **Supp. XVIII:** 11

American Radio Company, The (radio show, Keillor), **Supp. XVI:** 176–177

"American Realist Playwrights, The" (McCarthy), **II:** 562

American Register, or General Repository of History, Politics, and Science, The (Brown, ed.), **Supp. I Part 1:** 146

American Renaissance (Matthiessen), **I:** 259–260; **III:** 310; **Supp. XIII:** 93

"American Rendezvous, An" (Beauvoir), **Supp. IX:** 4

American Scene, The (James), **II:** 336; **III:** 460; **Retro. Supp. I:** 232, 235

American Scenes (Kozlenko, ed.), **IV:** 378

"American Scholar, The" (Emerson), **I:** 239; **II:** 8, 12–13; **Retro. Supp. I:** 62, 74–75, 149, 298; **Retro. Supp. II:** 155; **Supp. I Part 2:** 420; **Supp. IX:** 227, 271; **Supp. XIV:** 104

"American Scholar, The" (Pickering), **Supp. XXI:** 196

Americans in England; or, Lessons for Daughters (Rowson), **Supp. XV:** 240

"American Soldier, The" (Freneau), **Supp. II Part 1:** 269

American Songbag, The (Sandburg), **III:** 583

"American Student in Paris, An" (Farrell), **II:** 45

"American Sublime, The" (Stevens), **IV:** 74

"American Tar, The; or, The Press Gang Defeated" (Rowson and Taylor), **Supp. XV:** 238

"American Temperament, The" (Locke), **Supp. XIV:** 211

American Tragedy, An (Dreiser), **I:** 497, 498, 499, 501, 502, 503, 511–515, 517, 518, 519; **III:** 251; **IV:** 35, 484; **Retro. Supp. II:** 93, 95, **104–108;** **Supp. XVII:** 155

"American Triptych" (Kenyon), **Supp. VII:** 165

"American Use for German Ideals" (Bourne), **I:** 228

American Village, The (Freneau), **Supp. II Part 1:** 256, 257

"American Village, The" (Freneau), **Supp. II Part 1:** 256

America's Coming-of-Age (Brooks), **I:** 228, 230, 240, 245, 258; **IV:** 427

America's Humor: From Poor Richard to Doonesbury (Blair and Hill), **Retro. Supp. II:** 286

"America's Part in World Peace" (Locke), **Supp. XIV:** 208

America's Rome (Vance), **Supp. IV Part 2:** 684

America: The Story of a Free People (Commager and Nevins), **I:** 253

America Was Promises (MacLeish), **III:** 16, 17

"Amerika" (Snyder), **Supp. VIII:** 301

Ames, Christopher, **Supp. XVIII:** 242–243

Ames, Fisher, **Supp. I Part 2:** 486

Ames, Lois, **Supp. I Part 2:** 541, 547

Ames, William, **IV:** 158

Ames Stewart, Beatrice, **Supp. IX:** 200

Amichai, Yehuda, **Supp. XI:** 267

Amick, Steve, **Supp. XXII:** 205, 216

Amidon, Stephen, **Supp. XI:** 333

Amiel, Henri F., **I:** 241, 243, 250

Amis, Kingsley, **IV:** 430; **Supp. IV Part 2:** 688; **Supp. VIII:** 167; **Supp. XIII:** 93; **Supp. XV:** 117

Amis, Martin, **Retro. Supp. I:** 278

"Amish, The"(Thompson), **Supp. XXIII:** 295–296

"Amity Hills" (Skloot), **Supp. XX:** **204**

Ammons, A. R., **Supp. III Part 2:** 541; **Supp. VII: 23–38; Supp. IX:** 41, 42, 46; **Supp. XII:** 121; **Supp. XV:** 115; **Supp. XVII:** 242; **Supp. XIX:** 83

Ammons, Elizabeth, **Retro. Supp. I:** 364, 369; **Retro. Supp. II:** 140

Amnesia Moon (Lethem), **Supp. XVIII:** 136, **138–139**

"Among Children" (Levine), **Supp. V:** 192

Among Friends (M. F. K. Fisher), **Supp. XVII:** 89, 90–91, 92

Among My Books (Lowell), **Supp. I Part 2:** 407

"Among School Children" (Yeats), **III:** 249; **Supp. IX:** 52; **Supp. XIV:** 8

"Among the Hills" (Whittier), **Supp. I Part 2:** 703

Among the Isles of Shoals (Thaxter), **Supp. XIII:** 152

"Among Those Present" (Benét), **Supp. XI:** 53

"Amoral Moralist" (White), **Supp. I Part 2:** 648

Amory, Cleveland, **Supp. I Part 1:** 316

Amory, Fred, **Supp. III Part 1:** 2

Amos (biblical book), **II:** 166

Amos and Andy (television program), **Supp. XX:** **103**

Amran, David, **Supp. XIV:** 150

"Am Strand von Tanger" (Salter), **Supp. IX:** 257

"AMTRAK" (Baraka), **Supp. II Part 1:** 60

"Amulet, The" (Antin), **Supp. XX: 10**

"Amulets" (Hull), **Supp. XXI:** 139

Amy and Isabelle (film), **Supp. XXIII:** 275–276

Amy and Isabelle (Strout), **Supp. X:** 86; **Supp. XXIII:** 273, 274–275, **276–278,** 285

"Amy Lowell of Brookline, Mass." (Scott), **II:** 512

Amy Lowell: Portrait of the Poet in Her Time (Gregory), **II:** 512

"Amy Wentworth" (Whittier), **Supp. I Part 2:** 694, 696

Anabase (Perse), **III:** 12

"Anabasis (I)" (Merwin), **Supp. III Part 1:** 342, 346

"Anabasis (II)" (Merwin), **Supp. III Part 1:** 342, 346

Anagrams: A Novel (Moore), **Supp. X:** 163, 164, 167, **169–171,** 172

Analects (Confucius), **Supp. IV Part 1:** 14

Analects, The (Pound, trans.), **III:** 472

Analogy (J. Butler), **II:** 8

"Analysis of a Theme" (Stevens), **IV:** 81

Anarchiad, The, A Poem on the Restoration of Chaos and Substantial Night, in Twenty Four Books (Barlow), **Supp. II Part 1:** 70

Anarchist Woman, An (Hapgood), **Supp. XVII:** 102–103; **Supp. XXI:** 5

Anatomy Lesson, and Other Stories, The (Connell), **Supp. XIV:** 84, 87, 89

"Anatomy Lesson, The" (Connell), **Supp. XIV:** 84, 86, 87

Anatomy Lesson, The (P. Roth), **Retro. Supp. II:** 286, 290; **Supp. III Part 2:** 422–423, 425

"Anatomy Lesson of Dr. Nicholaas Tulp, Amsterdam, 1632, The" (Bierds), **Supp. XVII:** 27–28

Anatomy of Criticism (Frye), **Supp. XIII:** 19; **Supp. XIV:** 15

Anatomy of Melancholy (Burton), **III:** 78; **Supp. XVII:** 229

Anatomy of Nonsense, The (Winters), **Supp. II Part 2:** 811, 812

Anaya, Rudolfo A., **Supp. IV Part 2:** 502; **Supp. XIII:** 213, 220; **Supp. XIX:** 97

"Ancestor" (A. Finch), **Supp. XVII:** 72

Ancestors (Maxwell), **Supp. VIII:** 152, 168

"Ancestors, The" (Tate), **IV:** 128

Ancestral Voice: Conversations with N. Scott Momaday (Woodard), **Supp. IV Part 2:** 484, 485, 486, 489, 493

"Anchorage" (Harjo), **Supp. XII:** 220–221

Ancient Child, The: A Novel (Momaday), **Supp. IV Part 2:** 488, 489–491, 492, 493

"Ancient Egypt/Fannie Goldbarth" (Goldbarth), **Supp. XII:** 191–192

Ancient Evenings (Mailer), **Retro. Supp. II:** 206, 210, 213

Ancient Law, The (Glasgow), **II:** 179–180, 192

Ancient Musics (Goldbarth), **Supp. XII:** 191–192

"Ancient Semitic Rituals for the Dead" (Goldbarth), **Supp. XII:** 191–192

"Ancient World, The" (Doty), **Supp. XI:** 122

& (And) (Cummings), **I:** 429, 431, 432, 437, 445, 446, 448

Andersen, Hans Christian, **I:** 441; **Supp. I Part 2:** 622

Andersen, Hendrik Christian, **Supp. XX: 232**

Anderson, Charles R., **Supp. I Part 1:** 356, 360, 368, 371, 372

Anderson, Frances, **I:** 231

Anderson, Guy, **Supp. X:** 264, 265

Anderson, Henry J., **Supp. I Part 1:** 156

Anderson, Irwin M., **I:** 98–99

Anderson, Mrs. Irwin M., **I:** 98–99

Anderson, Jon, **Supp. V:** 338

Anderson, Judith, **III:** 399

Anderson, Karl, **I:** 99, 103

Anderson, Lorraine, **Supp. XVIII:** 189

Anderson, Margaret, **I:** 103; **III:** 471

Anderson, Margaret Bartlett, **III:** 171

Anderson, Marian, **Supp. XXII:** 283

Anderson, Mary Jane. *See* Lanier, Mrs. Robert Sampson (Mary Jane Anderson)

Anderson, Maxwell, **III:** 159

Anderson, Quentin, **Retro. Supp. I:** 392

Anderson, Robert, **Supp. I Part 1:** 277; **Supp. V:** 108

Anderson, Sally, **Supp. XIII:** 95

Anderson, Sherwood, **I: 97–120,** 211, 374, 375, 384, 405, 423, 445, 480, 487, 495, 506, 518; **II:** 27, 38, 44, 55, 56, 68, 250–251, 263, 271, 289, 451, 456–457; **III:** 220, 224, 382–383, 453, 483, 545, 576, 579; **IV:** 27, 40, 46,

190, 207, 433, 451, 482; **Retro. Supp. I:** 79, 80, 177; **Supp. I Part 2:** 378, 430, 459, 472, 613; **Supp. IV Part 2:** 502; **Supp. V:** 12, 250; **Supp. VIII:** 39, 152; **Supp. IX:** 14, 309; **Supp. XI:** 159, 164; **Supp. XII:** 343; **Supp. XV:** 298; **Supp. XVI:** 17, 20; **Supp. XVII:** 105; **Supp. XX: 69, 75; Supp. XXIII:** 68, 162, 164

Anderson, Mrs. Sherwood (Tennessee Mitchell), **I:** 100; **Supp. I Part 2:** 459, 460

Anderson, T. J., **Supp. XIII:** 132

Anderson, Wendy, **Supp. XXI:** 255

Anderssen, A., **III:** 252

"And Hickman Arrives" (Ellison), **Retro. Supp. II:** 118, 126; **Supp. II Part 1:** 248

And in the Hanging Gardens (Aiken), **I:** 63

"And It Came to Pass" (Wright), **Supp. XV:** 348

And I Worked at the Writer's Trade (Cowley), **Supp. II Part 1:** 137, 139, 141, 143, 147, 148

"...And Ladies of the Club" (J. W. Miller), **Supp. XX: 161**

And Live Apart (Peacock), **Supp. XIX: 196–197**

Andorra (Cameron), **Supp. XII:** 79, 81, **88–91**

"—and Other Poets" (column; Untermeyer), **Supp. XV:** 294

"—*and Other Poets" (Untermeyer), Supp. XV:* 297

Andral, Gabriel, **Supp. I Part 1:** 302

Andre, Michael, **Supp. XII:** 117–118, 129, 132, 133–134

"Andrea Is Changing Her Name" (Brockmeier), **Supp. XXII:** 61

Andre's Mother (McNally), **Supp. XIII:** 206

Andress, Ursula, **Supp. XI:** 307

"Andrew Jackson" (Masters), **Supp. I Part 2:** 472

Andrews, Bruce, **Supp. IV Part 2:** 426

Andrews, Peter, **Supp. XX: 87**

Andrews, Roy Chapman, **Supp. X:** 172

Andrews, Tom, **Supp. XI:** 317

Andrews, Wayne, **IV:** 310

Andrews, William L., **Supp. IV Part 1:** 13; **Supp. XIX:** 72; **Supp. XX: 105**

Andreyev, Leonid Nikolaevich, **I:** 53; **II:** 425

Andria (Terence), **IV:** 363

"Andromache" (Dubus), **Supp. VII:** 84

"And Summer Will Not Come Again" (Plath), **Retro. Supp. II:** 242

"And That Night Clifford Died" (Levine), **Supp. V:** 195

And the Band Played On (Shilts), **Supp. X:** 145

"And the Moon Be Still as Bright" (Bradbury), **Supp. IV Part 1:** 106

"And the Sea Shall Give up Its Dead" (Wilder), **IV:** 358

And Things That Go Bump in the Night (McNally), **Supp. XIII: 196–197,** 205, 208

And to Think That I Saw It on Mulberry Street (Geisel), **Supp. XVI:** 100, 101, 104

"And *Ut Pictura Poesis* Is Her Name" (Ashbery), **Supp. III Part 1:** 19

And We Are Millions (Ryan), **Supp. XVIII:** 225

"Anecdote and Storyteller" (Howe), **Supp. VI:** 127

"Anecdote of the Jar" (Stevens), **IV:** 83–84

"Anemone" (Rukeyser), **Supp. VI:** 281, 285

"Angel, The" (Buck), **Supp. II Part 1:** 127

"Angel and Unicorn and Butterfly" (Everwine), **Supp. XV:** 76

Angela's Ashes (McCourt), **Supp. XII: 271–279,** 283, 285; **Supp. XXII:** 94

"Angel at the Grave, The" (Wharton), **IV:** 310; **Retro. Supp. I:** 365

"Angel Butcher" (Levine), **Supp. V:** 181

Angel City (Shepard), **Supp. III Part 2:** 432, 445

Angelica (Holding), **Supp. XXII: 120–121**

"Angel Is My Watermark!, The" (H. Miller), **III:** 180

Angell, Carol, **Supp. I Part 2:** 655

Angell, Katharine Sergeant. *See* White, Katharine

Angell, Roger, **Supp. I Part 2:** 655; **Supp. V:** 22; **Supp. VIII:** 139

Angel Landing (Hoffman), **Supp. X: 82–83**

"Angel Levine" (Malamud), **Supp. I Part 2:** 431, 432, 433–434, 437

Angel of Bethesda, The (Mather), **Supp. II Part 2:** 464

"Angel of the Bridge, The" (Cheever), **Supp. I Part 1:** 186–187

"Angel of the Odd, The" (Poe), **III:** 425

Angelo Herndon Jones (Hughes), **Retro. Supp. I:** 203

"Angel on the Porch, An" (Wolfe), **IV:** 451

Angelou, Maya, **Supp. IV Part 1: 1–19; Supp. XI:** 20, 245; **Supp. XIII:** 185; **Supp. XVI:** 259; **Supp. XXI:** 172

"Angel Poem, The" (Stern), **Supp. IX:** 292

Angels and Earthly Creatures (Wylie), **Supp. I Part 2:** 709, 713, 724–730

Angels Flight (Connelly), **Supp. XXI:** 72, **72–73,** 75, 80

Angels in America: A Gay Fantasia on National Themes (Kushner), **Supp. IX:** 131, 134, **141–146**

"Angels of the Love Affair" (Sexton), **Supp. II Part 2:** 692

"Angel's Trumpet, The"(P. Benedict), **Supp. XXIII:** 48

"Angel Surrounded by Paysans" (Stevens), **IV:** 93

Angel That Troubled the Waters, The (Wilder), **IV:** 356, 357–358

"Anger" (Creeley), **Supp. IV Part 1:** 150–152

Anger (Sarton), **Supp. VIII: 256**

"Anger against Children" (R. Bly), **Supp. IV Part 1:** 73

Angle of Ascent (Hayden), **Supp. II Part 1:** 363, 367, 370

"Angle of Geese" (Momaday), **Supp. IV Part 2:** 485

Angle of Geese and Other Poems (Momaday), **Supp. IV Part 2:** 487, 491

Angle of Repose (Stegner), **Supp. IV Part 2:** 599, 605, 606, 610–611

"*Angle of Repose* and the Writings of Mary Hallock Foote: A Source Study" (Williams-Walsh), **Supp. IV Part 2:** 611

"Anglo-Mongrels and the Rose" (Loy), **Supp. XXII:** 156, 159, 166–167

Anglo-Saxon Century, The (Dos Passos), **I:** 474–475, 483

Angoff, Charles, **III:** 107

"Angola Question Mark" (Hughes), **Supp. I Part 1:** 344

Angry Hills, The (Uris), **Supp. XX: 246, 250**

Angry Wife, The (Sedges), **Supp. II Part 1:** 125

"Angry Women Are Building: Issues and Struggles Facing American Indian Women Today" (Gunn Allen), **Supp. IV Part 1:** 324

"Animal, Vegetable, and Mineral" (Bogan), **Supp. III Part 1:** 66

"Animal Acts" (Simic), **Supp. VIII:** 278

Animal and Vegetable Physiology Considered with Reference to Natural Theology (Roget), **Supp. I Part 1:** 312

"Animal Bodies: Corporeality, Class, and Subject Formation in *The Wide, Wide World*" (Mason), **Supp. XVIII:** 263

Animal Dreams (Kingsolver), **Supp. VII:** 199, 204–207

Animal Magnetism (Prose), **Supp. XVI:** 251, 260

"Animals, The" (Merwin), **Supp. III Part 1:** 348

"Animals Are Passing from Our Lives" (Levine), **Supp. V:** 181, 182

Animals in That Country, The (Atwood), **Supp. XIII:** 20, 33

Animals of the Soul: Sacred Animals of the Oglala Sioux (Brown), **Supp. IV Part 2:** 487

"Animals You Eat, The" (X. J. Kennedy), **Supp. XV:** 169

"Animula" (Eliot), **Retro. Supp. I:** 64

Anita Loos Rediscovered (M. A. Loos), **Supp. XVI:** 196

Ankor Wat (Ginsberg), **Supp. II Part 1:** 323

"Annabelle" (Komunyakaa), **Supp. XIII:** 117

"Annabel Lee" (Poe), **Retro. Supp. I:** 273; **Retro. Supp. II:** 266

Anna Christie (O'Neill), **III:** 386, 389, 390; **Supp. XXII:** 24

"Anna Grasa" (Weigl), **Supp. XIX:** 278

"Anna in Mourning" (Weigl), **Supp. XIX:** 288

Anna Karenina (Tolstoy), **I:** 10; **II:** 290; **Retro. Supp. I:** 225; **Supp. V:** 323

"Anna Karenina" (Trilling), Supp. III Part 2: 508

Annan, Noel, **Supp. XX: 240**

"Anna's Grace" (Weigl), **Supp. XIX:** 282–283

"Anna Who Was Mad" (Sexton), **Supp. II Part 2:** 692

"Ann Burlak" (Rukeyser), **Supp. VI:** 280

"Anne" (Oliver), **Supp. VII:** 232

"Anne" (R. H. Davis), **Supp. XVI:** 91, 92

"Anne at the Symphony" (Shields), **Supp. VII:** 310

"Anne Bradstreet's Poetic Voices" (Requa), **Supp. I Part 1:** 107

Anne of Geierstein: or, The Maiden of the Mist (Scott), **Supp. XX: 234**

Anne Sexton: The Artist and Her Critics (McClatchy), **Supp. XII:** 253

"Ann from the Street" (Dixon), **Supp. XII:** 146–147

"Ann Garner" (Agee), **I:** 27

"Anniad, The" (Brooks), **Supp. III Part 1:** 77, 78

Annie (musical), **Supp. IV Part 2:** 577

Annie Allen (Brooks), **Supp. III Part 1:** 76–79

Annie Dillard Reader, The (Dillard), **Supp. VI:** 23

Annie Hall (film; Allen), **Supp. IV Part 1:** 205; **Supp. XV:** 1, 2, 4, 5, **6–7**, 14

Annie John (Kincaid), **Supp. VII:** 184–186, 193

Annie Kilburn, a Novel (Howells), **II:** 275, 286, 287

"Annihilation" (X. J. Kennedy), **Supp. XV:** 168

"Annihilation of Matter, The" (Bronk), **Supp. XXI:** 30

Anniversary (Shields), **Supp. VII:** 320, 322, 323, 324

"Annunciation" (Nelson), **Supp. XVIII:** 174

"Annunciation, The" (Le Sueur), **Supp. V:** 130

Ann Vickers (Lewis), **II:** 453

"A No-Account Creole, A" (Chopin), **Retro. Supp. II:** 64

"Anodyne" (Komunyakaa), **Supp. XIII:** 130

Another America/Otra America (Kingsolver), **Supp. VII:** 207–209

"Another Animal" (Swenson), **Supp. IV Part 2:** 639

Another Animal: Poems (Swenson), **Supp. IV Part 2:** 639–641, 649

Another Antigone (Gurney), **Supp. V:** 97, 98, 100, 101, 102, 105

"Another August" (Merrill), **Supp. III Part 1:** 326

"Another Beer" (Matthews), **Supp. IX:** 158

Another Country (Baldwin), **Retro. Supp. II: 9–11**, 14; **Supp. I Part 1:** 51, 52, 56–58, 63, 67, 337; **Supp. II Part 1:** 40; **Supp. VIII:** 349

"Another Language" (Jong), **Supp. V:** 131

Another Mother Tongue: Gay Words, Gay Worlds (Grahn), **Supp. IV Part 1:** 330

"Another Night in the Ruins" (Kinnell), **Supp. III Part 1:** 239, 251

"Another Night with Snow" (W. V. Davis), **Supp. XXI:** 90, 91

"Another Old Woman" (W. C. Williams), **Retro. Supp. I:** 423

Another Part of the Forest (Hellman), **Supp. I Part 1:** 282–283, 297

Another Republic: 17 European and South American Writers (Strand, trans.), **Supp. IV Part 2:** 630

Another Roadside Attraction (Robbins), **Supp. X:** 259, 261, 262, 263, 264, 265–266, **267–269**, 274, 275, 277, 284

Another Side of Bob Dylan (album, Dylan), **Supp. XVIII:** 25

"Another Spring Uncovered" (Swenson), **Supp. IV Part 2:** 644

Another Thin Man (film), **Supp. IV Part 1:** 355

Another Time (Auden), **Supp. II Part 1:** 15

Another Turn of the Crank (Berry), **Supp. X:** 25, 35

"Another upon the Same" (Taylor), **IV:** 161

"Another Voice" (Wilbur), **Supp. III Part 2:** 557

"Another Wife" (Anderson), **I:** 114

"Another Winter Night" (Budbill), **Supp. XIX:** 10

Another Woman (film; Allen), **Supp. XV:** 11

Another You (Beattie), **Supp. V:** 29, 31, 33–34

Anouilh, Jean, **Supp. I Part 1:** 286–288, 297

Ansa, Tina McElroy, **Supp. XVIII:** 195

Ansen, Alan, **Supp. XXIII:** 112, 122, 123

Ansky, S., **IV:** 6

Ansky, Shloime, **Supp. IX:** 131, 138

"Answer, The" (Jeffers), **Supp. III Part 2:** 423

Answered Prayers: The Unfinished Novel (Capote), **Supp. III Part 1:** 113, 125, 131–132; **Supp. XVI:** 245

"Answering the Deer: Genocide and Continuance in the Poetry of American Indian Women" (Gunn Allen), **Supp. IV Part 1:** 322, 325

"Answer of Minerva, The: Pacifism and Resistance in Simone Weil" (Merton), **Supp. VIII:** 204

Antaeus (Wolfe), **IV:** 461

"Ante-Bellum Sermon, An" (Dunbar), **Supp. II Part 1:** 203–204

Antheil, George, **III:** 471, 472; **IV:** 404

Anthem (Rand), **Supp. IV Part 2:** 523

Anthology of Holocaust Literature (Glatstein, Knox, and Margoshes, eds.), **Supp. X:** 70

Anthology of Modern American Poetry (Nelson, ed.), **Supp. XXII:** 271

Anthology of Twentieth-Century Brazilian Poetry, An (Bishop and Brasil, eds.), **Retro. Supp. II:** 50; **Supp. I Part 1:** 94

Anthon, Kate, **I:** 452

Anthony, Adelina, **Supp. XXIII:** 197

Anthony, Andrew, **Supp. XVI:** 235, 245, 246

Anthony, Saint, **III:** 395

Anthony, Susan B., **Supp. XI:** 200

"Anthropologist as Hero, The" (Sontag), **Supp. III Part 2:** 451

"Anthropology of Water, The" (Carson), **Supp. XII: 102–103**

Anthropos: The Future of Art (Cummings), **I:** 430

Antichrist (Nietzsche), **III:** 176

"Anti-Father" (Dove), **Supp. IV Part 1:** 246

"Anti-Feminist Woman, The" (Rich), **Supp. I Part 2:** 550

Antigone (Sophocles), **Supp. I Part 1:** 284; **Supp. X:** 249

"Anti-Memoir"(Dybek), **Supp. XXIII:** 78

Antin, David, **Supp. VIII:** 292; **Supp. XII:** 2, 8

Antin, Mary, **Supp. IX:** 227; **Supp. XVI:** 148, 149; **Supp. XX: 1–16**

Anti-Oedipus: Capitalism and Schizophrenia (Deleuze and Guattari), **Supp. XII:** 4

Antiphon, The (Barnes), **Supp. III Part 1:** 43–44

"Antiquities" (Mather), **Supp. II Part 2:** 452

"Antiquity of Freedom, The" (Bryant), **Supp. I Part 1:** 168

"Antislavery Tocsin, An" (Douglass), **Supp. III Part 1:** 171

Antoine, Andre, **III:** 387

Antonioni, Michelangelo, **Supp. IV Part 1:** 46, 47, 48

Antony and Cleopatra (Shakespeare), **I:** 285

"Antony on Behalf of the Play" (Burke), **I:** 284

"An trentiesme de mon Eage, L" (MacLeish), **III:** 9

Antrim, Donald, **Supp. XX:** 90

"Ants" (R. Bly), **Supp. IV Part 1:** 71

Anxiety of Influence, The (Bloom), **Supp. XIII:** 46

"Any City" (Untermeyer), **Supp. XV:** 296

"Any Object" (Swenson), **Supp. IV Part 2:** 640

Anyplace but Here (Bontemps and Conroy), **Supp. XXII:** 11

"Any Porch" (Parker), **Supp. IX:** 194

Anything Else (film; Allen), **Supp. XV:** 2, 11

"Anywhere Out of This World" (Baudelaire), **II:** 552

Any Woman Can't (Wasserstein), **Supp. XV:** 322

Any Woman's Blues (Jong), **Supp. V:** 115, 123, 126

Anzaldúa, Gloria, **Supp. IV Part 1:** 330; **Supp. XIII:** 223; **Supp. XXIII:** 193, 194, 205

"Apache Tears" (Cliff), **Supp. XXII:** 76

"Aphorisms on Futurism" (Loy), **Supp. XXII:** 159

"Aphorisms on Society" (Stevens), **Retro. Supp. I:** 303

"Apiary IX" (C. Frost), **Supp. XV:** 106

"Apisculptures" (Bierds), **Supp. XVII:** 29

Apollinaire, Guillaume, **I:** 432; **II:** 529; **III:** 196; **IV:** 80; **Retro. Supp. II:** 326; **Supp. XV:** 182; **Supp. XXIII:** 208

Apologies to the Iroquois (Wilson), **IV:** 429

"Apology" (C. Frost), **Supp. XV:** 103

"Apology, An" (Malamud), **Supp. I Part 2:** 435, 437

"Apology for Bad Dreams" (Jeffers), **Supp. II Part 2:** 427, 438; **Supp. XVII:** 112

"Apology for Crudity, An" (Anderson), **I:** 109

Apology for Poetry (Sidney), **Supp. II Part 1:** 105

Apostle, The (Asch), **Supp. XXIII:** 2, 4, 9, **13–14**

"Apostle of the Tules, An" (Harte), **Supp. II Part 1:** 356

"Apostrophe to a Dead Friend" (Kumin), **Supp. IV Part 2:** 442, 451, 452

"Apostrophe to a Pram Rider" (White), **Supp. I Part 2:** 678

"Apostrophe to Man (on reflecting that the world is ready to go to war again)" (Millay), **III:** 127

"Apostrophe to Vincentine, The" (Stevens), **IV:** 90

"Apotheosis" (Kingsolver), **Supp. VII:** 208

"Apotheosis of Martin Luther King, The" (Hardwick), **Supp. III Part 1:** 203–204

Appalachia (Wright), **Supp. V:** 333, 345

Appalachia Inside Out (Miller, Higgs, and Manning, eds.), **Supp. XX: 166**

"Appalachian Book of the Dead III" (Wright), **Supp. V:** 345

"Appalachian Education: A Critique and Suggestions for Reform" (J. W. Miller), **Supp. XX: 165**

"Appalachian Literature: At Home in This World" (J. W. Miller), **Supp. XX: 165**

"Appalachian Values/American Values" (J. W. Miller), **Supp. XX: 165**

Appaloosa (Parker), **Supp. XIX:** 187

"Appeal to H. G. Wells" (Sturgis), **Supp. XX: 233, 240**

"Appeal to Progressives, An" (Wilson), **IV:** 429

Appeal to Reason (Paine), **I:** 490

Appeal to the World, An (Du Bois), **Supp. II Part 1:** 184

Appearance and Reality (Bradley), **I:** 572

"Appendix to 'The Anniad' " (Brooks), **Supp. III Part 1:** 77

"Applause, Applause"(Thompson), **Supp. XXIII:** 289, 291, 301

Apple, Max, **Supp. VIII:** 14; **Supp. XVII:** 1–11, 49–50

Apple, Sam, **Supp. XVII:** 8

"Apple, The" (Kinnell), **Supp. III Part 1:** 250

Applebaum, Anne, **Supp. XVI:** 153

Applebome, Peter, **Supp. XXI:** 38

Applegarth, Mabel, **II:** 465, 478

"Apple-Maggot Fly, The" (Major), **Supp. XXII:** 182

"Apple of Discord, The" (Humphrey), **Supp. IX:** 109

"Apple Peeler" (Francis), **Supp. IX:** 82

"Apple Rind" (C. Frost), **Supp. XV:** 102

"Apples" (Brockmeier), **Supp. XXII:** 51, 53

"Apples, The" (Di Piero), **Supp. XIX:** 46

Appleseed, Johnny (pseudonym). *See* Chapman, John (Johnny Appleseed)

Apple That Astonished Paris, The (Collins), **Supp. XXI:** 53, 57

Appleton, Nathan, **II:** 488

Appleton, Thomas Gold, **Supp. I Part 1:** 306; **Supp. I Part 2:** 415

"Apple Tree, The" (McCarriston), **Supp. XIV:** 263, 268

"Applicant, The" (Plath), **Retro. Supp. II:** 252; **Supp. I Part 2:** 535, 544, 545

"Application, The" (Neugeboren), **Supp. XVI:** 219, 220, 225

"Applications of the Doctrine" (Hass), **Supp. VI:** 100–101

Appointment, The (film), **Supp. IX:** 253

Appointment in Samarra (O'Hara), **III:** 361, 363–364, 365–367, 371, 374, 375, 383

Appreciation of Sarah Orne Jewett (Cary), **Retro. Supp. II:** 132

"Apprentice, The"(Dybek), **Supp. XXIII:** 71

"Approaches, The" (Merwin), **Supp. III Part 1:** 350

"Approaching Artaud" (Sontag), **Supp. III Part 2:** 470–471

"Approaching Prayer" (Dickey), **Supp. IV Part 1:** 175

"Approaching the Mohawk Village: Jogues' Journal"(Kenny), **Supp. XXIII:** 152

Approach to Literature, An: A Collection of Prose and Verse with Analyses and Discussions (Brooks, Warren, and Purser), **Supp. XIV:**4

"Approach to Thebes, The" (Kunitz), **Supp. III Part 1:** 265–267

Approach to Vedanta, An (Isherwood), **Supp. XIV:** 157, 163, 164

"Appropriation of Cultures, The" (Everett), **Supp. XVIII:** 66

Approximately Paradise (Skloot), **Supp. XX: 196, 202, 203–204**

"Après-midi d'un faune, L' " (Mallarmé), **III:** 8

"April" (Bierds), **Supp. XVII:** 29

"April" (W. C. Williams), **Retro. Supp. I:** 422

"April" (Winters), **Supp. II Part 2:** 788

April, Steve. *See* Lacy, Ed

April Galleons (Ashbery), **Supp. III Part 1:** 26

"April Galleons" (Ashbery), **Supp. III Part 1:** 26

April Hopes (Howells), **II:** 285, 289

"April Lovers" (Ransom), **III:** 489–490

"April Showers" (Wharton), **Retro. Supp. I:** 361

"April Today Main Street" (Olson), **Supp. II Part 2:** 581

April Twilights (Cather), **I:** 313; **Retro. Supp. I:** 5

"Apt Pupil" (King), **Supp. V:** 152

Arabian Nights, **I:** 204; **II:** 8; **Supp. I Part 2:** 584, 599; **Supp. IV Part 1:** 1

"Arabic Coffee" (Nye), **Supp. XIII:** 276

"Araby" (Joyce), **I:** 174; **Supp. VIII:** 15

Aragon, Louis, **I:** 429; **III:** 471; **Retro. Supp. II:** 85, 321

Arana-Ward, Marie, **Supp. VIII:** 84

Ararat (Glück), **Supp. V:** 79, 86–87

Aratani, Mariko, **Supp. XXIII:** 136

Arbre du voyageur, L' (W. J. Smith; Haussmann, trans.), Supp. XIII: 347

Arbus, Diane, **Supp. XII:** 188

Arbuthnott, John (pseudonym). *See* Henry, O.

"Arc, The" (Bidart), **Supp. XV:** 25–26, 27

Archaeologist of Morning (Olson), **Supp. II Part 2:** 557

Archaeology of the Circle: New and Selected Poems (Weigl), **Supp. XIX:** 282

"Archaic Maker, The" (Merwin), **Supp. III Part 1:** 357

"Archaic Torso of Apollo" (Rilke), **Supp. XV:** 148

"Archaischer Torso Apollos" (Rilke), **Supp. XVII:** 244

"Archbishop, The" (Gioia), **Supp. XV:** 126, 127

Archer (television show), **Supp. IV Part 2:** 474

Archer, William, **IV:** 131; **Retro. Supp. I:** 228

Archer at Large (Macdonald), **Supp. IV Part 2:** 473

Archer in Hollywood (Macdonald), **Supp. IV Part 2:** 474

"Archetype and Signature: The Relationship of Poet and Poem" (Fiedler), **Supp. XIII:** 101

"Archibald Higbie" (Masters), **Supp. I Part 2:** 461

"Architect, The" (Bourne), **I:** 223

Architect, The (Briggs and Ranlett), **Supp. XVIII:** 3

Arctic Dreams (Lopez), **Supp. V:** 211

Arctic Refuge: A Circle of Testimony (Haines), **Supp. XII:** 205

"Arcturus" (Connell), **Supp. XIV:** 88

À rebours (Huysmans), **Supp. XX: 239**

Arendt, Hannah, **II:** 544; **Retro. Supp. I:** 87; **Retro. Supp. II:** 28, 117; **Supp. I Part 2:** 570; **Supp. IV Part 1:** 386; **Supp. VIII:** 98, 99, 100, 243; **Supp. XII:** 166–167

Arensberg, Louise, **Supp. XXII:** 162

Arensberg, Walter, **IV:** 408; **Retro. Supp. I:** 416; **Supp. XXII:** 162

Aren't You Happy for Me? (Bausch), **Supp. VII:** 42, 51, 54

Areopagitica (Milton), **Supp. I Part 2:** 422

"Are You a Doctor?" (Carver), **Supp. III Part 1:** 139–141

"Are You Mr. William Stafford? (Stafford), **Supp. XI:** 317

Argall: The True Story of Pocahontas and Captain John Smith (Vollmann), **Supp. XVII:** 225, 226, 231, 232, 233

"Argonauts of 49, California's Golden Age" (Harte), **Supp. II Part 1:** 353, 355

"Arguments of Everlasting" (B. Kelly), **Supp. XVII:** 129

"Arguments with the Gestapo Continued: II" (Wright), **Supp. XV:** 344

"Arguments with the Gestapo Continued: Literary Resistance" (Wright), **Supp. XV:** 344

Ari (musical, Uris), **Supp. XX:** 247

Aria da Capo (Millay), **III:** 137–138

Ariadne's Thread: A Collection of Contemporary Women's Journals (Lifshin, ed.), **Supp. XVI:** 37–38

"Arias, 1971" (Hull), **Supp. XXI:** 135

Ariel (Plath), **Retro. Supp. II: 250–255; Supp. I Part 2:** 526, 539, 541; **Supp. V:** 79; **Supp. XXI:** 58; **Supp. XXII:** 93

"Ariel" (Plath), **Supp. I Part 2:** 542, 546

"Ariel Poems" (Eliot), **I:** 579

Ariosto, Ludovico, **Supp. XV:** 175

"Ariosto: Critical Notice of His Life and Genius" (Hunt), **Supp. XV:** 175

Arise, Arise (Zukofsky), **Supp. III Part 2:** 619, 629

Aristides. *See* Epstein, Joseph

"Aristocracy" (Emerson), **II:** 6

Aristocracy and Justice (More), **I:** 223

Aristocrat, The (Richter), **Supp. XVIII:** 220

Aristophanes, **I:** 436; **II:** 577; **Supp. I Part 2:** 406

Aristotle, **I:** 58, 265, 280, 527; **II:** 9, 12, 198, 536; **III:** 20, 115, 145, 157, 362, 422, 423; **IV:** 10, 18, 74–75, 89; **Supp. I Part 1:** 104, 296; **Supp. I Part 2:** 423; **Supp. IV Part 1:** 391; **Supp. IV Part 2:** 526, 530; **Supp. X:** 78; **Supp. XI:** 249; **Supp. XII:** 106; **Supp. XIV:** 242–243

Aristotle Contemplating the Bust of Homer (Rembrandt), **Supp. IV Part 1:** 390, 391

"Arkansas Traveller" (Wright), **Supp. V:** 334

Arlen, Harold, **Supp. XXII:** 6

"Arm, The" (X. J. Kennedy), **Supp. XV:** 169

"Armadillo, The" (Bishop), **Supp. I Part 1:** 93

Armadillo in the Grass (Hearon), **Supp. VIII: 58–59**

"Armageddon" (Ransom), **III:** 489, 492

Armageddon (Uris), **Supp. XX: 243, 247, 248, 252–253**

Armah, Aiy Kwei, **Supp. IV Part 1:** 373

Armenian Golgotha: A Memoir of the Armenian Genocide, 1915– 1918 (Grigoris Balakian; trans. Peter Balakian and Sevag), **Supp. XXIII: 28, 29–32**

Armies of the Night, The (Mailer), **III:** 39–40, 41, 42, 44, 45, 46; **Retro. Supp. II:** 205, 206–207, 208; **Supp. IV Part 1:** 207; **Supp. XIV:** 49, 162

"Arm in Arm" (Simpson), **Supp. IX:** 267–268

Arminius, Jacobus, **I:** 557

Armitage, Shelley, **Supp. IV Part 2:** 439

Arm of Flesh, The (Salter), **Supp. IX:** 251

"Armor" (Dickey), **Supp. IV Part 1:** 179

Armored Attack (film), **Supp. I Part 1:** 281

Arms, George W., **Supp. I Part 2:** 416–417

Armstrong, George, **Supp. I Part 2:** 386

Armstrong, Louis, **Retro. Supp. II:** 114

"'Arm the Paper Arm': Kenneth Koch's Postmodern Comedy" (Chinitz), **Supp. XV:** 180, 185

"Army" (Corso), **Supp. XII:** 117, 127

Army Brat (W. J. Smith), **Supp. XIII:** 331, 347

Arna Bontemps Langston Hughes: Letters 1925–1967 (Nichols), **Retro. Supp. I:** 194

"Arna Bontemps Talks About the Renaissance" (Collins), **Supp. XXII:** 7

Arner, Robert D., **Retro. Supp. II:** 62

"Arnie" (Budbill), **Supp. XIX:** 6

Arnold, Edwin T., **Supp. VIII:** 189

Arnold, George W., **Supp. I Part 2:** 411

Arnold, Marilyn, **Supp. IV Part 1:** 220

Arnold, Matthew, **I:** 222, 228, 275; **II:** 20, 110, 338, 541; **III:** 604; **IV:** 349; **Retro. Supp. I:** 56, 325; **Supp. I Part 2:** 416, 417, 419, 529, 552, 602; **Supp. IX:** 298; **Supp. XIV:** 11, 335; **Supp. XIX:** 41; **Supp. XXI:** 90

Arnold, Thurman, **Supp. I Part 2:** 645

Aronson, Steven M. L., **Supp. V:** 4

Around about America (Caldwell), **I:** 290

"Arrangement in Black and White" (Parker), **Supp. IX:** 198

"Arrival at Santos" (Bishop), **Retro. Supp. II:** 46; **Supp. IX:** 45–46

"Arrival of the Bee Box, The" (Plath), **Retro. Supp. II:** 255

Arrivistes, The: Poem 1940–1949 (Simpson), **Supp. IX:** 265, **267–268**

Arrogance (J. Scott), **Supp. XVII: 186–188,** 189, 191, 192, 194

"Arrow" (Dove), **Supp. IV Part 1:** 250

Arrowsmith (Lewis), **I:** 362; **II:** 445–446, 449

"Arsenal at Springfield, The" (Longfellow), **Retro. Supp. II:** 168

"Arson at Midnight" (Nelson), **Supp. XVIII:** 186

"Arson Plus" (Hammett), **Supp. IV Part 1:** 343; **Supp. XXI:** 68

"Ars Poetica" (Dove), **Supp. IV Part 1:** 250

"Ars Poetica" (Dunn), **Supp. XI:** 154

"Ars Poetica" (MacLeish), **III:** 9–10

"Ars Poetica" (X. J. Kennedy), **Supp. XV:** 154

"Ars Poetica: A Found Poem" (Kumin), **Supp. IV Part 2:** 455

"Ars Poetica; or, Who Lives in the Ivory Tower" (McGrath), **Supp. X:** 117

"Ars Poetica: Some Recent Criticism" (Wright), **Supp. III Part 2:** 603

"Art" (Emerson), **II:** 13

Art (Reza), **Supp. XXI:** 148

"Art and Architecture of the Double Ending, The"(Painter), **Supp. XXIII:** 295

"Art and Neurosis" (Trilling), **Supp. III Part 2:** 502

Art and Technics (Mumford), **Supp. II Part 2:** 483

Art & Ardor: Essays (Ozick), **Supp. V:** 258, 272

Art as Experience (Dewey), **I:** 266

Art by Subtraction (Reid), **IV:** 41

Art Chronicles 1954–1966 (O'Hara), **Supp. XXIII:** 220

Art de toucher le clavecin, L' (Couperin), III: 464

Artemis to Actaeon and Other Verse (Wharton), **Retro. Supp. I:** 372

Arte of English Poesie (Puttenham), **Supp. I Part 1:** 113

"Art"(Hadas), **Supp. XXIII:** 115–116

"Art History" (Cliff), **Supp. XXII:** 75–76

Arthur, Anthony, **Supp. IV Part 2:** 606

Arthur Mervyn; or, Memoirs of the Year 1793 (Brown), **Supp. I Part 1:** 137–140, 144

"Article of Faith" (Sobin), **Supp. XVI:** 291

Articles of Light & Elation (Sobin), **Supp. XVI:** 291

Articulation of Sound Forms in Time (Howe), **Supp. IV Part 2:** 419, 431–433

"Artificer" (X. J. Kennedy), **Supp. XV:** 160

"Artificial Nigger, The" (O'Connor), **III:** 343, 351, 356, 358; **Retro. Supp. II:** 229, 232

Artist, The: A Drama without Words (Mencken), **III:** 104

Artist as Revolutionary, The (Buhle), **Supp. XXI:** 172

"Artist of the Beautiful, The" (Hawthorne), **Retro. Supp. I:** 149

Artistry of Grief (Torsney), **Retro. Supp. I:** 224

"Artists' and Models' Ball, The" (Brooks), **Supp. III Part 1:** 72

Art of Detective Fiction, The (Swales), **Supp. XIX:** 183

"Art of Disappearing, The" (Nye), **Supp. XIII:** 287

Art of Drowning, The (Collins), **Supp. XXI:** 54, 60, 64

Art of Eating, The (M. F. K. Fisher), **Supp. XVII:** 87, 90, 91

Art of Fiction, The (Gardner), **Supp. VI:** 73

"Art of Fiction, The" (H. James), **Retro. Supp. I:** 226; **Retro. Supp. II:** 223

Art of Hunger, The (Auster), **Supp. XII:** 22

"Art of Keeping Your Mouth Shut, The" (Heller), **Supp. IV Part 1:** 383

"Art of Literature and Commonsense, The" (Nabokov), **Retro. Supp. I:** 271

Art of Living and Other Stories, The (Gardner), **Supp. VI:** 72

Art of Love, The (Koch), **Supp. XV:** 182

"Art of Love, The" (Koch), **Supp. XV:** 182

Art of Poetry, The (Koch), **Supp. XV:** 175–176, 178, 188

"Art of Poetry, The" (Koch), **Supp. XV:** 182

"Art of Poetry, The" (McClatchy), **Supp. XII:** 262

"Art of Romare Bearden, The" (Ellison), **Retro. Supp. II:** 123

"Art of Storytelling, The" (Simpson), **Supp. IX:** 277

Art of Sylvia Plath, The (Newman), **Supp. I Part 2:** 527

Art of the Moving Picture, The (Lindsay), **Supp. I Part 2:** 376, 391–392, 394; **Supp. XVI:** 185

Art of the Novel (H. James), **Retro. Supp. I:** 227

"Art of Theodore Dreiser, The" (Bourne), **I:** 235

Art of the Personal Essay, The (Lopate, comp.), **Supp. XIII:** 280–281; **Supp. XVI:** 266

Art of the Self, The: Essays a Propos "Steps" (Kosinski), *Supp. VII:* 222

Art of the Wasted Day, The (Hampl), **Supp. XXII:** 85

Arts and Sciences (Goldbarth), **Supp. XII: 184–186**

Arts and Sciences: A Seventies Seduction (Mallon), **Supp. XIX:** 132, 135

"Art's Bread and Butter" (Benét), **Retro. Supp. I:** 108

Artsybashev, Mikhail, **Supp. XXIII:** 1

Arvin, Newton, **I:** 259; **II:** 508; **Retro. Supp. I:** 19, 137

Asali, Muna, **Supp. XIII:** 121, 126

"As a Little Child" (Taggard), **Supp. XXII:** 272

Asbury, Herbert, **Supp. IV Part 1:** 353

Ascent of F6, The (Auden), **Supp. II Part 1:** 11, 13

Ascent to Truth, The (Merton), **Supp. VIII:** 208

Asch, Nathan, **Supp. XV:** 133, 134; **Supp. XXIII:** 4

Asch, Sholem, **IV:** 1, 9, 11, 14; **Retro. Supp. II:** 299; **Supp. XXIII:** 1–18

Ascherson, Neal, **Supp. XII:** 167

Ascher-Walsh, Rebecca, **Supp. XIX:** 54

"As Close as Breathing" (Jarman), **Supp. XVII:** 120

As David Danced (Bronk), **Supp. XXI:** 24

"As David Danced" (Bronk), **Supp. XXI:** 26

As Does New Hampshire and Other Poems (Sarton), **Supp. VIII:** 259

"As Evening Lays Dying" (Salinas), **Supp. XIII:** 319

"As Flowers Are" (Kunitz), **Supp. III Part 1:** 265

"Ash" (Sobin), **Supp. XVI:** 284–285

Ash, Nathan, **Supp. XXII:** 277

Ashbery, John, **Retro. Supp. I:** 313; **Supp. I Part 1:** 96; **Supp. III Part 1:** 1–29; **Supp. III Part 2:** 541; **Supp. IV Part 2:** 620; **Supp. VIII:** 272; **Supp. IX:** 52; **Supp. XI:** 139; **Supp. XIII:** 85; **Supp. XV:** 176, 177, 178,

188, 250; **Supp. XIX:** 40, 83; **Supp. XXI:** 227; **Supp. XXIII:** 207, 209, 210, 211, 215, 217, 220

"Ashes" (Lamott), **Supp. XX: 141**

"Ashes" (Levine), **Supp. V:** 188

"Ashes of the Beacon" (Bierce), **I:** 209

Ashes: Poems Old and New (Levine), **Supp. V:** 178, 188–189

Ashford, Margaret Mary (Daisy), **II:** 426

"Ash Wednesday" (Garrett), **Supp. VII:** 109–110

"Ash Wednesday" (Merton), **Supp. VIII:** 199

Ash Wednesday (T. S. Eliot), **I:** 570, 574–575, 578–579, 580, 582, 584, 585; **Retro. Supp. I:** 64

"Ash Wednesday" (T. S. Eliot), **Supp. IV Part 2:** 436

Asian American Authors (Hsu and Palubinskas, eds.), **Supp. X:** 292

Asian American Heritage: An Anthology of Prose and Poetry (Wand), **Supp. X:** 292

Asian Figures (Mervin), **Supp. III Part 1:** 341

Asian Journal of Thomas Merton, The (Merton), **Supp. VIII:** 196, 206, 208

"Asian Peace Offers Rejected without Publication" (R. Bly), **Supp. IV Part 1:** 61

"Asides on the Oboe" (Stevens), **Retro. Supp. I:** 305

"As I Ebb'd with the Ocean of Life" (Whitman), **IV:** 342, 345–346; **Retro. Supp. I:** 404, 405

As I Lay Dying (Faulkner), **II:** 60–61, 69, 73, 74; **IV:** 100; **Retro. Supp. I:** 75, 82, 84, 85, 86, 88, 89, 91, 92; **Supp. IV Part 1:** 47; **Supp. VIII:** 37, 178; **Supp. IX:** 99, 103, 251; **Supp. XIV:** 24

"As I Lay with My Head in Your Lap, Camerado" (Whitman), **IV:** 347

Asimov, Isaac, **Supp. IV Part 1:** 116; **Supp. XVI:** 122

Asinof, Eliot, **II:** 424

As I Remember It (PBS documentary), **Supp. XVIII:** 277

Asirvatham, Sandy, **Supp. XVI:** 249

"As Is the Daughter, So Is Her Mother" (Patchett), **Supp. XII:** 310

"As It Was in the Beginning" (Benét), **Supp. XI:** 56

"As I Walked Out One Evening" (Auden), **Supp. II Part 1:** 13; **Supp. XV:** 126; **Supp. XX:** 138

"As I Went Down by Havre de Grace" (Wylie), **Supp. I Part 2:** 723

Ask a Policeman (Hinojosa), **Supp. XIX:** 110–111

"Ask Me" (Stafford), **Supp. XI:** 326–327

Ask Me Tomorrow (Cozzens), **I:** 365–367, 379

Ask the Dust (Fante), **Supp. XI:** 159, 160, 166, **167–169,** 172, 173, 174

"Ask the Optimist!" (Saunders), **Supp. XIX:** 235

Ask Your Mama (Hughes), **Supp. I Part 1:** 339, 341–342

Ask Your Mama: 12 Moods for Jazz (Hughes), **Retro. Supp. I:** 210, 211

As Little Children (R. P. Smith), **Supp. XIV:** 333

"As One Put Drunk into the Packet Boat" (Ashbery), **Supp. III Part 1:** 18

"Asparagus" (Nelson), **Supp. XVIII:** 178

"Aspects of Robinson" (Kees), **Supp. XV:** 134

Aspects of the Novel (Forster), **Retro. Supp. I:** 232; **Supp. VIII:** 155; **Supp. XXI:** 233

"Aspen and the Stream, The" (Wilbur), **Supp. III Part 2:** 555, 556

Aspern Papers, The (James), **Supp. V:** 101, 102

"Aspern Papers, The" (James), **Retro. Supp. I:** 219, 227, 228

Asphalt Georgics (Carruth), **Supp. XVI:** 54

Asphalt Jungle (film, Huston), **Supp. XIII:** 174

"Asphodel" (Welty), **IV:** 265, 271

"Asphodel, That Greeny Flower" (W. C. Williams), **Retro. Supp. I:** 429

"Aspic and Buttermilk" (Olds), **Supp. X:** 213

Asquith, Herbert Henry, **Retro. Supp. I:** 59

"Ass" (Cisneros), **Supp. VII:** 67

Assante, Armand, **Supp. VIII:** 74

Assassin, The: A Play in Three Acts (Shaw), **Supp. XIX:** 248

Assassins, The (Oates), **Supp. II Part 2:** 512, 517–519

"Assault" (Millay), **III:** 130–131

"Assemblage of Husbands and Wives, An" (Lewis), **II:** 455–456

Assembly (O'Hara), **III:** 361

As She Climbed Across the Table (Lethem), **Supp. XVIII: 140–141,** 148

Assignment, Wildlife (LaBastille), **Supp. X: 99,** 104

"Assimiliation in Recent American Jewish Autobiographies" (Krupnick), **Supp. XVI:** 153

Assistant, The (Malamud), **Supp. I Part 2:** 427, 428, 429, 431, 435, 441–445, 451; **Supp. XVI:** 220

Assommoir, L' (Zola), **II:** 291; **III:** 318

Assorted Prose (Updike), **IV:** 215–216, 218; **Retro. Supp. I:** 317, 319, 327

Astaire, Adele, **Supp. XVI:** 187

As They Were (M. F. K. Fisher), **Supp. XVII:** 88, 89, 91

Astor, Mary, **Supp. IV Part 1:** 356; **Supp. XII:** 173

Astoria, or, Anecdotes of an Enterprise beyond the Rocky Mountains (Irving), **II:** 312

"Astounding News by Electric Express via Norfolk! The Atlantic Crossed in Three Days Signal Triumph of Mr. Monck's Flying-Machine . . ." (Poe), **III:** 413, 420

Astraea (Holmes), **III:** 82

Astro, Richard, **Supp. I Part 2:** 429, 445

"Astrological Fricassee" (H. Miller), **III:** 187

Astrophil and Stella (Sidney), **Supp. XIV:** 128

"As Weary Pilgrim" (Bradstreet), **Supp. I Part 1:** 103, 109, 122

As We Know (Ashbery), **Supp. III Part 1:** 9, 21–25

"As We Know" (Ashbery), **Supp. III Part 1:** 21–22

Aswell, Edward C., **IV:** 458, 459, 461

"Asylum, The" (Carruth), **Supp. XVI:** 48–49

"As You Like It" (Chopin), **Supp. I Part 1:** 217

As You Like It (Shakespeare), **Supp. I Part 1:** 308

"At a Bar in Charlotte Amalie" (Updike), **IV:** 214

"At a Lecture" (Brodsky), **Supp. VIII:** 33

"At a March against the Vietnam War" (R. Bly), **Supp. IV Part 1:** 61

"At a Reading" (McClatchy), **Supp. XII:** 256–257

"Atavism of John Tom Little Bear, The" (O. Henry), **Supp. II Part 1:** 410

"At Chênière Caminada" (Chopin), **Supp. I Part 1:** 220

"At Chinese Checkers" (Berryman), **I:** 182

Atchity, Kenneth John, **Supp. XI:** 227

"At Death's Window" (Lamott), **Supp. XX:** 144

At Eighty-Two (Sarton), **Supp. VIII:** 264

"At Every Gas Station There Are Mechanics" (Dunn), **Supp. XI:** 144

At Fault (Chopin), **Retro. Supp. II:** 57, 60, **62–63; Supp. I Part 1:** 207, 209–211, 220

"At Fifty" (Bronk), **Supp. XXI:** 31

At Heaven's Gate (Warren), **IV:** 243, 247–248, 251

Atheism Refuted: in a Discourse to Prove the Existence of God (Paine), **Supp. I Part 2:** 517

"Athénaïse" (Chopin), **Retro. Supp. II:** 66, 67; **Supp. I Part 1:** 219–220

Atherton, Gertrude, **I:** 199, 207–208

Athey, Jean L., **Supp. XI:** 184

At Home: Essays, 1982–1988 (Vidal), **Supp. IV Part 2:** 682, 687, 688

"At Home With" (column; Leland), **Supp. XV:** 69

"At Kino Viejo, Mexico" (Ríos), **Supp. IV Part 2:** 541

Atkinson, Brooks, **IV:** 288; **Supp. IV Part 2:** 683; **Supp. XIX:** 244

Atlantis (Doty), **Supp. XI:** 121, **126–129**

"Atlantis" (Doty), **Supp. XI:** 127–128

Atlas, James, **Supp. V:** 233; **Supp. XV:** 25

Atlas, The (Vollmann), **Supp. XVII:** 226, 227

Atlas Shrugged (Rand), **Supp. IV Part 2:** 517, 521, 523, 524–526, 528, 531

At Liberty (T. Williams), **IV:** 378

"At Melville's Tomb" (H. Crane), **I:** 393; **Retro. Supp. II:** 76, 78, 80, 82

"At Mother Teresa's" (Nye), **Supp. XIII:** 276

"At Nightfall" (Kooser), **Supp. XIX:** 122–123

At Night the Salmon Move (Carver), **Supp. III Part 1:** 142

At Night the States (Notley), **Supp. XXII:** 224, 231–232

"At night the states" (Notley), **Supp. XXII:** 232

"At North Farm" (Ashbery), **Supp. III Part 1:** 1–2

At Paradise Gate (Smiley), **Supp. VI:** 292, **293–294**

"At Paso Rojo" (Bowles), **Supp. IV Part 1:** 87

At Play in the Fields of the Lord (Matthiessen), **Supp. V:** 199, 202, 204–206, 212

"At Play in the Paradise of Bombs" (Sanders), **Supp. XVI:** 272–273, 274, 277

"At Pleasure By" (Pinsky), **Supp. VI:** 245

"A-Train / Ziggurat / Elegy"(Balakian), **Supp. XXIII:** 32

At Risk (Hoffman), **Supp. X:** 87

"At Sea" (Hemingway), **II:** 258

"At Shaft 11" (Dunbar), **Supp. II Part 1:** 212

"At Slim's River" (Haines), **Supp. XII:** 208–209

"At St. Croix" (Dubus), **Supp. VII:** 83, 87

At Sundown (Whittier), **Supp. I Part 2:** 704

"At Sunset" (Simic), **Supp. VIII:** 282

Attaway, William, **Supp. XXI:** 264

Attebery, Brian, **Supp. IV Part 1:** 101

Attendant, The (Bronk), **Supp. XXI:** 24

"Attendant, The" (Bronk), **Supp. XXI:** 26

"Attention"(Hadas), **Supp. XXIII:** 121

"At That Time, or The History of a Joke" (Paley), **Supp. VI:** 229–230

"At the Alhambra"(P. Benedict), **Supp. XXIII:** 40

At the Back of the North Wind (Macdonald), **Supp. XIII:** 75

"At the Birth of an Age" (Jeffers), **Supp. II Part 2:** 432

"At the Bomb Testing Site" (Stafford), **Supp. XI:** 317–318, 321, 323

At the Bottom of the River (Kincaid), **Supp. VII:** 182–184, 185

"At the 'Cadian Ball" (Chopin), **Retro. Supp. II:** 64, 65, 68

"At the Cancer Clinic" (Kooser), **Supp. XIX:** 127

"At the Chelton-Pulver Game" (Auchincloss), **Supp. IV Part 1:** 27

"At the Drugstore" (Taylor), **Supp. V:** 323

At the Edge of the Body (Jong), **Supp. V:** 115, 130

"At the End of the Curse, a Blessing" (Verducci), **Supp. XXII:** 209

At the End of the Open Road (Simpson), **Supp. IX:** 265, 269, **271–273,** 277

At the End of This Summer: Poems 1948–1954, **Supp. XII:** 211

"At the End of War" (Eberhart), **I:** 522–523

"At the Executed Murderer's Grave" (Wright), **Supp. III Part 2:** 595, 597

"At the Fishhouses" (Bishop), **Retro. Supp. II:** 45; **Supp. I Part 1:** 90, 92

At the Gates of the Animal Kingdom (Hempel), **Supp. XXI:** 115, **122–124**

"At the Grave of My Guardian Angel: St. Louis Cemetery, New Orleans" (Levis), **Supp. XI:** 268–269

"At the Gym" (Doty), **Supp. XI:** 135

"At the Indian Store" (McCarriston), **Supp. XIV:** 271

"At the Lake" (Oliver), **Supp. VII:** 244

"At the Landing" (Welty), **IV:** 265–266; **Retro. Supp. I:** 348

"At the Last" (Bynner), **Supp. XV:** 44

"At the Last Rites for Two Hot Rodders" (X. J. Kennedy), **Supp. XV:** 166

"At the Mountains of Madness" (Lovecraft), **Supp. XXII:** 58

"At the Owl Club, North Gulfport, Mississippi, 1950" (Trethewey), **Supp. XXI:** 249

"At the Premiere" (Keillor), **Supp. XVI:** 167

At the Rendezvous of Victory (C. L. R. James), **Supp. XXI:** 172

At the Root of Stars (Barnes), **Supp. III Part 1:** 34

"At the Slackening of the Tide" (Wright), **Supp. III Part 2:** 597

"At the Tomb of Walt Whitman" (Kunitz), **Supp. III Part 1:** 262

"At the Tourist Centre in Boston" (Atwood), **Supp. XIII:** 33

"At the Town Dump" (Kenyon), **Supp. VII:** 167

"At the Worcester Museum" (Pinsky), **Supp. VI:** 251

"At the Zoo in Spain" (Major), **Supp. XXII:** 182

"Atticus Finch and the Mad Dog: Harper Lee's *To Kill a Mockingbird*" (Jones), **Supp. VIII:** 128

"Atticus Finch—Right and Wrong" (Freedman), **Supp. VIII:** 127–128

"Attic Which Is Desire, The" (W. C. Williams), **Retro. Supp. I:** 422

"At Tikal" (Bronk), **Supp. XXI:** **28–29**

"At Times in Flight: A Parable" (H. Roth), **Supp. IX:** 234

Attitudes toward History (Burke), **I:** 274

Atwan, Robert, **Supp. XVI:** 273, 277

At Weddings and Wakes (McDermott), **Supp. XVIII:** 155, **160–162,** 166

"At White River" (Haines), **Supp. XII:** 208–209

Atwood, Margaret, **Supp. IV Part 1:** 252; **Supp. V:** 119; **Supp. XI:** 317; **Supp. XIII: 19–39,** 291, 306; **Supp. XXI:** 39, 42

"Atwood's Gorgon Touch" (Davey), **Supp. XIII:** 33

"Aubade" (McCarriston), **Supp. XIV:** 271

"Aubade: November" (McCarriston), **Supp. XIV:** 261–262

"Aubade of an Early Homo Sapiens" (C. Frost), **Supp. XV:** 97–98
"Aubade: Opal and Silver" (Doty), **Supp. XI:** 129
"Au Bal Musette" (Van Vechten), **Supp. II Part 2:** 735
Auchincloss, Hugh D., **Supp. IV Part 2:** 679
Auchincloss, Louis, **I:** 375; **III:** 66; **Retro. Supp. I:** 370, 373; **Supp. IV Part 1:** 21–38
"Auction" (Simic), **Supp. VIII:** 278
"Auction, The" (Crane), **I:** 411
"Auction Model 1934" (Z. Fitzgerald), **Supp. IX:** 61
Auden, W. H., **I:** 71, 381, 539; **II:** 367, 368, 371, 376, 586; **III:** 17, 134, 269, 271, 292, 476–477, 504, 527, 530, 542, 615; **IV:** 136, 138, 240, 430; **Retro. Supp. I:** 430; **Retro. Supp. II:** 183, 242, 244, 323; **Supp. I Part 1:** 270; **Supp. I Part 2:** 552, 610; **Supp. II Part 1:** 1–28; **Supp. III Part 1:** 2, 3, 14, 26, 60, 61, 64, 341; **Supp. III Part 2:** 591, 595; **Supp. IV Part 1:** 79, 84, 136, 225, 302, 313; **Supp. IV Part 2:** 440, 465; **Supp. V:** 337; **Supp. VIII:** 19, 21, 22, 23, 30, 32, 155, 190; **Supp. IX:** 94, 287, 288; **Supp. X:** 35, 57, 59, 115–116, 117, 118–119; **Supp. XI:** 243, 244; **Supp. XII:** 253, 264–265, 266, 269–270; **Supp. XIV:** 156, 158, 160, 162, 163; **Supp. XV:** 74, 117–118, 139, 144, 186; **Supp. XIX:** 147, 151; **Supp. XX: 138; Supp. XXI:** 60, 98; **Supp. XXIII:** 117, 207
"Auden's OED" (McClatchy), **Supp. XII:** 264–265
"Audition" (Alvarez), **Supp. VII:** 10
Audubon, John James, **III:** 210; **IV:** 265; **Supp. IX:** 171; **Supp. XVI: 1–14**
Audubon, John Woodhouse, **Supp. XVI:** 10
Audubon, Maria Rebecca, **Supp. XVI:** 11
Audubon, Victor Gifford, **Supp. XVI:** 10
Audubon and His Journals (M. Audubon, ed.), **Supp. XVI:** 11, 12
Audubon Reader, The: The Best Writings of John James Audubon (Sanders, ed.), **Supp. XVI:** 269
Auer, Jane. *See* Bowles, Jane
Auerbach, Eric, **III:** 453
Auerbach, Nina, **Supp. I Part 1:** 40
"August" (Oliver), **Supp. VII:** 235
"August" (Rich), **Supp. I Part 2:** 564
"August 1968" (Auden), **Supp. II Part 1:** 25
"August Darks, The" (Clampitt), **Supp. IX:** 43, **50–51,** 52
Augustine, Saint, **I:** 279, 290; **II:** 537; **III:** 259, 270, 292, 300; **IV:** 69, 126; **Retro. Supp. I:** 247; **Supp. VIII:** 203; **Supp. XI:** 245; **Supp. XIII:** 89; **Supp. XXI:** 83; **Supp. XXII:** 92–93
August Snow (Price), **Supp. VI:** 264
"Au Jardin" (Pound), **III:** 465–466
Aunt Carmen's Book of Practical Saints (Mora), **Supp. XIII: 227–229**
"Aunt Cynthy Dallett" (Jewett), **II:** 393

"Aunt Gladys" (Karr), **Supp. XI:** 241
"Aunt Granny Lith" (Offutt), **Supp. XIX:** 165, 166
"Aunties, The" (Lamott), **Supp. XX: 141**
"Aunt Imogen" (Robinson), **III:** 521
"Aunt Jemima of the Ocean Waves" (Hayden), **Supp. II Part 1:** 368, 379
"Aunt Jennifer's Tigers" (Rich), **Supp. XV:** 252
Aunt Jo's Scrapbooks (Alcott), **Supp. I Part 1:** 43
"Aunt Mary" (Oliver), **Supp. VII:** 232
"Aunt Mary" (Stowe), **Supp. I Part 2:** 587
"Aunt Moon's Young Man" (Hogan), **Supp. IV Part 1:** 400
"Aunt Rectita's Good Friday" (X. J. Kennedy), **Supp. XV:** 166
"Aunt Sarah" (Lowell), **II:** 554
"Aunt Sue's Stories" (Hughes), **Retro. Supp. I:** 197, 199
"Aunt Violet's Canadian Honeymoon/ 1932" (Shields), **Supp. VII:** 311
"Aunt Violet's Things" (Shields), **Supp. VII:** 311–312
"Aurelia: Moon Jellies" (Mora), **Supp. XIII:** 224
"Aurelio" (Di Piero), **Supp. XIX:** 38
Au revoir les enfants (film, Malle), **Supp. XXIII:** 122
Aurora 7 (Mallon), **Supp. XIX:** 132, **135–136**
Aurora Leigh (E. Browning), **Retro. Supp. I:** 33; **Supp. XI:** 197
Aurora Means Dawn (Sanders), **Supp. XVI:** 268
Auroras of Autumn, The (Stevens), **Retro. Supp. I:** 297, 300, **309–312**
"Auroras of Autumn, The" (Stevens), **Retro. Supp. I:** 311, 312; **Supp. III Part 1:** 12
Auschwitz: the Nazis and the "Final Solution" (television documentary), **Supp. XVII:** 40
Auslander, Joseph, **Supp. XIV:** 120
"Auspex" (Frost), **Retro. Supp. I:** 122
"Auspex" (Lowell), **Supp. I Part 2:** 424
Austen, Jane, **I:** 130, 339, 375, 378; **II:** 272, 278, 287, 568–569, 577; **IV:** 8; **Retro. Supp. I:** 354; **Supp. I Part 1:** 267; **Supp. I Part 2:** 656, 715; **Supp. IV Part 1:** 300; **Supp. VIII:** 125, 167; **Supp. IX:** 128; **Supp. XII:** 310; **Supp. XV:** 338; **Supp. XX: 108; Supp. XXII:** 206
Auster, Paul, **Supp. XII: 21–39; Supp. XIV:** 292; **Supp. XXI:** 20
Austerities (Simic), **Supp. VIII: 276–278,** 283
"Austerities" (Simic), **Supp. VIII:** 277
Austin, Mary Hunter, **Retro. Supp. I:** 7; **Supp. IV Part 2:** 503; **Supp. X:** 29; **Supp. XIII:** 154
"Authentic Unconscious, The" (Trilling), **Supp. III Part 2:** 512
Author and Agent: Eudora Welty and Diarmuid Russell (Kreyling), **Retro. Supp. I:** 342, 345, 347, 349–350
"Author at Sixty, The" (Wilson), **IV:** 426

"Author of 'Beltraffio,' The" (James), **Retro. Supp. I:** 227
"Author's Explanation, The" (Larsen), **Supp. XVIII:** 131
"Author's House" (Fitzgerald), **Retro. Supp. I:** 98
"Author's Reflections, An: Willie Loman, Walter Younger, and He Who Must Live" (Hansberry), **Supp. IV Part 1:** 370
"Author to Her Book, The" (Bradstreet), **Supp. I Part 1:** 119; **Supp. V:** 117–118; **Supp. XV:** 125–126
"Autism Poem #20: The Knot Garden"(Crooker), **Supp. XXIII:** 56–57
"Autobiographical Note" (H. Miller), **III:** 174–175
"Autobiographical Notes" (Baldwin), **Supp. I Part 1:** 54
"Autobiographical Notes" (Holmes), **Supp. I Part 1:** 301
"Autobiographic Chapter, An" (Bourne), **I:** 236
Autobiography (Franklin), **II:** 102, 103, 108, 121–122, 302
Autobiography (James), **I:** 462
"Autobiography" (MacLeish), **III:** 20
Autobiography (Van Buren), **III:** 473
Autobiography (W. C. Williams), **Supp. I Part 1:** 254
Autobiography (Zukofsky), **Supp. III Part 2:** 627
Autobiography by Jesus of Nazareth (Pettis), **Supp. XXIII:** 189
"Autobiography"(Dybek), **Supp. XXIII:** 78
"Autobiography in the Shape of a Book Review" (Bynner), **Supp. XV:** 40
"Autobiography of a Confluence, The" (Gunn Allen), **Supp. IV Part 1:** 321
Autobiography of Alice B. Toklas, The (Stein), **IV:** 26, 30, 35, 43; **Supp. IV Part 1:** 11, 81
Autobiography of an Ex-Colored Man, The (Johnson), **Supp. II Part 1:** 33, 194; **Supp. XVIII:** 127; **Supp. XXII:** 7
Autobiography of a Schizophrenic Girl (Renée), **Supp. XVI:** 64, 66
Autobiography of a Thief, The (Hapgood), **Supp. XVII:** 96, 101–102
Autobiography of Benjamin Franklin (Franklin), **Supp. IV Part 1:** 5
Autobiography of LeRoi Jones, The (Baraka), **Retro. Supp. I:** 411
Autobiography of Malcolm X (Little), **Supp. I Part 1:** 66; **Supp. X:** 27; **Supp. XIII:** 264; **Supp. XXII:** 95
Autobiography of Mark Twain, The (Twain), **IV:** 209
Autobiography of My Mother, The (Kincaid), **Supp. VII:** 182, 188 190, 191, 192, 193
Autobiography of Red: A Novel in Verse (Carson), **Supp. XII:** 97, **106–110**
Autobiography of Upton Sinclair, The (Sinclair), **Supp. V:** 276, 282
Autobiography of W. E. B. Du Bois, The (Du Bois), **Supp. II Part 1:** 159, 186

Autobiography of William Carlos Williams, The (W. C. Williams), **Retro. Supp. I:** 51, 428

Autocrat of the Breakfast-Table, The (Holmes), **Supp. I Part 1:** 306–307

"Automatic Gate, The" (Southern), **Supp. XI:** 294

"Automotive Passacaglia" (H. Miller), **III:** 186

"Autopsy Room, The" (Carver), **Supp. III Part 1:** 137

"Auto Wreck" (Shapiro), **Supp. II Part 2:** 706

"Autre Temps" (Wharton), **IV:** 320, 324

"Autumn, Mist" (Hull), **Supp. XXI:** 133

"Autumn Afternoon" (Farrell), **II:** 45

"Autumnal" (Eberhart), **I:** 540–541

"Autumn Begins in Martins Ferry, Ohio" (Wright), **Supp. III Part 2:** 599

"Autumn Courtship, An" (Caldwell), **I:** 309

"Autumn Equinox" (Skloot), **Supp. XX:** 202

Autumn Garden, The (Hellman), **Supp. I Part 1:** 285–286, 290

"Autumn Garden, The: Mechanics and Dialectics" (Felheim), **Supp. I Part 1:** 297

"Autumn Holiday, An" (Jewett), **II:** 391; **Retro. Supp. II:** 140–141

"Autumn Musings" (Harte), **Supp. II Part 1:** 336

Autumn Spring (Pickering), **Supp. XXI:** 204–205, 206

"Autumn Within" (Longfellow), **II:** 499

"Autumn Woods" (Bryant), **Supp. I Part 1:** 164

"Au Vieux Jardin" (Aldington), **Supp. I Part 1:** 257

"Aux Imagistes" (W. C. Williams), **Supp. I Part 1:** 266

Avakian, Aram, **Supp. XI:** 294, 295, 309

"Ave Atque Vale" (Bynner), Supp. XV: 49

Avedon, Richard, **Supp. I Part 1:** 58; **Supp. V:** 194; **Supp. X:** 15

Aveling, Edward, **Supp. XVI:** 85

"Avenue" (Pinsky), **Supp. VI:** 248

Avenue Bearing the Initial of Christ into the New World: Poems 1946–1964 (Kinnell), **Supp. III Part 1:** 235, 239–241

"Avenue of the Americas" (Simic), **Supp. VIII:** 278

"Average Torture" (Karr), **Supp. XI:** 243

Avery, George C., **Supp. XX:** 84

Avery, John, **Supp. I Part 1:** 153

"Avey" (Toomer), **Supp. IX:** 317

Avon's Harvest (Robinson), **III:** 510

Awake and Sing! (Odets), **Supp. II Part 2:** 530, 531, 536–538, 550; **Supp. IV Part 2:** 587

Awake at Midnight"(Schott), **Supp. XXIII:** 246

Awake in Spain (O'Hara), **Supp. XXIII:** 216

Awakening, The (Chopin), **Retro. Supp. I:** 10; **Retro. Supp. II:** 57, 59, 60, 67, **68–71,** 73; **Supp. I Part 1:** 200, 201, 202, 211, 220–225; **Supp. V:** 304; **Supp. VIII:** 198; **Supp. XII:** 170

Awakening Land, The (Richter), **Supp. XVIII:** 207, 215

Awful Rowing Toward God, The (Sexton), **Supp. II Part 2:** 694–696

Awiakta, Marilou, **Supp. IV Part 1:** 319, 335

Awkward Age, The (James), **II:** 332; **Retro. Supp. I:** 229, **230–231**

Axe Handles (Snyder), **Supp. VIII:** 303–305

Axel's Castle: A Study in the Imaginative Literature of 1870 to 1930 (Wilson), **I:** 185; **II:** 577; **IV:** 428, 431, 438, 439, 443; **Supp. VIII:** 101

"Ax-Helve, The" (Frost), **Retro. Supp. I:** 133

Azikewe, Nnamdi, **Supp. IV Part 1:** 361

"Aztec Angel" (Salinas), **Supp. XIII:** 314

Aztec Treasure House, The: New and Selected Essays (Connell), **Supp. XIV:** 80, 97

B

Babbitt (Lewis), **II:** 442, 443–445, 446, 447, 449; **III:** 63–64, 394; **IV:** 326

Babbitt, Irving, **I:** 247; **II:** 456; **III:** 315, 461, 613; **IV:** 439; **Retro. Supp. I:** 55; **Supp. I Part 2:** 423

Babcock, Elisha, **Supp. II Part 1:** 69

Babel, Isaac, **IV:** 1; **Supp. IX:** 260; **Supp. XII:** 308–309; **Supp. XVII:** 41; **Supp. XXIII:** 68

Babel, Isaak, **Supp. XIV:** 83, 84

Babel to Byzantium (Dickey), **Supp. IV Part 1:** 177, 185

Baber, Asa, **Supp. XXIII:** 52

Baber, Bob Henry, **Supp. XXIII:** 39

Babeuf, François, **Supp. I Part 2:** 518

"Babies, The" (Strand), **Supp. IV Part 2:** 625

Babouk (Endore), **Supp. XVII: 56–57,** 61, **64**

Baby, Come on Inside (Wagoner), **Supp. IX:** 335

"Baby, The" (Barthelme), **Supp. IV Part 1:** 49

Baby Doll (T. Williams), **IV:** 383, 386, 387, 389, 395

"Baby Face" (Sandburg), **III:** 584

"Babylon Revisited" (Fitzgerald), **II:** 95; **Retro. Supp. I:** 109

"Baby or the Botticelli, The" (Gass), **Supp. VI:** 92

"Baby Pictures of Famous Dictators" (Simic), **Supp. VIII:** 276

"Baby's Breath" (Bambara), **Supp. XI:** 15, 16

"Babysitter, The" (Coover), **Supp. V:** 43–44

"Baby Villon" (Levine), **Supp. V:** 182

Bacall, Lauren, **Supp. IV Part 1:** 130

"Baccalaureate" (MacLeish), **III:** 4

Bacchae, The (Euripides), **Supp. VIII:** 182

Bach, Johann Sebastian, **Supp. I Part 1:** 363; **Supp. III Part 2:** 611, 612, 619

Bachardy, Don, **Supp. XIV:** 166, 170, 172, 173

Bache, Richard, **Supp. I Part 2:** 504

Bachelard, Gaston, **Supp. XIII:** 225; **Supp. XVI:** 292

"Bachelor Girl, The" (Boyce), **Supp. XXI:** 3

Bachelor Girls (Wasserstein), **Supp. XV: 327–328,** 332

Bachman, John, **Supp. XVI:** 10, 11

Bachmann, Ingeborg, **Supp. IV Part 1:** 310; **Supp. VIII:** 272

Bachofen, J. J., **Supp. I Part 2:** 560, 567

Back Bog Beast Bait (Shepard), **Supp. III Part 2:** 437, 438

Backbone (C. Bly), **Supp. XVI: 34–36,** 37, 40, 41

Back Country, The (Snyder), **Supp. VIII: 296–299**

"Back from the Argentine" (Leopold), **Supp. XIV:** 186

"Background with Revolutionaries" (MacLeish), **III:** 14–15

"Back in the Saddle Again" (Swados), **Supp. XIX:** 259

Back in the World (Wolff), **Supp. VII:** 344, 345

Backis, Charles, **Supp. XXI:** 195

"Backlash Blues, The" (Hughes), **Supp. I Part 1:** 343

"Backlash of Kindness, A" (Nye), **Supp. XIII:** 285, 286

"Backslider, The" (R. Fisher), **Supp. XIX:** 70, 71

"Back Street Guy" (Halliday), **Supp. XIX:** 88

Back to China (Fiedler), **Supp. XIII: 102–103**

Back to Methuselah (Shaw), **IV:** 64

"Backwacking: A Plea to the Senator" (Ellison), **Retro. Supp. II:** 126; **Supp. II Part 1:** 248

Backward Glance, A (Wharton), **Retro. Supp. I:** 360, 363, 366, 378, 380, 382; **Supp. XX:** 229

"Backward Glance o'er Travel'd Roads, A" (Whitman), **IV:** 348

Bacon, Francis, **II:** 1, 8, 11, 15–16, 111; **III:** 284; **Retro. Supp. I:** 247; **Supp. I Part 1:** 310; **Supp. I Part 2:** 388; **Supp. IX:** 104; **Supp. XIV:** 22, 210

Bacon, Helen, **Supp. X:** 57

Bacon, Katie, **Supp. XXII:** 207; **Supp. XXIII:** 275

Bacon, Leonard, **II:** 530; **Supp. XXII:** 273

Bacon, Roger, **IV:** 69

"Bacterial War, The" (Nemerov), **III:** 272

Bad and the Beautiful, The (film), **Supp. XVIII:** 250

Bad Boy Brawly Brown (Mosley), **Supp. XIII:** 237, 239, 240–241

Bad Boys (Cisneros), **Supp. VII:** 58

"Bad Dream" (Taylor), **Supp. V:** 320

Badè, William Frederic, **Supp. IX:** 178

"Bad Fisherman, The" (Wagoner), **Supp. IX:** 328

Bad for Each Other (film), **Supp. XIII:** 174

"Badger" (Clare), **II:** 387

Badger, A. G., **Supp. I Part 1:** 356

Bad Government and Silly Literature (C. Bly), **Supp. XVI:** 37, 38, 40

Badlands (film; Malick), **Supp. XV:** 351

"Bad Lay" (McCarriston), **Supp. XIV:** 267

Badley, Linda, **Supp. V:** 148

Bad Man, A (Elkin), **Supp. VI: 47**

Bad Man Ballad (Sanders), **Supp. XVI:** 268

Bad Man Blues: A Portable George Garrett (Garrett), **Supp. VII:** 111

"Bad Music, The" (Jarrell), **II:** 369

"Bad People" (Halliday), **Supp. XIX:** 90, 91

"Bad Summer on K2, A" (Krakauer and Child), **Supp. XVIII:** 107, 108

"Bad Woman, A" (Fante), **Supp. XI:** 165

Baeck, Leo, **Supp. V:** 260

Baecker, Diann L., **Supp. VIII:** 128

Baer, William, **Supp. XIII:** 112, 118, 129; **Supp. XXIII:** 124

Baez, Joan, **Supp. IV Part 1:** 200; **Supp. VIII:** 200, 202; **Supp. XVIII:** 24, 25–26, 27

Bag of Bones (King), **Supp. V:** 139, 148, 151

"Bagpipe Music" (MacNeice), **Supp. X:** 117

"Baha'í Faith: Only Church in World That Does Not Discriminate" (Locke), **Supp. XIV:** 200

Bahá'u'lláh, **Supp. XX: 117, 121, 122**

"Bahá'u'lláh in the Garden of Ridwan" (Hayden), **Supp. II Part 1:** 370, 378

Bahr, David, **Supp. XV:** 66

Bahr, Thomas, **Supp. XXII:** 206, 214

"Bailbondsman, The" (Elkin), **Supp. VI:** 49, **50,** 58

Bailey, Gamaliel, **Supp. I Part 2:** 587, 590

Bailey, Peter, **Supp. XVI:** 69

Bailey, William, **Supp. IV Part 2:** 631, 634

Bailey's Café (Naylor), **Supp. VIII: 226–228**

Bailyn, Bernard, **Supp. I Part 2:** 484, 506

Bair, Deirdre, **Supp. X:** 181, 186, 187, 188, 192, 194, 195, 196, 197

Baird, Linnett, **Supp. XII:** 299

Baird, Peggy, **I:** 385, 401

Baiting the Void (Schott), **Supp. XXIII: 247–248**

Bakan, David, **I:** 59

Baker, Carlos, **II:** 259

Baker, Chet, **Supp. XXI:** 131

Baker, David, **Supp. IX:** 298; **Supp. XI:** 121, 142, 153; **Supp. XII:** 175, 191–192; **Supp. XIX:** 115

Baker, George Pierce, **III:** 387; **IV:** 453, 455

Baker, Gladys, **Supp. XIV:** 121

Baker, Houston, **Supp. XXII:** 6

Baker, Houston A., Jr., **Retro. Supp. II:** 121; **Supp. IV Part 1:** 365; **Supp. X:** 324

Baker, Katherine, **Supp. XX: 69**

Baker, Kevin, **Supp. XIV:** 96

Baker, Mabel, **Supp. XVIII:** 259, 263, 266–267, 269

Baker, Nicholson, **Supp. XIII: 41–57**

Baker, Robert, **Supp. XVI:** 288, 290

Bakerman, Jane S., **Supp. IV Part 2:** 468

Bakhtin, Mikhail, **Retro. Supp. II:** 273; **Supp. IV Part 1:** 301; **Supp. X:** 120, 239; **Supp. XXII:** 259

Bakst, Léon, **Supp. IX:** 66

Bakunin, Mikhail Aleksandrovich, **IV:** 429

Balaban, John, **Supp. XIX:** 281

Balakian, Anna, **Supp. XXIII:** 20

Balakian, Diran, **Supp. XXIII:** 28

Balakian, Grigoris, **Supp. XXIII:** 28, 29–32

Balakian, Jan, **Supp. XV:** 327

Balakian, Nona, **Supp. XXIII:** 20

Balakian, Peter, **Supp. XXIII: 19–34**

"Balance" (Bierds), **Supp. XVII:** 31

"Balance" (Nelson), **Supp. XVIII:** 174–175

Balbo, Ned, **Supp. XVII:** 120; **Supp. XIX:** 161

Balbuena, Bernado de, **Supp. V:** 11

Balch, Emily Greene, **Supp. I Part 1:** 25

Balcony, The (Genet), **I:** 84

Bald Soprano, The (Ionesco), **I:** 74

Baldwin, David, **Supp. I Part 1:** 47, 48, 49, 50, 51, 54, 65, 66

Baldwin, James, **Retro. Supp. II: 1–17; Supp. I Part 1: 47–71,** 337, 341; **Supp. II Part 1:** 40; **Supp. III Part 1:** 125; **Supp. IV Part 1:** 1, 10, 11, 163, 369; **Supp. V:** 201; **Supp. VIII:** 88, 198, 235, 349; **Supp. X:** 136, 324; **Supp. XI:** 288, 294; **Supp. XIII:** 46, 111, 181, 186, 294; **Supp. XIV:** 54, 71, 73, 306; **Supp. XVI:** 135, 141, 143; **Supp. XVIII:** 25; **Supp. XX: 147; Supp. XXI:** 245

Baldwin, Samuel, **Supp. I Part 1:** 48

Balitas, Vincent D., **Supp. XVI:** 222

Balkian, Nona, **Supp. XI:** 230

Balkun, Mary McAleer, **Supp. XX: 281**

Ball, Gordon, **Supp. XIV:** 148

Ball, John, **Supp. XV:** 202

"Ballad: Between the Box Cars" (Warren), **IV:** 245

"Ballade" (MacLeish), **III:** 4

"Ballade at Thirty-Five" (Parker), **Supp. IX:** 192

"Ballade for the Duke of Orléans" (Wilbur), **Supp. III Part 2:** 556

"Ballade of Broken Flutes, The" (Robinson), **III:** 505

"Ballade of Meaty Inversions" (White), **Supp. I Part 2:** 676

"Ballad of a Thin Man" (song, Dylan), **Supp. XVIII:** 30, 31

"Ballad of Aunt Geneva, The" (Nelson), **Supp. XVIII:** 175

"Ballad of Billie Potts, The" (Warren), **IV:** 241–242, 243, 253

"Ballad of Carmilhan, The" (Longfellow), **II:** 505

"ballad of chocolate Mabbie, the" (Brooks), **Supp. IV Part 1:** 15

"Ballad of Dead Ladies, The" (Villon), **Retro. Supp. I:** 286

Ballad of Dingus Magee, The (Markson), **Supp. XVII:** 139, 141

"Ballad of East and West, The" (Kipling), **Supp. IX:** 246; **Supp. XX:** 23

"Ballad of Jesse Neighbours, The" (Humphrey), **Supp. IX:** 100

"Ballad of Jesus of Nazareth, A" (Masters), **Supp. I Part 2:** 459

"Ballad of John Cable and Three Gentlemen" (Merwin), **Supp. III Part 1:** 342

"Ballad of Larry and Club" (Jarman), **Supp. XVII:** 115

"Ballad of Nat Turner, The" (Hayden), **Supp. II Part 1:** 378

"Ballad of Pearl May Lee, The" (Brooks), **Supp. III Part 1:** 74, 75

Ballad of Remembrance, A (Hayden), **Supp. II Part 1:** 367

"Ballad of Remembrance, A" (Hayden), **Supp. II Part 1:** 368, 372, 373

"Ballad of Ruby, The" (Sarton), **Supp. VIII:** 259–260

"Ballad of San Isidro, The" (Espaillat), **Supp. XXI:** 108

"Ballad of Sue Ellen Westerfield, The" (Hayden), **Supp. II Part 1:** 364

Ballad of the Brown Girl, The (Cullen), **Supp. IV Part 1:** 167, 168, 169–170, 173

"Ballad of the Brown Girl, The" (Cullen), **Supp. IV Part 1:** 168

"Ballad of the Children of the Czar, The" (Schwartz), **Supp. II Part 2:** 649

"Ballad of the Girl Whose Name Is Mud" (Hughes), **Retro. Supp. I:** 205

"Ballad of the Goodly Fere", **III:** 458

"Ballad of the Harp-Weaver" (Millay), **III:** 135

"Ballad of the Sad Cafe, The" (McCullers), **II:** 586, 587, 588, 592, 595, 596–600, 604, 605, 606

"Ballad of the Sixties" (Sarton), **Supp. VIII:** 259

"Ballad of Trees and the Master, A" (Lanier), **Supp. I Part 1:** 370

"Ballad of Typical Lovers" (Taggard), **Supp. XXII:** 277

"Ballad of William Sycamore, The" (Benét), **Supp. XI:** 44, 47

Ballads and Other Poems (Longfellow), **II:** 489; **III:** 412, 422; **Retro. Supp. II:** 157, 168

Ballads for Sale (Lowell), **II:** 527

"Ballads of Lenin" (Hughes), **Supp. I Part 1:** 331

Ballantyne, Sheila, **Supp. V:** 70

Ballard, J. G., **Supp. XVI:** 123, 124; **Supp. XVIII:** 136

Ballard, Josephine. *See* McMurtry, Josephine

"Ballena" (Mora), **Supp. XIII:** 224

"Ballet in Numbers for Mary Ellen, A" (Karr), **Supp. XI:** 241

"Ballet of a Buffoon, The" (Sexton), **Supp. II Part 2:** 693

"Ballet of the Fifth Year, The" (Schwartz), **Supp. II Part 2:** 650

Ball Four (Bouton), **Supp. XX: 274**

"Ball Game, The" (Creeley), **Supp. IV Part 1:** 140

Ballistics (Collins), **Supp. XXI:** 57, 65

"Ballistics" (Collins), **Supp. XXI:** 65

"Balloon Hoax, The" (Poe), **III:** 413, 420

"Balm of Recognition, The: Rectifying Wrongs through Generations" (E. Hoffman, lecture), **Supp. XVI:** 155

Balo (Toomer), **Supp. III Part 2:** 484

Balsan, Consuelo, **IV:** 313–314

Balthus, **Supp. IV Part 2:** 623

Balthus Poems, The (Dobyns), **Supp. XIII:** 87

Baltimore, Lord, **I:** 132

Balzac, Honoré de, **I:** 103, 123, 339, 376, 474, 485, 499, 509, 518; **II:** 307, 322, 324, 328, 336, 337; **III:** 61, 174, 184, 320, 382; **IV:** 192; **Retro. Supp. I:** 91, 217, 218, 235; **Retro. Supp. II:** 93; **Supp. I Part 2:** 647; **Supp. XVI:** 72

Bambara, Toni Cade, **Supp. XI: 1–23**

Bam opgrunt (At the abyss) (Asch), **Supp. XXIII:** 6

Banana Bottom (McKay), **Supp. X:** 132, **139–140**

Bananas (film; Allen), **Supp. XV:** 3, 4

Bancal, Jean, **Supp. I Part 2:** 514

Bancroft, George, **I:** 544; **Supp. I Part 2:** 479; **Supp. XXII:** 33

Band, Millen, **Supp. XVIII:** 238

Bandaged Nude, The (Ryan as Finnegan), **Supp. XVIII:** 233, **235–236**

Bandbox (Mallon), **Supp. XIX:** 132, 143

Band of Angels (Warren), **IV:** 245, 254–255

Bandung Files (television series), **Supp. XXI:** 170

Bang the Drum Slowly (Harris), **II:** 424–425

Banjo: A Story without a Plot (McKay), **Supp. X:** 132, **138–139**

"Banjo Song, A" (Dunbar), **Supp. II Part 1:** 197

Bank Director's Son, The: A Real and Intensely Interesting Revelation of City Life (Lippard), **Supp. XXIII:** 184

Bankhead, Tallulah, **IV:** 357; **Supp. IV Part 2:** 574

"Banking Potatoes" (Komunyakaa), **Supp. XIII:** 126

"Bank of England Restriction, The" (Adams), **I:** 4

Banks, Joanne Trautmann, **Supp. XIII:** 297

Banks, Russell, **Supp. V: 1–19,** 227; **Supp. IX:** 153; **Supp. X:** 85; **Supp. XI:** 178; **Supp. XII:** 295, 309, 343; **Supp. XX: 90**

"Banned Poem" (Nye), **Supp. XIII:** 282

Bannon, Barbara, **Supp. XI:** 228

"Banyan" (Swenson), **Supp. IV Part 2:** 651, 652

"Baptism" (Olsen). *See* "O Yes" (Olsen)

"Baptism" (Trethewey), **Supp. XXI:** 246

Baptism, The (Baraka), **Supp. II Part 1:** 40, 41–42, 43

Baptism of Desire (Erdrich), **Supp. IV Part 1:** 259

Barabtarlo, Gennady, **Retro. Supp. I:** 278

Baraka, Imamu Amiri (LeRoi Jones), **Retro. Supp. I:** 411; **Retro. Supp. II:** 280; **Supp. I Part 1:** 63; **Supp. II Part 1: 29–63,** 247, 250; **Supp. III Part 1:** 83; **Supp. IV Part 1:** 169,

244, 369; **Supp. VIII:** 295, 329, 330, 332; **Supp. X:** 324, 328; **Supp. XIII:** 94; **Supp. XIV:** 125, 144; **Supp. XXI:** 172, 227, 228; **Supp. XXIII:** 215

"Bar at the Andover Inn, The" (Matthews), **Supp. IX:** 168

"Barbados" (Marshall), **Supp. XI:** 281

"Barbara Frietchie" (Whittier), **Supp. I Part 2:** 695–696

Barbarella (film), **Supp. XI:** 293, **307–308**

"Barbarian Status of Women, The" (Veblen), **Supp. I Part 2:** 636–637

Barbarous Coast, The (Macdonald), **Supp. IV Part 2:** 472, 474

Barbary Shore (Mailer), **III:** 27, 28, 30–31, 33, 35, 36, 40, 44; **Retro. Supp. II: 199–200,** 207; **Supp. XIV:** 162

Barber, Charles, **Supp. XXIII:** 125

Barber, David, **Supp. IV Part 2:** 550; **Supp. XII:** 188–189

Barber, Rowland, **Supp. IV Part 2:** 581

Barber, Samuel, **Supp. IV Part 1:** 84

"Barber's Unhappiness, The" (Saunders), **Supp. XIX:** 229

"Barclay of Ury" (Whittier), **Supp. I Part 2:** 693

Barcott, Bruce, **Supp. XVII:** 32

Bard of Savagery, The: Thorstein Veblen and Modern Social Theory (Diggins), **Supp. I Part 2:** 650

"Barefoot Boy, The" (Whittier), **Supp. I Part 2:** 691, 699–700

Barefoot in the Park (Simon), **Supp. IV Part 2:** 575, 578–579, 586, 590

Bare Hills, The (Winters), **Supp. II Part 2:** 786, 788

"Bare Hills, The" (Winters), **Supp. II Part 2:** 790

Barely and Widely (Zukofsky), **Supp. III Part 2:** 627, 628, 635

Barenblat, Rachel, **Supp. XIII:** 274

Barfield, Owen, **III:** 274, 279

"Bargain Lost, The" (Poe), **III:** 411

Barillas, William, **Supp. XIV:** 177

Barillet, Pierre, **Supp. XVI:** 194

Barker, Arthur, **Supp. XIII:** 167

Barker, Clive, **Supp. V:** 142

Barking Dog (Budbill), **Supp. XIX:** 1, 5

"Barking Man" (Bell), **Supp. X:** 9

Barking Man and Other Stories (Bell), **Supp. X: 9**

Barksdale, Richard, **Retro. Supp. I:** 202, 205; **Supp. I Part 1:** 341, 346

Barlow, Joel, **Supp. I Part 1:** 124; **Supp. I Part 2:** 511, 515, 521; **Supp. II Part 1: 65–86,** 268

Barlow, Judith, **Supp. XXI:** 6

Barlow, Ruth Baldwin (Mrs. Joel Barlow), **Supp. II Part 1:** 69

"B.A.R. Man, The" (Yates), **Supp. XI:** 341

Barnaby Rudge (Dickens), **III:** 421

Barnard, Frederick, **Supp. I Part 2:** 684

Barnard, Rita, **Retro. Supp. II:** 324

Barn Blind (Smiley), **Supp. VI: 292–293**

"Barn Burning" (Faulkner), **II:** 72, 73; **Supp. IV Part 2:** 682; **Supp. XX:** 174

Barnes, Djuna, **Supp. III Part 1: 31–46; Supp. IV Part 1:** 79, 80; **Supp. XVI:** 282; **Supp. XXII:** 165, 167

Barnes, Kim, **Supp. XVIII:** 293

Barnet, Andrea, **Supp. XXII:** 159, 164

Barnett, Claudia, **Supp. XV:** 323, 330, 334

Barnett, Samuel, **Supp. I Part 1:** 2

Barnhardt, Wilton, **Supp. XXII:** 266

"Barn Owl" (Kooser), **Supp. XIX:** 123

Barnstone, Tony, **Supp. XIII:** 115, 126

Barnstone, Willis, **Supp. I Part 2:** 458

Barnum, P. T., **Supp. I Part 2:** 703

Baroja, Pío, **I:** 478

Baron, Zach, **Supp. XVIII:** 150

"Baroque Comment" (Bogan), **Supp. III Part 1:** 56, 58

"Baroque Sunburst, A" (Clampitt), **Supp. IX:** 49

"Baroque Wall-Fountain in the Villa Sciarra, A" (Wilbur), **Supp. III Part 2:** 553

Barr, Robert, **I:** 409, 424

Barracks Thief, The (Wolff), **Supp. VII:** 344–345

"Barred Owl" (Offutt), **Supp. XIX:** 170

Barren Ground (Glasgow), **II:** 174, 175, 178, 179, 184–185, 186, 187, 188, 189, 191, 192, 193, 194; **Supp. X:** 228

Barrés, Auguste M., **I:** 228

Barresi, Dorothy, **Supp. XV:** 100, 102

Barrett, Amy, **Supp. XVIII:** 136

Barrett, E. B., **Supp. XV:** 309

Barrett, Elizabeth, **Supp. IV Part 2:** 430

Barrett, George, **Supp. IX:** 250

Barrett, Ralph, **Supp. I Part 2:** 462

Barrie, J. M., **Supp. XX: 234**

Barrier, Rober G., **Supp. XXI:** 48–49

Barrier of a Common Language: An American Looks at Contemporary British Poetry (Gioia), **Supp. XV:** 112, **116–117**

"Barroco: An Essay" (Sobin), **Supp. XVI:** 291

Barron, Jonathan, **Supp. IX:** 299

Barrow, John, **II:** 18

Barrus, Clara, **I:** 220

Barry, Iris, **Supp. XIII:** 170

Barry, Philip, **Retro. Supp. I:** 104; **Supp. IV Part 1:** 83; **Supp. V:** 95

Barstow, Elizabeth Drew. *See* Stoddard, Elizabeth

Bartas, Seigneur du, **IV:** 157

Barth, John, **I: 121–143; Supp. I Part 1:** 100; **Supp. III Part 1:** 217; **Supp. IV Part 1:** 48, 379; **Supp. V:** 39, 40; **Supp. IX:** 208; **Supp. X:** 263, 301, 302, 307; **Supp. XI:** 309; **Supp. XII:** 29, 289, 316; **Supp. XIII:** 41, 101, 104; **Supp. XVII:** 183; **Supp. XVIII:** 136, 140, 141; **Supp. XX: 21; Supp. XXII:** 259, 261; **Supp. XXIII:** 42

Barth, Karl, **III:** 40, 258, 291, 303, 309; **IV:** 225; **Retro. Supp. I:** 325, 326, 327

Barth, Robert C., **Supp. XV:** 169

Barthé, Richmond, **Retro. Supp. II:** 115

Barthelme, Donald, **Supp. IV Part 1: 39–58,** 227; **Supp. V:** 2, 39, 44; **Supp.**

VIII: 75, 138; **Supp. X:** 263; **Supp. XI:** 25; **Supp. XII:** 29; **Supp. XIII:** 41, 46; **Supp. XVI:** 206; **Supp. XIX:** 235

Barthelme, Frederick, **Supp. XI: 25–41; Supp. XXI:** 38

Barthelme, Peter, **Supp. XI:** 25

Barthelme, Steven, **Supp. XI:** 25, 27, 37

Barthes, Roland, **Supp. IV Part 1:** 39, 119, 126; **Supp. XIII:** 83; **Supp. XVI:** 285, 294; **Supp. XVII:** 244

Bartholomew and the Oobleck (Geisel), **Supp. XVI:** 104

"Bar Time" (B. Collins), **Supp. XVII:** 245

"Bartleby, the Scrivener; A Story of Wall-Street" (Melville), **III:** 88–89; **Retro. Supp. I:** 255

Bartleby in Manhattan and Other Essays (Hardwick), **Supp. III Part 1:** 204, 210

"Bartleby the Scrivener" (Melville), **Supp. XVIII:** 4

Bartlet, Phebe, **I:** 562

Bartlett, Lee, **Supp. VIII:** 291

Bartlett, Mary Dougherty, **Supp. IV Part 1:** 335

Barton, Bruce, **III:** 14; **Retro. Supp. I:** 179

Barton, Priscilla. *See* Morison, Mrs. Samuel Eliot (Priscilla Barton)

Barton, Ralph, **Supp. XVI:** 195

Barton, Rev. William E., **Retro. Supp. I:** 179

Bartov, Omer, **Supp. XVI:** 153–154

Bartram, John, **Supp. I Part 1:** 244

Bartram, William, **II:** 313; **Supp. IX:** 171; **Supp. X:** 223

Barzun, Jacques, **Supp. XIV:** 54

"Basement" (Bambara), **Supp. XI:** 5

Basement Tapes, The (album, Dylan), **Supp. XVIII:** 27, 30, 32

"Base of All Metaphysics, The" (Whitman), **IV:** 348

"Base Stealer, The" (Francis), **Supp. IX:** 82

Bashevis, Isaac. *See* Singer, Isaac Bashevis

Bashir, Antonious, **Supp. XX: 116, 120**

Basil Stories, The (Fitzgerald), **Retro. Supp. I:** 109

Basin and Range (McPhee), **Supp. III Part 1:** 309

"Basin of Eggs, A" (Swenson), **Supp. IV Part 2:** 645

"Basket, The" (Lowell), **II:** 522

"Basketball and Beefeaters" (McPhee), **Supp. III Part 1:** 296

"Basketball and Poetry: The Two Richies" (Dunn), **Supp. XI:** 140

"Basketball Player" (L. Michaels), **Supp. XVI:** 209

"Basket of Trips"(Strout), **Supp. XXIII:** 283, 285

Baskin, Leonard, **Supp. X:** 58, 71; **Supp. XV:** 348

Bass, George, **Supp. XXII:** 6

Bass, Rick, **Supp. XIV:** 227; **Supp. XVI: 15–29; Supp. XXI:** 40, 45

Bassard, Katherine Clay, **Supp. XXII:** 148

Basso, Hamilton, **Retro. Supp. I:** 80

Bastard, The (Caldwell), **I:** 291, 292, 308

"Bastille Day" (Lamott), **Supp. XX: 143**

"Bat, The" (Kcnyon), **Supp. VII:** 168

Bataille, Georges, **Supp. VIII:** 4; **Supp. XII:** 1

"Batard" (London), **II:** 468–469

Batchelor, John Calvin, **Supp. XIX:** 142

Bate, W. J., **II:** 531

Bates, Arlo, **Retro. Supp. I:** 35

Bates, Blanche, **Supp. XVI:** 182

Bates, Kathy, **Supp. XIII:** 207

Bates, Lee, **Retro. Supp. II:** 46

Bates, Milton J., **Supp. XII:** 62

Bates, Sylvia Chatfield, **II:** 586

Bateson, Gregory, **Supp. XV:** 146

"Bath, The" (Carver), **Supp. III Part 1:** 144, 145

"Bath, The" (Snyder), **Supp. VIII:** 302

Bathwater Wine (Coleman), **Supp. XI:** 83, 90, **91**

"Batter my heart, three person'd God" (Donne), **Supp. I Part 2:** 726; **Supp. XVII:** 119

"Battle, The" (Simpson), **Supp. IX:** 268–269

Battle Cry (film), **Supp. XX: 246**

Battle Cry (Uris), **Supp. XX: 243, 246, 248–250, 255, 256**

Battlefield Where the Moon Says I Love You, The (Stanford), **Supp. XV:** 345

Battle for the Solomons (Wolfert), **Supp. XXI:** 267

Battle-Ground, The (Glasgow), **II:** 175, 176, 177, 178, 193

"Battle Hymn of the Republic" (Sandburg), **III:** 585

"Battle Hymn of the Republic, The" (Howe), **III:** 505

"Battle Hymn of the Republic, The" (Updike), **Retro. Supp. I:** 324

Battle of Angels (T. Williams), **IV:** 380, 381, 383, 385, 386, 387

"Battle of Lovell's Pond, The" (Longfellow), **II:** 493

Battle of the Atlantic, The (Morison), **Supp. I Part 2:** 490

"Battle of the Baltic, The" (Campbell), **Supp. I Part 1:** 309

"Battle of the Bunker, The" (Snodgrass), **Supp. VI:** 319–320

"***Battle of the Century!!!, The***" (Goldbarth), **Supp. XII:** 193

Battle of the Little Big Horn, The (Sandoz), **Supp. XXIII:** 146

Battle-Pieces and Aspects of the War (Melville), **II:** 538–539; **III:** 92; **IV:** 350; **Retro. Supp. I:** 257

"Battler, The" (Hemingway), **II:** 248; **Retro. Supp. I:** 175

"Baubles after Bombs" (Peacock), **Supp. XIX:** 200

"Baudelaire" (Schwartz), **Supp. II Part 2:** 663

Baudelaire, Charles, **I:** 58, 63, 384, 389, 420, 569; **II:** 543, 544–545, 552; **III:** 137, 141–142, 143, 409, 417, 418, 421, 428, 448, 466, 474; **IV:** 74, 79, 80, 87, 211, 286; **Retro. Supp. I:** 56, 90; **Retro. Supp. II:** 261, 262, 322, 326; **Supp. I Part 1:** 271; **Supp. III Part 1:** 4, 6, 105; **Supp. XIII:** 77, 284; **Supp. XV:** 165; **Supp. XXI:** 228

Baudrillard, Jean, **Supp. IV Part 1:** 45

Bauer, Dale, **Retro. Supp. I:** 381

Bauer, Douglas, **Supp. XII:** 290

Baum, L. Frank, **Supp. I Part 2:** 621; **Supp. IV Part 1:** 101, 113; **Supp. XII:** 42

Baumann, Walter, **III:** 478

Bausch, Richard, **Supp. VII: 39–56; Supp. XVII:** 21

Bawer, Bruce, **Supp. VIII:** 153; **Supp. IX:** 135; **Supp. X:** 187

Baxter, Charles, **Supp. XII:** 22; **Supp. XIV:** 89, 92; **Supp. XVII: 13–24; Supp. XXIII:** 289

Baxter, John, **Supp. XI:** 302

Baxter, Richard, **III:** 199; **IV:** 151, 153; **Supp. I Part 2:** 683

"Baxter's Procrustes" (Chesnutt), **Supp. XIV:** 76

"Bay City Blues" (Chandler), **Supp. IV Part 1:** 129

Baylies, William, **Supp. I Part 1:** 153

Baym, Nina, **Supp. IV Part 2:** 463; **Supp. X:** 229; **Supp. XVI:** 92; **Supp. XVIII:** 258, 259

"Bayou" (Di Piero), **Supp. XIX:** 37

Bayou Folk (Chopin), **Retro. Supp. II: 64–65,** 73; **Supp. I Part 1:** 200, 216, 218

Baziotes, William, **Supp. XV:** 144

"B.C." (Taggard), **Supp. XXII:** 278

Beach, Anna Hampstead, **Supp. XVII:** 75

Beach, Joseph Warren, **I:** 309, 500; **II:** 27; **III:** 319

Beach, Sylvia, **IV:** 404; **Retro. Supp. I:** 109, 422; **Supp. XXII:** 165

"Beach Women, The" (Pinsky), **Supp. VI:** 241

"Beaded Pear, The" (Simpson), **Supp. IX:** 276

Beagle, Peter, **Supp. X:** 24

Beam, Jeffrey, **Supp. XII:** 98

Beaman, E. O., **Supp. IV Part 2:** 604

Bean, Michael, **Supp. V:** 203

Bean, Robert Bennett, **Supp. II Part 1:** 170

Bean Eaters, The (Brooks), **Supp. III Part 1:** 79–81

Be Angry at the Sun (Jeffers), **Supp. II Part 2:** 434

"Beanstalk Country, The" (T. Williams), **IV:** 383

Bean Trees, The (Kingsolver), **Supp. VII:** 197, 199–201, 202, 207, 209

"Bear" (Hogan), **Supp. IV Part 1:** 412

Bear, The (Faulkner), **Supp. VIII:** 184

"Bear, The" (Faulkner), **II:** 71–72, 73, 228; **IV:** 203; **Supp. IV Part 2:** 434; **Supp. IX:** 95; **Supp. X:** 30; **Supp. XIV:** 32; **Supp. XXI:** 37

"Bear, The" (Kinnell), **Supp. III Part 1:** 244

"Bear, The" (Momaday), **Supp. IV Part 2:** 480, 487

Bear and His Daughter: Stories (Stone), **Supp. V:** 295, 308

Beard, Charles, **I:** 214; **IV:** 429; **Supp. I Part 2:** 481, 490, 492, 632, 640, 643, 647

Beard, James, **I:** 341; **Supp. XVII:** 89, 90

Beard, Mary, **Supp. I Part 2:** 481

"Bearded Oaks" (Warren), **IV:** 240

Bearden, Romare, **Retro. Supp. I:** 209; **Supp. VIII:** 337, 342; **Supp. XXI:** 249

"Beard of Bees, A" (X. J. Kennedy), **Supp. XV:** 171

Beardon, Romare, **Supp. XV:** 144

"Beards, The" (Lethem), **Supp. XVIII:** 148

Beardsley, Aubrey, **II:** 56; **IV:** 77

Beaser, Robert, **Supp. XV:** 259

"Beast" (Swenson), **Supp. IV Part 2:** 639

"Beast & Burden, The: Seven Improvisations" (Komunyakaa), **Supp. XIII:** 120, 121

Beast God Forgot to Invent, The (Harrison), **Supp. VIII:** 37, 46, **51–52**

Beast in Me, The (Thurber), **Supp. I Part 2:** 615

"Beast in the Jungle, The" (James), **I:** 570; **II:** 335; **Retro. Supp. I:** 235; **Supp. V:** 103–104

Beast in View (Rukeyser), **Supp. VI:** 272, 273, 279, 280

Beasts of Bethlehem, The (X. J. Kennedy), **Supp. XV:** 163

"Beat! Beat! Drums!" (Whitman), **III:** 585

Beat Down to Your Soul: What Was the Beat Generation? (Charters, ed.), **Supp. XIV:** 152

"Beatific Effigies" (Bronk), **Supp. XXI:** 31

Beaton, Cecil, **Supp. XVI:** 191

"Beatrice Palmato" (Wharton), **Retro. Supp. I:** 379

Beats, The (Krim, ed.), **Supp. XV:** 338

Beattie, Ann, **Supp. V:** 21–37; **Supp. XI:** 26; **Supp. XII:** 80, 139, 294; **Supp. XXI:** 118; **Supp. XXIII:** 289

Beattie, L. Elisabeth, **Supp. XX: 164, 165**

Beatty, General Sam, **I:** 193

Beaty, Jerome, **Supp. IV Part 1:** 331

"Beau Monde of Mrs. Bridge, The" (Connell), **Supp. XIV:** 88, 89

Beaumont, Francis, **Supp. I Part 2:** 422

"Beauties of Santa Cruz, The" (Freneau), **Supp. II Part 1:** 260

Beautiful and Damned, The (Fitzgerald), **II:** 88, 89–91, 93, 263; **Retro. Supp. I: 103–105,** 105, 106, 110; **Supp. IX:** 56, 57

Beautiful Changes, The (Wilbur), **Supp. III Part 2:** 544–550

"Beautiful Changes, The" (Wilbur), **Supp. III Part 2:** 549, 550

"Beautiful Child, A" (Capote), **Supp. III Part 1:** 113, 125

"Beautiful & Cruel" (Cisneros), **Supp. VII:** 63, 67

"Beautiful Wall, Machu Picchu, The" (Bronk), **Supp. XXI:** 31, 32

"Beautiful Woman Who Sings, The" (Gunn Allen), **Supp. IV Part 1:** 326

"Beauty" (Emerson), **II:** 2, 5

"Beauty" (Sanders), **Supp. XVI:** 277

"Beauty" (Wylie), **Supp. I Part 2:** 710

"Beauty and the Beast" (Dove), **Supp. IV Part 1:** 245

"Beauty and the Beast" (fairy tale), **IV:** 266; **Supp. X:** 88

"Beauty and the Shoe Sluts" (Karr), **Supp. XI:** 250

Beauty of the Husband, The: A Fictional Essay in Twenty-Nine Tangos (Carson), **Supp. XII: 113–114**

Beauty Queen, The (P. N. Warren), **Supp. XX: 268–269**

Beauty's Punishment (Rice), **Supp. VII:** 301

Beauty's Release: The Continued Erotic Adventures of Sleeping Beauty (Rice), **Supp. VII:** 301

Beauvoir, Simone de, **IV:** 477; **Supp. I Part 1:** 51; **Supp. III Part 1:** 200–201, 208; **Supp. IV Part 1:** 360; **Supp. IX:** 4

"Be Careful" (Zach; Everwine, trans.), **Supp. XV:** 86

Be Careful How You Live (Lacy), **Supp. XV:** 203–204

"Because I could not stop for Death—" (Dickinson), **Retro. Supp. I: 38–40,** 41, 43, 44

"Because It Happened" (Goldbarth), **Supp. XII:** 192

"Because of Libraries We Can Say These Things" (Nye), **Supp. XIII:** 283

"Because the Body Is a Flower"(Crooker), **Supp. XXIII:** 55

"Because You Mentioned the Spiritual Life" (Dunn), **Supp. XI:** 154

Bech: A Book (Updike), **IV:** 214; **Retro. Supp. I:** 329, 335

Beck, Dave, **I:** 493

Beck, Ervin, **Supp. XXIII:** 94, 95

Beck, Jack, **Supp. IV Part 2:** 560

Beck, Nicholas, **Supp. XVIII:** 252

Beck, Stefan, **Supp. XXII:** 268

Becker, Carl, **Supp. I Part 2:** 492, 493

Becker, Paula. *See* Modersohn, Mrs. Otto (Paula Becker)

Beckett, Samuel, **I:** 71, 91, 142, 298, 461; **III:** 387; **IV:** 95; **Retro. Supp. I:** 206; **Supp. IV Part 1:** 297, 368–369; **Supp. IV Part 2:** 424; **Supp. V:** 23, 53; **Supp. XI:** 104; **Supp. XII:** 21, 150–151; **Supp. XIII:** 74; **Supp. XIV:** 239; **Supp. XVII:** 185; **Supp. XX:** 17; **Supp. XXI:** 18; **Supp. XXII:** 263

Beckett, Tom, **Supp. IV Part 2:** 419

Beckford, William, **I:** 204

Beckonings (Brooks), **Supp. III Part 1:** 85

"Becky" (Toomer), **Supp. III Part 2:** 481, 483; **Supp. IX:** 312

Becky and Her Friends (Hinojosa), **Supp. XIX: 108–109**

Becoming a Man: Half a Life Story (Monette), **Supp. X:** 146, 147, 149, 151, 152, **155–157**

"Becoming a Meadow" (Doty), **Supp. XI:** 124–125

"Becoming and Breaking: Poet and Poem" (Ríos), **Supp. IV Part 2:** 539

Becoming Canonical in American Poetry (Morris), **Retro. Supp. I:** 40

Becoming Light: New and Selected Poems (Jong), **Supp. V:** 115

Bécquer, Gustavo Adolfo, **Supp. XIII:** 312

"Bed, The" (Dixon), **Supp. XII:** 154

Beddoes, Thomas Lovell, **III:** 469; **Retro. Supp. I:** 285

Bedichek, Roy, **Supp. V:** 225

Bedient, Calvin, **Supp. IX:** 298; **Supp. XII:** 98

"Bed in the Sky, The" (Snyder), **Supp. VIII:** 300

Bednarik, Joseph, **Supp. VIII:** 39

"Bedrock" (Proulx), **Supp. VII:** 253

"Bee, The" (Lanier), **Supp. I Part 1:** 364

Beecher, Catharine, **Supp. I Part 2:** 581, 582–583, 584, 586, 588, 589, 591, 599; **Supp. X:** 103; **Supp. XI:** 193

Beecher, Charles, **Supp. I Part 2:** 588, 589

Beecher, Edward, **Supp. I Part 2:** 581, 582, 583, 584, 588, 591

Beecher, Harriet. *See* Stowe, Harriet Beecher

Beecher, Henry Ward, **II:** 275; **Supp. I Part 2:** 581; **Supp. XI:** 193; **Supp. XVIII:** 4

Beecher, Lyman, **Supp. I Part 2:** 580–581, 582, 583, 587, 588, 599; **Supp. XI:** 193

Beecher, Mrs. Lyman (Roxanna Foote), **Supp. I Part 2:** 580–581, 582, 588, 599

Beeching, Jack, **Supp. X:** 114, 117, 118, 123, 125, 126

"Beehive" (Toomer), **Supp. IX:** 317

"Bee Hunt, The" (Irving), **II:** 313

"Beekeeper's Daughter, The" (Plath), **Retro. Supp. II:** 246–247

"Bee Meeting, The" (Plath), **Retro. Supp. II:** 254–255

Bee Poems (Plath), **Retro. Supp. II:** 254–255

Beer, John, **Supp. XVII:** 239

Beer, Thomas, **I:** 405

Beerbohm, Max, **III:** 472; **IV:** 436; **Supp. I Part 2:** 714

"Beer Bottle" (Kooser), **Supp. XIX:** 117

"Beer in the Sergeant Major's Hat, or The Sun Also Sneezes" (Chandler), **Supp. IV Part 1:** 121

Beers, Henry A., **Supp. XX: 68**

"Bees Bees Bees" (J. Scott), **Supp. XVII:** 188, 190

Beethoven, Ludwig van, **II:** 536; **III:** 118; **IV:** 274, 358; **Supp. I Part 1:** 363; **Supp. VIII:** 103

Beet Queen, The (Erdrich), **Supp. IV Part 1:** 259, 260, 264–265, 266, 273, 274, 275

Befo' de War: Echoes in Negro Dialect (Gordon), **Supp. II Part 1:** 201

"Before" (Goldbarth), **Supp. XII:** 175

"Before" (Snyder), **Supp. VIII:** 301

Before Adam (London), **II:** 466

Before Breakfast (O'Neill), **Supp. XXII:** 22

Before Disaster (Winters), **Supp. II Part 2:** 786, 800

"Before Disaster" (Winters), **Supp. II Part 2:** 801, 815

"Before I Knocked" (D. Thomas), **III:** 534

Beforelife, The (F. Wright), **Supp. XVII:** 240, 245–246

"Before March" (MacLeish), **III:** 15

Before My Life Began (Neugeboren), **Supp. XVI: 224–225**

"Before the Altar" (Lowell), **II:** 516

"Before the Birth of one of her children" (Bradstreet), **Supp. I Part 1:** 118

"Before the Sky Darkens" (Dunn), **Supp. XI:** 155

"Begat" (Sexton), **Supp. II Part 2: 693**

Beget, Philippe, **Supp. XXIII:** 74

Beggarman, Thief (Shaw), **Supp. XIX:** 251–252

Beggar on Horseback (Kaufman and Connelly), **III:** 394

"Beggar Said So, The" (Singer), **IV:** 12

Beggars in the House of Plenty (Shanley), **Supp. XIV:** 316, **327–328**

Beggar's Opera, The (Gay), **Supp. I Part 2:** 523

Begiebing, Robert, **Retro. Supp. II:** 210

Begin Again (Paley), **Supp. VI:** 221

"Beginning and the End, The" (Jeffers), **Supp. II Part 2:** 420–421, 424

"Beginning of Decadence, The" (Jeffers), **Supp. II Part 2:** 420

"Beginning of Enthusiasm, The" (Salinas), **Supp. XIII:** 327–328

Beginning of Wisdom, The (Benét), **I:** 358; **Supp. XI:** 44

"Beginnings of Sorrow, The"(P. Benedict), **Supp. XXIII:** 48

Be Glad You're Neurotic (Bisch), **Supp. I Part 2:** 608

"Begotten of the Spleen" (Simic), **Supp. VIII:** 277

"Behaving Like a Jew" (Stern), **Supp. IX: 290–291,** 294

"Behavior" (Emerson), **II:** 2, 4

Behavior of Titans, The (Merton), **Supp. VIII:** 201

Behind a Mask (Alcott), **Supp. I Part 1:** 36–37, 43–44

"Behind a Wall" (Lowell), **II:** 516

Behind the Movie Camera (radio show), **Supp. XV:** 147

"Behold the Key" (Malamud), **Supp. I Part 2:** 437

Behrendt, Stephen, **Supp. X:** 204

Behrman, S. N., **Supp. V:** 95

Beidler, Peter G., **Supp. IV Part 2:** 557

Beidler, Philip D., **Supp. XII:** 69

Beige Dolorosa (Harrison), **Supp. VIII:** 40, 51

Beiles, Sinclair, **Supp. XII:** 129

Beiliss, Mendel, **Supp. I Part 2:** 427, 446, 447, 448

"Being a Constellation" (A. Finch), **Supp. XVII:** 72

"Being a Lutheran Boy-God in Minnesota" (R. Bly), **Supp. IV Part 1:** 59, 67

Being and Race (Johnson), **Supp. VI:** 193, 199

Being and Time (Heidegger), **Supp. VIII:** 9

Being Busted (Fiedler), **Supp. XIII:** 95, 102, 104

Being John Malkovich (Kaufman), **Supp. XV:** 16

Being Perfect (Quindlen), **Supp. XVII:** 167, 179

Being There (Kosinski), **Supp. VII:** 215, 216, 222–223

Beiswanger, George, **Retro. Supp. II:** 220

Beka Lamb (Edgell), **Supp. XXIII:** 83, 85, **86–88,** 93–94, 95

Belasco, David, **Supp. XVI:** 182; **Supp. XXI:** 151

Bel Canto (Patchett), **Supp. XII:** 307, 310, **320–322**

Belchamber (Sturgis), **Supp. XX: 227, 233, 238–240**

"Beleaguered City, The" (Longfellow), **II:** 498

Belfry of Bruges, The, and Other Poems (Longfellow), **II:** 489; **Retro. Supp. II:** 157, 168

"Belief" (Levine), **Supp. V:** 186, 190

"Belief in the Self Abandoned, The" (Bronk), **Supp. XXI:** 30

"Beliefs of Writers, The" (Doctorow), **Supp. IV Part 1:** 235–236

Believeniks! (Lethem and Sorrentino), **Supp. XVIII:** 148–149

Believers (C. Baxter), **Supp. XVII:** 20–21, 22

"Believers" (C. Baxter), **Supp. XVII:** 21

"Believers, The/Los Creyentes" (Kingsolver), **Supp. VII:** 208

Belinda (Rice), **Supp. VII:** 301–302

"Belinda's Petition" (Dove), **Supp. IV Part 1:** 245

"Belita" (Ríos), **Supp. IV Part 2:** 541

Belitt, Ben, **Supp. XII:** 260

Bell, Archibald, **Supp. XX: 284, 285**

Bell, Bernard, **Supp. XXII:** 182

Bell, Clive, **IV:** 87

Bell, Daniel, **Supp. I Part 2:** 648

Bell, George Kennedy Allen, **Retro. Supp. I:** 65

Bell, Madison Smartt, **Supp. X: 1–20; Supp. XVII:** 236; **Supp. XIX:** 58–59, 60–61; **Supp. XXI:** 48; **Supp. XXIII:** 43

Bell, Marvin, **Supp. V:** 337, 339; **Supp. IX:** 152; **Supp. XI:** 316

Bell, Michael, **Retro. Supp. II:** 139

Bell, Pearl, **Supp. XI:** 233

Bell, Quentin, **Supp. I Part 2:** 636

Bell, Whitfield J., Jr., **II:** 123

Bellafante, Gina, **Supp. VIII:** 85

Bellamy, Edward, **II:** 276; **Supp. I Part 2:** 641; **Supp. XI:** 200, 203

Bellarosa Connection, The (Bellow), **Retro. Supp. II:** 31, 32

"Belle Dollinger" (Masters), **Supp. I Part 2:** 463

Belleforest, François de, **IV:** 370

"Belle Zoraïde, La" (Chopin), **Supp. I Part 1:** 215–216

Bell Jar, The (Plath), **Retro. Supp. II:** 242, **249–250; Supp. I Part 2:** 526, 527, 529, 531–536, 539, 540, 541, 542, 544

Belloc, Hilary, **III:** 176; **IV:** 432

"Bellocq" (Trethewey), **Supp. XXI:** 253

Bellocq, E. J., **Supp. XXI:** 246, 251

Bellocq's Ophelia (Trethewey), **Supp. XXI:** 243, 246, **251–254**

"Bellocq's Ophelia" (Trethewey), **Supp. XXI:** 254

Bellow, Saul, **I:** 113, 138–139, **144–166,** 375, 517; **II:** 579; **III:** 40; **IV:** 3, 19, 217, 340; **Retro. Supp. II: 19–36,** 118, 279, 307, 324; **Supp. I Part 2:** 428, 451; **Supp. II Part 1:** 109; **Supp. IV Part 1:** 30; **Supp. V:** 258; **Supp. VIII:** 98, 176, 234, 236–237, 245; **Supp. IX:** 212, 227; **Supp. XI:** 64, 233; **Supp. XII:** 159, 165, 170, 310; **Supp. XIII:** 106; **Supp. XV:** 143; **Supp. XVI:** 208; **Supp. XVIII:** 90; **Supp. XIX:** 157, 158, 261; **Supp. XX: 244; Supp. XXII:** 268; **Supp. XXIII:** 166

Bellows, George, **Supp. XV:** 295

"Bells, The" (Poe), **III:** 593; **Retro. Supp. II:** 266; **Supp. I Part 2:** 388

"Bells, The" (Sexton), **Supp. II Part 2:** 673

"Bells for John Whiteside's Daughter" (Ransom), **III:** 490

"Bells of Lynn, The" (Longfellow), **II:** 498

"Bells of San Blas, The" (Longfellow), **II:** 490–491, 493, 498

"Bell Tower, The" (Melville), **III:** 91

"Belly, The" (Dobyns), **Supp. XIII:** 87

'Bel of Prairie Eden (Lippard), **Supp. XXIII:** 178, 186

"Belonging" (Pickering), **Supp. XXI:** 202

"Belonging Kind, The" (W. Gibson and J. Shirley), **Supp. XVI:** 123

Beloved (Morrison), **Supp. III Part 1:** 364, 372–379; **Supp. IV Part 1:** 13–14; **Supp. V:** 259; **Supp. VIII:** 343; **Supp. XIII:** 60; **Supp. XXII:** 78, 109

Beloved, The (Gibran), **Supp. XX: 125**

"Beloved, The" (Halliday), **Supp. XIX:** 92

Beloved Lady: A History of Jane Addams' Ideas on Reform and Peace (Farrell), **Supp. I Part 1:** 24

Beloved Stranger, The (Bynner), **Supp. XV:** 44, 50

Bemorse, John, **Supp. XX: 62**

Benchley, Robert, **I:** 48, 482; **II:** 435; **III:** 53; **Supp. IX:** 190, 195, 204

Benda, W. T., **Retro. Supp. I:** 13

Bender, Aimee, **Supp. XXII:** 49

Bending of a Twig, The (Coke), **Supp. XX: 235**

Bend Sinister (Nabokov), **III:** 253–254; **Retro. Supp. I:** 265, 266, 270

"Beneath the Sidewalk" (Dunn), **Supp. XI:** 145

"Beneath the Smooth Skin of America" (Sanders), **Supp. XVI:** 275

Benedict, Elizabeth, **Supp. XVIII:** 289

Benedict, Laura, **Supp. XXIII:** 35, 36, 49

Benedict, Pinckney, **Supp. XXIII: 35–50**

Benedict, Ruth, **Supp. IX:** 229

Benefactor, The (Sontag), **Supp. III Part 2:** 451, 455, 468, 469

"Benefit Performance" (Malamud), **Supp. I Part 2:** 431

Benét, Laura, **Supp. XI:** 44

Benét, Rosemary, **Supp. XI:** 44, 51

Benét, Stephen Vincent, **I:** 358; **II:** 177; **III:** 22; **IV:** 129; **Supp. XI: 43–61**

Benét, William Rose, **II:** 530; **Retro. Supp. I:** 108; **Supp. I Part 2:** 709; **Supp. XI:** 43, 44; **Supp. XIV:** 119, 122, 129

Ben Franklin's Wit and Wisdom (Franklin), **II:** 111

Ben-Gurion, David, **Supp. XX: 243**

Ben-Hur (film), **Supp. IV Part 2:** 683

Benigna Machiavelli (Gilman), **Supp. XI:** 201, 208

Benitez, R. Michael, **Retro. Supp. II:** 264

Benito Cereno (Lowell), **II:** 546; **Retro. Supp. II:** 181

"Benito Cereno" (Melville), **III:** 91; **Retro. Supp. I:** 255; **Retro. Supp. II:** 188; **Supp. XVII:** 185

Benito's Dream Bottle (Nye), **Supp. XIII:** 278

"Bênitou's Slave, The" (Chopin), **Retro. Supp. II:** 64

Benjamin, Walter, **Supp. IX:** 133; **Supp. XVI:** 290, 291; **Supp. XXIII:** 28, 29, 30, 31

Benjamin Franklin (Van Doren), **Supp. I Part 2:** 486

"Benjamin Pantier" (Masters), **Supp. I Part 2:** 461

Bennett, Anne Virginia, **II:** 184

Bennett, Arnold, **I:** 103; **II:** 337; **Supp. XVI:** 190

Bennett, Elizabeth, **Supp. VIII:** 58

Bennett, Patrick, **Supp. V:** 225

Bennett, Paula, **Retro. Supp. I:** 29, 33, 42; **Supp. XX: 286**

Bennett, Reginald, **Supp. XXII:** 218

Bennett, William, **Supp. VIII:** 245

Benson, A. C., **Supp. XX: 238**

Benson, Arthur, **Supp. XX: 233**

Benson, E. F., **Supp. XX: 229**

Benson, Heidi, **Supp. XVIII:** 136

Benson, Jackson J., **Supp. IV Part 2:** 613

Benson, Martin, **Supp. XVIII:** 38

Benstock, Shari, **Retro. Supp. I:** 361, 368, 371, 382; **Supp. XX: 240**

Bentham, Jeremy, **I:** 279; **Supp. I Part 2:** 635

Bentley, Anna, **Supp. XXI:** 5

Bentley, Arthur, **Supp. XXI:** 4, 5

Bentley, Eric R., **IV:** 396

Bentley, Nelson, **Supp. IX:** 324

Bentley, Richard, **III:** 79, 86

Benton, Robert, **Supp. IV Part 1:** 236

"Bent Tones" (Wright), **Supp. XV:** 346

Benveniste, Emile, **Supp. XVI:** 292

Benzel, Jan, **Supp. XVI:** 112

Beowulf, **Supp. II Part 1:** 6; **Supp. XVII:** 70, 73

Beran, Carol, **Supp. XIII:** 25

"Berck-Plage" (Plath), **Retro. Supp. II:** 253–254

Bercovitch, Sacvan, **Retro. Supp. I:** 408; **Retro. Supp. II:** 325, 330; **Supp. I Part 1:** 99; **Supp. I Part 2:** 659

Berdyaev, Nikolai, **I:** 494; **III:** 292

"Bereaved Apartments" (Kingsolver), **Supp. VII:** 203

"Bereavement in their death to feel" (Dickinson), **Retro. Supp. I:** 43, 44

"Berenice" (Poe), **III:** 415, 416, 425; **Retro. Supp. II:** 270

Bérénice (Racine), **II:** 573

Berenson, Bernard, **Retro. Supp. I:** 381; **Supp. IV Part 1:** 314; **Supp. XIV:** 335, 336, 337; **Supp. XVII:** 99; **Supp. XXI:** 5

Berenson, Mary Smith, **Supp. XXI:** 4, 5, 6

Berg, James, **Supp. XIV:** 157, 159

Berg, Stephen, **Supp. IV Part 1:** 60

Berger, Alan, **Supp. XVII:** 39

Berger, Charles, **Retro. Supp. I:** 311

Berger, John, **Supp. XVI:** 284; **Supp. XXIII:** 167, 168–169

Berger, Roger, **Supp. XIII:** 237

Berger, Thomas, **III:** 258; **Supp. XII:** 171

Bergman, Ingmar, **I:** 291; **Supp. XV:** 7, 8, 12

Bergson, Henri, **I:** 224; **II:** 163, 165, 166, 359; **III:** 8, 9, 488, 619; **IV:** 86, 122, 466, 467; **Retro. Supp. I:** 55, 57, 80; **Supp. IV Part 1:** 42; **Supp. XXII:** 158

Berkeley, Anthony, **Supp. IV Part 1:** 341

Berkeley, George, **II:** 10, 349, 357, 480, 554

Berkman, Alexander, **Supp. XXIII:** 161

Berkman, Leonard, **Supp. XV:** 321

Berkowitz, Gerald, **Supp. IV Part 2:** 590

Berkson, Bill, **Supp. XXIII:** 217, 218

Berlin, Isaiah, **Supp. XXII:** 258

Berlin Alexanderplatz (Döblin), **Supp. XV:** 137

Berlin Stories (Isherwood), **Supp. IV Part 1:** 82; **Supp. XIV:** 155, 156, 161, 162, 164, 165

Berlioz, Hector, **Supp. XV:** 33

Berlyne, Daniel E., **Supp. I Part 2:** 672

Berman, Alexander, **Supp. XVII:** 103

Berman, Carolyn Vellenga, **Supp. XXII:** 147

Bernard Clare (Farrell), **II:** 38, 39

Bernard of Clairvaux, Saint, **I:** 22; **II:** 538

Bernays, Thekla, **Retro. Supp. II:** 65

Berne, Suzanne, **Supp. XII:** 320

Berne, Victoria (pseudonym). *See* Fisher, M. F. K.

Berneis, Peter, **IV:** 383

Bernhard, Brendan, **Supp. XIV:** 163

Bernhard, Thomas, **Supp. XX: 91**

Bernhardt, Sarah, **I:** 484; **Retro. Supp. I:** 377

Bernice (Glaspell), **Supp. III Part 1:** 179

"Bernice Bobs Her Hair" (Fitzgerald), **II:** 88; **Retro. Supp. I:** 103

Bernstein, Aline, **IV:** 455, 456

Bernstein, Andrea, **Supp. IX:** 146

Bernstein, Charles, **Supp. IV Part 2:** 421, 426

Bernstein, Elizabeth, **Supp. XII:** 318

Bernstein, Leonard, **I:** 28; **Supp. I Part 1:** 288, 289; **Supp. IV Part 1:** 83, 84

Bernstein, Melvin, **Supp. XIV:** 41, 46

Bernstein, Michael André, **Retro. Supp. I:** 427

Bernstein, Richard, **Supp. IX:** 253, 262; **Supp. XII:** 113; **Supp. XIV:** 33; **Supp. XXII:** 261

Berrett, Jesse, **Supp. XIII:** 241, 242

Berrigan, Ted, **Supp. XIV:** 150; **Supp. XXII:** 224, 225, 228, 231; **Supp. XXIII:** 218, 221

Berroa y Canelo, Quiterio, **Supp. XXI:** 104

"Berry" (Hughes), **Supp. I Part 1:** 329, 330

Berry, Eleanor, **Supp. XXIII:** 246

Berry, Faith, **Retro. Supp. I:** 194, 201

Berry, Walter, **IV:** 313–314, 326

Berry, Wendell, **Supp. VIII:** 304; **Supp. X: 21–39; Supp. XII:** 202; **Supp. XIII:** 1–2; **Supp. XIV:** 179; **Supp. XVI:** 39, 56; **Supp. XVIII:** 192; **Supp. XXI:** 90

"Berry Feast, A" (Snyder), **Supp. VIII:** 289, 297

Berryman, John, **I: 167–189,** 405, 441–442, 521; **II:** 554; **III:** 273; **IV:** 138, 430; **Retro. Supp. I:** 430; **Retro. Supp. II:** 175, 178; **Supp. I Part 2:** 546; **Supp. II Part 1:** 109; **Supp. III Part 2:** 541, 561, 595, 596, 603; **Supp. IV Part 2:** 620, 639; **Supp. V:** 179–180, 337; **Supp. IX:** 152; **Supp. XI:** 240; **Supp. XV:** 93; **Supp. XVII:** 111; **Supp. XXII:** 83

Berryman, Mrs. John, **I:** 168–169

Berryman's Sonnets (Berryman), **I:** 168, 175–178

"Berry Territory" (Snyder), **Supp. VIII:** 304

Berthoff, Warner, **Supp. I Part 1:** 133

Bertolucci, Bernardo, **Supp. IV Part 1:** 94

"Bertrand Hume" (Masters), **Supp. I Part 2:** 463–464

Besco, Glenn, **Supp. XXIII:** 125

"Best, the Most, The" (Carruth), **Supp. XVI:** 59

Best American Essays 1987, The (G. Talese and R. Atwan, eds.), **Supp. XVI:** 273

Best American Essays 1988, The (Dillard, ed.), **Supp. VIII:** 272

Best American Essays 1989, The (Wolff, ed.), **Supp. XVII:** 208

Best American Essays 1993, The (J. Epstein, ed.), **Supp. XVI:** 275

Best American Essays 1997, The (Frazier, ed.), **Supp. VIII:** 272; **Supp. XVII:** 207

Best American Essays 1999, The (E. Hoagland and R. Atwan, eds.), **Supp. XVI:** 277

Best American Essays for College Students, The (R. Atwan, ed.), **Supp. XVI:** 273

Best American Fantasy, 2010 (Brockmeier, ed.), **Supp. XXII:** 49–50

Best American New Voices 2001 (C. Baxter, ed.), **Supp. XVII:** 22

Best American Poetry, The: 1988 (Ashbery, ed.), **Supp. III Part 1:** 26

Best American Poetry 2000, The (Dove and Lehman, eds.), **Supp. XXI:** 246

Best American Poetry 2006, The (Collins, ed.), **Supp. XXI:** 54

Best American Short Stories, **I:**174; **II:** 587; **III:** 443; **Supp. IV Part 1:** 102, 315; **Supp. IX:** 114; **Supp. X:** 301

Best American Short Stories, 1915–1050, The, **Supp. IX:** 4

Best American Short Stories 1965, The (Foley, ed.), **Supp. XVI:** 225

Best American Short Stories 1979, The, **Supp. XXIII:** 290

Best American Short Stories 1982, The (Gardner, ed.), **Supp. XVII:** 16

Best American Short Stories 1983, The (A. Tyler, ed.), **Supp. XVI:** 37

Best American Short Stories 1986, The (Carver, ed.), **Supp. XVII:** 17

Best American Short Stories 1988, The (Helprin, ed.), **Supp. XVI:** 16

Best American Short Stories 1989, The (Atwood, ed.), **Supp. XVII:** 18; **Supp. XXI:** 39, 42

Best American Short Stories 1991, The (Adams and Kenison, eds.), **Supp. XVI:** 256

Best American Short Stories 1996, The, **Supp. XXIII:** 295

Best American Short Stories 1997, **Supp. XXII:** 75

Best American Short Stories 2001, The (Kenison and Kingsover, eds.), **Supp. XVI:** 24

Best American Short Stories 2007, The, **Supp. XXIII:** 290

Best American Short Stories of 1942, The, **Supp. V:** 316

Best American Short Stories of 1944, The, **Supp. IX:** 119

Best American Short Stories of the Century (Updike, ed.), **Supp. X:** 163

Best American Short Stories of the Eighties, The (Ravenal, ed.), **Supp. IV Part 1:** 93

Best American Sports Writing of the Century, The (Halberstam, ed.), **Supp. XVII:** 204

"Best China Saucer, The" (Jewett), **Retro. Supp. II:** 145–146

Bester, Alfred, **Supp. XVI:** 123

Best Hour of the Night, The (Simpson), **Supp. IX: 277–279**

Bestiaire, Le (Apollinaire), **IV:** 80

Bestiary, A (Wilbur), **Supp. III Part 2:** 552

"Bestiary for the Fingers of My Right Hand" (Simic), **Supp. VIII:** 274, 275

Best Man, The: A Play About Politics (Vidal), **Supp. IV Part 2:** 683

"Best of Everything, The" (Yates), **Supp. XI:** 341

Best of Pickering, The (Pickering), **Supp. XXI:** 192, 198

Best of Plimpton (Plimpton), **Supp. XVI:** 238, 239, 240

Best Short Plays, The (Mayorga), **IV:** 381

Best Short Stories, The (O'Brien, ed.), **I:** 289

Best Short Stories by Negro Writers, The (Hughes, ed.), **Supp. I Part 1:** 345

Best Short Stories of 1926, The (O'Brien, ed.), **Supp. XVIII:** 279

Best Short Stories of 1934 (O'Brien, ed.), **Supp. XVIII:** 227

Best Short Stories of 1938 (O'Brien, ed.), **Supp. XIX:** 256; **Supp. XX:** 34

Best That Ever Did It, The (Lacy), **Supp. XV:** 201–202

Best Times, The: An Informal Memoir (Dos Passos), **I:** 475, 482

Best Words, Best Order: Essays on Poetry (Dobyns), **Supp. XIII:** 74, **76–78,** 87

Best Years of Our Lives, The (film; Wyler), **Supp. XV:** 195

"BETANCOURT" (Baraka), **Supp. II Part 1:** 33, 34

Bête humaine, La (Zola), **III:** 316, 318

"Bethe" (Hellman), **Supp. I Part 1:** 293

Bethea, David, **Supp. VIII:** 27

Bethel Merriday (Lewis), **II:** 455

Bethke, Bruce, **Supp. XVI:** 121

Bethlehem in Broad Daylight (Doty), **Supp. XI:** 121, **122–123**

Bethune, Mary McLeod, **Retro. Supp. I:** 197; **Supp. I Part 1:** 333

Bethurum, Dorothy, **IV:** 121

"Betrayal" (Lanier), **Supp. I Part 1:** 364

"Betrothed" (Bogan), **Supp. III Part 1:** 49–51

Bettelheim, Bruno, **Supp. I Part 2:** 622; **Supp. X:** 77, 84; **Supp. XIV:** 126; **Supp. XVI:** 33

Better Days (Price), **Supp. VI:** 264

Better Sort, The (James), **II:** 335

"Better Things in Life, The" (Loos), **Supp. XVI:** 194

Betty Leicester (Jewett), **II:** 406

Betty Leicester's Christmas (Jewett), **II:** 406; **Retro. Supp. II:** 145

Between Angels (Dunn), **Supp. XI: 149–159**

"Between Angels" (Dunn), **Supp. XI:** 150

Between Fantoine and Agapa (Pinget), **Supp. V:** 39

"Between Memory and History: A Writer's Voice" (Kreisler), **Supp. XVI:** 155

Between Silences: A Voice from China (Jin), **Supp. XVIII:** 91, 92, 93

"Between the Porch and the Altar" (Lowell), **II:** 540–541

"Between the World and Me" (Wright), **Supp. II Part 1:** 228

Between Time and Timbuktu (Vonnegut), **Supp. II Part 2:** 753, 759

Between Two Rivers (Kenny), **Supp. XXIII:** 143

Beuka, Robert A., **Supp. XIX:** 263; **Supp. XXI:** 47

"Be Very Afraid—Of Loss of Liberty at Home" (P. N. Warren), **Supp. XX: 272–273**

Bevis, Howard L., **Supp. I Part 2:** 611

Bevis, John, **Supp. I Part 2:** 503

"Bewitched" (Wharton), **IV:** 316

Bewley, Marius, **I:** 336

Beyer, Werner, **Supp. XXIII:** 145

Beyle, Marie Henri. *See* Stendhal

Beyond (Goldbarth), **Supp. XII:** 192

Beyond a Boundary (C. L. R. James), **Supp. XXI:** 159, 170–171

Beyond Black Bear Lake (LaBastille), **Supp. X:** 95, **99–102,** 108

"Beyond Charles River to the Acheron" (Lowell), **II:** 541

Beyond Criticism (Shapiro), **Supp. II Part 2:** 703, 711

Beyond Culture (Trilling), **Supp. III Part 2:** 508–512

Beyond Desire (Anderson), **I:** 111

Beyond Document: The Art of Nonfiction Film (Warren, ed.), **Supp. IV Part 2:** 434

Beyond Good and Evil (Nietzsche), **Supp. IV Part 2:** 519

"Beyond Harm" (Olds), **Supp. X:** 210

Beyond Katrina: A Meditation on the Mississippi Gulf Coast (Trethewey), **Supp. XXI:** 248

"Beyond My Solitude" (Gibran), **Supp. XX:** 119

"Beyond the Alps" (Lowell), **II:** 547, 550

"Beyond the Bayou" (Chopin), **Supp. I Part 1:** 215

Beyond the Boom: New Voices on American Life, Culture and Politics (Teachout), **Supp. XIX:** 137

Beyond the Horizon (O'Neill), **III:** 389; **Supp. XXI:** 13; **Supp. XXII:** 22

Beyond the Hundredth Meridian: John Wesley Powell and the Second Opening of the West (Stegner), **Supp. IV Part 2:** 599, 603–604, 611

"Beyond the Kittery Bridge" (Hatlen), **Supp. V:** 138

Beyond the Law (film) (Mailer), **Retro. Supp. II:** 205

"Beyond the Sea (at the sanatorium)" (Salinas), **Supp. XIII:** 325

Beyond the Wall: Essays from the Outside (Abbey), **Supp. XIII:** 13

Beyond the Writers' Workshop: New Ways to Write Creative Nonfiction (C. Bly), **Supp. XVI:** 41

Beyond Tragedy (Niebuhr), **III:** 300–303

Bezner, Kevin, **Supp. XII:** 202

B. F.'s Daughter (Marquand), **III:** 59, 65, 68, 69

Bhagavad Gita, **III:** 566; **IV:** 183

"Biafra: A People Betrayed" (Vonnegut), **Supp. II Part 2:** 760

Bianchi, Martha Dickinson, **I:** 470; **Retro. Supp. I:** 35, 37, 38

Bible, **I:** 191, 280, 414, 421, 490, 506; **II:** 6, 12, 15, 17, 108, 231, 237, 238, 252, 267, 302; **III:** 28, 199, 308–309, 341, 343, 350, 356, 402, 492, 519, 565, 577; **IV:** 11, 13, 42, 57, 60, 67, 152, 153, 154, 155, 164, 165, 296, 337, 341, 367, 369, 370, 371, 438; **Retro. Supp. I:** 91; **Supp. I Part 1:** 4, 6, 63, 101, 104, 105, 113, 193, 369; **Supp. I Part 2:** 388, 433, 494, 515, 516, 517, 583, 584, 587, 589, 653, 689, 690, 691; **Supp. IV Part 1:** 284; **Supp. VIII:** 20; **Supp. IX:** 246; **Supp. XIV:** 225. *See also* names of biblical books; New Testament; Old Testament

Biblia Americana (Mather), **Supp. II Part 2:** 442

Biblical Dialogues between a Father and His Family (Rowson), **Supp. XV:** 245–246

"Bibliography of the King's Book, A, or, Eikon Basilike" (Howe), **Supp. IV Part 2:** 435

Bibliography of the King's Book, A; or, Eikon Basilike (Almack), **Supp. IV Part 2:** 435

Bickel, Freddy. *See* March, Fredric

Bidart, Frank, **Retro. Supp. II:** 48, 50, 52, 182, 183, 184; **Supp. XV:** 19–37; **Supp. XVIII:** 91,92; **Supp. XIX:** 82

Bid Me to Live (Doolittle), **Supp. I Part 1:** 258, 260, 268, 269, 270

"*Bien* Pretty" (Cisneros), **Supp. VII:** 70

"Bienvenidos" (Mora), **Supp. XIII:** 220

Bierce, Albert, **I:** 191, 209

Bierce, Ambrose, **I:** 190–213, 419; **II:** 74, 264, 271; **IV:** 350; **Retro. Supp. II:** 72

Bierce, Mrs. Ambrose, **I:** 194–195, 199

Bierce, Day, **I:** 195, 199

Bierce, Helen, **I:** 210

Bierce, Leigh, **I:** 195, 198, 208

Bierce, General Lucius Verus, **I:** 191

Bierce, Marcus, **I:** 190, 191

Bierce, Mrs. Marcus, **I:** 190, 191

Bierds, Linda, **Supp. XVII:** 25–37

Biffle, Kent, **Supp. V:** 225

"Bi-Focal" (Stafford), **Supp. XI:** 318, 321

Bigamist's Daughter, A (McDermott), **Supp. XVIII:** 155, **156–158**, 160, 166

Big as Life (Doctorow), **Supp. IV Part 1:** 231, 234

Big Bad Love (film, Howard), **Supp. XXI:** 39

Big Bad Love (L. Brown), **Supp. XXI:** 40, 42, **44–45**

"Big Bite" (Mailer), **Retro. Supp. II:** 204

"Big Blonde" (Parker), **Supp. IX:** 189, 192, 193, 195, 196, 203

Big Bozo, The (Glaspell), **Supp. III Part 1:** 182

Bigelow, Gordon, **Supp. X:** 222, 227, 229

Bigelow, Jacob, **Supp. I Part 1:** 302

Bigelow Papers, Second Series, The (Lowell), **Supp. I Part 2:** 406, 415–416

Bigelow Papers, The (Lowell), **Supp. I Part 2:** 406, 407, 408, 410, 411–412, 415, 417, 424

Big Fix, The (Lacy), **Supp. XV:** 204–205

Bigfoot Dreams (Prose), **Supp. XVI:** 253–254

Big Funk, The: A Casual Play (Shanley), **Supp. XIV:** 316, **327**

"Big Game" (Boyle), **Supp. XX: 20**

Big Game, The (film), **Supp. XIX:** 244

Big Gold Dream, The (C. Himes), **Supp. XVI:** 143, 144

"Bight, The" (Bishop), **Retro. Supp. II:** 38, 45

Big Hunger: Stories 1932–1959 (Fante), **Supp. XI:** 160

Big Knife, The (Odets), **Supp. II Part 2:** 546, 547, 548

Big Knockover, The (Hammett), **Supp. I Part 1:** 292; **Supp. IV Part 1:** 344, 345, 356

Big Laugh, The (O'Hara), **III:** 362, 373–375

Big Man (Neugeboren), **Supp. XVI:** 219, **220,** 221, 225

Big Money, The (Dos Passos), **I:** 482, 483, 486–487, 489; **Supp. I Part 2:** 646, 647

Big Picture (Everett), **Supp. XVIII:** 54, 66

"Big Picture" (Everett), **Supp. XVIII:** 66

"Big Picture" (Halliday), **Supp. XIX:** 93

"Big Rock Candy Figgy Pudding Pitfall, The" (Didion), **Supp. IV Part 1:** 195

Big Rock Candy Mountain, The (Stegner), **Supp. IV Part 2:** 596, 597, 598, 599, 600, 603, 604, 605, 606–607, 608, 610–611

Bigsby, C. W. E. (Christopher), **Supp. IX:** 137, 140; **Supp. XV:** 332

Big Sea, The (Hughes), **Retro. Supp. I:** 195, 197, 199, 201, 204; **Supp. I Part 1:** 322, 332, 333; **Supp. II Part 1:** 233–234; **Supp. XIX:** 77; **Supp. XXII:** 3

Big Sky, The (Mora), **Supp. XIII:** 221

Big Sleep, The (Chandler), **Supp. IV Part 1:** 122–125, 127, 128, 134

Big Sleep, The (film), **Supp. IV Part 1:** 130; **Supp. XVIII:** 148

Big Strike, The (Ryan as Quin), **Supp. XVIII:** 226,**232–233**

Big Sur (Kerouac), **Supp. III Part 1:** 230

Big Sur and the Oranges of Hieronymous Bosch (H. Miller), **III:** 189–190

Big Town, The (Lardner), **II:** 426, 429

"Big Two-Hearted River" (Hemingway), **II:** 249; **Retro. Supp. I:** 170–171; **Supp. IX:** 106; **Supp. XIV:** 227, 235

"Big Wind" (Roethke), **III:** 531

"Big Winner Rises Late, The" (Dunn), **Supp. XI:** 146

"Bilingual/*Bilingüe*" (essay; Espaillat), *Supp. XXI:* 103

"Bilingual/*Bilingüe*" (poem; Espaillat), *Supp. XXI:* 104

"Bilingual Christmas" (Mora), **Supp. XIII:** 216–217

"Bilingual Sestina" (Alvarez), **Supp. VII:** 10

"Bill" (Winters), **Supp. II Part 2:** 792

"Bill, The" (Malamud), **Supp. I Part 2:** 427, 430, 434

"Bill Collector's Vacation, The" (Hampl), **Supp. XXII:** 83

"Billie Holiday" (Carruth), **Supp. XVI:** 50

Billings, Gladys. *See* Brooks, Mrs. Van Wyck

Billings, Josh, **Supp. XVIII:** 1, 4

Bill of Rites, a Bill of Wrongs, a Bill of Goods, A (Morris), **III:** 237

"Bill's Beans" (Nye), **Supp. XIII:** 283

"Billy" (Gordon), **Supp. IV Part 1:** 306

"Billy" (McCarriston), **Supp. XIV:** 265

Billy Bathgate (Doctorow), **Supp. IV Part 1:** 217, 219, 222, 224, 227, 229–231, 231, 232, 233, 238

Billy Bathgate (film), **Supp. IV Part 1:** 236

Billy Budd, Sailor (Melville), **III:** 40, 93–95; **IV:** 105; **Retro. Supp. I:** 249, **258–260**

Billy Collins Live: A Performance at the Peter Norton Symphony Space April 20, 2005 (CD, Collins), **Supp. XXI:** 51

"Billy Gardner's Ground Out" (Skloot), **Supp. XX: 205, 207**

Billy Phelan's Greatest Game (W. Kennedy), **Supp. VII:** 131, 132, 134, 135, 142–147, 149, 151, 153, 155

Billy Ray's Farm: Essays from a Place Called Tula (L. Brown), **Supp. XXI:** 48, 49

Billy's Boy (P. N. Warren), **Supp. XX: 261, 265–267**

Billy the Kid, **Supp. IV Part 2:** 489, 490, 492

Biloxi Blues (Simon), **Supp. IV Part 2:** 576, 577, 584, 586–587, 590

"Bimini" (Hemingway), **II:** 258

Bingham, Anne, **Supp. XV:** 239

Bingham, Millicent Todd, **I:** 470; **Retro. Supp. I:** 36

Bingham, Remica L., **Supp. XXI:** 256

Bingo Palace, The (Erdrich), **Supp. IV Part 1:** 259, 260, 261, 263–264, 265, 266–267, 268–269, 270, 271–273, 274, 275

"Binsey Poplars" (Hopkins), **Supp. I Part 1:** 94; **Supp. IV Part 2:** 639

Binswanger, Ludwig, **Supp. XV:** 26

Biographia Literaria (Coleridge), **II:** 10; **Retro. Supp. I:** 308

"Biography" (Francis), **Supp. IX:** 77

"Biography" (Pinsky), **Supp. VI:** 235, 236, 239, 241, **243,** 249, 250

Biography and Poetical Remains of the Late Margaret Miller Davidson (Irving), **II:** 314

"Biography in the First Person" (Dunn), **Supp. XI:** 144

"Biography of an Armenian Schoolgirl" (Nye), **Supp. XIII:** 275, 280

"Biography of a Story" (Jackson), **Supp. IX:** 113

Biondi, Joann, **Supp. XI:** 103

"Biopoetics Sketch for *Greenfield Review*" (Harjo), **Supp. XII:** 216

"Biotherm"(O'Hara), **Supp. XXIII:** 208, 218–219

"Birchbrook Mill" (Whittier), **Supp. I Part 2:** 699

"Birches" (Frost), **II:** 154; **Retro. Supp. I:** 132; **Supp. XIII:** 147

Bird, Alan, **Supp. I Part 1:** 260

Bird, Gloria, **Supp. XII:** 216

Bird, Isabella, **Supp. X:** 103

Bird, Robert M., **III:** 423

"Bird, The" (Simpson), **Supp. IX:** 269–270

"Bird, the Bird, the Bird, The" (Creeley), **Supp. IV Part 1:** 149

"Bird, The"(Le Sueur), **Supp. XXIII:** 167

"Bird Banding with the Biologists" (Ray), **Supp. XVIII:** 194

Bird by Bird: Some Instructions on Writing and Life (Lamott), **Supp. XX:** 132, 137–138

"Bird came down the Walk, A" (Dickinson), **Retro. Supp. I:** 37

"Bird Frau, The" (Dove), **Supp. IV Part 1:** 245

"Bird in Hand" (screen story) (West and Ingster), **Retro. Supp. II:** 330

Bird Kingdom of the Mayas (LaBastille), **Supp. X:** 96

Birds and Beasts (W. J. Smith), **Supp. XIII:** 346

"Birds for Christmas, The" (Richard), **Supp. XIX:** 221

Bird's Nest, The (Jackson), **Supp. IX:** 124–125

Birds of America (McCarthy), **II:** 579–583; **Supp. X:** 177

Birds of America (Moore), **Supp. X:** 163, 165, 167, 168, 171, 177–179

Birds of America, The (Audubon), **Supp. XVI:** 5–6, 7, 9, 10, 12, 13

"Birds of Killingsworth, The" (Longfellow), **Retro. Supp. II:** 164

Birds of North America (Audubon Society), **Supp. V:** 177

"Birds of Vietnam, The" (Carruth), **Supp. XVI:** 55

"Bird-Witted" (Moore), **III:** 214

Birkelo, Cheryl, **Supp. XX:** 220–221

Birkerts, Sven, **Supp. IV Part 2:** 650; **Supp. V:** 212; **Supp. VIII:** 85; **Supp. X:** 311; **Supp. XX:** 92

Birkhead, L. M., **III:** 116

"Birmingham Sunday" (Hughes), **Supp. I Part 1:** 343

Birnbaum, Henry, **Supp. XII:** 128

Birnbaum, Robert, **Supp. X:** 13; **Supp. XVI:** 75; **Supp. XXIII:** 73, 75, 275

Birney, James G., **Supp. I Part 2:** 587, 588

Birstein, Ann, **Supp. VIII:** 100

"Birthday, A" (Untermeyer), **Supp. XV:** 296

Birthday Basket for Tía, A (Mora), **Supp. XIII:** 221

"Birthday Cake" (Carruth), **Supp. XVI:** 59

"Birthday Cake for Lionel, A" (Wylie), **Supp. I Part 2:** 721

"Birthday Girl: 1950" (McCarriston), **Supp. XIV:** 261

"Birthday of Mrs. Pineda, The" (Ríos), **Supp. IV Part 2:** 542, 546

"Birthday Poem, A" (Hecht), **Supp. X:** 64

"Birthday Present, A" (Plath), **Supp. I Part 2:** 531

"Birthmark, The" (Ellison), **Retro. Supp. II:** 116; **Supp. II Part 1:** 237–238

"Birth-mark, The" (Hawthorne), **Retro. Supp. I:** 152

Birth-mark, The: Unsettling the Wilderness in American Literary History (Howe), **Supp. IV Part 2:** 422, 431, 434

Birth of a Nation, The (film), **Supp. I Part 1:** 66

Birth of a World: Bolívar in Terms of His Peoples (W. Frank), **Supp. XX:** 80

Birth of the Poet, The (Gordon), **Supp. XII:** 7

Birth of Tragedy, The (Nietzsche), **Supp. IV Part 1:** 105, 110; **Supp. IV Part 2:** 519; **Supp. VIII:** 182

"Birth of Venus, The" (Botticelli), **IV:** 410

"Birth of Venus, The" (Rukeyser), **Supp. VI:** 281

"Birthplace Revisited" (Corso), **Supp. XII:** 123

"Birthright" (McKay), **Supp. X:** 136

Bisch, Louis E., **Supp. I Part 2:** 608

Bisco, John, **Supp. XVIII:** 11

"B is for Bachelors" (M. F. K. Fisher), **Supp. XVII:** 86

Bishop, Elizabeth, **Retro. Supp. I:** 140, 296, 303; **Retro. Supp. II:** 37–56, 175, 178, 189, 233, 234, 235; **Supp. I Part 1:** 72–97, 239, 320, 326; **Supp. III Part 1:** 6, 7, 10, 18, 64, 239, 320, 326; **Supp. III Part 2:** 541, 561; **Supp. IV Part 1:** 249, 257; **Supp. IV Part 2:** 439, 626, 639, 641, 644, 647, 651, 653; **Supp. V:** 337; **Supp. IX:** 40, 41, 45, 47, 48; **Supp. X:** 58; **Supp. XI:** 123, 136; **Supp. XIII:** 115, 348; **Supp. XV:** 20–21, 100, 101, 112, 119, 249, 251; **Supp. XVII:** 36, 76; **Supp. XXI:** 58, 84, 131; **Supp. XXIII:** 117

Bishop, James, Jr., **Supp. XIII:** 1, 5, 6, 7, 9, 11, 15

Bishop, John Peale, **I:** 432, 440; **II:** 81, 85, 86–87, 91, 209; **IV:** 35, 140, 427; **Retro. Supp. I:** 109; **Supp. I Part 2:** 709

Bishop, John W., **Supp. I Part 1:** 83

Bishop, Judith, **Supp. XVI:** 295

Bishop, Morris, **Supp. I Part 2:** 676

Bishop, William Thomas, **Supp. I Part 1:** 83

"Bishop Orders His Tomb at St. Praxed's Church, The" (R. Browning), **Supp. XV:** 127

"Bishop's Beggar, The" (Benét), **Supp. XI:** 56

"Bismarck" (Chapman), **Supp. XIV:** 52, 53

Bismark, Otto von, **Supp. I Part 2:** 643

"Bistro Styx, The" (Dove), **Supp. IV Part 1:** 250–251

Bitov, Andrei, **Retro. Supp. I:** 278

Bits of Gossip (R. H. Davis), **Supp. XVI:** 82–83, 84, 85, 89

"Bitter Drink, The" (Dos Passos), **Supp. I Part 2:** 647

"Bitter Farce, A" (Schwartz), **Supp. II Part 2:** 640, 657–658

"Bitter Pills for the Dark Ladies" (Jong), **Supp. V:** 118

Bitterroot (Burke), **Supp. XIV:** 34, 35

"Bittersweet Nightshade" (Skloot), **Supp. XX:** 202

Bitter Victory (Hardy; Kinnell, trans.), **Supp. III Part 1:** 235

Bittner, William, **Supp. XX:** 74, **Supp. XX:** 77, 76, 78, 80

Bitzer, G. W. "Billy", **Supp. XVI:** 183

Bixby, Horace, **IV:** 194

Bjerre, Thomas Aervold, **Supp. XXI:** 41, 47

Bjorkman, Frances Maule, **Supp. V:** 285

Bjorkman, Stig, **Supp. XV:** 6

Björnson, Björnstjerne, **II:** 275

Black, Cheryl, **Supp. XXI:** 6

Black 100, The (Salley), **Supp. XIV:** 195

Blackamerican Literature, 1760-Present (R. Miller), **Supp. X:** 324

Black American Literature Forum, **Supp. XI:** 86, 92, 93

Black and Blue (Quindlen), **Supp. XVII:** 166, 176–178

"Black and Tan" (Bell), **Supp. X:** 9

Black and White (Sorrentino), **Supp. XXI:** 228

Black Armour (Wylie), **Supp. I Part 2:** 708, 709, 712–714, 729

"Black Art" (Baraka), **Supp. II Part 1:** 49, 50–51, 59, 60

"Black Art, The" (Sexton), **Supp. II Part 2:** 682

"Black Ball, The" (Ellison), **Retro. Supp. II:** 124

Black Bart and the Sacred Hills (Wilson), **Supp. VIII:** 330, 331

Black Beetles in Amber (Bierce), **I:** 204, 209

"Blackberries" (Komunyakaa), **Supp. XIII:** 126

"Blackberry Eating" (Kinnell), **Supp. III Part 1:** 250

"Blackberrying" (D. West), **Supp. XVIII:** 283

Blackberry Winter (Warren), **IV:** 243, 251, 252

Black Betty (Mosley), **Supp. XIII:** 237, **Supp. XIII:** 240, 243

"Black Birch in Winter, A" (Wilbur), **Supp. III Part 2:** 561

Black Boy (Wright), **IV:** 477, 478, 479, 480–482, 488, 489, 494; **Retro. Supp. II:** 117; **Supp. II Part 1:** 235–236; **Supp. IV Part 1:** 11; **Supp. XVIII:** 286

"Black Boys and Native Sons" (Howe), **Retro. Supp. II:** 112

Blackburn, Alex, **Supp. XIII:** 112

Blackburn, Paul, **Supp. XXII:** 164, 169

Blackburn, William, **IV:** 100

"Black Buttercups" (Clampitt), **Supp. IX:** 42

Black Cargo, The (Marquand), **III:** 55, 60

Black Cargoes: A History of the Atlantic Slave Trade (Cowley), **Supp. II Part 1:** 140

"Black Cat, The" (Poe), **III:** 413, 414, 415; **Retro. Supp. II:** 264, 267, 269, 270

Black Cherry Blues (Burke), **Supp. XIV:** 30

"Black Christ, The" (Cullen), **Supp. IV Part 1:** 170, 171–172

Black Christ and Other Poems, The (Cullen), **Supp. IV Part 1:** 166, 170

"Black Clay Fish from Oaxaca, A" (Bronk), **Supp. XXI:** 31

"Black Cottage, The" (Frost), **Retro. Supp. I:** 128

"BLACK DADA NIHILISMUS" (Baraka), **Supp. II Part 1:** 39, 41

"Black Death" (Hurston), **Supp. VI:** 153

Black Dog, Red Dog (Dobyns), **Supp. XIII:** 87, **88–89**

"Black Dog, Red Dog" (Dobyns), **Supp. XIII:** 89

Black Dog of Fate: A Memoir (Balakian), **Supp. XXIII:** 19, **20–24**, 24, 25

"Black Earth" (Moore), **III:** 197, 212

Black Echo, The (Connelly), **Supp. XXI:** 67, 68, 75, 80

Black Fire (Jones and Neal, eds.), **Supp. X:** 324, 328

Black Fire: An Anthology of Afro American Writing (Baraka, ed.), **Supp. II Part 1:** 53

Black Flame, The (Du Bois), **Supp. II Part 1:** 159, 185–186

Black Folk, Then and Now: An Essay in the History and Sociology of the Negro Race (Du Bois), **Supp. II Part 1:** 159, 178, 183, 185

Blackford, Holly, **Supp. XXII:** 300

"Black Fox, The" (Whittier), **Supp. I Part 2:** 692

Black Freckles (Levis), **Supp. XI:** 257, 271

"Black Gang", **IV:** 406, 407

Black Genius (Mosley, ed.), **Supp. XIII:** 246

"Black Hood, The" (Francis), **Supp. IX:** 83, 91

Black House, The (Theroux), **Supp. VIII:** 319

Black Humor (Johnson), **Supp. VI:** 187, 199

Black Ice, The (Connelly), **Supp. XXI:** **70,** 75

Black Image in the White Mind, The (Fredrickson), **Supp. I Part 2:** 589

"Black Is My Favorite Color" (Malamud), **Supp. I Part 2:** 437

Black Jacobins, The (C. L. R. James), **Supp. XXI:** 159, 166–167

"Black Jewel, The" (Merwin), **Supp. III Part 1:** 355

Black Lamb and Grey Falcon (R. West), **Supp. XVI:** 152

"Black Laughter" (Taggard), **Supp. XXII:** 274

"Blacklegs" (B. Kelly), **Supp. XVII:** 131

Black Light (Kinnell), **Supp. III Part 1:** 235, 243

"Blacklist and the Cold War, The" (Kramer), **Supp. I Part 1:** 295

Black Literature in America (Baker), **Supp. X:** 324

Black Magic, A Pictorial History of the Negro in American Entertainment (Hughes), **Supp. I Part 1:** 345

Black Magic: Collected Poetry 1961– 1967 (Baraka), **Supp. II Part 1:** 45, 49–50

"Blackmailers Don't Shoot" (Chandler), **Supp. IV Part 1:** 121–122

Black Manhattan (Johnson), **Supp. IV Part 1:** 169

Black Mass, A (Baraka), **Supp. II Part 1:** 46, 48–49, 56, 57

"Black Mesa, The" (Merrill), **Supp. III Part 1:** 328

Black Metropolis (Cayton and Drake), **IV:** 475, 486, 488

Black Misery (Hughes), **Supp. I Part 1:** 336

Blackmur, Helen Dickson (Mrs. R. P. Blackmur), **Supp. II Part 1:** 90

Blackmur, Richard P., **I:** 50, 63, 67, 280, 282, 386, 455, 472; **II:** 320, 537; **III:** 194, 208, 462, 478, 497; **Supp. II Part 1:** **87–112,** 136; **Supp. II Part 2:** 543, 643; **Supp. XII:** 45

Black Music (Baraka), **Supp. II Part 1:** 47, 51

Black Nativity (Hughes), **Retro. Supp. I:** 196

Black No More (Schuyler), **Supp. XVI:** 142; **Supp. XIX:** 73

Black on Black: "Baby Sister" and Selected Writings (C. Himes), **Supp. XVI:** 145

"Black or White" (Major), **Supp. XXII:** 185

"Blackout" (Hay), **Supp. XIV:** 121

"Black Panther" (Hughes), **Retro. Supp. I:** 211

"Black Petal" (L.-Y. Lee), **Supp. XV:** 224–225

Black Power (Wright), **IV:** 478, 488, 494

"Black Rainbow, A: Modern Afro-American Poetry" (Dove and Waniek), **Supp. IV Part 1:** 244

Black Reconstruction (Du Bois), **Supp. II Part 1:** 159, 162, 171, 182

Black Riders and Other Lines, The (Crane), **I:** 406, 419

Black Riviera, The (Jarman), **Supp. XVII:** 109, 110, **115–116**

Blackrobe: Isaac Jogues (Kenny), **Supp. XXIII:** 143, 147, **151–152,** 153, 154

"Black Rook in Rainy Weather" (Plath), **Supp. I Part 2:** 543, 544; **Supp. XXIII:** 63

Blacks (Brooks), **Supp. III Part 1:** 69, 72, 86, 87

Blacks, The (Genet), **Supp. IV Part 1:** 8

Black Skin, White Masks (Fanon), **Retro. Supp. II:** 118

Black Sleuth, The (J. Bruce), **Supp. XVI:** 143

Black Spear, The (Hayden), **Supp. II Part 1:** 375

Black Spring (H. Miller), **III:** 170, 175, 178, 180–182, 183, 184; **Supp. X:** 187

"Black Stone Lying on a White Stone" (Vallejo), **Supp. XIII:** 324

Black Sun (Abbey), **Supp. XIII:** 4, **8–9,** 17

"Black Swan" (B. Kelly), **Supp. XVII:** 130–131

"Black Swan, The" (Jarrell), **II:** 382

Black Swan, The (Merrill), **Supp. III Part 1:** 319, 320

"Black Tambourine" (Crane), **I:** 387–388; **II:** 371

Black Thunder (Bontemps), **Supp. XXII:** 4, 9

"Black Tuesday" (Swenson), **Supp. IV Part 2:** 646

Black Virgin Mountain (Heinemann), **Supp. XXII:** 103, **114–116**

Black Voices (Chapman), **IV:** 485

"Blackwater Mountain" (Wright), **Supp. V:** 335, 340

"Black Wedding, The" (Singer), **IV:** 12–13

Blackwell, Alice Stone, **Supp. XI:** 195. 197

Blackwell, Elizabeth, **Retro. Supp. II:** 146

Black Woman, The (Bambara, ed.), **Supp. XI:** 1

"Black Workers" (Hughes), **Retro. Supp. I:** 202

"Black Writer and the Southern Experience, The" (Walker), **Supp. III Part 2:** 521

Black Zodiac (Wright), **Supp. V:** 333, 344, 345

Blade Runner (film), **Supp. XI:** 84

Blades, John, **Supp. XX: 87**

"Blades of Steel" (R. Fisher), **Supp. XIX:** 72

Blaine, Anita McCormick, **Supp. I Part 1:** 5

Blaine, Nell, **Supp. XV:** 179; **Supp. XXIII:** 217

Blair, Hugh, **II:** 8, 17; **Supp. I Part 2:** 422

Blair, Robert, **Supp. I Part 1:** 150

Blair, Walter, **II:** 20; **Retro. Supp. II:** 286

Blaisdell, Gus, **Supp. XIV:** 87

Blake, Casey Nelson, **Supp. XX: 69, 70, 78**

Blake, William, **I:** 381, 383, 389, 390, 398, 447, 476, 525, 526, 533; **II:** 321; **III:** 5, 19, 22, 195, 196, 197, 205, 485, 528, 540, 544–545, 567, 572; **IV:** 129; **Retro. Supp. II:** 76, 300; **Supp. I Part 1:** 80; **Supp. I Part 2:** 385, 514, 517, 539, 552, 708; **Supp. V:** 208, 257, 258; **Supp. VIII:** 26, 99, 103; **Supp. X:** 120; **Supp. XII:** 45; **Supp. XIV:** 344; **Supp. XVI:** 282; **Supp. XVII:** 119; **Supp. XX: 115, 116; Supp. XXII:** 225, 257

Blakely, Barbara, **Supp. XIII:** 32

Blanc, Marie Thérèse, **Retro. Supp. II:** 135

Blanc-Bentzon, Mme. Thérèse, **II:** 405

Blanchard, Paula, **Retro. Supp. II:** 131, 133–134, 135

Blanche, Jacques-Emile, **Supp. XX:** 232

Blanche of Brandywine (Lippard), **Supp. XXIII:** 178, 185

Blanchot, Maurice, **Supp. XVI:** 288

Blancs, Les (Hansberry), **Supp. IV Part 1:** 359, 364, 365, 369, 372–374

Blancs, Les: The Collected Last Plays of Lorraine Hansberry (Nemiroff, ed.), **Supp. IV Part 1:** 365, 368, 374

"'Blandula, Tenulla, Vagula'" (Pound), **III:** 463; **Supp. V:** 336, 337, 345

Blankenship, Tom, **IV:** 193

"Blank Paper" (Peacock), **Supp. XIX:** 198–199

Blank Wall, The (Holding), **Supp. XXII:** 119, 120, 121, 130, **131–133,** 134

Blanshard, Rufus A., **I:** 67

Blassingame, John, **Supp. XX:** 106

Blauvelt, William Satake, **Supp. V:** 171, 173

Blavatsky, Elena Petrovna, **III:** 176

"Blazing in Gold and Quenching in Purple" (Dickinson), **Retro. Supp. I:** 30

Bleak House (Dickens), **II:** 291; **Supp. IV Part 1:** 293

Blechman, Burt, **Supp. I Part 1:** 290

"Bleeder" (Dobyns), **Supp. XIII:** 88

"Bleeding" (Swenson), **Supp. IV Part 2:** 646–647

"Blessed Is the Man" (Moore), **III:** 215

"Blessed Man of Boston, My Grandmother's Thimble, and Fanning Island, The" (Updike), **IV:** 219

"Blessing, A" (Wright), **Supp. III Part 2:** 600, 606

Blessing on the Moon, A (Skibell), **Supp. XVII:** 48

Blessings (Quindlen), **Supp. XVII:** 167, **178–179**

"Blessing the Animals" (Komunyakaa), **Supp. XIII:** 129–130

"Blessing the Children" (Hogan), **Supp. IV Part 1:** 401

Bless Me, Ultima (Anya), **Supp. XIII:** 220

Blew, Mary Clearman, **Supp. XIV:** 227

Bligh, S. M., **I:** 226

"Blight" (Dybek), **Supp. XXIII:** 72

Blind Alleys (film), **Supp. XXI:** 146

Blind Assassin, The (Atwood), **Supp. XIII:** 20, **32**

Blind Bow-Boy, The (Van Vechten), **Supp. II Part 2:** 737, 740–742

"Blind Date" (Halliday), **Supp. XIX:** 85

Blind Date (Kosinski), **Supp. VII:** 215, 224–225

"Blinded by the Light" (Boyle), **Supp. XX:** 20

Blind Lion, The (Gunn Allen), **Supp. IV Part 1:** 324

"Blind Man's Holiday" (O. Henry), **Supp. II Part 1:** 401

Blind Man with a Pistol (C. Himes), **Supp. XVI:** 143, 144

Blindness and Insight (de Man), **Retro. Supp. I:** 67

"Blind Poet, The: Sidney Lanier" (Warren), **Supp. I Part 1:** 371, 373

"Blindsided" (P. E. Jones), **Supp. XXII:** 151–152

"Blind Tom" (R. H. Davis), **Supp. XVI:** 89, 90

Blithedale Romance, The (Hawthorne), **II:** 225, 231, 239, 241–242, 271, 282, 290; **IV:** 194; **Retro. Supp. I:** 63, 149, 152, 156–157, **162–163;** **Supp. I Part 2:** 579; **Supp. II Part 1:** 280; **Supp. VIII:** 153, 201

Blitzstein, Marc, **Supp. I Part 1:** 277

Blix (Norris), **III:** 314, 322, 327, 328, 333

Blixen, Karen Denisen Baroness. *See* Dinesen, Isak

"Blizzard in Cambridge" (Lowell), **II:** 554

Blizzard Voices, The (Kooser), **Supp. XIX:** 123

Bloch, Ernest, **Supp. XX:** 75

Block, Lawrence, **Supp. XXI:** 67

"Blocks" (O'Hara), **Supp. XXIII:** 214

Blok, Aleksandr Aleksandrovich, **IV:** 443

"Blond" (Trethewey), **Supp. XXI:** 244

Blonde Bait (Lacy), **Supp. XV:** 204

Blonde on Blonde (album, Dylan), **Supp. XVIII:** 20, 27, 30

Blondin, Antoine, **Supp. XVI:** 230

"Blood" (Hoffman), **Supp. XVIII:** 86

"Blood" (Singer), **IV:** 15, 19

Blood, Tin, Straw (Olds), **Supp. X:** 212–215

Blood and Guile (Hoffman), **Supp. XVIII:** 83–84

Blood and Guts in High School (Acker), **Supp. XII:** 5, 6, 11–12

"Blood Bay, The" (Proulx), **Supp. VII:** 262–263

"Blood-Burning Moon" (Toomer), **Supp. III Part 2:** 483; **Supp. IX:** 314–315

"Bloodchild" (O. Butler), **Supp. XIII:** 61, **69–70**

Bloodchild and Other Stories (O. Butler), **Supp. XIII:** 69

"Blood Donor" (Hay), **Supp. XIV:** 121

Blood for a Stranger (Jarrell), **II:** 367, 368–369, 370–371, 375, 377

Blood Issue (Crews), **Supp. XI:** 103

Bloodlines (Wright), **Supp. V:** 332, 335, 340

Blood Meridian (McCarthy), **Supp. XXIII:** 42

Blood Meridian; or, The Evening Redness in the West (McCarthy), **Supp. VIII:** 175, 177, **180–182,** 188, 190

Blood of My Blood (Gambino), **Supp. XX:** 35

"Blood of the Conquistadores, The" (Alvarez), **Supp. VII:** 7

"Blood of the Lamb, The" (hymn), **Supp. I Part 2:** 385

Blood of the Martyr (Crane), **I:** 422

"Blood of the Martyrs, The" (Benét), **Supp. XI:** 56, 58

Blood of the Prophets, The (Masters), **Supp. I Part 2:** 458, 459, 461

Blood on the Forge (Attaway), **Supp. II Part 1:** 234–235

Blood on the Tracks (album, Dylan), **Supp. XVIII:** 20, 27, 30

"Blood Relatives" (Apple), **Supp. XVII:** 6

"Blood Returns, The" (Kingsolver), **Supp. VII:** 209

"Bloodshed" (C. Ozick), **Supp. XVII:** 43

Bloodshed and Three Novellas (Ozick), **Supp. V:** 259–260, 261, 266–268

"Blood Soup" (Dybek), **Supp. XXIII:** 71

"Blood Stains" (Francis), **Supp. IX:** 86

Blood Work (Connelly), **Supp. XXI:** 72

Blood Work (film, Eastwood), **Supp. XXI:** 74

Bloody Crossroads, The: Where Literature and Politics Meet (Podhoretz), **Supp. VIII:** 241–242

Bloody News from My Friend (Samianto, trans. Balakian), **Supp. XXIII:** 28

Bloom, Alice, **Supp. IV Part 1:** 308

Bloom, Allan, **Retro. Supp. II:** 19, 30, 31, 33–34

Bloom, Claire, **Retro. Supp. II:** 281; **Supp. IX:** 125

Bloom, Harold, **Retro. Supp. I:** 67, 193, 299; **Retro. Supp. II:** 81, 210, 262; **Supp. IV Part 2:** 620, 689; **Supp. V:** 178, 272; **Supp. VIII:** 180; **Supp. IX:** 146, 259; **Supp. XII:** 261; **Supp. XIII:** 46, 47; **Supp. XIV:** 14; **Supp. XV:** 134; **Supp. XVII:** 70, 141; **Supp. XXIII:** 42

Bloom, Larry, **Supp. XIII:** 133

Bloom, Leopold, **I:** 27, 150; **III:** 10

Bloomfield, Leonard, **I:** 64

Bloomingdale Papers, The (Carruth), **Supp. XVI:** 48–50

"Blossom and Fruit" (Benét), **Supp. XI:** 52–53

Blotner, Joseph, **Retro. Supp. I:** 88

Blouin, Lenora, **Supp. VIII:** 266

"Blouse, The" (Rudman), **Supp. XXIII:** 124

"Blowing Soap Bubbles" (Crooker), **Supp. XXIII:** 56

"Blowin' in the Wind" (song, Dylan), **Supp. XVIII:** 24, 25, 26, 29

Blue Angel (Prose), **Supp. XVI:** 249, 259–260

Blue Angel, The (film), **Supp. XVIII:** 243

Blue Arabesque: A Search for the Sublime (Hampl), **Supp. XXII:** 86, 98–99

"Blue Battalions, The" (Crane), **I:** 419–420

"Blue Bead, The" (Hadas), **Supp. XXIII:** 118, 119

"Bluebeard" (Barthelme), **Supp. IV Part 1:** 47

"Bluebeard" (Millay), **III:** 130

"Blueberries" (Frost), **Retro. Supp. I:** 121, 128

"Blue Boy" (Dybek), **Supp. XXIII:** 76

Blue Calhoun (Price), **Supp. VI:** 265–266

Blue Caterpillar, The (Pickering), **Supp. XXI:** 202–203

Blue City (Macdonald, as Millar), **Supp. IV Part 2:** 466–467

Blue Devils of Nada, The: A Contemporary American Approach to Aesthetics (Murray), **Supp. XIX: 159–160**

Blue Estuaries, The: Poems, 1923–1968 (Bogan), **Supp. III Part 1:** 48, 57, 66

Blue Hammer, The (Macdonald), **Supp. IV Part 2:** 462

"Blue Hotel, The" (Crane), **I:** 34, 415–416, 423

"Blue Hour, The" (Komunyakaa), **Supp. XIII:** 130

Blue in the Face (Auster), **Supp. XII:** 21

Blue Jay's Dance, The: A Birth Year (Erdrich), **Supp. IV Part 1:** 259–260, 265, 270, 272

"Blue Juniata" (Cowley), **Supp. II Part 1:** 144

Blue Juniata: Collected Poems (Cowley), **Supp. II Part 1:** 140

"Blue Lick" (Offutt), **Supp. XIX:** 164, 165

Blue Light (Mosley), **Supp. XIII: 245–247,** 248, 249

"Blue Light Lounge Sutra for the Performance Poets at Harold Park Hotel" (Komunyakaa), **Supp. XIII:** 125

"Blue Meridian" (Toomer), **Supp. III Part 2:** 476, 487; **Supp. IX:** 320

"Blue Moles" (Plath), **Supp. I Part 2:** 539

Blue Mountain Ballads (music) (Bowles), **Supp. IV Part 1:** 84

Blue Movie (Southern), **Supp. XI:** 309

"Blue Notes" (Matthews), **Supp. IX:** 169

Blue Pastoral (Sorrentino), **Supp. XXI:** 226, 235–236

Blue Pastures (Oliver), **Supp. VII:** 229–230, 245

"Blueprint for Negro Writing" (Wright), **Supp. XVIII:** 282–283

"Blueprints" (Kingsolver), **Supp. VII:** 203

Blue Religion, The (Connelly, ed.), **Supp. XXI:** 74–75, 79

Blue Rhine, Black Forest (Untermeyer), **Supp. XV:** 310

"Blue Ribbon at Amesbury, A" (Frost), **Retro. Supp. I:** 138

"Blues Ain't No Mockin Bird" (Bambara), **Supp. XI:** 3

"Blues and the Fable in the Flesh, The" (lecture, Murray), **Supp. XIX:** 153

"Blues Chant Hoodoo Rival" (Komunyakaa), **Supp. XIII:** 117, 118

Blue Screen (Parker), **Supp. XIX:** 186

"Blues for Another Time" (Dunn), **Supp. XI:** 148

"Blues for Jimmy" (McGrath), **Supp. X:** 116

"Blues for John Coltraine, Dead at 41" (Matthews), **Supp. IX:** 157

Blues for Mister Charlie (Baldwin), **Retro. Supp. II:** 8; **Supp. I Part 1:** 48, 61–62, 63

"Blues for Warren" (McGrath), **Supp. X:** 116

Blue Shoe (Lamott), **Supp. XX: 138–140**

Blues If You Want (Matthews), **Supp. IX:** 155, **163–165**

"Blues I'm Playing, The" (Hughes), **Retro. Supp. I:** 204; **Supp. XIX:** 75

"Blue Sky, The" (Snyder), **Supp. VIII:** 306

"Blues on a Box" (Hughes), **Retro. Supp. I:** 208

"Blues People" (Ellison), **Retro. Supp. II:** 124

Blues People: Negro Music in White America (Baraka), **Retro. Supp. II:** 124; **Supp. II Part 1:** 30, 31, 33–35, 37, 41, 42, 53

"Blue Spruces in Pairs, a Bird Bath Between": (Bronk), **Supp. XXI:** 30

Bluest Eye, The (Morrison), **Supp. III Part 1:** 362, 363–367, 379; **Supp. IV Part 1:** 2, 253; **Supp. VIII:** 213, 214, 227; **Supp. XI:** 4, 91

Bluestone, George, **Supp. IX:** 7, 15

Blue Swallows, The (Nemerov), **III:** 269, 270, 271, 274–275, 278, 284, 286–288

"Blue Tattoo" (Nelson and Espeland), **Supp. XVIII:** 181

Blue Voyage (Aiken), **I:** 53, 56

Bluhm, Norman, **Supp. XXIII:** 217

Blum, Gustav, **Supp. XV:** 194

Blum, Morgan, **I:** 169

Blum, W. C (pseudonym). *See* Watson, James Sibley, Jr.

Blumenthal, Nathaniel. *See* Branden, Nathaniel

Blumenthal, Sidney, **Supp. VIII:** 241

Blunden, Edmund, **Supp. XIX:** 133

Blunt, Wilfrid Scawen, **III:** 459

Bly, Carol, **Supp. XVI: 31–43**

Bly, Robert, **I:** 291; **Supp. III Part 2:** 599; **Supp. IV Part 1: 59–77,** 177; **Supp. IV Part 2:** 623; **Supp. V:** 332; **Supp. VIII:** 279; **Supp. IX:** 152, 155, 265, 271, 290; **Supp. X:** 127; **Supp. XI:** 142; **Supp. XIII:** 284; **Supp. XV:** 74, 176; **Supp. XVI:** 32, 36, 39, 177, 212, 230; **Supp. XVII:** 243, 244; **Supp. XXI:** 83, 84–86, 87, 91, 93, 94, 95; **Supp. XXII:** 83; **Supp. XXIII:** 136

"B Negative" (X. J. Kennedy), **Supp. XV: 156–157**

"Boarder, The" (Simpson), **Supp. IX:** 269

Boarding House Blues (Farrell), **II:** 30, 43, 45

Boas, Franz, **I:** 214; **Supp. I Part 2:** 641; **Supp. VIII:** 295; **Supp. IX:** 329; **Supp. XIV:** 199, 209, 210

"Boat, The" (Oliver), **Supp. VII:** 247

"Boat, The" (Sexton), **Supp. II Part 2:** 692

Boating Party, The (Renoir), **Supp. XII:** 188

Boat of Quiet Hours, The (Kenyon), **Supp. VII:** 167–169, 171

"Boat of Quiet Hours, The" (Kenyon), **Supp. VII:** 168

"Bob and Spike" (Wolfe), **Supp. III Part 2:** 580

"Bobby Shafter's Gone to Sea" (Swados), **Supp. XIX:** 267

"Bob Dylan's 115th Dream" (song, Dylan), **Supp. XVIII:** 25

Bobrowski, Johannes, **Supp. XV:** 78

Bob the Gambler (F. Barthelme), **Supp. XI:** 30, 31, 32, 34–35, 36–37

Boccaccio, Giovanni, **III:** 283, 411; **IV:** 230

Bocock, Maclin, **Supp. X:** 79

Boddy, Kasia, **Supp. XXII:** 261

Bodelson, Anders, **Supp. XVI:** 33

Bodenheim, Maxwell, **II:** 42, 530; **Retro. Supp. I:** 417; **Supp. I Part 1:** 257

"Bodies" (Oates), **Supp. II Part 2:** 520

"Bodies and Souls: The Haitian Revolution and Madison Smartt Bell's *All Souls' Rising*" (Trouillot), **Supp. X:** 14

Bodies of Water (Cliff), **Supp. XXII:** 66–67, 74–75

Bodies of Work: Essays (Acker), **Supp. XII:** 7

Bodily Harm (Atwood), **Supp. XIII: 25–27**

Bodley Head Jack London (London), **II:** 483

Body (Crews), **Supp. XI: 108–109**

"Body, The" (Heldreth), **Supp. V:** 151

Body and Soul (Conroy), **Supp. XVI:** 63, **72–74,** 77

"Body and Soul: A Meditation" (Kumin), **Supp. IV Part 2:** 442, 452

Body and Soul: Essays on Poetry (Jarman), **Supp. XVII:** 110, **111–112**

"Body and Soul: Parts of a Life" (Jarman), **Supp. XVII:** 112, 113

Body and the Song, The (Bishop), **Retro. Supp. II:** 40

"Body Bright" (Sanders), **Supp. XVI:** 276

Body of Martin Aquilera, The (Everett), **Supp. XVIII:** 57

Body of Poetry, The: Essays on Women, Form, and the Poetic Self (A. Finch), **Supp. XVII:** 69–70, **77–78**

Body of This Death: Poems (Bogan), **Supp. III Part 1:** 47, 49–52, 58

Body of Waking (Rukeyser), **Supp. VI:** 274, 281

"Body of Waking" (Rukeyser), **Supp. VI:** 279

"Body on Fire, the Soul in Flight, The" (Jarman), **Supp. XVII:** 111, 112

Body Rags (Kinnell), **Supp. III Part 1:** 235, 236, 243–245, 250, 253, 254

"Body's Curse, The" (Dobyns), **Supp. XIII:** 87

"Body's Weight" (Espaillat), **Supp. XXI:** 111

"Body's Weight, The" (Dobyns), **Supp. XIII:** 89

Body Traffic (Dobyns), **Supp. XIII:** 87, 89

"'Body with the Lamp Lit Inside, The' " (Mills), **Supp. IV Part 1:** 64

Boehm, David, **Supp. XVII:** 58

Boehme, Jakob, **I:** 10

Bogan, Louise, **I:** 169, 185; **Retro. Supp. I:** 36; **Supp. I Part 2:** 707, 726; **Supp. III Part 1: 47–68; Supp. VIII:** 171,

265; **Supp. IX:** 229; **Supp. X:** 58, 102; **Supp. XIII:** 347; **Supp. XIV:** 129; **Supp. XVII:** 75; **Supp. XXIII:** 145

Bogan, Major Benjamin Lewis, **IV:** 120

Bogart, Humphrey, **Supp. I Part 2:** 623; **Supp. IV Part 1:** 130, 356

Bogdanovich, Peter, **Supp. V:** 226

Bogey Man, The (Plimpton), **Supp. XVI:** 241

Boggs, Francis W., **Supp. XVI:** 182

"Bogs" (Pickering), **Supp. XXI:** 198

"Bohemian, The" (Hapgood), **Supp. XVII:** 103

"Bohemian, The" (Harte), **Supp. II Part 1:** 339

"Bohemian Girl, The" (Cather), **Retro. Supp. I:** 7

"Bohemian Hymn, The" (Emerson), **II:** 19

"Bohemians" (Saunders), **Supp. XIX:** 234

"Boids and Beasties" (Geisel), **Supp. XVI:** 100

Boissevain, Eugen, **III:** 124

Boissière, Ralph de, **Supp. XXI:** 160

Boit, Edward, **Retro. Supp. I:** 366

Bojorquez, Jennifer, **Supp. XII:** 318

Boker, George, **Supp. XV:** 269

"Bold Words at the Bridge" (Jewett), **II:** 394

Boleslavsky, Richard, **Supp. XIV:** 240, 243

Boleyn, Anne, **Supp. I Part 2:** 461

Bolick, Katie, **Supp. XVI:** 167; **Supp. XXIII:** 135, 137, 138

Bolivar, Simon, **Supp. I Part 1:** 283, 284, 285

Bolonik, Kera, **Supp. XVIII:** 60

Bolton, Guy, **Supp. I Part 1:** 281

Bolts of Melody: New Poems of Emily Dickinson (Todd and Bingham, eds.), **I:** 470; **Retro. Supp. I:** 36

"Bomb" (Corso), **Supp. XII:** 117, 124, 125–126, 127

Bombeck, Erma, **Supp. XVII:** 168

Bombs Away (Steinbeck), **IV:** 51–52

"Bona and Paul" (Toomer), **Supp. IX:** 307, 318–319

Bonaparte, Marie, **III:** 418; **Retro. Supp. II:** 264, 266

"Bon-Bon" (Poe), **III:** 425

Bond, The (Boyce), **Supp. XXI:** 5, 11–12

Bond, The (N. Boyce), **Supp. XVII:** 99, 100

Bondage (Hwang), **Supp. XXI:** 147

Bondsman, The (Massinger), **Supp. XV:** 238

Bondwoman's Narrative, by Hannah Crafts, a Fugitive Slave, Recently Escaped from North Carolina, The, **Supp. XX:** 105

Bone, Martyn, **Supp. XXII:** 247

Bone, Robert, **Supp. IX:** 318–319; **Supp. XI:** 283; **Supp. XVIII:** 285

Bone by Bone (Matthiessen), **Supp. V:** 199, 212, 213, 214

"Bone Deposit" (Ray), **Supp. XVIII:** 194

Boners (Abingdon). *See Schoolboy Howlers* (Abingdon)

"Bones" (Goldbarth), **Supp. XII:** 173–174

"Bones and Jewels" (Monette), **Supp. X:** 159

"Bones and Shells" (Sanders), **Supp. XVI:** 271 272

"Bones of a House" (Cowley). *See* "Blue Juniata"

Bones on Black Spruce Mountain, The (Budbill), **Supp. XIX:** 11–12

Bonetti, Kay, **Supp. VIII:** 47, 152, 159, 160, 165, 168, 170, 223; **Supp. XII:** 61; **Supp. XIV:** 232, 234; **Supp. XXI:** 36

Bonfire of the Vanities, The (Wolfe), **Supp. III Part 2:** 584–586

Bonheur, Rosa, **Supp. XV:** 276

Bonhoeffer, Dietrich, **Supp. VIII:** 198

Boni, Charles, **Supp. XIV:** 288

Boni and Liveright, **Retro. Supp. I:** 59, 80, 178

Bonicelli, Vittorio, **Supp. XI:** 307

Bonifacius (Mather), **Supp. II Part 2:** 461, 464

Bonnefoy, Yves, **Supp. III Part 1:** 235, 243

Bonner, Robert, **Retro. Supp. I:** 246

Bonneville, Mme. Marguerite, **Supp. I Part 2:** 520, 521

Bonneville, Nicolas de, **Supp. I Part 2:** 511, 518, 519

Bonney, William. *See* Billy the Kid

Bontemps, Arna, **Retro. Supp. I:** 194, 196, 203; **Supp. I Part 1:** 325; **Supp. IV Part 1:** 170; **Supp. IX:** 306, 309; **Supp. XVIII:** 282; **Supp. XXII:** 1–16

Book, A (Barnes), **Supp. III Part 1:** 36, 39, 44

Book about Myself, A (Dreiser), **I:** 515; **Retro. Supp. II:** 104

"Book as a Container of Consciousness, The" (Gass), **Supp. VI:** 92

Booker, Keith, **Supp. XV:** 197

"Bookies, Beware!" (Heller), **Supp. IV Part 1:** 383

"Book Notes and News" (column, Boyce), **Supp. XXI:** 2

Book of American Negro Poetry, The (Johnson), **Supp. IV Part 1:** 165, 166; **Supp. XXII:** 11

Book of Americans, A (Benét), **Supp. XI:** 46, 47, 51

Book of Beb, The (Buechner), **Supp. XII:** 53

Book of Breeething, The (Burroughs), **Supp. III Part 1:** 97, 103

Book of Burlesques, A (Mencken), **III:** 104

Book of Common Prayer, A (Didion), **Supp. IV Part 1:** 196, 198, 203–205, 207, 208

Book of Daniel, The (Doctorow), **Supp. IV Part 1:** 218, 219, 220–222, 227, 231, 237–238, 238; **Supp. V:** 45

Book of Dreams (Kerouac), **Supp. III Part 1:** 225

"Book of Ephraim, The" (Merrill), **Supp. III Part 1:** 330–334

Book of Folly, The (Sexton), **Supp. II Part 2:** 691, 692–694

Book of Gods and Devils, The (Simic), **Supp. VIII:** 281

Book of Guys, The (Keillor), **Supp. XVI:** 177

"Book of Hours of Sister Clotilde, The" (Lowell), **II:** 522

Book of Jamaica, The (Banks), **Supp. V:** 11, 12, 16

"Book of Life" (Bidart), **Supp. XV:** 23

Book of Living Verse, The; English and American Poetry from the Thirteenth Century to the Present Day (Untermeyer, ed.), **Supp. XV:** 310

Book of Love, A (Vildrac; Bynner, trans.), **Supp. XV:** 50

Book of Lyrics (Bynner), **Supp. XV:** 51

Book of Martyrs (Fox). *See Acts and Monuments of These Latter and Perilous Days* (Fox)

Book of Medicines, The (Hogan), **Supp. IV Part 1:** 397, 410, 411–414

"Book of Medicines, The" (Hogan), **Supp. IV Part 1:** 412, 413

"Book of Memory, The" (Auster), **Supp. XII:** 21–22

Book of My Nights (L.-Y. Lee), **Supp. XV:** 215, **223–226**

Book of Negro Folklore, The (Hughes, ed.), **Supp. I Part 1:** 345; **Supp. XXII:** 11–12

Book of Nightmares, The (Kinnell), **Supp. III Part 1:** 235, 236, 243, 244, 246–254

Book of One's Own, A: People and Their Diaries (Mallon), **Supp. XIX:** 134

Book of Prefaces, A (Mencken), **III:** 99–100, 105

Book of Repulsive Women, The (Barnes), **Supp. III Part 1:** 33

Book of Revelation, **Supp. XXIII:** 44

Book of Roses, The (Parkman), **Supp. II Part 2:** 597, 598

Book of the Body, The (Bidart), **Supp. XV:** 21, **25–27**

"Book of the Dead, The" (Rukeyser), **Supp. VI:** 272, 278, 279; **Supp. XV:** 349

"Book of the Grotesque, The" (Anderson), **I:** 106

Book of the Homeless, The (Wharton), **Retro. Supp. I:** 377

Book of the Hopi (Waters), **Supp. X:** 124

Book of Tobit (Bible), **Supp. XII:** 54

Book of Verses, A (Masters), **Supp. I Part 2:** 458

Book of Yaak, The (Bass), **Supp. XVI:** **18–19**

"Book of Yolek, The" (Hecht), **Supp. X:** 69, **70–71**

"Books" (Collins), **Supp. XXI:** 55

"Books Considered" (Bloom), **Supp. I Part 1:** 96

"Books I Left Behind, The" (Pickering), **Supp. XXI:** 196

Books in My Life, The (H. Miller), **II:** 176, 189

"Books/P,L,E, The" (Goldbarth), **Supp. XII:** 190

Bookviews, **Supp. XI:** 216

"Book World Live", **Supp. XVIII:** 143–144
"Boolean Algebra: X2=X" (Bronk), **Supp. XXI:** 30
"Boom" (Nemerov), **III:** 278
Boom! (T. Williams), **IV:** 383
Boomer Girls: Poems by Women of the Baby Boom Generation (Gemin and Sergi, eds.), **Supp. XXI:** 246
Boom Town (Wolfe), **IV:** 456
"Boom Town" (Wolfe), **IV:** 469
Boone, Daniel, **II:** 207; **III:** 444; **IV:** 192, 193
Boorstin, Daniel, **I:** 253
Booth, Charles, **Supp. I Part 1:** 13
Booth, John Wilkes, **III:** 588
Booth, Philip, **I:** 522; **Supp. IX:** 269; **Supp. XI:** 141; **Supp. XIII:** 277; **Supp. XV:** 92
Booth, General William, **Supp. I Part 2:** 384, 386
"Booze"(P. Benedict), **Supp. XXIII:** 36
Borah, William, **III:** 475
Borden, Lizzie, **II:** 5
Borderlands/La Frontera: The New Mestiza (Anzaldúa), **Supp. XIII:** 223
Border Matters (Saldívar), **Supp. XIX:** 112–113
Borders (Mora), **Supp. XIII:** 213, **215–217**
Border Trilogy (McCarthy), **Supp. VIII:** 175, 182
"Border View, Hot Springs, Texas" (W. V. Davis), **Supp. XXI:** 95
Borel, Pétrus, **III:** 320
Borges, Jorge Luis, **I:** 123, 135, 138, 140, 142; **Supp. III Part 2:** 560; **Supp. IV Part 2:** 623, 626, 630; **Supp. V:** 238; **Supp. VIII:** 15, 348, 349; **Supp. XII:** 21, 147; **Supp. XV:** 34; **Supp. XVI:** 201, 206; **Supp. XVII:** 47; **Supp. XIX:** 131; **Supp. XXIII:** 68
"Borges and I" (Bidart), **Supp. XV:** 34, 35
"Borinken Blues" (Komunyakaa), **Supp. XIII:** 117
"Born, The" (Lamott), **Supp. XX: 143–144**
"Born a Square: The Westerner's Dilemma" (Stegner), **Supp. IV Part 2:** 595; **Supp. V:** 224
"Born Bad" (Cisneros), **Supp. VII:** 62
Born on the Fourth of July (Kovic), **Supp. XIX:** 17
"Borough of Cemeteries" (Shaw), **Supp. XIX:** 246
Borrowed Time: An AIDS Memoir (Monette), **Supp. X:** 145, 146, 147, 152, 154, 155
Bose, Sudip, **Supp. XXII:** 205, 206, 214
Bosmajian, Hamida, **Supp. XXII:** 290
"Bosque del Apache Wildlife Refuge" (Mora), **Supp. XIII:** 218
Boss Dog, The: A Story of Provence (M. F. K. Fisher), **Supp. XVII:** 91
Bost, Suzanne, **Supp. XXII:** 66, 70, 75, 78
"Boston" (Hardwick), **Supp. III Part 1:** 201
Boston (Sinclair), **Supp. V:** 282, 288–289

Boston, B. H., **Supp. XIII:** 312
Boston Adventure (Stafford), **Retro. Supp. II:** 177, 178
"Boston Common" (Berryman), **I:** 172
"Boston Hymn" (Emerson), **II:** 13, 19
Bostonians, The (H. James), **I:** 9; **II:** 282; **IV:** 202; **Retro. Supp. I:** 216, 225
Boston Marriage (Mamet), **Supp. XIV:** 247
"Boston Nativity, The" (Lowell), **II:** 538
Boswell, James, **IV:** 431; **Supp. I Part 2:** 656
Boswell: A Modern Comedy (Elkin), **Supp. VI:** 42, **44–45,** 57
Bosworth, Patricia, **Supp. IV Part 2:** 573, 591
"Bothersome Sex and O'Brien, The" (Ryan as Quin), **Supp. XVIII:** 238
Botticelli (McNally), **Supp. XIII:** 197
Botticelli, Sandro, **IV:** 410; **Retro. Supp. I:** 422
"Botticellian Trees, The" (W. C. Williams), **Retro. Supp. I:** 422
"Bottle of Milk for Mother, A" (Algren), **Supp. IX:** 3
"Bottle of Perrier, A" (Wharton), **IV:** 316
"Bottles" (Kenyon), **Supp. VII:** 171
"Bottom Line, The" (Elkin), **Supp. VI:** 52, **53**
Bottom: On Shakespeare (Zukofsky), **Supp. III Part 2:** 622, 624, 625, 626, 627, 629
Boublil, Alain, **Supp. XXI:** 155
Boucher, Anthony, **Supp. IV Part 2:** 473; **Supp. XV:** 203, 205
Boucicault, Dion, **Supp. XXII:** 70
Boughton, Henrietta Breckenridge. *See* Young, Barbara
Boukreev, Anatoli, **Supp. XVIII:** 112
Boulanger, Nadia, **Supp. IV Part 1:** 81
"Boulot and Boulette" (Chopin), **Supp. I Part 1:** 211
Boulton, Agnes, **III:** 403; **Supp. XXII:** 17–31
Bound East for Cardiff (O'Neill), **III:** 388
Bound for Glory (Guthrie), **Supp. XVIII:** 23
"Bounty" (Saunders), **Supp. XIX:** 226, 227
"Bounty"(P. Benedict), **Supp. XXIII:** 41
"Bouquet, The" (Stevens), **IV:** 90
"Bouquet of Dark Red Mums, The" (Notley), **Supp. XXII:** 230
"Bouquet of Roses in Sunlight" (Stevens), **IV:** 93
Bourdin, Henri L., **Supp. I Part 1:** 251
Bourgeois, Monique, **Supp. XXII:** 99–100
Bourgeois Poet, The (Shapiro), **Supp. II Part 2:** 701, 703, 704, 713, 714–716
Bourget, James, **IV:** 319
Bourget, Paul, **II:** 325, 338; **IV:** 311, 315; **Retro. Supp. I:** 224, 359, 373; **Supp. XX: 232**
Bourjaily, Vance, **III:** 43; **Supp. IX:** 260
Bourke-White, Margaret, **I:** 290, 293, 295, 297
Bourne, Charles Rogers, **I:** 215
Bourne, Mrs. Charles Rogers, **I:** 215

Bourne, Randolph, **I: 214–238,** 243, 245, 246–247, 251, 259; **Supp. I Part 2:** 524; **Supp. XV:** 141, 298, 301
Boursicot, Bernard, **Supp. XXI:** 152, 153, 154
Bouton, Jim "Bulldog", **Supp. XX: 274**
Bouton, John Bell, **Supp. XXIII:** 188, 189
Bowden, Charles, **Supp. XIII:** 17
Bowditch, Nathaniel, **Supp. I Part 2:** 482
Bowen, Barbara, **Supp. IX:** 311
Bowen, Elizabeth, **Retro. Supp. I:** 351; **Supp. IV Part 1:** 299; **Supp. VIII:** 65, 165, 251, 265; **Supp. IX:** 128
Bowen, Francis, **Supp. I Part 2:** 413
Bowen, Henry, **Supp. XVIII:** 4
Bowen, Louise de Koven, **Supp. I Part 1:** 5
Bowen, Michael, **Supp. VIII:** 73
Bowers, John, **Supp. XI:** 217–218
"Bowlers Anonymous" (Dobyns), **Supp. XIII:** 86
Bowles, Emily, **Supp. XVIII:** 200, 202
Bowles, Jane (Jane Auer), **II:** 586; **Supp. IV Part 1:** 89, 92
Bowles, Paul, **I:** 211; **II:** 586; **Supp. II Part 1:** 17; **Supp. IV Part 1: 79–99**
Bowles, Samuel, **I:** 454, 457; **Retro. Supp. I:** 30, 32, 33
"Bowl of Blood, The" (Jeffers), **Supp. II Part 2:** 434
"Bowls" (Moore), **III:** 196
Bowman, James, **I:** 193
"Bows to Drouth" (Snyder), **Supp. VIII:** 303
Box, Edgar (pseudonym). *See* Vidal, Gore
Box and Quotations from Chairman Mao Tse-tung (Albee), **I:** 89–91, 94
Boxer and the Spy, The (Parker), **Supp. XIX:** 190
Box Garden, The (Shields), **Supp. VII:** 314–315, 320
"Box of Pastels, A" (Kooser), **Supp. XIX:** 128
"Box Seat" (Toomer), **Supp. III Part 2:** 484; **Supp. IX:** 316, 318
Boy, A (Ashbery), **Supp. III Part 1:** 5
"Boy and Dog" (L. Brown), **Supp. XXI:** 38, 42, **43–44**
Boyce, Horace, **II:** 136
Boyce, Neith, **Supp. XVII:** 96, 97, 98–99, 100, 106; **Supp. XXI: 1–16**
Boyd, Brian, **Retro. Supp. I:** 270, 275
Boyd, Janet L., **Supp. X:** 229
Boyd, Kristen, **Supp. XXIII:** 246
Boyd, Nancy (pseudonym). *See* Millay, Edna St. Vincent
Boyd, Thomas, **I:** 99; **IV:** 427
Boyesen, H. H., **II:** 289
"Boyhood" (Collins), **Supp. XXI:** 64
"Boyhood" (Farrell), **II:** 28
"Boy in France, A" (Salinger), **III:** 552–553
Boy in the Water (Dobyns), **Supp. XIII:** 75, **84**
Boyle, Kay, **IV:** 404
Boyle, T. Coraghessan, **Supp. VIII:** **1–17; Supp. XX: 17–32; Supp. XXI:** 226; **Supp. XXII:** 262
Boyle, Thomas John. *See* Boyle, T. C.

Boynton, H. W., **Supp. IX:** 7

Boynton, Percy Holmes, **Supp. I Part 2:** 415

Boynton, Robert, **Supp. XVII:** 209; **Supp. XVIII:** 105, 107, 116

"Boy on a Train" (Ellison), **Retro. Supp. II:** 124

"Boy Riding Forward Backward" (Francis), **Supp. IX:** 82

"Boys and Girls" (Cisneros), **Supp. VII:** 59–60

Boy's Froissart, The (Lanier), **Supp. I Part 1:** 361

"Boys"(Kenny), **Supp. XXIII:** 149

Boy's King Arthur, The (Lanier), **Supp. I Part 1:** 361

Boy's Mabinogion, The (Lanier), **Supp. I Part 1:** 361

"Boys of '29, The" (Holmes), **Supp. I Part 1:** 308

Boys of '76, The (Coffin), **III:** 577

Boy's Percy, The (Lanier), **Supp. I Part 1:** 361

Boy's Town (Howells), **I:** 418

Boy's Will, A (Frost), **II:** 152, 153, 155–156, 159, 164, 166; **Retro. Supp. I:** 124, 127, 128, 131; **Retro. Supp. II:** 168

"Boy Up a Tree" (Hoffman), **Supp. XVIII:** 86

"Boy Who Wrestled with Angels, The" (Hoffman), **Supp. X:** 90

"Boy with One Shoe, The" (Jewett), **Retro. Supp. II:** 132

"Brace, The" (Bausch), **Supp. VII:** 48

Bracebridge Hall, or, The Humorists (Irving), **I:** 339, 341; **II:** 308–309, 313

Bracher, Frederick, **I:** 378, 380; **Supp. I Part 1:** 185

Brackenridge, Hugh Henry, **Supp. I Part 1:** 124, 127, 145; **Supp. II Part 1:** 65

Brackett, Leigh, **Supp. IV Part 1:** 130

Bradbury, John M., **I:** 288–289; **IV:** 130, 135

Bradbury, Malcolm, **Supp. VIII:** 124; **Supp. XVIII:** 140

Bradbury, Ray, **Supp. I Part 2:** 621–622; **Supp. IV Part 1: 101–118; Supp. XVI:** 122; **Supp. XVII:** 41; **Supp. XXIII:** 290

"Brad Carrigan, American" (Saunders), **Supp. XIX:** 233

Braddon, Mary E., **Supp. I Part 1:** 35, 36

Bradfield, Scott, **Supp. VIII:** 88

Bradford, Gamaliel, **I:** 248, 250

Bradford, Roark, **Retro. Supp. I:** 80

Bradford, William, **Retro. Supp. II:** 161, 162; **Supp. I Part 1:** 110, 112; **Supp. I Part 2:** 486, 494; **Supp. XXII: 33–47**

Bradlee, Ben, **Supp. V:** 201

Bradley, Bill, **Supp. VIII:** 47

Bradley, F. H., **Retro. Supp. I:** 57, 58

Bradley, Francis Herbert, **I:** 59, 567–568, 572, 573

Bradshaw, Barbara, **Supp. XIII:** 313

Bradstreet, Anne, **I:** 178–179, 180, 181, 182, 184; **III:** 505; **Retro. Supp. I:** 40; **Supp. I Part 1: 98–123,** 300;

Supp. I Part 2: 484, 485, 496, 546, 705; **Supp. V:** 113, 117–118; **Supp. XIII:** 152; **Supp. XIV:** 128; **Supp. XVIII:** 304; **Supp. XXII:** 46

Bradstreet, Elizabeth, **Supp. I Part 1:** 108, 122

Bradstreet, Simon, **I:** 178; **Supp. I Part 1:** 103, 110, 116

Bradstreet, Mrs. Simon. *See* Bradstreet, Anne

Brady, Alice, **III:** 399

Brady, Catherine, **Supp. XXIII:** 301

Brady, Matthew, **Supp. XVIII:** 4

Bragdon, Claude, **Supp. XX: 117**

"Bragdowdy and the Busybody, The" (Thurber), **Supp. I Part 2:** 617

Bragg, Rick, **Supp. XVIII:** 195

"Brahma" (Emerson), **II:** 19, 20

Brahms, Johannes, **III:** 118, 448

"Brahms in Delirium" (Skloot), **Supp. XX: 203**

Braided Creek (Kooser and Harrison), **Supp. XIX:** 126

"Braiding" (L.-Y. Lee), **Supp. XV:** 214

"Brain and the Mind, The" (James), **II:** 346

Brainard, Joe, **Supp. XV:** 33; **Supp. XXIII:** 217

"Brain Damage" (Barthelme), **Supp. IV Part 1:** 44

"Braindead Megaphone, The" (Saunders), **Supp. XIX:** 235

Braindead Megaphone, The: Essays (Saunders), **Supp. XIX: 234–236**

"Brain Scan" (Skloot), **Supp. XX: 200**

"Brain to the Heart, The" (Komunyakaa), **Supp. XIII:** 120

Braithwaite, Chris, **Supp. XXII:** 212

Braithwaite, William Stanley, **Retro. Supp. I:** 131; **Supp. IX:** 309; **Supp. XV:** 296–297, 301–302, 305, 306

Brakhage, Stan, **Supp. XII:** 2

Braly, Malcolm, **Supp. XVIII:** 147

"Bramble, The" (Wrigley), **Supp. XVIII:** 301

Brame, Gloria, **Supp. XV:** 113; **Supp. XXIII:** 122

Bramer, Monte, **Supp. X:** 152

Branch Will Not Break, The (Wright), **Supp. III Part 2:** 596, 598–601; **Supp. IV Part 1:** 60; **Supp. IX:** 159

Brancusi, Constantin, **III:** 201; **Retro. Supp. I:** 292

Brande, Dorothea, **Supp. I Part 2:** 608

Brandel, Marc, **Supp. XXI:** 276

Branden, Nathaniel, **Supp. IV Part 2:** 526, 528

"Branding Cities" (Greenberg), **Supp. XXII:** 244

"Brand-Name Blues" (Kaufmann), **Supp. XI:** 39

Brand New Life, A (Farrell), **II:** 46, 48

Brando, Marlon, **II:** 588; **Supp. IV Part 2:** 560; **Supp. XVIII:** 251

Brandon, Henry, **Supp. I Part 2:** 604, 612, 618

Brandt, Alice, **Supp. I Part 1:** 92

Brandt, Carl, **Supp. XI:** 45

Brant, Sebastian, **III:** 447, 448

Braque, Georges, **III:** 197; **Supp. IX:** 66

Brashford, Jake, **Supp. X:** 252

Brasil, Emanuel, **Supp. I Part 1:** 94

"Brasília" (Plath), **Supp. I Part 2:** 544, 545

"Brass Buttons" (McCoy), **Supp. XIII:** 161

"Brass Candlestick, The" (Francis), **Supp. IX:** 89

Brass Check, The (Sinclair), **Supp. V:** 276, 281, 282, 284–285

Brass Knuckles (Dybek), **Supp. XXIII: 68–69**

"Brass Ring, The" (Carver), **Supp. III Part 1:** 137

"Brass Spittoons" (Hughes), **Supp. I Part 1:** 326–327

Brass Verdict, The (Connelly), **Supp. XXI: 78–79**

Brats (X. J. Kennedy), **Supp. XV:** 163

Brautigan, Richard, **III:** 174; **Supp. VIII:** 42, 43; **Supp. XII:** 139; **Supp. XVI:** 172; **Supp. XXI:** 53

Brave Cowboy, The (Abbey), **Supp. XIII:** 4–5

Brave Men (Pyle), **Supp. XVII:** 61

Brave New World (Huxley), **II:** 454; **Supp. XIII:** 29; **Supp. XVIII:** 137

"Brave New World" (MacLeish), **III:** 18

Bravery of Earth, A (Eberhart), **I:** 522, 524, 525, 526, 530

"Brave Tailors of Maida, The" (Talese), **Supp. XVII:** 208

"Brave Words for a Startling Occasion" (Ellison), **Retro. Supp. II:** 118

Braving the Elements (Merrill), **Supp. III Part 1:** 320, 323, 325–327, 329

Bravo, The (Cooper), **I:** 345–346, 348

"Bravura" (Francis), **Supp. IX:** 90

Brawley, Benjamin, **Supp. I Part 1:** 327, 332

Brawl in a Tavern, A (Shaw), **Supp. XIX:** 241

Brawne, Fanny, **I:** 284; **II:** 531

Braxton, Joanne, **Supp. IV Part 1:** 12, 15

Brazil (Bishop), **Retro. Supp. II:** 45; **Supp. I Part 1:** 92

"Brazil" (Marshall), **Supp. XI:** 281

Brazil (Updike), **Retro. Supp. I:** 329, 330, 334

"Brazil, January 1, 1502" (Bishop), **Retro. Supp. II:** 47

Braziller, George, **Supp. X:** 24; **Supp. XXIII:** 214

Brazzi, Rossano, **Supp. IV Part 2:** 520

"Bread" (Dickey), **Supp. IV Part 1:** 182

"Bread" (Olds), **Supp. X:** 206

"Bread Alone" (Wylie), **Supp. I Part 2:** 727

Bread in the Wilderness (Merton), **Supp. VIII:** 197, 208

"Bread of Desire, The" (Nelson), **Supp. XVIII:** 177

Bread of Idleness, The (Masters), **Supp. I Part 2:** 460

"Bread of This World, The" (McGrath), **Supp. X:** 119, 127

Bread of Time, The (Levine), **Supp. V:** 180

Bread without Sugar (Stern), **Supp. IX: 297–298**

"Break, The" (Sexton), **Supp. II Part 2:** 689

"Breakaways, The" (Siddons), **Supp. XXII:** 244

Breakfast at Tiffany's (Capote), **Supp. III Part 1:** 113, 117, 119–121, 124, 126

Breakfast of Champions (Vonnegut), **Supp. II Part 2:** 755, 759, 769, 770, 777–778

Breaking and a Death, A (Kees), **Supp. XV:** 145

Breaking and Entering (X. J. Kennedy), **Supp. XV:** 153, **160–162**

Breaking Hard Ground (D. Hunter), **Supp. XVI:** 38

Breaking Ice (McMillan, ed.), **Supp. XIII:** 182–183

Breaking Open (Rukeyser), **Supp. VI:** 274, 281

"Breaking Open" (Rukeyser), **Supp. VI:** 286

Breaking Ranks: A Political Memoir (Podhoretz), **Supp. VIII: 239–241,** 245

"Breaking the Code of Silence: Ideology and Women's Confessional Poetry" (Harris), **Supp. XIV:** 269

"Breaking Up of the Winships, The" (Thurber), **Supp. I Part 2:** 616

Breast, The (P. Roth), **Retro. Supp. II:** 287–288; **Supp. III Part 2:** 416, 418

"Breast, The" (Sexton), **Supp. II Part 2:** 687

"Breasts" (Simic), **Supp. VIII:** 275

"Breasts"(Dybek), **Supp. XXIII:** 77

"Breath" (Espaillat), **Supp. XXI:** 109

"Breath" (Levine), **Supp. V:** 185

Breathe No More, My Lady (Lacy), **Supp. XV:** 203

Breathing Lessons (Tyler), **Supp. IV Part 2:** 669–670

Breathing the Water (Levertov), **Supp. III Part 1:** 274, 283, 284

"Breath of Life, The" (C. Baxter), **Supp. XVII:** 23

Breath's Burials (Sobin), **Supp. XVI: 288–289**

Breaux, Zelia, **Retro. Supp. II:** 114

Brecht, Bertolt, **I:** 60, 301; **III:** 161, 162; **IV:** 394; **Supp. I Part 1:** 292; **Supp. II Part 1:** 10, 26, 56; **Supp. IV Part 1:** 359; **Supp. IX:** 131, 133, 140; **Supp. X:** 112; **Supp. XIII:** 206, 286; **Supp. XIV:** 162; **Supp. XVIII:** 33

Breen, Joseph I., **IV:** 390

Breines, Ron, **Supp. XVIII:** 97

Breit, Harvey, **I:** 433; **III:** 575; **Retro. Supp. II:** 230; **Supp. XVIII:** 254; **Supp. XXI:** 277

Breman, Paul, **Supp. XXII:** 8

Bremer, Anne, **Supp. XXII:** 277

Bremer, Fredrika, **Supp. I Part 1:** 407

Bremer, Richard, **Supp. XXIII:** 236

Brendan: A Novel (Buechner), **Supp. XII:** 53

Brennan, Matthew C., **Supp. XV:** 113, 125; **Supp. XIX:** 121

Brent, David, **Supp. XXII:** 259

Brent, Linda, **Supp. IV Part 1:** 12, 13

Brentano, Franz, **II:** 350; **Supp. XIV:** 198, 199

Brer Rabbit (tales), **Supp. IV Part 1:** 11, 13; **Supp. XIV:** 88

Breslin, James E. B., **Retro. Supp. I:** 430

Breslin, John B., **Supp. IV Part 1:** 308

Breslin, Paul, **Supp. VIII:** 283

Bresson, Robert, **Supp. IV Part 1:** 156

"Bresson's Movies" (Creeley), **Supp. IV Part 1:** 156–157

Breton, André, **III:** 425; **Supp. XIII:** 114; **Supp. XVII:** 244

Brett, George, **II:** 466; **Supp. V:** 286

Brett, Reginald Baliol, **Supp. XX:** 230

Brevoort, Henry, **II:** 298

Brew, Kwesi, **Supp. IV Part 1:** 10, 16

Brewer, Gaylord, **Supp. XV:** 330

"Brewing of Soma, The" (Whittier), **Supp. I Part 2:** 704

Brewsie and Willie (Stein), **IV:** 27

Brewster, Martha, **Supp. I Part 1:** 114

"Brewsterville Croesus, A" (Briggs), **Supp. XVIII:** 16

Brewsterville letters (Briggs), **Supp. XVIII:** 1, 5, **15–16**

"Brian Age 7" (Doty), **Supp. XI:** 136

Briand, Paul, **Supp. XVIII:** 155

"Briar Patch, The" (Warren), **IV:** 237

Briar Rose (Coover), **Supp. V:** 52

"Briar Rose (Sleeping Beauty)" (Sexton), **Supp. II Part 2:** 690

Brice, Fanny, **II:** 427

"Brick, The" (Nye), **Supp. XIII:** 276

"Bricklayer in the Snow" (Fante), **Supp. XI:** 164–165

"Brick Layer's Lunch Hour, The" (Ginsberg), **Supp. II Part 1:** 318

Brickman, Marshall, **Supp. XV:** 5

"Bricks, The" (Hogan), **Supp. IV Part 1:** 413

"Bridal Ballad, The" (Poe), **III:** 428

"Bridal Bed, The" (Gibran), **Supp. XX:** 124

Bridal Dinner, The (Gurney), **Supp. V:** 109, 110

"Bride Comes to Yellow Sky, The" (Crane), **I:** 34, 415, 416, 423

Bridegroom, The (Jin), **Supp. XVIII: 97–98**

"Bridegroom, The" (Jin), **Supp. XVIII:** 98

Bridegroom Cometh, The (W. Frank), **Supp. XX:** 77

"Bride in the 30's, A" (Auden), **Supp. II Part 1:** 9

Bride of Lammermoor (Scott), **II:** 291

Bride of Samoa (film), **Supp. IV Part 1:** 82

"Bride of the Innisfallen, The" (Welty), **IV:** 278–279; **Retro. Supp. I:** 353

Bride of the Innisfallen, The, and Other Stories (Welty), **IV:** 261, 275–279; **Retro. Supp. I:** 352–353, 355

Brides of the South Wind: Poems 1917– 1922 (Jeffers), **Supp. II Part 2:** 419

Bridge, Horatio, **II:** 226

"BRIDGE, THE" (Baraka), **Supp. II Part 1:** 32, 36

Bridge, The (Crane), **Supp. XXIII:** 146

Bridge, The (H. Crane), **I:** 62, 109, 266, 385, 386, 387, 395–399, 400, 402; **IV:** 123, 341, 418, 419, 420; **Retro. Supp. I:** 427; **Retro. Supp. II:** 76, 77, 81, 83, **84–87; Supp. V:** 342; **Supp. IX:** 306

Bridge, The (Talese), **Supp. XVII:** 202, 203, 208

Bridge at Remagen, The (film), **Supp. XI:** 343

"Bridge Burners, The" (Van Vechten), **Supp. II Part 2:** 733

Bridgehead: The Drama of Israel (W. Frank), **Supp. XX:** 80

Bridge of San Luis Rey, The (Wilder), **I:** 360; **IV:** 356, 357, 360–363, 365, 366

"Bridge of Sighs"(P. Benedict), **Supp. XXIII:** 47–48

Bridge of Years, The (Sarton), **Supp. VIII:** 253

"Bridges" (Kingsolver), **Supp. VII:** 208

Bridges, Harry, **I:** 493; **Supp. XVIII:** 238; **Supp. XIX:** 264

Bridges, Lloyd, **Supp. XV:** 202

Bridges, Robert, **II:** 537; **III:** 527; **Supp. I Part 2:** 721; **Supp. II Part 1:** 21; **Supp. XIV:** 336, 341, 342, 343

"Bridging" (Apple), **Supp. XVII:** 5

Bridgman, P. W., **I:** 278

"Bridle, The" (Carver), **Supp. III Part 1:** 138

"Brief and Blameless Outline of the Ontogeny of Crow, A" (Wright), **Supp. XV:** 347

Brief and Frightening Reign of Phil, The (Saunders), **Supp. XIX: 230–231,** 233

"Brief Début of Tildy, The" (O. Henry), **Supp. II Part 1:** 408

"Brief Encounters on the Inland Waterway" (Vonnegut), **Supp. II Part 2:** 760

Brief History of the Dead, The (Brockmeier), **Supp. XXII: 57–59,** 61

Briefings (Ammons), **Supp. VII:** 29

Brief Interviews with Hideous Men (Wallace), **Supp. X: 308–310**

"Brief Interviews with Hideous Men" (Wallace), **Supp. X:** 309

"Briefly It Enters, and Briefly Speaks" (Kenyon), **Supp. VII:** 174

"Brief Study of the British, A" (Saunders), **Supp. XIX:** 235

Brier, His Book (J. W. Miller), **Supp. XX: 165, 168, 170**

"Brier Grows Wild, The" (J. W. Miller), **Supp. XX:** 170

"Brier Losing Touch with His Traditions, The" (J. W. Miller), **Supp. XX: 165,** 169

Brier Poems, The (J. W. Miller), **Supp. XX:** 168

"Brier Sermon, The—You Must Be Born Again" (J. W. Miller), **Supp. XX: 165, 169–170**

Briffault, Robert, **Supp. I Part 2:** 560, 567

"Brigade de Cuisine" (McPhee), **Supp. III Part 1:** 307–308

Brigadier and the Golf Widow, The (Cheever), **Supp. I Part 1:** 184–185, 192

Briggs, Charles Frederick, **Supp. I Part 2:** 411; **Supp. XVIII: 1–18**

brigham, besmilr, **Supp. XV:** 349

"Bright and Morning Star" (Wright), **IV:** 488

Bright Book of Life: American Novelists and Storytellers from Hemingway to Mailer (Kazin), **Supp. VIII:** 102, 104

Bright Center of Heaven (Maxwell), **Supp. VIII: 153–155,** 164

"Brightness from the North" (B. Kelly), **Supp. XVII:** 131

Brighton Beach Memoirs (Simon), **Supp. IV Part 2:** 576, 577, 584, 586–587, 590

Bright Procession (Sedges), **Supp. II Part 1:** 125

Bright Room Called Day, A (Kushner), **Supp. IX:** 133, **138–141,** 142

Brillat-Savarin, Jean Anthelme, **Supp. XVII:** 82, 86, 87

"Brilliance" (Doty), **Supp. XI:** 124, 128

"Brilliant Leaves" (Gordon), **II:** 199

"Brilliant Sad Sun" (W. C. Williams), **Retro. Supp. I:** 422

"Bringing Back the Trumpeter Swan" (Kumin), **Supp. IV Part 2:** 454

Bringing It All Back Home (album, Dylan), **Supp. XVIII:** 20, 25, 26, 30

Bringing It All Back Home (McNally), **Supp. XIII:** 197–198

Bringing the Devil to His Knees (C. Baxter), **Supp. XVII:** 22

"Bringing the Strange Home" (Dunn), **Supp. XI:** 141

"Bring the Day!" (Roethke), **III:** 536

Brinkley, Douglas, **Supp. XIII:** 9

Brinkmeyer, Robert H., Jr., **Supp. XI:** 38

Brinnin, John Malcolm, **IV:** 26, 27, 28, 42, 46; **Supp. XV:** 139

Brissot, Jacques Pierre, **Supp. I Part 2:** 511

"Britain's Negro Problem in Sierra Leone" (Du Bois), **Supp. I Part 1:** 176

"British Guiana" (Marshall), **Supp. XI:** 281–282

"British Poets, The" (Holmes), **Supp. I Part 1:** 306

"British Prison Ship, The" (Freneau), **Supp. II Part 1:** 261

Brittan, Gordon G., Jr., **Supp. XIV:** 234

Britten, Benjamin, **II:** 586; **Supp. II Part 1:** 17; **Supp. IV Part 1:** 84

Broadwater, Bowden, **II:** 562

Broadway, Broadway (McNally). *See It's Only a Play* (McNally)

Broadway, J. William, **Supp. V:** 316

Broadway Bound (Simon), **Supp. IV Part 2:** 576, 577, 584, 586–587, 590

Broadway Danny Rose (film; Allen), **Supp. XV:** 9

"Broadway Sights" (Whitman), **IV:** 350

Broccoli, Albert R. "Cubby", **Supp. XI:** 307

Brock

Bröck, Sabine, **Supp. XI:** 275, 277, 278

Brockmeier, Kevin, **Supp. XXII: 49–63**

Brodhead, Richard, **Retro. Supp. II:** 139; **Supp. XIV:** 61

Brodkey, Harold, **Supp. VIII:** 151; **Supp. X:** 160

Brodskii, Iosif Alexsandrovich. *See* Brodsky, Joseph

Brodsky, Joseph, **Supp. VIII: 19–35;** **Supp. X:** 65, 73; **Supp. XV:** 134, 135, 256; **Supp. XXIII:** 122

Brody, Alter, **Supp. XV:** 302, 307

Brodyar, Anatole, **Supp. XIV:** 106

Brokeback Mountain (film), **Supp. XX: 273**

"Brokeback Mountain" (Proulx), **Supp. VII:** 264–265

"Broken Balance, The" (Jeffers), **Supp. II Part 2:** 426

"Broken Field Running" (Bambara), **Supp. XI:** 10, 11

Broken Frieze, The (Everwine), **Supp. XV:** 74, 75, 89

Broken Ground, The (Berry), **Supp. X:** 30

"Broken Home, The" (Merrill), **Supp. III Part 1:** 319, 325

"Broken Oar, The" (Longfellow), **Retro. Supp. II:** 169

"Broken Promise" (MacLeish), **III:** 15

Broken Span, The (W. C. Williams), **IV:** 419; **Retro. Supp. I:** 424

"Broken Tower, The" (H. Crane), **I:** 385, 386, 400, 401–402; **Retro. Supp. II:** 89, 90

Broken Vessels (Dubus), **Supp. VII:** 90–91; **Supp. XI:** 347

"Broken Vessels" (Dubus), **Supp. VII:** 90

Broken Wings, The (al-Ajni&hudot;a al-Mutakassirah) (Gibran), **Supp. XX: 115, 124, 125**

"Broker" (H. Roth), **Supp. IX:** 234

Bromfield, Louis, **IV:** 380

"Brompton Cocktail" (Mamet), **Supp. XIV:** 252

Bromwich, David, **Retro. Supp. I:** 305; **Supp. XII:** 162

"Broncho That Would Not Be Broken, The" (Lindsay), **Supp. I Part 2:** 383

Bronk, William, **Supp. XV:** 115; **Supp. XXI: 17–34**

Brontë, Anne, **Supp. IV Part 2:** 430

Brontë, Branwell, **I:** 462

Brontë, Charlotte, **I:** 458; **II:** 175; **Supp. IV Part 2:** 430; **Supp. IX:** 128; **Supp. XII:** 104, 303; **Supp. XV:** 338; **Supp. XVI:** 158; **Supp. XX: 108**

Brontë, Emily, **I:** 458; **Retro. Supp. I:** 43; **Supp. IV Part 2:** 430; **Supp. IX:** 128; **Supp. X:** 78, 89; **Supp. XV:** 338

"Bronze" (Francis), **Supp. IX:** 76

"Bronze" (Merrill), **Supp. III Part 1:** 336

Bronze Booklets on the History, Problems, and Cultural Contributions of the Negro series, **Supp. XIV:** 202

"Bronze Buckaroo, The" (Baraka), **Supp. II Part 1:** 49

"Bronze Horses, The" (Lowell), **II:** 524

"Bronze Tablets" (Lowell), **II:** 523

Bronzeville Boys and Girls (Brooks), **Supp. III Part 1:** 79

"Bronzeville Mother Loiters in Mississippi. A. Meanwhile, a Mississippi Mother Burns Bacon" (Brooks), **Supp. III Part 1:** 80

"Brooch, The" (Singer), **IV:** 20

Brook, Peter, **Retro. Supp. II:** 182

Brooke, Rupert, **II:** 82; **III:** 3

Brook Evans (Glaspell), **Supp. III Part 1:** 182–185

"Brooking Likeness" (Glück), **Supp. V:** 85

"Brooklyn" (Marshall), **Supp. XI:** 281, 282

"Brooklyn" (Shaw), **Supp. XIX:** 239, 240

Brooks, Albert (Al Pew), **Supp. XXI:** 22

Brooks, Cleanth, **I:** 280, 282; **III:** 517; **IV:** 236, 279; **Retro. Supp. I:** 40, 41, 90; **Retro. Supp. II:** 235; **Supp. I Part 2:** 423; **Supp. III Part 2:** 542; **Supp. V:** 316; **Supp. IX:** 153, 155; **Supp. X:** 115, 123; **Supp. XIV: 1–20;** **Supp. XIX:** 246

Brooks, David, **Supp. IV Part 2:** 623, 626, 630; **Supp. VIII:** 232

Brooks, Gwendolyn, **Retro. Supp. I:** 208; **Supp. III Part 1: 69–90;** **Supp. IV Part 1:** 2, 15, 244, 251, 257; **Supp. XI:** 1, 278; **Supp. XIII:** 111, 112, 296; **Supp. XIV:** 73; **Supp. XVIII:** 175, 181, 185; **Supp. XXI:** 230

Brooks, Mel, **Supp. IV Part 1:** 390; **Supp. IV Part 2:** 591

Brooks, Paul, **Supp. IX:** 26, 31, 32

Brooks, Phillips, **II:** 542; **Retro. Supp. II:** 134; **Supp. XIII:** 142

Brooks, Van Wyck, **I:** 106, 117, 215, 222, 228, 230, 231, 233, 236, **239–263,** 266, 480; **II:** 30, 271, 285, 309, 337, 482; **III:** 394, 606; **IV:** 171, 312, 427, 433; **Retro. Supp. II:** 46, 137; **Supp. I Part 2:** 423, 424, 650; **Supp. II Part 1:** 137; **Supp. VIII:** 98, 101; **Supp. XIV:** 11; **Supp. XV:** 298, 301; **Supp. XX: 68**

Brooks, Mrs. Van Wyck (Eleanor Kenyon Stimson), **I:** 240, 245, 250, 252

Brooks, Mrs. Van Wyck (Gladys Billings), **I:** 258

Broom of the System, The (Wallace), **Supp. X:** 301, **302–305,** 310

"Brooms" (Simic), **Supp. VIII:** 275

Brosi, George, **Supp. XX: 166; Supp. XXIII:** 39

Brosnan, Jim, **II:** 424–425; **Supp. XX: 195**

Brossard, Chandler, **Supp. XXII:** 258

Brother Carl (Sontag), **Supp. III Part 2:** 452

"Brother Death" (Anderson), **I:** 114

Brother Fire (Di Piero), **Supp. XIX:** 35, 38, 45–47

Brotherhood of the Grape, The (Fante), **Supp. XI:** 160, **171–172**

Brother in Elysium, The: Ideas of Friendship and Society in the United States (Bronk), **Supp. XXI:** 21, 22, 25, 31

"Brothers" (Anderson), **I:** 114

Brothers, The (F. Barthelme), **Supp. XI:** 25, 28, 29, 30, 32 33

Brothers and Keepers (Wideman), **Supp. X:** 320, 321–322, 323, **325–327,** 328, 329–330, 331, 332

Brothers Ashkenazi, The (Singer), **IV:** 2

Brothers Karamazov, The (Dostoevsky), **II:** 60; **III:** 146, 150, 283; **Supp. IX:** 102, 106; **Supp. XI:** 172; **Supp. XII:** 322

Brothers of No Kin (Richter), **Supp. XVIII:** 209

"Brothers of No Kin" (Richter), **Supp. XVIII:** 208

Brother to Dragons: A Tale in Verse and Voices (Warren), **IV:** 243–244, 245, 246, 251, 252, 254, 257

Broughton, James, **Supp. XV:** 146

Broughton, Rhoda, **II:** 174; **IV:** 309, 310; **Supp. XX:** 232

Broun, Heywood, **I:** 478; **II:** 417; **IV:** 432; **Supp. IX:** 190; **Supp. XXII:** 277

Broussais, François, **Supp. I Part 1:** 302

Brouwer, Joel, **Supp. XXII:** 223, 237

Browder, Earl, **I:** 515; **Supp. XX: 76, 77**

Brower, David, **Supp. X:** 29

Brower, Reuben, **Supp. XV:** 20

Brown, Alice, **II:** 523; **Retro. Supp. II:** 136

Brown, Andrew, **Supp. XVI:** 150

Brown, Ashley, **Retro. Supp. II:** 48; **Supp. I Part 1:** 79, 80, 82, 84, 92

Brown, Charles Brockden, **I:** 54, 211, 335; **II:** 74, 267, 298; **III:** 415; **Supp. I Part 1: 124–149; Supp. II Part 1:** 65, 292; **Supp. XXIII:** 178

Brown, Mrs. Charles Brockden (Elizabeth Linn), **Supp. I Part 1:** 145, 146

Brown, Clifford, **Supp. V:** 195

Brown, Deborah, **Supp. XVII:** 75

Brown, Dee, **Supp. IV Part 2:** 504

Brown, Elijah, **Supp. I Part 1:** 125

Brown, Fleda, **Supp. XXIII:** 59

Brown, George Douglas, **III:** 473

Brown, Harry, **Supp. IV Part 2:** 560

Brown, Harvey, **Supp. XIV:** 148

Brown, Himan, **Supp. XIX:** 241, 242

Brown, H. Rap, **Supp. XXI:** 171

Brown, John, **II:** 13; **IV:** 125, 126, 172, 237, 249, 254; **Supp. I Part 1:** 345; **Supp. VIII:** 204

Brown, Joseph Epes, **Supp. IV Part 2:** 487

Brown, Larry, **Supp. XVIII:** 195; **Supp. XXI: 35–50**

Brown, Leonard, **Supp. IX:** 117

Brown, Mary Armitt, **Supp. I Part 1:** 125

Brown, Percy, **II:** 20

Brown, Robert E., **Supp. X:** 12

Brown, Scott, **Supp. XI:** 178

Brown, Slater, **IV:** 123; **Retro. Supp. II:** 79

Brown, Solyman, **Supp. I Part 1:** 156

Brown, Sterling, **Retro. Supp. I:** 198; **Supp. IV Part 1:** 169; **Supp. XIV:** 202; **Supp. XXII:** 1, 8, 12

Brown, Tina, **Supp. XVI:** 176–177

Brown, Wesley, **Supp. V:** 6

Brown, William Wells, **Supp. XXIII:** 184

Brown Decades, The (Mumford), **Supp. II Part 2:** 475, 478, 491–492

Brown Dog (Harrison), **Supp. VIII:** 51

Brown Dog of the Yaak: Essays on Art and Activism (Bass), **Supp. XVI:** 22

"Brown Dwarf of Rügen, The" (Whittier), **Supp. I Part 2:** 696

Browne, Charles Farrar, **II:** 289; **IV:** 193, 196; **Supp. XVIII:** 1, 4

Browne, Roscoe Lee, **Supp. VIII:** 345

Browne, Thomas, **II:** 15–16, 304; **III:** 77, 78, 198, 487; **IV:** 147; **Supp. IX:** 136; **Supp. XII:** 45; **Supp. XVI:** 292

Browne, William, **Supp. I Part 1:** 98

Brownell, W. C., **II:** 14

Brownell, William Crary, **Retro. Supp. I:** 365, 366

Browner, Stephanie P., **Supp. XVIII:** 17

Brown Girl, Brownstones (Marshall), **Supp. XI:** 275, 276, **278–280,** 282

Brownies' Book, The (Hughes), **Supp. I Part 1:** 321

Browning, Elizabeth Barrett, **I:** 458, 459; **Retro. Supp. I:** 33, 43; **Supp. XVIII:** 175–176; **Supp. XX: 108**

Browning, Oscar, **Supp. XX: 231**

Browning, Robert, **I:** 50, 66, 103, 458, 460, 468; **II:** 338, 478, 522; **III:** 5, 8, 467, 469, 484, 511, 521, 524, 606, 609; **IV:** 135, 245, 366, 416; **Retro. Supp. I:** 43, 55, 217; **Retro. Supp. II:** 188, 190; **Supp. I Part 1:** 2, 6, 79, 311; **Supp. I Part 2:** 416, 468, 622; **Supp. III Part 1:** 5, 6; **Supp. IV Part 2:** 430; **Supp. X:** 65; **Supp. XV:** 92, 250, 275

Brownmiller, Susan, **Supp. X:** 252

"Brown River, Smile" (Toomer), **Supp. IV Part 1:** 16

Brownstone Eclogues and Other Poems (Aiken), **I:** 65, 67

Brown: The Last Discovery of America (Rodriguez), **Supp. XIV:** 297, 298, 300, **305–309,** 310, 311–312

Broyard, Anatole, **Supp. IV Part 1:** 39; **Supp. VIII:** 140; **Supp. X:** 186; **Supp. XI:** 348; **Supp. XVI:** 213

Broyles, Yolanda Julia, **Supp. XIX:** 112

Bruccoli, Matthew, **Retro. Supp. I:** 98, 102, 105, 114, 115, 359; **Supp. IV Part 2:** 468, 470

Bruce, John Edward, **Supp. XVI:** 143

Bruce, Lenny, **Supp. VIII:** 198

Bruce, Virginia, **Supp. XII:** 173

Bruce-Novoa, Juan, **Supp. VIII:** 73, 74

Bruchac, Joseph, **Supp. IV Part 1:** 261, 319, 320, 321, 322, 323, 325, 328, 398, 399, 403, 408, 414; **Supp. IV Part 2:** 502, 506

Brueghel, Pieter, **I:** 174; **Supp. I Part 2:** 475

Brueghel, Pieter, the Elder, **Retro. Supp. I:** 430

Bruell, Edwin, **Supp. VIII:** 126

Brugh, Spangler Arlington. *See* Taylor, Robert

"Bruja: Witch" (Mora), **Supp. XIII:** 214, 220, 221, **Supp. XIII:** 222

Brulé, Claude, **Supp. XI:** 307

Brumer, Andy, **Supp. XIII:** 88

Brummels, J. V., **Supp. XIX:** 119

Brunner, Emil, **III:** 291, 303

"Brush Fire" (J. Wright), **Supp. XVII:** 241

Brustein, Robert, **Supp. VIII:** 331

Brutus, **IV:** 373, 374; **Supp. I Part 2:** 471

"Brutus and Antony" (Masters), **Supp. I Part 2:** 472

"Bryan, Bryan, Bryan, Bryan" (Lindsay), **Supp. I Part 2:** 394, 395, 398

Bryan, George, **Retro. Supp. II:** 76

Bryan, Sharon, **Supp. IX:** 154

Bryan, William Jennings, **I:** 483; **IV:** 124; **Supp. I Part 2:** 385, 395–396, 455, 456

Bryant, Austin, **Supp. I Part 1:** 152, 153

Bryant, Frances, **Supp. I Part 1:** 153

Bryant, Louise, **Supp. X:** 136

Bryant, Peter, **Supp. I Part 1:** 150, 151, 152, 153. *See also* George, Peter

Bryant, William Cullen, **I:** 335, 458; **II:** 311; **III:** 81; **IV:** 309; **Retro. Supp. I:** 217; **Retro. Supp. II:** 155; **Supp. I Part 1: 150–173,** 312, 362; **Supp. I Part 2:** 413, 416, 420; **Supp. IV Part 1:** 165; **Supp. XIII:** 145; **Supp. XIX:** 4

Bryant, Mrs. William Cullen (Frances Fairchild), **Supp. I Part 1:** 153, 169

Bryer, Jackson R., **Supp. IV Part 2:** 575, 583, 585, 586, 589, 591; **Supp. XIII:** 200, **Supp. XIII:** 205

Bryher, Jackson R. (pseudonym). *See* Ellerman, Winifred

Brynner, Witter, **Supp. XXII:** 273

Bubber Goes to Heaven (Bontemps), **Supp. XXII:** 4

"Bubbs Creek Haircut" (Snyder), **Supp. VIII:** 306

Buber, Martin, **II:** 228; **III:** 45, 308, 528; **IV:** 11; **Supp. I Part 1:** 83, 88; **Supp. XVI:** 291

Buccaneers, The (Wharton), **IV:** 327; **Retro. Supp. I:** 382

Buchanan Dying (Updike), **Retro. Supp. I:** 331, 335

Buchbinder, David, **Supp. XIII:** 32

Buchwald, Art, **Supp. XII:** 124–125; **Supp. XVI:** 110–111

Buchwald, Emilie, **Supp. XVI:** 35, 36

Buck, Dudley, **Supp. I Part 1:** 362

Buck, Gene, **II:** 427

Buck, Pearl S., **Supp. II Part 1: 113–134; Supp. XIV:** 274

Buckdancer's Choice (Dickey), **Supp. IV Part 1:** 176, 177, 178, 180

"Buckdancer's Choice" (Dickey), **Supp. IV Part 1:** 191

Bucke, Richard Maurice, **Retro. Supp. I:** 407

"Buckeyes"(P. Benedict), **Supp. XXIII:** 46

"Buck Fever" (Humphrey), **Supp. IX:** 109

"Buck in the Snow, The" (Millay), **III:** 135

Buckley, Christopher, **Supp. IX:** 169; **Supp. XI:** 257, 329; **Supp. XV:** 76–77, 86

Buckley, James, Jr., **Supp. XVII:** 220

Buckminster, Joseph, **Supp. II Part 1:** 66–67, 69

Bucknell, Katherine, **Supp. XIV:** 170

Bucolics (Auden), **Supp. II Part 1:** 21, 24

Budbill, David, **Supp. XIX: 1–16**

Budd, Louis J., **IV:** 210

Buddha, **I:** 136; **II:** 1; **III:** 173, 179, 239, 567; **Supp. I Part 1:** 363; **Supp. I Part 2:** 397

Buddha, The: The Story of Siddhartha (film, Grubin), **Supp. XXIII:** 138, 140

"Buddha Boy" (Saunders), **Supp. XIX:** 235

"Buddha's Last Instruction, The" (Oliver), **Supp. VII:** 239

"Buddies"(Kenny), **Supp. XXIII:** 150

Budding Prospects (Boyle), **Supp. VIII:** 8–9; **Supp. XX:** 27–28

Buechner, Frederick, **III:** 310; **Supp. XII: 41–59**

Buell, Lawrence, **Supp. V:** 209; **Supp. IX:** 29; **Supp. XV:** 269, 282

"Buffalo" (Peacock), **Supp. XIX:** 198

"Buffalo, The" (Moore), **III:** 215

"Buffalo Bill". *See* Cody, William

Buffalo Girls (screenplay) (McMurtry), **Supp. V:** 232

Buffalo Girls (McMurtry), **Supp. V:** 229

Buffett, Jimmy, **Supp. VIII:** 42

Buffon, Comte de, **II:** 101

Buford, Fanny McConnell, **Retro. Supp. II:** 117

Bugeja, Michael, **Supp. X:** 201

Bugged for Murder (Lacy), **Supp. XV:** 205

"Buglesong" (Stegner), **Supp. IV Part 2:** 606

Buhle, Paul, **Supp. XXI:** 172

"Buick" (Shapiro), **Supp. II Part 2:** 705

"Builders" (Yates), **Supp. XI: 342–343**

Builders, The (Glasgow), **II:** 183–184, 193

"Builders, The" (Hay), **Supp. XIV:** 125

Builders in Sand (W. Frank), **Supp. XX: 68**

Builders of the Bay Colony (Morison), **Supp. I Part 2:** 484–485

"Builders of the Bridge, The" (Mumford), **Supp. II Part 2:** 475

"Building" (Snyder), **Supp. VIII:** 305

"Building, Dwelling, Thinking" (Heidegger), **Retro. Supp. II:** 87

Building a Character (Stanislavsky), **Supp. XIV:** 243

" 'Building' Larry Brown(s) at Algonquin Books of Chapel Hill" (Perry), **Supp. XXI:** 42

"Building of the Ship, The" (Longfellow), **II:** 498; **Retro. Supp. II:** 159, 167, 168

"Build Soil" (Frost), **Retro. Supp. I:** 138, 139

"Build Soil" (Snyder), **Supp. VIII:** 304

Build-Up, The (W. C. Williams), **Retro. Supp. I:** 423

Bukiet, Melvin Jules, **Supp. XVII: 39–51**

Bukowski, Charles, **Supp. III Part 1:** 147; **Supp. XI:** 159, 161, 172, 173; **Supp. XVII:** 245

Bulgakov, Mikhail, **Supp. XIV:** 97

"Bulgarian Poetess, The" (Updike), **IV:** 215, 227; **Retro. Supp. I:** 329

Bull, Ole, **II:** 504

"Bulldozer, The" (Francis), **Supp. IX:** 87

"Bullet in the Brain" (Wolff), **Supp. VII:** 342–343

Bullet Park (Cheever), **Supp. I Part 1:** 185, 187–193, 194, 195

Bullets over Broadway (film; Allen), **Supp. XV:** 12, **12–13**

Bullfight, The (Mailer), **Retro. Supp. II:** 205

Bullins, Ed, **Supp. II Part 1:** 34, 42

Bullock, Sandra, **Supp. X:** 80

"Bull-Roarer, The" (Stern), **Supp. IX:** 297

"Bully, The" (Dubus), **Supp. VII:** 84

"Bulsh" (X. J. Kennedy), **Supp. XV:** 161

Bultmann, Rudolf, **III:** 309

Bulwark, The (Dreiser), **I:** 497, 506, 516–517; **Retro. Supp. II:** 95, 96, 105, 108

Bulwer-Lytton, Edward George, **IV:** 350

"Bums in the Attic" (Cisneros), **Supp. VII:** 62

Bunche, Ralph, **Supp. I Part 1:** 343; **Supp. XIV:** 202; **Supp. XXII:** 12

"Bunchgrass Edge of the World, The" (Proulx), **Supp. VII:** 263

Bunge, Nancy, **Supp. XVII:** 218; **Supp. XXII:** 175, 177, 178, 180, 183

"Bunner Sisters, The" (Wharton), **IV:** 317

Bunting, Basil, **Retro. Supp. I:** 422; **Supp. III Part 2:** 616, 620, 624; **Supp. XIV:** 286

Buntline, Ned, **Supp. XXIII:** 182

Buñuel, Luis, **III:** 184; **Retro. Supp. II:** 337

Bunyan, John, **I:** 445; **II:** 15, 104, 228; **IV:** 80, 84, 156, 437; **Supp. I Part 1:** 32

Bunyan, Paul, **Supp. XXII:** 203

Burana, Lily, **Supp. XI:** 253

Burbank, Luther, **I:** 483

Burbank, Rex, **IV:** 363

Burch, Michael, **Supp. XXI:** 99

Burchfield, Alice, **Supp. I Part 2:** 652, 660

Burden of Proof, The (Turow), **Supp. XVII: 216–217,** 218

Burden of Southern History, The (Woodward), **Retro. Supp. I:** 75

Burdens of Formality, The (Lea, ed.), **Supp. X:** 58

Burger, Gottfried August, **II:** 306

Burgess, Anthony, **Supp. IV Part 1:** 227; **Supp. IV Part 2:** 685; **Supp. V:** 128; **Supp. XXIII:** 42

Burgh, James, **Supp. I Part 2:** 522

"Burglar of Babylon, The" (Bishop), **Retro. Supp. II:** 47; **Supp. I Part 1:** 93

Burgum, E. B., **IV:** 469, 470

Burham, Philip, **Supp. XX:** 44

"Burial of Jonathan Brown, The"(Hadas), **Supp. XXIII:** 115

Buried Child (Shepard), **Supp. III Part 2:** 433, 447, 448; **Supp. XIV:** 327

"Buried Lake, The" (Tate), **IV:** 136

Burke, Carolyn, **Supp. XXII:** 156, 158, 162, 165, 167, 168

Burke, Edmund, **I:** 9; **III:** 310; **Supp. I Part 2:** 496, 511, 512, 513, 523; **Supp. II Part 1:** 80; **Supp. XVII:** 236

Burke, James Lee, **Supp. XIV: 21–38; Supp. XXI:** 67, 72, 80

Burke, Kenneth, **I: 264–287,** 291; **III:** 497, 499, 546; **IV:** 123, 408; **Retro. Supp. I:** 297; **Retro. Supp. II:** 117, 120; **Supp. I Part 2:** 630; **Supp. II Part 1:** 136; **Supp. VIII:** 105; **Supp. IX:** 229; **Supp. XIV:** 3; **Supp. XXI:** 89

Burke, William, **Supp. XXI:** 215

"Burl" (Mosher), **Supp. XXII:** 204, 211

Burley, Justin, **Supp. XVI:** 158

"Burly Fading One, The" (Hayden), **Supp. II Part 1:** 366

Burn, Stephen J., **Supp. XX: 85; Supp. XXII:** 266, 268

"Burned" (Levine), **Supp. V:** 186, 192

"Burned Diary, The" (Olds), **Supp. X:** 215

Burne-Jones, Edward, **Supp. XXII:** 156

Burnett, Allison, **Supp. XVII:** 22

Burnett, David, **Supp. XI:** 299

Burnett, Frances Hodgson, **Supp. I Part 1:** 44

Burnett, Whit, **III:** 551; **Supp. XI:** 294

Burney, Fanny, **Supp. XV:** 232; **Supp. XX:** 108

Burnham, James, **Supp. I Part 2:** 648

Burnham, John Chynoweth, **I:** 59

"Burning, The" (Welty), **IV:** 277–278; **Retro. Supp. I:** 353

Burning Angel (Burke), **Supp. XIV:** 30, 32

Burning Bright (Steinbeck), **IV:** 51, 61–62

Burning Bright: An Anthology of Sacred Poetry (Hampl, ed.), **Supp. XXII:** 87

"Burning Bush" (Cliff), **Supp. XXII:** 75

Burning Bush (Untermeyer), **Supp. XV: 309**

"Burning Bush" (Untermeyer), **Supp. XV:** 309

Burning Bush, The (Asch), **Supp. XXIII:** 7

Burning Bush, The (H. and G. Herczeg), **Supp. XVII:** 62

Burning Chrome (W. Gibson), **Supp. XVI:** 118, 122, **128**

"Burning Chrome" (W. Gibson), **Supp. XVI:** 117, 120, 123, 124, 128

Burning City (Benét), **Supp. XI:** 46, 58

Burning Daylight (London), **II:** 474, 481

Burning Down the House: Essays on Fiction (C. Baxter), **Supp. XVII:** 13, 20, 21

Burning House, The (Beattie), **Supp. V:** 29

"Burning Ladder, The" (Gioia), **Supp. XV:** 118

Burning Mystery of Anna in 1951, The (Koch), **Supp. XV:** 182–183

"Burning of Paper Instead of Children, The" (Rich), **Supp. I Part 2:** 558

"Burning Shit at An Khe" (Weigl), **Supp. XIX:** 279–280

Burning the Days (Salter), **Supp. XIX:** 252

Burning the Days: Recollections (Salter), **Supp. IX:** 245, 246, 248, 260, **261–262**

"Burning the Small Dead" (Snyder), **Supp. VIII:** 298

Burning Tigris, The: The Armenian Genocide and America's Response (Balakian), **Supp. XXIII:** 19, 21, 22, **25–28,** 30

"Burning Tobacco Beds" (J. W. Miller), **Supp. XX:** 167

Burns, Carol, **Supp. XVIII:** 162

Burns, David, **III:** 165–166

Burns, Ken, **Supp. XIV:** 14

Burns, Michael, **Supp. XV:** 339

Burns, Robert, **II:** 150, 306; **III:** 592; **IV:** 453; **Supp. I Part 1:** 158; **Supp. I Part 2:** 410, 455, 683, 685, 691, 692; **Supp. IX:** 173; **Supp. XII:** 171; **Supp. XIII:** 3; **Supp. XVIII:** 82

Burnshaw, Stanley, **Retro. Supp. I:** 298, 303; **Supp. III Part 2:** 615

"Burn the Cities" (West), **Retro. Supp. II:** 338

Burnt Mountain (Siddons), **Supp. XXII:** 253

Burnt Norton (T. S. Eliot), **I:** 575, 580–581, 582, 584, 585; **III:** 10

"Burnt Norton" (T. S. Eliot), **Retro. Supp. I:** 66; **Supp. XV:** 216

Burnt-Out Case, A (Greene), **Supp. VIII:** 4

"Burnt-out Spa, The" (Plath), **Retro. Supp. II:** 246

Burn Witch Burn (A. Merritt), **Supp. XVII:** 58

Burr, Aaron, **I:** 7, 549, 550; **II:** 300; **IV:** 264; **Supp. I Part 2:** 461, 483

Burr: A Novel (Vidal), **Supp. IV Part 2:** 677, 682, 684, 685, 687, 688, 689, 691

Burr Oaks (Eberhart), **I:** 533, 535

Burroughs, Edgar Rice, **Supp. IV Part 1:** 101

Burroughs, John, **I:** 220, 236, 506; **IV:** 346; **Supp. IX:** 171

Burroughs, William S., **III:** 45, 174, 258; **Supp. II Part 1:** 320, 328; **Supp. III Part 1:** **91–110,** 217, 226; **Supp. IV Part 1:** 79, 87, 90; **Supp. XI:** 297, 308; **Supp. XII:** 1, 3, 118, 121, 124, 129, 131, 136; **Supp. XIV:** 137, 140–141, 143–144, 150; **Supp. XVI:** 123, 135; **Supp. XVII:** 225; **Supp. XVIII:** 137; **Supp. XXIII:** 213

Burrow, Trigant, **Supp. II Part 1:** 6

Burrows, Ken, **Supp. V:** 115

Bursey, Jeff, **Supp. XXII:** 257

Burson, Claudia, **Supp. XV:** 343

Burstein, Janet, **Supp. XVII:** 41, 44, 48

"Bursts of Light" (Bronk), **Supp. XXI:** 33

Burt, Stephen, **Supp. XV:** 341, 342, 345, 347, 351; **Supp. XVII:** 18, 246

Burt, Steve, **Supp. V:** 83

Burtis, Thomson, **Supp. XIII:** 163

Burton, Robert, **II:** 535; **III:** 77, 78; **Supp. I Part 1:** 349

Burton, Sue D., **Supp. XIX:** 90

Burton, William Evans, **III:** 412

"Burying Ground by the Ties" (MacLeish), **III:** 14

Bury My Heart at Wounded Knee (Brown), **Supp. IV Part 2:** 504

Bury the Dead (Shaw), **IV:** 381; **Supp. XIX:** **242–244,** 249, 252

"Bus Along St. Clair: December, A" (Atwood), **Supp. XIII:** 33

Busch, Frederick, **Supp. X:** 78; **Supp. XII:** 343; **Supp. XVII:** 175

Bush, Barney, **Supp. XII:** 218, 222

Bush, Douglas, **Supp. I Part 1:** 268; **Supp. XIV:** 10

"Busher Comes Back, The" (Lardner), **II:** 422

"Busher's Letters Home, A" (Lardner), **II:** 418–419, 421

Bushrui, Suheil, **Supp. XX:** **113, 117, 120, 122, 126–127**

"Business and Poetry" (Gioia), **Supp. XV:** 113, 115

"Business Deal" (West), **IV:** 287

"Business Man, A" (Jewett), **Retro. Supp. II:** 132

Business of Memory, The: The Art of Remembering in an Age of Forgetting (C. Baxter, ed.), **Supp. XVII:** 21

"Business Trip" (Hoffman), **Supp. XVIII:** 86

Buss, Helen M., **Supp. IV Part 1:** 12

Butcher, Margaret Just, **Supp. XIV:** 203

"Butcher, The" (Southern), **Supp. XI:** 294

"Butcher Cock, The"(P. Benedict), **Supp. XXIII:** 46–47

"Butcher Shop" (Simic), **Supp. VIII:** 273

But Gentlemen Marry Brunettes (Loos), **Supp. XVI:** 190–191

"But He Says I Misunderstood" (Notley), **Supp. XXII:** 227

Butler, Benjamin, **I:** 457

Butler, Dorothy. *See* Farrell, Mrs. James T. (Dorothy Butler)

Butler, Elizabeth, **Supp. I Part 1:** 260

Butler, Ethel, **Supp. XIV:** 125

Butler, Hugo, **Supp. XVII:** 63

Butler, James D., **Supp. IX:** 175

Butler, Joseph, **II:** 8, 9

Butler, Judith, **Supp. XII:** 6

Butler, Maud. *See* Falkner, Mrs. Murray C. (Maud Butler)

Butler, Nicholas Murray, **I:** 223; **Supp. I Part 1:** 23; **Supp. III Part 2:** 499

Butler, Octavia, **Supp. XIII:** **59–72**

Butler, Robert Olen, **Supp. XII:** **61–78,** 319

Butler, Samuel, **II:** 82, 86; **IV:** 121, 440; **Supp. VIII:** 171

Butler-Evans, Elliot, **Retro. Supp. II:** 121

"But Only Mine" (Wright), **Supp. III Part 2:** 595

Butscher, Edward, **Supp. I Part 2:** 526

Butter Battle Book, The (Geisel), **Supp. XVI:** 110

"Buttercups" (Lowell), **Retro. Supp. II:** 187

Butterfield, R. W., **I:** 386

Butterfield, Stephen, **Supp. IV Part 1:** 3, 11

Butterfield 8 (O'Hara), **III:** 361

"Butterflies Under Persimmon" (Jarman), **Supp. XVII:** 120

Butterfly (Harvey), **Supp. XIII:** 184

"Butterfly, The" (Brodksy), **Supp. VIII:** 26

"Butterfly and the Traffic Light, The" (Ozick), **Supp. V:** 263, 265

Butterfly Plague, The (Findley), **Supp. XX:** **50, 52, 53**

Butterfly Stories (Vollmann), **Supp. XVII:** 226

"Butterfly-toed Shoes" (Komunyakaa), **Supp. XIII:** 126

Butter Hill and Other Poems (Francis), **Supp. IX:** 88, 89

"Button-Down Builders, The" (Siddons), **Supp. XXII:** 243–244

Buttons, Red, **Supp. IV Part 2:** 574

Buttrick, George, **III:** 301; **Supp. XII:** 47–48

"But What Is the Reader to Make of This?" (Ashbery), **Supp. III Part 1:** 25

Butz, Earl, **Supp. X:** 35

"Buz" (Alcott), **Supp. I Part 1:** 43

Buzinski, Jim, **Supp. XX:** **273**

"By an *Objibwa Female* Pen: Invitation to sisters to a walk in the Garden, after a shower"(J. Schoolcraft), **Supp. XXIII:** 230

Byatt, A. S., **Supp. XXI:** 147

By Avon River (Doolittle), **Supp. I Part 1:** 272

"By Blue Ontario's Shore" (Whitman), **Retro. Supp. I:** 399, 400

"By Candlelight" (Major), **Supp. XXII:** 185

"By Disposition of Angels" (Moore), **III:** 214

"By Earth" (Olds), **Supp. X:** 214

"By Fire" (Olds), **Supp. X:** 214

Bygones (Untermeyer), **Supp. XV:** 304, **308–309,** 312, 313

By Land, By Sea (Hoffman), **Supp. XVIII:** 86

By Land and by Sea (Morison), **Supp. I Part 2:** 492

Byles, Mather, **Supp. XX:** **279, 282**

By-Line: Ernest Hemingway (Hemingway), **II:** 257–258

By Love Possessed (Cozens), **I:** 358, 365, 372–374, 375, 376, 377, 378, 379

"By Morning" (Swenson), **Supp. IV Part 2:** 642

"By Night" (Francis), **Supp. IX:** 76

Bynner, Witter, **II:** 513, 527; **Supp. XIII:** 347; **Supp. XV:** **39–54**

Byrd, William, **Supp. IV Part 2:** 425; **Supp. XXI:** 35; **Supp. XXII:** 193

Byrne, Donn, **IV:** 67

Byron, George Gordon, Lord, **I:** 343, 568, 577; **II:** 135, 193, 296, 301, 303, 310, 315, 331, 566; **III:** 82, 137, 170, 409, 410, 412, 469; **IV:** 245, 435; **Supp. I**

Part 1: 150, 312, 349; **Supp. I Part 2:** 580, 591, 683, 685, 719; **Supp. XIII:** 139; **Supp. XVI:** 188, 203, 206, 210

"Byron's Cain" (L. Michaels), **Supp. XVI:** 203

"Bystanders" (Matthews), **Supp. IX:** 160

By the Bias of Sound (Sobin), **Supp. XVI:** 281

By the North Gate (Oates), **Supp. II Part 2:** 504

"By the People" (Stratton-Porter), **Supp. XX: 221**

By the Shores of Silver Lake (L. I. Wilder), **Supp. XXII:** 294, 295, 299

"By the Waters of Babylon" (Benét), **Supp. XI:** 56, 58

By the Waters of Manhattan (Reznikoff), **Supp. XIV:** 288, 293, 294

By the Waters of Manhattan: An Annual (Reznikoff), **Supp. XIV:** 277, 280, 289

By the Waters of Manhattan: Selected Verse (Reznikoff), **Supp. XIV:** 281, 291

By the Well of Living and Seeing and the Fifth Book of the Maccabees (Reznikoff), **Supp. XIV:** 281

By the Well of Living and Seeing: New and Selected Poems 1918–1973 (Reznikoff), **Supp. XIV:** 281, 287–288, 295

By Way of Orbit (O'Neill), **III:** 405

Byzantine Parables (Notley), **Supp. XXII:** 235, 237

C

"C 33" (H. Crane), **I:** 384; **Retro. Supp. II:** 76

Cabala, The (Wilder), **IV:** 356, 358–360, 369, 374

Cabaret (film), **Supp. XIV:** 155, 162

Cabaret (play), **Supp. XIV:** 162; **Supp. XVII:** 45

Cabbages and Kings (O. Henry), **Supp. II Part 1:** 394, 409

Cabell, James Branch, **II:** 42; **III:** 394; **IV:** 67, 359, 360; **Retro. Supp. I:** 80; **Supp. I Part 2:** 613, 714, 718, 721; **Supp. X:** 223

"Cabin, The" (Carver), **Supp. III Part 1:** 137, 146

Cabin, The: Reminiscence and Diversions (Mamet), **Supp. XIV:** 240

Cabinet of Dr. Caligari, The (film), **Retro. Supp. I:** 268

Cable, George Washington, **II:** 289; **Retro. Supp. II:** 65; **Supp. I Part 1:** 200; **Supp. II Part 1:** 198; **Supp. XIV:** 63

Cables to the Ace; or, Familiar Liturgies of Misunderstanding (Merton), **Supp. VIII:** 208

Cabot, James, **II:** 14; **IV:** 173

Cabot, John, **Supp. I Part 2:** 496, 497

Cachoeira Tales and Other Poems, The (Nelson), **Supp. XVIII: 178–179**

"Cachoiera Tales, The" (Nelson), **Supp. XVIII:** 179

Cactus Flower (Barillet and Grédy), **Supp. XVI:** 194

"Caddy's Diary, A" (Lardner), **II:** 421–422

"Cadence" (Dubus), **Supp. VII:** 84–85

Cadieux, Isabelle, **Supp. XIII:** 127

"Cadillac Flambé" (Ellison), **Retro. Supp. II:** 119, 126; **Supp. II Part 1:** 248

Cadillac Jack (McMurtry), **Supp. V:** 225

Cadillac Jukebox (Burke), **Supp. XIV:** 32

Cadle, Dean, **Supp. I Part 2:** 429

Cady, Edwin H., **II:** 272

"Caedmon" (Garrett), **Supp. VII:** 96–97

Caesar, Julius, **II:** 12, 502, 561–562; **IV:** 372, 373

Caesar, Sid, **Supp. IV Part 2:** 574, 591

"Cafeteria, The" (Singer), **Retro. Supp. II:** 316

Cage, John, **Supp. IV Part 1:** 84; **Supp. V:** 337, 341; **Supp. XXIII:** 211

"Cage and the Prairie: Two Notes on Symbolism, The" (Bewley), **Supp. I Part 1:** 251

Cage of Age, The (Bronk), **Supp. XXI:** 32

Cage of Spines, A (Swenson), **Supp. IV Part 2:** 641–642, 647

"Cage of the Body, The"(Schott), **Supp. XXIII:** 243–244

Cagney, James, **Supp. IV Part 1:** 236; **Supp. XIII:** 174

Cagney, William, **Supp. XIII:** 174

Cahalan, James, **Supp. XIII:** 1, 2, 3, 4, 12

Cahan, Abraham, **Supp. IX:** 227; **Supp. XIII:** 106; **Supp. XXI:** 3, 14; **Supp. XXIII:** 1, 2, 9, 16

Cahill, Tim, **Supp. XIII:** 13

Cain, James M., **III:** 99; **Supp. IV Part 1:** 130; **Supp. XI:** 160; **Supp. XIII:** 159, 165

Cain, Kathleen Shine, **Supp. XX: 247, 248**

Caird, G. B., **Supp. XXI:** 91–92

Cairns, Huntington, **III:** 103, 108, 114, 119

Cairo! Shanghai! Bombay! (Williams and Shapiro), **IV:** 380

Cake (Bynner), **Supp. XV:** 50

Cakes and Ale (Maugham), **III:** 64

Calabria, Frank, **Supp. XIII:** 164

Calamity Jane (Martha Jane Canary), **Supp. V:** 229–230; **Supp. X:** 103

"Calamus" (Whitman), **IV:** 342–343; **Retro. Supp. I:** 52, 403, 404, 407

Calasso, Roberto, **Supp. IV Part 1:** 301

Calder, William M., III, **Supp. XXIII:** 112

Calderón, Hector, **Supp. IV Part 2:** 544

Caldwell, Christopher, **Supp. IV Part 1:** 211

Caldwell, Erskine, **I:** 97, 211, **288–311;** **IV:** 286; **Supp. IV Part 2:** 601; **Supp. XXI:** 35; **Supp. XXII:** 196

Caldwell, Mrs. Erskine (Helen Lannegan), **I:** 289

Caldwell, Mrs. Erskine (Margaret Bourke-White), **I:** 290, 293–295, 297

Caldwell, Mrs. Erskine (Virginia Fletcher), **I:** 290

Caldwell, Reverend Ira Sylvester, **I:** 289, 305

Caldwell, Zoe, **Supp. XIII:** 207

Caleb Williams (Godwin), **III:** 415

"Calendar" (Creeley), **Supp. IV Part 1:** 158

Calendar of Saints for Unbelievers, A (Wescott), **Supp. XIV:** 342

Calendars (A. Finch), **Supp. XVII: 76–77**

Calhoun, John C., **I:** 8; **III:** 309

"Caliban in the Coal Mines" (Untermeyer), **Supp. XV:** 296

"California" (Carruth), **Supp. XVI:** 56

"California" (Didion), **Supp. IV Part 1:** 195

California and Oregon Trail, The (Parkman), **Supp. I Part 2:** 486

"California Hills in August" (Gioia), **Supp. XV:** 118–119

Californians (Jeffers), **Supp. II Part 2:** 415, 418, 420

"California Oaks, The" (Winters), **Supp. II Part 2:** 798

"California Plush" (Bidart), **Supp. XV:** 23

"California Republic" (Didion), **Supp. IV Part 1:** 205

"California Requiem, A" (Gioia), **Supp. XV:** 126

California Suite (film), **Supp. IV Part 2:** 589

California Suite (Simon), **Supp. IV Part 2:** 581, 582

"Caligula" (Lowell), **II:** 554

Callahan, John F., **Retro. Supp. II:** 119, 126, 127

"Call at Corazón" (Bowles), **Supp. IV Part 1:** 82, 87

Calle, Sophia, **Supp. XII:** 22

"Called Back" (Kazin), **Supp. VIII:** 104

Calley, Captain William, **II:** 579

Calley, John, **Supp. XI:** 305

Callicott, J. Baird, **Supp. XIV:** 184

Calligrammes (Apollinaire), **I:** 432

"Calling Jesus" (Toomer), **Supp. III Part 2:** 484

Calling Myself Home (Hogan), **Supp. IV Part 1:** 397, 399, 400, 401, 413

Calling the Wind: Twentieth Century African-American Short Stories (Major, ed.), **Supp. XXII:** 172

Calling Western Union (Taggard), **Supp. XXII:** 271–272, **281–283**

Call It Experience (Caldwell), **I:** 290–291, 297

"Call It Fear" (Harjo), **Supp. XII:** 220

Call It Sleep (H. Roth), **Supp. VIII:** 233; **Supp. IX:** 227, 228, **229–231;** **Supp. XIII:** 106

"Call Letters: Mrs. V. B." (Angelou), **Supp. IV Part 1:** 15

Call Me Ishmael (Olson), **Supp. II Part 2:** 556; **Supp. XXI:** 21

Call Me Shakespeare (Endore), **Supp. XVII:** 65

Call of the Gospel, The (Mather), **Supp. II Part 2:** 448

Call of the Wild, The (London), **II:** 466, 470–471, 472, 481

"Call of the Wild, The" (Snyder), **Supp. VIII:** 301

"Calloway's Code" (O. Henry), **Supp. II Part 1:** 404

"Call to Arms" (Mumford), **Supp. II Part 2:** 479

Call to Arms, The (film), **Retro. Supp. I:** 325

Calmer, Ned, **Supp. XI:** 219

Calvert, George H., **Supp. I Part 1:** 361

Calverton, V. F., **Supp. VIII:** 96

Calvin, John, **II:** 342; **IV:** 160, 490

Calvino, Italo, **Supp. IV Part 2:** 623, 678; **Supp. XIX:** 34; **Supp. XXI:** 225; **Supp. XXII:** 263

Cambridge Companion to Native American Literature, The (Porter and Roemer, eds.), **Supp. XX: 270**

Cambridge Edition of the Works of F. Scott Fitzgerald, The (Bruccoli, ed.), **Retro. Supp. I:** 115

Cambridge Film Handbook for *On the Waterfront* (Rapf), **Supp. XVIII:** 251

"Cambridge"(O'Hara), **Supp. XXIII:** 219

"Cambridge Thirty Years Ago" (Lowell), **Supp. I Part 2:** 419

Cambridge University Press, **Retro. Supp. I:** 115

"Camellia Sabina" (Moore), **III:** 208, 215

"Cameo" (Trethewey), **Supp. XXI:** 250

"Cameo Appearance" (Simic), **Supp. VIII:** 283

"Camera Notes" (column, Stratton-Porter), **Supp. XX: 217**

Camera Obscura (Nabokov), **III:** 255

Cameron, Angus, **Supp. XXI:** 268, 269, 275, 278

Cameron, Elizabeth, **I:** 10, 17

Cameron, Kenneth W., **II:** 16

Cameron, Peter, **Supp. XII: 79–95**

Cameron, Sharon, **Retro. Supp. I:** 43; **Retro. Supp. II:** 40

Camerson, Don, **I:** 10, 17

Camino, Léon Felipe, **Retro. Supp. II:** 89

Camino Real (T. Williams), **IV:** 382, 385, 386, 387, 388, 391, 392, 395, 398

Camões, Luiz Vaz de, **II:** 133; **Supp. I Part 1:** 94

"Camouflaging the Chimera" (Komunyakaa), **Supp. XIII: 122–123**

Camp, James, **Supp. XV:** 165

Camp, Walter, **II:** 423

Campana, Dino, **Supp. V:** 337

Campbell, Alan, **Supp. IV Part 1:** 353; **Supp. IX:** 196, 198, 201

Campbell, Alexander, **Supp. I Part 2:** 381, 395

Campbell, Donna, **Retro. Supp. II:** 139

Campbell, E. Simms, **Supp. XXII:** 12

Campbell, Helen, **Supp. XI:** 200, 206

Campbell, James, **Supp. XII:** 127

Campbell, James Edwin, **Supp. II Part 1:** 202

Campbell, Joanna (pseudonym). *See* Bly, Carol

Campbell, Joseph, **I:** 135; **IV:** 369, 370; **Supp. IX:** 245

Campbell, Lewis, **III:** 476

Campbell, Thomas, **II:** 8, 303, 314; **III:** 410; **Supp. I Part 1:** 309, 310

Campbell, Virginia, **Supp. XIII:** 114

Campbell, Will D., **Supp. XXI:** 247

Campbell (Hale), Janet, **Supp. IV Part 2:** 503

"Campers Leaving: Summer 1981" (Kenyon), **Supp. VII:** 169

"Camp Evergreen" (Kenyon), **Supp. VII:** 168

"Camping in Madera Canyon" (Swenson), **Supp. IV Part 2:** 649

Campion, Thomas, **I:** 439; **Supp. VIII:** 272

Campo, Rafael, **Supp. XVII:** 112

Camus, Albert, **I:** 53, 61, 292, 294, 494; **II:** 57, 244; **III:** 292, 306, 453; **IV:** 6, 211, 236, 442, 487; **Retro. Supp. I:** 73; **Retro. Supp. II:** 20; **Supp. I Part 2:** 621; **Supp. VIII:** 11, 195, 241; **Supp. XI:** 96; **Supp. XIII:** 74, 165, 233, 247; **Supp. XVII:** 137

Camuto, Christopher, **Supp. V:** 212–213

"Canada" (Di Piero), **Supp. XIX:** 39

Canada Fragrant with Resin, **Supp. XVI:** 149

Canadé, Eugene, **Supp. XXI:** 22, 23

"Canadian Mosaic, The" (Beran), **Supp. XIII:** 25

"Canadians and Pottawatomies" (Sandburg), **III:** 592–593

"Can a Good Wife Be a Good Sport?" (T. Williams), **IV:** 380

"Canal, The: A Poem on the Application of Physical Science to Political Economy" (Barlow), **Supp. II Part 1:** 73

Canary, Martha Jane. *See* Calamity Jane (Martha Jane Canary)

"Canary for One, A" (Hemingway), **Retro. Supp. I:** 170, 189

Canary in a Cat House (Vonnegut), **Supp. II Part 2:** 758

"Canary in Bloom" (Dove), **Supp. IV Part 1:** 248

Canby, Henry Seidel, **IV:** 65, 363

"Cancer" (McClatchy), **Supp. XII:** 266

"Cancer Match, The" (Dickey), **Supp. IV Part 1:** 182

"Cancíon y Glosa" (Merwin), **Supp. III Part 1:** 342

Candide (Hellman), **I:** 28; **Supp. I Part 1:** 288–289, 292

Candide (Voltaire), **Supp. I Part 1:** 288–289; **Supp. XI:** 297; **Supp. XVI:** 189

Candide (Voltaire; Wilbur, trans.), **Supp. III Part 2:** 560

"Candle Hat" (Collins), **Supp. XXI:** 60

Candle in the Cabin, The (Lindsay), **Supp. I Part 2:** 398, 400

"Candles" (Plath), **Retro. Supp. II:** 248, 257

Candles in Babylon (Levertov), **Supp. III Part 1:** 283

Candles in the Sun (T. Williams), **IV:** 381

Candles of Your Eyes, The (Purdy), **Supp. VII:** 278

Candy (Southern), **Supp. XI:** 297, **298–299, 305**

"Candy-Man Beechum" (Caldwell), **I:** 309

Cane (Toomer), **Supp. III Part 2:** 475, 481–486, 488; **Supp. IV Part 1:** 164, 168; **Supp. IX:** 305, 306, 307, **308–320; Supp. XIX:** 73; **Supp. XX:** 73

"Cane in the Corridor, The" (Thurber), **Supp. I Part 2:** 616

Canfield, Cass, **Supp. I Part 2:** 668

Canfield, Dorothy, **Retro. Supp. I:** 4, 11, 14, 18; **Supp. XX: 39**. *See also* Fisher, Dorothy Canfield

Can Grande's Castle (Lowell), **II:** 518, 524

"Canicula di Anna" (Carson), **Supp. XII:** 101–102

"Canis Major" (Frost), **Retro. Supp. I:** 137

"Canned Stuff" (Pickering), **Supp. XXI:** 198

Cannery Row (Steinbeck), **IV:** 50, 51, 64–65, 66, 68

Cannibal Galaxy, The (Ozick), **Supp. V:** 270

Cannibals and Christians (Mailer), **III:** 38–39, 40, 42; **Retro. Supp. II:** 203, 204, 205

Canning, George, **I:** 7, 8

Canning, Richard, **Supp. X:** 147

Cannon, Jimmy, **II:** 424

Cannon, Steve, **Retro. Supp. II:** 111

Cannon between My Knees, A (Gunn Allen), **Supp. IV Part 1:** 324

Canolle, Jean, **Supp. XVI:** 194

"Canonization, The" (Donne), **Supp. XIV:** 8

"Can Poetry Matter?" (Gioia), **Supp. XV:** 113, 114

Can Poetry Matter?: Essays on Poetry and American Culture (Gioia), **Supp. XV:** 112, **113–115**

"Canso" (Merwin), **Supp. III Part 1:** 344

Can Such Things Be? (Bierce), **I:** 203, 204, 205, 209

Canterbury Tales (Chaucer), **II:** 504; **III:** 411; **IV:** 65

Canterbury Tales, The (Chaucer), **Supp. XIX:** 4

"Canticle of Her Coming and Going" (Espaillat), **Supp. XXI:** 106

"Canto Amor" (Berryman), **I:** 173

Canto I (Pound), **III:** 469, 470; **Retro. Supp. I:** 286

Canto II (Pound), **III:** 470

Canto III (Pound), **III:** 470

Canto IV (Pound), **III:** 470

Canto VIII (Pound), **III:** 472

Canto IX (Pound), **III:** 472

Canto X (Pound), **III:** 472

Canto XIII (Pound), **III:** 472

Canto XXXIX (Pound), **III:** 468

Canto LXV (Pound), **Retro. Supp. I:** 292

Canto LXXXI (Pound), **III:** 459; **Retro. Supp. I:** 293

Cantor, Lois, **Supp. IV Part 1:** 285

Cantos (Pound), **I:** 482; **III:** 13–14, 17, 457, 462, 463, 466, 467, 469–470, 472–473, 474, 475, 476, 492; **Retro.**

Supp. I: 284, 292, **292–293**, 293, 427; **Supp. I Part 1:** 272; **Supp. II Part 1:** 5; **Supp. II Part 2:** 420, 557, 564, 644; **Supp. IV Part 1:** 153; **Supp. V:** 343, 345; **Supp. VIII:** 305; **Supp. XIV:** 55, 96; **Supp. XV:** 349

"Cantus Planis" (Pound), **III:** 466

Cantwell, Robert, **Retro. Supp. I:** 85; **Supp. VIII:** 96; **Supp. XIII:** 292

"Canyon de Chelly, Return, 1978"(Kenny), **Supp. XXIII:** 155

"Can You Carry Me" (O'Hara), **III:** 369

Can You See Me Yet? (Findley), **Supp. XX:** 52–53

Canzoneri, Robert, **IV:** 114, 116

Canzoni (Pound), **Retro. Supp. I:** 286, 288, 413

"Cap" (Shaw), **Supp. IV Part 1:** 345

"Cape Breton" (Bishop), **Supp. I Part 1:** 92; **Supp. IX:** 45

Cape Cod (Thoreau), **II:** 540

"Cape Cod, Rome, and Jerusalem" (Chapman), **Supp. XIV:** 55

Capitalism: The Unknown Ideal (Rand), **Supp. IV Part 2:** 518, 527, 531, 532

Caponi, Gena Dagel, **Supp. IV Part 1:** 95

Capote, Truman, **Supp. I Part 1:** 291, 292; **Supp. III Part 1: 111–133**; **Supp. III Part 2:** 574; **Supp. IV Part 1:** 198, 220; **Supp. VIII:** 105; **Supp. XII:** 43, 249; **Supp. XV:** 146; **Supp. XVI:** 245–246; **Supp. XVII:** 236

Capouya, Emile, **Supp. I Part 1:** 50

Cappetti, Carla, **Supp. IX:** 4, 8

Capra, Frank, **Supp. XVI:** 102

Capra, Fritjof, **Supp. X:** 261

Capron, Marion, **Supp. IX:** 193

"Capsule History of Conservation, A" (Stegner), **Supp. IV Part 2:** 600

"Captain Carpenter" (Ransom), **III:** 491

Captain Craig (Robinson), **III:** 508, 523; **Supp. II Part 1:** 192

"Captain Jim's Friend" (Harte), **Supp. II Part 1:** 337

"Captain Jones's Invitation" (Freneau), **Supp. II Part 1:** 261

"Captain's Son, The" (Taylor), **Supp. V:** 314, 325, 327

"Captain's Wife, The" (Salter), **Supp. IX:** 261

"Capt Christopher Levett (of York)" (Olson), **Supp. II Part 2:** 576, 577

Captive Israel (Reznikoff), **Supp. XIV:** 283

"Captivity and Restoration of Mrs. Mary Rowlandson, The" (Howe), **Supp. IV Part 2:** 419, 431, 434

"Captivity of the Fly" (MacLeish), **III:** 19

"Captured Goddess, The" (Lowell), **II:** 520

Caputi, Jane, **Supp. IV Part 1:** 334, 335

Caputo, Philip, **Supp. XI:** 234; **Supp. XIX:** 17–31; **Supp. XXII:** 104

Capuzzo, Michael, **Supp. XIII:** 254

Car (Crews), **Supp. XI: 110–111**

Carabi, Angels, **Supp. VIII:** 223; **Supp. XII:** 215

"Caramels" (Zinberg), **Supp. XV:** 195

"Caravaggio: Swirl & Vortex" (Levis), **Supp. XI:** 258, 269

Caravan (Bynner), **Supp. XV:** 50

Carby, Hazel B., **Supp. IV Part 1:** 13; **Supp. XXI:** 171

"Carcassonne" (Faulkner), **Retro. Supp. I:** 81

Card, Antha E., **Supp. I Part 2:** 496

Cárdenas, Lupe, **Supp. IV Part 2:** 538, 539, 540

Cardinale, Anthony, **Supp. XVII:** 239

Cardinale, Ernesto, **Supp. XII:** 225

"Cardinal Ideograms" (Swenson), **Supp. IV Part 2:** 645

"Cards" (Beattie), **Supp. V:** 31

"Career Woman" (Hay), **Supp. XIV:** 131

Carefree (film, Sandrich), **Supp. XVII:** 59

"Careful" (Carver), **Supp. III Part 1:** 138

Careful and Strict Enquiry into the Modern Prevailing Notions of That Freedom of Will, Which Is Supposed to be Essential to Moral Agency, Vertue and Vice, Reward and Punishment, Praise and Blame, A (Edwards), **I:** 549, 557, 558, 562

Carel: A Poem and Pilgrimage in the Holy Land (Melville), **III:** 92–93

Careless Love and Its Apostrophes (Bronk), **Supp. XXI:** 32

"Carentan O Carentan" (Simpson), **Supp. IX:** 267

Carew, Thomas, **IV:** 453

Carey, Gary, **Supp. XVI:** 186

Carey, Lynn, **Supp. XXIII:** 273

Carey, Mathew, **Supp. XV:** 238

"Car Games" (Conroy), **Supp. XVI:** 72

Cargill, Oscar, **Supp. II Part 1:** 117

Caribbean as Columbus Saw It (Morison and Obregon), **Supp. I Part 2:** 488

"Caribou Kitchen" (A. Finch), **Supp. XVII:** 76–77

Caribou Rising: Defending the Porcupine Herd, Gwich-'in Culture, and the Arctic National Wildlife Refuge (Bass), **Supp. XVI:** 27–28, 28

"Caring for the World"(Schott), **Supp. XXIII:** 249–250

Carl, K. A., **III:** 475

Carleton, George W., **Supp. XVIII:** 4

Carlin, George, **Supp. XXI:** 51

Carlin, Terry, **Supp. XXI:** 4, 5, 14

Carlisle, Harry, **Supp. XVIII:** 223, 233

Carl Krinken: His Christmas Stocking (S. and A. Warner), **Supp. XVIII:** 264

"Carlos Who Died, and Left Only This, The" (Ríos), **Supp. IV Part 2:** 547

Carlotta (empress of Mexico), **Supp. I Part 2:** 457

Carl Sandburg (Golden), **III:** 579

Carlson, Susan L., **Supp. XV:** 323

Carlyle, Thomas, **I:** 103, 279; **II:** 5, 7, 11, 15–16, 17, 20, 145, 315; **III:** 82, 84, 85, 87; **IV:** 169, 182, 338, 350; **Retro. Supp. I:** 360, 408; **Supp. I Part 1:** 2, 349; **Supp. I Part 2:** 410, 422, 482, 485, 552

"Carma" (Toomer), **Supp. III Part 2:** 481–483; **Supp. IX:** 312–313

"Carmen de Boheme" (Crane), **I:** 384

Carmen Jones (film), **Supp. I Part 1:** 66

Carmina Burana, **Supp. X:** 63

Carmon, Walt, **Supp. XXII:** 277

Carnegie, Andrew, **I:** 483; **IV:** 192; **Supp. I Part 2:** 639, 644; **Supp. V:** 285

Carnegie, Dale, **Supp. I Part 2:** 608

"Carnegie Hall: Rescued" (Moore), **III:** 215

Carne-Ross, D. S., **Supp. I Part 1:** 268, 269

Carnes, Mark C., **Supp. X:** 14

"Carnets" poems (Sobin), **Supp. XVI:** 286–287

Carnovsky, Morris, **III:** 154

"Carol for Carolyn, A" (A. Finch), **Supp. XVII:** 74, 75

Caroling Dusk: An Anthology of Verse by Negro Poets (Cullen), **Supp. IV Part 1:** 166, 169

"Carol of Occupations" (Whitman), **I:** 486

"Carolyn Kizer and the Chain of Women" (A. Finch), **Supp. XVII:** 74–75

Carolyn Kizer: Perspectives on Her Life and Work (A. Finch), **Supp. XVII: 74–75**

"Carpe Diem" (Frost), **Supp. XII:** 303

"Carpe Noctem, if You Can" (Thurber), **Supp. I Part 2:** 620

Carpenter, Dan, **Supp. V:** 250

Carpenter, David, **Supp. VIII:** 297

Carpenter, Edward, **Supp. XX: 230**

Carpenter, Frederic I., **II:** 20

"Carpenter Bee" (Trethewey), **Supp. XXI:** 250

Carpentered Hen and Other Tame Creatures, The (Updike), **IV:** 214; **Retro. Supp. I:** 320

Carpenter's Gothic (Gaddis), **Supp. IV Part 1:** 288, 289–291, 293, 294

Carr, Dennis W., **Supp. IV Part 2:** 560

Carr, Elias, **Supp. XIV:** 57

Carr, Rosemary. *See* Benét, Rosemary

Carrall, Aaron, **Supp. IV Part 2:** 499

Carrel, Alexis, **IV:** 240

"Carrell/Klee/and Cosmos's Groom" (Goldbarth), **Supp. XII:** 183

"Carriage from Sweden, A" (Moore), **III:** 212

Carrie (King), **Supp. V:** 137

Carried Away (Harrison), **Supp. VIII:** 39

Carrier of Ladders (Merwin), **Supp. III Part 1:** 339, 346, 350–352, 356, 357

"Carriers of the Dream Wheel" (Momaday), **Supp. IV Part 2:** 481

Carriers of the Dream Wheel: Contemporary Native American Poetry (Niatum, ed.), **Supp. IV Part 2:** 484, 505

Carrington, Carroll, **I:** 199

"Carrion Spring" (Stegner), **Supp. IV Part 2:** 604

Carroll, Charles, **Supp. I Part 2:** 525

Carroll, Lewis, **I:** 432; **II:** 431; **III:** 181; **Supp. I Part 1:** 44; **Supp. I Part 2:** 622, 656; **Supp. XVI:** 103

"Carrots, Noses, Snow, Rose, Roses" (Gass), **Supp. VI:** 87

Carrouges, Michel, **Supp. IV Part 1:** 104

"Carrousel, The" (Rilke), **III:** 558

Carruth, Hayden, **Supp. IV Part 1:** 66; **Supp. VIII:** 39; **Supp. IX:** 291; **Supp. XIII:** 112; **Supp. XIV:** 273–274; **Supp. XVI:** 45–61; **Supp. XIX:** 1; **Supp. XXI:** 31

Carruth, Joe-Anne McLaughlin, **Supp. XVI:** 47

"Carry" (Hogan), **Supp. IV Part 1:** 412

"Carrying On" (Dunn), **Supp. XI:** 145

Cars of Cuba (García), **Supp. XI:** 190

Carson, Anne, **Supp. XII:** 97–116; **Supp. XV:** 252

Carson, Johnny, **Supp. IV Part 2:** 526

Carson, Rachel, **Supp. V:** 202; **Supp. IX:** 19–36; **Supp. X:** 99; **Supp. XVI:** 36

Carson, Tom, **Supp. XI:** 227

Cart, Michael, **Supp. X:** 12

Carter, Elliott, **Supp. III Part 1:** 21

Carter, Hodding, **Supp. XIV:** 2

Carter, Jared, **Supp. XVII:** 110

Carter, Jimmy, **Supp. I Part 2:** 638; **Supp. XIV:** 107

Carter, Marcia, **Supp. V:** 223

Carter, Mary, **Supp. IV Part 2:** 444

Carter, Paul, **Supp. XX:** 77, 78

Carter, Peter, **Supp. XVIII:** 267

Carter, Stephen, **Supp. XI:** 220

Cartesian Sonata and Other Novellas (Gass), **Supp. VI:** 92–93

Cartier, Jacques, **Supp. I Part 2:** 496, 497

Cartier-Bresson, Henri, **Supp. VIII:** 98

"Cartographies of Silence" (Rich), **Supp. I Part 2:** 571–572

"Cartography" (Espaillat), **Supp. XXI:** 107

Cartwright, Louis, **Supp. XIV:** 147, 149, 151

Carver, Raymond, **Supp. III Part 1:** 135–151; **Supp. IV Part 1:** 342; **Supp. V:** 22, 23, 220, 326; **Supp. VIII:** 15; **Supp. X:** 85, 167; **Supp. XI:** 26, 65, 116, 153; **Supp. XII:** 79, 139, 289, 294; **Supp. XIX:** 209; **Supp. XXI:** 36, 115, 116, 118, 119; **Supp. XXIII:** 289, 296

Carver: A Life in Poems (Nelson), **Supp. XVIII:** 171, 172, **181–182,** 183

Carving Hawk (Kenny), **Supp. XXIII:** 143, 150

Cary, Alice, **Retro. Supp. II:** 145; **Supp. XV:** 273; **Supp. XXII:** 206

Cary, Phoebe, **Supp. XV:** 273

Cary, Richard, **Retro. Supp. II:** 132, 137

"Casabianca" (Bishop), **Retro. Supp. II:** 42; **Supp. I Part 1:** 86

Casablanca (film), **Supp. VIII:** 61; **Supp. XV:** 14

Casanova: His Known and Unknown Life (Endore), **Supp. XVII:** 54

"Casa solariega, La" ("The Family Mansion") (Espaillat), **Supp. XXI:** 107

"Case Against Mist, The" (Halliday), **Supp. XIX:** 91

Case for West-Indian Self-Government, The (C. L. R. James), **Supp. XXI:** 159, 161

Case of Rape, A (C. Himes), **Supp. XVI:** 143

Case of the Crushed Petunias, The (T. Williams), **IV:** 381

Case of the Officers of Excise (Paine), **Supp. I Part 2:** 503–504

Casey, Helen Marie, **Supp. XXIII:** 246

Casey, John, **Supp. X:** 164

Cash, Arthur, **Supp. IV Part 1:** 299

Cashman, Nellie, **Supp. X:** 103

Casiero, Robert, **Supp. XIV:** 167

Casino Royale (film), **Supp. XI:** 306–307

Caskey, William, **Supp. XIV:** 166

"Cask of Amontillado, The" (Poe), **II:** 475; **III:** 413; **Retro. Supp. II:** 268, 269, 270, 273

Caso, Frank, **Supp. XVIII:** 95

Caspary, Vera, **Supp. XIX:** 78

Casper, Robert N., **Supp. XV:** 339, 347

Casper and His Friends (S. and A. Warner), **Supp. XVIII:** 264

Cassada (Salter), **Supp. IX:** 251–252

Cassada, Jackie, **Supp. XXIII:** 291

Cassady, Carolyn, **Supp. XIV:** 150

Cassady, Neal, **Supp. II Part 1:** 309, 311; **Supp. XIV:** 137, 144

"Cassandra Southwick" (Whittier), **Supp. I Part 2:** 693

Cassell, Verlin, **Supp. XI:** 315

Cassill, Ronald Verlin, **Supp. V:** 323; **Supp. XVIII:** 72; **Supp. XIX:** 266

Cassirer, Ernst, **I:** 265; **IV:** 87, 89

Cass Timberlane (Lewis), **II:** 455–456

Cast a Cold Eye (McCarthy), **II:** 566

Castaway (Cozzens), **I:** 363, 370, 374, 375, 379

"Caste in America" (Du Bois), **Supp. II Part 1:** 169

Castiglione, Baldassare, **I:** 279; **III:** 282

"Castilian" (Wylie), **Supp. I Part 2:** 714

Castillo, Ana, **Supp. XI:** 177; **Supp. XXIII:** 194

"Castle in Lynn, A" (McCarriston), **Supp. XIV:** 265, 268

"Castles and Distances" (Wilbur), **Supp. III Part 2:** 550

Castle Sinister (Marquand), **III:** 58

Cast of Thousands (Loos), **Supp. XVI:** 192, 193, 195

Castro, Fidel, **II:** 261, 434; **Supp. XX:** 80

Cast the First Stone (C. Himes), **Supp. XVI:** 135, 137–138

"Casual Incident, A" (Hemingway), **II:** 44

"Casualty Report" (Halliday), **Supp. XIX:** 85

Caswell, Michelle, **Supp. XXII:** 262

"Cat, The" (Matthews), **Supp. IX:** 157–158

Cat, You Better Come Home (Keillor), **Supp. XVI:** 177

"Catbird Seat, The" (Thurber), **Supp. I Part 2:** 623

"Catch" (Francis), **Supp. IX:** 82

Catch-22 (Heller), **III:** 558; **Supp. IV Part 1:** 379, 380, 381–382, 383, 384–386, 387, 390, 391, 392, 393, 394; **Supp. V:** 244, 248; **Supp. XII:** 167–168; **Supp. XXIII:** 100

Catcher in the Rye, The (Salinger), **I:** 493; **III:** 551, 552, 553–558, 567, 571; **Retro. Supp. I:** 102; **Retro. Supp. II:** 222, 249; **Supp. I Part 2:** 535; **Supp. V:** 119; **Supp. VIII:** 242; **Supp. XI:** 65; **Supp. XVII:** 2; **Supp. XXIII:** 100

"Catching Frogs" (Kenyon), **Supp. VII:** 170

Catching the Mermother (A. Finch), **Supp. XVII:** 72

catechism of d neoamerican hoodoo church (Reed), **Supp. X:** 240, 241

Catered Affair, The (film), **Supp. IV Part 2:** 683

"Cathay" (Goldbarth), **Supp. XII:** 185, 186

Cathay (Pound), **II:** 527; **Retro. Supp. I:** 289

Cathedral (Carver), **Supp. III Part 1:** 144–146; **Supp. XII:** 139

"Cathedral" (Carver), **Supp. III Part 1:** 144–145

Cathedral, The (Lowell), **Supp. I Part 2:** 407, 416–417

Cather, Willa, **I:** 312–334, 405; **II:** 51, 96, 177, 404, 412; **III:** 453; **IV:** 190; **Retro. Supp. I:** 1–23, 355, 382; **Retro. Supp. II:** 71, 136; **Supp. I Part 2:** 609, 719; **Supp. IV Part 1:** 31; **Supp. VIII:** 101, 102, 263; **Supp. X:** 103; **Supp. XIII:** 253; **Supp. XIV:** 112; **Supp. XV:** 40, 51; **Supp. XVI:** 226; **Supp. XVIII:** 207; **Supp. XIX:** 131; **Supp. XXIII:** 290

Catherine, Saint, **II:** 211

Catherine II, **Supp. I Part 2:** 433

Catholic Art and Culture (Watkin), **Retro. Supp. II:** 187

"Catholic Novelist in the Protestant South, The" (O'Connor), **Retro. Supp. II:** 223, 224

"Cathy Queen of Cats" (Cisneros), **Supp. VII:** 59

Cat Inside, The (Burroughs), **Supp. III Part 1:** 105

Cat in the Hat, The (Geisel), **Supp. XVI:** 106–107, 112

Cat in the Hat Come Back, The (Geisel), **Supp. XVI:** 107

"Cat in the Hat for President, The" (Coover), **Supp. V:** 44, 46–47

Cat in The Hat Songbook, The (Geisel), **Supp. XVI:** 104

Cato, **II:** 114, 117

Cat on a Hot Tin Roof (T. Williams), **II:** 190; **IV:** 380, 382, 383, 386, 387, 389, 390, 391, 394, 395, 397–398

"Cat People: What Dr. Seuss Really Taught Us" (Menand), **Supp. XVI:** 106

Cat's Cradle (Vonnegut), **Supp. II Part 2:** 758, 759, 767–768, 770, 771, 772; **Supp. V:** 1

Cat's Eye (Atwood), **Supp. XIII:** 29–30

Catskill Eagle, A (Parker), **Supp. XIX:** 185

"Cat's Meow, A" (Brodsky), **Supp. VIII:** 31

Cat's Quizzer, The (Geisel), **Supp. XVI:** 111

"Catterskill Falls" (Bryant), **Supp. I Part 1:** 160

"Cattle Car Complex" (T. Rosenbaum), **Supp. XVII:** 48

Catullus, **Supp. XII:** 2, 13, **112; Supp. XV:** 23, 27, 35, 36

Catullus, Gaius Valerius, **I:** 381; **Supp. I Part 1:** 261; **Supp. I Part 2:** 728

Catullus (Gai Catulli Veronensis Liber) (Zukofsky), **Supp. III Part 2:** 625, 627, 628, 629

"*Catullus: Carmina*" (Carson), **Supp. XII:** **112**

"*Catullus: Excrucior*" (Bidart), **Supp. XV:** 32, 35

"Cat Walked Through the Casserole, The" (Nelson and Espeland), **Supp. XVIII:** **181**

Cat Walked Through the Casserole and Other Poems for Children (Nelson and Espeland), **Supp. XVIII:** 181

"Cat Who Aspired to Higher Things, The" (X. J. Kennedy), **Supp. XV:** 163

"Caucasian Storms Harlem, The" (R. Fisher), **Supp. XIX:** 78

Caudwell, Christopher, **Supp. X:** 112; **Supp. XXII:** 284

"Caul, The" (Banks), **Supp. V:** 10–11

Cause for Wonder (Morris), **III:** 232–233

"Causerie" (Tate), **IV:** 129

Causes and Consequences (Chapman), **Supp. XIV:** 41, 49, 51

"Causes of American Discontents before 1768, The" (Franklin), **II:** 120

Causley, Charles, **Supp. XV:** 117

Cavafy, Constantine P., **Supp. IX:** 275; **Supp. XI:** 119, 123; **Supp. XXI:** 131; **Supp. XXIII:** 150

Cavalcade of America, The (radio program), **III:** 146

Cavalcanti (Pound, opera), **Retro. Supp. I:** 287

Cavalcanti, Guido, **I:** 579; **III:** 467; **Supp. III Part 2:** 620, 621, 622, 623

Cavalieri, Grace, **Supp. IV Part 2:** 630, 631

"Cavalry Crossing the Ford" (Whitman), **IV:** 347

"Cave, The" (Bass), **Supp. XVI:** 23

Cave, The (Warren), **IV:** 255–256

Cavelieri, Grace, **Supp. XXIII:** 135

Cavell, Stanley, **Retro. Supp. I:** 306–307, 309

Cavender's House (Robinson), **III:** 510

Caver, Christine, **Supp. XXI:** 215

"Caviar" (Boyle), **Supp. XX:** **19**

Caviare at the Funeral (Simpson), **Supp. IX:** 266, **276–277**

"Cawdor" (Jeffers), **Supp. II Part 2:** 431

Caxton, William, **III:** 486

Cayton, Horace, **IV:** 475, 488

Cazamian, Louis, **II:** 529

"Ceiling, The" (Brockmeier), **Supp. XXII:** 52–53

Celan, Paul, **Supp. X:** 149; **Supp. XII:** 21, 110–111; **Supp. XVI:** 284–285, 288; **Supp. XVII:** 241

"Celebrated Jumping Frog of Calaveras County, The" (Twain), **IV:** 196

Celebrated Jumping Frog of Calaveras County, The, and Other Sketches (Twain), **IV:** 197

Celebration (Crews), **Supp. XI:** 103, **108**

Celebration (Swados), **Supp. XIX:** 269–270

Celebration at Dark (W. J. Smith), **Supp. XIII:** 332

"Celebration for June 24th" (McGrath), **Supp. X:** 116

Celebration of the Sound Through (Sobin), **Supp. XVI:** 284–285

Celebrations after the Death of John Brennan (X. J. Kennedy), **Supp. XV:** 165

Celebrity (film; Allen), **Supp. XV:** 11

"Celebrity" (Pickering), **Supp. XXI:** 198

"Celery" (Stein), **IV:** 43

"Celestial Games" (Conroy), **Supp. XVI:** 72

"Celestial Globe" (Nemerov), **III:** 288

Celestial Navigation (Tyler), **Supp. IV Part 2:** 662–663, 671

"Celestial Railroad, The" (Hawthorne), **Retro. Supp. I:** 152; **Supp. I Part 1:** 188

Celibate Season, A (Shields), **Supp. VII:** 323, 324

Cellini (Shanley), **Supp. XIV:** 316, **329–330**

"Cemetery at Academy, California" (Levine), **Supp. V:** 182

Cemetery Nights (Dobyns), **Supp. XIII:** 85, 87, 89

"Censors As Critics: *To Kill a Mockingbird* As a Case Study" (May), **Supp. VIII:** 126

"Census-Taker, The" (Frost), **Retro. Supp. I:** 129

"Centaur, The" (Swenson), **Supp. IV Part 2:** 641

Centaur, The (Updike), **IV:** 214, 216, 217, 218, 219–221, 222; **Retro. Supp. I:** 318, 322, 324, 331, 336

"Centennial Meditation of Columbia, The" (Lanier), **Supp. I Part 1:** 362

Centeno, Agusto, **IV:** 375

"Centipede" (Dove), **Supp. IV Part 1:** 246

"Central Man, The" (Bloom), **Supp. IV Part 2:** 689

"Central Park" (Lowell), **II:** 552

Central Park (Wasserstein and Drattel), **Supp. XV:** 333

Central Park West (Allen), **Supp. XV:** 13

Century of Dishonor, A (Jackson), **Retro. Supp. I:** 31

"Cerebral Snapshot, The" (Theroux), **Supp. VIII:** 313

"Ceremonies" (Rukeyser), **Supp. VI:** 279

Ceremony (Silko), **Supp. IV Part 1:** 274, 333; **Supp. IV Part 2:** 557–558, 558–559, 559, 561–566, 570; **Supp. XVIII:** 59

Ceremony (Wilbur), **Supp. III Part 2:** 550–551

"Ceremony, The" (Harjo), **Supp. XII:** 230

"Ceremony, The—Anatomy of a Massacre" (E. Hoffman, play), **Supp. XVI:** 160

Ceremony in Lone Tree (Morris), **III:** 229–230, 232, 238, 558

Ceremony of Brotherhood, A (Anaya and Ortiz, eds.), **Supp. IV Part 2:** 502

Cerf, Bennett, **III:** 405; **IV:** 288; **Retro. Supp. II:** 330; **Supp. XIII:** 172; **Supp. XIX:** 244

"Certain Attention to the World, A" (Haines), **Supp. XII:** 201

"Certain Beasts, Like Cats" (Bronk), **Supp. XXI:** 30

Certain Distance, A (Francis), **Supp. IX:** 85

"Certain Music, A" (Rukeyser), **Supp. VI:** 273

Certain Noble Plays of Japan (Pound), **III:** 458

Certain People (Wharton), **Retro. Supp. I:** 382

"Certain Poets" (MacLeish), **III:** 4

"Certain Testimony" (Bausch), **Supp. VII:** 48

Certificate, The (Singer), **IV:** 1; **Retro. Supp. II:** **314–315**

"Cerulean" (Everett), **Supp. XVIII:** 66

Cervantes, Lorna Dee, **Supp. IV Part 2:** 545

Cervantes, Miguel de, **I:** 130, 134; **II:** 8, 272, 273, 276, 289, 302, 310, 315; **III:** 113, 614; **IV:** 367; **Retro. Supp. I:** 91; **Supp. I Part 2:** 406; **Supp. V:** 277; **Supp. XIII:** 17; **Supp. XXIII:** 4

Césaire, Aimé, **Supp. X:** 132, 139; **Supp. XIII:** 114

"Cesarean" (Kenyon), **Supp. VII:** 173

Cézanne, Paul, **II:** 576; **III:** 210; **IV:** 26, 31, 407; **Supp. V:** 333, 341–342; **Supp. XIX:** 36

Chabon, Michael, **Supp. XI:** **63–81; Supp. XVI:** 259; **Supp. XIX:** 135, 138, 174, 223; **Supp. XX: 177; Supp. XXII:** 49

Chaboseau, Jean, **Supp. I Part 1:** 260

Chace, Bill, **Supp. XXI:** 256

Chagall, Marc, **Supp. XXIII:** 6

Chaikin, Joseph, **Supp. III Part 2:** 433, 436–437

"Chain, The" (Kumin), **Supp. IV Part 2:** 452

Chainbearer, The (Cooper), **I:** 351, 352–353

"Chain of Love, A" (Price), **Supp. VI:** **258–259,** 260

Chain Saw Dance, The (Budbill), **Supp. XIX:** 5–6

Chains of Dew (Glaspell), **Supp. III Part 1:** 181

Chalk Face (W. Frank), **Supp. XX: 73–74**

Challacombe, Robert Hamilton, **III:** 176

Challenge (Untermeyer), **Supp. XV:** 296, 303

"Challenge" (Untermeyer), **Supp. XV:** 296

Chalmers, George, **Supp. I Part 2:** 514, 521

"Chambered Nautilus, The" (Holmes), **Supp. I Part 1:** 254, 307, 312–313, 314

Chamberlain, John, **Supp. I Part 2:** 647; **Supp. IV Part 2:** 525

Chamberlain, Neville, **II:** 589; **Supp. I Part 2:** 664

Chamber Music (Joyce), **III:** 16

Chambers, Richard, **Supp. III Part 2:** 610, 611, 612

Chambers, Whittaker, **Supp. III Part 2:** 610; **Supp. IV Part 2:** 526; **Supp. XV:** 143

Chameleon (C. Baxter), **Supp. XVII:** 14–15

"Champ, The" (Zinberg), **Supp. XV:** 193

"Champagne Regions" (Ríos), **Supp. IV Part 2:** 553

"Champion" (Lardner), **II:** 420–421, 428, 430

Champion, Laurie, **Supp. VIII:** 128

Champollion-Figeac, Jean Jacques, **IV:** 426

"Chance" (Doolittle), **Supp. I Part 1:** 271

Chance, Frank, **II:** 418

Chance Acquaintance, A (Howells), **II:** 278

"Chance Encounter, A" (Swados), **Supp. XIX:** 261, 262

"Chanclas" (Cisneros), **Supp. VII:** 61

Chandler, Raymond, **Supp. III Part 1:** 91; **Supp. IV Part 1: 119–138,** 341, 344, 345; **Supp. IV Part 2:** 461, 464, 469, 470, 471, 472, 473; **Supp. XI:** 160, 228; **Supp. XII:** 307; **Supp. XIII:** 159, 233; **Supp. XIV:** 21; **Supp. XV:** 119; **Supp. XVI:** 122; **Supp. XVII:** 137; **Supp. XVIII:** 136,137, 137–138; **Supp. XIX:** 178, 189; **Supp. XXI:** 67; **Supp. XXII:** 119

Chandler, Sherry, **Supp. XXIII:** 247

Chaney, "Professor" W. H., **II:** 463–464

Chang, Leslie C., **Supp. IV Part 1:** 72

"Change, The: Kyoto-Tokyo Express" (Ginsberg), **Supp. II Part 1:** 313, 329

Changed Man, A (Prose), **Supp. XVI:** 261–262

"Changeling" (Espaillat), **Supp. XXI:** 100

Changeling (Middleton), **Retro. Supp. I:** 62

"Changeling, The" (Lowell), **Supp. I Part 2:** 409

"Changeling, The" (Whittier), **Supp. I Part 2:** 697

Change of World, A (Rich), **Supp. I Part 2:** 551, 552

"Changes of Mind" (Baker), **Supp. XIII:** 52

"Changes of the Soul" (Taggard), **Supp. XXII:** 280

"Change the Joke and Slip the Yoke" (Ellison), **Retro. Supp. II:** 118

Change Your Bedding! (O'Hara), **Supp. XXIII:** 210

Changing Light at Sandover, The (Merrill), **Supp. III Part 1:** 318, 319, 323, 327, 332, 335–336; **Supp. XII:** 269–270; **Supp. XV:** 264

"Changing Same, The" (Baraka), **Supp. II Part 1:** 47, 51, 53

Changing the Bully Who Rules the World: Reading and Thinking about Ethics (C. Bly), **Supp. XVI:** 32, **39–40,** 41

Chanler, Mrs. Winthrop, **I:** 22; **IV:** 325

Channing, Carol, **IV:** 357

Channing, Edward, **Supp. I Part 2:** 479–480

Channing, Edward Tyrrel, **Supp. I Part 1:** 155; **Supp. I Part 2:** 422

Channing, William Ellery, **I:** 336; **II:** 224, 495; **IV:** 172, 173, 176, 177; **Retro. Supp. I:** 54; **Supp. I Part 1:** 103; **Supp. I Part 2:** 589

Channing, William Henry, **IV:** 178; **Supp. II Part 1:** 280, 285

Chanson de Roland, La, **I:** 13

"Chanson un Peu Naïve" (Bogan), **Supp. III Part 1:** 50–51

"Chanteuse" (Doty), **Supp. XI:** 119

"Chant for May Day" (Hughes), **Supp. I Part 1:** 331

Chants (Mora), **Supp. XIII: 214–215**

Chaos (Dove), **Supp. IV Part 1:** 243

"Chaperone, The" (Van Vechten), **Supp. II Part 2:** 728

Chaplin, Charles Spencer "Charlie," **I:** 27, 32, 43, 386, 447; **III:** 403; **Supp. I Part 2:** 607; **Supp. IV Part 1:** 146; **Supp. IV Part 2:** 574; **Supp. XX: 75;** **Supp. XXI:** 170; **Supp. XXII:** 25, 26

"Chaplinesque" (H. Crane), **Retro. Supp. II:** 79

"Chapman" (Rukeyser), **Supp. VI:** 273

Chapman, Abraham, **IV:** 485

Chapman, George, **Supp. I Part 2:** 422

Chapman, John (Johnny Appleseed), **Supp. I Part 2:** 397

Chapman, John Jay, **IV:** 436; **Supp. XIV: 39–56**

Chapman, Stephen, **Supp. XIII:** 12

Chappell, Fred, **Supp. IV Part 1:** 69; **Supp. XI:** 317; **Supp. XVIII:** 87

Chapters in a Mythology: The Poetry of Sylvia Plath (Kroll), **Supp. I Part 2:** 541–543

Chapters on Erie (Adams and Adams), **Supp. I Part 2:** 644

Chapter Two (Simon), **Supp. IV Part 2:** 575, 586

"Chapter VI" (Hemingway), **II:** 252

Char, René, **Supp. XVI:** 282; **Supp. XVII:** 244

"Character" (Emerson), **II:** 6

"Character of Aboriginal Historical Tradition"(J. Schoolcraft), **Supp. XXIII:** 228–229

"Character of Presidents, The" (Doctorow), **Supp. IV Part 1:** 224

"Character of Socrates, The" (Emerson), **II:** 8–9

Character of the Poet, The (Simpson), **Supp. IX:** 273, 275, 278

"Characters in Fiction" (McCarthy), **II:** 562

"Charades" (Moore), **Supp. X:** 178

"Charge It" (Fante), **Supp. XI:** 164–165

Chariot in the Sky: A Story of the Jubilee Singers (Bontemps), **Supp. XXII:** 6, 13

"Charity" (Peacock), **Supp. XIX:** 221–222

Charity (Richard), **Supp. XIX: 220–222**

Charlatan, The (Singer), **IV:** 1

"Charles" (Jackson), **Supp. IX:** 125

Charles, Larry, **Supp. XVIII:** 21

"Charles Baxter, August Kleinzahler, Adrienne Rich: Contemporary Stevensians and the Problem of 'Other Lives' " (S. Burt), **Supp. XVII:** 18–19

Charles Goodnight: Cowman and Plainsman (Haley), **Supp. V:** 226

Charles Simic: Essays on the Poetry (Weigl), **Supp. VIII:** 269

Charles the Bold, Duke of Burgundy, **III:** 487

Charleville, Victoria Verdon, **Supp. I Part 1:** 200–201, 205, 206, 210

Charley's Aunt (B. Thomas), **II:** 138

Charlie Chan Is Dead: An Anthology of Contemporary Asian American Fiction (Hagedorn), **Supp. X:** 292

"Charlie Christian Story, The" (Ellison), **Retro. Supp. II:** 121

"Charlie Howard's Descent" (Doty), **Supp. XI:** 122

Charlotte: A Tale of Truth (Rowson), **Supp. I Part 1:** 128; **Supp. XV: 234–235,** 238. *See also Charlotte Temple* (Rowson)

Charlotte's Daughter; or, The Three Orphans (Rowson), **Supp. XV: 246**

Charlotte's Web (White), **Supp. I Part 2:** 655, 656, 658, 667, 670

Charlotte Temple (Rowson), **Supp. XV:** 229, **238–239.** *See also Charlotte: A Tale of Truth* (Rowson)

Charm, The (Creeley), **Supp. IV Part 1:** 139, 141, 144, 149–150

Charmed Life, A (McCarthy), **II:** 571–574

Charming Billy (McDermott), **Supp. XVIII:** 155, **162–164,** 166

Charms for the Easy Life (Gibbons), **Supp. X:** 45, **47–48**

Charnel Rose, The (Aiken), **I:** 50, 57, 62

Charney, Samuel, **Supp. XXIII:** 6

Charon's Cosmology (Simic), **Supp. VIII: 276–278**

Charterhouse, The (Percy), **Supp. III Part 1:** 388

Chart for Rough Water (W. Frank), **Supp. XX: 78**

Charvat, William, **II:** 244

Charyn, Jerome, **Supp. XVII:** 5

Chase, Mary Ellen, **Retro. Supp. II:** 243, 245

Chase, Richard, **IV:** 202, 443; **Retro. Supp. I:** 40, 395

Chase, Salmon P., **Supp. I Part 2:** 584

Chase, Stuart, **Supp. I Part 2:** 609

Chase, The (Foote), **Supp. I Part 1:** 281

Chasing the Dime (Connelly), **Supp. XXI:** 74

"Chaste Land, The" (Tate), **IV:** 122

Château, The (Maxwell), **Supp. VIII:** 152, 160, **165–167,** 168, 169

Chatham, Russell, **Supp. VIII:** 40

"Chattanooga Nights" (L. Brown), **Supp. XXI:** 39

Chatterdon, The Black Death, and Meriwether Lewis (Reznikoff), **Supp. XIV:** 288

Chatterton, Thomas, **Supp. I Part 1:** 349; **Supp. I Part 2:** 410, 716

Chatterton, Wayne, **Supp. IX:** 2, 4, 11–12

Chatwin, Bruce, **Supp. VIII:** 322

Chaucer, Geoffrey, **I:** 131; **II:** 11, 504, 516, 542, 543; **III:** 283, 411, 473, 492, 521; **Retro. Supp. I:** 135, 426; **Supp. I Part 1:** 356, 363; **Supp. I Part 2:** 422, 617; **Supp. V:** 259; **Supp. XII:** 197; **Supp. XVII:** 70; **Supp. XIX:** 4

Chauncy, Charles, **I:** 546–547; **IV:** 147

Chavez, César, **Supp. V:** 199

Chávez, Denise, **Supp. IV Part 2:** 544; **Supp. XI:** 316

Chavez, Lydia, **Supp. VIII:** 75

Chavkin, Allan, **Supp. IV Part 1:** 259

Chavkin, Nancy Feyl, **Supp. IV Part 1:** 259

Chawla, Louise, **Supp. XXI:** 24

Chayefsky, Paddy, **Supp. XI:** 306

Cheang, Shu Lea, **Supp. XI:** 20

"Cheat Takes Over" (Leopold), **Supp. XIV:** 189

"Cheers" (Carver), **Supp. III Part 1:** 138

Cheetham, James, **Supp. I Part 2:** 521

Cheever, Benjamin Hale, **Supp. I Part 1:** 175

Cheever, David W., **Supp. I Part 1:** 304

Cheever, Ezekiel, **Supp. I Part 1:** 174, 193

Cheever, Federico, **Supp. I Part 1:** 175

Cheever, Fred, **Supp. I Part 1:** 174

Cheever, Frederick L., **Supp. I Part 1:** 174

Cheever, John, **Retro. Supp. I:** 116, 333, 335; **Supp. I Part 1: 174–199; Supp. V:** 23, 95; **Supp. VIII:** 151; **Supp. IX:** 114, 208; **Supp. XI:** 65, 66, 99; **Supp. XII:** 140; **Supp. XIV:** 93; **Supp. XV:** 119, 142; **Supp. XXIII:** 104, 109, 275

Cheever, Mrs. John (Mary Winternitz), **Supp. I Part 1:** 175

Cheever, Mary Liley, **Supp. I Part 1:** 174

Cheever, Susan. *See* Cowley, Susan Cheever (Susan Cheever)

Cheever Evening, A (Gurney), **Supp. V:** 95

Chekhov, Anton, **I:** 52, 90; **II:** 27, 38, 44, 49, 198, 542; **III:** 362, 467; **IV:** 17, 53, 359, 446; **Retro. Supp. I:** 5, 355; **Retro. Supp. II:** 299; **Supp. I Part 1:** 196; **Supp. II Part 1:** 6; **Supp. IV Part 2:** 585; **Supp. V:** 265; **Supp. VIII:** 153, 332; **Supp. IX:** 260, 265, 274; **Supp. XI:** 66; **Supp. XII:** 94, 307; **Supp. XIII:** 79; **Supp. XIV:** 87, 242; **Supp. XV:** 320, 329; **Supp. XVIII:** 102; **Supp. XIX:** 172, 241; **Supp. XXII:** 60; **Supp. XXIII:** 162, 290

"Chekhov's Sense of Writing as Seen Through His Letters" (Dobyns), **Supp. XIII:** 77–78

"Chemin de Fer" (Bishop), **Retro. Supp. II:** 41; **Supp. I Part 1:** 80, 85, 86

Cheney, Brainard, **Retro. Supp. II:** 229

Cheney, Matthew, **Supp. XXII:** 50

Chenzira, Ayoka, **Supp. XI:** 19

Chéri (Colette; stage adaptation, Loos), **Supp. XVI:** 194

Cherkovski, Neeli, **Supp. XII:** 118, 132, 134

Chernyshevski, Nikolai, **III:** 261, 262, 263; **Retro. Supp. I:** 269

Cherokee Lottery, The: A Sequence of Poems (W. J. Smith), **Supp. XIII: 340–344**

"Cherríe Moraga's Radical Revision of *Death of a Salesman*"(Wiley), **Supp. XXIII:** 199

Cherry (Karr), **Supp. XI:** 239, **251–254**

"Cherrylog Road" (Dickey), **Supp. XVIII:** 191

Cherry Orchard, The (Chekhov), **IV:** 359, 426; **Supp. VIII:** 153

Cheslock, Louis, **III:** 99, 118, 119

Chesnutt, Charles Waddell, **Supp. II Part 1:** 174, 193, 211; **Supp. IV Part 1:** 257; **Supp. XIV: 57–78**

"Chess House, The" (Dixon), **Supp. XII:** 139

Chessman, Caryl, **Supp. I Part 2:** 446

Chester, Alfred, **Retro. Supp. II:** 111, 112; **Supp. X:** 192

Chesterfield, Lord, **II:** 36

Chesterton, Gilbert Keith, **I:** 226; **IV:** 432

Cheuse, Alan, **Supp. IV Part 2:** 570

Chevigny, Bell Gale, **Supp. XI:** 283

Cheyenne Autumn (Sandoz), **Supp. XXIII:** 146

"Chicago" (Sandburg), **III:** 581, 592, 596; **Supp. III Part 1:** 71

Chicago (Shepard), **Supp. III Part 2:** 439

Chicago: City on the Make (Algren), **Supp. IX:** 1, 3

"*Chicago Defender* Sends a Man to Little Rock, The" (Brooks), **Supp. III Part 1:** 80–81

"Chicago Hamlet, A" (Anderson), **I:** 112

Chicago Loop (Theroux), **Supp. VIII:** 324

"Chicago Picasso, The" (Brooks), **Supp. III Part 1:** 70–71, 84

Chicago Poems (Sandburg), **III:** 579, 581–583, 586

"Chicano/Borderlands Literature and Poetry" (Ríos), **Supp. IV Part 2:** 537, 538, 542, 545

Chick, Nancy, **Supp. IV Part 1:** 1

"Chickamauga" (Bierce), **I:** 201

"Chickamauga" (Wolfe), **IV:** 460

Chickamauga (Wright), **Supp. V:** 333, 343–344

"Chickamauga" (Wright), **Supp. V:** 334

"Chicken Market" (Skloot), **Supp. XX: 198, 200**

"Chiefly about War Matters" (Hawthorne), **II:** 227; **Retro. Supp. I:** 165

"Chiffon" (Hull), **Supp. XXI:** 138

"Child" (Plath), **Supp. I Part 2:** 544

Child, Greg, **Supp. XVIII:** 107

Child, Julia, **Supp. XVII:** 89, 90

Child, Lydia Maria, **Supp. XIII:** 141; **Supp. XVIII:** 11

"Child, The" (Ríos), **Supp. IV Part 2:** 543

"Child by Tiger, The" (Wolfe), **IV:** 451

"Childhood" (Wright), **Supp. V:** 341

Childhood, A: The Biography of a Place (Crews), **Supp. XI:** 102–103, 245

"Childhood, When You Are in It . . ." (Kenyon), **Supp. VII:** 160, 170

Childhood and Other Neighborhoods (Dybek), **Supp. XXIII:** 68, **69–70**

"Childhood Sketch" (Wright), **Supp. III Part 2:** 589

"Child Is Born, A" (Benét), **Supp. XI:** 46

"Child Is the Meaning of This Life, The" (Schwartz), **Supp. II Part 2:** 659–660

"Childlessness" (Merrill), **Supp. III Part 1:** 323

"Childless Woman" (Plath), **Supp. I Part 2:** 544

Child-Life (Whittier and Larcom, eds.), **Supp. XIII:** 142

Child-Life in Prose (Whittier and Larcom, eds.), **Supp. XIII:** 142

Childlike Life of the Black Tarantula, The (Acker), **Supp. XII:** 4, 6, **7–8**

"Child Margaret" (Sandburg), **III:** 584

"Child of Courts, The" (Jarrell), **II:** 378, 379, 381

Child of God (McCarthy), **Supp. VIII: 177–178**

Child of My Heart (McDermott), **Supp. XVIII:** 155, **164–166**

"CHILD OF THE THIRTIES" (Baraka), **Supp. II Part 1:** 60

"Child on Top of a Greenhouse" (Roethke), **III:** 531

Children (Gurney), **Supp. V:** 95, 96

"Children" (Stowe), **Supp. I Part 2:** 587

"Children, The" (Jarman), **Supp. XVII:** 116

Children, The (Wharton), **IV:** 321, 326; **Retro. Supp. I:** 381

"Children, the Sandbar, That Summer" (Rukeyser), **Supp. VI:** 274

Children and Others (Cozzens), **I:** 374

Children Is All (Purdy), **Supp. VII:** 277, 278, 282

"Children of Adam" (Whitman), **IV:** 342; **Retro. Supp. I:** 403, 405

Children of Job, The: American Second-Generation Witnesses to the Holocaust (A. Berger), **Supp. XVII:** 39

Children of Light (Stone), **Supp. V:** 304–306

Children of Light and the Children of Darkness, The (Niebuhr), **III:** 292, 306, 310

Children of the Frost (London), **II:** 469, 483

Children of the Holocaust (H. Epstein), **Supp. XVII:** 48; **Supp. XXII:** 95

"Children of the Lord's Supper, The" (Tegnér), **Retro. Supp. II:** 155, 157

Children of the Market Place (Masters), **Supp. I Part 2:** 471

"Children on Their Birthdays" (Capote), **Supp. III Part 1:** 114, 115

Children Playing Before a Statue of Hercules (Sedaris, ed.), **Supp. XXIII:** 289

"Children Selecting Books in a Library" (Jarrell), **II:** 371

Children's Hour, The (Hellman), **Supp. I Part 1:** 276–277, 281, 286, 297

"Children's Rhymes" (Hughes), **Supp. I Part 1:** 340

Childress, Mark, **Supp. X:** 89

Child's Garden of Verses, A (Stevenson), **Supp. IV Part 1:** 298, 314; **Supp. XIII:** 75

"Child's Nature, A" (Jin), **Supp. XVIII:** 93

"Child's Reminiscence, A" (Whitman), **IV:** 344

Childwold (Oates), **Supp. II Part 2:** 519–520

Chill, The (Macdonald), **Supp. IV Part 2:** 473

Chills and Fever (Ransom), **III:** 490, 491–492, 493

Chilly Scenes of Winter (Beattie), **Supp. V:** 21, 22, 23, 24, 26, 27

Chime of Words, A: The Letters of Logan Pearsall Smith (Tribble, ed.), **Supp. XIV:** 348–349

Chimera (C. Frost), **Supp. XV:** 94, 95, 100

"Chimes for Yahya" (Merrill), **Supp. III Part 1:** 329

Chin, Frank, **Supp. V:** 164, 172

Chin, Mei, **Supp. XVIII:** 95

"China" (Johnson), **Supp. VI:** 193–194

Chinaberry Tree, The (Fauset), **Supp. XIX:** 73

"Chinaman's Hat" (Kingston), **Supp. V:** 169

China Men (Kingston), **Supp. V:** 157, 158, 159, 160, 161, 164–169; **Supp. X:** 292; **Supp. XV:** 220

"China Poet, The" (Sturgis), **Supp. XX:** 233, 240

China Trace (Wright), **Supp. V:** 332, 340, 341, 342

"Chinese Apples" (Di Piero), **Supp. XIX:** 40

Chinese Apples: New and Selected Poems (Di Piero), **Supp. XIX:** 33, 36, 37, 38, 39, 40, 44, 45, 46, 47–48

Chinese Classics (Legge), **III:** 472

Chinese Materia Medica (P. Smith), **III:** 572

"Chinese New Year" (Hull), **Supp. XXI:** 135

"Chinese Nightingale, The" (Lindsay), **Supp. I Part 2:** 392–393, 394

Chinese Nightingale and Other Poems, The (Lindsay), **Supp. I Part 2:** 392

Chinese Siamese Cat, The (Tan), **Supp. X:** 289

Chinese Translations, The (Bynner), **Supp. XV:** 47, 52

Chinitz, David, **Supp. XV:** 180, 185

"Chinoiseries" (Lowell), **II:** 524–525

Chip (Untermeyer), **Supp. XV:** 310

Chirico, Giorgio de, **Supp. III Part 1:** 14

Chirico, Miriam M., **Supp. XV:** 323

"Chiron" (Winters), **Supp. II Part 2:** 801

"Chitlins at the Waldorf" (Crouch), **Supp. XIX:** 158

"Chloroform Jags" (J. Scott), **Supp. XVII:** 189

Chodorov, Jerome, **IV:** 274

"Choice, The" (Karr), **Supp. XI:** 251

"Choice of Accommodations, A" (Lahiri), **Supp. XXI:** 183

"Choice of Profession, A" (Malamud), **Supp. I Part 2:** 437

Choice of Wars, A (Shaw), **Supp. XIX:** 245

Chomei, Kamo No, **IV:** 170, 171, 184

Chomsky, Noam, **Supp. IV Part 2:** 679

Choosing not Choosing (Cameron), **Retro. Supp. I:** 43

Chopin, Felix, **Supp. I Part 1:** 202

Chopin, Frédéric, **Supp. I Part 1:** 363

Chopin, Jean, **Supp. I Part 1:** 206

Chopin, Kate, **II:** 276; **Retro. Supp. I:** 10, 215; **Retro. Supp. II: 57–74; Supp. I Part 1: 200–226; Supp. V:** 304; **Supp. X:** 227; **Supp. XVIII:** 194

"Chopin in Winter"(Dybek), **Supp. XXIII:** 72

"Choral: The Pink Church" (W. C. Williams), **Retro. Supp. I:** 428

"Chord" (Merwin), **Supp. III Part 1:** 356

"Chord"(Dybek), **Supp. XXIII:** 78

"Chords and Dischords" (column; Untermeyer), **Supp. XV:** 294

"Chorus, The"(Hadas), **Supp. XXIII:** 119–120

Choruses from Iphigenia in Aulis (Doolittle, trans.), **Supp. I Part 1:** 257, 268, 269

"Chosen Blindness" (Karr), **Supp. XI:** 251

Chosen Country (Dos Passos), **I:** 475, 490–491

Chosen Place, The Timeless People, The (Marshall), **Supp. XI:** 275, 276, **282–284**

Chosön (Lowell), **II:** 513

Choukri, Mohamed, **Supp. IV Part 1:** 92

Chovteau, Mane Thérèse, **Supp. I Part 1:** 205

"ChrisEaster" (Peacock), **Supp. XIX:** 198, 199

Chrisman, Robert, **Supp. IV Part 1:** 1

Christabel (Coleridge), **Supp. IV Part 2:** 465

"Christ for Sale" (Lowell), **II:** 538

Christian, Graham, **Supp. XII:** 193

Christian Dictionary, A (Wilson), **IV:** 153

"Christian in World Crisis, The" (Merton), **Supp. VIII:** 203

Christianity and Power Politics (Niebuhr), **III:** 292, 303

"Christianity and the Survival of Creation" (Berry), **Supp. X:** 30

Christianity of Sholem Asch, The: An Appraisal from the Jewish Viewpoint (Lieberman), **Supp. XXIII:** 3, 7

"Christian Minister, The" (Emerson), **II:** 10

Christian Philosopher, The (Mather), **Supp. II Part 2:** 463–464

Christian Realism and Practical Problems (Niebuhr), **III:** 292, 308

"Christian Roommates, The" (Updike), **IV:** 226–227; **Retro. Supp. I:** 319, 323

Christiansen, Carrie, **I:** 210

Christian's Secret of a Happy Life, The (H. W. Smith), **Supp. XIV:** 333–334

Christie, Agatha, **Supp. IV Part 1:** 341; **Supp. IV Part 2:** 469

Christ in Concrete (di Donato), **Supp. XX: 33, 34–40, 42, 43, 46**

"Christ in Concrete" (di Donato), **Supp. XX:** 34

Christine (King), **Supp. V:** 139, 148

"Christ Light, The" (Chopin), **Retro. Supp. II:** 61

"Christmas" (Saunders), **Supp. XIX:** 232

"Christmas, or the Good Fairy" (Stowe), **Supp. I Part 2:** 586

"Christmas 1944" (Levertov), **Supp. III Part 1:** 274

"Christmas Banquet, The" (Hawthorne), **II:** 227

Christmas Card, A (Theroux), **Supp. VIII:** 322

Christmas Carol, A (Dickens), **Retro. Supp. I:** 196; **Supp. I Part 2:** 409–410; **Supp. X:** 252, 253

"Christmas Eve at Johnson's Drugs N Goods" (Bambara), **Supp. XI:** 11–12

"Christmas Eve in the Time of War: A Capitalist Meditates by a Civil War Monument" (Lowell), **II:** 538

"Christmas Eve under Hooker's Statue" (Lowell), **II:** 539–540

"Christmas Gift" (Warren), **IV:** 252–253

"Christmas Greeting, A" (Wright), **Supp. III Part 2:** 601

"Christmas Hymn, A" (Wilbur), **Supp. III Part 2:** 557

Christmas Memory, A (Capote), **Supp. III Part 1:** 118, 119, 129

"Christmass Poem" (West), **Retro. Supp. II:** 338

Christmas Story (Mencken), **III:** 111

"Christmas to Me" (Lee), **Supp. VIII:** 113

Christographia (Taylor), **IV:** 164–165

Christ on a Clothesline (Loy), **Supp. XXII:** 168

"*Christ on the Cross*/Nuestro Señor Crucificado" (Mora), **Supp. XIII:** 229

Christopher, Mary (pseudonym). *See* West, Dorothy

Christopher and His Kind: 1929–1939 (Isherwood), **Supp. XIV:** 157, 163, 164, 171

"Christopher Cat" (Cullen), **Supp. IV Part 1:** 173

Christopher Columbus, Mariner (Morison), **Supp. I Part 2:** 488

Christopher Isherwood: A Critical Biography (Finney), **Supp. XIV:** 158

Christophersen, Bill, **Supp. IX:** 159, 167; **Supp. XI:** 155; **Supp. XIII:** 87; **Supp. XXI:** 103

"Christ's Passion" (Karr), **Supp. XI:** 251

Christus: A Mystery (Longfellow), **II:**
490, 493, 495, 505–507; **Retro. Supp.**
II: 161, 165, 166

Chroma (F. Barthelme), **Supp. XI:** 30,
33, 34

"Chroma" (F. Barthelme), **Supp. XI:** 31

"Chronicle of Race Relations, A" (Du
Bois), **Supp. II Part 1:** 182

Chronicle of the Conquest of Granada
(Irving), **II:** 310

Chronicles: Volume One (Dylan), **Supp.**
XVIII: 20, 21, 23, 24, 28, **32–33**

"Chronologues" (Goldbarth), **Supp. XII:**
183, 184

"Chrysanthemums, The" (Steinbeck), **IV:**
53

"Chrysaor" (Longfellow), **II:** 498

Chu, Louis, **Supp. X:** 291

Chuang, Hua, **Supp. X:** 291

Chuang-Tzu, **Supp. VIII:** 206

"Chunk of Amethyst, A" (R. Bly), **Supp.**
IV Part 1: 72

Church, Margaret, **IV:** 466

"Church and the Fiction Writer, The"
(O'Connor), **Retro. Supp. II:** 223,
233; **Supp. XVIII:** 161

"Church Going" (Larkin), **Supp. XXI:**
93

"Churchgoing" (Nelson), **Supp. XVIII:**
173

Churchill, Charles, **Supp. XV:** 232

Churchill, Winston, **I:** 9, 490; **Supp. I**
Part 2: 491

Church of Dead Girls, The (Dobyns),
Supp. XIII: 75, **83–84**

"Church of Omnivorous Light, The"
(Wrigley), **Supp. XVIII:** 306–307

"Church of the Latter Day Saints, The"
(Mosher), **Supp. XXII:** 208

"Church Porch, The" (Herbert), **IV:** 153

Church Psalmody, Selected from Dr.
Watts and Other Authors (Mason and
Greene, ed.), **I:** 458

Ciannic, Saint, **II:** 215

Ciano, Edda, **IV:** 249

Ciardi, John, **I:** 169, 179, 535; **III:** 268;
Supp. IV Part 1: 243; **Supp. IV Part**
2: 639; **Supp. IX:** 269, 324; **Supp.**
XII: 119

Cicada (Haines), **Supp. XII: 206–207**

"Cicadas" (Wilbur), **Supp. III Part 2:**
549

Cicero, **I:** 279; **II:** 8, 14–15; **III:** 23;
Supp. I Part 2: 405

Cider House Rules, The (Irving), **Supp.**
VI: 164, **173–175**

"Cigales" (Wilbur), **Supp. III Part 2:**
549

"Cigarette" (L. Michaels), **Supp. XVI:**
214

Cimarron, Rose (Burke), **Supp. XIV:** 22,
35

"Cimetière Marin, Le" (Valéry), **IV:**
91–92

Cimino, Michael, **Supp. X:** 126

Cincinnati Kid, The (film), **Supp. XI: 306**

"Cinderella" (Jarrell), **II:** 386

"Cinderella" (Perrault), **IV:** 266, 267

"Cinderella" (Sexton), **Supp. II Part 2:**
691

"Cinema, The" (Salter), **Supp. IX:** 257

Cinema of Tony Richardson, The: Essays
and Interviews (Phillips), **Supp. XI:**
306

Cinthio, **IV:** 370

Ciolkowski, Laura, **Supp. XVI:** 24

CIOPW (Cummings), **I:** 429

"Circe" (Welty), **Retro. Supp. I:** 353

Circle Game, The (Atwood), **Supp. XIII:**
20, 33

Circle in the Dirt (Moraga), **Supp.**
XXIII: 195, 202

"Circle in the Fire, A" (O'Connor), **III:**
344–345, 349–350, 351, 353, 354;
Retro. Supp. II: 229, 232

"Circle of Breath" (Stafford), **Supp. XI:**
318, 322

Circle of Hanh, The (Weigl), **Supp. XIX:**
273, 275, 282, **284–286**

"Circles" (Emerson), **I:** 455, 460

"Circles" (Lowell), **II:** 554

Circumference: Varieties of Metaphysical
Verse 1456–1928 (Taggard, ed.),
Supp. XXII: 279

"Circus, The" (Porter), **III:** 443, 445

"Circus Animals' Desertion" (Yeats), **I:**
389

"Circus in the Attic" (Warren), **IV:** 253

Circus in the Attic, The (Warren), **IV:**
243, 251–253

"Circus in Three Rings" (Plath), **Retro.**
Supp. II: 243; **Supp. I Part 2:** 536

Circus of Needs, A (Dunn), **Supp. XI:**
147–148

"Cirque d'Hiver" (Bishop), **Supp. I Part**
1: 85

Cisneros, Sandra, **Supp. IV Part 2:** 544;
Supp. VII: 57–73; Supp. XI: 177;
Supp. XVII: 71; **Supp. XXII:** 177

Cities of the Interior (Nin), **Supp. X:** 182

Cities of the Plain (McCarthy), **Supp.**
VIII: 175, **186–187**

Cities of the Red Night (Burroughs),
Supp. III Part 1: 106

"Citizen Cain" (Baraka), **Supp. II Part**
1: 49

Citizen Kane (film), **Retro. Supp. I:** 115;
Supp. V: 251; **Supp. XI:** 169

"Citizen of the World" (Goldsmith), **II:**
299

Citro, Joseph, **Supp. XXII:** 208, 218

"City" (Francis), **Supp. IX:** 87

"City and Country"(Hadas), **Supp.**
XXIII: 115, 116

City and the Pillar, The (Vidal), **Supp.**
IV Part 2: 677, 680–681; **Supp. XIV:**
170

"*City and the Pillar, The,* as Gay Fiction"
(Summers), **Supp. IV Part 2:** 680–
681

"City Articles" series (Briggs), **Supp.**
XVIII: 12

City Block (W. Frank), **Supp. XX: 71,**
72, 76

City Boy (L. Michaels), **Supp. XVI:** 212

"City Boy" (L. Michaels), **Supp. XVI:**
203–204

City Boy (Thompson), **Supp. XXIII:** 294,
298–299

City Dog (Di Piero), **Supp. XIX:** 33–34,
35, 38, 46, 48

"City Dog" (Di Piero), **Supp. XIX:** 47

City in History, The (Mumford), **Supp. II**
Part 2: 495

"City in the Sea, The" (Poe), **III:** 411;
Retro. Supp. II: 274

City in Which I Love You, The (L.-Y.
Lee), **Supp. XV:** 212, **215–220**

"City in Which I Love You, The" (L.-Y.
Lee), **Supp. XV:** 215, **217–218**

City Life (Barthelme), **Supp. IV Part 1:**
44, 47

City of Bones (Connelly), **Supp. XXI:**
74–75, 77

"City of Change, A" (Bynner), **Supp. XV:**
45

City of Dreadful Night (Siegel), **Supp.**
XXII: 258

City of Glass (Auster), **Supp. XII:** 22,
24–26

City of God, The (St. Augustine), **IV:** 126

City of Names (Brockmeier), **Supp.**
XXII: 55–56, 57

"City of Refuge, The" (R. Fisher), **Supp.**
XIX: 65, 66, **67–68**

City of Refuge, The: The Collected Stories
of Rudolph Fisher (McCluskey, ed.),
Supp. XIX: 68–69

City of the Living and Other Stories, The
(Stegner), **Supp. IV Part 2:** 599, 609,
613

City of Words: American Fiction 1950-
1970 (T. Tanner), **Supp. XVI:** 69

City of Your Final Destination, The
(Cameron), **Supp. XII:** 79, 82, **91–94**

"City on a Hill" (Lowell), **II:** 552

"City Person Encountering Nature, A"
(Kingston), **Supp. V:** 170

"City Planners, The" (Atwood), **Supp.**
XIII: 33

"City Winter, A"(O'Hara), **Supp. XXIII:**
210

City Winter and Other Poems, A
(O'Hara), **Supp. XXIII:** 210, 214

City Without Men (film), **Supp. XVIII:**
247

City Without Walls (Auden), **Supp. II**
Part 1: 24

Civil Disobedience (Thoreau), **IV:** 185;
Supp. I Part 2: 507

Civilization in the United States (Stearns),
I: 245

"Civil Rights" (Lanier), **Supp. I Part 1:**
357

CivilWarLand in Bad Decline (Saunders),
Supp. XIX: 224–227

"CivilWarLand in Bad Decline"
(Saunders), **Supp. XIX:** 224–225, 227

Civitatis Anthology of African American
Slave Narratives, The (H. L. Gates and
Andrews, eds.), **Supp. XX: 105**

Cixous, Hélène, **Supp. X:** 102; **Supp.**
XIII: 297; **Supp. XV:** 347

Claiborne, Craig, **Supp. XVII:** 89

Claiborne, William, **I:** 132

"Claim, The"(Balakian), **Supp. XXIII:**
20

Claiming an Identity They Taught Me to Despise (Cliff), **Supp. XXII:** 66, 67–68, 70

Claiming of Sleeping Beauty, The (Rice), **Supp. VII:** 301

Clampitt, Amy, **Supp. IX: 37–54; Supp. X:** 120; **Supp. XI:** 249; **Supp. XV:** 251, 256

Clancy's Wake, At (Crane), **I:** 422

"Clandeboye" (Leopold), **Supp. XIV:** 189

Clara Howard; or, The Enthusiasm of Love (Brown), **Supp. I Part 1:** 145

Clara's Ole Man (Bullins), **Supp. II Part 1:** 42

Clare, John, **II:** 387; **III:** 528; **Supp. XVI:** 295

Clarel: A Poem and Pilgrimage in the Holy Land (Melville), **Retro. Supp. I:** 257

Clarence Major and His Art (Bell), **Supp. XXII:** 182

Clarissa (Richardson), **II:** 111; **Supp. I Part 2:** 714; **Supp. V:** 127; **Supp. XV:** 231; **Supp. XX: 236**

Clark, Alex, **Supp. XII:** 307

Clark, Charles, **I:** 470

Clark, Eleanor. *See* Warren, Mrs. Robert Penn (Eleanor Clark)

Clark, Francis Edward, **II:** 9

Clark, Geoffrey, **Supp. XI:** 342

Clark, Harry Hayden, **Supp. I Part 2:** 423

Clark, John Bates, **Supp. I Part 2:** 633

Clark, Kenneth, **Supp. XIV:** 342, 348; **Supp. XIX:** 151

Clark, Lewis Gaylord, **Supp. XVIII:** 4, 7, 8

Clark, Shirley, **Supp. XXI:** 22

Clark, Thomas, **Supp. III Part 2:** 629; **Supp. IV Part 1:** 140, 145, 147

Clark, Walter, **Supp. XI:** 315

Clark, William, **III:** 14; **IV:** 179, 283

Clark, Willis Gaylord, **Supp. I Part 2:** 684

Clarke, Brock, **Supp. XXIII:** 109

Clarke, James Freeman, **Supp. II Part 1:** 280

Clarke, John, **Supp. IV Part 1:** 8

Clarke, John J., **III:** 356

Clarke, Samuel, **II:** 108

Clark Lectures, **Retro. Supp. I:** 65

Claros varones de Belken (Hinojosa). *See Fair Gentlemen of Belken County* (Hinojosa)

Clash by Night (Odets), **Supp. II Part 2:** 531, 538, 544 546, 550, 551

Classical Tradition, The (Highet), **Supp. I Part 1:** 268

Classic Ballroom Dances (Simic), **Supp. VIII:** 271, **276–278,** 283

Classics (Hadas), **Supp. XXIII: 124**

Classics and Commercials: A Literary Chronicle of the Forties (Wilson), **IV:** 433

"Classics"(Hadas), **Supp. XXIII:** 124

"CLASS STRUGGLE" (Baraka), **Supp. III Part 1:** 55

"Claude Glass, The: 1890" (Bierds), **Supp. XVII:** 27

Claudel, Paul, **I:** 60

Claudelle Inglish (Caldwell), **I:** 304

Clavel, Marcel, **I:** 343

"CLAY" (Baraka), **Supp. II Part 1:** 54

Clay, Henry, **I:** 8; **Supp. I Part 2:** 684, 686

Clay's Ark (O. Butler), **Supp. XIII:** 63

Clayton, John J., **Supp. IV Part 1:** 238

"Clean, Well Lighted Place, A" (Hemingway), **Retro. Supp. I:** 181

"Clear, with Light Variable Winds" (Lowell), **II:** 522

"Clear Days" (White), **Supp. I Part 2:** 664, 665

Clearing (Berry), **Supp. X:** 22

"Clearing, A" (Simpson), **Supp. IX:** 280

"Clearing, The" (Kenyon), **Supp. VII:** 174

"Clearing the Title" (Merrill), **Supp. III Part 1:** 336

"Clearing Up the Question of Stesichoros' Blinding by Helen" (Carson), **Supp. XII:** 107–108

"Clear Morning" (Glück), **Supp. V:** 88

"Clearness" (Wilbur), **Supp. III Part 2:** 544, 550

"Clear Night" (Wright), **Supp. V:** 341

Clear Pictures: First Loves, First Guides (Price), **Supp. VI:** 253, 254, 255, 256, 265

Clear Springs (Mason), **Supp. VIII:** 134–136, 137–138, 139, 147

Cleary, Rebecca Lauck, **Supp. XVIII:** 195

Cleaver, Eldridge, **Retro. Supp. II:** 12; **Supp. IV Part 1:** 206; **Supp. X:** 249

"Cleaving, The" (L.-Y. Lee), **Supp. XV:** 215, **218–220**

Cleland, John, **Supp. V:** 48, 127

Clemenceau, Georges, **I:** 490

"Clemency" (Wrigley), **Supp. XVIII:** 307–308

Clemens, Jane, **I:** 247

Clemens, Orion, **IV:** 193, 195

Clemens, Samuel Langhorne. *See* Twain, Mark

Clemens, Mrs. Samuel Langhorne (Olivia Langdon), **I:** 197, 208, 247; **Supp. I Part 2:** 457

Clemens, Susie, **IV:** 208

Clementine Recognitions (novel), **Supp. IV Part 1:** 280

Clements, Colin Campbell, **Supp. XVI:** 190

Clemons, Walter, **Supp. IV Part 1:** 305, 307

Cleopatra, **III:** 44; **IV:** 373; **Supp. I Part 1:** 114

"Clepsydra" (Ashbery), **Supp. III Part 1:** 10–15

"Clerks, The" (Robinson), **III:** 517–518

"Cleveland" (Halliday), **Supp. XIX:** 90

Cleveland, Carol, **Supp. IX:** 120, 125

Cleveland, Ceil, **Supp. V:** 222

Cleveland, Grover, **II:** 126, 128, 129, 130, 137, 138; **Supp. I Part 2:** 486

"Clever Magician Carrying My Heart, A" (Salinas), **Supp. XIII:** 323

Cliff, Michelle, **Supp. XXII: 65–80**

"Cliff, The" (C. Baxter), **Supp. XVII:** 16–17

Clifford, Craig, **Supp. IX:** 99

Clift, Montgomery, **III:** 161

Clifton, Lucille, **Supp. XVIII:** 177

Climate of Monastic Prayer, The (Merton), **Supp. VIII:** 205, 207

Climb, The (Boukreev), **Supp. XVIII:** 112

"Climber, The" (Mason), **Supp. VIII:** 140–141

Climbing High: A Woman's Account of Surviving the Everest Tragedy (Gammelgaard), **Supp. XVIII:** 112

"Climbing the Tower" (Crews), **Supp. XI:** 102

Clinton, De Witt, **I:** 338

"Clipped Wings" (H. Miller), **III:** 176–177

Clippinger, David, **Supp. XXI:** 24

Clive, Robert, **Supp. I Part 2:** 505

Clock Winder, The (Tyler), **Supp. IV Part 2:** 661–662, 670

Clock Without Hands (McCullers), **II:** 587–588, 604–606

Clockwork Orange, A (Burgess), **Supp. XIII:** 29

Clorindy (Cook), **Supp. II Part 1:** 199

"Close, The" (Jarman), **Supp. XVII:** 113

"Close Calls" (Wolff), **Supp. VII:** 332–333

"Closed Book, A" (Mosley), **Supp. XIII:** 237

Close Quarters (Heinemann), **Supp. XXII:** 103, **104–109,** 111, 115

Close Range: Wyoming Stories (Proulx), **Supp. VII:** 261–265

"Close Reading: Windows"(Hirshfield), **Supp. XXIII:** 131

Closers, The (Connelly), **Supp. XXI: 76–77**

Closest Possible Union, The (J. Scott), **Supp. XVII: 185–186,** 188, 191

Close the Book (Glaspell), **Supp. III Part 1:** 179

"Close the Book" (Lowell), **II:** 554

Close to Me & Closer ... (The Language of Heaven) and Désamère (Notley), **Supp. XXII:** 234

Close to Shore: A True Story of Terror in an Age of Innocence (Capuzzo), **Supp. XIII:** 254

Closet Writing & Gay Reading: The Case of Melville's Pierre (Creech), **Retro. Supp. I:** 254

Closing Circle, The (Commoner), **Supp. XIII:** 264

Closing of the American Mind, The (Bloom), **Retro. Supp. II:** 19, 30, 31

"Closing of the Rodeo, The" (W. J. Smith), **Supp. XIII:** 332

Closing Time (Heller), **Supp. IV Part 1:** 382, 386, 391–394

Closset, Marie, **Supp. VIII:** 251, 265

Clotel (Brown), **Supp. XXIII:** 184

"Cloud, The" (Shelley), **Supp. I Part 2:** 720

"Cloud and Fame" (Berryman), **I:** 173

Cloud Forest, The: A Chronicle of the South American Wilderness (Matthiessen), **Supp. V:** 202, 204

"Cloud on the Way, The" (Bryant), **Supp. I Part 1:** 171

"Cloud River" (Wright), **Supp. V:** 341

"Clouds" (Levine), **Supp. V:** 184

Cloudsplitter (Banks), **Supp. V:** 16

"Clover" (Lanier), **Supp. I Part 1:** 362–364

Clover and Other Poems (Lanier), **Supp. I Part 1:** 362

"Clown" (Corso), **Supp. XII:** 127

Clown in the Belfry, The: Writings on Faith and Fiction (Buechner), **Supp. XII:** 53

Cluck, Julia, **Supp. I Part 2:** 728

Clum, John M., **Supp. XIII: 200,** 201, 209

Cluny, Hugo, **IV:** 290

Clurman, Harold, **I:** 93; **IV:** 381, 385

Clytus, Radiclani, **Supp. XIII:** 128, **Supp. XIII:** 129, 132

"C.O." (Wrigley), **Supp. XVIII:** 298

"Coal: Beginning and End" (Winters), **Supp. II Part 2:** 791

Coale, Howard, **Supp. XIII:** 15

"Coals" (Hoffman), **Supp. XVIII:** 86

"Coast, The" (column), **Supp. IV Part 1:** 198

"Coast Guard's Cottage, The" (Wylie), **Supp. I Part 2:** 723

Coast of Chicago, The (Dybek), **Supp. XXIII: 72–74,** 75

Coast of Trees, A (Ammons), **Supp. VII:** 24, 34

"Coast-Range Christ, The" (Jeffers), **Supp. II Part 2:** 414, 419

"Coast-Road, The" (Jeffers), **Supp. II Part 2:** 425

"Coat, The" (Everwine), **Supp. XV:** 80

Coates, Joseph, **Supp. VIII:** 80; **Supp. XXII:** 205

Coates, Robert, **I:** 54; **IV:** 298

"Coatlicue's Rules: Advice from an Aztec Goddess" (Mora), **Supp. XIII:** 223

"Coats" (Kenyon), **Supp. VII:** 172

Cobb, Lee J., **III:** 153

Cobb, Ty, **III:** 227, 229

Cobbett, William, **Supp. I Part 2:** 517; **Supp. XV:** 237

"Cobbler Keezar's Vision" (Whittier), **Supp. I Part 2:** 699

"Cobweb, The" (Carver), **Supp. III Part 1:** 148

Cobwebs From an Empty Skull (Bierce), **I:** 195

Coccimiglio, Vic, **Supp. XIII:** 114

"Cock-a-Doodle-Doo!" (Melville), **III:** 89

"Cockayne" (Emerson), **II:** 6

"Cock-Crow" (Gordon), **II:** 219

Cock Pit (Cozzens), **I:** 359, 378, 379

Cockpit (Kosinski), **Supp. XII:** 21

Cockpit: A Novel (Kosinski), **Supp. VII:** 215, 223–224, 225

"Cock Robin Takes Refuge in the Storm House" (Snodgrass), **Supp. VI:** 319

Cocktail Hour, The (Gurney), **Supp. V:** 95, 96, 100, 101, 103, 105, 108

Cocktail Hour and Two Other Plays: Another Antigone and *The Perfect Party* (Gurney), **Supp. V:** 100

Cocktail Party, The (Eliot), **I:** 571, 582–583; **III:** 21; **Retro. Supp. I:** 65; **Supp. V:** 101, 103

Cocteau, Jean, **III:** 471; **Retro. Supp. I:** 82, 378; **Supp. IV Part 1:** 82; **Supp. XVI:** 135; **Supp. XX: 236**

"Coda: Wilderness Letter" (Stegner), **Supp. IV Part 2:** 595

"Code, The" (Frost), **Retro. Supp. I:** 121, 128

Codman, Florence, **Supp. II Part 1:** 92, 93

Codman, Ogden, Jr., **Retro. Supp. I:** 362, 363

Codrescu, Andrei, **Supp. XXII:** 155

Cody, William ("Buffalo Bill"), **I:** 440; **III:** 584; **Supp. V:** 230

Coffey, Michael, **Supp. V:** 243; **Supp. XV:** 65; **Supp. XX: 88**

Coffey, Warren, **III:** 358

Coffin, Charles, **III:** 577

Cogan, David J., **Supp. IV Part 1:** 362

Cogan, Joshua, **Supp. XXI:** 247

Coghill, Nevill, **Supp. II Part 1:** 4; **Supp. XIV:** 13

Cohan, George M., **II:** 427; **III:** 401

Cohen, Edward M., **Supp. XVI:** 212

Cohen, Esther, **Supp. XV:** 323

Cohen, Hettie, **Supp. II Part 1:** 30

Cohen, Joshua, **Supp. XXII:** 268

Cohen, Marty, **Supp. X:** 112

Cohen, Norman J., **Supp. IX:** 132, 143

Cohen, Rosetta, **Supp. XV:** 257

Cohen, Sarah Blacher, **Supp. V:** 273

Cohen, Victor, **Supp. XVIII:** 235, 236

"Coherent Decentering: Towards a New Model of the Poetic Self" (A. Finch), **Supp. XVII:** 76

"Coin" (Goldbarth), **Supp. XII:** 187

Coindreau, Maurice, **III:** 339

Coiner, Constance, **Supp. XIII:** 297, 302

Coit, Lille Hitchcock, **Supp. X:** 103

"Coitus" (Pound), **III:** 466

Coke, Desmond, **Supp. XX: 235**

Colburn, Nadia Herman, **Supp. XV:** 339, 341, 347

"Cold, The" (Kenyon), **Supp. VII:** 164

"Cold, The" (Winters), **Supp. II Part 2:** 790–791, 809, 811

"Cold-blooded Creatures" (Wylie), **Supp. I Part 2:** 729

Colden, Cadwallader, **Supp. I Part 1:** 250

"Colder the Air, The" (Bishop), **Supp. I Part 1:** 86

Cold Feet (Harrison), **Supp. VIII:** 39

Cold Frame (C. Frost), **Supp. XV:** 93, 96

Cold Ground Was My Bed Last Night (Garrett), **Supp. VII:** 98

"Cold Ground Was My Bed Last Night" (Garrett), **Supp. VII:** 100

"Cold Hill Side, The"(Hadas), **Supp. XXIII:** 121

"Cold Night, The" (W. C. Williams), **Retro. Supp. I:** 418

"Cold Plunge into Skin Diving, A" (Knowles), **Supp. XII:** 241

Cold Spring, A (Bishop), **Retro. Supp. II:** 45

Cold Springs Harbor (Yates), **Supp. XI:** 348

Cold War American Poetry, **Supp. V:** 182

Cold War and the Income Tax, The (Wilson), **IV:** 430

Cole, Bruce, **Supp. XX: 106**

Cole, Goody, **Supp. I Part 2:** 696–697

Cole, Lester, **Retro. Supp. II:** 329

Cole, Nat King, **Retro. Supp. I:** 334; **Supp. X:** 255

Cole, Thomas, **Supp. I Part 1:** 156, 158, 171

Cole, William, **Supp. XIX:** 120

"Coleman" (Karr), **Supp. XI:** 244

Coleman, Wanda, **Supp. XI: 83–98**

Coleridge, Samuel Taylor, **I:** 283, 284, 447, 522; **II:** 7, 10, 11, 19, 71, 169, 273, 301, 502, 516, 549; **III:** 77, 83–84, 424, 461, 488, 523; **IV:** 74, 173, 250, 349, 453; **Retro. Supp. I:** 65, 308; **Supp. I Part 1:** 31, 311, 349; **Supp. I Part 2:** 376, 393, 422; **Supp. IV Part 2:** 422, 465; **Supp. V:** 258; **Supp. IX:** 38, 50; **Supp. XIII:** 139; **Supp. XIV:** 21–22; **Supp. XV:** 250; **Supp. XXI:** 52, 55; **Supp. XXIII:** 231

Coles, Katharine, **Supp. IV Part 2:** 630

Colette, Sidonie-Gabrielle, **Supp. VIII:** 40, 171; **Supp. XVI:** 193–194

"Coliseum, The" (Poe), **III:** 411

Collage of Dreams (Spencer), **Supp. X:** 196

"Collapse of Tomorrow, The" (Mumford), **Supp. II Part 2:** 482

"Collected by a Valetudinarian" (E. Stoddard), **Supp. XV:** 286–287

Collected Earlier Poems (Hecht), **Supp. X:** 58, 59

Collected Earlier Poems (W. C. Williams), **Retro. Supp. I:** 414, 428

Collected Earlier Poems 1940–1960 (Levertov), **Supp. III Part 1:** 273, 275

Collected Essays (Tate), **IV:** 133–134

Collected Essays of Ralph Ellison, The (Ellison), **Retro. Supp. II:** 119

Collected Essays of Robert Creeley, The (Creeley), **Supp. IV Part 1:** 153, 154

Collected Later Poems (W. C. Williams), **Retro. Supp. I:** 428

Collected Plays (A. Miller), **III:** 158

Collected Plays, 1974–1983 (Gurney), **Supp. V:** 99

Collected Poems (Aiken), **I:** 50

Collected Poems (Burke), **I:** 269

Collected Poems (Cummings), **I:** 430, 439, 441

Collected Poems (Doolittle), **Supp. I Part 1:** 264–267, 269

Collected Poems (Frost), **Retro. Supp. I:** 136

Collected Poems (Hull), **Supp. XXI:** 141

Collected Poems (Kees; Justice, ed.), **Supp. XV:** 134

Collected Poems (Lindsay), **Supp. I Part 2:** 380, 387, 392, 396–397, 400

Collected Poems (Lowell), **Supp. XV:** 20

Collected Poems (Markson), **Supp. XVII:** 143

Collected Poems (Moore), **III:** 194, 215

Collected Poems (O'Hara), **Supp. XXIII:** 207, 211, 220

Collected Poems (Price), **Supp. VI:** 267

Collected Poems (Simpson), **Supp. IX:** 279

Collected Poems (W. C. Williams), **IV:** 415; **Retro. Supp. I:** 430

Collected Poems (Winters), **Supp. II Part 2:** 791, 810

Collected Poems (Wright), **Supp. III Part 2:** 602

Collected Poems (Yeats), **Supp. XV:** 152

Collected Poems, 1918–1938 (Taggard), **Supp. XXII:** 283

Collected Poems, 1923–1953 (Bogan), **Supp. III Part 1:** 64

Collected Poems, 1936–1976 (Francis), **Supp. IX:** 77, 80, **87**

Collected Poems, The (Stevens), **III:** 273; **IV:** 75, 76, 87, 93; **Retro. Supp. I:** 296, 309

Collected Poems 1909–1935 (Eliot), **I:** 580; **Retro. Supp. I:** 66

Collected Poems 1909–1962 (Eliot), **I:** 583

Collected Poems 1917–1952 (MacLeish), **III:** 3, 4, 19

Collected Poems 1921–1931 (W. C. Williams), **Retro. Supp. I:** 422; **Supp. XIV:** 285

Collected Poems 1930–1960 (Eberhart), **I:** 522, 525–526, 540, 541

Collected Poems: 1939–1989 (W. J. Smith), **Supp. XIII:** 332, 340, 343, 345

Collected Poems: 1940–1978 (Shapiro), **Supp. II Part 2:** 703, 717

Collected Poems: 1951–1971 (Ammons), **Supp. VII:** 24, 26–29, 32, 33

Collected Poems: 1956–1976 (Wagoner), **Supp. IX:** 323, **328–329**

Collected Poems of Amy Clampitt, The (Clampitt), **Supp. IX:** 37, 44, 53

Collected Poems of George Garrett (Garrett), **Supp. VII:** 109

Collected Poems of Hart Crane, The (Crane), **I:** 399–402

Collected Poems of James Agee, The (Fitzgerald, ed.), **I:** 27–28

Collected Poems of James T. Farrell, The (Farrell), **II:** 45

Collected Poems of Langston Hughes, The (Rampersad and Roessel, ed.), **Retro. Supp. I:** 194, 196, 212

Collected Poems of Muriel Rukeyser, The (Rukeyser), **Supp. VI:** 274

Collected Poems of Thomas Merton, The, **Supp. VIII:** 207, 208

Collected Poetry (Auden), **Supp. II Part 1:** 18

Collected Prose (Wright), **Supp. III Part 2:** 596

Collected Prose, The (Bishop), **Retro. Supp. II:** 51

Collected Recordings (W. C. Williams), **Retro. Supp. I:** 431

Collected Shorter Poems, 1946-1991 (Carruth), **Supp. XVI:** 47

Collected Short Stories, The (Wharton), **Retro. Supp. I:** 362, 363, 366

Collected Sonnets (Millay), **III:** 136–137

Collected Stories, 1939–1976 (Bowles), **Supp. IV Part 1:** 92

Collected Stories, The (Paley), **Supp. VI:** 218

Collected Stories, The (Price), **Supp. VI:** 266

Collected Stories, The (Theroux), **Supp. VIII:** 318

Collected Stories, The (Wharton), **Retro. Supp. I:** 361

Collected Stories of Amy Hempel, The (Hempel), **Supp. XXI:** 115, 117

Collected Stories of Eudora Welty, The (Welty), **Retro. Supp. I:** 355

Collected Stories of Isaac Bashevis Singer (Singer), **Retro. Supp. II: 307–308**

Collected Stories of Katherine Anne Porter (Porter), **III:** 454

Collected Stories of Peter Taylor (Taylor), **Supp. V:** 314, 320, 323–324, 325, 326

Collected Stories of Richard Yates, The, **Supp. XI:** 349

Collected Stories of Wallace Stegner (Stegner), **Supp. IV Part 2:** 599, 605

Collected Stories of William Faulkner (Faulkner), **II:** 72; **Retro. Supp. I:** 75

Collected Stories of William Humphrey, The (Humphrey), **Supp. IX:** 106

Collected Works (Bierce), **I:** 204, 208–210

Collected Works of Buck Rogers in the 25th Century, The (Bradbury), **Supp. IV Part 1:** 101

Collected Writings, The (Z. Fitzgerald; Bruccoli, ed.), **Supp. IX:** 65, 68

Collecting the Animals (Everwine), **Supp. XV:** 73, 75, **78–81,** 85, 88

Collection of Epigrams, **II:** 111

Collection of Poems, on American Affairs, and a Variety of Other Subjects . . . (Freneau), **Supp. II Part 1:** 274

Collection of Select Aphorisms and Maxims (Palmer), **II:** 111

"Collectors" (Carver), **Supp. III Part 1:** 141–142

Collette, **Supp. XVII:** 86

Collier, John, **Supp. XXI:** 8

Collier, Lucy Wood, **Supp. XXI:** 8

Collier, Michael, **Supp. XVII:** 23, 110

Collingwood, R. G., **I:** 278

Collins, Billy, **Supp. XI:** 143; **Supp. XIV:** 123; **Supp. XVII:** 245; **Supp. XXI: 51–66; Supp. XXIII:** 138

Collins, Doug, **Supp. V:** 5

Collins, Eddie, **II:** 416

Collins, L. M., **Supp. XXII:** 7

Collins, Richard, **Supp. XI:** 171

Collins, Ronald, **Supp. XXI:** 24

Collins, Wilkie, **Supp. I Part 1:** 35, 36; **Supp. IV Part 1:** 341; **Supp. XX: 236**

Collins, William, **Supp. I Part 2:** 714

Collinson, Peter , **II:** 114

Collinson, Peter (pseudonym). *See* Hammett, Dashiell

Colloff, Pamela, **Supp. XIII:** 281

Colloque Sentimental (ballet), **Supp. IV Part 1:** 83

"Colloquy" (Kees), **Supp. XV:** 133

"Colloquy in Black Rock" (Lowell), **II:** 535; **Retro. Supp. II:** 178

"Colloquy of Monos and Una, The" (Poe), **III:** 412

"Colloquy on a Bed" (Bronk), **Supp. XXI:** 31

Colonel's Dream, The (Chesnutt), **Supp. XIV:** 63, 75–76

Colônia, Regina, **Retro. Supp. II:** 53

Colony (Siddons), **Supp. XXII:** 239

Color (Cullen), **Supp. IV Part 1:** 164, 166, 167, 168

"Colorado" (Beattie), **Supp. V:** 27

Color and Democracy: Colonies and Peace (Du Bois), **Supp. II Part 1:** 184, 185

"Color-Blind Raspberry Picker, The"(Hadas), **Supp. XXIII:** 113

Color Curtain, The (Wright), **IV:** 478, 488

"Colored Americans" (Dunbar), **Supp. II Part 1:** 197

Colored People (H. L. Gates), **Supp. XX: 101, 103, 104–105, 109, 111**

"Color Line, The" (Douglass), **Supp. III Part 1:** 163–165

Color Line, The (W. B. Smith), **Supp. II Part 1:** 168

Color of a Great City, The (Dreiser), **Retro. Supp. II:** 104

Color of Darkness (Purdy), **Supp. VII:** 271

Color Purple, The (Walker), **Supp. III Part 2:** 517, 518, 520, 525–529, 532–537; **Supp. VIII:** 141; **Supp. X:** 252, 330; **Supp. XX: 107**

Color Schemes (Cheang; film), **Supp. XI:** 20

"Colors of Night, The" (Momaday), **Supp. IV Part 2:** 490

"Colors without Objects" (Swenson), **Supp. IV Part 2:** 645

"Color: The Unfinished Business of Democracy" (Locke), **Supp. XIV:** 202, 207

Colossus, The (Plath), **Retro. Supp. II: 245–247; Supp. I Part 2:** 529, 531, 536, 538, 540; **Supp. V:** 79; **Supp. XI:** 317

"Colossus, The" (Plath), **Retro. Supp. II:** 250; **Supp. XXIII:** 113

Colossus of Maroussi, The (H. Miller), **III:** 178, 185–186

"Colt, The" (Stegner), **Supp. IV Part 2:** 600

Coltelli, Laura, **Supp. IV Part 1:** 323, 330, 335, 409; **Supp. IV Part 2:** 493, 497, 559

Colter: The True Story of the Best Dog I Ever Had (Bass), **Supp. XVI:** 23

Coltrane, John, **Supp. VIII:** 197; **Supp. XXII:** 172

Colum, Mary, **I:** 246, 252, 256; **Supp. I Part 2:** 708, 709

"Columba" (Cliff), **Supp. XXII:** 74, 76

Columbiad, The (Barlow), **Supp. II Part 1:** 67, 72, 73, 74, 75–77, 79

Columbia History of the American Novel, **Supp. XV:** 270

Columbia Literary History of the United States, **Supp. XV:** 270

"Columbian Ode" (Dunbar), **Supp. II Part 1:** 199

"Columbia U Poesy Reading—1975" (Corso), **Supp. XII:** 134

Columbus, Christopher, **I:** 253; **II:** 6, 310; **III:** 8; **Supp. I Part 2:** 397, 479, 480, 483, 486–488, 491, 495, 497, 498

"Columbus to Ferdinand" (Freneau), **Supp. II Part 1:** 255

Comanche Moon (McMurtry), **Supp. V:** 232

"Come, Break With Time" (Bogan), **Supp. III Part 1:** 52

Come, Thief (Hirshfield), **Supp. XXIII:** 134, 138

Come Along with Me (Jackson), **Supp. IX:** 117, 118, 122

Come Back, Charleston Blue (film), **Supp. XVI:** 144

Comeback, The (Gurney), **Supp. V:** 97

"Come Back to the Raft Ag'in, Huck Honey!" (Fiedler), **Supp. XIII:** 93, **96–97,** 101

Come Blow Your Horn (Simon), **Supp. IV Part 2:** 574, 575, 577, 578, 586, 587, 591

Come By Here (Major), **Supp. XXII:** 171, 182

"Come Dance with Me in Ireland" (Jackson), **Supp. IX:** 119

"Comedian as the Letter C, The" (Stevens), **IV:** 84–85, 88; **Retro. Supp. I:** 297, 301, 302

"Comedy Cop" (Farrell), **II:** 45

Comedy of a Country House (J. Sturgis), **Supp. XX:** 238

"Comedy's Greatest Era" (Agee), **I:** 31

"Come In" (Frost), **Retro. Supp. I:** 139

"Come On, Baby" (Zinberg), **Supp. XV:** 195

"Come on Back" (Gardner), **Supp. VI:** 73

"Come Out into the Sun" (Francis), **Supp. IX:** 82

Come Out into the Sun: Poems New and Selected (Francis), **Supp. IX: 82–83**

"Come out the Wilderness" (Baldwin), **Supp. I Part 1:** 63

Comer, Anjanette, **Supp. XI:** 305

Comer, Cornelia, **I:** 214

"Come Rain or Come Shine" (song), **Supp. XXII:** 6

"Come Shining: The Spiritual South" (exhibition; Luster), **Supp. XV:** 350

Come with Me: Poems for a Journey (Nye), **Supp. XIII:** 279

"Comforts of Home, The" (O'Connor), **III:** 349, 351, 355; **Retro. Supp. II:** 237

Comic Artist, The (Glaspell and Matson), **Supp. III Part 1:** 182

"Comic Imagination of the Young Dickens, The" (Wright), **Supp. III Part 2:** 591

"Comic Textures and Female Communities 1937 and 1977: Clare Boothe and Wendy Wasserstein" (Carlson), **Supp. XV:** 323

Comic Tragedies (Alcott), **Supp. I Part 1:** 33

Coming After (Notley), **Supp. XXII:** 223, 227, 230, 232, 236

"Coming Close" (Levine), **Supp. V:** 192

Coming Forth by Day of Osiris Jones, The (Aiken), **I:** 59

"Coming Home" (Gordon), **Supp. IV Part 1:** 309

"Coming Home to Vermont" (McCarriston), **Supp. XIV:** 269

"Coming in From the Cold" (Walker), **Supp. III Part 2:** 526

Coming into Eighty (Sarton), **Supp. VIII:** 262

"Coming into Eighty" (Sarton), **Supp. VIII:** 262

Coming into the Country (McPhee), **Supp. III Part 1:** 298, 301–306, 309, 310

Coming Into Writing (Cixous), **Supp. X:** 102

Coming of Age in Mississippi (Moody), **Supp. IV Part 1:** 11

Comings Back (Goldbarth), **Supp. XII:** 180

"Coming to Canada--Age Twenty Two" (Shields), **Supp. VII:** 311

Coming to Canada: Poems (Shields), **Supp. VII:** 311–312

"Coming to Memoir as a Journalist" (Epstein), **Supp. XXII:** 95

"Coming to the Morning" (Merwin), **Supp. III Part 1:** 356

"Coming to This" (Strand), **Supp. IV Part 2:** 627

Comiskey, Charles, **II:** 422

Commager, Henry Steele, **I:** 253; **Supp. I Part 1:** 372; **Supp. I Part 2:** 484, 647, 650

Command the Morning (Buck), **Supp. II Part 1:** 125

"CommComm" (Saunders), **Supp. XIX:** 234

"Commencement Address, A" (Brodsky), **Supp. VIII:** 31

"Commencement Day Address, The" (Schwartz), **Supp. II Part 2:** 660

Commentaries (Caesar), **II:** 502, 561

"Commentary" (Auden), **Supp. II Part 1:** 13

"Comment on Curb" (Hughes), **Supp. I Part 1:** 340

"Comments/Questions" (Nelson), **Supp. XVIII:** 172

"Commerce" (Nye), **Supp. XIII:** 281

Commins, Saxe, **Retro. Supp. I:** 73; **Retro. Supp. II:** 337

Commodity of Dreams & Other Stories, A (Nemerov), **III:** 268–269, 285

Common Carnage (Dobyns), **Supp. XIII:** 87

"Common Ground, A" (Levertov), **Supp. III Part 1:** 277

"Common Life, The" (Auden), **Supp. IV Part 1:** 302, 313

"Common Meter" (R. Fisher), **Supp. XIX:** 71

Common Room, A: Essays 1954–1987 (Price), **Supp. VI:** 264–265, 267

Commons, John, **Supp. I Part 2:** 645

Common Sense (Paine), **II:** 117; **Supp. I Part 1:** 231; **Supp. I Part 2:** 505, 506–508, 509, 513, 516, 517, 521

Communal Cot (Loy), **Supp. XXII:** 168

"Communication" (Dobyns), **Supp. XIII:** 91

Communion (Mora), **Supp. XIII: 217–219**

Communist Manifesto, The (Marx and Engels), **II:** 463; **Supp. XXI:** 162–163

"Community Life" (Moore), **Supp. X:** 178

"Community of Glaciers, The" (Bass), **Supp. XVI:** 23

Comnes, Gregory, **Supp. IV Part 1:** 283, 284, 291

"Companions, The" (Nemerov), **III:** 269, 278, 287

Company of Poets, A (Simpson), **Supp. IX:** 265, 275

Company of Women, The (Gordon), **Supp. IV Part 1:** 302–304, 304, 306, 313

Company She Keeps, The (McCarthy), **II:** 562, 563–566

"Comparisons of Wonder" (Jarman), **Supp. XVII:** 114

Compass Flower, The (Merwin), **Supp. III Part 1:** 353, 357

"Compassionate Friendship" (Doolittle), **Supp. I Part 1:** 257, 258, 259, 260, 271

"Compatibility" (C. Frost), **Supp. XV:** 103

"Compendium" (Dove), **Supp. IV Part 1:** 248

"Complaint" (W. C. Williams), **Retro. Supp. I:** 418

"Complete Birth of the Cool, The" (Wright), **Supp. XV:** 343, 344

Complete Collected Poems of William Carlos Williams, 1906–1938, The (W. C. Williams), **Retro. Supp. I:** 424

"Complete Destruction" (W. C. Williams), **IV:** 413

"Complete Life of John Hopkins, The" (O. Henry), **Supp. II Part 1:** 405

Complete Poems (Frost), **II:** 155, 164

Complete Poems (Reznikoff), **Supp. XIV:** 281

Complete Poems (Sandburg), **III:** 590–592, 594, 596

Complete Poems, The (Bishop), **Retro. Supp. II:** 49; **Supp. I Part 1:** 72, 82, 94

Complete Poems, The (Bradbury), **Supp. IV Part 1:** 105

Complete Poems, The: 1927–1979 (Bishop), **Retro. Supp. II:** 51

Complete Poems of Emily Dickinson, The (Bianchi and Hampson, eds.), **Retro. Supp. I:** 35

Complete Poems of Emily Dickinson, The (Johnson, ed.), **I:** 470

Complete Poems of Frederick Goddard Tuckerman, The (Momaday), **Supp. IV Part 2:** 480

Complete Poems of Hart Crane, **Retro. Supp. II:** 81

Complete Poems to Solve, The (Swenson), **Supp. IV Part 2:** 652

Complete Poetical Works (Hulme), **III:** 464

Complete Poetical Works (Longfellow), **Retro. Supp. II:** 154

Complete Poetical Works (Lowell), **II:** 512, 516–517

Complete Poetical Works of Amy Lowell, The, **Supp. XV:** 295–296

Complete Stories (O'Connor), **Supp. X:** 1

Complete Tragedies, The: Euripedes II, **Supp. XV:** 50

"Complete with Starry Night and Bourbon Shots" (Goldbarth), **Supp. XII:** 192–193

Complete Works of Kate Chopin, The (Seyersted, ed.), **Supp. I Part 1:** 212, 225

Complete Works of the Gawain-Poet (Gardner), **Supp. VI:** 64, 65

"Complex Histories, Contested Memories: Some Reflections on Remembering Difficult Pasts" (E. Hoffman, lecture), **Supp. XVI:** 155

"Complicated Thoughts About a Small Son" (White), **Supp. I Part 2:** 678

"Compliments of the Season" (O. Henry), **Supp. II Part 1:** 392, 399

"Compline" (Auden), **Supp. II Part 1:** 23

"Composing a Life" (Pickering), **Supp. XXI:** 191, 196

Composition as Explanation (Stein), **IV:** 32, 33, 38

"Composition as Explanation" (Stein), **IV:** 27, 28

"Compounding of Consciousness" (James), **II:** 358–359

Comprehensive Bibliography (Hanneman), **II:** 259

Compton-Burnett, Ivy, **I:** 93; **II:** 580; **Supp. XXIII:** 209

"Comrade Laski, C.P.U.S.A. [M.L.]" (Didion), **Supp. IV Part 1:** 200

Comstock, Anthony, **Retro. Supp. II:** 95

Comus (Milton), **II:** 12; **Supp. I Part 2:** 622

Conan Doyle, Arthur. *See* Doyle, Arthur Conan

Conceptions of Reality in Modern American Poetry (Dembo), **Supp. I Part 1:** 272

"Concept of Character in Fiction, The" (Gass), **Supp. VI:** 85, **86**

Concept of Dread, The (Kierkegaard), **III:** 305

Concerning Children (Gilman), **Supp. XI:** 206

"Concerning Mold upon the Skin, Etc." (J. Scott), **Supp. XVII:** 188

"Concerning Necessity" (Carruth), **Supp. XVI:** 57

"Concerning Some Recent Criticism of His Work" (Doty), **Supp. XI:** 131

Concerning the End for Which God Created the World (Edwards), **I:** 549, 557, 559

"Concerning Things That Can Be Doubled"(Crooker), **Supp. XXIII:** 64

Concerto for Two Pianos, Winds, and Percussion (Bowles), **Supp. IV Part 1:** 83

Conchologist's First Book, The (Poe), **III:** 412

Conclusive Evidence (Nabokov), **III:** 247–250, 252

"Concord Hymn" (Emerson), **II:** 19

Concrete Blonde, The (Connelly), **Supp. XXI:** **70–71,** 78, **80**

"Concrete Universal, The: Observations on the Understanding of Poetry" (Ransom), **III:** 480

Concurring Beasts (Dobyns), **Supp. XIII:** 76

Condé, Maryse, **Supp. XXIII:** 94

Condensed Novels and Other Papers (Harte), **Supp. II Part 1:** 342

"Condition, The" (Karmi; Everwine, trans.), **Supp. XV:** 78

Condition of Man, The (Mumford), **Supp. II Part 2:** 483, 484, 486, 495–496, 498

"Condolence" (Parker), **Supp. IX:** 191

"Condominium, The" (Elkin), **Supp. VI:** 49, **50–51,** 55, 56

Condon, Charles R., **Supp. XIII:** 163

Condor and the Cows, The: A South American Travel Diary (Isherwood and Caskey), **Supp. XIV:** 166

"Condor and the Guests, The" (Connell), **Supp. XIV:** 86

Condorcet, Marquis de, **Supp. I Part 2:** 511

Conduct of Life, The (Emerson), **II:** 1–5, 8

Conduct of Life, The (Mumford), **Supp. II Part 2:** 485, 496–497

"Conductor of Nothing, The" (Levine), **Supp. V:** 189

Coney Island of the Mind, A (Ferlinghetti), **Supp. XIX:** 4; **Supp. XXI:** 53

"Conference Male, The" (Mora), **Supp. XIII:** 218

"Confession" (Peacock), **Supp. XIX:** 206

"Confessional" (Bidart), **Supp. XV:** 29–30, 31

"Confessional Poem" (Nelson), **Supp. XVIII:** 174

Confession de Claude, La (Zola), **I:** 411

"Confession of a House-Breaker, The" (Jewett), **Retro. Supp. II:** 146–147

Confession of Jereboam O. Beauchamp, The (pamphlet), **IV:** 253

Confessions (Augustine), **I:** 279; **Supp. XVI:** 288; **Supp. XXII:** 93

Confessions (Rousseau), **I:** 226

Confessions of a Barbarian: Selections from the Journals of Edward Abbey, 1951–1989 (Abbey; Petersen, ed.), **Supp. XIII:** 2, 4

"Confessions of a Latina Author" (Mora), **Supp. XIII:** 221

"Confessions of a Wannabe Negro" (McKnight), **Supp. XX: 152–153,** 158

Confessions of Nat Turner, The (Styron), **IV:** 98, 99, 105, 113–117; **Supp. X:** 16, 250

Confetti (Mora), **Supp. XIII:** 221

Confidence (James), **II:** 327, 328

Confidence-Man, The (Melville), **III:** 91; **Retro. Supp. I:** 255–256, 257; **Retro. Supp. II:** 121; **Supp. XIV:** 49

Confidence Man, The (Van Vechten), **Supp. II Part 2:** 737

Confidential Clerk, The (Eliot), **I:** 570, 571–572, 583, 584; **Retro. Supp. I:** 65

Confident Years, 1885–1915, The (Brooks), **I:** 257, 259; **Supp. I Part 2:** 650

"Configurations" (Ammons), **Supp. VII:** 28

Configurations: New and Selected Poems, 1958–1998 (Major), **Supp. XXII: 182**

Confronting the Horror: The Novels of Nelson Algren (Giles), **Supp. IX:** 11, 15

Confucius, **II:** 1; **III:** 456, 475; **Supp. IV Part 1:** 14

Confusion (Cozzens), **I:** 358, 359, 377, 378

"Confusion of Planes We Must Wander in Sleep, The" (Weigl), **Supp. XIX:** 283

Congdon, Don, **Supp. XXII:** 204

Congo (film), **Supp. IV Part 1:** 83

Congo (screenplay, Shanley), **Supp. XIV:** 316

"Congo, The" (Lindsay), **Supp. I Part 2:** 388–389, 392, 395

Congo and Other Poems, The (Lindsay), **Supp. I Part 2:** 379, 382, 389, 390, 391

"Congregation" (Trethewey), **Supp. XXI:** 245, 247

"Congregation of Grackles, A"(Crooker), **Supp. XXIII:** 63

"Congress of the Insomniacs, The" (Simic), **Supp. VIII:** 281–282

Congreve, William, **III:** 195; **Supp. V:** 101; **Supp. XVIII:** 12

Coningsby (Disraeli), **II:** 127

"Conjectural Reading" (Bronk), **Supp. XXI:** 31

Conjectures of a Guilty Bystander (Merton), **Supp. VIII:** 197, 206, 207

Conjugal Bliss: A Comedy of Marital Arts (Nichols), **Supp. XIII:** 269

"Conjugation of the Paramecium, The" (Rukeyser), **Supp. VI:** 271

Conjugations and Reiterations (Murray), **Supp. XIX:** 161

"Conjuration" (Wilbur), **Supp. III Part 2:** 551

Conjure (recording), **Supp. X:** 241

Conjure (Reed), **Supp. X:** 240, 242

Conjure-Man Dies, The: A Mystery Tale of Dark Harlem (R. Fisher), **Supp. XVI:** 143; **Supp. XIX:** 65, 71, **77–78**

Conjure Woman, The (Chesnutt), **Supp. II Part 1:** 193; **Supp. XIV:** 57, **58–61,** 62, 63
Conklin, Grof, **Supp. I Part 2:** 672
Conklin, Peggy, **Supp. XXII:** 27
Conkling, Hilda, **II:** 530
Conkling, Roscoe, **III:** 506
Conley, Robert J., **Supp. V:** 232
Conley, Susan, **Supp. XIII:** 111, 112
Connaroe, Joel, **Supp. IV Part 2:** 690
"Connecticut Lad, A" (White), **Supp. I Part 2:** 677
"Connecticut Valley" (Cowley), **Supp. II Part 1:** 141–142
Connecticut Yankee in King Arthur's Court, A (Twain), **I:** 209; **II:** 276; **IV:** 205
Connell, Evan S., **Supp. XIV:** 79–100; **Supp. XXIII:** 302
Connell, Norreys (pseudonym). *See* O'Riordan, Conal Holmes O'Connell
Connelly, Marc, **III:** 394; **Supp. I Part 2:** 679; **Supp. IX:** 190
Connelly, Michael, **Supp. XXI:** 67–82
Conner, Dan, **Supp. XXIII:** 125
Connery, Thomas B., **Supp. XVII:** 106
Connoisseur, The (Connell), **Supp. XIV:** 87
"Connoisseur of Chaos" (Stevens), **IV:** 89; **Retro. Supp. I:** 306
Connolly, Cyril, **Supp. XIV:** 158, 343, 348
Connors, Elizabeth. *See* Lindsay, Mrs. Vachel (Elizabeth Connors)
Connotations (Kenny), **Supp. XXIII:** 143, 144, 146, 150, 155
Conover, Roger, **Supp. I Part 1:** 95
Conover, Roger L., **Supp. XXII:** 155, 162
Conquering Horse (Manfred), **Supp. X:** 126
"Conqueror Worm, The" (Poe), **Retro. Supp. II:** 261
Conquest of Canaan (Dwight), **Supp. I Part 1:** 124
Conquistador (MacLeish), **III:** 2, 3, 13–14, 15
Conrad, Alfred, **Retro. Supp. II:** 245
Conrad, Alfred H., **Supp. I Part 2:** 552
Conrad, C. A., **Supp. XXII:** 155
Conrad, David, **Supp. I Part 2:** 552
Conrad, Jacob, **Supp. I Part 2:** 552
Conrad, Joseph, **I:** 123, 343, 394, 405, 409, 415, 421, 485, 506, 575–576, 578; **II:** 58, 73, 74, 91, 92, 144, 263, 320, 338, 595; **III:** 28, 102, 106, 328, 464, 467, 491, 512; **IV:** 476; **Retro. Supp. I:** 80, 91, 106, 108, 231, 274, 377; **Retro. Supp. II:** 222; **Supp. I Part 1:** 292; **Supp. I Part 2:** 621, 622; **Supp. IV Part 1:** 197, 341; **Supp. IV Part 2:** 680; **Supp. V:** 249, 251, 262, 298, 307, 311; **Supp. VIII:** 4, 310; **Supp. XIV:** 112; **Supp. XVI:** 158, 212; **Supp. XVIII:** 98, 102; **Supp. XIX:** 27; **Supp. XX:** 195
Conrad, Paul, **Supp. I Part 2:** 552
Conrad, Peter, **Supp. IV Part 2:** 688
"Conrad Aiken: From Savannah to Emerson" (Cowley), **Supp. II Part 1:** 43

Conrad Richter's Ohio Trilogy (Edwards), **Supp. XVIII:** 220
Conroy, Frank, **Supp. VIII:** 145; **Supp. XI:** 245; **Supp. XVI:** 63–78; **Supp. XXII:** 50
Conroy, Jack, **Supp. XXII:** 1, 5, 10
Conroy, Pat, **Supp. XVIII:** 193; **Supp. XXII:** 239
Cons, Scams, and Grifts (Gores), **Supp. XXI:** 70
Conscience with the Power and Cases thereof (Ames), **IV:** 158
"Conscientious Objector, The" (Shapiro), **Supp. II Part 2:** 710
"Consciousness and Dining" (Harrison), **Supp. VIII:** 46
"Conscription Camp" (Shapiro), **Supp. II Part 2:** 705
"Consejos de Nuestra Señora de Guadalupe: Counsel from the Brown Virgin" (Mora), **Supp. XIII:** 224
"Conservation Esthetic" (Leopold), **Supp. XIV:** 179, 181, 186, 189–190
"Conserving Natural and Cultural Diversity: The Prose and Poetry of Pat Mora" (Murphy), **Supp. XIII:** 214
Considerable Town, A (M. F. K. Fisher), **Supp. XVII:** 90
"Considerations by the Way" (Emerson), **II:** 2, 5
Consider the Oyster (M. F. K. Fisher), **Supp. XVII:** 84, 87
Considine, Bob, **II:** 424
"Consolation" (Bausch), **Supp. VII:** 48
"Consolations" (Stafford), **Supp. XI:** 329
"Conspiracy of History, The: E. L. Doctorow's *The Book of Daniel*" (Levine), **Supp. IV Part 1:** 221
Conspiracy of Kings, The (Barlow), **Supp. II Part 1:** 80
Conspiracy of Pontiac, The (Parkman), **Supp. II Part 2:** 590, 595, 596, 599–600
Constab Ballads (McKay), **Supp. X:** 131, 133
Constance (Kenyon), **Supp. VII:** 170–172
Constancy (Boyce), **Supp. XVII:** 100; **Supp. XXI:** 6, 7, 12
"Constellation Orion, The" (Kooser), **Supp. XIX:** 120
Construction of Boston, The (Koch), **Supp. XV:** 187
"Constructive Work" (Du Bois), **Supp. II Part 1:** 172
"Consumer's Report" (X. J. Kennedy), **Supp. XV:** 161–162
"Consumption" (Bryant), **Supp. I Part 1:** 169–170
Contact Collection of Contemporary Writers (McAlmon), **Supp. XXII:** 166
"Contagiousness of Puerperal Fever, The" (Holmes), **Supp. I Part 1:** 303–304
"Contemplation in a World of Action" (Merton), **Supp. VIII:** 204
"Contemplation of Poussin" (Sarton), **Supp. VIII:** 261
"Contemplations" (Bradstreet), **Supp. I Part 1:** 112, 113, 119–122

Contemporaries (Kazin), **Supp. VIII:** 102, **103–104**
Contemporary American Playwrights (Bigsby), **Supp. XV:** 332
Contemporary American Poetry (Poulin, ed.), **Supp. IX:** 272; **Supp. XI:** 259
Contemporary Authors Autobiography, **Supp. XXII:** 225
Contending Forces (Hopkins), **Supp. XVIII:** 284
"Contentment" (Holmes), **Supp. I Part 1:** 307
"Contents" (Halliday), **Supp. XIX:** 92
"Contest, The" (Paley), **Supp. VI:** 223, 230, 231
"Contest for Aaron Gold, The" (P. Roth), **Supp. III Part 2:** 403
Continental Drift (Banks), **Supp. V:** 13–14, 16, 227
Continental Op, The (Hammett), **Supp. IV Part 1:** 344
Continent's End: An Anthology of Contemporary California Poets (Taggard, Sterling, and Rorty, eds.), **Supp. XXII:** 276
Continuing Education, A (Pickering), **Supp. XXI:** 194, 195–196
Continuity of American Poetry, The (Pearce), **Supp. I Part 1:** 111; **Supp. I Part 2:** 475
Continuous Harmony, A: Essays Cultural and Agricultural (Berry), **Supp. X:** 33
Continuous Life, The (Strand), **Supp. IV Part 2:** 630, 631–633
Contoski, Victor, **Supp. XII:** 181
"Contract" (Lardner), **II:** 432
"Contraption, The" (Swenson), **Supp. IV Part 2:** 643
"Contrariness of the Mad Farmer, The" (Berry), **Supp. X:** 35
"Contrast, a Spenetic Effusion, The" (J. Schoolcraft), **Supp. XXIII:** 231–232
"Contrition" (Dubus), **Supp. VII:** 84
"Control Burn" (Snyder), **Supp. VIII:** 301
"Control Is the Mainspring" (Komunyakaa), **Supp. XIII:** 122, 124
"Controlling the 'Sloppiness of Things' in Frank Conroy's *Stop-Time*" (Strychacz), **Supp. XVI:** 69–70
Control of Nature, The (McPhee), **Supp. III Part 1:** 310–313
Controversial Sholem Asch, The (Siegel), **Supp. XXIII:** 3
"Conventional Wisdom, The" (Elkin), **Supp. VI:** 52–53
"Convergence" (Ammons), **Supp. VII:** 28
"Convergence of the Twain, The" (Hardy), **Supp. VIII:** 31, 32
Conversation (Aiken), **I:** 54
Conversation at Midnight (Millay), **III:** 138
"Conversation of Eiros and Charmion, The" (Poe), **III:** 412
"Conversation on Conversation" (Stowe), **Supp. I Part 2:** 587
"Conversations in Moscow" (Levertov), **Supp. III Part 1:** 282

Conversations on Some of the Old Poets (Lowell), **Supp. I Part 2:** 405

Conversations with Albert Murray (Maguire, ed.), **Supp. XIX:** 160–161

Conversations with Byron (Blessington), **Retro. Supp. II:** 58

Conversations with Eudora Welty (Prenshaw, ed.), **Retro. Supp. I:** 339, 340, 341, 342, 343, 352, 354

"Conversations with Helmholtz" (Allen), **Supp. XV:** 15

Conversations with Ishmael Reed (Dick and Singh, eds.), **Supp. X:** 244

Conversations with James Baldwin (Standley and Pratt, eds.), **Retro. Supp. II:** 6

Conversations with Richard Wilbur (Wilbur), **Supp. III Part 2:** 542–543

"Conversation with My Father, A" (Paley), **Supp. VI:** 220

"Conversion of the Jews, The" (P. Roth), **Retro. Supp. II:** 281; **Supp. III Part 2:** 404, 406

Convict, The: Stories (Burke), **Supp. XIV:** 25

"Convicta et Combusta" (J. Scott), **Supp. XVII:** 189

"Convolvulus" (Schott), **Supp. XXIII:** 248

"Convoy" (Weigl), **Supp. XIX:** 278

Conway, Jill, **Supp. I Part 1:** 19

Coode, John, **I:** 132

Cook, Bruce, **Supp. XII:** 130, 131, 133–134

Cook, Captain James, **I:** 2

Cook, Eleanor, **Retro. Supp. I:** 311

Cook, Elisha, **Supp. IV Part 1:** 356

Cook, Elizabeth Christine, **II:** 106

Cook, George Cram "Jig", **Supp. XXI:** 5, 6

Cook, Mercer, **Supp. IV Part 1:** 368

Cook, Richard, **Supp. XXII:** 158

Cooke, Alistair, **III:** 113, 119, 120

Cooke, Delmar G., **II:** 271

Cooke, Grace MacGowan, **Supp. V:** 285

Cooke, Philip Pendleton, **III:** 420

Cooke, Rose Terry, **II:** 401; **Retro. Supp. II:** 51, 136, 138; **Supp. XIII:** 152

"Cookie" (Taylor), **Supp. V:** 320

"Cookies, The" (Nye), **Supp. XIII:** 281

Cooking of Provincial France, The (M. F. K. Fisher), **Supp. XVII:** 89

Cook-Lynn, Elizabeth, **Supp. IV Part 1:** 325

Coolbrith, Ina, **I:** 193, 196

"Coole Park" (Yeats), **Supp. VIII:** 155, 159

"Coole Park and Ballylee" (Yeats), **Supp. VIII:** 156

Cooler by the Lake (Heinemann), **Supp. XXII:** 103, **114**

Cooley, John, **Supp. V:** 214

Cooley, Peter, **Supp. XIII:** 76

Coolidge, Calvin, **I:** 498; **II:** 95; **Supp. I Part 2:** 647

Cooling Time: An American Poetry Vigil (Wright), **Supp. XV:** 353

"Cool Million, A" (screen story) (West and Ingster), **Retro. Supp. II:** 330

Cool Million, A (West), **III:** 425; **IV:** 287, 288, 297–299, 300; **Retro. Supp. II:** 321, 322–323, 328, **335–337**

"Cool Tombs" (Sandburg), **III:** 554

Coon, Ross, **IV:** 196

Cooney, Seamus, **Supp. XIV:** 289

"Coon Hunt" (White), **Supp. I Part 2:** 669

Co-op (Sinclair), **Supp. V:** 290

Cooper, Bernard, **Supp. XI:** 129

Cooper, Frederic Taber, **Supp. XX: 219–220**

Cooper, Gary, **Supp. IV Part 2:** 524

Cooper, James Fenimore, **I:** 211, 257, **335–357; II:** 74, 277, 295–296, 302, 306, 309, 313, 314; **III:** 51; **IV:** 205, 333; **Retro. Supp. I:** 246; **Retro. Supp. II:** 160; **Supp. I Part 1:** 141, 155, 156, 158, 171, 372; **Supp. I Part 2:** 413, 495, 579, 585, 652, 660; **Supp. IV Part 1:** 80; **Supp. IV Part 2:** 463, 469; **Supp. V:** 209–210; **Supp. VIII:** 189; **Supp. XIV:** 227; **Supp. XVIII:** 4; **Supp. XXIII:** 178

Cooper, Mrs. James Fenimore (Susan A. De Lancey), **I:** 338, 351, 354

Cooper, Jane, **Supp. XV:** 259

Cooper, Rand Richards, **Supp. XVI:** 74

Cooper, Susan Fenimore, **I:** 337, 354

Cooper, William, **I:** 337–338, 351

Cooper, Mrs. William, **I:** 337

Cooperman, Robert, **Supp. XXIII:** 247

Coover, Robert, **Supp. IV Part 1:** 388; **Supp. V: 39–55; Supp. XII:** 152; **Supp. XIV:** 96; **Supp. XVII:** 6; **Supp. XXI:** 236; **Supp. XXII:** 259

Copacetic (Komunyakaa), **Supp. XIII:** 116–118, 126

Cope, Wendy, **Supp. XV:** 117

Copland, Aaron, **II:** 586; **Supp. I Part 1:** 281; **Supp. III Part 2:** 619; **Supp. IV Part 1:** 79, 80–81, 84; **Supp. XXII:** 283

Coplas de Don Jorge Manrique (Longfellow, trans.), **II:** 488, 492

Coppée, François Edouard Joachim, **II:** 325

Copperhead, The (Frederic), **II:** 134–135

Copperhead Cane (J. W. Miller), **Supp. XX: 163, 164, 166–167**

Copper Sun (Cullen), **Supp. IV Part 1:** 167, 168

Coppola, Francis Ford, **Supp. XI:** 171, 172; **Supp. XII:** 75

Coprolites (Goldbarth), **Supp. XII: 177–178,** 180, 183

Coral and Captive Israel (Reznikoff), **Supp. XIV:** 288

"Coral Ring, The" (Stowe), **Supp. I Part 2:** 586

"Cora Unashamed" (Hughes), **Supp. I Part 1:** 329, 330

"Corazón del Corrido" (Mora), **Supp. XIII:** 225

Corban Ephphata (Li Lin Lee), **Supp. XV:** 225

Corbett, Gentlemen Jim, **II:** 416

Corbett, William, **Supp. XI:** 248; **Supp. XVI:** 286, 295

Corbière, Jean Antoine, **II:** 354–355, 528

Cordiall Water, A: A garland of Odd & Old Receipts to Assuage the Ills of Man and Beast (M. F. K. Fisher), **Supp. XVII:** 88, 90

Cording, Robert, **Supp. IX:** 328; **Supp. XII:** 184

Core, George, **Supp. XVIII:** 86; **Supp. XXI:** 193

Corelli, Marie, **III:** 579

Corey, Lewis, **Supp. I Part 2:** 645

"Corinna's Going a-Maying" (Herrick), **Supp. XIV:** 8, 9

"Coriolan" (Eliot), **I:** 580

"Coriolanus and His Mother" (Schwartz), **Supp. II Part 2:** 643, 644–645

"Corkscrew" (Hammett), **Supp. IV Part 1:** 345, 347

Corkum, Gerald, **I:** 37

Corky's Brother (Neugeboren), **Supp. XVI:** 225

"Corky's Brother" (Neugeboren), **Supp. XVI:** 225

Corliss, Richard, **Supp. VIII:** 73

Corman, Cid, **Supp. III Part 2:** 624, 625, 626, 627, 628; **Supp. IV Part 1:** 144; **Supp. VIII:** 292; **Supp. XV:** 74, 153; **Supp. XXI:** 23, 27

"Corn" (Lanier), **Supp. I Part 1:** 352, 353, 354, 356–361, 364, 366

Corn, Alfred, **Supp. IX:** 156; **Supp. XV:** 250

Corneille, Pierre, **Supp. I Part 2:** 716; **Supp. IX:** 131

Cornell, Esther, **I:** 231

Cornell, Joseph, **Supp. XXI:** 131; **Supp. XXII:** 167, 168

Cornell, Katherine, **IV:** 356

Cornell, Valerie, **Supp. XX: 94–95**

"Corners" (Dunn), **Supp. XI:** 148

Cornhuskers (Sandburg), **III:** 583–585

"Corn-Planting, The" (Anderson), **I:** 114

"Corn story (or the origin of corn)"(J. Schoolcraft), **Supp. XXIII:** 234–235

Cornucopia: New and Selected Poems, 1975–2002 (Peacock), **Supp. XIX: 203–204**

Corn Village (Le Sueur), **Supp. XXIII:** 167

Coronation Murder-Mystery, The (O'Hara, Ashbery, and Koch), **Supp. XXIII:** 217

"Coroner's Report" (Wrigley), **Supp. XVIII:** 295

"Corporal of Artillery" (Dubus), **Supp. VII:** 84, 85

"Corpse Plant, The" (Rich), **Supp. I Part 2:** 555

Corpus Christi (McNally), **Supp. XIII: 205–206,** 209

Corradi, Juan, **Supp. IV Part 1:** 208

Corrections, The (Franzen), **Supp. XIX:** 54; **Supp. XX: 83, 84, 85, 90, 91, 91–93, 95**

"Correspondences" (Baudelaire), **I:** 63

"Corrido de Gregorio Cortez" (Mora), **Supp. XIII:** 225

"Corrigenda" (Komunyakaa), **Supp. XIII:** 115, 116

Corrosive Sublimate (Sorrentino), **Supp. XXI:** 226, 228

Corruption City (McCoy), **Supp. XIII:** 175

Corso, Gregory, **Supp. II Part 1:** 30; **Supp. IV Part 1:** 90; **Supp. XII: 117–138; Supp. XIV:** 150; **Supp. XVI:** 135; **Supp. XXI:** 53; **Supp. XXIII:** 215

Corsons Inlet (Ammons), **Supp. VII:** 25–26, 28–29, 36

"Corsons Inlet" (Ammons), **Supp. VII:** 25–26

Cortázar, Julio, **Retro. Supp. I:** 278; **Supp. XXII:** 265

"Cortège for Rosenbloom" (Stevens), **IV:** 81

Cortez, Hernando, **III:** 2

" 'Coruscating Glamour': Lynda Hull and the Movies" (Goldstein), **Supp. XXI:** 134

Cory, William Johnson, **Supp. XX: 230, 231**

Coser, Lewis, **Supp. I Part 2:** 650

Cosgrave, Patrick, **Retro. Supp. II:** 185

Cosmic Optimism: A Study of the Interpretation of Evolution by American Poets from Emerson to Robinson (Conner), **Supp. I Part 1:** 73

Cosmological Eye, The (H. Miller), **III:** 174, 184

"Cosmological Eye, The" (H. Miller), **III:** 183

"Cosmos" (Beattie), **Supp. V:** 35

"Cost, The" (Hecht), **Supp. X:** 62–63

Costello, Bonnie, **Retro. Supp. II:** 40

Costello, Mark, **Supp. XXIII:** 290

Costner, Kevin, **Supp. VIII:** 45

"Cost of Living, The" (Malamud), **Supp. I Part 2:** 429, 437

"Costume as Metaphor" (Bronk), **Supp. XXI:** 26

Cott, Jonathan, **Supp. XVI:** 104, 106

"Cottagers' Corner" column (D. West), **Supp. XVIII:** 286

"Cottage Street, 1953" (Wilbur), **Supp. III Part 2:** 543, 561

"Cottagette, The" (Gilman), **Supp. XI:** 207

Cotten, Joseph, **Supp. IV Part 2:** 524

Cotter, James Finn, **Supp. X:** 202

Cotton, John, **Supp. I Part 1:** 98, 101, 110, 111, 116

Cotton, Joseph, **Supp. XII:** 160

Cotton, Seaborn, **Supp. I Part 1:** 101

Cotton Club, The (Major), **Supp. XXII:** 174

"Cotton Club Classics" (Halliday), **Supp. XIX:** 92, 93

Cotton Comes to Harlem (C. Himes), **Supp. XVI:** 143, 144

Cotton Comes to Harlem (film, O. Davis), **Supp. XVI:** 144

"Cotton Song" (Toomer), **Supp. IX:** 312

Couch, W. T., **Supp. X:** 46

Coughlin, Ruth Pollack, **Supp. VIII:** 45

Coulette, Henri, **Supp. V:** 180; **Supp. XIII:** 312; **Supp. XV:** 74, 75

Coultrap-McQuin, Susan, **Supp. XVI:** 85, 92

"Council of State, A" (Dunbar), **Supp. II Part 1:** 211, 213

"Count Dracula" (Allen), **Supp. XV:** 15

"Countee Cullen at 'The Heights' " (Tuttleton), **Supp. IV Part 1:** 166

Counterfeiters, The (Gide), **Supp. IV Part 1:** 80; **Supp. IV Part 2:** 681

"Countering" (Ammons), **Supp. VII:** 28

Counterlife, The (P. Roth), **Retro. Supp. II:** 279, 280, 291; **Supp. III Part 2:** 424–426

Counter-Statement (Burke), **I:** 270–272; **IV:** 431

"Countess, The" (Whittier), **Supp. I Part 2:** 691, 694

Count Frontenac and New France Under Louis XIV (Parkman), **Supp. II Part 2:** 607, 609–610

"Counting Small-Boned Bodies" (R. Bly), **Supp. IV Part 1:** 62

"Counting the Body"(Schott), **Supp. XXIII:** 251–252

"Counting the Children" (Gioia), **Supp. XV: 122–123**

"Counting the Mad" (Justice), **Supp. VII:** 117

Count of Monte Cristo, The (Dumas), **III:** 386, 396; **Supp. XVII:** 64, 216

"Countries We Live In, The" (Zach; Everwine, trans.), **Supp. XV:** 87

"Country Boy in Boston, The" (Howells), **II:** 255

Country By-Ways (Jewett), **II:** 402

Country Doctor, A (Jewett), **II:** 391, 392, 396, 404–405; **Retro. Supp. II:** 131, 141, 146

"Country Full of Swedes" (Caldwell), **I:** 297, 309

Country Girl, The (Odets), **Supp. II Part 2:** 546, 547, 548–549

"Country House" (Kumin), **Supp. IV Part 2:** 446

"Country Husband, The" (Cheever), **Supp. I Part 1:** 184, 189

"Country Life" (Pickering), **Supp. XXI:** 197

"Country Marriage" (C. Frost), **Supp. XV:** 99

Countrymen of Bones (R. O. Butler), **Supp. XII:** 62, **65–66**

"Country Mouse, The" (Bishop), **Retro. Supp. II:** 37, 38, 51

Country Music: Selected Early Poems (Wright), **Supp. V:** 332, 335, 338, 342

Country of a Thousand Years of Peace, The (Merrill), **Supp. III Part 1:** 321, 322, 331

"Country of Elusion, The" (O. Henry), **Supp. II Part 1:** 407

Country Of Language, The (Sanders), **Supp. XVI:** 277

Country of Marriage, The (Berry), **Supp. X:** 33

Country of Strangers, A (Richter), **Supp. XVIII:** 217

Country of Survivors (Di Piero), **Supp. XIX:** 36

Country of the Pointed Firs, The (Jewett), **II:** 392, 399, 405, 409–411; **Retro. Supp. I:** 6; **Retro. Supp. II:** 134, 136, 139, 140, 141, 145, 146, 147; **Supp. VIII:** 126; **Supp. XIII:** 152; **Supp. XXIII:** 275, 278

"Country Printer, The" (Freneau), **Supp. II Part 1:** 269

"Country Wife, The" (Gioia), **Supp. XV:** 120

Count Your Bullets (film), **Supp. XVII:** 141

Count Zero (W. Gibson), **Supp. XVI:** 19, **126–127,** 129

Coup, The (Updike), **Retro. Supp. I:** 331, 334, 335

"Coup de Grâce, The" (Bierce), **I:** 202

Couperin, François, **III:** 464

"Couple, The" (Olds), **Supp. X:** 206

"Couple of Hamburgers, A" (Thurber), **Supp. I Part 2:** 616

"Couple of Nuts, A" (Z. Fitzgerald), **Supp. IX:** 58, 71, 72

"Couples" (Halliday), **Supp. XIX:** 89

Couples (Updike), **IV:** 214, 215, 216, 217, 227, 229–230; **Retro. Supp. I:** 320, 327, 330; **Supp. XII:** 296

Cournos, John, **III:** 465; **Supp. I Part 1:** 258

"Course in Creative Writing, A" (Stafford), **Supp. XI:** 327

"Course of a Particular, The" (Stevens), **Retro. Supp. I:** 312

"Coursier de Jeanne d'Arc, Le" (McCarriston), **Supp. XIV:** 267–268

Courtier, The (Castiglione), **III:** 282

" 'Courtin,' The" (Lowell), **Supp. I Part 2:** 415

"Courting of Sister Wisby, The" (Jewett), **Retro. Supp. II:** 134, 135, 146

"Courting the Famous Figures at the Grotto of Improbable Thought" (B. Kelly), **Supp. XVII:** 127–128

"Courtship" (Dove), **Supp. IV Part 1:** 248

"Courtship, A"(Thompson), **Supp. XXIII:** 293

"Courtship, Diligence" (Dove), **Supp. IV Part 1:** 248

Courtship of Miles Standish, The (Longfellow), **II:** 489, 502–503; **Retro. Supp. II:** 155, **161–162,** 163, 166, 168

"Cousin Aubrey" (Taylor), **Supp. V:** 328

Cousine Bette (Balzac), **Retro. Supp. II:** 98

Couturier, Maurice, **Supp. IV Part 1:** 44

Covarrubias, Miguel, **Supp. XVI:** 187

"Covered Bridges" (Kingsolver), **Supp. VII:** 203

"Cover Photograph" (Nelson), **Supp. XVIII:** 173

"Cover Stories" (Skloot), **Supp. XX: 195, 207**

"Cover Versions" (Halliday), **Supp. XIX:** 84

Cowan, Lester, **III:** 148

Cowan, Louise, **IV:** 120, 125

Coward, Noel, **Retro. Supp. I:** 65; **Supp. I Part 1:** 332; **Supp. V:** 101; **Supp. XV:** 329

"Cowardice" (Theroux), **Supp. VIII:** 313

Cowboy Mouth (Shepard), **Supp. III Part 2:** 441–442
"Cowboys" (Salter). *See* "Dirt" (Salter)
Cowboys (Shepard), **Supp. III Part 2:** 432
Cowboys #2 (Shepard), **Supp. III Part 2:** 437, 438
Cowell, Henry, **Supp. IV Part 1:** 80, 82
Cowen, Philip, **Supp. XX:** 2
Cowen, Wilson Walker, **Supp. IV Part 2:** 435
Cowie, Alexander, **IV:** 70
"Cow in Apple Time, The" (Frost), **II:** 154; **Retro. Supp. I:** 131
Cowl, Jane, **IV:** 357
Cowley, Abraham, **III:** 508; **IV:** 158; **Supp. I Part 1:** 357
Cowley, Malcolm, **I:** 246, 253, 254, 255, 256, 257, 283, 385; **II:** 26, 57, 94, 456; **III:** 606; **IV:** 123; **Retro. Supp. I:** 73, 91, 97; **Retro. Supp. II:** 77, 83, 89, 221, 330; **Supp. I Part 1:** 174; **Supp. I Part 2:** 609, 610, 620, 647, 654, 678; **Supp. II Part 1:** 103, **135–156;** **Supp. VIII:** 96; **Supp. XV:** 142; **Supp. XX:** 76
Cowley, Marguerite Frances Baird (Mrs. Malcolm Cowley), **Supp. I Part 2:** 615; **Supp. II Part 1:** 138, 139
Cowley, Muriel Maurer (Mrs. Malcolm Cowley), **Supp. II Part 1:** 139
Cowley, Susan Cheever (Susan Cheever), **Supp. I Part 1:** 175; **Supp. IX:** 133
Cowper, William, **II:** 17, 304; **III:** 508, 511; **Supp. I Part 1:** 150, 151, 152; **Supp. I Part 2:** 539
"Cow Wandering in the Bare Field, The" (Jarrell), **II:** 371, 388
Cox, Martha Heasley, **Supp. IX:** 2, 4, 11–12
Cox, Sidney, **Retro. Supp. I:** 131; **Supp. XXI:** 19, 21
Cox, Stephen, **Supp. IV Part 2:** 523, 524
Cox, Steve, **Supp. XIX:** 116, 128
Coxey, Jacob, **II:** 464
"Coxon Fund, The" (James), **Retro. Supp. I:** 228
"Coy Mistress" (A. Finch), **Supp. XVII:** 72
Coyne, Patricia, **Supp. V:** 123
"Coyote Ortiz: *Canis latrans latrans* in the Poetry of Simon Ortiz" (P. C. Smith), **Supp. IV Part 2:** 509
Coyote's Daylight Trip (Gunn Allen), **Supp. IV Part 1:** 320, 324
Coyote Was Here (Ortiz), **Supp. IV Part 2:** 499
Cozzens, James Gould, **I: 358–380; II:** 459
Crabbe, George, **II:** 304; **III:** 469, 508, 511, 521
"Crab-Boil" (Dove), **Supp. IV Part 1:** 249
"Cracked Looking-Glass, The" (Porter), **III:** 434, 435, 446
"Cracker Chidlings" (Rawlings), **Supp. X:** 224, 228
Cracks (Purdy), **Supp. VII:** 277–278

Crack-Up, The (Fitzgerald), **II:** 80; **III:** 35, 45; **Retro. Supp. I:** 113, 115; **Supp. V:** 276; **Supp. IX:** 61
"Crack-Up, The" (Fitzgerald), **I:** 509; **Retro. Supp. I:** 113, 114
"Crack-up of American Optimism, The: Vachel Lindsay, the Dante of the Fundamentalists" (Viereck), **Supp. I Part 2:** 403
"Cradle and the Bookcase, The"(Hadas), **Supp. XXIII:** 122
Cradle Will Rock, The (Blitzstein), **Supp. I Part 1:** 277, 278
Craft of Fiction, The (Lubbock), **I:** 504; **Supp. VIII:** 165
Craft of Peter Taylor, The (McAlexander, ed.), **Supp. V:** 314
Craig, David M., **Supp. XXII:** 187, 191, 192
Craig, Gordon, **III:** 394; **Supp. XXI:** 6
Crain, Jane Larkin, **Supp. V:** 123; **Supp. XII:** 167, 168
Crais, Robert, **Supp. XXI:** 70
Cram, Ralph Adams, **I:** 19
Cramer, Steven, **Supp. XI:** 139; **Supp. XV:** 26
Crandall, Reuben, **Supp. I Part 2:** 686
Crane, Agnes, **I:** 406
Crane, Edmund, **I:** 407
Crane, Hart, **I:** 61, 62, 97, 109, 116, 266, **381–404; II:** 133, 215, 306, 368, 371, 536, 542; **III:** 260, 276, 453, 485, 521; **IV:** 122, 123–124, 127, 128, 129, 135, 139, 140, 141, 341, 380, 418, 419; **Retro. Supp. I:** 427; **Retro. Supp. II: 75–91; Supp. I Part 1:** 86; **Supp. II Part 1:** 89, 152; **Supp. III Part 1:** 20, 63, 350; **Supp. V:** 342; **Supp. VIII:** 39; **Supp. IX:** 38, 229, 320; **Supp. X:** 115, 116, 120; **Supp. XI:** 123, 131; **Supp. XII:** 198; **Supp. XV:** 138; **Supp. XIX:** 35; **Supp. XX:** 80; **Supp. XXI:** 131, 132, 136, 230; **Supp. XXII:** 274; **Supp. XXIII:** 146, 174, 207
Crane, Jonathan, Jr., **I:** 407
Crane, Jonathan Townley, **I:** 406
Crane, Mrs. Jonathan Townley, **I:** 406
Crane, Luther, **I:** 406
Crane, Milton, **Supp. XV:** 144
Crane, Nellie, **I:** 407
Crane, R. S., **Supp. I Part 2:** 423
Crane, Stephen, **I:** 34, 169–170, 201, 207, 211, **405–427,** 477, 506, 519; **II:** 58, 144, 198, 262, 263, 264, 276, 289, 290, 291; **III:** 314, 317, 334, 335, 454, 505, 585; **IV:** 207, 208, 256, 350, 475; **Retro. Supp. I:** 231, 325; **Retro. Supp. II:** 97, 123; **Supp. I Part 2:** 314; **Supp. III Part 2:** 412; **Supp. IV Part 1:** 350, 380; **Supp. IV Part 2:** 680, 689, 692; **Supp. VIII:** 98, 105; **Supp. IX:** 1, 14; **Supp. X:** 223; **Supp. XI:** 95; **Supp. XII:** 50; **Supp. XIV:** 21, 50, 51, 227; **Supp. XVII:** 71, 228; **Supp. XVIII:** 74, 75; **Supp. XXIII:** 26
Crane, William, **I:** 407
Cranford (Gaskell), **Supp. IX:** 79
Crashaw, William, **IV:** 145, 150, 151, 165

"Crash Report" (McGrath), **Supp. X:** 116
Crater, The (Cooper), **I:** 354, 355
Cratylus (Plato), **II:** 10
Cravan, Arthur, **Supp. XXII:** 164, 169
"Craven Street Gazette" (Franklin), **II:** 119
"Crawdad, The" (F. Wright), **Supp. XVII:** 244
Crawdad Creek (Sanders), **Supp. XVI:** 269
Crawford, Brad, **Supp. XI:** 133
Crawford, Eva, **I:** 199
Crawford, F. Marion, **III:** 320
Crawford, Joan, **Supp. I Part 1:** 67
Crawford, John E., **Supp. XXIII:** 165
Crawford, Kathleen, **I:** 289
"Crayon House" (Rukeyser), **Supp. VI:** 273
Crayon Miscellany, The (Irving), **II:** 312–313
Crazed, The (Jin), **Supp. XVIII: 99–100**
"Crazy about her Shrimp" (Simic), **Supp. VIII:** 282
"Crazy Cock" (H. Miller), **III:** 177
Crazy Gypsy (Salinas), **Supp. XIII:** 311, **313–315,** 316
"Crazy Gypsy" (Salinas), **Supp. XIII:** 313–314
Crazy Horse, **Supp. IV Part 2:** 488, 489
Crazy Horse (McMurtry), **Supp. V:** 233
Crazy Horse in Stillness (Heyen), **Supp. XIII:** 344
"Crazy in the Stir" (C. Himes), **Supp. XVI:** 137
Crazy Kill, The (C. Himes), **Supp. XVI:** 143
Creating a Role (Stanislavsky), **Supp. XIV:** 243
"Creation, According to Coyote, The" (Ortiz), **Supp. IV Part 2:** 505
Creation: A Novel (Vidal), **Supp. IV Part 2:** 677, 685, 688
"Creation of Anguish" (Nemerov), **III:** 269
"Creation Story" (Gunn Allen), **Supp. IV Part 1:** 325
"Creative and Cultural Lag" (Ellison), **Retro. Supp. II:** 116; **Supp. II Part 1:** 229; **Supp. XVIII:** 283
Creative Criticism (Spingarn), **I:** 266
"Creative Democracy" (Locke), **Supp. XIV:** 208
Creative Present, The (Balkian and Simmons, eds.), **Supp. XI:** 230
Creatures in an Alphabet (illus. Barnes), **Supp. III Part 1:** 43
"Credences of Summer" (Stevens), **IV:** 93–94
"Credentials" (Halliday), **Supp. XIX:** 90
"Credo" (Bynner), **Supp. XV:** 50
"Credo" (Du Bois), **Supp. II Part 1:** 169
"Credo" (Jeffers), **Supp. II Part 2:** 424
"Credos and Curios" (Thurber), **Supp. I Part 2:** 606, 613
Creech, James, **Retro. Supp. I:** 254
"Creed for Americans, A" (Benét), **Supp. XI:** 52
"Creed of a Beggar, The" (Lindsay), **Supp. I Part 2:** 379
Creegan, Andy, **Supp. XIX:** 205

Creekmore, Hubert, **II:** 586
Creeley, Robert, **Retro. Supp. I:** 411; **Supp. II Part 1:** 30; **Supp. III Part 1:** 2; **Supp. III Part 2:** 622, 626, 629; **Supp. IV Part 1:** **139–161,** 322, 325; **Supp. XI:** 317; **Supp. XIII:** 104, 112; **Supp. XIV:** 150; **Supp. XVI:** 283; **Supp. XXI:** 23, 27, 227, 230; **Supp. XXII:** 227
Creelman, James Ashmore, **Supp. XVI:** 186–187
"Cremona Violin, The" (Lowell), **II:** 523
"Crêpe de Chine" (Doty), **Supp. XI:** 128
"Cressy" (Harte), **Supp. II Part 1:** 354, 356
"Cretan Woman, The" (Jeffers), **Supp. II Part 2:** 435
Crèvecoeur, Michel-Guillaume Jean de, **I:** 229; **Supp. I Part 1:** **227–252**
Crèvecoeur's Eighteenth-Century Travels in Pennsylvania and New York (Adams), **Supp. I Part 1:** 251
Crevel, René, **Supp. XIV:** 343
Crewe-Jones, Florence, **Supp. XVII:** 58
Crewe Train (Macaulay), **Supp. XII:** 88
Crews, Harry, **Supp. X:** 11, 12; **Supp. XI:** **99–117,** 245; **Supp. XVIII:** 195; **Supp. XXI:** 35, 38, 40, 44
Crews, James, **Supp. XXIII:** 134–135
Crichton, Michael, **Supp. XIV:** 316
Crick, Philip, **Supp. XVI:** 289
Cricket (C. L. R. James; Grimshaw, ed.), **Supp. XXI:** 172
"Cricket" (C. Miller), **Supp. XXII:** 199
"Crickets" (R. O. Butler), **Supp. XII:** 71
Criers and Kibitzers, Kibitzers and Criers (Elkin), **Supp. VI:** **45–46,** 57
Crime and Punishment (Dostoevsky), **II:** 60, 130; **IV:** 484; **Supp. IV Part 2:** 525; **Supp. VIII:** 282; **Supp. XII:** 281; **Supp. XVII:** 155; **Supp. XVIII:** 278; **Supp. XIX:** 276
Crime at Scottsboro, The (Endore), **Supp. XVII:** 59
Crime Beat (Connelly), **Supp. XXI:** 67, 79
Crimes and Misdemeanors (film; Allen), **Supp. XV:** 1, 2, **11,** 12
"Criminal"(Strout), **Supp. XXIII:** 283, 285
Crisis papers (Paine), **Supp. I Part 2:** 508–509, 510
"Criteria of Negro Art" (Du Bois), **Supp. II Part 1:** 181; **Supp. XIX:** 66–67
"Critiad, The" (Winters), **Supp. II Part 2:** 794, 799
Critical Anthology A (Untermeyer), **Supp. XV:** 310
Critical Essays on Charlotte Perkins Gilman (Karpinski, ed.), **Supp. XI:** 201
Critical Essays on Peter Taylor (McAlexander), **Supp. V:** 319, 320, 323–324
Critical Essays on Robert Bly (W. V. Davis), **Supp. IV Part 1:** 64, 69
Critical Essays on Wallace Stegner (Arthur), **Supp. IV Part 2:** 606
Critical Fable, A (Lowell), **II:** 511–512, 527, 529–530

Critical Guide to Leaves of Grass, A (J. Miller), **IV:** 352
Critical Response to Joan Didion, The (Felton), **Supp. IV Part 1:** 210
Critical Temper of Alain Locke, The: A Selection of His Essays on Art and Culture (Stewart, ed.), **Supp. XIV:** 196, **210–211,** 213
"Critic as Artist, The" (Wilde), **Supp. X:** 189
Criticism and Fiction (Howells), **II:** 288
Criticism and Ideology (Eagleton), **Retro. Supp. I:** 67
Criticism in the Borderlands (Calderón and Saldívar, eds.), **Supp. IV Part 2:** 544
"Critics, The" (Jong), **Supp. V:** 119
"Critics and Connoisseurs" (Moore), **III:** 209
Critic's Notebook, A (Howe), **Supp. VI:** 126–128
"Critic's Task, The" (Kazin), **Supp. VIII:** 103
"Critic Who Does Not Exist, The" (Wilson), **IV:** 431
"Critique de la Vie Quotidienne" (Barthelme), **Supp. IV Part 1:** 50
Critique of Pure Reason (Kant), **Supp. XVI:** 184
Croce, Benedetto, **I:** 58, 255, 265, 273, 281; **III:** 610
Crockett, Davy, **II:** 307; **III:** 227; **IV:** 266; **Supp. I Part 2:** 411
"Crocodilopolis" (Cliff), **Supp. XXII:** 76
Crofter and the Laird, The (McPhee), **Supp. III Part 1:** 301–302, 307
Croly, Herbert, **I:** 229, 231, 235; **IV:** 436
Cromwell, Oliver, **IV:** 145, 146, 156; **Supp. I Part 1:** 111
Cronenberg, David, **Supp. XXI:** 152, 154
Cronin, A. J., **Supp. XVII:** 59
Cronin, Dr. Archibald, **III:** 578
Cronin, Justin, **Supp. X:** 10
Crooke, Dr. Helkiah, **Supp. I Part 1:** 98, 104
Crooked Little Heart (Lamott), **Supp. XX:** 138
Crooker, Barbara, **Supp. XXIII:** **51–66,** 245, **246,** 251
Crooks, Alan, **Supp. V:** 226
Crooks, Robert, **Supp. XIII:** 237
"Crop, The" (O'Connor), **Retro. Supp. II:** 223–225
Crosby, Caresse, **I:** 385; **III:** 473; **Retro. Supp. II:** 85; **Supp. XII:** 198
Crosby, Harry, **I:** 385; **Retro. Supp. II:** 85
"Cross" (Hughes), **Supp. I Part 1:** 325; **Supp. XVIII:** 124
Crossan, John Dominic, **Supp. V:** 251
"Cross Country Snow" (Hemingway), **II:** 249
Cross Creek (Rawlings), **Supp. X:** 223, 226, 228, **231–232,** 233, 234, 235
Cross Creek Cookery (Rawlings), **Supp. X:** 233
Crossing, The (McCarthy), **Supp. VIII:** 175, **184–186**
"Crossing, The" (Swenson), **Supp. IV Part 2:** 644

"Crossing Brooklyn Ferry" (Whitman), **IV:** 333, 340, 341; **Retro. Supp. I:** 389, 396, 397, 400–401; **Supp. XXIII:** 109
"Crossing into Poland" (Babel), **Supp. XIV:** 84
Crossings (Chuang), **Supp. X:** 291
"Crossings" (Hogan), **Supp. IV Part 1:** 412
Crossing the Water (Plath), **Retro. Supp. II:** 248; **Supp. I Part 2:** 526, 538
Crossing to Safety (Stegner), **Supp. IV Part 2:** 599, 606, 612, 613–614
"Cross of Snow, The" (Longfellow), **II:** 490; **Retro. Supp. II:** 169–170
"Crossover" (O. Butler), **Supp. XIII:** 61
"Cross-Roads, The" (Lowell), **II:** 523
"Crossroads of the World Etc." (Merwin), **Supp. III Part 1:** 347, 348
Cross-Section (Seaver), **IV:** 485
Cross the Border, Close the Gap (Fiedler), **Supp. XIII:** 104
Cross Ties (X. J. Kennedy), **Supp. XV:** 165, **166–167**
"Cross Ties" (X. J. Kennedy), **Supp. XV:** 158
Crouch, Stanley, **Supp. XIX:** 158
"Croup" (Karr), **Supp. XI:** 243
Crouse, Russel, **III:** 284
"Crow" (Hogan), **Supp. IV Part 1:** 405
Crow (Hughes), **Supp. XV:** 347, 348
"Crow, The" (Creeley), **Supp. IV Part 1:** 148–149
Crow and the Heart,The (Carruth), **Supp. XVI:** 47–48
"Crowded Street, The" (Bryant), **Supp. I Part 1:** 168
Crowder, A. B., **Supp. XI:** 107
"Crow Jane" (Baraka), **Supp. II Part 1:** 38
Crow Mercies (Schott), **Supp. XXIII:** **252–254**
"Crow Mercies" (Schott), **Supp. XXIII:** 253
Crowninshield, Frank, **III:** 123; **Supp. IX:** 201
Crown of Columbus (Erdrich and Dorris), **Supp. IV Part 1:** 260
"Crows, The" (Bogan), **Supp. III Part 1:** 50, 51
Crucial Instances (Wharton), **Retro. Supp. I:** 365, 367
Crucible, The (A. Miller), **III:** 147, 148, 155, 156–158, 159, 166; **Supp. XIII:** 206
"Crucified" (Gibran), **Supp. XX:** 119
"Crucifix in the Filing Cabinet" (Shapiro), **Supp. II Part 2:** 712
"Crude Foyer" (Stevens), **Retro. Supp. I:** 310
"Cruel and Barbarous Treatment" (McCarthy), **II:** 562, 563
"Cruel Mother, The" (B. Kelly), **Supp. XVII:** 126
Cruise of the Dazzler, The (London), **II:** 465
Cruise of the Snark, The (London), **II:** 476–477
"Cruising with the Beach Boys" (Gioia), **Supp. XV:** 118

" 'Crumbling Idols' by Hamlin Garland" (Chopin), **Supp. I Part 1:** 217

"Crusade of the Excelsior, The" (Harte), **Supp. II Part 1:** 336, 354

"Crusoe in England" (Bishop), **Retro. Supp. II:** 50; **Supp. I Part 1:** 93, 95, 96; **Supp. III Part 1:** 10, 18

Cruz-Hacker, Alba, **Supp. XXI:** 107

Cry, the Beloved Country (Paton), **Supp. VIII:** 126

Cryer, Dan, **Supp. VIII:** 86, 88; **Supp. XII:** 164

Crying of Lot 49, The (Pynchon), **Supp. II Part 2:** 618, 619, 621, 630–633

"Crying Sisters, The" (Rand), **Supp. IV Part 2:** 524

"Crying Wolf" (C. Frost), **Supp. XV:** 101

"Cry of the Graves, The" (Gibran), **Supp. XX: 124**

Cryptogram, The (Mamet), **Supp. XIV:** 240, 247, 255

"Crystal, The" (Aiken), **I:** 60

"Crystal, The" (Lanier), **Supp. I Part 1:** 364, 370

"Crystal Cage, The" (Kunitz), **Supp. III Part 1:** 258

Crystal Vision (Sorrentino), **Supp. XXI:** 235, 236

"Crytal" (Sobin), **Supp. XVI:** 283

Cry to Heaven (Rice), **Supp. VII:** 300–301

"Cuba" (Hemingway), **II:** 258

"Cuba Libre" (Baraka), **Supp. II Part 1:** 33

Cuba: Prophetic Island (W. Frank), **Supp. XX: 80, 81**

"Cubism, Barcelona" (Hull), **Supp. XXI:** 137

Cudjoe, Selwyn, **Supp. IV Part 1:** 6

"Cudjo's Own Story of the Last American Slaver" (Hurston), **Supp. VI:** 153

Cudlipp, Thelma, **I:** 501

Cudworth, Ralph, **II:** 9, 10

"Cuentista" (Mora), **Supp. XIII:** 224

"Cuento de agua santa, Un" (Mora), **Supp. XIII:** 224

Cujo (King), **Supp. V:** 138–139, 143, 149, 152

Cukor, George, **Supp. XVI:** 192

Cullen, Countee, **Retro. Supp. I:** 207; **Retro. Supp. II:** 114; **Supp. I Part 1:** 49, 325; **Supp. III Part 1:** 73, 75, 76; **Supp. IV Part 1: 163–174; Supp. IX:** 306, 309; **Supp. X:** 136, 140; **Supp. XIII:** 186; **Supp. XVIII:** 122,131, 185, 279, 280, 282, 284; **Supp. XIX:** 78; **Supp. XXII:** 3, 6, 7, 8

"Cultivation of Christmas Trees, The" (Eliot), **I:** 579

"Cult of Personality in American Letters, The" (Swados), **Supp. XIX:** 265

"Cult of the Best, The" (Arnold), **I:** 223

"Cultural Exchange" (Hughes), **Supp. I Part 1:** 341

"Cultural Pluralism: A New American-ism" (Locke), **Supp. XIV:** 195

"Cultural Relativism and Ideological Peace" (Locke), **Supp. XIV:** 202, 212

"Culture" (Emerson), **III:** 2, 4

"Culture, Self, and Style" (Gass), **Supp. VI:** 88

"Culture and Religion" (Olds), **Supp. X:** 214

Culture of Cities, The (Mumford), **Supp. II Part 2:** 492, 494–495

Cummings, E. E., **I:** 44, 48, 64, 105, 176, **428–450,** 475, 477, 482, 526; **III:** 20, 196, 476; **IV:** 384, 402, 415, 427, 433; **Retro. Supp. II:** 178, 328; **Supp. I Part 2:** 622, 678; **Supp. III Part 1:** 73; **Supp. IV Part 2:** 637, 641; **Supp. IX:** 20; **Supp. XV:** 312, 338

Cummings, Robert, **Supp. IV Part 2:** 524

Cummins, Ann, **Supp. XXIII:** 280

Cummins, James, **Supp. XVII:** 74

Cunard, Lady, **III:** 459

Cunningham, J. V., **Supp. XV:** 169

Cunningham, Merce, **Supp. IV Part 1:** 83; **Supp. XV:** 187

Cunningham, Michael, **Supp. XII:** 80; **Supp. XV: 55–71**

Cunningham, Rodger, **Supp. XXIII:** 38–39

Cup of Gold (Steinbeck), **IV:** 51, 53, 61–64, 67

"Cupola, The" (Bogan), **Supp. III Part 1:** 53

"Curandera" (Mora), **Supp. XIII:** 214, 222

Curé de Tours, Le (Balzac), **I:** 509

Cure for Dreams, A: A Novel (Gibbons), **Supp. X: 45–47,** 48, 50

Curie, Marie, **IV:** 420, 421; **Supp. I Part 2:** 569

Curie, Pierre, **IV:** 420

Curiosa Americana (Mather), **Supp. II Part 2:** 463

Curiosities (Matthews), **Supp. IX:** 151, 152

"Curious Case of Sidd Finch, The" (Plimpton), **Supp. XVI:** 244

"Curious Shifts of the Poor" (Dreiser), **Retro. Supp. II:** 97

"Current" (Espaillat), **Supp. XXI:** 106

"Currents and Counter-Currents in Medical Science" (Holmes), **Supp. I Part 1:** 305

"Curried Cow" (Bierce), **I:** 200

Curry, Professor W. C., **IV:** 122

Curse of the Jade Scorpion, The (film; Allen), **Supp. XV:** 11

Curse of the Starving Class (Shepard), **Supp. III Part 2:** 433, 447–448

Curse of the Werewolf, The (film), **Supp. XVII:** 56

"Curse on a Thief, A" (X. J. Kennedy), **Supp. XV:** 171

"Curtain, The" (Chandler), **Supp. IV Part 1:** 122

Curtain Calls: British and American Women and the Theater, 1660–1820 (Saar), **Supp. XV:** 237

Curtain of Green, A (Welty), **IV:** 261–264, 268, 283

"Curtain of Green, A" (Welty), **IV:** 263–264

Curtain of Green and Other Stories, A (Welty), **Retro. Supp. I:** 343, 344, 345, 346, 347, 355

Curtain of Trees (opera), **Supp. IV Part 2:** 552

"Curtain Raiser, A" (Stein), **IV:** 43, 44

"Curtains" (Cisneros), **Supp. VII:** 66

Curtin, John, **Supp. IX:** 184

Curtis, George William, **Supp. I Part 1:** 307; **Supp. XVIII:** 3, 14

Curve (Goldbarth), **Supp. XII:** 181

Curve of Binding Energy, The (McPhee), **Supp. III Part 1:** 301

Curzon, Mary, **III:** 52

Cushing, Caleb, **Supp. I Part 2:** 684, 686

Cushman, Howard, **Supp. I Part 2:** 652

Cushman, Stephen, **Retro. Supp. I:** 430

"Custard Heart, The" (Parker), **Supp. IX:** 201

Custer, General George, **I:** 489, 491

Custer Died for Your Sins (Deloria), **Supp. IV Part 1:** 323; **Supp. IV Part 2:** 504

"Custody"(Schott), **Supp. XXIII:** 241

"Custom House, The" (Hawthorne), **II:** 223; **Retro. Supp. I:** 147–148, 157; **Supp. XXI:** 181

Custom of the Country, The (Wharton), **IV:** 318; **Retro. Supp. I:** 374, **375–376**

"Cut" (Plath), **Retro. Supp. II:** 253

"Cut-Glass Bowl, The" (Fitzgerald), **II:** 88

Cutting, Bronson, **III:** 600

Cutting Lisa (Everett), **Supp. XVIII:** 56

"Cuttings, *later*" (Roethke), **III:** 532

"Cyberpunk" (Bethke), **Supp. XVI:** 121

Cyberspace trilogy (W. Gibson). *See* Sprawl trilogy (W. Gibson)

"Cycles, The" (Pinsky), **Supp. VI:** 250–252

Cynic's Word Book, The (Bierce), **I:** 197, 205, 208, 209, 210

Cynthia Ozick (Lowin), **Supp. V:** 273

Cynthia Ozick's Comic Art (Cohen), **Supp. V:** 273

Cynthia Ozick's Fiction (Kauvar), **Supp. V:** 273

"Czeslaw Milosz and Memory" (Hampl), **Supp. XXII:** 92

D

Da Capo: Best Music Writing 2002 (Lethem, ed.), **Supp. XVIII:** 148

Dacey, Philip, **Supp. IV Part 1:** 70

Dacier, André, **II:** 10

"Dad" (Cullen), **Supp. IV Part 1:** 167

"Daddy" (Plath), **Retro. Supp. II:** 250–251; **Supp. I Part 2:** 529, 542, 545, 546; **Supp. II Part 2:** 688; **Supp. XXII:** 30; **Supp. XXIII:** 112, 113

"Daddy"(Hadas), **Supp. XXIII:** 112, 113

Daddy's Little Boy (Collins), **Supp. XXI:** 54

"Daemon, The" (Bogan), **Supp. III Part 1:** 58, 61

"Daemon Lover, The" (Jackson), **Supp. IX:** 116–117

"Daffodils" (Nelson and Espeland), **Supp. XVIII:** 181

"Daffodils" (Wordsworth), **Supp. XIII:** 284

"Daffy Duck in Hollywood" (Ashbery), **Supp. III Part 1:** 18

D'Agata, John, **Supp. XII:** 97, 98

Dago Red (Fante), **Supp. XI:** 160, 169

Dahl, Roald, **Supp. IX:** 114

Dahlberg, Edward, **I:** 231; **Retro. Supp. I:** 426; **Supp. III Part 2:** 624; **Supp. XIV:** 148; **Supp. XVIII:** 148; **Supp. XXII:** 257

Dahlberg, R'lene, **Supp. XIV:** 148

Daiches, David, **Retro. Supp. II:** 243; **Supp. I Part 2:** 536

Daily Horoscope (Gioia), **Supp. XV:** 112, **118–121,** 126

"Daily Horoscope" (Gioia), **Supp. XV:** 119

Daily Modernism (Podnieks), **Supp. X:** 189

Dain Curse, The (Hammett), **Supp. IV Part 1:** 348

"Daisies" (Glück), **Supp. V:** 88

"Daisy" (Oates), **Supp. II Part 2:** 523

Daisy (S. and A. Warner), **Supp. XVIII:** 268

Daisy-Head Mayzie (Geisel), **Supp. XVI:** 112

Daisy Miller (H. James), **Retro. Supp. I:** 216, 220, 222, 223, 228, 231; **Supp. XVIII:** 165

"Daisy Miller" (H. James), **II:** 325, 326, 327, 329; **IV:** 316

Dale, Charlie, **Supp. IV Part 2:** 584

Daley, Yvonne, **Supp. XXII:** 216

Dali, Salvador, **II:** 586; **Supp. IV Part 1:** 83; **Supp. XIII:** 317

Dalibard, Thomas-François, **II:** 117

"Dallas-Fort Worth: Redband and Mistletoe" (Clampitt), **Supp. IX:** 45

"Dalliance of Eagles, The" (Whitman), **IV:** 348

Dalva (Harrison), **Supp. VIII:** 37, 45, 46, **48–49**

Daly, Carroll John, **Supp. IV Part 1:** 343, 345

Daly, John, **II:** 25, 26

Daly, Julia Brown, **II:** 25, 26

"Dalyrimple Goes Wrong" (Fitzgerald), **II:** 88

"Dam, The" (Rukeyser), **Supp. VI:** 283

Damas, Leon, **Supp. X:** 139

Damascus Gate (Stone), **Supp. V:** 308–311

Damballah (Wideman), **Supp. X:** 319, 320, 321, 322, 323, 326, 327, 331, 333–334

Dameshek, Brandon, **Supp. XIX:** 273, 277, 287

Damnation of Theron Ware, The (Frederic), **II:** 140–143, 144, 146, 147; **Retro. Supp. I:** 325

Damned If I Do (Everett), **Supp. XVIII:** 66

"Damned Thing, The" (Bierce), **I:** 206

Damon, Matt, **Supp. VIII:** 175

Damon, S. Foster, **I:** 26; **II:** 512, 514, 515

"Damon and Vandalia" (Dove), **Supp. IV Part 1:** 252

Dana, H. W. L., **I:** 225

Dana, Richard Henry, **I:** 339, 351; **Supp. I Part 1:** 103, 154, 155; **Supp. I Part 2:** 414, 420

Dana, Richard Henry, Jr., **III:** 81; **Supp. XX:** 227

Dana, Robert, **Supp. V:** 178, 180

"Dana Gioia and Fine Press Printing" (Peich), **Supp. XV:** 117

"Dance" (Kenny), **Supp. XXIII:** 148

"Dance, The" (Crane), **I:** 109

"Dance, The" (Roethke), **III:** 541

"Dance, The" (W. C. Williams), **Supp. XVII:** 113

Dance and the Railroad, The (Hwang), **Supp. XXI:** 145, 146

Dance of Death, The (Auden), **Supp. II Part 1:** 10

Dance of Death, The (Bierce and Harcourt), **I:** 196

Dance of Life, The (Ellis), **Supp. XX:** **117**

Dance of the Sleepwalkers (Calabria), **Supp. XIII:** 164

"Dance of the Solids, The" (Updike), **Retro. Supp. I:** 323

"Dancer" (Hoffman), **Supp. XVIII:** 86

"Dancer, The" (Swados), **Supp. XIX:** 261, 263–264

"Dancers Work by Forgetting" (Espaillat), **Supp. XXI:** 102

"Dances of Madness" (Schott), **Supp. XXIII:** 245

Dances with Wolves (film), **Supp. X:** 124

Dance to the Music of Time, A (Powell), **Supp. XVIII:** 146

Dancing After Hours (Dubus), **Supp. VII:** 91

Dancing Back Strong the Nation (Kenny), **Supp. XXIII:** 144, **148**

Dancing Bears, The (Merwin), **Supp. III Part 1:** 343–344

Dancing on the Stones (Nichols), **Supp. XIII:** 256, 257, 259, 267, 269

"Dancing the Jig" (Sexton), **Supp. II Part 2:** 692

Dandelion Wine (Bradbury), **Supp. IV Part 1:** 101, 109–110

Dandurand, Karen, **Retro. Supp. I:** 30

"Dandy Frightening the Squatters, The" (Twain), **IV:** 193–194

Dangel, Mary Jo, **Supp. XVIII:** 156

Dangerous Crossroads (film), **Supp. XIII:** 163

Dangerous Moonlight (Purdy), **Supp. VII:** 278

"Dangerous Road Before Martin Luther King" (Baldwin), **Supp. I Part 1:** 52

"Dangerous Summer, The" (Hemingway), **II:** 261

Dangerous Thoughts (Ryan as Quin), **Supp. XVIII:** 226

"Dangers of Authorship, The" (Blackmur), **Supp. II Part 1:** 147

Dangling Man (Bellow), **I:** 144, 145, 147, 148, 150–151, 153–154, 158, 160, 161, 162, 163; **Retro. Supp. II:** 19, 20–21, 22, 23; **Supp. VIII:** 234; **Supp. XIX:** 157

"Dang Little Squirt" (Bontemps), **Supp. XXII:** 4

Daniel (biblical book), **Supp. I Part 1:** 105

Daniel (film), **Supp. IV Part 1:** 236

Daniel, Arnaut, **III:** 467

Daniel, Robert W., **III:** 76

Daniel, Samuel, **Supp. I Part 1:** 369

Daniel Deronda (G. Eliot), **I:** 458

Daniels, Frank, **Supp. XXII:** 196

Daniels, Kate, **Supp. XVII:** 112

Danielson, Linda, **Supp. IV Part 2:** 569

D'Annunzio, Gabriele, **II:** 515

Danny and the Deep Blue Sea: An Apache Dance (Shanley), **Supp. XIV:** 315, **318–319,** 320, 321, 323, 324

Danny O'Neill pentalogy (Farrell), **II:** 35–41

Danse Macabre (King), **Supp. IV Part 1:** 102; **Supp. V:** 144

"Danse Russe" (W. C. Williams), **IV:** 412–413

"Dans le Restaurant" (Eliot), **I:** 554, 578

Dans l'ombre des cathédrales (Ambelain), **Supp. I Part 1:** 273

Dante Alighieri, **I:** 103, 136, 138, 250, 384, 433, 445; **II:** 8, 274, 278, 289, 490, 492, 493, 494, 495, 504, 508, 524, 552; **III:** 13, 77, 124, 182, 259, 278, 448, 453, 467, 533, 607, 609, 610–612, 613; **IV:** 50, 134, 137, 138, 139, 247, 437, 438; **Retro. Supp. I:** 62, 63, 64, 66, 360; **Retro. Supp. II:** 330; **Supp. I Part 1:** 256, 363; **Supp. I Part 2:** 422, 454; **Supp. III Part 2:** 611, 618, 621; **Supp. IV Part 2:** 634; **Supp. V:** 277, 283, 331, 338, 345; **Supp. VIII:** 27, 219–221; **Supp. X:** 120, 121, 125; **Supp. XII:** 98; **Supp. XV:** 254; **Supp. XVII:** 227, 241

Danvis Tales: Selected Stories (Robinson; Budbill, ed.), **Supp. XIX:** 6

Danziger, Adolphe, **I:** 199–200

Danziger, Jeff, **Supp. XXII:** 208

Dar (Nabokov), **III:** 246, 255

D'Arcy, Randall, **Supp. XVII:** 76

Dardis, Tom, **Supp. XVIII:** 249

"Dare's Gift" (Glasgow), **II:** 190

Dark and Feeling, The: Black American Writers and Their Work (Major), **Supp. XXII:** 180

Dark Angel, The (Bolton), **Supp. I Part 1:** 281

"Dark Angel Travels With Us to Canada and Blesses Our Vacation, The" (Dunn), **Supp. XI:** 146

Dark Carnival (Bradbury), **Supp. IV Part 1:** 102

Darker (Strand), **Supp. IV Part 2:** 619, 626–628

Darker Face of the Earth, The (Dove), **Supp. IV Part 1:** 255–257

"Dark Fire" (Hadas), **Supp. XXIII:** 126

Dark Green, Bright Red (Vidal), **Supp. IV Part 2:** 677

Dark Half, The (King), **Supp. V:** 141

Dark Harbor: A Poem (Strand), **Supp. IV Part 2:** 633–634

"Dark Hills, The" (Robinson), **III:** 523

Dark Horses (X. J. Kennedy), **Supp. XV:** **167–170**

Dark Hours, The (W. V. Davis), **Supp. XXI: 91–92,** 93

Dark Laughter (Anderson), **I:** 111, 116; **II:** 250–251

"Darkling Alphabet, A" (Snodgrass), **Supp. VI:** 323

Darkling Child (Merwin and Milroy), **Supp. III Part 1:** 346

"Darkling Summer, Ominous Dusk, Rumorous Rain" (Schwartz), **Supp. II Part 2:** 661

"Darkling Thrush" (Hardy), **Supp. IX:** 40

"Dark Men, The" (Dubus), **Supp. VII:** 86

Dark Mirrors (Sobin), **Supp. XVI:** 295

Dark Mother, The (W. Frank), **Supp. XX:** 70–71

Dark Mountains, The (Hoffman), **Supp. XVIII:** 76–77

Darkness and the Light, The (Hecht), **Supp. X:** 58

Darkness at Noon (Koestler), **Supp. XXIII:** 1

Darkness More Than Night, A (Connelly), **Supp. XXI: 73–74,** 80

"Darkness on the Edge of Town" (O'Brien), **Supp. V:** 246

Darkness Surrounding Us, The (Sorrentino), **Supp. XXI:** 227, 228

Darkness under the Trees/Walking behind the Spanish (Salinas), **Supp. XIII:** 311, 319–324

"Dark Night" (St. John of the Cross), **Supp. XV:** 30

Dark Night of the Soul, The (St. John of the Cross), **I:** 1, 585

"Dark Ones" (Dickey), **Supp. IV Part 1:** 182

Dark Power (Holding), **Supp. XXII: 122–123,** 124

Dark Princess: A Romance (Du Bois), **Supp. II Part 1:** 179, 181–182

Dark Room, The (T. Williams), **IV:** 381

Dark Sacred Night (CD), **Supp. XXI:** 75

Dark Shadows (television show), **Supp. XIX:** 57

"Dark Summer" (Bogan), **Supp. III Part 1:** 51, 53

Dark Summer: Poems (Bogan), **Supp. III Part 1:** 52–53, 57

"Dark Tower, The" (column), **Supp. IV Part 1:** 168, 170

Dark Tower, The: The Gunslinger (King), **Supp. V:** 152

Dark Tower IV, The: Wizard and Glass (King), **Supp. V:** 139

Dark Tunnel, The (Macdonald as Millar), **Supp. IV Part 2:** 465, 466

"Dark TV Screen" (Simic), **Supp. VIII:** 282

"Dark Voyage, The" (McLay), **Supp. XIII:** 21

"Dark Walk, The" (Taylor), **Supp. V:** 320–321, 322, 326

Darkwater: Voices from Within the Veil (Du Bois), **Supp. II Part 1:** 178, 180, 183

Dark Waves and Light Matter (Goldbarth), **Supp. XII:** 176, 193

Dark World (Carruth), **Supp. XVI:** 55

"Darling" (Nye), **Supp. XIII:** 283–284

"Darling, The" (Chekhov), **Supp. IX:** 202

Darling-Darling (Barillet and Grédy; Loos, trans.), **Supp. XVI:** 194

Darnell, Linda, **Supp. XII:** 173

Darragh, Tina, **Supp. IV Part 2:** 427

Darreu, Robert Donaldson, **Supp. II Part 1:** 89, 98, 102

Darrow, Clarence, **Supp. I Part 1:** 5; **Supp. I Part 2:** 455

Dartmouth, Earl of, **Supp. XX: 284**

Darwin, Charles, **I:** 457; **II:** 323, 462, 481; **III:** 226, 231; **IV:** 69, 304; **Retro. Supp. I:** 254; **Retro. Supp. II:** 60, 65; **Supp. I Part 1:** 368; **Supp. IX:** 180; **Supp. XI:** 203; **Supp. XVI:** 13; **Supp. XX: 18**

"Darwin in 1881" (Schnackenberg), **Supp. XV:** 253, 254, 258

Daryush, Elizabeth, **Supp. V:** 180

Dasburg, Andrew, **Supp. XXI:** 6

Dash, Julie, **Supp. XI:** 17, 18, 20

Dashell, Alfred, **Supp. X:** 224

"DAS KAPITAL" (Baraka), **Supp. II Part 1:** 55

Datlow, Ellen, **Supp. XVI:** 123

"Datum Centurio" (Wallace), **Supp. X:** 309

Daudet, Alphonse, **II:** 325, 338

"Daughter" (Caldwell), **I:** 309

"Daughter in the House" (X. J. Kennedy), **Supp. XV:** 160

Daughter of Earth (Smedly), **Supp. XIII:** 295

Daughter of the Land, A (Stratton-Porter), **Supp. XX: 222**

Daughter of the Snows, A (London), **II:** 465, 469–470

"Daughters" (Anderson), **I:** 114

Daughters (Marshall), **Supp. XI:** 275, 276, 277, **286–288,** 289, 290

"Daughters, 1900" (Nelson), **Supp. XVIII:** 175

Daughters, I Love You (Hogan), **Supp. IV Part 1:** 397, 399, 401

"Daughters of Invention" (Alvarez), **Supp. VII:** 9

Daughters of the Dust (Dash; film), **Supp. XI:** 17, 18; **Supp. XX: 154**

Daumier, Honoré, **IV:** 412

Dave, R. A., **Supp. VIII:** 126

Davenport, Abraham, **Supp. I Part 2:** 699

Davenport, Gary, **Supp. IX:** 98

Davenport, Guy, **Supp. XIV:** 96; **Supp. XXI:** 235

Davenport, Herbert J., **Supp. I Part 2:** 642

Davenport, James, **I:** 546

Daves, E. G., **Supp. I Part 1:** 369

Davey, Frank, **Supp. XIII:** 33

"David" (Garrett), **Supp. VII:** 109–110

"David" (Gordon), **Supp. IV Part 1:** 298–299

David, Gray, **Supp. XX: 260**

"David and Agnes, a Romance" (Keillor), **Supp. XVI:** 175

David Blaize (Benson), **Supp. XX: 234**

David Copperfield (Dickens), **I:** 458; **II:** 290; **Retro. Supp. I:** 33; **Supp. XVI:** 65, 72; **Supp. XX: 234**

"David Crockett's Other Life" (Nye), **Supp. XIII:** 282

Davideis (Cowley), **IV:** 158

David Harum (Westcott), **I:** 216

"David Lynch Keeps His Head" (Wallace), **Supp. X:** 314

David Show, The (Gurney), **Supp. V:** 97

Davidson, Cathy, **Supp. XV:** 238

Davidson, Donald, **I:** 294; **III:** 495, 496; **IV:** 121, 122, 124, 125, 236; **Supp. II Part 1:** 139; **Supp. XIV:** 2; **Supp. XX: 164**

Davidson, James West, **Supp. XXII:** 218

Davidson, Jo, **Supp. XXI:** 7

Davidson, John, **Retro. Supp. I:** 55

Davidson, Michael, **Supp. VIII:** 290, 293, 294, 302–303

Davidson, Phebe, **Supp. XXIII:** 252

Davidson, Sara, **Supp. IV Part 1:** 196, 198, 203

Davidson, Sue, **Supp. XIX:** 260

Davidsz de Heem, Jan, **Supp. XI:** 133

Davie, Donald, **III:** 478; **Supp. IV Part 2:** 474; **Supp. V:** 331; **Supp. X:** 55, 59; **Supp. XVII:** 111, 112, 121

Davies, Arthur, **III:** 273

Davies, Sir John, **III:** 541

Davies, Marion, **Supp. XVI:** 186

Da Vinci, Leonardo, **I:** 274; **II:** 536; **III:** 210

Davis, Allen F., **Supp. I Part 1:** 1, 7

Davis, Allison, **Supp. I Part 1:** 327

Davis, Angela, **Supp. I Part 1:** 66; **Supp. X:** 249

Davis, Arthur B., **Supp. XVIII:** 119

Davis, Bette, **I:** 78; **Supp. I Part 1:** 67

Davis, Bill, **Supp. XIII:** 267

Davis, Christina, **Supp. XV:** 264

Davis, Cynthia, **Supp. XVIII:** 281, 286

Davis, Donald, **Supp. XIII:** 93

Davis, Elizabeth Gould, **Supp. I Part 2:** 567

Davis, George, **II:** 586

Davis, Glover, **Supp. V:** 180, 182, 186

Davis, Jefferson, **II:** 206; **IV:** 122, 125, 126

Davis, Jordan, **Supp. XV:** 178, 181, 186, 188

Davis, Katie, **Supp. VIII:** 83

Davis, L. J., **Supp. XI:** 234

Davis, Lydia, **Supp. XII:** 24; **Supp. XVII:** 21

Davis, Marcia, **Supp. XVIII:** 91, 100

Davis, Mary H., **Supp. XVIII:** 77

Davis, Miles, **Supp. XV:** 346; **Supp. XXII:** 172

Davis, Ossie, Jr., **Supp. IV Part 1:** 362; **Supp. XVI:** 144

Davis, Rebecca Harding, **Supp. I Part 1:** 45; **Supp. XIII:** 292, 295, 305; **Supp. XVI: 79–96**

Davis, Richard Harding, **III:** 328; **Supp. II Part 1:** 393; **Supp. XVI:** 85

Davis, Robert Gorham, **II:** 51; **IV:** 108

Davis, Stuart, **IV:** 409; **Supp. XV:** 295; **Supp. XXI:** 6

Davis, Thadious, **Supp. XVIII:** 120, 121, 123, 127, 129

Davis, Thulani, **Supp. XI:** 179; **Supp. XIII:** 233, 234, 239

Davis, William Virgil, **Supp. IV Part 1:** 63, 64, 68, 69, 70; **Supp. XXI: 83–96**

Davison, Peter, **Supp. XXI:** 91

Davy's Lake (M. Finch), **Supp. XVII:** 69

Dawn (Dreiser), **I:** 498, 499, 503, 509, 515, 519

Dawn (O. Butler), **Supp. XIII:** 63, **64**

"Dawnbreaker" (Hayden), **Supp. II Part 1:** 370

Dawn in Russia (W. Frank), **Supp. XX: 76**

Dawn Patrol, The (film), **Supp. XIV:** 81

"Dawn Patrol: A Review of the Literature of the Negro for 1948" (Locke), **Supp. XIV:** 211

Dawson, Edward, **IV:** 151

Dawson, Emma, **I:** 199

Dawson, Ruth, **Supp. XI:** 120

Day, Dorothy, **II:** 215; **Supp. I Part 2:** 524; **Supp. X:** 142

Day, Fred Holland, **Supp. XX: 114, 115**

Day, Georgiana, **Supp. I Part 2:** 585

Day, Richard, **Supp. XVIII:** 251

Dayan, Joan, **Retro. Supp. II:** 270

"Day Book" (Notley), **Supp. XXII:** 230

Day Book, A (Creeley), **Supp. IV Part 1:** 155

"Daybreak" (Kinnell), **Supp. III Part 1:** 250

"Daybreak Blues" (Kees), **Supp. XV:** 133

"Day-Breakers, The" (Bontemps), **Supp. XXII:** 8

"Daybreak in Alabama" (Hughes), **Retro. Supp. I:** 211; **Supp. I Part 1:** 344

Day by Day (Lowell), **Retro. Supp. II:** 184, 186, 191

"Day-Care Field Trip: Aquarium" (Karr), **Supp. XI:** 243

"Day-Dream, A" (Bryant), **Supp. I Part 1:** 160

"Day-Dream of a Grocer, The" (Twain), **Supp. XVIII:** 9

"Day for Poetry and Song, A" (Douglass), **Supp. III Part 1:** 172

"Day in the Life of Half of Rumpelstiltskin, A" (Brockmeier), **Supp. XXII:** 50, 52, 53

"Day Lady Died, The" (O'Hara), **Supp. XIX:** 85; **Supp. XXIII:** 216, 219

Day Late and a Dollar Short, A (McMillan), **Supp. XIII:** 184, **Supp. XIII:** 185, **191–192**

"Day longs for the evening, The" (Levertov), **Supp. III Part 1:** 274

Daynard, Jodi, **Supp. XVIII:** 97

Day of a Stranger (Merton), **Supp. VIII:** 203

"Day of Days, A" (James), **II:** 322

Day of Doom (Wigglesworth), **IV:** 147, 155, 156

Day of the Body (C. Frost), **Supp. XV:** 93, **98–100**, 106

Day of the Locust, The (West), **I:** 298; **IV:** 288, 299–306; **Retro. Supp. II:** 321, 323, 324, 329, **337–338; Supp.**

II Part 2: 626; **Supp. XI:** 296; **Supp. XII:** 173; **Supp. XIII:** 170; **Supp. XIV:** 328; **Supp. XVIII:** 246

"Day on the Big Branch, A" (Nemerov), **III:** 275–276

"Day on the Connecticut River, A" (Merrill), **Supp. III Part 1:** 336

Day Room, The (DeLillo), **Supp. VI:** 4

"Days" (Emerson), **II:** 19, 20

"Days and Nights" (Koch), **Supp. XV:** 179, 180

"Days and Nights: A Journal" (Price), **Supp. VI:** 265

Days Before, The (Porter), **III:** 433, 453

Days in the Yellow Leaf (Hoffman), **Supp. XVIII:** 75

"Days of 1935" (Merrill), **Supp. III Part 1:** 325, 328

"Days of 1941 and '44" (Merrill), **Supp. III Part 1:** 336

"Days of 1964" (Merrill), **Supp. III Part 1:** 328, 352

"Days of 1971" (Merrill), **Supp. III Part 1:** 328

"Days of 1981" (Doty), **Supp. XI:** 123

"Days of Awe: The Birth of Lucy Jane" (Wasserstein), **Supp. XV:** 332

"Days of Edward Hopper" (Haines), **Supp. XII:** 210

"Days of Heaven" (Bass), **Supp. XVI:** 20

Days of Obligation: An Argument with My Mexican Father (Rodriguez), **Supp. XIV:** 298, 300, **302–305,** 307, 310

Days of Our Lives (soap opera), **Supp. XI:** 83

Days of Our Lives Lie in Fragments: New and Old Poems (Garrett), **Supp. VII:** 109–110, 111

Days of the Phoenix (Brooks), **I:** 266

Days of Wine and Roses (J. P. Miller), **Supp. XIII:** 262

Days: Tangier Journal, 1987–1989 (Bowles), **Supp. IV Part 1:** 94

Days to Come (Hellman), **Supp. I Part 1:** 276, 277–278

Days without End (O'Neill), **III:** 385, 391, 397

"Day's Work, A" (Capote), **Supp. III Part 1:** 120

"Day's Work, A" (Porter), **III:** 443, 446

"Day the Presidential Candidate Came to Ciudad Tamaulipas, The" (Caldwell), **I:** 309

"Day the Singer Fell, The" (Swados), **Supp. XIX:** 258

Day the World ended, The (Coover), **Supp. V:** 1

"Day with Conrad Green, A" (Lardner), **II:** 428–429, 430

"Deacon's Masterpiece, The" (Holmes), **Supp. I Part 1:** 302, 307

"Dead, The" (Collins), **Supp. XXI:** 64

"Dead, The" (Joyce), **I:** 285; **III:** 343; **Supp. XXIII:** 71

Dead and the Living, The (Olds), **Supp. X:** 201, **204–206,** 207

"Dead Body, The" (Olds), **Supp. X:** 210

"Dead by the Side of the Road, The" (Snyder), **Supp. VIII:** 301

"Dead Doe" (B. Kelly), **Supp. XVII:** 128–129

Dead End (Kingsley), **Supp. I Part 1:** 277, 281

Dead Father, The (Barthelme), **Supp. IV Part 1:** 43, 47, 50–51

"Dead Fiddler, The" (Singer), **IV:** 20

Dead Fingers Talk (Burroughs), **Supp. III Part 1:** 103

"Dead Hand" series (Sinclair), **Supp. V:** 276, 277, 281

"Dead Languages, The" (Humphrey), **Supp. IX:** 109

Dead Lecturer, The (Baraka), **Supp. II Part 1:** 31, 33, 35–37, 49

Dead Letters Sent (Kenny), **Supp. XXIII:** 143, 145

"Dead Letters Sent (By the Ontario Shores)"(Kenny), **Supp. XXIII:** 145

Deadline at Dawn (Odets), **Supp. II Part 2:** 546

"Dead-Lock and Its Key, A" (E. Stoddard), **Supp. XV:** 286

"Dead Loon, The" (Bynner), **Supp. XV: 44–45**

Deadly Affair, A (Lacy), **Supp. XV:** 205–206

Deadly is the Female (film), **Supp. XVII:** 62

Dead Man's Walk (McMurtry), **Supp. V:** 231, 232

Dead Man's Walk (screenplay; McMurtry and Ossana), **Supp. V:** 231

Dead Man Walking (opera libretto, McNally), **Supp. XIII:** 207

Dead Poets Society (film), **Supp. XXI:** 192, 193, 194, 199

"Dead Reckoning" (Jarman), **Supp. XVII:** 113

"Dead Soldier's Talk, The" (Jin), **Supp. XVIII:** 92

Dead Souls (Gogol), **I:** 296

"Dead Souls on Campus" (Kosinski), **Supp. VII:** 222

"Dead Wingman, The" (Jarrell), **II:** 374

"Dead Wood, Green Wood" (Hadas), **Supp. XXIII:** 120

"Dead Yellow Women" (Hammett), **Supp. IV Part 1:** 345

Dead Zone, The (King), **Supp. V:** 139, 143, 144, 148, 152

Dean, James, **I:** 493

Dean, Man Mountain, **II:** 589

Deane, Silas, **Supp. I Part 2:** 509, 524

"Dean of Men" (Taylor), **Supp. V:** 314, 323

Dean's December, The (Bellow), **Retro. Supp. II:** 30–31

"Dear Adolph" (Benét), **Supp. XI:** 46

"Dear America" (Ortiz), **Supp. IV Part 2:** 503

"Dear Dark Continent" (Notley), **Supp. XXII:** 223

"Dearest M—" (Carruth), **Supp. XVI:** 59

"Dear Judas" (Jeffers), **Supp. II Part 2:** 431–432, 433

Dear Juliette (Sarton), **Supp. VIII:** 265

Dear Lovely Death (Hughes), **Retro. Supp. I:** 203; **Supp. I Part 1:** 328

Dear Rafe (Hinojosa), **Supp. XIX:** 98, **105–106**

"Dear Villon" (Corso), **Supp. XII:** 135

"Dear World" (Gunn Allen), **Supp. IV Part 1:** 321

Deasy, Philip, **Supp. XX: 42**

Death (Allen), **Supp. XV:** 3

"Death" (Corso), **Supp. XII:** 127

"Death" (Lowell), **II:** 536

"Death" (Mailer), **III:** 38

"Death" (W. C. Williams), **Retro. Supp. I:** 422

"Death" (West), **IV:** 286

"Death and Absence" (Glück), **Supp. V:** 82

Death and Birth of David Markand, The (W. Frank), **Supp. XX: 76–77**

Death and Taxes (Parker), **Supp. IX:** 192

"Death and the Child" (Crane), **I:** 414

"Death as a Society Lady" (Hecht), **Supp. X:** 71–72

Death before Bedtime (Vidal as Box), **Supp. IV Part 2:** 682

"Death Be Not Proud" (Donne), **Supp. XVI:** 158

"Death by Water" (Eliot), **I:** 395, 578

Death Comes for the Archbishop (Cather), **I:** 314, 327, 328–330; **Retro. Supp. I:** 16–18, 21; **Supp. XIII:** 253

Death in Paradise (Parker), **Supp. XIX:** 186

Death in the Afternoon (Hemingway), **II:** 253; **IV:** 35; **Retro. Supp. I:** 182; **Supp. VIII:** 182; **Supp. XVI:** 205; **Supp. XIX:** 246; **Supp. XX:** 76

"Death in the Country, A" (Benét), **Supp. XI:** 53–54

Death in the Family, A (Agee), **I:** 25, 29, 42, 45

Death in the Fifth Position (Vidal as Box), **Supp. IV Part 2:** 682

"Death in the Woods" (Anderson), **I:** 114, 115

Death in the Woods and Other Stories (Anderson), **I:** 112, 114, 115

Death in Venice (Mann), **III:** 231; **Supp. IV Part 1:** 392; **Supp. V:** 51

"Death in Viet Nam" (Salinas), **Supp. XIII:** 315

"Death in Winter" (C. Frost), **Supp. XV:** 98

Death Is a Lonely Business (Bradbury), **Supp. IV Part 1:** 102, 103, 111–112, 115

"Death Is Not the End" (Wallace), **Supp. X:** 309

Death Is the Place (Bronk), **Supp. XXI:** 32

Death Kit (Sontag), **Supp. III Part 2:** 451, 468–469

Death Likes It Hot (Vidal as Box), **Supp. IV Part 2:** 682

"*Death*/Muerta" (Mora), **Supp. XIII:** 228

Death Notebooks, The (Sexton), **Supp. II Part 2:** 691, 694, 695

"Death of a Columnist" (Siddons), **Supp. XXII:** 241–242

Death of Adam, The: Essays on Modern Thought (Robinson), **Supp. XXI:** 212

"Death of a Jazz Musician" (W. J. Smith), **Supp. XIII:** 334

Death of a Kinsman, The (Taylor), **Supp. V:** 324, 326

"Death of an Old Seaman" (Hughes), **Retro. Supp. I:** 199

"Death of a Pig" (White), **Supp. I Part 2:** 665–668

Death of a Salesman (A. Miller), **I:** 81; **III:** 148, 149, 150, 153–154, 156, 157, 158, 159, 160, 163, 164, 166; **IV:** 389; **Supp. IV Part 1:** 359; **Supp. XIV:** 102, 239, 254, 255; **Supp. XV:** 205; **Supp. XX: 27; Supp. XXIII:** 199

"Death of a Soldier, The" (Stevens), **Retro. Supp. I:** 299, 312. *see also* "Lettres d'un Soldat" (Stevens)

"Death of a Soldier, The" (Wilson), **IV:** 427, 445

"Death of a Toad" (Wilbur), **Supp. III Part 2:** 550

"Death of a Traveling Salesman" (Welty), **IV:** 261; **Retro. Supp. I:** 344

"Death of a Young Son by Drowning" (Atwood), **Supp. XIII:** 33

Death of Bessie Smith, The (Albee), **I:** 76–77, 92

Death of Billy the Kid, The (Vidal), **Supp. IV Part 2:** 683

Death of Cock Robin, The (Snodgrass), **Supp. VI:** 315, **317–319,** 324

Death of Dreams, A (Hoffman), **Supp. XVIII:** 79

"Death of General Wolfe, The" (Paine), **Supp. I Part 2:** 504

"Death of Halpin Frayser, The" (Bierce), **I:** 205

"Death of Justina, The" (Cheever), **Supp. I Part 1:** 184–185

Death of Life, The (Barnes), **Supp. III Part 1:** 34

Death of Malcolm X, The (Baraka), **Supp. II Part 1:** 47

"Death of Marilyn Monroe, The" (Olds), **Supp. X:** 205

"Death of Me, The" (Malamud), **Supp. I Part 2:** 437

"Death of Slavery, The" (Bryant), **Supp. I Part 1:** 168–169

"Death of St. Narcissus, The" (Eliot), **Retro. Supp. I:** 291

"Death of the Ball Turret Gunner, The" (Jarrell), **II:** 369–370, 372, 374, 375, 376, 378

"Death of the Fathers, The" (Sexton), **Supp. II Part 2:** 692

"Death of the Flowers, The" (Bryant), **Supp. I Part 1:** 170

Death of the Fox (Garrett), **Supp. VII:** 99, 101–104, 108

"Death of the Hat, The" (Collins), **Supp. XXI:** 59

"Death of the Hired Man, The" (Frost), **III:** 523; **Retro. Supp. I:** 121, 128; **Supp. IX:** 261

Death of the Kapowsin Tavern (Hugo), **Supp. VI:** 133–135

"Death of the Kapowsin Tavern" (Hugo), **Supp. VI:** 137, 141

"Death of the Lyric, The: The Achievement of Louis Simpson" (Jarman and McDowell), **Supp. IX:** 266, 270, 276

"Death of Venus, The" (Creeley), **Supp. IV Part 1:** 143, 144–145

"Death on All Fronts" (Ginsberg), **Supp. II Part 1:** 326

"Deaths" (Dunn), **Supp. XI:** 147

"Death Sauntering About" (Hecht), **Supp. X:** 72

Deaths for the Ladies (and Other Disasters) (Mailer), **Retro. Supp. II:** 203

Death's Jest-Book (Beddoes), **Retro. Supp. I:** 285

Death Song (McGrath), **Supp. X:** 127

"Death the Carnival Barker" (Hecht), **Supp. X:** 72

"Death the Film Director" (Hecht), **Supp. X:** 72

"Death the Judge" (Hecht), **Supp. X:** 72

"Death the Mexican Revolutionary" (Hecht), **Supp. X:** 72

"Death the Oxford Don" (Hecht), **Supp. X:** 72

"Death the Painter" (Hecht), **Supp. X:** 72

Death the Proud Brother (Wolfe), **IV:** 456

"Death to Van Gogh's Ear!" (Ginsberg), **Supp. II Part 1:** 320, 322, 323

"Death Warmed Over!" (Bradbury), **Supp. IV Part 1:** 104–105, 112

Death Wish, The (Holding), **Supp. XXII:** 120, **123,** 134, 135

Débâcle, La (Zola), **III:** 316

"Debate with the Rabbi" (Nemerov), **III:** 272

Debeljak, Aleš, **Supp. VIII:** 272

De Bellis, Jack, **Supp. I Part 1:** 366, 368, 372

Debo, Annette, **Supp. XXI:** 254

DeBoer-Langworthy, Carol, **Supp. XVII:** 98, 99, 100

De Bosis, Lauro, **IV:** 372

"Debriefing" (Sontag), **Supp. III Part 2:** 468–470

Debs, Eugene, **I:** 483, 493; **III:** 580, 581; **Supp. I Part 2:** 524; **Supp. IX:** 1, 15; **Supp. XXIII:** 161, 162

Debt to Pleasure, The (Lanchester), **Retro. Supp. I:** 278

Debussy, Claude, **Retro. Supp. II:** 266; **Supp. XIII:** 44

"Decades" (Sorrentino), **Supp. XXI:** 229

Decameron (Boccaccio), **III:** 283, 411; **Supp. IX:** 215

"Deceased" (Hughes), **Retro. Supp. I:** 208

"December" (Oliver), **Supp. VII:** 245

"December 1, 1994" (Stern), **Supp. IX:** 299

December 7 (film, Ford), **Supp. XVIII:** 247

"December 24" (Di Piero), **Supp. XIX:** 39

"December 28: Returning to Chicago" (Di Piero), **Supp. XIX:** 39

"December Dawn" (Skloot), **Supp. XX: 202**

"December Eclogue" (Winters), **Supp. II Part 2:** 794

"Decent Woman, A" (Boulton), **Supp. XXII:** 22–23

De Cenzo, Giorgia, **Supp. XXI:** 256

Deception (P. Roth), **Retro. Supp. II:** 291; **Supp. III Part 2:** 426–427

"Deceptions" (Dobyns), **Supp. XIII:** 77

De Chiara, Ann. *See* Malamud, Mrs. Bernard (Ann de Chiara)

De Chirico, Giorgio, **Supp. XIII:** 317

"Decided Loss, A" (Poe), **II:** 411

"Decisions to Disappear" (Dunn), **Supp. XI:** 144

"Decisive Moment, The" (Auster), **Supp. XIV:** 292

Decker, James A., **Supp. III Part 2:** 621

Declaration of Gentlemen and Merchants and Inhabitants of Boston, and the Country Adjacent, A (Mather), **Supp. II Part 2:** 450

"Declaration of Paris, The" (Adams), **I:** 4

Declaration of the Rights of Man and the Citizen, **Supp. I Part 2:** 513, 519

Declaration of Universal Peace and Liberty (Paine), **Supp. I Part 2:** 512

Declension in the Village of Chung Luong (Weigl), **Supp. XIX:** 287, 288

Decline and Fall (Waugh), **Supp. I Part 2:** 607; **Supp. XV:** 142

Decline and Fall of the English System of Finance, The (Paine), **Supp. I Part 2:** 518

Decline and Fall of the Roman Empire, The (Gibbons), **Supp. III Part 2:** 629

"Decline of Book Reviewing, The" (Hardwick), **Supp. III Part 1:** 201–202

Decline of the West, The (Spengler), **I:** 270; **IV:** 125

"Decolonizing the Tongue: Reading Speech and Aphasia in the Work of Michelle Cliff" (Aguiar), **Supp. XXII:** 68

Deconstructing Harry (film; Allen), **Supp. XV:** 12, **13**

"Décor" (X. J. Kennedy), **Supp. XV:** 171

"Decoration Day" (Jewett), **II:** 412; **Retro. Supp. II:** 138

Decoration of Houses, The (Wharton and Codman), **IV:** 308; **Retro. Supp. I:** 362, 363–364, 366

"Decoy" (Ashbery), **Supp. III Part 1:** 13–14

Decter, Midge, **Supp. XX:** 248

Dedalus, Stephen, **Supp. XIX:** 47

"De Daumier-Smith's Blue Period" (Salinger), **III:** 560–561

"Dedication" (Nelson), **Supp. XVIII:** 173, 180

"Dedication and Household Map" (Erdrich), **Supp. IV Part 1:** 272

"Dedication Day" (Agee), **I:** 34

"Dedication for a Book" (Hay), **Supp. XIV:** 125

"Dedication for a Book of Criticism" (Winters), **Supp. II Part 2:** 801

"Dedication in Postscript, A" (Winters), **Supp. II Part 2:** 801

Dedications and Other Darkhorses (Komunyakaa), **Supp. XIII:** 112, **113–114**

"Dedication to Hunger" (Glück), **Supp. V:** 83

"Dedication to My Wife, A" (Eliot), **I:** 583

Dee, Jonathan, **Supp. XXIII:** 302

Dee, Ruby, **Supp. IV Part 1:** 362

Deeds of Utmost Kindness (Gander), **Supp. XV:** 340

Deegan, Thomas, **Supp. XXIII:** 100, 107–108

"Deep Breath at Dawn, A" (Hecht), **Supp. X:** 58

Deep End, The (film), **Supp. XXII:** 120, 131, 133

Deeper into Movies: The Essential Kael Collection from '69 to '72 (Kael), **Supp. IX:** 253

"Deeper Wisdom, The" (Hay), **Supp. XIV:** 129

Deep Green Sea (R. O. Butler), **Supp. XII:** 62, **74**

Deephaven (Jewett), **II:** 398–399, 400, 401, 410, 411; **Retro. Supp. II:** 133, 134, 135, 136, 137, 138, 140, 141, 143, 144

"Deep Sight and Rescue Missions" (Bambara), **Supp. XI:** 18–19

Deep Sightings and Rescue Missions: Fiction, Essays, and Conversations (Bambara), **Supp. XI:** 1, 3, **14–20**

Deep Sleep, The (Morris), **III:** 224–225

Deep South (Caldwell), **I:** 305, 309, 310

Deepstep Come Shining (Wright), **Supp. XV:** 337, 341, 344, **349–350**, 351, 353

"Deep Water" (Marquand), **III:** 56

"Deep Woods" (Nemerov), **III:** 272–273, 275

"Deer at Providencia, The" (Dillard), **Supp. VI:** 28, 32

Deer Camp: Last Light in the Northeast Kingdom (Ostrum, ed.), **Supp. XXII:** 218

"Deer Dancer" (Harjo), **Supp. XII:** 224–225

"Deer Ghost" (Harjo), **Supp. XII:** 225

Deer Park, The (Mailer), **I:** 292; **III:** 27, 31–33, 35–36, 37, 39, 40, 42, 43, 44; **Retro. Supp. II: 200–202,** 205, 207, 211

Deer Park, The: A Play (Mailer), **Retro. Supp. II:** 205

Deer Pasture, The (Bass), **Supp. XVI:** 15, 16, 23

Deerslayer, The (Cooper), **I:** 341, 349, 350, 355; **Supp. I Part 1:** 251

Defence, The (Nabokov), **Supp. XXII:** 263

"Defence of Poesie, The" (Bronk), **Supp. XXI:** 32

"Defence of Poesy, The" (Sidney), **Supp. V:** 250

"Defence of Poetry" (Longfellow), **II:** 493–494

"Defender of the Faith" (P. Roth), **Retro. Supp. II:** 281; **Supp. III Part 2:** 404, 407, 420

"Defending *The Searchers* (Scenes in the Life of an Obsession)" *(Lethem),* **Supp. XVIII:** 136,141

"Defenestration in Prague" (Matthews), **Supp. IX:** 168

Defenestration of Prague (Howe), **Supp. IV Part 2:** 419, 426, 429–430

Defense, The (Nabokov), **III:** 251–252; **Retro. Supp. I:** 266, 268, **270–272**

"Defense of Poetry" (Francis), **Supp. IX:** 83–84

DeFeo, Ronald, **Supp. XXIII:** 106

Defiant Ones, The (film), **Supp. I Part 1:** 67

"Defining the Age" (W. V. Davis), **Supp. IV Part 1:** 64

"Definition" (Ammons), **Supp. VII:** 28

Defoe, Daniel, **I:** 204; **II:** 104, 105, 159, 304–305; **III:** 113, 423; **IV:** 180; **Supp. I Part 2:** 523; **Supp. V:** 127

De Forest, John William, **II:** 275, 280, 288, 289; **IV:** 350

DeFrees, Madeline, **Supp. XVIII:** 293

"Deganawidah: The Peacemaker" (Kenny), **Supp. XXIII:** 151

Degas, Brian, **Supp. XI:** 307

Degler, Carl, **Supp. I Part 2:** 496

"Degrees of Fidelity" (Dunn), **Supp. XI:** 148, 156

Deguy, Michel, **Supp. XV:** 178

De Haven, Tom, **Supp. XI:** 39; **Supp. XII:** 338–339

Deitch, Joseph, **Supp. VIII:** 125

"Dejection" (Coleridge), **II:** 97

DeJong, Constance, **Supp. XII:** 4

DeJong, David Cornel, **I:** 35

Dekker, Thomas, **Supp. XVII:** 232

de Kooning, Elaine de, **Supp. XXIII:** 210, 217

de Kooning, Willem, **Supp. XII:** 198; **Supp. XV:** 177, 178

de Kooning, Willem de, **Supp. XXIII:** 208, 210, 211, 217, 220

Delacroix, Henri, **I:** 227

De La Mare, Walter, **III:** 429; **Supp. II Part 1:** 4; **Supp. XVII:** 69

Delamotte, Eugenia C., **Supp. XI:** 279

De Lancey, James, **I:** 338

De Lancey, Mrs. James (Anne Heathcote), **I:** 338

De Lancey, Susan A. *See* Cooper, Mrs. James Fenimore

De Lancey, William Heathcote, **I:** 338, 353

Delano, Amasa, **III:** 90

Delattre, Roland A., **I:** 558

De Laurentiis, Dino, **Supp. XI:** 170, 307

De la Valdéne, Guy, **Supp. VIII:** 40, 42

Delbanco, Nicholas, **Supp. XXII:** 204

Del Cabral, Manuel, **Supp. XXI:** 104

DelCorso's Gallery (Caputo), **Supp. XIX:** 22–23

Delectorskaya, Lydia, **Supp. XXII:** 99

De l'éducation d'un homme sauvage (Itard), **Supp. I Part 2:** 564

"Delft" (Goldbarth), **Supp. XII:** 189

Delft: An Essay-Poem (Goldbarth), **Supp. XII:** 187

Delicate Balance, A (Albee), **I:** 86–89, 91, 93, 94

Delicate Balance, The (Hay), **Supp. XIV:** 121, 122, 124, 129, 133–134

"Delicate Balance, The" (Hay), **Supp. XIV:** 122

"Delicate Prey, The" (Bowles), **Supp. IV Part 1:** 86

Delicate Prey and Other Stories, The (Bowles), **Supp. IV Part 1:** 86–87

Délie (Scève), **Supp. III Part 1:** 11

Delights & Shadows (Kooser), **Supp. XIX:** 115, 116, 117, 121, **127–128**

DeLillo, Don, **Retro. Supp. I:** 278; **Retro. Supp. II:** 279; **Supp. VI:** 1–18; **Supp. IX:** 212; **Supp. XI:** 68; **Supp. XII:** 21, 152; **Supp. XVII:** 183; **Supp. XVIII:** 136, 140; **Supp. XIX:** 54; **Supp. XX: 83, 87, 91; Supp. XXIII:** 109

De Lint, Charles, **Supp. XXII:** 59

DeLisle, Anne, **Supp. VIII:** 175

Deliverance (Dickey), **Supp. IV Part 1:** 176, 186–188, 190; **Supp. X:** 30; **Supp. XX: 173–174; Supp. XXIII:** 43, 50

Deliverance, The (Glasgow), **II:** 175, 176, 177–178, 181

"Delivering" (Dubus), **Supp. VII:** 87

Dell, Floyd, **I:** 103, 105; **Supp. I Part 2:** 379; **Supp. XV:** 295; **Supp. XVII:** 96; **Supp. XXI:** 6; **Supp. XXII:** 275

Della Francesca, Piero, **Supp. XV:** 262

"Della Primavera Trasportata al Morale" (W. C. Williams), **Retro. Supp. I:** 419, 422

DeLoria, Philip J., **Supp. XIV:** 306

Deloria, Vine, Jr., **Supp. IV Part 1:** 323; **Supp. IV Part 2:** 504

"Delta Autumn" (Faulkner), **II:** 71

"Delta Factor, The" (Percy), **Supp. III Part 1:** 386

Delta of Venus: Erotica (Nin), **Supp. X:** 192, 195

Delta Wedding (Welty), **IV:** 261, 268–271, 273, 281; **Retro. Supp. I:** 349–350, 351

Delusions (Berryman), **I:** 170

De Man, Paul, **Retro. Supp. I:** 67; **Supp. XVII:** 70

DeMarinis, Rick, **Supp. XIV:** 22

DeMars, James, **Supp. IV Part 2:** 552

Dembo, L. S., **I:** 386, 391, 396, 397, 398, 402; **III:** 478; **Supp. I Part 1:** 272; **Supp. XIV:** 277, 282, 288, 290

"Dementia Translucida" (Bierds), **Supp. XVII:** 33

"Demeter"(Crooker), **Supp. XXIII:** 61

"Demeters"(Hadas), **Supp. XXIII:** 113

Demetrakopoulous, Stephanie A., **Supp. IV Part 1:** 12

DeMille, Cecil B., **Supp. IV Part 2:** 520; **Supp. XV:** 42

Demme, Jonathan, **Supp. V:** 14

Democracy (Adams), **I:** 9–10, 20; **Supp. IV Part 1:** 208; **Supp. XIX:** 139

Democracy (Didion), **Supp. IV Part 1:** 198, 208–210

"Democracy" (Lowell), **Supp. I Part 2:** 419

Democracy and Education (Dewey), **I:** 232

Democracy and Other Addresses (Lowell), **Supp. I Part 2:** 407

Democracy and Social Ethics (Addams), **Supp. I Part 1:** 8–11

Democracy in America (Tocqueville), **Retro. Supp. I:** 235; **Supp. XIV:** 306

Democratic Vistas (Whitman), **IV:** 333, 336, 348–349, 351, 469; **Retro. Supp. I:** 408; **Supp. I Part 2:** 456

Democritus, **II:** 480–481; **II:** 157; **III:** 606; **Retro. Supp. I:** 247

"Demon Lover, The" (Rich), **Supp. I Part 2:** 556

"Demonstrators, The" (Welty), **IV:** 280; **Retro. Supp. I:** 355

DeMott, Benjamin, **Supp. IV Part 1:** 35; **Supp. V:** 123; **Supp. XIII:** 95; **Supp. XIV: 106**

DeMott, Robert, **Supp. VIII:** 40, 41

Demuth, Charles, **IV:** 404; **Retro. Supp. I:** 412, 430; **Supp. XXI:** 6

"Demystified Zone" (Paley), **Supp. VI:** 227

Denmark Vesey (opera) (Bowles), **Supp. IV Part 1:** 83

Dennett, Daniel, **Supp. XXII:** 265

Denney, Joseph Villiers, **Supp. I Part 2:** 605

Denney, Reuel, **Supp. XII:** 121; **Supp. XXI:** 19

Dennie, Joseph, **II:** 298; **Supp. I Part 1:** 125

Denniston, Dorothy Hamer, **Supp. XI:** 276, 277

"Den of Lions" (Plath), **Retro. Supp. II:** 242

"Dental Assistant, The" (Simpson), **Supp. IX:** 280

Den Uyl, Douglas, **Supp. IV Part 2:** 528, 530

"Deodand, The" (Hecht), **Supp. X:** 65

"Departing" (Cameron), **Supp. XII:** 81

"Departure" (Glück), **Supp. V:** 89

"Departure" (Plath), **Supp. I Part 2:** 537

"Departure, The" (Freneau), **Supp. II Part 1:** 264

"Departure from Hydra, The" (Koch), **Supp. XV:** 180–181

Departures (Justice), **Supp. VII:** 124–127

Departures and Arrivals (Shields), **Supp. VII:** 320, 322

"Depressed by a Book of Bad Poetry, I Walk Toward an Unused Pasture and Invite the Insects to Join Me" (Wright), **Supp. III Part 2:** 600

"Depressed Person, The" (Wallace), **Supp. X:** 309

"Depression Days" (Mora), **Supp. XIII:** 224–225

"Deprived of Unhappiness" (Pickering), **Supp. XXI:** 203

De Puy, John, **Supp. XIII:** 12

D'Erasmo, Stacey, **Supp. IX:** 121

Derby, J. C., **Supp. XVIII:** 4

De Reilhe, Catherine, **Supp. I Part 1:** 202

De Rerum Natura (Lucretius), **II:** 162

"De Rerum Virtute" (Jeffers), **Supp. II Part 2:** 424

De Rioja, Francisco, **Supp. I Part 1:** 166

"Derivative Sport in Tornado Alley" (Wallace), **Supp. X:** 314

Derleth, August, **Supp. I Part 2:** 465, 472

Deronda, Daniel, **II:** 179

Derricotte, Toi, **Supp. XVIII:** 177

Derrida, Jacques, **Supp. IV Part 1:** 45; **Supp. XV:** 215, 224; **Supp. XVI:** 285, 288

Deruddere, Dominique, **Supp. XI:** 173

Der Wilde Jäger (Bürger), **II:** 306

Derzhavin, Gavrila Romanovich, **Supp. VIII:** 27

Desai, Anita, **Supp. XVI:** 156, 157, 158

Désamère (Notley), **Supp. XXII:** 226

De Santis, Christopher, **Retro. Supp. I:** 194

Descartes, René, **I:** 255; **III:** 618–619; **IV:** 133

"Descendant of Solomon and the Queen of Sheba" (Major), **Supp. XXII:** 182

Descendents, The (Glasgow), **II:** 173, 174–175, 176

Descending Figure (Glück), **Supp. V:** 83–84

"Descending Theology: Christ Human" (Karr), **Supp. XI:** 251

"Descending Theology: The Garden" (Karr), **Supp. XI:** 251

"Descent, The" (W. C. Williams), **Retro. Supp. I:** 428, 429

"Descent from the Cross" (Eliot), **Retro. Supp. I:** 57, 58

"Descent in the Maelström, A" (Poe), **Retro. Supp. II:** 274

"Descent into Proselito" (Knowles), **Supp. XII:** 237

"Descent into the Maelström, A" (Poe), **III:** 411, 414, 416, 424

Descent of Alette, The (Notley), **Supp. XXII:** 223, 224, 226, 227, 233–234

Descent of Man (Boyle), **Supp. VIII:** 1, 12–13; **Supp. XX: 17, 18, 20**

"Descent of Man" (Boyle), **Supp. VIII:** 14; **Supp. XX: 18**

Descent of Man, The (Darwin), **Supp. XIV:** 192

Descent of Man, The (Wharton), **IV:** 311; **Retro. Supp. I:** 367

Descent of Man and Other Stories, The (Wharton), **Retro. Supp. I:** 367

Descent of Winter, The (W. C. Williams), **Retro. Supp. I:** 419, 428

De Schloezer, Doris, **III:** 474

"Describers" (Halliday), **Supp. XIX:** 85

"Description" (Doty), **Supp. XI:** 126

"Description of the great Bones dug up at Clavarack on the Banks of Hudsons River A.D. 1705, The" (Taylor), **IV:** 163, 164

"Description without Place" (Stevens), **Retro. Supp. I:** 422

"Desert" (Hughes), **Retro. Supp. I:** 207

"Deserted Cabin" (Haines), **Supp. XII:** 203

Deserted Village, The (Goldsmith), **II:** 304

Desert Is My Mother, The/El desierto es mi madre (Mora), **Supp. XIII:** 214, 221

Desert Music, The (W. C. Williams), **IV:** 422; **Retro. Supp. I:** 428, 429

"Desert Music, The" (W. C. Williams), **Retro. Supp. I:** 428, 429

"Desert Places" (Frost), **II:** 159; **Retro. Supp. I:** 121, 123, 129, 138, 299; **Supp. XIV:** 229

Desert Rose, The (McMurtry), **Supp. V:** 225, 231

Desert Solitaire (Abbey), **Supp. X:** 30; **Supp. XIII:** 7–8, 12; **Supp. XIV:** 177, 179

"Design" (Frost), **II:** 158, 163; **Retro. Supp. I:** 121, 126, 138, 139; **Supp. IX:** 81; **Supp. XVII:** 132; **Supp. XVIII:** 298

"Designated National Park, A" (Ortiz), **Supp. IV Part 2:** 509

"Designs on a Point of View" (Everwine), **Supp. XV:** 76

DeSilva, Bruce, **Supp. XXII:** 205, 206, 217

Des Imagistes (Pound), **II:** 513; **Supp. I Part 1:** 257, 261, 262

Desire (album, Dylan), **Supp. XVIII:** 28

"Desire" (Beattie), **Supp. V:** 29

Desire (Bidart), **Supp. XV: 32–34,** 35

"Desire" (Everwine), **Supp. XV:** 85

"Desire and Denial" (Bronk), **Supp. XXI:** 26

"Désirée's Baby" (Chopin), **Retro. Supp. II:** 64, 65; **Supp. I Part 1:** 213–215

"Desire"(Hadas), **Supp. XXIII:** 117

Desire under the Elms (O'Neill), **III:** 387, 390

"Desolate Field, The" (W. C. Williams), **Retro. Supp. I:** 418

"Desolation, A" (Ginsberg), **Supp. II Part 1:** 313

Desolation Angels (Kerouac), **Supp. III Part 1:** 218, 225, 230

"Desolation Is a Delicate Thing" (Wylie), *Supp. I Part 2:* 729

"Desolation Row" (song, Dylan), **Supp. XVIII:** 30

Despair (Nabokov), **Retro. Supp. I:** 270, 274

Desperate Characters (Fox), **Supp. XX: 91**

"Despisals" (Rukeyser), **Supp. VI:** 282

Des Pres, Terrence, **Supp. X:** 113, 120, 124

"Destiny and the Lieutenant" (McCoy), **Supp. XIII:** 171

"Destruction of Kreshev, The" (Singer), **IV:** 13; **Retro. Supp. II:** 307

Destruction of the European Jews, The (Hilberg), **Supp. V:** 267

"Destruction of the Goetheanum, The" (Salter), **Supp. IX:** 257

"Destruction of the Long Branch, The" (Pinsky), **Supp. VI:** 239, 240, 243–244, 245, 247, 250

Destructive Element, The (Spender), **Retro. Supp. I:** 216

"Detail & Parody for the poem 'Paterson' " (W. C. Williams), **Retro. Supp. I:** 424

Detmold, John, **Supp. I Part 2:** 670

De Tolnay, Charles, **Supp. XXII:** 255

Detour at Night (Endore), **Supp. XVII:** 64

Deuce, The (R. O. Butler), **Supp. XII:** 62, **69–70,** 72

Deus Lo Volt! (Connell), **Supp. XIV:** 80, 81, 95

Deuteronomy (biblical book), **II:** 166

Deutsch, Andre, **Supp. XI:** 297, 301

Deutsch, Babette, **Supp. I Part 1:** 328, 341; **Supp. XV:** 305

Deutsch, Michel, **Supp. IV Part 1:** 104

"Devaluation Blues: Ruminations on Black Families in Crisis" (Coleman), **Supp. XI:** 87

Devane, William, **Supp. XI:** 234

Devasahayam, Madona, **Supp. XXII:** 260

"Development of My Mind and Character, The" (Notley), **Supp. XXII:** 227

"Development of the Literary West" (Chopin), **Retro. Supp. II:** 72

"Development of the Modern English Novel, The" (Lanier), **Supp. I Part 1:** 370–371

DeVeriante (Herbert of Cherbury), **II:** 108

"Devil and Daniel Webster, The" (Benét), **III:** 22; **Supp. XI:** 45–46, 47, 50–51, 52

Devil and Daniel Webster and Other Writings, The (Benét), **Supp. XI:** 48

"Devil and Tom Walker, The" (Irving), **II:** 309–310

Devil At Large, The: Erica Jong on Henry Miller (Jong), **Supp. V:** 115, 131

Devil-Doll, The (film, Browning), **Supp. XVII:** 58–59

Devil Finds Work, The (Baldwin), **Retro. Supp. II:** 14; **Supp. I Part 1:** 48, 52, 66–67

Devil in a Blue Dress (Mosley), **Supp. XIII:** 237, 239

"Devil in Manuscript, The" (Hawthorne), **II:** 226; **Retro. Supp. I:** 150–151

Devil in Paradise, A (H. Miller), **III:** 190

"Devil in the Belfry, The" (Poe), **III:** 425; **Retro. Supp. II:** 273

"Devil Is a Busy Man, The" (Wallace), **Supp. X:** 309

Devil's Dictionary, The (Bierce), **I:** 196, 197, 205, 208, 209, 210

Devil's Stocking, The (Algren), **Supp. IX:** 5, 16

"Devil's Thumb, The" (Krakauer), **Supp. XVIII:** 107

Devil's Tour, The (Karr), **Supp. XI:** 240, **242–244**

Devil Tree, The (Kosinski), **Supp. VII:** 215, 222, 223

"Devising" (Ammons), **Supp. VII:** 28

Devlin, Paul, **Supp. XIX:** 159

De Voto, Bernard, **I:** 247, 248; **II:** 446; **Supp. IV Part 2:** 599, 601

"Devout Meditation in Memory of Adolph Eichmann, A" (Merton), **Supp. VIII:** 198, 203

De Vries, Peter, **Supp. I Part 2:** 604

Dewberry, Elizabeth, **Supp. XII:** 62, 72

Dewey, John, **I:** 214, 224, 228, 232, 233, 266, 267; **II:** 20, 27, 34, 229, 361; **III:** 112, 294–295, 296, 303, 309–310, 599, 605; **IV:** 27, 429; **Supp. I Part 1:** 3, 5, 7, 10, 11, 12, 24; **Supp. I Part 2:** 493, 641, 647, 677; **Supp. V:** 290; **Supp. IX:** 179; **Supp. XIV:** 3; **Supp. XV:** 41

Dewey, Joseph, **Supp. IX:** 210

Dewey, Thomas, **IV:** 161

Dewey Defeats Truman (Mallon), **Supp. XIX:** 132, 137, **138**

Dexter, Peter, **Supp. XIV:** 221

De Young, Charles, **I:** 194

Dhairyam, Sagari, **Supp. IV Part 1:** 329, 330

Dharma Bums, The (Kerouac), **Supp. III Part 1:** 230, 231; **Supp. VIII:** 289, 305

"D. H. Lawrence" (Bynner), **Supp. XV:** 46

D. H. Lawrence: An Unprofessional Study (Nin), **Supp. X:** 182–183

D. H. Lawrence: The World of the Major Novels (Sanders), **Supp. XVI:** 267

D'Houdetot, Madame, **Supp. I Part 1:** 250

"Diabetes" (Dickey), **Supp. IV Part 1:** 182

Diaghilev, Sergei, **Supp. I Part 1:** 257

Dial (publication), **I:** 58, 109, 115, 116, 215, 231, 233, 245, 261, 384, 429; **II:** 8, 430; **III:** 194, 470, 471, 485; **IV:** 122, 171, 427; **Retro. Supp. I:** 58; **Retro. Supp. II:** 78; **Supp. I Part 2:** 642, 643, 647; **Supp. II Part 1:** 168, 279, 291; **Supp. II Part 2:** 474; **Supp. III Part 2:** 611

"Dialectical Materialism" (Weigl), **Supp. XIX:** 281

Dialectical Materialism and the Fate of Humanity (C. L. R. James), **Supp. XXI:** 169

"Dialectics of Love, The" (McGrath), **Supp. X:** 116

"Dialogue" (Rich), **Supp. I Part 2:** 560

Dialogue, A (Baldwin and Giovanni), **Supp. I Part 1:** 66

"Dialogue Between Franklin and the Gout" (Franklin), **II:** 121

"Dialogue Between General Wolfe and General Gage in a Wood near Boston, A" (Paine), **Supp. I Part 2:** 504

"Dialogue between Old England and New" (Bradstreet), **Supp. I Part 1:** 105–106, 110–111, 116

"Dialogue between the Writer and a Maypole Dresser, A" (Taylor), **IV:** 155

Dialogues (Bush, ed.), **III:** 4

Dialogues in Limbo (Santayana), **III:** 606

"Dialogue: William Harvey; Joan of Arc" (Goldbarth), **Supp. XII:** 178

Dialogue with a Dead Man (J. W. Miller), **Supp. XX: 163, 164, 167**

"Diamond as Big as the Ritz, The" (Fitzgerald), **II:** 88–89

Diamond Cutters and Other Poems, The (Rich), **Supp. I Part 2:** 551, 552, 553

"Diamond Guitar, A" (Capote), **Supp. III Part 1:** 124

Diamond Necklace, A (Notley), **Supp. XXII:** 228

"Diana and Persis" (Alcott), **Supp. I Part 1:** 32, 41

"Diaper Brigade, The" (Ryan as Quin), **Supp. XVIII:** 230

Diaries of Charlotte Perkins Gilman (Knight, ed.), **Supp. XI:** 201

"Diary–1903" (Boyce), **Supp. XXI:** 8

Diary of a Chambermaid, The (film; Renoir), **Supp. XVI:** 193

Diary of Anaïs Nin, The (1931–1974), **Supp. X:** 181, 185–189, 191, 192, 193, 195

Diary of Anne Frank, The, **Supp. XXI:** 245

Diary of a Rapist, The: A Novel (Connell), **Supp. XIV:** 80, 82, 94

Diary of a Yuppie (Auchincloss), **Supp. IV Part 1:** 31, 32–33

Diary of "Helena Morley", The (Bishop, trans.), **Retro. Supp. II:** 45, 51; **Supp. I Part 1:** 92

Dias, Robert Vas, **Supp. XXII:** 164, 169

Díaz del Castillo, Bernál, **III:** 13, 14

Dick, Philip K., **Supp. XVI:** 123; **Supp. XVIII:** 136, 137, 138, 139, 142; **Supp. XXII:** 49

Dickens, Charles, **I:** 152, 198, 505; **II:** 98, 179, 186, 192, 271, 273–274, 288, 290, 297, 301, 307, 316, 322, 559, 561, 563, 577, 582; **III:** 146, 247, 325, 368, 411, 421, 426, 572, 577, 613–614, 616; **IV:** 21, 192, 194, 211, 429; **Retro. Supp. I:** 33, 91, 218; **Retro. Supp. II:** 204; **Supp. I Part 1:** 13, 34, 35, 36, 41, 49; **Supp. I Part 2:** 409, 523, 579, 590, 622, 675; **Supp. IV Part 1:** 293, 300, 341; **Supp. IV Part 2:** 464; **Supp. VIII:** 180; **Supp. IX:** 246; **Supp. XI:** 277; **Supp. XII:** 335, 337; **Supp. XIII:** 233; **Supp. XV:** 62; **Supp. XVI:** 63, 65–66, 72–73, 202; **Supp. XVIII:** 7, 136, 146; **Supp. XX: 21, 87, 195; Supp. XXII:** 206; **Supp. XXIII:** 4, 85, 290

Dickey, James, **I:** 29, 535; **III:** 268; **Retro. Supp. II:** 233; **Supp. III Part 1:** 354; **Supp. III Part 2:** 541, 597; **Supp. IV Part 1: 175–194; Supp. V:** 333; **Supp. X:** 30; **Supp. XI:** 312, 317; **Supp. XV:** 115, 348; **Supp. XVIII:** 191, 299; **Supp. XIX:** 282; **Supp. XXI:** 35; **Supp. XXIII:** 43, 50

Dick Gibson Show, The (Elkin), **Supp. VI:** 42, **48–49**

Dickie, Margaret, **Retro. Supp. II:** 53, 84

Dickinson, Donald, **Retro. Supp. I:** 206, 212

Dickinson, Edward, **I:** 451–452, 453

Dickinson, Mrs. Edward, **I:** 451, 453

Dickinson, Emily, **I:** 384, 419, 433, **451–473; II:** 272, 276, 277, 530; **III:** 19, 194, 196, 214, 493, 505, 508, 556, 572, 576; **IV:** 134, 135, 331, 444; **Retro. Supp. I: 25–50; Retro. Supp. II:** 39, 40, 43, 45, 50, 76, 134, 155, 170; **Supp. I Part 1:** 29, 79, 188, 372; **Supp. I Part 2:** 375, 546, 609, 682, 691; **Supp. II Part 1:** 4; **Supp. III Part 1:** 63; **Supp. III Part 2:** 600, 622; **Supp. IV Part 1:** 31, 257; **Supp. IV Part 2:** 434, 637, 641, 643; **Supp. V:** 79, 140, 332, 335; **Supp. VIII:** 95, 104, 106, 108, 198, 205, 272; **Supp. IX:** 37, 38, 53, 87, 90; **Supp. XII:** 226; **Supp. XIII:** 153, 339; **Supp. XIV:** 45, 127–128, 133, 261, 284; **Supp. XV:** 287, 303, 309; **Supp. XVI:** 288; **Supp. XVII:** 71, 73, 74, 75, 132; **Supp. XVIII:** 301; **Supp. XIX:** 86; **Supp. XX: 106, 108; Supp. XXI:** 52, 61, 64, 132, 214; **Supp. XXII:** 81, 82, 225, 277–278; **Supp. XXIII:** 19, 165

Dickinson, Gilbert, **I:** 469

Dickinson, Goldsworthy Lowes, **Supp. XIV:** 336

Dickinson, Lavinia Norcross, **I:** 451, 453, 462, 470

Dickinson, Stephanie, **Supp. XXIII:** 250

Dickinson, Mrs. William A. (Susan Gilbert), **I:** 452, 453, 456, 469, 470

Dickinson, William Austin, **I:** 451, 453, 469

Dickinson and the Strategies of Reticence (Dobson), **Retro. Supp. I:** 29, 42

Dickson, Helen. *See* Blackmur, Helen Dickson

Dickstein, Morris, **Supp. XIII:** 106

"Dick Whittington and His Cat", **Supp. I Part 2:** 656

"DICTATORSHIP OF THE PROLETARIAT, THE" (Baraka), **Supp. II Part 1:** 54

Dictionary of Afro-American Slang (Major), **Supp. XXII:** 172, 174, 180

Dictionary of Literary Biography (Barron and Meyer, eds.), **Supp. XVIII:** 173; **Supp. XIX:** 195

Dictionary of Literary Biography (Gwynn, ed.), **Supp. XVIII:** 173; **Supp. XIX:** 121

Dictionary of Literary Biography (Kibler, ed.), **Supp. IX:** 94, 109; **Supp. XI:** 297

Dictionary of Literary Biography (Knight, ed.), **Supp. XIV:** 144

Dictionary of Literary Biography (Martine, ed.), **Supp. XXII:** 187

Dictionary of Literary Biography (Sicher, ed.), **Supp. XVII:** 41

Dictionary of Literary Biography (Twentieth-Century American Nature Poets, Bryson and Thompson, eds.), **Supp. XXIII:** 129

Dictionary of Modern English Usage, A (Fowler), **Supp. I Part 2:** 660

"Dictum: For a Masque of Deluge" (Merwin), **Supp. III Part 1:** 342–343

"Didactic Poem" (Levertov), **Supp. III Part 1:** 280

Diderot, Denis, **II:** 535; **IV:** 440; **Supp. XVI:** 293; **Supp. XVII:** 145

Did I Ever Tell You How Lucky You Are? (Geisel), **Supp. XVI:** 109

Didion, Joan, **Retro. Supp. I:** 116; **Retro. Supp. II:** 209; **Supp. I Part 1:** 196, 197; **Supp. III Part 1:** 302; **Supp. IV Part 1: 195–216; Supp. XI:** 221; **Supp. XII:** 307

Dido, **I:** 81

Di Donato, Peter, **Supp. XX: 34**

Di Donato, Pietro, **Supp. XX: 33–47**

"Did 'Paco's Story' Deserve Its Award" (Kakutani), **Supp. XXII:** 109

"Did You Ever Dream Lucky?" (Ellison), **Supp. II Part 1:** 246

Dieckmann, Katherine, **Supp. XXIII:** 295, 296

"Die-Hard, The" (Benét), **Supp. XI:** 54–55, 56

Diehl, Digby, **Supp. IV Part 1:** 204

Dien Cai Dau (Komunyakaa), **Supp. XIII:** 121, **122–124,** 125, 131, 132

Dies, Martin, **Supp. XVIII:** 229

"Dies Irae" (Lowell), **II:** 553

Die Zeit Ohne Beispiel, (Goebbels), **III:** 560

Difference Engine, The (W. Gibson and B. Sterling), **Supp. XVI:** 121, 124, **128–129**

Different Drummer, A (Larkin; film), **Supp. XI:** 20

Different Fleshes (Goldbarth), **Supp. XII:** 181–182, 188

Different Hours (Dunn), **Supp. XI:** 139, 142, 143, 155

"Different Road, A" (Strout), **Supp. XXIII:** 282–283

Different Seasons (King), **Supp. V:** 148, 152

Different Ways to Pray (Nye), **Supp. XIII:** 274, 275, 277, 285, 287

"Different Ways to Pray" (Nye), **Supp. XIII:** 275

"Difficulties of a Statesman" (Eliot), **I:** 580

"Difficulties of Modernism and the Modernism of Difficulty" (Poirier), **Supp. II Part 1:** 136

Diff'rent (O'Neill), **III:** 389; **Supp. XXII:** 22

Di Filippo, Paul, **Supp. XXII:** 260, 261

DiGaetani, John L., **Supp. XIII:** 200

Digges, Deborah, **Supp. XXIII:** 57

"Digging" (Sanders), **Supp. XVI:** 272

"Digging in the Garden of Age I Uncover a Live Root" (Swenson), **Supp. IV Part 2:** 649

Digging Up the Dirt (Moraga), **Supp. XXIII:** 197

Diggins, John P., **Supp. I Part 2:** 650

"Dignity of Life, The" (C. Bly), **Supp. XVI:** 34, 36–37

Digregorio, Charles, **Supp. XI:** 326

"Digression on *Number 1, 1948*" (O'Hara), **Supp. XXIII:** 214

"Dilemma" (Budbill), **Supp. XIX:** 2

"Dilemma of Determinism, The" (James), **II:** 347–348, 352

"Dilemma of the Negro Writer, The" (speech, C. Himes), **Supp. XVI:** 140

"Dilettante, The" (Wharton), **IV:** 311, 313

"Dilettante, The: A Modern Type" (Dunbar), **Supp. II Part 1:** 199

Dillard, Annie, **Supp. VI:** 19–39; **Supp. VIII:** 272; **Supp. X:** 31; **Supp. XIII:** 154

Dillard, R. H. W., **Supp. XII:** 16

Dillman, Bradford, **III:** 403; **Supp. XII:** 241

Dillon, Brian, **Supp. X:** 209

Dillon, George, **III:** 141; **Supp. III Part 2:** 621

Dillon, Millicent, **Supp. IV Part 1:** 95

Dilsaver, Paul, **Supp. XIII:** 112

Dilthey, Wilhelm, **I:** 58

Dime-Store Alchemy: The Art of Joseph Cornell, **Supp. VIII:** 272

"Diminuendo" (Dunn), **Supp. XI:** 152–153

"Dimout in Harlem" (Hughes), **Supp. I Part 1:** 333

"Dinah's Lament" (Nelson), **Supp. XVIII:** 183

Dinesen, Isak, **IV:** 279; **Supp. VIII:** 171; **Supp. XVI:** 250

Dining Room, The (Gurney), **Supp. V:** 105–106

"Dinner at ------, A" (O. Henry), **Supp. II Part 1:** 402

"Dinner at Sir Nigel's" (Bowles), **Supp. IV Part 1:** 94

Dinner at the Homesick Restaurant (Tyler), **Supp. IV Part 2:** 657, 667–668

"Dinner at Uncle Borris's" (Simic), **Supp. VIII:** 272

Dinner Bridge (Lardner), **II:** 435

Dinosaur Tales (Bradbury), **Supp. IV Part 1:** 103

"Diogenes Invents a Game" (Karr), **Supp. XI:** 240–241

"Diogenes Tries to Forget" (Karr), **Supp. XI:** 241

Diomede, Matthew, **Supp. XX: 46**

Dionysis in Doubt (Robinson), **III:** 510

Diop, Birago, **Supp. IV Part 1:** 16

Diop, David, **Supp. IV Part 1:** 16

Di Piero, W. S., **Supp. XVII:** 241; **Supp. XIX: 33–48**

Di Prima, Diane, **Supp. III Part 1:** 30; **Supp. XIV:** 125, 144, 148, 150

Dirda, Michael, **Supp. XXI:** 233

Direction of Poetry, The: An Anthology of Rhymed and Metered Verse Written in the English Language since 1975 (Richman, ed.), **Supp. XV:** 250, 251

Direction of Poetry, The: Rhymed and Metered Verse Written in the English Language since 1975 (Richman), **Supp. XI:** 249

"Directive" (Bishop), **Retro. Supp. II:** 42

"Directive" (Frost), **III:** 287; **Retro. Supp. I:** 140; **Supp. VIII:** 32, 33

"Dire Cure" (Matthews), **Supp. IX:** 168

"Dirge" (Dunbar), **Supp. II Part 1:** 199

"Dirge without Music" (Millay), **III:** 126

"Dirt" (Salter), **Supp. IX:** 257, 260, 261

"Dirt and Desire: Essay on the Phenomenology of Female Pollution in Antiquity" (Carson), **Supp. XII:** 111

Dirty Bird Blues (Major), **Supp. XXII: 180–181**

Dirty Dingus Magee (film), **Supp. XVII:** 139

"Dirty English Potatoes" (X. J. Kennedy), **Supp. XV:** 165

"Dirty Memories" (Olds), **Supp. X:** 211

Dirty Story (Shanley), **Supp. XIV:** 316, 331

"Dirty Word, The" (Shapiro), **Supp. II Part 2:** 710

Dirty Work (L. Brown), **Supp. XXI:** 37, 39, 40, 42, **45**

Disappearance of the Jews, The (Mamet), **Supp. XIV:** 249–250, 250–251, 252, 254

Disappearances (Auster), **Supp. XII:** 23

"Disappearances" (Hogan), **Supp. IV Part 1:** 401

Disappearances (Mosher), **Supp. XXII:** 204, 205, 206, 207, 208, 209, **210**

"Disappeared, The " (C. Baxter), **Supp. XVII:** 19

Disappearing Acts (McMillan), **Supp. XIII:** 182, 183, **188–189,** 192

Disappearing Ink: Poetry at the End of Print Culture (Gioia), **Supp. XV:** 112

"Disappointment, The" (Creeley), **Supp. IV Part 1:** 143

"Disappointment and Desire" (R. Bly), **Supp. IV Part 1:** 71

Disappointment Artist, The (Lethem), **Supp. XVIII:** 135, 141, **148**

"Discards" (Baker), **Supp. XIII:** 53, 55–56

Discerning the Signs of the Times (Niebuhr), **III:** 300–301, 307–308

Disch, Thomas M., **Supp. XIX:** 1

"Disciple of Bacon, The" (Epstein), **Supp. XII:** 163–164

"Discipline" (L. Brown), **Supp. XXI:** 44

Discomfort, Zone, The: A Personal History (Franzen), **Supp. XX: 83, 84, 95**

"Discordants" (Aiken), **I:** 65

Discourse on Method (Descartes), **I:** 255

"Discourtesies" (Kirsch), **Supp. XV:** 341

"Discovering Theme and Structure in the Novel" (Schuster), **Supp. VIII:** 126

"Discovery" (Freneau), **Supp. II Part 1:** 258

"Discovery of the Madeiras, The" (Frost), **Retro. Supp. I:** 139

"Discovery of What It Means to Be an American, The" (Baldwin), **Supp. I Part 1:** 54–55

Discovery! The Search for Arabian Oil (Stegner), **Supp. IV Part 2:** 599

"Discrete Series" (Zukofsky), **Supp. III Part 2:** 616

"Discretions of Alcibiades" (Pinsky), **Supp. VI:** 241

"Disease, The" (Rukeyser), **Supp. VI:** 279

Disenchanted, The (play, Schulberg and Breit), **Supp. XVIII:** 254

Disenchanted, The (Schulberg), **II:** 98; **Retro. Supp. I:** 113; **Supp. XVIII:** 247–250, 253

Disenchantments: An Anthology of Modern Fairy Tale Poetry (Mieder), **Supp. XIV:** 126

"Dish of Green Pears, A" (Ríos), **Supp. IV Part 2:** 552

"Disillusion and Dogma" (Untermeyer), **Supp. XV:** 306

Dismantling the Silence (Simic), **Supp. VIII:** 273–274, 275, 276

Disney, Walt, **III:** 275, 426

"Disney of My Mind" (Chabon), **Supp. XI:** 63

Disobedience (Notley), **Supp. XXII:** 235, 236

Dispatches (Herr), **Supp. XI:** 245; **Supp. XIX:** 17

"Displaced Person, The" (O'Connor), **III:** 343–344, 350, 352, 356; **Retro. Supp. II:** 229, 232, 236

"Disposal" (Snodgrass), **Supp. VI:** 314

Dispossessed, The (Berryman), **I:** 170, 172, 173, 174, 175, 176, 178

"Disquieting Muses, The" (Plath), **Supp. I Part 2:** 538

Disraeli, Benjamin, **II:** 127

Dissent (Didion), **Supp. IV Part 1:** 208

"Dissent in Ashcroft's America" (P. N. Warren), **Supp. XX: 273**

"Dissenting Opinion on Kafka, A" (Wilson), **IV:** 437–438

Dissent in Three American Wars (Morison, Merk, and Freidel), **Supp. I Part 2:** 495

Dissertation on Liberty and Necessity, Pleasure and Pain, A (Franklin), **II:** 108

Dissertations on Government; the Affairs of the Bank: and Paper Money (Paine), **Supp. I Part 2:** 510

"Distance" (Carver), **Supp. III Part 1:** 146

"Distance" (Everwine), **Supp. XV:** 85

"Distance" (Paley), **Supp. VI:** 222

"Distance, The" (Karr), **Supp. XI:** 241

"Distance from the Sea, A" (Kees), **Supp. XV:** 147

"Distance Nowhere" (Hughes), **Retro. Supp. I:** 207

"Distance Up Close, The" (Peacock), **Supp. XIX:** 196–197, 198

"Distant Episode, A" (Bowles), **Supp. IV Part 1:** 84–85, 86, 90

Distant Episode, A: The Selected Stories (Bowles), **Supp. IV Part 1:** 79

Distinguished Guest, The (Miller), **Supp. XII: 299–301**

Distortions (Beattie), **Supp. V:** 21, 23, 24, 25, 27

"Distrest Shepherdess, The" (Freneau), **Supp. II Part 1:** 258

District of Columbia (Dos Passos), **I:** 478, 489–490, 492

Disturber of the Peace (Manchester), **III:** 103

Disturbing the Peace (Yates), **Supp. XI:** 345, 346

"Diver, The" (Hayden), **Supp. II Part 1:** 368, 372, 373

"Divided Life of Jean Toomer, The" (Toomer), **Supp. III Part 2:** 488

Divided Self, The (Laing), **Supp. XX: 95**

Divina Commedia (Longfellow, trans.), **II:** 490, 492, 493

"Divina Pastora, La" (C. L. R. James), **Supp. XXI:** 160
"Divine, The" (Di Piero), **Supp. XIX:** 41
"Divine Collaborator" (Simic), **Supp. VIII:** 282
Divine Comedies (Merrill), **Supp. III Part 1:** 324, 329–332
Divine Comedy (Dante), **I:** 137, 265, 400, 446; **II:** 215, 335, 490, 492, 493; **III:** 13, 448, 453; **Supp. V:** 283, 331, 338, 345; **Supp. X:** 253; **Supp. XIV:** 6; **Supp. XIX:** 36, 39
"Divine Image, The" (Blake), **Supp. V:** 257
Divine Pilgrim, The (Aiken), **I:** 50, 55
Divine Right's Trip (Norman), **Supp. XXIII:** 42
Divine Tragedy, The (Longfellow), **II:** 490, 500, 505, 506, 507; **Retro. Supp. II:** 165, 166
Divine Weekes and Workes (Sylvester, trans.), **Supp. I Part 1:** 104
Divine Weeks (Du Bartas), **IV:** 157–158
Diving into the Wreck: Poems 1971–1972 (Rich), **Supp. I Part 2:** 550, 559–565, 569; **Supp. XV:** 252
"Diving Past African Violets" (A. Finch), **Supp. XVII:** 72
Diving Rock on the Hudson, A (H. Roth), **Supp. IX:** 236, **237–238**
"Divinity in Its Fraying Fact, A" (Levis), **Supp. XI:** 271
"Divinity School Address" (Emerson), **II:** 12–13
"Divisions upon a Ground" (Hecht), **Supp. X:** 58
"Divorce" (Karr), **Supp. XI:** 244
"Divorced Fathers and Pizza Crusts" (Halliday), **Supp. XIX:** 93
Divorced in America: Marriage in an Age of Possibility (Epstein), **Supp. XIV:** 113
"Divorce Dream" (Halliday), **Supp. XIX:** 90
Dix, Douglas Shields, **Supp. XII:** 14
Dixie City Jam (Burke), **Supp. XIV:** 32
Dixon, Ivan, **Supp. IV Part 1:** 362
Dixon, Stephen, **Supp. XII: 139–158**
Dixon, Terrell F., **Supp. XVI:** 21
Dixon, Thomas, Jr., **Supp. II Part 1:** 169, 171, 177
Djinn (Robbe-Grillet), **Supp. V:** 48
D'Lugoff, Burt, **Supp. IV Part 1:** 362, 370
Dmytryk, Edward, **Supp. XX:** 41
Do, Lord, Remember Me (Garrett), **Supp. VII:** 98–100, 110
"Doaksology, The" (Wolfe), **IV:** 459
Do Androids Dream of Electric Sheep? (Dick), **Supp. XVIII:** 137
Dobie, J. Frank, **Supp. V:** 225; **Supp. XIII:** 227
Döblin, Alfred, **Supp. XV:** 137
Dobriansky, Lev, **Supp. I Part 2:** 648, 650
Dobrin, Sidney I., **Supp. XVIII:** 192, 195
Dobson, Joanne, **Retro. Supp. I:** 29, 31, 42; **Supp. XVIII:** 259
Dobyns, Stephen, **Supp. XIII: 73–92**

"Docking at Palermo" (Hugo), **Supp. VI:** 137–138
"Dock Rats" (Moore), **III:** 213
"Dock-Witch, The" (Ozick), **Supp. V:** 262, 264
"Doc Mellhorn and the Pearly Gates" (Benét), **Supp. XI:** 55
"Doctor, The" (Dubus), **Supp. VII:** 80–81
"Doctor and the Doctor's Wife, The" (Hemingway), **II:** 248; **Retro. Supp. I:** 174, 175
Doctor Breen's Practice, a Novel (Howells), **I:** 282
Doctor Faustus (Mann), **III:** 283
Doctor Jazz (Carruth), **Supp. XVI:** 47, 59
"Doctor Jekyll" (Sontag), **Supp. III Part 2:** 469
"Doctor Leavis and the Moral Tradition" (Trilling), **Supp. III Part 2:** 512–513
Doctor Martino and Other Stories (Faulkner), **II:** 72; **Retro. Supp. I:** 84
"Doctor of the Heart, The" (Sexton), **Supp. II Part 2:** 692
Doctorow, E. L., **Retro. Supp. I:** 97; **Supp. III Part 2:** 590, 591; **Supp. IV Part 1: 217–240; Supp. V:** 45; **Supp. XVI:** 73; **Supp. XVII:** 183; **Supp. XX: 84, 90; Supp. XXI:** 18–19; **Supp. XXII:** 268
Doctor Sax (Kerouac), **Supp. III Part 1:** 220–222, 224–227
Doctor Sleep (Bell), **Supp. X: 9–11**
"Doctors' Row" (Aiken), **I:** 67
Doctor's Son and Other Stories, The (O'Hara), **III:** 361
Doctor Stories, The (W. C. Williams), **Retro. Supp. I:** 424
"Doctor's Wife, The" (Ozick), **Supp. V:** 262, 265
Doctor Zhivago (Pasternak), **IV:** 434, 438, 443
"Documentary" (Simic), **Supp. VIII:** 282
Dodd, Elizabeth, **Supp. V:** 77
Dodd, Wayne, **Supp. IV Part 2:** 625
Dodge, Mabel, **Supp. XX: 69; Supp. XXI:** 5, 6, 8, 12; **Supp. XXII:** 158, 161. *See also* Luhan, Mabel Dodge
Dodson, Owen, **Supp. I Part 1:** 54
Dodsworth (Lewis), **II:** 442, 449–450, 453, 456
Doenitz, Karl, **Supp. I Part 2:** 491
Does Civilization Need Religion? (Niebuhr), **III:** 293–294
"Does 'Consciousness' Exist?" (James), **II:** 356
"Does Education Pay?" (Du Bois), **Supp. II Part 1:** 159
"Dog" (B. Kelly), **Supp. XVII:** 126
Dog (Shepard), **Supp. III Part 2:** 434
"Dog Act, The" (Komunyakaa), **Supp. XIII:** 114–115
"Dog and the Playlet, The" (O. Henry), **Supp. II Part 1:** 399
Dog Beneath the Skin, The (Auden), **Supp. II Part 1:** 10
"Dog Creek Maidx1" (Wright), **Supp. V:** 340

"Dogfight" (W. Gibson and Swanwick), **Supp. XVI:** 128
Dog in the Manger, The (Vega; Merwin, trans.), **Supp. III Part 1:** 341, 347
Dog of the Marriage, The (Hempel), **Supp. XXI:** 115, 116, 117, 118, **126–127**
"Dog"(P. Benedict), **Supp. XXIII:** 36–37, 39
Dogs Bark, but the Caravan Rolls On (Conroy), **Supp. XVI:** 63, 70, 74, **75–76**
Dogs Bark, The: Public People and Private Places (Capote), **Supp. III Part 1:** 120, 132
"Dog's Eye" (J. W. Miller), **Supp. XX: 167**
Dogs of God (Benedict), **Supp. XXIII:** 35, **41–45,** 49–50
Dog Soldiers (Stone), **Supp. V:** 298, 299–301
Dog Star, The (Di Piero), **Supp. XIX:** 38, **40–41,** 43
"Dog Stories" (Prose), **Supp. XVI:** 256
Dog & the Fever, The (Quevedo), **Retro. Supp. I:** 423
"Dogtown Letters, The" (Jarman and R. McDowell), **Supp. XVII:** 111
"Dogwood, The" (Levertov), **Supp. III Part 1:** 276
"Dogwood Tree, The: A Boyhood" (Updike), **IV:** 218; **Retro. Supp. I:** 318, 319
Doig, Ivan, **Supp. XIV:** 227
"Doing Battle with the Wolf" (Coleman), **Supp. XI:** 87–88
"Doing Jigsaw Puzzles" (Crooker), **Supp. XXIII:** 56
Doing Literary Business: American Women Writers in the Nineteenth Century (Coultrap-McQuin), **Supp. XVI:** 85
Doings and Undoings (Podhoretz), **Supp. VIII: 236–237**
"Do-It-Yourself" (C. Baxter), **Supp. XVII:** 14–15
Dolan, Jill, **Supp. XV:** 327
Dolben, Digby Mackworth, **Supp. XX: 230**
"Dolce Far' Niente" (Humphrey), **Supp. IX:** 106
Dolci, Carlo, **III:** 474–475
Dollars and Cents (A. Warner), **Supp. XVIII:** 264
"Dollhouse, The" (Haines), **Supp. XII:** 204
Dollmaker's Ghost, The (Levis), **Supp. XI:** 259, 260, **264–268**
Doll's House, A (Ibsen), **III:** 523; **IV:** 357; **Supp. XVI:** 182
Dolmetsch, Arnold, **III:** 464
Dolores Claiborne (King), **Supp. V:** 138, 141, 147, 148, 149–150, 152
"Dolph Heyliger" (Irving), **II:** 309
Dolphin, The (Lowell), **Retro. Supp. II:** 183, 186, 188, **190–191; Supp. XII:** 253–254
"Dolphins" (Francis), **Supp. IX:** 83
Dome of Many-Coloured Class, A (Lowell), **II:** 515, 516–517

Domesday Book (Masters), **Supp. I Part 2:** 465, 466–469, 471, 473, 476

"Domestic Economy" (Gilman), **Supp. XI:** 206

"Domestic Manners" (Hardwick), **Supp. III Part 1:** 211

Domestic Work (Trethewey), **Supp. XXI:** 243, 244, **248–251,** 254

"Domestic Work, 1937" (Trethewey), **Supp. XXI:** 248

"Dominant White, The" (McKay), **Supp. X:** 134

Dominguez, Robert, **Supp. VIII:** 83

Domini, John, **Supp. XIX:** 45; **Supp. XXI:** 235

Dominique, Jean. *See* Closset, Marie

Donahoe, Edward, **Supp. XVIII:** 132

Donahue, Phil, **Supp. IV Part 2:** 526; **Supp. X:** 311

Donaldson, Susan, **Supp. XXII:** 148

Doña Perfecta (Galdós), **II:** 290

Dong, Stella, **Supp. XVI:** 222

Don Juan (Byron), **Supp. XV:** 259

"DON JUAN IN HELL" (Baraka), **Supp. II Part 1:** 33

Donkey of God, The (Untermeyer), **Supp. XV:** 310

"Donna mi Prega" (Cavalcanti), **Supp. III Part 2:** 620, 621, 622

Donn-Byrne, Brian Oswald. *See* Byrne, Donn

Donne, John, **I:** 358–359, 384, 389, 522, 586; **II:** 254; **III:** 493; **IV:** 83, 88, 135, 141, 144, 145, 151, 156, 165, 331, 333; **Retro. Supp. II:** 76; **Supp. I Part 1:** 80, 364, 367; **Supp. I Part 2:** 421, 424, 467, 725, 726; **Supp. III Part 2:** 614, 619; **Supp. VIII:** 26, 33, 164; **Supp. IX:** 44; **Supp. XII:** 45, 159; **Supp. XIII:** 94, 130; **Supp. XIV:** 122; **Supp. XV:** 92, 251; **Supp. XVI:** 158, 204; **Supp. XVIII:** 35, 39, 50–51, 307

Donne's Sermons: Selected Passages (L. P. Smith, ed.), **Supp. XIV:** 342

Donoghue, Denis, **I:** 537; **Supp. IV Part 1:** 39; **Supp. VIII:** 105, 189

Donohue, H. E. F., **Supp. IX:** 2, 3, 15, 16

Do Not Deny Me (Thompson), **Supp. XXIII: 300–301**

"Do Not Weep Maiden, For War Is Kind" (Crane), **Supp. XVIII:** 75

Donovan, Josephine, **Retro. Supp. II:** 138, 139, 147

Don Quixote (Cervantes), **I:** 134; **II:** 291, 434; **III:** 113, 614; **Supp. I Part 2:** 422; **Supp. IX:** 94

Don Quixote: Which Was a Dream (Acker), **Supp. XII:** 5, **12–14**

Don't Ask (Levine), **Supp. V:** 178

Don't Ask Questions (Marquand), **III:** 58

Don't Bet on the Prince: Contemporary Feminist Fairy Tales in North America and England (Zipes), **Supp. XIV:** 126

Don't Drink the Water (Allen), **Supp. XV:** 3, **14**

Don't Look Back (film, Pennebaker), **Supp. XVIII:** 19

"Don't Shoot the Warthog" (Corso), **Supp. XII:** 123

"Don't Tell Mother" (Wasserstein), **Supp. XV:** 319

"Don't Think Twice, It's All Right" (song, Dylan), **Supp. XVIII:** 24

Don't Worry About the Kids (Neugeboren), **Supp. XVI:** 226

"Don't Worry About the Kids" (Neugeboren), **Supp. XVI:** 226

Don't You Want to Be Free? (Hughes), **Retro. Supp. I:** 203; **Supp. I Part 1:** 339

"Doodler, The" (Merrill), **Supp. III Part 1:** 321

Doolan, Moira, **Retro. Supp. II:** 247

Doolittle, Hilda (H. D.), **II:** 517, 520–521; **III:** 194, 195–196, 457, 465; **IV:** 404, 406; **Retro. Supp. I:** 288, 412, 413, 414, 415, 417; **Supp. I Part 1: 253–275; Supp. I Part 2:** 707; **Supp. III Part 1:** 48; **Supp. III Part 2:** 610; **Supp. IV Part 1:** 257; **Supp. V:** 79; **Supp. XV:** 43, 249, 301, 302; **Supp. XVII:** 77; **Supp. XXII:** 88

Doolittle, Thomas, **IV:** 150

"Doomed by Our Blood to Care" (Orfalea), **Supp. XIII:** 278

"Doomsday" (Plath), **Retro. Supp. II:** 242

Doomsters, The (Macdonald), **Supp. IV Part 2:** 462, 463, 472, 473

"Door, The" (Creeley), **Supp. IV Part 1:** 145, 146, 156–157

"Door, The" (White), **Supp. I Part 2:** 651, 675–676

"Door in the Dark, The" (Frost), **II:** 156

Door in the Hive, A (Levertov), **Supp. III Part 1:** 283, 284

"Door of the Trap, The" (Anderson), **I:** 112

"Doors" (Dybek), **Supp. XXIII:** 69

Doors (Hoffman), **Supp. XVIII:** 86–87

"Doors" (Hoffman), **Supp. XVIII:** 86–87

"Doors, Doors, Doors" (Sexton), **Supp. II Part 2:** 681

Doors, The, **Supp. X:** 186

"Doorways into the Depths" (Sanders), **Supp. XVI:** 272

Doreski, William, **Retro. Supp. II:** 185

Dorfman, Ariel, **Supp. IX:** 131, 138

Dorfman, Joseph, **Supp. I Part 2:** 631, 647, 650

Dorman, Jen, **Supp. XI:** 240

Dorn, Edward, **Supp. IV Part 1:** 154

Dorn, Sarah, **Supp. XXI:** 243

"Dorothea Dix, Samaritan" (J. Scott), **Supp. XVII:** 189

Dorr, Julia, **Supp. XV:** 286

Dorris, Michael, **Supp. IV Part 1:** 260, 272

Dos Passos, John, **I:** 99, 288, 374, 379, **474–496,** 517, 519; **II:** 74, 77, 89, 98; **III:** 2, 28, 29, 70, 172, 382–383; **IV:** 340, 427, 433; **Retro. Supp. I:** 105, 113, 187; **Retro. Supp. II:** 95, 196; **Supp. I Part 2:** 646; **Supp. III Part 1:** 104, 105; **Supp. V:** 277; **Supp. VIII:** 101, 105; **Supp. XIV:** 24; **Supp. XV:** 135, 137, 182; **Supp. XVII:** 105, 107; **Supp. XXI:** 8; **Supp. XXIII:** 68

"Dos Passos: Poet Against the World" (Cowley), **Supp. II Part 1:** 143, 145

Dostoevsky, Fyodor, **I:** 53, 103, 211, 468; **II:** 60, 130, 275, 320, 587; **III:** 37, 61, 155, 174, 176, 188, 189, 267, 272, 283, 286, 354, 357, 358, 359, 467, 571, 572; **IV:** 1, 7, 8, 17, 21, 50, 59, 106, 110, 128, 134, 285, 289, 476, 485, 491; **Retro. Supp. II:** 20, 204, 299; **Supp. I Part 1:** 49; **Supp. I Part 2:** 445, 466; **Supp. IV Part 2:** 519, 525; **Supp. VIII:** 175; **Supp. X:** 4–5; **Supp. XI:** 161; **Supp. XII:** 322; **Supp. XVI:** 63; **Supp. XVII:** 225; **Supp. XVIII:** 278, 280; **Supp. XX:** 45; **Supp. XXIII:** 4

Doty, Mark, **Supp. IX:** 42, 300; **Supp. XI: 119–138; Supp. XXI:** 129, 130, 131, 139, 141; **Supp. XXIII:** 126, 221

Doty, M. R. *See* Dawson, Ruth; Doty, Mark

Double, The (Dostoevsky), **Supp. IX:** 105

"Double, The" (Levis), **Supp. XI:** 260, **261–263**

Double, The (Rank), **Supp. IX:** 105

Double Agent, The (Blackmur), **Supp. II Part 1:** 90, 108, 146

Double Axe, The (Jeffers), **Supp. II Part 2:** 416, 434

"Double Blind" (Skloot), **Supp. XX: 194, 208**

Doubleday, Frank, **I:** 500, 502, 515, 517; **III:** 327

Doubleday, Mrs. Frank, **I:** 500

Double Deuce (Parker), **Supp. XIX:** 183

Double Down (F. and S. Barthelme), **Supp. XI:** 27, 34, 35, 36–38

Double Dream of Spring, The (Ashbery), **Supp. III Part 1:** 11–13

Double Fold: Libraries and the Assault on Paper (Baker), **Supp. XIII:** 52, 56

Double Game (Calle), **Supp. XII:** 22

"Double Gap, The" (Auchincloss), **Supp. IV Part 1:** 33

"Double-Headed Snake of Newbury, The" (Whittier), **Supp. I Part 2:** 698

Double Honeymoon (Connell), **Supp. XIV:** 80, 87

Double Image, The (Levertov), **Supp. III Part 1:** 274, 276

"Double Image, The" (Sexton), **Supp. II Part 2:** 671, 677–678

Double Indemnity (film), **Supp. IV Part 1:** 130

Double Legacy: Reflections on a Pair of Deaths (Hadas), **Supp. XXIII:** 123, **126–127**

"Double Limbo" (Komunyakaa), **Supp. XIII:** 132

Double Man, The (Auden), **Supp. III Part 1:** 16; **Supp. X:** 118

"Double Ode" (Rukeyser), **Supp. VI:** 282–283, 286

Double Persephone (Atwood), **Supp. XIII:** 19

Double Play (Parker), **Supp. XIX: 189–190**

Doubles in Literary Psychology (Tymms), **Supp. IX:** 105

Double Vision: American Thoughts Abroad (Knowles), **Supp. XII:** 249

"Doubt on the Great Divide" (Stafford), **Supp. XI:** 322

Dougherty, Robin, **Supp. XXII:** 205

Dougherty, Steve, **Supp. X:** 262

Douglas, Aaron, **Supp. I Part 1:** 326

Douglas, Alfred, **Supp. X:** 151

Douglas, Ann, **Supp. XII:** 136; **Supp. XVIII:** 258; **Supp. XX: 69**

Douglas, Claire, **III:** 552

Douglas, Ellen, **Supp. XXI:** 38

Douglas, George (pseudonym). *See* Brown, George Douglas

Douglas, Kirk, **Supp. XIII:** 5–6

Douglas, Lloyd, **IV:** 434

Douglas, Marjory Stoneman, **Supp. XVIII:** 195

Douglas, Melvyn, **Supp. V:** 223

Douglas, Michael, **Supp. XI:** 67

Douglas, Paul, **III:** 294

Douglas, Stephen A., **III:** 577, 588–589; **Supp. I Part 2:** 456, 471

Douglas, William O., **III:** 581

Douglass, Frederick, **Supp. I Part 1:** 51, 345; **Supp. I Part 2:** 591; **Supp. II Part 1:** 157, 195, 196, 292, 378; **Supp. III Part 1: 153–174;** **Supp. IV Part 1:** 1, 2, 13, 15, 256; **Supp. VIII:** 202; **Supp. XVIII:** 16; **Supp. XX: 109, 281; Supp. XXIII:** 167

Douglass, Thomas E., **Supp. XXIII:** 36

Douglass Pilot, The (Baldwin, ed.), **Supp. I Part 1:** 49

Dove, Belle, **I:** 451

Dove, Rita, **Supp. IV Part 1: 241–258;** **Supp. XVII:** 71, 110; **Supp. XVIII:** 172, 174; **Supp. XXI:** 243, 246, 247, 249, 251

"Dover Beach" (Arnold), **Retro. Supp. I:** 325; **Supp. XIX:** 41

Dow, Lorenzo, **IV:** 265

Dowd, Douglas, **Supp. I Part 2:** 645, 650

"Do We Understand Each Other?" (Ginsberg), **Supp. II Part 1:** 311

Dowie, William, **Supp. V:** 199

Do with Me What You Will (Oates), **Supp. II Part 2:** 506, 515–517

Dowling, Eddie, **IV:** 394

Down and Out (Shanley), **Supp. XIV:** 317

"Down at City Hall" (Didion), **Supp. IV Part 1:** 211

"Down at the Cross" (Baldwin), **Retro. Supp. II:** 1, 2, 7, 12, 13, 15; **Supp. I Part 1:** 60, 61

"Down at the Dinghy" (Salinger), **III:** 559, 563

"Down by the Station, Early in the Morning" (Ashbery), **Supp. III Part 1:** 25

Downey, Sharon D., **Supp. XX: 244**

Downhill Racer (film), **Supp. IX:** 253

"Down Home" (J. W. Miller), **Supp. XX: 169**

"Down in Alabam" (Bierce), **I:** 193

Downing, Ben, **Supp. XII:** 175, 189, 190–191

Downing, Major Jack (pseudonym). *See* Smith, Seba

Down in My Heart (Stafford), **Supp. XI:** 313, 315

Down Mailer's Way (Solotaroff), **Retro. Supp. II:** 203

"Down the Highway" (song, Dylan), **Supp. XVIII:** 24

Down the Rabbit Hole: Adventures and Misadventures in the Realm of Children's Literature (Lanes), **Supp. XVI:** 104

Down There on a Visit (Isherwood), **Supp. XIV:** 159, 161, 164, **168–169,** 170, 171

Down the River (Abbey), **Supp. XIII:** 12–13

"Down the River with Henry Thoreau" (Abbey), **Supp. XIII:** 12–13

Down These Mean Streets (P. Thomas), **Supp. XIII:** 264

Down the Starry River (Purdy), **Supp. VII:** 278

Down to the River: Portraits of Iowa Musicians (Dyas), **Supp. XIX:** 174

Downtown (Siddons), **Supp. XXII:** 239, 240, 242, **247–249, 251–252,** 253

"Downtrodden Mary's Failed Campaign of Terror" (Saunders), **Supp. XIX:** 226

"Downward Path to Wisdom, The" (Porter), **III:** 442, 443, 446

"Down Where I Am" (Hughes), **Supp. I Part 1:** 344

Down with Starvation Wages in Southeast Missouri (C. L. R. James), **Supp. XXI:** 169

"Dowsing for Joy" (Skloot), **Supp. XX: 203**

Dowson, Ernest C., **I:** 384

Doyle, Arthur Conan, **Retro. Supp. I:** 270; **Supp. IV Part 1:** 128, 341; **Supp. IV Part 2:** 464, 469; **Supp. XI:** 63

Doyle, C. W., **I:** 199

"Draba" (Leopold), **Supp. XIV:** 186

Drabble, Margaret, **Supp. IV Part 1:** 297, 299, 305

Drabelle, Dennis, **Supp. XIII:** 13

Drach, Ivan, **Supp. III Part 1:** 268

Dracula (film), **Supp. IV Part 1:** 104; **Supp. XVII:** 57

"Draft Horse, The" (Frost), **Retro. Supp. I:** 141

"Draft Lyrics for *Candide*" (Agee), **I:** 28

Draft of XVI Cantos, A (Pound), **III:** 472; **Retro. Supp. I:** 292

Draft of XXX Cantos, A (Pound), **III:** 196; **Retro. Supp. I:** 292

Drafts & Fragments (Pound), **Retro. Supp. I:** 293

Dragon Country (T. Williams), **IV:** 383

Dragone, Nichole, **Supp. XXIII:** 157

Dragon Seed (Buck), **Supp. II Part 1:** 124

Dragon's Teeth (Sinclair), **Supp. V:** 290

Drake, Benjamin, **Supp. I Part 2:** 584

Drake, Daniel, **Supp. I Part 2:** 584

Drake, Sir Francis, **Supp. I Part 2:** 497

Drake, Robert, **Supp. XX: 274**

Drake, St. Clair, **IV:** 475

Drake, Sylvia, **Supp. XXI:** 155

Drake, William, **Supp. XV:** 295

Dramatic Duologues (Masters), **Supp. I Part 2:** 461

"Drapery Factory, Gulfport. Mississippi, 1956" (Trethewey), **Supp. XXI:** 246

Drattel, Deborah, **Supp. XV:** 333

Drat These Brats (X. J. Kennedy), **Supp. XV:** 163

"Draught" (Cowley), **Supp. II Part 1:** 141, 142

Drayton, Michael, **IV:** 135; **Retro. Supp. II:** 76

"Dr. Bergen's Belief" (Schwartz), **Supp. II Part 2:** 650

Dr. Bloodmoney (Dick), **Supp. XVIII:** 138

"Dreadful Has Already Happened, The" (Strand), **Supp. IV Part 2:** 627

Dread Road, The (Le Sueur), **Supp. XXIII:** 168, 169, **169–170,** 173

"Dream, A" (Ginsberg), **Supp. II Part 1:** 312

"Dream, A" (Tate), **IV:** 129

"Dream, The" (Hayden), **Supp. II Part 1:** 368, 377

Dream at the End of the World, The: Paul Bowles and the Literary Renegades in Tangier (Green), **Supp. IV Part 1:** 95

"Dream Avenue" (Simic), **Supp. VIII:** 282

"Dream Boogie" (Hughes), **Retro. Supp. I:** 208; **Supp. I Part 1:** 339–340

"Dreambook Bestiary" (Komunyakaa), **Supp. XIII:** 120

Dreamer (Johnson), **Supp. VI:** 186, **196–199**

dreamer examines his pillow, the (Shanley), **Supp. XIV:** 315, **327**

"Dreamer in a Dead Language" (Paley), **Supp. VI:** 217

Dreaming in Cuban (García), **Supp. XI:** 178, **179–185,** 190

"Dreaming of Hair" (L.-Y. Lee), **Supp. XV:** 214

"Dreaming the Breasts" (Sexton), **Supp. II Part 2:** 692

"Dreaming Water" (Espaillat), **Supp. XXI:** 102

"Dream Interpretation" (Hadas), **Supp. XXIII:** 113, 121

"Dream Interpreted, The" (Paine), **Supp. I Part 2:** 505

Dream Jumbo (Longo), **Supp. XVI:** 124

Dream Keeper, The (Hughes), **Supp. I Part 1:** 328, 332, 333, 334

Dream Keeper and Other Poems, The (Hughes), **Retro. Supp. I:** 201, 202

Dreamland (Baker), **Supp. XIV:** 96

"Dream-Land" (Poe), **Retro. Supp. II:** 274

Dream Life of Balso Snell, The (West), **IV:** 286, 287, 288–290, 291, 297; **Retro. Supp. II:** 321, 322, 327, 328, **330–332**

"Dream Machine, The" (Hadas), **Supp. XXIII:** 122–123

Dream Me Home Safely: Writers on Growing up in America (Shreve, ed.), **Supp. XXIII:** 284

Dream of a Common Language, The: Poems, 1974–1977 (Rich), **Supp. I Part 2:** 551, 554, 569–576

Dream of Arcadia: American Writers and Artists in Italy (Brooks), **I:** 254

Dream of Governors, A (Simpson), **Supp. IX:** 265, **269–270**

"Dream of Italy, A" (Masters), **Supp. I Part 2:** 458

"Dream of Mourning, The" (Glück), **Supp. V:** 84

"Dream of the Blacksmith's Room, A" (R. Bly), **Supp. IV Part 1:** 73

"Dream of the Cardboard Lover" (Haines), **Supp. XII:** 204

Dream of the Golden Mountains, The (Cowley), **Supp. II Part 1:** 139, 141, 142, 144

"Dream Pang, A" (Frost), **II:** 153

"Dreams About Clothes" (Merrill), **Supp. III Part 1:** 328–329

"Dreams"(Dybek), **Supp. XXIII:** 73

Dreams from Bunker Hill (Fante), **Supp. XI:** 160, 166, **172–173**

"Dreams"(Kenny), **Supp. XXIII:** 153

"Dreams of Adulthood" (Ashbery), **Supp. III Part 1:** 26

"Dreams of Glory on the Mound" (Plimpton), **Supp. XVI:** 238–239

"Dreams of Math" (Kenyon), **Supp. VII:** 160–161

"Dreams of the Animals" (Atwood), **Supp. XIII:** 33

"Dream Variations" (Hughes), **Retro. Supp. I:** 198; **Supp. I Part 1:** 323

"Dream Vision" (Olsen), **Supp. XIII:** 295–296

Dream Work (Oliver), **Supp. VII:** 234–235, 236–238, 240

Dred: A Tale of the Great Dismal Swamp (Stowe), **Supp. I Part 2:** 592

Dreiser, Theodore, **I:** 59, 97, 109, 116, 355, 374, 375, 475, 482, **497–520; II:** 26, 27, 29, 34, 38, 44, 74, 89, 93, 180, 276, 283, 428, 444, 451, 456–457, 467–468; **III:** 40, 103, 106, 251, 314, 319, 327, 335, 453, 576, 582; **IV:** 29, 35, 40, 135, 208, 237, 475, 482, 484; **Retro. Supp. I:** 325, 376; **Retro. Supp. II: 93–110,** 114, 322; **Supp. I Part 1:** 320; **Supp. I Part 2:** 461, 468; **Supp. III Part 2:** 412; **Supp. IV Part 1:** 31, 236, 350; **Supp. IV Part 2:** 689; **Supp. V:** 113, 120; **Supp. VIII:** 98, 101, 102; **Supp. IX:** 1, 14, 15, 308; **Supp. XI:** 207; **Supp. XIV:** 111; **Supp. XVII:** 95, 96–97, 105, 155; **Supp. XVIII:** 1, 6, 76, 226; **Supp. XXI:** 275; **Supp. XXIII:** 161, 164

"Drenched in Light" (Hurston), **Supp. VI:** 150–151

Drennen, Eileen M., **Supp. XXII:** 241, 243

Dresser, Paul, **Retro. Supp. II:** 94, 103

Dress Gray (teleplay), **Supp. IV Part 2:** 683

Dress Gray (Truscott), **Supp. IV Part 2:** 683

"Dressing for Dinner" (Ríos), **Supp. IV Part 2:** 548

Dressing Up for the Carnival (Shields), **Supp. VII:** 328

"Dress Rehearsal" (Skloot), **Supp. XX: 204**

Drew, Bettina, **Supp. IX:** 2, 4

Drew, Elizabeth, **Retro. Supp. II:** 242, 243

Drexler, Eric, **Supp. XVI:** 121

Dreyfus, Alfred, **Supp. I Part 2:** 446

"Dr. Hanray's Second Chance" (Richter), **Supp. XVIII:** 218

Drift and Mastery (Lippmann), **I:** 222–223

"Driftwood" (C. Frost), **Supp. XV:** 106–107

"Drinker, The" (Lowell), **II:** 535, 550

"Drinking Cold Water" (Everwine), **Supp. XV:** 80–81

"Drinking from a Helmet" (Dickey), **Supp. IV Part 1:** 180

Drinking Gourd, The (Hansberry), **Supp. IV Part 1:** 359, 365–367, 374

Drinks before Dinner (Doctorow), **Supp. IV Part 1:** 231, 234–235

Driscoll, David, **Supp. XIX:** 241, 242

Driskill, Qwo-Li, **Supp. XXIII:** 147, 148, 149

Drive, He Said (Larner), **Supp. XVI:** 220

"Drive Home, The" (Banks), **Supp. V:** 7

"Driver" (Merrill), **Supp. III Part 1:** 331

"Driving Alone in Winter" (W. V. Davis), **Supp. XXI:** 89, 90, 94

"Driving Through Minnesota During the Hanoi Bombings" (R. Bly), **Supp. IV Part 1:** 61; **Supp. XVII:** 243

"Driving through Oregon" (Haines), **Supp. XII:** 207

"Driving to Oregon"(Thompson), **Supp. XXIII:** 291

"Driving toward the Lac Qui Parle River" (R. Bly), **Supp. IV Part 1:** 61

"Dr. Jack-o'-Lantern" (Yates), **Supp. XI:** 340–341

Dr. Jekyll and Mr. Hyde (film), **Supp. XVII:** 57

"Drone" (Coleman), **Supp. XI:** 85–86

Drop City (Boyle), **Supp. XX: 30–31**

"Drowned Man, The: Death between Two Rivers" (McGrath), **Supp. X:** 116

"Drowning" (Boyle), **Supp. XX:** 18

"Drowning 1954" (Keillor), **Supp. XVI:** 172

Drowning Pool, The (film), **Supp. IV Part 2:** 474

Drowning Pool, The (Macdonald), **Supp. IV Part 2:** 470, 471

Drowning Season, The (Hoffman), **Supp. X: 82**

Drowning with Others (Dickey), **Supp. IV Part 1:** 176, 178, 179

"Drowsy Day, A" (Dunbar), **Supp. II Part 1:** 198

Dr. Seuss. *See* Geisel, Theodor Seuss (Dr. Seuss)

Dr. Seuss and Mr. Geisel (J. and N. Morgan), **Supp. XVI:** 103

Dr. Seuss Goes to War: The World War II Editorial Cartoons of Theodor Seuss Geisel (Minear), **Supp. XVI:** 101

Dr. Seuss's ABC (Geisel), **Supp. XVI:** 99

Dr. Strangelove; or, How I Learned to Stop Worrying and Love the Bomb (film), **Supp. XI:** 293, **301–305**

Drugiye Berega (Nabokov), **III:** 247–250, 252

"Drug Shop, The, or Endymion in Edmonstoun" (Benét), **Supp. XI:** 43

"Drug Store" (Shapiro), **Supp. II Part 2:** 705

"Drugstore in Winter, A" (Ozick), **Supp. V:** 272

Drukman, Steven, **Supp. XIII:** 195, 197, 202

"Drum" (Hogan), **Supp. IV Part 1:** 413

"Drum, The" (Alvarez), **Supp. VII:** 7

"Drumlin Woodchuck, A" (Frost), **II:** 159–160; **Retro. Supp. I:** 138

Drummond, William, **Supp. I Part 1:** 369

Drummond de Andrade, Carlos, **Supp. IV Part 2:** 626, 629, 630

Drums at Dusk (Bontemps), **Supp. XXII:** 5, 9–10

Drum-Taps (Whitman), **IV:** 346, 347, 444; **Retro. Supp. I:** 406

"Drunken Fisherman, The" (Lowell), **II:** 534, 550

"Drunken Sisters, The" (Wilder), **IV:** 374

Drunk in the Furnace, The (Merwin), **Supp. III Part 1:** 345–346

"Drunk in the Furnace, The" (Merwin), **Supp. III Part 1:** 346

Druten, John van, **Supp. XIV:** 162

"Dr. Williams' Position" (Pound), **Supp. XVII:** 226–227

Dryden, John, **II:** 111, 542, 556; **III:** 15; **IV:** 145; **Retro. Supp. I:** 56; **Supp. I Part 1:** 150; **Supp. I Part 2:** 422; **Supp. IX:** 68; **Supp. XIV:** 5; **Supp. XV:** 258; **Supp. XX:** 280

Drye, Captain Frank, **Retro. Supp. II:** 115

Dry Salvages, The (Eliot), **I:** 581

"Dry Salvages, The" (Eliot), **Retro. Supp. I:** 66

"Dry September" (Faulkner), **II:** 72, 73

"Dry Spring"(Thompson), **Supp. XXIII:** 291

Dry Sun, Dry Wind (Wagoner), **Supp. IX:** 323, 324

D'Souza, Dinesh, **Supp. X:** 255

"Dual" (Goldbarth), **Supp. XII:** 188

"Dual Curriculum" (Ozick), **Supp. V:** 270

"Dualism" (Reed), **Supp. X:** 242

Duane's Depressed (McMurtry), **Supp. V:** 233

Du Bartas, Guillaume, **Supp. I Part 1:** 98, 104, 111, 118, 119

Duberman, Martin, **Supp. I Part 2:** 408, 409

"Dubin's Lives" (Malamud), **Supp. I Part 2:** 451

Dubious Honors (M. F. K. Fisher), **Supp. XVII:** 91

"Dubliners" (J. Joyce), **Supp. XVI:** 41

Dubliners (Joyce), **I:** 130, 480; **III:** 471; **Supp. VIII:** 146

Dublin's Lives (Malamud), **Supp. XIX:** 142

Du Bois, Nina Gomer (Mrs. W. E. B. Du Bois), **Supp. II P art 1:** 158; **Supp. XIV:** 200

Du Bois, Shirley Graham, **Supp. II Part 1:** 186; **Supp. XXI:** 171. *See also* Graham, Shirley

Du Bois, W. E. B., **I:** 260; **Supp. I Part 1:** 5, 345; **Supp. II Part 1:** 33, 56, 61, **157–189,** 195; **Supp. IV Part 1:** 9, 164, 170, 362; **Supp. X:** 133, 134, 137, 139, 242; **Supp. XIII:** 185, **Supp. XIII:** 186, 233, 238, 243, 244, 247; **Supp. XIV:** 54, 69, 72, 201, 202; **Supp. XVI:** 135; **Supp. XVIII:** 119, 122, 126, 130; **Supp. XIX:** 67, 69, 77; **Supp. XX: 102, 105, 106; Supp. XXI:** 166, 277; **Supp. XXII:** 3

Dubreuil, Jean, **Supp. IV Part 2:** 425

Dubus, Andre, **Supp. VII: 75–93; Supp. XI:** 347,**Supp. XI:** 349; **Supp. XIV:** 21

Duchamp, Marcel, **IV:** 408; **Retro. Supp. I:** 416, 417, 418, 430; **Supp. IV Part 2:** 423, 424; **Supp. XII:** 124; **Supp. XV:** 157; **Supp. XXII:** 162, 163, 168

"Duchess at Prayer, The" (Wharton), **Retro. Supp. I:** 365

Duchess of Malfi, The (Webster), **IV:** 131

Duck Soup (film), **Supp. IV Part 1:** 384

Duck Variations, The (Mamet), **Supp. XIV:** 239, 240, 249

Ducornet, Rikki, **Supp. XXII:** 261

Dudley, Anne. *See* Bradstreet, Anne

Dudley, Joseph, **III:** 52

Dudley, Thomas, **III:** 52; **Supp. I Part 1:** 98, 99, 110, 116

"Duenna"(Schott), **Supp. XXIII:** 249

"Duet, With Muffled Brake Drums" (Updike), **Retro. Supp. I:** 319

Duet for Cannibals (Sontag), **Supp. III Part 2:** 452, 456

Duffey, Bernard, **Supp. I Part 2:** 458, 471

Duffield, Pitts, **Supp. XXI:** 3

Duffus, R. L., **Supp. I Part 2:** 650

Duffy, Martha, **Supp. IV Part 1:** 207; **Supp. XX: 244**

Duffy, William, **Supp. XVI:** 32

Du Fu (Tu Fu), **Supp. XV:** 217

Dufy, Raoul, **I:** 115; **IV:** 80

Dugan, Alan, **Supp. XIII:** 76

Dugan, James, **Supp. XV:** 197

"Dugout"(Kenny), **Supp. XXIII:** 155

Duhamel, Marcel, **Supp. XVI:** 135, 143

Dujardin, Edouard, **I:** 53

"Duke de l'Omelette, The" (Poe), **III:** 411, 425

"Duke in His Domain, The" (Capote), **Supp. III Part 1:** 113, 126

Duke of Deception, The (G. Wolff), **Supp. II Part 1:** 97; **Supp. XI:** 246

"Duke's Child, The" (Maxwell), **Supp. VIII:** 172

"Dulce et Decorum Est" (Owen), **Supp. XVIII:** 92

"Dulham Ladies, The" (Jewett), **II:** 407, 408; **Retro. Supp. II:** 143

Duluth (Vidal), **Supp. IV Part 2:** 677, 685, 689, 691–692

Dumas, Alexandre, **III:** 386; **Supp. XVII:** 64

"Dumb Oax, The" (Lewis), **Retro. Supp. I:** 170

"Dummy, The" (Sontag), **Supp. III Part 2:** 469

"Dump Ground, The" (Stegner), **Supp. IV Part 2:** 601

Dunant, Sarah, **Supp. XIX:** 186

Dunayevskaya, Raya, **Supp. XXI:** 169

Dunbar, Alice Moore (Mrs. Paul Laurence Dunbar), **Supp. II Part 1:** 195, 200, 217

Dunbar, Paul Laurence, **Supp. I Part 1:** 320; **Supp. II Part 1:** 174, **191–219; Supp. III Part 1:** 73; **Supp. IV Part 1:** 15, 165, 170; **Supp. X:** 136; **Supp. XI:** 277; **Supp. XIII:** 111; **Supp. XXII:** 11

Duncan, Harry, **Supp. XV:** 75

Duncan, Isadora, **I:** 483; **Supp. XV:** 42, 50

Duncan, Robert, **Retro. Supp. II:** 49; **Supp. III Part 2:** 625, 626, 630, 631; **Supp. VIII:** 304; **Supp. XVI:** 282–283; **Supp. XXIII:** 213

Dunciad, The (Pope), **I:** 204

Dunford, Judith, **Supp. VIII:** 107

Dunlap, William, **Supp. I Part 1:** 126, 130, 137, 141, 145

Dunn, Stephen, **Supp. XI: 139–158; Supp. XIX:** 85

Dunne, Finley Peter, **II:** 432

Dunne, John Gregory, **Supp. IV Part 1:** 197, 198, 201, 203, 207

"Dunnet Shepherdess, A" (Jewett), **II:** 392–393; **Retro. Supp. II:** 139

Dunning, Stephen, **Supp. XIV:** 126

Dunning, William Archibald, **Supp. II Part 1:** 170; **Supp. XIV:** 48

Dunnock, Mildred, **III:** 153

Dunster, Henry, **Supp. I Part 2:** 485

"Duo Tried Killing Man with Bacon" (Goldbarth), **Supp. XII:** 176

Dupee, F. W., **I:** 254; **II:** 548; **Supp. VIII:** 231; **Supp. IX:** 93, 96

DuPlessis, Rachel Blau, **Supp. IV Part 2:** 421, 426, 432; **Supp. XVI:** 284

Duplicate Keys (Smiley), **Supp. VI:** 292, **294–296**

Duplications, The (Koch), **Supp. XV:** 181, 183, 186

Durable Fire, A (Sarton), **Supp. VIII:** 260

Durand, Asher, B., **Supp. I Part 1:** 156, 157

Durand, Régis, **Supp. IV Part 1:** 44

"Durango Suite" (Gunn Allen), **Supp. IV Part 1:** 326

Durant, Kenneth, **Supp. XXII:** 278, 281

"Durations" (Matthews), **Supp. IX:** 152–153, 154

Dürer, Albrecht, **III:** 212; **Supp. XII:** 44

Durham, David Anthony, **Supp. XVIII:** 100

"During Fever" (Lowell), **II:** 547

Durkheim, Émile, **I:** 227; **Retro. Supp. I:** 55, 57; **Supp. I Part 2:** 637, 638

Durrell, Lawrence, **III:** 184, 190; **IV:** 430; **Supp. X:** 108, 187; **Supp. XVI:** 294

Dürrenmatt, Friedrich, **Supp. IV Part 2:** 683

Duse, Eleonora, **II:** 515, 528

Dusk and Other Stories (Salter), **Supp. IX: 260–261**

Dusk of Dawn: An Essay Toward an Autobiography of a Race Concept (Du Bois), **Supp. II Part 1:** 159, 183, 186

"Dust" (R. Fisher), **Supp. XIX:** 71

"Dusting" (Alvarez), **Supp. VII:** 4

"Dusting" (Dove), **Supp. IV Part 1:** 247, 248

"Dusting" (Schnackenberg), **Supp. XV:** 256

"Dust of Snow" (Frost), **II:** 154

Dust Tracks on a Road (Hurston), **Supp. IV Part 1:** 5, 11; **Supp. VI:** 149, 151, 158–159

"Dusty Braces" (Snyder), **Supp. VIII:** 302

Dutchman (Baraka), **Supp. II Part 1:** 38, 40, 42–44, 54, 55

"Dutch Nick Massacre, The" (Twain), **IV:** 195

"Dutch Picture, A" (Longfellow), **Retro. Supp. II:** 171

Dutton, Charles S., **Supp. VIII:** 332, 342

Dutton, Clarence Earl, **Supp. IV Part 2:** 598

Duvall, Robert, **Supp. V:** 227

"Duwamish" (Hugo), **Supp. VI:** 136

"Duwamish, Skagit, Hoh" (Hugo), **Supp. VI:** 136–137

"Duwamish No. 2" (Hugo), **Supp. VI:** 137

Duyckinck, Evert, **III:** 77, 81, 83, 85; **Retro. Supp. I:** 155, 247, 248; **Supp. I Part 1:** 122, 317

Duyckinck, George, **Supp. I Part 1:** 122

"Dvonya" (Simpson), **Supp. IX:** 274

Dwellings: A Spiritual History of the Living World (Hogan), **Supp. IV Part 1:** 397, 410, 415–416, 417

Dwight, Sereno E., **I:** 547

Dwight, Timothy, **Supp. I Part 1:** 124; **Supp. I Part 2:** 516, 580; **Supp. II Part 1:** 65, 69

Dworkin, Andrea, **Supp. XII:** 6

Dwyer, Jim, **Supp. XVI:** 16, 19

Dyas, Sandra, **Supp. XIX:** 174

Dybbuk, A, or Between Two Worlds: Dramatic Legend in Four Acts (Kushner), **Supp. IX:** 138

Dybbuk, The (Ansky), **IV:** 6

Dybek, Stuart, **Supp. XXIII: 67–81**

Dybuk, The (Ansky), **Supp. XXIII:** 8

Dyer, Geoff, **Supp. X:** 169

Dyer, Joyce, **Supp. XX: 166**

Dyer, R. C., **Supp. XIII:** 162

Dyer, Richard, **Supp. XXII:** 261

Dyer's Thistle (Balakian), **Supp. XXIII:** 25

Dying Animal, The (P. Roth), **Retro. Supp. II:** 288

"Dying Elm, The" (Freneau), **Supp. II Part 1:** 258

"Dying Indian, The" (Freneau), **Supp. II Part 1:** 262

"Dying Man, The" (Roethke), **III:** 540, 542, 543–545

Dykeman, Wilma, **Supp. XX: 163**

Dylan, Bob, **Supp. VIII:** 202; **Supp. XIII:** 114, 119; **Supp. XV:** 349, 350; **Supp. XVIII: 19–34; Supp. XXII:** 83

Dylan's Visions of Sin (Ricks), **Supp. XVIII:** 20

"Dynamics of Heroic Action, The" (lecture, Murray), **Supp. XIX:** 153

Dynamo (O'Neill), **III:** 396

"Dynasties" (Gibran), **Supp. XX: 118**

"Dysfunctional Narratives: Or, 'Mistakes Were Made' " (C. Baxter), **Supp. XVII:** 20

"Dysfunctional Nation" (Karr), **Supp. XI:** 245

Dyson, A. E., **Retro. Supp. II:** 247

Dyson, Freeman, **Supp. XVII:** 42

E

"Each and All" (Emerson), **II:** 19

Each Happiness Ringer by Lions (Hirshfield), **Supp. XXIII:** 135

Each in His Season (Snodgrass), **Supp. VI:** 324, 327

"Each Like a Leaf" (Swenson), **Supp. IV Part 2:** 644

Eads, Martha Greene, **Supp. XVIII:** 49

Eady, Cornelius, **Supp. XXI:** 246

Eager, Allen, **Supp. XI:** 294

"Eagle, The" (Tate), **IV:** 128

"Eagle and the Mole, The" (Wylie), **Supp. I Part 2:** 710, 711, 713, 714, 729

"Eagle and the Skylark, The" (Gibran), **Supp. XX: 124**

Eagle as Wide as the World, The (X. J. Kennedy), **Supp. XV:** 162, 164

"Eagle Poem" (Harjo), **Supp. XII:** 224, 226

"Eagles" (Dickey), **Supp. IV Part 1:** 186

Eagle's Mile, The (Dickey), **Supp. IV Part 1:** 178, 185–186

"Eagle That Is Forgotten, The" (Lindsay), **Supp. I Part 2:** 382, 387

Eagleton, Terry, **Retro. Supp. I:** 67

Eakin, Paul John, **Supp. VIII:** 167, 168; **Supp. XIII:** 225; **Supp. XVI:** 70

Eakins, Thomas, **Supp. XIV:** 338; **Supp. XXII:** 18–19

Eames, Emma, **Supp. XX: 232, 240**

Eames, Roscoe, **II:** 476

"Earl: My Life with a Louse" (Keillor), **Supp. XVI:** 176

"Earl Painter" (Banks), **Supp. V:** 14–15

"Early Adventures of Ralph Ringwood, The" (Irving), **II:** 314

Early Americana (Richter), **Supp. XVIII:** 208, 210, 211, 220

Early Autumn (Parker), **Supp. XIX:** 184–185

Early Ayn Rand, The: A Selection of Her Unpublished Fiction (Rand), **Supp. IV Part 2:** 520

Early Dark (Price), **Supp. VI:** 262

Early Diary of Anaïs Nin, The, **Supp. X:** 184, 192

Early Elkin (Elkin), **Supp. VI: 42–43,** 45

"Early Evenin' Blues" (Hughes), **Retro. Supp. I:** 205

"Early Evening, Frankfort, Kentucky" (Trethewey), **Supp. XXI:** 243, 250

"Early History of a Seamstress" (Reznikoff), **Supp. XIV:** 277, 289

Early History of a Sewing-Machine Operator (Reznikoff), **Supp. XIV:** 289

"Early History of a Sewing-Machine Operator" (Reznikoff), **Supp. XIV:** 277

"Early History of a Writer" (Reznikoff), **Supp. XIV:** 278, 290

"Early in the Morning" (L.-Y. Lee), **Supp. XV:** 214

Early Lectures of Ralph Waldo Emerson, The (Emerson), **II:** 11

Early Light (Di Piero), **Supp. XIX:** 38, **38–40**

Early Lives of Melville, The (Sealts), **Retro. Supp. I:** 257

"Early Marriage" (Richter), **Supp. XVIII:** 209

Early Martyr and Other Poems, An (W. C. Williams), **Retro. Supp. I:** 423

"Early Morning: Cape Cod" (Swenson), **Supp. IV Part 2:** 641

"Early Rooms"(Hirshfield), **Supp. XXIII:** 130

"Early Spring between Madison and Bellingham" (R. Bly), **Supp. IV Part 1:** 71

Early Writing (O'Hara), **Supp. XXIII:** 220

Earnhardt, Dale, **Supp. XII:** 310

Earnshaw, Doris, **Supp. IV Part 1:** 310

"Earth" (Bryant), **Supp. I Part 1:** 157, 164, 167

"Earth, The" (Sexton), **Supp. II Part 2:** 696

Earth Abides (Stewart), **Supp. XVIII:** 138

"Earth and Fire" (Berry), **Supp. X:** 27

Earth as Air, The: An Ars Poetica (Sobin), **Supp. XVI: 285–286**

"Earth Being" (Toomer), **Supp. IX:** 320

Earth Goat (online), **Supp. XXII:** 61

Earth Gods, The (Gibran), **Supp. XX: 116, 123**

"Earthly Care a Heavenly Discipline" (Stowe), **Supp. I Part 2:** 586

"Earthly City of the Jews, The" (Kazin), **Retro. Supp. II:** 286

Earthly Meditations (Wrigley), **Supp. XVIII:** 304–305

"Earthly Meditations" (Wrigley), **Supp. XVIII:** 304–306

Earthly Possessions (Tyler), **Supp. IV Part 2:** 665–666, 671

Earth Power Coming (Ortiz, ed.), **Supp. IV Part 2:** 502

"Earth's Holocaust" (Hawthorne), **II:** 226, 231, 232, 242; **III:** 82; **Retro. Supp. I:** 152

Earth Without You, The (F. Wright), **Supp. XVII:** 243

Eason, Laura, **Supp. XXIII:** 79

East Coker (Eliot), **I:** 580, 581, 582, 585, 587

"East Coker" (Eliot), **Retro. Supp. I:** 66; **Supp. VIII:** 195, 196

"Easter" (Toomer), **Supp. III Part 2:** 486

"Easter, an Ode" (Lowell), **II:** 536

"Easter 1916" (Yeats), **Supp. XXI:** 61

"Easter Morning" (Ammons), **Supp. VII:** 34

"Easter Morning" (Clampitt), **Supp. IX:** 45

"Easter Ode, An" (Dunbar), **Supp. II Part 1:** 196

"Easter"(O'Hara), **Supp. XXIII:** 211

Easter Parade, The (Yates), **Supp. XI:** 346, 349

"Easter Sermon, 1866" (Nelson), **Supp. XVIII:** 177

"Easter Service" (Di Piero), **Supp. XIX:** 39–40

"Easter Sunday: Recollection" (Gunn Allen), **Supp. IV Part 1:** 322

"Easter Wings" (Herbert), **Supp. IV Part 2:** 646

"East European Cooking" (Simic), **Supp. VIII:** 277

East Is East (Boyle), **Supp. VIII:** 1–3; **Supp. XX: 23–24, 25, 28**

Eastlake, William, **Supp. XIII:** 12

East Lynne (Wood), **Supp. I Part 1:** 35, 36; **Supp. I Part 2:** 459, 462; **Supp. XVI:** 182

Eastman, Elaine Goodale, **Supp. X:** 103

Eastman, Max, **Supp. III Part 2:** 620; **Supp. X:** 131, 134, 135, 137; **Supp. XV:** 295; **Supp. XVI:** 185; **Supp. XVII:** 96; **Supp. XXI:** 6; **Supp. XXII:** 274, 275, 277

East of Eden (Steinbeck), **IV:** 51, 56–57, 59

"East of the Sun and West of the Moon" (Merwin), **Supp. III Part 1:** 344

Easton, Alison, **Retro. Supp. II:** 143, 144, 145

Easton, Bret Ellis, **Supp. XI:** 65

Easton, Nina J., **Supp. XIX:** 137

Easton, Robert, **Supp. IV Part 2:** 461, 474

East River (Asch), **Supp. XXIII:** 1, 3, 7, **14–15**

East Wind (Lowell), **II:** 527

East Wind: West Wind (Buck), **Supp. II Part 1:** 114–115

Easy Rawlins mysteries, **Supp. XIII:** 236, **237–241,** 242

Easy Rider (film), **Supp. XI:** 293, **308,** 309

Eat a Bowl of Tea (Chu), **Supp. X:** 291

"Eating " (Bass), **Supp. XVI:** 23–24

"Eating Alone" (L.-Y. Lee), **Supp. XV:** 214

"Eating Barley Sugar and Waiting to Be Ninety"(Hadas), **Supp. XXIII:** 120–121

Eating Naked (Dobyns), **Supp. XIII: 78–79**

"Eating Out" (L. Michaels), **Supp. XVI:** 209

"Eating Poetry" (Strand), **Supp. IV Part 2:** 626

"Eating the Whole" (C. Frost), **Supp. XV:** 101

"Eating Together" (L.-Y. Lee), **Supp. XV:** 214

"Eating with My Fingers" (C. Frost), **Supp. XV:** 97

Eaton, Edith, **Supp. X:** 291

Eaton, Mark A., **Supp. XXIII:** 129, 130, 136

Eaton, Peggy, **Supp. I Part 2:** 461

Eaton, Winnifred, **Supp. X:** 291

"Eatonville Anthology, The" (Hurston), **Supp. VI:** 152

Eat Pray Love (Gilbert), **Supp. XXII:** 83, 90

Eat the Document (film, Pennebaker), **Supp. XVIII:** 19, 26, 27, 28

"Ebb and Flow, The" (Taylor), **IV:** 161

"Ebenezer Marsh, 1725" (Schnackenberg), **Supp. XV:** 256

Eben Holden (Bacheller), **I:** 216

Eberhardt, Isabelle, **Supp. IV Part 1:** 92

Eberhart, Mrs., **I:** 521–522, 530

Eberhart, Richard, **I: 521–543; II:** 535–536; **III:** 527; **IV:** 416; **Retro. Supp. II:** 176, 178; **Supp. I Part 1:** 83; **Supp. XII:** 119

Eble, Kenneth E., **Supp. I Part 1:** 201

"Ecce Homo" (Cliff), **Supp. XXII:** 76

Eccentricities of a Nightingale (T. Williams), **IV:** 382, 385, 397, 398

Ecclesiastica Historia Integram Ecclesiae (Taylor), **IV:** 163

"Echart" (Sobin), **Supp. XVI:** 289

"Echo, The" (Bowles), **Supp. IV Part 1:** 84, 86, 87

Echoes inside the Labyrinth (McGrath), **Supp. X:** 127

Echo Park (Connelly), **Supp. XXI: 77–78**

Eckehart, Meister, **Supp. XV:** 225

Eckhart, Maria, **Supp. V:** 212

Eclipse (Hogan), **Supp. IV Part 1:** 397, 400, 402

Eclipse, a Nightmare (Montalembert), **Supp. XV:** 349

"Eclipse"(Schott), **Supp. XXIII:** 252

Eclogues (Virgil), **Supp. VIII:** 31

"Ecologue" (Ginsberg), **Supp. II Part 1:** 326

"Ecologues of These States 1969–1971" (Ginsberg), **Supp. II Part 1:** 325

Ecology of a Cracker Childhood (Ray), **Supp. XVIII:** 189, 191, 192, **193**, **195–199**, 201, 202, 204

"Economics of Negro Emancipation in the United States, The" (Du Bois), **Supp. II Part 1:** 174

"Economics of the Cracker Landscape: Poverty as an Environmental Issue in Larry Brown's *Joe*" (Watson), *Supp. XXI:* 46

"Economic Theory of Women's Dress, The" (Veblen), **Supp. I Part 2:** 636

Economy of the Unlost: Reading Simonides of Keos with Paul Celan (Carson), **Supp. XII:** 110–111

Ecotactics: The Sierra Club Handbook for Environmental Activists (Mitchell and Stallings, eds.), **Supp. IV Part 2:** 488

"Ecstasy" (Bierds), **Supp. XVII:** 34

"Ecstasy" (Olds), **Supp. X:** 206

"Ecstasy of Influence, The" (Lethem), **Supp. XVIII:** 150

"Ecstatic" (Komunyakaa), **Supp. XIII:** 131

Edda, **Supp. X:** 114

Eddy, Mary Baker, **I:** 583; **III:** 506

Edel, Leon, **I:** 20; **II:** 338–339; **Retro. Supp. I:** 218, 224, 231

Edelberg, Cynthia, **Supp. IV Part 1:** 155

"Eden and My Generation" (Levis), **Supp. XI:** 270

Edenbaum, Robert, **Supp. IV Part 1:** 352

Eden Tree (Bynner), **Supp. XV:** 42, 51

Edenville Owls (Parker), **Supp. XIX:** 190

Eder, Richard, **Supp. XII:** 189; **Supp. XV:** 62, 187, 259, 261

Edgar Huntly; or, Memoirs of a Sleep-Walker (Brown), **Supp. I Part 1:** 140–144, 145

"Edge" (Plath), **Retro. Supp. II:** 256; **Supp. I Part 2:** 527, 547

Edge, Mary E., **II:** 316

Edgell, Zee, **Supp. XXIII: 83–96**

"Edge of Possibility, The: Susan Warner and the World of Sunday School Fiction" (S. Gates), **Supp. XVIII:** 267

"Edge of the Great Rift, The" (Theroux), **Supp. VIII:** 325

Edge of the Sea, The (Carson), **Supp. IX:** 19, **25–31,** 32

Edgers, Geoff, **Supp. XV:** 113

Edgeworth, Maria, **II:** 8; **Supp. XV:** 231; **Supp. XX:** 108

Edible Woman, The (Atwood), **Supp. XIII:** 19, 20, **20–21**

"Edict by the King of Prussia, An" (Franklin), **II:** 120

Edie: An American Biography (Stein), **Supp. XVI:** 245

Edinburgh Days: or, Doing What I Want to Do (Pickering), **Supp. XXI:** 200–201

Edison, Thomas A., **I:** 483; **Supp. I Part 2:** 392

Edith Wharton (Joslin), **Retro. Supp. I:** 376

Edith Wharton: A Biography (Lewis), **Retro. Supp. I:** 362

Edith Wharton: A Woman in Her Time (Auchincloss), **Retro. Supp. I:** 370

Edith Wharton: Matters of Mind and Spirit (Singley), **Retro. Supp. I:** 373

Edith Wharton's Argument with America (Ammons), **Retro. Supp. I:** 364

Edith Wharton's Brave New Politics (Bauer), **Retro. Supp. I:** 381

Edith Wharton's Letters from the Underworld (Waid), **Retro. Supp. I:** 360

Edith Wharton: Traveller in the Land of Letters (Goodwyn), **Retro. Supp. I:** 370

"Editing and Glosses" (Reznikoff), **Supp. XIV:** 283

Editing of Emily Dickinson, The (Franklin), **Retro. Supp. I:** 41

"Editor and the Schoolma'am, The" (Frederic), **II:** 130

"Editor's Easy Chair" (Howells), **II:** 276

"Editor's Study, The" (Howells), **II:** 275, 276, 285

"Editor Whedon" (Masters), **Supp. I Part 2:** 463

Edlin, Mari, **Supp. X:** 266

Edman, Irwin, **III:** 605

Edmond (Mamet), **Supp. XIV:** 241, 248, 249, 250

Edmonds, Dale, **Supp. XXIII:** 291

Edmondson, Belinda, **Supp. XXII:** 70

Edmundson, Mark, **Retro. Supp. II:** 262

Edsel (Shapiro), **Supp. II Part 2:** 703, 704, 717–719

Edson, Margaret, **Supp. XVIII:** 35–52

Edson, Russell, **Supp. VIII:** 279

"Educated American Woman, An" (Cheever), **Supp. I Part 1:** 194

"Education, An" (Ozick), **Supp. V:** 267

Education and Living (Bourne), **I:** 252

"Education by Poetry" (Frost), **Supp. XV:** 215

"Education of a Storyteller, The" (Bambara), **Supp. XI:** 20

Education of Black People, The (Du Bois), **Supp. II Part 1:** 186

Education of Harriet Hatfield, The (Sarton), **Supp. VIII:** 257–258

Education of Henry Adams, The (Adams), **I:** 1, 5, 6, 11, 14, 15–18, 19, 20–21, 111; **II:** 276; **III:** 504; **Retro. Supp. I:** 53, 59; **Supp. IX:** 19; **Supp. XIV:** 299

Education of H*y*m*a*n K*a*p*l*a*n, The (Rosten), **Supp. XVII:** 9

"Education of Mingo, The" (Johnson), **Supp. VI:** 193, 194

"Education of Norman Podhoretz, The" (Goldberg), **Supp. VIII:** 238

Education of Oscar Fairfax, The (Auchincloss), **Supp. IV Part 1:** 25, 36

"Education of the Poet" (Glück), **Supp. V:** 78, 80

Education sentimentale (Flaubert), **III:** 315

"Education the Imagination" (Koch), **Supp. XV:** 175–176, 177

Edwards, Clifford, **Supp. XVIII:** 220

Edwards, Eli. *See* McKay, Claude

Edwards, Esther, **I:** 545

Edwards, Harry Stillwell, **Supp. XXII:** 193

Edwards, John, **I:** 478

Edwards, Jonathan, **I: 544–566; II:** 432; **Retro. Supp. II:** 187; **Supp. I Part 1:** 301, 302; **Supp. I Part 2:** 552, 594, 700; **Supp. IV Part 2:** 430; **Supp. VIII:** 205

Edwards, Sarah, **I:** 545

Edwards, Thomas, **Supp. XV:** 20

Edwards, Thomas R., **Supp. XVI:** 207

Edwards, Timothy, **I:** 545

Edwards-Yearwood, Grace, **Supp. VIII:** 81; **Supp. XXII:** 213

"Edwin Arlington Robinson" (Cowley), **Supp. II Part 1:** 144

Edwin Arlington Robinson (Winters), **Supp. II Part 2:** 812

Edwin Booth (play), **Supp. IV Part 1:** 89

E. E. Cummings (Marks), **I:** 438

E. E. Cummings: A Miscellany (Cummings), **I:** 429, 441

E. E. Cummings: A Miscellany, Revised (Cummings), **I:** 429

"Effects of Analogy" (Stevens), **Retro. Supp. I:** 297

Effluences from the Sacred Caves; More Selected Essays and Reviews (Carruth), **Supp. XVI:** 46

"Effort at Speech between Two People" (Rukeyser), **Supp. VI:** 276, 284

"Efforts of Affection" (Moore), **III:** 214

"Efforts of Affection: A Memoir of Marianne Moore" (Bishop), **Retro. Supp. II:** 52

Egan, Jennifer, **Supp. XIX:** 49–63; **Supp. XXIII:** 299, 300

Egan, Leona, **Supp. XXI:** 6

"Egg, The" (Anderson), **I:** 113, 114

"Egg, The" (Snyder), **Supp. VIII:** 302

Eggleston, George Cary, **Supp. XVIII:** 15

"Eggplant Epithalamion, The" (Jong), **Supp. V:** 119

"Eggs" (Olds), **Supp. X:** 206

"Eggshell" (Stern), **Supp. IX:** 299

Egoist, The (Meredith), **II:** 186

Egorova, Lubov, **Supp. IX:** 58

"Egotism, or the Bosom Sergent" (Hawthorne), **II:** 227, 239

"Egyptian Pulled Glass Bottle in the Shape of a Fish, An" (Moore), **III:** 195, 213

Ehrenfels, Christian von, **Supp. XIV:** 198

Ehrenpreis, Irvin, **Supp. XII:** 128

Ehrenreich, Barbara, **Supp. XVII:** 210

Ehrhart, W. D., **Supp. XIX:** 281

Ehrlich, Gretel, **Supp. XIV:** 227; **Supp. XVIII:** 189

Eichmann, Adolf, **Supp. XII:** 166

Eichmann in Jerusalem (Arendt), **Retro. Supp. II:** 28; **Supp. VIII:** 243; **Supp. XII:** 166

"Eichmann in New York: The New York Intellectuals and the Hannah Arendt Controversy" (Rabinbach), **Supp. XII:** 166

"Eidolon" (Warren), **IV:** 239

"Eiger Dreams" (Krakauer), **Supp. XVIII:** 107

Eiger Dreams: Ventures Among Men and Mountains (Krakauer), **Supp. XVIII:** 105, 106, 107

Eight Cousins (Alcott), **Supp. I Part 1:** 29, 38, 42, 43

18 Poems from the Quechua (Strand, trans.), **Supp. IV Part 2:** 630

"18 West 11th Street" (Merrill), **Supp. III Part 1:** 323, 328

1876: A Novel (Vidal), **Supp. IV Part 2:** 677, 684, 688, 689, 691, 692; **Supp. XIX:** 141

"18,000 CDs" (Halliday), **Supp. XIX:** 92

"Eighth Air Force" (Jarrell), **II:** 373–374, 377

Eight Harvard Poets, **I:** 429, 475

"Eighth Avenue Incident" (Halliday), **Supp. XIX:** 89–90

"Eighth Day, The" (Apple), **Supp. XVII:** 6, 50

"Eighth Ditch, The" (Baraka), **Supp. II Part 1:** 40

"'80s Pastoral: Frederick Barthelme's *Moon Deluxe* Ten Years On" (Peters), **Supp. XI:** 39

Eight Men (Wright), **IV:** 478, 488, 494

80 Flowers (Zukofsky), **Supp. III Part 2:** 631

Eikon Basilike, The, **Supp. IV Part 2:** 435

Eileen (Masters), **Supp. I Part 2:** 460

Eimi (Cummings), **I:** 429, 433, 434, 439–440

"Einstein" (MacLeish), **III:** 5, 8, 10–11, 18–19

Einstein, Albert, **I:** 493; **III:** 8, 10, 21, 161; **IV:** 69, 375, 410, 411, 421; **Retro. Supp. I:** 63; **Supp. I Part 2:** 609, 643; **Supp. III Part 2:** 621; **Supp. V:** 290; **Supp. XII:** 45

Eiseley, Loren, **III:** 227–228

Eisenberg, Deborah, **Supp. XXIII:** 290

Eisenhower, Dwight D., **I:** 136, 376; **II:** 548; **III:** 215; **IV:** 75; **Supp. I Part 1:** 291; **Supp. III Part 2:** 624; **Supp. V:** 45

Eisenstadt, Jill, **Supp. XVIII:** 135

Eisenstein, Sergei, **I:** 481; **Supp. XXI:** 170

Eisinger, Chester E., **I:** 302; **II:** 604; **Supp. IX:** 15

Eisner, Douglas, **Supp. X:** 155

Elam, Angela, **Supp. XI:** 290

El Bernardo (Balbuena), **Supp. V:** 11

Elbert, Sarah, **Supp. I Part 1:** 34, 41

Elder, Donald, **II:** 417, 426, 435, 437; **Supp. XV:** 137

Elder, John, **Supp. IX:** 25

Elder, Lonne, III, **Supp. IV Part 1:** 362

Elder, Richard, **Supp. XII:** 172

"Elder Sister, The" (Olds), **Supp. X:** 205–206

Elder Statesman, The (Eliot), **I:** 572, 573, 583; **Retro. Supp. I:** 53, 65

E. L. Doctorow (Harter and Thompson), **Supp. IV Part 1:** 217

Eldredge, Kay, **Supp. IX:** 254, 259

Eldridge, Florence, **III:** 154, 403; **IV:** 357

Eleanor of Aquitaine, **III:** 470

Eleanor of Guienne, **I:** 14

Eleanor: or, Slave Catching in the Quaker City (Lippard), **Supp. XXIII:** 180, 185

"Elect, The" (Taylor), **Supp. V:** 323

"Elections, Nicaragua, 1984" (Kingsolver), **Supp. VII:** 208

Elective Affinities (Goethe; Bogan and Mayer, trans.), **Supp. III Part 1:** 63

Electra (Euripides), **III:** 398

Electra (Sophocles), **III:** 398; **IV:** 370; **Supp. IX:** 102

"Electra on Azalea Path" (Plath), **Supp. I Part 2:** 538

"Electrical Storm" (Bishop), **Supp. I Part 1:** 93

"Electrical Storm" (Hayden), **Supp. II Part 1:** 370

"Electric Arrows" (Proulx), **Supp. VII:** 256

"Electric Girl, The"(P. Benedict), **Supp. XXIII:** 40

"Electricity Saviour" (Olds), **Supp. X:** 215

Electric Kool-Aid Acid Test, The (Wolfe), **Supp. III Part 2:** 575–577, 582–584; **Supp. XI:** 239

Electric Lady, The (film), **Supp. XI:** 309

Electronic Book Review, **Supp. XXII:** 256, 257, 261

Elegant Extracts (Knox), **II:** 8

"Elegant Tom Dillar" (Briggs), **Supp. XVIII:** 17

Elegiac Feelings American (Corso), **Supp. XII:** 131–134

"Elegiac Fragments" (Everwine), **Supp. XV:** 89

Elegies (Rukeyser), **Supp. VI:** 273

"Elegies" (Rukeyser), **Supp. VI:** 272

"Elegies for Paradise Valley" (Hayden), **Supp. II Part 1:** 363

"Elegy" (Bidart), **Supp. XV:** 25, 29

Elegy (Levis), **Supp. XI:** 257, 259, 261, **271–272**

"Elegy" (Merwin), **Supp. III Part 1:** 351

"Elegy" (Stafford), **Supp. XI:** 322

"Elegy" (Tate), **IV:** 128

"Elegy, for the U.S.N. Dirigible, Macon, An" (Winters), **Supp. II Part 2:** 810

"Elegy Ending in the Sound of a Skipping Rope" (Levis), **Supp. XI:** 271–272

"Elegy for 41 Whales Beached in Florence, Oregon, June 1979" (Bierds), **Supp. XVII:** 27

"Elegy for D. H. Lawrence, An" (W. C. Williams), **Retro. Supp. I:** 421

"Elegy for My Father" (Strand), **Supp. IV Part 2:** 628

"Elegy for My Mother" (Wagoner), **Supp. IX:** 330

"Elegy for Redondo Beach" (Jarman), **Supp. XVII:** 112, 113

Elegy for September, An (Nichols), **Supp. XIII:** 268

"Elegy for Thelonious" (Komunyakaa), **Supp. XIII:** 118

"Elegy for the Lost Umbrella"(Stallings), **Supp. XXIII:** 124

"Elegy for the Native Guards" (Trethewey), **Supp. XXI:** 255

"Elegy for the U.S.N. Dirigible, Macon, A" (Winters), **Supp. II Part 2:** 810

"Elegy in Dialogue" (Taggard), **Supp. XXII:** 276

"Elegy"(J. Schoolcraft), **Supp. XXIII:** 231

"Elegy of Last Resort" (Nemerov), **III:** 271

"Elegy with a Thimbleful of Water in the Cage" (Levis), **Supp. XI:** 272

Elegy Written in a Country Churchyard (Gray), **I:** 68

"Elegy Written in a Country Churchyard" (Gray), **Supp. XIV:** 8
"Elementary Scene, The" (Jarrell), **II:** 387, 388, 389
"Elements" (M. Frank), **Supp. X:** 213
Elements of Style, The (Strunk), **Supp. I Part 2:** 670
"Elenita, Cards, Palm, Water" (Cisneros), **Supp. VII:** 64
"Eleonora" (Poe), **III:** 412
Eleothriambos (Lee), **IV:** 158
"Elephant & Ocean" (Notley), **Supp. XXII:** 230
"Elephants" (Moore), **III:** 203
"Elephant's Dance, The" (D. West), **Supp. XVIII:** 281
"Elevator, The" (Dixon), **Supp. XII:** 154
"Elevator Boy" (Hughes), **Retro. Supp. I:** 200; **Supp. I Part 1:** 326
"Eleven" (Cisneros), **Supp. VII:** 69
Eleven Essays in the European Novel (Blackmur), **Supp. II Part 1:** 91, 111
Eleven Kinds of Loneliness (Yates), **Supp. XI: 340–343,** 349
Eleven Poems on the Same Theme (Warren), **IV:** 239–241
"Eleven Times a Poem" (Corso), **Supp. XII:** 132, 133
El Greco (Doménikos Theotokópoulos), **I:** 387; **III:** 212
El-Hage, George N., **Supp. XX: 116**
"El-Hajj Malik El-Shabazz" (Hayden), **Supp. II Part 1:** 379
"Eli, the Fanatic" (P. Roth), **Supp. III Part 2:** 407–408
Elia, Nada, **Supp. XXII:** 73
Eliade, Mircea, **Supp. XVI:** 292
Elie, Paul, **Supp. XXII:** 91–92
Eliot, Charles William, **I:** 5; **II:** 345; **Retro. Supp. I:** 55; **Supp. I Part 2:** 479; **Supp. IX:** 94
Eliot, George, **I:** 375, 458, 459, 461, 467; **II:** 179, 181, 191–192, 275, 319, 324, 338, 577; **IV:** 311, 322; **Retro. Supp. I:** 218, 220, 225; **Supp. I Part 1:** 370; **Supp. I Part 2:** 559, 579; **Supp. IV Part 1:** 31, 297; **Supp. IV Part 2:** 677; **Supp. V:** 258; **Supp. IX:** 38, 43, 51; **Supp. XI:** 68; **Supp. XII:** 335; **Supp. XIV:** 344; **Supp. XX: 108**
Eliot, T. S., **I:** 48, 49, 52, 59, 60, 64, 66, 68, 105, 107, 215–216, 236, 243, 256, 259, 261, 266, 384, 386, 395, 396, 399, 403, 430, 433, 441, 446, 475, 478, 479, 482, 521, 522, 527, **567–591; II:** 65, 96, 158, 168, 316, 371, 376, 386, 529, 530, 532, 537, 542, 545; **III:** 1, 4, 5, 6, 7–8, 9, 10, 11, 14, 17, 20, 21, 23, 26, 34, 174, 194, 195–196, 205–206, 220, 236, 239, 269, 270–271, 277–278, 301, 409, 428, 435, 436, 453, 456–457, 459–460, 461–462, 464, 466, 471, 476, 478, 485, 488, 492, 493, 498, 504, 509, 511, 517, 524, 527, 539, 572, 575, 586, 591, 594, 600, 613; **IV:** 27, 74, 82, 83, 95, 122, 123, 127, 129, 134, 138, 140, 141, 191, 201, 237, 331, 379, 402, 403, 418, 419, 420, 430, 431, 439, 442, 491; **Retro. Supp. I:**
51–71, 74, 80, 89, 91, 171, 198, 210, 283, 289, 290, 292, 296, 298, 299, 311, 324, 359, 411, 413, 414, 416, 417, 420, 428; **Retro. Supp. II:** 79, 178, 189, 262, 326; **Supp. I Part 1:** 257, 264, 268, 270, 274, 299; **Supp. I Part 2:** 387, 423, 455, 536, 554, 624, 659, 721; **Supp. II Part 1:** 1, 4, 8, 20, 30, 91, 98, 103, 136, 314; **Supp. III Part 1:** 9, 10, 26, 31, 37, 41, 43, 44, 48, 62–64, 73, 91, 99–100, 105–106, 273; **Supp. III Part 2:** 541, 611, 612, 617, 624; **Supp. IV Part 1:** 40, 47, 284, 380, 404; **Supp. IV Part 2:** 436; **Supp. V:** 79, 97, 101, 338, 343, 344; **Supp. VIII:** 19, 21, 93, 102, 105, 182, 195, 205, 290, 292; **Supp. IX:** 158–159, 229; **Supp. X:** 59, 115, 119, 124, 187, 324; **Supp. XI:** 242; **Supp. XII:** 45, 159, 198, 308; **Supp. XIII:** 77, 104, 115, 332, 341–342, 344, 346; **Supp. XIV:** 5, 13, 107, 287, 290, 306, 347; **Supp. XV:** 20, 51, 139, 177, 181, 186, 216, 218, 250, 251, 258, 298, 302, 303, 306, 307; **Supp. XVI:** 158–159, 204, 207, 282; **Supp. XVII:** 36, 71, 75, 111, 240; **Supp. XVIII:** 136; **Supp. XIX:** 12; **Supp. XX: 86, 108, 199; Supp. XXIII:** 25, 60, 166
Eliot's Early Years (Gordon), **Retro. Supp. I:** 55
"Elizabeth" (Longfellow), **I:** 502
"Elizabeth, 1905" (Schnackenberg), **Supp. XV:** 253, 256
Elizabeth Appleton (O'Hara), **III:** 362, 364, 375–377
"Elizabeth Bishop (1911–1979)" (Merrill), **Retro. Supp. II:** 53
"Elizabeth Bishop in Brazil" (Brown), **Supp. I Part 1:** 96
"Elizabeth Bishop's *North & South*" (Lowell), **Retro. Supp. II:** 40–41
"Elizabeth Gone" (Sexton), **Supp. II Part 2:** 674, 681
Elizabeth Rex (Findley), **Supp. XX: 62–63**
Elizabeth Stoddard and the Boundaries of Bourgeois Culture (Mahoney), **Supp. XV:** 270
Elk Heads on the Wall (Ríos), **Supp. IV Part 2:** 540
Elkin, Stanley, **Supp. VI: 41–59**
Elkins, Andrew, **Supp. XXIII:** 131, 135
"Elk Song" (Hogan), **Supp. IV Part 1:** 406
Ella in Bloom (Hearon), **Supp. VIII: 70–71**
Elledge, Jim, **Supp. XIII:** 88
Ellen Foster: A Novel (Gibbons), **Supp. X:** 41, **42–44,** 46, 47, 49, 50
Ellen Montgomery's Bookshelf (S. and A. Warner), **Supp. XVIII:** 264
Ellen Rogers (Farrell), **II:** 42–43
"Ellen's Dream" (Gioia), **Supp. XV:** 128
"Ellen West" (Bidart), **Supp. XV: 26–27**
Eller, Ernest, **Supp. I Part 2:** 497
Ellerman, Winifred, **Supp. I Part 1:** 258–259. *See also* McAlmon, Mrs. Robert (Winifred Ellerman)
"El libro de la sexualidad" (Simic), **Supp. VIII:** 283
Ellington, Duke, **Retro. Supp. II:** 115; **Supp. IV Part 1:** 360; **Supp. IX:** 164
Elliot, Charles, **Supp. V:** 161
Elliot, George P., **Supp. XV:** 92
Elliott, George B., **III:** 478
Ellipse, The: Selected Poems of Leonardo Sinisgalli (Di Piero, trans.), **Supp. XIX:** 34
"Ellipsis" (C. Frost), **Supp. XV:** 107
Ellis, Albert, **Supp. IV Part 2:** 527
Ellis, Anne, **Supp. XVI:** 38
Ellis, Bret Easton, **Supp. XII:** 81; **Supp. XVIII:** 135
Ellis, Brett Easton, **Supp. X:** 7
Ellis, Charles, **Supp. I Part 1:** 99
Ellis, Havelock, **II:** 276; **Supp. XX: 117, 235; Supp. XXII:** 198
Ellis, John Harvard, **Supp. I Part 1:** 103
Ellis, Katherine, **IV:** 114
Ellis, Kelly, **Supp. XXI:** 249
Ellis, Ron, **Supp. XXII:** 209
Ellis, Thomas Sayers, **Supp. XXI:** 246
Ellison, Harlan, **Supp. XIII:** 61
Ellison, Ralph, **IV:** 250, 493; **Retro. Supp. II:** 3, **111–130; Supp. II Part 1:** 33, **221–252; Supp. IV, Part 1:** 374; **Supp. VIII:** 105, 245; **Supp. IX:** 114, 316; **Supp. X:** 324; **Supp. XI:** 18, 92, 275; **Supp. XIII:** 186, 233, 305; **Supp. XIV:** 306; **Supp. XV:** 194; **Supp. XVI:** 135, 139; **Supp. XVIII:** 59, 61, 62, 277, 283; **Supp. XIX:** 148, 149, 155
Ellmann, Maud, **Supp. IV Part 1:** 302
Ellmann, Richard, **Supp. VIII:** 105; **Supp. XV:** 74
Ellroy, James, **Supp. XIV:** 26; **Supp. XXI:** 71
Elman, Richard, **Supp. V:** 40
"Elmer" (Faulkner), **Retro. Supp. I:** 79, 80
Elmer Gantry (Lewis), **I:** 26, 364; **II:** 447–449, 450, 455
Elmer the Great (Lardner), **II:** 427
"Elms" (Glück), **Supp. V:** 85
"Elms Dying, The—And My Friend, Lew Stillwell, Dead" (Bronk), **Supp. XXI:** 31
Eloges (Perse), **Supp. XIII:** 344
"Eloquence of Grief, An" (Crane), **I:** 411
"El Paso Del Norte"(Kenny), **Supp. XXIII:** 150
"El Río Grande" (Mora), **Supp. XIII:** 224
"El Round up" (Alvarez), **Supp. VII:** 11
"El Salvador: Requiem and Invocation" (Levertov), **Supp. III Part 1:** 284
Elsasser, Henry, **I:** 226
"Elsa Wertman" (Masters), **Supp. I Part 2:** 462–463
Elsie John and Joey Martinez: Two Stories (Huncke), **Supp. XIV:** 148
Elsie Venner (Holmes), **Supp. I Part 1:** 243, 315–316
Elton, Charles, **Supp. XIV:** 192
Éluard, Paul, **III:** 528; **Supp. IV Part 1:** 80; **Supp. XVII:** 244
Elvins, Kells, **Supp. III Part 1:** 93, 101

Ely, Richard T., **Supp. I Part 1:** 5; **Supp. I Part 2:** 640, 645
"Emancipation. A Life Fable" (Chopin), **Retro. Supp. II:** 59; **Supp. I Part 1:** 207–208
"Emancipation in the British West Indies" (Emerson), **II:** 13
"Emancipation Proclamation, The" (Emerson), **II:** 13
Emanuel, James, **Supp. I Part 1:** 346
Embargo, The (Bryant), **Supp. I Part 1:** 152–153
Embarrassments (James), **Retro. Supp. I:** 229
Embezzler, The (Auchincloss), **Supp. IV Part 1:** 24, 30–31
"Embroidery, The" (C. Frost), **Supp. XV:** 97
"Emerald" (Doty), **Supp. XI:** 131
"Emerald, The" (Merrill), **Supp. III Part 1:** 328
Emerald City (Egan), **Supp. XIX:** 49, **52–53**
"Emerald City" (Egan), **Supp. XIX:** 52
"Emergence of Flight from Aristotle's Mud, The" (Goldbarth), **Supp. XII:** 190
Emergency Exit (Major), **Supp. XXII:** 174, **175,** 182
"Emergency Haying" (Carruth), **Supp. XVI:** 55
"Emergency Room" (Mora), **Supp. XIII:** 218
"Emerging Voices: The Teaching of Writing" (Mora), **Supp. XIII:** 220
Emerson, and Other Essays (Chapman), **Supp. XIV:** 41–44
Emerson, Ellen, **Supp. I Part 1:** 33
Emerson, John, **Supp. XVI:** 185, 186, 190, 192
Emerson, Ralph Waldo, **I:** 98, 217, 220, 222, 224, 228, 239, 246, 251, 252, 253, 257, 260, 261, 283, 386, 397, 402, 424, 433, 444, 447, 455, 458, 460–461, 463, 464, 485, 561; **II: 1–24,** 49, 92, 127–128, 169, 170, 226, 233, 237, 273–274, 275, 278, 289, 295, 301, 313, 315, 336, 338, 344, 402, 491, 503; **III:** 53, 82, 171, 174, 260, 277, 409, 424, 428, 453, 454, 507, 576–577, 606, 614; **IV:** 60, 167, 169, 170, 171, 172, 173–174, 176, 178, 183, 186, 187, 192, 201, 202, 211, 335, 338, 340, 342, 350; **Retro. Supp. I:** 34, 53, 54, 57, 62, 74–75, 76, 125, 148–149, 152–153, 159, 217, 250, 298, 392, 400, 403; **Retro. Supp. II:** 96, 113, 135, 142, 155, 207, 262; **Supp. I Part 1:** 2, 28–29, 31, 33, 188, 299, 308–309, 317, 358, 365, 366, 368; **Supp. I Part 2:** 374, 383, 393, 407, 413, 416, 420, 422, 474, 482, 580, 582, 602, 659, 679; **Supp. II Part 1:** 280, 288; **Supp. III Part 1:** 387; **Supp. IV Part 2:** 439, 597, 619; **Supp. V:** 118; **Supp. VIII:** 42, 105, 106, 108, 198, 201, 204, 205, 292; **Supp. IX:** 38, 90, 175, 176, 181; **Supp. X:** 42, 45, 121, 223; **Supp. XI:** 203; **Supp. XIII:** 141, 145, 233, 246,

Supp. XIII: 247; **Supp. XIV:** 41–44, 46, 54, 104, 177; **Supp. XV:** 219, 224; **Supp. XVI:** 84; **Supp. XVII:** 42, 236; **Supp. XX:** 115, 116; **Supp. XXI:** 217; **Supp. XXIII:** 161, 190
"Emerson and the Essay" (Gass), **Supp. VI:** 88
"Emerson the Lecturer" (Lowell), **Supp. I Part 2:** 420, 422
Emerson-Thoreau Award, **Retro. Supp. I:** 67
Emery, Clark, **III:** 478
Emery, Mary Lou, **Supp. XXII:** 73
E. M. Forster (Trilling), **Supp. III Part 2:** 496, 501, 504
"Emigre in Autumn, An" (Gioia), **Supp. XV:** 120
"Emily Dickinson and Class" (Erkkila), **Retro. Supp. I:** 42–43
Emily Dickinson Editorial Collective, **Retro. Supp. I:** 47
Emily Dickinson in Southern California (X. J. Kennedy), **Supp. XV: 164–165**
"Emily Dickinson's Defunct" (Nelson), **Supp. XVIII:** 173
Emily Dickinson: Woman Poet (Bennett), **Retro. Supp. I:** 42
Eminent Victorians (Strachey), **Supp. I Part 2:** 485
Emma (Austen), **Supp. XVIII:** 149
"Emma and Eginhard" (Longfellow), **III:** 505
"Emma Enters a Sentence of Elizabeth Bishop's" (Gass), **Supp. VI:** 93
Emmanuel Appodocca: or, A Blighted Life (Philip), **Supp. XXI:** 160
"Emmaus" (Di Piero), **Supp. XIX:** 42, 43
Emperor Jones, The (O'Neill), **II:** 278; **III:** 391, 392
Emperor of Haiti (Hughes), **Supp. I Part 1:** 339
"Emperor of Ice Cream, The" (Stevens), **IV:** 76, 80–81
"Emperors" (Dunn), **Supp. XI:** 155
"Emperor's New Clothes, The" (Anderson), **I:** 441
"Empire" (Ford), **Supp. V:** 69
Empire: A Novel (Vidal), **Supp. IV Part 2:** 677, 684, 686, 690; **Supp. XIX:** 132
"Empire Builders" (MacLeish), **III:** 14
Empire City, The: or, New York by Night and Day (Lippard), **Supp. XXIII:** 178, 180, 183, 184, 185
Empire Falls (Russo), **Supp. XII: 339–343**
Empire of Summer, The (Doty), **Supp. XI:** 120
Empire of the Senseless (Acker), **Supp. XII:** 5, **6, 14–16**
"Empires" (Simic), **Supp. VIII:** 282
"Emporium" (Shapiro), **Supp. II Part 2:** 705
Empress of the Splendid Season (Hijuelos), **Supp. VIII: 86–89**
Empson, William, **I:** 522, 533; **II:** 536; **III:** 286, 497, 498, 499; **IV:** 136, 431; **Retro. Supp. I:** 263; **Retro. Supp. II:** 253; **Supp. XVI:** 190

Empty Bed, The (Hadas), **Supp. XXIII: 117–118**
Empty Hands, The (Bronk), **Supp. XXI:** 31
"Empty Hills, The" (Winters), **Supp. II Part 2:** 792, 793, 796
Empty Mirror, Early Poems (Ginsberg), **Supp. II Part 1:** 308, 311, 313–314, 319, 329
"Empty Room" (Hughes), **Supp. I Part 1:** 337
"Empty Threat, An" (Frost), **II:** 159
Emshwiller, Ed, **Supp. XVIII:** 145
"Encantadas, The" (Melville), **III:** 89; **Supp. XVIII:** 4
Enchanter, The (Nabokov), **Retro. Supp. I:** 266
"Enclosed Dreams, Highways and Labyrinths: Jonathan Lethem's *Amnesia Moon*" (Rossi), *Supp. XVIII:* 139
"Encomium Twenty Years Later" (Tate), **I:** 381
"Encounter" (Espaillat), **Supp. XXI:** 107
"Encounter, The" (Pound), **III:** 466
Encounter in April (Sarton), **Supp. VIII:** 259
"Encounter in April" (Sarton), **Supp. VIII:** 259
"Encountering the Sublime" (McClatchy), **Supp. XII:** 261
"Encounter in Vindija Cave, Present-Day Croatia: Late October"(Schott), **Supp. XXIII:** 254
"Encounter on the Seine: Black Meets Brown" (Baldwin), **Retro. Supp. II:** 2
Encounters with Chinese Writers (Dillard), **Supp. VI:** 19, 23, 31
Encounters with the Archdruid (McPhee), **Supp. III Part 1:** 292–294, 301; **Supp. X:** 30
Encyclopedia of Arkansas History and Culture, The (online), **Supp. XXII:** 50
Encyclopedia of Scotland, The (A. Finch), **Supp. XVII: 70–71**
Encyclopedia of World Biography, The, **Supp. XXI:** 74
"End, The" (Olds), **Supp. X:** 205
"Endangered Species" (Mora), **Supp. XIII:** 219–220
Endecott and the Red Cross (Lowell), **II:** 545
Endgame (Beckett), **Supp. XIII:** 196; **Supp. XXII:** 263
"Endgame" (Tan), **Supp. X:** 290
"Endicott and the Red Cross" (Hawthorne), **Retro. Supp. II:** 181, 187–188
"End of Books, The" (Coover), **Supp. V:** 53
End of Books, The" (Coover), **Supp. XXII:** 259
End of Dreams, The (Skloot), **Supp. XX: 196, 202–203**
End of Education, The (Postman), **Supp. XI:** 275
"End of FIRPO in the World, The" (Saunders), **Supp. XIX:** 229
"End of Season" (Warren), **IV:** 239–240
"End of Something, The" (Hemingway), **II:** 248

End of the Affair, The (Greene), **Supp. XI:** 99

End of the Age of Innocence, The (Price), **Retro. Supp. I:** 377

"End of the Line, The" (Jarrell), **III:** 527

"End of the Rainbow, The" (Jarrell), **II:** 386

End of the Road (film), **Supp. XI:** 309

End of the Road, The (Barth), **I:** 121, 122, 126–131; **Supp. XI:** 309; **Supp. XVIII:** 140, 141

"End of the World, The" (Gioia), **Supp. XV:** 126

"End of the World, The" (MacLeish), **III:** 8

Endor (Nemerov), **III:** 269, 270, 279

Endore, Guy, **Supp. XVII: 53–67**

"Ends" (Dixon), **Supp. XII:** 153

End to Innocence, An: Essays on Culture and Politics (Fiedler), **Supp. XIII: 98–99**

Endure: The Diaries of Charles Walter Stetson (Stetson), **Supp. XI:** 196

"Enduring Chill, The" (O'Connor), **III:** 349, 351, 357; **Retro. Supp. II:** 236

Enduring Vision of Norman Mailer, The (Leeds), **Retro. Supp. II:** 204

Endymion (Keats), **IV:** 405; **Retro. Supp. I:** 412

End Zone (DeLillo), **Supp. VI:** 2, 3, 4, 10, 11, 12

Enemies (Boyce and Hapgood), **Supp. XVII:** 100; **Supp. XXI:** 7, 13

Enemies: A Love Story (Singer), **IV:** 1; **Retro. Supp. II: 310–311**

Enemy, The: Time (T. Williams), **IV:** 391

Enemy of the People, An (adapt. Miller), **III:** 154–156

"Energy Vampire" (Ginsberg), **Supp. II Part 1:** 326

"Enforcement of the Slave Trade Laws, The" (Du Bois), **Supp. II Part 1:** 161

"Engaging the Past" (Bell), **Supp. X:** 17

Engel, Bernard F., **I:** 532

Engels, Friedrich, **IV:** 429, 443–444; **Supp. I Part 1:** 13; **Supp. XXI:** 162

Engineer of Beasts, The (Sanders), **Supp. XVI:** 270

Engineer of Moonlight (DeLillo), **Supp. VI:** 4

Engineers and the Price System, The (Veblen), **I:** 475–476; **Supp. I Part 2:** 638, 642, 648

Engines of Creation: the Coming Era of Nanotechnology (Drexler), **Supp. XVI:** 121

"England" (Moore), **III:** 203, 207, 214

Englander, Nathan, **Supp. XX: 177, 179**

Engle, Paul, **III:** 542; **Retro. Supp. II:** 220, 221; **Supp. V:** 337; **Supp. XI:** 315; **Supp. XIII:** 76; **Supp. XVIII:** 72

English, Zoë, **Supp. XVI:** 293

English Elegy, The: Studies in the Genre from Spenser to Yeats (Sacks), **Supp. IV Part 2:** 450

English Hours (James), **II:** 337; **Retro. Supp. I:** 235

English Language, The (L. P. Smith), **Supp. XIV:** 341

English-Latin Gradus or Verse Dictionary, An (Ainger), **Supp. XX: 230**

"English Lesson"(Strout), **Supp. XXIII:** 273–274, 284

Englishmen of Letters (James), **II:** 327

English Notebooks, The (Hawthorne), **II:** 226, 227–228

English Novel, The (Lanier), **Supp. I Part 1:** 371

English Poets, The: Lessing, Rousseau (Lowell), **Supp. I Part 2:** 407

English Prosody and Modern Poetry (Shapiro), **Supp. II Part 2:** 710

English Traits (Emerson), **II:** 1, 5, 6–7, 8

"English Writers on America" (Irving), **II:** 308

Engstrand, Stuart, **Supp. I Part 1:** 51

"Enigma Variations" (Nelson), **Supp. XVIII:** 177

"Enoch and the Gorilla" (O'Connor), **Retro. Supp. II:** 225

Enormous Changes at the Last Minute (Paley), **Supp. VI:** 218

"Enormous Changes at the Last Minute" (Paley), **Supp. VI:** 226, 232

"Enormous Radio, The" (Cheever), **Supp. I Part 1:** 175–177, 195

Enormous Radio and Other Stories, The (Cheever), **Supp. I Part 1:** 175–177

Enormous Room, The (Cummings), **I:** 429, 434, 440, 445, 477; **Supp. XXI:** 277

"Enough for a Lifetime" (Buck), **Supp. II Part 1:** 127

Enough Rope (Parker), **Supp. IX:** 189, 192

Enquiry Concerning Political Justice (Godwin), **Supp. I Part 1:** 126, 146

"En Route" (Boulton), **Supp. XXII:** 25

Entered From the Sun (Garrett), **Supp. VII:** 105–106, 107–109

"Entering the Building" (Notley), **Supp. XXII:** 237

"Entering the Kingdom" (Oliver), **Supp. VII:** 234

Entertaining Strangers (Gurney), **Supp. V:** 98, 99

Enter without Desire (Lacy), **Supp. XV:** 201

Entranced, The (Lippard), **Supp. XXIII:** 178, 180, 190

Entrance: Four Chicano Poets, **Supp. XIII:** 316

Entrance to Porlock, The (Buechner), **Supp. XII:** 52

Entries (Berry), **Supp. X:** 23

"Entropy" (Pynchon), **Supp. II Part 2:** 619, 621

Entry in an Unknown Hand (F. Wright), **Supp. XVII:** 240, 244, 245

Environmental Imagination, The (Buell), **Supp. V:** 209; **Supp. IX:** 29

"Envoy" (Collins), **Supp. XXI:** 57

"Envoys, The" (Merrill), **Supp. III Part 1:** 326

"Envy; or, Yiddish in America" (Ozick), **Supp. V:** 263, 265–266

"Eolian Harp, The" (Coleridge), **I:** 284

"Eolian Harp, The"(Coleridge), **Supp. XXIII:** 231

"Eototo" (Sobin), **Supp. XVI:** 283–284

"Ephemera, The" (Franklin), **II:** 121

Ephesians (biblical book), **Supp. I Part 1:** 117

Epictetus, **III:** 566

"Epicurean, The" (Auchincloss), **Supp. IV Part 1:** 25

Epicurus, **I:** 59

Epidemic of Genius, An (Wolfert), **Supp. XXI:** 278

"Epigram" (Lowell), **II:** 550

"Epilogue" (Lowell), **Retro. Supp. II:** 191

"Epimanes" (Poe), **III:** 411

"Epimetheus" (Longfellow), **II:** 494

"Epiphany" (X. J. Kennedy), **Supp. XV:** 166, 167

"Epipsychidion" (Shelley), **Supp. I Part 2:** 718

Episode in Palmetto (Caldwell), **I:** 297, 307

"Epistle" (L.-Y. Lee), **Supp. XV:** 212

Epistle to a Godson (Auden), **Supp. II Part 1:** 24

"Epistle to Be Left in the Earth" (MacLeish), **III:** 13

"Epistle to George William Curtis" (Lowell), **Supp. I Part 2:** 416

"Epistle to Léon-Paul Fargue" (MacLeish), **III:** 15

"Epitaph Ending in And, The" (Stafford), **Supp. XI:** 321–322

Epitaph for a Dead Beat (Markson), **Supp. XVII: 136–138,** 141; 139

Epitaph for a Desert Anarchist (Bishop), **Supp. XIII:** 1

Epitaph for a Tramp (Markson), **Supp. XVII:** 136, 137, 139 142

"Epitaph for Fire and Flower" (Plath), **Supp. I Part 2:** 537

"Epitaph for the Race of Man" (Millay), **III:** 127–128

"Epithalamium" (Auden), **Supp. II Part 1:** 15

"Epstein" (P. Roth), **Retro. Supp. II:** 281; **Supp. III Part 2:** 404, 406–407, 412, 422

Epstein, Barbara, **Supp. XIX:** 268

Epstein, Helen, **Supp. XVII:** 47; **Supp. XXII:** 95

Epstein, Jacob, **Supp. XXIII:** 6

Epstein, Jason, **Supp. VIII:** 233

Epstein, Joseph, **Supp. IV Part 2:** 692; **Supp. VIII:** 236, 238; **Supp. XIV: 101–117; Supp. XVI:** 230, 275

Epstein, Leslie, **Supp. XII: 159–174; Supp. XVIII:** 92, 99

Epstein, Philip, **Supp. XII:** 159

"Equal in Paris" (Baldwin), **Retro. Supp. II:** 3; **Supp. I Part 1:** 52

"Equals" (Untermeyer), **Supp. XV:** 304

Equation for Evil (Caputo), **Supp. XIX:** 25–26

"Equations of the Light" (Gioia), **Supp. XV:** 125

"Equilibrists, The" (Ransom), **III:** 490, 494

"Equinox"(Crooker), **Supp. XXIII:** 55

"Equipment for Pennies" (H. Roth), **Supp. IX:** 233

Erasmus, Desiderius, **Supp. XV:** 258
Erasure (Everett), **Supp. XVIII:** 54, 60, **61–62**
"Erat Hora" (Pound), **III:** 463; **Retro. Supp. I:** 413
Erdrich, Louise, **Supp. IV Part 1: 259–278,** 333, 404; **Supp. X:** 290; **Supp. XVIII:** 189
"Erectus" (Karr), **Supp. XI:** 243
"Ere Sleep Comes Down to Soothe the Weary Eyes" (Dunbar), **Supp. II Part 1:** 199, 207–208
"Ergo Non Sum. Est." (Bronk), **Supp. XXI:** 31
"Ergotism"(Schott), **Supp. XXIII:** 245
Erikson, Erik, **I:** 58, 214, 218
Erisman, Fred, **Supp. VIII:** 126
Erkkila, Betsy, **Retro. Supp. I:** 42; **Supp. XX: 281, 287, 287–288**
Ernest, John, **Supp. XXI:** 24
"Ernest: or Parent for a Day" (Bourne), **I:** 232
Ernst, Max, **Retro. Supp. II:** 321
"Eros" (Komunyakaa), **Supp. XIII:** 130
"Eros and Anteros" (E. Stoddard), **Supp. XV:** 283
Eros and Civilization (Marcuse), **Supp. XII:** 2
"Eros at Temple Stream" (Levertov), **Supp. III Part 1:** 278–279
Eros the Bittersweet (Carson), **Supp. XII:** 97, **98–99**
"Eros Turannos" (Robinson), **III:** 510, 512, 513–516, 517, 518
"Eroticism in Women" (Nin), **Supp. X:** 195
"Errand" (Carver), **Supp. III Part 1:** 149
Erskine, Albert, **IV:** 261; **Retro. Supp. II:** 117
Erskine, John, **I:** 223; **Supp. X:** 183; **Supp. XIV:** 120
Erstein, Hap, **Supp. IV Part 2:** 589, 590
"Escape" (MacLeish), **III:** 4
Escape Artist, The (Wagoner), **Supp. IX:** 324, **334–335**
"Escape"(Thompson), **Supp. XXIII:** 301
Escher, M. C., **Supp. XII:** 26; **Supp. XVI:** 102
"Escudilla" (Leopold), **Supp. XIV:** 188
Eshleman, Clayton, **Supp. XVI:** 284
"Eskimo Love" (Apple), **Supp. XVII:** 5
Espaillat, Rhina P., **Supp. XXI: 97–114**
Esparza, Laura, **Supp. XXIII:** 197
Espeland, Pamela, **Supp. XVIII:** 180, 181
Espen, Hal, **Supp. X:** 15
Espey, John, **III:** 463, 468, 478
Esposito, Michael, **Supp. XX: 34, 40**
Esposito, Scott, **Supp. XVII:** 234
Esquibel, Catríona Rueda, **Supp. XXIII:** 202
Essais (Renouvier), **II:** 344–345
Essay Concerning Human Understanding, An (Locke), **I:** 554; **II:** 8, 348–349
Essay on American Poetry (Brown), **Supp. I Part 1:** 156
"Essay on Aristocracy" (Paine), **Supp. I Part 2:** 515

"Essay on Friendship, An" (McClatchy), **Supp. XII:** 258–259
"Essay on Love" (Carruth), **Supp. XVI:** 56
Essay on Man (Pope), **II:** 111; **Supp. I Part 2:** 516
"Essay on Marriage" (Carruth), **Supp. XVI:** 48
Essay on Our Changing Order (Veblen), **Supp. I Part 2:** 629, 642
"Essay on Poetics" (Ammons), **Supp. VII:** 29–31
Essay on Projects (Defoe), **II:** 104
"Essay on Psychiatrists" (Pinsky), **Supp. VI:** 237, 238, 241, 242, 249, 250
Essay on Rime (Shapiro), **I:** 430; **Supp. II Part 2:** 702, 703, 708–711
"Essay on Sanity" (Dunn), **Supp. XI:** 147
"Essay on the Character of Robespierre" (Paine), **Supp. I Part 2:** 515
Essay on the Chinese Written Character (Fenollosa), **III:** 474
"Essay on What I Think About Most" (Carson), **Supp. XII: 111–112**
Essays (Emerson), **II:** 1, 7, 8, 12–13, 15, 21
Essays, Speeches, and Public Letters by William Faulkner (Meriweather, ed.), **Retro. Supp. I:** 77
Essays in Anglo-Saxon Law (Adams), **I:** 5
Essays in London (James), **II:** 336
Essays in Radical Empiricism (James), **II:** 355, 356–357
Essays on Norman Mailer (Lucid), **Retro. Supp. II:** 195
Essays on the Nature and Principles of Taste (Alison), **Supp. I Part 1:** 151
Essays to Do Good (Mather), **II:** 104; **Supp. II Part 2:** 461, 467
"Essay: The Love of Old Houses" (Doty), **Supp. XI:** 136
"Essay Toward a Point of View, An" (Brooks), **I:** 244
"Essence, Absence, and Sobin's *Venus Blue*" (English), **Supp. XVI:** 293
Essential Haiku, The (Hass), **Supp. VI:** 102
Essential Keats (Levine, ed.), **Supp. V:** 179
"Essential Oils—are wrung" (Dickinson), **I:** 471; **Retro. Supp. I:** 43, 46
"Essentials" (Toomer), **Supp. III Part 2:** 486
Essentials: A Philosophy of Life in Three Hundred Definitions and Aphorisms (Toomer), **Supp. III Part 2:** 486
Essentials: Definitions and Aphorisms (Toomer), **Supp. IX:** 320
"Essentials of Spontaneous Prose" (Kerouac), **Supp. III Part 1:** 227–228
Estampas del valle y otras obras (Hinojosa). See *Valley, The* (Hinojosa)
Esta puente, mi espalda: Voces de mujeres tercermundistas en los Estados Unidos (Moraga, Castillo, and Alarcón, eds.), **Supp. XXIII:** 194
"Estate Sale" (Nye), **Supp. XIII:** 283
Estess, Sybil, **Supp. IV Part 2:** 449, 452
Esther (Adams), **I:** 9–10, 20

"Esther" (Toomer), **Supp. IX:** 313–314
"Esther Kahn" (Symons), **Supp. XX: 239**
"Esthétique du Mal" (Stevens), **IV:** 79; **Retro. Supp. I:** 300, 311, 312
"Estoy-eh-muut and the Kunideeyahs (Arrowboy and the Destroyers)" (film), **Supp. IV Part 2:** 560
Estrada, Genaro, **Retro. Supp. II:** 89
Estray, The (Longfellow, ed.), **Retro. Supp. II:** 155
Esty, William, **III:** 358
"Etching, An" (Masters), **Supp. I Part 2:** 458
"Eternal Goodness, The" (Whittier), **Supp. I Part 2:** 704
Eternal Spring, The (Boyce), **Supp. XVII:** 100; **Supp. XXI:** 4, 5, 11
"Eternity, An" (W. C. Williams), **Retro. Supp. I:** 423
"Eternity Is Now" (Roethke), **III:** 544–545
"Ethan Brand" (Hawthorne), **II:** 227
Ethan Frome (Wharton), **IV:** 316–317, 327; **Retro. Supp. I:** 372–373; **Supp. IX:** 108; **Supp. XVIII:** 216; **Supp. XXIII:** 275, 281
"Ethical Turn in Postcolonial Theory and Narrative, The: Michelle Cliff's *No Telephone to Heaven*" (Moynagh), **Supp. XXII:** 73
Ethics (Spinoza), **IV:** 12; **Retro. Supp. II:** 300
"Ethics of Culture, The" (Locke), **Supp. XIV:** 211
"Ethnics of Frank Costello, The" (Talese), **Supp. XVII:** 202
"Étiquettes Jaunes, Les"(O'Hara), **Supp. XXIII:** 214
"Etude" (Kooser), **Supp. XIX:** 115
Etulain, Richard, **Supp. IV Part 2:** 597, 601, 604, 606, 607, 608, 610, 611
"Etymology" (Nelson), **Supp. XVIII:** 185
Euclid, **III:** 6, 620
"Euclid Alone Has Looked on Beauty Bare" (Millay), **III:** 133
"Euclidean Spaces: Linear Time" (Bronk), **Supp. XXI:** 31
Eugene, Frank, **Supp. X:** 204
Eugene Onegin (Pushkin), **III:** 246, 263
Eugene Onegin (Pushkin; Nabokov, trans.), **Retro. Supp. I:** 266, 267, 272
Eugenides, Jeffrey, **Supp. XIX:** 138; **Supp. XXI:** 229
Eugénie, Empress, **IV:** 309
Eugénie Grandet (Balzac), **II:** 328
"Eugénie Grandet" (Barthelme), **Supp. IV Part 1:** 47
"Eulogy for Richard Hugo (1923–1982)" (Wagoner), **Supp. IX:** 330–331
"Eulogy on the Flapper" (Z. Fitzgerald), **Supp. IX:** 71
Eumenides (Aeschylus), **Retro. Supp. I:** 65
"E Unibus Pluram: Television and U.S. Fiction" (Wallace), **Supp. X:** 315–316
"Euphemisms" (Matthews), **Supp. IX: 167–168**
Eureka (Poe), **III:** 409, 424, 428–429
Eurekas (Goldbarth), **Supp. XII:** 181

Euripides, **I:** 325; **II:** 8, 282, 543; **III:** 22, 145, 398; **IV:** 370; **Supp. I Part 1:** 268, 269, 270; **Supp. I Part 2:** 482; **Supp. V:** 277

"Euripides and Professor Murray" (Eliot), **Supp. I Part 1:** 268

"Euripides—A Playwright" (West), **IV:** 286; **Retro. Supp. II:** 326

"Europe" (Ashbery), **Supp. III Part 1:** 7–10, 13, 18

European Discovery of America, The: The Northern Voyages (Morison), **Supp. I Part 2:** 496–497

Europeans, The (H. James), **I:** 452; **II:** 327, 328; **Retro. Supp. I:** 216, 220

Europe Central (Vollmann), **Supp. XVII:** 225, 226, 227, 229, 231, **233–235**, 236

"Europe! Europe!" (Ginsberg), **Supp. II Part 1:** 320, 322

Europe of Trusts, The: Selected Poems (Howe), **Supp. IV Part 2:** 420, 422, 426

Europe without Baedeker (Wilson), **IV:** 429

Eurydice in the Underworld (Acker), **Supp. XII:** 7

Eustace, Saint, **II:** 215

Eustace Chisholm and the Works (Purdy), **Supp. VII:** 273–274, 279–280

"Euthanasia" (Tate), **IV:** 122

"Evaluation" (Bronk), **Supp. XXI:** 32

Eva-Mary (McCarriston), **Supp. XIV:** 259, 260, **263–268**

"Evangeline" (Dixon), **Supp. XII:** 153

Evangeline (Longfellow), **II:** 489, 501–502; **Retro. Supp. II:** 155, **156–159**, 162, 164; **Supp. I Part 2:** 586

Evanier, David, **Supp. XVI:** 212

Evans, Alice, **Supp. XVII:** 71, 72

Evans, Mary Ann. *See* Eliot, George

Evans, Oliver, **Supp. IV Part 1:** 85, 91

Evans, Sandy, **Supp. XIII:** 129

Evans, Walker, **I:** 36, 38, 293; **Retro. Supp. II:** 85

Eve (A. Finch), **Supp. XVII: 72–74**

"Eve" (W. C. Williams), **Retro. Supp. I:** 423

Even Cowgirls Get the Blues (Robbins), **Supp. X:** 259, 260, 261, 262–263, 264, 266, **269–271**, 272, 274, 277, 284; **Supp. XIII:** 11

"Evening" (Carver), **Supp. III Part 1:** 148

Evening (Minot), **Supp. VI:** 204–205, 208, **213–215**

"Evening at a Country Inn" (Kenyon), **Supp. VII:** 167

"Evening in Advent, An" (W. V. Davis), **Supp. XXI:** 92

"Evening in a Lumber Yard" (Le Sueur), **Supp. XXIII:** 165

"Evening in a Sugar Orchard" (Frost), **Retro. Supp. I:** 133

"Evening in Nuevo Leon, An" (Caldwell), **I:** 309

"Evening in the Sanitarium" (Bogan), **Supp. III Part 1:** 61

Evening Light, The (Skloot), **Supp. XX: 196, 201–202**

"Evening Love-of-Self" (Taggard), **Supp. XXII:** 280–281

"Evening of the 4th of July, The" (Kees), **Supp. XV:** 140, 142

"Evening on the Cote d'Azur" (Yates), **Supp. XI:** 349

Evening Performance, An: New and Selected Short Stories (Garrett), **Supp. VII:** 109

"Evenings at Home" (Hardwick), **Supp. III Part 1:** 195–196

"Evening's at Seven, The" (Thurber), **Supp. I Part 2:** 616

"Evening Star" (Bogan), **Supp. III Part 1:** 56

Evening Star, The (McMurtry), **Supp. V:** 230

Evening Star, The (screenplay, McMurtry), **Supp. V:** 232

"Evening Sun" (Kenyon), **Supp. VII:** 168

Evening Sun Turned Crimson, The (Huncke), **Supp. XIV:** 140, 149–150

"Evening Sun Turned Crimson, The" (Huncke), **Supp. XIV:** 137–138, 139

"Evening Wind, The" (Bryant), **Supp. I Part 1:** 164

"Evening without Angels" (Stevens), **Retro. Supp. I:** 302

Evening with Richard Nixon, An (Vidal), **Supp. IV Part 2:** 683

"Even Sea, The" (Swenson), **Supp. IV Part 2:** 641

Even Stephen (Perelman and West), **Retro. Supp. II:** 328

"Event, An" (Wilbur), **Supp. III Part 2:** 547, 554

"Event, The" (Dove), **Supp. IV Part 1:** 242, 247–248

"Even the Vanishing Housed" (Hirshfield), **Supp. XXIII:** 132

"Eventide" (Brooks), **Supp. III Part 1:** 73

"Eventide" (Purdy), **Supp. VII:** 270

"Event Itself, The" (Carruth), **Supp. XVI:** 47

Eve of Saint Agnes, The (Keats), **II:** 82, 531

"Eve of St. Agnes, The" (Clampitt), **Supp. IX:** 40

"Ever a Bridegroom: Reflections on the Failure of Texas Literature" (McMurtry), **Supp. V:** 225

Everett, Alexander Hill, **Supp. I Part 1:** 152

Everett, Percival, **Supp. XVIII: 53–67**

Everlasting Story of Nory, The (Baker), **Supp. XIII:** 52, **Supp. XIII: 53–55**

"Everly Brothers, The" (Skloot), **Supp. XX: 199**

Ever-Present Past, The (Hamilton), **Supp. XVI:** 196

Evers, Medgar, **IV:** 280; **Retro. Supp. II:** 13; **Supp. I Part 1:** 52, 65

Everson, William, **Supp. XXII:** 276

Everwine, Peter, **Supp. V:** 180; **Supp. XIII:** 312; **Supp. XV: 73–90**

"Everybody's Protest Novel" (Baldwin), **Retro. Supp. II:** 4; **Supp. I Part 1:** 50, 51

"Everybody's Reading Li Po' Silk-screened on a Purple T-Shirt" (Komunyakaa), **Supp. XIII:** 120

Everybody's Story: Writing by Older Minnesotans (C. Bly, ed.), **Supp. XVI:** 38

"Everybody Was Very Nice" (Benét), **Supp. XI:** 53

"Everyday Alchemy" (Taggard), **Supp. XXII:** 274–275, 276, 279

"Every-Day Girl, A" (Jewett), **Retro. Supp. II:** 132

"Everyday Use" (Walker), **Supp. III Part 2:** 534

"Every-Day Work" (Jewett), **Retro. Supp. II:** 132

Everyman (Ashbery), **Supp. XXIII:** 210

Everyone Says I Love You (film; Allen), **Supp. XV:** 11

Every Pleasure (Goldbarth), **Supp. XII:** 181

Every Soul Is a Circus (Lindsay), **Supp. I Part 2:** 384, 394, 399

"Everything Is a Human Being" (Walker), **Supp. III Part 2:** 527

Everything Is Illuminated (Foer), **Supp. XII:** 169

Everything Is Now (Cliff), **Supp. XXII:** 67, 74, 76

"Everything Stuck to Him" (Carver), **Supp. III Part 1:** 143

Everything That Moves (Schulberg), **Supp. XVIII:** 254

Everything That Rises Must Converge (O'Connor), **III:** 339, 348–349, 350–351; **Retro. Supp. II:** 235, **236–237**

"Everything That Rises Must Converge" (O'Connor), **III:** 349, 352, 357; **Retro. Supp. II:** 236

Everything You Always Wanted to Know about Sex (film; Allen), **Supp. XV:** 4–5, 13

Eve's Diary (Twain), **IV:** 208–209

"Eve Speaks" (Untermeyer), **Supp. XV:** 300

"Eve the Fox" (Gunn Allen), **Supp. IV Part 1:** 331

"Evidence" (Harjo), **Supp. XII:** 219

"Evidence-cum-Witness: Subaltern History, Violence, and the (De)formation of a Nation in Michelle Cliff's *No Telephone to Heaven*" (Sethuraman), **Supp. XXII:** 73

Evidence of the Senses, The (Kelley), **Supp. IV Part 2:** 529

Evidence of Things Not Seen, The (Baldwin), **Retro. Supp. II:** 15

"Evil Seekers, The" (Sexton), **Supp. II Part 2:** 696

"Evolution" (Swenson), **Supp. IV Part 2:** 639

Evolving the Idol: The Poetry of Gustaf Sobin (Crick), **Supp. XVI:** 289

Ewing, Jon, **Supp. X:** 253

Ewings, The (O'Hara), **III:** 383

"Examination at the Womb Door" (Hughes), **Supp. XV:** 347

"Examination of the Hero in a Time of War" (Stevens), **Retro. Supp. I:** 305–306, 308

"Excavation of Troy" (MacLeish), **III:** 18

Excellent Becomes the Permanent, The (Addams), **Supp. I Part 1:** 25

"Excelsior" (Longfellow), **Retro. Supp. II:** 169

"Excerpts from Swan Lake" (Cameron), **Supp. XII:** 80, **84**

"Excerpts from the Epistemology Workshops" (Rand), **Supp. IV Part 2:** 529

"Excess of Charity" (Wylie), **Supp. I Part 2:** 720

"Exchange, The" (Swenson), **Supp. IV Part 2:** 644

"Excitement, The " (Jarman), **Supp. XVII:** 120–121

"Exclusive" (Olds), **Supp. X:** 206

"Excrement Poem, The" (Kumin), **Supp. IV Part 2:** 448

"Excursion" (Garrett), **Supp. VII:** 100

Excursions (Thoreau), **IV:** 188

"Excursion to Canada, An" (Thoreau), **Supp. XVIII:** 4

"Excursus of Reassurance in Begonia Time, An" (Carruth), **Supp. XVI:** 58

Executioner (Weigl), **Supp. XIX:** 277

Executioner's Song, The (Mailer), **Retro. Supp. II:** 108, 209

Exekiel, **Supp. XXI:** 91

"Exercise and Abstinence" (Swados), **Supp. XIX:** 265

Exercises in History, Chronology, and Biography, in Question and Answer (Rowson), **Supp. XV:** 245

Ex-Friends: Falling Out with Allen Ginsberg, Lionel and Diana Trilling, Lillian Hellman, Hannah Arendt, and Norman Mailer (Podhoretz), **Supp. VIII:** 239, **242–244**

"Exhausted Bug, The" (R. Bly), **Supp. IV Part 1:** 73

"Exhortation" (Bogan), **Supp. III Part 1:** 58

"Exhortation" (McKay), **Supp. X:** 135

"Ex-husband"(Schott), **Supp. XXIII:** 249

"Exile" (Gass), **Supp. VI:** 92

"Exile" (Oates), **Supp. II Part 2:** 523

Exile, The (Buck), **Supp. II Part 1:** 119, 131

"Exiles, The" (Bradbury), **Supp. IV Part 1:** 113

"Exiles, The" (Whittier), **Supp. I Part 2:** 692–693

Exiles and Fabrications (Scott), **II:** 512

Exile's Daughter, The (Spencer), **Supp. II Part 1:** 121

"Exile's Departure, The" (Whittier), **Supp. I Part 2:** 683

Exiles from Paradise: Zelda and Scott Fitzgerald (Mayfield), **Supp. IX:** 65

"Exile's Letter" (Karr), **Supp. XI:** 241

Exile's Return (Cowley), **Supp. III Part 1:** 136, 138, 140, 141, 144, 147, 148

"Exile's Return, The" (Lowell), **II:** 539; **Retro. Supp. II:** 187

Exiles: Three Short Novels (Caputo), **Supp. XIX:** 25, **26–27**

"Existences" (Stafford), **Supp. XI:** 324

Existentialism from Dostoevsky to Sartre (W. Kaufmann), **Supp. XVII:** 137

Exit into History (Hoffman), **Supp. XVI:** 148, 150, **151–153**

Exit to Eden (Rampling), **Supp. VII:** 301–302

Exley (Clarke), **Supp. XXIII:** 109

Exley, Frederick, **Supp. XVI:** 69; **Supp. XVII:** 135; **Supp. XXIII:** 78, **97–110**

Exodus (biblical book), **IV:** 300

Exodus (film), **Supp. XX: 246**

Exodus (Uris), **Supp. IV Part 1:** 379; **Supp. XX: 243–244**, **244**, **245**, **247**, **248**, **250–251**, **257**

Exodus Revisited (Uris), **Supp. XX: 247**

"Exorcism" (Snodgrass), **Supp. VI:** 314

"Exorcism, An" (Malamud), **Supp. I Part 2:** 435

Exorcist, The (film), **Supp. I Part 1:** 66

"Expanded Composition, The" (Major), **Supp. XXII:** 174

"Expanding Rooms" (Notley), **Supp. XXII:** 229

"Expanses" (Dickey), **Supp. IV Part 1:** 186

"Ex Parte" (Lardner), **II:** 432

"Expatiation on the Combining of Weathers at Thirty-seventh and Indiana Where the Southern More or Less Crosses the Dog, The" (Carruth), **Supp. XVI:**51–52

"Expectant Father Compares His Wife to a Rabbit, An" (White), **Supp. I Part 2:** 678

"Expedition to the Pole, An" (Dillard), **Supp. VI:** 32, 34

"Expelled" (Cheever), **Supp. I Part 1:** 174, 186

Expense of Greatness, The (Blackmur), **Supp. II Part 1:** 90, 107

Expense of Vision, The (Holland), **Retro. Supp. I:** 216

"Expensive Gifts" (Miller), **Supp. XII:** 294

"Expensive Moment, The" (Paley), **Supp. VI:** 222, **227–228**, 230

Expensive People (Oates), **Supp. II Part 2:** 509, 510–511

"Experience" (Emerson), **Supp. XIV:** 42

"Experience and Fiction" (Jackson), **Supp. IX:** 121

"Experience and the Objects of Knowledge in the Philosophy of F. H. Bradley" (Eliot), **I:** 572; **Retro. Supp. I:** 59

Experience of Literature, The (Trilling), **Supp. III Part 2:** 493

"Experiences and Principles of an Historian" (Morison), **Supp. I Part 2:** 492

Experimental Death Unit # 1 (Baraka), **Supp. II Part 1:** 46

"Experimental Life, The" (Bourne), **I:** 217, 220

"Experiment in Misery, An" (S. Crane), **I:** 411; **Retro. Supp. II:** 97

Experiments and Observations on Electricity (Franklin), **II:** 102, 114–115

"Expiation" (Hoffman), **Supp. XVIII:** 86

"Expiation" (Wharton), **Retro. Supp. I:** 367

"Explaining Evil" (Gordon), **Supp. IV Part 1:** 310

"Explaining Ted Kooser" (Gioia), **Supp. XIX:** 121

"Explanation" (Stevens), **IV:** 79

Explanation of America, An (Pinsky), **Supp. VI:** 237, **241–243**

Exploding Gravy (X. J. Kennedy), **Supp. XV:** 163

"Exploit" (Wharton), **IV:** 324

"Exploration in the Great Tuolumne Cañon" (Muir), **Supp. IX:** 181

"Explorer, The" (Brooks), **Supp. III Part 1:** 79–80

"Exploring the Magalloway" (Parkman), **Supp. II Part 2:** 591

Expositor's Bible, The (G. A. Smith), **III:** 199

Expressions of Sea Level (Ammons), **Supp. VII:** 24, 28, 36

Extract from Captain Stormfeld's Visit to Heaven (Twain), **IV:** 209–210

Extracts from Adam's Diary (Twain), **IV:** 208–209

"Exulting, The" (Roethke), **III:** 544

"Eye, The" (Bowles), **Supp. IV Part 1:** 93

Eye, The (Nabokov), **III:** 251

Eye-Beaters, Blood, Victory, Madness, Buckhead and Mercy, The (Dickey), **Supp. IV Part 1:** 178, 182–183

"Eye for an Eye, An" (Humphrey), **Supp. IX:** 108

"Eye in the Rock, The" (Haines), **Supp. XII:** 208, 209

Eye in the Sky (Dick), **Supp. XVIII:** 138

"Eye-Mote, The" (Plath), **Retro. Supp. II:** 246, 247

"Eye of Paris, The" (H. Miller), **III:** 183–184

Eye of the Poet, The: Six Views of the Art and Craft of Poetry (Citino, ed.), **Supp. XIII:** 115; **Supp. XXI:** 54

"Eye of the Rock, The" (Haines), **Supp. XII:** 208

"Eye of the Story, The" (Porter), **IV:** 279

Eye of the Story, The: Selected Essays and Reviews (Welty), **Retro. Supp. I:** 339, 342, 344, 345, 346, 351, 354, 355, 356

"Eyes, The" (Wharton), **IV:** 315

"Eyes like They Say the Devil Has" (Ríos), **Supp. IV Part 2:** 543, 544

Eyes of the Dragon, The (King), **Supp. V:** 139, 152

Eyes of the Heart: A Memoir of the Lost and Found (Buechner), **Supp. XII:** 53

"Eyes of Zapata" (Cisneros), **Supp. VII:** 70

"Eyes to See" (Cozzens), **I:** 374

Eye-to-Eye (Nye), **Supp. XIII:** 274

Eysturoy, Annie O., **Supp. IV Part 1:** 321, 322, 323, 328

Ezekiel (biblical book), **II:** 541

"Ezekiel" (R. Fisher), **Supp. XIX:** 71

Ezekiel, Mordecai, **Supp. I Part 2:** 645

"Ezekiel Learns" (R. Fisher), **Supp. XIX:** 71

"Ezra Pound" (Bynner), **Supp. XV:** 49

"Ezra Pound: His Cantos" (Zukofsky), **Supp. III Part 2:** 612, 619, 622

Ezra Pound's Mauberley (Espey), **III:** 463

"Ezra Pound's Very Useful Labors" (Schwartz), **Supp. II Part 2:** 644

F

Faas, Ekbert, **Supp. VIII:** 292

"Fabbri Tape, The" (Auchincloss), **Supp. IV Part 1:** 21–22

Faber, Geoffrey, **Retro. Supp. I:** 63

Faber Book of Movie Verse, The (French and Wlaschin, eds.), **Supp. XVI:** 294

"Fable" (Merwin), **Supp. III Part 1:** 343

"Fable" (Wylie), **Supp. I Part 2:** 714

Fable, A (Faulkner), **II:** 55, 73; **Retro. Supp. I:** 74

"Fable, A" (Glück), **Supp. V:** 86

"Fable, The" (Winters), **Supp. II Part 2:** 792, 793, 796

"Fable Containing a Reflection the Size of a Match Head in Its Pupil, A" (Brockmeier), **Supp. XXII:** 59

"Fable Ending in the Sound of a Thousand Parakeets, A" (Brockmeier), **Supp. XXII:** 59

Fable for Critics, A (Lowell), **Supp. I Part 2:** 406, 407–408, 409, 412–413, 416, 420, 422

"Fable for Critics, A" (Lowell), **Supp. XVIII:** 3, 8

"Fable of the War, A" (Nemerov), **III:** 272

Fables (Gay), **II:** 111

Fables and Distances: New and Selected Essays (Haines), **Supp. XII:** 197, 199, 207–208, 211

Fables for Our Time (Thurber), **Supp. I Part 2:** 610

Fables of Identity: Studies in Poetic Mythology (Frye), **Supp. X:** 80

Fables of La Fontaine, The (Moore), **III:** 194, 215

"Fables of Representation: Poetry of the New York School" (Hoover), **Supp. XV:** 179

"Fables of the Fallen Guy" (Rosaldo), **Supp. IV Part 2:** 544

"Fables of the Moscow Subway" (Nemerov), **III:** 271

"Fable with a Photograph of a Glass Mobile on the Wall, A" (Brockmeier), **Supp. XXII:** 59

"Fable with Slips of White Paper Spilling from the Pockets, A" (Brockmeier), **Supp. XXII:** 59

Fabulators, The (Scholes), **Supp. V:** 40

Fabulous Small Jews (Epstein), **Supp. XIV:** 112

Face against the Glass, The (Francis), **Supp. IX:** 80–81

Face in the Crowd, A (film, Kazan), **Supp. XVIII:** 252–253

Face of Time, The (Farrell), **II:** 28, 34, 35, 39

Faces of Jesus, The (Buechner), **Supp. XII:** 53

Face to the Wind (film), **Supp. XVII:** 141

Face Value (Hwang), **Supp. XXI:** 148, 154, 155

Fachinger, Petra, **Supp. XVI:** 153

"Facing It" (Komunyakaa), **Supp. XIII:** 117, 124, 125

Facing Shadows (Jin), **Supp. XVIII:** 92, 93

Facing the Music (L. Brown), **Supp. XXI:** 39, 42, **42–44**

"Facing the Music" (L. Brown), **Supp. XXI:** **38–39**, 41, 42, 43

"*Facing the Music:* What's Wrong with All Those Happy Endings" (Neal), **Supp. XXI:** 41

"Facing West from California's Shores" (Jeffers), **Supp. II Part 2:** 437–438

Fact, Fiction, and Representation: Four Novels by Gilbert Sorrentino (Mackey), **Supp. XXI:** 236

"Fact in Fiction, The" (McCarthy), **II:** 562

"Fact of Blackness, The" (Fanon), **Supp. XX:** 152

"Facts" (Franzen), **Supp. XX:** 85

"Facts" (Levine), **Supp. V:** 193

"Facts" (Oliver), **Supp. VII:** 231–232

"Facts" (Snyder), **Supp. VIII:** 301

"Facts, The" (Lardner), **II:** 431

Facts, The: A Novelist's Autobiography (P. Roth), **Retro. Supp. II:** 280, 291; **Supp. III Part 2:** 401, 405, 417, 426

"Facts and Traditions Respecting the Existence of Indigenous Intermittent Fever in New England" (Holmes), **Supp. I Part 1:** 303

"Facts in the Case of M. Valdemar, The" (Poe), **III:** 416

Faderman, Lillian, **Retro. Supp. II:** 135; **Supp. XIII:** 313

Fadiman, Clifton, **II:** 430, 431, 443, 591–592; **Supp. IX:** 8; **Supp. XVI:** 100, 106; **Supp. XVII:** 87, 90; **Supp. XXIII:** 2

Fading, My Parmacheene Belle (J. Scott), **Supp. XVII:** **184–185,** 188

"Fado" (McClatchy), **Supp. XII:** 265–266

Faerie Queene, The (Spenser), **III:** 487; **IV:** 253; **Supp. XIV:** 6; **Supp. XV:** 181

Faery, Rebecca Blevins, **Retro. Supp. I:** 374

Fagan, Kathy, **Supp. V:** 180; **Supp. XV:** 73

Fagan, Louise, **Supp. XIX:** 204, 205

Fahrenheit 451 (Bradbury), **Supp. IV Part 1:** 101, 102, 104, 107–109, 110, 113; **Supp. XIII:** 29

"Failure" (Gioia), **Supp. XV:** 125

"Failure" (Zach; Everwine, trans.), **Supp. XV:** 86

"Failure of David Barry, The" (Jewett), **Retro. Supp. II:** 132

Fainlight, Ruth, **Supp. XV:** 261, 264

Faint Perfume (Gale), **Supp. I Part 2:** 613

Fair, Bryan K., **Supp. VIII:** 128

Fairbanks, Douglas, **Supp. XVI:** 185, 186

Fairchild, Frances. *See* Bryant, Mrs. William Cullen (Frances Fairchild)

Fairchild, Hoxie, **Supp. XIV:** 120

Fairfield, Flora (pseudonym). *See* Alcott, Louisa May

Fair Gentlemen of Belken County (Hinojosa), **Supp. XIX:** 105

Fairly Conventional Woman, A (Shields), **Supp. VII:** 312, 316, 318

"Fairly Sad Tale, A" (Parker), **Supp. IX:** 192

Fair Warning (R. O. Butler), **Supp. XII:** 62, **75–76**

Faith (Goldbarth), **Supp. XII:** 181, **182–183**

Faith and History (Niebuhr), **III:** 308

Faith and the Good Thing (Johnson), **Supp. VI:** 187, **188–190,** 191, 193, 194, 196

Faith for Living (Mumford), **Supp. II Part 2:** 479–480

Faithful Narrative of the Surprising Works of God in the Conversion of Many Hundred Souls in Northampton, and the Neighboring Towns and Villages of New-Hampshire in New-England, A (Edwards), **I:** 545, 562

"Faith Healer" (Komunyakaa), **Supp. XIII:** 117

"Faith in a Tree" (Paley), **Supp. VI:** 217–218, 224, 230

"Faith in Search of Understanding" (Updike), **Retro. Supp. I:** 327

"Faith of an Historian" (Morison), **Supp. I Part 2:** 492

"Faith of Fishermen, The" (J. W. Miller), **Supp. XX: 170**

Faker's Dozen, A (Bukiet), **Supp. XVII:** 47

Falcoff, Mark, **Supp. VIII:** 88

Falcon (Hammett), **Supp. IV Part 1:** 351

Falconer (Cheever), **Supp. I Part 1:** 176, 193–195, 196

Falconer, A. F., **Supp. XIV:** 2

"Falcon of Ser Federigo, The" (Longfellow), **II:** 505

Falcon: Poems on Soviet Themes (Taggard), **Supp. XXII:** 284

Falk, Peter, **Supp. XI:** 174

Falkner, Dean, **II:** 55

Falkner, John, **II:** 55

Falkner, Murray, **II:** 55

Falkner, Murray C., **II:** 55

Falkner, Mrs. Murray C. (Maud Butler), **II:** 55

Falkner, William C., **II:** 55

"Fall" (Francis), **Supp. IX:** 76

"Fall, The" (Bass), **Supp. XVI:** 25

"Fall 1961" (Lowell), **II:** 550

"Fallen Western Star: The Decline of San Francisco as a Literary Region" (Gioia), **Supp. XV:** 112, **115–116**

"*Fallen Western Star*" *Wars, The: A Debate about Literary California* (Foley, ed.), **Supp. XV:** 112, 116

"Fall in Corrales" (Wilbur), **Supp. III Part 2:** 556

Falling (Dickey), **Supp. IV Part 1:** 178, 181–182

"Falling" (Dickey), **Supp. IV Part 1:** 182

"Falling Asleep over the Aeneid" (Lowell), **II:** 542; **Retro. Supp. II:** 188

Falling in Place (Beattie), **Supp. V:** 28–29

"Falling into Holes in Our Sentences" (R. Bly), **Supp. IV Part 1:** 71

"Fall Journey" (Stafford), **Supp. XI:** 322

Fall of America, The: 1965–1971 (Ginsberg), **Supp. II Part 1:** 323, 325, 327; **Supp. XV:** 264

Fall of Eve, The (Loos), **Supp. XVI:** 187

Fall of the City, The: A Verse Play for Radio (MacLeish), **III:** 20

"Fall of the House of Usher, The" (Poe), **III:** 412, 414, 415, 419; **Retro. Supp. II:** 270

Fall of the Magicians, The (Kees), **Supp. XV:** 144

Fall of the Year, The (Mosher), **Supp. XXII:** 205, 206, 208, 209, **214**

"Fall of Troy, Teh"(Hadas), **Supp. XXIII:** 113

Fallows, James, **Supp. VIII:** 241

Fall Quarter (Kees), **Supp. XV:** 141

Fall & Rise (Dixon), **Supp. XII:** 147–148, 148, 153, 157

Falls, Robert, **Supp. XXI:** 148

"Falls, The" (Olds), **Supp. X:** 215

"Falls, The" (Saunders), **Supp. XIX:** 229

"Falls Fight, The" (Howe), **Supp. IV Part 2:** 431–432

Falon, Janet Ruth, **Supp. IV Part 2:** 422

False Coin (Swados), **Supp. XIX: 260–261,** 263

"False Dawn" (Wharton), **Retro. Supp. I:** 381

"False Documents" (Doctorow), **Supp. IV Part 1:** 220, 236

"False Leads" (Komunyakaa), **Supp. XIII:** 116

Falwell, Jerry, **Supp. XX:** 273

Fame and Obscurity: Portraits by Gay Talese (Talese), **Supp. XVII:** 202, 203, 204

Fame & Folly: Essays (Ozick), **Supp. V:** 272

"Familiar Epistle to a Friend, A" (Lowell), **Supp. I Part 2:** 416

Familiar Territory: Observations on American Life (Epstein), **Supp. XIV: 106**

"Familiar Things" (Pickering), **Supp. XXI:** 204

"Family" (Sanders), **Supp. XVI:** 276

"Family" (Wilson), **IV:** 426

Family, Kinship, and Sympanthy in Nineteenth-Century America (Weinstein), **Supp. XVIII:** 261

"Family, The" (Taggard), **Supp. XXII:** 284

"Family Affair, A" (Chopin), **Retro. Supp. II:** 71

"Family and Socialism, The" (Ryan as Quin), **Supp. XVIII:** 238

Family Arsenal, The (Theroux), **Supp. VIII:** 322

"Family Barcus, The"(Thompson), **Supp. XXIII:** 299

Family Chronicle: An Odyssey from Russia to America (Reznikoff), **Supp. XIV:** 277, 288, 289

Family Devotions (Hwang), **Supp. XXI:** 145, 146

"Family History" (Mora), **Supp. XIII:** 217

"Family History, A" (R. H. Davis), **Supp. XVI:** 82

Family Honor (Parker), **Supp. XIX:** 186

Family Life (Banks), **Supp. V:** 7

"Family Matters" (Alvarez), **Supp. VII:** 10

Family Moskat, The (Singer), **IV:** 1, 17, 20, 46; **Retro. Supp. II:** 304

"Family of Little Feet, The" (Cisneros), **Supp. VII:** 61

Family Party, A (O'Hara), **III:** 362

Family Pictures (Brooks), **Supp. III Part 1:** 69, 85, 86

Family Pictures (Miller), **Supp. XII:** 291, **295–297,** 299

"Family Portrait" (Trethewey), **Supp. XXI:** 250

"Family Reunion" (J. W. Miller), **Supp. XX: 167**

"Family Reunion" (X. J. Kennedy), **Supp. XV:** 169

Family Reunion, The (Eliot), **I:** 570–571, 572, 581, 584, 588; **Retro. Supp. I:** 62, 65

"Family Secrets" (Kingsolver), **Supp. VII:** 208

"Family Sideshow, The" (Karr), **Supp. XI:** 245

"Family Story, The" (Skloot), **Supp. XX: 195**

"Family Ties" (Mora), **Supp. XIII:** 215

"Family Tree" (Komunyakaa), **Supp. XIII:** 117–118, 126

"Family Wasserstein, The" (Hoban), **Supp. XV:** 319, 325

Famous American Negroes (Hughes), **Supp. I Part 1:** 345

"Famous Gilson Bequest, The" (Bierce), **I:** 204

Famous Last Words (Findley), **Supp. XX: 49, 55–56**

Famous Negro Athletes (Bontemps), **Supp. XXII:** 6

Famous Negro Music Makers (Hughes), **Supp. I Part 1:** 345

"Famous New York Trials" (Ellison), **Supp. II Part 1:** 230

Fanatics, The (Dunbar), **Supp. II Part 1:** 213–214

Fancher, Edwin, **Retro. Supp. II:** 202

Fancher, Lou, **Supp. XVI:** 177

"Fancy and Imagination" (Poe), **III:** 421

Fancy Dancer, The (P. N. Warren), **Supp. XX: 267–268**

"Fancy Flights" (Beattie), **Supp. V:** 25

"Fancy's Show Box" (Hawthorne), **II:** 238

"Fancy Woman, The" (Taylor), **Supp. V:** 316–317, 319, 323

"Fang" (Goldbarth), **Supp. XII:** 190

Fanny: Being the True History of the Adventures of Fanny Hackabout-Jones (Jong), **Supp. V:** 115, 127

Fanny Hill (Cleland), **Supp. V:** 48, 127

Fan of Swords, The (al-Maghut), **Supp. XIII:** 278

Fanon, Frantz, **Retro. Supp. II:** 118; **Supp. X:** 131, 141; **Supp. XX: 152**

"Fan's Further Notes, A"(Exley), **Supp. XXIII:** 108

Fanshawe (Hawthorne), **II:** 223–224; **Retro. Supp. I:** 149, 151

Fan's Notes, A: A Fictional Memoir (Exley), **Supp. XVI:** 69; **Supp. XXIII:** 78, 97, 98, **99–103,** 106, 109

"Fantasia on 'The Nut-Brown Maid' " (Ashbery), **Supp. III Part 1:** 19

"Fantasia on the Relations between Poetry and Photography" (Strand), **Supp. IV Part 2:** 631

"Fantastic Fables" (Bierce), **I:** 209

"Fantasy"(O'Hara), **Supp. XXIII:** 220

Fante, John, **Supp. XI: 159–176**

Faraday, Michael, **I:** 480–481

Far and Away (Jarman), **Supp. XVII:** 110, 115

"Far and Away" (Jarman), **Supp. XVII:** 115

"Farewell" (Emerson), **II:** 13

"Farewell" (Ryan as Quin), **Supp. XVIII:** 229

Farewell, My Lovely (Chandler), **Supp. IV Part 1:** 122, 125–126, 127, 128, 130

"Farewell, My Lovely!" (White), **Supp. I Part 2:** 661–663, 665

Farewell, The (Gibran), **Supp. XX: 121**

"Farewell Performance" (Merrill), **Supp. III Part 1:** 336–337

Farewell-Sermon Preached at the First Precinct in Northampton, after the People's Publick Rejection of their Minister, A (Edwards), **I:** 548, 562

"Farewell Sweet Dust" (Wylie), **Supp. I Part 2:** 727–728

"Farewell to America, A" (Wheatley), **Supp. XX: 283**

Farewell to Arms, A (Hemingway), **I:** 212, 421, 476, 477; **II:** 68–69, 248–249, 252–253, 254, 255, 262, 265; **Retro. Supp. I:** 171, 178, **180–182,** 187, 189; **Retro. Supp. II:** 108; **Supp. IV Part 1:** 380–381, 381; **Supp. VIII:** 179; **Supp. XII:** 241–242; **Supp. XXI:** 277

"Farewell to Miles" (Berryman), **I:** 173

"Farewell to My Union Brothers" (Ryan as Quin), **Supp. XVIII:** 238

Farewell to Reform (Chamberlain), **Supp. I Part 2:** 647

Farewell to Sport (Gallico), **Supp. XVI:** 238

"Farewell to the Middle Class" (Updike), **Retro. Supp. I:** 321

Far Field, The (Roethke), **III:** 528, 529, 539, 545, 547–548

"Far Field, The" (Roethke), **III:** 537, 540

Far-Flung (Cameron), **Supp. XII:** 81

Far from the Madding Crowd (Hardy), **II:** 291

Faríd, 'Umar ibn al-, **Supp. XX: 117**

Faris, Athénaíse Charleville, **Supp. I Part 1:** 204

Farley, Abbie, **I:** 458

Farley, Harriet, **Supp. XIII:** 140

"Farm, The" (Creeley), **Supp. IV Part 1:** 155

Farmer (Harrison), **Supp. VIII:** 39, **44–45**

Farmer, Frances, **Supp. XV:** 196–197

Farmer, Richard, **Supp. XIV:** 2

"Farmer and the Fox, The" (Leopold), **Supp. XIV:** 188

Farmer Boy (L. I. Wilder), **Supp. XXII:** 294, 297, 299

"Farmers' Daughters, The" (W. C. Williams), **Retro. Supp. I:** 423

Farmers Hotel, The (O'Hara), **III:** 361

"Farmer's Sorrow, A" (Jewett), **Retro. Supp. II:** 132

"Farmer's Wife, The" (Sexton), **Supp. II Part 2:** 676

"Farm Garden" (Nelson), **Supp. XVIII:** 186

"Farm Implements and Rutabagas in a Landscape" (Ashbery), **Supp. III Part 1:** 13

Farming: A Hand Book (Berry), **Supp. X:** 31, 35

"Farmlights in Iowa" (Kooser), **Supp. XIX:** 120

"Farm on the Great Plains, The" (Stafford), **Supp. XI:** 322

Farnol, Jeffrey, **Supp. I Part 2:** 653

Far North (Shepard), **Supp. III Part 2:** 433, 435

"Far Northern Birch, The" (Francis), **Supp. IX:** 90

Farnsworth, Elizabeth, **Supp. XI:** 139

"Farrago" (Kees), **Supp. XV:** 145

Farrand, Max, **II:** 122

Farrar, Geraldine, **Retro. Supp. I:** 10

Farrar, John, **II:** 191; **Supp. XI:** 47

Farrell, Barry, **Supp. XIV:** 142

Farrell, James Francis, **II:** 25, 26

Farrell, James T., **I:** 97, 288, 475, 508, 517, 519; **II:** **25–53**, 416, 424; **III:** 28, 114, 116, 118, 119, 317, 382; **IV:** 211, 286; **Retro. Supp. II:** 196, 327; **Supp. I Part 2:** 679; **Supp. VIII:** 96, 97; **Supp. XIV:** 3; **Supp. XV:** 141

Farrell, Mrs. James T. (Dorothy Butler), **II:** 26

Farrell, Mrs. James T. (Hortense Alden), **II:** 26, 27, 45, 48

Farrell, John, **II:** 26

Farrell, John C., **Supp. I Part 1:** 24

Farrell, Kate, **Supp. XV:** 187–188,**Supp. XV:** 190

Farrell, Kevin, **II:** 26

Farrell, Mary, **II:** 25

"Far Rockaway" (Schwartz), **Supp. II Part 2:** 649

Farrow, Mia, **Supp. XV:** 8, 10

Far Side of the Dollar, The (Macdonald), **Supp. IV Part 2:** 473

Farther Off from Heaven (Humphrey), **Supp. IX:** 93, 96, 101, **103–104**, 105, 109

Far Tortuga (Matthiessen), **Supp. V:** 201, 206–207

"Fascinating Fascism" (Sontag), **Supp. III Part 2:** 465

"Fascination of Cities, The" (Hughes), **Supp. I Part 1:** 325

Fashion, Power, Guilt and the Charity of Families (Shields), **Supp. VII:** 323

Fasman, Jonathan, **Supp. V:** 253

Fast, Howard, **Supp. I Part 1:** 295; **Supp. XXI:** 277; **Supp. XXIII:** 165

Fast, Jonathan, **Supp. V:** 115

Fast and Loose (Wharton), **Retro. Supp. I:** 361

"Faster than Light" (Nelson), **Supp. XVIII:** 178–179

"Fastest Runner on Sixty-first Street, The" (Farrell), **II:** 45

Fast Lane on a Dirt Road (Sherman), **Supp. XXII:** 205

Fast Sooner Hound, The (Bontemps and Conroy), **Supp. XXII:** 5, 10–11

"Fat" (Carver), **Supp. III Part 1:** 141

Fatal Interview (Millay), **III:** 128–129, 130

"Fatality" (Bausch), **Supp. VII:** 54

Fatal Lady (film), **Supp. XIII:** 166

"Fate" (Emerson), **II:** 2–3, 4, 16; **Supp. XIV:** 42

"Fate" (Koch), **Supp. XV:** 183

"Fate" (Mailer), **Retro. Supp. II:** 207

"Fate of Pleasure, The" (Trilling), **Supp. III Part 2:** 510

Fate of the Jury, The (Masters), **Supp. I Part 2:** 466, 468, 469

"Fat Girl, The" (Dubus), **Supp. VII:** 84, 85

"Father" (Kooser), **Supp. XIX:** 117, 127

"Father" (Levine), **Supp. V:** 188

"Father" (Sanders), **Supp. XVI:** 277

"Father" (Trethewey), **Supp. XXI:** 253

"Father" (Walker), **Supp. III Part 2:** 522

"Father, The" (Carver), **Supp. III Part 1:** 137, 140

Father, The (Olds), **Supp. X:** **209–211**

"Father Abraham" (Faulkner), **Retro. Supp. I:** 81, 82

Fatheralong: A Meditation on Fathers and Sons, Race and Society (Wideman), **Supp. X:** 320, 332–333, 334, 335

"Father and Daughter" (Eberhart), **I:** 539

Father and Glorious Descendant (Lowe), **Supp. X:** 291

"Father and Son" (Eberhart), **I:** 539

Father and Son (Farrell), **II:** 34, 35, 290, 291

Father and Son (Gosse), **Supp. VIII:** 157

"Father and Son" (Hughes), **Retro. Supp. I:** 204; **Supp. I Part 1:** 329, 339

"Father and Son" (Kunitz), **Supp. III Part 1:** 262

Father and Son (L. Brown), **Supp. XXI:** 36, 40, 41, **46–47**

"Father and Son" (Schwartz), **Supp. II Part 2:** 650

Father Bombo's Pilgrimage to Mecca (Freneau), **Supp. II Part 1:** 254

Father Fisheye (Balakian), **Supp. XXIII:** 19

"Father Fisheye"(Balakian), **Supp. XXIII:** 19

"Father Fitzgerald" (Nelson and Espeland), **Supp. XVIII:** 181

"Father Guzman" (Stern), **Supp. IX:** **293,** 296

"Father John Melby and the Ghost of Amy Elizabeth" (Brockmeier), **Supp. XXII:** 60

Father of the Blues (Bontemps as Handy), **Supp. XXII:** 5

"Father out Walking on the Lawn, A" (Dove), **Supp. IV Part 1:** 246

"Fathers" (Creeley), **Supp. IV Part 1:** 157–158

Fathers, The (Tate), **IV:** 120, 127, 130, 131–133, 134, 141; **Supp. X:** 52

Fathers and Crows (Vollmann), **Supp. XVII:** 226, 231–232

"Fathers and Daughters, Mothers and Sons"(Hadas), **Supp. XXIII:** 119

"Fathers and Sons" (Hemingway), **II:** 249, 265–266; **Retro. Supp. I:** 175

"Father's Body, The" (Dickey), **Supp. IV Part 1:** 176

"Father's Day" (Connelly), **Supp. XXI:** 79–80

"Father's Story, A" (Dubus), **Supp. VII:** 88

"Father's Voice" (Stafford), **Supp. XI:** 322

"Fat Lady, The" (Carruth), **Supp. XVI:** 48

"Fat Man, Floating" (Dunn), **Supp. XI:** 144

"Fat Tuesday"(P. Benedict), **Supp. XXIII:** 38

Faulkner, Barry, **Supp. XV:** 41

Faulkner, William, **I:** 54, 97, 99, 105, 106, 115, 117, 118, 123, 190, 204–205, 211, 288, 289, 291, 292, 297, 305, 324, 374, 378, 423, 480, 517; **II:** 28, 51, **54–76,** 131, 174, 194, 217, 223, 228, 230, 259, 301, 306, 431, 458–459, 542, 594, 606; **III:** 45, 70, 108, 164, 218, 220, 222, 236–237, 244, 292, 334, 350, 382, 418, 453, 454, 482, 483; **IV:** 2, 4, 33, 49, 97, 98, 100, 101, 120, 131, 203, 207, 211, 217, 237, 257, 260, 261, 279, 280, 352, 461, 463; **Retro. Supp. I:** **73–95,** 215, 339, 347, 356, 379, 382; **Retro. Supp. II:** 19, 221, 326; **Supp. I Part 1:** 196, 197, 242, 372; **Supp. I Part 2:** 450, 621; **Supp. III Part 1:** 384–385, 396; **Supp. IV Part 1:** 47, 130, 257, 342; **Supp. IV Part 2:** 434, 463, 468, 502, 677, 682; **Supp. V:** 58, 59, 138, 210, 226, 237, 261, 262, 334–336; **Supp. VIII:** 37, 39, 40, 104, 105, 108, 175, 176, 180, 181, 183, 184, 188, 189, 215; **Supp. IX:** 20, 95; **Supp. X:** 44, 228, **Supp. XI:** 92, 247; **Supp. XII:** 16, 289, 310, 313; **Supp. XIII:** 100, 169; **Supp. XIV:** 1, 12–13, 21, 24, 93, 306; **Supp. XV:** 92, 135, 338; **Supp. XVI:** 148, 189; **Supp. XVII:** 225; **Supp. XVIII:** 76, 84, 90, 148, 249; **Supp. XIX:** 97, 154, 166; **Supp. XX:** **137, 162, 185, 195; Supp. XXI:** 36, 38, 256; **Supp. XXII:** 193, 203, 205; **Supp. XXIII:** 166

Faulkner: A Collection of Critical Essays (Warren), **Retro. Supp. I:** 73

Faulkner at Nagano (Jelliffe, ed.), **I:** 289; **II:** 63, 65

Faulkner-Cowley File, The: Letters and Memories 1944–1962 (Cowley, ed.), **Retro. Supp. I:** 73, 92; **Supp. II Part 1:** 140, 141

"Faultlines"(Hadas), **Supp. XXIII:** 117–118

"Faun" (Plath), **Supp. I Part 2:** 537

"Fauna" (Jeffers), **Supp. II Part 2:** 415

Fauset, Arthur Huff, **Supp. XVIII:** 126

Fauset, Jessie, **Supp. I Part 1:** 321, 325; **Supp. IV Part 1:** 164

Fauset, Jessie Redmon, **Supp. XVIII:** 122,127; **Supp. XIX:** 69, 78

Faust (Goethe), **I:** 396; **II:** 489; **III:** 395; **Supp. II Part 1:** 16; **Supp. IX:** 141

Faust, Beatrix Hapgood, **Supp. XXI:** 8

Faust, Clarence H., **II:** 20

Faute de l'Abbé Mouret, La (Zola), **III:** 322

Favor Island (Merwin), **Supp. III Part 1:** 346, 347

"Favor of Love, A" (Peacock), **Supp. XIX:** 203

"Favrile" (Doty), **Supp. XI:** 131

"Fawn, with a Bit of Green" (Swados), **Supp. XIX:** 258

Fay (L. Brown), **Supp. XXI:** 40, 41, 47

Fay, Bernard, **IV:** 41

"Fear, The" (Frost), **Retro. Supp. I:** 128

Fear and Trembling (Kierkegaard), **Supp. XX: 132**

"Fear & Fame" (Levine), **Supp. V:** 192

Fearful Child, The (C. Frost), **Supp. XV:** 96, 97, 106

"Fearful Child, The" (C. Frost), **Supp. XV:** 96

Fearing, Kenneth, **Supp. XV:** 138

"Fearless" (Mosley), **Supp. XIII:** 241

Fearless Jones (Mosley), **Supp. XIII: 241–242**

"Fear of Concrete" (Halliday), **Supp. XIX:** 91

Fear of Fifty: A Midlife Memoir (Jong), **Supp. V:** 114, 115, 116, 131

Fear of Flying (Jong), **Supp. V:** 113, 115, 116, 119–123, 124, 129

"Feast, The" (Kinnell), **Supp. III Part 1:** 239, 250

Feast of All Saints, The (Rice), **Supp. VII:** 299–301

Feast of Love, The (C. Baxter), **Supp. XVII:** 13, 21–22

Feast of Love, The (film, R. Benton), **Supp. XVII:** 22

Feast of Snakes, A (Crews), **Supp. XI:** 102, **107–108; Supp. XXI:** 40

"Feast of Stephen, The" (Hecht), **Supp. X:** 63–64

"Featherbed for Critics, A" (Blackmur), **Supp. II Part 1:** 93, 151

Feather Crowns (Mason), **Supp. VIII: 146–147**

"Feathers" (Carver), **Supp. III Part 1:** 145

Feathers (Van Vechten), **Supp. II Part 2:** 736, 749

"Feathers, The" (Hogan), **Supp. IV Part 1:** 416

"February" (Ellison), **Supp. II Part 1:** 229

"February 14th" (Levine), **Supp. V:** 194

February in Sydney (Komunyakaa), **Supp. XIII: 124–125,** 129

"February in Sydney" (Komunyakaa), **Supp. XIII:** 125

"February: Thinking of Flowers" (Kenyon), **Supp. VII:** 171

"Feces" (McClatchy), **Supp. XII:** 266, 267–268

Fechner, Gustav, **II:** 344, 355, 358, 359, 363

Feder, Lillian, **IV:** 136; **Supp. XVI:** 49, 50

Federal Arts Project, **Supp. III Part 2:** 618

Federigo, or, The Power of Love (Nemerov), **III:** 268, 276, 282, 283–284, 285

"Fedge, The" (Halliday), **Supp. XIX:** 93

"Fedora" (Chopin), **Supp. I Part 1:** 220

Fedorko, Kathy A., **Retro. Supp. I:** 361, 374

"Feeling and Precision" (Moore), **III:** 206

Feeling Italian: The Art of Ethnicity in America (Ferraro), **Supp. XX:** 43

"Feeling of Effort, The" (James), **II:** 349

Feeling Very Strange: The Slipstream Anthology (Kelly and Kessel, eds.), **Supp. XIX:** 231

"Feel Like a Bird" (Swenson), **Supp. IV Part 2:** 639

"Feel Me" (Swenson), **Supp. IV Part 2:** 647

Feeney, Mary, **Supp. IX:** 152, 154

Feinsilver, Pamela, **Supp. XX: 135**

Feinstein, Herbert, **Supp. XIX:** 260

Feinstein, Sascha, **Supp. XIII:** 125

Feldman, Charles K., **Supp. IX:** 307

Feldman, Morton, **Supp. XXIII:** 211

Fellini, Federico, **Supp. XII:** 172; **Supp. XV:** 8

"Fellini the Cat" (Peacock), **Supp. XIX:** 206

"Fellow Citizens" (Sandburg), **III:** 553

Fellows, John, **Supp. I Part 2:** 520

Fellow Travelers (Mallon), **Supp. XIX:** 132, **143–144**

"Felo de Se" (Wylie), **Supp. I Part 2:** 727, 729

Felton, Sharon, **Supp. IV Part 1:** 210

"Female Author" (Plath), **Retro. Supp. II:** 243

"Female Frailty" (Freneau), **Supp. II Part 1:** 258

"Female Laughter and Comic Possibilities: *Uncommon Women and Others*" (Chirico), **Supp. XV:** 323

Female Patriot, The; or, Nature's Rights (Rowson), **Supp. XV:** 237–238

Female Prose Writers of America (Hart), **Supp. XVIII:** 257, 264

"Female Voice in *To Kill a Mockingbird,* The: Narrative Strategies in Film and Novel" (Shakelford), **Supp. VIII:** 129

" 'Feminine' Epic, The" (Notley), **Supp. XXII:** 232, 234, 236

"Feminine Landscape of Leslie Marmon Silko's *Ceremony,* The" (Gunn Allen), **Supp. IV Part 1:** 324

Feminism and the Politics of Literary Reputation: The Example of Erica Jong (Templin), **Supp. V:** 116

"Feminismo" (Robbins), **Supp. X:** 272

"Feminist Criticism in the Wilderness" (Showalter), **Supp. X:** 97

"Feminist Manifesto" (Loy), **Supp. XXII:** 160

Feminization of American Culture, The (Douglas), **Supp. XVIII:** 258

"Fence, The" (Oliver), **Supp. VII:** 232

"Fence Posts" (Snyder), **Supp. VIII:** 304

Fences (Wilson), **Supp. VIII:** 329, 330, 331, **334–337,** 350

Fenick, Elizabeth, **Retro. Supp. II:** 221

"Fenimore Cooper's Literary Offenses" (Twain), **IV:** 204–205

Fennell, Frank L., **Supp. XVII:** 177–178

Fenollosa, Ernest, **III:** 458, 465, 466, 474, 475, 477; **Retro. Supp. I:** 289; **Supp. IV Part 1:** 154

Fenollosa, Mrs. Ernest, **III:** 458

"Fenstad's Mother" (C. Baxter), **Supp. XVII:** 18

Fenton, Charles, **Supp. XI:** 43

Fenton, James, **Supp. XV:** 117

Ferdinand: Including "It Was" (Zukofsky), **Supp. III Part 2:** 630

"Fergus" (Bourne), **I:** 229

Ferguson, James, **Supp. I Part 2:** 503

Ferguson, Otis, **Supp. IX:** 7

Ferguson, William, **Supp. XII:** 189

Ferguson Affair, The (Macdonald), **Supp. IV Part 2:** 473

Fergusson, Francis, **I:** 265, 440; **Supp. XV:** 20

Ferlinghetti, Lawrence, **Supp. IV Part 1:** 90; **Supp. VIII:** 290, 292; **Supp. XII:** 121, 125; **Supp. XIII:** 275; **Supp. XIX:** 4; **Supp. XXI:** 53; **Supp. XXIII:** 219

Fermata, The (Baker), **Supp. XIII: 49–52,** 54

"Fern" (Toomer), **Supp. III Part 2:** 481; **Supp. IX:** 313

Fern, Fanny, **Retro. Supp. I:** 246; **Supp. V:** 122

Fernández, Enrique, **Supp. VIII:** 73

Fernandez, Ramon, **Retro. Supp. I:** 302, 303; **Supp. XVI:** 214

"Fern-Beds in Hampshire Country" (Wilbur), **Supp. III Part 2:** 558

"Fern Hill" (D. Thomas), **IV:** 93; **Supp. XX: 204**

"Fern-Life" (Larcom), **Supp. XIII:** 143

Ferragammo, Salvatore, **Supp. XVI:** 192

Ferraro, Thomas J., **Supp. XX: 34, 43**

Ferreo, Guglielmo, **Supp. I Part 2:** 481

Ferris, Anthony, **Supp. XX: 124**

"Ferry, The" (Cliff), **Supp. XXII:** 74

Fessenden, Thomas Green, **II:** 300

Fessier, Michael, **Supp. XIII:** 164

"Festival Aspect, The" (Olson), **Supp. II Part 2:** 585

"Festival of Regrets, The" (Wasserstein), **Supp. XV:** 333

Festival of San Joaquin, The (Edgell), **Supp. XXIII:** 84, 85, **90–91,** 94

Fetching the Dead (Sanders), **Supp. XVI:** 269

Fêtes galantes (Verlaine), **IV:** 79
"Fetish" (McClatchy), **Supp. XII:** 256
Fetterley, Judith, **Retro. Supp. II:** 139
"Feud" (Zinberg), **Supp. XV:** 195
"Fever" (Carver), **Supp. III Part 1:** 145
"Fever 103'" (Plath), **Supp. I Part 2:** 541
Fever Pitch (Hornby), **Supp. XII:** 286;
　Supp. XXIII: 109
Fever: Twelve Stories (Wideman), **Supp.**
　X: 320
"Few Don'ts by an Imagiste, A" (Pound),
　III: 465; **Retro. Supp. I:** 288; **Supp.**
　I Part 1: 261–262
"Few Stray Comments on the Cultivation
　of the Lyric, A" (Sobin), **Supp. XVI:**
　285
"Few Words of Introduction, A"
　(McNally), **Supp. XIII:** 198–199
Fiamengo, Janice, **Supp. XIII:** 35
Fiber (Bass), **Supp. XVI:** 22
"*Fiber:* A Post-Pastoral Georgic"
　(Gifford), **Supp. XVI:** 22
Ficke, Arthur Davison, **Supp. XIII:** 347;
　Supp. XV: 40, 42, 43, 46, 48, 49
"Fiction" (Stafford), **Supp. XI:** 327
"Fiction: A Lens on Life" (Stegner),
　Supp. IV Part 2: 595, 596, 600
Fictional World of William Hoffman, The
　(Frank, ed.), **Supp. XVIII:** 74, 79, 80,
　87
Fiction and the Figures of Life (Gass),
　Supp. VI: 85
Fiction of Joseph Heller, The (Seed),
　Supp. IV Part 1: 391
Fiction of Paule Marshall, The
　(Denniston), **Supp. XI:** 276
Fiction of the Forties (Eisinger), **I:** 302;
　II: 604
*Fictions in Autobiography: Studies in the
　Art of Self-Invention* (Eakin), **Supp.**
　XVI: 70
"Fiction Writer and His Country, The"
　(O'Connor), **III:** 342; **Retro. Supp.**
　II: 223, 225; **Supp. II Part 1:** 148
Fiddler's Trance, The (Skloot), **Supp.**
　XX: 196, 202
Fidelity (Glaspell), **Supp. III Part 1:** 177
Fiedler, Leslie A., **II:** 27; **III:** 218; **Retro.**
　Supp. II: 280, 324; **Supp. II Part 1:**
　87; **Supp. IV Part 1:** 42, 86; **Supp.**
　IX: 3, 227; **Supp. X:** 80; **Supp. XIII:**
　93–110; Supp. XIV: 11; **Supp. XVIII:**
　146; **Supp. XIX:** 251; **Supp. XXIII:**
　42
*Fiedler on the Roof: Essays on Literature
　and Jewish Identity* (Fiedler), **Supp.**
　XIII: 106–107
"Fie! Fie! Fi-Fi!" (Fitzgerald), **Retro.**
　Supp. I: 100
Field, Eugene, **Supp. II Part 1:** 197
Field, John, **IV:** 179
"Field Events" (Bass), **Supp. XVI:** 19
"Field Full of Black Cats, A" (C. Frost),
　Supp. XV: 101
Field Guide, (Hass), **Supp. VI:** 97–98,
　99–101, 102, 103, 106
*Field Guide to Contemporary Poetry and
　Poetics* (Friebert and Young, eds.),
　Supp. XI: 270

"Field Guide to the Western Birds"
　(Stegner), **Supp. IV Part 2:** 609
Fielding, Henry, **I:** 134; **II:** 302, 304–
　305; **III:** 61; **Supp. I Part 2:** 421,
　422, 656; **Supp. IV Part 2:** 688;
　Supp. V: 127; **Supp. IX:** 128; **Supp.**
　XI: 277; **Supp. XVIII:** 2, 7
Fielding, Richard, **Supp. XV:** 232
"Field-larks and Blackbirds" (Lanier),
　Supp. I Part 1: 355
Field of Honor (Hay), **Supp. XIV:** 120–
　121, 125, 130
"Field of Honor" (Hay), **Supp. XIV:**
　120–121, 129–130
Field of Vision, The (Morris), **III:** 226–
　228, 229, 232, 233, 238
"Field Report" (Corso), **Supp. XII:** 124,
　136
"Fields" (Wright), **Supp. XV:** 342
Fields, Annie Adams, **II:** 401, 402, 403–
　404, 406, 412; **IV:** 177; **Retro. Supp.**
　II: 134, 135, 142; **Supp. I Part 1:**
　317; **Supp. XVI:** 84, 88
Fields, James T., **II:** 274, 279, 402–403;
　Retro. Supp. II: 135; **Supp. I Part 1:**
　317; **Supp. XIII:** 150; **Supp. XVI:**
　84, 88
Fields, Mrs. James T., **Supp. XIV:** 44,
　46. *See* Fields, Annie Adams
Fields, Joseph, **IV:** 274
Fields, The (Richter), **Supp. XVIII: 213–**
　214, 220
Fields, W. C., **II:** 427; **IV:** 335
"Fields at Dusk, The" (Salter), **Supp. IX:**
　260
Fields of Fire (Webb), **Supp. XXII:** 115
Fields of Praise, The (Nelson), **Supp.**
　XVIII: 171, 173, **177–178**
Fields of Wonder (Hughes), **Retro. Supp.**
　I: 206, 207; **Supp. I Part 1:** 333–334
Fierce Invalids Home from Hot Climates
　(Robbins), **Supp. X:** 267, 276–277,
　282–285
Fiery, Marion, **Supp. XXII:** 293
Fiery Chariot, The (Hurston), **Supp. VI:**
　155–156
15 Poems (Banks), **Supp. V:** 5
"Fifteenth Farewell" (Bogan), **Supp. III
　Part 1:** 51, 58
"Fifth Avenue, Uptown" (Baldwin),
　Supp. I Part 1: 52
"Fifth Avenue—Spring Afternoon"
　(Untermeyer), **Supp. XV:** 296
Fifth Book of Peace, The (Kingston),
　Supp. V: 173
Fifth Chinese Daughter (Wong), **Supp.**
　X: 291
Fifth Column, The (Hemingway), **II:** 254,
　258; **Retro. Supp. I:** 184
"Fifth Column of the Fencerow"
　(Leopold), **Supp. XIV:** 185
Fifth Decad of Cantos, The (Pound),
　Retro. Supp. I: 292
"Fifth Movement: *Autobiography*"
　(Zukofsky), **Supp. III Part 2:** 611
Fifth Sunday (Dove), **Supp. IV Part 1:**
　251, 252–253
"Fifth Sunday" (Dove), **Supp. IV Part 1:**
　252

50 Poems (Cummings), **I:** 430, 440, 442–
　443, 444–445, 446
Fifty Best American Short Stories
　(O'Brien), **III:** 56
"Fifty Dollars" (Elkin), **Supp. VI: 43–44**
"55 Miles to the Gas Pump" (Proulx),
　Supp. VII: 264
55 Poems (Zukofsky), **Supp. III Part 2:**
　611, 621
"Fifty Grand" (Hemingway), **II:** 250,
　424; **Retro. Supp. I:** 177
"Fifty Suggestions" (Poe), **Retro. Supp.
　II:** 266
"52 Oswald Street" (Kinnell), **Supp. III
　Part 1:** 251
*Fifty Years Among Authors, Editors, and
　Publishers* (Derby), **Supp. XVIII:** 4
"Fifty Years Among the Black Folk" (Du
　Bois), **Supp. II Part 1:** 169
"Fifty Years of American Poetry"
　(Jarrell), **Retro. Supp. I:** 52
Fig Connection, The (Franzen and
　Siebert), **Supp. XX:** 84
Fight, The (Mailer), **Retro. Supp. II:**
　207, 208
*Fight Back: For the Sake of the People,
　For the Sake of the Land* (Ortiz),
　Supp. IV Part 2: 497, 498, 499, 503,
　510–512, 514
"Fighters, The" (Zinberg), **Supp. XV:**
　193
Fight for Freedom (Hughes), **Supp. I
　Part 1:** 345
Fighting Angel (Buck), **Supp. II Part 1:**
　119, 131
*Fighting France; From Dunkerque to Bel-
　fort* (Wharton), **Retro. Supp. I:** 377,
　378
Fightin': New and Collected Stories
　(Ortiz), **Supp. IV Part 2:** 513
"Figlia che Piange, La" (Eliot), **I:** 570,
　584; **III:** 9
Figliola, Samantha, **Supp. V:** 143
"Figure a Poem Makes, The" (Frost),
　Retro. Supp. I: 139
"Figured Wheel, The" (Pinsky), **Supp.**
　VI: 243, 244, 245, 246
*Figured Wheel, The: New and Collected
　Poems* (Pinsky), **Supp. VI:** 247–248
"Figure in the Carpet, The" (James),
　Retro. Supp. I: 228, 229
"Figure in the Doorway, The" (Frost),
　Retro. Supp. I: 138
Figure of Fulfillment, The (Lerperger;
　Miller, trans.), **Supp. XX: 165, 167–**
　168
Figures from the Double World
　(McGrath), **Supp. X: 118–119**
*Figures in Black: Words, Signs, and the
　"Racial" Self* (H. L. Gates), **Supp.**
　XX: 99, 100, 106, 107
"Figures in the Clock, The" (McCarthy),
　II: 561–562
*Figures Made Visible in the Sadness of
　Time* (Everwine), **Supp. XV:** 75, 88
Figures of Time (Hayden), **Supp. II Part
　1:** 367
Filbin, Thomas, **Supp. XXIII:** 299
"Filling Out a Blank" (Wagoner), **Supp.**
　IX: 324

Fillmore, Millard, **III:** 101

Film Flam: Essays on Hollywood (McMurtry), **Supp. V:** 228

Films of Ayn Rand, The (Cox), **Supp. IV Part 2:** 524

Filo, John, **Supp. XII:** 211

Filreis, Alan, **Supp. XXI:** 262, 267, 268, 269, 271, 273, 275, 277, 278

Filson, John, **Retro. Supp. I:** 421

Final Beast, The (Buechner), **Supp. XII:** 49–51

"Finale" (Longfellow), **II:** 505, 506–507

"Final Fear" (Hughes), **Supp. I Part 1:** 338

Final Harvest: Emily Dickinson's Poems (Johnson, ed.), **I:** 470, 471

"Finally Harriet" (Wolfert), **Supp. XXI:** 265–267

Final Payments (Gordon), **Supp. IV Part 1:** 297, 299, 300–302, 304, 306, 314

"Final Report, A" (Maxwell), **Supp. VIII:** 169

"Final Soliloquy of the Interior Paramour" (Stevens), **Retro. Supp. I:** 312

Final Solution, The (Reitlinger), **Supp. XII:** 161

Financier, The (Dreiser), **I:** 497, 501, 507, 509; **Retro. Supp. II:** 94, 101–102, 105; **Supp. XVIII:** 246

Finch, Annie, **Supp. XVII:** 69–79

Finch, Henry Leroy, **Supp. XVII:** 69

Finch, Margaret Rockwell, **Supp. XVII:** 69

Finch, Robert, **Supp. XIV:** 186–187

"Finches, Little Pats of Butter on the Wing"(Crooker), **Supp. XXIII:** 62

Find a Victim (Macdonald), **Supp. IV Part 2:** 467, 472, 473

Fin de Chéri, La (Colette; stage adaptation, Loos), **Supp. XVI:** 194

Finder, Henry, **Supp. XX:** 90

"Fin de Saison Palm Beach" (White), **Supp. I Part 2:** 673

"Finding a Bible in an Abandoned Cabin" (Wrigley), **Supp. XVIII: 293–294,** 296, **297,** 300, 301, 303

Finding a Form (Gass), **Supp. VI:** 91–92, 93

Finding a Girl in America (Dubus), **Supp. VII:** 85–88

"Finding a Girl in America" (Dubus), **Supp. VII:** 87

"Finding Beads" (Hogan), **Supp. IV Part 1:** 400

Finding Losses (Bronk), **Supp. XXI:** 31, 32

"Finding of Zach, The" (Dunbar), **Supp. II Part 1:** 212

Findings and Keepings: Analects for an Autobiography (Mumford), **Supp. II Part 2:** 483

Finding the Center: Narrative Poetry of the Zuni Indians (Tedlock), **Supp. IV Part 2:** 509

Finding the Islands (Merwin), **Supp. III Part 1:** 353, 357

"Finding the Place: A Migrant Childhood" (Stegner), **Supp. IV Part 2:** 597

Findley, Timothy, **Supp. XX: 49–65**

"Find the Woman" (Macdonald, as Millar), **Supp. IV Part 2:** 466

Fine, David, **Supp. XI:** 160

Fine, Richard, **Supp. XVIII:** 248

Fine Clothes to the Jew (Hughes), **Retro. Supp. I:** 200, 201, 203, 205; **Supp. I Part 1:** 326–328

"Fine Old Firm, A" (Jackson), **Supp. IX:** 120

Fine Preserving (Plagemann), **Supp. XVII:** 91

Fine Preserving: M. F. K. Fisher's Annotated Edition of Catherine Plagemann's Cookbook (Plagemann; M. F. K. Fisher, ed.), **Supp. XVII:** 91

Finer Grain, The (James), **II:** 335

Fine Writing (L. P. Smith), **Supp. XIV:** 347

"Finis" (X. J. Kennedy), **Supp. XV:** 169

"Finished Basement" (Di Piero), **Supp. XIX:** 47

Finished Man, The (Garrett), **Supp. VII:** 96, 97–98

Fink, Jonathan, **Supp. XXI:** 244, 245, 248, 255, 256

Fink, Mike, **IV:** 266

Finkelstein, Norman, **Supp. XXI:** 24, 33

Finkle, David, **Supp. XXI:** 47

Finley, John H., **II:** 418

Finn, David, **Supp. VIII:** 106–107

Finnegan, Robert (pseudonym). *See* Ryan, Paul William

Finnegans Wake (Joyce), **III:** 7, 12, 14, 261; **IV:** 182, 369–370, 418, 421; **Supp. I Part 2:** 620; **Supp. II Part 1:** 2; **Supp. XIII:** 191; **Supp. XVIII:** 32

Finney, Brian, **Supp. XIV:** 158, 160, 161, 165, 166, 167, 169

"Finnish Rhapsody" (Ashbery), **Supp. III Part 1:** 26

Finster, Howard, **Supp. XV:** 349

Firbank, Ronald, **IV:** 77, 436; **Supp. XXIII:** 209

"Fire" (Hughes), **Supp. I Part 1:** 327

"Fire and Cloud" (Wright), **IV:** 488

"Fire and Ice" (Frost), **II:** 154; **Retro. Supp. I:** 133; **Supp. XIX:** 122

Fire and Ice (Stegner), **Supp. IV Part 2:** 598, 607–608

"Fire and the Cloud, The" (Hurston), **Supp. VI:** 158

"Fire and the Hearth, The" (Faulkner), **II:** 71

Firebird (Doty), **Supp. XI:** 119–120, 121, **132–133,** 134

"Firebombing, The" (Dickey), **Supp. IV Part 1:** 180–181, 187, 189–190

"Fireborn Are at Home in Fire, The" (Sandburg), **III:** 591

"Fire by Night" (R. Fisher), **Supp. XIX:** 70–71

"Fire Chaconne" (Francis), **Supp. IX:** 87

Firecrackers (Van Vechten), **Supp. II Part 2:** 740, 742–744, 749

"Fire Dreams"(Thompson), **Supp. XXIII:** 296

Fire: From "A Journal of Love," the Unexpurgated Diary of Anaïs Nin, 1934–1937, **Supp. X:** 184, 185, 189, 194, 195

"Fireman, The " (Bass), **Supp. XVI:** 24

Fireman's Wife and Other Stories, The (Bausch), **Supp. VII:** 48, 54

Fire Next Time, The (Baldwin), **Retro. Supp. II:** 5, 8, 9; **Supp. I Part 1:** 48, 49, 52, 60–61

"Fire Next Time, The" (Baldwin). *See* "Down at the Cross" (Baldwin)

"Fire of Driftwood, The" (Longfellow), **II:** 499; **Retro. Supp. II:** 159, 168

"Fire of Life" (McCullers), **II:** 585

Fire on the Mountain (Abbey), **Supp. XIII:** 6

"Fire Poem" (Merrill), **Supp. III Part 1:** 321

"Fires" (Bass), **Supp. XVI:** 20

"Fires" (Carver), **Supp. III Part 1:** 136–139, 147

Fire Screen, The (Merrill), **Supp. III Part 1:** 319, 325–329

"Fire Season" (Didion), **Supp. IV Part 1:** 199

"Fire Sequence" (Winters), **Supp. II Part 2:** 791, 796, 800

Fire Sermon (Morris), **III:** 238–239

"Fire Sermon, The" (Eliot), **Retro. Supp. I:** 60–61

Fires: Essays, Poems, Stories (Carver), **Supp. III Part 1:** 136, 140, 142, 146–147

Fireside Travels (Lowell), **Supp. I Part 2:** 407, 419–420

Firestarter (King), **Supp. V:** 140, 141, 144; **Supp. IX:** 114

"fire the bastards" (Green), **Supp. IV Part 1:** 285

"Fire-Truck, A" (Wilbur), **Supp. III Part 2:** 556

"Fireweed" (Clampitt), **Supp. IX: 44–45**

"Firewood" (Banks), **Supp. V:** 15

"Fireworks" (Ford), **Supp. V:** 69

"Fireworks" (Shapiro), **Supp. II Part 2:** 707

Fireworks: A History and Celebration (Plimpton), **Supp. XVI:** 245

Fir-Flower Tablets (Lowell), **II:** 512, 526–527

Firger, Jessica, **Supp. XIX:** 51, 58, 59, 62

Firkins, Oscar W., **II:** 271; **Supp. XV:** 297, 309

"Firmament, The" (Bryant), **Supp. I Part 1:** 162

Firmat, Gustavo Pérez, **Supp. VIII:** 76, 77, 79; **Supp. XI:** 184

"First American, The" (Toomer), **Supp. III Part 2:** 480, 487

"First Birth" (Olds), **Supp. X:** 212

First Book of Africa, The (Hughes), **Supp. I Part 1:** 344–345

First Book of Jazz, The (Hughes), **Supp. I Part 1:** 345

First Book of Negroes, The (Hughes), **Supp. I Part 1:** 345

First Book of Rhythms, The (Hughes), **Supp. I Part 1:** 345

First Book of the West Indies, The (Hughes), **Supp. I Part 1:** 345

Firstborn (Glück), **Supp. V:** 80, 81, 82, 84

"Firstborn" (Wright), **Supp. V:** 340
"First Chaldaic Oracle" (Carson), **Supp. XII: 111**
"First Communion" (Fante), **Supp. XI:** 160
"First Confession" (X. J. Kennedy), **Supp. XV: 154–155**
"First Day of School, The" (Gibbons), **Supp. X:** 41, 42
"First Death in Nova Scotia" (Bishop), **Supp. I Part 1:** 73
"First Formal" (Olds), **Supp. X:** 212
First Four Books of Poems, The (Glück), **Supp. V:** 81, 83
First Four Years, The (L. I. Wilder), **Supp. XXII:** 296, 298, 299–300
"First Grade" (Stafford), **Supp. XI:** 328
First Hand (Bierds), **Supp. XVII:** 32, 34–36
"First Hawaiian Bank" (Nye), **Supp. XIII:** 278
"First Heat" (Taylor), **Supp. V:** 323
First Hour, The (Di Piero), **Supp. XIX:** 36–37, 40
"First Hour of the Night, The" (Bidart), **Supp. XV: 30–32**
"First Hunters and the Last, The" (Sobin), **Supp. XVI:** 292
"First Job, The" (Cisneros), **Supp. VII:** 62
"1st Letter on Georges" (Olson), **Supp. II Part 2:** 578
First Light (C. Baxter), **Supp. XVII:** 15, **17–18,** 19, 22
First Light (Preston), **Supp. XVII:** 18
First Light (Wagoner), **Supp. IX:** 330
"First Love" (Welty), **IV:** 264; **Retro. Supp. I:** 347
First Love: A Lyric Sequence (Untermeyer), **Supp. XV:** 295
First Man, The (O'Neill), **III:** 390
First Manifesto (McGrath), **Supp. X:** 115
"First Meditation" (Roethke), **III:** 545–546
"First Noni Daylight, The" (Harjo), **Supp. XII:** 219
"First Passover" (Longfellow), **II:** 500–501
"First Person Female" (Harrison), **Supp. VIII:** 40, 41, 48
"First Place, The" (Wagoner), **Supp. IX:** 328
First Poems (Buechner), **Supp. XII:** 45
First Poems (Merrill), **Supp. III Part 1:** 318–321, 323
First Poems 1946–1954 (Kinnell), **Supp. III Part 1:** 235, 238–239
"First Praise" (W. C. Williams), **Retro. Supp. I:** 413
First Principles (Spencer), **Supp. I Part 1:** 368
"First Reader" (Collins), **Supp. XXI:** 55–56
"First Ride and First Walk" (Goldbarth), **Supp. XII:** 182–183
"First Seeing the St. Lawrence River"(Kenny), **Supp. XXIII:** 152
"First Seven Years, The" (Malamud), **Supp. I Part 2:** 431
"First Sex" (Olds), **Supp. X:** 208

"First Snow" (Mosher), **Supp. XXII:** 211
"First Snow in Alsace" (Wilbur), **Supp. III Part 2:** 545, 546, 559
"First Song" (Kinnell), **Supp. III Part 1:** 239
"First Spade in the West, The" (Fiedler), **Supp. XIII:** 103
"First Steps" (McClatchy), **Supp. XII:** 256
First There Is the Need (Reznikoff), **Supp. XIV:** 291
"First Things First" (Auden), **Supp. II Part 1:** 13
"First Thought, Best Thought" (Ginsberg), **Supp. II Part 1:** 327
"First Time I Saw Paris, The" (Fante), **Supp. XI:** 174
"First Travels of Max" (Ransom), **III:** 490–491
"First Tycoon of Teen, The" (Wolfe), **Supp. III Part 2:** 572
"First Views of the Enemy" (Oates), **Supp. II Part 2:** 508
"First Wife, The" (Buck), **Supp. II Part 1:** 127
First Words before Spring (Untermeyer), **Supp. XV:** 310
"First World War" (White), **Supp. I Part 2:** 665
"Fish" (F. Barthelme), **Supp. XI:** 26
"Fish" (Levis), **Supp. XI:** 259–260
Fish, Stanley, **Supp. IV Part 1:** 48; **Supp. XIV:** 14, 15
"Fish, The" (Bishop), **Supp. XV:** 100, 102
"Fish, The" (Moore), **III:** 195, 197, 209, 211, 213–214; **Supp. XXI:** 26
"Fish, The" (Oliver), **Supp. VII:** 236
"Fish, The/Lago Chapala" (Everwine), **Supp. XV:** 82–83
"Fish and Shadow" (Pound), **III:** 466
"Fishboy" (Richard), **Supp. XIX:** 212–213
Fishboy: A Ghost's Story (Richard), **Supp. XIX:** 209, **213–220,** 221
Fishburne, Laurence, **Supp. VIII:** 345
"Fish Cannery" (Fante), **Supp. XI:** 167
Fisher, Alexander Metcalf, **Supp. I Part 2:** 582
Fisher, Alfred, **Retro. Supp. II:** 243
Fisher, Barbara, **Supp. XXII:** 206
Fisher, Craig, **Supp. V:** 125
Fisher, Dorothy Canfield, **Retro. Supp. I:** 21, 133; **Supp. II Part 1:** 117. *See also* Canfield, Dorothy
Fisher, Mary, **Supp. I Part 2:** 455
Fisher, M. F. K., **Supp. XVII: 81–93**
Fisher, Phillip, **Retro. Supp. I:** 39
Fisher, Rudolph, **Retro. Supp. I:** 200; **Supp. I Part 1:** 325; **Supp. X:** 139; **Supp. XVI:** 143; **Supp. XIX: 65–80**
Fisher, Vardis, **Supp. IV Part 2:** 598
Fisher King, The (Marshall), **Supp. XI:** 275–276, **288–290**
"Fisherman, The" (Merwin), **Supp. II Part 1:** 346
"Fisherman and His Wife, The" (Welty), **IV:** 266
"Fisherman from Chihuahua, The" (Connell), **Supp. XIV:** 86

"Fishing" (Harjo), **Supp. XII:** 227–228
"Fishing Idyll, A" (Mosher), **Supp. XXII:** 209
"Fish in the Stone, The" (Dove), **Supp. IV Part 1:** 245, 257
"Fish in the unruffled lakes" (Auden), **Supp. II Part 1:** 8–9
"Fish R Us" (Doty), **Supp. XI:** 135
Fisk, James, **I:** 4, 474
Fiske, John, **Supp. I Part 1:** 314; **Supp. I Part 2:** 493
"Fit Against the Country, A" (Wright), **Supp. III Part 2:** 591–592, 601
Fitch, Clyde, **Supp. IV Part 2:** 573
Fitch, Elizabeth. *See* Taylor, Mrs. Edward (Elizabeth Fitch)
Fitch, James, **IV:** 147
Fitch, Noël Riley, **Supp. X:** 186, 187
"Fitting, The" (Hull), **Supp. XXI:** 134, 135
Fitts, Dudley, **I:** 169, 173; **Supp. I Part 1:** 342, 345; **Supp. XIII:** 346; **Supp. XXII:** 281
FitzGerald, Edward, **Supp. I Part 2:** 416; **Supp. III Part 2:** 610
Fitzgerald, Ella, **Supp. XIII:** 132
Fitzgerald, F. Scott, **I:** 107, 117, 118, 123, 188, 221, 288, 289, 358, 367, 374–375, 382, 423, 476, 482, 487, 495, 509, 511; **II: 77–100,** 257, 263, 272, 283, 415, 416, 417–418, 420, 425, 427, 430, 431, 432, 433, 434, 436, 437, 450, 458–459, 482, 560; **III:** 2, 26, 35, 36, 37, 40, 44, 45, 69, 106, 244, 284, 334, 350–351, 453, 454, 471, 551, 552, 572; **IV:** 27, 49, 97, 101, 126, 140, 191, 222, 223, 287, 297, 427, 471; **Retro. Supp. I:** 1, 74, **97–120,** 178, 180, 186, 215, 359, 381; **Retro. Supp. II:** 257, 321, 326, 328; **Supp. I Part 1:** 196, 197; **Supp. I Part 2:** 622; **Supp. III Part 2:** 409, 411, 585; **Supp. IV Part 1:** 123, 197, 200, 203, 341; **Supp. IV Part 2:** 463, 468, 607, 689; **Supp. V:** 23, 95, 226, 251, 262, 276, 313; **Supp. VIII:** 101, 103, 106, 137; **Supp. IX:** 15, 20, 55, 57–63, 199; **Supp. X:** 225; **Supp. XI:** 65, 221, 334; **Supp. XII:** 42, 173, 295; **Supp. XIII:** 170, 263; **Supp. XV:** 135; **Supp. XVI:** 64, 75, 191, 192, 294; **Supp. XVIII:** 148, 246, 248, 251, 254; **Supp. XX: 74; Supp. XXI:** 262; **Supp. XXII:** 82, 92; **Supp. XXIII:** 68, 101, 174
Fitzgerald, Robert, **I:** 27–28; **III:** 338, 348; **Retro. Supp. II:** 179, 221, 222, 223, 228, 229; **Supp. IV Part 2:** 631; **Supp. XV:** 112, 249; **Supp. XXII:** 281; **Supp. XXIII:** 112
Fitzgerald, Zelda (Zelda Sayre), **I:** 482; **II:** 77, 79, 82–85, 88, 90–91, 93, 95; **Supp. IV Part 1:** 310; **Supp. IX:** 55–73; **Supp. X:** 172. *See also* Sayre, Zelda
"Fitzgerald's Tragic Sense" (Schorer), **Retro. Supp. I:** 115
"Fitzgerald: The Romance of Money" (Cowley), **Supp. II Part 1:** 143
5 Detroits (Levine), **Supp. V:** 178

Five Came Back (West), **IV:** 287

Five Corners (screenplay, Shanley), **Supp. XIV:** 316

"Five-Dollar Bill, The" (D. West as Mary Christopher), **Supp. XVIII:** 282

"Five Dollar Guy, The" (W. C. Williams), **Retro. Supp. I:** 423

Five Easy Pieces (film), **Supp. V:** 26

"Five Elephants" (Dove), **Supp. IV Part 1:** 244–245

"Five Fucks" (Lethem), **Supp. XVIII:** 139

Five Groups of Verse (Reznikoff), **Supp. XIV:** 279, 282

Five Hundred Hats of Bartholomew Cubbins, The (Geisel), **Supp. XVI:** 100

Five Hundred Scorpions (Hearon), **Supp. VIII:** 57, 65, **66**

Five Indiscretions (Ríos), **Supp. IV Part 2:** 545–547

Five Men and Pompey (Benét), **Supp. XI:** 43, 44

Five Plays (Hughes), **Retro. Supp. I:** 197, 209

"Five Psalms" (Jarman), **Supp. XVII:** 120

Five Temperaments (Kalstone), **Retro. Supp. II:** 40

5,000 Fingers of Dr. T, The (film), **Supp. XVI:** 103

Five Young American Poets, **I:** 170; **II:** 367

Fixer, The (Malamud), **Supp. I Part 2:** 428, 435, 445, 446–448, 450, 451

"Fixin' Road" (Boulton), **Supp. XXII:** 23

"Fix It (Winter)"(Hadas), **Supp. XXIII:** 115

Fjellestad, Danuta Zadworna, **Supp. XVI:** 150

Flaccus, Kimball, **Retro. Supp. I:** 136

Flacius, Matthias, **IV:** 163

"Flagellant's Song" (X. J. Kennedy), **Supp. XV:** 165

Flag for Sunrise, A (Stone), **Supp. V:** 301–304

Flagg, Fannie, **Supp. XXII:** 213–214

Flag of Childhood, The: Poems from the Middle East (Nye, ed.), **Supp. XIII:** 280

"Flag of Summer" (Swenson), **Supp. IV Part 2:** 645

Flagons and Apples (Jeffers), **Supp. II Part 2:** 413, 414, 417–418

Flags in the Dust (Faulkner), **Retro. Supp. I:** 81, 82, 83, 86, 88

Flamel, Nicolas, **Supp. XII:** 178

Flaming Corsage, The (W. Kennedy), **Supp. VII:** 133, 153 156

Flammarion, Camille, **Supp. I Part 1:** 260

Flanagan, John T., **Supp. I Part 2:** 464, 465, 468

Flanner, Janet, **Supp. XVI:** 195

"Flannery O'Connor: Poet to the Outcast" (Sister Rose Alice), **III:** 348

Flappers and Philosophers (Fitzgerald), **II:** 88; **Retro. Supp. I:** 103; **Supp. IX:** 56

Flash and Filigree (Southern), **Supp. XI:** 295, **296–297**

"Flashcards" (Dove), **Supp. IV Part 1:** 250

Flash Fiction: Seventy-two Very Short Stories (J. Thomas, ed.), **Supp. XVI:** 268

"Flash in the Pan" (Shaw), **Supp. XIX:** 245

"Flat Sky of Summer"(Balakian), **Supp. XXIII:** 25

Flatt, Lester, **Supp. V:** 335

Flaubert, Gustave, **I:** 66, 123, 130, 272, 312, 314, 315, 477, 504, 506, 513, 514; **II:** 182, 185, 194, 198–199, 205, 209, 230, 289, 311, 316, 319, 325, 337, 392, 401, 577, 594; **III:** 196, 207, 251, 315, 461, 467, 511, 564; **IV:** 4, 29, 31, 37, 40, 134, 285, 428; **Retro. Supp. I:** 5, 215, 218, 222, 225, 235, 287; **Supp. III Part 2:** 411, 412; **Supp. XI:** 334; **Supp. XIV:** 87, 336; **Supp. XXIII:** 254

"Flavia and Her Artists" (Cather), **Retro. Supp. I:** 5

Flavoring of New England, The (Brooks), **I:** 253, 256

Flavor of Man, The (Toomer), **Supp. III Part 2:** 487

"Flaw, The" (Peacock), **Supp. XIX:** 206

Flaxman, Josiah, **Supp. I Part 2:** 716

"Flea, The" (Donne), **Supp. XVIII:** 307

"Flèche d'Or" (Merrill), **Supp. III Part 1:** 328

Flecker, James Elroy, **Supp. I Part 1:** 257

"Flee on Your Donkey" (Sexton), **Supp. II Part 2:** 683, 685

Fleming, Ian, **Supp. XI:** 307; **Supp. XX: 195**

Fleming, Rene, **Supp. XII:** 321

Fleming, Robert E., **Supp. XVII:** 155; **Supp. XXII:** 184

Flesch, Rudolf, **Supp. XVI:** 105, 106

Flesh and Blood (Cunningham), **Supp. XV:** **63–65**

Flesh and Blood (play; Cunnigham and Gaitens), **Supp. XV:** 65

"Fleshbody" (Ammons), **Supp. VII:** 27

Fletcher, H. D., **II:** 517, 529

Fletcher, John, **Supp. IV Part 2:** 621

Fletcher, John Gould, **I:** 243; **II:** 517, 529; **III:** 458; **Supp. I Part 1:** 263; **Supp. I Part 2:** 422; **Supp. XV:** 298, 302, 306, 307, 308

Fletcher, Phineas, **Supp. I Part 1:** 369

Fletcher, Virginia. *See* Caldwell, Mrs. Erskine (Virginia Fletcher)

Fleurs du mal, Les (Beaudelaire; Millay and Dillon, trans.), **III:** 141–142

"Flight" (Bierds), **Supp. XVII:** 36

"Flight" (Updike), **IV:** 218, 222, 224; **Retro. Supp. I:** 318

Flight (White), **Supp. XVIII:** 127

"Flight, The" (Haines), **Supp. XII:** 204–205

"Flight, The" (Roethke), **III:** 537–538

Flight 115; or, Pas de Fumer sur la Piste (O'Hara and Berkson), **Supp. XXIII:** 217, 218

Flight among the Tombs (Hecht), **Supp. X:** 58, **71–74**

"Flight for Freedom" (McCoy), **Supp. XIII:** 170

"Flight from Byzantium" (Brodsky), **Supp. VIII:** 30–31

"Flight of Besey Lane, The" (Jewett), **Retro. Supp. II:** 139

Flight of the Rocket, The (Fitzgerald), **II:** 89

Flights of the Harvest-Mare (Bierds), **Supp. XVII:** 26–27

Flight to Canada (Reed), **Supp. X:** 240, **249–252**

Flinn, Mary, **Supp. XVII:** 110

Flint, F. S., **II:** 517; **III:** 459, 464, 465; **Retro. Supp. I:** 127; **Supp. I Part 1:** 261, 262

Flint, Helen, **Supp. XXII:** 278

Flint, R. W., **Supp. XVI:** 47, 49, 57

"Flitting Flies" (X. J. Kennedy), **Supp. XV:** 166, **167**

Flivver King, The (Sinclair), **Supp. V:** 290

Floating House, The (Sanders), **Supp. XVI:** 269

Floating Light Bulb, The (Allen), **Supp. XV:** 2, 3, 13

Floating Opera, The (Barth), **I:** 121, 122–126, 127, 129, 130, 131

"Floating Poem, Unnumbered, The" (Rich), **Supp. I Part 2:** 572–573

"Floating Trees" (Wright), **Supp. XV:** 348

Flood (Matthews), **Supp. IX:** 154, **160–161**

Flood (Warren), **IV:** 252, 256–257

"Flood of Years, The" (Bryant), **Supp. I Part 1:** 159, 170, 171; **Supp. I Part 2:** 416

"Floor and the Ceiling, The" (W. J. Smith), **Supp. XIII:** 345, 346

"Floor Plans" (Komunyakaa), **Supp. XIII:** 114

"Floral Conversation" (Peacock), **Supp. XIX:** 200

"Floral Decorations for Bananas" (Stevens), **IV:** 8

Florida (Acker), **Supp. XII:** 5

"Florida" (Bishop), **Retro. Supp. II:** 43

"Florida Road Workers" (Hughes), **Retro. Supp. I:** 203

"Florida Sunday, A" (Lanier), **Supp. I Part 1:** 364, 366

Florist's Daughter, The (Hampl), **Supp. XXII:** 84, 85, 94, **95–98**

"Flossie Cabanis" (Masters), **Supp. I Part 2:** 461–462

"Flounder" (Trethewey), **Supp. XXI:** 244, 245, 246, 251

Flow Chart (Ashbery), **Supp. VIII:** 275

"Flowchart" (Ashbery), **Supp. III Part 1:** 26

Flower, Dean, **Supp. XXII:** 205, 212

Flower, Fruit, and Thorn Pieces (Richter), **Supp. XVI:** 182

Flower-de-Luce (Longfellow), **II:** 490

Flower Drum Song (Rodgers and Hammerstein), **Supp. XXI:** 148

Flower Drum Song, The (Lee), **Supp. XXI:** 148

Flower Fables (Alcott), **Supp. I Part 1:** 33

"Flower-Fed Buffaloes, The" (Lindsay), **Supp. I Part 2:** 398

"Flower Garden" (Jackson), **Supp. IX:** 119

"Flower-gathering" (Frost), **II:** 153

Flower Herding on Mount Monadnock (Kinnell), **Supp. III Part 1:** 235, 239, 241–244

"Flower Herding on Mount Monadnock" (Kinnell), **Supp. III Part 1:** 242

"Flowering Death" (Ashbery), **Supp. III Part 1:** 22

"Flowering Dream, The" (McCullers), **II:** 591

"Flowering Judas" (Porter), **III:** 434, 435–436, 438, 441, 445, 446, 450–451

Flowering Judas and Other Stories (Porter), **III:** 433, 434

Flowering of New England, The (Brooks), **IV:** 171–172; **Supp. VIII:** 101

Flowering of the Rod (Doolittle), **Supp. I Part 1:** 272

Flowering Peach, The (Odets), **Supp. II Part 2:** 533, 547, 549–550

"Flowering Plum" (Glück), **Supp. V:** 82

"Flowers for Marjorie" (Welty), **IV:** 262

"Flowers of the Fallow" (Larcom), **Supp. XIII:** 143, 145–146

"Flowers Well if anybody" (Dickinson), **Retro. Supp. I:** 30

"Fluff and Mr. Ripley" (D. West), **Supp. XVIII:** 284

"Fly, The" (Kinnell), **Supp. III Part 1:** 249

"Fly, The" (Shapiro), **Supp. II Part 2:** 705

"Fly, The" (Simic), **Supp. VIII:** 278

Flye, Father James Harold, **I:** 25, 26, 35–36, 37, 42, 46; **IV:** 215

"Fly in Buttermilk, A" (Baldwin), **Retro. Supp. II:** 8

Flying at Night: Poems 1965–1985 (Kooser), **Supp. XIX:** 128

"Flying High" (Levertov), **Supp. III Part 1:** 284

"Flying Home" (Ellison), **Retro. Supp. II:** 117, **125–126; Supp. II Part 1:** 235, 238–239

"Flying Home" (Kinnell), **Supp. III Part 1:** 250

"Flying Home" and Other Stories (Ellison), **Retro. Supp. II:** 119, 124

"Flying Home from Utah" (Swenson), **Supp. IV Part 2:** 645

"Flying over Clouds" (Gioia), **Supp. XV:** 118

"Flying to Hanoi" (Rukeyser), **Supp. VI:** 279

Flynn, Elizabeth Gurley, **Supp. XVIII:** 225

Flynn, Richard, **Supp. XVII:** 115; **Supp. XVIII:** 183

Fly-Truffler, The (Sobin), **Supp. XVI: 294–295,** 296

Foata, Anne, **Supp. XI:** 104

FOB (Hwang), **Supp. XXI:** 143, 144, 145, 146, **148–150**

Focillon, Henri, **IV:** 90

Focus (A. Miller), **III:** 150–151, 156

Foer, Jonathan Safran, **Supp. XII:** 169; **Supp. XX: 177**

Foerster, Norman, **I:** 222; **Supp. I Part 2:** 423, 424; **Supp. IV Part 2:** 598

"Fog" (Sandburg), **III:** 586

"Fog Galleon" (Komunyakaa), **Supp. XIII:** 127

"Foggy and dripping" (Kooser), **Supp. XIX:** 125

"Foggy Lane, The" (Simpson), **Supp. IX:** 274

"Fog Man, The" (Boyle), **Supp. XX:** 20

Folded Leaf, The (Maxwell), **Supp. III Part 1:** 62; **Supp. VIII:** 159–162

Folding Star, The (Hollinghurst), **Supp. XIII:** 52

Foley, Jack, **Supp. X:** 125; **Supp. XV:** 112, 116; **Supp. XVII:** 77

Foley, Martha, **II:** 587; **Supp. XVI:** 225

Folk-Lore in the Old Testament (Frazer), **Supp. XX: 116–117**

Folks from Dixie (Dunbar), **Supp. II Part 1:** 211–212

Folkways (Sumner), **III:** 102

Follain, Jean, **Supp. IX:** 152, 154

Follett, Wilson, **I:** 405; **Supp. XIII:** 173

Follower of Dusk (Salinas), **Supp. XIII:** 326

"Following the Bones" (W. V. Davis), **Supp. XXI:** 96

Following the Equator (Twain), **II:** 434; **IV:** 208

Follow Me Home (Hoffman), **Supp. XVIII:** 86

Folly (Minot), **Supp. VI:** 205, 208, **210–213**

Folly of Others, The (Boyce), **Supp. XVII:** 100; **Supp. XXI:** 10

Folsom, Charles, **Supp. I Part 1:** 156

Folsom, Ed, **Retro. Supp. I:** 392

Folson, Marcia McClintock, **Retro. Supp. II:** 139

Fonda, Henry, **Supp. I Part 1:** 67; **Supp. IV Part 1:** 236

Fonda, Jane, **III:** 284; **Supp. XI:** 307

Fonda, Peter, **Supp. VIII:** 42; **Supp. XI:** 293, 308

"Fondled Memories" (Molesworth), **Supp. XIX:** 121–122

"Fond Memories of a Black Childhood" (D. West), **Supp. XVIII:** 289

Foner, Eric, **Supp. I Part 2:** 523

Fong and the Indians (Theroux), **Supp. VIII:** 314, 315, **316–317**

Fontanne, Lynn, **III:** 397

Food and Drink (Untermeyer), **Supp. XV:** 310

Fool for Love (Shepard), **Supp. III Part 2:** 433, 447, 448

Fooling with Words (PBS special, Moyers), **Supp. XXIII:** 139

"Foolishness" (Pickering), **Supp. XXI:** 197

Fools (Simon), **Supp. IV Part 2:** 584–585

Fool's Progress, The: An Honest Novel (Abbey), **Supp. XIII:** 4, **13–15**

Foot Book, The (Geisel), **Supp. XVI:** 108

Foote, Horton, **Supp. I Part 1:** 281; **Supp. VIII:** 128, 129

Foote, Mary Hallock, **Retro. Supp. II:** 72; **Supp. IV Part 2:** 611

Foote, Roxanna. *See* Beecher, Mrs. Lyman (Roxanna Foote)

Foote, Samuel, **Supp. I Part 2:** 584

Foote, Stephanie, **Retro. Supp. II:** 139

"Foot Fault" (pseudonym). *See* Thurber, James

Footing on This Earth, A (Hay), **Supp. XIV:** 125, 126, 130

"Footing up a Total" (Lowell), **II:** 528

"Footnote to Howl" (Ginsberg), **Supp. II Part 1:** 316–317

"Footnote to Weather Forecasts, A" (Brodsky), **Supp. VIII:** 32

Footprints (Hearon), **Supp. VIII: 69–70**

Footprints (Levertov), **Supp. III Part 1:** 272, 281

"Footsteps of Angels" (Longfellow), **II:** 496

"For A, at Fourteen" (Weigl), **Supp. XIX:** 287

For a Bitter Season: New and Selected Poems (Garrett), **Supp. VII:** 99–100

"For a Dead Kitten" (Hay), **Supp. XIV:** 119–120

"For a Dead Lady" (Robinson), **III:** 508, 513, 517

"For a Ghost Who Once Placed Bets in the Park" (Levis), **Supp. XI:** 265

"For a Lamb" (Eberhart), **I:** 523, 530, 531

"For All" (Snyder), **Supp. VIII:** 304

"For All Tuesday Travelers" (Cisneros), **Supp. VII:** 67–68

"For a Lost Child" (Stafford), **Supp. XI:** 329

"For a Marriage" (Bogan), **Supp. III Part 1:** 52

"For an Emigrant" (Jarrell), **II:** 371

"For Anna Akmatova" (Lowell), **II:** 544

"For Anna Mae Pictou Aquash, Whose Spirit Is Present Here and in the Dappled Stars" (Harjo), **Supp. XII:** 225

"For Anne, at a Little Distance" (Haines), **Supp. XII:** 207

"For Annie" (Poe), **III:** 427; **Retro. Supp. II:** 263

"For an Old Friend Encountered Unexpectedly" (Espaillat), **Supp. XXI:** 111 112

"For a Southern Man" (Cisneros), **Supp. VII:** 67

"For Bailey" (Angelou), **Supp. IV Part 1:** 15

Forbes, Malcolm, **Supp. IV Part 1:** 94

"Forbidden, The" (Glück), **Supp. XIV:** 269

"For Bill Nestrick (1940–96)" (Bidart), **Supp. XV:** 35

For Bread Alone (Choukri), **Supp. IV Part 1:** 92

"Force" (Di Piero), **Supp. XIX:** 35–36, 42, 44

Force of Desire, The (Bronk), **Supp. XXI:** 31, 32

Force of Evil (film, Polonsky), **Supp. XXI:** 261, 272, 275

Force of Spirit, The (Sanders), **Supp. XVI:** 277 278

Forché, Carolyn, **Supp. IV Part 1:** 208; **Supp. XIX:** 193

Ford, Arthur, **Supp. IV Part 1:** 140

Ford, Ford Madox, **I:** 288, 405, 409, 417, 421, 423; **II:** 58, 144, 198, 257, 263, 265, 517, 536; **III:** 458, 464–465, 470–471, 472, 476; **IV:** 27, 126, 261; **Retro. Supp. I:** 127, 177, 178, 186, 231, 286–287, 418; **Supp. II Part 1:** 107; **Supp. III Part 2:** 617; **Supp. VIII:** 107; **Supp. XIV:** 3

Ford, Harrison, **Supp. VIII:** 323

Ford, Harry, **Supp. V:** 179; **Supp. XIII:** 76

Ford, Henry, **I:** 295, 480–481; **III:** 292, 293; **Supp. I Part 1:** 21; **Supp. I Part 2:** 644; **Supp. III Part 2:** 612, 613; **Supp. IV Part 1:** 223; **Supp. V:** 290

Ford, John, **Supp. I Part 2:** 422; **Supp. III Part 2:** 619; **Supp. XVIII:** 247

Ford, Mark, **Supp. XXIII:** 220

Ford, Mary K., **Supp. XX:** 239

Ford, Richard, **Supp. IV Part 1:** 342; **Supp. V:** 22, 57–75

Ford, Webster (pseudonym). *See* Masters, Edgar Lee

"Fording and Dread" (Harrison), **Supp. VIII:** 41

"Ford Madox Ford" (Lowell), **II:** 547; **Retro. Supp. II:** 188

"For Dudley" (Wilbur), **Supp. III Part 2:** 558

Fordyce, David, **II:** 113

For Eager Lovers (Taggard), **Supp. XXII:** 274–275

Foregone Conclusion, A (Howells), **II:** 278–279, 282

"Foreign Affairs" (Kunitz), **Supp. III Part 1:** 265

"Foreigner, A" (Bynner), **Supp. XV:** 46

"Foreigner, The" (Jewett), **II:** 409–410; **Retro. Supp. II:** 133, 142

"Foreigners" (Jarman), **Supp. XVII:** 113

"Foreign Language, The" (Franzen), **Supp. XX:** 84

"Foreign Shores" (Salter), **Supp. IX:** 260

Forensic and the Navigators (Shepard), **Supp. III Part 2:** 439

Forerunner, The (Boyce), **Supp. XXI:** 2, 4, **10–11**

Forerunner, The: His Parables and Poems (Gibran), **Supp. XX: 115, 118–119,** 119

Foreseeable Future, The (Price), **Supp. VI:** 265

Foreseeable Futures (Matthews), **Supp. IX:** 155, **163,** 169

"For Esmé with Love and Squalor" (Salinger), **III:** 560

"Forest" (Simic), **Supp. VIII:** 273

Forest, Jean-Claude, **Supp. XI:** 307

Forester's Letters (Paine), **Supp. I Part 2:** 508

"Forest Hymn, A" (Bryant), **Supp. I Part 1:** 156, 162, 163, 164, 165, 170

"Forest in the Seeds, The" (Kingsolver), **Supp. VII:** 203

Forest of the South, The (Gordon), **II:** 197

"Forest of the South, The" (Gordon), **II:** 199, 201

Forest without Leaves (Adams and Haines), **Supp. XII:** 209

"Forever, Said the Duck" (Lethem), **Supp. XVIII:** 139

"Forever and the Earth" (Bradbury), **Supp. IV Part 1:** 102

"Forever in That Year" (Carruth), **Supp. XVI:** 51

"Forever"(Thompson), **Supp. XXIII:** 296

"Forever Young" (Jarman and R. McDowell), **Supp. XVII:** 111

"For Fathers of Girls" (Dunn), **Supp. XI:** 146

For Frank O'Hara's Birthday (Notley), **Supp. XXII:** 224, 227

"For/From Lew" (Snyder), **Supp. VIII:** 303

"For Garrison Keillor, Fantasy Is a Lot More Fun then Reality" (Letofsky), **Supp. XVI:** 167

"For George Santayana" (Lowell), **II:** 547

"Forgetfulness" (Collins), **Supp. XXI:** 58

"Forgiveness" (Peacock), **Supp. XIX:** 200

Forgotten Helper, The: A Story for Children (Moore), **Supp. X:** 175

"Forgotten in an Old Notebook" (F. Wright), **Supp. XVII:** 244

Forgotten Village, The (Steinbeck), **IV:** 51

"For Grace, After a party"(O'Hara), **Supp. XXIII:** 214

"For Grizzel McNaught (1709–1792)" (A. Finch), **Supp. XVII:** 72

Forgue, Guy J., **III:** 118, 119

For Her Dark Skin (Everett), **Supp. XVIII:** 56, 60

"FOR HETTIE" (Baraka), **Supp. II Part 1:** 32

"FOR HETTIE IN HER FIFTH MONTH" (Baraka), **Supp. II Part 1:** 32, 38

"For Homer" (Corso), **Supp. XII:** 135

"For I'm the Boy" (Barthelme), **Supp. IV Part 1:** 47

"For James Dean"(O'Hara), **Supp. XXIII:** 214

"For Janice and Kenneth to Voyage"(O'Hara), **Supp. XXIII:** 214

"For Jeff" (Kooser), **Supp. XIX:** 125

"For Jessica, My Daughter" (Strand), **Supp. IV Part 2:** 629

"For John, Who Begs Me not to Enquire Further" (Sexton), **Supp. II Part 2:** 676

"For Johnny Pole on the Forgotten Beach" (Sexton), **Supp. II Part 2:** 675

"For Joy to Leave Upon" (Ortiz), **Supp. IV Part 2:** 508

"For Judy, Whose Husband Is Undergoing Surgery"(Crooker), **Supp. XXIII:** 61

"Fork" (Simic), **Supp. VIII:** 275

"For Karl Shapiro, Having Gone Back to the Sonnet" (Kooser), **Supp. XIX:** 118

For Lancelot Andrewes (Eliot), **Retro. Supp. I:** 64

For Lizzie and Harriet (Lowell), **Retro. Supp. II:** 183, 186, 190

"Forlorn Hope of Sidney Lanier, The" (Leary), **Supp. I Part 1:** 373

For Love (Creeley), **Supp. IV Part 1:** 139, 140, 142–145, 147–149, 150, 154

"For Love" (Creeley), **Supp. IV Part 1:** 145

For Love (Miller), **Supp. XII: 297–299,** 299

For Love of Imabelle (C. Himes), **Supp. XVI:** 135, 143, 144

Form, Cycle, Infinity: Landscape Imagery in the Poetry of Robert Frost and George Seferis (Hadas), **Supp. XXIII: 121–122**

"Formal Elegy" (Berryman), **I:** 170

Formal Feeling Comes, A (A. Finch, ed.), **Supp. XVII: 71–72**

"Formalist Criticism: Its Principles and Limits" (Burke), **I:** 282

Forman, Milos, **Supp. IV Part 1:** 236

"Form and Function of the Novel, The" (Goldbarth), **Supp. XII:** 183

"For Marse Chouchoute" (Chopin), **Retro. Supp. II:** 60

"For Mary Ann Youngren" (Bidart), **Supp. XV:** 29

"Format and Form" (A. Rich), **Supp. XVII:** 74

"Formation of a Separatist, I" (Howe), **Supp. IV Part 2:** 427

"Form Is Emptiness" (Baraka), **Supp. II Part 1:** 51

"For Mr. Death Who Stands with His Door Open" (Sexton), **Supp. II Part 2:** 695

Forms of Discovery (Winters), **Supp. II Part 2:** 812, 813

Forms of Fiction, The (Gardner and Dunlap), **Supp. VI:** 64

"For My Children" (Karr), **Supp. XI:** 254

"For My Daughter" (Kees), **Supp. XV:** 141, 147

"For My Daughter" (Olds), **Supp. X:** 206

"For My Former Wife, Watching TV, in the Past" (Kooser), **Supp. XIX:** 120

"For My Lover, Returning to His Wife" (Sexton), **Supp. II Part 2:** 688

Fornés, Maria Irene, **Supp. XXI:** 144; **Supp. XXIII:** 194, 200

"For Night to Come" (Stern), **Supp. IX:** 292

"For Once, Then, Something" (Frost), **II:** 156–157; **Retro. Supp. I:** 126, 133, 134

"For Peg: A Remnant of Song Still Distantly Sounding" (Carruth), **Supp. XVI:** 54

"For Pot-Boiling" (Hay), **Supp. XIV:** 128

"For Radicals" (Bourne), **I:** 221

"For Rainer Gerhardt" (Creeley), **Supp. IV Part 1:** 142–143, 147

Forrestal, James, **I:** 491; **Supp. I Part 2:** 489

Forrester, Fanny, **Supp. XVIII:** 13
"For Richard After All" (Kingsolver), **Supp. VII:** 208
"For Sacco and Vanzetti" (Kingsolver), **Supp. VII:** 208
"Forsaken Brother, The"(J. Schoolcraft), **Supp. XXIII:** 235
"Forsaken Merman" (Arnold), **Supp. I Part 2:** 529
"For S.F.S. 1875–1962" (J. W. Miller), **Supp. XX: 166**
For Spacious Skies (Buck), **Supp. II Part 1:** 131
Forster, E. M., **I:** 292; **IV:** 201; **Retro. Supp. I:** 59, 232; **Supp. III Part 2:** 503; **Supp. V:** 258; **Supp. VIII:** 155, 171; **Supp. IX:** 128; **Supp. XII:** 79, 81; **Supp. XIV:** 159, 160, 163; **Supp. XV:** 62; **Supp. XVI:** 236; **Supp. XVIII:** 143; **Supp. XX:** 229, 235, **239, 240; Supp. XXI:** 233
Forster, John, **II:** 315
Fort, Paul, **II:** 518, 528, 529; **Retro. Supp. I:** 55
"For the Ahkoond" (Bierce), **I:** 209
For the Body (Nelson), **Supp. XVIII:** 173
For the Century's End: Poems 1990–1999 (Haines), **Supp. XII: 211–213**
"For the Chinese New Year and Bill Berkson"(O'Hara), **Supp. XXIII:** 218
"For the Dedication of the New City Library, Boston" (Holmes), **Supp. I Part 1:** 308
"For the Fallen" (Levine), **Supp. V:** 188
For the Health of the Land: Previously Unpublished Essays and Other Writings (Leopold), **Supp. XIV:** 183
"For the Lady in the Black Raincoat Who Slept Through an Entire Poetry Reading" (Espaillat), **Supp. XXI:** 108
"For the Last Wolverine" (Dickey), **Supp. IV Part 1:** 182
"For the Lovers of the Absolute" (Simic), **Supp. VIII:** 278–279
"For the Man Cutting the Grass" (Oliver), **Supp. VII:** 235
"For the Marriage of Faustus and Helen" (H. Crane), **I:** 395–396, 399, 402; **Retro. Supp. II:** 78–79, 82
"For the Meeting of the National Sanitary Association, 1860" (Holmes), **Supp. I Part 1:** 307
For the New Intellectual (Rand), **Supp. IV Part 2:** 521, 526–527, 527, 532
"For the New Railway Station in Rome" (Wilbur), **Supp. III Part 2:** 554
"For the Night" (Kenyon), **Supp. VII:** 163
"For Theodore Roethke: 1908–1963" (Lowell), **II:** 554
"For the Poem *Patterson*" (W. C. Williams), **Retro. Supp. I:** 424
"For the Poets of Chile" (Levine), **Supp. V:** 188
"FOR THE REVOLUTIONARY OUTBURST BY BLACK PEOPLE" (Baraka), **Supp. II Part 1:** 55
"For the Sleepless" (Dunn), **Supp. XI:** 145

For the Time Being (Auden), **Supp. II Part 1:** 2, 17, 18
For the Time Being (Dillard), **Supp. VI:** 23, 27, 29, 32, **34–35**
"For the Twentieth Century" (Bidart), **Supp. XV:** 35
For the Union Dead (Lowell), **II:** 543, 550–551, 554, 555; **Retro. Supp. II:** 181, 182, 186, 189; **Supp. X:** 53
"For the Union Dead" (Lowell), **II:** 551; **Retro. Supp. II:** 189
"For the Walking Dead" (Komunyakaa), **Supp. XIII:** 121
"For the West" (Snyder), **Supp. VIII:** 299
"For the Word Is Flesh" (Kunitz), **Supp. III Part 1:** 262–264
"Fortress, The" (Glück), **Supp. V:** 82
"Fortress, The" (Sexton), **Supp. II Part 2:** 682
Fortress of Solitude, The (Lethem), **Supp. XVIII:** 135, 136, **145–148,** 150
"Fort Robinson" (Kooser), **Supp. XIX:** 120
"Fortunate Traveler" (Hull), **Supp. XXI:** 140
Fortune, T. Thomas, **Supp. II Part 1:** 159
Fortune's Bones: The Manumission Requiem (Nelson), **Supp. XVIII:** 171, 172–173, 182–183
Fortune's Daughter (Hoffman), **Supp. X:** 77, 85
"Fortune Spill, The" (Nelson), **Supp. XVIII:** 175
45 Mercy Street (Sexton), **Supp. II Part 2:** 694, 695, 697
Forty Poems Touching on Recent American History (Bly, ed.), **Supp. IV Part 1:** 61
42nd Parallel, The (Dos Passos), **I:** 482, 484–485
Forty Stories (Barthelme), **Supp. IV Part 1:** 47, 49, 53, 54
For Whom the Bell Tolls (Hemingway), **II:** 249, 254–255, 261; **III:** 18, 363; **Retro. Supp. I:** 115, 176–177, 178, **184,** 187; **Supp. XVII:** 229
Foscolo, Ugo, **II:** 543
Foss, Sam Walter, **Supp. II Part 1:** 197
"Fossils, The" (Kinnell), **Supp. III Part 1:** 244
Foster, Edward, **Supp. IV Part 2:** 431, 434; **Supp. XVI:** 281, 293; **Supp. XXI:** 33
Foster, Edward Halsey, **Supp. XII:** 120, 129, 130, 135; **Supp. XVIII:** 265, 268
Foster, Emily, **II:** 309
Foster, Frances Smith, **Supp. XX: 287**
Foster, Hannah, **Supp. XV:** 234
Foster, John Wilson, **Supp. XIII:** 32–33
Foster, Phil, **Supp. IV Part 2:** 574
Foster, Richard, **Supp. XV:** 269
Foster, Stephen, **Supp. I Part 1:** 100–101; **Supp. I Part 2:** 699
Foucault, Michel, **Supp. VIII:** 5; **Supp. XII:** 98; **Supp. XV:** 344; **Supp. XVI:** 285
"Founder, The" (Stern), **Supp. IX:** 297
Founding of Harvard College, The (Morison), **Supp. I Part 2:** 485

"Fountain, The" (Bryant), **Supp. I Part 1:** 157, 165, 166, 168
Fountain, The (O'Neill), **III:** 391
Fountain and Other Poems, The (Bryant), **Supp. I Part 1:** 157
Fountainhead, The (film), **Supp. IV Part 2:** 524
Fountainhead, The (Rand), **Supp. IV Part 2:** 517, 521–523, 525, 531
Fountainhead, The: A Fiftieth Anniversary Celebration (Cox), **Supp. IV Part 2:** 523
"Fountain Piece" (Swenson), **Supp. IV Part 2:** 641
4-H Club (Shepard), **Supp. III Part 2:** 439
"Four Ages of Man, The" (Bradstreet), **Supp. I Part 1:** 111, 115
Four American Indian Literary Masters (Velie), **Supp. IV Part 2:** 486
"Four Angers"(Hadas), **Supp. XXIII:** 115
"Four Beasts in One; the Homo Cameleopard" (Poe), **III:** 425
Four Black Revolutionary Plays (Baraka), **Supp. II Part 1:** 45; **Supp. VIII:** 330
"Four Brothers" (Di Piero), **Supp. XIX:** 37
"Four Brothers, The" (Sandburg), **III:** 585
Four Days (screenplay, P. Benedict), **Supp. XXIII:** 35
Four Dogs and a Bone and the Wild Goose (Shanley), **Supp. XIV:** 316, **328–329**
"Four Evangelists, The" (Komunyakaa), **Supp. XIII:** 131
"Four for Sir John Davies" (Roethke), **III:** 540, 541
"Four Girls, The" (Alvarez), **Supp. VII:** 7
"Four Horse Songs" (Harjo), **Supp. XII:** 220
"400-Meter Free Style" (Kumin), **Supp. IV Part 2:** 442
"400-Pound CEO, The" (Saunders), **Supp. XIX:** 225
Fourier, Charles, **II:** 342
"Four in a Family" (Rukeyser), **Supp. VI:** 272
Four in Hand: A Quartet of Novels (Warner), **Supp. VIII:** 164
"Four Lakes' Days" (Eberhart), **I:** 525
"Four Mad Studies" (Di Piero), **Supp. XIX:** 37
"Four Meetings" (James), **II:** 327
Four Million, The (O. Henry), **Supp. II Part 1:** 394, 408
"Four Monarchyes" (Bradstreet), **Supp. I Part 1:** 105, 106, 116
"Four Mountain Wolves" (Silko), **Supp. IV Part 2:** 561
Four of a Kind (Marquand), **III:** 54, 55
"Four of the Horsemen (Hypertense and Stroke, Coronary Occlusion and Cerebral Insult)" (Karr), **Supp. XI:** 250
"Four Poems" (Bishop), **Supp. I Part 1:** 92
"Four Poems at the End of Summer"(Hadas), **Supp. XXIII:** 117

"Four Preludes on Playthings of the Wind" (Sandburg), **III:** 586

Four Quartets (T. S. Eliot), **I:** 570, 576, 580–582, 585, 587; **II:** 537; **III:** 539; **Retro. Supp. I:** 66, 67; **Supp. II Part 1:** 1; **Supp. IV Part 1:** 284; **Supp. V:** 343, 344; **Supp. VIII:** 182, 195; **Supp. XIII:** 344; **Supp. XIV:** 167; **Supp. XV:** 216, 260, 266

Four Saints in Three Acts (Stein), **IV:** 30, 31, 33, 43, 44–45

"Four Seasons" (Bradstreet), **Supp. I Part 1:** 112–113

Four Seasons of Success, The (Schulberg), **Supp. XVIII:** 254

"Four Sides of One Story" (Updike), **Retro. Supp. I:** 328

"Four Skinny Trees" (Cisneros), **Supp. VII:** 64

"14: In A Dark Wood: Wood Thrushes" (Oliver), **Supp. VII:** 244

"14 Men Stage Head Winter 1624/ 25" (Olson), **Supp. II Part 2:** 574

14 Stories (Dixon), **Supp. XII:** 141, **145–147**

Fourteen Hundred Thousand (Shepard), **Supp. III Part 2:** 439

Fourteen Sisters of Emilio Montez O'Brien, The (Hijuelos), **Supp. VIII: 82–85**

Fourteen Stories (Buck), **Supp. II Part 1:** 126

"Fourteenth Ward, The" (H. Miller), **III:** 175

Fourth Book of Peace, The (Kingston), **Supp. V:** 173

"Fourth Down" (Marquand), **III:** 56

Fourth Group of Verse, A (Reznikoff), **Supp. XIV:** 282, 284

"Fourth of July in Maine" (Lowell), **II:** 535, 552–553

Fourth Wall, The (Gurney), **Supp. V:** 109–110

Fowler, Douglas, **Supp. IV Part 1:** 226, 227

Fowler, Gene, **Supp. VIII:** 290

Fowler, Henry Watson, **Supp. I Part 2:** 660

Fowler, Karen Joy, **Supp. XXII:** 49

Fowler, Singrid, **Supp. VIII:** 249, 258

Fowler, Virginia C., **Supp. VIII:** 224

Fox, Alan, **Supp. XIII:** 120

Fox, Dixon Ryan, **I:** 337

Fox, Joe, **Supp. IX:** 259, 261

Fox, John, **Supp. XIII:** 166; **Supp. XXII:** 36

Fox, Linda C., **Supp. XIII:** 217–218

Fox, Paula, **Supp. XX:** 91

Fox, Ruth, **Supp. I Part 2:** 619

"Fox, The" (Levine), **Supp. V:** 181, 189

Fox-Genovese, Elizabeth, **Supp. IV Part 1:** 286; **Supp. XXII:** 190, 192, 200

Fox in Socks (Geisel), **Supp. XVI:** 108, 112

"Fox Night" (Jarman), **Supp. XVII:** 120

Fox of Peapack, The (White), **Supp. I Part 2:** 676, 677–678

"Fox of Peapack, The" (White), **Supp. I Part 2:** 677

"Fox Point Health Clinic, 1974" (Halliday), **Supp. XIX:** 89, 93

Fox's Earth (Siddons), **Supp. XXII:** 239

Foye, Raymond, **Supp. XIV:** 150

Fradkin, Lori, **Supp. XIX:** 52

Fraenkel, Michael, **III:** 178, 183

"Fragging" (Komunyakaa), **Supp. XIII:** 123

Fragile Beauty, A: John Nichols' Milagro Country: Text and Photographs from His Life and Work (Nichols), **Supp. XIII:** 268

"Fragility" (Shields), **Supp. VII:** 318

"Fragment" (Ashbery), **Supp. III Part 1:** 11, 13, 14, 19, 20

"Fragment" (Lowell), **II:** 516

"Fragment" (Ortiz), **Supp. IV Part 2:** 507

"Fragment of a Meditation" (Tate), **IV:** 129

"Fragment of an Agon" (Eliot), **I:** 579–580

"Fragment of a Prologue" (Eliot), **I:** 579–580

"Fragment of New York, 1929" (Eberhart), **I:** 536–537

"Fragments" (Emerson), **II:** 19

"Fragments for Fall" (Salinas), **Supp. XIII:** 320–321

"Fragments of a Hologram Rose" (W. Gibson), **Supp. XVI:** 122, 123, 128

"Fragments of a Liquidation" (Howe), **Supp. IV Part 2:** 426

Fragonard, Jean Honoré, **III:** 275; **IV:** 79

Fraiman, Susan, **Supp. IV Part 1:** 324

"Frame for Poetry, A" (W. J. Smith), **Supp. XIII:** 333

France, Anatole, **IV:** 444; **Supp. I Part 2:** 631; **Supp. XIV:** 79

France and England in North America (Parkman), **Supp. II Part 2:** 596, 600–605, 607, 613–614

Franchere, Hoyt C., **II:** 131

Franchiser, The (Elkin), **Supp. VI: 51–52,** 58

Franciosi, Robert, **Supp. XIV:** 283

Francis, Lee, **Supp. IV Part 2:** 499

Francis, Richard, **Supp. XV:** 121

Francis, Robert, **Supp. IX: 75–92**

Francis of Assisi, Saint, **III:** 543; **IV:** 69, 375, 410; **Supp. I Part 2:** 394, 397, 441, 442, 443

Franco, Francisco, **II:** 261

Franco, Harry (pseudonym). *See* Briggs, Charles Frederick

Franconia (Fraser), **Retro. Supp. I:** 136

"Franconia" tales (Abbott), **Supp. I Part 1:** 38

Frank, Anne, **Supp. X:** 149; **Supp. XVII:** 39

Frank, Frederick S., **Retro. Supp. II:** 273

Frank, James M., **Supp. XIV:** 1

Frank, Jerome, **Supp. I Part 2:** 645

Frank, Joseph, **II:** 587

Frank, Mary, **Supp. X:** 213

Frank, Robert, **Supp. XI:** 295; **Supp. XII:** 127; **Supp. XIV:** 150

Frank, Sheldon, **Supp. XXII:** 210

Frank, Waldo, **I:** 106, 109, 117, 229, 236, 245, 259, 400; **Retro. Supp. II:** 77, 79, 83; **Supp. IX:** 308, 309, 311, 320; **Supp. XV:** 298; **Supp. XX: 67–82**

Frank, W. L., Jr., **Supp. XVIII:** 77

Frankel, Charles, **III:** 291

Frankel, Haskel, **Supp. I Part 2:** 448

Frankenberg, Lloyd, **I:** 436, 437, 445, 446; **III:** 194

Frankenheimer, John, **Supp. XI;** 343

Frankenstein (film), **Supp. IV Part 1:** 104; **Supp. XVII:** 57

Frankenstein (Gardner), **Supp. VI:** 72

Frankenstein (Shelley), **Supp. XII:** 79

Frankfurter, Felix, **I:** 489

"Frankie" (Keillor), **Supp. XVI:** 167

Frankie and Johnny (film), **Supp. XIII:** 206

Frankie and Johnny in the Clair de Lune (McNally), **Supp. XIII: 200,** 201

Franklin, Benjamin, **II:** 6, 8, 92, **101–125,** 127, 295, 296, 302, 306; **III:** 74, 90; **IV:** 73, 193; **Supp. I Part 1:** 306; **Supp. I Part 2:** 411, 503, 504, 506, 507, 510, 516, 518, 522, 524, 579, 639; **Supp. VIII:** 202, 205; **Supp. XIII:** 150; **Supp. XIV:** 306; **Supp. XVIII:** 12; **Supp. XX: 284**

Franklin, Cynthia, **Supp. IV Part 1:** 332

Franklin, Ruth, **Supp. XVI:** 160

Franklin, R. W., **Retro. Supp. I:** 29, 41, 43, 47

Franklin, Sarah, **II:** 122

Franklin, Temple, **II:** 122

Franklin, Walt, **Supp. XXIII:** 54

Franklin, Wayne, **Supp. XXII:** 205

Franklin, William, **II:** 122; **Supp. I Part 2:** 504

Franklin Evans (Whitman), **Retro. Supp. I:** 393

"Frank O'Connor and *The New Yorker*" (Maxwell), **Supp. VIII:** 172

Frank O'Hara: Poet Among Painters (Perloff), **Supp. XXIII:** 210

Franks, Lucinda, **Supp. XIII:** 12

"Frank Sinatra Has a Cold" (Talese), **Supp. XVII:** 203

"Frank Stanford of the Mulberry Family: An Arkansas Epilogue" (Wright), **Supp. XV:** 339–340

"Franny" (Salinger), **III:** 564, 565–566

Franny and Zooey (Salinger), **III:** 552, 564–567; **IV:** 216; **Supp. XIII:** 263

Franscell, Ron, **Supp. XXII:** 206, 216

Franzen, Jonathan, **Retro. Supp. II:** 279; **Supp. XIX:** 54; **Supp. XX: 83–97; Supp. XXII:** 255

Fraser, G. S., **Supp. XII:** 128; **Supp. XIV:** 162

Fraser, Joe, **III:** 46

Fraser, Marjorie Frost, **Retro. Supp. I:** 136

Frayn, Michael, **Supp. IV Part 2:** 582

Frazee, E. S., **Supp. I Part 2:** 381

Frazee, Esther Catherine. *See* Lindsay, Mrs. Vachel Thomas (Esther Catherine Frazee)

Frazer, Sir James G., **I:** 135; **II:** 204; **III:** 6–7; **IV:** 70; **Retro. Supp. I:** 80; **Supp. I Part 1:** 18; **Supp. I Part 2:** 541; **Supp. XX:** 117

Frazier, Ian, **Supp. VIII:** 272

Frazier, Kathleen, **Supp. XXI:** 22

"Freak Show, The" (Sexton), **Supp. II Part 2:** 695

Freaks: Myths and Images of the Secret Self (Fiedler), **Supp. XIII:** 106, 107

Freckles (film), **Supp. XX:** 223

Freckles (Stratton-Porter), **Supp. XX:** 211, 218, 218–219, 222

Freddy's Book (Gardner), **Supp. VI:** 72

Frederic, Harold, **I:** 409; **II:** 126–149, 175, 276, 289; **Retro. Supp. I:** 325

"Frederick Douglass" (Dunbar), **Supp. II Part 1:** 197, 199

"Frederick Douglass" (Hayden), **Supp. II Part 1:** 363

Frederick Douglass: Slave, Fighter, Freeman (Bontemps), **Supp. XXII:** 13

Frederick the Great, **II:** 103; **Supp. I Part 2:** 433

Fredrickson, George M., **Supp. I Part 2:** 589

"Free" (O'Hara), **III:** 369

Free, and Other Stories (Dreiser), **Retro. Supp. II:** 104

Free Agents (Apple), **Supp. XVII:** 5–6

Free Air (Lewis), **II:** 441

Freedman, Monroe H., **Supp. VIII:** 127

Freedman, Richard, **Supp. V:** 244

Freedom (Franzen), **Supp. XXII:** 255

"Freedom" (Larsen), **Supp. XVIII:** 124

"Freedom" (White), **Supp. I Part 2:** 659

"Freedom, New Hampshire" (Kinnell), **Supp. III Part 1:** 238, 239, 251

"Freedom and Discipline" (Carruth), **Supp. XVI:** 50

Freedom Business, The (Nelson), **Supp. XVIII:** 186

Freedom Is the Right to Choose: An Inquiry into the Battle for the American Future (MacLeish), **III:** 3

"Freedom's a Hard-Bought Thing" (Benét), **Supp. XI:** 47, 48

"Freedom's Plow" (Hughes), **Supp. I Part 1:** 346

Free Enterprise (Cliff), **Supp. XXII:** 66–67, 77–78

"Free Fantasia: Tiger Flowers" (Hayden), **Supp. II Part 1:** 363, 366

Freeing of the Dust, The (Levertov), **Supp. III Part 1:** 281–282

"Free Lance, The" (Mencken), **III:** 104, 105

Free-Lance Pallbearers, The (Reed), **Supp. X:** 240, 242–243, 244

Freeland (Lane), **Supp. XXII:** 297

Free Life, A (Jin), **Supp. XVIII:** 101–102

Freeloaders, The (Lacy), **Supp. XV:** 204

"Free Man" (Hughes), **Supp. I Part 1:** 333

Freeman, Chris, **Supp. XIV:** 157, 159

Freeman, Douglas Southall, **Supp. I Part 2:** 486, 493

Freeman, John, **Supp. XVIII:** 90

Freeman, Joseph, **II:** 26; **Supp. I Part 2:** 610; **Supp. XXII:** 274, 277

Freeman, Mary E. Wilkins, **II:** 401; **Retro. Supp. II:** 51, 136, 138; **Supp. IX:** 79

Freeman, Morgan, **Supp. XII:** 317

Freeman, Suzanne, **Supp. X:** 83

Free Man, The (Richter), **Supp. XVIII:** 215

"Free Man's Worship, A" (Russell), **Supp. I Part 2:** 522

Freewheelin' Bob Dylan, The (album, Dylan), **Supp. XVIII:** 20, 24, 29

Freilicher, Jane, **Supp. XV:** 178; **Supp. XXIII:** 209, 210, 212, 217

Freinman, Dorothy, **Supp. IX:** 94

Frémont, John Charles, **Supp. I Part 2:** 486

Fremont-Smith, Eliot, **Supp. XIII:** 263

Fremstad, Olive, **I:** 319; **Retro. Supp. I:** 10

French, Warren, **Supp. XII:** 118–119

French Chef, The (television program), **Supp. XVII:** 89

French Connection, The (film), **Supp. V:** 226

"French Informal Report, The"(Kenny), **Supp. XXIII:** 152

French Leave (X. J. Kennedy), **Supp. XV:** 165

French Poets and Novelists (James), **II:** 336; **Retro. Supp. I:** 220

"French Scarecrow, The" (Maxwell), **Supp. VIII:** 169, 170

French Ways and Their Meaning (Wharton), **IV:** 319; **Retro. Supp. I:** 378

Freneau, Eleanor Forman (Mrs. Philip Freneau), **Supp. II Part 1:** 266

Freneau, Philip M., **I:** 335; **II:** 295; **Supp. I Part 1:** 124, 125, 127, 145; **Supp. II Part 1:** 65, 253–277

Frenzy (Everett), **Supp. XVIII:** 59–60

Frescoes for Mr. Rockefeller's City (MacLeish), **III:** 14–15

"Fresh Air" (Koch), **Supp. XV:** 181, 185

Fresh Air Fiend: Travel Writings, 1985–2000 (Theroux), **Supp. VIII:** 325

Fresh Brats (X. J. Kennedy), **Supp. XV:** 163

"Freshman" (Sanders), **Supp. XVI:** 277

Freud, Sigmund, **I:** 55, 58, 59, 66, 67, 135, 241, 242, 244, 247, 248, 283; **II:** 27, 370, 546–547; **III:** 134, 390, 400, 418, 488; **IV:** 7, 70, 138, 295; **Retro. Supp. I:** 80, 176, 253; **Retro. Supp. II:** 104; **Supp. I Part 1:** 13, 43, 253, 254, 259, 260, 265, 270, 315; **Supp. I Part 2:** 493, 527, 616, 643, 647, 649; **Supp. IV Part 2:** 450; **Supp. VIII:** 103, 196; **Supp. IX:** 102, 155, 161, 308; **Supp. X:** 193, 194; **Supp. XII:** 14–15; **Supp. XIII:** 75; **Supp. XIV:** 83; **Supp. XV:** 219; **Supp. XVI:** 157–158, 161, 292; **Supp. XXII:** 165, 198

"Freud and Literature" (Trilling), **Supp. III Part 2:** 502–503

Freudian Psychology and Veblen's Social Theory, The (Schneider), **Supp. I Part 2:** 650

Freudian Wish and Its Place in Ethics, The (Holt), **I:** 59

"Freud's Room" (Ozick), **Supp. V:** 268

Freud: The Mind of the Moralist (Sontag and Rieff), **Supp. III Part 2:** 455

"Freud: Within and Beyond Culture" (Trilling), **Supp. III Part 2:** 508

Frey, Charles, **Supp. XXII:** 301

Frey, Hillary, **Supp. XIX:** 55; **Supp. XXII:** 53

Frey, James, **Supp. XXII:** 95; **Supp. XXIII:** 109

"Friday Morning Trial of Mrs. Solano, The" (Ríos), **Supp. IV Part 2:** 538, 548

Friebert, Stuart, **Supp. XIX:** 276

Frieburger, William, **Supp. XIII:** 239

Friede, Donald, **Supp. XVII:** 85, 86, 87, 90

Friedenberg, Edgar Z., **Supp. VIII:** 240

Friedman, Bruce Jay, **I:** 161; **Supp. IV Part 1:** 379

Friedman, Lawrence S., **Supp. V:** 273

Friedman, Milton, **Supp. I Part 2:** 648

Friedman, Norman, **I:** 431–432, 435, 439

Friedman, Stan, **Supp. XII:** 186

Friedmann, Georges, **Supp. I Part 2:** 645

"Fried Sausage" (Simic), **Supp. VIII:** 270

Friend, Julius, **Retro. Supp. I:** 80

Friend, The (Coleridge), **II:** 10

"Friend Husband's Latest" (Sayre), **Retro. Supp. I:** 104

"Friendly Debate between a Conformist and a Non-Conformist, A" (Wild), **IV:** 155

"Friendly Neighbor" (Keillor), **Supp. XVI:** 172

Friend of the Earth, A (Boyle), **Supp. VIII:** 12, 16; **Supp. XX:** 29–30

"Friend of the Fourth Decade, The" (Merrill), **Supp. III Part 1:** 327

"Friends" (Beattie), **Supp. V:** 23, 27

"Friends" (Paley), **Supp. VI:** 219, 226

"Friends" (Sexton), **Supp. II Part 2:** 693

Friend's Delight, The (Bierce), **I:** 195

"Friends from Philadelphia" (Updike), **Retro. Supp. I:** 319

"Friendship" (Emerson), **Supp. II Part 1:** 290

Friends: More Will and Magna Stories (Dixon), **Supp. XII:** 148, 149

"Friends of Heraclitus, The" (Simic), **Supp. VIII:** 284

"Friends of Kafka, The" (Singer), **Retro. Supp. II:** 308

"Friends of the Family, The" (McCarthy), **II:** 566

"Friend to Alexander, A" (Thurber), **Supp. I Part 2:** 616

"Frigate Pelican, The" (Moore), **III:** 208, 210–211, 215

"Frill, The" (Buck), **Supp. XIV:** 274

"Fringe, The" (Bass), **Supp. XVI:** 19

Frobenius, Leo, **III:** 475; **Supp. III Part 2:** 620

Froebel, Friedrich, **Supp. XIV:** 52–53

Frog (Dixon), **Supp. XII:** 151

"Frog Dances" (Dixon), **Supp. XII:** 151

"Frog Pond, The" (Kinnell), **Supp. III Part 1:** 254

"Frogs" (Nelson), **Supp. XVIII:** 176

"Frog Takes a Swim" (Dixon), **Supp. XII:** 152

Frohock, W. M., **I:** 34, 42

Frolic of His Own, A (Gaddis), **Supp. IV Part 1:** 279, 291, 292–294; **Supp. XX:** 91

"From a Mournful Village" (Jewett), **Retro. Supp. II:** 146

"From an Alabama Farm" (Nelson), **Supp. XVIII:** 182

"From an Old House in America" (Rich), **Supp. I Part 2:** 551, 565–567

From Another World (Untermeyer), **Supp. XV:** 293, 303, 310–311, 313

"From a Roadside Motel" (F. Wright), **Supp. XVII:** 245

"From a Survivor" (Rich), **Supp. I Part 2:** 563

From A to Z (musical review; Allen), **Supp. XV:** 3, 13

From a Work in Progress (Notley), **Supp. XXII:** 232

"From a Work in Progress" (Notley), **Supp. XXII:** 232

From a Writer's Notebook (Brooks), **I:** 254

From Bauhaus to Our House (Wolfe), **Supp. III Part 2:** 580, 581, 584

From Bondage (H. Roth), **Supp. IX:** 236, **238–240**

"From *Chants* to *Borders* to *Communion*" (Fox), *Supp. XIII:* 217, 217–218

"From Chicago" (Anderson), **I:** 108–109

From Colony to Nation: Women Activists and the Gendering of Politics in Belize, 1912–1982 (Macpherson), **Supp. XXIII:** 84

From Death to Morning (Wolfe), **IV:** 450, 456, 458

"From Dick to Lethem: The Dickian Legacy, Postmodernism, and Avant-Pop in Jonathan Lethem's *Amnesia Moon*" (Rossi), *Supp. XVIII:* 137, 138–139

"From Discord, a Wife Makes a Nice New Life—Too Nice" (Linfield), **Supp. XVII:** 177

From Down to the Village (Budbill), **Supp. XIX:** 6–7

"From Feathers to Iron" (Kunitz), **Supp. III Part 1:** 261

"From Fifth Avenue Up" (Barnes), **Supp. III Part 1:** 33, 44

"From Gorbunov and Gorchakov" (Brodsky), **Supp. VIII:** 26

"From Grand Canyon to Burbank" (H. Miller), **III:** 186

"From Hell to Breakfast", **Supp. IX:** 326–327

From Here to Eternity (film), **Supp. XI:** 221

From Here to Eternity (J. Jones), **I:** 477; **Supp. XI:** 215, 216, 217, 218, **219–221**, 223, 224, 226, 229, 230, 231, 232, 234; **Supp. XIX:** 248; **Supp. XX:** 248; **Supp. XXII:** 140

From Here to Eternity (miniseries), **Supp. XI:** 234

From Jordan's Delight (Blackmur), **Supp. II Part 1:** 91

"From Lumaghi Mine" (Wrigley), **Supp. XVIII:** 295

Fromm, Erich, **I:** 58; **Supp. VIII:** 196

From Morn to Midnight (Kaiser), **I:** 479

"From Native Son to Invisible Man" (Locke), **Supp. IX:** 306

"From Pico, the Women: A Life" (Creeley), **Supp. IV Part 1:** 149

From Plotzk to Boston (Antin), **Supp. XX:** 2

From Ritual to Romance (Weston), **II:** 540; **III:** 12; **Supp. I Part 2:** 439

From Room to Room (Kenyon), **Supp. VII:** 163–165, 166, 167

"From Room to Room" (Kenyon), **Supp. VII:** 159, 163–165

From Sand Creek: Rising in this Heart Which Is Our America (Ortiz), **Supp. IV Part 2:** 512–513

"From Sea Cliff, March" (Swenson), **Supp. IV Part 2:** 649

From Stone Orchard: A Collection of Memories (Findley), **Supp. XX: 57**

"From the Antigone" (Yeats), **III:** 459

From the Ashes: Voices of Watts (Schulberg, ed.), **Supp. XVIII:** 254

From the Barrio: A Chicano Anthology (Salinas and Faderman, eds.), **Supp. XIII:** 313

From the Beginning (Notley), **Supp. XXII:** 226, 235–236

From the Briarpatch File: On Context, Procedure, and American Identity (Murray), **Supp. XIX:** 161

"From the Childhood of Jesus" (Pinsky), **Supp. VI:** 244–245, 247

"From the Corpse Woodpiles, From the Ashes" (Hayden), **Supp. II Part 1:** 370

"From the Country to the City" (Bishop), **Supp. I Part 1:** 85, 86

"From the Cupola" (Merrill), **Supp. III Part 1:** 324–325, 331

"From the Dark Side of the Earth" (Oates), **Supp. II Part 2:** 510

"From the Diary of a New York Lady" (Parker), **Supp. IX:** 201

"From the Diary of One Not Born" (Singer), **IV:** 9

"From the Dreams" (Notley), **Supp. XXII:** 224

"From the East, Light" (Carver), **Supp. III Part 1:** 138

From the First Nine: Poems 1946–1976 (Merrill), **Supp. III Part 1:** 336

"From the Flats" (Lanier), **Supp. I Part 1:** 364

From the Flower Courtyard (Everwine), **Supp. XV:** 75

From the Heart of Europe (Matthiessen), **III:** 310

From the Meadow: Selected and New Poems (Everwine), **Supp. XV:** 75, **88–89**

"From the Memoirs of a Private Detective" (Hammett), **Supp. IV Part 1:** 343

"From the Nursery" (Kenyon), **Supp. VII:** 171

"From the Poets in the Kitchen" (Marshall), **Supp. XI:** 277

From the Terrace (O'Hara), **III:** 362

"From the Thirties: Tillie Olsen and the Radical Tradition" (Rosenfelt), **Supp. XIII:** 296, 304

"From Trollope's Journal" (Bishop), **Retro. Supp. II:** 47

"Front, A" (Jarrell), **II:** 374

Front, The (film), **Supp. I Part 1:** 295

"Front and the Back Parts of the House, The" (Maxwell), **Supp. VIII:** 169

Frontier Eden (Bigelow), **Supp. X:** 227

"Frontiers of Culture" (Locke), **Supp. XIV:** 213

"Front Lines" (Snyder), **Supp. VIII:** 301

Front Runner, The (P. N. Warren), **Supp. XX: 259, 262–264**

Frost, A. B., **Retro. Supp. II:** 72

Frost, Carol, **Supp. XV: 91–109**

Frost, Isabelle Moodie, **II:** 150, 151

Frost, Jeanie, **II:** 151

Frost, Richard, **Supp. XV:** 92

Frost, Robert, **I:** 26, 27, 60, 63, 64, 171, 229, 303, 326, 418; **II:** 55, 58, **150–172**, 276, 289, 388, 391, 471, 523, 527, 529, 535; **III:** 5, 23, 67, 269, 271, 272, 275, 287, 453, 510, 523, 536, 575, 581, 591; **IV:** 140, 190, 415; **Retro. Supp. I:** 67, **121–144**, 276, 287, 292, 298, 299, 311, 413; **Retro. Supp. II:** 40, 47, 50, 146, 178, 181; **Supp. I Part 1:** 80, 242, 263, 264; **Supp. I Part 2:** 387, 461, 699; **Supp. II Part 1:** 4, 19, 26, 103; **Supp. III Part 1:** 63, 74–75, 239, 253; **Supp. III Part 2:** 546, 592, 593; **Supp. IV Part 1:** 15; **Supp. IV Part 2:** 439, 445, 447, 448, 599, 601; **Supp. VIII:** 20, 30, 32, 98, 100, 104, 259, 292; **Supp. IX:** 41, 42, 75, 76, 80, 87, 90, 266, 308; **Supp. X:** 64, 65, 66, 74, 120, 172; **Supp. XI:** 43, 123, 150, 153, 312; **Supp. XII:** 130, 241, 303, 307; **Supp. XIII:** 143, 147, 334–335; **Supp. XIV:** 42, 122, 222, 229; **Supp. XV:** 21, 51, 65, 96, 212, 215, 250, 256, 293, 296, 299, 301, 302, 306, 348; **Supp. XVII:** 36, 110, 115–116; **Supp. XVIII:** 298, 300; **Supp. XIX:** 1, 123; **Supp. XX: 69, 199**; **Supp. XXI:** 19, 28, 51, 99, 104, 107, 205; **Supp. XXII:** 206; **Supp. XXIII:** 79, 145

Frost, William Prescott, **II:** 150–151

"Frost: A Dissenting Opinion" (Cowley), **Supp. II Part 1:** 143

Frost: A Time to Talk (Francis), **Supp. IX:** 76, **85–86**

"Frost at Midnight" (Coleridge), **Supp. X:** 71

"Frost Flowers" (Kenyon), **Supp. VII:** 168

"Frost: He Is Sometimes a Poet and Sometimes a Stump-Speaker" (News-Week), **Retro. Supp. I:** 137

Frothingham, Nathaniel, **I:** 3

Frothingham, Octavius B., **IV:** 173

"Frozen City, The" (Nemerov), **III:** 270

"Frozen Fields, The" (Bowles), **Supp. IV Part 1:** 80

"Fructifying a Cycle: Homage to Alan Ansen"(Hadas), **Supp. XXIII:** 123

"Fruit Garden Path, The" (Lowell), **II:** 516

"Fruit of the Flower" (Cullen), **Supp. IV Part 1:** 167

Fruit of the Tree, The (Wharton), **IV:** 314–315; **Retro. Supp. I:** 367, **370–371,** 373

"Fruit of Travel Long Ago" (Melville), **III:** 93

Fruits and Vegetables (Jong), **Supp. V:** 113, 115, 117, 118, 119

"Fruits of the Sea, The" (Di Piero), **Supp. XIX:** 47

Frumkes, Lewis Burke, **Supp. XII:** 335–336

Fry, Christopher, **Supp. I Part 1:** 270

Fry, Roger, **Supp. XIV:** 336

Fry, Stephen M., **Supp. XIX:** 159

Frye, Joanne, **Supp. XIII:** 292, 296, 298, 302

Frye, Northrop, **Supp. I Part 2:** 530; **Supp. II Part 1:** 101; **Supp. X:** 80; **Supp. XIII:** 19; **Supp. XIV:** 11, 15; **Supp. XVI:** 149, 156; **Supp. XX:** 50; **Supp. XXIII:** 42

Fryer, Judith, **Retro. Supp. I:** 379

F. Scott Fitzgerald: A Critical Portrait (Piper), **Supp. IX:** 65

"F. S. F., 1896–1996, R.I.P." (Doctorow), **Retro. Supp. I:** 97

Fuchs, Daniel, **Supp. XIII:** 106

Fuchs, Miriam, **Supp. IV Part 1:** 284

Fuehrer Bunker, The (Snodgrass), **Supp. VI:** 314, 315–317, 319–321

Fuel (Nye), **Supp. XIII:** 277, **282–284**

"Fuel" (Nye), **Supp. XIII:** 283

Fuertes, Gloria, **Supp. V:** 178

Fugard, Athol, **Supp. VIII:** 330; **Supp. XIII:** 205

Fugitive Group, The (Cowan), **IV:** 120

Fugitive Kind, The (T. Williams), **IV:** 381, 383

Fugitives, The (the group), **IV:** 122, 124, 125, 131, 237, 238

Fugitives, The: A Critical Account (Bradbury), **IV:** 130

"Fugitive Slave Law, The" (Emerson), **II:** 13

Fugitive's Return (Glaspell), **Supp. III Part 1:** 182–184

Fuller, B. A. G., **III:** 605

Fuller, Edmund, **Supp. XXII:** 211, 212

Fuller, Hiram, **Supp. XVIII:** 12,14

Fuller, Jesse "Lonecat", **Supp. XV:** 147

Fuller, Margaret, **I:** 261; **II:** 7, 276; **IV:** 172; **Retro. Supp. I:** 155–156, 163; **Retro. Supp. II:** 46; **Supp. I Part 2:** 524; **Supp. II Part 1:** 279–306; **Supp. IX:** 37; **Supp. XVIII:** 3, 11, 12, 16

Fuller, Thomas, **II:** 111, 112

Fullerton, Morton, **Supp. XX: 231**

Fullerton Street (Wilson), **Supp. VIII:** 331

"Full Fathom Five" (Plath), **Supp. I Part 2:** 538

Full Measure: Modern Short Stories on Aging (D. Sennett, ed.), **Supp. XVI:** 37

Full Monty, The (musical, McNally), **Supp. XIII:** 207

"Full Moon" (Hayden), **Supp. II Part 1:** 370

Full Moon and Other Plays (Price), **Supp. VI:** 266

"Full Moon and You're Not Here" (Cisneros), **Supp. VII:** 71–72

"Full Moon: New Guinea" (Shapiro), **Supp. II Part 2:** 707

"Fullness of Life, The" (Wharton), **Retro. Supp. I:** 363

Full of Life (Fante), **Supp. XI:** 160

Full of Life (film), **Supp. XI:** 170

Full of Lust and Good Usage (Dunn), **Supp. XI: 145–147**

"Full Summer" (Olds), **Supp. X:** 212

Fulton, Ben, **Supp. XXII:** 207

Fulton, Robert, **Supp. I Part 2:** 519; **Supp. II Part 1:** 73

Fun and Games (Major), **Supp. XXII:** 180

"Functional Poem" (Halliday), **Supp. XIX:** 85

Function of Criticism, The (Winters), **Supp. II Part 2:** 812, 813

"Fundamentalism" (Tate), **IV:** 125

"Fundamental Project of Technology, The" (Kinnell), **Supp. III Part 1:** 253

"Funeral of Bobò, The" (Brodsky), **Supp. VIII:** 27, 28

"Funnel" (Sexton), **Supp. II Part 2:** 675

"Furious Seasons, The" (Carver), **Supp. III Part 1:** 137

Furious Seasons and Other Stories (Carver), **Supp. III Part 1:** 142, 143, 146

"Furious Versions" (L.-Y. Lee), **Supp. XV:** 215–217, 218, 220

"Furnished Room, The" (Hayden), **Supp. II Part 1:** 386–387, 394, 397, 399, 406, 408

"Furor Scribendi" (O. Butler), **Supp. XIII:** 70

Furors Die (Hoffman), **Supp. XVIII: 80–81**

Fur Person, The (Sarton), **Supp. VIII: 264–265**

Further Adventures with You (Wright), **Supp. XV:** 339, 342, **343–345**

Further Fables for Our Time (Thurber), **Supp. I Part 2:** 612

"Further in Summer than the Birds" (Dickinson), **I:** 471

Further Poems of Emily Dickinson (Bianchi and Hampson, ed.), **Retro. Supp. I:** 35

Further Range, A (Frost), **II:** 155; **Retro. Supp. I:** 132, 136, 137, 138, 139

"Fury, The" (Skloot), **Supp. XX: 197**

"Fury of Aerial Bombardment, The" (Eberhart), **I:** 535–536

"Fury of Flowers and Worms, The" (Sexton), **Supp. II Part 2:** 694

"Fury of Rain Storms, The" (Sexton), **Supp. II Part 2:** 695

Fury of the Jungle (film), **Supp. XIII:** 163

Fussell, Paul, **Supp. V:** 241

"Future, if Any, of Comedy, The" (Thurber), **Supp. I Part 2:** 620

Future in the Present, The (C. L. R. James), **Supp. XXI:** 172

Future is Ours, Comrade, The: Conversations with the Russians (Kosinski), **Supp. VII:** 215

Futureland: Nine Stories of an Imminent World (Mosley), **Supp. XIII:** 247–249

"Future Life, The" (Bryant), **Supp. I Part 1:** 170

Future of Southern Letters, The (J. W. Miller), **Supp. XX: 161**

Future of the Race, The (H. L. Gates), **Supp. XX: 101, 104, 111**

Future Punishment of the Wicked, The (Edwards), **I:** 546

G

"Gabriel" (Rich), **Supp. I Part 2:** 557

Gabriel, Ralph H., **Supp. I Part 1:** 251

Gabriel, Trip, **Supp. V:** 212

Gabriel Conroy (Harte), **Supp. II Part 1:** 354

"Gabriel's Truth" (Kenyon), **Supp. VII:** 166

Gaddis, William, **Supp. IV Part 1: 279–296; Supp. IV Part 2:** 484; **Supp. V:** 52; **Supp. IX:** 208; **Supp. X:** 301, 302; **Supp. XX: 83, 91; Supp. XXI:** 226; **Supp. XXIII:** 107

Gadiot, Pud, **Supp. XI:** 295

Gain (Powers), **Supp. IX:** 212, **220–221**

Gaines, Ernest J., **Supp. X:** 24, 250

Gaines, James R., **Supp. IX:** 190

Gainor, J. Ellen, **Supp. XXI:** 6

Gaitens, Peter, **Supp. XV:** 65

Galamain, Ivan, **Supp. III Part 2:** 624

Galassi, Jonathan, **Supp. XVIII:** 92; **Supp. XIX:** 34; **Supp. XXII:** 177

Galatea 2.2 (Powers), **Supp. IX:** 212, **219–220**

"Galatea Encore" (Brodsky), **Supp. VIII:** 31

Galbraith, John Kenneth, **Supp. I Part 2:** 645, 650

Galdós, Benito Pérez. *See* Pérez Galdós, Benito

Gale, Zona, **Supp. I Part 2:** 613; **Supp. VIII:** 155

Galehouse, Maggie, **Supp. XXI:** 215

"Gale in April" (Jeffers), **Supp. II Part 2:** 423

Galignani, Giovanni Antonio, **II:** 315

Galileo Galilei, **I:** 480–481; **Supp. XII:** 180; **Supp. XIII:** 75

Gallagher, Tess, **Supp. XVI:** 36; **Supp. XVII:** 110; **Supp. XXI:** 246

Gallant, Mavis, **Supp. VIII:** 151

Gallatin, Albert, **I:** 5

"Gallery" (Goldbarth), **Supp. XII:** 188

"Gallery of Real Creatures, A" (Thurber), **Supp. I Part 2:** 619

Gallico, Paul, **Supp. XVI:** 238

Gallows Songs (Snodgrass), **Supp. VI:** 317

Gallup, Donald, **III:** 404, 478

Galsworthy, John, **III:** 70, 153, 382

Galton Case, The (Macdonald), **Supp. IV Part 2:** 463, 473, 474

Galvin, Frances, **Supp. XXI:** 5

"Gal Young 'Un" (Rawlings), **Supp. X:** 228

Gambino, Richard, **Supp. XX:** 35

"Gambler, the Nun, and the Radio, The" (Hemingway), **II:** 250

"Gambler's Wife, The" (Dunbar), **Supp. II Part 1:** 196

Gambone, Philip, **Supp. XII:** 81

"Gambrel Roof, A" (Larcom), **Supp. XIII:** 144

"Game at Salzburg, A" (Jarrell), **II:** 384, 389

Game Management (Leopold), **Supp. XIV:** 182

"Game of Catch, A" (Wilbur), **Supp. III Part 2:** 552

Game Players of Titan, The (Dick), **Supp. XVIII:** 138

"Games in Frank Conroy's *Stop-Time*" (T. Adams), **Supp. XVI:** 67

"Games Two" (Wilbur), **Supp. III Part 2:** 550

Gammelgaard, Lene, **Supp. XVIII:** 112

"Gamut, The" (Angelou), **Supp. IV Part 1:** 15

Gander, Forrest, **Supp. XV:** 339, 340, 342

Gandhi, Indira, **Supp. X:** 108

Gandhi, Mahatma, **III:** 179, 296–297; **IV:** 170, 185, 367; **Supp. VIII:** 203, 204; **Supp. X:** 27

Gandhi on Non-Violence (Merton, ed.), **Supp. VIII:** 204–205

Gang of Five: Leaders at the Center of the Conservative Crusade (Easton), **Supp. XIX:** 137

"Gang of Mirrors, The" (Simic), **Supp. VIII:** 283

Gansevoort, Guert, **III:** 94

Gansevoort, Peter, **III:** 92

"Gap" (Bierds), **Supp. XVII:** 35–36

Garabedian, Michael, **Supp. XIII:** 115

Garbage (Ammons), **Supp. VII:** 24, 35–36

Garbage (Dixon), **Supp. XII:** 147, 148

Garbage Man, The (Dos Passos), **I:** 478, 479, 481, 493

Garber, Frederick, **Supp. IX:** 294–295

Garbo, Greta, **Supp. I Part 2:** 616

García, Cristina, **Supp. VIII:** 74; **Supp. XI:** 177–192

García Lorca, Federico. *See* Lorca, Federico García

"García Lorca: A Photograph of the Granada Cemetery, 1966" (Levis), **Supp. XI:** 264

García Márquez, Gabriel, **Supp. V:** 244; **Supp. VIII:** 81, 82, 84, 85; **Supp. XII:** 147, 310, 316, 322; **Supp. XIII:** 226; **Supp. XVII:** 45

Gard, Claire, **Supp. XXIII:** 94

Gardaphe, Fred, **Supp. XX: 38, 41**

"Garden" (Marvell), **IV:** 161; **Supp. XVI:** 204

"Garden, The" (Glück), **Supp. V:** 83

"Garden, The" (Strand), **Supp. IV Part 2:** 629

"Garden Among Tombs" (B. Kelly), **Supp. XVII:** 126

"Garden by Moonlight, The" (Lowell), **II:** 524

"Gardener Delivers a Fawn, The" (C. Frost), **Supp. XV:** 99

Gardener's Son, The (McCarthy), **Supp. VIII:** 187

Garden God, The: A Tale of Two Boys (Reid), **Supp. XX: 235**

"Gardenias" (Doty), **Supp. XI:** 122

"Gardenias" (Monette), **Supp. X:** 159

"Garden Lodge, The" (Cather), **I:** 316, 317

Garden of Adonis, The (Gordon), **II:** 196, 204–205, 209

Garden of Earthly Delights, A (Oates), **Supp. II Part 2:** 504, 507–509

Garden of Earthly Delights, The (Bosch), **Supp. XXII:** 255, 261

"Garden of Eden" (Hemingway), **II:** 259

Garden of Eden, The (Hemingway), **Retro. Supp. I:** 186, **187–188**

"Garden of Flesh, Garden of Stone" (B. Kelly), **Supp. XVII:** 128

"Garden of the Moon, The" (Doty), **Supp. XI:** 122

Garden of the Prophet, The (Gibran), **Supp. XX: 119, 122**

"Garden of the Trumpet Tree, The" (B. Kelly), **Supp. XVII:** 131

"Gardens, The" (Oliver), **Supp. VII:** 236

"Gardens of Mont-Saint-Michel, The" (Maxwell), **Supp. VIII:** 169

"Gardens of the Villa D'Este, The" (Hecht), **Supp. X:** 59

"Gardens of Zuñi, The" (Merwin), **Supp. III Part 1:** 351

Garden Thieves, The: Twentieth Century African-American Poetry (Major, ed.), **Supp. XXII:** 172

Gardiner, Judith Kegan, **Supp. IV Part 1:** 205

Gardner, Erle Stanley, **Supp. IV Part 1:** 121, 345

Gardner, Isabella, **IV:** 127

Gardner, John, **Supp. I Part 1:** 193, 195, 196; **Supp. III Part 1:** 136, 142, 146; **Supp. VI: 61–76**

Gardner, Thomas, **Supp. XXI:** 214

Gardons, S. S. *See* Snodgrass, W. D.

"Gare de Lyon" (M. F. K. Fisher), **Supp. XVII:** 91

Garfield, John, **Supp. XII:** 160

Garibaldi, Giuseppe, **I:** 4; **II:** 284

Garibay, Angel M., **Supp. XV:** 77

Garland, Hamlin, **I:** 407; **II:** 276, 289; **III:** 576; **Retro. Supp. I:** 133; **Retro. Supp. II:** 72; **Supp. I Part 1:** 217; **Supp. IV Part 2:** 502; **Supp. XVIII:** 6

Garland Companion, The (Zverev), **Retro. Supp. I:** 278

"Garments" (Gibran), **Supp. XX: 124**

Garments the Living Wear (Purdy), **Supp. VII:** 278–279, 280–281

Garner, Dwight, **Supp. X:** 202; **Supp. XVIII:** 89

Garnett, Edward, **I:** 405, 409, 417; **III:** 27

Garrett, George P., **Supp. I Part 1:** 196; **Supp. VII: 95–113; Supp. X:** 3, 7; **Supp. XI:** 218; **Supp. XVIII:** 74, 75

Garrigue, Jean, **Supp. XII:** 260

Garrison, Deborah, **Supp. IX:** 299

Garrison, Fielding, **III:** 105

Garrison, William Lloyd, **Supp. I Part 2:** 524, 588, 683, 685, 686, 687; **Supp. XIV:** 54

"Garrison of Cape Ann, The" (Whittier), **Supp. I Part 2:** 691, 694

Garry Moore Show (television show), **Supp. IV Part 2:** 575

"Garter Motif" (White), **Supp. I Part 2:** 673

Gartner, Zsuzsi, **Supp. X:** 276

Garvey, Marcus, **Supp. III Part 1:** 175, 180; **Supp. IV Part 1:** 168; **Supp. X:** 135, 136; **Supp. XXI:** 166, 168; **Supp. XXII:** 7

Gas (Kaiser), **I:** 479

Gas-House McGinty (Farrell), **II:** 41–42

Gaskell, Elizabeth, A., **Supp. I Part 2:** 580

Gasoline (Corso), **Supp. XII:** 118, **121–123, 134**

Gasoline Wars, The (Thompson), **Supp. XXIII:** 290

"Gasoline Wars, The"(Thompson), **Supp. XXIII:** 291

Gass, William H., **Supp. V:** 44, 52, 238; **Supp. VI: 77–96; Supp. IX:** 208; **Supp. XII:** 152; **Supp. XIV:** 305; **Supp. XVII:** 183

Gassner, John, **IV:** 381; **Supp. I Part 1:** 284, 292

"Gas Stations" (Apple), **Supp. XVII:** 4

Gastronomical Me, The (M. F. K. Fisher), **Supp. XVII:** 84, 85, 87, 91, 92

Gates, David, **Supp. V:** 24; **Supp. XIII:** 93; **Supp. XVI:** 73, 74; **Supp. XX: 92**

Gates, Elmer, **I:** 515–516

Gates, Henry Louis, Jr., **Retro. Supp. I:** 194, 195, 203; **Supp. X:** 242, 243, 245, 247; **Supp. XVIII:** 287; **Supp. XIX:** 147, 149; **Supp. XX: 99–112, 279, 286**

Gates, Lewis E., **III:** 315, 330

Gates, Sondra Smith, **Supp. XVIII:** 267, 269

Gates, The (Rukeyser), **Supp. VI:** 271, 274, 281

"Gates, The" (Rukeyser), **Supp. VI:** 286

Gates, Tudor, **Supp. XI:** 307

Gates of Ivory, the Gates of Horn, The (McGrath), **Supp. X:** 118

Gates of Wrath, The; Rhymed Poems (Ginsberg), **Supp. II Part 1:** 311, 319

"Gathering" (Trethewey), **Supp. XXI:** 249

Gathering Forces, The (C. L. R. James), **Supp. XXI:** 171

"Gathering of Dissidents, A" (Applebaum), **Supp. XVI:** 153

Gathering of Fugitives, A (Trilling), **Supp. III Part 2:** 506, 512

Gathering of Zion, The: The Story of the Mormon Trail (Stegner), **Supp. IV Part 2:** 599, 602–603

Gather Together in My Name (Angelou), **Supp. IV Part 1:** 2, 3, 4–6, 11

Gathorne-Hardy, Robert, **Supp. XIV:** 344, 347, 348, 349

Gaudier-Brzeska, Henri, **III:** 459, 464, 465, 477

Gaughran, Richard, **Supp. XXI:** 47–48

Gauguin, Paul, **I:** 34; **IV:** 290; **Supp. IV Part 1:** 81; **Supp. XII:** 128

"Gauguin in Oregon" (Skloot), **Supp. XX:** 203

"Gauley Bridge" (Rukeyser), **Supp. VI:** 278

Gauss, Christian, **II:** 82; **IV:** 427, 439–440, 444

Gauthier, Jacquie, **Supp. XIX:** 204

Gautier, Théophile, **II:** 543; **III:** 466, 467; **Supp. I Part 1:** 277

Gay, John, **II:** 111; **Supp. I Part 2:** 523; **Supp. XIV:** 337

Gay, Peter, **I:** 560

Gay, Sydney Howard, **Supp. I Part 1:** 158; **Supp. XVIII:** 3

Gay, Walter, **IV:** 317

Gayatri Prayer, The, **III:** 572

Gay Canon, The (Drake), **Supp. XX:** 274

"Gay Chaps at the Bar" (Brooks), **Supp. III Part 1:** 74, 75

" 'Gay Culture': Still of the Wild Frontier" (P. N. Warren), **Supp. XX:** 272

Gaylord, Winfield R., **III:** 579–580

Gay Talese Reader, The: Portraits & Encounters (Talese), **Supp. XVII:** 202, 208

"Gaze, The"(Hadas), **Supp. XXIII:** 120

"Gazebo" (Carver), **Supp. III Part 1:** 138, 144, 145

Gazer's Spirit, The (Hollander), **Supp. XIX:** 121

Gazer Within, The, and Other Essays by Larry Levis, **Supp. XI:** 270

Gazzara, Ben, **Supp. VIII:** 319

Gazzo, Michael V., **III:** 155

"Geese Flying over Hamilton, New York"(Balakian), **Supp. XXIII:** 24

"Geese Gone Beyond" (Snyder), **Supp. VIII:** 304

Geffen, David, **Supp. XXI:** 154

"Gegenwart" (Goethe), **Supp. II Part 1:** 26

Geisel, Theodor Seuss (Dr. Seuss), **Supp. X:** 56; **Supp. XVI:** 97–115

Geismar, Maxwell, **II:** 178, 431; **III:** 71; **Supp. IX:** 15; **Supp. XI:** 223

Geist, Bill, **Supp. XXIII:** 298

Gelb, Arthur, **IV:** 380; **Supp. XXI:** 12

Gelb, Barbara, **Supp. XXI:** 12

Gelbart, Larry, **Supp. IV Part 2:** 591

Gelder, Robert Van, **Supp. XIII:** 166

Gelfant, Blanche H., **II:** 27, 41; **Supp. XVII:** 161

Gelfman, Jean, **Supp. X:** 3

Gellert, Hugo, **Supp. XXII:** 277

Gellhorn, Martha. *See* Hemingway, Mrs. Ernest (Martha Gellhorn)

Gelpi, Albert, **Supp. I Part 2:** 552, 554, 560

Gelpi, Barbara, **Supp. I Part 2:** 560

Gemin, Pamela, **Supp. XXI:** 246

Gemini: an extended autobiographical statement on my first twenty-five years of being a black poet (Giovanni), **Supp. IV Part 1:** 11

"Gen" (Snyder), **Supp. VIII:** 302

"Gender Norms" (Radinovsky), **Supp. XV:** 285

"Gender of Sound, The" (Carson), **Supp. XII:** 106

"Genealogies"(Hadas), **Supp. XXIII:** 116

"Genealogy" (Komunyakaa), **Supp. XIII:** 129

"General Aims and Theories" (Crane), **I:** 389

General Died at Dawn, The (Odets), **Supp. II Part 2:** 546

"General Gage's Confession" (Freneau), **Supp. II Part 1:** 257

"General Gage's Soliloquy" (Freneau), **Supp. II Part 1:** 257

General History of the Robberies and Murders of the Most Notorious Pyrates from Their First Rise and Settlement in the Island of New Providence to the Present Year, A (Johnson), **Supp. V:** 128

"General Returns from One Place to Another, The"(O'Hara), **Supp. XXIII:** 216–217

"General William Booth Enters into Heaven" (Lindsay), **Supp. I Part 2:** 374, 382, 384, 385–388, 389, 392, 399

General William Booth Enters into Heaven and Other Poems (Lindsay), **Supp. I Part 2:** 379, 381, 382, 387–388, 391

"Generation of the Dispossessed" (P. N. Warren), **Supp. XX:** 272

"Generations"(Kenny), **Supp. XXIII:** 154

"Generations of Men, The" (Frost), **Retro. Supp. I:** 128; **Supp. XIII:** 147

Generous Man, A (Price), **Supp. VI:** 259, 260, 261

Genesis (biblical book), **I:** 279; **II:** 540; **Retro. Supp. I:** 250, 256; **Supp. XII:** 54

"Genesis" (Stegner), **Supp. IV Part 2:** 604

Genesis: Book One (Schwartz), **Supp. II Part 2:** 640, 651–655

Gene Stratton-Porter (Richards), **Supp. XX:** 217–218

Gene Stratton-Porter, Naturalist and Novelist (Long), **Supp. XX:** 212

"Gene Stratton-Porter: Women's Advocate" (Obuchowski), **Supp. XX:** 222

Genet, Jean, **I:** 71, 82, 83, 84; **Supp. IV Part 1:** 8; **Supp. XI:** 308; **Supp. XII:** 1; **Supp. XIII:** 74; **Supp. XVII:** 95; **Supp. XXIII:** 213

"Genetic Coding" (Sorrentino), **Supp. XXI:** 227

"Genetic Expedition" (Dove), **Supp. IV Part 1:** 249, 257

"Genetics of Justice" (Alvarez), **Supp. VII:** 19

"Genial Host, The" (McCarthy), **II:** 564

"Genie in the Bottle, The" (Wilbur), **Supp. III Part 2:** 542

"Genius, The" (MacLeish), **III:** 19

Genius and Lust: A Journey through the Major Writings of Henry Miller (Mailer), **Retro. Supp. II:** 208

"Genius Child" (Hughes), **Retro. Supp. I:** 203

"Genius of Bob Dylan, The" (Lethem), **Supp. XVIII:** 146

"Genius," The (Dreiser), **I:** 497, 501, 509–511, 519; **Retro. Supp. II:** 94–95, **102–103,** 104, 105

Genova, Lisa, **Supp. XXIII:** 127

"Genteel Tradition in American Philosophy, The" (Santayana), **I:** 222

"Gentle Communion" (Mora), **Supp. XIII:** 218–219

Gentle Crafter, The (O. Henry), **Supp. II Part 1:** 410

"Gentle Lena, The" (Stein), **IV:** 37, 40

Gentleman Caller, The (T. Williams), **IV:** 383

"Gentleman from Cracow, The" (Singer), **IV:** 9

"Gentleman of Bayou Têche, A" (Chopin), **Supp. I Part 1:** 211–212

"Gentleman of Shalott, The" (Bishop), **Supp. I Part 1:** 85, 86

Gentleman's Agreement (Hobson), **III:** 151

"Gentleman's Agreement" (Richard), **Supp. XIX:** 220–221

Gentlemen Prefer Blondes (Loos; musical adaptation), **Supp. XVI:** 193

Gentlemen Prefer Blondes: The Illuminating Diary of a Professional Lady (Loos), **Supp. XVI:** 181, 183, 186, **188–189**

Gentlemen Prefer "Books" (J. Yeats), *Supp. XVI:* 190

Gentle People, The: A Brooklyn Fable (Shaw), **Supp. XIX:** 244–245, 249

Gentry, Marshall Bruce, **Supp. IV Part 1:** 236

"Genuine Man, The" (Emerson), **II:** 10

"Genus Narcissus" (Trethewey), **Supp. XXI:** 256

Geo-Bestiary (Harrison), **Supp. VIII:** 53

"Geode" (Frost), **II:** 161

Geographical History of America, The (Stein), **IV:** 31, 45; **Supp. XVIII:** 148

Geography and Plays (Stein), **IV:** 29–30, 32, 43, 44

Geography III (Bishop), **Retro. Supp. II:** 50; **Supp. I Part 1:** 72, 73, 76, 82, 93, 94, 95

Geography of a Horse Dreamer (Shepard), **Supp. III Part 2:** 432

Geography of Home, The: California's Poetry of Place (Bluckey and Young, eds.), **Supp. XIII:** 313

Geography of Lograire, The (Merton), **Supp. VIII:** 208

Geography of the Heart (Johnson), **Supp. XI:** 129

"Geometric Poem, The" (Corso), **Supp. XII:** 132, 133–134

George, Diana Hume, **Supp. IV Part 2:** 447, 449, 450

George, Henry, **II:** 276; **Supp. I Part 2:** 518

George, Jan, **Supp. IV Part 1:** 268

George, Lynell, **Supp. XIII:** 234–235, 237, 249

George, Peter, **Supp. XI:** 302, 303, 304

George and the Dragon (Shanley), **Supp. XIV:** 315

George Bernard Shaw: His Plays (Mencken), **III:** 102

George Mills (Elkin), **Supp. VI: 53–54**

George Palmer Putnam: Representative American Publisher (Greenspan), **Supp. XVIII:** 257

"George Robinson: Blues" (Rukeyser), **Supp. VI:** 279

George's Mother (Crane), **I:** 408

"George Thurston" (Bierce), **I:** 202

George Washington Crossing the Delaware (Koch), **Supp. XV:** 186

"George Washington"(Kenny), **Supp. XXIII:** 154

Georgia Boy (Caldwell), **I:** 288, 305–306, 308, 309, 310

"Georgia Dusk" (Toomer), **Supp. IX:** 309

"Georgia: Invisible Empire State" (Du Bois), **Supp. II Part 1:** 179

"Georgia Night" (Toomer), **Supp. III Part 2:** 481

Georgia Scenes (Longstreet), **II:** 70, 313; **Supp. I Part 1:** 352

Georgics (Virgil), **Retro. Supp. I:** 135; **Supp. XVI:** 22

Georgoudaki, Ekaterini, **Supp. IV Part 1:** 12

Gerald McBoing-Boing (film), **Supp. XVI:** 102

"Geraldo No Last Name" (Cisneros), **Supp. VII:** 60–61

Gerald's Game (King), **Supp. V:** 141, 148–150, 151, 152

Gerald's Party (Coover), **Supp. V:** 49–50, 51, 52

Gérando, Joseph Marie de, **II:** 10

"Geranium" (O'Connor), **Retro. Supp. II:** 221, 236

Gerard, Jeremy, **Supp. XXI:** 147

Gerber, Dan, **Supp. VIII:** 39

Gerhardt, Rainer, **Supp. IV Part 1:** 142

"German Girls! The German Girls!, The" (MacLeish), **III:** 16

"German Refugee, The" (Malamud), **Supp. I Part 2:** 436, 437

"Germany's Reichswehr" (Agee), **I:** 35

Germinal (Zola), **III:** 318, 322

Gernsback, Hugo, **Supp. IV Part 1:** 101

"Gernsback Continuum, The" (W. Gibson), **Supp. XVI:** 123, 128

"Gerontion" (Eliot), **I:** 569, 574, 577, 578, 585, 588; **III:** 9, 435, 436; **Retro. Supp. I:** 290; **Supp. XV:** 341; **Supp. XVI:** 158–159

Gerry, Elbridge, **Supp. I Part 2:** 486

"Gerry's Jazz" (Komunyakaa), **Supp. XIII:** 125

Gershwin, Ira, **Supp. I Part 1:** 281

"Gert" (Monette), **Supp. X:** 158

Gertrude of Stony Island Avenue (Purdy), **Supp. VII:** 281–282

Gertrude Stein (Sprigge), **IV:** 31

Gertrude Stein: A Biography of Her Work (Sutherland), **IV:** 38

"Gertrude Stein and the Geography of the Sentence" (Gass), **Supp. VI:** 87

Gesell, Silvio, **III:** 473

"Gestalt at Sixty" (Sarton), **Supp. VIII:** 260

"Gesture of a Woman-in-Process" (Trethewey), **Supp. XXI:** 249–250

"Gesture toward an Unfound Renaissance, A" (Stafford), **Supp. XI:** 323

"Get It Again" (Halliday), **Supp. XIX:** 85

Getlin, Josh, **Supp. V:** 22; **Supp. VIII:** 75, 76, 78, 79

"Getting Along" (Larcom), **Supp. XIII:** 144

"Getting Along with Nature" (Berry), **Supp. X:** 31–32

"Getting Away from Already Pretty Much Being Away from It All" (Wallace), **Supp. X:** 314–315

"Getting Born" (Shields), **Supp. VII:** 311

Getting Even (Allen), **Supp. XV:** 3, 14, 15

"Getting Lucky" (L. Michaels), **Supp. XVI:** 205, 209

"Getting Out of Jail on Monday" (Wagoner), **Supp. IX:** 327

"Getting Over Arnette"(P. Benedict), **Supp. XXIII:** 39

"Getting There" (Plath), **Supp. I Part 2:** 539, 542

"Getting to the Poem" (Corso), **Supp. XII:** 135

Getty, J. Paul, **Supp. X:** 108

Getty, Norris, **Supp. XV:** 136–137, 138, 139, 142, 143, 145, 146

Gettysburg, Manila, Acoma (Masters), **Supp. I Part 2:** 471

"Gettysburg: July 1, 1863" (Kenyon), **Supp. VII:** 172

Gevers, Nick, **Supp. XXII:** 59

Geyer, Bernadette, **Supp. XXIII:** 251

Ghachem, Malick, **Supp. X:** 17

Ghazálí, al-, **Supp. XX: 117**

"Ghazals: Homage to Ghalib" (Rich), **Supp. I Part 2:** 557

Ghost, The (Crane), **I:** 409, 421

"Ghost, The" (Peacock), **Supp. XIX:** 199

"Ghost Cat" (Peacock), **Supp. XIX:** 206

"Ghost Chant et alii" (Komunyakaa), **Supp. XIII:** 114

Ghost in the Music, A (Nichols), **Supp. XIII:** 267

"Ghost Jam"(Hadas), **Supp. XXIII:** 119

"Ghostlier Demarcations, Keener Sounds" (Vendler), **Supp. I Part 2:** 565

"Ghostly Father, I Confess" (McCarthy), **II:** 565–566

Ghostly Lover, The (Hardwick), **Supp. III Part 1:** 194–196, 208, 209

Ghost Money (Hull), **Supp. XXI:** 129, **132–135,** 136

Ghost of Meter, The (A. Finch), **Supp. XVII:** 71, 73

"Ghost of the Buffaloes, The" (Lindsay), **Supp. I Part 2:** 393

Ghost of Tradition, The (Walzer), **Supp. XVIII:** 174

Ghosts (Auster), **Supp. XII:** 22, **24, 26–27**

Ghosts (Ibsen), **III:** 152

Ghosts (Wharton), **IV:** 316, 327

Ghosts of Tsavo: Stalking the Mystery Lions of East Africa (Caputo), **Supp. XIX:** 28

Ghost Town (Coover), **Supp. V:** 52–53

Ghost Trio, The (Bierds), **Supp. XVII:** 29, **30**

Ghost Writer, The (P. Roth), **Retro. Supp. II:** 22, 290, 291; **Supp. III Part 2:** 420–421; **Supp. XVII:** 43

Giachetti, Fosco, **Supp. IV Part 2:** 520

"Giacometti" (Wilbur), **Supp. III Part 2:** 551

Giacometti, Alberto, **Supp. VIII:** 168, 169

Giacomo, Padre, **II:** 278–279

Giant's House, The: A Romance (McCracken), **Supp. X:** 86

"Giant Snail" (Bishop), **Retro. Supp. II:** 49

Giant Weapon, The (Winters), **Supp. II Part 2:** 810

"Giant Woman, The" (Oates), **Supp. II Part 2:** 523

Gibbon, Edward, **I:** 4, 378; **IV:** 126; **Supp. I Part 2:** 503; **Supp. III Part 2:** 629; **Supp. XIII:** 75; **Supp. XIV:** 97

Gibbons, James, **Supp. XVII:** 228

Gibbons, Kaye, **Supp. X: 41–54; Supp. XII:** 311

Gibbons, Reginald, **Supp. X:** 113, 124, 127; **Supp. XV:** 105; **Supp. XIX:** 40, 41–42, 281

Gibbons, Richard, **Supp. I Part 1:** 107

"Gibbs" (Rukeyser), **Supp. VI:** 273

Gibbs, Barbara, **Supp. IV Part 2:** 644

Gibbs, Wolcott, **Supp. I Part 2:** 604, 618; **Supp. VIII:** 151

Gibran, Kahlil, **Supp. XX: 69, 113–129**

"GIBSON" (Baraka), **Supp. II Part 1:** 54

Gibson, Charles Dana, **Supp. X:** 184

Gibson, Graeme, **Supp. XIII:** 20

Gibson, Wilfrid W., **Retro. Supp. I:** 128

Gibson, William, **Supp. XVI: 117–133; Supp. XXII:** 49

Giddins, Gary, **Supp. XIII:** 245

Gide, André, **I:** 271, 290; **II:** 581; **III:** 210; **IV:** 53, 289; **Supp. I Part 1:** 51; **Supp. IV Part 1:** 80, 284, 347; **Supp. IV Part 2:** 681, 682; **Supp. VIII:** 40; **Supp. X:** 187; **Supp. XIV:** 24, 348; **Supp. XVII:** 242

Gideon Planish (Lewis), **II:** 455

Gielgud, John, **I:** 82; **Supp. XI:** 305

Gierow, Dr. Karl Ragnar, **III:** 404

Gifford, Bill, **Supp. XI:** 38

Gifford, Terry, **Supp. XVI:** 22

"Gift, The" (Creeley), **Supp. IV Part 1:** 153

"Gift, The" (Doolittle), **Supp. I Part 1:** 267

Gift, The (Hyde), **Supp. XVIII:** 150

"Gift, The" (Jarman), **Supp. XVII:** 116

"Gift, The" (L.-Y. Lee), **Supp. XV:** 213, 214

Gift, The (Nabokov), **III:** 246, 255, 261–263; **Retro. Supp. I:** 264, 266, **268–270,** 273, 274–275, 278

"Gift from the City, A" (Updike), **Retro. Supp. I:** 320

"Gift of God, The" (Robinson), **III:** 512, 517, 518–521, 524

Gift of the Black Folk, The: The Negroes in the Making of America (Du Bois), **Supp. II Part 1:** 179

"Gift of the Magi, The" (O. Henry), **Supp. II Part 1:** 394, 406, 408

"Gift of the *Osuo,* The" (Johnson), **Supp. VI:** 194

"Gift of the Prodigal, The" (Taylor), **Supp. V:** 314, 326

"Gift Outright, The" (Frost), **II:** 152; **Supp. IV Part 1:** 15

Gigi (Colette; stage adaptation, Loos), **Supp. XVI:** 193

"Gigolo" (Plath), **Retro. Supp. II:** 257

"G.I. Graves in Tuscany" (Hugo), **Supp. VI:** 138

"Gila Bend" (Dickey), **Supp. IV Part 1:** 185–186

Gilbert, Elizabeth, **Supp. XXII:** 83, 90

Gilbert, Jack, **Supp. IX:** 287

Gilbert, Peter, **Supp. IX:** 291, 300

Gilbert, Roger, **Supp. XI:** 124

Gilbert, Sandra M., **Retro. Supp. I:** 42; **Retro. Supp. II:** 324; **Supp. IX:** 66; **Supp. XV:** 270

Gilbert, Susan. *See* Dickinson, Mrs. William A.

Gilbert and Sullivan, **Supp. IV Part 1:** 389

"Gilbert Stuart Portrait of Washington, The" (Kooser), **Supp. XIX:** 124

Gil Blas (Le Sage), **II:** 290

Gilded Age, The (Twain), **III:** 504; **IV:** 198

Gilded Lapse of Time, A (Schnackenberg), **Supp. XV:** 258, **260–263**

"Gilded Lapse of Time, A" (Schnackenberg), **Supp. XV:** 257

"Gilded Six-Bits, The" (Hurston), **Supp. VI:** 154–155

Gilder, R. W., **Retro. Supp. II:** 66; **Supp. I Part 2:** 418

Gildersleeve, Basil, **Supp. I Part 1:** 369

Gilead (Robinson), **Supp. XXI:** 212, **216–220,** 223

Giles, H. A., **Retro. Supp. I:** 289

Giles, James R., **Supp. IX:** 11, 15; **Supp. XI:** 219, 223–224, 228, 234

"Giles Corey of the Salem Farms" (Longfellow), **II:** 505, 506; **Retro. Supp. II:** 166, 167

Giles Goat-Boy (Barth), **I:** 121, 122–123, 129, 130, 134, 135–138; **Supp. V:** 39

Gill, Brendan, **Supp. I Part 2:** 659, 660

Gillespie, Nick, **Supp. XIV:** 298, 311

Gillette, Chester, **I:** 512

Gillian, Maria Mazziotti, **Supp. XXIII:** 248

Gilligan, Carol, **Supp. XIII:** 216; **Supp. XXII:** 18

Gillis, Jim, **IV:** 196

Gillis, Steve, **IV:** 195

Gilman, Charlotte Perkins, **Supp. I Part 2:** 637; **Supp. V:** 121, 284, 285; **Supp. XI:** **193–211;** **Supp. XIII:** 295, 306; **Supp. XVI:** 84; **Supp. XXIII:** 26

Gilman, Daniel Coit, **Supp. I Part 1:** 361, 368, 370

Gilman, Richard, **IV:** 115; **Supp. IV Part 2:** 577; **Supp. XIII:** 100; **Supp. XIX:** 251

Gilmore, Eddy, **Supp. I Part 2:** 618

Gilmore, Lyman, **Supp. XXI:** 20, 22, 24

Gilmore, Mikal, **Supp. XVI:** 123, 124

Gilpin, Charles, **III:** 392

Gilpin, Dewitt, **Supp. XV:** 197

Gilpin, Laura, **Retro. Supp. I:** 7

Gilpin, Sam, **Supp. V:** 213

Gilpin, William, **Supp. IV Part 2:** 603

"Gil's Furniture Bought & Sold" (Cisneros), **Supp. VII:** 61–62, 64

Gilyard, Keith, **Supp. XXI:** 246

"Gimcrackery" articles (Briggs), **Supp. XVIII:** 8–9

"Gimpel the Fool" (Singer), **IV:** 14; **Retro. Supp. II:** 22, 307

Gimpel the Fool and Other Stories (Singer), **IV:** 1, 7–9, 10, 12

"Gin" (Levine), **Supp. V:** 193

"Gingerbread House, The" (Coover), **Supp. V:** 42–43

Gingerbread Lady, The (Simon), **Supp. IV Part 2:** 580, 583–584, 588

Gingerich, Willard, **Supp. IV Part 2:** 510

Gingertown (McKay), **Supp. X:** 132, 139

Gingold, Hermione, **Supp. XV:** 13

Gingrich, Arnold, **Retro. Supp. I:** 113; **Supp. XVII:** 88; **Supp. XX:** 34

Ginna, Robert, **Supp. IX:** 259

Ginsberg, Allen, **I:** 183; **Retro. Supp. I:** 411, 426, 427; **Retro. Supp. II:** 280; **Supp. II Part 1:** 30, 32, 58, **307–333;** **Supp. III Part 1:** 2, 91, 96, 98, 100, 222, 226; **Supp. III Part 2:** 541, 627; **Supp. IV Part 1:** 79, 90, 322; **Supp. IV Part 2:** 502; **Supp. V:** 168, 336; **Supp. VIII:** 239, 242–243, 289; **Supp. IX:** 299; **Supp. X:** 120, 204; **Supp. XI:** 135, 297; **Supp. XII:** 118–119, 121–122, 124, 126, 130–131, 136, 182; **Supp. XIV:** 15, 53, 54, 125, 137, 141, 142, 143–144, 148, 150, 269, 280, 283; **Supp. XV:** 134, 177, 263; **Supp. XVI:** 123, 135; **Supp. XVII:** 138, 243; **Supp. XVIII:** 20, 27, 29, 30; **Supp. XXI:** 53; **Supp. XXII:** 172, 225; **Supp. XXIII:** 211, 213, 215

Gioia, Dana, **Supp. IX:** 279; **Supp. XII:** 209; **Supp. XIII:** 337; **Supp. XV:** **111–131,** 251; **Supp. XVII:** 69, 72, 112; **Supp. XIX:** 117, 144; **Supp. XXI:** 99; **Supp. XXIII:** 112

Giono, Jean, **Supp. XVI:** 135

Giordano, Tony J., **Supp. XXIII:** 125

Giotto di Bondone, **Supp. I Part 2:** 438; **Supp. XI:** 126

Giovani, Regula, **Supp. XV:** 270

Giovanni, Nikki, **Supp. I Part 1:** 66; **Supp. II Part 1:** 54; **Supp. IV Part 1:** 11; **Supp. VIII:** 214; **Supp. XXII:** 11

Giovanni's Room (Baldwin), **Retro. Supp. II:** 5, 6, **6–7,** 8, 10; **Supp. I Part 1:** 51, 52, 55–56, 57, 60, 63, 67; **Supp. III Part 1:** 125

Giovannitti, Arturo, **I:** 476; **Supp. XV:** 299, 301, 302, 307

"Giraffe" (Swenson), **Supp. IV Part 2:** 651

Giraldi, Giovanni Battista. *See* Cinthio

"Girl" (Kincaid), **Supp. VII:** 182–183

Girl, The (Le Sueur), **Supp. XXIII:** **172–174**

"Girl, The" (Olds), **Supp. X:** 207

"Girl Friend Poems" (Wright), **Supp. XV:** 349

"Girl from Lynn Bathes Horse!!" (McCarriston), **Supp. XIV:** 266

"Girl from Red Lion, P.A., A" (Mencken), **III:** 111

Girl in Glass, The: Love Poems (W. J. Smith), **Supp. XIII:** 335

Girl in Landscape (Lethem), **Supp. XVIII:** 136, **141–143**

"Girl in the Grave, The" (McCoy), **Supp. XIII:** 170

Girl Like I, A (Loos), **Supp. XVI:** 181, 183, 184, 187, 194, 196

"Girl of the Golden West" (Didion), **Supp. IV Part 1:** 195, 208, 211

Girl of the Golden West, The (Puccini), **III:** 139

Girl of the Limberlost (film), **Supp. XX:** **223**

Girl of the Limberlost (Stratton-Porter), **Supp. XX:** **211, 221–222**

"Girl on a Scaffold" (C. Frost), **Supp. XV:** 98

"Girl on the Baggage Truck, The" (O'Hara), **III:** 371–372

Girls at Play (Theroux), **Supp. VIII:** 314, 315, 316, **317**

"Girls at the Sphinx, The" (Farrell), **II:** 45

"Girls in Their Summer Dresses, The" (Shaw), **Supp. XIX:** 246

Girl Sleuth, The: A Feminist Guide (Mason), **Supp. VIII:** 133, 135, **139,** 142

"Girl's Story, A" (Bambara), **Supp. XI:** 10–11

"Girl the Prince Liked, The" (Z. Fitzgerald), **Supp. IX:** 71

Girl Who Had to Die, The (Holding), **Supp. XXII:** **126–127**

Girl Who Loved Tom Gordon, The (King), **Supp. V:** 138, 152

"Girl Who Raised Pigeons, The" (P. E. Jones), **Supp. XXII:** 143

Girl with Curious Hair (Wallace), **Supp. X:** 301, **305–308**

"Girl with Curious Hair" (Wallace), **Supp. X:** 306

"Girl with Silver Eyes, The" (Hammett), **Supp. IV Part 1:** 344, 345

"Girl with Talent, The" (Z. Fitzgerald), **Supp. IX:** 71

Girodias, Maurice, **III:** 171; **Supp. XI:** 297

Giroux, Robert, **Retro. Supp. II:** 177, 229, 235; **Supp. IV Part 1:** 280; **Supp. VIII:** 195; **Supp. XV:** 146

Gish, Dorothy, **Retro. Supp. I:** 103

Gish, Lillian, **Supp. XVI:** 184

Gissing, George, **II:** 138, 144

Gitagovinda, **Supp. XXII:** 258

Gita-govínda: Love Songs of Radha and Krishna (Jayadeva; Siegel, trans.), **Supp. XXII:** 258

Gittings, Robert, **II:** 531

"Given" (C. Frost), **Supp. XV:** 96

Given Sugar, Given Salt (Hirshfield), **Supp. XXIII:** 133

"Give Us Back Our Country" (Masters), **Supp. I Part 2:** 472

Give Us This Day (film, Dmytryk), **Supp. XX: 40–41**

"Give Way, Ye Gates" (Roethke), **III:** 536

"Give Your Heart to the Hawks" (Jeffers), **Supp. II Part 2:** 433

"Giving Blood" (Updike), **IV:** 226; **Retro. Supp. I:** 332

Giving Good Weight (McPhee), **Supp. III Part 1:** 307

"Giving in to You" (X. J. Kennedy), **Supp. XV:** 160

"Giving Myself Up" (Strand), **Supp. IV Part 2:** 627

Giving Up the Ghost (Moraga), **Supp. XXIII: 197–199**

G. K. the DJ (Keillor), **Supp. XVI:** 171

Glackens, William, **Retro. Supp. II:** 103

Gladden, Washington, **III:** 293; **Supp. I Part 1:** 5

Gladstone, William Ewart, **Supp. I Part 2:** 419

"Gladys Poem, The" (Alvarez), **Supp. VII:** 10

"Glance at German 'Kultur,' A" (Bourne), **I:** 228

Glance Away, A (Wideman), **Supp. X:** 320

"Glance from the Bridge, A" (Wilbur), **Supp. III Part 2:** 551

"Glance in the Mirror, A" (Swados), **Supp. XIX:** 261–262

Glance toward Shakespeare, A (Chapman), **Supp. XIV:** 44

Glancy, Diane, **Supp. XXI:** 246

Glanville-Hicks, Peggy, **Supp. IV Part 1:** 84

Glare (Ammons), **Supp. VII:** 35–36

Glasgow, Cary, **II:** 173, 182

Glasgow, Ellen, **II: 173–195; IV:** 328; **Supp. X:** 228, 234

Glasmon, Kubec, **Supp. XIII:** 166

Glaspell, Susan, **Supp. III Part 1: 175–191; Supp. X:** 46; **Supp. XVII:** 99; **Supp. XXI:** 5

"Glass" (Francis), **Supp. IX:** 80

Glass, Irony, and God (Carson), **Supp. XII:** 97, **104–106**

Glass, Philip, **Supp. XXI:** 146, 147

"Glass Ark, The" (Komunyakaa), **Supp. XIII:** 129

Glass Bees, The (Jünger; Bogan and Mayer, trans.), **Supp. III Part 1:** 63

"Glass Blower of Venice" (Malamud), **Supp. I Part 2:** 450

"Glass Essay, The" (Carson), **Supp. XII: 104–105**

"Glass Face in the Rain, A: New Poems" (Stafford), **Supp. XI: 327–328**

Glass Key, The (Hammett), **Supp. IV Part 1:** 351–353

"Glass Meadows" (Bausch), **Supp. VII:** 53–54

Glass Menagerie, The (T. Williams), **I:** 81; **IV:** 378, 379, 380, 382, 383, 385, 386, 387, 388, 389, 390, 391, 392, 393–394, 395, 398; **Supp. IV Part 1:** 84

"Glass Mountain, The" (Barthelme), **Supp. IV Part 1:** 47

"Glass Tent, The" (Everwine), **Supp. XV:** 76

Glatstein, Jacob, **Supp. X:** 70

Glazer, Nathan, **Supp. VIII:** 93, 243

"Gleaners, The" (Merwin), **Supp. III Part 1:** 346

Gleanings in Europe (Cooper), **I:** 346

Gleason, Ralph J., **Supp. IX:** 16

Glenday, Michael, **Retro. Supp. II:** 210

Glengarry Glen Ross (film), **Supp. XIV:** 242

Glengarry Glen Ross (Mamet), **Supp. XIV:** 239, 240, 242, 245, 246, 250, 254, 255

Glimcher, Arne, **Supp. VIII:** 73

"Glimpses" (Jones), **Supp. XI:** 218

Glimpses of the Moon, The (Wharton), **II:** 189–190; **IV:** 322–323; **Retro. Supp. I:** 381

"Glimpses of Vietnamese Life" (Levertov), **Supp. III Part 1:** 282

Glisson, J. T., **Supp. X:** 234

Gloria Mundi (Frederic), **II:** 144–145

Gloria Naylor (Fowler), **Supp. VIII:** 224

"Glorious Fourth, The" (Ryan as Quin), **Supp. XVIII:** 229

Glorious Ones, The (Prose), **Supp. XVI:** 251

Glory of Hera, The (Gordon), **II:** 196–197, 198, 199, 217–220

Glory of the Conquered, The (Glaspell), **Supp. III Part 1:** 176

Gloss, Molly, **Supp. XXIII:** 280

Glossary of Literary Terms (Abrams), **Supp. XVI:** 19

Glotfelty, Cheryll, **Supp. IX:** 25

Glover, Joyce Lee, **Supp. XIX:** 112

Glow, The (Wrigley), **Supp. XVIII:** 295

"Glow, The" (Wrigley), **Supp. XVIII:** 296–297, 307

Gluck, Christoph Willibald, **II:** 210, 211

Glück, Louise, **Supp. V: 77–94; Supp. VIII:** 272; **Supp. X:** 209; **Supp. XIV:** 269; **Supp. XV:** 19, 252; **Supp. XVII:** 241

"Glutton, The" (Shapiro), **Supp. II Part 2:** 705

"Glutton for Punishment, A" (Yates), **Supp. XI:** 341

Glyph (Everett), **Supp. XVIII: 60–61**

Gnädiges Fräulein, The (T. Williams), **IV:** 382, 395, 398

Gnomes and Occasions (Nemerov), **III:** 269

Gnomologia (Fuller), **II:** 111

"Gnothis Seauton" (Emerson), **II:** 11, 18–19

Go (Holmes), **Supp. XIV:** 144

"Go Ahead; Goodbye; Good Luck; and Watch Out" (Bronk), **Supp. XXI:** 31

"Goal of Intellectual Men, The" (Eberhart), **I:** 529–530

Go-Between, The (Hartley), **Supp. I Part 1:** 293

Gobineau, Joseph Arthur de, **Supp. XIV:** 209

God (Allen), **Supp. XV:** 3

God and the American Writer (Kazin), **Supp. VIII: 108–109**

Godard, Jean-Luc, **Supp. I Part 2:** 558

Godbey (Masters), **Supp. I Part 2:** 472

God Bless You, Mr. Rosewater (Vonnegut), **Supp. II Part 2:** 758, 767, 768, 769, 771, 772

Goddess Abides, The (Buck), **Supp. II Part 1:** 129, 131–132

Gödel, Kurt, **Supp. IV Part 1:** 43

Godfather (Puzo), **Supp. IV Part 1:** 390

Godfires (Hoffman), **Supp. XVIII: 81–82**

God in Ruins, A (Uris), **Supp. XX: 247, 256**

"God in the Doorway" (Dillard), **Supp. VI:** 28

"God is a distant-stately Lover" (Dickinson), **I:** 471

Godkin, E. L., **II:** 274

God Knows (Heller), **Supp. IV Part 1:** 386, 388–389

God Made Alaska for the Indians (Reed), **Supp. X:** 241

God of His Fathers, The (London), **II:** 469

God of Vengeance, The (Asch), **IV:** 11; **Supp. XXIII:** 5, **8–9**

Go Down, Moses (Faulkner), **Retro. Supp. I:** 75, 82, 85, 86, 88, 89, 90, 92; **Supp. XVIII:** 203

"Go Down, Moses" (Faulkner), **II:** 71–72

Go Down, Moses (Hayden), **Supp. II Part 1:** 365

Go Down, Moses and Other Stories (Faulkner), **II:** 71; **Supp. X:** 52

"Go Down Death A Funeral Sermon" (Johnson), **Supp. IV Part 1:** 7

"God Rest Ye Merry, Gentlemen" (Hemingway), **IV:** 122

Godric (Buechner), **Supp. XII:** 53

Gods, The (Goldbarth), **Supp. XII:** 189, 190

Gods Arrive, The (Wharton), **IV:** 326–327; **Retro. Supp. I:** 382

God Save the Child (Parker), **Supp. XIX:** 183–184

"God Save the Rights of Man" (Freneau), **Supp. I Part 1:** 268

"Gods|Children" (Swenson), **Supp. IV Part 2:** 645

"God's Christ Theory" (Carson), **Supp. XII: 106**

God's Country (Everett), **Supp. XVIII: 57–58,** 64, **65**

God's Country and My People (Morris), **III:** 238

Gods Determinations touching his Elect: and the Elects Combat in their Conversion, and Coming up to God in Christ together with the Comfortable Effects thereof (Taylor), **IV:** 155–160, 165

God-Seeker, The (Lewis), **II:** 456

God Sends Sunday (Bontemps), **Supp. XXII:** 2, 3, 9

God's Favorite (Simon), **Supp. IV Part 2:** 575, 586, 588, 590

"God's Fool" (Gibran), **Supp. XX: 118**

God's Little Acre (Caldwell), **I:** 288, 289, 290, 297, 298–302, 305–306, 309, 310; **Supp. XXII:** 196

God's Man: A Novel in Wood Cuts (Ward), **I:** 31

Gods of Winter, The (Gioia), **Supp. XV:** 112, **121–125**

"Gods of Winter, The" (Gioia), **Supp. XV:** 117

"God's Peace in November" (Jeffers), **Supp. II Part 2:** 420

God's Silence (F. Wright), **Supp. XVII:** 240, 246–247

"God Stiff" (Carson), **Supp. XII: 106**

God's Trombones (Johnson), **Supp. II Part 1:** 201

"God's Youth" (Untermeyer), **Supp. XV:** 296

"God the Father and the Empty House" (McCarriston), **Supp. XIV:** 273

Godwin, William, **II:** 304; **III:** 415; **Supp. I Part 1:** 126, 146; **Supp. I Part 2:** 512, 513–514, 522, 709, 719

God without Thunder (Ransom), **III:** 495–496, 499

Godwulf Manuscript, The (Parker), **Supp. XIX: 178–182**

Goebbels, Josef, **III:** 560

Goebel, Irma, **Supp. X:** 95

Goen, C. C., **I:** 560

Goethe, Johann Wolfgang von, **I:** 181, 396, 587–588; **II:** 5, 6, 320, 344, 488, 489, 492, 502, 556; **III:** 395, 453, 607, 612, 616; **IV:** 50, 64, 173, 326; **Retro. Supp. I:** 360; **Retro. Supp. II:** 94; **Supp. I Part 2:** 423, 457; **Supp. II Part 1:** 26; **Supp. III Part 1:** 63; **Supp. IX:** 131, 308; **Supp. X:** 60; **Supp. XI:** 169; **Supp. XVIII:** 278; **Supp. XX: 84**

Go for the Body (Lacy), **Supp. XV:** 201, 204

Gogan, Robert, **Supp. XXI:** 24

Gogol, Nikolai, **I:** 296; **IV:** 1, 4; **Retro. Supp. I:** 266, 269; **Supp. VIII:** 14; **Supp. XVII:** 45; **Supp. XVIII:** 102; **Supp. XXII:** 59

Goia, Dana, **Supp. XIX:** 121

Goines, Donald, **Supp. XXIII:** 174

"Going, Going, Gone" (Skloot), **Supp. XX: 207**

Going, William T., **Supp. VIII:** 126

Going After Cacciato (O'Brien), **Supp. V:** 237, 238, 239, 244–246, 248, 249

Going All the Way (Wakefield), **Supp. VIII:** 43

"Going Critical" (Bambara), **Supp. XI:** 14

Going Down (Markson), **Supp. XVII:** 136, 138, **139–140,** 141, 142–143, 144, 145

Going for the Rain (Ortiz), **Supp. IV Part 2:** 499, 505–508, 509, 514

"Going Home by Last Night" (Kinnell), **Supp. III Part 1:** 244

"Going Home in America" (Hardwick), **Supp. III Part 1:** 205

"Going Home"(Kenny), **Supp. XXIII:** 144, 148

"Going North" (Salinas), **Supp. XIII:** 316

Going Places (L. Michaels), **Supp. XVI:** 201, **203–206**

"Going Places" (L. Michaels), **Supp. XVI:** 203

"Going South" (J. W. Miller), **Supp. XX:** 169

Going South (Lardner and Buck), **II:** 427

Going To and Fro and Walking Up and Down (Reznikoff), **Supp. XIV:** 280, 282, 284, 285

Going to Meet the Man (Baldwin), **Supp. I Part 1:** 60, 62–63; **Supp. XX: 147**

"Going to Meet the Man" (Baldwin), **Retro. Supp. II:** 8, 9; **Supp. I Part 1:** 62–63

"Going to Naples" (Welty), **IV:** 278; **Retro. Supp. I:** 352, 353

"Going to Shrewsbury" (Jewett), **II:** 393

"Going to the Bakery" (Bishop), **Supp. I Part 1:** 93

Going-to-the-Stars (Lindsay), **Supp. I Part 2:** 398

Going-to-the-Sun (Lindsay), **Supp. I Part 2:** 397–398

Going to the Territory (Ellison), **Retro. Supp. II:** 119, 123–124

"Going towards Pojoaque, A December Full Moon/72" (Harjo), **Supp. XII:** 218

"Going Under" (Dubus), **Supp. VII:** 83

"Gold" (Francis), **Supp. IX:** 82

Gold (O'Neill), **III:** 391

Gold, Don, **Supp. XXII:** 258

Gold, Michael, **II:** 26; **IV:** 363, 364, 365; **Retro. Supp. II:** 323; **Supp. I Part 1:** 331; **Supp. I Part 2:** 609; **Supp. XIV:** 288; **Supp. XXII:** 277

Goldbarth, Albert, **Supp. XII: 175–195**

Goldbarth's Book of Occult Phenomena (Goldbarth), **Supp. XII:** 181

Goldberg, Carole, **Supp. XXII:** 207

Goldberg, Michael, **Supp. XXIII:** 210, 216, 217

Goldberg, S. L., **Supp. VIII:** 238

"Gold Bug, The" (Poe), **III:** 410, 413, 419, 420

Gold Bug Variations, The (Powers), **Supp. IX:** 210, 212, **216–217,** 219

Gold Cell, The (Olds), **Supp. X: 206–209**

Gold Diggers, The (Monette), **Supp. X:** 153

Golde, Miss (Mencken's Secretary), **III:** 104, 107

Golden, Harry, **III:** 579, 581; **Supp. VIII:** 244

Golden, Mike, **Supp. XI:** 294, 295, 297, 299, 303

Golden Age, The (Gurney), **Supp. V:** 101–103

Golden Apples (Rawlings), **Supp. X: 228–229,** 230, 234

Golden Apples, The (Welty), **IV:** 261, 271–274, 281, 293; **Retro. Supp. I:** 341, 342, 343, **350–351,** 352, 355

Golden Apples of the Sun, The (Bradbury), **Supp. IV Part 1:** 102, 103

Golden Book of Springfield, The (Lindsay), **Supp. I Part 2:** 376, 379, 395, 396

Golden Bough, The (Frazer), **II:** 204, 549; **III:** 6–7; **Supp. I Part 1:** 18; **Supp. IX:** 123; **Supp. X:** 124

Golden Bowl, The (James), **II:** 320, 333, 335; **Retro. Supp. I:** 215, 216, 218–219, 232, **234–235,** 374

Golden Boy (Odets), **Supp. II Part 2:** 538, 539, 540–541, 546, 551

Golden Calves, The (Auchincloss), **Supp. IV Part 1:** 35

Golden Child (Hwang), **Supp. XXI:** 147–148

Golden Day, The (Mumford), **Supp. II Part 2:** 471, 475, 477, 483, 484, 488–489, 493

Golden Fleece, The (Gurney), **Supp. V:** 97

Golden Gate (film, Madden), **Supp. XXI:** 147

Golden Gate, The (Seth), **Supp. XVII:** 117

Golden Grove, The: Selected Passages from the Sermons and Writings of Jeremy Taylor (L. P. Smith), **Supp. XIV:** 345

"Golden Heifer, The" (Wylie), **Supp. I Part 2:** 707

"Golden Honeymoon, The" (Lardner), **II:** 429–430, 431

Golden Journey, The (W. J. Smith and Bogan, comps.), **Supp. XIII:** 347

Golden Ladder series (S. and A. Warner), **Supp. XVIII:** 267

"Golden Lads" (Marquand), **III:** 56

Golden Legend, The (Longfellow), **II:** 489, 490, 495, 505, 506, 507; **Retro. Supp. II:** 159, 165, 166

Golden Mean and Other Poems, The (Tate and Wills), **IV:** 122

"Golden Retrievals" (Doty), **Supp. XI:** 132

Golden Shakespeare, The: An Anthology (L. P. Smith), **Supp. XIV:** 349

Golden Slippers: An Anthology of Negro Poetry for Young Readers (Bontemps, ed.), **Supp. XXII:** 5, 11

Goldensohn, Lorrie, **Retro. Supp. II:** 51

Golden State (Bidart), **Supp. XV:** 21, **23–25**

"Golden State" (Bidart), **Supp. XV:** 23, 24, 25

Golden States (Cunningham), **Supp. XV:** 55, **56–59,** 63

Golden Treasury of Best Songs and Lyrical Poems in the English Language (Palgrave), **Retro. Supp. I:** 124

Golden Treasury of the Best Songs and Lyrical Poems in the English Language (Palgrave), **Supp. XIV:** 340

Golden Whales of California and Other Rhymes in the American Language, The (Lindsay), **Supp. I Part 2:** 394–395, 396

"Goldfish Bowl, The" (Francis), **Supp. IX:** 78

Gold Fools (Sorrentino), **Supp. XXI:** 237

Goldin Boys, The (Epstein), **Supp. XIV:** 112

Golding, Arthur, **III:** 467, 468

Golding, William, **Supp. IV Part 1:** 297

Goldini, Carlo, **II:** 274

Goldkorn Tales (Epstein), **Supp. XII:** **163–164**

Goldman, Albert, **Supp. XI:** 299

Goldman, Arnold, **Supp. XXI:** 13

Goldman, Emma, **III:** 176, 177; **Supp. I Part 2:** 524; **Supp. XVII:** 96, 103, 104; **Supp. XXIII:** 162

Goldman, William, **Supp. IV Part 2:** 474

"Gold Mountain Stories" project (Kingston), **Supp. V:** 164

Gold of Chickaree, The (S. and A. Warner), **Supp. XVIII:** 267, 268, 269

Goldring, Douglas, **III:** 458

Goldsmith, Oliver, **II:** 273, 282, 299, 304, 308, 314, 315, 514; **Retro. Supp. I:** 335; **Supp. I Part 1:** 310; **Supp. I Part 2:** 503, 714, 716; **Supp. XVIII:** 12

Gold Standard and the Logic of Naturalism, The (W. B. Michaels), **Retro. Supp. I:** 369

Goldstein, Laurence, **Supp. XXI:** 134

Goldstein, Rebecca, **Supp. XVII:** 44

Goldwater, Barry, **I:** 376; **III:** 38

Goldwyn, Samuel, **Retro. Supp. II:** 199; **Supp. I Part 1:** 281

Golem, The (Leivick), **IV:** 6; **Supp. XXIII:** 8

"Golgotha Is a Mountain" (Bontemps), **Supp. XXII:** 3, 8

"Goliardic Song" (Hecht), **Supp. X:** 63

"Go Like This" (Moore), **Supp. X:** 165

Goll, Ivan, **Supp. III Part 1:** 235, 243–244; **Supp. III Part 2:** 621

Gomes, Albert, **Supp. XXI:** 160

Goncharova, Natalya, **Supp. IX:** 66

Goncourt, Edmond de, **II:** 325, 328; **III:** 315, 317–318, 321; **Retro. Supp. I:** 226

Goncourt, Jules de, **II:** 328; **III:** 315, 317–318, 321

Gone Fishin' (Mosley), **Supp. XIII:** 235–**236,** 240

"Gone to War" (E. Stoddard), **Supp. XV:** 282

"Gone West" (Rodriguez), **Supp. XIV:** 308

Gone with the Wind (film), **Retro. Supp. I:** 113

Gone with the Wind (Mitchell), **II:** 177; **Retro. Supp. I:** 340; **Supp. XX: 243;** **Supp. XXII:** 190, 195

Gongora y Argote, Luis de, **II:** 552

Gonzalez, David, **Supp. VIII:** 85

González, Jovita, **Supp. XIX:** 99

Gooch, Brad, **Supp. XII:** 121; **Supp. XXIII:** 218, 220

Good, George, **Supp. XI:** 306

"Good, the Plaid, and the Ugly, The" (Wasserstein), **Supp. XV:** 327

"Good and Not So Good, The" (Dunn), **Supp. XI:** 141

"Good Anna, The" (Stein), **IV:** 37, 40, 43

Good As Gold (Heller), **Supp. IV Part 1:** 386, 388, 394

Good as I Been to You (album, Dylan), **Supp. XVIII:** 28

Good Boys and Dead Girls and Other Essays (Gordon), **Supp. IV Part 1:** 309–310

Good Brother, The (Offutt), **Supp. XIX:** 163, **168–169**

"Good-by and Keep Cold" (Frost), **Retro. Supp. I:** 135

"Good-bye" (Emerson), **II:** 19

"Goodbye, Christ" (Hughes), **Retro. Supp. I:** 202, 203

Goodbye, Columbus (P. Roth), **Retro. Supp. II:** 280, 281, 290; **Supp. III Part 2:** 403–406; **Supp. XIV:** 112; **Supp. XX: 177**

"Goodbye, Columbus" (P. Roth), **Supp. III Part 2:** 401, 404, 408–409, 411

Goodbye, Columbus and Five Short Stories (P. Roth), **Retro. Supp. II:** 279

"Goodbye, Goldeneye" (Swenson), **Supp. IV Part 2:** 651

"Goodbye, Mr. Chipstein" (Epstein), **Supp. XIV:** 103, 108

"Goodbye, My Brother" (Cheever), **Supp. I Part 1:** 175, 177, 193

"Goodbye and Good Luck" (Paley), **Supp. VI:** 219, 223

Goodbye Girl, The (film), **Supp. IV Part 2:** 589

Goodbye Girl, The (musical), **Supp. IV Part 2:** 576, 588

Goodbye Girl, The (Simon), **Supp. IV Part 2:** 575

Goodbye Look, The (Macdonald), **Supp. IV Part 2:** 473, 474

"Good-Bye My Fancy" (Whitman), **IV:** 348

"Goodbye to All That" (Didion), **Supp. IV Part 1:** 197

Goodbye to All That (Graves), **I:** 477

Goodbye to Berlin (Isherwood), **Supp. XIV:** 159, 161, 162, 169

"Good-Bye to the Mezzogiorno" (Auden), **Supp. II Part 1:** 19

"Goodbye to the Poetry of Calcium" (Wright), **Supp. III Part 2:** 599

"Good Company" (Matthews), **Supp. IX:** 160

"Good Country People" (O'Connor), **III:** 343, 350, 351, 352, 358; **Retro. Supp. II:** 229, 232

Good Day to Die, A (Harrison), **Supp. VIII: 42–44,** 45, 47

Good Doctor, The (Simon), **Supp. IV Part 2:** 575, 585

Good Earth, The (Buck), **Supp. I Part 1:** 49; **Supp. II Part 1:** 115–175, 118, 125, 132

Good European, The (Blackmur), **Supp. II Part 1:** 91

Good Evening Mr. & Mrs. America, and All the Ships at Sea (Bausch), **Supp. VII:** 41, 47, 52

"Good Friday" (Jarman), **Supp. XVII:** 116

"Good Girl" (Peacock), **Supp. XIX:** 199

Good Gray Poet, The (O'Connor), **Retro. Supp. I:** 407

Good Health and How We Won It (Sinclair), **Supp. V:** 285–286

Good Hearts (Price), **Supp. VI:** 259, 265

"Good Job Gone, A" (Hughes), **Retro. Supp. I:** 204

Good Journey, A (Ortiz), **Supp. IV Part 2:** 497, 499, 503, 505, 509–510, 514

Good Luck in Cracked Italian (Hugo), **Supp. VI:** 133, 137–138

Goodman, Allegra, **Supp. XII:** 159; **Supp. XVI:** 205; **Supp. XX: 177**

Goodman, Ellen, **Supp. XVI:** 103

Goodman, Jack, **Supp. XXI:** 277

Goodman, Jenny, **Supp. XV:** 343, 344

Goodman, Paul, **I:** 218, 261; **III:** 39; **Supp. I Part 2:** 524; **Supp. VIII:** 239–240

Goodman, Philip, **III:** 105, 108

Goodman, Walter, **Supp. IV Part 2:** 532

Good Man Is Hard to Find, A (O'Connor), **III:** 339, 343–345

"Good Man Is Hard to Find, A" (O'Connor), **III:** 339, 344, 353; **Retro. Supp. II:** 230–231

Good Man Is Hard to Find and Other Stories, A (O'Connor), **Retro. Supp. II:** 229, **230–232**

Good Morning, America (Sandburg), **III:** 592–593

"Good Morning, Major" (Marquand), **III:** 56

Good Morning, Midnight (Rhys), **Supp. III Part 1:** 43

"Good Morning, Revolution" (Hughes), **Retro. Supp. I:** 201, 203

Good Morning Blues: The Autobiography of Count Basie (Murray), **Supp. XIX:** 159

Good Morning Revolution: Uncollected Writings of Social Protest (Hughes), **Retro. Supp. I:** 194, 201, 202, 209

Good Mother, The (Miller), **Supp. XII:** 289, **290–294,** 299, 301

Good News (Abbey), **Supp. XIII:** 11–12

"Good News from New-England" (Johnson), **Supp. I Part 1:** 115

Good News of Death and Other Poems (Simpson), **Supp. IX:** 265, **268–269**

"Goodnight, Saigon" (lecture, Caputo), **Supp. XIX:** 17, 30

Good Night, Willie Lee, I'll See You in the Morning (Walker), **Supp. III Part 2:** 520, 531

"Good Oak" (Leopold), **Supp. XIV:** 185, 187, 191

"Good Old Times, The: New York Fifty Years Ago" (Briggs), **Supp. XVIII:** 15

"Good Pine, A" (Offutt), **Supp. XIX:** 174

Goodrich, Chris, **Supp. XXII:** 206, 214

Goodrich, Samuel G., **Supp. I Part 1:** 38

Good Scent from a Strange Mountain, A (R. O. Butler), **Supp. XII:** 62, **70–72**

Good School, A (Yates), **Supp. XI:** 334, **346–347,** 348, 349

"*Good Shepherdess, The*/La Buena Pastora" (Mora), **Supp. XIII:** 228–229

Good Will (Smiley), **Supp. VI:** 292, **299–300**

Goodwin, K. L., **III:** 478

Goodwin, Stephen, **Supp. V:** 314, 316, 322, 323, 325

"Good Word for Winter, A" (Lowell), **Supp. I Part 2:** 420

Goodwyn, Janet, **Retro. Supp. I:** 370

Goody, Alex, **Supp. XXII:** 160

"Goophered Grapevine, The" (Chesnutt), **Supp. XIV:** 57, **58–61**

"Goose Fish, The" (Nemerov), **III:** 272, 284

"Goose Pond" (Kunitz), **Supp. III Part 1:** 262

Goose-Step, The (Sinclair), **Supp. V:** 276

Gordimer, Nadine, **Supp. XV:** 251

Gordon, Ambrose, **Supp. XV:** 144

Gordon, A. R., **III:** 199

Gordon, Caroline, **II: 196–222,** 536, 537; **III:** 454, 482; **IV:** 123, 126–127, 139, 282; **Retro. Supp. II:** 177, 222, 229, 233, 235; **Supp. II Part 1:** 139

Gordon, Charles G., **I:** 454

Gordon, Don, **Supp. X:** 119

Gordon, Eugene, **Supp. II Part 1:** 170; **Supp. XVIII:** 280

Gordon, Fran, **Supp. XIII:** 111

Gordon, James Morris, **II:** 197

Gordon, Lois, **Supp. IV Part 1:** 48; **Supp. V:** 46

Gordon, Lyndall, **Retro. Supp. I:** 55

Gordon, Mary, **Supp. IV Part 1: 297–317**

Gordon, Neil, **Supp. XVI:** 156

Gordon, Peter, **Supp. XII:** 3–4, 4–5, 8

Gordon, Ruth, **IV:** 357; **Supp. XX: 50**

Gore, Thomas Pryor, **Supp. IV Part 2:** 679

Gores, Joe, **Supp. XXI:** 70

Gorey, Edward, **IV:** 430, 436; **Supp. XXIII:** 209

Gorilla, My Love (Bambara), **Supp. XI:** 1, **2–7**

"Gorilla, My Love" (Bambara), **Supp. XI:** 2, 3–4

Gorki, Maxim, **I:** 478; **II:** 49; **III:** 402; **IV:** 299; **Supp. I Part 1:** 5, 51; **Supp. XIX:** 241

Gorky, Maxim, **Supp. XXIII:** 1, 4

Gorney, Cynthia, **Supp. XVI:** 112

Gorra, Michael, **Supp. V:** 71

Goslings, The (Sinclair), **Supp. V:** 276, 281

Go South to Sorrow (Rowan), **Supp. XIV:** 306

Gospel According to Joe, The (Gurney), **Supp. V:** 99

"Gospel According to Saint Mark, The" (Gordon), **Supp. IV Part 1:** 310

Gospel according to the Son (Mailer), **Retro. Supp. II:** 213

"Gospel for the Twentieth Century, The" (Locke), **Supp. XIV:** 206

"Gospel of Beauty, The" (Lindsay), **Supp. I Part 2:** 380, 382, 384, 385, 391, 396

Gospels, The (di Donato), **Supp. XX: 45–46**

Gospel Singer, The (Crews), **Supp. XI:** 102, **109**

Gosse, Edmund, **II:** 538; **IV:** 350; **Supp. VIII:** 157

"Gossip" (Conroy), **Supp. XVI:** 71–72

Gossips, Gorgons, and Crones: The Fates of the Earth (Caputi), **Supp. IV Part 1:** 335

Go Tell It on the Mountain (Baldwin), **Retro. Supp. II:** 1, 2, 3, **4–5,** 7, 14; **Supp. I Part 1:** 48, 49, 50, 51, 52, 53–54, 55, 56, 57, 59, 61, 63, 64, 67; **Supp. II Part 1:** 170

Gotera, Vince, **Supp. XIII:** 115, 116, 119, 121, 127

Gothic Revival, The: An Essay on the History of Taste (Clark), **Supp. XIV:** 348

Gothic Writers (Thomson, Voller, and Frank, eds.), **Retro. Supp. II:** 273

"Go to the Devil and Shake Yourself" (song), **Supp. I Part 2:** 580

"Go to the Shine That's on a Tree" (Eberhart), **I:** 523

Go to the Widow-Maker (Jones), **Supp. XI:** 214, **225–226,** 227, 229, 233

"Gots Is What You Got" (Di Piero), **Supp. XIX:** 35, 36, 38, 41, 42, 45–46

Gottfried, Alex, **Supp. XIX:** 260

Gottfried, Martin, **Supp. IV Part 2:** 584

Gotthelf, Allan, **Supp. IV Part 2:** 528

Gottlieb, Adolph, **Supp. XV:** 144

Gottlieb, Edward, **Supp. XX: 250**

Gottlieb, Leopold, **Supp. XXIII:** 6

Gottlieb, Morton, **Supp. XVI:** 196

Gottlieb, Robert, **Supp. IV Part 2:** 474

Gottschalk and the Grande Tarantelle (Brooks), **Supp. III Part 1:** 86

"Gottschalk and the Grande Tarantelle" (Brooks), **Supp. III Part 1:** 86–87

Gould (Dixon), **Supp. XII:** 152, **153**

Gould, Edward Sherman, **I:** 346

Gould, Janice, **Supp. IV Part 1:** 322, 327; **Supp. XII:** 229

Gould, Jay, **I:** 4

Gould, Joe, **Supp. XV:** 143

Gourd Dancer, The (Momaday), **Supp. IV Part 2:** 481, 487, 491, 493

Gourmont, Remy de, **I:** 270, 272; **II:** 528, 529; **III:** 457, 467–468, 477; **Retro. Supp. I:** 55

Gouverneurs de la Rosée (Roumain), **Supp. IV Part 1:** 360, 367

Government Girl (film, Nichols), **Supp. XVIII:** 247

"Governors of Wyoming, The" (Proulx), **Supp. VII:** 264

"Gowane"(Kenny), **Supp. XXIII:** 147–148

Goyen, William, **Supp. V:** 220

Grabhorn, Janet, **Supp. XV:** 142

"Grace" (Budbill), **Supp. XIX:** 2

"Grace" (Dubus), **Supp. VII:** 91

"Grace" (Harjo), **Supp. XII:** 224

Grace Notes (Dove), **Supp. IV Part 1:** 248–250, 252

Grace (Eventually): Thoughts on Faith (Lamott), **Supp. XX: 143–145**

Grade, Chaim, **Supp. XVII:** 41

"Graduation" (Dubus), **Supp. VII:** 84

Grady, Henry W., **Supp. I Part 1:** 370

Graeber, Laurel, **Supp. V:** 15

Graham, Billy, **I:** 308

Graham, David, **Supp. XV:** 104; **Supp. XIX:** 81

Graham, Don, **Supp. XI:** 252, 254

Graham, Jorie, **Supp. IX:** 38, 52; **Supp. X:** 73; **Supp. XII:** 209; **Supp. XIII:** 85; **Supp. XVII:** 110, 111, 133, 240, 241, 242

Graham, Martha, **Supp. XI:** 152

Graham, Maryemma, **Retro. Supp. I:** 201, 204

Graham, Nan, **Supp. XII:** 272

Graham, Sheilah, **II:** 94; **Retro. Supp. I:** 97, 113–114, 115; **Supp. IX:** 63

Graham, Shirley, **Supp. I Part 1:** 51; **Supp. XXI:** 277. *See also* Du Bois, Shirley Graham

Graham, Stephen, **Supp. I Part 2:** 397

Graham, Tom (pseudonym). *See* Lewis, Sinclair

"Graham House, April '76"(Balakian), **Supp. XXIII:** 24

Grahn, Judy, **Supp. IV Part 1:** 325, 330; **Supp. XXIII:** 195

"Grain Field" (Crapsey), **Supp. XVII:** 77

Grainger, Percy, **Supp. I Part 2:** 386

Grain of Mustard Seed, A (Sarton), **Supp. VIII: 259–260,** 263

Gramar (Lowth), **II:** 8

Grammar of Motives, A (Burke), **I:** 272, 275, 276–278, 283, 284

Gramsci, Antonio, **Supp. XX: 35–36**

Granados, Gabriel Bernal, **Supp. XV:** 350

Granath, Jack, **Supp. XVIII:** 93

Granberry, Edwin, **I:** 288

Grand Canyon, Inc. (Everett), **Supp. XVIII:** 66

Grand Design, The (Dos Passos), **I:** 489–490

"Grande Malade, The" (Barnes), **Supp. III Part 1:** 36

"Grandfather" (Dunn), **Supp. XI:** 147

"Grandfather and Grandson" (Singer), **Retro. Supp. II:** 307

Grandfathers, The (Richter), **Supp. XVIII: 219–220**

"Grandfather's Blessing" (Alvarez), **Supp. VII:** 2

"Grand Forks" (Bierds), **Supp. XVII:** 34

"Grand Forks" (Simpson), **Supp. IX:** 280–281

"Grand Inquisitor" (Dostoevsky), **IV:** 106

Grandissimes (Cable), **II:** 291

"Grand-Master Nabokov" (Updike), **Retro. Supp. I:** 317

"Grand Miracle, The" (Karr), **Supp. XI:** 251

"Grandmother" (Gunn Allen), **Supp. IV Part 1:** 320, 325
"Grandmother in Heaven" (Levine), **Supp. V:** 186
"Grandmother of the Sun: Ritual Gynocracy in Native America" (Gunn Allen), **Supp. IV Part 1:** 328
Grandmothers of the Light: A Medicine Woman's Sourcebook (Gunn Allen, ed.), **Supp. IV Part 1:** 332, 333–334
"Grandmother Songs, The" (Hogan), **Supp. IV Part 1:** 413
"Grandpa and the Statue" (A. Miller), **III:** 147
"Grandparents" (Lowell), **II:** 550
"Grandsire Bells, The" (Bierds), **Supp. XVII:** 28–29
"Grandstand Complex, The" (McCoy), **Supp. XIII:** 166
Grange, Red, **II:** 416
Granger's Index to Poetry (anthology), **Retro. Supp. I:** 37, 39
Granite & Cedar (Miller), **Supp. XXII:** 214
Grant, Gavin, **Supp. XIX:** 175
Grant, Lee, **Supp. XIII:** 295
Grant, Madison, **Supp. II Part 1:** 170
Grant, Richard, **Supp. X:** 282
Grant, Ulysses S., **I:** 4, 15; **II:** 542; **III:** 506, 584; **IV:** 348, 446; **Supp. I Part 2:** 418
Grantwood, **Retro. Supp. I:** 416, 417
"Grapes, The" (Hecht), **Supp. X:** 65–66
"Grape Sherbet" (Dove), **Supp. IV Part 1:** 246
Grapes of Wrath, The (Steinbeck), **I:** 301; **III:** 589; **IV:** 51, 53–55, 59, 63, 65, 67, 68, 69; **Supp. V:** 290; **Supp. XI:** 169; **Supp. XIV:** 181; **Supp. XV:** 351; **Supp. XX:** 28
"Grapevine, The" (Ashbery), **Supp. III Part 1:** 4
"Grass" (Sandburg), **III:** 584
Grass, Günter, **Supp. VIII:** 40
Grass County (Kooser), **Supp. XIX:** 119
"Grasse: The Olive Trees" (Wilbur), **Supp. III Part 2:** 550
Grass Harp, The (Capote), **Supp. III Part 1:** 114–117, 123
Grass Still Grows, The (A. Miller), **III:** 146
"Grating Parmesan"(Crooker), **Supp. XXIII:** 56
Gratitude to Old Teachers (R. Bly), **Supp. IV Part 1:** 73
Grattan, Bill, **Supp. XXIII:** 273, 274, 275, 276, 279, 280
Graupner, Gottlieb, **Supp. XV:** 240, 244
"Grave, A" (Moore), **III:** 195, 202, 208, 213
Grave, The (Blair), **Supp. I Part 1:** 150
"Grave, The" (Porter), **III:** 433, 443, 445–446
"Grave, The" (Winters), **Supp. II Part 2:** 795, 796
"Graven Image" (O'Hara), **III:** 320
Grave of Light: New and Selected Poems, 1970–2005 (Notley), **Supp. XXII:** 226, 235, 236

Grave of the Right Hand, The (Wright), **Supp. V:** 332, 338, 339
"Grave Piece" (Eberhart), **I:** 533
Graves, Billy, **Supp. I Part 2:** 607
Graves, John, **Supp. V:** 220
Graves, Morris, **Supp. X:** 264
Graves, Peter, **Supp. IV Part 2:** 474
Graves, Rean, **Supp. I Part 1:** 326
Graves, Robert, **I:** 437, 477, 523; **Supp. I Part 2:** 541; **Supp. IV Part 1:** 280, 348; **Supp. IV Part 2:** 685
"Graveyard Blues" (Trethewey), **Supp. XXI:** 245, 255, 256
Graveyard for Lunatics, A (Bradbury), **Supp. IV Part 1:** 102, 114–116
Gravity's Rainbow (Pynchon), **Supp. II Part 2:** 617, 618–619, 621–625, 627, 630, 633–636; **Supp. IV Part 1:** 279; **Supp. V:** 44; **Supp. XIV:** 49; **Supp. XVII:** 236; **Supp. XXII:** 255
Gray, Cecil, **Supp. I Part 1:** 258
Gray, Francine Du Plessix, **Supp. V:** 169
Gray, James, **III:** 207; **Supp. I Part 2:** 410
Gray, Jeffrey, **Supp. XV:** 27
Gray, Paul, **Supp. IV Part 1:** 305; **Supp. IV Part 2:** 639; **Supp. XVI:** 74; **Supp. XVIII:** 94
Gray, Thomas, **I:** 68; **Supp. I Part 1:** 150; **Supp. I Part 2:** 422, 716
Gray, Thomas A., **Supp. I Part 2:** 710
"Gray Heron, The" (Kinnell), **Supp. III Part 1:** 250
"Gray Mills of Farley, The" (Jewett), **Retro. Supp. II:** 132, 144
"Gray Poem" (Everwine), **Supp. XV:** 81
Grayson, Charles, **Supp. XIII:** 171
"Gray Squirrel" (Francis), **Supp. IX:** 90
"Gray Wolf's H 'ant, The" (Chesnutt), **Supp. XIV:** 60
Grealy, Lucy, **Supp. XII:** 310
Greasy Lake (Boyle), **Supp. VIII:** 14–15
"Greasy Lake" (Boyle), **Supp. VIII:** 15; **Supp. XX:** 18–19
Greasy Lake & Other Stories (Boyle), **Supp. XX:** 17, 18–19
"Great Adventure of Max Breuck, The" (Lowell), **II:** 522
Great American Novel, The (P. Roth), **Retro. Supp. II:** 283, 288–289; **Supp. III Part 2:** 414–416
Great American Short Novels (Phillips, ed.), **Supp. VIII:** 156
Great Battles of the World (Crane), **I:** 415
"Great Carousel, The" (Untermeyer), **Supp. XV:** 296
Great Christian Doctrine of Original Sin Defended, The . . . (Edwards), **I:** 549, 557, 559
Great Circle (Aiken), **I:** 53, 55, 57
"Great Class-Reunion Bazaar, The" (Theroux), **Supp. VIII:** 312
Great Day, The (Hurston), **Supp. VI:** 154
Great Days (Barthelme), **Supp. IV Part 1:** 39
Great Days, The (Dos Passos), **I:** 491
Great Digest (Pound, trans.), **III:** 472
"Great Divider, The" (Saunders), **Supp. XIX:** 235

"Great Elegy for John Donne" (Brodsky), **Supp. VIII:** 21, 23
"Greater Good, A" (Di Piero), **Supp. XIX:** 39
Greater Inclination, The (Wharton), **Retro. Supp. I:** 363, **364–365,** 366
Greater Sea, The (Gibran), **Supp. XX:** 118
"Greater Self, The" (Gibran), **Supp. XX:** 118
"Greater Torment, The" (Blackmur), **Supp. II Part 1:** 92
Greatest Hits 1969–1996 (Salinas), **Supp. XIII:** 311
"Greatest of These, The" (C. Miller), **Supp. XXII:** 188, 196
"Greatest Thing in the World, The" (Mailer), **Retro. Supp. II:** 196
Great Expectations (Acker), **Supp. XII:** 5, **9–11**
Great Expectations (Dickens), **III:** 247; **Supp. I Part 1:** 35; **Supp. XVI:** 73; **Supp. XVIII:** 146
"Great Expectations, No Satisfaction" (D. Gates), **Supp. XVI:** 73
"Great Figure, The" (W. C. Williams), **IV:** 414
"Great Fillmore Street Buffalo Drive, The" (Momaday), **Supp. IV Part 2:** 493
Great Gatsby, The (Fitzgerald) (Modern Library), **Retro. Supp. I:** 113
Great Gatsby, The (Fitzgerald), **I:** 107, 375, 514; **II:** 77, 79, 83, 84, 85, 87, 91–93, 94, 96, 98; **III:** 244, 260, 372, 572; **IV:** 124, 297; **Retro. Supp. I:** 98, 105, **105–108,** 110, 114, 115, 335, 359; **Retro. Supp. II:** 107, 201; **Supp. II Part 2:** 626; **Supp. III Part 2:** 585; **Supp. IV Part 2:** 468, 475; **Supp. IX:** 57, 58; **Supp. X:** 175; **Supp. XI:** 65, 69, 334; **Supp. XVI:** 64, 75; **Supp. XVIII:** 76, 148, 165; **Supp. XX: 59, 60, 61, 72; Supp. XXII:** 81, 82, 88; **Supp. XXIII:** 101
Great God Brown, The (O'Neill), **III:** 165, 391, **394–395**
Great Goodness of Life: A Coon Show (Baraka), **Supp. II Part 1:** 47
Great Heart: The History of a Labrador Adventure (Davidson and Rugge), **Supp. XXII:** 218
Great Inclination, The (Wharton), **IV:** 310
"Great Infirmities" (Simic), **Supp. VIII:** 277
Great Jones Street (DeLillo), **Supp. VI:** 2, 3, 8–9, 11, 12
"Great Lawsuit, The: Man *versus* Men: Woman *versus* Women" (Fuller), **Retro. Supp. I:** 156; **Supp. II Part 1:** 292
"Great Men and Their Environment" (James), **II:** 347
"Great Mississippi Bubble, The" (Irving), **II:** 314
Great Railway Bazaar, The: By Train through Asia (Theroux), **Supp. VIII:** 318, 319, **320–321,** 322

"Great Scott" (Conroy), **Supp. XVI:** 75, 77
"Great Sleigh-Ride of Brewsterville, The" (Briggs), **Supp. XVIII:** 16
Great Stories of Suspense (Millar, ed.), **Supp. IV Part 2:** 474
Great Topics of the World (Goldbarth), **Supp. XII:** 187, 189, 191
Great Valley, The (Masters), **Supp. I Part 2:** 465
Great World and Timothy Colt, The (Auchincloss), **Supp. IV Part 1:** 25, 31, 32
Grédy, Jean-Pierre, **Supp. XVI:** 194
"Greek Boy, The" (Bryant), **Supp. I Part 1:** 168
Greek Mind/Jewish Soul: The Conflicted Art of Cynthia Ozick (Strandberg), **Supp. V:** 273
"Greek Partisan, The" (Bryant), **Supp. I Part 1:** 168
"Greeks, The" (McCarriston), **Supp. XIV:** 271
"Greeks, the Chines, or Say the Mayans, The" (Bronk), **Supp. XXI:** 31
Greeley, Horace, **II:** 7; **IV:** 197, 286–287
Green, Ashbel, **Supp. IV Part 2:** 474
Green, Henry, **IV:** 279; **Retro. Supp. I:** 354; **Supp. III Part 1:** 3; **Supp. XI:** 294–295, 296, 297; **Supp. XII:** 315
Green, Jack, **Supp. IV Part 1:** 284–285
Green, Martin, **Supp. I Part 1:** 299
Green, Michelle, **Supp. IV Part 1:** 95
Green, Rose Basile, **Supp. XX:** 33, 41
"Green Automobile, The" (Ginsberg), **Supp. II Part 1:** 322
Greenberg, Clement, **Supp. XV:** 141, 143, 144, 145
Greenberg, Eliezer, **Supp. I Part 2:** 432; **Supp. XXIII:** 7
Greenberg, Hayim, **Supp. XXIII:** 3
Greenberg, Jonathan, **Supp. XII:** 285
Greenberg, Miriam, **Supp. XXII:** 244
Greenberg, Samuel, **I:** 393
Green Bough, A (Faulkner), **Retro. Supp. I:** 84
"Green Canoe" (Halliday), **Supp. XIX:** 88
Green Centuries (Gordon), **II:** 196, 197–207, 209
"Green Crab's Shell, A" (Doty), **Supp. XI:** 126
"Green Door, The" (O. Henry), **Supp. II Part 1:** 395
Greene, A. C., **Supp. V:** 223, 225
Greene, Graham, **I:** 480; **II:** 62, 320; **III:** 57, 556; **Retro. Supp. I:** 215; **Supp. I Part 1:** 280; **Supp. IV Part 1:** 341; **Supp. V:** 298; **Supp. IX:** 261; **Supp. XI:** 99,**Supp. XI:** 104; **Supp. XIII:** 233; **Supp. XVIII:** 79; **Supp. XIX:** 29–30
Greene, Helga, **Supp. IV Part 1:** 134, 135
Greene, J. Lee, **Retro. Supp. II:** 121
Greene, Nathanael, **Supp. I Part 2:** 508
Greene, Richard Tobias, **III:** 76
Greene, Robert, **Supp. XVII:** 232
Green Eggs and Ham (Geisel), **Supp. XVI:** 108, 109

"Greene-ing of the Portables, The" (Cowley), **Supp. II Part 1:** 140
"Greenest Continent, The" (Stevens), **Retro. Supp. I:** 304
Greenfeld, Josh, **III:** 364
Greenfield, Josh, **Supp. XIX:** 269
"Green Hell" (Boyle), **Supp. XX:** 18
Green Hills of Africa (Hemingway), **II:** 253; **Retro. Supp. I:** 182, 186
Greening of America, The (C. Reich), **Supp. XVII:** 3
"Green Lagoons, The" (Leopold), **Supp. XIV:** 188
"Green Lampshade" (Simic), **Supp. VIII:** 283
Greenlanders, The (Smiley), **Supp. VI:** 292, **296–298,** 299, 305, 307
Greenlaw, Edwin A., **IV:** 453
"Greenleaf" (O'Connor), **III:** 350, 351; **Retro. Supp. II:** 233, 237
Greenman, Walter F., **I:** 217, 222
Green Memories (Mumford), **Supp. II Part 2:** 474, 475, 479, 480–481
Green Mountain Ghosts, Ghouls, and Unsolved Mysteries (Citro), **Supp. XXII:** 208, 218
"Green Pasture, The" (Leopold), **Supp. XIV:** 184
Green Pastures, The (Connelly), **Supp. II Part 1:** 223
"Green Red Brown and White" (Swenson), **Supp. IV Part 2:** 639
"Green River" (Bryant), **Supp. I Part 1:** 155, 164
Green Shadows, White Whale (Bradbury), **Supp. IV Part 1:** 102, 103, 116
"Green Shirt, The" (Olds), **Supp. X:** 209
"Greensleeves" (Jarman), **Supp. XVII:** 113
"Greensleeves" (Notley), **Supp. XXII:** 228
Greenslet, Ferris, **I:** 19; **Retro. Supp. I:** 9, 10, 11, 13; **Retro. Supp. II:** 41
Greenspan, Alan, **Supp. IV Part 2:** 526
Greenspan, Ezra, **Supp. XVIII:** 257
Greenstreet, Sydney, **Supp. IV Part 1:** 356
"Green Thought, A" (L. Michaels), **Supp. XVI:** 204
"Green-Thumb Boy" (Nelson), **Supp. XVIII:** 182
Greenwald, Ted, **Supp. IV Part 2:** 423
Green Wall, The (Wright), **Supp. III Part 2:** 591, 593, 595
Green Wave, The (Rukeyser), **Supp. VI:** 273, 280
"Green Ways" (Kunitz), **Supp. III Part 1:** 265
Green with Beasts (Merwin), **Supp. III Part 1:** 340, 344–346
Greenwood, Grace, **Supp. XIII:** 141
"Greeting Card Verse" (Peacock), **Supp. XIX:** 200
Gregerson, Linda, **Supp. IV Part 2:** 651; **Supp. X:** 204–205; **Supp. XI:** 142
"Gregorio Valdes" (Bishop), **Retro. Supp. II:** 51
Gregory, Alyse, **I:** 221, 226, 227, 231

Gregory, Horace, **II:** 512; **Supp. III Part 2:** 614, 615; **Supp. IX:** 229; **Supp. XV:** 143
Gregory, Lady Isabella Augusta, **III:** 458
Gregory, Sinda, **Supp. X:** 260, 268
Grendel (Gardner), **Supp. VI:** 63, **67,** 68, 74
Grenstone Poems (Bynner), **Supp. XV:** 44
"Gretel in Darkness" (Glück), **Supp. V:** 82
Gretta (Caldwell), **I:** 301, 302
Greuze, Jean Baptiste, **Supp. I Part 2:** 714
Grey, Zane, **Supp. XIII:** 5
Greyhounding This America (Kenny), **Supp. XXIII: 155**
Gridley Firing (Hayford), **Supp. XXII:** 204
"Grief Has Stamped" (Pedersen; Nelson, trans.), **Supp. XVIII:** 180
Grieg, Michael, **Supp. XV:** 133, 148
Griffin, Bartholomew, **Supp. I Part 1:** 369
Griffin, John Howard, **Supp. VIII:** 208; **Supp. XXI:** 74
Griffin, Merv, **Supp. IV Part 2:** 526
Griffith, Albert J., **Supp. V:** 325
Griffith, D. W., **I:** 31, 481–482; **Retro. Supp. I:** 103, 325; **Supp. XI:** 45; **Supp. XVI:** 183, 184; **Supp. XXI:** 170
Griffith, Paul, **Supp. XVIII:** 173, 175
Griffiths, Clyde, **I:** 511
Grile, Dod (pseudonym). *See* Bierce, Ambrose
Grimm, Herman, **II:** 17
Grimm brothers, **II:** 378; **III:** 101, 491, 492; **IV:** 266; **Supp. I Part 2:** 596, 622; **Supp. X:** 78, 84, 86
Grimshaw, Anna, **Supp. XXI:** 172
Grinnell, George Bird, **Supp. XVI:** 13
Gris, Juan, **I:** 442; **Retro. Supp. I:** 430
Griswold, Rufus Wilmot, **III:** 409, 429; **Retro. Supp. II:** 261, 262; **Supp. XV:** 277, 278; **Supp. XVI:** 8, 10–11
Grogg, Sam, Jr., **Supp. IV Part 2:** 468, 471
Gromer, Crystal, **Supp. XII:** 297
Gronlund, Laurence, **II:** 276
Grooms, Red, **Supp. XV:** 178
Grooves: A Kind of Mystery (Brockmeier), **Supp. XXII:** 55, 56, 59
"Groping for Trouts" (Gass), **Supp. VI:** 87
Grosholz, Emily, **Supp. XII:** 185; **Supp. XIX:** 37–38, 278
Grosman un zun (Grosman and Son) (Asch), **Supp. XXIII:** 7
Gross, Robert A., **Supp. XIX:** 151
Gross, Terry, **Supp. XVI:** 167; **Supp. XXI:** 247, 255
"Grosse Fuge" (Doty), **Supp. XI:** 126–127
Grossman, Allen, **Retro. Supp. II:** 83; **Supp. XVIII:** 91; **Supp. XIX:** 82, 86, 94
Grosz, George, **III:** 172; **IV:** 438; **Retro. Supp. II:** 321; **Supp. X:** 137

"Grotesque in Modern Fiction, The" (E. Hoffman, Ph.D. dissertation), **Supp. XVI:** 147

"Groundhog, The" (Eberhart), **I:** 523, 530–532, 533

"Ground on Which I Stand, The" (Wilson), **Supp. VIII:** 331

"Ground Swell" (Jarman), **Supp. XVII:** 118

Group, The (McCarthy), **II:** 570, 574–578

"Group of Two, A" (Jarrell), **II:** 368

Group Therapy (Hearon), **Supp. VIII: 64–65**

"Grove" (Goldbarth), **Supp. XII:** 176

Groves of Academe, The (McCarthy), **II:** 568–571

Growing into Love (X. J. Kennedy), **Supp. XV:** 153, **158–160**

Growing Pains (J. S. Untermeyer), **Supp. XV:** 303

"Growing Season, The" (Caldwell), **I:** 309

Growing Up Gay: A Literary Anthology (Singer, ed.), **Supp. IV Part 1:** 330

"Growing Up Good in Maycomb" (Shaffer), **Supp. VIII:** 128

"Grown-Up" (Jewett), **Retro. Supp. II:** 134

"Growth" (Lowell), **II:** 554

"Growth and Decay in Recent Verse" (Untermeyer), **Supp. XV:** 299

Growth of the American Republic, The (Morison and Commager), **Supp. I Part 2:** 484

"Growtown Buggle, The" (Jewett), **Retro. Supp. II:** 132

Grubin, David, **Supp. XXIII:** 138

Gruenberg, Louis, **III:** 392

Grumbach, Doris, **II:** 560

"Gryphon" (C. Baxter), **Supp. XVII:** 14, 17

"Guacamaja" (Leopold), **Supp. XIV:** 188–189

Guardian Angel, The (Holmes), **Supp. I Part 1:** 315–316

"Guardian of the Law" (R. Fisher), **Supp. XIX:** 71

Guard of Honor (Cozzens), **I:** 370–372, 375, 376–377, 378, 379

Guardsman, The (Molnar), **Supp. XVI:** 187

Guare, John, **Supp. XIII:** 196, 207

Gubar, Susan, **Retro. Supp. I:** 42; **Retro. Supp. II:** 324; **Supp. IX:** 66; **Supp. XV:** 270

Guerard, Albert, Jr., **Supp. X:** 79; **Supp. XIII:** 172

Guérin, Maurice de, **I:** 241

"Guerrilla Handbook, A" (Baraka), **Supp. II Part 1:** 36

Guess and Spell Coloring Book, The (Swenson), **Supp. IV Part 2:** 648

Guess Who's Coming to Dinner (film), **Supp. I Part 1:** 67

Guest, Barbara, **Supp. XXIII:** 215

Guest, Judith, **Supp. XVI:** 36

Guest, Val, **Supp. XI:** 307

Guest Book (Bynner), **Supp. XV:** 51

"Guests of Mrs. Timms, The" (Jewett), **II:** 408; **Retro. Supp. II:** 135

Guevara, Martha, **Supp. VIII:** 74

Guevara, Fray Miguel de, **Supp. XXI:** 104

"Guevara . . .Guevara" (Salinas), **Supp. XIII:** 312–313, 315

Guggenheim, Peggy, **Supp. XXII:** 165

Guided Tours of Hell (Prose), **Supp. XVI:** 257, 261

"Guided Tours of Hell" (Prose), **Supp. XVI:** 257

Guide for the Perplexed (Maimonides), **Supp. XVII:** 46

Guide in the Wilderness, A (Cooper), **I:** 337

"Guidelines" (Espaillat), **Supp. XXI:** 99

"Guide to Dungeness Spit, A" (Wagoner), **Supp. IX:** 325–326, 329

Guide to Ezra Pound's Selected Cantos' (Kearns), Retro. Supp. I: 292

Guide to Kulchur (Pound), **III:** 475

Guide to the Ruins (Nemerov), **III:** 269, 270–271, 272

Guillén, Nicolás, **Retro. Supp. I:** 202; **Supp. I Part 1:** 345

Guillevic, Eugene, **Supp. III Part 1:** 283

"Guilt, The" (Peacock), **Supp. XIX:** 200

"Guilty Man, The" (Kunitz), **Supp. II Part 1:** 263

Guilty of Everything: The Autobiography of Herbert Huncke (Huncke), **Supp. XIV:** 138, 140, 141, 150

Guilty Pleasures (Barthelme), **Supp. IV Part 1:** 44, 45, 53

Guimond, James, **Supp. XXI:** 228

Guinness, Alec, **Retro. Supp. I:** 65; **Supp. XX:** 50

Gulag Archipelago, The (Solzhenitsyn), **Supp. XVII:** 229

"Gulf, The" (Dunn), **Supp. XI:** 149

Gulistan (Saadi), **II:** 19

Gullible's Travels (Lardner), **II:** 426, 427

Gulliver, Adelaide Cromwell, **Supp. XVIII:** 286

"Gulliver Found" (Bronk), **Supp. XXI:** 33

Gulliver's Travels (Swift), **I:** 209, 348, 366; **II:** 301; **Supp. I Part 2:** 656; **Supp. XI:** 209; **Supp. XVI:** 110

"Gulls" (Hayden), **Supp. II Part 1:** 367

"Gulls, The" (Nemerov), **III:** 272

"Gulls on Dumps" (Di Piero), **Supp. XIX:** 41

"Gun, The" (Dobyns), **Supp. XIII:** 88

Gun, with Occasional Music (Lethem), **Supp. XVIII: 137–138**

Günderode: A Translation from the German (Fuller), **Supp. II Part 1:** 293

Gundy, Jeff, **Supp. XI:** 315; **Supp. XVI:** 46, 265, 275

Gunfight at the O.K. Corral (film), **Supp. XX: 246**

Gunman's Rhapsody (Parker), **Supp. XIX:** 187

Gunn, Robin Wright, **Supp. XXI:** 243, 244

Gunn, Thom, **Supp. IX:** 269

Gunn, Thomas, **Supp. V:** 178

Gunn Allen, Paula, **Supp. IV Part 1: 319–340,** 404; **Supp. IV Part 2:** 499, 502, 557, 568; **Supp. XII:** 218

"Gunnar's Sword" (C. Bly), **Supp. XVI:** 34, 35, 37, 42

"Guns as Keys; and the Great Gate Swings" (Lowell), **II:** 524

Gurdjieff, Georges, **Supp. V:** 199; **Supp. IX:** 320

Gurganus, Allan, **Supp. XII:** 308–309, 310

Gurko, Leo, **III:** 62

Gurney, A. R., **Supp. V: 95–112; Supp. IX:** 261

Gurney, Mary (Molly) Goodyear, **Supp. V:** 95

Gussow, Mel, **Supp. IX:** 93; **Supp. XII:** 325, 328, 341

Gustavus Vassa, the African (Vassa), **Supp. IV Part 1:** 11

Gusto, Thy Name Was Mrs. Hopkins: A Prose Rhapsody (Francis), **Supp. IX:** 89

Guston, Philip, **Supp. XXIII:** 210

Gute Mensch von Sezuan, Der (Brecht), **Supp. IX:** 138

Gutenberg, Johann, **Supp. I Part 2:** 392

Guthrie, A. B., **Supp. X:** 103

Guthrie, Woody, **Supp. XVIII:** 23

Gutman, Herbert, **Supp. I Part 1:** 47

Guttenplan, D. D., **Supp. XI:** 38

"Gutting of Couffignal, The" (Hammett), **Supp. IV Part 1:** 345

Guy Domville (James), **II:** 331; **Retro. Supp. I:** 228

"Gwendolyn" (Bishop), **Retro. Supp. II:** 51

Gwynn, R. S., **Supp. XVIII:** 184

Gypsy Ballads (Hughes, trans.), **Supp. I Part 1:** 345

Gypsy's Curse, The (Crews), **Supp. XI: 110**

"Gyroscope, The" (Rukeyser), **Supp. VI:** 271

Gysin, Brion, **Supp. XII:** 129

H

Haardt, Sara. *See* Mencken, Mrs. H. L. (Sara Haardt)

Haas, Robert, **Supp. XXII:** 177

Habakkuk (biblical book), **III:** 200, 347

Habibi (Nye), **Supp. XIII:** 273, **279**

"Habit" (James), **II:** 351

Habitations of the Word (Gass), **Supp. VI:** 88

"Hack, The" (Swados), **Supp. XIX:** 267

"Hackberry"(P. Benedict), **Supp. XXIII:** 37–38, 39

Hacker, Marilyn, **Supp. XV:** 250; **Supp. XVII:** 71, 76, 112; **Supp. XVIII:** 177, 178

Hackett, David, **Supp. XII:** 236

Hadas, Rachel, **Supp. XXIII: 111–128**

Hadda, Janet, **Retro. Supp. II:** 317

Haddád, 'Abd al-Masíh, **Supp. XX: 116**

Haeckel, Ernst Heinrich, **II:** 480

Haegert, John, **Supp. XVI:** 69

Hafif, Marcia, **Supp. IV Part 2:** 423

Hagar's Daughter (P. Hopkins), **Supp. XVI:** 143

Hagedorn, Jessica, **Supp. X:** 292

Hagen, Beulah, **Supp. I Part 2:** 679

Hager, Kelly, **Supp. XVIII:** 183

Haggard, Rider, **III:** 189

Hagoromo (play), **III:** 466

Hagstrum, Jean, **Supp. XV:** 74

"Hail Mary" (Fante), **Supp. XI:** 160, 164

Haines, George, IV, **I:** 444

Haines, John, **Supp. XII: 197–214**

"Hair" (Corso), **Supp. XII:** 117, 126, 127

"Hair, The" (Carver), **Supp. III Part 1:** 137

"Haircut" (Lardner), **II:** 430, 436

"Hair Dressing" (Untermeyer), **Supp. XV:** 304, 305

Hairpiece: A Film for Nappy-Headed People (Chenzira; film), **Supp. XI:** 19–20

"Hairs" (Cisneros), **Supp. VII:** 59

Hairs/Pelitos (Cisneros), **Supp. VII:** 58

Hairy Ape, The (O'Neill), **III:** 391, 392, 393

"Haïta the Shepherd" (Bierce), **I:** 203

Haj, The (Uris), **Supp. XX: 244, 245, 247, 255–256**

Haldeman, Anna, **Supp. I Part 1:** 2

Hale, Edward Everett, **Supp. I Part 2:** 584; **Supp. XI:** 193, 200

Hale, John Parker, **Supp. I Part 2:** 685

Hale, Nancy, **Supp. VIII:** 151, 171

Haley, Alex, **Supp. I Part 1:** 47, 66

Haley, J. Evetts, **Supp. V:** 226

"Half a Century Gone" (Lowell), **II:** 554

Half-a-Hundred: Tales by Great American Writers (Grayson, ed.), **Supp. XIII:** 171

Half Asleep in Frog Pajamas (Robbins), **Supp. X:** 259, **279–282**

Half Breed, The (film), **Supp. XVI:** 185

Half-Century of Conflict, A (Parkman), **Supp. II Part 2:** 600, 607, 610

"Half Deity" (Moore), **III:** 210, 214, 215

"Half Hour of August" (Ríos), **Supp. IV Part 2:** 552

Half-Lives (Jong), **Supp. V:** 115, 119

Half Moon Street: Two Short Novels (Theroux), **Supp. VIII:** 322, 323

Half of Paradise (Burke), **Supp. XIV:** 22, 24

Half-Past Nation Time (Johnson), **Supp. VI:** 187

"Half-Skinned Steer, The" (Proulx), **Supp. VII:** 261–262

"Half Sonnets" (Jarman), **Supp. XVII:** 115

Half Sun Half Sleep (Swenson), **Supp. IV Part 2:** 645–646

Halfway (Kumin), **Supp. IV Part 2:** 441–442

"Halfway" (Rich), **Supp. I Part 2:** 553

Halfway Down the Hall: New and Selected Poems (Hadas), **Supp. XXIII: 118–119**

Halfway Home (Monette), **Supp. X:** 154

Halfway to Silence (Sarton), **Supp. VIII:** 261

Half You Don't Know, The: Selected Stories (Cameron), **Supp. XII:** 79, 80, 81

Haliburton, Thomas Chandler, **II:** 301; **IV:** 193; **Supp. I Part 2:** 411

Halifax, Lord, **II:** 111

Hall, Daniel, **Supp. XII:** 258

Hall, Donald, **I:** 567; **III:** 194; **Supp. IV Part 1:** 63, 72; **Supp. IV Part 2:** 621; **Supp. IX:** 269; **Supp. XIV:** 82, 126; **Supp. XV:** 21, 153, 176; **Supp. XVI:** 39, 230, 235; **Supp. XX: 194; Supp. XXI:** 86; **Supp. XXIII:** 209

Hall, Hazel, **Supp. XXII:** 275

Hall, James, **II:** 313; **Supp. I Part 2:** 584, 585

Hall, James Baker, **Supp. X:** 24

Hall, Rachel, **Supp. XXIII:** 301

Hall, Timothy L., **Supp. VIII:** 127, 128

Halleck, Fitz-Greene, **Supp. I Part 1:** 156, 158

"Hallelujah: A Sestina" (Francis), **Supp. IX:** 82

"Hallelujah on the Bum" (Abbey), **Supp. XIII:** 2

"Haller's Second Home" (Maxwell), **Supp. VIII:** 169

Halliday, Mark, **Supp. XV:** 19, 20, 21, 23, 25, 27, 30; **Supp. XIX: 81–95**

Hallock, Rev. Moses, **Supp. I Part 1:** 153

Hall of Mirrors, A (Stone), **Supp. V:** 295, 296–299, 300, 301

"Hallowe'en" (Huncke), **Supp. XIV:** 145

"Halloween Party, The" (Chabon), **Supp. XI:** 72

Halloween Tree, The (Bradbury), **Supp. IV Part 1:** 102, 112–113

"Halls, The" (Halliday), **Supp. XIX:** 90

Hallwas, John E., **Supp. I Part 2:** 454

Halpern, Daniel, **Supp. IV Part 1:** 94–95, 95

Halsey, Theresa, **Supp. IV Part 1:** 330, 331

"Halt in the Desert, A" (Brodsky), **Supp. VIII:** 24

"Halves" (Dunn), **Supp. XI:** 149

Hamburg, Victoria, **Supp. XVI:** 126

Hamerik, Asger, **Supp. I Part 1:** 356

Hamill, Pete, **Supp. XX: 244, 255**

Hamill, Sam, **Supp. X:** 112, 125, 126, 127

Hamilton, Alexander, **I:** 485; **Supp. I Part 2:** 456, 483, 509

Hamilton, Alice, **Supp. I Part 1:** 5

Hamilton, David, **Supp. IX:** 296

Hamilton, Edith, **Supp. XVI:** 196

Hamilton, Lady Emma, **II:** 524

Hamilton, Hamish, **Supp. I Part 2:** 617

Hamilton, Walton, **Supp. I Part 2:** 632

Hamilton Stark (Banks), **Supp. V:** 8, 9–10, 11

"Hamlen Brook" (Wilbur), **Supp. III Part 2:** 564

"Hamlet" (Laforgue), **I:** 573; **III:** 11

Hamlet (Miller and Fraenkel), **III:** 178, 183

Hamlet (Shakespeare), **I:** 53, 183, 205, 377, 586–587; **II:** 158, 531; **III:** 7, 11, 12, 183; **IV:** 116, 131, 227; **Supp. I Part 1:** 369; **Supp. I Part 2:** 422, 457, 471; **Supp. IV Part 2:** 612; **Supp. IX:** 14

Hamlet, The (Faulkner), **II:** 69–71, 73, 74; **IV:** 131; **Retro. Supp. I:** 82, 91, 92; **Supp. VIII:** 178; **Supp. IX:** 103; **Supp. XI:** 247

"Hamlet and His Problems" (Eliot), **I:** 586–587

Hamlet of A. MacLeish, The (MacLeish), **III:** 11–12, 14, 15, 18

Hamlin, Eva, **Retro. Supp. II:** 115

"Hammer" (Bidart), **Supp. XV:** 35

Hammer, Adam, **Supp. XIII:** 112

Hammer, Langdon, **Retro. Supp. II:** 45, 53; **Supp. X:** 65

"Hammer Man, The" (Bambara), **Supp. XI:** 4–5

Hammett, Dashiell, **IV:** 286; **Retro. Supp. II:** 327; **Supp. I Part 1:** 286, 289, 291, 292, 293, 294, 295; **Supp. III Part 1:** 91; **Supp. IV Part 1:** 120, 121, **341–357; Supp. IV Part 2:** 461, 464, 468, 469, 472, 473; **Supp. IX:** 200; **Supp. XI:** 228; **Supp. XIII:** 159; **Supp. XIV:** 21; **Supp. XVII:** 137; **Supp. XIX:** 178; **Supp. XXI:** 68

Hammon, Jupiter, **Supp. XXII:** 11

Hammond, John, **Supp. XVIII:** 24

Hammond, Karla, **Supp. IV Part 2:** 439, 442, 448, 637, 640, 644, 648

Hampl, Patricia, **Supp. IX:** 291; **Supp. XI:** 126; **Supp. XVII:** 21; **Supp. XXII: 81–101**

Hampson, Alfred Leete, **Retro. Supp. I:** 35–36, 38

"Hamrick's Polar Bear" (Caldwell), **I:** 309–310

Hamsun, Knut, **Supp. VIII:** 40; **Supp. XI:** 161, 167; **Supp. XII:** 21, 128

Hancock, John, **Supp. I Part 2:** 524; **Supp. XX: 282**

Hancock, Wade, **Supp. XVI:** 34

Handbook of North American Indians (Sando), **Supp. IV Part 2:** 510

Handcarved Coffins: A Nonfiction Account of an American Crime (Capote), **Supp. III Part 1:** 131

Handel, Georg Friedrich, **III:** 210; **IV:** 369

"Handfasting" (Wright), **Supp. XV:** 343

"Handfuls" (Sandburg), **III:** 584

"Handle with Care" (Fitzgerald), **Retro. Supp. I:** 114

Handley, William R., **Supp. XVIII:** 58

Handmaid's Tale, The (Atwood), **Supp. XIII:** 19, 20, **27–29**

"Hand of Casino, 1954, A" (Skloot), **Supp. XX: 194, 202**

"Hand of Emmagene, The" (Taylor), **Supp. V:** 314, 325–326

Hand of the Potter, The: A Tragedy in Four Acts (Dreiser), **Retro. Supp. II:** 104; **Supp. XVII:** 96

"Hands" (Anderson), **I:** 106, 107

"Hands" (Mora), **Supp. XIII:** 215

Hands of Orlac, The (M. Renard; Crewe-Jones, trans.), **Supp. XVII:** 58

Hand to Mouth (Auster), **Supp. XII:** 21

"Hand to Mouth" (Auster), **Supp. XII:** 31

Handy, Lowney, **Supp. XI:** 217, 220, 221, 225

Handy, W. C., **Supp. VIII:** 337

Handy Guide for Beggars, A (Lindsay), **Supp. I Part 2:** 376–378, 380, 382, 399

Haney, David, **Supp. XXI:** 253

"Hanged Man, A" (Cliff), **Supp. XXII:** 74

"Hanging Burley" (J. W. Miller), **Supp. XX:** 167

Hanging Garden, The (Wagoner), **Supp. IX:** 338–339

"Hanging Gardens of Tyburn, The" (Hecht), **Supp. X:** 58

"Hanging of the Crane, The" (Longfellow), **Retro. Supp. II:** 169, 171

Hanging On (Conroy), **Supp. XVI:** 69

"Hanging Pictures in Nanny's Room" (Kenyon), **Supp. VII:** 164

"Hanging the Wash" (Alvarez), **Supp. VII:** 4

"Hangman, The" (Sexton), **Supp. II Part 2:** 680, 691

Hangover Mass (X. J. Kennedy), **Supp. XV:** 165

Hangsaman (Jackson), **Supp. IX:** 116, 123, **124**

Hanh, Thich Nhat, **Supp. V:** 199

Hanks, Lucy, **III:** 587

Hanks, Nancy. *See* Lincoln, Mrs. Thomas (Nancy Hanks)

Hanley, Lynne T., **Supp. IV Part 1:** 208

"Hanlon Mountain in Mist" (J. W. Miller), **Supp. XX:** 164, 166–167

Hanna, Mark, **Supp. I Part 2:** 395

Hannah, Barry, **Supp. X:** 285; **Supp. XIX:** 209; **Supp. XXI:** 38, 118

Hannah and Her Sisters (film; Allen), **Supp. XV:** 9, 10–11

"Hannah Armstrong" (Masters), **Supp. I Part 2:** 461

"Hannah Binding Shoes" (Larcom), **Supp. XIII:** 141, 143

"Hannah Byde" (D. West), **Supp. XVIII:** 280

Hannah's House (Hearon), **Supp. VIII:** 58, **60–61**

Hanneman, Audre, **II:** 259

Hannibal Lecter, My Father (Acker), **Supp. XII:** 6

Hanoi (McCarthy), **II:** 579

"Hanoi Drifting, January 2003" (Weigl), **Supp. XIX:** 288

Hansberry, Lorraine, **Supp. IV Part 1:** 359–377; **Supp. VIII:** 329

Hanscom, Leslie, **Supp. XI:** 229

"Hansel and Gretel" (Prose), **Supp. XVI:** 256, 258

Hansen, Erik, **Supp. V:** 241

Hansen, Harry, **IV:** 366; **Supp. XXII:** 194, 277

Han-shan, **Supp. VIII:** 292

Hanson, Curtis, **Supp. XI:** 67

Han Suyin, **Supp. X:** 291

Hanzlicek, C. G., **Supp. XV:** 73

Hapgood, Charles H., II, **Supp. XXI:** 6

Hapgood, Hutchins, **Supp. XVII:** 95–108; **Supp. XXI:** 1, 3, 9, 10

Hapgood, Norman, **Supp. XXI:** 2

Hapgoods, The: Three Earnest Brothers (Marccaccio), **Supp. XVII:** 106

"Happenings: An Art of Radical Juxtaposition" (Sontag), **Supp. III Part 2:** 456

"Happenstance" (Komunyakaa), **Supp. XIII:** 130

Happenstance (Shields), **Supp. VII:** 315–318, 320, 323, 324, 326

Happersberger, Lucien, **Supp. I Part 1:** 51

"Happiest I've Been, The" (Updike), **IV:** 219

Happily Ever After (Quindlen), **Supp. XVII:** 167

"Happiness" (Oliver), **Supp. VII:** 236

"Happiness" (Sandburg), **III:** 582–583

"Happiness"(Hadas), **Supp. XXIII:** 117

Happiness of Getting It Down Right, The (Steinman, ed.), **Supp. VIII:** 172

"Happiness of the Garden Variety" (Richard), **Supp. XIX:** 212

"Happy Birthday" (Bambara), **Supp. XI:** 4

Happy Birthday (Loos), **Supp. XVI:** 193

Happy Birthday, Wanda June (Vonnegut), **Supp. II Part 2:** 759, 776–777

Happy Birthday of Death, The (Corso), **Supp. XII:** 127–129

Happy Childhood, A (Matthews), **Supp. IX:** 155, 160, **161–163**

Happy Days (Beckett), **Retro. Supp. I:** 206

Happy Days, 1880–1892 (Mencken), **III:** 100, 111, 120

"Happy End" (Simic), **Supp. VIII:** 276–277

"Happy Failure, The" (Melville), **III:** 90

Happy Families Are All Alike (Taylor), **Supp. V:** 322–323, 325

Happy Isles of Oceania, The: Paddling the Pacific (Theroux), **Supp. VIII:** 324

"Happy Journey to Trenton and Camden, The" (Wilder), **IV:** 366

"Happy Man, The" (Lethem), **Supp. XVIII:** 139

"Happy Marriage, The" (MacLeish), **III:** 15–16

Happy Marriage and Other Poems, The (MacLeish), **III:** 4

Happy to Be Here (Keillor), **Supp. XVI:** 165, 171

"Happy To Be Here" (Keillor), **Supp. XVI:** 168

"Hapworth 16, 1924" (Salinger), **III:** 552, 571–572

Haram, Karen, **Supp. XXIII:** 276

"Harbor Dawn, The" (H. Crane), **Supp. XXI:** 132, 136

"Harbor Lights" (Doty), **Supp. XI:** 122

Harcourt, Alfred, **II:** 191, 451–452; **III:** 587; **Retro. Supp. I:** 131; **Supp. XV:** 308

Harcourt, Lewis, **Supp. XX:** 232–233

Harcourt, T. A., **I:** 196

Hard Candy, a Book of Stories (T. Williams), **IV:** 383

"Hardcastle Crags" (Plath), **Supp. I Part 2:** 537

"Hard Daddy" (Hughes), **Retro. Supp. I:** 200

"Hardened Criminals, The" (Lethem), **Supp. XVIII:** 139

Harder They Fall, The (Schulberg), **Supp. XV:** 194, 201

Hard Facts (Baraka), **Supp. II Part 1:** 54, 55, 58

Hard Freight (Wright), **Supp. V:** 332, 339–340

Hard Hours, The (Hecht), **Supp. X:** 57, **59–62**, 63, 64

Hardie, Kier, **Supp. I Part 1:** 5

Harding, Walter, **IV:** 177, 178

Harding, Warren G., **I:** 486; **II:** 253, 433; **Supp. I Part 1:** 24

"Hard Kind of Courage, The" (Baldwin), **Supp. I Part 1:** 52

Hard Laughter (Lamott), **Supp. XX:** **132–133**

Hard Maple (S. and A. Warner), **Supp. XVIII:** 264

"Hard Rain's A-Gonna Fall, A" (song, Dylan), **Supp. XVIII:** 26, 29

"Hard Time Keeping Up, A" (Ellison), **Retro. Supp. II:** 124

Hard Times (Dickens), **Supp. I Part 2:** 675

"Hard Times in Elfland, The" (Lanier), **Supp. I Part 1:** 365

"Hard Traveling: *Fay*'s Deep South Landscape of Violence" (Beuka), **Supp. XXI:** 47

Hardwick, Elizabeth, **II:** 543, 554, 566; **Retro. Supp. II:** 179, 180, 183, 184, 190, 221, 228–229, 245; **Supp. I Part 1:** 196; **Supp. III Part 1:** 193–215; **Supp. IV Part 1:** 299; **Supp. V,** 319; **Supp. X,** 171; **Supp. XII:** 209; **Supp. XIV:** 89

"Hard Work 1956" (Dunn), **Supp. XI:** 147

Hardy, Barbara, **Supp. I Part 2:** 527

Hardy, Oliver, **Supp. I Part 2:** 607; **Supp. IV Part 1:** 574

Hardy, René, **Supp. III Part 1:** 235

Hardy, Thomas, **I:** 59, 103, 292, 317, 377; **II:** 181, 184–185, 186, 191–192, 271, 275, 372, 523, 542; **III:** 32, 453, 485, 508, 524; **IV:** 83, 135, 136; **Retro. Supp. I:** 141, 377–378; **Supp. I Part 1:** 217; **Supp. I Part 2:** 429, 512; **Supp. II Part 1:** 4, 26; **Supp. VIII:** 32; **Supp. IX:** 40, 78, 85, 108, 211; **Supp. X:** 228; **Supp. XI:** 311; **Supp. XIII:** 294, **Supp. XIII:** 130; **Supp. XIV:** 24; **Supp. XV:** 170; **Supp. XVIII:** 74; **Supp. XIX:** 86, 87; **Supp. XX:** 195; **Supp. XXI:** 109

Hardy and the Poetry of Truth-Seeking (Halliday), **Supp. XIX:** 82

Harjo, Joy, **Supp. IV Part 1:** 325, 404; **Supp. IV Part 2:** 499, 507; **Supp. XII:** 215–234; **Supp. XVIII:** 189

Harlan's Race (P. N. Warren), **Supp. XX:** 264–265

"Harlem" (Hughes), **Retro. Supp. I:** 194, 204; **Supp. I Part 1:** 340; **Supp. VIII:** 213

Harlem, Mecca of the New Negro (Locke), **Supp. XIV:** 201

"Harlem Dancer, The" (McKay), **Supp. X:** 134

Harlem Gallery (Tolson), **Retro. Supp. I:** 208, 209, 210

Harlem Glory: A Fragment of Aframerican Life (McKay), **Supp. X:** 132, **141–142**

Harlem: Negro Metropolis (McKay), **Supp. X:** 132, 141, 142

Harlem Renaissance Remembered, The (Bontemps, ed.), **Supp. XXII:** 7

"Harlem Runs Wild" (McKay), **Supp. X:** 140

Harlem Shadows (McKay), **Supp. X:** 131–132, 136

Harlem Underground (Lacy), **Supp. XV:** 206

"Harlequin of Dreams, The" (Lanier), **Supp. I Part 1:** 365

Harlot's Ghost (Mailer), **Retro. Supp. II:** 211–212

Harlow, Jean, **IV:** 256; **Retro. Supp. I:** 110

"Harm" (C. Frost), **Supp. XV:** 101

Harmon, William, **Retro. Supp. I:** 37; **Supp. XI:** 248

"Harmonic" (F. Barthelme), **Supp. XI:** 26

Harmonium (Stevens), **III:** 196; **IV:** 76, 77, 78, 82, 87, 89, 92; **Retro. Supp. I:** 296, 297, 299, **300–302,** 301, 302

"Harmony of the Gospels" (Taylor), **IV:** 149

Harmony of the World (C. Baxter), **Supp. XVII:** 16–17

"Harmony of the World" (C. Baxter), **Supp. XVII:** 16

Harnett, Vincent, **Supp. XV:** 198

"Harp, The" (Weigl), **Supp. XIX:** 278

Harper (film), **Supp. IV Part 2:** 473

Harper, Donna, **Retro. Supp. I:** 194, 195, 209

Harper, Frances E. Watkins, **Supp. II Part 1:** 201–202; **Supp. XVIII:** 284; **Supp. XXII:** 11

Harper, Gordon Lloyd, **Retro. Supp. II:** 23

Harper, Michael, **Supp. XV:** 74

Harper, Michael S., **Retro. Supp. II:** 116, 123

Harper, William Rainey, **Supp. I Part 2:** 631

Harper's Anthology of 20th Century Native American Poetry (Niatum, ed.), **Supp. IV Part 1:** 331

"Harriet" (Lowell), **II:** 554

Harrigan, Edward, **II:** 276; **III:** 14

Harrington, Michael, **I:** 306

Harrington, Ollie, **Supp. XVI:** 142–143

Harris, Celia, **Retro. Supp. I:** 9

Harris, Corra, **Supp. XXII:** 190, 193, 196

Harris, George, **II:** 70

Harris, George Washington, **Supp. XXII:** 193

Harris, Joel Chandler, **III:** 338; **Supp. I Part 1:** 352; **Supp. II Part 1:** 192, 201; **Supp. XIV:** 61; **Supp. XX:** 103

Harris, Judith, **Supp. XIV:** 269

Harris, Julie, **II:** 587, 601; **Supp. IX:** 125

Harris, Leonard, **Supp. XIV:** 196, 211–212

Harris, MacDonald, **Supp. XI:** 65

Harris, Marie, **Supp. IX:** 153

Harris, Peter, **Supp. X:** 206, 207

Harris, Susan K., **Supp. XV:** 269

Harris, Thomas, **Supp. XIV:** 26; **Supp. XXI:** 67, 78

Harris, Victoria Frenkel, **Supp. IV Part 1:** 68, 69

Harris, Violet J., **Supp. XXII:** 10, 13

Harris, Wilson, **Supp. XXI:** 170

Harrison, Colin, **Supp. XIV:** 26

Harrison, Hazel, **Retro. Supp. II:** 115

Harrison, Jim, **Supp. VIII: 37–56; Supp. XIX:** 125, 126

Harrison, Judy, **Supp. XXIII:** 278

Harrison, Kathryn, **Supp. X:** 191

Harrison, Ken, **Supp. IX:** 101

Harrison, Oliver (pseudonym). *See* Smith, Harrison

Harrod, Lois Marie, **Supp. XXIII:** 131–132

Harry: A Portrait (Boyce), **Supp. XVII:** 104; **Supp. XXI:** 7, **13–14**

Harryhausen, Ray, **Supp. IV Part 1:** 115

Harryman, Carla, **Supp. XV:** 344

"Harry of Nothingham" (Hugo), **Supp. VI:** 146–147

"Harry's Death" (Carver), **Supp. III Part 1:** 146

"Harsh Judgment, The" (Kunitz), **Supp. III Part 1:** 264

Hart, Albert Bushnell, **Supp. I Part 2:** 479, 480, 481

Hart, Bernard, **I:** 241, 242, 248–250, 256

Hart, Henry, **Retro. Supp. II:** 187; **Supp. XIV:** 97

Hart, James D., **Supp. XVIII:** 257

Hart, John Seely, **Supp. XVIII:** 257, 258, 264

Hart, Lorenz, **III:** 361

Hart, Moss, **Supp. IV Part 2:** 574; **Supp. XV:** 329

Hart, Pearl, **Supp. X:** 103

"Hart Crane" (Tate), **I:** 381

"Hart Crane and Poetry: A Consideration of Crane's Intense Poetics with Reference to 'The Return' " (Grossman), **Retro. Supp. II:** 83

Harte, Anna Griswold, **Supp. II Part 1:** 341

Harte, Bret, **I:** 193, 195, 203; **II:** 289; **IV:** 196; **Retro. Supp. II:** 72; **Supp. II Part 1: 335–359,** 399; **Supp. XV:** 115

Harte, Walter Blackburn, **I:** 199

Harter, Carol C., **Supp. IV Part 1:** 217

Hartigan, Grace, **Supp. XXIII:** 210, 212, 217

Hartley, David, **III:** 77

Hartley, Lois, **Supp. I Part 2:** 459, 464–465

Hartley, L. P., **Supp. I Part 1:** 293

Hartley, Marsden, **IV:** 409, 413; **Retro. Supp. I:** 430; **Supp. X:** 137; **Supp. XV:** 298

Hartman, Geoffrey, **Supp. IV Part 1:** 119; **Supp. XII:** 130, 253

Hartman, Saidiya, **Supp. XX: 154**

Harum, David, **II:** 102

"Harvard" (Lowell), **II:** 554

Harvard College in the Seventeenth Century (Morison), **Supp. I Part 2:** 485

"Harvest" (E. P. Jones), **Supp. XXII:** 141

"Harvest, The" (Hempel), **Supp. XXI:** 115, **122–123**

Harvester, The (Stratton-Porter), **Supp. XX: 211, 212, 218, 221**

"*Harvester, The:* The Natural Bounty of Gene Stratton-Porter" (Birkelo), **Supp. XX: 220–221**

"Harvesters of Night and Water" (Hogan), **Supp. IV Part 1:** 412

"Harvest Song" (Toomer), **Supp. III Part 2:** 483

Harvill Book of 20th Century Poetry in English, **Supp. X:** 55

Harvin, Emily, **Supp. XXIII:** 174

"Harv Is Plowing Now" (Updike), **Retro. Supp. I:** 318

Haselden, Elizabeth Lee, **Supp. VIII:** 125

Haskell, Mary, **Supp. XX: 115, 117**

Hass, Robert, **Supp. VI: 97–111; Supp. VIII:** 24, 28; **Supp. XI:** 142, 270; **Supp. XIV:** 83, 84; **Supp. XXI:** 60

Hassam, Childe, **Retro. Supp. II:** 136

Hassan, Ihab, **IV:** 99–100, 115; **Supp. XI:** 221

Hasse, Henry, **Supp. IV Part 1:** 102

Hasty-Pudding, The (Barlow), **Supp. II Part 1:** 74, 77–80

"Hater of Mediocrity, The" (Boulton), **Supp. XXII:** 23

Hate That Hate Produced, The (CBS documentary), **Supp. XX: 102**

Hatful of Rain, A (Gazzo), **III:** 155

Hatlen, Burton, **Supp. V:** 138, 139–140; **Supp. XXI:** 24

"Hatred"(O'Hara), **Supp. XXIII:** 212

"Hattie Bloom" (Oliver), **Supp. VII:** 232

Haunch, Paunch, and Jowl (Ornitz), **Supp. IX:** 227

"Haunted Landscape" (Ashbery), **Supp. III Part 1:** 22

Haunted Merchant, The (Briggs), **Supp. XVIII:** 2, 8

"Haunted Mind" (Simic), **Supp. VIII:** 282

"Haunted Mind, The" (Hawthorne), **II:** 230–231

"Haunted Oak, The" (Dunbar), **Supp. II Part 1:** 207, 208

"Haunted Palace, The" (Poe), **III:** 421

"Haunted Valley, The" (Bierce), **I:** 200

Haunting, The (film), **Supp. IX:** 125

Haunting of Hill House, The (Jackson), **Supp. IX:** 117, 121, 126

Hauptmann, Gerhart, **III:** 472

Haussmann, Sonja, **Supp. XIII:** 331, **Supp. XIII:** 347

"Havanna vanities come to dust in Miami" (Didion), **Supp. IV Part 1:** 210

Havel, Hippolyte, **Supp. XXI:** 4, 6

Haven, Cynthia, **Supp. XV:** 252, 264; **Supp. XXIII:** 134, 138, 139

Haven's End (Marquand), **III:** 55, 56, 63, 68

"Have You Ever Faked an Orgasm" (Peacock), **Supp. XIX:** 199

"Have You Ever Tried to Enter the Long Black Branches" (Oliver), **Supp. VII:** 247

"Having a Coke with You"(O'Hara), **Supp. XXIII:** 219

"Having Been Interstellar" (Ammons), **Supp. VII:** 25

"Having It Out With Melancholy" (Kenyon), **Supp. VII:** 171

"Having Lost My Sons, I Confront the Wreckage of the Moon: Christmas, 1960" (Wright), **Supp. III Part 2:** 600

"Having Snow" (Schwartz), **Supp. II Part 2:** 652

"Having Words"(Thompson), **Supp. XXIII:** 293–294

"Hawaii, Washington, Vermont: A Frame for the Verse" (Taggard), **Supp. XXII:** 281–282

Hawaiian Hilltop (Taggard), **Supp. XXII:** 275

Hawai'i One Summer (Kingston), **Supp. V:** 157, 160, 166, 169–170

Haweis, Stephen, **Supp. XXII:** 157, 158, 159, 161, 163, 165

"Hawk, The" (Francis), **Supp. IX:** 81

Hawke, David Freeman, **Supp. I Part 2:** 511, 516

Hawkes, John, **I:** 113; **Retro. Supp. II:** 234; **Supp. III Part 1:** 2; **Supp. V:** 40; **Supp. IX:** 212; **Supp. XVII:** 183; **Supp. XXI:** 210

Hawkins, Gary, **Supp. XXI:** 35, 39

Hawkins, William, **II:** 587

Hawk in the Rain, The (Hughes), **Retro. Supp. II:** 244; **Supp. I Part 2:** 537, 540

Hawk Is Dying, The (Crews), **Supp. XI:** 111

Hawk Moon (Shepard), **Supp. III Part 2:** 445

Hawks, Howard, **Supp. IV Part 1:** 130; **Supp. XVIII:** 148

"Hawk's Cry in Autumn, The" (Brodsky), **Supp. VIII:** 29

"Hawk's Shadow" (Glück), **Supp. V:** 85

Hawk's Well, The (Yeats), **III:** 459–460

Hawley, Adelaide, **Supp. XIV:** 207

Hawley, Joseph, **I:** 546

Hawthorne (James), **II:** 372–378; **Retro. Supp. I:** 220, 223–224

"Hawthorne" (Longfellow), **Retro. Supp. II:** 169

"Hawthorne" (Lowell), **II:** 550

Hawthorne, Julian, **II:** 225; **Supp. I Part 1:** 38; **Supp. XV:** 274

Hawthorne, Nathaniel, **I:** 106, 204, 211, 340, 355, 363, 384, 413, 458, 561, 562; **II:** 7, 8, 40, 60, 63, 74, 89, 127–128, 138, 142, 198, 223–246, 255, 259, 264, 267, 272, 274, 277, 281, 282, 295, 307, 309, 311, 313, 322, 324, 326, 402, 408, 446, 501, 545; **III:** 51, 81–82, 83, 84, 85, 87, 88, 91, 92, 113, 316, 359, 412, 415, 421, 438, 453, 454, 507, 565, 572; **IV:** 2, 4, 167, 172, 179, 194, 333, 345, 453; **Retro. Supp. I:** 1, 53, 59, 62, 63, 91, 145–167, 215, 218, 220, 223, 248–249, 252, 257, 258, 330, 331, 365; **Retro. Supp. II:** 136, 142, 153, 156–157, 158, 159, 187, 221; **Supp. I Part 1:** 38, 188, 197, 317, 372; **Supp. I Part 2:** 420, 421, 545, 579, 580, 582, 587, 595, 596; **Supp. III Part 2:** 501; **Supp. IV Part 1:** 80, 127, 297; **Supp. IV Part 2:** 463, 596; **Supp. V:** 152; **Supp. VIII:** 103, 105, 108, 153, 201; **Supp. IX:** 114; **Supp. X:** 78; **Supp. XI:** 51, 78; **Supp. XII:** 26; **Supp. XIII:** 102; **Supp. XIV:** 48; **Supp. XV:** 269, 272, 282; **Supp. XVI:** 83, 84, 157; **Supp. XVII:** 42; **Supp. XVIII:** 258, 260; **Supp. XXI:** 201; **Supp. XXIII:** 161, 190, 290

Hawthorne, Mrs. Nathaniel (Sophia Peabody), **II:** 224, 244; **III:** 75, 86

Hawthorne, Rose, **II:** 225

Hawthorne, Una, **II:** 225

"Hawthorne and His Mosses" (Melville), **Retro. Supp. I:** 254; **Supp. XIV:** 48

"Hawthorne Aspect [of Henry James], The" (Eliot), **Retro. Supp. I:** 63

"Hawthorne in Solitude" (Cowley), **Supp. II Part 1:** 143

Hay, John, **I:** 1, 10, 12, 14–15; **Supp. I Part 1:** 352

Hay, Mrs. John, **I:** 14

Hay, Sara Henderson, **Supp. XIV:** 119–135

Hayakawa, S. I., **I:** 448; **Supp. I Part 1:** 315; **Supp. XV:** 176

Hayden, Robert, **Supp. II Part 1:** 361–383; **Supp. IV Part 1:** 169; **Supp. XIII:** 115, 127; **Supp. XIV:** 119, 123

Hayden, Sterling, **Supp. XI:** 304

Haydn, Hiram, **IV:** 100, 358

Hayduke Lives! (Abbey), **Supp. XIII:** 16

Hayek, Friedrich A. von, **Supp. IV Part 2:** 524

Hayes, Helen, **Supp. XVI:** 193, 195

Hayes, Ira, **Supp. IV Part 1:** 326

Hayes, Richard, **Supp. V:** 320

Hayes, Rutherford B., **Supp. I Part 2:** 419

Hayford, James, **Supp. XXII:** 204, 218

Haygood, Wil, **Supp. VIII:** 79

"Haying While the Sun Shines" (L. I. Wilder), **Supp. XXII:** 290

Hayne, Paul Hamilton, **Supp. I Part 1:** 352, 354, 355, 360, 372

Haynes, Todd, **Supp. XVIII:** 23

Haynes-Smith, William, **Supp. XX: 231, 232, 233**

Hayward, Florence, **Retro. Supp. II:** 65

Hayward, John, **Retro. Supp. I:** 67

Hayward, Leland, **Supp. XIX:** 250

Haywood, "Big" Bill, **I:** 483; **Supp. V:** 286; **Supp. XXIII:** 162

Hazan, Joe, **Supp. XXIII:** 212

Hazard, Grace, **II:** 530

Hazard of Fortunes, A (Howells), **Retro. Supp. II:** 288

Hazard of New Fortunes, A (Howells), **II:** 275, 276, 286–297, 290

Hazel, Robert, **Supp. VIII:** 137, 138

Hazen, General W. B., **I:** 192, 193

Hazlitt, Henry, **Supp. IV Part 2:** 524

Hazlitt, William, **I:** 58, 378; **II:** 315; **Supp. XXI:** 205

Hazmat (McClatchy), **Supp. XII: 265–270**

Hazo, Samuel, **I:** 386; **Supp. XIV:** 123, 124

Hazzard, Shirley, **Supp. VIII:** 151

H.D. *See* Doolittle, Hilda

"He" (Porter), **III:** 434, 435

"Head and Shoulders" (Fitzgerald), **Retro. Supp. I:** 101

Headhunter (Findley), **Supp. XX: 57–59, 60, 61**

"Head-Hunter, The" (O. Henry), **Supp. II Part 1:** 403

"Headless Hawk, The" (Capote), **Supp. III Part 1:** 124

Headlines (T. Williams), **IV:** 381

Headlong Hall (Peacock), **Supp. I Part 1:** 307

Headmaster, The (McPhee), **Supp. III Part 1:** 291, 294, 298

"Head of Joaquín Murrieta, The" (Rodriguez), **Supp. XIV:** 303

Headsman, The (Cooper), **I:** 345–346

Heads of Grain (al-Sanábil) (Gibran), **Supp. XX: 124**

"Headwaters" (Momaday), **Supp. IV Part 2:** 486

"Head Wound" (Halliday), **Supp. XIX:** 92

Healy, Eloise Klein, **Supp. XI:** 121, 124, 126, 127, 129, 137

Healy, Tim, **II:** 129, 137

Heaney, Sally, **Supp. XVII:** 241

Heaney, Seamus, **Retro. Supp. II:** 245; **Supp. IX:** 41, 42; **Supp. X:** 67, 122; **Supp. XI:** 249; **Supp. XV:** 256; **Supp. XXI:** 54, 243

"Heard through the Walls of the Race-track Glen Motel" (X. J. Kennedy), **Supp. XV:** 170

Hearn, Lafcadio, **I:** 211; **II:** 311

Hearon, Shelby, **Supp. VIII: 57–72**

Hearst, Patty, **Supp. IV Part 1:** 195

Hearst, William Randolph, **I:** 198, 207, 208; **IV:** 298

Heart and Perimeter (Bierds), **Supp. XVII: 28–29**

"Heart and the Lyre, The" (Bogan), **Supp. III Part 1:** 65

"Heart as Origami, The (Hirshfield), **Supp. XXIII:** 132

"Heartbeat" (Harjo), **Supp. XII:** 221–222

Heartbreak Hotel (Siddons), **Supp. XXII:** 239, 241, 242

Heartbreak Kid, The (film), **Supp. IV Part 2:** 575, 589

"Heart Failure"(Schott), **Supp. XXIII:** 252

Heart for the Gods of Mexico, A (Aiken), **I:** 54

"Hear the Nightingale Sing" (Gordon), **II:** 200

Hear the Wind Blow (Sanders), **Supp. XVI:** 268

Heart is a Lonely Hunter, The (McCullers), **II:** 586, 588–593, 604, 605

Heart of a Woman, The (Angelou), **Supp. IV Part 1:** 2, 5, 7–9, 9, 14, 17
Heart of Darkness (Conrad), **Retro. Supp. II:** 292; **Supp. V:** 249, 311; **Supp. VIII:** 4, 316; **Supp. XIX:** 28; **Supp. XX:** 18, 57–58
"Heart of Darkness" (Conrad), **I:** 575, 578; **II:** 595; **Supp. XVI:** 212
Heart of Darkness (Didion), **Supp. IV Part 1:** 207
Heart of Dixie (film), **Supp. XXII:** 239, 241
Heart of Haiku, The (Hirshfield), **Supp. XXIII:** 137–138
Heart of Happy Hollow, The (Dunbar), **Supp. II Part 1:** 214
Heart of Knowledge, The: American Indians on the Bomb (Gunn Allen and Caputi, eds.), **Supp. IV Part 1:** 334–335
"Heart of Knowledge, The: Nuclear Themes in Native American Thought and Literature" (Caputi), **Supp. IV Part 1:** 335
Heart of the Earth (Moraga), **Supp. XXIII:** 196
"Heart of the Park, The " (O'Connor), **Retro. Supp. II:** 225
Heart of the West (O. Henry), **Supp. II Part 1:** 410
"Hearts, The" (Pinsky), **Supp. VI:** 245–247, 248
"'Hearts and Flowers' " (MacLeish), **III:** 8
"Hearts and Heads" (Ransom), **Supp. I Part 1:** 373
"Heart's Graveyard Shift, The" (Komunyakaa), **Supp. XIII:** 120
Heart-Shape in the Dust (Hayden), **Supp. II Part 1:** 365, 366
Heart's Needle (Snodgrass), **I:** 400
"Heart's Needle" (Snodgrass), **Supp. VI:** 311–313, 320
"Hearts of Oak" (Rowson), **Supp. XV:** 243
"Heart Songs" (Proulx), **Supp. VII:** 254
Heart Songs and Other Stories (Proulx), **Supp. VII:** 252–256, 261
Heart to Artemis, The (Bryher), **Supp. I Part 1:** 259
Heartwood (Burke), **Supp. XIV:** 35
Heath, Shirley, **Supp. XX: 90**
Heath Anthology of American Literature, The, **Supp. IX:** 4; **Supp. XV:** 270, 313
Heathcote, Anne. *See* De Lancey, Mrs. James
"Heathen Chinee, The" (Harte), **Supp. II Part 1:** 350–351, 352
Heathen Days, 1890–1936 (Mencken), **III:** 100, 111
Heath-Stubbs, John, **Supp. XV:** 153
Heat's On, The (C. Himes), **Supp. XVI:** 143, 144
"Heaven" (Dunn), **Supp. XI:** 154
"Heaven" (Levine), **Supp. V:** 182
"Heaven" (Patchett), **Supp. XII:** 309
Heaven and Earth: A Cosmology (Goldbarth), **Supp. XII: 187**
"Heaven and Earth in Jest" (Dillard), **Supp. VI:** 24, 28

"Heaven as Anus" (Kumin), **Supp. IV Part 2:** 448
Heavenly Conversation, The (Mather), **Supp. II Part 2:** 460
"Heavenly Feast, The" (Schnackenberg), **Supp. XV:** 257, 259
Heavens (Untermeyer), **Supp. XV:** 306
Heavens and Earth (Benét), **Supp. XI:** 44
Heaven's Coast (Doty), **Supp. XI:** 119, 121, **129–130,** 134; **Supp. XXIII:** 126
Heaven's Prisoners (Burke), **Supp. XIV:** 23, 29
"Heavy Angel, The" (Everwine), **Supp. XV:** 80
"Heavy Bear Who Goes with Me, The" (Schwartz), **Supp. II Part 2:** 646
"Heavy Trash" (Halliday), **Supp. XIX:** 92, 93
Hebert, Ernest, **Supp. XXII:** 207
"He Came Also Still" (Zukofsky), **Supp. III Part 2:** 612
Hecht, Anthony, **IV:** 138; **Supp. III Part 2:** 541, 561; **Supp. X: 55–75;** **Supp. XII:** 269–270; **Supp. XV:** 251, 256
Hecht, Ben, **I:** 103; **II:** 42; **Supp. I Part 2:** 646; **Supp. XI:** 307; **Supp. XIII:** 106
Hecht, S. Theodore, **Supp. III Part 2:** 614
Heckewelder, John, **II:** 503
"Hedge Island" (Lowell), **II:** 524
Hedges, William I., **II:** 311–312
"He 'Digesteth Harde Yron' " (Moore), **Supp. IV Part 2:** 454
Hedin, Robert, **Supp. XII:** 200, 202
Hedylus (Doolittle), **Supp. I Part 1:** 259, 270
"Heel & Toe To the End" (W. C. Williams), **Retro. Supp. I:** 430
Heffernan, Michael, **Supp. XII:** 177
"HEGEL" (Baraka), **Supp. II Part 1:** 53
Hegel, Georg Wilhelm Friedrich, **I:** 265; **II:** 358; **III:** 262, 308–309, 480, 481, 487, 607; **IV:** 86, 333, 453; **Supp. I Part 2:** 633, 635, 640, 645; **Supp. XVI:** 289
"Hegemony of Race, The" (Du Bois), **Supp. II Part 1:** 181
Hegger, Grace Livingston. *See* Lewis, Mrs. Sinclair (Grace Livingston Hegger)
"He Had Spent His Youth Dreaming" (Dobyns), **Supp. XIII:** 90
Heidegger, Martin, **II:** 362, 363; **III:** 292; **IV:** 491; **Retro. Supp. II:** 87; **Supp. V:** 267; **Supp. VIII:** 9; **Supp. XVI:** 283, 288
Heidenmauer, The (Cooper), **I:** 345–346
Heidi Chronicles, The (Wasserstein), **Supp. IV Part 1:** 309; **Supp. XV:** 319, **325–327**
"Height of the Ridiculous, The" (Holmes), **Supp. I Part 1:** 302
Heilbroner, Robert, **Supp. I Part 2:** 644, 648, 650
Heilbrun, Carolyn G., **Supp. IX:** 66; **Supp. XI:** 208; **Supp. XIV:** 161, 163; **Supp. XX: 108**

Heilman, Robert Bechtold, **Supp. XIV:** 11, 12
Heilpern, John, **Supp. XIV:** 242
Heim, Michael, **Supp. V:** 209
Heine, Heinrich, **II:** 272, 273, 277, 281, 282, 387, 544; **IV:** 5; **Supp. XV:** 293, 299; **Supp. XVI:** 188
Heineman, Frank, **Supp. III Part 2:** 619
Heinemann, Larry, **Supp. XXII: 103–117**
Heinlein, Robert, **Supp. IV Part 1:** 102; **Supp. XVI:** 122; **Supp. XVIII:** 149
Heinz, Helen. *See* Tate, Mrs. Allen (Helen Heinz)
Heiress, The (film), **Retro. Supp. I:** 222
"Heirs" (Nye), **Supp. XIII:** 284
"He Is Not Worth the Trouble" (Rowson), **Supp. XV:** 240
"He Knew" (C. Himes), **Supp. XVI:** 137
"Helas" (Creeley), **Supp. IV Part 1:** 150, 158
Helburn, Theresa, **IV:** 381
Heldreth, Leonard, **Supp. V:** 151
"Helen" (Lowell), **II:** 544
"Helen, Thy Beauty Is to Me" (Fante), **Supp. XI:** 169
"Helen: A Courtship" (Faulkner), **Retro. Supp. I:** 81
"Helen I Love You" (Farrell), **II:** 28, 45
Helen in Egypt (Doolittle), **Supp. I Part 1:** 260, 272, 273, 274; **Supp. XV:** 264
Helen Keller: Sketch for a Portrait (Brooks), **I:** 254
"Helen of Tyre" (Longfellow), **II:** 496
Heliodora (Doolittle), **Supp. I Part 1:** 266
"He Lives On the Landing" (Espaillat), **Supp. XXI:** 108
"Helix" (Sobin), **Supp. XVI:** 283
Hellbox (O'Hara), **III:** 361
Helle, Anita, **Supp. XXIII:** 117
Heller, Joseph, **III:** 2, 258; **IV:** 98; **Retro. Supp. II:** 324; **Supp. I Part 1:** 196; **Supp. IV Part 1: 379–396;** **Supp. V:** 244; **Supp. VIII:** 245; **Supp. XI:** 307; **Supp. XII:** 167–168; **Supp. XVI:** 322; **Supp. XVII:** 139; **Supp. XXIII:** 100
"Hell-Heaven" (Lahiri), **Supp. XXI: 181–183,** 183, 184–186, 188
Hellman, Lillian, **I:** 28; **III:** 28; **Supp. I Part 1: 276–298;** **Supp. IV Part 1:** 1, 12, 83, 353, 355, 356; **Supp. VIII:** 243; **Supp. IX:** 196, 198, 200–201, 204
Hellmann, Lillian, **Retro. Supp. II:** 327
Hello (Creeley), **Supp. IV Part 1:** 155, 157
"Hello, Hello Henry" (Kumin), **Supp. IV Part 2:** 446
"Hello, Stranger" (Capote), **Supp. III Part 1:** 120
Hello Dolly! (musical play), **IV:** 357
Hellyer, John, **Supp. I Part 2:** 468
Helm, Bob, **Supp. XV:** 147
Helm, Levon, **Supp. XVIII:** 26
Helmets (Dickey), **Supp. IV Part 1:** 175, 178, 180
"Helmsman, The" (Doolittle), **Supp. I Part 1:** 266
"Help" (Barth), **I:** 139

"Help Her to Believe" (Olsen). *See* "I Stand There Ironing" (Olsen)
Helprin, Mark, **Supp. XIX:** 142
"Helsinki Window" (Creeley), **Supp. IV Part 1:** 158
"Hema and Kaushik" (Lahiri), **Supp. XXI:** 183, 188
Hemenway, Robert E., **Supp. IV Part 1:** 6
Hemingway, Dr. Clarence Edwards, **II:** 248, 259
Hemingway, Ernest, **I:** 28, 64, 97, 99, 105, 107, 117, 150, 162, 190, 211, 221, 288, 289, 295, 367, 374, 378, 421, 423, 445, 476, 477, 478, 482, 484–485, 487, 488, 489, 491, 495, 504, 517; **II:** 27, 44, 51, 58, 68–69, 78, 90, 97, 127, 206, **247–270,** 289, 424, 431, 456, 457, 458–459, 482, 560, 600; **III:** 2, 18, 20, 35, 36, 37, 40, 61, 108, 220, 334, 363, 364, 382, 453, 454, 471–472, 476, 551, 575, 576, 584; **IV:** 27, 28, 33, 34, 35, 42, 49, 97, 108, 122, 126, 138, 190, 191, 201, 216, 217, 257, 297, 363, 404, 427, 433, 451; **Retro. Supp. I:** 74, 98, 108, 111, 112, 113, 115, **169–191,** 215, 292, 359, 418; **Retro. Supp. II:** 19, 24, 30, 68, 115, 123; **Supp. I Part 2:** 621, 658, 678; **Supp. II Part 1:** 221; **Supp. III Part 1:** 146; **Supp. III Part 2:** 617; **Supp. IV Part 1:** 48, 102, 123, 197, 236, 342, 343, 344, 348, 350, 352, 380–381, 383; **Supp. IV Part 2:** 463, 468, 502, 607, 679, 680, 681, 689, 692; **Supp. V:** 237, 240, 244, 250, 336; **Supp. VIII:** 40, 101, 105, 179, 182, 183, 188, 189, 196; **Supp. IX:** 16, 57, 58, 94, 106, 260, 262; **Supp. X:** 137, 167, 223, 225; **Supp. XI:** 214, 221; **Supp. XIII:** 96, 255, 270; **Supp. XIV:** 24, 83; **Supp. XV:** 69, 135; **Supp. XVI:** 203, 205–206, 208, 210, 233, 236–237, 281–282; **Supp. XVII:** 4, 105, 107, 137, 228, 229; **Supp. XVIII:** 74, 90, 102; **Supp. XIX:** 131, 154, 157, 246; **Supp. XX: 45, 74, 76; Supp. XXI:** 7, 8, 36, 262; **Supp. XXIII:** 4, 68, 166, 174, 275, 299
Hemingway, Mrs. Ernest (Hadley Richardson), **II:** 257, 260, 263
Hemingway, Mrs. Ernest (Martha Gellhorn), **II:** 260
Hemingway, Mrs. Ernest (Mary Welsh), **II:** 257, 260
Hemingway, Mrs. Ernest (Pauline Pfeiffer), **II:** 260
"Hemingway in Paris" (Cowley), **Supp. II Part 1:** 144
"Hemingway Story, A" (Dubus), **Supp. VII:** 91
"Hemingway: The Old Lion" (Cowley), **Supp. II Part 1:** 143
"Hemp, The" (Benét), **Supp. XI:** 44
Hempel, Amy, **Supp. XIX:** 209; **Supp. XXI: 115–128**
"Henchman, The" (Whittier), **Supp. I Part 2:** 696

Henderson, Alice Corbin, **Supp. I Part 2:** 387; **Supp. XV:** 302–303
Henderson, Darwin L., **Supp. XIII:** 213, 221–222
Henderson, Jane, **Supp. VIII:** 87; **Supp. XX: 84**
Henderson, Katherine, **Supp. IV Part 1:** 203, 207
Henderson, Linda. *See* Hogan, Linda
Henderson, Robert W., **Supp. VIII:** 124
Henderson, Stephen, **Supp. IV Part 1:** 365
Henderson, the Rain King (Bellow), **I:** 144, 147, 148, 152, 153, 154, 155, 158, 160, 161, 162–163; **Retro. Supp. II:** 19, **24–25,** 30
"Hen Flower, The" (Kinnell), **Supp. III Part 1:** 247–248
Henie, Sonja, **Supp. XII:** 165
Henkin, Joshua, **Supp. XXII:** 216
Henle, James, **II:** 26, 30, 38, 41; **Supp. IX:** 2
Henley, Beth, **Supp. XXI:** 145
Hennesy, Dale, **Supp. XV:** 5
Henninger, Katherine, **Supp. XXI:** 253
Henri, Robert, **IV:** 411; **Supp. I Part 2:** 376
Henry, Arthur, **I:** 515; **Retro. Supp. II:** 97
Henry, DeWitt, **Supp. XI:** 342
Henry, O., **I:** 201; **III:** 5; **Supp. I Part 2:** 390, 462; **Supp. II Part 1: 385–412; Supp. XV:** 40
Henry, Robert, **Retro. Supp. II:** 103
Henry, William A., III, **Supp. IV Part 2:** 574
Henry and Clara (Mallon), **Supp. XIX:** 132, **136–137,** 139, 141
Henry and June (film), **Supp. X:** 186
Henry and June: From the Unexpurgated Diary of Anaïs Nin, **Supp. X:** 184, 185, 187, 194
Henry Holt and Company, **Retro. Supp. I:** 121, 131, 133, 136
Henry IV (Shakespeare), **III:** 166; **Supp. VIII:** 164
"Henry James, Jr." (Howells), **II:** 289; **Retro. Supp. I:** 220
"Henry James and the Art of Teaching" (Rowe), **Retro. Supp. I:** 216
"Henry Manley, Living Alone, Keeps Time" (Kumin), **Supp. IV Part 2:** 451
"Henry Manley Looks Back" (Kumin), **Supp. IV Part 2:** 451
"Henry Manley" poems (Kumin), **Supp. IV Part 2:** 446
Henry Miller Reader, The (Durrell, ed.), **III:** 175, 190
"Henry's Confession" (Berryman), **I:** 186
Henry VIII (Shakespeare), **Supp. IX:** 235
Henslee, **Supp. IV Part 1:** 217
Henson, Josiah, **Supp. I Part 2:** 589
Hentoff, Margot, **Supp. IV Part 1:** 205
Hentz, Caroline Lee, **Supp. I Part 2:** 584
Henze, Hans Werner, **Supp. II Part 1:** 24
"He of the Assembly" (Bowles), **Supp. IV Part 1:** 90
Hepburn, Katharine, **Supp. IX:** 189; **Supp. XI:** 17

Heraclitus, **II:** 1, 163; **IV:** 86
Herakles: A Play in Verse (MacLeish), **III:** 21, 22
Herald of the Autochthonic Spirit (Corso), **Supp. XII:** 134–136
He Ran All the Way (film), **Supp. XVII:** 63
Herberg, Will, **III:** 291
Herbert, Edward, **II:** 11
Herbert, Francis (pseudonym), *See* Bryant, William Cullen
Herbert, George, **II:** 12; **IV:** 141, 145, 146, 151, 153, 156, 165; **Retro. Supp. II:** 40; **Supp. I Part 1:** 80, 107, 108, 122; **Supp. IV Part 2:** 646; **Supp. XV:** 92, 212, 251; **Supp. XXI:** 109
Herbert, Zbigniew, **Supp. VIII:** 20
Herbert Huncke Reader, The (Schafer, ed.), **Supp. XIV:** 137, 138, 139, 140, 145, 147, 150, 151–152
Herbert of Cherbury, Lord, **II:** 108
"Herbert White" (Bidart), **Supp. XV:** 24, 27
Herbst, Josephine, **Retro. Supp. II:** 325, 328; **Supp. XIII:** 295
"Her Choice" (Larcom), **Supp. XIII:** 144
"Her Dead Brother" (Lowell), **Retro. Supp. II:** 188
"Her Dream Is of the Sea" (Ríos), **Supp. IV Part 2:** 546
"Here" (Kenyon), **Supp. VII:** 164
Here and Beyond (Wharton), **Retro. Supp. I:** 382
Here and Now (Levertov), **Supp. III Part 1:** 275, 276
"Here and There" (Wallace), **Supp. X:** 305–306
Here Comes the Mystery Man (Sanders), **Supp. XVI:** 269
Heredia, Juanita, **Supp. XI:** 185, 190
Heredity and Variation (Lock), **Retro. Supp. I:** 375
Heredity: A Psychological Study of Its Phenomena, Laws, Causes, and Consequences (Ribot), **Supp. XX: 238**
"Here Inside My Forehead" (Rasmussen; Nelson and Espeland, trans.), **Supp. XVIII:** 180
Here is Your War (Pyle), **Supp. XVII:** 61
Here Let Us Feast (M. F. K. Fisher), **Supp. XVII:** 86, 87
Here Lies (Parker), **Supp. IX:** 192
Herendeen, Anne, **Supp. XXII:** 275
Here on Earth (Hoffman), **Supp. X:** 77, 89
Heresy and the Ideal: On Contemporary Poetry (Baker), **Supp. XI:** 142
"Here to Learn" (Bowles), **Supp. IV Part 1:** 93
"Here to Yonder" (Hughes), **Retro. Supp. I:** 205
"Her Father's Letters" (Milburn), **Supp. XI:** 242
"Her Favorite Story" (Richard), **Supp. XIX:** 211, 212
Herford, Reverend Brooke, **I:** 471
Herford, Will, **Supp. XXII:** 275
"Her Game" (Skloot), **Supp. XX: 196, 202**

Hergesheimer, Joseph, **Supp. I Part 2:** 620; **Supp. XVI:** 187

"Heritage" (Cullen), **Supp. IV Part 1:** 164–165, 168, 170, 171

"Heritage" (Hogan), **Supp. IV Part 1:** 413

"Her Kind" (Sexton), **Supp. II Part 2:** 687

Herland (Gilman), **Supp. XI:** 208–209

Herman, Florence. *See* Williams, Mrs. William Carlos (Florence Herman)

Herman, Jan, **Supp. XIV:** 150–151

Herman, William (pseudonym). *See* Bierce, Ambrose

"Her Management" (Swenson), **Supp. IV Part 2:** 642

"Herman Melville" (Auden), **Supp. II Part 1:** 14

Herman Melville (Mumford), **Supp. II Part 2:** 471, 476, 489–491

"Hermes of the Ways" (Doolittle), **Supp. I Part 1:** 266

"Hermes: Port Authority: His Song" (Di Piero), **Supp. XIX:** 47

Hermetic Definition (Doolittle), **Supp. I Part 1:** 271, 272, 273, 274

"Hermitage, The" (Haines), **Supp. XII:** 205–206

Hermit and the Wild Woman, The (Wharton), **IV:** 315; **Retro. Supp. I:** 371

"Hermit and the Wild Woman, The" (Wharton), **Retro. Supp. I:** 372

"Hermit Meets the Skunk, The" (Kumin), **Supp. IV Part 2:** 447

Hermit of 69th Street, The: The Working Papers or Norbert Kosky (Kosinski), **Supp. VII:** 215, 216, 223, 226–227

"Hermit of Saba, The" (Freneau), **Supp. II Part 1:** 259

"Hermit Picks Berries, The" (Kumin), **Supp. IV Part 2:** 447

Hermit's Story, The (Bass), **Supp. XVI:** 23–24

"Hermit Thrush, A" (Clampitt), **Supp. IX:** 40

Hernández, Miguel, **Supp. V:** 194; **Supp. XIII:** 315, 323; **Supp. XXI:** 104

Herne, James A., **II:** 276; **Supp. II Part 1:** 198

Hernton, Calvin, **Supp. X:** 240

"Hero, The" (Moore), **III:** 200, 211, 212

Hero, The: A Study in Tradition, Myth, and Drama (Raglan), **I:** 135; **Supp. XIX:** 147

Hero and the Blues, The (Murray), **Supp. XIX:** 153, 154

Hérodiade (Mallarmé), **I:** 66

Herodotus, **Supp. I Part 2:** 405

Heroes, The (Ashbery), **Supp. III Part 1:** 3

Heroes and Saints (Moraga), **Supp. XXIII:** 195, 196, 197, **203–204**

Heroes and Saints and Other Plays (Moraga), **Supp. XXIII:** 197

Hero in America, The (Van Doren), **II:** 103

"Heroines of Nature: Four Women Respond to the American Landscape" (Norwood), **Supp. IX:** 24

"Heron, The" (Roethke), **III:** 540–541

"Her One Bad Eye" (Karr), **Supp. XI:** 244

"Her Own People" (Warren), **IV:** 253

Her Place in These Designs (Espaillat), **Supp. XXI:** 99, 104

"Her Quaint Honour" (Gordon), **II:** 196, 199, 200

Herr, Michael, **Supp. XI:** 245; **Supp. XIX:** 17

Herreshoff, David, **Supp. XIX:** 265

Herrick, Robert, **II:** 11, 18, 444; **III:** 463, 592; **IV:** 453; **Retro. Supp. I:** 319; **Retro. Supp. II:** 101; **Supp. I Part 2:** 646; **Supp. XIII:** 334; **Supp. XIV:** 8, 9; **Supp. XV:** 155; **Supp. XXI:** 14

Herrmann, John, **Retro. Supp. II:** 328; **Supp. XXII:** 277

Herron, George, **Supp. I Part 1:** 7

"Hers" (column, Prose), **Supp. XVI:** 254

Herschdorfer, Helen, **Supp. XXI:** 262

Herschel, Sir John, **Supp. I Part 1:** 314

"Her Sense of Timing" (Elkin), **Supp. VI:** 56, 58

Hersey, John, **IV:** 4; **Supp. I Part 1:** 196; **Supp. XVI:** 105–106; **Supp. XX:** 251

"Her Sweet turn to leave the Homestead" (Dickinson), **Retro. Supp. I:** 44

"Her Untold Story"(Thompson), **Supp. XXIII:** 301

Herzog (Bellow), **I:** 144, 147, 149, 150, 152, 153, 154, 155, 156, 157, 158, 159–160; **Retro. Supp. II:** 19, **26–27;** **Supp. IV Part 1:** 30; **Supp. XIX:** 157

Herzog, Tobey C., **Supp. XXII:** 116

Heschel, Abraham, **Supp. XXI:** 110, 112

Hesford, Walter A., **Supp. XV:** 215, 217, 218

"He/She" (Dunn), **Supp. XI:** 149

"Hesitation Blues" (Hughes), **Retro. Supp. I:** 211

He Sleeps (McKnight), **Supp. XX: 151, 152–155, 158**

"He Sleeps" (McKnight), **Supp. XX: 152, 155**

Hesse, Hermann, **Supp. V:** 208

Hester, Carolyn, **Supp. XVIII:** 24

"Hetch Hetchy Valley" (Muir), **Supp. IX:** 185

He Who Gets Slapped (Andreyev), **II:** 425

"He Who Spits at the Sky" (Stegner), **Supp. IV Part 2:** 605

"He Will Not Leave a Note" (Ríos), **Supp. IV Part 2:** 548

Hewitt, James, **Supp. XV:** 240

Hewlett, Maurice, **I:** 359

Heyen, William, **Supp. XIII:** 285, 344; **Supp. XV:** 212

"Hey! Hey!" (Hughes), **Supp. I Part 1:** 327–328

Hey Rub-a-Dub-Dub (Dreiser), **I:** 515; **II:** 26; **Retro. Supp. II:** 104, 105, 108

"Hey Sailor, What Ship?" (Olsen), **Supp. XIII:** 293, 294, 298, **299**

Heyward, DuBose, **Supp. XVIII:** 281; **Supp. XIX:** 78

Hiawatha (Longfellow), **Supp. I Part 1:** 79; **Supp. III Part 2:** 609, 610; **Supp. XXI:** 53

"Hibernaculum" (Ammons), **Supp. VII:** 26–27

Hichborn, Philip, **Supp. I Part 2:** 707, 708

Hichborn, Mrs. Philip. *See* Wylie, Elinor

"Hic Jacet" (W. C. Williams), **Retro. Supp. I:** 414

Hickok, Guy, **Supp. XXI:** 7

Hickok, James Butler ("Wild Bill"), **Supp. V:** 229, 230

Hicks, Granville, **I:** 254, 259, 374; **II:** 26; **III:** 342, 355, 452; **Supp. I Part 1:** 361; **Supp. I Part 2:** 609; **Supp. IV Part 1:** 22; **Supp. IV Part 2:** 526; **Supp. VIII:** 96, 124; **Supp. XII:** 250; **Supp. XIII:** 263; **Supp. XXI:** 276; **Supp. XXII:** 279

Hicks, Sally, **Supp. XXI:** 255

Hicok, Bethany, **Retro. Supp. II:** 39

"Hidden" (Nye), **Supp. XIII:** 283

"Hidden Gardens" (Capote), **Supp. III Part 1:** 125

Hidden Law, The (Hecht), **Supp. X:** 58

"Hidden Name and Complex Fate" (Ellison), **Supp. II Part 1:** 245

Hiddenness, Uncertainty, Surprise: Three Generative Energies of Poetry (Hirshfield), **Supp. XXIII:** 137

Hidden Wound, The (Berry), **Supp. X:** 23, 25, 26–27, 29, 34, 35

"Hide-and-Seek" (Francis), **Supp. IX:** 81

"Hiding" (Minot), **Supp. VI:** 203, 206

Hiding Place (Wideman), **Supp. X:** 320, 321, 327, 329, 331–332, 333

"Hidin' Out in Honky Heaven: On Race Relations in Vermont" (Budbill), **Supp. XIX:** 5

Hienger, Jorg, **Supp. IV Part 1:** 106

Hieronymus Bosch (De Tolnay), **Supp. XXII:** 255

Higgins, George, **Supp. IV Part 1:** 356

Higginson, Thomas Wentworth, **I:** 451–452, 453, 454, 456, 458, 459, 463, 464, 465, 470; **Retro. Supp. I:** 26, 31, 33, 35, 39, 40; **Supp. I Part 1:** 307, 371; **Supp. IV Part 2:** 430

Higgs, Robert, **Supp. XX: 166**

"High Bridge above the Tagus River at Toledo, The" (W. C. Williams), **Retro. Supp. I:** 429

"High Dive: A Variant" (Kumin), **Supp. IV Part 2:** 442

"High Diver" (Francis), **Supp. IX:** 82

"Higher Keys, The" (Merrill), **Supp. III Part 1:** 335–336

Higher Learning in America, The (Veblen), **Supp. I Part 2:** 630, 631, 641, 642

Highet, Gilbert, **Supp. I Part 1:** 268

"High Heav'd my breast"(J. Schoolcraft), **Supp. XXIII:** 235

High Noon (film), **Supp. V:** 46

"High on Sadness" (Komunyakaa), **Supp. XIII:** 114

"High School Senior" (Olds), **Supp. X:** 212

Highsmith, Patricia, **Supp. IV Part 1:** 79, 94, 132; **Supp. XXII:** 136

"High Tide" (Marquand), **III:** 56

High Tide in Tucson: Essays from Now or Never (Kingsolver), **Supp. VII:** 198, 201, 209

"High-Toned Old Christian Woman, A" (Stevens), **Retro. Supp. I:** 301

"High Water" (Mosher), **Supp. XXII:** 205, 211

"Highway, The" (Merwin), **Supp. III Part 1:** 346

Highway 61 Revisited (album, Dylan), **Supp. XVIII:** 20, 27, 30, 32

"Highway 61 Revisited" (song, Dylan), **Supp. XVIII:** 30

"Highway 99E from Chico" (Carver), **Supp. III Part 1:** 136

"Highway Apple Trees" (Espaillat), **Supp. XXI:** 100–102

High Window, The (Chandler), **Supp. IV Part 1:** 127–129, 130, 131

"High Yaller" (R. Fisher), **Supp. XIX:** 72

Hijuelos, Oscar, **Supp. IV Part 1:** 54; **Supp. VIII:** 73–91

Hike and the Aeroplane (Lewis), **II:** 440–441

Hilberg, Raul, **Supp. V:** 267

Hildebrand, Al, **III:** 118

Hiler, Hilaire, **Retro. Supp. II:** 327; **Supp. III Part 2:** 617

"Hill, A" (Hecht), **Supp. X:** 59–60, 63

Hill, Abram, **Supp. XV:** 194

Hill, Anita, **Supp. XX:** 110

Hill, Hamlin, **Retro. Supp. II:** 286

Hill, James J., **Supp. I Part 2:** 644

Hill, Joe, **I:** 493; **Supp. XVIII:** 224; **Supp. XXIII:** 162

Hill, Lee, **Supp. XI:** 293, 294, 297, 299, 301, 305, 307

Hill, Pamela Smith, **Supp. XXII:** 295

Hill, Patti, **I:** 289

Hill, Peggy, **Supp. XIII:** 163

"Hill, The" (Strand), **Supp. IV Part 2:** 627

"Hill, The" (Toomer), **Supp. III Part 2:** 486

Hill, Vernon, **Supp. I Part 2:** 397

"Hillcrest" (Robinson), **III:** 504

Hill-Lubin, Mildred A., **Supp. IV Part 1:** 13

Hillman, Sidney, **Supp. I Part 1:** 5

Hillringhouse, Mark, **Supp. IX:** 286, 288, 299

Hills Beyond, The (Wolfe), **IV:** 450, 451, 460, 461

"Hills Beyond, The" (Wolfe), **IV:** 460

Hillside and Seaside in Poetry (Larcom, ed.), **Supp. XIII:** 142

"Hillside Thaw, A" (Frost), **Retro. Supp. I:** 133

"Hills Like White Elephants" (Hemingway), **Retro. Supp. I:** 170

Hills of the Shatemuc, The (S. Warner), **Supp. XVIII:** 266

"Hill-Top View, A" (Jeffers), **Supp. II Part 2:** 417

Hill Towns (Siddons), **Supp. XXII:** 239, 253

"Hill Wife, The" (Frost), **II:** 154; **Retro. Supp. I:** 131

Hillyer, Catherine, **Supp. XV:** 244

Hillyer, Robert, **I:** 475; **Supp. IX:** 75; **Supp. XIV:** 11

Hilton, James, **Supp. XIII:** 166

"Hiltons' Holiday, The" (Jewett), **II:** 391; **Retro. Supp. II:** 134

Him (Cummings), **I:** 429, 434–435

Himes, Chester Bomar, **Retro. Supp. II:** 117; **Supp. I Part 1:** 51, 325; **Supp. XIII:** 233; **Supp. XVI:** 135–146

Himes, Norman, **Supp. V:** 128

"Him on a Bicycle" (Weigl), **Supp. XIX:** 276

"Him with His Foot in His Mouth" (Bellow), **Retro. Supp. II:** 34

Him with His Foot in His Mouth and Other Stories (Bellow), **Retro. Supp. II:** 31

Hinchman, Sandra K., **Supp. IV Part 1:** 210

Hinckley, David, **Supp. XXII:** 215

Hindemith, Paul, **IV:** 357; **Supp. IV Part 1:** 81

Hindsell, Oliver, **Supp. XIII:** 162

Hindus, Milton, **Supp. XIV:** 288, 291, 292, 293; **Supp. XXIII:** 16

Hines, Suzanne, **Supp. XIV:** 151

Hinge Picture (Howe), **Supp. IV Part 2:** 423–424

Hinojosa, Rolando, **Supp. XIX:** 97–114

"Hinterlands" (W. Gibson), **Supp. XVI:** 123, 128

"Hippies: Slouching towards Bethlehem" (Didion), **Supp. IV Part 1:** 200

Hippolytus (Euripides), **II:** 543; **Supp. I Part 1:** 270

Hippolytus Temporizes (Doolittle), **Supp. I Part 1:** 270

"Hips" (Cisneros), **Supp. VII:** 61, 62

"Hipster's Hipster" (Ginsberg), **Supp. XIV:** 141

Hirsch, Edward D., **Supp. V:** 177; **Supp. IX:** 262; **Supp. XIV:** 15; **Supp. XV:** 78, 225; **Supp. XVII:** 23; **Supp. XIX:** 202; **Supp. XXIII:** 124

Hirsch, Sidney, **Supp. XIV:** 1. *See* Mttron-Hirsch, Sidney

Hirschfeld, Jane, **Supp. XVII:** 241

Hirschorn, Clive, **Supp. IV Part 2:** 577, 579

Hirshfield, Jane, **Supp. XXIII:** 129–141

Hirson, Roger, **Supp. XI:** 343

"His Bride of the Tomb" (Dunbar), **Supp. II Part 1:** 196

"His Chest of Drawers" (Anderson), **I:** 113, 114

"His Daily Journal"(Kenny), **Supp. XXIII:** 153

"His Father's Whistle" (Wrigley), **Supp. XVIII:** 299

His First, Best Country (J. W. Miller), **Supp. XX: 163, 166, 172–175**

"His Last Day" (C. Himes), **Supp. XVI:** 137

"His Lover" (Dubus), **Supp. VII:** 86

"His Music" (Dunn), **Supp. XI:** 149

"His Own Key" (Ríos), **Supp. IV Part 2:** 543

His Picture in the Papers (film; Emerson), **Supp. XVI:** 185

His Religion and Hers (Gilman), **Supp. XI:** 209

Hiss, Alger, **Supp. XV:** 143

"Hiss, Chambers, and the Age of Innocence" (Fiedler), **Supp. XIII:** 99

"His Shield" (Moore), **III:** 211

"His Story" (Cisneros), **Supp. VII:** 67

His Thought Made Pockets & the Plane Buckt (Berryman), **I:** 170

"His Three Women" (Gioia), **Supp. XV:** 119–120

Histoire comparée des systèmes de philosophie (Gérando), **II:** 10

Histoire de la brume, L' (Dybek; trans. Beget), **Supp. XXIII:** 74

Historical and Moral View of the Origin and Progress of the French Revolution (Wollstonecraft), **Supp. I Part 1:** 126

"Historical Conceptualization" (Huizinga), **I:** 255

Historical Evidence and the Reading of Seventeenth-Century Poetry (Brooks), **Supp. XIV:** 11

"Historical Interpretation of Literature, The" (Wilson), **IV:** 431, 433, 445

Historical Jesus, The: The Life of a Mediterranean Jewish Peasant (Crossan), **Supp. V:** 251

Historical Life of Jesus, The (Pettis), **Supp. XXIII:** 189

"Historical Value of Crèvecoeur's *Voyage . . .,*" (Adams), **Supp. I Part 1:** 251

"History" (Emerson), **II:** 13, 15

"History" (Hughes), **Supp. I Part 1:** 344

History (Lowell), **Retro. Supp. II:** 183, 190

"History" (Simic), **Supp. VIII:** 279

"History, Myth, and the Western Writer" (Stegner), **Supp. IV Part 2:** 596, 601

"History among the Rocks" (Warren), **IV:** 252

History as a Literary Art (Morison), **Supp. I Part 2:** 493

"History as Fate in E. L. Doctorow's Tale of a Western Town" (Arnold), **Supp. IV Part 1:** 220

"History Is the Memory of Time" (Olson), **Supp. II Part 2:** 574

"History Lesson" (Trethewey), **Supp. XXI:** 248, 249

"History Lessons" (Komunyakaa), **Supp. XIII:** 126

History Man, The (Bradbury), **Supp. XVIII:** 140

"History of a Literary Movement" (Nemerov), **III:** 270

"History of a Literary Radical, The" (Bourne), **I:** 215, 235, 236

History of a Radical: Essays by Randolph Bourne (Brooks), **I:** 245

"History of Armenia, The"(Balakian), **Supp. XXIII:** 23, 24

"History of Buttons, The" (Goldbarth), **Supp. XII:** 187

History of English Literature (Taine), **III:** 323

History of English Prosody (Saintsbury), **Supp. XV:** 181

History of Fortus, The (Emerson), **II:** 8

History of Henry Esmond, The (Thackeray), **II:** 91, 130

History of Modern Poetry, A (Perkins), **Supp. I Part 2:** 475; **Supp. XV:** 185

History of My Heart (Pinsky), **Supp. VI:** 243, 244, 245

History of New York, from the Beginning of the World to the End of the Dutch Dynasty, A (Irving), **II:** 300–303, 304, 310

History of Pendennis, The (Thackeray), **II:** 291

"History of Red, The" (Hogan), **Supp. IV Part 1:** 411

"History of Rodney, The" (Bass), **Supp. XVI:** 20

History of Roxbury Town (Ellis), **Supp. I Part 1:** 99

History of Southern Literature, The (Rubin), **Supp. XX:** 161

History of the African-American People (Proposed) by Strom Thurmond, The (Everett and Kincaid), **Supp. XVIII:** 62**, 63–64**

History of the Conquest of Mexico (Prescott), **Retro. Supp. I:** 123

History of the Conquest of Peru (Morison, ed.), **Supp. I Part 2:** 494

History of the Dividing Line betwixt Virginia and North Carolina (Byrd), **Supp. IV Part 2:** 425

History of the Life and Voyages of Christopher Columbus, A (Irving), **II:** 310, 314

History of the Navy of the United States of America (Cooper), **I:** 347

History of the Rise and Fall of the Slave-power in America (Wilson), **Supp. XIV:** 48, 49

History of the Russian Revolution, A (Trotsky), **Supp. XXI:** 161

History of the United States (Bancroft), **Supp. XXII:** 33

History of the United States of America during the Administrations of Thomas Jefferson and James Madison (Adams), **I:** 6–9, 10, 20, 21

History of the Work of Redemption, A (Edwards), **I:** 560

History of United States Naval Operations in World War II (Morison), **Supp. I Part 2:** 490–492

History of Womankind in Western Europe, The, **Supp. XI:** 197

"History Teacher, The" (Collins), **Supp. XXI:** 57

"History Through a Beard" (Morison), **Supp. I Part 2:** 490

His Toy, His Dream, His Rest (Berryman), **I:** 169, 170, 183, 184–186

"His Words" (Roethke), **III:** 544

Hitchcock, Ada. *See* MacLeish, Mrs. Archibald (Ada Hitchcock)

Hitchcock, Alfred, **IV:** 357; **Supp. IV Part 1:** 132; **Supp. VIII:** 177; **Supp. XX: 253; Supp. XXII:** 119

Hitchcock, George, **Supp. X:** 127; **Supp. XVII:** 110

"Hitch Haiku" (Snyder), **Supp. VIII:** 297

"Hitch-Hikers, The" (Welty), **IV:** 262

"Hitchhiking Is Illegal in Nevada" (Lethem), **Supp. XVIII:** 136

Hitchins, Christopher, **Supp. VIII:** 241

Hitler, Adolf, **I:** 261, 290, 492; **II:** 146, 454, 561, 565, 592; **III:** 2, 3, 110, 115, 140, 156, 246, 298, 446; **IV:** 5, 17, 18, 298, 372; **Supp. I Part 2:** 431, 436, 446, 664; **Supp. V:** 290

Hitler, Wendy, **III:** 404

Hitler Lives? (film), **Supp. XVI:** 102

Hix, H. L., **Supp. XV:** 114

H. L. Mencken, a Portrait from Memory (Angoff), **III:** 107

"H. L. Mencken Meets a Poet in the West Side Y.M.C.A." (White), **Supp. I Part 2:** 677

H. L. Mencken: The American Scene (Cairns), **III:** 119

H. M. Pulham, Esquire (Marquand), **II:** 482–483; **III:** 58, 59, 65, 68–69

Hnizdovsky, Jacques, **Supp. XIII:** 346

"Hoadley's Test Case in Indiana" (Neugeboren), **Supp. XVI:** 219

Hoagland, Edward, **Supp. XIV:** 80; **Supp. XVI:** 277; **Supp. XXII:** 204, 206

Hoagland, Tony, **Supp. XIX:** 81, 89

"Hoarder, The" (Sexton), **Supp. II Part 2:** 692

"Hoarfrost" (C. Baxter), **Supp. XVII:** 15

Hoban, Phoebe, **Supp. XV:** 319, 325

Hoban, Russell, **Supp. XXIII:** 42

Hobb, Gormley, **I:** 203

Hobbes, Thomas, **I:** 277; **II:** 9, 10, 540; **III:** 306; **IV:** 88; **Supp. XII:** 33; **Supp. XIV:** 5, 7

Hobson, Geary, **Supp. IV Part 1:** 321; **Supp. IV Part 2:** 502

Hobson, J. A., **I:** 232

Hobson, John A., **Supp. I Part 2:** 650

Hobson, Laura Z., **III:** 151

Hocking, Agnes, **Supp. VIII:** 251

Hocking, William Ernest, **III:** 303

Hodge, Merle, **Supp. XXIII:** 94

Hodges, Campbell B., **Supp. XIV:** 8

Hodgson, Captain Joseph, **III:** 328

Hoffa, Jimmy, **I:** 493

Hoffenberg, Mason, **Supp. XI:** 294, 297, 299, 305

Hoffer, Eric, **Supp. VIII:** 188; **Supp. XIX:** 264

Hoffman, Abbie, **Supp. XIV:** 150

Hoffman, Alice, **Supp. X: 77–94; Supp. XIII:** 13

Hoffman, Allen, **Supp. XVII:** 42, 44

Hoffman, Daniel, **Retro. Supp. II:** 265

Hoffman, Daniel G., **I:** 405; **II:** 307; **Supp. XI:** 152

Hoffman, Dustin, **Supp. IV Part 1:** 236

Hoffman, E. T. A., **Supp. XVI:** 157

Hoffman, Eva, **Supp. XVI: 147–164**

Hoffman, Frederick J., **I:** 60, 67; **II:** 443; **IV:** 113

Hoffman, Josiah Ogden, **II:** 297, 300

Hoffman, Matilda, **II:** 300, 314

Hoffman, Paul, **Supp. XV:** 141–142

Hoffman, Roy, **Supp. XX: 177**

Hoffman, Todd, **Supp. XVIII:** 101

Hoffman, William, **Supp. XVIII: 69–88**

Hoffman, William M., **Supp. X:** 153

Hoffmann, E. T. A., **III:** 415

Hofmann, Hans, **Supp. XV:** 144

Hofmeister, Tim, **Supp. XIX:** 115

Ho for a Hat (W. J. Smith), **Supp. XIII:** 346

Hofstadter, Richard, **Supp. VIII:** 98, 99, 108

Hogan, Linda, **Supp. IV Part 1:** 324, 325, **397–418; Supp. XVIII:** 189

Hogan, Randolph, **Supp. XVI:** 252–253

Hogan, Ron, **Supp. XVIII:** 138, 139

Hogarth, William, **Supp. XII:** 44

Hogg, James, **I:** 53; **Supp. I Part 1:** 349; **Supp. IX:** 275

Hoggart, Richard, **Supp. XIV:** 299

"Hog-Nosed Snake, The" (Kooser), **Supp. XIX:** 128

Hogue, W. Lawrence, **Supp. XXII:** 175–176

Hohne, Karen, **Supp. V:** 147

Hojoki (Chomei), **IV:** 170

Holbrook, David, **Supp. I Part 2:** 526–527, 546

Holcroft, Thomas, **Supp. I Part 2:** 514

Holden, Jonathan, **Supp. XI:** 143

Holden, Raymond, **Supp. XIV:** 121–122

Holden, William, **Supp. XI:** 307

Hölderlin, Friedrich, **Supp. XVI:** 48

Holding, Elisabeth Sanxay, **Supp. XXII: 119–137**

"Holding On" (Levine), **Supp. V:** 184

Holding the Line: Women in the Great Arizona Mine Strike of 1983 (Kingsolver), **Supp. VII:** 197, 201–202, 204

"Holding the Mirror Up to Nature" (Nemerov), **III:** 275, 276

"Hold Me" (Levine), **Supp. V:** 186

Hold the Press (film), **Supp. XIII:** 163

Hold with the Hares (Zinberg), **Supp. XV:** 197–198,**Supp. XV:** 203

"Hole in the Floor, A" (Wilbur), **Supp. III Part 2:** 556–557

Holiday (Barry), **Retro. Supp. I:** 104

"Holiday" (Porter), **III:** 454

Holiday (W. Frank), **Supp. XX: 72–73**

Holiday, Billie, **Supp. I Part 1:** 80; **Supp. IV Part 1:** 2, 7; **Supp. XIX:** 147

Holiday Song for Four-Part Chorus of Mixed Voices with Piano Accompaniment (Taggard and Schuman), **Supp. XXII:** 283

Holinshed, Raphael, **IV:** 370

Holladay, Polly, **Supp. XXI:** 6

Holland, Josiah, **Supp. I Part 2:** 420

Holland, Laurence Bedwell, **Retro. Supp. I:** 216

Holland, Theodore, **I:** 453

Holland, Mrs. Theodore, **I:** 453, 455, 465

Holland, William, **IV:** 381

Hollander, John, **Supp. III Part 2:** 541; **Supp. IV Part 2:** 642; **Supp. IX:** 50, 153, 155; **Supp. XII:** 254, 255, 260; **Supp. XV:** 256; **Supp. XVII:** 112; **Supp. XIX:** 121; **Supp. XXIII:** 112

Holley, Marietta, **Supp. XIII:** 152

Holliday, Billie, **Supp. XXI:** 131

Hollinghurst, Alan, **Supp. XIII:** 52

Hollins Critic (Nelson), **Supp. XIX:** 3

Hollis, Thomas Brand, **Supp. I Part 2:** 514

Hollow Men, The (T. S. Eliot), **I:** 574, 575, 578–579, 580, 585; **III:** 586; **Retro. Supp. I:** 63, 64

"Hollow Tree, A" (R. Bly), **Supp. IV Part 1:** 64, 66

Hollyberrys at the Shore, The, **Supp. X:** 42

"Hollywood!" (Vidal), **Supp. IV Part 2:** 688

Hollywood: American Movie-City (Rand, unauthorized), **Supp. IV Part 2:** 519

Hollywood: A Novel of America in the 1920s (Vidal), **Supp. IV Part 2:** 677, 684, 686, 688, 690, 691

Hollywood Ending (film; Allen), **Supp. XV:** 11

Hollywood on Trial (film), **Supp. I Part 1:** 295

Holmes, Abiel, **Supp. I Part 1:** 300, 301, 302, 310

Holmes, Mrs. Abiel (Sarah Wendell), **Supp. I Part 1:** 300

Holmes, John, **I:** 169; **Supp. II Part 1:** 87; **Supp. IV Part 2:** 440–441; **Supp. XIV:** 119

Holmes, John Clellon, **Supp. XII:** 118; **Supp. XIV:** 144, 150

Holmes, Martha Stoddard, **Supp. XX:** 205, 207

Holmes, Oliver Wendell, **I:** 487; **II:** 225, 273–274, 402, 403; **III:** 81–82, 590, 591–592; **IV:** 429, 436; **Retro. Supp. II:** 155; **Supp. I Part 1:** 103, 243, 254, 299–319; **Supp. I Part 2:** 405, 414, 415, 420, 593, 704, 705; **Supp. XI:** 194

Holmes, Oliver Wendell, Jr., **I:** 3, 19; **Supp. IV Part 2:** 422

Holmes, Mrs. Oliver Wendell (Amelia Jackson), **Supp. I Part 1:** 303

Holmes, Steven J., **Supp. IX:** 172, 177

Holmes, Ted, **Supp. V:** 180

Holmes, William Henry, **Supp. IV Part 2:** 603–604

Holocaust (Reznikoff), **Supp. XIV:** 281, 291–293

Holocaust in American Life, The (Novick), **Supp. XVI:** 154

Holt, Edwin E., **I:** 59

Holt, Felix, **II:** 179

Holt, Henry, **II:** 348; **III:** 587

Holt, Patricia, **Supp. XIV:** 89

Holtby, Winifred, **Supp. I Part 2:** 720

Holy Ghostly, The (Shepard), **Supp. III Part 2:** 437–438, 447

"Holy Innocents, The" (Lowell), **II:** 539

Holy Sonnets (Donne), **IV:** 145; **Supp. I Part 1:** 367; **Supp. III Part 2:** 619; **Supp. XIII:** 130–131; **Supp. XVIII:** 50–51

"Holy Terror, A" (Bierce), **I:** 203

"Holy Terror, The" (Maxwell), **Supp. VIII:** 169

Holy the Firm (Dillard), **Supp. VI:** 23, 29, 30, 31, 32

Holy War, The (Bunyan), **IV:** 156

"Holy Week"(Thompson), **Supp. XXIII:** 300

"Homage to Arthur Rimbaud" (Wright), **Supp. V:** 339

Homage to Baudelaire (Duncan, ed.), **Supp. XV:** 75

Homage to Catalonia (Orwell), **Supp. XVII:** 229

"Homage to Che Guevara" (Banks), **Supp. V:** 5

Homage to Clio (Auden), **Supp. II Part 1:** 24

"Homage to Elizabeth Bishop" (Ivask, ed.), **Supp. I Part 1:** 96

"Homage to Ezra Pound" (Wright), **Supp. V:** 339

Homage to Frank O'Hara (Ashbery), **Supp. III Part 1:** 2–3

"Homage to Franz Joseph Haydn" (Hecht), **Supp. X:** 69

"Homage to Hemingway" (Bishop), **IV:** 35

Homage to Mistress Bradstreet (Berryman), **I:** 168, 169, 170–171, 172, 174, 175, 178–183, 184, 186

"Homage to Paul Cézanne" (Wright), **Supp. V:** 341–342

Homage to Sextus Propertius (Pound), **Retro. Supp. I:** 290

"Homage to Sextus Propertius" (Pound), **III:** 462, 476; **Supp. III Part 2:** 622

"Homage to Shakespeare" (Cheever), **Supp. I Part 1:** 180

"Homage to the Empress of the Blues" (Hayden), **Supp. II Part 1:** 379

"Homage to the Memory of Wallace Stevens" (Justice), **Supp. VII:** 126

Homage to Theodore Dreiser (Warren), **I:** 517

Homans, Margaret, **Supp. X:** 229

"Home" (Hughes), **Supp. I Part 1:** 329, 330

"Home" (Mora), **Supp. XIII:** 217

Home (Robinson), **Supp. XXI:** 212, 220–223

Home (Updike), **Retro. Supp. I:** 320

"Home" (Weigl), **Supp. XIX:** 287

"Home, Home on the Strange" (J. D. Reed), **Supp. XVI:** 174

"Home, Sweet Home" (Fante), **Supp. XI:** 164, 165

Home, The (Gilman), **Supp. XI: 206–207**

"Home, The" (Jarman), **Supp. XVII:** 116

"Home Address" (Bronk), **Supp. XXI:** 27

"Home after Three Months Away" (Lowell), **II:** 547

Home and Colonial Library (Murray), **Retro. Supp. I:** 246

"Home and the Open Road: The Nonfiction of Larry Brown" (Barrier), **Supp. XXI:** 48–49

Home as Found (Cooper), **I:** 348, 349, 350, 351

Home at the End of the World, A (Cunningham), **Supp. XV: 59–62,** 63

"Home Away from Home, A" (Humphrey), **Supp. IX:** 101

Home Book of Shakespeare Quotations (Stevenson), **Supp. XIV:** 120

"Home Burial" (Frost), **Retro. Supp. I:** 124, 125, 128, **129–130; Supp. VIII:** 31; **Supp. XV:** 159; **Supp. XIX:** 9

Homecoming (Alvarez), **Supp. VII:** 1, 3–5, 9

"Homecoming" (Carruth), **Supp. XVI:** 55

"Homecoming" (McGrath), **Supp. X:** 116

"Homecoming, The" (Gioia), **Supp. XV:** 123, 124

Homecoming, The (Wilson), **Supp. VIII:** 330

Homecoming Game, The (Nemerov), **III:** 268, 282, 284–285

"Home during a Tropical Snowstorm I Feed My Father Lunch" (Karr), **Supp. XI:** 241–242, 248

Home Economics (Berry), **Supp. X:** 28, 31–32, 35, 36, 37

"Home Economics for Halfbacks" (Skloot), **Supp. XX: 195, 207**

Home from the Hill (film), **Supp. IX:** 95

Home from the Hill (Humphrey), **Supp. IX:** 93, 95, **96–98,** 104, 106, 109

"Home Grown" (Vital), **Supp. XVI:** 160

"Homeland" (Merwin), **Supp. III Part 1:** 351

Homeland and Other Stories (Kingsolver), **Supp. VII:** 199, 202–204, 207

Home on the Range (Baraka), **Supp. II Part 1:** 47

Homeplace (Siddons), **Supp. XXII:** 253

Home Place, The (Morris), **III:** 221, 222, 232

Homeplace, The (Nelson), **Supp. XVIII: 174–175**

Homer, **I:** 312, 433; **II:** 6, 8, 133, 302, 543, 544, 552; **III:** 14, 21, 278, 453, 457, 473, 567; **IV:** 54, 371; **Retro. Supp. I:** 59; **Supp. I Part 1:** 158, 283; **Supp. I Part 2:** 494; **Supp. X:** 36, 120, 122; **Supp. XIV:** 21; **Supp. XVII:** 70, 227

Homer, Louise, **Retro. Supp. I:** 10

Homer, Winslow, **Supp. XXI:** 243

"Home Range" (Leopold), **Supp. XIV:** 184, 185

"Home Repairs" (Skloot), **Supp. XX:** 204

Homer's Art (Notley), **Supp. XXII:** 232

"Homer's Art" (Notley), **Supp. XXII:** 232–233

"Homesick Blues" (Hughes), **Supp. I Part 1:** 327

Home: Social Essays (Baraka), **Supp. II Part 1:** 45, 61

"Homesteading on the Extraterrestrial Frontier" (Abbott), **Supp. XVIII:** 142

Home to Harlem (McKay), **Supp. X:** 132, 137–138, **138–139; Supp. XVIII:** 127

"Home Videos" (Brockmeier), **Supp. XXII:** 60

Homeward Bound (Cooper), **I:** 348

"Homeward Star, The" (Palmer), **Supp. XV:** 81–82

Homewood trilogy (Wideman), **Supp. X:** 319

"Homework" (Cameron), **Supp. XII:** 80, **83,** 84

"Homily" (Tate), **IV:** 121–122

Homing with the Birds (Stratton-Porter), **Supp. XX: 212, 216, 222**

"Homme Moyen Sensuel, L' " (Pound), **III:** 462

Homme révolté, L' (Camus), III: 306

"Homoeopathy and Its Kindred Delusions" (Holmes), **Supp. I Part 1:** 303–304, 305

Homo Ludens (Huizinga), **II:** 416–417, 425

"Homosexuality"(O'Hara), **Supp. XXIII:** 212

"Homosexual Villain, The" (Mailer), **III:** 36

"Homo Will Not Inherit" (Doty), **Supp. XI:** 128

"Homunculus, The: A Novel in One Chapter" (McKnight), **Supp. XX: 152**

Hone and Strong Diaries of Old Manhattan, The (Auchincloss, ed.), **Supp. IV Part 1:** 23

"Honey" (Beattie), **Supp. V:** 33

"Honey" (Wright), **Supp. III Part 2:** 589

"Honey, We'll Be Brave" (Farrell), **II:** 45

Honey and Salt (Sandburg), **III:** 594–596

"Honey and Salt" (Sandburg), **III:** 594

"Honey Babe" (Hughes), **Supp. I Part 1:** 334

"Honey Tree, The" (Oliver), **Supp. VII:** 236

Hong, Maxine. *See* Kingston, Maxine Hong

Hongo, Garrett, **Supp. X:** 292; **Supp. XIII:** 114; **Supp. XVII:** 112

"Honkytonk" (Shapiro), **Supp. II Part 2:** 705

"Honky Tonk in Cleveland, Ohio" (Sandburg), **III:** 585

Honorable Men (Auchincloss), **Supp. IV Part 1:** 23

Honor Thy Father (Talese), **Supp. XVII:** 204–205, 210

Hood, Tom, **I:** 195

"Hoodoo in America" (Hurston), **Supp. VI:** 153–154

"Hook" (Wright), **Supp. III Part 2:** 604

Hook, Sidney, **I:** 265; **Supp. IV Part 2:** 527; **Supp. VIII:** 96, 100; **Supp. XIV:** 3

Hooker, Adelaide. *See* Marquand, Mrs. John P. (Adelaide Hooker)

Hooker, Isabella Beecher, **Supp. XI:** 193

Hooker, Samuel, **IV:** 162, 165

Hooker, Thomas, **II:** 15–16; **IV:** 162

Hooper, Marian. *See* Adams, Mrs. Henry (Marian Hooper)

Hoosier Holiday, A (Dreiser), **Retro. Supp. II:** 104

Hoover, Herbert, **Supp. I Part 2:** 638

Hoover, J. Edgar, **Supp. XIII:** 170

Hoover, Paul, **Supp. XV:** 179

"Hope" (Bontemps), **Supp. XXII:** 2

"Hope" (Jarrell), **II:** 389

"Hope" (Matthews), **Supp. IX:** 163

Hope, A. D., **Supp. XIII:** 347

Hope, Lynn, **Supp. II Part 1:** 38

"Hope Atherton's Wanderings" (Howe), **Supp. IV Part 2:** 432

"Hopeless Kill, The"(Kenny), **Supp. XXIII:** 145

Hope of Heaven (O'Hara), **III:** 361

"Hopes Rise" (Boyle), **Supp. XX: 20**

"Hop-Frog" (Poe), **Retro. Supp. II:** 264, 268, 269

Hopkin, Pauline, **Supp. XVI:** 143

Hopkins, Anne Yale, **Supp. I Part 1:** 100, 102, 113

Hopkins, Gerard Manley, **I:** 171, 179, 397, 401, 522, 525, 533; **II:** 537; **III:** 197, 209, 523; **IV:** 129, 135, 141, 421; **Retro. Supp. II:** 40; **Supp. I Part 1:** 79, 81, 94; **Supp. III Part 2:** 551; **Supp. IV Part 1:** 178; **Supp. IV Part 2:** 637, 638, 639, 641, 643; **Supp. V:** 337; **Supp. IX:** 39, 42; **Supp. X:** 61, 115; **Supp. XIII:** 294; **Supp. XIV:** 83; **Supp. XV:** 250, 347; **Supp. XVI:** 282; **Supp. XVII:** 241; **Supp. XVIII:** 78, 79; **Supp. XX: 230; Supp. XXIII:** 121

Hopkins, Gerard Walter Sturgis, **Supp. XX: 229, 233, 240**

Hopkins, L. A., **I:** 502

Hopkins, Lemuel, **Supp. II Part 1:** 70

Hopkins, Miriam, **IV:** 381; **Supp. I Part 1:** 281

Hopkins, Pauline, **Supp. XVIII:** 284

Hopkins, Samuel, **I:** 547, 549

Hopkins, Vivian, **II:** 20

Hopkinson, Francis, **Supp. I Part 2:** 504

Hopler, Jay, **Supp. XXIII:** 132

Hopper (Strand), **Supp. IV Part 2:** 632

Hopper, Dennis, **Supp. XI:** 293, 308

Hopper, Edward, **IV:** 411, 413; **Supp. IV Part 2:** 619, 623, 631, 634; **Supp. XIX:** 117

Hopwood, Avery, **Supp. IV Part 2:** 573

Horace, **II:** 8, 154, 169, 543, 552, 568; **III:** 15; **IV:** 89; **Supp. I Part 2:** 423; **Supp. IX:** 152; **Supp. X:** 65; **Supp. XII:** 258, 260, 262

Horae Canonicae (Auden), **Supp. II Part 1:** 21

"Horatian Ode" (Marvell), **IV:** 135

"Horatian Ode upon Cromwell's Return from Ireland" (Marvell), **Supp. XIV:** 10

Horgan, Paul, **Supp. XV:** 46, 49, 52

Horkheimer, Max, **Supp. I Part 2:** 645; **Supp. IV Part 1:** 301

Horn, Dara, **Supp. XVII:** 50; **Supp. XX: 177**

Horn, Mother, **Supp. I Part 1:** 49, 54

Hornby, Nick, **Supp. XII:** 286; **Supp. XXIII:** 109

Horn of Africa (Caputo), **Supp. XIX:** 21–23

"Horn of Plenty" (Hughes), **Retro. Supp. I:** 210; **Supp. I Part 1:** 342

Horovitz, Israel, **Supp. XV:** 321

Horowitz, James. *See* Salter, James

Horowitz, Mark, **Supp. V:** 219, 231

"Horrible" (Halliday), **Supp. XIX:** 91

"Horse, The" (Levine), **Supp. V:** 182

"Horse, The" (Wright), **Supp. III Part 2:** 592, 601

"Horse, The"(Le Sueur), **Supp. XXIII:** 168

Horse Eats Hay (play), **Supp. IV Part 1:** 82

Horse Feathers (film), **Supp. IV Part 1:** 384

"Horseflies" (Wrigley), **Supp. XVIII:** 307

Horse Has Six Legs, The (Simic), **Supp. VIII:** 272

"Horselaugh on Dibber Lannon" (Fante), **Supp. XI:** 164

Horseman, Pass By (McMurtry), **Supp. V:** 220–221, 224

"Horses" (Doty), **Supp. XI:** 122

Horses and Men (Anderson), **I:** 112–113, 114

"Horses and Men in Rain" (Sandburg), **III:** 584

"Horse Show, The" (W. C. Williams), **Retro. Supp. I:** 423

Horses Make a Landscape More Beautiful (Walker), **Supp. III Part 2:** 521, 533

"Horse Thief" (Caldwell), **I:** 310

"Horseweed" (Offutt), **Supp. XIX:** 166, 167

Horse With a Green Vinyl Mane (P. N. Warren), **Supp. XX: 261**

"Horsie" (Parker), **Supp. IX:** 193

Horton, George Moses, **Supp. XXII:** 11

Horton, Philip, **I:** 383, 386, 387, 393, 441; **Supp. XV:** 138

Horton Hatches the Egg (Geisel), **Supp. XVI:** 100, 112

Horton Hears a Who! (Geisel), **Supp. XVI:** 102

"Horton's Ape"(P. Benedict), **Supp. XXIII:** 41

Horwitz, Tony, **Supp. XVIII:** 195–196

Hosea (biblical book), **II:** 166

Hospers, John, **Supp. IV Part 2:** 528

"Hospice" (Hull), **Supp. XXI:** 138

Hospital, Janette Turner, **Supp. IV Part 1:** 311–302

Hospital Sketches (Alcott), **Supp. I Part 1:** 34, 35

Hostages to Fortune (Humphrey), **Supp. IX:** 96, **104–106,** 109

Hostess to Murder (Holding), **Supp. XXII:** 126, **127**

"Hot Combs" (Trethewey), **Supp. XXI:** 249

"Hot Cross Bum" (Loy), **Supp. XXII:** 168

"Hot Dog" (Stern), **Supp. IX: 298–299**

"Hotel, The"(Hadas), **Supp. XXIII:** 121

"Hotel Bar" (McClatchy), **Supp. XII:** 269

Hotel Dwellers, The (Lacy), **Supp. XV:** 205

Hotel Insomnia (Simic), **Supp. VIII:** 280, **281–282**

Hotel Lambosa and Other Stories (Koch), **Supp. XV:** 186

Hotel New Hampshire, The (Irving), **Supp. VI:** 163, 164, **172–173,** 177, 179; **Supp. XIX:** 164

"Hot-Foot Hannibal" (Chesnutt), **Supp. XIV:** 60

"Hot Ice"(Dybek), **Supp. XXIII:** 72–73

"Hot Night on Water Street" (Simpson), **Supp. IX:** 269, 270

"Hot Time, A" (Gunn Allen), **Supp. IV Part 1:** 333

Houdini, Harry, **IV:** 437

"Hound of Heaven" (Thompson), **Retro. Supp. I:** 55

"Hourglass, The" (Kees), **Supp. XV:** 147

"Hour in Chartres, An" (Bourne), **I:** 228

"Hour of Peonies, The"(Crooker), **Supp. XXIII:** 58

Hours, The (Cunningham), **Supp. XII:** 80; **Supp. XV:** 65–68

"Hours before Eternity" (Caldwell), **I:** 291

House, Bridge, Fountain, Gate (Kumin), **Supp. IV Part 2:** 448, 449, 451, 454

House, Edward, **Supp. I Part 2:** 643

"House, The" (Merrill), **Supp. III Part 1:** 323

House at Pooh Corner, The (Milne), **Supp. IX:** 189

"House at the End of the World, The" (Brockmeier), **Supp. XXII:** 52, 53

House Behind the Cedars, The (Chesnutt), **Supp. XIV:** 69–71

Houseboat Days (Ashbery), **Supp. III Part 1:** 18–20

Housebreaker of Shady Hill and Other Stories, The (Cheever), **Supp. I Part 1:** 184

"House by the Sea, The" (E. Stoddard), **Supp. XV:** 277

House by the Sea, The (Sarton), **Supp. VIII:** 264

House Divided, A (Buck), **Supp. II Part 1:** 118

"House Divided, The/La Casa Divida" (Kingsolver), **Supp. VII:** 207

"House Guest" (Bishop), **Retro. Supp. II:** 49; **Supp. I Part 1:** 93

Household Saints (film), **Supp. XVI:** 256

Household Saints (Prose), **Supp. XVI:** 252–253, 254, 261

"House in Athens, The" (Merrill), **Supp. III Part 1:** 323

House in the Uplands, A (Caldwell), **I:** 297, 301, 306

"House in Turk Street, The" (Hammett), **Supp. IV Part 1:** 344

"House in Winter, The" (Sarton), **Supp. VIII:** 259

"House in Winter, The"(Hirshfield), **Supp. XXIII:** 132

"Housekeeping" (Alvarez), **Supp. VII:** 3–5, 10

Housekeeping (Robinson), **Supp. XXI:** 210–211, **212–216,** 218, 223

"Housekeeping" (Trethewey), **Supp. XXI:** 249

"Housekeeping for Men" (Bourne), **I:** 231

House Made of Dawn (Momaday), **Supp. IV Part 1:** 274, 323, 326; **Supp. IV Part 2:** 479, 480, 481–484, 485, 486, 504, 562

Houseman, John, **Supp. IV Part 1:** 173

House Next Door, The (Siddons), **Supp. XXII:** 239

House Next Door, The (television movie), **Supp. XXII:** 239

House of Dust, The: A Symphony (Aiken), **I:** 50

House of Earth trilogy (Buck), **Supp. II Part 1:** 118, 123

House of Five Talents, The (Auchincloss), **Supp. IV Part 1:** 21, 25–27

"House of Flowers" (Capote), **Supp. III Part 1:** 123

House of Games (Mamet), **Supp. XIV:** 243

House of Houses (Mora), **Supp. XIII:** 213, 215, 218, 219, 223–224, **225–227,** 228, 229

House of Incest (Nin), **Supp. III Part 1:** 43; **Supp. X:** 187, 190, 193

House of Life, The: Rachel Carson at Work (Brooks), **Supp. IX:** 26

House of Light (Oliver), **Supp. VII:** 238–240

House of Mirth, The (Wharton), **II:** 180, 193; **IV:** 311–313, 314, 316, 318, 323, 327; **Retro. Supp. I:** 360, 366, 367, **367–370,** 373, 380; **Supp. XX: 239, 240**

"House of Mist, The" (Rand), **Supp. IV Part 2:** 524

"House of My Own, A" (Cisneros), **Supp. VII:** 64

"House of Night, The" (Freneau), **Supp. II Part 1:** 259, 260

"House of Representatives and Me, The" (Conroy), **Supp. XVI:** 75

House of Sleeping Beauties, The (Hwang), **Supp. XXI:** 146

House of the Far and Lost, The (Wolfe), **IV:** 456

"House of the Injured, The" (Haines), **Supp. XII:** 203

"House of the One Father" (Antin), **Supp. XX: 3, 13**

House of the Prophet, The (Auchincloss), **Supp. IV Part 1:** 31

House of the Seven Gables (Hawthorne), **I:** 106; **II:** 60, 224, 225, 231, 237, 239, 240–241, 243, 244; **Retro. Supp. I:** 63, 149, **160–162,** 163, 164; **Supp. I Part 2:** 579

House of the Solitary Maggot, The (Purdy), **Supp. VII:** 274–275

"House on 15th S.W., The" (Hugo), **Supp. VI:** 140

"House on Main Street, The" (B. Kelly), **Supp. XVII:** 127

House on Mango Street, The (Cisneros), **Supp. VII:** 58, 59–64, 65, 66, 67, 68, 72

"House on Mango Street, The" (Cisneros), **Supp. VII:** 59

House on Marshland, The (Glück), **Supp. V:** 81–83, 84

"House on Moscow Street, The" (Nelson), **Supp. XVIII:** 174

"House on the Heights, A" (Capote), **Supp. III Part 1:** 120

"House on the Hill, The" (Robinson), **III:** 505, 524

"House Raising" (Offutt), **Supp. XIX:** 166

"Houses" (Hogan), **Supp. IV Part 1:** 402

"Houses, The" (Merwin), **Supp. III Part 1:** 354

"Houses of the Spirit" (Karr), **Supp. XI:** 250

"House Sparrows" (Hecht), **Supp. X: 68**

"House That Doesn't House, The" (Bronk), **Supp. XXI:** 34

House That Tai Maing Built, The (Lee), **Supp. X:** 291

"House Unroofed by the Gale" (Tu Fu), **II:** 526

"House Where Mark Twain Was Born, The" (Masters), **Supp. I Part 2:** 472

"Housewife" (Hempel), **Supp. XXI:** 124

"Housewife" (Sexton), **Supp. II Part 2:** 682

" 'Housing the Deliberations': New York, War, and Frank O'Hara"(Ward), **Supp. XXIII:** 218

Housman, A. E., **III:** 15, 136, 606; **Supp. II Part 1:** 4; **Supp. IV Part 1:** 165; **Supp. XV:** 40–41

Houston Trilogy (McMurtry), **Supp. V:** 223–225

How" (Ginsberg), **Supp. XIV:** 142, 143

"How" (Moore), **Supp. X:** 167

"How About This?" (Carver), **Supp. III Part 1:** 141

"How America Came to the Mountains" (J. W. Miller), **Supp. XX: 169**

"How Annandale Went Out" (Robinson), **III:** 513

Howard, Arliss, **Supp. XXI:** 39

Howard, Ben, **Supp. XVI:** 54

Howard, Gerald, **Supp. XII:** 21

Howard, Jane, **Retro. Supp. I:** 334

Howard, June, **Retro. Supp. II:** 139

Howard, Leon, **Supp. I Part 2:** 408, 422, 423

Howard, Maureen, **Supp. XII:** 285; **Supp. XVII:** 183

Howard, Richard, **Retro. Supp. II:** 43; **Supp. IV Part 2:** 624, 626, 640; **Supp. VIII:** 273; **Supp. IX:** 324, 326; **Supp. X:** 152; **Supp. XI:** 317; **Supp. XII:** 254; **Supp. XIII:** 76; **Supp. XV:** 23, 24

Howard, Vilma, **Retro. Supp. II:** 111, 112

Howards, J. Z., **Supp. VIII:** 178

Howards End (Forster), **Supp. XII:** 87

Howarth, Cora, **I:** 408, 409

Howbah Indians (Ortiz), **Supp. IV Part 2:** 513

"How Black Sees Green and Red" (McKay), **Supp. X:** 136

How Britain Rules Africa (Padmore), **Supp. XXI:** 166

"How David Did Not Care" (R. Bly), **Supp. IV Part 1:** 73

"How Did I Love Him?" (Nelson), **Supp. XVIII:** 176

"How Do I Love Thee?" (Browning), **Supp. XVIII:** 176

Howe, Darcus, **Supp. XXI:** 170

Howe, E.W., **I:** 106

Howe, Florence, **Supp. XIII:** 295, 306

Howe, Harriet, **Supp. XI:** 200, 201

Howe, Irving, **IV:** 10; **Retro. Supp. I:** 369; **Retro. Supp. II:** 112, 286; **Supp. I Part 2:** 432; **Supp. II Part 1:** 99; **Supp. VI: 113–129; Supp. VIII:** 93, 232; **Supp. IX:** 227; **Supp. X:** 203, 245; **Supp. XII:** 160; **Supp. XIII:** 98; **Supp. XIV:** 103–104, 104; **Supp. XVII:** 50; **Supp. XIX:** 257, 265; **Supp. XXIII:** 3, 7

Howe, James Wong, **Supp. I Part 1:** 281; **Supp. V:** 223

Howe, Julia Ward, **III:** 505; **Retro. Supp. II:** 135

Howe, M. A. DeWolfe, **I:** 258; **II:** 406; **Supp. XIV:** 54

Howe, Mary Manning, **Supp. IV Part 2:** 422

Howe, Samuel, **Supp. I Part 1:** 153

Howe, Susan, **Retro. Supp. I:** 33, 43; **Supp. IV Part 2: 419–438; Supp. XVI:** 284

Howell, Chris, **Supp. XIII:** 112

Howell, James, **II:** 111

Howells, Margaret, **II:** 271

Howells, William C., **II:** 273

Howells, William Dean, **I:** 109, 192, 204, 210, 211, 254, 355, 407, 411, 418, 459, 469; **II:** 127–128, 130, 131, 136, 137, 138, 140, **271–294,** 322, 331–332, 338, 397–398, 400, 415, 444, 451, 556; **III:** 51, 118, 314, 327–328, 461, 576, 607; **IV:** 192, 202, 342, 349; **Retro. Supp. I:** 220, 334, 362, 378; **Retro. Supp. II:** 93, 101, 135, 288; **Supp. I Part 1:** 306, 318, 357, 360, 368; **Supp. I Part 2:** 414, 420, 645–646; **Supp. II Part 1:** 198, 352; **Supp. IV Part 2:** 678; **Supp. VIII:** 98, 101, 102; **Supp. XI:** 198, 200; **Supp. XIV:** 45–46; **Supp. XV:** 269, 274, 285, 287; **Supp. XVIII:** 6

Howells, Mrs. William Dean (Elinor Mead), **II:** 273

Howells, Winifred, **II:** 271

"Howells as Anti-Novelist" (Updike), **Retro. Supp. I:** 334

Howells: His Life and World (Brooks), **I:** 254

Hower, Edward, **Supp. XII:** 330, 343

Howes, Barbara, **Supp. XIII:** 331

How Good Is David Mamet, Anyway? (Heilpern), **Supp. XIV:** 242

"How I Became a Shadow" (Purdy), **Supp. VII:** 269

"How I Came to Vedanta" (Isherwood), **Supp. XIV:** 164

"How I Come to You" (Peacock), **Supp. XIX:** 198

"How I Learned to Sweep" (Alvarez), **Supp. VII:** 4

"How I Spent My Forties" (Wasserstein), **Supp. XV:** 325, 330, 332

"How It Began" (Stafford), **Supp. XI:** 327

"How It Feels to Be Colored Me" (Hurston), **Supp. VI:** 152

"How It Is" (Budbill), **Supp. XIX:** 10

"How It Is" (Everwine), **Supp. XV:** 79, 86

"How I Told My Child About Race" (Brooks), **Supp. III Part 1:** 78

"How I Went to the Mines" (Harte), **Supp. II Part 1:** 336

"How I Write" (Franzen), **Supp. XX: 84**

"How I Write" (Welty), **IV:** 279, 280

"How I Wrote *The Promised Land*" (Antin), **Supp. XX:** 3

"How Jonah Did Not Care" (R. Bly), **Supp. IV Part 1:** 73

Howl (Ginsberg), **Retro. Supp. I:** 426; **Supp. III Part 1:** 92; **Supp. IV Part 1:** 90; **Supp. V:** 336; **Supp. VIII:** 290; **Supp. XIV:** 15, 126, 157; **Supp. XVIII:** 20, 29

"How Laddie and the Princess Spelled Down at the Christmas Bee" (Stratton-Porter), **Supp. XX: 216**

Howl and Other Poems (Ginsberg), **Supp. II Part 1:** 308, 317–318, 319; **Supp. X:** 123

Howlett, William, **Retro. Supp. I:** 17

Howl: Original Draft Facsimile, Transcript and Variant Versions (Gimsberg), **Supp. XIV:** 142

"How Many Midnights" (Bowles), **Supp. IV Part 1:** 86–87

"How Many Nights" (Kinnell), **Supp. III Part 1:** 245–246

How Much? (Blechman), **Supp. I Part 1:** 290

"How Much Are You Worth" (Salinas), **Supp. XIII:** 325–326

"How Much Earth" (Levine), **Supp. V:** 184

How Much Earth: The Fresno Poets (Buckley, Oliveira, and Williams, eds.), **Supp. XIII:** 313

"How Not to Forget" (Bartov), **Supp. XVI:** 153–154

"How Poetry Comes to Me" (Corso), **Supp. XII:** 122

"How Poetry Comes to Me" (Snyder), **Supp. VIII:** 305

How Reading Changed My Life (Quindlen), **Supp. XVII:** 167, 179–180

"How She Came By Her Name: An Interview with Louis Massiah" (Bambara), **Supp. XI:** 20

"How Soon Hath Time" (Ransom), **IV:** 123

How Spring Comes (Notley), **Supp. XXII:** 226, 229

How Stella Got Her Groove Back (McMillan), **Supp. XIII:** 185, **190–191**

How the Alligator Missed Breakfast (Kinney), **Supp. III Part 1:** 235, 253

"How the Devil Came Down Division Street" (Algren), **Supp. IX:** 3

How the García Girls Lost Their Accents (Alvarez), **Supp. VII:** 3, 5–9, 11, 15, 17, 18

How the Grinch Stole Christmas! (Geisel), **Supp. XVI:** 102

How the Other Half Lives (Riis), **I:** 293

"How the Saint Did Not Care" (R. Bly), **Supp. IV Part 1:** 73

"How the Women Went from Dover" (Whittier), **Supp. I Part 2:** 694, 696, 697

"How To" (Carruth), **Supp. XVI:** 51

How To Be Alone: Essays (Franzen), **Supp. XX: 83, 90, 93–94**

"How to Be an Other Woman" (Moore), **Supp. X:** 165, 167, 168

"How to Become a Writer" (Moore), **Supp. X:** 167, 168

"How to Be Happy: Another Memo to Myself" (Dunn), **Supp. XI:** 145

How To Cook a Wolf (M. F. K. Fisher), **Supp. XVII:** 84–85, 87

How to Develop Your Personality (Shellow), **Supp. I Part 2:** 608

How to Know God: The Yoga Aphorisms of Patanjali (Isherwood and Prabhavananda)), **Supp. XIV:** 164

"How To Like It" (Dobyns), **Supp. XIII: 85–86**

"How to Live on $36,000 a Year" (Fitzgerald), **Retro. Supp. I:** 105

"How to Live. What to Do" (Stevens), **Retro. Supp. I:** 302

"How Tom is Doin' " (Kees), **Supp. XV:** 143

How to Read (Pound), **Supp. VIII:** 291

How to Read a Novel (Gordon), **II:** 198

How to Read a Poem and Fall in Love with Poetry (Hirsch), **Supp. XIX:** 202

How to Read a Poem: And Fall in Love with Poetry (Hirsch), **Supp. XXIII:** 124

How to Read a Poem . . . and Start a Poetry Circle (Peacock), **Supp. XIX:** 194, 202–203, 205

How to Save Your Own Life (Jong), **Supp. V:** 115, 123–125, 130

"How to Study Poetry" (Pound), **III:** 474

"How to Talk to Your Mother" (Moore), **Supp. X:** 167, 172

How to Win Friends and Influence People (Carnegie), **Supp. I Part 2:** 608

How to Worry Successfully (Seabury), **Supp. I Part 2:** 608

How to Write (Stein), **IV:** 32, 34, 35

"How to Write a Blackwood Article" (Poe), **III:** 425; **Retro. Supp. II:** 273

"How to Write a Memoir Like This" (Oates), **Supp. III Part 2:** 509

"How to Write Like Somebody Else" (Roethke), **III:** 540

How to Write Short Stories (Lardner), **II:** 430, 431

"How Vincentine Did Not Care" (R. Bly), **Supp. IV Part 1:** 73

How We Became Human: New and Selected Poems (Harjo), **Supp. XII: 230–232**

"How We Danced" (Sexton), **Supp. II Part 2:** 692

How We Got Insipid (Lethem), **Supp. XVIII:** 149

"How We Got in Town and Out Again" (Lethem), **Supp. XVIII:** 149

"How You Sound??" (Baraka), **Supp. II Part 1:** 30

Hoy, Philip, **Supp. X:** 56, 58

Hoyer, Linda Grace (pseudonym). *See* Updike, Mrs. Wesley
Hoyt, Constance, **Supp. I Part 2:** 707
Hoyt, Elinor Morton. *See* Wylie, Elinor
Hoyt, Helen, **Supp. XXII:** 275
Hoyt, Henry (father), **Supp. I Part 2:** 707
Hoyt, Henry (son), **Supp. I Part 2:** 708
Hoyt, Henry Martyn, **Supp. I Part 2:** 707
Hsu, Kai-yu, **Supp. X:** 292
Hsu, Ruth Y., **Supp. XV:** 212
Hubba City (Reed), **Supp. X:** 241
Hubbard, Elbert, **I:** 98, 383
Hubbell, Jay B., **Supp. I Part 1:** 372
"Hubbub, The" (Ammons), **Supp. VII:** 35
Huber, François, **II:** 6
Huckins, Olga, **Supp. IX:** 32
Huckleberry Finn (Twain). *See Adventures of Huckleberry Finn, The* (Twain)
Hud (film), **Supp. V:** 223, 226
Hudgins, Andrew, **Supp. X:** 206; **Supp. XVII:** 111, 112; **Supp. XVIII:** 176
Hudson, Henry, **I:** 230
"Hudsonian Curlew, The" (Snyder), **Supp. VIII:** 302
Hudson River Bracketed (Wharton), **IV:** 326–327; **Retro. Supp. I:** 382
Huebsch, B. W., **III:** 110
Hueffer, Ford Madox, **Supp. I Part 1:** 257, 262. *See also* Ford, Ford Madox
Huene-Greenberg, Dorothee von, **Supp. XX:** 46
Huff (television series), **Supp. XIX:** 222
Hug Dancing (Hearon), **Supp. VIII:** 67–68
Huge Season, The (Morris), **III:** 225–226, 227, 230, 232, 233, 238
Hugging the Jukebox (Nye), **Supp. XIII:** 275–276, 277
"Hugging the Jukebox" (Nye), **Supp. XIII:** 276
Hughes, Brigid, **Supp. XVI:** 247
Hughes, Carolyn, **Supp. XII:** 272, 285
Hughes, Frieda, **Supp. I Part 2:** 540, 541
Hughes, Glenn, **Supp. I Part 1:** 255
Hughes, H. Stuart, **Supp. VIII:** 240
Hughes, James Nathaniel, **Supp. I Part 1:** 321, 332
Hughes, Ken, **Supp. XI:** 307
Hughes, Langston, **Retro. Supp. I:** 193–214; **Retro. Supp. II:** 114, 115, 117, 120; **Supp. I Part 1:** 320–348; **Supp. II Part 1:** 31, 33, 61, 170, 173, 181, 227, 228, 233, 361; **Supp. III Part 1:** 72–77; **Supp. IV Part 1:** 15, 16, 164, 168, 169, 173, 243, 368; **Supp. VIII:** 213; **Supp. IX:** 306, 316; **Supp. X:** 131, 136, 139, 324; **Supp. XI:** 1; **Supp. XIII:** 75, 111, 132, 233; **Supp. XVI:** 135, 138; **Supp. XVIII:** 90, 277, 279, 280, 281, 282; **Supp. XIX:** 72, 75, 77; **Supp. XXI:** 243; **Supp. XXII:** 3, 4, 5, 6, 8, 13–14
Hughes, Nicholas, **Supp. I Part 2:** 541
Hughes, Robert, **Supp. X:** 73
Hughes, Ted, **IV:** 3; **Retro. Supp. II:** 244, 245, 247, 257; **Supp. I Part 2:** 536, 537, 538, 539, 540, 541; **Supp. XV:** 117, 347, 348; **Supp. XXII:** 30

Hughes, Thomas, **Supp. I Part 2:** 406
"Hugh Harper" (Bowles), **Supp. IV Part 1:** 94
Hughie (O'Neill), **III:** 385, 401, 405
Hugh Selwyn Mauberley (Pound), **I:** 66, 476; **III:** 9, 462–463, 465, 468; **Retro. Supp. I:** 289–290, 291, 299; **Supp. XIV:** 272
Hugo, Richard, **Supp. VI:** 131–148; **Supp. IX:** 296, 323, 324, 330; **Supp. XI:** 315, 317; **Supp. XII:** 178; **Supp. XIII:** 112, 113, 133; **Supp. XVIII:** 293, 299; **Supp. XXI:** 243
Hugo, Victor, **II:** 290, 490, 543; **Supp. IV Part 2:** 518; **Supp. IX:** 308
Hui-neng, **III:** 567
Huis Clos (Sartre), **Supp. IV Part 1:** 84
Huizinga, Johan, **I:** 225; **II:** 416–417, 418, 425
Hulbert, Ann, **Supp. XI:** 38–39
Hull, Lynda, **Supp. XI:** 131; **Supp. XXI:** 129–142
Hulme, Thomas E., **I:** 68, 69, 475; **III:** 196, 209, 463–464, 465; **IV:** 122; **Supp. I Part 1:** 261, 262; **Supp. XV:** 43
Human, All Too Human (Nietzsche), **Supp. X:** 48
"Human Culture" (Emerson), **II:** 11–12
Human Factor, The (Greene), **Supp. V:** 298
"Human Figures" (Doty), **Supp. XI:** 123–124
"Human Fly, The" (Boyle), **Supp. XX:** 19
"Human Geography" (Jarman), **Supp. XVII:** 116
"Human Immortality" (James), **II:** 353–354
"Human Life" (Emerson), **II:** 11–12
"Human Pig" (Jin), **Supp. XVIII:** 99
Human Rights, Human Wrongs: The Oxford Amnesty Lectures, 2001, **Supp. XVI:** 155
"Human Soul as a Rube Goldberg Device, The: A Choose-Your-Own-Adventure-Story" (Brockmeier), **Supp. XXII:** 60–61
Human Stain, The (P. Roth), **Retro. Supp. II:** 279, 289, 294–295
"Human Things" (Nemerov), **III:** 279
Human Universe (Olson), **Supp. II Part 2:** 571
"Human Universe" (Olson), **Supp. II Part 2:** 565, 567
Human Vibration (Richter), **Supp. XVIII:** 209
Human Wishes (Hass), **Supp. VI:** 105–106, 107
Human Work (Gilman), **Supp. XI:** 206
Humbert, Humbert, **Supp. X:** 283
Humble Inquiry into the Rules of the Word of God, An, Concerning the Qualifications Requisite to a Complete Standing and Full Communion in the Visible Christian Church (Edwards), **I:** 548
Humboldt, Alexander von, **III:** 428
Humboldt's Gift (Bellow), **Retro. Supp. II:** 19, 28–29, 34; **Supp. XIII:** 320

Hume, David, **I:** 125; **II:** 349, 357, 480; **III:** 618
Humes, Harold, **Supp. V:** 201; **Supp. XIV:** 82
Humes, Harry, **Supp. XIX:** 281; **Supp. XXIII:** 54
Humes, H. L. "Doc", **Supp. XI:** 294
"Humility" (Hoffman), **Supp. XVIII:** 86
Hummer, T. R., **Supp. XIX:** 278; **Supp. XXI:** 91
"Hummingbirds, The" (Welty), **IV:** 273
Humors and/or Not So Humorous (Kenny), **Supp. XXIII:** 155
Humphrey, William, **Supp. IX:** 93–112; **Supp. XV:** 353
Humphreys, Christmas, **Supp. V:** 267
Humphreys, David, **Supp. II Part 1:** 65, 69, 70, 268
Humphreys, Josephine, **Supp. XII:** 311
Humphries, Rolfe, **III:** 124; **Retro. Supp. I:** 137
Hunchback of Notre Dame, The (film), **Supp. IV Part 1:** 101
Hunches in Bunches (Geisel), **Supp. XVI:** 111
Huncke, Herbert, **Supp. XII:** 118; **Supp. XIV:** 137–153
Huncke's Journal (Huncke), **Supp. XIV:** 139, 144, 145, 146
Hundred Camels in the Courtyard, A (Bowles), **Supp. IV Part 1:** 90
"Hundred Collars, A" (Frost), **Retro. Supp. I:** 128; **Supp. XIII:** 147
Hundred Secret Senses, The (Tan), **Supp. X:** 289, 293, 295, 297, 298, 299
Hundreds of Hens and Other Poems for Children by Halfdan Rasmussen (Nelson and Espeland, trans.), **Supp. XVIII:** 180
Hundred White Daffodils, A: Essays, Interviews, Newspaper Columns, and One Poem (Kenyon), **Supp. VII:** 160–162, 165, 166, 167, 174
Huneker, James, **III:** 102
Hunger (Hamsun), **Supp. XI:** 167
"Hunger" (Hogan), **Supp. IV Part 1:** 411
"Hunger . . ." (Rich), **Supp. I Part 2:** 571
"Hungerfield" (Jeffers), **Supp. II Part 2:** 416–417, 436
Hungerfield and Other Poems (Jeffers), **Supp. II Part 2:** 422
Hunger of Memory: The Education of Richard Rodriguez (Rodriguez), **Supp. XIV:** 297, 298, 298–302, 310
Hungry Ghosts, The (Oates), **Supp. II Part 2:** 504, 510
Hungry Hearts (Prose), **Supp. XVI:** 253
"Hungry Intellectual, A" (Le Sueur), **Supp. XXIII:** 164
Hungry Woman, The: A Mexican Medea (Moraga), **Supp. XXIII:** 196
Hunnewell, Susannah, **Supp. VIII:** 83
Hunt, Harriot K., **Retro. Supp. II:** 146
Hunt, Leigh, **II:** 515–516; **Supp. XV:** 175
Hunt, Richard Morris, **IV:** 312
Hunt, Robert, **Supp. XV:** 42, 49, 52
Hunt, William, **II:** 343
"Hunter" (Bierds), **Supp. XVII:** 30
Hunter, Dianna, **Supp. XVI:** 38

Ibn Sīná (Avicenna), **Supp. XX: 117**

Ibsen, Henrik, **II:** 27, 276, 280, 291–292; **III:** 118, 145, 148, 149, 150, 151, 152, 154–155, 156, 161, 162, 165, 511, 523; **IV:** 397; **Retro. Supp. I:** 228; **Retro. Supp. II:** 94; **Supp. IV Part 2:** 522; **Supp. XIV:** 89; **Supp. XVII:** 100; **Supp. XIX:** 241

"I Came Out of the Mother Naked" (R. Bly), **Supp. IV Part 1:** 62–63, 68

I Can Lick 30 Tigers Today! and Other Stories (Geisel), **Supp. XVI:** 108

"I Cannot Forget with What Fervid Devotion" (Bryant), **Supp. I Part 1:** 154

I Can Read with My Eyes Shut! (Geisel), **Supp. XVI:** 111

"I Can Speak!tm" (Saunders), **Supp. XIX:** 231

"I Can't Stand Your Books: A Writer Goes Home" (Gordon), **Supp. IV Part 1:** 314

"Icarium Mare" (Wilbur), **Supp. III Part 2:** 563

"Icarus in Winter" (C. Frost), **Supp. XV:** 94

Icarus's Mother (Shepard), **Supp. III Part 2:** 446

"Ice" (Bambara), **Supp. XI:** 16

"Ice Age" (Taggard), **Supp. XXII:** 276

Ice at the Bottom of the World, The (Richard), **Supp. XIX:** 209, **210–213,** 218, 220

"Iceberg, The" (Merwin), **Supp. III Part 1:** 345

Ice-Cream Headache, The, and Other Stories (Jones), **Supp. XI:** 215, 227

Ice Fire Water: A Leib Goldkorn Cocktail (Epstein), **Supp. XII: 164–166**

"Ice Fisherman, The" (C. Baxter), **Supp. XVII:** 15

"Ice House, The" (Gordon), **II:** 201

"Ice Man, The" (Di Piero), **Supp. XIX:** 40

Iceman Cometh, The (O'Neill), **I:** 81; **III:** 151, 385, 386, 401, 402–403; **Supp. VIII:** 345; **Supp. XVI:** 193; **Supp. XVII:** 103; **Supp. XXII:** 28

"Ice Palace, The" (Fitzgerald), **II:** 83, 88; **Retro. Supp. I:** 103

Ice-Shirt, The (Vollmann), **Supp. XVII:** 226, 231, 232, 233

"Ice Storm, The" (Ashbery), **Supp. III Part 1:** 26

"Ice-Storm, The" (Pinsky), **Supp. VI:** 247–248

"Ichabod" (Whittier), **Supp. I Part 2:** 687, 689–690; **Supp. XI:** 50

"I Chop Some Parsley While Listening to Art Blakey's Version of 'Three Blind Mice' " (Collins), **Supp. XXI:** 60

"Icicles" (Francis), **Supp. IX:** 83

"Icicles" (Gass), **Supp. VI:** 83

Ickes, Harold, **Supp. I Part 1:** 5

Iconographs (Swenson), **Supp. IV Part 2:** 638, 646–648, 651

"Icosaphere, The" (Moore), **III:** 213

"I Could Believe" (Levine), **Supp. V:** 189

"I Could Take" (Carruth), **Supp. XVI:** 56

I Could Tell You Stories: Sojourns in the Land of Memory (Hampl), **Supp. XXII:** 84, **92–94**

"I Cry, Love! Love!" (Roethke), **III:** 539–540

Ida (Stein), **IV:** 43, 45

"Idea, The" (Carver), **Supp. III Part 1:** 143

"Idea, The" (Strand), **Supp. IV Part 2:** 631

Ideal Husband (Wilde), **II:** 515

Idea of Florida in the American Literary Imagination, The (Rowe), **Supp. X:** 223

"Idea of Form at Spruce Creek, The" (Weigl), **Supp. XIX:** 283–284

"Idea of Ice, The" (C. Baxter), **Supp. XVII:** 15

"Idea of Order, An" (Wiman), **Supp. XVIII:** 173

"Idea of Order at Key West, The" (Stevens), **IV:** 89–90; **Retro. Supp. I:** 302, 303, 313

Ideas of Order (Stevens), **Retro. Supp. I:** 296, 298, **302–303,** 303, 305

"Identity Theft: True Memory, False Memory, and the Holocaust" (R. Franklin), **Supp. XVI:** 160

Ideograms in China (Michaux; Sobin, trans.), **Supp. XVI:** 288

"Ideographs" (Olds), **Supp. X:** 205

Ides of March, The (Wilder), **IV:** 357, 372

"I Did Not Learn Their Names" (Ellison), **Retro. Supp. II:** 124

"I Died with the First Blow & Was Reborn Wrong" (Coleman), **Supp. XI:** 91

"Idiom of a Self, The" (Pinsky), **Supp. VI:** 240

"Idiot, The" (Crane), **I:** 401

Idiot, The (Dostoevsky), **I:** 468

"Idiots First" (Malamud), **Supp. I Part 2:** 434–435, 437, 440–441

"Idiot Wind" (song, Dylan), **Supp. XVIII:** 30

I Don't Need You Any More (A. Miller), **III:** 165

Idoru (W. Gibson), **Supp. XVI:** 119, 124, **129–130**

"I Dream I'm the Death of Orpheus" (Rich), **Supp. I Part 2:** 557–558

I Dreamt I Became a Nymphomaniac! Imagining (Acker), **Supp. XII:** 4, 6, **8,** 11

"I Dreamt You Young" (Espaillat), **Supp. XXI:** 107

"Idyll" (Shaw), **Supp. XIX:** 241

Idylls of the King (Tennyson), **III:** 487; **Supp. I Part 2:** 410; **Supp. XIII:** 146

Idyl of Work, An (Larcom), **Supp. XIII:** 139, 142, 146–147, 150

"If" (Creeley), **Supp. IV Part 1:** 158

If Beale Street Could Talk (Baldwin), **Retro. Supp. II:** 13–14; **Supp. I Part 1:** 48, 59–60, 61

"If Biblical Law Ruled Modern Society . . . " (P. N. Warren), **Supp. XX: 272**

If Blessing Comes (Bambara), **Supp. XI:** 1

I Feel a Little Jumpy around You (Nye and Janeczko, eds.), **Supp. XIII:** 280

"I felt a Funeral, in my Brain" (Dickinson), **Retro. Supp. I:** 38

"If Grown-Ups Were Smart" (Nelson and Espeland), **Supp. XVIII:** 181

If He Hollers Let Him Go (C. Himes), **Supp. XVI:** 135, 138–139, 142

"If I Could Be Like Wallace Stevens" (Stafford), **Supp. XI:** 327

"If I Could Do Whatever I Wanted" (Nelson and Espeland), **Supp. XVIII:** 181

"If I Could Only Live at the Pitch That Is Near Madness" (Eberhart), **I:** 523, 526–527

If I Could Write This in Fire (Cliff), **Supp. XXII:** 67, 69

"If I Could Write This in Fire, I Would Write This in Fire" (Cliff), **Supp. XXII:** 65–66, 68–69

If I Die in a Combat Zone (O'Brien), **Supp. V:** 238, 239, 240, 245

"If I Had My Way" (Creeley), **Supp. IV Part 1:** 157

"If I Might Be" (Chopin), *Retro. Supp. II:* 61

"I Find the Real American Tragedy" (Dreiser), **Retro. Supp. II:** 105

If I Ran the Circus (Geisel), **Supp. XVI:** 105

If I Ran the Zoo (Geisel), **Supp. XVI:** 104–105

If It Die (Gide), **I:** 290

"If It Were Not for You" (Carruth), **Supp. XVI:** 57

"If I Were a Man" (Gilman), **Supp. XI:** 207

"If I Were the Wind" (Leopold), **Supp. XIV:** 184

If Morning Ever Comes (Tyler), **Supp. IV Part 2:** 658–659

If Mountains Die: A New Mexico Memoir (Nichols), **Supp. XIII:** 255, 257, 267

I Forgot to Go to Spain (Harrison), **Supp. VIII:** 39, **52–53**

If the River Was Whiskey (Boyle), **Supp. VIII:** 15–16; **Supp. XX: 17,** 19

"If They Knew Yvonne" (Dubus), **Supp. VII:** 81

"If We Had Bacon" (H. Roth), **Supp. IX:** 232, 234

"If We Had Known" (Francis), **Supp. IX:** 78

"If We Must Die" (McKay), **Supp. IV Part 1:** 3; **Supp. X:** 132, 134

"If We Take All Gold" (Bogan), **Supp. III Part 1:** 52

If You Call This a Cry Song (Carruth), **Supp. XVI:** 56

If You Want to Write (Ueland), **Supp. XVII:** 13

I Gaspiri (Lardner), **II:** 435

"I Gather the Limbs of Osiris" (Pound), **Retro. Supp. I:** 287

I Get on the Bus (McKnight), **Supp. XX: 148–150,** 152

"I Give You Back" (Harjo), **Supp. XII:** 223

Ignatius of Loyola, **IV:** 151; **Supp. XI:** 162

Ignatow, David, **Supp. XIII:** 275

"Ignis Fatuus" (Tate), **IV:** 128

"Ignorant Lust after Knowledge, The" (Bronk), **Supp. XXI:** 31

"I Go Back to May 1937" (Olds), **Supp. X:** 207

I Go Dreaming Serenades (Salinas), **Supp. XIII:** 316

I Got the Blues (Odets), **Supp. II Part 2:** 530

Iguana Killer, The (Ríos), **Supp. IV Part 2:** 542–544

"I Had Eight Birds Hatcht in One Nest" (Bradstreet), **Supp. I Part 1:** 102, 115, 117, 119

"I had no time to Hate" (Dickinson), **Retro. Supp. I:** 44–45, 46

I Had Trouble in Getting to Solla Sollew (Geisel), **Supp. XVI:** 108, 109

"I Have a Rendezvous with Life" (Cullen), **Supp. IV Part 1:** 168

"I Have Increased Power" (Ginsberg), **Supp. II Part 1:** 313

"I Have Moved West" (Taggard), **Supp. XXII:** 274

"I Have Seen Black Hands" (Wright), **Supp. II Part 1:** 228

"I Hear an Army" (Joyce), **Supp. I Part 1:** 262

"I heard a Fly buzz when I died" (Dickinson), **Retro. Supp. I:** 38

"I Heard Immanuel Singing" (Lindsay), **Supp. I Part 2:** 379

I Heard It Through the Grapevine (Turner), **Supp. XX:** 110

"I Hear It Was Charged against Me" (Whitman), **IV:** 343

I Hear Men Talking (Le Sueur), **Supp. XXIII:** 162, 167, **171–172**

"I Held a Shelley Manuscript" (Corso), **Supp. XII:** 128

"I Held His Name" (Ríos), **Supp. IV Part 2:** 547

"Ike and Nina" (Boyle), **Supp. XX:** 19

I Knew a Phoenix (Sarton), **Supp. VIII:** 249, 251–252

"I Know a Man" (Creeley), **Supp. IV Part 1:** 147–148, 149

I Know Some Things: Stories about Childhood by Contemporary Writers (Moore, ed.), **Supp. X:** 175

"I Know Why the Caged Bird Cannot Read" (Prose), **Supp. XVI:** 259

I Know Why the Caged Bird Sings (Angelou), **Supp. IV Part 1:** 2–4, 5, 7, 11, 12, 13, 14, 15, 17; **Supp. XVI:** 259

"Ikon: The Harrowing of Hell" (Levertov), **Supp. III Part 1:** 284

Ile (O'Neill), **III:** 388

"I Led Three Lives" (television program), **Supp. XX:** 195

"I Let Him Take Me" (Cisneros), **Supp. VII:** 71

Iliad (Bryant, trans.), **Supp. I Part 1:** 158

Iliad (Homer), **II:** 470; **Supp. IV Part 2:** 631; **Supp. IX:** 211; **Supp. X:** 114; **Supp. XVII:** 117; **Supp. XXI:** 36

Iliad (Pope, trans.), **Supp. I Part 1:** 152

"I like to see it lap the Miles" (Dickinson), **Retro. Supp. I:** 37

"I Live Up Here" (Merwin), **Supp. III Part 1:** 349

"I'll Be Doing More of Same" (Franzen), **Supp. XX: 89**

"Illegal Alien" (Mora), **Supp. XIII:** 215

"Illegal Days, The" (Paley), **Supp. VI:** 222

"Illegibility" (F. Wright), **Supp. XVII:** 244

Illig, Joyce, **Retro. Supp. II:** 20

"Illinois" (Masters), **Supp. I Part 2:** 458

"Illinois Bus Ride" (Leopold), **Supp. XIV:** 189

Illinois Poems (Masters), **Supp. I Part 2:** 472

"Illinois Village, The" (Lindsay), **Supp. I Part 2:** 381

"Ill-Lit" (F. Wright), **Supp. XVII:** 245

Ill-Lit: Selected & New Poems (F. Wright), **Supp. XVII:** 245

Illness as Metaphor (Sontag), **Supp. III Part 2:** 452, 461, 466

I'll Take My Stand ("Twelve Southerners"), **II:** 196; **III:** 496; **IV:** 125, 237; **Supp. X:** 25, 52–53; **Supp. XIV:** 3

"I'll Take You to Tennessee" (Connell), **Supp. XIV:** 82

Illumination (Frederic), **II:** 141

Illumination, The (Brockmeier), **Supp. XXII:** 61

Illumination Night (Hoffman), **Supp. X:** 85, **86,** 88, 89

Illuminations (Rimbaud), **Supp. XXI:** 233

Illusion and Reality (Caudwell), **Supp. XXII:** 284

Illusion comique, L' (Corneille), **Supp. IX:** 138

"Illusion of Eternity, The" (Eberhart), **I:** 541

"Illusion of Fiction in Frank Conroy's *Stop-Time,* The" (R. Ramsey), **Supp. XVI:** 69

Illusions (Dash; film), **Supp. XI:** 20

"Illusions" (Emerson), **II:** 2, 5, 14, 16

Illustrated Man, The (Bradbury), **Supp. IV Part 1:** 102, 103, 113

Illustrations of China and Its People (Thompson), **Supp. XXI:** 151

Illustrations of Political Economy (Martineau), **Supp. II Part 1:** 288

"I Look at My Hand" (Swenson), **Supp. IV Part 2:** 638, 647

I Love Gootie: My Grandmother's Story (Apple), **Supp. XVII:** 9–10

I Love Myself When I Am Laughing . . . : A Zora Neale Hurston Reader (Walker), **Supp. III Part 2:** 531, 532

"I Love the Way It Goes" (O'Hara), **Supp. XXIII:** 220

"I'm a Fool" (Anderson), **I:** 113, 114, 116; **Supp. I Part 2:** 430

Image and Idea (Rahv), **Supp. II Part 1:** 146

Image and the Law, The (Nemerov), **III:** 268, 269–271, 272

"Image in the Mirror, The" (Swados), **Supp. XIX:** 265

"Images" (Hass), **Supp. VI:** 103

"Images and 'Images' " (Simic), **Supp. VIII:** 274

"Images for Godard" (Rich), **Supp. I Part 2:** 558

"Images of Walt Whitman" (Fiedler), **IV:** 352

"Imaginary Dialogue, An" (Espaillat), **Supp. XXI:** 103

"Imaginary Friendships of Tom McGrath, The" (Cohen), **Supp. X:** 112

"Imaginary Iceberg, The" (Bishop), **Retro. Supp. II:** 42; **Supp. I Part 1:** 86, 88

"Imaginary Jew, The" (Berryman), **I:** 174–175

Imaginary Letters (Pound), **III:** 473–474

Imaginary Paintings (C. Baxter), **Supp. XVII:** 18–19

"Imaginary Prisons" (Schnackenberg), **Supp. XV:** 257, 258

Imagination and Fancy; or, Selections from the English Poets, illustrative of those first requisites of their art; with markings of the best passages, critical notices of the writers, and an essay in answer to the question'What is Poetry?' (Hunt), **II:** 515–516

"Imagination as Value" (Stevens), **Retro. Supp. I:** 298

"Imagination of Disaster, The" (Gordon), **Supp. IV Part 1:** 306

Imaginative Qualities of Actual Things (Sorrentino), **Supp. XXI:** 226, 230, 231–232, 234

"Imagine a Day at the End of Your Life" (Beattie), **Supp. V:** 33

Imagined London: A Tour of the World's Greatest Fictional City (Quindlen), **Supp. XVII:** 167, 180

Imagineering Atlanta (Rutheiser), **Supp. XXII:** 244

"Imagine Kissing Pete" (O'Hara), **III:** 372; **Supp. VIII:** 156

Imaging Robert: My Brother, Madness, and Survival (Neugeboren), **Supp. XVI:** 225, **226–229**

"Imagining How It Would Be to Be Dead" (Eberhart), **I:** 533

Imagining Los Angeles: A City in Fiction (Fine), **Supp. XI:** 160

"Imagining Their Own Hymns" (B. Kelly), **Supp. XVII:** 126–127

"Imagining the Midwest" (Sanders), **Supp. XVI:** 275–276

Imagining the Worst: Stephen King and the Representations of Women (Lant and Thompson), **Supp. V:** 141

"Imagisme" (Pound), **Retro. Supp. I:** 288

Imagistes, Des: An Anthology of the Imagists (Pound, ed.), **III:** 465, 471; **Retro. Supp. I:** 288

Imago (O. Butler), **Supp. XIII:** 63, **65–66**

"Imago" (Stevens), **IV:** 74, 89

Imagoes (Coleman), **Supp. XI:** 89–90

I Married a Communist (P. Roth), **Retro. Supp. II:** 289, 293–294

I Married an Angel (film), **Supp. XVI:** 193

"I May, I Might, I Must" (Moore), **III:** 215

Imbusch, Kevin, **Supp. XXIII:** 125

"I'm Crazy" (Salinger), **III:** 553

"I'm Here" (Roethke), **III:** 547

Imitations (Lowell), **II:** 543, 544–545, 550, 555; **Retro. Supp. II:** 181, 187

"Imitations of Drowning" (Sexton), **Supp. II Part 2:** 684, 686

"Immaculate Man" (Gordon), **Supp. IV Part 1:** 311

"Immanence of Dostoevsky, The" (Bourne), **I:** 235

"Immigrants" (Mora), **Supp. XIII:** 216

Immigrant Saint: The Life of Mother Cabrini (di Donato), **Supp. XX: 44**

"Immigrant Story, The" (Paley), **Supp. VI:** 230

Immobile Wind, The (Winters), **Supp. II Part 2:** 786

"Immobile Wind, The" (Winters), **Supp. II Part 2:** 788, 811

"Immolatus" (Komunyakaa), **Supp. XIII:** 126

"Immoral Proposition, The" (Creeley), **Supp. IV Part 1:** 144

"Immortal Autumn" (MacLeish), **III:** 13

"Immortality Ode" (Nemerov), **III:** 87

Immortality Ode (Wordsworth), **II:** 17; **Supp. I Part 2:** 673

"Immortal Woman, The" (Tate), **IV:** 130, 131, 137

"I'm Not Ready to Die Yet" (Harjo), **Supp. XII:** 231

I'm Not There (film, Haynes), **Supp. XVIII:** 23

"I'm on My Way" (Salinas), **Supp. XIII:** 320

"Impasse" (Hughes), **Supp. I Part 1:** 343

"Impatient Mary" (Taggard), **Supp. XXII:** 278

Imperative Duty, An, a Novel (Howells), **II:** 286

Imperial Eyes: Travel Writing and Transculturation (Pratt), **Retro. Supp. II:** 48

Imperial Germany and the Industrial Revolution (Veblen), **Supp. I Part 2:** 642, 643

Imperial Way, The: By Rail from Peshawar to Chittagong (Theroux), **Supp. VIII:** 323

"Implosions" (Rich), **Supp. I Part 2:** 556

"Imp of the Perverse, The" (Poe), **III:** 414–415; **Retro. Supp. II:** 267

Impolite Interviews, **Supp. XI:** 293

"Importance of Artists' Biographies, The" (Goldbarth), **Supp. XII:** 183, 184, 191

Importance of Being Earnest, The (Wilde), **Supp. XIV:** 324, 339

"Important Houses, The" (Gordon), **Supp. IV Part 1:** 315

"Impossible Indispensability of the Ars Poetica, The" (Carruth), **Supp. XVI:** 57

"Impossible to Tell" (Pinsky), **Supp. VI:** 247, 248

"Imposter, The" (West), **Retro. Supp. II:** 322, 327

"Impressionism and Symbolism in *Heart of Darkness*" (Watt), **Supp. VIII:** 4

"Impressionism"(Crooker), **Supp. XXIII:** 57

"Impressions of a European Tour" (Bourne), **I:** 225

"Impressions of a Plumber" (H. Roth), **Supp. IX:** 228, 234

"Impressions of Europe, 1913–1914" (Bourne), **I:** 225

"I Must Have Called and So He Comes" (Notley), **Supp. XXII:** 224

"I'm Walking behind the Spanish" (Salinas), **Supp. XIII:** 323–324

"I/Myself" (Shields), **Supp. VII:** 311

"In Absence" (Lanier), **Supp. I Part 1:** 364

"In Absentia" (Bowles), **Supp. IV Part 1:** 94

"In a Cab" (Untermeyer), **Supp. XV:** 296

"In a Country Cemetery" (Kooser), **Supp. XIX:** 120

Inada, Lawson Fusao, **Supp. V:** 180

"In a Dark Room, Furniture" (Nye), **Supp. XIII:** 274

"In a Dark Time" (Roethke), **III:** 539, 547, 548

In a Different Voice (Gilligan), **Supp. XXII:** 18

"In a Disused Graveyard" (Frost), **Retro. Supp. I:** 126, 133

In a Dusty Light (Haines), **Supp. XII:** 207

"In a Garden" (Lowell), **II:** 513

"In a Hard Intellectual Light" (Eberhart), **I:** 523

"In a Hollow of the Hills" (Harte), **Supp. II Part 1:** 354

In America (Sontag), **Supp. XIV:** 95–96

"In Amicitia" (Ransom), **IV:** 141

In a Narrow Grave: Essays on Texas (McMurtry), **Supp. V:** 220, 223

"Inanna" (A. Finch), **Supp. XVII:** 72

"In Another Country" (Hemingway), **I:** 484–485; **II:** 249

In April Once (Percy), **Retro. Supp. I:** 341

"In a Prominent Bar in Secaucus One Day" (X. J. Kennedy), **Supp. XV:** 154, 155–156

"In Armenia, 1987"(Balakian), **Supp. XXIII:** 25

In A Shallow Grave (Purdy), **Supp. VII:** 272

In a shlekhter tsayt (In a bad time) (Asch), **Supp. XXIII:** 4

"In a Station of the Metro" (Pound), **Retro. Supp. I:** 288; **Supp. I Part 1:** 265; **Supp. XIV:** 284–285

"In a Strange Town" (Anderson), **I:** 114, 115

"In Athens Once" (Rodriguez), **Supp. XIV:** 303

"In a Tub" (Hempel), **Supp. XXI:** 119

In Battle for Peace: The Story of My 83rd Birthday (Du Bois), **Supp. II Part 1:** 185

In Bed One Night & Other Brief Encounters (Coover), **Supp. V:** 49, 50

"In Bertram's Garden" (Justice), **Supp. VII:** 117

"In Blackwater Woods" (Oliver), **Supp. VII:** 244, 246

In Black & Whitey (Lacy), **Supp. XV:** 206–207

"In Broad Daylight" (Jin), **Supp. XVIII:** 94

In Broken Country (Wagoner), **Supp. IX:** 330

"In California" (Simpson), **Supp. IX:** 271

"In Camp" (Stafford), **Supp. XI:** 329

"Incant against Suicide" (Karr), **Supp. XI:** 249

"In Celebration of My Uterus" (Sexton), **Supp. II Part 2:** 689

"Incendiary, The" (Rowson), **Supp. XV:** 234

"In Certain Places and Certain Times There Can Be More of You" (Dunn), **Supp. XI:** 144

Incest: From "A Journal of Love," the Unexpurgated Diary of Anaïs Nin, 1932–1934 (Nin), **Supp. X:** 182, 184, 185, 187, 191

"In Chandler Country" (Gioia), **Supp. XV:** 119

Inchbald, Elizabeth, **II:** 8

"In Cheever Country" (Gioia), **Supp. XV:** 119

Inchiquin, the Jesuit's Letters (Ingersoll), **I:** 344

"Incident" (Cullen), **Supp. IV Part 1:** 165, 166

Incidental Numbers (Wylie), **Supp. I Part 2:** 708

Incidentals (Sandburg), **III:** 579

Incidentals in the Day World (Notley), **Supp. XXII:** 223, 226, 227

Incident at Vichy (A. Miller), **III:** 165, 166

Incidents in the Life of a Slave Girl (Brent), **Supp. IV Part 1:** 13

Incidents in the Life of a Slavegirl (Jacobs), **Supp. XVI:** 85

"Incipience" (Rich), **Supp. I Part 2:** 559

"In Clare" (McCarriston), **Supp. XIV:** 270–271

Including Horace (Untermeyer), **Supp. XV:** 301, 303–304

In Cold Blood: A True Account of a Multiple Murder and Its Consequences (Capote), **Retro. Supp. II:** 107–108; **Supp. I Part 1:** 292; **Supp. III Part 1:** 111, 117, 119, 122, 123, 125–131; **Supp. III Part 2:** 574; **Supp. IV Part 1:** 220; **Supp. XIV:** 162

In Cold Hell, in Thicket (Olson), **Supp. II Part 2:** 571

"In Cold Hell, in Thicket" (Olson), **Supp. II Part 2:** 558, 563–564, 566, 572, 580

"Incoming Tide"(Strout), **Supp. XXIII:** 282, 285

"Incomparable Light, The" (Eberhart), **I:** 541

Incorporative Consciousness of Robert Bly, The (Harris), **Supp. IV Part 1:** 68

In Country (Mason), **Supp. VIII:** 133, **142–143,** 146

"In Country of Conscience" (J. W. Miller), **Supp. XX: 165**

"Incredible Survival of Coyote, The" (Snyder), **Supp. VIII:** 297

"Increment" (Ammons), **Supp. VII:** 28

In Defense of Ignorance (Shapiro), **Supp. II Part 2:** 703, 704, 713–714

In Defense of Reason (Winters), **Supp. I Part 1:** 268

In Defense of Women (Mencken), **III:** 109

Indelible (Hadas), **Supp. XXIII:** 119

Independence Day (film), **Supp. X:** 80

Independence Day (Ford), **Supp. V:** 57, 62–63, 67–68

"Independent Candidate, The, a Story of Today" (Howells), **II:** 277

"Indestructible Mr. Gore, The" (Vidal), **Supp. IV Part 2:** 679

Index of American Design, **Supp. III Part 2:** 618

"India" (Rodriguez), **Supp. XIV:** 302

"Indian at the Burial-Place of His Fathers, An" (Bryant), **Supp. I Part 1:** 155–156, 167–168

"Indian Burying Ground, The" (Freneau), **Supp. II Part 1:** 264, 266

"Indian Camp" (Hemingway), **II:** 247–248, 263; **Retro. Supp. I:** 174–175, 176, 177, 181; **Supp. XVI:** 208

Indian Country (Caputo), **Supp. XIX:** 22–25

Indian Country (Matthiessen), **Supp. V:** 211

"Indian Country" (McCarriston), **Supp. XIV:** 271

"Indian Country" (Simpson), **Supp. IX:** 274

Indian Earth (Bynner), **Supp. XV:** 46

"Indian Girls" (McCarriston), **Supp. XIV:** 272–273

"Indian Manifesto" (Deloria), **Supp. IV Part 1:** 323

"Indian Names" (Sigourney), **Retro. Supp. II:** 47

"Indian Student, The" (Freneau), **Supp. II Part 1:** 264

"Indian Student, The" (Simpson), **Supp. IX:** 280

Indian Summer (Howells), **II:** 275, 279–281, 282

Indian Summer (Knowles), **Supp. XII:** 249, 250

Indian Summer: Musings on the Gift of Life (Pickering), **Supp. XXI:** 204

"Indian Uprising, The" (Barthelme), **Supp. IV Part 1:** 44

"Indian Wooing" (C. Miller), **Supp. XXII:** 197–198

Indifferent Children, The (Auchincloss), **Supp. IV Part 1:** 25

Indirections (Cox), **Supp. XXI:** 21

Indiscretions (Pound), **Retro. Supp. I:** 284

"Indispensability of the Eyes, The" (Olds), **Supp. X:** 202

"In Distrust of Merits" (Moore), **III:** 201, 214

"Individual and the State, The" (Emerson), **II:** 10

Individualism, Old and New (Dewey), **Supp. I Part 2:** 677

"Indolence" (Pickering), **Supp. XXI:** 203

In Dreams Begin Responsibilities (Schwartz), **Supp. II Part 2:** 642, 645–650

"In Dreams Begin Responsibilities" (Schwartz), **Supp. II Part 2:** 641, 649, 654

In Dubious Battle (Steinbeck), **IV:** 51, 55–56, 59, 63

"In Durance" (Pound), **Retro. Supp. I:** 285

"Industry of Hard Kissing, The" (Ríos), **Supp. IV Part 2:** 547

"In Duty Bound" (Gilman), **Supp. XI:** 196–197

"I Need, I Need" (Roethke), **III:** 535–536

"I Need Help" (Stern), **Supp. IX:** 290

"Ineffectual Marriage" (Loy), **Supp. XXII:** 165

"Inés in the Kitchen" (García), **Supp. XI:** 190

"I never saw a Moor" (Dickinson), **Retro. Supp. I:** 37

I Never Told Anybody: Teaching Poetry Writing in a Nursing Home (Koch), **Supp. XV:** 190

"I Never Will Be Married, I'd Rather Be Excus'd" (Rowson), **Supp. XV:** 240

Inevitable Exiles (Kielsky), **Supp. V:** 273

"Inevitable Trial, The" (Holmes), **Supp. I Part 1:** 318

"Inexhaustible Hat, The" (Wagoner), **Supp. IX:** 327

"In Extremis" (Berry), **Supp. X:** 23

Inez, Colette, **Supp. XXIII:** 54, 245

"Infancy" (Wilder), **IV:** 375

"Infant Boy at Midcentury" (Warren), **IV:** 244–245, 252

Infante, Guillermo Cabrera, **Retro. Supp. I:** 278

"Infant Sea Turtles" (F. Wright), **Supp. XVII:** 245

Infants of the Spring (Thurman), **Supp. XVIII:** 281; **Supp. XIX:** 73

Inferno (Dante), **IV:** 139; **Supp. V:** 338; **Supp. VIII:** 219–221

Inferno of Dante, The (Pinsky), **Supp. VI:** 235, 248

"Infidelity" (Komunyakaa), **Supp. XIII:** 130

Infidels (album, Dylan), **Supp. XVIII:** 28

"Infiltration of the Universe" (MacLeish), **III:** 19

Infinite Jest: A Novel (Wallace), **Supp. X:** 301, **310–314; Supp. XX: 91**

"Infinite Reason, The" (MacLeish), **III:** 19

"Infirmity" (Lowell), **II:** 554

"Infirmity" (Roethke), **III:** 548

In Five Years Time (Haines), **Supp. XII:** 206

"In Flower" (Snodgrass), **Supp. VI:** 325

"Influence of Landscape upon the Poet, The" (Eliot), **Retro. Supp. I:** 67

"In Football Season" (Updike), **IV:** 219

Informer, The (film), **Supp. III Part 2:** 619

Ingersoll, Charles J., **I:** 344

Ingersoll, Robert Green, **Supp. II Part 1:** 198

Ingraham, Lloyd, **Supp. XVI:** 184

Ingster, Boris, **Retro. Supp. II:** 330

Inhabitants, The (Morris), **III:** 221–222

"Inheritance and Invention in Li-Young Lee's Poetry" (Xiaojing), **Supp. XV:** 214

"Inheritance"(Kenny), **Supp. XXIII:** 154

"Inheritance of Tools, The" (Sanders), **Supp. XVI:** 273

Inheritors (Glaspell), **Supp. III Part 1:** 175, 179–181, 186, 189

"In Hollywood with the Zuni God of War" (Major), **Supp. XXII:** 180

"In Honor of David Anderson Brooks, My Father" (Brooks), **Supp. III Part 1:** 79

"Inhumanist, The" (Jeffers), **Supp. II Part 2:** 423, 426

"In Illo Tempore" (Karr), **Supp. XI:** 242

"In Interims: Outlyer" (Harrison), **Supp. VIII:** 38

"Initial" (F. Wright), **Supp. XVII:** 243

"Injudicious Gardening" (Moore), **III:** 198

"Injustice" (Paley), **Supp. VI:** 220

Injustice Collectors, The (Auchincloss), **Supp. IV Part 1:** 25

Ink, Blood, Semen (Goldbarth), **Supp. XII:** 181, 183

Ink Dark Moon, The: Love Poems by Ono no Komachi and Izumi Shikibu (Aratani and Hirshfield, trans.), **Supp. XXIII:** 136

Ink Truck, The (W. Kennedy), **Supp. VII:** 132, 133–138, 140, 141, 149, 152

In Life Sentences: Literary Essays (Epstein), **Supp. XIV:** 112

"In Limbo" (Wilbur), **Supp. III Part 2:** 544, 561

In Limestone Country (Sanders), **Supp. XVI:** 272

"In Line" (Major), **Supp. XXII:** 185

In Love and Trouble: Stories of Black Women (Walker), **Supp. III Part 2:** 520, 521, 530, 531, 532

In Mad Love and War (Harjo), **Supp. XII: 224–226**

"In Memoriam" (Emerson), **II:** 13

"In Memoriam" (Hay), **Supp. XIV:** 122, 127

"In Memoriam" (Tennyson), **Retro. Supp. I:** 325; **Supp. I Part 2:** 416

In Memoriam: 1933 (Reznikoff), **Supp. XIV:** 280, 285

In Memoriam to Identity (Acker), **Supp. XII:** 5, **16–18**

"In Memory of Arthur Winslow" (Lowell), **II:** 541, 547, 550; **Retro. Supp. II:** 187

"In Memory of Congresswoman Barbara Jordan" (Pinsky), **Supp. VI:** 250

"In Memory of Joe Brainard" (Bidart), **Supp. XV:** 33

"In Memory of My Feelings" (O'Hara), **Supp. XV:** 215–216

In Memory of My Feelings (O'Hara; Berkson, ed.), **Supp. XXIII:** 220

"In Memory of My Feelings"(O'Hara), **Supp. XXIII:** 208, 215–216

"In Memory of W. B. Yeats" (Auden), **Supp. VIII:** 19, 30; **Supp. XI:** 243, 244; **Supp. XIX:** 85

"In Memory of W. H. Auden" (Stern), **Supp. IX:** 288

"In Memory"(Schott), **Supp. XXIII:** 254

"In Mercy on Broadway" (Doty), **Supp. XI:** 132

In Morocco (Wharton), **Retro. Supp. I:** 380; **Supp. IV Part 1:** 81

Inmost Leaf, The: A Selection of Essays (Kazin), **Supp. VIII:** 102, 103

In Motley (Bierce), **I:** 209

In My Father's Court (Singer), **IV:** 16–17; **Retro. Supp. II: 301–302**

"In My Life" (Dubus), **Supp. VII:** 81

"In Navaho Country" (Bronk), **Supp. XXI:** 30

Inner Circle, The (Boyle), **Supp. XX: 24, 26**

Inner Landscape (Sarton), **Supp. VIII:** 259

Inner Room, The (Merrill), **Supp. III Part 1:** 336

"In Nine Sleep Valley" (Merrill), **Supp. III Part 1:** 328

Innocent Mrs. Duff, The (Holding), **Supp. XXII:** 119, 120, 123, **130–131,** 135, 136

Innocents, The: A Story for Lovers (Lewis), **II:** 441

Innocents Abroad, The; or, The New Pilgrim's Progress (Twain), **II:** 275, 434; **IV:** 191, 196, 197–198

Innocents at Cedro, The: A Memoir of Thorstein Veblen and Some Others (Duffus), **Supp. I Part 2:** 650

"In Off the Cliffs of Moher" (McCarriston), **Supp. XIV:** 270

In Old Plantation Days (Dunbar), **Supp. II Part 1:** 214

In Ole Virginia (Page), **Supp. II Part 1:** 201

In Orbit (Morris), **III:** 236

In Other Words (Swenson), **Supp. IV Part 2:** 650–652

In Other Words: Literature by Latinas of the United States (Fernandez, ed.), **Supp. XXI:** 104

In Our Terribleness (Some elements and meaning in black style) (Baraka), **Supp. II Part 1:** 52, 53

In Our Time (Hemingway), **I:** 117; **II:** 68, 247, 252, 263; **IV:** 42; **Retro. Supp. I:** 170, 173, 174, 178, 180; **Supp. IX:** 106

"In Our Time" (Wolfe), **Supp. III Part 2:** 584

"Inpatient" (Kenyon), **Supp. VII:** 169

In Persuasion Nation (Saunders), **Supp. XIX: 231–234**

"In Persuasion Nation" (Saunders), **Supp. XIX:** 233–234

In Pharaoh's Army: Memories of the Lost War (Wolff), **Supp. VII:** 331–334, 335, 338

"In Plaster" (Plath), **Supp. I Part 2:** 540

"In Prague, in Montmartre" (Bierds), **Supp. XVII:** 27

"In Praise of Johnny Appleseed" (Lindsay), **Supp. I Part 2:** 397

"In Praise of Limestone" (Auden), **Supp. II Part 1:** 20–21; **Supp. VIII:** 23

In Pursuit of a Vanishing Star (Sobin), **Supp. XVI: 294**

In Quest of the Ordinary (Cavell), **Retro. Supp. I:** 307

Inquiry into the Moral and Religious Character of the American Government, An (H. Warner), **Supp. XVIII:** 259

Inquiry into the Nature of Peace, An (Veblen), **Supp. I Part 2:** 642

Inquisitor, The (Rowson), **Supp. XV: 232,** 238

In Radical Pursuit (Snodgrass), **Supp. VI:** 312, 316, 318

In Reckless Ecstasy (Sandburg), **III:** 579

In Recognition of William Gaddis (Kuehl and Moore), **Supp. IV Part 1:** 279

"In Retirement" (Malamud), **Supp. I Part 2:** 437

"In Retrospect" (Angelou), **Supp. IV Part 1:** 15

"In Right" (Wolfert), **Supp. XXI:** 263, 264, 272

"Inroads of Time, The" (D. West), **Supp. XVIII:** 286–287

In Russia (A. Miller), **III:** 165

"In Sabine" (Chopin), **Supp. I Part 1:** 213

"In School-Days" (Whittier), **Supp. I Part 2:** 699–700

"Inscription for the Entrance to a Wood" (Bryant), **Supp. I Part 1:** 154, 155, 161–162

Inscriptions, 1944–1956 (Reznikoff), **Supp. XIV:** 281

In Search of America: The Image of the United States in Travel Writing of the 1980s and 1990s (Rutkowska), **Supp. XXII:** 208

"In Search of a Motif for Expressive Female Figuration" (Major), **Supp. XXII:** 184

In Search of Bisco (Caldwell), **I:** 296

In Search of Nella Larsen: A Biography of the Color Line (Hutchinson), **Supp. XVIII:** 120

"In Search of Our Mothers' Gardens" (Walker), **Supp. III Part 2:** 520–532, 524, 525, 527, 529, 532–533, 535, 536; **Supp. IX:** 306; **Supp. XVIII:** 200, 283

"In Search of Thomas Merton" (Griffin), **Supp. VIII:** 208

"In Search of Yage" (Burroughs), **Supp. III Part 1:** 98

"Insect Life in Florida" (Hull), **Supp. XXI:** 133

Insel (Loy), **Supp. XXII:** 167

"Insertion of Self into a Space of Borderless Possibilities, The" (Fjellestad), **Supp. XVI:** 150

"In Shadow" (Crane), **I:** 386

"In Sickness and in Health" (Auden), **Supp. II Part 1:** 15

"In Sickness and in Health" (Humphrey), **Supp. IX:** 94

Inside Diameter: The France Poems (Major), **Supp. XXII:** 182

Inside His Mind (A. Miller), **III:** 154

Inside Memory (Findley), **Supp. XX: 51, 63**

"Inside Norman Mailer" (Apple), **Supp. XVII:** 3, 4

"Insider Baseball" (Didion), **Supp. IV Part 1:** 211

Inside Sports magazine, **Supp. V:** 58, 61

"Insipid Profession of Jonathan Horneboom, The" (Lethem), **Supp. XVIII:** 149

"In So Many Dark Rooms" (Hogan), **Supp. IV Part 1:** 400

"Insomnia" (Bishop), **Supp. I Part 1:** 92

"Insomniac" (Plath), **Supp. I Part 2:** 539

"In Spain, Throwing Carnations" (P. N. Warren), **Supp. XX: 272**

"Inspiration for Greatness" (Caldwell), **I:** 291

"Instability of Race Types, The" (Boas), **Supp. XIV:** 209

"Installation #6" (Beattie), **Supp. V:** 33

Instinct of Workmanship and the State of the Industrial Arts, The (Veblen), **Supp. I Part 2:** 642

Instincts of the Herd in Peace and War, The (Trotter), **I:** 249

Institute (Calvin), **IV:** 158, 160

"Instruction Manual, The" (Ashbery), **Supp. III Part 1:** 6–7, 10, 12

Instructions, The (Levin), **Supp. XXII:** 268

"Instructions for the Afternoon" (Gioia), **Supp. XV:** 120

"Instruction to Myself" (Brooks), **Supp. III Part 1:** 87

Instrument, The (O'Hara), **III:** 362, 364

"In Such Times, Ties Must Bind" (Nye), **Supp. XIII:** 286

"Insurance and Social Change" (Stevens), **Retro. Supp. I:** 297

Insurgent Mexico (Reed), **I:** 476

In Suspect Terrain (McPhee), **Supp. III Part 1:** 309, 310

"In Tall Grass" (Sandburg), **III:** 585

"Integer Vitae" (Horace), **Supp. XV:** 304

Intellectual History, An (Senghor), **Supp. X:** 139

"Intellectual Pre-Eminence of Jews in Modern Europe, The" (Veblen), **Supp. I Part 2:** 643–644

Intellectual Things (Kunitz), **Supp. III Part 1:** 260, 262–264

Intellectual versus the City, The (White), **I:** 258

"In Temporary Pain" (Bynner), **Supp. XV:** 41–42

Intentions (Wilde), **Retro. Supp. I:** 56

"Interest in Life, An" (Paley), **Supp. VI:** 222, 224–225

Interest of Great Britain Considered, with Regard to Her Colonies and the Acquisition of Canada and Guadeloupe, The (Franklin), **II:** 119

Interior Landscapes (Vizenor), **Supp. IV Part 1:** 262

Interiors (film; Allen), **Supp. IV Part 1:** 205; **Supp. XV:** 1, 7, 10

Interlocking Lives (Koch), **Supp. XV:** 185

"Interlude" (A. Lowell), **Retro. Supp. II:** 46

Interlunar (Atwood), **Supp. XIII:** 35

"Intermezzo" (Schnackenberg), **Supp. XV:** 254

"In Terms of the Toenail: Fiction and the Figures of Life" (Gass), **Supp. VI:** 85

"International Episode, An" (James), **II:** 327

International Workers Order, **Retro. Supp. I:** 202

Interpretation of Christian Ethics, An (Niebuhr), **III:** 298–300, 301, 302

"Interpretation of Dreams, The" (Matthews), **Supp. IX:** 162–163

Interpretation of Music of the XVIIth and XVIIIth Centuries, The (Dolmetsch), **III:** 464

Interpretations and Forecasts: 1922–1972 (Mumford), **Supp. II Part 2:** 481

Interpretations of Poetry and Religion (Santayana), **III:** 611

Interpreter of Maladies (Lahiri), **Supp. XXI:** 175–176, **177–180,** 183

"Interpreter of Maladies" (Lahiri), **Supp. XXI:** 183, 184

Interpreters and Interpretations (Van Vechten), **Supp. II Part 2:** 729, 733–734

"Interrogate the Stones" (MacLeish), **III:** 9

Interrogations at Noon (Gioia), **Supp. XV:** 112, **125–127,** 128, 129

"Interrupted Conversation, An" (Van Vechten), **Supp. II Part 2:** 735

"Interrupted Elegy" (Peacock), **Supp. XIX:** 200

Intersect: Poems (Shields), **Supp. VII:** 310–311

Intersexes, The (Prime-Stevenson as Mayne), **Supp. XX: 235**

Interstate (Dixon), **Supp. XII:** 140, 152–153, 153, 156

"Interview" (Hay), **Supp. XIV:** 132

"Interview, The" (Thurber), **Supp. I Part 2:** 616

"Interview With a Lemming" (Thurber), **Supp. I Part 2:** 603

"Interview with Larry Rivers, An"(O'Hara), **Supp. XXIII:** 214

"Interview with Peter Everwine, An" (Veinberg and Buckley), **Supp. XV:** 76–77

"Interview with the Crab" (Lethem), **Supp. XVIII:** 148

Interview with the Vampire (Rice), **Supp. VII:** 287, 288–291, 297–298, 303

"Interview with the Vampire" (Rice), **Supp. VII:** 288

Interzone (Burroughs), **Supp. IV Part 1:** 90

"In the Absence of Bliss" (Kumin), **Supp. IV Part 2:** 453

"In the Afternoon" (Dunn), **Supp. XI:** 146

"In the Alley" (Elkin), **Supp. VI:** 46–47

In the American Grain (W. C. Williams), **Retro. Supp. I:** 420–421

In the American Jungle (W. Frank), **Supp. XX:** 76

In the American Tree (Silliman), **Supp. IV Part 2:** 426

In the Bank of Beautiful Sins (Wrigley), **Supp. XVIII: 300–302**

In the Bar of a Tokyo Hotel (T. Williams), **IV:** 382, 386, 387, 391, 393

In the Beauty of the Lilies (Updike), **Retro. Supp. I:** 322, 325, 326, 327, 333

"In the Beeyard" (Bierds), **Supp. XVII:** 29

"In the Beginning" (Quindlen), **Supp. XVII:** 166

"In the Beginning . . ." (Simic), **Supp. VIII:** 270, 271

In the Belly of the Beast: Letters from Prison (Abbott), **Retro. Supp. II:** 210

"In the Black Morning" (Wolfert), **Supp. XXI:** 265

"In the Black Museum" (Nemerov), **III:** 275

"In the Blink of God's Eye" (P. E. Jones), **Supp. XXII:** 150

"In the Bodies of Words" (Swenson), **Supp. IV Part 2:** 651

"In the Box"(Kenny), **Supp. XXIII:** 155

"In the Cage" (Gass), **Supp. VI:** 85

In the Cage (James), **Retro. Supp. I:** 229

"In the Cage" (James), **II:** 332; **Retro. Supp. I:** 231

"In the Cage" (Lowell), **Retro. Supp. II:** 187

"In the Cave at Lone Tree Meadow" (Haines), **Supp. XII:** 212

"In the Cemetery Where Al Jolson Is Buried" (Hempel), **Supp. XXI:** 115, **121–122**

"In the City Ringed with Giants" (Kingsolver), **Supp. VII:** 209

"In the Clearing" (Brodsky), **Supp. VIII:** 32

In the Clearing (Frost), **II:** 153, 155, 164; **Retro. Supp. I:** 121, 122, 141

"In the Closet of the Soul" (Walker), **Supp. III Part 2:** 526

"In the Cold Air Register" (W. V. Davis), **Supp. XXI:** 94

"In the Confidence of a Story-Writer" (Chopin), **Retro. Supp. II:** 66–67; **Supp. I Part 1:** 217

In the Country of Last Things (Auster), **Supp. XII:** 23, **29–30,** 31, 32

"In the Courtyard of the Isleta Missions" (R. Bly), **Supp. IV Part 1:** 71

"In the Dark" (Levine), **Supp. V:** 194

"In the Dark New England Days" (Jewett), **Retro. Supp. II:** 139

"In the Days of Prismatic Colour" (Moore), **III:** 205, 213

In the Days of the Comet (Wells), **Supp. XX:** 233, 240

In the Electric Mist with Confederate Dead (Burke), **Supp. XIV:** 30, 31–32

"In the Field" (Wilbur), **Supp. III Part 2:** 558

"In the First Stanza" (C. Kizer), **Supp. XVII:** 75

"In the Fleeting Hand of Time" (Corso), **Supp. XII:** 122–123

"In the Footsteps of Gutenberg" (Mencken), **III:** 101

"In the Forest" (Simpson), **Supp. IX:** 270

"In the Forest of the Laughing Elephant" (Caputo), **Supp. XIX:** 27

"In the Forties" (Lowell), **II:** 554

In the Garden of the North American Martyrs (Wolff), **Supp. VII:** 341–342

In the Garret (Van Vechten), **Supp. II Part 2:** 735

"In the Grove: The Poet at Ten" (Kenyon), **Supp. VII:** 160

"In the Hall of Mirrors" (Merrill), **Supp. III Part 1:** 322

In the Harbor (Longfellow), **II:** 491

In the Heart of the Heart of the Country (Gass), **Supp. VI: 82–83,** 84, 85, 93

In the Heat of the Night (Ball), **Supp. XV:** 202

In the Heat of the Night (film), **Supp. I Part 1:** 67

In the Hollow of His Hand (Purdy), **Supp. VII:** 278–280

In the House of Light (Everwine, trans.), **Supp. XV:** 73, 75, **76–78,** 82

In the Lake of the Woods (O'Brien), **Supp. V:** 240, 243, 250–252

In the Land of the White Death: A Epic Story of Survival in the Siberian Arctic (Albanov), **Supp. XVIII:** 114

"In the Last Days" (Everwine), **Supp. XV:** 88, 89

"In the Late Summer Garden"(Crooker), **Supp. XXIII:** 55

In the Loyal Mountains (Bass), **Supp. XVI: 19–20**

"In the Loyal Mountains" (Bass), **Supp. XVI:** 20

In the Mecca (Brooks), **Supp. III Part 1:** 74

"In the Mecca" (Brooks), **Supp. III Part 1:** 70, 83–84

In the Midst of Life (Bierce), **I:** 200–203, 204, 206, 208, 212

"In the Miro District" (Taylor), **Supp. V:** 323

In the Miro District and Other Stories (Taylor), **Supp. V:** 325–326

In the Money (W. C. Williams), **Retro. Supp. I:** 423

"In the Motel" (X. J. Kennedy), **Supp. XV:** 163

"In the Naked Bed, in Plato's Cave" (Schwartz), **Supp. II Part 2:** 646–649

In the Name of the Neither (Sobin), **Supp. XVI:** 291

"In the Night" (Kincaid), **Supp. VII:** 183

In the Night Season: A Novel (Bausch), **Supp. VII:** 52–53

"In the Old Neighborhood" (Dove), **Supp. IV Part 1:** 241, 257

"In the Old World" (Oates), **Supp. II Part 2:** 503, 504

"In the Park" (Huncke), **Supp. XIV:** 139

In the Pines (Notley), **Supp. XXII:** 236–237

"In the Pit" (Proulx), **Supp. VII:** 255, 261

In the Pond (Jin), **Supp. XVIII:** 95–96

In the Presence of the Sun (Momaday), **Supp. IV Part 2:** 489, 490, 491–493, 493

"In the Quiet Night" (Li Po), **Supp. XV:** 47

"In the Realm of the Fisher King" (Didion), **Supp. IV Part 1:** 211

"In the Red Room" (Bowles), **Supp. IV Part 1:** 93

"In the Region of Ice" (Oates), **Supp. II Part 2:** 520

In the Room We Share (Simpson), **Supp. IX:** 279

"In These Dissenting Times" (Walker), **Supp. III Part 2:** 522

"In the Shadow of Gabriel, A.D.1550" (Frederic), **II:** 139

In the Shadow of Memory (Skloot), **Supp. XX:** 193, 196, 205, 205–206

"In the Shadow of Memory" (Skloot), **Supp. XX:** 206

In the Shadow of the Morning: Essays on Wild Lands, Wild Waters, and a Few Untamed People (Caputo), **Supp. XIX:** 28–29

In the Spirit of Crazy Horse (Matthiessen), **Supp. V:** 211

"In the Subway" (Untermeyer), **Supp. XV:** 296

In the Summer House (Jane Bowles), **Supp. IV Part 1:** 83, 89

In the Tennessee Country (Taylor), **Supp. V:** 328

"In the Thick of Darkness" (Salinas), **Supp. XIII:** 325

"In the Time of the Blossoms" (Merwin), **Supp. III Part 1:** 352

In the Time of the Butterflies (Alvarez), **Supp. VII:** 1, 12–15, 18

In the Time of the Present (Kenny), **Supp. XXIII:** 146, **156**

"In the Tube" (Jarman), **Supp. XVII:** 121

"In the Tunnel Bone of Cambridge" (Corso), **Supp. XII:** 120–121

"In the Upper Pastures" (Kumin), **Supp. IV Part 2:** 453

In the Valley (Frederic), **II:** 133–134, 136, 137

"In the Village" (Bishop), **Retro. Supp. II:** 38; **Supp. I Part 1:** 73, 74–75, 76, 77, 78, 88

"In the Waiting Room" (Bishop), **Retro. Supp. II:** 50; **Supp. I Part 1:** 81, 94, 95; **Supp. IV Part 1:** 249

"In the Ward: The Sacred Wood" (Jarrell), **II:** 376, 377

In the Western Night: Collected Poems 1965–90 (Bidart), **Supp. XV:** 19, **30–32**

"In the White Night" (Beattie), **Supp. V:** 30–31

"In the Wind My Rescue Is" (Ammons), **Supp. VII:** 25

"In the Winter Dark" (Peacock), **Supp. XIX:** 206

In the Winter of Cities (T. Williams), **IV:** 383

"In the X-Ray of the Sarcophagus of Tapero" (Goldbarth), **Supp. XII:** 191

"In the Yard" (Swenson), **Supp. IV Part 2:** 647

In the Zone (O'Neill), **III:** 388

In This, Our Life (film), **Supp. I Part 1:** 67

"In This Country, but in Another Language, My Aunt Refuses to Marry the Men Everyone Wants Her To" (Paley), **Supp. VI:** 225

"In This Dream" (J. W. Miller), **Supp. XX:** 170

In This Hung-up Age (Corso), **Supp. XII:** 119–120, 129

In This Our Life (Glasgow), **II:** 175, 178, 189

In This Our World (Gilman), **Supp. XI:** 196, 200, 202

"In Those Days" (Jarrell), **II:** 387–388

"Intimately Connected to the Zeitgeist" (Franzen), **Supp. XX: 94**

"In Time of War" (Auden), **Supp. II Part 1:** 8, 13

In Times Like These (Edgell), **Supp. XXIII:** 84, **89–90,** 94

"Into Egypt" (Benét), **Supp. XI:** 56, 57–58

Intolerance (film; Griffith), **Supp. XVI:** 184

"Into My Own" (Frost), **II:** 153; **Retro. Supp. I:** 127

"Into Night" (McKnight), **Supp. XX: 151–152**

Into the Interior (Cliff), **Supp. XXII:** 67, 78–79

"Into the Night Life . . ." (H. Miller), **III:** 180, 184

"Into the Nowhere" (Rawlings), **Supp. X:** 220

Into the Stone (Dickey), **Supp. IV Part 1:** 178

"Into the Stone" (Dickey), **Supp. IV Part 1:** 179

Into the Stone and Other Poems (Dickey), **Supp. IV Part 1:** 176

Into the Wild (Krakauer), **Supp. XVIII:** 106, **107–108,** 116, 117

Into Thin Air: A Personal Account of the Mount Everest Disaster (Krakauer), **Supp. XVII:** 210, **Supp. XVIII:** 105, **109–113,** 117

In Touch: The Letters of Paul Bowles (J. Miller, ed.), **Supp. IV Part 1:** 95

"Intoxicated, The" (Jackson), **Supp. IX:** 116

"Intrigue" (Crane), **I:** 419

"Introducing the Fathers" (Kumin), **Supp. IV Part 2:** 452

Introductio ad Prudentiam (Fuller), **II:** 111

"Introduction"(Strout; *Ploughshares* spring 2010), **Supp. XXIII:** 284

"Introduction to a Haggadah" (Paley), **Supp. VI:** 219

Introduction to Objectivist Epistemology (Rand), **Supp. IV Part 2:** 527, 528–529

Introduction to Objectivist Epistemology 2nd ed. (Rand), **Supp. IV Part 2:** 529

"Introduction to Poetry" (Collins), **Supp. XXI:** 57

Introduction to Poetry, An (Gioia and X. J. Kennedy), **Supp. XV:** 113, 153

"Introduction to Some Poems, An" (Stafford), **Supp. XI:** 311, 324

Introduction to the Geography of Iowa, The (Doty), **Supp. XI:** 120

"Introduction to the Hoh" (Hugo), **Supp. VI:** 136–137

"Introduction to *The New Writing in the USA*" (Creeley), **Supp. IV Part 1:** 153–154

"Introduction to William Blake, An" (Kazin), **Supp. VIII:** 103

Introitus (Longfellow), **II:** 505, 506–507

"Intruder, The" (Dubus), **Supp. VII:** 76–78, 91

Intruder, The (Maeterlinck), **I:** 91

Intruder in the Dust (Faulkner), **II:** 71, 72; **Supp. XVI:** 148

"Invaders, The" (Haines), **Supp. XII:** 205

Invaders, The (W. Frank), **Supp. XX: 79–80**

Invasion of Privacy: The Cross Creek Trial of Marjorie Kinnan Rawlings (Acton), **Supp. X:** 233

Inventing Memory: A Novel of Mothers and Daughters (Jong), **Supp. V:** 115, 129

Inventing the Abbotts (Miller), **Supp. XII: 294–295**

"Invention of Autobiography. The" (Hampl), **Supp. XXII:** 93–94

"Invention of God in a Mouthful of Milk, The" (Karr), **Supp. XI:** 250

Invention of Solitude, The (Auster), **Supp. XII:** 21–22

Inventions of the March Hare (Eliot), **Retro. Supp. I:** 55–56, 58

"Inventions of the March Hare" (Eliot), **Retro. Supp. I:** 55

"Inventory" (Parker), **Supp. IX:** 192

"Inverted Forest, The" (Salinger), **III:** 552, 572

"Investigation" (Ryan as Quin), **Supp. XVIII:** 227–228

"Investigations of a Dog" (Kafka), **IV:** 438

"Investiture, The" (Banks), **Supp. V:** 7

"Investiture at Cecconi's" (Merrill), **Supp. III Part 1:** 336

"Invicibility"(O'Hara), **Supp. XXIII:** 214

"Invisible" (Pickering), **Supp. XXI:** 201

Invisible Circus, The (Egan), **Supp. XIX:** 49, **50–52**

Invisible Company, The (Sanders), **Supp. XVI:** 270–271

Invisible Man (Ellison), **IV:** 493; **Retro. Supp. II:** 3, 12, 111, 112, 113, 117, 119, **120–123,** 125; **Supp. II Part 1:**

40, 170, 221, 224, 226, 227, 230, 231–232, 235, 236, 241–245; **Supp. IX:** 306; **Supp. X:** 242; **Supp. XI:** 18, 92; **Supp. XVIII:** 59; **Supp. XIX:** 154, 155

Invisible: Poems (Nye), **Supp. XIII:** 277

Invisible Spectator, An (Sawyer-Lauçanno), **Supp. IV Part 1:** 95

Invisible Swords (Farrell), **II:** 27, 46, 48–49

Invisible Worm, The (Millar), **Supp. IV Part 2:** 465

Invitation to a Beheading (Nabokov), **III:** 252–253, 254, 257–258; **Retro. Supp. I:** 265, 270, 273

"Invitation to the Country, An" (Bryant), **Supp. I Part 1:** 160

"Invocation" (McKay), **Supp. X:** 134

"Invocation" (Untermeyer), **Supp. XV:** 296

"Invocation to Kali" (Sarton), **Supp. VIII:** 260

"Invocation: *To my Maternal Grandfather on hearing his descent from Chippewa ancestors misrepresented*"(J. Schoolcraft), Supp. XXIII: 232

"Invocation to the Social Muse" (MacLeish), **III:** 15

"In Weather" (Hass), **Supp. VI: 102–103**

"In Your Fugitive Dream" (Hugo), **Supp. VI:** 143

"In Your Good Dream" (Hugo), **Supp. VI:** 143–144

"Iola, Kansas" (Clampitt), **Supp. IX: 45–46**

Iola Leroy (Harper), **Supp. XVIII:** 284

Ion (Doolittle, trans.), **Supp. I Part 1:** 269, 274

Ion (Plato), **I:** 523

"Ione" (Dunbar), **Supp. II Part 1:** 199

Ionesco, Eugène, **I:** 71, 74, 75, 84, 295; **II:** 435; **Supp. VIII:** 201; **Supp. XIX:** 131

Ionica (Cory), **Supp. XX: 230**

Ionica II (Cory), **Supp. XX: 230**

"I Only Am Escaped Alone to Tell Thee" (Nemerov), **III:** 272, 273–274

"I Opened All the Portals Wide" (Chopin), **Retro. Supp. II:** 71

I Ought to Be in Pictures (Simon), **Supp. IV Part 2:** 584

Iphigenia (Notley), **Supp. XXII:** 226, 235

Iphigenia in Tauris (Euripedes), **Supp. XV:** 42, 50

I Promessi Sposi (Manzoni), **II:** 291

"I Put My Hand on My Son's Head" (Kooser), **Supp. XIX:** 120

Iram, Dhát al-'Imád (Gibran), **Supp. XX: 116**

"Iraq Drifting, July 2003" (Weigl), **Supp. XIX:** 288

"Irascibles, The" (Kees), **Supp. XV:** 145–146

Ireland: A Terrible Beauty (Uris), **Supp. XX: 244, 245–246, 246, 254**

"I Remember" (Sexton), **Supp. II Part 2:** 680

"Irenicon" (Shapiro), **Supp. II Part 2:** 704

Irigaray, Luce, **Supp. XII:** 6

Iris (Jarman), **Supp. XVII:** 110, **116–117**

"Iris by Night" (Frost), **Retro. Supp. I:** 132

"Irises" (L.-Y. Lee), **Supp. XV:** 214–215

Irish in America, The (Coffey, ed.), **Supp. XIX:** 133

Irish Stories of Sarah Orne Jewett, The (Jewett), **Retro. Supp. II:** 142

Irish Triangle, An (Barnes), **Supp. III Part 1:** 34

"Iron Characters, The" (Nemerov), **III:** 279, 282

"Iron Hans" (Sexton), **Supp. II Part 2:** 691

Iron Heel, The (London), **II:** 466, 480

Iron John: A Book about Men (R. Bly), **Supp. IV Part 1:** 59, 67; **Supp. XVI:** 177

"Iron Table, The" (Jane Bowles), **Supp. IV Part 1:** 82–83

"Iron Throat, The" (Olsen), **Supp. XIII:** 292, 297, 299

Ironweed (W. Kennedy), **Supp. VII:** 132, 133, 134, 135, 142, 144, 145–147, 148, 150, 153

"Irony as Art: The Short Fiction of William Humphrey" (Tebeaux), **Supp. IX:** 109

"Irony Is Not Enough: Essay on My Life as Catherine Deneuve" (Carson), **Supp. XII: 112–113**

Irony of American History, The (Niebuhr), **III:** 292, 306–307, 308

"Irrational Element in Poetry, The" (Stevens), **Retro. Supp. I:** 298, 301

"Irrevocable Diameter, An" (Paley), **Supp. VI:** 231–232

Irvine, Lorna, **Supp. XIII:** 26

Irving, Ebenezer, **II:** 296

Irving, Sir Henry, **IV:** 350

Irving, John, **Supp. VI: 163–183; Supp. X:** 77, 85

Irving, John Treat, **II:** 296

Irving, Peter, **II:** 296, 297, 298, 299, 300, 303

Irving, Washington, **I:** 211, 335, 336, 339, 343; **II: 295–318,** 488, 495; **III:** 113; **IV:** 309; **Retro. Supp. I:** 246; **Supp. I Part 1:** 155, 157, 158, 317; **Supp. I Part 2:** 377, 487, 585; **Supp. II Part 1:** 335; **Supp. IV Part 1:** 380; **Supp. XVIII:** 12; **Supp. XXIII:** 178

Irving, William, **II:** 296

Irving, William, Jr., **II:** 296, 297, 298, 299, 303

Irwin, Mark, **Supp. XII:** 21, 22, 24, 29

Irwin, Robert, **Supp. XX: 120**

Irwin, William Henry, **Supp. II Part 1:** 192

Is 5 (Cummings), **I:** 429, 430, 434, 435, 440, 445, 446, 447

"Isaac and Abraham" (Brodsky), **Supp. VIII:** 21

"Isaac and Archibald" (Robinson), **III:** 511, 521, 523

Isaacs, Neil D., **Supp. XIX:** 255

"Isabelle" (Saunders), **Supp. XIX:** 225

"Isabel Sparrow" (Oliver), **Supp. VII:** 232

Isaiah (biblical book), **Supp. I Part 1:** 236; **Supp. I Part 2:** 516; **Supp. XXI:** 107

"Isaiah Beethoven" (Masters), **Supp. I Part 2:** 461

I Sailed with Magellan (Dybek), **Supp. XXIII: 75–78,** 79

"I Saw in Louisiana a Live-Oak Growing" (Whitman), **I:** 220

"I Shall Be Released" (Dylan), **Supp. XV:** 349

I Shall Spit on Your Graves (film), **Supp. I Part 1:** 67

Isháq, Adib, **Supp. XX: 117**

Isherwood, Christopher, **II:** 586; **Supp. II Part 1:** 10, 11, 13; **Supp. IV Part 1:** 79, 82, 102; **Supp. XI:** 305; **Supp. XIV: 155–175; Supp. XVI:** 194

Isherwood Century, The (Berg and Freeman), **Supp. XIV:** 157, 159

Isherwood's Fiction (Schwerdt), **Supp. XIV:** 155

Ishiguro, Kazuo, **Supp. VIII:** 15

Ishi Means Man (Merton), **Supp. VIII:** 208

"Ishmael's Dream" (Stern), **Supp. IX:** 287

I Should Have Stayed Home (McCoy), **Supp. XIII:** 167, **168–170,** 171

"I Should Worry" (Kees), **Supp. XV:** 140

"I Sigh in the Afternoon" (Salinas), **Supp. XIII:** 318

"I Sing the Body Electric" (Whitman), **Retro. Supp. I:** 394, 395

"Isis: Dorothy Eady, 1924" (Doty), **Supp. XI:** 122

"Is It O.K. to Be a Luddite?" (Pynchon), **Supp. XVI:** 128

"Is It True?" (Hughes), **Supp. I Part 1:** 342

I: Six Nonlectures (Cummings), **I:** 430, 433, 434

"Island" (Hughes), **Supp. I Part 1:** 340

Island Garden, An (Thaxter), **Retro. Supp. II:** 136; **Supp. XIII:** 152

Island Holiday, An (Henry), **I:** 515

Island in the Atlantic (W. Frank), **Supp. XX: 79**

"Island of the Fay, The" (Poe), **III:** 412, 417

Islands (Siddons), **Supp. XXII:** 239

"Islands, The" (Hayden), **Supp. II Part 1:** 373

"Island Sheaf, An" (Doty), **Supp. XI:** 136

Islands in the Stream (Hemingway), **II:** 258; **Retro. Supp. I:** 186

Isn't It Romantic (Wasserstein), **Supp. XV: 323–325,** 327

Is Objectivism a Religion? (Ellis), **Supp. IV Part 2:** 527

"Isolation of Modern Poetry, The" (Schwartz), **Supp. II Part 2:** 644

"Israel" (Reznikoff), **Supp. XIV:** 283

Israel Potter, or Fifty Years of Exile (Melville), **III:** 90; **Supp. XVIII:** 4

"Israfel" (Poe), **III:** 411

Is Sex Necessary? (Thurber and White), **Supp. I Part 2:** 607, 612, 614, 653

"Issues, The" (Olds), **Supp. X:** 205
"Istanbul" (Collins), **Supp. XXI:** 60
"I Stand Here Ironing" (Olsen), **Supp. XIII:** 292, 294, 296, 298, 300, 305
I Stole a Million (West), **IV:** 287
"Is Verse a Dying Technique?" (Wilson), **IV:** 431
It (Creeley), **Supp. IV Part 1:** 157, 158
IT (King), **Supp. V:** 139, 140, 141, 146–147, 151, 152
"It" (Olds), **Supp. X:** 208
Italian American Reconciliation: A Folktale (Shanley), **Supp. XIV:** 315, **324–326,** 328, 330
Italian Backgrounds (Wharton), **Retro. Supp. I:** 370
Italian Hours (James), **I:** 12; **II:** 337; **Retro. Supp. I:** 235
Italian Journeys (Howells), **II:** 274
"Italian Morning" (Bogan), **Supp. III Part 1:** 58
Italian Villas and Their Gardens (Wharton), **IV:** 308; **Retro. Supp. I:** 361, 367
Italie, Hillel, **Supp. XV:** 128
It All Adds Up: From the Dim Past to the Uncertain Future (Bellow), **Retro. Supp. II:** 32
"It Always Breaks Out" (Ellison), **Retro. Supp. II:** 126; **Supp. II Part 1:** 248
Itard, Jean-Marc Gaspard, **Supp. I Part 2:** 564
"I taste a liquor never brewed" (Dickinson), **Retro. Supp. I:** 30, 37
It Came from Outer Space (film), **Supp. IV Part 1:** 102
It Can't Happen Here (Lewis), **II:** 454
"It Don't Mean a Thing If It Ain't Got That Swing" (Matthews), **Supp. IX: 164–165**
I Tell You Now (Ortiz), **Supp. IV Part 2:** 500
"Ithaca" (Glück), **Supp. V:** 89
It Happened One Night (Capra), **Supp. XV:** 197
It Has Come to Pass (Farrell), **II:** 26
"I think to live May be a Bliss" (Dickinson), **Retro. Supp. I:** 44
"I Thought It Was Harry" (Bronk), **Supp. XXI:** 31
I Thought of Daisy (Wilson), **IV:** 428, 434, 435
"Itinerary of an Obsession" (Kumin), **Supp. IV Part 2:** 450
"It Is a Strange Country" (Ellison), **Supp. II Part 1:** 238
"It Is Dangerous to Read Newspapers" (Atwood), **Supp. XIII:** 33
"It Must Be Abstract" (Stevens), **IV:** 95; **Retro. Supp. I:** 307
"It Must Change" (Stevens), **Retro. Supp. I:** 300, 307, 308
"It Must Give Pleasure" (Stevens), **Retro. Supp. I:** 307, 308, 309
"'It Out-Herods Herod. Pray You, Avoid It'" (Hecht), **Supp. X:** 62, 64
"It's All Over Now, Baby Blue" (song, Dylan), **Supp. XVIII:** 30
It's Loaded, Mr. Bauer (Marquand), **III:** 59

It's Nation Time (Baraka), **Supp. II Part 1:** 52, 53
"It's Nation Time" (Baraka), **Supp. II Part 1:** 53
It's Only a Play (McNally), **Supp. XIII:** 198
It Was (Zukofsky), **Supp. III Part 2:** 630
It Was the Nightingale (Ford), **III:** 470–471
"It Was When" (Snyder), **Supp. VIII:** 300
Ivanhoe (Scott), **I:** 216; **Supp. I Part 2:** 410
Ivens, Bryna, **Supp. XV:** 311, 312
Ivens, Joris, **I:** 488; **Retro. Supp. I:** 184
"Iverson Boy, The" (Simpson), **Supp. IX:** 280
"Ives" (Rukeyser), **Supp. VI:** 273, 283
Ives, George H., **Supp. I Part 1:** 153
Ivory Grin, The (Macdonald), **Supp. IV Part 2:** 471, 472
"Ivory Novel, The" (Halliday), **Supp. XIX:** 90
Ivory Tower, The (James), **II:** 337–338
"Ivory Tower, The: Louis Untermeyer as Critic" (Aiken), **Supp. XV:** 298
Ivry, Sara, **Supp. XX:** 179
"Ivy Winding" (Ammons), **Supp. VII:** 33
Iwamatsu, Mako, **Supp. XXI:** 150
"I Wandered Lonely as a Cloud" (Wordsworth), **Retro. Supp. I:** 121–122; **Supp. X:** 73; **Supp. XIV:** 184
"I want, I want" (Plath), **Retro. Supp. II:** 246
"I Wanted to Be There When My Father Died" (Olds), **Supp. X:** 210
"I Want to Be a Father Like the Men" (Cisneros), **Supp. VII:** 71
"I Want to Be Miss America" (Alvarez), **Supp. VII:** 18
"I Want to Know Why" (Anderson), **I:** 114, 115, 116; **II:** 263
"I Want You Women Up North To Know" (Olsen), **Supp. XIII:** 292, 297
"I Was Born in Lucerne" (Levine), **Supp. V:** 181, 189
"I Was Marching"(Le Sueur), **Supp. XXIII:** 167
"I Was Really Very Hungry" (M. F. K. Fisher), **Supp. XVII:** 91
"I Went into the Maverick Bar" (Snyder), **Supp. VIII:** 301
"I Will Lie Down" (Swenson), **Supp. IV Part 2:** 640
I Will Say Beauty (C. Frost), **Supp. XV:** 96, **105–107**
I Wonder As I Wander (Hughes), **Retro. Supp. I:** 196, 203; **Supp. I Part 1:** 329, 332–333
I Would Have Saved Them If I Could (L. Michaels), **Supp. XVI:** 203, 205, **206–210**
"Iyani: It goes this Way" (Gunn Allen), **Supp. IV Part 1:** 321
"I years had been from home" (Dickinson), **I:** 471
Iyer, Pico, **Supp. V:** 215
Izzo, David Garrett, **Supp. XIV:** 155, 156, 159, 160, 161, 163, 169, 171

J

Jab (Halliday), **Supp. XIX: 91–94**
"Jachid and Jechidah" (Singer), **IV:** 15
Jack and Jill (Alcott), **Supp. I Part 1:** 42
"Jack and the Beanstalk" (Hay), **Supp. XIV:** 124
"Jack in the Pot" (D. West), **Supp. XVIII:** 283
Jack Kelso (Masters), **Supp. I Part 2:** 456, 471–472
Jacklight (Erdrich), **Supp. IV Part 1:** 259, 270
Jack London, Hemingway, and the Constitution (Doctorow), **Supp. IV Part 1:** 220, 222, 224, 232, 235
Jackman, Harold, **Supp. XVIII:** 131
Jackpot (Caldwell), **I:** 304
"Jack Schmidt, Arts Administrator" (Keillor), **Supp. XVI:** 171
"Jack Schmidt on the Burning Sands" (Keillor), **Supp. XVI:** 171
Jackson, Amelia. *See* Holmes, Mrs. Oliver Wendell (Amelia Jackson)
Jackson, Andrew, **I:** 7, 20; **III:** 473; **IV:** 192, 248, 298, 334, 348; **Supp. I Part 2:** 456, 461, 473, 474, 493, 695
Jackson, Blyden, **Supp. I Part 1:** 337
Jackson, Charles, **Supp. I Part 1:** 303
Jackson, George, **Supp. I Part 1:** 66
Jackson, Helen Hunt, **I:** 459, 470; **Retro. Supp. I:** 26, 27, 30–31, 32, 33
Jackson, James, **Supp. I Part 1:** 302, 303
Jackson, J. O., **III:** 213
Jackson, Joe, **Supp. I Part 2:** 441
Jackson, Katherine Gauss, **Supp. VIII:** 124
Jackson, Lawrence, **Retro. Supp. II:** 113, 115
Jackson, Lawrence P., **Supp. XXII:** 140
Jackson, Melanie, **Supp. X:** 166
Jackson, Michael, **Supp. VIII:** 146
Jackson, Richard, **II:** 119; **Supp. IX:** 165
Jackson, Shelley, **Supp. XVIII:** 136
Jackson, Shirley, **Supp. IX: 113–130**
Jackson, Thomas J. ("Stonewall"), **IV:** 125, 126
"Jackson Hotel" (Hull), **Supp. XXI:** 134, 135
Jackson Pollock (O'Hara), **Supp. XXIII:** 214–215
"Jackson Square" (Levertov), **Supp. III Part 1:** 276
Jackstraws (Simic), **Supp. VIII:** 280, 282–283
"Jackstraws" (Simic), **Supp. VIII: 283**
Jack Tier (Cooper), **I:** 354, 355
"Jacob" (Garrett), **Supp. VII:** 109–110
"Jacob" (Schwartz), **Supp. II Part 2:** 663
Jacob, Max, **Supp. XV:** 178, 182
"Jacob and the Indians" (Benét), **Supp. XI:** 47–48
Jacobs, Catherine Haydon, **Supp. XXI:** 98
Jacobs, Harriet, **Supp. XVI:** 85
Jacobs, Jill Suzanne, **Supp. XX: 178, 186**
Jacobs, Rita D., **Supp. XII:** 339
Jacobsen, Josephine, **Supp. XIII:** 346; **Supp. XIV:** 260

"Jacob's Ladder" (Rawlings), **Supp. X:** 224, 228

Jacob's Ladder, The (Levertov), **Supp. III Part 1:** 272, 276–278, 281

"Jacob's Ladder, The" (Levertov), **Supp. III Part 1:** 278

Jacobson, Dale, **Supp. X:** 112

Jacobson, Kristin, **Supp. XVIII:** 113

Jacobson, Leslie, **Supp. XV:** 323

Jacoby, Russell, **Supp. IV Part 2:** 692

"Jacquerie, The" (Lanier), **Supp. I Part 1:** 355, 356, 360, 364, 370

Jacques le fataliste (D. Diderot), **Supp. XVII:** 145

Jade Mountain, The: A Chinese Anthology, Being Three Hundred Poems of the T'ang Dynasty (Bynner, trans.), **II:** 527; **Supp. XV:** 46, 47, 48

Jafsie and John Henry: Essays on Hollywood, Bad Boys, and Six Hours of Perfect Poker (Mamet), **Supp. XIV:** 252

Jaguar Totem (LaBastille), **Supp. X:** 99, 106, **107–109**

Jailbird (Vonnegut), **Supp. II Part 2:** 760, 779–780

Jaimes, M. Annette, **Supp. IV Part 1:** 330, 331

Jain, Manju, **Retro. Supp. I:** 53, 58

"Jake Flower, The" (Major), **Supp. XXII:** 182

Jake's Women (Simon), **Supp. IV Part 2:** 576, 588

"Jakie's Mother" (Fante), **Supp. XI:** 164

Jakobson, Roman, **Supp. IV Part 1:** 155

"Jamaica Kincaid's New York" (Kincaid), **Supp. VII:** 181

James, Alice, **I:** 454; **Retro. Supp. I:** 228, 235

James, A. Lloyd, **Supp. XIV:** 343

James, Caryn, **Supp. X:** 302, 303

James, C. L. R. (Cyril Lionel Robert), **Supp. XXI: 159–173**

James, Etta, **Supp. X:** 242

James, Henry, **I:** 4, 5, 9, 10, 12, 15, 16, 20, 52, 93, 109, 211, 226, 228, 244, 246, 251, 255, 258, 259, 336, 363, 374, 375, 379, 384, 409, 429, 436, 439, 452, 454, 459, 461–462, 463, 464, 485, 500, 504, 513, 514, 517–518, 571; **II:** 38, 58, 60, 73, 74, 95, 138, 140, 144, 147, 196, 198, 199, 228, 230, 234, 243, 259, 267, 271, 272, 275, 276, 278, 281, 282, 283, 284, 285, 286, 287, 288, 290, 306, 309, 316, **319–341**, 398, 404, 410, 415, 427, 444, 542, 544, 547–548, 556, 600; **III:** 44, 51, 136, 194–195, 199, 206, 208, 218, 228–229, 237, 281, 319, 325, 326, 334, 409, 453, 454, 457, 460, 461, 464, 511, 522, 576, 607; **IV:** 8, 27, 34, 37, 40, 53, 58, 73, 74, 134, 168, 172, 182, 198, 202, 285, 308, 309, 310, 311, 314, 316, 317, 318, 319, 321, 322, 323, 324, 328, 347, 352, 359, 433, 439, 476; **Retro. Supp. I:** 1, 8, 53, 56, 59, 108, 112, **215–242**, 272, 283, 284, 362, 366, 367, 368, 371, 373, 374, 375, 376, 377, 378, 379; **Retro. Supp.**

II: 93, 135, 136, 203, 223; **Supp. I Part 1:** 35, 38, 43; **Supp. I Part 2:** 414, 454, 608, 609, 612–613, 618, 620, 646; **Supp. II Part 1:** 94–95; **Supp. III Part 1:** 14, 200; **Supp. III Part 2:** 410, 412; **Supp. IV Part 1:** 31, 35, 80, 127, 197, 349, 353; **Supp. IV Part 2:** 613, 677, 678, 682, 689, 693; **Supp. V:** 97, 101, 103, 258, 261, 263, 313; **Supp. VIII:** 98, 102, 156, 166, 168; **Supp. IX:** 121; **Supp. XI:** 153; **Supp. XIII:** 102; **Supp. XIV:** 40, 110, 112, 335, 336, 348, 349; **Supp. XV:** 41; **Supp. XVII:** 5, 47; **Supp. XVIII:** 160, 258; **Supp. XX: 227, 228, 232, 233, 238, 240; Supp. XXI:** 225; **Supp. XXII:** 89

James, Henry (father), **II:** 7, 275, 321, 337, 342–344, 364; **IV:** 174; **Supp. I Part 1:** 300

James, Henry (nephew), **II:** 360

James, Horace, **Supp. XIV:** 57

James, P. D., **Supp. XIX:** 131

James, William, **I:** 104, 220, 224, 227, 228, 255, 454; **II:** 20, 27, 165, 166, 276, 321, 337, **342–366**, 411; **III:** 303, 309, 509, 599, 600, 605, 606, 612; **IV:** 26, 27, 28–29, 31, 32, 34, 36, 37, 43, 46, 291, 486; **Retro. Supp. I:** 57, 216, 227, 228, 235, 295, 300, 306; **Supp. I Part 1:** 3, 7, 11, 20; **Supp. XIV:** 40, 50, 197, 199, 212, 335; **Supp. XVII:** 97

James, William (grandfather), **II:** 342

James Baldwin: The Legacy (Troupe, ed.), **Retro. Supp. II:** 15

James Baldwin—The Price of the Ticket (film), **Retro. Supp. II:** 2

James Dickey and the Politics of Canon (Suarez), **Supp. IV Part 1:** 175

"James Dickey on Yeats: An Interview" (Dickey), **Supp. IV Part 1:** 177

James Hogg: A Critical Study (Simpson), **Supp. IX:** 269, 276

"James Is a Girl" (Egan), **Supp. XIX:** 61

James Jones: A Friendship (Morris), **Supp. XI:** 234

James Jones: An American Literary Orientalist Master (Carter), **Supp. XI:** 220

"James Jones and Jack Kerouac: Novelists of Disjunction" (Stevenson), **Supp. XI:** 230

James Jones: Reveille to Taps (television documentary), **Supp. XI:** 234

Jameson, Anna Brownell, **Supp. XXIII:** 225, 226, 232, 235

Jameson, F. R., **Supp. IV Part 1:** 119

Jameson, Sir Leander Starr, **III:** 327

James Shore's Daughter (Benét), **Supp. XI:** 48

"James Thurber" (Pollard), **Supp. I Part 2:** 468

"James Whitcomb Riley (From a Westerner's Point of View)" (Dunbar), **Supp. II Part 1:** 198

Jammes, Francis, **II:** 528; **Retro. Supp. I:** 55

"Jan, the Son of Thomas" (Sandburg), **III:** 593–594

Jan. 31 (Goldbarth), **Supp. XII:** 177, **178–179,** 180

"Jane Awake"(O'Hara), **Supp. XXIII:** 210

Janeczko, Paul, **Supp. XIII:** 280

Jane Eyre (Brontë), **Supp. XVI:** 158; **Supp. XXII:** 120

Janet, Pierre, **I:** 248, 249, 252; **Retro. Supp. I:** 55, 57

Jane Talbot: A Novel (Brown), **Supp. I Part 1:** 145–146

"Janet Waking" (Ransom), **III:** 490, 491

"Janice" (Jackson), **Supp. IX:** 117

Janowitz, Tama, **Supp. X:** 7

Jantz, Harold S., **Supp. I Part 1:** 112

"January" (Barthelme), **Supp. IV Part 1:** 54

"January" (W. V. Davis), **Supp. XXI:** 89, 90

January Man, The (screenplay, Shanley), **Supp. XIV:** 316

"January Thaw" (Leopold), **Supp. XIV:** 183–184

"Janus" (Beattie), **Supp. V:** 31

Janzen, Jean, **Supp. V:** 180

"Japan" (Collins), **Supp. XXI:** 56

Japanese Americans: The Formation and Transformations of an Ethnic Group (Spickard), **Supp. XXI:** 149

"Japanese Beetles" (X. J. Kennedy), **Supp. XV:** 161, 165

Japanese by Spring (Reed), **Supp. X:** 241, **253–255**

Japanese Cooking: A Simple Art (Tsuji), **Supp. XVII:** 90

"Japan's Young Dreams" (Geisel), **Supp. XVI:** 102

Jara, Victor, **Supp. IV Part 2:** 549

Jarecki, Dave, **Supp. XXIII:** 239

Jarman, Mark, **Supp. IV Part 1:** 68; **Supp. IX:** 266, 270, 276; **Supp. XII:** 209; **Supp. XV:** 251; **Supp. XVIII:** 178

Jarmon, Mark, **Supp. XVII: 109–122**

Jarrell, Randall, **I:** 167, 169, 173, 180; **II: 367–390**, 539–540; **III:** 134, 194, 213, 268, 527; **IV:** 352, 411, 422; **Retro. Supp. I:** 52, 121, 135, 140; **Retro. Supp. II:** 44, 177, 178, 182; **Supp. I Part 1:** 89; **Supp. I Part 2:** 552; **Supp. II Part 1:** 109, 135; **Supp. III Part 1:** 64; **Supp. III Part 2:** 541, 550; **Supp. IV Part 2:** 440; **Supp. V:** 315, 318, 323; **Supp. VIII:** 31, 100, 271; **Supp. IX:** 94, 268; **Supp. XI:** 311, 315; **Supp. XII:** 121, 260, 297; **Supp. XV:** 93, 153; **Supp. XVII:** 111

Jarrell, Mrs. Randall (Mary von Schrader), **II:** 368, 385

Jarry, Alfred, **Retro. Supp. II:** 326; **Supp. XV:** 177–178, 182, 188

Jarvis, John Wesley, **Supp. I Part 2:** 501, 520

Jaskoski, Helen, **Supp. IV Part 1:** 325; **Supp. XXII:** 166

"Jasmine" (Komunyakaa), **Supp. XIII:** 132

"Jason" (Hecht), **Supp. X:** 62

"Jason" (MacLeish), **III:** 4

Jason and Medeia (Gardner), **Supp. VI:** 63, **68–69**

Jaspers, Karl, **III:** 292; **IV:** 491

Jauss, David, **Supp. XXI:** 129, 132, 133, 134, 139

Jay, William, **I:** 338

Jayber Crow (Berry), **Supp. X:** 28, 34

"Jaz Fantasia" (Sandburg), **III:** 585

"Jazz Age Clerk, A" (Farrell), **II:** 45

Jazz Country: Ralph Ellison in America (Porter), **Retro. Supp. II:** 127

"Jazzonia" (Hughes), **Supp. I Part 1:** 324

Jazz Poetry Anthology, The (Komunyakaa and Feinstein, eds.), **Supp. XIII:** 125

"Jazztet Muted" (Hughes), **Supp. I Part 1:** 342

J. B.: A Play in Verse (MacLeish), **II:** 163, 228; **III:** 3, 21–22, 23; **Supp. IV Part 2:** 586

"Jealous" (Ford), **Supp. V:** 71

Jealousies, The: A Faery Tale, by Lucy Vaughan Lloyd of China Walk, Lambeth (Keats), **Supp. XII:** 113

Jean-Christophe (Rolland), **Supp. XX:** 70

"Jean Harlow's Wedding Night" (Wasserstein), **Supp. XV:** 328

Jean Huguenot (Benét), **Supp. XI:** 44

"Jeff Briggs's Love Story" (Harte), **Supp. II Part 1:** 355

Jeffers, Robinson, **I:** 66; **III:** 134; **Retro. Supp. I:** 202; **Supp. II Part 2: 413–440; Supp. VIII:** 33, 292; **Supp. IX:** 77; **Supp. X:** 112; **Supp. XI:** 312; **Supp. XV:** 113, 114, 115; **Supp. XVII:** 111, 112, 117; **Supp. XXI:** 87; **Supp. XXIII:** 145

Jeffers, Una Call Kuster (Mrs. Robinson Jeffers), **Supp. II Part 2:** 414

Jefferson, Blind Lemon, **Supp. VIII:** 349

Jefferson, Margo, **Supp. XX: 87**

Jefferson, Thomas, **I:** 1, 2, 5, 6–8, 14, 485; **II:** 5, 6, 34, 217, 300, 301, 437; **III:** 3, 17, 18, 294–295, 306, 310, 473, 608; **IV:** 133, 243, 249, 334, 348; **Supp. I Part 1:** 146, 152, 153, 229, 230, 234, 235; **Supp. I Part 2:** 389, 399, 456, 474, 475, 482, 507, 509, 510, 511, 516, 518–519, 520, 522; **Supp. X:** 26; **Supp. XIV:** 191; **Supp. XX: 285**

Jefferson and/or Mussolini (Pound), **Retro. Supp. I:** 292

"Jefferson Davis as a Representative American" (Du Bois), **Supp. II Part 1:** 161

J-E-L-L-O (Baraka), **Supp. II Part 1:** 47

"Jelly-Bean, The" (Fitzgerald), **II:** 88

"Jellyfish, A" (Moore), **III:** 215

Jemie, Onwuchekwa, **Supp. I Part 1:** 343

Jenkins, J. L., **I:** 456

Jenkins, Joe, **Supp. XX: 117, 120, 122**

Jenkins, Kathleen, **III:** 403

Jenkins, Susan, **IV:** 123

Jenks, Deneen, **Supp. IV Part 2:** 550, 554

Jenks, Tom, **Supp. XIX:** 51

Jennie Gerhardt (Dreiser), **I:** 497, 499, 500, 501, 504–505, 506, 507, 519; **Retro. Supp. II:** 94, **99–101**

"Jennie M'Grew" (Masters), **Supp. I Part 2:** 468

Jennifer Lorn (Wylie), **Supp. I Part 2:** 709, 714–717, 718, 721, 724

Jennison, Peter S., **Supp. XIX:** 268

"Jenny Garrow's Lover" (Jewett), **II:** 397

"Jerboa, The" (Moore), **III:** 203, 207, 209, 211–212

Jeremiah, **Supp. X:** 35

Jeremy's Version (Purdy), **Supp. VII:** 274

"Je Reviens"(Dybek), **Supp. XXIII:** 78

"Jericho" (Lowell), **II:** 536

Jerome, Judson, **Supp. XXIII:** 54

"Jerry's Garage" (Budbill), **Supp. XIX:** 7

"Jersey City Gendarmerie, Je T'aime" (Lardner), **II:** 433

Jersey Rain (Pinsky), **Supp. VI:** 235, **247–250**

"Jerusalem" (Nye), **Supp. XIII:** 287

Jerusalem: Song of Songs (Uris), **Supp. XX: 244–245, 246, 255**

Jerusalem the Golden (Reznikoff), **Supp. XIV:** 280, 285, 286

Jessup, Richard, **Supp. XI:** 306

"Je Suis Perdu" (Taylor), Supp. V: 314, 321–322

Jesuits in North America in the Seventeenth Century, The (Parkman), **Supp. II Part 2:** 597, 603–605

Jesus, **I:** 27, 34, 68, 89, 136, 552, 560; **II:** 1, 16, 197, 198, 214, 215, 216, 218, 219, 239, 373, 377, 379, 537, 538, 539, 549, 569, 585, 591, 592; **III:** 39, 173, 179, 270, 291, 296–297, 300, 303, 305, 307, 311, 339, 340, 341, 342, 344, 345, 346, 347, 348, 352, 353, 354, 355, 436, 451, 489, 534, 564, 566, 567, 582; **IV:** 51, 69, 86, 107, 109, 117, 137, 138, 141, 144, 147, 149, 150, 151, 152, 155, 156, 157, 158, 159, 163, 164, 232, 241, 289, 293, 294, 296, 331, 364, 392, 396, 418, 430; **Supp. I Part 1:** 2, 54, 104, 107, 108, 109, 121, 267, 371; **Supp. I Part 2:** 379, 386, 458, 515, 580, 582, 583, 587, 588, 683; **Supp. V:** 280

Jesus, the Son of Man (Gibran), **Supp. XX: 115–116, 117, 122–123**

"Jesus Asleep" (Sexton), **Supp. II Part 2:** 693

"Jesus of Nazareth, Then and Now" (Price), **Supp. VI:** 268

"Jesus Papers, The" (Sexton), **Supp. II Part 2:** 693

"Jesus Raises Up the Harlot" (Sexton), **Supp. II Part 2:** 693

"Jesus Stories, The" (Brockmeier), **Supp. XXII:** 52

Jetée, La (film), **Supp. IV Part 2:** 436

"Jeune Parque, La" (Valéry), **IV:** 92

"Jew as Writer/The Writer as Jew, The: Reflections on Literature and Identity" (Apple), **Supp. XVII:** 1, 9

"Jewbird, The" (Malamud), **Supp. I Part 2:** 435

"Jewboy, The" (P. Roth), **Supp. III Part 2:** 412

Jewett, Caroline, **II:** 396

Jewett, Katharine, **Retro. Supp. II:** 46

Jewett, Mary, **II:** 396, 403

Jewett, Rutger, **Retro. Supp. I:** 381

Jewett, Sarah Orne, **I:** 313; **II: 391–414; Retro. Supp. I:** 6, 7, 19; **Retro. Supp. II:** 51, 52, **131–151,** 156; **Supp. I Part 2:** 495; **Supp. VIII:** 126; **Supp. IX:** 79; **Supp. XIII:** 153; **Supp. XXIII:** 275, 278

Jewett, Theodore Furber, **II:** 395

Jewett, Dr. Theodore Herman, **II:** 396–397, 402

"Jew for Export, The" (Mamet), **Supp. XIV:** 251–252

Jew in Our Day, The (W. Frank), **Supp. XX: 79**

Jew in the American Novel, The (Fiedler), **Supp. XIII:** 106

"Jewish Graveyards, Italy" (Levine), **Supp. V:** 190

"Jewish Hunter, The" (Moore), **Supp. X:** 163, 165, **174**

Jewison, Norman, **Supp. XI:** 306; **Supp. XIV:** 316

Jews of Shklov (Schneour), **IV:** 11

Jews without Money (Gold), **Supp. XIV:** 288–289

JFK (film), **Supp. XIV:** 48

Jig of Forslin, The: A Symphony (Aiken), **I:** 50, 51, 57, 62, 66

"Jig Tune: Not for Love" (McGrath), **Supp. X:** 116

"Jihad" (McClatchy), **Supp. XII:** 266

"Jilting of Granny Weatherall, The" (Porter), **III:** 434, 435, 438

Jim Crow's Last Stand (Hughes), **Retro. Supp. I:** 205

Jiménez, Juan Ramón, **Supp. XIII:** 315, 323

Jimmie Higgins (Sinclair), **Supp. V:** 288

"Jimmy Harlow" (X. J. Kennedy), **Supp. XV:** 170

Jimmy's Blues (Baldwin), **Retro. Supp. II:** 8, 9, 15

Jim's Book: A Collection of Poems and Short Stories (Merrill), **Supp. III Part 1:** 319

Jin, Ha, **Supp. XVIII: 89–104**

Jitney (Wilson), **Supp. VIII:** 330, 331, 351

Jitterbug Perfume (Robbins), **Supp. X:** 273, **274–276,** 279

Joachim, Harold, **Retro. Supp. I:** 58

Joan, Pope, **IV:** 165

Joanna and Ulysses (Sarton), **Supp. VIII:** 254–255

Joan of Arc, **IV:** 241; **Supp. I Part 1:** 286–288; **Supp. I Part 2:** 469

Joans, Ted, **Supp. IV Part 1:** 169

Job (biblical book), **II:** 165, 166–167, 168; **III:** 21, 199, 512; **IV:** 13, 158; **Supp. I Part 1:** 125

Job, The (Burroughs and Odier), **Supp. III Part 1:** 97, 103

Job, The: An American Novel (Lewis), **II:** 441

"Job History" (Proulx), **Supp. VII:** 262

Jobim, Antonio Carlos, **Supp. IV Part 2:** 549

Jobim, Antônio Carlos, **Supp. XXI:** 100

"Job of the Plains, A" (Humphrey), **Supp. IX:** 101

"Jody Rolled the Bones" (Yates), **Supp. XI:** 335, 341

"Joe" (Alvarez), **Supp. VII:** 7–8

Joe (Brown), **Supp. XVIII:** 195

Joe (L. Brown), **Supp. XXI:** 41, **45–46,** 47

"Joe, the Vanishing American" (Swados), **Supp. XIX:** 258–259

Joe Hill: A Biographical Novel (Stegner), **Supp. IV Part 2:** 599

Joe Jones (Lamott), **Supp. XX: 134–135**

"Joe Louis: The King as a Middle-Aged Man" (Talese), **Supp. XVII:** 202

"Joe Messenger Is Dreaming"(P. Benedict), **Supp. XXIII:** 47

"Joe's Jitters" (Bronk), **Supp. XXI:** 27

Joe Turner's Come and Gone (Wilson), **Supp. VIII:** 334, **337–342,** 345

Joe versus the Volcano (screenplay, Shanley), **Supp. XIV:** 316

"Joey Martiney" (Huncke), **Supp. XIV:** 149

Johannes in Eremo (Mather), **Supp. II Part 2:** 453

John XXIII, Pope, **Supp. I Part 2:** 492

John (biblical book), **I:** 68; **Supp. XV:** 222, 224

"John" (Shields), **Supp. VII:** 310–311

John, Augustus, **Supp. XXII:** 157

John, Elton, **Supp. XXI:** 148

"John, John Chinaman" (Buck), **Supp. II Part 1:** 128

John Addington Symonds: A Biographical Study (Brooks), **I:** 240, 241

John-a Dreams: A Tale (J. Sturgis), **Supp. XX: 233**

"John Archer's Nose" (R. Fisher), **Supp. XIX:** 71–72, 78

John Barleycorn (London), **II:** 467, 481

John Brown (Du Bois), **Supp. II Part 1:** 171–172

"John Brown" (Emerson), **II:** 13

"John Brown" (Lindsay), **Supp. I Part 2:** 393

John Brown's Body (Benét), **II:** 177; **Supp. XI:** 45, 46, 47, **56–57**

John Brown: The Making of a Martyr (Warren), **IV:** 236

John Bull in America; or, The New Munchausen (Paulding), **I:** 344

"John Burke" (Olson), **Supp. II Part 2:** 579, 580

"John Burns of Gettysburg" (Harte), **Supp. II Part 1:** 343

"John Carter" (Agee), **I:** 27

John Chancellor Makes Me Cry (Siddons), **Supp. XXII:** 245

"John Coltrane: Where Does Art Come From?" (Baraka), **Supp. II Part 1:** 60

John Deth: A Metaphysical Legend and Other Poems (Aiken), **I:** 61

"John Endicott" (Longfellow), **II:** 505, 506; **Retro. Supp. II:** 165–166, 167

"John Evereldown" (Robinson), **III:** 524

John Fante Reader, The (Cooper, ed.), **Supp. XI:** 174

John Fante: Selected Letters, 1932–1981 (Cooney, ed.), **Supp. XI:** 170

"John Gardner: The Writer As Teacher" (Carver), **Supp. III Part 1:** 136, 146–147

John Gaunt (R. H. Davis), **Supp. XVI:** 89

John Jay Chapman and His Letters (Howe), **Supp. XIV:** 54

John Keats (Lowell), **II:** 530–531

"John Kinsella's Lament for Mrs. Mary Moore" (Yeats), **Supp. XVII:** 144

"John Lamar" (R. H. Davis), **Supp. XVI:** 89–90

John Lane, **Retro. Supp. I:** 59

"John L. Sullivan" (Lindsay), **Supp. I Part 2:** 394, 395

"John Marr" (Melville), **III:** 93

John Marr and Other Sailors (Melville), **III:** 93; **Retro. Supp. I:** 257

John Muir: A Reading Bibliography (Kimes and Kimes), **Supp. IX:** 178

Johnny Appleseed and Other Poems (Lindsay), **Supp. I Part 2:** 397

"Johnny Bear" (Steinbeck), **IV:** 67

Johnny Got His Gun (Trumbo), **Supp. XXI:** 45

"Johnny Mnemonic" (W. Gibson), **Supp. XVI:** 122, 123–125, 128, 131

"Johnny Panic and the Bible of Dreams" (Plath), **Retro. Supp. II:** 245

"Johnny Ray" (Ríos), **Supp. IV Part 2:** 543

Johnny Tremain (Forbes), **Supp. XIX:** 235

John of the Cross (Saint), **I:** 585; **Supp. IV Part 1:** 284; **Supp. XV:** 223; **Supp. XVII:** 112

John Paul Jones: A Sailor's Biography (Morison), **Supp. I Part 2:** 494–495

"John Redding Goes to Sea" (Hurston), **Supp. VI:** 150

Johns, George Sibley, **Retro. Supp. II:** 65

Johns, Jasper, **Supp. XXIII:** 217

Johns, Orrick, **Retro. Supp. II:** 71

John Sloan: A Painter's Life (Brooks), **I:** 254

"John Smith Liberator" (Bierce), **I:** 209

Johnson, Alexandra, **Supp. X:** 86

Johnson, Alvin, **I:** 236; **Supp. XV:** 304

Johnson, Ben, **Retro. Supp. I:** 56

Johnson, Buffie, **Supp. IV Part 1:** 94

Johnson, Caitlin, **Supp. XXIII:** 281

Johnson, Carol Siri, **Supp. XXIII:** 257, 258, 264, 269

Johnson, Charles, **Supp. I Part 1:** 325; **Supp. V:** 128; **Supp. VI: 185–201;** **Supp. X:** 239; **Supp. XIII:** 182; **Supp. XIX:** 160

Johnson, Charles S., **Supp. IX:** 309; **Supp. XXII:** 6, 7

Johnson, Claudia Durst, **Supp. VIII:** 126–127

Johnson, Clifton, **Supp. XXI:** 248, 250

Johnson, Denis, **Supp. XXI:** 118, 131

Johnson, Dennis, **Supp. XIX:** 209

Johnson, Diane, **Supp. XIII:** 127

Johnson, Dianne, **Retro. Supp. I:** 196

Johnson, Eastman, **IV:** 321

Johnson, Edward, **IV:** 157; **Supp. I Part 1:** 110, 115

Johnson, Fenton, **Supp. XI:** 129

Johnson, Georgia Douglas, **Supp. IV Part 1:** 164

Johnson, Helene, **Supp. XVIII:** 282

Johnson, James Weldon, **Retro. Supp. II:** 114; **Supp. I Part 1:** 324, 325; **Supp. II Part 1:** 33, 194, 200, 202–203, 206–207; **Supp. III Part 1:** 73; **Supp. IV Part 1:** 7, 11, 15, 16, 164, 165, 166, 169; **Supp. X:** 42, 136, **246;** **Supp. XVIII:** 122, 127, 282; **Supp. XIX:** 73

Johnson, Joyce, **Supp. XIV:** 150

Johnson, Kent, **Supp. XV:** 347

Johnson, Lady Bird, **Supp. IV Part 1:** 22

Johnson, Lyndon B., **I:** 254; **II:** 553, 582; **Retro. Supp. II:** 27

Johnson, Marguerite. *See* Angelou, Maya

Johnson, Maurice, **Supp. XV:** 136, 137, 138

Johnson, Michael K., **Supp. XVIII:** 59, 64

Johnson, Mordecai, **Supp. XIV:** 202

Johnson, Nunnally, **Supp. IV Part 1:** 355

Johnson, Pamela Hansford, **IV:** 469

Johnson, Rafer, **Supp. I Part 1:** 271

Johnson, Reed, **Supp. IV Part 2:** 589

Johnson, Richard, **Supp. XIII:** 132

Johnson, Robert, **Supp. IV Part 1:** 146; **Supp. VIII:** 15, 134

Johnson, Robert K., **Supp. IV Part 2:** 573, 584

Johnson, Robert Underwood, **Supp. IX:** 182, 184, 185

Johnson, Samuel, **II:** 295; **III:** 491, 503; **IV:** 452; **Retro. Supp. I:** 56, 65; **Supp. I Part 1:** 33; **Supp. I Part 2:** 422, 498, 503, 523, 656; **Supp. IV Part 1:** 34, 124; **Supp. XI:** 209; **Supp. XII:** 159; **Supp. XIII:** 55, 347; **Supp. XVI:** 204; **Supp. XVII:** 1

Johnson, Sarah Anne, **Supp. XVIII:** 145; **Supp. XIX:** 49, 50, 52, 54, 55, 56, 58, 59, 60, 61

Johnson, Steve, **Supp. XVI:** 177

Johnson, Thomas H., **I:** 470–471; **IV:** 144, 158; **Retro. Supp. I:** 26, 28, 36, 39, 40, 41, 43

Johnson, Walter, **II:** 422

Johnson, Willard "Spud", **Supp. XV:** 42, 46

"Johnson Girls, The" (Bambara), **Supp. XI:** 7

Johnsrud, Harold, **II:** 562

Johnston, Basil, **Supp. IV Part 1:** 269

Johnston, Mary, **II:** 194

Johnston, Robert M., **Supp. I Part 1:** 369

"John Sutter" (Winters), **Supp. II Part 2:** 810

John's Wife (Coover), **Supp. V:** 51–52

John the Baptist, **I:** 389; **II:** 537, 591

John Wesley Harding (album, Dylan), **Supp. XVIII:** 27

Jolas, Eugène, **Retro. Supp. II:** 85, 328; **Supp. IV Part 1:** 80

Jolie Blon's Bounce (Burke), **Supp. XIV:** 26, 33–34

Jolly (Mamet), **Supp. XIV:** 240, 254

"Jolly Corner, The" (James), **I:** 571; **Retro. Supp. I:** 235

"Ion" (Saunders), **Supp. XIX:** 232, 234

"Jonah" (Lowell), **II:** 536

Jonah's Gourd Vine (Hurston), **Supp. VI:** 149, 155

"Jonathan Edwards" (Holmes), **Supp. I Part 1:** 302, 315

"Jonathan Edwards in Western Massachusetts" (Lowell), **II:** 550

Jonathan Franzen at the End of Postmodernism (Burns), **Supp. XX:** 85

Jonathan Troy (Abbey), **Supp. XIII:** 4, 13

Jones, Anne, **Supp. X:** 8

Jones, Anne Goodwyn, **Supp. XXII:** 252

Jones, Carolyn M., **Supp. VIII:** 128; **Supp. XIX:** 160

Jones, Chuck, **Supp. XVI:** 102

Jones, David, **Supp. XVII:** 241

Jones, Dennis, **Supp. XXIII:** 228, 233

Jones, Derek Anson, **Supp. XVIII:** 38, 39

Jones, Edith Newbold. *See* Wharton, Edith

Jones, Edward P., **Supp. XXI:** 247; **Supp. XXII: 139–153**

Jones, E. Stanley, **III:** 297

Jones, Everett LeRoi. *See* Baraka, Imamu Amiri

Jones, George Frederic, **IV:** 309

Jones, Grover, **Supp. XIII:** 166

Jones, Harry, **Supp. I Part 1:** 337

Jones, Howard Mumford, **I:** 353; **Supp. IV Part 2:** 606; **Supp. XIV:** 11

Jones, James, **III:** 40; **IV:** 98; **Supp. XI: 213–237; Supp. XIX:** 248, 252; **Supp. XX:** 248

Jones, James Earl, **Supp. VIII:** 334; **Supp. XI:** 309

Jones, Jennifer, **Supp. IV Part 2:** 524

Jones, John Paul, **II:** 405–406; **Supp. I Part 2:** 479, 480, 494–495

Jones, Kirkland C., **Supp. XVIII:** 173, 174, 175; **Supp. XXII:** 9

Jones, LeRoi. *See* Baraka, Imamu Amiri

Jones, Louis B., **Supp. XVI:** 41

Jones, Loyal, **Supp. XX: 170**

Jones, Lucretia Stevens Rhinelander, **IV:** 309

Jones, Madison, **Retro. Supp. II:** 235; **Supp. X:** 1

Jones, Major (pseudonym). *See* Thompson, William T.

Jones, Malcolm, **Supp. V:** 219; **Supp. XX: 93, 138**

Jones, Mildred, **Supp. XVIII:** 281

Jones, Robert Edmond, **III:** 387, 391, 394, 399; **Supp. XXI:** 6, 12

Jones, Sharon L., **Supp. XVIII:** 280, 285, 286

Jones, Tommy Lee, **Supp. V:** 227

"Jones's Private Argyment" (Lanier), **Supp. I Part 1:** 352

"Jones's *The Thin Red Line:* The End of Innocence" (Michel-Michot), **Supp. XI:** 224–225

Jong, Allan, **Supp. V:** 115

Jong, Erica, **Supp. V: 113–135**

Jong-Fast, Molly Miranda, **Supp. V:** 115

Jonson, Ben, **I:** 58, 358; **II:** 11, 16, 17, 18, 436, 556; **III:** 3, 463, 575–576; **IV:** 395, 453; **Retro. Supp. II:** 76; **Supp. I Part 2:** 423; **Supp. IV Part 2:** 585; **Supp. XX: 197**

Jonsson, Thorsten, **Retro. Supp. I:** 73

Joplin, Janis, **Supp. IV Part 1:** 206; **Supp. XI:** 239

Joplin, Scott, **Supp. IV Part 1:** 223

Jordan, A. Van, **Supp. XVIII:** 172

Jordan, Barbara, **Supp. VIII:** 63; **Supp. XI:** 249

Jordan, David, **Supp. XIX:** 141

Jordan, June, **Supp. XII:** 217; **Supp. XXII:** 172

Jordan, Marie, **Supp. XV:** 224

Jo's Boys (Alcott), **Supp. I Part 1:** 32, 35, 40–41, 42

Joseph Heller (Ruderman), **Supp. IV Part 1:** 380

"Josephine Has Her Day" (Thurber), **Supp. I Part 2:** 606

Josephine Stories, The (Fitzgerald), **Retro. Supp. I:** 109

"Joseph Martinez" (Huncke), **Supp. XIV:** 149

"Joseph Pockets" (Stern), **Supp. IX:** 292

Josephson, Matthew, **I:** 259

"José's Country" (Winters), **Supp. II Part 2:** 789, 790

Joshua (biblical book), **Supp. I Part 2:** 515

"Joshua Clark"(Kenny), **Supp. XXIII:** 154

Joslin, Katherine, **Retro. Supp. I:** 376

Journal (Emerson), **Supp. I Part 1:** 309

"Journal" (L. Michaels), **Supp. XVI:** 213

Journal (Thoreau), **IV:** 175

Journal (Woolman), **Supp. VIII:** 202

"Journal for My Daughter" (Kunitz), **Supp. III Part 1:** 268

"Journal of an Airman" (Auden), **Supp. XIX:** 151

Journal of Arthur Stirling, The (Sinclair), **Supp. V:** 280

"Journal of a Solitary Man, The" (Hawthorne), **II:** 226

Journal of a Solitude (Sarton), **Supp. VIII:** 256, 262–263

Journal of My Other Self (Rilke), **Retro. Supp. II:** 20

Journal of the Fictive Life (Nemerov), **III:** 267, 268, 269, 272, 273, 274, 280–281, 284–285, 286, 287

Journal of the Plague Year, A (Defoe), **III:** 423

"Journal of the Year of the Ox, A" (Wright), **Supp. V:** 343

Journals (Thoreau), **Supp. I Part 1:** 299

Journals and Other Documents on the Life and Voyages of Christopher Columbus (Morison, ed.), **Supp. I Part 2:** 494

Journals of Ralph Waldo Emerson, The (Emerson), **II:** 8, 17, 21

Journals of Susanna Moodie, The: Poems (Atwood), **Supp. XIII:** 33

"Journey, A" (Wharton), **Retro. Supp. I:** 364

"Journey, The" (Winters), **Supp. II Part 2:** 795

"Journey, The" (Wright), **Supp. III Part 2:** 605–606

"Journey, the Arrival and the Dream, The" (Gioia), **Supp. XV:** 120

"Journey, The: For Jane at Thirteen" (Kumin), **Supp. IV Part 2:** 442

Journey and Other Poems, The (Winters), **Supp. II Part 2:** 786, 794, 795, 796, 799, 800, 801

Journey Around My Room: The Autobiography of Louise Bogan—A Mosaic (Bogan), **Supp. III Part 1:** 47, 48, 52, 53

Journey Down, The (Bernstein), **IV:** 455

Journey Home, The (Abbey), **Supp. XIII:** 2, 12

"Journey into Speech, A" (Cliff), **Supp. XXII:** 69

Journeyman (Caldwell), **I:** 297, 302–304, 307, 309

Journeyman: Travels of a Writer (Findley), **Supp. XX: 50**

Journey of Tai-me, The (Momaday), **Supp. IV Part 2:** 485

"Journey of the Magi" (Eliot), **Retro. Supp. I:** 64

Journey to a War (Auden and Isherwood), **Supp. II Part 1:** 13; **Supp. XIV:** 156, 158, 162

Journey to Love (W. C. Williams), **IV:** 422; **Retro. Supp. I:** 429

Journey to My Father; Isaac Bashevis Singer (Zamir), **Retro. Supp. II:** 317

"Journey to Nine Miles" (Walker), **Supp. III Part 2:** 527

"Journey to the Interior" (W. J. Smith), **Supp. XIII:** 339, 340

Journey with Genius: Recollections and Reflections Concerning the D. H. Lawrences (Bynner), **Supp. XV:** 46

Jowett, Benjamin, **Supp. XIV:** 335

"Joy" (Moore), **Supp. X:** 174

"Joy" (Singer), **IV:** 9; **Retro. Supp. II:** 307

Joyce, Cynthia, **Supp. X:** 194, 195, 196

Joyce, James, **I:** 53, 105, 108, 130, 174, 256, 285, 377, 395, 475–476, 478, 480, 483, 576; **II:** 27, 42, 58, 73, 74, 198, 209, 264, 320, 569; **III:** 7, 16, 26–27, 45, 174, 181, 184, 261, 273, 277, 343, 396, 398, 465, 471, 474; **IV:** 32, 73, 85, 95, 103, 171, 182, 211, 286, 370, 412, 418, 419, 428, 434, 456; **Retro. Supp. I:** 59, 63, 75, 80, 89, 91, 108, 109, 127, 287, 290, 292, 334, 335, 420; **Retro. Supp. II:** 221, 326; **Supp. I Part 1:** 257, 262, 270; **Supp. I Part 2:** 437, 546, 613, 620; **Supp. II Part 1:** 136; **Supp. III Part 1:** 35, 36, 65, 225, 229; **Supp. III Part 2:** 611, 617, 618; **Supp. IV Part 1:** 40, 47, 80, 227, 300, 310; **Supp. IV Part 2:** 424, 677; **Supp. V:** 261, 331; **Supp. VIII:** 14, 40, 103; **Supp. IX:** 211, 229, 235, 308; **Supp. X:** 115, 137, 194, 324; **Supp. XI:** 66; **Supp.**

XII: 139, 151, 165, 191, 289; **Supp. XIV:** 83; **Supp. XVI:** 41, 189, 282; **Supp. XVII:** 44; **Supp. XIX:** 151, 172; **Supp. XXI:** 7; **Supp. XXII:** 141, 143–144; **Supp. XXIII:** 162

Joy Comes in the Morning (J. Rosen), **Supp. XVII:** 50

Joy in the Morning (B. Smith), **Supp. XXIII:** 257, 258, **269–270**

Joy Luck Club, The (Tan), **Supp. X:** 289, 291, 293, 294, 296, 297, 298, 299

"Joy of Sales Resistance, The" (Berry), **Supp. X:** 36

J R (Gaddis), **Supp. IV Part 1:** 279, 280, 285–289, 291, 294; **Supp. IV Part 2:** 484; **Supp. XXI:** 226

Juana Inés de la Cruz, Sor, **Supp. XXI:** 94, 104

Juan de la Cruz (John of the Cross), **Supp. XXI:** 99, 104

"Juan's Song" (Bogan), **Supp. III Part 1:** 50

Juba to Jive: A Dictionary of African-American Slang (Major), **Supp. XXII:** 172, 180

Jubilate Agno (Smart), **Supp. IV Part 2:** 626

Judah, Hettie, **Supp. XIII:** 246

Judah the Pious (Prose), **Supp. XVI:** 249, 250, 262

"Judas Maccabaeus" (Longfellow), **II:** 506; **Retro. Supp. II:** 165, 167

Judd, Sylvester, **II:** 290; **Supp. I Part 2:** 420

Judd Rankin's Daughter (Glaspell), **Supp. III Part 1:** 186–188

Jude the Obscure (Hardy), **Supp. I Part 1:** 217

Judevine (Budbill), **Supp. XIX:** 4, **8–9,** 12

Judevine: A Play in Three Acts/Two Acts (Budbill), **Supp. XIX: 12–13**

Judge, Jane, **Supp. XXII:** 191

"Judgement Day" (O'Connor), **III:** 349, 350; **Retro. Supp. II:** 236

Judgment Day (Farrell), **II:** 29, 31, 32, 34, 39

"Judgment of Paris, The" (Merwin), **Supp. III Part 1:** 350

Judgment of Paris, The (Vidal), **Supp. IV Part 2:** 680, 682

"Judgment of the Sage, The" (Crane), **I:** 420

Judith (Farrell), **II:** 46, 48

"Judith" (Garrett), **Supp. VII:** 109–110

"Juggernaut" (Bass), **Supp. XVI:** 16–17

"Jug of Sirup, A" (Bierce), **I:** 206

"Jugurtha" (Longfellow), **II:** 499

"Juice or Gravy" (P. Roth), **Retro. Supp. II:** 279

"Juke Box Love Song" (Hughes), **Retro. Supp. I:** 209

"Julia" (Hellman), **Supp. I Part 1:** 280, 293

"Julia Miller" (Masters), **Supp. I Part 2:** 461

Julian (Vidal), **Supp. IV Part 2:** 677, 684–685, 685, 689

Julian the Apostate, **Retro. Supp. I:** 247

"Julian Vreden" (Bowles), **Supp. IV Part 1:** 94

Julie and Romeo (Ray), **Supp. XII:** 308, 310

Julien, Isaac, **Supp. XI:** 19

Julie; ou, La nouvelle Héloïse (Rousseau), **Supp. XVI:** 184

Julier, Laura, **Supp. IV Part 1:** 211

Julip (Harrison), **Supp. VIII: 51**

Julius Caesar (Shakespeare), **I:** 284

"July Midnight" (Lowell), **II:** 521

Jumel, Madame, **Supp. I Part 2:** 461

Jumping Out of Bed (R. Bly), **Supp. IV Part 1:** 71

"Jump-Up Day" (Kingsolver), **Supp. VII:** 203

"Junctions" (Lamott), **Supp. XX: 143**

"June 1940" (Kees), **Supp. XV:** 141

"June Light" (Wilbur), **Supp. III Part 2:** 545

June Moon (Lardner and Kaufman), **II:** 427

"June Recital" (Welty), **IV:** 272–273

Juneteenth (Ellison), **Retro. Supp. II:** 119, 124, **126–128**

"Juneteenth" (Ellison), **Retro. Supp. II:** 119, 126; **Supp. II Part 1:** 248

"June the Third" (Gander), **Supp. XV:** 340

June-Tree: New and Selected Poems, 1974–2000 (Balakian), **Supp. XXIII:** 19, **24–25,** 32

Jung, Carl, **I:** 58, 135, 241, 248, 252, 402; **III:** 400, 534, 543; **Supp. I Part 2:** 439; **Supp. IV Part 1:** 68, 69; **Supp. VIII:** 45; **Supp. X:** 193; **Supp. XV:** 214; **Supp. XX: 63, 117**

Junger, Ernst, **Supp. III Part 1:** 63

Jungle, The (Sinclair), **III:** 580; **Supp. V:** 281–284, 285, 289

Jungle Lovers (Theroux), **Supp. VIII:** 314, 315, 316, **317**

"Junior Addict" (Hughes), **Supp. I Part 1:** 343

"Juniper" (Francis), **Supp. IX:** 79

"Junk" (Wilbur), **Supp. III Part 2:** 556

Junker, Howard, **Supp. XV:** 116

Junkie: Confessions of an Unredeemed Drug Addict (Burroughs), **Supp. III Part 1:** 92, 94–96, 101

Junky (Burroughs), **Supp. XIV:** 143

Juno and the Paycock (O'Casey), **Supp. IV Part 1:** 361

"Jupiter Doke, Brigadier General" (Bierce), **I:** 204

Jupiter Laughs (A. Cronin), **Supp. XVII:** 59

Jurgen (Cabell), **III:** 394; **IV:** 286; **Retro. Supp. I:** 80; **Supp. I Part 2:** 718

Jury of Her Peers, A: American Women Writers from Anne Bradstreet to Annie Proulx (Showalter), **Supp. XX: 274**

Jusserand, Jules, **II:** 338

Just above My Head (Baldwin), **Retro. Supp. II:** 14–15

"Just a Little One" (Parker), **Supp. IX:** 191

Just and the Unjust, The (Cozzens), **I:** 367–370, 372, 375, 377, 378, 379

Just an Ordinary Day (Jackson), **Supp. IX:** 120

Just Before Dark: Collected Nonfiction (Harrison), **Supp. VIII:** 41, 45, 46, 53

"Just Before the War with the Eskimos" (Salinger), **III:** 559

"Just Boys" (Farrell), **II:** 45

"Just for the Thrill: An Essay on the Difference Between Women and Men" (Carson), **Supp. XII: 103–104**

"Justice" (Hughes), **Supp. I Part 1:** 331

"Justice, A" (Faulkner), **Retro. Supp. I:** 83

Justice, Donald, **Retro. Supp. I:** 313; **Supp. III Part 2:** 541; **Supp. V:** 180, 337, 338, 341; **Supp. VII: 115–130;** **Supp. XI:** 141, 315; **Supp. XIII:** 76, 312; **Supp. XV:** 74, 93, 118, 119, 134; **Supp. XVII:** 110, 120, 246; **Supp. XX: 199**

Justice and Expediency (Whittier), **Supp. I Part 2:** 686

"Justice Denied in Massachusetts" (Millay), **III:** 140

Justice for Salcido (Endore), **Supp. XVII:** 63

Justice of Gold in the Damnation of Sinners, The (Edwards), **I:** 559

"Justice to Feminism" (Ozick), **Supp. V:** 272

"Just Introduced" (Taggard), **Supp. XXII:** 274

Just Kids (Smith), **Supp. XXII:** 94

"Just Like a Woman" (Dylan), **Supp. XV:** 350

"Just Like Job" (Angelou), **Supp. IV Part 1:** 15

"Just One of the Boys" (Swados), **Supp. XIX:** 259

Just Whistle: A Valentine (Wright), **Supp. XV: 346–348**

Just Wild About Harry (H. Miller), **III:** 190

Juvenal, **II:** 8, 169, 552

K

"K, The" (Olson), **Supp. II Part 2:** 558, 563, 569

Kabir, **Supp. IV Part 1:** 74

"Kabnis" (Toomer), **Supp. III Part 2:** 481, 484; **Supp. IX:** 309, 310, **319–320**

Kachel, Elsie. *See* Stevens, Mrs. Wallace (Elsie Kachel)

"Kaddish" (Ginsberg), **Supp. II Part 1:** 319, 327

Kaddish and Other Poems, 1958–1960 (Ginsberg), **Supp. II Part 1:** 309, 319–320; **Supp. XIV:** 269

Kael, Pauline, **Supp. IX:** 253; **Supp. XV:** 147, 148

Kafka, Franz, **II:** 244, 565, 569; **III:** 51, 253, 418, 566, 572; **IV:** 2, 113, 218, 437–439, 442; **Retro. Supp. II:** 20, 221, 282; **Supp. I Part 1:** 197; **Supp. III Part 1:** 105; **Supp. III Part 2:** 413; **Supp. IV Part 1:** 379; **Supp. IV Part 2:** 623; **Supp. VIII:** 14, 15, 103; **Supp. XII:** 21, 37, 98, 168; **Supp.**

XIII: 305; **Supp. XVI:** 17, 201, 206, 209; **Supp. XVII:** 244; **Supp. XX: 18, 21, 85, 87; Supp. XXII:** 89, 90, 94; **Supp. XXIII:** 68
Kafka Americana (Lethem and Scholtz), **Supp. XVIII:** 144–145
Kaganoff, Penny, **Supp. XI:** 122
Kagan's Superfecta (A. Hoffman), **Supp. XVII:** 42
Kahane, Jack, **III:** 171, 178
Kahn, Otto, **I:** 385; **IV:** 123; **Retro. Supp. II:** 81, 84, 85; **Supp. XX: 75**
Kahn, R. T., **Supp. XI:** 216
"Kai, Today" (Snyder), **Supp. VIII:** 300
Kaiser, Georg, **I:** 479
Kaiser, Henry, **Supp. I Part 2:** 644
Kakutani, Michiko, **Supp. IV Part 1:** 196, 201, 205, 211, 212; **Supp. V:** 63; **Supp. VIII:** 81, 84, 86, 88, 141; **Supp. X:** 171, 301, 302, 310, 314; **Supp. XI:** 38, 179; **Supp. XII:** 165, 171, 172, 299; **Supp. XVI:** 71; **Supp. XVII:** 6; **Supp. XIX:** 142; **Supp. XX: 92, 94; Supp. XXII:** 109
Kalem, T. E., **Supp. IV Part 2:** 585
Kalevala (Finnish epic), **II:** 503, 504; **Retro. Supp. II:** 155
Kalevala (Lönnrot), **Retro. Supp. II:** 159, 160
Kalfus, Ken, **Supp. XVII:** 50
Kalki: A Novel (Vidal), **Supp. IV Part 2:** 677, 682, 685, 691, 692
Kallan, Richard A., **Supp. XX: 244**
Kallen, Horace, **I:** 229; **Supp. I Part 2:** 643; **Supp. XIV:** 195, 197, 198
Kallman, Chester, **II:** 586; **Supp. II Part 1:** 15, 17, 24, 26
"Kallundborg Church" (Whittier), **Supp. I Part 2:** 696
Kalstone, David, **Retro. Supp. II:** 40
Kamel, Rose, **Supp. XIII:** 306
Kamenev, Lev, **Supp. XXI:** 167
Kamera Obskura (Nabokov), **III:** 255
Kamhi, Michelle Moarder, **Supp. IV Part 2:** 529, 530
Kaminsky, Wally, **Supp. XVIII:** 72
Kamp, David, **Supp. XVIII:** 150
Kandy-Kolored Tangerine-Flake Streamline Baby, The (Wolfe), **Supp. III Part 2:** 569, 573–576, 580, 581
Kane, Julie, **Supp. XVII:** 78
Kane, Lesley, **Supp. XIV:** 250
Kanellos, Nicolás, **Supp. VIII:** 82; **Supp. XIII:** 213
Kanin, Garson, **Supp. IV Part 2:** 574
"Kansas City Coyote" (Harjo), **Supp. XII:** 219, 222
"Kansas Emigrants, The" (Whittier), **Supp. I Part 2:** 687
Kant, Immanuel, **I:** 61, 277, 278; **II:** 10–11, 362, 480, 580–581, 582, 583; **III:** 300, 480, 481, 488, 612; **IV:** 90; **Supp. I Part 2:** 640; **Supp. IV Part 2:** 527; **Supp. XIV:** 198, 199; **Supp. XVI:** 184
Kanter, Hal, **IV:** 383
Kapital, Das (Marx), **III:** 580; **Supp. XXI:** 161, 162, 163
Kaplan, Abraham, **I:** 277

Kaplan, Justin, **I:** 247–248; **Retro. Supp. I:** 392
Kaplan, Mary Jo, **Supp. XIX:** 266
Kaplan, Steven, **Supp. V:** 238, 241, 243, 248
Karate Is a Thing of the Spirit (Crews), **Supp. XI: 112–113**
Karbo, Karen, **Supp. X:** 259, 262
"Karintha" (Toomer), **Supp. IX:** 311
Karl, Frederick R., **Supp. IV Part 1:** 384; **Supp. XXI:** 234
"Karloff and the Rock" (Di Piero), **Supp. XIX:** 44
Karl Shapiro's America (film), **Supp. II Part 2:** 703
Karmi, T., **Supp. XV:** 78, 88
Karr, Mary, **Supp. XI: 239–256; Supp. XIII:** 285; **Supp. XV:** 223; **Supp. XVI:** 63, 70, 77; **Supp. XVII:** 242
Karyotakis, Konstantine, **Supp. XXIII:** 125
Kasabian, Linda, **Supp. IV Part 1:** 206
Kasper, Catherine, **Supp. XVI:** 294–295
Kate Chopin (Toth), **Retro. Supp. II:** 71
Kate Chopin: A Critical Biography (Seyersted), **Retro. Supp. II:** 65; **Supp. I Part 1:** 225
Kate Chopin and Edith Wharton: An Annotated Bibliographical Guide to Secondary Sources (Springer), **Supp. I Part 1:** 225
Kate Chopin and Her Creole Stories (Rankin), **Retro. Supp. II:** 57; **Supp. I Part 1:** 200, 225
"Kate Chopin's *The Awakening* in the Perspective of Her Literary Career" (Arms), **Supp. I Part 1:** 225
Kate Vaiden (Price), **Supp. VI:** 264, 265
"Käthe Kollwitz" (Rukeyser), **Supp. VI:** 283, 284
Katherine and Jean (Rice), **Supp. VII:** 288
"Kathleen" (Whittier), **Supp. I Part 2:** 693
Kathleen and Frank: The Autobiography of a Family (Isherwood), **Supp. XIV:** 158, 171
Kathy Goes to Haiti (Acker), **Supp. XII:** 5
Katz, Alan, **Supp. XXII:** 177
Katz, Alex, **Supp. XV:** 185
Katz, Jonathan, **Supp. XII:** 179
Katz, Steve, **Supp. V:** 44
Katz, Steven T., **Supp. XVI:** 154
Katzenberg, Jffrey, **Supp. XXI:** 154
Kauffman, Carol, **Supp. XI:** 295
Kauffmann, Stanley, **III:** 452; **Supp. I Part 2:** 391; **Supp. XVI:** 74
Kaufman, Boris, **Supp. XVIII:** 251
Kaufman, Charlie, **Supp. XV:** 16
Kaufman, Ellen, **Supp. XXIII:** 132, 133
Kaufman, George S., **II:** 427, 435, 437; **III:** 62, 71–72, 394; **Retro. Supp. II:** 327; **Supp. IV Part 2:** 574; **Supp. IX:** 190; **Supp. XV:** 329
Kaufman, James, **Supp. XI:** 39
Kaufmann, Walter, **Supp. XVII:** 137
Kauvar, Elaine M., **Supp. V:** 273

Kavanaugh (Longfellow), **I:** 458; **II:** 489, 491; **Retro. Supp. II:** 156; **Supp. I Part 2:** 420
Kaveney, Roz, **Supp. XI:** 39
Kawabata, Yasunari, **Supp. XV:** 186; **Supp. XXI:** 146
Kaye-Smith, Sheila, **Supp. XVIII:** 130–131
Kazan, Elia, **III:** 153, 163; **IV:** 383; **Supp. I Part 1:** 66, 295; **Supp. XVI:** 193; **Supp. XVIII:** 250–251, 252
Kazin, Alfred, **I:** 248, 417, 419, 517; **II:** 177, 459; **IV:** 236; **Retro. Supp. II:** 206, 243, 246, 286; **Supp. I Part 1:** 195, 196, 294, 295, 296; **Supp. I Part 2:** 536, 631, 647, 650, 678, 679, 719; **Supp. II Part 1:** 143; **Supp. IV Part 1:** 200, 382; **Supp. V:** 122; **Supp. VIII: 93–111; Supp. IX:** 3, 227; **Supp. XIII:** 98, 106; **Supp. XIV:** 11; **Supp. XV:** 142; **Supp. XXIII:** 2, 106
Keach, Stacey, **Supp. XI:** 309
Kean, Danuta, **Supp. XXI:** 80
Keane, Sarah, **Supp. I Part 1:** 100
Kearns, Cleo McNelly, **Retro. Supp. I:** 57
Kearns, George, **Retro. Supp. I:** 292
Keating, AnnLouise, **Supp. IV Part 1:** 330
Keaton, Buster, **I:** 31; **Supp. I Part 2:** 607; **Supp. IV Part 2:** 574
Keaton, Diane, **Supp. XV:** 5
Keats, John, **I:** 34, 103, 284, 314, 317–318, 385, 401, 448; **II:** 82, 88, 97, 214, 368, 512, 516, 530–531, 540, 593; **III:** 4, 10, 45, 122, 133–134, 179, 214, 237, 272, 275, 469, 485, 523; **IV:** 360, 405, 416; **Retro. Supp. I:** 91, 301, 313, 360, 395, 412; **Supp. I Part 1:** 82, 183, 266, 267, 312, 349, 362, 363, 365; **Supp. I Part 2:** 410, 422, 424, 539, 552, 675, 719, 720; **Supp. III Part 1:** 73; **Supp. IV Part 1:** 123, 168, 325; **Supp. IV Part 2:** 455; **Supp. VIII:** 41, 273; **Supp. IX:** 38, 39, 45; **Supp. XI:** 43, 320; **Supp. XII:** 9, 113, 255; **Supp. XIII:** 131, 281; **Supp. XIV:** 274; **Supp. XV:** 92; **Supp. XVII:** 76, 112; **Supp. XIX:** 33, 276; **Supp. XX: 115, 116; Supp. XXI:** 131
Keats, John (other), **Supp. IX:** 190, 195, 200
Keegan, Abigail, **Supp. XXIII:** 129, 130, 136
"Keela, the Outcast Indian Maiden" (Welty), **IV:** 263
Keeley, Mary Paxton, **Supp. XV:** 136
"Keen Scalpel on Racial Ills" (Bruell), **Supp. VIII:** 126
Keep, The (Egan), **Supp. XIX:** 49, **56–61**
"Keep A-Inchin' Along" (Van Vechten), **Supp. III Part 2:** 744
Keeping (Goldbarth), **Supp. XII:** 179–180, 180
"Keeping Informed in D.C." (Nemerov), **III:** 287
Keeping Slug Woman Alive: A Holistic Approach to American Indian Texts (Sarris), **Supp. IV Part 1:** 329

"'Keeping Their World Large' " (Moore), **III:** 201–202

Keeping the Night (Everwine), **Supp. XV:** 75, **81–85,** 86

"Keeping Things Whole" (Strand), **Supp. IV Part 2:** 624

Keep It Simple: A Defense of the Earth (Nichols), **Supp. XIII:** 268

"Keep the Saving Habit" (L. I. Wilder), **Supp. XXII:** 290

Kees, Weldon, **Supp. X:** 118; **Supp. XII:** 198; **Supp. XV:** 113, 114, 115, **133–149**

Keillor, Garrison, **Supp. XII:** 343; **Supp. XIII:** 274; **Supp. XVI: 165–179;** **Supp. XXI:** 53, 62; **Supp. XXII:** 83; **Supp. XXIII:** 57, 58, 138

Keillor, Gary Edward. *See* Keiller, Garrison

Keith, Brian, **Supp. IV Part 2:** 474

Keith, Minor C., **I:** 483

Kelleghan, Fiona, **Supp. XVIII:** 136, 139, 140

Keller, A. G., **III:** 108

Keller, Christopher J., **Supp. XVIII:** 192, 195

Keller, Helen, **I:** 254, 258; **Supp. XXIII:** 161

Keller, Lynn, **Supp. IV Part 2:** 423; **Supp. V:** 78, 80

Kelley, David, **Supp. IV Part 2:** 528, 529

Kelley, Florence, **Supp. I Part 1:** 5, 7

Kelley, Mary, **Supp. XVIII:** 257, 260

Kelley, Robin, **Supp. XVIII:** 231

Kellogg, Reverend Edwin H., **III:** 200

Kellogg, Paul U., **Supp. I Part 1:** 5, 7, 12

Kelly, **II:** 464

Kelly, Brigit Pegeen, **Supp. XVII: 123–134; Supp. XXIII:** 54

Kelly, Emmett, **Supp. XI:** 99, 106

Kelly, Gene, **Supp. XXI:** 148

Kelly, James Patrick, **Supp. XVIII:** 145; **Supp. XIX:** 231

Kelly, Walt, **Supp. XI:** 105

Kelly, William, **Supp. XV:** 75, 88

Kelsey, Penelope Myrtle, **Supp. XXIII:** 143, 153–164

Kelsh, Nick, **Supp. XVII:** 167, 179

Kemble, Fanny, **Retro. Supp. I:** 228

Kemble, Gouverneur, **II:** 298

Kemble, Peter, **II:** 298

Kempton, Murray, **Supp. VIII:** 104

Kempton-Wace Letters, The (London and Strunsky), **II:** 465

Kennan, George F., **Supp. VIII:** 241

Kennedy, Albert J., **Supp. I Part 1:** 19

Kennedy, Arthur, **III:** 153

Kennedy, Burt, **Supp. IV Part 1:** 236

Kennedy, Jeffery, **Supp. XXI:** 6

Kennedy, J. Gerald, **Retro. Supp. II:** 271

Kennedy, John F., **I:** 136, 170; **II:** 49, 152–153; **III:** 38, 41, 42, 234, 411, 415, 581; **IV:** 229; **Supp. I Part 1:** 291; **Supp. I Part 2:** 496; **Supp. VIII:** 98, 104, 203; **Supp. XII:** 132

Kennedy, Mrs. John F., **I:** 136

Kennedy, John Pendleton, **II:** 313; **Supp. XXII:** 193

Kennedy, Robert, **Supp. V:** 291

Kennedy, Robert F., **I:** 294; **Supp. I Part 1:** 52; **Supp. XI:** 343

Kennedy, Sarah, **Supp. XVIII:** 293, 299, 301

Kennedy, William, **Supp. VII: 131–157; Supp. XVII:** 135; **Supp. XIX:** 141; **Supp. XX:** 90

Kennedy, X. J., **Supp. V:** 178, 182; **Supp. XV:** 113, **151–173**

Kenner, Hugh, **III:** 475, 478; **IV:** 412; **Supp. I Part 1:** 255; **Supp. IV Part 2:** 474; **Supp. XV:** 147; **Supp. XXI:** 235

Kenneth Koch, a Tragedy (O'Hara and Rivers), **Supp. XXIII:** 217

"Kenneth Koch's 'Serious Moment' " (Spurr), **Supp. XV:** 183

Kenneth Millar/Ross Macdonald: A Checklist (Bruccoli), **Supp. IV Part 2:** 464, 469, 471

Kenney, Michael, **Supp. XIX:** 51, 52–53

Kenney, Susan, **Supp. XVIII:** 288, 289

Kenny, Maurice, **Supp. IV Part 2:** 502; **Supp. XXIII: 143–159**

Kent, George, **Supp. IV Part 1:** 11

Kent, Rockwell, **Supp. XV:** 41; **Supp. XXII:** 281

Kenton, Edna, **Supp. XXI:** 6

Kenton, Maxwell. *See* Burnett, David; Hoffenberg, Mason; Southern, Terry

"Kent State, May 1970" (Haines), **Supp. XII:** 211

Kentucky Straight (Offutt), **Supp. XIX: 163–167,** 171, 172

Kenya, the Land of Conflict (Kenyatta), **Supp. XXI:** 166

Kenyatta, Jomo, **Supp. X:** 135; **Supp. XXI:** 166

Kenyon, Jane, **Supp. VII: 159–177; Supp. VIII:** 272

Keogh, Tom, **Supp. XVI:** 230

Kepler, Johannes, **III:** 484; **IV:** 18

Keplinger, David, **Supp. XIX:** 273

Keppel, Frederick P., **I:** 214

"Kéramos" (Longfellow), **II:** 494; **Retro. Supp. II:** 167, 169

Kéramos and Other Poems (Longfellow), **II:** 490

Kercheval, Jesse Lee, **Supp. XIX:** 51

Kerim, Ussin, **Supp. IX:** 152

Kermode, Frank, **IV:** 133; **Retro. Supp. I:** 301

Kern, Jerome, **II:** 427

Kerouac, Jack, **III:** 174; **Retro. Supp. I:** 102; **Supp. II Part 1:** 31, 307, 309, 318, 328; **Supp. III Part 1:** 91–94, 96, 100, **217–234; Supp. IV Part 1:** 90, 146; **Supp. V:** 336; **Supp. VIII:** 42, 138, 289, 305; **Supp. IX:** 246; **Supp. XII:** 118, 121, 122, 123, 126, 131, 132; **Supp. XIII:** 275, 284; **Supp. XIV:** 137, 138, 141, 142, 143–144; **Supp. XV:** 134, 221; **Supp. XVI:** 123; **Supp. XVII:** 135, 138; **Supp. XX:** 17; **Supp. XXIII:** 100, 213

Kerr, Deborah, **Supp. XI:** 307

Kerr, Orpheus C. (pseudonym). *See* Newell, Henry

Kerr, Walter, **Supp. IV Part 2:** 575, 579

Kerridge, Richard, **Supp. XVI:** 26

Kesey, Ken, **III:** 558; **Supp. III Part 1:** 217; **Supp. V:** 220, 295; **Supp. X:** 24, 265; **Supp. XI:** 104; **Supp. XXIII:** 100

Kessel, John, **Supp. XVIII:** 145; **Supp. XIX:** 231

Kessler, Milton, **Supp. XIX:** 195

Kesten, Stephen, **Supp. XI:** 309

Ketchum, Liza, **Supp. XIX:** 266

Ketchup (Shanley), **Supp. XIV:** 315

Kevane, Bridget, **Supp. XI:** 185, 190

"Key, The" (Welty), **IV:** 262

"Keys" (Nye), **Supp. XIII:** 281

"Key to the Highway" (Halliday), **Supp. XIX:** 84

Key to Uncle Tom's Cabin, A (Stowe), **Supp. I Part 2:** 580

Key West (H. Crane), **Retro. Supp. II:** 84

"Key West" (H. Crane), **I:** 400

Key West: An Island Sheaf (Crane), **I:** 385, 399–402

"Khalil the Heretic" (Gibran), **Supp. XX:** 124

Khrushchev, Nikita, **I:** 136

Kiang Kang-hu, **Supp. XV:** 45, 47

Kick for a Bite, A (Cobbett), **Supp. XV:** 237

"Kicking the Candles Out" (Jarman), **Supp. XVII:** 113

Kid, The (Aiken), **I:** 61

Kid, The (Chaplin), **I:** 386

Kidder, Tracy, **Supp. III Part 1:** 302; **Supp. XVIII:** 106, 114

Kiddush Ha-Shem: An Epic of 1648 (Asch), **Supp. XXIII:** 3, 6, **10,** 11, 12, 16

Kidesh ha-Shem (Sanctification of the name) (Asch), **Supp. XXIII:** 6

Kidman, Nicole, **Supp. X:** 80

"Kidnapping in the Family, A" (Fante), **Supp. XI:** 164

"Kid's Guide to Divorce, The" (Moore), **Supp. X:** 167, 172

Kidwell, Clara Sue, **Supp. IV Part 1:** 333

Kielsky, Vera Emuma, **Supp. V:** 273

Kiely, Brendan, **Supp. XVII:** 75

Kieran, John, **II:** 417

Kierkegaard, Søren Aabye, **II:** 229; **III:** 292, 305, 309, 572; **IV:** 438, 491; **Retro. Supp. I:** 326; **Retro. Supp. II:** 222; **Supp. V:** 9; **Supp. VIII:** 7–8; **Supp. XX:** 132

Kiernan, Robert F., **Supp. IV Part 2:** 684

Kieseritsky, L., **III:** 252

Kilgo, Jim, **Supp. XVIII:** 192

"Kilim" (McClatchy), **Supp. XII:** 258

Kilina, Patricia (pseudonym). *See* Warren, Patricia Nell

"Killed at Resaca" (Bierce), **I:** 202

"Killed at the Ford" (Longfellow), **Retro. Supp. II:** 170–171

Killens, John Oliver, **Supp. IV Part 1:** 8, 369

"Killer in the Rain" (Chandler), **Supp. IV Part 1:** 122

"Killers, The" (Hemingway), **II:** 249; **Retro. Supp. I:** 188, 189

Killers, The: A Narrative of Real Life in Philadelphia (Lippard), **Supp. XXIII:** 178, 184

Killing Mister Watson (Matthiessen), **Supp. V:** 212, 214

"Killing of a State Cop, The" (Ortiz), **Supp. IV Part 2:** 499

Killing of Sister George, The (Marcus), **Supp. I Part 1:** 277

"Killings" (Dubus), **Supp. VII:** 85–86

"Killing the Ghost of Ripton" (Carruth), **Supp. XIX:** 1

"Killing the Plants" (Kenyon), **Supp. VII:** 167, 168

Kilmer, Joyce, **Supp. I Part 2:** 387; **Supp. XV:** 294

Kilpatrick, James K., **Supp. X:** 145

Kilvert, Francis, **Supp. VIII:** 172

Kim (Kipling), **Supp. X:** 230

Kim, Alfred, **Supp. XI:** 140

Kim, Sharon, **Supp. XVIII:** 267

Kimball, Frederic, **Supp. XXI:** 146

Kimball, J. Golden, **Supp. IV Part 2:** 602

Kimbrough, Mary Craig. *See* Sinclair, Mary Craig (Mary Craig Kimbrough)

Kimes, Maymie B., **Supp. IX:** 178

Kimes, William F., **Supp. IX:** 178

Kimmelman, Bert, **Supp. XXI:** 24

"Kin" (Welty), **IV:** 277; **Retro. Supp. I:** 353

Kinard, Agnes Dodds, **Supp. XIV:** 122, 123, 127

Kincaid, Jamaica, **Supp. VII: 179–196**

Kincaid, James, **Supp. XVIII:** 62, 63

"Kindness" (Dunn), **Supp. XI:** 149, 150

"Kindness" (Nye), **Supp. XIII:** 285

"Kindness" (Plath), **Retro. Supp. II:** 256

Kind of Light that Shines on Texas, The (McKnight), **Supp. XX: 151–152**

"Kind of Light that Shines on Texas, The" (McKnight), **Supp. XX: 151**

Kind of Order, A Kind of Folly, A: Essays and Conversations (Kunitz), **Supp. III Part 1:** 262, 268

Kindred (O. Butler), **Supp. XIII: 59–60,** 69

"Kind Sir: These Woods" (Sexton), **Supp. II Part 2:** 673

Kinds of Love (Sarton), **Supp. VIII: 253– 254,** 256

Kinfolk (Buck), **Supp. II Part 1:** 126

King, Alexander, **IV:** 287

King, Carole, **Supp. XII:** 308

King, Clarence, **I:** 1

King, Ernest, **Supp. I Part 2:** 491

King, Fisher, **II:** 425

King, Francis, **Supp. XIV:** 155, 156, 166, 169

King, Grace, **Retro. Supp. II:** 136

King, Martin Luther, Jr., **Retro. Supp. II:** 12, 13; **Supp. XVIII:** 24; **Supp. XX: 281**

King, Michael, **Supp. XII:** 182

King, Queen, Knave (Nabokov), **III:** 251; **Retro. Supp. I:** 270

King, Starr, **Supp. II Part 1:** 341, 342

King, Stephen, **Supp. IV Part 1:** 102, 104; **Supp. IV Part 2:** 467; **Supp. V: 137–155; Supp. IX:** 114; **Supp. XIII:** 53; **Supp. XXIII:** 290

King, Tabitha (Mrs. Stephen King), **Supp. V:** 137

King, The (Barthelme), **Supp. IV Part 1:** 47, 52

"King, The" (Gibran), **Supp. XX: 123– 124**

King Coffin (Aiken), **I:** 53–54, 57

"King David" (Benét), **Supp. XI:** 44

"King David" (Reznikoff), **Supp. XIV:** 283

Kingdom and the Power, The (Talese), **Supp. XVII:** 202, 203, 204, 210

Kingdom by the Sea, The: A Journey around Great Britain (Theroux), **Supp. VIII:** 323

"Kingdom County Come" (Mosher), **Supp. XXII:** 211–212

Kingdom of Earth (T. Williams), **IV:** 382, 386, 387, 388, 391, 393, 398

"Kingdom of Earth, The" (T. Williams), **IV:** 384

Kingfisher, The (Clampitt), **Supp. IX:** 38

"Kingfishers, The" (Olson), **Supp. II Part 2:** 557, 558–563, 582

King Jasper (Robinson), **III:** 523

King Kong (film), **Supp. IV Part 1:** 104; **Supp. XVII:** 58

King Lear (Shakespeare), **I:** 538; **II:** 540, 551; **Retro. Supp. I:** 248; **Supp. IV Part 1:** 31, 36; **Supp. IX:** 14; **Supp. XI:** 172; **Supp. XV:** 349

King Leopold's Soliloquy (Twain), **IV:** 208

King My Father's Wreck, The (Simpson), **Supp. IX:** 266, 267, 270, 275, 276

King of Babylon Shall Not Come Against You, The (Garrett), **Supp. VII:** 110– 111; **Supp. X:** 3

"King of Beasts" (P. N. Warren), **Supp. XX: 272**

"King of Folly Island, The" (Jewett), **II:** 394; **Retro. Supp. II:** 132, 133

King of Kings (film), **Supp. IV Part 2:** 520

King of Paris (Endore), **Supp. XVII:** 64

"King of the Bingo Game" (Ellison), **Retro. Supp. II:** 117, 125; **Supp. II Part 1:** 235, 238, 240–241

"King of the Cats, The" (Benét), **Supp. XI:** 49–50

"King of the Clock Tower" (Yeats), **III:** 473

"King of the Desert, The" (O'Hara), **III:** 369

King of the Fields, The (Singer), **Retro. Supp. II:** 317

King of the Jews (Epstein), **Supp. XII:** 161, **166–170,** 172

King of the Mountain (Garrett), **Supp. VII:** 96, 97

"King of the River" (Kunitz), **Supp. III Part 1:** 263, 267–268

"King of the Sea" (Marquand), **III:** 60

"King over the Water" (Blackmur), **Supp. II Part 1:** 107

"King Pandar" (Blackmur), **Supp. II Part 1:** 92, 102

"King Pest" (Poe), **Retro. Supp. II:** 273

Kingsblood Royal (Lewis), **II:** 456

Kingsbury, John, **Supp. I Part 1:** 8

"King's Daughters, Home for Unwed Mothers, 1948" (Stanford), **Supp. XV:** 345

King's Henchman, The (Millay), **III:** 138–139

Kingsley, Sidney, **Supp. I Part 1:** 277, 281

King's Mare, The (Canolle; Loos, trans.), **Supp. XVI:** 194

"King's Missive, The" (Whittier), **Supp. I Part 2:** 694

Kingsolver, Barbara, **Supp. VII: 197– 214; Supp. XIII:** 16; **Supp. XVIII:** 189

King's Stilts, The (Geisel), **Supp. XVI:** 100, 104

Kingston, Earll, **Supp. V:** 160

Kingston, Maxine Hong, **Supp. IV Part 1:** 1, 12; **Supp. V: 157–175,** 250; **Supp. X:** 291–292; **Supp. XI:** 18, 245; **Supp. XV:** 220, 223

"King Volmer and Elsie" (Whittier), **Supp. I Part 2:** 696

Kinkaid, Jamaica, **Supp. XXII:** 65

Kinmont, Alexander, **Supp. I Part 2:** 588–589

Kinnaird, John, **Retro. Supp. I:** 399

Kinnell, Galway, **Supp. III Part 1: 235– 256; Supp. III Part 2:** 541; **Supp. IV Part 2:** 623; **Supp. V:** 332; **Supp. VIII:** 39; **Supp. XI:** 139; **Supp. XII:** 241; **Supp. XV:** 212; **Supp. XVI:** 53; **Supp. XXII:** 83

Kinsella, Thomas, **Supp. XX: 195–196, 197, 207**

Kinsey, Alfred, **IV:** 230; **Supp. XIV:** 140

Kinzie, Mary, **Supp. XII:** 181; **Supp. XXIII:** 124

"Kipling" (Trilling), **Supp. III Part 2:** 495

Kipling, Rudyard, **I:** 421, 587–588; **II:** 271, 338, 404, 439; **III:** 55, 328, 508, 511, 521, 524, 579; **IV:** 429; **Supp. IV Part 2:** 603; **Supp. X:** 255; **Supp. XX: 23**

Kirby, David, **Supp. XIII:** 89; **Supp. XIX:** 81

Kirkland, Caroline, **Supp. XVIII:** 258

Kirkland, David, **Supp. XVI:** 186

Kirkland, Jack, **I:** 297

Kirkpatrick, Jeane, **Supp. VIII:** 241

Kirkus, Virginia, **Supp. XV:** 198

Kirkwood, Cynthia A., **Supp. XI:** 177, 178, 179

Kirp, David L., **Supp. XI:** 129

Kirsch, Adam, **Supp. XV:** 251, 260, 264, 266, 341, 347, 350–351

Kirstein, Lincoln, **Supp. II Part 1:** 90, 97; **Supp. IV Part 1:** 82, 83; **Supp. XXII:** 281

Kishef-makherin fun Kastilye, Di (The witch of Castle) (Asch), **Supp. XXIII:** 6

"Kiss, The" (Di Piero), **Supp. XIX:** 45, 47

Kiss, The (Harrison), **Supp. X:** 191

"Kiss, The" (Sexton), **Supp. II Part 2:** 687

"Kiss Away" (C. Baxter), **Supp. XVII:** 20

Kissel, Howard, **Supp. IV Part 2:** 580

Kiss Hollywood Good-by (Loos), **Supp. XVI:** 190, 195

Kissinger, Henry, **Supp. IV Part 1:** 388; **Supp. XII:** 9, 14

Kiss of the Spider Woman, the Musical (McNally), **Supp. XIII:** 207, **Supp. XIII:** 208

Kiss Tomorrow Good-bye (McCoy), **Supp. XIII:** 170, **172–173,** 174

"Kit and Caboodle" (Komunyakaa), **Supp. XIII:** 115

Kit Brandon: A Portrait (Anderson), **I:** 111

Kitchen, Judith, **Supp. IV Part 1:** 242, 245, 252; **Supp. IX:** 163; **Supp. XI:** 312, 313, 315, 317, 319, 320, 326, 329; **Supp. XV:** 215, 219

"Kitchenette" (Brooks), **Retro. Supp. I:** 208

Kitchen God's Wife, The (Tan), **Supp. X:** 289, 292, 293, 294–295, 296–297, 298–299

"Kitchen Terrarium: 1983" (McCarriston), **Supp. XIV:** 270

Kit O'Brien (Masters), **Supp. I Part 2:** 471

Kittel, Frederick August. See Wilson, August

Kittredge, Charmian. See London, Mrs. Jack (Charmian Kittredge)

Kittredge, William, **Supp. VIII:** 39; **Supp. XI:** 316; **Supp. XII:** 209; **Supp. XIII:** 16

"Kitty Hawk" (Frost), **II:** 164; **Retro. Supp. I:** 124, 141

Kizer, Carolyn, **Supp. XVII:** 71, 72, 73, 74

Klaidman, Stephen, **Supp. XIX:** 269

Klail City (Hinojosa), **Supp. XIX:** 97, **101–103**

Klail City Death Trip (Hinojosa). *See Ask a Policeman* (Hinojosa); *Becky and Her Friends* (Hinojosa); *Dear Rafe* (Hinojosa); *Fair Gentlemen of Belken County* (Hinojosa); *Klail City* (Hinojosa); *Korean Love Songs from Klail City Death Trip* (Hinojosa); *Partners in Crime: A Rafe Buenrostro Mystery* (Hinojosa); *Rites and Witnesses: A Comedy* (Hinojosa); *Useless Servants, The* (Hinojosa); *Valley, The* (Hinojosa)

Klein, Joe, **Supp. XII:** 67–68

Klein, Marcus, **Supp. I Part 2:** 432; **Supp. XI:** 233

Kleist, Heinrich von, **Supp. IV Part 1:** 224

Kline, Franz, **Supp. XII:** 198; **Supp. XXIII:** 210, 211, 217

Kline, George, **Supp. VIII:** 22, 28

Klinghoffer, David, **Supp. XVI:** 74

Klinkowitz, Jerome, **Supp. IV Part 1:** 40; **Supp. X:** 263; **Supp. XI:** 347; **Supp. XXI:** 233

Klise, James, **Supp. XXII:** 53

Kloefkorn, Bill, **Supp. XIX:** 119

Knapp, Adeline, **Supp. XI:** 200

Knapp, Friedrich, **III:** 100

Knapp, Samuel, **I:** 336

Knapp, Samuel Lorenzo, **Supp. XV:** 246

"Kneeling Down to Look into a Culvert" (R. Bly), **Supp. XXI:** 88

Kneel to the Rising Sun (Caldwell), **I:** 304, 309

"Knees/Dura-Europos" (Goldbarth), **Supp. XII:** 185

"Knife" (Simic), **Supp. VIII:** 275

Knight, Arthur, **Supp. XIV:** 144

Knight, Etheridge, **Supp. XI:** 239; **Supp. XXIII:** 174

Knight, Lania, **Supp. XXIII:** 273, 274, 275, 276, 279, 280

"Knight in Disguise, The" (Lindsay), **Supp. I Part 2:** 390

Knightly Quest, The (T. Williams), **IV:** 383

Knight's Gambit (Faulkner), **II:** 72

Knish, Anne. See Ficke, Arthur Davison

"Knit One, Purl Two" (K. Snodgrass), **Supp. XVI:** 42

"Knock" (Dickey), **Supp. IV Part 1:** 182

Knocked Out Loaded (album, Dylan), **Supp. XVIII:** 28

"Knocking Around" (Ashbery), **Supp. III Part 1:** 22

"Knocking on Heaven's Door" (Lamott), **Supp. XX:** **140–141**

"Knocking on Three, Winston" (Epstein), **Supp. XIV:** 109

Knock on Any Door (film, Ray), **Supp. XVII:** 150

Knock on Any Door (W. Motley), **Supp. XVII:** **150–155,** 159, 160; 158

Knockout Artist, The (Crews), **Supp. XI:** **113–114**

Knoll, Robert E., **Supp. XV:** 118

Knopf, Alfred A., **III:** 99, 105, 106, 107; **Retro. Supp. I:** 13, 19, 317; **Supp. I Part 1:** 324, 325, 327; **Supp. IV Part 1:** 125, 354; **Supp. XIII:** 172

Knopf, Blanche, **Supp. I Part 1:** 324, 325, 327, 328, 332, 341; **Supp. IV Part 1:** 128, 346, 348; **Supp. XIII:** 169

"Knot, The" (Rich), **Supp. I Part 2:** 555

Knotts, Kristina, **Supp. XIII:** 238

"Knowing, The" (Olds), **Supp. X:** 215

"Knowledge Forwards and Backwards" (Stern), **Supp. IX:** 296

"Knowledge of Plates" (Bronk), **Supp. XXI:** 33

Knowles, John, **Supp. IV Part 2:** 679; **Supp. XII:** **235–250; Supp. XX:** 84

Known World, The (E. P. Jones), **Supp. XXII:** 139, 140, 142, **146–150,** 150

Knox, Frank, **Supp. I Part 2:** 488, 489

Knox, Israel, **Supp. X:** 70

Knox, Vicesimus, **II:** 8

Knoxville: Summer of 1915 (Agee), **I:** 42–46

Knudson, R. Rozanne, **Supp. IV Part 2:** 648

Kober, Arthur, **Supp. I Part 1:** 292

Koch, Frederick, **IV:** 453

Koch, John, **Supp. VIII:** 88

Koch, Kenneth, **Supp. XV:** **175–192; Supp. XIX:** 81; **Supp. XXIII:** 124, 207, 209, 210, 211, 215, 217, 220

Koch, Vivienne, **III:** 194; **IV:** 136, 140; **Retro. Supp. I:** 428, 430

"Kochinnenako in Academe: Three Approaches to Interpreting a Keres Indian Tale" (Gunn Allen), **Supp. IV Part 1:** 329

"Kodachromes of the Island" (Hayden), **Supp. II Part 1:** 367, 380

Koestler, Arthur, **I:** 258; **Supp. I Part 2:** 671; **Supp. XXIII:** 1

Kokkinen, Eila, **Supp. XIV:** 146, 148

"Kola Street"(Asch), **Supp. XXIII:** 7

Kolba, Ellen D., **Supp. XVIII:** 257

Kolbenheyer, Dr. Frederick, **Supp. I Part 1:** 207

Kolodny, Annette, **Supp. X:** 97, 103, 229

Komisarjevsky, W. P., **Supp. XXIII:** 5

"Komodo" (C. Frost), **Supp. XV:** 95

Komunyakaa, Yusef, **Supp. XIII:** **111–136; Supp. XXI:** 129, 139; **Supp. XXIII:** 254

Konigsberg, Allan Stewart. See Allen, Woody

Kon-Tiki (Heyerdahl), **II:** 477

Koopman, Harry Lyman, **Retro. Supp. I:** 40

Ko; or, A Season on Earth (Koch), **Supp. XV:** 175, 180, 181, 183, 186

Kooser, Ted, **Supp. XV:** 113, 115; **Supp. XIX:** **115–130; Supp. XXI:** 243

Kootz, Samuel, **Supp. XV:** 144

Kora and Ka (Doolittle), **Supp. I Part 1:** 270

Kora in Hell (W. C. Williams), **Retro. Supp. I:** 416, **417–418,** 419, 430, 431; **Supp. XXI:** 232

Korb, Rena, **Supp. XI:** 2

Korczak, Janosz, **Supp. X:** 70

Korean Love Songs from Klail City Death Trip (Hinojosa), **Supp. XIX:** 98, **103–104**

Kornblatt, Joyce Reiser, **Supp. XV:** 62

Kornfield, Jack, **Supp. XX:** **142; Supp. XXIII:** 138

Korrektur (Bernhard), **Supp. XX:** 91

Kort, Amy, **Supp. XIII:** 148

Korwin, Yala, **Supp. XXI:** 99

Kosinski, Jerzy, **Supp. VII:** **215–228; Supp. XII:** 21

"Kostas Tympakianakis" (Merrill), **Supp. III Part 1:** 326

Koteliansky, S. S., **Supp. VIII:** 251, 265

Kouidis, Virginia M., **Supp. XXII:** 161, 162, 166, 167, 169

Kovic, Ron, **Supp. XIX:** 17; **Supp. XXII:** 104

Kowloon Tong (Theroux), **Supp. VIII:** 325

Kozlenko, William, **IV:** 378, 381

Krabbenhoft, Ken, **Supp. XVII:** 112

Kraft, James, **Supp. XV:** 40, 41, 42, 43, 52

Krakauer, Jon, **Supp. XVII:** 210; **Supp. XVIII:** **105–118**

Kramer, Dale, **Supp. I Part 2:** 669

Kramer, Glenn Philip, **Supp. XXIII:** 125

Kramer, Hilton, **III:** 537; **Supp. I Part 1:** 295, 296; **Supp. VIII:** 239; **Supp. XV:** 113; **Supp. XIX:** 269

Kramer, Lawrence, **Supp. IV Part 1:** 61, 65, 66; **Supp. IX:** 291

Kramer, Peter D., **Supp. XVI:** 229

Kramer, Stanley, **II:** 421, 587

Krapp's Last Tape (Beckett), **I:** 71; **III:** 387; **Retro. Supp. I:** 206

Krassner, Paul, **Supp. IV Part 1:** 385; **Supp. XI:** 293

Kraus, Karl, **Supp. XX:** 84

Krauth, Leland, **Supp. XVIII:** 58

Kreisler, Harry, **Supp. XVI:** 155

Kreitman, Esther, **IV:** 2

"Kremlin of Smoke" (Schnackenberg), **Supp. XV:** 257–258

Kreymborg, Alfred, **II:** 530; **III:** 465; **IV:** 76; **Retro. Supp. I:** 417; **Supp. XV:** 301, 306; **Supp. XXII:** 161–162

Krim, Seymour, **Supp. XV:** 338; **Supp. XVI:** 217; **Supp. XVIII:** 285

Krisak, Len, **Supp. XXI:** 99, 104

Kristeva, Julia, **Supp. XII:** 6

Kristofferson, Kris, **Supp. XIII:** 119

Kristol, Irving, **Supp. VIII:** 93, 244; **Supp. XIII:** 98

Krivak, Andrew, **Supp. XVII:** 242

Kroll, Jack, **Supp. IV Part 2:** 590; **Supp. XXIII:** 103

Kroll, Judith, **Supp. I Part 2:** 541–543, 544, 546

Kroll Ring, Frances. *See* Ring, Frances Kroll

Krondorfer, Björn, **Supp. XVI:** 160

Kronenberger, Louis, **Supp. XXII:** 191, 192

Krook, Dorothea, **Retro. Supp. II:** 243

Kropotkin, Peter, **I:** 493; **Supp. I Part 1:** 5; **Supp. IV Part 2:** 521

Kruif, Paul de, **II:** 446

Krupat, Arnold, **Supp. IV Part 2:** 500

Krupnick, Mark, **Supp. XVI:** 153

Krutch, Joseph Wood, **II:** 459; **III:** 425; **IV:** 70, 175

Krutikov, Mikhail, **Supp. XXIII:** 11

Kublai Khan, **III:** 395

"Kubla Khan" (Coleridge), **Supp. XIII:** 131, 283

Kubrick, Stanley, **Supp. IV Part 1:** 392; **Supp. XI:** 293, **Supp. XI:** 301, 302–303

"Kubuku Rides (This Is It) " (L. Brown), **Supp. XXI:** 39, 42–43

Kuehl, John, **Supp. IV Part 1:** 279, 284, 285, 287

Kuehl, Linda, **Supp. IV Part 1:** 199

"Kugelmass Episode, The" (Allen), **Supp. XV:** 15, 16

Kukachin, Princess, **III:** 395

"Ku Klux" (Hughes), **Retro. Supp. I:** 205

Kulshrestha, Chirantan, **Retro. Supp. II:** 21

Kumin, Maxine, **Supp. IV Part 2: 439–457; Supp. XIII:** 294; **Supp. XVII:** 71, 75–76; **Supp. XX:** 164

Kundera, Milan, **Supp. VIII:** 241

Kunerth, Jeff, **Supp. XXI:** 47

Kunitz, Stanley, **I:** 179, 180, 181, 182, 521; **II:** 545; **Supp. III Part 1:** 257–270; **Supp. V:** 79; **Supp. XI:** 259; **Supp. XIII:** 341

Kuo, Helena, **Supp. X:** 291

Kuropatkin, General Aleksei Nikolaevich, **III:** 247–248

Kurth, Peter, **Supp. XVIII:** 145

Kurzy of the Sea (Barnes), **Supp. III Part 1:** 34

Kushner, Tony, **Supp. IX: 131–149; Supp. XX: 177; Supp. XXI:** 145

Kussy, Bella, **IV:** 468

Kutnik, Jerzy, **Supp. XXII:** 177

Kuttner, Henry, **Supp. IV Part 1:** 102

Kuzma, Greg, **Supp. XV:** 118

L

LaBastille, Anne, **Supp. X: 95–110**

"Labor's Cultural Degradation" (Swados), **Supp. XIX:** 264–265

"Labours of Hercules, The" (Moore), **III:** 201

La Bruyère, Jean de, **I:** 58

La Bufera e Altro (Montale), **Supp. V:** 337

LaBute, Neil, **Supp. XXI:** 147

Labyrinth of Love (Untermeyer), **Supp. XV:** 312

Labyrinth of Solitude, The (Paz), **Supp. XIII:** 223

Lacan, Jacques, **Supp. IV Part 1:** 45; **Supp. VIII:** 5; **Supp. XII:** 98

La Casa en Mango Street (Cisneros), **Supp. VII:** 58–59

Lachaise, Gaston, **I:** 434

"Lackawanna" (Merwin), **Supp. III Part 1:** 350

Lackawanna Elegy (Goll; Kinnell, trans.), **Supp. III Part 1:** 235, 243–244

Laclède, Pierre, **Supp. I Part 1:** 205

"Lacquer Prints" (Lowell), **II:** 524–525

Lacy, Ed, **Supp. XV: 193–210**

Ladder, The (Rasmussen; Nelson, trans.), **Supp. XVIII:** 180–181

Ladder of Years (Tyler), **Supp. IV Part 2:** 657, 671–672

Ladders to Fire (Nin), **Supp. X:** 185

Laddie (Stratton-Porter), **Supp. XX: 211, 213**

"Laddie, the Princess and the Pie" (Stratton-Porter), **Supp. XX: 216**

"Ladies" (Coleman), **Supp. XI:** 93

Ladies Almanack (Barnes), **Supp. III Part 1:** 37–39, 42; **Supp. XXII:** 167

Ladies Auxiliary, The (Mirvis), **Supp. XX: 177, 179–185**

"Ladies in Spring" (Welty), **IV:** 276–277; **Retro. Supp. I:** 353

Lady, The (Richter), **Supp. XVIII: 211–212, 220**

Lady Audley's Secret (Braddon), **Supp. I Part 1:** 35, 36

"Lady Barberina" (James), **Retro. Supp. I:** 227

"Lady Bates" (Jarrell), **II:** 380–381

Lady Chatterley's Lover (Lawrence), **III:** 170; **IV:** 434; **Supp. XVI:** 267

Ladye Annabel (Lippard), **Supp. XXIII:** 178

Lady from Louisiana (film, Vorhaus), **Supp. XVII:** 59

"Lady from Redhorse, A" (Bierce), **I:** 203

Lady in Kicking Horse Reservoir, The (Hugo), **Supp. VI:** 134, **138–139**

Lady in the Lake, The (Chandler), **Supp. IV Part 1:** 127, 129–130

"Lady in the Lake, The" (Chandler), **Supp. IV Part 1:** 129

Lady in the Lake, The (film), **Supp. IV Part 1:** 130

"Lady in the Pink Mustang, The" (Erdrich), **Supp. IV Part 1:** 270

"Lady Is Civilized, The" (Taylor), **Supp. V:** 315

Lady Is Cold, The (White), **Supp. I Part 2:** 653

Lady Killer (Holding), **Supp. XXII:** 126, **127,** 130

"Lady Lazarus" (Plath), **Retro. Supp. II:** 250, 251, 255; **Supp. I Part 2:** 529, 535, 542, 545

Lady of Aroostook, The (Howells), **II:** 280

"Lady of Bayou St. John, A" (Chopin), **Retro. Supp. II:** 58

"Lady of the Lake, The" (Malamud), **Supp. I Part 2:** 437

Lady Oracle (Atwood), **Supp. XIII:** 21, **23–24**

"Lady Poverty" (Notley), **Supp. XXII:** 234–235

Lady Sings the Blues (film), **Supp. I Part 1:** 67

"Lady's Maid's Bell, The" (Wharton), **IV:** 316

"Lady Wentworth" (Longfellow), **II:** 505

"Lady with a Lamp" (Parker), **Supp. IX:** 193

"Lady with the Heron, The" (Merwin), **Supp. III Part 1:** 343

"Lady with the Pet Dog, The" (Chekov), **Supp. XXII:** 60

"Lady with the Pet Tribble, The" (Brockmeier), **Supp. XXII:** 60

La Farge, John, **I:** 1, 2, 20; **II:** 322, 338; **Retro. Supp. I:** 217

La Farge, Oliver, **Supp. IV Part 2:** 503

Lafayette, Marquis de, **I:** 344, 345; **II:** 405–406; **Supp. I Part 2:** 510, 511, 683

"La Figlia che Piange" (Eliot), **Retro. Supp. I:** 63

La Follette, Robert, **I:** 483, 485, 492; **III:** 580

La Fontaine, Jean de, **II:** 154; **III:** 194; **IV:** 80

Laforgue, Jules, **I:** 386, 569, 570, 572–573, 575, 576; **II:** 528; **III:** 8, 11, 466; **IV:** 37, 79, 80, 122; **Retro. Supp. I:** 55, 56; **Supp. XIII:** 332, 335, 346; **Supp. XV:** 165

La Gallienne, Eva, **Supp. VIII:** 251

"Lager Beer" (Dunbar), **Supp. II Part 1:** 193

"La Gringuita: On Losing a Native Language" (Alvarez), **Supp. VII:** 18

Laguna Woman (Silko), **Supp. IV Part 2:** 557, 560–561

Lahiri, Jhumpa, **Supp. XXI: 175–189; Supp. XXIII:** 289

Lahr, John, **Supp. XXI:** 18

Laing, R. D., **Supp. I Part 2:** 527; **Supp. XX:** 94

La kabbale pratique (Ambelain), **Supp. I Part 1:** 273

"Lake, The" (Bradbury), **Supp. IV Part 1:** 101

Lake, The (play), **Supp. IX:** 189

Lakeboat (Mamet), **Supp. XIV:** 240–241

"Lake Chelan" (Stafford), **Supp. XI:** 321

Lake Effect Country (Ammons), **Supp. VII:** 34, 35

"Lake Isle of Innisfree, The" (Yeats), **Retro. Supp. I:** 413; **Supp. XIX:** 92

"Lake Return" (Wright), **Supp. XV:** 345

Lake Wobegon Days (Keillor), **Supp. XVI:** 165, 166, **173–174**

Lake Wobegon Summer 1956 (Keillor), **Supp. XVI:** 178

Lalic, Ivan V., **Supp. VIII:** 272

Lamantia, Philip, **Supp. VIII:** 289

Lamb, Brian, **Supp. XIX:** 156; **Supp. XX:** 101

Lamb, Charles, **III:** 111, 207; **Supp. VIII:** 125

Lamb, Wendy, **Supp. IV Part 2:** 658

Lambardi, Marilyn May, **Retro. Supp. II:** 45–46

Lamb in His Bosom (C. Miller), **Supp. XXII:** 187, **189–191**, 193–194, 195, 197, 198, 199, 200

"Lame Feet of Salvation, The" (W. V. Davis), **Supp. XXI:** 87–88

"Lament" (Wilbur), **Supp. III Part 2:** 550

Lament and Chastisement (O'Hara), **Supp. XXIII:** 209

"Lamentation in Winter"(Schott), **Supp. XXIII:** 243

"Lamentations" (Glück), **Supp. V:** 83, 84

"Lament for Dark Peoples" (Hughes), **Retro. Supp. I:** 199

"Lament for Saul and Jonathan" (Bradstreet), **Supp. I Part 1:** 111

"Lament-Heaven" (Doty), **Supp. XI:** 125

"Lament of a New England Mother, The" (Eberhart), **I:** 539

Laments for the Living (Parker), **Supp. IX:** 192

"Lame Shall Enter First, The" (O'Connor), **III:** 348, 351, 352, 355, 356–357, 358; **Retro. Supp. II:** 237

Lamia (Keats), **II:** 512; **III:** 523

Lamming, George, **Supp. XXI:** 170

Lamott, Anne, **Supp. XX: 131–146**

La Motte-Fouqué, Friedrich Heinrich Karl, **III:** 77, 78

L'Amour, Louis, **Supp. XIII:** 5

Lamp for Nightfall, A (Caldwell), **I:** 297

Lamplit Answer, The (Schnackenberg), **Supp. XV:** 251, 254, **256–260**

"Lana Turner Has Collapsed!"(O'Hara), **Supp. XXIII:** 220

"Lance" (Nabokov), **Retro. Supp. I:** 266

Lancelot (Percy), **Supp. III Part 1:** 384, 395–396

Lancelot (Robinson), **III:** 513, 522

Lanchester, John, **Retro. Supp. I:** 278

"Land" (Emerson), **II:** 6

"Land Aesthetic, The" (Callicott), **Supp. XIV:** 184

Land and Freedom (film, Loach), **Supp. XXIII:** 163

"Land and Language" (J. W. Miller), **Supp. XX: 170**

Landau, Deborah, **Supp. XI:** 122, 123

"Land beyond the Blow, The" (Bierce), **I:** 209

"Land Ethic, The" (Leopold), **Supp. XIV:** 179, 180, 183, 191, 192

Landfall (Wagoner), **Supp. IX:** 330

"Landing in Luck" (Faulkner), **Retro. Supp. I:** 85

"Landing on the Moon" (Swenson), **Supp. IV Part 2:** 643

"Landings" (Hoffman), **Supp. XVIII:** 86

"Landing Under Water, I See Roots" (A. Finch), **Supp. XVII:** 76

"Land"(Kenny), **Supp. XXIII:** 147

Landlord at Lion's Head, The (Howells), **II:** 276, 287–288

Landmarks of Healing: A Study of House Made of Dawn (Scarberry-García), **Supp. IV Part 2:** 486

Land of Little Rain, The (Dillard), **Supp. VI: 27–28**

Land of Look Behind, The (Cliff), **Supp. XXII:** 65–66, 68–69

Land of the Free U.S.A. (MacLeish), **I:** 293; **III:** 16–17

Land of Unlikeness (Lowell), **II:** 537–538, 539, 547; **Retro. Supp. II:** 177, 178, **184–185**

Landor, Walter Savage, **III:** 15, 469; **Supp. I Part 2:** 422

"Landscape" (Sarton), **Supp. VIII:** 259

"Landscape #11" (Halliday), **Supp. XIX:** 93

Landscape and Journey (W. V. Davis), **Supp. XXI:** 83, 88, 90, **92–93**, 95

"Landscape as a Nude" (MacLeish), **III:** 14

Landscape at the End of the Century (Dunn), **Supp. XI:** 139, 143, **150–151**

"Landscape Chamber, The" (Jewett), **II:** 408–409

"Landscape for the Disappeared" (Komunyakaa), **Supp. XIII:** 120, 126

Landscape in American Poetry (Larcom), **Supp. XIII:** 142

"Landscape Painter, A" (James), **II:** 322; **Retro. Supp. I:** 219

"Landscape Symbolism in Kate Chopin's *At Fault*" (Arner), **Retro. Supp. II:** 62

"Landscape: The Eastern Shore" (Barth), **I:** 122

"Landscape with Boat" (Stevens), **Retro. Supp. I:** 306

"Landscape with Bottles"(Schott), **Supp. XXIII:** 242

"Landscape with the Fall of Icarus" (Brueghel), **Retro. Supp. I:** 430

Land's End: A Walk through Provincetown (Cunningham), **Supp. XV:** 69

Land That Drank the Rain, The (Hoffman), **Supp. XVIII:** 76, 80, 81, 82

"Land Where There Is No Death, The" (Benét), **Supp. XI:** 56

Lane, Ann, **Supp. XI:** 195, 208

Lane, Cornelia. *See* Anderson, Mrs. Sherwood

Lane, Homer, **Supp. II Part 1:** 6; **Supp. XIV:** 160

Lane, Nathan, **Supp. XIII:** 207

Lane, Rose Wilder, **Supp. IV Part 2:** 524; **Supp. XXII:** 293–294, 295, 296, 297, 301

Lanes, Selma G., **Supp. XVI:** 104, 107

Lang, Andrew, **Retro. Supp. I:** 127

Lang, Violet, **Supp. XII:** 119

Lang, V. R. "Bunny," **Supp. XXIII:** 209

Langdon, Olivia. *See* Clemens, Mrs. Samuel Langhorne (Olivia Langdon)

Lange, Carl Georg, **II:** 350

Lange, Dorothea, **I:** 293; **Supp. XIV:** 181

Langland, Joseph, **III:** 542

Langston Hughes, American Poet (Walker), **Supp. III Part 2:** 530–531

Langston Hughes and the "Chicago Defender": Essays on Race, Politics, and Culture (De Santis, ed.), **Retro. Supp. I:** 194

Langston Hughes: Modern Critical Views (Bloom, ed.), **Retro. Supp. I:** 193

Langston Hughes Reader, The (Hughes), **Retro. Supp. I:** 202; **Supp. I Part 1:** 345

Langston Hughes: The Poet and His Critics (Barksdale), **Retro. Supp. I:** 202

"Language, Visualization and the Inner Library" (Shepard), **Supp. III Part 2:** 436, 438, 449

Language and Imagery of the Bible, The (Caird), **Supp. XXI:** 91–92

"Language and the Writer" (Bambara), **Supp. XI:** 18

Language As Gesture (Blackmur), **Supp. II Part 1:** 108

Language as Symbolic Action (Burke), **I:** 275, 282, 285

Language Book, The (Andrews and Bernstein), **Supp. IV Part 2:** 426

"Language Divine!"(J. Schoolcraft), **Supp. XXIII:** 225

Language in Thought and Action (Hayakawa), **I:** 448

"Language of Being and Dying, The" (Gass), **Supp. VI:** 91

"Language of Home, The" (Wideman), **Supp. X:** 320, 323–324

Language of Life, The (Moyers, television series), **Supp. XIII:** 274, 276

Language of the American South, The (Brooks), **Supp. XIV:** 14

"Language of the Brag, The" (Olds), **Supp. X:** 204

"Language We Know, The" (Ortiz), **Supp. IV Part 2:** 500

Lanier, Clifford, **Supp. I Part 1:** 349, 350, 353, 355, 356, 371

Lanier, James F. D., **Supp. I Part 1:** 350

Lanier, Lyle H., **Supp. X:** 25

Lanier, Robert Sampson, **Supp. I Part 1:** 349, 351, 355, 356, 361

Lanier, Mrs. Robert Sampson (Mary Jane Anderson), **Supp. I Part 1:** 349

Lanier, Sidney, **IV:** 444; **Supp. I Part 1: 349 373; Supp. I Part 2:** 416; **Supp. IV Part 1:** 165

Lanier, Mrs. Sidney (Mary Day), **Supp. I Part 1:** 351, 355, 357, 361, 362, 364, 370, 371

"Lanier as Poet" (Parks), **Supp. I Part 1:** 373

"Lanier's Reading" (P. Graham), **Supp. I Part 1:** 373

"Lanier's Use of Science for Poetic Imagery" (Beaver), **Supp. I Part 1:** 373

Lankes, J. J., **Supp. XXII:** 275

Lannegan, Helen. *See* Caldwell, Mrs. Erskine

Lannin, Paul, **II:** 427

Lanny Budd novels (Sinclair), **Supp. V:** 290

Lant, Kathleen Margaret, **Supp. V:** 141

Lanterns on the Levee (Percy), **Supp. XXII:** 193

Lanthenas, François, **Supp. I Part 2:** 515

"Lanyard, The" (Collins), **Supp. XXI:** 56, **62–64**

Laotzu, **III:** 173, 189, 567; **Supp. XV:** 39, 46, 48

Lapine, James, **Supp. XXI:** 147–148

"Lapis Lazuli" (Yeats), **I:** 532; **III:** 40

Laplace, Pierre Simon de, **III:** 428

Lapouge, M. G., **Supp. I Part 2:** 633

Lappa, Katherine, **Supp. XV:** 176

Lapsing to Grace (Espaillat), **Supp. XXI:** 99, 100

Lapsley, Gaillard, **Supp. XX:** 231

Laqueur, Thomas, **Supp. XVI:** 154

Larbaud, Valery, **IV:** 404; **Supp. XIII:** 332; **Supp. XIV:** 338

Larcom, Lucy, **Retro. Supp. II:** 145; **Supp. XIII: 137–157**

Larcom's Poetical Works (Larcom), **Supp. XIII:** 142

Lardner, John, **II:** 437

Lardner, Ring, **I:** 487; **II:** 44, 91, 259, 263, **415–438**; **III:** 566, 572; **IV:** 433; **Retro. Supp. I:** 105; **Retro. Supp. II:** 222; **Supp. I Part 2:** 609; **Supp. IX:** 200; **Supp. XVI:** 189

Lardner, Ring, Jr., **Supp. XI:** 306

"Lardner, Shakespeare and Chekhov" (Matthews), **II:** 430

"Large Bad Picture" (Bishop), **Retro. Supp. II:** 43; **Supp. I Part 1:** 73, 80–82, 85, 86, 89, 90

"Large Coffee" (Lardner), **II:** 437

Large Glass, or The Bride Stripped Bare by Her Bachelors, Even (Duchamp), **Supp. IV Part 2:** 423, 424

Largo (Handel), **IV:** 369

"Lark" (Taggard), **Supp. XXII:** 280

Lark, The (Hellman), **Supp. I Part 1:** 286–288, 297

Lark: Four-Part Chorus for Mixed Voices (A Capella) with Baritone Solo (Taggard and Copland), **Supp. XXII:** 283

Larkin, Philip, **Supp. I Part 2:** 536; **Supp. XI:** 243, 249; **Supp. XIII:** 76, 85; **Supp. XV:** 117, 251; **Supp. XVII:** 110; **Supp. XVIII:** 173; **Supp. XX:** 199; **Supp. XXI:** 84, 93

Larkin, Sharon Alile, **Supp. XI:** 20

Larmore, Phoebe, **Supp. X:** 266

Larner, Jeremy, **Supp. XVI:** 220

La Rochefoucauld, François de, **I:** 279; **II:** 111; **Supp. XIV:** 130

"La Rose des Vents" (Wilbur), **Supp. III Part 2:** 550

"Larry Brown's *Dirty Work:* A Study of Man's Responsibility for Suffering" (Prevost), **Supp. XXI:** 45

"Larry"(O'Hara), **Supp. XXIII:** 212

Larry's Party (Shields), **Supp. VII:** 324, 326–327

Larsen, Nella, **Supp. I Part 1:** 325, 326; **Supp. IV Part 1:** 164; **Supp. XVIII: 119–134**

Larson, Charles, **Supp. IV Part 1:** 331

Larson, Clinton, **Supp. XI:** 328

Larson, Kelli, **Supp. XVIII:** 131

LaRue, Dorie, **Supp. XXI:** 43

"Larval Stage of a Bookworm" (Mencken), **III:** 101

La Salle and the Discovery of the Great West (Parkman), **Supp. II Part 2:** 595, 598, 605–607; **Supp. XVIII:** 114

Lasch, Christopher, **I:** 259

Lasher (Rice), **Supp. VII:** 299–300

Lask, Thomas, **III:** 576; **Supp. XVI:** 250

Laski, Harold, **Supp. I Part 2:** 632, 643

Lassalle, Ferdinand, **IV:** 429

Lasser, Louise, **Supp. XV:** 4

"Last Acts" (Olds), **Supp. X:** 210

Last Adam, The (Cozzens), **I:** 362–363, 364, 368, 375, 377, 378, 379

Last Analysis, The (Bellow), **I:** 152, 160, 161; **Retro. Supp. II:** 26

Last and Lost Poems of Delmore Schwartz (Phillips, ed.), **Supp. II Part 2:** 661, 665

Last Avant-Garde, The: The Making of the New York School of Poets (Lehman), **Supp. XV:** 178–179, 187

Last Beautiful Days of Autumn, The (Nichols), **Supp. XIII:** 254, 255, 267, 269

Last Blue (Stern), **Supp. IX: 299–300**

Last Book, The (Pickering), **Supp. XXI:** 203–204

Last Carousel, The (Algren), **Supp. IX:** 16

Last Centennial, The (P. N. Warren as Kilina), **Supp. XX: 261–262**

"Last Child" (X. J. Kennedy), **Supp. XV:** 162, 165

Last Clean Shirt, The (film, Leslie and O'Hara), **Supp. XXIII:** 217

Last Coyote, The (Connelly), **Supp. XXI:** 71

"Last Day in the Field, The" (Gordon), **II:** 200

"Last Day of the Last Furlough" (Salinger), **III:** 552–553

"Last Days of Alice" (Tate), **IV:** 129

"Last Days of August, The" (Nye), **Supp. XIII:** 284

"Last Days of John Brown, The" (Thoreau), **IV:** 185

Last Days of Louisiana Red, The (Reed), **Supp. X:** 240, **248–249**

Last Decade, The (Trilling), **Supp. III Part 2:** 493, 499

"Last Demon, The" (Singer), **IV:** 15, 21

Last Detective, The (Crais), **Supp. XXI:** 70

Last Exit to Brooklyn (Selby), **Supp. III Part 1:** 125; **Supp. XXI:** 227, 231

Last Flower, The (Thurber), **Supp. I Part 2:** 610

"Last Frontier" (McCarriston), **Supp. XIV:** 272

Last Generation, The (Moraga), **Supp. XXIII:** 201

Last Gentleman, The (Percy), **Supp. III Part 1:** 383–388, 392–393

"Last Good Country, The" (Hemingway), **II:** 258–259

Last Good Time, The (Bausch), **Supp. VII:** 45–46

"Last Great Saloon, The"(Exley), **Supp. XXIII:** 103

"Last Hiding Places of Snow, The" (Kinnell), **Supp. III Part 1:** 252

"Last Hours, The" (Dunn), **Supp. XI:** 141

Last House: Reflections, Dreams, and Observations, 1943–1991 (M. F. K. Fisher), **Supp. XVII:** 92

Last Husband and Other Stories, The (Humphrey), **Supp. IX:** 94

Last Jew in America, The (Fiedler), **Supp. XIII:** 103

"Last Jew in America, The" (Fiedler), **Supp. XIII:** 103

Last Laugh, Mr. Moto (Marquand), **III:** 57

"Last Leaf, The" (Holmes), **Supp. I Part 1:** 302, 309

"Last Leaf, The" (Porter), **III:** 444

"Last Lie, The" (Weigl), **Supp. XIX:** 279

"Last Light" (Major), **Supp. XXII:** 185

"Last Look at the Lilacs" (Stevens), **IV:** 74

Last Man, The (Kees), **Supp. XV:** 142, 143, 145

"Last May" (Dixon), **Supp. XII: 143**

"Last Mermother, The" (A. Finch), **Supp. XVII:** 72

"Last Mohican, The" (Malamud), **Supp. I Part 2:** 437–438, 450, 451

"Lastness" (Kinnell), **Supp. III Part 1:** 248–249

"Last Night" (Olds), **Supp. X:** 212

"Last Night at Tía's" (Alvarez), **Supp. VII:** 5

Last Night of Summer, The (Caldwell), **I:** 292–293

Last Notes from Home (Exley), **Supp. XXIII:** 97, 98, **106–108**

Last of Mr. Norris, The (Isherwood), **Supp. XIV:** 161

"Last of the Brooding Miserables, The" (Karr), **Supp. XI:** 250

"Last of the Caddoes, The" (Humphrey), **Supp. IX:** 101

Last of the Crazy People, The (Findley), **Supp. XX: 51–52**

"Last of the Gold Star Mothers, The" (C. Bly), **Supp. XVI:** 34, 35, 36

"Last of the Legions, The" (Benét), **Supp. XI:** 56, 57

Last of the Mohicans, The (Cooper), **I:** 341, 342, 349

Last of the Red Hot Lovers (Simon), **Supp. IV Part 2:** 575, 583, 589

"Last of the Valerii, The" (James), **II:** 327; **Retro. Supp. I:** 218

"Last One, The" (Merwin), **Supp. III Part 1:** 355

Last Picture Show, The (film), **Supp. V:** 223, 226

Last Picture Show, The (McMurtry), **Supp. V:** 220, 222–223, 233

Last Place on Earth, The: Scott and Amundsen's Race to the South Pole (Huntford), **Supp. XVIII:** 114

Last Puritan, The (Santayana), **III:** 64, 600, 604, 607, 612, 615–617

"Last Ride Together, The" (Browning), **I:** 468

"Last River, The" (Kinnell), **Supp. III Part 1:** 236

Last Song, The (Harjo), **Supp. XII:** 218

"Last Song for the Mend-It Shop" (Nye), **Supp. XIII:** 283

"Last Tango in Fresno" (Salinas), **Supp. XIII:** 318

"Last Trip to Greece"(Hadas), **Supp. XXIII:** 118–119

Last Tycoon, The: An Unfinished Novel (Fitzgerald), **II:** 84, 98; **Retro. Supp. I:** 109, 114, **114–115; Retro. Supp. II:** 337; **Supp. IV Part 1:** 203; **Supp. IX:** 63; **Supp. XII:** 173; **Supp. XIII:** 170; **Supp. XVIII:** 248, 250

"Last WASP in the World, The" (Fiedler), **Supp. XIII:** 103

"Last Watch, The" (Gibran), **Supp. XX:** 119

Last Watch of the Night: Essays Too Personal and Otherwise (Monette), **Supp. X:** 147, 148, 153, **157–159**

"Last Word, The" (column, Quindlen), **Supp. XVII:** 165, 167, 170

Last Word, The: Letters between Marcia Nardi and William Carlos Williams (O'Neil, ed.), **Retro. Supp. I:** 427

"Last Words" (Levine), **Supp. V:** 190

"Last Words" (Olds), **Supp. X:** 210

Last Worthless Evening, The (Dubus), **Supp. VII:** 87–88

"Las Vegas (What?) Las Vegas (Can't Hear You! Too Noisy) Las Vegas! ! ! !" (Wolfe), **Supp. III Part 2:** 572

"Late" (Bogan), **Supp. III Part 1:** 53

"Late Air" (Bishop), **Supp. I Part 1:** 89

"Late Autumn" (Sarton), **Supp. VIII:** 261

"Late Bronze, Early Iron: A Journey Book" (Sobin), **Supp. XVI:** 290

Late Child, The (McMurtry), **Supp. V:** 231

"Late Conversation" (Doty), **Supp. XI:** 122

"Late Elegy for John Berryman, A" (W. V. Davis), **Supp. XXI:** 91

"Late Encounter with the Enemy, A" (O'Connor), **III:** 345; **Retro. Supp. II:** 232

Late Fire, Late Snow (Francis), **Supp. IX: 89–90**

Late George Apley, The (Marquand), **II:** 482–483; **III:** 50, 51, 52, 56–57, 58, 62–64, 65, 66

Late George Apley, The (Marquand and Kaufman), **III:** 62

"Late Hour" (Everwine), **Supp. XV:** 85

Late Hour, The (Strand), **Supp. IV Part 2:** 620, 629–630

"Lately, at Night" (Kumin), **Supp. IV Part 2:** 442

"Late Moon" (Levine), **Supp. V:** 186

"Late Night Ode" (McClatchy), **Supp. XII:** 262–263

Later (Creeley), **Supp. IV Part 1:** 153, 156, 157

Later Life (Gurney), **Supp. V:** 103, 105

La Terre (Zola), **III:** 316, 322

Later the Same Day (Paley), **Supp. VI:** 218

"Late September in Nebraska" (Kooser), **Supp. XIX:** 120

Late Settings (Merrill), **Supp. III Part 1:** 336

"Late Sidney Lanier, The" (Stedman), **Supp. I Part 1:** 373

"Late Snow & Lumber Strike of the Summer of Fifty-Four, The" (Snyder), **Supp. VIII:** 294

"Late Start, A" (L. Brown), **Supp. XXI:** 40–41

"Latest Freed Man, The" (Stevens), **Retro. Supp. I:** 306

"Latest Injury, The" (Olds), **Supp. X:** 209

Latest Literary Essays and Addresses (Lowell), **Supp. I Part 2:** 407

"Late Subterfuge" (Warren), **IV:** 257

"Late Summer Lilies" (Weigl), **Supp. XIX:** 288

"Late Supper, A" (Jewett), **Retro. Supp. II:** 137

"Late Victorians" (Rodriguez), **Supp. XIV:** 303–304

"Late Walk, A" (Frost), **II:** 153; **Retro. Supp. I:** 127

Latham, Edyth, **I:** 289

Lathrop, George Parsons, **Supp. I Part 1:** 365

Lathrop, H. B., **Supp. III Part 2:** 612

Lathrop, Julia, **Supp. I Part 1:** 5

Latière de Trianon, La (Wekerlin), **II:** 515

"La Tigresse" (Van Vechten), **Supp. II Part 2:** 735, 738

Latimer, Hugh, **II:** 15

Latimer, Margery, **Supp. IX:** 320

La Traviata (Verdi), **III:** 139

"Latter-Day Warnings" (Holmes), **Supp. I Part 1:** 307

La Turista (Shepard), **Supp. III Part 2:** 440

Lauber, John, **Supp. XIII:** 21

Laud, Archbishop, **II:** 158

"Lauds" (Auden), **Supp. II Part 1:** 23

"Laughing Man, The" (Salinger), **III:** 559

Laughing Matters (Siegel), **Supp. XXII:** 260

Laughing to Keep From Crying (Hughes), **Supp. I Part 1:** 329–330

"Laughing with One Eye" (Schnackenberg), **Supp. XV:** 253

Laughlin, James, **III:** 171; **Retro. Supp. I:** 423, 424, 428, 430, 431; **Supp. VIII:** 195; **Supp. XV:** 140; **Supp. XVI:** 284; **Supp. XXI:** 29

Laughlin, Jay, **Supp. II Part 1:** 94

Laughlin, J. Laurence, **Supp. I Part 2:** 641

Laughter in the Dark (Nabokov), **III:** 255–258; **Retro. Supp. I:** 270

Laughter on the 23rd Floor (Simon), **Supp. IV Part 2:** 575, 576, 588, 591–592

"Launcelot" (Lewis), **II:** 439–440

"Laura Dailey's Story" (Bogan), **Supp. III Part 1:** 52

Laurel, Stan, **Supp. I Part 2:** 607; **Supp. IV Part 2:** 574

Laurel and Hardy Go to Heaven (Auster), **Supp. XII:** 21

Laurence, Alexander, **Supp. XVIII:** 138

Laurence, Dan H., **II:** 338–339

Laurens, John, **Supp. I Part 2:** 509

Lauter, Paul, **Supp. XV:** 313

Lautréamont, Comte de, **III:** 174

Lavender Locker Room, The (P. N. Warren), **Supp. XX: 261, 273–274**

Law, John, **Supp. XI:** 307

Law and Order (television), **Supp. XVII:** 153

Law and the Testimony, The (S. and A. Warner), **Supp. XVIII:** 264

Lawd Today (Wright), **IV:** 478, 492

Law for the Lion, A (Auchincloss), **Supp. IV Part 1:** 25

"Law Lane" (Jewett), **II:** 407

"Lawns of June, The" (Peacock), **Supp. XIX:** 196

"Law of Nature and the Dream of Man, The: Ruminations of the Art of Fiction" (Stegner), **Supp. IV Part 2:** 604

Lawrence, D. H., **I:** 291, 336, 377, 522, 523; **II:** 78, 84, 98, 102, 264, 517, 523, 532, 594, 595; **III:** 27, 33, 40, 44, 46, 172, 173, 174, 178, 184, 229, 261, 423, 429, 458, 546–547; **IV:** 138, 339, 342, 351, 380; **Retro. Supp. I:** 7, 18, 203, 204, 421; **Retro. Supp. II:** 68; **Supp. I Part 1:** 227, 230, 243, 255, 257, 258, 263, 329; **Supp. I Part 2:** 546, 613, 728; **Supp. II Part 1:** 1, 9, 20, 89; **Supp. IV Part 1:** 81; **Supp. VIII:** 237; **Supp. X:** 137, 193, 194; **Supp. XII:** 172; **Supp. XIV:** 310; **Supp. XV:** 45, 46, 158, 254; **Supp. XVI:** 267; **Supp. XX: 69; Supp. XXII:** 198; **Supp. XXIII:** 166, 275

Lawrence, Elizabeth, **Supp. XXIII:** 259, 264

Lawrence, Frieda, **Supp. XV:** 46

Lawrence, Rhoda, **Supp. I Part 1:** 45

Lawrence, Seymour, **Supp. IX:** 107; **Supp. XI:** 335, 346, 348

Lawrence, T. E., **Supp. XIV:** 159

Lawrence of Arabia (Aldington), **Supp. I Part 1:** 259

Lawrence of Arabia (film), **Supp. I Part 1:** 67

Laws (Hadas), **Supp. XXIII: 119–120,** 124

Laws (Plato), **Supp. IV Part 1:** 391

Laws of Ice, The (Price), **Supp. VI:** 264

Laws of Our Fathers, The (Turow), **Supp. XVII: 218–219**

Lawson, John Howard, **I:** 479, 482

Lawton Girl, The (Frederic), **II:** 132–133, 144

Layachi, Larbi (Driss ben Hamed Charhadi), **Supp. IV Part 1:** 92, 93

Layard, John, **Supp. XIV:** 160

Lay Down My Sword and Shield (Burke), **Supp. XIV:** 22, 25, 34

"Layers, The" (Kunitz), **Supp. III Part 1:** 260, 266–267

"Layers, The: Some Notes on 'The Abduction' " (Kunitz), **Supp. III Part 1:** 266

"Lay-mans Lamentation, The" (Taylor), **IV:** 162–163

Lay of the Land, The: Metaphor as Experience and History in American Life and Letters (Kolodny), **Supp. X:** 97

"Layover" (Hass), **Supp. VI:** 109

"Lay Preacher" (Dennie), **Supp. I Part 1:** 125

Layton, Irving, **Supp. XII:** 121

Lazar, Irving "Swifty", **Supp. XIX:** 250

Lazarillo de Tormes (Mendoza), **III:** 182

Lazar Malkin Enters Heaven (S. Stern), **Supp. XVII:** 42; **Supp. XX: 178**

Lazarus Laughed (O'Neill), **III:** 391, 395–396

Lazer, Hank, **Supp. IX:** 265

Lea, Luke, **IV:** 248

Leachman, Cloris, **Supp. XXI:** 146

Leacock, Stephen, **Supp. IV Part 2:** 464

"LEADBELLY GIVES AN AUTO-GRAPH" (Baraka), **Supp. II Part 1:** 49

Leaflets: Poems, 1965–1968 (Rich), **Supp. I Part 2:** 551, 556–557

"League of American Writers, The: Communist Organizational Activity among American Writers 1929–1942" (Wolfe), **Supp. II Part 2:** 568

League of Brightened Philistines and Other Papers, The (Farrell), **II:** 49

Leahy, Anna, **Supp. XXI:** 246

"Leakage" (Skloot), **Supp. XX: 202**

Leal, Luis, **Supp. XIX:** 98, 112

"Leaning" (Webb), **Supp. XX: 56**

Leaning Forward (Paley), **Supp. VI:** 221

"Leaning Tower, The" (Porter), **III:** 442, 443, 446–447

Leaning Tower and Other Stories, The (Porter), **III:** 433, 442, 443–447

"Leap, The" (Dickey), **Supp. IV Part 1:** 182

"Leaping Up into Political Poetry" (R. Bly), **Supp. IV Part 1:** 61, 63

Leap Year (Cameron), **Supp. XII:** 79–80, 81, **85–86,** 88

Lear, Edward, **III:** 428, 536; **Supp. XVI:** 103

Lear, Linda, **Supp. IX:** 19, 22, 25, 26

Learned Ladies, The (Molière; Wilbur, trans.), **Supp. III Part 2:** 560

"Learning a Dead Language" (Merwin), **Supp. III Part 1:** 345

Learning a Trade: A Craftsman's Notebooks, 1955–1997 (Price), **Supp. VI:** 254, 255, 267

"Learning Bones" (Espaillat), **Supp. XXI:** 107

Learning to Live in This World (Schott), **Supp. XXIII:** 248

Learning to Love: Exploring Solitude and Freedom (Merton), **Supp. VIII:** 200

"Learning to Read" (Harper), **Supp. II Part 1:** 201–202

"Learning to Speak" (Everwine), **Supp. XV:** 79

"Learning to Work Together" (L. I. Wilder), **Supp. XXII:** 290

Learning Tree, The (Park), **Supp. XIX:** 154

Leary, Lewis, **III:** 478

Leary, Paris, **Supp. IV Part 1:** 176

Leary, Timothy, **Supp. X:** 265; **Supp. XIV:** 150

Lease, Joseph, **Supp. XXI:** 246

Least Heat Moon, William, **Supp. V:** 169

Leather-Stocking Tales, The (Cooper), **I:** 335

Leatherwood God, The (Howells), **II:** 276, 277, 288

Leave It to Beaver (television show), **Supp. XX: 103**

"Leave Me Alone a Little" (Taggard), **Supp. XXII:** 274

"Leaves" (Updike), **Retro. Supp. I:** 323, 329, 335

Leaves and Ashes (Haines), **Supp. XII:** 206

Leaves from the Notebook of a Tamed Cynic (Niebuhr), **III:** 293

Leaves of Grass (1856) (Whitman), **Retro. Supp. I:** 399–402

Leaves of Grass (1860) (Whitman), **Retro. Supp. I:** 402–405

Leaves of Grass (Whitman), **II:** 8; **IV:** 331, 332, 333, 334, 335, 336, 340, 341–342, 348, 350, 405, 464; **Retro. Supp. I:** 387, 388, 389, 390, **392–395,** 406, 407, 408; **Retro. Supp. II:** 93; **Supp. I Part 1:** 365; **Supp. I Part 2:** 416, 579; **Supp. III Part 1:** 156; **Supp. V:** 170; **Supp. VIII:** 275; **Supp. IX:** 265; **Supp. X:** 120; **Supp. XIV:** 334; **Supp. XV:** 218; **Supp. XVIII:** 4; **Supp. XIX:** 276; **Supp. XXI:** 205; **Supp. XXII:** 92; **Supp. XXIII:** 165

"Leaves of Grass" (Whitman), **IV:** 463

Leaves of the Tree, The (Masters), **Supp. I Part 2:** 460

"Leaving" (Hogan), **Supp. IV Part 1:** 400

"Leaving" (Wilbur), **Supp. III Part 2:** 563

"Leaving, The" (B. Kelly), **Supp. XVII:** 127, 132

Leaving a Doll's House: A Memoir (C. Bloom), **Retro. Supp. II:** 281

Leaving Another Kingdom: Selected Poems (Stern), **Supp. IX:** 296

"Leaving Bartram's Garden in Southwest Philadelphia" (Di Piero), **Supp. XIX:** 46

"Leaving Brooklyn" (Neugeboren), **Supp. XVI:** 226

Leaving Cheyenne (McMurtry), **Supp. V:** 220, 221–222, 224, 229

Leaving Home (Keillor), **Supp. XVI:** 175

"Leaving One, The" (Offutt), **Supp. XIX:** 165–166

"Leaving the Island" (Olds), **Supp. X:** 214

"Leaving the Yellow House" (Bellow), **Retro. Supp. II:** 27, 32

"Leaving Town" (Kenyon), **Supp. VII:** 163

Leavis, F. R., **I:** 522; **III:** 462–463, 475, 478; **Retro. Supp. I:** 67; **Retro. Supp. II:** 243; **Supp. I Part 2:** 536; **Supp. VIII:** 234, 236, 245

Leavis, Queenie, **Supp. XX: 232**

"Leavis-Snow Controversy, The" (Trilling), **Supp. III Part 2:** 512

Leavitt, Caroline, **Supp. XX: 186**

Leavitt, David, **Supp. VIII:** 88

Lebanon (C. Miller), **Supp. XXII:** 198–199

Le Braz, Anatole, **Supp. XIII:** 253

Le Carre, John, **Supp. XX: 195**

Lecker, Robert, **Supp. XIII:** 21

LeClair, Thomas (Tom), **Supp. IV Part 1:** 286; **Supp. V:** 53; **Supp. XII:** 152; **Supp. XX: 93; Supp. XXII:** 206, 210, 261, 264

Le Conte, Joseph, **II:** 479; **III:** 227–228

"Lecture, The" (Singer), **IV:** 21

"LECTURE PAST DEAD CATS" (Baraka), **Supp. II Part 1:** 52

Lectures in America (Stein), **IV:** 27, 32, 33, 35, 36, 41, 42

"Lectures on Poetry" (Bryant), **Supp. I Part 1:** 159, 161

Lectures on Rhetoric (Blair), **II:** 8

"Leda and the Swan" (Yeats), **III:** 347; **Supp. IX:** 52

Ledger (Fitzgerald), **Retro. Supp. I:** 109, 110

Lee (Masters), **Supp. I Part 2:** 471

Lee, Baayork, **Supp. XXI:** 148

Lee, C. Y., **Supp. XXI:** 148

Lee, Don, **Supp. XII:** 295; **Supp. XVII:** 13, 14, 15, 16

Lee, Don L. *See* Madhubuti, Haki R.

Lee, Gypsy Rose, **II:** 586; **III:** 161; **Supp. IV Part 1:** 84

Lee, Harper, **Supp. VIII: 113–131**

Lee, Harriett, **Supp. XV:** 230

Lee, James Kyun-Jin, **Supp. XV:** 213

Lee, James W., **Supp. IX:** 94, 97, 109

Lee, James Ward, **Supp. VIII:** 57

Lee, Li Lin, **Supp. XV:** 211, 212

Lee, Li-Young, **Supp. XV: 211–228; Supp. XVII:** 241

Lee, Richard E., **Supp. XIX:** 226, 227

Lee, Robert E., **II:** 150, 206; **IV:** 126; **Supp. I Part 2:** 471, 486

Lee, Samuel, **IV:** 158

Lee, Spike, **Retro. Supp. II:** 12; **Supp. XI:** 19; **Supp. XIII:** 179, 186; **Supp. XVI:** 144; **Supp. XX:** 110

Lee, Virginia Chin-lan, **Supp. X:** 291

Leeds, Barry, **Retro. Supp. II:** 204

Leeds, Daniel, **II:** 110

Leeds, Titan, **II:** 110, 111

Leeming, David, **Retro. Supp. II:** 4, 10

"Lees of Happiness, The" (Fitzgerald), **II:** 88

"Le Filme" (Weigl), **Supp. XIX:** 288

Left Out in the Rain: New Poems 1947– 1985 (Snyder), **Supp. VIII:** 305

"Legacy" (Dunn), **Supp. XI:** 148

"Legacy" (Komunyakaa), **Supp. XIII:** 132

"Legacy" (W. V. Davis), **Supp. XXI:** 93–94

"Legacy of Aldo Leopold, The" (Stegner), **Supp. XIV:** 193

Legacy of Fear, A (Farrell), **II:** 39

"Legacy of the Ancestral Arts, The" (Locke), **Supp. XIV:** 201

Legacy of the Civil War, The: Meditations on the Centennial (Warren), **IV:** 236

"Legal Alien" (Mora), **Supp. XIII:** 215

"Legal Tender Act, The" (Adams), **I:** 5

Légende de la mort, La (Le Braz), **Supp. XIII:** 253

"Legend of Duluoz, The" (Kerouac), **Supp. III Part 1:** 218, 226, 227, 229

"Legend of Lillian Hellman, The" (Kazin), **Supp. I Part 1:** 297

"Legend of Monte del Diablo, The" (Harte), **Supp. II Part 1:** 339

"Legend of Paper Plates, The" (Haines), **Supp. XII:** 204

"Legend of Sammtstadt, A" (Harte), **Supp. II Part 1:** 355

"Legend of Sleepy Hollow, The" (Irving), **II:** 306–308

Legends (Lowell), **II:** 525–526

Legends and Dreams (P. N. Warren), **Supp. XX: 261**

Legends of Mexico (Lippard), **Supp. XXIII:** 178, 186

Legends of New England (Whittier), **Supp. I Part 2:** 684, 692

Legends of the Fall (Harrison), **Supp. VIII:** 38, 39, **45–46,** 48

"Legends of the Revolution" (series, Lippard), **Supp. XXIII:** 178

Legends of the West (Hall), **II:** 313

Léger, Fernand, **Retro. Supp. I:** 292

Legge, James, **III:** 472

Leggett, William, **Supp. I Part 1:** 157

"Legion, The" (Karr), **Supp. XI:** 243

"Legs" (Halliday), **Supp. XIX:** 90

Legs (W. Kennedy), **Supp. VII:** 133, 134, 138–142, 143, 151

Le Guin, Ursula K., **Supp. IV Part 1:** 333; **Supp. XXII:** 49

Lehan, Richard, **Retro. Supp. II:** 104

Lehman, David, **Supp. IX:** 161; **Supp. XIII:** 130; **Supp. XV:** 178–179, 180, 187, 190; **Supp. XXI:** 246

Lehmann, John, **Retro. Supp. II:** 243; **Supp. XIV:** 158, 159

Lehmann, Paul, **III:** 311

Lehmann-Haupt, Christopher, **Retro. Supp. II:** 291; **Supp. IV Part 1:** 205, 209, 306; **Supp. IX:** 95, 103; **Supp. XVI:** 73, 210, 294, 295; **Supp. XXII:** 205, 213; **Supp. XXIII:** 103

Lehrer, Jim, **Supp. XVIII:** 39

Leiber, Fritz, **Supp. XVI:** 123

Leibling, A. J., **Supp. XIV:** 112

Leibniz, Gottfried Wilhelm von, **II:** 103; **III:** 428

Leibowitz, Herbert A., **I:** 386; **Supp. XV:** 78

Leich, Roland, **Supp. XIV:** 123

Leichum, Laura, **Supp. XIX:** 197

Leighton, Betty, **Supp. XXI:** 42

Leimbach, Laura, **Supp. XXIII:** 54

Leithauser, Brad, **Retro. Supp. I:** 133; **Supp. XV:** 250; **Supp. XVII:** 112; **Supp. XXII:** 207

Leitz, Robert, **Supp. XIV:** 62

Leivick, H., **IV:** 6

Lekachman, Robert, **Supp. I Part 2:** 648

Leland, Charles, **Supp. II Part 1:** 193

Leland, Charles Godfrey, **I:** 257

Leland, John, **Supp. XV:** 69; **Supp. XIX:** 157

Lem, Stanislaw, **Supp. IV Part 1:** 103

"Le marais du cygne" (Whittier), **Supp. I Part 2:** 687

Lemay, Harding, **Supp. VIII:** 125; **Supp. IX:** 98

Lemercier, Eugène, **Retro. Supp. I:** 299

Lemkin, Raphael, **Supp. XXIII:** 31

"Lemorne *versus* Huell" (E. Stoddard), **Supp. XV:** 270, 273, 283

Le Morte D'Arthur Notes (Gardner), **Supp. VI:** 65, 66

Lenin, V. I., **I:** 366, 439, 440; **III:** 14–15, 262, 475; **IV:** 429, 436, 443–444; **Supp. I Part 2:** 647; **Supp. XXI:** 164

"Lenny Dying, Pacific Standard Time" (Thompson), **Supp. XXIII:** 294

"Lenore" (Poe), **III:** 411

"Lenox Avenue: Midnight" (Hughes), **Retro. Supp. I:** 198

"Lens of Poetry, The" (Bronk). *See Attendant, The* (Bronk)

Leonard, Elmore, **Supp. IV Part 1:** 356; **Supp. X:** 5; **Supp. XIV:** 26

Leonard, John, **Supp. IV Part 1:** 24; **Supp. IV Part 2:** 474; **Supp. V:** 164, 223–224; **Supp. XI:** 13; **Supp. XVIII:** 147, 148; **Supp. XIX:** 269; **Supp. XXI:** 233, 239

Leonardo da Vinci, **Supp. XII:** 44; **Supp. XXII:** 171

León-Portilla, Miguel, **Supp. XV:** 77

Leontiev, Constantine, **Supp. XIV:** 98

Leopard, The (Lampedusa), **Supp. XII:** 13–14

Leopardi, Giacomo, **II:** 543; **Supp. XIX:** 33, 43

"Leopard Man's Story, The" (London), **II:** 475

Leopard's Mouth Is Dry and Cold Inside, The (Levis), **Supp. XI:** 258

Leopold, Aldo, **Supp. V:** 202; **Supp. X:** 108; **Supp. XIV: 177–194; Supp. XXI:** 203

"Leper's Bell, the" (Komunyakaa), **Supp. XIII:** 118

Lerman, Leo, **Supp. X:** 188; **Supp. XVI:** 194

Lerner, Max, **III:** 60; **Supp. I Part 2:** 629, 630, 631, 647, 650, 654

Lerperger, Emil, **Supp. XX: 165, 167**

"Lesbos" (Plath), **Retro. Supp. II:** 254

Lesesne, Teri, **Supp. XIII:** 277

LeSieg, Theo (pseudonym). *See* Geisel, Theodor Seuss (Dr. Seuss)

Leskov, Nikolai, **IV:** 299

Leslie, Alfred, **Supp. XII:** 127; **Supp. XXIII:** 217

"Less and Less Human, O Savage Spirit" (W. Stevens), **Supp. XVI:** 64

Lesser, Wendy, **Supp. IV Part 2:** 453; **Supp. XII:** 297; **Supp. XVI:** 201

Lessing, Gotthold, **Supp. I Part 2:** 422

"Lesson, The" (Bambara), **Supp. XI:** 5–6

"Lesson, The" (Dunbar), **Supp. II Part 1:** 199

"Lesson, The" (Olsen), **Supp. XIII:** 297

"Lesson, The" (Schott), **Supp. XXIII:** 254

"Lesson for the Ill Clothed and Ill Fed, A" (Ryan as Quin), **Supp. XVIII:** 230–231

Lesson of the Master, The (James), **Supp. XVIII:** 248

"Lesson of the Master, The" (James), **Retro. Supp. I:** 227

Lesson of the Masters: An Anthology of the Novel from Cervantes to Hemingway (Cowley-Hugo, ed.), **Supp. II Part 1:** 140

"Lesson on Concealment, A" (Brown), **Supp. I Part 1:** 133

"Lessons" (Epstein), **Supp. XII:** 163

"Lessons from an Older Man" (Thompson), **Supp. XXIII:** 293

"Lessons of the Body" (Simpson), **Supp. IX:** 267

Less than One (Brodsky), **Supp. VIII:** 22, 29–31

Lester, Jerry, **Supp. IV Part 2:** 574

Lester, Ketty, **Supp. XV:** 133, 147

Le Style Apollinaire (Zukofsky), **Supp. III Part 2:** 616

Le Sueur, Arthur, **Supp. XXIII:** 161, 162

LeSueur, Joe, **Supp. XXIII:** 212, 216, 218, 220

Le Sueur, Meridel, **Supp. V:** 113, 130; **Supp. XII:** 217; **Supp. XXIII: 161– 176**

"Let America Be America Again" (Hughes), **Retro. Supp. I:** 202; **Supp. I Part 1:** 331

Let Evening Come (Kenyon), **Supp. VII:** 160, 169–171

Lethem, Jonathan, **Supp. IX:** 122; **Supp. XVIII: 135–153; Supp. XXII:** 49

Let It Come Down (Bowles), **Supp. IV Part 1:** 87

Let It Ride (Pickering), **Supp. XXI:** 198– 199

"Let Me Be" (Levine), **Supp. V:** 181, 189

"Let Me Begin Again" (Levine), **Supp. V:** 181, 189

"Let No Charitable Hope" (Wylie), **Supp. I Part 2:** 713–714, 729

Let No Man Write My Epitaph (film, Leacock), **Supp. XVII:** 150, 158

Let No Man Write My Epitaph (W. Motley), **Supp. XVII:** 150, **158–160**

Let Noon Be Fair (W. Motley), **Supp. XVII: 161**

Letofsky, Irv, **Supp. XVI:** 167

"Let one Eye his watches keep/While the Other Eye doth sleep" (Fletcher), **Supp. IV Part 2:** 621

Let's Balance the Books (radio show; Untermeyer), **Supp. XV:** 311

"Letter . . ." (Whittier), **Supp. I Part 2:** 687

"Letter, A" (Bogan), **Supp. III Part 1:** 54

"Letter, May 2, 1959" (Olson), **Supp. II Part 2:** 579, 580

"Letter, Much Too Late" (Stegner), **Supp. IV Part 2:** 613

"Letter, The" (Boulton), **Supp. XXII:** 22

"Letter, The" (Gioia), **Supp. XV:** 120

"Letter, The" (Malamud), **Supp. I Part 2:** 435–436

"Letter about Money, Love, or Other Comfort, If Any, The" (Warren), **IV:** 245

Letter Addressed to the People of Piedmont, on the Advantages of the French Revolution, and the Necessity of Adopting Its Principles in Italy, A (Barlow), **Supp. II Part 1:** 80, 81

"Letter for Marion, A" (McGrath), **Supp. X:** 116

"Letter from Aldermaston" (Merwin), **Supp. III Part 1:** 347

"Letter from a London Attic" (Pickering), **Supp. XXI:** 194

"Letter from a Region in My Mind" (Baldwin). *See* "Down at the Cross"

"Letter from Aunt Belle, A" (Kooser), **Supp. XIX:** 117

Letter from Li Po, A (Aiken), **I:** 68

"Letter from 'Manhattan' " (Didion), **Supp. IV Part 1:** 205

"Letter from the Country" (column, C. Bly), **Supp. XVI:** 33

Letter from the End of the Twentieth Century (Harjo), **Supp. XII:** 223

"Letter from the End of the Twentieth Century" (Harjo), **Supp. XII:** 227

"Letter Home" (Trethewey), **Supp. XXI:** 254

"Letter on Céline" (Kerouac), **Supp. III Part 1:** 232

Letters (Cato), **II:** 114

Letters (Landor), **Supp. I Part 2:** 422

Letters (White), **Supp. I Part 2:** 651, 653, 675, 680

Letters (Wolfe), **IV:** 462

"Letters, The" (Swados), **Supp. XIX:** 261, 262

Letters and Leadership (Brooks), **I:** 228, 240, 245, 246

"Letters for the Dead" (Levine), **Supp. V:** 186

Letters from an American Farmer (Crèvecoeur), **Supp. I Part 1:** 227–251

Letters from Maine (Sarton), **Supp. VIII: 261**

"Letters from Maine" (Sarton), **Supp. VIII:** 261

"Letters from My Father" (R. O. Butler), **Supp. XII:** 71

Letters from the Country (C. Bly), **Supp. XVI: 33–34,** 35, 37

Letters from the Earth (Twain), **IV:** 209

Letters from the East (Bryant), **Supp. I Part 1:** 158

"Letters from the Ming Dynasty" (Brodsky), **Supp. VIII:** 28

Letters of Angelicus and Fidelio Fobb (O'Hara and Berkson), **Supp. XXIII:** 218

Letters of a Traveller (Bryant), **Supp. I Part 1:** 158

Letters of a Traveller, Second Series (Bryant), **Supp. I Part 1:** 158

Letters of Emily Dickinson, The (Johnson and Ward, eds.), **I:** 470; **Retro. Supp. I:** 28

Letters of William James (Henry James, ed.), **II:** 362

Letters on Various Interesting and Important Subjects . . . (Freneau), **Supp. II Part 1:** 272

Letters to a Niece (Adams), **I:** 22

Letters to a Teacher (Pickering), **Supp. XXI:** 195, 201–202

Letters to a Young Poet (Rilke), **Supp. XIII:** 74; **Supp. XV:** 93

"Letters to Dead Imagists" (Sandburg), **I:** 421

"Letters Written on a Ferry While Crossing Long Island Sound" (Sexton), **Supp. II Part 2:** 683

"Letter to Abbé Raynal" (Paine), **Supp. I Part 2:** 510

Letter to a Man in the Fire: Does God Exist or Does He Care? (Price), **Supp. VI:** 267–268

"Letter to American Teachers of History, A" (Adams), **I:** 19

Letter to an Imaginary Friend (McGrath), **Supp. X:** 111, 112–113, 116, **119–125**

"Letter to a Reader" (Sanders), **Supp. XVI:** 266, 267, 268, 269, 275

"Letter to a Young Author" (P. N. Warren), **Supp. XX: 272**

"Letter to a Young Contributor" (Higginson), **Retro. Supp. I:** 31

"Letter to a Young Writer" (Price), **Supp. VI:** 267

"Letter to Bell from Missoula" (Hugo), **Supp. VI:** 142–143

"Letter to E. Franklin Frazier" (Baraka), **Supp. II Part 1:** 49

"Letter to Elaine Feinstein" (Olson), **Supp. II Part 2:** 561

"Letter to Freddy" (music) (Bowles), **Supp. IV Part 1:** 82

"Letter to Garber from Skye" (Hugo), **Supp. VI:** 146

"Letter to George Washington" (Paine), **Supp. I Part 2:** 517

"Letter to His Brother" (Berryman), **I:** 172, 173

Letter to His Countrymen, A (Cooper), **I:** 346, 347, 349

"Letter to Kizer from Seattle" (Hugo), **Supp. VI:** 142

Letter to Lord Byron (Auden), **Supp. II Part 1:** 11

"Letter to Lord Byron" (Mumford), **Supp. II Part 2:** 494

"Letter to Matthews from Barton Street Flats" (Hugo), **Supp. VI:** 133

"Letter to Minnesota" (Dunn), **Supp. XI:** 146

"Letter to Mr." (Poe), **III:** 411

"Letter Too Late to Vallejo" (Salinas), **Supp. XIII:** 313, 324

"Letter to Sister Madeline from Iowa City" (Hugo), **Supp. VI:** 142–143

"Letter to Soto" (Salinas), **Supp. XIII:** 325

"Letter to the Lady of the House" (Bausch), **Supp. VII:** 48

"Letter to the Rising Generation, A" (Comer), **I:** 214

"Letter to Walt Whitman" (Doty), **Supp. XI:** 135–136

"Letter to Wendell Berry, A" (Stegner), **Supp. IV Part 2:** 600

"Letter Writer, The" (Singer), **IV:** 20–21

"Let the Air Circulate" (Clampitt), **Supp. IX:** 45

Let the Hurricane Roar (Lane), **Supp. XXII:** 297

"Letting Down of the Hair, The" (Sexton), **Supp. II Part 2:** 692

Letting Go (P. Roth), **Retro. Supp. II:** 282, 283; **Supp. III Part 2:** 403, 404, 409–412

"Letting the Puma Go" (Dunn), **Supp. XI:** 149

"Lettres d'un Soldat" (Stevens), **Retro. Supp. I:** 299

Let Us Go into the Starry Night (Shanley), **Supp. XIV:** 317

Let Us Highly Resolve (Stratton-Porter), **Supp. XX: 223**

Let Us Now Praise Famous Men (Agee and Evans), **I:** 25, 27, 35, 36–39, 42, 45, 293

Let Your Mind Alone! (Thurber), **Supp. I Part 2:** 608

Leutze, Emanuel, **Supp. X:** 307

Levels of the Game (McPhee), **Supp. III Part 1:** 292, 294, 301

Levertov, Denise, **Retro. Supp. I:** 411; **Supp. III Part 1: 271–287; Supp. III Part 2:** 541; **Supp. IV Part 1:** 325; **Supp. VIII:** 38, 39; **Supp. XVI:** 39, 40; **Supp. XIX:** 282; **Supp. XXI:** 228; **Supp. XXII:** 83, 168, 177

Levi, Primo, **Supp. X:** 149; **Supp. XVII:** 48

Leviathan (Auster), **Supp. XII:** 27, **33–34**

"Leviathan" (Lowell), **II:** 537, 538

"Leviathan" (Merwin), **Supp. III Part 1:** 345

Levin, Adam, **Supp. XXII:** 268

Levin, Harry, **Supp. I Part 2:** 647

Levin, Jennifer, **Supp. X:** 305

Levin, Meyer, **Supp. XX: 34**

Lévinas, Emmanuel, **Supp. XVI:** 290, 291
Levine, Ellen, **Supp. V:** 4; **Supp. XI:** 178
Levine, Paul, **Supp. IV Part 1:** 221, 224
Levine, Philip, **Supp. III Part 2:** 541; **Supp. V: 177–197,** 337; **Supp. IX:** 293; **Supp. XI:** 123, 257, 259, 267, 271, 315; **Supp. XIII:** 312; **Supp. XV:** 73, 74, 212; **Supp. XIX:** 45
Levine, Rosalind, **Supp. XII:** 123
Levine, Sherry, **Supp. XII:** 4
Levis, Larry, **Supp. V:** 180; **Supp. IX:** 299; **Supp. XI: 257–274; Supp. XIII:** 312; **Supp. XV:** 73; **Supp. XVII:** 110
Lévi-Strauss, Claude, **Supp. I Part 2:** 636; **Supp. IV Part 1:** 45; **Supp. IV Part 2:** 490; **Supp. XVIII:** 190
Levitation: Five Fictions (Ozick), **Supp. V:** 268–270
"Levitation with Baby" (Nelson), **Supp. XVIII:** 173
Levitt, Saul, **Supp. XV:** 197
Levy, Alan, **Supp. IV Part 2:** 574, 589
Levy, D. A., **Supp. XXIII:** 174
Levy, G. Rachel, **Supp. I Part 2:** 567
Levy, Julien, **Supp. XXII:** 167, 168
Lévy-Bruhl, Lucien, **Retro. Supp. I:** 57
Levy Mayer and the New Industrial Era (Masters), **Supp. I Part 2:** 473
Lewes, George Henry, **II:** 569
Lewin, Albert, **Supp. XIV:** 279, 293
Lewis, C. Day, **III:** 527
Lewis, Dr. Claude, **II:** 442
Lewis, David Levering, **Supp. XVIII:** 127; **Supp. XIX:** 74, 75; **Supp. XXII:** 13
Lewis, Edith, **I:** 313; **Retro. Supp. I:** 19, 21, 22
Lewis, Edwin, J., **II:** 439, 442
Lewis, Jerry, **Supp. IV Part 2:** 575; **Supp. X:** 172
Lewis, John L., **I:** 493
Lewis, Lilburn, **IV:** 243
Lewis, Lorene, **Supp. IV Part 2:** 596, 597
Lewis, Lucy, **IV:** 243
Lewis, Maggie, **Supp. V:** 23
Lewis, Meriwether, **II:** 217; **III:** 14; **IV:** 179, 243, 283
Lewis, Merrill, **Supp. IV Part 2:** 596, 597
Lewis, Michael, **II:** 451, 452; **Supp. XVII:** 210
Lewis, Robert Q., **Supp. IV Part 2:** 574
Lewis, R. W. B., **I:** 386, 561; **II:** 457–458; **Retro. Supp. I:** 362, 367; **Supp. I Part 1:** 233; **Supp. XIII:** 93; **Supp. XXIII:** 42
Lewis, Sinclair, **I:** 116, 212, 348, 355, 362, 374, 378, 487, 495; **II:** 27, 34, 74, 79, 271, 277, 306, **439–461,** 474; **III:** 28, 40, 51, 60, 61, 63–64, 66, 70, 71, 106, 394, 462, 572, 606; **IV:** 53, 326, 366, 455, 468, 475, 482; **Retro. Supp. I:** 332; **Retro. Supp. II:** 95, 108, 197, 322; **Supp. I Part 2:** 378, 613, 709; **Supp. IV Part 2:** 678; **Supp. V:** 278; **Supp. IX:** 308; **Supp.**

X: 137; **Supp. XVII:** 41; **Supp. XVIII:** 278; **Supp. XXII:** 190; **Supp. XXIII:** 165, 166
Lewis, Mrs. Sinclair (Dorothy Thompson), **II:** 449–450, 451, 453
Lewis, Mrs. Sinclair (Grace Livingston Hegger), **II:** 441
Lewis, Wyndham, **III:** 458, 462, 465, 470; **Retro. Supp. I:** 59, 170, 292; **Supp. III Part 2:** 617
Lewisohn, Ludwig, **Supp. XXIII:** 1
Lexicon Tetraglotton (Howell), **II:** 111
"Lexington Avenue Musedog" (Peacock), **Supp. XIX:** 204
"Leyenda" (Mora), **Supp. XIII:** 214
Leyner, Mark, **Supp. XIX:** 223
Leyte (Morison), **Supp. I Part 2:** 491
"Liar, The" (Baraka), **Supp. II Part 1:** 36
"Liars, The" (Sandburg), **III:** 586
Liars' Club, The: A Memoir (Karr), **Supp. XI:** 239, 240, 241, 242, **244–248,** 252, 254; **Supp. XVI:** 70
Liar's Dice (C. Frost), **Supp. XV:** 93, 96
"Liar's Dice" (C. Frost), **Supp. XV:** 94, 107
Liars in Love (Yates), **Supp. XI:** 348, 349
Libation Bearers, The (Aeschylus), **III:** 398; **Supp. IX:** 103
Li Bay. *See* Li Po
Libby, Anthony, **Supp. XIII:** 87
Libera, Padre, **II:** 278
Liberal Imagination, The (Trilling), **III:** 308; **Retro. Supp. I:** 97, 216; **Supp. II Part 1:** 146; **Supp. III Part 2:** 495, 498, 501–504
Liberation (J. Scott), **Supp. XVII:** 192, **194–196**
"Liberation" (Winters), **Supp. II Part 2:** 791
Liber Brunenesis (yearbook), **IV:** 286
Liberties, The (Howe), **Supp. IV Part 2:** 426–428, 430, 432
Liberties of America, The (H. Warner), **Supp. XVIII:** 259
Liberty Jones (play), **Supp. IV Part 1:** 83
"Liberty Tree" (Paine), **Supp. I Part 2:** 505
Libra (DeLillo), **Supp. VI:** 2, **4, 5,** 6, **7,** 9, 10, 12, 13, 14, 16
Library for Juana, A (Mora), **Supp. XIII:** 218
Library of America, **Retro. Supp. I:** 2
"Library of Babel, The" (J. Borges), **Supp. XVII:** 47
"Library of Law, A" (MacLeish), **III:** 4
"Library of Moloch, The" (Bukiet), **Supp. XVII:** 47, 49
"Librettos for Eros" (Gander), **Supp. XV:** 340
Lice, The (Merwin), **Supp. III Part 1:** 339, 341–342, 346, 348, 349, 355
Lichtenberg, Georg Christoph, **Supp. XIV:** 339
Lichtenstein, Roy, **Supp. I Part 2:** 665; **Supp. XV:** 186
"Liddy's Orange" (Olds), **Supp. X:** 209
"Lie, The" (Antin), **Supp. XX:** 7, 9–10

Lieberman, Herman (Chaim), **Supp. XXIII:** 3, 7
Lieberman, Laurence, **Supp. XI:** 323–324
Liebestod (Wagner), **I:** 284, 395
Liebling, A. J., **IV:** 290; **Supp. VIII:** 151; **Supp. XVI:** 167
Lie Down in Darkness (Styron), **IV:** 98, 99, 100–104, 105, 111; **Supp. XI:** 343
Lie of the Mind, A (Shepard), **Supp. III Part 2:** 433, 435, 441, 447–449
"Lies" (Haines), **Supp. XII:** 204
Lies (Hoffman), **Supp. XVIII: 78–79**
"Lies and Consequences" (Pickering), **Supp. XXI:** 204
Lies Like Truth (Clurman), **IV:** 385
Lieutenant, The (Dubus), **Supp. VII:** 78
"Life" (Wharton), **Retro. Supp. I:** 372
Life along the Passaic River (W. C. Williams), **Retro. Supp. I:** 423
Life Among the Savages (Jackson), **Supp. IX:** 115, **125**
Life and Adventures of Charles Anderson Chester, The (Lippard), **Supp. XXIII:** 184
"Life and Death Kisses, The" (Grossman), **Supp. XIX:** 87
Life and Gabriella (Glasgow), **II:** 175, 176, 182–183, 184, 189
"Life and I" (Wharton), **Retro. Supp. I:** 360, 361, 362
"Life and Letters" (Epstein), **Supp. XIV:** 104–105
Life and Letters of Harrison Gray Otis, Federalist, 1765–1848, The (Morison), **Supp. I Part 2:** 480–481
Life and Letters of Sir Henry Wotton (L. P. Smith), **Supp. XIV:** 340–341
Life and Mind of Emily Dickinson, The (Taggard), **Supp. XXII:** 279
Life and Times of Frederick Douglass, Written by Himself, The (Douglass), **Supp. III Part 1:** 155, 159–163
Life and Writings of Horace McCoy, The (Wolfson), **Supp. XIII:** 172, 174
"Life as a Visionary Spirit" (Eberhart), **I:** 540, 541
"Life at Angelo's, A" (Benét), **Supp. XI:** 53
Life at Happy Knoll (Marquand), **III:** 50, 61
Life Before Man (Atwood), **Supp. XIII: 24–25**
"Life Cycle of Common Man" (Nemerov), **III:** 278
"Lifecycle Stairmaster" (Karr), **Supp. XI:** 250
Life Estates (Hearon), **Supp. VIII: 68–69**
Life for Life's Sake (Aldington), **Supp. I Part 1:** 256
Life Full of Holes, A (Layachi), **Supp. IV Part 1:** 92
"Lifeguard" (Updike), **IV:** 226; **Retro. Supp. I:** 325
"Lifeguard, The" (Dickey), **Supp. IV Part 1:** 179–180
"Life in the 30s" (column, Quindlen), **Supp. XVII:** 165, 167–169
Life in the Clearings (Shields), **Supp. VII:** 313

"Life in the Country: A City Friend Asks, 'Is It Boring?' " (Paley), **Supp. VI:** 231

Life in the Forest (Levertov), **Supp. III Part 1:** 282–283

Life in the Iron Mills (R. H. Davis), **Supp. XIII:** 292, 295, 299, 305; **Supp. XVI:** 79–82, **85–88,** 91

Life in the Iron Mills and Other Stories (T. Olson, ed.), **Supp. XVI:** 83

Life in the Theatre, A (Mamet), **Supp. XIV:** 241, 255

Life Is a Miracle: An Essay Against Modern Superstition (Berry), **Supp. X:** 35

"Life Is Fine" (Hughes), **Supp. I Part 1:** 334, 338

"Life Is Motion" (Stevens), **IV:** 74

Life & Letters of Gene Stratton-Porter (Meehan), **Supp. XX: 213**

Life of Albert Gallatin, The (Adams), **I:** 6, 14

"Life of a Man of the World, The"(Lippard), **Supp. XXIII:** 189

Life of an Ordinary Woman, The: Anne Ellis (A. Ellis), **Supp. XVI:** 38

Life of Captain Cipriani, The: An Account of British Government in the West Indies (C. L. R. James), **Supp. XXI:** 161

Life of Dryden (Johnson), **Retro. Supp. II:** 223

Life of Emily Dickinson, The (Sewall), **Retro. Supp. I:** 25

Life of Forms, The (Focillon), **IV:** 90

Life of Franklin Pierce (Hawthorne), **Retro. Supp. I:** 163

Life of George Cabot Lodge, The (Adams), **I:** 21

Life of George Washington (Irving), **II:** 314, 315–316

Life of Henry James (Edel), **Retro. Supp. I:** 224

"Life of Irony, The" (Bourne), **I:** 219

Life of Jesus (Renan), **Supp. XX: 122**

"Life of Lincoln West, The" (Brooks), **Supp. III Part 1:** 86

Life of Mary, The (Rilke; F. Wright, trans.), **Supp. XVII:** 244

Life of Michelangelo (Grimm), **II:** 17

"Life of Nancy, The" (Jewett), **Retro. Supp. II:** 133, 144

Life of Oliver Goldsmith, The, with Selections from His Writings (Irving), **II:** 315

Life of Phips (Mather), **Supp. II Part 2:** 451, 452, 459

Life of Poetry, The (Rukeyser), **Supp. VI:** 271, 273, 275–276, 282, 283, 286

Life of Samuel Johnson (Boswell), **Supp. I Part 2:** 656

Life of Savage (Johnson), **Supp. I Part 2:** 523

Life of the Drama, The (Bentley), **IV:** 396

"Life of the Mind, The" (Kees), **Supp. XV:** 140

Life of the Right Reverend Joseph P. Machebeuf, The (Howlett), **Retro. Supp. I:** 17

Life of Thomas Paine, author of Rights of Men, With a Defence of his Writings (Chalmers), **Supp. I Part 2:** 514

Life of Thomas Paine, The (Cobbett), **Supp. I Part 2:** 517

"Life of Towne, The" (Carson), **Supp. XII:** 102

"Life on Beekman Place, A" (Naylor), **Supp. VIII:** 214

"Life on the Black List" (Endore), **Supp. XVII:** 63

Life on the Hyphen: The Cuban-American Way (Firmat), **Supp. VIII:** 76; **Supp. XI:** 184

Life on the Mississippi (Twain), **I:** 209; **IV:** 198, 199; **Supp. I Part 2:** 440

"Life on the Rocks: The Galápagos" (Dillard), **Supp. VI:** 32

"Life Stories, East and West" (E. Hoffman), **Supp. XVI:** 157

Life Story (Baker), **II:** 259

Life Studies (Lowell), **I:** 400; **II:** 384, 386, 543, 546–550, 551, 555; **Retro. Supp. II:** 180, 185, 186, 188, 189, 191; **Supp. I Part 2:** 543; **Supp. XI:** 240, 244, 250, 317; **Supp. XII:** 255; **Supp. XIV:** 15; **Supp. XV:** 252

"Life Studies" (Lowell), **Retro. Supp. II:** 188

"Life Styles in the Golden Land" (Didion), **Supp. IV Part 1:** 200

Life Supports: New and Collected Poems (Bronk), **Supp. XXI:** 19, 31, 32

"Life That Is, The" (Bryant), **Supp. I Part 1:** 169

"Life Work" (Stafford), **Supp. XI:** 329–330

"Life You Save May Be Your Own, The" (O'Connor), **III:** 344, 350, 354; **Retro. Supp. II:** 229, 230, 233

Lifshin, Lyn, **Supp. XVI:** 37

"Lifting, The" (Olds), **Supp. X:** 210

"Ligeia" (Poe), **III:** 412, 414; **Retro. Supp. II:** 261, 270, 271, 275

Liggett, Walter W., **Supp. XIII:** 168

Light, James F., **IV:** 290; **Retro. Supp. II:** 325

Light, Kate, **Supp. XVII:** 109

Light and Dark (Bronk), **Supp. XXI:** 27–**29,** 31

"Light and the Sufferer" (Lethem), **Supp. XVIII:** 139–140

Light around the Body, The (R. Bly), **Supp. IV Part 1:** 61–62, 62; **Supp. XVII:** 243; **Supp. XXI:** 84–85

"Light Comes Brighter, The" (Roethke), **III:** 529–530

"Light from Above" (Eberhart), **I:** 541

Light in August (Faulkner), **II:** 63–64, 65, 74; **IV:** 207; **Retro. Supp. I:** 82, 84, 85, 86, 89, 92; **Supp. XIV:** 12

Light in the Forest, The (Richter), **Supp. XVIII: 216–217**

Light in the Morning (Baker), **Supp. XVIII:** 263, 269

"Light Man, A" (James), **II:** 322; **Retro. Supp. I:** 219

"Lightning" (Barthelme), **Supp. IV Part 1:** 53

"Lightning" (Bynner), **Supp. XV:** 44

"Lightning" (Oliver), **Supp. VII:** 235

"Lightning, The" (Swenson), **Supp. IV Part 2:** 645

"Lightning Flash, The" (Gibran), **Supp. XX: 123**

"Lightning Rod Man, The" (Melville), **III:** 90; **Supp. XVIII:** 4

"Light of the World, The" (Hemingway), **II:** 249

"Lights"(Dybek), **Supp. XXIII:** 72

"Lights in the Windows" (Nye), **Supp. XIII:** 280

"Lights Must Never Go Out, The"(Hadas), **Supp. XXIII:** 125

"Light Through the Window, The" (Brockmeier), **Supp. XXII:** 52, 59

Light Verse and Satires (Bynner), **Supp. XV:** 52

Light Years (Salter), **Supp. IX: 257–259**

"LIKE, THIS IS WHAT I MEANT!" (Baraka), **Supp. II Part 1:** 59

"Like All the Other Nations" (Paley), **Supp. VI:** 220

"Like a Rolling Stone" (song, Dylan), **Supp. XVIII:** 20, 30

"Like Decorations in a Nigger Cemetery" (Stevens), **IV:** 74, 79; **Retro. Supp. I:** 305

Like Ghosts of Eagles (Francis), **Supp. IX:** 86

"Like Life" (Moore), **Supp. X:** 163, 165, **172–173**

Like Life: Stories (Moore), **Supp. X:** 163, **171–175,** 177, 178

"Like Talk" (Mills), **Supp. XI:** 311

"Like the New Moon I Will Live My Life" (R. Bly), **Supp. IV Part 1:** 71

Li'l Abner (Capp), **IV:** 198

"Lilacs" (Lowell), **II:** 527

"Lilacs, The" (Wilbur), **Supp. III Part 2:** 557–558

"Lilacs for Ginsberg" (Stern), **Supp. IX:** 299

Liliom (Molnar), **Supp. XVI:** 187

Lilith's Brood (O. Butler), **Supp. XIII:** 63

Lillabulero Press, **Supp. V:** 4, 5

Lillian Hellman (Adler), **Supp. I Part 1:** 297

Lillian Hellman (Falk), **Supp. I Part 1:** 297

Lillian Hellman: Playwright (Moody), **Supp. I Part 1:** 280

Lillo, George, **II:** 111, 112

"Lily Daw and the Three Ladies" (Welty), **IV:** 262

Lima, Agnes de, **I:** 231, 232

Lima, Frank, **Supp. XXIII:** 217, 221

Lima, Maria Helena, **Supp. XXII:** 73

Lima Beans (Kreymborg), **Supp. XXII:** 163

"Limbo: Altered States" (Karr), **Supp. XI:** 249–250

"Limen" (Trethewey), **Supp. XXI:** 250

Lime Orchard Woman, The (Ríos), **Supp. IV Part 2:** 538, 547–550, 553

"Lime Orchard Woman, The" (Ríos), **Supp. IV Part 2:** 548

Limitations (Turow), **Supp. XVII: 222–223**

"Limits" (Emerson), **II**: 19

Lincoln, Abraham, **I**: 1, 4, 30; **II**: 8, 13, 135, 273, 555, 576; **III**: 576, 577, 580, 584, 587–590, 591; **IV**: 192, 195, 298, 347, 350, 444; **Supp. I Part 1**: 2, 8, 26, 309, 321; **Supp. I Part 2**: 379, 380, 382, 385, 390, 397, 399, 418, 424, 454, 456, 471, 472, 473, 474, 483, 579, 687; **Supp. VIII**: 108; **Supp. IX**: 15; **Supp. XIV**: 73

Lincoln, Kenneth, **Supp. IV Part 1**: 329; **Supp. IV Part 2**: 507

Lincoln, Thomas, **III**: 587

Lincoln, Mrs. Thomas (Nancy Hanks), **III**: 587

Lincoln: A Novel (Vidal), **Supp. IV Part 2**: 677, 684, 685, 688, 689–690, 691, 692

Lincoln Lawyer, The (Connelly), **Supp. XXI**: 77, 78

Lincoln on Race and Slavery (H. L. Gates), **Supp. XX**: 108–109

"Lincoln Relics, The" (Kunitz), **Supp. III Part 1**: 269

Lincoln: The Man (Masters), **Supp. I Part 2**: 471, 473–474

Lindbergh, Charles A., **I**: 482

"Linden Branch, The" (MacLeish), **III**: 19, 20

Linden Hills (Naylor), **Supp. VIII**: 214, 218, **219–223**

Linderman, Lawrence, **Supp. IV Part 2**: 579, 583, 585, 589

Lindner, April, **Supp. XV**: 111, 119

Lindsay, Howard, **III**: 284

Lindsay, John, **Supp. I Part 2**: 374

Lindsay, Olive, **Supp. I Part 2**: 374, 375, 392

Lindsay, Vachel, **I**: 384; **II**: 263, 276, 530; **III**: 5, 505; **Retro. Supp. I**: 133; **Supp. I Part 1**: 324; **Supp. I Part 2**: **374–403**, 454, 473, 474; **Supp. III Part 1**: 63, 71; **Supp. XV**: 293, 297, 299, 301, 306; **Supp. XVI**: 184–185

Lindsay, Mrs. Vachel (Elizabeth Connors), **Supp. I Part 2**: 398, 399, 473

Lindsay, Vachel Thomas, **Supp. I Part 2**: 374, 375

Lindsay, Mrs. Vachel Thomas (Esther Catherine Frazee), **Supp. I Part 2**: 374, 375, 384–385, 398

Lindsey, David, **Supp. XIV**: 26

"Line, The" (Olds), **Supp. X**: 206

Lineage of Ragpickers, Songpluckers, Elegiasts, and Jewelers, A (Goldbarth), **Supp. XII**: 191

"Line"(Crooker), **Supp. XXIII**: 58

Line Dance (Crooker), **Supp. XXIII**: 56, **58–60**

"Line Dance"(Crooker), **Supp. XXIII**: 59

"Line of Least Resistance, The" (Wharton), **Retro. Supp. I**: 366

Line Out for a Walk, A: Familiar Essays (Epstein), **Supp. XIV**: **107**

"Liner Notes for the Poetically Unhep" (Hughes), **Retro. Supp. I**: 210

"Lines After Rereading T. S. Eliot" (Wright), **Supp. V**: 343

"Lines Composed a Few Miles Above Tintern Abbey" (Wordsworth), **Supp. III Part 1**: 12

"Lines Composed Over Three Thousand Miles from Tintern Abbey" (Collins), **Supp. XXI**: 57–58

"Lines for an Interment" (MacLeish), **III**: 15

"Lines for My Father" (Cullen), **Supp. IV Part 1**: 167

"Lines from Israel" (Lowell), **II**: 554

"Lines from Pietro Longhi" (Sobin), **Supp. XVI**: 289

"Lines on Revisiting the Country" (Bryant), **Supp. I Part 1**: 164

"Lines Suggested by a Tennessee Song" (Agee), **I**: 28

"Lines to a Friend Asleep"(J. Schoolcraft), **Supp. XXIII**: 228, 230

"Line-Storm Song, A" (Frost), **Retro. Supp. I**: 127

"Lines written at Castle Island, Lake Superior"(J. Schoolcraft), **Supp. XXIII**: 229, 232, 233

"Lines Written at Port Royal" (Freneau), **Supp. II Part 1**: 264

"Lines Written in an Asylum" (Carruth), **Supp. XVI**: 48

"Lines Written in Manassas", **Supp. XV**: 99–100

Lineup, The (Connelly), **Supp. XXI**: 67, 68–69

"Line Written in the Dark Illegible Next Day" (F. Wright), **Supp. XVII**: 242

Linfield, Susie, **Supp. XVII**: 169, 177

Lingeman, Richard, **Supp. X**: 82; **Supp. XXII**: 104

Linn, Elizabeth. *See* Brown, Mrs. Charles Brockden (Elizabeth Linn)

Linn, John Blair, **Supp. I Part 1**: 145

Linnaeus, Carolus, **II**: 6; **Supp. I Part 1**: 245

"Linnets" (Levis), **Supp. XI**: 260, 261

"Linoleum Roses" (Cisneros), **Supp. VII**: 63, 66

Linotte: 1914–1920 (Nin), **Supp. X**: 193, 196, 197

Linschoten, Hans, **II**: 362, 363, 364

"Lion" (B. Kelly), **Supp. XVII**: 133

"Lion and Honeycomb" (Nemerov), **III**: 275, 278, 280

Lion and the Archer, The (Hayden), **Supp. II Part 1**: 366, 367

Lion and the Honeycomb, The (Blackmur), **Supp. II Part 1**: 91

Lion Country (Buechner), **Supp. XII**: 52, 53

Lionel Lincoln (Cooper), **I**: 339, 342

"Lion for Real, The" (Ginsberg), **Supp. II Part 1**: 320

Lionhearted, The: A Story about the Jews of Medieval England (Reznikoff), **Supp. XIV**: 280, 289

Lion in the Garden (Meriweather and Millgate), **Retro. Supp. I**: 91

"Lionizing" (Poe), **III**: 411, 425

"Lions, Harts, and Leaping Does" (Powers), **III**: 356

Lions and Shadows: An Education in the Twenties (Isherwood), **Supp. XIV**: 158, 159, 160, 162

"Lions in Sweden" (Stevens), **IV**: 79–80

Lipman, William R., **Supp. XIII**: 170

Li Po, **Supp. XI**: 241; **Supp. XII**: 218; **Supp. XV**: 47, 217

Lippard, George, **Supp. XXIII**: **177–192**

Lippmann, Walter, **I**: 48, 222–223, 225; **III**: 291, 600; **IV**: 429; **Supp. I Part 2**: 609, 643; **Supp. VIII**: 104

Lipschitz, Moryce, **Supp. XXIII**: 6

Lips Together, Teeth Apart (McNally), **Supp. XIII**: **201–202**, 208, 209

Lipsyte, Robert, **Supp. XVI**: 220

Lipton, James, **Supp. IV Part 2**: 576, 577, 579, 583, 586, 588

Lipton, Lawrence, **Supp. IX**: 3

Lisbon Traviata, The (McNally), **Supp. XIII**: 198, **199–200**, 201, 204, 208

Lish, Gordon, **Supp. XIX**: 209; **Supp. XXI**: 115, 121; **Supp. XXIII**: 274

Lisicky,Paul, **Supp. XI**: 120, 131, 135

Lisk, Thomas, **Supp. XXI**: 24

"Lisp, The" (Olds), **Supp. X**: 211

Listen, Ruben Fontanez (Neugeboren), **Supp. XVI**: **220–221**

"Listeners, The" (de la Mare), **Supp. XVII**: 69

"Listeners and Readers: The Unforgetting of Vachel Lindsay" (Trombly), **Supp. I Part 2**: 403

"Listening" (J. W. Miller), **Supp. XX**: **167**

"Listening" (Paley), **Supp. VI**: 218, 231, 232

"Listening" (Stafford), **Supp. XI**: 321, 322

Listening to Prozac (P. Kramer), **Supp. XVI**: 229

"Listening to the Desert" (Henderson), **Supp. XIII**: 221–222

"Listening to the Mockingbird" (Woodard), **Supp. VIII**: 128

Listening to Your Life: Daily Meditations with Frederick Buechner (Buechner), **Supp. XII**: 53

Listen to the Desert/Oye al desierto (Mora), **Supp. XIII**: 221

"Listen to the People" (Benét), **Supp. XI**: 51–52

Liston, Sonny, **III**: 38, 42

Li T'ai-po, **II**: 526

"Litany" (Ashbery), **Supp. III Part 1**: 21–22, 25, 26

"Litany" (Collins), **Supp. XXI**: 56–57

"Litany" (Sandburg), **III**: 593

"Litany, The" (Gioia), **Supp. XV**: 125, 126

"Litany for Dictatorships" (Benét), **Supp. XI**: 46, 58

"Litany for Survival, A" (Lorde), **Supp. XII**: 220

"Litany of the Dark People, The" (Cullen), **Supp. IV Part 1**: 170, 171

"Litany of the Heroes" (Lindsay), **Supp. I Part 2**: 397

"Litany of Washington Street, The" (Lindsay), **Supp. I Part 2**: 376, 398–399

Literary Anthropology (Trumpener and Nyce), **Retro. Supp. I:** 380

Literary Art and Activism of Rick Bass, The (Weltzien), **Supp. XVI:** 20–21

"Literary Blacks and Jews" (Ozick), **Supp. V:** 272

"Literary Career of Elizabeth Barstow Stoddard, The" (Matlack), **Supp. XV:** 269

Literary Criticism: A Short History (Brooks and Wimsatt), **Supp. XIV:** 12

"Literary Criticism of Georg Lukács, The" (Sontag), **Supp. III Part 2:** 453

Literary Disruptions (Klinkowitz), **Supp. XXI:** 233

Literary Essays of Thomas Merton, The, **Supp. VIII:** 207

"Literary Folk As They Came and Went with Ourselves" (E. Stoddard), **Supp. XV:** 274

Literary Friends and Acquaintance (Howells), **Supp. I Part 1:** 318; **Supp. XV:** 287

"Literary Heritage of Tennyson, The" (Locke), **Supp. XIV:** 197

Literary History of the United States (Spiller et al., ed.), **Supp. I Part 1:** 104; **Supp. II Part 1:** 95

"Literary Importation" (Freneau), **Supp. II Part 1:** 264

"Literary Life of America, The" (Brooks), **I:** 245

Literary Outlaw: The Life and Times of William S. Burroughs (Morgan), **Supp. XIV:** 141

Literary Situation, The (Cowley), **Supp. II Part 1:** 135, 140, 144, 146, 147, 148

"Literary Worker's Polonius, The" (Wilson), **IV:** 431, 432

"Literature" (Emerson), **II:** 6

Literature (X. J. Kennedy), **Supp. XV:** 153

Literature and American Life (Boynton), **Supp. I Part 2:** 415

Literature and Life (Howells), **Supp. XIV:** 45–46

Literature and Morality (Farrell), **II:** 49

"Literature and Place: Varieties of Regional Experience" (Erisman), **Supp. VIII:** 126

"Literature as a Symptom" (Warren), **IV:** 237

"Literature in Low Life" (Hapgood), **Supp. XVII:** 103

"Literature of Exhaustion, The" (Barth), **Supp. IV Part 1:** 48

"Lithuanian Nocturne" (Brodsky), **Supp. VIII:** 29

"Lit Instructor" (Stafford), **Supp. XI:** 321

Littauer, Kenneth, **Retro. Supp. I:** 114

Little Acts of Kindness (Budbill), **Supp. XIX:** 3, **14–15**

"Little Bernhardt" (Shaw), **Supp. XIX:** 246

Little Big Man (Berger), **Supp. XII:** 171

Little Big Man (film), **Supp. X:** 124

Littlebird, Harold, **Supp. IV Part 2:** 499

Littlebird, Larry, **Supp. IV Part 2:** 499, 505

Little Birds: Erotica (Nin), **Supp. X:** 192, 195

"Little Brown Baby" (Dunbar), **Supp. II Part 1:** 206

"Little Brown Jug" (Baraka), **Supp. II Part 1:** 51

"Little Burst, A" (Strout), **Supp. XXIII:** 282

"Little by Little" (Hadas), **Supp. XXIII:** 115

Little Casino (Sorrentino), **Supp. XXI:** 237, 238

"Little Clown, My Heart" (Cisneros), **Supp. VII:** 71

"Little Cosmic Dust Poem" (Haines), **Supp. XII:** 209–210

"Little Country Girl, A" (Chopin), **Retro. Supp. II:** 71

"Little Curtis" (Parker), **Supp. IX:** 193

Little Disturbances of Man, The (Paley), **Supp. VI:** 218

"Little Dog" (Hughes), **Supp. I Part 1:** 329

Little Dorrit (Dickens), **Supp. I Part 1:** 35

"Little Edward" (Stowe), **Supp. I Part 2:** 587

"Little Elegy" (X. J. Kennedy), **Supp. XV:** 155

"Little Elegy for Antonio Machado" (O'Hara), **Supp. XXIII:** 220

Little Essays Drawn from the Writings of George Santayana (L. P. Smith), **Supp. XIV:** 342

"Little Expressionless Animals" (Wallace), **Supp. X:** 305

"Little Fable" (Hay), **Supp. XIV:** 131

Little Face and Other Stories (Thompson), **Supp. XXIII: 293–294**

"Little Face" (Thompson), **Supp. XXIII:** 293

Littlefield, Catherine, **Supp. IX:** 58

Little Fling, A (Pickering), **Supp. XXI:** 203

Little Foxes, The (Hellman), **Supp. I Part 1:** 276, 278–279, 281, 283, 297

"Little Fred, the Canal Boy" (Stowe), **Supp. I Part 2:** 587

"Little French Mary" (Jewett), **II:** 400

Little Friend, Little Friend (Jarrell), **II:** 367, 372, 375–376

"Little Gidding" (Eliot), **I:** 582, 588; **II:** 539; **Retro. Supp. I:** 66

"Little Girl, My Stringbean, My Lovely Woman" (Sexton), **Supp. II Part 2:** 686

"Little Girl, The" (Paley), **Supp. VI:** 222, **228–229**

"Little Girl Tells a Story to a Lady, A" (Barnes), **Supp. III Part 1:** 36

"Little Goose Girl, The" (Grimm), **IV:** 266

Little Ham (Hughes), **Retro. Supp. I:** 203; **Supp. I Part 1:** 328, 339

Little House in the Big Woods (L. I. Wilder), **Supp. XXII:** 294, 295, 296, 297, 298–299, 300

Little House on the Prairie (L. I. Wilder), **Supp. XXII:** 294, 295–296, 297, 299, 301

Little House on the Prairie (television series), **Supp. XXII:** 289

"Little House" series (L. A. Wilder), **Supp. XXII:** 289

Little House Traveler, A (L. I. Wilder), **Supp. XXII:** 301

Little Ignorance, A (Schott), **Supp. XXIII:** 239, 241

Little King, The (Bynner), **Supp. XV:** 42, 50

Little Lady of the Big House, The (London), **II:** 481–482

Little Liar, The (film; Ingraham), **Supp. XVI:** 184–185

"Little Lion Face" (Swenson), **Supp. IV Part 2:** 651

"Little Lobelia's Song" (Bogan), **Supp. III Part 1:** 66

"Little Local Color, A" (Henry), **Supp. II Part 1:** 399

Little Lord Fauntleroy (Burnett), **Retro. Supp. I:** 188; **Supp. XVI:** 182

"Little Lyric" (Hughes), **Supp. I Part 1:** 334

Little Man, Little Man (Baldwin), **Supp. I Part 1:** 67

"Little Man at Chehaw Station, The" (Ellison), **Retro. Supp. II:** 123

Little Me (musical), **Supp. IV Part 2:** 575

Little Men (Alcott), **Supp. I Part 1:** 32, 39, 40

"Little Morning Music, A" (Schwartz), **Supp. II Part 2:** 662–663

Little Ocean (Shepard), **Supp. III Part 2:** 447

"Little Old Girl, A" (Larcom), **Supp. XIII:** 144

"Little Old Spy" (Hughes), **Supp. I Part 1:** 329

Little Orphan Annie (film), **Supp. XVIII:** 244

"Little Owl Who Lives in the Orchard" (Oliver), **Supp. VII:** 239

"Little Peasant, The" (Sexton), **Supp. II Part 2:** 690

"Little People" (Kenny), **Supp. XXIII:** 151

"Little Rapids, The" (Swenson), **Supp. IV Part 2:** 645

Little Red Song Book (Hill), **Supp. XVIII:** 224

Little Regiment and Other Episodes of the American Civil War, The (Crane), **I:** 408

Little River: New and Selected Poems (McCarriston), **Supp. XIV: 269–272**

"Little Road not made of Man , A" (Dickinson), **Retro. Supp. I:** 44

Little Sister, The (Chandler), **Supp. IV Part 1:** 122, 130, 131–132

"Little Sleep's-Head Sprouting Hair in the Moonlight" (Kinnell), **Supp. III Part 1:** 247

"Little Snow White" (Grimm), **IV:** 266

"Little Spirit, or Boy-Man, The: An Odjibwa Tale"(J. Schoolcraft), **Supp. XXIII:** 234

Little Star (Halliday), **Supp. XIX:** 82, **84–85,** 87

"Little Star" (Halliday), **Supp. XIX:** 83, 84, 93

"Little Testament of Bernard Martin, Aet. 30" (Mumford), **Supp. II Part 2:** 472, 473, 474

"Little Things" (Olds), **Supp. X:** 208

Little Tour in France (James), **II:** 337

Little Town, The (Asch), **Supp. XXIII:** 4, 5, **7–8**

"Little Travel Diary, A"(O'Hara), **Supp. XXIII:** 220

Little Women (Alcott), **Supp. I Part 1:** 28, 29, 32, 35, 37, 38, 39–40, 41, 43, 44; **Supp. IX:** 128

Little Yellow Dog, A (Mosley), **Supp. XIII:** 237, 241

"Liturgy and Spiritual Personalism" (Merton), **Supp. VIII:** 199

Litz, A. Walton, **Retro. Supp. I:** 306

"Liu Ch'e" (Pound), **III:** 466

"Live" (Sexton), **Supp. II Part 2:** 684, 686

Live from Baghdad (screenplay, Shanley), **Supp. XIV:** 316

Live from Golgotha (Vidal), **Supp. IV Part 2:** 677, 682, 691, 692

Live Now and Pay Later (Garrett), **Supp. VII:** 111

"Live-Oak with Moss" (Whitman), **Retro. Supp. I:** 403

Live or Die (Sexton), **Supp. II Part 2:** 670, 683–687

Liveright, Horace, **Retro. Supp. I:** 80, 81, 83; **Supp. I Part 2:** 464; **Supp. XX: 71, 75; Supp. XXII:** 25

Livermore, Elizabeth, **Supp. XXII:** 70

Lives (Plutarch), **II:** 5, 104

Lives of a Cell, The (L. Thomas), **Retro. Supp. I:** 322, 323

Lives of Distinguished American Naval Officers (Cooper), **I:** 347

"Lives of Gulls and Children, The" (Nemerov), **III:** 271, 272

Lives of the Animals (Wrigley), **Supp. XVIII: 306–308**

Lives of the Artists (Vasari), **Supp. I Part 2:** 450

"Lives of the Bohemians" (Lethem), **Supp. XVIII:** 135

Lives of the Heart, The (Hirshfield), **Supp. XXIII:** 132–133, 135

Lives of the Muses, The: Nine Women and the Artists They Inspired (Prose), **Supp. XVI:** 250, 260

"Lives of the Philosophers, The" (Brockmeier), **Supp. XXII:** 59, 61

Lives of the Poets (Doctorow), **Supp. IV Part 1:** 234

"Lives of the Poets" (Doctorow), **Supp. IV Part 1:** 234

"Lives of the—Wha'?, The" (Goldbarth), **Supp. XII:** 191

"Living" (Wright), **Supp. XV:** 345

Living, The (Dillard), **Supp. VI:** 23

"Living at Home" (Gordon), **Supp. IV Part 1:** 311

Living by Fiction (Dillard), **Supp. VI:** 23, 31, **32,** 33

Living by the Word (Walker), **Supp. III Part 2:** 521, 522, 526, 527, 535

Living End, The (Elkin), **Supp. VI: 54,** 58

Living Instead (Bronk), **Supp. XXI:** 32

"Living in the Flatlands" (Carruth), **Supp. XVI:** 54

Living in Time (Hadas), **Supp. XXIII:** 120, **122–123**

Living Is Easy, The (D. West), **Supp. XVIII:** 277, 280, **284–286,** 287

"Living Like Weasels" (Dillard), **Supp. VI:** 26, 33

Living Novel, The (Hicks), **III:** 342

Living of Charlotte Perkins Gilman, The (Gilman), **Supp. XI:** 193, 209

Living off the Country: Essays on Poetry and Place (Haines), **Supp. XII:** 199, 203, 207

"Living on a Giant" (X. J. Kennedy), **Supp. XV:** 163

Living Out Loud (Quindlen), **Supp. XVII:** 166, **167–169**

Living Reed, The (Buck), **Supp. II Part 1:** 129–130

Livingston, Myra Cohn, **Supp. XV:** 153, 162

Living Theater, **Retro. Supp. I:** 424

"Living There" (Dickey), **Supp. IV Part 1:** 182–183

Living the Spirit: A Gay American Indian Anthology (Roscoe, ed.), **Supp. IV Part 1:** 330

Living to Prowl (Pickering), **Supp. XXI:** 203

"Living with a Peacock" (O'Connor), **III:** 350

"Livvie" (Welty), **IV:** 265; **Retro. Supp. I:** 348–349

"Livvie Is Back" (Welty), **Retro. Supp. I:** 351

Livy, **II:** 8

Lizzie (film), **Supp. IX:** 125

"Llantos de La Llorona: Warnings from the Wailer" (Mora), **Supp. XIII:** 217, 224

"L'Lapse" (Barthelme), **Supp. IV Part 1:** 45–47, 48

Llosa, Mario Vargas, **Supp. XIX:** 131

Lloyd, Fabien. *See* Cravan, Arthur

Lloyd, Henry Demarest, **Supp. I Part 1:** 5

Lloyd George, Harold, **I:** 490

"LMFBR" (Snyder), **Supp. VIII:** 302

Loach, Ken, **Supp. XXIII:** 163

"Loaded Inflections" (Halliday), **Supp. XIX:** 90, 91

"Loam" (Sandburg), **III:** 584–585

"Loan, The" (Malamud), **Supp. I Part 2:** 427, 428, 431, 437

Loberer, Eric, **Supp. XV:** 339

"Local" (McCarriston), **Supp. XIV:** 270

Local Color (Capote), **Supp. III Part 1:** 120

"Local Color" (London), **II:** 475

"Local Family Keeps Son Happy" (Keillor), **Supp. XVI:** 168, 169

Local Girls (Hoffman), **Supp. X:** 77, **90–91,** 92

"Local Girls" (Hoffman), **Supp. X:** 90

Local Habitation & A Name, A (Kooser), **Supp. XIX:** 116, 118, **119–120**

Local Men (Whitehead), **Supp. XV:** 339

Local Time (Dunn), **Supp. XI:** 143, **148–149**

Local Wonders: Seasons in the Bohemian Alps (Kooser), **Supp. XIX:** 115, **126**

"Location" (Halliday), **Supp. XIX:** 87

Lock, Helen, **Supp. XIII:** 233, 237–238

Lock, Robert H., **IV:** 319; **Retro. Supp. I:** 375

Locke, Alain, **Retro. Supp. II:** 115; **Supp. I Part 1:** 323, 325, 341; **Supp. II Part 1:** 53, 176, 182, 228, 247; **Supp. IV Part 1:** 170; **Supp. IX:** 306, 309; **Supp. X:** 134, 137, 139; **Supp. XIV: 195–219; Supp. XVIII:** 122; **Supp. XIX:** 69, 75; **Supp. XXII:** 7, 13

Locke, Duane, **Supp. IX:** 273

Locke, John, **I:** 554–555, 557; **II:** 15–16, 113–114, 348–349, 480; **III:** 294–295; **IV:** 149; **Supp. I Part 1:** 130, 229, 230; **Supp. I Part 2:** 523

Locke, Sondra, **II:** 588

"Locked House, A" (Snodgrass), **Supp. VI:** 323

Locked Room, The (Auster), **Supp. XII:** 22, 24, **27–28**

Locket, The (Masters), **Supp. I Part 2:** 460

Lockridge, Ross, Jr., **Supp. XIX:** 263

"Locksley Hall" (Tennyson), **Supp. IX:** 19

Lockwood Concern, The (O'Hara), **III:** 362, 364, 377–382

"Locus" (Ammons), **Supp. VII:** 28

"Locus" (Hayden), **Supp. II Part 1:** 361–362, 381

"Locusts, the Plaza, the Room, The" (Kees), **Supp. XV:** 141

Loden, Barbara, **III:** 163

Lodge, Henry Cabot, **I:** 11–12, 21

Lodge, Mrs. Henry Cabot, **I:** 11–12, 19

Lodge, Thomas, **IV:** 370

Loeb, Gerald, **Supp. IV Part 2:** 523

Loeb, Jacques, **I:** 513; **Retro. Supp. II:** 104; **Supp. I Part 2:** 641

Loeffler, Jack, **Supp. XIII:** 1, 3, 12, 14, 16

Loftus, Mary J., **Supp. XXI:** 245

Lofty Dogmas (A. Finch, M. Kumin and D. Brown, eds.), **Supp. XVII:** 75–76

"Log" (Merrlll), **Supp. III Part 1:** 328

Logan, Rayford W., **Supp. II Part 1:** 171, 194; **Supp. XIV:** 73

Logan, William, **Supp. X:** 201, 213; **Supp. XI:** 131, 132; **Supp. XII:** 98, 107, 113, 184; **Supp. XV:** 212, 226, 251, 257, 260–261, 262, **Supp. XV:** 263, 266

Log Book of "The Loved One," The, **Supp. XI:** 306

Logenbach, James, **Supp. XVII:** 183

"Logging and Pimping and 'Your Pal, Jim' " (Maclean), **Supp. XIV:** 229

Logue, Christopher, **Supp. XIV:** 82

Lohengrin (Wagner), **I:** 216

Lohrfinck, Rosalind, **III:** 107, 117

Lolita (Nabokov), **III:** 246, 247, 255, 258–261; **Retro. Supp. I:** 263, 264, 265, 266, 269, 270, **272–274,** 275; **Supp. V:** 127, 252; **Supp. VIII:** 133; **Supp. XVI:** 294; **Supp. XXII:** 260

"Lolita" (Parker), **Supp. IX:** 193

Lolly Dinks' Doings (E. Stoddard), **Supp. XV:** 273, **Supp. XV:** 286

Lombardi, Marilyn May, **Retro. Supp. II:** 40

London, Eliza, **II:** 465

London, Jack, **I:** 209; **II:** 264, 440, 444, 451, **462–485; III:** 314, 580; **Supp. IV Part 1:** 236; **Supp. V:** 281; **Supp. IX:** 1, 14; **Supp. XIII:** 312; **Supp. XIV:** 227; **Supp. XV:** 115; **Supp. XVI:** 181; **Supp. XVIII:** 90; **Supp. XXII:** 203

London, Mrs. Jack (Bessie Maddern), **II:** 465, 466, 473, 478

London, Mrs. Jack (Charmian Kittredge), **II:** 466, 468, 473, 476, 478, 481

London, John, **II:** 464, 465

London, Scott, **Supp. XIV:** 301, 307, 311

London Embassy, The (Theroux), **Supp. VIII:** 323

London Fields (Amis), **Retro. Supp. I:** 278

"London Letter" (column; Eliot), **Supp. XV:** 306

London Magazine (Plath), **Supp. I Part 2:** 541

London Snow: A Christmas Story (Theroux), **Supp. VIII:** 322

London Suite (Simon), **Supp. IV Part 2:** 576, 581, 582, 588

London: The Biography (Ackroyd), **Supp. XVII:** 180

Loneliness of the Long Distance Runner, The (Sillitoe), **Supp. XX:** 195

Lonely Are the Brave (film), **Supp. XIII:** 6

"Lonely Coast, A" (Proulx), **Supp. VII:** 264

Lonely Crusade (C. Himes), **Supp. XVI:** 135, 139–140

Lonely for the Future (Farrell), **II:** 46, 47

"Lonely Gay Teen Seeking Same" (Egan), **Supp. XIX:** 61

Lonely Impulse of Delight, A (Shanley), **Supp. XIV:** 317–318

"Lonely Street, The" (W. C. Williams), **IV:** 413

"Lonely Worker, A" (Jewett), **Retro. Supp. II:** 132

Lonergan, Wayne, **Supp. I Part 1:** 51

Lonesome Boy (Bontemps), **Supp. XXII:** 6, 13–14

Lonesome Dove (McMurtry), **Supp. V:** 226–228, 231, 232, 233

Lonesome Traveler (Kerouac), **Supp. III Part 1:** 219, 225

"Lonesome Whistle Blowing" (Skow), **Supp. XVI:** 174

"Lone Striker, A" (Frost), **Retro. Supp. I:** 136, 137

Long, Ada, **Supp. V:** 178

Long, Haniel, **Supp. XV:** 46, 49

Long, Huey, **I:** 489; **II:** 454; **IV:** 249; **Supp. IV Part 2:** 679; **Supp. XIV:** 14

Long, John Luther, **Supp. XXI:** 150

Long, Judith Reick, **Supp. XX: 212, 215, 217, 223**

Long, Ray, **II:** 430; **III:** 54

Long after Midnight (Bradbury), **Supp. IV Part 1:** 102

Long Ago in France: The Years in Dijon (M. F. K. Fisher), **Supp. XVII:** 91

Long and Happy Life, A (Price), **Supp. VI:** 258, **259–260,** 262, 264, 265

Long Approach, The (Kumin), **Supp. IV Part 2:** 452–453, 453

Longbottom, Robert, **Supp. XXI:** 148

Long Christmas Dinner, The (Wilder), **IV:** 357, 365; **Supp. V:** 105

Long Christmas Dinner and Other Plays (Wilder), **IV:** 365–366

Long Day's Dying, A (Buechner), **Supp. XII:** 45–47

Long Day's Journey into Night (O'Neill), **III:** 385, 401, 403–404; **Supp. IV Part 1:** 359; **Supp. XIV:** 327; **Supp. XXI:** 13; **Supp. XXII:** 27, 29, 30

Long Desire, A (Connell), **Supp. XIV:** 79, 80, 97

"Long Distance" (Stafford), **Supp. XI:** 329

"Long-Distance Runner, The" (Paley), **Supp. VI:** 221–222, 228, 230

Long Dream, The (Wright), **IV:** 478, 488, 494

"Long Embrace, The" (Levine), **Supp. V:** 187

"Long Enough" (Rukeyser), **Supp. VI:** 274

"Longest Night of My Life, The " (Nichols), **Supp. XIII:** 269

Longfellow, Henry Wadsworth, **I:** 458, 471; **II:** 274, 277, 295–296, 310, 313, 402, **486–510; III:** 269, 412, 421, 422, 577; **IV:** 309, 371; **Retro. Supp. I:** 54, 123, 150, 155, 362; **Retro. Supp. II: 153–174; Supp. I Part 1:** 158, 299, 306, 317, 362, 368; **Supp. I Part 2:** 405, 406, 408, 409, 414, 416, 420, 586, 587, 602, 699, 704; **Supp. II Part 1:** 291, 353; **Supp. III Part 2:** 609; **Supp. IV Part 1:** 165; **Supp. IV Part 2:** 503; **Supp. XII:** 260; **Supp. XIII:** 141; **Supp. XIV:** 120; **Supp. XVIII:** 4; **Supp. XXI:** 51; **Supp. XXIII:** 223

"Long Feud" (Untermeyer), **Supp. XV:** 309

Long Feud: Selected Poems (Untermeyer), **Supp. XV:** 312

"Long Fourth, A" (Taylor), **Supp. V:** 313

Long Fourth and Other Stories, A (Taylor), **Supp. V:** 318–319

Long Gay Book, A (Stein), **IV:** 42

Long Goodbye, The (Chandler), **Supp. IV Part 1:** 120, 122, 132–134, 135

Long Goodbye, The (T. Williams), **IV:** 381

"Long Hair" (Snyder), **Supp. VIII:** 300

Longing for Home, The: Recollections and Reflections (Buechner), **Supp. XII:** 53

Longinus, Dionysius Cassius, **I:** 279

"Long-Legged House, The" (Berry), **Supp. X:** 21, 24–25, 27, 31

Long Live Man (Corso), **Supp. XII:** 129–130, 132

Long Love, The (Sedges), **Supp. II Part 1:** 125

Long Made Short (Dixon), **Supp. XII:** 152

Long March, The (Styron), **IV:** 97, 99, 104–107, 111, 113, 117

"Long Night, The" (Bambara), **Supp. XI:** 9

"Long Novel, A" (Ashbery), **Supp. III Part 1:** 6

Longo, Robert, **Supp. XVI:** 124

Long Patrol, The (Mailer), **III:** 46

"Long Point Light" (Doty), **Supp. XI:** 127

Long Road of Woman's Memory, The (Addams), **Supp. I Part 1:** 17–18

"Long Run, The" (Wharton), **IV:** 314

Long Season, The (Brosnan), **II:** 424, 425; **Supp. XX:** 195

"Long Shadow of Lincoln, The: A Litany" (Sandburg), **III:** 591, 593

Longshot O'Leary (McGrath), **Supp. X:** 117

"Long Shower, The" (Francis), **Supp. IX:** 90

"Long Stemmed Roses" (Jarman), **Supp. XVII:** 115

Longstreet, Augustus B., **II:** 70, 313; **Supp. I Part 1:** 352; **Supp. V:** 44; **Supp. X:** 227

"Long Summer" (Lowell), **II:** 553–554

"Long Term" (Dunn), **Supp. XI:** 149

"Long Thoughts, The"(Dybek), **Supp. XXIII:** 71

Longtime Companion (film), **Supp. X:** 146, 152

Long Valley, The (Steinbeck), **IV:** 51

Long View (Taggard), **Supp. XXII: 283–284**

Long Voyage Home, The (O'Neill), **III:** 388

"Long Wail, A" (Crews), **Supp. XI:** 101

"Long Walk, The" (Bogan), **Supp. III Part 1:** 61

Long Walks and Intimate Talks (Paley), **Supp. VI:** 221

Long Way from Home, A (McKay), **Supp. X:** 132, 140

Long Winter, The (L. I. Wilder), **Supp. XXII:** 291, 294, 295

Lönnrot, Elias, **Retro. Supp. II:** 159

Looby, Christopher, **Supp. XIII:** 96

Look, Stranger! (Auden), **Supp. II Part 1:** 11

"Look, The" (Olds), **Supp. X:** 210

Look at Me (Egan), **Supp. XIX:** 49, **53–56,** 60, 61

Look at the Harlequins (Nabokov), **Retro. Supp. I:** 266, 270

"Look for My White Self" (Ammons), **Supp. VII:** 25

Look Homeward, Angel (Wolfe), **II:** 457; **IV:** 450, 452, 453, 454, 455–456, 461, 462, 463, 464, 468, 471; **Supp. XI:** 216

"Looking" (Sanders), **Supp. XVI:** 277

"Looking a Mad Dog Dead in the Eyes" (Komunyakaa), **Supp. XIII:** 114

"Looking at Each Other" (Rukeyser), **Supp. VI:** 280, 285–286

"Looking at Kafka" (P. Roth), **Supp. III Part 2:** 402

"Looking at Women" (Sanders), **Supp. XVI:** 274

"Looking Back" (Harjo), **Supp. XII:** 218

"Looking Back" (Merwin), **Supp. III Part 1:** 352

"Looking Back at Girlhood" (Jewett), **Retro. Supp. II:** 131, 133

Looking Backward (Bellamy), **II:** 276; **Supp. I Part 2:** 641; **Supp. XI:** 200

"Looking for a Ship" (McPhee), **Supp. III Part 1:** 312–313

"Looking for Dragon Smoke" (R. Bly), **Supp. IV Part 1:** 60

Looking for Holes in the Ceiling (Dunn), **Supp. XI:** 139, **143–145**

Looking for Langston (Julien; film), **Supp. XI:** 19, 20

Looking for Lincoln (television production), **Supp. XX:** 99

Looking for Luck (Kumin), **Supp. IV Part 2:** 453, 454–455

"Looking for Mr. Green" (Bellow), **Retro. Supp. II:** 27

"Looking for the Buckhead Boys" (Dickey), **Supp. IV Part 1:** 182, 183

"Looking Forward to Age" (Harrison), **Supp. VIII:** 49

"Looking from Inside My Body" (R. Bly), **Supp. IV Part 1:** 71

"Looking Glass, The" (Wharton), **Retro. Supp. I:** 382

"Lookout's Journal" (Snyder), **Supp. VIII:** 291

"Looks Like They'll Never Learn" (McCoy), **Supp. XIII:** 166

"Look to the Woods" (P. N. Warren), **Supp. XX:** **272**

"Look to Thy Heart . . ." (Hay), **Supp. XIV:** 130

Loon, Hendrik Willem van, **Supp. XVI:** 185

Loon Lake (Doctorow), **Supp. IV Part 1:** 219, 222, 224–227, 230, 231, 232, 233

"Loon Point" (O'Brien), **Supp. V:** 237

Loos, Adolf, **Supp. XVI:** 187

Loos, Anita, **Supp. XVI:** **181–199**

Loos, Mary Anita, **Supp. XVI:** 196

Loose Canons (H. L. Gates), **Supp. XX:** **101, 108, 109–110, 111**

Loosestrife (Dunn), **Supp. XI:** **152–154**

"Loosestrife" (Dunn), **Supp. XI:** 154

"Loose Woman" (X. J. Kennedy), **Supp. XV:** 159

Loose Woman: Poems (Cisneros), **Supp. VII:** 58, 71–72

Lopate, Edward, **Supp. XVI:** 266

Lopate, Philip, **Supp. XII:** 184; **Supp. XIII:** 280–281; **Supp. XVI:** 230

Lopatnikoff, Nikolai, **Supp. XIV:** 123

Lopez, Barry, **Supp. IV Part 1:** 416; **Supp. V:** 211; **Supp. X:** 29, 31; **Supp. XIII:** 16; **Supp. XIV:** 227

Lopez, Rafael, **Supp. IV Part 2:** 602

Lorax, The (Geisel), **Supp. XVI:** 109–110

Lorca, Federico García, **IV:** 380; **Supp. I Part 1:** 345; **Supp. IV Part 1:** 83; **Supp. VIII:** 38, 39; **Supp. XIII:** 315, 323, 324; **Supp. XV:** 186; **Supp. XXI:** 100

Lord, Judge Otis P., **I:** 454, 457, 458, 470

Lorde, Audre, **Supp. I Part 2:** 550, 571; **Supp. IV Part 1:** 325; **Supp. XI:** 20; **Supp. XII:** 217, 220; **Supp. XIII:** 295; **Supp. XVII:** 71; **Supp. XXIII:** 194

Lord Jim (Conrad), **I:** 422; **II:** 26; **Retro. Supp. II:** 292; **Supp. I Part 2:** 623; **Supp. IV Part 2:** 680; **Supp. V:** 251

"Lord of Hosts" (Pinsky), **Supp. VI:** 244

Lord of the Flies (W. Golding), **Supp. XVI:** 65

Lord of the Rings (Tolkien), **Supp. V:** 140

Lords of Misrule, The (X. J. Kennedy), **Supp. XV:** 154, **170–171**

Lords of the Housetops (Van Vechten), **Supp. II Part 2:** 736

Lord's Prayer, **I:** 579

Lord Timothy Dexter of Newburyport, Mass. (Marquand), **III:** 55

Lord Weary's Castle (Lowell), **II:** 538, 542–551; **Retro. Supp. II:** 178, **186–187**, 188; **Supp. XV:** 252

"Lorelei" (Plath), **Retro. Supp. II:** 246; **Supp. I Part 2:** 538

"Lorenzo" (Bynner), **Supp. XV:** 46, 50

Lorimer, George Horace, **II:** 430; **Retro. Supp. I:** 101, 113

Lorre, Peter, **Supp. IV Part 1:** 356

"Los Alamos" (Momaday), **Supp. IV Part 2:** 482

Los Amigos de Becky (Hinojosa). *See Becky and Her Friends* (Hinojosa)

"Los Angeles, 1980" (Gunn Allen), **Supp. IV Part 1:** 325

"Los Angeles Days" (Didion), **Supp. IV Part 1:** 211

"Lo! School in Poetry, The" (Taggard), **Supp. XXII:** 276

"Loser, The" (Talese), **Supp. XVII:** 202, 208

Loser and Still Champion: Muhammad Ali (Schulberg), **Supp. XVIII:** 254

Losey, Joseph, **IV:** 383

Lose Your Mother: A Journey Along the Atlantic Slave Route (Hartman), **Supp. XX:** **154**

"Losing a Language" (Merwin), **Supp. III Part 1:** 356

Losing Battles (Welty), **IV:** 261, 281–282; **Retro. Supp. I:** 341, 352, **353–354**

"Losing the Marbles" (Merrill), **Supp. III Part 1:** 337

"Losing Track of Language" (Clampitt), **Supp. IX:** 38, 40

Losses (Jarrell), **II:** 367, 372, 373–375, 376, 377, 380–381

"Losses" (Jarrell), **II:** 375–376

Lossky, N. O., **Supp. IV Part 2:** 519

"Loss of Breath" (Poe), **III:** 425–426

"Loss of My Arms and Legs, The" (Kingsolver), **Supp. VII:** 208

"Loss of the Creature, The" (Percy), **Supp. III Part 1:** 387

"Lost" (Wagoner), **Supp. IX:** 328

"Lost, The/Los Perdidos" (Kingsolver), **Supp. VII:** 208

"Lost and Found" (Levine), **Supp. V:** 188

"Lost and Found" (Nelson), **Supp. XVIII:** 176

"Lost Bodies" (Wright), **Supp. V:** 342

"Lost Boy, The" (Wolfe), **IV:** 451, 460, 466–467

"Lost Children, The" (Crooker), **Supp. XXIII:** 54

"Lost Decade, The" (Fitzgerald), **II:** 98

"Lost Fugue for Chet" (Hull), **Supp. XXI:** 137–138, 141

Lost Galleon and Other Tales, The (Harte), **Supp. II Part 1:** 344

Lost Get-Back Boogie, The (Burke), **Supp. XIV:** 22, 25

"Lost Girls, The" (Hogan), **Supp. IV Part 1:** 406–407

Lost Grizzlies, The: A Search for Survivors in the Wilderness of Colorado (Bass), **Supp. XVI:** 25, 26

Lost Highway (film), **Supp. X:** 314

Lost Illusions (Balzac), **I:** 500

"Lost in Nostalgia: The Autobiographies of Eva Hoffman and Richard Rodriguez" (Fachinger), **Supp. XVI:** 153

Lost in the Bonewheel Factory (Komunyakaa), **Supp. XIII:** **114–115**, 116

Lost in the City (E. P. Jones), **Supp. XXII:** 140, 142, **143–146**, 148, 149

Lost in the Cosmos: The Last Self-Help Book (Percy), **Supp. III Part 1:** 397

Lost in the Funhouse (Barth), **I:** 122, 135, 139; **Supp. X:** 307

"Lost in the Whichy Thicket" (Wolfe), **Supp. III Part 2:** 573, 574

Lost in Translation (E. Hoffman), **Supp. XVI:** 147, **148–151**, 153, 154, 159

"Lost in Translation" (Hass), **Supp. VIII:** 28

"Lost in Translation" (Merrill), **Supp. III Part 1:** 324, 329–330

Lost in Yonkers (film), **Supp. IV Part 2:** 588

Lost in Yonkers (Simon), **Supp. IV Part 2:** 576, 577, 584, 587–588, 590–591

"Lost Jerusalem" (Untermeyer), **Supp. XV:** 307

Lost Lady, A (Cather), **I:** 323–325, 327; **Retro. Supp. I:** **15–16**, 20, 21, 382

Lost Light (Connelly), **Supp. XXI:** 72, **75–76**

"Lost Lives" (Sorrentino), **Supp. XXI:** 226

"Lost Lover, A" (Jewett), **II:** 400–401, 402; **Retro. Supp. II:** 137

"Lost Loves" (Kinnell), **Supp. III Part 1:** 237, 245

Lost Man's River (Matthiessen), **Supp. V:** 212, 213, 214, 215

"Lost on September Trail, 1967" (Ríos), **Supp. IV Part 2:** 540

Lost Puritan (Mariani), **Retro. Supp. II:** 189

Lost Roads Project, The: A Walk-In Book of Arkansas (exhibition; Wright and Luster), **Supp. XV:** 337, 348

"Lost Sailor, The" (Freneau), **Supp. II Part 1:** 264

Lost Son, The (Roethke), **III:** 529, 530–532, 533

"Lost Son, The" (Roethke), **III:** 536, 537–539, 542

"Lost Sons" (Salter), **Supp. IX:** 260

Lost Souls (Singer). *See* Meshugah (Singer)

"Lost"(Thompson), **Supp. XXIII:** 299, 300

Lost Weekend, The (Jackson), **Supp. XIII:** 262

"Lost World, A" (Ashbery), **Supp. III Part 1:** 9

"Lost World, The" (Chabon), **Supp. XI:** 72–73

Lost World, The (Jarrell), **II:** 367, 368, 371, 379–380, 386, 387

"Lost World, The" cycle (Chabon), **Supp. XI: 71–73**

"Lost World of Richard Yates, The: How the Great Writer of the Age of Anxiety Disappeared from Print" (O'Nan), **Supp. XI:** 348

"Lost Young Intellectual, The" (Howe), **Supp. VI:** 113, **115–116**

Lost Zoo, The: (A Rhyme for the Young, But Not Too Young) (Cullen), **Supp. IV Part 1:** 173

Loti, Pierre, **II:** 311, 325; **Supp. IV Part 1:** 81

"Lot of People Bathing in a Stream, A" (Stevens), **IV:** 93

Lotringer, Sylvère, **Supp. XII:** 4

"Lot's Wife" (Nemerov), **III:** 270

"Lottery, The" (Jackson), **Supp. IX:** 113, 114, 118, 120, **122–123**

Lottery, The; or, The Adventures of James Harris (Jackson), **Supp. IX:** 113, 115, 116, 124, 125

Lotze, Hermann, **III:** 600

Loud and Clear (Quindlen), **Supp. XVII:** 167, **170–172**

Louganis, Greg, **Supp. XX: 264**

"Louie, His Cousin & His Other Cousin" (Cisneros), **Supp. VII:** 60

Louis, Joe, **II:** 589; **Supp. IV Part 1:** 360

Louis, Pierre Charles Alexandre, **Supp. I Part 1:** 302, 303

"Louisa, Please Come Home" (Jackson), **Supp. IX:** 122

Louis Lambert (Balzac), **I:** 499

"Louis Simpson and Walt Whitman: Destroying the Teacher" (Lazer), **Supp. IX:** 265

"Louis Zukofsky: All: The Collected Short Poems, 1923–1958" (Creeley), **Supp. IV Part 1:** 154

"Lounge" (Francis), **Supp. IX:** 83

Lounsberry, Barbara, **Supp. XVII:** 208

Lounsbury, Thomas R., **I:** 335

Louter, Jan, **Supp. XI:** 173

"Love" (Collins), **Supp. XXI:** 61

"Love," (Gibran), **Supp. XX: 119**

"Love" (Olson), **Supp. II Part 2:** 571

"Love" (Paley), **Supp. VI:** 219, 222, 230

Love, Deborah, **Supp. V:** 208, 210

Love Alone: 18 Elegies for Rog (Monette), **Supp. X:** 146, 154

Love Always (Beattie), **Supp. V:** 29, 30, 35

Love among the Cannibals (Morris), **III:** 228, 230–231

"Love Among the Ruins" (Mosley), **Supp. XIII:** 247

Love and Death (film; Allen), **Supp. XV:** 2, **5–6**, 7, 11

Love and Death in the American Novel (Fiedler), **Supp. XIII:** 93, 96, **99–101**, 104

Love and Exile (Singer), **Retro. Supp. II: 302–304**, 315

Love and Fame (Berryman), **I:** 170

Love and Friendship (Bloom), **Retro. Supp. II:** 31, 33–34

Love and Glory (Parker), **Supp. XIX:** 189

"Love and How to Cure It" (Wilder), **IV:** 365

Love and Other Games of Chance (Siegel), **Supp. XXII:** 255, 256, **261–265**, 266, 267

Love and Scorn: New and Selected Poems (C. Frost), **Supp. XV:** 95, 96, 100, 103–105, 106

Love and Theft (album, Dylan), **Supp. XVIII:** 28, 31

"Love and the Hate, The" (Jeffers), **Supp. II Part 2:** 434–435

Love and the Incredibly Old Man (Siegel), **Supp. XXII: 267–268**

Love and Will (Dixon), **Supp. XII:** 148, 149

Love and Work (Price), **Supp. VI:** 261

"Love as a Great Power" (Bronk), **Supp. XXI:** 31

"Love Calls Us to the Things of This World" (Wilbur), **Supp. III Part 2:** 544, 552–553

Love Course, The (Gurney), **Supp. V:** 98

Lovecraft, H. P., **Supp. XXII:** 49

Loved One, The (film), **Supp. XI: 305–306**, 307

Loved One, The (Waugh), **Supp. XI:** 305

Love Expert, The (film; Kirkland), **Supp. XVI:** 186

Love Feast (Buechner), **Supp. XII:** 52

Love for Love (Congreve), **Supp. XVIII:** 12

"Love Fossil" (Olds), **Supp. X:** 203

"Love"(Hadas), **Supp. XXIII:** 117

Love in a Dead Language (Siegel), **Supp. XXII:** 255, **258–261**, 265–266, 267

Love in Buffalo (Gurney), **Supp. V:** 96

"Love—In Other Words" (Lee), **Supp. VIII:** 113

"Love in the Air" (Jin), **Supp. XVIII:** 93–94

"Love in the Morning" (Dubus), **Supp. VII:** 91

Love in the Ruins: The Adventures of a Bad Catholic at a Time near the End of the World (Percy), **Supp. III Part 1:** 385, 387, 393–394, 397–398

Love in the Western World (de Rougemont), **Retro. Supp. I:** 328

"Love Is a Deep and a Dark and a Lonely" (Sandburg), **III:** 595

Lovejoy, Elijah P., **Supp. I Part 2:** 588

Lovejoy, Owen R., **Supp. I Part 1:** 8

Lovejoy, Thomas, **Supp. X:** 108

Lovelace, Richard, **II:** 590

"Love Letter (Schnackenberg), **Supp. XV:** 258–259

Love Letters (film), **Supp. IV Part 2:** 524

Love Letters (Gurney), **Supp. V:** 105, 108–109

Love Letters, The (Massie), **Supp. IV Part 2:** 524

Love Letters and Two Other Plays: The Golden Age and What I Did Last Summer (Gurney), **Supp. V:** 100

"Love Lies Sleeping" (Bishop), **Retro. Supp. II:** 42

Love Life (Mason), **Supp. VIII:** 145–146

"Love Life" (Mason), **Supp. VIII: 145–146**

Lovell, Julia, **Supp. XVIII:** 101

Lovely Bones, The (Sebold), **Supp. XXII:** 55

Lovely Lady, The (Lawrence), **Retro. Supp. I:** 203

"Lovely Lady, The" (Lawrence), **Supp. I Part 1:** 329

Love Me (Keillor), **Supp. XVI:** 178

Love Medicine (expanded version) (Erdrich), **Supp. IV Part 1:** 263, 273, 274, 275

Love Medicine (Erdrich), **Supp. IV Part 1:** 259, 260, 261, 263, 265, 266, 267–268, 270, 271, 274–275; **Supp. X:** 290

"Love Minus Zero/No Limit" (song, Dylan), **Supp. XVIII:** 31

"Love Nest, The" (Lardner), **II:** 427, 429

Love Nest, The, and Other Stories (Lardner), **II:** 430–431, 436

Lovenheim, Barbara, **Supp. X:** 169

"Love of Annunziata, The" (di Donato), **Supp. XX: 40**

"Love of Elsie Barton: A Chronicle, The" (Warren), **IV:** 253

Love of Landry, The (Dunbar), **Supp. II Part 1:** 212

"Love of Morning, The" (Levertov), **Supp. III Part 1:** 284

Love of the Last Tycoon, The: A Western. See Last Tycoon, The

"Love on the Bon Dieu" (Chopin), **Supp. I Part 1:** 213

Love on the Hoof (O'Hara and Lima), **Supp. XXIII:** 217

Love Poems (Sexton), **Supp. II Part 2:** 687–689

Love Poems (Tentative Title) (O'Hara), **Supp. XXIII:** 219

Love Poems of May Swenson, The (Swenson), **Supp. IV Part 2:** 652, 653

"Love Poet" (Agee), **I:** 28

"Lover" (Hoffman), **Supp. XVIII:** 87

"Love Ritual" (Mora), **Supp. XIII:** 215

Loveroot (Jong), **Supp. V:** 115, 130
"Lovers, The" (Berryman), **I:** 174
"Lovers, The" (Buck), **Supp. II Part 1:** 128
"Lover's Garden, A" (Ginsberg), **Supp. II Part 1:** 311
"Lovers of the Poor, The" (Brooks), **Supp. III Part 1:** 81, 85
Lovers Should Marry (Martin), **Supp. IV Part 1:** 351
"Lover's Song" (Yeats), **Supp. I Part 1:** 80
"Love Rushes By" (Salinas), **Supp. XIII:** 326–327
"Love's Ghost" (Nelson), **Supp. XVIII:** 176
Lovesick (Stern), **Supp. IX: 295–296**
Love's Labour's Lost (Shakespeare), **III:** 263
Love's Old Sweet Song (Saroyan), **Supp. IV Part 1:** 83
"Love Song During Riot with Many Voices" (Hull), **Supp. XXI:** 136
"Love Song of J. Alfred Prufrock, The" (T. S. Eliot), **I:** 52, 66, 569–570; **III:** 460; **Retro. Supp. I:** 55, 56, 57, 60; **Supp. II Part 1:** 5; **Supp. XIII:** 346; **Supp. XVI:** 150
"Love Song of St. Sebastian" (Eliot), **Retro. Supp. I:** 57
"Love Songs" (Loy), **Supp. XXII:** 161
"Love Songs to Joannes" (Loy), **Supp. XXII:** 161, 163
Love's Pilgrimage (Sinclair), **Supp. V:** 286
"Love the Wild Swan" (Jeffers), **Supp. VIII:** 33
Love to Mamá: A Tribute to Mothers (Mora, ed.), **Supp. XIII:** 221
Lovett, Robert Morss, **II:** 43
"Love-Unknown" (Herbert), **Supp. I Part 1:** 80
Love! Valor! Compassion! (film), **Supp. XIII:** 206
Love! Valour! Compassion! (McNally), **Supp. XIII:** 199, **203–204**, 208, 209
"Love *versus* Law" (Stowe), **Supp. I Part 2:** 585–586
"Love Wall" (Peacock), **Supp. XIX:** 200
Love with a Few Hairs (Mrabet), **Supp. IV Part 1:** 92
Loving a Woman in Two Worlds (R. Bly), **Supp. IV Part 1:** 66, 67, 68–69, 71, 72
Loving in the War Years: Lo que nunca pasó por sus labios (Moraga), **Supp. XXIII:** 194, 195
"Loving on Borrowed Time" (J. W. Miller), **Supp. XX: 164**
"Loving Shepherdess, The" (Jeffers), **Supp. II Part 2:** 432
"Loving the Killer" (Sexton), **Supp. II Part 2:** 688
"Loving Wife" (C. Miller), **Supp. XXII:** 196–197, 199
Lovin' Molly (film), **Supp. V:** 223, 226
Low Country (Siddons), **Supp. XXII:** 239
Lowe, John, **Supp. XIII:** 238
Lowe, Pardee, **Supp. X:** 291

Lowell, Abbott Lawrence, **I:** 487; **II:** 513; **Supp. I Part 2:** 483
Lowell, Amy, **I:** 231, 384, 405, 475, 487; **II:** 174, **511–533**, 534; **III:** 465, 581, 586; **Retro. Supp. I:** 131, 133, 288; **Retro. Supp. II:** 46, 175; **Supp. I Part 1:** 257–259, 261–263, 265, 266; **Supp. I Part 2:** 465, 466, 707, 714, 729; **Supp. XIV:** 128; **Supp. XV:** 43, 293, 295, 297, 298, 299, 300, 301, 303, 306; **Supp. XX: 69; Supp. XXII:** 161
Lowell, Blanche, **Supp. I Part 2:** 409
Lowell, Harriet, **II:** 553, 554
Lowell, James Russell, **I:** 216, 458; **II:** 273, 274, 289, 302, 320, 402, 529, 530, 532, 534, 551; **III:** 409; **IV:** 129, 171, 175, 180, 182–183, 186; **Retro. Supp. I:** 228; **Retro. Supp. II:** 155, 175, 326; **Supp. I Part 1:** 168, 299, 300, 303, 306, 311, 312, 317, 318, 362; **Supp. I Part 2: 404–426; Supp. II Part 1:** 197, 291, 352; **Supp. XV:** 278, 279; **Supp. XVI:** 84; **Supp. XVIII:** 2–3, 4, 8, 12
Lowell, Mrs. James Russell (Maria White), **Supp. I Part 2:** 405, 406, 414, 424
Lowell, Percival, **II:** 513, 525, 534
Lowell, Robert, **I:** 172, 381, 382, 400, 442, 521, 544–545, 550; **II:** 371, 376, 377, 384, 386–387, 532, **534–557; III:** 39, 44, 142, 508, 527, 528–529, 606; **IV:** 120, 138, 402, 430; **Retro. Supp. I:** 67, 140, 411; **Retro. Supp. II:** 27, 40, 44, 46, 48, 50, **175–193,** 221, 228–229, 235, 245; **Supp. I Part 1:** 89; **Supp. I Part 2:** 538, 543, 554; **Supp. III Part 1:** 6, 64, 84, 138, 147, 193, 194, 197–202, 205–208; **Supp. III Part 2:** 541, 543, 555, 561, 599; **Supp. IV Part 2:** 439, 620, 637; **Supp. V:** 81, 179, 180, 315–316, 337, 344; **Supp. VIII:** 27, 100, 271; **Supp. IX:** 325; **Supp. X:** 53, 58; **Supp. XI:** 146, 240, 244, 250, 317; **Supp. XII:** 253–254, 255; **Supp. XIII:** 76; **Supp. XIV:** 15, 126, 269; **Supp. XV:** 20, 22, 93, 184, 249, 251, 253, 340; **Supp. XVII:** 239; **Supp. XIX:** 197; **Supp. XX: 199, 203; Supp. XXI:** 131; **Supp. XXIII:** 211, 220
Lowell, Rose, **Supp. I Part 2:** 409
"Lowell in the Classroom" (Vendler), **Retro. Supp. II:** 191
Lowenthal, Michael, **Supp. XII:** 82
Lower Depths, The (Gorki), **III:** 402
"Lower the Standard" (Shapiro), **Supp. II Part 2:** 715
Lowes, John Livingston, **II:** 512, 516, 532; **IV:** 453, 455
Lowin, Joseph, **Supp. V:** 273
"Low-Lands" (Pynchon), **Supp. II Part 2:** 620, 624
Lowle, Percival, **Supp. I Part 2:** 404
Lownsbrough, John, **Supp. IV Part 1:** 209, 211
Lowry, Beverly, **Supp. XXI:** 48
Lowry, Malcolm, **Supp. XVII:** 135, 136
Lowth, Richard, **II:** 8

Loy, Mina, **III:** 194; **Supp. XXII: 155–170**
Loy, Myrna, **Supp. IV Part 1:** 355
"Loyal Woman's No, A" (Larcom), **Supp. XIII:** 142, 143–144
"Luani of the Jungle" (Hughes), **Supp. I Part 1:** 328
Lubbock, Percy, **I:** 504; **II:** 337; **IV:** 308, 314, 319, 322; **Retro. Supp. I:** 366, 367, 373; **Supp. VIII:** 165; **Supp. XX: 231**
Lubin, Isidor, **Supp. I Part 2:** 632
Lubow, Arthur, **Supp. VIII:** 310
Lucas, Victoria (pseudonym). *See* Plath, Sylvia
Luce, Dianne C., **Supp. VIII:** 189
Lucid, Robert F., **Retro. Supp. II:** 195, 204
"Lucid Eye in Silver Town, The" (Updike), **IV:** 218
"Lucid Walking" (A. Finch), **Supp. XVII:** 72
"Lucinda Matlock" (Masters), **Supp. I Part 2:** 461, 465
"Luck" (Dunn), **Supp. XI:** 149
Luck of Barry Lyndon, The (Thackeray), **II:** 290
"Luck of Roaring Camp, The" (Harte), **Supp. II Part 1:** 335, 344, 345–347
"Luck of the Bogans, The" (Jewett), **Retro. Supp. II:** 142
Lucky Life (Stern), **Supp. IX: 290–291**
"Lucky Lucy's Daily Dream Book" (Di Piero), **Supp. XIX:** 38–39
Lucretius, **I:** 59; **II:** 162, 163; **III:** 600, 610–611, 612; **Supp. I Part 1:** 363
Lucy (Kincaid), **Supp. VII:** 180, 185, 186, 187–188, 194
Lucy, Saint, **II:** 211
Lucy Crown (Shaw), **Supp. XIX:** 251
Lucy Gayheart (Cather), **I:** 331; **Retro. Supp. I:** 19
"Lucy Tavish's Journey" (E. Stoddard), **Supp. XV:** 286
Lucy Temple (Rowson). *See Charlotte's Daughter; or, The Three Orphans*
Ludlow, Andrea, **Supp. XVIII:** 90
Ludvigson, Susan, **Supp. IV Part 2:** 442, 446, 447, 448, 451
Lueders, Edward, **Supp. XVI:** 265
"Luggage" (Bidart), **Supp. XV:** 35
Luhan, Mabel Dodge, **Retro. Supp. I:** 7; **Supp. XV:** 46, 50. *See also* Dodge, Mabel
Lu Ji, **Supp. VIII:** 303
Luke (biblical book), **III:** 606
"Luke Havergal" (E. A. Robinson), **Supp. XVII:** 69
"Luke Havergal" (Robinson), **III:** 524
Lukeman, Gary, **Supp. XV:** 221
Luks, George, **IV:** 411; **Retro. Supp. II:** 103
"Lullaby" (Auden), **Supp. II Part 1:** 9
"Lullaby" (Bishop), **Supp. I Part 1:** 85
"Lullaby" (Everwine), **Supp. XV:** 89
"Lullaby" (Silko), **Supp. IV Part 2:** 560, 568–569
"Lullaby for Amy" (Jarman), **Supp. XVII:** 113, 121

"Lullaby of Cape Cod" (Brodsky), **Supp. VIII:** 27–28

Lullaby Raft (Nye), **Supp. XIII:** 278

Lullaby Raft (Nye, album), **Supp. XIII:** 274

Lullaby: The Comforting of Cock Robin (Snodgrass), **Supp. VI:** 324

"Lulls" (Walker), **Supp. III Part 2:** 525

"Lulu" (Wedekind), **Supp. XII:** 14

Lulu on the Bridge (film), **Supp. XII:** 21

Lulu's Library (Alcott), **Supp. I Part 1:** 43

"Lumber" (Baker), **Supp. XIII:** 55, 56

"Lumens, The" (Olds), **Supp. X:** 209

Lume Spento, A (Pound), **III:** 470

Lumet, Sidney, **Supp. IV Part 1:** 236; **Supp. IX:** 253

Luminous Debris: Reflecting on Vestige in Provence and Languedoc (Sobin), **Supp. XVI:** 291–293, 293–294

"Lumumba's Grave" (Hughes), **Supp. I Part 1:** 344

"Luna, Luna" (Mora), **Supp. XIII:** 217

Lunar Baedecker (Loy), **Supp. XXII:** 165,**Supp. XXII:** 167, 166, 168

Lunar Baedecker and Time-Tables (Loy), **Supp. XXII:** 168

Lunar Follies (Sorrentino), **Supp. XXI:** 226, 237, 238–239

Lunch Poems (O'Hara), **Supp. XXIII:** 219–220, 220

Lunsford, Bascom Lamar, **Supp. XX:** 163

Lupercal (Hughes), **Retro. Supp. II:** 245; **Supp. I Part 2:** 540

Lupton, Mary Jane, **Supp. IV Part 1:** 7

Lure of the Labrador Wild, The (Wallace), **Supp. XXII:** 218

Luria, Isaac, **IV:** 7

Lurie, Alison, **Supp. X:** 166; **Supp. XVI:** 103, 111–112

Lust and Other Stories (Minot), **Supp. VI:** 205

Luster, Deborah, **Supp. XV:** 337,**Supp. XV:** 353, 348, 349, 350

Lustgarten, Edith, **III:** 107

Lustra (Pound), **Retro. Supp. I:** 289, 290

Luther, Martin, **II:** 11–12, 506; **III:** 306, 607; **IV:** 490

"Luther on Sweet Auburn" (Bambara), **Supp. XI:** 16–17

Lux, Thomas, **Supp. XI:** 270; **Supp. XIX:** 276

Luxury Girl, The (McCoy), **Supp. XIII:** 163

Lyall, Sarah, **Supp. XIII:** 247

Lycidas (Milton), **II:** 540; **IV:** 347; **Retro. Supp. I:** 60; **Retro. Supp. II:** 186; **Supp. I Part 1:** 370; **Supp. IX:** 41

Lycographia (Paullini), **Supp. XVII:** 55

"Lydia and Marian" (Rowson), **Supp. XV:** 234

Lydon, Susan, **Supp. XII:** 170

Lyell, Charles, **Supp. IX:** 180

Lyell, Frank H., **Supp. VIII:** 125

Lyford, Harry, **Supp. I Part 2:** 679

"Lying" (Wilbur), **Supp. III Part 2:** 547, 562

"Lying and Looking" (Swenson), **Supp. IV Part 2:** 652

"Lying in a Hammock at William Duffy's Farm in Pine Island, Minnesota" (Wright), **Supp. III Part 2:** 589, 599, 600

"Lying in the Pollen and Water" (C. Frost), **Supp. XV:** 96

Lying Ladies, The (Ryan as Finnegan), **Supp. XVIII:** 233–235, 237

Lyles, Lois F., **Supp. XI:** 7, 8

Lyly, John, **III:** 536; **Supp. I Part 1:** 369

Lynch, Anne, **Supp. XV:** 273

Lynch, Doris, **Supp. XVI:** 294

Lynchburg (Gander), **Supp. XV:** 340

"Lynched Man, The" (Karr), **Supp. XI:** 241

Lynchers, The (Wideman), **Supp. X:** 320

"Lynching, The" (McKay), **Supp. I Part 1:** 63

"Lynching of Jube Benson, The" (Dunbar), **Supp. II Part 1:** 214

"Lynching Song" (Hughes), **Supp. I Part 1:** 331

Lynd, Staughton, **Supp. VIII:** 240

Lynda Hull: Collected Poems (Hull), **Supp. XXI:** 129

Lynn, Kenneth, **Supp. XIII:** 96–97

Lynn, Kenneth S., **Supp. XIV:** 103

Lynn, Vera, **Supp. XI:** 304

Lyon, George Ella, **Supp. XX:** 161–162

Lyon, Kate, **I:** 409; **II:** 138, 143, 144

Lyon, Thomas, **Supp. IX:** 175

"Lyonnesse" (Plath), **Supp. I Part 2:** 541

Lyons, Bonnie, **Supp. V:** 58; **Supp. VIII:** 138

Lyotard, Jean-François, **Supp. IV Part 1:** 54

Lyrical Ballads (Wordsworth), **III:** 583; **IV:** 120; **Supp. IX:** 274; **Supp. XI:** 243; **Supp. XV:** 21; **Supp. XIX:** 1

Lyrics of Love and Laughter (Dunbar), **Supp. II Part 1:** 207

Lyrics of Lowly Life (Dunbar), **Supp. II Part 1:** 197, 199, 200, 207

Lyrics of the Hearthside (Dunbar), **Supp. II Part 1:** 206

Lytal, Tammy, **Supp. XI:** 102

Lytle, Andrew, **IV:** 125; **Retro. Supp. II:** 220, 221, 235; **Supp. II Part 1:** 139; **Supp. X:** 1, 25; **Supp. XI:** 101

Lyttelton, Alfred, **Supp. XX:** 230

Lytton of Knebworth. *See* Bulwer-Lytton, Edward George

M

Mabie, Hamilton W., **Supp. XVIII:** 257

MCabe, Susan, **Supp. XXII:** 234

McAlexander, Hubert H., **Supp. V:** 314, 319, 320, 323

McAlmon, Robert, **IV:** 404; **Retro. Supp. I:** 418, 419, 420; **Retro. Supp. II:** 328; **Supp. I Part 1:** 259; **Supp. III Part 2:** 614; **Supp. XXII:** 166, 215

McAlmon, Mrs. Robert (Winifred Ellerman), **III:** 194. *See also* Ellerman, Winifred

McAninch, Jerry, **Supp. XI:** 297, 298

Macaulay, Catherine, **Supp. I Part 2:** 522

Macaulay, Rose, **Supp. XII:** 88; **Supp. XIV:** 348

Macaulay, Thomas, **II:** 15–16; **III:** 113, 591–592

Macauley, Robie, **Retro. Supp. II:** 228; **Supp. X:** 56

Macbeth (Shakespeare), **I:** 271; **IV:** 227; **Retro. Supp. I:** 131; **Supp. I Part 1:** 67; **Supp. I Part 2:** 457; **Supp. IV Part 1:** 87; **Supp. XIV:** 8

Macbeth (silent film), **Supp. XVI:** 184

MacBeth, George, **Retro. Supp. II:** 250

MacBride, Roger, **Supp. XXII:** 297, 301

McCafferty, Larry, **Supp. XVII:** 227

McCaffery, Larry, **Supp. IV Part 1:** 217, 227, 234; **Supp. V:** 53, 238; **Supp. VIII:** 13, 14; **Supp. X:** 260, 268, 301, 303, 307; **Supp. XVI:** 117; **Supp. XXII:** 177

McCann, Janet, **Supp. XXIII:** 51, 53, 54, 64

McCann, Jannet, **Supp. XXI:** 92

McCarriston, Linda, **Supp. X:** 204; **Supp. XIV:** 259–275

McCarthy, Charles Joseph, Jr. *See* McCarthy, Cormac

McCarthy, Cormac, **Supp. VIII:** 175–192; **Supp. XII:** 310; **Supp. XVII:** 185; **Supp. XXI:** 38, 40; **Supp. XXII:** 49; **Supp. XXIII:** 42, 44

McCarthy, Eugene, **Retro. Supp. II:** 182

McCarthy, Joseph, **I:** 31, 492; **II:** 562, 568; **Supp. I Part 1:** 294, 295; **Supp. I Part 2:** 444, 611, 612, 620; **Supp. XV:** 198, 311–312; **Supp. XXIII:** 7

McCarthy, Mary, **II:** 558–584; **Supp. I Part 1:** 84; **Supp. IV Part 1:** 209, 297, 310; **Supp. VIII:** 96, 99, 100; **Supp. X:** 177; **Supp. XI:** 246; **Supp. XIV:** 3; **Supp. XV:** 142; **Supp. XVI:** 64, 70; **Supp. XVII:** 43

McCay, Maura, **Supp. XII:** 271, 276

McClanahan, Ed, **Supp. X:** 24

McClanahan, Thomas, **Supp. XII:** 125–126

McClatchy, J. D., **Supp. XII:** 253–270; **Supp. XV:** 185, 257, 258

McClaurin, Irma, **Supp. XXIII:** 84, 86, 93, 94

McClellan, John L., **I:** 493

McClung, Isabelle, **Retro. Supp. I:** 5

McClure, John, **Retro. Supp. I:** 80

McClure, Michael, **Supp. II Part 1:** 32; **Supp. VIII:** 289; **Supp. XVI:** 283

McClure, S. S., **I:** 313; **II:** 465; **III:** 327; **Retro. Supp. I:** 5, 6, 9; **Supp. XV:** 40

McCluskey, John, Jr., **Supp. XIX:** 65, 68, 71, 72, 78

McCombs, Judith, **Supp. XIII:** 33

McConagha, Alan, **Supp. XVI:** 166

McConnell, Frank, **Supp. X:** 260, 274

McCorkle, Jill, **Supp. X:** 6; **Supp. XVIII:** 195

McCourt, Frank, **Supp. XII:** 271–287

McCoy, Horace, **Supp. XIII:** 159–177

McCracken, Elizabeth, **Supp. X:** 86; **Supp. XII:** 310, 315–316, 321

McCrae, Fiona, **Supp. XVIII:** 60, 62

McCullers, Carson, **I:** 113, 190, 211; **II:** 585–608; **IV:** 282, 384, 385, 386; **Retro. Supp. II:** 324; **Supp. II Part 1:** 17; **Supp. IV Part 1:** 31, 84; **Supp.**

IV Part 2: 502; **Supp. VIII:** 124; **Supp. XII:** 309; **Supp. XIV:** 120; **Supp. XV:** 338
McCullers, Reeves, **III:** 585, 586, 587
McDavid, Raven I., **III:** 120; **Supp. XIV:** 14
McDermott, Alice, **Supp. XII:** 311; **Supp. XVIII: 155–169**
McDermott, John J., **II:** 364
MacDiarmid, Hugh, **Supp. X:** 112
Macdonald, C. G., **Supp. XVII:** 73–74
Macdonald, Dwight, **I:** 233, 372, 379; **III:** 39; **Supp. V:** 265; **Supp. XIV:** 340; **Supp. XV:** 140
McDonald, E. J., **Supp. I Part 2:** 670
Macdonald, George, **Supp. XIII:** 75
MacDonald, Jeanette, **II:** 589
Macdonald, Ross, **Supp. IV Part 1:** 116, 136; **Supp. IV Part 2: 459–477;** **Supp. XIII:** 233; **Supp. XVIII:** 137,136; **Supp. XXI:** 67
MacDonald, Ruth K., **Supp. XVI:** 102
McDonnell, Thomas P., **Supp. XX: 45**
MacDougall, Ruth Doan, **Supp. XV:** 58; **Supp. XVI:** 174
MacDowell, Edward, **I:** 228; **III:** 504, 508, 524
McDowell, Frederick P. W., **II:** 194
McDowell, Mary, **Supp. I Part 1:** 5
McDowell, Robert, **Supp. IX:** 266, 270, 276, 279
MacDowell, Robert, **Supp. XI:** 249
McDowell, Robert, **Supp. XVII:** 109, 110, 111
McDowell. Deborah, **Supp. XVIII:** 125, 129
McElderry, Margaret K., **Supp. XV:** 162
McElligot's Pool (Geisel), **Supp. XVI:** 104
McElrath, Joseph, **Supp. XIV:** 62
McElroy, Joseph, **Supp. IV Part 1:** 279, 285
McEuen, Kathryn, **II:** 20
McEwen, Arthur, **I:** 206
McFarland, Ron, **Supp. IX:** 323, 327, 328, 333
McGann, Jerome, **Retro. Supp. I:** 47
McGill, Meredith, **Supp. XVIII:** 17
McGillis, Ian, **Supp. XVIII:** 150
MacGillivray, William, **Supp. XVI:** 8
McGinity, Keren, **Supp. XX: 9**
McGovern, Edythe M., **Supp. IV Part 2:** 573, 582, 585
McGovern, George, **III:** 46
MacGowan, Christopher, **Retro. Supp. I:** 430
MacGowan, Kenneth, **III:** 387, 391
McGrath, Douglas, **Supp. XV:** 12
McGrath, Joseph, **Supp. XI:** 307, 309
McGrath, Patrick, **Supp. IX:** 113; **Supp. XXII:** 58
McGrath, Thomas, **Supp. X: 111–130**
"McGrath on McGrath" (McGrath), **Supp. X:** 119, 120
McGuane, Thomas, **Supp. V:** 53, 220; **Supp. VIII:** 39, 40, 42, 43
MacGuffin, The (Elkin), **Supp. VI: 55–56**
McGuiness, Daniel, **Supp. XV:** 261
Machado y Ruiz, Antonio, **Supp. XIII:** 315, 323

Machan, Tibor, **Supp. IV Part 2:** 528
McHaney, Pearl, **Supp. XXI:** 244, 255, 256, 257
McHaney, Thomas, **Supp. XVIII:** 199,203
Machen, Arthur, **IV:** 286
Machiavelli, Niccolò, **I:** 485; **Supp. XIX:** 34
"Machine-Gun, The" (Jarrell), **II:** 371
"Machine Song" (Anderson), **I:** 114
McHugh, Heather, **Supp. XIX:** 84
McHugh, Vincent, **Supp. XV:** 147
McInerney, Jay, **Supp. X:** 7, 166; **Supp. XI:** 65; **Supp. XII:** 81; **Supp. XVIII:** 148
"Mac in Love" (Dixon), **Supp. XII: 142**
McIntire, Holly, **Supp. V:** 338
McIntosh, Maria, **Retro. Supp. I:** 246
Mack, Maynard, **Supp. XIV:** 12
Mackail, John William, **Supp. I Part 1:** 268; **Supp. I Part 2:** 461
McKay, Claude, **Supp. I Part 1:** 63; **Supp. III Part 1:** 75, 76; **Supp. IV Part 1:** 3, 79, 164; **Supp. IX:** 306; **Supp. X: 131–144; Supp. XI:** 91; **Supp. XVII:** 74; **Supp. XVIII:** 122, 127, 280, 282; **Supp. XIX:** 73; **Supp. XX: 69; Supp. XXII:** 275
McKay, Donald, **Supp. I Part 2:** 482
McKay, Nellie Y., **Supp. XX: 105**
McKee, Elizabeth, **Retro. Supp. II:** 221, 222
McKee, Ellen, **Retro. Supp. II:** 67
McKenney, Eileen, **IV:** 288; **Retro. Supp. II:** 321, 330
McKenney, Ruth, **IV:** 288; **Retro. Supp. II:** 321; **Supp. XVIII:** 238
MacKenzie, Agnes, **I:** 199
Mackenzie, Captain Alexander, **III:** 94
Mackenzie, Compton, **II:** 82; **Retro. Supp. I:** 100, 102
McKenzie, Geraldine, **Supp. XII:** 107
MacKenzie, Margaret, **I:** 199
Mackey, Louis, **Supp. XXI:** 236, 237
McKibben, Bill, **Supp. XVIII:** 192
McKinley, William, **I:** 474; **III:** 506; **Supp. I Part 2:** 395–396, 707
MacKinnon, Catharine, **Supp. XII:** 6
McKnight, Reginald, **Supp. XX: 147–159**
MacLachlan, Suzanne L., **Supp. XII:** 300,**Supp. XVIII:** 299
McLaverty, Michael, **Supp. X:** 67
McLay, Catherine, **Supp. XIII:** 21
Maclean, Alasdair, **Supp. V:** 244
McLean, Carolyn (pseudonym). *See* Bly, Carol
Maclean, Norman, **Supp. XIV: 221–237; Supp. XVI:** 98
MacLeish, Archibald, **I:** 283, 293, 429; **II:** 165, 228; **III: 1–25,** 427; **Supp. I Part 1:** 261; **Supp. I Part 2:** 654; **Supp. IV Part 1:** 359; **Supp. IV Part 2:** 586; **Supp. X:** 120; **Supp. XIV:** 11
MacLeish, Mrs. Archibald (Ada Hitchcock), **III:** 1
MacLeish, Kenneth, **III:** 1
McLennan, Gordon Lawson, **Supp. IX:** 89
McLeod, A. W., **Supp. I Part 1:** 257

McLuhan, Marshall, **Supp. IV Part 2:** 474
McLure, Michael, **Supp. XIV:** 150
Macmahon, Arthur, **I:** 226
McMahon, Helen, **Supp. IV Part 2:** 579
McMichael, Barbara Lloyd, **Supp. XXII:** 206, 207, 215, 216
McMichael, George, **Supp. VIII:** 124
McMichael, Morton, **Supp. I Part 2:** 707
McMichaels, James, **Supp. XIII:** 114
McMillan, James B., **Supp. VIII:** 124
McMillan, Terry, **Supp. XIII: 179–193**
McMullan, Jim, **Supp. XIV:** 124
McMurtry, Josephine, **Supp. V:** 220
McMurtry, Larry, **Supp. V: 219–235; Supp. X:** 24; **Supp. XI:** 172
McNally, Terrence, **Supp. XIII: 195–211**
McNally, T. M., **Supp. XX: 92**
McNamee, Thomas, **Supp. XXII:** 218
McNamer, Deirdre, **Supp. XI:** 190
McNeese, Gretchen, **Supp. V:** 123
MacNeice, Louis, **II:** 586; **III:** 527; **Supp. II Part 1:** 17, 24; **Supp. IV Part 2:** 440; **Supp. X:** 116; **Supp. XIII:** 347
McNeil, Claudia, **Supp. IV Part 1:** 360, 362
M-a-c-n-o-l-i-a (Jordan), **Supp. XVIII:** 172
McPhee, John, **Supp. III Part 1: 289–316; Supp. X:** 29, 30; **Supp. XVIII:** 106–107, 114
MacPherson, Aimee Semple, **Supp. V:** 278
Macpherson, Anne, **Supp. XXIII:** 84
McPherson, Dolly, **Supp. IV Part 1:** 2, 3, 4, 6, 8, 11, 12
McPherson, James Alan, **Supp. XXII:** 141
McPherson, James Allen, **Retro. Supp. II:** 126
Macpherson, Jay, **Supp. XIII:** 19
MacPherson, Jennifer, **Supp. XXIII:** 248
MacPherson, Kenneth, **Supp. I Part 1:** 259
McPherson, Sandra, **Supp. XXIII:** 57
McPhillips, Robert, **Supp. XV:** 119, 250, 251, 252, 264, 266; **Supp. XXIII:** 111, 112, 114, 127
McQuade, Molly, **Supp. VIII:** 277, 281; **Supp. IX:** 151, 163; **Supp. XX: 90**
McQueen, Steve, **Supp. XI:** 306
Macrae, John, **I:** 252–253
McRobbie, Angela, **Supp. IV Part 2:** 691
MacShane, Frank, **Supp. IV Part 2:** 557; **Supp. XI:** 214, 216
"MacSwiggen" (Freneau), **Supp. II Part 1:** 259
McTaggart, John, **I:** 59
McTeague (Norris), **III:** 314, 315, 316–320, 322, 325, 327–328, 330, 331, 333, 335; **Retro. Supp. II:** 96; **Supp. IX:** 332
McWhorter, Dianne, **Supp. XXIII:** 38
McWilliams, Carey, **Supp. XI:** 169
Madama Butterfly (opera, Puccini), **III:** 139; **Supp. XXI:** 150, 155
"Madam and the Minister" (Hughes), **Supp. I Part 1:** 335

"Madam and the Wrong Visitor" (Hughes), **Supp. I Part 1:** 335

"Madame and Ahmad" (Bowles), **Supp. IV Part 1:** 93

"Madame Bai and the Taking of Stone Mountain" (Bambara), **Supp. XI:** 14–15

Madame Bovary (Flaubert), **II:** 185; **Retro. Supp. I:** 225; **Retro. Supp. II:** 70; **Supp. XI:** 334; **Supp. XX:** 58

"Madame Célestin's Divorce" (Chopin), **Supp. I Part 1:** 213

Madame Curie (film), **Retro. Supp. I:** 113

"Madame de Mauves" (James), **II:** 327; **Retro. Supp. I:** 218, 220

Madame de Treymes (Wharton), **IV:** 314, 323; **Retro. Supp. I:** 376

"Madame Rose Hanie" (Gibran), **Supp. XX:** 124

"Madame Swann at Home"(Hadas), **Supp. XXIII:** 113

"Madam's Calling Cards" (Hughes), **Retro. Supp. I:** 206

Madden, David, **Supp. IV Part 1:** 285

Maddern, Bessie. *See* London, Mrs. Jack (Bessie Maddern)

Mad Dog Black Lady (Coleman), **Supp. XI:** 85–89, 90

Mad Dog Blues (Shepard), **Supp. III Part 2:** 437, 438, 441

Maddox, Lucy, **Supp. IV Part 1:** 323, 325

Mad Ducks and Bears: Football Revisited (Plimpton), **Supp. XVI:** 243

Mademoiselle Coeur-Brisé (Sibon, trans.), **IV:** 288

Mademoiselle de Maupin (Gautier), **Supp. I Part 1:** 277

"Mad Farmer, Flying the Flag of Rough Branch, Secedes from the Union, The" (Berry), **Supp. X:** 35

"Mad Farmer Manifesto, The: The First Amendment" (Berry), **Supp. X:** 35

"Mad Farmer's Love Song, The" (Berry), **Supp. X:** 35

Madheart (Baraka), **Supp. II Part 1:** 47

Madhouse, The (Farrell), **II:** 41

Madhubuti, Haki R. (Don L. Lee), **Supp. II Part 1:** 34, 247; **Supp. IV Part 1:** 244

Madison, Charles, **Supp. XXIII:** 6, 13

Madison, Dolley, **II:** 303

Madison, James, **I:** 1, 2, 6–9; **II:** 301; **Supp. I Part 2:** 509, 524

"Madison Smartt Bell: *The Year of Silence*" (Garrett), **Supp. X:** 7

Mad Love (film, Freund), **Supp. XVII:** 58

"Madman, A" (Updike), **Retro. Supp. I:** 320

Madman, The: His Parables and Poems (Gibran), **Supp. XX:** 115, 118, 125

"Madman's Song" (Wylie), **Supp. I Part 2:** 711, 729

Madonick, Michael, **Supp. XVII:** 123

"Madonna" (Lowell), **II:** 535–536

"Madonna of the Evening Flowers" (Lowell), **II:** 524

"Madonna of the Future, The" (James), **Retro. Supp. I:** 219

"Mad Song" (Gioia), **Supp. XV:** 128

Madwoman in the Attic, The (Gilbert and Gubar), **Retro. Supp. I:** 42; **Supp. IX:** 66

"Maelzel's Chess-Player" (Poe), **III:** 419, 420

"Maestria" (Nemerov), **III:** 275, 278–279

Maeterlinck, Maurice, **I:** 91, 220; **Supp. XX:** 115, 116

"Magazine-Writing Peter Snook" (Poe), **III:** 421

Magdeburg Centuries (Flacius), **IV:** 163

Magellan, Ferdinand, **Supp. I Part 2:** 497

Maggie: A Girl of the Streets (S. Crane), **I:** 407, 408, 410–411, 416; **IV:** 208; **Retro. Supp. II:** 97, 107; **Supp. XVII:** 228; **Supp. XXIII:** 165

Maggie Cassidy (Kerouac), **Supp. III Part 1:** 220–221, 225, 227, 229, 232

Maggie-Now (B. Smith), **Supp. XXIII:** 258, 267–269

"Maggie of the Green Bottles" (Bambara), **Supp. XI:** 2–3

"Maggie's Farm" (song, Dylan), **Supp. XVIII:** 25, 26

"Magi" (Plath), **Supp. I Part 2:** 544–545

"Magi, The" (Garrett), **Supp. VII:** 97

"Magic" (Pickering), **Supp. XXI:** 202

"Magic" (Porter), **III:** 434, 435

"Magical Thinking" (Hull), **Supp. XXI:** 137, 139

Magic Barrel, The (Malamud), **Supp. I Part 2:** 427, 428, 430–434

"Magic Barrel, The" (Malamud), **Supp. I Part 2:** 427, 428, 431, 432–433

Magic Christian, The (film), **Supp. XI:** 309

Magic Christian, The (Southern), **Supp. XI:** 297, 299–301, 309

Magic City (Komunyakaa), **Supp. XIII:** 125–127, 128, 131

"Magic Flute, The" (Epstein), **Supp. XII:** 165

Magic Flute, The (Mozart), **III:** 164

Magician of Lublin, The (Singer), **IV:** 6, 9–10; **Retro. Supp. II:** 308–309

Magician's Assistant, The (Patchett), **Supp. XII:** 307, 310, 317–320, 322

"Magician's Wife, The" (Gordon), **Supp. IV Part 1:** 306

Magic Journey, The (Nichols), **Supp. XIII:** 266–267

Magic Keys, The (Murray), **Supp. XIX:** 157–158

Magic Kingdom, The (Elkin), **Supp. VI:** 42, 54–55, 56, 58

"Magic Mirror, The: A Study of the Double in Two of Doestoevsky's Novels" (Plath), **Supp. I Part 2:** 536

Magic Mountain, The (Mann), **III:** 281–282; **Supp. IV Part 2:** 522; **Supp. XII:** 321; **Supp. XVII:** 137

Magic Tower, The (Willams), **IV:** 380

Magnaghi, Ambrogio, **Supp. XVI:** 286

Magnalia Christi Americana (Mather), **II:** 302; **Supp. I Part 1:** 102; **Supp. I Part 2:** 584; **Supp. II Part 2:** 441, 442, 452–455, 460, 467, 468; **Supp. IV Part 2:** 434

Magnes, Judah, **Supp. XXIII:** 6

Magnificat (Nelson), **Supp. XVIII:** 176–177

"Magnificent Little Gift" (Salinas), **Supp. XIII:** 318

"Magnifying Mirror" (Karr), **Supp. XI:** 240

Magpie, The (Baldwin, ed.), **Supp. I Part 1:** 49

"Magpie Exhorts"(Schott), **Supp. XXIII:** 250

Magpie's Shadow, The (Winters), **Supp. II Part 2:** 786, 788

"Magpie's Song" (Snyder), **Supp. VIII:** 302

Magritte, René, **Supp. IV Part 2:** 623

Maguire, Roberta S., **Supp. XIX:** 160–161

Magus, The (Fowles), **Supp. XIX:** 58

Mahan, Albert Thayer, **Supp. I Part 2:** 491

Mahan, David C., **Supp. XXI:** 86

"Mahatma Joe" (Bass), **Supp. XVI:** 19

Mahlis, Kristen, **Supp. XXIII:** 90, 94

"Mahogany Tree, The" (M. F. K. Fisher), **Supp. XVII:** 88

Mahomet and His Successors (Irving), **II:** 314

Mahoney, Jeremiah, **IV:** 285

Mahoney, Lynn, **Supp. XV:** 270

"Maiden in a Tower" (Stegner), **Supp. IV Part 2:** 613

"Maiden Without Hands" (Sexton), **Supp. II Part 2:** 691

"Maid of St. Philippe, The" (Chopin), **Retro. Supp. II:** 63

"Maid's Shoes, The" (Malamud), **Supp. I Part 2:** 437

Mailer, Fanny, **III:** 28

Mailer, Isaac, **III:** 28

Mailer, Norman, **I:** 261, 292, 477; **III:** 26–49, 174; **IV:** 98, 216; **Retro. Supp. II:** 182, 195–217, 279; **Supp. I Part 1:** 291, 294; **Supp. III Part 1:** 302; **Supp. IV Part 1:** 90, 198, 207, 236, 284, 381; **Supp. IV Part 2:** 689; **Supp. VIII:** 236; **Supp. XI:** 104, 218, 222, 229; **Supp. XIV:** 49, 53, 54, 111, 162; **Supp. XVII:** 225, 228, 236; **Supp. XVIII:** 19–20; **Supp. XX:** 90; **Supp. XXIII:** 105, 106

"Maimed Man, The" (Tate), **IV:** 136

Maimonides, Moses, **Supp. XVII:** 46–47

Main Currents in American Thought: The Colonial Mind, 1625–1800 (Parrington), **I:** 517; **Supp. I Part 2:** 484

"Maine Roustabout, A" (Eberhart), **I:** 539

"Maine Speech" (White), **Supp. I Part 2:** 669–670

Maine Woods, The (Thoreau), **IV:** 188

Mains d'Orlac, Les (M. Renard), **Supp. XVII:** 58

Main Street (Lewis), **I:** 362; **II:** 271, 440, 441–442, 447, 449, 453; **III:** 394; **Supp. XIX:** 142; **Supp. XXII:** 282

"Maintenance" (Pickering), **Supp. XXI:** 204

Maitland, Margaret Todd, **Supp. XVI:** 292

Majdoubeh, Ahmad, **Supp. XX: 116**

Major, Clarence, **Supp. XXII: 171–186**

"Majorat, Das" (Hoffman), **III:** 415

Major Barbara (Shaw), **III:** 69

"Major Chord, The" (Bourne), **I:** 221

Majors and Minors (Dunbar), **Supp. II Part 1:** 197, 198

"Major's Tale, The" (Bierce), **I:** 205

Make Believe (J. Scott), **Supp. XVII: 191–192,** 193, 194, 195

Make-Believe Town: Essays and Remembrances (Mamet), **Supp. XIV:** 240, 251

Make It New (Pound), **III:** 470

Makers and Finders (Brooks), **I:** 253, 254, 255, 257, 258

Makers of the Modern World (Untermeyer), **Supp. XV:** 312

"Making a Change" (Gilman), **Supp. XI:** 207

"Making a Living" (Sexton), **Supp. II Part 2:** 695

"Making Changes" (L. Michaels), **Supp. XVI:** 204

"Making Do" (Hogan), **Supp. IV Part 1:** 406

Making Face, Making Soul: Haciendo Caras, Creative and Critical Perspectives by Feminists of Color (Anzaldúa, ed.), **Supp. IV Part 1:** 330

Making It (Podhoretz), **Supp. VIII:** 231, 232, 233, **237–238,** 239, 244

"Making Light of Auntie" (X. J. Kennedy), **Supp. XV:** 163

"Making of a Marginal Farm, The" (Berry), **Supp. X:** 22

Making of Americans, The (Stein), **IV:** 35, 37, 40–42, 45, 46; **Supp. III Part 1:** 37

"Making of Ashenden, The" (Elkin), **Supp. VI:** 49, 50

"Making of a Soldier USA, The" (Simpson), **Supp. IX:** 270

"Making of Garrison Keillor, The" (McConagha), **Supp. XVI:** 166"

Making of Modern Atlanta, The (documentary), **Supp. XXII:** 251

"Making of Paths, The" (Stegner), **Supp. IV Part 2:** 614

"Making of Poems, The" (W. J. Smith), **Supp. XIII:** 348

Making of the Modern Mind (Randall), **III:** 605

Making the Light Come: The Poetry of Gerald Stern (Somerville), **Supp. IX:** 296–297

"Making Up Stories" (Didion), **Supp. IV Part 1:** 196, 203, 205

Making Your Own Days: The Pleasures of Reading and Writing Poetry (Koch), **Supp. XV:** 188; **Supp. XXIII:** 124

Maladies de la volonté, Les (Ribot), **Supp. XX: 238**

Malady of the Ideal, The: Oberman, Maurice de Guérin, and Amiel (Brooks), **I:** 240, 241, 242

Malamud, Bernard, **I:** 144, 375; **II:** 424, 425; **III:** 40, 272; **IV:** 216; **Retro. Supp. II:** 22, 279, 281; **Supp. I Part 2: 427–453; Supp. IV Part 1:** 297, 382; **Supp. V:** 257, 266; **Supp. IX:** 114, 227; **Supp. XIII:** 106, 264, 265, 294; **Supp. XVI:** 220

Malamud, Mrs. Bernard (Ann de Chiara), **Supp. I Part 2:** 451

Malanga, Gerard, **Supp. III Part 2:** 629; **Supp. XXIII:** 221

Malaquais, Jean, **Retro. Supp. II:** 199

Malatesta, Sigismondo de, **III:** 472, 473

Malcolm (Purdy), **Supp. VII:** 270–273, 277

"Malcolm Cowley and the American Writer" (Simpson), **Supp. II Part 1:** 147

Malcolm Lowry's "Volcano": Myth Symbol Meaning (Markson), **Supp. XVII:** 142, 144

"MALCOLM REMEMBERED (FEB. 77)" (Baraka), **Supp. II Part 1:** 60

Malcolm X, **Retro. Supp. II:** 12, 13; **Supp. I Part 1:** 52, 63, 65, 66; **Supp. IV Part 1:** 2, 10; **Supp. VIII:** 330, 345; **Supp. X:** 240; **Supp. XIV:** 306

Malcolm X (film), **Retro. Supp. II:** 12

"Maldrove" (Jeffers), **Supp. II Part 2:** 418

Male, Roy, **II:** 239

Male Animal, The (Thurber), **Supp. I Part 2:** 605, 606, 610–611

"Malediction upon Myself" (Wylie), **Supp. I Part 2:** 722

Malefactors, The (Gordon), **II:** 186, 199, 213–216; **IV:** 139

"Malest Cornifici Tuo Catullo" (Ginsberg), **Supp. II Part 1:** 315

Malick, Terrence, **Supp. XI:** 234; **Supp. XV:** 351

Malin, Irving, **I:** 147; **Supp. XVI:** 71–72

"Malinche's Tips: Pique from Mexico's Mother" (Mora), **Supp. XIII:** 223

"Malinke's Atonement" (Antin), **Supp. XX: 10**

"Mallard" (C. Frost), **Supp. XV:** 98, 99

Mallarmé, Stéphane, **I:** 66, 569; **II:** 529, 543; **III:** 8, 409, 428; **IV:** 80, 86; **Retro. Supp. I:** 56; **Supp. I Part 1:** 261; **Supp. II Part 1:** 1; **Supp. III Part 1:** 319–320; **Supp. III Part 2:** 630; **Supp. XIII:** 114; **Supp. XV:** 158; **Supp. XVI:** 282, 285

Malle, Louis, **Supp. XXIII:** 122

Mallia, Joseph, **Supp. XII:** 26, 29, 37

Mallon, Anne-Marie, **Supp. XXI:** 215

Mallon, Thomas, **Supp. IV Part 1:** 200, 209; **Supp. XIX: 131–145**

Maloff, Saul, **Supp. VIII:** 238

Malory, Thomas, **II:** 302; **III:** 486; **IV:** 50, 61; **Supp. IV Part 1:** 47

"Mal Paso Bridge" (Jeffers), **Supp. II Part 2:** 415, 420

Malraux, André, **I:** 33–34, 127, 509; **II:** 57, 376; **III:** 35, 310; **IV:** 236, 247, 434; **Retro. Supp. I:** 73; **Retro. Supp. II:** 115–116, 119; **Supp. II Part 1:** 221, 232; **Supp. XIX:** 157

Maltese Falcon, The (film), **Supp. IV Part 1:** 342, 353, 355

Maltese Falcon, The (Hammett), **IV:** 286; **Supp. IV Part 1:** 345, 348–351

Mama (McMillan), **Supp. XIII:** 182, **187–188**

"Mama and Daughter" (Hughes), **Supp. I Part 1:** 334

Mama Day (Naylor), **Supp. VIII: 223–226,** 230

"Mama I Remember" (Nelson), **Supp. XVIII:** 173

Mama Poc: An Ecologist's Account of the Extinction of a Species (LaBastille), **Supp. X:** 99, **104–105,** 106

Mama Poems, The (Kenny), **Supp. XXIII:** 143, **154**

Mama's Bank Account (K. Forbes), **Supp. XVII:** 9

Mama's Promises (Nelson), **Supp. XVIII: 173–174**

"Mama Still Loves You" (Naylor), **Supp. VIII:** 214

Mambo Hips and Make Believe (Coleman), **Supp. XI: 94–96**

Mambo Kings, The (film), **Supp. VIII:** 73, 74

Mambo Kings Play Songs of Love, The (Hijuelos), **Supp. VIII:** 73–74, **79–82**

"Ma'me Pélagie" (Chopin), **Retro. Supp. II:** 64

Mamet, David, **Supp. XIV: 239–258,** 315

"Mamie" (Sandburg), **III:** 582

Mammedaty, Novarro Scott. *See* Momaday, N. Scott

"Mammon and the Archer" (O. Henry), **Supp. II Part 1:** 394, 408

Mammonart (Sinclair), **Supp. V:** 276–277

"Mammy" (D. West), **Supp. XVIII:** 283

"Mamouche" (Chopin), **Retro. Supp. II:** 66

Mamoulian, Rouben, **Supp. XVIII:** 281

"Man" (Corso), **Supp. XII:** 130

"Man" (Herbert), **II:** 12

"Man Against the Sky, The" (Robinson), **III:** 509, 523

"Man and a Woman Sit Near Each Other, A" (R. Bly), **Supp. IV Part 1:** 71

Man and Boy (Morris), **III:** 223, 224, 225

"Man and the Snake, The" (Bierce), **I:** 203

"Man and Woman" (Caldwell), **I:** 310

Manassas (Sinclair), **Supp. V:** 280, 281, 285

"Man Bring This Up Road" (T. Williams), **IV:** 383–384

"Man Carrying Thing" (Stevens), **IV:** 90

Manchester, William, **III:** 103

"Man Child, The" (Baldwin), **Supp. I Part 1:** 63

Man Could Stand Up, A (Ford), **I:** 423

"Mandarin's Jade" (Chandler), **Supp. IV Part 1:** 125

Mandel, Charlotte, **Supp. XVI:** 57

Mandelbaum, Maurice, **I:** 61

Mandelstam, Osip, **Retro. Supp. I:** 278; **Supp. III Part 1:** 268; **Supp. VIII:** 21, 22, 23, 27; **Supp. XIII:** 77; **Supp. XV:** 254, 261, 263

"Mandelstam: The Poem as Event" (Dobyns), **Supp. XIII:** 78

"Mandolin" (Dove), **Supp. IV Part 1:** 247

"Mandoline" (Verlaine), **IV:** 79

"Man Eating" (Kenyon), **Supp. VII:** 173

"Manet in Late Summer" (Skloot), **Supp. XX:** 201

"Man Feeding Pigeons" (Clampitt), **Supp. IX:** 49–50, 52

Manfred, Frederick, **Supp. X:** 126

Man From Limbo, The (Endore), **Supp. XVII:** 55

Man fun natseres, Der (Asch), **Supp. XXIII:** 6

"Mango Says Goodbye Sometimes" (Cisneros), **Supp. VII:** 64

Manhattan (film; Allen), **Supp. IV Part 1:** 205; **Supp. XV:** 5, 7–8, 13

"Manhattan Dawn" (Justice), **Supp. VII:** 117

"Manhattan: Luminism" (Doty), **Supp. XI:** 135

Manhattan Murder Mystery (film; Allen), **Supp. XV:** 5, 11

Manhattan Transfer (Dos Passos), **I:** 26, 475, 478, 479, 480, 481, 482–484, 487; **II:** 286; **Supp. I Part 1:** 57

"Mania" (Lowell), **II:** 554

"Manic in the Moon, The" (Thurber), **Supp. I Part 2:** 620

Manifest; and Furthermore (Bronk), **Supp. XXI:** 32

"Manifesto: A Press Release from PRKA" (Saunders), **Supp. XIX:** 235

Manikin, The (J. Scott), **Supp. XVII:** 189–191, 192, 194

"Man in Black" (Plath), **Supp. I Part 2:** 538

Man in Prehistory (Chard), **Supp. XII:** 177–178

Man in the Black Coat Turns, The (R. Bly), **Supp. IV Part 1:** 66–68, 71, 73

"Man in the Brooks Brothers Shirt, The" (McCarthy), **II:** 563–564

"Man in the Drawer, The" (Malamud), **Supp. I Part 2:** 437

Man in the Flying Lawn Chair and Other Excursions and Observations, The (Plimpton), **Supp. XVI:** 234

Man in the Gray Flannel Suit, The (Wilson), **Supp. IV Part 1:** 387

Man in the High Castle, The (Dick), **Supp. XVIII:** 138

Man in the Middle, The (Wagoner), **Supp. IX:** 324, 332–333

"Man in the Rain, The" (Ryan as Quin), **Supp. XVIII:** 226

"Man in the Toolhouse, The" (Swados), **Supp. XIX:** 263

Mankiewicz, Herman, **Supp. XVI:** 189

Mankiewicz, Joseph, **Retro. Supp. I:** 113

Mankowitz, Wolf, **Supp. XI:** 307

"Man Made of Words, The" (Momaday), **Supp. IV Part 2:** 481, 484–485, 486, 487, 488

Man-Made World, The (Gilman), **Supp. XI:** 207

"Man-Moth, The" (Bishop), **Retro. Supp. II:** 42; **Supp. I Part 1:** 85–87, 88

Mann, Charles, **Retro. Supp. II:** 40

Mann, Erika, **Supp. II Part 1:** 11

Mann, Seymour (Samuel Weisman), **Supp. V:** 113

Mann, Thomas, **I:** 271, 490; **II:** 42, 539; **III:** 231, 281–282, 283; **IV:** 70, 73, 85; **Supp. IV Part 1:** 392; **Supp. IV Part 2:** 522; **Supp. V:** 51; **Supp. IX:** 21; **Supp. XI:** 275; **Supp. XII:** 173, 310, 321; **Supp. XIV:** 87; **Supp. XVII:** 137; **Supp. XIX:** 147, 151, 157; **Supp. XX:** 85; **Supp. XXIII:** 4

Mannequins' Demise: A Play in Eight Scenes (Budbill), **Supp. XIX:** 12

Mannerhouse (Wolfe), **IV:** 460

Manner Music, The (Reznikoff), **Supp. XIV:** 293–295

"Manners" (Bishop), **Supp. I Part 1:** 73

"Manners" (Emerson), **II:** 4, 6

"Manners, Morals, and the Novel" (Trilling), **Supp. III Part 2:** 502, 503

Mannheim, Karl, **I:** 279; **Supp. I Part 2:** 644

Manning, Ambrose, **Supp. XX:** 166

Manning, Frederic, **III:** 459

Manning, Robert, **Supp. IX:** 236

Mannix, Daniel P., **Supp. II Part 1:** 140

Man Nobody Knows, The (B. Barton), **Retro. Supp. I:** 179

Mano, D. Keith, **Supp. XVI:** 250

Mano, Guy Levis, **Supp. XVI:** 282

"Man of Indeterminate Age on a Subway Grate, A" (DI Piero), **Supp. XIX:** 47

"Man of Letters" (Pickering), **Supp. XXI:** 192, 195–196

"Man of Letters as a Man of Business, The" (Howells), **Supp. XIV:** 45–46

"Man of No Account, The" (Harte), **Supp. II Part 1:** 339

"Man of the Crowd, The" (Poe), **III:** 412, 417; **Retro. Supp. I:** 154

Man on Spikes (Asinof), **II:** 424

Man on Stage (Dixon), **Supp. XII:** 141, 154–155

"Man on the Dump, The" (Stevens), **IV:** 74; **Retro. Supp. I:** 306

"Man on the Train, The" (Percy), **Supp. III Part 1:** 387

Manor, The (Singer), **IV:** 6, 17–19

Manrique, Jorge, **Retro. Supp. II:** 154

Mansart Builds a School (Du Bois), **Supp. II Part 1:** 185–186

Man's Fate (Malraux), **I:** 127; **Retro. Supp. II:** 121

"Man's Fate A Film Treatment of the Malraux Novel" (Agee), **I:** 33–34

Mansfield, June, **Supp. X:** 183, 194

Mansfield, Katherine, **III:** 362, 453

Mansfield, Stephanie, **Supp. IV Part 1:** 227

Man's Hope (Malraux), **IV:** 247

Mansion, The (Faulkner), **II:** 73; **Retro. Supp. I:** 74, 82

Man's Nature and His Communities (Niebuhr), **III:** 308

Manson, Charles, **Supp. IV Part 1:** 205

"Man Splitting Wood in the Daybreak, The" (Kinnell), **Supp. III Part 1:** 254

"Man's Pride" (Jeffers), **Supp. II Part 2:** 417

"Man's Story, The" (Anderson), **I:** 114

Man's Woman, A (Norris), **III:** 314, 322, 328, 329, 330, 332, 333

Man That Corrupted Hadleyburg, The (Twain), **I:** 204; **IV:** 208

"Man That Was Used Up, The" (Poe), **III:** 412, 425

"Mantis" (Zukofsky), **Supp. III Part 2:** 617

"'Mantis': An Interpretation" (Zukofsky), **Supp. III Part 2:** 617–618

"Man to Know in the Restaurants, The" (Siddons), **Supp. XXII:** 244

Man to Send Rain Clouds, The (Rosen, ed.), **Supp. IV Part 2:** 499, 505, 513

"Man to Send Rain Clouds, The" (Silko), **Supp. IV Part 2:** 559

Mantrap (Lewis), **II:** 447

Manuductio Ad Ministerium (Mather), **Supp. II Part 2:** 465–467

"Manuelzinho" (Bishop), **Retro. Supp. II:** 47–48

Manuscript Books of Emily Dickinson, The (Franklin, ed.), **Retro. Supp. I:** 29, 41

"Man Waiting for It to Stop, A" (Dunn), **Supp. XI:** 144

"Man Who Became a Woman, The" (Anderson), **I:** 114

"Man Who Carries the Desert Around Inside Himself, The: For Wally" (Komunyakaa), **Supp. XIII:** 125

"Man Who Closed Shop, The" (Dunn), **Supp. XI:** 149

Man Who Gave Up His Name, The (Harrison), **Supp. VIII:** 45, 52

Man Who Had All the Luck, The (A. Miller), **III:** 148, 149, 164, 166

"Man Who Knew Belle Star, The" (Bausch), **Supp. VII:** 46

"Man Who Knew Coolidge, The" (Lewis), **II:** 449

Man Who Knew Coolidge, The: Being the Soul of Lowell Schmaltz, Constructive and Nordic Citizen (Lewis), **II:** 450

Man Who Lived Underground, The (Wright), **Supp. II Part 1:** 40

"Man Who Lived Underground, The" (Wright), **IV:** 479, 485–487, 492; **Retro. Supp. II:** 121

"Man Who Made Me Love Him, The" (Weigl), **Supp. XIX:** 278

"Man Who Makes Brooms, The" (Nye), **Supp. XIII:** 276

"Man Who Studied Yoga, The" (Mailer), **III:** 35–36; **Retro. Supp. II:** 200

"Man Who Wanted to Win, The" (McCoy), **Supp. XIII:** 161

Man Who Was There, The (Morris), **III:** 220–221

"Man Who Writes Ants, The" (Merwin), **Supp. III Part 1:** 348

"Man with a Family" (Humphrey), **Supp. IX:** 94

Man without a Country, The (Hale), **I:** 488

"Man with the Blue Guitar, The" (Stevens), **I:** 266; **IV:** 85–87; **Retro. Supp. I:** 303–305, 306, 307, 309

Man with the Blue Guitar and Other Poems, The (Stevens), **IV:** 76; **Retro. Supp. I:** 303, 422

Man with the Golden Arm, The (Algren), **Supp. V:** 4; **Supp. IX:** 1, 3, **9–11,** 14, 15

Man with the Golden Arm, The (film), **Supp. IX:** 3

"Man with the Golden Beef, The" (Podhoretz), **Supp. IX:** 3

"Man with the Hoe, The" (Markham), **Supp. XV:** 115

Man with the Mask, The (Lippard), **Supp. XXIII:** 178, 183–184, 188

Many a Monster (Ryan as Finnegan), **Supp. XVIII:** 233, **236–238**

Manyan Letters (Olson), **Supp. II Part 2:** 571

Many Circles (Goldbarth), **Supp. XII:** 193

"Many Handles" (Sandburg), **III:** 594

"Many Happy Returns" (Auden), **Supp. II Part 1:** 15

Many Happy Returns (Berrigan), **Supp. XXII:** 224

Many Loves (W. C. Williams), **Retro. Supp. I:** 424

"Many Mansions" (H. Roth), **Supp. IX:** 233, 234

Many Marriages (Anderson), **I:** 104, 111, 113

"Many of Our Waters: Variations on a Poem by a Black Child" (Wright), **Supp. III Part 2:** 602

"Many Swans" (Lowell), **II:** 526

"Many Thousands Gone" (Baldwin), **Retro. Supp. II:** 4; **Supp. I Part 1:** 51

"Many Wagons Ago" (Ashbery), **Supp. III Part 1:** 22

Many-Windowed House, A (Cowley), **Supp. II Part 1:** 141, 143

"Many-Windowed House, A" (Cowley), **Supp. II Part 1:** 137

Mao II (DeLillo), **Supp. VI:** 2, 4, **5,** 6, **7,** 8, 9, 14, 16

"Map, The" (Bishop), **Retro. Supp. II:** 41; **Supp. I Part 1:** 72, 82, 85–88, 93

"Map, The" (Strand), **Supp. IV Part 2:** 623–624

"Maple Leaf, The" (Joplin), **Supp. IV Part 1:** 223

"Maple Tree, The" (D. West), **Supp. XVIII:** 284

Map of Another Town: A Memoir of Provence (M. F. K. Fisher), **Supp. XVII:** 88, 89, 92

"Map of Montana in Italy, A" (Hugo), **Supp. VI:** 139

Mapp and Lucia (Benson), **Supp. XX: 229**

Mapping American Culture (Franklin and Steiner), **Supp. XXII:** 205

"Maps" (Hass), **Supp. VI:** 103–104

Mapson, Jo-Ann, **Supp. IV Part 2:** 440, 454

Map to the Next World, A: Poems and Tales (Harjo), **Supp. XII: 228–230**

"Maquillage" (Hull), **Supp. XXI:** 133

"Mara" (Jeffers), **Supp. II Part 2:** 434

Ma Rainey's Black Bottom (Wilson), **Supp. VIII:** 331, **332–334,** 346, 349, 350

Maranen (Asch), **Supp. XXIII:** 10

Marat, Jean Paul, **IV:** 117; **Supp. I Part 2:** 514, 515, 521

"Marathon" (Glück), **Supp. V:** 85

Marble Faun, The (Faulkner), **II:** 55, 56; **Retro. Supp. I:** 79

Marble Faun, The; or, The Romance of Monte Beni (Hawthorne), **II:** 225, 239, 242–243, 290, 324; **IV:** 167; **Retro. Supp. I:** 63, 149, 163, **164–165; Supp. I Part 1:** 38; **Supp. I Part 2:** 421, 596; **Supp. XIII:** 102

Marbles (Brodsky), **Supp. VIII:** 26–27

Marburg, Anita, **Supp. XXII:** 281

Marcaccio, Michael, **Supp. XVII:** 97, 106

"March" (W. C. Williams), **Retro. Supp. I:** 418

March, Alan, **Supp. XVI:** 242

March, Fredric, **III:** 154, 403; **IV:** 357; **Supp. X:** 220

"March, March on Down the Field" (Shaw), **Supp. XIX:** 246

Marchalonis, Shirley, **Supp. XIII:** 138, 140, 141, 143, 147–148

"Marché aux Oiseaux" (Wilbur), **Supp. III Part 2:** 550

"Märchen, The" (Jarrell), **II:** 378–379

March Hares (Frederic), **II:** 143–144

Marching Men (Anderson), **I:** 99, 101, 103–105, 111

"Marching Music" (Simic), **Supp. VIII:** 281

"Marcia" (R. H. Davis), **Supp. XVI:** 91–92

Marcks, Greg, **Supp. XVIII:** 150

Marco Millions (O'Neill), **III:** 391, 395

Marcosson, Isaac, **III:** 322

Marcus, Greil, **Supp. XVIII:** 30, 53

Marcus, Steven, **Retro. Supp. II:** 196, 200

Marcus Aurelius, **II:** 1; **III:** 566; **Supp. XVIII:** 304

Marcuse, Herbert, **Supp. I Part 2:** 645; **Supp. VIII:** 196; **Supp. XII:** 2

Mardi and a Voyage Thither (Melville), **I:** 384; **II:** 281; **III:** 77–79, 84, 87, 89; **Retro. Supp. I:** 247, 254, 256

Margaret (Judd), **II:** 290

Margaret & Dusty (Notley), **Supp. XXII:** 231

"Margaret Fuller, 1847" (Clampitt), **Supp. IX:** 43

"Marginalia" (Wilbur), **Supp. III Part 2:** 544

Margin of Hope, A: An Intellectual Autobiography (Howe), **Supp. VI:** 113–114, 117, 125, 128

"Margins of Maycomb, The: A Rereading of *To Kill a Mockingbird*" (Phelps), **Supp. VIII:** 128

Margoshes, Samuel, **Supp. X:** 70

"Margrave" (Jeffers), **Supp. II Part 2:** 426

Margret Howth (R. H. Davis), **Supp. XVI:** 81, 83, 84, **88–89**

Margret Howth: A Story of Today (J. Yellin, ed.), **Supp. XVI:** 88

Margulies, Donald, **Supp. XXI:** 145

"Maria Concepción" (Porter), **III:** 434–435, 451

Mariani, Paul L., **Retro. Supp. I:** 412, 419; **Retro. Supp. II:** 189

Marianne Moore Reader, (Moore), **III:** 199

Marie Antoinette (film), **Retro. Supp. I:** 113

Marie Blythe (Mosher), **Supp. XXII:** 206, 209, **212**

Marie Laveau (Prose), **Supp. XVI:** 251

"Marijuana and a Pistol" (C. Himes), **Supp. XVI:** 137

"Marijuana Notation" (Ginsberg), **Supp. II Part 1:** 313

Maril, Herman, **Supp. XXI:** 22, 23

Marilyn: A Biography (Mailer), **Retro. Supp. II:** 208

"Marin" (Cisneros), **Supp. VII:** 60, 61

Marin, Jay, **Retro. Supp. II:** 325

"Marina" (Eliot), **I:** 584, 585; **Retro. Supp. I:** 64

Mariners, Renegades, and Castaways (C. L. R. James), **Supp. XXI:** 159, 169–170

"Marine Surface, Low Overcast" (Clampitt), **Supp. IX: 47–48**

Marinetti, F. T., **Supp. XXII:** 159, 160, 161, 163

Marinetti, Tommaso, **Retro. Supp. I:** 59

Marionettes, The (Faulkner), **Retro. Supp. I:** 79

Maritain, Jacques, **I:** 402

Maritime Compact (Paine), **Supp. I Part 2:** 519

Maritime History of Massachusetts, 1783–1860, The (Morison), **Supp. I Part 2:** 481–483

Marjolin, Jean-Nicolas, **Supp. I Part 1:** 302

Marjorie Kinnan Rawlings: Sojourner at Cross Creek (Silverthorne), **Supp. X:** 220, 234

"Mark, The" (Bogan), **Supp. III Part 1:** 52

Marker, Chris, **Supp. IV Part 2:** 434, 436

"Market" (Hayden), **Supp. II Part 1:** 368, 369

Marketplace, The (Frederic), **II:** 145–146

Markham, Edwin, **I:** 199, 207; **Supp. XV:** 115

Markings (Hammarskjold), **Supp. II Part 1:** 26

Mark of the Vampire (film, Browning), **Supp. XVII:** 58

Markopoulos, Gregory, **Supp. XII:** 2

Markowick-Olczakova, Hanna, **Supp. X:** 70

Marks, Alison, **Supp. I Part 2:** 660

Marks, Barry A., **I:** 435, 438, 442, 446

Markson, David, **Supp. XVII:** **135–147**

Mark Twain in Eruption (Twain), **IV:** 209

Mark Twain's America (De Voto), **I:** 248

Mark Twain's Autobiography (Twain), **IV:** 209

Marley, Bob, **Supp. IX:** 152

Marlowe, Christopher, **I:** 68, 368, 384; **II:** 590; **III:** 259, 491; **Retro. Supp. I:** 127; **Retro. Supp. II:** 76; **Supp. I Part 2:** 422; **Supp. XXI:** 227
Marlowe, Kimberly B., **Supp. XXII:** 214
"Marlowe Takes on the Syndicate" (Chandler), **Supp. IV Part 1:** 135
Marne, The (Wharton), **IV:** 319, 320; **Retro. Supp. I:** 378
Marquand, John, **Supp. XI:** 301
Marquand, Mrs. John P. (Adelaide Hooker), **III:** 57, 61
Marquand, Mrs. John P. (Christina Sedgwick), **III:** 54, 57
Marquand, J. P., **I:** 362, 375; **II:** 459, 482–483; **III:** 50–73, 383; **Supp. I Part 1:** 196; **Supp. IV Part 1:** 31; **Supp. V:** 95
Marquand, Philip, **III:** 52
Marquis, Don, **Supp. I Part 2:** 668
Marrásh, Francis al-, **Supp. XX:** 117
"Marriage" (Corso), **Supp. XII:** 117, 124, **127–128**
Marriage (Moore), **III:** 194
"Marriage" (Moore), **III:** 198–199, 213
"Marriage, A" (Untermeyer), **Supp. XV:** 305
Marriage A-la-Mode (Dryden), **Supp. IX:** 68
Marriage and Other Science Fiction (Goldbarth), **Supp. XII:** 189, 190
"Marriage in the Sixties, A" (Rich), **Supp. I Part 2:** 554
Marriage of Heaven and Hell (Blake), **Supp. XXII:** 257
"Marriage of Heaven and Hell, The" (Blake), **III:** 544–545; **Supp. VIII:** 99
"Marriage of Phaedra, The" (Cather), **Retro. Supp. I:** 5
"Marriage Rhapsody"(Hadas), **Supp. XXIII:** 114
Married (Strindberg), **Supp. XXII:** 23
"Married" (Taggard), **Supp. XXII:** 274
Married Men (Wolfert), **Supp. XXI:** 277
Marrow of Tradition, The (Chesnutt), **Supp. XIV:** 63, **71–75,** 76
Marryat, Captain Frederick, **III:** 423
"Marrying Absurd" (Didion), **Supp. IV Part 1:** 200
"Marrying Iseult?" (Updike), **Retro. Supp. I:** 329
Marrying Man (Simon), **Supp. IV Part 2:** 588
"Marrying the Hangman" (Atwood), **Supp. XIII:** 34
Marry Me: A Romance (Updike), **Retro. Supp. I:** 329, 330, 332
"Mars and Hymen" (Freneau), **Supp. II Part 1:** 258
Marsden, Dora, **III:** 471; **Retro. Supp. I:** 416
Marsena (Frederic), **II:** 135, 136–137
Marsh, Edward, **Supp. I Part 1:** 257, 263
Marsh, Frederick T., **Supp. XX:** **39, 46**
Marsh, Fred T., **Supp. IX:** 232
Marsh, John R., **Supp. XIX:** 187
Marsh, Mae, **Supp. I Part 2:** 391
Marshall, George, **III:** 3

Marshall, John, **Supp. I Part 2:** 455; **Supp. XVI:** 117; **Supp. XIX:** 62; **Supp. XXIII:** 275, 276
Marshall, Paule, **Supp. IV Part 1:** 8, 14, 369; **Supp. XI:** 18, **275–292;** **Supp. XIII:** 295; **Supp. XX:** **154**
Marshall, Tod, **Supp. XV:** 224; **Supp. XVII:** 25, 26, 29, 32
"Marshall Carpenter" (Masters), **Supp. I Part 2:** 463
"Marshes of Glynn, The" (Lanier), **Supp. I Part 1:** 364, 365–368, 370, 373
"'Marshes of Glynn, The': A Study in Symbolic Obscurity" (Ross), **Supp. I Part 1:** 373
Marsh Island, A (Jewett), **II:** 405; **Retro. Supp. II:** 134
"Marshland Elegy" (Leopold), **Supp. XIV:** 187, 189
"Mars Is Heaven!" (Bradbury), **Supp. IV Part 1:** 103, 106
Mars-Jones, Adam, **Supp. XXI:** 116
Marsman, Henrik, **Supp. IV Part 1:** 183
Marston, Ed, **Supp. IV Part 2:** 492
Marston, Elsa, **Supp. XXIII:** 241
Marta y Maria (Valdes), **II:** 290
"Martha's Lady" (Jewett), **Retro. Supp. II:** 140, 143
Marthe, Saint, **II:** 213
Martial, **II:** 1, 169; **Supp. IX:** 152
Martian Chronicles, The (Bradbury), **Supp. IV Part 1:** 102, 103, 106–107
Martian Time-Slip (Dick), **Supp. XVIII:** 142
Martin, Benjamin, **Supp. I Part 2:** 503
Martin, Charles, **Supp. XVII:** 112
Martin, Dick, **Supp. XII:** 44
Martin, Jay, **I:** 55, 58, 60, 61, 67; **III:** 307; **Retro. Supp. II:** 326, 327, 329; **Supp. XI:** 162
Martin, John, **Supp. XI:** 172
Martin, Judith, **Supp. V:** 128
Martin, Nell, **Supp. IV Part 1:** 351, 353
Martin, Reginald, **Supp. X:** 247, 249
Martin, Robert, **Supp. XX:** **165**
Martin, Stephen-Paul, **Supp. IV Part 2:** 430
Martin, Tom, **Supp. X:** 79
Martin du Gard, Roger, **Supp. I Part 1:** 51
Martineau, Harriet, **Supp. II Part 1:** 282, 288, 294; **Supp. XVIII:** 7
Martin Eden (London), **II:** 466, 477–481
Martinelli, Sheri, **Supp. IV Part 1:** 280
Martínez, Guillermo, **Supp. XIII:** 313
Martinez-Avila, Raul, **Supp. XXIII:** 125
Martini, Adrienne, **Supp. XVIII:** 35
Mart'nez, Rafael, **Retro. Supp. I:** 423
Martone, John, **Supp. V:** 179
Marty (Chayefsky), **Supp. XV:** 205
"Martyr, The" (Porter), **III:** 454
Martz, Louis L., **IV:** 151, 156, 165; **Supp. I Part 1:** 107; **Supp. XIV:** 12; **Supp. XXI:** 85
Marvell, Andrew, **IV:** 135, 151, 156, 161, 253; **Retro. Supp. I:** 62, 127; **Retro. Supp. II:** 186, 189; **Supp. I Part 1:** 80; **Supp. XII:** 159; **Supp. XIV:** 10; **Supp. XVI:** 204; **Supp. XXI:** 227; **Supp. XXIII:** 62

"Marvella, for Borrowing" (Ríos), **Supp. IV Part 2:** 551
"Marvelous Sauce, The", **Supp. XVII:** 189
Marvels and Masterpieces (al-Badá'i' wa'l Tará'if) (Gibran), **Supp. XX:** **116, 124**
Marx, Eleanor, **Supp. XVI:** 85
Marx, Karl, **I:** 60, 267, 279, 283, 588; **II:** 376, 462, 463, 483, 577; **IV:** 429, 436, 443–444, 469, **Retro. Supp. I:** 254; **Supp. I Part 2:** 518, 628, 632, 633, 634, 635, 639, 643, 645, 646; **Supp. III Part 2:** 619; **Supp. IV Part 1:** 355; **Supp. VIII:** 196; **Supp. IX:** 133; **Supp. X:** 119, 134; **Supp. XIII:** 75; **Supp. XXI:** 162, 263
Marx, Leo, **Supp. I Part 1:** 233
"Marxism and Monastic Perpectives" (Merton), **Supp. VIII:** 196
Mary (Asch), **Supp. XXIII:** 2, 7, **14**
Mary (Nabokov), **Retro. Supp. I:** **267–268,** 270, 277
"Mary" (Trethewey), **Supp. XXI:** 246
"Mary Karr, Mary Karr, Mary Karr, Mary Karr" (Harmon), **Supp. XI:** 248
Maryles, Daisy, **Supp. XII:** 271
Mary Magdalene, **I:** 303
Mary; or, The Test of Honour (Rowson), **Supp. XV:** **233,** 236
"Mary O'Reilly" (Anderson), **II:** 44
"Mary Osaka , I Love You" (Fante), **Supp. XI:** 169
"Mary Snorak the Cook, Skermo the Gardener, and Jack the Parts Man Provide Dinner for a Wandering Stranger" (Grossman), **Supp. XIX:** 87
"Mary's Song" (Plath), **Supp. I Part 2:** 541
"Mary Winslow" (Lowell), **Retro. Supp. II:** 187
Marzynski, Marian, **Supp. XVI:** 153
Masefield, John, **II:** 552; **III:** 523
Masked and Anonymous (film, Dylan and Charles), **Supp. XVIII:** 21, 28
Mask for Janus, A (Merwin), **Supp. III Part 1:** 339, 341, 342
Maslin, Janet, **Supp. XVI:** 213; **Supp. XXI:** 79
Maslow, Abraham, **Supp. I Part 2:** 540
Maso, Carole, **Supp. XXII:** 261
Mason, Bobbie Ann, **Supp. VIII:** **133–149;** **Supp. XI:** 26; **Supp. XII:** 294, 298, 311; **Supp. XX:** **162**
Mason, Charlotte, **Supp. XIV:** 201
Mason, David, **Supp. V:** 344; **Supp. XV:** 116, 251; **Supp. XVII:** 109, 110, 112, 121; **Supp. XVIII:** 182, 183
Mason, Jennifer, **Supp. XVIII:** 263
Mason, Lowell, **I:** 458
Mason, Margaret, **Supp. XXIII:** 209
Mason, Marsha, **Supp. IV Part 2:** 575, 586
Mason, Otis Tufton, **Supp. I Part 1:** 18
Mason, Walt, **Supp. XV:** 298
Mason & Dixon (Pynchon), **Supp. XVII:** 232
"Mason Jars by the Window" (Ríos), **Supp. IV Part 2:** 548

"Masque in Green and Black"(Hadas), **Supp. XXIII:** 121

Masque of Mercy, A (Frost), **II:** 155, 165, 167–168; **Retro. Supp. I:** 131, 140

"Masque of Mummers, The" (MacLeish), **III:** 18

"Masque of Pandora, The" (Longfellow), **Retro. Supp. II:** 167

Masque of Pandora, The, and Other Poems (Longfellow), **II:** 490, 494, 506; **Retro. Supp. II:** 169

Masque of Poets, A (Lathrop, ed.), **Retro. Supp. I:** 31; **Supp. I Part 1:** 365, 368

Masque of Reason, A (Frost), **II:** 155, 162, 165–167; **Retro. Supp. I:** 131, 140; **Retro. Supp. II:** 42

"Masque of the Red Death, The" (Poe), **III:** 412, 419, 424; **Retro. Supp. II:** 262, 268–269

"Masquerade" (Banks), **Supp. V:** 7

Massachusetts, Its Historians and Its History (Adams), **Supp. I Part 2:** 484

"Massachusetts 1932" (Bowles), **Supp. IV Part 1:** 94

"Massachusetts to Virginia" (Whittier), **Supp. I Part 2:** 688–689

"Massacre and the Mastermind, The" (Bausch), **Supp. VII:** 49

"Massacre at Scio, The" (Bryant), **Supp. I Part 1:** 168

"Massacre of the Innocents, The" (Simic), **Supp. VIII:** 282

Masses and Man (Toller), **I:** 479

"Masseur de Ma Soeur, Le" (Hecht), **Supp. X:** 58

Massey, Raymond, **Supp. IV Part 2:** 524

"Mass Eye and Ear: The Ward" (Karr), **Supp. XI:** 244

"Mass for the Day of St. Thomas Didymus" (Levertov), **Supp. III Part 1:** 283

Massie, Chris, **Supp. IV Part 2:** 524

Massing, Michael, **Supp. IV Part 1:** 208

Massinger, Philip, **Supp. I Part 2:** 422; **Supp. XV:** 238

Master Builder, The (Ibsen), **Supp. IV Part 2:** 522

Master Class (McNally), **Supp. XIII:** 204–205, 208

"Masterful" (Matthews), **Supp. IX:** 161–162

Mastering the Art of French Cooking (Child), **Supp. XVII:** 89

"Master Misery" (Capote), **Supp. III Part 1:** 117

Master of Dreams: A Memoir of Isaac Bashevis Singer (Telushkin), **Retro. Supp. II:** 317

"Master of Secret Revenges, The" (Gass), **Supp. VI:** 93

Master of the Crossroads (Bell), **Supp. X:** 16–17

"'Masterpiece of Filth, A': Portrait of Knoxville Forgets to Be Fair" (Howards), **Supp. VIII:** 178

Masterpieces of American Fiction, **Supp. XI:** 198

"Master Player, The" (Dunbar), **Supp. II Part 1:** 200

Masters, Edgar Lee, **I:** 106, 384, 475, 480, 518; **II:** 276, 529; **III:** 505, 576, 579; **IV:** 352; **Retro. Supp. I:** 131; **Supp. I Part 2:** 378, 386, 387, **454–478; Supp. III Part 1:** 63, 71, 73, 75; **Supp. IV Part 2:** 502; **Supp. IX:** 308; **Supp. XIV:** 282–283; **Supp. XV:** 256, 293, 297, 301, 306

Masters, Hardin W., **Supp. I Part 2:** 468

Masters, Hilary, **Supp. IX:** 96

Masters of Sociological Thought (Coser), **Supp. I Part 2:** 650

Masters of the Dew (Roumain), **Supp. IV Part 1:** 367

"Masters of War" (song, Dylan), **Supp. XVIII:** 24

"Master's Pieces, The" (H. L. Gates), **Supp. XX: 109**

Matchmaker, The (Wilder), **IV:** 357, 369, 370, 374; **Supp. XX: 50**

Mate of the Daylight, The, and Friends Ashore (Jewett), **II:** 404; **Retro. Supp. II:** 146–147

Materassi, Mario, **Supp. IX:** 233

Mather, Cotton, **II:** 10, 104, 302, 506, 536; **III:** 442; **IV:** 144, 152–153, 157; **Supp. I Part 1:** 102, 117, 174, 271; **Supp. I Part 2:** 584, 599, 698; **Supp. II Part 2: 441–470; Supp. IV Part 2:** 430, 434

Mather, Increase, **II:** 10; **IV:** 147, 157; **Supp. I Part 1:** 100

Mathews, Cornelius, **III:** 81; **Supp. I Part 1:** 317

Mathews, Shailer, **III:** 293

"Matinees" (Merrill), **Supp. III Part 1:** 319, 327

"Matins" (C. Frost), **Supp. XV:** 105

"Matins" (Glück), **Supp. V:** 88

"Matins" (Nelson), **Supp. XVIII:** 177

Matisse, Henri, **III:** 180; **IV:** 90, 407; **Supp. I Part 2:** 619; **Supp. VIII:** 168; **Supp. IX:** 66; **Supp. X:** 73, 74; **Supp. XXII:** 98, 99

"Matisse: Blue Interior with Two Girls–1947" (Hecht), **Supp. X: 73–74**

"Matisse: The Red Studio" (Snodgrass), **Supp. VI:** 316–317

Matlack, James, **Supp. XV:** 269, 271, 286

Matlock, Lucinda, **Supp. I Part 2:** 462

Matos, Juan, **Supp. XXI:** 104

Matrimaniac, The (film), **Supp. XVI:** 185, 186

Matrix Trilogy, The (film), **Supp. XVI:** 271

Matson, Harold, **Supp. XIII:** 164, 166, 167, 169, 172

Matson, Peter, **Supp. IV Part 1:** 299

Matson, Suzanne, **Supp. VIII:** 281

Matters of Fact and Fiction: Essays 1973–1976 (Vidal), **Supp. IV Part 2:** 687

Matters of Life and Death: New American Stories (Wolff, ed.), **Supp. XXIII:** 289

Matthew (biblical book), **IV:** 164; **Supp. XV:** 222

Matthew Arnold (Trilling), **Supp. III Part 2:** 500–501

Matthews, Jackson, **Supp. XVI:** 282

Matthews, T. S., **II:** 430; **Supp. XV:** 142

Matthews, William, **Supp. V:** 4, 5; **Supp. IX: 151–170; Supp. XIII:** 112; **Supp. XXI:** 87

Matthiessen, F. O., **I:** 254, 259–260, 517; **II:** 41, 554; **III:** 310, 453; **IV:** 181; **Retro. Supp. I:** 40, 217; **Retro. Supp. II:** 137; **Supp. IV Part 2:** 422; **Supp. XIII:** 93; **Supp. XIV:** 3; **Supp. XXI:** 277

Matthiessen, Peter, **Supp. V: 199–217,** 332; **Supp. XI:** 231, 294; **Supp. XIV:** 82; **Supp. XVI:** 230; **Supp. XIX:** 268

Mattingly, Garrett, **Supp. IV Part 2:** 601

Mattos, Anita, **Supp. XXIII:** 197

Mattu, Ravi, **Supp. XVI:** 124

"Maud Island" (Caldwell), **I:** 310

Maud Martha (Brooks), **Supp. III Part 1:** 74, 78–79, 87; **Supp. XI:** 278

"Maud Muller" (Whittier), **Supp. I Part 2:** 698

Maugham, W. Somerset, **III:** 57, 64; **Supp. IV Part 1:** 209; **Supp. X:** 58; **Supp. XIV:** 161

Maule's Curse: Seven Studies in the History of American Obscurantism (Winters), **Supp. II Part 2:** 807–808, 812

"Mau-mauing the Flak Catchers" (Wolfe), **Supp. III Part 2:** 577

Maupassant, Guy de, **I:** 309, 421; **II:** 191–192, 291, 325, 591; **IV:** 17; **Retro. Supp. II:** 65, 66, 67, 299; **Supp. I Part 1:** 207, 217, 223, 320; **Supp. XIV:** 336

"Maurice Barrès and the Youth of France" (Bourne), **I:** 228

Maurice Kenny: Celebrations of a Mohawk Writer (Kelsey, ed.), **Supp. XXIII:** 143

Maurier, George du, **II:** 338

Maurras, Charles, **Retro. Supp. I:** 55

Maus II: And Here My Troubles Began (A. Speigelman), **Supp. XVII:** 48

Mauve Gloves & Madmen, Clutter & Vine (Wolfe), **Supp. III Part 2:** 581

Maverick, Augustus, **Supp. XVIII:** 4

Maverick in Mauve (Auchincloss), **Supp. IV Part 1:** 26

"Mavericks, The" (play) (Auchincloss), **Supp. IV Part 1:** 34

"Mavericks, The" (story) (Auchincloss), **Supp. V Part 1:** 32

"Max" (H. Miller), **III:** 183

Max, D. T., **Supp. XXI:** 117

Max and the White Phagocytes (H. Miller), **III:** 178, 183–184

Maximilian (emperor of Mexico), **Supp. I Part 2:** 457–458

Maximilian: A Play in Five Acts (Masters), **Supp. I Part 2:** 456, 457–458

"Maximus, to Gloucester" (Olson), **Supp. II Part 2:** 574

"Maximus, to himself" (Olson), **Supp. II Part 2:** 565, 566, 567, 569, 570, 572

Maximus Poems, The (Olson), **Retro. Supp. I:** 209; **Supp. II Part 2:** 555, 556, 563, 564–580, 584; **Supp. VIII:** 305; **Supp. XV:** 170, 264, 349; **Supp. XVI:** 287

Maximus Poems 1–10, The (Olson), **Supp. II Part 2:** 571

Maximus Poems IV, V, VI (Olson), **Supp. II Part 2:** 555, 580, 582–584

Maximus Poems Volume Three, The (Olson), **Supp. II Part 2:** 555, 582, 584–585

"Maximus to Gloucester, Letter 19 (A Pastoral Letter)" (Olson), **Supp. II Part 2:** 567

"Maximus to Gloucester, Sunday July 19" (Olson), **Supp. II Part 2:** 580

"Maximus to himself June 1964" (Olson), **Supp. II Part 2:** 584

Maxwell, Glyn, **Supp. XV:** 252, 253, 260, 261, 263, 264

Maxwell, William, **Supp. I Part 1:** 175; **Supp. III Part 1:** 62; **Supp. VIII:** 151–174; **Supp. XVII:** 23

May, Abigail (Abba). *See* Alcott, Mrs. Amos Bronson (Abigail May)

May, Elaine Tyler, **Supp. XXII:** 81, 95

May, Jill, **Supp. VIII:** 126

"May 24, 1980" (Brodsky), **Supp. VIII:** 28

"May 1968" (Olds), **Supp. X:** 211–212

Mayakovsky, Vladimir, **Supp. XXIII:** 207

"Mayakovsky"(O'Hara), **Supp. XXIII:** 212, 214

"Mayan Glyphs Unread, The" (Bronk), **Supp. XXI:** 31

"Mayan Warning" (Mora), **Supp. XIII:** 214

Maybe (Hellman), **Supp. IV Part 1:** 12

"Maybe" (Oliver), **Supp. VII:** 239

"Maybe, Someday" (Ritsos), **Supp. XIII:** 78

May Blossom (Belasco), **Supp. XVI:** 182

"Mayday" (Faulkner), **Retro. Supp. I:** 80

"May Day" (Fitzgerald), **II:** 88–89; **Retro. Supp. I:** 103

"May Day Dancing, The" (Nemerov), **III:** 275

May Days (Pickering), **Supp. XXI:** 197–198

May Days: An Anthology of Verse from Masses-Liberator (Taggard, ed.), **Supp. XXII:** 275–276

"May Day Sermon to the Women of Gilmer County, Georgia, by a Woman Preacher Leaving the Baptist Church" (Dickey), **Supp. IV Part 1:** 182

Mayer, Elizabeth, **Supp. II Part 1:** 16; **Supp. III Part 1:** 63

Mayer, John, **Retro. Supp. I:** 58

Mayer, Louis B., **Supp. XII:** 160; **Supp. XVIII:** 250

Mayes, Wendell, **Supp. IX:** 250

Mayfield, Sara, **Supp. IX:** 65

Mayflower, The (Stowe), **Supp. I Part 2:** 585, 586

Mayle, Peter, **Supp. XVI:** 295

Maynard, Joyce, **Supp. V:** 23

Maynard, Tony, **Supp. I Part 1:** 65

Mayne, Xavier. *See* Prime-Stevenson, Edward Irenaeus

Mayo, Robert, **III:** 478

Mayor (Allen), **Supp. XXII:** 245

Mayorga, Margaret, **IV:** 381

"May-Pole of Merry Mount, The" (Hawthorne), **Supp. XXII:** 44

"Maypole of Merrymount, The" (Hawthorne), **II:** 229

"May Queen" (Di Piero), **Supp. XIX:** 41

May Sarton: Selected Letters 1916–1954, **Supp. VIII:** 265

"May Sun Sheds an Amber Light, The" (Bryant), **Supp. I Part 1:** 170

"May Swenson: The Art of Perceiving" (Stanford), **Supp. IV Part 2:** 637

May the Generations Die in the Right Order (Schott), **Supp. XXIII:** 248–250

"Maze" (Eberhart), **I:** 523, 525–526, 527

Mazel (R. Goldstein), **Supp. XVII:** 44

Mazower, David, **Supp. XXIII:** 4, 5

Mazur, Gail, **Supp. XVIII:** 92

Mazurkiewicz, Margaret, **Supp. XI:** 2

Mazzini, Giuseppe, **Supp. I Part 1:** 2, 8; **Supp. II Part 1:** 299

M. Butterfly (Hwang), **Supp. X:** 292; **Supp. XXI:** 143, 147, **150–154**

Mc. Names starting with Mc are alphabetized as if spelled Mac.

"M. Degas Teaches Art & Science at Durfee Intermediate School, Detroit, 1942" (Levine), **Supp. V:** 181, 193

"Me, Boy Scout" (Lardner), **II:** 433

Me, Vashya! (T. Williams), **IV:** 381

Mead, Elinor. *See* Howells, Mrs. William Dean (Elinor Mead)

Mead, George Herbert, **II:** 27, 34; **Supp. I Part 1:** 5; **Supp. I Part 2:** 641

Mead, Margaret, **Supp. I Part 1:** 49, 52, 66; **Supp. IX:** 229

Mead, Taylor, **Supp. XV:** 187

Meade, Frank, **Retro. Supp. II:** 114

Meade, Marion, **Supp. IX:** 191, 193, 194, 195

Meadow, Lynne, **Supp. XIII:** 198

"Meadow House" (Carruth), **Supp. XVI:** 48

Meadowlands (Glück), **Supp. V:** 88–90

"Mean, Mrs." (Gass), **Supp. VI:** 83

"Me and the Mule" (Hughes), **Supp. I Part 1:** 334

"Meaningless Institution, A" (Ginsberg), **Supp. II Part 1:** 313

"Meaning of a Literary Idea, The" (Trilling), **Supp. III Part 2:** 498

"Meaning of Birds, The" (C. Smith), **Supp. X:** 177

"Meaning of Death, The, An After Dinner Speech" (Tate), **IV:** 128, 129

"Meaning of Life, The" (Tate), **IV:** 137

"Meaning of Simplicity, The" (Ritsos), **Supp. XIII:** 78

Means of Escape (Caputo), **Supp. XIX:** 18, 21, 25

Mean Spirit (Hogan), **Supp. IV Part 1:** 397, 404, 407–410, 415, 416–417

Meantime, The (Bronk), **Supp. XXI:** 31

Mearns, Hughes, **III:** 220

"Measure" (Hass), **Supp. VI:** **99–100,** 101

"Measuring My Blood" (Vizenor), **Supp. IV Part 1:** 262

Meatyard, Gene, **Supp. X:** 30

Me: By Jimmy (Big Boy) Valente (Keillor), **Supp. XVI:** 177

Mechan, Dennis B., **Supp. XVI:** 267–268

Mechanic, The (Bynner and DeMille), **Supp. XV:** 42, 50

"Mechanism" (Ammons), **Supp. VII:** 28

"Mechanism in Thought and Morals" (Holmes), **Supp. I Part 1:** 314

Mecom, Mrs. Jane, **II:** 122

"Meddlesome Jack" (Caldwell), **I:** 309

Medea (Jeffers), **Supp. II Part 2:** 435

Medea and Some Poems, The (Cullen), **Supp. IV Part 1:** 169, 173

"Me Decade and the Third Great Awakening, The" (Wolfe), **Supp. III Part 2:** 581

"Médecin Malgré Lui, Le" (W. C. Williams), **IV:** 407–408

"Medfield" (Bryant), **Supp. I Part 1:** 157

Medical History of Contraception, A (Himes), **Supp. V:** 128

"Medicine Song" (Gunn Allen), **Supp. IV Part 1:** 326

Médicis, Marie de, **II:** 548

Medina (McCarthy), **II:** 579

"Meditation, A" (Eberhart), **I:** 533–535

"Meditation 1.6" (Taylor), **IV:** 165

"Meditation 1.20" (Taylor), **IV:** 165

"Meditation 2.68A" (Taylor), **IV:** 165

"Meditation 2.102" (Taylor), **IV:** 150

"Meditation 2.112" (Taylor), **IV:** 165

"Meditation 20" (Taylor), **IV:** 154–155

"Meditation 40" (Second Series) (Taylor), **IV:** 147

"Meditation at Lagunitas" (Hass), **Supp. VI:** 104–105; **Supp. XXI:** 60

"Meditation at Oyster River" (Roethke), **III:** 537, 549

Meditations (Descartes), **III:** 618

Meditations (Marcus Aurelius), **Supp. XVIII:** 304

"Meditations for a Savage Child" (Rich), **Supp. I Part 2:** 564–565

Meditations from a Movable Chair (Dubus), **Supp. VII:** 91

Meditations in an Emergency (O'Hara), **Supp. XXIII:** **213–214,** 219, 220

"Meditations in an Emergency"(O'Hara), **Supp. XXIII:** 212, 214

"Meditations in a Swine Yard" (Komunyakaa), **Supp. XIII:** 131

"Meditations of an Old Woman" (Roethke), **III:** 529, 540, 542, 543, 545–547, 548

"Meditations on Grass"(Crooker), **Supp. XXIII:** 55

Meditations on the Insatiable Soul (R. Bly), **Supp. IV Part 1:** 72–73

Meditative Poems, The (Martz), **IV:** 151

"Mediterranean, The" (Tate), **IV:** 129

"Medium of Fiction, The" (Gass), **Supp. VI:** 85–86

"Medley" (Bambara), **Supp. XI:** 9

"Medusa" (Bogan), **Supp. III Part 1:** 50, 51

Meehan, Jeannette Porter, **Supp. XX:** **213, 214, 217, 220, 224**

Meehan, Thomas, **Supp. IV Part 2:** 577–578, 586, 590

Meek, Martha, **Supp. IV Part 2:** 439, 440, 441, 442, 445, 447, 448

Meeker, Richard K., **II:** 190

Meese, Elizabeth, **Supp. XIII:** 297

"Meeting" (J. W. Miller), **Supp. XX: 167**

"Meeting, The" (F. Wright), **Supp. XVII:** 245

"Meeting and Greeting Area, The" (Cameron), **Supp. XII: 84–85**

Meeting by the River, A (Isherwood), **Supp. XIV:** 164, **170–171,** 172

"Meeting-House Hill" (Lowell), **II:** 522, 527

"Meeting in the Kitchen, The" (Schnackenberg), **Supp. XV:** 256

"Meeting South, A" (Anderson), **I:** 115

"Meeting the Mountains" (Snyder), **Supp. VIII:** 300

Meeting Trees (Sanders), **Supp. XVI:** 269

Meet Me at the Morgue (Macdonald), **Supp. IV Part 2:** 472

Mehta, Sonny, **Supp. XI:** 178

Mehta, Ved, **Supp. XX:** 87

Meine, Curt, **Supp. XIV:** 179

Meiners, R. K., **IV:** 136, 137, 138, 140

Meinong, Alexius, **Supp. XIV:** 198, 199

Meisner, Sanford, **Supp. XIV:** 240, 242

Meister, Charles W., **II:** 112

Mejia, Jaime, **Supp. XIX:** 97

"Melancholia" (Dunbar), **Supp. II Part 1:** 194

Melancholy Baby (Parker), **Supp. XIX:** 186

"Melanctha" (Stein), **IV:** 30, 34, 35, 37, 38–40, 45

"Melancthon" (Moore), **III:** 212, 215

Melbourne House (S. and A. Warner), **Supp. XVIII:** 268

Meliboeus Hipponax (Lowell). *See Bigelow Papers, The* (Lowell)

Melinda and Melinda (Allen), **Supp. XV:** 16

Mellaart, James, **Supp. I Part 2:** 567

Mellard, James, **Supp. IV Part 1:** 387

Mellon, Andrew, **III:** 14

Mellor, W. M., **Supp. XX:** 56

Melnick, Jeffrey, **Supp. X:** 252

Melnyczuk, Askold, **Supp. IV Part 1:** 70

Melodrama Play (Shepard), **Supp. III Part 2:** 440–441, 443, 445

Melodramatists, The (Nemerov), **III:** 268, 281–283, 284

Melopoeia (Espaillat and Tavano), **Supp. XXI:** 99–100

Melting-Pot, The (Zangwill), **I:** 229

"Melungeons" (Offutt), **Supp. XIX:** 171

Melville, Allan, **III:** 74, 77

Melville, Gansevoort, **III:** 76

Melville, Herman, **I:** 104, 106, 211, 288, 340, 343, 348, 354, 355, 561–562; **II:** 27, 74, 224–225, 228, 230, 232, 236, 255, 259, 271, 272, 277, 281, 295, 307, 311, 319, 320, 321, 418, 477, 497, 539–540, 545; **III:** 29, 45, 70, **74–98,** 359, 438, 453, 454, 507, 562–563, 572, 576; **IV:** 57, 105, 194, 199, 202, 250, 309, 333, 345, 350, 380, 444, 453; **Retro. Supp. I:** 54, 91, 160, 215, 220, **243–262; Retro. Supp. II:** 76; **Supp. I Part 1:** 147, 238, 242, 249, 309, 317, 372; **Supp. I Part 2:** 383, 495, 579, 580, 582, 602; **Supp. IV Part 2:** 463, 613; **Supp. V:** 279, 281, 298, 308; **Supp. VIII:** 48, 103, 104, 105, 106, 108, 156, 175, 181, 188; **Supp. XI:** 83; **Supp. XII:** 282; **Supp. XIII:** 294, 305; **Supp. XIV:** 48, 227; **Supp. XV:** 287; **Supp. XVII:** 42, 185; **Supp. XVIII:** 1, 4, 6, 7, 9; **Supp. XXI:** 169; **Supp. XXII:** 174, 262; **Supp. XXIII:** 164, 165, 174, 190

Melville, Mrs. Herman (Elizabeth Shaw), **III:** 77, 91, 92

Melville, Maria Gansevoort, **III:** 74, 77, 85

Melville, Thomas, **III:** 77, 79, 92; **Supp. I Part 1:** 309

Melville, Whyte, **IV:** 309

Melville Goodwin, USA (Marquand), **III:** 60, 65–66

Melville's Marginalia (Cowen), **Supp. IV Part 2:** 435

"Melville's Marginalia" (Howe), **Supp. IV Part 2:** 435

Member of the Wedding, The (McCullers), **II:** 587, 592, 600–604, 605, 606; **Supp. VIII:** 124

"Meme Ortiz" (Cisneros), **Supp. VII:** 60

Memmon (song cycle) (Bowles), **Supp. IV Part 1:** 82

Memnoch the Devil (Rice), **Supp. VII:** 289, 290, 294, 296–299

"Memoir" (Hempel), **Supp. XXI:** 118

"Memoir" (Untermeyer), **II:** 516–517

"Memoir, A" (Koch), **Supp. XV:** 184

"Memoirist's Apology, A" (Karr), **Supp. XI:** 245, 246

Memoir of Mary Ann, A (O'Connor), **III:** 357

Memoir of Thomas McGrath, A (Beeching), **Supp. X:** 114, 118

Memoirs (W. Frank), **Supp. XX: 67, 69, 70, 81**

Memoirs of a Preacher, a Revelation of the Church and the Home, The (Lippard), **Supp. XXIII:** 178, 183–184, 188, 190

Memoirs of Arii Taimai (Adams), **I:** 2–3

"Memoirs of Carwin, the Biloquist" (Brown), **Supp. I Part 1:** 132

Memoirs of Hecate County (Wilson), **IV:** 429

Memoirs of Margaret Fuller Ossoli (Fuller), **Supp. II Part 1:** 280, 283, 285

"Memoirs of Stephen Calvert" (Brown), **Supp. I Part 1:** 133, 144

Memorabilia (Xenophon), **II:** 105

Memorable Providences (Mather), **Supp. II Part 2:** 458

Memorial, The: Portrait of a Family (Isherwood), **Supp. XIV:** 156, 159, 160–161

"Memorial Day" (Cameron), **Supp. XII:** 80, **82–83**

"Memorial for the City" (Auden), **Supp. II Part 1:** 20

"Memorial Rain" (MacLeish), **III:** 15

"Memorial to Ed Bland" (Brooks), **Supp. III Part 1:** 77

"Memorial Tribute" (Wilbur), **Supp. IV Part 2:** 642

"Memories" (Whittier), **Supp. I Part 2:** 699

Memories of a Catholic Girlhood (McCarthy), **II:** 560–561, 566; **Supp. XI:** 246; **Supp. XVI:** 64, 70

"Memories of East Texas" (Karr), **Supp. XI:** 239

"Memories of Uncle Neddy" (Bishop), **Retro. Supp. II:** 38; **Supp. I Part 1:** 73, 93

"Memories of West Street and Lepke" (Lowell), **II:** 550

"Memory" (Epstein), **Supp. XII:** 163

"Memory" (Everwine), **Supp. XV:** 82

"Memory, A" (Welty), **IV:** 261–262; **Retro. Supp. I:** 344–345

"Memory, Narrative, and the Discourses of Identity in *Abeng* and *No Telephone to Heaven*" (Smith), **Supp. XXII:** 70

"Memory, The" (Gioia), **Supp. XV:** 119

Memory and Enthusiasm: Essays, 1975–1985 (Di Piero), **Supp. XIX:** 34, 41, 42

"Memory and Imagination" (Hampl), **Supp. XXII:** 94

Memory Gardens (Creeley), **Supp. IV Part 1:** 141, 157

"Memory Harbor" (Skloot), **Supp. XX:** 201

Memory of Murder, A (Bradbury), **Supp. IV Part 1:** 103

Memory of Old Jack, The (Berry), **Supp. X:** 34

Memory of Two Mondays, A (A. Miller), **III:** 153, 156, 158–159, 160, 166

"Memo to Non-White Peoples" (Hughes), **Retro. Supp. I:** 209

Men, Women and Ghosts (Lowell), **II:** 523–524

Menaker, Charlotte, **Supp. XIX:** 266

Menaker, Daniel, **Supp. VIII:** 151; **Supp. XXIII:** 276

Menand, Louis, **Supp. XIV:** 40, 197; **Supp. XVI:** 106, 107; **Supp. XXIII:** 104–105

Men and Angels (Gordon), **Supp. IV Part 1:** 304–305, 306, 308

Men and Brethen (Cozzens), **I:** 363–365, 368, 375, 378, 379

Men and Cartoons (Lethem), **Supp. XVIII:** 145, **148**

"Men and Women" (R. Bly), **Supp. IV Part 1:** 72

"Men at Forty" (Justice), **Supp. VII:** 126–127

Mencius (Meng-tzu), **IV:** 183

Mencken, August, **III:** 100, 108

Mencken, August, Jr., **III:** 99, 109, 118–119

Mencken, Mrs. August (Anna Abhau), **III:** 100, 109

Mencken, Burkhardt, **III:** 100, 108

Mencken, Charles, **III:** 99

Mencken, Gertrude, **III:** 99

Mencken, H. L., **I:** 199, 210, 212, 235, 245, 261, 405, 514, 515, 517; **II:** 25, 27, 42, 89, 90, 91, 271, 289, 430, 443, 449; **III:** **99–121,** 394, 482; **IV:** 76,

432, 440, 475, 482; **Retro. Supp. I:** 1, 101; **Retro. Supp. II:** 97, 98, 102, 265; **Supp. I Part 2:** 484, 629–630, 631, 647, 651, 653, 659, 673; **Supp. II Part 1:** 136; **Supp. IV Part 1:** 201, 314, 343; **Supp. IV Part 2:** 521, 692, 693; **Supp. XI:** 163–164, 166; **Supp. XIII:** 161; **Supp. XIV:** 111; **Supp. XV:** 297, 301, 303; **Supp. XVI:** 187–188, 189; **Supp. XVII:** 106; **Supp. XXII:** 23, 187, 277

Mencken, Mrs. H. L. (Sara Haardt), **III:** 109, 111

"Men Deified Because of Their Cruelty" (Simic), **Supp. VIII:** 282

Mendelbaum, Paul, **Supp. V:** 159

Mendele, **IV:** 3, 10

Mendelief, Dmitri Ivanovich, **IV:** 421

Mendelsohn, Daniel, **Supp. X:** 153, 154; **Supp. XV:** 257, 258, 261, 266

Mendelssohn, Moses, **Supp. XXIII:** 4

Mendes, Alfred, **Supp. XXI:** 160

"Mending Wall" (Frost), **II:** 153–154; **Retro. Supp. I:** 128, 130; **Supp. X:** 64

Men from the Boys, The (Lacy), **Supp. XV:** 202, 205

Men in the Off Hours (Carson), **Supp. XII:** 111–113

"Men in the Storm, The" (Crane), **I:** 411

"Men Loved Wholly Beyond Wisdom" (Bogan), **Supp. III Part 1:** 50

"Men Made Out of Words" (Stevens), **IV:** 88

Men Must Act (Mumford), **Supp. II Part 2:** 479

Mennes, John, **II:** 111

Mennoti, Gian Carlo, **Supp. IV Part 1:** 84

Men of Brewster Place, The (Naylor), **Supp. VIII:** 213, 228–230

"Men of Color, to Arms!" (Douglass), **Supp. III Part 1:** 171

Men of Good Hope: A Story of American Progressives (Aaron), **Supp. I Part 2:** 650

Mens' Club, The (film), **Supp. XVI:** 212–213

Men's Club, The (L. Michaels), **Supp. XVI:** 206, 210–212

"Menstruation at Forty" (Sexton), **Supp. II Part 2:** 686

"Mental Hospital Garden, The" (W. C. Williams), **Retro. Supp. I:** 428

Mental Radio (Sinclair), **Supp. V:** 289

Mentoria; or, The Young Lady's Friend (Rowson), **Supp. XV:** 233–234, 238

"Men We Carry in Our Minds, The" (Sanders), **Supp. XVI:** 273

Men Who Made the Nation, The (Dos Passos), **I:** 485

Men Without Women (Hemingway), **II:** 249; **Retro. Supp. I:** 170, 176; **Supp. IX:** 202

"Merced" (Rich), **Supp. I Part 2:** 563

"Mercedes" (E. Stoddard), **Supp. XV:** 278

"Mercedes Hospital" (Bishop), **Retro. Supp. II:** 51

"Mercenary, A" (Ozick), **Supp. V:** 267

Mercer, Johnny, **Supp. XXII:** 6

Merchandising (Hwang), **Supp. XXI:** 147

Merchant of Venice, The (Shakespeare), **IV:** 227; **Supp. XIV:** 325

Mercury Theatre, **Retro. Supp. I:** 65

Mercy, Pity, Peace, and Love (Ozick), **Supp. V:** 257, 258

Mercy, The (Levine), **Supp. V:** 194–195

"Mercy" (P. Benedict), **Supp. XXIII:** 49

Mercy Philbrick's Choice (Jackson), **Retro. Supp. I:** 26, 27, 33

Mercy Street (Sexton), **Supp. II Part 2:** 683, 689

"Mercy" (Thompson), **Supp. XXIII:** 295, 296

Meredith, George, **II:** 175, 186; **Supp. IV Part 1:** 300

Meredith, Mary. *See* Webb, Mary

Meredith, William, **II:** 545; **Retro. Supp. II:** 181

"Merely by Wilderness" (Peacock), **Supp. XIX:** 199

"Merely to Know" (Rich), **Supp. I Part 2:** 554

"Mère Pochette" (Jewett), **II:** 400

"Merger II, The" (Auchincloss), **Supp. IV Part 1:** 34

Meri (Asch), **Supp. XXIII:** 5, 11

"Mericans" (Cisneros), **Supp. VII:** 69

"Merida, 1969" (Matthews), **Supp. IX:** 151

"Meridian" (Clampitt), **Supp. IX:** 48–49

Meridian (Walker), **Supp. III Part 2:** 520, 524, 527, 528, 531–537

Mérimée, Prosper, **II:** 322

Meriwether, James B., **Retro Supp. I:** 77, 91

"Meriwether Connection, The" (Cowley), **Supp. II Part 1:** 142

Merker, Kim K., **Supp. XI:** 261; **Supp. XV:** 75, 77

"Merlin" (Emerson), **II:** 19, 20

Merlin (Robinson), **III:** 522

"Merlin Enthralled" (Wilbur), **Supp. III Part 2:** 544, 554

"Mermother" (A. Finch), **Supp. XVII:** 72

Merril, Judith, **Supp. XVI:** 123

Merrill, Cavafy, Poems, and Dreams (Hadas), **Supp. XXIII:** 123–124

Merrill, Christopher, **Supp. XI:** 329

Merrill, James, **Retro. Supp. I:** 296; **Retro. Supp. II:** 53; **Supp. III Part 1:** 317–338; **Supp. III Part 2:** 541, 561; **Supp. IX:** 40, 42, 48, 52; **Supp. X:** 73; **Supp. XI:** 123, 131, 249; **Supp. XII:** 44, 254, 255, 256, 261–262, 269–270; **Supp. XIII:** 76, 85; **Supp. XV:** 249, 250, 253; **Supp. XVII:** 123; **Supp. XXIII:** 112, 122, 123

Merrill, Mark (pseudonym). *See* Markson, David

Merrill, Robert, **Retro. Supp. II:** 201

Merrill, Ronald, **Supp. IV Part 2:** 521

Merritt, Abraham, **Supp. XVII:** 58

Merritt, Theresa, **Supp. VIII:** 332

Merritt, Vernon, **Supp. XXII:** 245

"Merry-Go-Round" (Hughes), **Retro. Supp. I:** 194, 205; **Supp. I Part 1:** 333

Merry-Go-Round, The (Van Vechten), **Supp. II Part 2:** 734, 735

Merry Month of May, The (Jones), **Supp. XI:** 227–228

Merry Widow, The (Lehar), **III:** 183

Merton, Thomas, **III:** 357; **Supp. VIII:** 193–212; **Supp. XXII:** 83, 90

Merwin, W. S., **Supp. III Part 1:** 339–360; **Supp. III Part 2:** 541; **Supp. IV Part 2:** 620, 623, 626; **Supp. V:** 332; **Supp. IX:** 152, 155, 290; **Supp. XIII:** 274, 277; **Supp. XV:** 222, 342; **Supp. XIX:** 82; **Supp. XXI:** 95

Meryman, Richard, **Supp. IV Part 2:** 579, 583

Meshiekhs tsaytn (Times of the Messiah) (Asch), **Supp. XXIII:** 5

Meshugah (Singer), **Retro. Supp. II:** 315–316

Mesic, Michael, **Supp. IV Part 1:** 175

Mesic, Penelope, **Supp. X:** 15

Message in the Bottle, The (Percy), **Supp. III Part 1:** 387–388, 393, 397

"Message in the Bottle, The" (Percy), **Supp. III Part 1:** 388

"Message of Flowers and Fire and Flowers, The" (Brooks), **Supp. III Part 1:** 69

Messengers Will Come No More, The (Fiedler), **Supp. XIII:** 103

Messerli, Douglas, **Supp. XVI:** 293

Messiah (Vidal), **Supp. IV Part 2:** 677, 680, 681–682, 685, 691, 692

"Messiah, The" (Wasserstein), **Supp. XV:** 328

Messiah of Stockholm, The (Ozick), **Supp. V:** 270–271; **Supp. XVII:** 42

Messud, Claire, **Supp. XVIII:** 98

Metamorphic Tradition in Modern Poetry (Quinn), **IV:** 421

Metamorphoses (Ovid), **II:** 542–543; **III:** 467, 468; **Supp. XV:** 33; **Supp. XVI:** 20; **Supp. XX:** 280

Metamorphoses (Pound, trans.), **III:** 468–469

Metamorphosis (Kafka), **Supp. XXI:** 89

Metamorphosis, The (Kafka), **IV:** 438; **Retro. Supp. II:** 287–288; **Supp. VIII:** 3

"Metamorphosis and Survival" (Woodcock), **Supp. XIII:** 33

"Metaphor as Mistake" (Percy), **Supp. III Part 1:** 387–388

Metaphor & Memory: Essays (Ozick), **Supp. V:** 272

Metaphor of Trees and Last Poems (Bronk), **Supp. XXI:** 32

"Metaphors of a Magnifico" (Stevens), **IV:** 92

Metaphysical Club, The (Menand), **Supp. XIV:** 40, 197

"Metaphysical Poets, The" (Eliot), **I:** 527, 586

"Metaphysics" (Ginsberg), **Supp. II Part 1:** 313

Metcalf, Paul, **Supp. XIV:** 96; **Supp. XXIII:** 163, 174

"Meteor, The" (Bradbury), **Supp. IV Part 1:** 102

Methinks the Lady...(Endore), **Supp. XVII:** 61–62

"Metonymy as an Approach to the Real World" (Bronk), **Supp. XXI:** 30

Metress, Christopher P., **Supp. V:** 314

Metrical History of Christianity, The (Taylor), **IV:** 163

Metropolis, The (Sinclair), **Supp. V:** 285

"Metterling Lists, The" (Allen), **Supp. XV:** 15

"Metzengerstein" (Poe), **III:** 411, 417

Mew, Charlotte, **Retro. Supp. II:** 247

Mewshaw, Michael, **Supp. V:** 57; **Supp. X:** 82

"Mexican Hands" (Ryan as Quin), **Supp. XVIII:** 227

"Mexico" (Lowell), **II:** 553, 554

"Mexico, Age Four" (Salinas), **Supp. XIII:** 315

Mexico City Blues (Kerouac), **Supp. III Part 1:** 225, 229

"Mexico Is a Foreign Country: Five Studies in Naturalism" (Warren), **IV:** 241, 252

"Mexico's Children" (Rodriguez), **Supp. XIV:** 302

Meyer, Carolyn, **Supp. XIX:** 194–195, 197

Meyer, Donald B., **III:** 298

Meyer, Ellen Hope, **Supp. V:** 123

Meyer, Robert, **Supp. XXI:** 23

Meyers, Jeffrey, **Retro. Supp. I:** 124, 138; **Retro. Supp. II:** 191

Meynell, Alice, **Supp. I Part 1:** 220

Mezey, Robert, **Supp. IV Part 1:** 60; **Supp. V:** 180; **Supp. XIII:** 312; **Supp. XV:** 74

Mezzanine, The (Baker), **Supp. XIII:** 41–43, 44, 45, 48, 55

"Mezzo Cammin" (Longfellow), **II:** 490

"Mi Abuelo" (Ríos), **Supp. IV Part 2:** 541

Miami (Didion), **Supp. IV Part 1:** 199, 210

Miami and the Siege of Chicago (Mailer), **Retro. Supp. II:** 206

Miasma (Holding), **Supp. XXII:** 121–122

"Michael" (Wordsworth), **III:** 523

Michael, Magali Cornier, **Supp. XIII:** 32

"Michael Angelo: A Fragment" (Longfellow), **II:** 490, 494, 495, 506; **Retro. Supp. II:** 167

"Michael Egerton" (Price), **Supp. VI:** 257–258, 260

Michael Kohlhaas (Kleist), **Supp. IV Part 1:** 224

Michael O'Halloran (Stratton-Porter), **Supp. XX: 222**

Michaels, Leonard, **Supp. XVI: 201–215**

Michaels, Walter Benn, **Retro. Supp. I:** 115, 369, 379

Michael Scarlett (Cozens), **I:** 358–359, 378

"Michael's Veterans Remember" (Espaillat), **Supp. XXI:** 110

Michaux, Henri, **Supp. XVI:** 288

Michelangelo, **I:** 18; **II:** 11–12; **III:** 124; **Supp. I Part 1:** 363; **Supp. XVII:** 112

Michel-Michot, Paulette, **Supp. XI:** 224–225

Michelson, Albert, **IV:** 27

Mickelsson's Ghosts (Gardner), **Supp. VI:** 63, **73–74**

Mickiewicz, Adam, **Supp. II Part 1:** 299

"Microscope" (Trethewey), **Supp. XXI:** 251

Midair (Conroy), **Supp. XVI:** 63, **71–72**

"Mid-Air" (Conroy), **Supp. XVI:** 69, 71

Mid-American Chants (Anderson), **I:** 109, 114

"Midas" (Winters), **Supp. II Part 2:** 801

"Mid-August at Sourdough Mountain Lookout" (Snyder), **Supp. VIII:** 292–293

Midcentury (Dos Passos), **I:** 474, 475, 478, 490, 492–494; **Supp. I Part 2:** 646

Mid-Century American Poets, **III:** 532

"Mid-Day" (Doolittle), **Supp. I Part 1:** 266–267

"Middle Age" (Lowell), **II:** 550

"Middle-Aged, Middle-Class Woman at Midnight, A" (Taggard), **Supp. XXII:** 282–283

"Middleaged Man, The" (Simpson), **Supp. IX:** 274–275

Middle Ages, The (Gurney), **Supp. V:** 96, 105, 108

Middlebrook, Diane Wood, **Supp. IV Part 2:** 444, 451

"Middle Daughter, The" (Kingsolver), **Supp. VII:** 209

Middlemarch (G. Eliot), **I:** 457, 459; **II:** 290, 291; **Retro. Supp. I:** 225; **Supp. I Part 1:** 174; **Supp. IX:** 43; **Supp. XI:** 68; **Supp. XII:** 335

Middle of My Tether, The: Familiar Essays (Epstein), **Supp. XIV: 106–107**

"Middle of Nowhere, The" (Wagoner), **Supp. IX:** 327–328

Middle of the Journey, The (Trilling), **Supp. III Part 2:** 495, 504–506

"Middle of the Way" (Kinnell), **Supp. III Part 1:** 242

"Middle Passage" (Hayden), **Supp. II Part 1:** 363, 375–376

Middle Passage (Johnson), **Supp. VI: 194–196,** 198, 199; **Supp. XIII:** 182

"Middle Toe of the Right Foot, The" (Bierce), **I:** 203

Middleton, Thomas, **Retro. Supp. I:** 62

"Middle Way, The"(Hadas), **Supp. XXIII:** 121

Middle Years, The (James), **II:** 337–338; **Retro. Supp. I:** 235

"Middle Years, The" (James), **Retro. Supp. I:** 228, 272

"Midnight" (Dunn), **Supp. XI:** 147

"Midnight Consultations, The" (Freneau), **Supp. II Part 1:** 257

Midnight Cry, A (Mather), **Supp. II Part 2:** 460

"Midnight Gladness" (Levertov), **Supp. III Part 1:** 284–285

"Midnight Magic" (Mason), **Supp. VIII:** 146

Midnight Magic: Selected Stories of Bobbie Ann Mason (Mason), **Supp. VIII:** 148

Midnight Mass (Bowles), **Supp. IV Part 1:** 93

"Midnight Postscript" (F. Wright), **Supp. XVII:** 245, 246

Midnight Queen, The (Lippard), **Supp. XXIII:** 180

"Midnight Show" (Shapiro), **Supp. II Part 2:** 705

"Midpoint" (Updike), **Retro. Supp. I:** 321, 323, 327, 330, 335

Midpoint and Other Poems (Updike), **IV:** 214

"Midrash on Happiness" (Paley), **Supp. VI:** 217

"Midsummer" (Bronk), **Supp. XXI:** 30

"Midsummer in the Blueberry Barrens" (Clampitt), **Supp. IX:** 40–41

"Midsummer Letter" (Carruth), **Supp. XVI:** 47

Midsummer Night's Dream, A (Shakespeare), **Supp. I Part 1:** 369–370; **Supp. X:** 69

Midsummer Night's Sex Comedy, A (film; Allen), **Supp. XV:** 8

"Midwest" (Stafford), **Supp. XI:** 317

"Midwest Poetics" (C. Baxter), **Supp. XVII:** 18

Mieder, Wolfgang, **Supp. XIV:** 126

Mies van der Rohe, Ludwig, **Supp. IV Part 1:** 40

Mighty Aphrodite (film; Allen), **Supp. XV:** 11

"Mighty Fortress, A" (Leopold), **Supp. XIV:** 185

"Mighty Lord, The (Rowson), **Supp. XV:** 243

"Migration, The" (Tate), **IV:** 130

Mihailovitch, Bata, **Supp. VIII:** 272

Mikado, The (Gilbert and Sullivan), **Supp. XXI:** 151

Miklitsch, Robert, **Supp. IV Part 2:** 628, 629

Mila 18 (Uris), **Supp. IV Part 1:** 379; **Supp. XX: 244, 247, 248, 251–252, 253**

Milagro Beanfield War, The (film), **Supp. XIII:** 267

Milagro Beanfield War, The (Nichols), **Supp. XIII:** 253, **265–266**

Milburn, Michael, **Supp. XI:** 239, 242

Milch, David, **Supp. XI:** 348

Mild Day, The (Bronk), **Supp. XXI:** 32

Miles, Barry, **Supp. XII:** 123

Miles, Jack, **Supp. VIII:** 86

Miles, Josephine, **Supp. XIII:** 275

Miles, Julie, **I:** 199

Miles, Kitty, **I:** 199

"Miles of Night, The" (Halliday), **Supp. XIX:** 91

Milestone, Lewis, **Supp. I Part 1:** 281

Miles Wallingford (Cooper). *See Afloat and Ashore* (Cooper)

Milford, Kate, **Supp. XVIII:** 150

Milford, Nancy, **II:** 83; **Supp. IX:** 60

Milhaud, Darius, **Supp. IV Part 1:** 81

Miligate, Michael, **IV:** 123, 130, 132

"Militant Nudes" (Hardwick), **Supp. III Part 1:** 210–211

Milk (film), **Supp. XX: 269**

"Milk Bottles" (Anderson), **I:** 114

"Milk Prose" (Weigl), **Supp. XIX:** 278

Milk Train Doesn't Stop Here Anymore, The (T. Williams), **IV:** 382, 383, 384, 386, 390, 391, 392, 393, 394, 395, 398

Mill, James, **II:** 357

Mill, John Stuart, **III:** 294–295; **Supp. XI:** 196, **Supp. XIV:** 22

Millar, Kenneth. *See* Macdonald, Ross

Millar, Margaret (Margaret Sturm), **Supp. IV Part 2:** 464, 465

Millay, Cora, **III:** 123, 133–134, 135–136

Millay, Edna St. Vincent, **I:** 482; **II:** 530; **III: 122–144; IV:** 433, 436; **Retro. Supp. II:** 48; **Supp. I Part 2:** 707, 714, 726; **Supp. IV Part 1:** 168; **Supp. IV Part 2:** 607; **Supp. V:** 113; **Supp. IX:** 20; **Supp. XIV:** 120, 121, 122, 127; **Supp. XV:** 42, 46, 51, 250, 293, 307; **Supp. XVII:** 69, 75, 96; **Supp. XXII:** 273; **Supp. XXIII:** 164

Millennium Approaches (Kushner), **Supp. IX:** 141, 142, 145

Miller, Arthur, **I:** 81, 94; **III: 145–169; Supp. IV Part 1:** 359; **Supp. IV Part 2:** 574; **Supp. VIII:** 334; **Supp. XIII:** 127; **Supp. XIV:** 102, 239; **Supp. XVI:** 194

Miller, Mrs. Arthur (Ingeborg Morath), **III:** 162–163

Miller, Mrs. Arthur (Marilyn Monroe), **III:** 161, 162–163

Miller, Mrs. Arthur (Mary Grace Slattery), **III:** 146, 161

Miller, Brown, **Supp. IV Part 1:** 67

Miller, Carol, **Supp. IV Part 1:** 400, 405, 409, 410, 411

Miller, Caroline, **Supp. XXII: 187–201**

Miller, Henry, **I:** 97, 157; **III:** 40, **170–192; IV:** 138; **Retro. Supp. II:** 327; **Supp. I Part 2:** 546; **Supp. V:** 119, 131; **Supp. X:** 183, 185, 187, 194, 195; **Supp. XIII:** 1, 17; **Supp. XXII:** 88, 256, 257, 258; **Supp. XXIII:** 100

Miller, Henry (actor), **Supp. XVI:** 182

Miller, Herman, **Supp. I Part 2:** 614, 617

Miller, James E., Jr., **IV:** 352

Miller, Jean Baker, **Supp. XXII:** 18

Miller, Jeffrey, **Supp. IV Part 1:** 95

Miller, J. Hillis, **Supp. IV Part 1:** 387

Miller, Jim Wayne, **Supp. XX: 161–176; Supp. XXIII:** 39

Miller, Joaquin, **I:** 193, 195, 459; **Supp. II Part 1:** 351

Miller, John Duncan, **Supp. I Part 2:** 604

Miller, John E., **Supp. XXII:** 295

Miller, John M., **Supp. XXII:** 214, 218

Miller, Jonathan, **Retro. Supp. II:** 181

Miller, Laura, **Supp. XIII:** 48; **Supp. XIX:** 53, 54, 56; **Supp. XXII:** 239

Miller, Marilyn, **Supp. XVI:** 187

Miller, Matt, **Supp. XV:** 211

Miller, Matthew, **Supp. XVI:** 47, 51

Miller, Orilla, **Supp. I Part 1:** 48

Miller, Perry, **I:** 546, 547, 549, 550, 560; **IV:** 186; **Supp. I Part 1:** 31, 104; **Supp. I Part 2:** 484; **Supp. IV Part 2:** 422; **Supp. VIII:** 101

Miller, R. Baxter, **Retro. Supp. I:** 195, 207

Miller, Robert Ellis, **II:** 588

Miller, Ruth, **Supp. X:** 324

Miller, Stuart, **Supp. XVI:** 242

Miller, Sue, **Supp. X:** 77, 85; **Supp. XI:** 190; **Supp. XII: 289–305**

Miller of Old Church, The (Glasgow), **II:** 175, 181

"Miller's Tale" (Chaucer), **III:** 283

Miller Williams and the Poetry of the Particular (Burns), **Supp. XV:** 339

Millett, Kate, **Supp. X:** 193, 196

Millgate, Michael, **Retro. Supp. I:** 91

Mill Hand's Lunch Bucket (Bearden), **Supp. VIII:** 337

Millhauser, Steven, **Supp. XXII:** 49

Millier, Brett C., **Retro. Supp. II:** 39

Milligan, Bryce, **Supp. XIII:** 274, 275, 277

Million Little Pieces, A (Frey), **Supp. XXII:** 95; **Supp. XXIII:** 109

Millions of Strange Shadows (Hecht), **Supp. X:** 57, **62–65**

"Million Young Workmen, 1915, A" (Sandburg), **III:** 585

Millroy the Magician (Theroux), **Supp. VIII:** 325

Mills, Alice, **Supp. XIII:** 233

Mills, Benjamin Fay, **III:** 176

Mills, C. Wright, **Supp. I Part 2:** 648, 650

Mills, Florence, **Supp. I Part 1:** 322

Mills, Ralph J., Jr., **III:** 530; **Supp. IV Part 1:** 64; **Supp. XI:** 311

Mills, Tedi López, **Supp. XVI:** 281

Mills of the Kavanaughs, The (Lowell), **II:** 542–543, 546, 550; **III:** 508; **Retro. Supp. II:** 178, 179, 188; **Supp. XXIII:** 211

"Mills of the Kavanaughs, The" (Lowell), **II:** 542–543

Milne, A. A., **Supp. IX:** 189

Milne, A. J. M., **I:** 278

Milosz, Czeslaw, **Supp. III Part 2:** 630; **Supp. VIII:** 20, 22; **Supp. XI:** 267, 312; **Supp. XVII:** 241; **Supp. XX: 165; Supp. XXI:** 132; **Supp. XXII:** 92; **Supp. XXIII:** 134, 140

Miltner, Robert, **Supp. XI:** 142

Milton, Edith, **Supp. VIII:** 79; **Supp. X:** 82

Milton, John, **I:** 6, 138, 273, 587–588; **II:** 11, 15, 113, 130, 411, 540, 542; **III:** 40, 124, 201, 225, 274, 468, 471, 486, 487, 503, 511; **IV:** 50, 82, 126, 137, 155, 157, 241, 279, 347, 422, 461, 494; **Retro. Supp. I:** 60, 67, 127, 360; **Retro. Supp. II:** 161, 295; **Supp. I Part 1:** 124, 150, 370; **Supp. I Part 2:** 412, 422, 491, 501, 522, 622, 722, 724; **Supp. IV Part 2:** 430, 634; **Supp. VIII:** 294; **Supp. X:** 22, 23, 36; **Supp. XII:** 180; **Supp. XIV:** 5, 7; **Supp. XX: 108; Supp. XXIII:** 122

Milton, John R., **Supp. IV Part 2:** 503

Milton and His Modern Critics (L. P. Smith), **Supp. XIV:** 347

"Milton by Firelight" (Snyder), **Supp. II Part 1:** 314; **Supp. VIII:** 294

"Miltonic Sonnet, A" (Wilbur), **Supp. III Part 2:** 558

Mimesis (Auerbach), **III:** 453

"Mimnermos and the Motions of Hedonism" (Carson), **Supp. XII: 99–100**

"Mimnermos Interviews, The" (Carson), **Supp. XII: 100–101**

Mims, Edwin, **Supp. I Part 1:** 362, 364, 365, 371

"Mind" (Wilbur), **Supp. III Part 2:** 554

"Mind, The" (Kinnell), **Supp. III Part 1:** 245

Mind Breaths: Poems 1972–1977 (Ginsberg), **Supp. II Part 1:** 326

Mindfield: New and Selected Poems (Corso), **Supp. XII: 136**

"Mind in the Modern World" (Trilling), **Supp. III Part 2:** 512

"Mind Is Shapely, Art Is Shapely" (Ginsberg), **Supp. II Part 1:** 327

Mindlin, Henrique, **Supp. I Part 1:** 92

Mind of My Mind (O. Butler), **Supp. XIII:** 62, 63

Mind of Primitive Man, The (Boas), **Supp. XIV:** 209

Mind-Reader, The (Wilbur), **Supp. III Part 2:** 560–562

"Mind-Reader, The" (Wilbur), **Supp. III Part 2:** 561–562

"Mind's Landscape on an Early Winter Day, The" (Bronk), **Supp. XXI:** 28

Mindwheel (Pinsky), **Supp. VI:** 235

Minear, Richard H., **Supp. XVI:** 101, 102

"Mined Country" (Wilbur), **Supp. III Part 2:** 546–548

"Minefields" (Espaillat), **Supp. XXI:** 106

"Mine Own John Berryman" (Levine), **Supp. V:** 179–180

Miner, Bob, **Supp. V:** 23

Miner, Earl, **III:** 466, 479

Miner, Madonne, **Supp. XIII:** 29

Miner, Valerie, **Supp. XXIII:** 295, 296

"Minerva Writes Poems" (Cisneros), **Supp. VII:** 63–64, 66

Mingus, Charles, **Supp. IX:** 152

"Mingus in Diaspora" (Matthews), **Supp. IX:** 166

"Mingus in Shadow" (Matthews), **Supp. IX:** 168–169

Ming Yellow (Marquand), **III:** 56

"Minimal, The" (Roethke), **III:** 531–532

Minimus Poems, The (X. J. Kennedy), **Supp. XV:** 169–170

"Mini-novela: *Rosa y sus espinas*" (Mora), **Supp. XIII:** 218

"Minions of Midas, The" (London), **II:** 474–475

Minister's Charge, The, or The Apprenticeship of Lemuel Barber (Howells), **II:** 285–286, 287

Minister's Wooing, The (Stowe), **II:** 541

"Minister's Wooing, The" (Stowe), **Supp. I Part 2:** 592–595

"Ministration of Our Departed Friends, The" (Stowe), **Supp. I Part 2:** 586–587

"Minneapolis Poem, The" (Wright), **Supp. III Part 2:** 601–602

Minnesota Grain Show, The (radio, Keillor), **Supp. XVI:** 170

"Minnesota Transcendentalist" (Peseroff), **Supp. IV Part 1:** 71

Minnie, Temple, **II:** 344

Minority Report: H. L. Mencken's Notebooks (Mencken), **III:** 112

Minor Pleasures of Life, The (Macaulay), **Supp. XIV:** 348

"Minor Poems" (Eliot), **I:** 579

"Minor Poet" (Hay), **Supp. XIV:** 127

"Minor Topics" (Howells), **II:** 274

Minot, Stephen, **Supp. XXIII:** 290

Minot, Susan, **Supp. VI: 203–215**

"Minotaur Loves His Labyrinth, The" (Simic), **Supp. VIII:** 270, 279, 281

"Minstrel Man" (Hughes), **Supp. I Part 1:** 325

Mint (Nye), **Supp. XIII:** 277

"Minting Time" (Sarton), **Supp. VIII:** 259

Mint Snowball (Nye), **Supp. XIII:** 277–278, **284–285**

"Mint Snowball" (Nye), **Supp. XIII:** 278, 284

"Mint Snowball II" (Nye), **Supp. XIII:** 284, 285

Minty Alley (C. L. R. James), **Supp. XXI:** 159, 161

Mintzlaff, Dorothy, **Supp. XV:** 153

Minus, Marian, **Supp. XVIII:** 282

Minutes to Go (Corso, Gysin, Beiles and Burroughs), **Supp. XII:** 129

Mi querido Rafa (Hinojosa). *See Dear Rafe* (Hinojosa)

Mirabai: Ecstatic Poems (Hirshfield and Bly, trans.), **Supp. XXIII:** 136

Mirabell: Books of Number (Merrill), **Supp. III Part 1:** 332–334

"Miracle" (Carver), **Supp. III Part 1:** 139–140

Miracle at Verdun (Chlumberg), **Supp. XIX:** 242

Miracle Boy and Other Stories (P. Benedict), **Supp. XXIII:** 35, **45–50**

"Miracle Boy"(P. Benedict), **Supp. XXIII:** 45–46, 50

"Miracle for Breakfast, A" (Bishop), **Retro. Supp. II:** 43

Miracle of Catfish, A (L. Brown), **Supp. XXI:** 39–40, 47, **48**

"Miracle of Lava Canyon, The" (Henry), **Supp. II Part 1:** 389, 390

Miracle of Mindfulness, The: A Manual on Meditation (Thich Nhat Hanh), **Supp. V:** 199–200

Mirage (Masters), **Supp. I Part 2:** 459, 470, 471

"Mirages, The" (Hayden), **Supp. II Part 1:** 373

"Miranda" (Buck), **Supp. II Part 1:** 128

Miranda, Carmen, **Supp. XII:** 165

Miranda, Francisco de, **Supp. I Part 2:** 522

"Miranda Over the Valley" (Dubus), **Supp. VII:** 81–83

"Miriam" (Capote), **Supp. III Part 1:** 117, 120, 122

"Miriam" (Whittier), **Supp. I Part 2:** 691, 703

"Miriam Tazewell" (Ransom), **Supp. X:** 58

"Mirror" (Merrill), **Supp. III Part 1:** 322

"Mirror" (Plath), **Retro. Supp. II:** 248–249, 257

"Mirror, The" (Glück), **Supp. V:** 83

"Mirror, The"(Hadas), **Supp. XXIII:** 116

"Mirroring Evil: Nazi Images/Recent Art" (Epstein), **Supp. XII:** 166

"Mirror of Leopold Leopoldovitch Siegelevsky, The" (Siegel), **Supp. XXII:** 257–258

Mirrors (Creeley), **Supp. IV Part 1:** 156

Mirrors and Windows (Nemerov), **III:** 269, 275–277

Mirrors of Astonishment (Hadas), **Supp. XXIII: 115–116**

"Mirrors of Chartres Street" (Faulkner), **II:** 56

Mirsky, Norman, **Supp. XX: 244**

Mirvis, Tova, **Supp. XX: 177–191**

Misanthrope, The (Molière; Wilbur, trans.), **Supp. III Part 2:** 552, 560

Miscellaneous Poems (Rowson), **Supp. XV:** 243

Miscellaneous Works of Mr. Philip Freneau, Containing His Essays and Additional Poems (Freneau), **Supp. II Part 1:** 263, 264, 266

Miscellany of American Poetry, A (Untermeyer, ed.), **Supp. XV:** 305, 310

Misérables, Les (Hugo), **II:** 179; **Supp. I Part 1:** 280

Misery (King), **Supp. V:** 140, 141, 142, 147–148, 151, 152

Mises, Ludwig von, **Supp. IV Part 2:** 524

Misfits, The (A. Miller), **III:** 147, 149, 156, 161–162, 163

Misfit: The Strange Life of Frederick Exley (Yardley), **Supp. XXIII:** 97

"Mishösha, or the Magician and his daughters: A Chippewa Tale"(J. Schoolcraft), **Supp. XXIII:** 234, 235

"Misogamist, The" (Dubus), **Supp. VII:** 86–87

Misread City, The: New Literary Los Angeles (Gioia and Timberg, eds.), **Supp. XV:** 116

Misrepresentations Corrected, and Truth Vindicated, in a Reply to the Rev. Mr. Solomon Williams's Book (Edwards), **I:** 549

Miss Crandall's School for Young Ladies & Little Misses of Color (Nelson and Alexander), **Supp. XVIII:** 171, 175, 181, **185–186**

"Miss Cynthie" (R. Fisher), **Supp. XIX:** 65, 69

Miss Doll, Go Home (Markson), **Supp. XVII:** 138

"Miss Ella" (Z. Fitzgerald), **Supp. IX:** 57, 59, **71–72**

"Miss Emily and the Bibliographer" (Tate), **Supp. II Part 1:** 103

"Miss Furr and Miss Skeene" (Stein), **IV:** 29–30

"Missing Child" (Simic), **Supp. VIII:** 282

"Missing in Action" (Komunyakaa), **Supp. XIII:** 123, 124

Missing/Kissing: Missing Marisa, Kissing Christine (Shanley), **Supp. XIV:** 316

Missing Link (X. J. Kennedy), **Supp. XV:** 165

"Missing Poem, The" (Halliday), **Supp. XIX:** 93–94

"Mission of Jane, The" (Wharton), **Retro. Supp. I:** 367

"Missions, The" (Rodriguez), **Supp. XIV:** 303

Mission to Moscow (film), **Supp. I Part 1:** 281

"Mississippi" (Bass), **Supp. XVI:** 17

"Mississippi" (Faulkner), **Retro. Supp. I:** 77

"Mississippi" (Simpson), **Supp. IX:** 271

"Miss Kate in H-1" (Twain), **IV:** 193

Miss Kelly (Holding), **Supp. XXII: 133–134**

Miss Leonora When Last Seen (Taylor), **Supp. V:** 323

Miss Lonelyhearts (West), **I:** 107; **II:** 436; **III:** 357; **IV:** 287, 288, 290–297, 300, 301, 305, 306; **Retro. Supp. II:** 321, 322, 325, 328, **332–335**

Miss Mamma Aimee (Caldwell), **I:** 308, 309, 310

"Miss Mary Pask" (Wharton), **IV:** 316; **Retro. Supp. I:** 382

"Miss McEnders" (Chopin), **Retro. Supp. II:** 67

"Missoula Softball Tournament" (Hugo), **Supp. VI:** 132

Miss Ravenel's Conversion from Secession to Loyalty (De Forest), **IV:** 350

Miss Saigon (musical), **Supp. XXI:** 155

"Miss Tempy's Watchers" (Jewett), **II:** 401; **Retro. Supp. II:** 139

"Miss Terriberry to Wed in Suburbs" (Updike), **Retro. Supp. I:** 335

"Miss Urquhart's Tiara" (Jarman), **Supp. XVII:** 116

"Mist, The" (King), **Supp. V:** 144

"Mistaken Charity, A" (Freeman), **Retro. Supp. II:** 138

"Mister Brother" (Cunningham), **Supp. XV:** 68

Misterioso (Sorrentino), **Supp. XXI:** 236, 237

"Mister Toussan" (Ellison), **Retro. Supp. II:** 124–125; **Supp. II Part 1:** 238

"Mistress of Sydenham Plantation, The" (Jewett), **Retro. Supp. II:** 141

Mitcham, Matthew, **Supp. XX: 264**

Mitchell, Burroughs, **Supp. XI:** 218, 222, 227

Mitchell, Don, **Supp. XXII:** 207, 211, 212

Mitchell, Joan, **Supp. XXIII:** 210

Mitchell, Margaret, **II:** 177; **Supp. XX: 243; Supp. XXII:** 195

Mitchell, Roger, **Supp. IV Part 1:** 70; **Supp. XV:** 213, 215

Mitchell, Dr. S. Weir, **IV:** 310

Mitchell, Tennessee. *See* Anderson, Mrs. Sherwood (Tennessee Mitchell)

Mitchell, Verner, **Supp. XVIII:** 281, 286
Mitchell, Wesley C., **Supp. I Part 2:** 632, 643
"Mitchie-Gawa" (Taggard), **Supp. XXII:** 272
Mitch Miller (Masters), **Supp. I Part 2:** 456, 466, 469–471, 474, 475, 476
Mitchum, Robert, **Supp. IX:** 95, 250
Mitgang, Herbert, **Supp. IV Part 1:** 220, 226, 307; **Supp. VIII:** 124; **Supp. XIX:** 251, **Supp. XX: 243**
Mitla Pass (Uris), **Supp. XX: 244, 247, 248, 256**
Mixed Company: Collected Short Stories (Shaw), **Supp. XIX:** 251
"Mixed Sequence" (Roethke), **III:** 547
Miyazawa Kenji, **Supp. VIII:** 292
Mizener, Arthur, **II:** 77, 81, 84, 94; **IV:** 132; **Supp. XVIII:** 249
Mizner, Addison, **Supp. XVI:** 191
Mizner, Wilson, **Supp. XVI:** 191, 195
Mladenoff, Nancy, **Supp. X:** 176
"M'liss: An Idyl of Red Mountain" (Harte), **Supp. II Part 1:** 339
"Mnemonic Devices" (Goldbarth), **Supp. XII:** 183
"Mobile in Back of the Smithsonian, The" (Swenson), **Supp. IV Part 2:** 646
Mobilio, Albert, **Supp. VIII:** 3; **Supp. XVIII:** 144; **Supp. XIX:** 45
Moby Dick (film), **Supp. IV Part 1:** 102, 116
Moby-Dick (Melville), **Supp. XXII:** 81, 268
Moby Dick; or, The Whale (Melville), **I:** 106, 354; **II:** 33, 224–225, 236, 539–540; **III:** 28–29, 74, 75, 77, 81, 82, 83–86, 87, 89, 90, 91, 93, 94, 95, 359, 453, 556; **IV:** 57, 199, 201, 202; **Retro. Supp. I:** 160, 220, 243, 244, 248, **249–253**, 254, 256, 257, 335; **Retro. Supp. II:** 121, 186, 275; **Supp. I Part 1:** 249; **Supp. I Part 2:** 579; **Supp. IV Part 2:** 613; **Supp. V:** 281; **Supp. VIII:** 106, 188, 198; **Supp. XXI:** 159
Mock, John, **Supp. XIII:** 174
"Mocking-Bird, The" (Bierce), **I:** 202
"Mock Orange" (Glück), **Supp. V:** 84–85
Modarressi, Mitra, **Supp. IV Part 2:** 657
Models of Misrepresentation: On the Fiction of E. L. Doctorow (Morris), **Supp. IV Part 1:** 231
Model World and Other Stories, A (Chabon), **Supp. XI:** 66
Modern American and British Poetry (Untermeyer, ed.), **Supp. XV:** 306
Modern American Poetry (Untermeyer, ed.), **Supp. XV:** 293, 303, 306, 312
Modern American Verse (Untermeyer, ed.), **Supp. XV:** 301
Modern Brazilian Architecture (Bishop, trans.), **Supp. I Part 1:** 92
Modern British Poetry (Untermeyer, ed.), **Supp. XV:** 305, 308, 312
Modern Fiction Studies, **Supp. V:** 238
Modern Fiction Studies (Haegert), **Supp. XVI:** 69

Modern Instance a Novel, A (Howells), **II:** 275, 279, 282–283, 285
Modern Library, The, **Retro. Supp. I:** 112, 113
Modern Mephistopheles, A (Alcott), **Supp. I Part 1:** 37–38
Modern Poetic Sequence, The (Rosenthal), **Supp. V:** 333
"Modern Poetry" (Crane), **I:** 390
Modern Poetry and the Tradition (Brooks), **Supp. XIV: 5–7**
"Modern Race Creeds and Their Fallacies" (Locke), **Supp. XIV:** 210
Modern Rhetoric, with Readings (Brooks and Warren), **Supp. XIV:** 11
"Modern Sorcery" (Simic), **Supp. VIII:** 283
Modern Times (album, Dylan), **Supp. XVIII:** 28, 31, 33
"Modern Times" (Zukofsky), **Supp. III Part 2:** 624
Modern Writer, The (Anderson), **I:** 117
Modersohn, Otto, **Supp. I Part 2:** 573
Modersohn, Mrs. Otto (Paula Becker), **Supp. I Part 2:** 573–574
"Modes of Being" (Levertov), **Supp. III Part 1:** 282
Modest Enquiry into the Nature and Necessity of a Paper-Currency, A (Franklin), **II:** 108–109
"Modest Proposal, A" (Swift), **I:** 295; **Retro. Supp. II:** 287
"Modest Proposal with Feline Feeling, A" (Neugeboren), **Supp. XVI:** 219
"Modest Self-Tribute, A" (Wilson), **IV:** 431, 432
Moeller, Philip, **III:** 398, 399
"Moench von Berchtesgaden, Der" (Voss), **I:** 199–200
Moers, Ellen, **Retro. Supp. II:** 99
Moe's Villa and Other Stories (Purdy), **Supp. VII:** 270, 280
Moffat, Juan, **Supp. XX: 52**
Mogen, David, **Supp. IV Part 1:** 106
Mohammed, **I:** 480; **II:** 1
Mohawk (Russo), **Supp. XII: 326–328**
Moir, William Wilmerding, **Supp. V:** 279
Mojo Hand (Phillips), **Supp. XXIII:** 174
Moldaw, Carol, **Supp. XV:** 264; **Supp. XVII:** 127, 130
"Moles" (Oliver), **Supp. VII:** 235
Molesworth, Charles, **Supp. IV Part 1:** 39; **Supp. VIII:** 292, 306; **Supp. XIX:** 121–122
Molière (Jean-Baptiste Poquelin), **III:** 113; **Supp. I Part 2:** 406; **Supp. III Part 2:** 552, 560; **Supp. IV Part 2:** 585; **Supp. V:** 101
"Molino Rojo, El" (Ríos), **Supp. IV Part 2:** 544
Moll Flanders (Defoe), **Supp. V:** 127; **Supp. XIII:** 43
"Molloch in State Street" (Whittier), **Supp. I Part 2:** 687
"Moll Pitcher" (Whittier), **Supp. I Part 2:** 684
"Molly Brant, Iroquois Matron" (Gunn Allen), **Supp. IV Part 1:** 331
"Molly Brant to Willie"(Kenny), **Supp. XXIII:** 153

Molnar, Ferenc, **Supp. XVI:** 187
"Moloch" (H. Miller), **III:** 177
Momaday, N. Scott, **Supp. IV Part 1:** 274, 323, 324, 404; **Supp. IV Part 2: 479–496,** 504, 557, 562; **Supp. XII:** 209; **Supp. XVIII:** 58
" 'Momentary Stay against Confusion,' A: Frank Conroy's *Stop-Time*" (T. Adams), **Supp. XVI:** 69
Moment of Untruth (Lacy), **Supp. XV:** 206, 207
Moments of the Italian Summer (Wright), **Supp. III Part 2:** 602
Moment to Moment: Poems of a Mountain Recluse (Budbill), **Supp. XIX:** 2, 7, **9–10**
"Momus" (Robinson), **III:** 508
Monaghan, Charles, **Supp. XIX:** 155
Monaghan, Pat, **Supp. XI:** 121
Monaghan, Patricia, **Supp. XVII:** 76, 123, 127, 129
Mona Lisa Overdrive (W. Gibson), **Supp. XVI:** 119, 120, **127–128**
"Mon Ami" (Bourne), **I:** 227
Monet, Claude, **Retro. Supp. I:** 378
"Monet's 'Waterlilies' " (Hayden), **Supp. II Part 1:** 361–362
Monette, Paul, **Supp. X: 145–161**
Money (Amis), **Retro. Supp. I:** 278
"Money" (Matthews), **Supp. IX:** 166
"Money" (Nemerov), **III:** 287
Money, Money, Money (Wagoner), **Supp. IX:** 324, **333–334**
Moneyball: The Art of Winning an Unfair Game (M. Lewis), **Supp. XVII:** 210
Moneychangers, The (Sinclair), **Supp. V:** 285
Money Writes! (Sinclair), **Supp. V:** 277
Monica, Saint, **IV:** 140
Monikins, The (Cooper), **I:** 348, 354
Monk, Thelonious, **Supp. XVIII:** 62
Monk and the Hangman's Daughter, The (Bierce), **I:** 199–200, 209
"Monkey" (Weigl), **Supp. XIX:** 278
"Monkey Garden, The" (Cisneros), **Supp. VII:** 63
"Monkey Puzzle, The" (Moore), **III:** 194, 207, 211
Monkeys (Minot), **Supp. VI:** 203–205, **206–210**
"Monkeys, The" (Moore), **III:** 201, 202
Monkey Wars, The (Weigl), **Supp. XIX:** 276, 278–280
Monkey Wrench Gang, The (Abbey), **Supp. VIII:** 42; **Supp. XIII: 9–11,** 16
"Monk of Casal-Maggiore, The" (Longfellow), **II:** 505
"Monocle de Mon Oncle, Le" (Stevens), **IV:** 78, 84; **Retro. Supp. I:** 301; **Supp. III Part 1:** 20; **Supp. X:** 58
"Monolog from a Mattress" (Untermeyer), **Supp. XV:** 307
"Monologue for Mothers" (Taggard), **Supp. XXII:** 279
Monro, Harold, **III:** 465; **Retro. Supp. I:** 127; **Supp. XV:** 296
Monroe, Harriet, **I:** 235, 384, 390, 393; **III:** 458, 581, 586; **IV:** 74; **Retro. Supp. I:** 58, 131; **Retro. Supp. II:** 82, 83; **Supp. I Part 1:** 256, 257, 258,

262, 263, 267; **Supp. I Part 2:** 374, 387, 388, 464, 610, 611, 613, 614, 615, 616; **Supp. XIV:** 286; **Supp. XV:** 43, 299, 302

Monroe, James, **Supp. I Part 2:** 515, 517

Monroe, Lucy, **Retro. Supp. II:** 70

Monroe, Marilyn, **III:** 161, 162–163

Monroe's Embassy; or, the Conduct of the Government in Relation to Our Claims to the Navigation of the Mississippi (Brown), **Supp. I Part 1:** 146

"Monsoon Season" (Komunyakaa), **Supp. XIII:** 122

Monsour, Leslie, **Supp. XV:** 125

"Monster, The" (Crane), **I:** 418

Monster, The, and Other Stories (Crane), **I:** 409

Montage of a Dream Deferred (Hughes), **Retro. Supp. I:** 194, **208–209; Supp. I Part 1:** 333, 339–341

Montagu, Ashley, **Supp. I Part 1:** 314

"Montaigne" (Emerson), **II:** 6

Montaigne, Michel de, **II:** 1, 5, 6, 8, 14–15, 16, 535; **III:** 600; **Retro. Supp. I:** 247; **Supp. XIV:** 105; **Supp. XXI:** 111, 205

Montale, Eugenio, **Supp. III Part 1:** 320; **Supp. V:** 337–338; **Supp. VIII:** 30; **Supp. XV:** 112

Montalembert, Hughes de, **Supp. XV:** 349

"Montana Memory" (Maclean), **Supp. XIV:** 221

"Montana; or the End of Jean-Jacques Rousseau" (Fiedler), **Supp. XIII: 97–98**

"Montana Ranch Abandoned" (Hugo), **Supp. VI:** 139

"Mont Blanc" (Shelley), **Supp. IX:** 52

Montcalm, Louis Joseph de, **Supp. I Part 2:** 498

Montcalm and Wolfe (Parkman), **Supp. II Part 2:** 596, 609, 610, 611–613

Montemarano, Nicholas, **Supp. XVI:** 227

Montgomery, Benilde, **Supp. XIII:** 202

Montgomery, George, **Supp. XXIII:** 209

Montgomery, Robert, **Supp. I Part 2:** 611; **Supp. IV Part 1:** 130

Month of Sundays, A (Updike), **Retro. Supp. I:** 325, 327, 329, 330, 331, 333, 335

Monti, Luigi, **II:** 504

Montoya, José, **Supp. IV Part 2:** 545

"Montrachet-le-Jardin" (Stevens), **IV:** 82

Mont-Saint-Michel and Chartres (Adams), **I:** 1, 9, 12–14, 18, 19, 21; **Supp. I Part 2:** 417

Montserrat (Hellman), **Supp. I Part 1:** 283–285

Montserrat (Robles), **Supp. I Part 1:** 283–285

"Monument, The" (Bishop), **Supp. I Part 1:** 89

Monument, The (Strand), **Supp. IV Part 2:** 629, 630

"Monument in Utopia, A" (Schnackenberg), **Supp. XV:** 261, 263

"Monument Mountain" (Bryant), **Supp. I Part 1:** 156, 162

"Monument to After-Thought Unveiled, A" (Frost), **Retro. Supp. I:** 124

Moo (Smiley), **Supp. VI:** 292, **303–305**

Moods (Alcott), **Supp. I Part 1:** 33, 34–35, 43

Moody, Anne, **Supp. IV Part 1:** 11

Moody, Richard, **Supp. I Part 1:** 280

Moody, Rick, **Supp. XXI:** 117

Moody, Ron, **Supp. XXII:** 49

Moody, William Vaughn, **III:** 507; **IV:** 26

Moody, Mrs. William Vaughn, **I:** 384; **Supp. I Part 2:** 394

Moody-Freeman, Julie, **Supp. XXIII:** 91, 94, 95

"Moon" (A. Finch), **Supp. XVII:** 77

Moon, Henry Lee, **Supp. XVIII:** 281, 285

"Moon and the Night and the Men, The" (Berryman), **I:** 172

"Moon Deluxe" (F. Barthelme), **Supp. XI:** 26, 27, 33, 36

Mooney, Tom, **I:** 505

"Moon-Face" (London), **II:** 475

Moon-Face and Other Stories (London), **II:** 483

"Moon Flock" (Dickey), **Supp. IV Part 1:** 186

Moon for the Misbegotten, A (O'Neill), **III:** 385, 401, 403, 404

Moon in a Mason Jar (Wrigley), **Supp. XVIII: 295–298**

Moon in Its Flight, The (Sorrentino), **Supp. XXI:** 226

"Moon in Its Flight, The" (Sorrentino), **Supp. XXI:** 229

Moon Is a Gong, The (Dos Passos). *See Garbage Man, The* (Dos Passos)

Moon Is Down, The (Steinbeck), **IV:** 51

Moon Lady, The (Tan), **Supp. X:** 289

"Moonlight Alert" (Winters), **Supp. II Part 2:** 801, 811, 815

"Moonlight: Chickens on a Road" (Wrigley), **Supp. XVIII:** 295–296, 297

"Moonlit Night" (Reznikoff), **Supp. XIV:** 285–286

Moon of the Caribbees, The (O'Neill), **III:** 388

Moon Palace (Auster), **Supp. XII:** 22, 27, **30–32**

"Moonshine" (Komunyakaa), **Supp. XIII:** 127, 128

"Moon Solo" (Laforgue), **Supp. XIII:** 346

Moonstone, The (Collins), **Supp. XX:** 236

Moonstruck (screenplay, Shanley), **Supp. XIV:** 315, 316, **321–324**

"Moon upon her fluent Route, The" (Dickinson), **I:** 471

Moony's Kid Don't Cry (T. Williams), **IV:** 381

Moore, Arthur, **Supp. I Part 1:** 49

Moore, Deborah Dash, **Supp. XX: 246**

Moore, George, **I:** 103

Moore, Hannah, **Supp. XV:** 231

Moore, John Milton, **III:** 193

Moore, Julie L., **Supp. XXIII:** 252

Moore, Lorrie, **Supp. VIII:** 145; **Supp. X: 163–180**

Moore, Marianne, **I:** 58, 285, 401, 428; **III: 193–217,** 514, 592–593; **IV:** 74, 75, 76, 91, 402; **Retro. Supp. I:** 416, 417; **Retro. Supp. II:** 39, 44, 48, 50, 82, 178, 179, 243, 244; **Supp. I Part 1:** 84, 89, 255, 257; **Supp. I Part 2:** 707; **Supp. II Part 1:** 21; **Supp. III Part 1:** 58, 60, 63; **Supp. III Part 2:** 612, 626, 627; **Supp. IV Part 1:** 242, 246, 257; **Supp. IV Part 2:** 454, 640, 641; **Supp. XIV:** 124, 130; **Supp. XV:** 306, 307; **Supp. XVII:** 131; **Supp. XXI:** 98; **Supp. XXII:** 273–274

Moore, Marie Lorena. *See* Moore, Lorrie

Moore, Mary Tyler, **Supp. V:** 107

Moore, Mary Warner, **III:** 193

Moore, Dr. Merrill, **III:** 506

Moore, Steven, **Supp. IV Part 1:** 279, 283, 284, 285, 287; **Supp. XII:** 151; **Supp. XVII:** 230, 231, 232; **Supp. XXII:** 261, 265

Moore, Sturge, **III:** 459

Moore, Thomas, **II:** 296, 299, 303; **Supp. IX:** 104; **Supp. X:** 114; **Supp. XXIII:** 138

Moore, Virginia, **Supp. XV:** 308

Moorehead, Caroline, **Supp. XIV:** 337

Moorepack, Howard, **Supp. XV:** 199

"Moorings" (Hoffman), **Supp. XVIII:** 87

Moos, Malcolm, **III:** 116, 119

"Moose, The" (Bishop), **Retro. Supp. II:** 50; **Supp. I Part 1:** 73, 93, 94, 95; **Supp. IX:** 45, 46

"Moose Wallow, The" (Hayden), **Supp. II Part 1:** 367

"Moowis, The Indian Coquette"(J. Schoolcraft), **Supp. XXIII:** 234

"Moquihuitzin's Answer" (Everwine), **Supp. XV:** 78

Mora, Pat, **Supp. XIII: 213–232**

Moraga, Cherríe, **Supp. XXIII: 193–206**

"Moral Bully, The" (Holmes), **Supp. I Part 1:** 302

"Moral Character, the Practice of Law, and Legal Education" (Hall), **Supp. VIII:** 127

"Moral Equivalent for Military Service, A" (Bourne), **I:** 230

"Moral Equivalent of War, The" (James), **II:** 361; **Supp. I Part 1:** 20

"Moral Imperatives for World Order" (Locke), **Supp. XIV:** 207, 213

Moralités Légendaires (Laforgue), **I:** 573

"Morality and Mercy in Vienna" (Pynchon), **Supp. II Part 2:** 620, 624

"Morality of Indian Hating, The" (Momaday), **Supp. IV Part 2:** 484

"Morality of Poetry, The" (Wright), **Supp. III Part 2:** 596–597, 599

Moral Man and Immoral Society (Niebuhr), **III:** 292, 295–297

"Morals Is Her Middle Name" (Hughes), **Supp. I Part 1:** 338

"Morals of Chess, The" (Franklin), **II:** 121

"Moral Substitute for War, A" (Addams), **Supp. I Part 1:** 20

"Moral Theology of Atticus Finch, The" (Shaffer), **Supp. VIII:** 127

"Moral Thought, A" (Freneau), **Supp. II Part 1:** 262

Moran, Thomas, **Supp. IV Part 2:** 603–604

Moran of the Lady Letty (Norris), **II:** 264; **III:** 314, 322, 327, 328, 329, 330, 331, 332, 333

Morath, Ingeborg. *See* Miller, Mrs. Arthur (Ingeborg Morath)

Moravec, Paul, **Supp. XIX:** 123

Moravia, Alberto, **I:** 301

More (Crooker), **Supp. XXIII:** 60–62

Moré, Gonzalo, **Supp. X:** 185

More, Henry, **I:** 132

More, Paul Elmer, **I:** 223–224, 247; **Supp. I Part 2:** 423

Moreau, Gustave, **I:** 66

"More Blues and the Abstract Truth" (Wright), **Supp. XV:** 345

More Boners (Abingdon), **Supp. XVI:** 99

More Conversations with Eudora Welty (Prenshaw, ed.), **Retro. Supp. I:** 340, 341, 342, 343, 344, 352, 353, 354

More Dangerous Thoughts (Ryan as Quin), **Supp. XVIII:** 226, **229–230,** 231, 238

More Die of Heartbreak (Bellow), **Retro. Supp. II:** 31, 33, 34

"More Girl Than Boy" (Komunyakaa), **Supp. XIII:** 117

"More Light! More Light! (Hecht), **Supp. X:** 60

"More Like an Extension of the Spirit: Clothing in Lyric Poems"(Hadas), **Supp. XXIII:** 124

"Morella" (Poe), **III:** 412; **Retro. Supp. II:** 270

"More Love in the Western World" (Updike), **Retro. Supp. I:** 327–328, 329

"Morels" (W. J. Smith), **Supp. XIII: 336–339**

Moreno, Gary, **Supp. XV:** 5

"More Observations Now" (Conroy), **Supp. XVI:** 75

"More of a Corpse Than a Woman" (Rukeyser), **Supp. VI:** 280

"More Pleasant Adventures" (Ashbery), **Supp. III Part 1:** 1

More Poems to Solve (Swenson), **Supp. IV Part 2:** 640, 642, 648

More Stately Mansions (O'Neill), **III:** 385, 401, 404–405

"More Than Human" (Chabon), **Supp. XI:** 71–72

More Things Change The More They Stay the Same, The (J. W. Miller), **Supp. XX: 164**

More Triva (L. P. Smith), **Supp. XIV:** 339

Morgan, Edmund S., **IV:** 149; **Supp. I Part 1:** 101, 102; **Supp. I Part 2:** 484

Morgan, Edwin, **Supp. IV Part 2:** 688

Morgan, Emanuel. *See* Bynner, Witter

Morgan, Henry, **II:** 432; **IV:** 63

Morgan, Jack, **Retro. Supp. II:** 142

Morgan, J. P., **I:** 494; **III:** 14, 15

Morgan, Judith, **Supp. XVI:** 103

Morgan, Neil, **Supp. XVI:** 103

Morgan, Robert, **Supp. V:** 5; **Supp. XX: 161, 162**

Morgan, Robin, **Supp. I Part 2:** 569

Morgan, Ted, **Supp. XIV:** 141

Morgan's Passing (Tyler), **Supp. IV Part 2:** 666 667, 668, 669

Morgenstern, Dan, **Supp. XIX:** 159

Morgenthau, Hans, **III:** 291, 309

Morgenthau, Henry, Sr., **Supp. XXIII:** 21, 22, 26, 30

Morgesons, The (E. Stoddard), **Supp. XV:** 270, 273, 274, 278, **279–282,** 283

Morgesons and Other Writings, Published and Unpublished, The (Buell and Zagarell), **Supp. XV:** 269

Moricand, Conrad, **III:** 190

Morison, Samuel Eliot, **Supp. I Part 2: 479–500; Supp. XXII:** 35

Morison, Mrs. Samuel Eliot (Elizabeth Shaw Greene), **Supp. I Part 2:** 483

Morison, Mrs. Samuel Eliot (Priscilla Barton), **Supp. I Part 2:** 493, 496, 497

Morita, Pat, **Supp. XXI:** 146

"Morituri Salutamus" (Longfellow), **II:** 499, 500; **Retro. Supp. II:** 169; **Supp. I Part 2:** 416

"Moriturus" (Millay), **III:** 126, 131–132

Morley, Christopher, **III:** 481, 483, 484; **Supp. I Part 2:** 653; **Supp. IX:** 124

Morley, Edward, **IV:** 27

Morley, Lord John, **I:** 7

Mormon Country (Stegner), **Supp. IV Part 2:** 598, 601–602

"Morning, The" (Updike), **Retro. Supp. I:** 329

"Morning after My Death, The" (Levis), **Supp. XI:** 260, 263–264

"Morning Arrives" (F. Wright), **Supp. XVII:** 244

Morning Face (Stratton-Porter), **Supp. XX: 223**

Morning for Flamingos, A (Burke), **Supp. XIV:** 30, 31, 32

"Morning Glory" (Merrill), **Supp. III Part 1:** 337

Morning Glory, The (R. Bly), **Supp. IV Part 1:** 63–65, 66, 71

"Morning Imagination of Russia, A" (W. C. Williams), **Retro. Supp. I:** 428

Morning in Antibes (Knowles), **Supp. XII:** 249

Morning in the Burned House (Atwood), **Supp. XIII:** 20, 34

Morning Is Near Us, The (Glaspell), **Supp. III Part 1:** 184–185

Morning Noon and Night (Cozzens), **I:** 374, 375, 376, 377, 379, 380

"Morning of the Day They Did It, The" (White), **Supp. I Part 2:** 663

"Morning Prayers" (Harjo), **Supp. XII:** 231

"Morning Roll Call" (Anderson), **I:** 116

"Morning Roudup" (Sorrentino), **Supp. XXI:** 228

"Morning Shadows" (Skloot), **Supp. XX: 199**

"Mornings in a New House" (Merrill), **Supp. III Part 1:** 327

"Mornings in Ormos"(Hadas), **Supp. XXIII:** 112, 113, 123

Mornings Like This (Dillard), **Supp. VI:** 23, 34

"Morning Song" (Plath), **Retro. Supp. II:** 252; **Supp. XXIII:** 115

Morning Watch, The (Agee), **I:** 25, 39–42

"Morning with Broken Window" (Hogan), **Supp. IV Part 1:** 405

Morrell, Ottoline, **Retro. Supp. I:** 60

Morris, Bernard E., **Supp. XV:** 154, 169

Morris, Christopher D., **Supp. IV Part 1:** 231, 236

Morris, Gary, **Supp. XXII:** 262

Morris, George Sylvester, **Supp. I Part 2:** 640

Morris, Gouverneur, **Supp. I Part 2:** 512, 517, 518

Morris, Lloyd, **III:** 458

Morris, Robert, **Supp. I Part 2:** 510

Morris, Timothy, **Retro. Supp. I:** 40

Morris, William, **II:** 323, 338, 523; **IV:** 349; **Supp. I Part 1:** 260, 356; **Supp. XI:** 202

Morris, Willie, **Supp. XI:** 216, 231, 234; **Supp. XIX:** 151, 252

Morris, Wright, **I:** 305; **III: 218–243,** 558, 572; **IV:** 211

Morrison, Charles Clayton, **III:** 297

Morrison, Jim, **Supp. IV Part 1:** 206

Morrison, Toni, **Retro. Supp. II:** 15, 118; **Supp. III Part 1: 361–381; Supp. IV Part 1:** 2, 13, 14, 250, 253, 257; **Supp. V:** 169, 259; **Supp. VIII:** 213, 214; **Supp. X:** 85, 239, 250, 325; **Supp. XI:** 4, 14, 20, 91; **Supp. XII:** 289, 310; **Supp. XIII:** 60, 185; **Supp. XVI:** 143; **Supp. XVII:** 183; **Supp. XX: 108; Supp. XXI:** 172, 243; **Supp. XXII:** 65, 78

"Morro Bay" (Jeffers), **Supp. II Part 2:** 422

Morrow, W. C., **I:** 199

Morse, Jedidiah, **Supp. XV:** 243

Morse, Robert, **Supp. XI:** 305

Morse, Samuel F. B., **Supp. I Part 1:** 156

Morse, Samuel French, **Supp. XXI:** 17, 19, 23, 27

Mortal Acts, Mortal Words (Kinnell), **Supp. III Part 1:** 235, 236, 237, 249–254

Mortal Antipathy, A (Holmes), **Supp. I Part 1:** 315–316

"Mortal Enemies" (Humphrey), **Supp. IX:** 109

"Mortal Eternal" (Olds), **Supp. X:** 214

Mortal No, The (Hoffman), **IV:** 113

Mortal Stakes (Parker), **Supp. XIX:** 183–184

Morte D'Arthur, Le (Malory), **Supp. IV Part 1:** 47

Mortmere Stories, The (Isherwood and Upward), **Supp. XIV:** 159

Morton, David, **Supp. IX:** 76

Morton, Jelly Roll, **Supp. X:** 242

Morton, Thomas, **Supp. XXII:** 44, 45, 46

"Mosaic of the Nativity: Serbia, Winter 1993" (Kenyon), **Supp. VII:** 173

Mosby's Memoirs and Other Stories (Bellow), **Retro. Supp. II:** 27

"Moscow, Idaho" (Offutt), **Supp. XIX:** 170

Moscow under Fire (Caldwell), **I:** 296

Moser, Barry, **Supp. XIV:** 223

Moses (Asch), **Supp. XXIII:** 7

Moses (Untermeyer), **Supp. XV: 309**

Moses, Man of the Mountain (Hurston), **Supp. VI:** 149, 158, 160

"Moses on Sinai" (Untermeyer), **Supp. XV:** 300

Mosher, Howard Frank, **Supp. XXII: 203–221**

Moskowitz, Alfred, **Supp. XXI:** 98, 106

Mosle, Sara, **Supp. XI:** 254

Mosley, Walter, **Supp. XIII: 233–252; Supp. XVI:** 143

Mosquito Coast, The (film), **Supp. VIII:** 323

Mosquito Coast, The (Theroux), **Supp. VIII:** 321, **322–323**

Mosquitos (Faulkner), **II:** 56; **Retro. Supp. I:** 79, 81

Moss, Howard, **III:** 452; **Supp. IV Part 2:** 642; **Supp. IX:** 39; **Supp. XIII:** 114; **Supp. XV:** 143, 152

Moss, Stanley, **Supp. XI:** 321

Moss, Thylias, **Supp. XI:** 248

Mosses from an Old Manse (Hawthorne), **I:** 562; **II:** 224; **III:** 82, 83; **Retro. Supp. I:** 157, 248

"Moss of His Skin" (Sexton), **Supp. II Part 2:** 676

Most, Doug, **Supp. XVIII:** 101

"Most Extraordinary Case, A" (James), **II:** 322; **Retro. Supp. I:** 218

"Most Girl Part of You, The" (Hempel), **Supp. XXI:** 116

Most Likely to Succeed (Dos Passos), **I:** 491

"Most of It, The" (Frost), **Retro. Supp. I:** 121, 125, 129, 139; **Supp. XVIII:** 300

"Most Popular Novels in America, The" (Mabie), **Supp. XVIII:** 257

Motel Chronicles (Shepard), **Supp. III Part 2:** 445

"Mother" (Kooser), **Supp. XIX:** 117, 126, 127

"Mother" (Paley), **Supp. VI: 222–223**

"Mother" (Snyder), **Supp. VIII:** 298

Mother (Whistler), **IV:** 369

Mother, The (Buck), **Supp. II Part 1:** 118–119

"Mother and Jack and the Rain" (Sexton), **Supp. II Part 2:** 686

"Mother and Son" (Tate), **IV:** 128, 137–138

Mother Country: Britain, the Welfare State and Nuclear Pollution (Robinson), **Supp. XXI:** 211

Mother Courage and Her Children (Brecht), **III:** 160; **Supp. IX:** 140; **Supp. XII:** 249

"Mother Earth: Her Whales" (Snyder), **Supp. VIII:** 302

"Motherhood" (Swenson), **Supp. IV Part 2:** 645

Mother Hubbard (Reed), **Supp. X:** 241

Motherless Brooklyn (Lethem), **Supp. XXII:** 49

Motherless in Brooklyn (Lethem), **Supp. XVIII:** 135, **143–144**

Mother Love (Dove), **Supp. IV Part 1:** 250–251, 254

"Mother Marie Therese" (Lowell), **Retro. Supp. II:** 188

Mother Night (Vonnegut), **Supp. II Part 2:** 757, 758, 767, 770, 771

"Mother Rosarine" (Kumin), **Supp. IV Part 2:** 442

"Mothers and Daughters in the Fiction of the New Republic" (Davidson), **Supp. XV:** 238

"Mother's lament for the absence of a child, A"(J. Schoolcraft), **Supp. XXIII:** 236

Mother's Recompense, The (Wharton), **IV:** 321, 324; **Retro. Supp. I:** 382

"Mother's Tale, A" (Agee), **I:** 29–30

"Mother's Things" (Creeley), **Supp. IV Part 1:** 141

"Mother Suite, The"(Crooker), **Supp. XXIII:** 61

"Mother's Voice" (Creeley), **Supp. IV Part 1:** 156

Mother to Daughter, Daughter to Mother (Olsen, ed.), **Supp. XIII:** 295

"Mother Tongue" (Simic), **Supp. VIII:** 283

"Mother to Son" (Hughes), **Retro. Supp. I:** 199, 203; **Supp. I Part 1:** 321–322, 323

Motherwell, Robert, **Supp. XV:** 145; **Supp. XXI:** 125

"Mother Writes to the Murderer, The: A Letter" (Nye), **Supp. XIII:** 276

Moths of the Limberlost (Stratton-Porter), **Supp. XX: 218**

"Motion, The" (Olson), **Supp. II Part 2:** 571

Motion of History, The (Baraka), **Supp. II Part 1:** 55, 56

"Motive for Metaphor, The" (Stevens), **IV:** 89; **Retro. Supp. I:** 310

Motiveless Malignity (Auchincloss), **Supp. IV Part 1:** 31

Motke ganef (Asch), **Supp. XXIII:** 5

Motley, John Lothrop, **Supp. I Part 1:** 299; **Supp. I Part 2:** 479; **Supp. XX: 228, 231**

Motley, Willard, **Supp. XVII: 149–163; Supp. XXIII:** 145

"Motor Car, The" (White), **Supp. I Part 2:** 661

Motor-Flight Through France (Wharton), **I:** 12; **Retro. Supp. I:** 372

Mott, Michael, **Supp. VIII:** 204, 208

Motta, Gustavo, **Supp. XXIII:** 125

Mottetti: Poems of Love: The Motets of Eugenio Montale (Montale; Gioia, trans.), **Supp. XV:** 112, **127–128**

Mottke, the Thief (Asch), **Supp. XXIII:** 9, 12

Mottke, the Thief (Asch; tr. Willa and Edwin Muir), **Supp. XXIII:** 5

Mouawad, Nelly, **Supp. XX: 126**

"Mountain, The" (Frost), **Retro. Supp. I:** 121

"Mountain Hermitage, The: Pages from a Japanese Notebook" (Passin), **Supp. XIII:** 337

Mountain Interval (Frost), **II:** 154; **Retro. Supp. I:** 131, 132, 133

"Mountain Lion" (Hogan), **Supp. IV Part 1:** 412

"Mountain Music" essays (Sanders), **Supp. XVI:** 276–277

Mountain on the Desert, The (Richter), **Supp. XVIII:** 216, 219

Mountainous Journey, A (Tuqan), **Supp. XIII:** 278

Mountains, The (Wolfe), **IV:** 461

Mountains and Rivers without End (Snyder), **Supp. VIII:** 295, **305–306**

"Mountains grow unnoticed, The" (Dickinson), **Retro. Supp. I:** 46

Mountains Have Come Closer, The (J. W. Miller), **Supp. XX: 165, 168, 169–170**

Mountains Look Down, The: A History of Chichester, a Company Town in the Catskills (Bennett), **Supp. XXII:** 218

Mountains of California, The (Muir), **Supp. IX:** 183

"Mountain Whippoorwill, The" (Benét), **Supp. XI:** 44–45, 46, 47

"Mount-Joy: or Some Passages Out of the Life of a Castle-Builder" (Irving), **II:** 314

"Mount Venus" (Wright), **Supp. XV:** 346

"Mourners" (Kooser), **Supp. XIX:** 127

"Mourners, The" (Malamud), **Supp. I Part 2:** 431, 435, 436–437

Mourners Below (Purdy), **Supp. VII:** 274, 280

"Mourning and Melancholia" (Freud), **Supp. IV Part 2:** 450; **Supp. XVI:** 161

Mourning Becomes Electra (O'Neill), **III:** 391, 394, 398–400

"Mourning Doves" (Pedersen; Nelson, trans.), **Supp. XVIII:** 180

"Mourning Poem for the Queen of Sunday" (Hayden), **Supp. II Part 1:** 379–380

"Mouse Elegy" (Olds), **Supp. X:** 209

Mouse Is Born, A (Loos), **Supp. XVI:** 193

"Mouse Roulette Wheel, The" (C. Bly), **Supp. XVI:** 34

Moustapha's Eclipse (McKnight), **Supp. XX: 147, 150**

"Mouth of Brass" (Humphrey), **Supp. IX:** 101

Moveable Feast, A (Hemingway), **II:** 257; **Retro. Supp. I:** 108, 171, **186–187**

Movement, The: Documentary of a Struggle for Equality (Student Nonviolent Coordinating Committee), **Supp. IV Part 1:** 369

"Move over Macho, Here Comes Feminismo" (Robbins), **Supp. X:** 272

Movers and Shakers (Sochen), **Supp. XXI:** 1

"Move to California, The" (Stafford), **Supp. XI:** 318, 321

"Movie" (Shapiro), **Supp. II Part 2:** 707

Movie at the End of the World, The (McGrath), **Supp. X:** 127

Moviegoer, The (Percy), **Supp. III Part 1:** 383–385, 387, 389–392, 394, 397

"Movie Magazine, The: A Low 'Slick' " (Percy), **Supp. III Part 1:** 385

Movies (Dixon), **Supp. XII:** 147

Movies About the Movies (Ames), **Supp. XVIII:** 242–243

"Moving Around" (Matthews), **Supp. IX:** 155

"Moving Finger, The" (Wharton), **Retro. Supp. I:** 365

"Moving Inward at Last" (Bly), **Supp. XXI:** 84–85

Moving On (McMurtry), **Supp. V:** 223–224

"Moving On" (Pickering), **Supp. XXI:** 197

Moving Pictures: Memoirs of a Hollywood Prince (Schulberg), **Supp. XVIII:** 242, 243, 254

Moving Target, The (Macdonald), **Supp. IV Part 2:** 462, 463, 467, 470, 471, 473, 474

Moving Target, The (Merwin), **Supp. III Part 1:** 346, 347–348, 352, 357

"Mowbray Family, The" (Farrell and Alden), **II:** 45

"Mowing" (Frost), **II:** 169–170; **Retro. Supp. I:** 127, 128

"Moxan's Master" (Bierce), **I:** 206

Moxley, Jennifer, **Supp. XVII:** 70

Moyers, Bill, **Supp. IV Part 1:** 267; **Supp. VIII:** 331; **Supp. XI:** 126, 132; **Supp. XII:** 217; **Supp. XIII:** 274, 276; **Supp. XV:** 212; **Supp. XXIII:** 129, 130, 131, 139

Moynagh, Maureen, **Supp. XXII:** 73

Moynihan, Daniel Patrick, **Retro. Supp. II:** 123; **Supp. VIII:** 241; **Supp. XIX:** 150–151

"Moyshele"(Asch), **Supp. XXIII:** 4

"Mozart" (C. Frost), **Supp. XV:** 94

Mozart, Wolfgang Amadeus, **I:** 479, 588; **IV:** 74, 358; **Supp. IV Part 1:** 284

"Mozart and the Gray Steward" (Wilder), **IV:** 358

Mrabet, Mohammed, **Supp. IV Part 1:** 92, 93

Mr. and Mrs. Baby and Other Stories (Strand), **Supp. IV Part 2:** 631

"Mr. and Mrs. Fix-It" (Lardner), **II:** 431

Mr. Arcularis (Aiken), **I:** 54, 56

"Mr. Big" (Allen), **Supp. XV:** 15

Mr. Bridge (Connell), **Supp. XIV:** 80, 82, 93; **Supp. XXIII:** 302

Mr. Brown Can Moo! Can You? (Geisel), **Supp. XVI:** 104

"Mr. Bruce" (Jewett), **II:** 397; **Retro. Supp. II:** 134, 143

"Mr. Burnshaw and the Statue" (Stevens), **Retro. Supp. I:** 298, 303

"Mr. Carson Death on His Nights Out" (McGrath), **Supp. X:** 118

Mr. Clemens and Mark Twain (Kaplan), **I:** 247–248

"Mr. Coffee and Mr. Fixit" (Carver), **Supp. III Part 1:** 145

"Mr. Cornelius Johnson, Office-Seeker" (Dunbar), **Supp. II Part 1:** 211, 213

"Mr. Costyve Duditch" (Toomer), **Supp. III Part 2:** 486

"Mr. Dajani, Calling from Jericho" (Nye), **Supp. XIII:** 286–287

"Mr. Edwards and the Spider" (Lowell), **I:** 544; **II:** 550; **Retro. Supp. II:** 187

Mr. Field's Daughter (Bausch), **Supp. VII:** 47–48, 51–52

"Mr. Flood's Party" (Robinson), **III:** 512

"Mr. Forster's Pageant" (Maxwell), **Supp. VIII:** 172

"Mr. Frost's Chickens" (Oliver), **Supp. VII:** 232–233

Mr. Hodge and Mr. Hazard (Wylie), **Supp. I Part 2:** 708, 709, 714, 721–724

"Mr. Hueffer and the Prose Tradition" (Pound), **III:** 465

Mr. Ives' Christmas (Hijuelos), **Supp. VIII: 85–86**

Mr. Kelso's Lion (Bontemps), **Supp. XXII:** 7

"Mr. Longfellow and His Boy" (Sandburg), **III:** 591

"Mr. Luna and History" (Ríos), **Supp. IV Part 2:** 551

"Mr. Mitochondria" (Stollman), **Supp. XVII:** 50

Mr. Moto Is So Sorry (Marquand), **III:** 57, 58

Mr. Norris Changes Trains (Isherwood), **Supp. XIV:** 161

"Mr. Preble Gets Rid of His Wife" (Thurber), **Supp. I Part 2:** 615

"Mr. Rat"(Thompson), **Supp. XXIII:** 301–302

"Mr. Rolfe" (Wilson), **IV:** 436

Mr. Rutherford's Children (S. and A. Warner), **Supp. XVIII:** 264

"Mrs. Adis" (Kaye-Smith), **Supp. XVIII:** 130–131

Mrs. Albert Grundy: Observations in Philistia (Frederic), **II:** 138–139

Mr. Sammler's Planet (Bellow), **I:** 144, 147, 150, 151, 152, 158; **Retro. Supp. II:** 19, 28, 30

"Mrs. Bilingsby's Wine" (Taylor), **Supp. V:** 323

Mrs. Bridge: A Novel (Connell), **Supp. XIV:** 79, 80, 81, 82, **89–94,** 95; **Supp. XXIII:** 302

"Mrs. Cassidy's Last Year" (Gordon), **Supp. IV Part 1:** 306

Mrs. Dalloway (Woolf), **Supp. IV Part 1:** 299; **Supp. VIII:** 5; **Supp. XV:** 55, 65–66

"Mr. Shelley Speaking" (Wylie), **Supp. I Part 2:** 719

"Mrs. Jellison" (Hay), **Supp. XIV:** 123

"Mrs. Krikorian" (Olds), **Supp. X:** 211

"Mrs. Maecenas" (Burke), **I:** 271

"Mrs. Mandrill" (Nemerov), **III:** 278

"Mrs. Manstey's View" (Wharton), **Retro. Supp. I:** 362, 363

"Mrs. Mobry's Reason" (Chopin), **Retro. Supp. I:** 61

Mr. Spaceman (R. O. Butler), **Supp. XII:** 62, **74–75**

Mrs. Reynolds (Stein), **IV:** 43

"Mrs. Sen's" (Lahiri), **Supp. XXI: 177–178,** 180–181

Mrs. Stevens Hears the Mermaids Singing (Sarton), **Supp. VIII:** 252–253, **256–257**

Mrs. Ted Bliss (Elkin), **Supp. VI: 56,** 58

"Mrs. Turner Cutting the Grass" (Shields), **Supp. VII:** 319–320

"Mrs. Walpurga" (Rukeyser), **Supp. VI:** 273

"Mr. Thompson's Prodigal" (Harte), **Supp. II Part 1:** 354

"Mr. Trumm's Eyes"(Schott), **Supp. XXIII:** 243

Mr. Vertigo (Auster), **Supp. XII: 34–35,** 36

"Mr. Vonnegut in Sumatra" (Saunders), **Supp. XIX:** 235

"Mr. Whittier" (Scott), **Supp. I Part 2:** 705

Mr. Wilson's War (Dos Passos), **I:** 485

"MS. Found in a Bottle" (Poe), **III:** 411, 416; **Retro. Supp. II:** 274

"Ms. Lot" (Rukeyser), **Supp. VI:** 281

Ms. Magazine, **Supp. V:** 259

Mttron-Hirsch, Sidney, **III:** 484–485

"Muchas Gracias Por Todo" (Nye), **Supp. XIII:** 282–283

"Much Madness is divinest Sense" (Dickinson), **Retro. Supp. I:** 37–38

"Muck-A-Muck" (Harte), **Supp. II Part 1:** 342

"Mud Below, The" (Proulx), **Supp. VII:** 262

Mudge, Alden, **Supp. XIV:** 35

"Mudman"(P. Benedict), **Supp. XXIII:** 47

Mudrick, Marvin, **Retro. Supp. II:** 289

"Mud Season" (Kenyon), **Supp. VII:** 167–168

Mueller, Lisel, **Supp. I Part 1:** 83, 88; **Supp. XIV:** 268

Muggli, Mark, **Supp. IV Part 1:** 207

Muhammad, Elijah, **Supp. I Part 1:** 60

Muir, Edwin, **I:** 527; **II:** 368; **III:** 20; **Supp. XXII:** 166; **Supp. XXIII:** 1

Muir, John, **Supp. VIII:** 296; **Supp. IX:** 33, **171–188;** **Supp. X:** 29; **Supp. XIV:** 177, 178, 181

Muir, Willa, **Supp. XXIII:** 1

Muirhead, Deborah, **Supp. XVIII:** 186

Mujica, Barbara, **Supp. VIII:** 89

Mulas, Franco, **Supp. XX: 38**

Mulatto (Hughes), **Retro. Supp. I:** 197, 203; **Supp. I Part 1:** 328, 339

Mulching of America, The (Crews), **Supp. XI:** 107

Muldoon, William, **I:** 500–501

Mule Bone (Hughes and Hurston), **Retro. Supp. I:** 194, 203; **Supp. VI:** 154

Mules and Men (Hurston), **Supp. VI:** 149, 153, 154, 160

Mulford, Prentice, **I:** 193

Mullennix, Joel, **Supp. XXIII:** 281

Mulligan, Robert, **Supp. VIII:** 128, 129

Mulligan Stew (Sorrentino), **Supp. XII:** 139; **Supp. XXI:** 233

Mullins, Eustace, **III:** 479

Mullins, Priscilla, **II:** 502–503

"Multiplication of Wool, The" (Sanders), **Supp. XVI:** 268

Multitudes, Multitudes (Clampitt), **Supp. IX:** 39

Mumbo Jumbo (Reed), **Supp. X:** 240, 242, **245–248,** 251

Mumford, Lewis, **I:** 245, 250, 251, 252, 259, 261; **II:** 271, 473–474; **Supp. I Part 2:** 632, 638; **Supp. II Part 2: 471–501**

Mumford, Sophia Wittenberg (Mrs. Lewis Mumford), **Supp. II Part 2:** 474, 475

"Mummers, The" (Di Piero), **Supp. XIX:** 44

Mummy, The (film), **Supp. IV Part 1:** 104; **Supp. XVII:** 57

Mundo y Palabra (Espaillat), **Supp. XXI:** 104

"Mundus et Infans" (Auden), **Supp. II Part 1:** 15

"Munich, 1938" (Lowell), **II:** 554

"Munich Mannequins, The" (Plath), **Retro. Supp. II:** 256

"Municipal Report, A" (Henry), **Supp. II Part 1:** 406–407

Munro, Alice, **Supp. IX:** 212; **Supp. X:** 290; **Supp. XII:** 289–290, 310; **Supp. XXIII:** 289, 296

Munsey, Frank, **I:** 501

Munson, Gorham, **I:** 252, 388, 432; **Retro. Supp. II:** 77, 78, 79, 82, 83; **Supp. I Part 2:** 454; **Supp. XX: 70, 74**

Münsterberg, Hugo, **Supp. XIV:** 197

Murakami, Haruki, **Supp. XVI:** 124

"Murano" (Doty), **Supp. XI:** 131

Murasaki, Lady, **II:** 577

Muratori, Fred, **Supp. XVI:** 281

Muray, Nicholas, **Supp. I Part 2:** 708

Murder, My Sweet (film), **Supp. IV Part 1:** 130

"Murderer Guest, The" (Gordon), **Supp. IV Part 1:** 306

"Murderers" (L. Michaels), **Supp. XVI:** 207–208

Murder in Mount Holly (Theroux), **Supp. VIII:** 315–316

Murder in the Cathedral (T. S. Eliot), **I:** 571, 573, 580, 581; **II:** 20; **Retro. Supp. I:** 65; **Retro. Supp. II:** 222

Murder of Lidice, The (Millay), **III:** 140

"Murders in the Rue Morgue, The" (Poe), **III:** 412, 416, 419–420; **Retro. Supp. II:** 271, 272; **Supp. XIX:** 77

Murdoch, Iris, **Supp. VIII:** 167; **Supp. XVIII:** 136,149

Murnau, F. W., **Supp. XV:** 128

Murphy, Brenda, **Supp. XXI:** 6

Murphy, Jacqueline Shea, **Retro. Supp. II:** 143

Murphy, Patrick, **Supp. XIII:** 214

Murphy, Richard, **Retro. Supp. II:** 250; **Supp. XXIII:** 75

Murray, Albert, **Retro. Supp. II:** 119, 120; **Supp. XIX: 147–162**

Murray, Bill, **Supp. XXI:** 51

Murray, Edward, **I:** 229

Murray, G. E., **Supp. X:** 201; **Supp. XI:** 143, 155

Murray, Gilbert, **III:** 468–469

Murray, Jan, **Supp. IV Part 2:** 574

Murray, John, **II:** 304; **III:** 76, 79; **Retro. Supp. I:** 246

Murray, Judith Sargent, **Supp. XV:** 236–237

Murray, Les, **Supp. XIX:** 131

Murray, Margaret A., **Supp. V:** 128

Murrell, John A., **IV:** 265

Mursell, James L., **Supp. I Part 2:** 608

"Muse" (Ammons), **Supp. VII:** 29

"Muse, Postmodern and Homeless, The" (Ozick), **Supp. V:** 272

"Musée des Beaux Arts" (Auden), **Retro. Supp. I:** 430; **Supp. II Part 1:** 14

"Musée des Beaux Arts Revisited" (Collins), **Supp. XXI:** 60

"Muse of Aboutness, The" (Baker), **Supp. XVI:** 288

Muses Are Heard, The (Capote), **Supp. III Part 1:** 126

"Muses of Terrence McNally, The" (Zinman), **Supp. XIII:** 207–208

"Muse's Tragedy, The" (Wharton), **Retro. Supp. I:** 364

Museum (Dove), **Supp. IV Part 1:** 245–247, 248

"Museum" (Hass), **Supp. VI:** 107

Museums and Women (Updike), **Retro. Supp. I:** 321

"Museum Vase" (Francis), **Supp. IX:** 83

"Mushrooms" (Plath), **Retro. Supp. II:** 246; **Supp. I Part 2:** 539

"Music" (Oliver), **Supp. VII:** 236

Music (al-Músíqá) (Gibran), **Supp. XX: 115, 124**

Music After the Great War (Van Vechten), **Supp. II Part 2:** 732

Music and Bad Manners (Van Vechten), **Supp. II Part 2:** 733

Music Appreciation (Skloot), **Supp. XX: 196, 197–201**

"Music for a Farce" (Bowles), **Supp. IV Part 1:** 83

Music for Chameleons (Capote), **Supp. III Part 1:** 120, 125–127, 131, 132

"Music for Museums?" (Van Vechten), **Supp. II Part 2:** 732

"Music for the Movies" (Van Vechten), **Supp. II Part 2:** 733

"Music from Spain" (Welty), **IV:** 272

Music Like Dirt (Bidart), **Supp. XV:** 35

"Music Like Dirt" (Bidart), **Supp. XV:** 35

Music of Chance, The (Auster), **Supp. XII:** 21, 23, **32–33**

"Music of My Own Kind Too, The" (Budbill), **Supp. XIX:** 10

"Music of Prose, The" (Gass), **Supp. VI:** 92

Music of Spain, The (Van Vechten), **Supp. II Part 2:** 734, 735

"Music of the Spheres" (Epstein), **Supp. XII:** 165

"Music School" (B. Kelly), **Supp. XVII:** 124

Music School, The (Updike), **IV:** 214, 215, 219, 226, 227; **Retro. Supp. I:** 320, 328, 329, 330

"Music School, The" (Updike), **Retro. Supp. I:** 326, 329, 335

"Music Swims Back to Me" (Sexton), **Supp. II Part 2:** 673

Muske, Carol, **Supp. IV Part 2:** 453–454

"Mussel Hunter at Rock Harbor" (Plath), **Supp. I Part 2:** 529, 537

Musset, Alfred de, **I:** 474; **II:** 543

Mussolini, Benito, **III:** 115, 473, 608; **IV:** 372, 373; **Supp. I Part 1:** 281, 282; **Supp. I Part 2:** 618; **Supp. V:** 290; **Supp. XVI:** 191

"Mustafa Ferrari" (X. J. Kennedy), **Supp. XV:** 170–171

Mustich, James, **Supp. XXI:** 52

"Must the Novelist Crusade?" (Welty), **IV:** 280

"Mutability of Literature, The" (Irving), **II:** 308

"Mutation of the Spirit" (Corso), **Supp. XII:** 132, 133

Mute, The (McCullers), **II:** 586

Mutilated, The (T. Williams), **IV:** 382, 386, 393

Mutiny of the Elsinore, The (London), **II:** 467

"Muttsy" (Hurston), **Supp. XVIII:** 279

Muyumba, Walton, **Supp. XIX:** 158

"My Adventures as a Social Poet" (Hughes), **Retro. Supp. I:** 194, 207

"My Alba" (Ginsberg), **Supp. II Part 1:** 320, 321

My Alexandria (Doty), **Supp. XI:** 119, 120, 121, **123–125,** 130

"My Amendment" (Saunders), **Supp. XIX:** 232

My Amputations (Major), **Supp. XXII:** 174, **175–176**

My Ántonia (Cather), **I:** 321–322; **Retro. Supp. I:** 1, 3, 4, **11–13,** 14, 17, 18, 22; **Supp. IV Part 2:** 608; **Supp. XVI:** 226

"My Appearance" (Wallace), **Supp. X:** 306–307

My Argument with the Gestapo: A Macaronic Journal (Merton), **Supp. VIII:** 207; **Supp. XV:** 344

"My Arkansas" (Angelou), **Supp. IV Part 1:** 15

"My Aunt" (Holmes), **Supp. I Part 1:** 302, 310

"My Beginnings" (Simpson), **Supp. IX:** 273

"My Bird Problem" (Franzen), **Supp. XX: 94**

"My Bodyguard" (Notley), **Supp. XXII:** 230

My Bondage and My Freedom (Douglass), **Supp. III Part 1:** 155, 173

My Brother (Kincaid), **Supp. VII:** 191–193

"My Brother Paul" (Dreiser), **Retro. Supp. II:** 94

"My Brothers the Silent" (Merwin), **Supp. III Part 1:** 349–350

"My Brother's Work" (Dunn), **Supp. XI:** 147

"My Brother Takes a Hammer to the Mirror" (F. Wright), **Supp. XVII:** 244

"My Butterfly" (Frost), **II:** 151; **Retro. Supp. I:** 124

"My Children, and a Prayer for Us" (Ortiz), **Supp. IV Part 2:** 507

"My College Sex Group" (Peacock), **Supp. XIX:** 199

"My Coney Island Uncle" (Swados), **Supp. XIX:** 267–268

"My Confession" (McCarthy), **II:** 562

"My Confessional Sestina" (Gioia), **Supp. XV:** 123

"My Corner" (Major), **Supp. XXII:** 184

My Country and My People (Yutang), **Supp. X:** 291

"My Country 'Tis of Thee" (Reznikoff), **Supp. III Part 2:** 616

"My Daughter Considers Her Body" (Skloot), **Supp. XX: 197–198, 200**

My Days of Anger (Farrell), **II:** 34, 35–36, 43

"My Dear Niece" (Boyce), **Supp. XXI:** 10

"My Dear Republican Mother" (C. Bly), **Supp. XVI:** 31–32

My Death My Life by Pier Paolo Pasolini (Acker), **Supp. XII:** 7

My Dog Stupid (Fante), **Supp. XI:** 160, **170–171**

My Dog Tulip (Ackerley), **Supp. XX: 237**

"My Ear-Rings"(J. Schoolcraft), **Supp. XXIII:** 226

My Emily Dickinson (Howe), **Retro. Supp. I:** 33, 43; **Supp. IV Part 2:** 430–431

"My English" (Alvarez), **Supp. VII:** 2

Myers, John Bernard, **Supp. XXIII:** 210, 219

Myers, Linda A., **Supp. IV Part 1:** 10

"My Extended Family" (Theroux), **Supp. VIII:** 311

"My Father" (Budbill), **Supp. XIX:** 5

"My Father" (L. Michaels), **Supp. XVI:** 214

"My Father" (Sterne), **IV:** 466

"My Father at Eighty-Five" (R. Bly), **Supp. IV Part 1:** 73

"My Father Is a Simple Man" (Salinas), **Supp. XIII:** 324

"My Father Is with Me" (Budbill), **Supp. XIX:** 15

"My Father: October 1942" (Stafford), **Supp. XI:** 323

My Father Photographed with Friends (Bronk), **Supp. XXI:** 26–27,**Supp. XXI:** 31

"My Father Photographed with Friends" (Bronk), **Supp. XXI:** 23, 27

"My Fathers Came From Kentucky" (Lindsay), **Supp. I Part 2:** 395

"My Father's Employment"(Schott), **Supp. XXIII:** 247

"My Father's Friends" (Maxwell), **Supp. VIII:** 171

"My Father's Ghost" (Wagoner), **Supp. IX:** 330

"My Father's God" (Fante), **Supp. XI:** 160, 174

"My Father's House" (L.-Y. Lee), **Supp. XV:** 225

"My Father's Love Letters" (Komunyakaa), **Supp. XIII:** 127

"My Father Speaks to me from the Dead" (Olds), **Supp. X:** 210

"My Father's Telescope" (Dove), **Supp. IV Part 1:** 246, 248

"My Father with Cigarette Twelve Years Before the Nazis Could Break His Heart" (Levine), **Supp. V:** 194

"My Favorite Murder" (Bierce), **I:** 205

My Favorite Plant: Writers and Gardeners on the Plants They Love (Kincaid), **Supp. VII:** 193–194

My Favorites in Suspense (Hitchcock, ed.), **Supp. XXII:** 119

"My Fifty-Plus Years Celebrate Spring" (Salinas), **Supp. XIII:** 327

"My First Book" (Harte), **Supp. II Part 1:** 343

My First Summer in the Sierra (Muir), **Supp. IX:** 172, 173, **178–181**, 183, 185; **Supp. XIV:** 177

"My Flamboyant Grandson" (Saunders), **Supp. XIX:** 231–232

"My Fountain Pen" (McClatchy), **Supp. XII:** 254, 260

My Friend, Henry Miller (Perlès), **III:** 189

My Friend, Julia Lathrop (Addams), **Supp. I Part 1:** 25

"My Friend, Walt Whitman" (Oliver), **Supp. VII:** 245

"My Garden Acquaintance" (Lowell), **Supp. I Part 2:** 420

My Garden [Book]: (Kincaid), **Supp. VII:** 193–194

"My Good-bye" (Weigl), **Supp. XIX:** 288

"My Grandfather" (Lowell), **II:** 554

"My Grandmother's Love Letters" (H. Crane), **Retro. Supp. II:** 78

My Grandparents Were Married for Sixty-five Years (Schott), **Supp. XXIII:** 240–241

"My Grandson, Home at Last" (Angelou), **Supp. IV Part 1:** 13

My Green Hills of Jamaica (McKay), **Supp. X:** 132, 142

My Guru and His Disciple (Isherwood), **Supp. XIV:** 157, 164, 172

"My Heart" (Collins), **Supp. XXI:** 58

My Heart's in the Highlands (Saroyan), **Supp. IV Part 1:** 83

"My High School Reunion" (Kingston), **Supp. V:** 169

"My House New-Painted" (Bronk), **Supp. XXI:** 30

"My Ideal Home" (Stratton-Porter), **Supp. XX: 222**

"My Indigo" (L.-Y. Lee), **Supp. XV:** 214

"My Kinsman, Major Molineux" (Hawthorne), **II:** 228, 229, 237–239, 243; **Retro. Supp. I:** 153–154, 158, 160, 161; **Retro. Supp. II:** 181, 187; **Supp. XVI:** 157

My Kinsman, Major Molineux (Lowell), **II:** 545–546

"My Last Afternoon with Uncle Devereux Winslow" (Lowell), **II:** 547–548; **Retro. Supp. II:** 189

"My Last Drive" (Hardy), **Supp. VIII:** 32

"My Last Duchess" (Browning), **Supp. XV:** 121

"My Life" (Strand), **Supp. IV Part 2:** 627

My Life, Starring Dara Falcon (Beattie), **Supp. V:** 31, 34–35

My Life a Loaded Gun: Dickinson, Plath, Rich, and Female Creativity (Bennett), **Retro. Supp. I:** 29

My Life and Hard Times (Thurber), **Supp. I Part 2:** 607, 609

My Life as a Man (P. Roth), **Retro. Supp. II:** 281, 286, 289; **Supp. III Part 2:** 401, 404, 405, 417–418

"My Life as a P.I.G., or the True Adventures of Smokey the Cop" (Abbey), **Supp. XIII:** 3

"My life closed twice before its close" (Dickinson), **Retro. Supp. I:** 38

"My Life had stood a Loaded Gun" (Dickinson), **Retro. Supp. I:** 42, 43, 45, 46; **Supp. IV Part 2:** 430

My Life of Absurdity (C. Himes), **Supp. XVI:** 145

"My Life with Medicine" (Nye), **Supp. XIII:** 282

"My Life with *Playboy*" (Plimpton), **Supp. XVI:** 246

"My Life with R. H. Macy" (Jackson), **Supp. IX:** 118

"My Little Utopia" (Simic), **Supp. VIII:** 283

My Lives and How I Lost Them (Cullen), **Supp. IV Part 1:** 173

"My Lord Bag of Rice" (C. Bly), **Supp. XVI:** 40

My Lord Bag of Rice: New and Selected Stories (C. Bly), **Supp. XVI:** 41

"My Lost City" (Fitzgerald), **Retro. Supp. I:** 102

"My Lost Youth" (Longfellow), **II:** 487, 499; **Retro. Supp. II:** 168

My Love Affair with America: The Cautionary Tale of a Cheerful Conservative (Podhoretz), **Supp. VIII:** 232, 233, 237, **244–246**

"My Lover Has Dirty Fingernails" (Updike), **Retro. Supp. I:** 332, 333

"My lover is tall and handsome"(J. Schoolcraft), **Supp. XXIII:** 235

"My Lucy Friend Who Smells Like Corn" (Cisneros), **Supp. VII:** 68–69

"My Mammogram" (McClatchy), **Supp. XII:** 263–264

"My Man Bovanne" (Bambara), **Supp. XI:** 2

"My Mariner" (Larcom), **Supp. XIII:** 147

My Mark Twain (Howells), **II:** 276

"My Metamorphosis" (Harte), **Supp. II Part 1:** 339

"My Moby Dick" (Humphrey), **Supp. IX:** 95

"My Monkey" (Nelson), **Supp. XVIII:** 178

"My Moral Life" (Halliday), **Supp. XIX:** 89

My Mortal Enemy (Cather), **I:** 327–328; **Retro. Supp. I:** 16–17; **Supp. I Part 2:** 719

My Mother, My Father and Me (Hellman), **Supp. I Part 1:** 290–291

"My Mother and My Sisters" (Ortiz), **Supp. IV Part 2:** 499

My Mother: Demonology (Acker), **Supp. XII:** 6

"My Mother Is Speaking from the Desert" (Gordon), **Supp. IV Part 1:** 309, 314

"My Mother's Goofy Song" (Fante), **Supp. XI:** 164

"My Mother's Memoirs, My Father's Lie, and Other True Stories" (Banks), **Supp. V:** 15

"My Mother's Nipples" (Hass), **Supp. VI:** 109

"My Mother's Story" (Kunitz), **Supp. III Part 1:** 259

"My Mother"(Taylor), **Supp. XXIII:** 231

"My Mother Then and Now" (Wasserstein), **Supp. XV:** 327

"My Mother with Purse the Summer They Murdered the Spanish Poet" (Levine), **Supp. V:** 194

My Movie Business: A Memoir (Irving), **Supp. VI:** 164

"My Name" (Cisneros), **Supp. VII:** 60

"My Negro Problem—And Ours" (Podhoretz), **Supp. VIII: 234–236**

"My Neighborhood"(Dybek), **Supp. XXIII:** 69

"My New Diet" (Karr), **Supp. XI:** 241

"My Number" (Collins), **Supp. XXI:** 64

"My Old Man" (Hemingway), **II:** 263

My Other Life (Theroux), **Supp. VIII:** 310, 324

"My Own Story" (E. Stoddard), **Supp. XV:** 273, 279, 283

My Own True Name: New and Selected Poems for Young Adults, 1984–1999 (Mora), **Supp. XIII:** 222

"My Parents Have Come Home Laughing" (Jarman), **Supp. XVII:** 113

"My Passion for Ferries" (Whitman), **IV:** 350

"My People" (Hughes), **Retro. Supp. I:** 197; **Supp. I Part 1:** 321–322, 323

"My Philosophy" (Allen), **Supp. XV:** 15

"My Playmate" (Whittier), **Supp. I Part 2:** 699–700

"My Priests" (Monette), **Supp. X:** 159

Myra Breckinridge (Vidal), **Supp. IV Part 2:** 677, 685–686, 689, 691

"My Raptor" (A. Finch), **Supp. XVII:** 72

"My Recollections of S. B. Fairchild" (Jackson), **Supp. IX:** 118–119

"My Religion" (Carson), **Supp. XII: 105–106**

"My Road to Hell Was Paved" (Patchett), **Supp. XII:** 310–311

Myron (Vidal), **Supp. IV Part 2:** 677, 685, 686, 691

"My Roomy" (Lardner), **II:** 420, 421, 428, 430

"My Sad Self" (Ginsberg), **Supp. II Part 1:** 320

My Secret History (Theroux), **Supp. VIII:** 310, 324

"Myself" (Audubon), **Supp. XVI:** 1–2, 5, 12

Myself Painting (Major), **Supp. XXII: 184–185**

"My Shoes" (Simic), **Supp. VIII:** 275

"My Side of the Matter" (Capote), **Supp. III Part 1:** 114, 115

My Silk Purse and Yours: The Publishing Scene and American Literary Art (Garrett), **Supp. VII:** 111; **Supp. X:** 7

My Sister Eileen (McKenney), **IV:** 288; **Retro. Supp. II:** 321

My Sister's Hand in Mine: The Collected Works of Jane Bowles, **Supp. IV Part 1:** 82–83

"My Son" (Strand), **Supp. IV Part 2:** 629

My Son, John (film), **Supp. I Part 1:** 67

"My Son, the Murderer" (Malamud), **Supp. I Part 2:** 437

"My Son the Man" (Olds), **Supp. X:** 212

"My Speech to the Graduates" (Allen), **Supp. XV:** 16

"Mysteries of Caesar, The" (Hecht), **Supp. X:** 73

"Mysteries of Eleusis, The" (Hardwick), **Supp. III Part 1:** 195

Mysteries of Paris, The (Sue), **Supp. XXIII:** 182

Mysteries of Pittsburgh, The (Chabon), **Supp. XI:** 65, 68, **69–71; Supp. XIX:** 135

Mysteries of Small Houses (Notley), **Supp. XXII:** 223, 224, 226, 234–235

"Mysterious Case of R, The" (Conroy), **Supp. XVI:** 72

Mysterious Stranger, The (Twain), **IV:** 190–191, 210

Mystery, A (Shields). *See Swann* (Shields)

"Mystery, The" (Dunbar), **Supp. II Part 1:** 199, 210

"Mystery, The" (Glück), **Supp. V:** 91

Mystery and Manners (O'Connor), **Retro. Supp. II:** 230

"'Mystery Boy' Looks for Kin in Nashville" (Hayden), **Supp. II Part 1:** 366, 372

"Mystery of Coincidence, The" (Conroy), **Supp. XVI:** 74

"Mystery of Heroism, A" (Crane), **I:** 414

"Mystery of Marie Rogêt, The" (Poe), **III:** 413, 419; **Retro. Supp. II:** 271

"Mystic" (Plath), **Retro. Supp. II:** 257; **Supp. I Part 2:** 539, 541

"Mystical Poet, A" (Bogan), **Retro. Supp. I:** 36

"Mystic of Sex, The—A First Look at D. H. Lawrence" (Nin), **Supp. X:** 188

"Mystic Vision in 'The Marshes of Glynn' " (Warfel), **Supp. I Part 1:** 366, 373

"Mystification" (Poe), **III:** 425

"My Strange New Poetry" (Halliday), **Supp. XIX:** 88, 94

My Study Windows (Lowell), **Supp. I Part 2:** 407

"My Teacher" (Conroy), **Supp. XVI:** 75

"Myth" (Rukeyser), **Supp. VI:** 281–282

"Myth" (Trethewey), **Supp. XXI:** 245, 255, 256

"Myth"(Hadas), **Supp. XXIII:** 119

"Mythmaker" (Trethewey), **Supp. XXI:** 243

Myth of Sisyphus, The (Camus), **I:** 294; **Supp. XIII:** 165

"Myth of the Happy Worker, The" (Swados), **Supp. XIX:** 265

"Myth of the Isolated Artist, The" (Oates), **Supp. II Part 2:** 520

Myth of the Machine, The (Mumford), **Supp. II Part 2:** 476, 478, 482, 483, 493, 497

"Myth of the Powerful Worker, The" (Swados), **Supp. XIX:** 265

Mythology and the Romantic Tradition in English Poetry (Bush), **Supp. I Part 1:** 268

Myths and Texts (Snyder), **Supp. VIII: 295–296**

"Myths of Bears, The" (Bass), **Supp. XVI:** 19, 20

"My *Tocaya*" (Cisneros), **Supp. VII:** 69

My Uncle Dudley (Morris), **I:** 305; **III:** 219–220

"My Uncle's Favorite Coffee Shop" (Nye), **Supp. XIII:** 283

"My Weariness of Epic Proportions" (Simic), **Supp. VIII:** 276

My Wicked Wicked Ways (Cisneros), **Supp. VII:** 58, 64–68, 71

"My Wicked Wicked Ways" (Cisneros), **Supp. VII:** 58, 64–66

My Wisdom (Thompson), **Supp. XXIII: 291–293**

"My Word-house" (Mora), **Supp. XIII:** 219, 225

My Works and Days (Mumford), **Supp. II Part 2:** 475, 477, 481

"My World and My Critics" (Stratton-Porter), **Supp. XX: 220**

My World and Welcome to It (Thurber), **Supp. I Part 2:** 610

N

Nabokov, Peter, **Supp. IV Part 2:** 490

Nabokov, Véra, **Retro. Supp. I:** 266, 270

Nabokov, Vladimir, **I:** 135; **III: 244–266,** 283, 286; **Retro. Supp. I: 263–281,** 317, 335; **Supp. I Part 1:** 196; **Supp. II Part 1:** 2; **Supp. IV Part 1:** 135; **Supp. V:** 127, 237, 251, 252, 253; **Supp. VIII:** 105, 133, 138; **Supp. IX:** 152, 212, 261; **Supp. X:** 283; **Supp. XI:** 66; **Supp. XII:** 310; **Supp. XIII:** 46, 52; **Supp. XVI:** 148, 294; **Supp. XVIII:** 98, 102; **Supp. XXII:** 263

Nabokov's Dozen (Nabokov), **Retro. Supp. I:** 266

Nabokov's Garden: A Guide to Ada (Mason), **Supp. VIII:** 138

Naca, Kristin, **Supp. XIII:** 133

Nadeau, Robert, **Supp. X:** 261, 270

Nadel, Alan, **Supp. IV Part 1:** 209

Naimy, Mikhail, **Supp. XX: 116, 119, 120**

Naipaul, V. S., **Supp. IV Part 1:** 297; **Supp. VIII:** 314; **Supp. X:** 131; **Supp. XIV:** 111; **Supp. XX: 87; Supp. XXI:** 170; **Supp. XXII:** 240, 241, 242, 246, 253

Naison, Mark, **Supp. XVIII:** 231

Naked and the Dead, The (Mailer), **I:** 477; **III:** 26, 27, 28–30, 31, 33, 35, 36, 44; **Retro. Supp. II: 197–199; Supp. IV Part 1:** 381; **Supp. XI:** 218; **Supp. XIX:** 248; **Supp. XX: 248; Supp. XXI:** 277

Naked Author (di Donato), **Supp. XX: 45**

Naked Babies (Quindlen and Kelsh), **Supp. XVII:** 167, 179

Naked in Garden Hills (Crews), **Supp. XI:** 102, **110**

Naked Lunch (Burroughs), **Supp. III Part 1:** 92–95, 97–105; **Supp. IV Part 1:** 90

"Naked Nude" (Malamud), **Supp. I Part 2:** 450

Naked Poetry (Berg and Mezey, eds.), **Supp. IV Part 1:** 60

Naked Poetry (Levine), **Supp. V:** 180

Naked Revenge (film), **Supp. XVII:** 141

Nall, Gus, **Supp. XXII:** 172, 184

Namedropping: Mostly Literary Memoirs (Coover), **Supp. V:** 40

"Name in the Papers" (Hughes), **Supp. I Part 1:** 330

Name Is Archer, The (Macdonald, under Millar), **Supp. IV Part 2:** 466

"Name Is Burroughs, The" (Burroughs), **Supp. III Part 1:** 93

Name Is Fogarty, The: Private Papers on Public Matters (Farrell), **II:** 49

"Names" (Carruth), **Supp. XVI:** 54, 56

"Names, The" (Collins), **Supp. XXI:** 54, 61–62

Names, The (DeLillo), **Supp. VI:** 3, 10, 13, 14

Names, The (Momaday), **Supp. IV Part 2:** 479, 480, 483, 486, 487, 488, 489

Namesake, The (Lahiri), **Supp. XXI:** 176, 184, **186–188**

Names and Faces of Heroes, The (Price), **Supp. VI:** 258, 260

Names of the Lost, The (Levine), **Supp. V:** 177–178, 179, 187–188

"Naming for Love" (Carruth), **Supp. XVI:** 48

"Naming Myself" (Kingsolver), **Supp. VII:** 208

"Naming of Names, The" (Sanders), **Supp. XVI:** 268

Naming of the Beasts, The (Stern). *See Rejoicings: Selected Poems, 1966–1972* (Stern)

Naming the Unseen (Ray), **Supp. XVIII:** 192, **193–195**

"Naming the Unseen" (Ray), **Supp. XVIII:** 203

Nana (Zola), **III:** 321

"Nancy Culpepper" (Mason), **Supp. VIII:** 141

Nancy Drew stories, **Supp. VIII:** 133, 135, 137, 142

"Nancy Knapp" (Masters), **Supp. I Part 2:** 461

"Naola Beauty Academy, New Orleans, 1943" (Trethewey), **Supp. XXI:** 246

"Naomi Counting Time"(Thompson), **Supp. XXIII:** 293

"Naomi Shihab Nye: U.S. Mideast-History a Harbinger of 9-11?" (Nye), **Supp. XIII:** 286

"Naomi Trimmer" (X. J. Kennedy), **Supp. XV:** 170

"Nap, The" (Banks), **Supp. V:** 7

"Napoleon" (Emerson), **II:** 6

Napoleon I, **I:** 6, 7, 8, 474; **II:** 5, 309, 315, 321, 523; **Supp. I Part 1:** 153; **Supp. I Part 2:** 518, 519

Napolitano, Louise, **Supp. XX: 35, 45, 46–47**

Narcissa and Other Fables (Auchincloss), **Supp. IV Part 1:** 21, 34

"Narcissus as Narcissus" (Tate), **IV:** 124

"Narcissus Leaves the Pool" (Epstein), **Supp. XIV:** 110

Narcissus Leaves the Pool: Familiar Essays (Epstein), **Supp. XIV:** 110

Nardal, Paulette, **Supp. X:** 139

Nardi, Marcia, **Retro. Supp. I:** 426, 427

"Narragansett Boulevard" (Halliday), **Supp. XIX:** 91

Narration (Stein), **IV:** 27, 30, 32, 33, 36

Narrative of a Four Months' Residence among the Natives of a Valley of the Marquesas Islands (Melville), **III:** 76

Narrative of Arthur Gordon Pym, The (Poe), **III:** 412, 416; **Retro. Supp. II:** 265, **273–275; Supp. XI:** 293

"Narrative of Arthur Gordon Pym, The" (Poe), **Supp. XXII:** 58

Narrative of the Life of Frederick Douglass, an American Slave, Written by Himself (Douglass), **Supp. III Part 1:** 154–159, 162, 165; **Supp. IV Part 1:** 13; **Supp. VIII:** 202

"Narrativity Scenes" (Wright), **Supp. XV:** 345

Narrenschiff, Das (Brant), **III:** 447

"Narrow Fellow in the Grass, A" (Dickinson), **Retro. Supp. I:** 30, 37

Narrow Heart, A: Portrait of a Woman (Gordon), **II:** 197, 217

Narrow Rooms (Purdy), **Supp. VII:** 274

Narrows, The (Connelly), **Supp. XXI:** 71, **76**

Nasby, Petroleum, **Supp. XVIII:** 1

Nash, Noreen, **Supp. XXII:** 256

Nash, Ogden, **Supp. XXI:** 51

Nash, Roderick, **Supp. IX:** 185; **Supp. XIV:** 191–192

Nash, Susan Smith, **Supp. XVI:** 274

Nash, Thomas, **Supp. III Part 1:** 387–388

Nashe, Thomas, **I:** 358; **Supp. XVII:** 232

Nashville (film), **Supp. IX:** 143

"Nashville Gone to Ashes" (Hempel), **Supp. XXI:** 115, 118, **120–121**

Nashville Skyline (album, Dylan), **Supp. XVIII:** 27

Nason, Elias, **Supp. XV:** 242

Nasser, Gamal Abdel, **IV:** 490

Natalie Mann (Toomer), **Supp. III Part 2:** 484–486

Nathan, George Jean, **II:** 91; **III:** 103, 104, 106, 107; **IV:** 432; **Supp. IV Part 1:** 343; **Supp. IX:** 56–57; **Supp. XIII:** 161; **Supp. XXII:** 23

"Nathanael West" (Herbst), **Retro. Supp. II:** 325

Nathanael West: The Art of His Life (Martin), **Retro. Supp. II:** 325

Nathan Coulter (Berry), **Supp. X:** 24, 33

National Dream, The: Building the Impossible Railway (Findley and Whitehead), **Supp. XX: 51**

"Nationalist, The" (Anderson), **I:** 115

"Nation Is Like Ourselves, The" (Baraka), **Supp. II Part 1:** 53

"Native, The" (Olds), **Supp. X:** 215

"Native American Attitudes to the Environment" (Momaday), **Supp. IV Part 2:** 481, 491

Native American Renaissance (Lincoln), **Supp. IV Part 2:** 507

Native American Testimony (Nabokov, ed.), **Supp. IV Part 2:** 490

"Native Blessing" (Ray), **Supp. XVIII:** 202

Native Guard (Trethewey), **Supp. XXI:** 243, 244, 247, **254–257**

"Native Guard" (Trethewey), **Supp. XXI:** 256

"Native Hill, A" (Berry), **Supp. X:** 21

Native in a Strange Land: Trials & Tremors (Coleman), **Supp. XI: 84–85,** 87

Native of Winby and Other Tales, A (Jewett), **II:** 396; **Retro. Supp. II:** 138

Native Son (Wright), **IV:** 476, 477, 478, 479, 481, 482–484, 485, 487, 488, 491, 495; **Retro. Supp. II:** 107, 116; **Supp. I Part 1:** 51, 64, 67, 337; **Supp. II Part 1:** 170, 235–236; **Supp. IX:** 306; **Supp. XIV:** 73; **Supp. XVII:** 155; **Supp. XVIII:** 283, 286; **Supp. XXI:** 169

"Native Trees" (Merwin), **Supp. III Part 1:** 355

Natorp, Paul, **Supp. XIV:** 198

Natural, The (Malamud), **II:** 424, 425; **Retro. Supp. II:** 288; **Supp. I Part 2:** 438–441, 443

"Natural, The: Malamud's World Ceres" (Wasserman), **Supp. I Part 2:** 439

"Natural History" (Olds), **Supp. X:** 210

"Natural History Note" (Hay), **Supp. XIV:** 124, 130

"Natural History of Some Poems, A" (Harrison), **Supp. VIII:** 53

"Natural History of the Dead" (Hemingway), **II:** 206; **Retro. Supp. I:** 176

"Naturally Superior School, A" (Knowles), **Supp. XII:** 235, 240–241

"Natural Method of Mental Philosophy" (Emerson), **II:** 14

"Natural Resources" (Rich), **Supp. I Part 2:** 575

Natural Selection (F. Barthelme), **Supp. XI:** 2, 28, 32, 33

Nature (Emerson), **I:** 463; **II:** 1, 8, 12, 16; **IV:** 171, 172–173

"Nature" (Emerson), **Retro. Supp. I:** 250; **Supp. I Part 2:** 383; **Supp. III Part 1:** 387; **Supp. IX:** 178

"Nature, Inc." (Lewis), **II:** 441

Nature and Destiny of Man, The (Niebuhr), **III:** 292, 303–306, 310

"Nature and Life" (Emerson), **II:** 19
"Nature and New America Painting"(O'Hara), **Supp. XXIII:** 212
"Nature and Nurture: When It Comes to Twins, Sometimes It's Hard to Tell the Two Apart" (Bausch), **Supp. VII:** 40
"Nature-Metaphors" (Lanier), **Supp. I Part 1:** 352
Nature Morte (Brodsky), **Supp. VIII:** 25
Nature of Evil, The (James), **II:** 343
Nature of Peace, The (Veblen), **Supp. I Part 2:** 642
Nature of Things, The (television show), **Supp. XX:** 51
Nature of True Virtue, The (Edwards), **I:** 549, 557–558, 559
Nature: Poems Old and New (Swenson), **Supp. IV Part 2:** 652
Nature's Economy: A History of Ecological Ideas (Worster), **Supp. IX:** 19
Naumburg, Margaret, **Supp. XX:** 68, 74–75
Nausea (Sartre), **Supp. VIII:** 7
"Navajo Blanket, A" (Swenson), **Supp. IV Part 2:** 649
Navarette, Don Martín de, **II:** 310
Navarro, Ramon, **Supp. IV Part 1:** 206
Navigator, The (film), **I:** 31
Navratilova, Martina, **Supp. XX:** 264
Naylor, Gloria, **Supp. VIII:** 213–230; **Supp. XX:** 108
Naylor, Paul Kenneth, **Supp. IV Part 2:** 420
Nazarene, The (Asch), **Supp. XXIII:** 2, 3, 4, 6, 9, 12–13, 14, 15, 16
Nazarene, The: or, The Last of the Washingtons (Lippard), **Supp. XXIII:** 183, 184, 187, 190
Nazimova, **III:** 399
Neal, Darlin', **Supp. XXI:** 41
Neal, Larry, **Retro. Supp. II:** 112, 128; **Supp. X:** 324, 328
Neal, Lawrence P., **Supp. II Part 1:** 53
Neal, Patricia, **Supp. I Part 1:** 286; **Supp. IV Part 2:** 524; **Supp. V:** 223
Neale, Walter, **I:** 192, 208
"Near Damascus" (Di Piero), **Supp. XIX:** 43
Nearer the Moon: From "A Journal of Love," the Unexpurgated Diary of Anaïs Nin, 1937–1939, **Supp. X:** 184, 185
Near-Johannesburg Boy and Other Poems, The (Brooks), **Supp. III Part 1:** 86
Near Klamath (Carver), **Supp. III Part 1:** 137
"Near Perigord" (Pound), **Retro. Supp. I:** 289, 290
"Near Spring" (Pickering), **Supp. XXI:** 198
Near the Ocean (Lowell), **II:** 543, 550, 551–553, 554, 555; **Retro. Supp. II:** 182, 186, 189–190
"Near View of the High Sierra, A" (Muir), **Supp. IX:** 183
Nebeker, Helen, **Supp. IX:** 122
"Nebraska Blizzard" (F. Wright), **Supp. XVII:** 247

Necessary Angel, The (Stevens), **IV:** 76, 79, 89, 90
Necessities of Life: Poems, 1962–1965 (Rich), **Supp. I Part 2:** 553, 555
"Necessity of Lemons, The"(Schott), **Supp. XXIII:** 247, 248
Nechayev, Sergey, **Supp. XXI:** 164
"Necrological" (Ransom), **III:** 486–489, 490, 492
Ned Christie's War (Conley), **Supp. V:** 232
"Need for a Cultural Base to Civil Rites & Bpower Mooments, The" (Baraka), **Supp. II Part 1:** 48
"Need for Christian Preaching, The" (Buechner), **Supp. XII:** 49
Needful Things (King), **Supp. V:** 139, 146
"Needle" (Simic), **Supp. VIII:** 275
"Needle Trade" (Reznikoff), **Supp. XIV:** 277, 289
"Need of Being Versed in Country Things, The" (Frost), **II:** 154; **Retro. Supp. I:** 133, 135
"Need to Say It, The" (Hampl), **Supp. XXII:** 94
Neel, Philippe, **Supp. XIV:** 338
Neelakantappa, Tara, **Supp. XV:** 104–105
Neeley, Barbara, **Supp. XVI:** 143
"Negative Capability" (Komunyakaa), **Supp. XIII:** 131
Negligible Tales (Bierce), **I:** 209
"Negotiating the Darkness, Fortified by Poets' Strength" (Karr), **Supp. XI:** 254; **Supp. XIII:** 285
Negotiating with the Dead (Atwood), **Supp. XIII:** 20, 35
Negritude movement, **Supp. X:** 131, 139
"Negro" (Hughes), **Supp. I Part 1:** 321–322
Negro, The (Du Bois), **Supp. II Part 1:** 178, 179, 185
Negro, The: The Southerner's Problem (Page), **Supp. II Part 1:** 168
Negro and His Music, The (Locke), **Supp. XIV:** 202
"Negro Artisan, The" (Du Bois), **Supp. II Part 1:** 166
"Negro Artist and the Racial Mountain, The" (Hughes), **Retro. Supp. I:** 200, 207; **Supp. I Part 1:** 323, 325; **Supp. IV Part 1:** 169
Negro Art: Past and Present (Locke), **Supp. XIV:** 202
"Negro Assays the Negro Mood, A" (Baldwin), **Supp. I Part 1:** 52
"Negro Citizen, The" (Du Bois), **Supp. II Part 1:** 179
"Negro Dancers" (Hughes), **Retro. Supp. I:** 199; **Supp. I Part 1:** 324
Negroes in America, The (McKay), **Supp. X:** 132, 136
"Negroes of Farmville, Virginia, The: A Social Study" (Du Bois), **Supp. II Part 1:** 166
Negro Family, The: The Case for National Action (Moynihan), **Retro. Supp. II:** 123
"Negro Farmer, The" (Du Bois), **Supp. II Part 1:** 167

"Negro Fight, The" (column, C. L. R. James), **Supp. XXI:** 169
"Negro Ghetto" (Hughes), **Supp. I Part 1:** 331
Negro in America, The (Locke), **Supp. XIV:** 208
Negro in American Civilization, The (Du Bois), **Supp. II Part 1:** 179
Negro in American Culture, The (Locke and Butcher), **Supp. XIV:** 202–203
Negro in Art, The: A Pictorial Record of the Negro Artist and of the Negro Theme in Art (Locke), **Supp. XIV:** 202
"Negro in Large Cities, The" (Du Bois), **Supp. II Part 1:** 169
"Negro in Literature and Art, The" (Du Bois), **Supp. II Part 1:** 174
Negro in New York, The (Ellison), **Supp. II Part 1:** 230
"Negro in the Black Belt, The: Some Social Sketches" (Du Bois), **Supp. II Part 1:** 166
Negro in the Caribbean, The (Williams), **Supp. XXI:** 166
"Negro in the Three Americas, The" (Locke), **Supp. XIV:** 211
"Negro in the Well, The" (Caldwell), **I:** 309
"Negro Love Song, A" (Dunbar), **Supp. II Part 1:** 204
"Negro Martyrs Are Needed" (C. Himes), **Supp. XVI:** 138
Negro Mother, The (Hughes), **Supp. I Part 1:** 328
Negro Mother and Other Dramatic Recitations, The (Hughes), **Retro. Supp. I:** 203
Negro Novel in America, The (Bone), **Supp. IX:** 318–319; **Supp. XVIII:** 285
Negro Publication Society of America, **Retro. Supp. I:** 205
"Negro Renaissance, The: Jean Toomer and the Harlem of the 1920s" (Bontemps), **Supp. IX:** 306
"Negro Schoolmaster in the New South, A" (Du Bois), **Supp. II Part 1:** 168
"Negro's Contribution to American Culture, The" (Locke), **Supp. XIV:** 210, 211
"Negro Sermon, A: Simon Legree" (Lindsay), **Supp. I Part 2:** 393
"Negro Sings of Rivers, The" (Hughes), **Supp. IV Part 1:** 16
"Negro Speaks of Rivers, The" (Hughes), **Retro. Supp. I:** 199; **Supp. I Part 1:** 321
"Negro Spirituals, The (Locke), **Supp. XIV:** 201
"Negro Takes Stock, The" (Du Bois), **Supp. II Part 1:** 180
"Negro Theatre, The" (Van Vechten), **Supp. II Part 2:** 735
"Negro Voter Sizes Up Taft, A" (Hurston), **Supp. VI:** 160
"Negro Writer and His Roots, The: Toward a New Romanticism" (Hansberry), **Supp. IV Part 1:** 364

"Negro Youth Speaks" (Locke), **Supp. XIV:** 201

"Nehemias Americanus" (Mather), **Supp. II Part 2:** 453

Nehru, Jawaharlal, **IV:** 490

"Neighbor" (Hugo), **Supp. VI:** 135–136

"Neighborhood Drunk"(Dybek), **Supp. XXIII:** 71

"Neighbors" (Carver), **Supp. III Part 1:** 135, 139, 141; **Supp. XI:** 153

"Neighbors" (Hogan), **Supp. IV Part 1:** 405

"Neighbors, The" (Hay), **Supp. XIV:** 126

"Neighbour Rosicky" (Cather), **I:** 331–332

Neil Simon (Johnson), **Supp. IV Part 2:** 573

"Neil Simon's Jewish-Style Comedies" (Walden), **Supp. IV Part 2:** 584, 591

"Neil Simon: Toward Act III?" (Walden), **Supp. IV Part 2:** 591

Neilson, Heather, **Supp. IV Part 2:** 681

Neiman, Gilbert, **Supp. XV:** 140

"Neither Out Far Nor In Deep" (Frost), **I:** 303; **Retro. Supp. I:** 121, 138

"Nellie Clark" (Masters), **Supp. I Part 2:** 461

Nelson, Alice Dunbar, **Supp. XVII:** 75

Nelson, Cary, **Supp. XVIII:** 226, 227, 230, 231; **Supp. XXII:** 271

Nelson, Ernest, **I:** 388

Nelson, Howard, **Supp. IV Part 1:** 66, 68; **Supp. XIX:** 3; **Supp. XXI:** 95

Nelson, Lord Horatio, **II:** 524

Nelson, Lynn (pseudonym). *See* Nelson, Marilyn

Nelson, Marilyn, **Supp. XVII:** 74, 112; **Supp. XVIII: 171–188**

Nelson, Shirley, **Supp. XII:** 293

Nelson, Steve, **Supp. XVIII:** 226

Nelson Algren (Cox and Chatterton), **Supp. IX:** 11–12

Nelson Algren: A Life on the Wild Side (Drew), **Supp. IX:** 2

Nemerov, David, **II:** 268

Nemerov, Howard, **III: 267–289; IV:** 137, 140; **Supp. III Part 2:** 541; **Supp. IV Part 2:** 455, 650; **Supp. IX:** 114

Nemiroff, Robert Barron, **Supp. IV Part 1:** 360, 361, 365, 369, 370, 374

Neoconservative Criticism: Norman Podhoretz, Kenneth S. Lynn, and Joseph Epstein (Winchell), **Supp. VIII:** 241; **Supp. XIV:** 103

"Neo-Formalism: A Dangerous Nostalgia" (Sadoff), **Supp. XXI:** 100

"Neo-Hoodoo Manifesto, The" (Reed), **Supp. X:** 242

Neon Rain, The (Burke), **Supp. XIV:** 22, 24, 26–27, 28–29, 30

Neon Vernacular (Komunyakaa), **Supp. XIII:** 121, **127–128,** 131

Neon Wilderness, The (Algren), **Supp. IX:** 3, 4

Neo-Slave Narratives (Rushdy), **Supp. X:** 250

Nepantla: Essays from the Land in the Middle (Mora), **Supp. XIII:** 213, **219–221,** 227

Nephew, The (Purdy), **Supp. VII:** 271, 273, 282

"Nereids of Seriphos, The" (Clampitt), **Supp. IX:** 41

Nericcio, William, **Supp. XIV:** 304–305

Neruda, Pablo, **Supp. I Part 1:** 89; **Supp. IV Part 2:** 537; **Supp. V:** 332; **Supp. VIII:** 272, 274; **Supp. IX:** 157, 271; **Supp. X:** 112; **Supp. XI:** 191; **Supp. XII:** 217; **Supp. XIII:** 114, 315, 323; **Supp. XXI:** 61, 100

Nesbit, Edith, **Supp. VIII:** 171

Nesbit, Lynn, **Supp. XXIII:** 100

Nesbitt, Robin, **Supp. VIII:** 89

Nessmuk (George Washington Sears), **Supp. XIX:** 10

Nesting Ground, The (Wagoner), **Supp. IX:** 324, **325–326**

Nest of Ninnies, A (Ashbery and Schuyler), **Supp. III Part 1:** 3; **Supp. XV:** 178

"Nests"(Le Sueur), **Supp. XXIII:** 165

Net of Cobwebs (Holding), **Supp. XXII:** 126, **129–130,** 134

Net of Magic: Wonders and Deceptions in India (Siegel), **Supp. XXII:** 262

Nets to Catch the Wind (Wylie), **Supp. I Part 2:** 709, 710–712, 714

Nettleton, Asahel, **I:** 458

"Net to Snare the Moonlight, A" (Lindsay), **Supp. I Part 2:** 387

Neubauer, Carol E., **Supp. IV Part 1:** 9

Neugeboren, Jacob Mordecai. *See* Neugeboren, Jay

Neugeboren, Jay, **Supp. XVI: 217–231**

Neugroschel, Joachim, **Supp. IX:** 138

Neuhaus, Richard John, **Supp. VIII:** 245; **Supp. XIX:** 144

Neumann, Erich, **Supp. I Part 2:** 567; **Supp. IV Part 1:** 68, 69

Neuromancer (W. Gibson), **Supp. XII:** 15; **Supp. XVI:** 117, 119–120, 122, 124, **125–126,** 127, 129, 131

Neurotica: Jewish Writers on Sex (Bukiet, ed.), **Supp. XVII:** 48

"Neurotic America and the Sex Impulse" (Dreiser), **Retro. Supp. II:** 105

Neutra, Richard, **Supp. XVI:** 192

"Never Bet the Devil Your Head" (Poe), **III:** 425; **Retro. Supp. II:** 273

Never Come Morning (Algren), **Supp. IX:** 3, **7–9**

Never in a Hurry: Essays on People and Places (Nye), **Supp. XIII:** 273, **280–282,** 286

"Never Marry a Mexican" (Cisneros), **Supp. VII:** 70

"Never Room with a Couple" (Hughes), **Supp. I Part 1:** 330

"Nevertheless" (Moore), **III:** 214

Nevins, Allan, **I:** 253; **Supp. I Part 2:** 486, 493

"Nevsky Prospekt" (Olds), **Supp. X:** 205

New Adam, The (Untermeyer), **Supp. XV:** 304, 305

New Addresses (Koch), **Supp. XV:** 177, 184

"New Age of the Rhetoricians, The" (Cowley), **Supp. II Part 1:** 135

New American Cyclopedia, **Supp. XVIII:** 4

New American Literature, The (Pattee), **II:** 456

New American Novel of Manners, The (Klinkowitz), **Supp. XI:** 347

"New American Ode, The" (Wright), **Supp. XV:** 346

New American Poetry, 1945–1960, The (Allen, ed.), **Supp. VIII:** 291, 292; **Supp. XIII:** 112; **Supp. XXIII:** 215–216

"New American Writer, A" (W. C. Williams), **Retro. Supp. II:** 335

New and Collected Poems (Reed), **Supp. X:** 241

New and Collected Poems (Wilbur), **Supp. III Part 2:** 562–564

New and Selected Poems (Nemerov), **III:** 269, 275, 277–279

New and Selected Poems (Oliver), **Supp. VII:** 240–241, 245

New and Selected Poems (W. J. Smith), **Supp. XIII:** 332

New and Selected Poems (Wagoner), **Supp. IX:** 326–327

New and Selected Poems, 1958–1998 (Sorrentino), **Supp. XXI:** 229

New and Selected Poems: 1974–1994 (Dunn), **Supp. XI: 151–152**

New and Selected Things Taking Place (Swenson), **Supp. IV Part 2:** 648–650, 651

"New Art Gallery Society, The" (Wolfe), **Supp. III Part 2:** 580

Newberger, Julee, **Supp. XVIII:** 168

New Black Poetry, The (Major, ed.), **Supp. XXII:** 172, 174, 176, 180

"New Capitalist Tool, The" (Wasserstein), **Supp. XV:** 328

Newcomb, Ralph, **Supp. XIII:** 12

Newcomb, Robert, **II:** 111

New Conscience and an Ancient Evil, A (Addams), **Supp. I Part 1:** 14–15, 16

"New Conservatism in American Poetry, The" (Wakoski), **Supp. XVII:** 112

"New Conservatives, The: Intellectuals in Retreat" (Epstein), **Supp. XIV:** 103

New Criticism, The (Ransom), **III:** 497–498, 499, 501

"New Day, A" (Levine), **Supp. V:** 182

Newdick, Robert Spangler, **Retro. Supp. I:** 138

Newdick's Season of Frost (Newdick), **Retro. Supp. I:** 138

New Dictionary of Quotations, A (Mencken), **III:** 111

New Directions Anthology in Prose and Poetry (Laughlin, ed.), **Supp. XVI:** 284

"New Directions in Poetry" (D. Locke), **Supp. IX:** 273

"New Dog, The: Variations on a Text by Jules Laforgue" (C. Frost), **Supp. XV:** 98

Newell, Henry, **IV:** 193

"New England" (Lowell), **II:** 536

"New England" (Robinson), **III:** 510, 524

"New England Bachelor, A" (Eberhart), **I:** 539

"New Englander, The" (Anderson), **I**: 114

New England Girlhood, A (Larcom), **Supp. XIII**: 137, 142, 143, 144, **147–154**

New England Gothic Literature (Ringel), **Supp. XXII**: 205

New England: Indian Summer (Brooks), **I**: 253, 256

New England Local Color Literature (Donovan), **Retro. Supp. II**: 138

"New England Sabbath-Day Chace, The" (Freneau), **Supp. II Part 1**: 273

New-England Tale, A (Sedgwick), **I**: 341

New England Tragedies, The (Longfellow), **II**: 490, 505, 506; **Retro. Supp. II**: 165, 167

New English Canaan (Morton), **Supp. XXII**: 45

New Era in American Poetry, The (Untermeyer, ed.), **Supp. XV**: 301, 303, 306

Newer Ideals of Peace (Addams), **Supp. I Part 1**: 11–12, 15, 16–17, 19, 20–21

"New Experience in Millinery, A" (Stratton-Porter), **Supp. XX: 216**

New Feminist Criticism, The: Essays on Women, Literature, and Theory (Showalter), **Supp. X**: 97

New Fire: To Put Things Right Again (Moraga), **Supp. XXIII**: 197

"New Folsom Prison" (Matthews), **Supp. IX**: 165

New Formalism, The: A Critical Introduction (McPhillips), **Supp. XV**: 250, 251, 252, 264

Newfound (J. W. Miller), **Supp. XX: 163, 166, 170–172**

New Found Land: Fourteen Poems (MacLeish), **III**: 12–13

"New Hampshire, February" (Eberhart), **I**: 536

New Hampshire: A Poem with Notes and Grace Notes (Frost), **II**: 154–155; **Retro. Supp. I**: 132, 133, 135

New Hard-Boiled Writers (Panek), **Supp. XIV**: 27

"New Home" (Richter), **Supp. XVIII**: 209

New Industrial State, The (Galbraith), **Supp. I Part 2**: 648

"New Journalism, The" (Wolfe), **Supp. III Part 2**: 571

New Journalism, The (Wolfe and Johnson, eds.), **Supp. III Part 2**: 570, 579–581, 583, 586

New Left, The. The Anti-Industrial Revolution (Rand), **Supp. IV Part 2**: 527

"New Letters from Thomas Jefferson" (Stafford), **Supp. XI**: 324

New Letters on the Air: Contemporary Writers on Radio, **Supp. X**: 165, 169, 173

"New Life" (Glück), **Supp. V**: 90

New Life, A (Malamud), **Supp. I Part 2**: 429–466

"New Life, The" (Bynner), **Supp. XV**: 44

"New Life, The"(Schott), **Supp. XXIII**: 242

"New Life at Kyerefaso" (Sutherland), **Supp. IV Part 1**: 9

"New Light on Veblen" (Dorfman), **Supp. I Part 2**: 650

"New Man, A" (P. E. Jones), **Supp. XXII**: 144

Newman, Charles, **Supp. I Part 2**: 527, 546–548

Newman, Edwin, **Supp. IV Part 2**: 526

Newman, Frances, **Supp. XXII**: 198

Newman, Judie, **Supp. IV Part 1**: 304, 305

Newman, Paul, **Supp. IV Part 2**: 473, 474

New Man, The (Merton), **Supp. VIII**: 208

"New Mecca, The" (Saunders), **Supp. XIX**: 235, 236

"New Medea, The" (Howells), **II**: 282

New Mexico trilogy (Nichols), **Supp. XIII**: 269

New Morning (album, Dylan), **Supp. XVIII**: 27, 33

"New Mother" (Olds), **Supp. X**: 206

"New Mothers, The" (Shields), **Supp. VII**: 310

New Music (Price), **Supp. VI**: 264, 265

"New Mutants, The" (Fiedler), **Supp. XIII**: 104

"New Name for Some Old Ways of Thinking, A" (James), **II**: 353

New Native American Novel, The: Works in Progress (Bartlett), **Supp. IV Part 1**: 335

"New Natural History, A" (Thurber), **Supp. I Part 2**: 619

New Negro, The (Locke), **Supp. XIX**: 69

"New Negro, The" (Locke), **Supp. XIV**: 201

New Negro, The (Locke, ed.), **Supp. II Part 1**: 176; **Supp. IX**: 309; **Supp. X**: 137; **Supp. XXII**: 8

New Negro, The: An Interpretation (Locke, ed.), **Retro. Supp. I**: 199; **Supp. IV Part 1**: 170; **Supp. XIV**: 195, 201–202

New Negro for a New Century, A (Washington, Wood, and Williams), **Supp. XIV**: 201

New New Journalism, The (R. Boynton), **Supp. XVII**: 209

"New Nomads, The" (E. Hoffman), **Supp. XVI**: 161

"New Orleans" (Carruth), **Supp. XVI**: 50

New Orleans Sketches (Faulkner), **Retro. Supp. I**: 80

New Path to the Waterfall, A (Carver), **Supp. III Part 1**: 138–140, 147, 149

"New Poem, The" (Wright), **Supp. V**: 339, 340

"New Poems" (MacLeish), **III**: 19

"New Poems" (Oliver), **Supp. VII**: 240

New Poems 1960 (Bynner), **Supp. XV**: 51

New Poems: 1980–88 (Haines), **Supp. XII: 209–210**

New Poetry, The (Monroe and Henderson, eds.), **Supp. I Part 2**: 387

"New Poetry Handbook, The" (Strand), **Supp. IV Part 2**: 626

New Poetry of Mexico (Strand, trans.), **Supp. IV Part 2**: 630

New Poets of England and America (Hall, Pack, and Simpson, eds.), **Supp. IV Part 2**: 621

"Newport of Anchuria" (Henry), **Supp. II Part 1**: 409

New Princeton Encyclopedia of Poetry and Poetics (Preminger and Brogan, eds.), **Supp. XV**: 250

"New Republic Moves Uptown, The" (Cowley), **Supp. II Part 1**: 142

"New Rose Hotel" (W. Gibson), **Supp. XVI**: 120, 122, 124

"News, The" (McClatchy), **Supp. XII**: 269

"New Season" (Levine), **Supp. V**: 188

New Seeds of Contemplation (Merton), **Supp. VIII**: 200, 208

News from the Glacier: Selected Poems 1960–1980 (Haines), **Supp. XII**: 207, 208–209

"News Item" (Parker), **Supp. IX**: 190

New Song, A (Hughes), **Retro. Supp. I**: 202; **Supp. I Part 1**: 328, 331–332

"New Song"(Kenny), **Supp. XXIII**: 156

Newson-Horst, Adele, **Supp. XXIII**: 95

"New South, The" (Lanier), **Supp. I Part 1**: 352, 354, 370

New Southern Girl, The: Female Adolescence in the Works of 12 Women Authors (Town), **Supp. XVIII**: 195

Newspaper Days, 1899–1906 (Mencken), **III**: 100, 102, 120

"New Spirit, The" (Ashbery), **Supp. III Part 1**: 14, 15

New Spoon River, The (Masters), **Supp. I Part 2**: 461–465, 473

New Star Chamber and Other Essays, The (Masters), **Supp. I Part 2**: 455–456, 459

New Tales of the Vampires (Rice), **Supp. VII**: 290

New Testament, **I**: 303, 457, 458; **II**: 167; **III**: 305; **IV**: 114, 134, 152; **Retro. Supp. I**: 58, 140, 360; **Supp. I Part 1**: 104, 106; **Supp. I Part 2**: 516; **Supp. XVII**: 155; **Supp. XXIII**: 13. *See also* names of New Testament books

New Testament, A (Anderson), **I**: 101, 114

"New Theory of Thorstein Veblen, A" (Galbraith), **Supp. I Part 2**: 650

Newton, Benjamin Franklin, **I**: 454

Newton, Huey P., **Supp. I Part 1**: 66; **Supp. IV Part 1**: 206

Newton, Isaac, **I**: 132, 557; **II**: 6, 103, 348–349; **III**: 428; **IV**: 18, 149

Newton, Maud, **Supp. XXIII**: 290

Newton, Sarah Emily, **Supp. XV**: 234

"New-Wave Format, A" (Mason), **Supp. VIII**: 141, 143, 147

New West of Edward Abbey, The (Ronald), **Supp. XIII**: 4

"New Wife" (Halliday), **Supp. XIX**: 89

New Wolves, The: The Return of the Mexican Wolf to the American Southwest (Bass), **Supp. XVI**: 26–27

New Woman's Survival Sourcebook, The (Rennie and Grimstead, eds.), **Supp. I Part 2:** 569

New World, The (Bronk), **Supp. XXI:** 25–26, 31

New World, The (Bynner), **Supp. XV:** 41, 42

New World, The: Tales (Banks), **Supp. V:** 8, 9, 10

New World Naked, A (Mariani), **Retro. Supp. I:** 419

New Worlds of Literature (Beaty and Hunter, eds.), **Supp. IV Part 1:** 331

New World Writing (Updike), **IV:** 217

New Year Letter (Auden), **Supp. II Part 1:** 14, 16

"New Year's Day" (Wharton), **Retro. Supp. I:** 381

"New Year's Eve" (Schwartz), **Supp. II Part 2:** 640, 656–657

New Year's Eve/1929 (Farrell), **II:** 43

"New Year's Eve 1968" (Lowell), **II:** 554

New Year's Eve: A Play (W. Frank), **Supp. XX:** 75

"New Year's Gift, The" (Stowe), **Supp. I Part 2:** 587

"New Year Two Thousand, The" (Weigl), **Supp. XIX:** 287–288

"New York" (Capote), **Supp. III Part 1:** 122

"New York" (Moore), **III:** 196, 198, 202, 206

"New York 1965" (Bowles), **Supp. IV Part 1:** 94

New York: A Serendipiter's Journey (Talese), **Supp. XVII:** 202, 203

"New York Breeze" (Halliday), **Supp. XIX:** 85

New York City Arts Project, **Supp. III Part 2:** 618

"New York City in 1979"(Acker), **Supp. XII:** 5

New York Edition, **Retro. Supp. I:** 235

"New York Edition" (James), **II:** 336, 337

"New York Gold Conspiracy, The" (Adams), **I:** 4

New York Hat, The (film; Griffith), **Supp. XVI:** 183

New York Intellectuals, **Supp. VIII:** 93

"New York Intellectuals, The" (Howe), **Supp. VI:** 120

"New York Is a City of Things Unnoticed" (Talese), **Supp. XVII:** 202, 209

New York: Its Upper Ten and Lower Million (Lippard), **Supp. XXIII:** 180, 183, 184

New York Jew (Kazin), **Supp. VIII:** 95, **97–100**

"New York Theater: Isn't It Romantic" (Wasserstein), **Supp. XV:** 320

New York Trilogy, The (Auster), **Supp. XII:** 21, **24–28**

Next (McNally), **Supp. XIII:** 197

"Next in Line, The" (Bradbury), **Supp. IV Part 1:** 102

Next Room of the Dream, The (Nemerov), **III:** 269, 275, 278, 279–280, 284

"Next Time I Crossed the Line into Oklahoma, The" (Wright), **Supp. XV:** 345

Next-to-Last Things: New Poems and Essays (Kunitz), **Supp. III Part 1:** 257–259, 261, 262, 265, 266, 268

"'Next to Reading Matter' " (Henry), **Supp. II Part 1:** 399

Nexus (H. Miller), **III:** 170, 187, 188, 189

Niatum, Duane, **Supp. IV Part 1:** 331; **Supp. IV Part 2:** 505

Nice and Noir (Schwartz), **Supp. XIV:** 23

"Nice Girl" (Nelson), **Supp. XVIII:** 178

Nice Jewish Boy, The (P. Roth), **Supp. III Part 2:** 412

Nicholas II, Tsar, **Supp. I Part 2:** 447

"Nicholas in the Park" (Halliday), **Supp. XIX:** 88

Nicholls, Peter, **Supp. XIX:** 232

Nichols, Charles, **Retro. Supp. I:** 194

Nichols, Dudley, **Supp. XVIII:** 247

Nichols, John Treadwell, **Supp. XIII:** **253–272**

Nichols, Luther, **Supp. X:** 265

Nichols, Mike, **Supp. IV Part 1:** 234; **Supp. IV Part 2:** 577

Nicholson, Colin, **Supp. VIII:** 129

Nicholson, Harold, **Supp. XIV:** 163

Nicholson, Jack, **Supp. V:** 26; **Supp. VIII:** 45; **Supp. XI:** 308

Nicholson, John, **Supp. XVI:** 293

Nick Adams Stories, The (Hemingway), **II:** 258; **Retro. Supp. I:** 174

"Nick and the Candlestick" (Plath), **Supp. I Part 2:** 544

Nickel and Dimed: On (Not) Getting By in America (Ehrenreich), **Supp. XVII:** 210

Nickel Mountain: A Pastoral Novel (Gardner), **Supp. VI:** 63, 64, 68, **69**

"Nicodemus" (Keillor), **Supp. XVI:** 167

Nicoll, Allardyce, **III:** 400

Nicoloff, Philip, **II:** 7

Niebuhr, Gustav, **III:** 292

Niebuhr, H. Richard, **I:** 494

Niebuhr, Lydia, **III:** 292

Niebuhr, Reinhold, **III:** **290–313;** **Supp. I Part 2:** 654; **Supp. XX:** 79

Niedecker, Lorine, **Supp. III Part 2:** 616, 623; **Supp. XIV:** 287; **Supp. XXIII:** 174

Nielsen, Ed, **Supp. IX:** 254

Nielson, Dorothy, **Supp. I Part 2:** 659

Nietzsche, Friedrich Wilhelm, **I:** 227, 283, 383, 389, 396, 397, 402, 509; **II:** 7, 20, 27, 42, 90, 145, 262, 462, 463, 577, 583, 585; **III:** 102–103, 113, 156, 176; **IV:** 286, 491; **Supp. I Part 1:** 254, 299, 320; **Supp. I Part 2:** 646; **Supp. IV Part 1:** 104, 105–106, 107, 110, 284; **Supp. IV Part 2:** 519; **Supp. V:** 277, 280; **Supp. VIII:** 11, 181, 189; **Supp. X:** 48; **Supp. XII:** 98; **Supp. XIV:** 339; **Supp. XX:** 117

Nieves, Felipe, **Supp. XVIII:** 90

Niflis, N. Michael, **Supp. IV Part 1:** 175

Niger, S. *See* Charney, Samuel

Nigger Heaven (Van Vechten), **Supp. II Part 2:** 739, 744–746; **Supp. XVIII:** 123, 127; **Supp. XIX:** 76

"Nigger Jeff" (Dreiser), **Retro. Supp. II:** 97

Nigger of the "Narcissus," The (Conrad), **II:** 91; **Retro. Supp. I:** 106; **Supp. XVIII:** 224

"NIGGY THE HO" (Baraka), **Supp. II Part 1:** 54

"Night, Death, Mississippi" (Hayden), **Supp. II Part 1:** 369

'Night, Mother (Norman), **Supp. VIII:** 141

"Night above the Avenue" (Merwin), **Supp. III Part 1:** 355

"Night among the Horses, A" (Barnes), **Supp. III Part 1:** 33–34, 39, 44

"Night and the Madman" (Gibran), **Supp. XX: 118**

Night at the Movies, A, or, You Must Remember This: Fictions (Coover), **Supp. V:** 50–51

"Night at the Opera, A" (Matthews), **Supp. IX:** 167

"Night before the Sentence Is Carried Out, The" (Wright), **Supp. XV:** 341

"Nightbird" (Komunyakaa), **Supp. XIII:** 132

Night-Blooming Cereus, The (Hayden), **Supp. II Part 1:** 367, 373

"Night-Blooming Cereus, The" (Hayden), **Supp. II Part 1:** 367

Night-Born, The (London), **II:** 467

"Nightbreak" (Rich), **Supp. I Part 2:** 556

"Nightclub" (Collins), **Supp. XXI:** 60

Night Dance (Price), **Supp. VI:** 264

"Night Dances, The" (Plath), **Supp. I Part 2:** 544

"Night Dream, The" (MacLeish), **III:** 15

"Night Ferry" (Doty), **Supp. XI:** 124

"Nightfishing" (Schnackenberg), **Supp. XV:** 254

"Nighthawks"(Dybek), **Supp. XXIII:** 73, 74

"Night I Met Little Floyd, The" (Wright), **Supp. XV:** 345–346

Night in Acadie, A (Chopin), **Retro. Supp. II: 66–67,** 73; **Supp. I Part 1:** 200, 219, 220, 224

"Night in Acadie, A" (Chopin), **Retro. Supp. II:** 66

"Night in June, A" (W. C. Williams), **Retro. Supp. I:** 424

"Night in New Arabia, A" (Henry), **Supp. II Part 1:** 402

Night in Question, The: Stories (Wolff), **Supp. VII:** 342–344

"Night Journey" (Roethke), **Supp. III Part 1:** 260

"Night Letter to the Reader" (Collins), **Supp. XXI:** 55

Night Light (Justice), **Supp. VII:** 126–127

"Nightmare" (Kumin), **Supp. IV Part 2:** 442

Nightmare Factory, The (Kumin), **Supp. IV Part 2:** 444–447, 451

"Nightmare Factory, The" (Kumin), **Supp. IV Part 2:** 445, 453

Nightmare on Main Street (Poe), **Retro. Supp. II:** 262

"Nightmare" poems (Benét), **Supp. XI:** 46, 58

"Night Mirror" (L.-Y. Lee), **Supp. XV:** 225

Night Music (Odets), **Supp. II Part 2:** 541, 543, 544

"Night of First Snow" (R. Bly), **Supp. IV Part 1:** 71

Night of January 16th (Rand), **Supp. IV Part 2:** 527

Night of the Iguana, The (T. Williams), **IV:** 382, 383, 384, 385, 386, 387, 388, 391, 392, 393, 394, 395, 397, 398

"Night of the Iguana, The" (T. Williams), **IV:** 384

"Night of the Living Beanfield: How an Unsuccessful Cult Novel Became an Unsuccessful Cult Film in Only Fourteen Years, Eleven Nervous Breakdowns, and $20 Million" (Nichols), **Supp. XIII:** 267

Night Passage (Parker), **Supp. XIX:** 185–186

Night Rider (Warren), **IV:** 243, 246–247

Nights (Doolittle), **Supp. I Part 1:** 270, 271

Nights and Days (Merrill), **Supp. III Part 1:** 319, 320, 322–325

"Nights and Days" (Rich), **Supp. I Part 2:** 574

"Night's for Cryin,' The" (C. Himes), **Supp. XVI:** 137

"Night Shift" (Plath), **Supp. I Part 2:** 538

Night-Side (Oates), **Supp. II Part 2:** 522

"Night-Side" (Oates), **Supp. II Part 2:** 523

Night-Side, The (Skloot), **Supp. XX: 193, 196, 205, 208**

Nights in the Gardens of Brooklyn (Swados), **Supp. XIX: 261–264**

"Nights in the Gardens of Brooklyn" (Swados), **Supp. XIX:** 261

"Night Sketches: Beneath an Umbrella" (Hawthorne), **II:** 235–237, 238, 239, 242; **Supp. XXI:** 201

"Night Sport" (Hoffman), **Supp. XVIII:** 86, 87

"Night-Sweat" (Lowell), **II:** 554

"Night-Talk" (Ellison), **Retro. Supp. II:** 126; **Supp. II Part 1:** 248

Night Thoughts (Young), **III:** 415

Night Traveler, The (Oliver), **Supp. VII:** 233

"Night Watch" (Gioia), **Supp. XV:** 117

"Night Watch, The" (Wright), **Supp. V:** 339

"Night We All Had Grippe, The" (Jackson), **Supp. IX:** 118

Nightwood (Barnes), **Supp. III Part 1:** 31, 32, 35–37, 39–43

Night World and the Word Night, The (F. Wright), **Supp. XVII:** 240, 244–245

"Nihilist as Hero, The" (Lowell), **II:** 554; **Retro. Supp. II:** 190

Nijinsky, Vaslav, **Supp. XV:** 28–29

Nikolai Gogol (Nabokov), **Retro. Supp. I:** 266

Niles, Thomas, **Retro. Supp. I:** 35

Niles, Thomas, Jr., **Supp. I Part 1:** 39

Nilsson, Christine, **Supp. I Part 1:** 355

Nilsson, Harry, **Supp. XI:** 309

Nilsson, Jenny Lind, **Supp. XVI:** 177

Nimitz, Chester, **Supp. I Part 2:** 491

"Nimram" (Gardner), **Supp. VI:** 73

Nims, John Frederick, **III:** 527; **Supp. XVII:** 112

Nin, Anaïs, **III:** 182, 184, 190; **Supp. III Part 1:** 43; **Supp. IV Part 2:** 680; **Supp. X: 181–200; Supp. XIX:** 134

"9" (Oliver), **Supp. VII:** 244

"9 Failures of the Imagination" (Lethem), **Supp. XVIII:** 148

"Nine-Ball" (Offutt), **Supp. XIX:** 166, 167

Nine Dragons (Connelly), **Supp. XXI:** 74, **79–80**

"Nine from Eight" (Lanier), **Supp. I Part 1:** 352–354

Nine Gates: Entering the Mind of Poetry (Hirshfield), **Supp. XXIII:** 136, 137

Nine Headed Dragon River: Zen Journals 1969–1982 (Matthiessen), **Supp. V:** 199

Nine Horses (Collins), **Supp. XXI:** 55, 60, 61, 62, 65

"Nine Horses" (Collins), **Supp. XXI:** 61

Ninemile Wolves,The (Bass), **Supp. XVI:** 24–25, 26

"Nine Nectarines" (Moore), **III:** 203, 209, 215

Nine Plays (Reznikoff), **Supp. XIV:** 288

"Nine Poems for the Unborn Child" (Rukeyser), **Supp. VI:** 280–281, 284

Nine Stories (Nabokov), **Retro. Supp. I:** 266

Nine Stories (Salinger), **III:** 552, 558–564

"19 Hadley Street" (Schnackenberg), **Supp. XV:** 253

19 Necromancers from Now (Reed), **Supp. X:** 240

19 Varieties of Gazelle (Nye), **Supp. XIII:** 275, **286–288**

"19 Varieties of Gazelle" (Nye), **Supp. XIII:** 286

1984 (Orwell), **Supp. XIII:** 29; **Supp. XVIII:** 137, 138

"1940" (Stafford), **Supp. XI:** 328–329

"1945–1985: Poem for the Anniversary" (Oliver), **Supp. VII:** 237

1919 (Dos Passos), **I:** 482, 485–486, 487, 489, 490, 492

"1975" (Wright), **Supp. V:** 341

"1973"(Hirshfield), **Supp. XXIII:** 130

"1910" (Mora), **Supp. XIII:** 215

"1938" (Komunyakaa), **Supp. XIII:** 114

"1939" (Taylor), **Supp. V:** 316

1933 (Levine), **Supp. V:** 185–187

"1933" (Levine), **Supp. V:** 188

"Nineteenth New York, The" (Doctorow), **Supp. IV Part 1:** 232

"1929" (Auden), **Supp. II Part 1:** 6

"1926" (Kees), **Supp. XV:** 135

"93990" (Saunders), **Supp. XIX:** 233

"90 North" (Jarrell), **II:** 370, 371

90 Trees (Zukofsky), **Supp. III Part 2:** 631

95 Poems (Cummings), **I:** 430, 433, 435, 439, 446, 447

"91 Revere Street" (Lowell), **II:** 547; **Retro. Supp. II:** 188; **Supp. XI:** 240

Ninety Percent of Everything (Lethem, Kelly and Kessel), **Supp. XVIII:** 145

"92 Days" (L. Brown), **Supp. XXI:** 44–45

"Nine Years Later" (Brodsky), **Supp. VIII:** 32

"Nirvana" (Lanier), **Supp. I Part 1:** 352

Nirvana Blues, The (Nichols), **Supp. XIII:** 266, 267

Nishikigi (play), **III:** 466

Niven, David, **Supp. XI:** 307

Nixon (film), **Supp. XIV:** 48

Nixon, Richard M., **I:** 376; **III:** 38, 46; **Supp. I Part 1:** 294, 295; **Supp. V:** 45, 46, 51; **Supp. XII:** 14; **Supp. XIV:** 306

"NJ Transit" (Komunyakaa), **Supp. XIII:** 132

Nketia, J. H., **Supp. IV Part 1:** 10

Nketsia, Nana, **Supp. IV Part 1:** 2, 10

Nkize, Julius, **Supp. IV Part 1:** 361

Nkrumah, Kwame, **I:** 490, 494; **Supp. IV Part 1:** 361; **Supp. X:** 135

Nkrumah and the Ghana Revolution (C. L. R. James), **Supp. XXI:** 159, 171–172

NO (Major), **Supp. XXII:** 174

Noailles, Anna de, **IV:** 328

Noa Noa (Gauguin), **I:** 34

Nobel Lecture (Singer), **Retro. Supp. II:** 300

"No Better Than a 'Withered Daffodil' " (Moore), **III:** 216

Noble, David W., **Supp. I Part 2:** 650

Noble, Marianne, **Supp. XVIII:** 267

"Noble Rider and the Sound of Words, The" (Stevens), **Retro. Supp. I:** 299

Noble Savage, The (Coover), **Supp. V:** 40

"No Bobolink reverse His Singing" (Dickinson), **Retro. Supp. I:** 45

Nobodaddy (MacLeish), **III:** 5–6, 8, 10, 11, 18, 19, 20

"Nobodaddy" (W. Blake), **Supp. XVII:** 245

"Nobody in Hollywood" (Bausch), **Supp. VII:** 54

Nobody Knows My Name (Baldwin), **Supp. XIII:** 111

"Nobody Knows My Name" (Baldwin), **Retro. Supp. II:** 8; **Supp. I Part 1:** 52

Nobody Knows My Name: More Notes of a Native Son (Baldwin), **Retro. Supp. II:** 6, 8; **Supp. I Part 1:** 47, 52, 55

"Nobody knows this little Rose" (Dickinson), **Retro. Supp. I:** 30

"Nobody Said Anything" (Carver), **Supp. III Part 1:** 141

"Nobody's Business" (Lahiri), **Supp. XXI:** 183

Nobody's Fool (Russo), **Supp. XII:** 326, **331–335,** 340

"No Change of Place" (Auden), **Supp. II Part 1:** 5

"Noche Triste, La" (Frost), **Retro. Supp. I:** 123

Nock, Albert Jay, **I:** 245; **Supp. IV Part 2:** 521, 524

"No Coward Soul Is Mine" (Brontë), **I:** 458

"No Crime in the Mountains" (Chandler), **Supp. IV Part 1:** 129

"Nocturne" (Komunyakaa), **Supp. XIII:** 126

"Nocturne" (MacLeish), **III:** 8

"Nocturne at Bethesda" (Bontemps), **Supp. XXII:** 3, 8

"Nocturne in a Deserted Brickyard" (Sandburg), **III:** 586

Nocturne of Remembered Spring (Aiken), **I:** 50

No Direction Home (documentary film, Scorsese), **Supp. XVIII:** 22, 23, 29

No Direction Home (Shelton), **Supp. XVIII:** 21

No Door (Wolfe), **IV:** 451–452, 456

"No Door" (Wolfe), **IV:** 456

"No Epitaph" (Carson), **Supp. XII:** 111

No Exit (Sartre), **I:** 82, 130; **Supp. XIV:** 320

No Exit (Sartre; Bowles, trans.), **Supp. IV Part 1:** 84

No Gifts from Chance (Benstock), **Retro. Supp. I:** 361

"No-Good Blues" (Komunyakaa), **Supp. XIII:** 130

No Hero (Marquand), **III:** 57

No Heroes: A Memoir of Coming Home (Offutt), **Supp. XIX:** 163, **172–174,** 175

No! In Thunder (Fiedler), **Supp. XIII:** 101

"Noiseless Patient Spider" (Whitman), **III:** 555; **IV:** 348; **Supp. IV Part 1:** 325

Noises Off (Frayn), **Supp. IV Part 2:** 582

Noi vivi. See We the Living (film)

"No Jury Would Convict" (Shaw), **Supp. XIX:** 245

"No Lamp Has Ever Shown Us Where to Look" (MacLeish), **III:** 9

Nolan, Sidney, **Retro. Supp. II:** 189

No Laughing Matter (Heller and Vogel), **Supp. IV Part 1:** 384, 389

No Love Lost, a Romance of Travel (Howells), **II:** 277

No Man Is an Island (Merton), **Supp. VIII:** 207

"No More This Home" (Taggard), **Supp. XXII:** 277, 280

No Mother to Guide Her (Loos), **Supp. XVI:** 194

No Name in the Street (Baldwin), **Retro. Supp. II:** 13, 14; **Supp. I Part 1:** 47, 48, 52, 65–66, 67

No Nature: New and Selected Poems (Snyder), **Supp. VIII:** 305

Nonconformist's Memorial, The (Howe), **Supp. IV Part 2:** 434, 435–436

Nonconformity (Algren), **Supp. IX:** 15

None but the Lonely Heart (film), **Supp. II Part 2:** 546

Nones (Auden), **Supp. II Part 1:** 21

"Nones" (Auden), **Supp. II Part 1:** 22–23

None Shall Look Back (Gordon), **II:** 205–207, 208

"No No, Bad Daddy" (Nelson), **Supp. XVIII:** 177, 178

"Non-Tenured" (Halliday), **Supp. XIX:** 90, 91

Nonverbal Communication: Notes on the Visual Perception of Human Relations (Kees and Ruesch), **Supp. XV:** 147

"Noon" (Bryant), **Supp. I Part 1:** 157

"No One Remembers" (Levine), **Supp. V:** 187

"Noon Walk on the Asylum Lawn" (Sexton), **Supp. II Part 2:** 673

"Noon Wine" (Porter), **III:** 436, 437–438, 442, 446

"No Pain Whatsoever" (Yates), **Supp. XI:** 341

"No Place for You, My Love" (Welty), **IV:** 278, 279; **Retro. Supp. I:** 353

No Plays of Japan, The (Waley), **III:** 466

No Pockets in a Shroud (McCoy), **Supp. XIII:** 166–168, 171, 172, 173, 174

"No Poem So Fine" (Francis), **Supp. IX:** 83

Norcross, Frances, **I:** 456, 462

Norcross, Louise, **I:** 456, 462

Nordfeldt, B. J. O., **Supp. XXI:** 6

Nordfeldt, Margaret, **Supp. XXI:** 6

Nordyke, Lewis, **Supp. XIII:** 5

No Relief (Dixon), **Supp. XII:** 139, **142–143**

No Resting Place (Humphrey), **Supp. IX:** 94, **106–108**

Norfolk Poems, The (Carruth), **Supp. XVI:** 47, 48

Norma (Bellini), **IV:** 309

Norma Ashe (Glaspell), **Supp. III Part 1:** 175, 186–187

"Normal Life, A" (Thompson), **Supp. XXIII:** 300

"Normal Motor Adjustments" (Stein and Solomons), **IV:** 26

Norman, Charles, **III:** 479

Norman, Gurney, **Supp. X:** 24; **Supp. XXIII:** 42

Norman, Jessye, **Supp. XX:** 110

Norman, Marsha, **Supp. VIII:** 141; **Supp. XXI:** 145

Norman Mailer (Poirier), **Retro. Supp. II:** 207–208

Norman Mailer: Modern Critical Views (Bloom), **Retro. Supp. II:** 205

Norman Mailer Revisited (Merrill), **Retro. Supp. II:** 201

Norna; or, The Witch's Curse (Alcott), **Supp. I Part 1:** 33

Norris, Charles, **III:** 320; **Retro. Supp. I:** 100; **Supp. XVIII:** 226

Norris, Frank, **I:** 211, 355, 500, 506, 517, 518, 519; **II:** 89, 264, 276, 289, 307; **III:** 227, **314–336,** 596; **IV:** 29; **Retro. Supp. I:** 100, 325; **Retro. Supp. II:** 96, 101; **Supp. III Part 2:** 412; **Supp. VIII:** 101, 102; **Supp. IX:** 14, 15; **Supp. XV:** 115

"North" (Budbill), **Supp. XIX:** 7–8

"North" (Hugo), **Supp. VI:** 135

North, Milou (pseudonym), **Supp. IV Part 1:** 260. *See also* Dorris, Michael; Erdrich, Louise

North, Sir Thomas, **IV:** 370

"North American Sequence" (Roethke), **I:** 171–172, 183; **III:** 529, 545, 547, 548

"North Beach" (Snyder), **Supp. VIII:** 289

North Country: A Personal Journey Through the Borderland (Mosher), **Supp. XXII:** 203–204, 206, 212, **217–218**

"North Country Sketches" (McClatchy), **Supp. XII:** 256

"Northeast Playground" (Paley), **Supp. VI:** 226–227, 229

Northern Borders (Mosher), **Supp. XXII:** 203, 204, 206, 207, 208, 209, **213–214**

Northern Lights (O'Brien), **Supp. V:** 237, 239, 241–244, 250

"Northern Motive" (Levine), **Supp. V:** 195

Northfield Poems (Ammons), **Supp. VII:** 29

"Northhanger Ridge" (Wright), **Supp. V:** 335, 340

"North Haven" (Bishop), **Retro. Supp. II:** 50

"North Labrador" (Crane), **I:** 386

North of Boston (Frost), **II:** 152, 153–154, 527; **Retro. Supp. I:** 121, 125, 127, **128–130,** 131; **Supp. I Part 1:** 263; **Supp. XIII:** 146

North of Jamaica (Simpson), **Supp. IV Part 2:** 448; **Supp. IX:** 275, 276

North of the Danube (Caldwell), **I:** 288, 290, 293, 294, 309, 310

North: Poems of Home (Kenny), **Supp. XXIII:** 147–148

Northrup, Cyrus, **Supp. I Part 1:** 350

North Sea (Jarman), **Supp. XVII:** 110, 113

"North Sea Undertaker's Complaint, The" (Lowell), **II:** 550

North & South (Bishop), **Retro. Supp. II:** 41–43; **Supp. I Part 1:** 72, 84, 85, 89

North Star, The (Hellman), **Supp. I Part 1:** 281

Northup, Solomon, **Supp. XIV:** 32

"North Winter" (Carruth), **Supp. XVI:** 53

Norton, Charles Eliot, **I:** 223, 568; **II:** 279, 322–323, 338; **Retro. Supp. I:** 371; **Retro. Supp. II;** 135; **Supp. I Part 1:** 103; **Supp. I Part 2:** 406, 479

Norton, Jody, **Supp. VIII:** 297

Norton, John, **Supp. I Part 1:** 99, 110, 112, 114

Norton Anthology of African American Literature, The (H. L. Gates and McKay, eds.), **Supp. X:** 325; **Supp. XX:** 105

Norton Anthology of American Literature, **Supp. X:** 325; **Supp. XV:** 270

Norton Anthology of Literature by Women (Gilbert and Gubar, eds.), **Supp. XV:** 270

Norton Anthology of Modern Poetry, The, **Supp. XI:** 259; **Supp. XV:** 258

Norton Anthology of Poetry, The, **Supp. XVIII:** 20

Norton Anthology of Short Fiction, The, **Supp. IX:** 4

Norton Book of Personal Essays, The, **Supp. XIV:** 105

Norton Lectures, **Retro. Supp. I:** 65

Norwood, Vera, **Supp. IX:** 24

No Safe Harbour (Porter), **III:** 447

Nosferatu: An Opera Libretto (Gioia), **Supp. XV:** 112, **128**

"Nosferatu's Serenade" (Gioia), **Supp. XV:** 128

No Siege Is Absolute (Char; version of F. Wright), **Supp. XVII:** 244

"No Snake" (A. Finch), **Supp. XVII:** 72

"No Speak English" (Cisneros), **Supp. VII:** 63

"Nostalgia" (Collins), **Supp. XXI:** 57

"Nostalgia" (Saunders), **Supp. XIX:** 235

Nostalgia for 70 (J. W. Miller), **Supp. XX:** 165

"Nostalgia of the Lakefronts" (Justice), **Supp. VII:** 118, 119, 120

"Nostalgic Mood" (Farrell), **II:** 45

No Star Is Lost (Farrell), **II:** 34, 35, 44

Nostrandt, Jeanne, **Supp. XVIII:** 80–81

Nostromo (Conrad), **II:** 600; **IV:** 245

"Nosty Fright, A" (Swenson), **Supp. IV Part 2:** 651

Not about Nightingales (T. Williams), **IV:** 381

"Not a Womb in the House" (Quindlen), **Supp. XVII:** 166, 171

Not Coming to Be Barked At (Kooser), **Supp. XIX:** 116, **120**

Not Dancing (Dunn), **Supp. XI:** 143, **148**

"Note about *Iconographs,* A" (Swenson), **Supp. IV Part 2:** 646

Notebook (Lowell), **Retro. Supp. II:** 186, 190; **Supp. V:** 343

Notebook 1967–68 (Lowell), **II:** 553–555; **Retro. Supp. II:** 182, 186, 190

Notebook of Malte Laurids Brigge, The (Rilke), **III:** 571

Notebooks (Fitzgerald), **Retro. Supp. I:** 110

Notebooks of Captain George, The (Renoir), **Supp. XXII:** 257

No Telephone to Heaven (Cliff), **Supp. XXII:** 66, 69, 71–72

"Note on Abraham Lincoln" (Vidal), **Supp. IV Part 2:** 688

"Note on Commercial Theatre" (Hughes), **Retro. Supp. I:** 207

"Note on Ezra Pound, A" (Eliot), **Retro. Supp. I:** 290

"Note on Lanier's Music, A" (P. Graham), **Supp. I Part 1:** 373

Note on Literary Criticism, A (Farrell), **II:** 26, 49

"Note on Poetry, A" (Doolittle), **Supp. I Part 1:** 254, 267–268

"Note on Realism, A" (Anderson), **I:** 110

"Note on the Limits of 'History' and the Limits of 'Criticism,' A" (Brooks), **Supp. XIV:** 11

"Note on the Poetry of Love, A" (Untermeyer), **Supp. XV:** 304

"Note on the Truth of the Tales, A" (Vollmann), **Supp. XVII:** 230

"Notes" (Dove), **Supp. IV Part 1:** 246

"Notes for a Moving Picture: The House" (Agee), **I:** 33, 34

"Notes for an Autobiography" (Van Vechten), **Supp. II Part 2:** 749

"Notes for a Novel About the End of the World" (Percy), **Supp. III Part 1:** 393

"Notes for a Preface" (Sandburg), **III:** 591, 596–597

"NOTES FOR A SPEECH" (Baraka), **Supp. II Part 1:** 33

Notes for the Green Box (Duchamp), **Supp. IV Part 2:** 423

Notes from a Bottle Found on the Beach at Carmel (Connell), **Supp. XIV:** 80, 87, 96, 97

Notes from a Sea Diary: Hemingway All the Way (Algren), **Supp. IX:** 16

"Notes from the Childhood and Girlhood" (Brooks), **Supp. III Part 1:** 77

"Notes from the River" (Stern), **Supp. IX:** 285, 287, 294, 295

Notes from Underground (Dostoevsky), **III:** 571; **IV:** 485; **Retro. Supp. II:** 121

Notes Left Behind: Last and Selected Poems (Hayford), **Supp. XXII:** 218

"Notes of a Faculty Wife" (Jackson), **Supp. IX:** 126

"Notes of a Native Daughter" (Didion), **Supp. IV Part 1:** 196, 197, 200, 201

Notes of a Native Son (Baldwin), **Retro. Supp. II:** 1, 2, 3, 5, 6; **Supp. I Part 1:** 50, 52, 54; **Supp. IV Part 1:** 163

"Notes of a Native Son" (Baldwin), **Supp. I Part 1:** 50, 54

Notes of a Son and Brother (James), **II:** 337; **Retro. Supp. I:** 235

"Notes on a Departure" (Trilling), **Supp. III Part 2:** 498

"Notes on Babbitt and More" (Wilson), **IV:** 435

"Notes on 'Camp' " (Sontag), **Supp. III Part 2:** 455–456; **Supp. XIV:** 167

Notes on Democracy (Mencken), **III:** 104, 107–108, 109, 116, 119

Notes on Dialectics (C. L. R. James), **Supp. XXI:** 169

"Notes on Free Verse" (Dobyns), **Supp. XIII:** 77

"Notes on 'Layover' " (Hass), **Supp. VI:** 109

"Notes on Memory and Enthusiasm" (Di Piero), **Supp. XIX:** 42

Notes on Novelists (James), **II:** 336, 337; **Retro. Supp. I:** 235

"Notes on Nukes, Nookie, and Neo-Romanticism" (Robbins), **Supp. X:** 272

"Notes on Poetry" (Eberhart), **I:** 524, 527–528, 529

"Notes on Teaching"(Hadas), **Supp. XXIII:** 122

"Notes on the Craft of Poetry" (Strand), **Supp. IV Part 2:** 626

"Notes on the Decline of Outrage" (Dickey), **Supp. IV Part 1:** 181

"Notes on the New Formalism" (Gioia), **Supp. XV:** 113, 114–115

"Notes on the Novel-as-Autobiography" (P. Bailey), **Supp. XVI:** 69

"Notes on 'The Poetry of Everday Life' " (Notley), **Supp. XXII:** 232

Notes on the State of Virginia (1781–1782) (Jefferson), **Supp. XIV:** 191

"Notes to Be Left in a Cornerstone" (Benét), **Supp. XI:** 46, 58

"Notes toward a Supreme Fiction" (Stevens), **IV:** 87–89; **Retro. Supp. I:** 300, 306, **306–309,** 311; **Supp. I Part 1:** 80

"Notes towards a Poem That Can Never Be Written" (Atwood), **Supp. XIII:** 34–35

"Not Exactly for Talia" (Halliday), **Supp. XIX:** 94

No Thanks (Cummings), **I:** 430, 431, 432, 436, 437, 441, 443, 446

Not Heaven: A Novel in the Form of Prelude, Variations, and Theme (W. Frank), **Supp. XX: 80**

"Nothing" (C. Frost), **Supp. XV:** 94

"Nothing Big" (Komunyakaa), **Supp. XIII:** 121

Nothing for Tigers (Carruth), **Supp. XVI:** 47, 48, 50

"Nothing Gold Can Stay" (Frost), **Retro. Supp. I:** 133

"Nothing in Heaven Functions as It Ought" (X. J. Kennedy), **Supp. XV:** 158–159

Nothing Makes You Free: Writings by Descendants of Jewish Holocaust Survivors (Bukiet, ed.), **Supp. XVII: 39–40,** 48–49

"Nothing Missing" (O'Hara), **III:** 369

Nothing Personal (Baldwin), **Supp. I Part 1:** 58, 60

Nothing Sacred (film), **Supp. XVIII:** 243

"Nothing Song, The" (Snodgrass), **Supp. VI:** 326

"Nothing Stays Put" (Clampitt), **Supp. IX:** 42

"Nothing Will Yield" (Nemerov), **III:** 279

No Third Path (Kosinski), **Supp. VII:** 215

"Not Ideas About the Thing but the Thing Itself" (Stevens), **IV:** 87

"No Time" (Collins), **Supp. XXI:** 61

Notions of the Americans: Picked up by a Travelling Bachelor (Cooper), **I:** 343, 345, 346

"Not-Knowing" (Barthelme), **Supp. IV Part 1:** 48

"Not Leaving the House" (Snyder), **Supp. VIII:** 300

Notley, Alice, **Supp. XXII: 223–238; Supp. XXIII:** 221

"'Not Marble nor the Gilded Monument' " (MacLeish), **III:** 12

Not Mine to Finish: Poems, 1928–1934 (Taggard), **Supp. XXII:** 280

"Not My Bones" (Nelson), **Supp. XVIII:** 183

Not Now But Now (M. F. K. Fisher), **Supp. XVII:** 86, 90
"Not Quite Social" (Frost), **II:** 156
"Not Sappho, Sacco" (Rukeyser), **Supp. VI:** 277
"Not Sixteen" (Anderson), **I:** 114
"Not Slightly" (Stein), **IV:** 44
Not So Deep as a Well (Parker), **Supp. IX:** 192
"Not Somewhere Else, but Here" (Rich), **Supp. I Part 2:** 552, 573
Not-So-Simple Neil Simon (McGovern), **Supp. IV Part 2:** 573
Not So Simple: The "Simple" Stories by Langston Hughes (Harper), **Retro. Supp. I:** 194, 209
"Not the Point" (Cameron), **Supp. XII:** 83
"Not They Who Soar" (Dunbar), **Supp. II Part 1:** 199
Not This Pig (Levine), **Supp. V:** 178, 181, 182–183
"Not to Be Satan nor to Deal with Him" (Bronk), **Supp. XXI:** 32
Not to Eat; Not for Love (Weller), **III:** 322
Not Wanted on the Voyage (Findley), **Supp. XX:** 50, 56–57, 59
Not Without Laughter (Hughes), **Retro. Supp. I:** 197, 198, 201; **Supp. I Part 1:** 328, 332; **Supp. XIX:** 73, 154
Nouvelle Héloïse, La (Rousseau), **Supp. XV:** 232
Nova Express (Burroughs), **Supp. III Part 1:** 93, 103, 104; **Supp. XVIII:** 137
Novel, The (Bulwer), **Retro. Supp. II:** 58
Novel, The: An Alternative History (Moore), **Supp. XXII:** 261
"Novel as a Function of American Democracy, The" (Ellison), **Retro. Supp. II:** 124
"Novel Démeublé, The" (Cather), **Retro. Supp. I:** 15
Novel History: Historians and Novelists Confront America's Past (and Each Other) (Carnes), **Supp. X:** 14
"Novelists of 2007" (Halliday), **Supp. XIX:** 90
Novella (Goethe; Bogan and Mayer, trans.), **Supp. III Part 1:** 63
Novellas and Other Writings (Wharton), **Retro. Supp. I:** 360
"Novel of the Thirties, A" (Trilling), **Supp. III Part 2:** 499
Novels and Other Writings (Bercovitch), **Retro. Supp. II:** 325
Novels and Tales of Henry James, The (James), **Retro. Supp. I:** 232
"Novel-Writing and Novel-Reading" (Howells), **II:** 276, 290
"November" (Larcom), **Supp. XIII:** 143
"November Cotton Flower" (Toomer), **Supp. IX:** 312
November Twenty Six Nineteen Sixty Three (Berry), **Supp. X:** 24
"Novices" (Moore), **III:** 200–201, 202, 213
Novick, Peter, **Supp. XVI:** 154–155

"Novogodnee" ("New Year's Greetings") (Tsvetayeva), **Supp. VIII:** 30
"Novotny's Pain" (P. Roth), **Supp. III Part 2:** 403
"No Voyage" (Oliver), **Supp. VII:** 231
No Voyage and Other Poems (Oliver), **Supp. VII:** 230–231, 232
Now and Another Time (Hearon), **Supp. VIII:** 58, 61–62
Now and Then (Buechner), **Supp. XII:** 49, 53
"Now and Then, America" (Mora), **Supp. XIII:** 217
"Nowhere" (J. Scott), **Supp. XVII:** 189
Nowhere Is a Place: Travels in Patagonia (Theroux and Chatwin), **Supp. VIII:** 322
"Now I Am Married" (Gordon), **Supp. IV Part 1:** 299
"Now I Lay Me" (Hemingway), **II:** 249; **Retro. Supp. I:** 175
"Now I Lay Me" (Olds), **Supp. X:** 208
"Now Is the Air Made of Chiming Balls" (Eberhart), **I:** 523
"No Word" (Kunitz), **Supp. III Part 1:** 263
"No Worst" (Nelson), **Supp. XVIII:** 177, 178
Now Sheba Sings the Song (Angelou), **Supp. IV Part 1:** 16
"Now That We Live" (Kenyon), **Supp. VII:** 165
"Now the Servant's Name Was Malchus" (Wilder), **IV:** 358
"Now We Know" (O'Hara), **III:** 368–369
NOW with Bill Moyers (television), **Supp. XIII:** 286
Noyes, Alfred, **IV:** 434
Nuamah, Grace, **Supp. IV Part 1:** 10
"Nuances of a Theme by Williams" (Stevens), **Retro. Supp. I:** 422
Nuclear Age, The (O'Brien), **Supp. V:** 238, 243, 244, 246–248, 249, 251
"Nuclear Arms and Morality" (Sanders), **Supp. XVI:** 266
"Nude at a Dressing Table" (Peacock), **Supp. XIX:** 204
Nude Croquet (Fiedler), **Supp. XIII:** 103
"Nude Descendig a Staircase" (X. J. Kennedy), **Supp. XV:** 168
Nude Descending a Staircase (Duchamp), **IV:** 408; **Retro. Supp. I:** 416; **Supp. XXII:** 162
Nude Descending a Staircase (X. J. Kennedy), **Supp. XV:** 153, **154–157**
Nugent, Bruce, **Retro. Supp. I:** 200
Nugent, Elliot, **Supp. I Part 2:** 606, 611, 613
Nuggets and Dust (Bierce), **I:** 195
"Nullipara" (Olds), **Supp. X:** 209
Number One (Dos Passos), **I:** 489
"Numbers" (Skloot), **Supp. XX: 196, 207**
"Numbers, Letters" (Baraka), **Supp. II Part 1:** 50
Nunc Dimittis (Brodsky), **Supp. VIII:** 25–26, 28
"Nun No More, A" (Fante), **Supp. XI:** 160
"Nun's Priest's Tale" (Chaucer), **III:** 492
Nunzio, Nanzia, **IV:** 89

Nuptial Flight, The (Masters), **Supp. I Part 2:** 460, 471
"Nuptials" (Tate), **IV:** 122
"Nurse Whitman" (Olds), **Supp. X:** 203
Nurture (Kumin), **Supp. IV Part 2:** 453–454, 455
Nussbaum, Emily, **Supp. XI:** 143
Nussbaum, Felicity A., **Supp. X:** 189
Nutcracker, The (Tchaikovsky), **Retro. Supp. I:** 196
"Nux Postcoenatica" (Holmes), **Supp. I Part 1:** 303
Nyce, James M., **Retro. Supp. I:** 380
Nye, Naomi Shihab, **Supp. XI:** 316; **Supp. XIII: 273–290; Supp. XXIII:** 253
Nyerere, Julius, **Supp. X:** 135
"Nympholepsy" (Faulkner), **Retro. Supp. I:** 81
Nymphs of the Valley ('Ará'is al-Murúj) (Gibran), **Supp. XX: 115, 124, 125**

O

"Ö" (Dove), **Supp. IV Part 1:** 245
Oak and Ivy (Dunbar), **Supp. II Part 1:** 98
"Oak Bluffs" column (D. West), **Supp. XVIII:** 286
Oak Openings, The (Cooper), **I:** 354, 355
Oandasan, Bill, **Supp. IV Part 2:** 499
Oasis, The (McCarthy), **II:** 566–568
Oates, Joyce Carol, **Supp. II Part 2: 503–527; Supp. IV Part 1:** 205; **Supp. IV Part 2:** 447, 689; **Supp. V:** 323; **Supp. XI:** 239; **Supp. XII:** 343; **Supp. XIII:** 306; **Supp. XIV:** 26, 109; **Supp. XXIII:** 35
"Oath, The" (Tate), **IV:** 127
Obbligati (Hecht), **Supp. X:** 57
Ober, Harold, **Retro. Supp. I:** 101, 103, 105, 110, 113
Oberndorf, Clarence P., **Supp. I Part 1:** 315
Obey, André, **IV:** 356, 375
"Obit" (Lowell), **II:** 554
"Obituaries" (Collins), **Supp. XXI:** 65
"Objective Value of a Social Settlement, The" (Addams), **Supp. I Part 1:** 4
"Objective Woman, The" (Jong), **Supp. V:** 119
Objectivist Anthology, An, **Supp. XIV:** 287
"Objectivist Ethics, The" (Rand), **Supp. IV Part 2:** 530–532
"Objectivists" Anthology, An (Zukofsky), **Supp. III Part 2:** 613, 615
Object Lessons (Quindlen), **Supp. XVII: 173–174**
"Objects" (Wilbur), **Supp. III Part 2:** 545–547
Oblique Prayers (Levertov), **Supp. III Part 1:** 283
"Oblivion" (Justice), **Supp. VII:** 121
Oblivion Seekers, The (Eberhardt), **Supp. IV Part 1:** 92
"Oblong Box, The" (Poe), **III:** 416
"Obnoxious Truth, The" (Notley), **Supp. XXII:** 234
Obregon, Maurice, **Supp. I Part 2:** 488

O'Briant, Don, **Supp. X:** 8
O'Brien, Edward, **Supp. XV:** 140
O'Brien, Edward J., **I:** 289; **III:** 56; **Supp. XVIII:** 227; **Supp. XIX:** 256; **Supp. XX:** 34
O'Brien, Edwin, **Supp. XVIII:** 208
O'Brien, Fitzjames, **I:** 211
O'Brien, Geoffrey, **Supp. IV Part 2:** 471, 473
O'Brien, Joe, **Supp. XXI:** 5, 6
O'Brien, John, **Supp. V:** 48, 49; **Supp. X:** 239, 244; **Supp. XXI:** 228, 229, 233
O'Brien, Tim, **Supp. V: 237–255; Supp. XI:** 234; **Supp. XVII:** 14; **Supp. XXI:** 122
"Obscene Poem, An" (Creeley), **Supp. IV Part 1:** 150
Obscure Destinies (Cather), **I:** 331–332; **Retro. Supp. I:** 19
"Observation Relative to the Intentions of the Original Founders of the Academy in Philadelphia" (Franklin), **II:** 114
"Observations" (Dillard), **Supp. VI:** 34
Observations (Moore), **III:** 194, 195–196, 197, 199, 203, 205, 215
"Observations Now" (Conroy), **Supp. XVI:** 75
Observations: Photographs by Richard Avedon: Comments by Truman Capote, **Supp. III Part 1:** 125–126
Obuchowski, Mary DeJong, **Supp. XX: 222**
O Canada: An American's Notes on Canadian Culture (Wilson), **IV:** 429–430
"O Carib Isle!" (Crane), **I:** 400–401
O'Casey, Sean, **III:** 145; **Supp. IV Part 1:** 359, 361, 364
"Occidentals" (Ford), **Supp. V:** 71–72
Occom, Samuel, **Supp. XX: 288**
"Occultation of Orion, The" (Longfellow), **Retro. Supp. II:** 168
"Occurrence at Owl Creek Bridge, An" (Bierce), **I:** 200–201; **II:** 264
"Ocean 1212-W" (Plath), **Supp. I Part 2:** 528
"Ocean of Words" (Jin), **Supp. XVIII:** 94
Ocean of Words: Army Stories (Jin), **Supp. XVIII:** 89, 92, **93–94**
O'Connell, Nicholas, **Supp. IX:** 323, 325, 334
O'Connell, Shaun, **Supp. XXI:** 231
O'Connor, Edward F., Jr., **III:** 337
O'Connor, Flannery, **I:** 113, 190, 211, 298; **II:** 606; **III: 337–360; IV:** 4, 217, 282; **Retro. Supp. II:** 179, **219–239,** 272, 324; **Supp. I Part 1:** 290; **Supp. III Part 1:** 146; **Supp. V:** 59, 337; **Supp. VIII:** 13, 14, 158; **Supp. X:** 1, 26, 69, 228, 290; **Supp. XI:** 104; **Supp. XIII:** 294; **Supp. XIV:** 93; **Supp. XV:** 338; **Supp. XVI:** 219; **Supp. XVII:** 43, 114; **Supp. XVIII:** 156, 161, 194; **Supp. XIX:** 166, 209, 223; **Supp. XXI:** 197; **Supp. XXIII:** 289

O'Connor, Frank, **III:** 158; **Retro. Supp. II:** 242; **Supp. I Part 2:** 531; **Supp. VIII:** 151, 157, 165, 167, 171; **Supp. XV:** 74
O'Connor, Philip F., **Supp. XXIII:** 290
O'Connor, Richard, **II:** 467
O'Connor, T. P., **II:** 129
O'Connor, William, **IV:** 346; **Retro. Supp. I:** 392, 407
O'Connor, William Van, **III:** 479; **Supp. I Part 1:** 195
"Octascope" (Beattie), **Supp. V:** 27, 28
"Octaves" (Robinson), **Supp. III Part 2:** 593
"Octet" (Wallace), **Supp. X:** 309
October (Isherwood), **Supp. XIV:** 157, 164
"October" (Oliver), **Supp. VII:** 241
"October" (Swenson), **Supp. IV Part 2:** 649
"October, 1866" (Bryant), **Supp. I Part 1:** 169
"October 1913" (McCarriston), **Supp. XIV:** 266
"October and November" (Lowell), **II:** 554
"October in the Railroad Earth" (Kerouac), **Supp. III Part 1:** 225, 227, 229
October Light (Gardner), **Supp. VI:** 63, **69–71,** 72
"October Maples, Portland" (Wilbur), **Supp. III Part 2:** 556
October Palace, The (Hirshfield), **Supp. XXIII:** 131
"October: With Rain" (W. V. Davis), **Supp. XXI:** 94
"Octopus, An" (Moore), **III:** 202, 207–208, 214
"Octopus, The" (Merrill), **Supp. III Part 1:** 321
Octopus, The (Norris), **I:** 518; **III:** 314, 316, 322–326, 327, 331–333, 334, 335
"O Daedalus, Fly Away Home" (Hayden), **Supp. II Part 1:** 377–378
"OD and Hepatitis Railroad or Bust, The" (Boyle), **Supp. VIII:** 1
Odd Couple, The (1985 version, Simon), **Supp. IV Part 2:** 580
Odd Couple, The (film), **Supp. IV Part 2:** 589
Odd Couple, The (Simon), **Supp. IV Part 2:** 575, 579–580, 585, 586; **Supp. XVII:** 8
Odd Jobs (Updike), **Retro. Supp. I:** 334
Odd Mercy (Stern), **Supp. IX: 298–299**
Odd Number (Sorrentino), **Supp. XXI:** 236
"Odds, The" (Hecht), **Supp. X:** 64–65
"Odds, The" (Salinas), **Supp. XIII:** 321
"Ode" (Emerson), **II:** 13
"Ode" (Sobin), **Supp. XVI:** 284–285
"Ode" (X. J. Kennedy), **Supp. XV:** 160
"Ode (Intimations of Immortality)" (Matthews), **Supp. IX:** 162
"Ode for Memorial Day" (Dunbar), **Supp. II Part 1:** 199
"Ode for the American Dead in Asia" (McGrath), **Supp. X:** 119

"Ode: For the Budding of Islands" (Sobin), **Supp. XVI:** 287
"Ode Inscribed to W. H. Channing" (Emerson), **Supp. XIV:** 46
"Ode: Intimations of Immortality" (Wordsworth), **Supp. I Part 2:** 729; **Supp. III Part 1:** 12; **Supp. XIV:** 8
"Ode in Time of Crisis" (Taggard), **Supp. XXII:** 271
Odell, Margeretta Matilda, **Supp. XX: 278, 284, 288**
"Ode: My 24th Year" (Ginsberg), **Supp. II Part 1:** 312
"Ode on a Grecian Urn" (Keats), **I:** 284; **III:** 472; **Supp. XII:** 113; **Supp. XIV:** 8, 9–10; **Supp. XV:** 100; **Supp. XXI:** 64
"Ode on Human Destinies" (Jeffers), **Supp. II Part 2:** 419
"Ode on Indolence" (Keats), **Supp. XII:** 113
"Ode on Melancholy" (Keats), **Retro. Supp. I:** 301
Ode Recited at the Harvard Commemoration (Lowell), **Supp. I Part 2:** 416–418, 424
"Ode Recited at the Harvard Commemoration" (Lowell), **II:** 551
Odes (O'Hara), **Supp. XXIII:** 216
"Ode: Salute to the French Negro Poets"(O'Hara), **Supp. XXIII:** 216
"Ode Secrète" (Valéry), **III:** 609
"Odes of Estrangement" (Sobin), **Supp. XVI:** 289
"Odes to Natural Processes" (Updike), **Retro. Supp. I:** 323
"Ode: The Capris" (Halliday), **Supp. XIX:** 88
"Ode to a Nightingale" (Keats), **II:** 368; **Retro. Supp. II:** 261; **Supp. IX:** 52
"Ode to Autumn" (Masters), **Supp. I Part 2:** 458
"Ode to Cervantes" (Salinas), **Supp. XIII:** 324
"Ode to Coit Tower" (Corso), **Supp. XII:** 122
"Ode to Ethiopia" (Dunbar), **Supp. II Part 1:** 199, 207, 208, 209
"Ode to Fear" (Tate), **IV:** 128
Ode to Harvard and Other Poems, An (Bynner), **Supp. XV:** 41, 44
"Ode to Joy"(O'Hara), **Supp. XXIII:** 208, 216
"Ode to Meaning" (Pinsky), **Supp. VI: 249–250,** 251
"Ode to Michael Goldberg ('s Birth and Other Births)"(O'Hara), **Supp. XXIII:** 209, 216, 218
"Ode to Night" (Masters), **Supp. I Part 2:** 458
"Ode to Our Young Pro-Consuls of the Air" (Tate), **IV:** 135
"Ode to the Austrian Socialists" (Benét), **Supp. XI:** 46, 58
"Ode to the Confederate Dead" (Tate), **II:** 551; **IV:** 124, 133, 137; **Supp. X:** 52
"Ode to the Johns Hopkins University" (Lanier), **Supp. I Part 1:** 370

"Ode to the Maggot" (Komunyakaa), **Supp. XIII:** 130

"Ode to the Mexican Experience" (Salinas), **Supp. XIII:** 316–317

"Ode to the Virginian Voyage" (Drayton), **IV:** 135

"Ode to the West Wind" (Shelley), **Retro. Supp. I:** 308; **Supp. I Part 2:** 728; **Supp. IX:** 52; **Supp. XII:** 117; **Supp. XIV:** 271–272; **Supp. XV:** 221

"Ode to Walt Whitman" (Benét), **Supp. XI:** 52

"Ode to Willem de Kooning" (O'Hara), **Supp. XXIII:** 208, 216

Odets, Clifford, **Supp. I Part 1:** 277, 295; **Supp. I Part 2:** 679; **Supp. II Part 2:** 529–554; **Supp. IV Part 2:** 587; **Supp. V:** 109; **Supp. VIII:** 96; **Supp. XVIII:** 238; **Supp. XX:** 34

Odier, Daniel, **Supp. III Part 1:** 97

"Odi et Amo" (Catullus), **Supp. XV:** 27, 32, 35

"Odom" (P. Benedict), **Supp. XXIII:** 41

O'Donnell, George Marion, **II:** 67

O'Donnell, Mary King, **Supp. XVIII:** 232

O'Donnell, Thomas F., **II:** 131

"Odor of Verbena" (Faulkner), **II:** 66

O'Doul, Lefty, **II:** 425

"Odysseus to Telemachus" (Brodsky), **Supp. VIII:** 25

Odyssey (Bryant, trans.), **Supp. I Part 1:** 158

Odyssey (Homer), **III:** 14, 470; **Retro. Supp. I:** 286, 290; **Retro. Supp. II:** 121; **Supp. I Part 1:** 185; **Supp. IV Part 2:** 631; **Supp. IX:** 211; **Supp. X:** 114; **Supp. XIV:** 191; **Supp. XVII:** 117; **Supp. XXI:** 36

"Odyssey of a Wop, The" (Fante), **Supp. XI:** 164, 165

Oedipus Rex (Sophocles), **I:** 137; **III:** 145, 151, 152, 332; **Supp. I Part 2:** 428

Oedipus Tyrannus (Sophocles), **II:** 203; **Supp. XV:** 265

Oehlschlaeger, Fritz, **Supp. IX:** 123

Oelze, Richard, **Supp. XXII:** 167

"Of Alexander Crummell" (Du Bois), **Supp. II Part 1:** 170

O'Faoláin, Seán, **Supp. II Part 1:** 101

Of a World That Is No More (Singer), **IV:** 16

"Of Booker T. Washington and Others" (Du Bois), **Supp. II Part 1:** 168

"Of Bright & Blue Birds & the Gala Sun" (Stevens), **IV:** 93

"Of Christian Heroism" (Ozick), **Supp. V:** 272

"Of Dying Beauty" (Zukofsky), **Supp. III Part 2:** 610

"Of Epiphanies and Poets" (Phillips), **Supp. XX:** 221

"Of 'Father and Son' " (Kunitz), **Supp. III Part 1:** 262

Offenbach, Jacques, **II:** 427

"Offering for Mr. Bluehart, An" (Wright), **Supp. III Part 2:** 596, 601

"Offerings" (Mason), **Supp. VIII:** 141

"Offertory" (Hempel), **Supp. XXI:** 126–127

Official Entry Blank (Kooser), **Supp. XIX:** 116, **117–118**

"Official Entry Form" (Kooser), **Supp. XIX:** 117

"Official Piety" (Whittier), **Supp. I Part 2:** 687

"Offloading for Mrs. Schwartz" (Saunders), **Supp. XIX:** 225–226

"Of Freemasons, Kings, and Constitutions" (P. N. Warren), **Supp. XX:** 273

"Off-Shore Pirates, The" (Fitzgerald), **II:** 88

Off the Beaten Path (Proulx), **Supp. VII:** 261

Off the Beaten Path: Stories of Place, **Supp. XVI:** 22

"Off the Cuff" (Simpson), **Supp. IX:** 278

"Off the Highway" (Wolfert), **Supp. XXI:** 265

Off the Map (Levine), **Supp. V:** 178

Offut, Chris, **Supp. XIX: 163–176**

Of Gravity and Angels (Hirshfield), **Supp. XXIII:** 131

O'Flaherty, George, **Supp. I Part 1:** 202, 205–206

O'Flaherty, Kate. *See* Chopin, Kate

O'Flaherty, Thomas, **Supp. I Part 1:** 202, 203–204, 205

O'Flaherty, Thomas, Jr., **Supp. I Part 1:** 202

"Of Maids and Other Muses" (Alvarez), **Supp. VII:** 11

"Of Margaret" (Ransom), **III:** 491

Of Mice and Men (Steinbeck), **IV:** 51, 57–58

"Of Modern Poetry" (Stevens), **IV:** 92

Of Plymouth Plantation (Bradford), **Retro. Supp. II:** 161, 162; **Supp. XXII:** 33, **35–47**

Of Plymouth Plantation (Morison, ed.), **Supp. I Part 2:** 494

"Ofrenda for Lobo" (Mora), **Supp. XIII:** 224

"Often" (Kenyon), **Supp. VII:** 171

"Often, in Dreams, He Moved through a City" (Dobyns), **Supp. XIII:** 90

"Of the Coming of John" (Du Bois), **Supp. II Part 1:** 170

"Of the Culture of White Folk" (Du Bois), **Supp. II Part 1:** 175

Of the Farm (Updike), **IV:** 214, 217, 223–225, 233; **Retro. Supp. I:** 318, 329, 332

"Of the Four-Winged Cherubim as Signature" (Sobin), **Supp. XVI:** 287

"Of 'The Frill' " (McCarriston), **Supp. XIV:** 274

"Of the Passing of the First-Born" (Du Bois), **Supp. II Part 1:** 170

"Of the Sorrow Songs" (Du Bois), **Supp. II Part 1:** 170

"Of the Wings of Atlanta" (Du Bois), **Supp. II Part 1:** 170

Of This Time, Of This Place (Trilling), **Supp. III Part 2:** 498, 504

Of Time and the River (Wolfe), **IV:** 450, 451, 452, 455, 456, 457, 458, 459, 462, 464–465, 467, 468, 469

Of Woman Born: Motherhood as Experience and Institution (Rich), **Supp. I Part 2:** 554, 567–569

Of Women and Their Elegance (Mailer), **Retro. Supp. II:** 209

Ogden, Archie, **Supp. XIII:** 174

Ogden, Henry, **II:** 298

Ogden, Uzal, **Supp. I Part 2:** 516

Ogle, Connie, **Supp. XXIII:** 300, 301

"Oh, Atonement" (Weigl), **Supp. XIX:** 287

"Oh, Fairest of the Rural Maids" (Bryant), **Supp. I Part 1:** 169

"Oh, Immobility, Death's Vast Associate" (Dobyns), **Supp. XIII:** 89

"Oh, Joseph, I'm So Tired" (Yates), **Supp. XI:** 348

Oh, the Places You'll Go! (Geisel), **Supp. XVI:** 111

Oh, the Thinks You can Think! (Geisel), **Supp. XVI:** 111

"O'Halloran's Luck" (Benét), **Supp. XI:** 47

O'Hara, Frank, **Supp. XII:** 121; **Supp. XV:** 93, 176, 177, 178, 179–180, 182, 186, 187, 215–216; **Supp. XIX:** 81, 85; **Supp. XXII:** 226, 236; **Supp. XXIII: 207–222**

O'Hara, J. D., **Supp. IV Part 1:** 43; **Supp. V:** 22; **Supp. XVI:** 221; **Supp. XXI:** 228

O'Hara, John, **I:** 375, 495; **II:** 444, 459; **III:** 66, **361–384**; **IV:** 59; **Retro. Supp. I:** 99, 112; **Supp. I Part 1:** 196; **Supp. II Part 1:** 109; **Supp. IV Part 1:** 31, 383; **Supp. IV Part 2:** 678; **Supp. V:** 95; **Supp. VIII:** 151, 156; **Supp. XX:** 208; **Supp. XIX:** 209

O'Hara's Choice (Uris), **Supp. XX: 247, 256–257**

O'Hehir, Andrew, **Supp. XII:** 280

O. Henry Biography (C. A. Smith), **Supp. II Part 1:** 395

"Ohio Pagan, An" (Anderson), **I:** 112, 113

Ohio trilogy (Richter), **Supp. XVIII:** 212–215

Oh Mercy (album, Dylan), **Supp. XVIII:** 28, 33

Oh Say Can You Say? (Geisel), **Supp. XVI:** 111

Oil! (Sinclair), **Supp. V:** 276, 277–279, 282, 288, 289

Oil Notes (Bass), **Supp. XVI:** 17

"Oil Painting of the Artist as the Artist" (MacLeish), **III:** 14

"O-jib-way Maid, The" (J. Schoolcraft), **Supp. XXIII:** 235

O'Keeffe, Georgia, **Supp. IX:** 62, 66; **Supp. XX:** 75

"Oklahoma" (Levis), **Supp. XI:** 267

Oktenberg, Adrian, **Supp. XVII:** 76; **Supp. XXI:** 253; **Supp. XXIII:** 133

"Old, Old, Old, Old Andrew Jackson" (Lindsay), **Supp. I Part 2:** 398

"Old Amusement Park, An" (Moore), **III:** 216

"Old Angel Midnight" (Kerouac), **Supp. III Part 1:** 229–230

"Old Apple Dealer, The" (Hawthorne), **II:** 227, 233–235, 237, 238

"Old Apple-Tree, The" (Dunbar), **Supp. II Part 1:** 198

"Old Army Game, The" (Garrett), **Supp. VII:** 100–101

"Old Aunt Peggy" (Chopin), **Retro. Supp. II:** 64

"Old Barn at the Bottom of the Fogs, The" (Frost), **Retro. Supp. I:** 138

Old Battle-Ax, The (Holding), **Supp. XXII: 128–129**

Old Beauty and Others, The (Cather), **I:** 331

"Old Boys, Old Girls" (P. E. Jones), **Supp. XXII:** 151

Old Bruin: Commodore Matthew C. Perry, 1794–1858 (Morison), **Supp. I Part 2:** 494–495

"Old Cracked Tune, An" (Kunitz), **Supp. III Part 1:** 264

Old Curiosity Shop, The (Dickens), **I:** 458; **Supp. I Part 2:** 409

Oldest Killed Lake in North America, The (Carruth), **Supp. XVI:** 51

"Oldest Man, The" (M. F. K. Fisher), **Supp. XVII:** 91

"Old Farmer, The" (Jeffers), **Supp. II Part 2:** 418

Old-Fashioned Girl, An (Alcott), **Supp. I Part 1:** 29, 41, 42

"Old Father Morris" (Stowe), **Supp. I Part 2:** 586

"Old Flame, The" (Lowell), **II:** 550

"Old Florist" (Roethke), **III:** 531

"Old Folsom Prison" (Matthews), **Supp. IX:** 165

Old Forest, The (Taylor), **Supp. V:** 320, 321, 326, 327

"Old Forest, The" (Taylor), **Supp. V:** 313, 321, 323, 326

Old Forest and Other Stories (Taylor), **Supp. V:** 326

Old Friends and New (Jewett), **II:** 402; **Retro. Supp. II:** 137, 140

Old Glory, The (Lowell), **II:** 543, 545–546, 555; **Retro. Supp. II:** 188

Old Helmet, The (S. and A. Warner), **Supp. XVIII:** 267

"Old Homestead, The" (Dunbar), **Supp. II Part 1:** 198

"Old House" (Espaillat), **Supp. XXI:** 112, 113

"Old Iron" (Nye), **Supp. XIII:** 276

"Old Ironsides" (Holmes), **Supp. I Part 1:** 302

"Old Lady We Saw, An" (Shields), **Supp. VII:** 310–311

"Old Love" (Singer), **Retro. Supp. II:** 307

"Old McGrath Place, The" (McGrath), **Supp. X:** 114

"Old Maid, The" (Wharton), **Retro. Supp. I:** 381, 382

"Old Man" (Faulkner), **II:** 68, 69

Old Man and the Sea, The (Hemingway), **II:** 250, 256–257, 258, 265; **III:** 40; **Retro. Supp. I:** 180, **185,** 186

"Old Man Drunk" (Wright), **Supp. III Part 2:** 595

"Old Man Feeding Hens" (Francis), **Supp. IX:** 78

"Old Man on the Hospital Porch" (Ríos), **Supp. IV Part 2:** 546–547

Old Man Rubbing His Eyes (R. Bly), **Supp. IV Part 1:** 65

"Old Manse, The" (Hawthorne), **II:** 224

"Old Man's Winter Night, An" (Frost), **Retro. Supp. I:** 126, 131

Old Man Who Love Cheese, The (Keillor), **Supp. XVI:** 177

"Old Man with a Dog" (Wright), **Supp. XV:** 346

Old Marriage and New (Kooser), **Supp. XIX: 120–121**

"Old Meeting House, The" (Stowe), **Supp. I Part 2:** 586

"Old Memory, An" (Dunbar), **Supp. II Part 1:** 198

"Old Men, Old Horses" (P. N. Warren as Kilina), **Supp. XX: 262**

"Old Men, The" (McCarthy), **II:** 566

"Old Men Pitching Horseshoes" (X. J. Kennedy), **Supp. XV:** 166

Old Money (Wasserstein), **Supp. XV: 333–334**

"Old Morgue, The" (Prose), **Supp. XVI:** 250

Old Morning Program, The (radio show, Keillor). *See Prairie Home Companion, A* (radio show, Keillor)

"Old Mortality" (Porter), **III:** 436, 438–441, 442, 445, 446

"Old Mrs. Harris" (Cather), **I:** 332; **Retro. Supp. I:** 19

Old Neighborhood, The (Mamet), **Supp. XIV:** 240, 241, 242, 249–250, 251, 252, 254

Old New York (Wharton), **IV:** 322; **Retro. Supp. I:** 381

"Ol' Doc Hyar" (Campbell), **Supp. II Part 1:** 202

"Old of the Moon" (Offutt), **Supp. XIX:** 165, 166

Old One-Two, The (Gurney), **Supp. V:** 98

"Old Order, The" (Porter), **III:** 443, 444–445, 451

"Old Osawatomie" (Sandburg), **III:** 584

Old Patagonia Express, The: By Train through the Americas (Theroux), **Supp. VIII:** 322

"Old People, The" (Faulkner), **II:** 71–72

"Old Photograph, An" (Kooser), **Supp. XIX:** 121

"Old Poet Moves to a New Apartment 14 Times, The" (Zukofsky), **Supp. III Part 2:** 628

Old Possum's Book of Practical Cats (T. S. Eliot), **Supp. XIII:** 228, 344

"Old Red" (Gordon), **II:** 199, 200, 203

Old Red and Other Stories (Gordon), **II:** 157

Old Régime in Canada, The (Parkman), **Supp. II Part 2:** 600, 607, 608–609, 612

Old Religion, The (Mamet), **Supp. XIV:** 253

Olds, Sharon, **Supp. X: 201–217; Supp. XI:** 139, 142, 244; **Supp. XII:** 229; **Supp. XIV:** 265; **Supp. XVII:** 114, 240; **Supp. XXI:** 249

"Old Saws" (Garrett), **Supp. VII:** 96–97

Old South, The: "A Summer Tragedy" and Other Stories (Bontemps), **Supp. XXII:** 7

"Old Stories" (Skloot), **Supp. XX: 200**

Old Testament, **I:** 109, 181, 300, 328, 401, 410, 419, 431, 457, 458; **II:** 166, 167, 219; **III:** 270, 272, 348, 390, 396; **IV:** 41, 114, 152, 309; **Retro. Supp. I:** 122, 140, 249, 311, 360; **Retro. Supp. II:** 299; **Supp. I Part 1:** 60, 104, 106, 151; **Supp. I Part 2:** 427, 515, 516; **Supp. IX:** 14. *See also* names of Old Testament books

"Old Things, The" (James), **Retro. Supp. I:** 229

"Old Times on the Mississippi" (Twain), **IV:** 199

Oldtown Folks (Stowe), **Supp. I Part 2:** 587, 596–598

"Old Town of Berwick, The" (Jewett), **Retro. Supp. II:** 132

"Old Trails" (Robinson), **III:** 513, 517

"Old Tyrannies" (Bourne), **I:** 233

"Old West" (Bausch), **Supp. VII:** 48

"Old Whorehouse, An" (Oliver), **Supp. VII:** 235

"Old Woman" (Pinsky), **Supp. VI:** 238

"Old Woman of Beare, The" (X. J. Kennedy), **Supp. XV:** 156

"Old Word, The" (Simic), **Supp. VIII:** 282

"Old-World Landowners" (Gogol), **Supp. XV:** 262

Oldys, Francis. *See* Chalmers, George

Oleanna (Mamet), **Supp. XIV:** 239, 241, 245, 248, 250

Olendorf, Donna, **Supp. IV Part 1:** 196

"Olga Poems, The" (Levertov), **Supp. III Part 1:** 279–281

"Olive Groves of Thasos, The" (Clampitt), **Supp. IX: 51–52**

Olive Kitteridge (Strout), **Supp. XXIII:** 273, 275, **280–284,** 285

Oliver, Bill, **Supp. VIII:** 138

Oliver, Douglas, **Supp. XXII:** 225, 226, 233, 235

Oliver, Mary, **Supp. VII: 229–248; Supp. X:** 31; **Supp. XVI:** 39; **Supp. XVII:** 111, 240; **Supp. XXIII:** 51

Oliver, Sydney, **I:** 409

Oliver Goldsmith: A Biography (Irving), **II:** 315

Oliver Twist (Dickens), **I:** 354; **Supp. IV Part 2:** 464

"Olivia" (Salinas), **Supp. XIII:** 316

"Olivier Bergmann" (Halliday), **Supp. XIX:** 93–94

Olivieri, David (pseudonym), **Retro. Supp. I:** 361. *See also* Wharton, Edith

Ollive, Samuel, **Supp. I Part 2:** 503

Olmsted, Frederick Law, **Supp. I Part 1:** 355

Olor de la memoria, El/The Scent of Memory (Espaillat), **Supp. XXI:** 104

Olsen, Lance, **Supp. IV Part 1:** 54; **Supp. IV Part 2:** 623

Olsen, Tillie, **Supp. V:** 114, 220; **Supp. XIII: 291–309; Supp. XVI:** 83, 90

Olshan, Joseph, **Supp. XIX:** 52

Olson, Charles, **Retro. Supp. I:** 209; **Supp. II Part 1:** 30, 328; **Supp. II Part 2: 555–587; Supp. III Part 1:** 9, 271; **Supp. III Part 2:** 542, 624; **Supp. IV Part 1:** 139, 144, 146, 153, 154, 322; **Supp. IV Part 2:** 420, 421, 423, 426; **Supp. VIII:** 290, 291; **Supp. XII:** 2, 198; **Supp. XIII:** 104; **Supp. XIV:** 96; **Supp. XV:** 177; **Supp. XXI:** 19, 21, 23

Olson, Clarence, **Supp. XX: 84, 85, 86**

Olson, Ray, **Supp. XVII:** 111, 112, 119

"Ol' Tunes, The" (Dunbar), **Supp. II Part 1:** 197

"O Lull Me, Lull Me" (Roethke), **III:** 536–537

O'Malley, Anne, **Supp. XXII:** 56

Omar Khayyam, **Supp. I Part 1:** 363

O'Meally, Robert, **Retro. Supp. II:** 112

Omega the Unknown (comic book series), **Supp. XVIII:** 149

"Omen" (Komunyakaa), **Supp. XIII:** 126, 127

Omensetter's Luck (Gass), **Supp. VI: 80–82,** 87

Omeros (Walcott), **Supp. XV:** 264

"Ominous Baby, An" (Crane), **I:** 411

Ommateum, with Doxology (Ammons), **Supp. VII:** 24–26, 27, 28, 36

Omni-Americans, The: New Perspectives on Black Experience and American Culture (Murray), **Supp. XIX:** 147, **149–151,** 154

"Omnibus Jaunts and Drivers" (Whitman), **IV:** 350

Omoo: A Narrative of Adventures in the South Seas (Melville), **III:** 76–77, 79, 84; **Retro. Supp. I:** 247

O My Land, My Friends (H. Crane), **Retro. Supp. II:** 76

"On Abrigador Hill" (Nelson), **Supp. XVIII:** 183

"On a Certain Condescension in Foreigners" (Lowell), **Supp. I Part 2:** 419

"On a Certain Engagement South of Seoul" (Carruth), **Supp. XVI:** 47

"On a Child Who Lived One Minute" (X. J. Kennedy), **Supp. XV:** 152, 155

"On Acquiring Riches" (Banks), **Supp. V:** 5

On a Darkling Plain (Stegner), **Supp. IV Part 2:** 598, 607

On a Fire on the Moon (Mailer), **Retro. Supp. II:** 206

"On a Hill Far Away" (Dillard), **Supp. VI:** 28

"On a Honey Bee, Drinking from a Glass and Drowned Therein" (Freneau), **Supp. II Part 1:** 273

"On a Monument to a Pigeon" (Leopold), **Supp. XIV:** 187–188

"On a Mountainside" (Wagoner), **Supp. IX:** 332

O'Nan, Stewart, **Supp. XI:** 348

"On an Old Photograph of My Son" (Carver), **Supp. III Part 1:** 140

"Onan's Soliloquy" (X. J. Kennedy), **Supp. XV:** 165

"On a Proposed Trip South" (W. C. Williams), **Retro. Supp. I:** 413

Onassis, Jacqueline Kennedy, **Supp. XVIII:** 287

"On a Tree Fallen across the Road" (Frost), **Retro. Supp. I:** 134

"On a View of Pasadena from the Hills" (Winters), **Supp. II Part 2:** 795, 796–799, 814

"On a Visit to a Halfway House after a Long Absence" (Salinas), **Supp. XIII:** 325

"On a Windy Night" (Dixon), **Supp. XII:** 155

On Becoming a Novelist (Gardner), **Supp. VI:** 64

"On Being an American" (Toomer), **Supp. III Part 2:** 479

"On Being Asked to Write a Poem against the War in Vietnam" (Carruth), **Supp. XVI:** 55–56

"On Being a Woman" (Parker), **Supp. IX:** 201

On Being Blue (Gass), **Supp. VI:** 77, 78, 86, 94; **Supp. XIV:** 305

"On Being Brought from Africa to America" (Wheatley), **Supp. XX: 280–281, 286–287**

"On Being Too Inhibited" (Hay), **Supp. XIV:** 130

"On Being Unable to Read" (Cornell), **Supp. XX: 94–95**

On Beyond Zebra! (Geisel), **Supp. XVI:** 105

"On Burroughs' Work" (Ginsberg), **Supp. II Part 1:** 320

Once (Walker), **Supp. III Part 2:** 519, 522, 530

Once at Antietam (Gaddis), **Supp. IV Part 1:** 285

"Once by the Pacific" (Frost), **II:** 155; **Retro. Supp. I:** 122, 137

"Once More, the Round" (Roethke), **III:** 529

Once More around the Block: Familiar Essays (Epstein), **Supp. XIV: 107**

"Once More to the Lake" (White), **Supp. I Part 2:** 658, 668, 673–675

"On Certain Political Measures Proposed to Their Consideration" (Barlow), **Supp. II Part 1:** 82

"Once There Was Light" (Kenyon), **Supp. VII:** 171–172

"On Credo Ut Intelligam" (Bronk), **Supp. XXI:** 31

Ondaatje, Michael, **Supp. IV Part 1:** 252

"On Dining Alone" (M. F. K. Fisher), **Supp. XVII:** 83

On Distant Ground (R. O. Butler), **Supp. XII:** 62, **66–68,** 69, 74

"On Divers Geometries" (Bronk), **Supp. XXI:** 31

"On Dreams"(Hadas), **Supp. XXIII:** 117

"One, The" (Weigl), **Supp. XIX:** 282–283

"1 January 1965" (Brodsky), **Supp. VIII:** 23–24

O'Neale, Sondra, **Supp. IV Part 1:** 2

"One A.M. with Voices" (X. J. Kennedy), **Supp. XV:** 157

"One Arm" (T. Williams), **IV:** 383

One Arm, and Other Stories (T. Williams), **IV:** 383

"One Art" (Bell), **Supp. X:** 2

One Art (Bishop), **Retro. Supp. II:** 51

"One Art" (Bishop), **Retro. Supp. II:** 50; **Supp. I Part 1:** 72, 73, 82, 93, 94–95, 96; **Supp. XV:** 126; **Supp. XXI:** 58; **Supp. XXIII:** 117

"One Art: The Poetry of Elizabeth Bishop, 1971–1976" (Schwartz), **Supp. I Part 1:** 81

One Big Self: Prisoners of Louisiana (Wright and Luster), **Supp. XV:** 337, 344, 350, **351–353**

"One Blessing had I than the rest" (Dickinson), **Retro. Supp. I:** 45

"One Body" (Hass), **Supp. VI:** 106

One Boy's Boston, 1887–1901 (Morison), **Supp. I Part 2:** 494

"One Coat of Paint" (Ashbery), **Supp. III Part 1:** 26

"One Dash-Horses" (Crane), **I:** 416

One Day (Morris), **III:** 233–236

One Day, When I Was Lost (Baldwin), **Retro. Supp. II:** 13; **Supp. I Part 1:** 48, 66, 67

"One Dead Friend" (Kumin), **Supp. IV Part 2:** 441

One Destiny: An Epistle to the Christians (Asch), **Supp. XXIII:** 2, 7

One Fish Two Fish Red Fish Blue Fish (Geisel), **Supp. XVI:** 108

One Flesh (Major), **Supp. XXII: 183–184**

One Flew Over the Cuckoo's Nest (Kesey), **III:** 558

One Flew Over the Cuckoo's Nest (Kesey), **Supp. XXIII:** 100

"One for the Road" (Swados), **Supp. XIX:** 259

One for the Rose (Levine), **Supp. V:** 178, 179, 181, 187, 189–191

"One for the Rose" (Levine), **Supp. V:** 181, 190

"One Friday Morning" (Hughes), **Supp. I Part 1:** 330

"One Holy Night" (Cisneros), **Supp. VII:** 69–70

"One Home" (Stafford), **Supp. XI:** 321

100 Faces of Death, The, Part IV (Boyle), **Supp. VIII:** 16

100 Great Poets of the English Language (Gioia, ed.), **Supp. XXI:** 99

100 Years of Negro Freedom (Bontemps), **Supp. XXII:** 6

$106,000 Blood Money (Hammett), **Supp. IV Part 1:** 345

"$106,000 Blood Money" (Hammett), **Supp. IV Part 1:** 345, 346

One Hundred Days in Europe (Holmes), **Supp. I Part 1:** 317

180 More: Extraordinary Poems for Every Day (Collins, ed.), **Supp. XXI:** 54

158-Pound Marriage, The (Irving), **Supp. VI:** 163, 164, **167–170**

O'Neil, Elizabeth Murrie, **Retro. Supp. I:** 427

O'Neill, Brendan, **Supp. XII:** 286

O'Neill, Eugene, **I:** 66, 71, 81, 94, 393, 445; **II:** 278, 391, 427, 585; **III:** 151, 165, **385–408; IV:** 61, 383; **Retro. Supp. II:** 82, 104; **Supp. III Part 1:** 177–180, 189; **Supp. IV Part 1:** 359; **Supp. IV Part 2:** 587, 607; **Supp. V:** 277; **Supp. VIII:** 332, 334; **Supp. XIV:** 239, 320, 328; **Supp. XVI:** 193; **Supp. XVII:** 96, 99–100, 103, 105, 107; **Supp. XX: 69; Supp. XXI:** 6, 13; **Supp. XXII:** 17, 18, 22, 28

O'Neill, Oona, **Supp. XXII:** 25, 26

"One Is a Wanderer" (Thurber), **Supp. I Part 2:** 616

One Is the Sun (P. N. Warren), **Supp. XX: 269–270**

One L (Turow), **Supp. XVII: 214,** 215, 217

"One Last Look at the Adige: Verona in the Rain" (Wright), **Supp. III Part 2:** 603

One Life (Rukeyser), **Supp. VI:** 273, 281, 283

One Life at a Time, Please (Abbey), **Supp. XIII:** 13

One Man in His Time (Glasgow), **II:** 178, 184

"One Man's Fortunes" (Dunbar), **Supp. II Part 1:** 211, 212–213

One Man's Initiation (Dos Passos), **I:** 476–477, 479, 488

One Man's Meat (White), **Supp. I Part 2:** 654, 669, 676

"One Man's Meat" (White), **Supp. I Part 2:** 655

One Matchless Time: A Life of William Faulkner (Parini), **Supp. XXII:** 205

"One Moment on Top of the Earth" (Nye), **Supp. XIII:** 282

One More July: A Football Dialogue with Bill Curry (Plimpton), **Supp. XVI:** 243

"One More"(Kenny), **Supp. XXIII:** 156

"One More Song" (Lindsay), **Supp. I Part 2:** 400–401

"One More Thing" (Carver), **Supp. III Part 1:** 138, 144

"One More Time" (Gordon), **II:** 200

One Nation (Stegner), **Supp. IV Part 2:** 599, 608

"One-Night Homecoming" (X. J. Kennedy), **Supp. XV:** 167

"ONE NIGHT STAND" (Baraka), **Supp. II Part 1:** 32

"One of Our Conquerors" (Bourne), **I:** 223

One of Ours (Cather), **I:** 322–323; **Retro. Supp. I:** 1, 3, **13–15,** 20

"One of the Missing" (Bierce), **I:** 201–202

"One of the Rooming Houses of Heaven" (Doty), **Supp. XI:** 131

"One of the Smallest" (Stern), **Supp. IX:** 299–300

"One of Us" (Fante), **Supp. XI:** 165

Oneóta: or, The Red Race of America (H. Schoolcraft), **Supp. XXIII:** 232

"One Out of Twelve: Writers Who Are Women in Our Century" (Olsen), **Supp. XIII:** 294

"One Part Humor, 2 Parts Whining" (Kakutani), **Supp. XI:** 38

"One Person" (Wylie), **Supp. I Part 2:** 709, 724–727

"One Sister have I in our house" (Dickinson), **Retro. Supp. I:** 34

165 Meeting House Lane (Notley), **Supp. XXII:** 224, 225, 226

"One Song, The" (Strand), **Supp. IV Part 2:** 619

"One Summer in Spain" (Coover), **Supp. V:** 40

One That Got Away, The (Everett), **Supp. XVIII:** 54

1000 Airplanes on the Roof (Glass, Hwang, and Sirlin), **Supp. XXI:** 147

One Thousand Avant-Garde Plays (Koch), **Supp. XV:** 187

"One Thousandth, The" (Weigl), **Supp. XIX:** 288

One Time, One Place: Mississippi in the Depression, a Snapshot Album (Welty), **Retro. Supp. I:** 339, 343, 344

1 x 1 (One Times One) (Cummings), **I:** 430, 436, 438–439, 441, 446, 447, 448

"One Touch of Nature" (McCarthy), **II:** 580

One Train (Koch), **Supp. XV:** 177, 184

"One Trip Abroad" (Fitzgerald), **II:** 95

One True Thing (film), **Supp. XVII:** 176

One True Thing (Quindlen), **Supp. XVII:** 166, **174–176**

"One Way" (Creeley), **Supp. IV Part 1:** 150–151

One Way or Another (Cameron), **Supp. XII:** 81

One-Way Ticket (Hughes), **Retro. Supp. I:** 206, 207, 208; **Supp. I Part 1:** 333–334

One Way to Heaven (Cullen), **Supp. IV Part 1:** 170, 172

One Way to Reconstruct the Scene (W. V. Davis), **Supp. XXI:** 83, **88–91**

"One Way to Reconstruct the Scene" (W. V. Davis), **Supp. XXI:** 88–89, 90, 91, 92, 93

One Way to Spell Man (Stegner), **Supp. IV Part 2:** 595, 598, 601, 609

"One Way to Spell Man" (Stegner), **Supp. IV Part 2:** 601

One Whose Eyes Open When You Close Your Eyes, The (F. Wright), **Supp. XVII:** 240, 243

"One Who Skins Cats, The" (Gunn Allen), **Supp. IV Part 1:** 331

"One Who Went Forth to Feel Fear" (Grimms), **Supp. X:** 86

"One Winter I Devise a Plan of My Own" (Ríos), **Supp. IV Part 2:** 549

One Winter Night in August (X. J. Kennedy), **Supp. XV:** 154, 162

One World at a Time (Kooser), **Supp. XIX:** 116, **122–123**

One Writer's Beginnings (Welty), **Retro. Supp. I:** 339, 340, 341, 343, 344, 355–356

"One Year" (Olds), **Supp. X:** 210

On Fire (L. Brown), **Supp. XXI:** 41, **48–49**

"On First Looking Into Chapman's Homer" (Keats), **Supp. XXI:** 64

"On First Looking Out through Juan de la Cosa's Eyes" (Olson), **Supp. II Part 2:** 565, 566, 570, 579

"On First Opening *The Lyric Year*" (W. C. Williams), **Retro. Supp. I:** 414

"On Freedom's Ground" (Wilbur), **Supp. III Part 2:** 562

On Glory's Course (Purdy), **Supp. VII:** 275–276, 279, 280

On Grief and Reason (Brodsky), **Supp. VIII: 31–32**

"On Hearing a Symphony of Beethoven" (Millay), **III:** 132–133

"On Hearing the Airlines Will Use a Psychological Profile to Catch Potential Skyjackers" (Dunn), **Supp. XI:** 144–145

On Human Finery (Bell), **Supp. I Part 2:** 636

"On *Imagerie:* Esther Williams, 1944" (Sobin), **Supp. XVI:** 294

"On Imagination" (Wheatley), **Supp. XX: 281**

"On Imminence: An Essay" (Sobin), **Supp. XVI:** 291

On Kingdom Mountain (Mosher), **Supp. XXII:** 203, 205, 206, 207, 208, 209, 212, 214, **216**

Onkl Mozes (Uncle Moses) (Asch), **Supp. XXIII:** 5

"On leaving my children John and Jane at School, in the Atlantic states, and preparing to return to the interior"(J. Schoolcraft), **Supp. XXIII:** 227, 228, 232, 233, 235, 236

On Liberty (Mill), **Supp. XI:** 196

"On Looking Alone at a Place" (M. F. K. Fisher), **Supp. XVII:** 91

"On Looking at a Copy of Alice Meynell's Poems, Given Me, Years Ago, by a Friend" (Lowell), **II:** 527–528

"On Lookout Mountain" (Hayden), **Supp. II Part 1:** 380

Only a Few of Us Left (Marquand), **III:** 55

"Only Animal, The" (F. Wright), **Supp. XVII:** 245

"Only a Pawn in Their Game" (song, Dylan), **Supp. XVIII:** 24

Only as Far as Brooklyn (Kenny), **Supp. XXIII: 148–151,** 152

"Only Bar in Dixon, The" (Hugo), **Supp. VI:** 140, 141

Only Dangerous Thing, The (Di Piero), **Supp. XIX: 37–38**

Only Dark Spot in the Sky, The (Dove), **Supp. IV Part 1:** 244

"Only Good Indian, The" (Humphrey), **Supp. IX:** 101

"Only Goodness" (Lahiri), **Supp. XXI:** 186, 188

Only in America (Golden), **Supp. VIII:** 244

"Only in the Dream" (Eberhart), **I:** 523

"Only Path to Tomorrow, The" (Rand), **Supp. IV Part 2:** 524

"Only Rose, The" (Jewett), **II:** 408

"Only Son of the Doctor, The" (Gordon), **Supp. IV Part 1:** 305, 306

"Only the Cat Escapes", **Supp. XII:** 150–151

"Only the Dead Know Brooklyn" (Wolfe), **IV:** 451

"Only When I Am Quiet and Do Not Speak"(Hirshfield), **Supp. XXIII:** 133

Only When I Laugh (Simon), **Supp. IV Part 2:** 575

Only World, The (Hull), **Supp. XXI:** 129, **138–141**

"On Meditation"(J. Schoolcraft), **Supp. XXIII:** 229

"On Messrs. Hussey and Coffin" (Wheatley), **Supp. XX: 280**

On Moral Fiction (Gardner), **Supp. VI:** 61, **71,** 72, 73

"On Morality" (Didion), **Supp. IV Part 1:** 196

"On Mt. Philo in November" (Di Piero), **Supp. XIX:** 37, 39

"On My Own" (Levine), **Supp. V:** 181, 189–190

"On My Own Work" (Wilbur), **Supp. III Part 2:** 541–542

On Native Grounds: An Interpretation of Modern American Prose Literature (Kazin), **I:** 517; **Supp. I Part 2:** 650; **Supp. VIII:** 93, 96–97, 98, **100–102**

"On Not Being a Dove" (Updike), **Retro. Supp. I:** 323

"On Open Form" (Merwin), **Supp. III Part 1:** 347–348, 353

On Photography (Sontag), **Supp. III Part 2:** 451, 458, 462–465

"On Poetry"(Hadas), **Supp. XXIII:** 115, 116

"On Political Poetry" (R. Bly), **Supp. IV Part 1:** 61

On Politics: A Carnival of Buncombe (Moos, ed.), **III:** 116

"On Pretentiousness" (Kushner), **Supp. IX:** 131–132

"On Quitting a Little College" (Stafford), **Supp. XI:** 321

"On Reading Eckerman's Conversations with Goethe" (Masters), **Supp. I Part 2:** 458

On Reading Shakespeare (L. P. Smith), **Supp. XIV:** 345–346

"On Reading to Oneself" (Gass), **Supp. VI:** 88, 89

"On Recollection" (Wheatley), **Supp. XX: 287**

On Revolution (Arendt), **Retro. Supp. I:** 87

On Second Thought (Kenny), **Supp. XXIII:** 144

"On Seeing Larry Rivers's *Washington Crossing the Delaware* at the Museum of Modern Art" (O'Hara), **Supp. XV:** 186; **Supp. XXIII:** 208, 214

"On Seeing Red" (Walker), **Supp. III Part 2:** 527

"On Social Plays" (A. Miller), **III:** 147, 148, 159

"On Steinbeck's Story 'Flight' " (Stegner), **Supp. IV Part 2:** 596

"On Style" (Sontag), **Supp. III Part 2:** 456–459, 465–466

"On Suicide" (Hay), **Supp. XIV:** 130, 132

"On Teaching the Young Laurel to Shoot" (Bynner), **Supp. XV:** 50

"On the Antler" (Proulx), **Supp. VII:** 252–253

"On the Avenue" (Espaillat), **Supp. XXI:** 112

On the Banks of Plum Creek (L. I. Wilder), **Supp. XXII:** 294, 299

"On the Banks of the Wabash" (Paul Dresser), **Retro. Supp. II:** 94

"On the Beach, at Night" (Whitman), **IV:** 348

"On the Bosom of This Grave and Wasted Land I Will Lay My Head" (Ray), **Supp. XVIII:** 189

On the Boundary (Tillich), **Retro. Supp. I:** 326

"On the Building of Springfield" (Lindsay), **Supp. I Part 2:** 381

"On the Coast of Maine" (Hayden), **Supp. II Part 1:** 381

On the Contrary: Articles of Belief (McCarthy), **II:** 559, 562

"On the Death of a Friend's Child" (Lowell), **Supp. I Part 2:** 409

"On the Death of Cardinal Tisserant" (Bronk), **Supp. XXI:** 32

"On the Death of General Wooster" (Wheatley), **Supp. XX: 287**

"On the Death of Rev. Mr. George Whitefield—1770" (Wheatley), **Supp. XX: 280,Supp. XX: 282–283**

"On the Death of Senator Thomas J. Walsh" (Winters), **Supp. II Part 2:** 802, 806

"On the Death of Yeats" (Bogan), **Supp. III Part 1:** 59

"On the Death of Zhukov" (Brodsky), **Supp. VIII:** 27

"On the Disadvantages of Central Heating" (Clampitt), **Supp. IX:** 41, 47, 52

"On the Doric Rock, Lake Superior"(J. Schoolcraft), **Supp. XXIII:** 232

On the Drumhead: A Selection from the Writing of Mike Quin (Carlisle, ed.), **Supp. XVIII:** 223, 226

"On the Edge" (Levine), **Supp. V:** 181–182

On the Edge and Over (Levine), **Supp. V:** 178, 180–182, 186

On the Edge of the Great Rift: Three Novels of Africa (Theroux), **Supp. VIII:** 316

"On the Edge of Visible Light"(Schott), **Supp. XXIII:** 242

"On the Eve of the Feast of the Immaculate Conception, 1942" (Lowell), **II:** 538; **Retro. Supp. II:** 185

"On the Eyes of an SS Officer" (Wilbur), **Supp. III Part 2:** 548

"On the Failure of Meaning in the Absence of Objective Analogs" (Bronk), **Supp. XXI:** 31

"On the Fall of General Earl Cornwallis" (Freneau), **Supp. II Part 1:** 261

"On the Folly of Writing Poetry" (Freneau), **Supp. II Part 1:** 263

On the Frontier (Auden and Isherwood), **Supp. II Part 1:** 13; **Supp. XIV:** 163

On the Great Atlantic Rainway: Selected Poems, 1950–1988 (Koch), **Supp. XV:** 177

"On the History of Poetry" (Halliday), **Supp. XIX:** 88, 89

"On the Hysterical Playground" (Watman), **Supp. XX: 93**

"On the Island" (Stern), **Supp. IX:** 290

"On the Late Eclipse" (Bryant), **Supp. I Part 1:** 152

On the Laws of the Poetic Art (Hecht), **Supp. X:** 58

On the Line (Swados), **Supp. XIX: 258–260**

"On the Line" (Swados), **Supp. XIX:** 259

"On the Marginal Way" (Wilbur), **Supp. III Part 2:** 558, 559

On the Mesa (Nichols), **Supp. XIII:** 268

"On the Moon and Matriarchal Consciousness" (Neumann), **Supp. IV Part 1:** 68

"On the Morning after the Sixties" (Didion), **Supp. IV Part 1:** 205, 206

On the Motion and Immobility of Douve (Bonnefoy; Kinnell, trans.), **Supp. III Part 1:** 235

"On the Mullica"(Schott), **Supp. XXIII:** 253

"On the Murder of Lieutenant José del Castillo by the Falangist Bravo Martinez, July 12, 1936" (Levine), **Supp. V:** 187

"On the Night of a Friend's Wedding" (Robinson), **III:** 524

"On the Occasion of a Poem: Richard Hugo" (Wright), **Supp. III Part 2:** 596

On the Occasion of My Last Afternoon (Gibbons), **Supp. X:** 46, **50–53**

On the Origin of Species (Darwin), **Supp. XIV:** 192

"On the Parapet" (Tanner), **Retro. Supp. II:** 205

"On the Platform" (Nemerov), **III:** 287

On the Poetry of Philip Levine: Stranger to Nothing (Levis), **Supp. XI:** 257

"On the Pottlecombe Cornice" (Sturgis), **Supp. XX: 233, 240**

"On the Powers of the Human Understanding" (Freneau), **Supp. II Part 1:** 274

On the Prejudices, Predilections, and Firm Beliefs of William Faulkner (Brooks), **Supp. XIV:** 13

"On the Pulse of Morning" (Angelou), **Supp. IV Part 1:** 15–17

"On the Railway Platform" (Jarrell), **II:** 370

"On the Rainy River" (O'Brien), **Supp. V:** 250

On the Rebound: A Story and Nine Poems (Purdy), **Supp. VII:** 276–277

"On the Religion of Nature" (Freneau), **Supp. II Part 1:** 275

"On the River" (Dunbar), **Supp. II Part 1:** 193

"On the River" (Levine), **Supp. V:** 193

On the River Styx and Other Stories (Matthiessen), **Supp. V:** 212

On the Road (Kerouac), **Retro. Supp. I:** 102; **Supp. III Part 1:** 92, 218, 222–224, 226, 230–231; **Supp. V:** 336; **Supp. X:** 269; **Supp. XIII:** 275; **Supp. XIV:** 138, 150; **Supp. XV:** 221; **Supp. XVIII:** 20, 138; **Supp. XXI:** 53

"On the Road Home" (Stevens), **Retro. Supp. I:** 306

On the Road with the Archangel (Buechner), **Supp. XII:** 54

"On the Rope" (Richard), **Supp. XIX:** 211–212

On These I Stand: An Anthology of the Best Poems of Countee Cullen (Cullen), **Supp. IV Part 1:** 173

"On the Skeleton of a Hound" (Wright), **Supp. III Part 2:** 593

"On the Staten Island Ferry"(Kenny), **Supp. XXIII:** 154

"On the Street" (Peacock), **Supp. XIX:** 199

"On the Street: Monument" (Gunn Allen), **Supp. IV Part 1:** 326

"On the Subway" (Olds), **Supp. X:** 207

"On the System of Policy Hitherto Pursued by Their Government" (Barlow), **Supp. II Part 1:** 82

"On the Teaching of Modern Literature" (Trilling), **Supp. III Part 2:** 509–510

"On the Uniformity and Perfection of Nature" (Freneau), **Supp. II Part 1:** 275

"On the Universality and Other Attributes of the God of Nature" (Freneau), **Supp. II Part 1:** 275

"On the Use of Trisyllabic Feet in Iambic Verse" (Bryant), **Supp. I Part 1:** 156

On the Verge: Emerging Poets (Ellis and Lease, eds.), **Supp. XXI:** 246

On the Waterfront (film, Kazan), **Supp. XVIII: 250–251,** 252, 253

"On the Way Home" (L. I. Wilder), **Supp. XXII:** 292

"On the Way to the San Remo"(O'Hara), **Supp. XXIII:** 212, 219

On the Way toward a Phenomenological Psychology: The Psychology of William James (Linschoten), **II:** 362

"On the Way to Work" (Dunn), **Supp. XI:** 149–150

"On the Wide Heath" (Millay), **III:** 130

"On the Writing of Novels" (Buck), **Supp. II Part 1:** 121

On the Yard (Braly), **Supp. XVIII:** 147

On This Island (Auden), **Supp. II Part 1:** 11

"On Time" (O'Hara), **III:** 369–370

"Ontological Episode of the Asylum" (Carruth), **Supp. XVI:** 48, 50

"Ontology of the Sentence, The" (Gass), **Supp. VI:** 77

"On Top" (Leopold), **Supp. XIV:** 188

"On Top" (Snyder), **Supp. VIII:** 304

"On Translating Akhmatova" (Kunitz), **Supp. III Part 1:** 268

"On Turning Ten" (Collins), **Supp. XXI:** 64

"On Waking to Old Debts" (Keillor), **Supp. XVI:** 167

On William Stafford: The Worth of Local Things (Andrews, ed.), **Supp. XI:** 311, 312, 317, 321, 324, 326

"On Writing" (Carver), **Supp. III Part 1:** 142–143

"On Writing" (Nin), **Supp. X:** 182

Opatoshu, Joseph, **IV:** 9

"Open Boat, The" (Crane), **I:** 408, 415, 416–417, 423; **Retro. Supp. I:** 325; **Supp. XIV:** 51

Open Boat and Other Stories (Crane), **I:** 408

Open Door, The (Skloot), **Supp. XX: 194, 196, 208**

Open Heart: A Patient's Story of Life-Saving Medicine and Life-Giving Friendship (Neugeboren), **Supp. XVI:** 217, **229–230**

Open House (Roethke), **III:** 529–530, 540

"Open House" (Roethke), **III:** 529

"Opening, An" (Swenson), **Supp. IV Part 2:** 639

Opening of the Field, The (Duncan), **Supp. III Part 2:** 625

Opening the Hand (Merwin), **Supp. III Part 1:** 341, 353, 355

"Open Letter" (Roethke), **III:** 532, 534

"Open Letter to Surrealists Everywhere, An" (H. Miller), **III:** 184

Open Meeting, The (Gurney), **Supp. V:** 98

Open Net (Plimpton), **Supp. XVI:** 241

"Open Road, The" (Dreiser), **II:** 44

Open Sea, The (Masters), **Supp. I Part 2:** 471

Open Season: Sporting Adventures (Humphrey), **Supp. IX:** 95

"Open Secret" (Nelson), **Supp. XVIII:** 185

"Open the Gates" (Kunitz), **Supp. III Part 1:** 264–265, 267

"Opera Company, The" (Merrill), **Supp. III Part 1:** 326

Operating Instructions: A Journal of My Son's First Year (Lamott), **Supp. XX: 136–137, 142**

"Operation, The" (Sanders), **Supp. XVI:** 266

"Operation, The" (Sexton), **Supp. II Part 2:** 675, 679

Operation Shylock: A Confession (P. Roth), **Retro. Supp. II:** 279, 280, 291

Operation Sidewinder (Shepard), **Supp. III Part 2:** 434–435, 439, 446–447

Operations in North African Waters (Morison), **Supp. I Part 2:** 490

Operation Wandering Soul (Powers), **Supp. IX:** 212, **217–219**

Opffer, Emil, **Retro. Supp. II:** 80

"Opinion" (Du Bois), **Supp. II Part 1:** 173

Opinionator, The (Bierce), **I:** 209

Opinions of Oliver Allston (Brooks), **I:** 254, 255, 256

O Pioneers! (Cather), **I:** 314, 317–319, 320; **Retro. Supp. I:** 1, 5, 6, **7–9,** 10, 13, 20; **Retro. Supp. II:** 136

Oppen, George, **IV:** 415; **Supp. III Part 2:** 614, 615, 616, 626, 628; **Supp. XIV:** 285, 286, 287; **Supp. XVI:** 282, 283; **Supp. XVII:** 243; **Supp. XXI:** 19,**Supp. XXI:** 29, 23; **Supp. XXIII:** 165–166, 168

Oppenheim, James, **I:** 106, 109, 239, 245; **Supp. XV:** 294, 296, 298, 299, 301, 302, 307, 313; **Supp. XX:** 68

Oppenheimer, J. Robert, **I:** 137, 492

Oppenheimer, Judy, **Supp. IX:** 115, 116, 118, 120, 126

"Opportunity for American Fiction, An" (Howells), **Supp. I Part 2:** 645–646

Opposing Self, The (Trilling), **Supp. III Part 2:** 506–507

"Opposition" (Lanier), **Supp. I Part 1:** 368, 373

Oprah's Roots: An African American Lives Special (television production), **Supp. XX:** 99

Opticks: A Poem in Seven Sections (Goldbarth), **Supp. XII:** 177, **178**

Optimist's Daughter, The (Welty), **IV:** 261, 280; **Retro. Supp. I:** 339, 355

"Optimist's Daughter, The" (Welty), **IV:** 280–281

Options (O. Henry), **Supp. II Part 1:** 410

Opus Posthumous (Stevens), **IV:** 76, 78

Opus Posthumous (W. Stevens), **Supp. XVII:** 241

Oracle at Stoneleigh Court, The (Taylor), **Supp. V:** 328

Orage, Alfred, **III:** 473

"O/Rain-in-the-Face"(Kenny), **Supp. XXIII:** 156

Orange, Max (pseudonym). *See* Heller, Joseph

Orange Fish, The (Shields), **Supp. VII:** 318, 320, 323, 328

Orangery, The (Sorrentino), **Supp. XXI:** 228

Oranges (exhibition, Hartigan), **Supp. XXIII:** 210

Oranges (McPhee), **Supp. III Part 1:** 298–299, 301, 309

Oranges: 12 Pastorals (O'Hara), **Supp. XXIII:** 210

"Oranging of America, The" (Apple), **Supp. XVII:** 3–4, 6

Oranging of America and Other Short Stories, The (Apple), **Supp. XVII:** 1–2, **3–4,** 7, 8

Oration Delivered at Washington, July Fourth, 1809 (Barlow), **Supp. II Part 1:** 80, 83

Orations and Addresses (Bryant), **Supp. I Part 1:** 158

Orators, The (Auden), **Supp. II Part 1:** 6, 7, 11, 18–19

Orbach, Jerry, **Supp. XXIII:** 103

Orb Weaver, The (Francis), **Supp. IX: 81–82**

"Orchard" (Doolittle), **Supp. I Part 1:** 263–264, 265, 266

"Orchard" (Eberhart), **I:** 539

Orchard, The (B. Kelly), **Supp. XVII:** 123, 127, **130–133**

"Orchard, The" (B. Kelly), **Supp. XVII:** 133

Orchard Keeper, The (McCarthy), **Supp. VIII: 175–176**

Orchestra (Davies), **III:** 541

"Orchids" (Roethke), **III:** 530–531

"Or Consider Prometheus" (Clampitt), **Supp. IX:** 44

Ordeal of Mansart, The (Du Bois), **Supp. II Part 1:** 185–186

Ordeal of Mark Twain, The (Brooks), **I:** 240, 247, 248; **II:** 482

Ordering the Façade: Photography and Contemporary Southern Women's Writing (Henninger), **Supp. XXI:** 253

"Order of Insects" (Gass), **Supp. VI:** 83

Order Out of Chaos (McPherson), **Supp. IV Part 1:** 2, 12

"Ordinary Afternoon in Charlottesville, An" (Wright), **Supp. V:** 344

"Ordinary Days" (Dunn), **Supp. XI:** 151

"Ordinary Evening in New Haven, An" (Stevens), **IV:** 91–92; **Retro. Supp. I:** 297, 300, 311, 312

Ordinary Heroes (Turow), **Supp. XVII: 221–222,** 223

Ordinary Life (Crooker), **Supp. XXIII: 56**

Ordinary Love (Smiley), **Supp. VI:** 292, **299–300**

Ordinary Love; and Good Will: Two Novellas (Smiley), **Supp. VI:** 292, **299–300**

Ordinary Miracles (Jong), **Supp. V:** 115, 130–131

"Ordinary Time: Virginia Woolf and Thucydides on War" (Carson), **Supp. XII: 111**

"Ordinary Women, The" (Stevens), **IV:** 81

Ordways, The (Humphrey), **Supp. IX:** 95, **98–100,** 109; **Supp. XV:** 353

"Oread" (Doolittle), **II:** 520–521; **Supp. I Part 1:** 265–266

Oregon Message, An (Stafford), **Supp. XI: 328–329**

Oregon Trail, The (Parkman), **II:** 312; **Supp. II Part 2:** 592, 595–596, 598, 606

Oresteia (Aeschylus), **Supp. IX:** 103

"Orestes at Tauris" (Jarrell), **II:** 376, 377

Orfalea, Gregory, **Supp. XIII:** 278

Orfeo ed Euridice (Gluck), **II:** 210, 211

Orff, Carl, **Supp. X:** 63

"Organizer's Wife, The" (Bambara), **Supp. XI:** 8–9

"Organmeister: Hasse After Marienkirche" (Bierds), **Supp. XVII:** 34

"Orgy" (Rukeyser), **Supp. VI:** 280

Orgy, The (Rukeyser), **Supp. VI:** 274, 283

"Orgy of Southerness, An" (Pickering), **Supp. XXI:** 203

"Oriental Rug"(Balakian), **Supp. XXIII:** 23, 24–25

"Orientation of Hope, The" (Locke), **Supp. XIV:** 212–213

Orient Express (Dos Passos), **I:** 480

"Orient Express, The" (Jarrell), **II:** 382, 383–384

Origen, Adamantius, **IV:** 153

"Origin" (Harjo), **Supp. XII:** 219

Original Child Bomb: Points for Meditation to Be Scratched on the Walls of a Cave (Merton), **Supp. VIII:** 203

Original Essays on the Poetry of Anne Sexton (George), **Supp. IV Part 2:** 450

"Original Follies Girl, The" (Z. Fitzgerald), **Supp. IX:** 71

Original Light (Goldbarth), **Supp. XII:** 181, **183–184,** 188

Original Love (Peacock), **Supp. XIX: 199–201,** 206

Original of Laura, The (Nabokov), **Retro. Supp. I:** 266

"Original Sin" (Jeffers), **Supp. II Part 2:** 426

"Original Sin" (Warren), **IV:** 245

Origin: Hawaii (Taggard), **Supp. XXII:** 272, 284

"Origin of Extermination in the Imagination, The" (Gass), **Supp. VI:** 89

Origin of Species, The (Darwin), **II:** 173, 462; **Supp. XVI:** 13

Origin of the Brunists, The (Coover), **Supp. V:** 39, 41, 52

"Origin of the Miscodeed, or the Maid of Taquimenon"(J. Schoolcraft), **Supp. XXIII:** 235

"Origin of the Robin, The"(J. Schoolcraft), **Supp. XXIII:** 234, 235

"Origins and History of Consciousness" (Rich), **Supp. I Part 2:** 570

"Origins of a Nonfiction Writer" (Talese), **Supp. XVII:** 208

"Origins of a Poem" (Levertov), **Supp. III Part 1:** 273

"Origins of the Beat Generation, The" (Kerouac), **Supp. III Part 1:** 231

Origo, Iris, **IV:** 328

"O'Riley's Late-Bloomed Little Son" (X. J. Kennedy), **Supp. XV:** 159

"Orion" (Rich), **Supp. I Part 2:** 557

O'Riordan, Conal Holmes O'Connell, **III:** 465

Orlacs Hände (film, Weine), **Supp. XVII:** 58

Orlando (V. Woolf), **Supp. XVII:** 86

Orlando (Woolf), **Supp. I Part 2:** 718; **Supp. VIII:** 263; **Supp. XII:** 9

Orlando Furioso (Ariosto), **Supp. XV:** 175

Orlik, Emil, **Supp. XXIII:** 6

Orloff, Chana, **Supp. XXIII:** 6

Orlovsky, Peter, **Supp. XII:** 121, 126; **Supp. XIV:** 150; **Supp. XVIII:** 27

Ormonde, Czenzi, **Supp. IV Part 1:** 132

Ormond; or, The Secret Witness (Brown), **Supp. I Part 1:** 133–137

Ornament and Crime (Loos), **Supp. XVI:** 187

Orne, Sarah. *See* Jewett, Sarah Orne

Ornithological Biography; or, An Account of the Habits of the Birds of the United States of America, and Interspersed with Delineations of American Scenery and Manners (Audubon), **Supp. XVI:**13; **7–10**

"Ornithology" (Hull), **Supp. XXI:** 138–139

Ornitz, Samuel, **Supp. IX:** 227; **Supp. XIII:** 166

Ornstein, Leo, **Supp. XX:** 75

O'Rourke, William, **Supp. XXII:** 213

Orphan Angel, The (Wylie), **Supp. I Part 2:** 707, 709, 714, 717, 719–721, 722, 724

Orphan's Tale, An (Neugeboren), **Supp. XVI:** 222, 223

Orpheus (Rukeyser), **Supp. VI:** 273

"Orpheus" (Winters), **Supp. II Part 2:** 801

"Orpheus, Eurydice, Hermes" (Rilke), **Supp. VIII:** 31, 32

"Orpheus (1)" (Atwood), **Supp. XIII:** 35

"Orpheus (2)" (Atwood), **Supp. XIII:** 35

"Orpheus Alone" (Strand), **Supp. IV Part 2:** 632

Orpheus Descending (T. Williams), **IV:** 380, 381, 382, 385, 386, 387, 389, 391–392, 395, 396, 398

Orr, David, **Supp. XXI:** 62

Orr, Peter, **Supp. I Part 2:** 538, 540, 543

Orse, Brian, **Supp. XX:** 264

Ortega y Gasset, José, **I:** 218, 222; **Supp. IV Part 2:** 521; **Supp. XXIII:** 165

Ortiz, Simon J., **Supp. IV Part 1:** 319, 404; **Supp. IV Part 2: 497–515,** 557; **Supp. XII:** 217, 218

"Ortlieb's Uptown Taproom" (Di Piero), **Supp. XIX:** 46, 47

O'Ruddy, The (Crane), **I:** 409, 424

Orwell, George, **I:** 489; **II:** 454, 580; **Supp. I Part 2:** 523, 620; **Supp. II Part 1:** 143; **Supp. IV Part 1:** 236; **Supp. V:** 250; **Supp. VIII:** 241; **Supp. XIV:** 112, 158; **Supp. XVII:** 228, 229; **Supp. XVIII:** 137, 138; **Supp. XX:** 86

Osborn, Dwight, **III:** 218–219, 223

"Osborn Look, The" (Morris), **III:** 221

Osgood, Frances, **Supp. XVII:** 75

Osgood, J. R., **II:** 283

O'Shea, Kitty, **II:** 137

O'Shea, Milo, **Supp. XI:** 308

"Oshkikwe's Baby" (traditional Chippewa story), **Supp. IV Part 1:** 333

Oshogay, Delia, **Supp. IV Part 1:** 333

Ossana, Diana, **Supp. V:** 230–231, 232

Ossian, **Supp. I Part 2:** 491

Ossip, Kathleen, **Supp. X:** 201

"Osso Bucco" (Collins), **Supp. XXI:** 60

Ostanovka v Pustyne (A halt in the wilderness) (Brodsky), **Supp. VIII:** 21

Oster, Judith, **Supp. XVI:** 151

Ostriker, Alicia, **Supp. I Part 2:** 540; **Supp. IV Part 2:** 439, 447, 449; **Supp. X:** 207, 208; **Supp. XI:** 143; **Supp. XV:** 251

Ostrom, Hans, **Retro. Supp. I:** 195

Oswald, Lee Harvey, **III:** 234, 235

Oswald II (DeLillo), **Supp. VI:** 16

Oswald's Tale (Mailer), **Retro. Supp. II:** 212–213

"Otagamiad, The"(J. Schoolcraft), **Supp. XXIII:** 223

O Taste and See (Levertov), **Supp. III Part 1:** 278–279, 281

Othello (Shakespeare), **I:** 284–285

"Other, The" (Sexton), **Supp. II Part 2:** 692

Other America, The (Harrington), **I:** 306

"Other American Renaissance, The" (Tompkins), **Supp. XVIII:** 258

Other Destinies: Understanding the American Indian Novel (Owens), **Supp. IV Part 1:** 404

"Other Frost, The" (Jarrell), **Retro. Supp. I:** 121

Other Gods: An American Legend (Buck), **Supp. II Part 1:** 123, 130–131

Other House, The (James), **Retro. Supp. I:** 229

"Other League of Nations, The" (Ríos), **Supp. IV Part 2:** 552

"Other Margaret, The" (Trilling), **Supp. III Part 2:** 504–505

"Other Miller, The" (Wolff), **Supp. VII:** 343–344

"Other Mothers" (Paley), **Supp. VI:** 225

"Other Night at Columbia, The" (Trilling), **Supp. XII:** 126

"Other People's Secrets" (Hampl), **Supp. XXII:** 94

"Other Robert Frost, The" (Jarrell), **Retro. Supp. I:** 135

Others (Shields), **Supp. VII:** 310

Other Side, The (Gordon), **Supp. IV Part 1:** 299, 306, 307–309, 310–311

Other Side, The/El Otro Lado (Alvarez), **Supp. VII:** 9–12

"Other Side, The"(Hadas), **Supp. XXIII:** 120

Other Side of the River, The (Wright), **Supp. V:** 332–333, 342

"Other Side of the River, The" (Wright), **Supp. V:** 335

"Other Tradition, The" (Ashbery), **Supp. III Part 1:** 15, 18

"Other Two, The" (Wharton), **Retro. Supp. I:** 367

Other Voices, Other Rooms (Capote), **Supp. III Part 1:** 113–118, 121, 123–124

"Other Wanderer, The" (Gibran), **Supp. XX: 124**

"Other War, The" (Cowley), **Supp. II Part 1:** 144

"Otherwise" (Kenyon), **Supp. VII:** 172, 174

Otherwise: New and Selected Poems (Kenyon), **Supp. VII:** 167, 172–174

Otherwise Than Being; or, Beyond Essence (Lévinas), **Supp. XVI:** 290, 291

"Other Woman, The" (Anderson), **I:** 114

"Other World, The" (Wrigley), **Supp. XVIII:** 307

Other Worlds Than This (Hadas), **Supp. XXIII:** 118, **124–125**

Otho the Great: A Tragedy in Five Acts (Keats), **Supp. XII:** 113

Otis, Harrison Gray, **Supp. I Part 2:** 479–481, 483, 486, 488

Otis, James, **III:** 577; **Supp. I Part 2:** 486; **Supp. XV:** 229

O to Be a Dragon (Moore), **III:** 215

Otto, Rudolf, **Supp. XVII:** 243

"Ouija" (McClatchy), **Supp. XII:** 269–270

Oupensky, Peter, **Supp. XIV:** 188

Our America (Michaels), **Retro. Supp. I:** 379

Our America (W. Frank), **I:** 229; **Supp. IX:** 308; **Supp. XX: 69–70, 75**

"Our Assistant's Column" (Twain), **IV:** 193

"Our Bourgeois Literature" (Sinclair), **Supp. V:** 281

Our Brains and What Ails Them (Gilman), **Supp. XI:** 207

Our Century (Wilder), **IV:** 374

"Our Christmas Party" (E. Stoddard), **Supp. XV:** 273, 278

Our Country (Strong), **Supp. XIV:** 64

"Our Countrymen in Chains!" (Whittier), **Supp. I Part 2:** 688

"Our Cultural Humility" (Bourne), **I:** 223, 228

Our Depleted Society (Seymour), **Supp. XIII:** 264

"Our Dust" (Wright), **Supp. XV:** 345, 346

"Our Father Who Drowns the Birds" (Kingsolver), **Supp. VII:** 208–209

"Our First House" (Kingston), **Supp. V:** 169

Our Gang (P. Roth), **Retro. Supp. II:** 287; **Supp. III Part 2:** 414; **Supp. IV Part 1:** 388

"Our Good Day" (Cisneros), **Supp. VII:** 60

Our Ground Time Here Will Be Brief (Kumin), **Supp. IV Part 2:** 450–452

Our House in the Last World (Hijuelos), **Supp. VIII:** 73, **76–79,** 87, 88

"Our Lady" (A. Finch), **Supp. XVII:** 77

"*Our Lady of the Annunciation*/Nuestra Señora de Anunciación" (Mora), **Supp. XIII:** 217, 224, 228

"Our Lady of Troy" (MacLeish), **III:** 3, 20

"Our Limitations" (Holmes), **Supp. I Part 1:** 314

"Our Martyred Soldiers" (Dunbar), **Supp. II Part 1:** 193

"Our Master" (Whittier), **Supp. I Part 2:** 704

"Our Mother Pocahontas" (Lindsay), **Supp. I Part 2:** 393

Our Mr. Wrenn: The Romantic Adventures of a Gentle Man (Lewis), **II:** 441

Our National Parks (Muir), **Supp. IX:** 181, 184

Our New York: A Personal Vision in Words and Photographs (Kazin), **Supp. VIII:** 106–107

Our Nig (Wilson), **Supp. XX: 105**

"Our Old Aunt Who Is Now in a Retirement Home" (Shields), **Supp. VII:** 310

Our Old Home: A Series of English Sketches (Hawthorne), **II:** 225; **Retro. Supp. I:** 163

"Our Own Movie Queen" (Z. Fitzgerald), **Supp. IX:** 71

"Our River Now" (L.-Y. Lee), **Supp. XV:** 224, 225

Our Selves (Bronk), **Supp. XXI:** 32

Ourselves to Know (O'Hara), **III:** 362, 365

Our Sister Killjoy: or, Reflections from a Black-Eyed Squint (Aidoo), **Supp. XXII:** 68

"Our Story Begins" (Wolff), **Supp. VII:** 345

"Our Sweating Selves" (Di Piero), **Supp. XIX:** 36

Our Town (Wilder), **IV:** 357, 364, 365, 366, 368–369

"Our Unplanned Cities" (Bourne), **I:** 229, 230

Our Wonder World, **Retro. Supp. I:** 341

Ouspensky, P. D., **I:** 383; **Supp. XX: 116**

"Out" (Harjo), **Supp. XII:** 219

"'Out, Out' " (Frost), **Retro. Supp. I:** 131

"Outcast" (McKay), **Supp. X:** 135

"Outcasts of Poker Flats, The" (Harte), **Supp. II Part 1:** 345, 347–348

Outcroppings (Harte), **Supp. II Part 1:** 343

Out Cry (T. Williams), **IV:** 383, 393

Outcry, The (James), **Retro. Supp. I:** 235

"Outdoor Shower" (Olds), **Supp. X:** 214

Outer Banks (Siddons), **Supp. XXII:** 239

Outerbridge Reach (Stone), **Supp. V:** 306–308

Outer Dark (McCarthy), **Supp. VIII: 176–177**

Outermost Dream, The: Essays and Reviews (Maxwell), **Supp. VIII: 171–172**

"Outing, The" (Baldwin), **Supp. I Part 1:** 63

"Out Like a Lamb" (Dubus), **Supp. VII:** 91

"Outline of an Autobiography" (Toomer), **Supp. III Part 2:** 478

Outlyer and Ghazals (Harrison), **Supp. VIII:** 41

"Out of Business" (Mora), **Supp. XIII:** 217

Out of Eden: Essays on Modern Art (Di Piero), **Supp. XIX:** 41, 42

"Out of My Deeper Heart" (Gibran), **Supp. XX: 118**

Out of My League (Plimpton), **Supp. XVI:** 233, 239

"Out of Nowhere into Nothing" (Anderson), **I:** 113

"Out of Season" (Hemingway), **II:** 263

"Out of the Cradle Endlessly Rocking" (Whitman), **IV:** 342, 343–345, 346, 351; **Retro. Supp. I:** 404, 406

"Out of the Deeps" (E. Stoddard), **Supp. XV:** 286

"Out of the Hospital and Under the Bar" (Ellison), **Retro. Supp. II:** 118–119; **Supp. II Part 1:** 246

"Out of the Rainbow End" (Sandburg), **III:** 594–595

"Out of the Sea, Early" (Swenson), **Supp. IV Part 2:** 645

"Out of the Snow" (Dubus), **Supp. VII:** 91

Out of the Stars (Purdy), **Supp. VII:** 281–282

"Out of the Woods" (Offutt), **Supp. XIX:** 169–170

Out of the Woods: Stories (Offutt), **Supp. XIX:** 163, 167, **169–172,** 175

"Out of Your Nakedness, Out of My Nakedness"(Hadas), **Supp. XXIII:** 125

"Outrageous" (Pickering), **Supp. XXI:** 202

Outre-Mer: A Pilgrimage beyond the Sea (Longfellow), **II:** 313, 491; **Retro. Supp. II:** 155, 165

"Outside" (Stafford), **Supp. XI:** 318

Outside, The (Glaspell), **Supp. III Part 1:** 179, 187

"Outside In" (Pickering), **Supp. XXI:** 197

Outsider, The (Wright), **IV:** 478, 481, 488, 491–494, 495

Outside World, The (Mirvis), **Supp. XX:** **177, 178, 185–190**

Out Went the Candle (Swados), **Supp. XIX:** 257

Out West (Shanley), **Supp. XIV:** 317

"Out with the Old" (Yates), **Supp. XI:** 342

"Ouzo for Robin" (Merrill), **Supp. III Part 1:** 326

"Oval Portrait, The" (Poe), **III:** 412, 415; **Retro. Supp. II:** 270

"Oven Bird, The" (Frost), **Retro. Supp. I:** 131; **Supp. XI:** 153; **Supp. XIX:** 15

"Over 2,000 Illustrations and a Complete Concordance" (Bishop), **Retro. Supp. II:** 45; **Supp. I Part 1:** 90–91

"Over by the River" (Maxwell), **Supp. VIII:** 169, 170

"Overcoat, The" (Gogol), **Supp. XXII:** 59

"Overgrown Pasture, The" (Lowell), **II:** 523

"Overheard through the Walls of the Invisible City" (Bidart), **Supp. XV:** 32

"Over Kansas" (Ginsberg), **Supp. II Part 1:** 320

Overland to the Islands (Levertov), **Supp. III Part 1:** 275, 276

Overlook, The (Connelly), **Supp. XXI:** 78

"Overlooking Lake Champlain" (Di Piero), **Supp. XIX:** 47

"Overnight Pass" (X. J. Kennedy), **Supp. XV:** 168

Overreachers, The (Talese), **Supp. XVII:** 202

"Over-Soul, The" (Emerson), **II:** 7

Over the Blue Mountain (Richter), **Supp. XVIII:** 220

"Over the Edge"(Hadas), **Supp. XXIII:** 115

"Over the Hill" (Dubus), **Supp. VII:** 76, 79–80

Overtime (Gurney), **Supp. V:** 104

"Overwhelming Question, An" (Taylor), **Supp. V:** 323

Ovid, **I:** 62; **II:** 542–543; **III:** 457, 467, 468, 470; **Retro. Supp. I:** 63; **Supp. IV Part 2:** 634; **Supp. XII:** 264

"Ovid in Exile" (Di Piero), **Supp. XIX:** 44

"Ovid's Farewell" (McClatchy), **Supp. XII:** 257–258

Owen, David, **II:** 34

Owen, Maureen, **Supp. IV Part 2:** 423

Owen, Wilfred, **II:** 367, 372; **III:** 524; **Supp. X:** 146; **Supp. XVII:** 245; **Supp. XVIII:** 92; **Supp. XIX:** 17

Owens, Hamilton, **III:** 99, 109

Owens, Louis, **Supp. IV Part 1:** 404

"O Where Are You Going?" (Auden), **Supp. X:** 116

"Owl, The" (Wrigley), **Supp. XVIII:** 297–298, 301

Owl in the Attic, The (Thurber), **Supp. I Part 2:** 614

Owl in the Mask of the Dreamer, The: Collected Poems (Haines), **Supp. XII:** 211

"Owl in the Sarcophagus, The" (Stevens), **Retro. Supp. I:** 300

Owl's Clover (Stevens), **Retro. Supp. I:** 298, **303–304**

"Owl's Clover" (Stevens), **IV:** 75

Owl's Insomnia, Poems by Rafael Alberti, The (Strand, trans.), **Supp. IV Part 2:** 630

Owlstone Crown, The (X. J. Kennedy), **Supp. XV:** 162, **164**

"Owl Who Was God, The" (Thurber), **Supp. I Part 2:** 610

Owning Jolene (Hearon), **Supp. VIII:** **66–67**

"Owning the Masters" (Nelson), **Supp. XVIII:** 171

Oxford Anthology of American Literature, The, **III:** 197; **Supp. I Part 1:** 254

Oxford Book of American Verse (Matthiessen, ed.), **Retro. Supp. I:** 40

Oxford Book of Children's Verse in America, The (Hall, ed.), **Supp. XIV:** 126

Oxford Companion to Twentieth-Century Poetry (Hamilton, ed.), **Supp. XVII:** 243

Oxford History of the American People, The (Morison), **Supp. I Part 2:** 495–496

Oxford History of the United States, 1783–1917, The (Morison), **Supp. I Part 2:** 483–484

"Oxford Town" (song, Dylan), **Supp. XVIII:** 24

Oxherding Tale (Johnson), **Supp. VI:** **190–192,** 193, 194, 196

Oxley, William, **Supp. XV:** 125

"O Yes" (Olsen), **Supp. XIII:** 294, 298, **299–300,** 301

"O Youth and Beauty!" (Cheever), **Retro. Supp. I:** 335

"Oysters" (Sexton), **Supp. II Part 2:** 692

"Ozark Odes" (Wright), **Supp. XV:** 346

Ozick, Cynthia, **Supp. V:** **257–274; Supp. VIII:** 141; **Supp. X:** 192; **Supp. XVII:** 42, 43, 49, 50

O-Zone (Theroux), **Supp. VIII:** 323–324

P

Pace, Patricia, **Supp. XI:** 245

Pacernik, Gary, **Supp. IX:** 287, 291

"Pacific Distances" (Didion), **Supp. IV Part 1:** 211

"Pacific Village" (M. F. K. Fisher), **Supp. XVII:** 83

Pack, Robert, **Supp. IV Part 2:** 621

"Packed Dirt, Churchgoing, a Dying Cat, a Traded Cat" (Updike), **IV:** 219

Packer, Nancy Huddleston, **Supp. XXIII:** 290

"Packing Mother's Things" (C. Frost), **Supp. XV:** 97

Pack of Lies (Sorrentino), **Supp. XXI:** 236, 237

Paco's Story (Heinemann), **Supp. XXII:** 103, **109–114,** 115

Paddock, Joe, **Supp. XVI:** 36

Paddock, Nancy, **Supp. XVI:** 36

Padel, Ruth, **Supp. XII:** 107

Padgett, Ron, **Supp. XV:** 190; **Supp. XXIII:** 218, 221

Padmore, Dorothy, **Supp. XXI:** 166

Padmore, George, **Supp. XXI:** 166

"Paesano with a Trowel" (*Time*), **Supp. XX:** 46

Pafko at the Wall (DeLillo), **Supp. VI:** 4

"Paganini and the Powers of Darkness" (Skloot), **Supp. XX:** **201**

"Pagan Prayer" (Cullen), **Supp. IV Part 1:** 170

"Pagan Rabbi, The" (Ozick), **Supp. V:** 262, 264, 265; **Supp. XVII:** 43

Pagan Rabbi and Other Stories, The (Ozick), **Supp. V:** 260, 261, 263–265

Pagan Spain (Wright), **IV:** 478, 488, 495

Page, Geraldine, **Supp. XV:** 7

Page, Kirby, **III:** 297

Page, Myra, **Supp. XXIII:** 166

Page, Thomas Nelson, **II:** 174, 176, 194; **Supp. XIV:** 61; **Supp. XXII:** 193

Page, Walter Hines, **II:** 174, 175; **Supp. I Part 1:** 370

Page, William, **Supp. XVIII:** 2, 11

Pages from a Cold Island (Exley), **Supp. XXIII:** 97, **103–106,** 108

"Pages from Cold Point" (Bowles), **Supp. IV Part 1:** 85, 86, 87

Paid on Both Sides: A Charade (Auden), **Supp. II Part 1:** 6, 18–19

Paige, Satchel, **Supp. I Part 1:** 234

Paige, T. D. D., **III:** 475

"Pail, The" (R. Bly), **Supp. XXI:** 85

Pain, Joseph, **Supp. I Part 2:** 502

Paine, Albert Bigelow, **I:** 249

Paine, Thomas, **I:** 490; **II:** 117, 302; **III:** 17, 148, 219; **Retro. Supp. I:** 390; **Supp. I Part 1:** 231; **Supp. I Part 2:** 501–525; **Supp. XI:** 55

"Pain has an Element of Blank" (Dickinson), **Retro. Supp. I:** 44

"Painstaking Historian, The" (Skloot), **Supp. XX: 205–206**

"Paint and Powder" (Z. Fitzgerald), **Supp. IX:** 71

Painted Bird, The (Kosinski), **Supp. VII:** 215–217, 219–221, 222, 227

Painted Desert (F. Barthelme), **Supp. XI:** 28–29, 32

Painted Dresses (Hearon), **Supp. VIII: 63**

"Painted Head" (Ransom), **III:** 491, 494; **Supp. II Part 1:** 103, 314

Painted Turtle: Woman with Guitar (Major), **Supp. XXII: 178–180,** 182

Painted Word, The (Wolfe), **Supp. III Part 2:** 580–581, 584; **Supp. XV:** 143

Painter, Pamela, **Supp. XXIII:** 295

"Painter, The" (Ashbery), **Supp. III Part 1:** 5–6, 13

Painter Dreaming in the Scholar's House, The (Nemerov), **III:** 269

"Painters" (Rukeyser), **Supp. VI:** 281

"Painting a Mountain Stream" (Nemerov), **III:** 275

"Pair a Spurs" (Proulx), **Supp. VII:** 263–264

"Pair of Bright Blue Eyes, A" (Taylor), **Supp. V:** 321

"Pajamas" (Olds), **Supp. X:** 206

Pakula, Alan, **Supp. XIII:** 264

Palace at 4 A.M. (Giacometti), **Supp. VIII:** 169

Palahniuk, Chuck, **Supp. XXI:** 116

"Palantine, The" (Whittier), **Supp. I Part 2:** 694, 696

Palatella, John, **Retro. Supp. II:** 48

"Palatski Man, The"(Dybek), **Supp. XXIII:** 70

Pale Fire (Nabokov), **III:** 244, 246, 252, 263–265; **Retro. Supp. I:** 264, 265, 266, 270, 271, 272, 276, 278, 335; **Supp. V:** 251, 253; **Supp. XXII:** 260

"Pale Horse, Pale Rider" (Porter), **III:** 436, 437, 441–442, 445, 446, 449

Pale Horse, Pale Rider: Three Short Novels (Porter), **III:** 433, 436–442; **Supp. VIII:** 157

"Pale Pink Roast, The" (Paley), **Supp. VI:** 217

"Pale Rider" (B. Kelly), **Supp. XVII:** 132–133

Paley, Grace, **Supp. VI: 217–233; Supp. IX:** 212; **Supp. X:** 79, 164; **Supp. XII:** 309; **Supp. XXI:** 118; **Supp. XXII:** 172

Paley, William, **II:** 9

Palgrave, Francis Turner, **Retro. Supp. I:** 124; **Supp. XIV:** 340

Palgrave's Golden Treasury (Palgrave), **IV:** 405

Palimpsest (Doolittle), **Supp. I Part 1:** 259, 268, 269, 270–271

Palimpsest (Vidal), **Supp. X:** 186

"Palingenesis" (Longfellow), **II:** 498

Pal Joey (O'Hara), **III:** 361, 367–368

"Pal Joey" stories (O'Hara), **III:** 361

Pallbearers Envying the One Who Rides (Dobyns), **Supp. XIII:** 89

Palm, Edward Frederick, **Supp. XXII:** 103

"Palm, The" (Merwin), **Supp. III Part 1:** 355

Palmer, Charles, **II:** 111

Palmer, Elihu, **Supp. I Part 2:** 520

Palmer, George Herbert, **Supp. XIV:** 197

Palmer, Michael, **Supp. IV Part 2:** 421; **Supp. XVI:** 284; **Supp. XVII:** 240

Palmer, Samuel, **Supp. XV:** 81

Palmerston, Lord, **I:** 15

Palm-of-the-Hand-Stories (Kawabata), **Supp. XV:** 186

"Palm Wine" (McKnight), **Supp. XX: 155**

"Palo Alto: The Marshes" (Hass), **Supp. VI:** 100

Palpable God, A: Thirty Stories Translated from the Bible with an Essay on the Origins and Life of Narrative (Price), **Supp. VI:** 262, 267

Palubinskas, Helen, **Supp. X:** 292

Pamela (Richardson), **Supp. V:** 127; **Supp. XX: 236; Supp. XXII:** 120

Pamela's First Musical (Wasserstein), **Supp. XV:** 333

Panache de bouquets (Komunyakaa; Cadieux, trans.), **Supp. XIII:** 127

Pan-African movement, **Supp. II Part 1:** 172, 175

Pancake, Breece D'J, **Supp. XXIII:** 35

Pandaemonium (Epstein), **Supp. XII:** 161, **172–173**

"Pandora" (Adams), **I:** 5

Pandora: New Tales of Vampires (Rice), **Supp. VII:** 295

Panek, LeRoy, **Supp. XIV:** 27

"Pangolin, The" (Moore), **III:** 210

Panic: A Play in Verse (MacLeish), **III:** 2, 20

Panic in Needle Park (film), **Supp. IV Part 1:** 198

Pankey, Eric, **Supp. XIX:** 44

Pantagruel (Rabelais), **II:** 112

"Pantaloon in Black" (Faulkner), **II:** 71

"Panther, The: A Bedtime Story"(P. Benedict), **Supp. XXIII:** 40

Panther and the Lash, The (Hughes), **Retro. Supp. I:** 204, 211; **Supp. I Part 1:** 342–344, 345–346

"Panthers, The" (Southern), **Supp. XI:** 295

"Panties and the Buddha" (Peacock), **Supp. XIX:** 199

"Pan *versus* Moses" (Ozick), **Supp. V:** 262

"Paolo Castelnuovo" (Everwine), **Supp. XV:** 83–84

"Papa and Mama Dance, The" (Sexton), **Supp. II Part 2:** 688

"Papago II"(Kenny), **Supp. XXIII:** 149–150

"Papago I"(Kenny), **Supp. XXIII:** 149–150

"Papa Who Wakes Up Tired in the Dark" (Cisneros), **Supp. VII:** 62

Pape, Greg, **Supp. V:** 180; **Supp. XIII:** 312; **Supp. XV:** 73

"Paper Covers Rock"(Thompson), **Supp. XXIII:** 291

Paper Doll (Parker), **Supp. XIX:** 184

"Paper Dolls Cut Out of a Newspaper" (Simic), **Supp. VIII:** 282

"Paper House, The" (Mailer), **III:** 42–43

Paper Lion (film, March), **Supp. XVI:** 242

Paper Lion: Confessions of a Last-String Quarterback (Plimpton), **Supp. XVI: 242–243**

Papernick, Jon, **Supp. XVII:** 50

Papers on Literature and Art (Fuller), **Supp. II Part 1:** 292, 299

Papini, Giovanni, **Supp. XVI:** 195; **Supp. XXII:** 159, 161, 163

Papp, Joseph, **Supp. IV Part 1:** 234; **Supp. XXI:** 145

"Paprika Johnson" (Barnes), **Supp. III Part 1:** 33

"Par" (Bausch), **Supp. VII:** 54

"Parable from a Christian" (Notley), **Supp. XXII:** 235

"Parable in the Later Novels of Henry James" (Ozick), **Supp. V:** 257

"Parable of the Gift" (Glück), **Supp. V:** 89

"Parable of the Hostages" (Glück), **Supp. V:** 89

"Parable of the King" (Glück), **Supp. V:** 89

Parable of the Sower (O. Butler), **Supp. XIII: 66–67,** 69

Parable of the Talents (O. Butler), **Supp. XIII:** 61,**Supp. XIII:** 66, **67–69**

"Parable of the Trellis" (Glück), **Supp. V:** 89

Parachutes & Kisses (Jong), **Supp. V:** 115, 123, 125–126, 129

"Paradelle for Susan" (Collins), **Supp. XXI:** 58

"Parade of Painters" (Swenson), **Supp. IV Part 2:** 645

"Paradigm, The" (Tate), **IV:** 128

Paradise (Barthelme), **Supp. IV Part 1:** 52

"Paradise" (Caputo), **Supp. XIX:** 26–27

"Paradise" (Doty), **Supp. XI:** 123

Paradise, Piece by Piece (Peacock), **Supp. XIX:** 193, 194–195, 195–196, **201–202**

Paradise Lost (Milton), **I:** 137; **II:** 168, 549; **IV:** 126; **Supp. XII:** 173, 297; **Supp. XV:** 181; **Supp. XX: 280**

Paradise Lost (Odets), **Supp. II Part 2:** 530, 531, 538–539, 550

"Paradise of Bachelors and the Tartarus of Maids, The" (Melville), **III:** 91

Paradise of Bombs, The (Sanders), **Supp. XVI:** 265, 272 273

Paradise Poems (Stern), **Supp. IX: 293–294,** 295

Paradiso (Dante), **Supp. IX:** 50

"Paradoxes and Oxymorons" (Ashbery), **Supp. III Part 1:** 23–24

Paradox of Progressive Thought, The (Noble), **Supp. I Part 2:** 650

Paragon, The (Knowles), **Supp. XII:** 249

"Paragraphs" (Carruth), **Supp. XVI:** 52–53

"Parameters" (Dunn), **Supp. XI:** 154

"Para Mi Tataranieto El Astropionero" (Espaillat), **Supp. XXI:** 104

"Paraphrase" (Crane), **I:** 391–392, 393
"Pardon, The" (Wilbur), **Supp. III Part 2:** 544, 550
Paredes, Américo, **Supp. XIII:** 225; **Supp. XIX:** 97, 98, 100
Paredes, Raymund A., **Supp. XIII:** 320, 321
"Parentage" (Stafford), **Supp. XI:** 321, 322
Parentheses: An Autobiographical Journey (Neugeboren), **Supp. XVI:** 217, 218, 219, 221, 226
"Parents" (F. Barthelme), **Supp. XI:** 34
"Parents Taking Shape" (Karr), **Supp. XI:** 243
"Parents' Weekend: Camp Kenwood" (Kenyon), **Supp. VII:** 169
Pareto, Vilfredo, **II:** 577
Paretsky, Sara, **Supp. IV Part 2:** 462; **Supp. XIV:** 26
Parini, Jay, **Supp. X:** 17; **Supp. XIX:** 120, 129; **Supp. XX: 243; Supp. XXI:** 192; **Supp. XXII:** 205
"Paris" (Collins), **Supp. XXI:** 60
"Paris" (Stern), **Supp. IX:** 300
"Paris, 7 A.M." (Bishop), **Retro. Supp. II:** 41, 42; **Supp. I Part 1:** 85, 89
Paris, Bob, **Supp. XX: 264**
Paris, Paris (Shaw), **Supp. XIX:** 240
Paris France (Stein), **IV:** 45
Park, Ed, **Supp. XXII:** 255
Park, Robert, **IV:** 475
"Park Bench" (Hughes), **Supp. I Part 1:** 331–332
Park City (Beattie), **Supp. V:** 24, 35–36
"Park City" (Beattie), **Supp. V:** 35
Parker, Charlie, **Supp. I Part 1:** 59; **Supp. X:** 240, 242, 246; **Supp. XIII:** 129
Parker, Dorothy, **Retro. Supp. II:** 327; **Supp. IV Part 1:** 353; **Supp. IX:** 62, 114, **189–206; Supp. X:** 164; **Supp. XI:** 28; **Supp. XVIII:** 242, 246, 252
Parker, Emily, **Supp. XVIII:** 102
Parker, Idella, **Supp. X:** 232, 234–235
Parker, Joan, **Supp. XIX:** 187
Parker, Lonnae O'Neal, **Supp. XXIII:** 276
Parker, Muriel, **Supp. IX:** 232
Parker, Patricia, **Supp. XV:** 242
Parker, Robert B., **Supp. IV Part 1:** 135, 136; **Supp. XIX: 177–192**
Parker, Robert Dale, **Supp. XXIII:** 223, 228, 229
Parker, Theodore, **Supp. I Part 1:** 38; **Supp. I Part 2:** 518
Parker, Thomas, **Supp. I Part 1:** 102
"Parker's Back" (O'Connor), **III:** 348, 352, 358
"Parkersburg" (Halliday), **Supp. XIX:** 92
Parkes, Henry Bamford, **Supp. I Part 2:** 617
Park-Fuller, Linda, **Supp. XIII:** 297
Parkman, Francis, **II:** 278, 310, 312; **IV:** 179, 309; **Supp. I Part 2:** 420, 479, 481–482, 486, 487, 493, 498; **Supp. II Part 2:** 589–616
Parkman Reader, The (Morison, ed.), **Supp. I Part 2:** 494
Parks, Gordon, Sr., **Supp. XI:** 17

Parks, Larry, **Supp. I Part 1:** 295
Parks, Rosa, **Supp. I Part 1:** 342
"Park Street Cemetery, The" (Lowell), **II:** 537, 538
Par le Détroit (cantata) (Bowles), **Supp. IV Part 1:** 82
Parliament of Fowls, The (Chaucer), **III:** 492
Parmenides (Plato), **II:** 10
Parnassus (Emerson), **II:** 8, 18
Parnell, Charles Stewart, **II:** 129, 137
Parole (film), **Supp. XIII:** 166
Parole Fixer (film), **Supp. XIII:** 170
Parrington, Vernon Louis, **I:** 254, 517, 561; **III:** 335, 606; **IV:** 173; **Supp. I Part 2:** 484, 640
Parrish, Dillwyn, **Supp. XVII:** 83–84, 90
Parrish, Robert, **Supp. XI:** 307
"Parrot, The" (Merrill), **Supp. III Part 1:** 320
"Parsley" (Dove), **Supp. IV Part 1:** 245, 246
Parson, Annie, **Supp. I Part 2:** 655
Parsons, Elsie Clews, **I:** 231, 235
Parsons, Ian, **Supp. IX:** 95
Parsons, Louella, **Supp. XII:** 173
Parsons, Talcott, **Supp. I Part 2:** 648
Parsons, Theophilus, **II:** 396, 504; **Retro. Supp. II:** 134; **Supp. I Part 1:** 155
"Parthian Shot, The" (Hammett), **Supp. IV Part 1:** 343
Partial Glossary, A (Bronk), **Supp. XXI:** 26
Partial Payments: Essays on Writers and Their Lives (Epstein), **Supp. XIV:** 111
Partial Portraits (James), **II:** 336
"Partial Relief" (Halliday), **Supp. XIX:** 91
Partial Truth (Nelson), **Supp. XVIII: 175–176,** 178
"Particulars" (Pickering), **Supp. XXI:** 197
Parties (Van Vechten), **Supp. II Part 2:** 739, 747–749
"Parting" (Kunitz), **Supp. III Part 1:** 263
"Parting Gift" (Wylie), **Supp. I Part 2:** 714
"Parting Glass, The" (Freneau), **Supp. II Part 1:** 273
"Partings" (Hogan), **Supp. IV Part 1:** 413
Partington, Blanche, **I:** 199
Partisans (Matthiessen), **Supp. V:** 201
"Partner, The" (Roethke), **III:** 541–542
Partners, The (Auchincloss), **Supp. IV Part 1:** 31, 34
Partners in Crime: A Rafe Buenrostro Mystery (Hinojosa), **Supp. XIX: 107–108**
"Part of a Letter" (Wilbur), **Supp. III Part 2:** 551
Part of a Long Story: Eugene O'Neill as a Young Man in Love (Boulton), **Supp. XXII:** 18, 21, 27–30
Part of Speech, A (Brodsky), **Supp. VIII:** 22
"Part of the Bee's Body Embedded in the Flesh, The" (C. Frost), **Supp. XV:** 105, 107

"Part of the Story" (Dobyns), **Supp. XIII:** 79
Part of Vermont, A (Taggard), **Supp. XXII:** 284
Parton, Sara, **Retro. Supp. I:** 246
Partridge, Jeffrey F., **Supp. XV:** 219
Partridge, John, **II:** 110, 111
"Parts of a Journal" (Gordon), **Supp. IV Part 1:** 310
Parts of a World (Stevens), **Retro. Supp. I: 305–306,** 307, 309, 313
"Parturition" (Loy), **Supp. XXII:** 159, 160–161
"Party, The" (Dunbar), **Supp. II Part 1:** 198, 205–206
"Party, The" (Taylor), **Supp. V:** 315
Party at Jack's, The (Wolfe), **IV:** 451–452, 469
"Party Down at the Square, A" (Ellison), **Retro. Supp. II:** 124
Party of Five (television series), **Supp. XIX:** 222
Pascal, Blaise, **II:** 8, 159; **III:** 292, 301, 304, 428; **Retro. Supp. I:** 326, 330
"Paskudnyak" (Pilcer), **Supp. XVII:** 50
"Pass, The" (Neugeboren), **Supp. XVI:** 225
"Passage" (Crane), **I:** 391
"Passage in the Life of Mr. John Oakhurst, A" (Harte), **Supp. II Part 1:** 353–354
Passage in the Night, A (Asch), **Supp. XXIII:** 7
"Passages" (Duncan), **Supp. XVI:** 287
"Passages from a Relinquished Work" (Hawthorne), **Retro. Supp. I:** 150
Passages toward the Dark (McGrath), **Supp. X:** 126, 127
"Passage to India" (Whitman), **IV:** 348
Passage to India, A (Forster), **II:** 600; **Supp. XVIII:** 143
Passaro, Vince, **Supp. X:** 167, 302, 309, 310
"Passenger, The" (Brockmeier), **Supp. XXII:** 52
"Passenger Pigeons" (Jeffers), **Supp. II Part 2:** 437
Passin, Herbert, **Supp. XIII:** 337
Passing (Larsen), **Supp. XVIII:** 119, 123, **127–130**
"Passing Beauty" (C. Frost), **Supp. XV:** 97
"Passing of Grandison, The" (Chesnutt), **Supp. XIV:** 62, **66–69**
"Passing of Sister Barsett, The" (Jewett), **Retro. Supp. II:** 138–139, 143
"Passing Show, The" (Bierce), **I:** 208
"Passing Through" (Kunitz), **Supp. III Part 1:** 265
"Passion, The" (Barnes), **Supp. III Part 1:** 36
"Passion, The" (Merwin), **Supp. III Part 1:** 343
Passionate, Accurate Story, The: Making Your Heart's Truth into Literature (C. Bly), **Supp. XVI: 41–42**
Passionate Pilgrim, A (James), **II:** 324; **Retro. Supp. I:** 219
"Passionate Pilgrim, A" (James), **II:** 322, 323–324; **Retro. Supp. I:** 218

Passion Play (Kosinski), **Supp. VII:** 215, 225–226

Passions of Uxport, The (Kumin), **Supp. IV Part 2:** 444

Pass It On (Hadas), **Supp. XXIII:** 115, 123

"Pass It On, I"(Hadas), **Supp. XXIII:** 115

"Pass It On, II"(Hadas), **Supp. XXIII:** 115

"Passive Resistance" (McKay), **Supp. X:** 133

Passport to the War (Kunitz), **Supp. III Part 1:** 261–264

Passwords (Stafford), **Supp. XI:** 329–330

"Past, The" (Bryant), **Supp. I Part 1:** 157, 170

Past, The (Kinnell), **Supp. III Part 1:** 235, 253–254

"Past, The" (Kinnell), **Supp. III Part 1:** 254

Past and Present (Carlyle), **Supp. I Part 2:** 410

Pasternak, Boris, **II:** 544; **Supp. XXIII:** 209

"Pastiches et Pistaches" (Van Vechten), **Supp. II Part 2:** 732

"Past Is the Present, The" (Moore), **III:** 199–200

"Pastoral" (Carver), **Supp. III Part 1:** 137, 146

"Pastoral" (Dove), **Supp. IV Part 1:** 249

"Pastoral" (Trethewey), **Supp. XXI:** 257

"Pastoral Hat, A" (Stevens), **IV:** 91

Pastoralia (Saunders), **Supp. XIX:** 227–229

"Pastoralia" (Saunders), **Supp. XIX:** 227, 229

"Pastor Dowe at Tacaté" (Bowles), **Supp. IV Part 1:** 87

Pastorela (ballet) (Kirstein), **Supp. IV Part 1:** 83

Pastorius, Francis Daniel, **Supp. I Part 2:** 700

"Pasture Poems" (Kumin), **Supp. IV Part 2:** 446

Pastures of Heaven, The (Steinbeck), **IV:** 51

Patch, Jerry, **Supp. XVIII:** 38

Patchen, Kenneth, **Supp. III Part 2:** 625

Patchett, Ann, **Supp. XII:** 307–324

Patchwork Planet (Lethem), **Supp. XVIII:** 150

Pater, Walter, **I:** 51, 272, 476; **II:** 27, 338; **III:** 604; **IV:** 74; **Retro. Supp. I:** 56, 79; **Retro. Supp. II:** 326; **Supp. I Part 2:** 552; **Supp. IX:** 66

Paterna (Mather), **Supp. II Part 2:** 451

"Paterson" (Ginsberg), **Supp. II Part 1:** 314–315, 321, 329

Paterson (W. C. Williams), **I:** 62, 446; **IV:** 418–423; **Retro. Supp. I:** 209, 284, 413, 419, 421, **424–428,** 428, 429, 430; **Retro. Supp. II:** 321, 328; **Supp. II Part 2:** 557, 564, 625; **Supp. VIII:** 275, 305; **Supp. XIV:** 96; **Supp. XV:** 264, 349

Paterson, Book Five (W. C. Williams), **IV:** 422–423

Paterson, Book One (W. C. Williams), **IV:** 421–422

Paterson, Isabel, **Supp. IV Part 2:** 524

Paterson, Part Three (W. C. Williams), **IV:** 420–421

Pat Garrett and Billy the Kid (film, Peckinpah), **Supp. XVIII:** 27

"Path, The" (Bryant), **Supp. I Part 1:** 169

Pathfinder, The (Cooper), **I:** 349, 350, 355

Pat Hobby Stories, The (Fitzgerald), **Retro. Supp. I:** 114

"Pathos of Low Life, The" (Hapgood), **Supp. XVII:** 103

"Patience of a Saint, The" (Humphrey), **Supp. IX:** 106

Patient 002 (Skloot), **Supp. XX: 194, 208**

Patinkin, Mandy, **Supp. IV Part 1:** 236

Paton, Alan, **Supp. VIII:** 126

Patria Mia (Pound), **III:** 460–461; **Retro. Supp. I:** 284

"Patria Mia" (Pound), **Retro. Supp. I:** 284

"Patriarch, The" (Alvares), **Supp. V:** 11

"Patrick Kavanagh at First Light" (Skloot), **Supp. XX:** 204

Patrimony: A True Story (P. Roth), **Retro. Supp. II:** 279, 280, 291; **Supp. III Part 2:** 427

Patriot, The (Buck), **Supp. II Part 1:** 122–123

Patriot, The (Connell), **Supp. XIV:** 94–95

Patriotic Gore: Studies in the Literature of the American Civil War (Wilson), **III:** 588; **IV:** 430, 438, 443, 445–445, 446; **Supp. VIII:** 100

"Patriotic Thing, The" (Ryan as Quin), **Supp. XVIII:** 229

"Patriots, The/Los Patriotas" (Kingsolver), **Supp. VII:** 209

Patron Saint of Liars, The (Patchett), **Supp. XII:** 307, 310, **311–314,** 317

Pattee, Fred L., **II:** 456

Patten, Gilbert, **II:** 423

Patten, Simon, **Supp. I Part 2:** 640

Patternmaster (O. Butler), **Supp. XIII:** 61, 62, 63

Patternmaster Series (O. Butler), **Supp. XIII: 62–63**

Pattern Recognition (W. Gibson), **Supp. XVI:** 124, **130–131**

"Patterns" (Lowell), **II:** 524

Patterson, Floyd, **III:** 38

Patterson, Margot, **Supp. XXII:** 85

Patterson, William M., **Supp. I Part 1:** 265

Patton, General George, **III:** 575; **Supp. I Part 2:** 664

"Patty-Cake, Patty-Cake...A Memoir" (Apple), **Supp. XVII:** 7

Paul, Saint, **I:** 365; **II:** 15, 494; **IV:** 122, 154, 164, 335; **Retro. Supp. I:** 247; **Supp. I Part 1:** 188

Paul, Sherman, **II:** 244; **IV:** 179

"Paula Becker to Clara Westhoff" (Rich), **Supp. I Part 2:** 573–574

"Paula Gunn Allen" (Ruppert), **Supp. IV Part 1:** 321

Paul Ardenheim, the Monk of Wissahikon (Lippard), **Supp. XXIII:** 178, 186, 187, 189, 190

Paul Bowles: Romantic Savage (Caponi), **Supp. IV Part 1:** 95

Paulding, James Kirke, **I:** 344; **II:** 298, 299, 303; **Supp. I Part 1:** 157

Pauley, Jane, **Supp. XXI:** 39

Paul Jones (Hapgood), **Supp. XVII:** 100–101

Paul Marchand, F.M.C. (Chesnutt), **Supp. XIV:** 76

"Paul Monette: The Brink of Summer's End" (film), **Supp. X:** 152

"Paul Revere" (Longfellow), **II:** 489, 501

"Paul Revere's Ride" (Longfellow), **Retro. Supp. II:** 163

"Paul's Case" (Cather), **I:** 314–315; **Retro. Supp. I:** 3, 5

Paulsen, Friedrich, **III:** 600

"Pauper Witch of Grafton, The" (Frost), **Retro. Supp. II:** 42

"Pause by the Water, A" (Merwin), **Supp. III Part 1:** 354

"Pavane for the Nursery, A" (W. J. Smith), **Supp. XIII:** 335

"Pavement, The" (Olson), **Supp. II Part 2:** 571

Pavese, Cesare, **Supp. XXI:** 132

Pavic, Milorad, **Supp. XXII:** 265

Pavilion of Women (Buck), **Supp. II Part 1:** 125–126

"Pawnbroker, The" (Kumin), **Supp. IV Part 2:** 442, 443–444, 451

Pawnbroker, The (Wallant), **Supp. XVI:** 220

"Paying Dues" (Bass), **Supp. XVI:** 16

Payne, Daniel, **Supp. V:** 202

Payne, John Howard, **II:** 309

Payne Tom, **Supp. XXII:** 266

Paz, Octavio, **Supp. III Part 2:** 630; **Supp. VIII:** 272; **Supp. XI:** 191; **Supp. XIII:** 223

P. D. Kimerakov (Epstein), **Supp. XII:** 160, **162**

Peabody, Elizabeth, **Retro. Supp. I:** 155–156, 225

Peabody, Francis G., **III:** 293; **Supp. I Part 1:** 5

Peabody, Josephine Preston, **III:** 507; **Supp. XX:** 115

Peaceable Kingdom, The (Prose), **Supp. XVI:** 256–257

Peace and Bread in Time of War (Addams), **Supp. I Part 1:** 21, 22–23

"Peace Between Black and White in the United States" (Locke), **Supp. XIV:** 205

Peace Breaks Out (Knowles), **Supp. XII:** 249

"Peacemaker"(Kenny), **Supp. XXIII:** 151

"Peace March, The" (Simpson), **Supp. IX:** 279

"Peace of Cities, The" (Wilbur), **Supp. III Part 2:** 545

"Peace of Mind" (Boyle), **Supp. XX:** 19

"Peaches—Six in a Tin Box, Sarajevo" (Cisneros), **Supp. VII:** 67

Peachtree Road (Siddons), **Supp. XXII:** 239, 240, 242, **246–247, 248–251,** 252

Peacock, Doug, **Supp. VIII:** 38; **Supp. XIII:** 12

Peacock, Gibson, **Supp. I Part 1:** 360

Peacock, Molly, **Supp. XVII:** 74; **Supp. XIX: 193–207**

"Peacock, The" (Merrill), **Supp. III Part 1:** 320

"Peacock, The" (Mosher), **Supp. XXII:** 211

Peacock, Thomas Love, **Supp. I Part 1:** 307; **Supp. VIII:** 125

"Peacock Room, The" (Hayden), **Supp. II Part 1:** 374–375

"Peacocks of Avignon, The" (Swados), **Supp. XIX:** 263

Pearce, Richard, **Supp. IX:** 254

Pearce, Roy Harvey, **II:** 244; **Supp. I Part 1:** 111, 114; **Supp. I Part 2:** 475

"Pearl" (Kooser), **Supp. XIX:** 127–128

Pearl, The (Steinbeck), **IV:** 51, 62–63

Pearlman, Daniel, **III:** 479

Pearlman, Mickey, **Supp. XIII:** 293, 306

Pearl of Orr's Island, The (Stowe), **Supp. I Part 2:** 592–593, 595

"Pearls" (A. Finch), **Supp. XVII:** 72

Pears, Peter, **II:** 586; **Supp. IV Part 1:** 84

Pearson, Drew, **Supp. XIV:** 126

Pearson, Norman Holmes, **Supp. I Part 1:** 259, 260, 273

"Pear Tree" (C. Frost), **Supp. XV:** 105

"Peasants' Way O' Thinkin' " (McKay), **Supp. X:** 133

Pease, Donald E., **Supp. IV Part 2:** 687

"Peboan and Seegwun (Winter and Spring): A Chippewa Allegory"(J. Schoolcraft), **Supp. XXIII:** 235

Peck, Gregory, **Supp. VIII:** 128, 129; **Supp. XII:** 160, 173

Peckinpah, Sam, **Supp. XI:** 306; **Supp. XVIII:** 27

"Peck of Gold, A" (Frost), **II:** 155

Peculiar Treasures: A Biblical Who's Who (Buechner), **Supp. XII:** 53

"Pedal Point" (Francis), **Supp. IX:** 87

Pedersen, Inge, **Supp. XVIII:** 179

"Pedersen Kid, The" (Gass), **Supp. VI:** 83

"Pedigree, The" (Creeley), **Supp. IV Part 1:** 150

Peebles, Melvin Van, **Supp. XI:** 17; **Supp. XVI:** 144

"Peed Onk" (Moore). *See* "People Like That Are the Only People Here: Canonical Babbling in Peed Onk" (Moore)

"Peeler, The" (O'Connor), **Retro. Supp. II:** 225

Peich, Michael, **Supp. XV:** 113, 117

Peikoff, Leonard, **Supp. IV Part 2:** 520, 526, 529

Peirce, Charles Sanders, **II:** 20, 352–353; **III:** 599; **Supp. I Part 2:** 640; **Supp. III Part 2:** 626

Pelagius, **III:** 295

"Pelican, The" (Merrill), **Supp. III Part 1:** 320

"Pelican, The" (Wharton), **IV:** 310; **Retro. Supp. I:** 364

Pellacchia, Michael, **Supp. XIII:** 16

Pelley, Denise, **Supp. XIX:** 205

Pelonero, Michael, **Supp. XXIII:** 125

Peltier, Leonard, **Supp. V:** 212

"Penance"(Dybek), **Supp. XXIII:** 69

"Pen and Paper and a Breath of Air" (Oliver), **Supp. VII:** 245

Pence, Amy, **Supp. XV:** 211, 223

"Pencil, The" (Chandler), **Supp. IV Part 1:** 135

Pencillings by the Way (Willis), **II:** 313; **Supp. XVIII:** 12

"Pencils" (Sandburg), **III:** 592

Pendleton, Devon, **Supp. XVIII:** 151

"Pendulum" (Bradbury and Hasse), **Supp. IV Part 1:** 102

"Penelope's Song" (Glück), **Supp. V:** 89

Penelope: The Story of the Half-Scalped Woman (Schott), **Supp. XXIII:** 240, **244–245**

Penhally (Gordon), **II:** 197, 199, 201–203, 204

"Penis" (McClatchy), **Supp. XII:** 266–267

Penitent, The (di Donato), **Supp. XX:** 44, 45

Penitent, The (Singer), **Retro. Supp. II:** **309–310,** 313

Penland, Nell Bates, **Supp. XXII:** 188

Penn, Robert, **I:** 489

Penn, Sean, **Supp. XI:** 107

Penn, Thomas, **II:** 118

Penn, William, **Supp. I Part 2:** 683

Penna, Sandro, **Supp. XIX:** 34

Pennebaker, D. A., **Supp. XVIII:** 19, 26

"Pennsylvania Pilgrim, The" (Whittier), **Supp. I Part 2:** 700

"Pennsylvania Planter, The" (Freneau), **Supp. II Part 1:** 268

Penny, Rob, **Supp. VIII:** 330

"Penny, The" (D. West), **Supp. XVIII:** 283–284

Penrod (Tarkington), **III:** 223

"Penseroso, Il" (Milton), **Supp. XIV:** 8

Pensieri (Leopardi; Di Piero, trans.), **Supp. XIX:** 34

"Pensive Hours"(J. Schoolcraft), **Supp. XXIII:** 230–231

Pentagon of Power, The (Mumford), **Supp. II Part 2:** 498

Pentimento (Hellman), **Supp. I Part 1:** 280, 292–294, 296; **Supp. IV Part 1:** 12; **Supp. VIII:** 243

"Peonies at Dusk" (Kenyon), **Supp. VII:** 171

People, The (Glaspell), **Supp. III Part 1:** 179

People, Yes, The (Sandburg), **III:** 575, 589, 590, 591

"PEOPLE BURNING, THE" (Baraka), **Supp. II Part 1:** 49

"People in Hell Just Want a Drink of Water" (Proulx), **Supp. VII:** 263

"People Like That Are the Only People Here: Canonical Babbling in Peed Onk" (Moore), **Supp. X:** 168, **178–179**

People Live Here: Selected Poems 1949–1983 (Simpson), **Supp. IX:** 269, 277

"People Next Door, The" (Simpson), **Supp. IX:** 279

People of the Abyss, The (London), **II:** 465–466

"People on the Roller Coaster, The" (Hardwick), **Supp. III Part 1:** 196

People Shall Continue, The (Ortiz), **Supp. IV Part 2:** 510

"People's Surroundings" (Moore), **III:** 201, 202, 203

"People v. Abe Lathan, Colored, The" (Caldwell), **I:** 309

"Peppermint Lounge Revisited, The" (Wolfe), **Supp. III Part 2:** 571

Peppis, Paul, **Supp. XXII:** 160

Pepys, Samuel, **Supp. I Part 2:** 653

"Perchance to Dream" (Franzen), **Supp. XX:** 90, 93

Perchance to Dream: Robert B. Parker's Sequel to Raymond Chandler's "Big Sleep" (Parker), **Supp. XIX:** 189

"Perch'io non spero di tornar giammai" (Cavalcanti), **Supp. III Part 2:** 623

Percy, Thomas, **Supp. XIV:** 2

Percy, Walker, **Supp. III Part 1: 383–400; Supp. IV Part 1:** 297; **Supp. V:** 334; **Supp. X:** 42; **Supp. XIV:** 21; **Supp. XIX:** 209

Percy, William, **Supp. V:** 334

Percy, William Alexander, **Retro. Supp. I:** 341; **Supp. XXII:** 193

Peregrin, Tony, **Supp. XV:** 69

"Peregrine" (Wylie), **Supp. I Part 2:** 712–713, 714

Perelman, Bob, **Supp. XII:** 23

Perelman, S. J., **IV:** 286; **Retro. Supp. I:** 342; **Retro. Supp. II:** 321, 322, 325, 326, 327, 336; **Supp. IV Part 1:** 353; **Supp. XI:** 66

Perestroika (Kushner), **Supp. IX:** 141, 142, 145

Péret, Benjamin, **Supp. VIII:** 272

Peretz, Isaac Leib, **IV:** 1, 3; **Retro. Supp. II:** 299; **Supp. XXIII:** 4, 7, 8–9

Pérez Galdós, Benito, **II:** 275

Perfect Analysis Given by a Parrot, A (T. Williams), **IV:** 395

"Perfect Couple, The" (Nelson), **Supp. XVIII:** 173

"Perfect Day for Bananafish, A" (Salinger), **III:** 563–564, 571

Perfect Fiction, The (Sorrentino), **Supp. XXI:** 228

Perfect Ganesh, A (McNally), **Supp. XIII: 202–203,** 208, 209

"Perfect Gerbil, The: Reading Barthelme's 'The School' " (Saunders), **Supp. XIX:** 235

"Perfect Knight, The" (Chandler), **Supp. IV Part 1:** 120

Perfect Mother, The (Schott), **Supp. XXIII: 241–242**

Perfect Party, The (Gurney), **Supp. V:** 100, 105, 106–107

"Perfect Things" (F. Barthelme), **Supp. XI:** 30, 33–34

"Performance, The" (Dickey), **Supp. IV Part 1:** 178–179, 181

"Perfume" (Mora), **Supp. XIII:** 218

"Perhaps the World Ends Here" (Harjo), **Supp. XII:** 228, 231

Perhaps Women (Anderson), **I:** 114

Pericles (Shakespeare), **I:** 585; **Supp. III Part 2:** 624, 627, 629

"Period Metaphor" (Bronk), **Supp. XXI:** 33

Period of Adjustment (T. Williams), **IV:** 382, 386, 387, 388, 389, 390, 392, 393, 394, 397

"Period Pieces from the Mid-Thirties" (Agee), **I:** 28

"Periphery" (Ammons), **Supp. VII:** 28

Perkins, David, **Supp. I Part 2:** 459, 475; **Supp. XV:** 185

Perkins, Maxwell, **I:** 252, 289, 290; **II:** 87, 93, 95, 252; **IV:** 452, 455, 457, 458, 461, 462, 463, 469; **Retro. Supp. I:** 101, 105, 108, 109, 110, 113, 114, 178; **Supp. IX:** 57, 58, 60, 232; **Supp. X:** 219, 224, 225, 229, 230, 233; **Supp. XI:** 218, 227

Perlès, Alfred, **III:** 177, 183, 187, 189

Perloff, Marjorie, **Supp. I Part 2:** 539, 542; **Supp. IV Part 1:** 68; **Supp. IV Part 2:** 420, 424, 432; **Supp. XXII:** 161, 271; **Supp. XXIII:** 210, 220

Permanence and Change (Burke), **I:** 274

Permanent Errors (Price), **Supp. VI:** 261

"Permanent Traits of the English National Genius" (Emerson), **II:** 18

Permit Me Voyage (Agee), **I:** 25, 27

"Perosa Canavese" (Everwine), **Supp. XV:** 84

Perrault, Charles, **IV:** 266; **Supp. I Part 2:** 622

Perrin, Noel, **Supp. XVI:** 34; **Supp. XXII:** 205, 207, 211, 218

Perrins, Carol. *See* Frost, Carol

Perry, Anne, **Supp. V:** 335

Perry, Bliss, **I:** 243

Perry, Donna, **Supp. IV Part 1:** 322, 327, 335

Perry, Edgar A., **III:** 410

Perry, Keith Ronald, **Supp. XXI:** 42

Perry, Lincoln, **Supp. V:** 24, 33

Perry, Matthew C., **Supp. I Part 2:** 494–495

Perry, Patsy Brewington, **Supp. I Part 1:** 66

Perry, Phyllis Alesia, **Supp. XVIII:** 96

Perry, Ralph Barton, **I:** 224; **II:** 356, 362, 364; **Supp. XIV:** 197

Perry, Dr. William, **II:** 395, 396

Perse, St.-John, **III:** 12, 13, 14, 17; **Supp. III Part 1:** 14; **Supp. IV Part 1:** 82; **Supp. XIII:** 344; **Supp. XV:** 178

"Persephone in Hell" (Dove), **Supp. IV Part 1:** 250, 251

"Persephone"(Le Sueur), **Supp. XXIII:** 162, 165, **170–171**

"Persimmons" (L.-Y. Lee), **Supp. XV:** 211, 213

"Persistence of Desire, The" (Updike), **IV:** 222–223, 228

"Persistence of Poetry, The" (Bynner), **Supp. XV:** 49

"Persistences" (Hecht), **Supp. X:** **68–69**

Person, Place, and Thing (Shapiro), **Supp. II Part 2:** 702, 705

Personae of Ezra Pound (Pound), **III:** 458

Personae: The Collected Poems (Pound), **Retro. Supp. I:** 285, 286; **Supp. I Part 1:** 255; **Supp. XVII:** 32

"Personal" (Stern), **Supp. IX:** 299

"Personal and Occasional Pieces" (Welty), **Retro. Supp. I:** 355

"Personal and the Individual, The" (L. Michaels), **Supp. XVI:** 201

Personal Injuries (Turow), **Supp. XVII:** **219–220,** 221, 223

"Personalities" (column, Briggs), **Supp. XVIII:** 15

Personal Narrative (Edwards), **I:** 545, 552, 553, 561, 562; **Supp. I Part 2:** 700

"Personal Poem"(O'Hara), **Supp. XXIII:** 219

Personal Recollection of Joan of Arc (Twain), **IV:** 208

Personals (Bontemps), **Supp. XXII:** 7, 8

"Personals" (Didion), **Supp. IV Part 1:** 200

"Personism" (O'Hara), **Supp. XV:** 181

"Personism: A Manifesto"(O'Hara), **Supp. XXIII:** 212, 215

Persons and Places (Santayana), **III:** 615

Persons in Hiding (film), **Supp. XIII:** 170

Persons in Hiding (Hoover), **Supp. XIII:** 170

Person Sitting in Darkness, A (Twain), **IV:** 208

"Perspective" (Francis), **Supp. IX:** 78

"Perspective: Anniversary D-Day" (Karr), **Supp. XI:** 241

Perspectives by Incongruity (Burke), **I:** 284–285

"Perspectives: Is It Out of Control?" (Gleason), **Supp. IX:** 16

Perspectives on Cormac McCarthy (Arnold and Luce, eds.), **Supp. VIII:** 189

Persse, Dudley Jocelyn, **Supp. XX:** **232**

Pertes et Fracas (McCoy), **Supp. XIII:** 175

"Peruvian Child" (Mora), **Supp. XIII:** 218

Peseroff, Joyce, **Supp. IV Part 1:** 71

"Pestilence" (Nelson), **Supp. XVIII:** 186

Pest Maiden, The (Schott), **Supp. XXIII:** **245–246**

"Peter" (Cather), **Retro. Supp. I:** 4

"Peter" (Moore), **III:** 210, 212

Peter, Saint, **III:** 341, 346; **IV:** 86, 294

Peterkin, Julia, **Supp. I Part 1:** 328; **Supp. XXII:** 12, 189

"Peter Klaus" (German tale), **II:** 306

Peter Pan (Barrie), **Supp. XV:** 319

"Peter Parley" works (Goodrich), **Supp. I Part 1:** 38

"Peter Pendulum" (Poe), **III:** 425

"Peter Quince at the Clavier" (Stevens), **IV:** 81, 82

Peter Rabbit tales, **Retro. Supp. I:** 335

Peters, Cora, **Supp. I Part 2:** 468

Peters, Jacqueline, **Supp. XII:** 225

Peters, Margot, **Supp. VIII:** 252

Peters, Robert, **Supp. XIII:** 114

Peters, S. H. (pseudonym). *See* Henry, O.

Peters, Timothy, **Supp. XI:** 39

"Peter's Avocado" (Rodriguez), **Supp. XIV:** 308–309

Petersen, David, **Supp. XIII:** 2

Petersen, Donald, **Supp. V:** 180; **Supp. XV:** 74, 92

Peterson, Dorothy, **Supp. XVIII:** 131, 132

Peterson, George, **Supp. XXII:** 250

Peterson, Houston, **I:** 60

Peterson, Roger Tory, **Supp. V:** 202

Peterson, Virgilia, **Supp. IV Part 1:** 30

Peter Whiffle: His Life and Works (Van Vechten), **Supp. II Part 2:** 728–729, 731, 735, 738–741, 749

"Petey and Yotsee and Mario" (H. Roth), **Supp. IX:** 234

"Petition, A" (Winters), **Supp. II Part 2:** 785

"Pet Milk"(Dybek), **Supp. XXIII:** 74

"'Pet Negro' System, The" (Hurston), **Supp. VI:** 159

"Petra and Its Surroundings" (Frost), **Retro. Supp. I:** 124

Petrarch, **I:** 176; **II:** 590; **III:** 4

"Petrarch, Shakespeare, and the Blues" (C. Frost), **Supp. XV:** 92, 104, 105

"Petrified Man" (Welty), **IV:** 262; **Retro. Supp. I:** 345, 351

"Petrified Man, The" (Twain), **IV:** 195

"Petrified Woman, The" (Gordon), **II:** 199

Petronius, **III:** 174, 179

Petry, Ann, **Supp. VIII:** 214; **Supp. XI:** 6, 85; **Supp. XVIII:** 286

Pet Sematary (King), **Supp. V:** 138, 143, 152

Pettengill, Richard, **Supp. VIII:** 341, 345, 348

Pettingell, Phoebe, **Supp. XV:** 251, 256–257, 262

Pettis, Joyce, **Supp. XI:** 276, 277, 278, 281

Pettis, Olive G., **Supp. XXIII:** 189

Petty, Jill, **Supp. XXI:** 244, 248, 249, 250

Pfaelzer, Jean, **Supp. XVI:** 88, 90

Pfaff, Timothy, **Supp. V:** 166

Pfeil, Fred, **Supp. XIV:** 36

Pfister, Karin, **IV:** 467, 475

Phaedo (Plato), **II:** 10

Phaedra (Lowell and Barzun, trans.), **II:** 543–544

"Phantasia for Elvira Shatayev" (Rich), **Supp. I Part 2:** 570

Phantasms of War (Lowell), **II:** 512

"Phantom of the Movie Palace, The" (Coover), **Supp. V:** 50–51

Phantom Ship, The (Marryat), **Supp. XVII:** 55

"Pharaoh, The" (Kenyon), **Supp. VII:** 172

"Pharmacy"(Strout), **Supp. XXIII:** 281

Pharr, Mary, **Supp. V:** 147

"Phases" (E. Stoddard), **Supp. XV:** 273

"Phases" (Stevens), **Retro. Supp. I:** 299

Phases of an Inferior Planet (Glasgow), **II:** 174–175

"Pheasant, The" (Carver), **Supp. III Part 1:** 146

Phelan, Alice, **Supp. XXII:** 193

Pheloung, Grant, **Supp. XI:** 39

Phelps, Donald, **Supp. XXIII:** 174

Phelps, Elizabeth Stuart, **Retro. Supp. II:** 146; **Supp. XIII:** 141; **Supp. XVI:** 80

Phelps, Teresa Godwin, **Supp. VIII:** 128

Phelps, William Lyon "Billy", **Supp. XX:** **68, 75, 220**

"Phenomena and Laws of Race Contacts, The" (Locke), **Supp. XIV:** 210

"Phenomenology of Anger, The" (Rich), **Supp. I Part 2:** 562–563, 571

Phenomenology of Moral Experience, The (Mandelbaum), **I:** 61

"Phenomenology of *On Moral Fiction*" (Johnson), **Supp. VI:** 188

Phidias, **Supp. I Part 2:** 482

Philadelphia Fire (Wideman), **Supp. X:** 320, 334

Philadelphia Negro, The (Du Bois), **Supp. II Part 1:** 158, 163–164, 166

Philbrick, Thomas, **I:** 343

"Philemon and Baucis"(Hadas), **Supp. XXIII:** 114

"Phil in the Marketplace" (Lethem), **Supp. XVIII:** 148

Philip, Jim, **Supp. XII:** 136

Philip, Maxwell, **Supp. XXI:** 160

Philip, Prince, **Supp. X:** 108

"Philip of Pokanoket" (Irving), **II:** 303

Philippians (biblical book), **IV:** 154

"Philippine Conquest, The" (Masters), **Supp. I Part 2:** 456

"Philip Roth Reconsidered" (Howe), **Retro. Supp. II:** 286

"Philistinism and the Negro Writer" (Baraka), **Supp. II Part 1:** 39, 44

Phillips, Adam, **Supp. XII:** 97–98

Phillips, Anne K., **Supp. XX:** **221**

Phillips, Carl, **Supp. XXI:** 246

Phillips, David Graham, **II:** 444; **Retro. Supp. II:** 101

Phillips, Gene D., **Supp. XI:** 306

Phillips, Jayne Anne, **Supp. XIV:** 21

Phillips, J. J., **Supp. XXIII:** 174

Phillips, J. O. C., **Supp. I Part 1:** 19

Phillips, Robert, **Supp. XIII:** 335, 344

Phillips, Wendell, **Supp. I Part 1:** 103; **Supp. I Part 2:** 524

Phillips, Willard, **Supp. I Part 1:** 154, 155

Phillips, William, **Supp. VIII:** 156

Phillips, William L., **I:** 106

"Philly Babylon" (Di Piero), **Supp. XIX:** 46

"Philoctetes"(Hadas), **Supp. XXIII:** 115

"Philosopher, The" (Farrell), **II:** 45

Philosopher of the Forest (pseudonym). *See* Freneau, Philip

Philosophes classiques, Les (Taine), **III:** 323

"Philosophical Cobbler, The" (Sanders), **Supp. XVI:** 268

"Philosophical Concepts and Practical Results" (James), **II:** 352

"Philosophical Investigation of Metaphor, A" (Gass), **Supp. VI:** 79

Philosophical Transactions (Watson), **II:** 114

"Philosophy, Or Something Like That" (P. Roth), **Supp. III Part 2:** 403

"Philosophy and Its Critics" (James), **II:** 360

"Philosophy and the Form of Fiction" (Gass), **Supp. VI:** 85

"Philosophy for People" (Emerson), **II:** 14

"Philosophy in Warm Weather" (Kenyon), **Supp. VII:** 168

"Philosophy Lesson" (Levine), **Supp. V:** 195

Philosophy of Alain Locke, The: Harlem Renaissance and Beyond (Harris, ed.), **Supp. XIV:** 196, 211–212

"Philosophy of Composition, The" (Poe), **III:** 416, 421; **Retro. Supp. II:** 266, 267, 271

Philosophy of Friedrich Nietzsche, The (Mencken), **III:** 102–103

"Philosophy of Handicap, A" (Bourne), **I:** 216, 218

"Philosophy of History" (Emerson), **II:** 11–12

Philosophy of Literary Form, The (Burke), **I:** 275, 281, 283, 291

Philosophy of the Human Mind, The (Stewart), **II:** 8

Philosophy: Who Needs It (Rand), **Supp. IV Part 2:** 517, 518, 527, 533

Philoxenes, **Supp. VIII:** 201

"Phineas" (Knowles), **Supp. XII:** 238–240

Phineas: Six Stories (Knowles), **Supp. XII:** 249

"Phocion" (Lowell), **II:** 536

Phoebe Light (Notley), **Supp. XXII:** 227

Phoenix and the Turtle, The (Shakespeare), **I:** 284

"Phoenix Lyrics" (Schwartz), **Supp. II Part 2:** 665

"Phone Booths, The" (Jarman), **Supp. XVII:** 112–113

"Phony War Films" (Jones), **Supp. XI:** 217, 232

"Photograph: Carlisle Indian School (1879–1918)"(Kenny), **Supp. XXIII:** 156

"Photograph: Migrant Worker, Parlier, California, 1967" (Levis), **Supp. XI:** 272

"Photograph of a Bawd Drinking Raleigh Rye" (Trethewey), **Supp. XXI:** 254

"Photograph of a Child on a Vermont Hillside" (Kenyon), **Supp. VII:** 168

"Photograph of My Mother as a Young Girl" (Gioia), **Supp. XV:** 119

"Photograph of the Girl" (Olds), **Supp. X:** 205

"Photograph of the Unmade Bed" (Rich), **Supp. I Part 2:** 558

Photographs (Welty), **Retro. Supp. I:** 343

"Photographs, The" (Barthelme), **Supp. IV Part 1:** 53

"Photography" (Levine), **Supp. V:** 194

Phyrrho, **Retro. Supp. I:** 247

"Physical Universe" (Simpson), **Supp. IX:** 278

"Physicist We Know, A" (Shields), **Supp. VII:** 310

"Physics and Cosmology in the Fiction of Tom Robbins" (Nadeau), **Supp. X:** 270

Physiologie du goût (Brillat-Savarin), **Supp. XVII:** 82, 86

Physiology of Taste, The; or, Meditations on Transcendent Gastronomy (Brillat-Savarin; M. F. K. Fisher, trans.), **Supp. XVII:** 86, 87, 91

"Physiology of Versification, The: Harmonies of Organic and Animal Life" (Holmes), **Supp. I Part 1:** 311

Physique de l'Amour (Gourmont), **III:** 467–468

Piaf, Edith, **Supp. IV Part 2:** 549

Piaget, Jean, **Supp. XIII:** 75

"Piano" (Lawrence), **Supp. XV:** 254

"Piano Fingers" (Mason), **Supp. VIII:** 146

Piano Lesson, The (Bearden), **Supp. VIII:** 342

Piano Lesson, The (Wilson), **Supp. VIII:** **342–345**

Piano Man's Daughter, The (Findley), **Supp. XX:** **59–61**

"Piano Player, The"(Strout), **Supp. XXIII:** 283, 285

Piatt, James, **Supp. I Part 2:** 420

Piatt, John J., **II:** 273

Piazza, Ben, **Supp. XIII:** 163

Piazza, Paul, **Supp. XIV:** 157, 160, 171

"Piazza de Spagna, Early Morning" (Wilbur), **Supp. III Part 2:** 553

Piazza Tales (Melville), **III:** 91

Picabia, Francis, **Retro. Supp. I:** 416; **Retro. Supp. II:** 331; **Supp. XXII:** 162

Picasso (Stein), **IV:** 28, 32, 45

Picasso, Pablo, **I:** 429, 432, 440, 442, 445; **II:** 602; **III:** 197, 201, 470; **IV:** 26, 31, 32, 46, 87, 407, 436; **Retro. Supp. I:** 55, 63; **Supp. IV Part 1:** 81; **Supp. IX:** 66

Piccione, Anthony, **Supp. XV:** 212

"Piccola Comedia" (Wilbur), **Supp. III Part 2:** 561

Pickard, Samuel T., **Supp. I Part 2:** 682

Picked-Up Pieces (Updike), **Retro. Supp. I:** 320, 322, 323, 335

Picker, Lauren, **Supp. VIII:** 78, 83

Picker, Tobias, **Supp. XII:** 253

Pickering, Sam, **Supp. XXI:** **191–207**

Pickford, Mary, **Retro. Supp. I:** 325; **Supp. I Part 2:** 391

"Picking and Choosing" (Moore), **III:** 205

"Picnic" (Peacock), **Supp. XIX:** 206

Picnic, Lightning (Collins), **Supp. XXI:** 54, 60

"Picnic, Lightning" (Collins), **Supp. XXI:** 64–65

Picnic Cantata (music) (Bowles), **Supp. IV Part 1:** 89

"Picnic Remembered" (Warren), **IV:** 240

Pictorial History of the Negro in America, A (Hughes), **Supp. I Part 1:** 345

"Picture, The" (Olson), **Supp. II Part 2:** 574

Picture Bride (Son), **Supp. X:** 292

"Picture I Want, The" (Olds), **Supp. X:** 209

Picture of Dorian Gray, The (Wilde), **Supp. IX:** 105

"Picture of Little J. A. in a Prospect of Flowers, A" (Ashbery), **Supp. III Part 1:** 3

Picture Palace (Theroux), **Supp. VIII:** 322

"Pictures" (Pickering), **Supp. XXI:** 197

"Pictures at an Extermination" (Epstein), **Supp. XII:** 161

"Pictures from an Expedition" (Duffy), **Supp. IV Part 1:** 207

Pictures from an Institution (Jarrell), **II:** 367, 385

Pictures from Brueghel (W. C. Williams), **Retro. Supp. I:** 429–431

"Pictures from Brueghel" (W. C. Williams), **Retro. Supp. I:** 419

"Pictures of Columbus, the Genoese, The" (Freneau), **Supp. II Part 1:** 258

Pictures of Fidelman: An Exhibition (Malamud), **Supp. I Part 2:** 450–451

"Pictures of the Artist" (Malamud), **Supp. I Part 2:** 450

Pictures of the Floating World (Lowell), **II:** 521, 524–525

Pictures of Travel (Heine), **II:** 281

Picturesque America; or, the Land We Live In (Bryant, ed.), **Supp. I Part 1:** 158

"Picturesque Ghetto, The" (Hapgood), **Supp. XVII:** 101

"Picturesque: San Cristóbal de las Casas" (Mora), **Supp. XIII:** 218

Picture This (Heller), **Supp. IV Part 1:** 386, 388, 390–391

Picturing Will (Beattie), **Supp. V:** 29, 31–32, 34

"Pie" (X. J. Kennedy), **Supp. XV:** 170

"Piece, A" (Creeley), **Supp. IV Part 1:** 155, 156

"Piece of Moon, A" (Hogan), **Supp. IV Part 1:** 407

Piece of My Heart, A (Ford), **Supp. V:** 57, 58–61, 62

Piece of My Mind, A: Reflections at Sixty (Wilson), **IV:** 426, 430, 438, 441

"Piece of News, A" (Welty), **IV:** 263; **Retro. Supp. I:** 345, 346

Pieces (Creeley), **Supp. IV Part 1:** 155

Pieces and Pontifications (Mailer), **Retro. Supp. II:** 209–210

Pieces of the Frame (McPhee), **Supp. III Part 1:** 293

"Pie of the Month" (Thompson), **Supp. XXIII:** 300

Pierce, Franklin, **II:** 225, 226, 227; **III:** 88; **Retro. Supp. I:** 150, 163, 164, 165

Pierce, Frederick, **Retro. Supp. I:** 136

Piercy, Josephine K., **Supp. I Part 1:** 103

"Pierian Handsprings" (column, Untermeyer), **Supp. XV:** 294

Pierpont, Claudia Roth, **Supp. X:** 192, 193, 196

Pierre et Jean (Maupassant), **I:** 421

Pierre: or The Ambiguities (Melville), **III:** 86–88, 89; **IV:** 194; **Retro. Supp. I:** 249, 253–254, 256; **Supp. I Part 2:** 579

Pierrepont, Sarah. *See* Edwards, Sarah

Pierrot qui pleure et Pierrot qui rit (Rostand), **II:** 515

Pierson, George W, **Supp. XXII:** 289

Pig Cookies (Ríos), **Supp. IV Part 2:** 537, 550, 552–554

Pigeon Feathers (Updike), **IV:** 214, 218, 219, 221–223, 226

"Pigeon Feathers" (Updike), **Retro. Supp. I:** 318, 322, 323

"Pigeons" (Rilke), **II:** 544

"Pigeons, The" (Espaillat), **Supp. XXI:** 98

"Pigeon Woman" (Swenson), **Supp. IV Part 2:** 644

"Pig Helmet and the Wall of Life" (P. Benedict), **Supp. XXIII:** 48–49

Pigs in Heaven (Kingsolver), **Supp. VII:** 197, 199, 209–210

Pike County Ballads, The (Hay), **Supp. I Part 1:** 352

Piket, Vincent, **Supp. IV Part 1:** 24

Pilar San-Mallafre, Maria del, **Supp. V:** 40

Pilcer, Sonya, **Supp. XVII:** 50

Pilgrim (Findley), **Supp. XX: 61–62**

"Pilgrim" (Freneau), **Supp. I Part 1:** 125

"Pilgrimage" (Ray), **Supp. XVIII:** 193

"Pilgrimage" (Sontag), **Supp. III Part 2:** 454–455

"Pilgrimage" (Trethewey), **Supp. XXI:** 255

"Pilgrimage, The" (Maxwell), **Supp. VIII:** 169, 171

Pilgrimage of Festus, The (Aiken), **I:** 50, 55, 57

Pilgrimage of Henry James, The (Brooks), **I:** 240, 248, 250; **IV:** 433

Pilgrim at Tinker Creek (Dillard), **Supp. VI:** 22, **23–26,** 28, 29, **30–31,** 34; **Supp. XVIII:** 189

"Pilgrim Makers" (Lowell), **II:** 541

Pilgrim's Harbor (Skloot), **Supp. XX: 196, 207**

Pilgrim's Progress (Bunyan), **I:** 92; **II:** 15, 168, 572; **Supp. I Part 1:** 32, 38; **Supp. I Part 2:** 599

Pili's Wall (Levine), **Supp. V:** 178, 183–184

"Pillar of Fire" (Bradbury), **Supp. IV Part 1:** 113–114

Pillars of Hercules, The: A Grand Tour of the Mediterranean (Theroux), **Supp. VIII:** 325

"Pillow" (L.-Y. Lee), **Supp. XV:** 224

Pilot, The (Cooper), **I:** 335, 337, 339, 342–343, 350

"Pilot from the Carrier, A" (Jarrell), **II:** 374

"Pilots, Man Your Planes" (Jarrell), **II:** 374–375

"Pilots, The" (Levertov), **Supp. III Part 1:** 282

Pilsudski, Joseph, **Supp. XXIII:** 6

"Pimp's Revenge, A" (Malamud), **Supp. I Part 2:** 435, 450, 451

Pinball (Kosinski), **Supp. VII:** 215, 226

Pinchot, Gifford, **Supp. IX:** 184; **Supp. XIV:** 178

Pindar, **I:** 381; **II:** 543; **III:** 610

"Pine" (Dickey), **Supp. IV Part 1:** 183

Pine Barrens, The (McPhee), **Supp. III Part 1:** 298–301, 309

"Pineys, The" (Stern), **Supp. IX:** 288, 296

Pinget, Robert, **Supp. V:** 39

Pinhook: Finding Wholeness in a Fragmented Land (Ray), **Supp. XVIII:** 189, 192, 202–204

"Pink Dog" (Bishop), **Retro. Supp. II:** 48

"Pink Dress, The" (Boulton), **Supp. XXII:** 19

Pinker, James B., **I:** 409; **Retro. Supp. I:** 231

Pinkerton, Jan, **Supp. V:** 323–324

"Pink Moon—The Pond" (Oliver), **Supp. VII:** 234

Pinktoes (C. Himes), **Supp. XVI:** 142

Pinocchio in Venice (Coover), **Supp. V:** 40, 51

Pinsker, Sanford, **Retro. Supp. II:** 23; **Supp. V:** 272; **Supp. IX:** 293, 327; **Supp. XI:** 251, 254, 317

Pinsky, Robert, **Retro. Supp. II:** 50; **Supp. VI: 235–251;** **Supp. IX:** 155, 158; **Supp. XIII:** 277, 285; **Supp. XXI:** 243; **Supp. XXIII:** 111, 124

Pinter, Harold, **I:** 71; **Supp. XIII:** 20, 196; **Supp. XIV:** 239; **Supp. XVI:** 207

Pinto, Ferdinand Mendes (pseudonym). *See* Briggs, Charles Frederick

Pinto and Sons (Epstein), **Supp. XII:** 170, **171–172**

Pinto letters (Briggs), **Supp. XVIII:** 3, **12–13**

"Pinup" (Collins), **Supp. XXI:** 59

"Pioneer Girl" (L. I. Wilder), **Supp. XXII:** 290, 293, 294, 295

Pioneers, The (Cooper), **I:** 336, 337, 339, 340–341, 342, 348; **II:** 313

Pioneers of France in the New World (Parkman), **Supp. III Part 2:** 599, 602

"Pioneers! O Pioneers!" (Whitman), **Retro. Supp. I:** 8

"Pioneer's Vision, The" (Larcom), **Supp. XIII:** 140

Pious and Secular America (Niebuhr), **III:** 308

Pipe Night (O'Hara), **III:** 361, 368

Piper, Dan, **Supp. IX:** 65

Pipers at the Gates of Dawn: The Wisdom of Children's Literature (Cott), **Supp. XVI:** 104

"Piper's Rocks" (Olson), **Supp. IV Part 1:** 153

"Pipistrelles" (B. Kelly), **Supp. XVII:** 129–130

Pipkin, Charles W., **Supp. XIV:** 3

Pippa Passes (Browning), **IV:** 128

Piquion, René, **Supp. I Part 1:** 346

Pirandello, Luigi, **Supp. IV Part 2:** 576, 588

Piranesi, Giovanni Battista, **Supp. XV:** 258

Pirate, The (Robbins), **Supp. XII:** 6

Pirate, The (Scott), **I:** 339

Pirates of Penzance, The (Gilbert and Sullivan), **IV:** 386

Pisan Cantos, The (Pound), **III:** 476; **Retro. Supp. I:** 140, 283, 285, 293; **Supp. III Part 1:** 63; **Supp. V:** 331, 337; **Supp. XIV:** 11; **Supp. XV:** 351

Pisarev, Dimitri, **Supp. XXI:** 164

Piscator, Erwin, **IV:** 394

"Pissaro: Tropical Impressions"(Kenny), **Supp. XXIII:** 146

Pissarro, Camille, **I:** 478

"Pissing off the Back of the Boat into the Nevernais Canal" (Matthews), **Supp. IX:** 160–161

Pistol, The (Jones), **Supp. XI:** 219, **223–224,** 227, 234

Pit, The (Norris), **III:** 314, 322, 326–327, 333, 334

"Pit, The" (Roethke), **III:** 538

"Pit and the Pendulum, The" (Poe), **III:** 413, 416; **Retro. Supp. II:** 264, 269–270, 273

"Pitcher" (Francis), **Supp. IX:** 82

"Pitcher, The" (Dubus), **Supp. VII:** 87

Pitchford, Nicola, **Supp. XII:** 13

"Pits, The" (D. Graham), **Supp. XI:** 252, 254

Pitt, William, **Supp. I Part 2:** 510, 518

Pitts, Rebecca, **Supp. XXII:** 280, 281

"Pittsburgh" (Carruth), **Supp. XVI:** 58

"Pity Me" (Wylie), **Supp. I Part 2:** 729

Pity the Monsters (Williamson), **Retro. Supp. II:** 185

Pius II, Pope, **III:** 472

Pius IX, Pope, **II:** 79

"Piute Creek" (Snyder), **Supp. VIII:** 293

Pixley, Frank, **I:** 196

Pizer, Donald, **III:** 321; **Retro. Supp. II:** 100, 199

"Place" (Hoffman), **Supp. XVIII:** 86

"Place at the Outskirts" (Simic), **Supp. VIII:** 282

Place Called Estherville, A (Caldwell), **I:** 297, 307

Place Called Freedom, A (Sanders), **Supp. XVI:** 269

Place for My Head, A (Hoffman), **Supp. XVIII:** 76

"Place in Fiction" (Welty), **IV:** 260, 279

Place of Dead Roads, The (Burroughs), **Supp. III Part 1:** 196

Place of Love, The (Shapiro), **Supp. II Part 2:** 702, 706

"Place of Poetry, The" (Stevens), **Retro. Supp. I:** 304

Place of Science in Modern Civilization and Other Essays, The (Veblen), **Supp. I Part 2:** 629, 642

"Place of Trumpets, The" (B. Kelly), **Supp. XVII:** 127

Place on Earth, A (Berry), **Supp. X:** 33–34, 36

Places Left Unfinished at the Time of Creation (Santos), **Supp. XIII:** 274

"Places to Look for Your Mind" (Moore), **Supp. X:** 174–175

"Place They'd Never Seen, A: The Theater" (Wasserstein), **Supp. XV:** 332

"Place to Live, A" (Levertov), **Supp. III Part 1:** 281

"Place to Stand, A" (Price), **Supp. VI:** 258

Place to Stand, A (Wagoner), **Supp. IX:** 324

"Place (Any Place) to Transcend All Places, A" (W. C. Williams), **Retro. Supp. I:** 422

"Place Where My Poems Are Coming From, The"(Crooker), **Supp. XXIII:** 64

Placi, Carlo, **IV:** 328

Plagemann, Catherine, **Supp. XVII:** 91

"Plagiarist, The" (Singer), **IV:** 19

Plague of Dreamers, A (Stern), **Supp. XX:** 178

Plainest Narrative, The (Bronk), **Supp. XXI:** 31

"Plain Language from Truthful James" (Harte). *See* "Heathen Chinee, The"

"Plain Sense of Things, The" (Stevens), **Retro. Supp. I:** 298, 299, 307, 312

"Plain Song" (Carruth), **Supp. XVI:** 54

Plain Song (Harrison), **Supp. VIII: 38–39**

"Plain Song" (Kooser), **Supp. XIX:** 120

"Plain Song for Comadre, A" (Wilbur), **Supp. III Part 2:** 554

"Plain Talk". *See Common Sense* (Paine)

Plaint of a Rose, The (Sandburg), **III:** 579

Plain Truth: Or, Serious Considerations on the Present State of the City of Philadelphia, and Province of Pennsylvania (Franklin), **II:** 117–119

Plainwater: Essays and Poetry (Carson), **Supp. XII:** 97, **99–104**

Plan B (C. Himes), **Supp. XVI:** 143, 144

Plan B: Further Thoughts on Faith (Lamott), **Supp. XX: 142–143**

"Planchette" (London), **II:** 475–476

"Planetarium" (Rich), **Supp. I Part 2:** 557

Planet News: 1961–1967 (Ginsberg), **Supp. II Part 1:** 321

Planet Waves (album, Dylan), **Supp. XVIII:** 27

"Plantation a beginning, a" (Olson), **Supp. II Part 2:** 573

Plant Dreaming Deep (Sarton), **Supp. VIII:** 250, 263

Plante, David, **Supp. IV Part 1:** 310

Planting a Sequoia (Gioia), **Supp. XV:** 117

"Planting a Sequoia" (Gioia), **Supp. XV:** 111, 112, 117, **121–122**

"Plants Fed On By Fawns" (B. Kelly), **Supp. XVII:** 133

Plarr, Victor, **III:** 459, 477

Plath, James, **Retro. Supp. I:** 334; **Supp. XXIII:** 73, 74, 80

Plath, Sylvia, **Retro. Supp. II:** 181, **241–260; Supp. I Part 2:** 526–549, 554, 571; **Supp. III Part 2:** 543, 561; **Supp. IV Part 2:** 439; **Supp. V:** 79,

81, 113, 117, 118, 119, 344; **Supp. X:** 201, 202, **203,** 215; **Supp. XI:** 146, 240, 241, 317; **Supp. XII:** 217, 308; **Supp. XIII:** 35, 76, 312; **Supp. XIV:** 269; **Supp. XV:** 123, 148, 184, 252, 253, 340; **Supp. XVII:** 239; **Supp. XXI:** 58; **Supp. XXII:** 30, 92, 93; **Supp. XXIII:** 63, 64, 112, 113, 254

Plath, Warren, **Supp. I Part 2:** 528

Plato, **I:** 224, 279, 383, 389, 485, 523; **II:** 5, 8, 10, 15, 233, 346, 391–392, 591; **III:** 115, 480, 600, 606, 609, 619–620; **IV:** 74, 140, 333, 363, 364; **Retro. Supp. I:** 247; **Retro. Supp. II:** 31; **Supp. I Part 2:** 595, 631; **Supp. IV Part 1:** 391; **Supp. IV Part 2:** 526; **Supp. X:** 78

"Plato" (Emerson), **II:** 6

"Platonic Relationship, A" (Beattie), **Supp. V:** 22

Platonic Scripts (Justice), **Supp. VII:** 115

Platonov, Dmitri, **Supp. VIII:** 30

Platt, Anthony M., **Supp. I Part 1:** 13–14

Platt, Edward, **Supp. XXIII:** 97

Platte River (Bass), **Supp. XVI:** 19

"Platte River" (Bass), **Supp. XVI:** 20

Plausible Prejudices: Essays on American Writing (Epstein), **Supp. XIV:** 111

Plautus, Titus Maccius, **IV:** 155; **Supp. III Part 2:** 630

Play and Other Stories, The (Dixon), **Supp. XII:** 148, 149

Playback (script) (Chandler), **Supp. IV Part 1:** 131

Playback (Chandler), **Supp. IV Part 1:** 134–135; **Supp. XVIII:** 138

"Play Ball!" (Francis), **Supp. IX:** 89

Playboy of the Western World, The (Synge), **Supp. III Part 1:** 34

Play Days (Jewett), **Retro. Supp. II:** 135

Play Days: A Book of Stories for Children (Jewett), **II:** 401–402

Player Piano (Vonnegut), **Supp. II Part 2:** 756, 757, 760–765

Players (DeLillo), **Supp. VI:** 3, 6, 8, 14

"Players, The" (W. J. Smith), **Supp. XIII:** 340, 343

"Playground, The" (Bradbury), **Supp. IV Part 1:** 104

Playing at Stillness (Espaillat), **Supp. XXI:** 112

Playing in the Dark (Morrison), **Retro. Supp. II:** 118; **Supp. XIII:** 185–186

"Playing the Bawd at Twenty" (Skloot), **Supp. XX: 204–205**

Play in Poetry (Untermeyer), **Supp. XV:** 310

"Playin with Punjab" (Bambara), **Supp. XI:** 6

Play It Again Sam (Allen), **Supp. XV:** 2, 3, 14

Play It as It Lays (Didion), **Supp. IV Part 1:** 198, 201–203, 203, 211

Play It as It Lays (film), **Supp. IV Part 1:** 198

"Plays and Operas Too" (Whitman), **IV:** 350

Plays of Negro Life: A Source-Book of Native American Drama (Locke and Gregory), **Supp. XIV:** 202

Plays: Winesburg and Others (Anderson), **I:** 113
"Playthings" (Komunyakaa), **Supp. XIII:** 126
"Playtime: Danish Fun" (Larsen), **Supp. XVIII:** 120, 122–123
"Playtime: Three Scandinavian Stories" (Larsen), **Supp. XVIII:** 122–123
Playwright's Voice, The (Savran), **Supp. XIII:** 209; **Supp. XV:** 321
Plaza Suite (Simon), **Supp. IV Part 2:** 575, 581–582, 583, 589
Pleading Guilty (Turow), **Supp. XVII:** **218,** 219
"Plea for Captain Brown, A" (Thoreau), **IV:** 185
"Please" (Komunyakaa), **Supp. XIII:** 122
"Please Don't Kill Anything" (A. Miller), **III:** 161
"Please Don't Take My Sunshine Away" (Conroy), **Supp. XVI:** 69
Pleasure Dome (Frankenberg), **I:** 436
Pleasure Dome (Komunyakaa), **Supp. XIII:** 113, 121, **131–133**
Pleasure of Hope, The (Emerson), **II:** 8
"Pleasure of Ruins, The" (McClatchy), **Supp. XII:** 256
"Pleasures of Formal Poetry, The" (Bogan), **Supp. III Part 1:** 51
"Pleasures of Peace, The" (Koch), **Supp. XV:** 180
"Plea to the Protestant Churches, A" (Brooks), **Supp. XIV:** 4
Plimpton, George, **Supp. IV Part 1:** 386; **Supp. V:** 201; **Supp. VIII:** 82, 157; **Supp. IX:** 256; **Supp. XI:** 294; **Supp. XIV:** 82; **Supp. XVI:** **233–248**
Pliny the Elder, **Supp. XVI:** 292
Pliny the Younger, **II:** 113
"Ploesti Isn't Long Island" (Zinberg), **Supp. XV:** 195
"Plot against the Giant, The" (Stevens), **IV:** 81
Plotinus, **Supp. XV:** 33; **Supp. XVI:** 291
Plough and the Stars, The (O'Casey), **III:** 159
"Ploughing on Sunday" (Stevens), **IV:** 74
Plowing the Dark (Powers), **Supp. IX:** 212–213, **221–224**
Plum Bun (Fauset), **Supp. XVIII:** 127; **Supp. XIX:** 73
Plumed Serpent, The (Lawrence), **Supp. XV:** 46
"Plumet Basilisk, The" (Moore), **III:** 203, 208, 215
Plumly, Stanley, **Supp. IV Part 2:** 625
Plummer, Amanda, **Supp. IV Part 1:** 236
Plunder (serial movie), **Supp. IV Part 2:** 464
Plunket, Robert, **Supp. XV:** 68
"Plunkville Patriot" (O'Henry), **Supp. II Part 1:** 389
"Pluralism and Ideological Peace" (Locke), **Supp. XIV:** 202, 212
"Pluralism and Intellectual Democracy" (Locke), **Supp. XIV:** 202, 208, 212
Pluralistic Universe, A (James), **II:** 342, 348, 357–358
Plutarch, **II:** 5, 8, 16, 555; **Retro. Supp. I:** 360; **Supp. XVI:** 292

Plymell, Charles, **Supp. XIV:** 149
Plymell, Pam, **Supp. XIV:** 149
Pnin (Nabokov), **III:** 246; **Retro. Supp. I:** 263, 265, 266, 275, 335
"Po' Boy Blues" (Hughes), **Supp. I Part 1:** 327
Pocahontas, **I:** 4; **II:** 296; **III:** 584
"Pocahontas to Her English Husband, John Rolfe" (Gunn Allen), **Supp. IV Part 1:** 331
"Pocketbook and Sauerkraut" (Di Piero), **Supp. XIX:** 35, 36, 41, 42, 45
"Pocket Poem" (Kooser), **Supp. XIX:** 128
Podhoretz, Norman, **IV:** 441; **Retro. Supp. II:** 323; **Supp. IV Part 1:** 382; **Supp. VIII:** 93, **231–247**; **Supp. IX:** 3; **Supp. XIV:** 103
Podnieks, Elizabeth, **Supp. X:** 189, 190, 191, 192
"Pod of the Milkweed" (Frost), **Retro. Supp. I:** 141
Poe, Edgar Allan, **I:** 48, 53, 103, 190, 194, 200, 210, 211, 261, 340, 459; **II:** 74, 77, 194, 255, 273, 295, 308, 311, 313, 421, 475, 482, 530, 595; **III:** 259, **409–432,** 485, 507, 593; **IV:** 123, 129, 133, 141, 187, 261, 345, 350, 432, 438, 439, 453; **Retro. Supp. I:** 41, 273, 365, 421; **Retro. Supp. II:** 102, 104, 160, 164, 220, **261–277,** 322; **Supp. I Part 1:** 36, 309; **Supp. I Part 2:** 376, 384, 385, 388, 393, 405, 413, 421, 474, 682; **Supp. II Part 1:** 385, 410; **Supp. III Part 2:** 544, 549–550; **Supp. IV Part 1:** 80, 81, 101, 128, 341, 349; **Supp. IV Part 2:** 464, 469; **Supp. VIII:** 105; **Supp. IX:** 115; **Supp. X:** 42, 78; **Supp. XI:** 85, 293; **Supp. XIII:** 100, 111; **Supp. XVI:** 294; **Supp. XVIII:** 3, 11; **Supp. XX:** 74; **Supp. XXIII:** 161, 164, 169, 177, 178
Poe, Edgar Allen, **Supp. XV:** 275; **Supp. XXI:** 51
Poe Abroad: Influence, Reputation, Affinities (Vines), **Retro. Supp. II:** 261
"Poem" (Bishop), **Retro. Supp. II:** 40; **Supp. I Part 1:** 73, 76–79, 82, 95
"Poem" (Harrison), **Supp. VIII:** 38
"Poem" (Justice), **Supp. VII:** 125
"Poem" (Kunitz), **Supp. III Part 1:** 263
"Poem" (Notley), **Supp. XXII:** 228–229
"Poem" (O'Hara), **Supp. XIX:** 85
"Poem" (Wright), **Supp. III Part 2:** 590
"Poem About George Doty in the Death House, A" (Wright), **Supp. III Part 2:** 594–595, 597–598
"Poem about People" (Pinsky), **Supp. VI:** **240–241,** 244, 248
"Poem as Mask, The" (Rukeyser), **Supp. VI:** 281, 285
"Poem Beginning 'The'" (Zukofsky), **Supp. III Part 2:** 610, 611, 614
"Poem Catching Up with an Idea" (Carruth), **Supp. XVI:** 56
"Poem for a Birthday" (Plath), **Supp. I Part 2:** 539

"POEM FOR ANNA RUSS AND FANNY JONES, A" (Baraka), **Supp. II Part 1:** 58
"Poem for Black Hearts, A" (Baraka), **Supp. II Part 1:** 50
"POEM FOR DEEP THINKERS, A" (Baraka), **Supp. II Part 1:** 55
"Poem for D. H. Lawrence" (Creeley), **Supp. IV Part 1:** 141
"Poem for Dorothy, A" (Merwin), **Supp. III Part 1:** 342
"Poem for Hemingway and W. C. Williams" (Carver), **Supp. III Part 1:** 147
"Poem for my Son" (Kumin), **Supp. IV Part 2:** 442
"Poem for People Who Are Understandably Too Busy to Read Poetry" (Dunn), **Supp. XI:** 147
"Poem for Someone Killed in Spain, A" (Jarrell), **II:** 371
"Poem for the Blue Heron, A" (Oliver), **Supp. VII:** 235–236
"Poem for Two Voices" (Everwine), **Supp. XV:** 89
"Poem For Willie Best, A" (Baraka), **Supp. II Part 1:** 36
"Poem in Prose" (Bogan), **Supp. III Part 1:** 58
"Poem in Which I Refuse Contemplation" (Dove), **Supp. IV Part 1:** 249
"Poem Is a Walk, A" (Ammons), **Supp. VII:** 36
"Poem Like a Grenade, A" (Haines), **Supp. XII:** 204
"Poem of Flight, The" (Levine), **Supp. V:** 189
"Poem of Liberation, The" (Stern), **Supp. IX:** 292
Poem of the Cid (Merwin, trans.), **Supp. III Part 1:** 347
"Poem of the Forgotten" (Haines), **Supp. XII:** 202–203
"Poem (V (F) W)"(O'Hara), **Supp. XXIII:** 219
"Poem on a Line by Anne Sexton, 'We Are All Writing God's Poem'"(Crooker), **Supp. XXIII:** 59
"Poem on the Memorable Victory Obtained by the Gallant Captain Paul Jones" (Freneau), **Supp. II Part 1:** 261
"Poem out of Childhood" (Rukeyser), **Supp. VI:** 272, 277
Poem-Paintings (O'Hara and Bluhm), **Supp. XXIII:** 217
"Poem Read at the Dinner Given to the Author by the Medical Profession" (Holmes), **Supp. I Part 1:** 310–311
Poems (Auden), **Supp. II Part 1:** 6
Poems (Berryman), **I:** 170
Poems (Bryant), **II:** 311; **Supp. I Part 1:** 155, 157
Poems (Cummings), **I:** 430, 447
Poems (E. Stoddard), **Supp. XV:** 274
Poems (Eliot), **I:** 580, 588; **IV:** 122; **Retro. Supp. I:** 59, 291
Poems (Emerson), **II:** 7, 8, 12–13, 17
Poems (Holmes), **Supp. I Part 1:** 303
Poems (Koch), **Supp. XV:** 179
Poems (Lowell), **Supp. I Part 2:** 405

Poems (Moore), **III:** 194, 205, 215

Poems (Poe), **III:** 411

Poems (Reznikoff), **Supp. XIV:** 282, 283, 284, 285

Poems (Tate), **IV:** 121

Poems (W. C. Williams), **Retro. Supp. I:** 412–413, 416, 424

Poems (W. J. Smith), **Supp. XIII:** 332

Poems (Winters), **Supp. II Part 2:** 809, 810

Poems (Wordsworth), **I:** 468

Poems, 1909–1925 (Eliot), **Retro. Supp. I:** 64

Poems, 1924–1933 (MacLeish), **III:** 7, 15

Poems, 1943–1956 (Wilbur), **Supp. III Part 2:** 554

Poems, The (Freneau), **Supp. II Part 1:** 263

Poems 1918–1975 : The Complete Poems of Charles Reznikoff (Cooney, ed.), **Supp. XIV:** 289

Poems 1940–1953 (Shapiro), **Supp. II Part 2:** 703, 711

Poems 1947–1954 (Kees), **Supp. XV:** 147

Poems: 1947–1957 (W. J. Smith), **Supp. XIII:** 333

Poems 1957–1967 (Dickey), **Supp. IV Part 1:** 178, 181

Poems about God (Ransom), **III:** 484, 486, 491; **IV:** 121

"Poems about Painting" (Snodgrass), **Supp. VI:** 316

Poems and Essays (Ransom), **III:** 486, 490, 492

Poems and New Poems (Bogan), **Supp. III Part 1:** 60–62

"Poems and Places" (Haines), **Supp. XII:** 203

Poems and Poetry of Europe, The (Longfellow, ed.), **Retro. Supp. II:** 155

Poems by Emily Dickinson (Todd and Higginson, eds.), **I:** 469, 470; **Retro. Supp. I:** 35, 39

Poems by Emily Dickinson, Second Series (Todd and Higginson, eds.), **I:** 454; **Retro. Supp. I:** 35

Poems by Emily Dickinson, The (Bianchi and Hampson, eds.), **Retro. Supp. I:** 35

Poems by Emily Dickinson, Third Series (Todd, ed.), **Retro. Supp. I:** 35

Poems by James Russell Lowell, Second Series (Lowell), **Supp. I Part 2:** 406, 409

Poems by Sidney Lanier, (Lanier), **Supp. I Part 1:** 364

Poems from Black Africa (Hughes, ed.), **Supp. I Part 1:** 344

"Poems I Have Lost, The" (Ortiz), **Supp. IV Part 2:** 507

Poems: North & South–A Cold Spring, (Bishop), **Supp. I Part 1:** 83, 89

Poems of a Jew (Shapiro), **Supp. II Part 2:** 703, 712–713

"Poems of a Mountain Recluse" (Budbill), **Supp. XIX:** 9, 10

Poems of Anna Akhmatova, The (Kunitz and Hayward, trans.), **Supp. III Part 1:** 269

Poems of Emily Dickinson, The (Bianchi and Hampson, eds.), **Retro. Supp. I:** 35

Poems of Emily Dickinson, The (Johnson, ed.), **I:** 470

Poems of François Villon (Kinnell, trans.), **Supp. III Part 1:** 235, 243, 249

"Poems of Our Climate, The" (Stevens), **Retro. Supp. I:** 313

Poems of Philip Freneau, Written Chiefly during the Late War (Freneau), **Supp. II Part 1:** 261

Poems of Places (Longfellow, ed.), **II:** 490; **Retro. Supp. II:** 155; **Supp. I Part 1:** 368

Poems of Stanley Kunitz, The (Kunitz), **Supp. III Part 1:** 258, 263, 264, 266, 268

"Poems of These States" (Ginsberg), **Supp. II Part 1:** 323, 325

Poems of Two Friends (Howells and Piatt), **II:** 273, 277

"POEM SOME PEOPLE WILL HAVE TO UNDERSTAND, A" (Baraka), **Supp. II Part 1:** 49

Poems on Slavery (Longfellow), **II:** 489; **Retro. Supp. II:** 157, 168; **Supp. I Part 2:** 406

Poems on Various Subjects (Rowson), **Supp. XV:** 232

Poems on Various Subjects, Religious and Moral (Wheatley), **Supp. XX: 277, 282, 284, 285, 289**

Poem Spoken at the Public Commencement at Yale College, in New Haven; September 1, 1781, A (Barlow), **Supp. II Part 1:** 67–68, 74, 75

Poems Retrieved (O'Hara), **Supp. XXIII:** 220

Poems to Solve (Swenson), **Supp. IV Part 2:** 642

Poems Written and Published during the American Revolutionary War (Freneau), **Supp. II Part 1:** 273, 274

Poems Written between the Years 1768 and 1794 (Freneau), **Supp. II Part 1:** 269

"Poem That Took the Place of a Mountain" (Olson), **Supp. II Part 2:** 582

"Poem to My First Lover" (Olds), **Supp. X:** 206

"Poem to the Reader" (Olds), **Supp. X:** 213

"Poem with No Ending, A" (Levine), **Supp. V:** 186, 190

"Poem You Asked For, The" (Levis), **Supp. XI:** 259–260

Poe Poe Poe Poe Poe Poe Poe (Hoffman), **Retro. Supp. II:** 265

Poesía Náhuatl, **Supp. XV:** 77

Poésies 1917–1920 (Cocteau), **Retro. Supp. I:** 82

"Poesis: A Conceit" (Sobin), **Supp. XVI:** 288

"Poet" (Taggard), **Supp. XXII:** 284

Poet, The (Connelly), **Supp. XXI: 71, 78**

"Poet, The" (Dunbar), **Supp. II Part 1:** 207, 209–210

"Poet, The" (Emerson), **II:** 13, 19, 20, 170

"Poet, The" (Ortiz), **Supp. IV Part 2:** 505

"Poet and His Book, The" (Millay), **III:** 126, 138

"Poet and His Public, The" (Jarrell), **Supp. I Part 1:** 96

"Poet and His Song, The" (Dunbar), **Supp. II Part 1:** 199

"Poet and the Person, The" (Kinard), **Supp. XIV:** 127

"Poet and the Queen, The" (Shaw), **Supp. XIX:** 241

"Poet and the World, The" (Cowley), **Supp. II Part 1:** 145

"Poet as Anti-Specialist, The" (Swenson), **Supp. IV Part 2:** 638, 643

"Poet as *Curandera*" (Mora), **Supp. XIII:** 214, 220

"Poet as Hero, The: Keats in His Letters" (Trilling), **Supp. III Part 2:** 506–507

"Poet as Religious Moralist, The" (Larson), **Supp. XI:** 328

"Poet at Seven, The" (Rimbaud), **II:** 545

Poet at the Breakfast-Table, The (Holmes), **Supp. I Part 1:** 313–314

"Poète contumace, Le" (Corbiere), **II:** 384–385

"Poet for President, A" (Mora), **Supp. XIII:** 220–221

Poetic Achievement of Ezra Pound, The (Alexander), **Retro. Supp. I:** 293

Poetic Diction: A Study in Meaning (Barfield), **III:** 274, 279

"Poetic Principle, The" (Poe), **III:** 421, 426; **Retro. Supp. II:** 266

"Poetics" (Ammons), **Supp. VII:** 29–30

Poetics (Aristotle), **III:** 422; **Supp. XI:** 249; **Supp. XIII:** 75; **Supp. XIV:** 243; **Supp. XV:** 265

Poetics of Space, The (Bachelard), **Supp. XIII:** 225; **Supp. XVI:** 292

"Poetics of the Periphery: Literary Experimentalism in Kathy Acker's *In Memoriam to Identity*" (Acker), **Supp. XII:** 17

"Poetics of the Physical World, The" (Kinnell), **Supp. III Part 1:** 239

"Poetics of Tourette Syndrome, The: Language, Neurobiology, and Poetry" (Schleifer), **Supp. XVIII:** 144

Poet in the World, The (Levertov), **Supp. III Part 1:** 271, 273, 278, 282

"Poet or the Growth of a Lit'ry Figure" (White), **Supp. I Part 2:** 676

Poetry (Barber), **Supp. IV Part 2:** 550

"Poetry" (Moore), **III:** 204–205, 215

"Poetry" (Nye), **Supp. XIII:** 282

"Poetry" (Wrigley), **Supp. XVIII:** 301–302

"Poetry, Community and Climax" (Snyder), **Supp. VIII:** 290

"Poetry, Pleasure, and the Hedonist Reader" (Collins), **Supp. XXI:** 54

"Poetry: A Metrical Essay" (Holmes), **Supp. I Part 1:** 310

"Poetry and Belief in Thomas Hardy" (Schwartz), **Supp. II Part 2:** 666

Poetry and Criticism (Nemerov, ed.), **III:** 269

"Poetry and Drama" (Eliot), **I:** 588

Poetry and Fiction: Essays (Nemerov), **III:** 269, 281

"Poetry and Place" (Berry), **Supp. X:** 22, 28, 31, 32

Poetry and Poets (Lowell), **II:** 512

"Poetry and Religion" (Jarman), **Supp. XVII:** 111

Poetry and the Age (Jarrell), **IV:** 352; **Retro. Supp. I:** 121; **Supp. II Part 1:** 135

"Poetry and the Primitive: Notes on Poetry as an Ecological Survival Technique" (Snyder), **Supp. VIII:** 291, 292, 299, 300

"Poetry and the Public World" (MacLeish), **III:** 11

Poetry and the World (Pinsky), **Supp. VI:** 236, 239, 244, 247

Poetry and Truth (Olson), **Supp. II Part 2:** 583

"Poetry and Uncertainty"(Hirshfield), **Supp. XXIII:** 137

"Poetry As a Way of Life" (Bishop interview), **Retro. Supp. II:** 53

"Poetry as Survival" (Harrison), **Supp. VIII:** 45

"Poetry Failure" (Halliday), **Supp. XIX:** 92

Poetry for Students (Taibl), **Supp. XV:** 255

"Poetry for the Advanced" (Baraka), **Supp. II Part 1:** 58

"Poetry Friendship on Earth" (Halliday), **Supp. XIX:** 90, 91

Poetry Handbook, A (Oliver), **Supp. VII:** 229, 245

Poetry Home Repair Manual, The (Kooser), **Supp. XIX:** 116, 128

Poetry in Motion: 100 Poems from the Subways and Buses (Peacock, ed.), **Supp. XIX:** 195

"Poetry of Barbarism, The" (Santayana), **IV:** 353

Poetry of Chaucer, The (Gardner), **Supp. VI: 63**

Poetry of Meditation, The (Martz), **IV:** 151; **Supp. I Part 1:** 107

Poetry of Mourning: The Modern Elegy from Hardy to Heaney (Ramazani), **Supp. IV Part 2:** 450

Poetry of Stephen Crane, The (Hoffman), **I:** 405

Poetry of the Negro, 1746–1949, The (Hughes and Bontemps), **Supp. I Part 1:** 345; **Supp. XXII:** 11

Poetry 180: A Turning Back to Poetry (Collins, ed.), **Supp. XXI:** 54

Poetry Reading against the Vietnam War, A (Bly and Ray, eds.), **Supp. IV Part 1:** 61, 63

"Poetry Workshop, The" (column, Kumin), **Supp. XX: 164**

"Poetry Wreck, The" (Shapiro), **Supp. II Part 2:** 717

Poetry Wreck, The: Selected Essays (Shapiro), **Supp. II Part 2:** 703, 704, 717

"Poets" (X. J. Kennedy), **Supp. XV:** 158

Poet's Alphabet, A: Reflections on the Literary Art and Vocation (Bogan), **Supp. III Part 1:** 55, 64

Poets and Poetry of America (Griswold), **Supp. XV:** 277

Poet's Choice (Engle and Langland, eds.), **III:** 277, 542

Poet's Guide to Poetry, A (Kinzie), **Supp. XXIII:** 124

"Poet's Husband Engages in Gourmet Cooking, The" (Espaillat), **Supp. XXI:** 99

Poets of the Old Testament, The (Gordon), **III:** 199

Poets of Today (Wheelock, ed.), **Supp. IV Part 2:** 639

Poets on Poetry (Nemerov, ed.), **III:** 269

"Poet's Tact, and a Necessary Tactlessness, The" (C. Frost), **Supp. XV:** 94–95

"Poet's View, A" (Levertov), **Supp. III Part 1:** 284

"Poet's Voice, The" (Oliver), **Supp. VII:** 245

"Poets with History and Poets Without History"(Tsvetaeva), **Supp. XXIII:** 168

"Poet Turns on Himself, The" (Dickey), **Supp. IV Part 1:** 177, 181, 185

Poganuc People (Stowe), **Supp. I Part 2:** 581, 596, 599–600

Pogo (comic strip), **Supp. XI:** 105

Pohrt, Tom, **Supp. XIX:** 123

Poincaré, Raymond, **IV:** 320

"Point, The" (Hayden), **Supp. II Part 1:** 373

"Point at Issue!, A" (Chopin), **Retro. Supp. II:** 61; **Supp. I Part 1:** 208

"Point of Age, A" (Berryman), **I:** 173

Point of No Return (Marquand), **III:** 56, 59–60, 65, 67, 69

Point Reyes Poems (R. Bly), **Supp. IV Part 1:** 71

"Points" (Hoffman), **Supp. XVIII:** 86

Points for a Compass Rose (Connell), **Supp. XIV:** 79, 80, 96

"Point Shirley" (Plath), **Supp. I Part 2:** 529, 538

Points in Time (Bowles), **Supp. IV Part 1:** 93

"Points West" (column), **Supp. IV Part 1:** 198

Poirier, Richard, **I:** 136, 239; **III:** 34; **Retro. Supp. I:** 134; **Retro. Supp. II:** 207–208; **Supp. I Part 2:** 660, 665; **Supp. IV Part 2:** 690

Poison Pen (Garrett), **Supp. VII:** 111

Poisonwood Bible, The (Kingsolver), **Supp. VII:** 197–198, 202, 210–213

Poitier, Sidney, **Supp. IV Part 1:** 360, 362

Pokerface (Collins), **Supp. XXI:** 53

"Polack Reverie" (Halliday), **Supp. XIX:** 88

Polanco, Richard, **Supp. XX: 260**

"Polar Bear" (Heller), **Supp. IV Part 1:** 383

"Polar Seas and Sir John Franklin, The" (Briggs), **Supp. XVIII:** 14

Pole, Rupert, **Supp. X:** 185

"Pole Star" (MacLeish), **III:** 16

Po Li, **Supp. I Part 1:** 262

Police (Baraka), **Supp. II Part 1:** 47

"Police" (Corso), **Supp. XII:** 117, 127

"Police Court Saturday Morning" (X. J. Kennedy), **Supp. XV:** 170

"Police Dreams" (Bausch), **Supp. VII:** 47

Politian (Poe), **III:** 412

"Political and Practical Conceptions of Race, The" (Locke), **Supp. XIV:** 209–210

Political Essays (Lowell), **Supp. I Part 2:** 407

Political Fable, A (Coover), **Supp. V:** 44, 46, 47, 49, 51

"Political Fables" (Mather), **Supp. II Part 2:** 450

"Political Interests" (Stevens), **Retro. Supp. I:** 295

"Political Litany, A" (Freneau), **Supp. II Part 1:** 257

"Political Migrations: A Family Story" (Mallon), **Supp. XIX:** 141–142

"Political Pastoral" (Frost), **Retro. Supp. I:** 139

"Political Poem" (Baraka), **Supp. II Part 1:** 36

Politics (Acker), **Supp. XII:** 3, 4

Politics (Macdonald), **I:** 233–234

"Politics" (Paley), **Supp. VI:** 217

"Politics, Structure, and Poetic Development" (McCombs), **Supp. XIII:** 33

"Politics and the English Language" (Orwell), **Retro. Supp. II:** 287; **Supp. I Part 2:** 620

Politics and the Novel (Howe), **Supp. VI:** 113

"Politics and the Personal Lyric in the Poetry of Joy Harjo and C. D. Wright" (Goodman), **Supp. XV:** 344

"Politics of Ethnic Authorship, The: Li-Young Lee, Emerson, and Whitman at the Banquet Table" (Partridge), **Supp. XV:** 219

"Politics of Silence, The" (Monette), **Supp. X:** 148

Polito, Robert, **Supp. XVIII:** 33

Politt, Katha, **Supp. XII:** 159

Polk, James, **Supp. XIII:** 20

Polk, James K., **I:** 17; **II:** 433–434

Pollack, Sydney, **Supp. XIII:** 159

"Pollen" (Nye), **Supp. XIII:** 284

Pollitt, Katha, **Supp. X:** 186, 191, 193; **Supp. XVI:** 39

Pollock, Jackson, **IV:** 411, 420; **Supp. XV:** 145, 177, 178; **Supp. XIX:** 33; **Supp. XXIII:** 208, 210, 211

"Polly" (Chopin), **Retro. Supp. II:** 72

Polo, Marco, **III:** 395

Polonsky, Abraham, **Supp. XXI:** 261, 275

Polybius, **Supp. I Part 2:** 491

"Polydore" (Chopin), **Retro. Supp. II:** 66

"Pomegranate" (Glück), **Supp. V:** 82

"Pomegranate Seed" (Wharton), **IV:** 316; **Retro. Supp. I:** 382

Ponce de Leon, Luis, **III:** 391

"Pond, The" (Nemerov), **III:** 272

"Pond at Dusk, The" (Kenyon), **Supp. VII:** 168

Ponder Heart, The (Welty), **IV:** 261, 274–275, 281; **Retro. Supp. I:** 351–352

"Ponderosa Pine" (Huncke), **Supp. XIV:** 146

Ponsot, Margaret, **Supp. XVII:** 241

"Pony" (Sanders), **Supp. XVI:** 277

"Pony Car"(P. Benedict), **Supp. XXIII:** 47

Poodle Springs (Parker and Chandler), **Supp. IV Part 1:** 135; **Supp. XIX:** 189

Poodle Springs Story, The (Chandler), **Supp. IV Part 1:** 135

"Pool, The" (Doolittle), **Supp. I Part 1:** 264–265

Poole, Ernest, **II:** 444

"Pool Lights" (F. Barthelme), **Supp. XI:** 25, 26–27, 36

"Pool Room in the Lions Club" (Merwin), **Supp. III Part 1:** 346

"Poolside" (Skloot), **Supp. XX: 202–203**

"Poor Black Fellow" (Hughes), **Retro. Supp. I:** 204

"Poor Bustard, The" (Corso), **Supp. XII:** 134

"Poor but Happy" (Mamet), **Supp. XIV:** 252, 253

"Poor Dead Feet of My First Husband, The"(Schott), **Supp. XXIII:** 241

Poore, Charles, **III:** 364; **Supp. XIX:** 257, 264; **Supp. XX:** 38

Poor Fool (Caldwell), **I:** 291, 292, 308

Poorhouse Fair, The (Updike), **IV:** 214, 228–229, 232; **Retro. Supp. I:** 317, 320

"Poor Joanna" (Jewett), **II:** 394

"Poor Man's Pudding and Rich Man's Crumbs" (Melville), **III:** 89–90

"Poor Richard" (James), **II:** 322

Poor Richard's Almanac (undated) (Franklin), **II:** 112

Poor Richard's Almanac for 1733 (Franklin), **II:** 108, 110

Poor Richard's Almanac for 1739 (Franklin), **II:** 112

Poor Richard's Almanac for 1758 (Franklin), **II:** 101

Poor White (Anderson), **I:** 110–111

"Poor Working Girl" (Z. Fitzgerald), **Supp. IX:** 71

Popa, Vasko, **Supp. VIII:** 272

Pope, Alexander, **I:** 198, 204; **II:** 17, 114; **III:** 263, 267, 288, 517; **IV:** 145; **Retro. Supp. I:** 335; **Supp. I Part 1:** 150, 152, 310; **Supp. I Part 2:** 407, 422, 516, 714; **Supp. II Part 1:** 70, 71; **Supp. X:** 32, 36; **Supp. XII:** 260; **Supp. XV:** 258; **Supp. XX:** 280

Pope, James, **Supp. XXII:** 196

Pope-Hennessy, James, **Supp. XIV:** 348

"Pope's Penis, The" (Olds), **Supp. X:** 207

"Poplar, Sycamore" (Wilbur), **Supp. III Part 2:** 549

Popo and Fifina: Children of Haiti (Hughes and Bontemps), **Retro. Supp. I:** 203; **Supp. XXII:** 4, 10, 12

"Poppies" (Oliver), **Supp. VII:** 240

"Poppies in July" (Plath), **Supp. I Part 2:** 544

"Poppies in July"(Crooker), **Supp. XXIII:** 61

"Poppies in October" (Plath), **Supp. I Part 2:** 544

"Poppycock" (Francis), **Supp. IX:** 87

"Poppy Juice" (Taggard), **Supp. XXII:** 276

"Poppy Seed" (Lowell), **II:** 523

"Popular Art and the Cultural Tradition" (C. L. R. James), **Supp. XXI:** 170

Popular Book, The: A History of America's Literary Taste (Hart), **Supp. XVIII:** 257, 258

Popular Culture (Goldbarth), **Supp. XII: 186**

Popular History of the United States (Gay), **Supp. I Part 1:** 158

"Popular Songs" (Ashbery), **Supp. III Part 1:** 6

"Populist Manifesto" (Ferlinghetti), **Supp. VIII:** 290

"Porcelain Bowl" (Glück), **Supp. V:** 83

Porcher, Frances, **Retro. Supp. II:** 71

Porco, Mike, **Supp. XVIII:** 24

"Porcupine, The" (Kinnell), **Supp. III Part 1:** 244

Porcupine's Kiss, The (Dobyns), **Supp. XIII: 89–90**

"Por esas coases que pasan" (Hinojosa), **Supp. XIX:** 101

Porgy and Bess (film), **Supp. I Part 1:** 66

Porgy and Bess (play), **Supp. IV Part 1:** 6

"Porn Bought my Football" (Offutt), **Supp. XIX:** 163

"Porphyria's Lover" (Browning), **II:** 522

Portable Beat Reader, The (Charters, ed.), **Supp. XIV:** 152

Portable Blake, The (Kazin, ed.), **Supp. VIII:** 103

Portable Faulkner, The (Cowley, ed.), **II:** 57, 59; **Retro. Supp. I:** 73

Portable Paul and Jane Bowles, The (Dillon), **Supp. IV Part 1:** 95

Portable Veblen, The (Veblen), **Supp. I Part 2:** 630, 650

"Porte-Cochere" (Taylor), **Supp. V:** 320

"Porter" (Hughes), **Supp. I Part 1:** 327

"Porter" (Nelson), **Supp. XVIII:** 175

Porter, Bern, **III:** 171

Porter, Cole, **Supp. IX:** 189

Porter, Eliot, **Supp. IV Part 2:** 599

Porter, Fairfield, **Supp. XV:** 178; **Supp. XXIII:** 209, 211, 212

Porter, Herman W., **Supp. I Part 1:** 49

Porter, Horace, **Retro. Supp. II:** 4, 127

Porter, Jacob, **Supp. I Part 1:** 153

Porter, Katherine Anne, **I:** 97, 385; **II:** 194, 606; **III: 433–455**, 482; **IV:** 26, 138, 246, 261, 279, 280, 282; **Retro. Supp. I:** 354; **Retro. Supp. II:** 233, 235; **Supp. IV Part 1:** 31, 310; **Supp. V:** 225; **Supp. VIII:** 156, 157; **Supp. IX:** 93, 94, 95, 98, 128; **Supp. X:** 50; **Supp. XIII:** 294; **Supp. XIV:** 3; **Supp. XV:** 338

Porter, Noah, **Supp. I Part 2:** 640

Porter, William Sydney. *See* Henry, O.

"Porter Paints a Picture"(O'Hara), **Supp. XXIII:** 212

Porteus, Beilby, **Supp. I Part 1:** 150

"Portland Going Out, The" (Merwin), **Supp. III Part 1:** 345

Portnoy's Complaint (P. Roth), **Retro. Supp. II: 282–286**, 291; **Supp. III Part 2:** 401, 404, 405, 407, 412–414, 426; **Supp. V:** 119, 122; **Supp. XI:** 140; **Supp. XVII:** 8, 43; **Supp. XX: 177**

Port of Saints (Burroughs), **Supp. III Part 1:** 106

"Portrait" (Dixon), **Supp. XII:** 154

"Portrait, A" (Parker), **Supp. IX:** 192–193

"Portrait, The" (Kunitz), **Supp. III Part 1:** 263

"Portrait, The" (Wharton), **Retro. Supp. I:** 364

"Portrait d'une Femme" (Pound), **Retro. Supp. I:** 288

Portrait in Brownstone (Auchincloss), **Supp. IV Part 1:** 21, 23, 27, 31

"Portrait in Georgia" (Toomer), **Supp. IX:** 314

"Portrait in Greys, A" (W. C. Williams), **Retro. Supp. I:** 416

"Portrait of a Girl in Glass" (T. Williams), **IV:** 383

"Portrait of a Jewelry Drummer" (Untermeyer), **Supp. XV:** 299–300

"Portrait of a Lady" (Eliot), **I:** 569, 570, 571, 584; **III:** 4; **Retro. Supp. I:** 55, 56, 62

Portrait of a Lady, The (James), **I:** 10, 258, 461–462, 464; **II:** 323, 325, 327, 328–329, 334; **Retro. Supp. I:** 215, 216, 217, 219, 220, 223, **224–225**, 232, 233, 381

"Portrait of an Artist" (P. Roth), **Supp. III Part 2:** 412

Portrait of an Eye: Three Novels (Acker), **Supp. XII:** 6, **7–9**

"Portrait of an Invisible Man" (Auster), **Supp. XII:** 21

"Portrait of a Supreme Court Judge" (Untermeyer), **Supp. XV:** 299

Portrait of Bascom Hawkes, A (Wolfe), **IV:** 451–452, 456

Portrait of Edith Wharton (Lubbock), **Retro. Supp. I:** 366

Portrait of Logan Pearsall Smith, Drawn from His Letters and Diaries, A (Russell, ed.), **Supp. XIV:** 349

Portrait of Picasso as a Young Man (Mailer), **Retro. Supp. II:** 213

"Portrait of the Artist as an Old Man, A" (Humphrey), **Supp. IX:** 109

Portrait of the Artist as a Young Man, A (Joyce), **I:** 475–476; **III:** 471, 561; **Retro. Supp. I:** 127; **Retro. Supp. II:** 4, 331; **Supp. IX:** 236; **Supp. XIII:** 53, 95

"Portrait of the Artist with Hart Crane" (Wright), **Supp. V:** 342

"Portrait of the Great White Hunter Fox-hunting in the Absence of Big Game" (Major), **Supp. XXII:** 183

"Portrait of the Intellectual as a Yale Man" (McCarthy), **II:** 563, 564–565

"Portrait of the Reader with a Bowl of Cereal, A" (Collins), **Supp. XXI:** 55

"Portrait of the Self . . . , A" (Sobin), **Supp. XVI:** 288

Portraits and Elegies (Schnackenberg), **Supp. XV:** 249, **253–256**

"Portraits of Grief" *(New York Times),* **Supp. XIX:** 142

"Port Town" (Hughes), **Retro. Supp. I:** 199

Portuguese Voyages to America in the Fifteenth Century (Morison), **Supp. I Part 2:** 488

"Po' Sandy" (Chesnutt), **Supp. XIV:** 60

Poseidon Adventure, The (film), **Supp. XII:** 321

Poseidon Adventure, The (Gallico), **Supp. XVI:** 238

"Poseidon and Company" (Carver), **Supp. III Part 1:** 137

"Positive Obsession" (O. Butler), **Supp. XIII:** 70

Poss, Stanley, **Supp. XIV:** 166

Possession (Byatt), **Supp. XXI:** 147

"Possessions" (H. Crane), **I:** 392–393; **Retro. Supp. II:** 78

Possible World, A (Koch), **Supp. XV:** 184

Postal Inspector (film), **Supp. XIII:** 166

Postcards (Proulx), **Supp. VII:** 249, 256–258, 262

"Postcard to Send to Sumer, A" (Bronk), **Supp. XXI:** 31

"Postcolonialism and Autobiography" (Skinner and Waller), **Supp. XXII:** 78

"Postcolonial Tale, A" (Harjo), **Supp. XII:** 227

"Posthumous Letter to Gilbert White" (Auden), **Supp. II Part 1:** 26

"Post-Larkin Triste" (Karr), **Supp. XI:** 242–243

Postlethwaite, Diana, **Supp. XII:** 317–318; **Supp. XVI:** 176

"Postlude" (W. C. Williams), **Retro. Supp. I:** 415

Postman, Neil, **Supp. XI:** 275

Postman Always Rings Twice, The (Cain), **Supp. XIII:** 165–166

Postman Always Rings Twice, The (film), **Supp. XIV:** 241

"Postmaster and the Clerk, The" (Budbill), **Supp. XIX:** 9

"Postmortem Guide, A" (Dunn), **Supp. XI:** 155

Postrel, Virginia, **Supp. XIV:** 298, 311

"Postscript" (Du Bois), **Supp. II Part 1:** 173

"Postscript" (Nye), **Supp. XIII:** 287

Postsouthern Sense of Place, The (Bone), **Supp. XXII:** 247

"Potato" (Wilbur), **Supp. III Part 2:** 545

"Potatoes' Dance, The" (Lindsay), **Supp. I Part 2:** 394

Pot of Earth, The (MacLeish), **III:** 5, 6–8, 10, 12, 18

"Pot Roast" (Strand), **Supp. IV Part 2:** 629

Potshot (Parker), **Supp. XIX:** 185

Pot Shots at Poetry (Francis), **Supp. IX:** **83–84**

Potter, Beatrix, **Supp. I Part 2:** 656; **Supp. XVI:** 100

Potter, Stephen, **IV:** 430

Potter's House, The (Stegner), **Supp. IV Part 2:** 598, 606

Poulenc, Francis, **Supp. IV Part 1:** 81

Poulin, Al, Jr., **Supp. IX:** 272; **Supp. XI:** 259

Pound, Ezra, **I:** 49, 58, 60, 66, 68, 69, 105, 236, 243, 256, 384, 403, 428, 429, 475, 476, 482, 487, 521, 578; **II:** 26, 55, 168, 263, 316, 371, 376, 513, 517, 520, 526, 528, 529, 530; **III:** 2, 5, 8, 9, 13–14, 17, 174, 194, 196, 278, 430, 453, **456–479**, 492, 504, 511, 523, 524, 527, 575–576, 586, 590; **IV:** 27, 28, 407, 415, 416, 433, 446; **Retro. Supp. I:** 51, 52, 55, 58, 59, 63, 82, 89, 127, 140, 171, 177, 178, 198, 216, **283–294**, 298, 299, 359, 411, 412, 413, 414, 417, 418, 419, 420, 423, 426, 427, 430, 431; **Retro. Supp. II:** 178, 183, 189, 326; **Supp. I Part 1:** 253, 255–258, 261–268, 272, 274; **Supp. I Part 2:** 387, 721; **Supp. II Part 1:** 1, 8, 20, 30, 91, 136; **Supp. III Part 1:** 48, 63, 64, 73, 105, 146, 225, 271; **Supp. III Part 2:** 542, **609–617**, 619, 620, 622, 625, 626, 628, 631; **Supp. IV Part 1:** 153, 314; **Supp. V:** 331, 338, 340, 343, 345; **Supp. VIII:** 39, 105, 195, 205, 271, 290, 291, 292, 303; **Supp. IX:** 291; **Supp. X:** 24, 36, 112, 120, 122; **Supp. XII:** 97; **Supp. XIV:** 11, 55, 83, 272, 284, 286, 287, 347; **Supp. XV:** 20, 42, 43, 51, 93, 161, 181, 297, 298, 299, 301, 302, 306; **Supp. XVI:** 47, 282; **Supp. XVII:** 111, 226–227; **Supp. XIX:** 42; **Supp. XXI:** 33; **Supp. XXII:** 165; **Supp. XXIII:** 26, 166, 174

Pound, Louise, **Retro. Supp. I:** 4; **Supp. XV:** 137

Pound, T. S., **I:** 428

"Pound Reweighed" (Cowley), **Supp. II Part 1:** 143

Powell, Anthony, **Supp. XVIII:** 136, 146; **Supp. XIX:** 131

Powell, Betty, **Retro. Supp. II:** 140

Powell, D. A., **Supp. XXIII:** 221

Powell, Dawn, **Supp. IV Part 2:** 678, 682; **Supp. XIX:** 143

Powell, Dick, **Supp. IX:** 250

Powell, John Wesley, **Supp. IV Part 2:** 598, 604, 611

Powell, Lawrence Clark, **III:** 189

Powell, William, **Supp. IV Part 1:** 355

"Power" (Corso), **Supp. XII:** 117, 126, 127, **128**

"Power" (Emerson), **II:** 2, 3

"Power" (Rich), **Supp. I Part 2:** 569

Power, Samantha, **Supp. XXIII:** 25, 26, 27

"Power and Light" (Dickey), **Supp. IV Part 1:** 182

Power and the Glory, The (Greene), **III:** 556

"Powerhouse" (Welty), **Retro. Supp. I:** 343, 346

"Power Never Dominion" (Rukeyser), **Supp. VI:** 281

"Power of Fancy, The" (Freneau), **Supp. II Part 1:** 255

Power of Myth, The (Campbell), **Supp. IX:** 245

"Power of Prayer, The" (Lanier), **Supp. I Part 1:** 357

"Power of Stories, The" (Sanders), **Supp. XVI:** 278

"Power of Suggestion" (Auchincloss), **Supp. IV Part 1:** 33

Power of Sympathy, The (Brown), **Supp. II Part 1:** 74

Power Politics (Atwood), **Supp. XIII:** 20, 33–34, 35

Powers, Catherine A., **Supp. XXII:** 217

Powers, J. F., **Supp. V:** 319; **Supp. XVII:** 43

Powers, Kim, **Supp. VIII:** 329, 340

Powers, Richard, **Supp. IX:** **207–225;** **Supp. XVII:** 183; **Supp. XX:** **93;** **Supp. XXII:** 49

Powers of Attorney (Auchincloss), **Supp. IV Part 1:** 31, 32, 33

"Powers of Darkness" (Wharton), **Retro. Supp. I:** 379

Powys, John Cowper, **Supp. I Part 2:** 454, 476; **Supp. IX:** 135

Poynton, Jerome, **Supp. XIV:** 147, 150

Pozorski, Aimee L., **Supp. XXII:** 160, 166

Practical Agitation (Chapman), **Supp. XIV:** 41

Practical Criticism: A Study of Literary Judgment (Richards), **Supp. XIV:** 3, 16

Practical Magic (film), **Supp. X:** 80

Practical Magic (Hoffman), **Supp. X:** 78, 82, **88–89**

"Practical Methods of Meditation, The" (Dawson), **IV:** 151

Practical Navigator, The (Bowditch), **Supp. I Part 2:** 482

Practice of Perspective, The (Dubreuil), **Supp. IV Part 2:** 425

Practice of Reading, The (Donoghue), **Supp. VIII:** 189

Pragmatism: A New Name for Some Old Ways of Thinking (James), **II:** 352

"Pragmatism's Conception of Truth" (James), **Supp. XIV:** 40

Prague Orgy, The (P. Roth), **Retro. Supp. II:** 280

"Praire, The" (Clampitt), **Supp. IX:** 42

"Prairie" (Sandburg), **III:** 583, 584

Prairie, The (Cooper), **I:** 339, 342

"Prairie Birthday" (Leopold), **Supp. XIV:** 185

Prairie Home Companion, A (Keillor, radio program), **Supp. XIII:** 274; **Supp. XVI:** 169–171, 173–178

Prairie Home Morning Show, A (Keillor, radio program), **Supp. XVI:** 171

"Prairie Life, A Citizen Speaks" (Dunn), **Supp. XI:** 145

"Prairies, The" (Bryant), **Supp. I Part 1:** 157, 162, 163, 166

Praise (Hass), **Supp. VI:** 104–105, 106

"Praise for an Urn" (Crane), **I:** 388

"Praise for Sick Women" (Snyder), **Supp. VIII:** 294

"Praise in Summer" (Wilbur), **Supp. III Part 2:** 546–548, 560, 562

"Praise of a Palmtree" (Levertov), **Supp. III Part 1:** 284

"Praise of the Committee" (Rukeyser), **Supp. VI:** 278

"Praises, The" (Goldbarth), **Supp. XII:** 185

"Praises, The" (Olson), **Supp. II Part 2:** 558, 560, 563, 564

Praises and Dispraises (Des Pres), **Supp. X:** 120

Praisesong for the Widow (Marshall), **Supp. IV Part 1:** 14; **Supp. XI:** 18, 276, 278, **284–286**, 287; **Supp. XX: 154**

"Praise to the End!" (Roethke), **III:** 529, 532, 539

Prajadhipok, King of Siam, **I:** 522

Prater Violet (Isherwood), **Supp. XIV: 164–166**, 169–170, 171

Pratt, Anna (Anna Alcott), **Supp. I Part 1:** 33

Pratt, Louis H., **Retro. Supp. II:** 6

Pratt, Mary Louise, **Retro. Supp. II:** 48

Pratt, Parley, **Supp. IV Part 2:** 603

"Prattler" (newspaper column), **I:** 207

"Prattler, The" (Bierce), **I:** 196

"Prayer" (Gioia), **Supp. XV:** 117

"Prayer" (Olds), **Supp. X:** 204

"Prayer" (Peacock), **Supp. XIX:** 198, 199, 200

"Prayer" (Toomer), **Supp. IX:** 318

"Prayer, A" (Kushner), **Supp. IX: 134**

"Prayer for Columbus" (Whitman), **IV:** 348

"Prayer for My Daughter" (Yeats), **II:** 598

"Prayer for My Grandfather to Our Lady, A" (Lowell), **II:** 541–542

"Prayer for my Son" (C. Frost), **Supp. XV:** 98–99

"Prayer for Our Daughters" (Jarman), **Supp. XVII:** 120

Prayer for Owen Meany, A (Irving), **Supp. VI:** 164, 165, 166, **175–176**

"PRAYER FOR SAVING" (Baraka), **Supp. II Part 1:** 52–53

"Prayer in Spring, A" (Frost), **II:** 153, 164

"Prayer Meeting" (Di Piero), **Supp. XIX:** 46, 47

"Prayer on All Saint's Day" (Cowley), **Supp. II Part 1:** 138, 153

Prayers for Dark People (Du Bois), **Supp. II Part 1:** 186

"Prayer to Hermes" (Creeley), **Supp. IV Part 1:** 156, 157

"Prayer to Masks" (Senghor), **Supp. IV Part 1:** 16

"Prayer to the Child of Prague" (Salinas), **Supp. XIII:** 327

"Prayer to the Good Poet" (Wright), **Supp. III Part 2:** 603

"Prayer to the Pacific" (Silko), **Supp. IV Part 2:** 560

"Pray without Ceasing" (Emerson), **II:** 9–10

Praz, Mario, **IV:** 430

"Preacher, The" (Whittier), **Supp. I Part 2:** 698–699

Preacher and the Slave, The (Stegner), **Supp. IV Part 2:** 599, 608, 609

Precaution (Cooper), **I:** 337, 339

"Precautions"(Karyotakis, trans. Hadas), **Supp. XXIII:** 125

"Preconceptions of Economic Science, The" (Veblen), **Supp. I Part 2:** 634

Predecessors, Et Cetera (Clampitt), **Supp. IX:** 37

"Predicament, A" (Poe), **Retro. Supp. II:** 273

Predilections (Moore), **III:** 194

Prefaces and Prejudices (Mencken), **III:** 99, 104, 106, 119

Preface to a Twenty Volume Suicide Note. . . . (Baraka), **Supp. II Part 1:** 31, 33–34, 51, 61

"Preference" (Wylie), **Supp. I Part 2:** 713

"Prejudice against the Past, The" (Moore), **IV:** 91

Prejudices (Mencken), **Supp. I Part 2:** 630

Prejudices: A Selection (Farrell, ed.), **III:** 116

Prejudices: First Series (Mencken), **III:** 105

"Preliminary Remarks on the Poetry in the First Person" (Wright), **Supp. XV:** 339

Prelude, A: Landscapes, Characters and Conversations from the Earlier Years of My Life (Wilson), **IV:** 426, 427, 430, 434, 445

Prelude, The (Wordsworth), **III:** 528; **IV:** 331, 343; **Supp. I Part 2:** 416, 676; **Supp. XI:** 248

Prelude and Liebestod (McNally), **Supp. XIII:** 201

"Preludes" (Eliot), **I:** 573, 576, 577; **Retro. Supp. I:** 55; **Supp. IV Part 2:** 436

Preludes for Memnon (Aiken), **I:** 59, 65

Preludes from Memnon (Aiken), **Supp. X:** 50

"Prelude to an Evening" (Ransom), **III:** 491, 492–493

Prelude to Darkness (Salinas), **Supp. XIII:** 311, **318–319**, 320

"Prelude to the Present" (Mumford), **Supp. II Part 2:** 471

"Premature Burial, The" (Poe), **III:** 415, 416, 418; **Retro. Supp. II:** 270

"Premeditations"(Schott), **Supp. XXIII:** 247

Preminger, Otto, **Supp. IX:** 3, 9; **Supp. XX: 246–247**

"Premonition" (Hay), **Supp. XIV:** 122

"Premonitions of the Bread Line" (Komunyakaa), **Supp. XIII:** 114, 115

Prenshaw, Peggy Whitman, **Supp. X:** 229

"Preparations" (Silko), **Supp. IV Part 2:** 560

Preparatory Meditations (Taylor), **IV:** 145, 148, 149, 150, 152, 153, 154–155, 164, 165

"Prepare" (Carruth), **Supp. XVI:** 59

Prepositions: The Collected Critical Essays of Louis Zukofsky (Zukofsky), **Supp. III Part 2:** 630

Prescott, Anne, **Supp. IV Part 1:** 299

Prescott, Orville, **Supp. IV Part 2:** 680; **Supp. XI:** 340; **Supp. XXIII:** 13

Prescott, Peter, **Supp. X:** 83

Prescott, Peter S., **Supp. XVI:** 212

Prescott, William, **Retro. Supp. I:** 123

Prescott, William Hickling, **II:** 9, 310, 313–314; **IV:** 309; **Supp. I Part 2:** 414, 479, 493, 494

"Prescription of Painful Ends" (Jeffers), **Supp. II Part 2:** 424

"Presence, The" (Gordon), **II:** 199, 200

"Presence, The" (Kumin), **Supp. IV Part 2:** 445, 455

Presence and Desire: Essays on Gender, Sexuality, Performance (Dolan), **Supp. XV:** 327

"Presence of Others, The" (Kenyon), **Supp. VII:** 164

Presences (Taylor), **Supp. V:** 325

"Present Age, The" (Emerson), **II:** 11–12

Present Danger, The: Do We Have the Will to Reverse the Decline of American Power? (Podhoretz), **Supp. VIII:** 241

"Present for the Boy, A" (Swados), **Supp. XIX:** 259

Present for Young Ladies, A (Rowson), **Supp. XV:** 245

"Present Hour" (Sandburg), **III:** 593–594

Present Philosophical Tendencies (Perry), **I:** 224

"Present State of Ethical Philosophy, The" (Emerson), **II:** 9

"Present State of Poetry, The" (Schwartz), **Supp. II Part 2:** 666

"Preservation of Innocence" (Baldwin), **Supp. I Part 1:** 51

"Preserving Wildness" (Berry), **Supp. X:** 28, 29, 32

"President and Other Intellectuals, The" (Kazin), **Supp. VIII:** 104

Presidential Papers, The (Mailer), **III:** 35, 37–38, 42, 45; **Retro. Supp. II:** 203, 204, 206

"Presidents" (Merwin), **Supp. III Part 1:** 351

Presnell, Robert, Sr., **Supp. XIII:** 166

Pressley, Nelson, **Supp. XVIII:** 37–38

"PRES SPOKE IN A LANGUAGE" (Baraka), **Supp. II Part 1:** 60

Presumed Innocent (Turow), **Supp. XVII:** 214–216, 223; 217

"Pretext, The" (Wharton), **Retro. Supp. I:** 371

Pretty Baby (film), **Supp. XXI:** 252

Pretty Boy Floyd (McMurtry), **Supp. V:** 231

"Pretty Girl, The" (Dubus), **Supp. VII:** 87–88

"Pretty Mouth and Green My Eyes" (Salinger), **III:** 560

"Previous Condition" (Baldwin), **Supp. I Part 1:** 51, 55, 63

"Previous Tenant, The" (Simpson), **Supp. IX:** 278–279

Prevost, Verbie Lovorn, **Supp. XXI:** 45

Priaulx, Allan, **Supp. XI:** 228

Price, Alan, **Retro. Supp. I:** 377

Price, Reynolds, **Supp. VI: 253–270; Supp. IX:** 256, 257

Price, Richard, **II:** 9; **Supp. I Part 2:** 522; **Supp. XX:** 85

Price, The (A. Miller), **III:** 165–166

"Price Is Right, The" (Skloot), **Supp. XX: 198–199**

"Price of the Harness, The" (Crane), **I:** 414

Pricksongs & Descants; Fictions (Coover), **Supp. V:** 39, 42, 43, 49, 50

"Pride" (Hughes), **Supp. I Part 1:** 331

Pride and Prejudice (Austen), **II:** 290

Prideaux, Tom, **Supp. IV Part 2:** 574, 590

"Priesthood, The" (Winters), **Supp. II Part 2:** 786

Priestly, Joseph, **Supp. I Part 2:** 522

Primary Colors, The (A. Theroux), **Supp. VIII:** 312

"Primary Ground, A" (Rich), **Supp. I Part 2:** 563

"Prime" (Auden), **Supp. II Part 1:** 22

"Primer Class" (Bishop), **Retro. Supp. II:** 38, 51

Primer for Blacks (Brooks), **Supp. III Part 1:** 85

"Primer for the Nuclear Age" (Dove), **Supp. IV Part 1:** 246

Primer mensaje a la América Hispana (W. Frank), **Supp. XX: 76**

Primer of Ignorance, A (Blackmur), **Supp. II Part 1:** 91

Prime-Stevenson, Edward Irenaeus, **Supp. XX: 235**

Primitive, The (C. Himes), **Supp. XVI:** 139, **141–142**

"Primitive Black Man, The" (Du Bois), **Supp. II Part 1:** 176

"Primitive Like an Orb, A" (Stevens), **IV:** 89; **Retro. Supp. I:** 309

Primitive People (Prose), **Supp. XVI:** 255, 256, 257

"Primitive Singing" (Lindsay), **Supp. I Part 2:** 389–390

Primitivism and Decadence (Winters), **Supp. II Part 2:** 786, 803–807, 812

Primrose, Archibald Philip, **Supp. XX: 230**

Prince, Richard, **Supp. XII:** 4

"Prince, The" (Jarrell), **II:** 379

"Prince, The" (Winters), **Supp. II Part 2:** 802

Prince and the Pauper, The (Twain), **IV:** 200–201, 206

Prince Hagen (Sinclair), **Supp. V:** 280

Prince of a Fellow, A (Hearon), **Supp. VIII:** 58, **62–63**

Princess, The (Tennyson), **Supp. I Part 2:** 410

Princess and the Goblins, The (Macdonald), **Supp. XIII:** 75

Princess Casamassima, The (James), **II:** 276, 291; **IV:** 202; **Retro. Supp. I:** 216, 221, 222, 225, **226–227**

"Princess Casamassima, The" (Trilling), **Supp. III Part 2:** 502, 503

Princess of Arcady, A (Henry), **Retro. Supp. II:** 97

"Principles" (Du Bois), **Supp. II Part 1:** 172

Principles of Literary Criticism (Richards), **I:** 274; **Supp. I Part 1:** 264; **Supp. XIV:** 3

Principles of Psychology, The (James), **II:** 321, 350–352, 353, 354, 357, 362, 363–364; **IV:** 28, 29, 32, 37

Principles of Psychology, The (W. James), **Supp. XVII:** 97

Principles of Zoölogy (Agassiz), **Supp. I Part 1:** 312

Prior, Sir James, **II:** 315

Prior, Matthew, **II:** 111; **III:** 521

"Prison, The" (Malamud), **Supp. I Part 2:** 431, 437

"Prisoned Love" (Boyce), **Supp. XXI:** 9

Prisoner of Ours, The (Weigl), **Supp. XIX:** 288

Prisoner of Second Avenue, The (Simon), **Supp. IV Part 2:** 583, 584

Prisoner of Sex, The (Mailer), **III:** 46; **Retro. Supp. II:** 206

Prisoner of Zenda, The (film), **Supp. I Part 2:** 615

Prisoner's Dilemma (Powers), **Supp. IX:** 212, **214–216,** 221

Prison Memoirs of an Anarchist (A. Berkman), **Supp. XVII:** 103–104

Pritchard, William, **Supp. XVI:** 71

Pritchard, William H., **Retro. Supp. I:** 131, 141; **Supp. IV Part 1:** 285; **Supp. IV Part 2:** 642; **Supp. XI:** 326

Pritchett, V. S., **II:** 587; **Supp. II Part 1:** 143; **Supp. VIII:** 171; **Supp. XIII:** 168

"Privatation and Publication" (Cowley), **Supp. II Part 1:** 149

Private Contentment (Price), **Supp. VI:** 263

"Private History of a Campaign That Failed" (Twain), **IV:** 195

Private I, The: Privacy in a Public World (Peacock, ed.), **Supp. XIX:** 193, 203

Private Life of Axie Reed, The (Knowles), **Supp. XII:** 249

Private Line (Major), **Supp. XXII:** 174

"Private Man Confronts His Vulgarities at Dawn, A" (Dunn), **Supp. XI:** 146

Private Memoirs and Confessions of a Justified Sinner, The (Hogg), **Supp. IX:** 276

"Private Property and the Common Wealth" (Berry), **Supp. X:** 25

Private Snafu series (Geisel), **Supp. XVI:** 102

"Private Theatricals" (Howells), **II:** 280

Private Women, Public Stage: Literary Domesticity in Nineteenth-Century America (Kelley), **Supp. XVIII:** 257

Privilege, The (Kumin), **Supp. IV Part 2:** 442–444, 451

Prize Stories 1918 : The O. Henry Awards, **Supp. XVI:** 16

"Probe" (Ryan as Quin), **Supp. XVIII:** 229

"Probing the Dark" (Komunyakaa), **Supp. XIII:** 131

"Problem from Hell, A": America and the Age of Genocide (Power), **Supp. XXIII:** 25, 27–28

"Problem from Milton, A" (Wilbur), **Supp. III Part 2:** 550

"Problem of Anxiety, The" (Koch), **Supp. XV:** 183

"Problem of Being, The" (James), **II:** 360

Problem of Classification in the Theory of Value, The (Locke), **Supp. XIV:** 199

"Problem of Evil into Cocoon" (Taggard), **Supp. XXII:** 284

"Problem of Housing the Negro, The" (Du Bois), **Supp. II Part 1:** 168

"Problem of the Religious Novel, The" (Isherwood), **Supp. XIV:** 172

Problems and Other Stories (Updike), **Retro. Supp. I:** 322, 329

Problems of Dostoevsky's Poetics (Bakhtin), **Supp. XXII:** 259

"Problem Solving" (Goldbarth), **Supp. XII:** 185

Procedures for Underground (Atwood), **Supp. XIII:** 33

"Procedures for Underground" (Atwood), **Supp. XIII:** 33

Procession, The (al-Mawákib) (Gibran), **Supp. XX: 116, 124**

Processional (Lawson), **I:** 479

"Procession at Candlemas, A" (Clampitt), **Supp. IX:** 41

"Proclamation" (Saunders), **Supp. XIX:** 235

Proclus, **Retro. Supp. I:** 247

"Prodigal" (Ammons), **Supp. VII:** 29

"Prodigal" (Hoffman), **Supp. XVIII:** 86

"Prodigal, The" (Bishop), **Supp. I Part 1:** 90, 92

Prodigal Parents, The (Lewis), **II:** 454–455

"Prodigy" (Simic), **Supp. VIII:** 278

Producers, The (film, M. Brooks), **Supp. XVII:** 45

"Proem" (Crane), **I:** 397

"Proem, The: By the Carpenter" (O. Henry), **Supp. II Part 1:** 409

"Professions for Women" (Woolf), **Supp. XIII:** 305

"Professor" (Hughes), **Supp. I Part 1:** 330

"Professor, The" (Bourne), **I:** 223

Professor at the Breakfast Table, The (Holmes), **Supp. I Part 1:** 313, 316

"Professor Clark's Economics" (Veblen), **Supp. I Part 2:** 634

Professor of Desire, The (P. Roth), **Retro. Supp. II:** 288; **Supp. III Part 2:** 403, 418–420

Professor's House, The (Cather), **I:** 325–336; **Retro. Supp. I:** 16

"Professor Veblen" (Mencken), **Supp. I Part 2:** 630

Proffer, Carl R., **Supp. VIII:** 22

Profile Makers, The (Bierds), **Supp. XVII:** 29, **30–32,** 33

"Profile of the Tenderloin Street Prostitute, A" (Vollmann), **Supp. XVII:** 230

Profits of Religion, The (Sinclair), **Supp. V:** 276

"Prognosis" (Warren), **IV:** 245

"Progress" (F. Wright), **Supp. XVII:** 247

"Progress Report" (Simic), **Supp. VIII:** 278

"Project for a Trip to China" (Sontag), **Supp. II Part 2:** 454, 469

"Project for *The Ambassadors*" (James), **Retro. Supp. I:** 229

"Projection" (Nemerov), **III:** 275

"Projective Verse" (Olson), **Supp. III Part 1:** 30; **Supp. III Part 2:** 555, 556, 557, 624; **Supp. IV Part 1:** 139, 153; **Supp. VIII:** 290

"Projector, The" (Baker), **Supp. XIII:** 53, 55

Prokofiev, Sergey Sergeyevich, **Supp. IV Part 1:** 81

"Prolegomena, Section 1" (Pound), **Supp. III Part 2:** 615–616

"Prolegomena, Section 2" (Pound), **Supp. III Part 2:** 616

"Prolegomenon to a Biography of Mailer" (Lucid), **Retro. Supp. II:** 195

Proletarian Literature in the United States (Hicks), **Supp. I Part 2:** 609–610

"Prologue" (MacLeish), **III:** 8, 14

Prologue, for Full Chorus of Mixed Voices and Orchestra (Taggard and Schuman), **Supp. XXII:** 283

"Prologue to a Life" (D. West), **Supp. XVIII:** 280

"Prologue to Our Time" (Mumford), **Supp. III Part 2:** 473

"Prometheus" (Longfellow), **II:** 494

Prometheus Bound (Lowell), **II:** 543, 544, 545, 555

Promise, The (Buck), **Supp. II Part 1:** 124

"Promise, The" (Olds), **Supp. X:** 213

"Promise and Fulfillment" (D. West), **Supp. XVIII:** 278

Promised Land (Parker), **Supp. XIX:** 183, 184, 190

Promised Land, The (M. Antin), **Supp. IX:** 227; **Supp. XVI:** 148, 149; **Supp. XX:** 1, 2, 3, **4–9,** 11

Promised Land, The (Porter), **III:** 447

"Promised Land, The" (R. Fisher), **Supp. XIX:** 72

Promised Lands (Sontag), **Supp. III Part 2:** 452

Promise of American Life, The (Croly), **I:** 229

"Promise of Blue Horses, The" (Harjo), **Supp. XII:** 228

Promise of Rest, The (Price), **Supp. VI:** 262, 266

Promises (Warren), **Supp. XIV:** 15

Promises, Promises (musical), **Supp. IV Part 2:** 575

Promises: Poems 1954–1956 (Warren), **IV:** 244–245, 249, 252

"Promise This When You Be Dying" (Dickinson), **Retro. Supp. I:** 44, 46

"Pronoun Variations"(Hadas), **Supp. XXIII:** 120

Proof, The (Winters), **Supp. II Part 2:** 786, 791, 792–794

Proofs and Theories: Essays on Poetry (Glück), **Supp. V:** 77, 79, 92; **Supp. XIV:** 269

"Propaganda of History, The" (Du Bois), **Supp. II Part 1:** 182

Propertius, Sextus, **III:** 467; **Retro. Supp. II:** 187; **Supp. XII:** 2

Property Of: A Novel (Hoffman), **Supp. X:** 77, 79, **80–82**

Property of Loss" (W. V. Davis), **Supp. XXI:** 95

"Prophecy of Samuel Sewall, The" (Whittier), **Supp. I Part 2:** 699

Prophet, The (Asch), **Supp. XXIII:** 7

Prophet, The (Gibran), **Supp. XX:** **113, 115, 119–121, 126**

"Prophet, The" (Notley), **Supp. XXII:** 229

"Prophet and the Child, The" (Gibran), **Supp. XX:** **123**

Propheteers, The (Apple), **Supp. XVII:** **6–7**

"Prophetic Pictures, The" (Hawthorne), **II:** 227

"Proportion" (Lowell), **II:** 525

"Proposal" (Carver), **Supp. III Part 1:** 149

Proposals Relating to the Education of Youth in Pensilvania (Franklin), **II:** 113

"Proposed New Version of the Bible" (Franklin), **II:** 110

Prose, Francine, **Supp. XII:** 333; **Supp. XVI:** **249–264; Supp. XIX:** 209; **Supp. XXIII:** 300

"Prose for Departure" (Merrill), **Supp. III Part 1:** 336

Prose Pieces (Bynner), **Supp. XV:** 52

"Prose Poem as an Evolving Form, The" (R. Bly), **Supp. IV Part 1:** 64

"Proserpina and the Devil" (Wilder), **IV:** 358

"Prosody" (Espaillat), **Supp. XXI:** 102

"Prosody" (Shapiro), **Supp. II Part 2:** 710

Prospect before Us, The (Dos Passos), **I:** 491

"Prospective Immigrants Please Note" (Rich), **Supp. I Part 2:** 555

Prospect of Peace, The (Barlow), **Supp. II Part 1:** 67, 68, 75

Prospects of Literature, The (L. P. Smith), **Supp. XIV:** 343

Prospects on the Rubicon (Paine), **Supp. I Part 2:** 510–511

Prospectus of a National Institution, to Be Established in the United States (Barlow), **Supp. II Part 1:** 80, 82

Prospice (Browning), **IV:** 366

"Protestant Easter" (Sexton), **Supp. II Part 2:** 684

"Prothalamion" (Schwartz), **Supp. II Part 2:** 649, 652

"Prothalamion" (Spenser), **Retro. Supp. I:** 62

Proud, Robert, **Supp. I Part 1:** 125

"Proud Farmer, The" (Lindsay), **Supp. I Part 2:** 381

Proud Flesh (Humphrey), **Supp. IX:** 94, 95, 96, **102–103,** 104, 105, 109

"Proud Flesh" (Warren), **IV:** 243

Proud Lady (Boyce), **Supp. XXI:** 7, 12

"Proud Lady" (Wylie), **Supp. I Part 2:** 711–712

Proulx, Annie, **Supp. VII:** **249–267**

Proust, Marcel, **I:** 89, 319, 327, 377, 461; **II:** 377, 514, 606; **III:** 174, 181, 184, 244–245, 259, 471; **IV:** 32, 201, 237, 301, 312, 328, 359, 428, 431, 434, 439, 443, 466, 467; **Retro. Supp. I:** 75, 89, 169, 335; **Supp. III Part 1:** 10, 12, 14, 15; **Supp. IV Part 2:** 600; **Supp. VIII:** 103; **Supp. IX:** 211; **Supp. X:** 193, 194; **Supp. XII:** 289; **Supp. XIV:** 24, 83, 95; **Supp. XVI:** 295; **Supp. XXI:** 231; **Supp. XXIII:** 122

Proverbs, **Supp. X:** 45

"Proverbs" (Jarman), **Supp. XVII:** 118

"Providence" (Komunyakaa), **Supp. XIII:** 132

"Provident Woman, A" (Boyce), **Supp. XXI:** 10

"Provincetown Postcards" (F. Wright), **Supp. XVII:** 244

"Provincia deserta" (Pound), **Retro. Supp. I:** 289

"Provisional Remarks on Being / A Poet / of Arkansas" (Wright), **Supp. XV:** 337

Pruette, Lorine, **Supp. IV Part 2:** 522

Prufrock and Other Observations (Eliot), **I:** 569–570, 571, 573, 574, 576–577, 583, 584, 585; **Retro. Supp. I:** 59, 62

"Prufrock's Perivigilium" (T. S. Eliot), **Retro. Supp. I:** 57

Pryor, Richard, **Supp. XIII:** 343

Pryse, Marjorie, **Retro. Supp. II:** 139, 146

"Psalm" (Ginsberg), **Supp. II Part 1:** 312

"Psalm" (Simic), **Supp. VIII:** 282

"Psalm, A, or Supplication for mercy, and confession of Sin, addressed to the Author of Life, in the Odjibway-Alqonquin tongue"(J. Schoolcraft), **Supp. XXIII:** 232

"Psalm and Lament" (Justice), **Supp. VII:** 116, 117–118, 120–122, 124

"Psalm for Pinhook" (Ray), **Supp. XVIII:** 202

"Psalm Jew, The"(Asch). *See Salvation* (Asch)

"Psalm of Life, A" (Longfellow), **II:** 489, 496; **Retro. Supp. II:** 164, 168, 169; **Supp. I Part 2:** 409

"Psalm of the West" (Lanier), **Supp. I Part 1:** 362, 364

"Psalm: Our Fathers" (Merwin), **Supp. III Part 1:** 350

Psalms (biblical book), **I:** 83; **II:** 168, 232; **Retro. Supp. I:** 62; **Supp. I Part 1:** 125

Psalms, Hymns, and Spiritual Songs of the Rev. Isaac Watts, The (Worcester, ed.), **I:** 458

Psychiatric Novels of Oliver Wendell Holmes, The (Oberndorf), **Supp. I Part 1:** 315

"Psychology and Form" (Burke), **I:** 270

Psychology: Briefer Course (James), **II:** 351–352

Psychology of Art (Malraux), **IV:** 434

Psychology of Insanity, The (Hart), **I:** 241–242, 248–250

Psychopathia Sexualis (Shanley), **Supp. XIV:** 316, **329**

Psychophysiks (Fechner), **II:** 358

"Pu-239" (Kalfus), **Supp. XVII:** 50

"Publication is the Auction" (Dickinson), **Retro. Supp. I:** 31

"Public Bath, The" (Snyder), **Supp. VIII:** 298

Public Burning, The (Coover), **Supp. IV Part 1:** 388; **Supp. V:** 44, 45, 46–47, 48, 51, 52; **Supp. XVII:** 6

"Public Burning of Julius and Ethel Rosenberg, The: An Historical Romance" (Coover), **Supp. V:** 44

"Public Figure" (Hay), **Supp. XIV:** 124

"Public Garden, The" (Lowell), **II:** 550

Public Good (Paine), **Supp. I Part 2:** 509–510

Public Poetry of Robert Lowell, The (Cosgrave), **Retro. Supp. II:** 185

"Public & Private" (column, Quindlen), **Supp. XVII:** 165, 167, 169–170

Public Speech: Poems (MacLeish), **III:** 15–16

Public Spirit (Savage), **II:** 111

"Public Woman, A" (Cliff), **Supp. XXII:** 76

Puccini, Giacomo, **Supp. XXI:** 150, 151

"Puck" (Monette), **Supp. X:** 157–158

Pudd'nhead Wilson (Twain), **I:** 197

"Pudd'nhead Wilson's Calendar" (Twain), **I:** 197

"Pueblo Revolt, The" (Sando), **Supp. IV Part 2:** 510

Puella (Dickey), **Supp. IV Part 1:** 178, 185

Pulitzer, Alfred, **Retro. Supp. I:** 257

Pull Down Vanity (Fiedler), **Supp. XIII:** 103

Pullman, George, **Supp. I Part 1:** 9

"Pullman Car Hiawatha" (Wilder), **IV:** 365–366

Pull My Daisy (film), **Supp. XII:** 126–127

"Pulp Cutters' Nativity, A" (Budbill), **Supp. XIX:** 9

"Pulpit and the Pew, The" (Holmes), **Supp. I Part 1:** 302

"Pulse-Beats and Pen-Strokes" (Sandburg), **III:** 579

"Pump, The" (Humphrey), **Supp. IX:** 101

Pump House Gang, The (Wolfe), **Supp. III Part 2:** 575, 578, 580, 581

Punch, Brothers, Punch and Other Sketches (Twain), **IV:** 200

Punch: The Immortal Liar, Documents in His History (Aiken), **I:** 57, 61

Punishment Without Vengeance (Vega; Merwin, trans.), **Supp. III Part 1:** 341, 347

"Pupil" (F. Barthelme), **Supp. XI:** 26

"Pupil, The" (H. James), **Supp. XX:** 233

"Pupil, The" (James), **II:** 331; **Retro. Supp. I:** 217, 219, 228

"Purchase" (Banks), **Supp. V:** 6

"Purchase of Some Golf Clubs, A" (O'Hara), **III:** 369

"Purdah" (Plath), **Supp. I Part 2:** 602

Purdy, Charles, **Supp. VIII:** 330

Purdy, James, **Supp. VII:** 269–285

Purdy, Theodore, **Supp. VIII:** 153

Pure (C. Frost), **Supp. XV:** 93, **101–102**, 104, 106

"Pure" (C. Frost), **Supp. XV:** 101–102

"Pure and the Good, The: On Baseball and Backpaking" (Maclean), **Supp. XIV:** 222

"Pure Good of Theory, The" (Stevens), **Retro. Supp. I:** 310

Purgatorio (Dante), **III:** 182

"Purim Parade" (Espaillat), **Supp. XXI:** 108

Puritan Family (Morgan), **Supp. I Part 1:** 101

"Puritanical Pleasures" (Hardwick), **Supp. III Part 1:** 213–214

Puritan Origins of the American Self, The (Bercovitch), **Supp. I Part 1:** 99

Puritan Pronaos, The: Studies in the Intellectual Life of New England in the Seventeenth Century (Morison), **Supp. I Part 2:** 485

"Puritan Realism: *The Wide, Wide World* and *Robinson Crusoe*" (Kim), **Supp. XVIII:** 267

Puritans, The (P. Miller), **Supp. VIII:** 101

"Puritan's Ballad, The" (Wylie), **Supp. I Part 2:** 723

"Purloined Letter, The" (Poe), **Retro. Supp. II:** 271, 272

Purple Cane Road (Burke), **Supp. XIV:** 32, 33

Purple Decades, The (Wolfe), **Supp. III Part 2:** 584

"Purple Hat, The" (Welty), **IV:** 264

Purple Rose of Cairo, The (film; Allen), **Supp. XV:** 1, **9–10**, 12, 14

Purser, John T., **Supp. XIV:** 4

"Pursuit of Happiness" (Simpson), **Supp. IX:** 279

"Pursuit of Happiness, The" (Ashbery), **Supp. III Part 1:** 23

Pursuit of the Prodigal, The (Auchincloss), **Supp. IV Part 1:** 25

Pushcart at the Curb, A (Dos Passos), **I:** 478, 479

"Pushcart Man" (Hughes), **Supp. I Part 1:** 330

Pushcart Prize, XIII, The (Ford), **Supp. V:** 58

Pushcart Prize VII, The (Hendeson, ed.), **Supp. XVII:** 16

Pushcart Prize XIV, The (Henderson, ed.), **Supp. XVII:** 18

Pushcart Prize XX, The (Henderson, ed.), **Supp. XVII:** 20

"Pushing 100" (Mora), **Supp. XIII:** 215

Pushkin, Aleksander, **III:** 246, 261, 262; **Retro. Supp. I:** 266, 269; **Supp. XVI:** 188

Pussy, King of the Pirates (Acker), **Supp. XII:** 6–7

"Pussycat and the Expert Plumber Who Was a Man, The" (A. Miller), **III:** 146–147

Pussycat Fever (Acker), **Supp. XII:** 6

Putnam, George Haven, **Supp. XVIII:** 257, 260

Putnam, George P., **II:** 314; **Supp. XVIII:** 3–4, 14, 260

Putnam, Phelps, **I:** 288

Putnam, Samuel, **II:** 26; **III:** 479; **Supp. III Part 2:** 615

"Put Off the Wedding Five Times and Nobody Comes to It" (Sandburg), **III:** 586–587

Puttenham, George, **Supp. I Part 1:** 113

Puttermesser Papers, The (Ozick), **Supp. V:** 269

"Putting a Burden Down" (Peacock), **Supp. XIX:** 199

"Putting on *Visit to a Small Planet*" (Vidal), **Supp. IV Part 2:** 683

Put Yourself in My Shoes (Carver), **Supp. III Part 1:** 139

"Put Yourself in My Shoes" (Carver), **Supp. III Part 1:** 139, 141

Putzi, Jennifer, **Supp. XV:** 284

Puzo, Mario, **Supp. IV Part 1:** 390

"Puzzle of Modern Society, The" (Kazin), **Supp. VIII:** 103

Pygmalion (Shaw), **Supp. XII:** 14

Pyle, Ernie, **III:** 148; **Supp. V:** 240; **Supp. XVII:** 61

Pylon (Faulkner), **II:** 64–65, 73; **Retro. Supp. I:** 84, 85

Pynchon, Thomas, **III:** 258; **Retro. Supp. I:** 278; **Retro. Supp. II:** 279, 324; **Supp. II Part 2:** 557, **617–638**; **Supp. III Part 1:** 217; **Supp. IV Part 1:** 53, 279; **Supp. IV Part 2:** 570; **Supp. V:** 40, 44, 52; **Supp. VIII:** 14; **Supp. IX:** 207, 208, 212; **Supp. X:** 260, 301, 302; **Supp. XI:** 103; **Supp. XII:** 289; **Supp. XIV:** 49, 53, 54, 96; **Supp. XVI:** 123, 126; **Supp. XVII:** 183, 225, 232, 236; **Supp. XIX:** 223; **Supp. XX:** 21, 83, 87; **Supp. XXIII:** 42, 101

Pyne, John, **Supp. XXI:** 7

Pyne, Mary, **Supp. XXI:** 7

Pyrah, Gill, **Supp. V:** 126

"Pyramid Club, The" (Doctorow), **Supp. IV Part 1:** 234

"Pyrography" (Ashbery), **Supp. III Part 1:** 18

Pythagoras, **I:** 332

Pythagorean Silence (Howe), **Supp. IV Part 2:** 426, 428–429

Q

QBVII (television movie), **Supp. XX: 247**

QBVII (Uris), **Supp. XX: 244, 247, 248, 251, 253–254**

"Qebehseneuf" (Goldbarth), **Supp. XII:** 186

"Quadroons, The" (Child), **Supp. XVIII:** 124

"Quai d'Orléans" (Bishop), **Supp. I Part 1:** 89

"Quail for Mr. Forester" (Humphrey), **Supp. IX:** 94

"Quail in Autumn" (W. J. Smith), **Supp. XIII:** 334–335, 339

Quaker City, The: or, The Monks of Monk Hall (Lippard), **Supp. XXIII:** 177, 178–179, **180–183,** 184, 187, 188–189, 190

"Quaker Graveyard in Nantucket, The" (Lowell), **II:** 54, 550; **Retro. Supp. II:** 178, 186–187

"Quake Theory" (Olds), **Supp. X:** 203

Qualey, Carlton C., **Supp. I Part 2:** 650

Quality of Hurt, The (C. Himes), **Supp. XVI:** 137, 145

"Quality of Wine" (Carruth), **Supp. XVI:** 59

"Quality Time" (Kingsolver), **Supp. VII:** 203

"Quandary" (F. Wright), **Supp. XVII:** 244

Quang-Ngau-chè, **III:** 473

Quarles, Francis, **I:** 178, 179

"Quarrel" (Taggard), **Supp. XXII:** 276

Quarry, The (Chesnutt), **Supp. XIV:** 76

"Quarry, The" (Nemerov), **III:** 272

Quarry, The: New Poems (Eberhart), **I:** 532, 539

Quartermain, Peter, **Supp. IV Part 2:** 423, 434

Quatermain, Peter, **Supp. XXII:** 163

"Quaternions, The" (Bradstreet), **Supp. I Part 1:** 104–106, 114, 122

"Quatrains for Ishi" (Komunyakaa), **Supp. XIII:** 129

Queechy (S. Warner as Wetherell), **Supp. XVIII:** 257, **264–266**

"Queen Elizabeth and the Blind Girl or Music for the Dead Children" (B. Kelly), **Supp. XVII:** 124, 125

"Queen of the Blues" (Brooks), **Supp. III Part 1:** 75

Queen of the Damned, The (Rice), **Supp. VII:** 290, 292–293, 297, 299

Queen of the Mob (film), **Supp. XIII:** 170

"Queens of France" (Wilder), **IV:** 365

"Queen's Twin, The" (Jewett), **Retro. Supp. II:** 138

Queen's Twin, The, and Other Stories (Jewett), **Retro. Supp. II:** 140

Queen Victoria (Strachey), **Supp. I Part 2:** 485, 494; **Supp. XIV:** 342

Queer (Burroughs), **Supp. III Part 1:** 93–102

"Queer Aztlán"(Moraga), **Supp. XXIII:** 201

"Queer Beer" (Hansberry), **Supp. IV Part 1:** 374

"Quelques considérations sur la méthode subjective" (James), **II:** 345–346

"Quest, The" (Gibran), **Supp. XX:** 124

"Question" (Swenson), **Supp. IV Part 2:** 640

"Question and Answer" (Hughes), **Retro. Supp. I:** 211

"Questioning Faces" (Frost), **Retro. Supp. I:** 141

"Question Mark in the Circle, The" (Stegner), **Supp. IV Part 2:** 597

"Questionnaire, The" (Snodgrass), **Supp. VI:** 318

"Question of Fidelity, A" (Beauvoir), **Supp. IX:** 4

"Question of Loneliness, A" (Swados), **Supp. XIX:** 262

"Question of Our Speech, The" (Ozick), **Supp. V:** 272

"Question of Simone de Beauvoir, The" (Algren), **Supp. IX:** 4

Questions About Angels (Collins), **Supp. XXI:** 54, 58, 59, 60, 64

Questions for Ecclesiastes (Jarman), **Supp. XVII:** 109, 110, **118–119**

"Questions of Geography" (Hollander), **Supp. I Part 1:** 96

Questions of Travel (Bishop), **Retro. Supp. II: 46–48; Supp. I Part 1:** 72, 83, 92, 94

"Questions of Travel" (Bishop), **Retro. Supp. II:** 47

"Questions to Tourists Stopped by a Pineapple Field" (Merwin), **Supp. III Part 1:** 355

"Questions without Answers" (T. Williams), **IV:** 384

"Quest of the Purple-Fringed, The" (Frost), **Retro. Supp. I:** 139

Quest of the Silver Fleece, The (Du Bois), **Supp. II Part 1:** 176–178

Quevedo y Villegas, Francisco Gómez, **Retro. Supp. I:** 423

Quickly: A Column for Slow Readers (Mailer), **Retro. Supp. II:** 202

Quicksand (Larsen), **Supp. XVIII:** 119, 121, 122, **124–127**

Quicksand and Passing (Larsen; McDowell, ed.), **Supp. XVIII:** 125

"Quies," (Pound), **Retro. Supp. I:** 413

Quiet American, The (Greene), **Supp. XIX:** 29

"Quiet and clear" (Kooser), **Supp. XIX:** 125

Quiet City (Shaw), **Supp. XIX:** 244

Quiet Days in Clichy (H. Miller), **III:** 170, 178, 183–184, 187

"Quiet Desperation" (Simpson), **Supp. IX:** 277–278

"Quiet Light, A" (Skloot), **Supp. XX: 203**

"Quiet of the Mind" (Nye), **Supp. XIII:** 284

"Quiet Woman, The" (Taggard), **Supp. XXII:** 274

"QUILLA" (Trethewey), **Supp. XXI:** 246

"Quilting" (D. West), **Supp. XVIII:** 283

Quin, Mike (pseudonym). *See* Ryan, Paul William

Quincy, Edmund, **Supp. XVIII:** 4

Quindlen, Anna, **Supp. XVI:** 108; **Supp. XVII: 165–181**

Quinlan, Kathleen, **Supp. X:** 80

Quinn, Anthony, **Supp. XXI:** 46

Quinn, John, **III:** 471

Quinn, Paul, **Supp. V:** 71

Quinn, Sister M. Bernetta, **III:** 479; **IV:** 421

Quinn, Vincent, **I:** 386, 401, 402; **Supp. I Part 1:** 270

"Quinnapoxet" (Kunitz), **Supp. III Part 1:** 263

Quinn's Book (W. Kennedy), **Supp. VII:** 133, 148–150, 153

Quintero, José, **III:** 403

Quintilian, **IV:** 123

Quinzaine for This Yule, A (Pound), **Retro. Supp. I:** 285

Quite Contrary: The Mary and Newt Story (Dixon), **Supp. XII: 144,** 153

Quod Erat Demonstrandum (Stein), **IV:** 34

Quo Vadis? (Sienkiewicz), **Supp. IV Part 2:** 518; **Supp. XVI:** 182

R

Raab, Max, **Supp. XI:** 309

"Rabbi, The" (Hayden), **Supp. II Part 1:** 363, 369

Rabbit, Run (Updike), **IV:** 214, 223, 230–234; **Retro. Supp. I:** 320, 325, 326, 327, 331, 333, 335; **Supp. XI:** 140; **Supp. XII:** 298; **Supp. XVI:** 220

"Rabbit, The" (Barnes), **Supp. III Part 1:** 34

Rabbit at Rest (Updike), **Retro. Supp. I:** 334

Rabbit Factory, The (L. Brown), **Supp. XXI:** 40, **47–48**

"*Rabbit Factory, The:* Escaping the Isolation of the Cage" (Gaughran), **Supp. XXI:** 47–48

Rabbit Is Rich (Updike), **Retro. Supp. I:** 334

Rabbit novels (Updike), **Supp. V:** 269

Rabbit Redux (Updike), **IV:** 214; **Retro. Supp. I:** 332, 333

Rabbit's Umbrella, The (Plimpton), **Supp. XVI:** 244

"Rabbits Who Caused All the Trouble, The" (Thurber), **Supp. I Part 2:** 610

Rabelais, and His World (Bakhtin), **Retro. Supp. II:** 273

Rabelais, François, **I:** 130; **II:** 111, 112, 302, 535; **III:** 77, 78, 174, 182; **IV:** 68; **Supp. I Part 2:** 461

Rabelais and His World (Bakhtin), **Supp. X:** 120

Rabinbach, Anson, **Supp. XII:** 166

Rabinowitz, Paula, **Supp. V:** 161

"Race" (Emerson), **II:** 6

"Race, Privilege, and the Politics of (Re)Writing History: An Analysis of the Novels of Michelle Cliff" (Edmondson), **Supp. XXII:** 70

"Race Contacts and Inter-Racial Relations" (Locke), **Supp. XIV:** 211

"Race Contacts and Inter-Racial Relations: A Study in the Theory and

Practice of Race" (lectures, Locke), **Supp. XIV:** 199, 209

Race Contacts and Interracial Relations: Lectures on the Theory and Practice of Race (Locke, Stewart, ed.), **Supp. XIV:** 196, **209–210**

"'RACE LINE' IS A PRODUCT OF CAPITALISM, THE" (Baraka), **Supp. II Part 1:** 61

"Race of Life, The" (Thurber), **Supp. I Part 2:** 614

"Race Problems and Modern Society" (Toomer), **Supp. III Part 2:** 486

Race Questions, Provincialism, and Other American Problems (Royce), **Supp. XIV:** 199

"Race Riot, Tulsa, 1921" (Olds), **Supp. X:** 205

Race Rock (Matthiessen), **Supp. V:** 201

"Races, The" (Lowell), **II:** 554

"Rachel" (D. West), **Supp. XVIII:** 289

Rachel Carson: Witness for Nature (Lear), **Supp. IX:** 19

Rachel River (film, Smolan), **Supp. XVI:** 36

"Racial Progress and Race Adjustment" (Locke), **Supp. XIV:** 210

Racine, Jean Baptiste, **II:** 543, 573; **III:** 145, 151, 152, 160; **IV:** 317, 368, 370; **Supp. I Part 2:** 716

Radcliffe, Ann, **Supp. XX:** 108

Radiance (Crooker), **Supp. XXIII:** 57–58

"Radical" (Moore), **III:** 211

"Radical Chic" (Wolfe), **Supp. III Part 2:** 577–578, 584, 585

Radical Chic & Mau-mauing the Flak Catchers (Wolfe), **Supp. III Part 2:** 577–578

Radical Empiricism of William James, The (Wild), **II:** 362, 363–364

Radicalism in America, The (Lasch), **I:** 259

"Radical Jewish Humanism: The Vision of E. L. Doctorow" (Clayton), **Supp. IV Part 2:** 238

"Radically Condensed History of Postindustrial Life, A" (Wallace), **Supp. X:** 309

Radical's America, A (Swados), **Supp. XIX:** 264–265

Radinovsky, Lisa, **Supp. XV:** 284, 285

"Radio" (O'Hara), **III:** 369

Radio Days (film; Allen), **Supp. XV:** 9

"Radio Pope" (Goldbarth), **Supp. XII:** 188, 192

Raditzer (Matthiessen), **Supp. V:** 201

Radkin, Paul, **Supp. I Part 2:** 539

"Rafaela Who Drinks Coconut & Papaya Juice on Tuesdays" (Cisneros), **Supp. VII:** 63

Rafelson, Bob, **Supp. XIV:** 241

Raffalovich, Marc-André, **Supp. XIV:** 335

Rafferty, Terence, **Supp. XX: 87, 92**

"Raft, The" (Lindsay), **Supp. I Part 2:** 393

Rag and Bone Shop of the Heart, The: Poems for Men (Bly, Hillman, and Meade, eds.), **Supp. IV Part 1:** 67

Rage in Harlem (C. Himes). *See For Love of Imabelle* (C. Himes)

Rage to Live, A (O'Hara), **III:** 361

Raglan, Lord, **I:** 135

Rago, Henry, **Supp. III Part 2:** 624, 628, 629

"Rag Rug"(Hadas), **Supp. XXIII:** 118

Ragtime (Doctorow), **Retro. Supp. II:** 108; **Supp. IV Part 1:** 217, 222–224, 231, 232, 233, 234, 237, 238; **Supp. V:** 45

"Ragtime" (Doctorow), **Supp. IV Part 1:** 234

Ragtime (film), **Supp. IV Part 1:** 236

Ragtime (musical, McNally), **Supp. XIII:** 207

Rahab (W. Frank), **Supp. XX: 71–72, 76**

Rahaim, Liz, **Supp. XVII:** 2

Rahv, Philip, **Retro. Supp. I:** 112; **Supp. II Part 1:** 136; **Supp. VIII:** 96; **Supp. IX:** 8; **Supp. XIV:** 3; **Supp. XV:** 140

"Raid" (Hughes), **Retro. Supp. I:** 208

Raids on the Unspeakable (Merton), **Supp. VIII:** 201, 208

Raikin, Judith, **Supp. XXII:** 66

Rail, DeWayne, **Supp. XIII:** 312

Rain and Other Fictions (Kenny), **Supp. XXIII:** 157

"Rain and the Rhinoceros" (Merton), **Supp. VIII:** 201

Rainbow, The (Lawrence), **III:** 27

"Rainbows" (Marquand), **III:** 56

Rainbow Stories, The (Vollmann), **Supp. XVII:** 226, 227, 230, 231, 233

Rainbow Tulip, The (Mora), **Supp. XIII:** 221

"Rain Country" (Haines), **Supp. XII:** 210

"Rain-Dream, A" (Bryant), **Supp. I Part 1:** 164

Raine, Kathleen, **I:** 522, 527

"Rain Falling Now, The" (Dunn), **Supp. XI:** 147

"Rain in the Heart" (Taylor), **Supp. V:** 317, 319

Rain in the Trees, The (Merwin), **Supp. III Part 1:** 340, 342, 345, 349, 354–356

"Rainmaker, The" (Humphrey), **Supp. IX:** 101

Raintree County (Lockridge), **Supp. XIX:** 263

Rainwater, Catherine, **Supp. V:** 272

"Rainy Day" (Longfellow), **II:** 498

"Rainy Day, The" (Buck), **Supp. II Part 1:** 127

"Rainy Mountain Cemetery" (Momaday), **Supp. IV Part 2:** 486

Rainy Mountain Christmas Doll (painting) (Momaday), **Supp. IV Part 2:** 493

"Rainy Season: Sub-Tropics" (Bishop), **Supp. I Part 1:** 93

"Rainy Sunday" (Espaillat), **Supp. XXI:** 106

"Raise High the Roof Beam, Carpenters" (Salinger), **III:** 567–569, 571

Raise High the Roof Beam, Carpenters; and Seymour: An Introduction (Salinger), **III:** 552, 567–571, 572

Raise Race Rays Raze: Essays Since 1965 (Baraka), **Supp. II Part 1:** 47, 52, 55

Raisin (musical), **Supp. IV Part 1:** 374

Raising Demons (Jackson), **Supp. IX: 125–126**

Raisin in the Sun, A (unproduced screenplay) (Hansberry), **Supp. IV Part 1:** 360

Raisin in the Sun, A (film: Columbia Pictures), **Supp. IV Part 1:** 360, 367

Raisin in the Sun, A (Hansberry), **Supp. IV Part 1:** 359, 360, 361, 362–364; **Supp. VIII:** 343

Raisin in the Sun, A (television film: American Playhouse), **Supp. IV Part 1:** 367, 374

Rajan, R., **I:** 390

"Rake, The" (Mamet), **Supp. XIV:** 240

Rake's Progress, The (opera), **Supp. II Part 1:** 24

Rakosi, Carl, **Supp. III Part 2:** 614, 615, 616, 617, 618, 621, 629; **Supp. XIV:** 286, 287

Ralegh, Sir Walter, **Supp. I Part 1:** 98

Raleigh, John Henry, **IV:** 366

Ralph, Brett, **Supp. XVII:** 245

Ramakrishna, Sri, **III:** 567

Ramakrishna and His Disciples (Isherwood), **Supp. XIV:** 164

Ramazani, Jahan, **Supp. IV Part 2:** 450

"Ramble of Aphasia, A" (O. Henry), **Supp. II Part 1:** 410

Ramey, Phillip, **Supp. IV Part 1:** 94

Ramírez, Juan, **Supp. XXIII:** 203

Rampersad, Arnold, **Retro. Supp. I:** 196, 200, 201, 204; **Supp. IV Part 1:** 244, 250

Rampling, Anne, **Supp. VII:** 201. *See also* Rice, Anne

Rampling, Charlotte, **Supp. IX:** 253

Ramsey, Priscilla R., **Supp. IV Part 1:** 15

Ramsey, Roger, **Supp. XVI:** 69

Ramsey, William, **Supp. XVIII:** 66

Ramus, Petrus, **Supp. I Part 1:** 104

Rand, Ayn, **Supp. I Part 1:** 294; **Supp. IV Part 2: 517–535**

Randall, Jarrell, 1914–1965 (Lowell, Taylor, and Warren, eds.), **II:** 368, 385

Randall, John H., **III:** 605

Randolph, John, **I:** 5–6

Randolph, Ladette, **Supp. XXIII:** 274

"Range-Finding" (Frost), **Retro. Supp. I:** 131

Range of the Possible (T. Marshall), **Supp. XVII:** 36

Rangoon (F. Barthelme), **Supp. XI:** 25

Rangus, Eric, **Supp. XXI:** 244, 254

Rank, Otto, **I:** 135; **Supp. IX:** 105; **Supp. X:** 183, 185, 193

Ranke, Leopold von, **Supp. I Part 2:** 492

Rankin, Daniel, **Retro. Supp. II:** 57, 72; **Supp. I Part 1:** 200, 203, 225

Rankin, Tom, **Supp. XXI:** 36

Rankine, Annette, **Supp. XX: 69**

Ranlett, William H., **Supp. XVIII:** 3

Ransohoff, Martin, **Supp. XI:** 305, 306

Ransom, John Crowe, **I:** 265, 301; **II:** 34, 367, 385, 389, 536–537, 542; **III:** 454, **480–502**, 549; **IV:** 121, 122, 123,

124, 125, 127, 134, 140, 141, 236, 237, 433; **Retro. Supp. I:** 90; **Retro. Supp. II:** 176, 177, 178, 183, 220, 228, 246; **Supp. I Part 1:** 80, 361; **Supp. I Part 2:** 423; **Supp. II Part 1:** 90, 91, 136, 137, 139, 318; **Supp. II Part 2:** 639; **Supp. III Part 1:** 318; **Supp. III Part 2:** 542, 591; **Supp. IV Part 1:** 217; **Supp. V:** 315, 331, 337; **Supp. X:** 25, 56, 58; **Supp. XIV:** 1; **Supp. XIX:** 123; **Supp. XXIII:** 145
"Rape" (Coleman), **Supp. XI:** 89–90
"Rape, The" (Baraka), **Supp. II Part 1:** 40
Rape of Bunny Stuntz, The (Gurney), **Supp. V:** 109
"Rape of Philomel, The" (Shapiro), **Supp. II Part 2:** 720
"Rape of the Lock, The" (Pope), **Supp. XIV:** 8
Rapf, Joanna, **Supp. XVIII:** 251
Raphael, **I:** 15; **III:** 505, 521, 524; **Supp. I Part 1:** 363
"Rapist" (Dunn), **Supp. XI:** 144
Rap on Race, A (Baldwin and Mead), **Supp. I Part 1:** 66
"Rappaccini's Daughter" (Hawthorne), **II:** 229
"Rapture of the Deep" (Hempel), **Supp. XXI: 123**
"Rapunzel" (Sexton), **Supp. II Part 2:** 691
Rare & Endangered Species: A Novella & Short Stories (Bausch), **Supp. VII:** 51, 54
"Raree Show" (MacLeish), **III:** 9
Rascoe, Burton, **III:** 106, 115
Raskin, Jonah, **Supp. XV:** 116
Raskin, Saul, **Supp. XXIII:** 6
"Raskolnikov" (Simic), **Supp. VIII:** 282
Rasmussen, Douglas, **Supp. IV Part 2:** 528, 530
Rasmussen, Halfdan, **Supp. XVIII:** 180
Rasselas (Johnson), **Supp. XI:** 209
Rathmann, Andrew, **Supp. XV:** 34
Ratiner, Steven, **Supp. XXIII:** 134
"Rat in the Engine" (Espaillat), **Supp. XXI:** 106
"Ration" (Baraka), **Supp. II Part 1:** 50
"Rationale of Verse, The" (Poe), **III:** 427–428; **Retro. Supp. II:** 266
Ratner, Rochelle, **Supp. XV:** 105
Ratner's Star (DeLillo), **Supp. VI:** 1, 2, 3, 4, 10, 12, 14; **Supp. XVIII:** 140
"Rat of Faith, The" (Levine), **Supp. V:** 192
Rattigan, Terence, **III:** 152
Raugh, Joseph, **Supp. I Part 1:** 286
Rauh, Ida, **Supp. XXI:** 6
Rauschenberg, Robert, **Supp. XV:** 187
Rauschenbusch, Walter, **III:** 293; **Supp. I Part 1:** 7
Ravelstein (Bellow), **Retro. Supp. II:** 19, **33–34**
Raven, Simon, **Supp. XII:** 241
Raven, The (film, Friedlander), **Supp. XVII:** 58
"Raven, The" (Poe), **III:** 413, 421–422, 426; **Retro. Supp. II:** 265, 266–267; **Supp. XVII:** 58

Raven, The, and Other Poems (Poe), **III:** 413
Ravenal, Shannon, **Supp. IV Part 1:** 93
"Raven Days, The" (Lanier), **Supp. I Part 1:** 351
Ravenel, Shannon, **Supp. XXI:** 39
Ravenna, Michael. *See* Welty, Eudora
"Ravens at Deer Creek" (Wrigley), **Supp. XVIII:** 299–300, 306
Raven's Road (Gunn Allen), **Supp. IV Part 1:** 330, 335
Raver, Anne, **Supp. XVIII:** 191
"Ravine, The" (Carruth), **Supp. XVI:** 53
Ravits, Martha, **Supp. XXI:** 215
Raw Heaven (Peacock), **Supp. XIX: 196–197**
Rawlings, Marjorie Kinnan, **Supp. X: 219–237; Supp. XVIII:** 194–195
Rawlins, C. L., **Supp. XVII:** 72, 73
Ray, David, **Supp. IV Part 1:** 61
Ray, Janisse, **Supp. XVIII: 189–206**
Ray, Jeanne Wilkinson, **Supp. XII:** 308, 310
Ray, John, **II:** 111, 112
Ray, Man, **IV:** 404; **Retro. Supp. I:** 416; **Supp. XII:** 124; **Supp. XXIII:** 6
Ray, Nicholas, **Supp. XVIII:** 253
Ray Bradbury Theatre, The (television show), **Supp. IV Part 1:** 103
Raymond, Henry J., **Supp. XVIII:** 4
"Raymond and Ann" (Budbill), **Supp. XIX:** 9
"Razor's Edge, The" (Wasserstein), **Supp. XV:** 328
Reactionary Essays on Poetry and Ideas (Tate), **Supp. II Part 1:** 106, 146
Read, Deborah, **II:** 122
Read, Forrest, **III:** 478
Read, Herbert, **I:** 523; **II:** 372–373, 377–378; **Retro. Supp. I:** 54; **Supp. III Part 1:** 273; **Supp. III Part 2:** 624, 626
Read, William A., **Supp. XIV:** 4
Reade, Charles, **Supp. I Part 2:** 580
Reader, Constant. *See* Parker, Dorothy
Reader, Dennis J., **Supp. I Part 2:** 454
"Reader, The" (F. Wright), **Supp. XVII:** 246
Reader's Block (Markson), **Supp. XVII: 143–145,** 146
Reader's Encyclopedia, The: An Encyclopedia of World Literature and the Arts (W. Benét), **Supp. XI:** 44
Reader's Guide to William Gaddis's The Recognitions, A (Moore), **Supp. IV Part 1:** 283
Reader's Map of Arkansas (Wright), **Supp. X:** 348
"Reader's Tale, A" (Doty), **Supp. XI:** 119, 120, 128, 129
"Reading" (Auden), **Supp. VIII:** 155
"Reading, The" (Di Piero), **Supp. XIX:** 41
"Reading, Writing, Region" (J. W. Miller), **Supp. XX: 165**
"Reading an Anthology of Chinese Poems of the Sung Dynasty, I Pause to Admire the Length and Clarity of Their Titles" (Collins), **Supp. XXI:** 56

"Reading at Forty" (Pickering), **Supp. XXI:** 196
"Reading Group Guide", **Supp. XI:** 244–245
"Reading Lao Tzu Again in the New Year" (Wright), **Supp. V:** 343
"Reading Late of the Death of Keats" (Kenyon), **Supp. VII:** 169
"Reading Myself" (Lowell), **II:** 555
Reading Myself and Others (P. Roth), **Retro. Supp. II:** 282; **Supp. V:** 45
"Reading *Ode to the West Wind* 25 Years Later" (McCarriston), **Supp. XIV:** 271–272
"Reading of the Psalm, The" (Francis), **Supp. IX:** 79
"Reading Ovid" (Di Piero), **Supp. XIX:** 44
"Reading Philosophy at Night" (Simic), **Supp. VIII:** 272
Reading Rilke: Reflections on the Problems of Translation (Gass), **Supp. VI:** 92, **93–94**
"Reading Rorty and Paul Celan One Morning in Early June" (Wright), **Supp. V:** 343
"Reading Sarcophagi: An Essay" (Sobin), **Supp. XVI:** 290
"Readings of History" (Rich), **Supp. I Part 2:** 554
"Reading the Signs, Empowering the Eye" (Bambara), **Supp. XI:** 17–18
Reading the Spirit (Eberhart), **I:** 525, 527, 530
Ready, Richard M., **Supp. XIX:** 154
"Ready Or Not" (Baraka), **Supp. II Part 1:** 50
Reagan, Ronald, **Supp. IV Part 1:** 224–225
"Real Bowery, The" (Hapgood), **Supp. XVII:** 103
"Real Class" (Vidal), **Supp. IV Part 1:** 35
Real Cool Killers, The (C. Himes), **Supp. XVI:** 143
Real Dope, The (Lardner), **II:** 422–423
"Real Estate" (Moore), **Supp. X:** 178
"Real Gone Guy, A" (McGrath), **Supp. X:** 117
"Real Horatio Alger Story, The" (Cowley), **Supp. II Part 1:** 143
"Realities" (MacLeish), **III:** 4
"Reality in America" (Trilling), **Supp. III Part 2:** 495, 502
"Reality! Reality! What Is It?" (Eberhart), **I:** 536
Reality Sandwiches, 1953–60 (Ginsberg), **Supp. II Part 1:** 315, 320
"Reality U.S.A." (Halliday), **Supp. XIX:** 89
Real Life of Sebastian Knight, The (Nabokov), **III:** 246; **Retro. Supp. I:** 266, 269, 270, 274
"Really Good Jazz Piano, A" (Yates), **Supp. XI:** 342
"Real Movie, with Stars, The" (Hull), **Supp. XXI:** 136
Real Presence: A Novel (Bausch), **Supp. VII:** 42–43, 50

"Real Revolution Is Love, The" (Harjo), **Supp. XII:** 224, 225–226

"Real Surrounding, The: On Canaletto's Venice" (Bronk), **Supp. XXI:** 32

"Real Thing, The" (H. James), **Retro. Supp. I:** 228; **Retro. Supp. II:** 223

"Real Two-Party System" (Vidal), **Supp. IV Part 2:** 679

Real West Marginal Way, The (Hugo), **Supp. VI:** 132, 134; **Supp. XVIII:** 299

"Real World around Us, The" (Carson), **Supp. IX:** 21

Reaper Essays, The (Jarman and McDowell), **Supp. IX:** 270; **Supp. XVII:** 110–111

"*Reaper* Interviews Jean Doh and Sean Dough, The" (Jarman and McDowell), **Supp. XVII:** 110

"Reapers" (Toomer), **Supp. III Part 2:** 481; **Supp. IX:** 312

Reason and Other Women (Notley), **Supp. XXII:** 224, 227, 235, 236, 237

"Reason and Race: A Review of the Literature of the Negro for 1946" (Locke), **Supp. XIV:** 206

"Reason for Moving, A" (Strand), **Supp. IV Part 2:** 624

"Reason for Stories, The: Toward a Moral Fiction" (Stone), **Supp. V:** 298, 300

Reasons for Moving (Strand), **Supp. IV Part 2:** 624–626, 626

"Reasons for Music" (MacLeish), **III:** 19

"Reasons of the Body" (Sanders), **Supp. XVI:** 274

Reasons to Live (Hempel), **Supp. XXI:** 115, 117, 118, **119–122**

Rebecca (du Maurier), **Supp. XIX:** 57–58; **Supp. XXII:** 120

Rebecca, or, The Fille de Chambre (Rowson), **Supp. XV:** 229, **235–236,** 238

Rebecca Harding Davis Reader, A (Pfaelzer, ed.), **Supp. XVI:** 88, 90

Rebel Angels: Twenty-five Poets of the New Formalism (Jarman and Mason, eds.), **Supp. XV:** 251; **Supp. XVII:** 109, 110, 112, 121

"Rebellion" (Lowell), **Retro. Supp. II:** 187

Rebel Powers (Bausch), **Supp. VII:** 41, 45–46, 49–51

Rebel without a Cause (film), **Supp. XII:** 9

"Rebirth" (McKnight), **Supp. XX:** **147, 157**

"Rebirth of God and the Death of Man, The" (Fiedler), **Supp. XIII:** 108

Rebolledo, Tey Diana, **Supp. XIII:** 214

Reb Shloyme nogid: A poeme fun yidishn leben (Shloyme the wealthy: A poem of Jewish life)(Asch), **Supp. XXIII:** 4, 5

Recapitulation (Stegner), **Supp. IV Part 2:** 598, 600, 612–613

"Recapitulation, The" (Eberhart), **I:** 522

"Recapitulations" (Shapiro), **Supp. II Part 2:** 701, 702, 708, 710–711

"Receding Horizons" (Lethem and Scholtz), **Supp. XVIII:** 145

"Recencies in Poetry" (Zukofsky), **Supp. III Part 2:** 615

Recent Killing, A (Baraka), **Supp. II Part 1:** 55

"Recent Negro Fiction" (Ellison), **Supp. II Part 1:** 233, 235

"Recessional" (A. Finch), **Supp. XVII:** 70–71

"Recital, The" (Ashbery), **Supp. III Part 1:** 14

"Recitative" (H. Crane), **I:** 390; **Retro. Supp. II:** 78

Reckless Eyeballing (Reed), **Supp. X:** 241

Reckless Moment, The (film), **Supp. XXII:** 120, 131, 132

Recognitions, The (Gaddis), **Supp. IV Part 1:** 279, 280–285, 286, 287, 288, 289, 291, 292, 294; **Supp. XX:** 91

"Recollection and Perhaps a Tribute, A" (Espaillat), **Supp. XXI:** 103–104

Recollections (R. H. Stoddard), **Supp. XV:** 271

Recollections of Logan Pearsall Smith: The Story of a Friendship (Gathorne-Hardy), **Supp. XIV:** 344

"Reconciliation" (Whitman), **IV:** 347

"Reconstructed but Unregenerate" (Ransom), **III:** 496

"Reconstruction and Its Benefits" (Du Bois), **Supp. II Part 1:** 171

Recovering (Sarton), **Supp. VIII:** 264

Recovering the U.S. Hispanic Literary Heritage (Paredes), **Supp. XIII:** 320

"Recovery" (Dove), **Supp. IV Part 1:** 248

Rector of Justin, The (Auchincloss), **Supp. IV Part 1:** 21, 23, 27–30, 36

"Recurrent Dream" (Nelson), **Supp. XVIII:** 176

"RED AUTUMN" (Baraka), **Supp. II Part 1:** 55

Red Badge of Courage, The (S. Crane), **I:** 201, 207, 212, 405, 406, 407, 408, 412–416, 419, 421, 422, 423, 477, 506; **II:** 264; **III:** 317; **IV:** 350; **Retro. Supp. II:** 108; **Supp. IV Part 1:** 380; **Supp. XIV:** 51; **Supp. XVII:** 228; **Supp. XVIII:** 75; **Supp. XXI:** 277

"Redbirds" (C. Frost), **Supp. XV:** 99

"Red Bow, The" (Saunders), **Supp. XIX:** 232–233, 234

"Redbreast in Tampa" (Lanier), **Supp. I Part 1:** 364

"Red Brocade" (Nye), **Supp. XIII:** 288

Redburn: His First Voyage (Melville), **III:** 79–80, 84; **Retro. Supp. I:** 245, 247–248, 249; **Supp. XVIII:** 6

Red Calico (Miller and Bowden), **Supp. XXII:** 188

"Red Carpet for Shelley, A" (Wylie), **Supp. I Part 2:** 724

Red Channels (Harnett), **Supp. XV:** 198

"Red Clowns" (Cisneros), **Supp. VII:** 63

Red Coal, The (Stern), **Supp. IX:** **291–292**

Red Coat, The (Shanley), **Supp. XIV:** 316–317

"Red Cords" (Lamott), **Supp. XX:** 142

"Red"(Crooker), **Supp. XXIII:** 63

"Red Cross" (Hughes), **Retro. Supp. I:** 205

Red Cross (Shepard), **Supp. III Part 2:** 440, 446

Red Death, A (Mosley), **Supp. XIII:** 237, 239, 240

"Red Deer" (C. Frost), **Supp. XV:** 101

Redding, Josephine, **Supp. XXI:** 2

Redding, Saunders, **Supp. I Part 1:** 332, 333

Reddings, J. Saunders, **Supp. IV Part 1:** 164

Red Dust (Levine), **Supp. V:** 178, 183–184, 188

"Red Dust" (Levine), **Supp. V:** 184

"Redemption" (Gardner), **Supp. VI:** 72

Redemption (Uris), **Supp. XX:** **244, 246, 247, 248, 254, 255**

"Redeployment" (Nemerov), **III:** 267, 272

Redfield, Robert, **IV:** 475

Redford, Robert, **Supp. IX:** 253, 259; **Supp. XIII:** 267; **Supp. XIV:** 223

Redgrave, Lynn, **Supp. V:** 107

Red Harvest (Hammett), **Supp. IV Part 1:** 346–348, 348; **Supp. IV Part 2:** 468; **Supp. XXI:** 272

"Red Hat, The"(Hadas), **Supp. XXIII:** 111, 113, 118, 119, 124, 128

Red-Headed Woman (film), **Retro. Supp. I:** 110; **Supp. XVI:** 191

"Red Horse Wind over Albuquerque" (Harjo), **Supp. XII:** 219

Red Hot Vacuum, The (Solotaroff), **Retro. Supp. II:** 281

Rediscovery of America, The (W. Frank), **Supp. XX:** 75

Rediscovery of Man, The (W. Frank), **Supp. XX:** **67–68, 80**

"Red Leaves" (Faulkner), **II:** 72

"Red Meat: What Difference Did Stesichoros Make?" (Carson), **Supp. XII:** 107

"Red Pawn" (Rand), **Supp. IV Part 2:** 520

Red Pony, The (Steinbeck), **IV:** 50, 51, 58, 70

Redrawing the Boundaries (Fisher), **Retro. Supp. I:** 39

Red Robins, The (Koch), **Supp. XV:** 185–186, 187

Red Roses for Bronze (Doolittle), **Supp. I Part 1:** 253, 268, 271

Red Rover, The (Cooper), **I:** 342–343, 355

"Red Silk Stockings" (Hughes), **Retro. Supp. I:** 200

Redskins, The (Cooper), **I:** 351, 353

"Red Sox Nation, North" (Mosher), **Supp. XXII:** 209

"Red Star, Winter Orbit" (W. Gibson and B. Sterling), **Supp. XVI:** 123

Red Suitcase (Nye), **Supp. XIII:** 277, 278, 287

Red the Fiend (Sorrentino), **Supp. XXI:** 227, 231, 237

Red Wallflower, A (S. Warner), **Supp. XVIII:** 260

"Red Wheelbarrow, The" (W. C. Williams), **IV:** 411–412; **Retro. Supp. I:** 419, 430

"Red Wind" (Chandler), **Supp. IV Part 1:** 122

"Red Wing Church, The" (Kooser), **Supp. XIX:** 119

"Redwings" (Wright), **Supp. III Part 2:** 603

Reed, Edward Bliss, **Supp. XV:** 297, 298, 300

Reed, Ishmael, **Retro. Supp. II:** 111, 324–325; **Supp. II Part 1:** 34; **Supp. X:** 239–257, 331; **Supp. XIII:** 181, 182; **Supp. XVI:** 143; **Supp. XX:** 107; **Supp. XXII:** 172

Reed, J. D., **Supp. XVI:** 174

Reed, John, **I:** 48, 476, 483; **Supp. X:** 136; **Supp. XV:** 295, 299; **Supp. XVII:** 96, 99, 100; **Supp. XVIII:** 225; **Supp. XXI:** 6, 12; **Supp. XXII:** 274, 275; **Supp. XXIII:** 161, 162

Reed, Lou, **Retro. Supp. II:** 266

"Reedbeds of the Hackensack, The" (Clampitt), **Supp. IX:** 41

"Reed of Pan, A" (McCullers), **II:** 585

Reedy, Billy, **Retro. Supp. II:** 65, 67, 71, 73

Reedy, William Marion, **Supp. I Part 2:** 456, 461, 465

Reef, The (Wharton), **IV:** 317–318, 322; **Retro. Supp. I:** 372, 373–374

Reena and Other Stories (Marshall), **Supp. XI:** 275, 277, 278

"Reese in Evening Shadow" (Skloot), **Supp. XX:** 204

Reeve, F. D., **Supp. XV:** 344, 349

Reeve's Tale (Chaucer), **I:** 131

"Refiguring the Postcolonial Imagination: Tropes of Visuality in Writing by Rhys, Kincaid, and Cliff" (Emery), **Supp. XXII:** 73

"Reflection from Anita Loos" (Empson), **Supp. XVI:** 190

"Reflections" (Carruth), **Supp. XVI:** 54

"Reflections" (Komunyakaa), **Supp. XIII:** 117

Reflections at Fifty and Other Essays (Farrell), **II:** 49

"Reflections by a Fire" (Sarton), **Supp. VIII:** 259

Reflections in a Golden Eye (McCullers), **II:** 586, 588, 593–596, 604; **IV:** 384, 396

Reflections of a Jacobite (Auchincloss), **Supp. IV Part 1:** 31

Reflections on a Gift of Watermelon Pickle (Dunning), **Supp. XIV:** 126

Reflections on Poetry and Poetics (Nemerov), **III:** 269

"Reflections on the Constitution of Nature" (Freneau), **Supp. II Part 1:** 274

"Reflections on the Death of the Reader" (Morris), **III:** 237

Reflections on the End of an Era (Niebuhr), **III:** 297–298

"Reflections on the Life and Death of Lord Clive" (Paine), **Supp. I Part 2:** 505

Reflections on the Revolution in France (Burke), **Supp. I Part 2:** 511, 512

Reflections: Thinking Part I (Arendt), **Supp. I Part 2:** 570

"Reflex Action and Theism" (James), **II:** 345, 363

Reflex and Bone Structure (Major), **Supp. XXII:** 174–175

"Refrains/Remains/Reminders" (Goldbarth), **Supp. XII:** 180–181, 181

"Refuge" (Kingsolver), **Supp. VII:** 208

"Refuge, A" (Goldbarth), **Supp. XII:** 190

Refugee Children: Theory, Research, and Services (Ahearn and Athey, eds.), **Supp. XI:** 184

"Refugees, The" (Jarrell), **II:** 371

"Refusal" (C. Frost), **Supp. XV:** 102

"Refusal to Publish Fifth Book" (Halliday), **Supp. XIX:** 94

Regarding Wave (Snyder), **Supp. VIII:** 299–300

Regina (Epstein), **Supp. XII:** 170–171

"Regional Literature of the South" (Rawlings), **Supp. X:** 228

"Regional Writer, The" (O'Connor), **Retro. Supp. II:** 223, 225

Régnier, Henri de, **II:** 528–529

Regulators, The (King), **Supp. V:** 141

Rehder, Robert, **Supp. IV Part 1:** 69

Rehearsing Absence (Espaillat), **Supp. XXI:** 99

Reich, Tova, **Supp. XVI:** 158

Reichel, Hans, **III:** 183

Reichl, Ruth, **Supp. X:** 79, 85

Reid, B. L., **II:** 41, 47

Reid, Forrest, **Supp. XX:** 235

Reid, Thomas, **II:** 9; **Supp. I Part 1:** 151

Reign of Snakes (Wrigley), **Supp. XVIII:** 293, **302–306**

"Reign of Snakes" (Wrigley), **Supp. XVIII:** 302–304

Reign of Wonder, The (Tanner), **I:** 260

Rein, Yevgeny, **Supp. VIII:** 22

Reinagle, Alexander, **Supp. XV:** 238, 240

"Reincarnation" (Dickey), **Supp. IV Part 1:** 181–182

Reine des pommes, La (C. Himes). *See For Love of Imabelle* (C. Himes)

Reiner, Carl, **Supp. IV Part 2:** 591

Reinfeld, Linda, **Supp. IV Part 2:** 421

Reinhardt, Max, **Supp. XV:** 307

Reinventing the Enemy's Language: Contemporary Native Women's Writing of North America (Bird and Harjo, eds.), **Supp. XII:** 216, 217

Reisman, Jerry, **Supp. III Part 2:** 618

Reiter, Amy, **Supp. XIX:** 54, 56

Reitlinger, Gerald, **Supp. XII:** 161

Reivers, The: A Reminiscence (Faulkner), **I:** 305; **II:** 57, 73; **Retro. Supp. I:** 74, 82, 91

"Rejoicings" (Stern), **Supp. IX:** 289–290

Rejoicings: Selected Poems, 1966–1972 (Stern), **Supp. IX:** 289–290

Relation of My Imprisonment, The (Banks), **Supp. V:** 8, 12–13

"Relations between Poetry and Painting, The" (Stevens), **Retro. Supp. I:** 312

Relations of the Alabama-Georgia Dialect to the Provincial Dialects of Great Britain, The (Brooks), **Supp. XIV:** 3

Relative Stranger, A (C. Baxter), **Supp. XVII:** 19, 22

"Relativity of Beauty, The" (Rawlings), **Supp. X:** 226

Relearning the Alphabet (Levertov), **Supp. III Part 1:** 280, 281

"Release" (C. Baxter), **Supp. XVII:** 15

"Release, The" (MacLeish), **III:** 16

Reles, Abe ("Kid Twist"), **Supp. IV Part 1:** 382

"Relevance of an Impossible Ethical Ideal, The" (Niebuhr), **III:** 298

"Religion" (Dunbar), **Supp. II Part 1:** 199

"Religion" (Emerson), **II:** 6

Religion of Nature Delineated, The (Wollaston), **II:** 108

"Religious Instruction" (Peacock), **Supp. XIX:** 200, 201

Religious Rebel, A: The Letters of "H. W. S." (Mrs. Pearsall Smith) (L. P. Smith), **Supp. XIV:** 349

"Reluctance" (Frost), **II:** 153

Reluctantly: Autobiographical Essays (Carruth), **Supp. XVI:** 45–46, 50

Remains (Snodgrass), **Supp. VI:** 311, **313–314**

"Remains, The" (Strand), **Supp. IV Part 2:** 627

"Remarks on Color" (Wright), **Supp. XV:** 346

"Remarks on Spencer's *Definition of Mind as Correspondence*" (James), **II:** 345

Remarque, Erich Maria, **Retro. Supp. I:** 113; **Supp. IV Part 1:** 380

Rembrandt, **II:** 536; **IV:** 310; **Supp. IV Part 1:** 390, 391

"Rembrandt, The" (Wharton), **IV:** 310

"Rembrandt's Hat" (Malamud), **Supp. I Part 2:** 435, 437

Rembrandt Takes a Walk (Strand), **Supp. IV Part 2:** 631

"Rembrandt to Rembrandt" (Robinson), **III:** 521–522

Remembered Earth, The: An Anthology of Contemporary Native American Literature (Hobson, ed.), **Supp. IV Part 1:** 321

Remembered Yesterdays (Johnson), **Supp. IX:** 184

"Remembering" (Angelou), **Supp. IV Part 1:** 15

"Remembering Allen Tate" (Cowley), **Supp. II Part 1:** 153

"Remembering Barthes" (Sontag), **Supp. III Part 2:** 451, 471

"Remembering Guston" (Kunitz), **Supp. III Part 1:** 257

"Remembering James Laughlin" (Karr), **Supp. XI:** 242

Remembering Laughter (Stegner), **Supp. IV Part 2:** 598, 606, 607, 608, 611, 614

"Remembering Lobo" (Mora), **Supp. XIII:** 220, 227

"Remembering My Father" (Berry), **Supp. X:** 23

"Remembering My Parents Remembering the Books They Read" (Espaillat), **Supp. XXI:** 107

"Remembering that Island" (McGrath), **Supp. X:** 116

"Remembering the Children of Auschwitz" (McGrath), **Supp. X:** 127

"Remembering the Lost World" (Jarrell), **II:** 388

"Remembering the Sixties" (Simpson), **Supp. IX:** 279

Remember Me to Tom (T. Williams), **IV:** 379–380

"Remember the Moon Survives" (Kingsolver), **Supp. VII:** 209

Remember to Remember (H. Miller), **III:** 186

"Remembrance, A" (Gioia), **Supp. XV:** 112

Remembrance of Things Past (Proust), **Supp. IV Part 2:** 600; **Supp. XII:** 9; **Supp. XIII:** 44

Remembrance Rock (Sandburg), **III:** 590

Reminiscence, A (Ashbery), **Supp. III Part 1:** 2

Remnick, David, **Supp. XVI:** 246

"Remora" (Merrill), **Supp. III Part 1:** 326

"Removal" (White), **Supp. I Part 2:** 664–665

"Removal, The" (Merwin), **Supp. III Part 1:** 350, 351

"Removal Service Request" (Halliday), **Supp. XIX:** 90

Removed from Time (Matthews and Feeney), **Supp. IX:** 154

Remsen, Ira, **Supp. I Part 1:** 369

"Rémy de Gourmont, A Distinction" (Pound), **III:** 467

"Renaissance" (Carruth), **Supp. XVI:** 56

Renaissance in the South (Bradbury), **I:** 288–289

Renaldo and Clara (film, Dylan and Shepard), **Supp. XVIII:** 21, 28, 31

"Renaming the Kings" (Levine), **Supp. V:** 184

Renan, Ernest, **Supp. XX: 122**

Renan, Joseph Ernest, **II:** 86; **IV:** 440, 444

Renard, Jules, **IV:** 79

"Renascence" (Millay), **III:** 123, 125–126, 128; **Supp. XV:** 42

Renault, Mary, **Supp. IV Part 2:** 685

"Rendezvous, The" (Kumin), **Supp. IV Part 2:** 455

René, Norman, **Supp. X:** 146, 152

Renée (anonymous author), **Supp. XVI:** 64, 66

"Renegade, The" (Jackson), **Supp. IX:** 120

Renewal of Life series (Mumford), **Supp. II Part 2:** 476, 479, 481, 482, 485, 495, 497

"Reno Hill ... Little Bighorn"(Kenny), **Supp. XXIII:** 155

Renoir, Jean, **Supp. XII:** 259; **Supp. XXII:** 256

Renouvrier, Charles, **II:** 344–345, 346

"Renunciation" (Banks), **Supp. V:** 10

Renza, Louis A., **Retro. Supp. II:** 142

"Repair" (Peacock), **Supp. XIX:** 204

"Repeating Dream" (Gander), **Supp. XV:** 340

Repent in Haste (Marquand), **III:** 59

Reperusals and Re-Collections (L. P. Smith), **Supp. XIV:** 346–347

"Repetitive Heart, The: Eleven Poems in Imitation of the Fugue Form" (Schwartz), **Supp. II Part 2:** 645–646

"Replacing Regionalism" (Murphy), **Retro. Supp. II:** 143

Replansky, Naomi, **Supp. X:** 119

"Reply to Mr. Wordsworth" (MacLeish), **III:** 19

"Report, A" (Jin), **Supp. XVIII:** 93

"Report from a Forest Logged by the Weyhaeuser Company" (Wagoner), **Supp. IX:** 328

"Report from North Vietnam" (Paley), **Supp. VI:** 227

Report from Part One (Brooks), **Supp. III Part 1:** 70, 72, 80, 82–85

Report from Part Two (Brooks), **Supp. III Part 1:** 87

Report on a Game Survey of the North Central States (Leopold), **Supp. XIV:** 182

"Report on the Barnhouse Effect" (Vonnegut), **Supp. II Part 2:** 756

"Report to an Academy, A" (Kafka), **Supp. XX:** 18

"Report to Crazy Horse" (Stafford), **Supp. XI: 324–325**

"Repose of Rivers" (H. Crane), **I:** 393; **Retro. Supp. II:** 78, 81

"Repossession of a Heritage, The" (Zagarell), **Supp. XV:** 270, 281

Repp, John, **Supp. XXIII:** 302

"Representation and the War for Reality" (Gass), **Supp. VI:** 88

Representative Men (Emerson), **II:** 1, 5–6, 8

"Representing Far Places" (Stafford), **Supp. XI:** 321

Repression and Recovery (Nelson), **Supp. XVIII:** 226

"REPRISE OF ONE OF A. G.'S BEST POEMS" (Baraka), **Supp. II Part 1:** 59

"Reproducing Ourselves Is All Very Well" (E. Hoffman), **Supp. XVI:** 155

Republic (Plato), **I:** 485

"Republican Manifesto, A" (Paine), **Supp. I Part 2:** 511

Republic of Love, The (Shields), **Supp. VII:** 323–324, 326, 327

"Requa" (Olsen), **Supp. XIII:** 294, **302–303,** 304

Requa, Kenneth A., **Supp. I Part 1:** 107

"Requa I" (Olsen). *See* "Requa" (Olsen)

"Request for Offering" (Eberhart), **I:** 526

"Requiem" (Akhmatova), **Supp. VIII:** 20

"Requiem" (LaBastille), **Supp. X:** 105

Requiem for a Nun (Faulkner), **II:** 57, 72–73

Requiem for Harlem (H. Roth), **Supp. IX:** 235, 236, **240–242**

"Rescue, The" (Updike), **IV:** 214

Rescued Year, The (Stafford), **Supp. XI: 321–322**

"Rescued Year, The" (Stafford), **Supp. XI:** 322, 323

"Rescue with Yul Brynner" (Moore), **III:** 215

"Rescuing Moon"(P. Benedict), **Supp. XXIII:** 40

"Resemblance" (Bishop), **Supp. I Part 1:** 86

"Resemblance between a Violin Case and a Coffin, A" (T. Williams), **IV:** 378–379

"Reservations" (Taylor), **Supp. V:** 323

"Reserved Memorials" (Mather), **Supp. II Part 2:** 446, 449

"Resignación" (Espaillat), **Supp. XXI:** 104

"Resignation"(J. Schoolcraft), **Supp. XXIII:** 228, 229–230

"Resistance to Civil Government" (Thoreau), **Supp. X:** 27, 28

Resist Much, Obey Little (Berry), **Supp. XIII:** 2

Resolution (Parker), **Supp. XIX:** 187

"Resolution and Independence" (Wordsworth), **Supp. XV:** 346

"Resort" (Hampl), **Supp. XXII:** 86–87

Resort and Other Poems (Hampl), **Supp. XXII:** 83, 86–87

Resources of Hope (R. Williams), **Supp. IX:** 146

"Respectable Place, A" (O'Hara), **III:** 369

"Respectable Woman, A" (Chopin), **Retro. Supp. II:** 66

"Respite" (Pedersen; Nelson, trans.), **Supp. XVIII:** 180

Responses (Wilbur), **Supp. III Part 2:** 541

"Response to a Rumor that the Oldest Whorehouse in Wheeling, West Virginia, Has Been Condemned" (Wright), **Supp. III Part 2:** 602

Restif de La Bretonne, Nicolas, **III:** 175

"Rest of Life, The" (Gordon), **Supp. IV Part 1:** 311

Rest of Life, The: Three Novellas (Gordon), **Supp. IV Part 1:** 310–312

Rest of the Way, The (McClatchy), **Supp. XII:** 255, **258–259**

Restoration comedy, **Supp. I Part 2:** 617

Restorers, The (Di Piero), **Supp. XIX:** 42–43, 44

"Restorers, The" (Di Piero), **Supp. XIX:** 43

"Restraint" (F. Barthelme), **Supp. XI:** 26

"Result" (Emerson), **II:** 6

"Résumé" (Parker), **Supp. IX:** 189

"Resurrecting Methuselah" (P. E. Jones), **Supp. XXII:** 151

Resurrection (Della Francesca), **Supp. XV:** 262

"Resurrection" (Harjo), **Supp. XII:** 224

"Resurrection" (Jin), **Supp. XVIII:** 94–95

Resurrection, The (Gardner), **Supp. VI:** 61, 63, **64–65,** 68, 69, 73, 74

"Retort" (Hay), **Supp. XIV:** 133

Retour amont (Char; Sobin, trans.), **Supp. XVI:** 282

Retrieval System, The (Kumin), **Supp. IV Part 2:** 449, 451, 452

"Retrievers in Translation" (Doty), **Supp. XI:** 132

"Retroduction to American History" (Tate), **IV:** 129

"Retrospects and Prospects" (Lanier), **Supp. I Part 1:** 352

"Return" (Corso), **Supp. XII:** 135

"Return" (Creeley), **Supp. IV Part 1:** 141, 145

"Return" (MacLeish), **III:** 12

"Return, The" (Bidart), **Supp. XV:** 32–33

"Return, The" (Bontemps), **Supp. XXII:** 3, 8

"Return, The" (Pound), **Retro. Supp. I:** 288

"Return, The" (Ray), **Supp. XVIII:** 194

"Return, The" (Roethke), **III:** 533

"Return, The: Orihuela, 1965" (Levine), **Supp. V:** 194

"Return: An Elegy, The" (Warren), **IV:** 239

"Return: Buffalo" (Hogan), **Supp. IV Part 1:** 411

"Returning" (Komunyakaa), **Supp. XIII:** 122

"Returning a Lost Child" (Glück), **Supp. V:** 81

"Returning from the Enemy" (Harjo), **Supp. XII:** 229–230

"Returning the Borrowed Road" (Komunyakaa), **Supp. XIII:** 113, 133

"Return of Alcibiade, The" (Chopin), **Retro. Supp. II:** 58, 64

Return of Ansel Gibbs, The (Buechner), **III:** 310; **Supp. XII: 48**

"Return of Eros to Academe, The" (Bukiet), **Supp. XVII:** 47

"Return of Spring" (Winters), **Supp. II Part 2:** 791

Return of the Native, The (Hardy), **II:** 184–185, 186

Return of the Vanishing American, The (Fiedler), **Supp. XIII:** 103

Return to a Place Lit by a Glass of Milk (Simic), **Supp. VIII:** 274, 276, 283

"Return to Lavinia" (Caldwell), **I:** 310

"Return to Thin Air: The Everest Disaster Ten Years Later" *(Outside),* **Supp. XVIII:** 113

Return to Zion, The (Asch), **Supp. XXIII:** 5

Reuben (Wideman), **Supp. X:** 320

Reuben and Rachel; or, Tales of Old Times (Rowson), **Supp. XV: 240–241**

Reunion (Mamet), **Supp. XIV:** 240, 247, 254

"Reunion in Brooklyn" (H. Miller), **III:** 175, 184

Reuther brothers, **I:** 493

"Reveille" (Kingsolver), **Supp. VII:** 208

"Reveille" (Untermeyer), **Supp. XV:** 300

"Reveille, The" (Harte), **Supp. II Part 1:** 342–343

Revelation (biblical book), **II:** 541; **IV:** 104, 153, 154; **Supp. I Part 1:** 105, 273

"Revelation" (O'Connor), **III:** 349, 353–354; **Retro. Supp. II:** 237

"Revelation" (Warren), **III:** 490

Revenge (Harrison), **Supp. VIII:** 39, 45

"Revenge of Hamish, The" (Lanier), **Supp. I Part 1:** 365

"Revenge of Hannah Kemhuff, The" (Walker), **Supp. III Part 2:** 521

"Revenge of Rain-in-the-Face, The" (Longfellow), **Retro. Supp. II:** 170

"Reverberation"(Kenny), **Supp. XXIII:** 155

Reverberator, The (James), **Retro. Supp. I:** 227

"Reverdure" (Berry), **Supp. X:** 22

Reverdy, Pierre, **Supp. XV:** 178, 182; **Supp. XXIII:** 208

"Reverend Father Gilhooley" (Farrell), **II:** 45

Reverse Transcription (Kushner), **Supp. IX:** 138

Reversible Errors (Turow), **Supp. XVII: 220–221**

"Rev. Freemont Deadman" (Masters), **Supp. I Part 2:** 463

Reviewer's ABC, A (Aiken), **I:** 58

Review of Contemporary Fiction, 1990 (Tabbi, ed.), **Supp. XVII:** 143

"Revolt, against the Crepuscular Spirit in Modern Poetry" (Pound), **Retro. Supp. I:** 286

"Revolution" (C. L. R. James), **Supp. XXI:** 160

"Revolution" (Taggard), **Supp. XXII:** 275

"Revolutionary Answer to the Negro Problem in the USA, The" (statement, C. L. R. James), **Supp. XXI:** 169

Revolutionary Petunias (Walker), **Supp. III Part 2:** 520, 522, 530

Revolutionary Road (Yates), **Supp. XI:** 334, **335–340**

"Revolutionary Symbolism in America" (Burke), **I:** 272

"Revolutionary Theatre, The" (Baraka), **Supp. II Part 1:** 42

Revolution in Taste, A: Studies of Dylan Thomas, Allen Ginsberg, Sylvia Plath, and Robert Lowell (Simpson), **Supp. IX:** 276

"Revolution in the Revolution in the Revolution" (Snyder), **Supp. VIII:** 300

Revon, Marcel, **II:** 525

"Rewaking, The" (W. C. Williams), **Retro. Supp. I:** 430

"Rewrite" (Dunn), **Supp. XI:** 147

Rexroth, Kenneth, **II:** 526; **Supp. II Part 1:** 307; **Supp. II Part 2:** 436; **Supp. III Part 2:** 625, 626; **Supp. IV Part 1:** 145–146; **Supp. VIII:** 289; **Supp. XIII:** 75; **Supp. XIV:** 287; **Supp. XV:** 140, 141, 146; **Supp. XXII:** 168

Reynolds, Ann (pseudonym). *See* Bly, Carol

Reynolds, Clay, **Supp. XI:** 254

Reynolds, David, **Supp. XV:** 269; **Supp. XXIII:** 187

Reynolds, Sir Joshua, **Supp. I Part 2:** 716

Reynolds, Quentin, **IV:** 286

Reza, Yasmina, **Supp. XXI:** 148

Reznikoff, Charles, **IV:** 415; **Retro. Supp. I:** 422; **Supp III Part 2:** 615, 616, 617, 628; **Supp. XIV: 277–296; Supp. XXIII:** 174

"Rhapsodist, The" (Brown), **Supp. I Part 1:** 125–126

"Rhapsody on a Windy Night" (Eliot), **Retro. Supp. I:** 55

Rhetoric of Motives, A (Burke), **I:** 272, 275, 278, 279

Rhetoric of Religion, The (Burke), **I:** 275, 279

"Rhobert" (Toomer), **Supp. IX:** 316–317

"Rhode Show" (Mallon), **Supp. XIX:** 137–138

"Rhododendrons" (Levis), **Supp. XI:** 260, 263

Rhubarb Show, The (radio, Keillor), **Supp. XVI:** 178

"Rhyme of Sir Christopher, The" (Longfellow), **II:** 501

Rhymes to Be Traded for Bread (Lindsay), **Supp. I Part 2:** 380, 381–382

Rhys, Ernest, **III:** 458

Rhys, Jean, **Supp. III Part 1:** 42, 43; **Supp. XVIII:** 131

"Rhythm & Blues" (Baraka), **Supp. II Part 1:** 37–38

Rhythms (Reznikoff), **Supp. XIV:** 279, 282, 283

Rhythms II (Reznikoff), **Supp. XIV:** 282, 283, 284

Ribalow, Harold, **Supp. IX:** 236

Ribbentrop, Joachim von, **IV:** 249

Ribicoff, Abraham, **Supp. IX:** 33

Ribot, Théodule Armand, **Supp. XX:** 238

Ricardo, David, **Supp. I Part 2:** 628, 634

Rice, Allen Thorndike, **Retro. Supp. I:** 362

Rice, Anne, **Supp. VII: 287–306**

Rice, Elmer, **I:** 479; **III:** 145, 160–161

Rice, Mrs. Grantland, **II:** 435

Rice, Philip Blair, **IV:** 141

Rice, Stan, **Supp. XII:** 2

Rice, Tim, **Supp. XXI:** 148

Rice, Tom, **Supp. XIV:** 125

Rich, Adrienne, **Retro. Supp. I:** 8, 36, 42, 47, 404; **Retro. Supp. II:** 43, 191, 245; **Supp. I Part 2:** 546–547, **550–578; Supp. III Part 1:** 84, 354; **Supp. III Part 2:** 541, 599; **Supp. IV Part 1:** 257, 325; **Supp. V:** 82; **Supp. VIII:** 272; **Supp. XII:** 217, 229, 255; **Supp. XIII:** 294; **Supp. XIV:** 126, 129; **Supp. XV:** 176, 252; **Supp. XVII:** 32, 74; **Supp. XIX:** 83, 193; **Supp. XXII:** 65, 66

Rich, Arnold, **Supp. I Part 2:** 552

Rich, Frank, **Supp. IV Part 2:** 585, 586; **Supp. V:** 106; **Supp. XXI:** 146

Richard, Mark, **Supp. XIX: 209–222**

Richard Cory (Gurney), **Supp. V:** 99–100, 105

"Richard Hunt's 'Arachne' " (Hayden), **Supp. II Part 1:** 374

Richard II (Shakespeare), **Supp. XVII:** 244

Richard III (Shakespeare), **Supp. I Part 2:** 422

Richards, Bertrand F., **Supp. XX: 217–218**

Richards, Constance S., **Supp. XXII:** 73

Richards, David, **Supp. IV Part 2:** 576

Richards, Grant, **I:** 515

Richards, I. A., **I:** 26, 273–274, 279, 522; **III:** 498; **IV:** 92; **Supp. I Part 1:** 264, 265; **Supp. I Part 2:** 647

Richards, Ivor Armonstrong, **Supp. XIV:** 2–3, 16

Richards, Laura E., **II:** 396; **III:** 505–506, 507

Richards, Leonard, **Supp. XIV:** 48

Richards, Lloyd, **Supp. IV Part 1:** 362; **Supp. VIII:** 331

Richards, Rosalind, **III:** 506

Richards, Tad, **Supp. XVII:** 77

Richardson, Alan, **III:** 295

Richardson, Charles, **Supp. XVIII:** 14, 15

Richardson, Dorothy, **I:** 53; **II:** 320; **Supp. III Part 1:** 65

Richardson, Helen Patges, **Retro. Supp. II:** 95

Richardson, Henry Hobson, **I:** 3, 10

Richardson, Maurice, **Supp. XII:** 241

Richardson, Samuel, **I:** 134; **II:** 104, 111, 322; **Supp. V:** 127; **Supp. IX:** 128; **Supp. XV:** 232; **Supp. XX:** 236

Richardson, Tony, **Supp. XI:** 305, 306

"Richard Wright and Recent Negro Fiction" (Ellison), **Retro. Supp. II:** 116

"Richard Wright's Blues" (Ellison), **Retro. Supp. II:** 117, 124

"Richard Yates: A Requiem" (Lawrence), **Supp. XI:** 335

"Rich Boy, The" (Fitzgerald), **II:** 94; **Retro. Supp. I:** 98, 108

Richer, the Poorer, The: Sketches and Reminiscences (D. West), **Supp. XVIII:** 277, 289

"Riches" (Bausch), **Supp. VII:** 54

Richler, Mordecai, **Supp. XI:** 294, 297

Rich Man, Poor Man (miniseries), **Supp. XIX:** 252

Rich Man, Poor Man (Shaw), **Supp. XIX:** 251–252

Richman, Robert, **Supp. XI:** 249; **Supp. XV:** 120–121, 251

Richmond (Masters), **Supp. I Part 2:** 471

Richmond, M. A., **Supp. XX: 277, 279, 282, 286, 289, 290**

Rich Relations (Hwang), **Supp. XXI:** 146–147

Richter, Conrad, **Supp. X:** 103; **Supp. XVIII: 207–222**

Richter, Jean Paul, **II:** 489, 492; **Supp. XVI:** 182

Rick Bass (Weltzien), **Supp. XVI:** 20

Rickman, Clio, **Supp. I Part 2:** 519

Ricks, Christopher, **Retro. Supp. I:** 56; **Supp. XVIII:** 20, 30, 32

Riddel, Joseph N., **IV:** 95

"Riddle, The" (Hay), **Supp. XIV:** 130

"Ride in an Omnibus, A" (Briggs), **Supp. XVIII:** 9, 16

"Riders to the Blood-Red Wrath" (Brooks), **Supp. III Part 1:** 82–83

Riders to the Sea (Synge), **III:** 157

Ridge, Lola, **Supp. IX:** 308; **Supp. XV:** 307

Riding, Alan, **Supp. XVI:** 294

Riding, Laura, **I:** 437

"Riding Out at Evening" (McCarriston), **Supp. XIV:** 262–263

Riding the Iron Rooster: By Train through China (Theroux), **Supp. VIII:** 324

Riesenberg, Felix, **I:** 360, 361

Riesman, David, **Supp. I Part 2:** 649, 650

"Rif, to Music, The" (Bowles), **Supp. IV Part 1:** 89

Riffs & Reciprocities (Dunn), **Supp. XI: 154–155**

Rifles, The (Vollmann), **Supp. XVII:** 226, 233

Riggs, Marlon, **Supp. XI:** 19

Right Distance, The (Pickering), **Supp. XXI:** 196–197

Right Madness on Skye, The (Hugo), **Supp. VI:** 145–147

Rights of Man (Paine), **Supp. I Part 2:** 508, 511, 512–514, 516, 519, 523

"Rights of Woman" (Rowson), **Supp. XV:** 243

"Rights of Women, The" (Brown). *See Alcuin: A Dialogue* (Brown)

Right Stuff, The (Wolfe), **Supp. III Part 2:** 581–584

Right Thoughts in Sad Hours (Mather), **IV:** 144

Rigney, Barbara Hill, **Supp. VIII:** 215

"Rigorists" (Moore), **III:** 198

Rihani, Ameen, **Supp. XX:** 115

Rihoku, **Supp. XXII:** 228

Riis, Jacob A., **I:** 293; **Supp. I Part 1:** 13; **Supp. XVII:** 101, 106

Riley, James Whitcomb, **I:** 205; **Supp. II Part 1:** 192, 193, 196, 197

Rilke, Rainer Maria, **I:** 445, 523; **II:** 367, 381, 382–383, 389, 543, 544; **III:** 552, 558, 563, 571, 572; **IV:** 380, 443; **Retro. Supp. II:** 20, 187; **Supp. I Part 1:** 264; **Supp. I Part 2:** 573; **Supp. III Part 1:** 239, 242, 246, 283, 319–320; **Supp. IV Part 1:** 284; **Supp. V:** 208, 343; **Supp. VIII:** 30, 40; **Supp. X:** 164; **Supp. XI:** 126; **Supp. XIII:** 74, 88; **Supp. XV:** 93, 212, 222,**Supp. XV:** 223, 225; **Supp. XVI:** 292; **Supp. XVII:** 244; **Supp. XXII:** 89, 90, 94; **Supp. XXIII:** 207

Rilke on Love and Other Difficulties (Rilke), **Supp. X:** 164

"Rilke's Growth as a Poet" (Dobyns), **Supp. XIII:** 77

"Rimbaud" (Kerouac), **Supp. III Part 1:** 232

Rimbaud, Arthur, **I:** 381, 383, 389, 391, 526; **II:** 528, 543, 545; **III:** 23, 174, 189; **IV:** 286, 380, 443; **Retro. Supp. I:** 56; **Retro. Supp. II:** 187, 326; **Supp. III Part 1:** 14, 195; **Supp. IV Part 2:** 624; **Supp. VIII:** 39, 40; **Supp. XII:** 1, 16, 128, 255; **Supp. XIII:** 284; **Supp. XIV:** 338; **Supp. XVIII:** 23, 33; **Supp. XXI:** 225, 233; **Supp. XXIII:** 207

Rindge, Debora, **Supp. XXI:** 246

Rinehart, Stanley, **III:** 36

Ring, Frances Kroll, **Supp. IX:** 63, 64

Ring and the Book, The (Browning), **Supp. I Part 2:** 416, 468

Ring cycle (Wagner), **Supp. IV Part 1:** 392

Ringe, Donald, **I:** 339, 343; **Retro. Supp. II:** 270

Ringel, Faye, **Supp. XXII:** 205, 207

"Ringing" (Bierds), **Supp. XVII:** 28

"Ringing the Bells" (Sexton), **Supp. II Part 2:** 672, 687

Ringle, Ken, **Supp. X:** 15

Ring of Heaven: Poems (Hongo), **Supp. X:** 292

Rink, The (musical, McNally), **Supp. XIII:** 207

Rio Lobo (film), **Supp. XVI:** 246

Ríos, Alberto Alvaro, **Supp. IV Part 2: 537–556**

"Riot" (Brooks), **Supp. III Part 1:** 71, 84–85

Ripening (Le Sueur), **Supp. XXIII:** 165

Ripley, Ezra, **II:** 8; **IV:** 172

Rip-off Red, Girl Detective (Acker), **Supp. XII:** 3–4

Ripostes (Pound), **Retro. Supp. I:** 287–288, 413

Ripostes of Ezra Pound, The, Whereunto Are Appended the Complete Poetical Works of T. E. Hulme, with Prefatory Note (Pound), **III:** 458, 464, 465

Riprap (Snyder), **Supp. VIII: 292–294,** 295

"Riprap" (Snyder), **Supp. VIII:** 293–294

"Rip Van Winkle" (Irving), **II:** 304–306; **Supp. I Part 1:** 185

Rischin, Moses, **Supp. XVII:** 101, 103, 106

Risco-Lozado, Eliezar, **Supp. XIII:** 313

Rise and Shine (Quindlen), **Supp. XVII:** 179

Rise of David Levinsky, The (Cahan), **Supp. IX:** 227; **Supp. XIII:** 106

Rise of Silas Lapham, The (Howells), **II:** 275, 279, 283–285; **IV:** 202; **Retro. Supp. II:** 93, 101

"Rise of the Middle Class" (Banks), **Supp. V:** 10

Rising and Falling (Matthews), **Supp. IX:** 154, **160**

"Rising Daughter, The" (Olds), **Supp. X:** 204

Rising from the Plains (McPhee), **Supp. III Part 1:** 309–310

Rising Glory of America, The (Brackenridge and Freneau), **Supp. I Part 1:** 124; **Supp. II Part 1:** 67, 253, 256, 263

"Rising of the Storm, The" (Dunbar), **Supp. II Part 1:** 199

Rising Sun in the Pacific, The (Morison), **Supp. I Part 2:** 490

Rising Up and Rising Down (Vollmann), **Supp. XVII:** 225, 226, **229–230,** 232, 233, 235–236

Risk Pool, The (Russo), **Supp. XII: 328–331**

Ristovic, Aleksandar, **Supp. VIII:** 272

"Rita Dove: Identity Markers" (Vendler), **Supp. IV Part 1:** 247, 257

Ritchey, John, **Supp. XIV:** 122

Ritchie, Anne Thackeray, **Supp. XX:** 231, 233

"Rite of Passage" (Olds), **Supp. X:** 206

"Rites and Ceremonies" (Hecht), **Supp. X:** 61

Rites and Witnesses: A Comedy (Hinojosa), **Supp. XIX:** 106–107

"Rites of Spring, The" (Morris), **III:** 223

Ritivoi, Andreea Deciu, **Supp. XVI:** 148

Ritschl, Albrecht, **III:** 309, 604

Ritsos, Yannis, **Supp. X:** 112

"Ritsos and the Metaphysical Moment" (Dobyns), **Supp. XIII:** 78

Rittenhouse, David, **Supp. I Part 2:** 507

Rittenhouse, Jessie, **Supp. XV:** 295

"Ritual, The" (Jarman), **Supp. XVII:** 114

"Ritual and Renewal: Keres Traditions in the Short Fiction of Leslie Silko" (Ruoff), **Supp. IV Part 2:** 559

Ritz, The (film), **Supp. XIII:** 206

Ritz, The (McNally), **Supp. XIII:** 198

"Rival, The" (Plath), **Retro. Supp. II:** 254

Riven Rock (Boyle), **Supp. VIII:** 5–6; **Supp. XX:** 25–26

"River" (Ammons), **Supp. VII:** 28

"River, The" (O'Connor), **III:** 344, 352, 353, 354, 356; **Retro. Supp. II:** 229, 231–232

Rivera, Tomás, **Supp. XIII:** 216, 221; **Supp. XIX:** 97, 102

Riverbed (Wagoner), **Supp. IX:** 327–328

"River Driftwood" (Jewett), **Retro. Supp. II:** 132, 133, 147

"River Jordan, The" (DeLillo), **Supp. VI:** 3, 4

River King, The (Hoffman), **Supp. X:** 78, 85, 90, 91–92

"River Merchant's Wife: A Letter, The" (Pound), **III:** 463

"River Now, The" (Hugo), **Supp. VI:** 144

River of Forgetfulness, The (Hadas), **Supp. XXIII:** 120

"River of Rivers in Connecticut, The" (Stevens), **Retro. Supp. I:** 313

River of the Mother of God and Other Essays by Aldo Leopold, The (Leopold), **Supp. XIV:** 180

"River"(O'Hara), **Supp. XXIII:** 212

"River Profile" (Auden), **Supp. II Part 1:** 26

"River Road" (Kunitz), **Supp. III Part 1:** 260

"River Runs Through It, A" (Maclean), **Supp. XIV:** 222–223, 223–229, 233, 234, 235; **Supp. XVI:** 98

River Runs Through It and Other Stories, A (Maclean), **Supp. XIV:** 221, 223

Rivers, Allison, **Supp. XXIII:** 51

Rivers, Larry, **Supp. III Part 1:** 3; **Supp. XV:** 177, 178, 186; **Supp. XXIII:** 209, 210, 211, 212, 215, 216, 217, 220

Rivers and Mountains (Ashbery), **Supp. III Part 1:** 10, 26

Riverside Drive (Simpson), **Supp. IX:** 275–276

Riverside Poetry (Auden, Moore, and Shapiro, eds.), **Supp. XXI:** 98

Rivers to the Sea (Teasdale), **Supp. XV:** 295

"River"(Strout), **Supp. XXIII:** 283

River Styx, Ohio, and Other Poems, The (Oliver), **Supp. VII:** 231, 232

"River That Is East, The" (Kinnell), **Supp. III Part 1:** 241–242

"River"(theater performance, Strout), **Supp. XXIII:** 281

"River Towns" (Masters), **Supp. I Part 2:** 473

Rives, Amélie, **II:** 194

Rivière, Jacques, **Retro. Supp. I:** 63

"Rivington's Last Will and Testament" (Freneau), **Supp. II Part 1:** 261

"Rivulet, The" (Bryant), **Supp. I Part 1:** 155, 162

Rix, Alice, **I:** 199

RL's Dream (Mosley), **Supp. XIII:** 234, 244–245, 249

Roach, Max, **Supp. X:** 239

"Road, Roadsides, and the Disparate Frames of a Sequence" (Sobin), **Supp. XVI:** 288

Road, The (McCarthy), **Supp. XXII:** 49

Road Between, The (Farrell), **II:** 29, 38, 39–40

"Road Between Here and There, The" (Kinnell), **Supp. III Part 1:** 254

"Road Home, The" (Hammett), **Supp. IV Part 1:** 343

Road Home, The (Harrison), **Supp. VIII:** 37, 45, 48, 49–50, 53

Road Is Before Us, The (Boulton), **Supp. XXII:** 17, 25–26

Roadless Yaak, The: Reflections and Observations about One of Our Last Great Wild Places (Bass, ed.), **Supp. XVI:** 23

"Road Not Taken, The" (R. Frost), **II:** 154; **Retro. Supp. I:** 131; **Supp. XI:** 150; **Supp. XV:** 127

"Roadside Flowers" (Collins), **Supp. XXI:** 61

Roadside Poems for Summer Travellers (Larcom, ed.), **Supp. XIII:** 142

"Roadside Resurrection, A" (L. Brown), **Supp. XXI:** 40, 42

Roads of Destiny (O. Henry), **Supp. II Part 1:** 410

Road through the Wall, The (Jackson), **Supp. IX:** 115, 118, 120, 123–124

"Road to Avignon, The" (Lowell), **II:** 516

"Road to Hell, The" (Fante), **Supp. XI:** 160

Road to Los Angeles, The (Fante), **Supp. XI:** 160, 166, 167, 168, 172

Road to Many a Wonder, The (Wagoner), **Supp. IX:** 327, 336

Road to the Temple, The (Glaspell), **Supp. III Part 1:** 175, 182, 186; **Supp. XXI:** 6

Road to Wellville, The (Boyle), **Supp. VIII:** 6–8; **Supp. XX:** 24–25, 26, 28

Road to Xanadu, The (Lowes), **IV:** 453

"Road Warrior" (Pickering), **Supp. XXI:** 204

"Roan Stallion" (Jeffers), **Supp. II Part 2:** 428–429

"Roast-beef" (Stein), **IV:** 43

Roast Leviatham (Untermeyer), **Supp. XV:** 307

"Roast Possum" (Dove), **Supp. IV Part 1:** 247, 248

Robards, Jason, Jr., **III:** 163, 403

Robb, Christina, **Supp. XV:** 251

Robbe-Grillet, Alain, **I:** 123; **IV:** 95; **Supp. IV Part 1:** 42; **Supp. V:** 47, 48; **Supp. XXIII:** 213

Robber Bride, The (Atwood), **Supp. XIII:** 30–31

Robber Bridegroom, The (Welty), **IV:** 261, 266–268, 271, 274; **Retro. Supp. I:** 347

Robbins, Harold, **Supp. XII:** 6

Robbins, Henry, **Supp. IV Part 1:** 198, 201, 210, 211

Robbins, Katherine Robinson, **Supp. X:** 264

Robbins, Thomas, **Supp. XV:** 271

Robbins, Tom, **Supp. IV Part 1:** 227; **Supp. VIII:** 14; **Supp. X:** 259–288; **Supp. XIII:** 11

"Robe, The" (Douglas), **IV:** 434

Robert Bly (Sugg), **Supp. IV Part 1:** 68

"Robert Bly" (W. V. Davis), **Supp. IV Part 1:** 70

"Robert Bly and the Trouble with America" (Mitchell), **Supp. IV Part 1:** 70

Robert Bly: An Introduction to the Poetry (Nelson), **Supp. IV Part 1:** 66

Robert Bly: The Poet and His Critics (W. V. Davis), **Supp. IV Part 1:** 63; **Supp. XXI:** 84, 85–86, 87, 95

Robert Coover: The Universal Fiction-making Process (Gordon), **Supp. V:** 46

Robert Creeley (Ford), **Supp. IV Part 1:** 140

Robert Creeley and the Genius of the American Common Place (Clark), **Supp. IV Part 1:** 140

Robert Creeley's Poetry: A Critical Introduction (Edelberg), **Supp. IV Part 1:** 155

Robert Frost (Meyers), **Retro. Supp. I:** 138

Robert Lowell (Meyers), **Retro. Supp. II:** 191

Robert Lowell and the Sublime (Hart), **Retro. Supp. II:** 187

Robert Lowell's Shifting Colors (Doreski), **Retro. Supp. II:** 185

Robert Lowell: The First Twenty years (Staples), **Retro. Supp. II:** 187

Roberts, Carol, **Supp. XX:** 53

Roberts, David, **Supp. XVIII:** 106

Roberts, Diane, **Supp. X:** 15

Roberts, J. M., **IV:** 454

Roberts, Leo, **II:** 449

Roberts, Margaret, **II:** 449; **IV:** 453, 454

Roberts, Matthew, **Retro. Supp. II:** 324

Roberts, Meade, **IV:** 383

Roberts, Michael, **I:** 527, 536

Roberts, Richard, **III:** 297

Roberts, Victoria, **Supp. XIX:** 205

Roberts, Wally, **Supp. XI:** 119, 120, 126
Roberts, William, **Supp. XI:** 343
Roberts Brothers, **Retro. Supp. I:** 31, 35
Robertson, David, **Supp. VIII:** 305
Robertson, D. B., **III:** 311
Robertson, Lisa, **Supp. XXII:** 155
Robertson, Nan, **Supp. IV Part 1:** 300
Robertson, William, **II:** 8
Robert the Devil (Merwin, trans.), **Supp. III Part 1:** 341, 346
Robeson, Paul, **III:** 392; **Supp. IV Part 1:** 360, 361; **Supp. X:** 137; **Supp. XIX:** 66; **Supp. XXI:** 167
Robeson, Susan L., **Supp. XVIII:** 268
Robespierre, Maximilien, **Supp. I Part 2:** 514, 515, 517
"Robinson" (Kees), **Supp. XV:** 143–144
Robinson, Christopher L., **Supp. XII:** 13, 14
Robinson, Dean, **III:** 506
Robinson, Edward, **III:** 505
Robinson, Edward G., **Supp. XI:** 306
Robinson, Edwin Arlington, **I:** 480; **II:** 388, 391, 529, 542; **III:** 5, **503–526,** 576; **Supp. I Part 2:** 699; **Supp. II Part 1:** 191; **Supp. III Part 1:** 63, 75; **Supp. III Part 2:** 592, 593; **Supp. IX:** 77, 266, 276, 308; **Supp. XV:** 256, 299, 300, 301, 306; **Supp. XVII:** 69; **Supp. XIX:** 123
Robinson, Forrest G., **Supp. IV Part 2:** 597, 601, 604
Robinson, Herman, **III:** 506–507
Robinson, H. M., **IV:** 369, 370
Robinson, Jackie, **Supp. I Part 1:** 338
Robinson, James Harvey, **I:** 214; **Supp. I Part 2:** 492
Robinson, James K., **Supp. IX:** 328
Robinson, Margaret G., **Supp. IV Part 2:** 597, 601, 604
Robinson, Marilynne, **Supp. XXI: 209–224; Supp. XXII:** 50
Robinson, Mary, **Supp. XI:** 26
Robinson, Rowland E., **Supp. XIX:** 6
Robinson, Sugar Ray, **Supp. IV Part 1:** 167
Robinson, Ted, **Supp. XIII:** 166
Robinson Crusoe (Defoe), **II:** 159; **III:** 113, 423; **IV:** 369; **Retro. Supp. II:** 274; **Supp. I Part 2:** 714; **Supp. IV Part 2:** 502
Robison, Mary, **Supp. V:** 22; **Supp. XXI:** 115, 116, 118
Roblès, Emmanuel, **Supp. I Part 1:** 283
"Robstown" (Salinas), **Supp. XIII:** 315
Rochefort, Christina, **Supp. XVI:** 143
Rochefoucauld, Louis Alexandre, **Supp. I Part 2:** 510
"Rock" (Nye), **Supp. XIII:** 287
Rock (Wagoner), **Supp. IX:** 324, **334,** 335
Rock, Catherine, **Supp. XII:** 17
Rock, The (Eliot), **Retro. Supp. I:** 65
Rock, The (Stevens), **Retro. Supp. I:** 309, 312
"Rock, The" (Stevens), **Retro. Supp. I:** 312
Rockaway (Shanley), **Supp. XIV:** 315
"Rock Climbers, The" (Francis), **Supp. IX:** 82

Rock-Drill (Pound), **Retro. Supp. I:** 293
Rockefeller, John D., **I:** 273; **III:** 580; **Supp. I Part 2:** 486; **Supp. V:** 286; **Supp. XXIII:** 26
Rockefeller, Nelson, **III:** 14, 15
Rockets and Rodeos and Other American Spectacles (Mallon), **Supp. XIX:** 137
Rocket to the Moon (Odets), **Supp. II Part 2:** 541–543, 544
Rock Garden, The (Shepard), **Supp. III Part 2:** 432, 447
"Rocking Horse Winner, The" (Lawrence), **Supp. I Part 1:** 329
Rocking the Boat (Vidal), **Supp. IV Part 2:** 683
"Rockpile, The" (Baldwin), **Supp. I Part 1:** 63
Rock Springs (Ford), **Supp. V:** 57, 58–59, 68–69
Rocky Mountains, The: or, Scenes, Incidents, and Adventures in the Far West; Digested from the Journal of Captain E. L. E Bonneville, of the Army of the United States, and Illustrated from Various Other Sources (Irving), **II:** 312
Rodden, John, **Supp. XVI:** 63, 69, 72
Roddenberry, Gene, **Supp. XXII:** 60
Roderick, David, **Supp. XV:** 223
Roderick Hudson (James), **II:** 284, 290, 324, 326, 328; **Retro. Supp. I:** 219, **220–221,** 221, 226; **Supp. IX:** 142
Rodgers, Richard, **III:** 361
Rodgers, Ronald, **Supp. IV Part 2:** 503
Rodker, John, **III:** 470
Rodman, Selden, **Supp. I Part 1:** 83; **Supp. X:** 115
Rodney, Walter, **Supp. XXI:** 171
"Rodrigo Returns to the Land and Linen Celebrates" (Cisneros), **Supp. VII:** 68
Rodríguez, Diane, **Supp. XXIII:** 203
Rodriguez, Randy A., **Supp. XIV:** 312
Rodriguez, Richard, **Supp. XIV: 297–313**
Roethke, Charles, **III:** 531
Roethke, Theodore, **I:** 167, 171–172, 183, 254, 285, 521; **III:** 273, **527–550;** **IV:** 138, 402; **Retro. Supp. II:** 178, 181, 246; **Supp. I Part 2:** 539; **Supp. III Part 1:** 47, 54, 56, 239, 253, 260–261, 350; **Supp. IV Part 2:** 626; **Supp. IX:** 323; **Supp. XV:** 140, 145, 212; **Supp. XVIII:** 90; **Supp. XX: 199; Supp. XXIII:** 19
"Roger Malvin's Burial" (Hawthorne), **II:** 243; **Retro. Supp. I:** 153
Rogers, Michael, **Supp. X:** 265, 266
Rogers, Pattiann, **Supp. XVIII:** 189
Rogers, Samuel, **II:** 303; **Supp. I Part 1:** 157
Rogers, Will, **I:** 261; **IV:** 388
Roger's Version (Updike), **Retro. Supp. I:** 325, 327, 330
Roget, Peter Mark, **Supp. I Part 1:** 312
"Rogue River Jet-Board Trip, Gold Beach, Oregon, July 4, 1977" (Carver), **Supp. III Part 1:** 140
"Rogue's Gallery" (McCarthy), **II:** 563
Rohr, Richard, **Supp. XX: 143**
Roland de La Platière, Jean Marie, **II:** 554

Rolando Hinojosa and the American Dream (Glover), **Supp. XIX:** 112
Rolando Hinojosa: A Reader's Guide (Zilles), **Supp. XIX:** 112
Rolando Hinojosa Reader, The (Saldívar, ed.), **Supp. XIX:** 112
Rôle du Nègre dans la culture des Amériques, La (Locke), **Supp. XIV:** 202
"Role of a Lifetime, The" (Skloot), **Supp. XX: 203**
"Role of Society in the Artist, The" (Ammons), **Supp. VII:** 34
Rolfe, Alfred, **IV:** 427
Rolfe, Frederick, **Supp. XX: 235**
"Roll, Jordan, Roll" (spiritual), **Supp. IV Part 1:** 16
Rolland, Romain, **Supp. XX: 70**
"Roll Call" (Hoffman), **Supp. XVIII:** 86
"Roll Call" (Komunyakaa), **Supp. XIII:** 123
Rolle, Esther, **Supp. IV Part 1:** 367
Rollin, Charles, **II:** 113
Rolling Stones (O. Henry), **Supp. II Part 1:** 410
Rolling Thunder Logbook (Shepard), **Supp. III Part 2:** 433
Rolling Thunder Logbook, The (Shepard), **Supp. XVIII:** 31
"Rolling Up" (Simpson), **Supp. IX:** 265, 274, 280
Rollins, Howard E., Jr., **Supp. IV Part 1:** 236
Rollins, Hyder E., **Supp. IV Part 1:** 168
Rollins, Sonny, **Supp. V:** 195
"Rollo" tales (Abbott), **Supp. I Part 1:** 38
"Roma I" (Wright), **Supp. V:** 338
"Roma II" (Wright), **Supp. V:** 338
Romains, Jules, **I:** 227
Román, David, **Supp. XIII:** 208
Romance, A (Weigl), **Supp. XIX: 277–278**
"Romance, A" (Weigl), **Supp. XIX:** 278
"Romance and a Reading List" (Fitzgerald), **Retro. Supp. I:** 101
Romance of a Plain Man, The (Glasgow), **II:** 175, 180–181
"Romance of Certain Old Clothes, The" (James), **II:** 322; **Retro. Supp. I:** 218
"Roman Elegies" (Brodsky), **Supp. VIII:** 29
"Roman Fever" (Wharton), **Retro. Supp. I:** 382
"Roman Fountain" (Bogan), **Supp. III Part 1:** 56
"*Romanitas* of Gore Vidal, The" (Tatum), **Supp. IV Part 2:** 684
Romaniuk, Zbigniew, **Supp. XVI:** 154
Romano, John, **Supp. XV:** 253
"Roman Sarcophagus, A" (Lowell), **II:** 544
Roman Spring of Mrs. Stone, The (T. Williams), **IV:** 383, 385
"Romantic, The" (Bogan), **Supp. III Part 1:** 50
Romantic Comedians, The (Glasgow), **II:** 175, 186, 190, 194
Romantic Education, A (Hampl), **Supp. XXII:** 82, 83, **87–90,** 91

Romantic Egoists, The (Auchincloss), **Supp. IV Part 1:** 25

Romantic Egotist, The (Fitzgerald), **II:** 82

"Romantic Egotist, The" (Fitzgerald), **Retro. Supp. I:** 100

"Romanticism and Classicism" (Hulme), **III:** 196

"Romanticism Comes Home" (Shapiro), **Supp. II Part 2:** 713

Romantic Manifesto, The: A Philosophy of Literature (Rand), **Supp. IV Part 2:** 521, 523, 527, 529–530

"Romantic Regionalism of Harper Lee, The" (Erisman), **Supp. VIII:** 126

"Rome" (W. C. Williams), **Retro. Supp. I:** 420

Rome Brothers, **Retro. Supp. I:** 393

Romeo and Juliet (Shakespeare), **Supp. V:** 252; **Supp. VIII:** 223

Romola (G. Eliot), **II:** 291; **IV:** 311

Romulus: A New Comedy (Vidal), **Supp. IV Part 2:** 683

Romulus der Grosse (Dürrenmatt), **Supp. IV Part 2:** 683

Ronald, Ann, **Supp. XIII:** 4, 5, 6, 7, 9, 11

"Rondel for a September Day" (White), **Supp. I Part 2:** 676

"Ron Narrative Reconstructions, The" (Coleman), **Supp. XI:** 83

"Ron Padgett's Visual Imagination" (Notley), **Supp. XXII:** 224

Ronsard, Pierre de, **Supp. X:** 65; **Supp. XV:** 165

Rood, John, **IV:** 261

"Roof, the Steeple, and the People, The" (Ellison), **Retro. Supp. II:** 118, 126; **Supp. II Part 1:** 248

"Room" (Levertov), **Supp. III Part 1:** 282

Roomates (film, P. Yates), **Supp. XVII:** 8, 9

Roomates: My Grandfather's Story (Apple), **Supp. XVII:** 2, 7–9

"Room at the Heart of Things, A" (Merrill), **Supp. III Part 1:** 337

Room Called Remember, A: Uncollected Pieces (Buechner), **Supp. XII:** 53

"Roomful of Hovings, A" (McPhee), **Supp. III Part 1:** 291, 294

Room of One's Own, A (Woolf), **Supp. V:** 127; **Supp. IX:** 19; **Supp. XIII:** 305

Room Rented by a Single Woman (Wright), **Supp. XV:** 340–341

"Rooms" (Collins), **Supp. XXI:** 61

Room Temperature (Baker), **Supp. XIII:** 41, **43–45,** 48, 50

Room to Swing (Lacy), **Supp. XV:** 202, 203, 205, 207

"Room Upstairs, The" (Gioia), **Supp. XV:** 120–121, 124

Roosevelt, Eleanor, **IV:** 371; **Supp. IV Part 2:** 679

Roosevelt, Franklin, **Supp. V:** 290

Roosevelt, Franklin Delano, **I:** 482, 485, 490; **II:** 553, 575; **III:** 2, 18, 69, 110, 297, 321, 376, 476, 580, 581; **Supp. I Part 2:** 488, 489, 490, 491, 645, 654, 655

Roosevelt, Kermit, **III:** 508

Roosevelt, Theodore, **I:** 14, 62; **II:** 130; **III:** 508; **IV:** 321; **Retro. Supp. I:** 377; **Supp. I Part 1:** 1, 21; **Supp. I Part 2:** 455, 456, 502, 707; **Supp. V:** 280, 282; **Supp. IX:** 184; **Supp. XIX:** 29; **Supp. XX:** 221; **Supp. XXIII:** 26

Roosevelt After Inauguration And Other Atrocities (Burroughs), **Supp. III Part 1:** 98

"Roosevelt Chair, The" (Skloot), **Supp. XX:** 205

"Roosters" (Bishop), **Retro. Supp. II:** 39, 43, 250; **Supp. I Part 1:** 89

Root, Abiah, **I:** 456

Root, Elihu, **Supp. IV Part 1:** 33

Root, Simeon, **I:** 548

Root, Timothy, **I:** 548

Rootabaga Stories (Sandburg), **III:** 583, 587

"Rootedness: The Ancestor as Foundation" (Morrison), **Supp. III Part 1:** 361

"Roots" (Halliday), **Supp. XIX:** 88

Roots in the Soil (film), **Supp. IV Part 1:** 83

"Rope" (Porter), **III:** 451

Rope, The (O'Neill), **III:** 388

Ropemakers of Plymouth, The (Morison), **Supp. I Part 2:** 494

"Ropes" (Nye), **Supp. XIII:** 276

"Rope's End, The" (Nemerov), **III:** 282

Roquelaure, A. N., **Supp. VII:** 301. *See also* Rice, Anne

Rorem, Ned, **Supp. IV Part 1:** 79, 84; **Supp. XXIII:** 217

Rorschach Test (F. Wright), **Supp. XVII:** 240, 245

Rorty, James, **Supp. XXII:** 276, 277

"Rosa" (Ozick), **Supp. V:** 271

Rosa, Rodrigo Rey, **Supp. IV Part 1:** 92

Rosaldo, Renato, **Supp. IV Part 2:** 544

"Rosalia" (Simic), **Supp. VIII:** 278

Roscoe, Will, **Supp. IV Part 1:** 330

"Roscoe in Hell" (McKnight), **Supp. XX:** 151

"Rose" (Dubus), **Supp. VII:** 88

Rose (L.-Y. Lee), **Supp. XV:** 211, **212–215,** 218

Rose, Alice, Sister, **III:** 348

Rose, Charlie, **Supp. XIX:** 26, 30

Rose, Mickey, **Supp. XV:** 3

Rose, Philip, **Supp. IV Part 1:** 362

"Rose, The" (Roethke), **III:** 537

"Rose, The" (W. C. Williams), **Retro. Supp. I:** 419

Rose, Where Did You Get That Red?: Teaching Great Poetry to Children (Koch), **Supp. XV:** 189

"Rose for Emily, A" (Faulkner), **II:** 72; **Supp. IX:** 96; **Supp. XX:** 179

Rose-Hued Cities (P. N. Warren), **Supp. XX:** 261

Rose in Bloom (Alcott), **Supp. I Part 1:** 42

"Rose-Johnny" (Kingsolver), **Supp. VII:** 203

Rose Madder (King), **Supp. V:** 141, 148, 150, 152

"Rose-Morals" (Lanier), **Supp. I Part 1:** 364

Rosen, Jonathan, **Supp. XVII:** 50; **Supp. XX:** 179

Rosen, Kenneth, **Supp. IV Part 2:** 499, 505, 513

Rosen, Norma, **Supp. XVII:** 49, 50

Rosenbaum, Alissa Zinovievna. *See* Rand, Ayn

Rosenbaum, Thane, **Supp. XVII:** 48

Rosenberg, Bernard, **Supp. I Part 2:** 650

Rosenberg, Harold, **Supp. XV:** 143; **Supp. XIX:** 159; **Supp. XXIII:** 211

Rosenberg, Julia, **Supp. XVIII:** 136

Rosenberg, Julius and Ethel, **Supp. I Part 1:** 295; **Supp. I Part 2:** 532; **Supp. V:** 45

Rosenberg, Liz, **Supp. XV:** 251

Rosenberg, Shlomo, **Supp. XXIII:** 6

Rosenbloom, Joel, **Supp. IV Part 2:** 527

Rosenfeld, Alvin H., **Supp. I Part 1:** 120

Rosenfeld, Isaac, **Supp. XII:** 160

Rosenfeld, Paul, **I:** 116, 117, 231, 245

Rosenfelt, Deborah, **Supp. XIII:** 296, 304

Rosenfield, Isaac, **IV:** 3

Rosengarten, Theodore, **Supp. XVIII:** 183

Rosenthal, Ira, **Supp. XIV:** 146–147

Rosenthal, Lois, **Supp. VIII:** 258

Rosenthal, M. L., **II:** 550; **III:** 276, 479; **Supp. V:** 333

Rosenthal, Peggy, **Supp. XVII:** 119

Rose of Wissahikon, The (Lippard), **Supp. XXIII:** 178

"Rose Pogonias" (Frost), **Retro. Supp. I:** 127

"Rose Red and Snow White" (Grimms), **Supp. X:** 82

"Rose Room" (Sorrentino), **Supp. XXI:** 228

"Roses" (Conroy), **Supp. XVI:** 72

"Roses" (Dove), **Supp. IV Part 1:** 246

"Roses and Skulls" (Goldbarth), **Supp. XII:** 192

"Roses for Lubbock" (Nye), **Supp. XIII:** 281

"Roses Only" (Moore), **III:** 195, 198, 200, 202, 215

Rose Tattoo, The (T. Williams), **IV:** 382, 383, 387, 388, 389, 392–393, 394, 397, 398

Rose Theatre (Sorrentino), **Supp. XXI:** 236

"Rosewood, Ohio" (Matthews), **Supp. IX:** 160

Rosie (Lamott), **Supp. XX:** 133–134

Rosinante to the Road Again (Dos Passos), **I:** 478

Roskies, David, **Supp. XVII:** 39, 44, 49–50

Roskolenko, Harry, **Supp. XV:** 179

Rosmersholm (Ibsen), **III:** 152

Rosmond, Babette, **II:** 432

Ross, Eleanor. *See* Taylor, Eleanor Ross

Ross, Harold, **Supp. I Part 1:** 174; **Supp. I Part 2:** 607, 617, 653, 654, 655, 660; **Supp. VIII:** 151, 170; **Supp. IX:** 190

Ross, Herbert, **Supp. XV:** 2

Ross, Jean, **Supp. XXI:** 144, 146
Ross, John F., **II:** 110
Ross, Lillilan, **Retro. Supp. II:** 198
Ross, Mary, **Supp. XXII:** 195
Ross, Mitchell S., **Supp. IV Part 2:** 692; **Supp. X:** 260
Rossen, Robert, **Supp. XI:** 306
Rosset, Barney, **III:** 171
Rossetti, Christina, **Supp. XIV:** 128
Rossetti, Dante Gabriel, **I:** 433; **II:** 323; **Retro. Supp. I:** 128, 286; **Supp. I Part 2:** 552; **Supp. XXII:** 156
Rossetti, William Michael, **Retro. Supp. I:** 407
Rossi, Umberto, **Supp. XVIII:** 137, 138–139
Rossini, Clare, **Supp. XVII:** 111
Rosskam, Edwin, **IV:** 477
Ross Macdonald (Bruccoli), **Supp. IV Part 2:** 468, 470
Rostand, Edmond, **II:** 515; **Supp. IV Part 2:** 518
Rosten, Leo, **Supp. XVII:** 9
Rosy Crucifixion, The (H. Miller), **III:** 170, 187, 188–189, 190
Rote Walker, The (Jarman), **Supp. XVII:** 110, **113–115**
Roth, Henry, **Supp. IV Part 1:** 314; **Supp. VIII:** 233; **Supp. IX: 227–243;** **Supp. XIII:** 106
Roth, Philip, **I:** 144, 161; **II:** 591; **Retro. Supp. II:** 22, **279–297; Supp. I Part 1:** 186, 192; **Supp. I Part 2:** 431, 441, 443; **Supp. II Part 1:** 99; **Supp. III Part 2: 401–429; Supp. IV Part 1:** 236, 379, 388; **Supp. V:** 45, 119, 122, 257, 258; **Supp. VIII:** 88, 236, 245; **Supp. IX:** 227; **Supp. XI:** 64, 68, 99, 140; **Supp. XII:** 190, 310; **Supp. XIV:** 79, 93, 111, 112; **Supp. XVI:** 206; **Supp. XVII:** 43, 48, 183; **Supp. XVIII:** 89; **Supp. XXI:** 234; **Supp. XXII:** 268
Roth, Rita, **Supp. XVI:** 112
Roth, William, **Supp. XV:** 142
Rothenberg, Jerome, **Supp. VIII:** 292; **Supp. XII:** 3
Rothermere, Lady Mary, **Retro. Supp. I:** 63
Rothko, Mark, **Supp. XV:** 144
Rothstein, Mervyn, **Supp. VIII:** 142
"Rouen, France"(Kenny), **Supp. XXIII:** 152
"Rouge High" (Hughes), **Supp. I Part 1:** 330
Rougemont, Denis de, **II:** 586; **IV:** 216; **Retro. Supp. I.** 328, 329, 330, 331
Rough Edges (Skloot), **Supp. XX: 196**
Roughing It (Twain), **II:** 312; **IV:** 195, 197, 198
Roughing It in the Bush (Shields), **Supp. VII:** 313
"Rough Outline" (Simic), **Supp. VIII:** 276
"Rough-Skinned Newt, The"(Schott), **Supp. XXIII:** 253–254
Rough South of Larry Brown, The (film, Hawkins), **Supp. XXI:** 39
Rougon-Macquart, Les (Zola), **II:** 175–176

Roumain, Jacques, **Retro. Supp. I:** 202; **Supp. IV Part 1:** 360, 367
"Round, The" (Kunitz), **Supp. III Part 1:** 268
"Roundelay Between Two Shepherdesses, A" (Notley), **Supp. XXII:** 229
"Round Trip" (Dunn), **Supp. XI:** 148–149
Round Up (Lardner), **II:** 426, 430, 431
Rourke, Constance, **I:** 258; **IV:** 339, 352
Rourke, Milton, **Retro. Supp. II:** 89
Rousseau, Jean-Jacques, **I:** 226; **II:** 8, 343; **III:** 170, 178, 259; **IV:** 80, 173, 440; **Supp. I Part 1:** 126; **Supp. I Part 2:** 637, 659; **Supp. IV Part 1:** 171; **Supp. XI:** 245; **Supp. XVI:** 292; **Supp. XXI:** 83
Roussel, Raymond, **Supp. III Part 1:** 6, 7, 10, 15, 16, 21; **Supp. XV:** 182
"Route 302" (Halliday), **Supp. XIX:** 93
"Routes" (Everwine), **Supp. XV:** 82
"Route Six" (Kunitz), **Supp. III Part 1:** 258
Route Two (Erdrich and Dorris), **Supp. IV Part 1:** 260
"Routine Things Around the House, The" (Dunn), **Supp. XI:** 148
Rover Boys (Winfield), **III:** 146
Rovit, Earl, **IV:** 102
Rowan, Carl T., **Supp. XIV:** 306
Rowe, Anne E., **Supp. X:** 223
Rowe, John Carlos, **Retro. Supp. I:** 216
Rowe, Kenneth Thorpe, **Supp. XXIII:** 258
Rowell, Charles, **Supp. XXI:** 250, 254, 255
"Rowing" (Sexton), **Supp. II Part 2:** 696
"Rowing Endeth, The" (Sexton), **Supp. II Part 2:** 696
Rowlandson, Mary, **Supp. IV Part 2:** 430, 431
"Rows of Cold Trees, The" (Winters), **Supp. II Part 2:** 790–791, 800
Rowson, Susanna, **Supp. I Part 1:** 128; **Supp. XV:** 229–248
Roxanna Slade (Price), **Supp. VI:** 267
Roxie Hart (Watkins), **Supp. XVI:** 188
Royal Family, The (Vollmann), **Supp. XVII:** 226, 230, 233
"Royal Palm" (Crane), **I:** 401
Royce, Josiah, **I:** 443; **III:** 303, 600; **IV:** 26; **Retro. Supp. I:** 57; **Supp. XIV:** 197, 199; **Supp. XVII:** 97
"Roy McInnes" (Budbill), **Supp. XIX:** 6–7
Royster, Sarah Elmira, **III:** 410, 429
Roytc, Elizabeth, **Supp. XV:** 59
Rózewicz, Tadeusz, **Supp. X:** 60
R. S. Thomas: Poetry and Theology (W. V. Davis), **Supp. XXI: 86–87**
Ruas, Charles, **Supp. IV Part 1:** 383
Ruback, Max, **Supp. XXIII:** 290
Rubáiyát (Khayyám), **I:** 568
Rubáiyát of Omar Khayyam (Fitzgerald), **Supp. I Part 2:** 416; **Supp. III Part 2:** 610; **Supp. XV:** 156
"Rubber Life" (Prose), **Supp. XVI:** 256
Rub from Snub, A (Swanwick), **Supp. XV:** 237
"Rubicon" (Cliff), **Supp. XXII:** 76

Rubin, Louis, **Supp. I Part 2:** 672, 673, 679; **Supp. X:** 42
Rubin, Louis D., Jr., **IV:** 116, 462–463
Rubin, Stan, **Supp. XIV:** 307, 310
Rubin, Stan Sanvel, **Supp. IV Part 1:** 242, 245, 252
Rubins, Josh, **Supp. XX: 89**
"Ruby Brown" (Hughes), **Supp. I Part 1:** 327
"Ruby Daggett" (Eberhart), **I:** 539
Rucker, Rudy, **Supp. X:** 302
Rudd, Hughes, **Supp. XII:** 141
"Rude Awakening, A" (Chopin), **Retro. Supp. II:** 64
Rudens (Plautus), **Supp. III Part 2:** 630
Ruderman, Judith, **Supp. IV Part 1:** 380
Rudge, Olga, **Supp. V:** 338
Rudikoff, Sonya, **Supp. XIV:** 113
Rudman, Mark, **Supp. XXIII:** 124
Rueckert, William, **I:** 264
Ruesch, Jurgen, **Supp. XV:** 147
Rugby Chapel (Arnold), **Supp. I Part 2:** 416
"Rugby Road" (Garrett), **Supp. VII:** 100
Rugge, John, **Supp. XXII:** 218
Ruining the New Road (Matthews), **Supp. IX:** 154, **155–157**
"Ruins of Italica, The" (Bryant, trans.), **Supp. I Part 1:** 166
Rukeyser, Muriel, **Retro. Supp. II:** 48; **Supp. VI: 271–289; Supp. XV:** 349; **Supp. XVII:** 74
"Rule of Phase Applied to History, The" (Adams), **I:** 19
Rule of the Bone (Banks), **Supp. V:** 16
"Rules by Which a Great Empire May Be Reduced to a Small One" (Franklin), **II:** 120
Rules For the Dance: A Handbook for Reading and Writing Metrical Verse (Oliver), **Supp. VII:** 229, 247
Rules of the Game, The (film), **Supp. XII:** 259
Rulfo, Juan, **Supp. IV Part 2:** 549
Rumba (film, Gering), **Supp. XVII:** 57
Rumbaut, Rubén, **Supp. XI:** 184
Rümelin-Oesterlen, Natalie, **Supp. XX: 235**
Rumens, Carol, **Supp. XI:** 14; **Supp. XVI:** 212
Rumi, **Supp. XX: 117**
"Rumination of Rivers, The" (Bronk), **Supp. XXI:** 32
Rumkowski, Chaim, **Supp. XII:** 168
Rummel, Mary Kay, **Supp. XIII:** 280
"Rumor and a Ladder" (Bowles), **Supp. IV Part 1:** 93
Rumor of War, A (Caputo), **Supp. XIX: 17–21,** 25, 30
Rumors (Simon), **Supp. IV Part 2:** 582–583, 591
Rumpelstiltskin (Gardner), **Supp. VI:** 72
"Rumpelstiltskin" (Grimm), **IV:** 266
"Rumpelstiltskin" (Sexton), **Supp. II Part 2:** 690
"Runagate Runagate" (Hayden), **Supp. II Part 1:** 377
"Runes" (Nemerov), **III:** 267, 277–278
Run Man Run (C. Himes), **Supp. XVI:** 142, 143

"Runner, The" (Grossman), **Supp. XIX:** 83

"Running" (Wilbur), **Supp. III Part 2:** 558–559

"RUNNING-AWAY"(Strout), **Supp. XXIII:** 274

Running Dog (DeLillo), **Supp. VI:** 3, 6, 8, 14

"Running in Church" (A. Finch), **Supp. XVII:** 72

"Running the Table" (Conroy), **Supp. XVI:** 75

"Run of Bad Luck, A" (Proulx), **Supp. VII:** 253–254

Run of Jacks, A (Hugo), **Supp. VI:** 131, 133, 134, 135, 136

Run River (Didion), **Supp. IV Part 1:** 197, 199–200, 201

Ruoff, A. LaVonne Brown, **Supp. IV Part 1:** 324, 327; **Supp. IV Part 2:** 559

Rupert, Jim, **Supp. XII:** 215

Ruppert, James, **Supp. IV Part 1:** 321

Rural Hours (Cooper), **Supp. XIII:** 152

"Rural Route" (Wright), **Supp. V:** 340

"Rural South, The" (Du Bois), **Supp. II Part 1:** 174

Rush, Benjamin, **Supp. I Part 2:** 505, 507

Rushdie, Salman, **Supp. IV Part 1:** 234, 297

Rushdy, Ashraf, **Supp. X:** 250

Rushing, Jimmy, **Retro. Supp. II:** 113

Rusk, Dean, **II:** 579

Ruskin, John, **II:** 323, 338; **IV:** 349; **Retro. Supp. I:** 56, 360; **Supp. I Part 1:** 2, 10, 87, 349; **Supp. I Part 2:** 410

Rusnak, Karl, **Supp. XVIII:** 149

Russell, Ada Dwyer, **II:** 513, 527

Russell, Bertrand, **II:** 27; **III:** 605, 606; **Retro. Supp. I:** 57, 58, 59, 60; **Supp. I Part 2:** 522; **Supp. V:** 290; **Supp. XII:** 45; **Supp. XIV:** 337

Russell, Diarmuid, **Retro. Supp. I:** 342, 345, 346–347, 349–350

Russell, George, **Retro. Supp. I:** 342

Russell, Herb, **Supp. I Part 2:** 465–466

Russell, John, **Supp. XIV:** 344, 347, 348

Russell, Peter, **III:** 479

Russell, Richard, **Supp. XI:** 102

Russell, Robert, **Supp. XX:** 195

Russell, Sue, **Supp. IV Part 2:** 653

Russert, Margaret, **Supp. XVIII:** 62

Russert, Tim, **Supp. XII:** 272

Russia at War (Caldwell), **I:** 296

"Russia Between Myth and Reality: From *Meri* to *Three Cities*"(Krutikov), *Supp. XXIII:* 11

Russian Journal, A (Steinbeck), **IV:** 52, 63

Russo, Richard, **Supp. XI:** 349; **Supp. XII:** 325–344; **Supp. XXIII:** 302

"Rusty Autumn" (Swenson), **Supp. IV Part 2:** 640

Rutabaga-Roo: I've Got a Song and It's for You (Nye, album), **Supp. XIII:** 274

Ruth (biblical book), **Supp. I Part 2:** 516

Ruth, George Herman ("Babe"), **II:** 423; **Supp. I Part 2:** 438, 440

Rutheiser, Charles, **Supp. XXII:** 244

Ruth Hall (Fern), **Supp. V:** 122

Ruthven, K. K., **Supp. XXII:** 261

Rutkowska, Malgorzata, **Supp. XXII:** 208

Rutledge, Ann, **III:** 588; **Supp. I Part 2:** 471

Ruwe, Donelle R., **Supp. XII:** 215

Ryan, Katy, **Supp. XXI:** 215

Ryan, Kay, **Supp. XXI:** 20

Ryan, Maureen, **Supp. XXI:** 215

Ryan, Paul William, **Supp. XVIII:** 223–239

Ryan, Paul William (Mike Quin), **Supp. XXI:** 264–265

Ryder (Barnes), **Supp. III Part 1:** 31, 36–38, 42, 43

"Ryder" (Rukeyser), **Supp. VI:** 273, 283

Ryle, Herbert Edward, **Supp. XX:** 230

Rymer, Thomas, **IV:** 122

"Ryōkan Says" (Budbill), **Supp. XIX:** 11

S

S. (Updike), **Retro. Supp. I:** 330, 331, 332, 333

S-1 (Baraka), **Supp. II Part 1:** 55, 57

Saadi, **II:** 19

Saar, Doreen Alvarez, **Supp. XV:** 237

Sabbatai Zevi (Asch), **Supp. XXIII:** 12

"Sabbath, The" (Stowe), **Supp. I Part 2:** 587

"Sabbath Mom" (White), **Supp. I Part 2:** 671–672

Sabbaths (Berry), **Supp. X:** 31

Sabbath's Theater (P. Roth), **Retro. Supp. II:** 279, 288

"Sabbioneta to Parma" (Di Piero), **Supp. XIX:** 36–37

Sabines, Jaime, **Supp. V:** 178

"Sabotage" (Baraka), **Supp. II Part 1:** 49, 53

"Saboteur" (Jin), **Supp. XVIII:** 97

Sacco, Nicola, **I:** 482, 486, 490, 494; **II:** 38–39, 426; **III:** 139–140; **Supp. I Part 2:** 446; **Supp. V:** 288–289; **Supp. IX:** 199; **Supp. XXII:** 277

Sachs, Hanns, **Supp. I Part 1:** 259; **Supp. X:** 186

Sack Full of Old Quarrels, A (Weigl), **Supp. XIX:** 277

"Sacks" (Carver), **Supp. III Part 1:** 143–144

Sacks, Oliver, **Supp. XVIII:** 143

Sacks, Peter, **Supp. IV Part 2:** 450

Sackville-West, Vita, **Supp. VIII:** 263

"Sacrament of Divorce, The" (Patchett), **Supp. XII:** 309

"Sacrament of Self: Catholic Roots of Contemporary Memoir" (lecture, Hampl), **Supp. XXII:** 81

"Sacraments" (Dubus), **Supp. VII:** 91

Sacred and Profane Memories (Van Vechten), **Supp. II Part 2:** 735, 749

"Sacred Chant for the Return of Black Spirit and Power" (Baraka), **Supp. II Part 1:** 51

"Sacred Factory, The" (Toomer), **Supp. IX:** 320

Sacred Fount, The (James), **II:** 332–333; **Retro. Supp. I:** 219, 228, 232

"Sacred Heart" (Egan), **Supp. XIX:** 52

"Sacred Hoop, The: A Contemporary Perspective" (Gunn Allen), **Supp. IV Part 1:** 324

Sacred Hoop, The: Recovering the Feminine in American Indian Traditions (Gunn Allen), **Supp. IV Part 1:** 319, 320, 322, 324, 325, 328–330, 331, 333, 334

Sacred Journey, The (Buechner), **Supp. XII:** 42, 53

"Sacred Thing, The" (Ryan as Quin), **Supp. XVIII:** 227

Sacred Wood, The (Eliot), **IV:** 431; **Retro. Supp. I:** 59, 60; **Supp. I Part 1:** 268; **Supp. II Part 1:** 136, 146

Sacrifice, The (Bidart), **Supp. XV:** 22, 27–30, 35

"Sacrifice, The" (Bidart), **Supp. XV:** 29

"Sacrifice, The" (Oates), **Supp. II Part 2:** 523

Sacrilege of Alan Kent, The (Caldwell), **I:** 291–292

"Sad Brazil" (Hardwick), **Supp. III Part 1:** 210

Sad Days of Light (Balakian), **Supp. XXIII:** 20

"Sad Dust Glories" (Ginsberg), **Supp. II Part 1:** 376

Sad Dust Glories: Poems Written Work Summer in Sierra Woods (Ginsberg), **Supp. II Part 1:** 326

Sade, Marquis de, **III:** 259; **IV:** 437, 442; **Supp. XII:** 1, 14–15

Sad-Faced Boy (Bontemps), **Supp. XXII:** 5, 12

Sad Flower in the Sand, A (film), **Supp. XI:** 173

Sad Heart at the Supermarket, A (Jarrell), **II:** 386

"Sadie" (Matthiessen), **Supp. V:** 201

"Sadie and Maud" (Brooks), **Supp. XVIII:** 175

Sadness and Happiness (Pinsky), **Supp. VI:** 235, 237–241

"Sadness of Brothers, The" (Kinnell), **Supp. III Part 1:** 237, 251

"Sadness of Days, The" (Salinas), **Supp. XIII:** 325

Sadness of Days, The: Selected and New Poems (Salinas), **Supp. XIII:** 311, 324–326

"Sadness of Lemons, The" (Levine), **Supp. V:** 184

Sadoff, Ira, **Supp. XVII:** 241; **Supp. XXI:** 100

"Sad Rite" (Karr), **Supp. XI:** 243

"Sad Strains of a Gay Waltz" (Stevens), **Retro. Supp. I:** 302

"Safe" (Gordon), **Supp. IV Part 1:** 299, 306

"Safe in their Alabaster Chambers" (Dickinson), **Retro. Supp. I:** 30

Safer, Morley, **Supp. XIX:** 25

"Safe Subjects" (Komunyakaa), **Supp. XIII:** 118

"Safeway" (F. Barthelme), **Supp. XI:** 26, 27, 36

Saffin, John, **Supp. I Part 1:** 115

Saffy, Edna, **Supp. X:** 227

Sagan, Miriam, **Supp. XXIII:** 133

"Saga of an American Ranch" (P. N. Warren), **Supp. XX:** 261

"Saga of Arturo Bandini" (Fante), **Supp. XI:** 159, **166–169**

"Saga of King Olaf, The" (Longfellow), **II:** 489, 505; **Retro. Supp. II:** 154, 155, 164

"Sage of Stupidity and Wonder, The" (Goldbarth), **Supp. XII:** 191

Sahl, Mort, **II:** 435–436

"Said" (Dixon), **Supp. XII:** 149–150

Said, Edward, **Supp. XXI:** 153

"Sailing after Lunch" (Stevens), **IV:** 73

Sailing Alone Around the Room: New and Selected Poems (Collins), **Supp. XXI:** 54, 56, 62

"Sailing Home from Rapallo" (Lowell), **Retro. Supp. II:** 189

Sailing through China (Theroux), **Supp. VIII:** 323

"Sailing to Byzantium" (Yeats), **III:** 263; **Supp. VIII:** 30; **Supp. X:** 74; **Supp. XI:** 281

"Sail Made of Rags, The" (Nye), **Supp. XIII:** 277

"Sailor off the Bremen" (Shaw), **Supp. XIX:** 247

"Sailors Lost at Sea" (Shields), **Supp. VII:** 318

"*St Anne*/Santa Ana" (Mora), **Supp. XIII:** 229

"*Saint Anthony of Padua*/San Antonio de Padua" (Mora), **Supp. XIII:** 228

"St. Augustine and the Bullfights" (Porter), **III:** 454

Sainte-Beuve, Charles Augustin, **IV:** 432

St. Elmo (Wilson), **Retro. Supp. I:** 351–352

"Saint Emmanuel the Good, Martyr" (Unamuno; Everwine, trans.), **Supp. XV:** 79

Sainte Vierge, La (Picabia), **Retro. Supp. II:** 331

Saint-Exupéry, Antoine de, **Supp. IX:** 247

"St. Francis Einstein of the Daffodils" (W. C. Williams), **IV:** 409–411

Saint-Gaudens, Augustus, **I:** 18, 228; **II:** 551

Saint-Gaudens, Homer, **Supp. XV:** 41

"St. George, the Dragon, and the Virgin" (R. Bly), **Supp. IV Part 1:** 73

St. George and the Godfather (Mailer), **III:** 46; **Retro. Supp. II:** 206, 208

Saint Jack (Theroux), **Supp. VIII:** 319

St. John, David, **Supp. V:** 180; **Supp. XI:** 270, 272; **Supp. XIII:** 312

St. John, Edward B., **Supp. IV Part 2:** 490

St. John, James Hector. *See* Crèvecoeur, Michel-Guillaume Jean de

"Saint John and the Back-Ache" (Stevens), **Retro. Supp. I:** 310

Saint Judas (Wright), **Supp. III Part 2: 595–599**

"Saint Judas" (Wright), **Supp. III Part 2:** 598–599

St. Louis Woman (Bontemps and Cullen), **Supp. IV Part 1:** 170

St. Mawr (Lawrence), **II:** 595

Saint Maybe (Tyler), **Supp. IV Part 2:** 670–671

"Saint Nicholas" (Moore), **III:** 215

"Saint"(O'Hara), **Supp. XXIII:** 219

St. Petersburg (Biely), **Supp. XII:** 13

Saint-Phalle, Niki de, **Supp. XV:** 187

"St. Roach" (Rukeyser), **Supp. VI:** 286

"Saint Robert" (Dacey), **Supp. IV Part 1:** 70

Saintsbury, George, **IV:** 440; **Supp. XV:** 181

Saints' Everlasting Rest, The (Baxter), **III:** 199; **IV:** 151, 153

Saint-Simon, Claude Henri, **Supp. I Part 2:** 648

"St. Thomas Aquinas" (Simic), **Supp. VIII:** 281

Saks, Gene, **Supp. IV Part 2:** 577, 588

Salamun, Tomaz, **Supp. VIII:** 272

Salazar, Dixie, **Supp. V:** 180; **Supp. XV:** 73

Saldívar, José David, **Supp. IV Part 2:** 544, 545; **Supp. XIX:** 110, 112–113

Sale, Richard, **Supp. IV Part 1:** 379

Sale, Roger, **Supp. V:** 244

Saleh, Dennis, **Supp. V:** 182, 186

"Salem" (Lowell), **II:** 550

Salemi, Joseph, **Supp. IV Part 1:** 284

Salem's Lot (King), **Supp. V:** 139, 144, 146, 151

"Sale of the Hessians, The" (Franklin), **II: 120**

Salick, Roydan, **Supp. XXIII:** 93, 94

Salinas, Luis Omar, **Supp. IV Part 2:** 545; **Supp. V:** 180; **Supp. XIII: 311–330; Supp. XV:** 73

"Salinas Is on His Way" (Salinas), **Supp. XIII:** 317

"Salinas Sends Messengers to the Stars" (Salinas), **Supp. XIII:** 317

"Salinas Summering at the Caspian and Thinking of Hamlet" (Salinas), **Supp. XIII:** 320

"Salinas Wakes Early and Goes to the Park to Lecture Sparrows" (Salinas), **Supp. XIII:** 320

Salinger, Doris, **III:** 551

Salinger, J. D., **II:** 255; **III: 551–574; IV:** 190, 216, 217; **Retro. Supp. I:** 102, 116, 335; **Supp. IV Part 2:** 502; **Supp. V:** 23, 119; **Supp. VIII:** 151; **Supp. XI:** 2, 66; **Supp. XIV:** 93; **Supp. XXIII:** 100

Salisbury, Harrison, **Supp. I Part 2:** 664

Salle, David, **Supp. XII:** 4

Salley, Columbus, **Supp. XIV:** 195

"Sally" (Cisneros), **Supp. VII:** 63

"Sally's Choice" (E. Stoddard), **Supp. XV:** 282

Salmagundi; or, The Whim-Whams and Opinions of Launcelot Langstaff Esq., and Others (Irving), **II:** 299, 300, 304

Salmon, Edward G., **Supp. XVIII:** 258

Salome (Strauss), **IV:** 316

Salon (online magazine), **Supp. VIII:** 310; **Supp. X:** 202

"Salt"(Crooker), **Supp. XXIII:** 62

Salt Eaters, The (Bambara), **Supp. XI:** 1, **12–14**

Salt Ecstasies, The (White), **Supp. XI:** 123

Salter, James, **Supp. IX: 245–263; Supp. XVI:** 237, 247; **Supp. XIX:** 252

Salter, Mary Jo, **Supp. IV Part 2:** 653; **Supp. IX:** 37, 292; **Supp. XV:** 251, 253; **Supp. XVII:** 112; **Supp. XXIII:** 112

Salt Garden, The (Nemerov), **III:** 269, 272–275, 277

"Salt Garden, The" (Nemerov), **III:** 267–268

Salting the Ocean (Nye, ed.), **Supp. XIII:** 280

Salt Lesson, The (C. Frost), **Supp. XV:** 92, 96

"Salt Lesson, The" (C. Frost), **Supp. XV:** 99

"Salts and Oils" (Levine), **Supp. V:** 190

Salt to the Devil (film, Dmytryk), **Supp. XX:** 41

Saltzman, Arthur, **Supp. XIII:** 48

Saltzman, Harry, **Supp. XI:** 307

"Salut au Monde!" (Whitman), **Retro. Supp. I:** 387, 396, 400

"Salute" (MacLeish), **III:** 13

Salute (Shaw), **Supp. XIX:** 244

"Salute to Mister Yates, A" (Dubus), **Supp. XI:** 347, 349

Salute to Spring (Le Sueur), **Supp. XXIII:** 164, 165, 166, 172

Salvador (Didion), **Supp. IV Part 1:** 198, 207–208, 210

"Salvage" (Clampitt), **Supp. IX:** 41

Salvation (Asch), **Supp. XXIII:** 3, 4, **12,** 13, 15

Salvos: An Informal Book About Books and Plays (W. Frank), **Supp. XX:** 75

Samain, Albert, **II:** 528

Same Door, The (Updike), **IV:** 214, 219, 226; **Retro. Supp. I:** 320

"Same in Blues" (Hughes), **Retro. Supp. I:** 208

Same River Twice, The (Offutt), **Supp. XIX:** 163, 164, **167–168,** 175

"Samhain" (A. Finch), **Supp. XVII:** 72

Sam Lawson's Oldtown Fireside Stories (Stowe), **Supp. I Part 2:** 587, 596, 598–599

Sam Patch, the High, Wide & Handsome Jumper (Bontemps and Conroy), **Supp. XXII:** 5, 11

"Sa'm Pèdi" (Bell), **Supp. X:** 17

"Sampler, A" (MacLeish), **III:** 4

Sampoli, Maria, **Supp. V:** 338

Sampson, Edward, **Supp. I Part 2:** 664, 673

Sampson, Martin, **Supp. I Part 2:** 652

"Sam's Dad" (Lamott), **Supp. XX: 142–143**

Sam's Legacy (Neugeboren), **Supp. XVI:** 221, 222

Samson Agonistes (Milton), **III:** 274

"Samson and Delilah" (Masters), **Supp. I Part 2:** 459

Samuel, Maurice, **Supp. XXIII:** 1, 7

Samuel de Champlain: Father of New France (Morison), **Supp. I Part 2:** 496–497

Samuels, Charles Thomas, **Retro. Supp. I:** 334

"Samuel Sewall" (Hecht), **Supp. X:** 58

"Samwheel" (Lamott), **Supp. XX: 144–145**

Sanborn, Franklin B., **IV:** 171, 172, 178

Sanborn, Kate, **Supp. XIII:** 152

Sanborn, Sara, **Supp. XIV:** 113

Sanchez, Carol Anne, **Supp. IV Part 1:** 335

Sanchez, Carol Lee, **Supp. IV Part 2:** 499, 557

Sanchez, Sonia, **Supp. II Part 1:** 34

Sánchez Beras, César, **Supp. XXI:** 100, 104

Sanctified Church, The (Hurston), **Supp. VI:** 150

"Sanction of the Victims, The" (Rand), **Supp. IV Part 2:** 528

Sanctuary (Faulkner), **II:** 57, 61–63, 72, 73, 74, 174; **Retro. Supp. I:** 73, 84, 86–87, 87; **Supp. I Part 2:** 614; **Supp. XII:** 16

"Sanctuary" (Larsen), **Supp. XVIII:** 119, 130–131

Sanctuary (Wharton), **IV:** 311

"Sanctuary" (Wylie), **Supp. I Part 2:** 711

"Sanctuary, The" (Nemerov), **III:** 272, 274

Sanctuary V (Schulberg), **Supp. XVIII:** 254

"Sanctus" (Nelson), **Supp. XVIII:** 183

Sand, George, **II:** 322; **Retro. Supp. I:** 235, 372; **Supp. XV:** 275

"Sandalphon" (Longfellow), **II:** 498

Sand and Foam: A Book of Aphorisms (Gibran), **Supp. XX: 115, 121–122**

Sandbox, The (Albee), **I:** 74–75, 89

Sandburg, Carl, **I:** 103, 109, 384, 421; **II:** 529; **III:** 3, 20, **575–598**; **Retro. Supp. I:** 133, 194; **Supp. I Part 1:** 257, 320; **Supp. I Part 2:** 387, 389, 454, 461, 653; **Supp. III Part 1:** 63, 71, 73, 75; **Supp. IV Part 1:** 169; **Supp. IV Part 2:** 502; **Supp. IX:** 1, 15, 308; **Supp. XIII:** 274, 277; **Supp. XV:** 293, 299, 300, 301, 302, 306; **Supp. XXII:** 275; **Supp. XXIII:** 161, 165

Sandburg, Mrs. Carl (Lillian Steichen), **III:** 580

Sandburg, Helga, **III:** 583

Sandburg, Janet, **III:** 583, 584

Sandburg, Margaret, **III:** 583, 584

Sand County Almanac and Sketches Here and There, A (Leopold), **Supp. XIV:** 177, 178, **182–192**

"Sand Creek, Colorado"(Kenny), **Supp. XXIII:** 155

"Sand Dabs" (Oliver), **Supp. VII:** 245

"Sand Dunes" (Frost), **Retro. Supp. I:** 137; **Retro. Supp. II:** 41

Sander, August, **Supp. IX:** 211

Sanders, Mark, **Supp. XIX:** 119, 121

Sanders, Scott Russell, **Supp. XVI: 265–280**

Sandlin, Tim, **Supp. XXII:** 114

"Sandman, The" (Barthelme), **Supp. IV Part 1:** 47

Sandman's Dust (Bukiet), **Supp. XVII:** 40, 41

Sando, Joe S., **Supp. IV Part 2:** 510

Sandoe, James, **Supp. IV Part 1:** 131; **Supp. IV Part 2:** 470

Sandoval, Chela, **Supp. XXIII:** 204

Sandoz, Mari, **Supp. XV:** 141; **Supp. XXIII:** 146

Sandperl, Ira, **Supp. VIII:** 200

"Sand-Quarry and Moving Figures" (Rukeyser), **Supp. VI:** 271, 278

Sand Rivers (Matthiessen), **Supp. V:** 203

"Sand Roses, The" (Hogan), **Supp. IV Part 1:** 401

Sands, Diana, **Supp. IV Part 1:** 362

Sands, Robert, **Supp. I Part 1:** 156, 157

"Sands at Seventy" (Whitman), **IV:** 348

"Sandstone Farmhouse, A" (Updike), **Retro. Supp. I:** 318

Sandy Bottom Orchestra,The (Keillor and Nilsson), **Supp. XVI:** 177

Sanford, John, **IV:** 286, 287

San Francisco (film), **Supp. XVI:** 181, 192

"San Francisco" (Hempel), **Supp. XXI:** 118

"San Francisco Blues" (Kerouac), **Supp. III Part 1:** 225

Sangamon County Peace Advocate, The (Lindsay), **Supp. I Part 2:** 379

Sanger, Margaret, **Supp. I Part 1:** 19; **Supp. XXI:** 6; **Supp. XXIII:** 161

Sankofa (film), **Supp. XX: 154**

Sansom, William, **IV:** 279

Sans Soleil (film), **Supp. IV Part 2:** 436

"Santa" (Sexton), **Supp. II Part 2:** 693

Santa Claus: A Morality (Cummings), **I:** 430, 441

"Santa Fe, New Mexico"(Kenny), **Supp. XXIII:** 150

"Santa Fé Trail, The" (Lindsay), **Supp. I Part 2:** 389

"Santa Lucia" (Hass), **Supp. VI:** 105–106

"Santa Lucia II" (Hass), **Supp. VI:** 105–106

Santayana, George, **I:** 222, 224, 236, 243, 253, 460; **II:** 20, 542; **III:** 64, **599–622**; **IV:** 26, 339, 351, 353, 441; **Retro. Supp. I:** 55, 57, 67, 295; **Retro. Supp. II:** 179; **Supp. I Part 2:** 428; **Supp. II Part 1:** 107; **Supp. X:** 58; **Supp. XIV:** 199, 335, 340, 342; **Supp. XVI:** 189; **Supp. XVII:** 97, 106; **Supp. XX: 228, 229, 231**

Santiago, Esmeralda, **Supp. XI:** 177

"Santorini: Stopping the Leak" (Merrill), **Supp. III Part 1:** 336

Santos, John Phillip, **Supp. XIII:** 274

Santos, Sherod, **Supp. VIII:** 270

Sapir, Edward, **Supp. VIII:** 295; **Supp. XVI:** 283

"Sapphics for Patience" (A. Finch), **Supp. XVII:** 72

Sapphira and the Slave Girl (Cather), **I:** 331; **Retro. Supp. I:** 2, **19–20**

Sappho, **II:** 544; **III:** 142; **Supp. I Part 1:** 261, 269; **Supp. I Part 2:** 458; **Supp. XII:** 98, 99; **Supp. XVII:** 74

"Sappho" (Wright), **Supp. III Part 2:** 595, 604

"Sappho, Keats"(Hadas), **Supp. XXIII:** 113

"Sara" (song, Dylan), **Supp. XVIII:** 28

"Sarah" (Schwartz), **Supp. II Part 2:** 663

Sarah; or, The Exemplary Wife (Rowson), **Supp. XV:** 242

"Saratoga" mysteries (Dobyns), **Supp. XIII:** 79–80

Sargent, John Singer, **II:** 337, 338; **Supp. XX: 231**

Sarlós, Robert K., **Supp. XXI:** 7, 12, 13

Saroyan, Aram, **Supp. XV:** 182

Saroyan, William, **III:** 146–147; **IV:** 393; **Supp. I Part 2:** 679; **Supp. IV Part 1:** 83; **Supp. IV Part 2:** 502; **Supp. XIII:** 280; **Supp. XXIII:** 20

Sarris, Greg, **Supp. IV Part 1:** 329, 330

Sarton, George, **Supp. VIII:** 249

Sarton, May, **Supp. III Part 1:** 62, 63; **Supp. VIII: 249–268;** **Supp. XIII:** 296; **Supp. XVII:** 71

Sartoris (Faulkner), **II:** 55, 56–57, 58, 62; **Retro. Supp. I:** 77, 81, 82, 83, 88

Sartor Resartus (Carlyle), **II:** 26; **III:** 82

Sartre, Jean-Paul, **I:** 82, 494; **II:** 57, 244; **III:** 51, 204, 292, 453, 619; **IV:** 6, 223, 236, 477, 487, 493; **Retro. Supp. I:** 73; **Supp. I Part 1:** 51; **Supp. IV Part 1:** 42, 84; **Supp. VIII:** 11; **Supp. IX:** 4; **Supp. XIII:** 74, 171; **Supp. XIV:** 24; **Supp. XVII:** 137

Sassone, Ralph, **Supp. X:** 171

Sassoon, Siegfried, **II:** 367; **Supp. XV:** 308; **Supp. XIX:** 18

Satan in Goray (Singer), **IV:** 1, 6–7, 12; **Retro. Supp. II:** 303, **304–305**

Satan Says (Olds), **Supp. X:** 201, 202, **202–204**, 215

"Satan Says" (Olds), **Supp. X:** 202; **Supp. XVII:** 114

Satanstoe (Cooper), **I:** 351–352, 355

"Sather Gate Illumination" (Ginsberg), **Supp. II Part 1:** 329

"Satire as a Way of Seeing" (Dos Passos), **III:** 172

Satires of Persius, The (Merwin, trans.), **Supp. III Part 1:** 347

Satirical Rogue on Poetry, The (Francis). *See Pot Shots at Poetry* (Francis)

Satori in Paris (Kerouac), **Supp. III Part 1:** 231

"Saturday" (Salinas), **Supp. XIII:** 315

"Saturday Matinee" (Trethewey), **Supp. XXI:** 251

Saturday Night at the War (Shanley), **Supp. XIV:** 315

"Saturday Rain" (Kees), **Supp. XV:** 136

"Saturday Route, The" (Wolfe), **Supp. III Part 2:** 580

Satyagraha (Gandhi), **IV:** 185

"Satyr's Heart, The" (B. Kelly), **Supp. XVII:** 132

Saucedo, José Guadalupe, **Supp. XXIII:** 197

Saul and Patsy (C. Baxter), **Supp. XVII:** 22–23
"Saul and Patsy" (C. Baxter), **Supp. XVII:** 17
"Saul and Patsy Are Getting Comfortable in Michigan" (C. Baxter), **Supp. XVII:** 22
"Saul and Patsy Are in Labor" (C. Baxter), **Supp. XVII:** 20, 22
"Saul and Patsy Are Pregnant" (C. Baxter), **Supp. XVII:** 22
Saunders, George, **Supp. XIX: 223–237; Supp. XXII:** 49
Saunders, Richard, **II:** 110
Savage, Augusta, **Retro. Supp. II:** 115
Savage, James, **II:** 111
Savage Holiday (Wright), **IV:** 478, 488
Savage in Limbo: A Concert Play (Shanley), **Supp. XIV:** 315, **319–321,** 323, 324
Savage Love (Shepard and Chaikin), **Supp. III Part 2:** 433
Savage Place, A (Parker), **Supp. XIX:** 185
Savage Wilds (Reed), **Supp. X:** 241
Save Me, Joe Louis (Bell), **Supp. X:** 7, 10, **11–12**
Save Me the Waltz (Z. Fitzgerald), **II:** 95; **Retro. Supp. I:** 110; **Supp. IX:** 58, 59, 65, **66–68**
Savers, Michael, **Supp. XI:** 307
Saving Lives (Goldbarth), **Supp. XII:** 192
Saving Private Ryan (film), **Supp. V:** 249; **Supp. XI:** 234
Savings (Hogan), **Supp. IV Part 1:** 397, 404, 405, 406, 410
Saving Sebastian (Taylor), **Supp. XXIII:** 57
Savo, Jimmy, **I:** 440
Savran, David, **Supp. IX:** 145; **Supp. XIII:** 209; **Supp. XV:** 321
"Sawdust" (Offutt), **Supp. XIX:** 164
Sawyer-Lauçanno, Christopher, **Supp. IV Part 1:** 95
Saxon, Lyle, **Retro. Supp. I:** 80
"Saxophone" (Di Piero), **Supp. XIX:** 38
"Sax's and Selves" (Halliday), **Supp. XIX:** 88
"Say All" (Ray), **Supp. XVIII:** 193
Say and Seal (S. and A. Warner), **Supp. XVIII:** 258, 266
Saye and Sele, Lord, **Supp. I Part 1:** 98
Sayer, Mandy, **Supp. XIII:** 118
Sayers, Dorothy, **Supp. IV Part 1:** 341; **Supp. IV Part 2:** 464
Sayers, Valerie, **Supp. XI:** 253; **Supp. XVIII:** 99
"Say Good-bye" (Weigl), **Supp. XIX:** 288
"Sayings/For Luck" (Goldbarth), **Supp. XII:** 176
"Saying What Needs To Be Said" (Skloot), **Supp. XX: 201**
Say! Is This the U.S.A.? (Caldwell), **I:** 293, 294–295, 304, 309, 310
Saylor, Bruce, **Supp. XII:** 253
Sayre, Joel, **Supp. XIII:** 166
Sayre, Nora, **Supp. XII:** 119

Sayre, Zelda, **Retro. Supp. I:** 101, 102–103, 104, 105, 108, 109, 110, 113, 114. *See also* Fitzgerald, Zelda (Zelda Sayre)
"Say Yes" (Wolff), **Supp. VII:** 344
"Say You Love Me" (Peacock), **Supp. XIX:** 198
Scafe, Suzanne, **Supp. XXIII:** 94, 95
"Scale" (Halliday), **Supp. XIX:** 92
"Scales of the Eyes, The" (Nemerov), **III:** 272, 273, 277
Scalpel (McCoy), **Supp. XIII: 174–175**
Scalpel (screen treatment, McCoy), **Supp. XIII:** 174
Scandalabra (Zelda Fitzgerald), **Supp. IX:** 60, 61, 65, 67, **68–70**
"Scandal Detectives, The" (Fitzgerald), **II:** 80–81; **Retro. Supp. I:** 99
Scarberry-García, Susan, **Supp. IV Part 2:** 486
Scarborough, Dorothy, **Supp. XVIII:** 279–280
Scarecrow, The (Connelly), **Supp. XXI:** 71, 74, 78, **79**
"Scarecrow, The" (Farrell), **II:** 45
"Scarf, A" (Shields), **Supp. VII:** 328
Scarlet Cabinet, The (Notley), **Supp. XXII:** 233
Scarlet Letter, The (Hawthorne), **II:** 63, 223, 224, 231, 233, 239–240, 241, 243, 244, 255, 264, 286, 290, 291, 550; **Retro. Supp. I:** 63, 145, 147, 152, **157–159,** 160, 163, 165, 220, 248, 330, 335; **Retro. Supp. II:** 100; **Supp. I Part 1:** 38; **Supp. II Part 1:** 386; **Supp. VIII:** 108, 198; **Supp. XII:** 11; **Supp. XVII:** 143; **Supp. XX: 178, 183; Supp. XXII:** 147
"Scarlet Letter Aleph, The" (Mirvis), **Supp. XX: 183**
Scarlet Plague, The (London), **II:** 467
Scarlet Sister Mary (Peterkin), **Supp. XXII:** 189
Scar Lover (Crews), **Supp. XI:** 103, 107, **114–115**
"Scarred Girl, The" (Dickey), **Supp. IV Part 1:** 180
Scates, Maxine, **Supp. XIV:** 264, 265, 274
"Scenario" (H. Miller), **III:** 184
"Scene" (Howells), **II:** 274
"Scene in Jerusalem, A" (Stowe), **Supp. I Part 2:** 587
"Scenes" (Shields), **Supp. VII:** 318
Scènes d'Anabase (chamber music) (Bowles), **Supp. IV Part 1:** 82
"Scenes from a Documentary History of Mississippi" (Trethewey), **Supp. XXI:** 255–256
Scenes from American Life (Gurney), **Supp. V:** 95, 96, 105, 108
Scenes from Another Life (McClatchy), **Supp. XII: 255–256**
"Scenes from Childhood" (W. V. Davis), **Supp. XXI:** 95
"Scenes of Childhood" (Merrill), **Supp. III Part 1:** 322, 323, 327
"Scented Herbage of My Breast" (Whitman), **IV:** 342–343

"Scent of a Woman's Ink" (Prose), **Supp. XVI:** 259
"Scent of Unbought Flowers, The" (Ríos), **Supp. IV Part 2:** 547
Scepticisms (Aiken), **I:** 58
Scève, Maurice, **Supp. III Part 1:** 11
Schad, Christian, **Supp. IV Part 1:** 247
Schafer, Benjamin G., **Supp. XIV:** 144
Schafer, William, **Supp. XIX:** 164, 172
Schaller, George, **Supp. V:** 208, 210–211
Schapiro, Meyer, **II:** 30
Scharmann, Hermann Balthazar, **Supp. XII:** 41
Scharper, Alice, **Supp. XXII:** 175
Scharper, Diane, **Supp. XXIII:** 134
Schary, Dore, **Supp. IV Part 1:** 365; **Supp. XIII:** 163
Schatz, Tom, **Supp. XVIII:** 242
Schaum, Melita, **Supp. XXII:** 166
Schaumbergh, Count de, **II:** 120
Scheele, Roy, **Supp. XVI:** 54; **Supp. XXI:** 103
Scheeman, George, **Supp. XXII:** 230
Scheffauer, G. H., **I:** 199
"Scheherazade" (Ashbery), **Supp. III Part 1:** 18
Scheick, William, **Supp. V:** 272
Schelberg, Budd, **Supp. XVIII: 241–256**
Scheler, Max, **I:** 58
Schelling, Friedrich, **Supp. I Part 2:** 422
Schenck, Joseph, **Supp. XVI:** 186
Schenk, Margaret, **I:** 199
Scheponik, Peter, **Supp. X:** 210
Scherer, Loline, **Supp. XIII:** 161
"Scherzo"(Hadas), **Supp. XXIII:** 113
Schevill, James, **I:** 116
Schickel, Richard, **Supp. XV:** 1
Schifano, Mario, **Supp. XXIII:** 217
Schilder, Paul, **Supp. I Part 2:** 622
Schildkraut, Rudolph, **Supp. XXIII:** 8
Schiller, Andrew, **II:** 20
Schiller, Frederick, **Supp. V:** 290
Schiller, Johann Christoph Friedrich von, **I:** 224; **Supp. IV Part 2:** 519; **Supp. XVI:** 292
Schiller, Lawrence, **Retro. Supp. II:** 208, 212, 214
Schimmel, Harold, **Supp. V:** 336
"Schizoid Nature of the Implied Author in Twentieth-Century American Ethnic Novels, The" (Nelson), **Supp. XVIII:** 172
Schlegel, Augustus Wilhelm, **III:** 422, 424
Schlegell, David von, **Supp. IV Part 2:** 423
Schleiermacher, Friedrich, **III:** 290–291, 309
Schleifer, Ronald, **Supp. XVIII:** 144
Schlepping Through the Alps (S. Apple), **Supp. XVII:** 8
Schlesinger, Arthur, Jr., **III:** 291, 297–298, 309
Schleuning, Neala, **Supp. XXIII:** 165
Schmidt, Jon Zlotnik, **Supp. IV Part 1:** 2
Schmidt, Kaspar. *See* Stirner, Max
Schmidt, Michael, **Supp. X:** 55
Schmitt, Carl, **I:** 386–387
Schmitz, Neil, **Supp. X:** 243

Schnackenberg, Gjertrud, **Supp. XV:** **249–268**
Schneider, Alan, **I:** 87
Schneider, Louis, **Supp. I Part 2:** 650
Schneider, Romy, **Supp. IV Part 2:** 549
Schneider, Steven, **Supp. IX:** 271, 274
Schnellock, Emil, **III:** 177
Schneour, Zalman, **IV:** 11
"Schnetzer Day" (Halliday), **Supp. XIX:** 93
Schnitzler, Arthur, **Supp. XV:** 307; **Supp. XVI:** 187
Schoerke, Meg, **Supp. XVII:** 110
"Scholar Gypsy, The" (Arnold), **II:** 541
"Scholastic and Bedside Teaching" (Holmes), **Supp. I Part 1:** 305
Schöler, Bo, **Supp. IV Part 1:** 399, 400, 403, 407, 409; **Supp. IV Part 2:** 499
Scholes, Robert, **Supp. V:** 40, 42
Scholtz, Carter, **Supp. XVIII:** 144
Schomburg, Arthur, **Supp. X:** 134; **Supp. XXII:** 6
Schomburg Library of Nineteenth-Century Black Women Writers (H. L. Gates, ed.), **Supp. XX:** **105**
Schönberg, Claude-Michel, **Supp. XXI:** 155
Schoolboy Howlers (Abingdon), **Supp. XVI:** 99
Schoolcraft, Henry Rowe, **II:** 503; **Retro. Supp. II:** 160; **Supp. XXIII:** 223, 227, 228, 232, 233–234
Schoolcraft, Jane Johnston (Bamewawagezhikaquay), **Supp. XXIII:** **223–238**
"School Daze" (Bambara), **Supp. XI:** 19
School Daze (film), **Supp. XI:** 19, 20
"Schoolhouse" (Levis), **Supp. XI:** 258
"School of Giorgione, The" (Pater), **I:** 51
"School Play, The" (Merrill), **Supp. III Part 1:** 336
"Schooner Fairchild's Class" (Benét), **Supp. XI:** 55
Schopenhauer, Arthur, **III:** 600, 604; **IV:** 7; **Retro. Supp. I:** 256; **Retro. Supp. II:** 94; **Supp. I Part 1:** 320; **Supp. I Part 2:** 457; **Supp. X:** 187; **Supp. XVI:** 184
Schorer, Mark, **II:** 28; **III:** 71; **Retro. Supp. I:** 115; **Supp. IV Part 1:** 197, 203, 211; **Supp. XVI:** 206
Schott, Penelope Scambly, **Supp. XXIII:** **239–256**
Schott, Webster, **Supp. IX:** 257
Schotts, Jeffrey, **Supp. XII:** 193
Schrader, Mary von. *See* Jarrell, Mrs. Randall (Mary von Schrader)
Schreiber, Jan, **Supp. XXI:** 105, 111
Schreiner, Olive, **I:** 419; **Supp. XI:** 203
Schroeder, Eric James, **Supp. V:** 238, 244
Schubert, Bernard L., **Supp. XVII:** 58
Schubert, Franz Peter, **Supp. I Part 1:** 363
Schubnell, Matthias, **Supp. IV Part 2:** 486
Schudel, Matt, **Supp. XXII:** 205, 214
Schulberg, Budd, **II:** 98; **Retro. Supp. I:** 113; **Supp. XIII:** 170; **Supp. XV:** 194
Schulberg, Stuart, **Supp. XVIII:** 254
Schulman, Grace, **Supp. XXIII:** 58

Schulman, Tom, **Supp. XXI:** 193, 194
Schulz, Bruno, **Supp. IV Part 2:** 623; **Supp. XVII:** 41
Schuman, William, **Supp. XII:** 253; **Supp. XXII:** 283
Schumann, Dr. Alanson Tucker, **III:** 505
Schuster, Edgar H., **Supp. VIII:** 126
Schuyler, George S., **III:** 110; **Supp. XVI:** 142; **Supp. XIX:** 78
Schuyler, James, **Supp. XV:** 177, 178; **Supp. XXIII:** 207, 212, 215, 217
Schuyler, William, **Supp. I Part 1:** 211
"Schuylkill, The" (Halliday), **Supp. XIX:** 92
Schwartz, Delmore, **I:** 67, 168, 188, 288; **IV:** 128, 129, 437; **Retro. Supp. II:** 29, 178; **Supp. II Part 1:** 102, 109; **Supp. II Part 2:** **639–668**; **Supp. VIII:** 98; **Supp. IX:** 299; **Supp. XIII:** 320; **Supp. XIV:** 3; **Supp. XV:** 184; **Supp. XIX:** 257
Schwartz, Leonard, **Supp. XVI:** 289
Schwartz, Lloyd, **Supp. I Part 1:** 81
Schwartz, Marilyn, **Supp. XII:** 126, 128, 130, 132
Schwartz, Meryl F., **Supp. XXII:** 65, 66
Schwartz, Richard B., **Supp. XIV:** 23, 27
Schwarz, A. B. Christa, **Supp. XIX:** 77, 79
Schwed, Peter, **Supp. XXII:** 119
Schweitzer, Albert, **Supp. IV Part 1:** 373
Schweitzer, Harold, **Supp. X:** 210
Schwerdt, Lisa M., **Supp. XIV:** 155, 171
Schwitters, Kurt, **III:** 197; **Retro. Supp. II:** 322, 331, 336; **Supp. IV Part 1:** 79
"Science" (Jeffers), **Supp. II Part 2:** 426
Science and Health with Key to the Scriptures (Eddy), **I:** 383
"Science Favorable to Virtue" (Freneau), **Supp. II Part 1:** 274
Science of English Verse, The (Lanier), **Supp. I Part 1:** 368, 369
"Science of the Night, The" (Kunitz), **Supp. III Part 1:** 258, 265
"Sci-Fi Floater Genius" (Halliday), **Supp. XIX:** 91
Sciolino, Martina, **Supp. XII:** 9
"Scissors" (C. Baxter), **Supp. XVII:** 19
Scofield, Sandra, **Supp. XXI:** 119
Scooter tetralogy (Murray). *See Magic Keys, The* (Murray); *Seven League Boots, The* (Murray); *Spyglass Tree, The* (Murray); *Train Whistle Guitar* (Murray)
Scopes, John T., **III:** 105, 495
"Scorched Face, The" (Hammett), **Supp. IV Part 1:** 344
"Scorn" (C. Frost), **Supp. XV:** 105
"Scorpion, The" (Bowles), **Supp. IV Part 1:** 84, 86
Scorsese, Martin, **Supp. IV Part 1:** 356; **Supp. XVIII:** 22
Scott, Anne Firor, **Supp. I Part 1:** 19
Scott, A. O., **Supp. X:** 301, 302; **Supp. XII:** 343
Scott, Evelyn, **Retro. Supp. I:** 73; **Supp. XXII:** 198
Scott, Gavin, **Supp. XXII:** 218

Scott, George C., **III:** 165–166; **Supp. XI:** 304
Scott, George Lewis, **Supp. I Part 2:** 503, 504
Scott, Hazel, **Supp. XXII:** 12
Scott, Herbert, **Supp. V:** 180
Scott, Howard, **Supp. I Part 2:** 645
Scott, Joanna, **Supp. XVII:** **183–197**
Scott, Lizabeth, **Supp. IV Part 2:** 524
Scott, Lynn Orilla, **Retro. Supp. II:** 12
Scott, Mark, **Retro. Supp. I:** 127
Scott, Nathan A., Jr., **II:** 27
Scott, Paul, **Supp. IV Part 2:** 690
Scott, Ridley, **Supp. XIII:** 268
Scott, Walter, **Supp. XVI:** 7, 13
Scott, Sir Walter, **I:** 204, 339, 341, 343, 354; **II:** 8, 17, 18, 217, 296, 301, 303, 304, 308; **III:** 415, 482; **IV:** 204, 453; **Retro. Supp. I:** 99; **Supp. I Part 2:** 579, 580, 685, 692; **Supp. IV Part 2:** 690; **Supp. IX:** 175; **Supp. X:** 51, 114
Scott, Winfield Townley, **II:** 512; **Supp. I Part 2:** 705; **Supp. XV:** 51
Scottsboro boys, **I:** 505; **Supp. I Part 1:** 330
Scottsboro Limited (Hughes), **Retro. Supp. I:** 203; **Supp. I Part 1:** 328, 330–331, 332
Scoundrel Time (Hellman), **Supp. I Part 1:** 294–297; **Supp. IV Part 1:** 12; **Supp. VIII:** 243
Scrambled Eggs Super! (Geisel), **Supp. XVI:** 105
Scrambled Eggs & Whiskey: Poems, 1991–1995 (Carruth), **Supp. XVI:** 47
Scratch (MacLeish), **III:** 22–23
"Scratch Music" (Wright), **Supp. XV:** 343
"Scream, The" (Lowell), **II:** 550
"Screamer, The" (Coleman), **Supp. XI:** **92–93**
"Screamers, The" (Baraka), **Supp. II Part 1:** 38
"Screen Guide for Americans" (Rand), **Supp. IV Part 2:** 524
"Screen Memory" (Cliff), **Supp. XXII:** 75
"Screeno" (Schwartz), **Supp. II Part 2:** 660
Screens, The (Genet), **Supp. XII:** 12
Screen Sirens Scream! (Parla and Mitchell), **Supp. XXII:** 256
Scribblers on the Roof: Contemporary American Jewish Fiction (Bukiet and Roskies, eds.), **Supp. XVII:** 39, 49–50
Scripts for the Pageant (Merrill), **Supp. III Part 1:** 332, 333, 335
Scrolls from the Dead Sea, The (Wilson), **IV:** 429
Scruggs, Earl, **Supp. V:** 335
Scudder, Horace Elisha, **II:** 400, 401; **Retro. Supp. II:** 67; **Supp. I Part 1:** 220; **Supp. I Part 2:** 410, 414
Scully, James, **Supp. XII:** 131
"Sculpting the Whistle" (Ríos), **Supp. IV Part 2:** 549
"Sculptor" (Plath), **Supp. I Part 2:** 538
"Sculptor's Funeral, The" (Cather), **I:** 315–316; **Retro. Supp. I:** 5, 6; **Supp. XV:** 40

Scum (Singer), **Retro. Supp. II:** 316–317

Scupoli, Lorenzo, **IV:** 156

"Scythe Song" (Lang), **Retro. Supp. I:** 128

Sea and the Mirror, The: A Commentary on Shakespeare's "The Tempest" (Auden), Supp. II Part 1: 2, 18

Sea around Us, The (Carson), **Supp. IX:** 19, **23–25**

Sea around Us, The (film), **Supp. IX:** 25

Sea Birds Are Still Alive, The (Bambara), **Supp. XI:** 1, 4, **7–12**

"Sea Birds Are Still Alive, The" (Bambara), **Supp. XI:** 8

"Sea-Blue and Blood-Red" (Lowell), **II:** 524

Seabrook, John, **Supp. VIII:** 157

"Sea Burial from the Cruiser Reve" (Eberhart), **I:** 532–533

Seabury, David, **Supp. I Part 2:** 608

"Sea Calm" (Hughes), **Retro. Supp. I:** 199

"Sea Chanty" (Corso), **Supp. XII:** 118

"Sea Dream, A" (Whitter), **Supp. I Part 2:** 699

"Seafarer, The" (Pound, trans.), **Retro. Supp. I:** 287

Seagall, Harry, **Supp. XIII:** 166

Sea Garden (Doolittle), **Supp. I Part 1:** 257, 259, 266, 269, 272

Seager, Allan, **IV:** 305

"Seagulls and Children" (C. Frost), **Supp. XV:** 95

Sea Lady, The (Boyce), **Supp. XXI:** 8, 13

"Sea Lily" (Doolittle), **Supp. I Part 1:** 266

Sea Lions, The (Cooper), **I:** 354, 355

Sealts, Merton M., Jr., **Retro. Supp. I:** 257

Seaman, Benjamin, **Supp. XXIII:** 69–70, 72

Seaman, Donna, **Supp. VIII:** 86; **Supp. X:** 1, 4, 12, 16, 213; **Supp. XV:** 65; **Supp. XVIII:** 102; **Supp. XIX:** 53, 55, 57, 58, 59, 60, 61; **Supp. XXI:** 236; **Supp. XXII:** 266; **Supp. XXIII:** 71, 74, 134, 135, 298

"Seamy Side, The"(Hadas), **Supp. XXIII:** 119

"Séance, The" (Singer), **IV:** 20

Séance and Other Stories, The (Singer), **IV:** 19–21

"Sea Oak" (Saunders), **Supp. XIX:** 228, 229, 231

Sea of Cortez (Steinbeck), **IV:** 52, 54, 62, 69

Sea of Grass, The (film), **Supp. XVIII:** 211

Sea of Grass, The (Richter), **Supp. XVIII:** 210–211, 215–216, 217, 220

"Sea Pieces" (Melville), **III:** 93

Searchers, The (film, Ford), **Supp. XVIII:** 57, 58, 135–136, 141

Searches and Seizures (Elkin), **Supp. VI:** 49

"Search for Southern Identity, The" (Woodward), **Retro. Supp. I:** 75; **Supp. XXII:** 194

Search for the King, A: A Twelfth-Century Legend (Vidal), **Supp. IV Part 2:** 681

Searching for Caleb (Tyler), **Supp. IV Part 2:** 663–665, 671

"Searching for Poetry: Real *vs.* Fake" (B. Miller), **Supp. IV Part 1:** 67

Searching for Survivors (Banks), **Supp. V:** 7

"Searching for Survivors (I)" (Banks), **Supp. V:** 8

"Searching for Survivors (II)" (Banks), **Supp. V:** 7, 8

Searching for the Ox (Simpson), **Supp. IX:** 266, **274–275**

"Searching for the Ox" (Simpson), **Supp. IX:** 275, 280

"Searching in the Britannia Tavern" (Wagoner), **Supp. IX:** 327

Searching Wing, The, (Hellman), **Supp. I Part 1:** 277, 278, 281–282, 283, 292, 297

Search-Light. *See* Frank, Waldo

"Search Party, The" (Matthews), **Supp. IX:** 156

Searle, Ronald, **Supp. I Part 2:** 604, 605

Sea Road to the Indies (Hart), **Supp. XIV:** 97

"Seascape" (Bishop), **Retro. Supp. II:** 42–43

"Sea's Green Sameness, The" (Updike), **IV:** 217

Seaside and the Fireside, The (Longfellow), **II:** 489; **Retro. Supp. II:** 159, 168

Season in Hell, A (Rimbaud), **III:** 189

Seasons, The (Thomson), **II:** 304; **Supp. I Part 1:** 151

Seasons' Difference, The (Buechner), **Supp. XII:** 47

Seasons of Celebration (Merton), **Supp. VIII:** 199, 208

Seasons of the Heart: In Quest of Faith (Kinard, comp.), **Supp. XIV:** 127

"Seasons of the Soul" (Tate), **IV:** 136–140

Seasons on Earth (Koch), **Supp. XV:** **183–184**

"Sea Surface Full of Clouds" (Stevens), **IV:** 82

"Sea Tides" (Hoffman), **Supp. XVIII:** 87

"Sea Treader" (Hoffman), **Supp. XVIII:** 87

"Sea Unicorns and Land Unicorns" (Moore), **III:** 202–203

Seaver, Richard, **Supp. XI:** 301

"Seaweed" (Longfellow), **II:** 498

Sea-Wolf, The (London), **II:** 264, 466, 472–473

Sebald, W. G., **Supp. XIV:** 96; **Supp. XXI:** 92

Sebold, Alice, **Supp. XXII:** 55

Seckler, David, **Supp. I Part 2:** 650

"2nd Air Force" (Jarrell), **II:** 375

Second American Revolution and Other Essays (1976–1982), The (Vidal), **Supp. IV Part 2:** 679, 687, 688

Secondary Colors, The (A. Theroux), **Supp. VIII:** 312

Second Avenue (O'Hara), **Supp. XXIII:** 216

"Second Avenue"(O'Hara), **Supp. XXIII:** 208, 211, 218

Second Blush, The (Peacock), **Supp. XIX:** 197, **205–206**

Second Chance (Auchincloss), **Supp. IV Part 1:** 33

"Second Chances" (Hugo), **Supp. VI:** 144, 145

Second Coming, The (Percy), **Supp. III Part 1:** 383, 384, 387, 388, 396–397

"Second Coming, The" (Yeats), **III:** 294; **Retro. Supp. I:** 290, 311; **Supp. VIII:** 24; **Supp. XVI:** 159; **Supp. XIX:** 85

Second Decade, The. See Stephen King, The Second Decade: "Danse Macabre" to "The Dark Half" (Magistrale)

Second Dune, The (Hearon), **Supp. VIII:** 58, **59–60**

Second Flowering, A: Works and Days of the Lost Generation (Cowley), **Retro. Supp. II:** 77; **Supp. II Part 1:** 135, 141, 143, 144, 147, 149

Second Growth (Stegner), **Supp. IV Part 2:** 599, 608

"Second Hour of the Night, The" (Bidart), **Supp. XV:** 32, **33–34**

Second Marriage (F. Barthelme), **Supp. XI:** 32, 33

"Second Marriage" (McCarriston), **Supp. XIV:** 262

"Second Mortgage" (Shaw), **Supp. XIX:** 245–246

Second Nature (Hoffman), **Supp. X:** 88, 89

Seconds, The (Bierds), **Supp. XVII:** **33–34**

Second Set, The (Komunyakaa and Feinstein, eds.), **Supp. XIII:** 125

Second Sex, The (Beauvoir), **Supp. IV Part 1:** 360

"Second Sight" (Mosher), **Supp. XXII:** 214

Second Stone, The (Fiedler), **Supp. XIII:** 102

"Second Swimming, The" (Boyle), **Supp. VIII:** 13, 14

Second Tree from the Corner (White), **Supp. I Part 2:** 654

"Second Tree from the Corner" (White), **Supp. I Part 2:** 651

Second Twenty Years at Hull-House, The: September 1909 to September 1929, with a Record of a Growing World Consciousness (Addams), **Supp. I Part 1:** 24–25

Second Voyage of Columbus, The (Morison), **Supp. I Part 2:** 488

Second Words, (Atwood), **Supp. XIII:** 35

Second World, The (Blackmur), **Supp. II Part 1:** 91

Secret, The (E. Hoffman), **Supp. XVI:** 151, **155–158**, 161

"Secret, The" (Levine), **Supp. V:** 195

Secret Agent, The (Conrad), **Supp. IV Part 1:** 341

Secret Agent X-9 (Hammett), **Supp. IV Part 1:** 355

"Secret Courts of Men's Hearts, The: Code and Law in Harper Lee's *To Kill a Mockingbird*" (Johnson), **Supp. VIII:** 126

"Secret Dog, The" (Cameron), **Supp. XII: 83–84**

Secret Garden, The (Burnett), **Supp. I Part 1:** 44

"Secret Garden, The" (Hoffman), **Supp. XVIII:** 86

"Secret Gladness, A" (C. Frost), **Supp. XV:** 91

Secret Historie (J. Smith), **I:** 131

Secret History of the Dividing Line (Howe), **Supp. IV Part 2:** 424, 425–426

"Secret Integration, The" (Pynchon), **Supp. II Part 2:** 624

"Secret Life of Musical Instruments, The" (Wright), **Supp. XV:** 343

"Secret Life of Walter Mitty, The" (Thurber), **Supp. I Part 2:** 623; **Supp. XVI:** 233

"Secret Lion, The" (Ríos), **Supp. IV Part 2:** 543, 544

"Secret Nature of the Mechanical Rabbit, The"(P. Benedict), **Supp. XXIII:** 49

"Secret Ocean, The" (Jarman), **Supp. XVII:** 120

Secret of Poetry, The: Essays (Jarman), **Supp. XVII:** 110, 111, 120

"Secret of the Russian Ballet, The" (Van Vechten), **Supp. II Part 2:** 732

"Secret Prune" (Ríos), **Supp. IV Part 2:** 549

Secret River, The (Rawlings), **Supp. X:** 233

Secrets and Surprises (Beattie), **Supp. V:** 23, 27, 29

Secrets from the Center of the World (Harjo), **Supp. XII: 223–224**

"Secret Sharer, The" (Conrad), **Supp. IX:** 105

"Secret Sharer, The" (J. Conrad), **Supp. XVI:** 158

"Secret Society, A" (Nemerov), **III:** 282

Secrets of the Heart (Gibran), **Supp. XX: 116**

Secrets of the Universe: Scenes from the Journey Home (Sanders), **Supp. XVI:** 273–274

"Secular" (Trethewey), **Supp. XXI:** 249

Secular Journal of Thomas Merton, The, **Supp. VIII:** 206

"Security" (Stafford), **Supp. XI:** 329

"Security"(Strout), **Supp. XXIII:** 283

Sedaris, David, **Supp. XXIII:** 289

Sedges, John (pseudonym). *See* Buck, Pearl S.

Sedgwick, Catherine Maria, **I:** 341; **Supp. I Part 1:** 155, 157

Sedgwick, Christina. *See* Marquand, Mrs. John P. (Christina Sedgwick)

Sedgwick, Ellery, **I:** 217, 229, 231; **III:** 54–55

Sedgwick, Eve, **Supp. XX: 267**

Sedgwick, Henry, **Supp. I Part 1:** 156

Sedgwick, Robert, **Supp. I Part 1:** 156

Sedore, Timothy, **Supp. XIV:** 312

"Seduction and Betrayal" (Hardwick), **Supp. III Part 1:** 207

Seduction and Betrayal: Women and Literature (Hardwick), **Supp. III Part 1:** 194, 204, 206–208, 212, 213; **Supp. XIV:** 89

See, Carolyn, **Supp. XXII:** 206, 217

Seed, David, **Supp. IV Part 1:** 391

"Seed Eaters, The" (Francis), **Supp. IX:** 82

"Seed Leaves" (Wilbur), **Supp. III Part 2:** 558

"Seeds" (Anderson), **I:** 106, 114

Seeds of Contemplation (Merton), **Supp. VIII:** 199, 200, 207, 208

Seeds of Destruction (Merton), **Supp. VIII:** 202, 203, 204, 208

"Seeing Red" (column, Ryan as Quin), **Supp. XVIII:** 226

"See(k)ing the Self: Mirrors and Mirroring in Bicultural Texts" (Oster), **Supp. XVI:** 151

Seeing through the Sun (Hogan), **Supp. IV Part 1:** 397, 400, 401–402, 402, 413

"See in the Midst of Fair Leaves" (Moore), **III:** 215

"Seekers, The" (McGrath), **Supp. X:** 117

"Seeking a Vision of Truth, Guided by a Higher Power" (Burke), **Supp. XIV:** 21, 23

"Seele im Raum" (Jarrell), **II:** 382–383

"Seele im Raum" (Rilke), **II:** 382–383

"See Naples and Die" (Hecht), **Supp. X:** 69, 70

"Seen from the 'L' " (Barnes), **Supp. III Part 1:** 33

"See the Moon?" (Barthelme), **Supp. IV Part 1:** 42, 49–50, 50

Sefarim, Mendele Mokher, **Supp. XXIII:** 4

Segal, D. (pseudonym). *See* Singer, Isaac Bashevis

Segal, George, **Supp. XI:** 343

Segal, Lore, **Supp. XVI:** 203

Segregation: The Inner Conflict in the South (Warren), **IV:** 237, 238, 246, 252

"*Se:* Hegel's Absolute and Heidegger's *Ereignis*" (Agamben), **Supp. XVI:** 289

Seidel, Frederick, **I:** 185

Seidman, Hugh, **Supp. XXI:** 228

Seize the Day (Bellow), **I:** 144, 147, 148, 150, 151, 152, 153, 155, 158, 162; **Retro. Supp. II:** 19, **23–24,** 27, 32, 34; **Supp. I Part 2:** 428

Selby, Hubert, **Supp. III Part 1:** 125

Selby, Hubert, Jr., **Supp. XXI:** 227

Selby, John, **Retro. Supp. II:** 221, 222

Selden, John, **Supp. XIV:** 344

Seldes, Gilbert, **II:** 437, 445; **Retro. Supp. I:** 108

Selected Criticism: Prose, Poetry (Bogan), **Supp. III Part 1:** 64

Selected Essays (Eliot), **I:** 572

Selected Essays and Reviews (Carruth), **Supp. XVI:** 46

Selected Journals and Other Writings (Audubon), **Supp. XVI:** 10, 12, 13

Selected Letters (Bynner), **Supp. XV:** 52

Selected Letters (W. C. Williams), **Retro. Supp. I:** 430

Selected Letters, 1940–1956 (Kerouac), **Supp. XIV:** 137, 144

Selected Letters of Robert Frost (Thompson, ed.), **Retro. Supp. I:** 125

Selected Levis, The (Levis), **Supp. XI:** 257, 272

Selected Plays (O'Hara), **Supp. XXIII:** 216

Selected Poems (Aiken), **I:** 69

Selected Poems (Ashbery), **Supp. III Part 1:** 25–26

Selected Poems (Brodsky), **Supp. VIII:** 22

Selected Poems (Brooks), **Supp. III Part 1:** 82–83

Selected Poems (Bynner), **Supp. XV:** 51, 52

Selected Poems (Corso), **Supp. XII:** 129

Selected Poems (Dove), **Supp. IV Part 1:** 241, 243, 250

Selected Poems (Frost), **Retro. Supp. I:** 133, 136

Selected Poems (Guillevic; Levertov, trans.), **Supp. III Part 1:** 283

Selected Poems (Hayden), **Supp. II Part 1:** 363, 364, 367

Selected Poems (Hughes), **Retro. Supp. I:** 202; **Supp. I Part 1:** 341, 345, 346

Selected Poems (Hugo), **Supp. VI:** 143

Selected Poems (Jarrell), **II:** 367, 370, 371, 374, 377, 379, 380, 381, 382, 384

Selected Poems (Justice), **Supp. VII:** 115

Selected Poems (Kinnell), **Supp. III Part 1:** 235, 253

Selected Poems (Levine, 1984), **Supp. V:** 178, 179

Selected Poems (Lowell), **II:** 512, 516; **Retro. Supp. II:** 184, 186, 188, 190

Selected Poems (Merton), **Supp. VIII:** 207, 208

Selected Poems (Moore), **III:** 193, 194, 205–206, 208, 215

Selected Poems (Notley), **Supp. XXII:** 234

Selected Poems (O'Hara; Allen, ed.), **Supp. XXIII:** 220

Selected Poems (O'Hara; Ford, ed.), **Supp. XXIII:** 220

Selected Poems (Pound), **Retro. Supp. I:** 289, 291

Selected Poems (R. Bly), **Supp. IV Part 1:** 60, 62, 65, 66, 68, 69–71

Selected Poems (Ransom), **III:** 490, 492

Selected Poems (Reznikoff), **Supp. XIV:** 288

Selected Poems (Rukeyser), **Supp. VI:** 274

Selected Poems (Sexton), **Supp. IV Part 2:** 449

Selected Poems (Sorrentino), **Supp. XXI:** 226

Selected Poems (Strand), **Supp. IV Part 2:** 630

Selected Poems, 1923–1943 (Warren), **IV:** 241–242, 243

Selected Poems, 1928–1958 (Kunitz), **Supp. III Part 1:** 261, 263–265

Selected Poems, 1938–1988 (McGrath), **Supp. X:** 127

Selected Poems, 1958–1980 (Sorrentino), **Supp. XXI:** 228

Selected Poems, 1963–1983 (Simic), **Supp. VIII:** 275

Selected Poems 1936–1965 (Eberhart), **I:** 541

Selected Poems: 1957–1987 (Snodgrass), **Supp. VI:** 314–315, 323, 324

Selected Poems 1965–1975 (Atwood), **Supp. XIII:** 32–34

Selected Poems: 1975–2005 (Skloot), **Supp. XX:** 196

Selected Poems II: Poems Selected and New, 1976–1986 (Atwood), **Supp. XIII:** 20, 34–35

Selected Poems of Ezra Pound (Pound), **Supp. V:** 336

Selected Poems of Gabriela Mistral (Hughes, trans.), **Supp. I Part 1:** 345

Selected Poetry of Amiri Baraka/LeRoi Jones (Baraka), **Supp. II Part 1:** 58

Selected Poetry of Hayden Carruth, The (Carruth), **Supp. XVI:** 53

Selected Stories (Dubus), **Supp. VII:** 88–89

Selected Stories of Richard Bausch, The (Bausch), **Supp. VII:** 42

Selected Translations (Snodgrass), **Supp. VI:** 318, 324, **325–326**

Selected Verse of Margaret Haskins Durber, The (Keillor), **Supp. XVI:** 171

Selected Witter Bynner, The, **Supp. XV:** 52

Selected Works of Djuna Barnes, The (Barnes), **Supp. III Part 1:** 44

Selected Writings 1950–1990 (Howe), **Supp. VI:** 116–117, 118, 120

Selected Writings of John Jay Chapman, The (Barzun), **Supp. XIV:** 54

Select Epigrams from the Greek Anthology (Mackail), **Supp. I Part 2:** 461

"Selecting a Reader" (Kooser), **Supp. XIX:** 119–120

"Selene Afterwards" (MacLeish), **III:** 8

"Self" (James), **II:** 351

Self, William, **Supp. XXII:** 172

Self and the Dramas of History, The (Niebuhr), **III:** 308

Self-Consciousness (Updike), **Retro. Supp. I:** 318, 319, 320, 322, 323, 324

"Self-Exposed, The" (X. J. Kennedy), **Supp. XV:** 159

Self-Help: Stories (Moore), **Supp. X:** 163, 166, **167–169,** 174, 175

"Self-Importance" (Halliday), **Supp. XIX:** 90

Self-Interviews (Dickey), **Supp. IV Part 1:** 179

"Self-Made Man, A" (Crane), **I:** 420

"Self Pity" (C. Frost), **Supp. XV:** 93, 94, 101, 102, 104

Self Portrait (album, Dylan), **Supp. XVIII:** 27

"Self-Portrait" (Creeley), **Supp. IV Part 1:** 156

"Self-Portrait" (Mumford), **Supp. II Part 2:** 471

"(Self) Portrait" (Trethewey), **Supp. XXI:** 253

"Self-Portrait" (Wylie), **Supp. I Part 2:** 729

"Self Portrait at Fifty-three" (Weigl), **Supp. XIX:** 288

Self-Portrait: Ceaselessly into the Past (Millar, ed. Sipper), **Supp. IV Part 2:** 464, 469, 472, 475

"Self-Portrait in a Convex Mirror" (Ashbery), **Supp. III Part 1:** 5, 7, 9, 16–19, 22, 24, 26

"Self-Portrait with 1911 NY Yankees Cap" (Skloot), **Supp. XX:** 202

"Self-Reliance" (Emerson), **II:** 7, 15, 17; **Retro. Supp. I:** 159; **Retro. Supp. II:** 155; **Supp. X:** 42, 45

Selfwolf (Halliday), **Supp. XIX:** 81, **89–91,** 93

Sélincourt, Ernest de, **Supp. I Part 2:** 676

Selinger, Eric, **Supp. XVI:** 47

Selinger, Eric Murphy, **Supp. XI:** 248

Sell, Henry, **Supp. XVI:** 188

Sellers, Isaiah, **IV:** 194–195

Sellers, Peter, **Supp. XI:** 301, 304, 306, 307, 309

Sellers, William, **IV:** 208

Seltzer, Mark, **Retro. Supp. I:** 227

Selznick, David O., **Retro. Supp. I:** 105, 113; **Supp. IV Part 1:** 353; **Supp. XVIII:** 242; **Supp. XXII:** 195

Semi, Allen (pseudonym). *See* Larsen, Nella

"Semi-Lunatics of Kilmuir, The" (Hugo), **Supp. VI:** 145

"Semiotics/The Doctor's Doll" (Goldbarth), **Supp. XII:** 183–184

Semmelweiss, Ignaz, **Supp. I Part 1:** 304

Senancour, Étienne Divert de, **I:** 241

Sendak, Maurice, **Supp. IX:** 207, 208, 213, 214; **Supp. XVI:** 110

Seneca, **II:** 14–15; **III:** 77

Senghor, Leopold Sédar, **Supp. IV Part 1:** 16; **Supp. X:** 132, 139

Senier, Siobhan, **Supp. IV Part 1:** 330

"Senility" (Anderson), **I:** 114

Senior, Olive, **Supp. XXIII:** 94

"Senior Partner's Ethics, The" (Auchincloss), **Supp. IV Part 1:** 33

Senlin: A Biography (Aiken), **I:** 48, 49, 50, 52, 56, 57, 64

Sennett, Dorothy, **Supp. XVI:** 43

Sennett, Mack, **III:** 442

"Señora X No More" (Mora), **Supp. XIII:** 218

"Señor Ong and Señor Ha" (Bowles), **Supp. IV Part 1:** 87

Sensational Designs: The Cultural Work of American Fiction, 1790–1860 (Tompkins), **Supp. XVIII:** 258–259

Sense of Beauty, The (Santayana), **III:** 600

Sense of Life in the Modern Novel, The (Mizener), **IV:** 132

"Sense of Shelter, A" (Updike), **Retro. Supp. I:** 318

"Sense of the Meeting, The" (Conroy), **Supp. XVI:** 72

Sense of the Past, The (James), **II:** 337–338

"Sense of the Past, The" (Trilling), **Supp. III Part 2:** 503

"Sense of the Present, The" (Hardwick), **Supp. III Part 1:** 210

"Sense of the Sleight-of-Hand Man, The" (Stevens), **IV:** 93

"Sense of Where You Are, A" (McPhee), **Supp. III Part 1:** 291, 296–298

"Sensibility! O La!" (Roethke), **III:** 536

"Sensible Emptiness, A" (Kramer), **Supp. IV Part 1:** 61, 66

"Sensuality Plunging Barefoot Into Thorns" (Cisneros), **Supp. VII:** 68

"Sentence" (Barthelme), **Supp. IV Part 1:** 47

Sent for You Yesterday (Wideman), **Supp. X:** 320, 321

"Sentimental Education, A" (Banks), **Supp. V:** 10

"Sentimental Journey" (Oates), **Supp. II Part 2:** 522, 523

"Sentimental Journey, A" (Anderson), **I:** 114

Sentimental Journey, A (Sterne), **Supp. I Part 2:** 714

"Sentimental Journeys" (Didion), **Supp. IV Part 1:** 211

Sentimental Journey through France and Italy, A (Sterne), **Supp. XV:** 232

"Sentiment of Rationality, The" (James), **II:** 346–347

"Separated Father" (Halliday), **Supp. XIX:** 92, 93

Separate Flights (Dubus), **Supp. VII:** 78–83

"Separate Flights" (Dubus), **Supp. VII:** 83

Separate Peace, A (Knowles), **Supp. IV Part 2:** 679; **Supp. XII:** 241–249

Separate Way (Reznikoff), **Supp. XIV:** 280

"Separating" (Updike), **Retro. Supp. I:** 321

"Separation, The" (Kunitz), **Supp. III Part 1:** 263

"Sepia High Stepper" (Hayden), **Supp. II Part 1:** 379

September (film; Allen), **Supp. XV:** 11

"September" (Komunyakaa), **Supp. XIII:** 130

"September" (Pickering), **Supp. XXI:** 198

"September 1, 1939" (Auden), **Supp. II Part 1:** 13; **Supp. IV Part 1:** 225; **Supp. VIII:** 30, 32; **Supp. XV:** 117–118

September 11, 2001: American Writers Respond (Heyen), **Supp. XIII:** 285

"September's Book" (Notley), **Supp. XXII:** 229

September Song (Humphrey), **Supp. IX:** 101, 102, **108–109**

"September Twelfth, 2001" (X. J. Kennedy), **Supp. XV:** 171

"Sept Vieillards, Les" (Millay, trans.), **III:** 142

Sequel to Drum-Taps (Whitman), **Retro. Supp. I:** 406

"Sequence, Sometimes Metaphysical" (Roethke), **III:** 547, 548

Sequence of Seven Plays with a Drawing by Ron Slaughter, A (Nemerov), **III:** 269

Sequoya, Jana, **Supp. IV Part 1:** 334

Seraglio, The (Merrill), **Supp. III Part 1:** 331

Seraphita (Balzac), **I:** 499

Seraph on the Suwanee (Hurston), **Supp. VI:** 149, 159–160

Serenissima: A Novel of Venice (Jong). *See Shylock's Daughter: A Novel of Love in Venice (Serenissima)* (Jong)

Sergeant, Elizabeth Shepley, **I:** 231, 236, 312, 319, 323, 328

Sergeant Bilko (television show), **Supp. IV Part 2:** 575

Sergi, Paula, **Supp. XXI:** 246

"Serious Talk, A" (Carver), **Supp. III Part 1:** 138, 144

Serly, Tibor, **Supp. III Part 2:** 617, 619

"Sermon by Doctor Pep" (Bellow), **I:** 151

Sermones (Horace), **II:** 154

"Sermon for Our Maturity" (Baraka), **Supp. II Part 1:** 53

"Sermon in the Cotton Field" (Nelson), **Supp. XVIII:** 177

Sermons and Soda Water (O'Hara), **III:** 362, 364, 371–373, 382

"Sermons on the Warpland" (Brooks), **Supp. III Part 1:** 84

"Serpent in the Wilderness, The" (Masters), **Supp. I Part 2:** 458

Servant of the Bones (Rice), **Supp. VII:** 298, 302

"Servant to Servants, A" (Frost), **Retro. Supp. I:** 125, 128; **Supp. X:** 66

Serve It Forth (M. F. K. Fisher), **Supp. XVII:** 83, 86, 87, 89, 92

Service, Robert W., **Supp. XXI:** 51; **Supp. XXII:** 203

Seshachari, Neila, **Supp. V:** 22

"Session, The" (Adams), **I:** 5

"Sestina" (Bishop), **Supp. I Part 1:** 73, 88

Set-angya, **Supp. IV Part 2:** 493

Seth, Vikram, **Supp. XVII:** 117

Seth's Brother's Wife (Frederic), **II:** 131–132, 137, 144

Sethuraman, Ramchandran, **Supp. XXII:** 73

Set This House on Fire (Styron), **IV:** 98, 99, 105, 107–113, 114, 115, 117

Setting Free the Bears (Irving), **Supp. VI:** 163, 166–167, 169–170

Setting the Tone (Rorem), **Supp. IV Part 1:** 79

Settle, Mary Lee, **Supp. IX:** 96

Settlement Horizon, The: A National Estimate (Woods and Kennedy), **Supp. I Part 1:** 19

"Settling the Colonel's Hash" (McCarthy), **II:** 559, 562

Setzer, Helen, **Supp. IV Part 1:** 217

"Seurat's Sunday Afternoon along the Seine" (Schwartz), **Supp. II Part 2:** 663–665

Sevag, Aris, **Supp. XXIII:** 28, 29

7 Years from Somehwere (Levine), **Supp. V:** 178, 181, 188–189

Seven against Thebes (Aeschylus; Bacon and Hecht, trans.), **Supp. X:** 57

Seven Ages of Man, The (Wilder), **IV:** 357, 374–375

Seven Deadly Sins, The (Wilder), **IV:** 357, 374–375

Seven Descents of Myrtle, The (T. Williams), **IV:** 382

"Seven Fat Brides, The" (P. Abraham), **Supp. XVII:** 50

Seven Guitars (Wilson), **Supp. VIII:** 331, 348–351

Seven Lady Godivas, The (Geisel), **Supp. XVI:** 100, 103

Seven League Boots, The (Murray), **Supp. XIX:** 156–157

Seven-League Crutches, The (Jarrell), **II:** 367, 372, 381, 382, 383–384, 389

Seven Mountains of Thomas Merton, The (Mott), **Supp. VIII:** 208

Seven-Ounce Man, The (Harrison), **Supp. VIII:** 51

"Seven Places of the Mind" (Didion), **Supp. IV Part 1:** 200, 210

Seven Plays (Shepard), **Supp. III Part 2:** 434

"Seven Selves, The" (Gibran), **Supp. XX:** 118

"Seven Sentences"(Dybek), **Supp. XXIII:** 74

"Seven Stanzas at Easter" (Updike), **IV:** 215

Seven Storey Mountain, The (Merton), **Supp. VIII:** 193, 195, 198, 200, 207, 208

Seventh Heaven (Hoffman), **Supp. X:** 87, 89

"Seventh of March" (Webster), **Supp. I Part 2:** 687

"7000 Romaine, Los Angeles 38" (Didion), **Supp. IV Part 1:** 200

"Seventh Street" (Toomer), **Supp. IX:** 316

Seven Types of Ambiguity (Empson), **II:** 536; **IV:** 431

77 Dream Songs (Berryman), **I:** 168, 169, 170, 171, 174, 175, 183–188

73 Poems (Cummings), **I:** 430, 431, 446, 447, 448

Seven Valleys and the Four Valleys, The (Bahá'u'lláh), **Supp. XX:** 121

"Several Short Questions About Crumbs"(Schott), **Supp. XXIII:** 249

Sevier, Jack, **IV:** 378

Sévigné, Madame de, **IV:** 361

Sewall, Richard, **Retro. Supp. I:** 25

Sewall, Samuel, **IV:** 145, 146, 147, 149, 154, 164; **Supp. I Part 1:** 100, 110

Sewell, Elizabeth, **Supp. XIII:** 344

"Sex" (Carruth), **Supp. XVI:** 58

Sex, Economy, Freedom and Community (Berry), **Supp. X:** 30, 36

"Sex Camp" (Mamet), **Supp. XIV:** 240

Sex Castle, The (Lacy), **Supp. XV:** 206

Sex & Character (Weininger), **Retro. Supp. I:** 416

"Sext" (Auden), **Supp. II Part 1:** 22

Sexton, Anne, **Retro. Supp. II:** 245; **Supp. I Part 2:** 538, 543, 546; **Supp. II Part 2: 669–700; Supp. III Part 2:** 599; **Supp. IV Part 1:** 245; **Supp. IV Part 2:** 439, 440–441, 442, 444, 447, 449, 451, 620; **Supp. V:** 113, 118, 124; **Supp. X:** 201, 202, 213; **Supp. XI:** 146, 240, 317; **Supp. XII:** 217, 253, 254, 256, 260, 261; **Supp. XIII:** 35, 76, 294, 312; **Supp. XIV:** 125, 126, 132, 269; **Supp. XV:** 123, 252, 340; **Supp. XVII:** 239; **Supp. XIX:** 82, 203; **Supp. XX:** 199

Sexual Behavior in the American Male (Kinsey), **Supp. XIII:** 96–97

Sexual Perversity in Chicago (Mamet), **Supp. XIV:** 239, 240, 246–247, 249

"Sexual Revolution, The" (Dunn), **Supp. XI:** 142

Sexus (H. Miller), **III:** 170, 171, 184, 187, 188

"Sex Without Love" (Olds), **Supp. X:** 206

"Sexy" (Lahiri), **Supp. XXI:** 183–184

Seyersted, Per E., **Retro. Supp. II:** 65; **Supp. I Part 1:** 201, 204, 211, 216, 225; **Supp. IV Part 2:** 558

Seyfried, Robin, **Supp. IX:** 324

Seymour, Miranda, **Supp. VIII:** 167

"Seymour: An Introduction" (Salinger), **III:** 569–571, 572

"Shack" (L. Brown), **Supp. XXI:** 49

Shacochis, Bob, **Supp. VIII:** 80

"Shadow" (Creeley), **Supp. IV Part 1:** 158

"Shadow, The" (Lowell), **II:** 522

Shadow and Act (Ellison), **Retro. Supp. II:** 119; **Supp. II Part 1:** 245–246

"Shadow and Shade" (Tate), **IV:** 128

"Shadow and the Flesh, The" (London), **II:** 475

"Shadow A Parable" (Poe), **III:** 417–418

Shadow Country (Gunn Allen), **Supp. IV Part 1:** 322, 324, 325–326

Shadow Man, The (Gordon), **Supp. IV Part 1:** 297, 298, 299, 312–314, 315

Shadow of a Dream, The, a Story (Howells), **II:** 285, 286, 290

Shadow of a Man (Moraga), **Supp. XXIII:** 195, 197, 199–203

"Shadow of the Crime, The: A Word from the Author" (Mailer), **Retro. Supp. II:** 214

Shadow on the Dial, The (Bierce), **I:** 208, 209

"Shadow Passing" (Merwin), **Supp. III Part 1:** 355

Shadowplay (C. Baxter), **Supp. XVII:** 15, 19–20

Shadows (Gardner), **Supp. VI:** 74

Shadows and Fog (film; Allen), **Supp. XV:** 11

Shadows Burning (Di Piero), **Supp. XIX:** 42, 43–44

Shadows by the Hudson (Singer), **IV:** 1

Shadows of Africa (Matthiessen), **Supp. V:** 203

Shadows on the Hudson (Singer), **Retro. Supp. II:** 311–313

Shadows on the Rock (Cather), **I:** 314, 330–331, 332; **Retro. Supp. I:** 18
Shadow Train (Ashbery), **Supp. III Part 1:** 23–24, 26
"Shad-Time" (Wilbur), **Supp. III Part 2:** 563
Shaffer, Thomas L., **Supp. VIII:** 127, 128
Shaft (Parks; film), **Supp. XI:** 17
Shaftesbury, Earl of, **I:** 559
Shahid, Irfan, **Supp. XX: 113, 127**
Shahn, Ben, **Supp. X:** 24
Shakedown for Murder (Lacy), **Supp. XV:** 203
Shakelford, Dean, **Supp. VIII:** 129
Shaker, Why Don't You Sing? (Angelou), **Supp. IV Part 1:** 16
Shakespear, Mrs. Olivia, **III:** 457; **Supp. I Part 1:** 257
"Shakespeare" (Emerson), **II:** 6
Shakespeare, William, **I:** 103, 271, 272, 284–285, 358, 378, 433, 441, 458, 461, 573, 585, 586; **II:** 5, 8, 11, 18, 72, 273, 297, 302, 309, 320, 411, 494, 577, 590; **III:** 3, 11, 12, 82, 83, 91, 124, 130, 134, 145, 153, 159, 183, 210, 263, 286, 468, 473, 492, 503, 511, 567, 575–576, 577, 610, 612, 613, 615; **IV:** 11, 50, 66, 127, 132, 156, 309, 313, 362, 368, 370, 373, 453; **Retro. Supp. I:** 43, 64, 91, 248; **Retro. Supp. II:** 114, 299; **Supp. I Part 1:** 79, 150, 262, 310, 356, 363, 365, 368, 369, 370; **Supp. I Part 2:** 397, 421, 422, 470, 494, 622, 716, 720; **Supp. II Part 2:** 624, 626; **Supp. IV Part 1:** 31, 83, 87, 243; **Supp. IV Part 2:** 430, 463, 519, 688; **Supp. V:** 252, 280, 303; **Supp. VIII:** 160, 164; **Supp. IX:** 14, 133; **Supp. X:** 42, 62, 65, 78; **Supp. XII:** 54–57, 277, 281; **Supp. XIII:** 111, 115, 233; **Supp. XIV:** 97, 120, 225, 245, 306; **Supp. XV:** 92; **Supp. XVIII:** 278; **Supp. XXII:** 206
Shakespeare and His Forerunners (Lanier), **Supp. I Part 1:** 369
Shakespeare in Harlem (Hughes), **Retro. Supp. I:** 194, 202, 205, 206, 207, 208; **Supp. I Part 1:** 333, 334, 345
Shalit, Gene, **Supp. VIII:** 73
Shalit, Wendy, **Supp. XX: 179, 182, 186**
Shall We Gather at the River (Wright), **Supp. III Part 2:** 601–602; **Supp. XVII:** 241
"Shame" (Oates), **Supp. II Part 2:** 520
"Shame" (Wilbur), **Supp. III Part 2:** 556
"Shame and Forgetting in the Information Age" (C. Baxter), **Supp. XVII:** 21
"Shameful Affair, A" (Chopin), **Retro. Supp. II:** 61
Shamela (Fielding), **Supp. V:** 127
"Shampoo, The" (Bishop), **Retro. Supp. II:** 46; **Supp. I Part 1:** 92
Shange, Ntozake, **Supp. VIII:** 214; **Supp. XVII:** 70; **Supp. XVIII:** 172; **Supp. XXI:** 172
Shank, Randy, **Supp. X:** 252
Shankaracharya, **III:** 567

Shanley, John Patrick, **Supp. XIV: 315–332**
Shannon, Sandra, **Supp. VIII:** 333, 348
"Shape of Flesh and Bone, The" (MacLeish), **III:** 18–19
Shape of Me and Other Stuff, The (Geisel), **Supp. XVI:** 111
Shape of the Journey, The (Harrison), **Supp. VIII:** 53
Shapes of Clay (Bierce), **I:** 208, 209
Shaping Joy, A: Studies in the Writer's Craft (Brooks), **Supp. XIV:** 13
Shapiro, Charles, **Supp. XIX:** 257, 259–260
Shapiro, David, **Supp. XII:** 175, 185
Shapiro, Dorothy, **IV:** 380
Shapiro, Karl, **I:** 430, 521; **II:** 350; **III:** 527; **Supp. II Part 2: 701–724; Supp. III Part 2:** 623; **Supp. IV Part 2:** 645; **Supp. X:** 116; **Supp. XI:** 315; **Supp. XIX:** 117, 118, 119; **Supp. XXI:** 98
Shapiro, Laura, **Supp. IX:** 120; **Supp. XX: 87, 89**
Sharif, Omar, **Supp. IX:** 253
"Shark Meat" (Snyder), **Supp. VIII:** 300
Shatayev, Elvira, **Supp. I Part 2:** 570
Shaviro, Steven, **Supp. VIII:** 189
Shaw, Chris, **Supp. XXIII:** 155–156
Shaw, Colonel Robert Gould, **II:** 551
Shaw, Elizabeth. *See* Melville, Mrs. Herman (Elizabeth Shaw)
Shaw, George Bernard, **I:** 226; **II:** 82, 271, 276, 581; **III:** 69, 102, 113, 145, 155, 161, 162, 163, 373, 409; **IV:** 27, 64, 397, 432, 440; **Retro. Supp. I:** 100, 228; **Supp. IV Part 1:** 36; **Supp. IV Part 2:** 585, 683; **Supp. V:** 243–244, 290; **Supp. IX:** 68, 308; **Supp. XI:** 202; **Supp. XII:** 94; **Supp. XIV:** 343; **Supp. XVII:** 100
Shaw, Irwin, **IV:** 381; **Supp. IV Part 1:** 383; **Supp. IX:** 251; **Supp. XI:** 221, 229, 231; **Supp. XIX: 239–254**
Shaw, Joseph Thompson ("Cap"), **Supp. IV Part 1:** 121, 345, 351; **Supp. XIII:** 161
Shaw, Judge Lemuel, **III:** 77, 88, 91
Shaw, Lytle, **Supp. XXIII:** 208
Shaw, Peter, **Supp. XVI:** 70
Shaw, Robert B., **Supp. XXIII:** 112
Shaw, Sarah Bryant, **Supp. I Part 1:** 169
Shaw, Wilbur, Jr., **Supp. XIII:** 162
Shawl, The (Mamet), **Supp. XIV:** 245
Shawl, The (Ozick), **Supp. V:** 257, 260, 271
"Shawl, The" (Ozick), **Supp. V:** 271–272
Shawl and Prarie du Chien, The: Two Plays (Mamet), **Supp. XIV:** 243–244
Shawn, William, **Supp. VIII:** 151, 170
"Shawshank Redemption, The" (King), **Supp. V:** 148
She (Haggard), **III:** 189
Shea, Renee, **Supp. XXIII:** 85, 86, 90, 95
Sheaffer, Louis, **Supp. XXI:** 6
Shearer, Flora, **I:** 199
"Sheaves, The" (Robinson), **III:** 510, 524
"She Came and Went" (Lowell), **Supp. I Part 2:** 409

"She-Devil" (Nelson), **Supp. XVIII:** 178
She-Devil Circus (Nelson), **Supp. XVIII:** 176, **178**
Sheed, Wilfrid, **IV:** 230; **Supp. XI:** 233; **Supp. XXI:** 233
Sheeler, Charles, **IV:** 409; **Retro. Supp. I:** 430
"Sheep Child" (B. Kelly), **Supp. XVII:** 131–132
"Sheep Child, The" (Dickey), **Supp. XVII:** 131–132
Sheeper (Rosenthal), **Supp. XIV:** 147
Sheffer, Jonathan, **Supp. IV Part 1:** 95
She Had Some Horses (Harjo), **Supp. XII: 220–223,** 231
"She Had Some Horses" (Harjo), **Supp. XII:** 215, 222
"Shell, The" (Humphrey), **Supp. IX:** 94
Shelley, Mary, **Supp. XX: 108**
Shelley, Percy Bysshe, **I:** 18, 68, 381, 476, 522, 577; **II:** 331, 516, 535, 540; **III:** 412, 426, 469; **IV:** 139; **Retro. Supp. I:** 308, 360; **Supp. I Part 1:** 79, 311, 349; **Supp. I Part 2:** 709, 718, 719, 720, 721, 722, 724, 728; **Supp. IV Part 1:** 235; **Supp. V:** 258, 280; **Supp. IX:** 51; **Supp. XII:** 117, 132, 136–137, 263; **Supp. XIV:** 271–272; **Supp. XV:** 92, 175, 182; **Supp. XX: 115; Supp. XXI:** 131
Shellow, Sadie Myers, **Supp. I Part 2:** 608
"Shelter" (C. Baxter), **Supp. XVII:** 19
"Shelter" (Doty), **Supp. XI:** 132
Sheltered Life, The (Glasgow), **II:** 174, 175, 179, 186, 187–188
Sheltering Sky, The (Bowles), **Supp. IV Part 1:** 82, 84, 85–86, 87
Sheltering Sky, The (film), **Supp. IV Part 1:** 94, 95
Shelton, Frank, **Supp. IV Part 2:** 658
Shelton, Richard, **Supp. XI:** 133; **Supp. XIII:** 7
Shelton, Robert, **Supp. XVIII:** 20, 21, 22, 23, 24, 25, 26
Shelton, Mrs. Sarah. *See* Royster, Sarah Elmira
Shenandoah (Schwartz), **Supp. II Part 2:** 640, 651–652
"Shenandoah" (Shapiro), **Supp. II Part 2:** 704
Shepard, Alice, **IV:** 287
Shepard, Gregory, **Supp. XXII:** 119
Shepard, Harvey, **Supp. XVII:** 240
Shepard, Jim, **Supp. XXI:** 115
Shepard, Odell, **II:** 508; **Supp. I Part 2:** 418
Shepard, Sam, **Supp. III Part 2: 431–450; Supp. XVIII:** 21, 28, 31; **Supp. XXI:** 144, 145
Shepard, Thomas, **I:** 554; **IV:** 158
"Shepherd of Resumed Desire, The" (Wright), **Supp. XV:** 349
Sheppard Lee (Bird), **III:** 423
"She Remembers the Future" (Harjo), **Supp. XII:** 222
Sheridan, Richard Brinsley, **Retro. Supp. I:** 127
Sherlock, William, **IV:** 152
Sherman, Joe, **Supp. XXII:** 205

Sherman, Sarah Way, **Retro. Supp. II:** 145

Sherman, Stuart Pratt, **I:** 222, 246–247; **Supp. I Part 2:** 423

Sherman, Susan, **Supp. VIII:** 265

Sherman, Tom, **IV:** 446

Sherman, William T., **IV:** 445, 446

Sherry, Denver William, **Supp. XXII:** 190

Sherwood, Robert, **II:** 435; **Supp. IX:** 190

Sherwood Anderson & Other Famous Creoles (Faulkner), **I:** 117; **II:** 56

Sherwood Anderson Reader, The (Anderson), **I:** 114, 116

Sherwood Anderson's Memoirs (Anderson), **I:** 98, 101, 102, 103, 108, 112, 116

Sherwood Anderson's Notebook (Anderson), **I:** 108, 115, 117

"She Sings" (Taggard), **Supp. XXII:** 272

She Stoops to Conquer (Goldsmith), **II:** 514

Shestov, Lev, **Supp. VIII:** 20, 24

Shetley, Vernon, **Supp. IX:** 292; **Supp. XI:** 123

"She Wept, She Railed" (Kunitz), **Supp. III Part 1:** 265

"Shiddah and Kuziba" (Singer), **IV:** 13, 15

Shidyak, Paris al-, **Supp. XX: 117**

Shield of Achilles, The (Auden), **Supp. II Part 1:** 21

"Shield of Achilles, The" (Auden), **Supp. II Part 1:** 21, 25

Shields, Carol, **Supp. VII: 307–330**

Shields, John C., **Supp. XX: 279, 280, 281, 286**

Shifting Landscape: A Composite, 1925–1987 (H. Roth), **Supp. IX: 233–235**

Shifts of Being (Eberhart), **I:** 525

Shigematsu, Soiko, **Supp. III Part 1:** 353

Shihab, Aziz, **Supp. XIII:** 273

Shih-hsiang Chen, **Supp. VIII:** 303

Shiksa Goddess; or, How I Spent My Forties (Wasserstein), **Supp. XV:** 319, 320, 325, 332, 333

"Shiloh" (Mason), **Supp. VIII:** 140

Shiloh and Other Stories (Mason), **Supp. VIII:** 133, **139–141,** 143, 145

Shilts, Randy, **Supp. X:** 145

Shimmering Verge, The (one-woman show, Peacock), **Supp. XIX:** 194, **204–205**

Shining, The (King), **Supp. V:** 139, 140, 141, 143–144, 146, 149, 151, 152

"Shining Ones, The" (P. N. Warren), **Supp. XX: 272**

Shining Victory (film, Rapper), **Supp. XVII:** 60

Shinn, Everett, **Retro. Supp. II:** 103

Shi Pei Pu, **Supp. XXI:** 152, 153, 154

"Ship in a Bottle"(Strout), **Supp. XXIII:** 283

"Ship of Death" (Lawrence), **Supp. I Part 2:** 728

Ship of Fools (Porter), **III:** 433, 447, 453, 454; **IV:** 138

Shipping News, The (Proulx), **Supp. VII:** 249, 258–259

"Ships" (O. Henry), **Supp. II Part 1:** 409

Ships Going into the Blue: Essays and Notes on Poetry (Simpson), **Supp. IX:** 275

Ship to America, A (Singer), **IV:** 1

"Shipwreck, The" (Merwin), **Supp. III Part 1:** 346

Shirley, John, **Supp. XVI:** 123, 128

"Shirt" (Pinsky), **Supp. VI: 236–237,** 239, 240, 241, 245, 247

"Shirt Poem, The" (Stern), **Supp. IX:** 292

"Shirts of a Single Color" (Ryan), **Supp. XVIII:** 227

"Shiva and Parvati Hiding in the Rain" (Pinsky), **Supp. VI:** 244

Shively, Charley, **Retro. Supp. I:** 391; **Supp. XII:** 181, 182

Shnayerson, Michael, **Supp. XIX:** 248

"Shock of Good Poetry, The"(Hirshfield), **Supp. XXIII:** 136

Shock of Recognition, The (Wilson), **II:** 530

Shock of the New, The (Hughes), **Supp. X:** 73

Shoe Bird, The (Welty), **IV:** 261; **Retro. Supp. I:** 353

Shoemaker of Dreams (Ferragammo), **Supp. XVI:** 192

"Shoes" (O. Henry), **Supp. II Part 1:** 409

"Shoes of Wandering, The" (Kinnell), **Supp. III Part 1:** 248

Sholem Asch: Zayn levn un zayne verk (Sholem Asch: His life and his work), **Supp. XXIII:** 6

Sholl, Betsy, **Supp. XXI:** 129, 131

"Shooters, Inc." (Didion), **Supp. IV Part 1:** 207, 211

"Shooting, The" (Dubus), **Supp. VII:** 84, 85

"Shooting Niagara; and After?" (Carlyle), **Retro. Supp. I:** 408

"Shooting Script" (Rich), **Supp. I Part 2:** 558; **Supp. IV Part 1:** 257

Shooting Star, A (Stegner), **Supp. IV Part 2:** 599, 608–609

"Shooting the Works" (Di Piero), **Supp. XIX:** 41–42

Shooting the Works: On Poetry and Pictures (Di Piero), **Supp. XIX: 41–42**

"Shooting Whales" (Strand), **Supp. IV Part 2:** 630

"Shopgirls" (F. Barthelme), **Supp. XI:** 26, 27, 33, 36

Shopping for Joe (O'Hara and Steven Rivers), **Supp. XXIII:** 217

"Shopping with Bob Berwick" (Halliday), **Supp. XIX:** 88

Shop Talk (P. Roth), **Retro. Supp. II:** 282

Shoptaw, John, **Supp. IV Part 1:** 247

Shore Acres (Herne), **Supp. II Part 1:** 198

Shorebirds of North America, The (Matthiessen), **Supp. V:** 204

"Shore House, The" (Jewett), **II:** 397

Shore Leave (Wakeman), **Supp. IX:** 247

"Shoreline Horses" (Ríos), **Supp. IV Part 2:** 553

"Shoreline Life" (Skloot), **Supp. XX: 201**

Shores of Light, The: A Literary Chronicle of the Twenties and Thirties (Wilson), **IV:** 432, 433

Shorey, Paul, **III:** 606

Short and the Long of It, The (Kenny), **Supp. XXIII.** 155–156

Short Cuts (film), **Supp. IX:** 143

"Short End, The" (Hecht), **Supp. X:** 65

"Shorter View, The" (X. J. Kennedy), **Supp. XV:** 160, 168

Short Fiction of Norman Mailer, The (Mailer), **Retro. Supp. II:** 205

Short Friday and Other Stories (Singer), **IV:** 14–16

Short Guide to a Happy Life, A (Quindlen), **Supp. XVII:** 167, 179

"Short Happy Life of Francis Macomber, The" (Hemingway), **II:** 250, 263–264; **Retro. Supp. I:** 182; **Supp. IV Part 1:** 48; **Supp. IX:** 106

Short Night, The (Turner), **Supp. XV:** 201

Short Novels of Thomas Wolfe, The (Wolfe), **IV:** 456

Short Poems (Berryman), **I:** 170

"SHORT SPEECH TO MY FRIENDS" (Baraka), **Supp. II Part 1:** 35

Short Stories (Rawlings), **Supp. X:** 224

Short Stories: Five Decades (Shaw), **Supp. XIX:** 252–253

"Short Story, The" (Welty), **IV:** 279

Short Story Masterpieces, **Supp. IX:** 4

Short Studies of American Authors (Higginson), **I:** 455

"Short-timer's Calendar" (Komunyakaa), **Supp. XIII:** 125

Shosha (Singer), **Retro. Supp. II: 313–314**

Shostakovich, Dimitri, **IV:** 75; **Supp. VIII:** 21

Shot of Love (album, Dylan), **Supp. XVIII:** 28

"Shots" (Ozick), **Supp. V:** 268

Shotts, Jeffrey, **Supp. XV:** 103, 104

"Should Wizard Hit Mommy?" (Updike), **IV:** 221, 222, 224; **Retro. Supp. I:** 335

Shoup, Barbara, **Supp. XV:** 55, 59, 62, 69

"Shoveling Snow with Buddha" (Collins), **Supp. XXI:** 60

"Shovel Man, The" (Sandburg), **III:** 553

Showalter, Elaine, **Retro. Supp. I:** 368; **Supp. IV Part 2:** 440, 441, 444; **Supp. X:** 97; **Supp. XVI:** 80, 92; **Supp. XX: 274**

"Shower of Gold" (Welty), **IV:** 271–272

Shribman, David M., **Supp. XXII:** 205, 218

"Shrike and the Chipmunks, The" (Thurber), **Supp. I Part 2:** 617

Shrimp Girl (Hogarth), **Supp. XII:** 44

"Shrine and the Burning Wheel, The" (Jarman), **Supp. XVII:** 116

"Shrine with Flowers" (Di Piero), **Supp. XIX:** 43, 44

"Shriveled Meditation" (X. J. Kennedy), **Supp. XV:** 170

Shropshire Lad, A (Housman), **Supp. XV:** 41

"Shrouded Stranger, The" (Ginsberg), **Supp. II Part 1:** 312

"Shroud of Color, The" (Cullen), **Supp. IV Part 1:** 166, 168, 170, 171

Shrunken Head of Pancho Villa, The (Valdez), **Supp. XXIII:** 203

Shtetl (film; Marzynski), **Supp. XVI:** 153

Shtetl: The Life and Death of a Small Town and the World of Polish Jews (E. Hoffman), **Supp. XVI:** 152, **153–155**

Shue, Elizabeth, **Supp. XXIII:** 276

Shuffle (L. Michaels), **Supp. XVI:** 202, 203, 213

Shuffle Along (musical), **Supp. I Part 1:** 322; **Supp. X:** 136

Shultz, George, **Supp. IV Part 1:** 234

Shurr, William, **Retro. Supp. I:** 43

Shuster, Joel, **Supp. XI:** 67

Shusterman, Richard, **Retro. Supp. I:** 53

"Shut a Final Door" (Capote), **Supp. III Part 1:** 117, 120, 124

Shut Up, He Explained (Lardner), **II:** 432

Shylock's Daughter: A Novel of Love in Venice (Serenissima) (Jong), **Supp. V:** 115, 127, 128–129

Siamanto (Atom Yarjanian), **Supp. XXIII:** 28

"Siasconset: How It Arose and What It Is" (Briggs), **Supp. XVIII:** 9

Siberian Village, The (Dove), **Supp. IV Part 1:** 255, 256

Sibley, Celestine, **Supp. XXII:** 194, 199

Sibley, Mulford Q., **Supp. I Part 2:** 524

"Sibling Mysteries" (Rich), **Supp. I Part 2:** 574

Siblings (Quindlen and Kelsh), **Supp. XVII:** 167, 179

Sibon, Marcelle, **IV:** 288

"Sicilian Emigrant's Song" (W. C. Williams), **Retro. Supp. I:** 413

Sicilian Miniatures (Sobin), **Supp. XVI:** 288

"Sick Wife, The" (Kenyon), **Supp. VII:** 173, 174

"'Sic transit gloria mundi' " (Dickinson), **Retro. Supp. I:** 30

Sid Caesar Show (television show), **Supp. IV Part 2:** 575

Siddons, Anne Rivers, **Supp. XXII: 239–254**

Siddons, Sarah, **II:** 298

Side Effects (Allen), **Supp. XV:** 3, 14, **15–16**

Side of Paradise, This (Fitgerald), **Supp. IX:** 56

Sidnee Poet Heroical, The (Baraka), **Supp. II Part 1:** 55

Sidney, Algernon, **II:** 114

Sidney, Mary, **Supp. I Part 1:** 98

Sidney, Philip, **II:** 470; **Supp. I Part 1:** 98, 111, 117–118, 122; **Supp. I Part 2:** 658; **Supp. II Part 1:** 104–105; **Supp. V:** 250; **Supp. XII:** 264; **Supp. XIV:** 128

Sidney, Sylvia, **Supp. I Part 1:** 67

Sidney Lanier: A Bibliographical and Critical Study (Starke), **Supp. I Part 1:** 371

Sidney Lanier: A Biographical and Critical Study (Starke), **Supp. I Part 1:** 371

Siebert, Kathy, **Supp. XX:** 84

Siege (Shaw), **Supp. XIX:** 244

Siegel, Barry, **Supp. XIV:** 82

Siegel, Ben, **Supp. XXIII:** 3, 4, 10, 11, 12, 14, 16

Siegel, Catherine, **Supp. XII:** 126

Siegel, Jerry, **Supp. XI:** 67

Siegel, Lee, **Supp. XXII: 255–269**

"Siege of London, The" (James), **Retro. Supp. I:** 227

Siegle, Robert, **Supp. XII:** 8

Sienkiewicz, Henryk, **Supp. IV Part 2:** 518; **Supp. XVI:** 182

"Sierra Kid" (Levine), **Supp. V:** 180–181

Sigal, Clancy, **Supp. XXI:** 44; **Supp. XXIII:** 166

Sigg, Eric, **Retro. Supp. I:** 53

"Sight" (Merwin), **Supp. III Part 1:** 356

Sighted Singer, The (Halliday), **Supp. XIX:** 82, **86–87**

"Sight in Camp in the Daybreak Gray and Dim, A" (Whitman), **II:** 373

Sights and Spectacles (McCarthy), **II:** 562

"Sights from a Steeple" (Hawthorne), **Retro. Supp. I:** 62; **Supp. XXI:** 201

Sights Unseen (Gibbons), **Supp. X: 49–50**

"Signals" (Carver), **Supp. III Part 1:** 143

"Signature for Tempo" (MacLeish), **III:** 8–9

"Signed Confession of Crimes against the State" (Merton), **Supp. VIII:** 201

Signifying Monkey, The (Hughes), **Retro. Supp. I:** 195

Signifying Monkey, The: A Theory of Afro-American Literary Criticism (H. L. Gates), **Supp. X:** 243; **Supp. XX: 99, 106–107**

"Signing, The (Dixon), **Supp. XII: 146**

Sign in Sidney Brustein's Window, The (Hansberry), **Supp. IV Part 1:** 359, 365, 369, 370–372

Sign of Jonas, The (Merton), **Supp. VIII:** 194–195, 195, 197, 200, 206, 207

"Sign of Saturn, The" (Olds), **Supp. X:** 206

"Signs, Oakvale, Mississippi, 1941" (Trethewey), **Supp. XXI:** 248–249

Signs and Wonders (Bukiet), **Supp. XVII: 45–46**

Sigourney, Lydia, **Supp. I Part 2:** 684

Sikora, Malgorzata, **Retro. Supp. II:** 324

Silas Marner (G. Eliot), **II:** 26

Silberg, Richard, **Supp. XV:** 116

"Silence" (Moore), **III:** 212

"Silence" (Poe), **III:** 416

"Silence" (Sanders), **Supp. XVI:** 278

"Silence, A" (Clampitt), **Supp. IX:** 53

"Silence—A Fable" (Poe), **III:** 416

Silence and Metaphor (Bronk), **Supp. XXI:** 31, 32

"Silence Before Harvest, The" (Merwin), **Supp. III Part 1:** 352

Silence Dogood Papers, The (Franklin), **II:** 106–107

Silence in the Snowy Fields (R. Bly), **Supp. IV Part 1:** 60–61, 62, 63, 65, 66, 72; **Supp. XXI:** 84, 85

Silence of History, The (Farrell), **II:** 46–47

Silence of the Lambs, The (T. Harris), **Supp. XXI:** 78

Silence Opens, A (Clampitt), **Supp. IX:** 53

Silences (Olsen), **Supp. XIII:** 293, 294, 295, 296, **304–306**

"Silences: When Writers Don't Write" (Olsen), **Supp. XIII:** 294

Silencing the Past: Power and the Production of History (Trouillot), **Supp. X:** 14

"Silent in America" (Levine), **Supp. V:** 183

Silent Life, The (Merton), **Supp. VIII:** 208

Silent Partner, The (Odets), **Supp. II Part 2:** 539

"Silent Poem" (Francis), **Supp. IX:** 86

"Silent Season of a Hero, The" (Talese), **Supp. XVII:** 203–204

"Silent Slain, The" (MacLeish), **III:** 9

"Silent Snow, Secret Snow" (Aiken), **I:** 52

Silent Spring (Carson), **Supp. V:** 202; **Supp. IX:** 19, 24, **31–34; Supp. XIV:** 177; **Supp. XVI:** 36; **Supp. XVIII:** 189

Silhouettes of American Life (R. H. Davis), **Supp. XVI:** 85

"Silken Tent, The" (Frost), **Retro. Supp. I:** 138–139; **Supp. IV Part 2:** 448

Silko, Leslie Marmon, **Supp. IV Part 1:** 274, 319, 325, 333–334, 335, 404; **Supp. IV Part 2:** 499, 505, **557–572; Supp. V:** 169; **Supp. XI:** 18; **Supp. XII:** 217; **Supp. XVIII:** 58

Silliman, Ron, **Supp. IV Part 2:** 426; **Supp. XV:** 344; **Supp. XVII:** 70, 77

Silliman's Blog (R. Silliman), **Supp. XVII:** 70

Silman, Roberta, **Supp. X:** 6

Silverblatt, Michael, **Supp. XV:** 224

"Silver Crown, The" (Malamud), **Supp. I Part 2:** 434–435, 437; **Supp. V:** 266

"Silver Dish, The" (Bellow), **Retro. Supp. II:** 30

"Silver Filigree" (Wylie), **Supp. I Part 2:** 707

"Silver Lake" (B. Kelly), **Supp. XVII:** 130

Silverman, Joseph, **Supp. XXIII:** 8

Silvers, Phil, **Supp. IV Part 2:** 574

Silverthorne, Elizabeth, **Supp. X:** 220, 221, 222, 226, 234

"Silver To Have and to Hurl" (Didion), **Supp. IV Part 1:** 197

Simic, Charles, **Supp. V:** 5, 332; **Supp. VIII:** 39, **269–287; Supp. XI:** 317; **Supp. XV:** 179, 185; **Supp. XIX:** 277, 282

"Similar Cases" (Gilman), **Supp. XI:** 200, 202

Similitudes, from the Ocean and Prairie (Larcom), **Supp. XIII:** 141

Simmel, Georg, **Supp. I Part 2:** 644; **Supp. XVII:** 98

Simmons, Charles, **Supp. XI:** 230

Simmons, Maggie, **Retro. Supp. II:** 21

Simms, Michael, **Supp. XII:** 184

Simms, William Gilmore, **I:** 211

Simon, John, **Supp. IV Part 2:** 691

Simon, Neil, **Supp. IV Part 2: 573–594; Supp. XVII:** 8

Simone, Nina, **Supp. XXI:** 243

"Simon Gerty" (Wylie), **Supp. I Part 2:** 713

Simonides, **Supp. XII:** 110–111

"Simon Ortiz" (Gingerich), **Supp. IV Part 2:** 510

Simon Ortiz (Wiget), **Supp. IV Part 2:** 509

Simonson, Lee, **III:** 396; **Supp. XXI:** 6

"Simple" (Peacock), **Supp. XIX:** 200

"Simple Art of Murder, The" (Chandler), **Supp. IV Part 1:** 121, 341

"Simple Autumnal" (Bogan), **Supp. III Part 1:** 52–53

Simple Heart (Flaubert), **I:** 504

Simple Honorable Man, A (Richter), **Supp. XVIII:** 208, 218, **219,** 220

"Simple Purchase, A" (Peacock), **Supp. XIX:** 199

Simple Speaks his Mind (Hughes), **Retro. Supp. I:** 209; **Supp. I Part 1:** 337

Simple Stakes a Claim (Hughes), **Retro. Supp. I:** 209; **Supp. I Part 1:** 337

Simple's Uncle Sam (Hughes), **Retro. Supp. I:** 209; **Supp. I Part 1:** 337

Simple Takes a Wife (Hughes), **Retro. Supp. I:** 209; **Supp. I Part 1:** 337

Simple Truth, The (Hardwick), **Supp. III Part 1:** 199, 200, 208

Simple Truth, The (Levine), **Supp. V:** 178, 179, 193–194

"Simple Widsom, The" (Skloot), **Supp. XX: 207**

"Simplicity" (Sanders), **Supp. XVI:** 276

Simply Heavenly (Hughes), **Retro. Supp. I:** 209; **Supp. I Part 1:** 338, 339

Simpson, Louis, **Supp. III Part 2:** 541; **Supp. IV Part 2:** 448, 621; **Supp. VIII:** 39, 279; **Supp. IX: 265–283,** 290; **Supp. XI:** 317; **Supp. XII:** 130; **Supp. XIII:** 337

Simpson, Mona, **Supp. XVI:** 206

"Sin" (C. Frost), **Supp. XV:** 96

Sinatra, Frank, **Supp. IX:** 3; **Supp. X:** 119; **Supp. XI:** 213

Sincere Convert, The (Shepard), **IV:** 158

Sincerely, Willis Wayde (Marquand), **III:** 61, 63, 66, 67–68, 69

Sincerity (Rowson), **Supp. XV:** 242

Sincerity and Authenticity (Trilling), **Supp. III Part 2:** 510–512

"Sincerity and Objectification: With Special Reference to the Work of Charles Reznikoff" (Zukofsky), **Supp. XIV:** 286

Sinclair, Mary Craig (Mary Craig Kimbrough), **Supp. V:** 275, 286, 287

Sinclair, Upton, **II:** 34, 440, 444, 451; **III:** 580; **Retro. Supp. II:** 95; **Supp. V: 275–293; Supp. VIII:** 11

Sinclair Lewis: An American Life (Schorer), **II:** 459

"Singapore" (Oliver), **Supp. VII:** 239, 240

Singer, Bennett L., **Supp. IV Part 1:** 330

Singer, Beth, **Supp. XIV:** 203

Singer, Isaac Bashevis, **I:** 144; **IV: 1–24; Retro. Supp. II:** 22, **299–320; Supp. IX:** 114; **Supp. XVIII:** 215, 220; **Supp. XXI:** 106; **Supp. XXII:** 258

Singer, Israel Joshua, **IV:** 2, 16, 17; **Retro. Supp. II:** 302; **Supp. XVII:** 41

Singer, Joshua, **IV:** 4

Singer, Rabbi Pinchos Menachem, **IV:** 16

Singin' and Swingin' and Gettin' Merry Like Christmas (Angelou), **Supp. IV Part 1:** 2, 5, 6–7, 9, 13, 14

"Singing & Doubling Together" (Ammons), **Supp. VII:** 34–35

Singing Jailbirds (Sinclair), **Supp. V:** 277

"Singing the Black Mother" (Lupton), **Supp. IV Part 1:** 7

Single Hound, The (Sarton), **Supp. VIII:** 251, 265

Single Hound, The: Poems of a Lifetime (Dickinson; Bianchi, ed.), **Retro. Supp. I:** 35

Single Man, A (Isherwood), **Supp. XIV:** 157, 164, **169–170,** 171

"Single Sonnet" (Bogan), **Supp. III Part 1:** 56–58

Singley, Carol, **Retro. Supp. I:** 373

Singular Family, A: Rosacoke and Her Kin (Price), **Supp. VI: 258–259,** 260

"Singular First Person, The" (Sanders), **Supp. XVI:** 274

Singularities (Howe), **Supp. IV Part 2:** 431

Sin in Their Blood (Lacy), **Supp. XV:** 200

"Sinister Adolescents, The" (Dos Passos), **I:** 493

Sinister Street (Mackenzie), **II:** 82

Sinking of Clay City, The (Wrigley), **Supp. XVIII: 294–295**

Sinners in the Hands of an Angry God (Edwards), **I:** 546, 552–553, 559, 562

Sinning with Annie, and Other Stories (Theroux), **Supp. VIII:** 318

"Sins of Kalamazoo, The" (Sandburg), **III:** 586

Sintram and His Companions (La Motte-Fouqué), **III:** 78

"Siope" (Poe), **III:** 411

"Sipapu: A Cultural Perspective" (Gunn Allen), **Supp. IV Part 1:** 323

Sipchen, Bob, **Supp. X:** 145

Sipper, Ralph B., **Supp. IV Part 2:** 475

"Sire" (Cisneros), **Supp. VII:** 62–63, 64

"Siren and Signal" (Zukofsky), **Supp. III Part 2:** 611, 612

Sirens of Titan, The (Vonnegut), **Supp. II Part 2:** 757, 758, 760, 765–767

"Sir Galahad" (Tennyson), **Supp. I Part 2:** 410

Sirin, V. (pseudonym), **Retro. Supp. I:** 266. *See also* Nabokov, Vladimir

Sirlin, Jerome, **Supp. XXI:** 147

Sir Vadia's Shadow: A Friendship across Five Continents (Theroux), **Supp. VIII:** 309, 314, 321, 325

"Sir William's Reply to Molly"(Kenny), **Supp. XXIII:** 153

"Sis" (F. Barthelme), **Supp. XI:** 26

"S is for Sad" (M. F. K. Fisher), **Supp. XVII:** 86

Sisley, Alfred, **I:** 478

Sissman, L. E., **Supp. X:** 69

"Sister" (Hughes), **Retro. Supp. I:** 208

"Sister" (Lamott), **Supp. XX: 142**

Sister Age (M. F. K. Fisher), **Supp. XVII:** 88, 91

Sister Carrie (Dreiser), **I:** 482, 497, 499, 500, 501–502, 503–504, 505, 506, 515, 519; **III:** 327; **IV:** 208; **Retro. Supp. I:** 376; **Retro. Supp. II:** 93, **96–99; Supp. XVIII:** 76, 243; **Supp. XXIII:** 165

"Sister of the Minotaur" (Stevens), **IV:** 89; **Supp. IX:** 332

"Sisters" (Boulton), **Supp. XXII:** 20

"Sisters" (Nelson), **Supp. XVIII:** 176

"Sisters, The" (Whittier), **Supp. I Part 2:** 696

Sister's Choice (Showalter), **Retro. Supp. I:** 368

Sisters of the Earth: Women's Prose and Poetry About Nature (Anderson, ed.), **Supp. XVIII:** 189

Sisters Rosensweig, The (Wasserstein), **Supp. XV:** 320, **328–330**

"Sisyphus" (Kumin), **Supp. IV Part 2:** 443, 444, 451

"Sitalkas" (Doolittle), **Supp. I Part 1:** 266

"Sites of Memory" (Cliff), **Supp. XXII:** 69, 74

Sitney, P. Adams, **Supp. XII:** 2

Sitting Bull, **Supp. IV Part 2:** 492

"Sitting in a Rocking Chair Going Blind" (Komunyakaa), **Supp. XIII:** 114

Sitting In: Selected Writings on Jazz, Blues, and Related Topics (Carruth), **Supp. XVI:** 46

"Sitting Up Late with My Father, 1977" (F. Wright), **Supp. XVII:** 247

Sitti's Secrets (Nye), **Supp. XIII:** 278

Situation Normal (A. Miller), **III:** 148, 149, 156, 164

Situation of Poetry, The: Contemporary Poetry and Its Traditions (Pinsky), **Supp. VI: 237–238,** 239, 241, 242

Sitwell, Edith, **IV:** 77; **Supp. I Part 1:** 271

"Six Brothers" (Cisneros), **Supp. VII:** 67

Six Characters in Search of an Author (Pirandello), **Supp. IV Part 2:** 576

"Six Days: Some Rememberings" (Paley), **Supp. VI:** 226

"65290" (Leopold), **Supp. XIV:** 184–185

Six French Poets (Lowell), **II:** 528–529

"Six in All" (Bierds), **Supp. XVII:** 31

Six Lips (Schott), **Supp. XXIII: 251–252**

"Six Persons" (Baraka), **Supp. II Part 1:** 53

Six Sections from Mountains and Rivers without End (Snyder), **Supp. VIII:** 305

"Sixteen Months" (Sandburg), **III:** 584

1601, or Conversation as It Was by the Fireside in the Time of the Tudors (Twain), **IV:** 201

"Sixth-Month Song in the Foothills" (Snyder), **Supp. VIII:** 297

Sixties, The (magazine) (R. Bly), **Supp. IV Part 1:** 60; **Supp. IX:** 271

"Sixty" (Dunn), **Supp. XI:** 155

"Sixty Acres" (Carver), **Supp. III Part 1:** 141

"64 Elmgrove" (Halliday), **Supp. XIX:** 88

"69 Hidebound Opinions, Propositions, and Several Asides from a Manila Folder concerning the Stuff of Poetry" (Wright), **Supp. XV:** 344–345

Sixty Stories (Barthelme), **Supp. IV Part 1:** 41, 42, 44, 47, 49, 50

63: Dream Palace (Purdy), **Supp. VII:** 270–271

"Six Variations" (Levertov), **Supp. III Part 1:** 277–278

"Six-Year-Old Boy" (Olds), **Supp. X:** 206

"Six Years Later" (Brodsky), **Supp. VIII:** 26, 28

"Size and Sheer Will" (Olds), **Supp. X:** 206

Size of Thoughts, The: Essays and Other Lumber (Baker), **Supp. XIII:** 52–53, 55, 56

Sizwe Bansi Is Dead (Fugard), **Supp. VIII:** 330

Sjöwall, Maj, **Supp. XX:** 87

"Skagway" (Haines), **Supp. XII:** 206

"Skaters, The" (Ashbery), **Supp. III Part 1:** 10, 12, 13, 18, 25

"Skaters, The" (Jarrell), **II:** 368–369

Skau, Michael, **Supp. XII:** 129, 130, 132, 134

Skeeters Kirby (Masters), **Supp. I Part 2:** 459, 470, 471

Skeleton Crew (King), **Supp. V:** 144

"Skeleton in Armor, The" (Longfellow), **Retro. Supp. II:** 168

"Skeleton's Cave, The" (Bryant), **Supp. I Part 1:** 157

Skelton, John, **III:** 521

Skepticisms (Aiken), **Supp. XV:** 298, 302

Sketch Book of Geoffrey Crayon, Gent., The (Irving), **II:** 295, 303, 304–308, 309, 311, 491; **Supp. I Part 1:** 155

Sketches of Art (Jameson), **Retro. Supp. II:** 58

Sketches of Eighteenth Century America (Crèvecoeur), **Supp. I Part 1:** 233, 240–241, 250, 251

"Sketches of Female Biography" (Rowson), **Supp. XV:** 245

Sketches of Switzerland (Cooper), **I:** 346

Sketches Old and New (Twain), **IV:** 198

"Sketch for a Job-Application Blank" (Harrison), **Supp. VIII:** 38

"Sketch"(Kenny), **Supp. XXIII:** 155

Sketch of Old England, by a New England Man (Paulding), **I:** 344

Skibell, Joseph, **Supp. XVII:** 48

"Skier and the Mountain, The" (Eberhart), **I:** 528–529

"Skin-Boats: 1830, The" (Bierds), **Supp. XVII:** 28

Skinker, Mary Scott, **Supp. IX:** 20

Skinner, Ewart, **Supp. XXII:** 78

Skinny Island (Auchincloss), **Supp. IV Part 1:** 33

Skinny Legs and All (Robbins), **Supp. X:** 267, 273, **276–279**

Skin of Our Teeth, The (Wilder), **IV:** 357, 358, 369–372; **Supp. IV Part 2:** 586; **Supp. XX: 50**

"Skins" (Wright), **Supp. V:** 340

Skins and Bones: Poems 1979–1987 (Gunn Allen), **Supp. IV Part 1:** 321, 331

"Skipper Ireson's Ride" (Whittier), **Supp. I Part 2:** 691, 693–694

"Skirmish at Sartoris" (Faulkner), **II:** 67

"Skirt" (Halliday), **Supp. XIX:** 90

Skirts and Slacks (Di Piero), **Supp. XIX:** 35, 36, 38, 45–47

Skloot, Floyd, **Supp. XX: 193–209**

Skotheim, Robert Allen, **Supp. XVII:** 104

Skow, John, **Supp. V:** 213; **Supp. XVI:** 174

Skube, Michael, **Supp. XVIII:** 96

"Skunk Cabbage" (Bronk), **Supp. XXI:** 31

"Skunk Cabbage" (Oliver), **Supp. VII:** 235, 236

"Skunk Hour" (Lowell), **II:** 548–550; **Retro. Supp. II:** 188, 189; **Supp. XIV:** 269; **Supp. XX: 203**

Sky, The Stars, The Wilderness, The (Bass), **Supp. XVI:** 19, 20

Sky Changes, The (Sorrentino), **Supp. XXI:** 228, 230, 231

"Sky Dance" (Leopold), **Supp. XIV:** 186

"Sky Line" (Taylor), **Supp. V:** 316

"Sky Line, The" (Mumford), **Supp. II Part 2:** 475

"Skyscraper" (Sandburg), **III:** 581–582

Sky's the Limit, The: A Defense of the Earth (Nichols), **Supp. XIII:** 268

"Sky Valley Rider" (Wright), **Supp. V:** 335, 340

Sky-Walk; or the Man Unknown to Himself (Brown), **Supp. I Part 1:** 127–128

"Slang in America" (Whitman), **IV:** 348

Slappy Hooper, the Wonderful Sign Painter (Bontemps and Conroy), **Supp. XXII:** 5, 11

Slapstick (Vonnegut), **Supp. II Part 2:** 753, 754, 778

Slapstick Tragedy (T. Williams), **IV:** 382, 393

Slate, Lane, **Supp. IX:** 251, 253

Slattery, Mary Grace. *See* Miller, Mrs. Arthur (Mary Grace Slattery)

"Slaughterer, The" (Singer), **IV:** 19

Slaughterhouse-Five (Vonnegut), **Supp. II Part 2:** 755, 758–759, 760, 770, 772–776; **Supp. V:** 41, 244; **Supp. XIX:** 235

Slaughter Rule, The (film; Alex and Andrew Smith), **Supp. XIX:** 174

Slave, The (Baraka), **Supp. II Part 1:** 42, 44, 56

Slave, The: A Novel (Singer), **IV:** 13; **Retro. Supp. II: 305–307**

"Slave Canal" (Ray), **Supp. XVIII:** 193

"Slave Coffle" (Angelou), **Supp. IV Part 1:** 16

"Slave of the Sky" (P. N. Warren), **Supp. XX: 261**

"Slave on the Block" (Hughes), **Supp. I Part 1:** 329

Slave Power, The: The Free North and Southern Domination, 1780–1860 (Richards), **Supp. XIV:** 48

"Slave Quarters" (Dickey), **Supp. IV Part 1:** 181

"Slave's Dream, The" (Longfellow), **Supp. I Part 2:** 409

Slave Ship: A Historical Pageant (Baraka), **Supp. II Part 1:** 47–49, 53, 56–57

"Slave-Ships, The" (Whittier), **Supp. I Part 2:** 687–688

Slaves in Algiers; or, A Struggle for Freedom (Rowson), **Supp. XV: 236–237**

"Slave Trade, The: View from the Middle Passage" (Major), **Supp. XXII:** 182

Slavs! Thinking about the Longstanding Problems of Virtue and Happiness (Kushner), **Supp. IX: 146**

Sledge, Eugene, **Supp. V:** 250

Sleek for the Long Flight (Matthews), **Supp. IX:** 154, 155, **157–158**

Sleep (Dixon), **Supp. XII:** 154

"Sleep, The" (Strand), **Supp. IV Part 2:** 627

Sleeper (film; Allen), **Supp. XV:** 5

"Sleeper, The" (Poe), **III:** 411

"Sleeper 1, The" (Hay), **Supp. XIV:** 132–133

"Sleeper 2, The" (Hay), **Supp. XIV:** 132–133

"Sleepers, The" (Whitman), **IV:** 336

"Sleepers in Jaipur" (Kenyon), **Supp. VII:** 172

Sleepers in Moon-Crowned Valleys (Purdy), **Supp. VII:** 274, 275

Sleepers Joining Hands (R. Bly), **Supp. XXI:** 85

"Sleepers Joining Hands" (R. Bly), **Supp. IV Part 1:** 63, 73

Sleeping Beauty (Macdonald), **Supp. IV Part 2:** 474, 475

Sleeping Beauty, The (Carruth), **Supp. XVI:** 53, 57–58

"Sleeping Beauty Syndrome, The: The New Agony of Single Men" (Wasserstein), **Supp. XV:** 328

"Sleeping Fury, The" (Bogan), **Supp. III Part 1:** 58

Sleeping Fury, The: Poems (Bogan), **Supp. III Part 1:** 55–58

Sleeping Gypsy and Other Poems, The (Garrett), **Supp. VII:** 96–98

Sleeping in the Forest (Oliver), **Supp. VII:** 233

"Sleeping in the Forest" (Oliver), **Supp. VII:** 233–234

Sleeping in the Woods (Wagoner), **Supp. IX: 328**

Sleeping on Fists (Ríos), **Supp. IV Part 2:** 540

Sleeping on the Wing: An Anthology of Modern Poetry (Koch and Farrell, eds.), **Supp. XV:** 187–188

"Sleeping on the Wing"(O'Hara), **Supp. XXIII:** 214

"Sleeping Standing Up" (Bishop), **Supp. I Part 1:** 85, 89, 93

"Sleeping with Animals" (Kumin), **Supp. IV Part 2:** 454

Sleeping with One Eye Open (Strand), **Supp. IV Part 2:** 621–624, 623, 628

Sleep in Thunder (Lacy), **Supp. XV:** 206

"Sleepless, The" (L.-Y. Lee), **Supp. XV:** 224

"Sleepless at Crown Point" (Wilbur), **Supp. III Part 2:** 561

Sleepless Nights (Hardwick), **Supp. III Part 1:** 193, 208–211

"Sleepless Nights" (Nelson), **Supp. XVIII:** 174

"Sleep-Walkers, The" (Gibran), **Supp. XX:** 118

Sleepy Lagoon Mystery, The (Endore), **Supp. XVII:** 60

"Sleepy People" (Lethem), **Supp. XVIII:** 140

Sleigh, Tom, **Supp. XIX:** 38, 40

Sleight, Ken, **Supp. XIII:** 12

Slick, Sam (pseudonym). *See* Haliburton, Thomas Chandler

"Slick Gonna Learn" (Ellison), **Retro. Supp. II:** 116; **Supp. II Part 1:** 237–238

"Slight Rebellion off Madison" (Salinger), **III:** 553

"Slight Sound at Evening, A" (White), **Supp. I Part 2:** 672

"Slim Graves Show, The" (Keillor), **Supp. XVI:** 172

"Slim Greer" series (Hayden), **Supp. II Part 1:** 369

"Slim in Hell" (Hayden), **Supp. II Part 1:** 369

"Slim Man Canyon" (Silko), **Supp. IV Part 2:** 560

"Slip, Shift, and Speed Up: The Influence of Robinson Jeffers's Narrative Syntax" (Jarman), **Supp. XVII:** 111, 112

"Slippery Fingers" (Hammett), **Supp. IV Part 1:** 343

Slipping-Down Life, A (Tyler), **Supp. IV Part 2:** 660–661

Sloan, Jacob, **IV:** 3, 6

Sloan, John, **I:** 254; **IV:** 411; **Retro. Supp. II:** 103; **Supp. XXII:** 277

Sloane, John, **Supp. XV:** 295

"Slob" (Farrell), **II:** 25, 28, 31

Slocum, Joshua, **Supp. I Part 2:** 497

Slonim, Véra. *See* Nabokov, Véra

Slopen, Beverly, **Supp. XX:** 59

Slouching towards Bethlehem (Didion), **Supp. IV Part 1:** 196, 197, 200–201, 202, 206, 210

Slovic, Scott, **Supp. XVI:** 277

"Slow Child with a Book of Birds" (Levis), **Supp. XI:** 268

"Slow Down for Poetry" (Strand), **Supp. IV Part 2:** 620

Slow Music (Taggard), **Supp. XXII:** 284

"Slow Pacific Swell, The" (Winters), **Supp. II Part 2:** 790, 793, 795, 796, 799

Slow Parade (Kees), **Supp. XV:** 137

Slow Train Coming (album, Dylan), **Supp. XVIII:** 28

Slow Transparency (Hadas), **Supp. XXIII:** 113–114

"Slum Church" (Espaillat), **Supp. XXI:** 110–111

"Slumgullions" (Olsen), **Supp. IV Part 1:** 54

Slumgullion Stew: An Edward Abbey Reader (Abbey), **Supp. XIII:** 4

Slung, Michelle, **Supp. XX:** 87

"S & M" (Komunyakaa), **Supp. XIII:** 114

"Small" (C. Frost), **Supp. XV:** 102

Small, Albion, **Supp. I Part 1:** 5

"Small, Good Thing, A" (Carver), **Supp. III Part 1:** 145, 147

Small, Miriam Rossiter, **Supp. I Part 1:** 319

Small Boy and Others, A (James), **II:** 337, 547; **Retro. Supp. I:** 235

"Small but Urgent Request to the Unknowable" (Karr), **Supp. XI:** 243

Small Ceremonies (Shields), **Supp. VII:** 312–315, 320

Small Craft Warnings (T. Williams), **IV:** 382, 383, 384, 385, 386, 387, 392, 393, 396, 398

"Small Degrees" (Brockmeier), **Supp. XXII:** 52, 59

"Small Fry" (Peacock), **Supp. XIX:** 206

Small Place, A (Kincaid), **Supp. VII:** 186–187, 188, 191

"Small Rain, The" (Pynchon), **Supp. II Part 2:** 620

Small Room, The (Sarton), **Supp. VIII:** 252, 255–256

Smalls, Bob, **II:** 128

"Small Song for Andrew" (Weigl), **Supp. XIX:** 280

Small Time Crooks (film; Allen), **Supp. XV:** 11

Small Town, A (Hearon), **Supp. VIII:** 65–66

"Small Vases from Hebron, The" (Nye), **Supp. XIII:** 283

"Small Vision, The" (Goldbarth), **Supp. XII:** 180

"Small Voice from the Wings" (Everwine), **Supp. XV:** 76

"Small Wire" (Sexton), **Supp. II Part 2:** 696

Small Worlds (A. Hoffman), **Supp. XVII:** 44

Smardz, Zofia, **Supp. XVI:** 155

Smart, Christopher, **III:** 534; **Supp. I Part 2:** 539; **Supp. IV Part 2:** 626

Smart, Joyce H., **Supp. XI:** 169

"Smart Cookie, A" (Cisneros), **Supp. VII:** 64

"Smash"(Thompson), **Supp. XXIII:** 301, 302

"Smashup" (Thurber), **Supp. I Part 2:** 616

Smedly, Agnes, **Supp. XIII:** 295

"Smell of a God, The" (Peacock), **Supp. XIX:** 199

"Smelt Fishing" (Hayden), **Supp. II Part 1:** 367

"Smile of the Bathers, The" (Kees), **Supp. XV:** 145

"Smile on the Face of a Kouros, The" (Bronk), **Supp. XXI:** 31

"Smiles" (Dunn), **Supp. XI:** 151

Smiles, Samuel, **Supp. X:** 167

Smiley, Jane, **Supp. VI:** 291–309; **Supp. XII:** 73, 297; **Supp. XIII:** 127; **Supp. XIX:** 54

Smith, Adam, **II:** 9; **Supp. I Part 2:** 633, 634, 639; **Supp. XVII:** 235

Smith, Annick, **Supp. XIV:** 223

Smith, Barbara, **Supp. XXIII:** 194

Smith, Benjamin, **IV:** 148

Smith, Bernard, **I:** 260

Smith, Bessie, **Retro. Supp. I:** 343; **Supp. VIII:** 330; **Supp. XIX:** 147

Smith, Betty, **Supp. XXIII:** 257–271

Smith, Charlie, **Supp. X:** 177

Smith, Dale, **Supp. XV:** 136, 138, 139

Smith, Dave, **Supp. V:** 333; **Supp. XI:** 152; **Supp. XII:** 178, 198; **Supp. XIX:** 277, 282

Smith, David, **Supp. XIII:** 246, 247

Smith, David Nichol, **Supp. XIV:** 2

Smith, Dinitia, **Supp. VIII:** 74, 82, 83; **Supp. XVIII:** 162

Smith, Elihu Hubbard, **Supp. I Part 1:** 126, 127, 130

Smith, Ernest J., **Supp. XXIII:** 111, 113, 117

Smith, George Adam, **III:** 199

Smith, Hannah Whitall, **Supp. XIV:** 333, 334, 338

Smith, Harrison, **II:** 61

Smith, Henry Nash, **IV:** 210; **Supp. I Part 1:** 233

Smith, Herbert F., **Supp. I Part 2:** 423

Smith, Iain Crichton, **Supp. XVIII:** 196

Smith, James, **II:** 111

Smith, Jedediah Strong, **Supp. IV Part 2:** 602

Smith, Jerome, **Supp. IV Part 1:** 369

Smith, Joe, **Supp. IV Part 2:** 584

Smith, John, **I:** 4, 131; **II:** 296

Smith, John Allyn, **I:** 168

Smith, Johnston (pseudonym). *See* Crane, Stephen

Smith, Katherine Capshaw, **Supp. XXII:** 10, 13–14

Smith, Kellogg, **Supp. I Part 2:** 660

Smith, Lamar, **II:** 585

Smith, Mrs. Lamar (Marguerite Walters), **II:** 585, 587

Smith, Lane, **Supp. XIX:** 231

Smith, Larry David, **Supp. XVIII:** 22

Smith, Lee, **Supp. XII:** 311; **Supp. XVIII:** 195; **Supp. XXII:** 206, 213

Smith, Lillian, **Supp. XXII:** 67

Smith, Logan Pearsall, **Supp. XIV:** 333–351

Smith, Lula Carson. *See* McCullers, Carson

Smith, Mark, **Supp. XVIII:** 155

Smith, Martha Nell, **Retro. Supp. I:** 33, 43, 46, 47

Smith, Mary Rozet, **Supp. I Part 1:** 5, 22

Smith, Oliver, **II:** 586

Smith, Patricia Clark, **Supp. IV Part 1:** 397, 398, 402, 406, 408, 410; **Supp. IV Part 2:** 509; **Supp. XII:** 218

Smith, Patrick, **Supp. VIII:** 40, 41

Smith, Patti, **Supp. XII:** 136; **Supp. XIV:** 151

Smith, Porter, **III:** 572

Smith, Red, **II:** 417, 424

Smith, Robert McClure, **Supp. XV:** 270

Smith, Robert Pearsall, **Supp. XIV:** 333

Smith, Sarah A., **Supp. XVIII:** 99

Smith, Seba, **Supp. I Part 2:** 411

Smith, Sidonie, **Supp. IV Part 1:** 11; **Supp. XXII:** 70

Smith, Stevie, **Supp. V:** 84

Smith, Sydney, **II:** 295; **Supp. XIV:** 112

Smith, Thorne, **Supp. IX:** 194

Smith, Valerie, **Supp. XXII:** 146

Smith, Wendy, **Supp. XII:** 330, 335; **Supp. XVIII:** 89, 92

Smith, Wilford Bascom "Pitchfork", **Supp. XIII:** 168

Smith, William, **II:** 114

Smith, William Gardner, **Supp. XVI:** 142–143

Smith, William Jay, **Supp. XIII:** 331–350

"Smoke" (Di Piero), **Supp. XIX:** 38

Smoke (film), **Supp. XII:** 21

Smoke and Steel (Sandburg), **III:** 585–587, 592

"Smokehouse" (Offutt), **Supp. XIX:** 166, 167

"Smokers" (Wolff), **Supp. VII:** 340–341

Smokey Bites the Dust (film, C. Griffith), **Supp. XVII:** 9

"Smoking My Prayers" (Ortiz), **Supp. IV Part 2:** 503

"Smoking Room, The" (Jackson), **Supp. IX:** 116

"Smoky Gold" (Leopold), **Supp. XIV:** 186

Smolan, Sandy, **Supp. XVI:** 36

Smollett, Tobias G., **I:** 134, 339, 343; **II:** 304–305; **III:** 61; **Supp. XVIII:** 7

Smooding, Robert, **Supp. XXIII:** 294

Smuggler's Bible, A (McElroy), **Supp. IV Part 1:** 285

Smuggler's Handbook, The (Goldbarth), **Supp. XII:** 181, 183

Smugglers of Lost Soul's Rock, The (Gardner), **Supp. VI: 70**

Smyth, Albert Henry, **II:** 123

Smyth, Jacqui, **Supp. XXI:** 215

"Snack Firm Maps New Chip Push" (Keillor), **Supp. XVI:** 168, 169

"Snail, The" (Hay), **Supp. XIV:** 124

"Snake, The" (Berry), **Supp. X:** 31

"Snake, The" (Crane), **I:** 420

"Snakecharmer" (Plath), **Supp. I Part 2:** 538

"Snakes, Mongooses" (Moore), **III:** 207

"Snakeskin" (Kooser), **Supp. XIX:** 123

"Snakes of September, The" (Kunitz), **Supp. III Part 1:** 258

"Snapshot of 15th S.W., A" (Hugo), **Supp. VI:** 141

"Snapshot Rediscovered, A" (X. J. Kennedy), **Supp. XV:** 170

"Snapshots in an Album" (Espaillat), **Supp. XXI:** 111

"Snapshots of a Daughter-in-Law" (Rich), **Supp. I Part 2:** 553–554

Snapshots of a Daughter-in-Law: Poems, 1954–1962 (Rich), **Supp. I Part 2:** 550–551, 553–554; **Supp. XII:** 255

Snaring the Flightless Birds (Bierds), **Supp. XVII:** 26

Sneetches and Other Stories, The (Geisel), **Supp. XVI:** 109

"Sneeze, The" (Chekhov), **Supp. IV Part 2:** 585

Snell, Ebenezer, **Supp. I Part 1:** 151

Snell, Thomas, **Supp. I Part 1:** 153

"Snob, The" (Boulton), **Supp. XXII:** 23

"Snob, The" (Shapiro), **Supp. II Part 2:** 705

Snobbery: The America Version (Epstein), **Supp. XIV:** 102, 114–115

Snodgrass, Kathleen, **Supp. XVI:** 42

Snodgrass, W. D., **I:** 400; **Retro. Supp. II:** 179; **Supp. III Part 2:** 541; **Supp. V:** 337; **Supp. VI: 311–328**; **Supp. XI:** 141, 315; **Supp. XIII:** 312; **Supp. XV:** 92, 153; **Supp. XVII:** 239

"Snow" (C. Baxter), **Supp. XVII:** 19

"Snow" (Frost), **Retro. Supp. I:** 133

"Snow" (Haines), **Supp. XII:** 212

"Snow" (Sexton), **Supp. II Part 2:** 696

"Snow" (W. V. Davis), **Supp. XXI:** 89, 90, 93

Snow, C. P., **Supp. I Part 2:** 536

Snow, Hank, **Supp. V:** 335

Snow Ball, The (Gurney), **Supp. V:** 99

"Snow-Bound" (Whittier), **Supp. I Part 2:** 700–703

"Snow Bound at Eagle's" (Harte), **Supp. II Part 1:** 356

"Snowflakes" (Longfellow), **II:** 498

"Snow Goose, The" (Gallico), **Supp. XVI:** 238

Snow-Image and Other Twice Told Tales, The (Hawthorne), **II:** 237; **Retro. Supp. I:** 160

"Snowing in Greenwich Village" (Updike), **IV:** 226; **Retro. Supp. I:** 321

"Snow in New York" (Swenson), **Supp. IV Part 2:** 644

Snow Leopard, The (Matthiessen), **Supp. V:** 199, 207–211

"Snow Man, The" (Stevens), **IV:** 82–83; **Retro. Supp. I:** 299, 300, 302, 306, 307, 312; **Supp. XXI:** 60

"Snowmass Cycle, The" (Dunn), **Supp. XI:** 152

Snow: Meditations of a Cautious Man in Winter (Banks), **Supp. V:** 6

Snow Poems, The (Ammons), **Supp. VII:** 32–34

Snowshoe Trek to Otter River (Budbill), **Supp. XIX:** 11

Snow's Music, The (Skloot), **Supp. XX: 196, 204–205**

"Snows of Kilimanjaro, The" (Hemingway), **II:** 78, 257, 263, 264; **Retro. Supp. I:** 98, 182; **Supp. XII:** 249

"Snows of Studiofiftyfour, The" (Plimpton), **Supp. XVI:** 245

"Snow Songs" (Snodgrass), **Supp. VI:** 324

"Snowstorm, The" (Oates), **Supp. II Part 2:** 523

"Snowstorm as It Affects the American Farmer, A" (Crèvecoeur), **Supp. I Part 1:** 251

Snow White (Barthelme), **Supp. IV Part 1:** 40, 47, 48–49, 50, 52; **Supp. V:** 39

"Snowy Egret" (Weigl), **Supp. XIX:** 280–281

"Snowy Mountain Song, A" (Ortiz), **Supp. IV Part 2:** 506

Snyder, Gary, **Supp. III Part 1:** 350; **Supp. IV Part 2:** 502; **Supp. V:** 168–169; **Supp. VIII:** 39, **289–307**; **Supp. XVI:** 283; **Supp. XXII:** 276

Snyder, Mike, **Supp. XIV:** 36

"So-and-So Reclining on Her Couch" (Stevens), **IV:** 90

"Soapland" (Thurber), **Supp. I Part 2:** 619

Soares, Lota de Macedo, **Retro. Supp. II:** 44; **Supp. I Part 1:** 89, 94

"Sobbin' Women, The" (Benét), **Supp. XI:** 47

Sobin, Gustaf, **Supp. XVI: 281–298**

Sochen, June, **Supp. XXI:** 1

Social Ethics (Gilman), **Supp. XI:** 207

"Social Function of the Story Teller, The" (lecture, Murray), **Supp. XIX:** 153

"Socialism and the Negro" (McKay), **Supp. X:** 135

"Socialism of the Skin, A (Liberation, Honey!)" (Kushner), **Supp. IX:** 135

Social Thought in America: The Revolt against Formalism (White), **Supp. I Part 2:** 648, 650

"Society, Morality, and the Novel" (Ellison), **Retro. Supp. II:** 118, 123–124

"Sociological Habit Patterns in Linguistic Transmogrification" (Cowley), **Supp. II Part 1:** 143

"Sociological Poet, A" (Bourne), **I:** 228

Socrates, **I:** 136, 265; **II:** 8–9, 105, 106; **III:** 281, 419, 606; **Supp. I Part 2:** 458; **Supp. XII:** 98

Socrates Fortlow stories (Mosley), **Supp. XIII: 242–243**

So Forth (Brodsky), **Supp. VIII:** 32–33

"So Forth" (Brodsky), **Supp. VIII:** 33

"Soft Flame" (Skloot), **Supp. XX: 203**

Soft Machine, The (Burroughs), **Supp. III Part 1:** 93, 103, 104

"Soft Mask" (Karr), **Supp. XI:** 243

Soft Side, The (James), **II:** 335; **Retro. Supp. I:** 229

"Soft Spring Night in Shillington, A" (Updike), **Retro. Supp. I:** 318, 319

"Soft Wood" (Lowell), **II:** 550–551

"So Help Me" (Algren), **Supp. IX:** 2

Soil and Survival: Land Stewardship and the Future of American Agriculture (C. Bly, J. Paddock and N. Paddock), **Supp. XVI:** 36–37

"Soirée in Hollywood" (H. Miller), **III:** 186

Sojourner, The (Rawlings), **Supp. X:** 233–234

"Sojourn in a Whale" (Moore), **III:** 211, 213

"Sojourns" (Didion), **Supp. IV Part 1:** 205

Sokolow, Jayme, **Supp. XIX:** 134

Solanus, Jane, **Supp. XVI:** 293

Solar Lottery (Dick), **Supp. XVIII:** 138

Solar Storms (Hogan), **Supp. IV Part 1:** 397, 410, 414–415

"Soldier, The" (Frost), **II:** 155

"Soldier Asleep at the Tomb" (Schnackenberg), **Supp. XV:** 262–263

Soldier Blue (film), **Supp. X:** 124

"Soldier of Fortune" (Wright), **Supp. XV:** 341

"Soldier's Home" (Hemingway), **Retro. Supp. I:** 189

Soldier's Joy (Bell), **Supp. X:** 7, **7–8,** 10, 11; **Supp. XXIII:** 43

Soldiers of the Storm (film), **Supp. XIII:** 163

Soldiers' Pay (Faulkner), **I:** 117; **II:** 56, 68; **Retro. Supp. I:** 80, 81

"Soldier's Testament, The" (Mumford), **Supp. II Part 2:** 473

"Soliloquy: Man Talking to a Mirror" (Komunyakaa), **Supp. XIII:** 116–117

"Solitary Confinement" (X. J. Kennedy), **Supp. XV:** 157

"Solitary Pond, The" (Updike), **Retro. Supp. I:** 323

So Little Time (Marquand), **III:** 55, 59, 65, 67, 69

"Solitude" (Maupassant), **Supp. I Part 1:** 223

Solo Faces (Salter), **Supp. IX: 259–260**

Solomon, Andy, **Supp. X:** 11

Solomon, Carl, **Supp. XIV:** 143, 150

Solomon, Charles, **Supp. VIII:** 82

Solomon, Deborah, **Supp. XXI:** 245

Solomon, Henry, Jr., **Supp. I Part 2:** 490

Solomons, Leon, **IV:** 26

So Long, See You Tomorrow (Maxwell), **Supp. VIII:** 156, 160, 162, **167–169; Supp. XVIII:** 23

"So Long Ago" (Bausch), **Supp. VII:** 41–42

Solotaroff, Robert, **Retro. Supp. II:** 203

Solotaroff, Theodore, **III:** 452–453; **Retro. Supp. II:** 281; **Supp. I Part 2:** 440, 445; **Supp. X:** 79; **Supp. XI:** 340; **Supp. XII:** 291; **Supp. XIX:** 268

Solstice (Di Piero), **Supp. XIX:** 36

"Solstice" (Jeffers), **Supp. II Part 2:** 433, 435

"Solstice, The" (Merwin), **Supp. III Part 1:** 356

"Solus Rex" (Nabokov), **Retro. Supp. I:** 274

"Solutions" (McCarthy), **II:** 578

"Solving the Puzzle" (Dunn), **Supp. XI:** 152

Solzhenitsyn, Alexandr, **Retro. Supp. I:** 278; **Supp. VIII:** 241

"Some Afternoon" (Creeley), **Supp. IV Part 1:** 150–151

Some American People (Caldwell), **I:** 292, 294, 295, 296, 304, 309

"Some Ashes Drifting above Piedra, California" (Levis), **Supp. XI:** 264–265

"Some Aspects of the Grotesque in Southern Fiction" (O'Connor), **Retro. Supp. II:** 223, 224

"Some Birds on a Dun Field" (Bronk), **Supp. XXI:** 27

"Somebody Always Grabs the Purple" (H. Roth), **Supp. IX:** 234

Somebody in Boots (Algren), **Supp. IX:** 3, **5–7,** 12

Somebody's Darling (McMurtry), **Supp. V:** 225

Some Came Running (film), **Supp. XI:** 213

Some Came Running (Jones), **Supp. XI:** 214, 215, 220, **222–223,** 226, 227, 232

Some Can Whistle (McMurtry), **Supp. V:** 229

"Some Children of the Goddess" (Mailer), **Retro. Supp. II:** 204

Someday, Maybe (Stafford), **Supp. XI: 323–325; Supp. XIII:** 281

"Some Dreamers of the Golden Dream" (Didion), **Supp. IV Part 1:** 200

Some Faces in the Crowd (Schulberg), **Supp. XVIII:** 252

"Some Foreign Letters" (Sexton), **Supp. II Part 2:** 674

"Some General Instructions" (Koch), **Supp. XV:** 182

"Some Good News" (Olson), **Supp. II Part 2:** 575, 576, 577

"Some Grass along a Ditch Bank" (Levis), **Supp. XI:** 266

"Some Greek Writings" (Corso), **Supp. XII:** 130

Some Honorable Men: Political Conventions, 1960–1972 (Mailer), **Retro. Supp. II:** 208

Some Imagist Poets (Lowell), **III:** 511, 518, 520; **Supp. I Part 1:** 257, 261

"Some keep the Sabbath going to Church" (Dickinson), **Retro. Supp. I:** 30; **Supp. VIII:** 301

"Some Laughed" (L. Michaels), **Supp. XVI:** 207

"Some Like Indians Endure" (Gunn Allen), **Supp. IV Part 1:** 330

"Some Like Them Cold" (Lardner), **II:** 427–428, 430, 431; **Supp. IX:** 202

"Some Lines from Whitman" (Jarrell), **IV:** 352

"Some Matters Concerning the Occupant" (Keillor), **Supp. XVI:** 167

"Some Musicians Play Chamber Music for Us" (Bronk), **Supp. XXI:** 27–28

"Some Negatives: X. at the Chateau" (Merrill), **Supp. III Part 1:** 322

"Some Neglected Points in the Theory of Socialism" (Veblen), **Supp. I Part 2:** 635

"Some Notes for an Autobiographical Lecture" (Trilling), **Supp. III Part 2:** 493, 497, 500

"Some Notes on French Poetry" (R. Bly), **Supp. IV Part 1:** 61

"Some Notes on Miss L." (West), **IV:** 290–291, 295; **Retro. Supp. II:** 322

"Some Notes on Organic Form" (Levertov), **Supp. III Part 1:** 272, 279

"Some Notes on Teaching; Probably Spoken" (Paley), **Supp. VI:** 225

"Some Notes on the Gazer Within" (Levis), **Supp. XI:** 270

"Some Notes on Violence" (West), **IV:** 304; **Retro. Supp. II:** 322, 323

"Some Observations Now" (Conroy), **Supp. XVI:** 75

Some Observations of a Stranger at Zuni in the Later Part of the Century (Major), **Supp. XXII:** 179–180

"Some Observations of a Stranger at Zuni in the Later Part of the Century" (Major), **Supp. XXII:** 179

Some of the Dharma (Kerouac), **Supp. III Part 1:** 225

"Someone Is Buried" (Salinas), **Supp. XIII:** 324

"Someone Puts a Pineapple Together" (Stevens), **IV:** 90–91

"Someone's Blood" (Dove), **Supp. IV Part 1:** 245

"Someone Talking" (Harjo), **Supp. XII:** 219–220

"Someone Talking to Himself" (Wilbur), **Supp. III Part 2:** 557

"Someone to Watch Over Me" (Stern), **Supp. IX:** 300

Someone to Watch Over Me: Stories (Bausch), **Supp. VII:** 53

Some People, Places, & Things That Will Not Appear in My Next Novel (Cheever), **Supp. I Part 1:** 184–185

"Some Poets' Criticism and the Age" (Yenser), **Supp. XV:** 113–114

Some Problems of Philosophy: A Beginning of an Introduction to Philosophy (James), **II:** 360–361

"Some Questions You Might Ask" (Oliver), **Supp. VII:** 238–239

"Some Remarks on Humor" (White), **Supp. I Part 2:** 672

"Some Remarks on Rhythm" (Roethke), **III:** 548–549

Somers, Fred, **I:** 196

Somerville, Jane, **Supp. IX:** 289, 296–297

"Some Secrets" (Stern), **Supp. IX:** 286, 287, 288, 289, 295

Some Sort of Epic Grandeur (Bruccoli), **Retro. Supp. I:** 115, 359

"Something" (Oliver), **Supp. VII:** 236

Something Happened (Heller), **Supp. IV Part 1:** 383, 386–388, 389, 392

"*Something Happened:* The Imaginary, the Symbolic, and the Discourse of the Family" (Mellard), **Supp. IV Part 1:** 387

Something in Common (Hughes), **Supp. I Part 1:** 329–330

Something Inside: Conversations with Gay Fiction Writers (Gambone), **Supp. XII:** 81

"Something Matters but We Don't " (Bronk), **Supp. XXI:** 32

"Something Might Be Gaining" (Mosher), **Supp. XXII:** 209

"Something New" (Stern), **Supp. IX:** 290

Something Said (Sorrentino), **Supp. XXI:** 226, 227, 229, 235

"Something's Going to Happen" (Zinberg), **Supp. XV:** 196

"Something Spurious from the Mindinao Deep" (Stegner), **Supp. IV Part 2:** 605

"Something to Believe In" (Pitts), **Supp. XXII:** 280

Something to Declare (Alvarez), **Supp. VII:** 1, 2, 11, 17–19

Something to Remember Me By (Bellow), **Retro. Supp. II:** 32

"Something to Remember Me By" (Bellow), **Retro. Supp. II:** 32

Something Wicked This Way Comes (Bradbury), **Supp. IV Part 1:** 101, 110–111

"Something Wild . . ." (T. Williams), **IV:** 381

"Some Thoughts" (McNally), **Supp. XIII:** 207

"Some Thoughts on the Line" (Oliver), **Supp. VII:** 238

"Sometimes, Reading" (Stafford), **Supp. XI:** 314

"Sometimes It Just Happens That Way, That's All" (Hinojosa), **Supp. XIX:** 101

"Sometimes I Wonder" (Hughes), **Supp. I Part 1:** 337

Sometimes Mysteriously (Salinas), **Supp. XIII:** 311, **326–328**

"Sometimes Mysteriously" (Salinas), **Supp. XIII:** 328

Some Trees (Ashbery), **Supp. III Part 1:** 3–7, 12

"Some Trees" (Ashbery), **Supp. III Part 1:** 2

"Some Views on the Reading and Writing of Short Stories" (Welty), **Retro. Supp. I:** 351

"Somewhere" (Nemerov), **III:** 279–280

"Somewhere Else" (Paley), **Supp. VI:** 227

"Somewhere in Africa" (Sexton), **Supp. II Part 2:** 684–685

"Somewhere Is Such a Kingdom" (Ransom), **III:** 492

"Somewhere near Phu Bai: (Komunyakaa), **Supp. XIII:** 123–124

Some Words (Bronk), **Supp. XXI:** 32

"Some Words with a Mummy" (Poe), **III:** 425

"Some Yips and Barks in the Dark" (Snyder), **Supp. VIII:** 291

Sommers, Michael, **Supp. IV Part 2:** 581

Sommers, William, **I:** 387, 388

"Somnambulisma" (Stevens), **Retro. Supp. I:** 310

"So Much Summer" (Dickinson), **Retro. Supp. I:** 26, 44, 45

"So Much the Worse for Boston" (Lindsay), **Supp. I Part 2:** 398

"So Much Water So Close to Home" (Carver), **Supp. III Part 1:** 143, 146

Son, Cathy, **Supp. X:** 292

"Son, The" (Dove), **Supp. IV Part 1:** 245

"Son and Father" (Pickering), **Supp. XXI:** 197

"Sonata" (Schnackenberg), **Supp. XV:** 259

"Sonata for the Invisible" (Harjo), **Supp. XII:** 228

Sonata for Two Pianos (Bowles), **Supp. IV Part 1:** 83

Son at the Front, A (Wharton), **II:** 183; **IV:** 320; **Retro. Supp. I:** 378

Sondheim, Stephen, **Supp. XII:** 260; **Supp. XVI:** 194

Son Excellence Eugène Rougon (Zola), **III:** 322

Son from Sleep, A (Hadas), **Supp. XXIII: 114–115**

Song (B. Kelly), **Supp. XVII:** 123, **127–130**

"Song" (B. Kelly), **Supp. XVII:** 127

"Song" (Bogan), **Supp. III Part 1:** 57

"Song" (Bryant). *See* "Hunter of the West, The"

"Song" (Dunbar), **Supp. II Part 1:** 199

"Song" (Espaillat), **Supp. XXI:** 106–107

"Song" (Ginsberg), **Supp. II Part 1:** 317

"Song" (Kenyon), **Supp. VII:** 169

"Song" (Rich), **Supp. I Part 2:** 560

"Song" (Wylie), **Supp. I Part 2:** 729

"Song, A" (Creeley), **Supp. IV Part 1:** 145

"Song, The" (Gioia), **Supp. XV:** 117

Song and Idea (Eberhart), **I:** 526, 529, 533, 539

"Song: Enlightenment" (X. J. Kennedy), **Supp. XV:** 169

"Song for a Lover Killed in Battle" (J. Schoolcraft), **Supp. XXIII:** 235

Song for My Father, A: A Play in Two Acts (Budbill), **Supp. XIX:** 3, **15–16**

"Song for Myself and the Deer to Return On" (Harjo), **Supp. XII:** 225

"Song for My Sixtieth Year" (Carruth), **Supp. XVI:** 54

"Song for Occupations, A" (Whitman), **Retro. Supp. I:** 394

"Song for Simeon, A" (Eliot), **Retro. Supp. I:** 64

"Song for the Coming of Smallpox" (Wagoner), **Supp. IX:** 329, 330

"Song for the End of Time" (Gioia), **Supp. XV:** 126–127

"Song for the First People" (Wagoner), **Supp. IX:** 328

"Song for the Last Act" (Bogan), **Supp. III Part 1:** 64

"Song for the Middle of the Night, A" (Wright), **Supp. III Part 2:** 594

"Song for the Rainy Season" (Bishop), **Supp. I Part 1:** 93–94, 96

"Song for the Romeos, A" (Stern), **Supp. IX:** 296

"Song for Woody" (song, Dylan), **Supp. XVIII:** 24

"Song from a Courtyard Window" (Gioia), **Supp. XV:** 119

"Song III" (Taggard), **Supp. XXII:** 284

"Song in the Front Yard, A" (Brooks), **Supp. XVIII:** 181

"Songline of Dawn" (Harjo), **Supp. XII:** 229

"Song: Love in Whose Rich Honor" (Rukeyser), **Supp. VI:** 285

"Song: Now That She Is Here" (Carruth), **Supp. XVI:** 59

"Song of Advent, A" (Winters), **Supp. II Part 2:** 789

"Song of a Man Who Rushed at the Enemy" (Wagoner), **Supp. IX:** 329, 330

"Song of Courage, A" (Masters), **Supp. I Part 2:** 458

Song of God, The: Bhagavad-Gita (Isherwood and Prabhavananda, trans.), **Supp. XIV:** 156, 157, 164

Song of Hiawatha, The (Longfellow), **II:** 501, 503–504; **Retro. Supp. II:** 155, **159–161,** 162, 163; **Supp. XXIII:** 223, 234–235

"Song of Innocence, A" (Ellison), **Retro. Supp. II:** 126; **Supp. II Part 1:** 248

"Song of My Fiftieth Birthday, The" (Lindsay), **Supp. I Part 2:** 399

"Song of Myself" (Whitman), **II:** 544; **III:** 572, 584, 595; **IV:** 333, 334, 337–339, 340, 341, 342, 344, 348, 349, 351, 405; **Retro. Supp. I:** 388, 389, 395–399, 400; **Supp. V:** 122; **Supp. IX:** 131, 136, 143, 328, 331; **Supp. XIV:** 139; **Supp. XVIII:** 194, 304; **Supp. XXII:** 81

Song of Napalm (Weigl), **Supp. XIX:** 278–282

"Song of Napalm" (Weigl), **Supp. XIX:** 276–277

Song of Russia (film), **Supp. I Part 1:** 281, 294; **Supp. XVII:** 60–61

"Song of Self" (Huncke), **Supp. XIV:** 138–139, 145

Song of Solomon (biblical book), **III:** 118; **IV:** 150

Song of Solomon (Morrison), **Supp. III Part 1:** 364, 368, 369, 372, 379; **Supp. XVIII:** 55

Song of Songs (biblical book), **II:** 538; **IV:** 153–154; **Supp. XV:** 221

"Song of the Answerer" (Whitman), **Retro. Supp. I:** 393, 399

Song of the Cardinal, The (Stratton-Porter), **Supp. XX: 217, 218, 219**

"Song of the Chattahoochee, The" (Lanier), **Supp. I Part 1:** 365, 368

"Song of the Degrees, A" (Pound), **III:** 466

"Song of the Dryads" (Taggard), **Supp. XXII:** 272

"Song of the Exposition" (Whitman), **IV:** 332

"Song of the Gavilan" (Leopold), **Supp. XIV:** 189

"Song of the Gourd" (Wright), **Supp. XV:** 348–349

"Song of the Greek Amazon" (Bryant), **Supp. I Part 1:** 168

Song of the Lark, The (Cather), **I:** 312, 319–321, 323; **Retro. Supp. I:** 1, 3, 7, **9–11,** 13, 19, 20

"Song of the Okogis, or Frog in Spring"(J. Schoolcraft), **Supp. XXIII:** 232, 233, 235

"Song of the Open Road" (McGrath), **Supp. X:** 127

"Song of the Open Road" (Whitman), **IV:** 340–341; **Retro. Supp. I:** 400; **Supp. IX:** 265

"Song of the Redwood Tree" (Whitman), **IV:** 348

"Song of the Scullery" (McCarriston), **Supp. XIV:** 272

"Song of the Sky Loom" (traditional Tewa poem), **Supp. IV Part 1:** 325

"Song of the Son" (Toomer), **Supp. III Part 2:** 482–483; **Supp. IX:** 313

"Song of the Sower, The" (Bryant), **Supp. I Part 1:** 169

"Song of the Stars" (Bryant), **Supp. I Part 1:** 163

"Song of the Swamp-Robin, The" (Frederic), **II:** 138

"Song of the Vermonters, The" (Whittier), **Supp. I Part 2:** 692

"Song of Three Smiles" (Merwin), **Supp. III Part 1:** 344

"Song of Wandering Aengus, The" (Yeats), **IV:** 271; **Retro. Supp. I:** 342, 350

"Song of Welcome" (Brodsky), **Supp. VIII:** 32

"Song on Captain Barney's Victory" (Freneau), **Supp. II Part 1:** 261

"Song/Poetry and Language-Expression and Perception" (Ortiz), **Supp. IV Part 2:** 500, 508

"Song: 'Rough Winds Do Shake the Darling Buds of May' " (Simpson), **Supp. IX:** 268

Songs (Boyce), **Supp. XXI:** 9

Songs and Satires (Masters), **Supp. I Part 2:** 465–466

Songs and Sonnets (L. P. Smith), **Supp. XIV:** 341

Songs and Sonnets (Masters), **Supp. I Part 2:** 455, 459, 461, 466

"Songs for a Colored Singer" (Bishop), **Supp. I Part 1:** 80, 85

Songs for a Summer's Day (A Sonnet Cycle) (MacLeish), **III:** 3

Songs for Eve (MacLeish), **III:** 3, 19

"Songs for Eve" (MacLeish), **III:** 19

"Songs for My Father" (Komunyakaa), **Supp. XIII:** 128

Songs for the Unborn Second Baby (Notley), **Supp. XXII:** 228

"Songs for Two Seasons" (C. Frost), **Supp. XV:** 95–96

Songs from This Earth on Turtle's Back: Contemporary American Indian Poetry (Bruchac, ed.), **Supp. IV Part 1:** 320, 328

"Songs of a Housewife" (Rawlings), **Supp. X:** 221–222

"Songs of Billy Bathgate, The" (Doctorow), **Supp. IV Part 1:** 230

Songs of Innocence (Blake), **Supp. I Part 2:** 708

Songs of Jamaica (McKay), **Supp. X:** 131, 133

"Songs of Maximus, The" (Olson), **Supp. II Part 2:** 567

"Songs of Parting" (Whitman), **IV:** 348

Songs of the North: A Sigurd Olson Reader (Mosher, ed.), **Supp. XXII:** 218

Songs of the Sierras (J. Miller), **I:** 459

Songs of Three Centuries (Whittier and Larcom, eds.), **Supp. XIII:** 142

"Song to David" (Smart), **III:** 534

"Song to No Music, A" (Brodsky), **Supp. VIII:** 26

"Song V" (Taggard), **Supp. XXII:** 284

Soniat, Katherine, **Supp. XXI:** 245

Sonneschein, Rosa, **Retro. Supp. II:** 65

"Sonnet" (Rukeyser), **Supp. VI:** 284

"Sonnet Crown for Two Voices" (Bierds), **Supp. XVII:** 35

"Sonnet"(J. Schoolcraft), **Supp. XXIII:** 229

"Sonnets" (Carruth), **Supp. XVI:** 56

Sonnets, The (Berrigan), **Supp. XXII:** 224

"Sonnets at Christmas" (Tate), **IV:** 135

Sonnets to Orpheus (Rilke), **Supp. XV:** 222

"Sonnet-To Zante" (Poe), **III:** 421

"Sonny's Blues" (Baldwin), **Retro. Supp. II:** 7, 8, 10, 14; **Supp. I Part 1:** 58–59, 63, 67; **Supp. XI:** 288

Son of Laughter, The: A Novel (Buechner), **Supp. XII:** 54

Son of Perdition, The (Cozzens), **I:** 359–360, 377, 378, 379

Son of the Circus, A (Irving), **Supp. VI:** 165, 166, **176–179**

"Son of the Gods, A" (Bierce), **I:** 202

Son of the Morning (Oates), **Supp. II Part 2:** 518, 519, 520–522

Son of the Morning Star: Custer and the Little Bighorn (Connell), **Supp. XIV:** 80, 82, 97

"Son of the Romanovs, A" (Simpson), **Supp. IX:** 273–274

Son of the Wolf, The (London), **II:** 465, 469

"Son of the Wolfman" (Chabon), **Supp. XI:** 76

"Sonrisas" (Mora), **Supp. XIII:** 216, 219

Sons (Buck), **Supp. II Part 1:** 117–118

Sons and Lovers (Lawrence), **III:** 27

Sontag, Kate, **Supp. XV:** 104

Sontag, Susan, **IV:** 13, 14; **Retro. Supp. II:** 279; **Supp. I Part 2:** 423; **Supp. III Part 2:** 451–473; **Supp. VIII:** 75; **Supp. XIV:** 14, 15, 95–96, 167; **Supp. XVI:** 201, 204, 206; **Supp. XX: 205;** **Supp. XXI:** 243

"Soonest Mended" (Ashbery), **Supp. III Part 1:** 1, 13

"Sootfall and Fallout" (White), **Supp. I Part 2:** 671

Sophocles, **I:** 274; **II:** 291, 385, 577; **III:** 145, 151, 152, 153, 159, 398, 476, 478, 609, 613; **IV:** 291, 363, 368, 370;

Supp. I Part 1: 153, 284; **Supp. I Part 2:** 491; **Supp. V:** 97; **Supp. VIII:** 332; **Supp. XV:** 265, 266

"Sophronsiba" (Bourne), **I:** 221

Sorayam, Aram, **Supp. XXII:** 25

Sorby, Angela, **Supp. XXIII:** 132

Sorcerer's Apprentice, The: Tales and Conjurations (Johnson), **Supp. VI: 192–193,** 194

"Sorcerer's Eye, The" (Nemerov), **III:** 283

Sordello (Browning), **III:** 467, 469, 470

"Sordid? Good God!" (Williams), **Retro. Supp. II:** 334

So Red the Rose (Young), **Supp. XXII:** 190, 193

"Sorghum" (Mason), **Supp. VIII:** 146

Sorokin, Pitirim, **Supp. I Part 2:** 679

Sorrentino, Christopher, **Supp. XVIII:** 148

Sorrentino, Gilbert, **Retro. Supp. I:** 426; **Supp. IV Part 1:** 286; **Supp. XII:** 139; **Supp. XXI: 225–241;** **Supp. XXII:** 261

Sorrento (Notley), **Supp. XXII:** 231

"Sorrow" (Komunyakaa), **Supp. XIII:** 119

Sorrow Dance, The (Levertov), **Supp. III Part 1:** 279–280, 283

"Sorrowful Guest, A" (Jewett), **Retro. Supp. II:** 137

Sorrows of Fat City, The: A Selection of Literary Essays and Reviews (Garrett), **Supp. VII:** 111

Sorrows of Young Werther, The (Goethe), **Supp. XI:** 169; **Supp. XX: 234, 236**

Sorrows of Young Werther, The (Goethe; Bogan and Mayer, trans.), **Supp. III Part 1:** 63

"Sorry Fugu" (Boyle), **Supp. XX: 19**

"Sorting Facts; or, Nineteen Ways of Looking at Marker" (Howe), **Supp. IV Part 2:** 434, 436

"Sort of Song, A" (W. C. Williams), **Supp. XVII:** 243

"S O S" (Baraka), **Supp. II Part 1:** 50

"So Sassafras" (Olson), **Supp. II Part 2:** 574

"So There" (Creeley), **Supp. IV Part 1:** 157

"So This Is Nebraska" (Kooser), **Supp. XIX:** 120

Sotirov, Vasil, **Supp. IX:** 152

Soto, Gary, **Supp. IV Part 2:** 545; **Supp. V:** 180; **Supp. XI:** 270; **Supp. XIII:** 313, 315, 316, 320, 323; **Supp. XV:** 73

"Soto Thinking of the Ocean" (Salinas), **Supp. XIII:** 321

"Sotto Voce" (Kunitz), **Supp. III Part 1:** 265

Sot-Weed Factor, The (Barth), **I:** 122, 123, 125, 129, 130, 131–134, 135; **Supp. XXII:** 259

Soul, The (Brooks), **I:** 244

Soul and Body of John Brown, The (Rukeyser), **Supp. VI:** 273

Soul Clap Hands and Sing (Marshall), **Supp. XI:** 276, 278, **280–282**

Soul Expeditions (Singer). *See Shosha* (Singer)

Soul Gone Home (Hughes), **Retro. Supp. I:** 203; **Supp. I Part 1:** 328

"Soul inside the Sentence, The" (Gass), **Supp. VI:** 88

Soul Is Here for Its Own Joy, The (Bly, ed.), **Supp. IV Part 1:** 74

Soul of Man under Socialism, The (Wilde), **Supp. IX:** 134–135

"Soul of Spain, The [In the manner of Gertrude Stein]" (Hemingway), **Supp. XX:** 74

Soul of the Far East, The (Lowell), **II:** 513

"Soul on Bench" (Halliday), **Supp. XIX:** 91

Soul on Ice (Cleaver), **Retro. Supp. II:** 12, 13

"Souls Belated" (Wharton), **Retro. Supp. I:** 364

"Soul selects her own Society, The" (Dickinson), **Retro. Supp. I:** 37

Souls of Black Folk, The (Du Bois), **Supp. II Part 1:** 33, 40, 160, 168–170, 176, 183; **Supp. IV Part 1:** 164; **Supp. IX:** 305, 306; **Supp. X:** 133; **Supp. XIII:** 185, 238, 243

Souls of Black Folk. The (Du Bois), **Supp. XX:** 102

"Sound, The" (Olds), **Supp. X:** 214

Sound and Beauty (Hwang), **Supp. XXI:** 146

"Sound and Fury" (O. Henry), **Supp. II Part 1:** 402

Sound and the Fury, The (Faulkner), **I:** 480; **II:** 55, 57, 58–60, 73; **III:** 237; **IV:** 100, 101, 104; **Retro. Supp. I:** 73, 75, 77, 82, **83–84,** 86, 88, 89, 90, 91, 92; **Supp. VIII:** 215; **Supp. IX:** 103; **Supp. X:** 44; **Supp. XII:** 33; **Supp. XIV:** 12; **Supp. XVII:** 138; **Supp. XVIII:** 84

"Sound Bites" (Alvarez), **Supp. VII:** 11

Sound I Listened For, The (Francis), **Supp. IX: 78–79,** 87

"Soundless Trumpet, The" (Antin), **Supp. XX:** 12

"Sound Mind, Sound Body" (Lowell), **II:** 554

Sound of a Voice, The (Hwang), **Supp. XXI:** 146

"Sound of Distant Thunder, A" (Elkin), **Supp. VI: 42–43,** 44

"Sound of Light, The" (Merwin), **Supp. III Part 1:** 356

Sound of Mountain Water, The (Stegner), **Supp. IV Part 2:** 595, 596, 598, 600, 608

"Sound of Talking" (Purdy), **Supp. VII:** 270

Sounds of Poetry (television special, Moyers), **Supp. XXIII:** 139

Sounds of Poetry, The (Pinsky), **Supp. VI:** 236, 247, 248; **Supp. XXIII:** 124

Sound the Stars Make Rushing Through the Sky, The: The Writings of Jane Johnston Schoolcraft (Parker, ed.), **Supp. XXIII:** 223–224, 227, 228

Soupault, Philippe, **IV:** 288, 404; **Retro. Supp. II:** 85, 321, 324

Source (Doty), **Supp. XI:** 121, **134–137**

"Source" (Doty), **Supp. XI:** 136

"Source, The" (Olds), **Supp. X:** 211

Source, The (Porter), **III:** 443

Source of Light, The (Price), **Supp. VI: 262,** 266

"Sources of Soviet Conduct, The" (Kennan), **Supp. VIII:** 241

Sour Grapes (W. C. Williams), **Retro. Supp. I:** 418

"Sour Grapes"(Moraga), **Supp. XXIII:** 202

"Sourwood Nocturne" (Skloot), **Supp. XX: 202**

"South" (Levis), **Supp. XI:** 266

"South" (Trethewey), **Supp. XXI:** 247, 256

"South, The" (Hughes), **Supp. I Part 1:** 321

South American Journey (W. Frank), **Supp. XX:** 79

"Southampton Variations"(O'Hara), **Supp. XXIII:** 212

"Southbound on the Freeway" (Swenson), **Supp. IV Part 2:** 643

South Dakota Guidebook, The (C. Baxter), **Supp. XVII:** 15

Southern, Terry, **Supp. IV Part 1:** 379; **Supp. V:** 40, 201; **Supp. XI: 293–310; Supp. XVI:** 230

Southern Cross, The (Wright), **Supp. V:** 332, 342

"Southern Cross, The" (Wright), **Supp. V:** 338

"Southerner's Problem, The" (Du Bois), **Supp. II Part 1:** 168

"Southern Girl" (Zelda Fitzgerald), **Supp. IX:** 71

"Southern Gothic" (Trethewey), **Supp. XXI:** 256

"Southern History" (Trethewey), **Supp. XXI:** 256, 257

"Southern Mode of the Imagination, A" (Tate), **IV:** 120

"Southern Romantic, A" (Tate), **Supp. I Part 1:** 373

"Southern Sojourn, A" (Hoffman), **Supp. XVIII:** 87

Southern Terry, **Supp. XIV:** 82

Southey, Robert, **II:** 304, 502; **Supp. I Part 1:** 154

"South Lingers On, The" (R. Fisher), **Supp. XIX:** 69–70

South Moon Under (Rawlings), **Supp. X: 225–226,** 229, 233

South Pacific Affair (Lacy), **Supp. XV:** 206

Southpaw, The (Harris), **II:** 424–425

"South Sangamon" (Cisneros), **Supp. VII:** 66

South to a Very Old Place (Murray), **Supp. XIX: 151–153**

Southwell, Robert, **IV:** 151

Southwick, Marcia, **Supp. XI:** 259

Southworth, E. D. E. N, **Retro. Supp. I:** 246

Souvenir of the Ancient World, Selected Poems of Carlos Drummond de Andrade (Strand, trans.), **Supp. IV Part 2:** 630

"Sow" (Plath), **Supp. I Part 2:** 537

"Sowing and Reaping in *Furors Die*" (Nostrandt), **Supp. XVIII:** 80–81

Soyinka, Wole, **Supp. XX: 100**

"Space" (Brockmeier), **Supp. XXII:** 51

Space between Our Footsteps, The: Poems and Paintings from the Middle East (Nye, ed.), **Supp. XIII:** 280

"Space Quale, The" (James), **II:** 349

"Spaces Between, The" (Kingsolver), **Supp. VII:** 209

"Space Where Sex Should Be, The: Toward a Definition of the Black Literary Tradition" (Nelson), **Supp. XVIII:** 172

Spackman, Peter, **Supp. XVI:** 221

Spacks, Patricia, **Supp. XVI:** 251

"Spain" (Auden), **Supp. II Part 1:** 12–13, 14

"Spain in Fifty-Ninth Street" (White), **Supp. I Part 2:** 677

"Spanish-American War Play" (Crane), **I:** 422

Spanish Ballads (Merwin, trans.), **Supp. III Part 1:** 347

Spanish Bayonet (Benét), **Supp. XI:** 45, 47

Spanish Earth, The (film), **Retro. Supp. I:** 184

Spanish Papers and Other Miscellanies (Irving), **II:** 314

"Spanish Revolution, The" (Bryant), **Supp. I Part 1:** 153, 168

Spanish Student, The (Longfellow), **II:** 489, 506; **Retro. Supp. II:** 165

"Spanish Winter" (Egan), **Supp. XIX:** 52

Spanking the Maid (Coover), **Supp. V:** 47, 48, 49, 52

Spare Change (Parker), **Supp. XIX:** 186–187

Spargo, John, **Supp. I Part 1:** 13

"Spark, The" (Wharton), **Retro. Supp. I:** 381

"Sparkles from the Wheel" (Whitman), **IV:** 348

Sparks, Debra, **Supp. X:** 177

Sparks, Jared, **Supp. I Part 1:** 156

"Sparrow" (Berry), **Supp. X:** 31

Sparrow, Henry, **III:** 587

Sparrow, Mrs. Henry, **III:** 587

"Sparrow's Gate, The" (B. Kelly), **Supp. XVII:** 133

Spaulding, William, **Supp. XVI:** 106

"Spawning Run, The" (Humphrey), **Supp. IX:** 95

"Speak, Gay Memory" (Kirp), **Supp. XI:** 129

"Speak, Hoyt-Schermerhorn" (Lethem), **Supp. XVIII:** 148

Speak, Memory (Nabokov), **III:** 247–250, 252; **Retro. Supp. I:** 264, 265, 266, 267, 268, 277; **Supp. XVI:** 148

Speak, Memory (V. Nabokov), **Supp. XVII:** 47

Speaking and Language (Shapiro), **Supp. II Part 2:** 721

Speaking for Nature: How Literary Naturalists from Henry Thoreau to Rachel Carson Have Shaped America (Brooks), **Supp. IX:** 31

Speaking for Ourselves: American Ethnic Writing (Faderman and Bradshaw, eds.), **Supp. XIII:** 313

Speaking of Accidents (Everwine), **Supp. XV:** 75, 88

"Speaking of Accidents" (Everwine), **Supp. XV:** 88–89

"Speaking of Counterweights" (White), **Supp. I Part 2:** 669

Speaking of Literature and Society (Trilling), **Supp. III Part 2:** 494, 496, 499

"Speaking of Love" (Gioia), **Supp. XV:** 124–125

Speaking of Race, Speaking of Sex: Hate Speech, Civil Rights, and Civil Liberties (H. L. Gates, Griffin, Lively, and Strossen), **Supp. XX:** 111

Speaking on Stage (Kolin and Kullman, eds.), **Supp. IX:** 145

Speaking on Stage: Interviews with Contemporary American Playwrights (Balakian), **Supp. XV:** 327

"Speaking Passions" (Kitchen), **Supp. XV:** 215

Speak of the Devil (Holding), **Supp. XXII:** 127

Speak What We Feel (Not What We Ought to Say): Reflections on Literature and Faith (Buechner), **Supp. XII:** 57

Spear, Roberta, **Supp. V:** 180; **Supp. XV:** 73

"Special Kind of Fantasy, A: James Dickey on the Razor's Edge" (Niflis), **Supp. IV Part 1:** 175

"Special Pleading" (Lanier), **Supp. I Part 1:** 364

"Special Problems in Teaching Leslie Marmon Silko's *Ceremony*" (Gunn Allen), **Supp. IV Part 1:** 333

Special Providence, A (Yates), **Supp. XI:** 342, **344–345**

"Special Time, a Special School, A" (Knowles), **Supp. XII:** 236

Special View of History, The (Olson), **Supp. II Part 2:** 566, 569, 572

Specimen Days (Whitman), **IV:** 338, 347, 348, 350; **Retro. Supp. I:** 408

Specimens of the American Poets, **Supp. I Part 1:** 155

"Spectacles, The" (Poe), **III:** 425

Spectator Bird, The (Stegner), **Supp. IV Part 2:** 599, 604, 606, 611–612

Spector, Robert, **Supp. XIII:** 87

Spectra: A Book of Poetic Experiments (Bynner and Ficke), **Supp. XV:** 43

"Spectre Bridegroom, The" (Irving), **II:** 304

"Spectre Pig, The" (Holmes), **Supp. I Part 1:** 302

"Speculating Woman" (X. J. Kennedy), **Supp. XV:** 168

"Speech Sounds" (O. Butler), **Supp. XIII:** 61, **70**

"Speech to a Crowd" (MacLeish), **III:** 16

"Speech to the Detractors" (MacLeish), **III:** 16

"Speech to the Young" (Brooks), **Supp. III Part 1:** 79, 86

"Speech to Those Who Say Comrade" (MacLeish), **III:** 16

Speedboat (Adler), **Supp. X:** 171

Speed of Darkness, The (Rukeyser), **Supp. VI:** 274, 281

Speed-the-Plow (Mamet), **Supp. XIV:** 241, 246, 249, 250, 251

"Speedy Gonzales Was the Fastest Mouse in Mexico" (P. N. Warren as Kilina), **Supp. XX:** 262

Speilberg, Steven, **Supp. XI:** 234

Speirs, Logan, **Supp. XIX:** 282

"Spell" (Francis), **Supp. IX:** 87

"Spell, The" (Peacock), **Supp. XIX:** 198, 200

"Spell for the Manufacture & Use of a Magic Carpet" (Hull), **Supp. XXI:** 132–133, 139, 141

Spelling Dictionary, A (Rowson), **Supp. XV:** 244

Spence, Thomas, **Supp. I Part 2:** 518

Spence + Lila (Mason), **Supp. VIII:** 133, **143–145**

Spencer, Edward, **Supp. I Part 1:** 357, 360

Spencer, Herbert, **I:** 515; **II:** 345, 462–463, 480, 483, 536; **III:** 102, 315; **IV:** 135; **Retro. Supp. II:** 60, 65, 93, 98; **Supp. I Part 1:** 368; **Supp. I Part 2:** 635

Spencer, Sharon, **Supp. X:** 185, 186, 195, 196

Spencer, Theodore, **I:** 433; **Supp. III Part 1:** 2

Spender, Natasha, **Supp. IV Part 1:** 119, 127, 134

Spender, Stephen, **II:** 371; **III:** 504, 527; **Retro. Supp. I:** 216; **Retro. Supp. II:** 243, 244; **Supp. I Part 2:** 536; **Supp. II Part 1:** 11; **Supp. IV Part 1:** 82, 134; **Supp. IV Part 2:** 440; **Supp. X:** 116

Spengler, Oswald, **I:** 255, 270; **II:** 7, 577; **III:** 172, 176; **Retro. Supp. II:** 324; **Supp. I Part 2:** 647

Spens, Sir Patrick, **Supp. I Part 2:** 404

Spenser, Edmund, **I:** 62; **III:** 77, 78, 89; **IV:** 155, 453; **Retro. Supp. I:** 62; **Supp. I Part 1:** 98, 152, 369; **Supp. I Part 2:** 422, 719

"Spenser's Ireland" (Moore), **III:** 211, 212

"Spermaceti Papers"(Lippard), **Supp. XXIII:** 178

Sperry, Margaret, **Supp. IV Part 1:** 169

Spheres of Existence (C. L. R. James), **Supp. XXI:** 172

Sphere: The Form of a Motion (Ammons), **Supp. VII:** 24, 32, 33, 35, 36

"Sphinx" (Hayden), **Supp. II Part 1:** 373

"Spiced Plums" (Ríos), **Supp. IV Part 2:** 553

Spickard, Paul, **Supp. XXI:** 149

"Spider and the Ghost of the Fly, The" (Lindsay), **Supp. I Part 2:** 375

Spider Bay (Van Vechten), **Supp. II Part 2:** 746

"Spider Heart, The" (Peacock), **Supp. XIX:** 200

"Spiders" (Schwartz), **Supp. II Part 2:** 665

Spider's House, The (Bowles), **Supp. IV Part 1:** 87–89, 90, 91

Spider Woman's Granddaughters: Traditional Tales and Contemporary Writing by Native American Women (Gunn Allen, ed.), **Supp. IV Part 1:** 320, 326, 332–333; **Supp. IV Part 2:** 567

Spiegel, Sam, **Supp. XVIII:** 251, 252

Spiegelman, Art, **Supp. XVII:** 48

Spiegelman, Willard, **Supp. XI:** 126

Spielberg, Steven, **Supp. XXI:** 154

Spillane, Mickey, **Supp. IV Part 2:** 469, 472; **Supp. XV:** 200; **Supp. XVIII:** 236, 237

Spiller, Robert E., **I:** 241; **Supp. I Part 1:** 104

Spillers, Hortense, **Supp. XX:** 109

"Spillikins: Gregor Mendel at the Table" (Bierds), **Supp. XVII:** 34–35

Spillville (Hampl), **Supp. XXII:** 98

Spillway (Barnes), **Supp. III Part 1:** 44

Spingarn, Amy, **Supp. I Part 1:** 325, 326

Spingarn, Joel, **I:** 266; **Supp. I Part 1:** 325

Spinoza, Baruch, **I:** 493; **II:** 590, 593; **III:** 600; **IV:** 5, 7, 11, 12, 17; **Retro. Supp. II:** 300; **Supp. I Part 1:** 274; **Supp. I Part 2:** 643; **Supp. XVI:** 184

"Spinoza of Market Street, The" (Singer), **IV:** 12–13; **Retro. Supp. II:** 307

"Spinster" (Plath), **Supp. I Part 2:** 536

"Spinster's Tale, A" (Taylor), **Supp. V:** 314–315, 316–317, 319, 323

Spiral of Memory, The: Interviews (Coltelli, ed.), **Supp. XII:** 215

Spires, Elizabeth, **Supp. X:** 8

"Spire Song" (Bowles), **Supp. IV Part 1:** 80

Spirit and Flame: An Anthology of African American Poetry (Gilyard, ed.), **Supp. XXI:** 246

Spirit and the Flesh, The: Sexual Diversity in American Indian Culture (W. L. Williams), **Supp. IV Part 1:** 330

"Spirit Birth" (Cullen), **Supp. IV Part 1:** 168

Spirit Brides (Gibran). *See Nymphs in the Valley*

Spirit in Man, The (Jung), **Supp. IV Part 1:** 68

"Spirit in Me, The" (Hoffman), **Supp. XVIII:** 87

"Spirit Made Visible" (art exhibit), **Supp. XXII:** 180

Spirit of Culver (West), **IV:** 287

Spirit of Labor, The (Hapgood), **Supp. XVII:** 96, 99, 101–102; **Supp. XXI:** 4

Spirit of Romance, The (Pound), **III:** 470; **Retro. Supp. I:** 286

Spirit of the Ghetto, The: Studies of the Jewish Quarter of New York (Hapgood), **Supp. XVII:** 96, 101, 103, 106

Spirit of Youth and the City Streets, The (Addams), **Supp. I Part 1:** 6–7, 12–13, 16, 17, 19
"Spirits" (Bausch), **Supp. VII:** 46–47
Spirits, and Other Stories (Bausch), **Supp. VII:** 46–47, 54
"Spirit Says, You Are Nothing, The" (Levis), **Supp. XI:** 265–266
Spirits Rebellious (al-Arwá&hudot; al-Mutamarrida) (Gibran), **Supp. XX: 115, 124, 125**
Spiritual Adventures (Symons), **Supp. XX: 239**
Spiritual Conflict, The (Scupoli), **IV:** 156
Spiritual Exercises, The (Loyola), **IV:** 151; **Supp. XI:** 162
"Spiritual Manifestation, A" (Whittier), **Supp. I Part 2:** 699
"Spirituals and Neo-Spirituals" (Hurston), **Supp. VI:** 152–153
Spits, Ellen Handler, **Supp. XII:** 166
"Spitzbergen Tales" (Crane), **I:** 409, 415, 423
Spitzer, Philip, **Supp. XIV:** 21
"Spleen" (Eliot), **I:** 569, 573–574
Spleen de Paris, Le (Baudelaire), **Supp. XIV:** 337
Splendid Drunken Twenties, The (Van Vechten), **Supp. II Part 2:** 739–744
Splendide-Hôtel (Sorrentino), **Supp. XXI:** 233
Splendid Table, The (radio show), **Supp. XXIII:** 138
"Splinters" (Bukiet), **Supp. XVII:** 47
"Split Infinitive" (Pickering), **Supp. XXI:** 204
"Splitting an Order" (Kooser), **Supp. XIX:** 128–129
"Splittings" (Rich), **Supp. I Part 2:** 570–571
"Splitting Wood at Six Above" (Kumin), **Supp. IV Part 2:** 449
Spofford, Harriet Prescott, **Supp. XIII:** 143
Spoils of Poynton, The (James), **I:** 463; **Retro. Supp. I:** 229–230
Spoken Page, The (Nye), **Supp. XIII:** 274
"Spokes" (Auster), **Supp. XII:** 23
Spokesmen (Whipple), **II:** 456
Spook Sonata, The (Strindberg), **III:** 387, 392
Spooky Art, The: A Book about Writing (Mailer), **Retro. Supp. II:** 214
"Spoon, The" (Simic), **Supp. VIII:** 275
Spoon River Anthology (Masters), **I:** 106; **III:** 579; **Supp. I Part 2:** 454, 455, 456, 460–465, 466, 467, 471, 472, 473, 476; **Supp. IX:** 306; **Supp. XIV:** 282–283; **Supp. XIX:** 121; **Supp. XXII:** 282
Sport and a Pastime, A (Salter), **Supp. IX: 254–257; Supp. XVI:** 237
Sporting Club, The (McGuane), **Supp. VIII:** 43
Sport of the Gods, The (Dunbar), **Supp. II Part 1:** 193, 200, 207, 214–217
Sports Illustrated Training with Weights (Parker and Marsh), **Supp. XIX:** 187

"Sportsman Born and Bred, A" (Plimpton), **Supp. XVI:** 241
Sportsman's Sketches, A (Turgenev), **I:** 106; **IV:** 277
Sportswriter, The (Ford), **Supp. V:** 57, 58, 62–67
"Spotted Horses" (Faulkner), **IV:** 260
Sprague, Morteza, **Retro. Supp. II:** 115
Spratling, William, **II:** 56; **Retro. Supp. I:** 80
Sprawl trilogy (W. Gibson), **Supp. XVI:** 117, 122, 124
"Spray, The" (Lethem), **Supp. XVIII:** 148
"Spray Paint King, The" (Dove), **Supp. IV Part 1:** 252–253
Spreading Fires (Knowles), **Supp. XII:** 249
Sprigge, Elizabeth, **IV:** 31
"Spring" (Kooser), **Supp. XIX:** 126
"Spring" (Millay), **III:** 126
"Spring" (Mora), **Supp. XIII:** 217
"Spring 1967" (Carruth), **Supp. XVI:** 55
Spring and All (W. C. Williams), **Retro. Supp. I:** 412, 418, **418–420,** 427, 430, 431
"Spring and All" (W. C. Williams), **Retro. Supp. I:** 419
Spring Awakening (Wedeking, trans. Franzen), **Supp. XX:** 85
"Spring Break-Up" (Carruth), **Supp. XVI:** 56
"Spring Bulletin" (Allen), **Supp. XV:** 15
Springer's Progress (Markson), **Supp. XVII: 141–142,** 143, 146
"Spring Evening" (Farrell), **II:** 45
"Spring Evening" (Kenyon), **Supp. VII:** 173
"Springfield Magical" (Lindsay), **Supp. I Part 2:** 379
Spring in New Hampshire and Other Poems (McKay), **Supp. X:** 131, 135
"Spring Notes from Robin Hill" (Carruth), **Supp. XVI:** 48
"Spring Pastoral" (Wylie), **Supp. I Part 2:** 707
"Spring Pools" (Frost), **II:** 155; **Retro. Supp. I:** 137
"Spring Snow" (Matthews), **Supp. IX:** 160
"SPRING SONG" (Baraka), **Supp. II Part 1:** 60
Springsteen, Bruce, **Supp. VIII:** 143
"Spring Strains" (W. C. Williams), **Retro. Supp. I:** 416
Spring Tides (Morison), **Supp. I Part 2:** 494
Springtime and Harvest (Sinclair), **Supp. V:** 280
"Springtime for You" (Halliday), **Supp. XIX:** 87
Spruance, Raymond, **Supp. I Part 2:** 479, 491
"Spruce Has No Taproot, The" (Clampitt), **Supp. IX:** 41–42
"Spunk" (Hurston), **Supp. VI:** 150, 151–152
Spunk: The Selected Stories (Hurston), **Supp. VI:** 150
Spurr, David, **Supp. XV:** 183

Spy, The (Cooper), **I:** 335, 336, 337, 339, 340; **Supp. I Part 1:** 155
"Spy, The" (Francis), **Supp. IX:** 81
Spy, The (Freneau), **Supp. II Part 1:** 260
Spyglass Tree, The (Murray), **Supp. XIX: 155–156**
Spy in the House of Love, A (Nin), **Supp. X:** 186
Squanto, **Supp. I Part 2:** 486
"Square Business" (Baraka), **Supp. II Part 1:** 49
Square Root of Wonderful, The (McCullers), **II:** 587–588
"Squash in Blossom" (Francis), **Supp. IX:** 81
"Squatter on Company Land, The" (Hugo), **Supp. VI:** 133
"Squatter's Children" (Bishop), **Retro. Supp. II:** 47
"Squeak, Memory" (Bukiet), **Supp. XVII:** 47
Squeeze Play (Auster), **Supp. XII:** 21
Squires, Radcliffe, **IV:** 127; **Supp. XV:** 118
Squirrels (Mamet), **Supp. XIV:** 240
S.S. Gliencairn (O'Neill), **III:** 387, 388, 405
S.S. San Pedro (Cozzens), **I:** 360–362, 370, 378, 379
"Ssshh" (Olds), **Supp. X:** 215
"Stacking the Straw" (Clampitt), **Supp. IX:** 41
Stade, George, **Supp. IV Part 1:** 286
Staël, Madame de, **II:** 298
"Staff of Life, The" (H. Miller), **III:** 187
Stafford, Jean, **II:** 537; **Retro. Supp. II:** 177; **Supp. V:** 316
Stafford, William, **Supp. IV Part 1:** 72; **Supp. IV Part 2:** 642; **Supp. IX:** 273; **Supp. XI: 311–332; Supp. XIII:** 76, 274, 276, 277, 281, 283; **Supp. XIV:** 119, 123; **Supp. XX: 161; Supp. XXI:** 246
"Stage All Blood, The" (MacLeish), **III:** 18
"Staggerlee Wonders" (Baldwin), **Retro. Supp. II:** 15
Stained White Radiance, A (Burke), **Supp. XIV:** 28, 31
Stalin, Joseph, **I:** 261, 490; **II:** 39, 40, 49, 564; **III:** 30, 298; **IV:** 372; **Supp. V:** 290; **Supp. XXI:** 164, 165, 167
"Stalking" (J. W. Miller), **Supp. XX:** 167
"Stalking the Billion-Footed Beast: A Literary Manifesto for the New Social Novel" (Wolfe), **Supp. III Part 2:** 586
Stallings, A. E., **Supp. XXIII:** 111, 124
Stallings, H. A., **Supp. XXII:** 194
Stallman, R. W., **I:** 405
Stamberg, Susan, **Supp. IV Part 1:** 201; **Supp. XII:** 193
Stamford, Anne Marie, **Supp. XII:** 162
Stanard, Mrs. Jane, **III:** 410, 413
Stand, The (King), **Supp. V:** 139, 140–141, 144–146, 148, 152
"Standard of Liberty, The" (Rowson), **Supp. XV:** 243
"Standard of Living, The" (Parker), **Supp. IX: 198–199**
Stander, Lionel, **Supp. I Part 1:** 289

"Standing and the Waiting, The" (M. F. K. Fisher), **Supp. XVII:** 83

Standing by Words (Berry), **Supp. X:** 22, 27, 28, 31, 32, 33, 35

Standing Fast (Swados), **Supp. XIX: 268–269**

"Standing Halfway Home" (Wagoner), **Supp. IX:** 324

"Standing In" (Caputo), **Supp. XIX:** 26

Standing Still and Walking in New York (O'Hara), **Supp. XXIII:** 220

Stand in the Mountains, A (Taylor), **Supp. V:** 324

Standish, Burt L. (pseudonym). *See* Patten, Gilbert

Standish, Miles, **I:** 471; **II:** 502–503

Standley, Fred L., **Retro. Supp. II:** 6

Stand Still Like the Hummingbird (H. Miller), **III:** 184

"Stand Up" (Salinas), **Supp. XIII:** 315

Stand with Me Here (Francis), **Supp. IX:** 76

Stanford, Ann, **Retro. Supp. I:** 41; **Supp. I Part 1:** 99, 100, 102, 103, 106, 108, 109, 113, 117; **Supp. IV Part 2:** 637

Stanford, Charles Villiers, **Supp. XX: 228**

Stanford, Donald E., **II:** 217

Stanford, Frank, **Supp. XV:** 338, 339, 341, 342–343, 343, 345, 348, 350

Stanford, Ginny (Crouch), **Supp. XV:** 339

Stanford, Leland, **I:** 196, 198

Stanislavsky, Konstantin, **Supp. XIV:** 240, 243

Stanley, Jodee, **Supp. XIX:** 52

"Stanley Kunitz" (Oliver), **Supp. VII:** 237

Stansell, Christine, **Supp. XVII:** 106; **Supp. XXI:** 4

Stanton, Frank L., **Supp. II Part 1:** 192

Stanton, Robert J., **Supp. IV Part 2:** 681

"Stanzas, Written in 1815 before going to hear my Father read religious services"(J. Schoolcraft), **Supp. XXIII:** 229

"Stanzas from the Grande Chartreuse" (Arnold), **Supp. I Part 2:** 417

Stanzas in Meditation (Stein), **Supp. III Part 1:** 13

Staples, Hugh, **Retro. Supp. II:** 187

Star, Alexander, **Supp. X:** 310

Starbuck, George, **Retro. Supp. II:** 53, 245; **Supp. I Part 2:** 538; **Supp. IV Part 2:** 440; **Supp. XIII:** 76

Star Child (Gunn Allen), **Supp. IV Part 1:** 324

"Star Dust" (Wrigley), **Supp. XVIII:** 296

Stardust Lounge, The (Digges), **Supp. XXIII:** 57

Stardust Memories (film; Allen), **Supp. XV:** 1, 4, **8**, 9, 13

"Stare, The" (Updike), **Retro. Supp. I:** 329

"Starfish, The" (R. Bly), **Supp. IV Part 1:** 72

"Staring at the Sea on the Day of the Death of Another" (Swenson), **Supp. IV Part 2:** 652

Star Is Born, A (film), **Supp. IV Part 1:** 198; **Supp. IX:** 198; **Supp. XVIII:** 242, 243

Stark, David, **Supp. XII:** 202

Stark, Heidi, **Supp. XXIII:** 228, 233

"Stark Boughs on the Family Tree" (Oliver), **Supp. VII:** 232

Starke, Aubrey Harrison, **Supp. I Part 1:** 350, 352, 356, 360, 362, 365, 370, 371

Starkey, David, **Supp. XII:** 180, 181

Star Ledger (Hull), **Supp. XXI:** 129, **136–138**

"Star Ledger" (Hull), **Supp. XXI:** 136

"Starlight" (Levine), **Supp. V:** 188

"Starlight Scope Myopia" (Komunyakaa), **Supp. XIII:** 123, 124

Starnino, Carmine, **Supp. XVII:** 74

"Star of the Nativity" (Brodsky), **Supp. VIII:** 33

Starr, Ellen Gates, **Supp. I Part 1:** 4, 5, 11

Starr, Jean. *See* Untermeyer, Jean Starr

Starr, Ringo, **Supp. XI:** 309

Star Rover, The (London), **II:** 467

"Starry Night, The" (Sexton), **Supp. II Part 2:** 681

"Stars" (Frost), **II:** 153

Stars, the Snow, the Fire, The: Twenty-five Years in the Northern Wilderness (Haines), **Supp. XII:** **199–201,** 206, 209

Star Shines over Mt. Morris Park, A (H. Roth), **Supp. IX:** 227, 236, **236–237**

"Stars of the Summer Night" (Longfellow), **II:** 493

"Stars over Harlem" (Hughes), **Retro. Supp. I:** 207

"Star-Spangled" (García), **Supp. XI:** 177, 178

Star-Spangled Girl, The (Simon), **Supp. IV Part 2:** 579

"Star-Splitter, The" (Frost), **Retro. Supp. I:** 123, 133

Stars Principal (McClatchy), **Supp. XII: 256–258**

"Star That Would Not Shine, The" (C. L. R. James), **Supp. XXI:** 160

"Starting from Paumanok" (Whitman), **IV:** 333

Starting from Troy (Hadas), **Supp. XXIII: 113**

Starting Out in the Thirties (Kazin), **Supp. VIII: 95–97**

Star Trek television series, **Supp. XXII:** 60

"Starved Lovers" (MacLeish), **III:** 19

Starved Rock (Masters), **Supp. I Part 2:** 465

"Starving Again" (Moore), **Supp. X:** 163, 172, 175

"Starving"(Strout), **Supp. XXIII:** 283, 285

"State, The" (Bourne), **I:** 233

State and Main (Mamet), **Supp. XIV:** 241

"Statement of Principles" (Ransom), **III:** 496

"Statement: Phillipa Allen" (Rukeyser), **Supp. VI:** 283–284

"Statements on Poetics" (Snyder), **Supp. VIII:** 291, 292

"Statement with Rhymes" (Kees), **Supp. XV:** 139

"State of the Art, The" (Elkin), **Supp. VI:** 52

"State of the Arts, The" (Wasserstein), **Supp. XV:** 332

State of the Nation (Dos Passos), **I:** 489

"State of the Union" (Vidal), **Supp. IV Part 2:** 678

Static Element, The: Selected Poems of Natan Zach (Everwine, trans.), **Supp. XV:** 73, 75, **85–88**

"Statue, The" (Berryman), **I:** 173

"Statue and Birds" (Bogan), **Supp. III Part 1:** 50

"Statue of an Unkown Soldier, The" (Kooser), **Supp. XIX:** 124

"Statues, The" (Schwartz), **Supp. II Part 2:** 654, 659

"Status Rerum" (Pound), **Supp. I Part 1:** 257

Stavans, Ilan, **Supp. XI:** 190

"Stave Church" (W. V. Davis), **Supp. XXI:** 93, 94

"Staying Afloat"(Strout), **Supp. XXIII:** 274

"Staying Alive" (Levertov), **Supp. III Part 1:** 281

Staying Alive (Wagoner), **Supp. IX:** 324, **326**

"Staying at Ed's Place" (Swenson), **Supp. IV Part 2:** 648

Staying Put : Making a Home in a Restless World (Sanders), **Supp. XVI:** 274–275

Stay Me, Oh Comfort Me: Journals and Stories, 1933–1941 (M. F. K. Fisher), **Supp. XVII:** 92

Stayton, Richard, **Supp. IX:** 133

Steadman, Goodman, **IV:** 147

"Steak" (Snyder), **Supp. VIII:** 301

Steal Away: Selected and New Poems (Wright), **Supp. XV:** 337, 340, 348, 350–351

Stealing Beauty (Minot), **Supp. VI:** 205

Stealing Glimpses (McQuade), **Supp. IX:** 151

Stealing the Language: The Emergence of Women's Poetry in America (Ostriker), **Supp. XV:** 251

"Stealing the Thunder: Future Visions for American Indian Women, Tribes, and Literary Studies" (Gunn Allen), **Supp. IV Part 1:** 331

"Steam Shovel Cut" (Masters), **Supp. I Part 2:** 468

Stearns, Harold, **I:** 245; **Supp. XVII:** 106

Stedman, Edmund Clarence, **Supp. I Part 1:** 372; **Supp. II Part 1:** 192; **Supp. XV:** 115, 269, 273, 274, 282, 286

Steel, Sharon, **Supp. XIX:** 61

Steele, Margaret, **Supp. XXI:** 5

Steele, Max, **Supp. XIV:** 82

Steele, Sir Richard, **I:** 378; **II:** 105, 107, 300; **III:** 430

Steele, Timothy, **Supp. XV:** 251; **Supp. XVII:** 112; **Supp. XXIII:** 111

Steele, Wilbur Daniel, **Supp. XXI:** 5
Steelwork (Sorrentino), **Supp. XXI:** 227, 230, 231, 232
Steenburgen, Mary, **Supp. IV Part 1:** 236
Steeple Bush (Frost), **II:** 155; **Retro. Supp. I:** 140; **Retro. Supp. II:** 42
"Steeple-Jack, The" (Moore), **III:** 212, 213, 215
"Steerage" (Goldbarth), **Supp. XII:** 187
Steers, Nina, **Retro. Supp. II:** 25
Stefans, Brian Kim, **Supp. XXII:** 226
Steffens, Lincoln, **II:** 577; **III:** 580; **Retro. Supp. I:** 202; **Retro. Supp. II:** 101; **Supp. I Part 1:** 7; **Supp. XVII:** 98, 101, 106–107; **Supp. XXI:** 2, 3, 5, 7, 10; **Supp. XXIII:** 162
Stegner, Page, **IV:** 114, 116; **Supp. IV Part 2:** 599
Stegner, Wallace, **Supp. IV Part 2: 595–618; Supp. V:** 220, 224, 296; **Supp. X:** 23, 24; **Supp. XIV:** 82, 193, 230, 233; **Supp. XVIII:** 192; **Supp. XXII:** 204, 205, 208
"Stegner's Short Fiction" (Ahearn), **Supp. IV Part 2:** 604
Steichen, Edward, **III:** 580, 594–595
Steichen, Lillian. *See* Sandburg, Mrs. Carl (Lillian Steichen)
Steiger, Rod, **Supp. VIII:** 269; **Supp. XI:** 305
Stein, Edith, **Supp. XXII:** 92–93, 167
Stein, Gertrude, **I:** 103, 105, 476; **II:** 56, 251, 252, 257, 260, 262–263, 264, 289; **III:** 71, 454, 471–472, 600; **IV: 24–48,** 368, 375, 404, 415, 443, 477; **Retro. Supp. I:** 108, 170, 176, 177, 186, 418, 422; **Retro. Supp. II:** 85, 207, 326, 331; **Supp. I Part 1:** 292; **Supp. III Part 1:** 13, 37, 225, 226; **Supp. III Part 2:** 626; **Supp. IV Part 1:** 11, 79, 80, 81, 322; **Supp. IV Part 2:** 468; **Supp. V:** 53; **Supp. IX:** 55, 57, 62, 66; **Supp. XII:** 1, 139; **Supp. XIV:** 336; **Supp. XVI:** 187; **Supp. XVII:** 98, 105, 107; **Supp. XVIII:** 148; **Supp. XXI:** 7, 33; **Supp. XXII:** 158, 159; **Supp. XXIII:** 166, 207
Stein, Jean, **Supp. XVI:** 245
Stein, Karen F., **Supp. XIII:** 29, 30
Stein, Leo, **IV:** 26; **Supp. XIV:** 336; **Supp. XV:** 298
Stein, Lorin, **Supp. XII:** 254; **Supp. XVIII:** 137, 139
Steinbeck, John, **I:** 107, 288, 301, 378, 495, 519; **II:** 272; **III:** 382, 453, 454, 589; **IV: 49–72; Retro. Supp. II:** 19, 196; **Supp. IV Part 1:** 102, 225; **Supp. IV Part 2:** 502; **Supp. V:** 290, 291; **Supp. VIII:** 10; **Supp. IX:** 33, 171; **Supp. XI:** 169; **Supp. XIII:** 1, 17; **Supp. XIV:** 21, 181; **Supp. XVII:** 228; **Supp. XVIII:** 90, 102, 254; **Supp. XIX:** 3
Steinbeck, Olive Hamilton, **IV:** 51
Steinberg, Saul, **Supp. VIII:** 272
Steinberg, Sybil, **Supp. XVII:** 165, 166; **Supp. XXIII:** 241
Steinem, Gloria, **Supp. IV Part 1:** 203; **Supp. XXIII:** 104, 105, 106

Steiner, George, **Retro. Supp. I:** 327; **Supp. IV Part 1:** 286; **Supp. XVI:** 230
Steiner, Michael, **Supp. XXII:** 205
Steiner, Nancy, **Supp. I Part 2:** 529
Steiner, Stan, **Supp. IV Part 2:** 505
Steinfels, Margaret, **Supp. XVII:** 170
Steinhoff, Eirik, **Supp. XVI:** 290
Steinman, Michael, **Supp. VIII:** 172
Steinmetz, Charles P., **Supp. XXIII:** 161
Steinmetz, Charles Proteus, **I:** 483
Steinway Quintet Plus Four, The (Epstein), **Supp. XII:** 159, **162–166**
Stekel, Wilhelm, **III:** 554
Stella (Goethe), **Supp. IX:** 133, 138
Stella (Kushner), **Supp. IX:** 133
Stella, Joseph, **I:** 387
"Stellaria" (Francis), **Supp. IX:** 83
Stelligery and Other Essays (Wendell), **Supp. I Part 2:** 414
St. Elmo (Evans), **Supp. XXII:** 120
Stendhal, **I:** 316; **III:** 465, 467; **Supp. I Part 1:** 293; **Supp. I Part 2:** 445
Stepanchev, Stephen, **Supp. XI:** 312
Stephen, Leslie, **IV:** 440
Stephen, Sir Leslie, **IV:** 440; **Supp. I Part 1:** 306
Stephen, Saint, **II:** 539; **IV:** 228
Stephen Crane (Berryman), **I:** 169–170, 405
Stephen King, The Second Decade: "Danse Macabre" to "The Dark Half" (Magistrale), Supp. V: 138, 146, 151
Stephen King: The Art of Darkness (Winter), **Supp. V:** 144
Stephens, Jack, **Supp. X:** 11, 14, 15, 17
Stephens, James, **Supp. XIX:** 204
Stephens, Uriah, **Supp. XXIII:** 187
Stephenson, Gregory, **Supp. XII:** 120, 123
Stephenson, Neal, **Supp. XXII:** 49
"Stepping Out" (Dunn), **Supp. XI:** 140, 141
Steps (Kosinski), **Supp. VII:** 215, 221–222, 225
"Steps" (Nye), **Supp. XIII:** 288
Steps to the Temple (Crashaw), **IV:** 145
"Steps Toward Poverty and Death" (R. Bly), **Supp. IV Part 1:** 60
Stepto, Robert B., **Retro. Supp. II:** 116, 120, 123
Sterile Cuckoo, The (Nichols), **Supp. XIII:** 258, **259–263,** 264
Sterling, Bruce, **Supp. XVI:** 118, 121, 123, 124, 128–129
Sterling, George, **I:** 199, 207, 208, 209; **II:** 440; **Supp. V:** 286, **Supp. XXII:** 276, 277
Sterling, Phillip, **Supp. XXIII:** 102
Stern, Bernhard J., **Supp. XIV:** 202, 213
Stern, Daniel, **Supp. VIII:** 238
Stern, Frederick C., **Supp. X:** 114, 115, 117
Stern, Gerald, **Supp. IX: 285–303; Supp. XI:** 139, 267; **Supp. XV:** 211, 212
Stern, Madeleine B., **Supp. I Part 1:** 35
Stern, Maurice, **IV:** 285
Stern, Philip Van Doren, **Supp. XIII:** 164
Stern, Richard, **Retro. Supp. II:** 291
Stern, Richard G., **Retro. Supp. II:** 204

Stern, Steven, **Supp. XVII:** 42, 48, 49; **Supp. XX: 178**
"Sterne" (Schwartz), **Supp. II Part 2:** 663
Sterne, Laurence, **II:** 302, 304–305, 308; **III:** 454; **IV:** 68, 211, 465; **Supp. I Part 2:** 714; **Supp. IV Part 1:** 299; **Supp. V:** 127; **Supp. X:** 324; **Supp. XV:** 232
Sterritt, David, **Supp. IV Part 2:** 574
Stetson, Caleb, **IV:** 178
Stetson, Charles Walter, **Supp. XI:** 195, 196, 197, 202, 204, 209
Steve Nelson, American Radical (Nelson), **Supp. XVIII:** 226
Stevens, Frances Simpson, **Supp. XXII:** 159, 162
Stevens, James, **Supp. XXIII:** 152
Stevens, Wallace, **I:** 60, 61, 266, 273, 462, 521, 528, 540–541; **II:** 56, 57, 530, 552, 556; **III:** 19, 23, 194, 216, 270–271, 272, 278, 279, 281, 453, 463, 493, 509, 521, 523, 600, 605, 613, 614; **IV: 73–96,** 140, 141, 332, 402, 415; **Retro. Supp. I:** 67, 89, 193, 284, 288, **295–315,** 335, 403, 411, 416, 417, 422; **Retro. Supp. II:** 40, 44, 326; **Supp. I Part 1:** 80, 82, 257; **Supp. II Part 1:** 9, 18; **Supp. III Part 1:** 2, 3, 12, 20, 48, 239, 318, 319, 344; **Supp. III Part 2:** 611; **Supp. IV Part 1:** 72, 393; **Supp. IV Part 2:** 619, 620, 621, 634; **Supp. V:** 337; **Supp. VIII:** 21, 102, 195, 271, 292; **Supp. IX:** 41; **Supp. X:** 58; **Supp. XI:** 123, 191, 312; **Supp. XIII:** 44, 45; **Supp. XV:** 39, 41, 92, 115, 250, 261, 298, 302, 306, 307; **Supp. XVI:** 64, 158, 202, 210, 288; **Supp. XVII:** 36, 42, 110, 129, 130, 240, 241; **Supp. XIX:** 7, 40, 86, 87; **Supp. XXI:** 19, 28, 60, 133; **Supp. XXII:** 162; **Supp. XXIII:** 53, 57, 65
Stevens, Mrs. Wallace (Elsie Kachel), **IV:** 75
"Stevens and the Idea of the Hero" (Bromwich), **Retro. Supp. I:** 305
Stevens and the Interpersonal (Halliday), **Supp. XIX: 85–86**
Stevenson, Adlai, **II:** 49; **III:** 581
Stevenson, Anne, **Supp. XV:** 121; **Supp. XVII:** 74
Stevenson, Burton E., **Supp. XIV:** 120
Stevenson, David, **Supp. XI:** 230
Stevenson, Robert Louis, **I:** 2, 53; **II:** 283, 290, 311, 338; **III:** 328; **IV:** 183–184, 186, 187; **Retro. Supp. I:** 224, 228; **Supp. I Part 1:** 49; **Supp. II Part 1:** 404–405; **Supp. IV Part 1:** 298, 314; **Supp. VIII:** 125; **Supp. XIII:** 75; **Supp. XIV:** 40; **Supp. XVII:** 69; **Supp. XXI:** 204
Stevick, Robert D., **III:** 509
Stewart, Dugald, **II:** 8, 9; **Supp. I Part 1:** 151, 159; **Supp. I Part 2:** 422
Stewart, George, **Supp. XVIII:** 138
Stewart, Jeffrey C., **Supp. XIV:** 196, 209, 210
Stewart, Randall, **II:** 244; **Supp. XX: 164**
Stewart, Robert E., **Supp. XI:** 216

"St. Francis of Assisi" (Di Piero), **Supp. XIX:** 43
Stickeen (Muir), **Supp. IX:** 182
"Sticks and Stones" (L. Michaels), **Supp. XVI:** 205
Sticks and Stones (Mumford), **Supp. II Part 2:** 475, 483, 487–488
Sticks & Stones (Matthews), **Supp. IX:** 154, 155, 157, 158
Stieglitz, Alfred, **Retro. Supp. I:** 416; **Retro. Supp. II:** 103; **Supp. VIII:** 98; **Supp. XVII:** 96; **Supp. XX: 74, 75**
"Stigmata" (Oates), **Supp. II Part 2:** 520
Stiles, Ezra, **II:** 108, 122; **IV:** 144, 146, 148
Still, James, **Supp. XX:** 163
Still, William Grant, **Retro. Supp. I:** 203
Still Alice (Genova), **Supp. XXIII:** 127
"Stillborn" (Plath), **Supp. I Part 2:** 544
"Still Here" (Hughes), **Retro. Supp. I:** 211
"Still Just Writing" (Tyler), **Supp. IV Part 2:** 658
"Still Life" (Hecht), **Supp. X:** 68
"Still Life" (Malamud), **Supp. I Part 2:** 450
Still Life (Pickering), **Supp. XXI:** 198
"Still Life" (Pickering), **Supp. XXI:** 198
"Still Life" (Sandburg), **III:** 584
"Still Life: Moonlight Striking up on a Chess-Board" (Lowell), **II:** 528
"Still Life Or" (Creeley), **Supp. IV Part 1:** 141, 150, 158
Still Life with Oysters and Lemon (Doty), **Supp. XI:** 119, 121, **133–134**
Still Life with Woodpecker (Robbins), **Supp. X:** 260, **271–274,** 282
"Still Moment, A" (Welty), **IV:** 265; **Retro. Supp. I:** 347
Stillness (Gardner), **Supp. VI:** 74
"Stillness in the Air" (Dickinson), **Supp. XV:** 261
Stillness of Dancing, The (Bierds), **Supp. XVII: 27–28**
"Still Small Voices, The" (Fante), **Supp. XI:** 164
Still Such (Salter), **Supp. IX:** 246
"Still the Place Where Creation Does Some Work on Itself" (W. V. Davis), **Supp. IV Part 1:** 68
Stimpson, Catharine R., **Supp. IV Part 2:** 686
Stimson, Eleanor Kenyon. *See* Brooks, Mrs. Van Wyck
"Stimulants, Poultices, Goads" (Wright), **Supp. XV:** 349
"Stings" (Plath), **Retro. Supp. II:** 255; **Supp. I Part 2:** 541
"Stirling Street September" (Baraka), **Supp. II Part 1:** 51
Stirner, Max, **II:** 27
"Stirrup-Cup, The" (Lanier), **Supp. I Part 1:** 364
Stitt, Peter, **Supp. IV Part 1:** 68; **Supp. IV Part 2:** 628; **Supp. IX:** 152, 163, 291, 299; **Supp. XI:** 311, 317; **Supp. XIII:** 87; **Supp. XV:** 98, 99; **Supp. XIX:** 121
Stivers, Valerie, **Supp. X:** 311
St. John, David, **Supp. XV:** 73, 253

St. Louis Woman (Bontemps and Cullen), **Supp. XXII:** 6
St. Mark, Tyler, **Supp. XX: 260**
Stock, Noel, **III:** 479
Stockton, Frank R., **I:** 201
Stoddard, Charles Warren, **I:** 193, 195, 196; **Supp. II Part 1:** 192, 341, 351
Stoddard, Elizabeth, **II:** 275; **Supp. XV: 269–291**
Stoddard, Richard, **Supp. I Part 1:** 372
Stoddard, Richard Henry, **Supp. XV:** 269, 271, 272, 273, 274, 278, 279, 286
Stoddard, Solomon, **I:** 545, 548; **IV:** 145, 148
Stoffman, Judy, **Supp. XVIII:** 97
Stoic, The (Dreiser), **I:** 497, 502, 508, 516; **Retro. Supp. II:** 95, 96, 101, 108
Stokes, Geoffrey, **Supp. XV:** 256
Stokes, Olivia Egleston Phelps, **Supp. XVIII:** 261
"Stolen Calf, The" (Dunbar), **Supp. II Part 1:** 196
Stolen Jew, The (Neugeboren), **Supp. XVI: 222–224,** 225
Stolen Past, A (Knowles), **Supp. XII:** 249
Stolen Words: Forays into the Origins and Ravages of Plagiarism (Mallon), **Supp. XIX: 134–135**
Stollman, Aryeh Lev, **Supp. XVII:** 49
Stolmar, Thomas, **Supp. XVIII:** 138
Stomping the Blues (Murray), **Supp. XIX: 158–159**
"Stone" (Ozick), **Supp. XVII:** 50
Stone, Edward, **III:** 479
Stone, Herbert S., **Supp. XXI:** 2
Stone, I. F., **Supp. XIV:** 3
Stone, Irving, **II:** 463, 466, 467
Stone, Oliver, **Supp. XIV:** 48, 316
Stone, Phil, **II:** 55
Stone, Richard, **Supp. XIV:** 54
Stone, Robert, **Supp. V: 295–312; Supp. X:** 1; **Supp. XIX:** 54
Stone, Rosetta (pseudonym). *See* Geisel, Theodor Seuss (Dr. Seuss)
Stone, Wilmer, **Supp. I Part 1:** 49
Stone and the Shell, The (Hay), **Supp. XIV:** 122, 123, 127, 130
"Stone Bear, The" (Haines), **Supp. XII:** 206–207, 212
"Stone City" (Proulx), **Supp. VII:** 251–253
Stone Country (Sanders), **Supp. XVI:** 271–272
Stone Diaries, The (Shields), **Supp. VII:** 307, 315, 324–326, 327
"Stone Dreams" (Kingsolver), **Supp. VII:** 203
Stone Harp, The (Haines), **Supp. XII:** **204,** 205, 206, 207
Stonemason, The (McCarthy), **Supp. VIII:** 175, 187
"Stones" (Hoffman), **Supp. XVIII:** 86
"Stones" (Kumin), **Supp. IV Part 2:** 447
Stones (lithograph series, O'Hara and Rivers), **Supp. XXIII:** 217
"Stones, The" (Plath), **Supp. I Part 2:** 535, 539
"Stones in My Passway, Hellhounds on My Trail" (Boyle), **Supp. VIII:** 15

Stones of Florence, The (McCarthy), **II:** 562
"Stone Walls" (Sarton), **Supp. VIII:** 259
"Stop" (Wilbur), **Supp. III Part 2:** 556
Stop-Loss (screenplay, Richard), **Supp. XIX:** 222
"Stop Me If You've Heard This One" (Lardner), **II:** 433
Stopover: Tokyo (Marquand), **III:** 53, 57, 61, 70
Stoppard, Tom, **Retro. Supp. I:** 189
"Stopping by Woods" (Frost), **II:** 154
"Stopping by Woods on a Snowy Evening" (Frost), **Retro. Supp. I:** 129, 133, 134, 135, 139
Stopping Westward (Richards), **II:** 396
"Stop Player. Joke No. 4" (Gaddis), **Supp. IV Part 1:** 280
Stop-Time (Conroy), **Supp. XVI: 63–71,** 72, 75, 76–77
"Store, The" (P. E. Jones), **Supp. XXII:** 144–145
Store, The (Stribling), **Supp. VIII:** 126; **Supp. XXII:** 195
"*Store* and *Mockingbird:* Two Pulitzer Novels about Alabama" (Going), **Supp. VIII:** 126
Store of a Million Items, The (Cliff), **Supp. XXII:** 67, 74, 75
"Store of a Million Items, The" (Cliff), **Supp. XXII:** 75
Storer, Edward, **Supp. I Part 1:** 261, 262
Stories, Fables and Other Diversions (Nemerov), **III:** 268–269, 285
Stories: Elizabeth Stoddard, **Supp. XV:** 270
"Stories for Sale" (Kolba), **Supp. XVIII:** 257
Stories for the Sixties (Yates, ed.), **Supp. XI:** 343
Stories from Our Living Past (Prose), **Supp. XVI:** 251
Stories from the Italian Poets (Hunt), **Supp. XV:** 175
Stories from the Old Testament Retold (L. P. Smith), **Supp. XIV:** 342
Stories from World Literature, **Supp. IX:** 4
"Stories in the Snow" (Leopold), **Supp. XIV:** 183
Stories of an Imaginary Childhood (Bukiet), **Supp. XVII: 41–44,** 45
Stories of F. Scott Fitzgerald, The (Cowley, ed.), **Retro. Supp. I:** 115
Stories of F. Scott Fitzgerald, The (Fitzgerald), **II:** 94
Stories of Modern America, **Supp. IX:** 4
Stories of Stephen Dixon, The (Dixon), **Supp. XII:** 152
Stories of the Spanish Civil War (Hemingway), **II:** 258
Stories Revived (James), **II:** 322
Stories that Could Be True (Stafford), **Supp. XI: 325–327**
Stories Toto Told Me (Rolfe), **Supp. XX:** 235
Storm, The (Buechner), **Supp. XII: 54–57**
"Storm, The" (Chopin), **Retro. Supp. II:** 60, 68; **Supp. I Part 1:** 218, 224

Storm, The (al-'Awásif) (Gibran), **Supp. XX: 116, 124, 125**
"Storm Fear" (Frost), **II:** 153; **Retro. Supp. I:** 127
"Storm Ship, The" (Irving), **II:** 309
"Storm Warnings" (Kingsolver), **Supp. VII:** 207–208
"Stormy Weather" (Ellison), **Supp. II Part 1:** 233
"Story" (Everwine), **Supp. XV:** 89
"Story, A" (Jarrell), **II:** 371
Story, Julian, **Supp. XX: 232**
Story, Richard David, **Supp. IV Part 2:** 575, 588
Story, William Wetmore, **Supp. XX: 228**
"Story about Chicken Soup, A" (Simpson), **Supp. IX:** 272–273
"Story about the Anteater, The" (Benét), **Supp. XI:** 53
"Story About the Body, A" (Hass), **Supp. VI: 107–108**
"Story for Teddy, A" (Swados), **Supp. XIX:** 266–267
Story for Teddy, A—and Others (Swados), **Supp. XIX: 266–268**
"Story Hearer, The" (Paley), **Supp. VI:** 230, 231
"Story Hour" (Hay), **Supp. XIV:** 124
"Story Hour" (Jarman), **Supp. XVII:** 116
Story Hour: A Second Look at Cinderella, Bluebeard, and Company (Hay), **Supp. XIV:** 119, 124, 125, 132, 133
Story of a Country Town, The (Howe), **I:** 106
Story of a Lover, The (Hapgood), **Supp. XVII:** 99, 100, 104; **Supp. XXI:** 3, 5, 7
Story of an American Family, The: Letters of the Hapgood Family, 1648–1917 (Boyce), **Supp. XVII:** 97; **Supp. XXI:** 9, 14
"Story of an Hour, The" (Chopin), **Retro. Supp. II:** 72; **Supp. I Part 1:** 212–213, 216
Story of a Novel, The (Wolfe), **IV:** 456, 458
Story of a Proverb, The (Lanier), **Supp. I Part 1:** 365
"Story of a Proverb, The: A Fairy Tale for Grown People" (Lanier), **Supp. I Part 1:** 365
Story of a Story and Other Stories, The: A Novel (Dixon), **Supp. XII:** 155
Story of a Wonder Man, The (Lardner), **II:** 433–434
"Story of a Year, The" (James), **Retro. Supp. I:** 218
Story of George Washington Carver, The (Bontemps), **Supp. XXII:** 13
Story of G.I. Joe, The (film, Wellman), **Supp. XVII:** 61, 62
"Story of Gus, The" (A. Miller), **III:** 147–148
"Story of How a Wall Stands, A" (Ortiz), **Supp. IV Part 2:** 499, 507
Story of Mist, The (Dybek), **Supp. XXIII: 74–75, 78**
"Story of Mist, The"(Dybek), **Supp. XXIII:** 74–75

Story of Mount Desert Island, Maine, The (Morison), **Supp. I Part 2:** 494
Story of My Boyhood and Youth, The (Muir), **Supp. IX:** 172–174, 176
Story of My Father, The: A Memoir (Miller), **Supp. XII:** 301
Story of O, The (Réage), **Supp. XII:** 9, 10
Story of Our Lives, The (Strand), **Supp. IV Part 2:** 620, 628–629, 629
"Story of Poppy Van Buster, The" (Briggs), **Supp. XVIII:** 8
Story of the Negro (Bontemps), **Supp. XXII:** 6, 12–13
Story of the Normans, The, Told Chiefly in Relation to Their Conquest of England (Jewett), **II:** 406
Story of the Telegraph, The (Briggs, and Maverick), **Supp. XVIII:** 4
"Story of Toby, The" (Melville), **III:** 76
"Story of To-day, A" (Davis). *See also Margret Howth*
"Story of To-day, A" (R. H. Davis), **Supp. XVI:** 88, 89
Story of Utopias, The (Mumford), **Supp. II Part 2:** 475, 483–486, 495
Story of Wine in California, The (M. F. K. Fisher), **Supp. XVII:** 88
Story on Page One, The (Odets), **Supp. II Part 2:** 546
Storyteller (Silko), **Supp. IV Part 2:** 558, 559, 560, 561, **566–570**
"Storyteller" (Silko), **Supp. IV Part 2:** 569
"*Storyteller:* Grandmother Spider's Web" (Danielson), **Supp. IV Part 2:** 569
"Storyteller's Notebook, A" (Carver), **Supp. III Part 1:** 142–143
Story Teller's Story, A: The Tale of an American Writer's Journey through His Own Imaginative World and through the World of Facts . . . (Anderson), **I:** 98, 101, 114, 117
"Story That Could Be True, A" (Stafford), **Supp. XI:** 326
"Stout Gentleman, The" (Irving), **II:** 309
Stover at Yale (Johnson), **III:** 321
Stowe, Calvin, **IV:** 445; **Supp. I Part 2:** 587, 588, 590, 596, 597
Stowe, Charles, **Supp. I Part 2:** 581, 582
Stowe, Eliza, **Supp. I Part 2:** 587
Stowe, Harriet Beecher, **II:** 274, 399, 403, 541; **Retro. Supp. I:** 34, 246; **Retro. Supp. II:** 4, 138, 156; **Supp. I Part 1:** 30, 206, 301; **Supp. I Part 2: 579–601; Supp. III Part 1:** 154, 168, 171; **Supp. IX:** 33; **Supp. X:** 223, 246, 249, 250; **Supp. XI:** 193; **Supp. XIII:** 141, 295; **Supp. XV:** 278; **Supp. XVI:** 82, 85
Stowe, Samuel Charles, **Supp. I Part 2:** 587
Stowe, William, **Supp. IV Part 1:** 129
Strachey, Lytton, **I:** 5; **IV:** 436; **Retro. Supp. I:** 59; **Supp. I Part 2:** 485, 494; **Supp. XIV:** 342; **Supp. XVI:** 191
"Stradivari" (Bierds), **Supp. XVII:** 28
Straight Cut (Bell), **Supp. X:** 5, **6–7,** 10
Straight Man (Russo), **Supp. XII: 335–339,** 340

Straits: Poems (Koch), **Supp. XV:** 184
Strand, Mark, **Supp. IV Part 2: 619–636; Supp. V:** 92, 332, 337, 338, 343; **Supp. IX:** 155; **Supp. XI:** 139, 145; **Supp. XII:** 254; **Supp. XIII:** 76; **Supp. XV:** 74
Strand, Paul, **Supp. VIII:** 272
Strandberg, Victor, **Supp. V:** 273
Strange, Sharan, **Supp. XXI:** 246
"Strange Beautiful Woman, A" (Nelson), **Supp. XVIII:** 173
Strange Bedfellows (Woods), **Supp. XXI:** 70
Strange Case of Dr. Jekyll and Mr. Hyde, The (Stevenson), **II:** 290
Strange Children, The (Gordon), **II:** 196, 197, 199, 211–213
Strange Commonplace, A (Sorrentino), **Supp. XXI:** 232, 237, 238
Strange Crime in Bermuda, The (Holding), **Supp. XXII: 124–125,** 127, 129
Strange Fire (Bukiet), **Supp. XVII: 46**
"Strange Fruit" (Harjo), **Supp. XII:** 224, 225
"Strange Fruit" (song), **Supp. I Part 1:** 80; **Supp. XVIII:** 228
Strange Interlude (O'Neill), **III:** 391, 397–398; **IV:** 61; **Supp. XXII:** 24
Stranger, The (Camus), **I:** 53, 292; **Supp. VIII:** 11; **Supp. XV:** 352
"Stranger, The" (Rich), **Supp. I Part 2:** 555, 560
"Stranger, The" (Salinger), **III:** 552–553
Strange Relation (Hadas), **Supp. XXIII:** 111, 113, 120, **127**
"Stranger in My Own Life, A: Alienation in American Indian Poetry and Prose" (Gunn Allen), **Supp. IV Part 1:** 10
Stranger in the Kingdom, A (Mosher), **Supp. XXII:** 204, 205, 206, 207, 208, 209, **212–213**
"Stranger in the Village" (Baldwin), **Retro. Supp. II:** 3; **Supp. I Part 1:** 54; **Supp. IV Part 1:** 10
"Stranger in Town" (Hughes), **Supp. I Part 1:** 334
"Strangers" (Howe), **Supp. VI:** 120
Strangers and Wayfarers (Jewett), **Retro. Supp. II:** 138
"Strangers from the Horizon" (Merwin), **Supp. III Part 1:** 356
Strangers on a Train (Highsmith), **Supp. IV Part 1:** 132
"Strange Story, A" (Taylor), **Supp. V:** 323
"Strange Story, A" (Wylie), **Supp. I Part 2:** 723
Strange Things (Atwood), **Supp. XIII:** 35
"Strato in Plaster" (Merrill), **Supp. III Part 1:** 328
Stratton-Porter, Gene, **Supp. XX: 211–225**
Straus, Ralph, **Supp. XIII:** 168
Straus, Roger, **Supp. VIII:** 82; **Supp. XV:** 59
Strauss, Harold, **Supp. XV:** 137
Strauss, Helen, **Supp. XXIII:** 258
Strauss, Johann, **I:** 66
Strauss, Richard, **IV:** 316

Strauss, Robert, **Supp. XI:** 141, 142

Stravinsky (De Schloezer), **III:** 474

Stravinsky, Igor, **Retro. Supp. I:** 378; **Supp. IV Part 1:** 81; **Supp. XI:** 133; **Supp. XV:** 265

"Stravinsky's Three Pieces 'Grotesques,' for String Quartet" (Lowell), **II:** 523

Straw, The (O'Neill), **III:** 390

"Strawberry Milkshake" (Halliday), **Supp. XIX:** 92, 94

"Stray Document, A" (Pound), **II:** 517

"Strays" (Richard), **Supp. XIX:** 210–211, 220

Streaks of the Tulip, The: Selected Criticism (W. J. Smith), **Supp. XIII:** 333, 334, 344, **347–348**

Streamline Your Mind (Mursell), **Supp. I Part 2:** 608

Strecker, Trey, **Supp. XXI:** 238

"Street, Cloud" (Ríos), **Supp. IV Part 2:** 549

Street, The (Petry), **Supp. XVIII:** 286

Streetcar Named Desire, A (T. Williams), **IV:** 382, 383, 385, 386, 387, 389–390, 395, 398; **Supp. IV Part 1:** 359

Street in Bronzeville, A (Brooks), **Retro. Supp. I:** 208; **Supp. III Part 1:** 74–78

"Street Moths" (X. J. Kennedy), **Supp. XV:** 170

"Street Musicians" (Ashbery), **Supp. III Part 1:** 18

"Street of Crocodiles" (Hull), **Supp. XXI:** 130

"Street off Sunset, A" (Jarrell), **II:** 387

"Streets" (Dixon), **Supp. XII: 145–146**

Streets in Their Own Ink (Dybek), **Supp. XXIII:** 78

Streets in the Moon (MacLeish), **III:** 5, 8–11, 15, 19

"Streets of Laredo" (screenplay) (McMurtry and Ossana), **Supp. V:** 226, 230

Streets of Laredo (McMurtry), **Supp. V:** 230

Streets of Night (Dos Passos), **I:** 478, 479–480, 481, 488

Streitfield, David, **Supp. XIII:** 234; **Supp. XVI:** 63

Strength of Fields, The (Dickey), **Supp. IV Part 1:** 178

"Strength of Fields, The" (Dickey), **Supp. IV Part 1:** 176, 184–185

"Strength of Gideon, The" (Dunbar), **Supp. II Part 1:** 212

Strength of Gideon and Other Stories, The (Dunbar), **Supp. II Part 1:** 211, 212

"Strenuous Artistry" (Zagarell), **Supp. XV:** 281

Strether, Lambert, **II:** 313

Stribling, T. S., **Supp. VIII:** 126

Strickland, Barbara, **Supp. XIX:** 102

Strickland, Joe (pseudonym). *See* Arnold, George W.

"Strictly Bucolic" (Simic), **Supp. VIII:** 278

Strictly Business (O. Henry), **Supp. II Part 1:** 410

"Strike, The" (Olsen), **Supp. XIII:** 292, 297

Strike at Shane's, The (Skloot), **Supp. XX:** 216

"Strikers" (Untermeyer), **Supp. XV:** 296

Strindberg, August, **I:** 78; **III:** 145, 165, 387, 390, 391, 392, 393; **IV:** 17; **Supp. XVII:** 100; **Supp. XXII:** 23

"String, The" (Dickey), **Supp. IV Part 1:** 179

String Light (Wright), **Supp. XV: 345–346**

"String Quartet, The" (Weigl), **Supp. XIX:** 278

"Strivings of the Negro People" (Du Bois), **Supp. II Part 1:** 167

Stroby, W. C., **Supp. XIV:** 26

Strohbach, Hermann, **Supp. XI:** 242

"Stroke of Good Fortune, A" (O'Connor), **III:** 344; **Retro. Supp. II:** 229, 232

Strom, Stephen, **Supp. XII:** 223

Strong, Anna Louise, **Supp. XVIII:** 238; **Supp. XXIII:** 166

Strong, George Templeton, **IV:** 321

Strong, Josiah, **Supp. XIV:** 64

"Strong Draughts of Their Refreshing Minds" (Dickinson), **Retro. Supp. I:** 46

Strong Motion (Franzen), **Supp. XX: 85, 88–89, 92, 95**

Strong Opinions (Nabokov), **Retro. Supp. I:** 263, 266, 270, 276

"Strong Room of the House, The" (Bronk), **Supp. XXI:** 32

"Strong Women" (Dorman), **Supp. XI:** 240

Strout, Elizabeth, **Supp. X:** 86; **Supp. XXIII: 273–287**

Structure of Nations and Empires, The (Niebuhr), **III:** 292, 308

"Structure of Rime, The" (Duncan), **Supp. XVI:** 287

Structuring the Void (Klinkowitz), **Supp. XXI:** 233

Struggle, The (film; Griffith), **Supp. XVI:** 191

"Strumpet Song" (Plath), **Retro. Supp. II:** 246; **Supp. I Part 2:** 536

Strunk, William, **Supp. I Part 2:** 652, 662, 670, 671, 672

Strunsky, Anna, **II:** 465

"Strut for Roethke, A" (Berryman), **I:** 188

Strychacz, Thomas F., **Supp. XVI:** 69–70

Stuart, Dabney, **Supp. XVIII:** 79

Stuart, Gilbert, **I:** 16

Stuart, J. E. B., **III:** 56

Stuart, Jesse, **Supp. XX: 162–163, 165**

Stuart, Michael, **Supp. XV:** 140

Stuart Little (White), **Supp. I Part 2:** 655–658

Stuckey, W. J., **Supp. XXII:** 191–192

"Student, The" (Moore), **III:** 212, 215

"Student of Clouds" (Collins), **Supp. XXI:** 60

"Student of Salmanaca, The" (Irving), **II:** 309

"Student's Wife, The" (Carver), **Supp. III Part 1:** 141

Studies in American Indian Literature: Critical Essays and Course Designs (Gunn Allen), **Supp. IV Part 1:** 324, 333

Studies in Classic American Literature (Lawrence), **II:** 102; **III:** 33; **IV:** 333; **Retro. Supp. I:** 421

Studies in Short Fiction (Edmonds), **Supp. XXIII:** 291

Studies in Short Fiction (Malin), **Supp. XVI:** 71

Studies in the Psychology of Sex (Ellis), **Supp. XX: 235**

"Studs" (Farrell), **II:** 25, 28, 31

Studs Lonigan: A Trilogy (Farrell), **II:** 25, 26, 27, 31–34, 37, 38, 41–42

"Study in Orange and White" (Collins), **Supp. XXI:** 60

"Study of Images" (Stevens), **IV:** 79

"Study of Lanier's Poems, A" (Kent), **Supp. I Part 1:** 373

Study of Milton's Prosody (Bridges), **II:** 537

"Study of the Negro Problems, The" (Du Bois), **Supp. II Part 1:** 165

Stuewe, Paul, **Supp. IV Part 1:** 68

Stuhlmann, Gunther, **Supp. X:** 182, 184, 185, 187

Stultifera Navis (Brant), **III:** 447

Sturak, John Thomas, **Supp. XIII:** 162, 163, 165, 168

Sturgeon, Theodore, **Supp. XVIII:** 145

Sturgis, George, **III:** 600

Sturgis, Howard, **IV:** 319; **Retro. Supp. I:** 367, 373

Sturgis, Howard Overing, **Supp. XX: 227–242**

Sturgis, Julian Russell, **Supp. XX: 228, 233, 238**

Sturgis, Susan, **III:** 600

Sturm, Margaret. *See* Millar, Margaret

Stuttaford, Genevieve, **Supp. IX:** 279

Stuyvesant, Peter, **II:** 301

"Style" (Nemerov), **III:** 275

Styles of Radical Will (Sontag), **Supp. III Part 2:** 451, 459, 460–463

"Stylist, The" (Egan), **Supp. XIX:** 51, 52

Styne, Jule, **Supp. XVI:** 193

Styron, William, **III:** 40; **IV:** 4, **97–119,** 216; **Supp. V:** 201; **Supp. IX:** 208; **Supp. X:** 15–16, 250; **Supp. XI:** 229, 231, 343; **Supp. XIV:** 82; **Supp. XVI:** 235–236; **Supp. XXIII:** 107, 109

Suares, J. C., **Supp. IV Part 1:** 234

Suarez, Ernest, **Supp. IV Part 1:** 175; **Supp. V:** 180

Suarez, Ray, **Supp. XXI:** 243

"Sub, The" (Dixon), **Supp. XII:** 146

Subjection of Women, The (Mill), **Supp. XI:** 196, 203

"Subjective Necessity for Social Settlements" (Addams), **Supp. I Part 1:** 4

"Subject of Childhood, A" (Paley), **Supp. VI:** 221; **Supp. XXI:** 118

"Submarginalia" (Howe), **Supp. IV Part 2:** 422

Substance and Shadow (James), **II:** 344

"Subterranean Homesick Blues" (song, Dylan), **Supp. XVIII:** 25

Subterraneans, The (Kerouac), **Supp. III Part 1:** 225, 227–231

"Subtitle" (Kees), **Supp. XV:** 139

Subtreasury of American Humor, A (White and White), **Supp. I Part 2:** 668

"Suburban Culture, Imaginative Wonder: The Fiction of Frederick Barthelme" (Brinkmeyer), **Supp. XI:** 38

Suburban Sketches (Howells), **II:** 274, 277

"Subversive Element, The" (Ryan as Quin), **Supp. XVIII:** 230

"Subverted Flower, The" (Frost), **Retro. Supp. I:** 139

"Subway, The" (Tate), **IV:** 128

"Subway Singer, The" (Clampitt), **Supp. IX:** 45

"Success" (Mora), **Supp. XIII:** 217

Successful Love and Other Stories (Schwartz), **Supp. II Part 2:** 661, 665

Succession, The: A Novel of Elizabeth and James (Garrett), **Supp. VII:** 104–107, 108

"Success is counted sweetest" (Dickinson), **Retro. Supp. I:** 30, 31–32, 38; **Supp. XV:** 126

Success Stories (Banks), **Supp. V:** 14–15

"Success Story" (Banks), **Supp. V:** 15

"Such Counsels You Gave to Me" (Jeffers), **Supp. II Part 2:** 433

Such Silence (Milburn), **Supp. XI:** 242

"Such Things Happen Only in Books" (Wilder), **IV:** 365

Such Was the Season (Major), **Supp. XXII: 177–178,** 179, 182

Suddenly, Last Summer (film) (Vidal), **Supp. IV Part 2:** 683

Suddenly Last Summer (T. Williams), **I:** 73; **IV:** 382, 383, 385, 386, 387, 389, 390, 391, 392, 395–396, 397, 398

Suder (Everett), **Supp. XVIII: 54–55**

Sudermann, Hermann, **I:** 66

Sue, Eugène, **Supp. XXIII:** 182

Sugg, Richard P., **Supp. IV Part 1:** 68

"Suggestion from a Friend" (Kenyon), **Supp. VII:** 171

"Suicide" (Barnes), **Supp. III Part 1:** 33

"Suicide off Egg Rock" (Plath), **Supp. I Part 2:** 529, 538

Suicides and Jazzers (Carruth), **Supp. XVI:** 46

"Suicide's Note" (Hughes), **Retro. Supp. I:** 199

"Suitable Surroundings, The" (Bierce), **I:** 203

"Suitcase, The" (Ozick), **Supp. V:** 262, 264

"Suite for Augustus, A" (Dove), **Supp. IV Part 1:** 245

"Suite for Emily" (Hull), **Supp. XXI:** 139–140

"Suite for Lord Timothy Dexter" (Rukeyser), **Supp. VI:** 283, 285

"Suite from the Firebird" (Stravinsky), **Supp. XI:** 133

"Suitor, The" (Kenyon), **Supp. VII:** 164–165

Sukarno, **IV:** 490

Sukenick, Ronald, **Supp. V:** 39, 44, 46; **Supp. XII:** 139

Sula (Morrison), **Supp. III Part 1:** 362, 364, 367, 368, 379; **Supp. VIII:** 219

Sullivan, Andrew, **Supp. IX:** 135

Sullivan, Arthur, **Supp. XX: 228**

Sullivan, Frank, **Supp. IX:** 201

Sullivan, Harry Stack, **I:** 59

Sullivan, Jack, **Supp. X:** 86; **Supp. XII:** 331

Sullivan, Noel, **Retro. Supp. I:** 202; **Supp. I Part 1:** 329, 333

Sullivan, Richard, **Supp. VIII:** 124

Sullivan, Walter, **Supp. VIII:** 168

"Sullivan County Sketches" (Crane), **I:** 407, 421

"Sumach and Goldenrod: An American Idyll" (Mumford), **Supp. II Part 2:** 475

Suma Genji (Play), **III:** 466

Sumerian Vistas (Ammons), **Supp. VII:** 34, 35

"Summa Lyrica" (Grossman), **Supp. XIX:** 86

"Summer" (Emerson), **II:** 10

Summer (Gioia), **Supp. XV:** 117

"Summer" (Lowell), **II:** 554

Summer (Wharton), **IV:** 317; **Retro. Supp. I:** 360, 367, 374, **378–379,** 382; **Supp. XXIII:** 275, 281

Summer, Bob, **Supp. X:** 1, 5, 6, 42

Summer and Smoke (T. Williams), **IV:** 382, 384, 385, 386, 387, 395, 397, 398; **Supp. IV Part 1:** 84

Summer Anniversaries, The (Justice), **Supp. VII:** 115, 117

Summer Blue (Skloot), **Supp. XX: 196, 207–208**

"Summer Commentary, A" (Winters), **Supp. II Part 2:** 808

"Summer Day" (O'Hara), **III:** 369

"Summer Days, The" (Oliver), **Supp. VII:** 239

Summer Never Ends (W. Frank), **Supp. XX:** 78

"Summer Night" (Hughes), **Supp. I Part 1:** 325

"Summer Night, A" (Auden), **Supp. II Part 1:** 8

"Summer Night—Broadway" (Untermeyer), **Supp. XV:** 296

"Summer Noon: 1941" (Winters), **Supp. II Part 2:** 811

"Summer of '82" (Merwin), **Supp. III Part 1:** 355–356

Summer on the Lakes in 1843 (Fuller), **Supp. II Part 1:** 279, 295–296

"Summer People" (Hemingway), **II:** 258–259

"Summer People, The" (Jackson), **Supp. IX:** 120

"Summer People, The" (Merrill), **Supp. III Part 1:** 325–326

"Summer Perdu" (Halliday), **Supp. XIX:** 89

"Summer Planning" (Halliday), **Supp. XIX:** 92

"Summer Ramble, A" (Bryant), **Supp. I Part 1:** 162, 164

Summers, Claude J., **Supp. IV Part 2:** 680–681; **Supp. XIV:** 161, 169

Summers, Robert, **Supp. IX:** 289

"Summer Solstice, New York City" (Olds), **Supp. X:** 207

"Summer's Reading, A" (Malamud), **Supp. I Part 2:** 430–431, 442

"Summer Storm" (Gioia), **Supp. XV:** 127

"Summer Storm" (Simpson), **Supp. IX:** 268

"'Summertime and the Living . . .' " (Hayden), **Supp. II Part 1:** 363, 366

Summertime Island (Caldwell), **I:** 307–308

"Summer Tragedy" (Bontemps), **Supp. XXII:** 9

"Summer: West Side" (Updike), **Retro. Supp. I:** 320

"Summer with Tu Fu, A" (Carruth), **Supp. XVI:** 55, 58

"Summit Beach, 1921" (Dove), **Supp. IV Part 1:** 249

Summoning of Stones, A (Hecht), **Supp. X:** 57, 58, **58–59**

"Summons" (Untermeyer), **Supp. XV:** 296

Summons to Memphis, A (Taylor), **Supp. V:** 313, 314, 327

Summons to the Free, A (Benét), **Supp. XI:** 47

Sumner, Charles, **I:** 3, 15; **Supp. I Part 2:** 685, 687

Sumner, John, **Retro. Supp. II:** 95

Sumner, John B., **I:** 511

Sumner, William Graham, **III:** 102, 108; **Supp. I Part 2:** 640

"Sumptuous Destination" (Wilbur), **Supp. III Part 2:** 553

"Sun" (Moore), **III:** 215

"Sun" (Swenson), **Supp. IV Part 2:** 640

"Sun, Sea, and Sand" (Marquand), **III:** 60

Sun Also Rises, The (Hemingway), **I:** 107; **II:** 68, 90, 249, 251–252, 260, 600; **III:** 36; **IV:** 35, 297; **Retro. Supp. I:** 171, **177–180,** 181, 189; **Supp. I Part 2:** 614; **Supp. XIII:** 263; **Supp. XVIII:** 74

"Sun and Moon" (Kenyon), **Supp. VII:** 168

"Sun and the Still-born Stars, The" (Southern), **Supp. XI:** 295

Sun at Midnight (Soseki; Merwin and Shigematsu, trans.), **Supp. III Part 1:** 353

"Sun Crosses Heaven from West to East Bringing Samson Back to the Womb, The" (R. Bly), **Supp. IV Part 1:** 73

"Sun Dance Shield" (Momaday), **Supp. IV Part 2:** 491

Sunday, Billy, **II:** 449

"Sunday Afternoons" (Komunyakaa), **Supp. XIII:** 127

Sunday after the War (H. Miller), **III:** 184

"Sunday at Home" (Hawthorne), **II:** 231–232

"Sunday Following Mother's Day. The" (P. E. Jones), **Supp. XXII:** 145

"Sunday Morning" (Stevens), **II:** 552; **III:** 278, 463, 509; **IV:** 92–93; **Retro. Supp. I:** 296, 300, 301, 304, 307, 313;

Supp. XV: 120; **Supp. XVI:** 210; **Supp. XVII:** 42; **Supp. XIX:** 40; **Supp. XXI:** 28, 133; **Supp. XXIII:** 57

"Sunday Morning Apples" (Crane), **I:** 387

"Sunday Morning Prophecy" (Hughes), **Supp. I Part 1:** 334

"Sunday Morning with the Sensational Nightingales" (Collins), **Supp. XXI:** 60

"Sundays" (B. Kelly), **Supp. XVII:** 124–125

"Sundays" (Salter), **Supp. IX:** 257

"Sundays, They Sleep Late" (Rukeyser), **Supp. VI:** 278

"Sundays of Satin-Legs Smith, The" (Brooks), **Supp. III Part 1:** 74, 75

"Sundays Visiting" (Ríos), **Supp. IV Part 2:** 541

Sundial, The (Jackson), **Supp. IX: 126–127**

Sundog (Harrison), **Supp. VIII: 46–48**

Sun Dogs (R. O. Butler), **Supp. XII: 64–65**

Sun Do Move, The (Hughes), **Supp. I Part 1:** 339

Sundquist, Eric, **Supp. XIV:** 66, 71

"Sunfish" (C. Frost), **Supp. XV:** 100–101, 102

"Sunflower Sutra" (Ginsberg), **Supp. II Part 1:** 317, 321; **Supp. XV:** 215

Sunlight Dialogues, The (Gardner), **Supp. VI:** 63, **68,** 69, 70

"Sunlight Is Imagination" (Wilbur), **Supp. III Part 2:** 549

"Sunny Ridge, The" (Halliday), **Supp. XIX:** 92

Sun Out: Selected Poems, 1952–1954 (Koch), **Supp. XV:** 179

"Sunrise" (Lanier), **Supp. I Part 1:** 370

"Sunrise and the Bomb" (Halliday), **Supp. XIX:** 84, 85, 92

"Sunrise runs for Both, The" (Dickinson), **Retro. Supp. I:** 45

Sunrise with Seamonsters: Travels and Discoveries, 1964–1984 (Theroux), **Supp. VIII:** 311, 313, 323, 325

"Sun Rising" (Donne), **Supp. VIII:** 164

"Sunset" (Ransom), **III:** 484

"Sunset from Omaha Hotel Window" (Sandburg), **III:** 584

Sunset Gun (Parker), **Supp. IX:** 192

Sunset Limited (Burke), **Supp. XIV:** 32, 33

Sunset Limited (Harrison), **Supp. VIII:** 51

"Sunset Maker, The" (Justice), **Supp. VII:** 123

Sunset Maker, The: Poems, Stories, a Memoir (Justice), **Supp. VII:** 116, 118, 119, 123–124

Sunshine Boys, The (film), **Supp. IV Part 2:** 589

Sunshine Boys, The (Simon), **Supp. IV Part 2:** 575, 584–585

"Sunthin' in the Pastoral Line" (Lowell), **Supp. I Part 2:** 415–416

Sun to Sun (Hurston), **Supp. VI:** 154

Sun Tracks (Ortiz), **Supp. IV Part 2:** 499, 500

Sun Under Wood (Hass), **Supp. VI:** 103, 108–109

"Superb Lily, The" (Pinsky), **Supp. VI:** 250

"Super Goat Man" (Lethem), **Supp. XVIII:** 148

"Superman Comes to the Supermarket" (Mailer), **Retro. Supp. II:** 204

"Supermarket in California, A" (Ginsberg), **Supp. XI:** 135

"Supernatural Love" (Schnackenberg), **Supp. XV:** 257, 259–260

Supernatural Love: Poems 1976–1992 (Schnackenberg), **Supp. XV:** 253, 256, 260, 263

Suplee, Curt, **Supp. XVI:** 202

"Supper After the Last, The" (Kinnell), **Supp. III Part 1:** 239

"Supposedly Fun Thing I'll Never Do Again, A" (Wallace), **Supp. X:** 315

Supposedly Fun Thing I'll Never Do Again, A: Essays and Arguments (Wallace), **Supp. X: 314–316**

Suppressed Desires (Glaspell and Cook), **Supp. III Part 1:** 178; **Supp. XXI:** 6

Suppression of the African Slave Trade to the United States of America, 1638–1870 (Du Bois), **Supp. II Part 1:** 157, 162

Supreme Fiction, The (Stevens), **Supp. XVI:** 158

"Supremes, The" (Jarman), **Supp. XVII:** 115

Sure Hand of God, The (Caldwell), **I:** 297, 302

Sure Signs: New and Selected Poems (Kooser), **Supp. XIX:** 116, 117, **121–122**

"Surety and Fidelity Claims" (Stevens), **Retro. Supp. I:** 296, 309

Surface of Earth, The (Price), **Supp. VI:** 261–262

"Surfaces" (Ammons), **Supp. VII:** 36

Surfaces and Masks (Major), **Supp. XXII:** 180

Surfacing (Atwood), **Supp. XIII:** 20, 21, **22–23,** 24, 33, 35

"Surgeon at 2 A.M." (Plath), **Supp. I Part 2:** 545

Summer Knowledge (Schwartz), **Supp. II Part 2:** 662, 665

"Surprise" (Kenyon), **Supp. VII:** 173

Surprised by Sin: The Reader in Paradise Lost (Fish), **Supp. XIV:** 15

Surreal South (eds. P. Benedict and L. Benedict), **Supp. XXIII:** 35

"Surround, The Imagining Herself as the Environment,/She Speaks to James Wright at Sundow" (Dickey), **Supp. IV Part 1:** 185

"Survey of Literature" (Ransom), **III:** 480

"Survey of the Literature, A" (Saunders), **Supp. XIX:** 235

"Surveyor, The" (H. Roth), **Supp. IX:** 233, 234

Survival (Atwood), **Supp. XIII:** 20, 22, 35

"Survival as Tao, Beginning at 5:00 A.M." (Carruth), **Supp. XVI:** 56

Survival of the Bark Canoe, The (McPhee), **Supp. III Part 1:** 301, 302, 308, 313

Survival This Way: Interviews with American Indian Poets (Bruchac), **Supp. IV Part 2:** 506

"Surviving Love" (Berryman), **I:** 173

Survivor (O. Butler), **Supp. XIII:** 62, 63

Susan and Anna Warner (Foster), **Supp. XVIII:** 265

Susan and God (film; Cukor), **Supp. XVI:** 192

Susanna Moodie: Voice and Vision (Shields), **Supp. VII:** 313

Susan Warner ("Elizabeth Wetherell") (A. Warner), **Supp. XVIII:** 259, 260

Suspect in Poetry, The (Dickey), **Supp. IV Part 1:** 177

"Sustained by Fiction" (Hoffman), **Supp. X:** 90, 92

"Susto" (Ríos), **Supp. IV Part 2:** 553

Sutherland, Donald, **IV:** 38, 44; **Supp. IX:** 254

Sutherland, Efua, **Supp. IV Part 1:** 9, 16

Sutherland-Smith, James, **Supp. X:** 211, 212

Sut Lovingood (Harris), **II:** 70; **Supp. XXII:** 193

Sutton, Roger, **Supp. X:** 266

Sutton, Walter, **III:** 479

"Sutton Pie Safe, The"(P. Benedict), **Supp. XXIII:** 36

Suttree (McCarthy), **Supp. VIII: 178–180,** 189

Suvero, Mark di, **Supp. IX:** 251

Svevo, Italo, **Supp. XIV:** 112

Swados, Harvey, **Supp. XI:** 222; **Supp. XIX: 255–271**

Swales, Martin, **Supp. XIX:** 183

Swallow, Alan, **Supp. X:** 112, 115, 116, 120, 123

Swallow Barn (J. P. Kennedy), **II:** 313

Swallow Barn (Kennedy), **Supp. XXII:** 193

Swallow the Lake (Major), **Supp. XXII:** 174

"Swamp Boy" (Bass), **Supp. XVI:** 20

Swan, Barbara, **Supp. IV Part 2:** 447

Swan, Jon, **Supp. IV Part 1:** 176

Swan Lake (Tchaikovsky), **Supp. IX:** 51

"Swan Legs" (Stern), **Supp. IX:** 299

Swann (Shields), **Supp. VII:** 315, 318–323, 326

Swann, Brian, **Supp. IV Part 2:** 500

Swanson, Gloria, **II:** 429

Swanson, Stevenson, **Supp. XIV:** 111

Swanton, John Reed, **Supp. VIII:** 295

Swan Watch (Schulberg), **Supp. XVIII:** 254

Swanwick, John, **Supp. XV:** 237

Swanwick, Michael, **Supp. XVI:** 128

"Swarm, The" (Plath), **Retro. Supp. II:** 255

"Sway" (Simpson), **Supp. IX:** 276

Sweat (Hurston), **Supp. VI:** 152

Swedenborg, Emanuel, **II:** 5, 10, 321, 342, 343–344, 396

Sweeney Agonistes (Eliot), **I:** 580; **Retro. Supp. I:** 64, 65; **Retro. Supp. II:** 247

"Sweeney Among the Nightingales" (Eliot), **III:** 4

"Sweeper, The" (Kooser), **Supp. XIX:** 125

Sweet, Blanche, **Supp. I Part 2:** 391

Sweet, Timothy, **Supp. IV Part 1:** 330

Sweet and Lowdown (film; Allen), **Supp. XV:** 11

Sweet and Sour (O'Hara), **III:** 361

"Sweet Armageddon" (Hoffman), **Supp. XVIII:** 85, 86

Sweet Bird of Youth (T. Williams), **IV:** 382, 383, 385, 386, 387, 388, 389, 390, 391, 392, 395, 396, 398; **Supp. IV Part 1:** 84, 89

Sweet Charity (musical), **Supp. IV Part 2:** 575

Sweet Flypaper of Life, The (Hughes), **Supp. I Part 1:** 335–336

"Sweetgrass"(Kenny), **Supp. XXIII:** 148

"Sweetheart" (Notley), **Supp. XXII:** 231

"Sweetheart of the Song Tra Bong, The" (O'Brien), **Supp. V:** 243, 249

"Sweethearts" (Ford), **Supp. V:** 69

Sweet Hereafter, The (Banks), **Supp. V:** 15–16

Sweet Lorain (Weigl), **Supp. XIX:** 282

Sweet Machine (Doty), **Supp. XI:** 121, **131–132,** 135

Sweet Sue (Gurney), **Supp. V:** 105, 107–108

Sweet Sweetback's Baadasss Song (Peebles; film), **Supp. XI:** 17

Sweet Thursday (Steinbeck), **IV:** 50, 52, 64–65

Sweet Will (Levine), **Supp. V:** 178, 187, 189, 190

"Sweet Will" (Levine), **Supp. V:** 190

"Sweet Willy"(J. Schoolcraft), **Supp. XXIII:** 226, 231

"Sweet Words on Race" (Hughes), **Retro. Supp. I:** 211

Sweezy, Paul, **Supp. I Part 2:** 645

"Swell-Looking Girl, A" (Caldwell), **I:** 310

Swenson, May, **Retro. Supp. II:** 44; **Supp. IV Part 2: 637–655; Supp. XIX:** 123

Swetman, Glenn R., **Supp. XXI:** 91

"Swift" (Schwartz), **Supp. II Part 2:** 663

Swift, Jonathan, **I:** 125, 194, 209, 441; **II:** 110, 302, 304–305, 577; **III:** 113; **IV:** 68; **Retro. Supp. I:** 66; **Supp. I Part 2:** 406, 523, 603, 656, 665, 708, 714; **Supp. IV Part 1:** 51; **Supp. IV Part 2:** 692; **Supp. XI:** 105, 209; **Supp. XII:** 276; **Supp. XV:** 258; **Supp. XVI:** 110; **Supp. XVIII:** 2, 12

"Swimmer" (Francis), **Supp. IX:** 82

"Swimmer" (Skloot), **Supp. XX: 199, 200**

"Swimmer, The" (Cheever), **Supp. I Part 1:** 185, 187

"Swimmer, The" (Glück), **Supp. V:** 82

"Swimmers" (Untermeyer), **Supp. XV:** 300

"Swimmers, The" (Fitzgerald), **Retro. Supp. I:** 110, 111

"Swimmers, The" (Tate), **IV:** 136

"Swimming" (Harjo), **Supp. XII:** 218

"Swimming Pool, The"(Strout), **Supp. XXIII:** 284

Swinburne, Algernon C., **I:** 50, 384, 568; **II:** 3, 4, 129, 400, 524; **IV:** 135; **Retro. Supp. I:** 100; **Supp. I Part 1:** 79; **Supp. I Part 2:** 422, 552; **Supp. XIV:** 120, 344

"Swinburne as Poet" (Eliot), **I:** 576

Swinger of Birches, A: A Portrait of Robert Frost (Cox), **Retro. Supp. I:** 132

"Swinging an Arc Before Him As He Goes" (Espaillat), **Supp. XXI:** 108

"Swinging on a Birch-Tree" (Larcom), **Supp. XIII:** 147

Swiss, Tom, **Supp. XIX:** 40

Switch, The (Dixon), **Supp. XII:** 141

Swope, D. B., **Supp. IX:** 95

Sword Blades and Poppy Seed (Lowell), **II:** 518, 520, 522, 532

Sword of God, The: Jeanne D'Arc (Endore), **Supp. XVII:** 55

Sybil (Auchincloss), **Supp. IV Part 1:** 25

Sybil and Chryssa (S. and A. Warner), **Supp. XVIII:** 264

"Sycamore" (Stern), **Supp. IX:** 294

"Sycamore, The" (Moore), **III:** 216

"Sycamores, The" (Whittier), **Supp. I Part 2:** 699

Sylvester, Johnny, **Supp. I Part 2:** 438

Sylvester, Joshua, **I:** 178, 179; **II:** 18; **III:** 157; **Supp. I Part 1:** 98, 104, 114, 116

Sylvia (Gurney), **Supp. V:** 105

"Sylvia" (L. Michaels), **Supp. XVI:** 202, 213

"Sylvia" (Larcom), **Supp. XIII:** 144

"Sylvia" (Stern), **Supp. IX:** 297

Sylvia: A Fictional Memoir (L. Michaels), **Supp. XVI:** 202, 213

Sylvia Plath: Method and Madness (Butscher), **Supp. I Part 2:** 526

Sylvia Plath: Poetry and Existence (Holbrook), **Supp. I Part 2:** 526–527

"Sylvia's Death" (Sexton), **Supp. II Part 2:** 671, 684, 685

"Symbol and Image in the Shorter Poems of Herman Melville" (Dickey), **Supp. IV Part 1:** 176

Symbolist Movement in Literature, The (Symons), **I:** 50, 569; **Retro. Supp. I:** 55

Symonds, John Addington, **I:** 241, 242, 251, 259; **IV:** 334; **Supp. XIV:** 329, 335; **Supp. XX: 230**

Symons, Arthur, **I:** 50, 569; **Retro. Supp. I:** 55; **Supp. XX: 239**

Symons, Julian, **Supp. IV Part 1:** 343, 351

"Sympathy" (Dunbar), **Supp. IV Part 1:** 15

Sympathy of Souls, A (Goldbarth), **Supp. XII:** 175, 176, **186–187**

"Symphony, The" (Lanier), **Supp. I Part 1:** 352, 360–361, 364; **Supp. I Part 2:** 416

Symposium (Plato), **Retro. Supp. II:** 31; **Supp. IV Part 1:** 391

Symposium: To Kill a Mockingbird (Alabama Law Review), **Supp. VIII:** 127, 128

Symptoms and Madness (Major), **Supp. XXII:** 174

Symptoms of Being 35 (Lardner), **II:** 434

Synanon (Endore), **Supp. XVII:** 65

Synanon (film, Quine), **Supp. XVII:** 65

Synanon City (Endore), **Supp. XVII:** 65

Syncopated Cakewalk, The (Major), **Supp. XXII:** 174

Synge, John Millington, **I:** 434; **III:** 591–592; **Supp. III Part 1:** 34; **Supp. VIII:** 155

Synthetic Philosophy (Spencer), **II:** 462–463

"Syringa" (Ashbery), **Supp. III Part 1:** 19–21, 25

"Syrinx" (Clampitt), **Supp. IX:** 53

"Syrinx" (Merrill), **Supp. III Part 1:** 328

Syrkin, Marie, **Supp. XIV:** 279, 288, 291

"System, The" (Ashbery), **Supp. III Part 1:** 14, 15, 18, 21–22

System of Dante's Hell, The (Baraka), **Supp. II Part 1:** 39–41, 55

"System of Dante's Inferno, The" (Baraka), **Supp. II Part 1:** 40

"System of Doctor Tarr and Professor Fether, The" (Poe), **III:** 419, 425

System of General Geography, A (Brown), **Supp. I Part 1:** 146

Szaylay, Michael, **Supp. XXI:** 267

Sze, Mai-mai, **Supp. X:** 291

Szentgyorgyi, Tom, **Supp. IX:** 135, 136, 140, 141–142

Szulc, Tad, **Supp. XVI:** 154

Szymborka, Wislawa, **Supp. XI:** 267

Szymborska, Wislawa, **Supp. XVIII:** 29

T

"T-2 Tanker Blues" (Snyder), **Supp. VIII:** 294

Tabios, Eileen, **Supp. XV:** 214, 225, 226

"Table of Delectable Contents, The" (Simic), **Supp. VIII:** 276

Tabloid Dreams (R. O. Butler), **Supp. XII:** 70–72, 74

Tacey Cromwell (Richter), **Supp. XVIII: 211,** 215, 217

Tacitus, Cornelius, **I:** 485; **II:** 113

Tadic, Novica, **Supp. VIII:** 272

Taft (Patchett), **Supp. XII:** 307, 312, **314–317**

"Tag" (Hughes), **Supp. I Part 1:** 341

Taggard, Genevieve, **IV:** 436; **Supp. XXII: 271–287**

Taggart, John, **Supp. IV Part 2:** 421

Tagore, Rabindranath, **I:** 383; **Supp. XX: 117**

"Taibele and Her Demon" (Singer), **Retro. Supp. II:** 307

Taibl, Erika, **Supp. XV:** 255

"Tailor Shop, The" (H. Miller), **III:** 175

"Tails" (Dixon), **Supp. XII:** 154

Taine, Hippolyte, **I:** 503; **II:** 271; **III:** 323; **IV:** 440, 444

"Tain't So" (Hughes), **Supp. I Part 1:** 330

"Taipei Tangle" (Halliday), **Supp. XIX:** 91

Takasago (play), **III:** 466

Takazauckas, Albert, **Supp. XXIII:** 203

Take Away the Darkness (Bynner), **Supp. XV:** 51

Take Heart (Peacock), **Supp. XIX: 197– 199,** 206

Take Me Back: A Novel (Bausch), **Supp. VII:** 41, 43–45, 46, 49

"Take My Saddle from the Wall: A Valediction" (McMurtry), **Supp. V:** 219

"'Take No for an Answer' " (Didion), **Supp. IV Part 1:** 203

"Take Pity" (Malamud), **Supp. I Part 2:** 427, 428, 435, 436, 437

"Takers, The" (Olds), **Supp. X:** 205

"Take the I Out" (Olds), **Supp. X:** 213

Take the Money and Run (film; Allen), **Supp. XV: 3–4,** 6

"Taking Away the Name of a Nephew" (Ríos), **Supp. IV Part 2:** 545–546

Taking Care of Mrs. Carroll (Monette), **Supp. X:** 153

"Taking of Captain Ball, The" (Jewett), **Retro. Supp. II:** 134

"Taking Off Emily Dickinson's Clothes" (Collins), **Supp. XXI:** 59, 60

"Taking Out the Lawn Chairs" (Karr), **Supp. XI:** 241

"Taking the Bypass" (J. Epstein), **Supp. XIV:** 110; **Supp. XVI:** 230

"Taking the Forest" (Howe), **Supp. IV Part 2:** 433

"Taking the Lambs to Market" (Kumin), **Supp. IV Part 2:** 455

Talbot, Daniel, **Supp. XIX:** 264

"Tale, A" (Bogan), **Supp. III Part 1:** 50, 51

Taleb-Khyar, Mohamed, **Supp. IV Part 1:** 242, 243, 244, 247, 257

Talented Mr. Ripley, The (Highsmith), **Supp. XXII:** 119

"Tale of Jerusalem, A" (Poe), **III:** 411

Tale of Possessors Self-Dispossessed, A (O'Neill), **III:** 404

Tale of the Body Thief, The (Rice), **Supp. VII:** 290, 293–294, 297

Tale of Two Cities, A (film), **Supp. I Part 1:** 67

"Tale of Two Liars, A" (Singer), **IV:** 12

Tales (Baraka), **Supp. II Part 1:** 39, 55

Tales (Poe), **III:** 413

Tales and Stories for Black Folks (Bambara, ed.), **Supp. XI:** 1

Tales before Midnight (Benét), **Supp. XI:** 46, 53, 57

Talese, Gay, **Supp. XVI:** 273; **Supp. XVII: 199–211**

Tales of a Traveller (Irving), **II:** 309–310

Tales of a Wayside Inn (Longfellow), **II:** 489, 490, 501, 502, 504–505; **Retro. Supp. II:** 154, **162–165**

Tales of Glauber-Spa (Bryant, ed.), **Supp. I Part 1:** 157

Tales of Manhattan (Auchincloss), **Supp. IV Part 1:** 23

Tales of Men and Ghosts (Wharton), **IV:** 315; **Retro. Supp. I:** 372

Tales of My People (Asch), **Supp. XXIII:** 7

Tales of Rhoda, The (Rice), **Supp. VII:** 288

Tales of Soldiers and Civilians (Bierce), **I:** 200–203, 204, 206, 208, 212

Tales of the Argonauts (Harte), **Supp. II Part 1:** 337, 348, 351

Tales of the Fish Patrol (London), **II:** 465

Tales of the Grotesque and Arabesque (Poe), **II:** 273; **III:** 412, 415; **Retro. Supp. II:** 270

Tales of the Jazz Age (Fitzgerald), **II:** 88; **Retro. Supp. I:** 105; **Supp. IX:** 57

Tales You Won't Believe (Stratton-Porter), **Supp. XX:** 217

Taliaferro, Frances, **Supp. XXII:** 210

"Talisman, A" (Moore), **III:** 195–196

Talisman, The (King), **Supp. V:** 140, 144, 152

"Talkin Bout Sonny" (Bambara), **Supp. XI:** 6–7

"Talking" (Merwin), **Supp. III Part 1:** 354

Talking All Morning (R. Bly), **Supp. IV Part 1:** 59, 60, 61, 62, 64, 65

Talking Dirty to the Gods (Komunyakaa), **Supp. XIII: 130–131**

Talking History (television program), **Supp. XXI:** 172

"Talking Horse" (Malamud), **Supp. I Part 2:** 435

Talking Soft Dutch (McCarriston), **Supp. XIV: 260–263,** 266, 270, 271

"Talking to Barr Creek" (Wagoner), **Supp. IX:** 328

"Talking to Sheep" (Sexton), **Supp. II Part 2:** 695

Talking to the Sun: An Illustrated Anthology of Poems for Young People (Koch and Farrell, eds.), **Supp. XV:** 188

"Talking Water" (Taggard), **Supp. XXII:** 276

"Talk of Heroes" (C. Bly), **Supp. XVI:** 34

"Talk of the Town" (*The New Yorker* column), **IV:** 215; **Supp. IV Part 1:** 53, 54

"Talk on Guadalcanal" (Wolfert), **Supp. XXI:** 264

Talk Talk (Boyle), **Supp. XX:** 24

"Talk with the Yellow Kid, A" (Bellow), **I:** 151

Tallent, Elizabeth, **Supp. IV Part 2:** 570

Tallman, Warren, **Supp. IV Part 1:** 154

TallMountain, Mary, **Supp. IV Part 1:** 324–325

Talma, Louise, **IV:** 357

Talmadge, Constance, **Supp. XVI:** 186, 187, 196

Talmadge, Norma, **Supp. XVI:** 186, 187, 196

Talmadge Girls, The (Loos), **Supp. XVI:** 186, 196

Talmey, Allene, **Supp. IV Part 1:** 197; **Supp. XIII:** 172

Talmud, **IV:** 8, 17

Taltos: Lives of the Mayfair Witches (Rice), **Supp. VII:** 299–300

"Tamar" (Jeffers), **Supp. II Part 2:** 427– 428, 436

Tamar and Other Poems (Jeffers), **Supp. II Part 2:** 416, 419

Tambourines to Glory (Hughes), **Supp. I Part 1:** 338–339

"Tame Indians" (Jewett), **Retro. Supp. II:** 141

"Tamerlane" (Poe), **III:** 426

Tamerlane and Other Poems (Poe), **III:** 410

"Tammany Man, The" (Hapgood), **Supp. XVII:** 103

"Tam O'Shanter" (Burns), **II:** 306

Tamsen Donner: A Woman's Journey (Whitman), **Supp. XXI:** 246

Tan, Amy, **Supp. X: 289–300**

Tangential Views (Bierce), **I:** 209

"Tangier 1975" (Bowles), **Supp. IV Part 1:** 94

Tanguay, Pablo, **Supp. XXIII:** 299

"Tankas" (McClatchy), **Supp. XII:** 266

Tanner, Laura E., **Supp. X:** 209; **Supp. XXI:** 217

Tanner, Obour, **Supp. XX: 281, 288**

Tanner, Tony, **I:** 260, 261; **Retro. Supp. II:** 205; **Supp. IV Part 1:** 285; **Supp. XVI:** 65, 69

Tannhäuser (Wagner), **I:** 315

"Tan Ta Ra, Cries Mars...," (Wagoner), **Supp. IX:** 325

Tao of Physics, The (Capra), **Supp. X:** 261

Tao Teh Ching (Bynner, trans.), **Supp. XV:** 46, 47

Tapahonso, Luci, **Supp. IV Part 1:** 404; **Supp. IV Part 2:** 499, 508

Tape for the Turn of the Year (Ammons), **Supp. VII:** 31–33, 35

"Tapestry" (Ashbery), **Supp. III Part 1:** 22–23

"Tapestry" (P. E. Jones), **Supp. XXII:** 152

"Tapiama" (Bowles), **Supp. IV Part 1:** 89–90

"Tapiola" (W. C. Williams), **Retro. Supp. I:** 429

Tappan, Arthur, **Supp. I Part 2:** 588

Tapping the White Cane of Solitude (F. Wright), **Supp. XVII:** 243

Taps at Reveille (Fitzgerald), **II:** 94, 96; **Retro. Supp. I:** 113

Tar: A Midwest Childhood (Anderson), **I:** 98, 115; **II:** 27

Tarantino, Quentin, **Supp. IV Part 1:** 356

Tarantula (Dylan), **Supp. XVIII:** 21, 29, **31–32**

Tar Baby (Morrison), **Supp. III Part 1:** 364, 369–372, 379; **Supp. IV Part 1:** 13

Tarbell, Ida, **III:** 322, 580; **Retro. Supp. II:** 101

"Target Practice" (Offutt), **Supp. XIX:** 171

"Target Study" (Baraka), **Supp. II Part 1:** 49–50, 54

Tarkington, Booth, **II:** 444; **III:** 70; **Retro. Supp. I:** 100; **Supp. XV:** 41

Tarnawsky, Yuriy (George) Orest, **Supp. XX: 259**

Tarpon (film), **Supp. VIII:** 42

Tarr, Rodger L., **Supp. X:** 222, 224, 226

Tárrega, Francisco, **Supp. XXI:** 100

Tartt, Donna, **Supp. XVIII:** 135

Tartuffe (Molière; Wilbur, trans.), **Supp. III Part 2:** 560

Tarumba, Selected Poems of Jaime Sabines (Levine and Trejo, trans.), **Supp. V:** 178

Tarzan Finds a Son (film, Weismuller), **Supp. XX:** 18

"Tarzan Is an Expatriate" (Theroux), **Supp. VIII:** 313

Tasis, Juan de, **Supp. XXI:** 104

Task, The (Cowper), **II:** 304

Tasker Street (Halliday), **Supp. XIX:** 82, **87–89**

Tasso, Torquato, **I:** 276

Taste of Palestine, A: Menus and Memories (Shihab), **Supp. XIII:** 273

Tate, Alan, **Supp. XV:** 141

Tate, Allen, **I:** 48, 49, 50, 67, 69, 381, 382, 386, 390, 396, 397, 399, 402, 441, 468; **II:** 197–198, 367, 536, 537, 542, 551, 554; **III:** 424, 428, 454, 482, 483, 485, 493, 495, 496, 497, 499, 500, 517; **IV: 120–143,** 236, 237, 433; **Retro. Supp. I:** 37, 41, 90; **Retro. Supp. II:** 77, 79, 82, 83, 89, 176, 178, 179; **Supp. I Part 1:** 364, 371; **Supp. I Part 2:** 423; **Supp. II Part 1:** 90–91, 96, 98, 103–104, 136, 139, 144, 150, 151, 318; **Supp. II Part 2:** 643; **Supp. III Part 2:** 542; **Supp. V:** 315, 331; **Supp. X:** 1, 52; **Supp. XIV:** 2; **Supp. XXI:** 256; **Supp. XXII:** 277

Tate, Mrs. Allen (Caroline Gordon). *See* Gordon, Caroline

Tate, Mrs. Allen (Helen Heinz), **IV:** 127

Tate, Mrs. Allen (Isabella Gardner), **IV:** 127

Tate, Benjamin Lewis Bogan, **IV:** 127

Tate, Greg, **Supp. XIII:** 233, 237

Tate, James, **Supp. V:** 92, 338; **Supp. VIII:** 39, 279; **Supp. XV:** 250; **Supp. XVII:** 242

Tate, John Allen, **IV:** 127

Tate, Michael Paul, **IV:** 127

Tate, Nancy, **II:** 197

Tatonetti, Lisa, **Supp. XXIII:** 149–150

Tattooed Countess, The (Van Vechten), **I:** 295; **Supp. II Part 2:** 726–728, 738, 742

Tattooed Feet (Nye), **Supp. XIII:** 274

"Tattoos" (McClatchy), **Supp. XII:** 266–267, 268

"Tattoos" (Wright), **Supp. V:** 335, 340

Tatum, Anna, **I:** 516

Tatum, James, **Supp. IV Part 2:** 684

Taupin, René, **II:** 528, 529; **Supp. III Part 2:** 614, 615, 617, 621

Tavano, John, **Supp. XXI:** 99

Tawney, Richard Henry, **Supp. I Part 2:** 481

Taylor, Ann, **Supp. XXIII:** 231

Taylor, Bayard, **II:** 275; **Supp. I Part 1:** 350, 361, 362, 365, 366, 372; **Supp. XV:** 269

Taylor, Chuck, **Supp. XXIII:** 57

Taylor, Cora. *See* Howarth, Cora

Taylor, Deems, **III:** 138

Taylor, Edward, **III:** 493; **IV: 144–166;** **Supp. I Part 1:** 98; **Supp. I Part 2:** 375, 386, 546

Taylor, Mrs. Edward (Elizabeth Fitch), **IV:** 147, 165

Taylor, Mrs. Edward (Ruth Wyllys), **IV:** 148

Taylor, Eleanor Ross, **Supp. V:** 317, 318

Taylor, Elizabeth, **II:** 588

Taylor, Frank, **III:** 81

Taylor, Frederick Winslow, **Supp. I Part 2:** 644

Taylor, Graham, **Supp. I Part 1:** 5

Taylor, Henry, **Retro. Supp. I:** 212; **Supp. XI:** 317; **Supp. XIII:** 333

Taylor, Henry W., **IV:** 144

Taylor, Jeremy, **II:** 11; **III:** 487; **Supp. I Part 1:** 349; **Supp. XII:** 45; **Supp. XIV:** 344, 345

Taylor, John, **IV:** 149

Taylor, Katherine, **Supp. VIII:** 251

Taylor, Kezia, **IV:** 148

Taylor, Nathaniel W., **Supp. I Part 2:** 580

Taylor, Paul, **I:** 293

Taylor, Peter, **Retro. Supp. II:** 179; **Supp. V: 313–329; Supp. XIV:** 3

Taylor, Raynor, **Supp. XV:** 238

Taylor, Richard, **IV:** 146

Taylor, Robert, **Supp. I Part 1:** 294; **Supp. XV:** 135, 138; **Supp. XVI:** 277

Taylor, Samuel A., **Supp. XX:** 253

Taylor, Stephan, **Supp. XVI:** 203

Taylor, Thomas, **II:** 10

Taylor, William, **IV:** 145–146

Taylor, Zachary, **I:** 3; **II:** 433–434

Tchelitchew, Peter, **II:** 586

Tea and Sympathy (Anderson), **Supp. I Part 1:** 277; **Supp. V:** 108

"Tea at the Palaz of Hoon" (Stevens), **Retro. Supp. I:** 300, 302, 306

"Teacher's Pet" (Thurber), **Supp. I Part 2:** 605–606

"Teaching and Story Telling" (Maclean), **Supp. XIV:** 234

Teaching a Stone to Talk: Expeditions and Encounters (Dillard), **Supp. VI:** 23, 26, 28, 32, 33, 34–35

"Teaching Emily Dickenson"(Hadas), **Supp. XXIII:** 115

"Teaching Hanh the Blues" (Weigl), **Supp. XIX:** 287

Teachings of Don B., The (Barthelme), **Supp. IV Part 1:** 53

Teachout, Terry, **Supp. XIX:** 137

Teale, Edwin Way, **Supp. XIII:** 7

Teall, Dorothy, **I:** 221

Team Team Team (film), **Supp. IX:** 251

"Tea on the Mountain" (Bowles), **Supp. IV Part 1:** 90

"Tea Party, The" (MacLeish), **III:** 11

Tear and a Smile, A (Dam'a wa Ibtisáma) (Gibran), **Supp. XX: 116, 118, 124**

Teare, Brian, **Supp. XXII:** 236

"Tears, Idle Tears" (Lord Tennyson), **Supp. XIV:** 8

"Tears of the Pilgrims, The" (McClatchy), **Supp. XII:** 256

Teasdale, Sara, **Retro. Supp. I:** 133; **Supp. I Part 2:** 393, 707; **Supp. XIV:** 127; **Supp. XV:** 295, 297, 301, 305, 307, 308; **Supp. XVII:** 69, 75

"Tease" (Swados), **Supp. XIX:** 267

Tebeaux, Elizabeth, **Supp. IX:** 109

"Technical Manifesto of Futurist Literature" (Marinetti), **Supp. XXII:** 161

Technics and Civilization (Mumford), **Supp. I Part 2:** 638; **Supp. II Part 2:** 479, 493, 497

Technics and Human Development (Mumford), **Supp. I Part 2:** 638; **Supp. II Part 2:** 497

"Technology, The" (Egan), **Supp. XIX:** 61

"Teddy" (Salinger), **III:** 561–563, 571

"Te Deum" (Reznikoff), **Supp. XIV:** 281

Tedlock, Dennis, **Supp. IV Part 2:** 509

"Teeth Mother Naked at Last, The" (R. Bly), **Supp. IV Part 1:** 63, 68, 73

Teggart, Richard, **Supp. I Part 2:** 650

Tegnér, Esaias, **Retro. Supp. II:** 155

Teilhard de Chardin, Pierre, **Supp. I Part 1:** 314

Tekonwatonti/Molly Brant (Kenny), **Supp. XXIII:** 143, 147, 151, **152–153,** 154

Telephone, The (film), **Supp. XI:** 309

"Telephone Call, A" (Parker), **Supp. IX: 202–203**

"Telephone Number of the Muse, The" (Justice), **Supp. VII:** 124–125

Telephone Poles and Other Poems (Updike), **IV:** 214, 215

"Television" (Beattie), **Supp. V:** 33

Teller, Edward, **I:** 137

"Telling" (Ortiz), **Supp. IV Part 2:** 509

"Telling It in Black and White: The Importance of the Africanist Presence in *To Kill a Mockingbird*" (Baecker), **Supp. VIII:** 128

Telling Secrets (Buechner), **Supp. XII:** 53–54

Telling Stories (Didion), **Supp. IV Part 1:** 197

"Telling Stories" (Didion), **Supp. IV Part 1:** 197

"Telling the Bees" (Whittier), **Supp. I Part 2:** 694–695

Telling the Little Secrets (J. Burstein), **Supp. XVII:** 44

Telling the Truth: The Gospel as Tragedy, Comedy, and Fairy Tale (Buechner), **Supp. XII:** 53

"Tell Me" (Hughes), **Supp. VIII:** 213

"Tell Me, Sir, ... What Is 'Black' Literature?" (H. L. Gates), **Supp. XX: 108**

Tell Me, Tell Me (Moore), **III:** 215

Tell Me Again (Notley), **Supp. XXII:** 224, 230–231

Tell Me Again How the White Heron Rises and Flies across the Nacreous River at Twilight toward the Distant Islands (Carruth), **Supp. XVI:**56

Tell Me a Riddle (film), **Supp. XIII:** 295

Tell Me a Riddle (Olsen), **Supp. XIII:** 294, 296, **298–302,** 303, 305

"Tell Me a Riddle" (Olsen), **Supp. XIII:** 294, 297, 298, **300–302,** 305

"Tell Me a Story" (McDermott), **Supp. XVIII:** 177

Tell Me How Long the Train's Been Gone (Baldwin), **Retro. Supp. II:** 9, **11–12,** 14; **Supp. I Part 1:** 48, 52, 63–65, 67

"Tell Me My Fortune" (Epstein), **Supp. XII:** 163

Tell Me True: Memoir, History, and Writing a Life (Hampl and May, eds.), **Supp. XXII:** 81–82, 84, **94–95**

Tell Me Your Answer True (Sexton), **Supp. II Part 2:** 683

Tell My Horse (Hurston), **Supp. VI:** 149, 156, 158

"Tell-Tale Heart, The" (Poe), **III:** 413, 414–415, 416; **Retro. Supp. II:** 267, 269, 270

"Tell the Women We're Going" (Carver), **Supp. III Part 1:** 138, 144

"Telluride Blues—A Hatchet Job" (Abbey), **Supp. XIII:** 10

Telushkin, Dvorah, **Retro. Supp. II:** 317

Temblor (Howe), **Supp. IV Part 2:** 431

Tempering of Eugene O'Neill, The (D. Alexander), **Supp. XVII:** 99

"Temper of Steel, The" (Jones), **Supp. XI:** 218

Tempers, The (W. C. Williams), **Retro. Supp. I:** **413–414,** 415, 416, 424

Tempest, The (Shakespeare), **I:** 394; **II:** 12; **III:** 40, 61, 263; **Retro. Supp. I:** 61; **Supp. IV Part 2:** 463; **Supp. V:** 302–303; **Supp. XII:** 54–57; **Supp. XV:** 255, 256

Temple, Minnie, **II:** 323

Temple, The (Herbert), **IV:** 145, 153

Temple, William, **III:** 303

Temple House (E. Stoddard), **Supp. XV:** 273, **284–286**

Temple of My Familiar, The (Walker), **Supp. III Part 2:** 521, 527, 529, 535, 537; **Supp. IV Part 1:** 14

"Temple of the Holy Ghost, A" (O'Connor), **III:** 344, 352; **Retro. Supp. II:** 232

Templin, Charlotte, **Supp. V:** 116

Temporary Shelter (Gordon), **Supp. IV Part 1:** 299, 305–307

"Temporary Shelter" (Gordon), **Supp. IV Part 1:** 306

Temptation Game, The (Gardner), **Supp. VI:** 72

"Temptation of St. Anthony, The" (Barthelme), **Supp. IV Part 1:** 47

Temptations, The, **Supp. X:** 242

"10 Best Weathers of 1983, The" (Notley), **Supp. XXII:** 224

"10 Things I Do Every Day" (Berrigan), **Supp. XXII:** 224

"Tenancy, A" (Merrill), **Supp. III Part 1:** 322, 323

"Tenant" (Hoffman), **Supp. XVIII:** 86

Tenants, The (Malamud), **Supp. I Part 2:** 448–450

"Ten Best Issues of Comic Books, The" (Notley), **Supp. XXII:** 224

Ten Commandments (McClatchy), **Supp. XII: 262–265**

Ten Days That Shook the World (Reed), **II:** 577; **Supp. X:** 136; **Supp. XVIII:** 225

Tendencies in Modern American Poetry (Lowell), **II:** 529

"Tender, Hilarious Reminiscences of Life in Mythical Lake Wobegon" (MacDougall), **Supp. XVI:** 174

Tender Buttons (G. Stein), **I:** 103, 105; **IV:** 27, 42–43; **Retro. Supp. II:** 331; **Supp. XV:** 347

"Tenderfoot" (Haines), **Supp. XII:** 209

Tender Is the Night (Fitzgerald), **I:** 375; **II:** 79, 84, 91, 95–96, 97, 98, 420; **Retro. Supp. I:** 105, 108, 109, **110–112,** 114; **Supp. IX:** 59, 60, 61; **Supp. XV:** 197; **Supp. XXI:** 11

"Tenderloin" (Crane), **I:** 408

"Tenderly" (Dobyns), **Supp. XIII:** 86–87

'Tender Man, A" (Bambara), **Supp. XI:** 9–10

"Tenderness" (Dunn), **Supp. XI:** 149, 150

"Tender Offer, The" (Auchincloss), **Supp. IV Part 1:** 34

"Tender Organizations, The" (C. Bly), **Supp. XVI:** 40, 42

"Tenebrae" (Komunyakaa), **Supp. XIII:** 132

Tenenbaum, Joseph, **Supp. XX:** 253

"Ten Forty-Four" (Kingsolver), **Supp. VII:** 208

Ten Indians (Bell), **Supp. X:** 7, **12**

Ten Introductions: A Collection of Modern Verse (Taggard and Fitts, ed.), **Supp. XXII:** 281

Tennant, Agnieszka, **Supp. XX: 140**

"Ten Neglected American Writers Who Deserve to Be Better Known" (Cantor), **Supp. IV Part 1:** 285

Tennent, Gilbert, **I:** 546

Tennessee Day in St. Louis (Taylor), **Supp. V:** 324

"Tennessee's Partner" (Harte), **Supp. II Part 1:** 345, 348–350

"Tennis" (Pinsky), **Supp. VI:** 241, 242

Tennis Court Oath, The (Ashbery), **Supp. III Part 1:** 7, 9, 12, 14, 26

Ten North Frederick (O'Hara), **III:** 361

Tennyson, Alfred, Lord, **I:** 587–588; **II:** 18, 82, 273, 338, 404, 439, 604; **III:** 5, 409, 469, 485, 511, 521, 523; **Retro. Supp. I:** 100, 325; **Retro. Supp. II:** 135; **Supp. I Part 1:** 349, 356; **Supp. I Part 2:** 410, 416, 552; **Supp. IX:** 19; **Supp. X:** 157; **Supp. XIII:** 111; **Supp. XIV:** 40, 120; **Supp. XV:** 275; **Supp. XVIII:** 78

"Tenochtitlan" (Bronk), **Supp. XXI:** 31

"Ten O'Clock News" (Ortiz), **Supp. IV Part 2:** 503–504

"Te-Non-An-At-Che"(Kenny), **Supp. XXIII:** 151

Ten Poems (Dove), **Supp. IV Part 1:** 244

Ten Poems of Francis Ponge Translated by Robert Bly and Ten Poems of Robert Bly Inspired by the Poems by Francis Ponge (R. Bly), **Supp. IV Part 1:** 71

"Tension in Poetry" (Tate), **IV:** 128, 129, 135

Tenth Muse, The (Bradstreet), **Supp. I Part 1:** 102, 103, 114

10,000 Days of Thunder: A History of the Vietnam War (Caputo), **Supp. XIX:** 29

"Tent on the Beach, The" (Whittier), **Supp. I Part 2:** 703

"Teodoro Luna Confesses after Years to His Brother, Anselmo the Priest, Who Is Required to Understand, But Who Understands Anyway, More Than People Think" (Ríos), **Supp. IV Part 2:** 552

Teodoro Luna's Two Kisses (Ríos), **Supp. IV Part 2:** 550–552, 553

"Tepeyac" (Cisneros), **Supp. VII:** 69

"Terce" (Auden), **Supp. II Part 1:** 22

Terence, **IV:** 155, 363; **Supp. I Part 2:** 405

Terkel, Studs, **Supp. IV Part 1:** 364

"Term" (Merwin), **Supp. III Part 1:** 356–357

"Terminal Days at Beverly Farms" (Lowell), **Retro. Supp. II:** 189

Terminating, or Sonnet LXXV, or "Lass Meine Schmerzen nicht verloren sein, or Ambivalence" (Kushner), *Supp. IX:* 132

Terminations (James), **Retro. Supp. I:** 229

"Terminus" (Emerson), **II:** 13, 19

"Terminus" (Wharton), **Retro. Supp. I:** 371

"Terms in Which I Think of Reality, The" (Ginsberg), **Supp. II Part 1:** 311

Terms of Endearment (film), **Supp. V:** 226

Terms of Endearment (McMurtry), **Supp. V:** 224–225

"Terrace, The" (Wilbur), **Supp. III Part 2:** 550

Terrarium (Sanders), **Supp. XVI:** 270

"Terrence McNally" (Bryer), **Supp. XIII:** 200

"Terrence McNally" (Di Gaetani), **Supp. XIII:** 200

Terrence McNally: A Casebook (Zinman), **Supp. XIII:** 209

"Terrestrial Cuckoo"(O'Hara), **Supp. XXIII:** 210

"Terrible Peacock, The" (Barnes), **Supp. III Part 1:** 33

Terrible Threes, The (Reed), **Supp. X:** 241, 253

Terrible Twos, The (Reed), **Supp. X:** 241, **252–253**

"Terrific Mother" (Moore), **Supp. X:** 178

Territory Ahead, The (Morris), **III:** 228–229, 236

Terrorism (Wright), **Supp. XV:** 341, 342

"Terrorism" (Wright), **Supp. XV:** 341

Terry, Edward A., **II:** 128, 129

Terry, Rose, **Supp. I Part 2:** 420

Tertium Organum (Ouspensky), **I:** 383; **Supp. XX: 116**

Tess of the d'Ubervilles (Hardy), **II:** 181; **Retro. Supp. II:** 100

"Testament" (Berry), **Supp. X:** 36

"Testament" (Carruth), **Supp. XVI:** 59
"Testament (Or, Homage to Walt Whitman)" (Jong), **Supp. V:** 130
"Testament of Flood" (Warren), **IV:** 253
Testament of François Villon, The (Pound, opera), **Retro. Supp. I:** 287
"Testament: Vermeer in December" (Bierds), **Supp. XVII:** 33
"Testimonia on the Question of Stesichoros' Blinding by Helen" (Carson), **Supp. XII:** 107
"Testimonies of a Roasted Chicken" (Jarman), **Supp. XVII:** 120
"Testimony" (Komunyakaa), **Supp. XIII:** 129
"Testimony of James Apthorp, The" (Kees), **Supp. XV:** 146
Testimony: The United States (1885–1890): Recitative (Reznikoff), **Supp. XIV:** 279, 280, 281, 285, **289–291**
Testimony: The United States (1891–1900): Recitative (Reznikoff), **Supp. XIV:** 291
Testing-Tree, The (Kunitz), **Supp. III Part 1:** 260, 263, 264, 267, 268
"Testing-Tree, The" (Kunitz), **Supp. III Part 1:** 269
Test of Poetry, A (Zukofsky), **Supp. III Part 2:** 618, 622
"Teutonic Scholar" (X. J. Kennedy), **Supp. XV:** 161
"Texas Moon, and Elsewhere, The" (McMurtry), **Supp. V:** 225
Texas Poets in Concert: A Quartet (Gwynn, ed.), **Supp. XIII:** 277
Texas Summer (Southern), **Supp. XI:** 309
Texasville (McMurtry), **Supp. V:** 228, 233
Thacher, Molly Day, **IV:** 381
Thackeray, William Makepeace, **I:** 194, 354; **II:** 182, 271, 282, 288, 316, 321, 322; **III:** 64, 70; **IV:** 326; **Retro. Supp. I:** 218; **Supp. I Part 1:** 307; **Supp. I Part 2:** 421, 495, 579; **Supp. IV Part 1:** 297; **Supp. IX:** 200; **Supp. XI:** 277; **Supp. XIV:** 306; **Supp. XX:** **228**
Thaddeus, Janice Farrar, **Supp. IV Part 1:** 299
"Thailand" (Barthelme), **Supp. IV Part 1:** 41
Thalberg, Irving, **Retro. Supp. I:** 109, 110, 114; **Supp. XVI:** 191, 192
Thales, **I:** 480–481
Thalia Trilogy (McMurtry), **Supp. V:** 220–223, 234
Tham, Claire, **Supp. VIII:** 79
"Thanatopsis" (Bryant), **Supp. I Part 1:** 150, 154, 155, 170
Thanatos Syndrome, The (Percy), **Supp. III Part 1:** 385, 397–399
"Thanks Can Be Named to Death" (Peacock), **Supp. XIX:** 199
"Thanksgiving" (Glück), **Supp. V:** 83
"Thanksgiving, A" (Auden), **Supp. II Part 1:** 26
"Thanksgiving for a Habitat" (Auden), **Supp. II Part 1:** 24
Thanksgivings (Traherne), **Supp. XVI:** 288

"Thanksgiving Spirit" (Farrell), **II:** 45
Thanksgiving Visitor, The (Capote), **Supp. III Part 1:** 116, 118, 119
"Thank You, Esther Forbes" (Saunders), **Supp. XIX:** 235
Thank You, Fog (Auden), **Supp. II Part 1:** 24
"Thank You, Lord" (Angelou), **Supp. IV Part 1:** 15
Thank You, Mr. Moto (Marquand), **III:** 57, 58
Thank You and Other Poems (Koch), **Supp. XV:** 180–181
"Thank You in Arabic" (Nye), **Supp. XIII:** 273, 281
"Thar's More in the Man Than Thar Is in the Land" (Lanier), **Supp. I Part 1:** 352–353, 359–360
"That Evening Sun" (Faulkner), **II:** 72; **Retro. Supp. I:** 75, 83
That Horse (Hogan), **Supp. IV Part 1:** 397, 404, 405
"That House, This Room" (W. V. Davis), **Supp. XXI:** 90
"That I Had the Wings" (Ellison), **Supp. II Part 1:** 238
That Night (McDermott), **Supp. XVIII:** 155, **158–160,** 162, 163, 166
"That's the Place Indians Talk About" (Ortiz), **Supp. IV Part 2:** 511
That Tantalus (Bronk), **Supp. XXI:** 31
"That the Soul May Wax Plump" (Swenson), **Supp. IV Part 2:** 650
"That the Universe Is Chrysalid" (Sobin), **Supp. XVI:** 284
"That Tree" (Porter), **III:** 434–435, 446, 451
That Was the Week That Was (television program), **Supp. XIV:** 125
"That Year" (Olds), **Supp. X:** 203
"Thaw" (C. Frost), **Supp. XV:** 93, 104, 105
Thaxter, Celia, **Retro. Supp. II:** 136, 147; **Supp. XIII:** 143, 153
Thayer, Abbott, **I:** 231
Thayer, Scofield, **I:** 231; **Retro. Supp. I:** 58
Thayer and Eldridge, **Retro. Supp. I:** 403
"Theater" (Toomer), **Supp. IX:** 309, 317–318
"Theater Chronicle" (McCarthy), **II:** 562
"Theater Problems? Call Dr. Chekhov" (Wasserstein), **Supp. XV:** 320
Theatricals (James), **Retro. Supp. I:** 228
The Blacker the Berry: A Novel of Negro Life (Thurman), **Supp. XVIII:** 281; **Supp. XIX:** 73
"Theft" (Porter), **III:** 434, 435
Theft, A (Bellow), **Retro. Supp. II:** 31–32, 34
The Harder They Fall (Schulberg), **Supp. XVIII:** **247,** 253
The Harder They Fall: Celebrities Tell Their Real-Life Stories of Addiction and Recovery (F. Wright), **Supp. XVII:** 240
Their Eyes Were Watching God (Hurston), **Supp. VI:** 149, 152, 156–157; **Supp. XX:** **107**

Their Heads Are Green and Their Hands Are Blue: Scenes from the Non-Christian World (Bowles), **Supp. IV Part 1:** 89
"Their Losses" (Taylor), **Supp. V:** 320
"Their Sleep" (W. V. Davis), **Supp. XXI:** 93
Their Wedding Journey (Howells), **II:** 277–278; **Retro. Supp. I:** 334
them (Oates), **Supp. II Part 2:** 503, 511–514
Theme Is Freedom, The (Dos Passos), **I:** 488–489, 492, 494
Theme Time Radio Hour (radio show, Dylan), **Supp. XVIII:** 28
"Theme with Variations" (Agee), **I:** 27
"Then" (Barthelme), **Supp. IV Part 1:** 48
"Then as Now" (Cliff), **Supp. XXII:** 76
"The Night Rhonda Ferguson Was Killed" (P. E. Jones), **Supp. XXII:** 144
"Then It All Came Down" (Capote), **Supp. III Part 1:** 125, 131
Theocritus, **II:** 169; **Retro. Supp. I:** 286
Theodore Roethke's Far Fields: The Evolution of His Poetry (Balakian), **Supp. XXIII:** 19
"Theodore the Poet" (Masters), **Supp. I Part 2:** 461
Theological Position, A (Coover), **Supp. V:** 44
Theophrastus, **I:** 58
"Theoretical and Scientific Conceptions of Race, The" (Locke), **Supp. XIV:** 209
"Theoretical Subject(s) of *This Bridge Called My Back,* The" (Alarcón), **Supp. XXIII:** 204–205
"Theories of Time and Space" (Trethewey), **Supp. XXI:** 255
Theory and Practice of Rivers and Other Poems, The (Harrison), **Supp. VIII:** 47, 49
Theory of Business Enterprise, The (Veblen), **Supp. I Part 2:** 638, 641, 644
Theory of Flight (Rukeyser), **Supp. VI:** 272, 275, **277–278,** 284
"Theory of Flight" (Rukeyser), **Supp. VI:** 277–278
Theory of Moral Sentiments, The (A. Smith), **Supp. I Part 2:** 634
Theory of the Leisure Class, The (Veblen), **I:** 475–476; **Supp. I Part 2:** 629, 633, 641, 645; **Supp. IV Part 1:** 22
"There" (Taylor), **Supp. V:** 323
"There Are No Such Trees in Alpine California" (Haines), **Supp. XII:** 207
"There Goes (Varoom! Varoom!) That Kandy-Kolored Tangerine-Flake Streamline Baby" (Wolfe), **Supp. III Part 2:** 569–571
"There Have Been Changes" (Pickering), **Supp. XXI:** 202–203
"There Is a Lesson" (Olsen), **Supp. XIII:** 292, 297
"There is a Man" (Espaillat), **Supp. XXI:** 108–109
"There Is Only One of Everything" (Atwood), **Supp. XIII:** 34

There Is Something Out There (McNally). *See And Things That Go Bump in the Night* (McNally)

"There Must Be" (Peacock), **Supp. XIX:** 199

"There's a certain Slant of light" (Dickinson), **Retro. Supp. I:** 38

There's a Wocket in My Pocket! (Geisel), **Supp. XVI:** 111

Thérèse de Lisieux, Saint, **Supp. VIII:** 195

"There She Is She Is Taking Her Bath" (Anderson), **I:** 113, 114

"There Was a Child Went Forth" (Whitman), **IV:** 348

"There Was a Man, There Was a Woman" (Cisneros), **Supp. VII:** 70

"There Was an Old Woman She Had So Many Children She Didn't Know What to Do" (Cisneros), **Supp. VII:** 60

"There Was a Youth Whose Name Was Thomas Granger" (Olson), **Supp. II Part 2:** 558, 560, 563

There Were Giants in the Land (Benét), **Supp. XI:** 50

There You Are (Simpson), **Supp. IX:** 279–280

"There You Are" (Simpson), **Supp. IX:** 279

"Thermopylae" (Clampitt), **Supp. IX:** 43

Theroux, Alexander, **Supp. VIII:** 312

Theroux, Marcel, **Supp. VIII:** 325

Theroux, Paul, **Supp. V:** 122; **Supp. VIII: 309–327**

"These Are My People" (Hayden), **Supp. II Part 1:** 365

These Are My Same Hands (Schott), **Supp. XXIII:** 241, 242

"These are the days when Birds come back" (Dickinson), **Retro. Supp. I:** 30

"These Days" (Olds), **Supp. X:** 215

"These Flames and Generosities of the Heart: Emily Dickinson and the Illogic of Sumptuary Values" (Howe), **Supp. IV Part 2:** 431

"These Hands" (Brockmeier), **Supp. XXII:** 51, 52, 53

These Happy Golden Years (L. I. Wilder), **Supp. XXII:** 294, 297, 299

These Low Grounds (Turpin), **Supp. XVIII:** 283

"These saw Visions" (Dickinson), **Retro. Supp. I:** 46

These Thirteen (Faulkner), **II:** 72

These Three (film), **Supp. I Part 1:** 281

These Times (Untermeyer), **Supp. XV: 299–300**, 303

"These Times" (Untermeyer), **Supp. XV:** 300

"Thessalonica: A Roman Story" (Brown), **Supp. I Part 1:** 133

Thévenaz, Paul, **Supp. XV:** 42

Thew, Harvey, **Supp. XIII:** 166

"They Ain't the Men They Used To Be" (Farrell), **II:** 45

"They Burned the Books" (Benét), **Supp. XI:** 46

They Came Like Swallows (Maxwell), **Supp. VIII: 155–159**, 168, 169

"They Can't Turn Back" (Baldwin), **Supp. I Part 1:** 52

They Do Not: The Letters of a Non-Professional Lady Arranged for Public Consumption (Clements), **Supp. XVI:** 190

They Feed They Lion (Levine), **Supp. V:** 178, 179, 181, 184–185, 186

"They Feed They Lion" (Levine), **Supp. V:** 188

"They Lion Grow" (Levine), **Supp. V:** 184–185

"They're Not Your Husband" (Carver), **Supp. III Part 1:** 141, 143

They're Playing Our Song (musical), **Supp. IV Part 2:** 589

They Seek a City (Bontemps and Conroy), **Supp. XXII:** 5, 11

They Shall Inherit the Laughter (Jones), **Supp. XI:** 217, 218, 232

"They Shall Not Die" (Ryan as Quin), **Supp. XVIII:** 228–229

They Shoot Horses (film), **Supp. XIII:** 159

They Shoot Horses, Don't They? (McCoy), **Supp. XIII:** 159, **164–166**, 168, 171, 172, 174

"They Sing, They Sing" (Roethke), **III:** 544

They Stooped to Folly (Glasgow), **II:** 175, 186–187

They Were Expendable (film), **Supp. XVIII:** 247

They Whisper (R. O. Butler), **Supp. XII: 72–73**

They Who Knock at Our Gates: A Complete Gospel of Immigration (Antin), **Supp. XX: 2–3, 10–11,** 12

"Thick and Thin"(Hadas), **Supp. XXIII:** 119

Thidwick the Big-Hearted Moose (Geisel), **Supp. XVI:** 104

"Thief's Philosophy of Life, The" (Hapgood), **Supp. XVII:** 103

"Thief's Wife, The" (B. Kelly), **Supp. XVII:** 125–126

"Thieves" (Yates), **Supp. XI:** 349

Thieves of Paradise (Komunyakaa), **Supp. XIII:** 113, **128–130,** 132

"Thimble, The" (Kenyon), **Supp. VII:** 164

"Thing and Its Relations, The" (James), **II:** 357

"Things" (Haines), **Supp. XII:** 207

"Things" (Kenyon), **Supp. VII:** 169

"Things, The" (Kinnell), **Supp. III Part 1:** 246

Things As They Are (Stein), **IV:** 34, 37, 40

"Things Can Be Named to Death" (Peacock), **Supp. XIX:** 199

"Things Don't Stop" (Nye), **Supp. XIII:** 287

Things Gone and Things Still Here (Bowles), **Supp. IV Part 1:** 91

"Things of August" (Stevens), **Retro. Supp. I:** 309

Things of This World (Wilbur), **Supp. III Part 2:** 552–555

Things That Fall from the Sky (Brockmeier), **Supp. XXII: 50–53**

"Things That Fall from the Sky" (Brockmeier), **Supp. XXII:** 51, 53

Things Themselves: Essays and Scenes (Price), **Supp. VI:** 261

Things They Carried, The (T. O'Brien), **Supp. V:** 238, 239, 240, 243, 248–250; **Supp. XVII:** 14; **Supp. XXI:** 122

"Things to Do in New York City" (Berrigan), **Supp. XXII:** 224

"Thing That Killed My Father Off, The" (Carver), **Supp. III Part 1:** 143

Thingy World!: or, How We Got to Where We Are: A Satire in One Act (Budbill), **Supp. XIX: 13–14**

"Think about It" (Conroy), **Supp. XVI:** 75

Think Back on Us . . . (Cowley), **Supp. II Part 1:** 139, 140, 142

Think Fast, Mr. Moto (Marquand), **III:** 57, 58

"Thinking about Barbara Deming" (Paley), **Supp. VI:** 227

"Thinking about Being Called Simple by a Critic" (Stafford), **Supp. XI:** 328

Thinking about the Longstanding Problems of Virtue and Happiness: Essays, a Play, Two Poems, and a Prayer (Kushner), **Supp. IX:** 131, 134, 135

"Thinking about the Past" (Justice), **Supp. VII:** 123–124

"Thinking about Western Thinking" (Didion), **Supp. IV Part 1:** 204, 206

"'Thinking against Oneself': Reflections on Cioran" (Sontag), **Supp. III Part 2:** 459–460

"Thinking Back Through Our Mothers: Traditions in Canadian Women's Writing" (Shields), **Supp. VII:** 307–308

"Thinking for Berky" (Stafford), **Supp. XI:** 320

"Thinking like a Mountain" (Leopold), **Supp. XIV:** 188, 189

"Thinking of the Lost World" (Jarrell), **II:** 338–389

Thinking Out Loud (Quindlen), **Supp. XVII:** 167, **169–170**

Thin Man, The (film), **Supp. IV Part 1:** 342, 355

Thin Man, The (Hammett), **Supp. IV Part 1:** 354–355

"Thinnest Shadow, The" (Ashbery), **Supp. III Part 1:** 5

"Thin People, The" (Plath), **Supp. I Part 2:** 538, 547

Thin Red Line, The (film; Malick), **Supp. V:** 249; **Supp. XV:** 351

Thin Red Line, The (Jones), **Supp. XI:** 219, **224–225,** 229, 231, 232, 233, 234

"Thin Strips" (Sandburg), **III:** 587

"Third and Final Continent, The" (Lahiri), **Supp. XXI: 178–180**

"Third Avenue in Sunlight" (Hecht), **Supp. X:** 61

"Third Body, A" (R. Bly), **Supp. IV Part 1:** 71

Third Circle, The (Norris), **III:** 327

"Third Expedition, The" (Bradbury), **Supp. IV Part 1:** 103, 106

Third Generation, The (C. Himes), **Supp. XVI:** 135, **140–141**

Third Life of Grange Copeland, The (Walker), **Supp. III Part 2:** 520, 527–536

Third Mind, The (Burroughs), **Supp. XII:** 3

Third Rose, The (Brinnin), **IV:** 26

"Third Sermon on the Warpland, The" (Brooks), **Supp. III Part 1:** 85

"Third Thing That Killed My Father Off, The" (Carver), **Supp. III Part 1:** 144

Third Violet, The (Crane), **I:** 408, 417–418

Thirlwall, John C., **Retro. Supp. I:** 430

"Thirst: Introduction to Kinds of Water" (Carson), **Supp. XII:** 103

"13, 1977, 21" (Lethem), **Supp. XVIII:** 148

13 by Shanley (Shanley), **Supp. XIV:** 316

13 Seconds: A Look Back at the Kent State Shootings (Caputo), **Supp. XIX:** 29

Thirteen Hands: A Play in Two Acts (Shields), **Supp. VII:** 322–323

Thirteen O'Clock (Benét), **Supp. XI:** 46

Thirteen Other Stories (Purdy), **Supp. VII:** 278

Thirteen Stories and Thirteen Epitaphs (Vollmann), **Supp. XVII:** 226

"Thirteenth and Pennsylvania" (Stafford), **Supp. XI:** 324

Thirteenth Month, The (Pedersen; Nelson, trans.), **Supp. XVIII:** 179–180

"Thirteen Ways of Looking at a Blackbird" (Stevens), **IV:** 94; **Supp. IX:** 47; **Supp. XVII:** 130; **Supp. XXIII:** 253

"Thirteen Ways of Looking at a Blackbird" (W. Stevens), **Supp. XX:** 110

Thirteen Ways of Looking at a Black Man (H. L. Gates), **Supp. XX:** 102, 110

30/6 (poetry chapbook), **Supp. V:** 5, 6

"30. Meditation. 2. Cor. 5.17. He Is a New Creature" (Taylor), **IV:** 144

30: Pieces of a Novel (Dixon), **Supp. XII:** 152, **153–154**

"Thirty Bob a Week" (Davidson), **Retro. Supp. I:** 55

"Thirty Delft Tiles" (Doty), **Supp. XI:** 131

"35/10" (Olds), **Supp. X:** 206

"35,000 Feet—The Lanterns" (Goldbarth), **Supp. XII:** 182

31 Letters and 13 Dreams (Hugo), **Supp. VI:** 141–144

Thirty Poems (Bryant), **Supp. I Part 1:** 157, 158

Thirty-Six Poems (Warren), **IV:** 236, 239, 240

"33" (Alvarez), **Supp. VII:** 4

"3275" (Monette), **Supp. X:** 148, 159

Thirty Years (Marquand), **III:** 56, 60–61

Thirty Years of Treason (Bentley), **Supp. I Part 1:** 297

This, My Letter (Hay), **Supp. XIV:** 121, 122, 129, 131

"This, That & the Other" (Nemerov), **III:** 269

This Body Is Made of Camphor and Gopherwood (R. Bly), **Supp. IV Part 1:** 63–65, 66, 71; **Supp. XXI:** 85

This Boy's Life: A Memoir (T. Wolff), **Supp. VII:** 334–339, 340, 343; **Supp. XI:** 246, 247

This Bridge Called My Back: Writings by Radical Women of Color (Moraga and Anzaldúa, eds.), **Supp. XXIII:** 193, 194, 196, **204–205**

"This Bright Dream" (Benét), **Supp. XI:** 55

This Coffin Has No Handles (McGrath), **Supp. X:** 117

"This Configuration" (Ashbery), **Supp. III Part 1:** 22

"This Corruptible" (Wylie), **Supp. I Part 2:** 727, 729

"This Crazy Wickedness, Little Nests of Light" (Notley), **Supp. XXII:** 228

"This Crutch That I Love" (Nye), **Supp. XIII:** 288

"This Gentile World" (H. Miller), **III:** 177

"This Hand" (Wylie), **Supp. I Part 2:** 713

"This Hour" (Olds), **Supp. X:** 212

"This House I Cannot Leave" (Kingsolver), **Supp. VII:** 208

This Hunger (Nin), **Supp. X:** 185

"This Is a Photograph of Me" (Atwood), **Supp. XIII:** 33

"This Is a Poem, Good Afternoon" (Keillor), **Supp. XVI:** 167

"This Is It" (Stern), **Supp. IX:** 290

"This Is Just to Say" (W. C. Williams), **Supp. XI:** 328

"This Is My Heart" (Harjo), **Supp. XII:** 230

This Is Not a Novel (Markson), **Supp. XVII:** 145–146

"This Is Not Who We Are" (Nye), **Supp. XIII:** 285, 286

This Is Our Time: Secular Cantata No. 1, Mixed Voice Chorus and Orchestra (Taggard, Schuman and Weissleder), **Supp. XXII:** 283

"This Is Us, Excellent" (Richard), **Supp. XIX:** 212

"This Is What I Said" (Salinas), **Supp. XIII:** 322

This Journey (Wright), **Supp. III Part 2:** 605–606

"This Lime-Tree Bower My Prison" (Coleridge), **Supp. XXI:** 52, 55

This Man and This Woman (Farrell), **II:** 42

"This Monkey, My Back" (Boyle), **Supp. XX:** 17

"This Morning" (Kenyon), **Supp. VII:** 164

"This Morning, This Evening, So Soon" (Baldwin), **Supp. I Part 1:** 63

"This Morning Again It Was in the Dusty Pines" (Oliver), **Supp. VII:** 240

This Music Crept by Me upon the Waters (MacLeish), **III:** 21

"This New England: Newport, Vermont" (Mosher), **Supp. XXII:** 209

This People Israel: The Meaning of Jewish Existence (Baeck), **Supp. V:** 260

"This Personal Maze Is Not the Prize" (Selinger), **Supp. XI:** 248

"This Place in the Ways" (Rukeyser), **Supp. VI:** 273–274

This Property Is Condemned (T. Williams), **IV:** 378

This Proud Heart (Buck), **Supp. II Part 1:** 119–120

This Same Sky: A Collection of Poems from around the World (Nye, ed.), **Supp. XIII:** 280

"This Sandwich Has No Mayonnaise" (Salinger), **III:** 552–553

This Shape We're In (Lethem), **Supp. XVIII:** 145

"This Shape We're In" (Lethem), **Supp. XVIII:** 148

This Side of Paradise (Fitzgerald), **I:** 358; **II:** 77, 80, 81, 82–83, 84, 85–87, 88; **Retro. Supp. I:** 99–100, **101–102,** 103, 105, 106, 110, 111; **Supp. XVIII:** 248

This Singing World: An Anthology of Modern Poetry for Young People (Untermeyer, ed.), **Supp. XV:** 306

This Strange Joy: Selected Poems of Sandro Penna (Di Perio, trans.), **Supp. XIX:** 34

This Stubborn Self: Texas Autobiographies (Almon), **Supp. XIII:** 288

This Thing Don't Lead to Heaven (Crews), **Supp. XI:** 112

This Time: New and Selected Poems (Stern), **Supp. IX:** 290–291, **299**

"Thistle Seed in the Wind" (Francis), **Supp. IX:** 81

"Thistles in Sweden, The" (Maxwell), **Supp. VIII:** 169

"This Tokyo" (Snyder), **Supp. VIII:** 298

This Tree Will Be Here for a Thousand Years (revised edition) (R. Bly), **Supp. IV Part 1:** 66

This Tree Will Be Here for a Thousand Years (R. Bly), **Supp. IV Part 1:** 65–66, 71, 72

This Very Earth (Caldwell), **I:** 297, 302

This Wheel's on Fire: Levon Helm and the Story of the Band (Helm), **Supp. XVIII:** 26

This Woman (di Donato), **Supp. XX: 33, 41–42, 46**

Thoens, Karen, **Supp. V:** 147

Thomas, Brandon, **II:** 138

Thomas, Debra, **Supp. XIII:** 114

Thomas, D. M., **Supp. VIII:** 5

Thomas, Dylan, **I:** 49, 64, 382, 432, 526, 533; **III:** 21, 521, 528, 532, 534; **IV:** 89, 93, 136; **Supp. I Part 1:** 263; **Supp. III Part 1:** 42, 47; **Supp. V:** 344; **Supp. VIII:** 21; **Supp. IX:** 114; **Supp. X:** 115; **Supp. XV:** 74; **Supp. XVII:** 135; **Supp. XX: 199, 204**

Thomas, Edna Lewis, **Supp. XVIII:** 281

Thomas, Edward, **II:** 154; **Retro. Supp. I:** 127, 131, 132; **Supp. I Part 1:** 263; **Supp. II Part 1:** 4

Thomas, James, **Supp. XVI:** 268

Thomas, Joseph, **Supp. XVIII:** 183

Thomas, J. Parnell, **Supp. I Part 1:** 286; **Supp. XV:** 198

Thomas, Lewis, **Retro. Supp. I:** 323

Thomas, Louisa, **Supp. XXIII:** 280, 283

Thomas, Rob, **Supp. XVIII:** 100, 101

Thomas, R. S., **Supp. XXI:** 83, 86 87, 93, 95, 96

Thomas, William I., **Supp. I Part 2:** 641

Thomas-a-Kempis, **Retro. Supp. I:** 247

Thomas and Beulah (Dove), **Supp. IV Part 1;** 242, 247–248, 249; **Supp. XVIII:** 174; **Supp. XXI:** 249

Thomas Aquinas (Saint), **I:** 13, 14, 265, 267; **III:** 270; **Retro. Supp. II:** 222; **Supp. IV Part 2:** 526

"Thomas at the Wheel" (Dove), **Supp. IV Part 1:** 248

"Thomas Eakins and the Photograph of a Man in Motion" (Major), **Supp. XXII:** 183

"Thomas Eakins' Delaware River Paintings" (Major), **Supp. XXII:** 183

"Thomas McGrath: Words for a Vanished Age" (Vinz), **Supp. X:** 117

Thomas Merton on Peace, **Supp. VIII:** 208

Thomas Merton Studies Center, The, **Supp. VIII:** 208

Thompson, Barbara, **Supp. V:** 322

Thompson, Caroline, **Supp. XXIII:** 291

Thompson, Cy, **I:** 538

Thompson, Daniel, **Supp. XXIII:** 174

Thompson, Dorothy, **II:** 449–450, 451, 453; **Supp. XV:** 307

Thompson, Edward, **Supp. XXI:** 172

Thompson, E. P., **Supp. X:** 112, 117

Thompson, Francis, **Retro. Supp. I:** 55

Thompson, Frank, **II:** 20

Thompson, George, **Supp. I Part 2:** 686; **Supp. XXIII:** 182

Thompson, Hunter S., **Supp. VIII:** 42; **Supp. XI:** 105; **Supp. XIII:** 1, 17; **Supp. XVII:** 95, 102, 228

Thompson, James R., **Supp. IV Part 1:** 217

Thompson, Jean, **Supp. XXIII: 289–305**

Thompson, John, **Supp. V:** 323; **Supp. XXI:** 151

Thompson, Juliet, **Supp. XX:** 117

Thompson, Lawrance, **II:** 508

Thompson, Lawrance Roger, **Retro. Supp. I:** 138, 141

Thompson, Lisa B., **Supp. XXIII:** 202

Thompson, Morton, **Supp. XIII:** 170

Thompson, Theresa, **Supp. V:** 141

Thompson, William T., **Supp. I Part 2:** 411

Thomson, James, **II:** 304; **Supp. I Part 1:** 150, 151

Thomson, Virgil, **IV:** 45; **Supp. IV Part 1:** 81, 83, 84, 173; **Supp. XVI:** 195

"Thoreau" (Lowell), **Supp. I Part 2:** 420, 422

Thoreau, Henry David, **I:** 98, 104, 228, 236, 257, 258, 261, 305, 433; **II:** 7, 8, 13, 17, 101, 159, 224, 273–274, 295, 312–313, 321, 457–458, 540, 546–547; **III:** 171, 174, 186–187, 189, 208, 214–215, 453, 454, 507, 577; **IV: 167–189,** 191, 341; **Retro. Supp. I:** 51, 62,

122; **Retro. Supp. II:** 13, 96, 142, 158; **Supp. I Part 1:** 29, 34, 116, 188, 299, 358; **Supp. I Part 2:** 383, 400, 420, 421, 507, 540, 579, 580, 655, 659, 660, 664, 678; **Supp. III Part 1:** 340, 353, **Supp. IV Part 1:** 236, 392, 416; **Supp. IV Part 2:** 420, 430, 433, 439, 447; **Supp. V:** 200, 208; **Supp. VIII:** 40, 42, 103, 105, 198, 201, 204, 205, 292, 303; **Supp. IX:** 25, 90, 171; **Supp. X:** 21, 27, 28–29, 101, 102, **Supp. XI:** 155; **Supp. XIII:** 1, 17; **Supp. XIV:** 40, 54, 106, 177, 181; **Supp. XVIII:** 4; **Supp. XX: 116, 221;** **Supp. XXI:** 203, 217; **Supp. XXII:** 206; **Supp. XXIII:** 174

Thoreau, John, **IV:** 171, 182

Thoreau, Mrs. John, **IV:** 172

"Thoreau's Hound: On Hiddenness"(Hirshfield), **Supp. XXIII:** 137

"Thorn, The" (Gordon), **Supp. IV Part 1:** 314

Thorne, Francis, **Supp. XII:** 253

"Thorn Merchant, The" (Komunyakaa), **Supp. XIII:** 119–120

Thornton, Billy Bob, **Supp. VIII:** 175

Thornton, Lionel, **III:** 291

"Thorofare" (Minot), **Supp. VI: 209–210**

"Thorow" (Howe), **Supp. IV Part 2:** 419, 420, 421, 431, 433–434

Thorp, Willard, **Supp. XIII:** 101

Thorslev, Peter L., Jr., **I:** 524

Thorstein Veblen (Dowd), **Supp. I Part 2:** 650

Thorstein Veblen (Qualey, ed.), **Supp. I Part 2:** 650

Thorstein Veblen: A Chapter in American Economic Thought (Teggart), **Supp. I Part 2:** 650

Thorstein Veblen: A Critical Interpretation (Riesman), **Supp. I Part 2:** 649, 650

Thorstein Veblen: A Critical Reappraisal (Dowd, ed.), **Supp. I Part 2:** 650

Thorstein Veblen and His America (Dorfman), **Supp. I Part 2:** 631, 650

Thorstein Veblen and the Institutionalists: A Study in the Social Philosophy of Economics (Seckler), **Supp. I Part 2:** 650

"Those before Us" (Lowell), **II:** 550

"Those Being Eaten by America" (R. Bly), **Supp. IV Part 1:** 62

Those Bones Are Not My Child (Bambara), **Supp. XI:** 1, 14, **20–22**

Those Extraordinary Twins (Twain), **IV:** 205–206

"Those Graves in Rome" (Levis), **Supp. XI:** 266

"Those of Us Who Think We Know" (Dunn), **Supp. XI:** 146

Those That Be in Bondage (Webber), **Supp. XXI:** 160

"Those Times . . ." (Sexton), **Supp. II Part 2:** 670, 684

"Those Various Scalpels" (Moore), **III:** 202

"Those Were the Days" (Levine), **Supp. V:** 190

"Those Who Don't" (Cisneros), **Supp. VII:** 60

"Those Who Thunder" (Hogan), **Supp. IV Part 1:** 406

"Thought, A" (Sarton), **Supp. VIII:** 262

Thought and Character of William James (Perry), **II:** 362

Thoughtbook of Francis Scott Key Fitzgerald (Fitzgerald), **Retro. Supp. I:** 99

"Thought Experiment" (Saunders), **Supp. XIX:** 235

"Thoughtful Roisterer Declines the Gambit, The" (Hecht), **Supp. X:** 63

"Thought of Heaven, The" (Stern), **Supp. IX:** 297

"Thoughts after Lambeth" (Eliot), **I:** 587; **Retro. Supp. I:** 324

Thoughts and Reflections (Lord Halifax), **II:** 111

Thoughts in Solitude (Merton), **Supp. VIII:** 207

"Thoughts on Being Bibliographed" (Wilson), **IV:** 435

"Thoughts on the Establishment of a Mint in the United States" (Paine), **Supp. I Part 2:** 512

"Thoughts on the Gifts of Art" (Kenyon), **Supp. VII:** 167

Thousand Acres, A (Smiley), **Supp. VI:** 292, **301–303**

"Thousand and Second Night, The" (Merrill), **Supp. III Part 1:** 324

"Thousand Dollar Vagrant, The" (Olsen), **Supp. XIII:** 292, 297

"Thousand Faces of Danny Torrance, The" (Figliola), **Supp. V:** 143

"Thousand Genuflections, A" (McCarriston), **Supp. XIV:** 266

Thousand-Mile Walk to the Gulf, A (Muir), **Supp. IX: 177–178**

"Thou Shalt Not Steal" (McClatchy), **Supp. XII:** 264

"Thread, The" (Merwin), **Supp. III Part 1:** 351

Three (film), **Supp. IX:** 253

3-3-8 (Marquand), **III:** 58

"Three Academic Pieces" (Stevens), **IV:** 90

"Three Agee Wards, The" (Morris), **III:** 220–221

"Three American Singers" (Cather), **Retro. Supp. I:** 10

"Three Around the Old Gentleman" (Berryman), **I:** 188

"Three Avilas, The" (Jeffers), **Supp. II Part 2:** 418

"Three Black Women Writers" (C. L. R. James), **Supp. XXI:** 172

Three Books of Song (Longfellow), **II:** 490

"Three Bushes" (Yeats), **Supp. I Part 1:** 80

Three Cantos (Pound), **Retro. Supp. I:** 290

Three Centuries of Harvard (Morison), **Supp. I Part 2:** 485

Three Circles of Light (di Donato), **Supp. XX: 33, 42–43, 44, 46**

Three Cities: A Trilogy (Asch), **Supp. XXIII:** 1, 5, **10–12**

Three Comrades (Remarque), **Retro. Supp. I:** 113

"Three Corollaries of Cultural Relativism" (Locke), **Supp. XIV:** 202

"Three-Day Blow, The" (Hemingway), **II:** 248

Three Essays on America (Brooks), **I:** 246

Three Farmers on Their Way to a Dance (Powers), **Supp. IX:** 211–212, **213–214,** 222

"Three Fates, The" (Benét), **Supp. XI:** 48–49, 50

"Three Generations of Secrets" (A. Finch), **Supp. XVII:** 73

"Three Gifts, The" (Gibran), **Supp. XX: 124**

Three Gospels (Price), **Supp. VI:** 267

"Three Kings, The: Hemingway, Faulkner, and Fitzgerald" (Ford), **Supp. V:** 59

Three Lives (Auchincloss), **Supp. IV Part 1:** 25

Three Lives (Stein), **I:** 103; **IV:** 26, 27, 31, 35, 37–41, 42, 45, 46; **Supp. IX:** 306; **Supp. XXIII:** 166

"THREE MOVEMENTS AND A CODA" (Baraka), **Supp. II Part 1:** 50

Three One Act Plays (Riverside Drive, Old Saybrook, and *Central Park West)* (Allen), **Supp. XV:** 3

Three on the Tower: The Lives and Works of Ezra Pound, T. S. Eliot, and William Carlos Williams (Simpson), **Supp. IX:** 276

Three Papers on Fiction (Welty), **IV:** 261

Three-Penny Opera (Brecht), **I:** 301; **Supp. XIV:** 162

"Three Percent Own All the Wealth" (Ryan as Quin), **Supp. XVIII:** 231–232

Three Philosophical Poets (Santayana), **III:** 610–612

"Three Pigs in Five Days" (Prose), **Supp. XVI:** 257, 258

"Three Players of a Summer Game" (T. Williams), **IV:** 383

Three Poems (Ashbery), **Supp. III Part 1:** 2, 3, 14, 15, 18, 24–26

"Three Poems for my Daughter" (Di Piero), **Supp. XIX:** 40

"Three Pokes of a Thistle" (Nye), **Supp. XIII:** 281

Three Roads, The (Macdonald, under Millar), **Supp. IV Part 2:** 466, 467

"Three Silences of Molinos, The" (Longfellow), **Retro. Supp. II:** 169

Three Sisters, The (Chekhov), **Supp. XV:** 323

"Three Sisters, The" (Cisneros), **Supp. VII:** 64

Three Soldiers (Dos Passos), **I:** 477–478, 480, 482, 488, 493–494; **Supp. XXI:** 277

"Three Songs at the End of Summer" (Kenyon), **Supp. VII:** 169–170

"Three Steps to the Graveyard" (Wright), **Supp. III Part 2:** 593, 596

Three Stories and Ten Poems (Hemingway), **II:** 68, 263; **Supp. XVII:** 105

Three Taverns, The (Robinson), **III:** 510

"Three Taverns, The" (Robinson), **III:** 521, 522

Three Tenant Families (Agee), **I:** 37–38

Three Tenors, One Vehicle: A Book of Songs (X. J. Kennedy, Camp, and Waldrop), **Supp. XV:** 165

"Three Types of Poetry" (Tate), **IV:** 131

"Three Vagabonds of Trinidad" (Harte), **Supp. II Part 1:** 338

"Three Waterfalls, The" (Lanier), **Supp. I Part 1:** 350

"Three-Way Mirror" (Brooks), **Supp. III Part 1:** 69–70

Three Weeks in Spring (Parker and Parker), **Supp. XIX:** 187

"Three Women" (Plath), **Supp. I Part 2:** 539, 541, 544, 545, 546

Three Young Poets (Swallow, ed.), **Supp. X:** 116

Threnody (Emerson), **Supp. I Part 2:** 416

"Threnody" (Emerson), **II:** 7

"Threnody for a Brown Girl" (Cullen), **Supp. IV Part 1:** 166

"Threshing-Floor, The" (Baldwin), **Supp. I Part 1:** 50

Threshold (film), **Supp. IX:** 254

"Threshold" (Goldbarth), **Supp. XII:** 175

Threshold (Jackson), **Supp. IX:** 117

"Throat" (Goldbarth), **Supp. XII:** 177–178

Throne of Labdacus, The (Schnackenberg), **Supp. XV:** 260, **263–266**

Thrones (Pound), **Retro. Supp. I:** 293

Through Dooms of Love (Kumin), **Supp. IV Part 2:** 444

"Through the Black Curtain" (Kingston), **Supp. V:** 169

Through the Forest: New and Selected Poems, 1977–1987 (Wagoner), **Supp. IX:** 330–331

"Through the Hills of Spain" (Salinas), **Supp. XIII:** 315

"Through the Hole in the Mundane Millstone" (West), **Retro. Supp. II:** 321, 322

Through the Ivory Gate (Dove), **Supp. IV Part 1:** 242, 243, 251, 252, 253–254, 254

"Through the Kitchen Window, Chiapas" (Nye), **Supp. XIII:** 277

Through the Safety Net (C. Baxter), **Supp. XVII:** 17, 22

"Through the Smoke Hole" (Snyder), **Supp. VIII:** 299

Throw Like a Girl (Thompson), **Supp. XXIII: 299–300**

"Throw Like a Girl"(Thompson), **Supp. XXIII:** 299, 300

"Thrush Relinquished, The" (Grossman), **Supp. XIX:** 83

Thucydides, **II:** 418; **IV:** 50; **Supp. I Part 2:** 488, 489, 492; **Supp. IV Part 1:** 391; **Supp. XIII:** 233

Thunderbolt and Lightfoot (film), **Supp. X:** 126

"Thunder from a Cloudless Sky" (Mosher), **Supp. XXII:** 209

"Thunderhead" (MacLeish), **III:** 19

Thurber, James, **I:** 487; **II:** 432; **IV:** 396; **Supp. I Part 2:** 602–627, 653, 654, 668, 672, 673, 679; **Supp. II Part 1:** 143; **Supp. IV Part 1:** 349; **Supp. IX:** 118; **Supp. XIV:** 104; **Supp. XVI:** 167; **Supp. XVII:** 4

Thurber, Mrs. James (Althea Adams), **Supp. I Part 2:** 613, 615, 617

Thurber, Mrs. James (Helen Muriel Wismer), **Supp. I Part 2:** 613, 617, 618

Thurber, Robert, **Supp. I Part 2:** 613, 617

Thurber, Rosemary, **Supp. I Part 2:** 616

Thurber, William, **Supp. I Part 2:** 602

Thurber Album, The (Thurber), **Supp. I Part 2:** 611, 619

Thurber Carnival, The (Thurber), **Supp. I Part 2:** 620; **Supp. XIV:** 104

Thurman, Judith, **Supp. IV Part 1:** 309

Thurman, Wallace, **Retro. Supp.:** 200; **Supp. I Part 1:** 325, 326, 328, 332; **Supp. IV Part 1:** 164; **Supp. X:** 136, 139; **Supp. XVI:** 135; **Supp. XVIII:** 279, 281; **Supp. XIX:** 78; **Supp. XXII:** 2

"Thursday" (Millay), **III:** 129

"Thurso's Landing" (Jeffers), **Supp. II Part 2:** 433

"Thus Do I Refute Gioia" (Junker), **Supp. XV:** 116

"Thus Far by Faith" (Nelson), **Supp. XVIII:** 177

Thus Spake Zarathustra (Nietzsche), **II:** 463; **Supp. IV Part 1:** 110; **Supp. IV Part 2:** 519

Thwaite, Lady Alicia. *See* Rawlings, Marjorie Kinnan

Thy Neighbor's Wife (Talese), **Supp. XVII:** 204, 205–206, 207, 208, 210

"Tiara" (Doty), **Supp. XI:** 122

"Tibetan Time" (Prose), **Supp. XVI:** 255

Ticket for a Seamstitch, A (Harris), **II:** 424–425

Tickets for a Prayer Wheel (Dillard), **Supp. VI:** 22, 34

Ticket That Exploded, The (Burroughs), **Supp. III Part 1:** 93, 103, 104

Tickless Time (Glaspell), **Supp. III Part 1:** 179

Ticknor, George, **II:** 488; **Supp. I Part 1:** 313

Ticknor, William, **Supp. XVIII:** 258

"Ti Démon" (Chopin), **Supp. I Part 1:** 225

Tide of Time, The (Masters), **Supp. I Part 2:** 471

"Tide of Voices" (Hull), **Supp. XXI:** 132, 133–134, 136

"Tide Rises, the Tide Falls, The" (Longfellow), **I:** 498

"Tides" (Hoffman), **Supp. XVIII:** 86

Tidewater Blood (Hoffman), **Supp. XVIII: 82–83**

Tidyman, Ernest, **Supp. V:** 226

Tietjens, Eunice, **Supp. XV:** 47, 297

"Tiger" (Blake), **Supp. I Part 1:** 80; **Supp. VIII:** 26

Tiger (Bynner), **Supp. XV:** 42, 50

"Tiger, The" (Buechner), **Supp. XII:** 48

Tiger in the House, The (Van Vechten), **Supp. II Part 2:** 736

Tiger Joy (Benét), **Supp. XI:** 45

Tiger-Lilies (Lanier), **Supp. I Part 1:** 350–351, 357, 360, 371

Tiger Who Wore White Gloves, The: or, What You Are, You Are (Brooks), **Supp. III Part 1:** 86

Till, Emmett, **Supp. I Part 1:** 61

Till, Eric, **Supp. XXIII:** 103

Tillich, Paul, **II:** 244; **III:** 291, 292, 303, 309; **IV:** 226; **Retro. Supp. I:** 325, 326, 327; **Supp. V:** 267; **Supp. XIII:** 74, 91

Tillie Olsen: A Study of the Short Fiction (Frye), **Supp. XIII:** 292, 296, 298, 299, 302

Tillman, Lynne, **Supp. XII:** 4

Tillotson, John, **II:** 114

Tillotson, Kristen, **Supp. XVII:** 23

Tillstrom, Burr, **Supp. XIV:** 125

Till the Day I Die (Odets), **Supp. II Part 2:** 530, 533–536, 552

Tilton, Eleanor, **Supp. I Part 1:** 317

Tilton, Theodore, **Supp. XVIII:** 4

Timaeus (Plato), **II:** 10; **III:** 609

Tim: A Story of School Life (Sturgis), **Supp. XX:** 227, 230, 232, **233–235**

Timber (Jonson), **II:** 16

Timberg, Scott, **Supp. XV:** 116

"Timberwolf" (Halliday), **Supp. XIX:** 91

Timbuktu (Auster), **Supp. XII:** 34, **35–36**

"Time" (Matthews), **Supp. IX: 165–166**

"Time" (Merrill), **Supp. III Part 1:** 325

"Time and Again" (Sanders), **Supp. XVI:** 269

Time and a Place, A (Humphrey), **Supp. IX:** 95, 98, **100–102**

"Time and the Garden" (Winters), **Supp. II Part 2:** 801, 809

"Time and the Liturgy" (Merton), **Supp. VIII:** 199

Time and the River (Edgell), **Supp. XXIII:** 84, 85, **91–93**

Time and Tide: A Walk through Nantucket (Conroy), **Supp. XVI:** 63, 71, **76–77**

"Time Exposure" (C. Baxter), **Supp. XVII:** 20–21

Time Exposures, by Search-Light (W. Frank), **Supp. XX: 75**

Time in the Rock (Aiken), **I:** 65

Time Is Noon, The (Buck), **Supp. II Part 1:** 129, 130–131

Time & Money (Matthews), **Supp. IX:** 155, **165–167**

"Time of Friendship, The" (Bowles), **Supp. IV Part 1:** 90–91

"Time of Her Time, The" (Mailer), **III:** 37, 45; **Retro. Supp. II:** 200

Time of Our Time, The (Mailer), **Retro. Supp. II:** 213–214

Time of the Assassins, The: A Study of Rimbaud (H. Miller), **III:** 189

Time Out of Mind (album, Dylan), **Supp. XVIII:** 28

"Time Past" (Morris), **III:** 232

"Time Present" (Morris), **III:** 232

"Times" (Beattie), **Supp. V:** 31

"Times, The" (Emerson), **II:** 11–12

Times Are Never So Bad, The (Dubus), **Supp. VII:** 87–88

Time's Arrow (Amis), **Retro. Supp. I:** 278

"Time Shall Not Die" (Chandler), **Supp. IV Part 1:** 120

Times of Melville and Whitman, The (Brooks), **I:** 257

Times They Are A-Changin', The (album, Dylan), **Supp. XVIII:** 20, 25

"Times They Are A-Changin,' The" (song, Dylan), **Supp. XVIII:** 30

"Timesweep" (Sandburg), **III:** 595–596

Time to Act, A (MacLeish), **III:** 3

Time to Be Born, A (Powell), **Supp. XIX:** 143

Time to Go (Dixon), **Supp. XII:** 147

Time to Kill (film), **Supp. IV Part 1:** 130

Time to Speak, A (MacLeish), **III:** 3

Time Will Darken It (Maxwell), **Supp. VIII:** 159, **162–164,** 169

"Timing of Sin, The" (Dubus), **Supp. VII:** 91

Tim O'Brien (Herzog), **Supp. V:** 239

Timoleon (Melville), **III:** 93; **Retro. Supp. I:** 257

Timothy Dexter Revisited (Marquand), **III:** 55, 62, 63

Timothy Findley: Stories from a Life (Roberts), **Supp. XX:** 53

Timrod, Henry, **Supp. XVIII:** 31, 33

Tin Can, The (W. J. Smith), **Supp. XIII:** 334, **Supp. XIII:** 336, 337

"Tin Can, The" (W. J. Smith), **Supp. XIII:** **337–339**

Tin Can Tree, The (Tyler), **Supp. IV Part 2:** 659–660

Tinguely, Jean, **Supp. XV:** 187

Tinker, Chauncey Brewster, **Supp. XIV:** 12

"Tinseled Bucks: A Historical Study of Indian Homosexuality"(Kenny), **Supp. XXIII:** 149

Tintern Abbey (Wordsworth), **Supp. I Part 2:** 673, 675

Tiny Alice (Albee), **I:** 81–86, 87, 88, 94

"Tiny Mummies! The True Story of the Ruler of 43rd Street's Land of the Walking Dead" (Wolfe), **Supp. III Part 2:** 573, 574

Tip on a Dead Jockey and Other Stories (Shaw), **Supp. XIX:** 251

"Tip-Top Club, The" (Keillor), **Supp. XVI:** 172

"Tired" (Hughes), **Supp. I Part 1:** 331

"Tired and Unhappy, You Think of Houses" (Schwartz), **Supp. II Part 2:** 649

"Tiresias" (Garrett), **Supp. VII:** 96–97

'Tis (McCourt), **Supp. XII:** 271, **279–286**

Tisch (Dixon), **Supp. XII:** 141, **155–156**

Titan, The (Dreiser), **I:** 497, 501, 507–508, 509, 510; **Retro. Supp. II:** 94, 101, 102

Titian, **Supp. I Part 2:** 397, 714

"Tito's Goodbye" (García), **Supp. XI:** 190

"To a Bird, Seen Under My Window in the Garden"(J. Schoolcraft), **Supp. XXIII:** 230

To a Blossoming Pear Tree (Wright), **Supp. III Part 2:** 602–605

"To a Blossoming Pear Tree" (Wright), **Supp. III Part 2:** 604

"To Abolish Children" (Shapiro), **Supp. II Part 2:** 717

To Abolish Children and Other Essays (Shapiro), **Supp. II Part 2:** 703

"To a Caty-Did, the Precursor of Winter" (Freneau), **Supp. II Part 1:** 274–275

"To a Chameleon" (Moore), **III:** 195, 196, 215

"To a Conscript of 1940" (Read), **II:** 372–373, 377–378

"To a Contemporary Bunk Shooter" (Sandburg), **III:** 582

"To a Cough in the Street at Midnight" (Wylie), **Supp. I Part 2:** 727, 729–730

"To a Defeated Savior" (Wright), **Supp. III Part 2:** 593–594, 596

"To a Face in the Crowd" (Warren), **IV:** 239

"To a Fish Head Found on the Beach near Malaga" (Levine), **Supp. V:** 185

"To a Friend" (Nemerov), **III:** 272

"To a Friend"(O'Hara), **Supp. XXIII:** 212

"To a Friend Whose Work Has Come to Triumph" (Sexton), **Supp. II Part 2:** 683

To a God Unknown (Steinbeck), **I:** 107; **IV:** 51, 59–60, 67

"To a Greek Marble" (Aldington), **Supp. I Part 1:** 257

"To a Locomotive in Winter" (Whitman), **IV:** 348

"To a Military Rifle" (Winters), **Supp. II Part 2:** 810, 811, 815

"To a Mouse" (Burns), **Supp. IX:** 173

"To an American Workman Dying of Starvation" (Taggard), **Supp. XXII:** 282

"To an Athlete Dying Young" (Houseman), **Supp. XVII:** 121

"To a Negro Jazz Band in a Parisian Cabaret" (Hughes), **Supp. I Part 1:** 325

"To an Old Philosopher in Rome" (Stevens), **III:** 605; **Retro. Supp. I:** 312

"To an Old Poet in Peru" (Ginsberg), **Supp. II Part 1:** 322

"To a Now-Type Poet" (X. J. Kennedy), **Supp. XV:** 161

"To Answer Your Question" (Jarman), **Supp. XVII:** 114–115

"To Any Would-Be Terrorists" (Nye), **Supp. XIII:** 285, 286

"To a Poet" (Rich), **Supp. I Part 2:** 571; **Supp. XIX:** 83

"To a Prize Bird" (Moore), **III:** 215

"To a Republican, with Mr. Paine's Rights of Man" (Freneau), **Supp. II Part 1:** 267

"To a Shade" (Yeats), **III:** 18

"To a Skylark" (Shelley), **Supp. I Part 2:** 720; **Supp. X:** 31

"Toast to Harlem, A" (Hughes), **Supp. I Part 1:** 338

"To Aunt Rose" (Ginsberg), **Supp. II Part 1:** 320

"To Autumn" (Keats), **Supp. IX:** 50

"To a Waterfowl" (Bryant), **Supp. I Part 1:** 154, 155, 162, 171

"To a Young Poet" (X. J. Kennedy), **Supp. XV:** 161

"To a Young Writer" (Stegner), **Supp. X:** 24

Tobacco Road (Caldwell), **I:** 288, 289, 290, 295–296, 297, 298, 302, 307, 309, 310; **IV:** 198; **Supp. XXII:** 196

"To Be a Monstrous Clever Fellow" (Fante), **Supp. XI:** 167

"To Become Music or Break" (Jauss), **Supp. XXI:** 133

To Bedlam and Part Way Back (Sexton), **Retro. Supp. II:** 245; **Supp. II Part 2:** 672–678; **Supp. IV Part 2:** 441; **Supp. XI:** 317

"To Beethoven" (Lanier), **Supp. I Part 1:** 364

To Begin Again: Stories and Memoirs, 1908–1929 (M. F. K. Fisher), **Supp. XVII:** 92

Tobey, Mark, **Supp. X:** 264

To Be Young, Gifted, and Black: Lorraine Hansberry in Her Own Words (Nemiroff), **Supp. IV Part 1:** 372, 374

"To Big Mary from an Ex-Catholic" (Mora), **Supp. XIII:** 217, 224, 228

"Tobin's Palm" (O. Henry), **Supp. II Part 1:** 408; **Supp. XV:** 40

Tobit (apocryphal book), **I:** 89

"To Build a Fire" (London), **II:** 468

Toby Tyler: or, Ten Weeks with a Circus (Otis), **III:** 577

"To Change in a Good Way" (Ortiz), **Supp. IV Part 2:** 511

"To Charlotte Cushman" (Lanier), **Supp. I Part 1:** 364

"To Cole, the Painter, Departing for Europe" (Bryant), **Supp. I Part 1:** 157, 161

Tocqueville, Alexis de, **III:** 261; **IV:** 349; **Retro. Supp. I:** 235; **Supp. I Part 1:** 137; **Supp. I Part 2:** 659, 660; **Supp. II Part 1:** 281, 282, 284; **Supp. XIV:** 306, 312

"To Crispin O'Conner" (Freneau), **Supp. II Part 1:** 268

"To Da-Duh, In Memoriam" (Marshall), **Supp. XI:** 276

"TODAY" (Baraka), **Supp. II Part 1:** 55

"Today" (Ginsberg), **Supp. II Part 1:** 328

"Today Is a Good Day To Die" (Bell), **Supp. X:** 7

"Today"(O'Hara), **Supp. XXIII:** 210–211

"Today Will Be a Quiet Day" (Hempel), **Supp. XXI:** 117,**Supp. XXI:** 118

Todd, Mabel Loomis, **I:** 454, 470; **Retro. Supp. I:** 33, 34, 35, 39, 47

"To Death" (Levertov), **Supp. III Part 1:** 274

"To Delmore Schwartz" (Lowell), **II:** 547; **Retro. Supp. II:** 188

"to disembark" (Brooks), **Supp. III Part 1:** 86

"To Dorothy on Her Exclusion from The Guinness Book of Records" (X. J. Kennedy), **Supp. XV:** 166

"To Dr. Thomas Shearer" (Lanier), **Supp. I Part 1:** 370

"To Earthward" (Frost), **II:** 154

"To Edwin V. McKenzie" (Winters), **Supp. II Part 2:** 801

"To Eleonora Duse" (Lowell), **II:** 528

"To Elizabeth Ward Perkins" (Lowell), **II:** 516

"To Elsie" (W. C. Williams), **Retro. Supp. I:** 419

"To Emily Dickinson" (H. Crane), **Retro. Supp. II:** 76

"To E. T." (Frost), **Retro. Supp. I:** 132

To Feel These Things (L. Michaels), **Supp. XVI:** 205, **213–214**

"To Feel These Things" (L. Michaels), **Supp. XVI:** 214

Toffler, Alvin, **Supp. IV Part 2:** 517

"To Fill" (Moore), **Supp. X:** 168, 169

"To Gabriela, a Young Writer" (Mora), **Supp. XIII:** 220

To Have and Have Not (film), **Supp. XV:** 347

To Have and Have Not (Hemingway), **I:** 31; **II:** 253–254, 264; **Retro. Supp. I:** 182, **183,** 187

"To Helen" (Poe), **III:** 410, 411, 427; **Retro. Supp. II:** 102

"To Hell With Dying" (Walker), **Supp. III Part 2:** 523

"To His Coy Mistress"(Marvell), **Supp. XXIII:** 62

"To His Excellency General Washington" (Wheatley), **Supp. XX: 289**

"To His Father" (Jeffers), **Supp. II Part 2:** 415

Toilet, The (Baraka), **Supp. II Part 1:** 37, 40–42

"To James Russell Lowell" (Holmes), **Supp. I Part 1:** 311

To Jerusalem and Back (Bellow), **Retro. Supp. II:** 29

"To Jesus on His Birthday" (Millay), **III:** 136–137

"To John Keats" (Lowell), **II:** 516

"To Judge Faolain, Dead Long Enough: A Summons" (McCarriston), **Supp. XIV:** 264–265

"To Justify My Singing" (Wright), **III Part 2:** 590

"To Kill a Deer" (C. Frost), **Supp. XV:** 102

To Kill a Mockingbird (film), **Supp. VIII:** 128–129

To Kill a Mockingbird (Lee), **Supp. VIII: 113–129; Supp. XVI:** 259; **Supp. XIX:** 142

"To Kill a Mockingbird: Harper Lee's Tragic Vision" (Dave), **Supp. VIII:** 126

To Kill a Mockingbird: Threatening Boundaries (Johnson), **Supp. VIII:** 126

Toklas, Alice B., **IV:** 27; **Supp. IV Part 1:** 81, 91; **Supp. XVI:** 187

"Tokyo Story" (Wasserstein), **Supp. XV:** 328

"To Larry Rivers"(O'Hara), **Supp. XXIII:** 212

"To Light" (Hogan), **Supp. IV Part 1:** 402

"To Live and Diet" (Wasserstein), **Supp. XV:** 328

Tolkien, J. R. R., **Supp. V:** 140

Tolkin, Michael, **Supp. XI:** 160

Toller, Ernst, **I:** 479

"To Lose the Earth" (Sexton), **Supp. II Part 2:** 684, 685

Tolson, Melvin, **Retro. Supp. I:** 208, 209, 210

Tolstoy, Leo, **I:** 6, 7, 58, 103, 312, 376; **II:** 191–192, 205, 271, 272, 275, 276, 281, 285, 286, 320, 407, 542, 559, 570, 579, 606; **III:** 37, 45, 61, 323, 467, 572; **IV:** 17, 21, 170, 285; **Retro. Supp. I:** 91, 225; **Retro. Supp. II:** 299; **Supp. I Part 1:** 2, 3, 6, 20; **Supp. IV Part 1:** 392; **Supp. V:** 277, 323; **Supp. IX:** 246; **Supp. XI:** 68; **Supp. XII:** 310, 322; **Supp. XIV:** 87, 97, 98; **Supp. XIX:** 241; **Supp. XXIII:** 4, 11, 275

"To Lu Chi" (Nemerov), **III:** 275

Tom (Cummings), **I:** 430

"Tom" (Oliver), **Supp. VII:** 232

"Tom, Tom, the Piper's Son" (Ransom), **Supp. X:** 58

"To M, with a Rose" (Lanier), **Supp. I Part 1:** 364

To Make a Prairie (Kumin), **Supp. IV Part 2:** 440, 441

"To Make Words Disappear" (Simpson), **Supp. IX:** 265–266

Tomás and the Library Lady (Mora), **Supp. XIII:** 216, 221

"Tomatoes" (Francis), **Supp. IX:** 82

"Tom Ball's Barn" (Kooser), **Supp. XIX:** 119

"Tom Brown at Fisk" (Du Bois), **Supp. II Part 1:** 160

Tom Brown's School Days (Hughes), **Supp. I Part 2:** 406

"Tomb Stone" (Dickey), **Supp. IV Part 1:** 185

"Tombstone Blues" (song, Dylan), **Supp. XVIII:** 30

Tomcat in Love (O'Brien), **Supp. V:** 238, 240, 243, 252–254

"Tomcat's Wife, The" (C. Bly), **Supp. XVI:** 40

Tomcat's Wife and Other Stories, The (C. Bly), **Supp. XVI:** 40–41

"Tom Fool at Jamaica" (Moore), **III:** 215

To Mix with Time (Swenson), **Supp. IV Part 2:** 637, 643–645, 645

Tom Jones (Fielding), **I:** 131; **Supp. V:** 127

Tomlinson, Charles, **Supp. XVI:** 284

Tommy Gallagher's Crusade (Farrell), **II:** 44

Tommyknockers, The (King), **Supp. V:** 139, 144

"Tommy's Burglar" (Henry), **Supp. II Part 1:** 399, 401

"Tommy Stames" (Budbill), **Supp. XIX:** 8

Tomo Cheeki (pseudonym). *See* Freneau, Philip

Tomorrow Is Another Day (E. P. Jones), **Supp. XXII:** 252

Tomorrow is Another Day (film, Feist), **Supp. XVII:** 62

"Tomorrow the Moon" (Dos Passos), **I:** 493

Tomorrow Will Be Better (B. Smith), **Supp. XXIII:** 258, **264–267**

"Tom Outland's Story" (Cather), **I:** 325–326

Tompkins, Jane, **Supp. XVI:** 89; **Supp. XVIII:** 258, 259, 263

Tompson, Benjamin, **Supp. I Part 1:** 110, 111

"Tom-Rock Through Eels" (Hempel), **Supp. XXI:** 116, 118, **123–124**

Tom Sawyer (musical) (Gurney), **Supp. V:** 96

Tom Sawyer (Twain). *See Adventures of Tom Sawyer, The* (Twain)

Tom Sawyer Abroad (Twain), **II:** 482; **IV:** 19, 204

Tom Sawyer Detective (Twain), **IV:** 204

"Tom's Husband" (Jewett), **Retro. Supp. II:** 132, 141

Tom Swift (Stratemeyer), **III:** 146

"Tom Wolfe's Guide to Etiquette" (Wolfe), **Supp. III Part 2:** 578

"To My Brother Killed: Haumont Wood: October, 1918" (Bogan), **Supp. III Part 1:** 58

"To My Class, on Certain Fruits and Flowers Sent Me in Sickness" (Lanier), **Supp. I Part 1:** 370

"To my ever beloved & lamented son William Henry"(J. Schoolcraft), **Supp. XXIII:** 226, 231

"To My Father's Ghost" (Everwine), **Supp. XV:** 76

"To My Ghost Reflected in the Auxvasse River" (Levis), **Supp. XI:** 265

"To My Greek" (Merrill), **Supp. III Part 1:** 326

"To My Mother" (Berry), **Supp. X:** 23

"To My Sister—Ernestine Kealoha Taggard, 1900–1943" (Taggard), **Supp. XXII:** 284

"To My Small Son, at the Photographer's" (Hay), **Supp. XIV:** 121

"To My Small Son, on Certain Occasions" (Hay), **Supp. XIV:** 121

"To My Students" (Taggard), **Supp. XXII:** 280

"To Name is to Possess" (Kincaid), **Supp. VII:** 194

Tone, Aileen, **I:** 21–22

"Tongue Is, The" (Komunyakaa), **Supp. XIII:** 113

"Tongue of the Jews" (Bukiet), **Supp. XVII:** 47

Tongues (Shepard and Chaikin), **Supp. III Part 2:** 433

Tongues of Angels, The (Price), **Supp. VI:** 265

Tongues Untied (Riggs; film), **Supp. XI:** 19, 20

"Tonight" (Lowell), **II:** 538

"Tonight Is Part of the Struggle"(Le Sueur), **Supp. XXIII: 172**

Tonight Is the Night of the Prom (Jarman), **Supp. XVII:** 110, **112–113**

"Tonight Is the Night of the Prom" (Jarman), **Supp. XVII:** 113

Tony Kushner in Conversation (Vorlicky, ed.), **Supp. IX:** 132

"Too Anxious for Rivers" (Frost), **II:** 162

"Too Blue" (Hughes), **Retro. Supp. I:** 207

"Too Damn Close: Thresholds and Their Maintenance in Rick Bass's Work" (Kerridge), **Supp. XVI:** 26

"Too Early" (Leopold), **Supp. XIV:** 186

"Too Early Spring" (Benét), **Supp. XI:** 53

"Too Far from Home" (Bowles), **Supp. IV Part 1:** 94–95

Too Far from Home: Selected Writings of Paul Bowles (Halpern, ed.), **Supp. IV Part 1:** 94, 95

Too Far to Go: The Maples Stories (Updike), **Retro. Supp. I:** 321

"Too Good To Be True": The Life and Art of Leslie Fiedler (Winchell), **Supp. XIII:** 94, 98, 99, 101

Toohey, John Peter, **Supp. IX:** 190

Toolan, David, **Supp. IV Part 1:** 308

Too Late (Dixon), **Supp. XII: 143–144**

"Too Late" (Pickering), **Supp. XXI:** 197

"Too-Late Born, The" (Hemingway), **III:** 9

Toole, John Kennedy, **Supp. XIV:** 21

"Toolless" (Pickering), **Supp. XXI:** 204

Too Many Bottles (Holding), **Supp. XXII:** 126, **134–135**

Toomer, Jean, **Retro. Supp. II:** 79; **Supp. I Part 1:** 325, 332; **Supp. III Part 2: 475–491; Supp. IV Part 1:** 16, 164, 168; **Supp. IX: 305–322; Supp. XIII:** 305; **Supp. XVIII:** 122; **Supp. XX:** 73; **Supp. XXII:** 6

Toomer, Nathan Eugene Pinchback. *See* Toomer, Jean

Too Much Johnson (film), **Supp. IV Part 1:** 83

"To One Who Said Me Nay" (Cullen), **Supp. IV Part 1:** 166

"Tooth, The" (Jackson), **Supp. IX:** 122

Tooth and Claw (Boyle), **Supp. XX:** 20

Tooth of Crime, The (Shepard), **Supp. III Part 2:** 432, 441–445, 447

"Too Young" (O'Hara), **III:** 369

Topaz (film), **Supp. XX:** 253

Topaz (Uris), **Supp. XX:** 247, 248, 253

"Top Israeli Official Hints at 'Shared' Jerusalem" (Nye), **Supp. XIII:** 287

"To P. L., 1916–1937" (Levine), **Supp. V:** 185

"To Please a Shadow" (Brodsky), **Supp. VIII:** 30

"Top of the Food Chain" (Boyle), **Supp. XX: 20**

"Top of the Hill" (Jewett), **II:** 406

"Topography" (Olds), **Supp. X:** 208

Topper (T. Smith), **Supp. IX:** 194

To Praise the Music (Bronk), **Supp. XXI:** 31, 32

Torah, **IV:** 19

"Torch Songs" (Wrigley), **Supp. XVIII:** 296

Torday, Daniel, **Supp. XXII:** 151

Torpedo 8: The Story of Swede Larsen's Bomber Squadron (Wolfert), **Supp. XXI:** 267

"Torquemada" (Bukiet), **Supp. XVII:** 44

"Torquemada" (Longfellow), **II:** 505; **Retro. Supp. II:** 164

Torrence, Ridgely, **III:** 507

Torrent and the Night Before, The (Robinson), **III:** 504

Torrents of Spring, The (Hemingway), **I:** 117; **II:** 250–251

Torres, Héctor A., **Supp. XIII:** 225

Torres, Louis, **Supp. IV Part 2:** 529, 530

Torres-Saillant, Silvio, **Supp. XXI:** 104, 105, 108, 109

Torsney, Cheryl, **Retro. Supp. I:** 224

Tortilla Curtain, The (Boyle), **Supp. VIII: 9–10; Supp. XX: 28–29**

Tortilla Flat (Steinbeck), **IV:** 50, 51, 61, 64

Tortilla Flats (Steinbeck), **Supp. XX: 28**

Tortured Skins, and Other Fictions (Kenny), **Supp. XXIII:** 150, 156, 157

Tory Lover, The (Jewett), **II:** 406; **Retro. Supp. II:** 144–145

"Toscana" (Dixon), **Supp. XII:** 154

"To Sir Toby" (Freneau), **Supp. II Part 1:** 269

"To Sophy, Expectant" (Mumford), **Supp. II Part 2:** 475

"To Speak of Woe That Is in Marriage" (Lowell), **II:** 550

"To Statecraft Embalmed" (Moore), **III:** 197

To Stay Alive (Levertov), **Supp. III Part 1:** 280–282

"Total Eclipse" (Dillard), **Supp. VI:** 28

"Total Eclipse of the Moon"(Crooker), **Supp. XXIII:** 55

Toth, Emily, **Retro. Supp. II:** 71

Toth, Susan Allan, **Retro. Supp. II:** 138

"To the Americans of the United States" (Freneau), **Supp. II Part 1:** 271

"To the Apennines" (Bryant), **Supp. I Part 1:** 157, 164

"To the Bleeding Hearts Association of American Novelists" (Nemerov), **III:** 281

"To the Botequim & Back" (Bishop), **Retro. Supp. II:** 51

To the Bright and Shining Sun (Burke), **Supp. XIV:** 22, 25

"To the Citizens of the United States" (Paine), **Supp. I Part 2:** 519–520

"To the Dandelion" (Lowell), **Supp. I Part 2:** 424

"To the End" (Haines), **Supp. XII:** 212–213

To the Ends of the Earth: The Selected Travels of Paul Theroux, **Supp. VIII:** 324

"To the Film Industry in Crisis"(O'Hara), **Supp. XXIII:** 214

To the Finland Station: A Study in the Writing and Acting of History (Wilson), **IV:** 429, 436, 443–444, 446

"To the Governor & Legislature of Massachusetts" (Nemerov), **III:** 287

To the Green Man (Jarman), **Supp. XVII:** 110, 120–121

"To the Harbormaster"(O'Hara), **Supp. XXIII:** 208, 212, 214

To the Holy Spirit (Winters), **Supp. II Part 2:** 810

"To the Keeper of the King's Water Works" (Freneau), **Supp. II Part 1:** 269

"To the Lacedemonians" (Tate), **IV:** 134

"To the Laodiceans" (Jarrell), **Retro. Supp. I:** 121, 140

To the Lighthouse (Woolf), **I:** 309; **II:** 600; **Retro. Supp. II:** 337; **Supp. VIII:** 155

"To the Man on Trail" (London), **II:** 466

"To the Memory of the Brave Americans Under General Greene" (Freneau), **Supp. II Part 1:** 262, 274

"To the Miscodeed"(J. Schoolcraft), **Supp. XXIII:** 230

"To the Muse" (Wright), **Supp. III Part 2:** 601

"To the Natural World: at 37" (Taggard), **Supp. XXII:** 279–280

"To the Nazi Leaders" (Hay), **Supp. XIV:** 121

"To the New World" (Jarrell), **II:** 371

"To the One of Fictive Music" (Stevens), **IV:** 89; **Retro. Supp. I:** 297, 300

"To the One Upstairs" (Simic), **Supp. VIII:** 283

"To the Peoples of the World" (Du Bois), **Supp. II Part 1:** 172

"To the Pine Tree on first seeing it on returning from Europe"(J. Schoolcraft), **Supp. XXIII:** 225, 228, 232–233

To the Place of Trumpets (B. Kelly), **Supp. XVII: 123–127;** 132

"To the Pliocene Skull" (Harte), **Supp. II Part 1:** 343–344

"To the Powers of Darkness" (Taggard), **Supp. XXII:** 279, 280

"To the Powers of Desolation" (Taggard), **Supp. XXII:** 280

"To the Queen of Heaven" (Taggard), **Supp. XXII:** 280

"To the Reader" (Baudelaire), **II:** 544–545

"To The Reader" (Jarman), **Supp. XVII:** 115

"To the Reader" (Levertov), **Supp. III Part 1:** 277

"To the Right Honourable William, Earl of Dartmouth" (Wheatley), **Supp. XX: 278, 284, 287–288**

"To the River Arve" (Bryant), **Supp. I Part 1:** 163

"To the Snake" (Levertov), **Supp. III Part 1:** 277

"To the Stone-Cutters" (Jeffers), **Supp. II Part 2:** 420

"To the Unseeable Animal" (Berry), **Supp. X:** 31

"To the Western World" (Simpson), **Supp. IX:** 269, 270

To the White Sea (Dickey), **Supp. IV Part 1:** 186, 190–191

"To the Young Who Want to Die" (Brooks), **Supp. III Part 1:** 85–86

"To Tlaoc of the Rain" (Everwine), **Supp. XV:** 77

"To Train a Writer" (Bierce), **I:** 199

"Touch, The" (Sexton), **Supp. II Part 2:** 687

Touch and Go (M. F. K. Fisher and D. Parrish), **Supp. XVII:** 84

"Touching the Tree" (Merwin), **Supp. III Part 1:** 355

Touching the World (Eakin), **Supp. VIII:** 167

Touch of Danger, A (Jones), **Supp. XI:** 226, **228–229**

Touch of the Poet, A (O'Neill), **III:** 385, 401, 404

Touchstone, The (Wharton), **Retro. Supp. I:** 365

"Touch-up Man" (Komunyakaa), **Supp. XIII:** 119

Tough Guys Don't Dance (Mailer), **Retro. Supp. II:** 211

"Tough People" (Offutt), **Supp. XIX:** 170–171

Toulet, Paul Jean, **IV:** 79

Tour (McNally), **Supp. XIII:** 197

"Tour 5" (Hayden), **Supp. II Part 1:** 381

To Urania (Brodsky), **Supp. VIII:** 22, 28–29

Tourgée, Albion W., **Supp. XIV:** 63

"Tour Guide" (Komunyakaa), **Supp. XIII:** 114

"Tourist Death" (MacLeish), **III:** 12

Tourmaline (J. Scott), **Supp. XVII: 192–194,** 195

Tour of Duty (Dos Passos), **I:** 489

Touron the Prairies, A (Irving), **II:** 312–313

Toussaint L'Ouverture, **Supp. XXI:** 166

Toussaint L'Ouverture (C. L. R. James), **Supp. XXI:** 167

Tovey, Donald Francis, **Supp. XIV:** 336

To Walk a Crooked Mile (McGrath), **Supp. X:** 117

Toward a New Synthesis (Begiebing), **Retro. Supp. II:** 210

"Toward Nightfall" (Simic), **Supp. VIII:** 277

Towards a Better Life (Burke), **I:** 270

"Towards a Chicano Poetics: The Making of the Chicano Subject, 1969–1982" (Saldívar), **Supp. IV Part 2: 544**

Towards an Enduring Peace (Bourne), **I:** 232

"Towards Morning" (Pedersen; Nelson, trans.), **Supp. XVIII:** 180

Toward the Blanched Alphabets (Sobin), **Supp. XVI:** 290

Toward the Gulf (Masters), **Supp. I Part 2:** 465–466

"Toward the Solstice" (Rich), **Supp. I Part 2:** 575–576

Toward Wholeness in Paule Marshall's Fiction (Pettis), **Supp. XI:** 276

"Tower" (Merwin), **Supp. III Part 1:** 343

"Tower Beyond Tragedy, The" (Jeffers), **Supp. II Part 2:** 429–430

Tower of Ivory (MacLeish), **III:** 3–4

Towers, Robert, **Supp. IX:** 259; **Supp. XVI:** 211

"To What Red Hell" (C. Himes), **Supp. XVI:** 137

"To Whistler, American" (Pound), **III:** 465–466

"To Wine" (Bogan), **Supp. III Part 1:** 57, 58

Towle, Tony, **Supp. XXIII:** 221

Town, Caren J., **Supp. XVIII:** 195, 199

Town, The (Faulkner), **II:** 57, 73; **Retro. Supp. I:** 74, 82

Town, The (Richter), **Supp. XVIII:** 207, **214–215,** 217

Town and the City, The (Kerouac), **Supp. III Part 1:** 222–224; **Supp. XIV:** 143

"Town Crier" (Bierce), **I:** 193, 194, 195, 196

"Town Crier Exclusive, Confessions of a Princess Manqué: 'How Royals Found Me "Unsuitable" to Marry Their Larry' " (Elkin), **Supp. VI:** 56

Town Down the River, The (Robinson), **III:** 508

"Town Dump, The" (Nemerov), **III:** 272, 275, 281

Towne, Robert, **Supp. XI:** 159, 172, 174

"Townhouse Interior with Cat" (Clampitt), **Supp. IX:** 40

"Townies" (Dubus), **Supp. VII:** 86

Town in the Forest, The: Life Story of Richmond, New Hampshire (Boyce; Faust, ed.), **Supp. XXI:** 8

"Town of the Sound of a Twig Breaking" (Carson), **Supp. XII: 102**

"Town Poor, The" (Jewett), **Retro. Supp. II:** 138, 139, 143

Townsend, Alison, **Supp. XIII:** 222; **Supp. XXIII:** 132, 139

Townsend, Ann, **Supp. V:** 77

Townsend, Jim, **Supp. XXII:** 243

"Towns in Colour" (Lowell), **II:** 523–524

Townsman, The (Sedges), **Supp. II Part 1:** 124–125

Town Smokes (P. Benedict), **Supp. XXIII: 35–39**

"Town Smokes"(P. Benedict), **Supp. XXIII:** 37

"To World War Two" (Koch), **Supp. XV:** 184

Toys in a Field (Komunyakaa), **Supp. XIII: 121–122**

"Toys in a Field" (Komunyakaa), **Supp. XIII.** 122

Toys in the Attic (Hellman), **Supp. I Part 1:** 289–290

Toyter mentsh, Der (The dead man) (Asch), **Supp. XXIII:** 9

Tracer (F. Barthelme), **Supp. XI:** 31–32, 33

Traces of Thomas Hariot, The (Rukeyser), **Supp. VI:** 273, 274, 283

"Tracing Life with a Finger" (Caldwell), **I:** 291

Tracker (Wagoner), **Supp. IX:** 329, **336–337**

"Tracking" (Wagoner), **Supp. IX:** 329

"Track Meet, The" (Schwartz), **Supp. II Part 2:** 665

Tracks (Erdrich), **Supp. IV Part 1:** 259, 262–263, 269, 272, 273–274, 274, 275

"Tract" (W. C. Williams), **Retro. Supp. I:** 414

"Tract against Communism, A" (Twelve Southerners), **IV:** 125, 237

Tractatus (Wittgenstein), **Supp. XVII:** 143

Tracy, Benjamin, **Supp. XVIII:** 4

Tracy, D. H., **Supp. XVIII:** 178

Tracy, Lee, **IV:** 287, 288

Tracy, Steven, **Retro. Supp. I:** 195

"Trade, The" (Levine), **Supp. V:** 193

Trading Twelves (Callahan and Murray, eds.), **Retro. Supp. II:** 119

Trading Twelves: The Selected Letters of Ralph Ellison and Albert Murray (Murray and Callahan, eds.), **Supp. XIX:** 148, 158

" 'Traditional' Marriage: A Secular Affair" (P. N. Warren), **Supp. XX: 273**

"Tradition and Industrialization" (Wright), **IV:** 489–490

"Tradition and Mythology: Signatures of Landscape in Chicana Poetry" (Rebolledo), **Supp. XIII:** 214

"Tradition and the Individual Talent" (Eliot), **I:** 441, 574, 585; **Retro. Supp. I:** 59, 286

Tragedies, Life and Letters of James Gates Percival (Swinburne), **Supp. I Part 2:** 422

Tragedy of Bees, A (P. N. Warren), **Supp. XX: 261**

"Tragedy of Bees, A" (P. N. Warren), **Supp. XX: 272**

Tragedy of Don Ippolito, The (Howells), **II:** 279

"Tragedy of Error, A" (James), **II:** 322; **Retro. Supp. I:** 218

Tragedy of Pudd'nhead Wilson, The (Twain), **IV:** 206–207

Tragic America (Dreiser), **Retro. Supp. II:** 95

"Tragic Dialogue" (Wylie), **Supp. I Part 2:** 724

Tragic Ground (Caldwell), **I:** 297, 306

Tragic Muse, The (James), **Retro. Supp. I:** 227

Traherne, Thomas, **IV:** 151; **Supp. III Part 1:** 14; **Supp. V:** 208; **Supp. XV:** 212; **Supp. XVI:** 282, 288, 295

"Trail, The" (W. J. Smith), **Supp. XIII:** 342

Trailerpark (Banks), **Supp. V:** 12

"Trailing Arbutus, The" (Whittier), **Supp. I Part 2:** 691

Trail of the Lonesome Pine, The (Fox), **Supp. XIII:** 166

"Train, The" (O'Connor), **Retro. Supp. II:** 225

"Train Rising Out of the Sea" (Ashbery), **Supp. III Part 1:** 22

"Trains" (Banks), **Supp. V:** 8

"Train Tune" (Bogan), **Supp. III Part 1:** 64

Train Whistle Guitar (Murray), **Supp. XIX: 153–155,** 157

"Traits of Indian Character" (Irving), **II:** 303

Trakl, Georg, **Supp. XVII:** 241

Tramp Abroad, A (Twain), **IV:** 200

Tramping With a Poet in the Rockies (S. Graham), **Supp. I Part 2:** 397

Tramp's Excuse, The (Lindsay), **Supp. I Part 2:** 379, 380, 382

"Trance, The" (Taggard), **Supp. XXII:** 280

"Transaction" (Cliff), **Supp. XXII:** 75

"Transatlantic" (Toomer), **Supp. III Part 2:** 486

Transatlantic Sketches (James), **II:** 324; **Retro. Supp. I:** 219

"Transcendental Etude" (Rich), **Supp. I Part 2:** 576

"Transcontinental Highway" (Cowley), **Supp. II Part 1:** 141

"Transducer" (Ammons), **Supp. VII:** 28

"Transfiguration" (Jarman), **Supp. XVII:** 118, 119

"Transfigured Bird" (Merrill), **Supp. III Part 1:** 320–321

"Transformations" (Harjo), **Supp. XII:** 226

Transformations (Sexton), **Supp. II Part 2:** 689–691; **Supp. IV Part 2:** 447; **Supp. XIV:** 125

Transforming Madness: New Lives for People Living with Mental Illness (Neugeboren), **Supp. XVI:** 229

"Transit" (Conroy), **Supp. XVI:** 72

Transit to Narcissus, A (Mailer), **Retro. Supp. II:** 196

"Translation" (Espaillat), **Supp. XXI:** 107

"Translation and Transposition" (Carne-Ross), **Supp. I Part 1:** 268–269

"Translation of a Fragment of Simonides" (Bryant), **Supp. I Part 1:** 153, 155

"Translations" (Rich), **Supp. I Part 2:** 563

Translations of Ezra Pound, The (Kenner, ed.), **III:** 463

Translations of the Gospel Back into Tongues (Wright), **Supp. XV: 342–343,** 346

"Translator's Task, The"(Benjamin), **Supp. XXIII:** 28

"Trans-National America" (Bourne), **I:** 229, 230

"Transparency" (X. J. Kennedy), **Supp. XV:** 159–160

"Transparent Itineraries: 1983" (Sobin), **Supp. XVI:** 287

"Transparent Itineraries: 1984" (Sobin), **Supp. XVI:** 287

"Transparent Itineraries: 1992" (Sobin), **Supp. XVI:** 289

"Transparent Itineraries" poems (Sobin), **Supp. XVI:** 290

Transparent Man, The (Hecht), **Supp. X:** 57, **69–71**

"Transparent Man, The" (Hecht), **Supp. X: 69–70**

Transparent Things (Nabokov), **Retro. Supp. I:** 266, 270, 277

"Transport" (Simic), **Supp. VIII:** 282

Transport to Summer (Stevens), **IV:** 76, 93; **Retro. Supp. I:** 309–312

Tranströmer, Thomas, **Supp. IV Part 2:** 648

"Traps for the Unwary" (Bourne), **I:** 235

Trash Trilogy (McMurtry), **Supp. V:** 225–226, 231

Traubel, Horace, **IV:** 350

"Travel: After a Death" (Kenyon), **Supp. VII:** 169

Travel Alarm (Nye), **Supp. XIII:** 277

"Traveled World, The" (Pickering), **Supp. XXI:** 203

"Traveler, The" (Haines), **Supp. XII:** 203–204, 210

"Traveler, The" (Stegner), **Supp. IV Part 2:** 605

Traveler at Forty, A (Dreiser), **I:** 515

Traveler from Altruria, a Romance A, (Howells), **II:** 285, 287

Traveler's Tree, The: New and Selected Poems (W. J. Smith), **Supp. XIII:** 332, 347

"Traveling" (Paley), **Supp. VI:** 230

"Traveling Light" (Wagoner), **Supp. IX:** 329

Traveling Mercies: Some Thoughts on Faith (Lamott), **Supp. XX: 132, 140–142**

"Traveling Onion, The" (Nye), **Supp. XIII:** 276

Traveling through the Dark (Stafford), **Supp. XI:** 311, 316, **318–321**

"Traveling through the Dark" (Stafford), **Supp. XI:** 318–320, 321, 323, 329

Travelling in Amherst: A Poet's Journal, 1931–1954, **Supp. IX: 88–89**

Travelling Standing Still: Poems, 1918–1928 (Taggard), **Supp. XXII:** 278

Travels in Alaska (Muir), **Supp. IX:** 182, 185–186

"Travels in Georgia" (McPhee), **Supp. III Part 1:** 293–294

"Travels in North America" (Kees), **Supp. XV:** 133–134

Travels in the Congo (Gide), **III:** 210

"Travels in the South" (Ortiz), **Supp. IV Part 2:** 506

Travels with Charley (Steinbeck), **IV:** 52

"Travel Writing: Why I Bother" (Theroux), **Supp. VIII:** 310

Travis, Merle, **Supp. V:** 335

Travisano, Thomas, **Retro. Supp. II:** 40

Treadway, Jessica, **Supp. XXIII:** 280

Treasure Hunt (Buechner), **Supp. XII:** 52

Treasure Island (Stevenson), **Supp. X:** 230

Treasure of the Humble, The (Maeterlinck), **Supp. XX: 116**

"Treasure of the Redwoods, A" (Harte), **Supp. II Part 1:** 337

Treasury of Art Masterpieces, A: From the Renaissance to the Present Day (Craven), **Supp. XII:** 44

Treasury of English Aphorisms, A (L. P. Smith), **Supp. XIV:** 344

Treasury of English Prose, A (L. P. Smith, ed.), **Supp. XIV:** 341

Treasury of the Theatre, A (Gassner), **Supp. I Part 1:** 292

Treasury of Yiddish Stories, A (Howe and Greenberg, eds.), **Supp. I Part 2:** 432; **Supp. XXIII:** 7

Treat 'Em Rough (Lardner), **II:** 422–423

Treatise Concerning Religious Affections (Edwards), **I:** 547, 552, 554, 555, 557, 558, 560, 562

Treatise Concerning the Lord's Supper (Doolittle), **IV:** 150

"Treatise on Poetry" (Milosz), **Supp. VIII:** 20

Treatise on Right and Wrong, A (Mencken), **III:** 110, 119

"Treatise on Tales of Horror, A" (Wilson), **IV:** 438

Treatise on the Gods, A (Mencken), **III:** 108–109, 119

"Treatment" (Wright), **Supp. XV:** 343

Trece poetas del mundo azteca (León-Portilla), **Supp. XV:** 77

Tre Croce (Tozzi), **Supp. III Part 2:** 616

"Tree, a Rock, a Cloud, A" (McCullers), **II:** 587

"Tree, The" (Pound), **Retro. Supp. I:** 286; **Supp. I Part 1:** 255

"Tree, the Bird, The" (Roethke), **III:** 548

"Tree at My Window" (Frost), **II:** 155

Tree Grows in Brooklyn, A (B. Smith), **Supp. XVII:** 9; **Supp. XXIII:** 257, 259–264, 265, 271

Tree Grows in Brooklyn, A (film; Kazan), **Supp. XVI:** 193

"Tree House at Night, The" (Dickey), **Supp. IV Part 1:** 179

"Tree House"(Thompson), **Supp. XXIII:** 301

Tree Is Older Than You Are, The (Nye, ed.), **Supp. XIII:** 280

"Tree of Laughing Bells, The" (Lindsay), **Supp. I Part 2:** 376

"Tree of Life, The" (Swados), **Supp. XIX:** 268

"Tree of Night, A" (Capote), **Supp. III Part 1:** 114, 120

Tree of Night and Other Stories, A (Capote), **Supp. III Part 1:** 114

"Trees, The" (Rich), **Supp. I Part 2:** 555

Trees, The (Richter), **Supp. XVIII:** 212–213, 220

"Trees Listening to Bach" (Merrill), **Supp. III Part 1:** 336

Tree That Came to Stay, The (Quindlen), **Supp. XVII:** 167

Tree Where Man Was Born, The (Matthiessen), **Supp. V:** 199, 203, 204

Trejo, Ernesto, **Supp. V:** 178, 180; **Supp. XIII:** 313, 316; **Supp. XV:** 73

Trelawny, Edward John, **Supp. I Part 2:** 721

"Trellis for R., A" (Swenson), **Supp. IV Part 2:** 647

Tremblay, Bill, **Supp. XIII:** 112

Tremble (Wright), **Supp. XV:** 348–349

"Trespass" (Frost), **Retro. Supp. I:** 139

Trespassing (Pickering), **Supp. XXI:** 202

"Trespassing" (Pickering), **Supp. XXI:** 202

Trethewey, Eric, **Supp. XXI:** 243, 244

Trethewey, Natasha, **Supp. XXI:** 243–259

"Tretitoli, Where the Bomb Group Was" (Hugo), **Supp. VI:** 138

Trevelyan, Robert C., **Supp. XIV:** 334

Trevor-Roper, Hugh, **Supp. XIV:** 348

Trial, The (Kafka), **IV:** 113; **Retro. Supp. II:** 20

"Trial, The" (Rukeyser), **Supp. VI:** 278

"Trial by Existence, The" (Frost), **II:** 166

"Trial for Arson, The"(Hadas), **Supp. XXIII:** 114

Trial of a Poet, The (Shapiro), **Supp. II Part 2:** 710

Trial of the Hawk, The: A Comedy of the Seriousness of Life (Lewis), **II:** 441

Trials of the Human Heart (Rowson), **Supp. XV:** 237, 239

Tribal Secrets: Recovering American Indian Intellectual Traditions (Warrior), **Supp. IV Part 1:** 329

"Tribute" (A. Finch), **Supp. XVII:** 72, 73–74

"Tribute, A" (Easton), **Supp. IV Part 2:** 461

"Tribute, The" (Doolittle), **Supp. I Part 1:** 267

Tribute (To My Mother)" (Cullen), **Supp. IV Part 1:** 166

Tribute to Freud (Doolittle), **Supp. I Part 1:** 253, 254, 258, 259, 260, 268

Tribute to the Angels (Doolittle), **Supp. I Part 1:** 272

"Trick on the World, A" (Ríos), **Supp. IV Part 2:** 553

"Tricks" (Olds), **Supp. X:** 203–204

"Trick Scenery" (F. Barthelme), **Supp. XI:** 26

Trifler, The (Masters), **Supp. I Part 2:** 459–460

Trifles (Glaspell), **Supp. III Part 1:** 175, 178, 179, 182, 186, 187; **Supp. X:** 46; **Supp. XXI:** 12

Trifonov, Iurii V., **Retro. Supp. I:** 278

Triggering Town, The: Lectures and Essays on Poetry and Writing (Hugo), **Supp. VI:** 133, 140

Trilling, Diana, **II:** 587, 600; **Supp. I Part 1:** 297; **Supp. XII:** 126; **Supp. XXI:** 271, 275

Trilling, Lionel, **I:** 48; **II:** 579; **III:** 308, 310, 319, 327; **IV:** 201, 211; **Retro. Supp. I:** 19, 97, 121, 216, 227; **Supp. III Part 2: 493–515; Supp. V:** 259; **Supp. VIII:** 93, 98, 190, 231, 236, 243; **Supp. IX:** 266, 287; **Supp. XIII:** 100–101; **Supp. XIV:** 280, 288–289; **Supp. XV:** 20, 140, 152

Trilogy (Doolittle), **Supp. I Part 1:** 271, 272

Trilogy of Desire (Dreiser), **I:** 497, 508; **Retro. Supp. II:** 94, 96, **101–102**

Trimberger, Ellen Kay, **Supp. XVII:** 96, 106; **Supp. XXI:** 12

Trimmed Lamp, The (O. Henry), **Supp. II Part 1:** 410

"Trinc" (McGrath), **Supp. X:** 127

Trinity (Uris), **Supp. XX: 243, 244, 245, 246, 247, 248, 253, 254–255**

Trio (Baker), **Supp. I Part 1:** 277

Trio (Saroyan), **Supp. XXII:** 25

"Triolets for Triolet" (Nelson), **Supp. XVIII:** 179

"Trip" (F. Barthelme), **Supp. XI:** 26

Triple Thinkers, The: Ten Essays on Literature (Wilson), **IV:** 428, 431; **Supp. II Part 1:** 146

"Triplex" (Doolittle), **Supp. I Part 1:** 271

Tripmaster Monkey: His Fake Book (Kingston), **Supp. V:** 157, 158, 169, 170–173

Trippings in Authorland (Forrester), **Supp. XVIII:** 13

Trippings of Tom Pepper, The (Briggs), **Supp. XVIII:** 3, **13–14**

"Trip to Hanoi" (Sontag), **Supp. III Part 2:** 460–462

Trip to Parnassus, A; or, The Judgement of Apollo on Dramatic Authors and Performers (Rowson), **Supp. XV: 232–233**

"Triptych" (Eberhart), **I:** 522, 539

Tristam Shandy (Sterne), **Supp. XXII:** 267

Tristan and Iseult, **Retro. Supp. I:** 328, 329, 330, 331

Tristessa (Kerouac), **Supp. III Part 1:** 225, 227, 229

Tristram (Robinson), **III:** 521, 522, 523

Tristram Shandy (Sterne), **I:** 299; **IV:** 465–466; **Supp. V:** 127; **Supp. XVIII:** 60

"Triumph" (C. L. R. James), **Supp. XXI:** 160

"Triumphal March" (Eliot), **I:** 580; **III:** 17; **Retro. Supp. I:** 64

Triumph of Achilles, The (Glück), **Supp. V:** 79, 84–86, 92

"Triumph of a Modern, The, or, Send for the Lawyer" (Anderson), **I:** 113, 114

"Triumph of the Egg, The" (Anderson), **I:** 113

Triumph of the Egg, The: A Book of Impressions from American Life in Tales and Poems (Anderson), **I:** 112, 114

Triumph of the Spider Monkey, The (Oates), **Supp. II Part 2:** 522

Triumphs of the Reformed Religion in America (Mather), **Supp. II Part 2:** 453

Trivial Breath (Wylie), **Supp. I Part 2:** 709, 722–724

Trivia; or, the Art of Walking the Streets of London (Gay), **Supp. XIV:** 337

Trivia: Printed from the Papers of Anthony Woodhouse, Esq. (L. P. Smith), **Supp. XIV:** 336, **337–340**

"Trivia Tea" (Skloot), **Supp. XX: 205**

Trocchi, Alexander, **Supp. XI:** 294, 295, 301

Troilus and Criseyde (Chaucer), **Retro. Supp. I:** 426

Trois contes (Flaubert), **IV:** 31, 37

Trojan Horse, The: A Play (MacLeish), **III:** 21

"Trojan Women, The" (Maxwell), **Supp. VIII:** 169

Troll Garden, The (Cather), **I:** 313, 314–316, 322; **Retro. Supp. I:** 5, 6, 8, 14

"Trolling for Blues" (Wilbur), **Supp. III Part 2:** 563–564

Trollope, Anthony, **I:** 10, 375; **II:** 192, 237; **III:** 51, 70, 281, 382; **Retro. Supp. I:** 361

Trombly, Albert Edmund, **Supp. I Part 2:** 403

Trombold, John, **Supp. XVIII:** 111

"Trompe L'Oeil" (Collins), **Supp. XXI:** 60

"Troop Train" (Shapiro), **Supp. II Part 2:** 707

"Tropes of the Text" (Gass), **Supp. VI:** 88

Tropic of Cancer (H. Miller), **III:** 170, 171, 174, 177, 178–180, 181, 182, 183, 187, 190; **Supp. V:** 119; **Supp. X:** 187; **Supp. XXII:** 230, 257

Tropic of Capricorn (H. Miller), **III:** 170, 176–177, 178, 182, 183, 184, 187, 188–189, 190

"Tropic of Cuba" (di Donato), **Supp. XX:** 45

Trotsky, Leon, **I:** 366; **II:** 562, 564; **IV:** 429; **Supp. XXI:** 161, 164, 165, 167, 168

Trotter, W., **I:** 249

Troubled Air, The (Shaw), **Supp. XIX:** 249–250

Troubled Island (opera; Hughes and Still), **Retro. Supp. I:** 203

Troubled Lovers in History (Goldbarth), **Supp. XII:** 176, **192–193**

Trouble Follows Me (Macdonald, under Millar), **Supp. IV Part 2:** 466

Trouble in July (Caldwell), **I:** 297, 304–305, 306, 309

Trouble Island (Hughes), **Supp. I Part 1:** 328

"Trouble of Marcie Flint, The" (Cheever), **Supp. I Part 1:** 186

Trouble with Francis, The: An Autobiography (Francis), **Supp. IX:** 76, 77, 82, **84–85**

Trouble with God, The (Francis), **Supp. IX:** 88

"Trouble with Poetry, The" (Collins), **Supp. XXI:** 57

Trouble with Poetry and Other Poems, The (Collins), **Supp. XXI:** 55, 57, 62

"Trouble with the Stars and Stripes" (Nye), **Supp. XIII:** 277

Trouillot, Michel-Rolphe, **Supp. X:** 14–15

Troupe, Quincy, **Retro. Supp. II:** 15, 111; **Supp. X:** 242

"Trout" (Hugo), **Supp. VI:** 135

Trout Fishing in America (Brautigan), **Supp. VIII:** 43

"Trouvée" (Bishop), **Retro. Supp. II:** 49

Troy (film), **Supp. XX:** **273**

"Truce" (Taggard), **Supp. XXII:** 276–277

"Truce of the Bishop, The" (Frederic), **II:** 139–140

"Truck Stop: Minnesota" (Dunn), **Supp. XI:** 145–146

True Account, The: A Novel of the Lewis & Clark & Kinneson Expeditions (Mosher), **Supp. XXII:** 206, 207, 208, **214–215**

True and False: Heresy and Common Sense for the Actor (Mamet), **Supp. XIV:** 241, 243

True Blood (television series), **Supp. XIX:** 174

Trueblood, Valerie, **Supp. XIII:** 306

True Confessions (Dunne), **Supp. IV Part 1:** 198

True Confessions (film), **Supp. IV Part 1:** 198

Trueheart, Charles, **Supp. XXI:** 238

True History of the Conquest of New Spain, The (Castillo), **III:** 13

True Intellectual System of the Universe, The (Cuddleworth), **II:** 10

"True Love" (Olds), **Supp. X:** 212

Trueman, Matthew (pseudonym). *See* Lowell, James Russell

"True Morality" (Bell), **Supp. X:** 13

"True Romance" (Everett), **Supp. XVIII:** 65

Truesdale, C. W., **Supp. XXI:** 246

True Stories (Atwood), **Supp. XIII:** 34–35

"True Stories" (Atwood), **Supp. XIII:** 34

"True Stories of Bitches" (Mamet), **Supp. XIV:** 246, 252

"Truest Sport, The: Jousting with Sam and Charlie" (Wolfe), **Supp. III Part 2:** 581–582

"True Vine" (Wylie), **Supp. I Part 2:** 723

True West (Shepard), **Supp. III Part 2:** 433, 441, 445, 447, 448

Truman, Harry, **III:** 3

Truman Capote: In Which Various Friends, Enemies, Acquaintances, and Detractors Recall His Turbulent Career (Plimpton), **Supp. XVI:** 245

Truman Show, The (film), **Supp. XVI:** 271

Trumbo, Dalton, **Supp. I Part 1:** 295; **Supp. XIII:** 6; **Supp. XVII:** 63; **Supp. XX:** 246; **Supp. XXI:** 45

Trumbull, John, **Supp. II Part 1:** 65, 69, 70, 268

Trump, Donald, **Supp. IV Part 1:** 393

Trumpener, Katie, **Retro. Supp. I:** 380

"Trumpet Player" (Hughes), **Supp. I Part 1:** 333

"Trumpet Player, 1963" (Halliday), **Supp. XIX:** 92

Trumpet Shall Sound, The (Wilder), **IV:** 356

Trumpet Unblown, The (Hoffman), **Supp. XVIII:** 71, **74–75**

Trunk Music (Connelly), **Supp. XXI:** 72, 75

"Truro Bear, The" (Oliver), **Supp. VII:** 234

Truscott, Lucian K., **Supp. IV Part 2:** 683

Trust (Ozick), **Supp. V:** 257–258, 259, 260–263, 270, 272

Trust Me (Updike), **Retro. Supp. I:** 322

"Trust Yourself" (Emerson), **II:** 10

"Truth" (Emerson), **II:** 6

"Truth, The" (Halliday), **Supp. XIX:** 87, 88, 94

"Truth, The" (Jarrell), **II:** 381–382

Truth About Celia, The (Brockmeier), **Supp. XXII:** **53–55**

"Truth about God, The" (Carson), **Supp. XII:** **105–106**

"Truth be told" (Trethewey), **Supp. XXI:** 255, 256

"Truthful James" (Harte), **IV:** 196

"Truth Is, The" (Hogan), **Supp. IV Part 1:** 401–402

"Truth Is Forced, The" (Swenson), **Supp. IV Part 2:** 652

"Truth of the Matter, The" (Nemerov), **III:** 270

Truth Serum (Cooper), **Supp. XI:** 129

"Truth the Dead Know, The" (Sexton), **Supp. II Part 2:** 681

"Trying to Evangelize a Cut Flower" (Peacock), **Supp. XIX:** 199

Trying to Find Chinatown (Hwang), **Supp. XXI:** 147

Trying to Save Piggy Sneed (Irving), **Supp. VI:** **19–165**

"Trying to Talk with a Man" (Rich), **Supp. I Part 2:** 559

"Tryptich I" (Bell), **Supp. X:** 7

"Tryst, The" (Wharton), **Retro. Supp. I:** 378

"Try the Girl" (Chandler), **Supp. IV Part 1:** 125

Try! Try! (O'Hara), **Supp. XXIII:** 209, 210, 216

"Ts'ai Chih" (Pound), **III:** 466

T. S. Eliot and American Philosophy (Jain), **Retro. Supp. I:** 58

T. S. Eliot's Silent Voices (Mayer), **Retro. Supp. I:** 58

Tsuji, Shizuo, **Supp. XVII:** 90

Tsurikgekumen (The return) (Asch), **Supp. XXIII:** 5

Tsvetaeva, Marina, **Supp. VIII:** 30; **Supp. XXIII:** 168

"Tuberoses" (E. Stoddard), **Supp. XV:** 282

Tubert, Susana, **Supp. XXIII:** 203

Tucker, Benjamin R., **Supp. XXI:** 9

Tuckerman, Frederick Goddard, **IV:** 144

Tucker's People (Wolfert), **Supp. XXI:** 261, 262, 263, 267, **267–275**, 278

"Tuesday, November 5th, 1940" (Benét), **Supp. XI:** 46, 52

"Tuesday April 25th 1966" (Olson), **Supp. II Part 2:** 585

"Tuesday Night at the Savoy Ballroom" (Komunyakaa), **Supp. XIII:** 132

Tuffield, Aviva, **Supp. XVI:** 147, 148

"Tuft of Flowers, The" (Frost), **II:** 153; **Retro. Supp. I:** 126, 127

Tufts, James Hayden, **Supp. I Part 2:** 632

Tu Fu, **II:** 526; **Supp. XV:** 47

Tu Fu (Ayscough), **II:** 527

Tugwell, Rexford Guy, **Supp. I Part 2:** 645

"Tulip" (Hammett), **Supp. IV Part 1:** 356

"Tulip Man, The" (McCarriston), **Supp. XIV:** 261

"Tulips" (Nye), **Supp. XIII:** 281

"Tulips" (Plath), **Retro. Supp. II:** 252–253; **Supp. I Part 2:** 540, 542, 544

"Tulips" (Snodgrass), **Supp. VI:** 325

Tulips and Chimneys (Cummings), **I:** 436, 437, 440, 445, 447

"Tulips"(Strout), **Supp. XXIII:** 283, 285

"Tulips"(theater performance, Strout), **Supp. XXIII:** 281

Tully, Jim, **III:** 103, 109

Tumble Home (Hempel), **Supp. XXI:** 115, **124–125**

"Tumble Home" (Hempel), **Supp. XXI:** 115, 116, **124–125**, 126

Tumble Tower (Modarressi and Tyler), **Supp. IV Part 2:** 657

"Tuned in Late One Night" (Stafford), **Supp. XI:** 327–328

Tunnel, The (Gass), **Supp. V:** 44; **Supp. VI: 89–91,** 94

"Tunnel, The" (Strand), **Supp. IV Part 2:** 622

"Tunnels" (Komunyakaa), **Supp. XIII:** 123

Tuqan, Fadwa, **Supp. XIII:** 278

Tura, Cosimo, **III:** 474–475

Turandot and Other Poems (Ashbery), **Supp. III Part 1:** 3

Turco, Lewis, **Supp. XV:** 118

Turgenev, Ivan Sergeevich, **I:** 106; **II:** 263, 271, 275, 280, 281, 288, 319, 320, 324–325, 338, 407; **III:** 461; **IV:** 17, 277; **Retro. Supp. I:** 215, 222; **Supp. VIII:** 167

Turgot, Anne Robert Jacques, **II:** 103; **Supp. I Part 1:** 250

"Turkey and Bones and Eating and We Liked It" (Stein), **IV:** 44

Turman, Glynn, **Supp. IV Part 1:** 362

Turnbull, Dr. George, **II:** 113

Turnbull, Lawrence, **Supp. I Part 1:** 352

"Turned" (Gilman), **Supp. XI:** 207

Turner, Addie, **IV:** 123

Turner, Darwin, **Supp. I Part 1:** 339; **Supp. IV Part 1:** 165

Turner, Frederick Jackson, **Supp. I Part 2:** 480, 481, 632, 640; **Supp. IV Part 2:** 596

Turner, Nat, **IV:** 113–114, 115, 116, 117

Turner, Patricia A., **Supp. XIII:** 237; **Supp. XX:** 110

Turner, Russell. *See* Lacy, Ed

Turner, Victor, **Supp. IV Part 1:** 304

"Turning Away Variations on Estrangement" (Dickey), **Supp. IV Part 1:** 183

Turning Point, The (McCoy), **Supp. XIII:** 175

"Turning Thirty, I Contemplate Students Bicycling Home" (Dove), **Supp. IV Part 1:** 250

Turning Wind, A (Rukeyser), **Supp. VI:** 272–273, 279–280

Turn in the South, A (Naipaul), **Supp. XXII:** 240

Turn of the Screw, The (H. James), **Retro. Supp. I:** 219, 231; **Supp. IV Part 2:** 682

"Turn of the Screw, The" (H. James), **II:** 331–332; **Retro. Supp. I:** 228, 229, 231, 232; **Supp. XVII:** 143

Turns and Movies and Other Tales in Verse (Aiken), **I:** 65

"Turn with the Sun, A" (Knowles), **Supp. XII:** 237–238

"Turn Your Radio On" (J. W. Miller), **Supp. XX: 169**

Turow, Scott, **Supp. V:** 220; **Supp. XVII: 213–224**

Turpin, E. Walters, **Supp. XVIII:** 283

Turrinus, Lucius Mamilius, **IV:** 373

"Turtle" (Hogan), **Supp. IV Part 1:** 401

Turtle, Swan (Doty), **Supp. XI: 121–122**

"Turtle, Swan" (Doty), **Supp. XI:** 121–122

Turtle Island (Snyder), **Supp. VIII: 300–303**

Turtle Moon (Hoffman), **Supp. X:** 77, **87–88,** 89

"Turtle Shrine near Chittagong, The" (Nye), **Supp. XIII:** 277

Turtotte, James, **Supp. XXIII:** 125

Turturro, John, **Supp. XI:** 174

Tuscan Cities (Howells), **II:** 280

Tuskegee movement, **Supp. II Part 1:** 169, 172

Tuten, Frederic, **Supp. VIII:** 75, 76; **Supp. XIII:** 237, 249

Tuten, James, **Supp. XVIII:** 195

Tuthill, Louisa Cavolne, **Supp. I Part 2:** 684

"Tutored Child, The" (Kunitz), **Supp. III Part 1:** 264

Tuttleton, James W., **Supp. IV Part 1:** 166, 168

"T.V.A." (Agee), **I:** 35

Tvedten, Brother Benet, **Supp. IV Part 2:** 505

"TV Men" (Carson), **Supp. XII: 105, 112**

Twain, Mark, **I:** 57, 103, 107, 109, 190, 192, 193, 195, 197, 203, 209, 245, 246, 247–250, 255, 256, 257, 260, 261, 292, 342, 418, 469, 485; **II:** 70, 140, 259, 262, 266–268, 271, 272, 274–275, 276, 277, 280, 285–286, 287, 288, 289, 301, 304, 306, 307, 312, 415, 432, 434, 436, 446, 457, 467, 475, 476, 482; **III:** 65, 101, 102, 112–113, 114, 220, 347, 357, 409, 453, 454, 504, 507, 554, 558, 572, 575, 576; **IV: 190–213,** 333, 349, 451; **Retro. Supp. I:** 169, 194, 195; **Retro. Supp. II:** 123; **Supp. I Part 1:** 37, 39, 44, 247, 251, 313, 317; **Supp. I Part 2:** 377, 385, 393, 410, 455, 456, 457, 473, 475, 579, 602, 604, 618, 629, 651, 660; **Supp. II Part 1:** 193, 344, 354, 385; **Supp. IV Part 1:** 386, 388; **Supp. IV Part 2:** 463, 468, 603, 607, 693; **Supp. V:** 44, 113, 131; **Supp. VIII:** 40, 189; **Supp. IX:** 14, 171; **Supp. X:** 51, 227; **Supp. XII:** 343; **Supp. XIII:** 1, 17; **Supp. XV:** 41; **Supp. XVI:** 66, 208; **Supp. XVIII:** 1, 9, 13; **Supp. XXI:** 205; **Supp. XXII:** 89, 203, 205, 206; **Supp. XXIII:** 85

"Twa Sisters, The" (ballad), **Supp. I Part 2:** 696

Twelfth Night (Shakespeare), **Supp. IV Part 1:** 83; **Supp. IX:** 14; **Supp. XXII:** 229

"12 O'Clock News" (Bishop), **Retro. Supp. II:** 48

Twelve Men (Dreiser), **Retro. Supp. II:** 94, 104

Twelve Moons (Oliver), **Supp. VII:** 231, 233–236, 238, 240

Twelve Southerners, **IV:** 125; **Supp. X:** 25

Twelve Years a Slave (Northup), **Supp. XIV:** 32

Twentieth Century Authors, **I:** 376, 527

"Twentieth Century Fiction and the Black Mask of Humanity" (Ellison), **Retro. Supp. II:** 118

Twentieth Century Pleasures (Hass), **Supp. VI:** 103, 106, 109

Twenty Drawings (Gibran), **Supp. XX: 116**

"28" (Levine), **Supp. V:** 187, 191

"Twenty-Four Poems" (Schwartz), **Supp. II Part 2:** 646, 649

"2433 Agnes, First Home, Last House in Missoula" (Hugo), **Supp. VI:** 139–140

"Twenty Hill Hollow" (Muir), **Supp. IX:** 178

"Twenty Minutes" (Salter), **Supp. IX:** 260

"Twenty-One Love Poems" (Rich), **Supp. I Part 2:** 572–573

"Twenty-One Poems" (MacLeish), **III:** 19

Twenty Poems (Haines), **Supp. XII:** 204, **205–206**

Twenty Poems of Anna Akhmatova (Kenyon), **Supp. VII:** 165–166

Twenty Questions: (Posed by Poems) (McClatchy), **Supp. XII:** 254, **259–262**

27 Wagons Full of Cotton and Other One-Act Plays (T. Williams), **IV:** 381, 383

Twenty-seventh City, The (Franzen), **Supp. XX: 83–84, 84, 85, 86–88, 88, 89, 91, 92, 95**

Twenty Thousand Leagues under the Sea (Verne), **I:** 480; **Supp. XI:** 63

"Twenty Years Ago" (Lindsay), **Supp. I Part 2:** 384, 399

Twenty Years at Hull-House (Addams), **Supp. I Part 1:** 3, 4, 11, 16

Twersky, David, **Supp. XX: 244**

Twice over Lightly: New York Ten and Now (Hayes and Loos), **Supp. XVI:** 195

Twice-Told Tales (Hawthorne), **I:** 354; **II:** 224; **III:** 412, 421; **Retro. Supp. I:** 154–155, 160

Twichell, Chase, **Supp. V:** 16; **Supp. XVII:** 110, 112

Twilight (Frost), **II:** 151

"Twilight's Last Gleaming" (Burroughs and Elvins), **Supp. III Part 1:** 93, 94, 101

Twilight Sleep (Wharton), **IV:** 320–322, 324–325, 327, 328; **Retro. Supp. I:** 381

"Twin, The" (Olds), **Supp. X:** 207

"Twin Beds in Rome" (Updike), **Retro. Supp. I:** 332

"Twins of Table Mountain, The" (Harte), **Supp. II Part 1:** 355

"Twist, The" (Olson), **Supp. II Part 2:** 570

Twitch and Shout (film), **Supp. XVIII:** 143

Twitchell-Waas, Jeffrey, **Supp. XVIII:** 99; **Supp. XXII:** 163

Two Admirals, The (Cooper), **I:** 350

Two against One (F. Barthelme), **Supp. XI:** 32, 33, 36

"Two and One"(Hadas), **Supp. XXIII:** 114–115

"Two Boys" (Moore), **Supp. X:** 173

"Two Brothers, The" (Jewett), **Retro. Supp. II:** 132

Two-Character Play, The (T. Williams), **IV:** 382, 386, 393, 398

Two Citizens (Wright), **Supp. III Part 2:** 602–604

"Two Deer" (Bass), **Supp. XVI:** 24

"Two Domains, The" (Goldbarth), **Supp. XII:** 192

"Two-Eleven All Around" (Offutt), **Supp. XIX:** 170

"Two Environments, The" (Trilling), **Supp. III Part 2:** 510

"Two-Fisted Self Pity" (Broyard), **Supp. XI:** 348

Two for Texas (Burke), **Supp. XIV:** 25, 34

"Two Friends" (Cather), **I:** 332

"Two Gardens in Linndale" (Robinson), **III:** 508

Two Gentlemen in Bonds (Ransom), **III:** 491–492

Two: Gertrude Stein and Her Brother (Stein), **IV:** 43

"Two Ghosts" (Francis), **Supp. IX:** 87

"Two Hangovers" (Wright), **Supp. III Part 2:** 596

Two-Headed Poems (Atwood), **Supp. XIII:** 34

Two Hot to Handle (Lacy), **Supp. XV:** 206

Two Hours to Doom (Bryant), **Supp. XI:** 302

"Two Hundred Years in an Hour" (Boyce), **Supp. XXI:** 8

"Two Kitchens in Provence" (M. F. K. Fisher), **Supp. XVII:** 88, 91

"Two Ladies in Retirement" (Taylor), **Supp. V:** 320

Two Letters to the Citizens of the United States, and One to General Washington (Barlow), **Supp. II Part 1:** 80

"Two Lives, The" (Hogan), **Supp. IV Part 1:** 400, 402, 403, 406, 411

Two Long Poems (Stern), **Supp. IX:** 296

"Two Look at Two" (Frost), **Supp. XXI:** 26

"Two Lovers and a Beachcomber by the Real Sea" (Plath), **Supp. I Part 2:** 536

"Two Men" (McClatchy)", **Supp. XII:** 269

Two Men (E. Stoddard), **Supp. XV:** 272, 273, **283–284**

Two Men of Sandy Bar (Harte), **Supp. II Part 1:** 354

Twomey, Jay, **Supp. XVII:** 111

"Two Moods of Love" (Cullen), **Supp. IV Part 1:** 166

Two Moons (Mallon), **Supp. XIX:** 132, **138–141**

"Two Morning Monologues" (Bellow), **I:** 150; **Retro. Supp. II:** 20

"Two Nations of Black America, The" (*Frontline*), **Supp. XX:** **99**

Two-Ocean War, The (Morison), **Supp. I Part 2:** 491

"Two of Hearts" (Hogan), **Supp. IV Part 1:** 410

"Two on a Party" (T. Williams), **IV:** 388

"Two or Three Things I Dunno About John Cassavetes" (Lethem), **Supp. XVIII:** 148

"Two Pendants: For the Ears" (W. C. Williams), **Retro. Supp. I:** 423

"Two Poems of Going Home" (Dickey), **Supp. IV Part 1:** 182–183

"Two Portraits" (Chopin), **Supp. I Part 1:** 218

"Two Presences, The" (R. Bly), **Supp. IV Part 1:** 65

"Two Rivers" (Stegner), **Supp. IV Part 2:** 605

Tworkov, Jack, **Supp. XII:** 198

"Two Scenes" (Ashbery), **Supp. III Part 1:** 4

Two Serious Ladies (Jane Bowles), **Supp. IV Part 1:** 82

"Two Silences" (Carruth), **Supp. XVI:** 55

"Two Sisters" (Farrell), **II:** 45

Two Sisters: A Memoir in the Form of a Novel (Vidal), **Supp. IV Part 2:** 679

"Two Sisters of Persephone" (Plath), **Retro. Supp. II:** 246

"Two Songs on the Economy of Abundance" (Agee), **I:** 28

Two Sons, The (Boyce), **Supp. XXI:** 7, 13

"Two Tales of Clumsy" (Schnackenberg), **Supp. XV:** 258

"Two Temples, The" (Melville), **III:** 89–90

Two Thousand Seasons (Armah), **Supp. IV Part 1:** 373

Two Towns in Provence (M. F. K. Fisher), **Supp. XVII:** 91

Two Trains Running (Wilson), **Supp. VIII:** **345–348**

"Two Tramps in Mudtime" (Frost), **II:** 164; **Retro. Supp. I:** 137; **Supp. IX:** 261

"Two Views of a Cadaver Room" (Plath), **Supp. I Part 2:** 538

"Two Villages" (Paley), **Supp. VI:** 227

"Two Voices in a Meadow" (Wilbur), **Supp. III Part 2:** 555

Two Weeks in Another Town (Shaw), **Supp. XIX:** 251

"Two Witches" (Frost), **Retro. Supp. I:** 135

"Two Words" (Francis), **Supp. IX:** 81

Two Worlds Walking: A Mixed-Blood Anthology (Glancy and Truesdale, eds.), **Supp. XXI:** 246

Two Years before the Mast (Dana), **I:** 351

"Tyger, The" (Blake), **Supp. XVII:** 128

Tyler, Anne, **Supp. IV Part 2: 657–675; Supp. V:** 227, 326; **Supp. VIII:** 141; **Supp. X:** 1, 77, 83, 85; **Supp. XII:** 307; **Supp. XVI:** 37; **Supp. XVIII:** 157, 195; **Supp. XXIII:** 298

Tyler, Royall, **I:** 344; **Retro. Supp. I:** 377

Tymms, Ralph, **Supp. IX:** 105

Tyndale, William, **II:** 15

Tyndall, John, **Retro. Supp. II:** 93

Typee: A Peep at Polynesian Life (Melville), **III:** 75–77, 79, 84; **Retro. Supp. I:** 245–246, 249, 252, 256

Types From City Streets (Hapgood), **Supp. XVII:** 103

"Typewriter, The" (D. West), **Supp. XVIII:** 279

Typewriter Town (W. J. Smith), **Supp. XIII:** 332

"Typhus" (Simpson), **Supp. IX:** 277

Tyranny of the Normal (Fiedler), **Supp. XIII:** **107–108**

"Tyranny of the Normal" (Fiedler), **Supp. XIII:** 107–108

"Tyrant of Syracuse" (MacLeish), **III:** 20

"Tyrian Businesses" (Olson), **Supp. II Part 2:** 567, 568, 569

Tytell, John, **Supp. XIV:** 140

Tzara, Tristan, **Supp. III Part 1:** 104, 105

U

U and I (Baker), **Supp. XIII:** **45–47,** 48, 52, 55

Überdie Seelenfrage (Fechner), **II:** 358

Ubik (Dick), **Supp. XVIII:** 136

Ubu Roi (Jarry), **Supp. XV:** 178, 186

Ueland, Brenda, **Supp. XVII:** 13

Uhry, Alfred, **Supp. XX:** **177**

ukanhavyrfuckinciti back (Phillips), **Supp. XXIII:** 174

Ukrainian Dumy (P. N. Warren as Kilina and Tarnawsky, trans.), **Supp. XX:** **261**

"Ulalume" (Poe), **III:** 427; **Retro. Supp. II:** 264, 266

Ulin, David, **Supp. XIII:** 244; **Supp. XVI:** 74

Ullman, Leslie, **Supp. IV Part 2:** 550; **Supp. XVIII:** 175

Ultimate Good Luck, The (Ford), **Supp. V:** 57, 61–62

Ultimate Punishment: A Lawyer's Reflections on Dealing with the Death Penalty (Turow), **Supp. XVII:** 220–221

Ultima Thule (Longfellow), **II:** 490; **Retro. Supp. II:** 169

"Ultima Thule" (Nabokov), **Retro. Supp. I:** 274

Ultramarine (Carver), **Supp. III Part 1:** 137, 138, 147, 148

Ulysses (Joyce), **I:** 395, 475–476, 478, 479, 481; **II:** 42, 264, 542; **III:** 170, 398; **IV:** 103, 418, 428, 455; **Retro.**

Supp. I: 59, 63, 290, 291; **Retro. Supp. II:** 121; **Supp. I Part 1:** 57; **Supp. III Part 2:** 618, 619; **Supp. IV Part 1:** 285; **Supp. IV Part 2:** 424; **Supp. V:** 261; **Supp. IX:** 102; **Supp. X:** 114; **Supp. XIII:** 43, 191; **Supp. XV:** 305; **Supp. XVII:** 140, 227

"*Ulysses,* Order and Myth" (Eliot), **Retro. Supp. I:** 63

"Umbrella, The" (Peacock), **Supp. XIX:** 203–204

Unaccountable Worth of the World, The (Price), **Supp. VI:** 267

Unaccustomed Earth (Lahiri), **Supp. XXI:** 176, **181–183,** 183, 188

"Unaccustomed Earth" (Lahiri), **Supp. XXI:** 186

Unamuno y Jugo, Miguel de, **III:** 310; **Supp. XV:** 79

"Unattached Smile, The" (Crews), **Supp. XI:** 101

"Unbelievable Thing Usually Goes to the Heart of the Story, The: Magic Realism in the Fiction of Rick Bass" (Dwyer), **Supp. XVI:** 16

"Unbeliever, The" (Bishop), **Retro. Supp. II:** 43

"Unborn Song" (Rukeyser), **Supp. VI:** 274

Unbought Spirit: A John Jay Chapman Reader (Stone, ed.), **Supp. XIV:** 54

Uncalled, The (Dunbar), **Supp. II Part 1:** 200, 211, 212

Uncentering the Earth: Copernicus and The Revolutions of the Heavenly Spheres (Vollmann), **Supp. XVII:** 226

Uncertain Certainty, The: Interviews, Essays, and Notes on Poetry (Simic), **Supp. VIII:** 270, 273, 274

Uncertainty and Plenitude: Five Contemporary Poets (Stitt), **Supp. IX:** 299

"Uncle" (Levine), **Supp. V:** 186

"Uncle Adler" (Kooser), **Supp. XIX:** 120

"Uncle Christmas" (Ríos), **Supp. IV Part 2:** 552

"Uncle Jim's Baptist Revival Hymn" (Lanier and Lanier), **Supp. I Part 1:** 353

"Uncle Lot" (Stowe), **Supp. I Part 2:** 585–586

Uncle Moses (Asch), **Supp. XXIII:** 14

"Uncle Moustapha's Eclipse" (McKnight), **Supp. XX:** 148

Uncle Remus Tales (Harris), **Supp. II Part 1:** 201

"Uncle Tomitudes" (Briggs), **Supp. XVIII:** 14

Uncle Tom's Cabin (Stowe), **II:** 291; **Supp. I Part 1:** 49; **Supp. I Part 2:** 410, 579, 582, 589–592; **Supp. II Part 1:** 170; **Supp. III Part 1:** 154, 171; **Supp. IX:** 19; **Supp. X:** 246, 249, 250; **Supp. XIII:** 95; **Supp. XVI:** 82, 85, 88; **Supp. XVIII:** 14

Uncle Tom's Children (Wright), **IV:** 476, 478, 488; **Supp. II Part 1:** 228, 235; **Supp. XVIII:** 283

"Uncle Wiggily in Connecticut" (Salinger), **III:** 559–560, 563

"Unclouded Day, The" (Proulx), **Supp. VII:** 254–255

"Uncommon Visage" (Brodsky), **Supp. VIII:** 31

"Uncommon Woman: An Interview with Wendy Wasserstein" (Cohen), **Supp. XV:** 323

Uncommon Women and Others (Wasserstein), **Supp. XV:** 320–321, **322–323**

Uncompromising Fictions of Cynthia Ozick (Pinsker), **Supp. V:** 272

"Unconscious Came a Beauty" (Swenson), **Supp. IV Part 2:** 646

"Uncreation, The" (Pinsky), **Supp. VI:** 245

"Undead, The" (Wilbur), **Supp. III Part 2:** 556

"Undefeated, The" (Hemingway), **II:** 250; **Retro. Supp. I:** 180

Under a Glass Bell (Nin), **Supp. X:** 186

"Under Ben Bulben" (Yeats), **Supp. V:** 220

Undercliff: Poems 1946–1953 (Eberhart), **I:** 528, 536–537

Under Cover (Goldbarth), **Supp. XII:** 177, 180, 193

Undercover Doctor (film), **Supp. XIII:** 170

"Under Cygnus" (Wilbur), **Supp. III Part 2:** 558

"Under Forty" (Trilling), **Supp. III Part 2:** 494

Underground, The Story of a People (Tenenbaum), **Supp. XX: 253**

Underground Man, The (film), **Supp. IV Part 2:** 474

Underground Man, The (Macdonald), **Supp. IV Part 2:** 474, 475

"Under Libra: Weights and Measures" (Merrill), **Supp. III Part 1:** 328

Under Milk Wood (D. Thomas), **III:** 21

"Undersea" (Carson), **Supp. IX:** 21

Understanding Cynthia Ozick (Friedman), **Supp. V:** 273

Understanding Drama (Brooks and Heilman), **Supp. XIV:** 12

Understanding E. L. Doctorow (Fowler), **Supp. IV Part 1:** 226

Understanding Fiction (Brooks and Warren), **IV:** 279; **Supp. XIV:** 11

Understanding Fiction (Brooks and Warren, eds.), **Supp. XIX:** 246

Understanding Flannery O'Connor (Whitt), **Retro. Supp. II:** 226

Understanding Nicholson Baker (Saltzman), **Supp. XIII:** 48

Understanding Poetry: An Anthology for College Students (Brooks and Warren), **IV:** 236; **Retro. Supp. I:** 40, 41; **Supp. XIV:** 4–5

Understanding Robert Bly (W. V. Davis), **Supp. XXI: 84–85,** 88

Understanding Tim O'Brien (Kaplan), **Supp. V:** 241

Understanding To Kill a Mockingbird: A Student Casebook to Issues, Sources, and Documents (Johnson), **Supp. VIII:** 127

Undertaker's Garland, The (Wilson and Bishop), **IV:** 427

Under Taos Mountain: The Terrible Quarrel of Magpie and Tía (Schott), **Supp. XXIII: 250–251**

Under the Banner of Heaven: A Story of Violent Faith (Krakauer), **Supp. XVIII:** 105, **114–116,** 117

"Under the Cedarcroft Chestnut" (Lanier), **Supp. I Part 1:** 364

"Under the Harbour Bridge" (Komunyakaa), **Supp. XIII:** 125

"Under the Influence" (Sanders), **Supp. XVI:** 274, 277

Under the Lilacs (Alcott), **Supp. I Part 1:** 42–43, 44

"Under the Maud Moon" (Kinnell), **Supp. III Part 1:** 246–247

Under the Mountain Wall: A Chronicle of Two Seasons in the Stone Age (Matthiessen), **Supp. V:** 202

Under the Red Flag (Jin), **Supp. XVIII:** 89, **94–95**

"Under the Rose" (Pynchon), **Supp. II Part 2:** 620

Under the Sea-Wind: A Naturalist's Picture of Ocean Life (Carson), **Supp. IX:** 19, **22–23**

Under the Shadow (Sorrentino), **Supp. XXI:** 236–237

Under the Sign of Saturn (Sontag), **Supp. III Part 2:** 451, 452, 458, 470–471

"Under the Sign of Saturn" (Sontag), **Supp. III Part 2:** 470

"Under the Sky" (Bowles), **Supp. IV Part 1:** 87

"Under the Sun"(Schott), **Supp. XXIII:** 247, 248

" 'Under the Umbrella of Black Civilization': A Conversation with Reginald McKnight" (Ashe), **Supp. XX:** 154

Under the Volcano (M. Lowry), **Supp. XVII:** 135, 139, 140

"Under the Willows" (Lowell), **Supp. I Part 2:** 416

Under the Willows and Other Poems (Lowell), **Supp. I Part 2:** 424

"Undertow" (Boyce), **Supp. XXI:** 10

Underwood, Wilbur, **Retro. Supp. II:** 79

Underworld (DeLillo), **Supp. VI:** 2, 4–5, 6–7, 8, 9, 10, 11, **13–15; Supp. XI:** 68; **Supp. XX:** 91

Underworld, The (Wolfert). See *Tucker's World* (Wolfert)

Undine (La Motte-Fouqué), **II:** 212; **III:** 78

Undiscovered Country, The (Howells), **II:** 282

"Undressing, The" (C. Frost), **Supp. XV:** 98

Uneasy Chair, The (Stegner), **Supp. IV Part 2:** 599

"Unemployed, Disabled, and Insane, The" (Haines), **Supp. XII:** 211–212

Unending Blues (Simic), **Supp. VIII: 278–279**

Unending Dialogue: Voices from an AIDS Poetry Workshop (Hadas, Barber, et al), **Supp. XXIII:** 118, **125–126**

"Unexpected Freedom" (Peacock), **Supp. XIX:** 199

"Unexpressed" (Dunbar), **Supp. II Part 1:** 199

"Unfinished Bronx, The" (Paley), **Supp. VI:** 228

Unfinished Crime, The (Holding), **Supp. XXII:** 120, **123–124,** 135, 136

"Unfinished Poems" (Eliot), **I:** 579

"Unfinished Song" (C. Frost), **Supp. XV:** 97

Unfinished Woman, An (Hellman), **Supp. I Part 1:** 292, 293, 294; **Supp. IV Part 1:** 12, 353–354; **Supp. IX:** 196, 200–201

Unforeseen Wilderness, The: An Essay on Kentucky's Red River Gorge (Berry), **Supp. X:** 28, 29, 30, 36

Unforgotten Years (L. P. Smith), **Supp. XIV:** 333, 334, 335, 336, 347

"Unfortunate Coincidence" (Parker), **Supp. IX:** 190

Unframed Originals (Merwin), **Supp. III Part 1:** 341

Ungar, Sanford, **Supp. XI:** 228

Ungaretti, Giuseppe, **Supp. V:** 337

Unguided Tour (Sontag), **Supp. III Part 2:** 452

"Unheimliche, Das" (The Uncanny) (Freud), **Supp. XVI:** 157–158

Unholy Sonnets (Jarman), **Supp. XVII:** 109, 110, **119–120; Supp. XVIII:** 178

"Unholy Sonnets" (Jarman), **Supp. XVII:** 118, 119–120

"Unidentified Flying Object" (Hayden), **Supp. II Part 1:** 368

"Unifying Principle, The" (Ammons), **Supp. VII:** 28

"Unimportant Man, An" (D. West), **Supp. XVIII:** 280

"Union" (Hughes), **Supp. I Part 1:** 331

"Union Street: San Francisco, Summer 1975" (Carver), **Supp. III Part 1:** 138

"United"(Kenny), **Supp. XXIII:** 149

United States Army in World War II (Morison), **Supp. I Part 2:** 490

United States Constitution, **I:** 6, 283

United States Essays, 1951–1991 (Vidal), **Supp. IV Part 2:** 678, 687

"United States of Huck, The: Introduction to *Adventures of Huckleberry Finn*" (Saunders), *Supp.* **XIX:** 235

United States of Poetry, The (television series), **Supp. XIII:** 274

"Unity through Diversity" (Locke), **Supp. XIV:** 212, 213

Universal Baseball Asociation, Inc., J. Henry Waugh, Prop., The (Coover), **Supp. V:** 39, 41–42, 44, 46

Universal Passion (Young), **III:** 111

"Universe of Death, The" (H. Miller), **III:** 184

Universe of Time, A (Anderson), **II:** 27, 28, 45, 46, 48, 49

"Universities" (Emerson), **II:** 6

"Universities: A Mirage? " (Mora), **Supp. XIII:** 219

"University" (Shapiro), **Supp. II Part 2:** 704–705, 717

"University Avenue" (Mora), **Supp. XIII:** 216

"University Days" (Thurber), **Supp. I Part 2:** 605

"University Hospital, Boston" (Oliver), **Supp. VII:** 235

"University's Peril, The" (Taggard), **Supp. XXII:** 273

"Unknowable, The" (Levine), **Supp. V:** 195

"Unknown Girl in the Maternity Ward" (Sexton), **Supp. II Part 2:** 676

"Unknown Love, The" (Chandler), **Supp. IV Part 1:** 120

Unknown Rilke, The (Rilke; F. Wright, trans.), **Supp. XVII:** 244

"Unknown War, The" (Sandburg), **III:** 594

Unkown Constellations, The (Swados), **Supp. XIX:** 256

Unleashed (anthology), **Supp. XI:** 132

Unleashed: Poems by Writers' Dogs (Hempel and Shepard, eds.), **Supp. XXI:** 115

"Unlighted Lamps" (Anderson), **I:** 112

Unlit Lamp, The (Holding), **Supp. XXII:** 121, 130

Unloved Wife, The (Alcott), **Supp. I Part 1:** 33

Unmarried Woman, An (film), **Supp. IV Part 1:** 303

"Unnatural Mother, The" (Gilman), **Supp. XI:** 207

"Unnatural State of the Unicorn" (Komunyakaa), **Supp. XIII:** 119

"Unparalleled Adventure of One Hans Pfaall, The" (Poe), **III:** 424

"Unpleasant Profession of Jonathan Hoag, The" (Heinlein), **Supp. XVIII:** 149

Unprecedented Era, The (Goebbels), **III:** 560

"Unprofitable Servant, The" (O. Henry), **Supp. II Part 1:** 403

Unpublished Poems of Emily Dickinson (Bianchi and Hampson, ed.), **Retro. Supp. I:** 35

Unpunished (Gilman), **Supp. XI:** 208

Unraveling Strangeness, The (Weigl), **Supp. XIX: 287–288**

"Unreal City" (Eliot), **Supp. XV:** 218

"Unreasoning Heart" (Untermeyer), **Supp. XV:** 309

"Unsaid (Gioia), **Supp. XV:** 129

"Unseen, The" (Pinsky), **Supp. VI:** 243–244

"Unseen, The" (Singer), **Retro. Supp. II:** 307

Unseen Hand, The (Shepard), **Supp. III Part 2:** 439, 445–446

Unselected Poems (Levine), **Supp. V:** 179

Unsettling of America, The: Culture and Agriculture (Berry), **Supp. X:** 22, 26, 29, 32, 33, 35; **Supp. XIV:** 177, 179

Unspeakable Gentleman, The (Marquand), **III:** 53–54, 60, 63

Unspeakable Practices, Unnatural Acts (Barthelme), **Supp. IV Part 1:** 39

"Unspeakable Things Unspoken: The Afro-American Presence in American Literature" (Morrison), **Supp. III Part 1:** 375, 377–379

Unspoken and Other Poems, The (Bremer), **Supp. XXII:** 277

"Untelling, The" (Strand), **Supp. IV Part 2:** 629

Unterecker, John, **I:** 386

Untermeyer, Jean Starr, **II:** 530; **Supp. XV:** 294, 295, 303, 307, 308, 310

Untermeyer, Louis, **II:** 516–517, 530, 532; **III:** 268; **Retro. Supp. I:** 124, 133, 136; **Supp. III Part 1:** 2; **Supp. IX:** 76; **Supp. XIV:** 119, 123; **Supp. XV: 293–318; Supp. XXI:** 277

Untimely Papers (Bourne), **I:** 218, 233

"Untitled" (C. Frost), **Supp. XV:** 103

"Untitled Blues" (Komunyakaa), **Supp. XIII:** 117

Unto the Sons (Talese), **Supp. XVII:** 199–200, **206–207,** 208, 209, 210

"Untrustworthy Speaker, The" (Glück), **Supp. V:** 86

"Unused" (Anderson), **I:** 112, 113

Unvanquished, The (Faulkner), **II:** 55, 67–68, 71; **Retro. Supp. I:** 84; **Supp. I Part 2:** 450

"Unvexed Isles, The" (Warren), **IV:** 253

"Unwedded" (Larcom), **Supp. XIII:** 144

"Unweepables, The" (Karr), **Supp. XI:** 243

"Unwelcome Guest, An" (Papernick), **Supp. XVII:** 50

Unwelcome Man, The (W. Frank), **Supp. XX: 70, 76**

Unwelcome Words (Bowles), **Supp. IV Part 1:** 93, 94

"Unwelcome Words" (Bowles), **Supp. IV Part 1:** 94, 95

Unwin, T. Fisher, **Supp. XI:** 202

"Unwithered Garland, The" (Kunitz), **Supp. III Part 1:** 265

Unwobbling Pivot, The (Pound, trans.), **III:** 472

"Unwritten, The" (Merwin), **Supp. III Part 1:** 352

"Unwritten Law" (Glück), **Supp. V:** 91

Up (Sukenick), **Supp. V:** 39

Up Above the World (Bowles), **Supp. IV Part 1:** 82, 91, 92

"Up and Down" (Merrill), **Supp. III Part 1:** 328

Upanishads, **IV:** 183

Up Country: Poems of New England (Kumin), **Supp. IV Part 2:** 446, 447–448, 453

"Update" (Dunn), **Supp. XI:** 150–151

Updike, John, **I:** 54; **III:** 572; **IV: 214–235; Retro. Supp. I:** 116, **317–338; Retro. Supp. II:** 213, 279, 280; **Supp. I Part 1:** 186, 196; **Supp. IV Part 2:** 657; **Supp. V:** 23, 43, 95, 119; **Supp. VIII:** 151, 167, 236; **Supp. IX:** 208; **Supp. XI:** 65, 66, 99, 140; **Supp. XII:** 140, 296, 298, 310; **Supp. XIII:** 45–46, 47, 52; **Supp. XIV:** 79, 93, 111; **Supp. XVI:** 205, 207, 220; **Supp. XX: 17; Supp. XXI:** 116, 226; **Supp. XXIII:** 109

Updike, Mrs. Wesley, **IV:** 218, 220
Up from Slavery (Washington), **Supp. II Part 1:** 169; **Supp. IX:** 19
Upham, Thomas Goggswell, **II:** 487
"Upholsterers, The" (Lardner), **II:** 435
"Up in Michigan" (Hemingway), **II:** 263; **Supp. XIX:** 241
Upjohn, Richard, **IV:** 312
"Upon a Spider Catching a Fly" (Taylor), **IV:** 161
"Upon a Wasp Child with Cold" (Taylor), **IV:** 161
"Upon Meeting Don L. Lee, in a Dream" (Dove), **Supp. IV Part 1:** 244
"Upon My Dear and Loving Husband His Going into England, Jan. 16, 1661" (Bradstreet), **Supp. I Part 1:** 110
"Upon My Mother's Death"(Hadas), **Supp. XXIII:** 118
"Upon Returning to the Country Road" (Lindsay), **Supp. I Part 2:** 382
"Upon the Burning of Our House, July 10th, 1666" (Bradstreet), **Supp. I Part 1:** 107–108, 122
"Upon the Sweeping Flood" (Taylor), **IV:** 161
"Upon Wedlock, and Death of Children" (Taylor), **IV:** 144, 147, 161
"Upset, An" (Merrill), **Supp. III Part 1:** 336
Upstairs and Downstairs (Vonnegut), **Supp. II Part 2:** 757
Upstate (Wilson), **IV:** 447
Upton, Lee, **Supp. X:** 209
"Upturned Face" (Crane), **I:** 423
Upward, Allen, **Supp. I Part 1:** 262
Upward, Edward, **Supp. XIV:** 159, 160
"Upward Moon and the Downward Moon, The" (R. Bly), **Supp. IV Part 1:** 71
Urania: A Rhymed Lesson (Holmes), **Supp. I Part 1:** 300
"Urban Convalescence, An" (Merrill), **Supp. III Part 1:** 322–324
"Urban Renewal" (Komunyakaa), **Supp. XIII:** 113
Urdang, Constance, **Supp. XV:** 74
"Urganda and Fatima" (Rowson), **Supp. XV:** 234
Urial Accosta: A Play (Reznikoff), **Supp. XIV:** 282, 288
Urich, Robert, **Supp. V:** 228
"Uriel" (Emerson), **II:** 19
Uris, Leon, **Supp. IV Part 1:** 285, 379; **Supp. XX: 243–258**
Uroff, Margaret D., **Supp. I Part 2:** 542
"Us" (Sexton), **Supp. II Part 2:** 687
U.S. 1 (Rukeyser), **Supp. VI:** 272, 278, 283, 285
U.S.A. (Dos Passos), **I:** 379, 475, 478, 482–488, 489, 490, 491, 492, 493, 494, 495; **Retro. Supp. II:** 197; **Supp. I Part 2:** 646; **Supp. III Part 1:** 104, 105; **Supp. XIV:** 24
"U.S.A. School of Writing, The" (Bishop), **Retro. Supp. II:** 43
"U.S. Commercial Orchid, The" (Agee), **I:** 35
"Used-Boy Raisers, The" (Paley), **Supp. VI:** 218, 228

"Used Cars on Oahu" (Nye), **Supp. XIII:** 282
"Used Side of the Sofa, The" (Ríos), **Supp. IV Part 2:** 551
Useless Servants, The (Hinojosa), **Supp. XIX:** 98, 103, 104, **109–110**
Use of Fire, The (Price), **Supp. VI:** 265
"Use of Force, The" (W. C. Williams), **Retro. Supp. I:** 424
Use of Poetry and the Use of Criticism, The (Eliot), **Retro. Supp. I:** 65
Uses of Enchantment, The: The Meaning and Importance of Fairy Tales (Bettelheim), **Supp. X:** 77; **Supp. XIV:** 126
"Uses of Hell, The" (E. Hoffman), **Supp. XVI:** 154
"Uses of Hell, The: An Exchange"(Novick, Katz, and Szulc), **Supp. XVI:** 154
Uses of Literacy, The (Hoggart), **Supp. XIV:** 299
Uses of Literature, The (Calvino), **Supp. XXII:** 263
"Uses of Poetry, The" (W. C. Williams), **Retro. Supp. I:** 412
"Uses of the Blues, The" (Baldwin), **Retro. Supp. II:** 8
"Use-Unuse of Us, The" (Bronk), **Supp. XXI:** 32
"USFS 1919: The Ranger, the Cook, and a Hole in the Sky" (Maclean), **Supp. XIV:** 230, 234
Ushant: An Essay (Aiken), **I:** 49, 54, 55, 56, 57
"Usher 11" (Bradbury), **Supp. I Part 2:** 622
"Using Parrots to Kill Mockingbirds: Yet Another Racial Prosecution and Wrongful Conviction in Maycomb" (Fair), **Supp. VIII:** 128
Ustedes y Nosotros: Nuevo Mensaje a Ibero-América (W. Frank), **Supp. XX: 79**
"Usual Objects"(Schott), **Supp. XXIII:** 248
Usual Star, The (Doolittle), **Supp. I Part 1:** 270
"Usurpation (Other People's Stories)" (Ozick), **Supp. V:** 268, 271
Utopia 14 (Vonnegut), **Supp. II Part 2:** 757

V

V. (Pynchon), **Supp. II Part 2:** 618, 620–622, 627–630; **Supp. IV Part 1:** 279
"Vacation" (Stafford), **Supp. XI:** 321, 322
"Vacation Trip" (Stafford), **Supp. XI:** 322
Vachel Lindsay: A Poet in America (Masters), **Supp. I Part 2:** 473, 474
"Vachel Lindsay: The Midwest as Utopia" (Whitney), **Supp. I Part 2:** 403
"Vachel Lindsay Writes to Floyd Dell" (Tanselle), **Supp. I Part 2:** 403
"Vacillation" (Yeats), **Supp. XV:** 253
Vadim, Roger, **Supp. XI:** 293, 307
"Vag" (Dos Passos), **I:** 487–488
Vagina Monologues, The (Ensler), **Supp. XIX:** 204–205

Valdez, Luis, **Supp. XXIII:** 203
Valediction (Parker), **Supp. XIX:** 185
Valentine, Jean, **Supp. V:** 92
Valentine, Saint, **IV:** 396
Valentines (Kooser), **Supp. XIX:** 116, 123, **128–129**
Valentino, Rudolph, **I:** 483
Valéry, Paul, **II:** 543, 544; **III:** 279, 409, 428, 609; **IV:** 79, 91, 92, 428, 443; **Retro. Supp. II:** 187
"Valhalla" (Francis), **Supp. IX:** 77
Valhalla and Other Poems (Francis), **Supp. IX:** 76
Validity in Interpretation (Hirsch), **Supp. XIV:** 15
Valitsky, Ken, **Supp. XII:** 7
Vallejo, César, **Supp. V:** 332; **Supp. IX:** 271; **Supp. XIII:** 114, 315, 323; **Supp. XXI:** 132
"Valley, The" (Bass), **Supp. XVI:** 20, 22
Valley, The (Hinojosa), **Supp. XIX:** 97, 99, **100–101**
"Valley Between, The" (Marshall), **Supp. XI:** 278
Valley of Decision, The (Wharton), **IV:** 311, 315; **Retro. Supp. I:** 365–367
"Valley of the Monsters, The" (Peacock), **Supp. XIX:** 198
Valley of the Moon, The (London), **II:** 467, 481
"Valley of Unrest, The" (Poe), **III:** 411
Valli, Alida, **Supp. IV Part 2:** 520
"Valor" (Bausch), **Supp. VII:** 54
Valparaiso (DeLillo), **Supp. VI:** 4, 12
"Value of a Place, The" (Bass), **Supp. XVI:** 18
"Values and Fictions" (Toomer), **Supp. III Part 2:** 485–486
"Values and Imperatives" (Locke), **Supp. XIV:** 199, 202, 212
Values of Veblen, The: A Critical Appraisal (Rosenberg), **Supp. I Part 2:** 650
"Vampire" (Karr), **Supp. XI:** 241
Vampire Armand, The (Rice), **Supp. VII:** 290, 294–295
Vampire Chronicles, The (Rice), **Supp. VII:** 290
Vampire Lestat, The (Rice), **Supp. VII:** 290–292, 298, 299
Van Aalst, Mariska, **Supp. XIX:** 50, 51
Van Buren, Martin, **II:** 134, 312; **III:** 473
Vande Kieft, Ruth M., **IV:** 260
Vanderbilt, Cornelius, **III:** 14
Van Dine, S. S., **Supp. IV Part 1:** 341
Van Doren, Carl, **I:** 252–253, 423; **II:** 103, 111, 112; **Supp. I Part 2:** 474, 486, 707, 709, 717, 718, 727; **Supp. II Part 1:** 395; **Supp. VIII:** 96–97
Van Doren, Mark, **I:** 168; **III:** 4, 23, 589; **Supp. I Part 2:** 604; **Supp. III Part 2:** 626; **Supp. VIII:** 231; **Supp. IX:** 266, 268; **Supp. XV:** 152, 305, 307; **Supp. XXII:** 275
Vandover and the Brute (Norris), **III:** 314, 315, 316, 320–322, 328, 333, 334
Van Duyn, Mona, **Supp. IX:** 269
Van Dyke, Annette, **Supp. IV Part 1:** 327
Van Dyke, Henry, **I:** 223; **II:** 456

Van Gogh, Vincent, **I:** 27; **IV:** 290; **Supp. I Part 2:** 451; **Supp. IV Part 1:** 284; **Supp. XXII:** 171–172

Van Gogh's Room at Arles (Elkin), **Supp. VI:** 56

"Vanilla Dunk" (Lethem), **Supp. XVIII:** 139

"Vanisher, The" (Whittier), **Supp. I Part 2:** 691

Vanishing Point (Markson), **Supp. XVII:** 135, 137, 138, 145–146

"Vanishing Red, The" (Frost), **Retro. Supp. II:** 47

"Vanity" (B. Diop), **Supp. IV Part 1:** 16

Vanity Fair (Thackeray), **I:** 354; **II:** 91; **III:** 70; **Supp. IX:** 200

"Vanity of All Wordly Things, The" (Bradstreet), **Supp. I Part 1:** 102, 119

Vanity of Duluoz (Kerouac), **Supp. III Part 1:** 221, 222

"Vanity of Existence, The" (Freneau), **Supp. II Part 1:** 262

Van Matre, Lynn, **Supp. V:** 126

Vann, Barbara, **Supp. XV:** 187

Vanquished, The (Faulkner), **I:** 205

Van Rensselaer, Stephen, **I:** 351

Van Vechten, Carl, **I:** 295; **IV:** 76; **Retro. Supp. I:** 199; **Supp. I Part 1:** 324, 327, 332; **Supp. I Part 2:** 715; **Supp. II Part 2: 725–751**; **Supp. X:** 247; **Supp. XVI:** 135; **Supp. XVII:** 96, 97, 101, 104; **Supp. XVIII:** 123, 131, 132, 279, 280; **Supp. XIX:** 76; **Supp. XX: 69**; **Supp. XXI:** 5, 8; **Supp. XXII:** 5, 158, 160

Van Vliet, Don, **Supp. XXIII:** 174

Vanzetti, Bartolomeo, **I:** 482, 486, 490, 494; **II:** 38–39, 426; **III:** 139–140; **Supp. I Part 2:** 446, 610, 611; **Supp. V:** 288–289; **Supp. IX:** 199; **Supp. XXII:** 277

"Vapor Trail Reflected in the Frog Pond" (Kinnell), **Supp. III Part 1:** 242–243

"Vapor Trails" (Snyder), **Supp. VIII:** 298

"Variation: Ode to Fear" (Warren), **IV:** 241

"Variation on a Sentence" (Bogan), **Supp. III Part 1:** 60

"Variation on Gaining a Son" (Dove), **Supp. IV Part 1:** 248

"Variation on Pain" (Dove), **Supp. IV Part 1:** 248

"Variations: The air is sweetest that a thistle guards" (Merrill), **Supp. III Part 1:** 321

"Variations: White Stag, Black Bear" (Merrill), **Supp. III Part 1:** 321

"Varick Street" (Bishop), **Supp. I Part 1:** 90, 92

Varieties of Metaphysical Poetry, The (Eliot), **Retro. Supp. I:** 65

Varieties of Religious Experience, The (William James), **II:** 344, 353, 354, 359–360, 362; **IV:** 28, 291; **Supp. IX:** 19

Variety (film), **Supp. XII:** 7

Variorum (Whitman), **Retro. Supp. I:** 406

Various Antidotes (J. Scott), **Supp. XVII: 188–189**

Various Miracles (Shields), **Supp. VII:** 318–320, 323, 324

"Various Miracles" (Shields), **Supp. VII:** 318–319, 324

Various Poems (Zach), **Supp. XV:** 86

"Various Tourists" (Connell), **Supp. XIV:** 79

"Varmint Question, The" (Leopold), **Supp. XIV:** 180–181

Varno, David, **Supp. XIX:** 205

Vasari, Giorgio, **Supp. I Part 2:** 450; **Supp. III Part 1:** 5

Vasquez, Robert, **Supp. V:** 180

Vassall Morton (Parkman), **Supp. II Part 2:** 595, 597–598

Vasse, W. W., **III:** 478

Vaudeville for a Princess (Schwartz), **Supp. II Part 2:** 661–662

Vaughan, Henry, **IV:** 151; **Supp. XV:** 251

Vaughn, Robert, **Supp. XI:** 343

"Vaunting Oak" (Ransom), **III:** 490

Vazirani, Reetika, **Supp. XIII:** 133

Veblen (Hobson), **Supp. I Part 2:** 650

Veblen, Andrew, **Supp. I Part 2:** 640

Veblen, Oswald, **Supp. I Part 2:** 640

Veblen, Thorstein, **I:** 104, 283, 475–476, 483, 498, 511; **II:** 27, 272, 276, 287; **Supp. I Part 2: 628–650**; **Supp. IV Part 1:** 22

Veblen, Mrs. Thorstein (Ellen Rolfe), **Supp. I Part 2:** 641

Veblenism: A New Critique (Dobriansky), **Supp. I Part 2:** 648, 650

"Veblen's Attack on Culture" (Adorno), **Supp. I Part 2:** 650

Vectors and Smoothable Curves (Bronk), **Supp. XXI: 24–26,** 32

Vedanta for Modern Man (Isherwood, ed.), **Supp. XIV:** 164

Vedanta for the Western World (Isherwood, ed.), **Supp. XIV:** 164

Vedas, **IV:** 183

Vega, Janine Pommy, **Supp. XIV:** 148

Vega, Lope de, **Retro. Supp. I:** 285; **Supp. III Part 1:** 341, 347

Vegetable, The (Fitzgerald), **Retro. Supp. I:** 105; **Supp. IX:** 57

Vegetable, The, or From President to Postman (Fitzgerald), **II:** 91

"Vegetable Love" (Apple), **Supp. XVII:** 4

"Vegetable Love" (Crooker), **Supp. XXIII:** 62

"Vegetable Wisdom" (Halliday), **Supp. XIX:** 88

Veg tsu zikh, Der (The road to one's self) (Asch), **Supp. XXIII:** 5, 11

Veinberg, Jon, **Supp. V:** 180; **Supp. XIII:** 313; **Supp. XV:** 76–77, 86

Vein of Iron (Glasgow), **II:** 175, 186, 188–189, 191, 192, 194

Vein of Riches, A (Knowles), **Supp. XII:** 249

Vein of Words (J. W. Miller), **Supp. XX: 165**

Velie, Alan R., **Supp. IV Part 2:** 486

Velocities: New and Selected Poems, 1966–1992 (Dobyns), **Supp. XIII:** 86–87, 87, 88

"Velocity" (Collins), **Supp. XXI:** 61

"Velorio" (Cisneros), **Supp. VII:** 66

"Velvet Gentleman, The" (Skloot), **Supp. XX:** 201

"Velvet Shoes" (Wylie), **Supp. I Part 2:** 711, 714

Venant, Elizabeth, **Supp. XI:** 343

Vencloca, Thomas, **Supp. VIII:** 29

Vendler, Helen H., **Retro. Supp. I:** 297; **Retro. Supp. II:** 184, 191; **Supp. I Part 1:** 77, 78, 92, 95; **Supp. I Part 2:** 565; **Supp. IV Part 1:** 245, 247, 249, 254, 257; **Supp. IV Part 2:** 448; **Supp. V:** 78, 82, 189, 343; **Supp. XII:** 187, 189; **Supp. XV:** 20, 184

"Venetian Blind, The" (Jarrell), **II:** 382–383

Venetian Glass Nephew, The (Wylie), **Supp. I Part 2:** 707, 709, 714, 717–719, 721, 724

Venetian Life (Howells), **II:** 274, 277, 279

Venetian Vespers, The (Hecht), **Supp. X:** 57, **65–69**

"Venetian Vespers, The" (Hecht), **Supp. X:** 65, **66–67**

Venice Observed (McCarthy), **II:** 562

Ventadorn, Bernard de, **Supp. IV Part 1:** 146

"Ventriloquists' Conversations" (Gentry), **Supp. IV Part 1:** 236

"Venus, Cupid, Folly and Time" (Taylor), **Supp. V:** 322–323

Venus and Adonis (film), **Supp. IV Part 1:** 82

Venus and Don Juan (C. Frost), **Supp. XV:** 93, **102–103,** 104, 107

"Venus and Don Juan" (C. Frost), **Supp. XV:** 103

Venus Blue (Sobin), **Supp. XVI: 293–294,** 294

Venus in Sparta (Auchincloss), **Supp. IV Part 1:** 25

"Venus Pandemos" (Halliday), **Supp. XIX:** 85, 89, 90, 93

"Venus's-flytraps" (Komunyakaa), **Supp. XIII:** 126, 127

"Veracruz" (Hayden), **Supp. II Part 1:** 371, 373

Verducci, Tom, **Supp. XXII:** 209

Verga, Giovanni, **II:** 271, 275

Verghese, Abraham, **Supp. X:** 160

Verhaeren, Emile, **I:** 476; **II:** 528, 529

Verlaine, Paul, **II:** 529, 543; **III:** 466; **IV:** 79, 80, 86, 286; **Retro. Supp. I:** 56, 62; **Retro. Supp. II:** 326

"Vermeer" (Nemerov), **III:** 275, 278, 280

Vermeer, Jan, **Retro. Supp. I:** 335

"Vermont" (Carruth), **Supp. XVI:** 54

Vermont Notebook, The (Ashbery), **Supp. III Part 1:** 1

Vermont Writers: A State of Mind (Daley), **Supp. XXII:** 216

"Vernal Ague, The" (Freneau), **Supp. II Part 1:** 258

Verne, Jules, **I:** 480; **Retro. Supp. I:** 270; **Supp. XI:** 63

Vernon, John, **Supp. X:** 15

Verplanck, Gulian C., **Supp. I Part 1:** 155, 156, 157, 158

Verrazano, Giovanni da, **Supp. I Part 2:** 496, 497

Verse (Zawacki), **Supp. VIII:** 272
"Verse for Urania" (Merrill), **Supp. III Part 1:** 329, 330
Verses (Wharton), **Retro. Supp. I:** 362
Verses, Printed for Her Friends (Jewett), **II:** 406
"Verses for Children" (Lowell), **II:** 516
"Verses Made at Sea in a Heavy Gale" (Freneau), **Supp. II Part 1:** 262
"Verses on the Death of T. S. Eliot" (Brodsky), **Supp. VIII:** 19
"Version of a Fragment of Simonides" (Bryant), **Supp. I Part 1:** 153, 155
Verulam, Baron. *See* Bacon, Francis
Very, Jones, **III:** 507
"Very Hot Sun in Bermuda, The" (Jackson), **Supp. IX:** 126
Very Old Bones (W. Kennedy), **Supp. VII:** 133, 148, 150–153
Very Persistent Gappers of Frip, The (Saunders), **Supp. XIX: 229–230**
"Very Proper Gander, The" (Thurber), **Supp. I Part 2:** 610
"Very Short Story, A" (Hemingway), **II:** 252; **Retro. Supp. I:** 173
"Vesalius in Zante" (Wharton), **Retro. Supp. I:** 372
Vesey, Denmark, **Supp. I Part 2:** 592
Vesey, Desmond, **Supp. XIV:** 162
"Vespers" (Auden), **Supp. II Part 1:** 23
"Vespers" (Glück), **Supp. V:** 88
"Vespers"(Dybek), **Supp. XXIII:** 78
Vestal Lady on Brattle, The (Corso), **Supp. XII:** 119, **120–121,** 134
Vested Interests and the Common Man, The (Veblen), **Supp. I Part 2:** 642
"Vesuvius at Home" (Rich), **Retro. Supp. I:** 42
"Veteran, The" (Crane), **I:** 413
"Veterans' Cemetery" (Gioia), **Supp. XV:** 117
"Veteran Sirens" (Robinson), **III:** 512, 524
"Veterinarian" (X. J. Kennedy), **Supp. XV:** 168
"Vetiver" (Ashbery), **Supp. III Part 1:** 26
Vetter, Lara, **Supp. XXII:** 166
"Via Dieppe-Newhaven" (H. Miller), **III:** 183
"Via Negativa" (Salter), **Supp. IX:** 257
Vicar of Wakefeld, The (Goldsmith), **I:** 216
Vicious Circle, The (film, Wilder), **Supp. XVII:** 62
"Vicissitudes of the Avant-Garde, The" (Gass), **Supp. VI:** 91
Vico, Giambattista, **Supp. XX: 38**
Victim, The (Bellow), **I:** 144, 145, 147, 149, 150, 151, 152, 153, 155, 156, 158, 159, 164; **IV:** 19; **Retro. Supp. II:** 21, 22, 34
"Victor" (Mumford), **Supp. II Part 2:** 476
Victoria (Rowson), **Supp. XV:** 231
Victorian in the Modern World, A (Hapgood), **Supp. XVII:** 95, 97, 100, 101, 103, 105, 106; **Supp. XXI:** 8
"Victoria's Secret" (Collins), **Supp. XXI:** 58–59

"Victories" (Untermeyer), **Supp. XV:** 300
"Victory at Sea" (television series), **Supp. I Part 2:** 490
"Victory comes late" (Dickinson), **Retro. Supp. I:** 45
"Victory of the Moon, The" (Crane), **I:** 420
Vida, Vendela, **Supp. XIX:** 49, 50, 53, 57, 58, 59, 61, 62
Vidal, Gore, **II:** 587; **IV:** 383; **Supp. IV Part 1:** 22, 35, 92, 95, 198; **Supp. IV Part 2: 677–696; Supp. IX:** 96; **Supp. X:** 186, 195; **Supp. XIV:** 156, 170, 338; **Supp. XIX:** 131, 132
Video Poems (Collins), **Supp. XXI:** 53
Viebahn, Fred, **Supp. IV Part 1:** 248
Viera, Joseph M., **Supp. XI:** 178, 186
Viereck, Peter, **Supp. I Part 2:** 403
Viertel, Berthold, **Supp. XIV:** 165
Viertel, Salka, **Supp. XVI:** 192
Viet Journal (Jones), **Supp. XI: 230–231**
Vietnam (McCarthy), **II:** 578–579
"Vietnam in Me, The" (O'Brien), **Supp. V:** 241, 252
Vie unanime, La (Romains), **I:** 227
"View, The" (Roussel), **Supp. III Part 1:** 15, 16, 21
View from 80, The (Cowley), **Supp. II Part 1:** 141, 144, 153
"View from an Institution" (F. Wright), **Supp. XVII:** 244
"View from the Backyard" (W. V. Davis), **Supp. XXI:** 96
View from the Bridge, A (A. Miller), **III:** 147, 148, 156, 158, 159–160
View from the Seventh Layer, The (Brockmeier), **Supp. XXII: 59–61**
"View from the Seventh Layer, The" (Brockmeier), **Supp. XXII:** 61
View of My Own, A: Essays in Literature and Society (Hardwick), **Supp. III Part 1:** 194, 200
"View of the Capital from the Library of Congress" (Bishop), **Retro. Supp. II:** 45
View of the Soil and Climate of the United States, A (Brown, trans.), **Supp. I Part 1:** 146
"View of the Woods, A" (O'Connor), **III:** 349, 351, 358; **Retro. Supp. II:** 237
"Viewpoint" (column, Siddons), **Supp. XXII:** 240, 245
"Views of the Mysterious Hill: The Appearance of Parnassus in American Poetry" (Strand), **Supp. IV Part 2:** 631
"Vigil" (Karr), **Supp. XI:** 241
"Vigil, The" (Dante), **III:** 542
"Vigil at Heiligenkreuz" (W. V. Davis), **Supp. XXI:** 93
"Vigil"(Dybek), **Supp. XXIII:** 78
"Vignette" (Trethewey), **Supp. XXI:** 253, 254
Vigny, Alfred Victor de, **II:** 543
Vildrac, Charles, **Supp. XV:** 50
Vile Bodies (Waugh), **Supp. I Part 2:** 607
Villa, Pancho, **I:** 210; **III:** 584
"Village Blacksmith, The" (Longfellow), **Retro. Supp. II:** 167, 168; **Supp. I Part 2:** 409

Village Hymns, a Supplement to Dr. Watts's Psalms and Hymns (Nettleton), **I:** 458
"Village Improvement Parade, The" (Lindsay), **Supp. I Part 2:** 388, 389
Village Magazine, The (Lindsay), **Supp. I Part 2:** 379–380, 382
Village Virus, The (Lewis), **II:** 440
"Villanelle at Sundown" (Justice), **Supp. VII:** 119, 122–123
"Villanelle of Change" (Robinson), **III:** 524
Villard, Oswald, **Supp. I Part 1:** 332
"Villa Selene" (Simpson), **Supp. IX:** 279
Villon, François, **II:** 544; **III:** 9, 174, 592; **Retro. Supp. I:** 286; **Supp. I Part 1:** 261; **Supp. III Part 1:** 235, 243, 249, 253; **Supp. III Part 2:** 560; **Supp. IX:** 116
"Villonaud for This Yule" (Pound), **Retro. Supp. I:** 286
"Vincenzo Tailor" (Di Piero), **Supp. XIX:** 38
Vindication of the Rights of Woman (Wollstonecraft), **Supp. I Part 1:** 126; **Supp. XI:** 203
Vines, Lois Davis, **Retro. Supp. II:** 261
Vintage Book of Amnesia, The (Lethem, ed.), **Supp. XVIII:** 138
"Vintage Thunderbird, A" (Beattie), **Supp. V:** 27
Vinz, Mark, **Supp. X:** 117
Viol de Lucrèce, Le (Obey), **IV:** 356
Violence (Bausch), **Supp. VII:** 48–49, 54
Violent Bear It Away, The (O'Connor), **III:** 339, 345–348, 350, 351, 354, 355, 356, 357; **Retro. Supp. II:** 233, **234–236**
Violent Hero, Wilderness Heritage and Urban Reality, The: A Study of the Private Eye in the Novels of Dashiell Hammett, Raymond Chandler and Ross Macdonald (Parker), **Supp. XIX:** 177
"Violent Vet, The" (O'Brien), **Supp. V:** 238
Violin (Rice), **Supp. VII:** 302
Viorst, Judith, **Supp. X:** 153
Viper Run (Karr), **Supp. XI: 248–251**
Virgil, **I:** 312, 322, 587; **II:** 133, 542; **IV:** 137, 359; **Retro. Supp. I:** 135; **Supp. I Part 1:** 153; **Supp. I Part 2:** 494; **Supp. IV Part 2:** 631
"Virgin and Child with Music and Numbers" (Bronk), **Supp. XXI:** 30
"Virgin and the Dynamo" (Adams), **III:** 396
"Virgin Carrying a Lantern, The" (Stevens), **IV:** 80
Virgin Huntress, The (Holding), **Supp. XXII:** 119, 124, **135–136**
Virginia (Glasgow), **II:** 175, 178, 181–182, 193, 194
"Virginia" (Lindsay), **Supp. I Part 2:** 398
"Virginia Britannia" (Moore), **III:** 198, 208–209
"Virginians Are Coming Again, The" (Lindsay), **Supp. I Part 2:** 399
Virginia Reels (Hoffman), **Supp. XVIII:** 79, 86

Virgin Spain (W. Frank), **Supp. XX: 76**
"Virgins Plus Curtains Minus Dots" (Loy), **Supp. XXII:** 161
Virgin Time: In Search of the Contemplative Life (Hampl), **Supp. XXII:** 82, 83 84, **90–92**
"Virgin Violeta" (Porter), **III:** 454
"Virility" (Ozick), **Supp. V:** 262, 265
Virtual Light (W. Gibson), **Supp. XVI:** 124, **129**, 130
Virtue of Selfishness, The: A New Concept of Egoism (Rand), **Supp. IV Part 2:** 527, 530–532
"Virtuoso" (Francis), **Supp. IX:** 82
Virtuous Woman, A (Gibbons), **Supp. X: 44–45**, 46, 50
Visconti, Luchino, **Supp. V:** 51
Viscusi, Robert, **Supp. XX:** 46
Visible Saints: The History of a Puritan Idea (Morgan), **IV:** 149
"Vision, A" (Olds), **Supp. X:** 214
"Vision, A" (Winters), **Supp. II Part 2:** 785, 795
"Vision and Prayer" (D. Thomas), **I:** 432
"Visionary, The" (Poe), **III:** 411
Visionary Farms, The (Eberhart), **I:** 537–539
Visioning, The (Glaspell), **Supp. III Part 1:** 175–177, 180, 187, 188
Vision in Spring (Faulkner), **Retro. Supp. I:** 79
Vision of Columbus (Barlow), **Supp. I Part 1:** 124; **Supp. II Part 1:** 67, 68, 70–75, 77, 79
Vision of Sir Launfal, The (Lowell), **Supp. I Part 1:** 311; **Supp. I Part 2:** 406, 409, 410
"Vision of the World, A" (Cheever), **Supp. I Part 1:** 182, 192
"Visions of Budhardin"(Dybek), **Supp. XXIII:** 70–71
Visions of Cody (Kerouac), **Supp. III Part 1:** 225–227
Visions of Gerard (Kerouac), **Supp. III Part 1:** 219–222, 225, 227, 229
"Visions of the Daughters of Albion" (Blake), **III:** 540
"Visit" (Ammons), **Supp. VII:** 28–29
"Visit, The" (Kenyon), **Supp. VII:** 169
"Visitant, The" (Dunn), **Supp. XI:** 147
"Visitation, The/La Visitación" (Mora), **Supp. XIII:** 217, 224, 228
"Visitation"(Kenny), **Supp. XXIII:** 157
"Visit Home, A" (Stafford), **Supp. XI:** 318
Visit in 2001, The (musical, McNally), **Supp. XIII:** 207
"Visiting My Own House in Iowa City" (Stern), **Supp. IX:** 300
"Visit of Charity, A" (Welty), **IV:** 262
"Visitors" (J. W. Miller), **Supp. XX:** 167
"Visitors" (Salinas), **Supp. XIII:** 318
"Visitors, The/Los Visitantes" (Kingsolver), **Supp. VII:** 208
"Visits to St. Elizabeths" (Bishop), **Retro. Supp. II:** 47
"Visit to a Small Planet" (teleplay) (Vidal), **Supp. IV Part 2:** 682

Visit to a Small Planet: A Comedy Akin to Vaudeville (Vidal), **Supp. IV Part 2:** 682–683
"Visit to Avoyelles, A" (Chopin), **Supp. I Part 1:** 213
"Visit to Manafon, A" (W. V. Davis), **Supp. XXI:** 96
"Vissi d'Arte" (Moore), **Supp. X: 173–174**
Vistas of History (Morison), **Supp. I Part 2:** 492
"Vita" (Stafford), **Supp. XI:** 330
"Vita Brevis" (Hull), **Supp. XXI:** 138
Vital, David, **Supp. XVI:** 160
Vital Provisions (Price), **Supp. VI:** 262–263
"Vitamins" (Carver), **Supp. III Part 1:** 138
Vita Nova (Glück), **Supp. V:** 90–92
Vitruvius, **Supp. XVI:** 292
Vittorio, the Vampire (Rice), **Supp. VII:** 295–296
Viudas (Dorfman), **Supp. IX:** 138
"Vivaldi"(Dybek), **Supp. XXIII:** 68
"Viva Vargas!" (Allen), **Supp. XV:** 15
Viviparous Quadrupeds of North America, The (Audubon and Bachman), **Supp. XVI:** 10
Vivisections (Siegel), **Supp. XXII:** 257
Vizenor, Gerald, **Supp. IV Part 1:** 260, 262, 329, 404; **Supp. IV Part 2:** 502
Vladimir Nabokov: The American Years (Nabokov), **Retro. Supp. I:** 275
Vlag, Piet, **Supp. XV:** 295
"Vlemk, the Box Painter" (Gardner), **Supp. VI:** 73
"V-Letter" (Shapiro), **Supp. II Part 2:** 707
V-Letter and Other Poems (Shapiro), **Supp. II Part 2:** 702, 706
"Vocabulary of Dearness" (Nye), **Supp. XIII:** 284
"Vocation" (Stafford), **Supp. XI:** 312, 321
Vocation and a Voice, A (Chopin), **Retro. Supp. II:** 67, 72
"Vocation and a Voice, A" (Chopin), **Retro. Supp. II:** 72; **Supp. I Part 1:** 200, 220, 224, 225
Vogel, David, **Supp. XV:** 88
Vogel, Speed, **Supp. IV Part 1:** 390
"Vogue Vista" (Peacock), **Supp. XIX:** 200
"Voice" (F. Wright), **Supp. XVII:** 245
"Voice" (Notley), **Supp. XXII:** 230
"Voice, The" (Dunn), **Supp. XI:** 152
Voiced Connections of James Dickey, The (Dickey), **Supp. IV Part 1:** 177
"Voice from the Wilderness" (Ray), **Supp. XVIII:** 202
"Voice from the Woods, A" (Humphrey), **Supp. IX:** 101
"Voice from Under the Table, A" (Wilbur), **Supp. III Part 2:** 553, 554
Voice of Reason, The: Essays in Objectivist Thought (Rand), **Supp. IV Part 2:** 527, 528, 532
"Voice of Rock, The" (Ginsberg), **Supp. II Part 1:** 313

Voice of the Butterfly, The (Nichols), **Supp. XIII:** 270
Voice of the City, The (O. Henry), **Supp. II Part 1:** 410
"Voice of the Mountain, The" (Crane), **I:** 420
Voice of the Negro (Barber), **Supp. II Part 1:** 168
"Voice of the Past, The" (Skloot), **Supp. XX:** 207
Voice of the People, The (Glasgow), **II:** 175, 176
Voice of the Turtle: American Indian Literature 1900–1970 (Gunn Allen, ed.), **Supp. IV Part 1:** 332, 334
Voices from the Moon (Dubus), **Supp. VII:** 88–89
"Voices from the Other World" (Merrill), **Supp. III Part 1:** 331
Voices in the House (Sedges), **Supp. II Part 1:** 125
Voices of a Summer Day (Shaw), **Supp. XIX:** 251
Voices of the Night (Longfellow), **II:** 489, 493; **Retro. Supp. II:** 154, 157, 168
"Voices of Village Square, The" (Wolfe), **Supp. III Part 2:** 571–572
Voice That Is Great within Us, The (Caruth, ed.), **Supp. XIII:** 112
Void Moon (Connelly), **Supp. XXI: 73**, 74
Voigt, Ellen Bryan, **Supp. XIII:** 76
Voix humaine, La (Cocteau), **Supp. XX: 236**
Volkening, Henry, **Retro. Supp. II:** 117; **Supp. XV:** 142
Vollmann, William T., **Supp. XIV:** 96; **Supp. XVII: 225–237; Supp. XX:** 93
Volney, Constantin François de Chasseboeuf, **Supp. I Part 1:** 146
Voltaire, **I:** 194; **II:** 86, 103, 449; **III:** 420; **IV:** 18; **Retro. Supp. II:** 94; **Supp. I Part 1:** 288–289; **Supp. I Part 2:** 669, 717; **Supp. XV:** 258; **Supp. XX: 285**
Voltaire! Voltaire! (Endore), **Supp. XVII:** 65
Volunteers, The (Rowson and Reinagle), **Supp. XV:** 238
Volynsky, Akim (Chaim Flekser), **Supp. XXIII:** 11
Vonnegut, Kurt, **Retro. Supp. I:** 170; **Supp. II Part 2:** 557, 689, **753–784; Supp. IV Part 1:** 227, 392; **Supp. V:** 40, 42, 237, 244, 296; **Supp. X:** 260; **Supp. XI:** 104; **Supp. XII:** 139, 141; **Supp. XVIII:** 242, 252; **Supp. XXI:** 226; **Supp. XXIII:** 42, 101, 109
Vonnegut, Kurt, Jr., **Supp. XVII:** 41, 135; **Supp. XIX:** 223
"Voracities and Verities" (Moore), **III:** 214
Vore, Nellie, **I:** 199
Vorlicky, Robert, **Supp. IX:** 132, 135, 136, 141, 144, 147
Vorse, Mary Heaton, **Supp. XVII:** 99; **Supp. XX: 76; Supp. XXI:** 5, 6, 9, 13
"Vorticism" (Pound), **Retro. Supp. I:** 288
Vosjoli, Philippe de, **Supp. XX:** 253

Voss, Richard, **I:** 199–200

"Vow, The" (Hecht), **Supp. X:** 64

"Vowels 2" (Baraka), **Supp. II Part 1:** 51

Vow of Conversation, A: Journal, 1964–1965 (Merton), **Supp. VIII:** 206

Vox (Baker), **Supp. XIII: 47–49,** 50, 52, 53

"Voyage" (MacLeish), **III:** 15

Voyage, The (Caputo), **Supp. XIX:** 25, 27–28

"Voyage, The" (Irving), **II:** 304

Voyage, The, and Other Versions of Poems by Baudelaire (Lowell), **Retro. Supp. II:** 187

Voyage dans la Haute Pennsylvanie et dans l'état de New-York (Crèvecoeur), **Supp. I Part 1:** 250–251

Voyage of the Beagle (Darwin), **Supp. IX:** 211

Voyage Out, The (Woolf), **Supp. XV:** 65

"Voyager, The" (Everwine), **Supp. XV:** 75

"Voyages" (H. Crane), **I:** 393–395; **Retro. Supp. II:** 78, 80, 81

"Voyages" (Levine), **Supp. V:** 190

Voyages and Discoveries of the Companions of Columbus (Irving), **II:** 310

Voyage to Pagany, A (W. C. Williams), **IV:** 404; **Retro. Supp. I:** 418–419, **420–421,** 423

Voyaging Portraits (Sobin), **Supp. XVI:** 282, 287

"Voyeur, The" (Gioia), **Supp. XV:** 125

"Voz de America" (column, W. Frank), **Supp. XX:** 80

Voznesensky, Andrei, **II:** 553; **Supp. III Part 1:** 268; **Supp. III Part 2:** 560

Vrbovska, Anca, **Supp. IV Part 2:** 639

V. S. Naipaul: An Introduction to His Work (Theroux), **Supp. VIII:** 314, 318

"V. S. Pritchett's Apprenticeship" (Maxwell), **Supp. VIII:** 172

Vukelich, James, **Supp. XXIII:** 228, 233

"Vulgarity in Literature" (Huxley), **III:** 429–430

"Vultures" (Oliver), **Supp. VII:** 235

"V. V." (Alcott), **Supp. I Part 1:** 37

W

W (Viva) (Cummings), **I:** 429, 433, 434, 436, 443, 444, 447

Wabash (R. O. Butler), **Supp. XII:** 61, **68–69**

Wade, Grace, **I:** 216

"Wading at Wellfleet" (Bishop), **Retro. Supp. II:** 42, 43; **Supp. I Part 1:** 80, 85, 86

Wadsworth, Charles, **I:** 454, 470; **Retro. Supp. I:** 32, 33

Wagenknecht, Edward, **II:** 508; **Supp. I Part 2:** 408, 584; **Supp. IV Part 2:** 681

"Wages of Poetry, The" (Wright), **Supp. XV:** 337

Wagner, Erica, **Supp. XXI:** 117

Wagner, Jean, **Supp. I Part 1:** 341, 346; **Supp. IV Part 1:** 165, 167, 171

Wagner, Richard, **I:** 284, 395; **II:** 425; **III:** 396, 507; **Supp. IV Part 1:** 392

Wagner, Robert, **Supp. IX:** 250

"Wagnerians, The" (Auchincloss), **Supp. IV Part 1:** 23

"Wagner Matinee, A" (Cather), **I:** 315–316; **Retro. Supp. I:** 5, 8

Wagoner, David, **Supp. IX: 323–340; Supp. XII:** 178; **Supp. XX: 200**

Wahlöö, Per, **Supp. XX: 87**

Waid, Candace, **Retro. Supp. I:** 360, 372, 373

Waif, The (Longfellow, ed.), **Retro. Supp. II:** 155

"Waif of the Plains, A" (Harte), **Supp. II Part 1:** 354

Wain, John, **Supp. XIV:** 166

"Wait" (Kinnell), **Supp. III Part 1:** 250

"Waiter in a California Vietnamese Restaurant" (Major), **Supp. XXII:** 182

"Waiting" (Dubus), **Supp. VII:** 87

Waiting (Jin), **Supp. XVIII:** 89, **96–97,** 99

"Waiting" (W. C. Williams), **Retro. Supp. I:** 418

"Waiting, The" (L.-Y. Lee), **Supp. XV:** 218

"Waiting, The" (Olds), **Supp. X:** 209

"Waiting between the Trees" (Tan), **Supp. X:** 290

"Waiting by the Gate" (Bryant), **Supp. I Part 1:** 171

Waiting for God (Weil), **I:** 298

Waiting for Godot (Beckett), **I:** 78, 91, 298; **Supp. IV Part 1:** 368–369; **Supp. XXIII:** 213

Waiting for Lefty (Odets), **Supp. I Part 1:** 277; **Supp. II Part 2:** 529, 530–533, 540; **Supp. V:** 109; **Supp. XIX:** 242

Waiting for Sweet Betty (Major), **Supp. XXII: 183**

Waiting for Teddy Williams (Mosher), **Supp. XXII:** 205, 206, 207, 208, 209, **215–216**

Waiting for the End of the World (Bell), **Supp. X: 4–5,** 11

"Waiting for the Ladies" (L. Brown), **Supp. XXI:** 44

Waiting for the Verdict (R. H. Davis), **Supp. XVI:** 85, 89, 90

"Waiting in a Rain Forest" (Wagoner), **Supp. IX:** 329

Waiting in the Wings (Loraga), **Supp. XXIII:** 195

Waiting Room, The (Kees), **Supp. XV:** 133, 148

Waiting to Exhale (McMillan), **Supp. XIII:** 184, 185, **189–190,** 191

"Waiting to Freeze" (Banks), **Supp. V:** 5, 6

Waiting to Freeze: Poems (Banks), **Supp. V:** 6, 8

Waits, Tom, **Supp. VIII:** 12

Wait until Spring, Bandini (Fante), **Supp. XI:** 160, 161, 164, 165, **166–167**

Wait until Spring, Bandini (film), **Supp. XI:** 173

"Wake, The" (Dove), **Supp. IV Part 1:** 250

"Wakefield" (Hawthorne), **Retro. Supp. I:** 154, 159

Wakefield, Dan, **Supp. VIII:** 43; **Supp. XVI:** 220; **Supp. XIX:** 257, 258

Wakefield, Richard, **Supp. IX:** 323

"Wake Island" (Rukeyser), **Supp. VI:** 273

"Wake"(Kenny), **Supp. XXIII:** 155

Wakeman, Frederic, **Supp. IX:** 247

Wake Up and Live! (Brande), **Supp. I Part 2:** 608

"Waking" (C. Frost), **Supp. XV:** 93

Waking, The (Roethke), **III:** 541

"Waking Early Sunday Morning" (Lowell), **II:** 552; **Retro. Supp. II:** 190

"Waking in the Blue" (Lowell), **II:** 547; **Retro. Supp. II:** 180

"Waking in the Dark" (Rich), **Supp. I Part 2:** 559

"Waking Up the Rake" (Hogan), **Supp. IV Part 1:** 415–416, 416

Wakoski, Diane, **Supp. V:** 79; **Supp. XII:** 184; **Supp. XV:** 252; **Supp. XVII:** 112; **Supp. XXIII:** 52

Walbridge, John, **Supp. XX: 125**

Walcott, Charles C., **II:** 49

Walcott, Derek, **Supp. VIII:** 28; **Supp. X:** 122, 131; **Supp. XV:** 256

Walcott, Jersey Joe, **Supp. V:** 182

Wald, Alan, **Supp. XV:** 202; **Supp. XVIII:** 223; **Supp. XXI:** 261, 262, 271, 275–276, 277, 278

Wald, Lillian, **Supp. I Part 1:** 12

Walden (Thoreau), **Supp. XIV:** 177, 227; **Supp. XV:** 275; **Supp. XVIII:** 14, 80, 189

Walden, Daniel, **Supp. IV Part 2:** 584, 591; **Supp. V:** 272

Walden; or, Life in the Woods (Thoreau), **I:** 219, 305; **II:** 8, 142, 159, 312–313, 458; **IV:** 168, 169, 170, 176, 177–178, 179–182, 183, 187; **Retro. Supp. I:** 62; **Supp. I Part 2:** 579, 655, 664, 672; **Supp. VIII:** 296; **Supp. X:** 27, 101; **Supp. XIII:** 152

Waldman, Anne, **Supp. XIV:** 150; **Supp. XXIII:** 221

Waldmeir, Joseph, **III:** 45

Waldmeir, Joseph J., **Supp. I Part 2:** 476

Waldo (Theroux), **Supp. VIII:** 313, 314, **314–315**

Waldo Frank: A Study (Munson), **Supp. XX: 74**

Waldron, Jeremy, **Supp. XVII:** 235

Waldrop, Keith, **Supp. XV:** 153, 165

Waley, Arthur, **II:** 526, **III:** 466, **Supp. V:** 340

"Walk, A" (Snyder), **Supp. VIII:** 297

Walkabout Year: Twelve Months in Australia (Pickering), **Supp. XXI:** 199, 200

"Walk at Sunset, A" (Bryant), **Supp. I Part 1:** 155

"Walk before Mass, A" (Agee), **I:** 28–29

Walker, Alice, **Retro. Supp. I:** 215; **Supp. I Part 2:** 550; **Supp. III Part 2:** 488, **517–540; Supp. IV Part 1:** 14; **Supp. VIII:** 141, 214; **Supp. IX:** 306, 311; **Supp. X:** 85, 228, 252, 325,

330; **Supp. XIII:** 179, 185, 291, 295; **Supp. XVI:** 39; **Supp. XVIII:** 200, 283; **Supp. XX: 84, 107, 108; Supp. XXI:** 172; **Supp. XXII:** 172

Walker, Cheryl, **Supp. XI:** 145

Walker, David, **Supp. V:** 189, **Supp. XVII:** 246

Walker, Franklin D., **III:** 321

Walker, Gue, **Supp. XII:** 207

Walker, Margaret, **Supp. XVIII:** 282; **Supp. XX: 106**

Walker, Marianne, **Supp. VIII:** 139

Walker, Obadiah, **II:** 113

Walker, Scott, **Supp. XV:** 92

Walker in the City, A (Kazin), **Supp. VIII: 93–95,** 99

Walk Hard (Blum and Hill), **Supp. XV:** 194

Walk Hard-Talk Loud (Zinberg), **Supp. XV:** 194, 202

"Walking" (Hogan), **Supp. IV Part 1:** 416

"Walking" (Thoreau), **Supp. IV Part 1:** 416; **Supp. IX:** 178

"Walking Along in Winter" (Kenyon), **Supp. VII:** 167

"Walking around the Block with a Three-Year-Old" (Wagoner), **Supp. IX:** 331–332

"Walking at Noon Near the Burlington Depot in Lincoln, Nebraska" (Kooser), **Supp. XIX:** 122

"Walking Backwards into the Future" (R. Williams), **Supp. IX:** 146

Walking Down the Stairs: Selections from Interviews (Kinnell), **Supp. III Part 1:** 235, 249

"Walking Home" (Schnackenberg). *See* "Laughing with One Eye" (Schnackenberg)

"Walking Home at Night" (Ginsberg), **Supp. II Part 1:** 313

"Walking Is Almost Falling" (Peacock), **Supp. XIX:** 196, 197

Walking Light (Dunn), **Supp. XI:** 140, 141, 153

"Walking Man of Rodin, The" (Sandburg), **III:** 583

"Walking Sticks and Paperweights and Water Marks" (Moore), **III:** 215

Walking Tall (Dunn), **Supp. XI:** 140

Walking the Black Cat (Simic), **Supp. VIII:** 280, **282–284**

Walking to Gatlinburg (Mosher), **Supp. XXII:** 204, 205, 206, 207, 208, 209, 215, **216–217**

Walking to Martha's Vineyard (F. Wright), **Supp. XVII:** 240, 241, 245, 246

Walking to Sleep (Wilbur), **Supp. III Part 2:** 557–560

"Walking to Sleep" (Wilbur), **Supp. III Part 2:** 544, 557, 559, 561, 562

"Walking Wounded" (Shaw), **Supp. XIX:** 248

Walkin' the Dog (Mosley), **Supp. XIII:** 242

"Walk in the Moonlight, A" (Anderson), **I:** 114

Walk Me to the Distance (Everett), **Supp. XVIII: 55–56,** 57

Walk on the Wild Side, A (Algren), **Supp. V:** 4; **Supp. IX:** 3, **12–13,** 14

"Walks in Rome" (Merrill), **Supp. III Part 1:** 337

Walk to the River, A (Hoffman), **Supp. XVIII: 77–78**

Walk with Tom Jefferson, A (Levine), **Supp. V:** 179, 187, 190–191

"Wall, The" (Bronk), **Supp. XXI:** 31

"Wall, The" (Brooks), **Supp. III Part 1:** 70, 71, 84

Wall, The (Hersey), **IV:** 4; **Supp. XX: 251**

"Wall, The" (Roethke), **III:** 544

"Wall, The" (Sexton), **Supp. II Part 2:** 696

Wallace, Daniel, **Supp. XXII:** 49

Wallace, David, **Supp. XXI:** 277

Wallace, David Foster, **Retro. Supp. II:** 279; **Supp. X: 301–318; Supp. XVII:** 226; **Supp. XIX:** 223; **Supp. XX: 91, 93; Supp. XXII:** 260, 261

Wallace, Henry, **I:** 489; **III:** 111, 475; **Supp. I Part 1:** 286; **Supp. I Part 2:** 645

Wallace, Jim, **Supp. XX: 143**

Wallace, Mike, **Supp. IV Part 1:** 364; **Supp. IV Part 2:** 526; **Supp. XX: 102**

Wallace, Richard, **Supp. XVIII:** 101–102

Wallace Stevens (Kermode), **Retro. Supp. I:** 301

Wallace Stevens: The Poems of our Climate (Bloom), **Retro. Supp. I:** 299

Wallace Stevens: Words Chosen out of Desire (Stevens), **Retro. Supp. I:** 297

Wallach, Eli, **III:** 161

Wallant, Edward Lewis, **Supp. XVI:** 220

Wallas, Graham, **Supp. I Part 2:** 643

"Walled City" (Oates), **Supp. II Part 2:** 524

Wallenstein, Anna. *See* Weinstein, Mrs. Max (Anna Wallenstein)

Waller, Edmund, **III:** 463

Waller, Fats, **IV:** 263

Waller, Nicole, **Supp. XXII:** 78

Walling, William English, **Supp. I Part 2:** 645; **Supp. XV:** 295

"Wall of Paintings, The" (Notley), **Supp. XXII:** 230

Wall of the Sky, the Wall of the Eye, The (Lethem), **Supp. XVIII:** 139

Walls Do Not Fall, The (Doolittle), **Supp. I Part 1:** 271, 272

Walls of Jericho, The (R. Fisher), **Supp. XIX:** 65, 67, 70, **72–77,** 78

"Wall Songs" (Hogan), **Supp. IV Part 1:** 413

Wall Writing (Auster), **Supp. XII:** 23–24

Walpole, Horace, **I:** 203; **Supp. I Part 2:** 410, 714

Walpole, Hugh, **Retro. Supp. I:** 231; **Supp. XX: 232**

Walpole, Robert, **IV:** 145

Walsh, David M., **Supp. XV:** 5

Walsh, Ed, **II:** 424

Walsh, George, **Supp. IV Part 2:** 528

Walsh, Raoul, **Supp. XIII:** 174

Walsh, Richard J., **Supp. II Part 1:** 119, 130

Walsh, William, **Supp. IV Part 1:** 242, 243, 246, 248, 252, 254, 257

"Walt, the Wounded" (Di Piero), **Supp. XIX:** 37

"Walt and Will" (Apple), **Supp. XVII:** 6

Walter, Eugene, **Supp. XVI:** 230

Walter, Joyce, **Supp. XV:** 121

Walter Benjamin at the Dairy Queen: Reflections at Sixty and Beyond (McMurtry), **Supp. V:** 232

Walters, Barbara, **Supp. XIV:** 125

Walters, Marguerite. *See* Smith, Mrs. Lamar (Marguerite Walters)

"Walter T. Carriman" (O'Hara), **III:** 368

Walton, Izaak, **Supp. I Part 2:** 422

"Walt Whitman" (Kooser), **Supp. XIX:** 118

"Walt Whitman" (Masters), **Supp. I Part 2:** 458

"Walt Whitman at Bear Mountain" (Simpson), **Supp. IX:** 265

Walt Whitman Bathing (Wagoner), **Supp. IX: 331–332**

Walt Whitman Handbook (Allen), **IV:** 352

Walt Whitman Reconsidered (Chase), **IV:** 352

"Waltz, The" (Parker), **Supp. IX:** 204

"Waltzer in the House, The" (Kunitz), **Supp. III Part 1:** 258

Waltzing Matilda (Notley), **Supp. XXII:** 229–230

"Waltzing Matilda" (Notley), **Supp. XXII:** 230

Waltzing the Magpies: A Year in Australia (Pickering), **Supp. XXI:** 199, 200

Walzer, Kevin, **Supp. XII:** 202; **Supp. XV:** 118; **Supp. XVIII:** 174

Wambaugh, Joseph, **Supp. X:** 5; **Supp. XXI:** 67

Wampeters, Foma, & Granfalloons (Vonnegut), **Supp. II Part 2:** 758, 759–760, 776, 779

Wand, David Hsin-fu, **Supp. X:** 292

"Wanderer, The" (W. C. Williams), **Retro. Supp. I:** 414, 421

Wanderer, The: His Parables and His Sayings (Gibran), **Supp. XX: 116, 123–124**

"Wanderers, The" (Welty), **IV:** 273–274

"Wandering Jew, The" (Robinson), **III:** 505, 516–517

Wanderings of Oisin (Yeats), **Supp. I Part 1:** 79

Wang, Dorothy, **Supp. X:** 289

Wang Wei, **Supp. XV:** 47

Waniek, Marilyn Nelson, **Supp. IV Part 1:** 244. *See also* Nelson, Marilyn

"Wan Lee, the Pagan" (Harte), **Supp. II Part 1:** 351

"Want, The" (Olds), **Supp. X:** 210

Want Bone, The (Pinsky), **Supp. VI:** 236–237, 244–245, 247

"Wanted: An Ontological Critic" (Ransom), **III:** 498

"Wanting to Die" (Sexton), **Supp. II Part 2:** 684, 686; **Supp. XIV:** 132

"Wants" (Paley), **Supp. VI:** 219

Waples, Dorothy, **I:** 348

Wapshot Chronicle, The (Cheever), **Supp. I Part 1:** 174, 177–180, 181, 196

Wapshot Scandal, The (Cheever), **Supp. I Part 1:** 180–184, 187, 191, 196
"War" (Findley), **Supp. XX: 49**
"War" (Jin), **Supp. XVIII:** 93
"War" (Kingston), **Supp. V:** 169
"War" (Simic), **Supp. VIII:** 282
"War, Response, and Contradiction" (Burke), **I:** 283
"War and Peace" (Sanders), **Supp. XVI:** 277
War and Peace (Tolstoy), **I:** 6, 7; **II:** 191, 205, 291; **IV:** 446; **Supp. V:** 277; **Supp. XI:** 68; **Supp. XIV:** 97; **Supp. XXIII:** 11
War and Remembrance (Wouk), **Supp. XX: 243**
"War and the Small Nations" (Gibran), **Supp. XX: 127**
War and War (F. Barthelme), **Supp. XI:** 25
"War Between Men and Women, The" (Thurber), **Supp. I Part 2:** 615
War Bulletins (Lindsay), **Supp. I Part 2:** 378–379
Ward, Aileen, **II:** 531
Ward, Artemus (pseudonym). *See* Browne, Charles Farrar
Ward, Douglas Turner, **Supp. IV Part 1:** 362
Ward, Geoff, **Supp. XXIII:** 218
Ward, Henry, **Supp. I Part 2:** 588
Ward, Mrs. Humphry, **II:** 338
Ward, Leo R., **Supp. VIII:** 124
Ward, Lester F., **Supp. I Part 2:** 640; **Supp. XI:** 202, 203
Ward, Lynn, **I:** 31
Ward, Nathaniel, **Supp. I Part 1:** 99, 102, 111, 116
Ward, Susan, **Supp. XXIII:** 146
Ward, Theodora, **I:** 470; **Retro. Supp. I:** 28
Ward, William Hayes, **Supp. I Part 1:** 371
"War Debt, A" (Jewett), **Retro. Supp. II:** 138, 141
"War Diary" (Boyce), **Supp. XVII:** 104; **Supp. XXI:** 6
"War Diary, A" (Bourne), **I:** 229
War Dispatches of Stephen Crane, The (Crane), **I:** 422
"Ward Line, The" (Morris), **III:** 220
Warfel, Harry R., **Supp. I Part 1:** 366
War Games (Morris), **III:** 238
War Goes On, The (Asch), **Supp. XXIII:** 6
"Warhol / Blue Jackie"(Balakian), **Supp. XXIII:** 32
War in Heaven, The (Shepard and Chaikin), **Supp. III Part 2:** 433
War Is Kind (Crane), **I:** 409; **III:** 585
"War Is Kind" (Crane), **I:** 419
Warlock (Harrison), **Supp. VIII:** 45, **46**
Warm as Wool (Sanders), **Supp. XVI:** 269
"Warming" (Trethewey), **Supp. XXI:** 245
Warner, Anna, **Supp. XVIII:** 258–275
Warner, Charles Dudley, **II:** 405; **IV:** 198
Warner, Jack, **Supp. XII:** 160–161; **Supp. XVIII:** 249
Warner, John R., **III:** 193

Warner, Oliver, **I:** 548
Warner, Susan, **Retro. Supp. I:** 246; **Supp. XV:** 275; **Supp. XVIII: 257–275**
Warner, Sylvia Townsend, **Supp. VIII:** 151, 155, 164, 171
Warner, W. Lloyd, **III:** 60
Warner Family and the Warner Books, The (Baker), **Supp. XVIII:** 259, 267
"Warning" (Hughes), **Supp. I Part 1:** 343
"Warning" (Pound), **III:** 474
"Warning, The" (Creeley), **Supp. IV Part 1:** 150
"Warning, The" (Longfellow), **II:** 498
Warning Hill (Marquand), **III:** 55–56, 60, 68
"War of Eyes, A" (Coleman), **Supp. XI:** 93–94
War of Eyes and Other Stories, A (Coleman), **Supp. XI: 91–92**
War of the Classes (London), **II:** 466
"War of the Wall, The" (Bambara), **Supp. XI:** 15–16
"War of Vaslav Nijinsky, The" (Bidart), **Supp. XV:** 21–22, **27–29**
"War Poems" (Sandburg), **III:** 581
Warren, Austin, **I:** 265, 268, 271; **Supp. I Part 2:** 423
Warren, Earl, **III:** 581
Warren, Gabriel, **IV:** 244
Warren, Mercy Otis, **Supp. XV:** 230
Warren, Patricia Nell, **Supp. XX: 259–276**
Warren, Robert Penn, **I:** 190, 211, 517; **II:** 57, 217, 228, 253; **III:** 134, 310, 382–383, 454, 482, 485, 490, 496, 497; **IV:** 121, 122, 123, 125, 126, **236–259**, 261, 262, 279, 340–341, 458; **Retro. Supp. I:** 40, 41, 73, 90; **Retro. Supp. II:** 220, 235; **Supp. I Part 1:** 359, 371; **Supp. I Part 2:** 386, 423; **Supp. II Part 1:** 139; **Supp. III Part 2:** 542; **Supp. V:** 261, 316, 318, 319, 333; **Supp. VIII:** 126, 176; **Supp. IX:** 257; **Supp. X:** 1, 25, 26; **Supp. XI:** 315; **Supp. XII:** 254, 255; **Supp. XIV:** 1, 2, 3, 4, 11, 14, 15; **Supp. XVIII:** 77, 78–79; **Supp. XIX:** 246; **Supp. XXI:** 256
Warren, Mrs. Robert Penn (Eleanor Clark), **IV:** 244
Warren, Rosanna, **IV:** 244; **Supp. XV:** 251, 261, 262, 263; **Supp. XIX:** 34
Warren, Vincent, **Supp. XXIII:** 218, 219
Warrington Poems, The (Ríos), **Supp. IV Part 2:** 540
Warrior, Robert Allen, **Supp. IV Part 1:** 329
"Warrior, The" (Gunn Allen), **Supp. IV Part 1:** 326
"Warrior: 5th Grade" (Olds), **Supp. X:** 214
"Warrior Road" (Harjo), **Supp. XII:** 217
Wars, The (Findley), **Supp. XX: 53–54**
Warshavsky, Isaac (pseudonym). *See* Singer, Isaac Bashevis
Warshow, Robert, **Supp. I Part 1:** 51
Wars I Have Seen (Stein), **IV:** 27, 36, 477
Wartime (Fussell), **Supp. V:** 241

War Trash (Jin), **Supp. XVIII:** 89, **100–101**
"War Widow, The" (Frederic), **II:** 135–136
"Was" (Creeley), **Supp. IV Part 1:** 155
"Was" (Faulkner), **II:** 71
"Wash" (Faulkner), **II:** 72
Wash, Richard, **Supp. XII:** 14
"Washboard Wizard" (Nelson), **Supp. XVIII:** 182
"Washed in the Rain" (Fante), **Supp. XI:** 165
"Washing of Hands, A" (Kooser), **Supp. XIX:** 115
Washington, Booker T., **Supp. I Part 2:** 393; **Supp. II Part 1:** 157, 160, 167, 168, 171, 225; **Supp. XIV:** 198, 199, 201; **Supp. XVIII:** 121–122
Washington, D.C. (Vidal), **Supp. IV Part 2:** 677, 684, 686–687, 690
Washington, George, **I:** 453; **II:** 313–314; **Supp. I Part 2:** 399, 485, 508, 509, 511, 513, 517, 518, 520, 599
Washington, Mary Helen, **Supp. XVIII:** 119, 284
Washington and His Generals (Lippard), **Supp. XXIII:** 178, **185–186,** 187
Washington Crossing the Delaware (Rivers), **Supp. XV:** 186
Washington Post Book World (Lesser), **Supp. IV Part 2:** 453; **Supp. VIII:** 80, 84, 241; **Supp. X:** 282
Washington Square (James), **II:** 327, 328; **Retro. Supp. I:** 215, 220, **222–223**
"Washington Square, 1946" (Ozick), **Supp. V:** 272
Washington Square Ensemble, The (Bell), **Supp. X:** 1, **3–4**
"Washman"(P. Benedict), **Supp. XXIII:** 40
"Was Lowell an Historical Critic?" (Altick), **Supp. I Part 2:** 423
Wasserman, Earl R., **Supp. I Part 2:** 439, 440
Wasserman, Jakob, **Supp. I Part 2:** 669
Wasserstein, Wendy, **Supp. IV Part 1:** 309; **Supp. XV: 319–336**
Wasson, Ben, **Retro. Supp. I:** 79, 83
"Waste Carpet, The" (Matthews), **Supp. IX: 158–159**
Waste Land, The (T. S. Eliot), **I:** 107, 266, 298, 395, 396, 482, 570–571, 572, 574–575, 577–578, 580, 581, 584, 585, 586, 587; **III:** 6–8, 12, 196, 277–278, 453, 471, 492, 586; **IV:** 122, 123, 124, 140, 418, 419, 420; **Retro. Supp. I:** 51, 60, **60–62,** 63, 64, 66, 210, 290, 291, 299, 311, 420, 427; **Retro. Supp. II:** 85, 121, 190; **Supp. I Part 1:** 272; **Supp. I Part 2:** 439, 455, 614; **Supp. II Part 1:** 4, 5, 11, 96; **Supp. III Part 1:** 9, 10, 41, 63, 105; **Supp. IV Part 1:** 47, 284; **Supp. V:** 338; **Supp. IX:** 158, 305; **Supp. X:** 125; **Supp. XIII:** 341–342, 344, 346; **Supp. XIV:** 6, 284; **Supp. XV:** 21, 181, 261, 306; **Supp. XVI:** 204; **Supp. XVII:** 140–141, 144, 227; **Supp. XVIII:** 78, 79–80; **Supp. XIX:** 288; **Supp. XXIII:** 23, 25, 79, 165

"Waste Land, The": A Facsimile and Transcript of the Original Drafts Including the Annotations of Ezra Pound (Eliot, ed.), **Retro. Supp. I:** 58

Waste Land and Other Poems, The (T. S. Eliot), **Supp. XV:** 305

Wat, Alexander, **Supp. XVI:** 155, 161

Watch, The (Bass), **Supp. XVI:** 16–17

"Watch, The, —" (Bass), **Supp. XVI:** 17

Watch and Ward (James), **II:** 323; **Retro. Supp. I:** 218, **219,** 220

"Watcher" (Trethewey), **Supp. XXI:** 247

"Watcher, The" (R. Bly), **Supp. IV Part 1:** 71

"Watcher by the Dead, A" (Bierce), **I:** 203

Watchfires (Auchincloss), **Supp. IV Part 1:** 23

"Watching Crow, Looking toward the Manzano Mountains" (Harjo), **Supp. XII:** 219

"Watching the Oregon Whale" (A. Finch), **Supp. XVII:** 77

"Watching the Sunset" (Coleman), **Supp. XI:** 92

Watch on the Rhine (Hellman), **Supp. I Part 1:** 276, 278, 279–281, 283–284; **Supp. IV Part 1:** 83

"Water" (Emerson), **II:** 19

"Water" (Komunyakaa), **Supp. XIII:** 132

"Water" (Lowell), **II:** 550

"Waterbird" (Swenson), **Supp. IV Part 2:** 651

"Water Borders" (Dillard), **Supp. VI:** 27

"Water Buffalo" (Komunyakaa), **Supp. XIII:** 122

"Watercolor of Grantchester Meadows" (Plath), **Supp. I Part 2:** 537

Water Cure, The (Everett), **Supp. XVIII: 64–66**

"Water Drum"(Kenny), **Supp. XXIII:** 144

"Waterfall, The" (Clampitt), **Supp. IX:** 44

Waterfront (Schulberg), **Supp. XVIII: 251–252**

"Water Hose Is on Fire, The" (Simic), **Supp. XV:** 185

Waterhouse, Keith, **Supp. VIII:** 124

"Waterlily Fire" (Rukeyser), **Supp. VI:** 285, 286

Waterlily Fire: Poems 1935–1962 (Rukeyser), **Supp. VI:** 274, 283, 285

Watermark (Brodsky), **Supp. VIII:** 29

Water-Method Man, The (Irving), **Supp. VI:** 163, **167–179,** 180

Water Music (Boyle), **Supp. VIII:** 1, 3–5, 8, 14; **Supp. XX: 20–22**

"Water Music for the Progress of Love in a Life-Raft Down the Sammamish Slough" (Wagoner), **Supp. IX:** 326

"Water People" (Burke), **Supp. XIV:** 21

"Water Picture" (Swenson), **Supp. IV Part 2:** 641

"Water Rising" (Hogan), **Supp. IV Part 1:** 400

Waters, Ethel, **II:** 587

Waters, Frank, **Supp. X:** 124

Waters, Muddy, **Supp. VIII:** 345

Watershed (Everett), **Supp. XVIII: 58–59, 64**

"Watershed" (Kingsolver), **Supp. VII:** 208

"Watershed" (Warren), **IV:** 239

"Watershed, The" (Auden), **Supp. II Part 1:** 5

Waters of Kronos, The (Richter), **Supp. XVIII:** 207, 208, **218–219,** 220

Waters of Siloe, The (Merton), **Supp. VIII:** 196, 208

Waterston, Sam, **Supp. IX:** 253

Water Street (Merrill), **Supp. III Part 1:** 321–323

"Water Walker" (Wilbur), **Supp. III Part 2:** 548, 560

Water-Witch, The (Cooper), **I:** 342–343

"Water Witch"(P. Benedict), **Supp. XXIII:** 38

Waterworks, The (Doctorow), **Supp. IV Part 1:** 218, 222, 223, 231–233, 234

"Water Works, The" (Doctorow), **Supp. IV Part 1:** 234

Watkin, E. I., **Retro. Supp. II:** 187

Watkins, Floyd C., **IV:** 452

Watkins, James T., **I:** 193, 194

Watkins, Maureen, **Supp. XVI:** 188

Watkins, Mel, **Supp. X:** 330; **Supp. XIII:** 246

Watman, Max, **Supp. XX: 92**

Watrous, Peter, **Supp. VIII:** 79

Watson, Brook, **Supp. XX: 284**

Watson, Burton, **Supp. XV:** 47

Watson, James Sibley, Jr., **I:** 261

Watson, Jay, **Supp. XVIII:** 195; **Supp. XXI:** 46

Watson, J. B., **II:** 361

Watson, Richard, **Supp. I Part 2:** 516, 517

Watson, William, **II:** 114

Watsonville: Some Place Not Here (Moraga), **Supp. XXIII:** 195, 196, 202, 203

Watt, Ian, **Supp. VIII:** 4

Watteau, Jean Antoine, **III:** 275; **IV:** 79

Watts, Emily Stipes, **Supp. I Part 1:** 115

Waugh, Evelyn, **I:** 480; **III:** 281; **Supp. I Part 2:** 607; **Supp. IV Part 2:** 688; **Supp. XI:** 305, 306; **Supp. XIX:** 131

"Wave" (Snyder), **Supp. VIII:** 299

Wave, A (Ashbery), **Supp. III Part 1:** 1, 4, 24–26

"Wave, A" (Ashbery), **Supp. III Part 1:** 9, 19, 24–25

"Wave, The" (MacLeish), **III:** 19

"Wave, The" (Untermeyer), **Supp. XV:** 300

Wave Amplitude in the Mona Passage (Schott), **Supp. XXIII: 242–243**

"Wavemaker Falters, The" (Saunders), **Supp. XIX:** 225

"Waxwings" (Francis), **Supp. IX:** 82

Way, The (Steiner and Witt, eds.), **Supp. IV Part 2:** 505

"Way Down, The" (Kunitz), **Supp. III Part 1:** 263

"Way It Is, The" (Ellison), **Supp. II Part 1:** 245

"Way It Is, The" (Jones), **Supp. XI:** 229

"Way It Is, The" (Stafford), **Supp. XIII:** 274

"Way It Is, The" (Strand), **Supp. IV Part 2:** 627

"Wayland" (Sanders), **Supp. XVI:** 275

Wayne, John, **Supp. IV Part 1:** 200

Way of Chuang-Tzu, The (Merton), **Supp. VIII:** 208

"Way of Exchange in James Dickey's Poetry, The" (Weatherby), **Supp. IV Part 1:** 175

Way of Life According to Laotzu, The (Bynner), **Supp. XV:** 46, 48

Way Out, A (Frost), **Retro. Supp. I:** 133

Wayside Motor Inn, The (Gurney), **Supp. V:** 96, 105, 109

"Ways of Breaking: Lynda Hull's 'Ornithology' " (Jauss), **Supp. XXI:** 139

"Ways of Talking" (Jin), **Supp. XVIII:** 93

Ways of the Hour, The (Cooper), **I:** 354

Ways of White Folks, The (Hughes), **Retro. Supp. I:** 203, 204; **Supp. I Part 1:** 329, 330, 332

Way Some People Die, The (Macdonald), **Supp. IV Part 2:** 470, 471, 472, 474

Way Some People Live, The (Cheever), **Supp. I Part 1:** 175

"Way the Cards Fall, The" (Komunyakaa), **Supp. XIII:** 117

"Way the Luck Runs, The" (Wolfert), **Supp. XXI:** 265

"Way Things Are, The" (Turow, unpub.), **Supp. XVII:** 215, 218

Way to Rainy Mountain, The (Momaday), **Supp. IV Part 2:** 485–486, 487–489, 491, 493

Way to Wealth, The (Franklin), **II:** 101–102, 110; **Supp. XX: 27**

Wayward and the Seeking, The: A Collection of Writings by Jean Toomer (Toomer), **Supp. III Part 2:** 478–481, 484, 487

Wayward Bus, The (Steinbeck), **IV:** 51, 64–65

"Way We Live Now, The" (Sontag), **Supp. III Part 2:** 467–468

"Way You'll Never Be, A" (Hemingway), **II:** 249

"W. D. Sees Himself Animated" (Snodgrass), **Supp. VI:** 327

"W. D. Sits in Kafka's Chair and Is Interrogated Concerning the Assumed Death of Cock Robin" (Snodgrass), **Supp. VI:** 319

"W. D. Tries to Warn Cock Robin" (Snodgrass), **Supp. VI:** 319

"We" (Alexander), **Supp. XVIII:** 185

Weaks, Mary Louise, **Supp. X:** 5

Weales, Gerald, **II:** 602

"Wealth," from Conduct of Life, The (Emerson), **II:** 2, 3–4

"Wealth," from English Traits (Emerson), **II:** 6

Wealth of Nations, The (A. Smith), **II:** 109

"We Are Looking at You, Agnes" (Caldwell), **I:** 309

We Are Still Married: Stories and Letters (Keillor), **Supp. XVI:** 176, 177

"We Are the Crazy Lady and Other Feisty Feminist Fables" (Ozick), **Supp. V:** 259

Weary Blues, The (Hughes), **Retro. Supp. I:** 195, 197, 198, 199, 200, 203, 205; **Supp. I Part 1:** 325

"Weary Blues, The" (Hughes), **Retro. Supp. I:** 198, 199; **Supp. I Part 1:** 324, 325

"Weary Kingdom" (Irving), **Supp. VI:** 163

Weasels and Wisemen: Ethics and Ethnicity in the Work of David Mamet (Kane), **Supp. XIV:** 250

Weather and the Women Treat Me Fair, The (Everett), **Supp. XVIII:** 66

Weatherby, H. L., **Supp. IV Part 1:** 175

Weather Central (Kooser), **Supp. XIX:** 116, **123–125**

"Weathering Out" (Dove), **Supp. IV Part 1:** 248

"Weather Within, The" (M. F. K. Fisher), **Supp. XVII:** 88, 91

Weaver, Harriet, **III:** 471

Weaver, James, **Supp. XVIII:** 72

Weaver, Michael, **Supp. XVIII:** 176, 177

Weaver, Mike, **Retro. Supp. I:** 430

Weaver, Will, **Supp. XVI:** 39

"Weaving" (Larcom), **Supp. XIII:** 142, **Supp. XIII:** 144–145, 150, 151

"Web" (Oliver), **Supp. VII:** 236

Web and the Rock, The (Wolfe), **IV:** 451, 455, 457, 459–460, 462, 464, 467, 468

Webb, Beatrice, **Supp. I Part 1:** 5

Webb, Mary, **I:** 226

Webb, Phyllis, **Supp. XX: 56**

Webb, Sidney, **Supp. I Part 1:** 5

Webb, W. P., **Supp. V:** 225

Webber, A. R. F., **Supp. XXI:** 160

Weber, Brom, **I:** 383, 386

Weber, Carl, **Supp. IX:** 133, 138, 141

Weber, Max, **I:** 498; **Supp. I Part 2:** 637, 648

Weber, Sarah, **Supp. I Part 1:** 2

Weberman, A. J., **Supp. XVIII:** 27

Web of Earth, The (Wolfe), **IV:** 451–452, 456, 458, 464, 465

"Web of Life, The" (Nemerov), **III:** 282

Webster, Brenda, **Supp. XVI:** 157, 161

Webster, Daniel, **II:** 5, 9; **Supp. I Part 2:** 659, 687, 689, 690

Webster, John, **I:** 384; **Supp. I Part 2:** 422

Webster, Noah, **Supp. I Part 2:** 660; **Supp. II Part 1:** 77

Wector, Dixon, **II:** 103

Wedding, The (D. West), **Supp. XVIII:** 277, **287–289**

"Wedding, The" (Everwine), **Supp. XV:** 83

"Wedding, The" (Major), **Supp. XXII:** 185

Wedding, The (television miniseries), **Supp. XVIII:** 277, 289

"Wedding Cake" (Nye), **Supp. XIII:** 283

"Wedding Dance, The" (Di Piero), **Supp. XIX:** 47

"Wedding in Brownsville, A" (Singer), **IV:** 15

Wedding in Hell, A (Simic), **Supp. VIII:** 280, **282**

"Wedding of the Rose and Lotus, The" (Lindsay), **Supp. I Part 2:** 387

"Wedding Supper, The" (Rowson), **Supp. XV:** 243

"Wedding Toast, A" (Wilbur), **Supp. III Part 2:** 561

Wedekind, Frank, **III:** 398; **Supp. XX: 85; Supp. XXII:** 23

Wedge, The (W. C. Williams), **Retro. Supp. I:** 424

"We Didn't"(Dybek), **Supp. XXIII:** 77–78

"Wednesday at the Waldorf" (Swenson), **Supp. IV Part 2:** 647

"We Don't Live Here Anymore" (Dubus), **Supp. VII:** 78–79, 85

"Weed" (McCarriston), **Supp. XIV:** 259, 273

"Weed, The" (Bishop), **Supp. I Part 1:** 80, 88–89

"Weed, The" (Taggard), **Supp. XXII:** 284

"Weeds, The" (McCarthy), **II:** 566

"Weekend" (Beattie), **Supp. V:** 27

"Weekend" (Hempel), **Supp. XXI:** 124

Weekend, The (Cameron), **Supp. XII:** 80, 81, **86–88**

"Weekend at Ellerslie, A" (Wilson), **IV:** 431

Weekend Edition (National Public Radio), **Supp. IX:** 299; **Supp. XVII:** 240, 242

Weekend in Dinlock (Sigal), **Supp. XXIII:** 166

"Week in the Word, A" (Hampl), **Supp. XXII:** 85

Week on the Concord and Merrimack Rivers, A (Thoreau), **IV:** 168, 169, 177, 182–183; **Supp. I Part 2:** 420; **Supp. XIV:** 227

Weeks, Edward, **III:** 64

Weeks, Jerome, **Supp. VIII:** 76

"Weeping Burgher" (Stevens), **IV:** 77

"Weeping Women" (Levertov), **Supp. III Part 1:** 282

We Fished All Night (W. Motley), **Supp. XVII: 155–158,** 159, 160

We Fly Away (Francis), **Supp. IX: 79–80,** 84

We Happy Few (Hinojosa), **Supp. XIX:** 99, **111–112**

We Have Always Lived in the Castle (Jackson), **Supp. IX:** 121, 126, **127–128**

"We Have Our Arts So We Won't Die of Truth" (Bradbury), **Supp. IV Part 1:** 105

We Have Tomorrow (Bontemps), **Supp. XXII:** 6, 12

Weich, Dave, **Supp. XII:** 321; **Supp. XVIII:** 91

"Weighing In" (Espaillat), **Supp. XXI:** 111

"Weight" (Wideman), **Supp. X:** 321

"Weights" (C. Baxter), **Supp. XVII:** 16

Weigl, Bruce, **Supp. VIII:** 269, 274; **Supp. XV:** 342; **Supp. XIX: 273–290**

Weil, Dorothy, **Supp. XV:** 231

Weil, James L., **Supp. XXI:** 23, 31

Weil, Robert, **Supp. IX:** 236

Weil, Simone, **I:** 298; **Supp. XV:** 259; **Supp. XXII:** 93

Weiland (C. B. Brown), **Supp. XIII:** 100

Weinauer, Ellen, **Supp. XV:** 270, 284

Weinberger, Eliot, **Supp. IV Part 1:** 66; **Supp. VIII:** 290, 292; **Supp. XVI:** 284

Weinberger, Eric, **Supp. XXII:** 264

Weinfield, Henry, **Supp. XXI:** 24, 28, 33

Weininger, Otto, **Retro. Supp. I:** 416

Weinraub, Judith, **Supp. XXI:** 39

Weinreb, Mindy, **Supp. X:** 24

Weinreich, Regina, **Supp. XIV:** 22

Weinstein, Cindy, **Supp. XVIII:** 261

Weinstein, Hinda, **IV:** 285

Weinstein, Max, **IV:** 285

Weinstein, Mrs. Max (Anna Wallenstein), **IV:** 285, 287

Weinstein, Nathan. *See* West, Nathanael

Weinstein, Selma, **Supp. XXI:** 170

Weisheit, Rabbi, **IV:** 76

Weismuller, Johnny, **Supp. X:** 264; **Supp. XX: 18**

Weiss, David, **Supp. XVI:** 55

Weiss, Jane, **Supp. XVIII:** 267, 269

Weiss, Peter, **IV:** 117

Weiss, Theodore, **Supp. IV Part 2:** 440; **Supp. IX:** 96

Weissleder, Paul, **Supp. XXII:** 283

Weist, Dianne, **Supp. X:** 80

Weithas, Art, **Supp. XI:** 231

Welch, Dave, **Supp. XXI:** 118

Welch, Don, **Supp. XIX:** 119

Welch, James, **Supp. IV Part 1:** 404; **Supp. IV Part 2:** 503, 513, 557, 562

Welch, Lew, **Supp. V:** 170; **Supp. VIII:** 303; **Supp. XXII:** 276

"Welcome from War" (Rukeyser), **Supp. VI:** 286

"Welcome Morning" (Sexton), **Supp. II Part 2:** 696

"Welcome the Wrath" (Kunitz), **Supp. III Part 1:** 261

Welcome to Hard Times (Doctorow), **Supp. IV Part 1:** 218, 219–220, 222, 224, 230, 238

Welcome to Hard Times (film), **Supp. IV Part 1:** 236

"Welcome to New Dork" (Leonard), **Supp. XVIII:** 148

Welcome to Our City (Wolfe), **IV:** 461

Welcome to the Monkey House (Vonnegut), **Supp. II Part 2:** 758

Welcome to the Moon (Shanley), **Supp. XIV:** 318

Welcome to the Moon and Other Plays (Shanley), **Supp. XIV:** 315, **316–319**

Weld, Theodore, **Supp. I Part 2:** 587, 588

Weld, Tuesday, **Supp. XI:** 306

Welded (O'Neill), **III:** 390; **Supp. XXII:** 24

"Welfare Worker, Disenchanted, Contemplates Friday Afternoon, The" (Trethewey), **Supp. XXI:** 246

"Well, The" (Momaday), **Supp. IV Part 2:** 483

"Well Dressed Man with a Beard, The" (Stevens), **Retro. Supp. I:** 297

Wellek, René, **I:** 253, 261, 282; **II:** 320; **Supp. XIV:** 12, 14

Weller, George, **III:** 322

Welles, Gideon, **Supp. I Part 2:** 484

Welles, Orson, **IV:** 476; **Supp. I Part 1:** 67; **Supp. IV Part 1:** 82, 83; **Supp. V:** 251; **Supp. VIII:** 46; **Supp. XI:** 169, 307

"Wellfleet Whale, The" (Kunitz), **Supp. III Part 1:** 263, 269

Wellfleet Whale and Companion Poems, The (Kunitz), **Supp. III Part 1:** 263

Wellink, Yvonne, **Supp. XVIII:** 257

Wellman, Flora, **II:** 463–464, 465

"Well Rising, The" (Stafford), **Supp. XI:** 318

Wells, H. G., **I:** 103, 226, 241, 243, 253, 405, 409, 415; **II:** 82, 144, 276, 337, 338, 458; **III:** 456; **IV:** 340, 455; **Retro. Supp. I:** 100, 228, 231; **Supp. XVI:** 190; **Supp. XXI:** 8

Wellspring, The (Olds), **Supp. X:** 211–212

Well Wrought Urn, The: Studies in the Structure of Poetry (Brooks), **Supp. XIV:** 1, **8–9**, 14, 15, 16

Welsh, Mary, **Supp. XIX:** 248. *See also* Hemingway, Mrs. Ernest (Mary Welsh)

Welty, Eudora, **II:** 194, 217, 606; **IV:** **260–284**; **Retro. Supp. I:** 339–358; **Retro. Supp. II:** 235; **Supp. IV Part 2:** 474; **Supp. V:** 59, 315, 336; **Supp. VIII:** 94, 151, 171; **Supp. X:** 42, 290; **Supp. XII:** 310, 322; **Supp. XIV:** 3; **Supp. XV:** 338

Welty, Eurora, **Supp. XIX:** 151

Weltzien, O. Alan, **Supp. XVI:** 20–21, 28

"We miss Her, not because We see—" (Dickinson), **Retro. Supp. I:** 46

We Must Dance My Darlings (Trilling), **Supp. I Part 1:** 297

Wendell, Barrett, **III:** 507; **Supp. I Part 2:** 414; **Supp. XIV:** 197

Wendell, Sarah. *See* Holmes, Mrs. Abiel (Sarah Wendell)

Wendy Wasserstein: A Casebook (Barnett), **Supp. XV:** 323, 330

"Wendy Wasserstein's Three Sisters: Squandered Privilege" (Brewer), **Supp. XV:** 330

Wept of Wish-ton-Wish, The (Cooper), **I:** 339, 342, 350

Werbe, Peter, **Supp. XIII:** 236

"We Real Cool" (Brooks), **Supp. III Part 1:** 80

We're Back! A Dinosaur's Story (screenplay, Shanley), **Supp. XIV:** 316

"We're Friends Again" (O'Hara), **III:** 372–373

"Were the Whole Realm of Nature Mine" (Watts), **I:** 458

Werewolf (M. Sommers), **Supp. XVII:** 55

Were-Wolf, The (C. Housman), **Supp. XVII:** 55

Werewolf of Paris, The (Endore), **Supp. XVII:** 55–56

Werewolves in Their Youth (Chabon), **Supp. XI:** 66, **76–77**

Werlock, Abby, **Supp. XIII:** 293

Werthman, Michael, **Supp. V:** 115

"Wer-Trout, The" (Proulx), **Supp. VII:** 255–256

Wescott, Glenway, **I:** 288; **II:** 85; **III:** 448, 454; **Supp. VIII:** 156; **Supp. XIV:** 342; **Supp. XVI:** 195

"We Shall All Be Born Again But We Shall Not All Be Saved" (Matthews), **Supp. IX:** 162

West, Anthony, **Supp. IV Part 1:** 284

West, Benjamin, **Supp. I Part 2:** 511

West, Dorothy, **Supp. XIII:** 295; **Supp. XVIII: 277–291; Supp. XIX:** 72

West, James, **II:** 562

West, Nathanael, **I:** 97, 107, 190, 211, 298; **II:** 436; **III:** 357, 425; **IV:** **285–307; Retro. Supp. II: 321–341; Supp. IV Part 1:** 203; **Supp. VIII:** 97; **Supp. XI:** 85, 105, 159, 296; **Supp. XII:** 173, 310; **Supp. XIII:** 106, 170; **Supp. XVIII:** 251, 253, 254

West, Nathaniel, **Supp. XIX:** 223

West, Ray, **Supp. XV:** 142

West, Rebecca, **II:** 412, 445; **Supp. XVI:** 152, 153

Westall, Julia Elizabeth. *See* Wolfe, Mrs. William Oliver (Julia Elizabeth Westall)

"We Stand United" (Benét), **Supp. XI:** 46

"West Authentic, The: Willa Cather" (Stegner), **Supp. IV Part 2:** 608

"West Coast, The: Region with a View" (Stegner), **Supp. IV Part 2:** 608–609

"West Coast Waterfront: End of an Era" (Swados), **Supp. XIX:** 264

Westcott, Edward N., **II:** 102

"Western Association of Writers" (Chopin), **Supp. I Part 1:** 217

"Western Ballad, A" (Ginsberg), **Supp. II Part 1:** 311

Western Borders, The (Howe), **Supp. IV Part 2:** 424–425

Western Canon: The Books and Schools of the Ages (Bloom), **Supp. IX:** 146

Western Lands, The (Burroughs), **Supp. III Part 1:** 106

"Western North Carolina" (Halliday), **Supp. XIX:** 85

Western Star (Benét), **Supp. XI:** 46, 47, 57

"Westland" (C. Baxter), **Supp. XVII:** 18, 19

"West Marginal Way" (Hugo), **Supp. VI:** 131, 135

West of Eden: Writers in Hollywood, 1928–1940 (Fine), **Supp. XVIII:** 248

West of Yesterday, East of Summer: New and Selected Poems, 1973–1993 (Monette), **Supp. X:** 159

West of Your City (Stafford), **Supp. XI:** 316, **317–318**, 321, 322

Weston, Jessie L., **II:** 540; **III:** 12; **Supp. I Part 2:** 438

"West Real" (Ríos), **Supp. IV Part 2:** 539, 540

West-running Brook (Frost), **II:** 155; **Retro. Supp. I:** 136, 137

"West-running Brook" (Frost), **II:** 150, 162–164

"West Wall" (Merwin), **Supp. III Part 1:** 355

"Westward Beach, A" (Jeffers), **Supp. II Part 2:** 418

Westward Ho (Harrison), **Supp. VIII:** 51, **52**

Westward the Course of Empire (Leutze), **Supp. X:** 307

"Westward the Course of Empire Takes Its Way" (Wallace), **Supp. X: 307–308; Supp. XXII:** 260

"West Wind" (Oliver), **Supp. VII:** 246

"West Wind, The" (Bryant), **Supp. I Part 1:** 155

West Wind: Poems and Prose Poems (Oliver), **Supp. VII:** 243, 246–248

"Wet Casements" (Ashbery), **Supp. III Part 1:** 18–20

We the Living (film), **Supp. IV Part 2:** 520

We the Living (Rand), **Supp. IV Part 2:** 520–521

Wetherell, Elizabeth (pseudonym). *See* Warner, Susan

Wet Parade (Sinclair), **Supp. V:** 289

Wetzsteon, Ross, **Supp. XXI:** 12

"We've Adjusted Too Well" (O'Brien), **Supp. V:** 247

Wevill, David, **Retro. Supp. II:** 247, 249

"We Wear the Mask" (Dunbar), **Supp. II Part 1:** 199, 207, 209–210

Weybright, Victor, **Supp. XIII:** 172

Weyden, Rogier van der, **Supp. IV Part 1:** 284

Whalen, Marcella, **Supp. I Part 1:** 49

Whalen, Philip, **Supp. VIII:** 289; **Supp. XXII:** 226

Whalen-Bridge, John, **Retro. Supp. II:** 211–212

"Whales off Wales, The" (X. J. Kennedy), **Supp. XV:** 163

"Whales Weep" (Boyle), **Supp. XX:** 19

"Whales Weep Not!" (D. H. Lawrence), **Supp. XVII:** 77

Wharton, Edith, **I:** 12, 375; **II:** 96, 180, 183, 186, 189–190, 193, 283, 338, 444, 451; **III:** 69, 175, 576; **IV:** 8, 53, 58, **308–330; Retro. Supp. I:** 108, 232, **359–385; Supp. IV Part 1:** 23, 31, 35, 36, 80, 81, 310; **Supp. IX:** 57; **Supp. XII:** 308; **Supp. XIV:** 337, 347; **Supp. XVI:** 189; **Supp. XVIII:** 278; **Supp. XX: 227, 229, 232, 239, 240; Supp. XXIII:** 275

Wharton, Edward Robbins, **IV:** 310, 313–314, 319

"What" (Dunn), **Supp. XI:** 144

What a Kingdom It Was (Kinnell), **Supp. III Part 1:** 235, 238, 239

"What America Would Be Like without Blacks" (Ellison), **Retro. Supp. II:** 123

What Are Masterpieces (Stein), **IV:** 30–31

What Are Years (Moore), **III:** 208–209, 210, 215

"What Are Years?" (Moore), **III:** 211, 213

What a Way to Go (Morris), **III:** 230–232

"What a Wonder among the Instruments Is the Walloping Trombone!" (Carruth), **Supp. XVI:** 51

"What Became of the Flappers?" (Zelda Fitzgerald), **Supp. IX:** 71

"What Can I Tell My Bones?" (Roethke), **III:** 546, 549

What Century? (O'Hara), **Supp. XXIII:** 216

"What Child Is This?" (Jarman), **Supp. XVII:** 113–114, 115

"What Do We Have Here" (Carson), **Supp. XII: 101**

"What Do We See" (Rukeyser), **Supp. VI:** 282

What Do Women Want? Bread Roses Sex Power (Jong), **Supp. V:** 115, 117, 129, 130

"What Do You Do in San Francisco?" (Carver), **Supp. III Part 1:** 143

What D'Ya Know for Sure (Zinberg), **Supp. XV:** 196

Whatever Happened to Gloomy Gus of the Chicago Bears? (Coover), **Supp. V:** 51, 52

Whatever Happened to Jacy Farrow? (Cleveland), **Supp. V:** 222

"What Every Boy Should Know" (Maxwell), **Supp. VIII:** 169

"What Feels Like the World" (Bausch), **Supp. VII:** 46

"What Fort Sumter Did for Me" (E. Stoddard), **Supp. XV:** 282

"What Girls Read" (Salmon), **Supp. XVIII:** 258

"What God Is Like to Him I Serve" (Bradstreet), **Supp. I Part 1:** 106–107

"What Happened Here Before" (Snyder), **Supp. VIII:** 302

"What Happened to Georgia" (Ray), **Supp. XVIII:** 194

What Happens (Herrmann), **Supp. XXII:** 277

What Have I Ever Lost by Dying? (R. Bly), **Supp. IV Part 1:** 71–72

What Have You Lost? (Nye, ed.), **Supp. XIII:** 280

What I Believe (Asch), **Supp. XXIII:** 2

"What I Believe" (Mumford), **Supp. II Part 2:** 479

"What I Call What They Call Onanism" (Goldbarth), **Supp. XII:** 175

What I Did Last Summer (Gurney), **Supp. V:** 96, 100, 107, 108

"What if God" (Olds), **Supp. X:** 208

What I Have Done with Birds: Character Studies of Native American Birds (Stratton-Porter), **Supp. XX: 218**

"What I Have to Defend, What I Can't Bear Losing" (Stern), **Supp. IX:** 286, 287, 288, 298

"What I Knew" (Nelson), **Supp. XVIII:** 178

"What I Know about Being a Playwright" (McNally), **Supp. XIII:** 195, 207

"What I Mean" (Ortiz), **Supp. IV Part 2:** 497

"What Is an Emotion" (James), **II:** 350

What Is Art? (Tolstoy), **I:** 58

"What Is Civilization? Africa's Answer" (Du Bois), **Supp. II Part 1:** 176

"What Is College For?" (Bourne), **I:** 216

"What Is Exploitation?" (Bourne), **I:** 216

What Is Found There: Notebooks on Poetry and Politics (A. Rich), **Supp. XVII:** 74

"What Is It?" (Carver), **Supp. III Part 1:** 139

What Is Man? (Twain), **II:** 434; **IV:** 209

"What Is Poetry" (Ashbery), **Supp. III Part 1:** 19

"What Is Seized" (Moore), **Supp. X:** 164, 168, 169, 172, 175

"What Is the Earth?" (Olds), **Supp. X:** 213

"What Is This Poet" (Stern), **Supp. IX:** 295

What Is To Be Done? (Lenin), **Supp. XXI:** 164

"What I Think" (Hogan), **Supp. IV Part 1:** 406

What Maisie Knew (H. James), **II:** 332; **Retro. Supp. I:** 229, **230; Supp. XVIII:** 160

What Makes Sammy Run? (NBC broadcast, Schulberg and Schulberg), **Supp. XVIII:** 254

What Makes Sammy Run? (Schulberg), **Supp. XIII:** 170; **Supp. XVIII:** 241, **244–247,** 248, 249, 253

"What Makes Sammy Run?" (Schulberg), **Supp. XVIII:** 241

What Moon Drove Me to This? (Harjo), **Supp. XII: 218–220**

"What Must" (MacLeish), **III:** 18

What My Father Believed (Wrigley), **Supp. XVIII:** 298–300

"What My Father Believed" (Wrigley), **Supp. XVIII: 298–299**

What Price Hollywood? (film), **Supp. XVIII:** 243

"What Sally Said" (Cisneros), **Supp. VII:** 63

What Saves Us (Weigl), **Supp. XIX:** 282

"What's Happening in America" (Sontag), **Supp. III Part 2:** 460–461

"What She Couldn't Tell" (Hampl), **Supp. XXII:** 92

"What's in Alaska?" (Carver), **Supp. III Part 1:** 141, 143

"What's in a Name" (H. L. Gates), **Supp. XX: 101**

What's New, Pussycat? (film; Allen), **Supp. XI:** 307; **Supp. XV:** 1, 2, 14

"What's New in American and Canadian Poetry" (R. Bly), **Supp. IV Part 1:** 67

What's O'Clock (Lowell), **II:** 511, 527, 528

What's Up, Tiger Lily? (film; Allen), **Supp. XV:** 2, **3**

"What the Arts Need Now" (Baraka), **Supp. II Part 1:** 47

"What the Bed Knows"(Schott), **Supp. XXIII:** 249

"What the Body Can Say" (Trethewey), **Supp. XXI:** 255

"What the Brand New Freeway Won't Go By" (Hugo), **Supp. VI:** 132–133

"What the Gypsies Told My Grandmother While She Was Still a Young Girl" (Simic), **Supp. VIII:** 283

"What the Prose Poem Carries with It" (R. Bly), **Supp. IV Part 1:** 64

"What They Wanted" (Dunn), **Supp. XI:** 151

What Thou Lovest Well (Hugo), **Supp. VI:** 140, 141

"What Thou Lovest Well Remains American" (Hugo), **Supp. VI:** 140, 141

What Time Collects (Farrell), **II:** 46, 47–48

What to Do? (Chernyshevsky), **Retro. Supp. I:** 269

"What to Keep, What to Discard" (Taggard), **Supp. XXII:** 280

"What to the Slave is Your Fourth of July?"(Douglass), **Supp. XXIII:** 167

What Use Are Flowers? (Hansberry), **Supp. IV Part 1:** 359, 368–369, 374

What Was Literature? (Fiedler), **Supp. XIII:** 96–97, **105–106**

What Was Mine (Beattie), **Supp. V:** 33, 35

What Was the Relationship of the Lone Ranger to the Means of Production? (Baraka), **Supp. II Part 1:** 58

"What We Came Through" (Goldbarth), **Supp. XII:** 179–180

"What Were the White Things?" (Hempel), **Supp. XXI:** 126

What We Talk About When We Talk About Love (Carver), **Supp. III Part 1:** 142–146; **Supp. XII:** 139

"What Why When How Who" (Pinsky), **Supp. VI:** 244

What Will Suffice: Contemporary American Poets on the Art of Poetry (Buckley and Young, eds.), **Supp. XIII:** 313

What Work Is (Levine), **Supp. V:** 181, 187, 192–193

"What You Hear from Em" (Taylor), **Supp. V:** 314, 320, 324

"What You Want" (O. Henry), **Supp. II Part 1:** 402

"What You Would Do" (Weigl), **Supp. XIX:** 288

Wheatley, Phillis, **Supp. XIII:** 111; **Supp. XVII:** 74–75; **Supp. XX: 106, 277–291**

Whedon, Tony, **Supp. XXI:** 131, 132

Wheeler, David, **Supp. XVI:** 277

Wheeler, John, **II:** 433

Wheeler, Monroe, **Supp. XV:** 295

Wheelock, John Hall, **IV:** 461; **Supp. IX:** 268; **Supp. XIV:** 120; **Supp. XV:** 301

Wheel of Life, The (Glasgow), **II:** 176, 178, 179, 183

Wheelwright, Philip, **Supp. XV:** 20

"When" (Olds), **Supp. X:** 207

When Boyhood Dreams Come True (Farrell), **II:** 45

"When Death Came April Twelve 1945" (Sandburg), **III:** 591, 593

"When Death Comes" (Oliver), **Supp. VII:** 241

"When De Co'n Pone's Hot" (Dunbar), **Supp. II Part 1:** 202 203

"When God First Said" (Zach; Everwine trans.), **Supp. XV:** 87

"When Grandma Died—1942" (Shields), **Supp. VII:** 311

"When Howitzers Began" (Carruth), **Supp. XVI:** 55

"When I Buy Pictures" (Moore), **III:** 205

"When I Came from Colchis" (Merwin), **Supp. III Part 1:** 343

"When I Have Fears I May Cease to Be" (Keats), **Supp. XIX:** 92

"When I Left Business for Literature" (Anderson), **I:** 101

"When I Love You" (Peacock), **Supp. XIX:** 199

"When in Rome—Apologia" (Komunyakaa), **Supp. XIII:** 120

"When It Comes" (Olds), **Supp. X:** 213

"When It's Clear and Hot" (Trethewey), **Supp. XXI:** 246

When I Was Alive (Notley), **Supp. XXII:** 228

"When I Was Alive" (Notley), **Supp. XXII:** 229

"When I Was Seventeen" (Kincaid), **Supp. VII:** 181

"When I Was Twenty-five" (Talese), **Supp. XVII:** 202

When Knighthood Was in Flower (Major), **III:** 320

"[When] Let by rain" (Taylor), **IV:** 160–161

"When Lilacs Last in the Dooryard Bloom'd" (Whitman), **IV:** 347–348, 351; **Retro. Supp. I:** 406; **Supp. IV Part 1:** 16; **Supp. XV:** 215

"When Malindy Sings" (Dunbar), **Supp. II Part 1:** 200, 204–205

When Peoples Meet: A Study of Race and Culture (Locke and Stern), **Supp. XIV:** 202, 213

When She Was Good (P. Roth), **Retro. Supp. II:** 282, 283, 284; **Supp. III Part 2:** 403, 405, 410–413

"When Sue Wears Red" (Hughes), **Retro. Supp. I:** 195, 204

"When the Acacia Blooms"(Crooker), **Supp. XXIII:** 60

"When the Dead Ask My Father about Me" (Olds), **Supp. X:** 210

"When the Frost Is on the Punkin" (Riley), **Supp. II Part 1:** 202

When the Jack Hollers (Hughes), **Retro. Supp. I:** 203; **Supp. I Part 1:** 328

"When the Last Riders" (Zach; Everwine, trans.), **Supp. XV:** 75, 86

"When the Light Gets Green" (Warren), **IV:** 252

"When the Model Does Not Show" (Major), **Supp. XXII:** 184

"When the Peace Corps Was Young" (Theroux), **Supp. VIII:** 314

When the Sun Tries to Go On (Koch), **Supp. XV:** 185

"When the Sun Tries to Go On" (Koch), **Supp. XV:** 179, 180

"When the World Ended as We Knew It" (Harjo), **Supp. XII:** 231

When Time Was Born (Farrell), **II:** 46, 47

"When We Dead Awaken: Writing as Re-Vision" (Rich), **Supp. I Part 2:** 552–553, 560

"When We Gonna Rise" (Baraka), **Supp. II Part 1:** 48

"When We Have To" (Salinas), **Supp. XIII:** 322–323

"WHEN WE'LL WORSHIP JESUS" (Baraka), **Supp. II Part 1:** 54

"When We Sold the Tent" (Espaillat), **Supp. XXI:** 102

"When we speak of God, is it God we speak of?" (J. Logan), **Supp. XVII:** 113

"When Women Throw Down Bundles: Strong Women Make Strong Nations" (Gunn Allen), **Supp. IV Part 1:** 328

"'When You Finally See Them': The Unconquered Eye in *To Kill a Mockingbird*" (Champion), **Supp. VIII:** 128

"When You Lie Down, the Sea Stands Up" (Swenson), **Supp. IV Part 2:** 643

"Where Blue Is Blue" (Richard), **Supp. XIX:** 221

Where Does One Go When There's No Place Left to Go? (Crews), **Supp. XI:** 103

"Where Go the Boats" (R. Stevenson), **Supp. XVII:** 69

Where Horizons Go (Espaillat), **Supp. XXI:** 99, 103, 104

"Where I Come from Is Like This" (Gunn Allen), **Supp. IV Part 1:** 319

"Where I'm Calling From" (Carver), **Supp. III Part 1:** 145

Where I'm Calling From: New and Selected Stories (Carver), **Supp. III Part 1:** 138, 148

"Where I Ought to Be" (Erdrich), **Supp. IV Part 1:** 265

Where Is My Wandering Boy Tonight? (Wagoner), **Supp. IX: 335–336**

"Where Is the Island?" (Francis), **Supp. IX:** 78

"Where Is the Voice Coming From?" (Welty), **IV:** 280; **Retro. Supp. I:** 355

Where Joy Resides (Isherwood), **Supp. XIV:** 156

"Where Knock Is Open Wide" (Roethke), **III:** 533–535

"Where My Sympathy Lies" (H. Roth), **Supp. IX:** 234

Where's My Money? (Shanley), **Supp. XIV:** 316, 328, **330–331**

Where the Bluebird Sings to the Lemonade Springs (Stegner), **Supp. IV Part 2:** 596, 597, 598, 600, 604, 606, 613; **Supp. XXII:** 205

"Where the Bones Move" (W. V. Davis), **Supp. XXI:** 92

Where the Cross Is Made (O'Neill), **III:** 388, 391

Where the Rivers Flow North (Mosher), **Supp. XXII:** 205, 207, 208, **210–212**

"Where the Rivers Flow North" (Mosher), **Supp. XXII:** 204, 206, 207, 208, 209, **210–211**

Where the Sea Used to Be (Bass), **Supp. XVI:** 21

"Where the Sea Used to Be" (Bass), **Supp. XVI:** 20, 21

"*Where the Sea Used to Be*: Rick Bass and the Novel of Ecological Education" (Dixon), **Supp. XVI:** 21

"Where the Soft Air Lives" (Nye), **Supp. XIII:** 275

Where the Twilight Never Ends (Haines), **Supp. XII:** 211

Where the Wild Grape Grows: Selected Writings, 1930–1950 (D. West; Mitchell and Davis, eds.), **Supp. XVIII:** 283, 286

Where the Wild Things Are (Sendak), **Supp. IX:** 207

"Wherever Home Is" (Wright), **Supp. III Part 2:** 605, 606

Where Water Comes Together With Other Water (Carver), **Supp. III Part 1:** 147, 148

"Where We Crashed" (Hugo), **Supp. VI:** 138

"Where We Must Look for Help" (R. Bly), **Supp. XXI:** 84

"Where You Are" (Doty), **Supp. XI:** 131

Where You'll Find Me, and Other Stories (Beattie), **Supp. V:** 30–31

Whicher, Stephen, **II:** 20

"Which Is More Than I Can Say for Some People" (Moore), **Supp. X:** 177, 178

Which Ones Are the Enemy? (Garrett), **Supp. VII:** 98

"Which Theatre Is the Absurd One?" (Albee), **I:** 71

"Which Way to the Future?" (Rehder), **Supp. IV Part 1:** 69

While I Was Gone (Miller), **Supp. XII:** 290, **301–303**

"While Seated in a Plane" (Swenson), **Supp. IV Part 2:** 645

While the Messiah Tarries (Bukiet), **Supp. XVII:** 43, **46–47**

While We've Still Got Feet (Budbill), **Supp. XIX:** 5, 7, **10–11**, 15

Whilomville Stories (Crane), **I:** 414

"Whip, The" (Robinson), **III:** 513

Whipple, Thomas K., **II:** 456, 458; **IV:** 427

"Whippoorwill, The" (Francis), **Supp. IX:** 90

"Whip-poor-will, The" (Thurber), **Supp. I Part 2:** 616

Whirlpool (film, Preminger), **Supp. XVII:** 62

"Whispering Gallery, The" (Komunyakaa), **Supp. XIII:** 132

"Whispering Leaves" (Glasgow), **II:** 190

Whispering to Fool the Wind (Ríos), **Supp. IV Part 2:** 540–541, 544, 545

"Whispers in the Next Room" (Simic), **Supp. VIII:** 278

"Whispers of Heavenly Death" (Whitman), **IV:** 348

"Whispers of Immortality" (Eliot), **Supp. XI:** 242

Whistle (Jones), **Supp. XI:** 219, 224, **231–234**

"Whistle, The" (Franklin), **II:** 121

"Whistle, The" (Komunyakaa), **Supp. XIII:** 111, 126

"Whistle, The" (Welty), **IV:** 262

Whistler, James, **I:** 484; **III:** 461, 465, 466; **IV:** 77, 369

Whistler, James Abbott McNeill, **Supp. XIV:** 335–336

"Whistling Dick's Christmas Stocking" (O. Henry), **Supp. II Part 1:** 390, 392

Whistling in the Dark (Garrett), **Supp. VII:** 111

Whistling in the Dark: True Stories and Other Fables (Garrett), **Supp. VII:** 95

Whitcher, Frances Miriam Berry, **Supp. XIII:** 152

"White" (Simic), **Supp. VIII: 275–276**

White, Barbara, **Retro. Supp. I:** 379

White, Dana, **Supp. XXII:** 251

White, E. B., **Retro. Supp. I:** 335; **Supp. I Part 2:** 602, 607, 608, 612, 619, 620, **651–681; Supp. II Part 1:** 143; **Supp. VIII:** 171; **Supp. IX:** 20, 32; **Supp. XVI:** 167

White, Elizabeth Wade, **Supp. I Part 1:** 100, 103, 111

White, Henry Kirke, **Supp. I Part 1:** 150

White, James L., **Supp. XI:** 123

White, Joel, **Supp. I Part 2:** 654, 678

White, Katharine. (Katharine Sergeant Angell), **Supp. I Part 2:** 610, 653, 655, 656, 669; **Supp. VIII:** 151, 171

White, Lillian, **Supp. I Part 2:** 651

White, Lucia, **I:** 258

White, Maria. *See* Lowell, Mrs. James Russell (Maria White)

White, Morton, **I:** 258; **Supp. I Part 2:** 647, 648, 650

White, Roberta, **Supp. XII:** 293

White, Stanford, **Supp. IV Part 1:** 223

White, Stanley, **Supp. I Part 2:** 651, 655

White, T. H., **III:** 522

White, T. W., **III:** 411, 415

White, Walter, **Supp. I Part 1:** 345; **Supp. XVIII:** 123, 127; **Supp. XIX:** 73

White, William, **Retro. Supp. II:** 326

White, William A., **I:** 252

White Album, The (Didion), **Supp. IV Part 1:** 198, 202, 205–207, 210

"White Album, The" (Didion), **Supp. IV Part 1:** 205, 206

"White Angel" (Cunningham), **Supp. XV:** 59

"White Apache" (Markson), **Supp. XVII:** 136

White Boys (McKnight), **Supp. XX: 155–157**

"White Boys, The" (McKnight), **Supp. XX: 155–157**

White Buildings (H. Crane), **I:** 385, 386, 390–395, 400; **Retro. Supp. II:** 77–78, **80–81,** 82, 83, 85

White Butterfly (Mosley), **Supp. XIII:** 237, 238, 240

White Center (Hugo), **Supp. VI:** 144–145

"White Center" (Hugo), **Supp. VI:** 144, 146

Whited, Stephen, **Supp. XI:** 135

White Deer, The (Thurber), **Supp. I Part 2:** 606

White Doves at Morning (Burke), **Supp. XIV:** 22–23, 32, 35–36

"White Eagle, The" (Chopin), **Retro. Supp. II:** 72

White Fang (London), **II:** 471–472, 481

Whitefield, George, **I:** 546; **Supp. XX: 280**

White-Footed Deer and Other Poems (Bryant), **Supp. I Part 1:** 157

White Goddess, The (Graves), **Supp. IV Part 1:** 280

White-Haired Lover (Shapiro), **Supp. II Part 2:** 703, 717

Whitehead, Alfred North, **III:** 605, 619, 620; **IV:** 88; **Supp. I Part 2:** 554, 647

Whitehead, Mrs. Catherine, **IV:** 116

Whitehead, Colson, **Supp. XIII:** 233, 241

Whitehead, James, **Supp. XV:** 339

Whitehead, Margaret, **IV:** 114, 115, 116

Whitehead, William, **Supp. XX: 50–51, 53**

White Heat (Walsh), **Supp. XIII:** 174

"White Heron, A" (Jewett), **II:** 409; **Retro. Supp. II:** 17

White Heron and Other Stories, A (Jewett), **II:** 396

White Horses (Hoffman), **Supp. X: 83–85,** 90, 92

White House Diary, A (Lady Bird Johnson), **Supp. IV Part 1:** 22

White-Jacket; or, The World in a Man-of-War (Melville), **III:** 80, 81, 84, 94; **Retro Supp. I:** 248, 249, 254; **Supp. XVIII:** 7, 9

White Lantern, The (Connell), **Supp. XIV:** 97

"White Lies" (Trethewey), **Supp. XXI:** 244, 246, 251

"White Lights, The" (Robinson), **III:** 524

"White Lilies, The" (Glück), **Supp. V:** 88

White Man, Listen! (Wright), **IV:** 478, 488, 489, 494

"White Mulberry Tree, The" (Cather), **I:** 319; **Retro. Supp. I:** 7, 9, 17

White Mule (W. C. Williams), **Retro. Supp. I:** 423

"White Negro, The" (Mailer), **III:** 36–37; **Retro. Supp. II:** 202

"Whiteness of the Whale, The" (Melville), **III:** 84, 86

"White Night" (Oliver), **Supp. VII:** 236

"White Nights" (Auster), **Supp. XII:** 23–24

White Noise (DeLillo), **Supp. VI:** 1, 3–4, 5–7, 10, 11–12, 16; **Supp. XVIII:** 140; **Supp. XX: 91**

White Oxen and Other Stories, The (Burke), **I:** 269, 271

White Paper on Contemporary American Poetry (McClatchy), **Supp. XII:** 253, **259–260**

"White Phosphorous" (Notley), **Supp. XXII:** 232, 233

"White Pine" (Oliver), **Supp. VII:** 244

White Pine: Poems and Prose Poems (Oliver), **Supp. VII:** 243–246

White Poems, The (Crooker), **Supp. XXIII: 54–55**

White Sail (Sorrentino), **Supp. XXI:** 228

"White Silence, The" (London), **II:** 468

"White Silk" (Nye), **Supp. XIII:** 275

"White Snake, The" (Sexton), **Supp. II Part 2:** 691

"White Spot" (Anderson), **I:** 116

"White-Tailed Hornet, The" (Frost), **Retro. Supp. I:** 138

"White Trash Cowboys of *Father and Son,* The" (Bjerre), **Supp. XXI:** 41

Whitfield, Raoul, **Supp. IV Part 1:** 345

Whitfield, Stephen J., **Supp. XX: 243, 244**

Whitlock, Brand, **II:** 276

Whitman (Masters), **Supp. I Part 2:** 473, 475, 476

Whitman, George, **IV:** 346, 350

Whitman, Ruth, **Supp. XXI:** 246

Whitman, Sarah Wyman, **Retro. Supp. II:** 136

Whitman, Walt, **I:** 61, 68, 98, 103, 104, 109, 219, 220, 227, 228, 242, 246, 250, 251, 260, 261, 285, 381, 384, 386, 396, 397, 398, 402, 419, 430, 459, 460, 483, 485, 486, 577; **II:** 7, 8, 18, 127, 140, 273–274, 275, 289, 295, 301, 320, 321, 373, 445, 446, 451, 457, 494, 529, 530, 552; **III:** 171, 175, 177, 181–182, 189, 203, 234, 260, 426, 430, 453, 454, 461, 505, 507–508, 511, 528, 548, 552, 555, 559, 567, 572, 576, 577, 579, 584, 585, 595, 606, 609; **IV:** 74, 169, 191, 192, 202, **331–354,** 405, 409, 416, 444, 450–451, 457, 463, 464, 469, 470, 471; **Retro. Supp. I:** 8, 52, 194, 254, 283, 284, 333, **387–410,** 412, 417, 427; **Retro. Supp. II:** 40, 76, 93, 99, 155, 156, 158, 170, 262; **Supp. I Part 1:** 6, 79, 167, 311, 314, 325, 365, 368, 372; **Supp. I Part 2:** 374, 384, 385, 387, 389, 391, 393, 399, 416, 436, 455, 456, 458, 473, 474, 475, 525, 540, 579, 580, 582, 682, 691; **Supp. III Part 1:** 6, 20, 156, 239–241, 253, 340; **Supp. III Part 2:** 596; **Supp. IV Part 1:** 16, 169, 325; **Supp. IV Part 2:** 597, 625; **Supp. V:** 113, 118, 122, 130, 170, 178, 183, 277, 279, 332; **Supp. VIII:** 42, 95, 105, 126, 198, 202, 269; **Supp. IX:** 8, 9, 15, 38, 41, 44, 48, 53, 131, 292, 298, 299, 308, 320; **Supp. X:** 36, 112, 203, 204; **Supp. XI:** 83, 123, 132, 135, 203, 321; **Supp. XII:** 132, 185, 190, 256; **Supp. XIII:** 1, 77, 115, 153, 221, 304, 335; **Supp. XIV:** 89, 312, 334, 335, 338; **Supp. XV:** 41, 93, 181, 183, 212, 213, 218, 250, 275, 301, 302, 303, 309, 352; **Supp. XVI:** 209; **Supp. XVII:** 42, 71, 112, 133; **Supp. XVIII:** 4, 194, 196, 304; **Supp. XIX:** 118, 276; **Supp. XX: 69, 115, 116, 221;**

Supp. XXI: 169, 217, 227, 256; **Supp. XXII:** 81, 82, 86, 92; **Supp. XXIII:** 19, 109, 166, 207

"Whitman Pinch Hits, 1861" (Skloot), **Supp. XX: 203**

"Whitman: The Poet and the Mask" (Cowley), **Supp. II Part 1:** 143

Whitmarsh, Jason, **Supp. VIII:** 283

Whitmer, Peter, **Supp. X:** 264, 265

Whitney, Blair, **Supp. I Part 2:** 403

Whitney, Josiah, **Supp. IX:** 180, 181

Whitt, Margaret Earley, **Retro. Supp. II:** 226

Whittemore, Reed, **III:** 268; **Supp. XI:** 315

Whittier, Elizabeth, **Supp. I Part 2:** 700, 701, 703; **Supp. XIII:** 141, 142

Whittier, John Greenleaf, **I:** 216; **II:** 275; **III:** 52; **Retro. Supp. I:** 54; **Retro. Supp. II:** 155, 163, 169; **Supp. I Part 1:** 168, 299, 313, 317, 372; **Supp. I Part 2:** 420, 602, **682–707**; **Supp. VIII:** 202, 204; **Supp. XI:** 50; **Supp. XIII:** 140, 145; **Supp. XV:** 246; **Supp. XXIII:** 156

Whittier, Mary, **Supp. I Part 2:** 683

"Whittier Birthday Speech" (Twain), **Supp. I Part 1:** 313

"Who" (Kenyon), **Supp. VII:** 174

"Who" (Sobin), **Supp. XVI:** 284–285

"Who Am I—Who I Am" (Corso), **Supp. XII:** 134

"Who Be Kind To" (Ginsberg), **Supp. II Part 1:** 323

Who Do You Love (Thompson), **Supp. XXIII:** 289, **295–296**

"Whoever Was Using This Bed" (Carver), **Supp. III Part 1:** 148

"Whoever You Are Holding Me Now in Hand" (Whitman), **IV:** 342; **Retro. Supp. I:** 52

Who Gathered and Whispered behind Me (Goldbarth), **Supp. XII:** 181, 182

"Who in One Lifetime" (Rukeyser), **Supp. VI:** 276, 279

Who Is Witter Bynner? (Kraft), **Supp. XV:** 40, 52

"Who Is Your Mother? Red Roots of White Feminism" (Gunn Allen), **Supp. IV Part 1:** 329

Whole Hog (Wagoner), **Supp. IX: 337–338**

"Whole Mess…Almost, The" (Corso), **Supp. XII:** 135

"Whole Moisty Night, The" (R. Bly), **Supp. IV Part 1:** 69

Whole New Life, A (Price), **Supp. VI:** 265, **266**, 267

"Whole Self, The" (Nye), **Supp. XIII:** 275

"Whole Soul, The" (Levine), **Supp. V:** 192

"Whole Story, The" (Strand), **Supp. IV Part 2:** 622

Whole Town's Talking, The (Loos), **Supp. XVI:** 187

"Whole World Knows, The" (Welty), **IV:** 272; **Retro. Supp. I:** 343

Who'll Stop the Rain (film), **Supp. V:** 301

Who Lost an American? (Algren), **Supp. IX: 15–16**

Who Owns America? (symposium), **Supp. XIV:** 4

"Who Puts Together" (Hogan), **Supp. IV Part 1:** 403, 405, 412–413

"Whore of Mensa, The" (Allen), **Supp. XV:** 15

Whores for Gloria (Vollmann), **Supp. XVII:** 226, 230

Whorf, Benjamin Lee, **Supp. XVI:** 283

Who's Afraid? (Holding), **Supp. XXII:** 120, **125–126**

Who's Afraid of Virginia Woolf? (Albee), **I:** 71, 77–81, 83, 85, 86, 87, 94; **IV:** 230

Who Shall Be the Sun? Poems Based on the Lore, Legends, and Myths of the Northwest Coast and Plateau Indians (Wagoner), **Supp. IX:** 328, **329–330**, 337

"Whosis Kid, The" (Hammett), **Supp. IV Part 1:** 344

"Who Sit Watch in Daylight" (Wright), **Supp. XV:** 342

"Who's Passing for Who?" (Hughes), **Supp. I Part 1:** 330

"Who Speak on the Page?" (Sanders), **Supp. XVI:** 278

Who Will Run the Frog Hospital?: A Novel (Moore), **Supp. X:** 163, 165, 169, **175–177**

Who Wrote the Book of Love? (Siegel), **Supp. XXII: 265–267**, 267

Why Are We in Vietnam? (Mailer), **III:** 27, 29, 30, 33, 34–35, 39, 42, 44; **Retro. Supp. II:** 205–206

"Why Bother?" (Franzen). *See* "Perchance to Dream" (Franzen)

"Why China?" (Egan), **Supp. XIX:** 51, 52

"Why Did the Balinese Chicken Cross the Road?" (Walker), **Supp. III Part 2:** 527

"Why Do the Heathens Rage?" (O'Connor), **III:** 351

"Why Do You Write About Russia?" (Simpson), **Supp. IX:** 277

"Why I Am a Danger to the Public" (Kingsolver), **Supp. VII:** 204

Why I Am Not a Christian (Russell), **Supp. I Part 2:** 522

"Why I Am Not a Painter" (O'Hara), **Supp. XXIII:** 208

Why I Came to Judevine (Budbill), **Supp. XIX:** 2, **7–8**, 15

"Why I Do Not Wish to Float in Space" (Schott), **Supp. XXIII:** 251

"Why I Entered the Gurdjieff Work" (Toomer), **Supp. III Part 2:** 481

"Why I Like Laurel" (Patchett), **Supp. XII:** 309

"Why I Live at the P.O." (Welty), **IV:** 262; **Retro. Supp. I:** 345

"Why I Make Sam Go to Church" (Lamott), **Supp. XX: 141**

"Why Is Economics Not an Evolutionary Science?" (Veblen), **Supp. I Part 2:** 634

"Why I Write" (Didion), **Supp. IV Part 1:** 201, 203

"Why I Wrote *Phil:* An Exclusive Essay for Amazon.com" (Saunders), **Supp. XIX:** 230–231

Why Johnny Can't Read: And What You Can Do About It (Flesch), **Supp. XVI:** 105

"Why Negro Women Leave Home" (Brooks), **Supp. III Part 1:** 75

Why Poetry Matters (Parini), **Supp. XIX:** 120, 129

"Why Resign from the Human Race?" (Swados), **Supp. XIX:** 265

"Why the Little Frenchman Wears His Hand in a Sling" (Poe), **III:** 425

"Why We Are Forgiven" (Weigl), **Supp. XIX:** 282–283

Why We Behave Like Microbe Hunters (Thurber), **Supp. I Part 2:** 606

Why We Were in Vietnam (Podhoretz), **Supp. VIII:** 241

"Why Write?" (Updike), **Retro. Supp. I:** 317

"Wichita Vortex Sutra" (Ginsberg), **Supp. II Part 1:** 319, 321, 323–325, 327

Wickenden, Dorothy, **Supp. XXIII:** 291

Wickes, George, **Supp. XIV:** 165

Wickford Point (Marquand), **III:** 50, 58, 64–65, 69

Wicks, Robert Russell, **Supp. XII:** 49

Wide, Wide World, The (S. Warner as Wetherell), **Supp. XV:** 275; **Supp. XVIII:** 257, 260, **262–264**, 265

Wide Blue Yonder (Thompson), **Supp. XXIII:** 289, **296–298**

"Wide Empty Landscape with a Death in the Foreground" (Momaday), **Supp. IV Part 2:** 492

Wideman, John Edgar, **Retro. Supp. II:** 123; **Supp. X:** 239, 250, **319–336**; **Supp. XI:** 245; **Supp. XIII:** 247; **Supp. XVIII:** 89; **Supp. XXI:** 246

Widener, Jeff, **Supp. XVIII:** 91

"Wideness" (Pickering), **Supp. XXI:** 203

"Wide Net, The" (Welty), **IV:** 266

Wide Net and Other Stories, The (Welty), **IV:** 261, 264–266, 271; **Retro. Supp. I: 347–349**, 352, 355

Widening Spell of the Leaves, The (Levis), **Supp. XI:** 258, 259, 261, **268–269**, 271

"Wide Prospect, The" (Jarrell), **II:** 376–377

Wide Sargasso Sea (Rhys), **Supp. XVIII:** 131

"Widow" (Peacock), **Supp. XIX:** 206

"Widower" (Robison), **Supp. XXI:** 118

Widow for One Year, A (Irving), **Supp. VI:** 165, **179–181**

Widow's Mite (Holding), **Supp. XXII: 136**

Widows of Thornton, The (Taylor), **Supp. V:** 320, 321

"Widow's Wish, The" (Briggs), **Supp. XVIII:** 15

Wieland; or, The Transformation. An American Tale (Brown), **Supp. I Part 1:** 128–132, 133, 137, 140

Wiene, Robert, **Retro. Supp. I:** 268

Wiener, John, **Supp. IV Part 1:** 153
Wieners, John, **Supp. II Part 1:** 32; **Supp. XXIII:** 215
Wiesel, Elie, **Supp. XVII:** 47, 48, 49
Wiest, Dianne, **Supp. XV:** 12
"Wife, Forty-five, Remembers Love, A" (Shields), **Supp. VII:** 310
"Wifebeater, The" (Sexton), **Supp. II Part 2:** 693
"Wife for Dino Rossi, A" (Fante), **Supp. XI:** 165
"Wife of His Youth, The" (Chesnutt), **Supp. XIV: 63–66**
Wife of His Youth and Other Stories of the Color Line, The (Chesnutt), **Supp. XIV:** 62, 63
"Wife of Jesus Speaks, The" (Karr), **Supp. XI:** 250–251
"Wife of Nashville, A" (Taylor), **Supp. V:** 320
"Wife's Story, The" (R. H. Davis), **Supp. XVI:** 85, 91, 92–93
Wife's Story, The (Shields), **Supp. VII:** 316. *See also* Happenstance
"Wife-Wooing" (Updike), **IV:** 226
Wigan, Gareth, **Supp. XI:** 306
Wiget, Andrew, **Supp. IV Part 2:** 509
Wigglesworth, Michael, **IV:** 147, 156; **Supp. I Part 1:** 110, 111
Wilbur, Richard, **III:** 527; **Retro. Supp. II:** 50; **Supp. III Part 1:** 64; **Supp. III Part 2: 541–565; Supp. IV Part 2:** 626, 634, 642; **Supp. V:** 337; **Supp. VIII:** 28; **Supp. X:** 58, 120; **Supp. XII:** 258; **Supp. XIII:** 76, 336; **Supp. XV:** 51, 251, 256; **Supp. XVII:** 26; **Supp. XVIII:** 178; **Supp. XX: 199; Supp. XXI:** 247
Wilcocks, Alexander, **Supp. I Part 1:** 125
Wilcox, Ella Wheeler, **Supp. II Part 1:** 197
Wilcox, Kirstin, **Supp. XX:** 283, 284, 285
Wild, John, **II:** 362, 363–364
Wild, Peter, **Supp. V:** 5
Wild, Robert, **IV:** 155
"Wild, The" (Berry), **Supp. X:** 30
Wild 90 (film) (Mailer), **Retro. Supp. II:** 205
Wild and Woolly (film), **Supp. XVI:** 185
Wild Boy of Aveyron, The (Itard). *See* De l'éducation d'un homme sauvage
Wild Boys, The: A Book of the Dead (Burroughs), **Supp. III Part 1:** 106–107
Wild Card Quilt: Taking A chance on Home (Ray), **Supp. XVIII:** 189, 192, 193, 196, 198, **200–202,** 204
Wilde, Oscar, **I:** 50, 66, 381, 384; **II:** 515; **IV:** 77, 350; **Retro. Supp. I:** 56, 102, 227; **Retro. Supp. II:** 76, 326; **Supp. IV Part 2:** 578, 679, 683; **Supp. V:** 106, 283; **Supp. IX:** 65, 66, 68, 189, 192; **Supp. X:** 148, 151, 188–189; **Supp. XIV:** 324, 334; **Supp. XV:** 350
Wilder, Amos Parker, **IV:** 356
Wilder, Mrs. Amos Parker (Isabella Thornton Niven), **IV:** 356
Wilder, Billy, **Supp. IV Part 1:** 130; **Supp. XI:** 307
Wilder, Isabel, **IV:** 357, 366, 375

Wilder, Laura Ingalls, **Supp. XXI:** 2; **Supp. XXII: 289–303**
Wilder, Thornton, **I:** 360, 482; **IV: 355–377,** 431; **Retro. Supp. I:** 109, 359; **Supp. I Part 2:** 609; **Supp. IV Part 2:** 586; **Supp. V:** 105; **Supp. IX:** 140; **Supp. XII:** 236–237; **Supp. XX:** 50
"Wilderness" (Leopold), **Supp. XIV:** 190
Wilderness (Parker), **Supp. XIX:** 177, **188–189**
"Wilderness" (Sandburg), **III:** 584, 595
Wilderness (Warren), **IV:** 256
"Wilderness, The" (Merwin), **Supp. III Part 1:** 340, 345
"Wilderness, The" (Robinson), **III:** 524
Wilderness of Vision, The: On the Poetry of John Haines (Bezner and Walzer, eds.), **Supp. XII:** 202
Wilderness Plots: Tales about the Settlement of the American Land (Sanders), **Supp. XVI:** 267–268, 269
"Wilderness"(Thompson), **Supp. XXIII:** 301
Wilderness World of Anne LaBastille, The (LaBastille), **Supp. X: 105,** 106
Wild Flag, The (White), **Supp. I Part 2:** 654
"Wildflower, The" (W. C. Williams), **Retro. Supp. I:** 420
"Wild Flowers" (Caldwell), **I:** 310
"Wildflowers" (Minot), **Supp. VI:** 208
"Wild Geese" (Oliver), **Supp. VII:** 237
"Wild Honey Suckle, The" (Freneau), **Supp. II Part 1:** 253, 264, 266
Wild in the Country (Odets), **Supp. II Part 2:** 546
"Wild in the Woods" (Skloot), **Supp. XX:** 206
Wild Iris, The (Glück), **Supp. V:** 79, 87–89, 91
Wildlife (Ford), **Supp. V:** 57, 69–71
Wildlife in America (Matthiessen), **Supp. V:** 199, 201, 204
"Wildlife in American Culture" (Leopold), **Supp. XIV:** 190, 191
"Wild Light" (Skloot), **Supp. XX: 200**
Wild Man, The (P. N. Warren), **Supp. XX: 260, 270–272**
"Wildness" (Sanders), **Supp. XVI:** 276
Wild Old Wicked Man, The (MacLeish), **III:** 3, 20
Wild Palms, The (Faulkner), **II:** 68–69; **Retro. Supp. I:** 85
"Wild Palms, The" (Faulkner), **II:** 68
"Wild Peaches" (Wylie), **Supp. I Part 2:** 707, 712
Wild Roses of Cape Ann and Other Poems (Larcom), **Supp. XIII:** 142, 147
Wild Seed (O. Butler), **Supp. XIII:** 62, 63
"Wild Swans at Coole, The " (W. B. Yeats), **Supp. XVI:** 48
"Wild Swans at Norfolk, The" (Carruth), **Supp. XVI:** 48
"Wild Thing" (L. Brown), **Supp. XXI:** 44
Wild Thorn (Hoffman), **Supp. XVIII: 84–85**
Wild to the Heart (Bass), **Supp. XVI:** 16

"Wild Turkeys: Dignity of the Damned" (B. Kelly), **Supp. XVII:** 129
"Wildwest" (MacLeish), **III:** 14
Wiley, Catherine, **Supp. XXIII:** 199
Wiley, Craig, **Supp. VIII:** 313
Wilhelm Meister (Goethe), **II:** 291
Wilkes, John, **Supp. I Part 2:** 503, 519, 522
Wilkie, Curtis, **Supp. V:** 11
Wilkins, Roy, **Supp. I Part 1:** 345
Wilkinson, Alec, **Supp. VIII:** 164, 168, 171
Wilkinson, Max, **Supp. IX:** 251
Will, The (Swados), **Supp. XIX: 265–266**
Willard, Nancy, **Supp. XIX:** 138
Willard, Samuel, **IV:** 150
Willard Gibbs (Rukeyser), **Supp. VI:** 273, 283, 284
Willcutts, Tim, **Supp. XVII:** 239, 241, 246
Willett, Ralph, **Supp. XIV:** 27
Willey, Basil, **Retro. Supp. II:** 243
"William Butler Yeats Among the Ghosts" (Skloot), **Supp. XX:** 204–205
William Carlos Williams (Koch), **Retro. Supp. I:** 428
William Carlos Williams: An American Artist (Breslin), **Retro. Supp. I:** 430
William Carlos Williams and Alterity (Ahearn), **Retro. Supp. I:** 415
William Carlos Williams and the Meanings of Measure (Cushman), **Retro. Supp. I:** 430
William Carlos Williams: The American Background (Weaver), **Retro. Supp. I:** 430
William Faulkner: A Critical Study (Howe), **Supp. VI:** 119–120, 125
William Faulkner: Early Prose and Poetry (Faulkner), **Retro. Supp. I:** 80
William Faulkner: First Encounters (Brooks), **Supp. XIV:** 13
"William Faulkner's Legend of the South" (Cowley), **Supp. II Part 1:** 143
"William Faulkner: The Stillness of *Light in August*" (Kazin), *Supp. VIII:* 104
William Faulkner: The Yoknapatawpha Country (Brooks), **Supp. XIV: 12–13,** 16
William Faulkner: Toward Yoknapatawpha and Beyond (Brooks), **Supp. XIV:** 13
"William Humphrey, 73, Writer of Novels about Rural Texas" (Gussow), **Supp. IX:** 93
William Humphrey, Destroyer of Myths (Almon), **Supp. IX:** 93
William Humphrey. Boise State University Western Writers Series (Winchell), **Supp. IX:** 109
"William Humphrey Remembered" (Masters), **Supp. IX:** 96
William Humphrey. Southwestern Series (Lee), **Supp. IX:** 109
"William Ireland's Confession" (A. Miller), **III:** 147–148

William James and Phenomenology: A Study of the "Principles of Psychology" (Wilshire), **II:** 362
William Lloyd Garrison (Chapman), **Supp. XIV:** 46–51, 52, 53, 55
William Maxwell Portrait, A: Memories and Appreciations (C. Baxter, Collier, and Hirsch, eds.), **Supp. XVII:** 23
Williams, Annie Laurie, **Supp. IX:** 93
Williams, Blanch Colton, **Supp. XVIII:** 279
Williams, Cecil, **II:** 508
Williams, Charles, **Supp. II Part 1:** 15, 16
Williams, C. K., **Supp. XIII:** 114; **Supp. XVII:** 112
Williams, Cratis, **Supp. XX: 163**
Williams, Dakin, **IV:** 379
Williams, David Reichard, **Supp. XIII:** 162
Williams, Edward, **IV:** 404
Williams, Edwina Dakin, **IV:** 379
Williams, Eric, **Supp. XXI:** 166, 170, 171
Williams, Esther, **Supp. XII:** 165
Williams, Fannie Barrier, **Supp. XIV:** 201
Williams, Garth, **Supp. XXII:** 301
Williams, George, **Supp. V:** 220
Williams, Henry Sylvester, **Supp. XXI:** 166
Williams, Horace, **IV:** 453
Williams, Joan, **Supp. IX:** 95
Williams, John A., **Supp. XVI:** 143
Williams, John Alexander, **Supp. XXIII:** 39
Williams, John Sharp, **IV:** 378
Williams, Jonathan, **Supp. XXII:** 168
Williams, Kenny J., **Supp. XX: 281, 286**
Williams, Lyle, **Supp. XIV:** 22
Williams, Michael, **Supp. V:** 286
Williams, Miller, **Supp. XIV:** 126; **Supp. XV:** 339; **Supp. XVIII:** 177
Williams, Paul, **IV:** 404
Williams, Raymond, **Supp. IX:** 146
Williams, Roger, **Supp. I Part 2:** 699; **Supp. XXIII:** 15
Williams, Rose, **IV:** 379
Williams, Sherley Anne, **Supp. V:** 180
Williams, Solomon, **I:** 549
Williams, Stanley T., **II:** 301, 316; **Supp. I Part 1:** 251
Williams, Stephen, **IV:** 148
Williams, Ted, **IV:** 216; **Supp. IX:** 162
Williams, Tennessee, **I:** 73, 81, 113, 211; **II:** 190, 194; **III:** 145, 147; **IV:** 4, **378–401; Supp. I Part 1:** 290, 291; **Supp. IV Part 1:** 79, 83, 84, 359; **Supp. IV Part 2:** 574, 682; **Supp. IX:** 133; **Supp. XI:** 103; **Supp. XIII:** 331; **Supp. XIV:** 250, 315; **Supp. XVI:** 194
Williams, Terry Tempest, **Supp. XIII:** 16; **Supp. XVIII:** 189
Williams, Walter L., **Supp. IV Part 1:** 330, 331
Williams, William, **IV:** 404, 405
Williams, William Carlos, **I:** 61, 62, 229, 255, 256, 261, 285, 428, 438, 446, 539; **II:** 133, 536, 542, 543, 544, 545; **III:** 194, 196, 198, 214, 269, 409, 453, 457, 458, 464, 465, 591; **IV:** 30, 74, 75, 76, 94, 95, 286, 287, **402–425; Retro. Supp. I:** 51, 52, 62, 209, 284, 285, 288, 296, 298, 411, **411–433; Retro. Supp. II:** 178, 181, 189, 250, 321, 322, 326, 327, 328, 334, 335; **Supp. I Part 1:** 254, 255, 259, 266; **Supp. II Part 1:** 9, 30, 308, 318; **Supp. II Part 2:** 421, 443; **Supp. III Part 1:** 9, 147, 239, 271, 275, 276, 278, 350; **Supp. III Part 2:** 542, 610, 613, 614, 615, 616, 617, 621, 622, 626, 628; **Supp. IV Part 1:** 151, 153, 246, 325; **Supp. V:** 180, 337; **Supp. VIII:** 195, 269, 272, 277, 292; **Supp. IX:** 38, 268, 291; **Supp. X:** 112, 120, 204; **Supp. XI:** 311, 328; **Supp. XII:** 198; **Supp. XIII:** 77, 90, 335; **Supp. XIV:** 280, 284, 285, 293; **Supp. XV:** 42, 51, 182, 250, 306, 307; **Supp. XVI:** 48, 282; **Supp. XVII:** 36, 113, 227, 243; **Supp. XIX:** 1, 42, 117, 119, 121; **Supp. XXI:** 226, 227, 230, 233; **Supp. XXII:** 162, 165, 168, 226, 227, 228; **Supp. XXIII:** 164, 207, 211
Williams, Mrs. William Carlos (Florence Herman), **IV:** 404
Williams, Wirt, **Supp. XIV:** 24
Williamson, Alan, **Retro. Supp. II:** 185; **Supp. XIX:** 91
Williamson, J. W., **Supp. XX: 164**
William Styron's Nat Turner: Ten Black Writers Respond (Clarke, ed.), **IV:** 115
Williams-Walsh, Mary Ellen, **Supp. IV Part 2:** 611
William the Conqueror, **Supp. I Part 2:** 507
William Wetmore Story and His Friends (James), **Retro. Supp. I:** 235; **Supp. XX:** 228
William Wilson (Gardner), **Supp. VI:** 72
"William Wilson" (Poe), **II:** 475; **III:** 410, 412; **Retro. Supp. II:** 269; **Supp. IX:** 105
"Willie" (Angelou), **Supp. IV Part 1:** 15
Willie Masters' Lonesome Wife (Gass), **Supp. VI:** 77, **84–85, 86–87**
"Willing" (Moore), **Supp. X:** 178
Willis, Bruce, **Supp. IV Part 1:** 236
Willis, Dail, **Supp. XXIII:** 298
Willis, Gordon, **Supp. XV:** 7
Willis, Mary Hard, **Supp. V:** 290–291
Willis, Nathaniel Parker, **II:** 313; **Supp. I Part 2:** 405; **Supp. XVIII:** 12
Williwaw (Vidal), **Supp. IV Part 2:** 677, 680, 681
"Willow Woman" (Francis), **Supp. IX:** 78
Wills, Garry, **Supp. I Part 1:** 294; **Supp. IV Part 1:** 355
Wills, Ridley, **IV:** 122
Wills, Ross B., **Supp. XI:** 169
"Will to Believe, The" (James), **II:** 352; **Supp. XIV:** 50
Will to Believe, The, and Other Essays in Popular Philosophy (James), **II:** 356; **IV:** 28
Will to Change, The: Poems, 1968–1970 (Rich), **Supp. I Part 2:** 551, 557–559
"Will We Plug Chips into Our Brains?" (W. Gibson), **Supp. XVI:** 117–118
Will You Please Be Quiet, Please? (Carver), **Supp. III Part 1:** 138, 140, 144
"Will You Please Be Quiet, Please?" (Carver), **Supp. III Part 1:** 137, 141
"Will You Tell Me?" (Barthelme), **Supp. IV Part 1:** 42, 47
Wilsdorf, Anne, **Supp. XVI:** 177
Wilshire, Bruce, **II:** 362, 364
Wilshire, Gaylord, **Supp. V:** 280
Wilson, Adrian, **Supp. XV:** 147
Wilson, Alexander, **Supp. XVI:** 4, 6
Wilson, Angus, **IV:** 430, 435
Wilson, August, **Supp. VIII: 329–353; Supp. XIX:** 132
Wilson, Augusta Jane Evans, **Retro. Supp. I:** 351
Wilson, Earl, **Supp. X:** 264
Wilson, Edmund, **I:** 67, 185, 236, 247, 260, 434, 482; **II:** 79, 80, 81, 86, 87, 91, 97, 98, 146, 276, 430, 530, 562, 587; **III:** 588; **IV:** 308, 310, **426–449; Retro. Supp. I:** 1, 97, 100, 101, 103, 104, 105, 115, 274; **Retro. Supp. II:** 321, 327, 329; **Supp. I Part 1:** 372; **Supp. I Part 2:** 407, 646, 678, 709; **Supp. II Part 1:** 19, 90, 106, 136, 137, 143; **Supp. III Part 2:** 612; **Supp. IV Part 2:** 693; **Supp. VIII:** 93, 95, 96, 97, 98–99, 100, 101, 103, 105, 162; **Supp. IX:** 55, 65, 190; **Supp. X:** 186; **Supp. XI:** 160; **Supp. XIII:** 170; **Supp. XIV:** 338; **Supp. XV:** 142, 308; **Supp. XVI:** 194; **Supp. XX: 76, 81; Supp. XXII:** 278; **Supp. XXIII:** 104–105, 106
Wilson, Edmund (father), **IV:** 441
Wilson, E. O., **Supp. X:** 35
Wilson, Harriet, **Supp. XX: 105**
Wilson, Henry, **Supp. XIV:** 48
Wilson, Reuel, **II:** 562
Wilson, Robert, **Supp. XI:** 144
Wilson, Robley, **Supp. XXIII:** 290
Wilson, Sloan, **Supp. IV Part 1:** 387
Wilson, Thomas, **IV:** 153
Wilson, Tracy, **Supp. XVIII:** 101
Wilson, Victoria, **Supp. X:** 166
Wilson, Woodrow, **I:** 245, 246, 490; **II:** 183, 253; **III:** 105, 581; **Supp. I Part 1:** 21; **Supp. I Part 2:** 474, 643; **Supp. V:** 288
Wilton, David, **IV:** 147
Wiman, Christian, **Supp. XV:** 251, 253, 264; **Supp. XVII:** 74; **Supp. XVIII:** 173, 174
Wimberly, Lowry, **Supp. XV:** 136, 137
Wimsatt, William K., **Supp. XIV:** 12
Winch, Terence, **Supp. XXIII:** 291
Winchell, Mark, **Supp. VIII:** 176, 189
Winchell, Mark Royden, **Supp. VIII:** 241; **Supp. IX:** 97, 98, 109; **Supp. XIII:** 94, 98, 99, 101; **Supp. XIV:** 103, 106, 111
Winckelmann, Johann Joachim, **Supp. XII:** 178
Wind, Sand, and Stars (Saint-Exupéry), **Supp. IX:** 247

Wind Across the Everglades (film, Ray), **Supp. XVIII:** 253

Wind Chrysalid's Rattle (Sobin), **Supp. XVI:** 283

"Windfall" (B. Kelly), **Supp. XVII:** 132

Windflower Home Almanac of Poetry, The (Kooser, ed.), **Supp. XIX:** 119

Windham, Donald, **IV:** 382

"Windhover" (Hopkins), **I:** 397; **II:** 539; **Supp. IX:** 43

Winding Stair and Other Poems, The (Yeats), **Supp. XV:** 253

"Winding Street, The" (Petry), **Supp. XI:** 6

"Window" (Pinsky), **Supp. VI:** 237, 247

"Window, The" (Hull), **Supp. XXI:** 140–141

Windows (Creeley), **Supp. IV Part 1:** 157, 158

"Windows" (Jarrell), **II:** 388, 389

"Window Seat, A" (Goldbarth), **Supp. XII:** 185

Wind Remains, The (opera) (Bowles), **Supp. IV Part 1:** 83

"Winds, The" (Welty), **IV:** 265; **Retro. Supp. I:** 348, 350

"Winds and Clouds over a Funeral" (Jin), **Supp. XVIII:** 94

Winds of War (Wouk), **Supp. XX: 243**

"Wind up Sushi" (Goldbarth), **Supp. XII:** 186–187

"Windy Day at the Reservoir, A" (Beattie), **Supp. V:** 33

Windy McPherson's Son (Anderson), **I:** 101, 102–103, 105, 111

"Wine" (Carver), **Supp. III Part 1:** 138

"Wine Menagerie, The" (H. Crane), **I:** 389, 391; **Retro. Supp. II:** 82

Wine of the Puritans, The: A Study of Present-Day America (Brooks), **I:** 240

"Wine of Wizardry, A" (Sterling), **I:** 208

Winer, Linda, **Supp. IV Part 2:** 580; **Supp. XV:** 332

Winesburg, Ohio: A Group of Tales of Ohio Small Town Life (Anderson), **I:** 97, 102, 103, 104, 105–108; **III:** 112, 113, 114, 116, 224, 579; **Supp. V:** 12; **Supp. IX:** 306, 308; **Supp. XI:** 164; **Supp. XVI:** 17; **Supp. XXII:** 282

Winfrey, Oprah, **Supp. XIX:** 194, 204; **Supp. XX: 83, 93**

Wing-and-Wing, The (Cooper), **I:** 350, 355

Winged Seed, The: A Remembrance (L.-Y. Lee), **Supp. XV:** 211, **220–223**

Winged Words: American Indian Writers Speak (Coltelli), **Supp. IV Part 2:** 493, 497

"Wingfield" (Wolff), **Supp. VII:** 341–342

"Wings, The" (Doty), **Supp. XI:** 124

Wings of the Dove, The (James), **I:** 436; **II:** 320, 323, 333, 334–335; **Retro. Supp. I:** 215, 216, 217, 232, **233–234**; **Supp. II Part 1:** 94–95; **Supp. IV Part 1:** 349

"Wink of the Zenith, The" (Skloot), **Supp. XX: 207**

Wink of the Zenith, The: The Shaping of a Writer's Life (Skloot), **Supp. XX: 195, 196, 207**

"Winkte"(Kenny), **Supp. XXIII:** 148–149

"Winky" (Saunders), **Supp. XIX:** 228–229, 229

Winner Names the Age, The: A Collection of Works by Lillian Smith (Cliff, ed.), **Supp. XXII:** 67

Winner Take Nothing (Hemingway), **II:** 249; **Retro. Supp. I:** 170, 175, 176, 181

"Winnie" (Brooks), **Supp. III Part 1:** 86

Winokur, Maxine. *See* Kumin, Maxine

Winslow, Art, **Supp. XVIII:** 102

Winslow, Devereux, **II:** 547

Winslow, Harriet, **II:** 552–553

Winslow, Ola Elizabeth, **I:** 547

Winslow, Warren, **II:** 540

Winston, Andrew, **Supp. XII:** 189

Winston, Michael R., **Supp. XIV:** 197

Winter, Douglas, **Supp. V:** 144

Winter, Johnny and Edgar, **Supp. V:** 334

Winter, Kate, **Supp. X:** 104

"Winter Branch, A" (Irving), **Supp. VI:** 163

"Winter Burial, A" (Clampitt), **Supp. IX:** 48

Winter Carnival (film), **Retro. Supp. I:** 113

"Winter Concert"(Strout), **Supp. XXIII:** 283

"Winter Daybreak at Vence, A" (Wright), **Supp. III Part 1:** 249–250

Winter Diary, A (Van Doren), **I:** 168

"Winter Dreams" (Fitzgerald), **II:** 80, 94; **Retro. Supp. I:** 108

"Winter Drive, A" (Jewett), **Retro. Supp. II:** 147

"Winter Eden, A" (Frost), **Retro. Supp. I:** 137

"Winter Father, The" (Dubus), **Supp. VII:** 83, 87

Winter Hours: Prose, Prose Poems, and Poems (Oliver), **Supp. VII:** 230, 247

"Winter in Dunbarton" (Lowell), **II:** 547; **Retro. Supp. II:** 187

"Wintering" (Plath), **Retro. Supp. II:** 255

Winter Insomnia (Carver), **Supp. III Part 1:** 138

Winter in the Blood (Welch), **Supp. IV Part 2:** 562

"Winter Landscape" (Berryman), **I:** 174; **Retro. Supp. I:** 430

Winter Light (W. V. Davis), **Supp. XXI: 92, 93**

"Winter Light" (W. V. Davis), **Supp. XXI:** 90, 92

Winter Lightning (Nemerov), **III:** 269

Winter Morning Walks: One Hundred Postcards to Jim Harrison (Kooser), **Supp. XIX:** 116, **125–126**

Winter News (Haines), **Supp. XII:** 199, **201–204,** 207–208, 208

Winternitz, Mary. *See* Cheever, Mrs. John (Mary Winternitz)

Winter: Notes from Montana (Bass), **Supp. XVI:** 17–18

Winter of Our Discontent, The (Steinbeck), **IV:** 52, 65–66, 68

"Winter on Earth" (Toomer), **Supp. III Part 2:** 486

"Winter Piece, A" (Bryant), **Supp. I Part 1:** 150, 155

"Winter Rains, Cataluña" (Levine), **Supp. V:** 182

"Winter Remembered" (Ransom), **III:** 492–493

"Winter Roses" (W. V. Davis), **Supp. XXI:** 94

Winterrowd, Prudence, **I:** 217, 224

Winters, Jonathan, **Supp. XI:** 305

Winters, Yvor, **I:** 59, 63, 386, 393, 397, 398, 402, 471; **III:** 194, 498; **IV:** 153; **Retro. Supp. II:** 76, 77, 78, 82, 83, 85, 89; **Supp. I Part 1:** 268; **Supp. II Part 2:** 416, 666, **785–816; Supp. IV Part 2:** 480; **Supp. V:** 180, 191–192; **Supp. XIV:** 287; **Supp. XV:** 74, 341

"Winter Sacrament" (Bronk), **Supp. XXI:** 33

"Winter Scenes" (Bryant). *See* "Winter Piece, A"

Winterset (Anderson), **III:** 159

"Winter Shrub, A" (Bronk), **Supp. XXI:** 28

"Winter Skyline Late" (F. Wright), **Supp. XVII:** 245

"Winter Sleep" (Wylie), **Supp. I Part 2:** 711, 729

Winter's Night (Boyce), **Supp. XXI:** 7, **12–13**

Winter's Tale, The (Shakespeare), **Supp. XIII:** 219

Winter Stars (Levis), **Supp. XI:** 259, **266–268**

"Winter Stars" (Levis), **Supp. XI:** 267–268

Winter Stop-Over (Everwine), **Supp. XV:** 74, 76

"Winter Stop-Over" (Everwine), **Supp. XV:** 76

Winter Studies and Summer Rambles in Canada (Jameson), **Supp. XXIII:** 225, 226

"Winter Swan" (Bogan), **Supp. III Part 1:** 52

Winter Thunder (X. J. Kennedy), **Supp. XV:** 167

"Winter Thunder" (X. J. Kennedy), **Supp. XV:** 169

"Winter Trees" (Pedersen; Nelson, trans.), **Supp. XVIII:** 180

Winter Trees (Plath), **Retro. Supp. II:** 257; **Supp. I Part 2:** 526, 539, 541

"Winter Walk" (W. V. Davis), **Supp. XXI:** 92

"Winter Weather Advisory" (Ashbery), **Supp. III Part 1:** 26

"Winter Wheat" (Hoffman), **Supp. XVIII:** 86, 87

"Winter without Snow, The" (C. Frost), **Supp. XV:** 96, 105–106

"Winter Words" (Levine), **Supp. V:** 192

Winthrop, John, **Supp. I Part 1:** 99, 100, 101, 102, 105; **Supp. I Part 2:** 484, 485

Winthrop Covenant, The (Auchincloss), **Supp. IV Part 1:** 23

"Wires of the Night, The" (Collins), **Supp. XXI:** 64

Wirt, William, **I:** 232

Wirth, Louis, **IV:** 475

Wisconsin Death Trip (Levy), **Supp. XIX:** 102

"Wisdom Cometh with the Years" (Cullen), **Supp. IV Part 1:** 166

Wisdom of the African World (McKnight, ed.), **Supp. XX:** 157–158

Wisdom of the Desert, The: Sayings from the Desert Fathers of the Fourth Century (Merton), **Supp. VIII:** 201

Wisdom of the Heart, The (H. Miller), **III:** 178, 184

Wise Blood (O'Connor), **III:** 337, 338, 339–343, 344, 345, 346, 350, 354, 356, 357; **Retro. Supp. II:** 219, 221, 222, 223, **225–228**

Wise Men, The (Price), **Supp. VI:** 254

"Wiser Than a God" (Chopin), **Retro. Supp. II:** 61; **Supp. I Part 1:** 208

Wishes, Lies, and Dreams: Teaching Children to Write Poetry (Koch), **Supp. XV:** 176, 189

"Wish for a Young Wife" (Roethke), **III:** 548

Wishful Thinking: A Theological ABC (Buechner), **Supp. XII:** 53

Wishing Tree, The: Christopher Isherwood on Mystical Religion (Adjemian, ed.), **Supp. XIV:** 164, 173

Wismer, Helen Muriel. *See* Thurber, Mrs. James (Helen Muriel Wismer)

Wisse, Ruth, **Supp. XII:** 167, 168

Wister, Owen, **I:** 62; **Retro. Supp. II:** 72; **Supp. XIV:** 39

Wit (Edson), **Supp. XVIII:** 35–36, 37, **38–51**

"Witchbird" (Bambara), **Supp. XI:** 11

"Witch Burning" (Plath), **Supp. I Part 2:** 539

Witchcraft of Salem Village, The (Jackson), **Supp. IX:** 121

"Witch Doctor" (Hayden), **Supp. II Part 1:** 368, 380

Witches of Eastwick, The (Updike), **Retro. Supp. I:** 330, 331

Witch from Castile, The (Asch), **Supp. XXIII:** 6, 10

Witching Hour, The (Rice), **Supp. VII:** 299–300

"Witch of Coös, The" (Frost), **II:** 154–155; **Retro. Supp. I:** 135; **Retro. Supp. II:** 42

"Witch of Owl Mountain Springs, The: An Account of Her Remarkable Powers" (Taylor), **Supp. V:** 328

"Witch of Wenham, The" (Whittier), **Supp. I Part 2:** 694, 696

Witek, Terri, **Supp. XVII:** 117

"With a Little Help from My Friends" (Kushner), **Supp. IX:** 131

With Bold Knife and Fork (M. F. K. Fisher), **Supp. XVII:** 89, 91

"With Che at Kitty Hawk" (Banks), **Supp. V:** 6

"With Che at the Plaza" (Banks), **Supp. V:** 7

"With Che in New Hampshire" (Banks), **Supp. V:** 6

"With Child" (Taggard), **Supp. XXII:** 276, 278

"Withdrawal Symptoms" (Mora), **Supp. XIII:** 216

"Withered Skins of Berries" (Toomer), **Supp. III Part 2:** 485; **Supp. IX:** 320

Withers, Harry Clay, **Supp. XIII:** 161

Witherspoon, John, **Supp. I Part 2:** 504

With Eyes at the Back of Our Heads (Levertov), **Supp. III Part 1:** 276–277

With Her in Ourland (Gilman), **Supp. XI:** 208–209

With His Pistol in His Hand (Paredes), **Supp. XIII:** 225; **Supp. XIX:** 98

"Within the Words: An Apprenticeship" (Haines), **Supp. XII:** 197

"With Kit, Age 7, at the Beach" (Stafford), **Supp. XI:** 323

With Love to Lesbia (Kenny), **Supp. XXIII:** 145

"With Mercy for the Greedy" (Sexton), **Supp. II Part 2:** 680

With My Trousers Rolled (Epstein), **Supp. XIV:** 101, 105

Without a Hero (Boyle), **Supp. VIII:** 16; **Supp. XX:** 20

Without Feathers (Allen), **Supp. XV:** 3, 14, 15

Without Stopping (Bowles), **Supp. IV Part 1:** 79, 81, 85, 90, 91, 92

"Without Tradition and within Reason: Judge Horton and Atticus Finch in Court" (Johnson), **Supp. VIII:** 127

With Shuddering Fall (Oates), **Supp. II Part 2:** 504–506

"With the Dog at Sunrise" (Kenyon), **Supp. VII:** 170

With the Empress Dowager of China (Carl), **III:** 475

"With the Horse in the Winter Pasture" (McCarriston), **Supp. XIV:** 262

With the Old Breed: At Peleliu and Okinawa (Sledge), **Supp. V:** 249–250

"With the Violin" (Chopin), **Retro. Supp. II:** 61

"Witness" (Clampitt), **Supp. IX:** 42–43, 45, 46

"Witness" (Dubus), **Supp. VII:** 89

"Witness" (Harjo), **Supp. XII:** 227–228

Witness (McNally), **Supp. XIII:** 197

"Witness" (Nelson), **Supp. XVIII:** 186

"Witness, The" (Porter), **III:** 443–444

"Witness for Poetry, A" (Stafford), **Supp. XI:** 324

"Witness for the Defense" (Hay), **Supp. XIV:** 124

"Witnessing My Father's Will" (Karr), **Supp. XI:** 241

"Witnessing to a Shared World" (Sanders), **Supp. XVI:** 278

Witness to the Times! (McGrath), **Supp. X:** 118

Witness Tree, A (Frost), **II:** 155; **Retro. Supp. I:** 122, 137, 139

Wit's End: Days and Nights of the Algonquin Round Table (Gaines), **Supp. IX:** 190

Wits Recreations (Mennes and Smith), **II:** 111

Witt, Shirley Hill, **Supp. IV Part 2:** 505

Witte, John, **Supp. XX:** 200

Wittels, Anne F., **Supp. XV:** 59

Wittenberg, Judith Bryant, **Retro. Supp. II:** 146

Wittgenstein, Ludwig, **Retro. Supp. I:** 53; **Supp. III Part 2:** 626–627; **Supp. X:** 304; **Supp. XII:** 21; **Supp. XV:** 344, 346

Wittgensteins' Mistress (Markson), **Supp. XVII:** 135, 142, 143, 145

Wittliff, William, **Supp. V:** 227

"Witty War, A" (Simpson), **Supp. IX:** 268

Witz (Cohen), **Supp. XXII:** 268

"Wives and Mistresses" (Hardwick), **Supp. III Part 1:** 211–212

Wizard of Loneliness, The (Nichols), **Supp. XIII:** 259, 263, 264

Wizard of Oz, The (Baum), **Supp. IV Part 1:** 113

Wizard of Oz, The (film), **Supp. X:** 172, 214

Wizard's Tide, The: A Story (Buechner), **Supp. XII:** 54

"WLT (The Edgar Era)" (Keillor), **Supp. XVI:** 172

WLT: A Radio Romance (Keillor), **Supp. XVI:** 176

Wobegon Boy (Keillor), **Supp. XVI:** 177

Wodehouse, P. G., **Supp. IX:** 195; **Supp. XXI:** 204–205

Woiwode, Larry, **Supp. VIII:** 151; **Supp. XVI:** 206

Wojahn, David, **Supp. IX:** 161, 292, 293; **Supp. XXI:** 130, 131, 132, 138, 139, 141

Wolcott, James, **Supp. IX:** 259

Wolf, Christa, **Supp. IV Part 1:** 310, 314

Wolf, Daniel, **Retro. Supp. II:** 202

Wolf, Robert L., **Supp. XXII:** 274, 277, 279, 280

Wolf: A False Memoir (Harrison), **Supp. VIII:** 40, **41–42**, 45

Wolfe, Ben, **IV:** 454

Wolfe, Gregory, **Supp. XIV:** 307

Wolfe, James, **Supp. I Part 2:** 498

Wolfe, Linnie, **Supp. IX:** 176

Wolfe, Mabel, **IV:** 454

Wolfe, Thomas, **I:** 288, 289, 374, 478, 495; **II:** 457; **III:** 40, 108, 278, 334, 482; **IV:** 52, 97, 357, **450–473; Retro. Supp. I:** 382; **Supp. I Part 1:** 29; **Supp. IV Part 1:** 101; **Supp. IX:** 229; **Supp. X:** 225; **Supp. XI:** 213, 216, 217, 218; **Supp. XIII:** 17; **Supp. XIV:** 122; **Supp. XVIII:** 78; **Supp. XX:** 163

Wolfe, Tom, **Supp. III Part 2:** 567–588; **Supp. IV Part 1:** 35, 198; **Supp. V:** 296; **Supp. X:** 264; **Supp. XI:** 239; **Supp. XV:** 143; **Supp. XVII:** 202; **Supp. XVIII:** 72, 117

Wolfe, William Oliver, **IV:** 454

Wolfe, Mrs. William Oliver (Julia Elizabeth Westall), **IV:** 454

"Wolfe Homo Scribens" (Cowley), **Supp. II Part 1:** 144

Wolfert, Ira, **Supp. XXI:** 261–279

Wolfert's Roost (Irving), **II:** 314

Wolff, Cynthia Griffin, **Retro. Supp. I:** 379; **Supp. IV Part 1:** 203

Wolff, Donald, **Supp. XIII:** 316, 317, 326

Wolff, Geoffrey, **Supp. II Part 1:** 97; **Supp. XI:** 239, 245, 246; **Supp. XXII:** 206, 211

Wolff, Tobias, **Retro. Supp. I:** 190; **Supp. V:** 22; **Supp. VII: 331–346; Supp. X:** 1; **Supp. XI:** 26, 239, 245, 246, 247; **Supp. XV:** 223; **Supp. XVI:** 39, 41, 63, 70, 77; **Supp. XXIII:** 289

"Wolf in the Bed, The"(Hadas), **Supp. XXIII:** 118

Wolfreys, Julian, **Supp. XVIII:** 61

Wolfson, P. J., **Supp. XIII:** 172

"Wolf Town" (Carson), **Supp. XII: 102**

Wolf Willow: A History, a Story, and a Memory of the Last Plains Frontier (Stegner), **Supp. IV Part 2:** 595, 596, 597, 598, 599, 600, 601, 604, 606, 611, 613, 614

Wolitzer, Hilma, **Supp. XV:** 55; **Supp. XXIII:** 108

Wolitzer, Meg, **Supp. XV:** 65

Wolkomir, Richard, **Supp. XXII:** 218

Wollaston, William, **II:** 108

Wollstonecraft, Mary, **Supp. I Part 1:** 126; **Supp. I Part 2:** 512, 554

Womack, Craig, **Supp. XXIII:** 147, 153, 154–155

"Woman" (Bogan), **Supp. X:** 102

"Woman, I Got the Blues" (Komunyakaa), **Supp. XIII:** 117

"Woman, Why Are You Weeping?" (Kenyon), **Supp. VII:** 174–175

"Woman, Young and Old, A" (Paley), **Supp. VI:** 222, 225

Woman Aroused, The (Lacy), **Supp. XV:** 199–200

Woman at the Washington Zoo, The (Jarrell), **II:** 367, 386, 387, 389

Woman Before an Aquarium (Hampl), **Supp. XXII:** 83, 86, 98

"Woman Before an Aquarium" (Hampl), **Supp. XXII:** 85, 98

"Womand and the Woman's Movement" (Briggs), **Supp. XVIII:** 14

"Woman Dead in Her Forties, A" (Rich), **Supp. I Part 2:** 574–575

Woman Driver, The (Thompson), **Supp. XXIII:** 291, **294–295**

"Woman Hanging from the Thirteenth Floor Window, The" (Harjo), **Supp. XII:** 216, 221

"Woman Hollering Creek" (Cisneros), **Supp. VII:** 70

Woman Hollering Creek and Other Stories (Cisneros), **Supp. VII:** 58, 68–70

"Womanhood" (Brooks), **Supp. III Part 1:** 77

"Woman in Rain" (X. J. Kennedy), **Supp. XV:** 168

Woman in the Dark (Hammett), **Supp. IV Part 1:** 343

"Woman in the House, A" (Caldwell), **I:** 310

Woman in the Nineteenth Century (Fuller), **Retro. Supp. I:** 156; **Supp. II Part 1:** 279, 292, 294–296; **Supp. XI:** 197, 203; **Supp. XVIII:** 3, 11

"Woman in the Shoe, The" (Ryan as Quin), **Supp. XVIII:** 231

Woman in White, The (Collins), **Supp. I Part 1:** 35, 36

"Woman Is Talking to Death, A"(Grahn), **Supp. XXIII:** 195

"Womanizer, The" (Ford), **Supp. V:** 71, 72

"Woman Like Yourself, A" (C. Frost), **Supp. XV:** 107

Woman Lit by Fireflies, The (Harrison), **Supp. VIII: 50–51**

"Woman Loses Cookie Bake-Off, Sets Self on Fire" (R. O. Butler), **Supp. XII:** 72

Woman of Andros, The (Wilder), **IV:** 356, 363–364, 367, 368, 374

Woman of Means, A (Taylor), **Supp. V:** 319–320

Woman on the Edge of Time (Piercy), **Supp. XIII:** 29

Woman on the Porch, The (Gordon), **II:** 199, 209–211

"Woman on the Stair, The" (MacLeish), **III:** 15–16

"Woman's Dream, A" (E. Stoddard), **Supp. XV:** 278

Woman's Fiction: A Guide to Novels By and About Women in America, 1820–1870 (Baym), **Supp. XVIII:** 258

"Woman's Heartlessness" (Thaxter), **Retro. Supp. II:** 147

Woman's Honor (Glaspell), **Supp. III Part 1:** 179

"Woman Singing" (Ortiz), **Supp. IV Part 2:** 513

Woman's Place, A (C. L. R. James and Weinstein), **Supp. XXI:** 170

Woman's Share in Primitive Culture (Mason), **Supp. I Part 1:** 18

"Woman Struck by Car Turns into Nymphomaniac" (R. O. Butler), **Supp. XII:** 72

"Woman's Work" (Alvarez), **Supp. VII:** 4

"Woman Taken in Adultery, A"(Thompson), **Supp. XXIII:** 300

"Woman Uses Glass Eye to Spy on Philandering Husband" (R. O. Butler), **Supp. XII:** 70, 72

Woman Warrior (Kingston), **Supp. IV Part 1:** 12; **Supp. V:** 157, 158, 159, 160–164, 166, 169; **Supp. X:** 291–292; **Supp. XIV:** 162

Woman Warrior, The (Kingston), **Supp. XV:** 220

Woman Who Fell from the Sky, The (Harjo), **Supp. XII: 226–228**

"Woman Who Fell From the Sky, The" (Iroquois creation story), **Supp. IV Part 1:** 327

Woman Who Owned the Shadows, The (Gunn Allen), **Supp. IV Part 1:** 320, 322, 326, 327–328

"Woman Who Plays Trumpet Is Deported, A" (Cliff), **Supp. XXII:** 74

"Woman Who Went Backwards, The"(Schott), **Supp. XXIII:** 241

Woman Within, The (Glasgow), **II:** 183, 190–191

"Womanwork" (Gunn Allen), **Supp. IV Part 1:** 326

Women (Bukowski), **Supp. XI:** 172

"Women" (Didion), **Supp. IV Part 1:** 205

"Women" (Swenson), **Supp. IV Part 2:** 647

Women, The (Boyle), **Supp. XX: 24, 26–27**

Women, The (film), **Retro. Supp. I:** 113

Women, The (film; Cukor), **Supp. XVI:** 181, 192

"Women and Children First" (Prose), **Supp. XVI:** 254

Women and Children First: Stories (Prose), **Supp. XVI:** 254

Women and Economics (Gilman), **Supp. I Part 2:** 637; **Supp. V:** 284; **Supp. XI:** 200, **203–204,** 206

"Women and Poetry" (Notley), **Supp. XXII:** 236

Women and Thomas Harrow (Marquand), **III:** 50, 61, 62, 66, 68, 69–70, 71

Women and Vodka (Markson as Merrill, ed.), **Supp. XVII:** 136

Women and Wilderness (LaBastille), **Supp. X:** 97, **102–104**

"Women as They Are" (Rowson), **Supp. XV:** 243

Women at Point Sur, The (Jeffers), **Supp. II Part 2:** 430–431

Women in Love (Lawrence), **III:** 27, 34

Women in Praise of the Sacred: 43 Centuries of Spiritual Poetry by Women (Hirshfield, ed.), **Supp. XXIII:** 136, 137

Women of Belize: Gender and Change in Central America (McClaurin), **Supp. XXIII:** 84

Women of Brewster Place, The: A Novel in Seven Stories (Naylor), **Supp. VIII:** 213, **214–218**

Women of Manhattan: An Upper West Side Story (Shanley), **Supp. XIV:** 315, **326–327**

"Women of My Color" (Coleman), **Supp. XI:** 88–89

Women of Trachis (Pound, trans.), **III:** 476

"Women on the Breadlines"(Le Sueur), **Supp. XXIII:** 166, 167

Women on the Wall, The (Stegner), **Supp. IV Part 2:** 599, 605, 606

Women Poets in English (Stanford, ed.), **Retro. Supp. I:** 41

"Women Reformers and American Culture, 1870–1930" (Conway), **Supp. I Part 1:** 19

"Women's Movement, The" (Didion), **Supp. IV Part 1:** 206

"Women Waiting" (Shields), **Supp. VII:** 320

"Women We Love Whom We Never See Again" (R. Bly), **Supp. IV Part 1:** 66

"Women We Never See Again" (R. Bly), **Supp. IV Part 1:** 66

Women with Men (Ford), **Supp. V:** 57, 71–72

"Wonder" (Olds), **Supp. X:** 210

Wonder Boys (Chabon), **Supp. XI:** 67, **73–75,** **Supp. XI:** 78; **Supp. XVI:** 259

Wonder Boys (film), **Supp. XI:** 67

Wonderful O, The (Thurber), **Supp. I Part 2:** 612

"Wonderful Old Gentleman, The" (Parker), **Supp. IX:** 197

"Wonderful Pen, The" (Swenson), **Supp. IV Part 2:** 650

Wonderful Words, Silent Truth: Essays on Poetry and a Memoir (Simic), **Supp. VIII:** 270

Wonderland (Oates), **Supp. II Part 2:** 511, 512, 514–515

Wonders Hidden (Sanders), **Supp. XVI:** 269

Wonders of the African World (television series), **Supp. XX: 99**

Wonders of the Invisible World, The (Mather), **Supp. II Part 2:** 456–459, 460, 467

Wonder-Working Providence (Johnson), **IV:** 157

Wong, Hertha, **Supp. IV Part 1:** 275

Wong, Jade Snow, **Supp. X:** 291

Wong, Nellie, **Supp. XVII:** 72

Wong, Shawn, **Supp. XV:** 221

Wong, Timothy, **Supp. XVIII:** 94

"Wood" (Nye), **Supp. XIII:** 276

Wood, Audrey, **IV:** 381

Wood, Charles Erskine Scott, **Supp. XV:** 301

Wood, Clement, **Supp. XV:** 298

Wood, Clement Biddle, **Supp. XI:** 307

Wood, Harrison, **Supp. XXII:** 283

Wood, Mrs. Henry, **Supp. I Part 1:** 35

Wood, James, **Supp. XIV:** 95–96; **Supp. XIX:** 138

Wood, Mabel, **I:** 199

Wood, Michael, **Supp. IV Part 2:** 691

Wood, Norman Barton, **Supp. XIV:** 201

Wood, Susan, **Supp. XVI:** 123

Woodard, Calvin, **Supp. VIII:** 128

Woodard, Charles L., **Supp. IV Part 2:** 484, 493

Woodard, Deborah, **Supp. XIII:** 114

Woodberry, George Edward, **III:** 508

Woodbridge, Frederick, **I:** 217, 224

Woodbridge, John, **Supp. I Part 1:** 101, 102, 114

"Wood-Choppers, The" (Chopin), **Retro. Supp. II:** 72

Woodcock, George, **Supp. XIII:** 33

Woodcome, Beth, **Supp. XVII:** 240

"Wood Dove at Sandy Spring, The" (MacLeish), **III:** 19

"Wooden Spring" (Rukeyser), **Supp. VI:** 285

"Wooden Umbrella, The" (Porter), **IV:** 26

Woodhull, Victoria, **Supp. XVIII:** 4

"Woodnotes" (Emerson), **II:** 7, 19

"Wood-Pile, The" (Frost), **Retro. Supp. I:** 128; **Supp. IV Part 2:** 445

Woodrow, James, **Supp. I Part 1:** 349, 366

"Woods, Books, and Truant Officers, The" (Maclean), **Supp. XIV:** 221, 225

"Woods, New York, The" (Bronk), **Supp. XXI:** 27

Woods, Paula L., **Supp. XXI:** 70

Woods, Robert A., **Supp. I Part 1:** 19

Woods, The (Mamet), **Supp. XIV:** 241, 254–255

Woodswoman (LaBastille), **Supp. X:** 95, **96–99,** 108

Woodswoman III: Book Three of the Woodswoman's Adventures (LaBastille), **Supp. X:** 95, **106–107**

"Wood Thrush" (Kenyon), **Supp. VII:** 172

Woodward, C. Vann, **IV:** 114, 470–471; **Retro. Supp. I:** 75, 76; **Supp. XIX:** 152; **Supp. XXII:** 194

"Woof: A Plea of Sorts" (Saunders), **Supp. XIX:** 235

"Wooing the Inanimate" (Brodsky), **Supp. VIII:** 32

Woolcott, Alexander, **Supp. IX:** 197

Wooley, Bryan, **Supp. V:** 225

Woolf, Douglas, **Supp. XXIII:** 174

Woolf, Leonard, **Supp. IX:** 95

Woolf, Virginia, **I:** 53, 79, 112, 309; **II:** 320, 415; **IV:** 59; **Retro. Supp. I:** 59, 75, 170, 215, 291, 359; **Supp. I Part 2:** 553, 714, 718; **Supp. IV Part 1:** 299; **Supp. V:** 127; **Supp. VIII:** 5, 155, 251, 252, 263, 265; **Supp. IX:** 66, 109; **Supp. XI:** 134, 193; **Supp. XII:** 81, 98, 289; **Supp. XIII:** 305; **Supp. XIV:** 341–342, 342, 343, 346, 348; **Supp. XV:** 55, 65; **Supp. XIX:** 134; **Supp. XXIII:** 275

Woollcott, Alexander, **IV:** 432; **Retro. Supp. II:** 327; **Supp. I Part 2:** 664; **Supp. IX:** 190, 194

Woolley, Leonard, **Supp. XXIII:** 33

Woollstonecraft, Mary, **Supp. XVI:** 184

"Woolly Mammoth" (X. J. Kennedy), **Supp. XV:** 163–164

Woolman, John, **Supp. VIII:** 202, 204, 205

Woolson, Constance Fenimore, **Retro. Supp. I:** 224, 228

Woolverton, Linda, **Supp. XXI:** 148

Wooster, David, **Supp. XX: 288**

Worcester, Samuel, **I:** 458

Word and Idioms: Studies in the English Language (L. P. Smith), **Supp. XIV:** 343

"Word by Word" (column, Lamott), **Supp. XX: 140**

Word of God and the Word of Man, The (Barth), **Retro. Supp. I:** 327

"Word out of the Sea, A" (Whitman), **IV:** 344

Words (Creeley), **Supp. IV Part 1:** 139, 150–153, 154, 155, 158

"Words" (Creeley), **Supp. IV Part 1:** 152

"Words" (Gioia), **Supp. XV:** 125

"Words" (Merwin), **Supp. III Part 1:** 352

"Words" (Plath), **Supp. I Part 2:** 547

"Words" (Shields), **Supp. VII:** 323

"Words, The" (Wagoner), **Supp. IX:** 326

"Words above a Narrow Entrance" (Wagoner), **Supp. IX:** 325

"Words for a Bike-Racing, Osprey-Chasing Wine-Drunk Squaw Man" (Gunn Allen), **Supp. IV Part 1:** 325

Words for Dr. Y (Sexton), **Supp. II Part 2:** 698

"Words for Hart Crane" (Lowell), **I:** 381; **II:** 547; **Retro. Supp. II:** 188

"Words for Maria" (Merrill), **Supp. III Part 1:** 327

"Words for My Grandmother"(Balakian), **Supp. XXIII:** 19, 20

Words for the Chisel (Taggard), **Supp. XXII:** 276–277

"Words for the Unknown Makers" (Kunitz), **Supp. III Part 1:** 264

Words for the Wind (Roethke), **III:** 529, 533, 541, 543, 545

"Words for the Wind" (Roethke), **III:** 542–543

Words in the Mourning Time (Hayden), **Supp. II Part 1:** 361, 366, 367

"Words in the Mourning Time" (Hayden), **Supp. II Part 1:** 370–371

"Words into Fiction" (Welty), **IV:** 279

"Words into Worlds Won't Go" (Major), **Supp. XXII:** 174

"Words Like Freedom" (Hughes), **Retro. Supp. I:** 207

"Words of a Young Girl" (Lowell), **II:** 554

Words under the Words: Selected Poems (Nye), **Supp. XIII:** 277

Wordsworth, Dorothy, **Supp. IX:** 38

Wordsworth, William, **I:** 283, 522, 524, 525, 588; **II:** 7, 11, 17, 18, 97, 169, 273, 303, 304, 532, 549, 552; **III:** 219, 263, 277, 278, 511, 521, 523, 528, 583; **IV:** 120, 331, 343, 453, 465; **Retro. Supp. I:** 121, 196; **Supp. I Part 1:** 150, 151, 154, 161, 163, 312, 313, 349, 365; **Supp. I Part 2:** 375, 409, 416, 422, 607, 621, 622, 673, 674, 675, 676, 677, 710–711, 729; **Supp. II Part 1:** 4; **Supp. III Part 1:** 12, 15, 73, 279; **Supp. IV Part 2:** 597, 601; **Supp. V:** 258; **Supp. VIII:** 273; **Supp. IX:** 38, 41, 265, 274; **Supp. X:** 22, 23, 65, 120; **Supp. XI:** 248, 251, 312; **Supp. XIII:** 214; **Supp. XIV:** 184; **Supp. XV:** 93, 250; **Supp. XIX:** 1; **Supp. XX: 108, 116; Supp. XXI:** 131

" 'Word Which Made All Clear, The': The Silent Close of *The House of Mirth*" (Benstock), **Supp. XX: 240**

Work (Alcott), **Supp. I Part 1:** 32–33, 42

Work (Dixon), **Supp. XII:** 141, **143**

"Work" (Halliday), **Supp. XIX:** 85

"Work" (Oliver), **Supp. VII:** 243

Work and Love (Dunn), **Supp. XI: 147–148**

"Worker" (Coleman), **Supp. XI:** 89

Worker Writers (Le Sueur), **Supp. XXIII:** 165

Working a Passage; or, Life on a Liner (Briggs), **Supp. XVIII:** 2, **9–10**

Working Class Movement in America, The (E. Marx and E. Aveling), **Supp. XVI:** 85

Working Papers: Selected Essays and Reviews (Carruth), **Supp. XVI:** 46

"Working Roots: A Collection of Poetry and Prose" (Trethewey), **Supp. XXI:** 245

"Working the Landscape" (Dunn), **Supp. XI:** 151

Workin' on the Chain Gang: Shaking Off the Dead Hand of History (Mosley), **Supp. XIII:** 247, 248

"Work Notes '66" (Baraka), **Supp. II Part 1:** 47

Work of Art (Lewis), **II:** 453–454

"Work of Shading, The" (Simic), **Supp. VIII:** 277–278

Work of Stephen Crane, The (Follett, ed.), **I:** 405

"Work on Red Mountain, The" (Harte), **Supp. II Part 1:** 339

"Workshop" (Espaillat), **Supp. XXI:** 105

Works of Love, The (Morris), **III:** 223–224, 225, 233

Works of Witter Bynner, The (Kraft, ed.), **Supp. XV:** 52

"World, The" (Bronk), **Supp. XXI:** 32

"World, The" (Simic), **Supp. VIII:** 282

"World, the Flesh, and the Devil, The"(P. Benedict), **Supp. XXIII:** 48

World, the Worldless, The (Bronk), **Supp. XXI:** 29–31

World According to Garp, The (Irving), **Supp. VI:** 163, 164, **170–173,** 181

World and Africa, The: An Inquiry into the Part Which Africa Has Played in World History (Du Bois), **Supp. II Part 1:** 184–185

"World and All Its Teeth, The" (Nye), **Supp. XIII:** 282

"World and the Door, The" (O. Henry), **Supp. II Part 1:** 402

"World and the Jug, The" (Ellison), **Retro. Supp. II:** 112, 119, 123

"World as We Know It, The" (Barresi), **Supp. XV:** 100

World Authors 1950–1970, **Supp. XIII:** 102

World Below, The (Miller), **Supp. XII:** **303–304**

World Below the Window, The: Poems 1937–1997 (W. J. Smith), **Supp. XIII:** 332, 340, 345

World Doesn't End, The (Simic), **Supp. VIII:** 272, **279–280**

World Elsewhere, A: The Place of Style in American Literature (Poirier), **I:** 239

"World Ends Here, The" (Harjo), **Supp. XII:** 227–228

World Enough and Time (Warren), **IV:** 243, 253–254

World Gone Wrong (album, Dylan), **Supp. XVIII:** 28

"World I Live In, The" (T. Williams), **IV:** 388

World I Never Made, A (Farrell), **II:** 34, 35, 424

World in the Attic, The (Morris), **III:** 222–223, 224

World in the Evening, The (Isherwood), **Supp. XIV:** 157, 164, 165, **166–167,** 170

World Is a Wedding, The (Schwartz), **Supp. II Part 2:** 643, 654–660

"World Is a Wedding, The" (Schwartz), **Supp. II Part 2:** 655–656, 657

"World Is Too Much with Us, The" (Wordsworth), **Supp. I Part 1:** 312

Worldly Hopes (Ammons), **Supp. VII:** 34

Worldly Philosophers, The (Heilbroner), **Supp. I Part 2:** 644, 650

World of Apples, The (Cheever), **Supp. I Part 1:** 191, 193

World of David Wagoner, The (McFarland), **Supp. IX:** 323

"World of Easy Rawlins, The" (Mosley), **Supp. XIII:** 234, 236

World of Gwendolyn Brooks, The (Brooks), **Supp. III Part 1:** 83, 84

World of H. G. Wells, The (Brooks), **I:** 240, 241, 242

World of Light, A (Skloot), **Supp. XX:** **196, 205, 206–207**

"World of Light, A" (Skloot), **Supp. XX:** **194, 207**

World of Light, A: Portraits and Celebrations (Sarton), **Supp. III Part 1:** 62; **Supp. VIII:** 249, 253, 262

World of Our Fathers: The Journey of the Eastern European Jews to America and the Life They Found and Made (Howe), **Supp. VI:** 113, 114, 116, 118, 119, **120–125; Supp. XIV:**104; **Supp. XXIII:** 3

"World of Pure Experience, A" (James), **II:** 356–357

World of Raymond Chandler, The (Spender), **Supp. IV Part 1:** 119

World of Sex, The (H. Miller), **III:** 170, 178, 187

"World of the Perfect Tear, The" (McGrath), **Supp. X:** 116, 118

World of the Ten Thousand Things, The: Selected Poems (Wright), **Supp. V:** 333

"World of Tomorrow, The" (White), **Supp. I Part 2:** 663

World of Washington Irving, The (Brooks), **I:** 256–257

World Over, The (Wharton), **Retro. Supp. I:** 382

World Revolution (C. L. R. James), **Supp. XXI:** 167

"Worlds" (Goldbarth), **Supp. XII:** 183, 189

World's Body, The (Ransom), **III:** 497, 499; **Supp. II Part 1:** 146

World's End (Boyle), **Supp. VIII:** 11–12; **Supp. XX:** 22–23

World's End and Other Stories (Theroux), **Supp. VIII:** 322

"World's Fair" (Berryman), **I:** 173

World's Fair (Doctorow), **Supp. IV Part 1:** 217, 224, 227–229, 234, 236–237

World's Fair, The (Fitzgerald), **II:** 93

Worlds of Color (Du Bois), **Supp. II Part 1:** 185–186

"Worlds of Color" (Du Bois), **Supp. II Part 1:** 175

World So Wide (Lewis), **II:** 456

"World's Worst Boyfriends, The" (Wasserstein), **Supp. XV:** 328

"World-Telegram" (Berryman), **I:** 173

World to Come, The (D. Horn), **Supp. XVII:** 50

"World Trade Center / Mail runner / '73"(Balakian), **Supp. XXIII:** 32–33

World View on Race and Democracy: A Study Guide in Human Group Relations (Locke), **Supp. XIV:** 205, 206

World within the Word, The (Gass), **Supp. VI:** 77

"World Without Objects Is a Sensible Place, A" (Wilbur), **Supp. III Part 2:** 550

"World Without Rodrigo, The" (Cisneros), **Supp. VII:** 68

"Worm Moon" (Oliver), **Supp. VII:** 234

Wormser, Baron, **Supp. XXIII:** 57

"Worn Path, A" (Welty), **IV:** 262; **Retro. Supp. I:** 345–346

"Worsening Situation" (Ashbery), **Supp. III Part 1:** 17–18

"Worship" (Emerson), **II:** 2, 4–5

"Worship and Church Bells" (Paine), **Supp. I Part 2:** 521

Worster, Donald, **Supp. IX:** 19

Worthington, Marjorie, **Supp. XII:** 13

Wouk, Herman, **Supp. XX: 243**

Wouldn't Take Nothing for My Journey Now (Angelou), **Supp. IV Part 1:** 10, 12, 14, 15, 16

"Wound" (Pedersen; Nelson, trans.), **Supp. XVIII:** 180

Wound and the Bow, The: Seven Studies in Literature (Wilson), **IV:** 429

Wounded (Everett), **Supp. XVIII:** 54, **64,** 65

Wounds in the Rain (Crane), **I:** 409, 414, 423

Woven Stone (Ortiz), **Supp. IV Part 2:** 501, 514

Woven Stories (Ortiz), **Supp. IV Part 2:** 503

"Wraith, The" (Roethke), **III:** 542

"Wrath of God, The" (Fante), **Supp. XI:** 160, 164

"Wreath for a Bridal" (Plath), **Supp. I Part 2:** 537

"Wreath for Emmet Till, A" (Nelson), **Supp. XVIII:** 177

Wreath for Emmett Till, A (Nelson), **Supp. XVIII:** 171, 173, 175, 181, **183–185**

Wreath for Garibaldi and Other Stories, A (Garrett), **Supp. VII:** 99–101

"Wreath of Women" (Rukeyser), **Supp. VI:** 280

Wreckage (Jin), **Supp. XVIII: 98–99**

Wreckage of Agathon, The (Gardner), **Supp. VI:** 63, **65–66**

Wrecking Crew (Levis), **Supp. XI: 259–260**

Wrecking Yard, The (Benedict), **Supp. XXIII:** 35, **39–41**

"Wrecking Yard, The (P. Benedict), **Supp. XXIII:** 39–40

"Wreck of Rivermouth, The" (Whittier), **Supp. I Part 2:** 694, 696–697

"Wreck of the Deutschland" (Hopkins), **Supp. X:** 61

"Wreck of the Hesperus, The" (Longfellow), **Retro. Supp. II:** 168, 169

Wrestler's Cruel Study, The (Dobyns), **Supp. XIII:** 82–83

"Wrestler with Sharks, A" (Yates), **Supp. XI:** 341

Wright, Bernie, **I:** 191, 193

Wright, C. D. (Carolyn Doris), **Supp. XV: 337–355**

Wright, Charles, **Supp. V:** 92, **331–346; Supp. VIII:** 272; **Supp. XIII:** 114; **Supp. XVII:** 71; **Supp. XXI:** 95, 255

Wright, Chauncey, **II:** 344

Wright, Frank Lloyd, **I:** 104, 483

Wright, Franz, **Supp. XVII: 239–249**

Wright, George, **III:** 479

Wright, Harold Bell, **II:** 467–468

Wright, Holly, **Supp. VIII:** 272

Wright, James, **I:** 291; **Supp. III Part 1:** 249; **Supp. III Part 2:** 541, **589–607; Supp. IV Part 1:** 60, 72; **Supp. IV Part 2:** 557, 558, 561, 566, 571, 623; **Supp. V:** 332; **Supp. IX:** 152, 155, 159, 265, 271, 290, 293, 296; **Supp. X:** 69, 127; **Supp. XI:** 150; **Supp. XII:** 217; **Supp. XIII:** 76; **Supp. XV:** 79, 93, 212; **Supp. XVII:** 239, 241, 243, 244; **Supp. XIX:** 122, 273

Wright, Nathalia, **IV:** 155

Wright, Philip Green, **III:** 578, 579, 580

Wright, Richard, **II:** 586; **IV:** 40, **474–497; Retro. Supp. II:** 4, 111, 116, 120; **Supp. I Part 1:** 51, 52, 64, 332, 337; **Supp. II Part 1:** 17, 40, 221, 228, 235, 250; **Supp. IV Part 1:** 1, 11, 84, 374; **Supp. VIII:** 88; **Supp. IX:** 131, 245, 254; **Supp. XI:** 85; **Supp. XII:** 316; **Supp. XIII:** 46, 233; **Supp. XIV:** 73; **Supp. XVI:** 135, 139, 141, 143; **Supp. XVIII:** 277, 282, 286; **Supp. XXI:** 169; **Supp. XXIII:** 166

Wright, Mrs. Richard (Ellen Poplar), **IV:** 476

Wright, Sarah, **Supp. IV Part 1:** 8; **Supp. XIII:** 295

Wright, William, **Retro. Supp. II:** 76, 77

Wrigley, Robert, **Supp. XVIII: 293–308**

"Writer" (Sanders), **Supp. XVI:** 277

"Writer, The" (Wilbur), **Supp. III Part 2:** 561, 562

"Writer as Alaskan, The" (Haines), **Supp. XII:** 199

Writer in America, The (Brooks), **I:** 253, 254, 257

Writer in America, The (Stegner), **Supp. IV Part 2:** 597, 599, 607

"Writers" (Lowell), **II:** 554

Writer's Almanac, The (Keillor, radio program), **Supp. XIII:** 274; **Supp. XVI:** 178; **Supp. XXIII:** 138

Writer's America, A: Landscape in Literature (Kazin), **Supp. VIII:** 106

Writers and Their Craft (Delbanco, ed.), **Supp. XXII:** 204

"Writer's Bed, A" (Mirvis), **Supp. XX: 179**

Writer's Capital, A (Auchincloss), **Supp. IV Part 1:** 21, 23, 24, 31

"Writer's Credo, A" (Abbey), **Supp. XIII:** 1, 17

Writer's Eye, A: Collected Book Reviews (Welty), **Retro. Supp. I:** 339, 354, 356

Writers in America (Schulberg), **Supp. XVIII:** 242, 243, 250, 254

Writers in Revolt (Southern, Seaver, and Trocchi, eds.), **Supp. XI:** 301

Writer's Life, A (Talese), **Supp. XVII:** 208–209, 210

Writer's Notebook, A (Maugham), **Supp. X:** 58

Writers on America (U.S. Department of State, ed.), **Supp. XIII:** 288

Writers on the Left (Aaron), **IV:** 429; **Supp. II Part 1:** 137

Writers on Writing (Prose), **Supp. XVI:** 259

"Writer's Prologue to a Play in Verse" (W. C. Williams), **Retro. Supp. I:** 424

"Writer's Quest for a Parnassus, A" (T. Williams), **IV:** 392

Writers' Workshop (University of Iowa), **Supp. V:** 42

"Writers Workshop, The" (Conroy), **Supp. XVI:** 76

"Writing" (Nemerov), **III:** 275

"Writing About the Universe" (Mosley), **Supp. XIII:** 247

"Writing American Fiction" (P. Roth), **Retro. Supp. II:** 279; **Supp. I Part 1:** 192; **Supp. I Part 2:** 431; **Supp. III Part 2:** 414, 420, 421; **Supp. V:** 45

"Writing and a Life Lived Well" (Patchett), **Supp. XII:** 308

"Writing and Writers: *Disjecta Membra*" (Sorrentino), *Supp. XXI:* 235

Writing a Woman's Life (Heilbrun), **Supp. IX:** 66

"Writing Between Worlds" (Mirvis), **Supp. XX: 177, 178, 179**

Writing Brave and Free: Encouraging Words for People Who Want to Start Writing (Kooser and Cox), **Supp. XIX:** 116, 128

Writing Chicago: Modernism, Ethnography, and the Novel (Cappetti), **Supp. IX:** 4, 8

Writing Creative Nonfiction: The Literature of Reality (Talese and Lounsberry, eds.), **Supp. XVII:** 208

Writing Dylan: The Songs of a Lonesome Traveler (Smith), **Supp. XVIII:** 22

Writing from the Center (Sanders), **Supp. XVI:** 266, 275–276

"Writing from the Inside Out: Style Is Not the Frosting; It's the Cake" (Robbins), **Supp. X:** 266

"Writing here last autumn of my hopes of seeing a hoopoe" (Updike), **Retro. Supp. I:** 335

Writing Home (Crooker), **Supp. XXIII:** 54

Writing in Restaurants (Mamet), **Supp. XIV:** 246

"Writing Lesson, The" (Gordon), **Supp. IV Part 1:** 306

Writing Life, The (Dillard), **Supp. VI:** 23, 31

"Writing of Apollinaire, The" (Zukofsky), **Supp. III Part 2:** 616, 617

"Writing of *Fearless Jones,* The" (Mosley), **Supp. XIII:** 242

Writing on the Wall, The, and Literary Essays (McCarthy), **II:** 579

Writings to an Unfinished Accompaniment (Merwin), **Supp. III Part 1:** 352

"Writing the Universe-Mind" (Tabios), **Supp. XV:** 225

Writing the World (Stafford), **Supp. XI:** 314

"Writing to Save Our Lives" (Milligan), **Supp. XIII:** 274

Writing Vietnam, Writing Life: Caputo, Heinemann, O'Brien, Butler (Herzog), **Supp. XXII:** 116

Writin' Is Fightin' (Reed), *Supp. X:* 241

"Writ on the Eve of My 32nd Birthday" (Corso), **Supp. XII:** 129–130

"Written History as an Act of Faith" (Beard), **Supp. I Part 2:** 492

"Written on the Land" (J. W. Miller), **Supp. XX: 170**

"Wrong Man, The" (Larsen), **Supp. XVIII:** 124

"Wrong Notes" (S. Kauffmann), **Supp. XVI:** 74

"Wrought Figure" (McCarriston), **Supp. XIV:** 272

Wrozynski, Henryk, **Supp. XXIII:** 64

"Wunderkind" (McCullers), **II:** 585

Wunderlich, Mark, **Supp. XI:** 119, 132

Wundt, Wilhelm, **II:** 345

Wurster, William Wilson, **Supp. IV Part 1:** 197

WUSA (film), **Supp. V:** 301

Wuthering Heights (E. Brontë), **Supp. V:** 305; **Supp. X:** 89

WWII (Jones), **Supp. XI:** 219, 231

Wyandotté (Cooper), **I:** 350, 355

Wyatt, Robert B., **Supp. V:** 14

Wyatt, Thomas, **Supp. I Part 1:** 369

Wycherly Woman, The (Macdonald), **Supp. IV Part 2:** 473

Wych Hazel (S. and A. Warner), **Supp. XVIII:** 267, **268–269**

Wydra, Ewa. *See* Hoffman, Eva

Wyeth, Andrew, **Supp. XIX:** 117

Wyler, William, **Supp. XV:** 195

Wylie, Elinor, **IV:** 436; **Supp. I Part 2:** **707–730; Supp. III Part 1:** 2, 63, 318–319; **Supp. XI:** 44; **Supp. XIV:** 127; **Supp. XV:** 307

Wylie, Horace, **Supp. I Part 2:** 708, 709

Wylie, Philip, **III:** 223

Wyllys, Ruth. *See* Taylor, Mrs. Edward (Ruth Wyllys)

"Wyoming Valley Tales" (Crane), **I:** 409

Wyzewa, Théodore de, **Supp. XIV:** 336

X

Xaipe (Cummings), **I:** 430, 432–433, 447

Xenogenesis trilogy (O. Butler), **Supp. XIII: 63–66,** 69

Xenophon, **II:** 105

X Factor, The: A Quest for Excellence" (Plimpton), *Supp. XVI:* 241

X Files (television series), **Supp. XVI:** 125

Xiaojing, Zhou, **Supp. XV:** 214

Xicana Codex of Changing Consciousness, A: Writings, 2000–2010 (Moraga), **Supp. XXIII:** 197

Xingu and Other Stories (Wharton), **IV:** 314, 320; **Retro. Supp. I:** 378
Xionia (Wright), **Supp. V:** 333
XLI Poems (Cummings), **I:** 429, 432, 440, 443

Y

Yabroff, Jennie, **Supp. XIX:** 50, 58, 61
Yacoubi, Ahmed, **Supp. IV Part 1:** 88, 92, 93
Yage Letters, The (Burroughs), **Supp. III Part 1:** 94, 98, 100
Yagoda, Ben, **Supp. VIII:** 151
Yamamoto, Isoroku, **Supp. I Part 2:** 491
Yancey's War (Hoffman), **Supp. XVIII:** 71, **75–76**
Yankee City (Warner), **III:** 60
Yankee Clipper (ballet) (Kirstein), **Supp. IV Part 1:** 82
Yankee in Canada, A (Thoreau), **IV:** 188
Yankey in London (Tyler), **I:** 344
"Yánnina" (Merrill), **Supp. III Part 1:** 329
"Yanosz Korczak's Last Walk" (Markowick-Olczakova), **Supp. X:** 70
Yarboro, Chelsea Quinn, **Supp. V:** 147
Yarbro-Bejarano, Yvonne, **Supp. XXIII:** 196, 201
Yardley, Jonathan, **Supp. V:** 326; **Supp. XI:** 67; **Supp. XXIII:** 97, 99, 103, 104, 107, 108, 109
"Yard Sale" (Kenyon), **Supp. VII:** 169
Yates, Richard, **Supp. XI:** 333–350; **Supp. XXIII:** 289
"Year, The" (Sandburg), **III:** 584
Year at the Races, A (Parker and Parker), **Supp. XIX:** 187
"Year Between, The" (Neugeboren), **Supp. XVI:** 226
Year in Provence, A (Mayle), **Supp. XVI:** 295
Yearling, The (Rawlings), **Supp. X:** 219, **230–231**, 233, 234; **Supp. XXII:** 195
"Year of Grace" (Swados), **Supp. XIX:** 262–263
Year of Happy, A (Goldbarth), **Supp. XII:** 180
"Year of Mourning, The" (Jeffers), **Supp. II Part 2:** 415
Year of Silence, The (Bell), **Supp. X:** 1, **5–6**, 7
"Year of Silence, The" (Brockmeier), **Supp. XXII:** 59
"Year of the Double Spring, The" (Swenson), **Supp. IV Part 2:** 647
Year's Best Fantasy and Horror, 2004, **Supp. XXII:** 55
Year's Best Science Fiction, The (Merril, ed.), **Supp. XVI:** 123
Year's Life, A (Lowell), **Supp. I Part 2:** 405
"Years of Birth" (Cowley), **Supp. II Part 1:** 149
Years of Conscience: The Muckrakers: An Anthology of Reform Journalism (Swados, ed.), **Supp. XIX:** 264
Years of My Youth (Howells), **II:** 276
"Years of Wonder" (White), **Supp. I Part 2:** 652, 653

"Years Without Understanding, The" (Weigl), **Supp. XIX:** 282–283
Years With Ross, The (Thurber), **Supp. I Part 2:** 619
Year We Left Home, The (Thompson), **Supp. XXIII:** 301, **302–303**
Yeats, Jack, **Supp. XVI:** 190
Yeats, Jack B., **Supp. XX:** 201
Yeats, John Butler, **III:** 458; **Supp. XX:** 69
Yeats, William Butler, **I:** 69, 172, 384, 389, 403, 434, 478, 494, 532; **II:** 168–169, 566, 598; **III:** 4, 5, 8, 18, 19, 20, 23, 29, 40, 205, 249, 269, 270–271, 272, 278, 279, 294, 347, 409, 457, 458–460, 472, 473, 476–477, 521, 523, 524, 527, 528, 533, 540, 541, 542, 543–544, 591–592; **IV:** 89, 93, 121, 126, 136, 140, 271, 394, 404; **Retro. Supp. I:** 59, 66, 127, 141, 270, 283, 285, 286, 288, 290, 311, 342, 350, 378, 413; **Retro. Supp. II:** 185, 331; **Supp. I Part 1:** 79, 80, 254, 257, 262; **Supp. I Part 2:** 388, 389; **Supp. II Part 1:** 1, 4, 9, 20, 26, 361; **Supp. III Part 1:** 59, 63, 236, 238, 253; **Supp. IV Part 1:** 81; **Supp. IV Part 2:** 634; **Supp. V:** 220; **Supp. VIII:** 19, 21, 30, 155, 156, 190, 239, 262, 292; **Supp. IX:** 43, 119; **Supp. X:** 35, 58, 119, 120; **Supp. XI:** 140; **Supp. XII:** 132, 198, 217, 266; **Supp. XIII:** 77, **Supp. XIII:** 87; **Supp. XIV:** 7; **Supp. XV:** 36, 41, 181, 186; **Supp. XVI:** 47–48, 159; **Supp. XVII:** 36; **Supp. XXI:** 61
Yee, Amy, **Supp. XVIII:** 93, 94
Yellin, Jean Fagan, **Supp. XVI:** 88, 89
Yellow Back Radio Broke-Down (Reed), **Supp. X:** 240, 242, **243–245**
"Yellow Dog Café" (Komunyakaa), **Supp. XIII:** 126
Yellow Face (Hwang), **Supp. XXI:** 143, 148, **154–156**
"Yellow Girl" (Caldwell), **I:** 310
Yellow Glove (Nye), **Supp. XIII:** 275, **276–277**
"Yellow Glove" (Nye), **Supp. XIII:** 276
"Yellow Gown, The" (Anderson), **I:** 114
Yellow House on the Corner, The (Dove), **Supp. IV Part 1:** 244, 245, 246, 254
"Yellow Raft, The" (Connell), **Supp. XIV:** 85–86
"Yellow River" (Tate), **IV:** 141
"Yellowstone, The"(Kenny), **Supp. XXIII:** 155
"Yellow Violet, The" (Bryant), **Supp. I Part 1:** 154, 155
"Yellow Wallpaper, The" (Gilman), **Supp. XI:** **198–199**, 207; **Supp. XVI:** 84
"Yellow Woman" (Keres stories), **Supp. IV Part 1:** 327
"Yellow Woman" (Silko), **Supp. IV Part 2:** 567–568
Yelverton, Theresa, **Supp. IX:** 181
Yenser, Stephen, **Supp. X:** 207, 208; **Supp. XV:** 113–114
"Yentl the Yeshiva Boy" (Singer), **IV:** 15, 20
Yerkes, Charles E., **I:** 507, 512

Yerma (opera) (Bowles), **Supp. IV Part 1:** 89
Yertle the Turtle and Other Stories (Geisel), **Supp. XVI:** 109
"Yes" (Stafford), **Supp. XI:** 329
Yes, Mrs. Williams (W. C. Williams), **Retro. Supp. I:** 423
Yes, Yes, No, No (Kushner), **Supp. IX:** 133
"Yes and It's Hopeless" (Ginsberg), **Supp. II Part 1:** 326
"Yes"(Crooker), **Supp. XXIII:** 62
Yesenin, Sergey, **Supp. VIII:** 40
"Yes: I Mean So OK–Love" (Bronk), **Supp. XXI:** 31
"Yes! No!" (Oliver), **Supp. VII:** 243–244
Yesterday and Today: A Comparative Anthology of Poetry (Untermeyer, ed.), **Supp. XV:** 309
Yesterday's Self: Nostalgia and the Immigrant Identity (Ritivoi), **Supp. XVI:** 148
Yesterday Will Make You Cry (C. Himes), **Supp. XVI:** 137
"Yet Another Example of the Porousness of Certain Borders" (Wallace), **Supp. X:** 309
"Yet Do I Marvel" (Cullen), **Supp. IV Part 1:** 165, 169
Yet Other Waters (Farrell), **II:** 29, 38, 39, 40
"Yevtushenko" (Kooser), **Supp. XIX:** 124
Yevtushenko, Yevgeny, **Supp. III Part 1:** 268
Yezzi, David, **Supp. XII:** 193
Yiddish Policemen's Union, The (Chabon), **Supp. XXII:** 49
Yizkor Book, **Supp. XVI:** 154
...y no se lo tragó la tierra (Rivera), **Supp. XIX:** 99, 101
Y no se lo trago la tierra (And the Earth Did Not Cover Him) (Rivera), **Supp. XIII:** 216
¡Yo! (Alvarez), **Supp. VII:** 1, 15–17
"Yogurt of Vasirin Kefirovsky, The" (Apple), **Supp. XVII:** 3, 4
Yohannan, J. D., **II:** 20
"Yoke, The" (Bidart), **Supp. XV:** 33
Yonge, Charlotte, **II:** 174
"Yonnondio" (Whitman), **Supp. XIII:** 304
Yonnondio: From the Thirties (Olsen), **Supp. XIII:** 295, 295, **Supp. XIII:** 292, 296, **303–304**, 305
"Yore" (Nemerov), **III:** 283
York, Jake Adam, **Supp. XXI:** 257
York, Lorraine, **Supp. XX:** 51
"York Beach" (Toomer), **Supp. III Part 2:** 486
Yorke, Dorothy, **Supp. I Part 1:** 258
Yorke, Henry Vincent. *See* Green, Henry
"York Garrison, 1640" (Jewett), **Retro. Supp. II:** 141
Yosemite, The (Muir), **Supp. IX:** 185
"Yosemite Glaciers: Ice Streams of the Great Valley" (Muir), **Supp. IX:** 181
Yoshe Kalb (Singer), **IV:** 2
"You, Andrew Marvell" (MacLeish), **III:** 12–13

"You, Dr. Martin" (Sexton), **Supp. II Part 2:** 673

You, Emperors, and Others: Poems 1957–1960 (Warren), **IV:** 245

"You, Genoese Mariner" (Merwin), **Supp. III Part 1:** 343

"You, Reader" (Collins), **Supp. XXI:** 55

"You All Know the Story of the Other Woman" (Sexton), **Supp. II Part 2:** 688

"You Are Gorgeous and I'm Coming"(O'Hara), **Supp. XXIII:** 219

You Are Happy (Atwood), **Supp. XIII:** 34

"You Are Happy" (Atwood), **Supp. XIII:** 34

"You Are in Bear Country" (Kumin), **Supp. IV Part 2:** 453, 455

"You Are Not I" (Bowles), **Supp. IV Part 1:** 87

"You Begin" (Atwood), **Supp. XIII:** 34

You Bright and Risen Angels (Vollmann), **Supp. XVII:** 225, 226

"You Bring Out the Mexican in Me" (Cisneros), **Supp. VII:** 71

You Came Along (film), **Supp. IV Part 2:** 524

"You *Can* Go Home Again" (TallMountain), **Supp. IV Part 1:** 324–325

"You Can Have It" (Levine), **Supp. V:** 188–189

You Can't Go Home Again (Wolfe), **IV:** 450, 451, 454, 456, 460, 462, 468, 469, 470

You Can't Keep a Good Woman Down (Walker), **Supp. III Part 2:** 520, 525, 531

You Can't Pet a Possom (Bontemps), **Supp. XXII:** 4, 12

You Can't Take It with You (Kaufman and Hart), **Supp. XIV:** 327

"You Can't Tell a Man by the Song He Sings" (P. Roth), **Supp. III Part 2:** 406

"You Don't Know What Love Is" (Carver), **Supp. III Part 1:** 147

You Don't Love Me Yet (Lethem), **Supp. XVIII: 149–150**

"You Have Left Your Lotus Pods on the Bus" (Bowles), **Supp. IV Part 1:** 91

You Have Seen Their Faces (Caldwell), **I:** 290, 293–294, 295, 304, 309

You Know Me, Al: A Busher's Letters (Lardner), **Supp. XVI:** 189

You Know Me Al (comic strip), **II:** 423

You Know Me Al (Lardner), **II:** 26, 415, 419, 422, 431

"You Know More Than You Think You Do"(Hadas), **Supp. XXIII:** 124

"You Know What" (Beattie), **Supp. V:** 33

"You Know Who You Are" (Nye), **Supp. XIII:** 275

You Might As Well Live: The Life and Times of Dorothy Parker (Keats), **Supp. IX:** 190

"You Must Relax!" (J. Scott), **Supp. XVII:** 189

You Must Revise Your Life (Stafford), **Supp. XI:** 312–313, 313–314, 315

"Young" (Sexton), **Supp. II Part 2:** 680

Young, Al, **Supp. X:** 240

Young, Art, **IV:** 436

Young, Barbara, **Supp. XX: 119, 123**

Young, Brigham, **Supp. IV Part 2:** 603

Young, Courtland, **Supp. XXII:** 21

Young, David, **Supp. XIX:** 276

Young, Dianne, **Supp. XXII:** 252

Young, Edward, **II:** 111; **III:** 415, 503

Young, Gary, **Supp. XV:** 88

Young, Mary, **Supp. XIII:** 236, 238, 239, 240

Young, Philip, **II:** 306; **Retro. Supp. I:** 172

Young, Stark, **Supp. XXII:** 193

Young Adventure (Benét), **Supp. XI:** 44

"Young America" (Brooks), **Supp. XV:** 298

"Young Child and His Pregnant Mother, A" (Schwartz), **Supp. II Part 2:** 650

Young Christian, The (Abbott), **Supp. I Part 1:** 38

"Young Dr. Gosse" (Chopin), **Supp. I Part 1:** 211, 216

Younger Choir, The (anthology), **Supp. XV:** 294

Younger Quire, The (Untermeyer), **Supp. XV:** 294, 297

"Young Folks, The" (Salinger), **III:** 551

Young Folk's Cyclopaedia of Persons and Places (Champlin), **III:** 577

"Young Girl's Lament, A" (Jin), **Supp. XVIII:** 99

"Young Goodman Brown" (Hawthorne), **II:** 229; **Retro. Supp. I:** 151–152, 153, 154; **Supp. XI:** 51; **Supp. XIV:** 48, 50

Young Harvard: First Poems of Witter Bynner (Bynner), **Supp. XV:** 41

Young Hearts Crying (Yates), **Supp. XI:** 348

"Young Housewife, The" (W. C. Williams), **Retro. Supp. I:** 415

Young Immigrants, The (Lardner), **II:** 426

"Young Lady's Friend, The: Verses, Addressed to a Young Lady, on Her Leaving School" (Rowson), **Supp. XV:** 234

"Young Lions" (P. E. Jones), **Supp. XXII:** 145

Young Lions, The (Shaw), **Supp. XIX: 248–249**

Young Lonigan: A Boyhood in Chicago Streets (Farrell), **II:** 31, 41

Young Manhood of Studs Lonigan, The (Farrell), **II:** 31, 34

"Young Man on the Go" (column, Siddons), **Supp. XXII:** 244

Young Men and Fire (Maclean), **Supp. XIV:** 221, **231–233**

Young People's Pride (Benét), **Supp. XI:** 44

Young Poet's Primer (Brooks), **Supp. III Part 1:** 86

Youngren, J. Alan, **Supp. XVI:** 174

"Young Sammy's First Wild Oats" (Santayana), **III:** 607, 615

"Young Sor Juana, The" (Mora), **Supp. XIII:** 218

"Your Arkansas Traveler" (Schulberg), **Supp. XVIII:** 252

"Your Dailiness" (Notley), **Supp. XXII:** 227

"Your Death" (Dove), **Supp. IV Part 1:** 250

"You're History" (Hampl), **Supp. XXII:** 84, 95

You're Only Old Once! (Geisel), **Supp. XVI:** 111

"You're Ugly, Too" (Moore), **Supp. X:** 171

"Your Face on the Dog's Neck" (Sexton), **Supp. II Part 2:** 686

"Your Hand, Your Hand" (Hoffman), **Supp. XVIII:** 79

Your Job in Germany (film, Capra), **Supp. XVI:** 102

Your Job in Japan (film, Capra), **Supp. XVI:** 102

"Your Life" (Stafford), **Supp. XI:** 329

"Your Mother's Eyes" (Kingsolver), **Supp. VII:** 209

"You Take a Train through a Foreign Country" (Dobyns), **Supp. XIII:** 90

"Youth" (Hughes), **Supp. I Part 1:** 321; **Supp. XXII:** 12

"Youth" (Huncke), **Supp. XIV:** 145

Youth and Life (Bourne), **I:** 217–222, 232

Youth and the Bright Medusa (Cather), **I:** 322; **Retro. Supp. I:** 14

"Youthful Religious Experiences" (Corso), **Supp. XII:** 117

Youth of Parnassus, and Other Stories, The (L. P. Smith), **Supp. XIV:** 336

Youth's First Steps in Geography (Rowson), **Supp. XV:** 243

You Touched Me! (Williams and Windham), **IV:** 382, 385, 387, 390, 392–393

"You Touch Me" (X. J. Kennedy), **Supp. XV:** 166

You Went Away (Findley), **Supp. XX: 49**

"You Who Sleep Soundly Through Our Bleakest Hour" (Espaillat), **Supp. XXI:** 110

Yurchenco, Henrietta, **Supp. XVIII:** 20

Yurka, Blanche, **Supp. I Part 1:** 67

Yutang, Adet, **Supp. X:** 291

Yutang, Anor, **Supp. X:** 291

Yutang, Lin, **Supp. X:** 291; **Supp. XVI:** 190

Yutang, Mei-mei, **Supp. X:** 291

Yvernelle: A Legend of Feudal France (Norris), **III:** 314

Y & X (Olson), **Supp. II Part 2:** 556

Z

Zabel, Morton Dauwen, **II:** 431; **III:** 194, 215; **Supp. I Part 2:** 721

Zach, Natan, **Supp. XV:** 75, 82, 85

Zaehner, R. C., **Supp. XXII:** 258

Zagajewski, Adam, **Supp. XVII:** 241

Zagarell, Sandra, **Supp. XV:** 269, 270, 278, 281, 282

Zagarell, Sandra A., **Retro. Supp. II:** 140, 143

"Zagrowsky Tells" (Paley), **Supp. VI:** 229

Zaino, Nick, **Supp. XXII:** 207
Zakrzewska, Marie, **Retro. Supp. II:** 146
Zaleski, Jeff, **Supp. XI:** 143; **Supp. XIX:** 54
Zall, Paul, **Supp. XIV:** 156
Zaltzberg, Charlotte, **Supp. IV Part 1:** 374
"Zambesi and Ranee" (Swenson), **Supp. IV Part 2:** 647
Zamir, Israel, **Retro. Supp. II:** 303, 317
Zamora, Bernice, **Supp. IV Part 2:** 545
Zamoyski, Adam, **Supp. XV:** 257
Zangwill, Israel, **I:** 229; **Supp. XX:** 2
Zanita: A Tale of the Yosemite (Yelverton), **Supp. IX:** 181
Zanuck, Darryl F., **Supp. XI:** 170; **Supp. XII:** 165
Zapata, Emiliano, **Supp. XIII:** 324
"Zapatos" (Boyle), **Supp. VIII:** 15
Zapruder, Matthew, **Supp. XVI:** 55
Zarathustra, **III:** 602
Zawacki, Andrew, **Supp. VIII:** 272
"Zaydee" (Levine), **Supp. V:** 186
Zebra-Striped Hearse, The (Macdonald), **Supp. IV Part 2:** 473
Zechariah (biblical book), **IV:** 152
Zeidner, Lisa, **Supp. IV Part 2:** 453; **Supp. XXIII:** 297
"Zeitl and Rickel" (Singer), **IV:** 20
Zeke and Ned (McMurtry and Ossana), **Supp. V:** 232
Zeke Proctor, Cherokee Outlaw (Conley), **Supp. V:** 232
Zelazo, Suzanne, **Supp. XXII:** 158, 167
Zelda: A Biography (Milford), **Supp. IX:** 60
"Zelda and Scott: The Beautiful and Damned" (National Portrait Gallery exhibit), **Supp. IX:** 65
Zelig (film; Allen), **Supp. XV:** 4, 6, **8–9**

Zen and the Birds of Appetite (Merton), **Supp. VIII:** 205–206, 208
Zend-Avesta (Fechner), **II:** 358
Zeno, **Retro. Supp. I:** 247
Zero db and Other Stories (Bell), **Supp. X:** 1, 5, 6
"Zeus over Redeye" (Hayden), **Supp. II Part 1:** 380
Zevi, Sabbatai, **IV:** 6
Ziegfeld, Florenz, **II:** 427–428
Ziegler, Cyd, **Supp. XX: 273**
Ziegler, Heidi, **Supp. XXII:** 260
Ziggurat (Balakian), **Supp. XXIII:** 19, **32–33**
Zigrosser, Carl, **I:** 226, 228, 231
Zilles, Klaus, **Supp. XIX:** 112
Zimmerman, Paul D., **Supp. IV Part 2:** 583, 589, 590
Zimmerman, Robert. *See* Dylan, Bob
Zimmerman, Robert Allen. *See* Dylan, Bob
Zinberg, Leonard S. *See* Lacy, Ed
Zinman, Toby Silverman, **Supp. XIII:** 207–208, 209
Zinn, Howard, **Supp. V:** 289
Zinovyev, Grigory, **Supp. XXI:** 167
Zinsser, Hans, **I:** 251, 385
Zip: A Novel of the Left and Right (Apple), **Supp. XVII: 4–5**
Zipes, Jack, **Supp. XIV:** 126
"Zipper, The" (L. Michaels), **Supp. XVI:** 214
"Zizi's Lament" (Corso), **Supp. XII:** 123
Zodiac, The (Dickey), **Supp. IV Part 1:** 178, 183–184, 185
"Zog-19: A Scientific Romance"(P. Benedict), **Supp. XXIII:** 49
Zola, Émile, **I:** 211, 411, 474, 500, 502, 518; **II:** 174, 175–176, 182, 194, 275, 276, 281, 282, 319, 325, 337, 338; **III:** 315, 316, 317–318, 319–320, 321,

322, 323, 393, 511, 583; **IV:** 326; **Retro. Supp. I:** 226, 235; **Retro. Supp. II:** 93; **Supp. I Part 1:** 207; **Supp. II Part 1:** 117
Zolotow, Maurice, **III:** 161
"Zone" (Bogan), **Supp. III Part 1:** 60–61
Zone Journals (Wright), **Supp. V:** 332–333, 342–343
"Zooey" (Salinger), **III:** 564–565, 566, 567, 569, 572
"Zoo Revisited" (White), **Supp. I Part 2:** 654
Zoo Story, The (Albee), **I:** 71, 72–74, 75, 77, 84, 93, 94; **III:** 281
Zorach, William, **I:** 260
Zuccotti, Susan, **Supp. XVI:** 154
Zuckerman Bound: A Trilogy and Epilogue (P. Roth), **Supp. III Part 2:** 423
Zuckerman Unbound (P. Roth), **Retro. Supp. II:** 283; **Supp. III Part 2:** 421–422
Zueblin, Charles, **Supp. I Part 1:** 5
Zuger, Abigail, **Supp. X:** 160
Zukofsky, Celia (Mrs. Louis), **Supp. III Part 2:** 619–621, 623, 625, 626–629, 631
Zukofsky, Louis, **IV:** 415; **Retro. Supp. I:** 422; **Supp. III Part 2: 619–636;** **Supp. IV Part 1:** 154; **Supp. XIV:** 279, 282, 285, 286–287
Zukofsky, Paul, **Supp. III Part 2:** 622, 623–626, 627, 628
Zuleika Dobson (Beerbohm), **Supp. I Part 2:** 714
Zulus (Everett), **Supp. XVIII:** 54, **56–57**
"Zuni Potter: Drawing the Heartline" (Bierds), **Supp. XVII:** 26
Zverev, Aleksei, **Retro. Supp. I:** 278
Zwinger, Ann, **Supp. X:** 29
Zyda, Joan, **Retro. Supp. II:** 52

ORLAND PARK PUBLIC LIBRARY